Leslie Halliwell was born in London. He buys most of the feature films and series screened by the ITV network and goes twice a year to Hollywood in search of them; he has been an enthusiast for the medium since childhood. He has managed several Rank Organisation and specialist cinemas and is a member of two National Film Archive committees.

Mr Halliwell spent several years as film reviewer for *Picturegoer* and *Sight and Sound* and has contributed to other national publications, including *The Spectator* and *Films and Filming*. He has also had two plays professionally staged. He was the man behind Granada's long-running *Cinema* series, and still advises on its junior version, *Clapperboard*.

HALLIWELL'S FILM GUIDE

A Survey of 8000 English-Language Movies

Leslie Halliwell

PALADIN
GRANADA PUBLISHING
London Toronto Sydney New York

Published by Granada Publishing Limited
in Paladin Books 1979

ISBN 0 586 08340 5

First published by Hart-Davis, MacGibbon Ltd 1977

Granada Publishing Limited
Frogmore, St Albans, Herts AL2 2NF
and
3 Upper James Street, London W1R 4BP
866 United Nations Plaza, New York, NY 10017, USA
117 York Street, Sydney, NSW 2000, Australia
100 Skyway Avenue, Rexdale, Ontario, M9W 3A6, Canada
PO Box 84165, Greenside, 2034 Johannesburg, South Africa
CML Centre, Queen & Wyndham, Auckland 1, New Zealand

Made and printed in Great Britain by
Richard Clay (The Chaucer Press) Ltd
Bungay, Suffolk

Contents

This book is dedicated
to the memory of

MY MOTHER

who first took me to the pictures

and to everyone who has
since joined me there

also to all the people mentioned
in the following 1081 pages

especially those who refrained from
making the following films, which
I have over the years anticipated with
dread but which never actually arrived:
I WAS AN INFANT FRANKENSTEIN
THE DANCING NUN
I MARRIED A MARTIAN
CITIZEN NIXON, or EXPLETIVE DELETED
RETURN TO LOST HORIZON
MEET ME IN ST HELEN'S*
THE BRIDE OF SHERLOCK HOLMES
THAT'S MONOGRAM!
THE PRIVATE LIVES OF
ELIZABETH AND RICHARD
ALL THE PRESIDENT'S WOMEN
SON OF PSYCHO
I WAS A CANNIBAL FOR THE F.B.I.
THE BAWDY BARD OF STRATFORD
THE GHOUL NEXT DOOR
TWO FLEW OVER THE CUCKOO'S NEST
THE KEEFE BRASSELLE STORY
Jerry Lewis in ME, MYSELF AND I
ABBOTT AND COSTELLO MEET THE EXORCIST

Even the epic threatened in SULLIVAN'S TRAVELS
—ANTS IN YOUR PANTS OF 1939—
would have been preferable

*odd that so many American place names have successfully formed film titles. Why have the British not responded to OKLAHOMA! with ACCRINGTON!, to THUNDER BAY with WIGAN PIER, to BAD DAY AT BLACK ROCK with SUNDAY IN SCUNTHORPE?

Introduction

During the twelve years which have elapsed since *The Filmgoer's Companion* first appeared, I have often been asked why I do not produce a complete compendium of all the films ever made, giving a minimum of useful information for each title. Some people even complain because the *Companion* does not provide all this. Plainly, with more than 25,000 English-speaking titles alone to contend with – and I am speaking here of feature-length films only – no one volume could hope to be comprehensive, and even if it were possible the attempt would be fairly pointless, for the book would be cluttered up with endless lists of routine second features of long ago, which no one in his right mind would even wish to remember, let alone see again.

In the *Companion* I do treat separately some seven or eight hundred titles which I consider significant either historically or as pure entertainment, and some readers have been annoyed when looking up films they consider memorable to discover that their titles have not accorded with my prejudices. Ever anxious to please, I have rearranged and amplified the information given in these entries, and multiplied the number of entries tenfold: hence the volume you hold in your hand, which I hope will provide an instant reference when what you want to look up is a movie rather than a person, a theme or a technical expression.

The key to the volume must still be selection, even with a goal of eight thousand entries. To some extent the selection must be personal, but readers of the *Companion* will be helped by having sensed the extent of my memory and the balance of my inclinations. (I think I may claim to have as reasonable a set of hang-ups as anyone now writing about films, except that I tend to hark back towards the old rather than the new, which is not a bad qualification for the job in hand.) I did feel it necessary, however, to restrict myself, at least in the first edition, to films wholly or partly financed in America or Britain. Obviously there are many foreign-language films which demanded inclusion, but it would have been impossible to select them on the same level: I could have given only a smattering of the better-known ones, which seemed unfair. The same is true of silent films, so I firmly put both problems aside for another day and limited myself to English-speaking talking films, which gave me fifty years of product to play with.

I have tried to include every film which seemed likely or worthy of remembrance by the keen filmgoer or student, whether with affection for its own sake as good entertainment, for showcasing memorable work by a particular talent, for sheer curiosity value or for box office success. This brings in virtually everything which played as a main feature in Britain or America. Co-features, 'programmers' and second features are included if they are known to have special merit or to show promise in some department; I have tried to omit the absolutely routine, and specifically excluded a few hundred westerns on the Audie Murphy and Randolph Scott level or below. Another way of looking at my choice is to say that the main studios to suffer are Republic, Monogram, PRC, Nettlefold and Mancunian. Other deliberate exclusions are porno films (hard or soft);

underground films; documentaries and shorts; features below fifty-five minutes: exploitation and horror films from independent sources; from-the-stalls versions of ballet, opera and Shakespeare; and pop concerts on film.

After much thought I did make an effort to include all TV movies made for ninety-minute or longer slots. This is a form which began in the fifties, then disappeared until the late sixties and now seems to average more than one hundred items a year. As it has strong links with the old Hollywood, it seemed that someone should keep a record, and it might as well be me while the task is still not too onerous. It would of course be quite impossible to cope with all the thirty- and sixty-minute episodes of film series, excellent though a few of them are.

I shall be disappointed if the regular reader of the *Companion* cannot find in this volume any film he is likely to require, unless he is a specialist in the early work of Edgar G. Ulmer, Maurice Elvey, or Harry d'Abbabie d'Arrast. Complaints of omissions will nevertheless be welcome: if only one reader sees merit in an excluded film, it has to be worthy of reconsideration next time. Be assured, however, that I already have another three thousand titles half researched . . .

Here is a note of the information given for each film:

Title, with alternatives if used
Italicizing, as in the *Companion*, of any talent involved who makes a particularly outstanding or typical contribution
A rating system
Country of origin
Date of completion/release
Production company, with producer bracketed if named. (Distributor precedes production company if different)
Colour, including name of process, or black and white, and wide-screen or 3-D systems if applicable
Brief synopsis
Brief appraisal (intended as an amalgam of the general view)
Writer, including original source
Director
Photographer
Composer of music score
Other credits as available and applicable
Principal cast with comments
Brief quotes from well-known critics (for about a fifth of the titles)

On reflection I decided to omit all awards, which are readily available elsewhere and in any case are seldom of real significance.

The compilation of such a tome is an enterprise both daunting and challenging. I could not have accomplished it without the help of many predecessors on whose research I have leaned. I salute especially the work of Leonard Maltin, James Robert Parish, Denis Gifford, Douglas Eames and the unsung anonymous heroes who compiled the reviews of the BFI's *Monthly Film Bulletin* during the fifties and sixties.

The least the reader will derive from this book, I hope, is a notion of the enormous variety of talent which has been poured into the film business during the last half-century. It is often said with justice that far too many film books are published: I hope this may be one of the most useful and comprehensive. I have certainly tried to pour a quart of information into a pint pot of paper, and any corrections or additions will certainly be welcomed. They should be sent to me, please, care of Granada TV, 36 Golden Square, London W.1.

August 1976* L.H.

*The above date is roughly the stopping place for new entries: I have tried to include everything released before then. TV movies for the 1976–7 season are not included.

Explanatory Notes

Title The complete title is given, though the definite and indefinite articles are not of course counted in the alphabetical arrangement. The spelling of the country of origin is used, e.g. *My Favorite Blonde* rather than *My Favourite Blonde.*

Alphabetical order Hyphenated or apostrophized words are counted as one word, and as usual in reference books the order is taken not by the complete title but a word at a time, e.g. *No Room at the Inn* comes before *Nob Hill.* Mac and Mc are regarded as interchangeable under Mac.

Ratings It would be absurd to classify films selected from a period of forty-five years as to which are the best or the worst. Techniques improve, standards change, and personal preferences have to be accounted for. I have tried, however, to give credit for what seemed excellent or innovative at the time, even though it may have been overtaken by imitators; I have tried to judge each film by its own standards (how could one sensibly compare *Frankenstein Meets the Wolf Man* with *Gone with the Wind*?), and I have rescrutinized it now to see what historical or artistic interest it retains. Mere entertainment value has not been derided, nor have films which may seem naïve but give an accurate picture of the standards of their own time. To sum up in one word, the ratings indicate how much *interest* a film is thought to have for the modern viewer, whether he be a student or a reasonably alert seeker of entertainment.

Four stars, then, indicate a film outstanding in many ways, a milestone in cinema history, remarkable for acting, direction, writing, photography or some other aspect of technique. Three stars indicates a very high standard of professional excellence or high historical interest: or if you like, three strong reasons for admiring it. Two stars indicate a good level of competence and a generally entertaining film. One star draws attention to minor points of merit, usually in a film not very satisfactory as a whole; it could be a failed giant or a second feature with a few interesting ideas among the dross. No stars at all indicates a totally routine production or worse; such films may be watchable but are at least equally missable.

It will be seen that my judgements are fairly harsh, but I hope they are consistent. For further elucidation of my personal prejudices see the essay, 'The Decline and Fall of the Movie', on p. 1066.

Country of origin First item on second line; usually either British or American, though some co-productions are included.

Year of release Comes after country of origin, and is intended to be the year in which the film was first shown. If it was made earlier and held back, I have tried to indicate the fact.

Running time In minutes, signified by 'm'. As far as possible this is the original release time. Very many films are cut when they cross the water, sometimes by twenty minutes or more, but I have not tried to indicate this, as when the film appears on television the new print is usually taken from the original negative (but may be cut again). Remember, however, that an engineering function of British television results in an imperceptible speeding-up of projection and a consequent loss of one minute in every twenty-five. A hundred-minute film, therefore, will run only ninety-six minutes on the box, so check your facts before complaining.

Black and white or colour I have given the colour process where known (it is not always stated these days, and almost never on TV movies), and have coined the single word Eastmancolor to equate with Technicolor.

Other notable points are given at the end of the second line: Whether the film is in some special process (3-D, Vistavision, etc), or if it was made for television (TVM).

A word about TV movies Less information is given for TV movies because less is available, even on the credits, and these flip past so quickly that they are difficult to catch unless one can examine the print on the bench. I have aimed to give the writer and director, the cast, and where possible the producer. The production company is given but not always the distributor, which tends to change from country to country. The colour process used by TV movies is usually anonymous except in the case of Universal, which has the world's biggest Technicolor plant on the lot and always uses it. TV movie ratings should be compared with other TV movies, not with theatrical ratings: movies made for the box are put together slickly and simply, with old-fashioned values and old-fashioned censorship as befits the home audience; they are a training ground for behind-the-camera talent comparable with the second features which used to be made by young directors such as Zinnemann and Wise for MGM or RKO (*Eyes in the Night, The Body Snatcher*, and so on).

Most TV movies are too long because they must be padded to the required slot length, normally 74 minutes (90-minute slot) or 98 minutes (2-hour slot). Almost all of them, moreover, are disfigured by being conceived as 'pilots' for series which may or may not emerge; this may help to explain undue attention to one particular character who has been conceived as the hero of a continuing series. All kinds of abuses occur: one producer, Twentieth Century Fox, regularly adds 16 minutes of out-takes to its 74-minute movies when they are sent out after networking for American syndication in slots for which no advertising may have been gathered.

Production credit The central credit on the third line is the production company. To the left, however, comes the distributor if different from the production company, in brackets if his rights subsequently lapsed. To the right is the actual producer, except for early thirties films in which he was seldom credited. He is also in brackets unless he has a stake in the production.

Alternative title This is given on a separate line, usually with a note of the country in which it was used. If no such fine line exists, I have used the formula *aka* (also known as). An index of alternative titles is at the end of the book, and should be consulted if any film for which the reader is looking cannot at first be found.

Synopsis Self-explanatory, with brevity and accuracy the keynote.

Assessment Again very brief, so flippancy will inevitably be suspected. Not so, but for more considered judgements look for books which have more space.

Writer credit It seems to me that this is, at least sometimes, more important than the director credit, and as script in any case precedes direction, it comes first in this book. The author of the screenplay is always given; if this derives from a novel, play or story, this is given next, together with the original author.

Director credit *d.*

Photography credit *ph.*

Music credit *(m)* This means the composer of the background music score. Sometimes there is only a music director (*md*) who orchestrates library or classical music.

Other credits Production designer (*pd*), music and lyrics (*m/ly*), art director (*ad*), special effects (*sp*), montage, etc., are given when they seem important and can be found. In some cases it has not been possible to track down all the credits one would wish.

Cast The principal actors are given where possible, roughly in order of importance. I have stopped before the bit parts.

Additional notes Any other significant remarks about the film are given after the symbol †.

Comments from critics To about a fifth of the items I have appended brief quotes from well-known professional critics, sometimes because they wittily confirm my own findings, and sometimes because they disagree with me entirely. I hope these will be enjoyable and illuminating; the absence of a quote casts no reflection whatever on the film, only on my own ability as a researcher.

Italics These denote a contribution of a particularly high standard. Arguments are expected and additions welcomed.

A

A-Haunting We Will Go*
US 1942 68m bw
TCF (Sol M. Wertzel)

Gangsters dupe Laurel and Hardy into escorting a coffin, which is accidentally switched with one used in a magic act.
Nothing whatever to do with haunting: a poor comedy with no typical material for the stars, but interesting as a record of the touring show of Dante the Magician.

w Lou Breslow *d* Alfred Werker *ph* Glen Macdonald

Stan Laurel, Oliver Hardy, *Dante*, Sheila Ryan, John Shelton, Elisha Cook Jnr

Aaron Slick from Punkin Crick*
US 1952 95m Technicolor
Paramount (William Perlberg, George Seaton)
GB title: *Marshmallow Moon*

A small-town girl is tricked into selling her farm and moving to the city, but eventually marries the simple farmer who rescues her.
Homespun entertainment based on a staple success of the American provincial theatre, with pleasant songs added.

wd Claude Binyon, *play* Walter Benjamin Hare *ph* Charles B. Lang Jnr *m/ly* Jay Livingston, Ray Evans *ch* Charles O'Curran

Alan Young, Dinah Shore, Robert Merrill, Adele Jergens, Minerva Urecal

Abbott and Costello Go to Mars
US 1953 76m bw
U-I (Howard Christie)

Two incompetents accidentally launch a space ship and land first in Louisiana, then on Venus.
Dismal knockabout, badly made.

w John Grant, D. D. Beauchamp *d* Charles Lamont
ph Clifford Stine *m* Joseph Gershenson

Bud Abbott, Lou Costello, Mari Blanchard, Robert Paige, Martha Hyer

Abbott and Costello in Hollywood*
US 1945 85m bw
MGM (Martin Gosch)

Two agents have hectic adventures in a film studio.
Tolerable star romp on one of their biggest budgets, climaxing in a roller coaster ride.

w Nat Perrin, Lou Breslow *d* S. Sylvan Simon *ph* Charles Schoenbaum

Bud Abbott, Lou Costello, Francis Rafferty, Warner Anderson, Robert Z. Leonard

Abbott and Costello in the Foreign Legion
US 1950 80m bw
U-I (Robert Arthur)

Incompetent legionaires become heroes to the fury of their sergeant.
Dull star vehicle on ramshackle sets, with no memorable routines.

w John Grant, Leonard Stern, Martin Ragaway *d* Charles Lamont *ph* George Robinson *m* Joseph Gershenson

Bud Abbott, Lou Costello, Patricia Medina, Walter Slezak, Douglass Dumbrille

Abbott and Costello Lost in Alaska
US 1952 76m bw
U-I (Howard Christie)

Two San Francisco firemen take a melancholy prospector back to Alaska to find a gold mine.
Sub-standard comedy vehicle with poor production.

w Martin Ragaway, Leonard Stern *d* Jean Yarbrough *ph* George Robinson *m* Joseph Gershenson

Bud Abbott, Lou Costello, *Tom Ewell*, Mitzi Green, Bruce Cabot

Abbott and Costello Meet Captain Kidd*
US 1952 70m Supercinecolor
Warner / Woodley (Alex Gottlieb)

Two servants have a treasure map, and a fearsome pirate wants it.
Crude knockabout: the stars are way below their best, and a famous actor is embarrassed.

w Howard Dimsdale, John Grant *d* Charles Lamont
ph Stanley Cortez *m* Raoul Kraushaar

Bud Abbott, Lou Costello, Charles Laughton, Hillary Brooke, Leif Erickson

Abbott and Costello Meet Dr Jekyll and Mr Hyde*
US 1953 77m bw
U-I (Howard Christie)

In Victorian London, two rookie policemen catch a monster.
Quite a lively spoof with some well-paced comedy sequences.

w John Grant, Lee Loeb *d* Charles Lamont *ph* George Robinson *m* Joseph Gershenson

Bud Abbott, Lou Costello, Boris Karloff, Reginald Denny, Craig Stevens, Helen Westcott, John Dierkes
'Gracious Boris Karloff is superior to his surroundings.'—*MFB*. (Though it is doubtful whether he ever got behind the Hyde make-up.)
† In Britain, the film was given an 'X' certificate, though it later played on children's television.

Abbott and Costello Meet Frankenstein**
US 1948 83m bw
U-I (Robert Arthur)
GB title: *Abbott and Costello Meet the Ghosts*

Two railway porters deliver crates containing the Frankenstein monster, Dracula, and the Wolf Man.
Fairly lively spoof which put an end to Universal's monsters for a while. Good typical sequences for the stars, a few thrills, and some good lines. (Dracula to Costello, lovingly: 'What we need is young blood . . . and brains . . .')

w Robert Lees, Frederic I. Rinaldo, John Grant *d* Charles Barton *ph* Charles van Enger *m* Frank Skinner

Bud Abbott, Lou Costello, Bela Lugosi, Lon Chaney Jnr, Glenn Strange, Lenore Aubert, Jane Randolph
† Probably the Abbott and Costello film which survives best.

Abbott and Costello Meet the Invisible Man*
US 1951 82m bw
U-I (Howard Christie)

A boxer accused of murder makes himself invisible while two detectives clear him.
Quite a bright comedy with good trick effects.

w Robert Lees, Frederic I. Rinaldo, John Grant *d* Charles Lamont *ph* George Robinson *m* Joseph Gershenson

Bud Abbott, Lou Costello, Arthur Franz, Nancy Guild, Adele Jergens, Sheldon Leonard

Abbott and Costello Meet the Keystone Kops*
US 1954 79m bw
U-I (Howard Christie)

In pioneer film days, two incompetents are sold a dud studio by a con man, but succeed as stunt men.
Flabby comedy which never seems to get going until the chase finale; notable chiefly for a guest appearance by Mack Sennett.

w John Grant *d* Charles Lamont *ph* Reggie Lanning *m* Joseph Gershenson

Bud Abbott, Lou Costello, Lynn Bari, Fred Clark, Frank Wilcox, Maxie Rosebloom

Abbott and Costello Meet the Killer, Boris Karloff*
US 1948 84m bw
U-I (Robert Arthur)

Two bellboys help to solve mysterious murders in a remote hotel.
This clumsily titled comedy really does not work until the last sequence in a cavern. Boris Karloff is not the killer and appears very little.

w Hugh Wedlock Jnr, Howard Snyder, John Grant *d* Charles Barton *ph* Charles van Enger *m* Milton Schwarzwald

Bud Abbott, Lou Costello, Boris Karloff, Gar Moore, Lenore Aubert, Alan Mowbray

Abbott and Costello Meet the Mummy*
US 1955 77m bw
U-I (Howard Christie)

A missing medallion leads to a lost tomb and a living mummy.
The comedians show their age in this one, but there is some typical if predictable humour and a thrill or two.

w John Grant *d* Charles Lamont *ph* George Robinson *m* Joseph Gershenson

Bud Abbott, Lou Costello, Kurt Katch, Marie Windsor, Michael Ansara, Dan Seymour

The Abdication
GB 1974 102m Technicolor
Warner (Robert Fryer, James Cresson)

17th-century Queen Christina of Sweden journeys to Rome to embrace the Catholic church and falls in love with a cardinal.
Sombre historical fantasia, more irritating than interesting.

w Ruth Wolff from her play *d* Anthony Harvey *ph* Geoffrey Unsworth *m* Nino Rota

Liv Ullman, Peter Finch, Cyril Cusack, Paul Rogers, Graham Crowden, Michael Dunn, Lewis Fiander, Harold Goldblatt

'Dainty debauchery and titillating tease straight from twenties women's pulp magazines.'—*Variety*

The Abduction of St Anne*
US 1975 74m colour TVM
Quinn Martin

A private eye is asked by a bishop to investigate the reported sainthood of a gangster's daughter. This is called having it all ways. Oddly, the mixture works well enough in the revered Hollywood manner.

w Edward Hume, *novel* The Issue of the Bishop's Blood by Thomas Patrick McMahon *d* Harry Falk

Robert Wagner, E. G. Marshall, Lloyd Nolan, William Windom, Kathleen Quinlan, James Gregory

The Abductors*
US 1957 80m bw Regalscope
TCF / Regal (Ray Wander)

Around 1870, criminals steal Lincoln's body as ransom to effect a convict's release.
Interesting minor melodrama, but not sufficiently well made.

w Ray Wander *d* Andrew V. McLaglen *ph* Joseph La Shelle

Victor McLaglen, Gavin Muir, George Macready

Abdul the Damned**
GB 1935 111m bw
BIP / Capitol (Max Schach)

In 1900 Turkey, an opera star gives herself to a villainous sultan to protect her fiancé.
Thoroughgoing hokum, well produced, which pleased a lot of people at the time.

w Ashley Dukes, Warren Chetham Strode, Roger Burford *d* Karl Grune

Fritz Kortner, Adrienne Ames, Nils Asther, John Stuart, Esme Percy, Walter Rilla, Patric Knowles, Eric Portman

Abdulla the Great
GB / Egypt 1954 103m Technicolor
(Gregory Ratoff)

A pleasure-loving European potentate sets his sights on an English girl.
Feeble satire on King Farouk, inept and relentlessly boring.

w George St George, Boris Ingster *d* Gregory Ratoff *ph* Lee Garmes

Gregory Ratoff, Kay Kendall, Sydney Chaplin

Abe Lincoln in Illinois**
US 1939 110m bw
RKO (Max Gordon)
GB title: *Spirit of the People*

Episodes in the political and domestic life of Abraham Lincoln.
Pleasant, muted, careful film based on a Broadway success: generally informative and interesting.

w Grover Jones, *play* Robert E. Sherwood *d* John Cromwell *ph James Wong Howe* *m* Roy Webb

Raymond Massey, Ruth Gordon, Gene Lockhart, Mary Howard, Dorothy Tree, Minor Watson, Howard da Silva

Abie's Irish Rose
US 1946 96m bw
(UA) Bing Crosby Productions

Flat filming of the twenties Broadway play about Irish girl marrying Jewish boy, leading to a clash of families.

w Anne Nichols, from her play *d* Edward A. Sutherland *ph* William Mellor *m* John Scott Trotter

Joanne Dru, Richard Norris, Michael Chekhov, Eric Blore, Art Baker

† There had been a silent version in 1928, and the plot was borrowed, to say the least, for the 1972 TV series *Bridget Loves Bernie.*

The Abominable Dr Phibes**
GB 1971 94m Movielab
AIP (Louis M. Heyward, Ron Dunas)

A disfigured musical genius devises a series of horrible murders, based on the ten curses of Pharaoh, for the surgeons who failed to save his wife.
Brisk but uninspired treatment of a promising theme, with more unintended nastiness than intended laughs. Some good moments and interesting low-budget thirties sets.

w James Whiton, William Goldstein *d* Robert Fuest *ph* Norman Warwick *m* Basil Kirchen, Jack Nathan *pd* Brian Eatwell

Vincent Price, Joseph Cotten, Hugh Griffith,

Terry-Thomas, Peter Jeffrey, Virginia North, Aubrey Woods
† Sequel: *Dr Phibes Rises Again* (1973).

The Abominable Snowman*
GB 1957 91m bw Hammerscope
Hammer / Clarion (Aubrey Baring)

Himalayan explorers are attacked one by one by the Yeti and their own fear.
A thin horror film with intelligent scripting: more philosophizing and characterization than suspense. The briefly glimpsed Yeti are disappointing creations.

w Nigel Kneale, from his TV play *d* Val Guest *ph* Arthur Grant *m* John Hollingsworth

Peter Cushing, Forrest Tucker, Maureen Connell, Richard Wattis, Robert Brown, *Arnold Marle*

About Face
US 1952 96m Technicolor
Warner (William Jacobs)

Moronic remake of *Brother Rat* (qv), shorn of all wit, pace and style.

w Peter Milne *d* Roy del Ruth *ph* Bert Glennon *songs* Charles Tobias, Peter de Rose

Eddie Bracken, Gordon Macrae, Dick Wesson, Virginia Gibson, Phyllis Kirk, Joel Grey

About Mrs Leslie*
US 1954 104m bw
Paramount (Hal B. Wallis)

An ageing nightclub singer has a platonic affair with a mysterious wealthy man, who leaves her enough money to buy a boarding house.
Odd, likeable romantic drama tailored for an unusual star; but its plot is too thin and its direction too drab for real success.

w Ketti Frings, Hal Kanter *d* Daniel Mann *ph* Ernest Laszlo *m* Victor Young

Shirley Booth, Robert Ryan, Alex Nicol, Marjie Miller, Eilene Janssen

'This quiet and curious film has an unexpectedly gentle, civilized flavour.'—*Gavin Lambert*

'It's all sunny disposition and sweet sadness for Miss Booth.'—*Judith Crist*

'One is reminded alternately of Chekhov and of *Back Street*.'—*Sight and Sound*

Above and Beyond*
US 1952 122m bw
MGM (Melvin Frank, Norman Panama)

The training of Colonel Paul Tibbetts, who dropped the first atomic bomb on Japan.
Overstretched flagwaver with laborious domestic interludes. Of little real interest then or now.

w Melvin Frank, Norman Panama, Beirne Lay Jnr *d* Melvin Frank, Norman Panama *ph* Ray June *m* Hugo Friedhofer

Robert Taylor, Eleanor Parker, James Whitmore, Larry Keating, Larry Gates

Above Suspicion*
US 1943 91m bw
MGM (Victor Saville)

Just before World War II, an Oxford professor on a continental honeymoon is asked to track down a missing agent.
Patchy, studio-bound spy comedy-drama with a couple of good sequences. Notable also for Mr MacMurray's impersonation of a professor who hails a Nazi as 'Hiya, dope!'

w Keith Winter, Melville Baker, Patricia Coleman, *novel* Helen MacInnes *d* Richard Thorpe *ph* Robert Planck *m* Bronislau Kaper

Fred MacMurray, Joan Crawford, Conrad Veidt, *Basil Rathbone*, Reginald Owen, Felix Bressart, Richard Ainley

Above Us the Waves*
GB 1955 99m bw
(Rank) London Independent Producers (William Macquitty)

In World War II, midget submarines attack a German battleship in a Norwegian fjord.
Archetypal stiff-upper-lip war drama with good action sequences.

w Robin Estridge *d* Ralph Thomas *ph* Ernest Steward *m* Arthur Benjamin

John Mills, John Gregson, Donald Sinden, James Robertson Justice, Michael Medwin, Lee Patterson, Lyndon Brook

Abraham Lincoln**
US 1930 97m bw
UA / D. W. Griffith

An account of Lincoln's entry into politics and his years of power.
Rather boring even at the time, this straightforward biopic has the virtues of sincerity and comparative fidelity to the facts.

w Stephen Vincent Benet, Gerrit Lord *d D. W. Griffith* *ph* Karl Struss *m* none *pd* William Cameron Menzies

Walter Huston, Una Merkel, Edgar Dearing, Russell Simpson, Henry B. Walthall

Abroad with Two Yanks*
US 1944 80m bw
Edward Small

Adventures around the Pacific with two woman-chasing sailors.
This simple-minded farce with its punny title was a great success in its day, and still generates a laugh or two.

w Charles Rogers, Wilkie Maholey, Fred Redsills *d* Allan Dwan *ph* Charles Lawton *m* Lud Gluskin

Dennis O'Keefe, William Bendix, Helen Walker, John Abbott, John Loder

The Absent-Minded Professor*
US 1960 97m bw
Walt Disney (Bill Walsh)

A lighter-than-air substance called flubber enables its inventor to drive his Model-T through the sky and catch some spies.
Foolishly engaging fantasy comedy with goodish trick effects.

w Bill Walsh *d* Robert Stevenson *ph* Edward Colman *m* George Bruns *sp* Robert A. Mattey, Peter Ellenshaw, Eustace Lycett

Fred MacMurray, Tommy Kirk, Keenan Wynn, Nancy Olson, Leon Ames, Ed Wynn, Edward Andrews
† Sequel: *Son of Flubber* (1964).

Accent on Youth*
US 1935 77m bw
Paramount (Douglas Maclean)

A secretary falls in love with her middle-aged playwright employer.
Reasonably sparkling comedy from a popular play, later remade as *Mr Music* and *But Not for Me*.

w Herbert Fields, Claude Binyon, *play* Samson Raphaelson *d* Wesley Ruggles *ph* Leon Shamroy

Herbert Marshall, Sylvia Sidney, Philip Reed, Astrid Allwyn, Holmes Herbert

Accident**
GB 1967 105m Eastmancolor
London Independent Producers (Joseph Losey, Norman Priggen)

An Oxford undergraduate is killed in a car crash; his tutor looks back over the tangle of personal relationships that contributed to his death.
Ascetic drama in which the audience is too often left to observe at length and draw its own conclusions; good characterizations nevertheless.

w Harold Pinter, *novel* Nicholas Mosley *d* Joseph Losey *ph* Gerry Fisher *m* Johnny Dankworth

Dirk Bogarde, Stanley Baker, Jacqueline Sassard, Vivien Merchant, Michael York

'The whole thing is such a teapot tempest, and it is so assiduously underplayed that it is neither strong drama nor stinging satire. It is just a sad little story of a wistful don.'—*Bosley Crowther*

'Everything is calm, unruffled, lacquered in a veneer of civilization, yet underneath it all, one gradually begins to realize, the characters are tearing each other emotionally to shreds.'—*Monthly Film Bulletin, 1973*

The Accused*
US 1948 101m bw
Paramount (Hal B. Wallis)

In self-defence a lady professor kills a student who has sexually attacked her.
Dullish suspenser with the outcome never in doubt, though the production values are beyond reproach.

w Ketti Frings *d* William Dieterle *ph* Milton Krasner *m* Victor Young

Loretta Young, Robert Cummings, Wendell Corey, Sam Jaffe, Douglas Dick

Ace Eli and Rodger of the Skies
US 1973 92m De Luxe Panavision
TCF (Robert Fryer, James Cresson)

Adventures of a father-and-son aerial barnstorming act after World War I.
Poorly written melodrama, very tame apart from the flying shots.

w Claudia Salter, *story* Steven Spielberg *d* John Erman *ph* David M. Walsh, Bill Birch, Don Morgan *m* Jerry Goldsmith

Cliff Robertson, Pamela Franklin, Eric Shea, Rosemary Murphy, Bernadette Peters, Alice Ghostley

'A tediously inane flop. Nostalgia isn't what it used to be.'—*Variety*

Ace in the Hole****
US 1951 111m bw
Paramount (Billy Wilder)

In order to prolong the sensation and boost newspaper sales, a self-seeking journalist delays the rescue of a man trapped in a cave.
An incisive, compelling melodrama taking a sour look at the American scene; one of its director's masterworks.

w Billy Wilder, Lesser Samuels, Walter Newman *d* *Billy Wilder* *ph* Charles B. Lang Jnr *m* Hugo Friedhofer

Kirk Douglas, Jan Sterling, Porter Hall, Bob Arthur, Frank Cady, Ray Teal

'Few of the opportunities for irony, cruelty and horror are missed.'—*Gavin Lambert*

'Style and purpose achieve for the most part a fusion even more remarkable than in *Sunset Boulevard*.'—*Penelope Houston*

† Alternative title intended to draw the crowds: *The Big Carnival.*

Aces High*

GB 1976 114m Technicolor

EMI / S. Benjamin Fisz / Jacques Roitfeld

In the air force during World War I, young pilots are needlessly sacrificed.

Spirited if rather unnecessary remake of *Journey's End* transposed to the air war, which makes it almost identical to *The Dawn Patrol.*

w Howard Barker *d* Jack Gold *ph* Gerry Fisher, Peter Allwork *m* Richard Hartley

Malcolm McDowell, Christopher Plummer, Simon Ward, Peter Firth, John Gielgud, Trevor Howard, Richard Johnson, Ray Milland

Across 110th Street*

US 1972 102m De Luxe

UA / Film Guarantors (Fouad Said, Ralph Serpe)

A tough New York cop loses his own life tracking down three Harlem criminals who have robbed the Mafia.

Brutish, noisy, incoherent police melodrama, with fashionable sadism and predictable performances. Good location work, though.

w Luther Davis, *novel* Wally Ferris *d* Barry Shear *ph* Jack Priestley *m* J. J. Johnson

Anthony Quinn, Anthony Franciosa, Yaphet Kotto, Paul Benjamin, Ed Bernard

'Not for the squeamish . . . a virtual blood bath, leaving no relief from depression and oppression.'—*Variety*

Across the Bridge*

GB 1957 103m bw

Rank / IPF (John Stafford)

A fugitive financier kills his pursuer, finds he was a murderer, and tries to hide out across the Mexican border.

This star *tour de force* is unconvincing in detail and rather unattractive to watch (British films never could cope with American settings), but the early sequences have suspense.

w Guy Elmes, Denis Freeman, *novel* Graham Greene *d* Ken Annakin *ph* Reg Wyer *m* James Bernard

Rod Steiger, David Knight, Marla Landi, Noel Willman, Bernard Lee

Across the Pacific***

US 1942 99m bw

Warner (Hal. B. Wallis)

Just before Pearl Harbor, an army officer is cashiered by arrangement in order to contact pro-Japanese sympathizers.

Hasty, easy-going and very enjoyable hokum, partly ship-set and successfully reteaming three stars of *The Maltese Falcon.*

w Richard Macauley, *serial* Aloha Means Goodbye by Robert Carson *d* John Huston *ph* Arthur Edeson *m* Adolph Deutsch

Humphrey Bogart, Mary Astor, Sydney Greenstreet, Sen Yung, Richard Loo, Monte Blue

'A spy picture which tingles with fearful uncertainties and glints with the sheen of blue steel.'—*Bosley Crowther*

Across the Wide Missouri*

US 1951 77m Technicolor

MGM (Robert Sisk)

In the 1820s, a trapper marries an Indian girl and lives with her people.

Promising credits produce an unsatisfactory western: despite honest efforts, the elements do not jell into a convincing whole.

w Talbot Jennings *d* William Wellman *ph* William C. Mellor *m* David Raksin

Clark Gable, Ricardo Montalban, John Hodiak, Adolphe Menjou, Maria Elena Marques, J. Carrol Naish, Jack Holt, Alan Napier

Act of Love*

US 1954 104m bw

UA / Benagoss (Anatole Litvak)

In Paris in 1944, an American with the liberation army falls in love with a French girl, who commits suicide when he is posted and cannot make their rendezvous.

Cheerless romantic drama, rather thin and unmemorable despite the efforts of all concerned.

w Irwin Shaw, *novel* The Girl on the Via Flaminia by Alfred Hayes *d* Anatole Litvak *ph* Armand Thirard *m* Michael Emer, Joe Hajos *pd* Alexander Trauner

Kirk Douglas, Dany Robin, Barbara Laage, Robert Strauss, Gabrielle Dorziat, Gregoire Aslan, Fernand Ledoux, Serge Reggiani, Brigitte Bardot

† Made in France, an early Hollywood foreign location film.

An Act of Murder**
US 1948 90m bw
U-I (Jerry Bresler)
aka: *Live Today for Tomorrow*

A judge insists on being tried for the mercy killing of his incurably ill wife.
Earnest social drama which despite excellent acting can only reach an inconclusive ending.

w Michael Blankfort, Ernest Thoeren, *novel* The Mills of God by Ernst Lothar *d* Michael Gordon *ph* Hal Mohr *m* Daniele Amfitheatrof

Fredric March, Florence Eldridge, Edmond O'Brien, Geraldine Brooks

Act of Murder**
GB 1964 62m bw
Merton Park (Jack Greenwood)

A couple arrange a holiday by swapping houses with strangers, and a complex plot ensues.
Slick, superior example of the Edgar Wallace second feature series.

w Lewis Davidson *d Alan Bridges* *ph* James Wilson *m* Bernard Ebbinghouse

John Carson, Anthony Bate, Justine Lord, Duncan Lewis, Dandy Nichols

'This uncommonly intelligent little thriller is just the sort of film which is likely to arouse critical sneers for reaching too high on a low budget.'—*Tom Milne*

Act of Violence**
US 1948 82m bw
MGM (William Wright)

After the war, an ex-GI tracks down a prison camp informer.
Moody, glossy melodrama with tension well sustained, though the sentimental ending is a cop-out.

w Robert I. Richards, *story* Collier Young *d Fred Zinnemann* *ph Robert Surtees* *m* Bronislau Kaper

Van Heflin, *Robert Ryan*, Janet Leigh, Mary Astor

'Strong characterization, fine direction and good photography combine to put this film high among its kind.'—*MFB*

'An effortless narrative control and a real power to maintain tension.'—*Richard Winnington*

Act One*
US 1963 110m bw
Warner (Dore Schary)

Poor Brooklyn boy Moss Hart rises to Broadway eminence via his writing partnership with George S. Kaufman.
Incredibly stilted film version of an excellent autobiography, notable only for fragments of acting and the fact that a film so totally uncommercial was made at all.

wd Dore Schary *ph* Arthur J. Ornitz *m* Skitch Henderson

George Hamilton (Hart), Jason Robards Jnr (Kaufman), Jack Klugman, Sam Levene, George Segal, Ruth Ford, Eli Wallach

'From the moment young Hart takes pencil in hand, we have nowhere to go except to that happy ending; and despite all the painstaking detail, we don't believe a word of it.'—*Judith Crist*

Action for Slander*
GB 1937 83m bw
London Films / Saville (Victor Saville)

A bankrupt officer, accused of cheating at cards, defends his honour with a writ.
Lively melodrama of the old school.

w Ian Dalrymple, Miles Malleson, *novel* Mary Borden *d* Tim Whelan

Clive Brook, Ann Todd, Margaretta Scott, Arthur Margetson, Ronald Squire, Athole Stewart, Percy Marmont, Frank Cellier, Morton Selten

Action in the North Atlantic*
US 1943 127m bw
Warner (Jerry Wald)

An American convoy bound for Russia comes under U-boat attack.
Efficient propaganda potboiler; studio bound, but still works as a war actioner.

w John Howard Lawson *d* Lloyd Bacon *ph* Ted McCord *m* Adolph Deutsch

Humphrey Bogart, Raymond Massey, Alan Hale, Julie Bishop, Ruth Gordon, Sam Levene, Dane Clark

'The production has interludes of tremendous power. What is lacking is dramatic cohesion.'—*Howard Barnes*

'Directly in line of descent from *The Perils of Pauline*.'—*Time*

Action of the Tiger
GB 1957 93m Technicolor
Cinemascope
MGM / Claridge (Kenneth Harper)

An adventurer helps a French girl to rescue her brother from political imprisonment in Albania.
Dull and poorly constructed action melodrama.

w Robert Carson *d* Terence Young *ph* Desmond Dickinson *m* Humphrey Searle

Van Johnson, Martine Carol, Herbert Lom, Gustavo Rocco, Anthony Dawson, Helen Haye, Sean Connery

Actors and Sin*
US 1952 91m bw
(UA) Sid Kuller (Ben Hecht)

Two short stories. When an unsuccessful actress commits suicide, her father makes it look like murder so that for once she shall get attention. The authoress of a romantic script bought by Hollywood is discovered to be a horrid little 9-year-old.
Interesting but incompetent compendium which descends almost to the home movie level and leaves the actors struggling.

wd Ben Hecht *ph* Lee Garmes *m* George Antheil

Edward G. Robinson, Marsha Hunt, Dan O'Herlihy, Rudolph Anders, Eddie Albert, Alan Reed, Jenny Hecht

'A depressing double bill.'—*Lindsay Anderson*

The Actress
US 1953 91m bw
MGM (Lawrence Weingarten)

Ruth Jones becomes an actress against the wishes of her stubborn seafaring father.
Episodes from Ruth Gordon's early life, based on her Broadway play *Years Ago*, make a pleasant though scarcely engrossing film: it is all a shade too discreet and wanly winning, and the few key events take place offscreen.

w Ruth Gordon *d* George Cukor *ph* Harold Rosson *m* Bronislau Kaper *ad* Cedric Gibbons, Arthur Lonergan

Jean Simmons, Spencer Tracy, Teresa Wright, Anthony Perkins, Ian Wolfe, Mary Wickes

Ada*
US 1961 109m Metrocolor Cinemascope
MGM / Avon / Chalmar (Lawrence Weingarten)

A political candidate marries a call girl who becomes his strong right arm and weathers a threat to reveal her past.
Indecisive romantic drama which pulls too many punches but has interesting background detail.

w Arthur Sheekman, William Driskill, *novel* Ada Dallas by Wirt Williams *d* Daniel Mann *ph* Joseph Ruttenberg *m* Bronislau Kaper

Susan Hayward, Dean Martin, Wilfrid Hyde White, Ralph Meeker, Martin Balsam

'A bonanza for connoisseurs of perfectly awful movies.'—*Judith Crist*

Adam and Evelyne
GB 1949 92m bw
Rank / Two Cities (Harold French)

A society playboy adopts his dead friend's daughter, and falls in love with her.
Undernourished romantic drama, a mild variation on *Daddy Longlegs*.

w Noel Langley, Lesley Storm, George Barraud, Nicholas Phipps *d* Harold French *ph* Guy Green *m* Mischa Spoliansky

Stewart Granger, Jean Simmons, Helen Cherry, Edwin Styles, Beatrice Varley, Wilfrid Hyde White

Adam Had Four Sons*
US 1941 81m bw
Columbia (Robert Sherwood)

A widower's family is cared for by a governess.
Modest magazine fiction which established Ingrid Bergman as an American star.

w Michael Blankfort, William Hurlbut, *novel* Legacy by Charles Bonner *d* Gregory Ratoff *ph* Peverell Marley *m* W. Franke Harling

Warner Baxter, *Ingrid Bergman*, Susan Hayward, Richard Denning, Fay Wray

Adam's Rib***
US 1949 101m bw
MGM (Lawrence Weingarten)

Husband and wife lawyers are on opposite sides of an attempted murder case.
A superior star vehicle which also managed to introduce four promising personalities; slangily written and smartly directed, but perhaps a shade less funny than it once seemed.

w Ruth Gordon, Garson Kanin d George Cukor ph George J. Folsey *m* Miklos Rozsa

Spencer Tracy, Katharine Hepburn, David Wayne, Tom Ewell, Judy Holliday, Jean Hagen, Hope Emerson, Clarence Kolb
† A 1972 TV series of the same title provided a boring imitation, with Ken Howard and Blythe Danner.

The Adding Machine*
GB 1968 99m Technicolor
Universal / Associated London (Jerome Epstein)

Downtrodden clerk Mr Zero rebels against society by murdering his boss. Tried and executed, he spends thirty years in heaven before

being 'laundered' and sent back to start again as another nonentity.
Elmer Rice's satirical fantasy of the twenties is here robbed of its expressionist staging and presented naturalistically, a fatal error from which the film never for one moment recovers.

wd Jerome Epstein *ph* Walter Lassally *m* Mike Leander, Lambert Williamson

Phyllis Diller, Milo O'Shea, Billie Whitelaw, Sydney Chaplin, Julian Glover, Raymond Huntley, Phil Brown, Libby Morris

Address Unknown*
US 1944 72m bw
Columbia (William Cameron Menzies)

A German-American becomes a Nazi and is incriminated by false letters from his one-time friend.
Reasonably engrossing, cheaply-made adaptation of a slim little thriller which was widely read during World War II.

w Kressman Taylor, Herbert Dalmass, *novel* Kressman Taylor *d* William Cameron Menzies *ph* Rudolf Maté *m* Ernst Toch

Paul Lukas, Peter Van Eyck, Mady Christians, Emory Parnel

The Admirable Crichton*
GB 1957 93m Technicolor Vistavision
Columbia / Modern Screenplays (Ian Dalrymple)
US title: *Paradise Lagoon*

Lord Loam and his family are shipwrecked on a desert island, where his manservant proves the undisputed leader.
Few laughs are to be had from this blunt, sentimental version of a famous play, but the photography and decor are excellent.

w Vernon Harris, *play* J. M. Barrie *d* Lewis Gilbert *ph* Wilkie Cooper *m* Richard Addinsell *ad* William Kellner *costumes* Bernard Nevill *devices* Emmett

Kenneth More, Cecil Parker, Sally Ann Howes, Diane Cilento, Martita Hunt, Jack Watling, Peter Graves, Gerald Harper

'Barrie's play now seems more remote than Gammer Gurton.'—*David Robinson*

Adolf Hitler—My Part in His Downfall*
GB 1972 102m Technicolor
UA / Norcon (Gregory Smith, Norman Cohen)

Episodes in the life of a conscript at the beginning of World War II.
Lumbering anarchic comedy based on Spike Milligan's own sidesplitting memoirs; an enfeebled British *M*A*S*H*.

w Johnny Byrne *d* Norman Cohen *ph* Terry Maher *m* Wilfred Burns

Jim Dale, Spike Milligan (as his own father), Arthur Lowe, Bill Maynard, Windsor Davies, Pat Coombs, Tony Selby, Geoffrey Hughes

'A convincing period shabbiness and sleaziness which are endearing when they're not being overstated.'—*MFB*

Advance to the Rear*
US 1964 97m bw Panavision
MGM / Ted Richmond
GB title: *Company of Cowards?*

After the Civil War, a troop of misfits is sent west out of harm's way, but manages to capture a rebel spy and save a gold shipment.
Semi-satirical western action comedy with a farcical climax; quite sharply made.

w Samuel A. Peeples, William Bowers *d* George Marshall *ph* Milton Krasner *m* Randy Sparks

Glenn Ford, *Melvyn Douglas,* Stella Stevens, Jim Backus, Joan Blondell, Andrew Prine, Alan Hale, James Griffith, Preston Foster

Adventure*
US 1945 126m bw
MGM (Sam Zimbalist)

A roughneck sailor marries a librarian, but only settles down to love her when their child is born.
Uniquely embarrassing (and fascinating) mishmash of pretentious dialogue and cardboard characters. 'Gable's back and Garson's got him!' squealed the posters, but the stars would have done better not to meet.

w Frederick Hazlitt Brennan, Vincent Lawrence, *novel* Clyde Brion Davis *d* Victor Fleming *ph* Joseph Ruttenberg *m* Herbert Stothart

Clark Gable, Greer Garson, Thomas Mitchell, Joan Blondell, John Qualen, Richard Haydn

'MGM proudly announce *Adventure* as the meeting of a red-blooded man with a blue-blooded woman. Its impact on the bloodstream of your critic was a chilling one. Fifty years of the cinema, he thought, and this is where we've landed.'—*Richard Winnington*

Adventure in Baltimore
US 1949 89m bw
RKO (Richard H. Berger)
GB title: *Bachelor Bait*

In 1905, a young society girl becomes a suffragette.
Inconsequential period comedy which did nothing for its young star's fading career.

w Lionel Houser, *story* Christopher Isherwood,

Lesser Samuels *d* Richard Wallace *ph* Robert de Grasse *m* Constantin Bakaleinikoff

Shirley Temple, Robert Young, John Agar, Albert Sharpe, Josephine Hutchinson, Johnny Sands, John Miljan, Norma Varden

Adventure in Diamonds
US 1940 76m bw
Paramount (George Fitzmaurice)

A British adventurer in South Africa falls in love with a lady diamond thief.
Acceptable romantic comedy-drama.

w Leonard Lee, Franz Schultz *d* George Fitzmaurice *ph* Charles Lang

George Brent, Isa Miranda, John Loder, Nigel Bruce, Elizabeth Patterson, Matthew Boulton, Cecil Kellaway, Ernest Truex, E. E. Clive

The Adventure of Sherlock Holmes' Smarter Brother
GB 1975 91m De Luxe
TCF / Jouer (Richard A. Roth)

More by good luck than good management, Sherlock's younger brother solves one of his cases.
Infuriating parody with little sense of the original and a hit-or-miss style all of its own. Amusing moments fail to atone for the general waste of opportunity.

wd Gene Wilder *ph* Gerry Fisher *m* John Morris *pd* Terry Marsh

Gene Wilder, Marty Feldman, Madeleine Kahn, Leo McKern, Dom De Luise, Roy Kinnear, John Le Mesurier, Douglas Wilmer, Thorley Walters

'Like a compilation of the kind of numbers actors like to do at parties.'—*Howard Kissel*

'He has bitten off more than he can chew or I can swallow.'—*John Simon*

The Adventurers
GB 1950 86m bw
Rank / Mayflower (Maxwell Setton, Aubrey Baring)
US title: *The Great Adventure*

In 1902, two Boers and a cashiered English officer set out to recover stolen diamonds.
Lethargic South African western in the wake of *Treasure of the Sierra Madre*; clumsy and unconvincing, with cardboard characters.

w Robert Westerby *d* David MacDonald *ph* Oswald Morris *m* Cedric Thorpe Davie

Dennis Price, Jack Hawkins, Siobhan McKenna, Peter Hammond, Bernard Lee, Grégoire Aslan

The Adventurers*
US 1970 170m Technicolor Panavision
Paramount / Avco Embassy / Adventurers Film (Lewis Gilbert)

A sensualist brought up amid Europe's luxuries returns to his Central American homeland to take vengeance on the brutal security chief who raped and murdered his mother.
Sprawling, sexy, bloodstained extravaganza from a Harold Robbins novel. Expensive to look at and riddled with sensation, but that's about all.

w Michael Hastings, Lewis Gilbert *d* Lewis Gilbert *ph* Claude Renoir *m* Antonio Carlos Jobim *pd* Tony Masters

Bekim Fehmiu, Alan Badel, Candice Bergen, Ernest Borgnine, Olivia de Havilland, Rossano Brazzi, Charles Aznavour, Sidney Tafler, Fernando Rey, Leigh Taylor-Young, Thommy Berggren, John Ireland

'A three-hour slog through every imaginable cliché of writing and direction . . . in addition to an abundance of flaccid sex and violence, it offers drugs, sadism, orchids, fireworks, orgies, lesbianism, a miscarriage, a private torture chamber, and the hell of several fashion shows with loud pop music accompaniment. This might well be described as the film with everything; trouble is, it is difficult to imagine anybody wanting any of it.'—*MFB*

'Lovers of rotten movies and close-up violence can revel in it.'—*Judith Crist*

Adventures of a Young Man*
US 1962 145m De Luxe Cinemascope
TCF (Jerry Wald)
GB title: *Hemingway's Adventures of a Young Man*

Young Nick Adams leaves Michigan for various Hemingwayesque adventures around the world.
A curious composite of stories and autobiography by Ernest Hemingway, too patchy to maintain interest but with good moments along the way.

w A. E. Hotchner *d* Martin Ritt *ph* Lee Garmes *m* Franz Waxman

Richard Beymer, Diane Baker, Corinne Calvet, Fred Clark, Dan Dailey, James Dunn, Juano Hernandez, Arthur Kennedy, Ricardo Montalban, Susan Strasberg, Paul Newman, Jessica Tandy, Eli Wallach, Tullio Carminati, Michael Pollard

'Obviously designed as a tribute to the Great Man of American Letters, this film offends in its inability to be faithful to the quality of its finest moments.'—*MFB*

The Adventures of Barry Mackenzie*
Australia 1972 114m Eastmancolor
Columbia / Longford (Philip Adams)

A sex-hungry Australian gets into all kinds of trouble on a visit to the Old Country.
Occasionally funny, defiantly crude and tasteless, but poorly produced comedy-misadventure from the *Private Eye* comic strip. Australian slang combines with bad sound recording to make much of the film unintelligible.

w Barry Humphries, Bruce Beresford *d* Bruce Beresford *ph* Don McAlpine *m* Peter Best

Barry Crocker, Barry Humphries (as Aunt Edna Everage), Peter Cook, Spike Milligan, Dennis Price, Avice Landon, Dick Bentley, Joan Bakewell, William Rushton

'A wildly uneven concoction of antipodean bad taste, probably only fully appreciated by Earls Court exiles.'—*Sight and Sound*

† Sequel 1974: *Barry Mackenzie Holds His Own.*

The Adventures of Bullwhip Griffin**
US 1965 110m Technicolor
Walt Disney (Bill Anderson)

In the 1849 California Gold Rush, two aristocrats and their butler head west.
Rather splendid spoof western with careful attention to detail and comedy pointing, well above the average Disney standard.

w Lowell S. Hawley, novel By the Great Horn Spoon by Sid Fleischman *d* James Neilson *ph* Edward Colman *m* George Bruns *titles Ward Kimball*

Roddy McDowall, Suzanne Pleshette, Bryan Russell, Karl Malden, Harry Guardino, Richard Haydn, Mike Mazurki, Hermione Baddeley, Cecil Kellaway

The Adventures of Captain Fabian
US 1951 100m bw
Republic / Silver (William Marshall)

A sea captain returns to New Orleans to revenge himself on the family which had defrauded his father.
Stilted, old-fashioned *Monte Cristo*ish melodrama with some curiosity value but little verve in the playing or production. An awful warning to independent producers.

w Errol Flynn, *novel* Fabulous Ann Medlock by Robert Shannon *d* William Marshall *ph* Marcel Grignon *m* René Cloerec

Errol Flynn, Micheline Presle, Agnes Moorehead, Vincent Price, Victor Francen, Jim Gerald

† Made in France.

The Adventures of Don Juan**
US 1949 110m Technicolor
Warner (Jerry Wald)
GB title: *The New Adventures of Don Juan*

A reformed 17th-century rake saves his queen from the machinations of her first minister.
Expensive, slightly uneasy, but generally very entertaining swashbuckler with elements of self-spoofery. Flynn's last big-budget extravaganza.

w George Oppenheimer, Harry Kurnitz *d* Vincent Sherman *ph* Elwood Bredell *m* Max Steiner

Errol Flynn, Viveca Lindfors, Romney Brent, Robert Douglas, Alan Hale, Ann Rutherford, Robert Warwick, Jerry Austin, Douglas Kennedy, Una O'Connor, Aubrey Mather, Raymond Burr

The Adventures of Gerard**
GB 1970 91m De Luxe Panavision
UA / Sir Nigel Films (Peter Beale)

A hussar of Napoleon becomes involved in a double spy game but comes out trumps and wins a fair lady.
A lighthearted historical spoof of military pomp, with plenty of attractive elements which unfortunately fail to jell into a satisfying film.

w H. A. L. Craig and others, from stories by Arthur Conan Doyle *d* Jerzy Skolimowski *ph* Witold Sobocinski *m* Riz Ortolani

Peter McEnery, Claudia Cardinale, Eli Wallach, Jack Hawkins, Mark Burns, Norman Rossington, John Neville

'Enormously graceful and witty . . . picks its way with amazing delicacy through the reefs of facetiousness.'—*Tom Milne*

The Adventures of Huckleberry Finn: see Huckleberry Finn

The Adventures of Hajji Baba*
US 1954 93m De Luxe Cinemascope
Allied Artists / Walter Wanger

In ancient Arabia, a barber helps and falls in love with an escaping princess.
A reasonably dashing sword and sandal romp which no one takes very seriously.

w Richard Collins *d* Don Weis *ph* Harold Lipstein *m* Dmitri Tiomkin *pd* Gene Allen

John Derek, Elaine Stewart, Thomas Gomez, Amanda Blake, Paul Picerni, Rosemarie Bowe

The Adventures of Marco Polo*
US 1938 100m bw
Samuel Goldwyn

The medieval Italian explorer discovers China, fireworks, and a beautiful maiden.
One gets the impression that this began as a standard adventure and that during production it switched to comedy; whatever the cause, lively and amusing scenes fail to add up to more than a thinly scripted pantomime.

w Robert E. Sherwood *d* Archie Mayo
ph Rudolph Maté *m* Alfred Newman
ad Richard Day

Gary Cooper, Sigrid Gurie, Basil Rathbone, Ernest Truex, Binnie Barnes, Alan Hale, George Barbier

The Adventures of Mark Twain**
US 1944 130m bw
Warner (Jesse L. Lasky)

The life of America's foremost humorous writer, from a Mississippi riverboat to his becoming an honorary fellow of Oxford University.
Conventional biopic, quite watchable and with unusual side turnings, but eventually lacking the zest of the subject.

w Harold M. Sherman, Alan le May, Harry Chandler *d* Irving Rapper *ph Sol Polito*
m Max Steiner

Fredric March, Alexis Smith, Donald Crisp, Alan Hale, C. Aubrey Smith, John Carradine, William Henry, Robert Barrat, Walter Hampden

The Adventures of Nick Carter
US 1972 73m Technicolor TVM
Universal (Stanley Kallis)
aka: *Nick Carter*

A private detective gets into colourful company when investigating the death of a friend.
Another attempt to revivify one of the longest-lasting detectives of all; plot and cast are uneasy, the nineties setting really does not help.

w Ken Pettus *d* Paul Krasny

Robert Conrad, Shelley Winters, Brooke Bundy, Dean Stockwell, Pat O'Brien, Broderick Crawford, Neville Brand, Pernell Roberts

The Adventures of Quentin Durward**
GB 1955 100m Eastmancolor
Cinemascope
MGM (Pandro S. Berman)
aka: *Quentin Durward*

The Duke of Burgundy's nephew is sent to bring back a runaway princess.
Busy, amusing simplification of Sir Walter Scott's costume novel, worth watching for the action set-pieces, the castles, and the supporting cast.

w Robert Ardrey *d* Richard Thorpe
ph Christopher Challis *m* Bronislau Kaper

Robert Taylor, Kay Kendall, Robert Morley, Alec Clunes, Duncan Lamont, Marius Goring, Wilfrid Hyde White, Ernest Thesiger, Harcourt Williams, George Cole

Adventures of the Queen
US 1975 99m colour TVM
TCF (Irwin Allen)

A mad bomber is loose on an ocean liner.
Overstretched failed pilot shot on the *Queen Mary* at Long Beach. Plot and performances make it very ho-hum.

w John Gay *d* David Lowell Rich

Robert Stack, Ralph Bellamy, David Hedison, Bradford Dillman, Sorrell Booke, Burr de Benning, John Randolph

The Adventures of Robin Hood****
US 1938 102m Technicolor
Warner (Hal B. Wallis)

Rebel outlaw Robin Hood outwits Guy of Gisbourne and the Sheriff of Nottingham, and saves the throne for the absent King Richard.
A splendid adventure story, rousingly operatic in treatment, with dashing action highlights, fine comedy balance, and incisive acting all round. Historically notable for its use of early three-colour Technicolor; also for convincingly recreating Britain in California.

w Seton I. Miller, Norman Reilly Raine *d William Keighley, Michael Curtiz* *ph Tony Gaudio, Sol Polito, Howard Green* *m Erich Wolfgang Korngold* *ad Carl Jules Weyl*

Errol Flynn, Olivia de Havilland, *Basil Rathbone, Claude Rains,* Eugene Pallette, Alan Hale, Patric Knowles, Melville Cooper, Una O'Connor, Ian Hunter, Herbert Mundin, Montagu Love

'Magnificent, unsurpassable . . . the film is lavish, brilliantly photographed, and has a great Korngold score.'—*NFT, 1974*

'Has the supreme virtue of a movie . . . it keeps moving.'–*James Shelley Hamilton*

The Adventures of Sherlock Holmes***
US 1939 83m bw
TCF (Gene Markey)
GB title: *Sherlock Holmes*

Moriarty sends Holmes on a false trail while he plots to steal the Crown jewels.

Highly engaging piece of Hollywood Victoriana, with all elements perfect except for an unconvincing plot.

w Edwin Blum, William Drake *d* Alfred Werker *ph Leon Shamroy* *m* Cyril Mockridge

Basil Rathbone, Nigel Bruce, George Zucco, Ida Lupino, Alan Marshal, E. E. Clive, Mary Gordon

† This was the second and last of Rathbone's costume outings as Holmes, and the one in which he sang a comic song in disguise.

The Adventures of Tartu*
GB 1943 103m bw
MGM (Irving Asher)
US title: *Tartu*

During World War II, a British spy goes to Czechoslovakia to dismantle a poison gas factory.
Halting and artificial comedy-thriller, saved only by a graceful star performance.

w Howard Emmett Rogers, John Lee Mahin, Miles Malleson *d* Harold S. Bucquet *ph* John J. Cox *m* Louis Levy

Robert Donat, Valerie Hobson, Walter Rilla, Glynis Johns, Martin Miller

The Adventures of Tom Sawyer***
US 1938 91m Technicolor
David O. Selznick (William H. Wright)

Small-town Mississippi boy tracks down a murderer, Injun Joe.
Set-bound but excellent version of the children's classic by Mark Twain.

w John Weaver *d* Norman Taurog *ph* James Wong Howe, Wilfrid Cline *m* Lou Forbes *ad William Cameron Menzies*

Tommy Kelly, Ann Gillis, *May Robson,* Victor Jory, Jackie Moran, Walter Brennan, Spring Byington, Margaret Hamilton, Victor Kilian

Advise and Consent**
US 1962 139m bw Panavision
Columbia / Otto Preminger

The President's choice of an unpopular secretary of state leads to divisions in the Senate and the blackmail and suicide of a senator.
Absorbing political melodrama from a novel which aimed to lift the lid off Washington. Many character actors make their mark, but the harsh-contrast photography seems misjudged.

w Wendell Mayes, *novel* Allen Drury *d* Otto Preminger *ph* Sam Leavitt *m* Jerry Fielding *titles* Saul Bass

Don Murray, *Charles Laughton,* Henry Fonda, Walter Pidgeon, Lew Ayres, Edward Andrews, Burgess Meredith, Gene Tierney, Franchot Tone, George Grizzard, Paul Ford, Peter Lawford, Inga Swenson, Will Geer

'The result is supremely ambivalent, a battle between fascinatingly real props and procedures and melodramatically unreal characters and situations.'—*Peter John Dyer*

The Affair*
US 1973 74m colour TVM
ITC / Spelling–Goldberg

Extrovert lawyer falls in love with reclusive polio victim, but it doesn't work.
Watchable modern soap opera.

w Barbara Turner *d* Gilbert Cates *ph* Jerry Hirschfeld

Natalie Wood, Robert Wagner, Bruce Davison, Kent Smith, Pat Harrington

† A theatrical version was released at 92m.

Affair in Trinidad*
US 1952 98m bw
Columbia / Beckworth (Vincent Sherman)

A nightclub singer whose husband is killed by gangsters works undercover for the police and routs the gang with the help of her husband's brother.
A tired tropical melodrama intended to follow up the success of *Gilda*, but without the verve. Some routine pleasures, though.

w Oscar Saul, James Gunn *d* Vincent Sherman *ph* Joseph Walker *m* Morris Stoloff, George Dunning

Rita Hayworth, Glenn Ford, Alexander Scourby, Torin Thatcher, Valerie Bettis, Steve Geray, Karel Stepanek, George Voskovec

'Improbable, foolish, but glossy.'—*Penelope Houston*

An Affair to Remember**
US 1957 114m Eastmancolor Cinemascope
TCF (Leo McCarey)

An ex-nightclub singer falls in love with a wealthy bachelor on a transatlantic liner, but an accident prevents her from attending their subsequent rendezvous.
Remake of *Love Affair*, a surprisingly successful mixture of smart lines, sentiment and tears, all applied with style and assurance.

w Delmer Daves, Leo McCarey *d* Leo McCarey *ph* Milton Krasner *m* Hugo Freidhofer

Cary Grant, Deborah Kerr, Cathleen Nesbitt, Richard Denning, Neva Patterson

'A lush slice of Hollywood romanticism.'—*MFB*

Affair with a Stranger*
US 1953 87m bw
RKO (Robert Sparks)

Five friends reminisce about a marriage which seems about to break up.
This would-be-smart comedy has a good idea unsatisfactorily worked out, and could have used a more sparkling cast.

w Richard Flournoy *d* Roy Rowland *ph* Harry J. Wild *m* Roy Webb

Jean Simmons, Victor Mature, Mary Jo Tarola, Monica Lewis, Jane Darwell, Nicholas Joy, Wally Vernon, Dabbs Greer

The Affairs of Annabel*
US 1938 69m bw
RKO (Lee Marcus, Lou Lusty)

A crackpot Hollywood press agent sends his star to jail as a publicity stunt.
An amusing frenetic comedy of its time, successful enough to warrant a sequel, *Annabel Takes a Tour*, in the same year.

w Bert Granet, Paul Yawitz *d* Lew Landers *ph* Russell Metty *m* Roy Webb

Lucille Ball, Jack Oakie, Ruth Donnelly, Bradley Page, Fritz Feld, Thurston Hall, Elizabeth Risdon, Granville Bates, James Burke

The Affairs of Cellini*
US 1934 90m bw
Twentieth Century (Darryl F. Zanuck)

The complex amours of a 16th-century Florentine rake.
Lively period bedroom farce somewhat hampered by censorship.

w Bess Meredyth, *play* The Firebrand by Edwin Justus Mayer *d* Gregory La Cava *ph* Charles Rosher

Fredric March, Constance Bennett, *Frank Morgan*, Fay Wray, Vince Barnett, Louis Calhern, Jessie Ralph

'Gay and entertaining though whipped up synthetically like circus ice cream.'—*Variety*

The Affairs of Susan**
US 1945 110m bw
Paramount (Hal B. Wallis)

Four men in Susan's life see her differently.
Occasionally witty comedy designed as a champagne vehicle for its star. It seemed quite good at the time.

w Richard Flournoy, Laszlo Gorog, T. Monroe *d* William A. Seiter *ph* David Abel *m* Frederick Hollander

Joan Fontaine, George Brent, Walter Abel, Don Defore, Dennis O'Keefe

'The cast enters into the irresponsibilities with gusto.'—*MFB*

Affectionately Yours
US 1941 88m bw
Warner (Mark Hellinger)

A foreign correspondent hurries home when he hears that his wife plans to divorce him.
Thin lightweight comedy, unsuitably cast.

w Edward Kaufman *d* Lloyd Bacon *ph* Tony Gaudio *m* Heinz Roemheld

Merle Oberon, Dennis Morgan, *Rita Hayworth*, George Tobias, Ralph Bellamy, James Gleason, Hattie McDaniel

Africa Texas Style*
GB 1967 109m Eastmancolor
Paramount / Vantors (Andrew Marton)

A Kenyan settler hires two Texas cowboys to help in his scheme of wild game ranching.
Excellent location sequences are dragged down by a very boring script, but it's a good family film nevertheless.

w Andy White *d* Andrew Marton *ph* Paul Beeson *m* Malcolm Arnold

John Mills, Hugh O'Brian, Nigel Green, Tom Nardini, Adrienne Corri, Ronald Howard
† Forerunner of TV series, *Cowboy in Africa*.

The African Queen****
GB 1951 103m Technicolor
IFD / Romulus–Horizon (Sam Spiegel)

In 1915, a gin-drinking river trader and a prim missionary make odd companions for a boat trip down a dangerous river, culminating in an attack on a German gunboat.
Despite some unfortunate studio sets mixed in with real African footage achieved through great hardship by all concerned, this is one of those surprising films that really work, a splendidly successful mixture of comedy, character and adventure.

w James Agee, novel C. S. Forester *d John Huston ph Jack Cardiff m Allan Gray*

Humphrey Bogart, Katharine Hepburn, Robert Morley, Peter Bull

'Entertaining but not entirely plausible or original.'—*Robert Hatch*

After Office Hours*
US 1935 75m bw
MGM (Bernard H. Hyman)

A newspaperman and his socialite reporter solve a murder mystery.
Crisply-written, fast-moving comedy melodrama; good stuff of its time and type.

w Herman J. Mankiewicz *d* Robert Z. Leonard *ph* Charles Rosher

Clark Gable, Constance Bennett, Stuart Erwin, Billie Burke, Harvey Stephens, Katherine Alexander, Henry Travers, Henry Armetta

'One of the best balanced pix of the season; it has practically everything.'—*Film Daily*

After the Ball*
GB 1957 89m Eastmancolor
IFD / Beaconsfield (Peter Rogers)

The life and loves of music-hall singer Vesta Tilley, who married into the nobility.
Adequate if uninspired biopic with entertaining detail and songs.

w Hubert Gregg *d* Compton Bennett

Pat Kirkwood, Laurence Harvey, Clive Morton, Jerry Verno, June Clyde

After the Fox*
US / Italy 1966 103m Technicolor Panavision
UA / Nancy / CCM (John Bryan)

The Fox escapes from jail to execute a gold bullion caper and save his young sister from the streets.
Unlikeable and unfunny farce which sets its star among excitable Italians and hopes for the best, adding a few wild stabs at satire on movie-making styles.

w Neil Simon, Cesare Zavattini *d* Vittorio de Sica *ph* Leonida Barboni *m* Burt Bacharach

Peter Sellers, *Victor Mature* (agreeably sending up his old image), Britt Ekland, Lilia Brazzi, Paola Stoppa, Akim Tamiroff, Martin Balsam

'Never even begins to get off the ground.'—*MFB*

After the Thin Man**
US 1936 113m bw
MGM (Hunt Stromberg)

Nick and Nora Charles, not forgetting Asta, solve another murder.
Overlong but well-carpentered sequel to *The Thin Man*, developing the thesis that a married couple, even if they are detectives and drink too much, can be interesting and lovable.

w Frances Goodrich, Albert Hackett *d* W. S. Van Dyke II *ph* Oliver T. Marsh *m* Herbert Stothart

William Powell, Myrna Loy, James Stewart, Elissa Landi, Joseph Calleia, Jessie Ralph, Alan Marshal, Sam Levene

Against All Flags*
US 1952 83m Technicolor
U-I (Howard Christie)

A daring British seaman routs Spanish ships at the request of the king.
Standard pirate yarn, almost Flynn's last swashbuckler; production below par.

w Aeneas Mackenzie, Joseph Hoffman *d* George Sherman *ph* Russell Metty *m* Hans Salter

Errol Flynn, Maureen O'Hara, Anthony Quinn, Mildred Natwick

† Remade as *The King's Pirate* (qv).

Against the Wind**
GB 1947 96m bw
Ealing (Sidney Cole)

In London during World War II, men and women are trained as saboteurs, and one of them is a traitor.
Thoughtful, well-made spy thriller with good performances.

w T. E. B. Clarke, Michael Pertwee *d* Charles Crichton *ph* Lionel Banes *m* Leslie Bridgewater

Simone Signoret, Robert Beatty, Jack Warner, Gordon Jackson, Paul Dupuis, Gisele Preville, John Slater, Peter Illing, James Robertson Justice

Age of Consent*
Australia 1969 103m colour
Columbia / Nautilus (James Mason, Michael Powell)

An artist seduces the granddaughter of a drunken harridan with whom he shares a Barrier Reef island.
Mildly likeable but self-conscious and overlong South Pacific idyll.

w Peter Yeldham, *novel* Norman Lindsay *d* Michael Powell *ph* Hannes Staudinger *m* Stanley Myers

James Mason, Helen Mirren, Jack McGowran, Neva Carr-Glyn, Frank Thring

The Agitator*
GB 1944 98m bw
British National (Louis H. Jackson)

An embittered mechanic becomes a loud-mouthed union spokesman, but fate eventually takes him into management.
Fairly absorbing, modest narrative of the flaws of socialism.

w Edward Dryhurst, *novel* Peter Pettinger by William Riley *d* John Harlow

William Hartnell (then being built into a star), Mary Morris, John Laurie, Moore Marriott, George Carney, Edward Rigby, Elliot Mason, Frederick Leister, Cathleen Nesbitt, Moira Lister

The Agony and the Ecstasy*
US 1965 140m De Luxe Todd-AO
TCF / International Classics Inc (Carol Reed)

Pope Julius II persuades Michelangelo to leave his sculptures and paint the ceiling of the Sistine Chapel.
Dully reverent comic strip approach to art and history; generally heavy going, but good looking.

w Philip Dunne, *novel* Irving Stone *d* Carol Reed *ph* Leon Shamroy *m* Alex North *pd* John de Cuir

Charlton Heston, Rex Harrison, Diane Cilento, Harry Andrews, Alberto Lupo, Adolfo Celi

'The vulgarity of the whole concept has none of the joyfully enthusiastic philistinism of a de Mille; rather its tone is a dry, almost cynical, condescension.'—*Brenda Davies*

'All agony, no ecstasy.'—*Judith Crist*

Ah, Wilderness**
US 1935 101m bw
MGM (Hunt Stromberg)

Problems of a small-town family at the turn of the century.
Well-acted, affectionately remembered version of a play later musicalized as *Summer Holiday*. The commercial success of this film led to the Hardy family series.

w Albert Hackett, Frances Goodrich, *play* Eugene O'Neill *d* Clarence Brown *ph* Clyde de Vinna *m* Herbert Stothart

Wallace Beery, Lionel Barrymore, Eric Linden, Spring Byington, Mickey Rooney, Aline MacMahon, Charley Grapewin, Cecilia Parker, Frank Albertson, Bonita Granville

Ain't Misbehavin'*
US 1955 81m Technicolor
U-I (Samuel Marx)

A young millionaire marries a cabaret girl, who determines to improve her mind and manners.
Lively American version of *Pygmalion*, with musical numbers and some bright lines.

w Edward Buzzell, Philip Rapp, Devery Freeman *d* Edward Buzzell *ph* Wilfrid Cline *m* Joseph Gershenson *ch* Kenny Williams, Lee Scott

Rory Calhoun, *Piper Laurie, Reginald Gardiner,* Jack Carson, Barbara Britton, Mamie Van Doren

Ain't No Time for Glory
US 1957 74m bw TVM
Columbia / Playhouse 90

During the Battle of the Bulge, an American officer talks a German commander into surrender.
Dull, respectable early TV movie.

d Oscar Rudolph

Barry Sullivan, Gene Barry, John Drew Barrymore, Bruce Bennett

Air Force*
US 1943 124m bw
Warner (Hal B. Wallis)

A Flying Fortress and its crew see action in Manila, Pearl Harbor and the Coral Sea.
Propaganda piece concentrating on the characters of the crew members, with action setpieces largely provided by newsreel; but skilled direction still conveys plenty of punch.

w Dudley Nichols *d Howard Hawks* *ph* James Wong Howe, Elmer Dyer, Charles Marshall *m* Franz Waxman

John Garfield, Gig Young, Arthur Kennedy, Charles Drake, John Ridgley, Harry Carey, George Tobias, Stanley Ridges, Moroni Olsen, Edward Brophy

Air Raid Wardens*
US 1943 67m bw
MGM (B. F. Zeidman)

Rejected by the armed services, two incompetent air raid wardens accidentally round up Nazi spies.
Well below par star comedy: their incomparable dignity has disappeared.

w Jack Jevne, Martin Rackin, Charles Rogers, Harry Crane *d* Edward Sedgwick *ph* Charles Rogers, Harry Crane *m* Edwin Willis, Alfred Spencer

Stan Laurel, Oliver Hardy, Edgar Kennedy, Jacqueline White, Stephen McNally, Nella Walker, Donald Meek

Airport***
US 1969 136m Technicolor Todd-AO
Universal / Ross Hunter (Jaque Mapes)

Events of one snowy night at a midwestern international airport, culminating in airborne melodrama when a mad bomber is killed and the damaged plane has to be talked down.
Glossy, undeniably entertaining, all-star version

of a popular novel, with cardboard characters skilfully deployed in Hollywood's very best style.

w George Seaton, *novel* Arthur Hailey *d* George Seaton *ph* Ernest Laszlo *m* Alfred Newman

Burt Lancaster, Dean Martin, Jean Seberg, *Helen Hayes*, Van Heflin, Jacqueline Bisset, George Kennedy, Maureen Stapleton, Barry Nelson, Dana Wynter, Lloyd Nolan, Barbara Hale, Gary Collins, Jessie Royce Landis

'The best film of 1944.'—*Judith Crist*

Airport 1975
US 1974 105m Technicolor
Panavision
Universal (Jennings Lang, William Frye)

A private aircraft collides with a jet plane and kills or immobilizes its crew, so a stewardess has to manoeuvre the jumbo to safety.
Inept airborne suspenser loaded with stars who do nothing and marred by continuity lapses and boring dialogue.

w Don Ingalls *d* Jack Smight *ph* Philip Lathrop *m* John Cacavas

Charlton Heston, *Karen Black*, George Kennedy, Helen Reddy, Efrem Zimbalist Jnr, Susan Clark, Myrna Loy, Gloria Swanson, Linda Blair, Dana Andrews, Roy Thinnes, Sid Caesar, Ed Nelson, Nancy Olson, Martha Scott

'Aimed squarely for the yahoo trade.'—*Variety*

Al Capone**
US 1959 105m bw
Allied Artists (John H. Burrows, Leonard J. Ackerman)

An account of Chicago's most famous gangster, up to his arrest for income tax evasion.
Only slightly overplayed, semi-documentary retelling of a larger-than-life true story.

w Marvin Wald, Henry Greenberg *d* Richard Wilson *ph* Lucien Ballard *m* David Raksin

Rod Steiger (a clever impersonation on the border of caricature), Fay Spain, Murvyn Vye, Nehemiah Persoff, Martin Balsam, James Gregory, Joe de Santis

The Alamo*
US 1960 193m Technicolor Todd-AO
UA / John Wayne

In 1836 a small southern fort becomes the centre of Texas' fight for independence, but it is suddenly annihilated by a Mexican raid, and all its defenders killed.
Sprawling historical epic with many irrelevant episodes and distracting changes of mood.

w James Edward Grant *d* John Wayne *ph* William H. Clothier *m* Dmitri Tiomkin

John Wayne (as Crockett), Richard Widmark (Bowie), Laurence Harvey (Travis), Richard Boone (Houston), Frankie Avalon, Patrick Wayne, Linda Cristal, Chill Wills, Joseph Calleia

'Its sole redeeming feature lies in one of those crushing climaxes of total massacre which Hollywood can still pull off thunderingly well.'—*Peter John Dyer*

Albert RN**
GB 1953 88m bw
Dial (Daniel M. Angel)
US title: *Break to Freedom*

Prisoners of war construct a lifelike dummy to cover the absence of escaping prisoners.
Competent, entertaining version of a successful play: an archetypal POW comedy drama.

w Guy Morgan, Vernon Harris, *play* Guy Morgan, Edward Sammis *d* Lewis Gilbert *ph* Jack Asher *m* Philip Martell

Jack Warner, Anthony Steel, Robert Beatty, William Sylvester, Anton Diffring, Eddie Byrne, Guy Middleton, Paul Carpenter, Frederick Valk

Alcatraz Express**
US 1960 96m bw TVM
Paramount / Desilu / Quinn Martin
aka: *The Big Train*

An attempt is made to rescue Al Capone on his way by train to Alcatraz.
Excellent suspense thriller made from two episodes of *The Untouchables*.

w William Spier *d* John Peyser

Robert Stack, Neville Brand, Bruce Gordon, Paul Picerni, Nicholas Georgiade, Abel Fernandez

Alexander Hamilton*
US 1931 73m bw
Warner

Stagey star vehicle concerning episodes in the life of one of America's early political figures.

w Julian Josephson, Maude Howell *d* John G. Adolfi *ph* James Van Trees

George Arliss, Doris Kenyon, Montagu Love, Dudley Digges, Lionel Belmore, Ralf Harolde, Alan Mowbray, June Collyer

Alexander the Great*
US 1956 135m Technicolor
Cinemascope
UA / Robert Rossen

The life and early death at thirty-three of the

Macedonian warrior who conquered the entire known world.
Dour impassive epic which despite good intelligent stretches makes one long for Hollywood's usual more ruthless view of history.

wd Robert Rossen *m* Mario Nascimbene *ph* Robert Krasker *ad* André Andrejew

Richard Burton, Fredric March, Danielle Darrieux, Claire Bloom, Barry Jones, Harry Andrews, Peter Cushing, Stanley Baker, Michael Hordern, Niall MacGinnis

'Not a scene is held for a second longer than it is worth; greatness is pictured in constant dissolve.'—*Alexander Walker*

Alexander's Ragtime Band***
US 1938 106m bw
TCF (Darryl F. Zanuck, Harry Joe Brown)

Between 1911 and 1939, two songwriters vie for the affections of a rising musical comedy star.
Archetypal chronicle musical with 26 songs: well-paced, smartly made, and bursting with talent.

w Kathryn Scola, Lamar Trotti, Richard Sherman *d Henry King ph Peverell Marley m/ly Irving Berlin*

Tyrone Power, *Alice Faye*, Don Ameche, *Ethel Merman, Jack Haley*, Jean Hersholt, Helen Westley, John Carradine, Paul Hurst, Wally Vernon, Ruth Terry, Eddie Collins, Douglas Fowley, Chick Chandler

The Alf Garnett Saga
GB 1972 90m colour
Columbia / Associated London Films (Ned Sherrin, Terry Glinwood)

Bigoted Alf is exasperated by his council flat, his son-in-law, and the possibility that his daughter is pregnant by a black man.
Second inflation of the TV series, *Till Death Us Do Part*, even cruder and less funny than the first; listlessly written and developed.

w Johnny Speight *d* Bob Kellett *ph* Nic Knowland *m* Georgie Fame

Warren Mitchell, Dandy Nichols, Adrienne Posta, Mike Angelis, John Le Mesurier, Joan Sims, John Bird, Roy Kinnear

'One long, repetitive and unfunny diatribe.'—*MFB*

Alfie**
GB 1966 114m Techniscope
Paramount / Sheldrake (Lewis Gilbert)

A Cockney Lothario is proud of his amorous conquests, but near-tragedy finally makes him more mature.
Garish sex comedy, an immense box office success because of its frankness and an immaculate performance from its star.

w Bill Naughton, from his play *d* Lewis Gilbert *ph* Otto Heller *m* Sonny Rollins

Michael Caine, Vivien Merchant, Shirley Anne Field, Millicent Martin, Jane Asher, Julia Foster, Shelley Winters, Eleanor Bron, Denholm Elliott

Alfred the Great*
GB 1969 122m Metrocolor Panavision
MGM / Bernard Smith

In AD 871 Alfred takes over kingship from his weak elder brother.
A 'realistic' youth-oriented view of history: blood and four-letter words alternate with cliché to make a dispiriting, disunified whole, though the background detail is interesting and the battle scenes vivid.

w Ken Taylor, James R. Webb *d* Clive Donner *ph* Alex Thomson *m* Ray Leppard *pd* Michael Stringer

David Hemmings, Michael York, Prunella Ransome, Colin Blakely, Julian Glover, Ian McKellen, Alan Dobie

Alf's Button Afloat**
GB 1938 89m bw
Gainsborough (Edward Black)

Six itinerants encounter a genie, whose granting of their wishes brings riches and embarrassment.
Archetypal music hall farce descending at moments into surrealism (the lovers are eaten by a bear). All concerned are on top form.

w Marriott Edgar, Val Guest, Ralph Smart, novel Alf's Button by W. A. Darlington *d Marcel Varnel*

Bud Flanagan, Chesney Allen, Jimmy Nervo, Toddy Knox, Charles Naughton, Jimmy Gold (the six original members of the Crazy Gang), *Alastair Sim*, Wally Patch, Peter Gawthorne

Algiers**
US 1938 95m bw
Walter Wanger

A romantic Casbah thief makes the mistake of falling in love.
Seminal Hollywood romantic drama based closely on a French original, *Pepe le Moko*; laughed at for years because of the alleged line 'Come with me to the Casbah' (which is never actually said), it holds up remarkably well in its fashion.

w John Howard Lawson, James M. Cain *d John*

Cromwell ph James Wong Howe m Vincent Scott, Mohammed Igorbouchen

Charles Boyer, Hedy Lamarr, Sigrid Gurie, Gene Lockhart, Joseph Calleia, Alan Hale, Johnny Downs

'Few films this season, or any other, have sustained their mood more brilliantly.'—*New York Times*

† Remake: *Casbah* (qv).

Ali Baba and the Forty Thieves*
US 1944 87m Technicolor
U-I (Paul Malvern)

A deposed prince pretending to be a bandit regains his rightful throne.
Absurd but likeable wartime pantomime without much humour: a typical big-budget production of its studio and period.

w Edmund L. Hartmann *d* Arthur Lubin *ph* George Robinson *m* Edward Ward

Jon Hall, Maria Montez, Scotty Beckett, Turhan Bey, Frank Puglia, Andy Devine, Kurt Katch
† Remake: *Sword of Ali Baba*, which over twenty years later used much of the same footage.

Ali Baba Goes to Town*
US 1937 81m bw
TCF (Lawrence Schwab)

A hobo falls off a train into a film set and thinks he is back in the Arabian Nights.
Rather flat star vehicle with a few compensations.

w Harry Tugend, Jack Yelten *d* David Butler *ph* Ernest Palmer

Eddie Cantor, Tony Martin, Roland Young, John Carradine, June Lang

Alias Jesse James*
US 1958 92m Technicolor
Hope Enterprises (Jack Hope)

An incompetent insurance salesman sells a policy to Jesse James and has to protect his client until he can get it back.
Ho-hum star comedy saved by a climax in which Hope is protected by every cowboy star in Hollywood.

w William Bowers, D. D. Beauchamp *d* Norman Z. McLeod *ph* Lionel Lindon *m* Joseph J. Lilley

Bob Hope, Rhonda Fleming, Wendell Corey, Jim Davis, Will Wright

Alias Nick Beal***
US 1949 93m bw
Paramount (Endre Boehm)
GB title: *The Contact Man*

A politician is nearly corrupted by a mysterious stranger offering wealth and power.
Highly satisfactory modern version of *Faust*, done in gangster terms but not eschewing a supernatural explanation. Acting, photography and direction all in the right key.

w Jonathan Latimer, story Mindret Lord *d John Farrow ph Lionel Lindon m* Franz Waxman

Ray Milland, Thomas Mitchell, Audrey Totter, George Macready, Fred Clark

Alias Smith and Jones*
US 1970 74m Technicolor TVM
Universal (Frank Price, Glen Larson)

Two bandits come to an arrangement with the government.
Comedy western, clearly modelled on *Butch Cassidy and the Sundance Kid*; it spawned a successful series.

w Glen Larson *d* Gene Levitt *m* Billy Goldenberg

Pete Duel, Ben Murphy, Susan St James, James Drury, Forrest Tucker, Earl Holliman

Alibi*
GB 1942 82m bw
Corona (Josef Somlo)

A nightclub mindreader forces the lady owner to give him a murder alibi.
Interesting but disappointing minor suspenser copied from a sharper French original.

w uncredited, *novel* Marcel Achard *d* Brian Desmond Hurst *ph* Otto Heller *m* Jack Beaver

Margaret Lockwood, Hugh Sinclair, James Mason, *Raymond Lovell,* Enid Stamp-Taylor, Hartley Power, Jane Carr, Rodney Ackland, Edana Romney, Elizabeth Welch, Olga Lindo, Muriel George

Alibi Ike**
US 1935 73m bw
Warner

A baseball pitcher gets involved in all kinds of trouble.
Above average star comedy vehicle.

w William Wister Haines, *story* Ring Lardner *d* Ray Enright *ph* Arthur Todd *m* Leo Forbstein

Joe E. Brown, Olivia de Havilland, Ruth Donnelly, Roscoe Karns, William Frawley

Alice Adams**
US 1935 99m bw
RKO (Pandro S. Berman)

A social-climbing small-town girl falls in love. Dated but interesting star vehicle with good production values.

w Dorothy Yost, Mortimer Offner, *novel* Booth Tarkington *d George Stevens* *ph* Robert de Grasse *m* Max Steiner

Katharine Hepburn, Fred MacMurray, Evelyn Venable, Frank Albertson, Fred Stone, Ann Shoemaker, Charles Grapewin, Grady Sutton, Hedda Hopper

'A nice middle-class film, as trivial as a schoolgirl's diary, and just about as pathetically true.'—*C. A. Lejeune*

Alice Doesn't Live Here Any More**
US 1975 112m Technicolor
Warner (David Susskind, Audrey Maas)

A widow sets off with her young son for Monterey and a singing career.
Realistically squalid and foul-mouthed but endearing look at a slice of America today, with firm handling and excellent performances in a surprisingly old-fashioned theme.

w Robert Getchell d Martin Scorsese *ph* Kent L. Wakeford *m* various *pd* Toby Carr Rafelson

Ellen Burstyn, Alfred Lutter, Kris Kristofferson, Billy Green Bush, *Diane Ladd,* Lelia Goldoni, Jodie Foster

'What Scorsese has done is to rescue an American cliché from the bland, flat but much more portentous naturalism of such as *Harry and Tonto* and restore it to an emotional and intellectual complexity through his particular brand of baroque realism.'—*Richard Combs*

'Full of funny malice and breakneck vitality.'—*New Yorker*

Alice in Wonderland**
US 1933 90m bw
Paramount

Intriguing but disappointing version of the nonsense classic, keeping to the Tenniel drawings by dressing an all-star cast in masks, thereby rendering them ineffective.

w Joseph L. Mankiewicz, William Cameron Menzies, *novel* Lewis Carroll *d* Norman Z. McLeod *ph* Henry Sharp, Bert Glennon *m* Dmitri Tiomkin

Charlotte Henry, W. C. Fields (Humpty Dumpty), Cary Grant (Mock Turtle), Gary Cooper (White Knight), Edward Everett Horton (Mad Hatter), Edna May Oliver (Red Queen), Jack Oakie (Tweedledum), Leon Errol (Uncle), Charles Ruggles (March Hare), May Robson (Queen of Hearts), Louise Fazenda (White Queen), Ned Sparks (Caterpillar), Alison Skipworth (Duchess)

Alice in Wonderland*
US 1951 75m Technicolor
Walt Disney

Fully animated cartoon version which has good moments but modernizes and Americanizes the familiar characters.

w various *d* Clyde Geronomi, Hamilton Luske, Wilfred Jackson *supervisor* Ben Sharpsteen

Alice's Adventures in Wonderland*
GB 1972 101m Eastmancolor Todd-AO
TCF / Josef Shaftel (Derek Horne)

Live-action version which starts amiably enough but soon becomes flat and uninventive, with a star cast all at sea and tedium replacing the wit of the original.

wd William Sterling *ph* Geoffrey Unsworth *m* John Barry *pd* Michael Stringer

Fiona Fullerton, Michael Crawford (White Rabbit), Robert Helpmann (Mad Hatter), Dudley Moore (Dormouse), Spike Milligan (Gryphon), Peter Sellers (March Hare), Dennis Price (King of Hearts), Flora Robson (Queen of Hearts), Rodney Bewes (Knave of Hearts), Peter Bull (Duchess), Michael Hordern (Mock Turtle), Ralph Richardson (Caterpillar), etc

Alice's Restaurant*
US 1969 110m De Luxe
UA / Florin (Harold Levanthal)

Folk singer Arlo Guthrie, on the verge of being drafted, gets some varied experience of life among the drop-outs of Montana, Massachusetts and New York.
Typical of the freakish, anti-Vietnam, do-as-you-please movies which splurged from Hollywood in the wake of *Easy Rider*, this has the minor benefits of good production values and a few jokes.

w Venable Herndon, Arthur Penn *d* Arthur Penn *ph* Michael Nebbia *m/songs* Arlo Guthrie

Arlo Guthrie, Pat Quinn, James Broderick, Michael McClanathan, Geoff Outlaw

Alive and Kicking*
GB 1958 94m bw
ABP (Victor Skuzetsky)

Three old ladies escape from a home to an Irish island.

Agreeable minor comedy, a showcase for its elderly but vigorous stars.

w Denis Cannan *d* Cyril Frankel *ph* Gilbert Taylor *m* Philip Green

Sybil Thorndike, Kathleen Harrison, Estelle Winwood, Stanley Holloway, Joyce Carey, Eric Pohlmann, Colin Gordon

All About Eve****
US 1950 138m bw
TCF (Darryl F. Zanuck)

An ageing Broadway star suffers from the hidden menace of a self-effacing but secretly ruthless and ambitious young actress.
A basically unconvincing story with thin characters is transformed by a screenplay scintillating with savage wit and a couple of waspish performances into a movie experience to treasure.

wd Joseph L. Mankiewicz ph Milton Krasner m Alfred Newman

Bette Davis (a supremely bitchy performance), *George Sanders* (caricaturing his usual image), Anne Baxter, Celeste Holm, Gary Merrill, Hugh Marlowe, Gregory Ratoff, Thelma Ritter, Marilyn Monroe, Barbara Bates

'The wittiest, the most devastating, the most adult and literate motion picture ever made that had anything to do with the New York Stage.'—*Leo Mishkin*

'The dialogue and atmosphere are so peculiarly remote from life that they have sometimes been mistaken for art.'—*Pauline Kael, 1968*

'Plenty of surface cynicism, but no detachment, no edge and no satire. Boiled down it is a plush backstage drama.'—*Richard Winnington*

The All-American
US 1952 83m bw
U-I (Aaron Rosenberg)
GB title: *The Winning Way*

When his parents are killed on the way to a match, a college football hero rejects sport for the *groves of academe*.
Very modest formula drama.

w D. D. Beauchamp *d* Jesse Hibbs *ph* Maury Gertsman *m* Joseph Gershenson

Tony Curtis, Mamie Van Doren, Lori Nelson, Gregg Palmer, Richard Long, Paul Cavanagh

All Creatures Great and Small*
GB1974 92m Eastmancolor
EMI / Venedon (David Susskind, Duane Bogie)

The pre-war Yorkshire life of a country vet.
Simple-minded popular entertainment of a long-forgotten kind, oddly sponsored by American TV in the shape of Readers' Digest and the Hallmark Hall of Fame.

w Hugh Whitemore, *novel* James Herriot *d* Claude Whatham *ph* Peter Suschitzky *m* Wilfred Josephs

Anthony Hopkins, Simon Ward, Lisa Harrow, Freddie Jones, Brian Stirner, T. P. McKenna, Brenda Bruce, John Collin

†1976 sequel: *It Shouldn't Happen to a Vet.*

All Fall Down*
US 1962 111m bw
MGM (John Houseman)

A young man reveres his ne'er-do-well elder brother but determines to shoot him when he causes a girl's death.
Another gallery of middle American failures, competently portrayed by a writer and actors very practised at this sort of thing.

w William Inge, *novel* James Leo Herlihy *d* John Frankenheimer *ph* Lionel Lindon *m* Alex North

Warren Beatty, Brandon de Wilde, Angela Lansbury, Karl Malden, Eva Marie Saint

All for Mary*
GB 1956 82m Eastmancolor
Rank / Paul Soskin

Two rivals for the hand of the pretty daughter of a Swiss hotelier are struck down by chicken pox and cared for by the old nanny of one of them.
Simple-minded farce in which two grown men quail like children before a forceful old lady; on the strength of the latter characterization and a few funny lines the original play was a considerable West End success.

w Peter Blackmore, Paul Soskin, *play* Harold Brooke, Kay Bannerman *d* Wendy Toye *ph* Reg Wyer *m* Robert Farnon

Kathleen Harrison, Nigel Patrick, David Tomlinson, Jill Day, David Hurst, Leo McKern

All Hands on Deck
US 1961 98m De Luxe Cinemascope
TCF (Oscar Brodney)

Romantic and farcical adventures of sailors on leave.
Tired musical comedy romp with a second team cast.

w Jay Sommars, *novel* Donald R. Morris *d* Norman Taurog *ph* Leo Tover *m* Cyril Mockridge *songs* Jay Livingston, Ray Evans

Pat Boone, Buddy Hackett, Dennis O'Keefe, Barbara Eden, Warren Berlinger, Gale Gordon, Joe E. Ross

All I Desire
US 1953 79m bw
U-I (Ross Hunter)

A woman who had deserted her husband and family for a life on the stage returns for her daughter's graduation and is reconciled.
Resilient star melodrama with all stops out.

w James Gunn, Robert Blees *d* Douglas Sirk *ph* Carl Guthrie *m* Joseph Gershenson

Barbara Stanwyck, Richard Carlson, Lyle Bettger, Maureen O'Sullivan, Richard Long, Lori Nelson

All in a Night's Work
US 1961 94m Technicolor
Paramount / Hal B. Wallis–Joseph Hazen

A publishing heir falls for a girl he suspects of having been his uncle's mistress.
Unpolished and not very amusing comedy which falters after an intriguing start.

w Edmund Beloin, Maurice Richlin, Sidney Sheldon *d* Joseph Anthony *ph* Joseph La Shelle *m* André Previn

Shirley Maclaine, Dean Martin, Charles Ruggles, Cliff Robertson, Norma Crane, Gale Gordon, Jerome Cowan, Jack Weston

'Tame and aimless sex-and-big-business comedy.'—*MFB*

All Mine To Give*
US 1956 102m Technicolor RKOscope
RKO (Sam Wiesenthal)
GB title: *The Day They Gave Babies Away*

In 1856, a pioneer couple in Wisconsin train their children to carry on the family after their own deaths.
Weird sentimental sob story, even odder under its English title. Surprisingly, some of it works quite well.

w Dale and Katherine Eunson (apparently about their own ancestors) *d* Allen Reisner *ph* William Skall *m* Max Steiner

Glynis Johns, Cameron Mitchell, Patty McCormack, Rex Thompson, Ernest Truex, Hope Emerson, Alan Hale

'A strong mood folksy western reminiscence.'—*MFB*

All My Darling Daughters*
US 1973 74m Technicolor TVM
Universal (David Victor, David J. O'Connell)

A widower discovers that his four daughters want to get married at the same time.
Amiable sentimental nonsense which needed firmer control.

w John Gay *d* David Lowell Rich

Robert Young, Raymond Massey, Eve Arden, Darleen Carr, Judy Strangis, Sharon Gless

All My Darling Daughters' Anniversary
US 1974 74m Technicolor TVM
Universal (David Victor, David J. O'Connell)
aka: *My Darling Daughters' Anniversary*

Inevitable sequel to the above: all the girls have babies at the same time.
Dim.

w John Gay *d* Joseph Pevney

Robert Young, Raymond Massey, Ruth Hussey, Darleen Carr, Judy Strangis, Sharon Gless

All My Sons*
US 1948 94m bw
U-I (Chester Erskine)

A young man establishes that his father sold defective airplanes during the war.
Heady family melodrama from a taut and topical stage play. The film is well-meaning but artificial and unconvincing.

w Chester Erskine, *play* Arthur Miller *d* Irving Reis *ph* Russell Metty *m* Leith Stevens

Edward G. Robinson, Burt Lancaster, Mady Christians, Howard Duff

All Neat in Black Stockings
GB 1969 99m Eastmancolor
Anglo Amalgamated / Miton (Leon Clore)

Sex adventures of an amorous window cleaner.
Modish comedy drama with surface entertainment of a sort, but no depth.

w Jane Gaskell, Hugh Whitemore *d* Christopher Morahan *ph* Larry Pizer *m* Robert Cornford

Victor Henry, Susan George, Jack Shepherd, Anna Cropper, Clare Kelly, Terence de Marney

All Night Long*
GB 1961 95m bw
Rank / Bob Roberts (Michael Relph, Basil Dearden)

Because of rumour set about by a jealous rival, a jazz trumpeter at an all-night party tries to strangle his wife.
Cheeky updating of *Othello* with jazz accompaniment, played a shade too grimly by an excellent cast. An interesting misfire.

w Nel King, Peter Achilles *d* Basil Dearden *ph* Ted Scaife *m* John Guthridge

Patrick McGoohan, Richard Attenborough, Keith Michell, Betsy Blair, Marti Stevens, Paul Harris, Bernard Braden; and on the sound track Dave Brubeck, Tubby Hayes, Johnny Dankworth etc

All Over the Town*
GB 1949 88m bw
Rank / Wessex (Ian Dalrymple)

Two reporters revivify a West of England local newspaper, and expose local corruption.
Fresh, agreeable romantic comedy on sub-Ealing lines.

w Derek Twist and others *d* Derek Twist *ph* C. Pennington-Richards *m* Temple Abady

Norman Wooland, Sarah Churchill, *Fabia Drake* (as a local gorgon), Cyril Cusack, James Hayter

All Quiet on the Western Front****
US 1930 130m approx. bw
Universal (Carl Laemmle Jnr)

In 1914, a group of German teenagers volunteer for action on the Western Front, but they become disillusioned, and none of them survive.
A landmark of American cinema and Universal's biggest and most serious undertaking until the sixties, this highly emotive war film with its occasional outbursts of bravura direction fixed in millions of minds the popular image of what it was like in the trenches, even more so than *Journey's End* which had shown the allied viewpoint. Despite dated moments, it retains its overall power and remains a great pacifist work.

w Lewis Milestone, Maxwell Anderson, Del Andrews, George Abbott, *novel* Erich Maria Remarque *d* Lewis Milestone (in a manner reminiscent of Eisenstein and Lang) *ph* Arthur Edeson *m* David Broekman

'A trenchant and imaginative audible picture . . . most of the time the audience was held to silence by its realistic scenes.'—*New York Times*

'The sound and image mediums blend as one, as a form of artistic expression that only the motion screen can give.'—*National Board of Review*

All That Heaven Allows
US 1955 89m Technicolor
U-I (Ross Hunter)

A sad widow falls in love with the gardener at her winter home, and marries him despite local prejudice.
Standard tearjerker in the tradition of *Magnificent Obsession*, reuniting the same stars, producer and director in the same rich musical and photographic sauce.

w Peg Fenwick *d* Douglas Sirk *ph* Russell Metty *m* Joseph Gershenson

Jane Wyman, Rock Hudson, Agnes Moorehead, Conrad Nagel, Virginia Grey, Charles Drake

'As laboriously predictable as it is fatuously unreal.'—*MFB*

All That Money Can Buy****
US 1941 106m bw
RKO / William Dieterle (Charles L. Glett)
aka: *The Devil and Daniel Webster; Daniel and the Devil*

A hard-pressed farmer gives in to the Devil's tempting, but is saved from the pit by a famous lawyer's pleading at his 'trial'.
A brilliant Germanic Faust set in 19th-century New Hampshire and using historical figures, alienation effects, comedy asides and the whole cinematic box of tricks which Hollywood had just learned again through *Citizen Kane*. A magic act in more ways than one.

w Dan Totheroh, based on The Devil and Daniel Webster by Stephen Vincent Benet *d William Dieterle ph Joseph August m Bernard Herrmann ad Van Nest Polglase sp Vernon L. Walker*

Walter Huston ('Mr Scratch', a great performance), James Craig, Anne Shirley, Simone Simon, *Edward Arnold* (Daniel Webster), Jane Darwell, Gene Lockhart, John Qualen, H. B. Warner

All the Brothers Were Valiant*
US 1953 94m Technicolor
MGM (Pandro S. Berman)

Rivalry between brothers on a whaling schooner.
Remake of a silent melodrama with predictable vengefulness and formula heroism, capably but unmemorably portrayed.

w Harry Brown, *novel* Ben Ames Williams *d* Richard Thorpe *ph* George Folsey *m* Miklos Rozsa

Stewart Granger, Robert Taylor, Ann Blyth, Betta St John, Keenan Wynn, James Whitmore, Kurt Kasznar, Lewis Stone

All the Fine Young Cannibals
US 1960 122m Metrocolor
Cinemascope
MGM / Avon (Pandro S. Berman)

The son of a country clergyman loves the daughter of another clergyman; they both find the realities of life in New York a horrid shock.
The glum joys of sex and dope in the big city are revealed in this boring rather than daring farrago which is not even unintentionally funny.

w Robert Thom, *novel* The Bixby Girls by Rosamond Marshall *d* Michael Anderson *ph* William H. Daniels *m* Jeff Alexander

Robert Wagner, Natalie Wood, Pearl Bailey, Susan Kohner, George Hamilton, Jack Mullaney, Onslow Stevens, Anne Seymour

All the Kind Strangers
US 1974 74m colour TVM
Cinemation / Jerry Gross

Seven orphans decoy strangers to their lonely farmhouse: some of the adults disappear.
Nuthatch melodrama with a certain amount of pizazz.

w Clyde Ware d Burt Kennedy

Stacy Keach, Samantha Eggar, John Savage, Robby Benson

All the King's Men***
US 1949 109m bw
Columbia (Robert Rossen)

An honest man from a small town is elected mayor and then governor, but power corrupts him absolutely and he ruins his own life and those of his friends before being assassinated.
Archetypal American political melodrama based on the life of southern senator Huey Long. The background is well sketched in and there are excellent performances, but the overall narrative is rather flabby.

w Robert Rossen, *novel* Robert Penn Warren *d Robert Rossen ph* Burnett Guffey *m* Louis Gruenberg *ad* Sturges Carne

Broderick Crawford, John Ireland, Mercedes McCambridge, Joanne Dru, John Derek, Anne Seymour, Shepperd Strudwick

'More conspicuous for scope and worthiness of intention than for inspiration.'—*Gavin Lambert*

'A superb pictorialism which perpetually crackles and explodes.'—*Bosley Crowther*

All the President's Men***
US 1976 138m Technicolor
Warner / Wildwood (Robert Redford, Walter Coblenz)

A reconstruction of the discovery of the White House link with the Watergate affair by two young reporters from the Washington Post.
An absorbing drama from the headlines which despite its many excellences would have been better with a more audible dialogue track, less murky photography and a clearer introduction of the characters concerned. The acting however is a treat.

w William Goldman, *book* Carl Bernstein, Bob Woodward *d* Alan J. Pakula *ph* Gordon Willis *m* David Shire *pd* George Jenkins

Robert Redford, Dustin Hoffman, Jason Robards Jnr, Martin Balsam, Hal Holbrook, Jack Warden, Jane Alexander, Meredith Baxter

All the Right Noises*
GB 1969 91m Eastmancolor
(TCF) Trigon (Anthony Hope)

The electrician of a touring company has an affair with a 15-year-old actress, but finally returns to his wife.
Sharp, sensible treatment of a cliché situation, as watchable as a superior television play.

wd Gerry O'Hara ph Gerry Fisher *m* John Cameron

Tom Bell, Judy Carne, Olivia Hussey, John Standing

'Built on a solid framework of disciplined direction and animated performances.'—*MFB*

All the Way Home**
US 1963 107m bw
Paramount / Talent Associates (David Susskind)

In 1916 Tennessee, the beloved father of a family is killed in a car crash, and after the trauma wears off, mother helps the children to rebuild their lives.
Tactful, charming though finally depressing slice of small town period Americana, with generally eloquent performances.

w Philip Reisman Jnr, *play* Tad Mosel, *novel* A Death in the Family by James Agee *d* Alex Segal *ph Boris Kaufman m* Bernard Green

Robert Preston, Jean Simmons, Aline MacMahon, Pat Hingle, Michael Kearney

'A heart-wrenching blend of nostalgia and sorrow.'—*Judith Crist*

All the Way Up*
GB 1970 97m Technicolor
Granada / EMI (Philip Mackie)

Social-climbing Dad makes his way by treachery and blackmail, but gets his come-uppance when his son takes after him.
Crudely farcical adaptation of a thoughtful comedy of its time; the treatment works in fits and starts but leaves one in no mood for the talkative finale.

w Philip Mackie, *play* Semi Detached by David Turner *d* James MacTaggart *ph* Dick Bush *m* Howard Blake

Warren Mitchell, Pat Heywood, Elaine Taylor, Kenneth Cranham, Vanessa Howard, Richard Briers, Adrienne Posta, Bill Fraser

All the Young Men
US 1960 87m bw
Columbia (Hall Bartlett / Jaguar)

A marine patrol in Korea is commanded by a black man, and racial tensions take precedence over fighting the enemy.
Simple-minded, parsimoniously-budgeted war melodrama.

wd Hall Bartlett *ph* Daniel Fapp *m* George Duning

Alan Ladd, Sidney Poitier, Ingemar Johansson, Glenn Corbett, James Darren, Mort Sahl

'Strenuously engaged in exploiting the entertainment values of nostalgia, fear, suspense, hatred and sex.'—*MFB*

All This and Heaven Too**
US 1940 143m bw
Warner (Jack L. Warner, Hal B. Wallis)

A 19th-century French nobleman falls in love with his governess and murders his wife.
Romantic, melodramatic soap opera from a mammoth best seller; well made for those who can stomach it, with excellent acting and production values.

w Casey Robinson, *novel* Rachel Field *d* Anatole Litvak *ph* Ernest Haller *m* Max Steiner

Charles Boyer, Bette Davis, Barbara O'Neil, Virginia Weidler, Jeffrey Lynn, Helen Westley, Henry Daniell, Harry Davenport, Walter Hampden, George Coulouris, Janet Beecher, Montagu Love

All Through the Night**
US 1942 107m bw
Warner (Jerry Wald)

Gangsters help to track down fifth columnists in World War II New York.
Highly entertaining muddle of several styles which somehow works well and allows several favourites to do their thing.

w Leonard Spiegelgass, Edwin Gilbert *d* Vincent Sherman *ph* Sid Hickox *m* Adolph Deutsch

Humphrey Bogart, Conrad Veidt, Peter Lorre, Karen Verne, Judith Anderson, Jane Darwell, Frank McHugh, Jackie Gleason, William Demarest, Phil Silvers

All Together Now
US 1975 74m colour TVM
RSO (Ron Bernstein)

A teenage boy proves to the court that he and his young brother and sisters can make it on their own.
Adequate sentimental stuff.

w Jeff Andrus, Rubin Carson d Randall Kleiser

John Rubenstein, Glynnis O'Connor, Brad Savage, Bill Macy, Jane Withers, Helen Hunt

Allegheny Uprising
US 1939 81m bw
RKO (P. J. Wolfson)
GB title: *The First Rebel*

A young frontiersman smashes liquor traffic with the Indians.
Modestly efficient western with an impressive cast.

w P. J. Wolfson, *story* Neil Swanson *d* William A. Seiter *ph* Nicholas Musuraca

John Wayne, Claire Trevor, Brian Donlevy, George Sanders, Wilfrid Lawson, Robert Barrat, Moroni Olsen, Eddie Quillan, Chill Wills

An Alligator Named Daisy
GB 1955 88m Technicolor Vistavision
Rank (Raymond Stross)

A young songwriter finds himself saddled with a pet alligator.
The ultimate in silly animal comedies, this does score a few laughs.

w Jack Davies, *novel* Charles Terrot *d* J. Lee-Thompson *ph* Reg Wyer *m* Stanley Black

Donald Sinden, Diana Dors, Jean Carson, James Robertson Justice, Stanley Holloway, Roland Culver, Margaret Rutherford, Avice Landone, Richard Wattis, Frankie Howerd, Jimmy Edwards, Gilbert Harding

'Apart from a fairly Kafkaesque scene in which Daisy is discovered in an upright piano, the situation is treated with little wit or comic invention.'—*MFB*

Aloha Means Goodbye
US 1974 100m Technicolor TVM
Universal (Sam Strangis)

A girl in hospital discovers that if she dies she may become a heart donor for the surgeon's son.
Icky medical melodrama.

w Dean Riesner, Joseph Stefano, *novel* Naomi A. Hentze *d* David Lowell Rich

Sally Struthers, James Franciscus, Joanna Miles, Henry Darrow, Larry Gates

Aloma of the South Seas
US 1941 77m Technicolor
Paramount (Monte Bell)

A young Polynesian chieftain returns to quell trouble on his island after being educated in the US.

Hoary goings-on in gory colour, a remake of a silent epic devised to display the star's sarong and the backlot's expensive volcano.

w Frank Butler, Seena Owen, Lillie Hayward *d* Alfred Santell *ph* Karl Struss *m* Andrea Setaro *sp* Gordon Jennings

Dorothy Lamour, Jon Hall, Lynne Overman, Philip Reed, Katherine de Mille, Fritz Leiber, Dona Drake, Esther Dale

'The mountain has the privilege of belching when it is dissatisfied, which is something no well-bred critic should do.'—*C. A. Lejeune*

Along Came a Spider**
US 1972 74m colour TVM
TCF (Alan A. Armer)

The widow of a scientist killed in an accident plots revenge on his careless colleague.
Efficient suspenser shot on a university campus.

w Barry Oringer *d* Lee H. Katzin

Suzanne Pleshette, Ed Nelson, Andrew Prine, Richard Anderson, Brooke Bundy

Along Came Jones*
US 1945 90m bw
(UA) Cinema Artists Corporation (Gary Cooper)

Two cowboys are mistaken for killers.
Very mild western comedy melodrama, with the star at his most self-effacing and production only mediocre.

w Nunnally Johnson, *novel* Alan le May *d* Stuart Heisler *ph* Milton Krasner *m* Charles Maxwell

Gary Cooper, Loretta Young, William Demarest, Dan Duryea, Russell Simpson

Along the Great Divide*
US 1950 88m bw
Warner (Anthony Veiller)

A marshal prevents an old man from being hanged for murder, and eventually discovers the real culprit.
Adequate, modest western with an unusual detective element.

w Walter Doniger, Lewis Meltzer *d* Raoul Walsh *ph* Sid Hickox *m* David Buttolph

Kirk Douglas, Virginia Mayo, Walter Brennan, John Agar, Ray Teal

The Alpha Caper*
US 1973 74m Technicolor TVM
Universal / Silverton (Aubrey Schenck)
GB theatrical title: *Inside Job*

A parole officer, unjustly retired, plots a thirty million dollar robbery with one of his protégés.
Reasonably entertaining comedy drama.

w Elroy Schwartz *d* Robert Michael Lewis *ph* Enzo Martinelli *m* Oliver Nelson

Henry Fonda, Leonard Nimoy, James McEachin, Larry Hagman, Elena Verdugo, John Marley, Noah Beery

'There's a good thesis to be written on the hermetic aesthetics of the TV movie: every element seems to follow a pre-ordained pattern whose points of reference are always other movies rather than real experience.'—*MFB*

The Alphabet Murders
GB 1965 90m bw
MGM (Ben Arbeid)

Hercule Poirot solves a series of murders by an apparent lunatic choosing his victims in alphabetical order.
Ruination of a classic whodunnit novel, misguided both in its attempt to mix slapstick with detection and in its terrible central performance.

w David Pursall, Jack Seddon, *novel* The ABC Murders by Agatha Christie *d* Frank Tashlin *ph* Desmond Dickinson *m* Ron Goodwin

Tony Randall, Robert Morley, Anita Ekberg, Maurice Denham, Guy Rolfe, James Villiers, Clive Morton

Alvarez Kelly*
US 1966 116m Technicolor Panavision
Columbia / Ray David (Sol C. Siegel)

The owner of a herd of 2500 cattle finds himself between two sides in the American Civil War.
Unusual if rather tepid western which balances historical interest against social conscience and throws in a variety of other elements.

w Franklin Coen *d* Edward Dmytryk *ph* Joseph MacDonald *m* John Green

William Holden, Richard Widmark, Janice Rule, Patrick O'Neal, Victoria Shaw, Roger C. Carmel, Richard Rust

Always Goodbye
US 1938 75m bw
TCF (Raymond Griffith)

An unwed mother gives up her baby and later wants it back.
Tired sentimental warhorse, a remake of *Gallant Lady* (qv).

w Kathryn Scola, Edith Skouras *d* Sidney Lanfield *ph* Robert Planck *m* Louis Silvers

Barbara Stanwyck, Herbert Marshall, Ian

Hunter, Cesar Romero, Lynn Bari, Binnie Barnes

Always in My Heart*
US 1942 92m bw
Warner (Walter McEwen, William Jacobs)

A convict returns home to find his daughter a stranger and his wife about to marry again.
Well acted sentimental drama.

w Adele Commandini, *play* Fly Away Home by Dorothy Bennett, Irving White *d* Joe Graham *ph* Sid Hickox *m* Heinz Roemheld

Walter Huston, Kay Francis, Gloria Warren, Frankie Thomas, Sidney Blackmer, Una O'Connor

Always Leave Them Laughing*
US 1949 116m bw
Warner (Jerry Wald)

A vaudeville comedian craves the spotlight at the expense of his private life.
Raucous backstage vehicle, crammed with sentimental and melodramatic cliché but affording tantalizing glimpses of the stage acts of its two stars.

w Jack Rose, Mel Shavelson *d* Roy del Ruth *ph* Ernest Haller *m* Sammy Cahn

Milton Berle, Bert Lahr, Virginia Mayo, Ruth Roman, Alan Hale, Jerome Cowan

The Amateur Gentleman*
GB 1936 102m bw
Criterion (Marcel Hellman, Douglas Fairbanks Jnr)

A Regency innkeeper's son poses as a travelling pugilist in order to clear his father's name of theft.
Dated but rather fascinating period adventure, quite a lively production of its time.

w Clemence Dane, Edward Knoblock, Sergei Nolbandov *d* Thornton Freeland

Douglas Fairbanks Jnr, Elissa Landi, Gordon Harker, Basil Sydney, Hugh Williams, Irene Browne, Margaret Lockwood, Coral Browne, Frank Pettingell, Athole Stewart, Esmé Percy

The Amazing Colossal Man*
US 1957 80m bw
AIP / Malibu (Bert I. Gordon)

A plutonium explosion causes an army colonel to grow at the rate of ten feet a day.
Modest, quite well written sci-fi let down by shaky trick work.

w Bert I. Gordon, Mark Hanna *d* Bert I. Gordon *ph* Joe Biroc *m* Albert Glasser

Glenn Langan, Cathy Downs, William Hudson, James Seay
† Sequel: *Revenge of the Colossal Man* (GB: *The Terror Strikes*).

The Amazing Dr Clitterhouse**
US 1938 87m bw
Warner (Robert Lord)

A criminologist researcher joins a gangster's mob and becomes addicted to crime.
Amusing, suspenseful, well acted comedy-melodrama.

w John Huston, John Wexley, *play* Barre Lyndon *d* Anatole Litvak *ph* Tony Gaudio *m* Max Steiner

Edward G. Robinson, Humphrey Bogart, Claire Trevor, Allen Jenkins, Gale Page, Donald Crisp, Maxie Rosebloom

The Amazing Mr Blunden**
GB 1972 99m Eastmancolor
Hemdale / Hemisphere (Barry Levinson)

In 1918, a widow and her two children meet a kindly gentleman who offers them work in his old mansion. Here they meet two ghost children, discover that he is a ghost too, and travel a hundred years back in time to right a wicked wrong.
Involved ghost story for intellectual children, made generally palatable by oodles of period charm and good acting.

wd Lionel Jeffries, story The Ghosts by Antonio Barker *ph* Gerry Fisher *m* Elmer Bernstein *pd* Wilfrid Shingleton

Laurence Naismith, Diana Dors, James Villiers, David Lodge, Lynne Frederick, Dorothy Alison, Rosalyn Lander, Marc Granger

'Easy period charm . . . fills every crevice.'—*Clyde Jeavons*

The Amazing Mr Williams*
US 1939 86m bw
Columbia (Everett Riskin)

About-to-be-marrieds investigate a murder.
Brisk comedy-thriller on *Thin Man* lines.

w Dwight Taylor, Sy Bartlett, Richard Maibaum *d* Alexander Hall *ph* Arthur Todd *m* Morris Stoloff

Melvyn Douglas, Joan Blondell, Ruth Donnelly, Clarence Kolb, Ed Brophy, Donald MacBride, Don Beddoe

The Amazing Mrs Holliday
US 1943 98m bw
Universal (Bruce Manning, Frank Shaw)

Torpedoed in mid-Pacific, a missionary's

daughter arrives in San Francisco with eight Chinese orphans.
Unusual sentimental vehicle for its star; of no particular interest or merit in itself, but with the usual interludes for song.

w Frank Ryan, John Jacoby *d* Bruce Manning *ph* Elwood Bredell *md* Charles Previn

Deanna Durbin, Edmond O'Brien, Frieda Inescort, Barry Fitzgerald

The Amazing Quest of Ernest Bliss
GB 1936 80m bw
Garrett–Klement (Robert Garrett, Otto Klement)
US title: *Romance and Riches*

A millionaire accepts a wager that he can live independently of his riches for one year.
Formulary comedy drama of its era on the theme that money isn't everything. Very dated.

w John L. Balderston *d* Alfred Zeisler *ph* Otto Heller

Cary Grant (on home leave after his first Hollywood success), Mary Brian, Henry Kendall, Leon M. Lion, Garry Marsh, Moore Marriott, Peter Gawthorne, Ralph Richardson

The Ambassador's Daughter*
US 1956 102m Technicolor Cinemascope
UA / Norman Krasna

An American senator in Paris decides that the presence of US forces in Paris constitutes a moral danger. The ambassador's daughter decides to investigate.
Thin comedy of the old-fashioned type: smart lines and intimate playing not helped by the vast screen.

wd Norman Krasna *ph* Michael Kelber *m* Jacques Metehen

Olivia de Havilland, John Forsythe, Edward Arnold, Adolphe Menjou, Myrna Loy, Francis Lederer, Tommy Noonan, Minor Watson

'An experienced cast approach the story's frivolities with poise and style.'—*MFB*

Ambush*
US 1949 89m bw
MGM (Armand Deutsch)

An army scout leads a posse to capture an Indian chief who is holding a white woman hostage.
Good, clean, robust western, well produced and acted.

w Marguerite Roberts *d* Sam Wood *ph* Harold Lipstein *m* Rudolph Kopp

Robert Taylor, John Hodiak, Arlene Dahl, Don Taylor, Jean Hagen, Leon Ames

Ambush Bay
US 1966 109m De Luxe
UA / Aubrey Schenck

In 1944, nine Marines try to escape from a Japanese-held island.
Routine, lengthy, sub-standard heroics for action addicts.

w Marve Feinberg, Ib Melchior *d* Ron Winston *ph* Emanuel Rojas *m* Richard La Salle

Hugh O'Brian, Mickey Rooney, James Mitchum, Tisa Chang, Harry Lauter

The Ambushers
US 1967 102m Technicolor
Columbia / Meadway / Claude (Irving Allen)

An experimental flying disc disappears on a test run, and the trail leads Matt Helm to the Mexican jungle.
The third Matt Helm adventure had such a stupid script that all concerned decided to send it up, unfortunately with too obvious a tendency to smirk at their own bravado.

w Herbert Baker *d* Henry Levin *ph* Burnett Guffey, Edward Colman *m* Hugo Montenegro

Dean Martin, Senta Berger, Janice Rule, Kurt Kasznar, James Gregory, Albert Salmi

'Plot, jokes and gadgets all well below par.'—*MFB*

America, America*
US 1963 177m bw
Warner (Elia Kazan)
GB title: *The Anatolian Smile*

In 1896 Turkey, a young Greek dreams of emigrating to America, and finally does so.
A massive piece of self-indulgence by a one-man band, fascinating for his family circle but so poorly constructed as to be of very limited interest elsewhere.

wd Elia Kazan *ph* Haskell Wexler *m* Manos Hadjidakis

Stathis Giallelis, Frank Wolff, Harry Davis, Elena Karam, Estelle Hemsley, Lou Antonio

'Kazan has failed to film the adventure implicit in his material, and a potentially exciting story has gone to waste.'–*MFB*

'If he sinks his teeth in a scene or a sequence that he enjoys, the audience can just sit around and be damned.'—*Stanley Kauffmann*

An American Dream
US 1966 103m Technicolor
Warner (William Conrad)
GB title: *See You in Hell, Darling*

A TV commentator is goaded into murdering his wife, becomes involved with gangsters and,

tortured by guilt, allows them to kill him for shielding the girl friend of one of them.
Ludicrously heavy-handed version of a semi-surrealist book which presumably had something to say about modern America, at least in its author's mind. Nothing comes through but relentless boredom at watching sordid and unlikely events, and sympathy for those involved.

w Mann Rubin, *novel* Norman Mailer *d* Robert Gist *ph* Sam Leavitt *m* Johnny Mandel

Stuart Whitman, Janet Leigh, Eleanor Parker (in a one-scene role of screaming bitchery that has to be seen to be believed), J. D. Cannon, Lloyd Nolan, Barry Sullivan, Murray Hamilton

American Graffiti***
US 1973 110m Techniscope
Universal / Lucasfilm / Coppola Company (Francis Ford Coppola, Gary Kurtz)

In 1962 California, four young men about to leave for college gather for a night's girl-chasing and police-baiting.
Nostalgic comedy recalling many sights and sounds of the previous generation and carefully crystallizing a particular time and place. Successful in itself, it led to many imitations.

wd George Lucas *ph* Ron Eveslage, Jan D'Alquen *m* popular songs

Richard Dreyfuss, Ronny Howard, Paul le Mat, Charlie Martin Smith, Cindy Williams, Candy Clark, Mackenzie Philips

An American Guerrilla in the Philippines*
US 1950 105m Technicolor
TCF (Lamar Trotti)
GB title: *I Shall Return*

World War II, Pacific Zone: two American sailors try to make their way to Australia after MacArthur's surrender at Bataan.
Rather dull adventure story shot in the actual locations.

w Lamar Trotti, *novel* Ira Wolfert *d* Fritz Lang *ph* Harry Jackson *m* Cyril Mockridge

Tyrone Power, Micheline Presle, Tom Ewell, Bob Pattern, Tommy Cook, Robert Barrat (as MacArthur), Jack Elam

'Cannot be regarded as a serious war film.'—*Penelope Houston*

An American in Paris****
US 1951 113m Technicolor
MGM (*Arthur Freed*)

A carefree young artist scorns a rich woman's patronage and wins the love of a gamin.
Altogether delightful musical holiday, one of the highspots of the Hollywood genre, with infectious enthusiasm and an unexpected sense of the Paris that was.

w Alan Jay Lerner *d Vincente Minnelli* *ph Al Gilks, John Alton* *m George Gershwin* *ly Ira Gershwin* *ch Gene Kelly* *ad Cedric Gibbons, Preston Ames*

Gene Kelly, Oscar Levant, Nina Foch, Leslie Caron, Georges Guetary

American Madness**
US 1932 80m bw
Columbia

When a bank failure threatens, hundreds of small savers increase their deposits to save the situation.
Vivid, overstressed topical melodrama with crowd scenes typical of its director's later output.

w Robert Riskin *d Frank Capra* *ph* Joseph Walker

Walter Huston, Pat O'Brien, Kay Johnson, Constance Cummings, Gavin Gordon, Berton Churchill

An American Romance*
US 1944 151m Technicolor
MGM (King Vidor)

The life of a European immigrant who becomes a master of industry.
Mind-boggling pageant of the American dream, coldly presented and totally humourless. Its saving grace is its smooth physical presentation.

w Herbert Dalmas, William Ludwig *d* King Vidor *ph* Harold Rosson *m* Louis Gruenberg

Brian Donlevy, Ann Richards, John Qualen, Walter Abel, Stephen McNally

'A thousand chances to inform, excite or even interest have been flung away.'—*Richard Winnington*

An American Tragedy**
US 1931 95m bw
Paramount

An ambitious young man murders his pregnant fiancée when he has a chance to marry a rich girl.
Dated but solidly satisfying adaptation of a weighty novel, more compelling than the 1951 remake *A Place in the Sun*.

wd Josef Von Sternberg, novel Theodore Dreiser *ph* Lee Garmes *ad* Hans Dreier

Phillips Holmes, *Sylvia Sidney*, Frances Dee, Irving Pichel, Frederick Burton, Claire McDowell

'It is the first time, I believe, that the subjects of sex, birth control and murder have been put into a picture with sense, taste and reality.'—*Pare Lorentz*

The Americanization of Emily*
US 1964 115m bw
MGM / Filmways (John Calley)

World War II: just before the Normandy landings, a war widow driver falls for an American commander who is a self-confessed coward.
Bizarre comedy full of eccentric characters, an uneasy choice for its female star but otherwise successful in patches in its random distillation of black comedy, sex and the tumbling of old-fashioned virtues.

w Paddy Chayevsky, *novel* William Bradford Huie *d* Arthur Hiller *ph* Philip Lathrop, Chris Challis *m* Johnny Mandel

Julie Andrews, James Garner, *Melvyn Douglas*, James Coburn, Liz Fraser, Joyce Grenfell, Edward Binns, Keenan Wynn, William Windom
'Out of it all there comes the definite feeling that Hitler's war is incidental to Paddy Chayevsky's war of ideas . . . no plot synopsis could begin to suggest how much the characters talk.'—*MFB*

Among the Living*
US 1941 68m bw
Paramount (Sol C. Siegel)

In a small town live twin brothers, one of whom is a murderer.
Offbeat suspenser with effective performances.

w Lester Cole, Garrett Fort *d* Stuart Heisler *ph* Theodor Sparkuhl

Albert Dekker, Susan Hayward, Frances Farmer, Harry Carey, Gordon Jones

The Amorous Adventures of Moll Flanders
GB 1965 125m Technicolor Panavision
Paramount / Winchester (Marcel Hellman)

An ambitious servant girl loses her virtue to a succession of rich gentlemen but finally settles for a highwayman.
The aim was to make a female *Tom Jones*, but this bawdy romp never achieves the freewheeling fluency of that surprise success, and a vacuous central performance makes the constant couplings more boring than exciting.

w Dennis Cannan, Roland Kibbee, *novel* Daniel Defoe *d* Terence Young *ph* Ted Moore *m* John Addison *pd* Syd Cain

Kim Novak, Richard Johnson, George Sanders, Lilli Palmer, Angela Lansbury, Leo McKern, Vittorio De Sica, Cecil Parker, Daniel Massey
'Further from Defoe than *Tom Jones* was from Fielding, but with much the same combination of crude table manners and clean sets to stand in for period flavour.'—*MFB*

The Amorous Prawn*
GB 1962 89m bw
BL / Covent Garden (Leslie Gilliat)
US title: *The Playgirl and the War Minister* (an attempt to cash in on the Profumo case)

A hard-up general's wife invites American paying guests to their official highland home.
This film version of a stage success seems very mild, but the cast is eager to please: the result is a frantic high class farce.

w Anthony Kimmins, Nicholas Phipps, *play* Anthony Kimmins *d* Anthony Kimmins *ph* Wilkie Cooper *m* John Barry

Joan Greenwood, Ian Carmichael, Cecil Parker, Dennis Price, Robert Beatty, Finlay Currie, Liz Fraser, Derek Nimmo

Amsterdam Affair
GB 1968 91m Eastmancolor
LIP / Trio / Group W (Gerry Willoughby)

Inspector Van der Valk investigates when a writer is accused of murdering his mistress.
Tolerable *roman policier*.

w Edmund Ward, *novel* Love in Amsterdam by Nicholas Freeling *d* Gerry O'Hara *ph* Gerry Fisher *m* Patrick John Scott

Wolfgang Kieling, William Marlowe, Caterina Von Schell

Amy Prentiss: see Mystery Movie

Anastasia**
US 1956 105m Eastmancolor Cinemascope
TCF (Buddy Adler)

In 1928 Paris, a group of exiled White Russians claim to have found the living daughter of the Tsar, presumed executed in 1918; but the claimant is a fake schooled by a general, with whom she falls in love.
Slick, highly theatrical entertainment for the upper classes; it dazzles and satisfies without throwing any light on history.

w Arthur Laurents, *play* Marcelle Maurette, Guy Bolton *d* Anatole Litvak *ph* Jack Hildyard *m* Alfred Newman *ad* Andrei Andreiev, Bill Andrews

Ingrid Bergman (her Hollywood comeback after some years in Europe under a cloud for her 'immoral' behaviour), Yul Brynner, *Helen*

Hayes, Martita Hunt, Akim Tamiroff, Felix Aylmer, Ivan Desny

'Little weight but considerable and urbane charm.'—*John Cutts*

Anatomy of a Murder**

US 1959 161m bw Cinemascope

Columbia / Otto Preminger

A small-town lawyer successfully defends an army officer accused of murdering a bartender who had assaulted his wife.

Overlong and over-faithful version of a highly detailed courtroom bestseller. The plot is necessarily equivocal, the characterizations overblown, but the trial commands some interest, and the use of 'daring' words in evidence caused controversy at the time.

w Wendell Mayes, *novel* Robert Traver *d* Otto Preminger *ph* Sam Leavitt *m* Duke Ellington *pd* Boris Leven

James Stewart, Ben Gazzara, Lee Remick, *Eve Arden,* Arthur O'Connell, *George C. Scott* (his first notable role, as the prosecutor), Kathryn Grant, Orson Bean, Murray Hamilton

† The trial judge was played by Joseph N. Welch, a real-life judge who had gained fame by his supervision of the McCarthy hearings.

Anchors Aweigh**

US 1945 139m Technicolor

MGM (Joe Pasternak)

Two sailors on leave in Los Angeles get involved with a small boy who wants to join the navy.

Rather droopy musical most notable as a forerunner of *On the Town,* though on much more conventional lines. Amiable performances, and a brilliant dance with a cartoon mouse, save the day.

w Isobel Lennart *d* George Sidney *ph* Robert Planck, Charles Boyle *principal songs* Jule Styne *ly* Sammy Cahn *m* George Stoll *pd* Cedric Gibbons

Frank Sinatra, Gene Kelly, Kathryn Grayson, Jose Iturbi, Sharon McManus, Carlos Ramirez, Dean Stockwell, Pamela Britton

And No One Could Save Her

GB 1972 73m colour TVM

Associated London (Robert Stigwood)

An American girl seeks her husband in Dublin; but there is no trace of him, so could he be a figment of her imagination?

Bunny Lake Is Missing all over again; not badly done.

w Anthony Skene *d* Kevin Billington

Lee Remick, Milo O'Shea, Frank Grimes, Jennie Linden

And Now For Something Completely Different**

GB 1971 88m colour

(Columbia) Kettledrum / Python (Victor Lowndes / GSF) (Patricia Casey)

Useful round-up of the more famous sketches from BBC TV's zany comedy series *Monty Python.*

Side-splitting for those who want Groucho Marx updated; baffling for reactionaries; movie presentation perfunctory.

written by and starring *John Cleese, Graham Chapman, Terry Gilliam, Eric Idle, Michael Palin, Terry Jones*

d Ian Macnaughton *ph* David Muir

And Now Miguel*

US 1965 95m Technicolor

Universal / Robert B. Radnitz

A 10-year-old Mexican boy proves himself worthy to work on the mountain with the sheep.

A children's film typical of its producer: good to look at, documentarily convincing, but too slight and too slow.

w Ted Sherdeman, Jane Clove, *novel* Joseph Krumgold *d* James B. Clark *ph* Clifford Stine *m* Phillip Lambro

Pat Cardi, Guy Stockwell, Clu Gulager, Michael Ansara, Joe de Santis

And Now Tomorrow*

US 1944 86m bw

Paramount (Fred Kohlmar)

A rich girl goes deaf, loses her fiancé, but wins the poor doctor who cares for her.

Bestselling slush turned into a routine star romance.

w Frank Partos, Raymond Chandler (!), *novel* Rachel Field *d* Irving Pichel *ph* Daniel L. Fapp *m* Victor Young

Loretta Young, Alan Ladd (his first film in confirmed top-star status after a meteoric rise interrupted by war service) Susan Hayward, Beulah Bondi, Cecil Kellaway, Barry Sullivan.

'A vernal sign of the boys getting back to one of their favourite legends after the wintry days of war.'—*Richard Winnington*

And So They Were Married

US 1935 74m bw

Columbia (B. P. Schulberg)

A widow and a widower try to get married

despite the ill-feeling of their children.
Predictable romantic farce.

w Doris Anderson, Joseph Anthony *d* Elliott Nugent *ph* Henry Freulich *m* Howard Jackson

Melvyn Douglas, Mary Astor, Edith Fellows, Jackie Moran, Donald Meek, Dorothy Stickney

And Soon the Darkness*
GB 1970 99m Technicolor
Associated British (Albert Fennell, Brian Clemens)

Of two young nurses on a cycling holiday in France, one is murdered by a local sex maniac and the other almost shares her fate.
Slow, overstretched, often risible suspenser on vanishing lady lines; long on red herrings and short on humour, but with some pretension to style. The action all takes place along a mile or two of sunlit country road.

w Brian Clemens, Terry Nation *d* Robert Fuest *ph* Ian Wilson *m* Laurie Johnson

Pamela Franklin, Michele Dotrice, Sandor Eles, John Nettleton

And the Angels Sing*
US 1944 95m bw
Paramount (E. D. Leshin)

Four singing sisters have hectic adventures with a bandleader.
Mildly disarming romantic comedy with music, more firmly set in a recognizable social milieu than the usual fan product from this studio.

w Melvin Frank, Norman Panama *d* Claude Binyon *ph* Karl Struss *m* Victor Young *songs* Johnny Burke, Jimmy Van Heusen

Dorothy Lamour, Diana Lynn, Betty Hutton, Mimi Chandler, Fred MacMurray, Raymond Walburn, Eddie Foy Jnr, Frank Albertson, Mikhail Rasumny

'Slapstick sophistication in a sub-Sturges manner.'—*MFB*

And Then There Were None****
US 1945 97m bw
Harry M. Popkin
GB title: *Ten Little Niggers*

Ten people are invited to a house party on a lonely island, and murdered one by one.
A classic mystery novel is here adapted and directed with the utmost care to provide playful black comedy, stylish puzzlement, and some splendid acting cameos.

w Dudley Nichols, novel Agatha Christie (aka Ten Little Niggers) *d René Clair ph Lucien Andriot m Mario Castelnovo-Tedesco*

Walter Huston, Barry Fitzgerald, Louis Hayward, June Duprez, *Roland Young, Richard Haydn,* C. Aubrey Smith, Judith Anderson, Queenie Leonard, Mischa Auer

And Then There Were None
GB 1974 98m Technicolor
EMI / Filibuster (Harry Alan Towers)

Ten people are lured to an isolated Persian hotel and murdered one by one.
Listless remake, often so inept you could scream.

w Peter Welbeck (Harry Alan Towers) *d* Peter Collinson *ph* Fernando Arribas *m* Bruno Nicolai

Oliver Reed, Richard Attenborough, Elke Sommer, Herbert Lom, Gert Froebe, Stéphane Audran, Charles Aznavour, Adolfo Celi, Alberto de Mendoza, Maria Rohm

The Anderson Tapes*
US 1971 98m Technicolor Panavision
Columbia / Robert M. Weitman

An ex-con forms a gang to rob a building, not knowing that police and others, for various purposes, are making tape recordings of his conversations.
Superficially slick and fashionable crime thriller, marred by unnecessarily flashy direction, a failure to explain enough about the tapes, and a climax which oddly mixes bloodshed and farce.

w Frank R. Pierson, *novel* Lawrence Sanders *d* Sidney Lumet *ph* Arthur J. Ornitz *m* Quincy Jones

Sean Connery, *Martin Balsam,* Dyan Cannon, Alan King, Ralph Meeker

Androcles and the Lion**
US 1952 96m bw
RKO (Gabriel Pascal)

A slave takes a thorn from the paw of a lion which later, in the arena, refuses to eat him.
Shavian drollery, with interpolated discussions on faith, is scarcely ideal cinema material, but gusto in the performances keeps it going despite stolid direction.

w Chester Erskine, *play* Bernard Shaw *d* Chester Erskine *ph* Harry Stradling *m* Frederick Hollander *ad* Harry Horner

Alan Young, Jean Simmons, Robert Newton, Victor Mature, Maurice Evans (as Caesar), Reginald Gardiner, Elsa Lanchester, Alan Mowbray, Gene Lockhart

The Andromeda Strain**
US 1970 131m Technicolor Panavision
Universal / Robert Wise

Scientists work frantically to neutralize an infected village, knowing that the least infection will cause their laboratory to self-destruct.
Solemn and over-detailed but generally suspenseful thriller, with a sense of allegory about man's inhumanity to man.

w Nelson Gidding, *novel* Michael Crichton *d* Robert Wise *ph* Richard H. Kline *m* Gil Melle *ad* Boris Leven

Arthur Hill, David Wayne, James Olson, Kate Reid, Paula Kelly

Andy Hardy Comes Home*
US 1958 81m bw
MGM (Red Doff)

Fortyish Andy returns to Carvel, his home town, to negotiate a land deal.
Rather dismal sequel to the celebrated series of *Hardy* (qv) family comedies which were enormously popular in the early forties: a thirteen-year gap is too long, and although most of the family is reunited the old Judge is sadly missed.

w Edward Everett Hutshing, Robert Morris Donley *d* Howard W. Koch *ph* William W. Spencer, Harold E. Wellman *m* Van Alexander

Mickey Rooney, Fay Holden, Cecilia Parker, Patricia Breslin, Sara Haden, Jerry Colonna

Angel**
US 1937 98m bw
Paramount (Ernst Lubitsch)

The wife of an English diplomat finds herself neglected and almost has an affair with his old friend.
A curious romantic comedy in many ways typical of its time, yet with very few laughs, showing none of its director's usual cinematic sense, and compromised by the censor's refusal to let a spade be called a spade. Underplaying, and a sense that we watch a way of life about to be swept away, just about save it.

w Samson Raphaelson, *play* Melchior Lengyel *d* Ernst Lubitsch *ph* Charles Lang *m* Frederick Hollander

Marlene Dietrich, Herbert Marshall, Melvyn Douglas, Edward Everett Horton, Laura Hope Crews, Ernest Cossart

Angel and the Badman*
US 1947 100m bw
Republic (John Wayne)

The love of a Quaker girl converts a wounded gunslinger to an honourable life.
Thoughtful western with good background detail and a fair measure of action.

wd James Edward Grant *ph* Archie Stout *m* Richard Hageman *pd* Ernest Fegte

John Wayne, Gail Russell, Harry Carey, Bruce Cabot, Irene Rich, Tom Powers

Angel Baby*
US 1960 97m bw
Madera (Thomas F. Woods)

A mute girl is cured by an evangelist, and renounces her sins.
Strident, vigorous low-budget melodrama.

w Oris Borstem, Samuel Roeca, Paul Mason, *novel* Jenny Angel by Elsie Oaks Barbour *d Paul Wendkos ph* Haskell Wexler, Jack Marta *m* Wayne Shanklin

Salome Jens, George Hamilton, Joan Blondell, Mercedes McCambridge, Henry Jones, Burt Reynolds

Angel Face*
US 1952 91m bw
RKO (Otto Preminger)

A demented girl murders her father and stepmother, involving her chauffeur, whom she finally kills, and commits suicide.
Outrageous melodrama, so absurd as to be almost endearing.

w Frank Nugent, Oscar Millard *d* Otto Preminger *ph* Harry Stradling *m* Dmitri Tiomkin

Jean Simmons, Robert Mitchum, Herbert Marshall, Barbara O'Neil, Leon Ames, Mona Freeman, Kenneth Tobey, Raymond Greenleaf

'The one lyrical nightmare in the cinema.'—*Ian Cameron*

An Angel from Texas*
US 1940 69m bw
Warner

Misadventures of a country boy in New York.
Modest revamping of a much filmed farce, also made as *The Tenderfoot* (1928) and *Dance Charlie Dance* (1937).

w Fred Niblo Jnr, Bertram Millhauser, *play* The Butter and Egg Man by George F. Kaufman *d* Ray Enright *ph* Arthur L. Todd

Eddie Albert, Rosemary Lane, Wayne Morris, Ronald Reagan, Milburn Stone

Angel in Exile
US 1948 90m bw
Republic

An ex-con heads for an abandoned Arizona mine to recover stolen gold.
Modest, effective western about a baddie who reforms.

w Charles Larson *d* Allan Dwan, Philip Ford *ph* Reggie Lanning *m* Nathan Scott

John Carroll, Adele Mara, Thomas Gomez

The Angel Levine*
US 1970 105m De Luxe
UA / Belafonte Enterprises (Chiz Schultz)

An elderly Jewish tailor complains to God of his bad luck; a black angel appears and seems to help him for a while.
Muddled and seemingly pointless parable with occasional felicities.

w Bill Gunn, Ronald Ribman, *story* Bernard Malamud *d* Jan Kadar *ph* Richard Kratina *pd* George Jenkins *m* Zdenek Linka

Zero Mostel, Harry Belafonte, Ida Kaminska, Milo O'Shea, Eli Wallach, Anne Jackson, *Gloria Foster*

'A prolonged variation on the theme that faith can produce miracles, but only if there is enough of it.'—*John Gillett*

Angel on My Shoulder**
US 1946 101m bw
UA / Charles R. Rogers

The devil promises leniency to a dead gangster if he will return to earth and take over the body of a judge who is stamping out evil.
Crude but lively fantasy on the tail-end of the *Here Comes Mr Jordan* cycle, and by the same author.

w Harry Segall, Roland Kibbee *d* Archie Mayo *ph* James Van Trees *m* Dmitri Tiomkin

Paul Muni, Claude Rains, Anne Baxter, Erskine Sanford, Hardie Albright

'The story is so imitative that it's hard to feel any more towards it than a mildly nostalgic regard.'—*Bosley Crowther*

Angel on the Amazon
US 1948 86m bw
Republic (John H. Auer)

An elderly white lady resident of the Amazon jungle looks only 25 after being scared by a panther . . .
Ludicrous melodrama which the actors take seriously.

w Lawrence Kimble *d* John H. Auer *ph* Reggie Lanning *m* Morton Scott

George Brent, Constance Bennett, Vera Hruba Ralston, Brian Aherne, Fortunio Bonanova, Alfonso Bedoya, Gus Schilling

The Angel Who Pawned Her Harp*
GB 1954 76m bw
Group Three (Sidney Cole)

A real angel arrives on a goodwill visit to seamy Islington, and manages to right a few wrongs.
Simple-minded whimsy, spottily effective, with good performances.

w Charles Terrot, Sidney Cole *d* Alan Bromly *ph* Arthur Grant *m* Antony Hopkins

Diane Cilento, Felix Aylmer, Robert Eddison, Jerry Desmonde, Sheila Sweet, Alfie Bass

The Angel with the Trumpet
GB 1949 98m bw
British Lion / London Films (Karl Hartl)

An Austrian lady has an affair with a crown prince but marries for security and dies in defiance of the Nazis.
Curious European cavalcade, dully directed to keep the budget down and accommodate long stretches of an Austrian original. An eccentricity.

w Karl Hartl, Franz Tassie, *novel* Ernst Lothar *d* Anthony Bushell *ph* Robert Krasker *m* Willy Schmidt-Gentner

Eileen Herlie, Basil Sydney, Norman Wooland, Anthony Bushell, Maria Schell, John Justin, Oskar Werner, Andrew Cruickshank

The Angel Wore Red
US 1960 105m bw
MGM / Titanus / Spectator (Gottfredo Lombardo)

The love story of a priest and a prostitute in the Spanish Civil War.
Turgid farrago, unsatisfactory both romantically and politically.

wd Nunnally Johnson *ph* Giuseppe Rotunno *m* Bronislau Kaper

Ava Gardner, Dirk Bogarde, Joseph Cotten, Vittorio De Sica, Aldo Fabrizi, Finlay Currie

'The stars show no apparent surprise that a film so empty of reward should take itself so seriously.'—*Peter John Dyer*

Angels in the Outfield
US 1952 99m bw
MGM (Clarence Brown)
GB title: *Angels and the Pirates*

The profane and bad-tempered manager of an unsuccessful baseball team gets help from an angel.
Unamusing, saccharine whimsy which does not deserve its excellent production values.

w Dorothy Kingsley, George Wells *d* Clarence Brown *ph* Paul C. Vogel *m* Daniele Amfitheatrof

Paul Douglas, Janet Leigh, Keenan Wynn,

Lewis Stone, Donna Corcoran, Spring Byington, Bruce Bennett

Angels One Five*
GB 1952 98m bw
Associated British (John W. Gossage, Derek Twist)

A slice of life in an RAF fighter station during the Battle of Britain.
Underplayed semi-documentary drama with stiff upper lips all round and the emphasis on characterization rather than action. A huge commercial success in Britain.

w Derek Twist *d* George More O'Ferrall *ph* Christopher Challis *m* John Wooldridge

Jack Hawkins, John Gregson, Michael Denison, Andrew Osborn, Cyril Raymond, Humphrey Lestocq, Dulcie Gray, Veronica Hurst

Angels Over Broadway*
US 1940 80m bw
Columbia (Ben Hecht, Douglas Fairbanks Jnr)

During one rainy New York night, three of life's failures have one last stab at success.
Would-be poetic, moralizing melodrama very typical of its author; interesting but not a success.

w Ben Hecht *d* Ben Hecht, Lee Garmes *ph* Lee Garmes

Douglas Fairbanks Jnr, Rita Hayworth, Thomas Mitchell, John Qualen, George Watts, Ralph Theodore

Angels Wash Their Faces*
US 1939 86m bw
Warner (Max Siegel)

A bad boy joins the Dead End Kids, but they all reform in the end.
Routine programmer, hastily concocted after the success of *Angels with Dirty Faces*.

w Michael Fessier, Niven Busch, Robert Buckner *d* Ray Enright *ph* Arthur Todd *m* Adolph Deutsch

Ann Sheridan, Ronald Reagan, the Dead End Kids, Bonita Granville, Frankie Thomas, Henry O'Neill, Berton Churchill, Eduardo Ciannelli

Angels with Dirty Faces****
US 1938 97m bw
Warner (Sam Bischoff)

A Brooklyn gangster is admired by slum boys, but for their sake pretends to be a coward when he goes to the electric chair.
A shrewd, slick entertainment package and a seminal movie for all kinds of reasons. It combined gangster action with fashionable social conscience; it confirmed the Dead End Kids as stars; it provided archetypal roles for its three leading players and catapulted the female lead into stardom. It also showed the Warner style of film-making, all cheap sets and shadows, at its most effective.

w John Wexley, Warren Duff, Rowland Brown *d Michael Curtiz ph Sol Polito* *m* Max Steiner

James Cagney (gangster with redeeming features), *Pat O'Brien* (priest), *Humphrey Bogart* (gangster with no redeeming features), *The Dead End Kids, Ann Sheridan*, George Bancroft, Edward Pawley

'A rousing, bloody, brutal melodrama.'—*New York Mirror*

The Angry Hills
GB 1959 105m bw
MGM / Raymond Stross

In 1940, an American war correspondent is helped by Greek freedom fighters.
Laboured war melodrama with pretentious dialogue but little characterization.

w A. I. Bezzerides, *novel* Leon Uris *d* Robert Aldrich *ph* Stephen Dade *m* Richard Rodney Bennett *ad* Ken Adam

Robert Mitchum, Gia Scala, Elisabeth Mueller, Stanley Baker, Donald Wolfit, Kieron Moore, Theodore Bikel, Sebastian Cabot, Peter Illing, Marius Goring, Leslie Phillips

The Angry Silence*
GB 1960 94m bw
British Lion / Beaver (Richard Attenborough, Bryan Forbes)

A worker who refuses to join an unofficial strike is 'sent to Coventry' by his mates; the matter hits national headlines, and the communists use it to their own advantage.
Irresistibly reminding one of a po-faced *I'm All Right Jack*, this remains a fresh and urgent film which unfortunately lost excitement in its domestic scenes.

w Bryan Forbes *d* Guy Green *ph* Arthur Ibbetson *m* Malcolm Arnold

Richard Attenborough, Michael Craig, Pier Angeli, Bernard Lee, Alfred Burke, Laurence Naismith, Geoffrey Keen

Animal Crackers***
US 1930 98m bw
Paramount

Thieves covet a valuable oil painting unveiled at a swank party.
An excuse for the Marx Brothers, and a lively

one in patches, though sedate and stage bound in treatment. The boys are all in top form, and many of the dialogue exchanges are classics.

w Morrie Ryskind, from musical play by himself and *George F. Kaufman* *d* Victor Heerman *ph* George Folsey *m/ly Bert Kalmar, Harry Ruby*

Groucho, Chico, Harpo, Zeppo, *Margaret Dumont*, Lillian Roth, Louis Sorin, Robert Greig, Hal Thompson

Animal Farm**
GB 1955 75m Technicolor
Louis de Rochemont / Halas and Batchelor

Oppressed by the cruelty and inefficiency of their master, the animals take over a farm but find fresh tyrants among themselves.
George Orwell's political fable—'all animals are equal but some animals are more equal than others'—is faithfully followed in this ambitious but rather disappointingly flat cartoon version.

w/pd John Halas and Joy Batchelor
voices Maurice Denham

The Animal Kingdom*
US 1932 95m bw
RKO (Darryl F. Zanuck)
GB title: *The Woman in His House*

An intellectual publisher tries to justify keeping both a wife and a mistress.
Smart comedy-drama from a Broadway success, later bowdlerized as *One More Tomorrow* (qv).

w Horace Jackson, *play* Philip Barry *d* Edward H. Griffith *ph* Lucien Andriot

Leslie Howard, Ann Harding, Myrna Loy, Neil Hamilton, William Gargan, Henry Stephenson, Ilka Chase

The Animal World*
US 1956 80m Technicolor
Warner / Windsor (Irwin Allen)

The evolution of animals from their primitive beginnings.
Ambitious documentary with a popular science approach; very variable, with poorish model work.

wd Irwin Allen *ph* Harold Wellman *m* Paul Sawtell *sp* Willis O'Brien, Ray Harryhausen

Ann Vickers*
US 1933 72m bw
RKO (Pandro S. Berman)

A feminist social worker is taught a thing or two by life and settles down with a corrupt judge.
Reasonably effective version of a popular though heavy-going novel of the time.

w Jane Murfin, *novel* Sinclair Lewis *d* John Cromwell *ph* David Abel, Edward Cronjager *m* Max Steiner

Irene Dunne, Walter Huston, Conrad Nagel, Bruce Cabot, Edna May Oliver, Mitchell Lewis, Murray Kinnell

Anna and the King of Siam**
US 1946 128m bw
TCF (Louis D. Lighton)

In 1862 an English governess arrives in Bangkok to teach the 67 children of the king.
Unusual and lavish drama, tastefully handled and generally absorbing despite miscasting and several slow passages.

w Talbot Jennings, Sally Benson, *book* Margaret Landon *d* John Cromwell *ph Arthur Miller* *m* Bernard Herrmann *ad Lyle Wheeler, William Darling*

Irene Dunne, Rex Harrison, Linda Darnell, Gale Sondergaard, Lee J. Cobb, Mikhail Rasumny
'A film that never touches the imagination, a film that leaves the mind uninformed and the memory unburdened.'—*Richard Winnington*

Anna Christie**
US 1930 74m bw
MGM

A waterfront prostitute falls in love with a young seaman.
Primitive sound version of an earthy theatrical warhorse: it has a niche in history as the film in which Garbo first talked.

w Frances Marion, *play* Eugene O'Neill *d* Clarence Brown *ph* William Daniels

Greta Garbo, Charles Bickford, *Marie Dressler*, James T. Mack, Lee Phelps
'A very talkie, uncinematic affair, more old-fashioned than the silent movies. If it were not so well acted it would be pretty tiresome.'—*National Board of Review*

Anna Karenina**
US 1935 95m bw
MGM (David O. Selznick)

The wife of a Russian aristocrat falls for a dashing cavalry officer.
Well-staged but finally exasperating romantic tragedy, sparked by good performances and production.

w Clemence Dane, Salka Viertel, *novel* Leo Tolstoy *d Clarence Brown* *ph William Daniels* *m* Herbert Stothart

Greta Garbo, Fredric March, *Basil Rathbone*, Freddie Bartholemew, Maureen O'Sullivan, May Robson, Reginald Owen, Reginald Denny

† Previously filmed as a 1928 silent called *Love*, with Garbo and John Gilbert.

Anna Karenina*
GB 1947 139m bw
London Films (Alexander Korda)

Tiresomely overlong but very handsomely staged remake marred by central miscasting.

w Jean Anouilh, Guy Morgan, Julien Duvivier *d* Julien Duvivier *ph Henri Alekan* *m* Constant Lambert

Vivien Leigh, Kieron Moore, *Ralph Richardson*, Marie Lohr, Sally Ann Howes, Niall MacGinnis, Michael Gough, Helen Haye, Mary Kerridge

Anna Lucasta*
US 1949 86m bw
Columbia / Security (Philip Yordan)

The bad girl of a farming family comes home to marry, but her past catches up with her.
Polish immigrant melodrama, a touring company staple, adequately transferred to the screen.

w Philip Yordan, Arthur Laurents, *play* Philip Yordan *d* Irving Rapper *ph* Sol Polito *m* David Diamond

Paulette Goddard, Oscar Homolka, Broderick Crawford, William Bishop, Gale Page, Mary Wickes

Anna Lucasta*
US 1958 97m bw
(UA) Longridge Enterprises (Sidney Harmon)

Black version of the long-running play; performances standard.

w Philip Yordan *d* Arnold Laven *ph* Lucien Ballard *m* Elmer Bernstein

Eartha Kitt, Frederick O'Neal, Sammy Davis Jnr, Henry Scott, Rex Ingram, James Edwards

Anne of Green Gables*
US 1934 79m bw
RKO (Kenneth MacGowan)

An orphan girl goes to the country to live with her aunt.
Standard version of the classic for young girls.

w Sam Mintz, *novel* L. M. Montgomery *d* George Nicholls Jnr *ph* Lucien Andriot

Anne Shirley (who had been known as Dawn O'Day and legally adopted the name of her character in this, her first starring role), Tom Brown, O. P. Heggie, Helen Westley, Sara Haden, Charley Grapewin

Anne of the Indies*
US 1951 87m Technicolor
TCF (George Jessel)

Lady pirate Anne Bonney, the terror of the Caribbean, is at odds with her former master Blackbeard.
Routine swashbuckler, generally well handled.

w Philip Dunne, Arthur Caesar *d* Jacques Tourneur *ph* Harry Jackson *m* Franz Waxman

Jean Peters, Louis Jourdan, Debra Paget, Herbert Marshall, Thomas Gomez, James Robertson Justice, Sean McClory, Francis Pierlot

Anne of the Thousand Days*
GB 1969 146m Technicolor Panavision
Universal / Hal B. Wallis

Henry VIII divorces his wife to marry Anne Boleyn, but soon finds evidence of adultery.
A somewhat unlikely view of history, rather boringly presented on a woman's magazine level, but with occasional good moments from a cast of British notables.

w John Hale, Bridget Boland, *play* Maxwell Anderson *d* Charles Jarrott *ph* Arthur Ibbetson *pd* Maurice Carter *m* Georges Delerue

Richard Burton, Geneviève Bujold, John Colicos (as Cromwell), Irene Papas, Anthony Quayle, Michael Hordern, Katharine Blake, Peter Jeffrey, William Squire, Esmond Knight, Nora Swinburne

'The costumes, beautiful in themselves, have that unconvincing air of having come straight off the rack at Nathan's.'—*Brenda Davies*

Annie Get Your Gun*
US 1950 107m Technicolor
MGM (Arthur Freed)

A young female hillbilly joins Frank Butler's sharpshooting act, and is sophisticated by her love for him.
Gaudy, stagey, generally uninspired screen version of the famous musical show based remotely on a historical character of post-wild-west days. There is a lack of dancing, the direction is stodgy, and in general flair the production falls disappointingly below MGM's usual standard.

w Sidney Sheldon, *musical play* Herbert and Dorothy Fields *d* George Sidney *ph* Charles Rosher *m/ly Irving Berlin* *ch* Robert Alton *ad* Cedric Gibbons, Paul Grosse

Betty Hutton (who took over when temperament ousted Judy Garland), *Howard Keel*, Edward Arnold, J. Carrol Naish, Louis Calhern

Annie Oakley*
US 1935 90m bw
RKO (Cliff Reid)

The historical story, more or less, of the lady later immortalized in *Annie Get Your Gun*. Lively semi-western with good dialogue but gluey plot development.

w Joel Sayre, John Twist *d George Stevens* *ph* J. Roy Hunt *m* Alberto Columbo *ad* Van Nest Polglase

Barbara Stanwyck, Preston Foster, Melvyn Douglas, Moroni Olsen, Pert Kelton, Andy Clyde, Chief Thunderbird

The Anniversary*
GB 1968 95m Technicolor
Hammer (Jimmy Sangster)

A malevolent one-eyed widow will stop at nothing to prevent her grown sons from leaving the family orbit, and they meet each year to mourn the death of the husband she really hated. Agreeable but over-talkative black comedy with a splendid role for its star and some good scattered moments, marred by a general lack of style.

w Jimmy Sangster, *play Bill MacIlwraith* *d* Roy Ward Baker *ph* Harry Waxman *m* Philip Martell

Bette Davis, Jack Hedley, *James Cossins*, Sheila Hancock, Elaine Taylor, Christian Roberts, Timothy Bateson

'Magisterially grotesque in elegantly tailored eye-patch and exotic gown, she snaps out her bitchy insults with all 57 varieties of relish.'—*MFB*

Another Dawn
US 1937 73m bw
Warner (Harry Joe Brown)

In a British army post in Africa, a wife is torn between duty and romance.
Absurdly sudsy melodrama, a potboiler for stars between more important assignments.

w Laird Doyle *d* William Dieterle *ph* Tony Gaudio *m* Erich Wolfgang Korngold

Errol Flynn, Kay Francis, Ian Hunter, Frieda Inescort, Herbert Mundin

† In every Warner film where a cinema canopy was shown, the title advertised was *Another Dawn*, so its use here as an actual title is presumably a piece of cynicism.

Another Language
US 1933 75m bw
MGM (Walter Wanger)

A young wife does not fit in with her husband's snobby family and falls in love with his nephew. Flat treatment of a dated play.

w Herman J. Mankiewicz, Gertrude Purcell, Donald Ogden Stewart, *play* Rose Franken *d* Edward H. Griffith *ph* Ray June

Helen Hayes, Robert Montgomery, John Beal, Louise Closser Hale, Henry Travers, Margaret Hamilton

Another Man's Poison*
GB 1951 89m bw
Douglas Fairbanks Jnr / Daniel M. Angel

A lady novelist poisons her husband and lover, then unwittingly takes a fatal dose herself. Hysterical vehicle for a fading Hollywood star reduced to repeating her tantrums in an English studio on a low budget; she should have stayed home, as should her director.

w Val Guest, *play* Deadlock by Leslie Sands *d* Irving Rapper *ph* Robert Krasker *m* John Greenwood

Bette Davis, Anthony Steel, Gary Merrill, Emlyn Williams, Barbara Murray, Reginald Beckwith, Edna Morris

'Barnstormers as rich and improbable as this are rare . . . the general atmosphere takes one back to 1935.'—*Gavin Lambert*

'Like reading Ethel M. Dell by flashes of lightning.'—*Frank Hauser*

Another Part of the Forest*
US 1948 108m bw
U-I (Jerry Bresler)

In the post-Civil War years, Marcus Hubbard leads his family to worldly success by cheating and the misuse of power: he lives to regret it, as the children learn their lessons all too well.
This backwards sequel to *The Little Foxes*, showing how the characters of that play got to be their nasty selves, is quite absorbingly acted but stagily presented, with plenty of care but no style.

w Vladimir Pozner, *play Lillian Hellman* *d* Michael Gordon *ph* Hal Mohr *m* Daniele Amfitheatrof

Fredric March, Florence Eldridge, Ann Blyth, Dan Duryea, Edmond O'Brien, John Dall

Another Shore*
GB 1948 77m bw
Ealing (Hal Mason)

A young Irishman dreams of life in the South Seas but gives up his fancies for love.
Curiously whimsical, artificial and unconvincing comedy drama from a famous studio, but not without its moments of interest.

w Walter Meade, *novel* Kenneth Reddin

d Charles Crichton *ph* Douglas Slocombe *m* Georges Auric

Robert Beatty, Stanley Holloway, Moira Lister

Another Time, Another Place
GB 1958 98m bw Vistavision
Paramount / Kaydor (Lewis Allen, Smedley Aston)

During World War II an American newspaperwoman has an affair with a British war correspondent; when he is killed in action, she consoles his widow.
Drippy romance, unsympathetically played and artificially set in a Cornish village.

w Stanley Mann, *novel* Lenore Coffee *d* Lewis Allen *ph* Jack Hildyard *m* Douglas Gamley

Lana Turner, Barry Sullivan, Glynis Johns, Sean Connery, Sidney James

Anthony Adverse*
US 1936 141m bw
Warner (Henry Blanke)

Adventures of an ambitious young man in early 19th-century America.
A rousing spectacle of its day, from a bestselling novel, this award-winning movie quickly dated and now seems very thin and shadowy despite the interesting talents involved.

w Sheridan Gibney, *novel* Hervey Allen *d* Mervyn Le Roy *ph Tony Gaudio ad Anton Grot m Erich Wolfgang Korngold*

Fredric March, Olivia de Havilland, Gale Sondergaard, Edmund Gwenn, Claude Rains, Anita Louise, Louis Hayward, Steffi Duna, Donald Woods, Akim Tamiroff, Ralph Morgan, Henry O'Neill

'A bulky, rambling and indecisive photoplay which has not merely taken liberties with the letter of the original but with its spirit.'—*Frank S. Nugent, New York Times*

Antony and Cleopatra*
GB 1972 170m Technicolor Todd-AO 35
Transac (Zurich) / Izaro (Madrid) / Folio Films (London) (Peter Snell)

Well-meaning, well-mounted, but quite uninspired rendering.

wd Charlton Heston, *play* William Shakespeare *ph* Rafael Pacheco *m* John Scott *pd* Maurice Pelling

Charlton Heston, Hildegarde Neil, Eric Porter, *John Castle* (as Octavius), Fernando Rey, Freddie Jones, Peter Arne, Roger Delgado

Any Number Can Play*
US 1949 103m bw
MGM (Arthur Freed)

A gambling casino owner has health problems, is reconciled with his son and retires from the game.
Rather boring drama redeemed by slightly offbeat dialogue and excellent star acting, albeit in routine roles.

w Richard Brooks, *novel* E. H. Heth *d* Mervyn Le Roy *ph* Harold Rosson *m* Lennie Hayton

Clark Gable, Alexis Smith, Mary Astor, Wendell Corey, Audrey Totter, Lewis Stone, Frank Morgan, *Marjorie Rambeau*, Barry Sullivan

Any Second Now
US 1959 98m Technicolor TVM
Universal (Gene Levitt)

A would-be wife murderer is on the run in Mexico.
Thinly stretched suspenser with attractive backgrounds.

wd Gene Levitt

Stewart Granger, Lois Nettleton, Joseph Campanella, Dana Wynter, Katy Jurado, Tom Tully

Any Wednesday*
US 1966 109m Technicolor
Warner (Julius J. Epstein)
GB title: *Bachelor Girl Apartment*

A millionaire businessman spends every Wednesday with his mistress, but complications arise when his young associate is accidentally sent to use the company flat.
Overlong screen version of a thinly scripted Broadway success in which yawns gradually overtake laughs.

w Julius J. Epstein, *play* Muriel Resnik *d* Robert Ellis Miller *ph* Harold Lipstein *m* George Duning

Jane Fonda, Dean Jones, Jason Robards Jnr, *Rosemary Murphy* (a breath of air as the deceived wife who doesn't mind), Ann Prentiss, King Moody

Anything Can Happen*
US 1952 93m bw
Paramount / William Perlberg, George Seaton

Adventures of a Russian immigrant family in New York.
A standard Hollywood product based on a sentimental best-seller.

w George Seaton, George Oppenheimer, *book* George and Helen Papashvily *d* George Seaton *ph* Daniel L. Fapp *m* Victor Young

Jose Ferrer, Kim Hunter, Kurt Kasznar, Alex Danaroff, Oscar Beregi

'Exploits to the hilt the somewhat limited possibilities of quaintness and whimsicality with a broken accent.'—*Penelope Houston*

Anything Goes**
US 1936 92m bw
Paramount (Benjamin Glazer)
TV title: *Tops is the Limit*

Romantic adventures on board a transatlantic liner.
Amiably batty musical comedy, zestfully directed and blithely performed.

w Guy Bolton, P. G. Wodehouse, Howard Lindsay, Russell Crouse, from their Broadway show *d* Lewis Milestone *songs* Cole Porter *m* Victor Young *ph* Karl Struss *ad* Hans Dreier

Bing Crosby, Ethel Merman, Charles Ruggles, Grace Bradley, Ida Lupino, Chill Wills, the Avalon Boys, Arthur Treacher

Anything Goes*
US 1956 106m Technicolor Vistavision
Paramount (Robert Emmett Dolan)

The male stars of a musical comedy each sign a girl to play the female lead; resulting complications are ironed out during a transatlantic voyage.
Below-par reworking of the 1936 film in which technical gloss and dull sets virtually reduce the characters to puppets. A few good moments transcend the general lack of imagination.

w Sidney Sheldon, from show as credited in 1936 version *d* Robert Lewis *songs* Cole Porter *m* Joseph J. Lilley *ph* John F. Warren *ch* Nick Castle, Roland Petit *ad* Hal Pereira, Joseph M. Johnson

Bing Crosby, Donald O'Connor, Zizi Jeanmaire, Mitzi Gaynor, Phil Harris, Kurt Kasznar

Anzio
Italy 1968 117m Technicolor Panavision
(Columbia) Dino de Laurentiis (Marcel Bebert)
GB title: *The Battle for Anzio*

A war correspondent joins American and British troops preparing for the 1944 landing in Italy.
Threadbare war film which wastes an all-star American cast.

w H. A. L. Craig, *book* Anzio by Wynford Vaughan Thomas *d* Edward Dmytryk *ph* Giuseppe Rotunno *m* Riz Ortolani

Robert Mitchum, Peter Falk, Arthur Kennedy, Robert Ryan, Earl Holliman, Mark Damon, Reni Santoni, Anthony Steel, Patrick Magee

'It must be a long time since a script managed to pack in so many crassly portentous statements about why men fight wars.'—*MFB*

Apache*
US 1954 91m Technicolor
UA / Hecht–Lancaster (Harold Hecht)

After the surrender of Geronimo, one Apache leader is unconquered; after creating much havoc, he settles for domesticity, and the white men let him go unharmed.
Sober western in the wake of *Broken Arrow*, with a predictably sympathetic star performance and a surprising happy ending. More decency than excitement along the way.

w James R. Webb, *novel* Bronco Apache by Paul I. Wellman *d* Robert Aldrich *ph* Ernest Laszlo *m* David Raksin

Burt Lancaster, Jean Peters, John McIntire, Charles Bronson, John Dehner, Paul Guilfoyle, Walter Sande, Monte Blue

The Apartment***
US 1960 125m bw Panavision
UA / Mirisch (Billy Wilder)

A lonely, ambitious clerk rents out his apartment to philandering executives and finds that one of them is after his own girl.
Overlong and patchy but agreeably mordant and cynical comedy with a sparkling view of city office life and some deftly handled individual sequences.

w Billy Wilder, I. A. L. Diamond d Billy Wilder ph Joseph La Shelle *m* Adolph Deutsch *ad* Alexander Trauner

Jack Lemmon, Shirley Maclaine, Fred MacMurray, Ray Walston, Jack Kruschen, Edie Adams, David Lewis

'Without either style or taste, shifting gears between pathos and slapstick without any transition.'—*Dwight MacDonald*

Apartment for Peggy*
US 1948 98m Technicolor
TCF (William Perlberg)

A retired professor finds a new lease of life through caring for the homeless family of an ex-GI.
Sentimental comedy with serious undertones (the professor twice attempts suicide). Signs of enterprise are smothered by regulation charm.

wd George Seaton, *story* Faith Baldwin *ph* Harry Jackson *m* David Raksin

Edmund Gwenn, Jeanne Crain, William Holden, Gene Lockhart, Henri Letondal, Charles Lane, Houseley Stevenson

The Appaloosa*
US 1966 99m Techniscope
Universal (Alan Miller)
GB title: *Southwest to Sonora*

A cowboy's plan to start a stud farm with his magnificent horse is interrupted by badmen who think he has molested their girl.
Mannered, slow western set on the Mexican border, with star and director apparently striving to upstage each other.

w James Bridges, Roland Kibbee, *novel* Robert MacLeod *d* Sidney J. Furie *ph Russell Metty* *m* Frank Skinner

Marlon Brando, Anjanette Comer, John Saxon, Rafael Campos, Frank Silvera

'Seems intent less on telling a story than in carving out the incidental details.'—*MFB*

'The camerawork concentrates on beady eyes, sweaty foreheads, spurred boots and anonymous midriffs being studied through a variety of frames, ranging from tequila bottles to cook fires to grillwork to fingers to feet.'—*Judith Crist*

Applause***
US 1929 78m bw
Paramount (Jesse L. Lasky, Walter Wanger)

A vaudeville star gradually loses the love of her daughter.
Absorbing treatment of a hasbeen tearjerking theme, full of cinematic touches and with unusual use of New York locations.

w Garrett Fort, *novel* Beth Brown *d Rouben Mamoulian* *ph* George Folsey

Helen Morgan, Joan Peers, Henry Wadsworth, Fuller Mellish Jnr

'An oasis of filmic sophistication in a desert of stage-bound early talkies.'—*William Everson, 1966*

The Appointment*
US 1969 100m colour
MGM (Martin Poll)

A businessman suspects his wife of spare time prostitution.
Unusual sophisticated fable, dressed to kill but rather stretched out for its substance. Shades of *El* and *The Chinese Room.*

w James Salter *d* Sidney Lumet *m* John Barry

Omar Sharif, Anouk Aimée, Lotte Lenya

Appointment in Berlin
US 1943 77m bw
Columbia (Sam Bischoff)

An RAF wing commander expresses unpopular views and is recruited by the Nazis as a 'voice of truth' broadcaster.
World War II potboiler.

w Horace McCoy, Michael Hogan *d* Alfred E. Green *ph* Franz Planer *m* Anthony Collins

George Sanders, Marguerite Chapman, Gale Sondergaard, Onslow Stevens, Alan Napier, H. P. Sanders (the star's father)

Appointment in London*
GB 1952 96m bw
Mayflower (Aubrey Baring, Maxwell Setton)

The exploits of a squadron of Bomber Command during one month in 1943.
Dullish war film with standard credits.

w John Wooldridge, Robert Westerby *d* Philip Leacock *ph* Stephen Dade *m* John Wooldridge

Dirk Bogarde, Ian Hunter, Dinah Sheridan, Bill Kerr, Bryan Forbes, William Sylvester, Charles Victor

Appointment with Danger*
US 1949 89m bw
Paramount (Robert Fellows)

A nun becomes the government's chief witness in identifying the murderers of a US postal inspector.
Routine but entertaining star thick-ear.

w Richard Breen, Warren Duff *d* Lewis Allen *ph* John Seitz *m* Victor Young

Alan Ladd, Phyllis Calvert, Paul Stewart, Jan Sterling, Jack Webb, Henry Morgan

Appointment with Venus**
GB 1951 89m bw
GFD / British Film Makers (Betty E. Box)
US title: *Island Rescue*

During World War II, a pedigree cow is rescued from the German-occupied Channel Islands.
Curious but generally agreeable mixture of comedy and war adventure, pleasantly shot on Sark.

w Nicholas Phipps, *novel* Jerrard Tickell *d* Ralph Thomas *ph* Ernest Steward *m* Benjamin Frankel

David Niven, Glynis Johns, George Coulouris, Barry Jones, Kenneth More, Noel Purcell, Bernard Lee, Jeremy Spenser

The Apprenticeship of Duddy Kravitz*
Canada 1974 121m Bellevue–Pathe Panavision
Duddy Kravitz Syndicate (Gerald Schneider)

An ambitious young Jew finds that it is best to be liked.
Amusing adventures of an anti-hero; good scenes but rather patchy technique.

w Mordecai Richler, from his novel *d* Ted Kotcheff *ph* Miklos Lente *m* Stanley Myers

Richard Dreyfuss, Micheline Lanctot, Jack Warden, Randy Quaid, Denholm Elliott, Joseph Wiseman

The April Fools*
US 1969 95m Technicolor Panavision
Cinema Center / Jalem (Gordon Carroll)

An unhappy New York husband elopes to Paris with an unhappy wife.
Whimsical romantic comedy which rather strains its resources without giving full value for money in romance, humour or simple charm. Good moments, though.

w Hal Dresner *d* Stuart Rosenberg *ph* Michel Hugo *m* Marvin Hamlisch *pd* Richard Sylbert

Jack Lemmon, Catherine Deneuve, Myrna Loy, Charles Boyer, Peter Lawford, Jack Weston, Harvey Korman, Sally Kellerman
'Painfully modish, from the opening party in an apartment filled with fashionable objets d'art to the final mad dash to the airport in an expensive sports car.'—*MFB*

April in Paris*
US 1952 100m Technicolor
Warner (William Jacobs)

A chorus girl is mistakenly invited to a US Arts Festival in Paris, and bewitches the bureaucrat in charge.
Poorly produced star musical with a thin plot and a few redeeming wisps of wit.

w Jack Rose, Melville Shavelson *d* David Butler *ph* Wilfrid Cline *m* Ray Heindorf *ch* Le Roy Prinz *songs* Sammy Cahn, Vernon Duke, E. Y. Harburg

Doris Day, *Ray Bolger*, Claude Dauphin, Eve Miller, George Givot

April Love
US 1957 99m Eastmancolor
Cinemascope
TCF (David Weisbart)

For stealing a car, a teenager is sent on probation to his uncle's stud farm, where circumstances seem once again to put him in trouble with the law.
Easygoing star vehicle with little to recommend it to adults.

w Winston Miller, *novel* George Agnew Chamberlain *d* Henry Levin *ph* Wilfrid Cline *songs* Sammy Fain, Paul Francis Webster

Pat Boone, Shirley Jones, Dolores Michaels, Arthur O'Connell, Jeanette Nolan

April Showers*
US 1948 94m bw
Warner (William Jacobs)

In a family vaudeville act, Dad takes to drink.
Hoary musical melodrama enlivened by occasional acts.

w Peter Milne *d* James V. Kern *ph* Carl Guthrie *m* Ray Heindorf

Jack Carson, Robert Alda, Ann Sothern, Robert Ellis, S. Z. Sakall

The Aquarians
US 1970 96m Technicolor TVM
Universal (Ivan Tors)

Underwater scientists fight sharks, earthquakes, and each other.
Routine ocean depths hokum, professionally but boringly handled.

w Leslie Stevens, Winston Miller *d* Don McDougall *m* Lalo Schifrin

Ricardo Montalban, Jose Ferrer, Leslie Nielsen, Kate Woodville

Arabesque**
US 1966 118m Technicolor
Panavision
Universal (Stanley Donen)

An Oxford professor is asked by Middle Eastern oil magnates to decipher a hieroglyphic, and finds afterwards that he is marked for assassination.
The ultimate in sixties spy kaleidoscopes, in which the working out of the plot matters much less than the stars, the jokes and the lavish backgrounds. Fast moving, amusing and utterly forgettable.

w Julian Mitchell, Stanley Price, Pierre Marton *d* Stanley Donen *ph Christopher Challis* *ad* Reece Pemberton *m* Henry Mancini

Gregory Peck, Sophia Loren, *Alan Badel*, Kieron Moore, Carl Duering
'Nothing could look more "with it", or somehow matter less.'—*MFB*

Arabian Nights*
US 1942 86m Technicolor
Universal (Walter Wanger)

The Caliph of Baghdad is deposed by his half-brother but wins back his throne with the help of a dancer and an acrobat.
Well presented oriental adventure which has nothing to do with its source material but entertained multitudes in search of relief from total war and was followed by several vaguely similar slices of hokum with the same stars.

w Michael Hogan *d John Rawlins* *ph* Milton Krasner *m* Frank Skinner

Jon Hall, Maria Montez, Sabu, Leif Erickson, Thomas Gomez, Turhan Bey, John Qualen, Billy Gilbert, Shemp Howard

Arch of Triumph*
US 1948 120m bw
Enterprise (Lewis Milestone)

In postwar Paris, an embittered refugee seeks his former Nazi tormentor and has a tragic romance with a would-be suicide.
Doleful, set-bound melodrama knee-deep in misery and artificial melodramatics. An expensive, ambitious failure, both commercially and artistically, but an interesting one.

w Lewis Milestone, Harry Brown, *novel* Erich Maria Remarque *d* Lewis Milestone *ph* Russell Metty

Ingrid Bergman, Charles Boyer, Charles Laughton, Louis Calhern

Are Husbands Necessary?
US 1942 79m bw
Paramount

A bickering couple decide to kiss and make up.
Mild marital comedy in a familiar mould.

w Tess Slesinger, Frank Davis, *novel* Mr and Mrs Cugat by Isabel Scott Rorick *d* Norman Taurog *ph* Charles Lang

Ray Milland, Betty Field, Patricia Morison, Eugene Pallette, Charles Dingle, Cecil Kellaway, Leif Erickson, Richard Haydn, Elizabeth Risdon

Arena
US 1953 83m Anscocolor 3-D
MGM (Arthur M. Loew Jnr)

A rodeo rider regains his wife and his sense when his best friend is killed.
Routine actioner, distinguished by 3-D camerawork.

w Harold Jack Bloom *d* Richard Fleischer *ph* Paul C. Vogel *m* Rudolph G. Kopp

Gig Young, Jean Hagen, Polly Bergen, Henry Morgan, Barbara Lawrence, Robert Horton, Lee Van Cleef

Aren't Men Beasts!*
GB 1937 66m bw
BIP (Walter Mycroft)

A dentist poses as his aunt to stop a plot to prevent his son's marriage.
Archetypal British star farce.

w Marjorie Deans, William Freshman, *play* Vernon Sylvaine *d* Graham Cutts

Robertson Hare, Alfred Drayton, June Clyde, Billy Milton, Judy Kelly

Arise My Love***
US 1940 113m bw
Paramount (Arthur Hornblow Jnr)

American reporters in Europe and in love survive the Spanish Civil War, a wrathful editor in Paris and the sinking of the *Athenia*.
Unique sophisticated entertainment gleaned from the century's grimmest headlines, ending with a plea against American isolationism. A significant and stylish comedy melodrama.

w Charles Brackett, Billy Wilder d Mitchell Leisen *ph* Charles Lang *m* Victor Young

Claudette Colbert, Ray Milland, Walter Abel (who as the harassed editor inaugurated his celebrated line 'I'm not happy. I'm not happy at all . . .'), Dennis O'Keefe, George Zucco, Dick Purcell

The Aristocats**
US 1970 78m Technicolor
Walt Disney

Two cats are deliberately lost by a butler who fears they will inherit his mistress's wealth; but a variety of animal friends restore them to their rightful place.
Cartoon feature, a moderate example of the studio's work after Disney's death, with rather too few felicitous moments.

d Wolfgang Reitherman

Arizona
US 1941 125m bw
Columbia (Wesley Ruggles)

A Tucson wildcat meets her match in a travelling Missourian who helps her outwit villains who are sabotaging her wagon trains.
Loosely built, deliberately paced western which for all its pretensions makes very little impact.

w Claude Binyon *d* Wesley Ruggles *ph* Joseph Walker, Harry Hollenberger, Fayte Brown *m* Victor Young

Jean Arthur, William Holden, Warren William, Porter Hall, Paul Harvey, George Chandler, Byron Foulger, Regis Toomey, Edgar Buchanan

'Lacks the sweep and dramatic impulse that would have made it a great picture.'—*Variety*

Arizona Bushwhackers
US 1968 86m Techniscope
Paramount (A. C. Lyles)

A Confederate prisoner is given a chance as a western sheriff.
Stolid western, notable only, as is usual with this

producer, for its gallery of ageing but still reliable familiar faces.

w Steve Fisher *d* Lesley Selander *ph* Lester Shorr *m* Jimmie Haskell

Howard Keel, Yvonne de Carlo, Brian Donlevy, John Ireland, Marilyn Maxwell, Scott Brady, Barton Maclane, James Craig

Armored Car Robbery*
US 1950 67m bw
RKO (Herman Schlom)

A police lieutenant leads the recovery of half a million dollars stolen by gangsters.
Good competent second feature with Los Angeles locations and detailed observation of police methods.

w Earl Felton, Gerald Drayson Adams *d* Richard Fleischer *ph* Guy Roe *m* Constantin Bakaleinikoff

Charles McGraw, Adele Jergens, William Talman, Douglas Fowley, Steve Brodie

Armored Command
US 1961 105m bw
Allied Artists (Ron W. Alcorn)

During the Battle of the Bulge, a ravishing Nazi spy is infiltrated into an American army outpost.
Incredible Mata Hari melodrama posing as a war film, nicely shot in bleak snowscapes. Not exactly rewarding, but unusual.

w Ron W. Alcorn *d* Byron Haskin *ph* Ernest Haller *m* Bert Grund

Howard Keel, Tina Louise, Burt Reynolds, Earl Holliman, Warner Anderson, Carleton Young, Marty Ingels

Around the World
US 1943 81m bw
RKO (Allan Dwan)

Kay Kyser's band goes on a world tour to entertain troops overseas.
Typical wartime patriotic musical, now of sociological interest.

w Ralph Spence *d* Allan Dwan *ph* Russell Metty *md* Constantin Bakaleinikoff

Kay Kyser, Ish Kabibble, Ginny Simms, Joan Davis, Mischa Auer

Around the World in Eighty Days***
US 1956 178m Technicolor
Todd-AO
UA / *Michael Todd*

A Victorian gentleman and his valet win a bet that they can go round the world in eighty days.
Amiable large-scale pageant resolving itself into a number of sketches, which could have been much sharper, separated by wide screen spectacle. What was breathtaking at the time seems generally slow and blunted in retrospect, but the fascination of recognising 44 cameo stars remains. The film is less an exercise in traditional skills than a tribute to its producer's energy.

w James Poe, John Farrow, S. J. Perelman, *novel* Jules Verne *d* Michael Anderson, Kevin McClory *ph Lionel Lindon m Victor Young titles Saul Bass*

David Niven, Cantinflas, Robert Newton, Shirley Maclaine, Charles Boyer, Joe E. Brown, Martine Carol, John Carradine, Charles Coburn, *Ronald Colman*, Melville Cooper, *Noel Coward*, Finlay Currie, Reginald Denny, Andy Devine, Marlene Dietrich, Luis Dominguin, Fernandel, *John Gielgud*, Hermione Gingold, Jose Greco, Cedric Hardwicke, Trevor Howard, Glynis Johns, *Buster Keaton*, Evelyn Keyes, Beatrice Lillie, Peter Lorre, Edmund Lowe, A. E. Matthews, Mike Mazurki, Tim McCoy, Victor McLaglen, John Mills, Alan Mowbray, Robert Morley, Jack Oakie, George Raft, Gilbert Roland, Cesar Romero, Frank Sinatra, *Red Skelton*, Ronald Squire, Basil Sidney, *Harcourt Williams*, Ed Murrow

'Michael Todd's "show", shorn of the ballyhoo and to critics not mollified by parties and sweetmeats, is a film like any other, only twice as long as most . . . the shots of trains and boats seem endless.'—*David Robinson*

Around the World under the Sea
US 1966 110m Metrocolor
Panavision
MGM / Ivan Tors (Andrew Marton)

An ultra-modern underwater craft travels around the seabed fixing sensors to give early warning of volcanoes.
Earnest, dullish, elementary sci-fi with cardboard characters providing routine five men-one woman skirmishes.

w Arthur Weiss, Art Arthur *d* Andrew Marton, Ricou Browning *ph* Clifford Poland, Lamar Boren *m* Harry Sukman

Lloyd Bridges, Shirley Eaton, Brian Kelly, David McCallum, Keenan Wynn, Marshall Thompson, Gary Merrill

The Arrangement**
US 1969 127m Technicolor
Panavision
Warner / Athena (Elia Kazan)

A wealthy advertising man fails in a suicide attempt and spends his convalescence reflecting on his unsatisfactory emotional life.
A lush, all-American melodrama, rich in

technique but peopled by characters who have nothing to say; the film makes no discernible point except as a well-acted tirade against the compromises of modern urban living.

wd Elia Kazan, from his own novel *ph Robert Surtees* *m* David Amram *pd* Malcolm C. Bert

Kirk Douglas, Faye Dunaway, Deborah Kerr, Richard Boone, Hume Cronyn

'The sort of collage that won't fit together, no matter where you stand.'—*PS*

Arrest Bulldog Drummond: see Bulldog Drummond

Arrowhead
US 1953 105m Technicolor
Paramount (Nat Holt)

Enmity between an army scout and an Indian chief is resolved by single combat.
Standard western, good-looking but rather lifeless.

w Charles Marquis Warren, *novel* W. R. Burnett *d* Charles Marquis Warren *ph* Ray Rennahan *m* Paul Sawtell

Charlton Heston, Jack Palance, Katy Jurado, Brian Keith, Milburn Stone

Arrowsmith*
US 1932 108m bw
Samuel Goldwyn

The self-sacrificing career of a doctor.
Emotionally satisfactory, dramatically slow and unsurprising variation on a theme which has since been treated far too often.

w Sidney Howard, *novel* Sinclair Lewis *d* John Ford *ph* Ray June *m* Alfred Newman

Ronald Colman, Helen Hayes, Richard Bennett, Myrna Loy, Charlotte Henry, Beulah Bondi, A. E. Anson

Arsene Lupin**
US 1932 75m bw
MGM

The Parisian gentleman thief accomplishes some daring robberies and is almost caught stealing the Mona Lisa.
Amusing crook comedy with a few flat passages but much sparkle in between, and a lively finale.

w Carey Wilson, Lenore Coffee, Bayard Veiller *d* Jack Conway *ph* Oliver Marsh

John Barrymore, Lionel Barrymore, Karen Morley, Tully Marshall, John Miljan

Arsenic and Old Lace***
US 1942 (released 1944) 118m bw
Warner (Frank Capra)

Two dear, well-meaning old ladies invite lonely old men to their Brooklyn home, poison them with elderberry wine, and have their mad brother, who believes the corpses are yellow fever victims, bury them in the cellar. A homicidal nephew then turns up with bodies of his own.
A model for stage play adaptations, this famous black farce provided a frenzy of hilarious activity, and its flippant attitude to death was better received in wartime than would have been the case earlier or later. The director coaxes some perfect if overstated performances from his star cast, and added his own flair for perpetuating a hubbub.

w Julius J. and Philip G. Epstein, from the play by Joseph Kesselring with help from Howard Lindsay and Russell Crouse *d Frank Capra* *ph Sol Polito* *m* Max Steiner

Cary Grant (registering nineteen double takes to the minute), *Josephine Hull, Jean Adair, Raymond Massey, Peter Lorre, Priscilla Lane, Edward Everett Horton, James Gleason, John Alexander, Jack Carson, Grant Mitchell*

The Art of Crime
US 1975 100m colour TVM
Brut

A girl is kidnapped by an escaped mental inmate, and falls in love with him.
Wouldn't you just know?

novel Welcome to Xanadu by Nathaniel Benchley *d* Lee Phillips

Linda Blair, Martin Sheen, Jeanne Cooper

The Art of Love
US 1965 99m Technicolor
Universal / Ross Hunter

To stimulate interest in his work, a penniless artist fakes suicide, subsequently becoming so famous that he finds it difficult to reappear.
A pleasant black comedy idea is buried under lush production, dull direction and a host of unattractive Parisian sets.

w Carl Reiner *d* Norman Jewison *ph* Russell Metty *m* Cy Coleman

James Garner, Dick Van Dyke, Angie Dickinson, Elke Sommer, Ethel Merman, Pierre Olaf

Artists and Models*
US 1937 97m bw
Paramount (Lewis E. Gensler)

An advertising man has to find the right girl as symbol for a silverware company.
Fairly stylish comedy musical with many elements typical of its studio.

w Walter de Leon, Francis Martin *d* Raoul Walsh *ph* Victor Milner *m* Victor Young *songs* various

Jack Benny, Ida Lupino, Richard Arlen, Gail Patrick, Ben Blue, Judy Canova, Martha Raye, Donald Meek, Hedda Hopper, André Kostelanetz and his Orchestra, Louis Armstrong and his Orchestra

Artists and Models*
US 1955 109m Technicolor Vistavision
Paramount / Hal B. Wallis

A goonish young man receives telepathic top secret information in his nightmares, which are used by his artist friend in comic strips; foreign agents and the CIA get interested.
A good zany idea is worked into an overlong dyspeptic comedy which neither the stars nor frantic treatment can hope to save.

w Frank Tashlin, Don McGuire *d* Frank Tashlin *ph* Daniel Fapp *m* Walter Scharf

Dean Martin, Jerry Lewis, Shirley Maclaine, Dorothy Malone, Eddie Mayehoff, Eva Gabor, Anita Ekberg, George 'Foghorn' Winslow, Jack Elam

Artists and Models Abroad*
US 1938 90m bw
Paramount (Arthur Hornblow Jnr)
GB title: *Stranded in Paris*

Stranded in Paris, a troupe of girls and their manager are helped by a Texas oil millionaire.
Generally agreeable comedy musical with emphasis on fashion.

w Howard Lindsay, Russell Crouse, Ken Englund *d Mitchell Leisen* *ph* Ted Tetzlaff *md* Borris Morros *songs* various *ad Hans Dreier, Ernest Fegte*

Jack Benny, Joan Bennett, Mary Boland, Charley Grapewin, Joyce Compton, the Yacht Club Boys, Fritz Feld, G. P. Huntley, Monty Woolley

As Long as They're Happy*
GB 1955 91m Eastmancolor
Rank / Group (Raymond Stross)

The suburban home of a London stockbroker is invaded by an American sob singer.
Frantic farce expanded from a stage satire of the Johnnie Ray cult; a patchy but sometimes funny star vehicle.

w Alan Melville, *play* Vernon Sylvaine *d* J. Lee-Thompson

Jack Buchanan, Brenda de Banzie, Diana Dors, Jean Carson, Janette Scott, Susan Stephen, Jerry Wayne, Hugh McDermott

As You Desire Me*
US 1931 71m bw
MGM (George Fitzmaurice)

The amnesiac mistress of a novelist rediscovers her real husband and falls in love with him again.
Interesting star vehicle with good cast and production.

w Gene Markey, *play* Luigi Pirandello *d* George Fitzmaurice *ph* William Daniels

Greta Garbo, Melvyn Douglas, Erich Von Stroheim, Owen Moore, Hedda Hopper, Rafaela Ottiano

As You Like It*
GB 1936 96m bw
TCF / Inter-Allied (Joseph M. Schenck, Paul Czinner)

The fortunes of an exiled king take a turn in the Forest of Arden.
Stylized, rather effete but often amusing version of Shakespeare's pastoral comedy.

w J. M. Barrie, Robert Cullen, *play* William Shakespeare *d* Paul Czinner

Elisabeth Bergner, Laurence Olivier, Sophie Stewart, Leon Quartermaine, Henry Ainley, Richard Ainley, Felix Aylmer, Mackenzie Ward, Aubrey Mather, John Laurie, Peter Bull

As Young as You Feel*
US 1951 77m bw
TCF (Lamar Trotti)

An elderly employee, forced to retire, impersonates the company president, saves the firm from bankruptcy, and proves his continued worth.
Good-natured comedy, ably presented.

w Lamar Trotti, *story* Paddy Chayevsky *d* Harmon Jones *ph* Joe MacDonald *m* Cyril Mockridge

Monty Woolley, Constance Bennett, Thelma Ritter, David Wayne, Jean Peters, Marilyn Monroe, Allyn Joslyn, Albert Dekker

Ash Wednesday*
US 1973 99m Technicolor
Sagittarius (Dominick Dunne)

An ageing American beauty rejuvenates herself via plastic surgery, leads a vivid sex life, and leaves her stolid husband.
The bloodthirsty operation scenes are revolting,

yet this joyless saga seems meant as a celebration of the wonders of cosmetic surgery and Sex for the Aged. Hypnotic but hardly rewarding.

w Jean Claude Tramont *d* Larry Peerce *ph* Ennio Guarnieri *m* Maurice Jarre

Elizabeth Taylor, Henry Fonda, Helmut Berger, Keith Baxter, Maurice Teynac

Ask a Policeman**
GB 1938 82m bw
Gainsborough (Edward Black)

In a small coastal village, incompetent policemen accidentally expose smugglers who are scaring the locals with a headless horseman legend.
One of the best comedies of an incomparable team, with smart dialogue, good situations and a measure of suspense.

w Marriott Edgar, Val Guest, J. O. C. Orton d Marcel Varnel

Will Hay, Moore Marriott, Graham Moffatt, Glennis Lorimer, *Peter Gawthorne, Herbert Lomas,* Charles Oliver

Ask Any Girl*
US 1959 98m Metrocolor Cinemascope
MGM / Euterpe (Joe Pasternak)

A husband-hunting receptionist in New York catches the eye of a wealthy playboy but finally settles for his elder brother.
Predictable Cinderella story with a lively but forgettable script and actors going through familiar paces.

w George Wells, *novel* Winifred Wolfe *d* Charles Walters *ph* Robert Bronner *m* Jeff Alexander

David Niven, Shirley Maclaine, Gig Young, Rod Taylor, Jim Backus, Claire Kelly

'Like a comic strip transposed to the glossy pages of *Vogue*'.—*MFB*

The Asphalt Jungle***
US 1950 112m bw
MGM (Arthur Hornblow Jnr)

An elderly crook comes out of prison and assembles a gang for one last robbery.
Probably the very first film to show a 'caper' from the criminals' viewpoint (a genre which has since been done to death several times over), this is a clever character study rather than a thriller, extremely well executed and indeed generally irreproachable yet somehow not a film likely to appear on many top ten lists; perhaps the writer-director stands too far back from everybody, or perhaps he just needed Humphrey Bogart.

w Ben Maddow, John Huston, *novel* W. R. Burnett *d John Huston ph* Harold Rosson *m* Miklos Rozsa

Sterling Hayden, *Sam Jaffe, Louis Calhern,* Jean Hagen, Marilyn Monroe, James Whitmore, John McIntire, Marc Lawrence, Barry Kelley

'Where this film excels is in the fluency of its narration, the sharpness of its observation of character and the excitement of its human groupings.'—*Dilys Powell*

'I wouldn't walk across the room to see a thing like that.'—*Louis B. Mayer*

† Apart from imitations, the film has been directly remade as *The Badlanders, Cairo* and *A Cool Breeze.*

The Assassination Bureau*
GB 1968 110m Technicolor
Paramount / Heathfield (Michael Relph)

In 1906 a lady journalist breaks up an international gang of professional killers by falling in love with their leader.
Black comedy period pastiche which resolves itself into a series of sketches leading up to a spectacular zeppelin climax. Plenty going on, but the level of wit is not high.

w Michael Relph, with Wolf Mankowitz *d* Basil Dearden *ph Geoffrey Unsworth m* Ron Grainer

Oliver Reed, Diana Rigg, Telly Savalas, Curt Jurgens, Philippe Noiret, Warren Mitchell, Clive Revill, Beryl Reid, Kenneth Griffith

The Assassination of Trotsky*
Italy / GB / France 1972 103m Technicolor
Dino de Laurentiis / Josef Shaftel / Cinetel (Norman Priggen, Joseph Losey)

In 1940, Trotsky is hiding out in Mexico; a Stalinist infiltrates his presence and kills him with an ice pick.
Glum historical reconstruction with much fictitious padding; basically undramatic.

w Nicholas Mosley, Masolino d'Amico *d* Joseph Losey *ph* Pasquale de Santis *m* Egisto Macchi

Richard Burton, Alain Delon, Romy Schneider, Valentina Cortese, Jean Desailly

Assault
GB 1970 91m Eastmancolor
Rank / Peter Rogers (George H. Brown)

An art mistress helps police to solve a case of multiple rape in an English village.
Old-fashioned police mystery with new-fangled shock treatment. Routine excitements.

w John Kruse, *novel* Kendal Young *d* Sidney Hayers *ph* Ken Hodges *m* Eric Rogers

Frank Finlay, Suzy Kendall, James Laurenson, Lesley-Anne Down, Freddie Jones, Tony Beckley, Anthony Ainley, Dilys Hamlett

Assault on a Queen
US 1966 106m Technicolor Panavision
Paramount / Seven Arts / Sinatra Enterprises (William Goetz)

Crooks dredge up a submarine and use it to hi-jack the *Queen Mary*.
Strained caper film which remains uncertain whether to play for drama or thrills, and achieves neither. Special effects unconvincing.

w Rod Serling, *novel* Jack Finney *d* Jack Donohue *ph* William Daniels *m* Duke Ellington

Frank Sinatra, Virna Lisi, Tony Franciosa, Alf Kjellin, Errol John, Richard Conte, Murray Matheson, Reginald Denny
'Just about as enthralling as plastic boats in the bath.'—*MFB*

Assault on the Wayne
US 1970 74m colour TVM
Paramount

Enemy agents try to seize a top secret device from an atomic submarine.
Standard excitements, quite professionally put together.

d Marvin Chomsky

Joseph Cotten, Leonard Nimoy, Lloyd Haynes, Dewey Martin, Kenan Wynn, William Windom

Assignment K
GB 1968 97m Techniscope
Columbia / Mazurka (Ben Arbeid, Maurice Foster)

The European head of a toy firm is also head of a special spy unit.
Dreary espionage thriller, instantly forgettable, and only watchable at odd moments while it's on.

w Val Guest, Bill Strutton, Maurice Foster, *novel* Hartley Howard *d* Val Guest *ph* Ken Hodges *m* Basil Kirchen

Stephen Boyd, Michael Redgrave, Camilla Sparv, Leo McKern, Jeremy Kemp

Assignment Munich
US 1972 96m colour TVM
MGM

A shady American saloon owner in Germany helps the US Army find loot stolen during World War II.
Pilot for a short-lived series which turned up as *Assignment Vienna*. (Vienna gave more facilities.) The aim was for a cross between *Casablanca* and *The Third Man*, but what came on the screen was pure hokum.

w Eric Bercovici, Jerry Ludwig *d* David Lowell Rich

Roy Scheider, Richard Basehart, Lesley Warren, Werner Klemperer, Robert Reed, Pernell Roberts, Keenan Wynn

Assignment to Kill
US 1967 99m Technicolor Panavision
Warner Seven Arts (William Conrad)

A New York insurance company hires a private eye to investigate a dubious European financier.
Routine international intrigue with muddled plot and unusual cast. A nice production wasted.

wd Sheldon Reynolds *ph* Harold Lipstein *m* William Lava

Patrick O'Neal, John Gielgud, Peter Van Eyck, Joan Hackett, Herbert Lom, Eric Portman, Oscar Homolka, Leon Greene

The Astonished Heart*
GB 1949 89m bw
Gainsborough / Sydney Box (Antony Darnborough)

A psychiatrist is permitted by his wife to fall in love with another woman but finds the situation intolerable and kills himself.
The star, looking like a Chinese mandarin, reached his nadir in this unwise screen adaptation, inelegantly directed, of one of his slightest short plays about boring and effete people. It sank without trace.

w Noel Coward, from his play *d* Terence Fisher, Antony Darnborough *ph* Jack Asher *m* Noel Coward

Noel Coward, Margaret Leighton, Celia Johnson, Graham Payn, Joyce Carey, Ralph Michael, Michael Hordern

The Astronaut*
US 1971 74m Technicolor TVM
Universal

A civilian is asked to double for a famous astronaut who has been injured.
Tense melodrama which eventually runs out of plot.

w Gerald di Pego, Charles R. Kuenstle *d* Robert Michael Lewis

Jackie Cooper, Monte Markham, Susan Clark, Robert Lansing, Richard Anderson, John Lupton

Asylum*
GB 1972 88m Eastmancolor
Amicus (Max J. Rosenberg, Milton Subotsky)

A doctor applies for a job at an asylum, hears weird stories from four patients, and finds himself in the middle of a weirder one.
Lively horror compilation with echoes of *Caligari* and *Dead of Night*. Gruesomeness sometimes overdone.

w Robert Bloch *d* Roy Ward Baker *ph* Denys Coop *m* Douglas Gamley

Patrick Magee, Robert Powell, Geoffrey Bayldon, Barbara Parkins, Sylvia Syms, Richard Todd, Peter Cushing, Barry Morse, Britt Ekland, Charlotte Rampling, James Villiers, Megs Jenkins, Herbert Lom

Asylum for a Spy
US 1967 74m Technicolor TVM
Universal

A spy suffers a mental breakdown and a counterspy goes undercover in the hospital to pick his brains.
Tedious, talky suspenser, originally a Chrysler Theatre two-parter

w Robert L. Joseph *d* Stuart Rosenberg

Robert Stack, Felicia Farr, Martin Milner, George Macready

At Long Last Love
US 1975 114m Technicolor
TCF / Copa de Oro

The 1935 romance of a New York millionaire and a musical star.
An attempt to recapture the simple pleasures of an Astaire-Rogers musical; unfortunately true professionalism is lacking and the wrong kind of talent is used. The result is awful to contemplate.

wd Peter Bogdanovich *ph* Laszlo Kovacs *m* Cole Porter *pd* Gene Allen

Burt Reynolds, Cybill Shepherd, Eileen Brennan, Madeleine Kahn, Duilio del Prete, John Hillerman, Mildred Natwick

'He works hard at reducing all his sets and costumes to variations of black against silver or white on white, and uncovers in his most oft-repeated visual motif—the elegant mirrors before which his cast seem at all times to be posed—the perfect metaphor for this endlessly narcissistic, thoroughly calcified enterprise.'—*Richard Combs*

'It just lies there, and it dies there.'—*Variety*

At Sword's Point*
US 1951 81m Technicolor
RKO (Jerrold T. Brandt)
GB title: *Sons of the Musketeers*

The sons of the three musketeers rally round their ageing queen to prevent her daughter's marriage to a villain.
Adequate swashbuckler with plenty of pace and a sound cast.

w Walter Ferris, Joseph Hoffman *d* Lewis Allen *ph* Ray Rennahan *m* Roy Webb

Cornel Wilde, Maureen O'Hara, Gladys Cooper, Robert Douglas, Dan O'Herlihy, Alan Hale Jnr, Blanche Yurka, Nancy Gates

At the Circus**
US 1939 87m bw
MGM (Mervyn Le Roy)

A shyster lawyer and two incompetents save a circus from bankruptcy.
This film began the decline of the Marx Brothers; in it nothing is ill done but nothing is very fresh either apart from the rousing finale which shows just what professionalism meant in the old Hollywood. Highlights include Groucho singing about Lydia the tattooed lady, his seduction of Mrs Dukesbury, and the big society party.

w Irving Brecher *d* Edward Buzzell *ph* Leonard M. Smith *m* Harold Arlen

Groucho, Chico, Harpo, Margaret Dumont, Florence Rice, Kenny Baker, Eve Arden, Nat Pendleton, Fritz Feld

At War with the Army
US 1951 93m bw
Paramount / Fred K. Finklehoffe

A couple of song and dance men have trouble as army recruits.
American service farce, based on a play and confined largely to one set; rather untypical of Martin and Lewis, yet oddly enough the film which sealed their success.

w Fred K. Finklehoffe, *play* James Allardice *d* Hal Walker *ph* Stuart Thompson *m* Joseph Lilley

Dean Martin, Jerry Lewis, Mike Kellin, Polly Bergen, Jimmie Dundee

Athena
US 1954 96m Eastmancolor
MGM (Joe Pasternak)

A young lawyer falls in love with the eldest of seven sisters brought up to high standards of moral conduct and physical fitness.
Promising but unfulfilling light musical which smothers a good idea in routine treatment.

w William Ludwig, Leonard Spiegelgass *d* Richard Thorpe *ph* Robert Planck *songs* Hugh Martin, Ralph Blane

Edmund Purdom, Jane Powell, Debbie Reynolds, Louis Calhern, Evelyn Varden, Vic Damone, Linda Christian, Ray Collins

Atlantic Ferry*
GB 1941 108m Technicolor
Warner (Max Milder)
US title: *Sons of the Sea*

In 1837 Liverpool, two brothers build the first steamship to cross the Atlantic.
Ponderous historical romance with points of interest.

w Gordon Wellesley, Edward Dryhurst, Emeric Pressburger *d* Walter Forde

Michael Redgrave, Valerie Hobson, Griffith Jones, Margaretta Scott, Hartley Power, Bessie Love, Milton Rosmer

Atlantis, the Lost Continent
US 1961 91m Metrocolor
MGM / Galaxy / George Pal

A Greek fisherman is imprisoned when he returns a maiden he has rescued to her island home of Atlantis, but escapes just before volcanic eruption overtakes the decadent nation.
Penny-pinching fantasy spectacle with very little entertainment value.

w Daniel Mainwaring, *play* Sir Gerald Hargreaves *d* George Pal *ph* Harold E. Wellman *m* Russell Garcia

Anthony Hall, Joyce Taylor, John Dall, Edward Platt, Frank de Kova, Jay Novello

The Atomic City*
US 1952 85m bw
Paramount (Joseph Sistrom)

The young son of a leading atomic scientist is kidnapped but his father and the FBI rescue him.
Routine but well-paced thriller with a documentary background of research at Los Alamos.

w Sydney Boehm *d* Jerry Hopper *ph* Charles B. Lang Jnr *m* Leith Stevens

Gene Barry, Lydia Clarke, Lee Aaker, Nancy Gates, Milburn Stone

Attack**
US 1956 104m bw
UA / Associates and Aldrich

In 1944 Belgium, an American infantry command is led by a coward.
High-pitched, slick, violent and very effective war melodrama, even though by the end we seem to be in the company of raving lunatics rather than soldiers.

w James Poe, play Fragile Fox by Norman Brooks *d Robert Aldrich ph Joseph Biroc* *m* Frank de Vol

Jack Palance, Eddie Albert, Lee Marvin, Buddy Ebsen, Robert Strauss, Richard Jaeckel, William Smithers, Peter Van Eyck

'The film does not so much tackle a subject as hammer it down.'—*Penelope Houston*

Attack on the Iron Coast
GB 1967 90m De Luxe
US / Mirisch (John Champion)

In World War II, a Canadian commando unit destroys a German installation on the French coast.
Stagey low-budgeter with modest action sequences.

w Herman Hoffman *d* Paul Wendkos *ph* Paul Beeson *m* Gerard Schurmann

Lloyd Bridges, Andrew Keir, Mark Eden, Sue Lloyd

Attack on Terror
US 1975 198m (two parts) colour TVM
Warner / Quinn Martin
aka: *The FBI versus the Ku Klux Klan*

The alternative title says it all.
Flat, overlong cops and robbers in a very familiar vein.

w Calvin Clements *d* Marvin Chomsky

George Grizzard, Rip Torn, Dabney Colman, Andrew Duggan, L. Q. Jones, Marlyn Mason, Peter Strauss, Wayne Rogers, Ed Flanders

Aunt Clara
GB 1954 84m bw
London Films (Colin Lesslie, Anthony Kimmins)

A pious old person inherits from a reprobate uncle five greyhounds, a pub and a brothel.
Extremely mild star vehicle with a gallery of comedy character cameos.

w Kenneth Horne, *novel* Noel Streatfield *d* Anthony Kimmins *ph* C. Pennington-Richards *m* Benjamin Frankel

Margaret Rutherford, Ronald Shiner, A. E. Matthews, Fay Compton, Nigel Stock, Jill Bennett, Reginald Beckwith, Raymond Huntley

Auntie Mame*
US 1958 144m Technirama
Warner (Morton da Costa)

An orphan boy is adopted by his volatile extravagant aunt, whose giddy escapades fill his memory of the twenties and thirties.
A rather unsatisfactory star revue from a book and play later turned into a musical, *Mame*. A few splendid moments, otherwise rather dull and irritating.

w Betty Comden, Adolph Green, *novel* Patrick Dennis, *play* Jerome Lawrence, Robert E. Lee *d* Morton da Costa *ph* Harry Stradling *m* Bronislau Kaper *ad* Malcolm Bert

Rosalind Russell, Forrest Tucker, *Coral Browne, Fred Clark*, Roger Smith, Patric Knowles, Peggy Cass, Lee Patrick, Joanna Barnes

The Autobiography of Miss Jane Pittman**
US 1973 109m Eastmancolor TVM
Tomorrow (Robert W. Christiansen, Rick Rosenberg)

In 1962, a 110-year-old negress in a southern state reflects on her early life as a slave and takes a drink from the 'Whites Only' fountain.
Ambitious and careful TV movie which did much in America to raise the sights of the genre.

w Tracy Keenan Wynn *n* Ernest J. Gaines *d* John Korty *ph* James Crabe *m* Fred Karlin *pd* Michael Haller

Cicely Tyson, Michael Murphy, Richard A. Dysart, Katherine Helmond

Autumn Leaves*
US 1956 108m bw
Columbia / William Goetz

A middle-aged spinster marries a young man who turns out to be a pathological liar and tries to murder her.
Skilfully tailored star vehicle for female audiences.

w Jack Jevne, Lewis Meltzer, Robert Blees *d* Robert Aldrich *ph* Charles Lang *m* Hans Salter

Joan Crawford, Cliff Robertson, Lorne Greene, Vera Miles, Ruth Donnelly, Shepperd Strudwick

Avanti!**
US 1972 144m De Luxe
UA / Mirisch / Phalanx / Jalem (Billy Wilder)

A young American goes to Ischia to collect the body of his father who has died on holiday. He finds that the fatal accident had also killed his father's mistress, and amid overwhelming bureaucratic problems proceeds to fall in love with her daughter.
Absurdly overlong black comedy, with compensations in the shape of a generally witty script and some fine breakneck sequences of culminating confusion.

w Billy Wilder, I. A. L. Diamond, play Samuel Taylor *d Billy Wilder ph* Luigi Kuveiller *m* Carlo Rustichelli

Jack Lemmon, Juliet Mills, Clive Revill, Edward Andrews, Gianfranco Barra

Away All Boats!
US 1956 114m Technicolor Vistavision
U-I (Howard Christie)

Adventures of a small transport boat during the Pacific War.
Competent drum-beating war heroics with expensive action sequences.

w Ted Sherdeman *d* Joseph Pevney *ph* William Daniels, Clifford Stine *m* Frank Skinner

Jeff Chandler, George Nader, Julie Adams, Lex Barker, Keith Andes, Richard Boone, Frank Faylen

The Awful Truth***
US 1937 90m bw
Columbia (Leo McCarey)

A divorcing couple endure various adventures which lead to reconciliation.
Classic crazy comedy of the thirties, marked by a mixture of sophistication and farce and an irreverent approach to plot.

wd Leo McCarey, play Arthur Richman *ph* Joseph Walker *m* Morris Stoloff

Irene Dunne, Cary Grant, Ralph Bellamy, Alexander D'Arcy, Cecil Cunningham, Molly Lamont, Esther Dale, Joyce Compton
† Remade 1953 as *Let's Do It Again* (qv).

B

B.F.'s Daughter*
US 1948 106m bw
MGM (Edwin A. Knopf)
GB title: *Polly Fulton*

The wife of a penniless lecturer secures her husband's rise to fame without his knowing that she is the daughter of a millionaire.
Solid upper class romantic drama with a touch of Peg's Paper.

w Luther Davis, *novel* John P. Marquand
d Robert Z. Leonard *ph* Joseph Ruttenberg
m Bronislau Kaper

Barbara Stanwyck, Van Heflin, Charles Coburn, Richard Hart, Keenan Wynn, Margaret Lindsay, Spring Byington, Marshall Thompson

Babbitt*
US 1934 74m bw
Warner (Sam Bischoff)

Problems of a middle-aged man in a small American town.
A minor attempt to film a major novel: quite tolerable but lacking density.

w Mary McCall Jnr, *novel* Sinclair Lewis
d William Keighley *ph* Arthur Todd

Guy Kibbee, Aline MacMahon, Claire Dodd, Maxine Doyle, Minor Watson, Minna Gombell, Alan Hale, Berton Churchill, Russell Hicks, Nan Grey

Babe*
US 1975 100m colour TVM
MGM / Norman Felton, Stanley Rubin

The story of woman athlete Babe Didrikson and her battle with cancer.
Careful but essentially tedious American hero-worship in the wake of *Sunshine, It's Good to be Alive*, etc.

Susan Clark, Alex Karras, Slim Pickens, Jeanette Nolan, Ellen Geer

The Babe Ruth Story
US 1948 107m bw
Allied Artists

The biography of a baseball player who was thought of as something of a saint.
Dim, sentimental and faintly mystical biopic, throughout which the star presents his familiar image.

w Bob Considine, George Callahan *d* Roy del Ruth *ph* Philip Tunnura, James Van Trees
m Edward Ward

William Bendix, Claire Trevor, Charles Bickford

Babes in Arms**
US 1939 96m bw
MGM (Arthur Freed)

The teenage sons and daughters of retired vaudevillians put on a big show.
Simple-minded backstage musical which marked the first enormously successful teaming of its two young stars.

w Jack McGowan, Kay Van Riper, from the Broadway show by Rodgers and Hart
d/ch Busby Berkeley *ph* Ray June
songs Rodgers and Hart

Judy Garland, Mickey Rooney, Charles Winninger, Douglas Macphail, Leni Lynn, June Preisser

Babes in Toyland**
US 1934 77m bw
Hal Roach
aka: *Wooden Soldiers, Laurel and Hardy in Toyland*

Santa Claus's incompetent assistants accidentally make some giant wooden soldiers, which come in useful when a villain tries to take over Toyland.
Comedy operetta in which the stars have pleasant but not outstanding material; the style and decor are however sufficient to preserve the film as an eccentric minor classic.

w Nick Grinde, Frank Butler, *original book/ly* Glen MacDonough *d* Gus Meins, Charles Rogers *ph* Art Lloyd, Francis Corby
m Victor Herbert

Stan Laurel, Oliver Hardy, Charlotte Henry, Henry Brandon, Felix Knight, Florence Roberts, Johnny Downs, Marie Wilson

Babes in Toyland
US 1961 105m Technicolor
Walt Disney

A misfiring remake, all charm and no talent apart from some excellent special effects at the climax.

w Ward Kimball, Joe Rinaldi, Lowell S. Hawley *d* Jack Donohue *ph* Edward Colman *sp* Eustace Lycett, Robert A. Mattey, Bill Justice, Xavier Atencio, Yale Gracey

Ray Bolger (miscast as the villain), Annette Funicello, Tommy Kirk, Gene Sheldon (imitating Stan Laurel), Henry Calvin (imitating Oliver Hardy), Ed Wynn, Kevin Corcoran

Babes on Broadway**
US 1941 118m bw
MGM (Arthur Freed)

A sequel to *Babes in Arms*, in which the kids get to Broadway and share some disillusion.
Inflated and less effective than the original, but with good numbers.

w Fred Finkelhoffe, Elaine Ryan *d/ch* Busby Berkeley *ph* Lester White *songs* Burton Lane and Ralph Freed

Judy Garland, Mickey Rooney, Virginia Weidler, Ray Macdonald, Richard Quine, Fay Bainter

The Baby and the Battleship
GB 1956 96m Eastmancolor
Jay Lewis / British Lion (Antony Darnborough)

Two sailors hide an Italian baby on their battleship.
Simple-minded lower decks farce, with lots of confusion and cooing over the baby, but not much to laugh at.

w Jay Lewis, Gilbert Hackforth-Jones, Bryan Forbes *d* Jay Lewis *ph* Harry Waxman

John Mills, Richard Attenborough, André Morell, Bryan Forbes, Michael Howard, Lisa Gastoni, Ernest Clark, Lionel Jeffries, Thorley Walters

Baby Blue Marine*
US 1976 90m Metrocolor
Columbia / Spelling–Goldberg (Robert LaVigne)

In 1943, a failed marine returns home and pretends to be a war hero.
Careful small-town drama with good period feel but not much dramatic punch: *Hail the Conquering Hero* did it better.

w Stanford Whitmore *d* John Hancock *ph* Laszlo Kovacs *m* Fred Karlin

Jan-Michael Vincent, Glynnis O'Connor, Katherine Helmond, Dana Elcar, Bert Remsen, Richard Gere

Baby Doll**
US 1956 116m bw
Warner / Elia Kazan

In the deep South, the child wife of a broken-down cotton miller is seduced by her husband's revenge-seeking rival.
An incisive, cleverly-worked-out study of moral and physical decay; whether it was worth doing is another question, for it's a film difficult to remember with affection.

wd Elia Kazan, play Tennessee Williams *ph Boris Kaufman* *m* Kenyon Hopkins *ad* Richard Sylbert

Karl Malden, Eli Wallach, Carroll Baker, Mildred Dunnock, Lonny Chapman

'Just possibly the dirtiest American-made motion picture that has ever been legally exhibited, with Priapean detail that might well have embarrassed Boccaccio.'—*Time*

'He views southern pretensions with sardonic humor, and builds an essentially minor story into a magnificently humorous study of the grotesque and the decadent.'—*Hollis Alpert*

'A droll and engrossing carnal comedy.'—*Pauline Kael, 1968*

Baby Face**
US 1933 70m bw
Warner (Ray Griffith)

Amorous adventures of an ambitious working girl.
Sharp melodrama very typical of its time, with fast pace and good performances.

w Gene Markey, Kathryn Scola, Mark Canfield (Darryl F. Zanuck) *d* Alfred E. Green *ph* James Van Trees

Barbara Stanwyck, George Brent, Donald Cook, Margaret Lindsay, Arthur Hohl, John Wayne, Henry Kolker, Douglass Dumbrille

Baby Face Nelson*
US 1957 85m bw
UA / Fryman–ZS (Al Zimbalist)

Fragmentary account of the life of a thirties public enemy, with the star over the top and the technicians doing what they can on an obviously low budget.

w Irving Shulman, Daniel Mainwaring *d* Don Siegel *ph* Hal Mohr *m* Van Alexander

Mickey Rooney, Cedric Hardwicke, Carolyn Jones, Chris Dark, Ted de Corsia, Leo Gordon, John Hoyt, Anthony Caruso, Jack Elam

Baby Love
GB 1968 93m Eastmancolor
(Avco) Avton / Michael Klinger (Guido Coen)

An orphaned nymphet causes trouble among the men in her foster home.
Ludicrous sexploiter which embarrasses a good cast and descends into bathos.

w Alastair Reid, Guido Coen, Michael Klinger, *novel* Tina Chad Christian *d* Alastair Reid *ph* Desmond Dickinson *m* Max Harris

Linda Hayden, Ann Lynn, Keith Barron, Derek Lamden, Diana Dors, Patience Collier, Dick Emery

Baby, the Rain Must Fall
US 1964 100m bw
Columbia / Pakula–Mulligan (Alan Pakula)

A parolee rejoins his wife and daughter in a Southern town, but his outbursts of violence separate them again.
Hard work by all concerned scarcely produces absorbing interest in this filmed play of the Tennessee Williams school.

w Horton Foote, from his play The Travelling Lady *d* Robert Mulligan *ph* Ernest Laszlo *m* Elmer Bernstein

Steve McQueen, Lee Remick, Don Murray, Paul Fix, Josephine Hutchinson, Ruth White, Charles Watts

The Bachelor and the Bobbysoxer***
US 1947 95m bw
RKO (Dore Schary)
GB title: *Bachelor Knight*

A lady judge allows her impressionable young sister to get over her crush on an errant playboy by forcing them together.
Simple but unexpectedly delightful vehicle for top comedy talents, entirely pleasant and with several memorable moments.

w Sidney Sheldon *d* Irving Reis *ph* Robert de Grasse, Nicholas Musuraca *m* Constantin Bakaleinikoff

Cary Grant, Myrna Loy, Shirley Temple, *Ray Collins*, Rudy Vallee, *Harry Davenport*, Johnny Sands, Don Beddoe

Bachelor Father
US 1931 90m bw
MGM

A much-married elderly man visits his grown children.
Unremarkable star comedy of its day.

w Laurence E. Johnson, *play* Edward Childs Carpenter *d* Robert Z. Leonard *ph* Oliver T. Marsh

Marion Davies, *C. Aubrey Smith*, Ray Milland, Ralph Forbes, Halliwell Hobbes, Guinn Williams, David Torrence

Bachelor in Paradise
US 1961 109m Metrocolor
Cinemascope
MGM / Ted Richmond

A famous writer of advice to the lovelorn settles incognito in a well-heeled Californian community to observe its social habits.
Mildly amusing satire is too frequently interrupted by unsuitable romantic interludes in this rather ill-considered star comedy.

w Valentine Davies, Hal Kanter *d* Jack Arnold *ph* Joseph Ruttenberg *m* Henry Mancini

Bob Hope, Lana Turner, Janis Paige, Don Porter, Paula Prentiss, Jim Hutton, Virginia Grey, Reta Shaw, John McGiver, Agnes Moorehead

Bachelor Mother***
US 1939 82m bw
RKO (B. G. De Sylva)

A shopgirl finds an abandoned baby and is thought to be its mother; the department store owner's son is then thought to be the father.
Blithely-scripted comedy which stands the test of time and provided several excellent roles.

w Norman Krasna d Garson Kanin ph Robert de Grasse

Ginger Rogers, David Niven, Charles Coburn, Frank Albertson, E. E. Clive, Ernest Truex
† Remade as *Bundle of Joy* (qv).

Bachelor of Hearts
GB 1958 94m Technicolor
Rank / Independent Artists (Vivian A. Cox)

Adventures of a German student at Cambridge University.
Sometimes agreeable, sometimes annoying, especially when romance gets in the way of the possibilities for fun.

w Leslie Bricusse, Frederic Raphael *d* Wolf Rilla *ph* Geoffrey Unsworth

Hardy Kruger, Sylvia Syms, Ronald Lewis, Eric Barker, Newton Blick

The Bachelor Party***
US 1957 93m bw
UA / Norma (Harold Hecht)

New York book-keepers throw a wedding eve party for one of their fellows, but drink only brings to the fore their own private despairs.
Though the last half-hour lets it down, most of this is a brilliantly observed social study of New

York life at its less attractive, and the acting matches the incisiveness of the script.

w Paddy Chayevsky, from his TV play *d* Delbert Mann *ph* Joseph La Shelle *m* Paul Madeira

Don Murray, E. G. Marshall, Jack Warden, Philip Abbott, Larry Blyden, Patricia Smith, Carolyn Jones

The Bachelor's Daughters*
US 1946 90m bw
UA / Andrew Stone
GB title: *Bachelor Girls*

Four shopgirls and a floorwalker rent a Long Island house and pass themselves off as a wealthy family in order to lure suitable husbands for the girls.
Mildly amusing comedy with good performances.

wd Andrew Stone *ph* Theodor Sparkuhl

Adolphe Menjou, Gail Russell, Claire Trevor, Billie Burke

Back from Eternity
US 1956 97m bw
RKO (John Farrow)

An airliner is forced to crashland in headhunter country, and when repairs are made only five of the eight survivors can be carried.
Remake by the same producer-director of his own 1939 'B', *Five Came Back*, this time to considerably less effect despite superior production.

w Jonathan Latimer *d* John Farrow *ph* William Mellor *m* Franz Waxman

Robert Ryan, Anita Ekberg, Rod Steiger, Phyllis Kirk, Gene Barry, Keith Andes, Beulah Bondi, Fred Clark, Cameron Prud'homme, Jesse White

Back Street*
US 1932 93m bw
Universal (Carl Laemmle Jnr)

A married man has a sweet-tempered mistress who effaces herself for twenty years.
Popular version of a sudsy bestselling novel.

w Gladys Lehman, Lynn Starling, *novel* Fannie Hurst *d* John M. Stahl *ph* Karl Freund

Irene Dunne, John Boles, June Clyde, George Meeker, Zasu Pitts, Doris Lloyd

Back Street*
US 1941 89m bw
Universal (Bruce Manning)

Competent remake.

w Bruce Manning, Felix Jackson *d* Robert Stevenson *ph* William Daniels *m* Frank Skinner

Margaret Sullavan, Charles Boyer, Richard Carlson, Frank McHugh, Tim Holt, Frank Jenks, Esther Dale, Samuel S. Hinds

Back Street*
US 1961 107m Technicolor
U-I / Ross Hunter / Carrollton

Glossy remake typical of its producer: unfortunately it fails to work because the heroine suffers too luxuriously.

w Eleanore Griffin, William Ludwig *d* David Miller *ph* Stanley Cortez *m* Joseph Gershenson

Susan Hayward, John Gavin, Vera Miles, Virginia Grey, Charles Drake, Reginald Gardiner

'Though there is a lot to be said for this new version's thesis that one can be just as lonely in a series of apartments and lovers' nests apparently never less than a hundred yards wide, the illusion is quickly shattered the moment one gets the impression that the lovers prefer to keep much the same distance during their moments of passion.'—*Peter John Dyer*

Back to Bataan
US 1945 97m bw
RKO (Robert Fellows)

When Bataan is cut off, a Marine colonel organizes guerrilla resistance.
Modestly made and rather dislikeable flagwaver.

w Ben Barzman, Richard Landau *d* Edward Dmytryk *ph* Nicholas Musuraca *m* Roy Webb

John Wayne, Anthony Quinn, Beulah Bondi, Fely Franquelli, Leonard Strong, Richard Loo, Philip Ahn, Lawrence Tierney, Paul Fix

Background*
GB 1953 82m bw
Group Three (Herbert Mason)
US title: *Edge of Divorce*

Two people decide on divorce, but thoughts of their children bring them together again.
Low budget, stiff-upper-lip marriage guidance tract, well acted but more well-intentioned than memorable.

w Warren Chetham Strode, from his play, with Don Sharp *d* Daniel Birt *ph* Arthur Grant

Valerie Hobson, Philip Friend, Norman Wooland, Janette Scott, Mandy Miller, Jeremy Spenser, Richard Wattis

Background to Danger**
US 1943 80m bw
Warner (Jerry Wald)

An adventurer thwarts Nazi intrigue in Turkey.

Good routine war action yarn, well presented and performed.

w W. R. Burnett, *novel* Uncommon Danger by Eric Ambler *d* Raoul Walsh *ph* Tony Gaudio

George Raft, Brenda Marshall, Sydney Greenstreet, Peter Lorre, Osa Massen, Turhan Bey, Kurt Katch

'You could use this film for one kind of measurement of the unconquerable difference between a good job by Hitchcock and a good job of the Hitchcock type.'—*James Agee*

Backlash*
US 1956 84m Technicolor
U-I (Aaron Rosenberg)

A gunman seeks the father he has never met, who turns out to be a villain who sold his partners for gold to attacking Indians.
Rather unusual suspense western, very watchable for its mystery elements.

w Borden Chase d John Sturges ph Irving Glassberg *m* Joseph Gershenson

Richard Widmark, Donna Reed, John McIntire, William Campbell, Barton Maclane

Backtrack
US 1968 97m Technicolor TVM
Universal

Adventures of four Texas Rangers.
Poor pilot for *Laredo.*

d Earl Bellamy

Neville Brand, Doug McClure, Peter Brown, James Drury

The Bad and the Beautiful**
US 1952 118m bw
MGM (John Houseman)

A director, a star, a screenwriter and an executive recall their experiences at the hands of a go-getting Hollywood producer.
Very much a Hollywood 'in' picture, this rather obvious flashback melodrama offers good acting chances and a couple of intriguing situations; never quite finding the style it seeks, it offers good bitchy entertainment along the way, and there are references back to it in *Two Weeks in Another Town*, made ten years later.

w Charles Schnee *d* Vincente Minnelli *ph* Robert Surtees *m* David Raksin

Kirk Douglas, Walter Pidgeon, Lana Turner, Dick Powell, Barry Sullivan, Gloria Grahame, Gilbert Roland, Leo G. Carroll, Vanessa Brown, Paul Stewart

'For all the cleverness of the apparatus, it lacks a central point of focus.'—*Penelope Houston*

Bad Bascomb*
US 1946 110m bw
MGM (Orville Dull)

A sentimental bank robber becomes the hero of a group of travelling Mormons.
Pleasing though overlong star western, with good production values.

w William Lipman, Grant Garrett *d* S. Sylvan Simon *ph* Charles Schoenbaum *m* David Snell

Wallace Beery, Margaret O'Brien, Marjorie Main, J. Carrol Naish, Russell Simpson, Sara Haden

Bad Company**
US 1972 92m Technicolor
Paramount (Stanley R. Jaffe)

During the Civil War, two youths on the run team up and become outlaws.
A successful attempt to recreate the feeling of past time, by the writers of another criminal myth, *Bonnie and Clyde.*

w David Newman, Robert Benton d Robert Benton *ph* Gordon Willis *m* Harvey Schmidt

Jeff Bridges, Barry Brown, Jim Davis, David Huddleston, John Savage

Bad Day at Black Rock****
US 1954 81m Eastmancolor Cinemascope
MGM (Dore Schary)

A one-armed stranger gets off the train at a sleepy desert hamlet and is greeted with hostility by the townsfolk, who have something to hide.
Seminal suspense thriller—the guilty town motif became a cliché—with a terse script and professional presentation. The moments of violence, long awaited, are electrifying.

w Millard Kaufman d John Sturges ph William C. Mellor m André Previn

Spencer Tracy, Robert Ryan, Dean Jagger, Walter Brennan, Ernest Borgnine, Lee Marvin, Anne Francis, John Ericson, Russell Collins

'A very superior example of motion picture craftsman- ship.'—*Pauline Kael*

Bad for Each Other
US 1954 83m bw
Columbia (William Fadiman)

A doctor back from the army scorns his home town for high society, but a mine disaster reverses his decision.
Misleadingly titled cliché drama, patterned after *The Citadel.* Actors ill at ease, handling competent but routine.

w Irving Wallace, Horace McCoy, from the

latter's novel *d* Irving Rapper *ph* Franz Planer *m* Mischa Bakaleinikoff

Charlton Heston, Lizabeth Scott, Dianne Foster, Mildred Dunnock, Arthur Franz, Ray Collins, Marjorie Rambeau

The Bad Lord Byron*
GB 1948 85m bw
Rank / Sydney Box (Aubrey Baring)

Byron lies dying, and imagines his life and loves under review in a heavenly court.
Thought risible at the time, this historical romance in flashback now seems no worse and even a little more stylish than most, though the script suffers from too many cooks.

w Terence Young, Anthony Thorne, Peter Quennell, Laurence Kitchin, Paul Holt *d* David MacDonald *ph* Stephen Dade *m* Cedric Thorpe Davie

Dennis Price, Mai Zetterling, Linden Travers, *Joan Greenwood*, Sonia Holm, Raymond Lovell, Leslie Dwyer
† The end of the British costume cycle which began with *The Man in Grey*.

Bad Ronald
US 1974 74m colour TVM
Lorimar

A teenage killer is hidden in the attic by his mother. When she dies, new tenants find him still there.
Silly, tasteless melodrama, put over with some style.

w Andrew Peter Marin, *novel* John Holbrook Vance *d* Buzz Kulik

Kim Hunter, Scott Jacoby, Pippa Scott, Anita Sorsaut, John Larch

The Bad Seed*
US 1956 129m bw
Warner (Mervyn Le Roy)

A sweet-looking 8-year-old girl is a liar and a murderess; her mother finds out and attempts to kill her and commit suicide.
A real curiosity from an unexpected stage hit: absurd melodrama treated with astonishing high literary style and some censor-induced levity: at the end, after the little villainess has been struck by lightning, a curtain call shows her being soundly spanked.

w John Lee Mahin, *play* Maxwell Anderson, *novel* William March *d* Mervyn Le Roy *ph* Harold Rosson *m* Alex North

Nancy Kelly (rather uneasily recreating her stage role as the mother), *Patty McCormack*, Henry Jones, Eileen Heckart, Evelyn Varden, William Hopper, Paul Fix, Jesse White

Bad Sister
US 1931 71m bw
Universal (Carl Laemmle Jnr)

A small-town coquette falls for a city slicker, and her quiet sister gets her steady boy friend.
A teenage potboiler of its day, remarkable only for its cast.

w Raymond L. Schrock, Tom Reed, *story* The Flirt by Booth Tarkington *d* Hobart Henley *ph* Karl Freund

Conrad Nagel, Sidney Fox, Bette Davis, Humphrey Bogart, Zasu Pitts, Slim Summerville, Emma Dunn, Bert Roach

Badge 373
US 1973 116m Technicolor
Paramount (Howard W. Koch)

A police detective is enraged by the murder of his partner and his own suspension after the death of a suspect.
'Realistic' (i.e. violent and foul-mouthed) cop thriller in the wake of *The French Connection*, tolerable only for action highlights.

w Pete Hamill, from the exploits of Eddie Egan *d* Howard W. Koch *ph* Arthur J. Ornitz *m* J. J. Jackson

Robert Duvall, Verna Bloom, Henry Darrow, Eddie Egan, Felipe Luciano, Tina Christiana, Marina Durell

'A deeply divided and scarcely reassuring addition to the movies' composite portrait of the American police force.'—*John Gillett*

'Nasty, violent and humourless.'—*Sight and Sound*

The Badge or the Cross
US 1971 98m Technicolor TVM
Universal (David Levy)
aka: *Sarge: The Badge or the Cross*

When his fiancée is killed by a bomb meant for him, a cop becomes a priest, in which guise he later solves the crime.
Heavy-going pilot for a short-lived series. Another pilot was *The Priest-Killer* (qv).

w Don M. Mankiewicz *d* Richard A. Colla

George Kennedy, Ricardo Montalban, Diane Baker, Larry Gates

The Badlanders*
US 1958 83m Metrocolor Cinemascope
MGM / Arcola (Aaron Rosenberg)

Crooked westerners plan to rob a goldmine.

Rather sloppy western remake of *The Asphalt Jungle.*

w Richard Collins *d* Delmer Daves *ph* John Seitz

Alan Ladd, Ernest Borgnine, Katy Jurado, Claire Kelly, Kent Smith, *Nehemiah Persoff,* Robert Emhardt

Badlands***
US 1973 94m Consolidated Color
(Columbia) Pressman / Williams / Badlands (Terrence Malick)

A teenage girl and a young garbage collector wander across America leaving a trail of murder behind them.
A violent folk tale for moderns; very well put together if somewhat lacking in point, it quickly became a cult film.

wd Terrence Malick ph Brian Probyn, Tak Fujimoto, Stevan Larner *m* George Tipton

Martin Sheen, Sissy Spacek, Warren Oates, Ramon Bieri

'One of the finest literate examples of narrated cinema since the early days of Welles and Polonsky.'—*Jonathan Rosenbaum*

'So preconceived that there's nothing left to respond to.'—*New Yorker*

Baffled!
GB 1971 96m Eastmancolor TVM
ITC / Arena (Philip Leacock)

A racing driver has a prophetic dream which leads him into a very involved murder plot.
Weird and fathomless hotchpotch which wastes a lot of talent.

w Theodore Apstein *d* Philip Leacock *ph* Ken Hodges *m* Richard Hill

Leonard Nimoy, Susan Hampshire, Vera Miles, Jewel Blanch, Rachel Roberts, Valerie Taylor, Ray Brooks, Angharad Rees

Bahama Passage
US 1941 82m Technicolor
Paramount (Edward H. Griffith)

A sophisticated girl is determined to live on a salt-mining island in the West Indies.
Forgettable tropical romance in very pleasing early colour.

w Nelson Hayes *d* Edward H. Griffith *ph* Leo Tover

Madeleine Carroll, Sterling Hayden, Flora Robson, Leo G. Carroll, Cecil Kellaway, Dorothy Dandridge

The Bait*
US 1972 74m colour TVM
Spelling – Goldberg

An undercover policewoman lures a girl killer into a trap.
Smart suspenser which oddly failed as a pilot; two years later along came *Police Woman.*

w Don M. Mankiewicz, Gordon Botler
d Leonard Horn

Donna Mills, Michael Constantine, William Devane, June Lockhart

Balalaika*
US 1939 102m bw
MGM (Lawrence Weingarten)

Russian exiles gather in Paris.
Mildly pleasing star musical.

w Jacques Deval, Leon Gordon, *play* Eric Maschwitz *d* Reinhold Schunzel *ph* Joseph Ruttenberg, Karl Freund *m* Herbert Stothart *songs* various

Nelson Eddy, Ilona Massey, Charles Ruggles, Frank Morgan, C. Aubrey Smith, Lionel Atwill, Walter Woolf King, Joyce Compton

The Balcony*
US 1963 86m bw
Walter Reade / Sterling / Allen Hodgdon / City Film
(Joseph Strick, Ben Maddow)

In a war-torn world, a brothel continues to attract customers of every variety.
Low-budget adaptation of a rather confused allegorical play: vivid moments hardly atone for reels of surrealist groping.

w Ben Maddow, *play* Jean Genet *d* Joseph Strick *ph* George Folsey *m* Igor Stravinsky

Shelley Winters, Peter Falk, Lee Grant, Peter Brocco, Kent Smith, Ruby Dee, Jeff Corey, Leonard Nimoy

Ball of Fire*
US 1942 111m bw
Samuel Goldwyn

Seven professors compiling a dictionary give shelter to a stripteaser on the run from gangsters.
Rather overstretched but fitfully amusing romp inspired by *Snow White and the Seven Dwarfs.*

w Charles Brackett, Billy Wilder d Howard Hawks *ph* Gregg Toland *m* Alfred Newman

Barbara Stanwyck, Gary Cooper, Oscar Homolka, Henry Travers, S. Z. Sakall, Tully Marshall, Leonid Kinskey, Richard Haydn, Aubrey Mather, Allen Jenkins, Dana Andrews, Dan Duryea

Ballad in Blue
GB 1964 88m bw
(Warner) Alexander and Miguel Salkind (Herman Blaser)
US title: *Blues for Lovers*

A famous pianist becomes friendly with a blind boy and helps reconcile his parents.
Curious sentimental drama with the star playing himself; competent but hardly rousing.

w Burton Wohl *d* Paul Henreid *ph* Ron Taylor *m* Ray Charles, Stanley Black

Ray Charles, Mary Peach, Dawn Addams, Tom Bell, Piers Bishop, Betty McDowell

The Ballad of Andy Crocker
US 1967 74m colour TVM
Thomas – Spelling

A Vietnam veteran finds his home town changed.
Rather tiresome, would-be poetic, *Best Years of Our Lives*-style folksiness.

w Stuart Margolin *d* George McCowan

Lee Majors, Pat Hingle, Jimmy Dean, Agnes Moorehead, Joey Heatherton, Jill Haworth, Bobby Hatfield

The Ballad of Cable Hogue*
US 1970 121m Technicolor
Warner (Sam Peckinpah)

A gold prospector takes a lengthy and ineffectual revenge on men who robbed him, and dies trying to be a hero.
Curious peripatetic western with the director in uncharacteristically experimental and comparatively non-violent mood. All concerned seem to be enjoying themselves, but the fun is not always communicated.

w John Crawford, Edward Penney *d Sam Peckinpah ph Lucien Ballard m* Jerry Goldsmith

Jason Robards, David Warner, Strother Martin, Slim Pickens, L. Q. Jones, Peter Whitney, R. G. Armstrong, Gene Evans

The Ballad of Josie
US 1967 102m Techniscope
Universal (Marty Melcher)

Cleared of the manslaughter of her husband, a western widow renovates a derelict ranch and sets up as a sheep farmer.
Tediously whimsical, unsuitably cast women's lib comedy with so few laughs that it may require to be taken seriously.

w Harold Swanton *d* Andrew V. McLaglen *ph* Milton Krasner *m* Frank de Vol

Doris Day, Peter Graves, George Kennedy, William Talman, Andy Devine, Audrey Christie

Bambi****
US 1942 72m Technicolor
Walt Disney

The story of a forest deer, from the book by Felix Salten.
Anthropomorphic cartoon feature, one of Disney's most memorable and brilliant achievements, with a great comic character in Thumper the rabbit and a climactic forest fire sequence which is genuinely thrilling. A triumph of the animator's art.

supervisor David Hand

Banacek see Detour to Nowhere and Mystery Movie

Bananas*
US 1971 81m De Luxe
UA / Rollins and Joffe (Jack Grossberg)

A meek and mild product tester for a New York corporation accidentally becomes a South American rebel hero.
Disjointed anarchic comedy with a few good jokes typical of their author.

w Woody Allen with Mickey Rose *d* Woody Allen *ph* Andrew M. Costikyan *m* Marvin Hamlisch

Woody Allen, Louise Lasser, Carlos Montalban, Jacobo Morales
'Full of hilarious comic ideas and lines, supplied by Allen and his collaborator; then Allen, the director and actor, murders them.'—*Stanley Kauffmann*
† Asked why his film was called *Bananas*, Allen replied: 'Because there are no bananas in it.'

Band of Angels
US 1957 127m Warnercolor
Warner (no producer credited)

In 1865, a Kentucky girl learns that her mother was black and is sold as a slave, but quickly becomes her owner's mistress.
Long-winded romantic adventure, rather lamely scripted and developed. The star's presence reinforces the impression of sitting through the ghost of *Gone with the Wind*.

w John Twist, Ivan Goff, Ben Roberts, *novel* Robert Penn Warren *d* Raoul Walsh *ph* Lucien Ballard *m* Max Steiner

Clark Gable, Yvonne de Carlo, Sidney Poitier, Efrem Zimbalist Jnr, Patric Knowles, Rex Reason, Torin Thatcher, Andrea King
'Too absurd to be dislikeable.'—*MFB*

Band Waggon*
GB 1939 85m bw
Gainsborough (Edward Black)

Comedians running a pirate TV station in a ghostly castle round up a gang of spies.
Film version of a long-running radio comedy series; quite a serviceable record of a phenomenon.

w Marriott Edgar, Val Guest *d* Marcel Varnel

Arthur Askey, Richard Murdoch, Jack Hylton and his band, Pat Kirkwood, Moore Marriott, Peter Gawthorne, Wally Patch, Donald Calthrop

The Band Wagon***
US 1953 112m Technicolor
MGM (Arthur Freed)

A has-been Hollywood dancer joins forces with a temperamental stage producer to put on a Broadway musical.
Simple but sophisticated musical with the bare minimum of plot, told mostly in jokes, and the maximum of music and song. Numbers include 'Shine on My Shoes', 'Triplets', 'Dancing in the Dark', 'I Guess I'll Have to Change My Plan', 'Louisiana Hayride' and 'That's Entertainment', and there is a spoof Mickey Spillane ballet finale. Level of technical accomplishment very high.

w Adolph Green, Betty Comden songs Howard Dietz, Arthur Schwarz d Vincente Minnelli ph Harry Jackson *ad Cedric Gibbons, Preston Ames*

Fred Astaire, Jack Buchanan, Oscar Levant, Cyd Charisse, Nanette Fabray

Bandido
US 1956 92m De Luxe Cinemascope
UA / Robert L. Jacks

Mexico 1916: an American adventurer helps a rebel leader to defeat a gun runner.
Standard action fare, rather slackly handled.

w Earl Felton *d* Richard Fleischer *ph* Ernest Laszlo *m* Max Steiner

Robert Mitchum, Gilbert Roland, Zachary Scott, Ursula Thiess

The Bandit of Sherwood Forest**
US 1946 87m Technicolor
Columbia (Leonard S. Picker, Clifford Sanforth)

Robin Hood frustrates the Regent who plans to usurp the throne from the boy king.
A lively romp through Sherwood Forest with a capable cast.

w Wilfrid H. Pettit, Melvin Levy, *novel* Son of Robin Hood by Paul A. Castleton *d* George Sherman, Henry Levin *ph* Tony Gaudio, William Snyder, George Meehan *m* Hugo Friedhofer

Cornel Wilde, Anita Louise, Edgar Buchanan, Jill Esmond, Henry Daniell, George Macready, Russell Hicks, John Abbott, Lloyd Corrigan

Bandolero!*
US 1968 108m De Luxe Panavision
TCF (Robert L. Jacks)

In Texas, fugitive outlaw brothers run into trouble with their Mexican counterparts.
Dour and downbeat but well-staged western with emphasis on hanging and rape; an unusual mixture but smoothly assembled.

w James Lee Barrett *d* Andrew V. McLaglen *ph* William H. Clothier *m* Jerry Goldsmith

James Stewart, Dean Martin, Raquel Welch, George Kennedy, Will Geer, Andrew Prine

Bang the Drum Slowly
US 1973 96m Movielab
Paramount (Maurice and Lois Rosenfield)

A baseball star finds that he is dying of leukemia.
Cliché-ridden tearjerker in the modern style.

w Mark Harris, from his novel *d* John Hancock *ph* Richard Shore *m* Stephen Lawrence

Michael Moriarty, Robert de Niro, Vincent Gardenia, Phil Foster

Banjo Hackett
US 1976 99m colour TVM
Columbia

Adventures of a wandering cowboy and a small orphan boy.
A failed pilot, and no wonder: aimless, slow-moving sentimental goo.

w Ken Trevey *d* Andrew V. McLaglen

Don Meredith

Banjo on my Knee**
US 1936 95m bw
TCF (Nunnally Johnson)

In a Mississippi riverboat shanty town, a wedding night is interrupted when the groom is arrested during a brawl.
Unusual, easy-going comedy in which the stars sing and dance as well as fool around.

w Nunnally Johnson, novel Harry Hamilton *d John Cromwell ph* Ernest Palmer *m* Arthur Lange

Barbara Stanwyck, Joel McCrea, Buddy Ebsen, Walter Brennan, Helen Westley, Walter Catlett, Tony Martin, Katherine de Mille

The Bank Dick**
US 1940 73m bw
Universal
GB title: *The Bank Detective*

In Lompoc, California, a ne'er-do-well accidentally stops a hold-up, is made a bank detective, acquires deeds to a worthless mine and interferes in the production of a film.
Imperfect, but probably the best Fields vehicle there is: the jokes sometimes end in mid-air, but there are delicious moments and very little padding. The character names are sometimes funnier than the script: they include Egbert Sousè (*accent grave* over the 'e'), J. Pinkerton Snoopington, Ogg Oggilbie and Filthy McNasty.

w Mahatma Kane Jeeves (W. C. Fields) *d* Eddie Cline *ph* Milton Krasner *m* Charles Previn

W. C. Fields, Franklin Pangborn, Shemp Howard, Jack Norton, Grady Sutton, Cora Witherspoon
'One of the great classics of American comedy.'—*Robert Lewis Taylor*

Bank Holiday*
GB 1938 86m bw
Gainsborough (Edward Black)
US title: *Three on a Weekend*

The lives of various people intertwine during a day out in Brighton.
Simple but effective slice-of-life comedy-drama, establishing several actors and a director. Still quite refreshing.

w Hans Wilhelm, Rodney Ackland, Roger Burford *d Carol Reed*

Margaret Lockwood, Hugh Williams, Kathleen Harrison, Wally Patch, Rene Ray, Linden Travers, Garry Marsh, Wilfrid Lawson

The Bank Shot*
US 1974 83m De Luxe
UA / Hal Landers, Bobby Roberts

Using house-moving equipment, an escaped convict steals a whole bank.
Extended chase comedy with scenes of gleeful destruction. Acceptable for those in the mood, but a shade overdone.

w Wendell Mayes, *novel* Donald E. Westlake *d* Gower Champion *ph* Harry Stradling Jnr *m* John Morris

George C. Scott, Joanna Cassidy, Sorrell Brooke, G. Wood, Clifton James

Bannerline*
US 1951 87m bw
MGM (Henry Berman)

To comfort a dying old man, a young reporter prints a fake newspaper showing the indictment of the old man's gangster enemy. By an odd chain of events, the story becomes true.
Worthy but rather dull MGM 'B', typical of the regime of Dore Schary, boasting a pleasing small-town atmosphere and a remarkable cast of old actors.

w Charles Schnee, *story* Samson Raphaelson *d* Don Weis *ph* Harold Lipstein *m* Rudolph Kopp

Lionel Barrymore, Keefe Brasselle, Sally Forrest, Lewis Stone, Elizabeth Risdon, J. Carrol Naish, Spring Byington, Larry Keating

Banning
US 1967 102m Techniscope
Universal (Dick Berg)

A tennis pro has sporting and amorous adventures at a country club.
Tedious, complexly plotted melodrama of life among the idle rich; handling generally laboured. A showcase for the studio's young contract talent.

w James Lee *d* Ron Winston *ph* Loyal Griggs *m* Quincy Jones

Robert Wagner, Anjanette Comer, Jill St John, Guy Stockwell, James Farentino, Susan Clark, Howard St John, Mike Kellin, Sean Garrison, Gene Hackman

Banyon*
US 1971 97m colour TVM
Warner (Richard Alan Simmons)
aka: *Walk Up and Die*

Adventures of a Los Angeles private eye of the thirties.
Smart-looking nostalgia and not a bad plot for a pilot; but the hero is humourless and the show was short-lived, as four years later was its almost indistinguishable successor *City of Angels*, which even used the same building for the hero's office.

w Ed Adamson *d* Robert Day

Robert Forster, Jose Ferrer, Darren McGavin, Herb Edelman

Barabbas*
Italy / US 1962 144m Technirama
Columbia / Dino de Laurentiis

Pardoned instead of Christ, Barabbas is sentenced to the silver mines, turns Christian, and becomes a gladiator.
Overblown epic which starts with a genuine eclipse of the sun and has nowhere to go but down. The cast sparks a few moments, but it is generally a gaudy display of carnage.

w Christopher Fry, Nigel Balchin, Diego Fabbri,

Ivo Perilli, *novel* Pär Lagerkvist *d* Richard Fleischer *ph* Aldo Tonti *m* Mario Nascimbene *ad* Mario Chiari

Anthony Quinn, Silvana Mangano, Vittorio Gassman, Ernest Borgnine, Jack Palance, Arthur Kennedy, Norman Wooland, Valentina Cortese, Harry Andrews, Katy Jurado, Michael Gwynn

'Unacceptable in its pain-preoccupation and its religiosity.'—*Peter John Dyer*

Barbarella*
France / Italy 1967 98m Technicolor Panavision
Marianne / Dino de Laurentiis

A beautiful young 40th-century astronaut prevents the positronic ray from getting into the wrong hands.
Campy and slightly sick adventures with angels and other space people, from a highly censorable comic strip; some ingenious gadgetry and design, but not much of interest in the foreground.

w Terry Southern, *book* Jean-Claude Forest *d* Roger Vadim *ph* Claude Renoir *m* Maurice Jarre *pd Mario Garbuglia*

Jane Fonda, John Phillip Law, Anita Pallenberg, Milo O'Shea, David Hemmings, Marcel Marceau, Ugo Tognazzi, Claude Dauphin

'A leading science fiction authority has claimed that if Lewis Carroll were alive today he would inevitably have written not *Alice's Adventures in Wonderland* but *Lolita*. He might perhaps equally well have written *Barbarella*.'—*Jack Ibberson*

The Barbarian and the Geisha*
US 1958 105m Eastmancolor Cinemascope
TCF (Eugene Frenke)

In 1856 the first US diplomat to visit Japan meets local opposition but is helped by a geisha.
Episodic semi-historical romance which scarcely suits the talents of those involved.

w Charles Grayson *d* John Huston *ph* Charles G. Clarke *m* Hugo Friedhofer

John Wayne, Eiko Ando, Sam Jaffe, So Yamamura

Barbary Coast**
US 1935 91m bw
Samuel Goldwyn

During San Francisco's gold rush days a ruthless club owner builds a lonely girl into a star attraction but cannot win her love.
Juicy melodrama tailored for its stars, but with excellent background detail, sets and lighting.

w Ben Hecht, Charles MacArthur *d Howard Hawks* *ph* Ray June *m* Alfred Newman

Edward G. Robinson, Miriam Hopkins, Joel McCrea, Walter Brennan, Frank Craven, Brian Donlevy, Donald Meek

† David Niven made his first screen appearance as an extra.

Barbary Coast*
US 1975 74m or 98m colour TVM
Paramount (Douglas Heyes)
GB title: *In Old San Francisco*

A police detective with a penchant for disguise blackmails a saloon proprietor into helping him.
Ambitious pilot for a rumbustious nineties series. Alas, the elements did not jell even with Doug McClure subbed for Dennis Cole, and the show was pensioned off after thirteen weeks.

w Douglas Heyes d Bill Bixby

William Shatner, Dennis Cole, Lynda Day George, Charles Aidman, Michael Ansara

The Barefoot Contessa**
US 1954 128m Technicolor
UA / Figaro (Forrest E. Johnston)

A glamorous barefoot dancer in a Spanish cabaret is turned into a Hollywood star, but her sexual frustrations lead to a tragic end.
A fascinating farrago of addled philosophy and lame wisecracks, very typical of a writer-director here not at his best, decorated by a splendid gallery of actors and some attractive settings.

wd Joseph L. Mankiewicz *ph Jack Cardiff* *m* Mario Nascimbene

Humphrey Bogart, Ava Gardner, Edmond O'Brien, Marius Goring, Valentina Cortese, Rossano Brazzi, Elizabeth Sellars, Warren Stevens

'This example of the Higher Lunacy must vie with *Johnny Guitar* for the silliest film of the year.'—*Gavin Lambert*

'A trash masterpiece: a Cinderella story in which the prince turns out to be impotent.'—*Pauline Kael, 1968*

The Barefoot Executive*
US 1970 96m Technicolor
Walt Disney (Bill Anderson)

A TV network discovers that its most infallible average viewer is a chimpanzee.
Quite a beguiling little farcical comedy with mild doses of satire.

w Joseph L. McEveety *d* Robert Butler *ph* Charles F. Wheeler *m* Robert F. Brunner

Kurt Russell, Harry Morgan, Joe Flynn, Wally

Cox, Heather North, Alan Hewitt, Hayden Rorke

Barefoot in the Park**
US 1967 109m Technicolor
Paramount / Hal B. Wallis

A pair of New York newlyweds rent a cold water flat at the top of a liftless building, and manage to marry the bride's mother to an eccentric neighbour.
Breezy but overlong adaptation of a stage play which succeeded through audience response to its one-liners, which on the screen sometimes fall flat. The people are nice, though.

w Neil Simon, from his play *d* Gene Saks *ph* Joseph La Shelle *m* Neal Hefti

Robert Redford, Jane Fonda, *Mildred Natwick*, Charles Boyer, Herb Edelmann, Mabel Albertson

The Bargee*
GB 1964 106m Techniscope
AB / Galton–Simpson (W. A. Whitaker)

A canal barge Casanova is trapped into marriage.
The long-awaited comedy which was supposed to make a film star out of TV's Young Steptoe turned out to be rough and vulgar but not very funny.

w Ray Galton, Alan Simpson *d* Duncan Wood *ph* Harry Waxman *m* Frank Cordell

Harry H. Corbett, Ronnie Barker, Hugh Griffith, Eric Sykes, Julia Foster, Miriam Karlin, Eric Barker, Derek Nimmo, Norman Bird, Richard Briers

The Barkleys of Broadway*
US 1949 109m Technicolor
MGM (Arthur Freed)

A quarrelling couple of musical comedy stars split up, and she becomes a serious actress.
A rather flat and unattractive reunion for a famous pair, with a witless script, poorish numbers and very little style. The compensations are minor.

w Adolph Green, Betty Comden *d* Charles Walters *ph* Harry Stradling *songs* Harry Warren, Ira Gershwin

Fred Astaire, Ginger Rogers, Oscar Levant, Jacques François, Billie Burke

Barnacle Bill
US 1941 90m bw
MGM (Milton Bren)

A fishing boat skipper gets romantic in the hope of financing his enterprises.
Adequate waterfront comedy on *Min and Bill* lines, consolidating a popular star teaming.

w Jack Jevne, Hugo Butler *d* Richard Thorpe *ph* Clyde de Vinna

Wallace Beery, Marjorie Main, Leo Carrillo, Virginia Weidler, Donald Meek, Barton Maclaine, Connie Gilchrist, Sara Haden

Barnacle Bill*
GB 1957 87m bw
Ealing (Michael Balcon)
US title: *All at Sea*

The last of a long line of sailors suffers from seasickness, and takes command of a decaying Victorian pier at an English seaside resort.
Quite an amusing comedy which had the misfortune to come at the tag-end of the Ealing classics and so seemed too mild and predictable. Perhaps it was a little staid.

w T. E. B. Clarke *d* Charles Frend *ph* Douglas Slocombe *m* John Addison

Alec Guinness, Irene Browne, Percy Herbert, Harold Goodwin, Maurice Denham, George Rose, Lionel Jeffries, Victor Maddern

The Baroness and the Butler
US 1938 75m bw
TCF (Raymond Griffith)

The Hungarian prime minister's butler is loved by a princess.
Thin mittel-European romantic star whimsy.

w Sam Hellman, Lamar Trotti, Kathryn Scola, *play* The Lady Has a Heart by Ladislaus Bus-Fekete *d* Walter Lang *ph* Arthur Miller *md* Louis Silvers

William Powell, Annabella, Henry Stephenson, Nigel Bruce, Helen Westley, Joseph Schildkraut, J. Edward Bromberg, Lynn Bari

The Barretts of Wimpole Street**
US 1934 109m bw
MGM (Irving Thalberg)
TV title: *Forbidden Alliance*

Invalid Elizabeth Barrett plans to marry poet Robert Browning, against her tyrannical father's wishes.
Claustrophobic but well-acted adaptation of a stage play which has become more forceful than history. Stilted now, but still better than the remake.

w Ernst Vajda, Claudine West, Donald Ogden Stewart, *play* Rudolf Besier *d* Sidney Franklin *ph* William Daniels *m* Herbert Stothart

Norma Shearer, Fredric March, *Charles Laughton*, Maureen O'Sullivan, Katherine

Alexander, Ralph Forbes, Una O'Connor, Ian Wolfe

The Barretts of Wimpole Street
GB 1956 105m Metrocolor Cinemascope
MGM (Sam Zimbalist)

Dreadful, miscast remake of the above, with emphasis on the Freudian father-daughter relationship. An unattractive and boring film.

w John Dighton *d* Sidney Franklin *ph* Frederick A. Young *m* Bronislau Kaper

Jennifer Jones, Bill Travers, John Gielgud, Virginia McKenna

Barricade
US 1939 71m bw
TCF (Edward Kaufman)

A newsman and a girl with a past fight Mongolian bandits in North China.
A bagful of clichés which does not quite add up to entertainment.

w Granville Walker *d* Gregory Ratoff *ph* Karl Freund

Warner Baxter, Alice Faye, Charles Winninger, Arthur Treacher, Keye Luke, Willie Fung, Doris Lloyd

Barricade
US 1949 75m Technicolor
Warner (Saul Elkins)

A tough mine-owner who runs a camp miles from civilization meets his come-uppance when three strangers are forced to accept his hospitality.
Rough western only notable as an (almost) scene-for-scene steal from *The Sea Wolf*: a text-book adaptation.

w William Sackheim *d* Peter Godfrey *ph* Carl Guthrie *m* William Lava

Raymond Massey, Dane Clark, Ruth Roman, Robert Douglas, Morgan Farley

Barry Lyndon**
GB 1975 187m Eastmancolor
Warner / Hawk / Peregrine (Stanley Kubrick)

Adventures of an 18th-century Irish gentleman of fortune.
A curiously cold-hearted enterprise, like an art gallery in which the backgrounds are sketched in loving detail and the human figures totally neglected; there is much to enjoy, but script and acting are variable to say the least, and the point of it all is obscure, as it certainly does not tell a rattling good story.

wd Stanley Kubrick, novel W. M. Thackeray *ph John Alcott md* Leonard Rosenman *pd Ken Adam*

Ryan O'Neal, Marisa Berenson, Patrick Magee, Hardy Kruger, Steven Berkoff, Gay Hamilton, Marie Kean, Murray Melvin, André Morell, Leonard Rossiter, Philip Stone *narrator* Michael Hordern

'The motion picture equivalent of one of these very large, very expensive, very elegant and very dull books that exist solely to be seen on coffee tables.'—*Charles Champlin*

'Watching the movie is like looking at illustrations for a work that has not been supplied.'—*John Simon*

Bartleby*
GB 1970 79m Eastmancolor
Pantheon (Rodney Carr-Smith)

A young clerk gradually refuses to take part in life.
A non-action film from an independent source, praiseworthy but overlong and fairly lacking in any kind of appeal except to literary connoisseurs.

w Anthony Friedmann, Rodney Carr-Smith, *story* Herman Melville *d* Anthony Friedmann *ph* Ian Wilson *m* Roger Webb

Paul Scofield, John McEnery, Thorley Walters, Colin Jeavons

The Bat
US 1959 78m bw
AA / Liberty (C. J. Tevlin)

A lady mystery writer rents a spooky old house and finds herself and her guests at the mercy of a maniac in search of hidden loot.
Poor remake of a standard twenties stage thriller; everyone chews the scenery.

wd Crane Wilbur, *play* Mary Roberts Rinehart *ph* Joseph Biroc *m* Louis Forbes

Vincent Price, Agnes Moorehead, Gavin Gordon, John Sutton, Lenita Lane, Darla Hood

The Bat Whispers**
US 1930 70m bw
UA / Roland West

Classic early sound version of *The Bat* (qv) by the director of the 1926 silent version. Excellent use of camera, sets, and unusual models.

wd Roland West ph Ray June, Robert Planck

Chester Morris, Una Merkel, Chancer Ward, Grayce Hampton, Maude Eburne, Spencer Charters, Gustav Von Seyffertitz

Bataan*
US 1943 114m bw
MGM (Irving Starr)

Thirteen soldiers holding a bridge against the Japanese die one by one.
Uncredited remake of *The Lost Patrol* (qv) transposed to the Pacific war, with stereotyped characters and much flagwaving. Very dated, but a big box office film of its time, despite its studio jungles.

w Robert D. Andrews *d* Tay Garnett *ph* Sidney Wagner *m* Bronislau Kaper

Robert Taylor, George Murphy, Thomas Mitchell, Lloyd Nolan, Lee Bowman, Robert Walker, Desi Arnaz, Barry Nelson, Philip Terry

Bathing Beauty
US 1944 101m Technicolor
MGM (Jack Cummings)

A songwriter plans to retire and settle down, but his publisher schemes to set his fiancée against him.
Witless, artificial aqua-musical, with plenty of unpersuasive high jinks but no real style despite a capable cast.

w Dorothy Kingsley, Allen Boretz, Frank Waldman *d* George Sidney *ch* John Murray Anderson

Esther Williams, Red Skelton, Basil Rathbone, Keenan Wynn, Ethel Smith, Xavier Cugat, Bill Goodwin

Batman*
US 1966 105m De Luxe
TCF / Greenlawn / National Periodical Publications (William Dozier)

The cloaked avenger saves an important executive from the clutches of four of the world's most notorious criminals.
Glossy feature version of the old and new serials about the comic strip hero who scurries around in his Batmobile making sure that justice is done. The scriptwriter's invention unfortunately flags halfway, so that despite a fairly sharp production the result is more childish than camp.

w Lorenzo Semple Jnr *d* Leslie Martinson *ph* Howard Schwarz *m* Nelson Riddle

Adam West, Burt Ward, Cesar Romero, Frank Gorshin, Burgess Meredith, Lee Meriwether, Alan Napier, Neil Hamilton

The Battle*
France 1934 85m bw
Gaumont (Leon Garganoff)
English language version aka: *Thunder in the East, Hara Kiri*

A Japanese aristocrat urges his wife to befriend an English naval attaché and steal secrets from him; she does, and falls in love.
Stagey but discreet melodrama of the old school, quite well made and acted.

w Nicolas Farkas, Bernard Zimmer, Robert Stevenson, *novel* Claude Farrère *d* Nicolas Farkas

Charles Boyer, Merle Oberon, John Loder, Betty Stockfield, Miles Mander

Battle beneath the Earth*
GB 1967 92m Technicolor
MGM / Reynolds / Vetter (Charles Reynolds)

Enemy agents burrow under the US by means of a giant laser.
Agreeable schoolboy science fiction with fair special effects.

w L. Z. Hargeaves *d* Montgomery Tully *ph* Kenneth Talbot *m* Ken Jones *sp* Tom Howard

Kerwin Mathews, Vivienne Ventura, Robert Ayres, Peter Arne, Martin Benson

Battle Circus
US 1952 90m bw
MGM (Pandro S. Berman)

A patriotic nurse and a disillusioned major fall in love at a mobile army hospital in Korea.
A flat, studio-bound potboiler with miscast stars, bound to provoke hilarity now as a serious version of *M*A*S*H*.

wd Richard Brooks *ph* John Alton *m* Lennie Hayton

Humphrey Bogart, June Allyson, Keenan Wynn, Robert Keith, William Campbell

Battle Cry
US 1954 148m Warnercolor Cinemascope
Warner (producer not credited)

During World War II, marines endure tough training before combat in Saipan; their sex lives come a close second to the war.
Interminable cheapie epic with both eyes on the box office: the cast salvages an odd moment or two, but violence of all kinds is the key to the entertainment.

w Leon Uris, from his novel *d* Raoul Walsh *ph* Sid Hickox *m* Max Steiner

Van Heflin, Aldo Ray, Mona Freeman, Dorothy Malone, Raymond Massey, Nancy Olson, James Whitmore, Tab Hunter, Anne Francis, William Campbell

Battle for Music*
GB 1943 87m bw
Strand Films (Donald Taylor)

The story of the wartime ups and downs of the London Philharmonic Orchestra.
Not many films feature a classical orchestra, and this simple tribute, a mediocre production at best, has considerable historical interest.

w St John L. Clowes *d* Donald Taylor

Hay Petrie, Joss Ambler, Charles Carson, Jack Hylton, J. B. Priestley, Eileen Joyce, Moiseiwitch, Sir Adrian Boult, Sir Malcolm Sargent

Battle Hymn
US 1957 108m Technicolor Cinemascope
U-I (Ross Hunter)

An American preacher with a guilt complex volunteers to help the South Koreans and after many adventures founds an orphanage.
Earnest, somnolent biopic of one Dean Hess; its mixture of drama, comedy, religion and war heroics is indigestible despite professional handling.

w Charles Grayson, Vincent B. Evans *d* Douglas Sirk *ph* Russell Metty *m* Frank Skinner

Rock Hudson, Anna Kashfi, Dan Duryea, Don Defore, Martha Hyer, Jock Mahoney, James Edwards, Carl Benton Reid

'The film seems to infer that heroic self-sacrifice, a little homely Eastern philosophy and a capacity for còmbining battle experience with an awareness of spiritual values are enough to overcome all emergencies.'—*John Gillett*

Battle of Britain*
GB 1969 131m Technicolor Panavision
UA / Spitfire (Harry Saltzman, Ben Fisz)

Summer 1940: England defends itself against aerial onslaught.
Plodding attempt to cover an historic event from too many angles and with too many guest stars, all indistinguishable from each other when masked in the cockpit during the repetitive and interminable dogfight sequences. On the ground, things are even duller.

w James Kennaway, Wilfrid Greatorex *d* Guy Hamilton *ph Frederick A. Young* *m* William Walton, Ron Skinner

Laurence Olivier (as Dowding), Robert Shaw, Michael Caine, Christopher Plummer, Kenneth More, Susannah York, Trevor Howard, Ralph Richardson, Patrick Wymark, Curt Jurgens, Michael Redgrave, Nigel Patrick, Robert Flemyng, Edward Fox

The Battle of Paris
US 1929 71m bw
Paramount

A lady music seller teams up with a pickpocket and falls for an American artist.
Primitive sound musical notable chiefly for its cast.

w Gene Markey *d* Robert Florey *ph* Bill Steiner *songs* Cole Porter

Gertrude Lawrence, Charles Ruggles, Walter Petrie, Arthur Treacher, Gladys du Bois

Battle of the Bulge**
US 1965 167m Technicolor Ultra Panavision
Warner / United States Pictures (Sidney Harmon, Milton Sperling, Philip Yordan)

In December 1944, the Allies take longer than expected to win a land battle in the Ardennes because of a crack Nazi Panzer commander.
Bloody and unbowed war spectacle, quite literate and handsome but deafeningly noisy and with emphasis on strategy rather than character.

w Philip Yordan, Milton Sperling, John Melson *d* Ken Annakin *ph* Jack Hildyard *m* Benjamin Frankel

Henry Fonda, Robert Shaw, Robert Ryan, Telly Savalas, Dana Andrews, George Montgomery, Ty Hardin, Pier Angeli, Barbara Werle, Charles Bronson, James MacArthur, Werner Peters

The Battle of the River Plate*
GB 1956 119m Technicolor Vistavision
Rank / Powell and Pressburger
US title: *Pursuit of the Graf Spee*

Semi-documentary account of the 1939 trapping of the German pocket battleship *Graf Spee* in Montevideo Harbour, and of her subsequent scuttling.
A sympathetic view of a German hero, Commander Langsdorff (not unexpected from these producers) is the most notable feature of this disappointingly patchy and studio-bound war epic, with too many actors in ill-defined bit parts, too undisciplined a storyline, and too confusing scenes of battle.

wd Michael Powell, Emeric Pressburger *ph* Christopher Challis *m* Brian Easdale

John Gregson, Anthony Quayle, Peter Finch, Bernard Lee, Ian Hunter, Jack Gwillim, Lionel Murton, Anthony Bushell, Peter Illing

'It is difficult to understand how English film-makers can have done thus badly with material so apt to their gifts.'—*Stanley Kauffmann*

The Battle of the Sexes*
GB 1960 83m bw
Prometheus (Monja Danischewsky)

A lady efficiency expert upsets the even tenor of life at an Edinburgh tweed manufactory, and the chief accountant plans to eliminate her.
Sub-Ealing black comedy which tends to misfire despite effort all round.

w Monja Danischewsky, from James Thurber's story The Catbird Seat *d* Charles Crichton *ph* Freddie Francis *m* Stanley Black

Peter Sellers, Constance Cummings, Robert Morley, Jameson Clark, Moultrie Kelsall, Alex Mackenzie, Roddy McMillan, Donald Pleasance, Ernest Thesiger

The Battle of the V1
GB 1958 109m bw
Maynard–Sewell (George Maynard)
US title: *Unseen Heroes*

Polish patriots sabotage the German rocket installation at Peenemunde.
Effective though schoolboyish war adventure shot on a low budget: story development reasonably brisk though predictable.

w Jack Hanley, Eryk Wlodek, *book* Bernard Newman *d* Vernon Sewell *ph* Basil Emmott *m* Robert Sharples

Michael Rennie, Patricia Medina, Milly Vitale, David Knight, Esmond Knight, Christopher Lee

The Battle of the Villa Fiorita
GB 1964 111m Technicolor Panavision
Warner (Delmer Daves)
US title: *Affair at the Villa Fiorita*

Two children aim to break up their mother's romance with an Italian concert pianist.
Quite lively, old-fashioned romantic comedy-drama largely set in a splendid Mediterranean villa; happy ending never in doubt.

wd Delmer Daves *novel* Rumer Godden *ph* Oswald Morris *m* Mischa Spoliansky

Maureen O'Hara, Rossano Brazzi, Richard Todd, Phyllis Calvert, Olivia Hussey, Martin Stephens, Elizabeth Dear

Battleground*
US 1949 118m bw
MGM (Dore Schary)

How a group of American soldiers in 1944 endured the Battle of the Bulge.
Enormously successful at the box office, this studio-bound production now seems stilted and unpersuasive, despite some good writing and direction

w Robert Pirosh *d* William Wellman *ph* Paul C. Vogel *m* Lennie Hayton

Van Johnson, John Hodiak, Ricardo Montalban, George Murphy, Marshall Thompson, Jerome Courtland, Don Taylor, Bruce Cowling, James Whitmore, Douglas Fowley, Leon Ames

The Bawdy Adventures of Tom Jones
GB 1976 94m Technicolor
Universal / Robert Sadoff

See *Tom Jones*, of which this is a musical version.
Not quite as bad as one would expect, but not up to the original.

w Jeremy Lloyd, *play* Don McPherson *m/ly* Paul Holden *d* Cliff Owen *ph* Douglas Slocombe *m* Ron Grainer

Nicky Henson, Trevor Howard, Terry-Thomas, Arthur Lowe, Georgia Brown, Joan Collins, William Mervyn, Murray Melvin, Geraldine McEwan, Michael Bates, James Hayter, Isabel Dean, Gladys Henson

Baxter*
GB 1972 100m Technicolor
(EMI) Performing Arts (Arthur Lewis)

An American son of divorced parents comes to London with his mother, meets tragedy in the shape of a friend's death, and responds to treatment for a speech defect.
Slight, appealing case history of a maladjusted 12-year-old; a rather unnecessarily uncommercial slice of life with no easy solution offered.

w Reginald Rose *d* Lionel Jeffries *ph* Geoffrey Unsworth *m* Michael J. Lewis

Patricia Neal (as the therapist), Scott Jacoby, Britt Ekland, Jean-Pierre Cassel, Lynn Carlin, Paul Eddington

Beach Party*
US 1963 104m Pathecolor Panavision
AIP / Alta Vista (James H. Nicholson)

An anthropologist sets up house on a California beach to study the mating habits of young people but becomes personally involved when one of them falls for him.
Vaguely satirical pop musical with relaxed performances; quite tolerable in itself, it started an excruciating trend.

w Lou Rusoff *d* William Asher *ph* Kay Norton *m* Les Baxter

Robert Cummings, Dorothy Malone, Annette Funicello, Frankie Avalon, Vincent Price, Harvey Lembeck, Morey Amsterdam, Jody McCrea

Beach Red*
US 1967 105m Technicolor
UA / Theodora (Cornel Wilde)

In 1943, American assault craft take a Jap-held Pacific island.
Brutal, pacifist war film, simply and clearly portrayed but not exactly entertaining.

w Clint Johnston, Donald A. Peters, Jefferson Pascal *d Cornel Wilde* *ph* Cecil R. Cooney *m* Antonio Buenaventura

Cornel Wilde, Rip Torn, Burr de Benning, Jean Wallace

The Beachcomber*
GB 1954 90m Technicolor
GFD / London Independent (William MacQuitty)

An alcoholic ne'er-do-well in the Dutch East Indies reforms after an unexpected adventure with a lady missionary.
Styleless remake of *Vessel of Wrath* (qv); the acting just about holds the interest, but all other contributions are flat.

w Sydney Box, from Somerset Maugham's story *d* Muriel Box *ph* Reg Wyer *m* Francis Chagrin

Robert Newton, Glynis Johns, Donald Sinden, Paul Rogers, Donald Pleasance, Walter Crisham, Michael Hordern, Ronald Lewis

The Bears and I
US 1974 89m Technicolor
Walt Disney (Winston Hibler)

An army veteran goes to live near an Indian settlement and adopts three bear cubs, later becoming a Park Ranger.
Simple, pleasing outdoor family film.

w John Whedon, *novel* Robert Franklin Leslie *d* Bernard McEveety *ph* Ted D. Landon *m* Buddy Baker

Patrick Wayne, Chief Dan George, Andrew Duggan, Michael Ansara

The Beast from Twenty Thousand Fathoms
US 1953 80m bw
Warner (Hal Chester, Jack Dietz)

Heat generated by an atomic bomb test in the Arctic thaws out a prehistoric rhedosaurus which travels down the American coast to cause havoc in New York until cornered and destroyed on Coney Island.
Flat-footed addition to the monster cycle, with an interminable wait for the beast's appearance and inferior trick work when he goes on the rampage.

w Lou Morheim, Fred Freiburger *d* Eugène Lourié *ph* Jack Russell *m* David Buttolph *sp* Ray Harryhausen

Paul Christian, Paula Raymond, Cecil Kellaway (as a professor gobbled up in a bathysphere), Kenneth Tobey, Donald Woods, Lee Van Cleef

The Beast Must Die*
GB 1974 93m Technicolor
BL / Amicus (Milton Subotsky)

A millionaire big game hunter holds a weekend party to track down a werewolf, but his guest list rapidly gets smaller . . .
A savage variation on *Ten Little Niggers*, not badly done, with such gimmicks as a 'guess who' break near the end.

w Michael Winder, *story* James Blish *d* Paul Annett *ph* Jack Hildyard *m* Douglas Gamley

Calvin Lockhart, Peter Cushing, Charles Gray, Anton Diffring, Marlene Clark, Ciaran Madden, Michael Gambon

Beast of the City
US 1932 80m bw
MGM

A police captain is determined to get a ruthless racketeer by fair means or foul.
Curiously dour little crime melodrama with a high death rate; the cast does not quite save it.

w John Lee Mahin, *story* W. R. Burnett *d* Charles Brabin *ph* Barney McGill

Walter Huston, Jean Harlow, Wallace Ford, Jean Hersholt, Dorothy Petersen, Tully Marshall, John Miljan

'Endowed with vitality and realism.'—*New York Times*

The Beast with Five Fingers*
US 1946 88m bw
Warner (William Jacobs)

A famous pianist dies and his severed hand returns to commit murder.
Slow-moving, Italian-set horror thriller which wastes an excellent original; a superb central performance and clever trick effects can hardly redeem the stodgy script or the ending which reveals the hauntings as an hallucination.

w Curt Siodmak, *story* W. F. Harvey *d* Robert Florey *ph* Wesley Anderson *m* Max Steiner

Peter Lorre, Andrea King, Robert Alda, J. Carrol Naish, Victor Francen, Charles Dingle

Beat the Devil*
GB 1953 100m bw
Romulus / Santana (Jack Clayton)

In a small Mediterranean port, and subsequently on a boat bound for the African coast, oddly assorted travellers plan to acquire land known to contain uranium deposits.
Unsatisfactory, over-talkative and inconsequential burlesque of the director's own *The Maltese Falcon* and *Across the Pacific*. Good fun was obviously had by the cast, but audiences were mostly baffled by the in-jokes, the extra-strange characters, and the lack of attention to pace, suspense and plot development.

w Truman Capote, John Huston, *novel* James Helvick *d* John Huston *ph* Oswald Morris *m* Franco Mannino

Humphrey Bogart, Gina Lollobrigida, Jennifer Jones, *Edward Underdown, Peter Lorre*, Robert Morley, *Ivor Barnard,* Bernard Lee

'A potential treat emerged as a wet firecracker . . . the incidents remain on a naggingly arch and lagging verbal keel.'—*New York Times*

'Each of its cinematic clichés appears to be placed in the very faintest of mocking quotation marks.'—*Time*

Beau Brummell*
GB 1954 111m Eastmancolor
MGM (Sam Zimbalist)

A Regency dandy enjoys a close relationship with the Prince of Wales, and when this is eventually withdrawn he dies in penury.
Stodgy historical romance with entertaining patches; the main story is too graceful and conventional to be believed.

w Karl Tunberg, *play* Clyde Fitch *d* Curtis Bernhardt *ph* Oswald Morris *m* Richard Addinsell *ad* Alfred Junge

Stewart Granger, Elizabeth Taylor, *Peter Ustinov* (as the Prince), *Robert Morley* (as George III), James Donald, James Hayter, Rosemary Harris, Paul Rogers, Noel Willman, Peter Bull, Peter Dyneley

Beau Geste**
US 1939 120m bw
Paramount (William Wellman)

The secret of who stole the family jewel is not revealed until the Geste brothers have fought and died in the Foreign Legion.
Spirited remake of the famous silent adventure, with the famous flashback opening of the desert fort defended by corpses. Style and acting generally satisfactory.

w Robert Carson, *novel* P. C. Wren *d* William Wellman *ph* Theodor Sparkuhl, Archie Stout *m* Alfred Newman

Gary Cooper, Ray Milland, Robert Preston, *Brian Donlevy, J. Carrol Naish*

Beau Geste
US 1966 105m Techniscope
Universal (Walter Seltzer)

The central desert section of the story is here augmented, with violence stressed, and Beau allowed to survive at the end.
A cheap leery melodrama is what results from the jettisoning of all the romantic portions of the original.

wd Douglas Heyes *ph* Bud Thackery *m* Hans Salter

Telly Savalas (rampant as the sadistic sergeant), Guy Stockwell, Doug McClure, Leslie Nielsen, Leon Gordon, Michael Constantine

Beau Ideal
US 1931 75m bw
RKO (William Le Baron)

John Geste and a new legionaire friend become involved in a religious war started by a rascally emir.
Lame sequel to *Beau Geste*, fettered by primitive dialogue.

w Paul Schofield, *novel* P. C. Wren *d* Herbert Brenon *ph* J. Roy Hunt

Lester Vail, Ralph Forbes, Don Alvarado, Loretta Young, Irene Rich

Beau James*
US 1957 107m Technicolor Vistavision
Paramount / Hope Enterprises (Jack Rose)

The vaguely crooked career of Jimmy Walker, mayor of New York in the twenties.
Romanticized biopic with few funny moments: Hope cannot cope with the drama, and the result is a creaking vehicle apart from a well-recreated twenties atmosphere and excellent production values.

w Jack Rose, Melville Shavelson, *book* Gene Fowler *d* Melville Shavelson *ph* John F. Warren

Bob Hope, Paul Douglas, Vera Miles, Alexis Smith, Darren McGavin, Joe Mantell, Walter Catlett *guest stars* Jack Benny, George Jessel, Jimmy Durante *narrator* Alistair Cooke

The Beautiful Blonde from Bashful Bend*
US 1949 77m Technicolor
TCF (Preston Sturges)

A temperamental saloon entertainer accidentally shoots the sheriff and takes refuge as a schoolmistress.
A dishevelled western farce unworthy of its creator, but with the advantage of appearances by many of his usual repertory of players.

wd Preston Sturges *ph* Harry Jackson *m* Cyril Mockridge

Betty Grable, Cesar Romero, El Brendel, Hugh Herbert, Rudy Vallee, Olga San Juan, Sterling Holloway, Porter Hall, Esther Howard, Margaret Hamilton

'Somehow the ramshackle air of Bashful Bend itself seems to have permeated the whole film.'—*MFB*

Beautiful Stranger
GB 1954 89m bw
Maxwell Setton, John R. Sloan
US title: *Twist of Fate*

On the Riviera, an actress discovers that her fiancé is a criminal.
Tawdry star melodrama of virtually no interest.

w Robert Westerby, Carl Nystrom *d* David Miller *ph* Robert Day, Ted Scaife *m* Malcolm Arnold

Ginger Rogers, Jacques Bergerac, Herbert Lom, Stanley Baker, Margaret Rawlings, Eddie Byrne, Coral Browne

The Beauty Jungle*
GB 1964 114m Eastmancolor
Cinemascope
Rank / Val Guest
US title: *Contest Girl*

A typist enters a beauty contest and step by step becomes Miss Globe; but her descent is equally rapid.
Wicked show biz and the road to ruin in one glossy package, predictable, but not badly done; always something going on, and performed with gusto.

w Robert Muller, Val Guest *d Val Guest*
ph Arthur Grant *m* Laurie Johnson

Janette Scott, Ian Hendry, Ronald Fraser, Edmund Purdom, Kay Walsh, Norman Bird, Janina Faye, Tommy Trinder, Francis Matthews

Because of Him*
US 1946 88m bw
U-I

A waitress pesters a Broadway author and actor for a leading role in their new show.
Moderately sprightly star vehicle with bonuses in the leading men; handling disappointingly routine.

w Edmund Beloin *d* Richard Wallace *ph* Hal Mohr

Deanna Durbin, Charles Laughton, Franchot Tone

Because of You
US 1952 95m bw
U-I (Albert J. Cohen)

A female ex-convict marries on parole but does not tell her husband of her past. Her old associates involve her innocently in another crime, and her husband divorces her; but years later she gets him and their child back.
Soap opera of the stickiest kind, made quite tolerable by good production.

w Ketti Frings *d* Joseph Pevney *ph* Russell Metty *m* Frank Skinner

Loretta Young, Jeff Chandler, Alex Nicol, Frances Dee, Lynne Roberts, Alexander Scourby, Mae Clarke

'Shows the most whole-hearted devotion to woman's magazine conventions.'—*MFB*

Because You're Mine
US 1952 103m Technicolor
MGM (Joe Pasternak)

An opera singer becomes a GI and wins the sergeant's sister.
Lumberingly inept star vehicle, giving the impression of nothing at all happening between the songs.

w Leonard Spiegelgass, Karl Tunberg
d Alexander Hall *ph* Joseph Ruttenberg
md Johnny Green

Mario Lanza, Doretta Morrow, James Whitmore, Dean Miller, Paula Corday, Jeff Donnell, Spring Byington

Becket**
GB 1964 149m Technicolor
Panavision
Paramount / Hal B. Wallis

Henry II leans on his boisterous Saxon friend Thomas à Becket, but when the latter is made first chancellor and then archbishop a rift between them widens and ends in Becket's assassination by Henry's over-eager knights.
Jean Anouilh's bitter stage comedy is filmed literally and soberly as a rather anaemic epic, so that the point is lost and the edge blunted. The paucity of physical action causes good scenes to alternate with long stretches of tedium.

w Edward Anhalt *d* Peter Glenville *ph Geoffrey Unsworth* *m* Laurence Rosenthal

Richard Burton, Peter O'Toole, Donald Wolfit, *John Gielgud*, Martita Hunt, Pamela Brown, Sian Phillips, Paola Stoppa

'Handsome, respectable and boring.'—*John Simon*

Becky Sharp**
US 1935 83m Technicolor
(RKO) Kenneth MacGowan

An ambitious girl makes her way into Regency society.
Chiefly notable as the first feature in three-colour Technicolor, this rather theatrical piece has its civilized enjoyments and the director made a few predictable cinematic experiments; the overall effect, however, is patchy.

w Francis Edward Faragoh, *play* Landon Mitchell, *novel* Vanity Fair by W. M. Thackeray *d Rouben Mamoulian* *ph Ray Rennahan* *m* Roy Webb *pd Robert Edmond Jones*

Miriam Hopkins, *Cedric Hardwicke*, Frances Dee, Billie Burke, Alison Skipworth, Nigel Bruce, Alan Mowbray, Colin Tapley, G. P. Huntley Jnr

The Bed Sitting Room*
GB 1969 91m De Luxe
UA / Oscar Lewenstein (Richard Lester)

Surrealist romance; after a nuclear war, motley survivors in the waste lands turn into bed sitting rooms, cupboards and parakeets.
Arrogantly obscure fantasy, a commercial flop which kept its director in the wilderness for four years. Fans of Monty Python may salvage a joke or two.

w John Antrobus, from the play by himself and Spike Milligan *d* Richard Lester *ph* David Watkin *m* Ken Thorne *pd* Assheton Gorton

Ralph Richardson, Rita Tushingham, Michael Hordern, Arthur Lowe, Mona Washbourne, Peter Cook, Dudley Moore, Spike Milligan, Harry Secombe, Marty Feldman, Jimmy Edwards

Bedazzled*
GB 1968 96m De Luxe Panavision
TCF / Stanley Donen

A short order cook is saved from suicide by Mr Spiggott, who offers him seven wishes in exchange for his soul.
A camped-up version of Faust which resolves itself into a series of threadbare sketches for the stars. All rather desperate apart from the leaping nuns.

w Peter Cook *d* Stanley Donen *ph* Austin Dempster *m* Dudley Moore

Peter Cook, Dudley Moore, Michael Bates, Raquel Welch, Eleanor Bron

Bedelia
GB 1946 90m bw
John Corfield (Isadore Goldsmith)

A psychotic woman is discovered to have poisoned three husbands.
Dreary upper-class British murder drama, totally devoid of style or suspense but a big star hit of the time.

w Vera Caspary, Moie Charles, Herbert Victor, Roy Ridley, Isadore Goldsmith, *novel* Vera Caspary *d* Lance Comfort

Margaret Lockwood, Ian Hunter, Barry K. Barnes, Anne Crawford, Jill Esmond, Ellen Pollock

Bedevilled
US 1955 86m Eastmancolor Cinemascope
MGM (Henry Berman)

In Paris, a novice priest befriends a girl on the run from gangsters. She turns out to be a murderess and is shot by her victim's brother.
Absurd high-flown bosh, unsuitably cinemascoped in ugly colour, and surprisingly badly handled by old professionals.

w Jo Eisinger *d* Mitchell Leisen *ph* Frederick A. Young *m* William Alwyn

Anne Baxter, Steve Forrest, Simone Renant, Victor Francen, Maurice Teynac, Joseph Tomelty

'This mixture of melodrama and religion provides a most unedifying entertainment.' —*MFB*

The Bedford Incident***
GB 1965 102m bw
Columbia / Bedford Productions (James B. Harris)

A ruthlessly efficient US destroyer captain in the Arctic chases a Russian submarine and accidentally fires an atomic weapon.
Gripping mixture of themes from *Dr Strangelove* and *The Caine Mutiny*, very tense and forceful, with excellent acting.

w James Poe, *novel* Mark Rascovitch *d James B. Harris* *ph* Gilbert Taylor *m* Gerald Schurrmann

Richard Widmark, *Sidney Poitier* (his first role with no reference to his colour), James MacArthur, Eric Portman, Wally Cox, Martin Balsam, Phil Brown, Michael Kane, Garry

Cockrell, Donald Sutherland
'Strong on virtues of a rather negative kind.'—*Penelope Houston*

Bedknobs and Broomsticks
US 1971 117m Technicolor
Walt Disney (Bill Walsh)

In 1940 three evacuee children and a kindly witch ride on a magic bedstead and defeat the invasion of England.
Extraordinarily dishevelled and incompetent Disney follow-up to *Mary Poppins*, a very muddled narrative with few high points and evidence of much cutting. Redeemed occasionally by camera trickery.

w Bill Walsh, Don DaGradi *d* Robert Stevenson *ph* Frank Philips *m/ly* Richard M. Sherman, Robert B. Sherman *sp* Eustace Lycett, Alan Maley, Danny Lee

Angela Lansbury, David Tomlinson, Roy Smart, Cindy O'Callaghan, Sam Jaffe, Roddy McDowall, Bruce Forsyth, Tessie O'Shea, Reginald Owen

Bedlam**
US 1946 80m bw
RKO (*Val Lewton*)

In 18th-century London, a sane girl is confined by the malevolent asylum master.
Interesting but rather flatly handled addition to the Val Lewton gallery of horrors, perhaps too carefully and discreetly done for pace or suspense.

w Mark Robson, Carlos Keith *d* Mark Robson *ph* Nicholas Musuraca *m* Roy Webb

Boris Karloff, Anna Lee, Billy House, Richard Fraser, Glenn Vernon

Bedtime for Bonzo
US 1951 83m bw
U-I (Michael Kraike)

To prove that environment determines character, a chimpanzee is brought up as a human baby.
Very moderate fun and games which proved successful enough for a sequel, *Bonzo Goes to College*.

w Val Burton, Lou Breslow *d* Frederick de Cordova *ph* Carl Guthrie *m* Frank Skinner

Ronald Reagan, Diana Lynn, Walter Slezak, Lucille Berkely, Herbert Heyes

A Bedtime Story*
US 1933 89m bw
Paramount (Emmanuel Cohen)

A breezy Frenchman has to interrupt his romances to look after an abandoned baby.
Mild star vehicle in which the agreeable comedy is largely supplanted by sentimental cooing.

w Benjamin Glazer, *novel* Bellamy the Magnificent by Roy Horniman *d* Norman Taurog *ph* Charles Lang *songs* Ralph Rainger, Leo Robin

Maurice Chevalier, Helen Twelvetrees, Baby LeRoy, Edward Everett Horton, Adrienne Ames

Bedtime Story*
US 1941 85m bw
Columbia (B. P. Schulberg)

A playwright's wife wants to retire instead of acting in his next play.
Pleasantly sparkling comedy with good performances.

w Horace Jackson, Grant Garrett, Richard Flournoy *d* Alexander Hall *ph* Joseph Walker

Fredric March, Loretta Young, Robert Benchley, Allyn Joslyn, Eve Arden, Helen Westley, Joyce Compton, Tim Ryan

Bedtime Story*
US 1964 99m Eastmancolor
U-I / Lankershim / Pennebaker (Stanley Shapiro)

Two Riviera confidence tricksters outwit each other.
A fairly lively script is defeated by dull handling, but performances and backgrounds are attractive.

w Stanley Shapiro, Paul Henning *d* Ralph Levy *ph* Clifford Stine *m* Hans Salter

David Niven, Marlon Brando, Shirley Jones, Dody Goodman, Aram Stephan, Marie Windsor

Before I Hang*
US 1940 71m bw
Columbia

A research scientist experiments with a new serum which turns him into a murderer.
Archetypal Karloff mad doctor flick, Jekyll and Hyde model: still quite tolerable.

w Robert D. Andrews *d* Nick Grinde *ph* Benjamin Kline

Boris Karloff, Evelyn Keyes, Bruce Bennett, Pedro de Cordoba, Edward Van Sloan, Don Beddoe

Before Winter Comes*
GB 1968 107m Technicolor
Columbia / Windward (Robert Emmett Ginna)

Austria 1945: a British major in charge of displaced persons is helped and hindered by a cheerful Yugoslav refugee who turns out to be a Russian deserter.

Likeable, well-produced drama hampered by a plot which becomes unnecessarily schematic, coincidental and downbeat in its attempts to tug at the heartstrings.

w Andrew Sinclair, *novel* The Interpreter by Frederick L. Keefe *d* J. Lee-Thompson *ph* Gilbert Taylor *m* Ron Grainer

David Niven, Topol, Ori Levi, Anna Karina, John Hurt, Anthony Quayle

'One of those films with a message on every page of its script.'—*MFB*

Beg Borrow or Steal
US 1973 74m Technicolor TVM
Universal (Stanley Kallis)

Three disabled men plan a museum heist.
Modest caper yarn which becomes tasteless in its effort to be different.

w Paul Playdon *d* David Lowell Rich

Mike Connors, Kent McCord, Michael Cole, Russell Johnson, Joel Fabiani, Henry Beckman

The Beggar's Opera**
GB 1952 94m Technicolor
British Lion / Imperadio (Herbert Wilcox, Laurence Olivier)

A highwayman in Newgate jail devises an opera based on his own exploits.
Exuberant potted version of the 1728 low opera, generally likeable but lacking a strong coherent approach and marred by violent colour and raggedly theatrical presentation. It nearly but not quite comes off.

w Dennis Cannan, Christopher Fry, *opera* John Gay *d* Peter Brook *ph* Guy Green *ad* George Wakhevitch, William C. Andrews *musical arrangement and additions* Arthur Bliss

Laurence Olivier, Stanley Holloway, Dorothy Tutin, Daphne Anderson, Mary Clare, George Devine, Athene Seyler, Hugh Griffith, Margot Grahame, Sandra Dorne, Laurence Naismith

'The failure is equalled only by the ambition.'—*Gavin Lambert*

The Beginning or the End
US 1947 112m bw
MGM (Samuel Marx)

During World War II American scientists continue to perfect the atom bomb despite their own misgivings, and one dies in an explosion.
Semi-documentary marred by sentimental personal asides and of very little continuing interest.

w Robert Considine *d* Norman Taurog *ph* Ray June

Brian Donlevy, Robert Walker, Tom Drake, Beverly Tyler, Hume Cronyn, Audrey Totter, *Godfrey Tearle* (as Roosevelt)

The Beguiled*
US 1971 109m Technicolor
Universal / Malpaso (Don Siegel)

A wounded Unionist soldier hides out in a Confederate ladies' school; the teachers fend for him until he causes trouble among the sexually frustrated women, who eventually kill him.
Eccentric melodrama which does not really work despite its credentials and patient work all round.

w John B. Sherry, Grimes Grice, *novel* Thomas Cullinan *d* Don Siegel *ph* Bruce Surtees *m* Lalo Schifrin *pd* Ted Haworth

Clint Eastwood, Geraldine Page, Elizabeth Hartman, Jo Ann Harris, Darleen Carr, Mae Mercer

'A must for sadists and woman-haters.'—*Judith Crist*

Behave Yourself*
US 1951 81m bw
RKO (Jerry Wald, Norman Krasna)

A young married couple and their dog get mixed up in a chain of murders.
Zany black comedy in the wake of *A Slight Case of Murder* and *The Thin Man.* The humour is spread too thin for success.

wd George Beck *ph* James Wong Howe *m* Leigh Harline

Farley Granger, Shelley Winters, William Demarest, Francis L. Sullivan, Margalo Gillmore, Lon Chaney, Hans Conried, Elisha Cook Jnr

Behind the Mask*
GB 1958 99m Eastmancolor
BL / GW Films (Sergei Nolbandov, Josef Somlo)

Political infighting causes tension on the board of a local hospital.
Oddly titled social drama with interesting detail but not much tension or conclusion.

w John Hunter, *novel* The Pack by John Rowan Wilson *d* Brian Desmond Hurst *ph* Robert Krasker *m* Geoffrey Wright

Michael Redgrave, Tony Britton, Carl Mohner, Niall MacGinnis, Vanessa Redgrave, Ian Bannen, Brenda Bruce, Lionel Jeffries, Miles Malleson, John Welsh, Ann Firbank

Behind the Rising Sun*
US 1943 88m bw
RKO

An American-educated Japanese goes home in

the thirties, comes under the influence of warmongers, and causes his father to commit hara-kiri.
Outrageous wartime flagwaver designed to vilify 'Uncle Tojo's dogs', from the writer and director of the similar *Hitler's Children* (qv).

w Emmet Lavery *d* Edward Dmytryk *ph* Russell Metty *m* Roy Webb

J. Carrol Naish, Tom Neal, Margo, Robert Ryan, Gloria Holden, Don Douglas, Adeline de Walt Reynolds

Behold a Pale Horse*
US 1964 121m bw
Columbia / Highland / Brentwood (Fred Zinnemann, Alexander Trauner)

A Spanish guerrilla goes into exile at the end of the Civil War. Twenty years later he is persuaded to return and kill a brutal police chief.
An action film which unfortunately insists on saying something significant about morality, destiny and death. Impeccably made, but somehow not very interesting apart from the action sequences.

w J. P. Miller, *novel* Killing a Mouse on Sunday by Emeric Pressburger *d Fred Zinnemann* *ph* Jean Badal *m* Maurice Jarre *ad* Alexander Trauner

Gregory Peck, Omar Sharif, Anthony Quinn, Raymond Pellegrin, Paola Stoppa, Mildred Dunnock, Daniela Rocca, Christian Marquand
'A fine example of a high class failure.'—*Judith Crist*

Behold My Wife
US 1934 79m bw
Paramount (B. P. Schulberg)

A wealthy young man brings back and marries a New Mexico Indian girl to show up his snobbish family.
Dated melodrama, of interest solely for its racial theme.

w William R. Lippman, Oliver LaFarge, *novel* The Translation of a Savage by Sir Gilbert Parker *d* Mitchell Leisen *ph* Leon Shamroy

Sylvia Sidney, Gene Raymond, Juliette Compton, Laura Hope Crews, H. B. Warner, Monroe Owsley, Ann Sheridan

Bell, Book and Candle*
US 1958 103m Technicolor
Columbia / Phoenix (Julian Blaustein)

A publisher slowly becomes aware that his new girl friend is a witch.
A gossamer stage comedy has been fatally flattened in translation; most of the actors are miscast, and sentiment soaks the script. But it remains a civilized entertainment.

w Daniel Taradash, *play* John Van Druten *d* Richard Quine *ph* James Wong Howe *m* George Duning

James Stewart, Kim Novak, Jack Lemmon, Ernie Kovacs, *Hermione Gingold*, Elsa Lanchester, Janice Rule

A Bell for Adano*
US 1945 104m bw
TCF (Louis D. Lighton, Lamar Trotti)

An American major takes over an Italian town and wins affection by replacing the local bell.
Slight end-of-war mood piece, still quite pleasant but without the undercurrents of feeling it had at the time.

w Lamar Trotti, Norman Reilly Raine, *novel* John Hersey *d* Henry King *ph* Joseph La Shelle *m* Alfred Newman

John Hodiak, Gene Tierney, William Bendix, Glenn Langan, Richard Conte, Stanley Prager, Henry Morgan

The Bellboy*
US 1960 72m bw
Paramount / Jerry Lewis Productions (Jerry Lewis)

An incompetent bellboy causes havoc in a Miami hotel.
Plotless essence of a comedian who divides opinion and will never be better than variable. This ragbag of old gags at least prevents his usual sentimental excesses, and is mercifully short.

wd Jerry Lewis *ph* Haskell Boggs *m* Walter Scharf

Jerry Lewis, Alex Gerry, Bob Clayton, Herkie Styles, Milton Berle

The Belle of New York*
US 1952 82m Technicolor
MGM (Arthur Freed)

A nineties playboy falls for a Salvation Army girl.
A rather dreary version of the old musical, with undistinguished additions.

w Robert O'Brien, Irving Elinson *d* Charles Walters *ph* Robert Planck *m/ly* Johnny Mercer, Harry Warren *ad Jack Martin Smith*

Fred Astaire, Vera-Ellen, Marjorie Main, Keenan Wynn, Alice Pearce, Clinton Sundberg, Gale Robbins

Belle of the Nineties*
US 1934 75m bw
Paramount (William Le Baron)

A saloon entertainer loves two men, one of whom is a crook.
Much-laundered star vehicle which despite superior production seems a pale shadow of the star's better pieces.

w Mae West *d* Leo McCarey *ph* Karl Struss

Mae West, Roger Pryor, John Miljan, John Mack Brown, Katherine de Mille, Duke Ellington and his Orchestra

Belle of the Yukon*
US 1944 84m Technicolor
International

A troupe of saloon entertainers in the Yukon become involved with a bank robbery.
Threads of plot support comedy, dancing and songs in this thin but reasonably fresh musical imitation of *The Spoilers*.

w James Edward Grant *d* William A. Seiter *ph* Ray Rennahan *md* Arthur Lange

Gypsy Rose Lee, Randolph Scott, Dinah Shore, Charles Winninger, Bob Burns

Belle Starr
US 1941 87m Technicolor
TCF (Kenneth MacGowan)

Absurdly laundered version of the life of the west's most notorious female outlaw, with the star laughably miscast.

w Lamar Trotti *d* Irving Cummings *ph* Ernest Palmer, Ray Rennahan *m* Alfred Newman

Gene Tierney, Randolph Scott, Dana Andrews, Shepperd Strudwick, Elizabeth Patterson, Chill Wills, Louise Beavers

The Belles of St Trinian's*
GB 1954 91m bw
BL / London Films / Launder and Gilliat

At an unruly and bankrupt school for girls, more time is spent backing horses than studying subjects, and the headmistress's bookmaker brother has a scheme or two of his own.
Fairly successful film version of Ronald Searle's awful schoolgirl cartoons, the emphasis shifted to a grotesque older generation with the star in drag. An enormous commercial success, but the three sequels *Blue Murder at St Trinian's*, *The Pure Hell of St Trinian's*, *The Great St Trinian's Train Robbery* went from bad to awful.

w Frank Launder, Sidney Gilliat, Val Valentine *d* Frank Launder *ph* Stan Pavey *m* Malcolm Arnold

Alastair Sim, George Cole, Joyce Grenfell, Hermione Baddeley, Betty Ann Davies, Renée Houston, Beryl Reid, Irene Handl, Mary Merrall

'Not so much a film as an entertainment on celluloid, a huge charade, a rich pile of idiot and splendidly senseless images.'—*David Robinson*

Belles on Their Toes
US 1952 89m Technicolor
TCF (Samuel G. Engel)

Further adventures in the growing up of the twelve Gilbreth children.
Flat sequel to *Cheaper by the Dozen* (qv) with sentimentality instead of Clifton Webb. Period atmosphere attractive.

w Phoebe and Henry Ephron, *book* Frank B. Gilbreth Jnr and Ernestine Gilbreth Carey *d* Henry Levin *ph* Arthur E. Arling *m* Cyril Mockridge

Myrna Loy, Jeanne Crain, Debra Paget, Jeffrey Hunter, Edward Arnold, Hoagy Carmichael, Barbara Bates, Robert Arthur

Bells are Ringing*
US 1960 126m Metrocolor
Cinemascope
MGM (Arthur Freed)

A telephone answering service operator becomes passionately involved in the lives of her clients.
Dull, rather ugly and boring transcription of a Broadway musical, with all talents below par, not enough dancing and too much plot.

w/ly Betty Comden, Adolph Green, from their play *d* Vincente Minnelli *ph* Milton Krasner *m* Jule Styne *ad* George W. Davis, Preston Ames *ch* Charles O'Curran

Judy Holliday, Dean Martin, Fred Clark, Eddie Foy Jnr, Jean Stapleton, Ruth Storey, Frank Gorshin

The Bells Go Down**
GB 1943 89m bw
Ealing (Michael Balcon)

The exploits of a London firefighting unit during World War II.
Tragi-comedy with lively scenes, a good record of the historical background of the blitz.

w Roger Macdougall, Stephen Black *d* Basil Dearden *ph* Ernest Palmer *m* Roy Douglas

Tommy Trinder, James Mason, Mervyn Johns, Philippa Hyatt, Finlay Currie, Philip Friend, Meriel Forbes, Beatrice Varley, Billy Hartnell

The Bells of St Mary's**
US 1945 126m bw
RKO (Leo McCarey)

At a big city Catholic school, Father O'Malley and Sister Benedict indulge in friendly rivalry, and succeed in extending the school through the gift of a building.

Sentimental and very commercial sequel to *Going My Way*, with the stars at their peak and the handling as cosy and well-paced as might be expected.

w Dudley Nichols *d* Leo McCarey *ph* George Barnes *m* Robert Emmett Dolan

Bing Crosby, Ingrid Bergman, Henry Travers, William Gargan, Ruth Donnelly, Rhys Williams, Una O'Connor, Eva Novak

Beloved Enemy*
US 1936 90m bw
Samuel Goldwyn (George Haight)

During the 1921 Irish rebellion, the fiancée of a British army officer falls in love with the leading revolutionary.
Dreamy-eyed romance with little relevance to the real situation; not badly done of its kind.

w John Balderston, Rose Franken, William Brown Meloney, David Hart *d* H. C. Potter *ph* Gregg Toland

Brian Aherne, Merle Oberon, David Niven, Karen Morley, Jerome Cowan, Henry Stephenson, Donald Crisp

Beloved Infidel*
US 1959 123m De Luxe Cinemascope
TCF / Company of Artists (Jerry Wald)

Sheilah Graham, a British chorus girl turned Hollywood columnist, marries Scott Fitzgerald but fails to cure him of alcoholism.
A bitter and even sordid true story becomes a slice of Hollywood romance, with stars unsuitably cast. On all levels it falls between two stools, satisfying nobody.

w Sy Bartlett, *book* Sheilah Graham and Gerald Frank *d* Henry King *ph* Leon Shamroy *m* Franz Waxman

Gregory Peck, Deborah Kerr, Eddie Albert, Philip Ober, Herbert Rudley, Karin Booth, Ken Scott

'Catastrophically misguided.'—*Penelope Houston*

The Beloved Vagabond*
GB 1936 78m bw
Ludovico Toeplitz

At the turn of the century, a jilted French artist becomes a vagabond and falls in love with an orphan girl.
Mildly amusing bi-lingual production from a bestselling picaresque novel; production quite lively.

w Wells Root, Arthur Wimperis, Hugh Mills, Walter Creighton, *novel* W. J. Locke *d* Curtis Bernhardt

Maurice Chevalier, Margaret Lockwood, Betty Stockfield, Desmond Tester, Austin Trevor, Peter Haddon, Cathleen Nesbitt

The Belstone Fox*
GB 1973 103m Eastmancolor Todd-AO 35
Rank / Independent Artists (Sally Shuter)

A fox and a hound grow up together but the fox leads to tragedy for its masters.
Good animal and countryside photography barely compensate for a fragmentary story with unpleasant moments or for a muddled attitude towards humans and animals; one is not clear what audience the result is supposed to appeal to.

wd James Hill, *novel* David Rook *ph* John Wilcox, James Allen *m* Laurie Johnson

Eric Porter, Rachel Roberts, Jeremy Kemp, Bill Travers, Dennis Waterman

Ben
US 1972 92m De Luxe
Cinerama / Bing Crosby (Mort Briskin)

A sickly boy inherits an army of trained rats.
Boring reprise of *Willard* in which the audience knows only too well what to expect. Production and development quite routine.

w Gilbert A. Ralston *d* Phil Karlson *ph* Russell Metty *m* Walter Scharf

Lee Harcourt Montgomery, Arthur O'Connell, Rosemary Murphy, Meredith Baxter, Kaz Garas, Paul Carr, Kenneth Tobey

Ben Hur**
US 1959 217m Technicolor Camera 65
MGM (Sam Zimbalist)

A Jew about the age of Christ is freed from the Roman galleys when he saves the life of a nobleman; he defeats his old enemy in a chariot race, joins the Christians after Calvary, and sees his mother's sister miraculously healed of leprosy.
Solid, expensive, surprisingly unimaginative epic from the Victorian novel; generally less sprightly than the silent version with Ramon Novarro.

w Karl Tunberg, *novel* General Lew Wallace *d* William Wyler, *Andrew Marton* *ph* Robert L. Surtees *m* Miklos Rozsa *ad* William A. Horning, Edward Carfagno

Charlton Heston, Haya Harareet, Jack Hawkins, Stephen Boyd, Hugh Griffith, Martha Scott, Sam Jaffe, Cathy O'Donnell, Finlay

Currie, Frank Thring, Terence Longdon, André Morell, George Relph

Bend of the River**
US 1952 91m Technicolor
U-I (Aaron Rosenberg)
GB title: *Where the River Bends*

1880 wagon trains arrive in Oregon, and the pioneers have trouble with the local bad man.
Good standard western with pace and period feeling.

w Borden Chase, *novel* Bend of the Snake by William Gulick *d* Anthony Mann *ph* Irving Glassberg *m* Hans Salter

James Stewart, Arthur Kennedy, Rock Hudson, Julia Adams, Lori Nelson, Jay C. Flippen, Henry Morgan, Royal Dano, Stepin Fetchit

Beneath the Twelve Mile Reef
US 1953 102m Technicolor
Cinemascope
TCF (Robert Bassler)

Jealousy, tragedy and romance among the Florida sponge fishers.
Fox's second Cinemascope production involved much underwater shooting, a trick octopus, and predictable plot devices.

w A. I. Bezzerides *d* Robert D. Webb *ph* Edward Cronjager *m* Bernard Herrmann

Robert Wagner, Terry Moore, Gilbert Roland, Peter Graves, J. Carrol Naish, Richard Boone, Angela Clarke, Jay Novello

'The dead weight of a melodramatic script overtaxes the gallant attempts at conviction.'—*MFB*

Benji*
US 1974 86m CFI color
Mulberry Square (Joe Camp)

A stray mongrel dog saves two kidnapped children.
Family film par excellence which rang the box office bell in a big way in the US. Its modest merits are rather beside the point.

wd Joe Camp *ph* Don Reddy *m* Evel Box

Peter Breck, Edgar Buchanan, Terry Carter, Christopher Connelly

The Benny Goodman Story*
US 1955 117m Technicolor
U-I (Aaron Rosenberg)

A clarinettist from the Jewish section of Chicago becomes internationally famous.
Sentimental biopic of a familiar figure w comes to life when the sound track is gi /en i.s head (and the real Goodman's clarinet).

wd Valentine Davies *ph* William Daniels *md* Joseph Gershenson

Steve Allen, Donna Reed, *Berta Gersten*, Herbert Anderson, Robert F. Simon, Sammy Davis Snr, Harry James, Martha Tilton, Gene Krupa

'The customary fictional liberties appear to have been taken.'—*MFB*

Bequest to the Nation*
GB 1973 116m Technicolor
Universal / Hal B. Wallis
US title: *The Nelson Affair*

The story of Nelson's long affair with the tempestuous Lady Hamilton.
Undistinguished historical drama from a thin play which despite hard work all round makes very ordinary screen entertainment.

w Terence Rattigan, from his play *d* James Cellan Jones *ph* Gerry Fisher *pd* Carmen Dillon *m* Michel Legrand

Peter Finch, Glenda Jackson (way over the top), Michael Jayston, Anthony Quayle, Margaret Leighton, Dominic Guard, Nigel Stock, Roland Culver

'As empty as an out-of-town matinee.'—*MFB*

Berkeley Square**
US 1933 87m bw
Fox (Jesse L. Lasky)

A London house reincarnates its owner as his 18th-century ancestor.
Romantic fantasy on a time lapse theme, the first of many and perhaps the most stylish and self-assured. Remade as *I'll Never Forget You* (qv).

w Sonya Levien, John Balderston, from Balderston's play *d* Frank Lloyd *ph* Ernest Palmer *m* Louis de Francesco *ad* William Carling

Leslie Howard, Heather Angel, Valerie Taylor, Irene Browne, Beryl Mercer, Colin Keith-Johnson, Alan Mowbray

Berlin Affair
US 1970 97m Technicolor TVM
Universal (E. Jack Neuman, Paul Donnelly)

A professional killer loses his value when he falls in love.
Complex, rather unpleasant international suspenser.

w Peter Penduik, E. Jack Neuman *d* David Lowell Rich

Darren McGavin, Fritz Weaver, Brian Kelly, Claude Dauphin, Pascale Petit

Berlin Correspondent
US 1942 70m bw
TCF (Bryan Foy)

In pre-war Germany an American reporter is kidnapped by the Nazis and replaced by a double . . .
Preposterous melodrama, so silly as to be often quite funny.

w Steve Fisher, Jack Andrews *d* Eugene Forde *ph* Virgil Miller *m* Emil Newman

Dana Andrews, Virginia Gilmore, Mona Maris, Martin Kosleck, Sig Rumann, Kurt Katch, Torben Meyer

Berlin Express*
US 1948 87m bw
RKO (Bert Granet)

Police of four nations guard a German VIP on a crack train to Berlin.
Rather muddled suspenser with attempts at political moralizing; the cast provides some good moments.

w Harold Medford *d* Jacques Tourneur *ph* Lucien Ballard *m* Frederick Hollander

Merle Oberon, Robert Ryan, Charles Korvin, Paul Lukas, Robert Coote

Bernardine*
US 1957 95m Eastmancolor Cinemascope
TCF (Samuel G. Engel)

A college student forced to swat for exams asks a friend's elder brother to look after his girl.
Henry Aldrich-style high school comedy, showing the lighter side of *Rebel without a Cause*. Notable for the clean-living hero played by a clean-living singing star, and the reappearance of Janet Gaynor for the only time since 1939, in a routine mother role.

w Theodore Reeves, *play* Mary Chase *d* Henry Levin *ph* Paul Vogel *m* Lionel Newman

Pat Boone, Richard Sargent, Terry Moore, *Janet Gaynor*, Walter Abel, Dean Jagger, Natalie Schaefer, James Drury

Berserk!
GB 1968 96m Technicolor
Columbia (Herman Cohen)

A lady circus owner revels in the publicity brought about by a series of murders.
Grisly and unattractive thriller with an ageing star in a series of unsuitably abbreviated costumes; the script is beyond redemption.

w Herman Cohen, Aben Kandel *d* Jim O'Connolly *ph* Desmond Dickinson *m* Patrick John Scott

Joan Crawford, Diana Dors, Ty Hardin, Judy Geeson, Michael Gough, Robert Hardy, Geoffrey Keen, Sidney Tafler, Philip Madoc

Best Foot Forward
US 1943 94m Technicolor
MGM (Arthur Freed)

A glamorous publicity-seeking film star accepts an invitation to a military college ball.
Old-fashioned formula musical based on a lightweight Broadway success.

w Irving Brecher, Fred Finklehoffe, *play* John Cecil Holmes *d* Edward Buzzell *ph* Leonard Smith *md* Lennie Hayton *ch* Charles Walters

Lucille Ball, William Gaxton, Virginia Weidler, Harry James and his Orchestra, June Allyson, Gloria de Haven

The Best House in London*
GB 1968 96m Eastmancolor
MGM / Bridge / Carlo Ponti (Philip Breen, Kurt Unger)

A Victorian publicity agent tries to organize a government-sponsored brothel.
Cheerful slam-bang historical send-up with as many dull thuds of banality as pleasant witticisms.

w Denis Norden *d* Philip Savile *ph* Alex Thompson *m* Mischa Spoliansky *pd* Wilfrid Shingleton

David Hemmings, George Sanders, Joanna Pettet, Warren Mitchell, Dany Robin, William Rushton

The Best Man***
US 1964 104m bw
UA / Stuart Millar, Lawrence Turman

Two contenders for a presidential nomination seek the support of the dying ex-president.
Brilliant political melodrama, ingeniously adapted on a low budget from an incisive play, with splendid dramatic scenes, memorable performances and good convention detail.

w Gore Vidal from his play *d Franklin Schaffner* *ph* Haskell Wexler *m* Mort Lindsey

Henry Fonda, Cliff Robertson, *Lee Tracy*, Margaret Leighton, Edie Adams, Kevin McCarthy, *Shelley Berman*, Ann Sothern, Gene Raymond, Mahalia Jackson

'A fine opportunity to watch pros at work in a hard-hitting and cogent drama that seems to become more topical and have more relevance with each showing.'—*Judith Crist*

'Some of the wittiest lines since *Strangelove* . . . the acting fairly crackled with authenticity.' —*Isabel Quigly*

The Best of Enemies
Italy / US 1961 104m Technirama
Columbia / Dino de Laurentiis

During the Abyssinian campaign of 1941, an Italian and a British officer learn mutual respect.
Mild satirical comedy drama with a few points to make about war; the elements blend rather obviously and dispiritingly.

w Jack Pulman *d* Guy Hamilton *ph Giuseppe Rotunno* *m* Nino Rota

David Niven, Alberto Sordi, Michael Wilding, Amedeo Nazzari, Harry Andrews, David Opatoshu, Kenneth Fortescue, Duncan Macrae

The Best of Everything*
US 1959 121m De Luxe Cinemascope
TCF (Jerry Wald)

Personal problems of a New York publisher's female staff.
Slick novelette on the lines of a naughty Peg's Paper; pure Hollywood gossamer.

w Edith Sommer, Mann Rubin, *novel* Rona Jaffe *d* Jean Negulesco *ph* William C. Mellor *m* Alfred Newman

Hope Lange, Stephen Boyd, Joan Crawford, Louis Jourdan, Suzy Parker, Martha Hyer, Diane Baker, Brian Aherne, Robert Evans, Brett Halsey, Donald Harron

Best of the Badmen*
US 1951 84m Technicolor
RKO (Herman Schlom)

At the end of the Civil War Jeff Clanton organizes the break-up of Quantrell's Raiders, but is himself arrested on a trumped-up charge and needs the Raiders' help.
Standard western notable for a good cast and for bringing in a remarkable number of historical outlaws, doing rather unhistorical things.

w Robert Hardy Andrews, John Twist *d* William D. Russell *ph* Edward Conjager

Robert Ryan, Claire Trevor, Jack Buetel, Robert Preston, Walter Brennan, Bruce Cabot, John Archer, Lawrence Tierney

The Best Things in Life Are Free*
US 1956 103m Eastmancolor Cinemascope
TCF (Henry Ephron)

From Broadway to Hollywood in the twenties, the story of songwriting team De Sylva, Brown and Henderson.
Gangsters, movie studios and the writing of 'Sonny Boy' for Al Jolson all figure in this amiable musical which spends more time on jokes than romance; the numbers are disappointing despite good tunes.

w William Bowers, Phoebe Ephron *d* Michael Curtiz *ph* Leon Shamroy *m* Lionel Newman

Ernest Borgnine, Gordon Macrae, Dan Dailey, Sheree North, Jacques d'Amboise, Norman Brooks, Murvyn Vye

The Best Years of Our Lives****
US 1946 182m bw
Samuel Goldwyn

Three men come home from war to a small middle-American community, and find it variously difficult to pick up where they left off.
The situations and even some of the characters now seem a little obvious, but this was a superb example of high-quality film-making in the forties, with smiles and tears cunningly spaced, and a film which said what was needed on a vital subject.

w Robert Sherwood, novel Glory for Me by Mackinlay Kantor *d William Wyler* *ph Gregg Toland*

Fredric March, Myrna Loy, Teresa Wright, Dana Andrews, Virginia Mayo, Cathy O'Donnell, *Hoagy Carmichael, Harold Russell* (a handless veteran whose only film this was), Gladys George, Roman Bohnen, Ray Collins

'The result is a work of provocative and moving insistence and beauty.'—*Howard Barnes*

The Betrayal
US 1974 74m colour TVM
Metromedia
aka: *The Companion*

A girl takes a job as companion to a lonely widow and sets her up as a robbery victim.
Fairly well characterized suspenser which runs out of steam.

w James Miller *d* Gordon Hessler

Amanda Blake, Tisha Sterling, Dick Haymes, Sam Groom

Betrayal from the East
US 1945 83m bw
RKO (Herman Schlom)

Japanese out to sabotage the Panama Canal are thwarted by a carnival showman.
Extravagant but penny-pinching flagwaver.

w Kenneth Gamet, Aubrey Wisberg, *novel* Alan Hynd *d* William Berke *ph* Russell Metty *m* Roy Webb

Lee Tracy, Nancy Kelly, Richard Loo, Abner Biberman, Regis Toomey, Addison Richards, Sen Yung

Betrayed
US 1954 108m Eastmancolor
MGM (Gottfried Reinhardt)

In 1943 a Dutch intelligence officer works with a resistance leader who turns out to be a traitor.
Slow-moving, studio-set romantic melodrama of the old school; not very lively.

w Ronald Millar, George Froeschel *d* Gottfried Reinhardt *ph* Frederick A. Young *m* Walter Goehr

Clark Gable, Victor Mature, Lana Turner, Louis Calhern,
O. E. Hasse, Wilfrid Hyde White, Ian Carmichael, Niall MacGinnis, Nora Swinburne

Between Heaven and Hell
US 1956 94m Eastmancolor Cinemascope
TCF (David Weisbart)

After Pearl Harbor a young southern landowner is called up and finds himself on active service with mixed racial types.
Vaguely anti-war, pro-understanding action thriller which ends up going through predictable heroics in a professional but not too sympathetic manner.

w Harry Brown, *novel* The Day the Century Ended by Francis Gwaltney *d* Richard Fleischer *ph* Leo Tover *m* Hugo Friedhofer

Robert Wagner, Buddy Ebsen, Broderick Crawford, Brad Dexter, Mark Damon, Robert Keith, Ken Clark, Skip Homeier, Harvey Lembeck

Between Two Worlds*
US 1944 112m bw
Warner (Mark Hellinger)

A number of air-raid victims, and two lovers who have committed suicide, find themselves on a luxury ship en route to the next world.
Nice-looking but slow and turgid remake of *Outward Bound* (qv), largely sunk in its own misery but redeemed by two performances.

w Daniel Fuchs, *play* Sutton Vane *d* Edward A. Blatt *ph* Carl Guthrie *m* Erich Wolfgang Korngold

John Garfield, *Edmund Gwenn*, Eleanor Parker, Paul Henreid, *Sydney Greenstreet*, Sara Allgood, George Tobias, Faye Emerson, George Coulouris, Dennis King, Isobel Elsom

Between Us Girls
US 1942 89m bw
Universal

A mother and daughter are both involved in romances which tend to cross.
Mild comedy, a disappointing debut for a disappointing young star.

w Myles Connolly, True Boardman, *play* Le Fruit Vert by Regis Gignoux, Jacques Thery *d* Henry Koster *ph* Joseph Valentine *m* Charles Previn

Diana Barrymore, Kay Francis, Robert Cummings, John Boles, Scotty Beckett, Ethel Griffies

Beware My Lovely
US 1952 77m bw
RKO / Filmmakers (Collier Young)

A handyman employed by a widow turns out to be a mental defective who imprisons and threatens to rape and murder her.
Dismal suspenser with a lot of screaming and running around but very little flair.

w Mel Dinelli, from his play The Man *d* Harry Horner *ph* George E. Diskant *m* Leith Stevens

Ida Lupino, Robert Ryan, Taylor Holmes, Barbara Whiting

'Inept characterization and ludicrously repetitive situations will surely rank this among the silliest films of the year.'—*MFB*

Beware of Pity*
GB 1946 106m bw
Two Cities (W. P. Lipscomb)

An officer courts a crippled girl out of pity. She finds out and kills herself.
Ambitious but rather artificial and dreary drama, a shade too pleased with its own literariness; performances straitjacketed by production.

w W. P. Lipscomb, Elizabeth Baron, Margaret Steen, *novel* Stefan Zweig *d* Maurice Elvey *ph* Derick Williams

Lilli Palmer, Albert Lieven, Cedric Hardwicke, Gladys Cooper, Linden Travers, Ernest Thesiger, Emrys Jones

Bewitched
US 1945 65m bw
MGM (Arch Oboler)

A girl with twin personalities has her murderous element exorcised by a spiritualist.
Hilarious nonsense, ancestor of the Eve/Lizzie schizos of the fifties.

wd Arch Oboler, from his story Alter Ego *ph* Charles Salerno Jnr

Phyllis Thaxter, Edmund Gwenn, Addison Richards, Kathleen Lockhart

Beyond the Bermuda Triangle
US 1975 74m colour TVM
Playboy (Ron Roth)

Sequel to *Satan's Triangle* (qv): a businessman searches for friends who have disappeared in the fatal area.
Open-air-melodramatic nonsense: quite watchable.

w Charles A. McDaniel *d* William A. Graham

Fred MacMurray, Sam Groom, Donna Mills, Suzanne Reed

Beyond the Blue Horizon*
US 1942 76m Technicolor
Paramount (Monta Bell)

An orphan white girl grows up on a tropical island with a chimpanzee and a swimming tiger; when rescued and her story doubted, she leads an expedition back to prove it.
The most tongue-in-cheek of the Lamour jungle extravaganzas, with plenty of simple fun.

w Frank Butler *d* Alfred Santell *ph* Charles Boyle *m* Victor Young

Dorothy Lamour, Richard Denning, Jack Haley, Patricia Morison, Walter Abel, Helen Gilbert, Elizabeth Patterson

Beyond the Forest*
US 1949 96m bw
Warner (Henry Blanke)

The discontented wife of a small-town doctor has an affair with a wealthy Chicagoan, murders a witness, attempts suicide, and dies of fever.
The star caricatures herself in this overblown melodrama which marked the unhappy end of her association with the studio. The rest of the cast suffer more dumbly from the script's unintentional hilarities.

w Lenore Coffee, *novel* Stuart Engstrandt *d* King Vidor *ph* Robert Burks *m* Max Steiner

Bette Davis, Joseph Cotten, David Brian, Ruth Roman, Minor Watson, Dona Drake, Regis Toomey

'Miss Davis makes a regrettably melodramatic mess of what is undoubtedly one of the most unfortunate stories she has ever tackled.'—*Newsweek*

Beyond Glory
US 1948 82m bw
Paramount

The honour of a West Point cadet is vindicated.
Proficient but dramatically turgid vehicle for an absurdly over-age star.

w Jonathan Latimer, Charles Marquis Warren, William Wister Haines *d* John Farrow *ph* John F. Seitz

Alan Ladd, Donna Reed, George Coulouris, George Macready, Audie Murphy

Beyond a Reasonable Doubt*
US 1956 80m bw
RKO (Bert Friedlob)

A novelist is persuaded by a crusading newspaper proprietor to fake circumstantial evidence incriminating himself in a murder, thus proving the uselessness of such evidence. He does it so well that he is convicted . . . but that doesn't matter as he was guilty all the time.
Ingenious but rather cheerless and mechanical thriller. The actors extract what they can from a script intent on sleight of hand, but the distinguished director is at his most flatulent.

w Douglas Morrow *d* Fritz Lang *ph* William Snyder *m* Herschel Burke Gilbert

Dana Andrews, Joan Fontaine, Sidney Blackmer, Philip Bourneuf, Shepperd Strudwick, Arthur Franz, Edward Binns

Beyond This Place*
GB 1959 90m bw
Renown / Georgefield (Maxwell Setton, John R. Sloan)
US title: *Web of Evidence*

An American visiting London finds his supposedly dead father in prison serving a life sentence for murder; he delves into history and finds the real culprit.
Spiritless murder mystery with less serious intent than the original novel; tolerable entertainment.

w Kenneth Taylor, *novel* A. J. Cronin *d* Jack Cardiff *ph* Wilkie Cooper *m* Douglas Gamley *ad* Ken Adam

Van Johnson, Vera Miles, Bernard Lee, Emlyn Williams, Jean Kent, Moultrie Kelsall, Leo McKern, Ralph Truman

Beyond the Valley of the Dolls
US 1970 109m De Luxe Panavision
TCF (Russ Meyer)

Three girls in Hollywood enjoy the wilder reaches of show biz high life.
The skinflick director's first film for a major studio, with positively no connection with *Valley of the Dolls*, is not explicitly pornographic but pussyfoots around with as many general excesses as can be crammed into two hours. If taken as high camp it provides a laugh or two, but is chiefly notable as marking a major studio's deepest dip into muddy waters.

w Roger Ebert *d* Russ Meyer *ph* Fred J. Koenekamp *m* Stu Phillips

Dolly Read, Cynthia Myers, Marcia McBroom, John La Zar, Michael Blodgett, Edy Williams

'If one can resist walking out, the last half hour is quite manic.'—*MFB*

Bhowani Junction*
GB 1955 110m Eastmancolor
Cinemascope
MGM (Pandro S. Berman)

Adventures of an Anglo-Indian girl during the last years of British India.
Disappointingly anaemic semi-epic from a gutsy novel, variably handled by all concerned.

w Sonya Levien, Ivan Moffat, *novel* John Masters *d* George Cukor *ph* Frederick A. Young *m* Miklos Rozsa

Ava Gardner, Stewart Granger, *Francis Matthews*, Bill Travers, Abraham Sofaer, Marne Maitland, Peter Illing, Freda Jackson, Edward Chapman

'An unwieldy, flatly-conceived charade.'—*MFB*

The Bible*
US / Italy 1966 174m De Luxe
Dimension 150 (70mm)
TCF / Dino de Laurentiis (Luigi Luraschi)

Through the Old Testament from Adam to Isaac.
A portentous creation with whispered commentary gives way to a dull misty Eden with decorous nudes, a sprightly Noah's Ark, a spectacular Babel, a brooding Sodom and a turgid Abraham. The pace is killingly slow and the script has little religious sense, but the pictures are often pretty.

w Christopher Fry and others *d* John Huston *ph Giuseppe Rotunno* *m* Toshiro Mayuzumi *ad* Mario Chiari

Michael Parks (Adam), Ulla Bergryd (Eve), Richard Harris (Cain), *John Huston* (Noah), Stephen Boyd (Nimrod), George C. Scott (Abraham), Ava Gardner (Sarah), Peter O'Toole (the three angels)

'An Old Testament spectacular like any other.'—*David Robinson*

'At a time when religion needs all the help it can get, John Huston may have set its cause back a couple of thousand years.'—*Rex Reed*

Big Bad Mama
US 1974 85m Metrocolor
Santa Cruz (Roger Corman)

In 1932 Texas, a desirable widow becomes a bank robber.
Fast moving, violent nonsense, like a caricature of *Bonnie and Clyde*, which was itself a caricature.

w William Norton, Frances Doel *d* Steve Carver *ph* Bruce Logan *m* David Grisman

Angie Dickinson, William Shatner, Tom Skerritt, Susan Sennett, Robbie Lee

The Big Blockade*
GB 1941 73m bw
Ealing (Alberto Cavalcanti)

A semi-documentary showing the importance of blockading Germany in winning the war.
A curious all-star propaganda revue with some sketches more effective than others.

w Charles Frend, Angus Macphail *d* Charles Frend

Leslie Banks, Michael Redgrave, John Mills, Will Hay (his only serious role), Frank Cellier, Robert Morley, Alfred Drayton, Michael Rennie, Marius Goring, Bernard Miles

The Big Boodle
US 1957 83m bw
UA / Monteflor (Lewis F. Blumberg)
GB title: *Night in Havana*

A croupier in an Havana gambling casino is suspected of knowing where counterfeit plates are hidden . . .
An undistinguished chase film with the star very tired and a long way from home.

w Jo Eisinger, *novel* Robert Sylvester *d* Richard Wilson *ph* Lee Garmes *m* Roaul Lavista

Errol Flynn, Pedro Armendariz, Gia Scala, Rossana Rory

The Big Bounce
US 1969 102m Technicolor
Panavision
Warner / Greenway (William Dozier)

An ex-GI with a criminal record gets into sexual and criminal trouble while working at a California motel.
Unattractive melodrama with no discernible point, certainly not to entertain.

w William Dozier, *novel* Elmore Leonard *d* Alex March *ph* Howard R. Schwartz *m* Michael Curb

Ryan O'Neal, Leigh Taylor-Young, Van Heflin, James Daly, Robert Webber, Lee Grant

The Big Broadcast**
US 1932 78m bw
Paramount

A failing radio station is saved by an all-star show.
Revue-style show with a minimum of plot, valuable as archive material covering many stars of the time.

w George Marion Jnr, *novel* Wild Horses by William Ford Manley *d* Frank Tuttle *ph* George Folsey

Bing Crosby, Kate Smith, George Burns, Gracie

Allen, Stuart Erwin, Leila Hyams, Cab Calloway, the Mills Brothers, the Boswell Sisters

The Big Broadcast of 1936**
US 1935 97m bw
Paramount (Ben Glazer)

The 'radio lover' of a small radio station is kidnapped by a man-hungry countess.
Zany comedy with interpolated variety acts and a totally Marxian climax.

w Walter de Leon, Francis Martin, Ralph Spence *d* Norman Taurog *ph* Leo Tover *songs* various *ch* LeRoy Prinz

Jack Oakie, George Burns, Gracie Allen, Henry Wadsworth, Wendy Barrie, Lyda Roberti, C. Henry Gordon, Benny Baker, Bing Crosby, Ethel Merman, Richard Tauber, Amos 'n Andy, Mary Boland, Charles Ruggles, Virginia Weidler, Guy Standing, Gail Patrick, Bill Robinson, the Nicholas Brothers, the Vienna Boys Choir, Akim Tamiroff

The Big Broadcast of 1937**
US 1936 100m bw
Paramount (Lewis Gensler)

A radio station manager has trouble with his sponsors.
More recorded acts separated by a measure of plot.

w Edwin Gelsey, Arthur Kober, Barry Travers, Walter de Leon, Francis Martin *d* Mitchell Leisen *ph* Theodor Sparkuhl *songs* various

Jack Benny, George Burns, Gracie Allen, Bob Burns, Martha Raye, Shirley Ross, Ray Milland, Benny Fields, Benny Goodman and his Orchestra, Leopold Stokowski and the Philadelphia Orchestra, Eleanore Whitney, Larry Adler, Louis da Pron

The Big Broadcast of 1938**
US 1937 90m bw
Paramount (Harlan Thompson)

A steamship owner engaged in a transatlantic race is hampered by his practical joking twin brother.
Glamorous, empty-headed all-star nonsense with the expected bevy of interpolated acts.

w Walter de Leon, Francis Martin, Ken Englund, Frederick Hazlitt Brennan *d* Mitchell Leisen *ph* Harry Fischbeck *songs* various

W. C. Fields, Bob Hope (debut), Martha Raye, Dorothy Lamour, Shirley Ross, Lynne Overman, Ben Blue, Leif Erickson, Kirsten Flagstad, Tito Guizar, Shep Fields and his Rippling Rhythm Orchestra

Big Brown Eyes
US 1936 76m bw
Paramount (Walter Wanger)

A private detective and his wisecracking girl friend catch a jewel thief.
Minor league Thin Man stuff, quite acceptably done.

w Raoul Walsh, Bert Hanlon *d* Raoul Walsh *ph* George Clemens *m* Boris Morros

Cary Grant, Joan Bennett, Walter Pidgeon, Lloyd Nolan, Alan Baxter, Marjorie Gateson, Isabel Jewell, Douglas Fowley

The Big Bus
US 1976 88m Movielab Panavision
Paramount (Fred Freeman, Lawrence J. Cohen)

Misadventures of a giant atomic-powered bus on its first cross-country trip.
Rather feeble spoof on disaster pictures, with some good moments.

w Fred Freeman, Lawrence J. Cohen *d* James Frawley *ph* Harry Stradling Jnr *m* David Shire *pd* Joel Schiller

Joseph Bologna, Stockard Channing, John Beck, René Auberjonois, Ned Beatty, Bob Dishy, Jose Ferrer, Ruth Gordon, Harold Gould, Larry Hagman, Sally Kellerman, Richard Mulligan, Lynn Redgrave

The Big Circus*
US 1959 109m Technicolor Cinemascope
AA (Irwin Allen)

A bankrupt circus owner tries to get his show back on the road despite the murderous schemes of his ex-partners.
Fast-paced melodrama which makes little sense but generally provides the expected thrills.

w Irwin Allen, Charles Bennett, Irving Wallace *d* Joseph Newman *ph* Winton C. Hoch *m* Paul Sawtell, Bert Shefter

Victor Mature, Red Buttons, Rhonda Fleming, Kathryn Grant, Vincent Price, Peter Lorre, *Gilbert Roland*, David Nelson, Adele Mara, Steve Allen

The Big City*
US 1937 80m bw
MGM (Norman Krasna)

An honest cab driver and his wife hold out against corruption.
Sentimental realism of the type expected of its director. Smooth and syrupy.

w Dore Schary, Hugo Butler *d* Frank Borzage *ph* Joseph Ruttenberg *m* William Axt

Spencer Tracy, Luise Rainer, Charley Grapewin, Janet Beecher, Irving Bacon, William Demarest, Eddie Quillan

Big City
US 1948 103m bw
MGM (Joe Pasternak)

In New York's East Side, a little girl is the adopted daughter of three bachelors, but trouble looms when they all get ideas of romance.
Later-day star vehicle for which the young star is really too old and all else is excessively sentimental and sprawling.

w Whitfield Cook, Ann Morrison *d* Norman Taurog *ph* Robert Surtees

Margaret O'Brien, Robert Preston, Danny Thomas, George Murphy, Karin Booth, Jackie Butch Jenkins, Betty Garrett

The Big Clock*
US 1947 95m bw
Paramount (John Farrow)

A publishing magnate murders his mistress and assigns one of his editors to solve the crime.
Slick but rather empty thriller with judicious use of adequate talent.

w Jonathan Latimer, from his novel *d* John Farrow *ph* John Seitz *m* Victor Young

Charles Laughton, Ray Milland, Maureen O'Sullivan, Rita Johnson, Elsa Lanchester

The Big Combo*
US 1955 80m bw
Allied Artists / Security-Theodora (Sidney Harmon)

The police crush a crime syndicate.
An otherwise uninspired thriller memorable for starting the new violence, with some ugly scenes of torture which suffered at the time from the censor.

w Philip Yordan *d* Joseph H. Lewis *ph* John Alton *m* David Raksin

Cornel Wilde, Richard Conte, Jean Wallace, Brian Donlevy, Robert Middleton, Lee Van Cleef, Ted de Corsia, Helen Walker, John Hoyt

The Big Country***
US 1958 165m Technirama
US / Anthony / Worldwide (William Wyler, Gregory Peck)

The Terrills and the Hannesseys feud over water rights, and peace is brought about only with the deaths of the family heads.
Big-scale western with a few pretensions to say something about the Cold War. All very fluent, star-laden and easy to watch.

w James R. Webb, Sy Bartlett, Robert Wilder, *novel* Donald Hamilton *d William Wyler ph Franz Planer m Jerome Moross*

Gregory Peck, Jean Simmons, Charlton Heston, Carroll Baker, *Burl Ives, Charles Bickford*, Alfonso Bedoya, Chuck Connors

Big Fella*
GB 1937 73m bw
Fortune (J. Elder Wills)

In Marseilles, a black man returns a lost child to his English parents.
Pleasant light vehicle with the star in typical easy form.

w Fenn Sherie, Ingram d'Abbes, *novel* Banjo by Claude McKay *d* J. Elder Wills

Paul Robeson, Elizabeth Welch, Roy Emerton, Marcelle Rogez

The Big Fisherman
US 1959 166m Technicolor Panavision
Centurion (Rowland V. Lee)

An Arab princess meets disciple Simon Peter, who dissuades her from her plan to assassinate her stepfather Herod.
Well-meaning but leaden adaptation of a bestselling novel which followed on from *The Robe*. Too reverent by half, and in many respects surprisingly incompetent.

w Howard Estabrook, Rowland V. Lee, *novel* Lloyd C. Douglas *d* Frank Borzage *ph* Lee Garmes *m* Albert Hay Malotte *pd* John de Cuir

Howard Keel, Alexander Scourby, Susan Kohner, John Saxon, Martha Hyer, Herbert Lom, Ray Stricklyn, Beulah Bondi

'Its overall flatness of conception and execution is a stiff price to pay for the lack of spectacular sensationalism characterizing its fellow-epics.'—*MFB*

The Big Gamble*
US 1960 100m De Luxe Cinemascope
TCF / Darryl F. Zanuck

Three people drive an ailing truck to a remote African township where they hope to start a haulage business.
Curious comedy-drama-adventure which starts off with family matters in Dublin and gradually develops into a lighter-hearted *Wages of Fear*. It has its moments.

w Irwin Shaw *d* Richard Fleischer, Elmo Williams *ph* William Mellor, Henri Persin *m* Maurice Jarre

Stephen Boyd, Juliette Greco, David Wayne, *Gregory Ratoff*, Sybil Thorndike, Fernand Ledoux

A Big Hand for the Little Lady**
US 1966 96m Technicolor
Warner / Eden (Fielder Cook)
GB title: *Big Deal at Dodge City* (though the action clearly takes place in Laredo)

Five rich poker players are outwitted by a family of confidence tricksters.
Diverting but thinly stretched acting-piece from a much shorter TV original; still, suspense builds nicely until the disappointingly handled revelation.

w Sidney Carroll, from his own TV play *d Fielder Cook* *ph* Lee Garmes *m* David Raksin

Henry Fonda, *Joanne Woodward*, Jason Robards, Paul Ford, Kevin McCarthy, *Charles Bickford*, Robert Middleton, *Burgess Meredith*, John Qualen

The Big Heat**
US 1953 90m bw
Columbia (Robert Arthur)

A police detective's wife is killed by a bomb meant for himself; he goes undercover to track down the gangsters responsible.
Considered at the time to reach a new low in violence (boiling coffee in the face), this dour little thriller also struck a new note of realism in crime films and produced one of Glenn Ford's most typical performances.

w Sydney Boehm, *novel* William P. McGivern *d* Fritz Lang *ph* Charles Lang *m* Mischa Bakaleinikoff

Glenn Ford, Gloria Grahame, Alexander Scourby, Jocelyn Brando, Lee Marvin, Jeanette Nolan, Peter Whitney

'The main impression is of violence employed arbitrarily, mechanically and in the long run pointlessly.'—*Penelope Houston*

The Big House**
US 1930 88m bw
MGM

Tensions in prison lead to an attempted breakout and a massacre.
Archetypal prison melodrama and a significant advance in form for early talkies. Its sets were re-used by Laurel and Hardy in *Pardon Us*.

w Frances Marion *d George Hill* *ph* Harold Wenstrom

Chester Morris, Wallace Beery, Robert Montgomery, Lewis Stone, Leila Hyams, George F. Marion, J. C. Nugent, Karl Dane

Big Jake*
US 1971 110m Technicolor Panavision
Batjac / Cinema Center (Michael A. Wayne)

An elderly Texas cattleman swings into action when his grandson is kidnapped.
Satisfactory example of the star's later vehicles, with efficient production and familiar cast and brawling.

w Harry Julian Fink, R. M. Fink *d* George Sherman *ph* William Clothier *m* Elmer Bernstein

John Wayne, Richard Boone, Maureen O'Hara, Patrick Wayne, Chris Mitchum, Bobby Vinton, Bruce Cabot, Glenn Corbett, Harry Carey Jnr, John Agar

'Another genial celebration of Big John's ability to carry a film practically single-handed.'—*MFB*

Big Jim McLain
US 1952 90m bw
Wayne / Fellows (Robert Fellows)

A special agent for the House of Unamerican Activities Committee routs communists in Hawaii.
Curious and rather offensive star vehicle in which the right-wing political shading interferes seriously with the entertainment value.

w James Edward Grant *d* Edward Ludwig *ph* Archie Stout *m* Emil Newman

John Wayne, Nancy Olson, James Arness, Alan Napier, Veda Ann Borg, Hans Conried, Gayne Whitman

'Brings to the screen all the unattractively hysterical mentality of the witch hunt.'—*Penelope Houston*

The Big Knife*
US 1955 111m bw
UA / Aldrich and Associates

A depressed Hollywood star who wants better things for himself is blackmailed into signing a new contract.
Overheated argument between Art and Mammon, with rather disagreeable people shouting at each other, for too long a time. Limited interest is provided by the acting.

w James Poe, *play* Clifford Odets *d* Robert Aldrich *ph* Ernest Laszlo *m* Frank de Vol

Jack Palance, Ida Lupino, *Rod Steiger*, Everett Sloane, Jean Hagen, Shelley Winters, Wendell Corey, Ilka Chase, Wesley Addy

'Everything in it is garish and overdone: it's paced too fast and pitched too high, immorality is attached with almost obscene relish, the knife turns into a buzz saw.'—*Pauline Kael, 1968*

The Big Land
US 1957 92m Warnercolor
(Warner) Jaguar
GB title: *Stampeded*

Cattlemen encourage the building of a rail link for Texas.
Undistinguished star western.

w David Dortort, Martin Rackin, *novel* Buffalo Grass by Frank Gruber *d* Gordon Douglas

Alan Ladd, Virginia Mayo, Edmond O'Brien, Anthony Caruso, Julie Bishop, John Qualen

'Hackneyed, humdrum western.'—*Howard Thompson*

The Big Lift*
US 1949 119m bw
TCF (William Perlberg)

When the Russians blockade Berlin, British and American airmen get supplies there via a massive airlift; two men on one plane hold opposite views of the matter, and both have chastening experiences.
Rather heavy-going fiction based on fact, with earnest performances and good production.

wd George Seaton *ph* Charles G. Clarke *m* Alfred Newman

Montgomery Clift, Paul Douglas, Cornell Borchers, O. E. Hasse, Bruni Lobel

'There are some acute touches . . . just enough to make the slick evasions of the rest all the more regrettable.'—*Gavin Lambert*

The Big Night
US 1951 75m bw
(UA) Philip A. Waxman

A 17-year-old youth goes on the rampage in the underworld to avenge the beating up of his father by gangsters.
Hysterical melodrama presenting a rather false and dismal view of the world. Amazingly typical of its director's later output.

w Stanley Ellin, Joseph Losey, *novel* Dreadful Summit by Stanley Ellin *d* Joseph Losey *ph* Hal Mohr *m* Edward Mann

John Barrymore Jnr, Preston Foster, Howard St John, Philip Bourneuf, Howland Chamberlin, Emile Meyer, Dorothy Comingore, Joan Lorring

'We are in that familiar underworld of the American cinema: dark streets gleaming with rain, sleazy apartments, garish night clubs, with Negro singers, drunks who spout philosophy, discontented blondes and fierce pock-marked thugs.'—*Gavin Lambert*

The Big Noise
US 1944 74m bw
TCF (Sol M. Wurtzel)

Two incompetent detectives accidentally round up a spy gang.
Very thin star vehicle consisting largely of poorly staged and warmed up versions of a few old routines.

w Scott Darling *d* Mal St Clair *ph* Joe MacDonald

Stan Laurel, Oliver Hardy, Doris Merrick, Arthur Space, Jack Norton

The Big Pond*
US 1930 79m bw
Paramount (Monta Bell)

The son of an important French family acts as a tourist guide in Venice.
Reasonably lively, semi-satirical early musical with Americans the butt of the jokes.

w Robert Presnell, Garrett Fort, Preston Sturges, *play* George Middleton, A. E. Thomas *d* Hobart Henley *ph* George Folsey *songs* various

Maurice Chevalier, Claudette Colbert, George Barbier, Nat Pendleton, Marion Ballou

Big Red
US 1962 89m Technicolor
Walt Disney (Winston Hibler)

An orphan boy protects a dog which later saves him from a mountain lion.
Simple boy-and-dog yarn with impressive Canadian settings.

w Louis Pelletier *d* Norman Tokar *ph* Edward Colman

Walter Pidgeon, Gilles Payant, Emile Genest

The Big Rip Off
US 1974 97m Technicolor TVM

A gambling con-man confounds his enemies and solves a murder.
Slick, fairly entertaining pilot for a *Mystery Movie* (qv) segment (McCoy).
w Roland Kibbee, Dean Hargrove *d* Dean Hargrove

Tony Curtis, Roscoe Lee Browne, Larry Hagman, John Dehner, Brenda Vaccaro

Big Rose
US 1974 74m colour TVM
TCF

Adventures of a middle-aged lady private eye.
Not unentertaining for a failed pilot.

w Andy Lewis *d* Paul Krasny

Shelley Winters, Barry Primus, Lonny Chapman, Peggy Walton, Joan Van Ark

The Big Shot*
US 1942 82m bw
Warner (Walter MacEwen)

An ill-fated criminal has trouble with women and his former companions.
Dullish star vehicle.

w Bertram Millhauser, Aben Finkel, Daniel Fuchs *d* Lewis Seiler *ph* Sid Hickox

Humphrey Bogart, Irene Manning, Richard Travis, Donald Crisp, Stanley Ridges, Henry Hull, Arthur Kennedy, Susan Peters, Howard da Silva

The Big Show
US 1961 113m De Luxe Cinemascope
TCF / API (Ted Sherdeman)

A circus proprietor dominates his sons; after his death they fight for supremacy.
Another remake of *House of Strangers*, which was also remodelled as *Broken Lance*. Not too bad as circus melodramas go.

w Ted Sherdeman *d* James B. Clark *ph* Otto Heller *m* Paul Sawtell, Bert Shefter

Esther Williams, Cliff Robertson, *Nehemiah Persoff*, Robert Vaughn, Carol Christensen, Margia Dean, David Nelson

The Big Sky*
US 1952 122m bw
RKO (Howard Hawks)

In 1830 two Kentucky mountain men join an exploration up the Missouri and become preoccupied with Indian trouble.
A large-scale adventure, loaded with talent, which becomes oddly tedious.

w Dudley Nichols, *novel* A. B. Guthrie Jnr *d* Howard Hawks *ph* Russell Harlan *m* Dmitri Tiomkin

Kirk Douglas, Arthur Hunnicutt, Elizabeth Threatt, Dewey Martin, Buddy Baer, Steve Geray, Jim Davis

'It has the timeless, relentless quality of the long American historical novel.'—*Penelope Houston*

The Big Sleep***
US 1946 114m bw
Warner (Howard Hawks)

Private eye Philip Marlowe is hired to protect General Sternwood's wild young daughter from her own indiscretions, and finds several murders later that he has fallen in love with her elder sister.
Inextricably complicated, moody thriller from a novel whose author claimed that even he did not know 'who done it'. The film is nevertheless vastly enjoyable along the way for its slangy script, star performances and outbursts of violence, suspense and sheer fun.

w William Faulkner, Leigh Brackett, Jules Furthman, novel Raymond Chandler d Howard Hawks ph Sid Hickox *m Max Steiner*

Humphrey Bogart, Lauren Bacall, Martha Vickers, John Ridgely, Dorothy Malone, Regis Toomey, Charles Waldron, Elisha Cook Jnr

'A sullen atmosphere of sex saturates the film, which is so fast and complicated you can hardly catch it.'—*Richard Winnington*

'A violent, smoky cocktail shaken together from most of the printable misdemeanours and some that aren't.'—*James Agee*

'Harder, faster, tougher, funnier and more laconic than any thriller since.'—*NFT, 1974*

'Wit, excitement and glamour in generous doses.'—*Francis Wyndham*

The Big Steal**
US 1949 72m bw
RKO (Jack J. Gross)

An army officer is framed for the theft of a payroll, and sets off across Mexico in hectic pursuit of the real culprit.
Unexpectedly enjoyable comedy melodrama with a plethora of twists and a pace that never lets up. Routine Hollywood at a level seldom achieved, and short enough to leave one asking for more.

w Gerald Drayson Adams, Geoffrey Homes, story The Road to Carmichael's by Richard Wormser *d Don Siegel ph* Harry J. Wild *m* Leigh Harline

Robert Mitchum, Jane Greer, William Bendix, Ramon Novarro, Patric Knowles, Don Alvarado, John Qualen

'Vigour and excellent craftsmanship.'—*Gavin Lambert*

The Big Store*
US 1941 83m bw
MGM (Louis K. Sidney)

An eccentric private eye saves a department store from the hands of crooks.
Reckoned to be the Marx Brothers' weakest MGM vehicle, but it has its moments, especially the first reel and the bedding department scene,

also Groucho's rendering of 'Sing While You Sell'.

w Sid Kuller, Hal Fimberg, Ray Golden *d* Charles Reisner *ph* Charles Lawton *m* Hal Borne

Groucho, Chico, Harpo, Margaret Dumont, Douglass Dumbrille, Tony Martin, Virginia Grey, Virginia O'Brien, Henry Armetta

The Big Street*
US 1942 88m bw
RKO (Damon Runyon)

A Broadway nightclub waiter falls in love with a crippled singer who selfishly accepts his help without loving him in return.
Unusual but mawkish material from an author who never really suited the screen; a mixture of laughs, tears and sentimentality, with a comic gangster background.

w Leonard Spiegelgass, *story* Little Pinks by Damon Runyon *d* Irving Reis *ph* Russell Metty *m* Constantin Bakaleinikoff

Henry Fonda, Lucille Ball, Eugene Pallette, Virginia Weidler, Agnes Moorehead, Barton MacLane, Ozzie Nelson and his Orchestra, Sam Levene, Ray Collins, Marion Martin

The Big Trail*
US 1930 125m bw
Fox

A wagon train struggles along the Oregon trail.
Simple-minded early talkie western spectacular with a new young star who took another nine years to make it big. Originally shown on a giant 70mm gauge and intended for big screens.

w Jack Peabody, Marie Boyle, Florence Postal *d* Raoul Walsh *ph* Lucien Andriot, Arthur Edeson

John Wayne, Marguerite Churchill, El Brendel, Tully Marshall, Tyrone Power Snr, David Rollins, Ward Bond, Helen Parrish

The Big Trees**
US 1952 89m Technicolor
Warner (Louis F. Edelmann)

An unscrupulous lumberman tries to exploit California's giant redwood forests but is won over by the local Quakers who hold the trees in awe.
Pleasing, old-fashioned outdoor drama with a plot which allows the star much opportunity for derring-do.

w John Twist, James R. Webb *d* Felix Feist *ph* Bert Glennon *m* Heinz Roemheld

Kirk Douglas, Eve Miller, Patrice Wymore, Edgar Buchanan, John Archer, Alan Hale Jnr

The Bigamist*
US 1953 80m bw
Filmmakers (Collier Young)

A travelling salesman has two wives.
Minor melodrama which took its subject seriously but failed to make absorbing drama of it. Very much a family affair, starring the producer's present and past wives, the latter also directing.

w Collier Young *d* Ida Lupino *ph* George Diskant *m* Leith Stevens

Edmond O'Brien, Joan Fontaine, Ida Lupino, Edmund Gwenn, Jane Darwell

'The film seems to have summoned all its energy to shout defiantly that bigamous marriages exist and, finding no one to defy, retires deflated.'—*MFB*

Bigger than Life*
US 1956 95m Eastmancolor
Cinemascope
TCF / James Mason

A small-town schoolteacher is prescribed cortisone for arthritis; it gradually turns him into a bullying megalomaniac full of grandiose schemes.
Exaggerated and sensationalized but still not very dramatic expansion of a genuine case hisotry. A curious choice for all concerned.

w Cyril Hume, Richard Maibaum *d* Nicholas Ray *ph* Joe MacDonald *m* David Raksin

James Mason, Barbara Rush, Walter Matthau, Robert Simon, Roland Winters

The Biggest Bundle of Them All
US 1967 110m Metrocolor
Panavision
MGM / Shaftel–Stewart

A retired gangster is kidnapped by other gangsters and shows them how to steal five million dollars worth of platinum.
Very moderately amusing international comedy caper.

w Josef Shaftel, Sy Salkowitz *d* Ken Annakin *ph* Piero Portalupi *m* Riz Ortolani

Raquel Welch, Robert Wagner, Vittorio De Sica, Edward G. Robinson, Godfrey Cambridge, Davy Kaye

'It begins like one of these really bad movies that are unintentionally funny. Then it becomes clear that it intends to be funny, and it isn't.'—*Renata Adler*

A Bill of Divorcement**
US 1932 76m bw
David O. Selznick

A middle-aged man, released from a mental institution, comes home and meets his strong-willed daughter.
Pattern play which became a celebrated star vehicle; now very dated but the performances survive.

w Howard Estabrook, Harry Wagstaff Gribble, *play* Clemence Dane *d* George Cukor *ph* Sid Hickox

John Barrymore, Katharine Hepburn (her debut), Billie Burke, David Manners, Paul Cavanagh, Henry Stephenson, Elizabeth Patterson

A Bill of Divorcement*
US 1940 69m bw
David O. Selznick
GB title: *Never To Love*

Virtually a scene-for-scene remake of the above. Again the acting holds the material together.

w Dalton Trumbo *d* John Farrow *ph* Nicholas Musuraca

Adolphe Menjou, Maureen O'Hara, Patric Knowles, Herbert Marshall, C. Aubrey Smith, Dame May Whitty

Billie
US 1965 87m Techniscope
UA / Peter Lawford (Don Weis)

A teenage tomboy runs into trouble because she is better at sport than her boy friends.
Routine American college/domestic comedy with a young star and good comedy support.

w Ronald Alexander, from his play Time Out for Ginger *d* Don Weis *ph* John Russell *m* Dominic Frontière

Patty Duke, Jim Backus, Jane Greer, Warren Berlinger, Billy de Wolfe, Charles Lane, Dick Sargent, Richard Deacon

Billion Dollar Brain
GB 1967 111m Technicolor Panavision
UA / Lowndes (Harry Saltzman)

Ex-secret agent Harry Palmer agrees to take a mysterious canister to Finland and becomes involved in an American megalomaniac's bid to take over the world.
Incomprehensible spy story smothered in the kind of top dressing now expected from this director, but which almost killed his career at the time. Occasional pictorial pleasures, but the total kaleidoscopic effect is enough to drive most audiences to the exit.

w John McGrath, *novel* Len Deighton *d* Ken Russell *ph Billy Williams m* Richard Rodney Bennett *pd* Syd Cain

Michael Caine, *Oscar Homolka*, Françoise Dorléac, Karl Malden, Ed Begley

Billy Budd*
GB 1962 125m bw Cinemascope
Anglo-Allied (A. Ronald Lubin, Peter Ustinov)

In 1797 the sadistic master at arms of a British warship terrorizes the crew and is killed by young Billy Budd, who must hang for his unpremeditated crime.
Handsomely photographed but obtusely scripted and variously acted attempt at the impossible, an allegory of good and evil more suited to opera or the printed page than film: in any case, a hopelessly and defiantly uncommercial enterprise. Some actors bore, others chew the scenery.

w Peter Ustinov, Robert Rossen, *novel* Herman Melville *d* Peter Ustinov *ph* Robert Krasker *m* Anthony Hopkins

Peter Ustinov, Robert Ryan, Terence Stamp, Melvyn Douglas, Paul Rogers, John Neville, Ronald Lewis, David McCallum, Lee Montague, John Meillon, Thomas Heathcote, Niall MacGinnis, Cyril Luckham

Billy Jack*
US 1971 113m Technicolor
Warner / National Student Film Corporation (Mary Rose Solti)

A half-breed Vietnam veteran roams the Arizona desert protecting wild mustangs and a runaway teenager.
A trendy radical drama, virtually a one-man show which had an enormous success in the US and led to a sequel, *The Trial of Billy Jack* (qv).

w Tom Laughlin, Delores Taylor *d* Tom Laughlin (T. C. Frank) *ph* Fred Koenekamp, John Stephens *m* Mundell Lowe

Tom Laughlin, Delores Taylor, Bert Freed, Clark Howat, Julie Webb, Ken Tobey, Victor Izay

'A plea for the alternative society with a format of the crudest melodrama.'—*MFB*

Billy the Kid*
US 1930 90m bw
MGM

A young western outlaw is relentlessly pursued by Sheriff Pat Garrett.
Mildly interesting early talkie western with the usual romanticized view of Billy. Originally made and shown in 70mm.

w Wanda Tuchock, Laurence Stallings, Charles MacArthur *d* King Vidor

Johnny Mack Brown, Wallace Beery, Kay Johnson, Karl Dane, Roscoe Ates

Billy the Kid*
US 1941 95m Technicolor

Remake of the above, equally false and rather less well acted, but a striking outdoor colour film of its period.

w Gene Fowler *d* David Miller *ph* Leonard Smith, William V. Skall *m* David Snell

Robert Taylor, Brian Donlevy, Ian Hunter, Mary Howard, Gene Lockhart, Henry O'Neill, Frank Puglia, Cy Kendall, Ethel Griffies

Billy Liar***
GB 1963 98m bw Cinemascope
Vic Films (Joe Janni)

In a drab North Country town, an undertaker's clerk lives in a world of fantasy.
Flawed only by its unsuitable Cinemascope ratio, this is a brilliant urban comedy of its time, seminal in acting, theme, direction and permissiveness. From a novel and play no doubt inspired by Thurber's Walter Mitty, it was later turned into a TV series and a successful stage musical, making Billy a universal figure of the period.

w Keith Waterhouse, Willis Hall, from KW's novel and their play *d John Schlesinger* *ph* Denys Coop *m* Richard Rodney Bennett

Tom Courtenay, Julie Christie, Wilfred Pickles, Mona Washbourne, *Ethel Griffies*, Finlay Currie, Rodney Bewes, Leonard Rossiter

Billy Two Hats
US 1973 99m Technicolor
UA / Algonquin (Norman Jewison, Patrick Palmer, Mitchell Lifton)

The friendship of an old Scottish outlaw and a young half-breed is broken only by the old man's death.
Curiously miscast western shot in Israel; it makes no discernible point and is not very entertaining.

w Alan Sharp *d* Ted Kotcheff *ph* Brian West *m* John Scott

Gregory Peck, Desi Arnez Jnr, Jack Warden, Sian Barbara Allen, David Huddleston

Billy Rose's Diamond Horseshoe see Diamond Horseshoe

Billy Rose's Jumbo see Jumbo

The Bingo Long Traveling All-Stars and Motor Kings
US 1976 111m Technicolor
Universal (Rob Cohen)

Adventures of a black baseball team in the 1940s.
High-spirited japes and exhibitions of athleticism which dramatically do not add up to very much.

w Hal Barwood, Matthew Robbins, *novel* William Brashler *d* John Badham *ph* Bill Butler *m* William Goldstein

Billy Dee Williams, James Earl Jones, Richard Pryor, Rico Dawson

Biography (of a Bachelor Girl)*
US 1935 84m bw
MGM

The biography of a sophisticated lady portrait painter reveals surprising details of her love life.
Leaden, bowdlerized screen version of a sparkling Broadway play, fragments of which do however survive.

w Anita Loos, *play* S. N. Behrman *d* Edward H. Griffith *ph* James Wong Howe

Ann Harding (miscast), Robert Montgomery, Edward Everett Horton, Edward Arnold, Una Merkel, Charles Richman, Donald Meek

Bird of Paradise
US 1932 80m bw
RKO

An adventurer on a South Sea island marries a native girl and causes trouble.
Never-never romance which remains stilted despite care obviously taken.

w Wells Root *d* King Vidor *ph* Clyde de Vinna *m* Max Steiner

Joel McCrea, John Halliday, *Dolores del Rio*, Skeets Gallagher

Bird of Paradise
US 1951 100m Technicolor
TCF (Harmon Jones)

Opulent remake of the above; the trappings make it even more absurd, and the ritual sacrifice of the heroine seems misplaced in what is otherwise a pantomime.

wd Delmer Daves *ph* Winton Hoch *m* Daniele Amfitheatrof

Louis Jourdan, Jeff Chandler, Debra Paget, Maurice Schwartz, Everett Sloane, Jack Elam
'The Kahuna is a naively grotesque figure, with a Central European accent and carrying what appears to be an outsize radish: he personifies the film's dubious approach to Polynesian myth and culture.'—*Gavin Lambert*

Birdman of Alcatraz**
US 1961 148m bw
UA / Hecht–Lancaster (Stuart Millar, Guy Trosper)

An imprisoned murderer makes a name for himself as an ornithologist.
Overlong and rather weary biopic of Robert Stroud, who spent nearly sixty years in prison and became *a cause célèbre*. One cannot deny many effective moments, notably of direction, but it's a long haul.

w Guy Trosper, *book* Thomas E. Gaddis *d John Frankenheimer ph* Burnett Guffey *m* Elmer Bernstein

Burt Lancaster, Karl Malden, Thelma Ritter, Edmond O'Brien, Betty Field, Neville Brand, Hugh Marlowe, Telly Savalas, James Westerfield

The Birdmen
US 1971 96m Technicolor TVM
Universal (Harve Bennett)
aka: *Escape of the Birdmen*

Prisoners of war escape from the Nazis by building a glider and soaring down from the castle parapets into Switzerland.
By *Colditz* out of *The Flight of the Phoenix*: phoney-looking but otherwise passable fantasy.

w David Kidd *d* Philip Leacock

Doug McClure, Chuck Connors, Richard Basehart, René Auberjonois, Don Knight, Max Baer, Tom Skerritt

The Birds***
US 1963 119m Technicolor
Universal / Alfred Hitchcock

In a Californian coastal area, flocks of birds unaccountably make deadly attacks on human beings.
A curiously absorbing work which begins as light comedy and ends as apocalyptic allegory, this piece of Hitchcockery has no visible point except to tease the audience and provide plenty of opportunity for shock, offbeat humour and special effects (which despite the drumbeating are not quite as good as might be expected). The actors are pawns in the master's hand.

w Evan Hunter, *story* Daphne du Maurier *d Alfred Hitchcock ph Robert Burks m* Bernard Herrmanns *sp* Lawrence A. Hampton

Rod Taylor, Tippi Hedren, Jessica Tandy, Suzanne Pleshette, Ethel Griffies

'Enough to make you kick the next pigeon you come across.'—*Judith Crist*

'The dialogue is stupid, the characters insufficiently developed to rank as clichés, the story incohesive.'—*Stanley Kauffmann*

The Birds and the Bees
US 1956 94m Technicolor Vistavision
Paramount (Paul Jones)

On a transatlantic voyage a wealthy simpleton is fleeced by a card sharp and his daughter; but the latter falls in love with her victim.
Competent but uninspired reworking of *The Lady Eve* as a vehicle for a rather charmless comic. Lacking Preston Sturges at the helm, the mixture of slapstick and sentiment fails to jell.

w Sidney Sheldon after Preston Sturges *d* Norman Taurog *ph* Daniel Fapp *m* Walter Scharf

George Gobel, David Niven, Mitzi Gaynor, Fred Clark, Reginald Gardiner, Harry Bellaver, Hans Conried

Birds Do It
US 1966 88m colour
Columbia (Ivan Tors, Stanley Colbert)

A janitor at an atomic plant is accidentally ionized and finds he can fly, which enables him to catch a spy or two.
Childish stunt comedy.

w Arnie Kogen *d* Andrew Marton *ph* Howard Winner *m* Samuel Maltovsky

Soupy Sales, Tab Hunter, Arthur O'Connell, Edward Andrews, Doris Dowling, Beverly Adams, Louis Quinn

Birds of Prey**
US 1972 81m colour TVM
Tomorrow (Alan A. Armer)

A helicopter pilot on traffic duty tracks down an armoured car hold-up.
Smoothly-made actioner with pretensions.

w Robert Boris *d* William Graham

David Janssen, Ralph Meeker, Elayne Heilveil

The Birth of the Blues*
US 1941 85m bw
Paramount (B. G. De Sylva, Monta Bell)

Trials and tribulations of a jazz band in New Orleans.
Thin fiction on which is strung a multitude of dark brown musical entertainment. Not bad, even now.

w Harry Tugend, Walter de Leon *d* Victor Schertzinger *ph* William C. Mellor *m* Robert Emmett Dolan

Bing Crosby, Mary Martin, Brian Donlevy, Jack Teagarden, Eddie Rochester Anderson, Carolyn Lee

The Birthday Party**

GB 1968 126m Technicolor
Palomar (Max Rosenberg, Milton Subotsky)

The down-at-heel lodger in a seaside boarding house is menaced by two mysterious strangers, who eventually take him away.
Overlong but otherwise satisfactory film record of an entertaining if infuriating play, first of the black absurdities which proliferated in the sixties to general disadvantage, presenting structure without plot and intelligence without meaning.

w Harold Pinter, from his play *d* William Friedkin *ph* Denys Coop *m* none *pd* Edward Marshall

Sidney Tafler, Patrick Magee, Robert Shaw, *Dandy Nichols*, Moultrie Kelsall

The Birthday Present*

GB 1957 100m bw
BL / Jack Whittingham

A toy salesman's life is changed when he is charged with smuggling a watch through the customs.
Downcast, prolonged and rather uninteresting domestic drama; attention is held by generally good acting.

w Jack Whittingham *d* Pat Jackson *ph* Ted Scaife *m* Clifton Parker

Tony Britton, Sylvia Syms, Jack Watling, Walter Fitzgerald, Geoffrey Keen, Howard Marion Crawford, John Welsh

The Bishop's Wife**

US 1947 108m bw
Samuel Goldwyn

An angel is sent down to mend the ways of a bishop whose absorption with cathedral buildings has put him out of touch with his wife and parishioners.
Whimsical, stolid and protracted light comedy saved by its actors and its old-fashioned Hollywood style.

w Robert E. Sherwood, Leonardo Bercovici, *novel* Robert Nathan *d* Henry Koster *ph* Gregg Toland *m* Hugo Friedhofer

Cary Grant, Loretta Young, David Niven, Monty Woolley, James Gleason, Gladys Cooper, Elsa Lanchester, Sara Haden, Regis Toomey

Bite the Bullet*

US 1975 131m Metrocolor
Panavision
Columbia / Persky–Bright / Vista
(Richard Brooks)

Several cowboys compete in a 700-mile endurance horse race.
Episodic adventure story with too much muddled chat and a very thin connecting story line; good to look at, though.

wd Richard Brooks *ph* Harry Stradling *m* Alex North

Gene Hackman, Candice Bergen, James Coburn, Ben Johnson, Ian Bannen, Jan-Michael Vincent, Paul Stewart

Bitter Harvest

GB 1963 96m Eastmancolor
Rank / Independent Artists (Albert Fennell)

An innocent Welsh girl comes to London, is deflowered, and sets off in search of wealth and luxury at any price.
Naive sixties version of the road to ruin, quite well done if you like that kind of thing.

w Ted Willis *d* Peter Graham Scott *ph* Ernest Steward *m* Laurie Johnson

Janet Munro, John Stride, Anne Cunningham, Alan Badel, Thora Hird, Vanda Godsell, Terence Alexander

Bitter Springs*

GB 1950 89m bw
Ealing (Leslie Norman)

A pioneer family in Australia buys a patch of ground but has trouble with aborigines.
Thinnest of the Ealing attempts to make movies down under, suffering from a lack of pace and sharpness as well as obvious studio settings.

w Monja Danischewsky, W. P. Lipscomb *d* Ralph Smart *ph* George Heath *m* Vaughan Williams

Chips Rafferty, Tommy Trinder, Gordon Jackson, Jean Blue, Charles Tingwell

Bitter Sweet

GB 1933 93m bw
British and Dominion (Herbert Wilcox)

In 1875 Vienna, a violinist marries a girl dancer and is later killed by a gambler.
Rather feeble filming of Noel Coward's operetta: it pleased a lot of people at the time.

w Lydia Hayward, Herbert Wilcox, Monckton Hoffe *d* Herbert Wilcox

Anna Neagle, Fernand Gravet, Ivy St Helier, Miles Mander, Esmé Percy, Hugh Williams, Pat Peterson, Kay Hammond

Bitter Sweet

US 1940 94m Technicolor
MGM (Victor Saville)

Remake of the above, retailored for unsuitable leads and with the story and music unattractively rearranged.

w Lesser Samuels, *operetta* Noel Coward *d* W. S. Van Dyke II

Jeanette Macdonald, Nelson Eddy, George Sanders, Felix Bressart, Ian Hunter, Fay Holden, Sig Rumann, Herman Bing, Curt Bois

The Bitter Tea of General Yen**
US 1933 89m bw
Columbia (Walter Wanger)

An American lady missionary in Shanghai is captured by a Chinese warlord and falls in love with him.
Arty miscegenation story which bids fair to become a cult film and certainly has a number of interesting sequences.

w Edward Paramore, *story* Grace Zaring Stone *d Frank Capra* *ph* Joseph Walker *m* W. Frank Harling

Barbara Stanwyck, Nils Asther, Toshia Mori, Walter Connolly, Gavin Gordon, Lucien Littlefield

Bitter Victory
US / France 1957 100m bw Cinemascope
Columbia / Transcontinental / Robert Laffont

Two officers sent on a document raid in Libya during World War II become poor soldiers because one suspects the other of an affair with his wife.
Glum desert melodrama, turgidly scripted and boringly made.

w René Hardy, Nicholas Ray, Gavin Lambert, *novel* Bitter Victory by René Hardy *d* Nicholas Ray *ph* Michel Kelber *m* Maurice Le Roux

Richard Burton, Curt Jurgens, Ruth Roman, Raymond Pellegrin, Anthony Bushell, Andrew Crawford, Nigel Green, Christopher Lee

Black Angel*
US 1946 80m bw
U-I (Roy William Neill, Tom McKnight)

A drunk sets out to find the murderer of his wife, and finds it was himself.
Stylish but empty version of a tired theme, interesting for performances and atmosphere.

w Roy Chanslor, *novel* William Irish *d* Roy William Neill *ph* Paul Ivano *m* Frank Skinner

Dan Duryea, Peter Lorre, Broderick Crawford, June Vincent, Wallace Ford, Hobart Cavanaugh, Constance Dowling

Black Beauty
US 1946 74m bw
(TCF) Edward L. Alperson

In Victorian England, a girl searches for her lost colt.
Stilted children's film with little relation to the book.

w Lillie Hayward, Agnes Christie Johnson, *novel* Anna Sewell *d* Max Nosseck *m* Dmitri Tiomkin

Mona Freeman, Richard Denning, Evelyn Ankers, J. M. Kerrigan, Terry Kilburn

Black Beauty*
GB 1971 106m colour
Tigon / Chilton (Tony Tenser)

A luckless horse passes from hand to hand but is finally restored to its original young master and has a happy retirement.
Pleasant, episodic animal story which stays pretty close to the book. A shade yawn-inducing for adults, but fine for children.

w Wolf Mankowitz, *novel* Anna Sewell *d* James Hill *ph* Chris Menges *m* Lionel Bart

Mark Lester, Walter Slezak, Peter Lee Lawrence, Patrick Mower, John Nettleton, Maria Rohm

The Black Bird
US 1975 98m colour
Columbia / Rastar (Michael Levee, Lou Lombardo)

Sam Spade's son finds himself beset by crooks still after the Maltese falcon.
Dismal, witless, boring parody of a classic crime film, with none of the humour of the original.

wd David Giler *ph* Philip Lathrop *m* Jerry Fielding

George Segal, Stéphane Audran, *Lee Patrick*, Elisha Cook Jnr, Lionel Stander, John Abbott, Signe Hasso, Felix Silla

The Black Book*
US 1949 88m bw
Eagle–Lion
GB title: *Reign of Terror*

A member of a secret organization which plans to replace Robespierre with a moderate goes undercover with the French Revolutionaries.
Moderate period melodrama with an attractive though artificial look.

w Philip Yordan, Aeneas Mackenzie *d* Anthony Mann *ph* John Alton *m* Sol Kaplan

Robert Cummings, Arlene Dahl, Richard Basehart, Richard Hart, Arnold Moss

The Black Cat*
US 1934 65m bw
Universal
GB title: *House of Doom*

A revengeful doctor seeks out the Austrian architect and devil-worshipper who betrayed his country in World War I.
Absurd and dense farrago set in a modernistic but crumbling castle which is eventually blown to bits just as its owner is skinned alive. Mostly rather dull despite the extraordinary plot, but the thing has moments of style, a delightful cod devil worship sequence (especially for audiences with a rudimentary knowledge of Latin) and nothing at all to do with the title or Edgar Allan Poe.

w Peter Ruric *d* Edgar G. Ulmer *ph John Mescall* *m* Heinz Roemheld *ad* Charles D. Hall

Boris Karloff, *Bela Lugosi*, David Manners, Jacqueline Wells, Egon Brecher

The Black Cat*
US 1941 70m bw
Universal

Murder follows the summoning of the family to the spooky house of a cat-loving recluse.
Disappointing mystery which squanders a splendid cast on a script full of non-sequiturs and makes heavy weather of its light relief.

w Robert Lees, Fred Rinaldo, Eric Taylor, Robert Neville *d* Albert S. Rogell *ph* Stanley Cortez

Basil Rathbone, Gladys Cooper, Broderick Crawford, Hugh Herbert, Gale Sondergaard, Anne Gwynne, Alan Ladd, Cecilia Loftus, Bela Lugosi

Black Fury*
US 1935 95m bw
Warner (Robert Lord)

A coal miner comes up against union problems, unsafe conditions and corruption.
Typical Warner social drama, good for its time but now very obvious.

w Abem Finkel, Carl Erickson, *play* Bohunk by Harry R. Irving *d* Michael Curtiz *ph* Byron Haskin

Paul Muni, Karen Morley, William Gargan, Barton MacLane, John Qualen, J. Carrol Naish, Vince Barnett, Tully Marshall, Henry O'Neill

Black Hand*
US 1949 92m bw
MGM (William H. Wright)

In New York at the turn of the century, an Italian boy avenges his father's death at the hands of the Mafia.
Neatly produced, studio-set melodrama, unusual in subject but very stereotyped and artificial in treatment.

w Luther Davis *d* Richard Thorpe *ph* Paul C. Vogel *m* Alberto Colombo

Gene Kelly, J. Carrol Naish, Teresa Celli, Marc Lawrence, Frank Puglia, Barry Kelley

The Black Knight
GB 1954 85m Technicolor
Warwick (Irving Allen, Albert R. Broccoli)

A humble swordmaker reveals a traitor to King Arthur.
Hilarious travesty of English historical legend, meant seriously for Anglo-American consumption. Shades of *Zorro, Babes in the Wood* and *1066 and All That.*

w Alec Coppel *d* Tay Garnett *ph* John Wilcox *m* John Addison

Alan Ladd, Peter Cushing, Patricia Medina, Harry Andrews, André Morell, Anthony Bushell, Patrick Troughton, Laurence Naismith, John Laurie

'Alan Ladd galahads with wild west *gentilesse* in this Technicolored rampage through British history.'—*MFB*

Black Legion**
US 1936 83m bw
Warner (Robert Lord)

A factory worker becomes involved with the Ku Klux Klan.
Social melodrama typical of its studio, and good of its kind.

w Robert Lord, Abem Finkel, William Wister Haines *d* Archie Mayo *ph* George Barnes

Humphrey Bogart, Erin O'Brien Moore, Dick Foran, Ann Sheridan, Robert Barrat, John Litel, Charles Halton

Black Magic*
US 1949 105m bw
Edward Small (Gregory Ratoff)

Cagliostro the magician becomes involved in a plot to supply a double for Marie Antoinette.
Deliriously complicated historical romp which unfortunately suffers from a stolid script and production which kill all the flights of fancy.

w Charles Bennett *d* Gregory Ratoff *ph* Ubaldo Arata, Anchise Brizzi *m* Paul Sawtell

Orson Welles, Nancy Guild, Akim Tamiroff, Valentina Cortese, Margot Grahame, Charles Goldner, Frank Latimore, Stephen Bekassy

Black Narcissus***
GB 1946 100m Technicolor
GFD / The Archers (Michael Powell, Emeric Pressburger)

Anglo-Catholic nuns in the Himalayas have trouble with climate, morale, and one of their number who goes mad of sex frustration.
An unlikely theme produces one of the cinema's most beautiful films, a visual and emotional stunner despite some narrative uncertainty.

wd Michael Powell, Emeric Pressburger, *novel* Rumer Godden *ph Jack Cardiff*

Deborah Kerr, David Farrar, Sabu, Jean Simmons, Kathleen Byron, Flora Robson, Esmond Knight, Jenny Laird, May Hallatt, Judith Furse

Black Noon*
US 1971 73m colour TVM
Columbia (Andrew Fenady)

In the old west, a young minister and his wife arrive at a remote town run by diabolists.
Preposterous nonsense with a winning way.

w Andrew J. Fenady *d* Bernard Kowalski

Roy Thinnes, Ray Milland, Yvette Mimieux, Gloria Grahame, Lynn Loring, Henry Silva

The Black Orchid*
US 1958 95m bw Vistavision
Paramount (Carlo Ponti, Marcello Girosi)

A widower incurs hostility from his daughter when he plans to marry a gangster's widow.
Rather solemn New York/Italian romantic melodrama, with much gesticulation all round.

w Joseph Stefano *d* Martin Ritt *ph* Robert Burks *m* Alessandro Cicognini

Sophia Loren, Anthony Quinn, Ina Balin, Jimmy Baird, Mark Richman

The Black Room*
US 1935 70m bw
Columbia

A nobleman's power is claimed by his evil twin brother.
Rather splendid old barnstormer with touches of horror, a neatly produced star vehicle.

w Henry Myers, from the writings of Arthur Strawn *d Roy William Neill ph* Al Siegler

Boris Karloff, Marian Marsh, Katherine de Mille, Thurston Hall

The Black Rose*
US 1950 120m Technicolor
TCF (Louis D. Lighton)

A 13th-century English scholar journeys to the land of the Mongols, and after many adventures returns to a knighthood for his scientific discoveries.
Portentous and slow-moving adventure with good things along the way.

w Talbot Jennings, *novel* Thomas B. Costain *d* Henry Hathaway *ph Jack Cardiff m* Richard Addinsell *ad* Paul Sheriff

Tyrone Power, Orson Welles, Cecile Aubry, Jack Hawkins, Finlay Currie, Henry Oscar, Michael Rennie

The Black Scorpion
US 1957 88m bw
Warner (Frank Melford, Jack Dietz)

Volcanic explosions uncover a nest of prehistoric giant scorpions near a Mexican village.
Apart from a genuinely terrifying sequence in the scorpion's lair, this is a poor monster movie in which excessively dark photography seems intended to cover up very variable trick work.

w David Duncan, Robert Bless *d* Edward Ludwig *ph* Lionel Lindon *m* Paul Sawtell *sp* Willis O'Brien

Richard Denning, Mara Corday, Carlos Rivas, Mario Navarro

The Black Sheep of Whitehall*
GB 1941 80m bw
Ealing (S. C. Balcon)

An incompetent teacher is mistaken for an economics expert and saves the real expert from spies who run a nursing home.
Pretty good wartime star comedy, with a succession of briskly timed gags.

w Angus Macphail, John Dighton *d* Basil Dearden, Will Hay

Will Hay, John Mills, Basil Sydney, Frank Cellier, Felix Aylmer

The Black Shield of Falworth*
US 1954 99m Technicolor Cinemascope
U-I (Robert Arthur, Melville Tucker)

The film in which Tony Curtis says 'Yonda lies the castle of my fodda' (or something like it) is an amiable romp which alternates between comic strip dialogue and a surprisingly convincing sense of medieval custom. The training scenes are as sharp as the romantic asides are pallid.

w Oscar Brodney, *novel* Men of Iron by Howard Pyle *d* Rudolph Maté *ph* Irving Glassberg *m* Joseph Gershenson

Tony Curtis, Janet Leigh, David Farrar, Barbara Rush, Herbert Marshall, Rhys Williams, Dan O'Herlihy, Torin Thatcher

'A straightforward piece of hokum with no pretensions, and spoken in a variety of accents that only Hollywood could muster.'—*John Gillett*

The Black Sleep
US 1956 81m bw
UA / Bel Air (Howard W. Koch)

A Victorian brain surgeon experiments on human beings and produces freaks who eventually turn on him.
Gruesome and humourless horror film notable only for its gallery of wasted talent.

w John C. Higgins *d* Reginald Le Borg *ph* Gordon Avil *m* Les Baxter

Basil Rathbone, Bela Lugosi, Lon Chaney Jnr, John Carradine, Akim Tamiroff, Tor Johnson, Herbert Rudley, Patricia Blake

The Black Swan***
US 1942 85m Technicolor
TCF (Robert Bassler)

Morgan the pirate is made governor of Jamaica and enlists the help of his old friends to rid the Caribbean of buccaneers.
Rousing adventure story with comic asides: just what action hokum always aimed to be, with a spirited gallery of heroes and villains and an entertaining narrative taken at a spanking pace.

w Ben Hecht, Seton I. Miller, novel Rafael Sabatini *d Henry King ph Leon Shamroy m* Alfred Newman

Tyrone Power, Maureen O'Hara, *Laird Cregar, Thomas Mitchell, George Sanders*, Anthony Quinn, George Zucco, Edward Ashley

The Black Tent
GB 1956 93m Technicolor Vistavision
Rank / William MacQuitty

During a Libyan battle a wounded army captain is cared for by Arabs and marries the sheik's daughter. Ten years later, after his death, his son elects to live with the tribe.
Pleasantly shot but otherwise dull, formless and interminable romantic drama, all very stiff upper lip.

w Robin Maugham, Bryan Forbes *d* Brian Desmond Hurst *ph Desmond Dickinson m* William Alwyn

Anthony Steel, Donald Sinden, *André Morell*, Anna Maria Sandri, Ralph Truman, Donald Pleasance, Anthony Bushell, Michael Craig

Black Tuesday*
US 1954 80m bw
UA / Leonard Goldstein (Robert Goldstein)

A killer escapes from Death Row and hides out with hostages in a disused warehouse.
Starkly melodramatic gangster vehicle with the star up to his oldest tricks. Good tension, but generally rather unpleasant.

w Sydney Boehm *d* Hugo Fregonese *ph* Stanley Cortez *m* Paul Dunlap

Edward G. Robinson, Jean Parker, Peter Graves, Milburn Stone, Warren Stevens, Jack Kelly, James Bell

Black Water Gold
US 1969 75m colour TVM
Metromedia

A scuba diver finds lost treasure from a Spanish galleon, but has trouble profiting from it.
Naively made and written adventure piece.

wd Alan Landsburg

Bradford Dillman, Aron Kincaid, Keir Dullea, Ricardo Montalban, France Nuyer

Black Widow*
US 1954 95m De Luxe Cinemascope
TCF (Nunnally Johnson)

A Broadway producer is suspected of the murder of an ambitious young girl.
Reasonably classy whodunnit with glamorous settings and an able cast, but a little lacking in wit and pace.

wd Nunnally Johnson, *novel* Fatal Woman by Patrick Quentin *ph* Charles G. Clarke *m* Leigh Harline

Ginger Rogers, Van Heflin, George Raft, Gene Tierney, Peggy Ann Garner, Reginald Gardiner, Virginia Leith, Otto Kruger, Hilda Simms, Cathleen Nesbitt

The Black Windmill*
GB 1974 106m Technicolor Panavision
Universal / Zanuck–Brown (Don Siegel)

A secret service agent has to fight a lone battle when his young son is kidnapped by spies.
Unconvincing variant on *The Man Who Knew Too Much*, with an unwieldy and incoherent plot and more borrowings from Hitchcock than you can count. It ends up as fair predictable fun despite its jaded air.

w Leigh Vance, *novel* Seven Days to a Killing by Clive Egleton *d* Don Siegel *ph* Ousama Rawi *m* Roy Budd

Michael Caine, Janet Suzman, Joseph O'Conor, Donald Pleasance, Delphine Seyrig, John Vernon, Joss Ackland

'A flaccid spy thriller, vaguely reminiscent of Hitchcock and *Foreign Correspondent*, with direction as blank as the expression on Michael Caine's face throughout.'—*Sight and Sound*

Blackbeard the Pirate*
US 1952 99m Technicolor
RKO (Edmund Grainger)

In the 17th century, reformed pirate Sir Henry Morgan is commissioned to rid the Caribbean of the rascally Blackbeard.
A farrago of action clichés with the star giving his eye-rolling all. The romantic element is dreary and the whole a shade bloodthirsty for family fare.

w Alan le May *d* Raoul Walsh *ph* William E. Snyder *m* Victor Young

Robert Newton, Linda Darnell, Keith Andes, William Bendix, Torin Thatcher, Irene Ryan, Alan Mowbray, Richard Egan

Blackbeard's Ghost
US 1967 107m Technicolor
Walt Disney (Bill Walsh)

The famous pirate returns as a ghost to help the old ladies who own a hotel he loved.
Ponderous and lengthy comedy, partially salvaged by performances.

w Bill Walsh, Ben Da Gradi *d* Robert Stevenson *ph* Edward Colman *m* Robert F. Brunner

Peter Ustinov, Dean Jones, Suzanne Pleshette, Elsa Lanchester, Richard Deacon

The Blackboard Jungle*
US 1955 101m bw
MGM (Pandro S. Berman)

In a slum school, a teacher finally gains the respect of his class of young hooligans.
Seminal fifties melodrama more notable for its introduction of 'Rock Around the Clock' behind the credits than for any intrinsic interest.

wd Richard Brooks, *novel* Evan Hunter *ph* Russell Harlan *m Bill Haley and the Comets*

Glenn Ford, Anne Francis, Louis Calhern, Margaret Hayes, John Hoyt, Richard Kiley, Emile Meyer, Warner Anderson, Basil Ruysdael, *Sidney Poitier, Vic Morrow*, Rafael Campos

Blackmail***
GB 1929 78m bw
BIP (John Maxwell)

A Scotland Yard inspector finds that his girl is involved in a murder; he conceals the fact and is blackmailed.
Hitchcock's first talkie is now a very hesitant entertainment but fully bears the director's stamp and will reward patient audiences in several excitingly staged sequences.

w Alfred Hitchcock, Benn W. Levy, Charles Bennett, *play* Charles Bennett *d Alfred Hitchcock* *ph* Jack Cox *m* Campbell and Connelly

Anny Ondra, Sara Allgood, John Longden, Charles Paton, Donald Calthrop, Cyril Ritchard

Blackmail
US 1939 81m bw
MGM (John Considine Jnr)

A man is released from prison after serving a sentence for a crime he did not commit. Immediately a blackmailer pounces . . .
Co-feature drama for a star marking time; not bad in its way.

w David Hertz, William Ludwig *d* H. C. Potter *ph* Clyde de Vinna

Edward G. Robinson, Ruth Hussey, Gene Lockhart, Guinn Williams, Esther Dale

Blackmailed
GB 1950 85m bw
GFD / Harold Huth

Several victims of a blackmailer are involved in his murder.
Interestingly plotted and well cast melodrama which suffers from a flat script and production.

w Hugh Mills, Roger Vadim, *novel* Mrs Christopher by Elizabeth Myers *d* Marc Allégret *ph* George Stretton *m* John Wooldridge

Dirk Bogarde, Mai Zetterling, Fay Compton, Robert Flemyng, Michael Gough, James Robertson Justice, Joan Rice, Wilfrid Hyde White, Harold Huth

The Blackwell Story
US 1957 74m bw TVM
Columbia / Playhouse 90

In the 1830s America's first woman doctor gains respect.

d James Neilson

Joanne Dru, Dan O'Herlihy, Marshall Thompson, Charles Korvin, Keith Larsen

Blacula
US 1972 93m Movielab
AIP (Joseph T. Naar)

In 1815 in Transylvania, an African prince falls victim to Dracula. A hundred and fifty years later, his body is shipped to Los Angeles and accidentally revivified.

Jaded semi-spoof notable chiefly as the first black horror film. The star's performance is as stately as could be wished in the circumstances.

w Joan Torres, Raymond Koenig *d* William Crain *ph* John Stevens *m* Gene Page

William Marshall, Vonetta McGee, Denise Nicholas, Gordon Pinsent, Charles Macaulay

Blanche Fury
GB 1948 95m Technicolor
GFD / Cineguild (Anthony Havelock-Allan)

A governess marries a wealthy heir, then with a steward connives at his murder.
Chilly Victorian melodrama without much interest outside the decor: the actors have unplayable roles and the handling is very flat.

w Audrey Erskine Lindop, Hugh Mills, Cecil McGivern, *novel* Joseph Shearing *d* Marc Allégret *ph* Guy Green, Geoffrey Unsworth *m* Clifton Parker

Valerie Hobson, Stewart Granger, Walter Fitzgerald, Michael Gough, Maurice Denham, Sybilla Binder

Blaze of Noon
US 1947 91m bw
Paramount (John Farrow)

Three stunt flier brothers in the twenties leave their circus to start a commercial air-line.
Predictable romantic drama with little flying: tragic pretensions, routine performances.

w Frank Wead, Arthur Sheekman *d* John Farrow

William Holden, Anne Baxter, Sonny Tufts, Sterling Hayden, William Bendix, Howard da Silva

The Blazing Forest
US 1952 90m Technicolor
Paramount / Pine–Thomas (William H. Pine, William C. Thomas)

A lady landowner has trouble with her rival timber bosses.
Fair period programmer.

w Lewis R. Foster, Winston Miller *d* Edward Ludwig *ph* Lionel Lindon *m* Lucien Caillet

John Payne, Agnes Moorehead, William Demarest, Richard Arlen, Susan Morrow, Roscoe Ates, Lynne Roberts

Blazing Saddles*
US 1974 93m Technicolor Panavision
Warner / Crossbow (Michael Herzberg)

A black railroad worker and an alcoholic ex-gunfighter foil a crooked attorney and his henchmen.
Wild western parody in which the action eventually shifts to the Warner backlot, after which the actors repair to Grauman's Chinese Theatre to find out what happened at the end of the story. At least as many misses as hits, and all aimed squarely at film buffs.

w Norman Steinberg, Mel Brooks, Andrew Bergman, Richard Pryoy, Alan Unger *d* Mel Brooks *ph* Joseph Biroc *m* John Morris

Cleavon Little, Gene Wilder, Slim Pickens, Harvey Korman, Madeleine Kahn, Mel Brooks, Burton Gilliam, Alex Karras

'One suspects that the film's gradual disintegration derives not from the makers' inability to end it, so much as from their inability to stop laughing at their own jokes.'—*Jan Dawson*

'A surfeit of chaos and a scarcity of comedy.'—*Judith Crist*

Bless the Beasts and Children*
US 1973 110m colour
Columbia / Stanley Kramer

Six boys on an adventure holiday try to free a herd of buffalo earmarked for destruction.
Rather obviously pointed melodrama, well enough done but not very interesting.

w Mac Benoff, *novel* Glendon Swarthout *d* Stanley Kramer

Bill Mumy, Barry Robins, Miles Chapin, Jesse White, Ken Swofford

Blessed Event**
US 1932 84m bw
Warner (Ray Griffith)

A gossip columnist gets himself into hot water.
Amusing vehicle for a fast-talking star, and quite an interesting historical document.

w Howard Green, *play* Manuel Seff, Forest Wilson *d* Roy del Ruth *ph* Sol Polito

Lee Tracy, Ned Sparks, Mary Brian, Dick Powell, Ruth Donnelly, Frank McHugh, Allen Jenkins

Blind Alley**
US 1939 61m bw
Columbia

An escaped killer takes refuge in the home of a psychiatrist, who explores his subconscious and tames him.
Unusual lowercase thriller with effective dream sequences; it was much imitated.

w Philip MacDonald, Albert Blankfort, Michael Duffy, *play* James Warwick *d Charles Vidor* *ph* Lucien Ballard *m* Morris Stoloff

Chester Morris, Ralph Bellamy, Ann Dvorak, Melville Cooper, Rose Stradner, Marc Lawrence

'As un-Hollywood as anything that has come from France this year.'—*New York Daily News*

† Remake: *The Dark Past* (qv).

Blind Date*

GB 1959 95m bw

Rank / Sydney Box / Independent Artists (David Deutsch)

A young Dutch painter in London discovers his mistress's body and finds himself in a web of deceit.

Tolerable, comparatively sophisticated murder puzzle; rather glum looking, but the plot holds the interest.

w Ben Barzman, Millard Lampell, *novel* Leigh Howard *d* Joseph Losey *ph* Christopher Challis *m* Richard Rodney Bennett

Hardy Kruger, Stanley Baker, Micheline Presle, Robert Flemyng, Gordon Jackson, John Van Eyssen

The Blind Goddess

GB 1947 88m bw

Gainsborough (Betty Box)

The private secretary to a public figure finds that his idol has feet of clay, and suffers in court for his discovery.

Courtroom drama from an old-fashioned stage play: surefire for addicts, but routine as a film.

w Muriel and Sydney Box, *play Patrick Hastings* *d* Harold French

Eric Portman, Anne Crawford, Hugh Williams, Michael Denison, Nora Swinburne, Claire Bloom, Raymond Lovell, Frank Cellier

Blind Terror

GB 1971 89m colour

Columbia / Filmways / Genesis (Basil Appleby)

US title: *See No Evil*

A blind girl is the sole, hunted survivor of a maniac's rampage on a lonely estate.

Shocks, screams and starts fill a cliché-ridden but still effective script which is faithfully turned into a competent but routine heart-stopper.

w Brian Clemens *d* Richard Fleischer *ph* Gerry Fisher *m* Elmer Bernstein

Mia Farrow, Robin Bailey, Dorothy Alison, Diane Grayson, Norman Eshley, Brian Rawlinson

'For those who like to watch folks pull the wings off flies.'—*Judith Crist*

Blindfold**

US 1965 102m Technicolor Panavision

Universal (Marvin Schwarz)

A society psychiatrist is enlisted by the CIA to make regular blindfold journeys to a secret destination where he treats a neurotic physicist. Discovering that his contacts are really enemy agents, he tracks down the destination by sound and guesswork, and routs the villains.

Lively spy spoof with rather too much knockabout between the Hitchcockian suspense sequences; it has indeed the air of a script which Hitchcock rejected, but provides reliable entertainment.

w Philip Dunne, W. H. Menger, *novel* Lucile Fletcher *d* Philip Dunne *ph* Joseph MacDonald *m* Lalo Schifrin

Rock Hudson, Claudia Cardinale, Jack Warden, Guy Stockwell, Brad Dexter

The Bliss of Mrs Blossom

GB 1968 93m Technicolor

Paramount (Josef Shaftel)

The wife of a bra manufacturer keeps her lover in the attic.

Silly, wild-eyed sex comedy decorated with the flashy tinsel of swinging London's dying fall.

w Alec Coppel, Denis Norden *d* Joe McGrath *ph* Geoffrey Unsworth *m* Riz Ortolani *pd* Assheton Gorton

Richard Attenborough, Shirley Maclaine, James Booth, Freddie Jones, William Rushton, Bob Monkhouse, Patricia Routledge

Blithe Spirit***

GB 1945 96m Technicolor

Two Cities / Cineguild (Anthony Havelock-Allan)

A cynical novelist's second marriage is disturbed when the playful ghost of his first wife materializes during a séance.

Direction and acting carefully preserve a comedy which on its first West End appearance in 1941 achieved instant classic status. The repartee scarcely dates, and altogether this is a most polished job of film-making.

w Noel Coward, from his play *scenario* David Lean, Anthony Havelock-Allan, Ronald Neame *d* David Lean *ph* Ronald Neame *m* Richard Addinsell

Rex Harrison, Kay Hammond, Constance Cummings, Margaret Rutherford, Hugh Wakefield, Joyce Carey, Jacqueline Clark

The Blob
US 1958 83m De Luxe
Tonylyn / Jack H. Harris

A small town combats a slimy space invader.
Padded hokum for drive-ins, with a few effective moments.

w Theodore Simonson, Kate Phillips *d* Irwin S. Yeaworth Jnr *ph* Thomas Spalding *m* Ralph Carmichael

Steve McQueen, Aneta Corseaut, Olin Howlin, Earl Rowe
† Sequel 1971: *Beware! The Blob* (GB: *Son of Blob*).

Blockade*
US 1938 84m bw
Walter Wanger

During the Spanish Civil War, a peace-loving young farmer has to take up arms to defend his land.
Much touted as Hollywood's first serious contribution to international affairs, this dogged drama was in fact so bland that audiences had difficulty ascertaining which side it was on, especially as neither Franco nor the Fascists were mentioned. As a romantic action drama, however, it passed muster.

w John Howard Lawson *d* William Dieterle

Henry Fonda, Madeleine Carroll, Leo Carrillo, John Halliday, Vladimir Sokoloff, Robert Warwick, Reginald Denny
'The film has a curious unreality considering the grim reality behind it.'—*Frank S. Nugent*

Blockheads***
US 1938 60m bw
Hal Roach / Stan Laurel

Twenty years after World War I, Stan is still guarding a trench because nobody told him to stop. Olly takes him home to meet the wife, with disastrous consequences.
The last first-class Laurel and Hardy comedy is shapeless but hilarious, a fragmented reworking of earlier ideas, all of which work beautifully. Gags include encounters with a tip-up truck and an automatic garage, and a brilliantly worked out sequence up and down several flights of stairs.

w James Parrott, Harry Langdon, Felix Adler, Charles Rogers, Arnold Belgard *d* John G. Blystone *ph* Art Lloyd

Stan Laurel, Oliver Hardy, Billy Gilbert, Patricia Ellis, Minna Gombell, James Finlayson

Blonde Bombshell see Bombshell

Blonde Crazy*
US 1931 74m bw
Warner
GB title: *Larceny Lane*

A bellhop and a chambermaid set out to fleece all-comers.
Smart con man comedy with the star in excellent form.

w Kubec Glasmon, John Bright *d* Roy del Ruth *ph* Sid Hickox

James Cagney, Joan Blondell, Ray Milland, Louis Calhern, Guy Kibbee, Polly Walters, Charles Lane, Maude Eburne
'A chipper, hard-boiled, amusing essay in petty thieving.'—*Time*

Blonde Venus*
US 1932 97m bw
Paramount

A German café singer marries an American research chemist, but their marriage doesn't run smoothly.
Rather dreary, fragmented star vehicle with good moments, notably the star's opening appearance as a gorilla.

w Jules Furthman, S. K. Lauren *d* Josef Von Sternberg *ph* Bert Glennon *m* Oscar Poteker

Marlene Dietrich, Herbert Marshall, Cary Grant, Dickie Moore
'The story has all the dramatic integrity of a sashweight murderer's tabloid autobiography.'—*Pare Lorentz*

Blondie*
US 1938 68m bw
Columbia

Misadventures of a harassed suburban family man.
Dagwood Bumstead and his wife Blondie were Mr and Mrs Small Town America throughout the thirties and forties, and received their perfect screen incarnations in this unambitious but quite watchable series, which provided familiar and often quite observant fun.

w Richard Flournoy, from the comic strip by *Chic Young* *d* Frank R. Strayer

Arthur Lake, Penny Singleton, Larry Simms, Daisy the Dog, *Jonathan Hale* (as the boss, Mr Dithers), Gene Lockhart, Ann Doran, Irving Bacon (as the mailman)

Other episodes were as follows:
1939: BLONDIE MEETS THE BOSS
BLONDIE TAKES A VACATION
BLONDIE BRINGS UP BABY
1940: BLONDIE ON A BUDGET, BLONDIE

HAS SERVANT TROUBLE, BLONDIE PLAYS CUPID
1941: BLONDIE GOES LATIN, BLONDIE IN SOCIETY
1942: BLONDIE GOES TO COLLEGE, BLONDIE'S BLESSED EVENT, BLONDIE FOR VICTORY
1943: IT'S A GREAT LIFE, FOOTLIGHT GLAMOUR
1945: LEAVE IT TO BLONDIE
1946: BLONDIE KNOWS BEST, LIFE WITH BLONDIE, BLONDIE'S LUCKY DAY
1947: BLONDIE'S BIG MOMENT, BLONDIE'S HOLIDAY, BLONDIE IN THE DOUGH, BLONDIE'S ANNIVERSARY
1948: BLONDIE'S REWARD
1949: BLONDIE'S SECRET, BLONDIE'S BIG DEAL, BLONDIE HITS THE JACKPOT
1950: BLONDIE'S HERO, BEWARE OF BLONDIE
† TV series were started in the fifties and sixties, but both failed.

Blondie of the Follies*
US 1932 97m bw
MGM (Marion Davies)

Two New York showgirls graduate from tenements to luxury.
Adequate comedy-melodrama with an interesting cast and good dialogue.

w Frances Marion, Anita Loos *d* Edmund Goulding *ph* George Barnes *m* William Axt

Marion Davies, Jimmy Durante, Robert Montgomery, Billie Dove, James Gleason, Zasu Pitts, Sidney Toler, Douglass Dumbrille

Blood Alley
US 1955 115m Warnercolor Cinemascope
Warner / Batjac (no producer credited)

An American sailor is helped by local people to escape from a Chinese jail; he then escorts them to Hong Kong.
Rudimentary anti-Red heroics with expensive spectacle punctuating a tacky script.

w A. S. Fleischmann, from his novel *d* William Wellman *ph* William H. Clothier *m* Roy Webb *pd* Alfred Ybarra

John Wayne, Lauren Bacall, Paul Fix, Joy Kim, Berry Kroger, Mike Mazurki, Anita Ekberg

Blood and Sand*
US 1941 123m Technicolor
TCF (Darryl F. Zanuck, Robert T. Kane)

A Spanish bullfighter comes to grief through love of a society lady.
Rather boring remake of the Valentino vehicle, fine to look at but dramatically deadly.

w Jo Swerling, *novel* Vincente Blasco Ibanez *d* Rouben Mamoulian *ph* Ernest Palmer, Ray Rennahan *m* Alfred Newman *ad Richard Day, Joseph C. Wright*

Tyrone Power, Rita Hayworth, Linda Darnell, Nazimova, Anthony Quinn, J. Carrol Naish, John Carradine, Lynn Bari, Laird Cregar, Monty Banks

Blood from the Mummy's Tomb*
GB 1971 94m Technicolor
Hammer (Howard Brandy)

Twenty years after a female mummy is brought back to England, members of the expedition are killed one by one, and their leader's daughter is possessed by the spirit of the dead princess.
Interesting but over-complicated and hard-to-enjoy attempt to maintain the mummy saga without an actual marauding mummy.
Intelligently handled but sadly lacking in a sense of humour.

w Christopher Wicking, *novel* Jewel of the Seven Stars by Bram Stoker *d Seth Holt* *ph* Arthur Grant *m* Tristam Cary

Andrew Keir, Valerie Leon, James Villiers, Hugh Burden, George Coulouris, Mark Edwards, Rosalie Crutchley, Aubrey Morris, David Markham

'Makes the genre seem like new.'—*Tony Rayns*

Blood on the Moon*
US 1948 88m bw
RKO

A homesteader finds that his best friend is the villainous leader of a group of cattlemen.
Good-looking but rather pedestrian western, generally well handled.

w Lillie Hayward *d* Robert Wise *ph* Nicholas Musuraca *m* Constantin Bakaleinikoff

Robert Mitchum, Barbara Bel Geddes, Robert Preston, Walter Brennan

Blood on the Sun*
US 1945 94m bw
William Cagney

In the twenties, the American editor of a Tokyo newspaper reveals a Japanese militarist plan for world conquest.
Satisfactory star actioner with good production and exciting highlights.

w Lester Cole *d* Frank Lloyd *ph* Theodor Sparkuhl *m* Miklos Rozsa

James Cagney, Sylvia Sidney, Wallace Ford,

Rosemary de Camp, Robert Armstrong, John Emery, Leonard Strong, Frank Puglia

'It ought to be fine for those who enjoy a good ninety-minute massacre.'—*New Yorker*

Blood Sport
US 1973 74m colour TVM
Danny Thomas

A college boy fights his father's wish to make him a football star.
Predictable character melodrama.

wd Jerrold Friedman

Ben Johnson, Gary Busey, David Doyle, Larry Hagman

Bloodhounds of Broadway*
US 1952 90m Technicolor
TCF (George Jessel)

With the help of a gangster, an orphan girl and her pet bloodhounds make a big hit in cabaret.
Absurd but sporadically amusing gangster burlesque, typical of its author. Lively production values.

w Sy Gomberg, *story* Damon Runyon
d Harmon Jones *ph* Edward Cronjager
md Lionel Newman

Mitzi Gaynor, Scott Brady, Mitzi Green, Marguerite Chapman, Michael O'Shea, Wally Vernon, George E. Stone

Bloody Mama*
US 1971 90m Movielab
AIP (Roger Corman)

In the thirties, outlaw Kate Barker and her four sons conduct a reign of terror until what's left of the gang is riddled with machine gun bullets.
Violent gangster story with a star on the rampage; the attempt to philosophize is more than the facts will bear, but the production moves smartly enough.

w Robert Thom *d* Roger Corman *ph* John Alonzo *m* Don Randi

Shelley Winters, Pat Hingle, Don Stroud, Diane Varsi, Bruce Dern, Clint Kimbrough, Robert de Niro, Robert Walden, Alex Nicol

Blossoms in the Dust**
US 1941 99m Technicolor
MGM (Irving Asher)

A woman who loses her husband and child founds a state orphanage.
Archetypal tearjerker of the forties, a glossy 'woman's picture' which distorts the facts into a star vehicle. Excellent colour helped to make it enormous success.

w Anita Loos, based on the life of Edna Gladney
d Mervyn Le Roy *ph* Karl Freund, W. Howard Greene *m* Herbert Stothart

Greer Garson, Walter Pidgeon, Felix Bressart, Marsha Hunt, Fay Holden, Samuel S. Hinds

Blow Up**
GB 1966 110m Eastmancolor
MGM / Carlo Ponti

A London fashion photographer thinks he sees a murder, but the evidence disappears.
Not a mystery but a fashionable think-in on the difference (if any) between fantasy and reality. Agreeable to look at for those who can stifle their irritation at the non-plot and non-characters; a huge audience was lured by flashes of nudity and the trendy 'swinging London' setting.

wd Michelangelo Antonioni *ph* Carlo di Palma
m Herbert Hancock *ad* Assheton Gorton

David Hemmings, Sarah Miles, Vanessa Redgrave

Blowing Wild*
US 1953 88m bw
(Warner) United States (Milton Sperling)

A Mexican oil driller becomes involved with the psychotic wife of an old friend; the triangle leads to murder and retribution.
Pot-boiling star vehicle with adequate melodramatic interest, full of reminiscences of other movies, with a wicked lady to end them all.

w Philip Yordan *d* Hugo Fregonese *ph* Sid Hickox *m* Dmitri Tiomkin

Gary Cooper, Barbara Stanwyck, Anthony Quinn, Ruth Roman, Ward Bond

Blue
US 1968 113m Technicolor Panavision
Paramount / Kettledrum (Judd Bernard, Irwin Winkler)

The white adopted son of a Mexican bandit prevents his cohorts from raping a white girl, and falls in love with her.
Pretentious, self-conscious, literary western without much zest.

w Meade Roberts, Ronald M. Cohen *d* Silvio Narizzano *ph* *Stanley Cortez* *m* Manos Hadjidakis

Terence Stamp, Joanna Pettet, Karl Malden, Ricardo Montalban

'I don't know which is worse—bad cowboy movies or bad *arty* cowboy movies. *Blue* is both.'—*Rex Reed*

The Blue Angel****
Germany 1930 98m bw
UFA (Erich Pommer)

A fuddy-duddy professor is infatuated with a tawdry night-club singer. She marries him but is soon bored and contemptuous; humiliated, he leaves her and dies in his old classroom.
A masterwork of late twenties German grotesquerie, and after a slowish beginning an emotional powerhouse, set in a dark nightmare world which could be created only in the studio. Shot also in English, it was highly popular and influential in Britain and America.

w Robert Liebmann, Karl Zuckmayer, Karl Vollmoeller, *novel* Professor Unrath by Heinrich Mann *d* Josef Von Sternberg *ph* Gunthĕr Rittau, Hans Schneeberger *m* Frederick Hollander (inc 'Falling in Love Again', 'They Call Me Wicked Lola') *ad* Otto Hunte, Emil Hasler

Emil Jannings, Marlene Dietrich (who was instantly catapulted to international stardom), Kurt Gerron, Hans Albers

The Blue Angel
US 1959 107m De Luxe Cinemascope
TCF (Jack Cummings)

Ill-advised attempt at a 'realistic', updated remake of the above; the result is a total travesty, with the actors aware that stylized melodrama is turning before their eyes into unintentional farce.

w Nigel Balchin *d* Edward Dmytryk *ph* Leon Shamroy *m* Hugo Friedhofer

Curt Jurgens, May Britt, Theodore Bikel, John Banner

'It totally lacks the stifling atmosphere of sordid and oppressive sexuality which is essential to give conviction to the German sadism of the story.'—*Brenda Davies*

The Blue Dahlia**
US 1946 99m bw
Paramount (John Houseman)

A returning war veteran finds his faithless wife murdered and himself suspected.
Hailed on its first release as sharper than average, this mystery suspenser is now only moderately compelling despite the screenplay credit; direction and editing lack urgency and the acting lacks bounce.

w Raymond Chandler d George Marshall *ph* Lionel Lindon *m* Victor Young

Alan Ladd, Veronica Lake, William Bendix, Howard da Silva, Doris Dowling, Tom Powers, Hugh Beaumont, Howard Freeman, Will Wright

'It threatens to turn into something, but it never does.'—*New Yorker*, 1976

Blue Denim*
US 1959 89m bw Cinemascope
TCF (Charles Brackett)
GB title: *Blue Jeans*

Teenagers confronted with the prospect of illegitimate parenthood consult an abortionist, but all ends with wedding bells.
First of its rather dreary kind but better than most, this only slightly mawkish domestic drama has its heart in the right place and steers surprisingly towards a nick-of-time chase climax.

w Edith Sommer, Philip Dunne, *play* James Leo Herlihy, William Noble *d* Philip Dunne *ph* Leo Tover *m* Bernard Herrmann

Carol Lynley, Brandon de Wilde, Macdonald Carey, Marsha Hunt, Nina Shipman, Warren Berlinger

The Blue Gardenia
US 1953 90m bw
Warner (Alex Gottlieb)

A girl gets drunk and wakes up in a strange apartment with a dead man by her side.
Totally undistinguished mystery which leaves egg on the actors' faces.

w Charles Hoffman *d* Fritz Lang *ph* Nicholas Musuraca *m* Raoul Krashaar

Anne Baxter, Richard Conte, Ann Sothern, Raymond Burr, Jeff Donnell, Richard Erdman, Nat King Cole

Blue Hawaii
US 1961 101m Technicolor Panavision
Hal B. Wallis

A GI comes home to Honolulu and becomes a beachcomber.
Lifeless star vehicle shot on glamorous locations.

w Hal Kanter *d* Norman Taurog *ph* Charles Lang Jnr *m* Joseph J. Lilley

Elvis Presley, Joan Blackman, Nancy Walters, Roland Winters, Angela Lansbury, John Archer, Howard McNear

The Blue Knight*
US 1973 195m approx colour TVM
Lorimar (Walter Coblenz)

The life of a Los Angeles cop on the beat.
The first superlength TV movie: the length is wasted on this mundane material, which resists all efforts to give it status.

w E. Jack Neuman, *novel* Joseph Wambaugh *d* Robert Butler *ph* Michael Margulies

William Holden, Lee Remick, Sam Elliott, Eileen Brennan, Joe Santos

The Blue Knight
US 1975 74m colour TVM
Lorimar

Second try for the above: this time the pilot, though shorter, was even slower and duller, and the consequent series had a brief life.

w Albert Rueben *d* J. Lee-Thompson

George Kennedy, Alex Rocco, Glynn Turman, Verna Bloom

The Blue Lagoon*
GB 1949 103m Technicolor
GFD / Individual (Frank Launder, Sidney Gilliat)

A shipwrecked boy and girl grow up on a desert island, ward off smugglers, have a baby, and eventually sail away in search of civilization.
Rather lifeless, though pretty, treatment of a famous novel: the story never becomes vivid despite splendid Fijian locations.

w Frank Launder, John Baines, Michael Hogan, *novel* H. de Vere Stacpoole *d* Frank Launder *ph Geoffrey Unsworth* *m* Clifton Parker

Jean Simmons, Donald Houston, Noel Purcell, Cyril Cusack, James Hayter

The Blue Lamp***
GB 1949 84m bw
Ealing (Michael Relph)

A young man joins London's police force. The elderly copper who trains him is killed in a shootout, but the killer is apprehended.
Seminal British police film which spawned not only a long line of semi-documentary imitations but also the twenty-year TV series *Dixon of Dock Green* for which the shot PC was happily revived. As an entertainment, pacy but dated; more important, it burnished the image of the British copper for a generation or more.

w T. E. B. Clarke *d Basil Dearden* *ph* Gordon Dines *m* Ernest Irving

Jack Warner, Jimmy Hanley, Dirk Bogarde, Meredith Edwards, Robert Flemyng, Bernard Lee, Patric Doonan, Peggy Evans, Gladys Henson, Dora Bryan

'The mixture of coyness, patronage and naive theatricality which has vitiated British films for the last ten years.'—*Gavin Lambert*

The Blue Max**
US 1966 156m De Luxe Cinemascope
TCF (Christian Ferry)

In Germany after World War I an ambitious and skilful pilot causes the death of his comrades and steals the wife of his High Command superior, who eventually finds a means of revenge.
For once, an action spectacular not too badly let down by its connecting threads of plot, apart from some hilarious and unnecessary bedroom scenes in which the female star's bath towel seems to become conveniently adhesive.

w David Pursall, Jack Seddon, Gerald Hanley, *novel* Jack Hunter *d John Guillermin* *ph* Douglas Slocombe *m* Jerry Goldsmith

George Peppard, *James Mason*, Ursula Andress, Jeremy Kemp, Karl Michael Vogler, Anton Diffring, Derren Nesbitt

Blue Skies*
US 1946 104m Technicolor
Paramount (Sol C. Siegel)

A dancing star and a nightclub owner fight for years over the same girl.
Thin musical with splendid Irving Berlin tunes and lively individual numbers.

w Arthur Sheekman *d* Stuart Heisler *ph* Lionel Lindon *md* Robert Emmett Dolan

Fred Astaire (dancing 'Putting On the Ritz'), Bing Crosby, Joan Caulfield, Billy de Wolfe, Olga San Juan, Robert Benchley, Frank Faylen, Victoria Horne, Jack Norton

The Blue Veil*
US 1951 114m bw
(RKO) Wald–Krasna (Raymond Hakim)

The vocational career of a children's nurse who descends into poverty but is rescued by one of her own charges, now grown up.
Sober American remake of a French tearjerker (*Le Voile bleu*) with the star suffering nobly but being upstaged by the cameo players.

w Norman Corwin, from the original by François Campaux *d* Curtis Bernhardt *ph* Franz Planer *m* Franz Waxman

Jane Wyman, Charles Laughton, Richard Carlson, Joan Blondell, Agnes Moorehead, Don Taylor, Audrey Totter, Everett Sloane, Cyril Cusack, Natalie Wood, Warner Anderson

Bluebeard's Eighth Wife*
US 1938 80m bw
Paramount (Ernst Lubitsch)

The daughter of an impoverished French aristocrat marries for money a millionaire who

has had seven previous wives, and determines to teach him a lesson.
Very thin sophisticated comedy with unsympathetic characters and little wit after the first scene; a disappointment from the talent involved.

w Charles Brackett, Billy Wilder, *story* Alfred Savoir *d* Ernst Lubitsch *ph* Leo Tover

Claudette Colbert, Gary Cooper, David Niven, Edward Everett Horton, Elizabeth Patterson, Herman Bing, Warren Hymer, Franklin Pangborn

The Bluebird***
US 1940 98m Technicolor
TCF (Gene Markey)

In a Grimm's Fairy Tale setting, the two children of a poor woodcutter seek the bluebird of happiness in the past, the future and the Land of Luxury, but eventually discover it in their own back yard.
An imaginative and often chilling script clarifies Maurice Maeterlinck's fairy play, and the art direction is outstanding, but the children are necessarily unsympathetic and the expensive production paled beside the success of the more upbeat *Wizard of Oz*, which was released almost simultaneously. Slashed for re-release, the only existing prints now open with confusing abruptness and no scene-setting before the adventures begin.

w Ernest Pascal d Walter Lang ph Arthur Miller m Alfred Newman

Shirley Temple, Johnny Russell, *Gale Sondergaard* (as the cat), *Eddie Collins* (as the dog), Nigel Bruce, Jessie Ralph, Spring Byington, Sybil Jason, Helen Ericson, Russell Hicks, Al Shean, Cecilia Loftus

A Blueprint for Murder*
US 1953 77m bw
TCF (Michael Abel)

After the death of his brother and nephew, a man proves that his sister-in-law is a murderess.
Unpleasant but efficient murder story with enough twists to keep one watching.

wd Andrew Stone *ph* Leo Tover *m* Lionel Newman

Jean Peters, Joseph Cotten, Gary Merrill, Catherine McLeod, Jack Kruschen

Blueprint for Robbery*
US 1960 87m bw
Paramount (Bryan Foy)

Crooks plan and execute a robbery, agreeing not to touch the proceeds for two and a half years. But some get tired of waiting...
Minor but effective crime melodrama in semi-documentary vein.

w Irwin Winehouse, A. Sanford Wolf *d* Jerry Hopper *ph* Loyal Griggs *m* Van Cleave

J. Pat O'Malley, Robert Gist, Romo Vincent, Marion Ross, Tom Duggan

'A not uninteresting entry in the screen log-book on crime.'—*MFB*

Blues in the Night*
US 1941 88m bw
Warner (Henry Blanke)

Career and romantic problems for the members of a travelling jazz band.
Atmospheric little melodrama with good score and smart dialogue.

w Robert Rossen, play Hot Nocturne by Edwin Gilbert *d* Anatole Litvak *ph* Ernest Haller

Priscilla Lane, Richard Whorf, Lloyd Nolan, Betty Field, Jack Carson, Elia Kazan, Wallace Ford, Billy Halop, Peter Whitney

Blume in Love**
US 1973 116m Technicolor
Warner (Paul Mazursky)

A divorced American lawyer in Venice reminisces about his love life.
Shapeless but enjoyable 'serious comedy' with star and director in good form.

wd Paul Mazursky ph Bruce Surtees *m* various

George Segal, Susan Anspach, Kris Kristofferson, Marsha Mason, Shelley Winters

The Boatniks*
US 1970 100m Technicolor
Walt Disney (Ron Miller)

An accident-prone coastguard officer creates havoc at a yachting marina but is acclaimed a hero after catching three jewel thieves.
Simple fresh-air farce for the family, pleasantly set but flatly directed.

w Arthur Julian *d* Norman Tokar *ph* William Snyder *m* Robert F. Brunner

Phil Silvers, Robert Morse, Stefanie Powers, Norman Fell, Mickey Shaughnessey, Wally Cox, Don Ameche, Joey Forman

Bob and Carol and Ted and Alice**
US 1969 105m Technicolor
Columbia (Larry Tucker)

Two California couples, influenced by a group therapy session advocating natural spontaneous behaviour, decide to admit their extra-marital

affairs and narrowly avoid a wife-swapping party.
Fashionable comedy without the courage of its convictions: it starts and finishes very bashfully, but there are bright scenes in the middle. An attempt to extend it into a TV series was a failure.

w Paul Mazursky, Larry Tucker *d* Paul Mazursky *ph* Charles E. Lang *m* Quincy Jones

Natalie Wood, Robert Culp, Elliott Gould, Dyan Cannon, Horst Ebersberg

'An old-fashioned romantic comedy disguised as a blue picture.'—*Arthur Schlesinger Jnr*

The Bobo
US 1967 105m Technicolor
Warner / Gina (Elliott Kastner, Jerry Gershwin) (David R. Schwarz)

An unsuccessful and timid bullfighter is offered a contract if within three days he can seduce the local belle.
Stylized, silly and boring comedy from an obviously dated play; hopefully the star's last attempt to provide Chaplinesque pathos.

w David R. Schwarz, from his play and the novel *Olimpia* by Burt Cole *d* Robert Parrish *ph* Gerry Turpin *m* Francis Lai

Peter Sellers, Britt Ekland, Rossano Brazzi, Adolfo Celi, Hattie Jacques, Ferdy Mayne, Kenneth Griffith, John Wells

Body and Soul*
US 1947 104m bw
Enterprise (Bob Roberts)

A young boxer fights his way unscrupulously to the top.
Melodramatic but absorbing study of prizefighting's seamy side. (Is there any other?) Inventively studio-bound and almost impressionist in treatment.

w Abraham Polonsky d Robert Rossen ph James Wong Howe md Rudolph Polk

John Garfield, Lilli Palmer, Hazel Brooks, Anne Revere, William Conrad, Joseph Pevney, Canada Lee

The Body Snatcher***
US 1945 77m bw
RKO (Val Lewton)

In 19th-century Edinburgh a doctor obtains 'specimens' from grave-robbers, and murder results when supplies run short.
A familiar theme very imaginatively handled, and well acted, though the beginning is slow. The best of the Lewton thrillers.

w Philip MacDonald, Carlos Keith (Val Lewton), *story* R. L. Stevenson *d Robert Wise ph Robert de Grasse m* Roy Webb

Henry Daniell, Boris Karloff, Bela Lugosi, Edith Atwater, Russell Wade

'A humane sincerity and a devotion to good cinema . . . However, most of the picture is more literary than lively.'—*Time*

Boeing-Boeing
US 1965 102m Technicolor
(Paramount) Hal B. Wallis

By successfully juggling with plane schedules, a Paris journalist manages to live with three air hostesses at the same time.
Frenetic, paper-thin sex comedy from a one-joke play; film style generally undistinguished.

w Edward Anhalt, *play* Marc Camoletti *d* John Rich *ph* Lucien Ballard *m* Neal Hefti

Tony Curtis, Jerry Lewis (his only 'straight' part), Dany Saval, Christiane Schmidtner, Suzanna Leigh, *Thelma Ritter*

'A sort of jet-age French farce.'—*Judith Crist*

The Bofors Gun**
GB 1968 105m Technicolor
Rank / Everglades (Robert A. Goldson, Otto Plaschkes)

In 1954 Germany a British army unit runs into trouble when a violent and unstable Irish sergeant picks on a weakly National Service corporal.
Keen, fascinating, but often crude and eventually rather silly expansion of a TV play chiefly notable for the excellent acting opportunities provided by its unattractive but recognizable characters.

w John McGrath *d* Jack Gold *ph* Alan Hume *m* none

Nicol Williamson, John Thaw, *David Warner*, Ian Holm

The Bohemian Girl*
US 1936 74m bw
Hal Roach

Gypsies kidnap a nobleman's daughter and bring her up as their own.
One of several operettas reworked for Laurel and Hardy, this is an inoffensive entertainment which devotes too little care to their need for slowly built-up gag structure; their sequences tend to fizzle out and the singing is a bore.

w Alfred Bunn, *operetta* William Balfe *d* James Horne, Charles Rogers *ph* Art Lloyd, Francis Corby

Stan Laurel, Oliver Hardy, Mae Busch, Antonio Moreno, Jacqueline Wells, Darla Hood, Zeffie

Tilbury, James Finlayson, Thelma Todd (for one song, apparently dubbed: presumably before her sudden death she had been cast as the heroine)

The Bold and the Brave
US 1956 87m bw Superscope
RKO / Hal E. Chester

An assortment of American types come together in the Italian campaign of 1944.
Routine war heroics chiefly remembered (if at all) for a crap game sequence.

w Robert Lewin *d* Lewis Foster *ph* Sam Leavitt *m* Herschel Burke Gilbert

Wendell Corey, *Mickey Rooney*, Nicole Maurey, Don Taylor

Bolero*
US 1934 85m bw
Paramount

A New York dancer neglects his personal life to become king of the European night club circuit.
Lively romantic drama which performed remarkably at the box office and led to a kind of sequel, *Rumba*.

w Carey Wilson, Kubec Glasmon, Ruth Ridenour, Horace Jackson *d Wesley Ruggles ph* Leo Tover

George Raft, Carole Lombard, Sally Rand (doing her fan dance), Frances Drake, William Frawley, Ray Milland, Gertrude Michael

Bomba the Jungle Boy
US 1949 65m bw or sepia
Monogram (Walter Mirisch)

Photographers in Africa meet a junior Tarzan who rescues their girl friend.
Cut-rate hokum starring the lad who had played Johnny Weissmuller's 'son' in earlier Tarzan movies; it led to several tedious sequels.

w Jack de Witt, from the comic strip by Roy Rockwell *d* Ford Beebe *ph* William Sickner *m* Edward Kay

Johnny Sheffield, Peggy Ann Garner, Onslow Stevens, Charles Irwin

Bombers B-52
US 1957 106m Warnercolor Cinemascope
Warner (Richard Whorf)
GB title: *No Sleep till Dawn*

A USAF sergeant considers applying for a discharge so that he can earn more money in civilian life.
Glossy domestic melodrama punctuated by aircraft shots.

w Irving Wallace *d* Gordon Douglas *ph* William Clothier *m* Leonard Rosenman

Karl Malden, Marsha Hunt, Natalie Wood, Efrem Zimbalist Jnr, Don Kelly

'No one questions the basic assumption—that the good life consists of servicing bigger and better bombers.'—*MFB*

Bombshell***
US 1933 91m bw
MGM (Hunt Stromberg)
GB and aka title: *Blonde Bombshell*

A glamorous film star yearns for a new image.
Crackpot farce which even by today's standards moves at a fair clip and enabled the star to give her best comedy performance.

w Jules Furthman, John Lee Mahin, play Caroline Francke, Mack Crane *d Victor Fleming ph* Chester Lyons, Hal Rosson

Jean Harlow, Lee Tracy, Frank Morgan, Franchot Tone, Pat O'Brien, Ivan Lebedeff, Una Merkel, Ted Healy, Isabel Jewell, C. Aubrey Smith, Louise Beavers, Leonard Carey, Mary Forbes

Bon Voyage*
US 1962 133m Technicolor
Walt Disney (Bill Walsh, Ron Miller)

An American family spends a holiday in Paris.
Simple-minded, overlong comedy of mishaps, with daddy finally trapped in the sewer.
Smoothly done of its kind.

w Bill Walsh, *novel* Marrijane and Joseph Hayes *d* James Neilson *ph* William Snyder *m* Paul Smith

Fred MacMurray, Jane Wyman, Michael Callan, Deborah Walley, Jessie Royce Landis, Tommy Kirk, Ivan Desny

Bond Street
GB 1948 107m bw
ABP / World Screenplays (Anatole de Grunwald)

Four stories, each concerning an item of an expensive wedding trousseau.
Mild and laboured short story compendium.

w Anatole de Grunwald *d* Gordon Parry *ph* Otto Heller *m* Benjamin Frankel

Roland Young, Jean Kent, Paula Valenska, Kathleen Harrison, Derek Farr, *Kenneth Griffith*, Hazel Court, Ronald Howard

'Even a glimpse of actual Bond Street makes little contact with reality.'—*MFB*

Bonjour Tristesse*
GB 1957 93m Technicolor
Cinemascope
(Columbia) Wheel Films (Otto Preminger)

A teenage girl becomes involved with her sophisticated father's amours and causes the death of his would-be mistress.
The novel's rather repellent characters are here played like royal personages against a background of Riviera opulence. The result is very odd but often entertaining, especially when it slips into self-parody.

w Arthur Laurents, *novel* Françoise Sagan
d Otto Preminger *ph Georges Périnal*
m Georges Auric *pd* Roger Furse

David Niven, Deborah Kerr, Jean Seberg, Mylene Demongeot, Geoffrey Horne, Juliette Greco, Martita Hunt, Walter Chiari, Jean Kent, Roland Culver

'An elegant, ice-cold charade of emotions.'—*Judith Crist*

† Shot in monochrome for Paris, colour for the Riviera.

Bonnie and Clyde****
US 1967 111m Technicolor
Warner Seven Arts / Tatira / Hiller
(*Warren Beatty*)

In the early thirties, a car thief and the daughter of his intended victim team up to become America's most feared and ruthless bank robbers.
Technically brilliant evocation of sleepy mid-America at the time of the public enemies, using every kind of cinematic trick including fake snapshots, farcical interludes, dreamy soft-focus and a jazzy score. For all kinds of reasons a very influential film which even made extreme violence quite fashionable (and very bloody it is).

w David Newman, Robert Benton d Arthur Penn ph Burnett Guffey m Charles Strouse, using 'Foggy Mountain Breakdown' by Flatt and Scruggs

Warren Beatty, Faye Dunaway, Gene Hackman, Estelle Parsons, *Michael J. Pollard,* Dub Taylor, Denver Pyle, Gene Wilder

'It is a long time since we have seen an American film so perfectly judged.'—*MFB*

'. . . all to the rickety twang of a banjo and a saturation in time and place.'—*Judith Crist*

'The formula is hayseed comedy bursting sporadically into pyrotechnical bloodshed and laced with sentimental pop-Freudianism.'—*John Simon*

Bonnie Prince Charlie
GB 1948 140m approx (later cut to 118m)
Technicolor
British Lion / London Films (Edward Black)

The hope of the Stuarts returns from exile but is eventually forced to flee again.
Good highland photography combines with appalling studio sets, an initially confused narrative, a draggy script and uneasy performances to produce an ill-fated attempt at a British historical epic. Alexander Korda, who masterminded it, sulked in public at the critical roasting, but on this occasion the critics were right.

w Clemence Dane *d* Anthony Kimmins
ph Robert Krasker *m* Ian Whyte

David Niven, Margaret Leighton, Jack Hawkins, Judy Campbell, Morland Graham, Finlay Currie, John Laurie

'I have a sense of wonder about this film, beside which *The Swordsman* seems like a dazzling work of veracity and art. It is that London Films, having surveyed the finished thing, should not have quietly scrapped it.'—*Richard Winnington*

Bonnie Scotland**
US 1935 80m bw
MGM / Hal Roach

Two Americans journey to Scotland to collect a non-existent inheritance, then follow their friend in the army and wind up in India.
Generally disappointing star comedy which still contains excellent sequences when it is not vainly trying to preserve interest in a boring plot. An obvious parody on *Lives of a Bengal Lancer,* released earlier that year; Scotland has almost nothing to do with it.

w Frank Butler, Jeff Moffitt *d* James Horne
ph Art Lloyd, Walter Lundin

Stan Laurel, Oliver Hardy, James Finlayson, Daphne Pollard, William Janney, June Lang

The Boogie Man Will Get You
US 1944 66m bw
Columbia

Bodies accumulate when mad doctors get to work creating supermen in a small village.
Desperately unfunny spoof notable only for the fact that it was attempted with these players and at that time.

w Edwin Blum *d* Lew Landers *ph* Henry Freulich

Boris Karloff, Peter Lorre, Maxie Rosenbloom, Jeff Donnell, Larry Parks, Maude Eburne, Don Beddoe

Boom!
GB 1968 113m Technicolor Panavision
Universal / World Film Services / Moon Lake Productions (John Heyman, Norman Priggen)

On the volcanic Mediterranean island which she owns, a dying millionairess plans to take as her last lover a wandering poet who is the angel of death.
Pretentious, boring nonsense, showing that when talent goes awry it certainly goes boom.

w Tennessee Williams, from his play *The Milk Train Doesn't Stop Here Any More* *d* Joseph Losey *ph* Douglas Slocombe *m* John Barry

Elizabeth Taylor, Richard Burton, *Noel Coward*, Michael Dunn, Joanna Shimkus

Boom Town**
US 1940 120m bw
MGM (Sam Zimbalist)

Two friendly oil drillers strike it rich.
Enjoyable four-star, big-studio product of its time: world-wide entertainment of assured success, with a proven mix of romance, action, drama and comedy.

w John Lee Mahin, *story* James Edward Grant *d Jack Conway* *ph* Elwood Bredell *m* Franz Waxman *ad* Cedric Gibbons

Clark Gable, Spencer Tracy, Claudette Colbert, Hedy Lamarr, *Frank Morgan,* Lionel Atwill, Chill Wills

Boomerang***
US 1947 88m bw
TCF (Louis de Rochemont)

In a New England town, a clergyman is shot dead on the street. The DA prevents an innocent man from being convicted, but cannot track down the guilty party.
Incisive real life thriller: based on a true case, it was shot in an innovative documentary style which was much copied, and justice is not seen to be done, though the murderer is known to the audience. A milestone movie of its kind.

w Richard Murphy *d Elia Kazan* *ph* Norbert Brodine *m* David Buttolph

Dana Andrews, Jane Wyatt, Lee J. Cobb, Cara Williams, Arthur Kennedy, Sam Levene, Taylor Holmes, Robert Keith, Ed Begley

'A study of integrity, beautifully developed by Dana Andrews against a background of political corruption and chicanery that is doubly shocking because of its documentary understatement.'—*Richard Winnington*

Boots Malone
US 1952 103m bw
Columbia (Milton Holmes)

A would-be jockey tags along with a down-at-heel agent who gets him work and finally persuades him not to throw a crooked race.
Dullish racetrack melodrama bogged down by repetitive and unsympathetic plot twists.

w Milton Holmes *d* William Dieterle *ph* Charles Lawton *m* Elmer Bernstein

William Holden, Johnny Stewart, Stanley Clements, Basil Ruysdael, Carl Benton Reid, Ed Begley, Henry Morgan

Bordertown*
US 1935 90m bw
Warner (Robert Lord)

In a North Mexican town, a shabby lawyer becomes infatuated with the neurotic wife of a businessman.
Satisfying melodrama whose plot climax was later borrowed for *They Drive by Night*.

w Laird Doyle, Wallace Smith, *novel* Carroll Graham *d* Archie Mayo *ph* Tony Gaudio

Paul Muni, Bette Davis, Margaret Lindsay, Eugene Pallette, Robert Barrat, Henry O'Neill, Hobart Cavanaugh

The Borgia Stick**
US 1967 98m Technicolor TVM
Universal (Richard Lewis)

An innocent-seeming suburban couple are blackmailed employees of a powerful and mysterious crime syndicate.
Well-paced and intriguingly unfolded thriller, one of the best of the early TV movies.

w A. J. Russell *d* David Lowell Rich

Don Murray, Inger Stevens, Fritz Weaver, Barry Nelson, Sorrell Booke
† A TV movie which was also released theatrically.

Born Free**
GB 1965 95m Technicolor Panavision
Columbia / Open Road (Carl Foreman)

A Kenyan game warden and his wife rear three lion cubs, one of which eventually presents them with a family.
Irresistible animal shots salvage this rather flabbily put together version of a bestselling book. An enormous commercial success, it was followed by the even thinner *Living Free*, by a TV series, and by several semi-professional documentaries.

w Gerald L. C. Copley, *book* Joy Adamson *d* James Hill *ph* Kenneth Talbot *m John Barry*

Virginia McKenna, Bill Travers, Geoffrey Keen

Born Innocent
US 1974 74m colour TVM
Tomorrow

Problems of a 14-year-old girl in a tough detention centre.
Television thought it had grown up because the heroine was raped with a broom handle. Ho hum.

w Gerald di Pego *d* Donald Wrye

Linda Blair, Joanna Miles, Kim Hunter, Richard Jaeckel, Mitch Vogel

Born to be Bad
US 1934 61m bw
Twentieth Century (William Goetz, Raymond Griffith)

A girl schemes to seduce the man who has adopted her illegitimate son.
Batty mother-love melodrama.

w Ralph Graves *d* Lowell Sherman *ph* Barney McGill *m* Alfred Newman

Loretta Young, Cary Grant, Jackie Kelk, Henry Travers, Russell Hopton, Andrew Tombes, Harry Green

Born to be Bad
US 1950 94m bw
RKO (Robert Sparks)

An ambitious girl marries a millionaire but continues her affair with a novelist; finally both men discover her true character.
Tentative bad girl novelette, just about passable.

w Edith Sommer, *novel* All Kneeling by Anne Parrish *d* Nicholas Ray *ph* Nicholas Musuraca *m* Constantin Bakaleinikoff

Joan Fontaine, Robert Ryan, Zachary Scott, Joan Leslie, Mel Ferrer

Born to Dance*
US 1936 108m bw
MGM (Jack Cummings)

A sailor meets a girl in New York.
Well remembered musical with good numbers but a rather lame look.

w Jack McGowan, Sid Silvers, B. G. De Sylva *d* Roy del Ruth *ph* Ray June *songs* Cole Porter

Eleanor Powell, James Stewart, Virginia Bruce, Una Merkel, Sid Silvers, Frances Langford, Raymond Walburn, *Reginald Gardiner*, Buddy Ebsen

Born to Kill*
US 1947 92m bw
RKO
GB title: *Lady of Deceit*

A psychotic involves his new wife in his criminal pursuits.
Unusual, heavy-going, well acted melodrama.

w Eve Greene, Richard Macauley *d* Robert Wise *ph* Robert de Grasse

Lawrence Tierney, Claire Trevor, Walter Slezak, Philip Terry, Elisha Cook Jnr

Born Yesterday**
US 1950 103m bw
Columbia (S. Sylvan Simon)

The ignorant ex-chorus girl mistress of a scrap iron tycoon takes English lessons, falls for her tutor, and politically outmanoeuvres her bewildered lover.
Pleasant film version of a cast-iron box office play, subtle and intelligent in all departments yet with a regrettable tendency to wave the flag.

w Albert Mannheimer, *play Garson Kanin d George Cukor ph* Joseph Walker *m* Morris Stoloff

Judy Holliday, Broderick Crawford, William Holden, Howard St John

The Boss*
US 1956 89m bw
UA / Frank N. Seltzer

After World War I, a ne'er-do-well becomes a corrupt small town political boss.
Low budgeted, complexly plotted, occasionally quite powerful and efficient crime melodrama.

w Ben L. Parry *d* Byron Haskin *ph* Hal Mohr

John Payne, William Bishop, Gloria McGhee, Doe Avedon, Joe Flynn

Boston Blackie

An American second feature series made by Columbia between 1941 and 1949. There had been silent films about the character, a reformed crook and con man who has to solve crimes because he is suspected by the law. Cheap but sometime vigorous productions, they had a loyal following, and starred Chester Morris with George E. Stone as his assistant the Runt.

The titles were:

1941: MEET BOSTON BLACKIE
CONFESSIONS OF BOSTON BLACKIE
1942: ALIAS BOSTON BLACKIE, BOSTON BLACKIE GOES TO HOLLYWOOD
1943: AFTER MIDNIGHT WITH BOSTON BLACKIE
1944: ONE MYSTERIOUS NIGHT

1945: BOSTON BLACKIE BOOKED ON SUSPICION, BOSTON BLACKIE'S RENDEZVOUS
1946: A CLOSE CALL FOR BOSTON BLACKIE, THE PHANTOM THIEF
1947: BOSTON BLACKIE AND THE LAW
1948: TRAPPED BY BOSTON BLACKIE
1949: BOSTON BLACKIE'S CHINESE VENTURE
† A television series starring Kent Taylor followed in 1951.

The Boston Strangler**
US 1968 118m De Luxe Panavision
TCF (Robert Fryer)

A semi-factual account of the sex maniac who terrified Boston in the mid-sixties.
Ambitious *policier* rendered less effective by pretentious writing and flashy treatment, including multi-image sequences; the investigation is more interesting than the psychoanalysis.

w Edward Anhalt, *book* Gerold Frank *d* Richard Fleischer *ph* Richard Kline *m* Lionel Newman

Henry Fonda, *Tony Curtis* (as the murderer), George Kennedy, Mike Kellin, Hurd Hatfield, Murray Hamilton, Sally Kellerman, Jeff Corey, George Voskovec

Botany Bay
US 1952 94m Technicolor
Paramount (Joseph Sistrom)

On a convict ship in 1787 an American student unjustly accused of robbery clashes with the brutal captain for the favours of the only woman aboard.
Cramped and brutal action melodrama, a let-down considering the talent involved.

w Jonathan Latimer, *novel* Charles Nordhof and James Hall *d* John Farrow *ph* John Seitz *m* Franz Waxman

James Mason, Alan Ladd, Patricia Medina, Cedric Hardwicke, Murray Matheson, Jonathan Harris

The Bottom of the Bottle
US 1956 86m Eastmancolor Cinemascope
TCF (Buddy Adler)
GB title: *Beyond the River*

A wealthy attorney is visited by his drunken brother, on the run from the police and needing help to escape into Mexico.
Dreary drama in muddy colour, a clearly mis-guided enterprise.

w Sydney Boehm, *novel* Georges Simenon *d* Henry Hathaway *ph* Lee Garmes

Joseph Cotten, Van Johnson, Ruth Roman, Jack Carson

Bottoms Up
US 1934 85m bw
Fox (B. G. De Sylva)

A slick promoter in Hollywood disguises his pals as British nobility and gets them lucrative jobs.
Mild musical with a rather interesting cast.

w B. G. De Sylva, David Butler, Sid Silvers *d* David Butler *ph* Arthur Miller *md* Constantin Bakaleinikoff

Spencer Tracy, Pat Patterson, John Boles, Harry Green, Herbert Mundin, Sid Silvers, Thelma Todd, Robert Emmett O'Connor

Bought
US 1931 70m bw
Warner

An ambitious working girl rebels against her slum existence and seeks a rich man.
Typical star vehicle of its time, with a predictable and unlikely change of heart for a finale.

w Charles Kenyon, Raymond Griffith, *novel* Jackdaw's Strut by Harriet Henry *d* Archie Mayo *ph* Ray June

Constance Bennett, Ben Lyon, Richard Bennett, Dorothy Peterson, Ray Milland, Doris Lloyd, Maude Eburne

The Bounty Man
US 1972 74m colour TVM
Spelling–Goldberg

A hunter falls for the girl friend of his quarry.
Glum pocket western.

w Jim Byrnes *d* John Llewellyn Moxey

Clint Walker, Richard Basehart, John Ericson, Margot Kidder, Gene Evans, Arthur Hunnicutt

The Bowery***
US 1933 92m bw
Twentieth Century (Darryl F. Zanuck) (Raymond Griffith, William Goetz)

In nineties New York, two boisterous rivals settle their differences after one has jumped off the Brooklyn Bridge for a bet.
Roistering saga of cross and double cross on the seamy side, splendidly vigorous in acting and treatment.

w Howard Estabrook, James Gleason d Raoul Walsh ph Barney McGill *m* Alfred Newman *ad* Richard Day

Wallace Beery, George Raft, Pert Kelton, Jackie Cooper, Fay Wray, Herman Bing

The Bowery Boys

A cheap and cheerful series of American second features, immensely popular between 1946 and 1958, these adventures of a group of ageing Brooklyn layabouts had their origin in the 1937 film *Dead End*, from which the Dead End Kids graduated to other features at Warner: *Crime School, They Made Me a Criminal, Angels with Dirty Faces, Angels Wash their Faces*, etc. A couple of the 'boys' then defected to Universal and made *Little Tough Guy* and a series of half a dozen subsequent pictures; while in 1940 Monogram took a couple more and built up another group called the East Side Kids. In 1946 a formal merger of talent at Monogram consolidated the remaining members into the Bowery Boys. The members were Leo Gorcey, Huntz Hall, Bobby Jordan, Gabriel Dell (all from the Dead End Kids), Bernard Gorcey, David Gorcey, Billy Benedict, and Bennie Bartlett.

The films are:

1946: IN FAST COMPANY, BOWERY BOMBSHELL, LIVE WIRES, SPOOK BUSTERS, MR HEX
1947: BOWERY BUCKAROOS, HARD BOILED MAHONEY, NEWS HOUNDS, ANGELS' ALLEY
1948: JINX MONEY, SMUGGLER'S COVE, TROUBLE MAKERS
1949: ANGELS IN DISGUISE, FIGHTING FOOLS, HOLD THAT BABY, MASTER MINDS
1950: BLONDE DYNAMITE, BLUES BUSTERS, LUCKY LOSERS, TRIPLE TROUBLE
1951: BOWERY BATALLION, CRAZY OVER HORSES, GHOST CHASERS, LET'S GO NAVY
1952: FEUDIN' FOOLS, HERE COME THE MARINES, HOLD THAT LINE, NO HOLDS BARRED
1953: CLIPPED WINGS, JALOPY, LOOSE IN LONDON, PRIVATE EYES
1954: THE BOWERY BOYS MEET THE MONSTERS, JUNGLE GENTS, PARIS PLAYBOYS
1955: BOWERY TO BAGDAD, HIGH SOCIETY, JAIL BUSTERS, SPY CHASERS
1956: DIG THAT URANIUM, CRASHING LAS VEGAS, FIGHTING TROUBLE, HOT SHOTS
1957: SPOOK CHASERS, HOLD THAT HYPNOTIST, LOOKING FOR DANGER
1958: UP IN SMOKE, IN THE MONEY

Bowery to Broadway
US 1944 94m bw
Universal (John Grant)

In the nineties, a Bowery songstress makes it to the big time.
Simple-minded musical in which the drama has no drive and the guest stars are given inferior material.

w Joseph Lytton, Arthur T. Horman *d* Charles Lamont *ph* Charles Van Enger *md* Edward Ward

Maria Montez, Turhan Bey, Susanna Foster, Jack Oakie, Donald Cook, Louise Allbritton, Andy Devine, Rosemary de Camp, Ann Blyth, Donald O'Connor, Peggy Ryan, Frank McHugh, Leo Carrillo, Evelyn Ankers, Mantan Moreland

Boxcar Bertha*
US 1972 88m De Luxe
AIP (Roger Corman)

In early thirties Arkansas, an unhappy girl falls in with gangsters and train robbers.
Competent imitation of *Bonnie and Clyde*.

w Joyce H. and John W. Corrington *d Martin Scorsese ph* John Stephens *m* Gilb Guilbeau, Thad Maxwell

Barbara Hershey, David Carradine, Barry Primus, Bernie Casey, John Carradine

A Boy a Girl and a Bike
GB 1947 92m bw
Gainsborough (Ralph Keene)

Romantic jealousies arise between members of a Yorkshire cycling club.
Mild comedy drama with the advantage of fresh air locations.

w Ted Willis *d* Ralph Smart

John McCallum, Honor Blackman, Patrick Holt, Diana Dors, Leslie Dwyer, Thora Hird, Anthony Newley, Megs Jenkins, Maurice Denham

The Boy and the Bridge
GB 1959 91m bw
Xanadu (Kevin McClory)

A boy who believes he has committed a murder hides in the ramparts of Tower Bridge.
This tiny fable adds up to very weak entertainment, despite inventive photography, because it has virtually no plot development.

w Geoffrey Orme, Kevin McClory, Desmond O'Donovan *d* Kevin McClory *ph Ted Scaife* *m* Malcolm Arnold

Ian MacLaine, Liam Redmond, James Hayter,

Norman Macowan, Geoffrey Keen, Jack MacGowran, Royal Dano, Rita Webb

Boy, Did I Get a Wrong Number
US 1966 99m De Luxe
UA / Edward Small (George Beck)

Trying to phone his wife, an estate agent gets involved with a runaway actress.
Lifeless and generally resistible star comedy, the first of several hard and unfunny vehicles for an ageing Bob Hope seeming to hark back to the least attractive aspects of burlesque rather than the sympathetic wisecracking which suits him best.

w Burt Styler, Albert E. Lewin, George Kennett *d* George Marshall *ph* Lionel Lindon *m* Richard Lasalle, By Dunham

Bob Hope, Elke Sommer, Phyllis Diller, Marjorie Lord, Cesare Danova, Benny Baker

The Boy Friend*
GB 1971 125m Metrocolor Panavision
MGM / Russflix (Ken Russell)

On a wet Wednesday afternoon in Portsmouth in the late twenties, a tatty company with backstage problems puts on an empty-headed musical.
Russell the mastermind effectively destroys Sandy Wilson's charming period pastiche, sending up all the numbers (via badly staged dream sequences on the wrong shape screen) in a Busby Berkeley manner which had not yet been invented. Moments do work, but a non-star doesn't help, and the whole thing is an artistic disaster of some significance both to Russell's career and to the cinema of the early seventies.

w Ken Russell, from Sandy Wilson's musical play *d* Ken Russell *ph* David Watkin *md* Ian Whittaker *pd* Tony Walton

Twiggy, Christopher Gable, *Max Adrian*, Tommy Tune, Barbara Windsor, Moyra Fraser, Bryan Pringle, Vladek Sheybal, *Antonia Ellis*, *Glenda Jackson*

The Boy from Oklahoma*
US 1953 88m Warnercolor
Warner (David Weisbart)

A genial plainsman studying law becomes sheriff of a small town and uncovers its mayor as a killer.
Modest, pleasing western with the star imitating his father.

w Frank David, Winston Miller *d* Michael Curtiz *ph* Robert Burks *m* Max Steiner

Will Rogers Jnr, Nancy Olson, Lon Chaney Jnr, Anthony Caruso, Wallace Ford, Clem Bevans, Merv Griffin

Boy Meets Girl**
US 1938 86m bw
Warner (George Abbott)

Two crazy Hollywood scenario writers make a star of an infant yet unborn.
Freewheeling film version of a hilarious play: fine crazy comedy and excellent Hollywood satire.

w Bella and Sam Spewack, from their play *d* Lloyd Bacon *ph* Sol Polito *m* Leo Forbstein

James Cagney, Pat O'Brien, Marie Wilson, Ralph Bellamy, Frank McHugh, Dick Foran, Bruce Lester, Ronald Reagan, James Stephenson

Boy on a Dolphin*
US 1957 111m Eastmancolor Cinemascope
TCF (Samuel G. Engel)

A Greek girl diver discovers a sunken artifact of great value and the news spreads to an American archaeologist and an unscrupulous collector.
Likeable, sunswept Mediterranean adventure romance marred by the miscasting of the male lead.

w Ivan Moffatt, Dwight Taylor, *novel* David Divine *d* Jean Negulesco *ph Milton Krasner* *m* Lionel Newman

Alan Ladd, Sophia Loren, *Clifton Webb*, Laurence Naismith, Alexis Minotis, Jorge Mistral

The Boy with Green Hair
US 1948 82m Technicolor
RKO (Dore Schary)

When he hears that his parents were killed in an air raid, a boy's hair turns green; other war orphans encourage him to parade himself publicly as an image of the horror and futility of war.
Muddled, pretentious and unpersuasive fantasy, typical of this producer's do-goodery. One of those oddities which make Hollywood endearing, but not very entertaining apart from Pat O'Brien's garrulous grandpa.

w Ben Barzman, Alfred Lewis Levitt, *story* Betsy Beaton *d* Joseph Losey *ph* George Barnes *m* Leigh Harline

Dean Stockwell, Pat O'Brien, Robert Ryan, Barbara Hale

The Boys
GB 1962 123m Cinemascope
Gala / Columbia (Sidney J. Furie)

Four boys are on trial for killing a garage attendant.
Elaborate courtroom drama with flashbacks,

stars for counsel, a tricksy director, and about forty minutes too much footage.

w Stuart Douglass *d* Sidney J. Furie *ph* Gerald Gibbs *m* The Shadows

Richard Todd, Robert Morley, Felix Aylmer, Dudley Sutton, Ronald Lacey, Tony Garnett, Jess Conrad, Wilfrid Brambell, Allan Cuthbertson, Colin Gordon

The Boys from Syracuse*
US 1940 74m bw
Universal (Jules Levey)

The Comedy of Errors with modern wisecracks, and a few songs.
Predictable well-drilled confusion arises from master and slave having identical twins, but the general tone is a bit flat for an adaptation from a hilarious Broadway success. Still, the songs are lively and the chariot race finale shows spirit.

w Leonard Spiegelgass, Charles Grayson, Paul Gerard Smith, from the play by George Abbott and William Shakespeare *d* Edward A. Sutherland *ph* Joseph Valentine *m* Charles Previn *songs* Rodgers and Hart

Allan Jones, Joe Penner, Charles Butterworth, Rosemary Lane, Irene Hervey, Martha Raye, Alan Mowbray
† The writing credit on screen ends: 'After a play by William Shakespeare . . . long, long after!'

Boys in Brown
GB 1949 84m bw
Gainsborough (Antony Darnborough)

Life in a Borstal institution.
The stars make elderly boys, but Jack Warner is a cuddly governor. Boring and unpersuasive non-documentary fiction in Britain's most tiresome style.

wd Montgomery Tully, *play* Reginald Beckwith *ph* Gordon Lang, Cyril Bristow *m* Doreen Carwithen

Jack Warner, Dirk Bogarde, Michael Medwin, Jimmy Hanley, Richard Attenborough, Alfie Bass, Barbara Murray, Thora Hird
† Made by the Independent Frame method, which blended real backgrounds with studio sets.

The Boys in the Band*
US 1970 120m Technicolor
Cinema Center / Leo (Mart Crowley, Kenneth Utt)

Tempers fray and true selves are revealed when a heterosexual is accidentally invited to a homosexual party.
Careful but claustrophobic filming of a Broadway play, which at the screen's closer quarters becomes overpowering well before the end.

w Mart Crowley, from his play *d* William Friedkin *ph* Arthur J. Ornitz *m* none

Leonard Frey, Kenneth Nelson, Cliff Gorman, Frederick Combs, Reuben Greene, Robert La Tourneaux, Laurence Luckinbill, Keith Prentice, Peter White

'They crack jokes while their hearts are breaking.'—*New Yorker*

Boys' Night Out
US 1962 115m Metrocolor Cinemascope
MGM / Filmways (Martin Ransohoff)

Three married men and their bachelor friend share a flat and a 'mistress'.
Would-be saucy comedy in which nothing sexy ever happens and the helpless players are as witless as the script.

w Ira Wallach *d* Michael Gordon *ph* Arthur E. Arling *m* Frank de Vol

James Garner, Kim Novak, Tony Randall, Howard Duff, Howard Morris, Oscar Homolka, Janet Blair, Patti Page, Jessie Royce Landis

Boys' Town**
US 1938 93m bw
MGM (John W. Considine Jnr)

The story of Father Flanagan and his school for juvenile delinquents.
Well-made, highly successful, but sentimental crowd pleaser.

w John Meehan, Dore Schary *d* Norman Taurog *ph* Sidney Wagner

Spencer Tracy, Mickey Rooney, Henry Hull, Gene Reynolds, Sidney Miller, Frankie Thomas, Bobs Watson, Tommy Noonan

The Brain
France / US 1969 115m colour
Paramount (Alain Poire)

A British colonel leads an international crew in an attempt to rob NATO.
Exhausting and generally misfiring international crook comedy.

w Gerard Oury, Marcel Julian, Daniele Thompson *d* Gerard Oury *ph* Vladimir Ivanov, Armand Thirard *m* Georges Delerue

David Niven, Jean-Paul Belmondo, Bourvil, Eli Wallach, Silvia Monti

Brainstorm
US 1965 110m bw Panavision
Warner / Kodima (William Conrad)

A passer-by saves a married woman from suicide, has an affair with her, and conspires to murder her husband. This accomplished, she leaves him and he goes insane.
Overlong thriller which starts off agreeably in the *Double Indemnity* vein; but goes slow and solemn around the half way mark.

w Mann Rubin *d* William Conrad *ph* Sam Leavitt *m* George Duning

Jeffrey Hunter, Anne Francis, Dana Andrews, Viveca Lindfors, Stacy Harris

'A sub-B potboiler for those who find comic books too intellectual.'—*Judith Crist*

The Bramble Bush
US 1960 105m Technicolor
Warner / United States (Milton Sperling)

A doctor returns to his home town and finds himself involved in old tragedies including the mercy killing of his friend.
Sordid small-town melodrama in the *Peyton Place* vein, with adequate production values but dispiriting treatment.

w Milton Sperling, Philip Yordan, *novel* Charles Mergendahl *d* Daniel Petrie *ph* Lucien Ballard *m* Leonard Rosenman

Richard Burton, Barbara Rush, Jack Carson, Angie Dickinson, James Dunn, Tom Drake, Henry Jones, Frank Conroy, Carl Benton Reid, William Hansen

A Brand New Life*
US 1972 74m colour TVM
Tomorrow

A middle-aged wife discovers she is pregnant.
Well acted but fairly predictable domestic drama.

w Jerome Kass, Peggy Chantler Dick *d* Sam O'Steen *m* Billy Goldenberg

Cloris Leachman, Martin Balsam, Wilfrid Hyde White, Mildred Dunnock, Gene Nelson, Marge Redmond

Branded
US 1950 104m Technicolor
Paramount (Mel Epstein)

A gunman poses as a rancher's lost heir, but redeems himself by finding the real one.
Competent, brisk western.

w Sydney Boehm, Cyril Hume *d* Rudolph Maté *ph* Charles Lang Jnr *m* Roy Webb

Alan Ladd, Charles Bickford, Mona Freeman, Robert Keith, Joseph Calleia, Peter Hansen, Selena Royle, Tom Tully

Brandy for the Parson*
GB 1951 79m bw
Group Three (Alfred O'Shaughnessy)

A couple on a yachting holiday find themselves unwittingly smuggling brandy into Britain.
Pleasant little sub-Ealing comedy with agreeable locations but not much drive.

w John Dighton, Walter Meade, *story* Geoffrey Household *d* John Eldridge *ph* Martin Curtis *m* John Addison

James Donald, Kenneth More, Jean Lodge, Frederick Piper, Charles Hawtrey, Michael Trubshawe, Alfie Bass, Reginald Beckwith

Brannigan*
GB 1975 111m De Luxe Panavision
UA / Wellborn (Jules Levy, Arthur Gardner)

A Chicago policeman is sent to London to pick up a gangster.
Cheerful crime pastiche and tour of London, quite an agreeable entertainment despite its obviously over-age star.

w Christopher Trumbo, Michael Butler, William P. McGivern, William Norton *d* Douglas Hickox *ph* Gerry Fisher *m* Dominic Frontière

John Wayne, Richard Attenborough, Judy Geeson, Mel Ferrer, John Vernon, Daniel Pilon, John Stride, James Booth, Barry Dennen

The Brasher Doubloon*
US 1946 72m bw
TCF
GB title: *The High Window*

Philip Marlowe investigates the theft of a rare coin and finds himself involved in a series of murders.
The poorest of the Chandler adaptations, previously filmed as *Time to Kill*, still contains good moments, though the star is lightweight and the production low-budget.

w Dorothy Bennett, *novel* The High Window by Raymond Chandler *d* John Brahm *ph* Lloyd Ahern

George Montgomery, Nancy Guild, Florence Bates, Conrad Janis, Fritz Kortner

The Brass Bottle
US 1964 89m Eastmancolor
U-I / Scarus (Robert Arthur)

A young architect finds an old brass bottle which contains a troublesome genie.
Simple-minded farce with little invention and poor trickwork.

w Oscar Brodney, *novel* F. Anstey *d* Harry Keller *ph* Clifford Stine *m* Bernard Green *sp* Roswell Hoffman

Tony Randall, Burl Ives, Barbara Eden, Edward Andrews, Ann Doran

The Bravados*
US 1958 98m Eastmancolor Cinemascope
TCF (Herbert B. Swope)

A widower chases four killers who, he believes, raped and murdered his wife.
Dour western with a downbeat ending; production good, but entertainment uneasy.

w Philip Yordan, *novel* Frank O'Rourke
d Henry King *ph* Leon Shamroy *m* Lionel Newman

Gregory Peck, Stephen Boyd, Joan Collins, Albert Salmi, Henry Silva, George Voskovec, Barry Coe, Lee Van Cleef

The Brave Bulls
US 1951 108m bw
Columbia (Robert Rossen)

A Mexican matador regains his courage but loses his girl in a car crash.
Muddled narrative with dollops of bull-fighting mystique; a rather miserable movie despite effort all round.

w John Bright, *novel* Tom Lea *d* Robert Rossen *ph* James Wong Howe, Floyd Crosby

Mel Ferrer, Miroslava, Anthony Quinn, Eugene Iglesias

The Brave Don't Cry*
GB 1952 90m bw
Group Three (John Baxter)

Over a hundred men are rescued in a Scottish mine disaster.
Semi-documentary based on a real incident: well done on a small budget, but hardly memorable.

w Montagu Slater *d* Philip Leacock *ph* Arthur Grant *m* none

John Gregson, Meg Buchanan, John Rae, Fulton Mackay, Andrew Keir, Russell Waters, Jameson Clark, Jean Anderson, Eric Woodburn

The Brave One*
US 1956 100m Technicolor Cinemascope
King Brothers

A small boy saves the life of his pet bull when it is sent into the ring.
Mildly beguiling minor drama for those who adore small boys and bulls.

w Harry Franklin, Merrill G. White, Robert Rich (Dalton Trumbo) *d* Irving Rapper *ph* Jack Cardiff *m* Victor Young

Michael Ray, Rodolfo Hoyos, Elsa Cardenas, Joi Lansing, Carlos Navarro

The Bravos
US 1971 100m colour TVM
Universal

Post-Civil War problems of an army officer.
Adequate, overlong mini-western.

w Christopher Knopf *d* Ted Post

George Peppard, Pernell Roberts, Belinda Montgomery,
L. Q. Jones, Bo Svenson

Break of Hearts
US 1935 80m bw
RKO (Pandro S. Berman)

A girl composer falls in love with a distinguished conductor who becomes a dipsomaniac.
Well acted soap opera, not really worthy of its stars.

w Sarah Y. Mason, Victor Heerman, Anthony Veiller *d* Philip Moeller *ph* Robert de Grasse *m* Max Steiner

Katharine Hepburn, Charles Boyer, Jean Hersholt, John Beal, Sam Hardy

Break the News*
GB 1938 78m bw
GFD / Jack Buchanan

A dancer arranges his partner's 'death' for publicity reasons but is sent to jail when the partner disappears.
Thin but lively comedy with a remarkable couple of song and dance men. Negative apparently lost.

w Geoffrey Kerr, *novel* Le Mort en Fuite by Loid de Gouriadec *d* René Clair

Jack Buchanan, Maurice Chevalier, June Knight, Marta Labarr, Garry Marsh, Felix Aylmer, Robb Wilton

† Various remakes include *The Art of Love* (qv).

Breakfast at Tiffany's*
US 1961 115m Technicolor
Paramount (Martin Jurow, Richard Shepherd)

A young New York writer has as neighbour the volatile Holly Golightly, a slightly crazy call girl with an exotic social and emotional life.
Impossibly cleaned up and asexual version of a light novel which tried to be the American *I Am a Camera*. Wild parties, amusing scenes and good cameos, but the pace is slow, the atmosphere is unconvincingly clean and luxurious, and the sentimentality kills it.

w George Axelrod, *novel* Truman Capote

d Blake Edwards *ph* Franz Planer *m Henry Mancini*

Audrey Hepburn, George Peppard, Patricia Neal, Buddy Ebsen, Martin Balsam, *John McGiver* (as the Tiffany salesman), Mickey Rooney

Breakfast for Two*
US 1937 65m bw
RKO (Edward Kaufman)

A Texas heiress turns a playboy into a businessman.
Star crazy comedy with some wildly funny scenes.

w Charles Kaufman, Paul Yawitz, Viola Brothers Shore *d* Alfred Santell *ph* J. Roy Hunt

Barbara Stanwyck, Herbert Marshall, Donald Meek, Glenda Farrell, Eric Blore, Etienne Girardot

Breakheart Pass*
US 1975 94m De Luxe
UA / Elliott Kastner (Jerry Gershwin)

Various mysterious passengers on an 1873 train across the frozen west to Fort Humboldt turn out to have smuggling and murder in mind.
Botched murder mystery on wheels: there are some exciting scenes, but the plot makes little sense and the 'action finale' is muddled.

w Alistair MacLean, from his book *d* Tom Gries *ph* Lucien Ballard *m* Jerry Goldsmith

Charles Bronson, Ben Johnson, Richard Crenna, Jill Ireland, Charles Durning, Archie Moore, Ed Lauter

The Breaking Point*
US 1950 97m bw
Warner (Jerry Wald)

A charterboat owner becomes involved with crooks but turns them in when they have killed his friend.
Adequate if slightly humdrum attempt by Warners to atone for what they had done to a Hemingway novel, the infidelity of *To Have and Have Not* and the unauthorized variation of *Key Largo*. (See also: *The Gun Runners*.)

w Ranald MacDougall, *novel* To Have and Have Not by Ernest Hemingway *d* Michael Curtiz *ph* Ted McCord *m* Ray Heindorf

John Garfield, Patricia Neal, Phyllis Thaxter, Juano Hernandez, Wallace Ford, Edmon Ryan, William Campbell

Breaking Point
Canada 1976 92m colour Panavision
TCF / Astral Belle Vue (Harold Greenberg, Harold Pariser)

An innocent witness against the Mafia takes off against them vigilante style when his partner is murdered and his own life threatened.
Comic strip thuggery with performances to match; plenty of excitement for toughies.

w Roger E. Swaybill, Stanley Mann *d* Bob Clark *ph* Marc Champion *m* David McLey

Bo Svenson, Robert Culp, John Colicos, Belinda J. Montgomery, Stephen Young

Breakout
US 1967 97m Technicolor TVM
Universal (Richard Irving)

Escaped convicts in a blizzard stop to help a small boy.
Ripe Hollywood corn and not much action.

w Sy Gomberg *d* Richard Irving

James Drury, Kathryn Hays, Woody Strode, Sean Garrison

Breakthrough
US 1950 91m bw
Warner (Bryan Foy)

Adventures of a US army unit in Normandy after D-Day.
Routine low-budgeter which improves after a slow start.

w Bernard Girard, Ted Sherdeman, Joseph I. Breen Jnr *d* Lewis Seiler *ph* Edwin DuPar *m* William Lava

David Brian, John Agar, Frank Lovejoy, William Campbell, Paul Picerni, Greg McClure, Edward Norris, Matt Willis, Dick Wesson

A Breath of Scandal
US 1960 98m Technicolor
Paramount / Titanus / Ponti–Gorosi (Carlo Ponti, Marcello Girosi)

A spirited Ruritanian princess falls for an American industrialist.
Exceedingly flat-footed and boring international co-production of an old Molnar play; if anyone concerned had bright ideas, they don't show.

w Sidney Howard (presumably in the thirties, for he died in 1939), *play* Olimpia by Ferenc Molnar *d* Michael Curtiz, Mario Russo *ph* Mario Montuori *m* Allessandro Cicognini

Sophia Loren, Maurice Chevalier, John Gavin, Isabel Jeans, Angela Lansbury, Roberto Risso, Frederick Ledebur, Tullio Carminati, Milly Vitale

Breezy
US 1973 107m Technicolor
Universal / Malpaso (Robert Daley)

A divorced 50-year-old real estate agent is rejuvenated by an affair with a young girl hippy. An abrasive veneer covers the most stereotyped of January–May love stories. Technically an attractive piece of work.

w Jo Heims *d* Clint Eastwood *ph* Frank Stanley *m* Michel Legrand

William Holden, Kay Lenz, Roger C. Carmel, Marj Dusay, Joan Hotchkis

Brenda Starr, Girl Reporter*
US 1975 74m colour TVM
David Wolper

An intrepid newspaperwoman defends a millionaire from voodoo villains.
Comic strip derivative which did not quite take, but provides some fair fun along the way.

w George Kirgo, *comic strip* Dale Messick *d* Mel Stuart

Jill St John, Jed Allan, Victor Buono, Sorrell Booke, Joel Fabiani

Brewster's Millions*
GB 1935 84m bw
British and Dominion (Herbert Wilcox)

If he can spend a million pounds within two months, a playboy will inherit many millions more.
Artless but lively version of a famous comedy which provided a good role for its star.

w Arthur Wimperis, Paul Gangelin, Douglas Furber, Clifford Grey, Donovan Pedelty, Wolfgang Wilhelm, *play* George Barr McCutcheon and Winchell Smith, *original novel* George Barr McCutcheon *d* Thornton Freeland

Jack Buchanan, Lili Damita, Nancy O'Neil, Amy Veness, Sydney Fairbrother, Fred Emney, Sebastian Shaw

Brewster's Millions*
US 1945 79m bw
Edward Small

Competent American remake of the above.

w Winchell Smith, Cryon Ongley *d* Allan Dwan *ph* Charles Lawton Jnr

Dennis O'Keefe, Eddie 'Rochester' Anderson, Helen Walker
† Remade as *Three on a Spree* (GB 1961).

Brewster McCloud
US 1970 105m Metrocolor Panavision
MGM / Adler–Phillips / Lion's Gate (Lou Adler)

A man hides out under the roof of the Houston Astrodrome, prepares to learn to fly with man-made wings, and refuses all offers of help; when he launches himself, he falls to his death.
Anarchic, allegorical fantasy, a delight no doubt for connoisseurs of way-out humour. Everyone else, forget it.

w Doran William Cannon *d* Robert Altman *ph* Lamar Boren, Jordan Cronenweth *m* Gene Page

Bud Cort, Sally Kellerman, Michael Murphy, William Windom, Shelley Duvall, René Auberjonois, Stacy Keach, John Shuck, Margaret Hamilton

'Amorphous and rather silly . . . the idea seems to be left over from a Victorian fable, but the style is like a Road Runner cartoon.'—*New Yorker, 1974*

Brian's Song*
US 1971 73m colour TVM
Columbia (Paul Junger Witt)

The true story of Brian Piccolo, a baseball star who died of cancer.
In the tradition of *The Pride of the Yankees*, this earnest sentimental piece was a big hit in its home country, and won a few plaudits for telemovies, but other countries saw it as one long cliché.

w William Blinn *d* Buzz Kulik *m Michel Legrand*

James Caan, Jack Warden, Billy Dee Williams, Bud Furillo, Shelley Fabares, Judy Pace

The Bribe*
US 1949 98m bw
MGM (Robert Z. Leonard)

A US agent tracks down a group of criminals in Central America.
Steamy melodrama with pretensions but only moderate entertainment value despite high gloss. The rogues' gallery, however, is impressive.

w Marguerite Roberts *d* Robert Z. Leonard *ph* Joseph Ruttenberg *m* Miklos Rozsa

Robert Taylor, Ava Gardner, Charles Laughton, Vincent Price, John Hodiak

The Bridal Path*
GB 1959 95m Technicolor
British Lion / Sidney Gilliat, Frank Launder

A stalwart Hebridean islander journeys to the mainland in search of a wife.

Mild, episodic, very pleasant open-air comedy set amid splendid locations.

w Frank Launder, Geoffrey Willans, *novel* Nigel Tranter *d* Frank Launder *ph* Arthur Ibbetson *m* Cedric Thorpe Davie

Bill Travers, Fiona Clyne, George Cole, Duncan Macrae, Gordon Jackson, Dilys Laye, Bernadette O'Farrell

The Bride Came C.O.D.*
US 1941 92m bw
Warner (Hal B. Wallis)

A charter pilot agrees to kidnap a temperamental heiress, but is stuck with her when they crashland in the desert.
Feeble comedy with a script totally unworthy of its stars. The mass of talent does however provide a smile or two towards the end.

w Julius J. and Philip G. Epstein *d* William Keighley *ph* Ernest Haller

Bette Davis, James Cagney, Harry Davenport, Stuart Erwin, Eugene Pallette, Jack Carson, George Tobias, William Frawley, Edward Brophy, Chick Chandler

'Neither the funniest comedy ever made, nor the shortest distance between two points, but for the most part a serviceable romp.'—*Theodore Strauss*

The Bride Comes Home*
US 1935 82m bw
Paramount (Wesley Ruggles)

A penniless socialite helps a wealthy man and his roughneck bodyguard in a magazine venture.
Slight but freshly handled romantic comedy, still worth a look.

w Elizabeth Sanxay Holding, Claude Binyon *d* Wesley Ruggles *ph* Leo Tover

Claudette Colbert, Robert Young, Fred MacMurray, William Collier Snr, Donald Meek, Edgar Kennedy, Richard Carle, Jimmy Conlin

Bride for Sale
US 1949 87m bw
RKO (Jack H. Skirball)

A practical-minded businesswoman has two admirers.
Skittish romantic comedy for ageing stars.

w Bruce Manning, Islin Auster *d* William D. Russell *ph* Joseph Valentine *m* Constantin Bakaleinikoff

Claudette Colbert, George Brent, Robert Young, Max Baer, Gus Schilling, Charles Arnt, Thurston Hall

The Bride Goes Wild
US 1948 98m bw
MGM (William H. Wright)

As his lady illustrator finds out, a writer of children's books is not quite the sober uncle she expected, especially when he has to pretend to adopt an unruly orphan.
Scatty comedy with farcical interludes, quite pleasantly played but lacking style.

w Albert Beich *d* Norman Taurog *ph* Ray June *m* Rudolf Kopp

June Allyson, Van Johnson, Jackie 'Butch' Jenkins, Hume Cronyn, Richard Derr

Bride of Frankenstein****
US 1935 80m bw
Universal (Carl Laemmle Jnr)

Baron Frankenstein is blackmailed by Dr Praetorious into reviving his monster and building a mate for it.
Frankenstein was startlingly good in a primitive way; this sequel is the screen's sophisticated masterpiece of black comedy, with all the talents working deftly to one end. Every scene has its own delights, and they are woven together into a superb if wilful cinematic narrative which, of its gentle mocking kind, has never been surpassed.

w John L. Balderston, William Hurlbut d James Whale ph John Mescall m Franz Waxman

Boris Karloff, Colin Clive, *Ernest Thesiger*, Valerie Hobson, *E. E. Clive*, Dwight Frye, O. P. Heggie, Una O'Connor, *Elsa Lanchester* (as Mary Shelley and the monster's mate), Gavin Gordon (as Byron), Douglas Walton (as Shelley)

'It is perhaps because Whale was by now master of the horror film that this production is the best of them all.'—*John Baxter, 1968*

'An extraordinary film, with sharp humour, macabre extravagance, and a narrative that proceeds at a fast, efficient pace.'—*Gavin Lambert, 1948*

Bride of Vengeance*
US 1948 91m bw
Paramount (Richard Maibaum)

The story of the Borgias (whitewashing Lucretia) and the Duke of Ferrara.
Superb looking but appallingly acted and rather stodgily directed piece of historical melodrama. Totally studio-bound, but one of these days it could find a sympathetic audience.

w Cyril Hume, Michael Hogan *d* Mitchell Leisen *ph* Daniel L. Fapp *m* Hugo Friedhofer *ad* Hans Dreier, Roland Anderson, Albert Nozaki

Paulette Goddard, John Lund, Macdonald Carey, Albert Dekker, Raymond Burr

The Bride Walks Out
US 1936 81m bw
RKO (Edward Small)

A successful mannequin tries to manage on her engineer husband's lowly salary.
Thin, pleasant marital comedy with no surprises.

w P. J. Wolfson, Philip G. Epstein *d* Leigh Jason *ph* J. Roy Hunt *m* Roy Webb

Barbara Stanwyck, Gene Raymond, Robert Young, Ned Sparks, Helen Broderick, Willie Best, Robert Warwick, Billy Gilbert, Hattie McDaniel, Irving Bacon

The Bride Wore Boots
US 1946 86m bw
Paramount (Seton I. Miller)

A woman who loves horses is married to a man who does not.
Flimsy, silly, but mainly quite tolerable light comedy sustained by its stars.

w Dwight Mitchell Wiley *d* Irving Pichel *ph* Stuart Thompson *m* Frederick Hollander

Barbara Stanwyck, Robert Cummings, Diana Lynn, Patric Knowles, Peggy Wood, Robert Benchley, Willie Best, Natalie Wood

The Bride Wore Red*
US 1937 103m bw
MGM (Joseph L. Mankiewicz)

A whimsical count arranges for a chorus girl to spend two weeks at an aristocratic Tyrol resort, where she is pursued by two rich men.
Cinderella retold in fancy dress; a typically unreal but quite entertaining star confection of its day.

w Tess Slesinger, Bradbury Foote, *play* The Girl from Trieste by Ferenc Molnar *d* Dorothy Arzner *ph* George Folsey *m* Franz Waxman

Joan Crawford, Robert Young, Franchot Tone, Billie Burke, Reginald Owen, George Zucco, Lynne Carver, Mary Phillips, Paul Porcasi

Brides of Dracula**
GB 1960 85m Technicolor
U-I / Hammer / Hotspur (Anthony Hinds)

Baron Meinster, a disciple of Dracula, is locked up by his mother; but a servant lets him out and he goes on the rampage in a girls' school.
The best of the Hammer *Draculas*, with plenty of inventive action, some classy acting and a good sense of place and period.

w Jimmy Sangster, Peter Bryan, Edward Percy *d Terence Fisher ph* Jack Asher *m* John Hollingsworth

David Peel (as Meinster), *Peter Cushing*, Freda Jackson, *Martita Hunt*, Yvonne Monlaur, Andrée Melly, Mona Washbourne, Henry Oscar, Miles Malleson

The Bridge at Remagen*
US 1968 116m De Luxe Panavision
UA / Wolper (David L. Wolper)

February 1945: Germans and Americans fight over a Rhine bridge.
Disenchanted, violent war film in which incessant bang-bang, adroitly staged, is all that matters.

w Richard Yates, William Roberts *d* John Guillermin *ph* Stanley Cortez *m* Elmer Bernstein

George Segal, Robert Vaughn, Ben Gazzara, Bradford Dillman, E. G. Marshall, Peter Van Eyck

'Viable viewing if explosions and clichés are your shtick and exciting if you're not sure who won that war.'—*Judith Crist*

The Bridge of San Luis Rey*
US 1944 85m bw
(UA) Benedict Bogeaus

Five people die when a Peruvian rope bridge collapses; the film investigates why they were each on the bridge at the time.
An intriguing novel is turned into tedious film drama, with actors, director, scenarist and production designer all making heavy weather.

w Dmitri, *novel* Thornton Wilder *d* Rowland V. Lee *ph* John Boyle *m* Dmitri Tiomkin

Lynn Bari, Francis Lederer, Nazimova, Louis Calhern, Akim Tamiroff, Blanche Yurka, Donald Woods

The Bridge on the River Kwai***
GB 1957 161m Technicolor Cinemascope
Columbia / Sam Spiegel

British POWs in Burma are employed by the Japs to build a bridge; meanwhile British agents seek to destroy it.
Ironic adventure epic with many fine moments but too many centres of interest and an unforgivably confusing climax. It is distinguished by Guinness' portrait of the English CO who is heroic in his initial stand against the Japs but finally cannot bear to see his bridge blown up: and the physical detail of the production is beyond criticism.

w Carl Foreman, *novel* Pierre Boulle *d David Lean ph* Jack Hildyard *m* Malcolm Arnold

Alec Guinness, Jack Hawkins, William Holden, Sessue Hayakawa, Percy Herbert, *James Donald*, Geoffrey Horne, André Morell

Bridge to the Sun*
France / US 1961 112m bw
MGM / Cité Films (Jacques Bar)

Just before Pearl Harbor, an American girl marries a Japanese diplomat and goes to live in Tokyo.
Romantic drama which oddly sides with the Japanese and shows America in a poor light. Interesting if not very compelling, with some unfamiliar views of Japan.

w Charles Kaufman, *autobiography* Gwendolen Terasaki *d* Etienne Périer *ph* Marcel Weiss, Seiichi Kizuka, Bill Kelly *m* Georges Auric

Carroll Baker, James Shigeta, James Yagi, Tetsuro Tamba

'In yet another burst of national flagellation, Hollywood turns on itself and unthinking Americans for being so beastly about the wartime Japanese.'—*MFB*

Bridger
US 1976 100m colour TVM
Universal (David Lowell Rich)

Adventures of a mountain man around 1830.
Fairly pleasing western pilot which didn't make it.

w Merwin Gerard *d* David Lowell Rich

James Wainwright, Ben Murphy, Dirk Blocker, Sally Field, William Windom

The Bridges at Toko-Ri*
US 1954 104m Technicolor
Paramount / Perlberg–Seaton

The comradeship and death of two jet pilots during the Korean War.
Ambitiously staged action thriller with points to make about war, death and politics: a well-worn American formula pitched very hard.

w Valentine Davies, *novel* James E. Michener *d* Mark Robson *ph* Loyal Griggs *m* Lyn Murray

William Holden, Mickey Rooney, Grace Kelly, Fredric March, Robert Strauss, Charles McGraw, Earl Holliman, Willis Bouchey

Brief Encounter****
GB 1945 86m bw
Cineguild (Anthony Havelock-Allan, Ronald Neame)

A suburban housewife on her weekly shopping visits develops a love affair with a local doctor; but he gets a job abroad and they agree not to see each other again.
An outstanding example of good middle-class cinema turned by sheer professional craft into a masterpiece; even those bored by the theme must be riveted by the treatment, especially the use of a dismal railway station and its trains.

w Noel Coward, from his one-act play Still Life *d David Lean ph Robert Krasker*
m Rachmaninov

Celia Johnson, Trevor Howard, Stanley Holloway, Joyce Carey, Cyril Raymond

'Both a pleasure to watch as a well-controlled piece of work, and deeply touching.'—*James Agee*

'Polished as is this film, its strength does not lie in movie technique, of which there is plenty, so much as in the tight realism of its detail.'—*Richard Winnington*

Brief Encounter
GB 1975 74m colour TVM
ITC / Carlo Ponti / Cecil Clarke (Duane C. Bogie)

Almost a word-for-word remake, but with the wrong talent off form. A disaster.

w John Bowen d Alan Bridges

Richard Burton, Sophia Loren, Jack Hedley, Rosemary Leach, Anne Firbank, John Le Mesurier

Brigadoon*
US 1954 108m Anscocolor Cinemascope
MGM (Arthur Freed)

Two Americans in Scotland find a ghost village which awakens only once every hundred years.
Likeable but disappointing adaptation of a Lost Horizonish Broadway musical, marred by artificial sets and jaded direction.

w Alan Jay Lerner, from his play
songs Frederick Loewe, Alan Jay Lerner
d Vincente Minnelli *ph* Joseph Ruttenberg
md Johnny Green

Gene Kelly, Cyd Charisse, Van Johnson, Jimmy Thompson, Elaine Stewart, Barry Jones, Eddie Quillan

'The whimsical dream world it creates holds no compelling attractions.'—*Penelope Houston*

Brigham Young**
US 1940 112m bw
TCF (Kenneth MacGowan)

The story of the Mormon trek to Utah.
Ambitious but rather dull interpretation of history, seen as a western with romantic fictional trimmings.

w Lamar Trotti, *story* Louis Bromfield *d* Henry Hathaway *ph Arthur Miller m* Alfred Newman

Dean Jagger, Tyrone Power, Linda Darnell, Brian Donlevy, Jane Darwell, John Carradine, Mary Astor, Vincent Price, Moroni Olsen

Bright Eyes*
US 1934 84m bw
TCF

An orphan finds herself torn between foster-parents.
The first of Shirley Temple's genuine star vehicles has a liveliness and cheerfulness hard to find today. As a production, however, it is decidedly economical.

w William Conselman *d* David Butler *ph* Arthur Miller *m* Samuel Kaylin

Shirley Temple, James Dunn, Lois Wilson, *Jane Withers*, Judith Allen

Bright Leaf
US 1950 110m bw
Warner (Henry Blanke)

A 19th-century tobacco farmer builds a cigarette empire.
Quite agreeable but disjointed fictional biopic, more about love than tobacco.

w Ranald MacDougall *d* Michael Curtiz *ph* Karl Freund *m* Max Steiner

Gary Cooper, Lauren Bacall, Patricia Neal, Jack Carson, Donald Crisp, Gladys George, Elizabeth Patterson, Jeff Corey, Taylor Holmes

Bright Road*
US 1953 69m bw
MGM (Sol Baer Fielding)

In an all-black school, a problem child finds himself when he helps to rid the school of a swarm of bees.
Slight but attractive second feature, unostentatiously set in a black community.

w Emmet Lavery *d* Gerald Mayer *ph* Alfred Gilks *m* David Rose

Dorothy Dandridge, Harry Belafonte, Robert Horton, Philip Hepburn, Barbara Ann Sanders

Bright Victory*
US 1951 97m bw
Universal (Robert Buckner)
GB title: *Lights Out*

A blinded soldier adjusts to civilian life.
Well-meaning if rather slow and sticky, this drama is more sentimental than realistic but has good performances.

w Robert Buckner, *novel* Bayard Kendrick *d* Mark Robson *ph* William Daniels *m* Frank Skinner

Arthur Kennedy, Peggy Dow, Julia Adams, James Edwards, Will Geer, Minor Watson, Jim Backus

Brighton Rock***
GB 1947 92m bw
Associated British / The Boultings
US title: *Young Scarface*

The teenage leader of a racetrack gang uses a waitress as alibi to cover a murder, and marries her. He later decides to be rid of her, but fate takes a hand in his murder plot.
A properly 'seedy' version of Graham Greene's 'entertainment', very flashily done for the most part but with a trick ending which allows the heroine to keep her illusions.

w Graham Greene, Terence Rattigan *d John Boulting ph* Harry Waxman *m* Hans May

Richard Attenborough, Hermione Baddeley, *Harcourt Williams*, William Hartnell, Alan Wheatley, Carol Marsh

'The film is slower, much less compelling, and, if you get me, less cinematic than the book, as a child's guide to which I hereby offer it.'—*Richard Winnington*

Bring Me the Head of Alfredo Garcia
US 1974 112m De Luxe
UA / Optimus / Churubusco (Martin Baum)

A wealthy Mexican offers a million dollars for the head of a man who seduced his daughter, and claimants find that grave robbing is involved.
Gruesome, sickly action melodrama with revolting detail; the nadir of a director obsessed by violence.

w Gordon Dawson, Sam Peckinpah *d* Sam Peckinpah *ph* Alex Phillips Jnr *m* Jerry Goldsmith

Warren Oates, Gig Young, Isela Vega, Robert Webber, Helmut Dantine, Emilio Fernandez, Kris Kristofferson

Bring On the Girls
US 1945 92m Technicolor
Paramount (Fred Kohlmar)

A millionaire joins the navy in the hope that a girl will love him for himself.
A good example of the gaily-coloured but witless drivel which occasionally came out of the big studios towards the end of the war.

w Karl Tunberg, Darrell Ware *d* Sidney Lanfield *ph* Karl Struss *md* Robert Emmett Dolan

Veronica Lake, Eddie Bracken, Sonny Tufts,

Marjorie Reynolds, Grant Mitchell, Alan Mowbray, Porter Hall

Bringing Up Baby***
US 1938 102m bw
RKO (Howard Hawks)

A zany girl causes a zoology professor to lose a dinosaur bone and a pet leopard in the same evening.
Outstanding crazy comedy which barely pauses for romance and ends up with the whole splendid cast in jail.

w Dudley Nichols, Hagar Wilde d Howard Hawks ph Russell Metty *m* Roy Webb

Katharine Hepburn, Cary Grant, May Robson, Charles Ruggles, Walter Catlett, Fritz Feld, Jonathan Hale, Barry Fitzgerald

'I am happy to report that it is funny from the word go, that it has no other meaning to recommend it . . . and that I wouldn't swap it for practically any three things of the current season.'—*Otis Ferguson*

'It may be the American movies' closest equivalent to Restoration comedy.'—*Pauline Kael*

'Crazy comedies continue to become crazier, and there will soon be few actors and actresses left who have no straw in their hair.'—*Basil Wright*

Britannia Mews
GB 1948 91m bw
TCF (William Perlberg)
US title: *The Forbidden Street*

In Victorian times, the widow of a puppetmaster eventually marries his lookalike who rebuilds their puppet theatre.
Curious and uncertain comedy drama set among yesterday's high society, with poorly played leads but an interesting supporting cast and technical assurance.

w Ring Lardner Jnr, *novel* Margery Sharp *d* Jean Negulesco *ph* Georges Périnal *ad* Andrei Andrejew *m* Malcolm Arnold

Dana Andrews, Maureen O'Hara, Sybil Thorndike Wilfrid Hyde White, Fay Compton, A. E. Matthews

British Agent*
US 1934 81m bw
Warner (Henry Blanke)

In 1910 Russia, a Britisher falls in love with a lady spy.
Sluggish and dated romantic melodrama, notable only for Howard's performance and some directional felicities.

w Laird Doyle, *novel* H. Bruce Lockhart *d* Michael Curtiz *ph* Ernest Haller *ad* Anton Grot

Leslie Howard, Kay Francis, William Gargan, *Irving Pichel*, Philip Reed, Walter Byron, J. Carrol Naish, Halliwell Hobbes

British Intelligence
US 1940 63m bw
Warner

During World War I a German lady spy becomes a guest in the house of a British war official, the butler of which is the leader of a German spy ring.
Second feature remake of *Three Faces East* (qv); still quite an entertaining melodrama.

w Lee Katz, *play* Anthony Paul Kelly *d* Terry Morse *ph* Sid Hickox

Boris Karloff, Margaret Lindsay, Maris Wrixon, Bruce Lester, Leonard Mudie, Holmes Herbert

Broadway
US 1942 90m bw
Universal (Bruce Manning)

George Raft recalls his days as a hoofer in a New York speakeasy, and in particular a murder involving gangsters and chorus girls.
Minor crime melodrama which after interminable scene-setting paints an effective picture of the twenties but has too slack a grip on narrative.

w Felix Jackson, John Bright, *play* Philip Dunning, George Abbott *d* William A. Seiter *ph* George Barnes *md* Charles Previn

George Raft, Pat O'Brien, S. Z. Sakall, Janet Blair, Broderick Crawford, Marjorie Rambeau

Broadway Bill**
US 1934 104m bw
Columbia (Frank Capra)
GB title: *Strictly Confidential*

A cheerful horse trainer finds he has a winner.
Easygoing romantic comedy with the energetic Capra style in fairly full bloom.

w Robert Riskin, *story* Mark Hellinger *d Frank Capra ph* Joseph Walker

Warner Baxter, Myrna Loy, Walter Connolly, Helen Vinson, Douglass Dumbrille, Raymond Walburn, Lynne Overman, Clarence Muse, Margaret Hamilton, Paul Harvey, Claude Gillingwater, Charles Lane, Ward Bond
† Remade as *Riding High* (qv).

Broadway Limited*
US 1941 75m bw
Hal Roach
GB title: *The Baby Vanishes*

On an express train, a Hollywood publicity stunt backfires.
Wild farce which is not very funny as a whole but has entertaining comic performances.

w Rian James *d* Gordon Dougl *ph* Henry Sharp *m* Charles Previn

Victor McLaglen, Patsy Kelly, *Leonid Kinskey*, Marjorie Woodworth, Dennis O'Keefe, Zasu Pitts, George E. Stone

Broadway Melody*
US 1929 110m bw (Technicolor scenes)
MGM

Chorus girls try to make it big on Broadway.
The screen's very first musical, exceedingly primitive by the standards of even a year later, but rather endearing and with a splendid score.

w James Gleason, Norman Houston, Edmund Goulding *d* Harry Beaumont *ph* John Arnold *songs Nacio Herb Brown, Arthur Freed*

Charles King, Anita Page, Bessie Love, Jed Prouty, Kenneth Thomson, Mary Doran, Eddie Kane

Broadway Melody of 1936*
US 1935 103m bw
MGM (John W. Considine Jnr)

A Broadway producer is at loggerheads with a columnist.
Fairly lively musical with lavish numbers.

w Jack McGowan, Sid Silvers, Moss Hart *d* Roy del Ruth *ph* Charles Rosher *songs Nacio Herb Brown, Arthur Freed*

Jack Benny, Robert Taylor, Una Merkel, *Eleanor Powell*, June Knight, Vilma and Buddy Ebsen, Nick Long Jnr

Broadway Melody of 1938*
US 1937 110m bw
MGM (Jack Cummings)

Backstage problems threaten the opening of a musical show.
Lavish but fairly forgettable musical with top talent.

w Jack McGowan, Sid Silvers *d* Roy del Ruth *ph* William Daniels *songs* Nacio Herb Brown, Arthur Freed

Eleanor Powell, George Murphy, *Sophie Tucker*, Judy Garland, Robert Taylor, Buddy Ebsen, Sid Silvers, Billy Gilbert, Raymond Walburn

Broadway Melody of 1940*
US 1939 102m bw
MGM (Jack Cummings)

A dance team gets to the top.
Splendidly produced but thinly plotted extravaganza with good numbers.

w Leon Gordon, George Oppenheimer *d* Norman Taurog *ph* Oliver T. Marsh, Joseph Ruttenberg *songs* Cole Porter

Fred Astaire, Eleanor Powell, George Murphy, Douglas Macphail, Florence Rice, Frank Morgan, Ian Hunter

Broadway Rhythm*
US 1943 113m Technicolor
MGM (Jack Cummings)

Originally intended as *Broadway Melody of 1944*, this putting-on-a-show extravaganza had only the numbers to commend it.

w Dorothy Kingsley, Harry Clark, from the Kern/Hammerstein operetta Very Warm for May *d* Roy del Ruth *ph* Leonard Smith *songs* various

George Murphy, Ginny Simms, Charles Winninger, Gloria de Haven, Lena Horne, Nancy Walker, Hazel Scott, Eddie Anderson, Ben Blue, Tommy Dorsey and his Orchestra

Broadway Serenade
US 1939 114m bw
MGM (Robert Z. Leonard)
GB title: *Serenade*

Career problems split the marriage of a songwriter and his singing wife.
Lavish but rather dull romantic drama with music.

w Lew Lipton, John T. Foote, Hans Kraly *d* Robert Z. Leonard *md* Herbert Stothart

Jeanette MacDonald, Lew Ayres, Frank Morgan, Ian Hunter, Rita Johnson, Virginia Grey, William Gargan, Katherine Alexander

Broadway thru a Keyhole*
US 1933 90m bw
UA / William Goetz, Raymond Griffith

A tough New York gangster falls for a singer in his nightclub.
Reputed acid observation of the New York scene distinguishes this low-budget gangster drama.

w Gene Town, *story* Walter Winchell *d* Lowell Sherman *ph* Barney McGill *songs* Mack Gordon, Harry Revel

Constance Cummings, Russ Columbo, Paul Kelly, *Blossom Seeley*, Gregory Ratoff, *Texas Guinan*, Hobart Cavanaugh, C. Henry Gordon

Brock's Last Case*
US 1972 98m Technicolor TVM
Universal (Roland Kibbee)

A New York police detective retires to a Californian citrus ranch but finds himself still up to his neck in murder.
Competent telemovie serving as the pilot for a series which later switched back to New York and the title of its original inspiration, *Madigan*.

w Martin Donaldson, Alex Gordon *d* David Lowell Rich *m* Charles Gross

Richard Widmark, Will Geer, John Anderson, Michael Burns, Henry Darrow

Broken Arrow*
US 1950 92m Technicolor
TCF (Julian Blaustein)

A US army scout brings about peace between white man and Apache.
Solemn western which at the time was acclaimed for giving the Indian's point of view (something which had scarcely happened since silent days). As entertainment it was not exciting, but it set Jeff Chandler off on a career playing Cochise with variations, and a TV series of the same name surfaced in 1956.

w Michael Blankfort, *novel* Blood Brother by Elliott Arnold *d* Delmer Daves *ph* Ernest Palmer *m* Alfred Newman

James Stewart, Jeff Chandler, Debra Paget, Basil Ruysdael, Will Geer, Arthur Hunnicutt, Jay Silverheels

'It has probably done more to soften racial hostilities than most movies designed to instruct, indict and inspire.'—*Pauline Kael*

Broken Blossoms*
GB 1936 78m bw
Twickenham (Julius Hagen)

In old Limehouse, a brutal boxer kills his daughter when she falls in love with a Chinaman.
A curiosity based on D. W. Griffith's 1919 classic, always an absurd melodrama in a never-never setting and now made even more so, but with a fairly handsome production and interesting acting.

w Emlyn Williams, *novel* The Chink and the Child by Thomas Burke *d* John Bra (Hans Brahm)

Emlyn Williams, Dolly Haas, Arthur Margetson, Gibb McLaughlin, Donald Calthrop, Ernest Sefton, Jerry Verno, Bertha Belmore, Ernest Jay, Kathleen Harrison, Basil Radford, C. V. France

Broken Journey
GB 1948 89m bw
Gainsborough (Sydney Box)

A plane crashes in the Alps, and the survivors take different attitudes to their situation.
Unpersuasive and stagey melodrama which wastes some good talent.

w Robert Westerby *d* Ken Annakin *ph* Jack Cox *m* John Greenwood

Phyllis Calvert, James Donald, Margot Grahame, Francis L. Sullivan, Raymond Huntley, Derek Bond, Guy Rolfe, David Tomlinson

Broken Lance*
US 1954 96m De Luxe Cinemascope
TCF (Sol C. Siegel)

An autocratic cattle baron causes dissension among his sons.
Western remake of *House of Strangers*, quite well done.

w Richard Murphy *d* Edward Dmytryk *ph* Joe MacDonald *m* Leigh Harline

Spencer Tracy, Richard Widmark, Robert Wagner, Jean Peters, Katy Jurado, Earl Holliman, Hugh O'Brian, Eduard Franz, E. G. Marshall

Broken Lullaby*
US 1932 77m bw
Paramount
GB and original title: *The Man I Killed*

A young Frenchman goes to Germany to seek out the family of the man he killed in the war, and is accepted by them as a friend.
This most untypical Lubitsch film now seems very dated but was deeply felt at the time and has plenty of cinematic grip.

w Ernest Vajda, Samson Raphaelson, *play* L'Homme que J'ai Tué by Maurice Rostand *d Ernst Lubitsch* *ph* Victor Milner *ad* Hans Dreier

Lionel Barrymore, Phillips Holmes, Nancy Carroll, Tom Douglas, Zasu Pitts, Lucien Littlefield, Lois Carver, Emma Dunn

'The best talking picture that has yet been seen and heard.'—*Robert E. Sherwood*

Bronk
US 1975 74m colour TVM
MGM

A homicide detective on suspension tracks down a narcotics ring.
Utterly predictable crime hokum resting on its star, who carried the subsequent series for a year.

w Ed Waters, Al Martinez, Carroll O'Connor, Bruce Geller *d* Richard Donner

Jack Palance, David Birney, Tony King, Joanna Moore, Henry Beckman

Brother John*
US 1970 94m Eastmancolor
Columbia / E and R (Joel Glickman)

A mysterious black man comes to town for a family funeral and is suspected by the townsfolk of various sinister motives, but when they imprison him he is freed by a sympathizer.
The humans are all mean-minded, the saintly visitor is either Christ or an emissary from another planet. Either way, we have been here before, but although this little fantasy has nothing clear to say it is quite enjoyable on the surface.

w Ernest Kinoy *d* James Goldstone *ph* Gerald Perry Finnerman *m* Quincy Jones

Sidney Poitier, Bradford Dillman, Will Geer, Beverly Todd, Ramon Pieri, Warren J. Kemmerling, Paul Winfield, Lincoln Kilpatrick

Brother Orchid*
US 1940 91m bw
Warner (Hal B. Wallis)

A gangster, 'taken for a ride' by his former friends, escapes and becomes a monk.
Rather uneasy blend of comedy, drama and religion, with some good scenes.

w Earl Baldwin, *story* Richard Connell *d* Lloyd Bacon *ph* Tony Gaudio

Edward G. Robinson, Humphrey Bogart, Donald Crisp, Ann Sothern, Ralph Bellamy, Allen Jenkins, Cecil Kellaway

Brother Rat*
US 1938 89m bw
Warner (Robert Lord)

Fun and games with the cadets at a military academy.
Brisk but dated farce from a highly successful Broadway original; remade as *About Face*.

w Richard Macauley, Jerry Wald, *play* Fred Finklehoffe, John Monks *d* William Keighley *ph* Ernest Haller

Wayne Morris, Eddie Albert, Ronald Reagan, Priscilla Lane, Jane Bryan, Jane Wyman, Johnnie Davis, Henry O'Neill

Brother Rat and a Baby
US 1939 87m bw
Warner (Robert Lord)
GB title: *Baby Be Good*

Scatty follow-up to the above, with the cadets graduating.

w Jerry Wald, Richard Macauley *d* Ray Enright *ph* Charles Rosher

Wayne Morris, Eddie Albert, Ronald Reagan, Priscilla Lane, Jane Wyman, Jane Bryan, Arthur Treacher, Moroni Olsen

Brother Sun, Sister Moon
GB / Italy
1972 122m Technicolor Panavision
Paramount / Vic Films / Euro International (Luciano Perugia)

The life of Francis of Assisi.
Good-looking but relentlessly boring view of a medieval saint as a kind of early flower person.

w Suso Cecchi d'Amico, Kenneth Ross, Lina Wertmuller, Franco Zeffirelli *d* Franco Zeffirelli *ph* Ennio Guarnieri *m* Donovan

Graham Faulkner, Judi Bowker, Alec Guinness (as Pope Innocent III), Leigh Lawson, Kenneth Cranham, Lee Montague, Valentina Cortese

'If I were Pope, I would burn it.'—*Stanley Kauffmann*

The Brotherhood*
US 1968 96m Technicolor
Paramount / Brotherhood Company

A Mafia executive welcomes his younger brother into the syndicate, but is finally executed by him.
Dour melodrama with tragic pretensions: well made but rather tedious and violent.

w Lewis John Carlino *d* Martin Ritt *ph* Boris Kaufman *m* Lalo Schifrin

Kirk Douglas, Alex Cord, *Luther Adler*, Irene Papas, Susan Strasberg, Murray Hamilton, Eduardo Ciannelli

The Brotherhood of Satan*
US 1970 93m Techniscope
Columbia / LQJAF / Four Star Excelsior (L. Q. Jones, Alvy Moore)

A village is isolated by an outbreak of diabolism.
Fresh and intriguing minor horror film with imaginative touches.

w William Welch *d Bernard McEveety* *ph* John Arthur Morril *m* Jaime Mendoza-Nava

Strother Martin, L. Q. Jones, Charles Bateman, Anna Capri, Charles Robinson, Alvy Moore, Geri Reischl

The Brotherhood of the Bell*
US 1971 100m colour TVM
Cinema Center (Hugh Benson)

A secret fraternity takes stern measures against the enemies of its members.
Unusual mystery, quite watchable and well done.

w David Karp *d* Paul Wendkos

Glenn Ford, Dean Jagger, Maurice Evans, Rosemary Forsyth

Brotherly Love see Country Dance

The Brothers**
GB 1947 98m bw
GFD / Sydney Box

An orphan girl comes to a Skye fishing family at the turn of the century, and causes superstition, sexual jealousy and tragedy.
Wildly melodramatic but good-looking open-air melodrama, a surprising and striking British film of its time.

w Muriel and Sydney Box, *novel* L. A. G. Strong *d David Macdonald ph Stephen Dade*

Patricia Roc, Maxwell Reed, *Duncan Macrae* (a splendidly malevolent performance), Will Fyffe, Andrew Crawford, Finlay Currie

Brothers in Law*
GB 1957 97m bw
British Lion / the Boultings

A young barrister has comic misdemeanours in and out of court.
The lighter side of the law, from a bestseller by a judge; mechanically amusing and not in the same street as its predecessor *Private's Progress*, though it seemed hilarious at the time.

w Roy Boulting, Frank Harvey, Jeffrey Dell, *novel Henry Cecil d* John Boulting *ph* Max Greene *m* Benjamin Frankel

Ian Carmichael, Terry-Thomas, Richard Attenborough, *Miles Malleson, Eric Barker*, Irene Handl, John Le Mesurier, Olive Sloane, Kynaston Reeves

The Brothers Karamazov*
US 1958 146m Metrocolor
MGM (Pandro S. Berman)

In 19th-century Russia, the father of three sons is murdered and the wrong brother is found guilty.
Decent but decidedly unenthralling Hollywood compression of a classic, faithful to the letter but not the spirit of the book, and with few memorable moments or performances.

w Richard Brooks, *novel* Fedor Dostoievsky *d* Richard Brooks *ph* John Alton *m* Bronislau Kaper *ad* William A. Horning, Paul Groesse

Yul Brynner, Maria Schell, Richard Basehart, Claire Bloom, Lee J. Cobb, Albert Salmi, William Shatner, Judith Evelyn

The Brothers Rico
US 1957 91m bw
Columbia / William Goetz (Lewis J. Rachmil)

An accountant fails to retrieve his brothers from a life of crime.
Moderate gangster fare with good credentials but more talk than action.

w Lewis Meltzer, Ben Perry, *novel* Georges Simenon *d* Phil Karlson *ph* Burnett Guffey *m* George Duning

Richard Conte, James Darren, Dianne Foster, Kathryn Grant, Larry Gates, Lamont Johnson, Harry Bellaver

Brown on Resolution*
GB 1935 80m bw
Gaumont (Michael Balcon)
Later retitled: *Forever England*; US title: *Born for Glory*

In the 1914 war in the Mediterranean, a seaman holds a German warship at bay with a rifle.
Uneasy amalgam of adventure heroics and character study, interesting for its effort.
Remade as *Singlehanded* (qv).

w Michael Hogan, Gerard Fairlie, J. O. C. Orton, *novel* C. S. Forester *d* Walter Forde

John Mills, Betty Balfour, Barry Mackay, Jimmy Hanley, Howard Marion Crawford, H. G. Stoker

The Browning Version*
GB 1951 90m bw
GFD / Javelin (Teddy Baird)

Retiring through ill health, a classics master finds that he is hated by his unfaithful wife, his headmaster and his pupils. An unexpected act of kindness gives him courage to face the future.
A rather thin extension of a one-act play, capped by a thank-you speech which is wildly out of character. Dialogue and settings are smooth, but the actors are not really happy with their roles.

w Terence Rattigan, from his play *d* Anthony Asquith *ph* Desmond Dickinson

Michael Redgrave, Jean Kent, Nigel Patrick, Wilfrid Hyde White, Bill Travers, Ronald Howard

Brute Force**
US 1947 96m bw
U-I

Six violent convicts revolt against a sadistic warden and try to escape.
Vivid and rather repellent prison melodrama leading up to an explosive climax; its savagery seemed at the time to break fresh ground.

w Richard Brooks d Jules Dassin ph William Daniels *m* Miklos Rozsa

Burt Lancaster, Charles Bickford, Hume Cronyn, Ella Raines, Yvonne de Carlo

The Buccaneer*
US 1938 90m bw
Paramount (Cecil B. de Mille)

During the 1812 war, pirate Jean Lafitte helps president Andrew Jackson to repel the British. Sprightly adventure romance with generally good production and acting.

w Jeanie Macpherson, Edwin Justus Mayer, Harold Lamb, C. Gardner Sullivan *d* Cecil B. de Mille *ph* Victor Milner *m* Boris Morros

Fredric March, Franciska Gaal, *Akim Tamiroff*, Margot Grahame, Walter Brennan, Ian Keith, Spring Byington, Douglass Dumbrille, Robert Barrat, Hugh Sothern, Beulah Bondi, Anthony Quinn, Montagu Love

The Buccaneer
US 1958 121m Technicolor Vistavision
Paramount / Cecil B. de Mille (Henry Wilcoxon)

Slow, slack and stolid remake of the 1938 film, with practically no excitement or interest and very obvious studio sets.

w Jesse L. Lasky Jnr, Berenice Mosk, from the earlier screenplay *d* Anthony Quinn *ph* Loyal Griggs *m* Elmer Bernstein

Yul Brynner, Claire Bloom, Charles Boyer, Inger Stevens, Henry Hull, Charlton Heston, E. G. Marshall, Douglass Dumbrille, Lorne Greene, Ted de Corsia, Robert F. Simon

Buck and the Preacher
US 1971 103m colour
Columbia / E and R / Belafonte (Joel Glickman)

Nightriders chasing escaped slaves are outwitted by a wagon train guide and a con man.
Lively, easygoing western with a largely black cast, and a message of militancy sugar-coated by Hollywood hokum.

w Ernest Kinoy *d* Sidney Poitier *ph* Alex Phillips *m* Benny Carter

Sidney Poitier, Harry Belafonte, Ruby Dee, Cameron Mitchell, Denny Miller, Nita Talbot, John Kelly

Buck Privates*
US 1941 84m bw
Universal (Alex Gottlieb)
GB title: *Rookies*

Two incompetents in the army accidentally become heroes.
Abbott and Costello's first starring vehicle is a tired bundle of army jokes and old routines separated by plot and romance, but it sent the comedians right to the top, where they stayed for ten years.

w Arthur T. Horman *d* Arthur Lubin *ph* Milton Krasner *m* Charles Previn

Bud Abbott, Lou Costello, Lee Bowman, Alan Curtis, Jane Frazee, *The Andrews Sisters, Nat Pendleton*, Samuel S. Hinds, Shemp Howard

Buck Privates Come Home
US 1946 77m bw
U-I
GB title: *Rookies Come Home*

Incompetent war veterans are demobilized and find civilian life tough.
Thin star comedy with a good final chase.

w John Grant, Frederic I. Rinaldo, Robert Lees *d* Charles T. Barton *ph* Charles Van Enger

Bud Abbott, Lou Costello, Beverly Simmons, Tom Brown, Nat Pendleton

Buckskin
US 1968 97m Pathecolor
Paramount / A. C. Lyles

In the frontier town of Gloryhole a gambler is routed by the new marshal.
Routine old-fashioned western with this producer's predictable gallery of weatherbeaten familiar faces.

w Michael Fisher *d* Michael Moore *ph* W. Wallace Kelley *m* Jimmie Haskell

Barry Sullivan, Joan Caulfield, Lon Chaney Jnr, John Russell, Richard Arlen, Barbara Hale, Bill Williams, Barton Maclane

Buffalo Bill*
US 1944 89m Technicolor
TCF (Harry Sherman)

A moderately fictitious account of the life of William Cody, from buffalo hunter to wild west showman.
Easygoing entertainment which turns from western excitements to domestic drama. Generally watchable.

w Aeneas Mackenzie, Clements Ripley, Cecile Kramer *d* William Wellman *ph* Leon Shamroy *m* David Buttolph

Joel McCrea, Maureen O'Hara, Linda Darnell, Thomas Mitchell, Edgar Buchanan, Anthony Quinn, Moroni Olsen

Buffalo Bill and the Indians, or Sitting Bull's History Lesson*
US 1976 118m colour Panavision
UA / Robert Altman

During winter camp for his wild west show,

Buffalo Bill Cody and his friends discuss life and his own myth.
Anti-action, alienation-effect talk piece which has some points of interest for sophisticates but is likely to set western addicts asking for their money back.

w Alan Rudolph, Robert Altman, *play* Indians by Arthur Kopit *d* Robert Altman *ph* Paul Lohmann *m* Richard Baskin

Paul Newman, Burt Lancaster, Joel Grey, Kevin McCarthy, Geraldine Chaplin, Harvey Keitel, John Considine, Denver Pyle

'The western is an enormously resilient form, but never has that resilience been tested quite so much as in this movie . . . it isn't really a movie, it's a happening.'—*Arthur Knight*

Bug
US 1975 101m · Movielab
Paramount / William Castle

Large rocklike insects appear after an earthquake and set fire to themselves and their victims.
Absurd, overlong and rather nasty horror film with no visible redeeming features.

w William Castle, Thomas Page, *novel* The Hephaestus Plague by Thomas Page *d* Jeannot Szwarc *ph* Michel Hugo, Ken Middleham *m* Charles Fox

Bradford Dillman, Joanna Miles, Richard Gilliland, Jamie Smith Jackson, Alan Fudge, Patty McCormack

'The finer scientific points are to say the least elusive.'—*David Robinson*

Bugles in the Afternoon
US 1952 85m Technicolor
William Cagney

In the US army at the time of Custer's last stand, a young officer is victimized by a jealous rival.
Modest, adequate western with nice scenery but no surprises.

w Geoffrey Homes, Harry Brown, *novel* Ernest Haycox *d* Roy Rowland *ph* Wilfrid Cline *m* Dmitri Tiomkin

Ray Milland, Hugh Marlowe, Helena Carter, Forrest Tucker, Barton Maclane, George Reeves, James Millican, Gertrude Michael

Bulldog Drummond*
US 1929 90m bw
Samuel Goldwyn

After advertising for adventure, ex-war hero Drummond is approached by an American girl whose uncle is being held prisoner in a fake nursing home by villainous Carl Petersen.
This is the closest the screen ever came to the original Drummond character, debonair yet taking personal and unnecessary vengeance on the chief villain. A fairly primitive talkie with little movement, yet consistently interesting.

w Sidney Howard, *play* 'Sapper' (H. C. McNeile) *d* F. Richard Jones *ph* George Barnes, Gregg Toland *ad William Cameron Menzies*

Ronald Colman, Joan Bennett, *Claud Allister* (as Algy), Lilyan Tashman, Montagu Love, Lawrence Grant

Bulldog Drummond Strikes Back*
US 1934 83m bw
Samuel Goldwyn

Drummond gets married, but delays his honeymoon to investigate a mysterious London house with a disappearing body.
Slow-starting, then intriguing light mystery which becomes repetitive and silly. Performances and production enjoyable.

w Nunnally Johnson *d* Roy del Ruth *ph* Peverell Marley

Ronald Colman, Loretta Young, C. Aubrey Smith, *Charles Butterworth* (Algy), Warner Oland, Mischa Auer, Una Merkel

† Later Drummond films included a few from Paramount in the late thirties with John Howard, three in the late forties with Tom Conway, and two totally unrecognizable sixties personifications by Richard Johnson, *Deadlier than the Male* and *Some Girls Do.*

Bulldog Jack*
GB 1935 72m bw
Gaumont (Michael Balcon)
US title: *Alias Bulldog Drummond*

A playboy poses as Bulldog Drummond when the real man is injured, and manages to foil the thieves and save the girl.
After a slowish start, this comedy thriller works up into a fine frenzy with exciting scenes on the London Underground and in the British Museum.

w H. C. McNeile, Gerard Fairlie, J. O. C. Orton, Sidney Gilliat *d Walter Forde*

Jack Hulbert, Ralph Richardson, Claude Hulbert, Fay Wray, Athole Fleming, Paul Graetz

'There is . . . a mad train ride towards the terminus and destruction, as good as anything in screen melodrama.'—*Peter John Dyer*

A Bullet for Joey
US 1955 85m bw
UA / Sam Bischoff David Diamond

A Canadian policeman prevents the murder of an atomic scientist.
Listless low-budgeter with familiar stars below par.

w Geoffrey Homes, A. I. Bezzerides *d* Lewis Allen *ph* Harry Neumann *m* Harry Sukman

Edward G. Robinson, George Raft, Audrey Totter, George Dolenz, Peter Hanson, Peter Van Eyck

A Bullet is Waiting
US 1954 82m Technicolor
Columbia / Welsch (Howard Welsch)

A plane accident brings a policeman and his prisoner to a lonely farm, where a girl and her father bring a fresh twist to the situation.
Disappointing melodrama full of pretentious moralizing and fey characterization.

w Thames Williamson, Casey Robinson *d* John Farrow *ph* Franz Planer *m* Dmitri Tiomkin

Jean Simmons, Rory Calhoun, Stephen McNally, Brian Aherne

Bullets or Ballots*
US 1936 81m bw
Warner (Lou Edelman)

A city cop goes undercover to break the mob.
Vivid routine gangster thriller, not quite of the top flight, but nearly.

w Seton I. Miller *d* William Keighley *ph* Hal Mohr *m* Heinz Roemheld

Edward G. Robinson, Joan Blondell, Humphrey Bogart, Barton Maclane, Frank McHugh, Dick Purcell, George E. Stone

The Bullfighter and the Lady
US 1950 87m bw
Republic / John Wayne (Budd Boetticher)

A young American in Mexico is fascinated by bullfighting but during training accidentally causes the death of a great matador.
Predictable, rather boring plot given routine treatment: for aficionados only.

w James Edward Grant *d* Budd Boetticher *ph* Jack Draper *m* Victor Young

Robert Stack, Gilbert Roland, Joy Page, Katy Jurado, Virginia Grey, John Hubbard

The Bullfighters*
US 1945 60m bw
TCF (William Girard)

Two detectives in Mexico find that one of them resembles a famous matador.
Laurel and Hardy's last American feature is poor enough as a whole, but at least has a few sequences in their earlier style.

w Scott Darling *d* Mal St Clair *ph* Norbert Brodine

Stan Laurel, Oliver Hardy, Richard Lane, Carol Woode

Bullitt***
US 1968 113m Technicolor
Warner / Solar (Philip D'Antoni)

A San Francisco police detective conceals the death of an underground witness in his charge, and goes after the killers himself.
Routine cop thriller with undoubted charisma, distinguished by a splendid car chase which takes one's mind off the tedious plot. Technical credits first class.

w Harry Kleiner, Alan R. Trustman, *novel* Mute Witness by Robert L. Pike *d Peter Yates* *ph William A. Fraker* *m* Lalo Schifrin

Steve McQueen, Jacqueline Bisset, Robert Vaughn, Don Gordon, Robert Duvall, Simon Oakland

'It has energy, drive, impact, and above all, style.'—*Hollis Alpert*

Bundle of Joy
US 1956 98m Technicolor RKOscope
RKO / Edmund Grainger

A shopgirl finds an abandoned baby and everyone thinks it is hers.
Tame musical remake of *Bachelor Mother*; some laughs, but poor numbers.

w Norman Krasna, Arthur Sheekman, Robert Carson *d* Norman Taurog *ph* William Snyder *m* Josef Myrow

Debbie Reynolds, Eddie Fisher, Adolphe Menjou, Melville Cooper, Tommy Noonan, Nita Talbot, Una Merkel, Robert H. Harris

Bunny Lake is Missing**
GB 1965 107m bw Panavision
Columbia / Wheel (Otto Preminger)

The 4-year-old illegitimate daughter of an American girl in London disappears, and no one can be found to admit that she ever existed.
A nightmarish gimmick story, with more gimmicks superimposed along the way to say nothing of a *Psycho*ish ending; some of the decoration works and makes even the unconvincing story compelling, while the cast is alone worth the price of admission.

w John and Penelope Mortimer, *novel* Evelyn Piper *d* Otto Preminger *ph* Denys Coop *m* Paul Glass *pd* Don Ashton *titles* Saul Bass

Laurence Olivier, Carol Lynley, Keir Dullea, Noel Coward, Martita Hunt, Finlay Currie, Clive Revill, Anna Massey, Lucie Mannheim

'It has the enjoyable hallmarks of really high calibre professionalism.'—*Penelope Houston*

Bunny O'Hare
US 1971 92m Movielab
AIP (Gerd Oswald, Norman T. Herman)

A middle-aged widow and an ex-con plumber become bank robbers, dressed as hippies and escaping on a motor cycle.
Unappealing, ill-thought-out comedy with pretensions to satire, an unhappy venture for both stars.

w Stanley Z. Cherry, Coslough Johnson *d* Gerd Oswald *ph* Loyal Griggs, John Stephens *m* Billy Strange

Bette Davis, Ernest Borgnine, Jack Cassidy, Joan Delaney, Jay Robinson, John Astin

Buona Sera Mrs Campbell*
US 1968 113m Technicolor
UA / Connaught (Melvin Frank)

Wartime USAF comrades reassemble twenty years later in an Italian village, and three find that they have been paying paternity money to the same local glamour girl.
Agreeably cast, pleasantly set and photographed, quite funny in parts, this comedy of middle age unfortunately outstays its welcome and lets its invention peter out.

w Melvin Frank, Denis Norden, Sheldon Keller *d* Melvin Frank *ph* Gabor Pogany *m* Riz Ortolani

Gina Lollobrigida, Telly Savalas, Phil Silvers, Peter Lawford, Lee Grant, Marian Moses, Shelley Winters

Bus Riley's Back in Town*
US 1965 93m Eastmancolor
U-I (Elliott Kastner)

An ex-sailor wants to settle back into small-town life but finds that his girl friend has married.
Watchable, middling, routine small-town drama in the style of *Picnic*.

w Walter Gage (William Inge) *d Harvey Hart* *ph* Russell Metty *m* Richard Markowitz

Michael Parks, Ann-Margret, Jocelyn Brando, Janet Margolin, Kim Darby, Brad Dexter, Larry Storch, Crahan Denton, Mimsy Farmer, David Carradine

Bus Stop**
US 1956 96m Eastmancolor
Cinemascope
TCF (Buddy Adler)

In a rodeo town, a simple-thinking cowboy meets a café singer and asks her to marry him.
Sex comedy-drama, a modest entertainment in familiar American vein, very well done but rather over-inflated by its star.

w George Axelrod, *play* William Inge *d* Joshua Logan *ph* Milton Krasner *m* Alfred Newman, Cyril Mockridge

Marilyn Monroe, Don Murray, Betty Field, Arthur O'Connell, Eileen Heckart, Robert Bray, Hope Lange, Hans Conried, Casey Adams

'The film demands of its principal performers a purely physical display of their bodies viewed as sexual machinery.'—*David Robinson*

Busman's Honeymoon*
GB 1940 99m bw
MGM (Harold Huth)
US title: *Haunted Honeymoon*

Lord Peter Wimsey finds a murder to be solved in his honeymoon cottage.
Pleasant, slightly flat film version of a favourite old-fashioned detective novel.

w Monckton Hoffe, Angus Macphail, Harold Goldman, *novel* Dorothy L. Sayers *d* Arthur Woods

Robert Montgomery, Constance Cummings, Leslie Banks, *Seymour Hicks*, Robert Newton, Googie Withers, Frank Pettingell, Joan Kemp-Welch

The Buster Keaton Story*
US 1957 91m bw Vistavision
Paramount (Sidney Sheldon, Robert Smith)

A biopic of the great silent comedian, with the emphasis on his years of downfall through drink.
An interesting recreation of Hollywood in the twenties and thirties is the main asset of this otherwise dismal tribute to a man whose greatness the star is unable to suggest apart from a few acrobatic moments.

w Robert Smith, Sidney Sheldon *d* Sidney Sheldon *ph* Loyal Griggs *m* Victor Young

Donald O'Connor, Rhonda Fleming, Ann Blyth, Peter Lorre, Larry Keating, Richard Anderson, Dave Willock

The Busy Body
US 1966 102m Techniscope
Paramount / William Castle

A gangster is buried in a suit with a million dollar lining which various people are out to get.
Unfunny black comedy; laboured handling makes it a joke in poor taste.

w Ben Starr, *novel* Donald E. Westlake *d* William Castle *ph* Hal Stine *m* Vic Mizzy

Robert Ryan, Sid Caesar, Arlene Golonka, Anne Baxter, Kay Medford, Charles McGraw

But I Don't Want to Get Married
US 1970 72m colour TVM
Aaron Spelling

A widower is inundated with candidates to be the mother of his family.
Pleasant comedy which is neither quite funny nor quite moving enough.

w Roland Wolpert *d* Jerry Paris

Herschel Bernardi, Kay Medford, Shirley Jones, Sue Lyon, Nanette Fabray

But Not for Me
US 1959 105m bw
Paramount (William Perlberg, George Seaton)

An ageing, washed-up Broadway producer is loved by his young drama student secretary.
Rather heavy-going remake of *Accent on Youth*, efficiently performed but lacking the original gaiety.

w John Michael Hayes *d* Walter Lang *ph* Robert Burks *m* Leith Stevens

Clark Gable, Carroll Baker, Lilli Palmer, Lee J. Cobb, Barry Coe, Thomas Gomez

Butch Cassidy and the Sundance Kid***
US 1969 110m De Luxe Panavision
TCF / Campanile (John Foreman)

A hundred years ago, two western train robbers keep one step ahead of the law until finally tracked down to Bolivia.
Humorous, cheerful, poetic, cinematic account of two semi-legendary outlaws, winningly acted and directed. One of the decade's great commercial successes, not least because of the song 'Raindrops Keep Fallin' on My Head'.

w William Goldman d George Roy Hill ph Conrad Hall m Burt Bacharach

Paul Newman, Robert Redford, Katharine Ross, Strother Martin, Henry Jones, Jeff Corey, Cloris Leachman, Ted Cassidy, Kenneth Mars

Butley*
US / GB 1973 130m Eastmancolor
American Express / Ely Landau / Cinevision

Personal problems assail an English lecturer at a university college.
Adequate but not outstanding transcription (for the American Film Theatre) of a successful and percipient play.

w Simon Gray, from his play *d* Harold Pinter *ph* Gerry Fisher *m* none

Alan Bates, Jessica Tandy, Richard Callaghan, Susan Engel, Michael Byrne

The Buttercup Chain*
GB 1970 95m Technicolor Panavision
Columbia (Leslie Gilliat, John Whitney, Philip Waddilove)

A hothouse sex quartet changes partners with bewildering rapidity against a background of European splendour.
Chi-chi romance with a fashionably disillusioned and tragic ending. As watchable as the best TV commercials, but totally empty.

w Peter Draper, *novel* Janice Elliott *d* Robert Ellis Miller *ph* Douglas Slocombe *m* Richard Rodney Bennett

Hywel Bennett, Leigh Taylor-Young, Jane Asher, Sven-Bertil Taube, Clive Revill, Roy Dotrice

Butterfield Eight
US 1960 108m Metrocolor Cinemascope
MGM / Afton / Linebrook (Pandro S. Berman)

A society call girl has a complex love life.
This coy sex drama seemed mildly daring in 1960, but has since been well outclassed in that field and certainly has nothing else going for it except good production values.

w Charles Schnee, John Michael Hayes, *novel* John O'Hara *d* Daniel Mann *ph* Joseph Ruttenberg, Charles Harten *m* Bronislau Kaper

Elizabeth Taylor, Laurence Harvey, Eddie Fisher, Dina Merrill, Mildred Dunnock, Betty Field, Jeffrey Lynn, Kay Medford, Susan Oliver

'The mixture resolutely refuses to come to the boil.'—*John Gillett*

Butterflies are Free
US 1972 109m Eastmancolor
Columbia / M. J. Frankovich

An aspiring actress falls for a blind neighbour but is handicapped by his possessive mother.
Three-character comedy-drama from a slight, sentimental but successful Broadway play.

w Leonard Gershe, from his play *d* Milton Katselas *ph* Charles B. Lang *m* Bob Alcivar

Goldie Hawn, Edward Albert, Eileen Heckart

Buy Me That Town*
US 1941 70m bw
Paramount (Sol C. Siegel)

Gangsters take over a small town and pull the community out of bankruptcy.
Unusual comedy-drama, quite well done for a second feature.

w Gordon Kahn *d* Eugene Forde *ph* Theodor Sparkuhl

Lloyd Nolan, Albert Dekker, Constance Moore,

Sheldon Leonard, Vera Vague, Edward Brophy, Horace MacMahon, Warren Hymer

Bwana Devil
US 1952 79m Anscocolor
(UA) Arch Oboler

At the turn of the century, two man-eating lions threaten an African railroad.
Inept actioner notable only as the first film in 3-D ('Natural Vision'), advertised with the famous slogan 'A lion in your lap'.

wd Arch Oboler *ph* Joseph Biroc *m* Gordon Jenkins

Robert Stack, Barbara Britton, Nigel Bruce, Ramsay Hill

By Love Possessed*
US 1961 116m De Luxe Panavision
UA / Miral (Walter Mirisch)

A Massachusetts lawyer reflects on the outlandish sexual mores of himself, his family and friends.
Peyton Place moved up in the social scale; a reasonably absorbing melodrama but hardly memorable.

w John Dennis, *novel* James Gould Cozzens *d* John Sturges *ph* Russell Metty *m* Elmer Bernstein

Lana Turner, Efrem Zimbalist Jnr, Jason Robards Jnr, Barbara Bel Geddes, George Hamilton, Susan Kohner, Thomas Mitchell, Yvonne Craig, Everett Sloane

By the Light of the Silvery Moon*
US 1953 101m Technicolor
Warner (William Jacobs)

In a small American town in 1918, the Winfield family has several problems arising from the return of daughter Marjorie's soldier boyfriend.
A sequel to *On Moonlight Bay*, presenting further situations from the Penrod stories retailored for Doris Day. Inoffensive, well-made, old-fashioned entertainment with nostalgic songs and an archetypal family.

w Robert O'Brien, Irving Elinson, from stories by Booth Tarkington *d* David Butler *ph* Wilfrid M. Cline *m* Max Steiner

Doris Day, Gordon Macrae, *Leon Amis, Rosemary de Camp, Mary Wickes*

Bye Bye Birdie
US 1963 112m Eastmancolor
Panavision
Columbia / Fred Kohlmar / George Sidney

Havoc suffuses the last TV show of a pop star before he goes into the army.
Noisy, frenetic musical, hard to follow and even harder to like, with all the satire of the stage original subtracted. For young audiences who enjoy incoherence.

w Irving Brecher, from musical by Michael Stewart *d* George Sidney *ph* Joseph Biroc *m* Johnny Green

Janet Leigh, Dick Van Dyke, Maureen Stapleton, Ann-Margret, Bobby Rydell, Jesse Pearson, Ed Sullivan, Paul Lynde, Robert Paige

Bye Bye Braverman*
US 1968 92m Technicolor
Warner / Sidney Lumet

New Yorkers get drunk and disillusioned on their way home from the funeral of a friend.
Witty, downbeat Jewish comedy which does not quite come off and would in any case be caviare to the general.

w Herbert Sargent, *novel* To an Early Grave by Wallace Markfield *d* Sidney Lumet *ph* Boris Kaufman *m* Peter Matz

George Segal, Jack Warden, Joseph Wiseman, Sorrell Booke, Jessica Walter, Phyllis Newman, Zohra Lampert, Alan King, Godfrey Cambridge

C

Cabaret***
US 1972 123m Technicolor
ABC Pictures / Allied Artists (Cy Feuer)

In the early thirties, Berlin is a hotbed of vice and anti-semitism. In the Kit Kat Klub, singer Sally Bowles shares her English lover with a homosexual German baron, and her Jewish friend Natasha has troubles of her own.
This version of Isherwood's Berlin stories regrettably follows the plot line of the play *I Am a Camera* rather than the Broadway musical on which it is allegedly based, and it lacks the incisive remarks of the MC, but the very smart direction creates a near-masterpiece of its own, and most of the songs are intact.

w Jay Presson Allen, from Goodbye to Berlin by Christopher Isherwood *d/ch Bob Fosse m John Kander ly Fred Ebb ph Geoffrey Unsworth pd Rolf Zehetbauer*

Liza Minnelli, Joel Grey, Michael York, Helmut Griem, Fritz Wepper, Marisa Berenson

'A stylish, sophisticated entertainment for grown-up people.'—*John Russell Taylor*

'Film journals will feast for years on shots from this picture; as it rolled along, I saw page after illustrated page from a not-too-distant book called *The Cinema of Bob Fosse*.'—*Stanley Kauffmann*

Cabin in the Cotton*
US 1932 79m bw
Warner (Hal B. Wallis)

A sharecropper is almost ruined by a southern belle.
Dated melodrama with interesting style and performances.

w Paul Green, *novel* Harry Harrison Knoll
d Michael Curtiz *ph* Barney McGill

Richard Barthelmess, Dorothy Jordan, Bette Davis, David Landau, Tully Marshall, Henry B. Walthall, Hardie Albright

Cabin in the Sky**
US 1943 99m bw
MGM (Arthur Freed)

An idle, gambling husband is reformed by a dream of his own death, with God and Satan battling for his soul.
Consistently interesting, often lively, but generally rather stilted all-black musical which must have seemed a whole lot fresher on the stage. Still, a good try.

w Joseph Schrank, *musical play* Lynn Root
d Vincente Minnelli *ph Sidney Wagner*
m George Stoll *ly/m E. Y. Harburg, Harold Arlen*

Eddie 'Rochester' Anderson, Ethel Waters, Lena Horne, Cab Calloway, Louis Armstrong, John W. Bublett

The Cabinet of Caligari
US 1962 105m bw Cinemascope
TCF / Lippert (Roger Kay)

A young woman whose car breaks down near a country house is held prisoner by the sinister Caligari. Eventually it transpires that the mystery is all in her imagination: he is a psychiatrist and she an old lady whose sexual fantasies he has been curing.
Interminably talkative and frequently (unintentionally) funny trick film with the odd moment of effective suspense. The original ending, which cast some doubt on who was mad and who sane, is no longer available. The actors do not entirely escape absurdity.

w Robert Bloch *d* Roger Kay *ph* John Russell
m Gerald Fried

Glynis Johns, Dan O'Herlihy, Constance Ford, Dick Davalos, Lawrence Dobkin

'It is impossible to be grateful for the film on any of its levels.'—*MFB*

† The fact that the story is told by a mad person is the only link with the 1919 classic.

Cactus Flower*
US 1969 103m Technicolor
Columbia / M. J. Frankovich

To deceive his mistress, a dentist employs his starchy secretary to pose as his wife, and falls for her when she loosens up.
Amusing sophisticated comedy, generally well handled.

w I. A. L. Diamond, *play* Abe Burrows, French

original by Pierre Barillet, Jean Pierre Gredy *d* Gene Saks *ph* Charles E. Lang *m* Quincy Jones *pd* Robert Clatworthy

Ingrid Bergman, Walter Matthau, Goldie Hawn, Jack Weston, Rick Lenz, Vito Scotti, Irene Hervey

The Caddy
US 1953 95m bw
Paramount (Paul Jones)

A music hall comedy act recall how they got together.
Less a feature than a series of short sketches, this ragbag has its choice moments, but they are few.

w Edmund Hartmann, Danny Arnold *d* Norman Taurog *ph* Daniel L. Fapp *m* Joseph L. Lilley

Dean Martin, Jerry Lewis, Donna Reed, Barbara Bates, Joseph Calleia, Fred Clark, Clinton Sundberg, Marshall Thompson

Caesar and Cleopatra**
GB 1945 135m Technicolor
Rank / Gabriel Pascal

An elaborate screen treatment of Bernard Shaw's comedy about Caesar's years in Alexandria.
Britain's most expensive film is an absurd extravaganza for which the producer actually took sand to Egypt to get the right colour. It has compensations however in the sets, the colour, the performances and the witty lines, though all its virtues are theatrical rather than cinematic and the play is certainly not a major work.

w Bernard Shaw *d* Gabriel Pascal *ph* F. A. Young, Robert Krasker, Jack Hildyard, Jack Cardiff *m* Georges Auric *decor, costumes Oliver Messel sets John Bryan*

Claude Rains, Vivien Leigh, Cecil Parker, Stewart Granger, Flora Robson, Francis L. Sullivan, Raymond Lovell, Anthony Harvey, Anthony Eustrel, Basil Sydney, Ernest Thesiger, Stanley Holloway, Leo Genn, Jean Simmons, Esmé Percy, Michael Rennie

'It cost over a million and a quarter pounds, took two and a half years to make, and well and truly bored one spectator for two and a quarter hours.'—*Richard Winnington*

Café Metropole
US 1937 83m bw
TCF (Nunnally Johnson)

An heiress in Paris romances a Russian nobleman who is actually a penniless American.
Lighter-than-air romance which passed the time at the time.

w Jacques Duval *d* Edward H. Griffith *ph* Lucien Andriot *md* Louis Silvers

Loretta Young, Adolphe Menjou, Tyrone Power, Charles Winninger, Gregory Ratoff, Christian Rub, Helen Westley

Café Society
US 1939 84m bw
Paramount

A publicity-seeking socialite impulsively marries a reporter who has annoyed her, but instead of making a fool of him she falls in love.

w Virginia Van Upp *d* Edward H. Griffith

Madeleine Carroll, Fred MacMurray, Shirley Ross, Claude Gillingwater

Cage of Gold*
GB 1950 83m bw
Ealing (Michael Relph)

A girl's philandering ex-husband comes back into her life and is murdered.
Mild mystery melodrama in which the puzzle comes too late.

w Jack Whittingham *d* Basil Dearden *ph* Douglas Slocombe *m* Georges Auric

Jean Simmons, David Farrar, James Donald, Madeleine Lebeau, Maria Mauban, Herbert Lom, Bernard Lee, Gladys Henson, Harcourt Williams, Grégoire Aslan

Cage without a Key
US 1975 100m colour TVM
Columbia / Douglas S. Cramer

A girl teenager is wrongly convicted of murder and sent to a penal institution.
By *Born Innocent*, out of *Caged* and *Woman's Prison* . . . every scene has been seen before.

w Joanna Lee *d* Buzz Kulik

Susan Dey, Michael Brandon, Jonelle Allen, Sam Bottoms

Caged*
US 1950 96m bw
Warner (Jerry Wald)

After being involved in a robbery a 19-year-old girl is sent to prison, and finds the staff more terrifying than the inmates.
Slick, superficial, hysterically harrowing women-in-prison melodrama; predictably overblown but also effective and powerful.

w Virginia Kellogg, Bernard Schoenfeld *d* John Cromwell *ph* Carl Guthrie *m* Max Steiner

Eleanor Parker, Agnes Moorehead, Ellen Corby, *Hope Emerson*, Betty Garde, Jan Sterling, Lee Patrick, Olive Deering, Jane Darwell, Gertrude Michael, Joan Miller

Cahill, US Marshal*
US 1973 103m Technicolor Panavision
Warner / Batjac (Michael A. Wayne)

A stalwart western marshal finds that his own young sons are involved in a robbery he is investigating.
Satisfactory but sentimental John Wayne vehicle with the star too often yielding place to the rather boring young folk.

w Harry Julian Fink, Rita M. Fink *d* Andrew V. McLaglen *ph* Joseph Biroc *m* Elmer Bernstein

John Wayne, George Kennedy, Gary Grimes, Neville Brand, Clay O'Brien, Marie Windsor, Royal Dano, Denver Pyle, Jackie Coogan

Cain and Mabel*
US 1936 90m bw
Warner (Sam Bischoff)

Tribulations of a prizefighter in love with a showgirl.
Generously produced but weakly written comedy drama with rather unexpected musical numbers; not a successful whole, but interesting.

w Laird Doyle, H. C. Witwer *d* Lloyd Bacon *ph* George Barnes

Clark Gable, Marion Davies, Allen Jenkins, Roscoe Karns, Walter Catlett, Hobart Cavanaugh, Pert Kelton, Ruth Donnelly, E. E. Clive

The Caine Mutiny**
US 1954 125m Technicolor
Columbia / Stanley Kramer

Jealousies and frustrations among the officers of a peacetime destroyer come to a head when the neurotic captain panics during a typhoon and is relieved of his post. At the resulting trial the officers learn about themselves.
Decent if lamely paced version of a bestseller which also made a successful play; the film skates too lightly over the characterizations and even skimps the courtroom scene, but there are effective scenes and performances.

w Stanley Roberts, *novel* Herman Wouk *d* Edward Dmytryk *ph* Franz Planer *m* Max Steiner

Humphrey Bogart, Jose Ferrer, Van Johnson, Fred MacMurray, Robert Francis, May Wynn, Tom Tully, E. G. Marshall, Lee Marvin, Arthur Franz

Cairo*
US 1941 100m bw
MGM

An American war reporter in Egypt meets a screen star and thinks she is a spy.
Mildly pleasing light comedy-drama with self-spoofing elements.

w John McClain *d* W. S. Van Dyke II *ph* Ray June *md* Herbert Stothart

Jeanette MacDonald, Robert Young, Ethel Waters, Reginald Owen, Lionel Atwill, Mona Barrie, Eduardo Ciannelli, Dennis Hoey, Dooley Wilson

Cairo
GB 1963 91m bw
MGM (Ronald Kinnoch)

Crooks plan to steal Tutankhamun's jewels from the Cairo Museum.
Spiritless remake of *The Asphalt Jungle* (qv).

w Joanne Court *d* Wolf Rilla *ph* Desmond Dickinson *m* Kenneth V. Jones

George Sanders, Richard Johnson, Faten Hamama, John Meillon, Eric Pohlmann, Walter Rilla

Cairo Road
GB 1950 95m bw
ABP (Aubrey Baring)

An Egyptian police chief lays traps for drug smugglers.
Oddly cast, reasonably lively but routine police adventure in an unfamiliar setting.

w Robert Westerby *d* David MacDonald *ph* Oswald Morris *m* Robert Gill

Eric Portman, Laurence Harvey, Maria Mauban, Karel Stepanek, Harold Lang, Camelia, Grégoire Aslan, Oscar Quitak

Calamity Jane**
US 1953 101m Technicolor
Warner (William Jacobs)

Calamity helps a saloon owner friend find a star attraction, and wins the heart of Wild Bill Hickok.
Agreeable, cleaned-up, studio-set western musical patterned after *Annie Get Your Gun*, but a much friendlier film, helped by an excellent score.

w James O'Hanlon *d* David Butler *ph* Wilfrid Cline *songs Sammy Fain, Paul Francis Webster* *ch* Jack Donohue

Doris Day, Howard Keel, Allyn McLerie, Phil Carey, Dick Wesson, Paul Harvey

Calcutta
US 1948 83m bw
Paramount (Seton I. Miller)

Two fliers seek the murderer of their friend in the hotels and bazaars of Calcutta.
Studio-bound action potboiler, simple-minded but quite good fun.

w Seton I. Miller *d* John Farrow *ph* John F. Seitz *m* Victor Young

Alan Ladd, Gail Russell, William Bendix, June Duprez, Lowell Gilmore

California
US 1946 97m Technicolor
Paramount (Seton I. Miller)

An army deserter joins the 1848 California gold rush.
Standard glamorized star western; not bad if you accept the conventions.

w Frank Butler, Theodore Strauss *d* John Farrow *ph* Ray Rennahan *m* Victor Young

Ray Milland, Barbara Stanwyck, Barry Fitzgerald, Albert Dekker, George Coulouris, Anthony Quinn

The California Kid*
US 1974 74m Technicolor TVM
Universal (Paul Mason)

The brother of a victim corners a psychotic small-town sheriff who forces speeders off the road to their deaths.
Oddball mixture of *Duel* and *Bad Day at Black Rock*; not unentertaining.

w Richard Compton *d* Richard Heffron

Martin Sheen, Vic Morrow, Michele Phillips, Stuart Margolin, Nick Nolte

California Split*
US 1974 109m Metrocolor Panavision
Columbia / Won World (Robert Altman, Joseph Walsh)

Two cheerful gamblers get drunk, laid, cheated and happy.
Sporadically entertaining character comedy sunk in a sea of chatter.

w Joseph Walsh *d* Robert Altman *ph* Paul Lohmann

Elliott Gould, George Segal, Gwen Welles, Ann Prentiss, Joseph Walsh

'The film seems to be being improvised . . . we catch at events and personalities by the ends of threads.'—*New Yorker*

California Straight Ahead*
US 1937 67m bw
Universal (Trem Carr)

A nationwide race is held between a special train and a convoy of high-powered trucks.
Unusual and quite lively second feature shot on location.

w Herman Boxer *d* Arthur Lubin *ph* Harry Neumann

John Wayne, Louise Latimer, Robert McWade, Tully Marshall

Call Her Mom
US 1972 74m colour TVM
Columbia (Herb Wallerstein)

A glamorous waitress becomes house mother for a college fraternity and sharpens up the ideas of the members.
Easy-going collegiate nonsense.

w Kenny Solms, Gail Parent *d* Jerry Paris

Connie Stevens, Van Johnson, Charles Nelson Reilly, Jim Hutton, Cyd Charisse, Corbett Monica, Gloria de Haven

Call Her Savage
US 1932 88m bw
Paramount (Sam E. Rork)

Trials and tribulations of a half-breed Indian girl who marries a cad and later takes to the streets.
Rough and ready melodrama for female audiences; the penultimate appearance of a star who did not take to talkies.

w Edwin Burke, *novel* Tiffany Thayer *d* John Francis Dillon *ph* Lee Garmes

Clara Bow, Gilbert Roland, Monroe Owsley, Thelma Todd, Estelle Taylor

Call It a Day*
US 1937 89m bw
Warner (Henry Blanke)

An upper-class British family has problems during a single day.
Surprising, and not very effective, Hollywood treatment of a very British comedy.

w Casey Robinson, *play* Dodie Smith *d* Archie Mayo *ph* Ernest Haller

Olivia de Havilland, Ian Hunter, Anita Louise, Alice Brady, Roland Young, Frieda Inescort, Bonita Granville, Peggy Wood, Walter Woolf King, Una O'Connor, Beryl Mercer

Call Me Bwana*
GB 1962 93m Eastmancolor
Rank / Eon (Harry Saltzman, Albert R. Broccoli)

A fake African explorer is sent to the jungle to recover a space capsule.
Moderate star farce with occasional bright moments.

w Nate Monaster, Johanna Harwood *d* Gordon Douglas *ph* Ted Moore *m* Monty Norman

Bob Hope, Anita Ekberg, Edie Adams, Lionel Jeffries, Percy Herbert, Paul Carpenter, Orlando Martins

Call Me Madam***
US 1953 114m Technicolor
TCF (Sol C. Siegel)

A Washington hostess is appointed Ambassador to Lichtenberg and marries the foreign minister.
Studio-bound but thoroughly lively transcription of Irving Berlin's last big success, with most of the performers at their peak and some topical gags which may now be mystifying.

w Arthur Sheekman, *play* Howard Lindsay, Russell Crouse *m/ly Irving Berlin md* Alfred Newman *ph* Leon Shamroy *d* Walter Lang *ch* Robert Alton

Ethel Merman, Donald O'Connor, George Sanders, Vera-Ellen, Billy de Wolfe, Helmut Dantine, Walter Slezak, Steve Geray, Ludwig Stossel

Call Me Mister
US 1951 95m Technicolor
TCF (Fred Kohlmar)

A husband-and-wife dance team entertain the troops in Japan and after the war.
Passable musical of a very predictable kind.

w Albert E. Lewin, Burt Styler *d* Lloyd Bacon *ph* Arthur E. Arling *m* Leigh Harline *ch* Busby Berkeley *songs* various

Betty Grable, Dan Dailey, Danny Thomas, Dale Robertson, Richard Boone

Call Northside 777**
US 1948 111m bw
TCF (Otto Lang)

A Chicago reporter helps a washerwoman prove her son not guilty of murdering a policeman.
Overlong semi-documentary crime thriller based on a real case. Acting and detail excellent, but the sharp edge of *Boomerang* is missing.

w Jerome Cady, Jay Dratler *d* Henry Hathaway *ph Joe MacDonald*

James Stewart, Lee J. Cobb, Helen Walker, *Kazia Orzazewski*, Betty Garde

Call of the Wild*
TCF (Darryl F. Zanuck)
US 1935 81m bw

A young widow falls in love with a wild Yukon prospector.
Inaccurate but pleasing adaptation of an adventure novel with dog interest.

w Gene Fowler, Leonard Praskins, *novel* Jack London *d* William Wellman *ph* Charles Rosher

Clark Gable, Loretta Young, Jack Oakie, Reginald Owen, Frank Conroy

Call of the Wild
GB / Ger / Sp / It / Fr 1972 105m Eastmancolor
Massfilms / CCC / Izaro / Oceania / UPF (Harry Alan Towers)

During the Klondike gold rush, a stolen dog becomes a miner's best friend before joining the wolf-pack.
Closer to the book than the previous version, but curiously scrappy and unsatisfactory.

w Harry Alan Towers, Wyn Wells, Peter Yeldman *d* Ken Annakin *ph* John Vabrera, Dudley Lovell *m* Carlo Rustichelli

Charlton Heston, Michèle Mercier, Raimund Harmstorf, George Eastman

Call to Danger
US 1972 74m colour TVM
Paramount

Adventures of an elite squad for the Justice Department.
Warmed-over crime busting in a failed pilot designed as a follow-up to *Mission Impossible.*

w Laurence Heath *d* Tom Gries

Peter Graves, Clu Gulager, Diana Muldaur, John Anderson, Tina Louise

Callan*
GB 1974 106m Eastmancolor
EMI / Magnum (Derek Horne)

A former secret agent is seconded to a government section devoted to the elimination of undesirables.
Expanded rewrite of the first episode of a long-running TV series, quite fresh and vivid in the circumstances, especially as it comes at the tail end of ten years of similar bouts of blood and thunder.

w James Mitchell, from A Magnum for Schneider *d Don Sharp ph* Ernest Steward *m* Marcus Dods

Edward Woodward, Eric Porter, Carl Mohner, Catherine Schell, Peter Egan, Russell Hunter, Kenneth Griffith

Callaway Went Thataway*
US 1951 81m bw
MGM (Melvin Frank, Norman Panama)
GB title: *The Star Said No*

The old movies of a Hollywood cowboy become popular on TV, but the star has become a hopeless drunk and an actor is hired to pose as him for public appearances.

Reasonably engaging comedy using charm rather than acid.

wd Melvin Frank, Norman Panama *ph* Ray June *m* Marlin Skiles

Dorothy McGuire, Fred MacMurray, Howard Keel, Jesse White, Natalie Schaefer

Calling Bulldog Drummond
GB 1951 80m bw
MGM (Hayes Goetz)

Drummond goes undercover to catch a gang of thieves.
Minor-league quota quickie addition to the exploits of a long-running character (see *Bulldog Drummond*).

w Howard Emmett Rogers, Gerard Fairlie, Arthur Wimperis *d* Victor Saville *ph* Graham Kelly *m* Rudolph Kopp

Walter Pidgeon, Margaret Leighton, Robert Beatty, David Tomlinson, Peggy Evans, Charles Victor, Bernard Lee, James Hayter

Camelot**
US 1967 181m Technicolor
Panavision 70
Warner (Jack L. Warner)

King Arthur marries Guinevere, loses her to Lancelot, and is forced into war.
A film version of a long-running Broadway show with many excellent moments. Unfortunately the director cannot make up his mind whether to go for style or realism, and has chosen actors who cannot sing. The result is cluttered and overlong, with no real sense of period or sustained imagination, but the photography and the music linger in the mind.

w Alan Jay Lerner m Frederick Loewe
d Joshua Logan *ph Richard H. Kline*
pd/costumes John Truscott ad Edward Carere

Richard Harris, Vanessa Redgrave, David Hemmings, Lionel Jeffries, Laurence Naismith, Franco Nero

'One wonders whether the fashion for musicals in which only the chorus can actually sing may be reaching its final stage.'—*MFB*

'Three hours of unrelieved glossiness, meticulous inanity, desperate and charmless striving for charm.'—*John Simon*

Camille**
US 1936 108m bw
MGM

A dying courtesan falls for an innocent young man who loves her, and dies in his arms.
This old warhorse is an unsuitable vehicle for Garbo but magically she carries it off, and the production is elegant and pleasing.

w Frances Marion, James Hilton, Zoe Akins, *novel* Alexandre Dumas *d George Cukor*
ph William Daniels m Herbert Stothart

Greta Garbo, Robert Taylor, Lionel Barrymore, *Henry Daniell*, Elizabeth Allan, Lenore Ulric, Laura Hope Crews, Rex O'Malley, Jessie Ralph, E. E. Clive

'The slow, solemn production is luxuriant in its vulgarity: it achieves that glamor which MGM traditionally mistook for style.'—*Pauline Kael, 1968*

The Camp on Blood Island
GB 1958 81m bw Megascope
Columbia / Hammer (Anthony Hinds)

The sadistic commandant of a Japanese POW camp swears to kill all the inmates. Japan surrenders, and a great effort is made to prevent the news from reaching him.
Dubious melodrama parading sadism and brutality as entertainment.

w Jon Manchip White, Val Guest *d* Val Guest *ph* Jack Asher *m* Gerard Schurmann

André Morell, Carl Mohner, Edward Underdown, Michael Goodliffe, Ronald Radd, Walter Fitzgerald, Phil Brown, Barbara Shelley, Michael Gwynn, Richard Wordsworth, Marne Maitland, Mary Merrall

Campbell's Kingdom*
GB 1957 102m Eastmancolor
Rank (Betty E. Box)

A young man who thinks he is dying arrives in the Canadian Rockies to take over his father's oil valley, but a scheming contractor opposes him.
Competent and entertaining romantic thick-ear.

w Robin Estridge, *novel* Hammond Innes
d Ralph Thomas *ph* Ernest Steward

Dirk Bogarde, Stanley Baker, Barbara Murray, Athene Seyler, Mary Merrall, James Robertson Justice

Can Can
US 1960 131m De Luxe Todd-AO
TCF (Jack Cummings)

A Parisian nightclub dancer in the nineties is sued for performing the Can Can.
Flat film of a dull musical, with just a few plums in the pudding.

w Dorothy Kingsley, Charles Lederer, *play* Abe Burrows *songs* Cole Porter *d* Walter Lang
ph William Daniels *ch* Hermes Pan

Frank Sinatra, Shirley Maclaine, Maurice

Chevalier, Louis Jourdan, Juliet Prowse, Marcel Dalio, Leon Belasco

Can Ellen Be Saved?
US 1974 74m colour TVM
ABC Circle

A private eye rescues a teenager from a strange religious sect.
Adequate melodrama, treated rather more weirdly than it warrants.

w Emmett Roberts *d* Harvey Hart

Leslie Nielsen, Michael Parks, John Saxon, Kathy Cannon, Louise Fletcher

Can Heironymus Merkin Ever Forgive Mercy Humppe and Find True Happiness?
GB 1969 117m Technicolor
Universal / Taralex (Anthony Newley)

A performer on a beach assembles a huge pile of personal bric-à-brac and reminisces about his life in the style of a variety show.
Obscure and pointless personal fantasy, financed at great expense by a major film company as a rather seedy monument to Anthony Newley's totally uninteresting sex life, and to the talent which he obviously thinks he possesses. The few mildly amusing moments are not provided by him.

w Herman Raucher, Anthony Newley
d Anthony Newley *ph* Otto Heller *m* Anthony Newley

Anthony Newley, Joan Collins, George Jessel, Milton Berle, Bruce Forsyth, Stubby Kaye, Patricia Hayes, Victor Spinetti

'If I'd been Anthony Newley I would have opened it in Siberia during Christmas week and called it a day.'—*Rex Reed*

The Candidate**
US 1972 110m Technicolor
Warner / Redford–Ritchie (Walter Coblenz)

A young Californian lawyer is persuaded to run for senator; in succeeding, he alienates his wife and obscures his real opinions.
Put together in a slightly scrappy but finally persuasive style, this joins a select band of rousing, doubting American political films.

w Jeremy Larner *d Michael Ritchie ph* Victor J. Kemper *m* John Rubinstein

Robert Redford, Peter Boyle, *Don Porter*, Allen Garfield, Karen Carlson, Quinn Redeker, Morgan Upton, *Melvyn Douglas*

'Decent entertainment . . . it is never boring, but it is never enlarging, informationally or emotionally or thematically.'—*Stanley Kauffmann*

Candy
US 1968 124m Technicolor
Selmur / Dear / Corona (Robert Haggiag)

An innocent girl defends herself from a fate worse than death in a variety of international situations.
Witless and charmless perversion of a sex satire in which the point (if any) was that the nymphet gladly surrendered herself to all the gentlemen for their own good. A star cast flounders helplessly in a morass of bad taste, bad film-making, and boredom.

w Buck Henry, *novel* Terry Southern
d Christian Marquand *ph* Giuseppe Rotunno
m Dave Grusin

Ewa Aulin, Richard Burton, Marlon Brando, James Coburn, Walter Matthau, Charles Aznavour, John Huston, Elsa Martinelli, Ringo Starr, John Astin

'Hippy psychedelics are laid on with the self-destroying effect of an overdose of garlic.'—*MFB*

'As an emetic, liquor is dandy, but *Candy* is quicker.'—*John Simon*

Cannon
US 1970 100m colour TVM
Quinn Martin

A fat private eye investigates a murder and finds small-town corruption.
Adequate, padded mystery serving as pilot for a successful series.

w Edward Hume *d* George McCowan

William Conrad, Barry Sullivan, Vera Miles, J. D. Cannon, Lynda Day, Earl Holliman

Cannon for Cordoba
US 1970 104m De Luxe Panavision
UA / Mirisch (Stephen Kandel, Vincent Fenelly)

In 1912, the Mexican bandit Cordoba is outgunned and outwitted by a US army captain.
Fast-moving but rather uninteresting action adventure.

w Stephen Kandel *d* Paul Wendkos *ph* Antonio Macasoli *m* Elmer Bernstein

George Peppard, Raf Vallone, Giovanna Ralli, Pete Duel, Don Gordon, Nico Minardos, John Russell

Cannonball
US 1976 93m Metrocolor
New World (Samuel W. Gelfman)

Violence is the chief result of a no-holds-barred cross country car race for a prize of a hundred thousand dollars.

Vaguely written, action-packed extravaganza for the youth market.

w Paul Bartel, Donald W. Simpson *d* Paul Bartel *ph* Tak Fujimoto *m* David A. Axelrod

David Carradine, Bill McKinney, Veronica Hamel, Gerrit Graham

Can't Help Singing*
US 1944 90m Technicolor
Universal (Frank Ross)

A Washington heiress chases her army lieutenant lover across the wild west to California.
Lively star musical which could have used a little more wit in its lighthearted script.

w Lewis Foster, Frank Ryan *d* Frank Ryan *ph* Woody Bredell, W. Howard Greene *m* Jerome Kern *ly* E. Y. Harburg

Deanna Durbin, David Bruce, Robert Paige, *Akim Tamiroff, Leonid Kinskey*, Ray Collins, Thomas Gomez

'This could have been a beautiful and gay picture, but it is made without much feeling for beauty or gaiety.'—*James Agee*

A Canterbury Tale*
GB 1944 124m bw
Rank / Archers (Michael Powell, Emeric Pressburger)

A batty magistrate is unmasked by a land girl, an army sergeant and a GI.
Curious would-be propaganda piece with Old England bathed in a roseate wartime glow, but the plot seems to have little to do with Chaucer. Indeed, quite what Powell and Pressburger thought they were up to is hard to fathom, but the detail is interesting.

wd Michael Powell and Emeric Pressburger

Eric Portman, Sheila Sim, John Sweet, Dennis Price, Esmond Knight, Charles Hawtrey, Hay Petrie, George Merritt, Edward Rigby

The Canterville Ghost*
US 1943 95m bw
MGM (Arthur Field)

The young girl heiress of an English castle introduces GIs to the resident ghost.
Leaden comedy a long way after Oscar Wilde, sunk by slow script and direction, but partly salvaged by the respective roguishness and infant charm of its stars.

w Edwin Blum *d* Jules Dassin *m* George Bassman

Charles Laughton, Margaret O'Brien, Robert Young, William Gargan, Rags Ragland, Peter Lawford, Una O'Connor, Mike Mazurki

Canyon Passage*
US 1946 99m Technicolor
Universal (Walter Wanger)

In the 1850s along the pioneering tracks the west's first towns were being built . . .
Simple, scrappy but generally pleasing film which gives a vivid picture of pioneering life while minimizing its hardships.

w Ernest Pascal, William Fosche *d* Jacques Tourneur *ph* Edward Cronjager *m* Frank Skinner

Dana Andrews, Patricia Roc, Hoagy Carmichael, Brian Donlevy, Susan Hayward, Ward Bond, Andy Devine, Lloyd Bridges

Cape Fear
US 1962 106m bw
U-I / Melville–Talbot (Sy Bartlett)

An ex-convict blames a lawyer for his sentence and threatens to rape the lawyer's wife.
Unpleasant and drawn out suspenser with characters of cardboard and situations from stock.

w James R. Webb, *novel* The Executioners by John D. MacDonald *d* J. Lee-Thompson *ph* Sam Leavitt *m* Bernard Herrmann

Gregory Peck, Robert Mitchum, Polly Bergen, Martin Balsam, Lori Nelson, Jack Kruschen, Telly Savalas

The Caper of the Golden Bulls
US 1966 104m Pathecolor
Embassy (Clarence Greene)
GB title: *Carnival of Thieves*

Ex-air-aces rob banks in order to pay for the restoration of a French cathedral they had to bomb; to avoid incrimination they are blackmailed into doing one last job in Pamplona.
Ingeniously plotted, flatly executed suspenser set in Pamplona during the bull run.

w Ed Waters, William Moessinger, *novel* William P. McGivern *d* Russel Rouse *ph* Hal Stine *m* Vic Mizzy

Stephen Boyd, Giovanna Ralli, Yvette Mimieux, Walter Slezak, Vito Scotti

Capetown Affair
US / SA 1967 100m De Luxe
TCF / Killarney (Robert D. Webb)

A pickpocket on a South African bus steals a purse containing secret microfilm.
Flatulent remake of *Pickup on South Street* with nothing but the unfamiliar locale to recommend it.

w Harold Medford, Samuel Fuller *d* Robert D. Webb *ph* David Millin *m* Bob Adams

James Brolin, Jacqueline Bisset, Claire Trevor, Bob Courtney, Jon Whiteley

Caprice*
US 1967 98m De Luxe Cinemascope
TCF / Aaron Rosenberg, Marty Melcher

A career girl investigating the death of her boss discovers that a cosmetics empire is the front for international drug smuggling.
Incoherent kaleidoscope which switches from farce to suspense and Bond-style action, scattering in-jokes along the way. Bits of it however are funny, and it looks good.

w Jay Jayson, Frank Tashlin *d* Frank Tashlin *ph* Leon Shamroy (who also appears) *m* Frank de Vol

Doris Day, Richard Harris, Edward Mulhare, Ray Walston, Jack Kruschen, Lilia Skala, Irene Tsu, Michael Romanoff, Michael J. Pollard

Captain Blood**
US 1935 119m bw
Warner (Harry Joe Brown)

A young British surgeon, wrongly condemned by Judge Jeffreys for helping rebels, escapes and becomes a Caribbean pirate.
Modestly produced but quite exhilarating pirate adventure notable for making a star of Errol Flynn. Direction makes the most of very limited production values.

w Casey Robinson, *novel* Rafael Sabatini *d Michael Curtiz ph Hal Mohr ad Anton Grot*

Errol Flynn, Olivia de Havilland, *Basil Rathbone*, Lionel Atwill, Guy Kibbee, Ross Alexander, Henry Stephenson, Forrester Harvey, Hobart Cavanaugh, Donald Meek

Captain Boycott*
GB 1947 93m bw
GFD / Individual (Frank Launder, Sidney Gilliat)

In 1880, poor Irish farmers rebel against their tyrannical English landlords.
Modest historical drama in which a splendid cast is rather subdued.

w Wolfgang Wilhelm, Frank Launder, Paul Vincent Carroll, Patrick Campbell *d* Frank Launder *ph* Wilkie Cooper

Stewart Granger, Kathleen Ryan, Alastair Sim, Robert Donat (a cameo as Parnell), Cecil Parker, Mervyn Johns, Noel Purcell, Niall MacGinnis

Captain Carey USA
US 1951 83m bw
Paramount (Richard Maibaum)
GB title: *After Midnight*

After the war, a military officer returns to an Italian village to expose the informer who betrayed his comrades.
Muddled and rather boring melodrama with a labyrinthine plot which seems to have stultified all concerned. It did produce a hit song, 'Mona Lisa'.

w Robert Thoeren, *novel* Dishonoured by Martha Albrand *d* Mitchell Leisen *ph* John F. Seitz *m* Hugo Friedhofer

Alan Ladd, Francis Lederer, Wanda Hendrix, Joseph Calleia, Celia Lovsky, Angela Clarke, Jane Nigh, Frank Puglia, Luis Alberni

Captain Caution
US 1940 84m bw
Hal Roach

In 1812, a girl takes over her dead father's ship and fights the British.
Lively though unconvincing adventure with emphasis on comedy.

w Grover Jones *d* Richard Wallace *ph* Norbert Brodine *m* Phil Ohman

Victor Mature, Louise Platt, Bruce Cabot, Leo Carrillo, Robert Barrat, Vivienne Osborne, Alan Ladd

Captain Clegg*
GB 1962 82m Technicolor
Universal / Hammer (John Temple-Smith)
US title: *Night Creatures*

The vicar of an 18th-century village in Romney Marsh is really a retired pirate, now doing a little smuggling on the side.
Mild remake of *Dr Syn* with a few moments of violence added; watchable for those who like totally predictable plot development.

w John Elder *d* Peter Graham Scott *ph* Arthur Grant *m* Don Banks

Peter Cushing, Patrick Allen, Michael Ripper, Oliver Reed, Derek Francis, Milton Reid, Martin Benson, David Lodge

Captain Eddie
US 1945 107m bw
TCF / Eureka

Eddie Rickenbacker, adrift on a life raft after a plane crash in the Pacific, thinks back on his adventurous life in aviation.
Flat and surprisingly poorly made biopic with little to hold the attention.

w John Tucker Battle *d* Lloyd Bacon *ph* Joe MacDonald

Fred MacMurray, Lynn Bari, Thomas Mitchell, Lloyd Nolan, Charles Bickford

Captain from Castile
US 1947 140m Technicolor
TCF (Lamar Trotti)

A young 15th-century Spaniard hopes for fame and fortune in the New World.
Rather empty and boring adventure epic from a bestseller; high production values produce moments of interest.

w Lamar Trotti, *novel* Samuel Shellabarger *d* Henry King *ph* Charles Clarke, Arthur E. Arling *m* Alfred Newman *ad* Richard Day, James Basevi

Tyrone Power, Jean Peters, Lee J. Cobb, Cesar Romero, John Sutton, Antonio Moreno, Thomas Gomez, Alan Mowbray, Barbara Lawrence, George Zucco, Roy Roberts, Marc Lawrence

Captain Fury*
US 1939 91m bw
Hal Roach

In 19th-century Australia, an adventurer fights the evil head of a penal colony.
Shades of Zorro and Robin Hood in a brawling, comic actioner typical of this producer.

w Grover Jones, Jack Jevne, William de Mille *d* Hal Roach *ph* Norbert Brodine *m* Marvin Hatley

Brian Aherne, Victor McLaglen, Paul Lukas, June Lang, John Carradine

The Captain Hates the Sea*
US 1934 92m bw
Columbia

Crime and comedy on an ocean voyage.
Zany, rather endearing comedy which gave the star his last role.

w Wallace Smith *d* Lewis Milestone *ph* Joseph August

John Gilbert, Victor McLaglen, Walter Connolly, Alison Skipworth, Wynne Gibson, Helen Vinson, Leon Errol, Walter Catlett

Captain Horatio Hornblower RN
GB 1951 117m Technicolor
Warner (Raoul Walsh)

Events from the adventure novels about a 19th-century sailor who outwits the Spaniards and the French and marries his admiral's widow.
Sprawling, plotless sea saga with the cast ill at ease in highly unconvincing sets: no air seems to blow across the decks of the *Lydia*.

w Ivan Goff, Ben Roberts, Aeneas Mackenzie, *novels* C. S. Forester *d* Raoul Walsh *ph* Guy Green *m* Robert Farnon *ad* Tom Morahan

Gregory Peck, Virginia Mayo, Robert Beatty, James Robertson Justice, Terence Morgan, Moultrie Kelsall, Richard Hearne, Denis O'Dea

Captain January*
US 1936 74m bw
TCF (Darryl F. Zanuck)

A little girl is rescued from a shipwreck by a lighthouse keeper.
Standard Shirley Temple vehicle with pleasing dialogue and numbers.

w Sam Hellman, Gladys Lehman, Harry Tugend, *novel* Laura E. Richards *d* David Butler *ph* John F. Seitz

Shirley Temple, Guy Kibbee, Buddy Ebsen, Slim Summerville, June Lang, Sara Haden, Jane Darwell

Captain Kidd
US 1945 90m bw
Benedict Bogeaus

A pirate tricks King William III into giving him royal orders, but enemies he believes dead return to see him hanged.
Rather poorly produced vehicle for a star who however rants and raves to some effect.

w Norman Reilly Raine *d* Rowland V. Lee *ph* Archie Stout

Charles Laughton, Randolph Scott, Barbara Britton, Reginald Owen, John Carradine, Gilbert Roland, Sheldon Leonard

Captain Lightfoot
US 1955 92m Technicolor print Cinemascope
U-I (Ross Hunter)

Adventures of a 19th-century Irish rebel.
Dullish adventure story with the star ill at ease.

w W. R. Burnett, Oscar Brodney *d* Douglas Sirk *ph* Irving Glassberg *m* Joseph Gershenson

Rock Hudson, Barbara Rush, Jeff Morrow, Kathleen Ryan, Finlay Currie, Denis O'Dea, Geoffrey Toone

Captain Nemo and the Underwater City
GB 1969 106m Metrocolor Panavision
MGM / Omnia (Steven Pallos, Bertram Ostrer)

Six survivors from an Atlantic shipwreck are picked up by a mysterious submarine and have

adventures in a spectacular underwater city.
Further adventures of Jules Verne's engaging Victorian character from *Twenty Thousand Leagues under the Sea.* Here however the general production values are stolid rather than solid, and the script makes heavy weather.

w Pip Baker, Jane Baker, R. Wright Campbell *d* James Hill *ph* Alan Hume, Egil Woxholt *m* Walter Stott *ad* Bill Andrews

Robert Ryan, Chuck Connors, Bill Fraser, Kenneth Connor, Nanette Newman, John Turner, Luciana Paluzzi, Allan Cuthbertson

Captain Newman MD*
US 1963 126m Eastmancolor
Universal–Brentwood–Reynard (Robert Arthur

At an army air base during World War II, a psychiatrist has varied success with his patients.
A decidedly curious comedy drama on the fringe of bad taste; it should have turned out better than it does, but will entertain those who like hospital heroics drenched in bitter-sweet sentimentality.

w Richard L. Breen, Phoebe and Henry Ephron, *novel* Leo Rosten *d* David Miller *ph* Russell Metty *m* Joseph Gershenson

Gregory Peck, Tony Curtis, Angie Dickinson, Eddie Albert, Bobby Darin, James Gregory, Jane Withers, Bethel Leslie, Robert Duvall, Larry Storch, Robert F. Simon, Dick Sargent

Captain Sinbad*
US / Germany 1963 88m Eastmancolor Wonderscope
King Brothers

Sinbad returns to Baristan and by means of magic deposes a sultan.
Rather splendid adventure fantasy with a European flavour, good trick effects and full-blooded performances.

w Samuel B. West, Harry Relis *d* Byron Haskin *ph* Gunther Senftleben, Eugen Shuftan *m* Michel Michelet *sp* Tom Howard *ad* Werner and Isabell Schlicting

Guy Williams, Pedro Armendariz, Heidi Bruhl, Abraham Sofaer

Captains Courageous**
US 1937 116m bw
MGM (Louis D. Lighton)

A spoiled rich boy falls off a cruise liner and lives for a while among fisherfolk who teach him how to live.
Semi-classic Hollywood family film which is not all that enjoyable while it's on but is certainly a good example of the prestige picture of the thirties. (It also happened to be good box office.)

w John Lee Mahin, Marc Connelly, Dale Van Every, *novel* Rudyard Kipling *d* Victor Fleming *ph* Harold Rosson *m* Franz Waxman

Spencer Tracy, Lionel Barrymore, Freddie Bartholemew, Mickey Rooney, Melvyn Douglas, Charley Grapewin, Christian Rub, John Carradine, Walter Kingsford, Leo G. Carroll, Charles Trowbridge

'Another of those grand jobs of movie-making we have come to expect from Hollywood's most profligate studio.'—*Frank S. Nugent, New York Times*

Captains of the Clouds
US 1942 113m Technicolor
Warner (Hal. B. Wallis, William Cagney)

A flippant Canadian Air Force pilot proves his worth under fire.
Recruiting poster heroics, reasonably well done but lacking the vital spark.

w Arthur T. Horman, Richard Macaulay, Norman Reilly Raine *d* Michael Curtiz *ph* Sol Polito, Wilfrid M. Cline *m* Max Steiner

James Cagney, Brenda Marshall, George Tobias, Alan Hale, Reginald Gardiner, Reginald Denny, Paul Cavanagh, Clem Bevans, J. M. Kerrigan

'Pure tribute to the unchanging forcefulness of James Cagney.'—*New York Post*

The Captain's Paradise*
GB 1953 89m bw
BL / London (Anthony Kimmins)

The captain of a steamer plying between Gibraltar and Tangier has a wife in each port, one to suit each of his personalities.
Over-dry comedy in which the idea is much funnier than the script. One is left with the memory of a pleasant star performance.

w Alec Coppel, Nicholas Phipps *d* Anthony Kimmins *ph* Ted Scaife *m* Malcolm Arnold

Alec Guinness, Celia Johnson, Yvonne de Carlo, Charles Goldner, Miles Malleson, Bill Fraser, Nicholas Phipps, Ferdy Mayne, George Benson

The Captain's Table*
GB 1958 89m Eastmancolor
Rank (Joseph Janni)

A cargo skipper is given command of a luxury liner and has to watch his manners.
Lively adaptation of a frivolous book of obvious jokes, most of which come up quite funny amid the luxurious surroundings.

w John Whiting, Bryan Forbes, Nicholas Phipps, *novel* Richard Gordon *d* Jack Lee *ph* Christopher Challis *m* Frank Cordell

John Gregson, Peggy Cummins, *Donald Sinden*, *Reginald Beckwith*, Nadia Gray, Richard Wattis, Maurice Denham, Nicholas Phipps, Joan Sims, Miles Malleson

The Captive City**
US 1951 91m bw
UA / Aspen (Theron Warth)

Small-town corruption imposed by the Mafia is revealed by a crusading editor who defies threats to his wife and family and tells all to the Kefauver Commission.
Excellent documentary melodrama made in a style then original, also notable for use of the Hoge deep focus lens.

w Karl Lamb, Alvin Josephy Jnr d Robert Wise ph Lee Garmes m Jerome Moross

John Forsythe, Joan Camden, Harold J. Kennedy, Marjorie Crossland, Victor Sutherland, Ray Teal, Martin Milner, Hal K. Dawson

The Captive Heart**
GB 1946 108m bw
Ealing (Michael Relph)

Stories of life among British officers in a German POW camp, especially of a Czech who has stolen the papers of a dead Britisher.
Archetypal POW drama lacing an almost poetic treatment with humour and melodrama.

w Angus Macphail, Guy Morgan *d Basil Dearden ph* Lionel Banes, Douglas Slocombe *m* Alan Rawsthorne

Michael Redgrave, *Jack Warner*, Basil Radford, Mervyn Johns, Jimmy Hanley, Gordon Jackson, Ralph Michael, Derek Bond, Karel Stepanek, Guy Middleton, Jack Lambert, Gladys Henson, Rachel Kempson, Meriel Forbes

Caravan
US 1934 101m bw
Fox

A countess marries a gypsy.
Odd romantic drama with music: too whimsical to succeed.

w Samson Raphaelson *d* Erik Charell *ph* Ernest Palmer, Theodor Sparkuhl *songs* Werner B. Heymann, Gus Kahn

Loretta Young, Charles Boyer, Jean Parker, Phillips Holmes, Louise Fazenda, Eugene Pallette, C. Aubrey Smith, Charley Grapewin, Noah Beery, Dudley Digges

Caravan
GB 1946 122m bw
Gainsborough (Harold Huth)

A young man on a mission in Spain is left for dead by emissaries of his rival in love; he is nursed back to health by a gypsy girl who falls in love with him.
Artificial, romantic, high-flown period tosh without the courage of its lack of convictions. At the time, an exhibitor's dream.

w Roland Pertwee, *novel* Lady Eleanor Smith *d* Arthur Crabtree *ph* Stephen Dade

Stewart Granger, Jean Kent, Anne Crawford, *Robert Helpmann*, Dennis Price, Gerard Heinz, Enid Stamp-Taylor, David Horne, John Salew

Caravan to Vaccares
GB / France 1974 98m Eastmancolor Panavision
Crowndale (Geoffrey Reeve)

An American drifter on the Riviera is employed to escort a mysterious Hungarian to New York.
Lumpy Alistair McLean action thriller, all a bit *déjà vu*.

w Paul Wheeler *d* Geoffrey Reeve *ph* Frederic Tammes *m* Stanley Myers

David Birney, Charlotte Rampling, Michel Lonsdale, Marcel Bozzuffi, Michael Bryant

'An undernourished plot advanced only by a series of venerable clichés.'—*MFB*

Carbine Williams
US 1952 93m bw
MGM (Armand Deutsch)

An imprisoned bootlegger perfects a new gun and is pardoned.
Flat fictionalization of a true story, with the star miscast.

w Art Cohn *d* Richard Thorpe *ph* William Mellor *m* Conrad Salinger

James Stewart, Jean Hagen, Wendell Corey, Carl Benton Reid, Paul Stewart, Otto Hulett, James Arness

The Card**
GB 1952 91m bw
Rank / British Film Makers (John Bryan)
US title: *The Promoter*

A bright young clerk from the potteries finds many ingenious ways of improving his bank account and his place in society.
Pleasing period comedy with the star in a made-to-measure role and excellent production values.

w Eric Ambler, *novel* Arnold Bennett *d Ronald Neame ph* Oswald Morris *ad T. Hopwell Ash m* William Alwyn

Alec Guinness, Glynis Johns, Petula Clark, *Valerie Hobson*, Edward Chapman, Veronica Turleigh, Gibb McLaughlin, Frank Pettingell

Cardboard Cavalier*
GB 1949 96m bw
Rank / Two Cities

In Cromwellian England, royalists commission a barrow boy to carry a secret letter. Helped by Nell Gwynn, he succeeds after encounters with a castle ghost and custard pies.
A pantomime crossed with an Aldwych farce in a period setting. It failed at the time but now seems a brave try, with nice judgment all round.

w Noel Langley *d Walter Forde ph* Jack Hildyard *m* Lambert Williamson

Sid Field, Margaret Lockwood, Mary Clare, Jerry Desmonde, Claude Hulbert, Irene Handl, Brian Worth, Edmund Willard (as Cromwell)

The Cardinal*
US 1963 175m Technicolor
Panavision 70
Gamma / Otto Preminger

A 1917 ordinand becomes a Boston curate, a fighter of the Ku Klux Klan, a Rome diplomat, and finally gets a cardinal's hat.
Heavy-going documentary melodrama with many interesting sequences marred by lack of cohesion, too much grabbing at world problems, and over-sensational personal asides.

w Robert Dozier, *novel* Henry Morton Robinson *d Otto Preminger ph* Leon Shamroy *m* Jerome Moross *pd* Lyle Wheeler *titles* Saul Bass

Tom Tryon, *Carol Lynley*, Dorothy Gish, Maggie Macnamara, Cecil Kellaway, John Saxon, *John Huston*, Robert Morse, Burgess Meredith, Jill Haworth, Raf Vallone, Tullio Carminati, Ossie Davis, Chill Wills, Arthur Hunnicutt, Murray Hamilton, Patrick O'Neal, Romy Schneider

'Very probably the last word in glossy dishonesty posturing as serious art.'—*John Simon*

'Mere and sheer wide screen Technicolor movie.'—*Stanley Kauffmann*

Cardinal Richelieu*
US 1935 83m bw
Twentieth Century (Darryl F. Zanuck)

Fictionalized biography of the unscrupulous cardinal who was the grey eminence behind Louis XIII.
One of George Arliss' better star vehicles, with not much conviction but excellent production values.

w Maude Howell, Cameron Rogers, W. P. Lipscomb *d* Rowland V. Lee *ph* Peverell Marley *m* Alfred Newman

George Arliss, Maureen O'Sullivan, Edward Arnold, Cesar Romero

Career*
US 1959 105m bw
Paramount / Hal B. Wallis (Paul Nathan)

An actor from the midwest finally gets his chance in New York.
A location melodrama with the feel of a documentary, well played but slow and rather indeterminate.

w James Lee, from his play *d* Joseph Anthony *ph* Joseph La Shelle *m* Franz Waxman

Anthony Franciosa, Dean Martin, Shirley Maclaine, Carolyn Jones, Joan Blackman, Robert Middleton, Frank McHugh, Donna Douglas

Carefree*
US 1938 85m bw
RKO (Pandro S. Berman)

A humourless lawyer sends his undecided girl friend to an alienist, with whom she falls in love.
Slight, frothy comedy musical; quite palatable, but it signalled the end of the Astaire–Rogers series.

w Allan Scott, Ernest Pagano *d* Mark Sandrich *ph* Robert de Grasse *m/ly* Irving Berlin *ch* Hermes Pan

Fred Astaire, Ginger Rogers, Ralph Bellamy, Luella Gear, Clarence Kolb, Jack Carson, Franklin Pangborne, Walter Kingsford, Hattie McDaniel

Careful, Soft Shoulder*
US 1942 69m bw
TCF (Walter Morosco)

A Washington socialite becomes a spy for both sides.
Modest, slightly unusual second feature which over the years has gathered for itself more reputation than it really deserves.

wd Oliver H. P. Garrett *ph* Charles Clarke

Virginia Bruce, James Ellison, Aubrey Mather, Sheila Ryan, Ralph Byrd

The Caretaker*
GB 1964 105m bw
Caretaker Films (Michael Birkett)
US title: *The Guest*

Two brothers invite a revolting tramp to share their attic.
Rather doleful filming of the fashionable play with its non-plot, irregular conceits and interesting interplay of character. It remains a theatrical experience.

w Harold Pinter *d* Clive Donner *ph* Nicolas Roeg *m* Ron Grainer

Alan Bates, Robert Shaw, Donald Pleasance

The Caretakers*
US 1963 97m bw
UA / Hall Bartlett
GB title: *Borderlines*

The interrelationship of several cases in a state mental hospital.
Rather hysterical melodrama, lacking in the stature required for its subject, but sometimes perversely entertaining.

w Henry F. Greenberg, *novel* Daniel Telfer *d* Hall Bartlett *ph* *Lucien Ballard* *m* Elmer Bernstein

Polly Bergen, Robert Stack, Joan Crawford, Diane McBain, Janis Paige, Van Williams, Robert Vaughn, Herbert Marshall, Constance Ford

The Carey Treatment*
US 1972 101m Metrocolor Panavision
MGM (William Belasco)

A Boston pathologist investigating the death of an abortion victim becomes the potential murder victim of a father turned killer.
Pretentious thriller with a tendency to make moral points among the bloodshed; vigorously but variably made.

w James P. Bonner, *novel* A Case of Need by Jeffrey Hudson *d* Blake Edwards *ph* Frank Stanley *m* Roy Budd

James Coburn, Jennifer O'Neill, Skye Aubrey, Pat Hingle, Dan O'Herlihy, Elizabeth Allen, Alex Dreier, Regis Toomey

Caribbean
US 1952 94m Technicolor
(Paramount) Pine–Thomas (William H. Pine, William C. Thomas)
GB title: *Caribbean Gold*

An 18th-century pirate captures the nephew of his old enemy.
Adequate but not very exciting swashbuckler with fair production values.

w Frank L. Moss, Edward Ludwig *d* Edward Ludwig *ph* Lionel Lindon *m* Lucien Cailliet

John Payne, Arlene Dahl, Cedric Hardwicke (incredibly cast as the pirate), Francis L. Sullivan, Dennis Hoey

Carlton-Browne of the FO
GB 1958 88m bw
British Lion / Charter Films (John Boulting)
US title: *Man in a Cocked Hat*

When valuable mineral deposits are found in a small British colony, the diplomat sent to cement good relations does quite the reverse.
Hit-or-miss farcical comedy several rungs below the Ealing style, with all concerned in poor form.

wd Jeffrey Dell, Roy Boulting *ph* Max Greene *m* John Addison

Terry-Thomas, Peter Sellers, Ian Bannen, Thorley Walters, Raymond Huntley, John Le Mesurier. Luciana Paluzzi, Miles Malleson, Kynaston Reeves, Marie Lohr

Carmen Jones*
US 1954 105m De Luxe Cinemascope
TCF (Otto Preminger)

A factory girl marries a pilot, and is strangled by him for infidelity.
Black American updating of Bizet's opera, not really satisfactory but given full marks for trying, though the main singing is dubbed and the effect remains doggedly theatrical.

w Harry Kleiner *d* Otto Preminger *ph* Sam Leavitt *ly* Oscar Hammerstein II *titles Saul Bass*

Dorothy Dandridge, Harry Belafonte, *Pearl Bailey*, Olga James, Joe Adams, Roy Glenn, Nick Stewart, Diahann Carroll, Brock Peters

'All one regrets is that the director has been unable to impose a unifying style on this promising material.'—*Gavin Lambert*

Carnal Knowledge*
US 1971 97m Technicolor Panavision
Avco Embassy / Icarus (Mike Nichols)

A college student embarks on an enthusiastic and varied sex life but by middle age is bored and empty.
Hampered by an unsuitable wide screen, this pretentious but fragmented comedy drama is embarrassingly conscious of its own daring in subject and language, and good performances are weighed down by an unsubtle script and tricksy direction.

w Jules Feiffer *d* Mike Nichols *ph* Giuseppe Rotunno *m* various songs *pd* Richard Sylbert

Jack Nicholson, *Arthur Garfunkel*, Candice Bergen, *Ann-Margret*, Rita Moreno

Carnegie Hall
US 1947 134m bw
Federal Films

The story of New York's music centre, based on a fiction about a cleaner who finally becomes a concert organizer when her son is a famous pianist.
Slim and risible excuse for a classical concert, featuring among others Bruno Walter, Leopold Stokowski, Artur Rubenstein, Jascha Heifitz, Lily Pons, Rise Stevens, Ezio Pinza, Jan Peerce, Harry James, Vaughn Monroe and the New York Philharmonic Symphony Orchestra.

w Karl Lamb *d* Edgar G. Ulmer *ph* William Miller

'The thickest and sourest mess of musical mulligatawny I have yet had to sit down to.'—*James Agee*

Carnival
GB 1946 93m bw
Rank / Two Cities

In the nineties, a ballet dancer marries a dour Cornish farmer, who shoots her when her erstwhile lover comes after her.
Flimsy screen version of a solidly old-fashioned romantic drama.

w Eric Maschwitz, *novel* Compton Mackenzie *d* Stanley Haynes *ph* Guy Green

Sally Gray, Michael Wilding, Bernard Miles, Cathleen Nesbitt

Carnival Story
US / Germany 1954 95m Technicolor
The King Brothers

A starving girl becomes a trapezist at a German circus and stirs up jealousy among her partners.
Bleak reworking of *The Three Maxims* (qv), reworked again with more expertise in *Trapeze* (qv); this version is a cheap and unattractive co-production.

w Kurt Neumann, Hans Jacoby *d* Kurt Neumann *ph* Ernest Haller *m* Willi Schmidt-Genter

Anne Baxter, Steve Cochran, Lyle Bettger, George Nader, Jay C. Flippen

Carolina
US 1934 85m bw
Fox (Darryl F. Zanuck)

A Yankee farmer's daughter falls in love with a Southern plantation owner.
Mildly pleasing period piece.

w Reginald Berkeley, *play* The House of Connelly by Paul Green *d* Henry King *ph* Hal Mohr

Janet Gaynor, Lionel Barrymore, Robert Young, Henrietta Crosman, Mona Barrie, Richard Cromwell

Carousel*
US 1956 128m Eastmancolor
Cinemascope 55
TCF (Henry Ephron)

A ne'er-do-well dies while committing a hold-up. Fifteen years later he returns from heaven to set his family's affairs in order.
Based on a fantasy play with an honourable history, this super-wide-screen version of an effective stage musical is hollow and boring, a humourless whimsy in which even the songs seem an intrusion.

w Phoebe and Henry Ephron, from the musical based on Ferenc Molnar's play Liliom *d* Henry King *ph* Charles G. Clarke *m/ly* Rodgers and Hammerstein *ch* Rod Alexander, Agnes de Mille

Gordon Macrae, Shirley Jones, Cameron Mitchell,Gene Lockhart, Barbara Ruick, Robert Rounseville

The Carpetbaggers**
US 1964 150m Technicolor
Panavision
Paramount / Embassy (Joseph E. Levine)

A young playboy inherits an aircraft business, becomes a megalomaniac tycoon, and moves to Hollywood in his search for power.
Enjoyable pulp fiction clearly suggested by the career of Howard Hughes. Lashings of old-fashioned melodrama, quite well pointed by all concerned.

w John Michael Hayes, *novel* Harold Robbins *d Edward Dmytryk* *ph* Joseph Macdonald *m* Elmer Bernstein *ad* Hal Pereira, Walter Tyler

George Peppard, Carroll Baker, *Alan Ladd* (his last film), *Martin Balsam*, Bob Cummings, Martha Hyer, Elizabeth Ashley, Lew Ayres, Ralph Taeger, Archie Moore, Leif Erickson, Audrey Totter

'One of those elaborate conjuring tricks in which yards and yards of coloured ribbon are spread all over the stage merely to prove that the conjuror has nothing up his sleeve.'—*Tom Milne*

Carrie**
US 1952 122m bw
Paramount (William Wyler)

In the early 1900s a country girl comes to Chicago, loses her innocence and goes on the stage, meanwhile reducing a wealthy restaurant manager to penury through love for her.
A famous satirical novel is softened into an unwieldy narrative with scarcely enough dramatic power to sustain interest despite splendid production values. Heavy pre-release

cuts remain obvious, and the general effect is depressing; but it is very good to look at.

w Ruth and Augustus Goetz, *novel* Sister Carrie by Theodore Dreiser *d William Wyler ph Victor Milner m* David Raksin *ad Hal Pereira, Roland Anderson*

Laurence Olivier, Jennifer Jones, Miriam Hopkins, Eddie Albert, Basil Ruysdael, Ray Teal, Barry Kelley, Mary Murphy

Carrington VC*
GB 1954 106m bw
British Lion / Romulus (Teddy Baird)
US title: *Court Martial*

An army major is courtmartialled for embezzling mess funds.
Good courtroom drama with a few plot surprises, convincing characters, and very serviceable acting and direction.

w John Hunter, *play* Dorothy and Campbell Christie *d* Anthony Asquith *ph* Desmond Dickinson

David Niven, Margaret Leighton, Noelle Middleton, Laurence Naismith, Clive Morton, Mark Dignam, Allan Cuthbertson, Victor Maddern, John Glyn-Jones, Raymond Francis, Newton Blick, John Chandos

Carry on Sergeant
GB 1958 83m bw
Anglo Amalgamated / Insignia (Peter Rogers)

An army training sergeant accepts a bet that his last platoon of raw recruits will win the Star Squad award.
Shabby farce with humdrum script and slack direction, saved by energetic performances.

w Norman Hudis, *play* The Bull Boys by R. F. Delderfield *d* Gerald Thomas *ph* Peter Hennessy *m* Bruce Montgomery

Bob Monkhouse, William Hartnell, Kenneth Williams, Charles Hawtrey, Shirley Eaton, Eric Barker, Dora Bryan, Bill Owen, Kenneth Connor

† From this unlikely beginning sprang almost twenty years of *Carry Ons*, their plots gradually disappearing under an accumulation of old jokes which grew steadily bluer. Colour did little to disguise their makeshift construction, and they never raised their sights as high as satire, but they became a British institution like fish and chips, and many of the regulars became stars. Apart from Williams, Hawtrey and Connor, those most regularly featured in the sequels were Sid James, Bernard Bresslaw, Jim Dale, Joan Sims, Hattie Jacques, Peter Butterworth, and Jack Douglas, with occasional guests such as Harry H. Corbett, Juliet Mills and even Phil Silvers. All were produced by Peter Rogers and directed by Gerald Thomas; most were written (or recollected) by Talbot Rothwell. Delivered at the rate of roughly two a year, the sequence of titles was CARRY ON NURSE (a surprising hit in the US), CARRY ON TEACHER, CARRY ON CONSTABLE, CARRY ON REGARDLESS, CARRY ON CRUISING, CARRY ON CABBY, CARRY ON JACK, CARRY ON SPYING, CARRY ON CLEO, CARRY ON COWBOY, CARRY ON SCREAMING, FOLLOW THAT CAMEL (Beau Geste), DON'T LOSE YOUR HEAD (the Scarlet Pimpernel), CARRY ON DOCTOR, CARRY ON UP THE KHYBER, CARRY ON CAMPING, CARRY ON AGAIN DOCTOR, CARRY ON LOVING, CARRY ON UP THE JUNGLE, CARRY ON HENRY (Henry VIII), CARRY ON AT YOUR CONVENIENCE, CARRY ON MATRON, CARRY ON ABROAD, CARRY ON GIRLS, CARRY ON DICK, CARRY ON BEHIND, CARRY ON ENGLAND.
†CARRY ON ADMIRAL and WHAT A CARRY ON are not part of the series.

Carter's Army
US 1969 72m colour TVM
Thomas–Spelling

During World War II a white southern officer is given a black platoon to help in a dangerous assignment.
Formula action hokum.

w Aaron Spelling, David Kidd *d* George McCowan

Stephen Boyd, Robert Hooks, Susan Oliver, Roosevelt Grier, Moses Gunn, Richard Pryor, Billy Dee Williams

Carve Her Name with Pride*
GB 1958 119m bw
Rank / Keyboard (Daniel M. Angel)

In 1940, the young British widow of a French officer is enlisted as a spy, and after various adventures dies before a German firing squad.
Slightly muddled if ultimately moving biopic in which initial light comedy gives way to romance, documentary, character study, blazing war action and finally tragedy. Generally well made.

w Vernon Harris, Lewis Gilbert, *book* R. J. Minney *d Lewis Gilbert ph* John Wilcox *m* William Alwyn

Virginia McKenna (as Violette Szabo), *Paul Scofield*, Jack Warner, Sidney Tafler, Denise Grey, Alain Saury, Maurice Ronet, Nicole Stéphane, Noel Willman, Bill Owen, William Mervyn, Anne Leon

'What is missing is the deeply charged passion which would have gone beyond the quietly decent statement intermittently achieved.'—*John Gillett*

Casablanca****
US 1942 102m bw
Warner *(Hal B. Wallis)*

Rick's Café in Casablanca is a centre for war refugees awaiting visas for America. Rick abandons his cynicism to help an old love escape the Nazis with her underground leader husband.
Cinema par excellence: a studio-bound Hollywood melodrama which after various chances just fell together impeccably into one of the outstanding entertainment experiences of cinema history, with romance, intrigue, excitement, suspense and humour cunningly deployed by master technicians and a perfect cast.

w Julius J. Epstein, Philip G. Epstein, Howard Koch, from an unproduced play, Everybody Comes to Rick's, by Murray Burnett and Joan Alison *d Michael Curtiz ph Arthur Edeson m Max Steiner*

Humphrey Bogart, Ingrid Bergman, Claude Rains, Paul Henreid, Conrad Veidt, S. Z. Sakall, Sydney Greenstreet, Peter Lorre, Dooley Wilson (singing 'As Time Goes By'), *Marcel Dalio, Leonid Kinskey*

'A picture which makes the spine tingle and the heart take a leap . . . they have so combined sentiment, humour and pathos with taut melodrama and bristling intrigue that the result is a highly entertaining and even inspiring film.'—*New York Times*

'Its humour is what really saves it, being a mixture of Central European irony of attack and racy Broadway–Hollywood Boulevard cynicism.'—*Herman G. Weinberg*

'The happiest of happy accidents, and the most decisive exception to the *auteur* theory.'—*Andrew Sarris, 1968*

'A film which seems to have been frozen in time . . . the sum of its many marvellous parts far exceeds the whole.'—*NFT, 1974*

Casanova Brown
US 1944 99m bw
International / Christie (Nunnally Johnson)

Just as his divorce comes through, a man discovers that his wife is pregnant.
Very mild star comedy which tiptoes round its subject.

w Nunnally Johnson, *play* Bachelor Father by Floyd Dell, Thomas Mitchell *d* Sam Wood *ph* John F. Seitz *m* Arthur Lange

Gary Cooper, Teresa Wright, Frank Morgan, Anita Louise, Patricia Collinge, Edmond Breon, Jill Esmond, Isobel Elsom, Mary Treen, Halliwell Hobbes

Casanova's Big Night
US 1954 86m Technicolor
Paramount (Paul Jones)

In old Italy, the great lover is fleeing from his creditors and changes places with a tailor's apprentice.
The last of Bob Hope's big-budget, big-studio burlesques is a lumbering vehicle which wastes its star cast and mistimes its laughs.

w Hal Kanter, Edmund Hartmann *d* Norman Z. McLeod *ph* Lionel Lindon

Bob Hope, Joan Fontaine (an unhappy comedy foil), Basil Rathbone, Vincent Price, Audrey Dalton, Hugh Marlowe, John Carradine, Primo Carnera, Arnold Moss, Lon Chaney Jnr

Casbah
US 1948 94m bw
Universal (Erik Charell)

Remake of *Algiers* (qv) with songs added.
Not too bad in the circumstances, but a wholly artificial exercise, and another version was really not needed. The sets seem overlit and claustrophobic.

w (not credited) *d* John Berry *ph* Irving Glassberg *m* Harold Arlen

Tony Martin, Yvonne de Carlo, Marta Toren, *Peter Lorre,* Hugo Haas

The Case against Mrs Ames
US 1936 85m bw
Paramount (Walter Wanger)

The prosecutor in a murder case is convinced of the defendant's innocence.
Tired rehash of a familiar theme.

w Gene Towne, Graham Baker *d* William A. Seiter *ph* Lucien Andriot

Madeleine Carroll, George Brent, Arthur Treacher, Alan Baxter, Beulah Bondi, Alan Mowbray, Esther Dale, Ed Brophy

A Case of Rape*
US 1974 98m colour TVM
Universal

A rape victim finds the legal system works against her.
Spirited warming over of documentary facts.

w Robert E. Thompson *d* Boris Sagal

Elizabeth Montgomery, Ronnie Cox, Cliff Potts, William Daniels, Rosemary Murphy

Cash McCall
US 1960 102m Technicolor
Warner (Henry Blanke)

A Napoleon of the stock market gets into trouble for the first time when love interferes with business.
Slightly unusual comedy drama, quite sharply made and played, but not adding up to much.

w Lenore Coffee, Marion Hargrove, *novel* Cameron Hawley *d* Joseph Pevney *ph* George Folsey *m* Max Steiner

James Garner, Natalie Wood, Nina Foch, Dean Jagger, E. G. Marshall, Henry Jones, Otto Kruger, Roland Winters

Cash on Demand*
GB 1963 86m bw
Columbia / Woodpecker / Hammer (Michael Carreras)

A fussy bank manager outwits a classy robber.
Quietly effective suspenser with an admirable middle-aged cast and no love interest.

w Lewis Greifer, David T. Chantler, from Jacques Gillies' TV play *d* Quentin Lawrence *ph* Arthur Grant *m* Wilfred Josephs

Peter Cushing, André Morell, Richard Vernon, Norman Bird, Edith Sharpe

Casino Royale
GB 1967 130m Technicolor Panavision
Columbia / Famous Artists (Charles K. Feldman, Jerry Bresler)

The heads of the allied spy forces call Sir James Bond out of retirement to fight the power of *SMERSH.*
Woeful all-star kaleidoscope, a way-out spoof which generates far fewer laughs than the original. One of the most shameless wastes of time and talent in screen history.

w Wolf Mankowitz, John Law, Michael Sayers, *novel* Ian Fleming *d* John Huston, Ken Hughes, Val Guest, Robert Parrish, Joe McGrath, Richard Talmadge *ph* Jack Hildyard *m* Burt Bacharach *pd* Michael Stringer

David Niven, Deborah Kerr, Orson Welles, Peter Sellers, Ursula Andress, Woody Allen, William Holden, Charles Boyer, John Huston, Joanna Pettet, Daliah Lavi, Kurt Kasznar, Jacqueline Bisset, Derek Nimmo, George Raft, Ronnie Corbett, Peter O'Toole, Jean-Paul Belmondo, Geoffrey Bayldon, Duncan Macrae

'One of those wild wacky extravaganzas in which the audience is expected to have a great time because everybody making the film did. It seldom works out that way, and certainly doesn't here.'—*John Russell Taylor*

Cass Timberlane*
US 1947 119m bw
MGM (Arthur Hornblow Jnr)

A judge marries a working class girl, who is unsettled at first but finally comes to realize her good fortune.
Solid drama with an understanding star performance and good production values.

w Donald Ogden Stewart, *novel* Sinclair Lewis *d* George Sidney *ph* Robert Planck *m* Roy Webb

Spencer Tracy, Lana Turner, Zachary Scott, Tom Drake, Mary Astor, Albert Dekker, Selena Royle, Josephine Hutchinson, Margaret Lindsay

Cast a Dark Shadow*
GB 1955 82m bw
Frobisher / Daniel M. Angel (Herbert Mason)

A wife-murderer marries an ex-barmaid and tries again.
Unambitious but enjoyable melodrama, well acted though with directorial opportunities missed.

w John Cresswell, *play* Murder Mistaken by Janet Green *d* Lewis Gilbert *ph* Jack Asher *m* Antony Hopkins

Dirk Bogarde, *Margaret Lockwood* (her last film to date), Kay Walsh, Kathleen Harrison, Robert Flemyng, Mona Washbourne, Walter Hudd

Cast a Giant Shadow*
US 1966 141m De Luxe Panavision
UA / Mirisch / Llenroc / Batjac (Melville Shavelson)

An American military lawyer and ex-colonel goes to Israel in 1947 to help in the fight against the Arabs.
Spectacular war biopic with all concerned in good form but lacking the clarity and narrative control of a real smash.

w Melville Shavelson, from Ted Berkman's biography of Col. David Marcus *d* Melville Shavelson *ph Aldo Tonti* *m* Elmer Bernstein *pd* Michael Stringer

Kirk Douglas, Angie Dickinson, Senta Berger, Luther Adler, Stathis Giallelis, Chaim Topol, John Wayne, Frank Sinatra, Yul Brynner, James Donald, Gordon Jackson, Michael Hordern, Gary Merrill, Allan Cuthbertson, Jeremy Kemp

The Castaway Cowboy*
US 1974 91m Technicolor
Walt Disney (Ron Miller, Winston Hibler)

In 1850, a Shanghaied sailor on Hawaii helps a lady potato farmer to turn her land into a cattle ranch.

Unexciting and unexceptional family fare.

w Don Tait *d* Vincent McEveety *ph* Andrew Jackson *m* Robert F. Brunner

James Garner, Vera Miles, Robert Culp, Eric Shea, Elizabeth Smith

Castle Keep*
US 1969 107m Technicolor Panavision
Columbia / Filmways (Martin Ransohoff, John Calley)

During World War II seven battle-weary American soldiers occupy a 10th-century castle filled with art treasures, then die defending it. Or are they dead all the time? The film version of this fantastic novel never seems quite sure, and the uncertainty finally deadens it despite careful work all round.

w Daniel Taradash, David Rayfiel, *novel* William Eastlake *d* Sydney Pollack *ph* Henri Decae *m* Michel Legrand

Burt Lancaster, Peter Falk, Jean Pierre Aumont, Patrick O'Neal, Al Freeman Jnr, Scott Wilson, Tony Bill, Bruce Dern, Astrid Heeren

Castle on the Hudson*
US 1940 77m bw
Warner (Sam Bischoff)
GB title: *Years without Days*

A hardened criminal is not helped by his years in prison.
Adequate, gloomy remake of *Twenty Thousand Years in Sing Sing*.

w Seton I. Miller, Brown Holmes, Courtney Terrett *d* Anatole Litvak *ph* Arthur Edeson

John Garfield, Pat O'Brien, Ann Sheridan, Burgess Meredith, Jerome Cowan, Henry O'Neill, Guinn Williams, John Litel

Cat and Mouse*
GB 1958 79m bw
(Eros) Anvil (Paul Rotha)

The daughter of a man executed for murder is threatened by criminals seeking hidden loot.
Interesting rather than exciting second feature thriller directed by a documentary maker.

wd Paul Rotha, *novel* Michael Halliday *ph* Wolfgang Suschitsky

Lee Patterson, Ann Sears, Hilton Edwards, Victor Maddern, George Rose, Roddy McMillan

The Cat and the Canary***
US 1939 72m bw
Paramount (Arthur Hornblow Jnr)

Heirs to an eccentric's will gather at midnight in his gloomy mansion in the swamps, and are menaced by a maniac who turns out to be one of their number.
The 'classic' spooky house thriller, previously filmed as a 1927 silent and (as *The Cat Creeps*) in 1930 by Rupert Julian, is here superbly staged, briskly paced, perfectly cast and lusciously photographed. The comedy-thriller par excellence, with Bob Hope fresh and sympathetic in his first big star part.

w Walter de Leon, Lynn Starling, play John Willard *d Elliott Nugent ph Charles Lang m Dr Ernst Toch ad* Hans Dreier, Robert Usher

Bob Hope, Paulette Goddard, Gale Sondergaard, John Beal, Douglass Montgomery, Nydia Westman, *Elizabeth Patterson*, John Wray, *George Zucco*

'Beautifully shot, intelligently constructed.'—*Peter John Dyer, 1966*

Cat Ballou**
US 1965 96m Technicolor
Columbia (Harold Hecht)

Young Catherine Ballou hires a drunken gunfighter to protect her father from a vicious gunman, but despite her efforts he is shot, so she turns outlaw.
Sometimes lively, sometimes somnolent western spoof which considering the talent involved should have been funnier than it is. The linking ballad helps.

w Walter Newman, Frank R. Pierson, *novel* Roy Chanslor *d* Eliot Silverstein *ph* Jack Marta *m* Frank de Vol

Jane Fonda, *Lee Marvin*, Michael Callan, Dwayne Hickman, Nat King Cole, Stubby Kaye, Tom Nardini, John Marley, Reginald Denny

'Uneven, lumpy, coy and obvious.' —*Pauline Kael*

The Cat Creature
US 1973 74m colour TVM
Columbia / Douglas S. Cramer

Death from a supernatural feline follows a stolen Egyptian amulet.
Poorly made, sluggishly written horror hokum which wastes its cast.

w Robert Bloch *d* Curtis Harrington

Meredith Baxter, Stuart Whitman, Gale Sondergaard, Keye Luke, David Hedison, John Carradine

Cat on a Hot Tin Roof**
US 1958 108m Metrocolor Cinemascope
MGM (Lawrence Weingarten)

A rich plantation owner, dying of cancer, finds his two sons unsatisfactory: one is a conniver, the other a neurotic who refuses to sleep with his wife.
Slightly bowdlerized version of Tennessee Williams' most straightforward melodrama, watchable for the acting but still basically a theatrical experience.

w Richard Brooks, James Poe *d* Richard Brooks *ph* William Daniels *m* none

Paul Newman, Burl Ives, Elizabeth Taylor, Jack Carson, Judith Anderson, Madeleine Sherwood, Larry Gates

Cat People**
US 1942 73m bw
RKO (*Val Lewton*)

A beautiful Yugoslavian girl believes she can turn into a panther; before she is found mysteriously dead, several of her acquaintances are attacked by such a beast.
The first of Lewton's famous horror series for RKO is a slow starter but has some notable suspense sequences. It was also the first monster film to refrain from showing its monster.

w De Witt Bodeen *d Jacques Tourneur* *ph* Nicholas Musuraca *m* Roy Webb

Simone Simon, Kent Smith, Tom Conway, Jane Randolph, Jack Holt

'(Lewton) revolutionized scare movies with suggestion, imaginative sound effects and camera angles, leaving everything to the fear-filled imagination.'—*Pauline Kael, 1968*

† *Curse of the Cat People* (qv) was a very unrelated sequel.

Catch Me a Spy
GB 1971 94m Technicolor
Rank / Ludgate / Capitol / Films de la Pleiade (Steven Pallos)

A British agent smuggling Russian manuscripts into England falls for the wife of a Russian spy and finally gets his money as well.
Complex, patchy comedy thriller with dispirited action scenes in Bucharest and Scotland. Technical credits rather dim.

w Dick Clement, Ian La Frenais, *novel* George Marton, Tibor Meray *d* Dick Clement *ph* Christopher Challis *m* Claude Bolling

Kirk Douglas, Trevor Howard, Tom Courtenay, Marlene Jobert, Patrick Mower, Bernadette Lafont, Bernard Blier

Catch 22*
US 1970 122m Technicolor Panavision
Paramount (John Calley, Martin Ransohoff)

At a US Air Force base in the Mediterranean during World War II, one by one the officers are distressingly killed; a survivor paddles towards neutral Sweden.
Intensely black comedy, more so than *M*A*S*H* and less funny, effectively mordant in places but too grisly and missing several tricks.

w Buck Henry, *novel* Joseph Heller *d* Mike Nichols *ph* David Watkin *m* none *pd* Richard Sylbert

Alan Arkin, Martin Balsam, Richard Benjamin, Art Garfunkel, Jack Gilford, Buck Henry, Bob Newhart, Anthony Perkins, Paula Prentiss, Jon Voight, Martin Sheen, Orson Welles

The Catcher
US 1971 98m colour TVM
Columbia / Herbert B. Leonard

An ex-police detective offers his services in tracking down fugitives.
Tedious pilot which not surprisingly didn't get anywhere.

w David Freeman *d* Allen H. Miner

Michael Witney, Jan-Michael Vincent, Tony Franciosa, Catherine Burns, David Wayne, Alf Kjellin, Anne Baxter

The Catered Affair*
US 1956 93m bw
MGM (Sam Zimbalist)
GB title: *Wedding Breakfast*

When the daughter of a New York taxi driver gets married, her mother insists on a bigger function than they can afford.
Rather heavy-going comedy with amusing dialogue, from the period when Hollywood was seizing on TV plays like *Marty* and *Twelve Angry Men.*

w Gore Vidal, TV play Paddy Chayevsky *d* Richard Brooks *ph* John Alton *m* André Previn

Bette Davis Ernest Borgnine, Debbie Reynolds, Barry Fitzgerald, Rod Taylor, Robert Simon, Madge Kennedy, Dorothy Stickney

Catherine the Great*
GB 1934 93m bw
Alexander Korda

How Catherine married the mad prince and slowly conquered the Russian court.
Dated but well acted and written account, sober by comparison with *The Scarlet Empress* which came out at the same time.

w Lajos Biro, Arthur Wimperis, Marjorie Deans, *play* The Czarina by Melchior Lengyel, Lajos Biro *d* Paul Czinner

Elisabeth Bergner, Douglas Fairbanks Jnr, Flora Robson, Gerald du Maurier, Irene Vanbrugh, Griffiths Jones, Joan Gardner, Diana Napier

Catholics***
GB 1973 74m colour TVM
CBS / Harlech TV

A remote abbey insists on sticking to the Latin mass and a young priest is sent to talk to the abbot.
Absorbing drama of ideas with splendid Scottish island backgrounds.

w Brian Moore d Jack Gold ph Gerry Fisher *m* Carl Davis

Trevor Howard, Martin Sheen, Cyril Cusack, Andrew Keir, Michael Gambon

Catlow*
GB 1971 101m Metrocolor Panavision
MGM / Euan Lloyd

A maverick cattleman tricks his enemies and winds up as sheriff.
Light-hearted, cheerfully cast, fast-moving, Spanish-located western.

w Scot Finch, J. J. Griffith, *novel* Louis L'Amour *d* Sam Wanamaker *ph* Ted Scaife *m* Roy Budd

Yul Brynner, Leonard Nimoy, Richard Crenna, Daliah Lavi, Jo Ann Pflug, Jeff Corey, Bessie Love, David Ladd

Caught*
US 1948 88m bw
Enterprise (Wolfgang Reinhardt)

The ill-treated wife of a vicious millionaire leaves him for a doctor, but finds she is to have the millionaire's baby.
Pretentious *film noir*, rather typical of its time, with much talent squandered on a very boring plot.

w Arthur Laurents, *novel* Wild Calendar by Libbie Block *d Max Ophuls ph Lee Garmes m* Frederick Hollander

James Mason (the doctor), Robert Ryan (the millionaire), Barbara Bel Geddes, Natalie Schaefer, Curt Bois

Caught in the Draft**
US 1941 82m bw
Paramount (B. G. De Sylva)

A nervous film star cannot avoid being drafted into the army.
Sprightly comedy from the star's best period, with gags and supporting cast well up to form.

w Harry Tugend *d* David Butler *ph* Karl Struss *m* Victor Young

Bob Hope, Lynne Overman, Dorothy Lamour, Clarence Kolb, Eddie Bracken, Paul Hurst, Irving Bacon

Cause for Alarm*
US 1951 74m bw
MGM (Tom Lewis)

A housewife tries frantically to retrieve a posted letter containing manufactured evidence which may put her on a murder charge.
Minor-league suspenser, watchable but disappointingly handled.

w Mel Dinelli, Tom Lewis *d* Tay Garnett *ph* Joe Ruttenberg *m* André Previn

Loretta Young, Barry Sullivan, Bruce Cowling, Margalo Gillmore, Irving Bacon

Cavalcade**
US 1933 109m bw
Fox (Winfield Sheehan)

The story of an upper-class English family between the Boer War and World War I.
Rather static version of the famous stage spectacular, very similar in setting and style to TV's later *Upstairs Downstairs*. Good performances, flat handling.

w Reginald Berkeley, *play Noel Coward d* Frank Lloyd *ph* Ernest Palmer *war scenes* William Cameron Menzies *ad* William Darling

Clive Brook, Diana Wynyard, Ursula Jeans, Herbert Mundin, Una O'Connor, Irene Browne, Merle Tottenham, Beryl Mercer, Frank Lawton, Billy Bevan

'If there is anything that moves the ordinary American to uncontrollable tears, it is the plight—the constant plight—of dear old England . . . a superlative newsreel, forcibly strengthened by factual scenes, good music, and wonderful photography.'—*Pare Lorentz*

Ceiling Zero**
US 1935 95m bw
Warner / Cosmopolitan (Harry Joe Brown)

Amorous and airborne adventures of an irresponsible but brilliant civil airlines pilot.
Splendid star vehicle which turns maudlin in the last reel but until then provides crackling entertainment.

w Frank 'Spig' Wead, from his play *d Howard Hawks ph* Arthur Edeson

James Cagney, Pat O'Brien, June Travis, Stuart Erwin, Henry Wadsworth, Isabel Jewell, Barton Maclane

'The best of all airplane pictures.'—*Otis Ferguson, 1939*

'Directed at a breakneck pace which emphasizes its lean fibre and its concentration on the essentials of its theme.'—*Andrew Sarris, 1963*

Cell 2455 Death Row
US 1955 77m bw
Columbia (Wallace MacDonald)

A convicted murderer staves off execution with appeal after appeal.
Cheap run-off of the case of Caryl Chessman, who was executed ten years after his trial for rape and murder.

w Jack de Witt *d* Fred F. Sears *ph* Fred Jackman Jnr *m* Mischa Bakaleinikoff

William Campbell, Kathryn Grant, Harvey Stephens, Marian Carr

Centennial Summer**
US 1946 102m Technicolor
TCF (Otto Preminger)

A Philadelphia family responds to the Great Exposition of 1876.
Pleasing family comedy with music, the kind of harmless competence Hollywood used to throw off with ease but can no longer manage.

w Michael Kanin, *novel* Albert E. Idell *d* Otto Preminger *ph* Ernest Palmer *m* Alfred Newman *songs* Jerome Kern, Oscar Hammerstein II, E. Y. Harburg, Leo Robin

Jeanne Crain, Cornel Wilde, Linda Darnell, William Eythe, Walter Brennan, *Constance Bennett*, Dorothy Gish

The Century Turns
US 1971 97m Technicolor TVM
Universal (Jack Webb, William Finnegan)
aka: *Hec Ramsey*

An ex US marshal solves the double murder of a homesteading couple.
Tolerable pilot for a series which became part of *Mystery Movie* (qv), about a western detective using scientific methods.

w Harold Jack Bloom *d* Daniel Petrie

Richard Boone, Rick Lenz, Sharon Acker, Harry Morgan, Robert Pratt

The Ceremony
US / Spain 1963 107m bw
UA / Magla (Laurence Harvey)

In a Tangier jail, a bank robber awaits the firing squad, but he and his brother have an escape plan.
Murky and pretentious melodrama with aspirations to high style and symbolism. A bore.

w Ben Barzman, *novel* Frederic Grendel
d Laurence Harvey *ph* Oswald Morris
m Gerard Schurmann

Laurence Harvey, Sarah Miles, Robert Walker, John Ireland, Ross Martin, Lee Patterson, Jack McGowran, Murray Melvin, Fernando Rey

A Certain Smile*
US 1958 105m Eastmancolor Cinemascope
TCF (Henry Ephron)

A girl student falls in love with her philandering uncle.
Another sordid novella by Françoise Sagan (see *Bonjour Tristesse*), transformed by Hollywood into a glowing romantic saga of life among the Riviera rich. On this level, very competent.

w Francis Goodrich, Albert Hackett *d* Jean Negulesco *ph* Milton Krasner *m* Alfred Newman

Christine Carere, Rossano Brazzi, Joan Fontaine, Bradford Dillman, Eduard Franz, Kathryn Givney, Steve Geray

Chad Hanna*
US 1940 86m Technicolor
TCF (Darryl F. Zanuck, Nunnally Johnson)

Life in a Pennsylvania circus in the 1840s.
Mild romantic drama from a bestseller; local colour excellent, dramatic interest thin.

w Nunnally Johnson, *novel* Red Wheels Rolling by Walter D. Edmonds *d* Henry King
ph Ernest Palmer *m* David Buttolph

Henry Fonda, Dorothy Lamour, Linda Darnell, Guy Kibbee, Jane Darwell, John Carradine, Ted North, Roscoe Ates

The Chadwick Family
US 1974 74m Technicolor TVM
Universal (David Victor)

A writer discovers family problems when he is offered an important new job which involves a move.
Ho-hum domestic drama.

w John Gay *d* David Lowell Rich

Fred MacMurray, Kathleen Maguire, Darleen Carr, Barry Bostwick, John Larch, Margaret Lindsay

Chain Lightning
US 1950 94m bw
Warner (Anthony Veiller)

After World War II a bomber pilot learns how to control the new jets.

Absolutely routine romance and heroics.

w Liam O'Brien, Vincent Evans *d* Stuart Heisler *ph* Ernest Haller *m* David Buttolph

Humphrey Bogart, Eleanor Parker, Raymond Massey, Richard Whorf, James Brown, Roy Roberts, Morris Ankrum

Chained*
US 1934 77m bw
MGM (Hunt Stromberg)

A devoted wife has a shipboard romance with another man.
Moderate star romantic drama.

w John Lee Mahin *d* Clarence Brown *ph* George Folsey *m* Herbert Stothart

Joan Crawford, Clark Gable, Otto Kruger, Stuart Erwin, Una O'Connor, Akim Tamiroff

The Chalk Garden*
GB 1964 106m Technicolor
U-I / Quota Rentals (Ross Hunter)

The governess in a melancholy household has an effect on the lives of her aged employer and the young granddaughter.
Sub-Chekhovian drama in a house by the sea, flattened by routine handling into something much less interesting than it was on the stage.

w John Michael Hayes, *novel* Enid Bagnold *d* Ronald Neame *ph* Arthur Ibbetson *m* Malcolm Arnold

Edith Evans, Deborah Kerr, Hayley Mills, John Mills, Felix Aylmer, Elizabeth Sellars, Lally Bowers, Toke Townley

'Crashing symbolism, cracker-motto sententiousness.'—*MFB*

The Challenge
US 1970 74m colour TVM
TCF

To avoid a nuclear war, two countries poised to strike each other agree to settle their differences by an unarmed contest between one man from each side.
Silly panic button melodrama.

w Marc Norman *d* Alan Smithee

Darren McGavin, Mako, Broderick Crawford, Paul Lukas, James Whitmore, Skip Homeier

A Challenge for Robin Hood*
GB 1967 96m Technicolor
Hammer (Clifford Parkes)

A retelling of the original Robin Hood legend.
Unassuming, lively, predictable adventure hokum.

w Peter Bryan *d* C. Pennington-Richards *ph* Arthur Grant *m* Gary Hughes

Barrie Ingham, James Hayter, Leon Greene, John Arnatt

The Challengers
US 1968 96m colour TVM
Universal (Roy Huggins)

International racing drivers compete in the Grand Prix.
You can compute this one before you switch on.

w Dick Nelson *d* Leslie H. Martinson

Darren McGavin, Sean Garrison, Nico Minardos, Anne Baxter, Richard Conte, Farley Granger, Juliet Mills, Sal Mineo, Susan Clark

Chamber of Horrors
US 1966 99m Warnercolor
Warner (Hy Averback)

A maniacal murderer is finally trapped by two amateur criminologists who run a wax museum in Baltimore.
Zany horror thriller originally meant for TV; it turned out a shade too harrowing. Advertised as 'the picture with the Fear Flasher and the Horror Horn', shock gimmicks which proved much more startling than the crude events they heralded.

w Stephen Kandel *d* Hy Averback *ph* Richard Kline *m* William Lava

Patrick O'Neal, Cesare Danova, Wilfrid Hyde White, Laura Devon, Patrice Wymore, Suzy Parker, Jeanette Nolan, Tony Curtis (guest)

The Champ*
US 1931 87m bw
MGM

A young boy has faith in a washed-up prizefighter.
Maudlin drama, highly commercial in its day and a box office tonic for its two stars. Remade as *The Clown* (qv).

w Leonard Praskins, Frances Marion *d* King Vidor *ph* Gordon Avil

Wallace Beery, Jackie Cooper, Irene Rich, Roscoe Ates, Edward Brophy

Champagne Charlie*
GB 1944 107m bw
Ealing (John Croydon)

The life of Victorian music hall singer George Leybourne and his rivalry with the Great Vance.
Careful period reconstruction and good songs and acting are somehow nullified by unsympathetic handling and photography.

w Austin Melford, Angus Macphail, John Dighton *d* Alberto Cavalcanti

Tommy Trinder, Stanley Holloway, Betty Warren, Austin Trevor, Jean Kent, Guy Middleton, Frederick Piper, Harry Fowler

Champagne for Caesar*
US 1950 99m bw
Cardinal (George Moskov)

A self-confessed genius with a grudge against a soap company determines to win astronomical sums on its weekly radio quiz.
Agreeable, mildly satirical star comedy which tends to peter out halfway.

w Hans Jacoby, Fred Brady *d* Richard Whorf *ph* Paul Ivano *m* Dmitri Tiomkin

Ronald Colman, Vincent Price, Celeste Holm, Barbara Britton, Art Linkletter

Champion**
US 1949 99m bw
Stanley Kramer

An ambitious prizefighter alienates his friends and family, and dies of injuries received in the ring.
Interesting exposé of the fight racket, presented in good cinematic style and acted with great bravura.

w Carl Foreman, story Ring Lardner *d Mark Robson ph* Franz Planer *m* Dmitri Tiomkin

Kirk Douglas, Arthur Kennedy, Marilyn Maxwell, Paul Stewart, Ruth Roman, Lola Albright, Luis Van Rooten

Chance of a Lifetime*
GB 1950 93m bw
Pilgrim Pictures (Bernard Miles)

The owner of a small engineering works, impatient with the unionism of his men, gives them a chance to run the factory themselves.
Quiet comedy-drama on sub-Ealing lines; always interesting, it never quite catches fire despite a reliable cast.

w Walter Greenwood, Bernard Miles *d* Bernard Miles *ph* Eric Cross

Bernard Miles, Basil Radford, Niall MacGinnis, Geoffrey Keen, Julien Mitchell, Josephine Wilson, Kenneth More, Hattie Jacques

Chandu the Magician*
US 1932 74m bw
Fox

A spiritualist battles against a madman with a death ray which could destroy the world.
Rather dim serial-like thriller, with interesting talent not at its best.

w Philip Klein, Barry Conners *d* Marcel Varnel, William Cameron Menzies *ph* James Wong Howe

Edmund Lowe, Bela Lugosi, Irene Ware, Herbert Mundin, Henry B. Walthall

Change of Heart
US 1934 74m bw
Fox

Four young California students make good in New York.
Minor fairy tale which marked the last of twelve teamings for Gaynor and Farrell.

w Sonya Levien, James Gleason, Samuel Hoffenstein, *novel* Kathleen Norris *d* John G. Blystone *ph* Joseph Aiken

Janet Gaynor, Charles Farrell, Ginger Rogers, James Dunn, Beryl Mercer, Gustav Von Seyffertitz, Shirley Temple

Change of Mind
US 1969 98m Eastmancolor
Sagittarius (Seeleg Lester, Richard Wesson)

The life of a liberal white DA can only be 'saved' by transplanting his brain into the body of a dead black man.
Fantasy melodrama with a social conscience, about a half-and-half which is acceptable to neither whites nor blacks. Very obvious and rather boring.

w Seeleg Lester, Richard Wesson *d* Robert Stevens *ph* Arthur J. Ornitz *m* Duke Ellington

Raymond St Jacques, Susan Oliver, Janet McLachlan, Leslie Nielsen

The Chapman Report
US 1962 125m Technicolor
(Warner) Darryl F. Zanuck (Richard D. Zanuck)

Dr Chapman conducts a study of female sex behaviour in an American suburb.
Influenced by the Kinsey report, this melodramatic compendium takes itself far too seriously, and the director's smooth style is barely in evidence.

w Wyatt Cooper, Don M. Mankiewicz, *novel* Irving Wallace *d* George Cukor *ph* Harold Lipstein *m* Leonard Rosenman

Shelley Winters, Claire Bloom, *Glynis Johns*, Efrem Zimbalist Jnr, Jane Fonda, Ray Danton, Ty Hardin, Andrew Duggan, John Dehner, Henry Daniell, Corey Allen, Harold J. Stone

'We had a preview which went very well, and then it was sent over to Mr Zanuck, who did what I thought was a most horrendous job of cutting it up.'—*George Cukor*

Charade***
US 1964 113m Technicolor
Universal / Stanley Donen

A Parisienne finds her husband murdered. Four strange men are after her, and she is helped by a handsome stranger . . . but is he hero, spy or murderer?
Smoothly satisfying sub-Hitchcock nonsense, effective both as black romantic comedy and macabre farce.

w Peter Stone d Stanley Donen ph Charles Lang Jnr *m* Henry Mancini

Cary Grant (sixty but concealing the fact by taking a shower fully clothed), *Audrey Hepburn, Walter Matthau*, James Coburn, George Kennedy, Ned Glass, Jacques Marin

The Charge at Feather River*
US 1953 96m Warnercolor
Warner (David Weisbart)

An army platoon composed of men from the guardhouse tries to rescue two women kidnapped by Indians.
Formula western distinguished by 3-D photography, probably the best to be achieved in the brief life of the medium. Warnerphonic sound was less successfully added; the sum total would be trying for nervous people.

w James R. Webb *d* Gordon Douglas *ph Peverell Marley m* Max Steiner

Guy Madison, Frank Lovejoy, Vera Miles, Helen Westcott, Dick Wesson, Onslow Stevens, Steve Brodie

'From the start we are involved in a whirl of frenzied activity: a cavalry charge, knife throwing, sabre practice, flaming arrows—not a trick missed.'—*MFB*

The Charge of the Light Brigade***
US 1936 115m bw
Warner (Hal B. Wallis, Sam Bischoff)

An army officer deliberately starts the Balaclava charge to even an old score with Surat Khan, who's on the other side.
Though allegedly 'based on the poem by Alfred Lord Tennyson', this is no more than a travesty of history, most of it taking place in India. As pure entertainment however it is a most superior slice of Hollywood hokum and the film which set the seal on Errol Flynn's superstardom.

w Michael Jacoby, Rowland Leigh *d Michael Curtiz ph Sol Polito, Fred Jackman m Max Steiner*

Errol Flynn, Olivia de Havilland, Patric Knowles, Donald Crisp, C. Aubrey Smith, David Niven, Henry Stephenson, Nigel Bruce, *C. Henry Gordon*, Spring Byington, E. E. Clive, Lumsden Hare, Robert Barrat, J. Carrol Naish

The Charge of the Light Brigade
GB 1968 141m De Luxe Panavision
US / Woodfall (Neil Hartley)

An historical fantasia with comic, sociological and cartoon embellishments.
This version for the swinging sixties has a few splendid moments but apes *Tom Jones* all too obviously and leaves audiences with an even dimmer view of history than they started with.

w Charles Wood *d* Tony Richardson *ph* David Watkin, Peter Suschitsky *m* John Addison *animation Richard Williams ad* Edward Marshall

Trevor Howard, John Gielgud, David Hemmings, Vanessa Redgrave, Jill Bennett, Harry Andrews, Peter Bowles, Mark Burns

'Considering the lucid book on which it is largely based, it is almost as inexcusably muddled as the British commanders at Balaclava.'—*John Simon*

'The point of the film is to recreate mid-Victorian England in spirit and detail.' —*Stanley Kauffmann*

'Notions for at least three interesting films are on view . . . what seems signally lacking is a guiding hand, an overriding purpose.'—*John Coleman*

Charley and the Angel*
US 1974 93m Technicolor
Walt Disney (Bill Anderson)

A small-town sporting goods storekeeper in the thirties escapes death three times and finds an impatient angel waiting for him.
Mild sentimental whimsy on the lines of *On Borrowed Time*, but with a happy ending and attractive period trappings.

w Roswell Rogers, *novel* The Golden Evenings of Summer by Will Stanton *d* Vincent McEveety *ph* Charles F. Wheeler *m* Buddy Baker

Fred MacMurray, Cloris Leachmann, Harry Morgan, Kurt Russell, Kathleen Cody, Edward Andrews, Barbara Nichols

Charley Moon*
GB 1956 92m Eastmancolor
Colin Lesslie, Aubrey Baring

A music hall comic becomes swollen-headed but returns to his home village and marries his childhood sweetheart.
Faltering musical lacking the gusto of its background, but providing a generally believable impression of life on the halls.

w/songs Leslie Bricusse, *novel* Reginald Arkell *d* Guy Hamilton *ph* Jack Hildyard

Max Bygraves, Dennis Price, Michael Medwin, Florence Desmond, Shirley Eaton, Patricia Driscoll, Reginald Beckwith

Charley's Aunt**
US 1941 81m bw
TCF (William Perlberg)
GB title: *Charley's American Aunt*

For complicated reasons, an Oxford undergraduate has to impersonate his own rich aunt from Brazil (where the nuts come from).
Very adequate version of the Victorian farce, with all concerned in excellent form.

w George Seaton, *play* Brandon Thomas *d* Archie Mayo *ph* Peverell Marley *m* Alfred Newman *ad* Richard Day, Nathan Juran

Jack Benny, Kay Francis, James Ellison, Anne Baxter, *Laird Cregar*, Edmund Gwenn, Reginald Owen, Richard Haydn, Arleen Whelan, Ernest Cossart
† See also: *Where's Charley?*

Charley's Big-Hearted Aunt
GB 1940 76m bw
Gainsborough (Edward Black)

Rather disappointing British version of the famous farce, dully assembled and rather unsuitably cast.

w Marriott Edgar, Val Guest *d* Walter Forde

Arthur Askey, Phyllis Calvert, Moore Marriott, Graham Moffatt, Richard Murdoch, Jeanne de Casalis, J. H. Roberts, Felix Aylmer, Wally Patch

Charley Varrick**
US 1973 111m Technicolor
Universal (Don Siegel)

A bank robber discovers he has stolen Mafia money, and devises a clever scheme to get himself off the hook.
Sharp, smart, well-observed but implausible thriller, astringently handled and agreeably set in Californian backlands. Accomplished, forgettable entertainment.

w Howard Rodman, Dean Reisner, *novel* The Looters by John Reese *d Don Siegel* *ph* Michael Butler *m* Lalo Schifrin

Walter Matthau, Joe Don Baker, Felicia Farr, Andy Robinson, John Vernon, Sheree North, Norman Fell

'It proves there is nothing wrong with an *auteur* director that a good script can't cure.'—*Stanley Kauffmann*

'The narrative line is clean and direct, the characterizations economical and functional, and the triumph of intelligence gloriously satisfying.'—*Andrew Sarris*

Charlie Bubbles***
GB 1968 91m Technicolor
Universal / Memorial (Michael Medwin, George Pitcher)

A successful novelist loathes the pointlessness of the good life and tries unsuccessfully to return to his northern working class background.
A little arid and slow in its early stages, and with a rather lame end (our hero escapes by air balloon), this is nevertheless a fascinating, fragmentary character study with a host of wry comedy touches and nimbly sketched characters; in its unassuming way it indicts many of the symbols people lived by in the sixties.

w Shelagh Delaney d Albert Finney ph Peter Suschitsky m Mischa Donat

Albert Finney, Billie Whitelaw, Liza Minnelli, Colin Blakely, Timothy Garland, Diana Coupland, Alan Lake, Yootha Joyce, Joe Gladwin

'A modest thing, but like all good work in minor keys it has a way of haunting the memory.'—*Richard Schickel*

Charlie Chan
The Oriental detective created by Earl Derr Biggers began his film career as a minor character (played by George Kuwa) in a 1926 serial called HOUSE WITHOUT A KEY. In 1928 Kamiyama Sojin had a bigger role in THE CHINESE PARROT, but in 1929 E. L. Park did almost nothing in BEHIND THAT CURTAIN. In 1931 however began the fully-fledged Chan movies, which entertained a generation. Chan, based on a real-life Chinese detective named Chang Apana, became a citizen of Honolulu and was developed as a polite family man, aided by his impulsive number one or number two son (out of a family of fourteen), in solving murder puzzles. He had a treasury of aphorisms (a whole book of which has been published), and his technique was to gather all the suspects into one room before unmasking one as the murderer. The films built to a peak around 1936–9, but tailed off disastrously in the mid-forties. They were never noted for production values, but many retain interest for their scripts, their puzzles, and their casts of budding stars, as well as the central character. This is a complete list:

For Fox (later Twentieth Century Fox), with *Warner Oland* as Chan:

1931: CHARLIE CHAN CARRIES ON*, THE BLACK CAMEL
1932: CHARLIE CHAN'S CHANCE
1933: CHARLIE CHAN'S GREATEST CASE
1934: CHARLIE CHAN'S COURAGE, CHARLIE CHAN IN LONDON
1935: CHARLIE CHAN IN PARIS*, CHARLIE CHAN IN EGYPT, CHARLIE CHAN IN SHANGHAI
1936: CHARLIE CHAN'S SECRET*, CHARLIE CHAN AT THE CIRCUS*, CHARLIE CHAN AT THE RACE TRACK, CHARLIE CHAN AT THE OPERA**
1937: CHARLIE CHAN AT THE OLYMPICS, CHARLIE CHAN ON BROADWAY*, CHARLIE CHAN AT MONTE CARLO

For Twentieth Century Fox, with *Sidney Toler*:
1938: CHARLIE CHAN IN HONOLULU
1939: CHARLIE CHAN IN RENO, CHARLIE CHAN ON TREASURE ISLAND**, CITY OF DARKNESS
1940: CHARLIE CHAN IN PANAMA, CHARLIE CHAN'S MURDER CRUISE, CHARLIE CHAN AT THE WAX MUSEUM*, MURDER OVER NEW YORK
1941: DEAD MEN TELL, CHARLIE CHAN IN RIO, CASTLE IN THE DESERT*

For Monogram, with Sidney Toler:
1944: CHARLIE CHAN IN THE SECRET SERVICE, THE CHINESE CAT, BLACK MAGIC
1945: THE SCARLET CLUE, THE JADE MASK, SHANGHAI COBRA, RED DRAGON
1946: SHADOWS OVER CHINATOWN, DANGEROUS MONEY
1947: THE TRAP

For Monogram, with Roland Winters:
1947: THE CHINESE RING
1948: DOCKS OF NEW ORLEANS, SHANGHAI CHEST, THE GOLDEN EYE, THE FEATHERED SERPENT
1949: SKY DRAGON

In the late fifties J. Carrol Naish appeared in a half-hour TV series as Chan, but the episodes were dull. In 1971 Universal tried to revive the character in a 96-minute pilot film *Happiness is a Warm Clue*, but Ross Martin was woefully miscast.

Charlie Chan: Happiness is a Warm Clue
US 1971 96m Technicolor TVM
Universal (Jack Laird)

A famous detective emerges from retirement to solve murders aboard a yacht.
Dismal comeback for a famous screen character: desperately poor writing, total lack of pace and unsuitable casting made sure that no series ensued.

w Gene Kearney *d* Daryl Duke

Ross Martin, Leslie Nielsen, Virginia Lee, Rocky Gunn

Charlie's Angels**
US 1976 74m colour TVM
Spelling–Goldberg (Ivan Goff, Ben Roberts)

Three gorgeous girls with special skills work undercover on expensive, impossible cases for an employer they never see.
If it's smooth Hitchcockian hokum you are after, a very good pilot for a series that did make it. The plot is borrowed from all kinds of other movies including *Dark Waters*, the pace is snappy and the spirit of *The Avengers* and *Mission Impossible* hovers at hand.

w Ivan Goff, Ben Roberts *d* John Llewellyn Moxey

Kate Jackson, Farrah Fawcett-Majors, Jacklyn Smith, Diana Muldaur, Bo Hopkins, David Doyle, David Ogden Stiers

Charly*
US 1968 106m Techniscope
Selmur / Robertson Associates (Ralph Nelson)

New methods of surgery cure a mentally retarded young man, who becomes a genius, but the effects wear off.
Smooth, unconvincing, rather pointless fantasy which ultimately leaves a bad taste in the mouth.

w Sterling Silliphant, *novel* Flowers for Algernon by Daniel Keyes *d* Ralph Nelson *ph* Arthur J. Ornitz *m* Ravi Shankar

Cliff Robertson, Claire Bloom, Leon Janney, Lilia Skala

'The most distressing thing about *Charly* is not its ticklish subject, nor yet its clumsily modish surface, but its insistent, persistent sentimentality.'—*Tom Milne*

Charro
US 1969 98m Technicolor Panavision
National General (Charles Marquis Warren)

A reformed outlaw is framed for the theft of a cannon.
Dismal western with a singing star playing straight. A bad experience.

wd Charles Marquis Warren *ph* Ellsworth Fredericks *m* Hugo Montenegro

Elvis Presley, Ina Balin, Barbara Werle, Lynn Kellogg, Victor French, Solomon Sturges

Chase
US 1973 74m Technicolor TVM
Universal / Jack Webb

Four Los Angeles police officers, with special skills and motor cycles, form an elite squad.
The mixture as before; it doesn't rise.

w Stephen J. Cannell *d* Jack Webb

Mitch Ryan, Reid Smith, Michael Richardson, Brian Fong

The Chase*
US 1947 84m bw
Nero Pictures (Seymour Nebenzal)

A shell-shocked ex-serviceman foils a criminal and falls for his wife.
Weird Cuban-set *film noir* with a strange cast and stranger atmosphere. A genuine bomb, but worth a look for its pretensions, its cast, and its trick ending.

w Philip Yordan, *novel* The Black Path of Fear by Cornell Woolrich *d Arthur Ripley ph* Franz Planer *m* Michel Michelet

Robert Cummings, Michèle Morgan, Peter Lorre, Steve Cochran, Lloyd Corrigan, Jack Holt

The Chase*
US 1966 135m Technicolor Panavision
Columbia / Sam Spiegel

When a convict escapes and heads for his small Texas home town, almost all the inhabitants are affected in one way or another.
Expensive but shoddy essay in sex and violence, with Brando as a masochistic sheriff lording it over Peyton-Place-in-all-but-name. Literate moments do not atone for the general pretentiousness, and we have all been here once too often.

w Lillian Hellman, *novel* Horton Foote *d* Arthur Penn *ph* Joseph La Shelle *pd* Richard Day *m* John Barry

Marlon Brando, Jane Fonda, Robert Redford, Angie Dickinson, Janice Rule, James Fox, Robert Duvall, E. G. Marshall, Miriam Hopkins, Henry Hull

'The worst thing that has happened to movies since Lassie played a war veteran with amnesia.'—*Rex Reed*

'Considering all the talent connected with it, it is hard to imagine how *The Chase* went so haywire.'—*Philip T. Hartung*

Chase a Crooked Shadow**
GB 1957 87m bw
ABP / Associated Dragon Films (Douglas Fairbanks Jnr)

An heiress finds her home invaded by a stranger posing as her dead brother.
Tricksy, lightly controlled suspense melodrama with a perfectly fair surprise ending. Handling equivocal but competent.

w David D. Osborn, Charles Sinclair *d Michael Anderson ph* Erwin Hillier *m* Matyas Seiber

Richard Todd, Anne Baxter, Faith Brook, Herbert Lom, Alexander Knox, Alan Tilvern
† The plot was borrowed from an episode in *The Whistler* TV series, and later reversed for a 1975 TV film, *One of my Wives is Missing.*

Chato's Land
GB 1971 100m Technicolor
UA / Scimitar (Michael Winner)

An Apache half-breed kills a man in self-defence, subsequently eluding and destroying the sheriff's posse.
Exhaustingly violent western in which the audience is spared no gory detail; efficiently put together for those who like this kind of fracas.

w Gerald Wilson *d* Michael Winner *ph* Robert Paynter *m* Jerry Fielding

Charles Bronson, Jack Palance, Richard Basehart, James Whitmore, Simon Oakland, Richard Jordan, Ralph Waite, Victor French, Lee Patterson

Che!
US 1969 94m De Luxe Panavision
TCF (Sy Bartlett)

Fidel Castro is helped in his subversion of Batista's Cuban regime by an Argentinian doctor named Che Guevara.
Fictionalized biography, and a dull one, of a man who became a myth.

w Michael Wilson, Sy Bartlett *d* Richard Fleischer *ph* Charles Wheeler *m* Lalo Schifrin

Omar Sharif, Jack Palance (as Castro), Cesare Danova, Robert Loggia, Woody Strode, Barbara Luna

Cheaper by the Dozen**
US 1950 86m Technicolor
TCF (Lamar Trotti)

Efficiency expert Frank Gilbreth and his wife Lillian have twelve children, a fact which requires mathematical conduct of all their lives.
Amusing family comedy set in the twenties, unconvincing in detail though based on a book by two of the children. A great commercial

success and a Hollywood myth-maker. Sequel: *Belles on their Toes* (qv).

w Lamar Trotti, *book* Frank B. Gilbreth Jnr, Ernestine Gilbreth Carey *d Walter Lang* *ph* Leon Shamroy *m* Lionel Newman *ad* Lyle Wheeler, Leland Fuller

Clifton Webb, Myrna Loy, Jeanne Crain, Edgar Buchanan, Barbara Bates, Betty Lynn, Mildred Natwick, Sara Allgood

The Cheaters*
US 1945 86m bw
Republic

A selfish and ostentatious family is reformed by the ministrations of a down-and-out actor.
Fairly engaging variation on *The Passing of the Third Floor Back*, with sweetness and light brought into people's lives by a fireside recital of *A Christmas Carol.*

w Francis Hyland *d* Joseph Kane

Joseph Schildkraut, Billie Burke, Eugene Pallette, Ona Munson, Raymond Walburn

Check and Double Check
US 1932 71m bw
RKO

Comic adventures of a couple of black handymen.
Feeble comedy notable only for the film appearance of radio's immensely popular Amos 'n Andy, played by white actors in blackface.

w Bert Kalmar, Harry Ruby, J. Walter Ruben *d* Melville Brown *ph* William Marshall

Freeman F. Gosden, Charles V. Correll, Sue Carol, Charles Morton, Irene Rich, Ralf Harolde, Duke Ellington and his Orchestra

Checkpoint*
GB 1956 84m Eastmancolor
Rank (Betty Box)

A tycoon sends an industrial spy to Italy in search of new motor racing car designs.
Acceptable hokum, cleanly assembled, with motor race highlights.

w Robin Estridge *d* Ralph Thomas *ph* Ernest Steward *m* Bruce Montgomery

Anthony Steel, Stanley Baker, James Robertson Justice, Odile Versois, Maurice Denham, Michael Medwin, Lee Patterson

Cheers for Miss Bishop*
US 1941 94m bw
Paramount (Richard A. Rowland)

The life of a schoolmistress in a small midwestern town.
Acceptable sentimental hokum, quite pleasantly done.

w Adelaide Heinbron, *novel* Bess Streeter Aldrich *d* Tay Garnett *ph* Hal Mohr *m* Edmund Ward

Martha Scott, William Gargan, Edmund Gwenn, Sterling Holloway, Sidney Blackmer, Mary Anderson, Dorothy Petersen

Cheyenne Autumn*
US 1964 170m Technicolor Panavision 70
Warner / Ford-Smith (Bernard Smith)

In the 1860s, Cheyenne Indians are moved to a new reservation 1500 miles away; wanting aid, they begin a trek back home, and various battles follow.
Dispirited, shapeless John Ford western with little of the master's touch; good to look at, however, with effective cameos, notably an irrelevant and out-of-key comic one featuring James Stewart as Wyatt Earp.

w James R. Webb, *novel* Mari Sandoz *d* John Ford *ph William H. Clothier* *m* Alex North

Richard Widmark, Carroll Baker, Karl Malden, *Dolores del Rio*, Sal Mineo, Edward G. Robinson, *James Stewart*, Ricardo Montalban, Gilbert Roland, Arthur Kennedy, Patrick Wayne, Elizabeth Allen, Victor Jory, John Carradine, Mike Mazurki, John Qualen, George O'Brien

'Although one would like to praise the film for its high-minded aims, it is hard to forget how ponderous and disjointed it is.'—*Moira Walsh*

'The acting is bad, the dialogue trite and predictable, the pace funereal, the structure fragmented and the climaxes puny.'—*Stanley Kauffmann*

The Cheyenne Social Club*
US 1970 102m Technicolor Panavision
National General (James Lee Barrett, Gene Kelly)

Two itinerant cowboys inherit a high-class brothel.
Disappointing star comedy western with pleasing moments and a lively climactic shoot-out. Perhaps the girls are just a shade too winsome.

w James Lee Barrett *d* Gene Kelly *ph* William H. Clothier *m* Walter Scharf

James Stewart, Henry Fonda, Shirley Jones, Sue Anne Langdon, Robert Middleton, Arch Johnson

'Co-starring Shirley Jones and Rigor Mortis,

who enters early and stays through the very last scene.'—*Rex Reed*

Chicago Calling*
US 1951 75m bw
UA / Arrowhead / Joseph Justman (Peter Berneis)

A drunk cannot pay his phone bill and is waiting for a vital call about his daughter's involvement in a car crash.
Moderate, location-shot minor melodrama with a few good ideas.

w John Reinhardt, Peter Berneis *d* John Reinhardt *ph* Robert de Grasse

Dan Duryea, Mary Anderson, Gordon Gebert, Ross Elliot

Chicago Deadline
US 1949 87m bw
Paramount (Robert Fellows)

A reporter researches the life of a lonely girl who died of tuberculosis.
Flat star vehicle consisting mainly of overplayed cameos.

w Warren Duff, Tiffany Thayer *d* Lewis Allen *ph* John F. Seitz *m* Victor Young

Alan Ladd, Donna Reed, *June Havoc*, Berry Kroeger, Arthur Kennedy, Gavin Muir, Shepperd Strudwick

Chicken Every Sunday*
US 1949 94m bw
TCF

The Hefferans have run a boarding house for twenty years, but dad's wild schemes run away with any possible profit.
Archetypal, folksy, American small-town chronicle, reasonably well made, for an audience that now watches *The Waltons*.

w George Seaton, Valentine Davies *d* George Seaton *ph* Harry Jackson *m* Alfred Newman

Dan Dailey, Celeste Holm, Colleen Townsend, Alan Young, Natalie Wood

Chief Crazy Horse
US 1954 86m ✝ Technicolor Cinemascope
U-I (William Alland)
GB title: *Valley of Fury*

The tribal problems of the Indian chief who defeated Custer at Little Big Horn.
Competent pro-Indian western.

w Franklin Coen, Gerald Drayson Adams *d* George Sherman *ph* Harold Lipstein *m* Frank Skinner

Victor Mature, Suzan Ball, John Lund, Ray Danton, Keith Larsen, Paul Guilfoyle, David Janssen

A Child is Born
US 1939 79m bw
Warner (Sam Bischoff)

A slice of life in the maternity ward.
Adequately dramatic sequence of cameos, with mothers-to-be including a gangster's moll: a remake of *Life Begins*.

w Robert Rossen, *play* Mary M. Axelson *d* Lloyd Bacon *ph* Charles Rosher

Geraldine Fitzgerald, Jeffrey Lynn, Gladys George, Gale Page, Spring Byington, Henry O'Neill, John Litel, Gloria Holden, Eve Arden, Nanette Fabares, Hobart Cavanaugh, Johnny Downs, Johnnie Davis

A Child is Waiting**
US 1963 104m bw
UA / Stanley Kramer

A mixed-up spinster joins the staff of a school for mentally handicapped children.
Worthy semi-documentary marred by having a normal boy play the central character (albeit very well). A little over-dramatized but cogent and unsentimental.

w Abby Mann *d* John Cassavetes *ph* Joseph La Shelle *m* Ernest Gold

Burt Lancaster, *Judy Garland, Bruce Ritchey*, Steven Hill, Gena Rowlands, *Paul Stewart*, Lawrence Tierney

Children of the Damned*
GB 1964 90m bw
MGM (Ben Arbeid)

Six super-intelligent children of various nations are brought to London by UNESCO, and turn out to be invaders from another planet.
Moderate sequel to *Village of the Damned*, well made but with no new twists.

w John Briley *d* Anton M. Leader *ph* David Boulton *m* Ron Goodwin

Ian Hendry, Alan Badel, Barbara Ferris, Alfred Burke, Sheila Allen, Ralph Michael, Martin Miller, Harold Goldblatt

The Children's Hour*
US 1961 108m bw
UA / Mirisch (William Wyler)
GB title: *The Loudest Whisper*

A spoilt schoolgirl spreads a rumour that her schoolmistresses are lesbians.
Frank sixties version of a play originally filmed

in a much bowdlerized version as *These Three*. Unfortunately frankness in this case leads to dullness, as nothing is done with the theme once it is stated, and the treatment is heavy-handed.

w Lillian Hellman, from her play *d* William Wyler *ph* Franz Planer *m* Alex North

Audrey Hepburn, Shirley Maclaine, James Garner, Miriam Hopkins, Fay Bainter, Karen Balkin

'All very exquisite, and dead as mutton.'—*Tom Milne*

Child's Play*
US 1972 100m Movielab
Paramount (David Merrick)

In a Catholic boarding school for boys, an unpopular master is hounded and discredited by another whose motives may be diabolic.
Enjoyable overblown melodrama with hints of many nasty goings on, rather spoiled by too much talk and too little local colour.

w Leon Prochnik, *play* Robert Marasco *d* Sidney Lumet *ph* Gerald Hirschfeld *m* Michael Small

James Mason, Robert Preston, Beau Bridges, Ronald Weyand

The Chiltern Hundreds*
GB 1949 84m bw
Rank / Two Cities (George H. Brown)

An aged earl is bewildered when his son fails to be elected to parliament as a socialist but his butler gets in as a tory.
Satisfactory filming of an amusing stage comedy, with the aged A. E. Matthews repeating his delightful if irrelevant act as the dotty earl.

w William Douglas Home, Patrick Kirwan, *play William Douglas Home* *d* John Paddy Carstairs *ph* Jack Hildyard *m* Benjamin Frankel

A. E. Matthews, Cecil Parker, David Tomlinson, Marjorie Fielding, Joyce Carey

Chimes at Midnight*
Spain / Switz 1966 119m bw
Internacional Films Espanola / Alpine (Alessandro Tasca)
aka *Falstaff*

Prince Hal becomes King Henry V and rejects his old friend Falstaff.
Clumsy adaptation of Shakespeare with brilliant flashes and the usual Welles vices of hasty production, poor synchronization and recording, etc. One wonders why, if he wanted to make a telescoped version of the plays, he did not spare the time and patience to make it better.

w Orson Welles *d* Orson Welles *ph* Edmond Richard *m* Angelo Francesco Lavagnino

Orson Welles, Keith Baxter, John Gielgud (Henry IV), Margaret Rutherford (Mistress Quickly), Jeanne Moreau (Doll Tearsheet), Norman Rodway, Alan Webb, Marina Vlady, Tony Beckley, Fernando Rey

China
US 1943 79m bw
Paramount (Richard Blumenthal)

An oil salesman joins a Chinese guerrilla force and sacrifices himself.
Solemnly hilarious propaganda piece tailored to its star, showing the immense superiority of one lone American to the entire Japanese army.

w Frank Butler, *novel* The Fourth Brother by Reginald Forbes *d* John Farrow *ph* Leo Tover

Alan Ladd, Loretta Young, William Bendix, Philip Ahn, Iris Wong, Sen Yung, Richard Loo, Tala Birell

China Clipper*
US 1936 89m bw
Warner (Sam Bischoff)

An aviator neglects his wife while building up a trans-Pacific civil aviation link.
Solid entertainment feature of its day, with adequate production and performance.

w Frank 'Spig' Wead *d* Ray Enright *ph* Arthur Edeson

Pat O'Brien, Beverly Roberts, Ross Alexander, Humphrey Bogart, Marie Wilson, Henry B. Walthall, Joseph Crehan, Addison Richards

China Doll
US 1958 99m bw
Romina / Batjac (Frank Borzage)

In 1943 an American air force officer accidentally buys the services of a young Chinese housekeeper. He marries her but they are both killed in action; years later their daughter is welcomed to America by members of his old air crew.
Incurably sentimental and icky romantic drama in the style of the director's silent films; something of a curiosity for historians.

w Kitty Buhler *d* Frank Borzage *ph* William H. Clothier *m* Henry Vars

Victor Mature, Li Li Hua, Bob Mathias, Ward Bond, Stuart Whitman

China Gate
US 1957 90m bw Cinemascope
TCF (Samuel Fuller)

A Eurasian girl guides her American husband to a communist arms dump.
Anti-Red thick ear, slick but undistinguished.

wd Samuel Fuller *ph* Joseph Biroc *m* Victor Young, Max Steiner

Gene Barry, Angie Dickinson, Nat King Cole, Paul Dubov, Lee Van Cleef, George Givot

China Girl
US 1943 95m bw
TCF (Ben Hecht)

A newsreel cameraman in China falls in love with a Eurasian schoolteacher.
Routine adventure romance with splodges of love and self-sacrifice.

w Ben Hecht *d* Henry Hathaway *ph* Lee Garmes *m* Hugo Friedhofer

Gene Tierney, George Montgomery, *Lynn Bari*, Victor McLaglen, Alan Baxter, Sig Rumann, Myron McCormick, Philip Ahn

China Seas**
US 1935 89m bw
MGM (Albert Lewin)

Luxury cruise passengers find themselves involved with piracy.
Omnibus shipboard melodrama, tersely scripted and featuring a splendid cast all somewhere near their best; slightly dated but very entertaining.

w Jules Furthman, James Kevin McGuinness, *novel* Crosbie Garstin *d Tay Garnett ph* Ray June

Clark Gable, Jean Harlow, Wallace Beery, Rosalind Russell, Lewis Stone, C. Aubrey Smith, Dudley Digges, Robert Benchley

China Sky
US 1945 78m bw
RKO (Maurice Geraghty)

Two American doctors live with Chinese guerrillas; the jealousy of the wife of one of them causes problems.
Routine adventure romance with generally unconvincing production and performance.

w Brenda Weisberg, Joseph Hoffman, *novel* Pearl Buck *d* Ray Enright *ph* Nicholas Musuraca *m* Roy Webb

Randolph Scott, Ellen Drew, Ruth Warrick, Anthony Quinn, Carol Thurston, Richard Loo, Philip Ahn

Chinatown***
US 1974 131m Technicolor Panavision
Paramount / Long Road (Robert Evans)

In 1937, a Los Angeles private eye takes on a simple case and burrows into it until it leads to murder and a public scandal.
Pretentious melodrama which is basically no more serious than the Raymond Chandler mysteries from which it derives; the tragic ending is merely an irritation, and the title only allusive. Superficially, however, it is eminently watchable, with effective individual scenes and performances and photography which is lovingly composed though tending to suggest period by use of an orange filter.

w Robert Towne d Roman Polanski ph John A. Alonso m Jerry Goldsmith *pd Richard Sylbert*

Jack Nicholson, Faye Dunaway, John Huston, Perry Lopez, John Hillerman, Roman Polanski, Darrell Zwerling, Diane Ladd

The Chinatown Murders
US 1974 98m Technicolor TVM
Universal

Kojak tangles with Chinese tongs when a top gangster is kidnapped.
Tedious Kojak double entry.

w Jack Laird *d* Jeannot Szwarc

Telly Savalas, Dan Frazer, Kevin Dobson, George Savalas, Michael Constantine, Sheree North

The Chinese Bungalow
GB 1939 72m bw
George King

A Chinese merchant plots to kill the lover of his English wife.
Stolid version of an old melodrama which can hardly fail; previously filmed in 1926 with Matheson Lang and Genevieve Townsend (directed by Sinclair Hill) and in 1930 with Matheson Lang and Anna Neagle (directed by J. B. Williams).

w A. R. Rawlinson, George Wellesley, *play* Matheson Lang, Marian Osmond *d* George King

Paul Lukas, Jane Baxter, Robert Douglas, Kay Walsh, Jerry Verno

Chisum*
US 1970 110m Technicolor Panavision
Warner / Batjac (Michael Wayne, Andrew J. Fenady)

A corrupt businessman plots against the head of a vast cattle empire, who is saved by the intervention of numerous friends including Pat Garrett and Billy the Kid.
Desultory, overlong, friendly western in the Ford manner. Easy to watch and easier to forget.

w Andrew J. Fenady *d* Andrew V. McLaglen *ph William H. Clothier m* Dominic Frontière

John Wayne, Forrest Tucker, Christopher George, Ben Johnson, Glenn Corbett, Bruce Cabot, Andrew Prine, Patric Knowles, Richard Jaeckel, Linda Day George, John Agar, Ray Teal, Glenn Langan, Alan Baxter, Abraham Sofaer

'A curious mixture of styles and myths.'—*John Gillett*

Chitty Chitty Bang Bang
GB 1968 145m Technicolor Super Panavision 70
UA / Warfield / DFI (Albert R. Broccoli)

An unsuccessful inventor rescues a derelict car and gives it magical properties, then helps the children who own it to overthrow the government of a country which hates children.
A bumpy ride. Sentiment, slapstick, whimsy and mild scares do not combine but are given equal shares of the limelight, while poor trickwork prevents the audience from being transported.

w Roald Dahl, Ken Hughes *d* Ken Hughes *ph* Christopher Challis *m* Irwin Kostal *songs* the Sherman Brothers *ad* Ken Adam *decor* Rowland Emmett

Dick Van Dyke, Sally Ann Howes (as Truly Scrumptious), Lionel Jeffries, Robert Helpmann, Gert Frobe, Benny Hill, James Robertson Justice

The Chocolate Soldier*
US 1941 102m bw
MGM (Victor Saville)

Married opera singers fall out backstage.
Talky musical remake of *The Guardsman*: nearly comes off but not quite.

w Keith Winter, Leonard Lee *d* Roy del Ruth *ph* Karl Freund *m* Oscar Straus

Nelson Eddy, Rise Stevens, Nigel Bruce, Florence Bates, Nydia Westman

Chosen Survivors
US 1974 98m colour
Alpine / Metromedia (Charles Fries)

Ten people with special skills are chosen to test human reaction to thermo-nuclear war, but find themselves at the mercy of vampire bats.
Another misfit group united by disaster; more shocks than suspense, and not much characterization, but for adventure/horror addicts it will pass the time.

w H. B. Cross, Joe Red Moffly *d* Sutton Roley *ph* Gabriel Torres *m* Fred Karlin

Jackie Cooper, Alex Cord, Richard Jaeckel, Dina Muldaur, Lincoln Kilpatrick, Bradford Dillman, Pedro Armendariz Jnr, Gwen Mitchell, Barbara Babcock, Christina Moreno

A Christmas Carol*
US 1938 69m bw
MGM (Joseph L. Mankiewicz)

Scrooge the miser is reformed when four ghosts visit him on Christmas Eve.
Standard Dickensian frolic, quite well mounted.

w Hugo Butler *d* Edwin L. Marin *ph* Sidney Wagner *m* Franz Waxman

Reginald Owen, Gene Lockhart, Kathleen Lockhart, Terry Kilburn, Leo G. Carroll, Lynne Carver
† See also *Scrooge.*

Christmas Eve*
US 1947 92m bw
Benedict Bogeaus
aka: *Sinners' Holiday*

An old lady needs the help of her three adopted sons to prevent herself from being swindled.
Basically three short stories sealed by a Christmas Eve reunion, this is old-fashioned sentimental stuff, but it works on its level and the cast is interesting.

w Lawrence Stallings *d* Edwin L. Marin *ph* Gordon Avil *m* Heinz Roemheld

Ann Harding, George Raft, Randolph Scott, George Brent, Joan Blondell, Virginia Field, Reginald Denny

Christmas Holiday
US 1944 93m bw
Universal (Felix Jackson)

A young girl marries a murderer, and later, as a shady songstress in a nightclub, is forced to help him escape.
A weird change of pace for Deanna Durbin, whose forte had been sweetness and light, this relentlessly grim and boring melodrama was also a travesty of the novel on which it was based.

w Herman J. Mankiewicz, *novel* Somerset Maugham *d* Robert Siodmak *ph* Elwood Bredell *m* Hans Salter

Deanna Durbin, Gene Kelly, Dean Harens, Gladys George, Richard Whorf, Gale Sondergaard

Christmas in Connecticut*
US 1945 101m bw
Warner (William Jacobs)
GB title: *Indiscretion*

The spinster writer of a successful column about

love and marriage has to conjure up a family for herself in the cause of publicity.
Predictable but fairly brisk comedy with excellent talent well deployed.

w Lionel Houser, Adele Commandini *d* Peter Godfrey *ph* Carl Guthrie *m* Frederick Hollander

Barbara Stanwyck, Dennis Morgan, Sydney Greenstreet, Reginald Gardiner, S. Z. Sakall, Robert Shayne, Una O'Connor, Frank Jenks

Christmas in July**
US 1940 67m bw
Paramount

A young clerk and his girl win first prize in a big competition.
Slightly unsatisfactory as a whole, this Preston Sturges comedy has echoes of Clair and a dully predictable plot line, but is kept alive by inventive touches and a gallery of splendid character comedians.

wd Preston Sturges *ph* Victor Milner *m* Sigmund Krumgold

Dick Powell, Ellen Drew, Ernest Truex, *Al Bridge*, Raymond Walburn, William Demarest

'The perfect restorative for battered humors and jangled nerves.'—*Bosley Crowther*

The Christmas Tree
France / Italy 1969 110m Eastmancolor
Corona / Jupiter (Robert Dorfmann)

The small son of a millionaire widower is fatally infected by radioactivity.
Painfully sentimental and overdrawn weepie, the most lachrymose film of the sixties.

wd Terence Young, *novel* Michel Bataille *ph* Henri Alekan *m* Georges Auric

William Holden, Virna Lisi, Brook Fuller, Bourvil

'Depending on your taste threshold, there may not be a dry eye—nor a full stomach—in the house.'—*Judith Crist*

Christopher Columbus
GB 1948 104m Technicolor
Rank (Betty Box)

Columbus seeks and receives the patronage of the Spanish court for his voyage to the west.
An extraordinarily tediously paced historical account of basically undramatic events; interesting without being stimulating.

w Muriel and Sydney Box, Cyril Roberts *d* David MacDonald *ph* Stephen Dade *m* Arthur Bliss

Fredric March, Florence Eldridge, Francis L. Sullivan, Linden Travers

Christopher Strong*
US 1955 72m bw
RKO (Pandro S. Berman)

A daring lady aviator has an affair with a married businessman and commits suicide when she finds herself pregnant.
A curious and unsatisfactory yarn for Hepburn's second film; well enough made, it died at the box office.

w Zoe Akins, *novel* Gilbert Frankau *d* Dorothy Arzner *ph* Bert Glennon *m* Max Steiner

Katharine Hepburn, Colin Clive, Billie Burke, Helen Chandler, Ralph Forbes, Irene Browne, Jack La Rue

Chu Chin Chow*
GB 1934 102m bw
Gainsborough (Michael Balcon)

In old Arabia, a slave girl foils a robber posing as a dead mandarin.
Second screen version (the first was silent) of the old Arabian Nights stage musical. A curiosity.

w Edward Knoblock, L. DuGarde Peach, Sidney Gilliat, *play* Oscar Asche and Frederick Norton *d* Walter Forde

George Robey, Fritz Kortner, Anna May Wong, John Garrick, Pearl Argyle, Malcolm MacEachern, Dennis Hoey, Francis L. Sullivan, Sydney Fairbrother

Chubasco
US 1967 100m Technicolor Panavision
Warner Seven Arts (William Conrad)

A wild beach boy takes a job on a tuna fishing boat.
Old-fashioned boy-makes-good melodrama à la Captains Courageous. Excellent action sequences at sea.

wd Allen H. Miner *ph* Louis Jennings, Paul Ivano *m* William Lava

Chris Jones, Richard Egan, Susan Strasberg, Ann Sothern, Simon Oakland, Preston Foster, Audrey Totter, Peter Whitney

Chuka
US 1967 105m Technicolor
Paramount / Rod Taylor

A wandering gunfighter defends the inhabitants of a fort against Indian attack.
Ill-assorted characters under stress is the theme of this rather pedestrian and slightly pretentious western.

w Richard Jessup *d* Gordon Douglas *ph* Harold Stine *m* Leith Stevens

Rod Taylor, Ernest Borgnine, John Mills, Luciana Paluzzi, James Whitmore, Louis Hayward, Angela Dorian

A Chump at Oxford**
US 1939 63m bw
Hal Roach

Two street cleaners foil a bank hold-up and are presented with an Oxford education.
Patchy but endearing Laurel and Hardy romp, starting with an irrelevant two reels about their playing butler and maid, but later including Stan's burlesque impersonation of Lord Paddington.

w Charles Rogers, Harry Langdon, Felix Adler *d* Alfred Goulding *ph* Art Lloyd

Stan Laurel, Oliver Hardy, James Finlayson, Forrester Harvey, Wilfrid Lucas, Peter Cushing

'Ranks with their best pictures—which, to one heretic, are more agreeable than Chaplin's. Their clowning is purer; they aren't out to better an unbetterable world; they've never wanted to play Hamlet.'—*Graham Greene*

Cimarron*
US 1931 130m bw
RKO (Louis Sarecky)

The life of an Oklahoma homesteader from 1890 to 1915.
Sprawling western family saga; a big early talkie, it dates badly.

w Howard Estabrook, *novel* Edna Ferber *d* Wesley Ruggles *ph* Edward Cronjager

Richard Dix, Irene Dunne, Estelle Taylor, Nance O'Neill, William Collier Jnr, Roscoe Ates, George E. Stone, Stanley Fields, Edna May Oliver

Cimarron
US 1961 147m Metrocolor Cinemascope
MGM (Edmund Grainger)

Flabby, relentlessly boring remake of the above.

w Arnold Schulman *d* Anthony Mann *ph* Robert L. Surtees *m* Franz Waxman

Glenn Ford, Maria Schell, Anne Baxter, Lili Darvas, Russ Tamblyn, Henry Morgan, David Opatoshu, Charles McGraw, Aline MacMahon, Edgar Buchanan, Arthur O'Connell, Mercedes McCambridge, Vic Morrow, Robert Keith, Mary Wickes, Royal Dano, Vladimir Sokoloff

The Cincinnati Kid**
US 1965 113m Metrocolor
MGM / Filmways (Martin Ransohoff, John Calley)

In New Orleans in the late thirties, stud poker experts compete for supremacy.
This is to poker what *The Hustler* was to pool, a fascinating suspense study of experts at work; as before, the romantic asides let down the effectiveness of the others.

w Ring Lardner Jnr, Terry Southern, *novel* Richard Jessup *d Norman Jewison ph* Philip Lathrop *m* Lalo Schifrin

Steve McQueen, *Edward G. Robinson*, Karl Malden, Ann-Margret, Tuesday Weld, Joan Blondell, Rip Torn, Jack Weston, Cab Calloway, Jeff Corey

Cinderella**
US 1950 75m Technicolor
Walt Disney

The Perrault fairy tale embroidered with animal characters.
A feature cartoon rather short on inspiration, though with all Disney's solid virtues. The mice are lively and the villainous cat the best character.

supervisor Ben Sharpsteen *d* Wilfred Jackson, Hamilton Luske, Clyde Geronomi

Cinderella Jones
US 1946 89m bw
Warner (Alex Gottlieb)

To collect an inheritance, a girl must marry a brainy man.
Witless comedy for the easily pleased.

w Charles Hoffman, *story* Philip Wylie *d* Busby Berkeley *ph* Sol Polito *m* Frederick Hollander

Joan Leslie, Robert Alda, S. Z. Sakall, Edward Everett Horton, Julie Bishop, William Prince, Charles Dingle, Ruth Donnelly, Elisha Cook Jnr, Hobart Cavanaugh, Chester Clute

Cinderella Liberty
US 1974 117m De Luxe Panavision
TCF / Sanford (Mark Rydell)

A sailor on shore leave picks up a prostitute and falls in love with her.
Assertively 'modern' yet glutinously sentimental love story in squalid settings. It presumably has an audience.

w Darryl Ponicsan from his novel *d* Mark Rydell *ph* Vilmos Zsigmond *m* John Williams

James Caan, Marsha Mason, Eli Wallach, Kirk Calloway, Allyn Ann McLerie

'A sordid, messy affair which wants to jerk tears but just doesn't have the knack.'—*New Yorker*

Cinderfella
US 1960 91m Technicolor
Paramount / Jerry Lewis

Luxury pantomime featuring a male Cinderella.
Annoyingly lavish and empty star vehicle with precious little to laugh at: Lewis' own jokes are strung out to snapping point and no one else gets a look in.

wd Frank Tashlin *ph* Haskell Boggs *m* Walter Scharf

Jerry Lewis, Ed Wynn, Judith Anderson, Anna Maria Alberghetti, Henry Silva, Robert Hutton, Count Basie

'A drought of comic inspiration, followed by a flood of mawkish whimsy, gradually increases one's early misgivings to a degree which finally verges on revulsion.'—*Peter John Dyer*

Circle of Danger*
GB 1951 89m bw
Coronado / David Rose (Joan Harrison)

An American in England investigates the strange death some years earlier of his brother during a commando raid.
Individual scenes are well milked for suspense and dramatic emphasis, but the plot line has virtually no mystery and absolutely no danger. It all seems mildly reminiscent of several Hitchcock films.

w Philip MacDonald *d Jacques Tourneur*
ph Oswald Morris *m* Robert Farnon

Ray Milland, Patricia Roc, Marius Goring, Hugh Sinclair, Naunton Wayne, Marjorie Fielding, Edward Rigby, Colin Gordon, Dora Bryan

Circle of Deception
GB 1960 100m bw Cinemascope
TCF (T. H. Morahan)

An officer is parachuted into Germany with the intention that he should crack under interrogation and reveal false information.
Depressing World War II tall tale, with suspense sacrificed by flashback structure.

w Nigel Balchin, Robert Musel, *novel* Alec Waugh *d* Jack Lee *ph* Gordon Dines *m* Clifton Parker

Bradford Dillman, Harry Andrews, Suzy Parker, Robert Stephens, John Welsh, Paul Rogers, Duncan Lamont, Michael Ripper

Circus of Horrors
GB 1960 91m Eastmancolor
Anglo Amalgamated / Lynx / Independent Artists (Norman Priggen)

A plastic surgeon staffs a semi-derelict circus with criminals whose faces he has altered, and murders any who try to flee.
Stark horror comic; quite professionally made, but content-wise a crude concoction of sex and sadism.

w George Baxt *d* Sidney Hayers *ph* Douglas Slocombe *m* Franz Reizenstein, Muir Mathieson

Anton Diffring, Erika Remberg, Yvonne Monlaur, Donald Pleasance, Jane Hylton, Kenneth Griffith, Conrad Phillips, Jack Gwyllim

Circus World
US 1964 138m Super Technirama
Bronston / Midway (Samuel Bronston)
GB title: *The Magnificent Showman*

An American circus owner tours Europe in search of his alcoholic ex-wife who left him when her lover fell to death from the trapeze.
Lethargic big-screen epic which exhausts its spectacle in the first hour and then settles down to a dreary will-daughter-guess-who-the-strange-lady-is plot, without even the plus of an exciting finale.

w Ben Hecht, Julian Halevy, James Edward Grant *d* Henry Hathaway *ph* Jack Hildyard *pd* John de Cuir *m* Dmitri Tiomkin

John Wayne, *Rita Hayworth*, Claudia Cardinale, John Smith, Lloyd Nolan, Richard Conte, Wanda Rotha, Kay Walsh

The Cisco Kid
The Cisco Kid, a ruthless Mexican bandit originally created by O. Henry in a short story, was turned by Hollywood into a dashing wild western Robin Hood in twenty-three sound features (following a few silent ones) and a long-running TV series. In most of them he was accompanied by his fat side-kick Pancho.

For Fox:
1929: IN OLD ARIZONA (Warner Baxter)
1931: THE CISCO KID (Baxter)

For Twentieth Century Fox:
1939: THE RETURN OF THE CISCO KID (Baxter), THE CISCO KID AND THE LADY (Cesar Romero: who played the role in all the remaining TCF movies).
1940: VIVA CISCO KID, LUCKY CISCO KID, THE GAY CABALLERO
1941: ROMANCE OF THE RIO GRANDE, RIDE ON, VAQUERO

For Monogram:
1945: THE CISCO KID RETURNS (Duncan Renaldo), THE CISCO KID IN OLD NEW MEXICO (Renaldo), SOUTH OF THE RIO GRANDE (Renaldo)
1946: THE GAY CAVALIER (Gilbert

Roland), SOUTH OF MONTEREY (Roland), BEAUTY AND THE BANDIT (Roland)
1947: RIDING THE CALIFORNIA TRAIL (Roland), ROBIN HOOD OF MONTEREY (Roland), KING OF THE BANDITS (Roland)
For United Artists (all with Renaldo):
1949: THE VALIANT HOMBRE, THE GAY AMIGO, THE DARING CABALLERO, SATAN'S CRADLE
1950: THE GIRL FROM SAN LORENZO
The fifties TV series starred Renaldo with Leo Carrillo.

Cisco Pike
US 1971 94m Eastmancolor
Columbia / Acrobat (Gerald Ayres)

A former pop group leader and drug pusher is blackmailed by a cop into selling heroin.
Low-key, would-be realistic study of a section of life in seventies LA. Flashy, boring and almost plotless.

wd Bill L. Norton *ph* Vilis Lapenieks *m* various

Kris Kristofferson, Gene Hackman, Karen Black, Harry Dean Stanton

'A moody, melancholy little film whose strength lies in its evocation of the rootless, aimless, irresponsible life-style of the pop/drug culture.'—*Brenda Davies*

The Citadel**
GB 1938 113m bw
MGM (Victor Saville)

A young doctor has a hard time in the mining villages but is later swayed by the easy rewards of a Mayfair practice.
Solidly produced adaptation of a bestseller; the more recent deluge of doctors on television make it appear rather elementary, but many scenes work in a classical way. One of the first fruits of MGM's British studios which were closed by World War II.

w Elizabeth Hill, Ian Dalrymple, Emlyn Williams, Frank Wead, *novel* A. J. Cronin
d King Vidor *m* Louis Levy

Robert Donat, Rosalind Russell, Ralph Richardson, Emlyn Williams, Penelope Dudley Ward, Francis L. Sullivan

'I think any doctor will agree that here is a medical picture with no *Men in White* hokum, no hysterical, incredible melodrama, but with an honest story, honestly told. And that's a rare picture.'—*Pare Lorentz*

Citizen Kane****
US 1941 119m bw
RKO (Orson Welles)

A newspaper tycoon dies, and a magazine reporter interviews his friends in an effort to discover the meaning of his last words.
A brilliant piece of Hollywood cinema using all the resources of the studio; despite lapses of characterization and gaps in the narrative, almost every shot and every line is utterly absorbing both as entertainment and as craft. See *The Citizen Kane Book* by Pauline Kael, and innumerable other writings.

w Herman J. Mankiewicz, Orson Welles
d Orson Welles ph Gregg Toland m Bernard Herrmann ad Van Nest Polglase sp Vernon L. Walker

Orson Welles, Joseph Cotten, Dorothy Comingore, Everett Sloane, Paul Stewart, Ray Collins, Ruth Warrick, *Erskine Sanford, Agnes Moorehead, George Coulouris*, William Alland, Fortunio Bonanova

'On seeing it for the first time, one got a conviction that if the cinema could do that, it could do anything.'—*Penelope Houston*

'What may distinguish *Citizen Kane* most of all is its extracting the mythic from under the humdrum surface of the American experience.'—*John Simon, 1968*

'Probably the most exciting film that has come out of Hollywood for twenty-five years. I am not sure it isn't the most exciting film that has ever come out of anywhere.'—*C. A. Lejeune*

'At any rate Orson Welles has landed in the movies, with a splash and a loud yell.'—*James Shelley Hamilton*

'More fun than any great movie I can think of.'—*Pauline Kael, 1968*

The City*
US 1971 95m Technicolor TVM
Universal (Frank Price)

The Indian mayor of a southwestern city wages a political war while he pursues a mad bomber.
Well made telemovie set in Albuquerque, the pilot for a short-lived series.

w Howard Rodman *d* Daniel Petrie *m* Alex North

Anthony Quinn, Skye Aubrey, Robert Reed, E. G. Marshall, Pat Hingle

City across the River
US 1949 91m bw
U-I (Howard Christie)

Brooklyn delinquents get involved in murder.
Semi-documentary throwback to the Dead End Kids, with location shooting influenced by *The Naked City*. Dull.

w Maxwell Shane, Dennis Cooper, *novel* The

Amboy Dukes by Irving Shulman *d* Maxwell Shane *ph* Maury Gertsman *m* Walter Scharf

Stephen McNally, Barbara Whiting, Peter Fernandez, Al Ramsen, Joshua Shelley, Anthony Curtis (Tony Curtis in his first film role)

City beneath the Sea
US 1953 87m Technicolor
U-I (Albert J. Cohen)

Deep sea divers fall out over a sunken treasure. Adequate double-biller with little to stir the interest.

w Jack Harvey, Ramon Romero *d* Budd Boetticher *ph* Charles P. Boyle

Robert Ryan, Anthony Quinn, Mala Powers, Suzan Ball, George Mathews, Karel Stepanek, Lalo Rios

City beneath the Sea
US 1970 98m De Luxe TVM
Warner / Kent / Motion Pictures International (Irwin Allen)
GB theatrical release title: *One Hour to Doomsday*

An undersea city is threatened by an errant planetoid.
Futuristic adventure from a familiar stable; it will satisfy followers of *Voyage to the Bottom of the Sea*.

w John Meredyth Lucas *d* Irwin Allen *ph* Kenneth Peach *m* Richard La Salle *ad* Roger E. Maus, Stan Jolley

Stuart Whitman, Robert Wagner, Rosemary Forsyth, Robert Colbert, Burr de Benning, Richard Basehart, Joseph Cotten, James Darren, Sugar Ray Robinson, Paul Stewart

City for Conquest**
US 1940 106m bw
Warner (Anatole Litvak)

An East Side truck driver becomes a boxer but is blinded in a fight; meanwhile his composer brother gives up pop music for symphonies.
Phony but oddly persuasive melodrama set in a studio in New York and heavily influenced by the pretensions of the Group theatre.

w John Wexley, *novel* Aben Kandel *d Anatole Litvak* *ph* Sol Polito, James Wong Howe *m* Max Steiner

James Cagney, Ann Sheridan, Frank Craven, Donald Crisp, *Arthur Kennedy*, Frank McHugh, George Tobias, Anthony Quinn, Jerome Cowan, Lee Patrick, Blanche Yurka, Thurston Hall

'Sometimes we wonder whether it wasn't really the Warner brothers who got New York from the Indians, so diligent and devoted have they been in feeling the great city's pulse, picturing its myriad facets and recording with deep compassion the passing life of its seething population.'—*Bosley Crowther*

City Lights***
US 1931 85m bw
Charles Chaplin

A tramp meets a millionaire who when drunk treats him as a great friend but ignores him when sober; he also wins the love of a blind girl.
Mainly sentimental Chaplin vehicle with splendid high spots; silent but with a music track.

wd/m Charles Chaplin

Charles Chaplin, Virginia Cherrill

City of Bad Men*
US 1953 82m Technicolor
TCF (Leonard Goldstein)

In Carson City during the Corbett–Fitzsimmons boxing match, outlaws plan to rob the arena of its receipts.
Slightly unusual western suspenser with generally accomplished handling.

w George W. George, George Slavin *d* Harmon Jones *ph* Charles G. Clarke *m* Lionel Newman

Dale Robertson, Jeanne Crain, Richard Boone, Lloyd Bridges, Carl Betz, Carole Mathews, Whitfield Connor

City of Fear*
US 1958 81m bw
Columbia / Orbit (Leon Chooluck)

A convict escapes with a canister of radioactive cobalt, which he believes to be heroin. After terrifying the city, he finally dies of exposure to it.
Rough-edged but occasionally gripping minor thriller from an independent company.

w Steven Ritch, Robert Dillon *d Irving Lerner* *ph* Lucien Ballard *m Jerry Goldsmith*

Vince Edwards, John Archer, Patricia Blair, Steven Ritch, Lyle Talbot

City of the Dead*
GB 1960 78m bw
Vulcan (Donald Taylor)
US title: *Horror Hotel*

In Massachusetts, a woman burned as a witch 250 years ago is still 'alive', running a local hotel and luring unwary strangers into becoming sacrificial victims.
A deadly first half gives way to splendid cinematic terror when the scene shifts to the village by night, all dry ice and limpid fog, and

the heroine becomes a human sacrifice. A superior horror comic.

w George Baxt *d John Moxey ph Desmond Dickinson m* Douglas Gamley, Ken Jones

Patricia Jessel, Betta St John, Christopher Lee, Dennis Lotis, Valentine Dyall, Venetia Stevenson, Norman Macowan, Fred Johnson

City Streets**
US 1931 86m bw
Paramount

A gangster's daughter is sent to jail for a murder she did not commit, and on release narrowly escapes being 'taken for a ride'.
Tense, dated gangland melodrama of primary interest because of its director's very cinematic treatment.

w Max Marcin, Oliver H. P. Garrett, Dashiell Hammett *d Rouben Mamoulian ph Lee Garmes*

Sylvia Sidney, Gary Cooper, Paul Lukas, Guy Kibbee, William (Stage) Boyd, Stanley Fields, Wynne Gibson

City That Never Sleeps
US 1953 90m bw
Republic (John H. Auer)

The work of the Chicago police force during one night.
Adequate minor semi-documentary police yarn.

w Steve Fisher *d* John H. Auer *ph* John I. Russell *m* R. Dale Butts

Gig Young, Mala Powers, William Talman, Edward Arnold, Chill Wills, Paula Raymond, Marie Windsor

City under the Sea
GB 1965 84m Eastmancolor Colorscope
Bruton / AIP (Daniel Haller)
US title: *War Gods of the Deep*

An American heiress in Cornwall meets Victorian smugglers who have lived a hundred years under the sea in Lyonesse.
Childlike, unpersuasive nonsense which wastes some good talent.

w Charles Bennett, Louis M. Heyward *d* Jacques Tourneur *ph* Stephen Dade *m* Stanley Black

Vincent Price, David Tomlinson, Susan Hart, Tab Hunter, Henry Oscar, John Le Mesurier

The Clairvoyant*
GB 1934 80m bw
Gainsborough (Michael Balcon)

A fraudulent mindreader predicts a disaster which comes true.
Effective minor suspenser on predictable but enjoyable lines.

w Charles Bennett, Bryan Edgar Wallace, Robert Edmunds *d* Maurice Elvey

Claude Rains, Fay Wray, Jane Baxter, Mary Clare, Athole Stewart, Ben Field, Felix Aylmer, Donald Calthrop

Clambake
US 1967 98m Techniscope
UA / Rhodes (Laven–Gardner–Levy)

The son of an oil millionaire sets out to see life.
Painless, forgettable star vehicle.

w Arthur Browne Jnr *d* Arthur H. Nadel *ph* William Margulies *m* Jeff Alexander

Elvis Presley, Shelley Fabares, Bill Bixby, James Gregory, Will Hutchins, Gary Merrill

Clarence the Cross-Eyed Lion
US 1965 98m Technicolor
MGM (Leonard Kaufman)

Adventures of animal farmers in Africa.
Amiable theatrical 'pilot' for the *Daktari* TV series.

w Alan Caillou, Marshall Thompson, Art Arthur *d* Andrew Marton

Marshall Thompson, Betsy Drake, Richard Haydn, Cheryl Miller

Clash by Night*
US 1952 105m bw
RKO (Harriet Parsons) (A Wald–Krasna Production)

In a northern fishing village, jealousy and near-tragedy are occasioned by the return home of a hardened girl from the big city.
Absurdly overblown melodrama of the *Anna Christie* school, burdened with significance and doggedly acted by a remarkable cast.

w Alfred Hayes, *play* Clifford Odets *d* Fritz Lang *ph* Nicholas Musuraca *m* Constantin Bakaleinikoff

Barbara Stanwyck, Paul Douglas, Robert Ryan, Marilyn Monroe, J. Carrol Naish, Keith Andes

Class of '44
US 1973 95m Technicolor Panavision
Warner (Paul Bogart)

Sex problems of college students during World War II.
Thin sequel to *Summer of '42*, nostalgic to Americans over forty but not much of a trip for anyone else.

w Herman Raucher *d* Paul Bogart *ph* Andrew Laszlo *m* David Shire

Gary Grimes, Jerry Houser, Oliver Conant, William Atherton, Sam Bottoms, Deborah Winters

Class of '63
US 1973 74m colour TVM
Metromedia / Stonehenge (Dick Berg)

Old passions flare up at a college reunion.
Adequate mini-drama.

w Lee Kalcheim *d* John Korty

Joan Hackett, James Brolin, Cliff Gorman, Ed Lauter

Claudelle Inglish
US 1961 99m bw
Warner (Leonard Freeman)
GB title: *Young and Eager*

A poor farmer's daughter scorns a wealthy man for a succession of young studs.
Would-be sensational novelette from the author of *Tobacco Road*; it does not begin to be interesting.

w Leonard Freeman, *novel* Erskine Caldwell *d* Gordon Douglas *ph* Ralph Woolsey *m* Howard Jackson

Diane McBain, Arthur Kennedy, Constance Ford, Chad Everett, Claude Akins, Will Hutchins, Robert Colbert, Ford Rainey, James Bell

Claudia***
US 1943 92m bw
TCF (William Perlberg)

A middle-class husband helps his child-wife to mature.
Typical of the best of Hollywood's 'woman's pictures' of the period, this is a pleasant domestic comedy-drama featuring recognizably human characters in an agreeable setting.

w Morrie Ryskind, *novel* and *play Rose Franken* *d* Edmund Goulding *ph* Leon Shamroy *m* Alfred Newman

Dorothy McGuire (her film debut), *Robert Young, Ina Claire*, Reginald Gardiner, Olga Baclanova, Jean Howard, Elsa Janssen

Claudia and David*
US 1946 78m bw
TCF

Claudia and her husband survive assorted crises including their son's illness and David's involvement in a car crash.
Patchwork sequel to *Claudia*, quite pleasant but obviously contrived quickly from scraps.

w Rose Franken, William Brown Meloney *d* Walter Lang *ph* Joseph La Shelle

Dorothy McGuire, Robert Young, Mary Astor, John Sutton, Gail Patrick, Florence Bates

The Clay Pigeon**
US 1949 63m bw
RKO (Herman Schlom)

An amnesiac sailor finds himself courtmartialled for treason, but discovers the real culprit.
Tidily efficient second feature thriller; good enjoyable stuff of its kind.

w Carl Foreman d Richard Fleischer *ph* Robert de Grasse *m* Paul Sawtell

Bill Williams, Barbara Hale, Richard Quine, Richard Loo, Frank Fenton

A Clear and Present Danger*
US 1969 100m Technicolor TVM
Universal (William Sackheim)

A senator's son determines to do something about smog.
Enjoyable socially-conscious drama.

w A. J. Russell, Henri Simoun *d* James Goldstone

Hal Holbrook, E. G. Marshall, Jack Albertson, Joseph Campanella, Pat Hingle, Sharon Acker, Mike Kellin

Cleaver and Haven
US 1976 74m colour TVM
Paramount (Anthony Wilson)
aka: *Future Cop*

A tough cop is assigned a robot for a partner.
Moderately silly comedy pilot.
Holmes and Yoyo was signed instead.

w Anthony Wilson *d* Jud Taylor *m* Billy Goldenberg

Ernest Borgnine, Michael Shannon, John Amos, John Larch

Cleopatra**
US 1934 101m bw
Paramount / Cecil B. de Mille

After Julius Caesar's death, Cleopatra turns her attention to Mark Antony.
More of the virtues than the vices of its producer are notable in this fustian epic, which is almost but not quite unwatchable because of its stolid pace and miscasting. Some of the action montages and the barge scene, however, are superb cinema.

w Waldemar Young, Vincent Lawrence *d Cecil B. de Mille ph Victor Milner* *m* Rudolph Kopp

Claudette Colbert, Henry Wilcoxon (Antony),

Warren William (Caesar), Gertrude Michael, Joseph Schildkraut, Ian Keith, C. Aubrey Smith, Leonard Mudie, Irving Pichel, Arthur Hohl

'It is remarkable how Cecil B. de Mille can photograph so much on such a vast scale and still say nothing . . . it reeks of so much pseudo-artistry, vulgarity, philistinism, sadism, that it can only be compared with the lowest form of contemporary culture: Hitlerism. This is the type of 'culture' that will be fed to the audience of Fascist America.'—*Irving Lerner, 1968*

'He has certainly made the most sumptuous of Roman circuses out of Roman history . . . a constant succession of banquets, dancers, triumphs, and a fleet set on fire.'—*The Times*

Cleopatra

US 1963 243m De Luxe Todd-AO
TCF (Walter Wanger)

The unsurprising story is told at inordinate length and dullness in this ill-starred epic, one of the most heralded, and mismanaged, in film history. (Its story is best told in the producer's *My Life with Cleopatra*.) The most expensive film ever made, for various reasons which do not appear on the screen.

w Joseph L. Mankiewicz, Ranald MacDougall, Sidney Buchman, and others *d* Joseph L. Mankiewicz (and others) *ph* Leon Shamroy *m* Alex North *ad* John de Cuir, Jack Martin Smith, and others

Elizabeth Taylor, Richard Burton, Rex Harrison, Pamela Brown, George Cole, Hume Cronyn, Cesare Danova, Kenneth Haigh, Andrew Keir, Martin Landau, Roddy McDowall, Robert Stephens, Francesca Annis, Martin Benson, Herbert Berghof, Grégoire Aslan, Richard O'Sullivan

'Whatever was interesting about it clearly ended up somewhere else: on the cutting room floor, in various hotel rooms, in the newspaper columns . . . it lacks not only the intelligent spectacle of *Lawrence of Arabia* but the spectacular unintelligence of a Cecil B. de Mille product . . .'—*John Simon*

'The small screen does more than justice to this monumental mouse.'—*Judith Crist*

'I only came to see the asp.'—*Charles Addams*

The Climax*

US 1944 86m Technicolor
Universal (George Waggner)

A young opera singer is hypnotized by a mad doctor, who has kept his murdered mistress embalmed for ten years.
Gothic romantic melodrama invented to capitalize on the success—and the sets—of *Phantom of the Opera*. Curiously endearing, with a good eye-rolling part for Karloff.

w Curt Siodmak, Lynn Starling, *play* Edward Cochran *d* George Waggner *ph* Hal Mohr, W. Howard Greene *m* Edward Ward

Boris Karloff, Susanna Foster, Gale Sondergaard, Turhan Bey, Thomas Gomez, Scotty Beckett

Climb an Angry Mountain*

US 1972 97m colour TVM
Warner / Herb Solow

A local sheriff trails an Indian escaped convict to the top of Mount Shasta.
Overlong but generally enjoyable location melodrama which failed to spark a series.

w Joseph Calvelli, Sam Rolfe *d* Leonard Horn

Fess Parker, Arthur Hunnicutt, Marj Dusay, Barry Nelson, Stella Stevens

Clipper Ship

US 1957 74m bw TVM
Columbia / Playhouse 90

On a ship returning to South America a girl falls for a condemned prisoner.
Talky melodrama with back-projected sails.

d Oscar Rudolph

Charles Bickford, Jan Sterling, Steve Forrest, Helmut Dantine, Evelyn Ankers

Clive of India*

US 1935 90m bw
TCF (Darryl F. Zanuck, William Goetz, Raymond Griffith)

The life of the 18th-century empire builder, with special emphasis on his marriage.
A very tame and now faded epic, with more romance than adventure. The production relies more on stars than technique, but it works.

w W. P. Lipscomb, R. J. Minney, from their play *d* Richard Boleslawski *ph* Peverell Marley *m* Alfred Newman

Ronald Colman, Loretta Young, Colin Clive, Francis Lister, Montagu Love, Robert Greig, Leo G. Carroll, C. Aubrey Smith, Mischa Auer

'Patriotic pageantry, undistorted by facts.'—*J. R. Parish*

Cloak and Dagger*

US 1946 106m bw
United States Pictures (Milton Sperling)

A physics professor joins the secret service and is parachuted into Germany to interview a kidnapped scientist.
Supposedly authoritative espionage adventure

which turned out dull and humourless; plot routine, direction absent-minded.

w Albert Maltz, Ring Lardner Jnr *d* Fritz Lang *ph* Sol Polito *m* Max Steiner

Gary Cooper, Lilli Palmer, Robert Alda, Vladimir Sokoloff, J. Edward Bromberg, Ludwig Stossel, Helene Thimig, Marc Lawrence

The Clock**
US 1945 90m bw
MGM (Arthur Freed)
GB title: *Under the Clock*

A girl meets a soldier at New York's Grand Central Station and marries him during his 24-hour leave.
Everyone now seems far too nice in this winsome romance full of comedy cameos and real New York locations, but if you can relive the wartime mood it still works as a corrective to the Betty Grable glamour pieces.

w Robert Nathan, Joseph Schrank, *story* Paul and Pauline Gallico *d Vincente Minnelli* *ph* George Folsey *m* George Bassman

Judy Garland, Robert Walker, James Gleason, Lucile Gleason, Keenan Wynn, Marshall Thompson, Chester Clute

A Clockwork Orange*
GB 1971 136m colour
Warner / Polaris (Bernard Williams)

In a future Britain of desolation and violence, a young gangster guilty of rape and murder obtains a release from prison after being experimentally brainwashed: he finds society more violent than it was in his time.
A repulsive film in which intellectuals have found acres of social and political meaning; the average judgement is likely to remain that it is pretentious and nasty rubbish for sick minds who do not mind jazzed-up images and incoherent sound.

wd Stanley Kubrick, *novel* Anthony Burgess *ph* John Alcott *m* Walter Carlos *pd* John Barry

Malcolm McDowell, Michael Bates, Adrienne Corri, Patrick Magee, Warren Clarke

'Very early there are hints of triteness and insecurity, and before half an hour is over it begins to slip into tedium . . . Inexplicably the script leaves out Burgess' reference to the title.'—*Stanley Kauffmann*

Close to My Heart
US 1951 90m bw
Warner (William Jacobs)

An adopted baby is discovered to have a murderer for a father; but environment is proved to be more important than heredity.
Routine sentimental drama.

wd William Keighley, *story* A Baby for Midge by James R. Webb *ph* Robert Burks *m* Max Steiner

Ray Milland, Gene Tierney, Fay Bainter, Howard St John, Mary Beth Hughes

The Clouded Yellow*
GB 1950 96m bw
Sydney Box (Betty Box)

A sacked secret service agent gets work tending a butterfly collection and finds that this involves him in a murder plot.
Implausible but quite engaging thriller in the Hitchcock style, involving a chase across the Lake District.

w Janet Green, Eric Ambler *d* Ralph Thomas

Trevor Howard, Jean Simmons, Barry Jones, Sonia Dresdel, Maxwell Reed, Kenneth More, André Morell

The Clown
US 1952 91m bw
MGM (William H. Wright)

A drunken clown, once a great star, is idolized by his son who believes in a comeback.
Maudlin reworking of *The Champ* (qv), with not a surprise in the plot and a star way over the top.

w Martin Rackin *d* Robert Z. Leonard *ph* Paul C. Vogel *m* David Rose

Red Skelton, Jane Greer, Tim Considine, Loring Smith, Philip Ober

Cluny Brown**
US 1946 100m bw
TCF (Ernst Lubitsch)

A plumber's niece goes into service and falls for a Czech refugee guest.
Romantic comedy in a never-never pre-war England; it does no more than poke casual fun at upper-class conventions, but the smooth direction and some excellent character comedy keep it well afloat.

w Samuel Hoffenstein, Elizabeth Reinhardt, *novel* Margery Sharp *d Ernst Lubitsch* *ph* Joseph La Shelle *m* Cyril Mockridge, Emil Newman

Jennifer Jones, Charles Boyer, *Richard Haydn*, *Una O'Connor*, Peter Lawford, Helen Walker, Reginald Gardiner, Reginald Owen, C. Aubrey Smith, Sara Allgood, Ernest Cossart, Florence Bates, Billy Bevan

Cobra Woman
US 1944 71m Technicolor
U-I (George Waggner)

A South Seas girl is abducted by snake worshippers ruled by her evil twin.
A monument of undiluted hokum with some amusing sets and performances but not enough self-mockery in the script.

w Richard Brooks, Gene Lewis *d* Robert Siodmak *ph* George Robinson, Howard Greene *m* Edward Ward

Maria Montez, Jon Hall, Sabu, Lon Chaney Jnr, Mary Nash, Edgar Barrier, Lois Collier, Samuel S. Hinds, Moroni Olsen

The Cobweb
US 1955 124m Eastmancolor
Cinemascope
MGM (John Houseman)

Tensions among the staff of a private mental clinic reach a new high over the purchase of curtains.
The patients seem saner than the doctors in this strained and verbose character drama which despite its cast and big studio look never begins to engage the interest.

w John Paxton, *novel* William Gibson *d* Vincente Minnelli *ph* George Folsey *m* Leonard Rosenman

Richard Widmark, Lauren Bacall, Charles Boyer, *Lillian Gish*, Gloria Grahame, John Kerr, Susan Strasberg, *Oscar Levant*, Tommy Rettig, Paul Stewart, Adèle Jergens

'An overwrought and elaborately artificial exercise, made scarcely more plausible by reliance on the basic jargon of psychiatry.'—*Penelope Houston*

The Cockeyed World*
US 1929 115m bw
Fox

Further adventures of Sergeants Flagg and Quirt, the boisterous heroes of *What Price Glory*.
Lively early talkie; the adventure comedy remains interesting, though the technique is badly faded.

w William K. Wells, Laurence Stallings, Michael Anderson, Wilson Mizner, Tom Barry *d* Raoul Walsh *ph* Arthur Edeson

Victor McLaglen, Edmund Lowe, Lili Damita, Lelia Karnelly, El Brendel, Bobby Burns, Stuart Erwin

Cockleshell Heroes
GB 1955 97m Technicolor
Cinemascope
Columbia / Warwick (Phil C. Samuel)

During World War II, ten marines are trained to travel by canoe into Bordeaux harbour and attach limpet mines to German ships.
Absolutely predictable semi-documentary war heroics, with barrack-room humour turning eventually into tragedy. The familiar elements, including a display of stiff upper lips, ensured box office success.

w Bryan Forbes, Richard Maibaum *d* Jose Ferrer *ph* John Wilcox, Ted Moore *m* John Addison

Jose Ferrer, *Trevor Howard*, Dora Bryan, Victor Maddern, Anthony Newley, Peter Arne, David Lodge, Walter Fitzgerald, Beatrice Campbell

Coconut Grove
US 1938 85m bw
Paramount (George Arthur)

A band is fired from an excursion boat but makes it big in a Los Angeles night club.
Vacuous comedy musical with a watchable number or two.

w Sy Bartlett, Olive Cooper *d* Alfred Santell *ph* Leo Tover *songs* various

Fred MacMurray, Harriet Hilliard, The Yacht Club Boys, Ben Blue, Eve Arden, Billy Lee, Rufe Davis

The Coconuts**
US 1929 96m bw
Paramount (Walter Wanger, James R. Cown)

A chiselling hotel manager tries to get in on the Florida land boom.
Considering its age and the dismal prints which remain, this is a remarkably lively if primitive first film by the Marxes, with some good routines among the excess footage.

w George S. Kaufman, Morrie Ryskind *d* Robert Florey *ph* George Folsey *m/ly* Irving Berlin

The Four Marx Brothers, Margaret Dumont, Oscar Shaw, Mary Eaton, Kay Francis, Basil Ruysdael

'The camerawork showed all the mobility of a concrete fire hydrant caught in a winter freeze.'—*Paul D. Zimmermann*

Code Name: Heraclitus
GB 1967 88m colour TVM
Universal

A war veteran dies briefly on the operating table; revived, he is emotionless and so makes an ideal spy.
So who said the six million dollar man was a new idea?

w Alvin Sapinsley

Stanley Baker, Ricardo Montalban, Jack

Weston, Leslie Nielsen, Sheree North, Kurt Kasznar

Coffee, Tea or Me?*
US 1973 74m colour TVM
Mark Carliner
An airline stewardess has one lover in London and another in Los Angeles.
So what else is new? Agreeable daffy comedy.
d Norman Panama
Karen Valentine, John Davidson, Michael Anderson Jnr

A Cold Night's Death*
US 1972 73m colour TVM
Spelling–Goldberg (Paul Junger Witt)
In a snowbound laboratory scientists are experimenting on apes . . . and someone is experimenting on *them*.
Reasonably tart and chilling sci-fi.
w Jarrold Freeman *d* Christopher Knopf
Robert Culp, Eli Wallach, Michael C. Gwynne

Cold Turkey*
US 1970 102m De Luxe
UA / Tandem / DFI (Bud Yorkin, Norman Lear)
A tobacco company offers 25 million dollars to any town which can give up smoking for thirty days.
Rather wild and strained but sporadically amusing satirical comedy, aggressively littered with unpleasant detail.
w Norman Lear, *novel* I'm Giving Them Up for Good by Margaret and Neil Rau *d* Norman Lear *ph* Charles F. Wheeler *m* Randy Newman
Dick Van Dyke, Pippa Scott, Tom Poston, Edward Everett Horton, Bob Newhart, Vincent Gardenia, Jean Stapleton
'An eager desire to debunk and shock at the same time.'—*David McGillivray*

A Cold Wind in August*
US 1960 77m bw
UA / Troy Films (Robert L. Ross, Philip Hazleton)
An ageing stripper seduces a 17-year-old janitor but the affair ends when he sees her do her act.
Roughly-made, well-acted sex drama which at the time seemed mildly shocking but can only survive for its central acting performance.
w Burton Wohl, from his novel *d* Alexander Singer *ph* Floyd Crosby *m* Gerald Fried
Lola Albright, Scott Marlowe, Joe de Santis, Herschel Bernardi

The Colditz Story**
GB 1954 97m bw
British Lion / Ivan Foxwell
Adventures of British POWs in the German maximum security prison in Saxony's Colditz Castle during World War II.
Probably the most convincing of the British accounts of POW life, with a careful balance of tragedy and comedy against a background of humdrum, boring daily existence. A TV series followed in 1972.
w Guy Hamilton, Ivan Foxwell, *book* P. R. Reid *d* Guy Hamilton *ph* Gordon Dines *m* Francis Chagrin
John Mills, Eric Portman, Christopher Rhodes, Lionel Jeffries, Bryan Forbes, Ian Carmichael, Richard Wattis, Frederick Valk, Anton Diffring, Eugene Deckers, Theodore Bikkel

The Collector*
US 1965 119m Technicolor
Columbia (Jud Kinberg, John Kohn)
An inhibited young butterfly specialist kidnaps a girl to add to his collection.
Talkative and unrewarding suspenser with pretensions, sluggishly handled and not very interestingly acted.
w Stanley Mann, John Kohn, *novel* John Fowles *d* William Wyler *ph* Robert L. Surtees, Robert Krasker *m* Maurice Jarre
Terence Stamp, Samantha Eggar, Mona Washbourne

Colleen*
US 1936 89m bw
Warner (Robert Lord)
Boy meets Irish girl in New York.
Typical light musical of the period with standard studio talent.
w Peter Milne, F. Hugh Herbert, Sig Herzig *d* Alfred E. Green *ph* Byron Haskin, Sol Polito *m/ly* Harry Warren, Al Dubin *ch* Bobby Connolly *gowns* Orry-Kelly
Dick Powell, Ruby Keeler, Jack Oakie, Joan Blondell, Hugh Herbert, Louise Fazenda, Paul Draper, Marie Wilson, Luis Alberni, Hobart Cavanaugh, Berton Churchill

College Holiday
US 1936 87m bw
Paramount (Harlan Thompson)
Bright young specimens are invited to spend a summer with a lady hotelier interested in eugenics.
Boisterous fun and games which may have seemed funny at the time.

w J. P. McEvoy, Harlan Ware, Jay Gorney, Henry Myers *d* Frank Tuttle *ph* Theodor Sparkuhl *songs* various

Jack Benny, George Burns, Gracie Allen, Mary Boland, Martha Raye, Etienne Girardot, Marsha Hunt, Leif Erickson, Eleanore Whitney, Johnny Downs, Olympe Bradna, Ben Blue, Jed Prouty

College Humor
US 1933 84m bw
Paramount

A freshman discovers that football and necking are at least as important as studies.
Easy-going comedy-musical which helped to establish its star.

w Dean Fales *d* Wesley Ruggles

Bing Crosby, Jack Oakie, George Burns, Gracie Allen, Richard Arlen, Mary Carlisle

College Swing
US 1938 86m bw
Paramount (Lewis Gensler)
GB title: *Swing, Teacher, Swing*

A dumb girl must graduate if a college is to inherit a fortune.

w Walter de Leon, Francis Martin *d* Raoul Walsh *ph* Victor Milner *songs* various

George Burns, Gracie Allen, Martha Raye, Bob Hope, Edward Everett Horton, Florence George, Ben Blue, Betty Grable, Jackie Coogan, John Payne, Cecil Cunningham, Robert Cummings

Collision Course**
US 1976 100m colour TVM (tape)
David Wolper

The conflict between President Truman and General MacArthur which led to the latter's resignation.
Dogged dramatized documentary with some splendid moments between the padding.

w Ernest Kinoy d Anthony Page

E. G. Marshall, Henry Fonda, John Randolph, Andrew Duggan, Barry Sullivan, Lloyd Bochner, Lucille Benson, Ann Shoemaker

Colorado Territory*
US 1949 93m Technicolor
Warner (Anthony Veiller)

An outlaw escapes from prison planning one last robbery but is shot in the attempt.
Moderate western remake of *High Sierra*.

w John Twist, Edmund H. North *d* Raoul Walsh *ph* Sid Hickox *m* David Buttolph

Joel McCrea, Virginia Mayo, Dorothy Malone, Henry Hull, John Archer, James Mitchell, Morris Ankrum, Basil Ruysdael, Frank Puglia

Columbo see Mystery Movie

The Comancheros**
US 1961 107m De Luxe Cinemascope
TCF (George Sherman)

A Texas Ranger and his gambler prisoner join forces to clean up renegade gunmen operating from a remote armed compound.
Easy-going, cheerfully violent western with lively roughhouse sequences.

w James Edward Grant, Clair Huffaker *d* Michael Curtiz *ph* William H. Clothier *m* Elmer Bernstein

John Wayne, Stuart Whitman, Nehemiah Persoff, Lee Marvin, Ina Balin, Bruce Cabot

Come and Get It*
US 1935 99m bw
Samuel Goldwyn (Merritt Hulburd)

The life and loves of a lumber tycoon in 19th-century Wisconsin.
Disappointingly conventional, mainly studio-bound action drama using top talent of the period.

w Jules Furthman, Jane Murfin, *novel* Edna Ferber *d* Howard Hawks, William Wyler *ph* Gregg Toland, Rudolph Maté

Edward Arnold, Joel McCrea, Frances Farmer, Walter Brennan, Andrea Leeds

Come Back Little Sheba*
US 1952 99m bw
Paramount (Hal B. Wallis)

An ex-alcoholic is let down not only by his slovenly wife but by the young girl he idolizes.
Stagey but theatrically effective transcription of a popular domestic drama, with one outstanding performance.

w Ketti Frings, *play William Inge d* Daniel Mann *ph* James Wong Howe *m* Franz Waxman

Shirley Booth, Burt Lancaster, Terry Moore, Richard Jaeckel

Come Blow Your Horn*
US 1962 112m Technicolor Panavision
Paramount / Lear and Yorkin

A country boy in New York is envious of his older brother's sophisticated life.
Amusing characters and funny lines permeate

this stolid transcription of an early Neil Simon success; the big screen is not the place for them.

w Norman Lear, *play Neil Simon* *d* Bud Yorkin *ph* William Daniels *m* Nelson Riddle

Frank Sinatra, Tony Bill, Lee J. Cobb, Molly Picon, Jill St John, Barbara Rush, Dan Blocker

Come Fill the Cup*
US 1951 113m bw
Warner (Henry Blanke)

An alcoholic newspaperman cures himself, then his boss's alcoholic son who is involved with gangsters.
Unlikely but solidly entertaining melodrama, powerfully cast.

w Ivan Goff, Ben Roberts, *novel* Harlan Ware *d* Gordon Douglas *ph Robert Burks* *m* Ray Heindorf

James Cagney, Gig Young, Raymond Massey, Phyllis Thaxter, James Gleason, Selena Royle, Larry Keating

Come Fly with Me
US 1962 109m Metrocolor Panavision
MGM / Anatole de Grunwald

The romantic adventures of three air hostesses.
Good-looking girls and airplanes but little else make thin entertainment.

w William Roberts *d* Henry Levin *ph* Oswald Morris

Hugh O'Brian, Dolores Hart, Karl Malden, Pamela Tiffin, Lois Nettleton, Karl Boehm

Come Live with Me*
US 1941 86m bw
MGM (Clarence Brown)

In order to stay in America, a girl refugee from Vienna arranges a strictly platonic marriage with a struggling author.
Hypnotically predictable comedy, quite well presented and performed.

w Patterson McNutt, Virginia Van Upp *d* Clarence Brown *ph* George Folsey *m* Herbert Stothart

James Stewart, Hedy Lamarr, Ian Hunter, Verree Teasdale, Donald Meek, Barton MacLane, *Adeline de Walt Reynolds*

Come Next Spring*
US 1955 92m Trucolor
Republic

A drunkard returns to his Arkansas farm family and wins the respect of them and the community.
D. W. Griffith-type pastoral melodrama which surprisingly works pretty well and leaves one with the intended warm glow.

w Montgomery Pittman *d* R. G. Springsteen *ph* Jack Marta *m* Max Steiner

Ann Sheridan, Steve Cochran, Walter Brennan, Sherry Jackson, Richard Eyer, Edgar Buchanan, Sonny Tufts, Mae Clarke
'An unpretentious film with a good deal of charm.'—*MFB*

Come on George*
GB 1939 88m bw
ATP (Jack Kitchin)

A stableboy calms a nervous racehorse and rides him to victory.
Standard comedy vehicle, well mounted, with the star at his box office peak.

w Anthony Kimmins, Leslie Arliss, Val Valentine *d* Anthony Kimmins

George Formby, Pat Kirkwood, Joss Ambler, Meriel Forbes, Cyril Raymond, George Carney, Ronald Shiner

Come September
US 1961 112m Technicolor Cinemascope
Universal (Robert Arthur)

A wealthy American discovers that his Italian villa is being used as a hotel by his once-a-year mistress, who is about to marry.
Clumsy sex farce with lush trimmings and generation gap asides; effort more noticeable than achievement.

w Stanley Shapiro, Maurice Richlin *d* Robert Mulligan *ph* William Daniels *m* Hans J. Salter

Rock Hudson, Gina Lollobrigida, Sandra Dee, Bobby Darin, Walter Slezak, Brenda de Banzie, Joel Grey, Rosanna Rory, Ronald Howard

Come to the Stable*
US 1949 94m bw
TCF (Samuel G. Engel)

Two French nuns arrive in New England to build a local hospital, and melt the hearts of the local grumps.
This old-time charmer simply brims with sweetness and light and is produced with high-class studio efficiency.

w Oscar Millard, Sally Benson, *story* Clare Boothe Luce *d* Henry Koster *ph* Joseph La Shelle *m* Lionel Newman

Loretta Young, Celeste Holm, Hugh Marlowe, Elsa Lanchester, Thomas Gomez, Dorothy Patrick, Basil Ruysdael, Dooley Wilson, Regis Toomey, Henri Letondal

The Comedians*
US / Bermuda / France 1967 160m
Metrocolor Panavision
MGM / Maximilian / Trianon (Peter Glenville)

A variety of English-speaking eccentrics are caught up in the violent events of Haiti under Papa Doc Duvalier.
Clumsy and heavy-going compression of a too-topical novel, with most of the plot left in at the expense of character. Neither entertaining nor instructive, but bits of acting please.

w Graham Greene, from his novel *d* Peter Glenville *ph* Henri Decae *m* Laurence Rosenthal

Richard Burton, Elizabeth Taylor, *Alec Guinness*, Peter Ustinov, Lillian Gish, Paul Ford, Roscoe Lee Browne, James Earl Jones, Raymond St Jacques, Cicely Tyson

'So thick and fast do the clichés come that one feels the script can only have been salvaged from some *New Statesman* competition.'—*Tom Milne*

'It's pleasant to spend two hours again in Greeneland, still well-stocked with bilious minor crucifixions, furtive fornication, cynical politics, and reluctant hope.'—*Stanley Kauffmann*

The Comedy Man*
GB 1964 92m bw
British Lion–Gray–Consort (Jon Pennington)

A middle-aged actor on the skids desperately rounds up his contacts and becomes the star of a TV commercial.
Determinedly depressing satirical melodrama with engaging moments; comedy emphasis would have better suited the talents.

w Peter Yeldham, *novel* Douglas Hayes *d* Alvin Rakoff *ph* Ken Hodges *m* Bill McGuffie

Kenneth More, Cecil Parker, Dennis Price, Billie Whitelaw, Norman Rossington, Angela Douglas, Edmund Purdom, Frank Finlay, Alan Dobie

The Comedy of Terrors*
US 1963 88m Pathecolor Panavision
Alta Vista / AIP (Anthony Carras, Richard Matheson)

Two impecunious funeral directors decide to speed up the demise of their prospective clients.
Disappointingly slackly-handled and rather tiresome macabre frolic, notable for a few splendid moments and an imperishable cast.

w Richard Matheson *d* Jacques Tourneur *ph* Floyd Crosby *m* Les Baxter

Vincent Price, Peter Lorre, Boris Karloff, Basil Rathbone, Joe E. Brown, Joyce Jameson

The Comic**
US 1969 95m Technicolor
Columbia (Carl Reiner)

The success, downfall and old age of a silent film comedian in Hollywood.
Remarkably bright and cinematic tragi-comedy obviously based on Buster Keaton, with a *Citizen Kane*-type framework. Not a commercial success, but a must for professionals.

w Carl Reiner, Aaron Rubin *d* Carl Reiner *ph* W. Wallace Kelley *m* Jack Elliott

Dick Van Dyke, Mickey Rooney (more or less playing Ben Turpin), Cornel Wilde, Carl Reiner, Michele Lee, Pert Kelton

'Offers a variety of delights.'—*Judith Crist*

The Command
US 1954 94m Warnercolor
Cinemascope
Warner (David Weisbart)

A cavalry troop escorts a wagon train through Indian country.
Competent but unsurprising 'second team' western.

w Russell Hughes, *novel* James Warner Bellah *d* David Butler *ph* Wilfrid M. Cline *m* Dmitri Tiomkin

Guy Madison, Joan Weldon, James Whitmore, Carl Benton Reid, Harvey Lembeck, Ray Teal, Bob Nichols

Command Decision*
US 1949 111m bw
MGM (Sidney Franklin)

War among the back-room boys; a general, his staff and his peers debate the aerial bombardment of Germany.
Plainly reproduced version of a determinedly serious play, with a remarkable cast partly at sea.

w William R. Laidlaw, George Froeschel, *play* William Wister Haines *d* Sam Wood *ph* Harold Rosson *m* Miklos Rozsa

Clark Gable, Walter Pidgeon, Van Johnson, Brian Donlevy, John Hodiak, Charles Bickford, Edward Arnold, Marshall Thompson, Richard Quine, Cameron Mitchell, Clinton Sundberg, Ray Collins, Warner Anderson, John McIntire, Moroni Olsen

The Commandos Strike at Dawn*
US 1942 98m bw
Columbia (Lester Cowan)

Norwegian commandos outwit the Nazis with the help of the British navy.

Standard war adventure shot in Newfoundland.

w Irwin Shaw, *story* C. S. Forester *d* John Farrow *ph* William C. Mellor *m* Louis Gruenberg

Paul Muni, Anna Lee, Lillian Gish, Cedric Hardwicke, Robert Coote, Ray Collins, Rosemary de Camp, Richard Derr, Alexander Knox, Rod Cameron

The Common Touch*
GB 1941 104m bw
British National (John Baxter)

A rich young man poses as a tramp to save a dosshouse from destruction.
Naive drama with a social conscience, remade from the 1932 talkie *Dosshouse*. A brave try.

w Barbara K. Emery, Geoffrey Orme, *novel* Herbert Ayres *d* John Baxter

Geoffrey Hibbert, Greta Gynt, Joyce Howard, Harry Welchman, Edward Rigby, George Carney, Bransby Williams, Wally Patch, Eliot Makeham, Bernard Miles, Bill Fraser, John Longden; *guests* Sandy Macpherson, Scott Sanders, Mark Hambourg, Carrol Gibbons

Companions in Nightmare*
US 1967 99m Technicolor TVM
Universal (Norman Lloyd)

Murder at a group therapy session.
Slightly offbeat, rather pretentious whodunnit.

w Robert L. Joseph *d* Norman Lloyd

Melvyn Douglas, Gig Young, Anne Baxter, Patrick O'Neal, Dana Wynter, Leslie Nielsen

Company of Killers
US 1969 87m Technicolor TVM
Universal

A psychopathic killer is at large in the city.
Adequate chase thriller.

w E. Jack Neuman *d* Jerry Thorpe

Van Johnson, Ray Milland, Robert Middleton, John Saxon, Susan Oliver, Clu Gulager, Brian Kelly, Fritz Weaver, Diana Lynn

The Company She Keeps
US 1950 83m bw
RKO (John Houseman)

A self-sacrificing parole officer allows a parolee to steal her fiancé.
Considering the credits, a dismally novelettish drama of almost no interest.

w Ketti Frings *d* John Cromwell *ph* Nicholas Musuraca *m* Leigh Harline

Lizabeth Scott, *Jane Greer*, Dennis O'Keefe, Fay Baker, John Hoyt, James Bell, Don Beddoe, Bert Freed

Compulsion**
US 1959 103m bw Cinemascope
TCF (Richard D. Zanuck)

In the twenties, two Chicago students kidnap and murder a young boy for kicks.
Rather dogged but earnest fictionalization of the Leopold-Loeb case with solid performances and production.

w Richard Murphy, *play* Meyer Levin *d* Richard Fleischer *ph* William C. Mellor *m* Lionel Newman

Dean Stockwell, Bradford Dillman, Orson Welles (in a cameo court appearance as Clarence Darrow), Diane Varsi, E. G. Marshall, Martin Milner, Richard Anderson, Robert Simon

Comrade X*
US 1940 89m bw
MGM (Gottfried Reinhardt)

An American correspondent in Russia is blackmailed into smuggling a girl out of the country.
Lame satirical comedy in the wake of *Ninotchka*; a few good moments, but generally heavy-handed.

w Ben Hecht, Charles Lederer, Walter Reisch *d* King Vidor *m* Bronislau Kaper

Clark Gable, Hedy Lamarr, Felix Bressart, Oscar Homolka, Eve Arden, Sig Rumann

Condemned*
US 1930 86m bw
Samuel Goldwyn

A bank robber is sent to Devil's Island and falls in love with the wife of the brutal warden.
Slow-moving but pictorially attractive melodrama with old-style performances.

w Sidney Howard, *novel* Condemned to Devil's Island by Blair Niles *d* Wesley Ruggles *ph George Barnes, Gregg Toland sets William Cameron Menzies*

Ronald Colman, Ann Harding, Louis Wolheim, Dudley Digges, William Elmer

The Condemned of Altona*
Italy / France 1962 113m bw
(TCF) Titanus / SGC (Carlo Ponti)

The head of a German shipping empire discovers he has only a few months to live and tries to bring his family to order.
Strident intellectual melodrama whose credits tell all. Watchable for the acting, but very glum.

w Abby Mann, Cesare Zavattini, *play* Jean-Paul Sartre *d* Vittorio De Sica *ph* Roberto Gerardi *m* Dmitri Shostakovich

Fredric March, Sophia Loren, Robert Wagner, Maximilian Schell, Françoise Prévost, Alfredo Franchi

'This film is such a hopeless mess that it is difficult to know where to begin criticizing it.'—*Tom Milne*

Conduct Unbecoming*

GB 1975 107m Technicolor
British Lion / Crown (Michael Deeley, Barry Spikings)

In an officers' mess in India in the nineties, a cadet is accused of assault on a lady but the real culprit is a paranoic who has taken to pigsticking in quite the wrong way.
Disappointingly flatly-handled and quite unatmospheric picturization of an absorbing West End melodrama. The cast is largely wasted, but stretches of dialogue maintain their interest.

w Robert Enders, *play* Barry England *d* Michael Anderson *ph* Bob Huke *m* Stanley Myers

Michael York, Stacy Keach, Trevor Howard, Christopher Plummer, Richard Attenborough, Susannah York, James Faulkner, James Donald

Cone of Silence*

GB 1960 92m bw
British Lion / Bryanston (Aubrey Baring)

A seasoned pilot is condemned for an error which caused a crash and later dies in similar circumstances. A flying examiner discovers scientific reasons for exonerating him.
Tolerable suspense drama let down by thin dialogue and confused characterization.

w Robert Westerby, *novel* David Beaty *d* Charles Frend *ph* Arthur Grant *m* Gerhard Schurmann

Michael Craig, Bernard Lee, Peter Cushing, George Sanders, Elizabeth Seal, André Morell, Gordon Jackson, Delphi Lawrence, Noel Willman, Charles Tingwell

Coney Island**

US 1943 96m Technicolor
TCF (William Perlberg)

Two fairground showmen vie for the affections of a songstress.
Brassy, simple-minded, entertaining musical. Very typical of its time; later remade as *Wabash Avenue* (qv).

w George Seaton *d Walter Lang ph* Ernest Palmer *songs* Leo Robin, Ralph Rainger *ch* Hermes Pan *ad* Richard Day, Joseph C. Wright

Betty Grable, George Montgomery, Cesar Romero, Charles Winninger, Phil Silvers, Matt Briggs, Paul Hurst, Frank Orth, Andrew Tombes, Alec Craig, Hal K. Dawson

Confession

US 1937 90m bw
Warner (Henry Blanke)

An errant mother shoots her former lover to protect her daughter.
Stilted romantic melodrama copied scene for scene from a 1936 German film *Mazurka*.

w Julius J. Epstein, Margaret Le Vino, *original screenplay* Hans Rameau *d* Joe May *ph* Sid Hickox *m* Leo F. Forbstein, Peter Kreuder *ad* Anton Grot

Kay Francis, Ian Hunter, Basil Rathbone, Jane Bryan, Donald Crisp, Dorothy Peterson, Laura Hope Crews, Robert Barrat

Confession

US 1957 74m bw TVM
Columbia / Playhouse 90

A reporter discovers that the public idol who is his subject had feet of clay.
Familiar exposé stuff, adequately put over.

d Anton M. Leader

Dennis O'Keefe, June Lockhart, Paul Stewart, Romney Brent

Confessions of a Nazi Spy***

US 1939 102m bw
Warner (Robert Lord)

How G-men ferreted out Nazis in the United States.
Topical exposé with all concerned in top form; a semi-documentary very typical of Warner product throughout the thirties and forties, from *G-Men* to *Mission to Moscow* and *I Was a Communist for the FBI*: well made, punchy, and smartly edited, with a loud moral at the end.

w Milton Krims, John Wexley, from materials gathered by former FBI agent Leon G. Turrou *d Anatole Litvak ph Sol Polito m* Max Steiner

Edward G. Robinson, Paul Lukas, George Sanders, Francis Lederer, Henry O'Neill, Lya Lys, James Stephenson, Sig Rumann, Dorothy Tree, Joe Sawyer

'The Warner brothers have declared war on Germany with this one . . . with this precedent there is no way any producer could argue against dramatizing any social or political theme on the grounds that he's afraid of domestic or foreign censorship. Everybody duck.'—*Pare Lorentz*

'Has a remarkable resemblance to a full-length *Crime Does Not Pay*.'—*David Wolff*

Confessions of an Opium Eater
US 1962 85m bw
Albert Zugsmith
GB title: *Evils of Chinatown*

In San Francisco in the nineties, a seaman falls into the clutches of a tong.
The hero is called De Quincey, but that is the only association with the famous book of the same title. This absurd melodrama is just about bad enough to be funny, but not very.

w Robert Hill *d* Albert Zugsmith *ph* Joseph Biroc *m* Albert Glasser *ad Eugene Lourié*

Vincent Price, Linda Ho, Richard Loo, Philip Ahn, June Kim

'Has to be seen to be believed . . . starved girls captive in cages, secret panels, sliding doors, sewer escape routes, opium dens and nightmares . . .'—*MFB*

Confidential Agent**
US 1945 122m bw
Warner (Robert Buckner)

An emissary of Franco's Spain comes to England in the late thirties to make a munitions deal, and falls in love with the tycoon's daughter.
Heavy-going simplification of Graham Greene's lowering novel, with cast and (especially) set designers all at sea but nevertheless providing striking moments.

w Robert Buckner *d* Herman Shumlin *ph James Wong Howe* *m* Franz Waxman

Charles Boyer, Lauren Bacall, Katina Paxinou, Peter Lorre, Victor Francen, George Coulouris, Wanda Hendrix, George Zucco, Miles Manderrer

Confidential Report*
Spain 1955 99m bw
Sevilla Studios (Louis Dolivet, Orson Welles)
aka: *Mr Arkadin*

A wealthy and powerful financier employs a young American to seek out figures from his own past, who are soon found dead . . .
Silly melodrama which might have been suspenseful if done by Hitchcock, or even by Welles at his peak; as it is, weak writing and sloppy production remove most of the interest and reveal it as a very obvious bag of tricks.

wd Orson Welles *ph* Jean Bourgoin *m* Paul Misraki

Orson Welles, Michael Redgrave, Katina Paxinou, Akim Tamiroff, Mischa Auer, Patricia Medina, Jack Watling, Peter Van Eyck, Paola Mori, Robert Arden, Grégoire Aslan, Suzanne Flon

'Tilted camera angles, heavy atmospheric shots, overlapping dialogue—all the trademarks are here, sometimes over-used to an almost hysterical degree, but they have little significance . . . (the film) springs not from life but from the earlier cinematic world of Welles himself and from the kind of thriller written about thirty years ago by E. Philips Oppenheim.'—*Gavin Lambert*

Confirm or Deny*
US 1941 78m bw
TCF (Len Hammond)

An American reporter falls for a wireless operator in wartime London.
Artificial but watchable minor romantic melodrama.

w Jo Swerling, Henry Wales, Samuel Fuller *d* Archie Mayo *ph* Leon Shamroy

Don Ameche, Joan Bennett, Roddy McDowall, Arthur Shields, Raymond Walburn, John Loder

Conflict*
US 1945 86m bw
Warner (William Jacobs)

A man murders his wife and is apparently haunted by her; but the odd happenings have been arranged by a suspicious psychiatrist.
Leaden and artificial melodrama with both stars miscast; a few effective moments.

w Arthur T. Horman, Dwight Taylor *d* Curtis Bernhardt *ph* Merritt Gerstad *m* Frederick Hollander

Humphrey Bogart, Sydney Greenstreet, Alexis Smith, Rose Hobart, Charles Drake, Grant Mitchell

Conflict of Wings*
GB 1953 84m Eastmancolor
Group Three (Herbert Mason)
US title: *Fuss over Feathers*

East Anglian villagers fight to save a bird sanctuary from being taken over by the RAF as a rocket range.
Sub-Ealing comedy-drama with a highly predictable outcome; generally pleasant but without much bite.

w Don Sharp, John Pudney *d* John Eldridge *ph* Arthur Grant *m* Philip Green

John Gregson, Muriel Pavlow, Kieron Moore, Niall MacGinnis, Sheila Sweet, Harry Fowler, Barbara Hicks, Charles Lloyd Pack

Congo Crossing
US 1956 85m Technicolor
U-I (Howard Christie)

Assorted fugitives from justice gather at Congotanga, which has no extradition laws. The poor man's *Casablanca*, quite good looking but dully written and presented.

w Richard Alan Simmons *d* Joseph Pevney *ph* Russell Metty *m* Joseph Gershenson

George Nader, Virginia Mayo, *Peter Lorre*, Michael Pate, Rex Ingram

Congratulations, It's a Boy
US 1971 73m colour TVM
Aaron Spelling

A swinging bachelor's life changes when his grown son turns up.
Modest comedy with a few laughs.

w Stanley Cherry *d* William A. Graham

Bill Bixby, Diane Baker, Jack Albertson, Ann Sothern, Karen Jensen

A Connecticut Yankee*
US 1931 96m bw
Fox

A man dreams himself back to the court of King Arthur, and teaches the Middle Ages a thing or two about modern living.
First sound version of Mark Twain's classic fantasy, also filmed in 1921 and 1949. Creaky now, but amiable.

w William Conselman *d* David Butler *ph* Ernest Palmer

Will Rogers, Maureen O'Sullivan, Myrna Loy, Frank Albertson, William Farnum

A Connecticut Yankee in King Arthur's Court*
US 1949 106m Technicolor
Paramount
GB title: *A Yankee in King Arthur's Court*

Gossamer musical version of the above with the emphasis on song and knockabout. Palatable, with the 'Busy Doin' Nothin' ' sequence the most memorable.

w Edmund Beloin *d* Tay Garnett *ph* Ray Rennahan *md* Victor Young

Bing Crosby, Rhonda Fleming, William Bendix, *Cedric Hardwicke*, Murvyn Vye

Connecting Rooms
GB 1969 103m Technicolor
Telstar / Franklin Gollings (Harry Field)

In a seedy Bayswater boarding house, a dismissed schoolmaster befriends a failed cellist whose protégé is a sponging songwriter.
Aggressively dismal melodrama which would be hilarious if it were not so sadly slow and naive.

wd Franklin Gollings, *play* The Cellist by Marion Hart *ph* John Wilcox *m* Joan Shakespeare

Bette Davis, Michael Redgrave, Alexis Kanner, Kay Walsh, Gabrielle Drake, Leo Genn, Olga Georges-Picot, Richard Wyler, Brian Wilde

The Connection*
US 1973 74m colour TVM
Phil D'Antoni / Metromedia

A tough reporter mediates between jewel thieves and insurance companies.
Complex, New York based thriller which resolves itself into a pretty good chase comparable with the same producer's *The French Connection.*

w Albert Ruben *d* Tom Gries

Charles Durning, Ronnie Cox, Zohra Lampert, Dennis Cole, Dana Wynter, Howard Cosell, Mike Kellin

The Conqueror
US 1955 112m Technicolor Cinemascope
Howard Hughes (Dick Powell)

A romance of the early life of Genghis Khan, who captures and is enamoured by the daughter of an enemy.
Solemn pantomime with a measure of bloodthirsty action and dancing girls, but featuring too many dull spots between, especially as the star is the most unlikely of eastern warriors and the production values careful but not too steady.

w Oscar Millard *d* Dick Powell *ph* Joseph La Shelle, Leo Tover, Harry J. Wild *m* Victor Young

John Wayne, Susan Hayward, Pedro Armendariz, Agnes Moorehead, Thomas Gomez, John Hoyt, William Conrad, Ted de Corsia, Lee Van Cleef

Conquest**
US 1937 115m bw
MGM (Bernard Hollyman)
GB title: *Marie Walewska*

The life of Napoleon's most enduring mistress.
Measured, dignified, and often rather dull historical fiction, lightened by excellent performances and production.

w Samuel Hoffenstein, Salka Viertel, S. N. Behrman, from a Polish play dramatized by Helen Jerome *d* Clarence Brown *ph* Karl Freund

Greta Garbo, *Charles Boyer*, Reginald Owen, Alan Marshal, Henry Stephenson, Dame May Whitty, Leif Erickson

Conquest of Space
US 1955 80m Technicolor
Paramount (George Pal)

In 1980, the Americans have built a space station in the atmosphere, and plan a voyage to the moon but are sent to Mars instead.
So history catches up with science fiction. This sober prophecy looks good but very little happens and the result is as dull as it is bright and shiny.

w James O'Hanlon *d* Byron Haskin *ph* Lionel Lindon *m* Van Cleeve *ad* Hal Pereira, James McMillan Johnson *sp* John P. Fulton, Irmin Roberts, Paul Lerpae, Ivyl Burks, Jan Domella

Eric Fleming, Walter Brooke, Mickey Shaughnessy, William Hopper, Ross Martin

Conrack*
US 1974 106m De Luxe Panavision
TCF (Martin Ritt, Irving Ravetch)

A young white teacher is assigned to an all-black school in South Carolina, and after some difficulty makes friends with children and parents.
Nostalgically mellow happy-film, lit by bright smiles all round.

w Irving Ravetch, Harriet Frank Jnr, *novel* The Water Is Wide by Pat Conroy *d* Martin Ritt *ph* John Alonzo *m* John Williams

Jon Voight, Paul Winfield, Hume Cronyn, Madge Sinclair, Tina Andrews

'For all its craftsman-like virtues, it seems a conscious turning aside from the complexities of modern cinema to the simpler alternatives of yesteryear. Indeed, with underprivileged white children instead of black and Greer Garson substituting for Jon Voight, the film might have been made all of thirty years ago.'—*John Raisbeck*

Conspiracy of Hearts*
GB 1960 113m bw
Rank (Betty E. Box)

During World War II, Italian nuns smuggle Jewish children across the border from a nearby prison camp.
Highly commercial combination of exploitable sentimental elements: Germans, Jews, nuns, children, war, suspense. Remarkably, it gets by without causing nausea.

w Robert Presnell Jnr *d* Ralph Thomas *ph* Ernest Steward *m* Angelo Lavagnino

Lilli Palmer, Sylvia Syms, Yvonne Mitchell, Albert Lieven, Ronald Lewis, Peter Arne, Nora Swinburne, Michael Goodliffe, Megs Jenkins, David Kossoff, Jenny Laird, George Coulouris, Phyllis Neilson-Terry

Conspiracy of Terror*
US 1975 74m colour TVM
Lorimar
aka: *Enter Horowitz*

A man-and-wife detective team encounter diabolism in the suburbs.
Curious mix of Jewish humour and macabre goings-on; a failed pilot.

w Howard Rodman *d* John Llewellyn Moxey *m* Neal Hefti

Michael Constantine, Barbara Rhoades, Mariclare Costello, Logan Ramsay

Conspiracy to Kill*
US 1970 97m Technicolor TVM
Universal / Jack Webb
aka: *The DA: Conspiracy to Kill*

The DA of a small community tries a case involving a local chemist who is also a fence.
One of two failed pilots for the same non-series (see *Murder One*). Quite watchable.

w Stanford Whitmore, Joel Oliansky *d* Paul Krasny

Robert Conrad, William Conrad, Belinda Montgomery, Don Stroud, Steve Ihnat

Conspirator
GB 1949 87m bw
MGM (Arthur Hornblow Jnr)

A guards officer, unknown to his young wife, is a communist spy.
Singularly awful romantic melodrama which never convinces or entertains for a moment.

w Sally Benson, Gerard Fairlie, *novel* Humphrey Slater *d* Victor Saville *ph* E. A. Young *m* John Wooldridge

Robert Taylor, Elizabeth Taylor, Harold Warrender, Robert Flemyng, Marie Ney

The Conspirators*
US 1944 101m bw
Warner (Jack Chertok)

A Dutch underground leader escapes to Lisbon and clears up international intrigue.
Interestingly cast but often listless wartime melodrama, a doomed attempt to reprise *Casablanca* without Humphrey Bogart.

w Vladimir Pozner, Leo Rosten, *novel* City of

Shadows by Frederick Prokosch *d* Jean Negulesco *ph* Arthur Edeson *m* Max Steiner

Hedy Lamarr, Paul Henreid, Sydney Greenstreet, Peter Lorre, *Victor Francen*, Carol Thurston, Vladimir Sokoloff, Joseph Calleia, Edward Ciannelli, Steve Geray, Kurt Katch, George Macready

The Constant Husband*
GB 1954 88m Technicolor print
British Lion / London Films (Frank Launder, Sidney Gilliat)

An amnesiac discovers that he is a multiple bigamist, still wanted by each of his five wives.
Flimsy comedy which never really gets going despite an attractive cast.

w Sidney Gilliat, Val Valentine *d* Sidney Gilliat *ph* Ted Scaife *m* Malcolm Arnold

Rex Harrison, Kay Kendall, Margaret Leighton, Cecil Parker, Nicole Maurey, George Cole, Raymond Huntley, Michael Hordern, Eric Pohlmann, Robert Coote

The Constant Nymph*
GB 1933 98m bw
Gaumont (Michael Balcon)

In the Tyrol, a composer leaves his rich wife for a schoolgirl suffering from a heart condition.
Archetypal romantic drama from Margaret Kennedy's book, first filmed in 1928 by the same producer (directed by Adrian Brunel, with Ivor Novello and Mabel Poulton). A standard production of its time, which seems to have vanished with the literary copyright.

w Margaret Kennedy, Basil Dean, from their play based on her novel *d* Basil Dean

Brian Aherne, Victoria Hopper, Leonora Corbett, Lyn Harding, Mary Clare, Jane Baxter

The Constant Nymph*
US 1943 112m bw
Warner (Henry Blanke)

Artificially well-produced, overlong Hollywood version of the above.

w Kathryn Scola *d* Edmund Goulding *ph* Tony Gaudio *m* Erich Wolfgang Korngold

Charles Boyer, *Joan Fontaine*, Alexis Smith, Brenda Marshall, Charles Coburn, Dame May Whitty, Peter Lorre, Joyce Reynolds, Jean Muir, Edward Ciannelli, Montagu Love, André Charlot

Contraband**
GB 1940 92m bw
British National (John Corfield)
US title: *Blackout*

A Danish merchant captain and a girl in wartime London expose a gang of spies using a cinema as headquarters.
Enjoyable lightweight comedy melodrama on Hitchcock lines, reuniting the unlikely star team from *The Spy in Black*.

w Emeric Pressburger, Michael Powell, Brock Williams *d* Michael Powell

Conrad Veidt, Valerie Hobson, Esmond Knight, Hay Petrie, Raymond Lovell, Harold Warrender, Charles Victor, Manning Whiley

Convention City*
US 1933 78m bw
Warner (Henry Blanke)

Extra-marital fun and games at a Chicago convention.
Amusing and rather risqué comedy which helped to bring down on Hollywood the wrath of the Legion of Decency.

w Robert Lord *d* Archie Mayo *ph* William Rees

Joan Blondell, Guy Kibbee, Adolphe Menjou, Dick Powell, Mary Astor, Frank McHugh, Ruth Donnelly, Hugh Herbert, Hobart Cavanaugh

The Conversation**
US 1974 113m Technicolor
Paramount / Francis Ford Coppola

A bugging device expert lives only for his work, but finally develops a conscience.
Absorbing but extremely difficult to follow in detail, this personal, timely (in view of Watergate), Kafkaesque suspense story centres almost entirely on director and leading actor, who have a field day.

wd Francis Ford Coppola *ph* Bill Butler *m* David Shire

Gene Hackman, John Cazale, Allen Garfield, Frederick Forrest

'A private, hallucinatory study in technical expertise and lonely guilt.'—*Sight and Sound*

Convict 99**
GB 1938 91m bw
Gainsborough (Edward Black)

A seedy schoolmaster accidentally becomes a prison governor and lets the convicts run the place.
Patchily funny if overlong and in some ways rather serious Will Hay comedy, not quite typical of him.

w Marriott Edgar, Val Guest, Ralph Smart, Jack Davies *d* Marcel Varnel

Will Hay, Graham Moffatt, Moore Marriott,

Googie Withers, Garry Marsh, Peter Gawthorne, Basil Radford, Kathleen Harrison

Convicted*
US 1950 91m bw
Columbia (Jerry Bresler)

When a prison informer is killed, one convict knows who did it.
Routine, over-plotted, strongly cast prison melodrama.

w William Bowers, Fred Niblo Jnr, Seton I. Miller, *play* Martin Flavin *d* Henry Levin *ph* Burnett Guffey *m* Morris Stoloff

Glenn Ford, Broderick Crawford, Millard Mitchell, Dorothy Malone, Frank Faylen, Carl Benton Reid, Will Geer

Convicts Four*
US 1962 106m bw
Allied Artists–Lubin–Kaufman (A. Ronald Lubin)
Original and GB title: *Reprieve*

A convict reprieved from the electric chair spends eighteen years in prison, becomes a painter, and is rehabilitated.
Odd and unsatisfactory mixture of documentary, melodrama, sentimentality and character study, with stars unexpectedly popping in for cameo appearances. Something worthier was obviously intended.

wd Millard Kaufman, from the autobiography of John Resko *ph* Joseph Biroc *m* Leonard Rosenman

Ben Gazzara, Vincent Price, Rod Steiger, Broderick Crawford, Stuart Whitman, Ray Walston, Jack Kruschen, Sammy Davis Jnr

Convoy*
GB 1941 90m bw
Ealing (Sergei Nolbandov)

A German pocket battleship menaces a British convoy, and a merchant ship sacrifices itself to prevent disaster.
Fluent British war film of the early days, the only substantial work of a much vaunted director who was subsequently killed.

w Pen Tennyson, Patrick Kirwan *d Pen Tennyson*

Clive Brook, John Clements, Edward Chapman, Judy Campbell, Penelope Dudley Ward, Edward Rigby, Allan Jeayes, Albert Lieven

Coogan's Bluff**
US 1968 94m Technicolor
Universal (Don Siegel)

An Arizona sheriff takes an escaped killer back to New York, and when the man escapes uses western methods to recapture him.
Violent, well-done police story which inspired the TV series *McCloud*.

w Herman Miller, Dean Riesner, Howard Rodman *d Don Siegel ph* Bud Thackery *m* Lalo Schifrin

Clint Eastwood, Lee J. Cobb, Susan Clark, Don Stroud, Tisha Sterling, Betty Field, Tom Tully

Cool Breeze
US 1972 102m Metrocolor
MGM / Penelope (Gene Corman)

A miscellaneous gang of crooks is rounded up to commit a robbery, which ultimately fails.
Third, all-black remake of *The Asphalt Jungle* (the others being *The Badlanders* and *Cairo*). Fashionable violence against a Los Angeles backdrop, but not at all memorable.

wd Barry Pollack *ph* Andy Davis *m* Solomon Burke

Thalmus Rasulala, Judy Pace, Jim Watkins, Raymond St Jacques, Lincoln Kilpatrick

Cool Hand Luke**
US 1967 126m Technicolor Panavision
Jalem / Warner (Gordon Carroll)

Sentenced to two years' hard labour with the chain gang, a convict becomes a legend of invulnerability but is eventually shot during an escape.
Allegedly a Christ-allegory, this well-made and good-looking film is only partially successful as an entertainment; slow stretches of soul-searching alternate with brutality, and not much acting is possible.

w Donn Pearce, Frank R. Pierson, *novel* Donn Pearce *d Stuart Rosenberg ph Conrad Hall m* Lalo Schifrin

Paul Newman, George Kennedy, Jo Van Fleet, J. D. Cannon, Lou Antonio, Robert Drivas, Strother Martin, Clifton James

Cool Million
US 1971 97m Technicolor TVM
Universal (David J. O'Connell)

A private eye whose fee per case is one million dollars locates a missing heiress.
Slick, glamorous and empty pilot for a short-lived addition to *Mystery Movie* (qv).

w Larry Cohen *d* Gene Levitt

James Farentino, Lila Kedrova, Patrick O'Neal, Christine Belford, Barbara Bouchet, John Vernon, Jackie Coogan

The Cool Ones
US 1967 96m Technicolor Panavision
Warner (William Conrad)

Former pop singer makes a comeback.
Zazzy showbiz saga with ear-splitting track, quite professionally assembled.

w Joyce Geller *d* Gene Nelson *ph* Floyd Crosby *m* Ernie Freeman

Roddy McDowall, Debbie Watson, Robert Coote, Phil Harris, Nita Talbot

The Co-Optimists*
GB 1929 83m bw
New Era (Gordon Craig)

A revue by a popular pierrot troupe of the time.
Famous as Britain's first musical, this is a dated but valuable record of a stage performance of the kind long vanished.

d Edwin Greenwood, Laddie Cliff

Davy Burnaby, Stanley Holloway, Laddie Cliff, Phyllis Monkman, Melville Gideon, Gilbert Childs, Betty Chester, Elsa MacFarlane, Peggy Petronella, Harry S. Pepper

Copacabana
US 1947 91m bw
(UA) Sam Coslow

A quick-thinking agent forms two acts out of one client, which makes things awkward when both are needed at once.
Thinly produced comedy with both stars doing what is expected of them in surroundings less glamorous than those to which they were previously accustomed.

w Laslo Vadnay, Allen Boretz, Howard Harris *d* Alfred E. Green

Groucho Marx, Carmen Miranda, Steve Cochran, Gloria Jean, Andy Russell

Cops and Robbers*
US 1973 89m De Luxe
UA / EK Corp (Elliott Kastner)

Two New York cops turn crook and pull off a job for the Mafia.
Trendily anti-establishment comedy, quite snappy and smart when you can follow it.

w Donald E. Westlake *d* Aram Avakian *ph* David L. Quaid *m* Michel Legrand

Cliff Gorman, Joe Bologna, Dick Ward, Shepperd Strudwick, Ellen Holly, John P. Ryan

The Corn is Green*
US 1945 118m bw
Warner (Jack Chertok)

In 1895 Miss Moffat starts a village school for Welsh miners, and after some tribulations sees one of them off to Oxford.
A very theatrical production with unconvincing sets and mannered acting, but the original play has its felicities.

w Casey Robinson, Frank Cavett, *play Emlyn Williams* *d* Irving Rapper *ph* Sol Polito *m* Max Reiner *ad* Carl Jules Weyl

Bette Davis, John Dall, Nigel Bruce, Joan Lorring, Rhys Williams, Rosalind Ivan, Mildred Dunnock, Arthur Shields

Cornered*
US 1945 102m bw
RKO

After demobilization, a French-Canadian pilot tracks down the collaborationist responsible for the death of his wife.
Well-made but humourless revenge thriller.

w John Paxton, *story* John Wexley *d Edward Dmytryk* *ph* Harry J. Wild

Dick Powell, Micheline Cheirel, Walter Slezak, Morris Carnovsky

The Corpse Came COD
US 1947 87m bw
Columbia (Sam Bischoff)

Rival reporters try to solve the mystery of a wandering body.
Routine crime comedy with too few smart lines.

w George Bricker, Dwight Babcock, *novel* Jimmy Starr *d* Henry Levin *ph* Lucien Andriot *m* George Duning

George Brent, Joan Blondell, Adele Jergens, Jim Bannon, Leslie Brooks, Grant Mitchell, Una O'Connor

Corridor of Mirrors
GB 1948 105m bw
Cartier–Romney–Apollo (Rudolph Cartier)

An eccentric art collector believes that he and his mistress are reincarnations of 400-year-old lovers in a painting; but they are separated by murder.
Pretentious melodrama of no urgent narrative interest, with all concerned sadly at sea.

w Rudolph Cartier, Edana Romney *d* Terence Young *ph* André Thomas *m* Georges Auric

Eric Portman, Edana Romney, Barbara Mullen, Hugh Sinclair

'It has aimed at Art. It is, in fact, Effect. Some members of the cast wander in and out of the scenes as if they are not quite sure what has happened to them. Their confusion is not beyond comprehension.'—*MFB*

Corridors of Blood*
GB 1958 86m bw
Producers' Associates (John Croydon)

Seeking to discover anaesthetics, a Victorian doctor falls a prey to resurrection men.
Unpleasant but well-mounted semi-horror backed by strong cast and art direction.

w Jean Scott Rogers *d Robert Day ph Geoffrey Faithfull m* Buxton Orr *ad Anthony Masters*

Boris Karloff, Christopher Lee, Finlay Currie, Frank Pettingell, Betta St John, Francis Matthews, Adrienne Corri, Marian Spencer

Corruption
GB 1967 91m Technicolor
Columbia / Titan (Peter Newbrook)

A surgeon kills for pituitary gland fluid to restore his fiancée's beauty.
Highly derivative shocker with no inspiration of its own except an accumulation of gory detail.

w Donald and Derek Ford *d* Robert Hartford Davis *ph* Peter Newbrook *m* Bill McGuffie

Peter Cushing, Sue Lloyd, Noel Trevarthen, Kate O'Mara, Daviid Lodge

The Corsican Brothers*
US 1941 111m bw
Edward Small

Siamese twins are separated but remain spiritually tied through various adventures.
Adequately exciting picturization of the Dumas swashbuckler.

w George Bruce, Howard Estabrook *d* Gregory Ratoff *ph* Harry Stradling *m* Dmitri Tiomkin

Douglas Fairbanks Jnr, Akim Tamiroff, Ruth Warrick, J. Carrol Naish, H. B. Warner, Henry Wilcoxon

Corvette K 225*
US 1943 97m bw
Universal (Howard Hawks)
GB title: *The Nelson Touch*

A Canadian corvette commander encounters submarines and bombers in mid-Atlantic.
Good war film of its period, marred by romantic interest.

w Lt John Sturdy *d* Richard Rosson *ph* Tony Gaudio *m* David Buttolph

Randolph Scott, James Brown, Ella Raines, Barry Fitzgerald, Andy Devine, Richard Lane

Cosa Nostra, Arch Enemy of the FBI
US 1966 97m colour TVM
Quinn Martin

A contract killer murders a grand jury witness.
Muddled cops and robbers, as cumbersome as its title, put together from two episodes of *The FBI.*

w Norman Jolley *d* Don Medford

Efrem Zimbalist Jnr, Walter Pidgeon, Celeste Holm, Philip Abbott, Telly Savalas, Susan Strasberg

Cottage on Dartmoor
GB 1929 75m bw
BIP (Bruce Woolfe)

A farmer's wife shelters her ex-lover when he breaks jail.
Crude early talkie notable only as an immature work of its director.

wd Anthony Asquith

Norah Baring, Uno Hemming, Hans Schlettow, Judd Green

Cottage to Let*
GB 1941 90m bw
Gainsborough (Edward Black)
US title: *Bombsight Stolen*

Evacuated to Scotland, a Cockney helps prevent spies from kidnapping his inventor foster-father.
Stagey but often amusing comedy-thriller which after a shaky start becomes agreeably Hitchcockian.

w Anatole de Grunwald, J. O. C. Orton, *play* Geoffrey Kerr *d* Anthony Asquith

Leslie Banks, *Alastair Sim, John Mills*, Jeanne de Casalis, George Cole, Carla Lehmann, Michael Wilding, Frank Cellier, Wally Patch, Muriel Aked, Muriel George, Catherine Lacey, Hay Petrie

Count Five and Die*
GB 1957 92m bw Cinemascope
TCF / Zonic (Ernest Gartside)

British intelligence seeks to give the Nazis false information about the 1944 invasion, but conviction grows that a double agent is among them.
Terse, downbeat war suspenser, gripping in parts but quite forgettable.

w Jack Seddon, David Pursall *d* Victor Vicas *ph* Arthur Grant *m* John Wooldridge

Nigel Patrick, Jeffrey Hunter, Anne-Marie Duringer, David Kossoff

The Count of Monte Cristo***
US 1934 114m bw
Edward Small / Reliance

After spending years in prison, Edmond Dantes escapes and avenges himself on those who framed him.

Classic swashbuckler, extremely well done with due attention to dialogue as well as action; a model of its kind and period.

w Philip Dunne, Dan Totheroh, Rowland V. Lee, *novel* Alexandre Dumas *d Rowland V. Lee* *ph* Peverell Marley *m* Alfred Newman

Robert Donat, Elissa Landi, Louis Calhern, Sidney Blackmer, Raymond Walburn, O. P. Heggie, William Farnum

Count Three and Pray
US 1955 92m Technicolor Cinemascope
Columbia (Ted Richmond)

After the Civil War a roistering Southerner comes home to rebuild his town and become its parson.
Moderate semi-western, fresh and pleasing but not memorable.

w Herb Meadow *d* George Sherman *ph* Burnett Guffey *m* George Duning

Van Heflin, Joanne Woodward (debut), Phil Carey, Raymond Burr, Allison Hayes, Myron Healey, Nancy Kulp, James Griffiths

Count Your Blessings
US 1959 102m Metrocolor Cinemascope
MGM (Karl Tunberg)

An English girl marries an aristocratic Frenchman, but the war and other considerations make them virtual strangers until their son is nine years old, when it becomes clear that daddy is a philanderer.
Slight upper-crust comedy, basically rather tedious but kept buoyant by Chevalier as commentator.

w Karl Tunberg, *novel* The Blessing by Nancy Mitford *d* Jean Negulesco *ph* Milton Krasner, George Folsey *m* Franz Waxman

Deborah Kerr, *Maurice Chevalier*, Rossano Brazzi, Martin Stephens, Tom Helmore, Ronald Squire, Patricia Medina, Mona Washbourne

'Negulesco's aspirations to elegance are now familiar . . . this is far too absurd an example of Hollywood's infatuation with Old Europe to arouse much interest.'—*MFB*

Countdown*
US 1967 101m Technicolor Panavision
Warner (William Conrad)

Russian and American spaceships race for the moon.
Earnest, simply-plotted science-fiction in which technology is the centre of interest.

w Loring Mandel *d* Robert Altman *ph* William W. Spencer *m* Leonard Rosenman *ad* Jack Poplin

James Caan, Robert Duvall, Barbara Baxley, Joanna Moore, Charles Aidman, Steve Ihnat

Counterattack
US 1945 89m bw
Columbia
GB title: *One against Seven*

Resistance fighters go behind enemy lines for purposes of sabotage.
Standard World War II actioner, the star appearing above his surroundings.

w John Howard Lawson, *play* Janet and Philip Stevenson *d* Zoltan Korda *m* Louis Gruenberg

Paul Muni, Marguerite Chapman, Larry Parks, George Macready, Roman Bohnen

The Counterfeit Killer
US 1968 95m Technicolor TVM
Universal
aka: *The Faceless Man*

A cop with a criminal background goes undercover to solve the mystery of corpses being washed ashore.
Underdeveloped and rather boring mystery pilot.

w Harold Clements, Stephen Bochco *d* Josef Leytes

Jack Lord, Shirley Knight, Charles Drake, Jack Weston, Mercedes McCambridge, Joseph Wiseman

The Counterfeit Traitor*
US 1962 140m Technicolor
Paramount / Perlberg–Seaton

An oil importer, a naturalized Swede born in America, is blackmailed by the Allies into becoming a spy.
Heavy-going espionage drama which divides its time between action and moralizing. Excellent production does not quite make it exciting.

wd George Seaton, *book* Alexander Klein *ph Jean Bourgoin* *m* Alfred Newman

William Holden, Lilli Palmer, Hugh Griffith, Werner Peters, Eva Dahlbeck

Counterpoint*
US 1967 107m Techniscope
Universal (Dick Berg)

In 1944, an American symphony orchestra is captured by the Germans and threatened with execution.
Bizarre war suspenser, quite unconvincing but with effectively suspenseful moments and an old-

fashioned portrayal of the Nazis as sadistic music-loving Huns.

w James Lee, Joel Oliansky, *novel* The General by Alan Sillitoe *d* Ralph Nelson *ph* Russell Metty *m* Bronislau Kaper

Charlton Heston, Maximilian Schell, Anton Diffring, Kathryn Hays, Leslie Nielsen

A Countess from Hong Kong
GB 1967 120m Technicolor
Universal (Jerome Epstein)

An American millionaire diplomat is followed from Hong Kong by his Russian émigrée girl friend, and complications mount when his wife boards the ship at Hawaii.
Flatulent comedy with neither the sparkle of champage nor even the fizz of lemonade: Chaplin's writing, direction and music are alike soporific, and commiserations are due to the cast.

wd/m Charles Chaplin *ph* Arthur Ibbetson *pd* Don Ashton

Marlon Brando, Sophia Loren, *Patrick Cargill*, Margaret Rutherford, Charles Chaplin, Sydney Chaplin, Oliver Johnston, John Paul

Country Dance
GB 1969 112m Metrocolor
MGM / Keep–Windward (Robert Emmett Ginna)
aka: *Brotherly Love*

An eccentric baronet's incestuous love for his sister finally breaks up her marriage.
Rambling melodrama with O'Toole going mad in squire's tweeds; tediously fashionable but too pallid for general success, it was barely released.

w James Kennaway, from his novel Household Ghosts *d* J. Lee-Thompson *ph* Ted Moore *m* John Addison

Peter O'Toole, Susannah York, Michael Craig, Harry Andrews, Cyril Cusack, Judy Cornwell, Brian Blessed

The Country Doctor*
US 1936 94m bw
TCF (Darryl F. Zanuck)

A rural physician becomes famous when quintuplets are born to one of his patients.
Fictionalization of the birth of the Dionne Quintuplets; pleasantly nostalgic even forty years after its *raison d'être*.

w Sonya Levien *d* Henry King *ph* John F. Seitz, Daniel B. Clark

Jean Hersholt, the Dionne Quins, Dorothy Petersen, June Lang, Slim Summerville, Michael Whalen, Robert Barrat

† Sequels: *Reunion* (1936), *Five of a Kind* (1938).

The Country Girl*
US 1954 104m bw
Paramount (William Perlberg)

The wife of an alcoholic singer blossoms when he is stimulated into a comeback.
Theatrically effective but highly unconvincing, this rather glum stage success made a cold film, miscast with an eye on the box office.

w George Seaton, *play* Clifford Odets *d* George Seaton *ph* John F. Warren *m* Victor Young *songs* Ira Gershwin, Harold Arlen

Bing Crosby, Grace Kelly, William Holden, Anthony Ross, Gene Reynolds

'The dramatic development is not really interesting enough to sustain a film of the intensity for which it strives.'—*Karel Reisz*

The Country Husband*
US 1957 74m bw TVM
Columbia / Playhouse 90

A middle-aged executive wonders whether to leave his wife and family for a young girl.
Routine domestic drama, quite well acted.

w Paul Monash, *story* John Cheever *d* James Neilson

Frank Lovejoy, Barbara Hale, Felicia Farr, Kerwin Mathews

The Couple Takes a Wife
US 1972 73m Technicolor TVM
Universal (George Eckstein)

An au pair girl becomes rather too well entrenched.
Simple domestic comedy.

w Susan Silver *d* Jerry Paris

Bill Bixby, Paula Prentiss, Myrna Loy, Nanette Fabray, Valerie Perrine, Robert Goulet, Larry Storch

The Court Jester***
US 1955 101m Technicolor Vistavision
Paramount / Dena (Melvin Frank, Norman Panama)

Opposition to a tyrannical king is provided by the Fox, but it is one of the rebel's meekest men who, posing as a jester, defeats the usurper.
One of the star's most delightful vehicles, this medieval romp has good tunes and lively action, not to mention an exceptional cast and the memorable 'chalice from the palace' routine.

wd Norman Panama, Melvin Frank *ph* Ray

June *songs* Sylvia Fine, Sammy Cahn *ad* Hal Pereira, Roland Anderson

Danny Kaye, Glynis Johns, *Basil Rathbone*, Cecil Parker, *Mildred Natwick*, Angela Lansbury, Edward Ashley, Robert Middleton, Michael Pate, Alan Napier

The Court Martial of Billy Mitchell*
US 1955 100m Warnercolor
Cinemascope
United States Pictures (Milton Sperling)
GB title: *One Man Mutiny*

In the early twenties, an American general of the Army Air Service is court-martialled for accusing the war department of criminal negligence.
Adequate recreation of a historical incident, with a cast of excellent actors converging for a courtroom scene of some effectiveness.

w Milton Sperling, Emmet Lavery *d* Otto Preminger *ph* Sam Leavitt *m* Dmitri Tiomkin

Gary Cooper, *Rod Steiger*, Ralph Bellamy, Charles Bickford, Elizabeth Montgomery, Fred Clark, Darren McGavin, James Daly

The Courtneys of Curzon Street*
GB 1947 120m bw
British Lion / Herbert Wilcox
US title: *The Courtney Affair*

In Victorian times, a baronet's son marries a lady's maid . . . and many years later, their grandson marries a factory worker.
Unbelievable upstairs-downstairs romantic drama spanning three generations; all to be taken with a gigantic pinch of salt, but a huge success when released.

w Nicholas Phipps, *novel* Florence Tranter *d* Herbert Wilcox *ph* Max Greene

Anna Neagle, Michael Wilding, Gladys Young, Coral Browne, Michael Medwin, Daphne Slater, Jack Watling, Helen Cherry, Bernard Lee

'The dignity of Curzon Street is Hollywoodized, and it is rare in 1945 that people in their sixties look as though they have one foot in the grave. —*MFB*

The Courtship of Eddie's Father*
US 1962 117m Metrocolor
Panavision
MGM / Joe Pasternak

The small son of a widower tries to interest Dad in another woman.
Fairly icky American-style sentimental comedy with most of the stops pulled out; way over-length and too self-indulgently solemn in the last part, but with professional touches.

w John Gay, *novel* Muriel Toby *d* Vincente Minnelli *ph* Milton Krasner *m* George Stoll

Glenn Ford, Ronnie Howard, Shirley Jones, Stella Stevens, Dina Merrill
† A TV series starring Bill Bixby followed in 1976.

A Covenant with Death
US 1966 97m Technicolor
Warner (William Conrad)

A half-Mexican judge in a border town convicts a man who accidentally kills the hangman just as the real murderer confesses.
Dreary moral melodrama with accents, nicely photographed but cold, remote and drawn out.

w Larry Marcus, Saul Levitt, *novel* Stephen Becker *d* Lamont Johnson *ph Robert Burks* *m* Leonard Rosenman

George Maharis, Katy Jurado, Earl Holliman, Sidney Blackmer, Laura Devon, Gene Hackman

Cover Girl**
US 1944 107m Technicolor
Columbia (Arthur Schwartz)

The road to success for magazine cover models.
Wartime glamour musical with a stronger reputation than it really deserves apart from Kelly's solos; it does however manage a certain *joie de vivre* which should not be despised.

w Virginia Van Upp *d* Charles Vidor *ph* Rudolph Maté *m* Morris Stoloff *songs* Jerome Kern, Ira Gershwin

Rita Hayworth, Gene Kelly, Phil Silvers, Lee Bowman, Jinx Falkenberg, Otto Kruger, Eve Arden, Ed Brophy

Cowboy*
US 1957 92m Technicolor
Columbia (Julian Blaustein)

Frank Harris becomes a cattle herder for love of a lady but is quickly disillusioned with the outdoor life.
Fashioned from a lively autobiography, this has interesting moments but is never as fascinating as one would expect.

w Edmund H. North, *book* On the Trail by Frank Harris *d* Delmer Daves *ph* Charles Lawton Jnr *m* George Duning

Jack Lemmon, Glenn Ford, Brian Donlevy, Anna Kashfi, Dick York, Richard Jaeckel, King Donovan

The Cowboy and the Lady
US 1938 91m bw
Samuel Goldwyn

The daughter of a presidential candidate

becomes infatuated with a rodeo cowboy.
Insubstantial and witless romantic comedy which suffered many sea changes from script to screen.

w Leo McCarey, S. N. Behrman, Sonya Levien *d* H. C. Potter *ph* Gregg Toland *m* Alfred Newman

Gary Cooper, Merle Oberon, Patsy Kelly, Walter Brennan, Fuzzy Knight, Henry Kolker, Harry Davenport

The Cowboys*
US 1972 128m Technicolor Panavision 70
Sanford / Warner (Mark Rydell)

Deserted by his ranch hands, a cattle drover on a long trail enlists the help of eleven schoolboys, who later avenge his death.
Ambling, climactically violent, extremely unlikely western with good scenes along the way.

w Irving Ravetch, Harriet Frank Jnr, *novel* William Dale Jennings *d* Mark Rydell *ph Robert Surtees* *m* John Williams

John Wayne, Roscoe Lee Browne, Bruce Dern, Colleen Dewhurst, Slim Pickens, Sarah Cunningham

† A TV series followed in 1974 but was shortlived.

Crack in the Mirror
US 1960 97m bw Cinemascope
TCF / Darryl F. Zanuck

A young lawyer and his ageing mentor are at opposite sides of a murder case.
Pointless Paris-set melodrama in which for no obvious reason each of the three stars plays two roles. Relentlessly boring.

w Mark Canfield (Darryl F. Zanuck) *d* Richard Fleischer *ph* William C. Mellor *m Maurice Jarre*

Orson Welles, Bradford Dillman, Juliette Greco, William Lucas, Alexander Knox, Catherine Lacey

Crack in the World
US 1965 96m Technicolor
Paramount / Security (Philip Yordan, Bernard Glasser, Lester A. Sansom)

A dying scientist fires a missile into the earth's centre, and nearly blows the planet apart.
Jaded science-fiction melodrama, overburdened with initial chat but waking up when the special effects take over.

w Jon Manchip White, Julian Halevy *d* Andrew Marton *ph* Manuel Berenguer *m* John Douglas *ad Eugene Lourié sp John Douglas*

Dana Andrews, Janette Scott, Kieron Moore, Alexander Knox, Peter Damon, Gary Lasdun

Crack Up*
US 1946 93m bw
RKO

A museum curator with an eye for forgery is discredited by crooks who make him appear drunk or half-crazed when he recounts a set of strange events which have happened to him . . .
The intriguing mystery of the opening reels, when solved, is replaced by rather dull detection, but this remains a thriller with a difference, generally well presented.

w John Paxton *d* Irving Reis *ph* Robert de Grasse

Pat O'Brien, Claire Trevor, Herbert Marshall, Ray Collins

Craig's Wife*
US 1936 77m bw
Columbia

A middle-class wife lets her house take precedence over her husband.
Capable picturization of a Broadway success, later remade as *Harriet Craig* (qv).

w Mary McCally Jnr, George Kelly, *play* George Kelly *d* Dorothy Arzner *ph* Lucien Ballard *m* Morris Stoloff

Rosalind Russell, John Boles, Billie Burke, Jane Darwell, Dorothy Wilson, Alma Kruger, Thomas Mitchell, Elizabeth Risdon, Raymond Walburn

Crash Dive*
US 1943 105m Technicolor
TCF (Milton Sperling)

A submarine lieutenant and his commander love the same girl.
Well-staged war thrills in the final reels are prefaced by a long romantic comedy build-up, which probably seemed good propaganda at the time.

w Jo Swerling, *story* W. R. Burnett *d* Archie Mayo *ph* Leon Shamroy *m* Emil Newman *sp Fred Sersen*

Tyrone Power, Anne Baxter, Dana Andrews, James Gleason, Dame May Whitty, Henry Morgan, Frank Conroy, Minor Watson

'One of those films which have no more sense of reality about this war than a popular song.'—*Bosley Crowther*

Crawlspace*
US 1971 74m colour TVM
Viacom / Titus

A lonely middle-aged couple take in a dangerous young man who comes to repair their furnace. Unusual suspenser which keeps the interest.

w Ernest Kinoy, *novel* Jerbert Lieberman *d* John Newland

Teresa Wright, Arthur Kennedy, Tom Harper, Gene Roche

Craze
GB 1973 95m Technicolor
(EMI) Harbour (Herman Cohen)

An African idol accidentally causes a death which brings money to its owner, who kills again and again in the hope of more loot.
Crude shocker from the bottom of even this producer's barrel, notable for the star cast which was surprisingly roped in.

w Aben Kandel, Herman Cohen, *novel* Infernal Idol by Henry Seymour *d* Freddie Francis *ph* John Wilcox *m* John Scott

Jack Palance, Diana Dors, Julie Ege, Edith Evans, Hugh Griffith, Trevor Howard, Michael Jayston, Suzy Kendall, Martin Potter, Percy Herbert, Kathleen Byron

Crazy House
US 1943 80m bw
Universal (Erle C. Kenton)

Olsen and Johnson go to Hollywood to make a film.
Lame sequel to *Hellzapoppin;* after an explosively well edited first reel of panic in the studio, it degenerates into a slew of below-par variety turns.

w Robert Lees, Frederic I. Rinaldo *d* Edward Cline *ph* Charles Van Enger *md* George Hale

Ole Olsen, Chic Johnson, Martha O'Driscoll, Patric Knowles, Percy Kilbride, Cass Daley, Thomas Gomez, Edgar Kennedy
† Sherlock Holmes fans may or may not wish to record a two-line comic bit by Basil Rathbone and Nigel Bruce in character.

The Creature from the Black Lagoon
US 1954 79m bw 3-D
U-I (William Alland)

Up the Amazon, scientists encounter a fearful fanged creature who is half man, half fish.
Unpersuasive and unsuspenseful horror hokum from the bottom drawer of imagination: it did, however, coin enough pennies to generate two even worse sequels, *Revenge of the Creature* (1955) and *The Creature Walks Among Us* (1956). And the underwater photography is super.

w Harry Essex, Arthur Ross *d* Jack Arnold *ph* William E. Snyder

Richard Carlson, Julie Adams, Richard Denning, Antonio Moreno, Nestor Paiva, Ricou Browning (in the rubber suit)

Creatures the World Forgot
GB 1970 95m Technicolor
Columbia / Hammer (Michael Carreras)

Quarrels break out between rival tribes of Stone Age men.
Feeble follow-up to *One Million Years BC* and *When Dinosaurs Ruled the Earth*: someone forgot to order any monsters.

w Michael Carreras *d* Don Chaffey *ph* Vincent Cox *m* Mario Nascimbene

Julie Ege, Brian O'Shaughnessy, Robert John, Marcia Fox, Rosalie Crutchley

The Creeping Flesh*
GB 1972 91m Eastmancolor
Tigon / World Film Services (Michael Redbourn)

A Victorian scientist discovers that water causes the recomposing of tissue on the skeleton of a Neanderthal man.
Absurd but persuasive horror film, quite well done in all departments.

w Peter Spenceley, Jonathan Rumbold *d* Freddie Francis *ph* Norman Warwick *m* Paul Ferris

Peter Cushing, Christopher Lee, Lorna Heilbron, George Benson, Kenneth J. Warren, Duncan Lamont, Michael Ripper

Crescendo*
GB 1969 95m Technicolor
Warner / Hammer (Michael Carreras)

A girl researcher goes to stay with the widow of a famous composer, and finds herself in mortal danger . . .
Lunatic Hammer horror with the courage of its shameless borrowings from *Taste of Fear, Fanatic, Nightmare, Maniac* and all the films about mad twin brothers, to which this chaotic brew adds dollops of sex and heroin addiction.

w Jimmy Sangster, Alfred Shaughnessy *d Alan Gibson* *ph* Paul Beeson *m* Malcolm Williamson

Stefanie Powers, James Olson, Margaretta Scott, Jane Lapotaire, Joss Ackland

Crime and Punishment*
US 1935 88m bw
Columbia

A student kills a pawnbroker and is tortured by remorse.

Heavy-going rendering of Dostoievsky with some pictorial interest.

w S. K. Lauren, Joseph Anthony *d Josef Von Sternberg ph* Lucien Ballard *m* Arthur Honegger

Peter Lorre, Edward Arnold, Tala Birell, Marian Marsh, Elizabeth Risdon, Mrs Patrick Campbell

Crime and Punishment USA
US 1958 96m bw
Allied Artists / Sanders Associates (Terry Sanders)

A student murders an old pawnbroker and is driven mad by guilt.
Pointless updating of Dostoievsky by two young film-makers who seemed for years to be on the brink of a masterpiece but never actually produced it. Some points of interest, but the low budget is cramping.

w Walter Newman *d* Denis Sanders *ph* Floyd Crosby *m* Herschel Burke Gilbert

George Hamilton, Frank Silvera, Mary Murphy, John Harding, Marian Seldes
'There is about it a strange quality of aimlessness which nullifies much of its effect.'—*MFB*

Crime by Night*
US 1944 72m bw
Warner (William Jacobs)

A private detective reluctantly solves a small-town murder, and finds a spy.
Second feature which was thought at the time to have established a new pair of married detectives in the tradition of *The Thin Man*. However, one poor sequel, *Find the Blackmailer*, put paid to the idea.

w Richard Weil, Joel Malone, *novel* Forty Whacks by Geoffrey Homes *d* William Clemens *ph* Henry Sharpe

Jerome Cowan, Jane Wyman, Faye Emerson, Charles Lang, Eleanor Parker, Cy Kendall, Creighton Hale

Crime Club*
US 1972 74m colour TVM
CBS / Glicksman–Larson

A private detective investigates the fatal car crash of an old friend.
Entertaining mystery pilot which never got anywhere.

d David Lowell Rich

Lloyd Bridges, Barbara Rush, Victor Buono, Paul Burke, William Devane, David Hedison, Cloris Leachman, Belinda Montgomery, Martin Sheen

Crime Club
US 1975 74m Technicolor TVM
Universal (Matthew Rapf)
aka: *The Last Key*

A Washington DC club comprises specialists who band together to combat crime.
Another failed attempt to promote this famous title into a series.

w Gene R. Kearney *d* Jeannot Szwarc

Robert Lansing, Scott Thomas, Eugene Roche, Barbara Rhoades, Biff McGuire

Crime Doctor*
US 1943 66m bw
Columbia

An amnesiac becomes a successful psychiatrist, then discovers that he was once a wanted gangster.
Time-passing second feature from a popular radio series. Ten *Crime Doctor* films were made between 1943 and 1949, all starring Warner Baxter, all except the first being locked room mysteries which seldom played fair with the audience.

w Graham Baker, Louise Lantz *d* Michael Gordon

Warner Baxter, Margaret Lindsay, John Litel, Ray Collins, Harold Huber, Leon Ames, Don Costello

The sequels:
1943: CRIME DOCTOR'S STRANGEST CASE
1944: SHADOWS IN THE NIGHT, CRIME DOCTOR'S COURAGE
1945: CRIME DOCTOR'S WARNING
1946: CRIME DOCTOR'S MANHUNT, JUST BEFORE DAWN
1947: THE MILLERSON CASE
1948: CRIME DOCTOR'S GAMBLE
1949: CRIME DOCTOR'S DIARY

Crime in the Streets*
US 1956 91m bw
Allied Artists (Vincent M. Fenelly)
GB title: *Killer Dino*

Rival knife gangs bring havoc to tenement dwellers.
Lively semi-documentary low-life melodrama; routine subject, excellent credits.

w Reginald Rose, from his TV play *d Don Siegel ph Sam Leavitt*

John Cassavetes, James Whitmore, Sal Mineo, Mark Rydell

Crime of Passion
US 1956 86m bw
UA / Bob Goldstein (Herman Cohen)

An executive's wife sleeps his way to the top, but when the boss doesn't come through with promotion she shoots him.
Old-fashioned star melodrama on a low budget.

w Jo Eisinger *d* Gerd Oswald *ph* Joseph La Shelle *m* Paul Dunlap

Barbara Stanwyck, Sterling Hayden, Raymond Burr, Fay Wray, Royal Dano, Virginia Grey

Crime School*
US 1938 86m bw
Warner (Bryan Foy)

Problems of the warden of a reform school.
Predictable vehicle for the Dead End Kids; watchable at the time.

w Crane Wilbur, Vincent Sherman *d* Lewis Seiler *ph* Arthur Todd

Humphrey Bogart, Gale Page, Billy Halop, Huntz Hall, Leo Gorcey, Bobby Jordan, Gabriel Dell, Bernard Punsley, Paul Porcasi, Al Bridge

Crime without Passion**
US 1934 82m bw
Paramount (Ben Hecht, Charles MacArthur)

A lawyer is driven to commit murder.
Effective melodrama notable for then-new techniques which were blended into the mainstream of movie-making, and for the first appearance in Hollywood of a smart new writer-producer-director team.

wd Ben Hecht, Charles MacArthur, from their story Caballero of the Law *ph Lee Garmes* *sp* Slavko Vorkapitch

Claude Rains, Margo, Whitney Bourne, Stanley Ridges

'The whole venture seems to take a long stride forward for the movies.'—*Otis Ferguson*

'A flamboyant, undisciplined, but compulsively fascinating film classic.'—*Peter John Dyer, 1966*

The Criminal*
GB 1960 97m bw
Merton Park (Jack Greenwood)
US title: *The Concrete Jungle*

Sent to jail for a racecourse snatch, a gangster comes out fifteen years later to regain the loot and is followed by other criminals who kill him.
Relentlessly grim saga of prison life, with a few sensational trimmings.

w Alun Owen, Jimmy Sangster *d* Joseph Losey *ph Robert Krasker* *m* Johnny Dankworth

Stanley Baker, Sam Wanamaker, Margit Saad, *Patrick Magee*, Noel Willman, Grégoire Aslan, Jill Bennett, Kenneth J. Warren, Nigel Green, Patrick Wymark, Murray Melvin

'A savage, almost expressionistic picture of English underworld life.'—*NFT, 1973*

The Criminal Code*
US 1931 97m bw
Columbia (Harry Cohn)

A young man kills in self-defence, is railroaded into jail and becomes involved in another murder.
Impressive melodrama with good performances and sharp handling.

w Seton I. Miller, Fred Niblo Jnr, *play* Martin Flavin *d Howard Hawks* *ph* James Wong Howe, William O'Connell

Walter Huston, Phillips Holmes, Constance Cummings, Mary Doran, De Witt Jennings, John Sheehan, Boris Karloff

The Crimson Pirate*
GB 1952 104m Technicolor
Warner / Harold Hecht

An 18th-century pirate and an eccentric inventor lead an island's people in rebellion against a tyrant.
One suspects that this started off as a straight adventure and was turned halfway through production into a spoof; at any rate, the effect is patchy but with spirited highlights, and the star's acrobatic training is put to good use.

w Roland Kibbee *d* Robert Siodmak *ph* Otto Heller *m* William Alwyn

Burt Lancaster, Nick Cravat, Eva Bartok, Torin Thatcher, James Hayter, Margot Grahame, Noel Purcell, Frank Pettingell

Crisis*
US 1950 96m bw
MGM (Arthur Freed)

A brain surgeon is forced to operate secretly on a South American dictator, and his wife is kidnapped by revolutionaries.
Dour intellectual suspense piece, in key with the genteel enlightenment of the Dore Schary regime at MGM. Well made but cold.

wd Richard Brooks, *story* George Tabori *ph* Ray June *m* Miklos Rozsa

Cary Grant, Jose Ferrer, Signe Hasso, Paula Raymond, Ramon Navarro, Antonio Moreno, Leon Ames, Gilbert Roland

Criss Cross*
US 1948 87m bw
U-I (Michael Draike)

An armoured car guard and his double-crossing ex-wife get mixed up with vicious gangsters.
Sordid *film noir* with a poor plot but suspenseful sequences.

w Daniel Fuchs *d Robert Siodmak ph Franz Planer m* Miklos Rozsa

Burt Lancaster, Yvonne de Carlo, Dan Duryea, Stephen McNally, Richard Long, Tom Pedi, Alan Napier

'Siodmak's talent for brooding violence and the sombre urban setting gives the film a relentlessly mounting tension.'—*Peter John Dyer*

Critic's Choice
US 1963 100m Technicolor Panavision
Warner / Frank P. Rosenberg

A ruthless Broadway critic is forced by his scruples to write a bad review of his wife's play.
Unsuitable vehicle for stars who have shorn a good comedy of wit and strive vainly for sentiment, wisecracks and pratfalls.

w Jack Sher, *play* Ira Levin *d* Don Weis *ph* Charles Lang *m* George Duning

Bob Hope, Lucille Ball, Marilyn Maxwell, Rip Torn, Jessie Royce Landis, John Dehner, Jim Backus, Marie Windsor

'For instant stultification.'—*Judith Crist*

Cromwell*
GB 1970 141m Technicolor Panavision
Columbia / Irving Allen (Andrew Donally)

An account of the rise of Cromwell to power, the execution of Charles I, and the Civil War.
Disappointingly dull schoolbook history, with good production values but glum handling.

wd Ken Hughes *ph Geoffrey Unsworth m* Frank Cordell *pd John Stoll*

Richard Harris, Alec Guinness, Robert Morley, Dorothy Tutin, Frank Finlay, Timothy Dalton, Patrick Wymark, Patrick Magee, Nigel Stock, Charles Gray, Michael Jayston, Anna Cropper, Michael Goodliffe

'It tries to combine serious intentions with the widest kind of popular appeal and falls unhappily between the two. It will offend the purists and bore the kiddies.'—*Brenda Davies*

The Crooked Hearts
US 1972 74m colour TVM
Lomar

A policewoman goes undercover to catch a suave murderer who preys on wealthy members of a lonelyhearts club.
Rather unattractive comedy-drama, interesting for its stars.

w A. J. Russell *d* Jay Sandrich

Douglas Fairbanks Jnr, Rosalind Russell, Maureen O'Sullivan, Ross Martin

Crooks and Coronets
GB 1969 106m Technicolor
Warner Seven Arts / Herman Cohen

American gangsters plan to rob a stately home but are taken over by the dowager in charge.
Overlong and mainly flatulent comedy, with a good climax involving a vintage plane.

wd Jim O'Connelly *ph* Desmond Dickinson *m* Patrick John Scott

Telly Savalas, Edith Evans, Warren Oates, Nicky Henson, Cesar Romero, Harry H. Corbett

Crooks Anonymous*
GB 1962 87m bw
Anglo Amalgamated (Nat Cohen)

A petty thief joins an organization for reforming criminals, but is tempted again . . . and so are they.
Amusingly devised and plotted minor comedy with an exceptional cast.

w Jack Davies, Henry Blyth *d* Ken Annakin

Leslie Phillips, Stanley Baxter, Wilfrid Hyde White, Julie Christie, James Robertson Justice, Robertson Hare, Charles Lloyd Pack

Crooks' Tour*
GB 1940 84m bw
British National (John Corfield)

English tourists are mistaken for spies by Nazis in Baghdad.
Amusing vehicle for two comic actors who excelled at portraying the English abroad.

w John Watt, Max Kester, from their radio serial *d* John Baxter

Basil Radford, Naunton Wayne, Greta Gynt, Abraham Sofaer, Gordon McLeod

Cross My Heart*
US 1945 83m bw
Paramount (Harry Tugend)

A romantic girl confesses to murder, is acquitted, and finds the real murderer.
Modest remake of *True Confession* (qv), with frenetic pace but not much style.

w Claude Binyon, Harry Tugend, Charles Schnee *d* John Berry *ph* Charles Lang Jnr *m* Robert Emmett Dolan

Betty Hutton, Sonny Tufts, Michael Chekhov,

Rhys Williams, Ruth Donnelly, Al Bridge, Howard Freeman, Iris Adrian

The Cross of Lorraine*
US 1944 91m bw
MGM (Edwin Knopf)

In a German camp for French prisoners, an escape leads to a rising by local villagers.
Standard war propaganda piece, made with enthusiasm on unconvincing sets.

w Michael Kanin, Ring Lardner Jnr, Alexander Esway, Robert Andrews *d* Tay Garnett *ph* Sidney Wagner *m* Bronislau Kaper

Gene Kelly, Jean-Pierre Aumont, Cedric Hardwicke, Peter Lorre, Joseph Calleia, Richard Whorf, Hume Cronyn

Crosscurrent*
US 1971 96m colour TVM
Warner (E. Jack Neuman)
aka: *The Cable Car Murders*

The San Francisco police investigate when a man is found dead on a cable car.
Good competent police mystery.

w Herman Miller *d* Jerry Thorpe

Robert Hooks, Jeremy Slate, Robert Wagner, Carol Lynley, Jose Ferrer, Simon Oakland, John Randolph

Crossfire****
US 1947 86m bw
RKO (Adrian Scott)

A Jew is murdered in a New York hotel, and three soldiers are suspected.
Tense, talky thriller shot entirely at night with pretty full expressionist use of camera technique; notable for style, acting, experimentation, and for being the first Hollywood film to hit out at racial bigotry.

w John Paxton, novel The Brick Foxhole by Richard Brooks *ph J. Roy Hunt d Edward Dmytryk m* Constantin Bakaleinikoff

Robert Young, Robert Mitchum, *Robert Ryan*, Gloria Grahame, *Paul Kelly*, Sam Levene, Jacqueline White, Steve Brodie

Crossfire
US 1975 75m colour TVM
Quinn Martin

A police volunteer for undercover work is 'caught' peddling drugs and ostracized by his colleagues.
Routine hokum, well enough made.

w Philip Saltzman *d* William Hale

James Farentino, John Saxon, Roman Bieri, Patrick O'Neal, Pamela Franklin, Frank de Kova

Crossplot
GB 1969 97m Eastmancolor
UA / Tribune (Robert S. Baker)

An advertising executive gets involved in a spy ring.
Old-fashioned, London-set amalgam of secret codes, disappearing bodies, helicopter attacks, and a finale frustrating the assassination of a statesman in Hyde Park.

w Leigh Vance *d* Alvin Rakoff *ph* Brendan J. Stafford *m* Stanley Black

Roger Moore, Martha Hyer, Alexis Kanner, Francis Matthews, Bernard Lee

Crossroads*
US 1942 84m bw
MGM (Edwin Knopf)

A French diplomat who once lost his memory is blackmailed by crooks who claim he was once a criminal.
Smooth mystery melodrama adapted from the French film *Carrefour*.

w Howard Emmett Rogers, John Kafka *d* Jack Conway *ph* Joseph Ruttenberg *m* Bronislau Kaper

William Powell, Hedy Lamarr, Basil Rathbone, Claire Trevor, Margaret Wycherly, Felix Bressart, Sig Rumann

The Crowd Roars*
US 1932 85m bw
Warner

A star motor-racing driver tries to prevent his young brother from following in his footsteps.
Typical early Cagney vehicle, still spectacularly pacy but dated in its dialogue scenes.

w Kubec Glasmon, John Bright, Niven Busch *d* Howard Hawks *ph* Sid Hickox, John Stumar *m* Leo Forbstein

James Cagney, Joan Blondell, Ann Dvorak, Eric Linden, Guy Kibbee, Frank McHugh, Regis Toomey

'As so often Hawks seems bitter at the world men have created but respects those who have to attempt to live it to the full.'—*NFT, 1963*

† Remade in 1939 as *Indianapolis Speedway*.

The Crowd Roars*
US 1938 90m bw
MGM (Sam Zimbalist)

A young boxer becomes involved with the underworld.
Standard star vehicle with efficient trimmings.

w Thomas Lennon, George Bruce, George Oppenheimer *d* Richard Thorpe *ph* John Seitz *m* Edward Ward

Robert Taylor, Frank Morgan, Edward Arnold, Maureen O'Sullivan, William Gargan, Frank Craven, Jane Wyman, Lionel Stander, Nat Pendleton

The Crowded Sky
US 1960 104m Technicolor
Warner (Michael Garrison)

As two planes fly unwittingly towards each other, the passengers muse on their personal problems. An emergency landing averts total disaster.
The format goes back as far as *Friday the Thirteenth*, and forward to *Airport 75*, but this was in fact a cut-rate rehash of *The High and the Mighty*, with dull characters and insufficiently tense handling, not to mention a second team cast.

w Charles Schnee *d* Joseph Pevney *ph* Harry Stradling *m* Leonard Rosenman

Dana Andrews, Rhonda Fleming, Efrem Zimbalist Jnr, John Kerr, Anne Francis, Keenan Wynn, Troy Donahue, Joe Mantell, Patsy Kelly

Crowhaven Farm*
US 1970 72m colour TVM
Aaron Spelling (Walter Grauman)

Local witches terrify a New York wife when she inherits a Connecticut farm.
Genuinely frightening supernatural high jinks in the *Rosemary's Baby* area.

w John McGreevey *d* Walter Grauman

Hope Lange, Paul Burke, Lloyd Bochner, John Carradine, Virginia Gregg

The Cruel Sea**
GB 1952 126m bw
Ealing (Leslie Norman)

Life and death on an Atlantic corvette during World War II.
Competent transcription of a bestselling book, cleanly produced and acted; a huge box office success.

w Eric Ambler, *novel* Nicholas Monsarrat *d Charles Frend* *ph* Gordon Dines, Jo Jago, Paul Beeson *m* Alan Rawsthorne

Jack Hawkins, Donald Sinden, Stanley Baker, John Stratton, Denholm Elliott, John Warner, Bruce Seton, Virginia McKenna, Moira Lister, June Thorburn

'One is grateful nowadays for a film which does not depict war as anything but a tragic and bloody experience, and it is this quality which gives the production its final power to move.'—*John Gillett*

The Crusades**
US 1935 127m bw
Paramount / Cecil B. de Mille

Spurred by his wife Berengaria, Richard the Lionheart sets off on his holy wars.
Heavily tapestried medieval epic, spectacular sequences being punctuated by wodges of uninspired dialogue. A true de Mille pageant.

w Harold Lamb, Waldemar Young, Dudley Nichols *d Cecil B. de Mille* *ph Victor Milner* *sp* Gordon Jennings

Henry Wilcoxon, Loretta Young, C. Aubrey Smith, Ian Keith, Katherine de Mille, Joseph Schildkraut, Alan Hale, C. Henry Gordon, George Barbier, Montagu Love, Lumsden Hare, William Farnum, Hobart Bosworth, Pedro de Cordoba, Mischa Auer

'Mr de Mille's evangelical films are the nearest equivalent today to the glossy German colour prints which decorated mid-Victorian bibles. There is the same lack of a period sense, the same stuffy horsehair atmosphere of beards and whiskers, and, their best quality, a childlike eye for detail.'—*Otis Ferguson*

Cry for Happy
US 1961 110m Eastmancolor Cinemascope
Columbia (William Goetz)

Four navy cameramen in Japan help geishas to found an orphanage.
As bad as it sounds, a repellent mixture of sentiment and knockabout.

w Irving Brecher *d* George Marshall *ph* Burnett Guffey *m* George Duning

Glenn Ford, Donald O'Connor, Miiko Taka, James Shigeta, Mikoshi Umeki, Joe Flynn, Howard St John

'Any film which expends most of its energies on a protracted joke about how far you can go with a geisha could hardly fail to be as charmless and witless as this.'—*MFB*

A Cry for Help**
US 1975 74m Technicolor TVM
Universal / Fairmont–Foxcroft (Richard Levinson, William Link)
aka: *End of the Line*

A cynical disc jockey desperately tries to help a suicidal girl who phones in.
Character drama with sufficient suspense.

w Peter S. Fischer *d Daryl Duke*

Robert Culp, Elayne Heilveil, Ken Swofford, Chuck McCann

A Cry from the Streets
GB 1958 100m bw
Film Traders (Ian Dalrymple)

Episodes from the work of child welfare officers. Mildly pleasing but unconvincing semi-documentary, with children competing with the star at scene-stealing.

w Vernon Harris, *novel* The Friend in Need by Elizabeth Coxhead *d* Lewis Gilbert *ph* Harry Gillan *m* Larry Adler

Max Bygraves, Barbara Murray, Colin Petersen, Dana Wilson, Elizabeth Harrison, Eleanor Summerfield, Mona Washbourne

Cry Havoc
US 1943 97m bw
MGM (Edwin Knopf)

War nurses are caught up in the Bataan retreat. An all-woman cast adequately handles a stagey melodrama about a tragic situation.

w Paul Osborn, *play* Proof thro' the Night by Allen R. Kenward *d* Richard Thorpe

Margaret Sullavan, Joan Blondell, Ann Sothern, Fay Bainter, Marsha Hunt, Ella Raines, Frances Gifford, Diana Lewis, Heather Angel, Connie Gilchrist

'A sincere fourth-rate film made from a sincere fifth-rate play.'—*James Agee*

A Cry in the Night
US 1956 75m bw
Warner / Jaguar (George C. Bertholon)

A peeping Tom, caught by a teenage couple, abducts the girl and threatens rape.
Odd little domestic thriller, with parents and police working together. Watchable, but a bit over the top.

w David Dortort *d* Frank Tuttle *ph* John Seitz *m* David Buttolph

Edmond O'Brien, Brian Donlevy, Natalie Wood, Raymond Burr, Richard Anderson, Irene Hervey, Anthony Caruso

A Cry in the Wilderness
US 1974 74m Technicolor TVM
Universal / Lou Morheim

Bitten by a rabid skunk, a man chains himself in the barn while his wife fetches medical help. His home is then threatened by a flood . . .
Absurd piling-up of disaster situations: more laughs than suspense.

w Stephen and Elinor Karpf *d* Gordon Hessler

George Kennedy, Joanna Pettet, Lee H. Montgomery, Collin Wilcox-Horne

Cry of the Banshee
GB 1970 87m Movielab
AIP (Gordon Hessler)

A 16th-century magistrate is cursed by a witch, who sends a devil in the form of a young man to destroy him.
Modest horror film which fails to do justice to its interesting plot.

w Tim Kelly, Christopher Wicking *d* Gordon Hessler *ph* John Coquillon *m* Les Baxter

Vincent Price, Elisabeth Bergner, Patrick Mower, Essy Persson, Hugh Griffith, Hilary Dwyer, Sally Geeson

Cry of the City**
US 1948 96m bw
TCF

A ruthless gangster on the run is pursued by a policeman who was once his boyhood friend.
Very well produced but relentlessly miserable New York thriller on the lines of *Manhattan Melodrama* and *Angels with Dirty Faces.*

w Richard Murphy *d Robert Siodmak ph Lloyd Aherne m* Alfred Newman

Victor Mature, Richard Conte, Mimi Agulia, Shelley Winters, Tommy Cook, Fred Clark, Debra Paget

Cry Panic*
US 1974 74m colour TVM
Spelling–Goldberg

In an unfamiliar town, a motorist accidentally kills a pedestrian. The body then disappears . . .
Efficient what-the-hell-happened melodrama with echoes of *Bad Day at Black Rock.*

w Jack Sowards *d* James Goldstone

John Forsythe, Earl Holliman, Anne Francis, Ralph Meeker, Claudia McNeil

Cry Rape*
US 1974 74m colour TVM
Warner

Various points of view on the trying of rape cases.
Dramatized documentary: nothing new, but persuasive.

w Will Lorin *d* Corey Allen

Peter Coffield, Andrea Marcovicci, Patricia Mattick

Cry Terror**
US 1958 96m bw
MGM / Andrew Stone

As security against ransom money being delivered, an airline bomber kidnaps a family.

Unabashed suspenser which screws panic situations as far as they will go and farther.

wd Andrew Stone *ph* Walter Strenge *m* Howard Jackson

James Mason, Rod Steiger, Inger Stevens, Neville Brand, Angie Dickinson, Kenneth Tobey, Jack Klugman, Jack Kruschen

Cry the Beloved Country*
GB 1951 96m bw
London Films (Alan Paton)
US title: *African Fury*

In South Africa, a white farmer and a black preacher find friendship through linked family tragedies.
Well-intentioned, earnest, rather high-flown racial drama.

w Alan Paton, from his novel *d* Zoltan Korda *ph* Robert Krasker *m* native themes

Canada Lee, Sidney Poitier, Charles Carson, Charles McRae, Joyce Carey, Geoffrey Keen, Michael Goodliffe, Edric Connor

Cry Wolf
US 1947 83m bw
Warner (Henry Blanke)

A widow claims her husband's estate and finds his mysterious uncle very difficult to deal with . . .
Rather obvious old dark house mystery with a not very interesting solution, all relying too heavily on star performances.

w Catherine Turney, *novel* Marjorie Carleton *d* Peter Godfrey *ph* Carl Guthrie *m* Franz Waxman

Barbara Stanwyck, Errol Flynn (as the apparent heavy), Geraldine Brooks, Richard Basehart, Helene Thimig

The Crystal Ball*
US 1943 82m bw
(Richard Blumenthal)

A failed beauty contestant becomes a fortune teller and is involved in a land swindle.
Pleasant comedy with fanciful moments, ending with a pie-throwing contest.

w Virginia Van Upp *d* Elliott Nugent *ph* Leo Tover *m* Victor Young

Paulette Goddard, Ray Milland, Gladys George, Virginia Field, Cecil Kellaway, William Bendix, Ernest Truex

Cuban Love Song
US 1931 86m bw
MGM

A marine on leave in Cuba falls in love; years later he returns to retrieve his illegitimate child, whose mother has died.
Pathetic musical melodrama which did not advance its singing star's film career.

w John Lynch *d* W. S. Van Dyke *ph* Harold Rosson *songs* various

Lawrence Tibbett, Lupe Velez, Jimmy Durante, Ernest Torrence, Karen Morley, Louise Fazenda

A Cuckoo in the Nest*
GB 1933 85m bw
Gaumont (Ian Dalrymple, Angus MacPhail)

A newlywed husband is forced to spend a night at an inn with an old flame pretending to be his wife.
Classic Aldwych farce with the stage company in excellent form.

w Ben Travers, A. R. Rawlinson, *play Ben Travers* *d* Tom Walls

Ralph Lynn, Tom Walls, Yvonne Arnaud, Mary Brough, Veronica Rose, Gordon James, Cecil Parker, Roger Livesey

Cul de Sac
GB 1966 111m bw
Compton–Tekli (Gene Gutowski)

Two gangsters on the run take refuge in an old castle on a desolate Northumbrian island, but find their nemesis in the effeminate owner and his voluptuous wife.
Overlong, eccentric black comedy, more perplexing than entertaining.

w Roman Polanski, Gerard Brach *d* Roman Polanski *ph* Gilbert Taylor *m* Komeda

Lionel Stander, Donald Pleasance, Jack MacGowran, Françoise Dorléac, William Franklyn, Robert Dorning, Renée Houston

The Culpeper Cattle Company*
US 1972 92m De Luxe
TCF (Paul A. Helmick)

A 16-year-old would-be cowboy joins a cattle trail but is shocked at the harsh realities of western life.
Excellent moody photography helps to convince us that the old west was really like this, but the story is more brutal than interesting.

w Eric Bercovici, Gregory Prentiss *d* Dick Richards *ph Lawrence Edward Williams, Ralph Woolsey* *m* Tom Scott, Jerry Goldsmith

Gary Grimes, Billy 'Green' Bush, Luke Askew, Bo Hopkins, Geoffrey Lewis, Wayne Sutherlin

The Cure for Love
GB 1949 98m bw
London Films (Robert Donat)

An ex-soldier goes home and tries to get married. Thin Lancashire comedy which seemed an astonishing choice for Robert Donat, whose acting and direction are equally ill at ease.

w Robert Donat, Alexander Shaw, Albert Fennell, *play* Walter Greenwood *d* Robert Donat *ph* Jack Cox *m* William Alwyn

Robert Donat, Renée Asherson, Dora Bryan, Marjorie Rhodes, Charles Victor, Thora Hird, Gladys Henson

'Antediluvian regional farce.'—*MFB*

Curly Top*
US 1935 78m bw
TCF (Darryl F. Zanuck, Winfield Sheehan)

An orphan waif is adopted by a playboy, and not only sets his business right but fixes his romantic interest in her sister.
Archetypal Temple vehicle, a loose remake of *Daddy Longlegs*.

w Patterson McNutt, Arthur Beckhard *d* Irving Cummings *ph* John Seitz

Shirley Temple, John Boles, Rochelle Hudson, Jane Darwell, Rafaela Ottiano, Esther Dale, Arthur Treacher, Etienne Girardot

The Curse of Frankenstein**
GB 1957 83m Eastmancolor
Warner / Hammer

A lurid revamping of the 1931 *Frankenstein*, this time with severed eyeballs and a peculiarly unpleasant and uncharacterized creature, all in gory colour. It set the trend in nasty horrors from which we have all suffered since, and launched Hammer Studios on a long and profitable career of charnelry. But it did have a gruesome sense of style.

w Jimmy Sangster d Terence Fisher ph Jack Asher *m James Bernard ad* Ted Marshall

Peter Cushing, Christopher Lee, Hazel Court, Robert Urquhart, Valerie Gaunt, Noel Hood

The Curse of the Cat People*
US 1944 70m bw
RKO (*Val Lewton*)

A child is haunted by the spirit of the cat people.
A gentle film ordered by the studio as a sequel to *Cat People* but turned by Lewton into a fantasy of childhood. Slow to start but finally compelling, it's a pleasing and unusual film in a minor key.

w De Witt Bodeen *d* Robert Wise, Gunther Fritsch *ph* Nicholas Musuraca *m* Roy Webb

Kent Smith, Simone Simon, Jane Randolph, Julia Dean, Ann Carter, Elizabeth Russell

'Full of the poetry and danger of childhood.'—*James Agee*

Curse of the Crimson Altar
GB 1968 89m Eastmancolor
Tigon / AIP (Tony Tenser)

Witchcraft, diabolism and mystery in an English country house.
A derivative, muddled scribble of a horror film, making no sense and wasting much talent.

w Mervyn Haisman, Henry Lincoln *d* Vernon Sewell *ph* John Coquillon *m* Peter Knight

Boris Karloff (his last appearance), Christopher Lee, Rupert Davies, Mark Eden, Barbara Steele, Michael Gough

Curse of the Werewolf
GB 1961 92m Technicolor
U-I / Hammer (Anthony Hinds)

A beggar rapes a servant girl and their offspring grows up to be a werewolf.
Doleful Hammer horror in a Spanish setting, with an absurd but predictable plot and a lack of sympathy for its fancy, hairy hero.

w John Elder (Anthony Hinds) *d* Terence Fisher *ph* Arthur Grant *m* Benjamin Frankel

Oliver Reed, Clifford Evans, Catherine Feller, Yvonne Romain, Anthony Dawson, Richard Wordsworth, Warren Mitchell

Curtain Call*
US 1940 63m bw
RKO

Two Broadway producers buy an awful play in order to get even with a temperamental star, but she likes it.
Amusing second feature, a kind of flashforward to *The Producers*. A reprise the following year, *Footlight Fever*, did not work.

w Dalton Trumbo *d* Frank Woodruff *ph* Russell Metty *m* Roy Webb

Alan Mowbray, Donald MacBride, Helen Vinson, Barbara Read, John Archer

Curtain Call at Cactus Creek*
US 1949 83m Technicolor
U-I (Robert Arthur)
GB title: *Take the Stage*

A travelling repertory company in the old west exposes a gang of bank robbers.
Cheerful minor comedy with good pace and amusing burlesques of old melodramas.

w Oscar Brodney *d* Charles Lamont *ph* Russell Metty

Donald O'Connor, Gale Storm, Eve Arden, Vincent Price, Walter Brennan, Chick Chandler

Curtain Up*
GB 1952 85m bw
Rank / Constellation (Robert Garrett)

A seaside repertory company runs into trouble when the producer is at loggerheads with the author of next weeks's play.
Fairly amusing farce which has now acquired historical value for the light it throws on the old weekly reps.

w Michael Pertwee, Jack Davies, *play* On Monday Next by Philip King *d* Ralph Smart *ph* Stanley Pavey *m* Malcolm Arnold

Margaret Rutherford, Robert Morley, Olive Sloane, Joan Rice, Charlotte Mitchell, Kay Kendall, Liam Gaffney, Michael Medwin

Custer of the West
US 1968 146m Super Technirama 70
Cinerama / Security (Louis Dolivet, Philip Yordan, Irving Lerner)

After the Civil War, Custer is offered a cavalry command, becomes disillusioned, and is massacred with his troops at Little Big Horn.
Gloomily inaccurate spectacular with pauses for Cinerama carnival thrills and dour bits of melodrama.

w Bernard Gordon, Julian Halevy *d* Robert Siodmak *ph* Cecilio Paniagua *m* Bernardo Segall

Robert Shaw, Mary Ure, Robert Ryan, Jeffrey Hunter, Ty Hardin, Lawrence Tierney, Kieron Moore

Cutter*
US 1973 74m colour TVM
Universal (Richard Irving)

Private eye seeks missing football player.
Snazzy black-oriented mystery pilot that didn't make it.

wd Dean Hargrove

Peter De Anda, Cameron Mitchell, Barbara Rush, Gabriel Dell, Robert Webber, Archie Moore

Cutter's Trail*
US 1969 100m colour TVM
CBS / John Mantley

Adventures of the Marshal of Santa Fe in 1873.
Standard western pilot that wasn't picked up.

w Paul Savage *d* Vincent McEveety

Rohn Gavin, Marisa Pavan, Joseph Cotten, Beverly Garland

The Cyclops
US 1956 65m bw
B and H (Bert I. Gordon)

Explorers in Mexico find animals turned by radiation into monsters, plus a one-eyed 25-foot-tall human.
Modest monster movie, quite palatable of its kind.

wd Bert I. Gordon *ph* Ira Morgan *m* Albert Glasser

James Craig, Lon Chaney Jnr, Gloria Talbot, Tom Drake

Cynara**
US 1933 78m bw
Samuel Goldwyn

A London barrister has an affair with a young girl who commits suicide when he goes back to his wife.
Solidly carpentered, effective star vehicle of the old school, now dated but preserving its dignity.

w Frances Marion, Lynn Starling, *novel* An Imperfect Lover by Robert Gore Brown *d* King Vidor *ph* Ray June

Ronald Colman, Kay Francis, Phyllis Barry, *Henry Stephenson*, Paul Porcasi

Cyrano de Bergerac*
US 1950 112m bw
Stanley Kramer

In the 17th century a long-nosed poet, philospher and buffoon writes letters enabling a friend to win the lady he loves himself.
The classic romantic verse play does not take kindly to a hole-in-corner black-and-white production, but at the time it was lapped up as a daring cultural breakthrough.

w Brian Hooker, *play* Edmond Rostand *d* Michael Gordon *ph* Franz Planer *m* Dmitri Tiomkin

Jose Ferrer, Mala Powers, William Prince, Morris Carnovsky, Ralph Clanton, Virginia Farmer, Edgar Barrier, Elena Verdugo

D

Daddy Longlegs*
US 1931 73m bw
Fox

An orphan girl grows up to fall in love with her mysterious benefactor.
Cinderella-like romance, adequately adapted from a novel which became the classic American version of the January–May romance.

w Sonya Levien, *novel* Jean Webster *d* Alfred Santell *ph* Lucien Andriot

Janet Gaynor, Warner Baxter, Una Merkel, John Arledge, Claude Gillingwater, Louise Closser Hale
† Other versions were made in 1919 with Mary Pickford and Mahlon Hamilton, directed by Marshal Neilan; in 1935 disguised as *Curly Top* (qv) and in 1955 (see below).

Daddy Longlegs*
US 1955 126m Technicolor
Cinemascope
TCF (Samuel G. Engel)

Overlong and unsuitably wide-screened musical version of a popular story (see above). Generally clumsy and dispirited, but Astaire is always worth watching and a couple of the dances are well staged.

w Phoebe and Henry Ephron *d* Jean Negulesco *ph* Leon Shamroy *m* Alex North *songs* Johnny Mercer

Fred Astaire, Leslie Caron, *Fred Clark*, Thelma Ritter, Terry Moore, Charlotte Austin, Larry Keating

Daddy's Gone A-Hunting
US 1969 108m Technicolor
Warner / Red Lion (Mark Robson)

A child and its mother are threatened by her deranged ex-husband.
Unpleasant and protracted suspenser with the emphasis on sex rather than thrills.

w Larry Cohen, Lorenzo Semple Jnr *d* Mark Robson *ph* Ernest Laszlo *m* John Williams

Carol White, Paul Burke, Scott Hylands, Mala Powers, Andrea King

Dad's Army**
GB 1971 95m Technicolor
Columbia / Norcon (John R. Sloan)

Misadventures of a number of elderly gents in Britain's wartime Home Guard.
Expanded big-screen version of the long-running TV series, a pleasant souvenir but rather less effective than was expected because everything is shown—the town, the Nazis, the wives—and thus the air of gentle fantasy disappears, especially in the face of much coarsened humour.

w Jimmy Perry, David Croft *d* Norman Cohen *ph* Terry Maher *m* Wilfred Burns

Arthur Lowe, John Le Mesurier, John Laurie, James Beck, Ian Lavender, *Arnold Ridley*, Liz Fraser, *Clive Dunn*, Bill Pertwee, Frank Williams, Edward Sinclair

Daisy Kenyon
US 1947 99m bw
TCF (Otto Preminger)

A fashion designer has two men in her life.
Adequate woman's picture which hardly justifies its cast.

w David Hertz, *novel* Elizabeth Janeway *d* Otto Preminger *ph* Leon Shamroy *m* David Raksin

Joan Crawford, Henry Fonda, Dana Andrews, Ruth Warrick, Martha Stewart, Peggy Ann Garner

Daisy Miller*
US 1974 92m Technicolor
Paramount / Copa de Oro (Peter Bogdanovich)

In the 19th century, an American girl tourist in Europe falls in love but dies of the Roman fever.
Curious attempt to film a very mild and uneventful Henry James story, with careful production but inadequate leads. The first sign that Bogdanovich was getting too big for his boots.

w Frederic Raphael *d* Peter Bogdanovich *ph* Alberto Spagnoli *m* classical themes *ad* Ferdinando Scarfiotti

Cybill Shepherd, Barry Brown, Cloris

Leachman, Mildred Natwick, Eileen Brennan, James MacMurtry

'A historical film bereft of any feeling for history, and a literary adaptation which reveals a fine contempt for literary subtlety.'—*Jan Dawson*

Dakota
US 1945 82m bw
Republic (Joseph Kane)

The daughter of a railroad tycoon elopes with a cowboy and becomes involved in a land war.
Adequate star western.

w Lawrence Hazard, *story* Carl Foreman *d* Joseph Kane *ph* Jack Marta *m* Walter Scharf

John Wayne, Vera Hruba Ralston, Walter Brennan, Ward Bond, Ona Munson, Hugo Haas, Mike Mazurki, Paul Fix, Grant Withers, Jack La Rue

Dallas*
US 1950 94m Technicolor
Warner (Anthony Veiller)

A renegade ex-Confederate colonel is pardoned for bringing law and order to Dallas.
Routinely competent top-of-the-bill western.

w John Twist *d* Stuart Heisler *ph* Ernest Haller *m* Max Steiner

Gary Cooper, Ruth Roman, Raymond Massey, Steve Cochran, Barbara Payton, Leif Erickson, Antonio Moreno, Jerome Cowan

The Dam Busters**
GB 1954 125m bw
ABPC (Robert Clark)

In 1943 the Ruhr dams are destroyed by Dr Barnes Wallis' bouncing bombs.
Understated British war epic with additional scientific interest and good acting and model work, not to mention a welcome lack of love interest.

w R. C. Sheriff, books by Guy Gibson and Paul Brickhill *d* Michael Anderson *ph* Erwin Hillier *m* Leighton Lucas, *Eric Coates* *sp* George Blackwell

Michael Redgrave, Richard Todd, Basil Sydney, Derek Farr, Patrick Barr, Ernest Clark, Raymond Huntley, Ursula Jeans

Dames**
US 1935 90m bw
Warner (Robert Lord)

A millionaire purity fanatic tries to stop the opening of a Broadway show.
Typical Warner musical of the period: its real *raison d'être* is to be found in the splendidly imaginative numbers at the finale, but it also gives very full rein to the roster of comic actors under contract at the time.

w Delmer Daves *d* Ray Enright *ch Busby Berkeley* *ph* Sid Hickox, George Barnes *m* various

Joan Blondell, Hugh Herbert, Guy Kibbee, Zasu Pitts, Dick Powell, Ruby Keeler

Damn Yankees**
US 1958 110m Technicolor
Warner (George Abbott, Stanley Donen)
GB title: *What Lola Wants*

The devil interferes in the fortunes of a failing baseball team.
Smartly-styled but very American musical based on *Faust*; brilliant moments but some tedium.

w George Abbott, *novel* Douglas Wallop *d* George Abbott, Stanley Donen *ph Harold Lipstein* *m/ly* Richard Adler, Jerry Ross

Gwen Verdon, Tab Hunter, Ray Walston, Russ Brown, Shannon Bolin

The Damned*
GB 1961 87m bw Hammerscope
Columbia / Hammer–Swallow (Anthony Hinds)
US title: *These Are the Damned*

A scientist keeps radioactive children in a cliff cave, sealed off from the world's corruption.
Absurdly pompous, downcast and confused sci-fi melodrama set in Weymouth, with a secondary plot about motor-cycling thugs.

w Evan Jones, *novel* The Children of Light by H. L. Lawrence *d* Joseph Losey *ph* Arthur Grant *m* James Bernard

Macdonald Carey, Shirley Ann Field, Alexander Knox, Viveca Lindfors, Oliver Reed, Walter Gotell, James Villiers

'A *folie de grandeur*.'—*Tom Milne*

'Out of this wild mishmash some really magnificent images loom.'—*John Coleman*

The Damned Don't Cry
US 1950 103m bw
Warner (Jerry Wald)

A middle-class housewife leaves her husband for a gambler, and becomes involved with gangsters, but eventually reforms.
Rather dreary stimulation for female audiences who like safe dreams of danger.

w Harold Medford, Jerome Weidman, *novel* Case History by Gertrude Walker *d* Vincent Sherman *ph* Ted McCord *m* Daniele Amfitheatrof

Joan Crawford, Kent Smith, David Brian, Steve

Cochran, Hugh Sanders, Selena Royle, Morris Ankrum, Richard Egan

A Damsel in Distress*
US 1937 101m bw
RKO (Pandro S. Berman)

An American dancing star falls for an aristocratic young Englishwoman.
Astaire without Rogers, but the style is the same and there are some very good numbers.

w P. G. Wodehouse, S. K. Lauren, Ernest Pagano *d* George Stevens *ph* Joseph H. August *m/ly* George and Ira Gershwin *ch* Hermes Pan

Fred Astaire, George Burns, Gracie Allen, Joan Fontaine, Reginald Gardiner, Constance Collier, Ray Noble, Montagu Love
† Rogers had demanded a break from musicals, so she was replaced by the demure Miss Fontaine, who was generally thought disappointing.

Dance Fools Dance
US 1931 82m bw
MGM

A lady reporter in Chicago proves her worth.
Bizarrely-titled gangster thriller based on the Jake Lingle killing. Very moderate of its kind.

w Richard Schayer, Aurania Rouverol *d* Harry Beaumont *ph* Charles Rosher

Joan Crawford, Lester Vail, Cliff Edwards, William Bakewell, William Holden (the other one), Clark Gable, Earle Foxe, Joan Marsh

Dance Girl Dance*
US 1940 88m bw
RKO (Erich Pommer)

Private problems of the members of a nightclub dance troupe.
Competent and sometimes interesting formula drama with a harder edge than usual.

w Tess Slesinger, Frank Davis, *story* Vicki Baum *d Dorothy Arzner ph* Russell Metty

Maureen O'Hara, Louis Hayward, Lucille Ball, Maria Ouspenskaya, Ralph Bellamy, Virginia Field, Mary Carlisle, Walter Abel, Edward Brophy, Harold Huber

Dance Hall*
GB 1950 80m bw
Ealing (E. V. H. Emmett)

Four factory girls seek relaxation and various kinds of romance at the local palais.
Untypically flat Ealing slice of life, now watchable only with a smile as musical nostalgia.

w E. V. H. Emmett, Diana Morgan, Alexander Mackendrick *d* Charles Crichton *ph* Douglas Slocombe *md* Ernest Irving

Natasha Parry, Donald Houston, Diana Dors, Bonar Colleano, Jane Hylton, Petula Clark, Gladys Henson, Sydney Tafler; the bands of Geraldo and Ted Heath

The Dance of Death*
GB 1968 149m Technicolor
BHE / National Theatre (John Brabourne)

Edgar and Alice live alone on an island, their marriage having become a constant war.
Too-literal film transcription of an applauded theatrical production, with the camera anchored firmly in the middle of the stalls.

w August Strindberg (*translation* by C. D. Locock) *d* David Giles *ph* Geoffrey Unsworth

Laurence Olivier, Geraldine McEwan, Robert Lang, Carolyn Jones

Dancing in the Dark*
US 1949 92m Technicolor
TCF (George Jessel)

A silent movie idol makes a comeback as a talent scout, and spots his own daughter.
Thin but unusual Hollywood drama with music; in the long run too sentimental.

w Mary C. McCall Jnr, *play* The Band Wagon by George F. Kaufman, Howard Dietz, Arthur Schwarz *d* Irving Reis *ph* Harry Jackson *m* Alfred Newman

William Powell, Adolphe Menjou, Mark Stevens, Betsy Drake, Hope Emerson, Lloyd Corrigan, Walter Catlett, Jean Hersholt

Dancing Lady*
US 1933 94m bw
MGM (David O. Selznick)

A successful dancer chooses between a playboy and her stage manager.
Routine backstage semi-musical with interesting talent applied.

w Allen Rivkin, P. J. Wolfson, *novel* James Warner Bellah *d* Robert Z. Leonard *ph* Oliver T. Marsh *m* various

Joan Crawford, Clark Gable, *Fred Astaire*, Franchot Tone, May Robson, Ted Healy and his Stooges (the Three Stooges), Winnie Lightner, Robert Benchley, Nelson Eddy

The Dancing Masters
US 1943 63m bw
TCF (Lee Marcus)

Laurel and Hardy run a ballet school, and get involved with gangsters and inventors.
Insubstantial star comedy featuring reworkings

of old routines, and a back-projected runaway bus climax.

w Scott Darling, George Bricker *d* Mal St Clair *ph* Norbert Brodine

Stan Laurel, Oliver Hardy, Trudy Marshall, Bob Bailey, Margaret Dumont, Matt Briggs, Robert Mitchum

The Dancing Years

GB 1949 97m Technicolor
ABPC (Warwick Ward)

A composer loves a singer who leaves him after a misunderstanding but later bears his son . . . all in the Alps pre-1914.
Lamentable transcription of an operetta; precisely the ingredients which worked so well on stage seem embarrassing on film, and the performances and direction do not help.

w Warwick Ward, Jack Whittingham, from Ivor Novello's operetta *d* Harold French *ph* Stephen Dade *m Ivor Novello*

Dennis Price, Gisèle Préville, Patricia Dainton, Anthony Nicholls, Grey Blake, Muriel George, Olive Gilbert

A Dandy in Aspic

GB 1968 107m Technicolor Panavision
Columbia (Anthony Mann)

A double agent in Berlin is given orders to kill himself.
Muddled, pretentious spy thriller; flat, nebulous and boring.

w Derek Marlowe, from his novel *d* Anthony Mann *ph* Christopher Challis *m* Quincy Jones

Laurence Harvey, Tom Courtenay, Lionel Stander, Mia Farrow, Harry Andrews, Peter Cook, Per Oscarsson
† Anthony Mann died during shooting, and Laurence Harvey completed the direction.

Danger Has Two Faces

US 1967 89m colour TVM
TCF

A much disliked executive in Berlin is shot in mistake for an American agent, who promptly takes his place.
Re-edited episodes from *The Man Who Never Was*, a series which had nothing except the title to do with its movie namesake.

w Merwin Gerard, Robert C. Dennis, Judith and Robert Guy Barrows *d* John Newland

Robert Lansing, Dana Wynter, Murray Hamilton

Danger Route

GB 1967 92m De Luxe
UA / Amicus (Max J. Rosenberg, Milton Subotsky)

An 'eliminator' for the British secret service finds after a series of adventures that he must dispose of his own girl friend.
Dour sub-Bondian thriller with little to commend it.

w Meade Roberts, *novel* The Eliminator by Andrew York *d* Seth Holt *ph* Harry Waxman *m* John Mayer

Richard Johnson, Diana Dors, Sylvia Syms, Carol Lynley, Barbara Bouchet, Gordon Jackson, Sam Wanamaker, Maurice Denham, Harry Andrews

Danger Within**

GB 1958 101m bw
British Lion / Colin Lesslie
US title: *Breakout*

Escape plans of officers in a prisoner-of-war camp are threatened by an informer.
Familiar comedy and melodrama with an added whodunnit element, smartly handled and very entertaining.

w Bryan Forbes, Frank Harvey, novel Michael Gilbert *d Don Chaffey ph* Arthur Grant *m* Francis Chagrin

Richard Todd, Bernard Lee, Michael Wilding, Richard Attenborough, Dennis Price, Donald Houston, William Franklyn, Vincent Ball, Peter Arne

Dangerous*

US 1935 78m bw
Warner (Harry Joe Brown)

An alcoholic actress is rehabilitated.
Unconvincing and only adequately handled melodrama which won the star her first Oscar, presumably from sympathy at her losing it the previous year for *Of Human Bondage*.

w Laird Doyle *d* Alfred E. Green *ph* Ernest Haller

Bette Davis, Franchot Tone, Margaret Lindsay, Alison Skipworth, John Eldridge, Dick Foran
† Remade 1941 as *Singapore Woman*.

Dangerous Corner*

US 1934 67m bw
RKO

After dinner conversation reveals what might have been if friends had spoken the truth about a long-ago suicide.
A fascinating trick play makes interesting but scarcely sparkling cinema.

w Anne Morrison Chapin, Madeleine Ruthven, *play* J. B. Priestley *d* Phil Rosen *ph* J. Roy Hunt

Melvyn Douglas, Conrad Nagel, Virginia Bruce, Erin O'Brien Moore, Ian Keith, Betty Furness, Henry Wadsworth

Dangerous Crossing*
US 1953 75m bw
TCF (Robert Bassler)

At the start of an Atlantic sea voyage a woman's husband disappears, and she is assured that he never existed. He does, and is trying to murder her.
Adequately handled twist on the vanishing lady story: grade A production covers lapses of grade B imagination.

w Leo Townsend, *story* John Dickson Carr *d* Joseph M. Newman *ph* Joseph La Shelle *m* Lionel Newman

Jeanne Crain, Michael Rennie, Carl Betz, Casey Adams, Mary Anderson, Willis Bouchey

Dangerous Curves
US 1929 75m bw
Paramount

A bareback rider loves a high wire artist.
Obvious circus melodrama, a modest star vehicle.

w Donald David, Florence Ryerson *d* Lothar Mendes *ph* Harry Fischbeck

Clara Bow, Richard Arlen, Kay Francis, David Newell, Anders Randolf

The Dangerous Days of Kiowa Jones
US 1966 100m colour TVM
MGM / Max E. Youngstein, David Karr

Adventures of an ex-lawman in the old west.
Dreary, talkative western which seems desperate to fill up its alotted time and go home.

w Frank Fenton, Robert E. Thompson, *novel* Clinton Adams *d* Alex March *ph* Ellsworth Fredericks *m* Samuel Matlovsky

Robert Horton, Diane Baker, Sal Mineo, Nehemiah Persoff, Gary Merrill, Robert H. Harris, Royal Dano

Dangerous Exile
GB 1957 90m Eastmancolor Vistavision
Rank (George H. Brown)

After the French Revolution, the young would-be Louis XVII is brought across the Channel and hidden in Pembrokeshire, where enemies attack him.
Historical romance, ineptly plotted but quite well produced.

w Robin Estridge, *novel* Vaughan Wilkins *d* Brian Desmond Hurst *ph Geoffrey Unsworth* *m* Georges Auric

Louis Jourdan, Belinda Lee, Keith Michell, Richard O'Sullivan, Martita Hunt, Finlay Currie, Anne Heywood, Jacques Brunius

Dangerous Moonlight*
GB 1941 98m bw
RKO (William Sistrom)
US title: *Suicide Squadron*

A Polish pianist escapes from the Nazis and loses his memory after flying in the Battle of Britain.
Immensely popular wartime romance which introduced Richard Addinsell's Warsaw Concerto. Production values and script somewhat below par.

w Shaun Terence Young, Brian Desmond Hurst, Rodney Ackland *d* Brian Desmond Hurst

Anton Walbrook, Sally Gray, Derrick de Marney, Cecil Parker, Percy Parsons, Keneth Kent, Guy Middleton, John Laurie, Frederick Valk

Dangerous to Know*
US 1938 70m bw
Paramount

A ruthless Chicago gangster comes a cropper when his Chinese mistress discovers he has fallen for a socialite.
Flatly handled but mildly interesting adaptation of a highly successful play, the potential of which seems to have been thrown away.

w William R. Lippmann, Horace McCoy, *play* On the Spot by Edgar Wallace *d* Robert Florey *ph* Theodor Sparkuhl

Akim Tamiroff, Anna May Wong, Gail Patrick, Lloyd Nolan, Harvey Stephens, Anthony Quinn, Porter Hall

Dangerous When Wet**
US 1953 95m Technicolor
MGM (George Wells)

An entire Arkansas family is sponsored to swim the English Channel.
A bright and lively vehicle for an aquatic star, who in one sequence swims with Tom and Jerry. Amusing sequences give opportunities to a strong cast.

w Dorothy Kingsley *d* Charles Walters *ph* Harold Rosson *songs* Johnny Mercer, Arthur Schwarz

Esther Williams, Charlotte Greenwood, William Demarest, Fernando Lamas, Jack Carson, Denise Darcel, Barbara Whiting

Dangerously They Live
US 1941 77m bw
Warner (Ben Stoloff)

American Nazi agents try to get a secret memorized by a British girl agent injured in a car crash.
Watchable, routine spy propaganda fare.

w Marion Parsonnet *d* Robert Florey *ph* William O'Connell

John Garfield, Raymond Massey, Nancy Coleman, Moroni Olsen, Lee Patrick, Christian Rub, Frank Reicher

Dante's Inferno**
US 1935 89m bw
TCF (Sol M. Wurtzel)

A ruthless carnival owner gets too big for his boots, and has a vision of hell induced by one of his own attractions.
Curiously unpersuasive melodrama with a moral, but the inferno sequence is one of the most unexpected, imaginative and striking pieces of cinema in Hollywood's history.

w Philip Klein, Robert Yost *d Harry Lachman* *ph Rudolph Maté*

Spencer Tracy, Claire Trevor, Henry B. Walthall, Alan Dinehart, Scotty Beckett, Rita Hayworth (her first appearance, as a dancer)

'We depart gratefully, having seen papier maché photographed in more ways than we had thought possible.'—*Robert Herring*

'One of the most unusual and effectively presented films of the thirties.'—*John Baxter, 1968*

Darby O'Gill and the Little People*
US 1959 90m Technicolor
Walt Disney

An Irish caretaker falls down a well and is captured by leprechauns, who allow him three wishes to rearrange his life.
Pleasantly barmy Irish fantasy with brilliant trick work but some tedium in between.

w Lawrence Edward Watkin, *stories* H. T. Kavanagh *d* Robert Stevenson *ph* Winton C. Hoch *m* Oliver Wallace *sp Peter Ellenshaw, Eustace Lycett, Joshua Meador*

Albert Sharpe, *Jimmy O'Dea*, Sean Connery, Janet Munro, Kieron Moore, Estelle Winwood, Walter Fitzgerald, Denis O'Dea, J. G. Devlin, Jack MacGowran

'One of the best fantasies ever put on film.'—*Leonard Maltin*

Darby's Rangers
US 1957 121m bw
Warner (Martin Rackin)

A tough American commando unit is trained in Britain before seeing action in Africa and Sicily.
Standard World War II actioner, adequately executed.

w Guy Trosper, *book* Major James Altieri *d* William Wellman *ph* William H. Clothier *m* Max Steiner

James Garner, Etchika Choureau, Jack Warden, Edward Byrnes, Venetia Stevenson, Torin Thatcher, Stuart Whitman, Andrea King, Frieda Inescort, Reginald Owen, Adam Williams

The Daring Game
US 1967 101m Eastmancolor
Paramount / Tors (Gene Levitt)

A commercial group experiments with airborne and underwater inventions, and rescues a scientist from a police state.
Well photographed but haphazardly assembled adventures, aimed at TV.

w Andy White *d* Laslo Benedek *ph* Edmund Gibson *m* George Bruns

Lloyd Bridges, Nico Minardos, Joan Blackman, Michael Ansara

The Dark Angel*
US 1935 105m bw
Samuel Goldwyn

During World War I, a blinded officer tries to dismiss his fiancée without her learning of his infirmity.
Tearstained melodrama from another age, neatly packaged for the romantic 1935 public.

w Lillian Hellman, Mordaunt Shairp, *play* Guy Bolton *d* Sidney Franklin *ph* Gregg Toland *m* Alfred Newman

Merle Oberon, Fredric March, Herbert Marshall, Janet Beecher, John Halliday, Henrietta Crosman, Frieda Inescort, George Breakston, Claud Allister

† A 1925 silent version had starred Ronald Colman and Vilma Banky.

The Dark at the Top of the Stairs**
US 1960 124m Technicolor
Warner (Michael Garrison)

Twenties small town drama about a young boy's awakening to the sexual tensions around him.
Archetypal family drama set in that highly familiar American street. The perfect essence of this playwright's work, with high and low spots, several irrelevancies, but a real feeling for the people and the place.

w Harriet Frank Jnr, Irving Ravetch, *play William Inge* *d* Delbert Mann *ph* Harry Stradling *m* Max Steiner

Robert Preston, Dorothy McGuire, Angela Lansbury, *Eve Arden*, Shirley Knight, Frank Overton, Lee Kinsolving, Robert Eyer

† The curious title turns out to be a synonym for life, which one should never be afraid of.

The Dark Avenger*
GB 1955 85m Eastmancolor Cinemascope
Allied Artists
US title: *The Warriors*

The Black Prince quells some French rebels.
Good-humoured historical romp with the ageing star in his last swashbuckling role, helped by a good cast and brisk pace.

w Daniel B. Ullman *d* Henry Levin *ph* Guy Green *m* Cedric Thorpe Davie

Errol Flynn, Peter Finch, Joanne Dru, Yvonne Furneaux, Patrick Holt, Michael Hordern, Moultrie Kelsall, Robert Urquhart, Noel Willman

Dark City
US 1950 97m bw
Paramount / Hal B. Wallis

A bookmaker finds himself on the run from a revenge-seeking psychopath.
Unattractive and heavily-handled underworld melodrama, a disappointment from the talents involved.

w John Meredyth Lucas, Larry Marcus *d* William Dieterle *ph* Victor Milner *m* Franz Waxman

Charlton Heston (his first Hollywood appearance), Lizabeth Scott, Viveca Lindfors, Dean Jagger, Don Defore, Jack Webb, Ed Begley, Henry Morgan, Mike Mazurki

'A jaded addition to a type of thriller which has become increasingly tedious and unreal.'—*MFB*

Dark Command*
US 1940 92m bw
Republic (Sol C. Siegel)

In pre-Civil War Kansas, an ambitious ex-schoolteacher named Cantrill organizes guerrilla bands to pillage the countryside.
Semi-historical hokum, quite well done with a good cast.

w Grover Jones, Lionel Houser, F. Hugh Herbert, *novel* W. R. Burnett *d* Raoul Walsh *ph* Jack Marta *m* Victor Young

John Wayne, Claire Trevor, Walter Pidgeon, Roy Rogers, George 'Gabby' Hayes, Porter Hall, Marjorie Main

The Dark Corner*
US 1946 98m bw
TCF (Fred Kohlmar)

A private eye with a criminal record thinks he is being menaced by an old adversary, but the latter is found murdered.
Moody, brutish, well-made thriller with a plot put together from bits and pieces of older, better movies, notably Clifton Webb's reprise of his *Laura* performance and William Bendix ditto *The Glass Key*.

w Jay Dratler, Bernard Schoenfeld, *story* Leo Rosten *d Henry Hathaway ph Joe MacDonald* *m* Cyril Mockridge

Mark Stevens, Clifton Webb, Lucille Ball, William Bendix, Kurt Kreuger, Cathy Downs, Reed Hadley, Constance Collier

'Not so much a whodunnit as a whodunnwhat . . . all seem bent on "getting" each other and their internecine plottings add up to an alpha thriller.'—*Daily Mail*

Dark Eyes of London*
GB 1939 75m bw
Pathe / Argyle (John Argyle)
US title: *The Human Monster*

The proprietor of a home for the blind uses a mute giant to drown insured victims.
Reasonably effective British horror, a rarity at the time.

w John Argyle, Walter Summers, Patrick Kirwan, *novel* Edgar Wallace *d* Walter Summers

Bela Lugosi, Hugh Williams, Greta Gynt, Wilfrid Walter, Edmon Ryan

Dark Journey*
GB 1937 82m bw
London Films / Victor Saville

In 1915 Stockholm, a French woman spy masquerading as a traitor falls in love with her German spy contact.
Unconvincing but entertaining romantic adventure with good star performances.

w Lajos Biro, Arthur Wimperis, *play* Lajos Biro *d* Victor Saville *ph* Georges Périnal, Harry Stradling

Conrad Veidt, Vivien Leigh, Joan Gardner, Anthony Bushell, Ursula Jeans, Eliot Makeham, Austin Trevor, Edmund Willard

The Dark Mirror***
US 1946 85m bw
International

A police detective works out which of identical twin girls is a murderer.
Unconvincing but highly absorbing thriller with all credits plus; the best brand of Hollywood moonshine.

w Nunnally Johnson d Robert Siodmak
ph Milton Krasner

Olivia de Havilland, Lew Ayres, Thomas Mitchell, Garry Owen

Dark Passage**
US 1947 106m bw
Warner (Jerry Wald)

A convicted murderer escapes from jail and proves his innocence.
Loosely assembled, totally unconvincing star thriller which succeeds because of its professionalism, some good cameos, and a number of narrative tricks including subjective camera for the first half hour.

w Delmer Daves, *novel* David Goodis *d Delmer Daves ph Sid Hickox m* Franz Waxman

Humphrey Bogart, Lauren Bacall, Agnes Moorehead, Bruce Bennett, *Tom D'Andrea, Houseley Stevenson*

The Dark Past**
US 1948 75m bw
Columbia

A psychiatrist turns the tables on convicts who break into his home.
Tense, economical remake of *Blind Alley* (qv); a fresh look at a familiar situation (*The Small Voice, The Desperate Hours,* etc) helped by excellent performances.

w Philip Macdonald, Malvin Wald, Oscar Saul *d Rudolph Maté ph* Joseph Walker *m* George Duning

William Holden, Lee J. Cobb, Nina Foch, Adele Jergens, Stephen Dunne

Dark Victory**
US 1939 106m bw
Warner (David Lewis)

A good-time society girl discovers she is dying of a brain tumour.
A highly commercial tearjerker of its day, this glutinous star vehicle now works only fitfully. Remade as *Stolen Hours* (qv) and as a 1975 TV movie under its original title.

w Casey Robinson, *play* George Brewer Jnr, Bertram Bloch *d* Edmund Goulding *ph* Ernest Haller

Bette Davis, George Brent, Humphrey Bogart, Ronald Reagan, Geraldine Fitzgerald, Henry Travers, Cora Witherspoon, Dorothy Peterson

'A completely cynical appraisal would dismiss it all as emotional flim-flam . . . but it is impossible to be that cynical about it.'—*Frank S. Nugent*

'A gooey collection of clichés, but Davis slams through them in her nerviest style.'—*New Yorker, 1976*

Dark Victory
US 1975 150m Technicolor TVM
Universal

A socialite finds she is dying of a brain tumour.
Absurdly extended remake of the 1939 film, which proved to be way out of fashion when remade in 1963 as *Stolen Hours.*

w M. Charles Cohen *d* Jules Irving

Elizabeth Montgomery, Anthony Hopkins, Michele Lee

Dark Waters**
US 1944 90m bw
Benedict Bogeaus

Recovering from being torpedoed, an orphan girl visits her aunt and uncle in Louisiana and has some terrifying experiences.
Competent frightened-lady melodrama helped by its bayou surroundings.Possibly discarded by Hitchcock, but with sequences well in his manner.

w Joan Harrison, Marian Cockrell *d André de Toth ph John Mescall*

Merle Oberon, Franchot Tone, *Thomas Mitchell, Fay Bainter, John Qualen,* Elisha Cook Jnr, Rex Ingram

Darker than Amber
US 1970 96m Technicolor
Cinema Center / Major Films

A Florida private eye rescues a girl who is subsequently murdered and turns out to be part of a confidence racket.
Routine suspenser from the Travis McGee books; not very stimulating.

w Ed Waters, *novel* John D. MacDonald *d* Robert Clouse *ph* Frank Phillips *m* John Parker

Rod Taylor, Suzy Kendall, Theodore Bikel, James Booth, Jane Russell, Janet McLachlan, William Smith

Darling**
GB 1965 127m bw
Anglo-Amalgamated / Vic / Appia (Joseph Janni, Victor Lyndon)

An ambitious young woman deserts her journalist mentor for a company director, an effeminate photographer and an Italian prince.
Fashionable mid-sixties concoction of smart swinging people and their amoral doings. Influential, put over with high style, and totally tiresome in retrospect.

w Frederic Raphael *d John Schlesinger* *ph* Ken Higgins *m* John Dankworth

Julie Christie, Dirk Bogarde, Laurence Harvey, Roland Curram, Alex Scott, Basil Henson, Pauline Yates

'As empty of meaning and mind as the empty life it's exposing.'—*Pauline Kael*

Darling How Could You
US 1951 96m bw
Paramount (Harry Tugend)
GB title: *Rendezvous*

Children long separated from their parents have fantasies about them.
Faded-looking Edwardian comedy which does not quite have the style or the cast for success. (Or the title, come to that.)

w Dodie Smith, Lesser Samuels, *play* Alice Sit by the Fire by J. M. Barrie *d* Mitchell Leisen *ph* Daniel L. Fapp *m* Frederick Hollander

Joan Fontaine, John Lund, Mona Freeman, Peter Hanson, David Stollery, Lowell Gilmore, Robert Barrat, Gertrude Michael

Darling Lili*
US 1970 136m Technicolor Panavision
Paramount / Geoffrey (Owen Crump)

During World War I, an American air ace falls for a German lady spy, and waits till the war is over to marry her.
Farce and romance mix oddly with aerial acrobatics in this expensive and dull extravaganza which bore the sub-title *Where Were You the Night I Shot Down Baron Von Richthofen?* (which probably sums up its aims and its failure). A coffee table film, good to look at and with occasional striking moments.

wd Blake Edwards *ph Russell Harlan, Harold E. Wellman* *m* Henry Mancini *pd* Fernando Carrere

Julie Andrews, Rock Hudson, Jeremy Kemp, Lance Percival, Michael Witney, Jacques Marin, André Maranne

The Darwin Adventure*
GB 1971 91m Eastmancolor
(TCF) Palomar (Joseph Strick, Irving Lerner)

In 1831, Charles Darwin becomes ship's naturalist on the *Beagle* and studies wild life in South America.
Rather naive biopic of Darwin which tries to cover too much with too slender resources but makes a pleasant introduction to the subject.

w William Fairchild *d* Jack Couffer *ph* Denys Coop, Jack Couffer *m* Marc Wilkinson

Nicholas Clay, Susan Macready, Ian Richardson, Christopher Martin, Robert Flemyng, Aubrey Woods, Hugh Morton

'The biopic plague, which has ravaged the screen lives of Pasteur, Juarez, Cole Porter and countless others, has now struck down the memory of famed naturalist Charles Darwin. The filmgoing public's own version of Darwin's natural selection theory will immediately weed out this inferior species.'—*Variety*

A Date with Judy
US 1948 113m Technicolor
MGM (Joe Pasternak)

A teenager wrongly suspects her friend of an illicit affair.
Ambitious but flat comedy musical which neatly wraps up all kinds of forties people and institutions: teenagers, small towns, families, Carmen Miranda and Miss Taylor, not to mention the producer.

w Dorothy Cooper, Dorothy Kingsley *d* Richard Thorpe *ph* Robert Surtees *m/ly* various

Wallace Beery, Elizabeth Taylor, Jane Powell, Carmen Miranda, Xavier Cugat, Robert Stack, Selena Royle, Scotty Beckett, Leon Ames

Daughter of Darkness
GB 1947 91m bw
Kenilworth–Alliance (Victor Hanbury)

A murderous Irish servant girl has a fatal flair for men.
Absurd melodrama, almost Grand Guignol, louringly set on the Yorkshire moors but lethargically handled all round.

w Max Catto, from his play They Walk Alone *d* Lance Comfort

Siobhan McKenna, Anne Crawford, Maxwell Reed, George Thorpe, Barry Morse, Honor Blackman, Liam Redmond, David Greene

The Daughter of Rosie O'Grady*
US 1950 104m Technicolor
Warner (William Jacobs)

A girl determines to follow in her dead mother's musical comedy footsteps against the wishes of her still-grieving father.
Absolutely standard period musical, quite pleasantly handled but with below-par musical numbers.

w Jack Rose, Mel Shavelson, Peter Milne *d* David Butler *ph* Wilfred M. Cline *md* David Buttolph

June Haver, Gordon Macrae, *James Barton*, S. Z. Sakall, Gene Nelson, Debbie Reynolds, Sean McClory, Jane Darwell

Daughter of the Mind**
US 1969 74m colour TVM
TCF (Walter Grauman)

An international scientist believes that the ghost of his dead daughter is appearing to him, but the FBI exposes the trickery as the work of foreign agents.
Chilling little mystery which plays reasonably fair with the audience and works up quite a bit of excitement.

w Luther Davis, *novel* The Hand of Mary Constable by Paul Gallico *d* Walter Grauman

Ray Milland, Gene Tierney, Don Murray, George Macready

Daughters Courageous*
US 1939 107m bw
Warner (Hal B. Wallis)

A prodigal father returns to his family and sorts out their problems.
Following the success of *Four Daughters* (qv) the cast was reassembled to make this amiable rehash about a different family.

w Julius and Philip Epstein, *play* Fly Away Home by Dorothy Bennett, Irving White *d* Michael Curtiz *ph James Wong Howe*

Claude Rains, John Garfield, Jeffrey Lynn, Fay Bainter, Priscilla Lane, Rosemary Lane, Lola Lane, Gale Page, Donald Crisp, May Robson, Frank McHugh, Dick Foran, Berton Churchill

'For its intelligent use of small town locations, its skilled acting, fine camerawork and evenly paced, sympathetic direction, it surpasses everything of its type.'—*John Baxter, 1968*

The Daughters of Joshua Cabe
US 1972 74m colour TVM
Spelling–Goldberg

A grizzled westerner finds that he will lose his property unless his three daughters to whom it is entailed come to live on it. He cannot reach them, so he recruits three more . . .
Rather boring open-air comedy drama, like a heavy-handed *Petticoat Junction*.

w Paul Savage *d* Philip Leacock

Buddy Ebsen, Sandra Dee, Karen Valentine, Lesley Warren, Jack Elam, Leif Erickson
† Sequels (qv): *The Daughters of Joshua Cabe Return, The New Daughters of Joshua Cabe.*

The Daughters of Joshua Cabe Return
US 1975 74m colour TVM
Spelling–Goldberg

One of the daughters is blackmailed by her own father.
Another attempt to turn a pilot into a series, with a new cast. No livelier than the first. (A third pilot appeared in 1976, and again failed: see *The New Daughters of Joshua Cabe.*)

w Kathleen Hite *d* David Lowell Rich

Dan Dailey, Christine Hart, Dub Taylor, Carl Betz, Ronne Troup, Brooke Adams, Kathleen Freeman

David and Bathsheba*
US 1952 116m Technicolor
TCF (Darryl F. Zanuck)

King David loves the wife of one of his captains, and ensures that the latter is killed in battle.
Deliberately sober bible-in-pictures, probably intended as a riposte to Cecil B. de Mille. Somewhat lacking in excitement, but you can't call it gaudy.

w Philip Dunne *d* Henry King *ph* Leon Shamroy *m* Alfred Newman

Gregory Peck, Susan Hayward, James Robertson Justice, Raymond Massey, Kieron Moore, Jayne Meadows, John Sutton, Dennis Hoey, Francis X. Bushman, George Zucco

David and Lisa*
US 1963 94m bw
Continental (Paul M. Heller)

Two disturbed adolescents at a special school fall in love.
Case history drama, earnest and well meaning rather than exciting.

w Eleanor Perry, book Theodore Isaac Rubin *d Frank Perry ph* Leonard Hirschfield *m* Mark Lawrence

Keir Dullea, Janet Margolin, Howard da Silva, Neva Patterson, Clifton James, Richard McMurray

David Copperfield****
US 1935 132m bw
MGM (David O. Selznick)

Disliked by his cruel stepfather and helped by his

eccentric aunt, orphan David grows up to become an author and eventually to marry his childhood sweetheart.
Only slightly faded after forty years, this small miracle of compression not only conveys the spirit of Dickens better than the screen has normally managed but is a particularly pleasing example of Hollywood's handling of literature and of the deployment of a great studio's resources. It also overflows with memorable character cameos, and it was a box office giant.

w Hugh Walpole, Howard Estabrook, *novel* Charles Dickens *d George Cukor* *ph* Oliver T. Marsh *m* Herbert Stothart *montages* Slavko Vorkapitch *ad Cedric Gibbons*

Freddie Bartholemew (young David), *Frank Lawton* (David as a man), *W. C. Fields* (Micawber), *Roland Young* (Uriah Heep), *Edna May Oliver* (Aunt Betsy), *Lennox Pawle* (Mr Dick), *Basil Rathbone* (Mr Murdstone), Violet Kemble Cooper (Miss Murdstone), Maureen O'Sullivan (Dora), Madge Evans (Agnes), Elizabeth Allan (Mrs Copperfield), *Jessie Ralph* (Peggotty), Lionel Barrymore (Dan Peggotty), Hugh Williams (Steerforth), Lewis Stone (Mr Wickfield), *Herbert Mundin* (Barkis), Elsa Lanchester (Clickett), Jean Cadell (Mrs Micawber), Una O'Connor (Mrs Gummidge), John Buckler (Ham), Hugh Walpole (the Vicar), Arthur Treacher (donkey man)

'Though half the characters are absent, the whole spectacle of the book, Micawber always excepted, is conveyed.'—*James Agee*

'The most profoundly satisfying screen manipulation of a great novel that the camera has ever given us.'—*André Sennwald*

David Copperfield*
GB/US 1969 118m Technicolor TVM
TCF / Omnibus Productions (Hugh Attwooll)

The story rearranged for a TV format, beginning and ending with David's self doubt on the Yarmouth sands.
Flatly directed and boringly written, this is a stultifying reduction of a great novel to meaningless narrative.

w Jack Pulman *d* Delbert Mann *ph* Ken Hodges *m* Malcolm Arnold

Alistair Mackenzie (young David), Robin Phillips (David as a man), *Ralph Richardson* (Micawber), Ron Moody (Uriah Heep), Edith Evans (Aunt Betsy), Emlyn Williams (Mr Dick), James Donald (Mr Murdstone), Anna Massey (Miss Murdstone), Pamela Franklin (Dora), Susan Hampshire (Agnes Wickfield), Isobel Black (Mrs Copperfield), Megs Jenkins (Peggotty), Michael Redgrave (Dan Peggotty), Corin Redgrave (Steerforth), Donald Layne-Smith (Mr Wickfield), Cyril Cusack (Barkis), Wendy Hiller (Mrs Micawber), *Laurence Olivier* (Mr Creakle), Richard Attenborough (Mr Tungay)

Davy*
GB 1957 84m Technirama
Ealing (Basil Dearden)

A member of a family music hall act auditions at Covent Garden.
Curiously unsuccessful vehicle for a popular singing comic; the script and continuity are simply poor, and swamped by the wide screen.

w William Rose *d* Michael Relph *ph* Douglas Slocombe *m* various classics

Harry Secombe, Ron Randell, George Relph, Alexander Knox, Susan Shaw, Bill Owen

Davy Crockett*
US 1955 93m Technicolor TVM
Walt Disney

Episodes in the career of the famous Tennessee hunter and Indian scout who died at the Alamo.
Disjointed and naive but somehow very fresh and appealing adventures; made for American television but elsewhere an enormous hit in cinemas.

w Tom Blackburn *d* Norman Foster *ph* Charles Boyle *m* George Bruns

Fess Parker, Buddy Ebsen, Basil Ruysdael, William Bakewell, Hans Conried, Kenneth Tobey, Nick Cravat
† 1956 sequel on similar lines: *Davy Crockett and the River Pirates.*

The Dawn Patrol**
US 1930 82m bw
Warner

In France during World War I, flying officers wait their turn to leave on missions which may mean death.
The second version (see below) is more watchable today, but this early talkie was highly effective in its time, and much of its aerial footage was re-used.

w John Monk Saunders, Dan Totheroh, Seton I. Miller *d Howard Hawks* *ph* Ernest Haller

Richard Barthelmess, Douglas Fairbanks Jnr, Neil Hamilton, William Hanney, *James Finlayson*, Clyde Cook, Edmund Breon, Frank McHugh

'Bare, cleancut, uncluttered technique, a stark story line, terse dialogue . . . and a pervasive atmosphere of hopelessness captured with economy and incisiveness.'—*Andrew Sarris, 1963*

The Dawn Patrol**
US 1938 103m bw
Warner (Hal B. Wallis)

A remarkably early but trim and competent remake of the 1930 film, using much of the same aerial footage.

w Seton I. Miller, Dan Totheroh *d Edmund Goulding ph* Tony Gaudio

Errol Flynn, Basil Rathbone, David Niven, Melville Cooper, Donald Crisp, Barry Fitzgerald, Carl Esmond

A Day at the Races****
US 1937 109m bw
MGM (Max Siegel)

The Marxes help a girl who owns a sanatorium and a racehorse.
Fashions in Marxism change, but this top quality production, though lacking their zaniest inspirations, does contain several of their funniest routines and a spectacularly well integrated racecourse climax. The musical and romantic asides are a matter of taste but delightfully typical of their time.

w Robert Pirosh, George Seaton, George Oppenheimer d Sam Wood ph Joseph Ruttenberg m Franz Waxman

Groucho, Chico, Harpo, Margaret Dumont, Maureen O'Sullivan, Allan Jones, *Douglass Dumbrille, Esther Muir, Sig Rumann*

A Day in the Death of Joe Egg**
GB 1971 106m Eastmancolor
Columbia / Domino (David Deutsch)

A teacher and his wife are frustrated by their own inability to cope with the problem of their spastic daughter.
A well-filmed version of a sincerely human play, with humour and fantasy sequences leavening the gloom.

w Peter Nichols, from his play *d Peter Medak ph* Ken Hodges *m* Elgar

Alan Bates, Janet Suzman, Peter Bowles, Sheila Gish, *Joan Hickson*

'It's unsatisfying, and it's not to be missed.'—*Stanley Kauffmann*

The Day of the Dolphin*
US 1973 104m Technicolor Panavision
Avco–Embassy / Icarus (Robert E. Relyea)

A marine biologist researching dolphins off the Florida coast discovers they are being used in a plot to blow up the President's yacht.
A strangely unexpected and unsuccessful offering from the talent involved: thin and repetitive as scientific instruction (the dolphins' language in any case topples it into fantasy), and oddly childlike as spy adventure.

w Buck Henry, *novel* Robert Merle *d* Mike Nichols *ph William A. Fraker m* Georges Delerue *pd* Richard Sylbert

George C. Scott, Trish Van Devere, Paul Sorvino, Fritz Weaver

'The whole thing seems to have been shoved through the cameras as glibly as possible, so that everyone concerned could grab the money and run.'—*Stanley Kauffmann*

The Day of the Evil Gun*
US 1968 93m Metrocolor Panavision
MGM (Jerry Thorpe)

Returning home after three years, a rancher finds that his wife and child have been carried off by Indians.
Competent standard western which resolves itself into a duel of wits between the hero and his rival.

w Charles Marquis Warren, Eric Bercovici *d* Jerry Thorpe *ph* W. Wallace Kelley *m* Jeff Alexander

Glenn Ford, Arthur Kennedy, Dean Jagger, Paul Fix, John Anderson, Nico Minardos

The Day of the Jackal**
GB / France 1973 142m Technicolor
Universal / Warwick / Universal France (John Woolf, David Deutsch)

British and French police combine to prevent an OAS assassination attempt on de Gaulle by use of a professional killer.
An incisive, observant and professional piece of work based on a rather clinical bestseller. Lack of a channel for sympathy, plus language confusions, are its main drawbacks.

w Kenneth Ross, *novel* Frederick Forsyth *d Fred Zinnemann ph Jean Tournier m* Georges Delerue

Edward Fox, Michel Lonsdale, Alan Badel, Eric Porter, Cyril Cusack, Delphine Seyrig, Donald Sinden, Tony Britton, Timothy West, Olga Georges-Picot, Barrie Ingham, Maurice Denham, Anton Rodgers

'Before *Jackal* is five minutes old, you know it's just going to be told professionally, with no flavour and no zest.'—*Stanley Kauffmann*

The Day of the Locust**
US 1975 143m Technicolor
Paramount / Long Road (Jerome Hellman, Sheldon Shrager)

In Hollywood in the 1930s, a novice art director

is bewildered by the eccentricities of life and an innocent man is martyred by the crowd.
A curious and interesting work from a savagely satirical novel; full of stimulating scenes and characters, it barely succeeds as a whole and was a disaster at the box office.

w Waldo Salt, *novel* Nathanael West *d John Schlesinger ph* Conrad Hall *m* John Barry *pd* Richard MacDonald

Donald Sutherland, William Atherton, Karen Black, Burgess Meredith, Geraldine Page, Richard A. Dysart, Bo Hopkins, Lelia Goldoni

The Day of the Outlaw**
US 1958 96m bw
US / Security Pictures (Sidney Harmon)

Two rival cattlemen forget their differences to fight six outlaws who ride into town.
Bleak and wintry western, well done and sufficiently unusual to stick in the mind.

w Philip Yordan, *novel* Lee Wells *d André de Toth ph Russell Harlan m* Alexander Courage

Robert Ryan, Burl Ives, Tina Louise, Nehemiah Persoff, David Nelson, Venetia Stevenson, Jack Lambert, Lance Fuller

'In the best William S. Hart tradition.'—*MFB*

The Day of the Triffids*
GB 1962 95m Eastmancolor Cinemascope
Philip Yordan

Almost everyone in the world is blinded by meteorites prior to being taken over by intelligent plants.
Rough and ready adaptation of a famous sci-fi novel, sometimes blunderingly effective and with moments of good trick work.

w Philip Yordan, *novel* John Wyndham *d* Steve Sekely *ph* Ted Moore *m* Ron Goodwin

Howard Keel, Nicole Maurey, Kieron Moore, Janette Scott, Alexander Knox

The Day the Earth Caught Fire**
GB 1961 99m bw with filters Dyaliscope
British Lion / Pax (Val Guest)

Nuclear tests knock the world off its axis and send it careering towards the sun.
A smart piece of science fiction told through the eyes of Fleet Street journalists and showing a sharp eye for the London scene. Rather exhaustingly talkative, but genuinely frightening at the time.

w Wolf Mankowitz, Val Guest d Val Guest ph Harry Waxman *m* Stanley Black

Edward Judd, Janet Munro, Leo McKern, *Arthur Christiansen* (ex-editor of the Daily Express), Michael Goodliffe, Bernard Braden, Reginald Beckwith, Austin Trevor, Renée Asherson, Edward Underdown

The Day the Earth Moved*
US 1974 74m colour TVM
ABC Circle

Aerial photographers track an incipient earthquake and try to persuade local townfolk to evacuate.
Fairly smart low-budget disaster movie.

w Jack Turley, Max Jack *d* Robert Michael Lewis

Jackie Cooper, Stella Stevens, Cleavon Little, William Windom, Beverly Garland

The Day the Earth Stood Still**
US 1951 92m bw
TCF (Julian Blaustein)

A flying saucer arrives in Washington and its alien occupant, aided by a robot, demonstrates his intellectual and physical power, warns the world what will happen if wars continue, and departs.
Cold-war wish-fulfilment fantasy, impressive rather than exciting but very capably put over with the minimum of trick work and the maximum of sober conviction.

w Edmund H. North *d Robert Wise ph Leo Tover m Bernard Herrmann*

Michael Rennie, Patricia Neal, Hugh Marlowe, Sam Jaffe, Billy Gray

The Day the Fish Came Out
GB / Greece 1967 109m De Luxe
TCF / Michael Cacoyannis

Atomic material contaminates a Mediterranean island.
Addle-pated, would-be satirical mod fantasy with establishment figures cast as world villains.

wd Michael Cacoyannis *ph* Walter Lassally *m* Mikis Theodorakis

Tom Çourtenay, Colin Blakely, Sam Wanamaker, Candice Bergen, Ian Ogilvy, Patricia Burke

The Day They Robbed the Bank of England*
GB 1960 85m bw
MGM / Summit (Jules Buck)

In 1901 Irish patriots plan a coup against the British government . . .
Small-scale, well-detailed period caper story, marred by a slow-starting script and unsympathetic acting.

w Howard Clewes, Richard Maibaum, *novel* John Brophy *d* John Guillermin *ph* Georges Périnal *m* Edwin Astley

Peter O'Toole, Aldo Ray, Elizabeth Sellars, Kieron Moore, Albert Sharpe, Hugh Griffith, John Le Mesurier, Joseph Tomelty, Miles Malleson, Colin Gordon

The Day Will Dawn*
GB 1942 98m bw
Paul Soskin
US title: *The Avengers*

Norwegian freedom fighters destroy a U-boat base and are saved by commandos.
Dated propaganda piece with an interesting cast.

w Terence Rattigan, Anatole de Grunwald, Patrick Kirwan *d* Harold French

Ralph Richardson, Deborah Kerr, Hugh Williams, Griffith Jones, Francis L. Sullivan, Roland Culver, Niall MacGinnis, Finlay Currie, Bernard Miles, Patricia Medina

Daybreak
GB 1946 81m bw
GFD / Triton (Sydney Box)

A barber and part-time hangman marries a destitute girl, loses her to a Swedish seaman, and kills himself in such a way as to implicate the other man.
Dockside melodrama of extraordinary pretentious gloominess; laughable in most respects. A curious follow-up from the *Seventh Veil* team.

w Muriel and Sydney Box, *play* Monckton Hoffe *d* Compton Bennett

Ann Todd, Eric Portman, Maxwell Reed, Edward Rigby, Bill Owen, Jane Hylton, Maurice Denham

Days of Glory
US 1944 86m bw
RKO (Casey Robinson)

Russian peasants fight the invading Nazis.
Lower-berth wartime propaganda piece chiefly notable for introducing Gregory Peck to the screen.

w Casey Robinson, *story* Melchior Lengyel *d* Jacques Tourneur *ph* Tony Gaudio *m* Daniele Amfitheatrof

Tamara Toumanova, Gregory Peck, Alan Reed, Maria Palmer, Lowell Gilmore, Hugo Haas

Days of Wine and Roses**
US 1962 117m bw
Warner (Martin Manulis)

A PR man becomes an alcoholic; his wife gradually reaches the same state, but he recovers and she does not.
Smart satirical comedy confusingly gives way to melodrama, then sentimentality; quality is evident throughout, but all concerned are happiest with the first hour.

w J. P. Miller *d* Blake Edwards *ph Philip Lathrop m Henry Mancini*

Jack Lemmon, Lee Remick, Charles Bickford, Jack Klugman, Alan Hewitt, Debbie Megowan, Jack Albertson

Dayton's Devils
US 1968 103m Eastmancolor
Madison / Harold Goldman (Robert W. Stabler)

A former USAF colonel assembles a group of misfits and adventurers to steal an army payroll.
Overlong, routine caper film with a surprisingly crisp climax (when it comes).

w Fred de Gorter *d* Jack Shea *ph* Brick Marquard *m* Martin Skiles

Leslie Nielsen, Rory Calhoun, Lainie Kazan, Hans Gudegast

D-Day the Sixth of June
US 1956 106m Eastmancolor Cinemascope
TCF (Charles Brackett)

On the way to invade France in 1944, a British colonel and an American captain reminisce about their love for the same woman.
Turgid war romance with some good action scenes and the usual hilarious Hollywood view of London. General effect very wooden.

w Ivan Moffat, Harry Brown, *novel* Lionel Shapiro *d* Henry Koster *ph* Lee Garmes *m* Lyn Murray

Robert Taylor, Richard Todd, Dana Wynter, Edmond O'Brien, John Williams, Jerry Paris, Richard Stapley

'Reminiscent of *Mrs Miniver* in style and feeling.'—*MFB*

De Sade*
US / Germany 1969 113m Movielab
AIP / CCC / Transcontinental (Louis M. Heyward, Artur Brauner)

The unbalanced Marquis de Sade is tormented by his wicked uncle with thoughts of his past.
Mildly interesting attempt by AIP at European debauchery, with a good theatrical framework for the fantasies but too much flailing about by all concerned, especially in the slow motion orgy sequences, which are relentlessly boring, as is the film.

w Richard Matheson *d* Cy Endfield *ph Heinz Pehlke ad Jurgen Kiebach m* Billy Strange

Keir Dullea, *John Huston*, Lilli Palmer, Senta Berger, Anna Massey, Uta Levka

The Dead Don't Die*
US 1975 74m colour TVM
Douglas S. Cramer

A man wrongly executed becomes a zombie and helps find the real murderer.
Interesting low-budget attempt to reproduce a thirties horror thriller such as *The Walking Dead*. Script not quite good enough.

w Robert Bloch *d* Curtis Harrington

George Hamilton, Ray Milland, Ralph Meeker, Linda Cristal, Joan Blondell, James McEachin

Dead End***
US 1937 92m bw
Samuel Goldwyn

A slice of life in New York's east side, where slum kids and gangsters live in a river street next to a luxury apartment block.
Highly theatrical film of a highly theatrical play, more or less preserving the single set and overcoming the limitations of the script and setting by sheer cinematic expertise. It is chiefly remembered, however, for introducing the Dead End Kids to a delighted world.

w Lillian Hellman, *play Sidney Kingsley d William Wyler ph Gregg Toland ad Richard Day m* Alfred Newman

Joel McCrea, Sylvia Sidney, *Humphrey Bogart*, Wendy Barrie, Claire Trevor, Allen Jenkins, *Marjorie Main*, James Burke, Ward Bond, *The Dead End Kinds* (Billy Halop, Leo Gorcey, Bernard Punsley, Huntz Hall, Bobby Jordan, Gabriel Dell)

The Dead End Kids
The films in which the original gang of young 'hooligans' (see above) appeared were as follows:

1937: DEAD END
1938: CRIME SCHOOL, ANGELS WITH DIRTY FACES
1939: THEY MADE ME A CRIMINAL, HELL'S KITCHEN, ANGELS WASH THEIR FACES
1940: THE DEAD END KIDS ON DRESS PARADE
Subsequently they broke up into the LITTLE TOUGH GUYS, the EAST SIDE KIDS, and the BOWERY BOYS (all qv)

Dead Heat on a Merry Go Round
US 1968 108m Technicolor
Columbia (Carter de Haven)

An ex-con breaks parole and plans to rob Los Angeles Airport.
Boringly arty caper comedy-melodrama, concentrating less on the robbery than on its hero's sexual prowess. All very superficially flashy, and what the title means is anybody's guess.

wd Bernard Girard *ph* Lionel Lindon
m Stu Phillips

James Coburn, Camilla Sparv, Aldo Ray, Nina Wayne, Robert Webber, Rose Marie, Todd Armstrong, Marian Moses, Severn Darden

'Just fills the space between a frisky title and a tricky TV-comedy ending, but doesn't fill it with any revels that require a viewer's complete attention.'—*Time*

Dead Man on the Run
US 1975 74m colour TVM
Bob Sweeney
aka: *New Orleans Force*

The head of an elite squad of federal investigators investigates his predecessor's murder.
Unnecessarily muddled and unrefreshing cop show.

w Ken Pettus *d* Bruce Bilson

Peter Graves, Pernell Roberts, Diana Douglas, Katherine Justice

Dead Men Tell No Tales*
US 1971 74m colour TVM
TCF (Walter Grauman)

A travelling photographer in Los Angeles is hunted by professional killers who have mistaken him for someone else.
Quite smartly-made chase mystery.

w Robert Dozier, *novel* Kelly Roos *d* Walter Grauman

Christopher George, Judy Carne, Patricia Barry, Richard Anderson

Dead of Night****
GB 1945 104m bw
Ealing (Michael Balcon)

An architect is caught up in an endless series of recurring dreams, during which he is told other people's supernatural experiences and finally murders the psychiatrist who is trying to help him.
Chillingly successful and influential compendium of the macabre, especially effective in its low-key handling of the linking sequence with its circular ending.

w John Baines, Angus Macphail, based on stories by themselves, H. G. Wells, E. F. Benson *d Cavalcanti, Charles Crichton, Robert Hamer, Basil Dearden* *ph* Douglas Slocombe, Stan Pavey *m Georges Auric* *ad Michael Relph*

Mervyn Johns, Roland Culver, Mary Merrall, Judy Kelly, Anthony Baird, *Sally Ann Howes, Frederick Valk, Googie Withers*, Ralph Michael, Esmé Percy, Basil Radford, Naunton Wayne, Miles Malleson, *Michael Redgrave*, Hartley Power, Elizabeth Welch

'In a nightmare within a nightmare are contained five separate ghost stories . . . they have atmosphere and polish, they are eerie, they are well acted.'—*Richard Winnington*

'One of the most successful blends of laughter, terror and outrage that I can remember.'—*James Agee*

'The five ghost stories accumulate in intensity until the trap closes in the surrealist climax.'—*Pauline Kael, 1968*

Dead or Alive
Italy / US 1967 89m Eastmancolor
Documento / Selmur (Albert Band)

A gunman with a paralysed right arm helps a state governor rid a town of bandits.
Semi-spaghetti western with a strong cast and violent action scenes.

w Ugo Liberatore, Louis Garfinkle *d* Franco Giraldi *ph* Aiace Parolin *m* Carlo Rustichelli

Robert Ryan, Arthur Kennedy, Alex Cord, Nicoletta Machiavelli

Dead Reckoning*
US 1947 100m bw
Columbia (Sidney Biddell)

Two war veterans are on their way to be decorated in Washington when one disappears.
Dour, complexly plotted thriller, a typical Hollywood *film noir* of the post-war years but a long way behind *Gilda* in likeability. The hero confesses the plot to a priest, and all the way it is more glum than fun.

w Oliver H. P. Garrett, Steve Fisher *d John Cromwell* *ph* Leo Tover *m* Morris Stoloff

Humphrey Bogart, Lizabeth Scott, *Morris Carnovsky*, Charles Cane, William Prince, Marvin Miller, Wallace Ford, James Bell

Dead Ringer*
US 1964 116m bw
Warner (William H. Wright)
GB title: *Dead Image*

A woman shoots her rich twin sister and assumes her identity.
High camp star vehicle, full of memories of long ago but rather drearily assembled and far too long, though Miss Davis as ever is in fighting form.

w Albert Beich, Oscar Millard *d* Paul Henreid *ph* Ernest Haller *m* André Previn

Bette Davis, Karl Malden, Peter Lawford, Philip Carey, Jean Hagen, Estelle Winwood, George Chandler, Cyril Delevanti

Deadfall
GB 1968 120m De Luxe
TCF / Salamanda (Paul Monash, Jack Rix)

Robbery turns sour when a cat burglar falls in love with the wife of his homosexual partner.
Drearily fashionable romantic melodrama with far too few high spots and generally dull performances.

w Bryan Forbes, *novel* Desmond Cory *d* Bryan Forbes *ph* Gerry Turpin *m* John Barry

Michael Caine, Eric Portman, Giovanna Ralli, Nanette Newman, David Buck

'Exhausted no doubt by their past passions and childhood traumas, the principal protagonists move like so many somnambulists through the turgid labyrinth . . . whatever the intention, *Deadfall* merely falls flat on its somewhat ludicrous face.'—*MFB*

Deadlier Than the Male
GB 1967 101m Techniscope
Rank / Sydney Box (Betty E. Box)

Bulldog Drummond traces the death of oil company executives to a master criminal using glamorous female assassins.
Just about tolerable recreation of Drummond in the modern world, with too little style, too much violence and sex, and an almost total lack of self-mockery. A sequel *Some Girls Do* (qv), was an unmitigated disaster.

w Jimmy Sangster, David Osborn, Liz Charles-Williams *d* Ralph Thomas *ph* Ernest Steward *m* Malcolm Lockyer *ad* Alex Vetchinsky

Richard Johnson, Nigel Green, Elke Sommer, Sylva Koscina, Suzanna Leigh, Zia Mohyeddin, Steve Carlson

'The original Drummond would have found the whole thing rather distasteful.'—*MFB*

Deadline at Dawn
US 1946 82m bw
RKO

A sailor on leave passes out, finds the girl he was with has been murdered, and is helped by a philosophical taxi driver and a girl.
This could have been another *Crossfire*, but is smothered by pretentious writing and uncertain direction. The credits are interesting, though.

w Clifford Odets *d* Harold Clurman
ph Nicholas Musuraca

Paul Lukas, Bill Williams, Susan Hayward, Osa Massen, Lola Lane

Deadline USA*
US 1952 87m bw
TCF (Sol C. Siegel)
GB title: *Deadline*

Despite threats and the killing of a witness, a crusading newspaper editor goes ahead with a story about the crimes of a powerful gangster.
Watchable newspaper melodrama with nothing much to say except that America must wake up to the enemy within. Smooth production, but too much semi-pretentious talk.

wd Richard Brooks *ph* Milton Krasner *m* Cyril Mockridge

Humphrey Bogart, Kim Hunter, Ethel Barrymore, Ed Begley, Paul Stewart, Warren Stevens, Martin Gabel, Joe de Santis, Audrey Christie, Jim Backus

Deadlock
US 1969 96m Technicolor TVM
Universal (William Sackheim)

The police chief and district attorney of a large city disagree violently over the best means of solving local murders and preventing mob action.
Sobersided, socially conscious pilot for a series that did not go.

w Chester Krumholtz, Robert E. Thompson, William Sackheim *d* Lamont Johnson

Leslie Nielsen, Hari Rhodes, Aldo Ray, Ruby Dee

The Deadly Affair**
GB 1966 106m Technicolor
Columbia / Sidney Lumet

A Foreign Office man apparently commits suicide; his colleague is unconvinced and finally uncovers a spy ring.
Compulsive if heavy-going thriller from the sour-about-spies era, deliberately glum, photographed against the shabbiest possible London backgrounds in muddy colour. Solidly entertaining for sophisticated grown-ups.

w Paul Dehn, novel Call for the Dead by John Le Carré *d Sidney Lumet* *ph* Frederick A. Young *m* Quincy Jones

James Mason, Simone Signoret, Harry Andrews, Maximilian Schell, Harriet Andersson, Kenneth Haigh, *Max Adrian*, Robert Flemyng, Roy Kinnear, Lynn Redgrave

The Deadly Companions*
US 1961 90m Pathecolor Panavision
Warner / Pathe America (Charles B. Fitzsimmons)

An army sergeant, a deserter, a trigger-happy gunman and a saloon hostess join forces to rob a bank.
Disjointed but rather attractive little western let down by corny moments in the script.

w A. S. Fleishman *d Sam Peckinpah*
ph William H. Clothier

Brian Keith, Maureen O'Hara, Chill Wills, Steve Cochran

The Deadly Dream*
US 1971 73m Technicolor TVM
Universal (Stan Shpetner)

A weird dream about a death sentence begins to turn into reality.
A sufficiently engaging suspenser with an unconvincing outcome.

w Barry Oringer *d* Alf Kjellin

Lloyd Bridges, Janet Leigh, Leif Erickson, Carl Betz, Don Stroud, Richard Jaeckel

Deadly Harvest*
US 1972 73m colour TVM
CBS / Anthony Wilson

An East European defector in California finds himself the target for an assassin's bullet.
Efficient suspenser.

w Anthony Wilson, *novel* Watcher in the Shadows by Geoffrey Household *d* Michael O'Herlihy

Richard Boone, Patty Duke, Michael Constantine, Murray Hamilton

The Deadly Hunt*
US 1971 74m colour TVM
Four Star

A young couple on a forest holiday become unwitting targets for paid killers, and a forest fire helps them escape.
Silly but watchable action suspenser.

w Eric Bercovici *d* John Newland

Tony Franciosa, Peter Lawford, Anjanette Comer, Jim Hutton

Deadly Strangers
GB 1974 93m Eastmancolor
Rank / Silhouette (Peter Miller)

A girl accepts a lift from a motorist at a time when a mad strangler is on the loose.
Sub-Hitchcock melo-thriller with enough red

herrings to sink a ship. Smartly enough done, but the grisliness needed balancing by humour.

w Philip Levene *d* Sidney Hayers *ph* Graham Edgar *m* Ron Goodwin

Hayley Mills, Simon Ward, Sterling Hayden, Ken Hutchison, Peter Jeffrey

The Deadly Tide
US 1975 98m colour TVM
Spelling–Goldberg

Jewel thieves vanish into thin air from a waterfront warehouse . . . they become scuba divers.
Fragmented adventures of the *SWAT* team originally shown in two parts.

w Ben Masselink *d* Gene Levitt

Steve Forrest, Christopher George, Lesley Warren, Sal Mineo, Don Stroud, Susan Dey, Phil Silvers

The Deadly Tower*
US 1975 100m colour TVM
MGM

The capture of the University of Texas sniper who in 1966 caused many casualties before being caught by a single policeman.
Good documentary-style re-creation of an awesome event.

w William Douglas Lansford *d* Jerry Jameson

Kurt Russell, Richard Yniguez, Ned Beatty, John Forsythe, Pernell Roberts

The Deadly Trackers
US 1973 104m Technicolor
Warner / Cine Film (Ed Rosen, Fouad Said)

A sheriff stalks the bandits who have killed his wife and son.
Lurid and ludicrous western started, and abandoned, by Samuel Fuller; the challenge need not have been taken up.

w Lukas Heller *d* Barry Shear *ph* Gabriel Torres *m* various

Rod Taylor, Richard Harris, Al Lettieri, Neville Brand, William Smith
'It is no more than the outline of a shadow.'—*Tony Rayns*

Dear Brigitte
US 1965 100m De Luxe Cinemascope
TCF / Fred Kohlmar

The small son of an American professor writes a love letter to Brigitte Bardot, and when they finally go to Paris she is charming to them.
Mild family comedy quaintly set around a decaying Mississippi riverboat home; despite assured performances, it all gets a bit icky at times.

w Hal Kanter, *novel* Erasmus with Freckles by John Haase *d* Henry Koster *ph* Lucien Ballard *m* George Duning

James Stewart, Glynis Johns, Fabian, Cindy Carol, Billy Mumy, John Williams, Jack Kruschen, Brigitte Bardot, Ed Wynn, Alice Pearce

Dear Heart*
US 1964 114m bw
Warner (Martin Manulis)

At a postmasters' convention in New York, two middle-aged delegates fall in love.
Charming, understated, overlong romantic drama in the *Marty* tradition; all quite professional and satisfying.

w Tad Mosel *d* Delbert Mann *ph* Russell Harlan *m* Henry Mancini

Glenn Ford, Geraldine Page, Angela Lansbury, Michael Anderson Jnr, Barbara Nichols, Patricia Barry, Charles Drake, Ruth McDevitt, Neva Patterson, Alice Pearce, Richard Deacon

Dear Mr Prohack
GB 1949 91m bw
GFD / Wessex (Ian Dalrymple, Dennis Van Thal)

A treasury official copes admirably with public money but is helpless when he comes into a private fortune.
Flat little comedy in which the minor amusements are incidental to the story.

w Ian Dalrymple, Donald Bull, *novel* Arnold Bennett *d* Thornton Freeland *ph* H. E. Fowle *m* Temple Abady

Cecil Parker, Hermione Baddeley, Dirk Bogarde, Sheila Sim, Glynis Johns, Heather Thatcher, Henry Edwards, Judith Furse

Dear Murderer
GB 1947 94m bw
GFD / Gainsborough (Betty E. Box)

Plot and counterplot among an adulterous triangle.
Thoroughly artificial pattern play set among the unreal rich, from one of those unaccountable West End successes, here boringly filmed.

w Muriel and Sydney Box, Peter Rogers, *play* St John L. Clowes *d* Arthur Crabtree *ph* Stephen Dade

Eric Portman, Greta Gynt, Dennis Price, Maxwell Reed, Jack Warner, Hazel Court, Andrew Crawford, Jane Hylton

Dear Octopus**
GB 1943 86m bw
GFD / Gainsborough (Edward Black)
US title: *The Randolph Family*

Members of a well-to-do British family reunite for Golden Wedding celebrations.
Traditional upper-class British comedy drama, and very well done too, with opportunities for excellent character acting.

w R. J. Minney, Patrick Kirwan, *play Dodie Smith* *d* Harold French

Margaret Lockwood, Michael Wilding, *Helen Haye, Frederick Leister, Celia Johnson, Roland Culver, Athene Seyler*, Basil Radford, Nora Swinburne, Jean Cadell, Kathleen Harrison, Ann Stephens, Muriel George, Antoinette Cellier, Graham Moffatt

Dear Ruth*
US 1947 95m bw
Paramount (Paul Jones)

A schoolgirl causes confusion when she writes love letters to a soldier using her elder sister's photograph.
Smoothly amusing family comedy from a Broadway success.

w Arthur Sheekman, *play* Norman Krasna
d William D. Russell *ph* Ernest Laszlo
m Robert Emmett Dolan

Joan Caulfield, William Holden, Mona Freeman, Billy de Wolfe, Edward Arnold, Mary Philips, Virginia Welles
† Two less amusing sequels were made using virtually the same cast: *Dear Wife* (1949, 88m, *d* Richard Haydn); *Dear Brat* (1951, 82m, *d* William A. Seiter).

Death Among Friends
US 1975 74m colour TVM
Warner / Douglas S. Kramer
aka: *Mrs R*

A lady cop solves a Beverly Hills murder
Talkative whodunnit.

w Stanley Ralph Ross *d* Paul Wendkos

Kate Reid, Martin Balsam, Jack Cassidy, Paul Henreid, Lynda Day George

Death at Broadcasting House*
GB 1934 71m bw
ABFD / Phoenix (Hugh Perceval)

A radio actor is murdered during a broadcast.
Intriguing little murder mystery with an unusual background.

w Basil Mason, *novel* Val Gielgud *d* Reginald Denham

Ian Hunter, Austin Trevor, Mary Newland, Henry Kendall, Val Gielgud, Peter Haddon, Betty Ann Davies, Jack Hawkins, Donald Wolfit

Death at Love House*
US 1976 74m colour TVM
Spelling–Goldberg (Hal Sitowitz)

A long-dead silent film star appears to haunt her Beverly Hills mansion.
Engaging supernatural nonsense with a most agreeable cast entering into the spirit of the thing.

w Jim Barnett *d* E. W. Swackhamer

Robert Wagner, Kate Jackson, Marianna Hill, Sylvia Sydney, Joan Blondell, Dorothy Lamour, John Carradine

Death Be Not Proud**
US 1975 100m colour TVM
Westfall Productions / Good Housekeeping (Donald Wrye)

An account of the death of journalist John Gunther's son from a brain tumour.
Extremely well-made and acted wallow in a real-life tragedy, for those who can take it.

wd Donald Wrye, *book* John Gunther

Arthur Hill, Jane Alexander, *Robby Benson*, Linden Chiles

Death Cruise
US 1974 74m colour TVM
Spelling–Goldberg

Holidaymakers on a luxurious cruise are systematically murdered.
Mildly engrossing murder mystery on the lines of *And Then There Were None*.

w Jack Sowards *d* Ralph Senensky

Edward Albert, Kate Jackson, Richard Long, Polly Bergen, Celeste Holm, Tom Bosley, Michael Constantine, Cesare Danova

Death of a Gunfighter*
US 1969 100m Technicolor
Universal (Richard E. Lyons)

An unpopular marshal refuses to resign, and the situation leads to gunplay.
Downcast character western set in the early years of the century.

w Joseph Calvelli *d* Robert Totten, Don Siegel
ph Andrew Jackson *m* Oliver Nelson

Richard Widmark, Lena Horne, John Saxon, Carroll O'Connor, Larry Gates, Kent Smith

Death of a Salesman***
US 1952 112m bw
Columbia (Stanley Kramer)

An ageing travelling salesman recognizes the emptiness of his life and commits suicide.
A very acceptable screen version of a milestone play which has become an American classic; stage conventions and tricks are cleverly adapted to cinematic use, especially when the hero walks from the present into the past and back again.

w Stanley Roberts, *play Arthur Miller d Laslo Benedek ph* Franz Planer *m* Morris Stoloff

Fredric March, Kevin McCarthy, Cameron Mitchell, Mildred Dunnock, Howard Smith, Royal Beal, Jesse White

'Its time shifts with light, which were poetic in the theatre, seemed shabby in a medium that can dissolve time and space so easily.'—*Stanley Kauffmann*

Death of a Scoundrel*
US 1956 119m bw
RKO / Charles Martin

A Czech in New York becomes rich by fraud.
Unconvincing but intermittently entertaining melodrama, a vehicle for a male Bette Davis.

wd Charles Martin *ph* James Wong Howe *m* Max Steiner

George Sanders, Yvonne de Carlo, Coleen Gray, Victor Jory, Zsa Zsa Gabor, Nancy Gates, John Hoyt, Tom Conway

'Vague moralizing and some attempts at social comment scarcely enliven this protracted study in megalomania.'—*MFB*

A Death of Innocence*
US 1971 74m colour TVM
Mark Carliner

A small town woman goes to New York for her daughter's murder trial.
Emotional character drama, well presented.

w Zelda Popkin, her novel, *d* Paul Wendkos

Shelley Winters, Arthur Kennedy, Tisha Sterling, Ann Sothern

The Death of Me Yet*
US 1971 74m colour TVM
Aaron Spelling

A Russian spy who has apparently defected to California turns out to have been a US agent all the time.
Confused but watchable suspense drama.

w A. J. Russell, *novel* Whit Masterson *d* John Llewellyn Moxey

Richard Basehart, Doug McClure, Darren McGavin, Rosemary Forsyth, Meg Foster

Death Race*
US 1973 74m Technicolor TVM
Universal (Harve Bennett)

In the Libyan desert during World War II, two grounded US pilots are relentlessly pursued by a German tank commander.
Fairly gripping war action suspenser.

w Charles Kuenstle *d* David Lowell Rich

Lloyd Bridges, Roy Thinnes, Eric Braeden, Doug McClure, Brendan Boone

Death Race 2000*
US 1975 79m colour
New World (Roger Corman)

In the year 2000, the world's most popular sport involves motor racers who compete for the highest total of human casualties.
Cheaply made macabre satire, quite well enough made to please addicts of the blackest of black comedy.

w Robert Thom, Charles Griffith, Ib Melchior *d* Paul Bartel *ph* Tak Fujimoto *m* Paul Chihara

David Carradine, Simone Griffeth, Sylvester Stallone, Mary Woronov

Death Scream*
US 1975 100m colour TVM
RSO (Ron Bernstein)

The case history of a woman who was fatally stabbed in view of neighbours who ignored her cries for help.
Dramatized documentary about an American malaise—the 'don't get involved' syndrome.

d Richard T. Heffron

Raul Julia, Cloris Leachman, John Ryan, Nancy Walker, Philip Clark, Lucie Arnaz, Art Carney, Diahann Carroll, Kate Jackson, Tina Louise

Death Sentence*
US 1974 74m colour TVM
Spelling–Goldberg

A woman juror who discovers the truth about a murder case is threatened by the real killer—her husband.
Good watchable suspenser.

w John Neufeld, *novel* After the Trial by Eric Roman
d E. W. Swackhamer

Cloris Leachman, Laurence Luckinbill, Nick Nolte, Alan Oppenheimer, William Schallert

Death Squad*
US 1973 74m colour TVM
Spelling–Goldberg

The police commissioner hires a tough ex-cop as

undercoverman to expose a renegade policeman. Good tough cop show.

w James David Buchanan, Ronald Austin *d* Harry Falk

Robert Forster, Melvyn Douglas, Michelle Phillips, Claude Akins

Death Stalk*
US 1974 80m colour TVM
David Wolper / Herman Rush (Richard Caffey)

Escaped convicts abduct the wives of two campers, and an overland chase ensues.

w Stephen Kandel, John W. Bloch d Robert Day

Vince Edwards, Anjanette Comer, Robert Webber, Carol Lynley

Death Takes a Holiday**
US 1934 78m bw
Paramount (E. Lloyd Sheldon)

In the form of a mysterious prince, Death visits an Italian noble family to see why men fear him so.
A somewhat pretentious classic from a popular play of the twenties; interesting handling and performances, but a slow pace by modern standards.

w Maxwell Anderson, Gladys Lehman, Walter Ferris based on plays by Maxwell Anderson and Alberto Casella *d Mitchell Leisen ph* Charles Lang *ad* Ernst Fegte

Fredric March, Evelyn Venable, Sir Guy Standing, Katherine Alexander, Gail Patrick, Helen Westley, Kathleen Howard, Henry Travers, Kent Taylor

Death Takes a Holiday
US 1971 73m Technicolor TVM
Universal (George Eckstein)

Curious, would-be fashionable, tricksily photographed and mainly flat-footed updating of the above.

w Rita Lakin *d* Robert Butler

Melvyn Douglas, Myrna Loy, Monte Markham, Yvette Mimieux, Maureen Reagan

Death Wish*
US 1974 94m Technicolor
Paramount / Dino de Laurentiis (Hal Landers, Bobby Roberts, Michael Winner)

When his wife dies and his daughter becomes a vegetable after an assault by muggers, a New York businessman takes the law into his own hands.
After a highly unpleasant and sensational opening, this curious and controversial film settles down into what amounts to black comedy, with the audience well on the vigilante's side. It's not very good, but it keeps one watching.

w Wendell Mayes, *novel* Brian Garfield *d* Michael Winner *ph* Arthur J. Ornitz *m* Herbie Hancock

Charles Bronson, Hope Lange, Vincent Gardenia, Stuart Margolin, Stephen Keats, William Redfield

Decameron Nights
GB 1952 94m Technicolor
Film Locations (M. J. Frankovich)

Young Boccaccio entertains a glamorous widow and her three guests with stories.
Feeble costume charade with all the cuckolding off-screen: insipid and artificial.

w George Oppenheimer *d* Hugo Fregonese *ph* Guy Green *m* Antony Hopkins

Louis Jourdan, Joan Fontaine, Binnie Barnes, Joan Collins, Godfrey Tearle, Eliot Makeham, Noel Purcell

'The sort of hybrid international production of which experience has made one mistrustful.'—*Gavin Lambert*

Deception**
US 1946 112m bw
Warner (Henry Blanke)

A European cellist returning to America after the war finds that his former girl friend has a rich and jealous lover.
Downcast melodrama made when its star was beginning to slide; today it seems irresistible bosh with a background of classical music, done with intermittent style especially by Claude Rains as the egomaniac lover.

w John Collier, *play* Monsieur Lamberthier by Louis Verneuil *d* Irving Rapper *ph* Ernest Haller *m* Erich Wolfgang Korngold

Bette Davis, *Claude Rains*, Paul Henreid, John Abbott, Benson Fong

'It's like grand opera, only the people are thinner . . . I wouldn't have missed it for the world.'—*Cecelia Ager*

Decision before Dawn*
US 1951 119m bw
TCF (Anatole Litvak, Frank McCarthy)

In 1944, anti-Nazi German POWs are parachuted into Germany to obtain information.
Meticulous, well made but unexciting spy story which seldom comes vividly to life.

w Peter Viertel, *novel* Call It Treason by George

Howe *d* Anatole Litvak *ph* Franz Planer *m* Franz Waxman

Oskar Werner, Richard Basehart, Gary Merrill, Hildegarde Neff, Dominique Blanchar, Helene Thimig, O. E. Hasse, Hans Christian Blech

The Decision of Christopher Blake
US 1948 75m bw
Warner (Ranald MacDougall)

A 12-year-old boy reunites his divorcing parents.
Sentimental slop, surprisingly ill done, but with a few good lines.

w Ranald MacDougall, *play* Moss Hart *d* Peter Godfrey *ph* Karl Freund *m* Max Steiner

Alexis Smith, Robert Douglas, *Cecil Kellaway*, Ted Donaldson, *Harry Davenport*, John Hoyt, Mary Wickes, Art Baker, Lois Maxwell

The Decks Ran Red
US 1958 84m bw
MGM / Andrew and Virginia Stone

Unscrupulous sailors plan to murder the entire crew of a freighter and claim the salvage money.
Solidly crafted but basically uninteresting melodrama.

w Andrew and Virginia Stone *d* Andrew Stone *ph* Meredith M. Nicholson

James Mason, Broderick Crawford, Dorothy Dandridge, Stuart Whitman

Decline and Fall
GB 1968 113m De Luxe
TCF / Ivan Foxwell

An innocent, accident-prone Oxford undergraduate is expelled and after various adventures in high and low society is convicted as a white slaver.
Flabby, doomed attempt to film a satirical classic which lives only on the printed page. Odd moments amuse.

w Ivan Foxwell, *novel* Evelyn Waugh *d* John Krish *ph* Desmond Dickinson *m* Ron Goodwin

Robin Phillips, Donald Wolfit, Genevieve Page, Robert Harris, Leo McKern, Colin Blakely, Felix Aylmer, Donald Sinden, Griffith Jones

The Deep Blue Sea*
GB 1955 99m Eastmancolor
Cinemascope
TCF / London Films (Anatole Litvak)

A judge's wife attempts suicide when jilted by her ex-RAF lover.
Undistinguished adaptation of a very good play, hampered by wide screen and muddy colour, helped by thoughtful performances.

w Terence Rattigan, from his play *d* Anatole Litvak *ph* Jack Hildyard *m* Malcolm Arnold

Vivien Leigh, Kenneth More, Eric Portman, *Emlyn Williams*, Moira Lister, Arthur Hill, Dandy Nichols, Jimmy Hanley, Miriam Karlin

Deep in My Heart*
US 1954 132m Eastmancolor
MGM (Roger Edens)

Sigmund Romberg, a composer-waiter in New York, is helped by writer Dorothy Donnelly and showman Florenz Ziegfeld to become a famous writer of musicals.
Standard fictionalized biopic with plenty of good turns and a sharper script than usual.

w Leonard Spiegelgass *d* Stanley Donen *ph* George Folsey *m* Sigmund Romberg *ad* Cedric Gibbons, Edward Carfagno *ch* Eugene Loring

Jose Ferrer, Merle Oberon, Paul Henreid (as Ziegfeld), Walter Pidgeon, Helen Traubel, Doe Avedon, Tamara Toumanova, Paul Stewart, Isobel Elsom, David Burns, Jim Backus . . . and Gene Kelly, Fred Kelly, Rosemary Clooney, Jane Powell, Ann Miller, Cyd Charisse, James Mitchell, Howard Keel, Tony Martin, Joan Weldon

The Deep Six
US 1958 110m Warnercolor
Jaguar (Martin Rackin)

A Quaker is unhappy at being drafted into the submarine service, but after initial unpopularity becomes a hero.
An ageing star contends with many hazards: slipshod production, poor colour, a dull script, and an unplayable part.

w John Twist, Martin Rackin, Harry Brown *d* Rudolph Maté *ph* John Seitz *m* David Buttolph

Alan Ladd, William Bendix, Efrem Zimbalist Jnr, Dianne Foster, Keenan Wynn, James Whitmore, Joey Bishop, Jeanette Nolan

Deep Valley
US 1947 104m bw
Warner (Henry Blanke)

The daughter of a poor California farmer falls for a convict on a work gang.
Downright peculiar melodrama, a cross between Tobacco Road and Cold Comfort Farm, with touches of High Sierra. For collectors.

w Salka Viertel, Stephen Morehouse Avery, *novel* Dan Totheroh *d* Jean Negulesco *ph* Ted McCord *m* Max Steiner

Ida Lupino, Dane Clark, Wayne Morris, Henry Hull, Fay Bainter, Willard Robertson

The Defiant Ones**

US 1958 96m bw
US / Stanley Kramer

A black and a white convict escape from a chain gang, still linked together but hating each other. Schematic melodrama with a moral, impeccably done and with good performances.

w Nathan E. Douglas, Harold Jacob Smith *d Stanley Kramer ph Sam Leavitt m* Ernest Gold

Tony Curtis, Sidney Poitier, Theodore Bikel, Charles McGraw, Lon Chaney Jnr, King Donovan, Claude Akins, Lawrence Dobkin, Whit Bissell, Carl 'Alfalfa' Switzer

'Probably Kramer's best picture. The subject matter is relatively simple, though 'powerful'; the action is exciting; the acting is good. But the singleness of purpose behind it all is a little offensive.'—*Pauline Kael*

Delancey Street: The Crisis Within

US 1975 74m colour TVM
Paramount (Emmet Lavery Jnr)

A dramatized account of a San Francisco hostel for people in trouble.
Glum do-goodery which dramatically just doesn't take off despite obvious earnestness all round.

w Robert Foster *d* James Frawley

Walter McGinn, Carmine Caridi, Lou Gossett, Michael Conrad, Mark Hamill

A Delicate Balance*

US 1975 134m colour
American Express / Ely Landau / Cinevision

A quarrelsome Connecticut family is dominated by an ageing matriarch, and tensions mount to a climax of fear and threats.
Honourable but slightly boring film version of an essentially theatrical play: the acting is the thing.

w Edward Albee, from his play *d* Tony Richardson *ph* David Watkin *m* none

Katharine Hepburn, Paul Scofield, Joseph Cotten, Lee Remick, Kate Reid, Betsy Blair

The Delicate Delinquent

US 1956 101m bw Vistavision
Paramount / Jerry Lewis

A New York policeman tries to make friends with an eccentric youth who mixes with thugs; the boy decides to train as a policeman.
Jerry Lewis' first film without Dean Martin: a sobering experience combining zany comedy, sentiment, pathos and social comment. The mixture fails to rise.

wd Don McGuire *ph* Haskell Boggs *m* Buddy Bregman

Jerry Lewis, Darren McGavin, Martha Hyer, Robert Ivers, Horace McMahon

Delicious

US 1931 106m bw
Fox

An Irish girl in New York falls for a rich man.
Early musical, very thin, but an agreeable museum piece for collectors.

w Guy Bolton, Sonya Levien *d* David Butler *ph* Ernest Palmer *songs George and Ira Gershwin*

Janet Gaynor, Charles Farrell, El Brendel, Lawrence O'Sullivan, Virginia Cherrill, Mischa Auer

Deliver Us from Evil*

US 1973 74m colour TVM
Warner / Playboy

Five men recover a fortune from a skyjacker and fight their own greed and each other.
Smartly made open-air fable with predictable outcome.

w Jack Sowards *d* Boris Sagal

George Kennedy, Jan-Michael Vincent, Bradford Dillman, Jack Weston, Charles Aidman

Deliverance***

US 1972 109m Technicolor Panavision
Warner / Elmer Enterprises (John Boorman),

Four men spend a holiday weekend canoeing down a dangerous river, but find that the real danger to their lives comes from themselves and other humans.
Vigorous, meaningful, almost apocalyptic vision of man's inhumanity, disguised as a thrilling adult adventure.

w James Dickey, from his novel *d John Boorman ph* Vilmos Zsigmond *m* Eric Weissberg

Burt Reynolds, Jon Voight, Ned Beatty, Ronny Cox, James Dickey

'There is fundamentally no view of the material, just a lot of painful grasping and groping.'—*Stanley Kauffmann*

Della

US 1964 66m colour TVM
Four Star

An attorney visits a small town to negotiate land purchase with a wealthy lady recluse.
Peyton Place-style pilot for a projected series called *Royal Bay*.

d Robert Gist

Joan Crawford, Diane Baker, Paul Burke, Charles Bickford, Richard Carlson

The Delphi Bureau
US 1972 99m colour TVM
Warner

An agency of gifted people with total recall is responsible only to the President.
Ingenuous spy capers with the usual high gloss and nonsense plot. This pilot led to a series of eight.

w Sam Rolfe *d* Paul Wendkos

Laurence Luckinbill, Joanna Pettet, Celeste Holm, Bob Crane, Cameron Mitchell, Bradford Dillman, Dean Jagger

Dementia 13*
US / Eire 1963 81m bw
Filmgroup / AIP (Roger Corman)
GB title: *The Haunted and the Hunted*

An axe murderer attacks members of a noble Irish family at their lonely castle.
Nastily effective macabre piece with interesting credits.

wd Francis Ford Coppola ph Charles Hannawalt *m* Ronald Stein

Luana Anders, William Campbell, Bart Patton, Mary Mitchell, Patrick Magee, Eithne Dunn

Demetrius and the Gladiators**
US 1954 101m Technicolor Cinemascope
TCF (Frank Ross)

A Greek slave who keeps Christ's robe after the crucifixion is sentenced to be one of Caligula's gladiators and becomes involved in Messalina's wiles.
Lively, efficient sequel to *The Robe*, with emphasis less on religiosity than on the brutality of the arena and our hero's sexual temptations and near-escapes. Good Hollywood hokum.

w Philip Dunne d Delmer Daves ph Milton Krasner *m* Franz Waxman

Victor Mature, Susan Hayward, Michael Rennie (as Peter), Debra Paget, Anne Bancroft, Jay Robinson, Barry Jones, William Marshall, Richard Egan, Ernest Borgnine

The Demi-Paradise**
GB 1943 114m bw
Two Cities (Anatole de Grunwald)
US title: *Adventure for Two*

In 1939, a Russian inventor is sent to observe the British way of life.
Pleasant, aimless little satirical comedy in which this blessed plot seems to be peopled entirely by eccentrics.

w Anatole de Grunwald *d* Anthony Asquith

Laurence Olivier, Penelope Dudley Ward, *Margaret Rutherford*, Leslie Henson, Marjorie Fielding, Felix Aylmer, Guy Middleton, Michael Shepley, George Thorpe, Edie Martin, Muriel Aked, Joyce Grenfell

'A backhanded way of showing us poor juvenile-minded cinemagoers that the England of Mr Punch and Mrs Malaprop lives forever.'—*Richard Winnington*

The Deputies
US 1976 98m colour TVM
Quinn Martin
aka: *Law of the Land*

Three young deputies and their elderly boss solve murders of local prostitutes.
Downbeat western detection, very dark, very slow and very boring. A failed pilot.

Jim Brown, Barbara Parkins

The Desert Fox**
US 1951 88m bw
TCF (Nunnally Johnson)
GB title: *Rommel, Desert Fox*

Rommel returns, disillusioned, to Hitler's Germany after his North African defeat, and is involved in the July plot.
Vivid but scrappy account of the last years of a contemporary hero. At the time it seemed to show a new immediacy in film-making, and was probably the first film to use an action sequence to arrest attention before the credit titles.

w Nunnally Johnson, book Rommel by Desmond Young *d Henry Hathaway ph Norbert Brodine*

James Mason, Jessica Tandy, Cedric Hardwicke, Luther Adler (as Hitler), Everett Sloane, *Leo G. Carroll, George Macready*, Richard Boone, Eduard Franz, Desmond Young

Desert Fury
US 1947 96m Technicolor
Paramount (Hal B. Wallis)

Against advice, a girl is attracted to a neurotic gambler who may have murdered his first wife.
Muddled melodrama slightly helped by Arizona

colour settings; unconvincing characters mouth unspeakable lines in an airless tedium.

w Robert Rossen *d* Lewis Allen *ph* Charles Lang, Edward Cronjager *m* Miklos Rozsa

Lizabeth Scott, Wendell Corey, Burt Lancaster, John Hodiak, Mary Astor, Kristine Miller

'The only fury I could sense was in my corner of the balcony.'—*C. A. Lejeune*

Desert Legion
US 1953 86m Technicolor
Universal (Ted Richmond)

A Foreign Legion captain rids a lost city of menacing bandits.
Schoolboy stuff, impudent in its silly story and its unconvincing Shangri-La, but quite entertaining for those prepared to let their hair down.

w Irving Wallace, Lewis Meltzer *d* Joseph Pevney *ph* John Seitz *m* Frank Skinner

Alan Ladd, Richard Conte, Arlene Dahl, Akim Tamiroff, Leon Askin

The Desert Rats*
US 1953 88m bw
TCF (Robert L. Jacks)

An English captain commands an Australian detachment in the siege of Tobruk, and survives an encounter with Rommel.
Actioner made to cash in on the success of *The Desert Fox* (qv). Stars and battle scenes survive a studio look.

w Richard Murphy *d* Robert Wise *ph* Lucien Ballard *m* Leigh Harline

James Mason (as Rommel), Richard Burton, Robert Newton, Robert Douglas, Torin Thatcher, Chips Rafferty

The Desert Song
US 1929 106m bw
Warner

A romantic and mysterious figure leads North African natives against evil Arabs.
Primitive sound version of the highly successful operetta.

w Harvey Gates, *play* Otto Harbach, Lawrence Schwab, Frank Mandel *d* Roy del Ruth *ph* Barney McGill *m Sigmund Romberg* *ly* Oscar Hammerstein II

John Boles, Carlotta King, Louise Fazenda, Johnny Arthur, Edward Martindel, Jack Pratt

The Desert Song
US 1943 96m Technicolor
Warner (Robert Florey)

Updated version with Nazis as the real villains.

adaptation Robert Buckner *d* Robert Florey *ph* Bert Glennon

Dennis Morgan, Irene Manning, Bruce Cabot, Lynne Overman, Gene Lockhart, Victor Francen, Faye Emerson, Curt Bois, Jack La Rue, Marcel Dalio, Nestor Paiva, Gerald Mohr

The Desert Song
US 1953 110m Technicolor
Warner (Rudi Fehr)

Well staged straight version of the musical, with full score.

adaptation Roland Kibbee *d* Bruce Humberstone *ph* Robert Burks *m adaptation* Max Steiner

Gordon Macrae, Kathryn Grayson, Steve Cochran, Raymond Massey, Dick Wesson, Allyn McLerie, Ray Collins, Paul Picerni, William Conrad

Design for Living**
US 1933 88m bw
Paramount (Ernst Lubitsch)

Two friends love and are loved by the same worldly woman, and they set up house together.
Elegant but miscast version of a scintillating play, with all the sex and the sting removed (at the insistence of the Legion of Decency, then coming into power). Ben Hecht claimed to have removed all but one line of Coward's dialogue.

w Ben Hecht, *play* Noel Coward *d Ernst Lubitsch* *ph* Victor Milner *m* Nathaniel Finston *ad* Hans Dreier

Gary Cooper, Fredric March, Miriam Hopkins, Edward Everett Horton, Franklin Pangborn, Isabel Jewell

Designing Woman*
US 1957 118m Metrocolor
Cinemascope
MGM (Dore Schary)

A sports reporter marries a dress designer and finds that their common interests are few.
Lumbering comedy which aims for sophistication but settles for farce: tolerable for star watchers who have dined well.

w George Wells *d* Vincente Minnelli *ph* John Alton *m* André Previn

Gregory Peck, Lauren Bacall, Dolores Gray, Sam Levene, Tom Helmore, Mickey Shaughnessey, Jesse White, Chuck Connors, Jack Cole

Desire**
US 1936 89m bw
Paramount (Ernst Lubitsch)

In Spain, an American car designer falls for a glamorous jewel thief.
Romantic comedy which the producer should have worked on longer: it begins brilliantly and keeps its style, but the pace and wit ebb away.

w Edwin Justus Mayer, Waldemar Young, Samuel Hoffenstein, from a German film Die schonen Tage von Aranjuez and a play by Hans Szekely and R. A. Stemmle *d Frank Borzage* *ph* Charles Lang, Victor Milner *m* Frederick Hollander *ad* Hans Dreier, Robert Usher

Marlene Dietrich, Gary Cooper, *John Halliday*, William Frawley, Ernest Cossart, Akim Tamiroff, Alan Mowbray, Zeffie Tilbury

'It sparkles and twinkles . . . one of the most engaging pictures of the season.'—*Frank S. Nugent, New York Times*

Desire in the Dust
US 1960 102m De Luxe Cinemascope
TCF / Associated Producers (William F. Claxton)

A wealthy southern aristocrat is involved in a fatal car crash and persuades a young farmhand to take the blame.
Derivative hothouse drama, a little better than its title, with a cast breathing heavily in imitation of refugees from Tennessee Williams or William Faulkner.

w Charles Lang, *novel* Harry Whittington *d* William F. Claxton *ph* Lucien Ballard *m* Paul Dunlap

Raymond Burr, Martha Hyer, Joan Bennett, Ken Scott, Brett Halsey, Anne Helm, Jack Ging, Edward Binns

Desire Me
US 1947 91m bw
MGM (Arthur Hornblow Jnr)

The wife of a Normandy villager hears that he has died in a concentration camp. She marries the bearer of the news, who turns out to be a psychotic who has left her husband for dead . . . but he is not.
Dreary drama, troubled during production and offering little for the actors to chew on.

w Marguerite Roberts, Zoe Akins, Casey Robinson, *novel* Leonhard Frank *d* not credited, but partly by George Cukor *ph* Joseph Ruttenberg *m* Herbert Stothart

Greer Garson, Robert Mitchum, Richard Hart, George Zucco, Morris Ankrum

'The supporting cast includes a number of characters who give the appearance of having come out of a dusty cupboard marked "French Types—Assorted".'—*MFB*

Desire under the Elms
US 1958 111m bw Vistavision
Paramount (Don Hartman)

A New England farmer brings home a young bride and causes friction with his son.
This bid for culture turns out like a hoary and very slow melodrama, not exactly risible but annoying because it teeters between several styles.

w Irwin Shaw, *play* Eugene O'Neill *d* Delbert Mann *ph* Daniel L. Fapp *m* Elmer Bernstein

Sophia Loren, Burl Ives, Anthony Perkins, Frank Overton, Pernell Roberts, Anne Seymour

'The film is consistently and unhappily out of its depth.'—*Penelope Houston*

Desirée
US 1954 110m De Luxe Cinemascope
TCF (Julian Blaustein)

Fictionalized biopic of one of Napoleon's mistresses.
Heavy-going costume piece, with all contributors distinctly uncomfortable.

w Daniel Taradash, *novel* Annemarie Selinko *d* Henry Koster *ph* Milton Krasner *m* Alex North

Jean Simmons, Marlon Brando, Merle Oberon, Michael Rennie, Cameron Mitchell, Elizabeth Sellars, Cathleen Nesbitt, Isobel Elsom

The Desk Set**
US 1957 103m Eastmancolor Cinemascope
TCF (Henry Ephron)
GB title: *His Other Woman*

Ladies in a broadcasting company's reference section are appalled when an electronics expert is sent to improve their performance.
Thin comedy, altered from a Broadway success; patchy as a whole, but with several splendid dialogue scenes for the principals.

w Phoebe and Henry Ephron, *play* William Marchant *d* Walter Lang *ph* Leon Shamroy *m* Cyril Mockridge

Spencer Tracy, Katharine Hepburn, Joan Blondell, Gig Young, Dina Merrill, Neva Patterson

The Desperados
US 1968 90m Technicolor
Columbia / Meadway (Irving Allen)

After the Civil War, a fanatic 'parson' leads a tribe of violent outlaws including his three sons.
Rough-and-tumble western in the modern savage manner; made in Spain.

w Walter Brough *d* Henry Levin *ph* Sam Leavitt *m* David Whitaker

Vince Edwards, Jack Palance, George Maharis, Neville Brand, Sylvia Syms, Christian Roberts, Kate O'Mara, Kenneth Cope, John Paul

Desperate Characters*
US 1971 88m colour
ITC (Frank D. Gilroy)

Residents of New York's east side find the rigours of life hard to take.
Curious but interesting suburban drama, a kind of deglamorized and updated *City for Conquest.*

wd Frank D. Gilroy, *novel* Paula Fox *ph* Urs Furrer

Shirley Maclaine, Gerald S. O'Loughlin, Kenneth Mars, Sada Thompson, Jack Somack

'The most blistering indictment of New York City since *Midnight Cowboy.*'—*Rex Reed*

'A film of authenticity, of delicately realized intangibles.'—*Stanley Kauffmann*

The Desperate Hours*
US 1955 112m bw Vistavision
Paramount (William Wyler)

Three escaped convicts take over a suburban house but are finally outwitted by the family.
Ponderous treatment of an over-familiar situation with only the acting and an 'A' picture look to save it.

w Joseph Hayes, from his novel and play *d* William Wyler *ph* Lee Garmes *m* Gail Kubik

Fredric March, Humphrey Bogart, Martha Scott, Arthur Kennedy, Gig Young, Dewey Martin, Mary Murphy, Robert Middleton, Richard Eyer

'A solid, deliberate and long-drawn-out exercise in the mechanics of suspense.'—*Penelope Houston*

Desperate Journey**
US 1942 109m bw
Warner (Hal B. Wallis)

Three POWs in Nazi Germany fight their way back to freedom.
When you pit Errol Flynn against the Nazis, there's no doubt who wins; and the last line is 'Now for Australia and a crack at those Japs!' Exhilarating adventure for the totally uncritical; professional standards high.

w Arthur Horman *d Raoul Walsh ph* Bert Glennon

Errol Flynn, Alan Hale, Ronald Reagan, Nancy Coleman, Raymond Massey, Arthur Kennedy, Ronald Sinclair, Albert Basserman, Sig Rumann, Ilka Gruning, Pat O'Moore

The Desperate Miles*
US 1975 74m Technicolor TVM
Universal / Joel Rogosin

To prove his independence, a disabled war veteran undertakes a 130-mile road trip by wheelchair.
Impressive or foolish according to one's point of view: well enough put together and acted.

w Joel Rogosin, Arthur Ross *d* Daniel Haller

Tony Musante, Joanna Pettet, Jeanette Nolan, Lynn Loring, John Larch

Desperate Mission
US 1971 98m colour TVM
TCF / Ricardo Montalban

Episodes in the career of Joaquin Murieta.
Moderate western fare fictionalized from the exploits of a real-life outlaw.

w Jack Guss *d* Earl Bellamy

Ricardo Montalban, Slim Pickens, Earl Holliman, Ina Balin, Rosie Greer

Destination Gobi*
US 1953 90m Technicolor
TCF (Stanley Rubin)

American soldiers get Mongol help against the Japanese in the Gobi desert.
A curious war adventure, a kind of camel opera, apparently based on fact; mildly enjoyable, though the outlandish is gradually replaced by the predictable.

w Everett Freeman *d* Robert Wise *ph* Charles G. Clarke *m* Sol Kaplan

Richard Widmark, Don Taylor, Casey Adams, Murvyn Vye, Darryl Hickman, Martin Milner, Ross Badgasarian, Rodolfo Acosta

Destination Moon*
US 1950 91m Technicolor
Universal / George Pal

An American inventor gets private backing to build a rocket so that the US can reach the moon before the Russians.
Semi-documentary prophecy with impressive gadgetry encased in a tedious and totally unsurprising script.

w Rip Van Ronkel, Robert Heinlan, James O'Hanlon *d* Irving Pichel *ph Lionel Lindon m* Leith Stevens

Warner Anderson, John Archer, Tom Powers, Dick Wesson

'Heavy-handed, unimaginative and very badly acted.'—*MFB*

Destination Tokyo*
US 1943 135m bw
Warner (Jerry Wald)

A US submarine is sent into Tokyo harbour.
Solid, well acted war suspenser, but overlong.

w Delmer Daves, Albert Maltz *d* Delmer Daves *ph* Bert Glennon *m* Franz Waxman

Cary Grant, John Garfield, Alan Hale, John Ridgely, Dane Clark, Warner Anderson, William Prince, Robert Hutton, Tom Tully, Peter Whitney, Faye Emerson, John Forsythe

'We don't say it is credible; we don't even suggest that it makes sense. But it does make a pippin of a picture from a purely melodramatic point of view.'—*Bosley Crowther*

Destiny*
US 1944 65m bw
Universal (Roy William Neill)

An escaped convict on the run finds refuge with a blind girl on a lonely farm.
Curious second feature, interesting because it began as a story eliminated from *Flesh and Fantasy* (qv); extra footage was added to bring it up to the required length. The original footage is mainly the nightmare suffered by the girl.

w Roy Chanslor (*F and F* Ernest Pascal)
d Reginald Le Borg (*F and F* Julien Duvivier)
ph George Robinson (*F and F* Paul Ivano)

Gloria Jean, Alan Curtis (who died in the original but here survives), Frank Craven, Grace McDonald

Destiny of a Spy
GB 1969 99m Technicolor TVM
Universal

Spies on opposite sides fall in love.
Competent, forgettable espionage stuff.

w Stanford Whitmore, *novel* John Blackburn *d* Boris Sagal

Lorne Greene, Harry Andrews, Anthony Quayle, Rachel Roberts, Patrick Magee, James Donald

Destroyer
US 1943 99m bw
Columbia (Louis F. Edelmann)

An old sea dog talks himself into a job on a World War II destroyer but works his men too hard.
Flat propaganda piece, not too well made.

w Frank Wead, Lewis Meltzer, Borden Chase
d William A. Seiter ph Franz Planer
m Anthony Collins

Edward G. Robinson, Glenn Ford, Marguerite Chapman, Edgar Buchanan, Leo Gorcey, Regis Toomey, Ed Brophy

Destry*
US 1954 95m Technicolor
U-I (Stanley Rubin)

Almost scene-for-scene remake of *Destry Rides Again* (qv). Well enough made and tolerably acted, but it doesn't have the sparkle, despite employing the same director.

w Edmund H. North, D. D. Beauchamp
d George Marshall *ph* George Robinson
m Joseph Gershenson

Audie Murphy, Mari Blanchard, Lyle Bettger, Thomas Mitchell, Edgar Buchanan, Wallace Ford, Lori Nelson, Alan Hale Jnr, Mary Wickes

'The impression is of a school revival of the original production.'—*MFB*

Destry Rides Again****
US 1939 94m bw
Universal (Joe Pasternak)

A mild-mannered sheriff finally gets mad at local corruption and straps on his guns.
Classic western which manages to encompass suspense, comedy, romance, tenderness, vivid characterization, horseplay, songs and standard western excitements, without moving for more than a moment from a studio main street set. It starts with a sign reading 'Welcome to Bottleneck' and an outburst of gunfire; it ends with tragedy followed by a running joke. Hollywood expertise at its very best.

w Felix Jackson, Gertrude Purcell, Henry Myers, novel Max Brand *d George Marshall ph Hal Mohr ly Frank Loesser m Frederick Hollander*

James Stewart, Marlene Dietrich, Brian Donlevy, Charles Winninger, Samuel S. Hinds, Mischa Auer, Irene Hervey, Jack Carson, *Una Merkel*, Allen Jenkins, Warren Hymer, *Billy Gilbert*

† An early sound version in 1932 starred Richard Dix; *Frenchie* (1950) was a slight variation. See also *Destry*.

The Detective**
US 1968 114m De Luxe Panavision
TCF / Arcola / Millfield (Aaron Rosenberg)

A New York police detective fights crime and corruption.
Determinedly sleazy and 'frank' cop stuff, quite arrestingly narrated and with something to say about police methods. Good violent entertainment, with just a shade too many homosexuals and nymphomaniacs for balance.

w Abby Mann, novel Roderick Thorp *d Gordon Douglas ph* Joseph Biroc *m* Jerry Goldsmith

Frank Sinatra, Lee Remick, Jacqueline Bisset, Ralph Meeker, Jack Klugman, Horace MacMahon, Lloyd Bochner, William Windom, Tony Musante, Al Freeman Jnr, Robert Duvall

'It vacillates uncertainly between murder mystery, political allegory, and a psychological study of the hero.'—*Jan Dawson*

Detective Story***
US 1951 103m bw
Paramount (William Wyler)

A day in a New York precinct police station, during which a detective of almost pathological righteousness discovers a stain on his family and himself becomes a victim of violence.
Clever, fluent transcription of a Broadway play with some of the pretensions of Greek tragedy; it could have been the negation of cinema, but professional handling makes it the essence of it.

w Philip Yordan, Robert Wyler, play Sidney Kingsley d William Wyler ph Lee Garmes

Kirk Douglas, Eleanor Parker, William Bendix, Cathy O'Donnell, George Macready, Horace MacMahon, Gladys George, *Joseph Wiseman, Lee Grant*, Gerald Mohr, Frank Faylen, Luis Van Rooten

Detour to Nowhere*
US 1971 98m Technicolor TVM
Universal (George Eckstein)
aka: *Banacek*

A wealthy Polish Bostonian collects lost and valuable property for insurance companies . . . at a ten per cent finder's fee.
Overlong but fairly ingenious pilot about a gold heist in the desert with no getaway tracks. It made a rather boring addition to *Mystery Movie* (qv).

w Anthony Wilson *d* Jack Smight

George Peppard, Christine Belford, Ed Nelson

The Devil and Miss Jones**
US 1941 97m bw
RKO / Frank Ross, Norman Krasna

A millionaire masquerades as a clerk in his own department store to investigate worker complaints.
Attractive comedy with elements of the crazy thirties and the more socially conscious forties.

w Norman Krasna d Sam Wood *ph* Harry Stradling

Jean Arthur, *Charles Coburn*, Robert Cummings, Spring Byington, S. Z. Sakall, William Demarest

The Devil and Miss Sarah*
US 1971 73m Technicolor TVM
Universal (Stan Shpetner)

A man captures an outlaw and brings him to justice, but the outlaw—who may be the devil—turr s the mind of the wife his way.
Oddball western semi-fantasy which drags more often than it sparkles.

w Calvin Clements *d* Michael Caffey

Gene Barry, James Drury, Janice Rule, Charles McGraw, Slim Pickens

Devil and the Deep*
US 1932 73m bw
Paramount

A submarine commander goes mad with jealousy of his faithless wife.
A turgid melodrama notable for its stars.

w Benn Levy *d* Marion Gering *ph* Charles Lang

Tallulah Bankhead, Charles Laughton, Gary Cooper, Cary Grant, Paul Porcasi

The Devil at Four o'Clock
US 1961 126m Eastmancolor
Columbia / Leroy / Kohlmar (Fred Kohlmar)

A drunken missionary and three convicts save a colony of leper children from a South Seas volcano.
Muddled adventure melodrama with a downbeat ending long delayed.

w Liam O'Brien, *novel* Max Catto *d* Mervyn Le Roy *ph* Joseph Biroc *m* George Duning

Spencer Tracy, Frank Sinatra, Kerwin Mathews, Jean-Pierre Aumont, Grégoire Aslan, Alexander Scourby, Barbara Luna

The Devil Commands*
US 1941 65m bw
Columbia

An electrical scientist tries to communicate with his dead wife through a medium.
Modestly effective horror thriller, though rather too deliberately paced.

w Robert D. Andrews, Milton Gunzberg, *story* The Edge of Running Water by William Sloane *d* Edward Dmytryk *ph* Allan G. Siegler

Boris Karloff, Richard Fiske, Amanda Duff, Anne Revere, Ralph Penney

Devil Dogs of the Air**
US 1935 86m bw
Warner (Lou Edelman)

Rivalry and romance in the Marine Flying Corps.

Standard, lively vehicle for Cagney and O'Brien, with excellent stunt flying sequences.

w Malcolm Stuart Boylan, Earl Baldwin, *novel* John Monk Saunders *d* Lloyd Bacon *ph* Arthur Edeson *m* Leo F. Forbstein

James Cagney, Pat O'Brien, Margaret Lindsay, Frank McHugh, Helen Lowell, John Arledge, Robert Barrat, Russell Hicks, Ward Bond

'A loud and roughneck screen comedy, both amusing and exciting.'—*André Sennwald*

The Devil Doll**
US 1936 79m bw
MGM

A refugee from Devil's Island disguises himself as an old lady who sells human dolls which murder those responsible for his imprisonment.
Interesting rather than exciting tall tale with a Paris backdrop; despite impressive moments it does not quite have the right *frisson*.

w Tod Browning, Garrett Fort, Erich Von Stroheim, Guy Endore, *novel* Burn Witch Burn by A. A. Merritt *d Tod Browning ph Leonard Smith m* Franz Waxman *ad* Cedric Gibbons

Lionel Barrymore, Maureen O'Sullivan, Frank Lawton, Henry B. Walthall, Rafaela Ottiano, Grace Ford, Arthur Hohl

The Devil Is a Sissy
US 1936 92m bw
MGM (Frank Davis)

The young son of divorcing parents gets into bad company.
Adequate juvenile melodrama

w John Lee Mahin, Richard Schayer, Roland Brown *d* W. S. Van Dyke *ph* Harold Rosson, George Schneidermann *m* Herbert Stothart

Freddie Bartholomew, Jackie Cooper, Mickey Rooney, Ian Hunter, Peggy Conklin, Katherine Alexander, Gene Lockhart, Dorothy Peterson

The Devil Is a Woman*
US 1935 82m bw
Paramount

In Seville in th 1890s a *femme fatale* has several admirers.
The last Dietrich vehicle to be directed by Von Sternberg, and rather splendid in its highly decorative and uncommercial way; a treat for addicts.

w John Dos Passos, S. K. Winston, *novel* La Femme et le Pantin by Pierre Louÿs *d Josef Von Sternberg ph Josef Von Sternberg, Lucien Ballard ad Hans Dreier*

Marlene Dietrich, Lionel Atwill, Cesar Romero, Edward Everett Horton, Alison Skipworth, Don Alvarado, Morgan Wallace, Tempe Pigott

'One of the most sophisticated films ever produced in America.'—*André Sennwald, New York Times*

'Light and shadow are splashed liberally around over the white-painted sets; cafés, tobacco factories, stairs and balconies are decorated with every conceivable device and camera-level.'—*Peter John Dyer, 1964*

The Devil Makes Three
US 1952 90m bw
MGM (Richard Goldstone)

An American intelligence officer in post-war Germany becomes involved with neo-Nazis.
A curious break from dancing for Gene Kelly, this obscurely titled thriller has little to commend it but authentic locations.

w Jerry Davis, *story* Lawrence Bachmann *d* Andrew Marton *ph* Vaclav Vich *m* Rudolph G. Kopp

Gene Kelly, Pier Angeli, Richard Rober, Richard Egan, Claus Clausen

The Devil Rides Out*
GB 1967 95m Technicolor
Hammer (Anthony Nelson Keys)
US title: *The Devil's Bride*

The Duc de Richleau rescues a friend from a group of Satanists.
Rather stodgy adaptation of a frightening novel; moments of suspense.

w Richard Matheson, *novel* Dennis Wheatley *d* Terence Fisher *ph* Arthur Grant *m* James Bernard

Christopher Lee, *Charles Gray*, Leon Greene, Patrick Mower, Gwen Frangcon Davies

A Devil with Women
US 1930 76m bw
Fox (George Middleton)

Soldiers of fortune in a banana republic end the regime of a notorious bandit and compete for a fair señorita.
Primitive Flagg-and-Quirt knockabout.

w Dudley Nichols, Henry M. Johnson, *novel* Dust and Sun by Clements Ripley *d* Irving Cummings *ph* Arthur Todd *m* Peter Brunelli

Victor McLaglen, Humphrey Bogart, Mona Maris, Michael Vavitch

The Devils*
GB 1970 111m Technicolor
Panavision
Warner / Russo (Robert H. Solo, Ken Russell)

An account of the apparent demoniacal possession of the 17th-century nuns of Loudun, climaxing in the burning of their priest as a sorcerer.
Despite undeniable technical proficiency this is its writer-director's most outrageously sick film to date, campy, idiosyncratic and in howling bad taste from beginning to end, full of worm-eaten skulls, masturbating nuns, gibbering courtiers, plague sores, rats and a burning to death before our very eyes . . . plus a sacreligious dream of Jesus. A pointless pantomime for misogynists.

wd Ken Russell, *play* John Whiting, *book* The Devils of Loudun by Aldous Huxley *ph David Watkin* *m* Peter Maxwell Davies *ad* Robert Cartwright

Vanessa Redgrave, Oliver Reed, Dudley Sutton, Max Adrian, Gemma Jones, Murray Melvin, Michael Gothard, Graham Armitage

'Ken Russell doesn't report hysteria, he markets it.'—*New Yorker, 1976*

'Russell's swirling multi-colored puddle . . . made me glad that both Huxley and Whiting are dead, so that they are spared this farrago of witless exhibitionism.'—*Stanley Kauffmann*

The Devil's Brigade
US 1968 132m De Luxe Panavision
UA / David L. Wolper

For combat in Norway and Italy during World War II a US officer assembles a platoon of thugs and misfits to work with crack Canadian commandos.
Flagrant but routine imitation of *The Dirty Dozen*, quite undistinguished.

w William Roberts *d* Andrew V. McLaglen *ph* William Clothier *m* Alex North

William Holden, Cliff Robertson, Vince Edwards, Andrew Prine, Claude Akins, Carroll O'Connor, Richard Jaeckel

Devil's Canyon
US 1953 92m Technicolor 3-D
RKO / Edmund Grainger

Life in a notorious Arizona prison in the eighties; a marshal is unjustly convicted but wins his pardon.
Fair, brutal western, quite unmemorable.

w Frederick Hazlitt Brennan *d* Alfred Werker *ph* Nicholas Musuraca *m* Daniele Amfitheatrof

Dale Robertson, Virginia Mayo, Stephen McNally, Arthur Hunnicutt, Robert Keith, Jay C. Flippen, Whit Bissell

The Devil's Daughter*
US 1972 74m colour TVM
Paramount (Edward J. Mikis)

When a girl turns 21, she finds that her dead mother had sold her soul to the devil.
Moderately creepy black magic mumbo jumbo sparked by its star performance.

w Colin Higgins *d* Jeannot Szwarc

Shelley Winters, Robert Foxworth, Belinda Montgomery, Joseph Cotten, Jonathan Frid, Martha Scott, Diane Ladd

The Devil's Disciple*
GB 1959 82m bw
UA / Hecht–Hill–Lancaster / Brynaprod (Harold Hecht)

In 1777 an American ne'er-do-well almost allows himself to be hanged by the British in mistake for a rebel pastor.
Star-studded but indifferently staged adaptation of a minor Shavian frolic. Patchy, with good moments.

w John Dighton, Roland Kibbee, *play* Bernard Shaw *d* Guy Hamilton *ph* Jack Hildyard *m* Richard Rodney Bennett *ad* Terence Verity, Edward Carere

Burt Lancaster, Kirk Douglas, *Laurence Olivier* (as General Burgoyne), Eva Le Gallienne, Janette Scott, Harry Andrews, Basil Sidney, George Rose, Neil McCallum, David Horne, Mervyn Johns

Devil's Doorway
US 1950 84m bw
MGM (Nicholas Nayfack)

A Shoshone Indian fights valiantly in the Civil War but on his return to Wyoming finds himself hated and threatened by his former colleagues.
Dull pro-Indian western with a most unsuitable star.

w Guy Trosper *d* Anthony Mann *ph* John Alton *m* Daniele Amfitheatrof

Robert Taylor, Louis Calhern, Paula Raymond, Marshall Thompson, James Mitchell, Edgar Buchanan, Rhys Williams, Spring Byington

The Devil's Hairpin
US 1957 83m Technicolor Vistavision
Paramount / Cornel Wilde

A former motor racing champion makes a comeback, and redeems his past boorish behaviour.
Efficient routine melodramatics with good action sequences.

w James Edmiston, Cornel Wilde *d* Cornel Wilde *ph* Daniel Fapp *m* Van Cleave, Cornel Wilde

Cornel Wilde, Jean Wallace, Arthur Franz, *Mary Astor*, Paul Fix

The Devil's Rain
US 1975 86m colour Todd-AO 35
Sandy Howard

Witchcraft in the modern west causes victims to melt; the son of one of them takes arms against the leading Satanist.
Interestingly cast example of the low-budget seventies exploitation picture, with more nastiness than logic.

w Gabe Essoe, James Ashton, Gerald Hopman *d* Robert Fuest *ph* Alex Phillips Jnr *m* Al de Lory

Ernest Borgnine, Ida Lupino, Eddie Albert, William Shatner, Keenan Wynn, Tom Skerritt

Devotion**
US 1944 107m bw
Warner (Robert Buckner)

A highly romanticized account of the lives of the Brontë sisters and their brother Branwell.
An enjoyably bad example of a big-budget Hollywood production which tampers with things it cannot understand, in this case life in a Yorkshire parsonage in Victorian times. An excuse is found to give the curate an Austrian accent to fit the available actor, but this and other *faux pas* are atoned for by the vividness of Emily's recurrent dream of death as a silhouetted man on horseback. In general, an interesting period piece in more senses than one.

w Keith Winter *d Curtis Bernhardt ph Ernest Haller* *m* Erich Wolfgang Korngold

Ida Lupino (Emily), Olivia de Havilland (Charlotte), Nancy Coleman (Anne), Arthur Kennedy (Branwell), Montagu Love (Revd Brontë), Paul Henreid (Revd Nicholls), Ethel Griffies (Aunt Branwell), Sidney Greenstreet (Thackeray), Eily Malyon, Forrester Harvey, Victor Francen

'I found it painless. It never got nearer to the subject than names and consequently didn't hurt. But I would like to know who was devoted to whom and why.'—*Richard Winnington*

The DI
US 1957 106m bw
Warner / Mark VII (Jack Webb)

A tough marine drill instructor takes a special interest in a backward member of his platoon.
Noisy recruiting poster heroics in which the producer gives himself a loud but boring part. The drill sequences are well done, but the film is overlong and repetitive.

w James Lee Barrett *d* Jack Webb *ph* Edward Colman *m* David Buttolph

Jack Webb, Don Dubbins, Jackie Loughery, Lin McCarthy, Monica Lewis

Diagnosis: Murder
GB 1974 90m Eastmancolor
Silhouette (Patrick Dromgoole, Peter Miller)

A psychiatrist's wife disappears, and the police suspect her husband.
Well-upholstered but sadly old-fashioned domestic crime thriller; one is vaguely surprised to see it in colour, having seen it so often in black-and-white.

w Philip Levene *d* Sidney Hayers *ph* Bob Edwards *m* Laurie Johnson

Jon Finch, Judy Geeson, Christopher Lee, Tony Beckley, Dilys Hamlett, Jane Merrow, Colin Jeavons

Dial Hot Line
US 1970 98m Technicolor TVM
Universal (William Sackheim)

A psychiatric social worker starts a clinic for those in desperate mental straits.
Ho-hum do-gooder which sparked a very short series.

w Carol Sobieski *d* Jerry Thorpe

Vince Edwards, Chelsea Brown, Kim Hunter, June Harding

Dial M For Murder**
US 1954 105m Warnercolor 3-D
Warner (Alfred Hitchcock)

An ageing tennis champion tries to arrange the death of his wife so that he will inherit, but his complex plan goes wrong.
Hitchcock did not try very hard to adapt this highly commercial play for the cinema, nor did he exploit the possibilities of 3-D. But for a one-room film with a not very exciting cast the film holds its grip pretty well.

w Frederick Knott, from his play *d Alfred Hitchcock* *ph* Robert Burks *m* Dmitri Tiomkin

Ray Milland, John Williams, Grace Kelly, Robert Cummings, Anthony Dawson

'All this is related with Hitchcock's ghoulish chic but everyone in it seems to be walking around with tired blood.'—*Pauline Kael, 1968*

Dial 1119*
US 1950 75m bw
MGM (Richard Goldstone)
GB title: *The Violent Hour*

An assortment of people are held up in a bar by a maniac.
Suspenseful thriller when it sticks to its central

theme; dullish when it tries characterization. A good second feature.

w John Monks Jnr *d Gerald Mayer ph* Paul Vogel *m* André Previn

Marshall Thompson, Virginia Field, Andrea King, Leon Ames, Keefe Brasselle, Richard Rober, James Bell, William Conrad

Diamond City
GB 1949 90m bw
GFD / Gainsborough (A. Frank Bundy)

Law and order is maintained during the working of a South African diamond field.
British imitation of a Wyatt Earp western; very milk-and-water.

w Roger Bray, Roland Pertwee *d* David MacDonald *ph* Reginald Wyer *m* Clifton Parker

David Farrar, Honor Blackman, Diana Dors, Niall MacGinnis, Andrew Crawford, Mervyn Johns, Bill Owen, Phyllis Monkman

Diamond Head
US 1962 107m Eastmancolor Panavision
Columbia (Jerry Bresler)

A domineering Hawaiian landowner almost ruins the lives of his family.
Predictable, heavy-going transcription of a bestseller.

w Marguerite Roberts, *novel* Peter Gilman *d* Guy Green *ph* Sam Leavitt *m* Johnny Williams

Charlton Heston, Yvette Mimieux, George Chakiris, France Nuyen, James Darren, Aline MacMahon, Eliizabeeeth Allen, Richard Loo

Diamond Horseshoe
US 1945 104m Technicolor
TCF (William Perlberg)

A nightclub singer gives up her career for a medical student.
Lavish but humourless star vehicle with standard numbers.

wd George Seaton, *play* The Barker by Kenyon Nicholson *ph* Ernest Palmer *songs* Mack Gordon, Harry Warren

Betty Grable, Dick Haymes, *William Gaxton*, Phil Silvers, Beatrice Kay, Carmen Cavallero, Margaret Dumont

Diamond Jim*
US 1935 93m bw
Universal (Edmund Grainger)

A fantasia on the life of the nineties millionaire who sailed pretty close to the wind in business, adored Lillian Russell, and developed a gargantuan appetite.
Cheerful period comedy drama with plenty of gusto.

w Preston Sturges *d* A. Edward Sutherland *ph* George Robinson *m* Ferde Grofe, Franz Waxman

Edward Arnold, Jean Arthur, Binnie Barnes, Cesar Romero, Eric Blore

Diamonds
US 1975 108m Eastmancolor
Avco Embassy / AmeriEuro (Menahem Golan)

A London diamond merchant sets himself up to be robbed so that he can blackmail the culprits into a raid on the Tel Aviv diamond repository.
Cheerful but unremarkable caper movie with an upbeat ending.

w David Paulsen, Menahem Golan *d* Menahem Golan *ph* Adam Greenberg *m* Roy Budd

Robert Shaw, Richard Roundtree, Barbara Seagull, Shelley Winters

Diamonds Are Forever*
GB1971 120m Technicolor Panavision
UA / Eon / Danjaq (Harry Saltzman, Albert R. Broccoli)

Seeking a diamond smuggler, James Bond has adventures in Amsterdam, a Los Angeles crematorium, various Las Vegas gambling parlours, and a secret installation in the desert.
Campy, rather vicious addition to a well-worn cycle, with an element of nastiness which big-budget stunts cannot conceal. Panavision does not help, and Connery's return to the role for a final throw is disappointing.

w Richard Maibaum, Tom Mankiewicz, *novel* Ian Fleming *d* Guy Hamilton *ph* Ted Moore *m* John Barry *pd* Ken Adam

Sean Connery, Jill St John, Charles Gray, Lana Wood, Jimmy Dean, Bruce Cabot, Bernard Lee, Lois Maxwell

Diamonds for Breakfast
GB 1968 102m Eastmancolor
Paramount / Bridge Films (Carlo Ponti, Pierre Rouve)

An impoverished Russian aristocrat decides to retrieve from a museum the crown jewels of his ancestors, and seduces seven female accomplices.
Yawning caper yarn embellished with sex and slapstick.

w N. F. Simpson, Pierre Rouve, Ronald Harwood *d* Christopher Morahan *ph* Gerry Turpin *m* Norman Kay

Marcello Mastroianni, Rita Tushingham, Elaine Taylor, Warren Mitchell, Nora Nicholson, Bill Fraser, Leonard Rossiter

Diane

US 1956 110m Eastmancolor Cinemascope

MGM (Edwin H. Knopf)

Diane de Poitier becomes a consultant to the king and falls in love with his son.

Solidly boring slice of Hollywood history, with all concerned out of their depth.

w Christopher Isherwood *d* David Miller *ph* Robert Planck

Lana Turner, Roger Moore, Cedric Hardwicke, Pedro Armendariz, Marisa Pavan

The Diary of a Chambermaid*

US 1946 86m bw

Benedict Bogeaus (Burgess Meredith, Paulette Goddard)

A 19th-century serving girl causes sexual frustration and other troubles in two households.

Hollywood notables were all at sea in this wholly artificial and unpersuasive adaptation of a minor classic.

w Burgess Meredith, *novel* Octave Mirabeau *d Jean Renoir* *ph* Lucien Andriot *pd* Eugene Lourié

Paulette Goddard, Burgess Meredith, Hurd Hatfield, Francis Lederer, Judith Anderson, Florence Bates, Irene Ryan, Reginald Owen, Almira Sessions

Diary of a Mad Housewife**

US 1970 95m Technicolor

Universal / Frank Perry

The bored and repressed wife of a lawyer tries an affair, walks out on her husband, and opts for group therapy.

An agreeably mordant view of the contemporary American scene, with good dialogue and performances, but the little bits of satire do not really add up to a satisfactory film.

w Eleanor Perry, novel Sue Kaufman *d Frank Perry* *ph* Gerald Hirschfeld

Carrie Snodgress, Richard Benjamin, Frank Langella, Lorraine Cullen, Frannie Michel

'A prototypical contemporary American artifact . . . all its assorted talents and technological smartness are turned to the varnishing of mediocrity.'—*Stanley Kauffmann*

The Diary of a Madman

US 1962 96m Technicolor

UA / Admiral (Robert E. Kent)

A murderer explains to a magistrate that he was possessed by an evil spirit.

Ponderous transcription of a Maupassant story with a few moments of horror.

w Robert E. Kent *d* Reginald Le Borg *ph* Ellis W. Carter *m* Richard La Salle

Vincent Price, Nancy Kovack, Chris Warfield, Stephen Roberts

The Diary of Anne Frank**

US 1959 170m bw Cinemascope

TCF / George Stevens

In 1942, a family of Dutch Jews hides in an attic from the Nazis; just before the war ends they are found and sent to concentration camps.

Based on the famous diaries of a girl who died at Auschwitz, this solemn adaptation is elephantine in its length, its ponderousness and its use of Cinemascope when the atmosphere is supposed to be claustrophobic.

w Frances Goodrich, Albert Hackett, from their play based on Anne Frank's diaries *d* George Stevens *ph William C. Mellor* *m* Alfred Newman

Millie Perkins, *Joseph Schildkraut, Shelley Winters, Ed Wynn*, Richard Beymer, Gusti Huber, Lou Jacobi, Diane Baker

Dick Tracy

US 1945 61m bw

RKO (Herman Schlom)

The jut-jawed detective routs a disfigured criminal named Splitface.

Vigorous second feature from the comic strip.

w Eric Taylor, *strip* Chester Gould *d* William Berke *ph* Frank Redman *m* Roy Webb

Morgan Conway, Jane Greer, Mike Mazurki, Anne Jeffreys, Lyle Latell, Joseph Crehan, Trevor Bardette

† Sequels: *Dick Tracy vs Cueball* (1946) with Morgan Conway, *d* John Rawlins; *Dick Tracy Meets Gruesome* (1947) with Ralph Byrd, Boris Karloff, *d* John Rawlins; *Dick Tracy's Dilemma* (1947), with Ralph Byrd, *d* John Rawlins. There had been several Republic serials featuring Tracy, and in the fifties a cartoon series appeared.

Did You Hear the One about the Travelling Saleslady?

US 1967 96m Techniscope

Universal (Si Rose)

In a Kansas town in 1910 an eccentric saleslady offers pianolas which tend to go berserk.
Cornbelt comedy vehicle for an unappealing star.

w John Fenton Murray *d* Don Weis *ph* Bud Thackery *m* Vic Mizzy

Phyllis Diller, Bob Denver, Joe Flynn, Jeanette Nolan

Dillinger*
US 1945 70m bw
Monogram

The life of American public enemy number one who was shot by the police in 1934.
Slick, speedy gangster thriller, possibly the most tolerable movie to come from this low-budget studio.

w Philip Yordan *d Max Nosseck ph* Jackson Rose

Lawrence Tierney, Edmund Lowe, Anne Jeffreys

Dillinger*
US 1973 107m Movielab
AIP (Buzz Feitshans)

Violence-soaked version, with black comedy touches, of the last year of Dillinger's life. Not badly done, with a style reminiscent of *Bonnie and Clyde.*

wd John Milius ph Jules Brenner *m* Barry Devorzon

Warren Oates, Ben Johnson (as Melvin Purvis), Michelle Philips, Cloris Leachman, Harry Dean Stanton, Richard Dreyfuss

Dimples**
US 1936 82m bw
TCF (Darryl F. Zanuck, Nunnally Johnson)

In the New York Bowery in pre-Civil War days, a child and her reprobate grandfather win the hearts of high society.
Excellent Temple vehicle with good period flavour.

w Arthur Sheekman, Nat Perrin *d* William A. Seiter *ph* Bert Glennon *m* Louis Silvers

Shirley Temple, Frank Morgan, Helen Westley, Berton Churchill, Robert Kent, Delma Byron, Astrid Allwyn

Dinner at Eight***
US 1933 113m bw
MGM

Guests at a society dinner party all find themselves in dramatic circumstances.
Artificial but compelling pattern play from a Broadway success.

w Frances Marion, Herman J. Mankiewicz, *play* George S. Kaufman, Edna Ferber *d George Cukor ph* William Daniels

Marie Dressler, John Barrymore, Lionel Barrymore, Billie Burke, Wallace Beery, *Jean Harlow*, Lee Tracy, Edmund Lowe, Madge Evans, Jean Hersholt, Karen Morley, Louise Closser Hale, Phillips Holmes, May Robson, Grant Mitchell, Elizabeth Patterson

Dinner at the Ritz*
GB 1937 77m bw
New World (Robert T. Kane)

A French girl exposes swindlers who faked her father's suicide.
Diverting comedy melodrama with an international cast.

w Roland Pertwee, Romney Brent *d* Harold Schuster

Annabella, Paul Lukas, David Niven, Romney Brent, Stewart Rome, Francis L. Sullivan, Nora Swinburne, Frederick Leister

The Dion Brothers
US 1974 96m colour TVM
Tomorrow (Roger Gimbel)
GB theatrical title: *The Gravy Train*

Two coal miners seek a quick fortune in the city as armed robbers.
Adequate modern gangster stuff.

w Bill Kerby, David Whitney (Terrence Malick) *d* Jack Starrett *m* Fred Karlin

Stacy Keach, Frederic Forrest, Margot Kidder, Barry Primus

Diplomatic Courier*
US 1952 98m bw
TCF (Casey Robinson)

American and Russian agents clash on a train between Salzburg and Trieste; an unexpected master spy is revealed after several chases.
Lively cold war intrigue, well produced and played with relish.

w Casey Robinson, Liam O'Brien, *novel* Sinister Errand by Peter Cheyney *d* Henry Hathaway *ph* Lucien Ballard *m* Lionel Newman

Tyrone Power, Patricia Neal, Stephen McNally, Hildegarde Neff, Karl Malden, James Millican, Herbert Berghof

'A reversion to the oldest tradition of spy fiction.'—*Penelope Houston*

Dirigible*
US 1931 102m bw
Columbia

The story of an airship disaster.
Economical epic with a few Capra touches.

w Jo Swerling, Dorothy Howell, *story* 'Spig' Wead *d* Frank Capra *ph* Joe Wilbur, Elmer Dyer

Jack Holt, Fay Wray, Ralph Graves, Hobart Bosworth, Roscoe Karns

Dirty Dingus Magee
US 1970 91m Metrocolor Panavision
MGM (Burt Kennedy)

A likeable western outlaw crosses swords with an old enemy.
Fair burlesque western often stooping to vulgarity.

w Tom Waldman, Frank Waldman, Joseph Heller, *novel* David Markson *d* Burt Kennedy *ph* Harry Stradling *m* Jeff Alexander

Frank Sinatra, George Kennedy, Anne Jackson, Lois Nettleton, Jack Elam, John Dehner, Henry Jones, Harry Carey Jnr, Paul Fix

'Skittish burlesque, scripted in the brash and undisciplined style of a TV show . . . heavily reliant on the *Carry On* brand of humour.'—*David McGillivray*

The Dirty Dozen**
US/Spain 1967 150m Metrocolor 70mm
MGM / Kenneth Hyman (Raymond Anzarut)

In 1944, twelve convicts serving life sentences are recruited for a commando suicide mission.
Professional, commercial but unlikeable slice of wartime thick ear; pretensions about capital punishment are jettisoned early on in favour of frequent and violent bloodshed. Much imitated, e.g. by *The Devil's Brigade, A Reason to Live, a Reason to Die*, etc.

w Nunnally Johnson, Lukas Heller *d Robert Aldrich ph* Edward Scaife *m* Frank de Vol

Lee Marvin, Ernest Borgnine, Robert Ryan, Charles Bronson, Jim Brown, John Cassavetes, George Kennedy, Richard Jaeckel, Trini Lopez, Telly Savalas, Ralph Meeker, Clint Walker, Robert Webber, Donald Sutherland

Dirty Harry**
US 1971 103m Technicolor Panavision
Warner / Malpaso (Don Siegel)

A violently inclined San Francisco police inspector is the only cop who can bring to book a mad sniper. When the man is released through lack of evidence, he takes private revenge.
A savage cop show which became a cult and led to a spate of dirty cop movies, including two sequels, *Magnum Force*.and *The Enforcer*. Well done for those who can take it.

w Harry Julian Fink, Rita M. Fink, Dean Riesner *d Don Siegel ph* Bruce Surtees *m* Lalo Schifrin

Clint Eastwood, Harry Guardino, Reni Santoni, John Vernon, Andy Robinson, John Larch, John Mitchum

Dirty Little Billy
US 1972 92m Eastmancolor
Columbia / WRG / Dragoti (Jack L. Warner)

The violent young life of Billy the Kid.
Squalid little western with few attractive aspects except that it presents its hero as the mentally retarded delinquent which history says he was.

w Charles Moss, Stan Dragoti *d* Stan Dragoti *ph* Ralph Woolsey *m* Sascha Burland

Michael J. Pollard, Lee Purcell, Richard Evans, Charles Aidman

'The gap between its ostensible aims and its manner of realizing them continually leaves the film bogged down in its own scrupulously realistic mud.'—*Tony Rayns*

Dirty Mary, Crazy Larry
US 1974 92m De Luxe
Academy Pictures Corporation (Norman T. Herman)

Two racing drivers and a kooky groupie rob a supermarket and almost elude their police pursuers.
Elaborately stunted chase film, agreeable enough to watch if the characters were not so disagreeable.

w Leigh Chapman, Antonio Santean, *novel* The Chase by Richard Unekis *d* John Hough *ph* Mike Margulies *m* Jimmie Haskell

Peter Fonda, Susan George, Adam Roarke, Vic Morrow, Kenneth Tobey, Roddy McDowall, Eugene Daniels

The Disappearance of Flight 412
US 1974 74m colour TVM
Cinemobile

Two air force jets disappear while chasing a UFO.
Milk-and-water science fiction which adds up to very little.

w George Simpson, Neal Burger *d* Jud Taylor

Glenn Ford, Bradford Dillman, Guy Stockwell, David Soul, Robert F. Lyons, Kent Smith

Dishonored**
US 1931 91m bw
Paramount

An officer's widow turned streetwalker is hired by the German government as a spy.
Rather gloomy melodrama which helped to establish its star as a top American attraction; but the heavy hand of her Svengali, Von Sternberg, was already evident.

w Daniel H. Rubin *d Josef Von Sternberg ph Lee Garmes m* Karl Hajos

Marlene Dietrich, Victor McLaglen, Lew Cody, Gustav Von Seyffertitz, Warner Oland, Barry Norton, Wilfred Lucas

'The most exciting movie I have seen in several months . . . yet I hope I may die young if I ever again have to listen to a manuscript so full of recusant, stilted, outmoded theatrical mouthings.'—*Pare Lorentz*

'The whole film has a kind of magnificent grandeur embellished, of course, by its shining central performance.'—*John Gillett, 1964*

Dishonored Lady
US 1947 85m bw
Mars Film (Hedy Lamarr)

A girl with a past is cleared of a murder charge by her psychiatrist.
Melodramatic showpiece designed for herself by a glamorous star; OK for the silly season.

w Edmund H. North, *play* Edward Sheldon, Margaret Ayer Barnes *d* Robert Stevenson *ph* Lucien Andriot

Hedy Lamarr, John Loder, Dennis O'Keefe, Paul Cavanagh, William Lundigan, Natalie Schaefer, Morris Carnovsky

A Dispatch from Reuters**
US 1940 90m bw
Warner (Hal B. Wallis)
GB title: *This Man Reuter*

The story of the man who provided Europe's first news service.
Acceptable if slightly dull addition to Warner's prestige biopics; well made and acted.

w Milton Krims *d William Dieterle ph James Wong Howe*

Edward G. Robinson, Edna Best, Eddie Albert, Albert Basserman, Gene Lockhart, Otto Kruger, Montagu Love, Nigel Bruce, James Stephenson

Disputed Passage*
US 1939 90m bw
Paramount (Harlan Thompson)

A young scientist who wants to marry meets resistance from his mentor.
Adequate screen version of a bestseller.

w Anthony Veiller, Sheridan Gibney, *novel* Lloyd C. Douglas *d* Frank Borzage *ph* William C. Mellor *m* Frederick Hollander, James Leopold

Dorothy Lamour, John Howard, Akim Tamiroff, Judith Barrett, William Collier Snr, Victor Varconi, Keye Luke, Elizabeth Risdon

Disraeli*
US 1929 89m bw
Warner

Fictionalized episodes in the life of the Victorian statesman, including his activities as a matchmaker.
Very early star talkie, of primarily archival interest; Arliss had appeared in a silent version in 1921.

w Julian Josephson, *play* Louis N. Parker *d* Alfred E. Green *ph* Lee Garmes

George Arliss, Joan Bennett, Florence Arliss, Anthony Bushell, David Torrence, Ivan Simpson, Doris Lloyd

Distant Drums
US 1951 101m Technicolor
United States Pictures (Milton Sperling)

In 1840 Florida, an army officer rescues prisoners from an Indian fort and decimates the Seminoles who threaten their return journey.
Overlong action saga, with dull stretches compensated by a dominating star and some lively incident.

w Niven Busch, Martin Rackin *d* Raoul Walsh *ph* Sid Hickox *m* Max Steiner

Gary Cooper, Mari Aldon, Richard Webb, Ray Teal, Arthur Hunnicutt, Robert Barrat

A Distant Trumpet
US 1964 116m Technicolor Panavision
Warner (William H. Wright)

The new commander of a cavalry outpost tightens up discipline, which serves him well when Indian trouble erupts.
Moderate western, quite well staged but with a second team cast.

w John Twist, *novel* Paul Horgan *d* Raoul Walsh *ph* William Clothier *m* Max Steiner

Troy Donahue, Suzanne Pleshette, James Gregory, Diane McBain, William Reynolds, Claude Akins, Kent Smith, Judson Pratt

Dive Bomber*
US 1941 133m Technicolor
Warner (Hal B. Wallis)

Aviation scientists work to eliminate pilot blackout.
Somewhat rarefied propaganda piece with too

many reels of romantic banter but tense climactic scenes and good star performances.

w Frank 'Spig' Wead, Robert Buckner *d* Michael Curtiz *ph* Bert Glennon, Winton C. Hoch *m* Leo F. Forbstein

Errol Flynn, Fred MacMurray, Ralph Bellamy, Alexis Smith, Regis Toomey, Robert Armstrong, Allen Jenkins, Craig Stevens, Moroni Olsen, Gig Young, William Hopper, Charles Drake, Russell Hicks, Addison Richards, Ann Doran, Herbert Anderson

The Divided Heart**
GB 1954 89m bw
Ealing (Michael Truman)

A boy believed to be a war orphan is lovingly brought up by foster parents; then his real mother turns up and wants him back.
Effective 'woman's picture' set in Europe and giving a genuine sense of post-war feelings and problems.

w Jack Whittingham d Charles Crichton ph Otto Heller *m* Georges Auric

Cornell Borchers, Yvonne Mitchell, Armin Dahlen, Alexander Knox, Geoffrey Keen, Michel Ray, Liam Redmond, Eddie Byrne

Divorce American Style**
US 1967 109m Technicolor
Columbia / Tandem (Norman Lear)

Well-heeled Los Angeles suburbanites toy with divorce but eventually resume their domestic bickering.
Rather arid and patchy but often sharply sardonic comedy about a society in which people can't afford to divorce.

w Norman Lear d Bud Yorkin *ph* Conrad Hall *m David Grusin pd* Edward Stephenson

Dick Van Dyke, Debbie Reynolds, Jean Simmons, Jason Robards Jnr, Van Johnson, Joe Flynn, Shelley Berman, Martin Gabel, Lee Grant, Tom Bosley, Dick Gautier

Divorce His, Divorce Hers
GB 1972 74m × 2 colour TVM
Harlech TV / John Heyman

Two films showing aspects of a divorce, one from the wife's viewpoint and one from the husband's.
Abysmally dull regurgitation of their own lives by the world's most boring showbiz couple.

w John Hopkins *d* Waris Hussein *m* Stanley Myers

Richard Burton, Elizabeth Taylor

The Divorce of Lady X**
GB 1937 92m Technicolor
London Films (Alexander Korda)

A nobleman's daughter wins a barrister by posing as a divorce client.
Pleasing comedy with high production standards of its time, deftly performed by a distinguished cast.

w Lajos Biro, Arthur Wimperis, Ian Dalrymple, *play* Counsel's Opinion by Gilbert Wakefield *d Tim Whelan*

Laurence Olivier, Merle Oberon, Binnie Barnes, Ralph Richardson, Morton Selten, J. H. Roberts

The Divorcee*
US 1930 83m bw
MGM

A woman's past affects her future.
Dated but sociologically interesting drama about attitudes to divorce.

w John Meehan, Nick Grinde, Zelda Sears, *novel* Ex-Wife by Ursula Parrott *d* Robert Z. Leonard *ph* Norbert Brodine *ad* Cedric Gibbons

Norma Shearer, Chester Morris, Conrad Nagel, Robert Montgomery, Florence Eldridge

Dixie*
US 1943 90m Technicolor
Paramount (Paul Jones)

The life of old-time minstrel man Dan Emmett.
Lighter-than-air fictionalized biography with pleasing mid-19th-century settings.

w Karl Tunberg, Darrell Ware *d* A. Edward Sutherland *ph* William C. Mellor *songs* Johnny Burke, Jimmy Van Heusen

Bing Crosby, Dorothy Lamour, Marjorie Reynolds, *Lynne Overman, Eddie Foy Jnr, Billy de Wolfe, Raymond Walburn*, Grant Mitchell

DOA**
US 1949 81m bw
Cardinal Pictures (Leo C. Popkin)

A businessman discovers that he has effectively been murdered by a slow-acting poison. In the few hours left to him he tracks down and kills his murderer, and confesses to the police.
Unusual and effective thriller, well photographed on location in San Francisco and Los Angeles.

w Russel Rouse, Clarence Greene d Rudolph Maté ph Ernest Laszlo m Dmitri Tiomkin

Edmond O'Brien, Luther Adler, Pamela Britton, William Ching
† Remade 1970 as *Colour Me Dead*, with Tom Tryon.

Do Not Disturb
US 1965 102m De Luxe Cinemascope
TCF / Melcher / Arcola (Aaron Rosenberg, Martin Melcher)

An American wool executive is posted to London; his dizzy wife makes him jealous by flirting with a French antique dealer.
Silly farce which paints a lunatic picture of English and French life but occasionally raises a wild laugh or two. Thin script and production.

w Milt Rosen, Richard Breen, *play* William Fairchild *d* Ralph Levy *ph* Leon Shamroy *m* Lionel Newman

Doris Day, Rod Taylor, *Sergio Fantoni*, Reginald Gardiner, Hermione Baddeley, Leon Askin

Do Not Fold, Spindle or Mutilate**
US 1971 73m colour TVM
Aaron Spelling (Robert L. Jacks)

Four old biddies answer a computer dating service as one fictitious glamorous girl, but one of the applicants is a homicidal maniac.
Lively four-star comedy-thriller.

w John D. F. Black, *novel* Doris Miles Disney *d* Ted Post

Myrna Loy, Helen Hayes, Sylvia Sidney, Mildred Natwick, Vince Edwards

Do You Love Me?
US 1946 91m Technicolor
TCF (George Jessel)

The lady dean of a music school gets herself glamorized.
Thin, mildly agreeable but forgettable musical.

w Robert Ellis, Helen Logan *d* Gregory Ratoff *ph* Edward Cronjager *songs* various

Maureen O'Hara, Dick Haymes, Harry James and his Orchestra, Reginald Gardiner, Richard Gaines, Stanley Prager

Do You Take This Stranger?
US 1970 95m Technicolor TVM
Universal / Roy Huggins

In order to inherit a million dollars, a desperate man must engineer a switch of identities.
Complex puzzle melodrama, good fun for addicts.

w Matthew Howard *d* Richard Heffron

Gene Barry, Lloyd Bridges, Diane Baker, Joseph Cotten, Sidney Blackmer, Susan Oliver

Doc**
US 1971 96m De Luxe
UA / Frank Perry

Doc Holliday goes to Tombstone to die of TB, but is drawn into the feud between the Clantons and his friend Wyatt Earp, whose motives are not of the highest.
A somewhat glum debunking of the west's most heroic myth, backing dour character study with grubby pictures. The result lacks excitement but maintains interest.

w Pete Hamill *d* Frank Perry *ph Gerald Hirschfeld* *m* Jimmy Webb

Stacy Keach (Doc), Harris Yulin (Earp), Faye Dunaway (Kate Elder), Mike Witney, Denver John Collins, Dan Greenberg

'The physical realism that *Doc* is at pains to establish becomes simply a convention of its own.'—*Richard Combs*

Doc Savage, Man of Bronze
US 1975 100m Technicolor
Warner (George Pal)

A thirties superman and his assistants the Amazing Five fly to South America to avenge the death of Doc's father.
Stolid, humourless adaptation from a comic strip, totally lacking in the necessary panache.

w George Pal, Joe Morhaim, *stories* Kenneth Robeson *d* Michael Anderson *ph* Fred Koenekamp *m* John Philip Sousa

Ron Ely, Paul Gleason, Bill Lucking, Michael Miller, Eldon Quick

'A slick, ultra-self-conscious camp that denies the material its self-respect.'—*Colin Pahlow*

'Nothing in this unfortunate enterprise is likely to please anyone: former Savage fans will be enraged, newcomers bored, and children will probably feel superior to the whole mess . . .' —*New Yorker*

The Dock Brief
GB 1962 88m bw
(MGM) Dimitri de Grunwald
US title: *Trial and Error*

An incompetent barrister defends his client on a murder charge. The client is found guilty but the sentence is quashed on the grounds of inadequate defence.
Flat filming of a TV play which was a minor milestone; the film is twice the length and half as funny, and both stars quickly become tiresome.

w John Mortimer, Pierre Rouve, *play* John Mortimer *d* James Hill *ph* Ted Scaife *m* Ron Grainer

Peter Sellers, Richard Attenborough

Dr Christian
Following the success of THE COUNTRY DOCTOR (qv), a rival studio (RKO) made a

series of second features about a fictional country doctor, the rights to Dr Dafoe's life story being unavailable. Jean Hersholt again played the leading role and the films were immensely popular in small towns. A TV series followed in the fifties, starring Macdonald Carey.

1939: MEET DR CHRISTIAN
1940: THE COURAGEOUS DR CHRISTIAN, DR CHRISTIAN MEETS THE WOMEN, REMEDY FOR RICHES
1941: MELODY FOR THREE, THEY MEET AGAIN

Dr Cook's Garden*
US 1970 74m colour TVM
Paramount (Bob Markell)

A small-town doctor nurtures the healthy and weeds out the sick.
Macabre comedy melodrama which tries hard but does not quite come off.

w Arthur Wallace, *play* Ira Levin *d* Ted Post

Bing Crosby, Frank Converse, Bethel Leslie, Blythe Danner

Dr Crippen*
GB 1962 98m bw
ABP / John Clein

A quiet doctor murders his wife and elopes with a typist.
Straightforward account of a famous and rather unsurprising Edwardian murder case; well enough made but with no special *raison d'être.*

w Leigh Vance *d* Robert Lynn *ph* Nicolas Roeg

Donald Pleasance, Coral Browne, Samantha Eggar, Donald Wolfit

Dr Cyclops*
US 1940 76m Technicolor
Paramount (Menan C. Cooper)

Jungle travellers are captured and miniaturized by a mad scientist.
Splendid special effects and an appropriately sombre atmosphere are hampered by a slow-paced narrative in this minor horror classic.

w Tom Kilpatrick *d* Ernest Schoedsack *ph Henry Sharp, Winton Hoch m* Ernst Toch, Gerard Carbonera, Albert Hay Malotte

Albert Dekker, Janice Logan, Victor Kilian, Thomas Coley, Charles Halton

Dr Dolittle
US 1967 152m De Luxe Todd-AO
TCF / APJAC (Arthur P. Jacobs)

In a Victorian English village, Dr Dolittle is a veterinary surgeon who talks to his patients; escaping from a lunatic asylum, he travels with friends to the South Seas in search of the Great Pink Sea Snail.
Lumpish family spectacular with no imagination whatever, further handicapped by charmless performances and unsingable songs.

w/songs Leslie Bricusse, *novels* Hugh Lofting *d* Richard Fleischer *ph* Robert Surtees *pd* Mario Chiari

Rex Harrison, Anthony Newley, Samantha Eggar, *Richard Attenborough*, William Dix, Peter Bull

Dr Ehrlich's Magic Bullet***
US 1940 103m bw
Warner (Wolfgang Reinhardt)
aka: *The Story of Dr Ehrlich's Magic Bullet*

A German scientist develops a cure for venereal disease.
Excellent period biopic: absorbing, convincing and extremely well put together.

w John Huston, Heinz Herald, Norman Burnside *d William Dieterle ph James Wong Howe*

Edward G. Robinson, Ruth Gordon, Otto Kruger, Donald Crisp, Maria Ouspenskaya, Montagu Love, Sig Rumann, Donald Meek, Henry O'Neill, Albert Basserman, Edward Norris, Harry Davenport, Louis Calhern, Louis Jean Heydt

'A superb motion picture.'—*Pare Lorentz*

Dr Faustus
GB 1967 93m Technicolor
Columbia / Oxford University Screen Productions / Nassau Films / Venfilms (Richard Burton, Richard McWhorter)

A medieval scholar conjures up Mephistopheles and offers his soul in exchange for a life of voluptuousness.
Marlowe's play has been adapted and 'improved', and there is some good handling of the poetry, but the production is flat, dingy and uninspired, as well as ludicrous when Miss Taylor makes her silent appearances.

w Nevill Coghill, *play* Christopher Marlowe *d* Richard Burton, Nevill Coghill *ph* Gabor Pogany *m* Mario Nascimbene *pd* John de Cuir

Richard Burton, Andreas Teuber, Ian Marter, Elizabeth Donovan, Elizabeth Taylor (as Helen of Troy)

'It is of an awfulness that bends the mind. The whole enterprise has the immense vulgarity of a collaboration in which academe would sell its soul for a taste of the glamour of Hollywood, and the stars are only too happy to appear a while in academe.'—*John Simon*

'It turns out to be the story of a man who sold his soul for Elizabeth Taylor.'—*Judith Crist*

Dr Goldfoot and the Bikini Machine
US 1965 90m Pathecolor Panavision
AIP (Anthony Carras)

Dr G. makes girl robots programmed to lure wealthy men into their clutches.
Way-out farce for the jaded end of the teenage market; a few lively touches and a climactic chase partly atone for the general tastelessness.

w Elwood Ullman, Robert Kaufman *d* Norman Taurog *ph* Sam Leavitt *m* Les Baxter *ad* Daniel Haller

Vincent Price, Fred Clark, Frankie Avalon, Dwayne Hickman, Susan Hart, Jack Mullaney

Doctor in the House**
GB 1954 91m Eastmancolor
Rank (Betty Box)

Amorous and other misadventures of medical students at St Swithin's Hospital.
A comedy with much to answer for: several sequels and an apparently endless TV series. The original is not bad, as the students, though plainly over age, constitute a formidable mass of British talent at its peak.

w Nicholas Phipps, book Richard Gordon d Ralph Thomas *ph* Ernest Steward *m* Bruce Montgomery

Dirk Bogarde, Kenneth More, Donald Sinden, Donald Houston, Kay Kendall, Muriel Pavlow, *James Robertson Justice*, Geoffrey Keen

'Works its way with determined high spirits through the repertoire of medical student jokes.'—*MFB*

† Sequels: *Doctor at Sea* (1955) with Dirk Bogarde, *Doctor at Large* (1957) with Dirk Bogarde, *Doctor in Love* (1960) with Michael Craig, *Doctor in Distress* (1963) with Dirk Bogarde, *Doctor in Clover* (1966) with Leslie Phillips, *Doctor in Trouble* (1970) with Leslie Phillips.

Doctor Jekyll and Mr Hyde****
US 1932 90m bw
Paramount (Rouben Mamoulian)

A Victorian research chemist finds a formula which separates the good and evil in his soul; when the latter predominates, he becomes a rampaging monster.
The most exciting and cinematic version by far of the famous horror story; the make-up is slightly over the top, but the gas-lit London settings, the pace, the performances and clever camera and sound tricks make it a film to enjoy over and over again. Subjective camera is used at the beginning, and for the first transformation the actor wore various layers of make up which were sensitive to different colour filters and thus produced instant change.

w Samuel Hoffenstein, Percy Heath, novel Robert Louis Stevenson d Rouben Mamoulian ph Karl Struss ad Hans Dreier

Fredric March, Miriam Hopkins, Rose Hobart, Holmes Herbert, Halliwell Hobbes, Edgar Norton

'As a work of cinematic imagination this film is difficult to fault.'—*John Baxter, 1968*

Dr Jekyll and Mr Hyde**
US 1941 122m bw
MGM (Victor Saville, Victor Fleming)

Curiously misconceived, stately, badly cast version with elaborate production including Freudian dream sequences. Always worth watching, but not a success.

w John Lee Mahin *d* Victor Fleming *m* Franz Waxman

Spencer Tracy, Ingrid Bergman, Lana Turner, Ian Hunter,
C. Aubrey Smith, Donald Crisp, Sara Allgood
† Other versions: *The Two Faces of Dr Jekyll* (1960),
I Monster (1970). Variations: *Daughter of Dr Jekyll* (1957), *Abbott and Costello Meet Dr Jekyll and Mr Hyde* (1954), *Son of Dr Jekyll* (1951), *The Ugly Duckling* (1960), *House of Dracula* (1945), *The Nutty Professor* (1963), *Dr Jekyll and Sister Hyde* (1970).

Dr Jekyll and Sister Hyde*
GB 1971 97m Technicolor
Hammer

A twist: Jekyll now turns into a young and beautiful woman, and kills prostitutes so that he can continue his research.
Half-successful attempt to link the legend with Jack the Ripper, killed by gore and overlength.

w Brian Clemens *d* Roy Ward Baker *ph* Norman Warwick *m* David Whitaker

Ralph Bates, Martine Beswick, Gerald Sim, Lewis Fiander, Dorothy Alison

Dr Kildare
This long-running screen hero was a young intern at Blair Hospital, under the cranky tutelage of old Dr Gillespie. Created by Max Brand in a series of novels, he first appeared on the screen in a 1937 Paramount double-biller called INTERNS CAN'T TAKE MONEY, played by Joel McCrea with Barbara Stanwyck, no less, providing the love interest. Kildare came up against gangsters; Gillespie did not appear.

MGM then took over the property and went to town with it, making fifteen films in nine years. They were as follows:

1938: YOUNG DR KILDARE
1939: CALLING DR KILDARE, THE SECRET OF DR KILDARE
1940: DR KILDARE'S STRANGEST CASE, DR KILDARE GOES HOME, DR KILDARE'S CRISIS
1941: DR KILDARE'S WEDDING DAY
1942: DR KILDARE'S VICTORY, CALLING DR GILLESPIE
1943: DR GILLESPIE'S NEW ASSISTANT, DR GILLESPIE'S CRIMINAL CASE
1944: THREE MEN IN WHITE, BETWEEN TWO WOMEN
1947: DARK DELUSION

Lew Ayres played Kildare, but in 1942 declared himself a conscientious objector and was dropped. The emphasis shifted to Gillespie, played by Lionel Barrymore from a wheelchair, and he proceeded to deal with a whole series of interns. The films were well enough made on medium budgets; nine were directed by Harold S. Buquet and the last five by Willis Goldbeck, one by W. S. Van Dyke. In 1961 a TV series began with Richard Chamberlain and Raymond Massey, and ran for seven years.

Dr Max
US 1974 74m colour TVM
CBS / James Goldstone

A small-town doctor neglects his family to look after his patients.
Modest domestic drama.

Lee J. Cobb, Robert Lipton, David Sheiner, Janet Ward

Doctor No***
GB 1962 111m Technicolor
UA / Eon (Harry Saltzman, Albert R. Broccoli)

A British secret service agent foils a master criminal operating in the West Indies.
First of the phenomenally successful James Bond movies, mixing sex, violence and campy humour against expensive sets and exotic locales. Toned down from the original novels, they expressed a number of sixties attitudes, and proved unstoppable box office attractions for nearly fifteen years. The first was, if not quite the best, reasonably representative of the series.

w Richard Maibaum, Johanna Harwood, Berkely Mather, *novel* Ian Fleming *d* Terence Young *ph* Ted Moore *m Monty Norman*

Sean Connery, Ursula Andress, Jack Lord, Joseph Wiseman, John Kitzmiller, Bernard Lee, Lois Maxwell, Zena Marshall, Eunice Gayson, Anthony Dawson

† The subsequent titles, all qv, were *From Russia with Love* (1963), *Goldfinger* (1964), *Thunderball* (1965), *You Only Live Twice* (1967), *On Her Majesty's Secret Service* (1969), *Diamonds Are Forever* (1971), *Live and Let Die* (1973), *The Man with the Golden Gun* (1974). *Casino Royale* (1967) was a Bond spoof made by other hands.

Dr Socrates**
US 1935 70m bw
Warner (Robert Lord)

A-small town doctor is forced to help wounded gangsters, and becomes involved.
Good star melodrama.

w Robert Lord, *novel* W. R. Burnett *d* William Dieterle ph Tony Gaudio *m* Leo F. Forbstein

Paul Muni, Ann Dvorak, Barton Maclane, Robert Barrat, John Eldridge, Hobart Cavanaugh, Mayo Methot, Samuel S. Hinds, Henry O'Neill

Dr Strangelove; or, How I Learned to Stop Worrying and Love the Bomb***
GB 1963 93m bw
Columbia / Stanley Kubrick (Victor Lyndon)

A mad USAF general launches a nuclear attack on Russia, and when recall attempts fail, and retaliation is inevitable, all concerned sit back to await the destruction of the world.
Black comedy resolving itself into a series of sketches, with the star playing three parts (for no good reason): the US president, an RAF captain, and a mad German-American scientist. Historically an important film in its timing, its nightmares being those of the early sixties, artistically it clogs its imperishable moments by untidy narrative and unattractively contrasty photography.

w Stanley Kubrick, Terry Southern, Peter George, *novel* Red Alert by Peter George *d* Stanley Kubrick *ph* Gilbert Taylor *m* Laurie Johnson *ad Ken Adam*

Peter Sellers, George C. Scott, Peter Bull, Sterling Hayden, Keenan Wynn, Slim Pickens, James Earl Jones, Tracy Reed

† *Fail Safe* (qv), which took the same theme more seriously, was released almost simultaneously.

Dr Syn*
GB 1937 80m bw
Gaumont

The vicar of Dymchurch in 1780 is really a pirate believed dead.

This now obscure, lively pirate yarn was its star's last film.

w Michael Hogan, Roger Burford, *novel* Russell Thorndike *d Roy William Neill*

George Arliss, Margaret Lockwood, John Loder, Roy Emerton, Graham Moffatt, Frederick Burtwell, Meinhart Maur, George Merritt
† Remakes: *Captain Clegg (Night Creatures)* (1962), *Dr Syn Alias the Scarecrow* (1963).

The Doctor Takes a Wife*
US 1940 89m bw
Columbia (William Perlberg)

A young doctor has to pretend to be the husband of a socialite.
Typical high life comedy of its period, quite brisk and diverting.

w George Seaton, Ken Englund *d* Alexander Hall *ph* Sid Hickox *m* Morris Stoloff

Loretta Young, Ray Milland, Edmund Gwenn, Reginald Gardiner, Gail Patrick, Frank Sully, George Metaxa, Charles Halton, Chester Clute

Dr Terror's House of Horrors
GB 1965 98m Techniscope
Amicus (Milton Subotsky)

An eccentric, who turns out to be Death himself, tells the fortunes of five men in a railway carriage.
One of the first Amicus horror compendiums and a weak one, not helped by wide screen, a couple of naïve scripts and ho-hum acting. The book-ends are quite pleasant, though.

w Milton Subotsky *d* Freddie Francis *ph* Alan Hume *m* Elisabeth Lutyens

Peter Cushing, Ursula Howells, Max Adrian, Roy Castle, Alan Freeman, Bernard Lee, Jeremy Kemp, Kenny Lynch, Christopher Lee, Michael Gough, Donald Sutherland
† Later collections from the same stable include *Torture Garden, Tales from the Crypt, Vault of Horror* and *Asylum*.

Doctor You've Got to be Kidding
US 1967 93m Metrocolor Panavision
MGM / Trident (Douglas Laurence)

A girl arrives at a maternity hospital chased by three prospective husbands.
Wild and wacky farce which leaves little impression.

w Phillip Shuken, *novel* Patte Wheat Mahan *d* Peter Tewkesbury *ph* Fred Koenekamp *m* Kenyon Hopkins

Sandra Dee, George Hamilton, Celeste Holm, Bill Bixby, *Dwayne Hickman*, Dick Kallman, Mort Sahl, Allen Jenkins

Dr X**
US 1932 82m Technicolor
Warner

A reporter investigates a series of moon murders and narrows his search to one of several doctors at a medical college.
Fascinating, German-inspired, overblown and generally enjoyable horror mystery whose armless villain commits murders by growing limbs from 'synthetic flesh'.

w Earl Baldwin, Robert Tasker, *play* Howard W. Comstock, Allen C. Miller *d Michael Curtiz ph Richard Tower, Ray Rennahan*

Lee Tracy, Lionel Atwill, Preston Foster, Fay Wray, George Rosener, Mae Busch, Arthur Edmund Carewe, John Wray

'The settings, lighting and final battle with the man-monster are quite stunning.'—*NFT, 1974*

Doctor Zhivago***
US 1965 192m Technicolor Panavision 70
MGM / Carlo Ponti

A Moscow doctor is caught up in World War I, exiled for writing poetry, forced into partisan service and separated from his only love.
Beautifully photographed and meticulously directed, this complex epic has been so reduced from the original novel that many parts of the script simply do not make any kind of sense. What remains is a collection of expensive set pieces, great for looking if not listening.

w Robert Bolt, *novel* Boris Pasternak *d David Lean ph Frederick A. Young m* Maurice Jarre

Omar Sharif, Julie Christie, Rod Steiger, Alec Guinness, Rita Tushingham, Ralph Richardson, Tom Courtenay, Geraldine Chaplin, Siobhan McKenna, Noel Willman, Geoffrey Keen, Adrienne Corri

'A long haul along the road of synthetic lyricism.'—*MFB*

'David Lean's *Doctor Zhivago* does for snow what his *Lawrence of Arabia* did for sand.'—*John Simon*

'It isn't shoddy (except for the music); it isn't soap opera; it's stately, respectable, and dead.'—*Pauline Kael*

The Doctor's Dilemma*
GB 1958 99m Metrocolor
MGM / Anatole de Grunwald

Eminent Harley Street surgeons debate the case

of a devoted wife and her tubercular artist husband.
Well acted but curiously muffled filming of Shaw's Edwardian play about ethics and human values.

w Anatole de Grunwald, *play* Bernard Shaw *d* Anthony Asquith *ph* Robert Krasker *m* Joseph Kosma *ad* Paul Sheriff

Leslie Caron, Dirk Bogarde, *John Robinson*, Alastair Sim, Felix Aylmer, Robert Morley, Michael Gwynn, Maureen Delany, Alec McCowen

Doctors' Wives
US 1970 102m Eastmancolor
Columbia / M. J. Frankovich

When Dr Dellman shoots his unfaithful wife, his colleagues reconsider their sex lives.
Adult soap opera from talents who at other times have found better things to do. In the sensational circumstances, two sanguinary operation sequences are tastelessly irrelevant.

w Daniel Taradash, *novel* Frank G. Slaughter *d* George Schaefer *ph* Charles B. Lang *m* Elmer Bernstein

Richard Crenna, Janice Rule, Gene Hackman, John Colicos, Dyan Cannon, Diana Sands, Rachel Roberts, Carroll O'Connor, Cara Williams, Ralph Bellamy, Richard Anderson
'Crisis follows hard on crisis to breathlessly ludicrous effect.'—*Tom Milne*

Dodge City***
US 1939 104m Technicolor
Warner (Robert Lord)

An ex-soldier and trail boss helps clean up the west's great railroad terminus.
Standard, satisfying big-scale western with all clichés intact and very enjoyable, as is the soft, rich early colour. The story is plainly inspired by the exploits of Wyatt Earp.

w Robert Buckner *d Michael Curtiz ph Sol Polito, Ray Rennahan m* Max Steiner

Errol Flynn, Olivia de Havilland, Ann Sheridan, Bruce Cabot, Alan Hale, Frank McHugh, John Litel, Victor Jory, William Lundigan, Henry Travers, Henry O'Neill, Guinn Williams, Gloria Holden

Dodsworth***
US 1936 101m bw
Samuel Goldwyn

An American businessman takes his wife on a tour of Europe, and their lives are changed.
Satisfying, well-acted drama from a bestselling novel; production values high.

w Sidney Howard, novel Sinclair Lewis d William Wyler ph Rudolph Maté *m* Alfred Newman

Walter Huston, Mary Astor, Ruth Chatterton, David Niven, Paul Lukas, Gregory Gaye, Maria Ouspenskaya, Odette Myrtil, Spring Byington, John Payne

Dog Day Afternoon**
US 1975 130m Technicolor
Warner / AEC (Martin Bregman, Martin Elfand)

Two incompetent robbers are cornered in a Brooklyn bank.
Recreation of a tragi-comic episode from the newspaper headlines; for half its length a fascinating and acutely observed film which then bogs itself down in a surplus of talk and excessive sentiment about homosexuality.

w Frank Pierson *d Sidney Lumet ph* Victor J. Kemper *m* none

Al Pacino, John Cazale, *Charles Durning*, Sully Boyar, James Broderick, *Chris Sarandon*
'There is plenty of Lumet's vital best here in a film that at least glancingly captures the increasingly garish pathology of our urban life.'—*Jack Kroll*
'Scattered moments of wry humour, sudden pathos and correct observation.'—*John Simon*
'The mask of frenetic cliché doesn't spoil moments of pure reporting on people in extremity.'—*New Yorker*

Dollars*
US 1971 120m Technicolor
Columbia / M. J. Frankovich
GB title: *The Heist*

An American security expert installs an electronic system in a Hamburg bank which he plans to rob himself.
Overlong caper comedy-drama which is quite good to watch when it starts moving, though the quick cutting, short takes and deliberately obscure narrative leave one breathless.

wd Richard Brooks *ph* Petrus Schloemp *m* Quincy Jones

Warren Beatty, Goldie Hawn, Gert Frobe, Robert Webber, Scott Brady, Arthur Brauss
'An essay in virtuoso film construction . . . rather as if one were watching a perfect machine in full throttle but with nowhere to go.'—*John Gillet*

A Doll's House*
GB 1973 95m Eastmancolor
Elkins / Freeward (Hillard Elkins)

A wife begins to resist her husband's will.

Ibsen's feminist play was always good value; set in Norway in the nineties, it was taken up eighty years later as a precursor of women's lib, which accounts for two film versions in one year. This one is simply staged and well performed, but suffers from a bad translation.

w Christopher Hampton, *play* Henrik Ibsen *d* Patrick Garland *ph* Arthur Ibbetson *m* John Barry

Claire Bloom, Anthony Hopkins, Ralph Richardson, Denholm Elliott, Anna Massey, Edith Evans

A Doll's House
GB / France 1973 106m Eastmancolor
World Film Services / Les Films de la Boétie (Joseph Losey)

Opened out but less effective version of the above, with too much solemnity and the central part miscast.

w David Mercer, *play* Henrik Ibsen *d* Joseph Losey *ph* Gerry Fisher *m* Michel Legrand

Jane Fonda, David Warner, Trevor Howard, Edward Fox, Delphine Seyrig, Anna Wing

The Dolly Sisters**
US 1945 114m Technicolor
TCF (George Jessel)

The lives of a Hungarian sister act in American vaudeville.
Fictionalized biographical musical, only fair in the script department but glittering to look at in superb colour, and enriched by splendid production values. Undoubtedly among the best of its kind.

w John Larkin, Marian Spitzer *d* Irving Cummings *ph Ernest Palmer* *md* Alfred Newman, Charles Henderson *songs* various *ch* Seymour Felix *ad Lyle Wheeler, Leland Fuller*

Betty Grable, June Haver, John Payne, S. Z. Sakall, Reginald Gardiner, Frank Latimore, Gene Sheldon, Sig Rumann, Trudy Marshall

The Don is Dead
US 1973 117m Technicolor
Universal / Hal B. Wallis (Paul Nathan)

Cross and double cross among Mafia families.
A failed attempt to cash in on *The Godfather*, this endless melodrama is boringly violent and totally predictable.

w Marvin H. Albert, from his novel *d* Richard Fleischer *ph* Richard H. Kline *m* Jerry Goldsmith

Anthony Quinn, Frederic Forrest, Robert Forster, Al Lettieri, Angel Tompkins, Charles Cioffi

Donovan's Brain*
US 1953 81m bw
UA / Dowling (Tom Gries)

An unscrupulous tycoon is fatally injured, but his brain is kept alive by a surgeon who finds himself dominated by it.
Modest competence marks this version of a much filmed novel, with quiet suspense and a firm central performance.

w Felix Feist, *novel* Curt Siodmak *d* Felix Feist *ph* Joseph Biroc *m* Eddie Dunstedter

Lew Ayres, Gene Evans, Nancy Davis, Steve Brodie,
Lisa K. Howard

Donovan's Reef
US 1963 108m Technicolor
Paramount (John Ford)

War veterans settle down on a South Sea island; when the daughter of one of them comes to visit, his reputation must be protected.
Good-humoured but finally enervating mixture of rough-house and slapstick, with the appearance of an old friends' benefit and the director in familiar sub-standard form.

w Frank Nugent, James Edward Grant *d* John Ford *ph* William H. Clothier *m* Cyril Mockridge

John Wayne, Lee Marvin, Jack Warden, Elizabeth Allen, Dorothy Lamour, Cesar Romero, Mike Mazurki

Don't Be Afraid of the Dark*
US 1973 74m colour TVM
Lorimar / Allen Epstein

A young couple move into an old house and find supernatural creatures already in occupation.
Foolish but effective ghost story.

w Nigel McKeand *d* John Newland

Jim Hutton, Kim Darby, Barbara Anderson, William Demarest, Pedro Armendariz Jnr

Don't Bother to Knock*
US 1952 76m bw
TCF (Julian Blaustein)

A deranged girl gets a baby-sitting job in a hotel and terrifies all concerned by threatening to kill her charge.
Curious vehicle for the emergent Monroe, who is not up to it, as who would be? Technical credits par, but entertainment value small.

w Daniel Taradash, *novel* Charlotte Armstrong

d Roy Baker *ph* Lucien Ballard *m* Lionel Newman

Marilyn Monroe, Richard Widmark, Anne Bancroft, Donna Corcoran, Jeanne Cagney, Lurene Tuttle, Jim Backus, Elisha Cook Jnr

Don't Bother to Knock
GB 1961 89m Technicolor Cinemascope
ABP / Haileywood (Frank Godwin)

A Casanova travel agent gives each of his girl friends a key to his Edinburgh flat.
Poorly developed and self-conscious sex farce.

w Dennis Cannan, Frederick Gotfurt, Frederic Raphael, *novel* Clifford Hanley *d* Cyril Frankel *ph* Geoffrey Unsworth *m* Elisabeth Lutyens

Richard Todd, *Judith Anderson*, Elke Sommer, June Thorburn, Nicole Maurey, Rik Battaglia, Eleanor Summerfield, John Le Mesurier

Don't Go Near the Water*
US 1957 107m Metrocolor Cinemascope
MGM (Lawrence Weingarten)

The US Navy sets up a public relations unit on a South Pacific island.
Loosely cemented service farce full of fumbling lieutenants and bumbling commanders, a more light-hearted *M*A*S*H*. Boring romantic interludes separate some very funny farcical sequences.

w Dorothy Kingsley, George Wells, *novel* William Brinkley *d* Charles Walters *ph* Robert Bronner *m* Bronislau Kaper

Glenn Ford, Fred Clark, Gia Scala, Romney Brent, Mickey Shaughnessey, Earl Holliman, Anne Francis, Keenan Wynn, Eva Gabor, Russ Tamblyn, Jeff Richards, Mary Wickes

Don't Just Stand There
US 1967 99m Techniscope
Universal (Stan Margulies)

A mild-mannered watch smuggler gets himself involved with kidnapping, murder, and finishing a sex novel.
Frantic but ineffective farce which keeps on the move but does not arrive anywhere.

w Charles Williams, from his novel The Wrong Venus *d* Ron Winston *ph* Milton Krasner *m* Nick Perito

Mary Tyler Moore, Robert Wagner, *Barbara Rhoades*, Glynis Johns, Harvey Korman

Don't Look Now***
GB 1973 110m Technicolor
BL / Casey / Eldorado (Peter Katz)

After the death of their small daughter, the Baxters meet in Venice two old sisters who claim mediumistic connection with the dead girl. The husband scorns the idea, but repeatedly sees a little red-coated figure in shadowy passages by the canals. When he confronts it, it proves to be a maniac dwarf who stabs him to death.
A macabre short story has become a pretentious and puzzling piece of high cinema art full of vague suggestions and unexplored avenues. Whatever its overall deficiencies, it is too brilliant in surface detail to be dismissed. Depressingly but fascinatingly set in wintry Venice, it has to be seen to be appreciated.

w Allan Scott, Chris Bryant, *story* Daphne du Maurier *d Nicolas Roeg ph Anthony Richmond m* Pino D'Onnagio *ad* Giovanni Soccol

Donald Sutherland, Julie Christie, Hilary Mason, Clelia Matania, Massimo Serrato

'The fanciest, most carefully assembled enigma yet seen on the screen.'—*New Yorker*

'A powerful and dazzling visual texture.'—*Penelope Houston*

Don't Make Waves
US 1967 97m Metrocolor Panavision
MGM / Filmways (Julian Bercovici)

A swimming-pool salesman attempts to get his own back on an impulsive young woman who has wrecked his car.
Malibu beach farce for immature adults, made by professionals helpless in the face of a weak script, but boasting a funny climax with a house teetering on the edge of a cliff.

w Ira Wallach, George Kirgo, *novel* Muscle Beach by Ira Wallach *d* Alexander Mackendrick *ph* Philip Lathrop *m* Vic Mizzy

Tony Curtis, Claudia Cardinale, Robert Webber, Joanna Barnes, Sharon Tate, Jim Backus, Mort Sahl

Don't Push, I'll Charge When I'm Ready
US 1969 97m Technicolor TVM
Universal

Adventures of an Italian POW in the US.
Drawn-out farce over-exploiting Italian volubility.

w Al Ramus, John Shaner *d* Nathaniel Lande

Enzo Cerusico, Cesar Romero, Soupy Sales, Sue Lyon

Don't Raise the Bridge Lower the River
GB 1967 100m Technicolor
Columbia / Walter Shenson

An American turns his English wife's home into a discotheque.
Dreary comedy apparently intent on proving that its star can be just as unfunny abroad as at home.

w Max Wilk *d* Jerry Paris *ph* Otto Heller *m* David Whitaker

Jerry Lewis, Terry-Thomas, Jacqueline Pearce, Bernard Cribbins, Patricia Routledge, Nicholas Parsons, Michael Bates

Don't Take it to Heart*
GB 1944 90m bw
GFD / Two Cities (Sydney Box)

A genial castle ghost is unleashed by a bomb and affects the love affair of a researcher with the daughter of the house.
Amiably lunatic British-upper-class extravaganza with eccentric characters and some felicitous moments.

wd Jeffrey Dell

Richard Greene, *Edward Rigby*, Patricia Medina, Alfred Drayton, Richard Bird, Wylie Watson, Moore Marriott, Brefni O'Rourke, Amy Veness, Claude Dampier, Joan Hickson, Joyce Barbour, Ronald Squire, Ernest Thesiger

The Doomsday Flight*
US 1966 97m Technicolor TVM
Universal

A mad bomber is discovered on a jet plane between Los Angeles and New York.
Obvious but effective suspenser.

w Rod Serling *d* William Graham

Jack Lord, Edmond O'Brien, Katherine Crawford, Van Johnson, John Saxon

Double Dynamite
US 1951 (produced 1948) 80m bw
RKO (Irving Cummings)
aka: *It's Only Money*

A bank teller wins a fortune at the race track but is afraid his winnings will be thought the proceeds of a bank robbery.
Insultingly mild comedy, nearly saved by a few quips from Groucho.

w Melville Shavelson, Harry Crane, Leo Rosten *d* Irving Cummings *ph* Robert de Grasse *m* Leigh Harline

Frank Sinatra, Jane Russell, Groucho Marx, Don McGuire, Howard Freeman

Double Indemnity****
US 1944 107m bw
Paramount (Joseph Sistrom)

An insurance agent connives with the glamorous wife of a client to kill her husband and collect.
Archetypal *film noir* of the forties, brilliantly filmed and incisively written, perfectly capturing the decayed Los Angeles atmosphere of a Chandler novel but using a simpler story and more substantial characters. The hero/villain was almost a new concept.

w Billy Wilder, Raymond Chandler, novel James M. Cain d Billy Wilder ph John Seitz m Miklos Rozsa

Fred MacMurray, Barbara Stanwyck, Edward G. Robinson, Tom Powers, Porter Hall, Jean Heather, Byron Barr, Richard Gaines

'The sort of film which revives a critic from the depressive effects of bright epics about the big soul of America or the suffering soul of Europe and gives him a new lease of faith.'—*Richard Winnington*

'Masturbation fantasy triple distilled.'—*James Agee*

'The most pared-down and purposeful film ever made by Billy Wilder.'—*John Coleman, 1966*

Double Indemnity
US 1973 74m Technicolor TVM
Universal (David Victor)

A fair copy of the above without any of its character or effectiveness

w from the original screenplay *d* Jack Smight

Richard Crenna, Samantha Eggar, Lee J. Cobb, Robert Webber

A Double Life**
US 1947 103m bw
Kanin Productions

An actor playing Othello is obsessed by the role and murders a woman he imagines to be Desdemona.
An old theatrical chestnut (cf *Men Are Not Gods*) is decked out with smartish backstage dialogue but despite a pleasant star performance remains unrewarding if taxing, and the entertainment value of the piece is on the thin side considering the mighty talents involved

w Ruth Gordon, Garson Kanin *d* George Cukor *ph* Milton Krasner *m* Miklos Rozsa

Ronald Colman, Shelley Winters, Signe Hasso, Edmond O'Brien, Millard Mitchell

The Double Man*
GB 1968 105m Technicolor
Warner / Hal E. Chester

A CIA agent investigates the death of his son on a Swiss skiing holiday and finds the murder was a lure to get him there so that an enemy lookalike can substitute for him.

Rather ruthless but good-looking and generally watchable spy melodrama.

w Frank Tarloff, Alfred Hayes, *novel* Henry S. Maxfield *d* Franklin Schaffner *ph* *Denys Coop*

Yul Brynner, Clive Revill, Anton Diffring, Britt Ekland, Moira Lister

Double Wedding
US 1937 87m bw
MGM (Joseph L. Mankiewicz)

A bohemian artist makes a play for the lady of his choice by romancing her sister.
Zany star comedy which doesn't quite come off.

w Jo Swerling, *play* Great Love by Ferenc Molnar *d* Richard Thorpe *ph* William Daniels *m* Edward Ward

William Powell, Myrna Loy, John Beal, Florence Rice, Jessie Ralph, Edgar Kennedy, Sidney Toler, Barnett Parker, Katherine Alexander, Donald Meek

The Doughgirls*
US 1944 102m bw
Warner (Mark Hellinger)

In a crowded wartime Washington hotel, a honeymoon is frustrated by constant interruption, not to mention the discovery that the wedding was not legal.
Frantic farce, generally well adapted, and certainly played with gusto.

w James V. Kern, Sam Hellman, *play* Joseph Fields *d* James V. Kern *ph* Ernest Haller *m* Adolph Deutsch

Alexis Smith, Jane Wyman, Jack Carson, Ann Sheridan, Irene Manning, *Eve Arden*, Charlie Ruggles, John Alexander, John Ridgely, Craig Stevens, Alan Mowbray, Donald MacBride

'There's nothing so good in it that you must attend, just as there is nothing bad enough to keep you away.'—*Archer Winsten*

The Dove*
US 1974 104m Technicolor Panavision
St George Productions (Gregory Peck)

Yachtsman Robin Lee Graham makes a five-year voyage around the world.
Bland, rather stolid adventure story for boatniks, based on real incidents; good to look at.

w Peter Beagle, Adam Kennedy *d* Charles Jarrott *ph* *Sven Nykvist* *m* John Barry

Joseph Bottoms, Deborah Raffin, John McLiam, Dabney Coleman

'Postcard views flick by to the strains of a saccharine score.'—*David McGillivray*

Down Argentine Way*
US 1940 94m Technicolor
TCF (Harry Joe Brown)

A wealthy American girl falls in love with an Argentinian horse-breeder.
A very moderate musical which happened to bring both Grable and Miranda to star stature and set Fox off on their successful run of forties extravaganzas, reasonably pleasant to look at but empty-headed.

w Karl Tunberg, Darrell Ware *d* Irving Cummings *ph* Ray Rennahan, Leon Shamroy *songs* Harry Warren, Mack Gordon

Betty Grable, Carmen Miranda, Don Ameche, Charlotte Greenwood, J. Carrol Naish, Henry Stephenson, Leonid Kinskey, The Nicholas Brothers

'I dislike Technicolor in which all pinks resemble raspberry sauce, reds turn to sealing wax, blues shriek of the washtub, and yellows become suet pudding.'—*James Agate*

'So outrageous—that it's hard to believe it isn't at least partly intentional—but why would anybody make this picture on purpose.'—*New Yorker, 1976*

Down Three Dark Streets*
US 1954 85m bw
UA / Edward Small (Arthur Gardner, Jules V. Levy)

An FBI agent is shot on duty, and his friend avenges him in the course of clearing up three cases in which he was involved.
Competent, enjoyable police film with three cases for the price of one.

w The Gordons, Bernard C. Schoenfeld, *book* Case File FBI by the Gordons *d* *Arnold Laven* *ph* Joseph Biroc *m* Paul Sawtell

Broderick Crawford, Ruth Roman, Martha Hyer, Marisa Pavan, Casey Adams, Kenneth Tobey

† One of the first collaborations of the prolific production company Laven-Gardner-Levy.

Down to Earth*
US 1947 101m Technicolor
Columbia

The muse Terpsichore comes down to help a Broadway producer fix a new show in which she is featured.
Pleasant but undistinguished musical fantasy, a sequel to *Here Comes Mr Jordan*. The heavenly sequences promise more amusement than they produce.

w Edwin Blum, Don Hartman *d* Alexander Hall *ph* Rudolph Maté *m* Heinz Roemheld

Rita Hayworth, Larry Parks, Roland Culver (as Mr Jordan), *Edward Everett Horton* (repeating as Messenger 7013), Marc Platt, James Gleason

'Just the film to make the spectator forget the troubles of life.'—*MFB*

Down to the Sea in Ships*
US 1948 120m bw
TCF

An old whaling skipper wants his grandson to follow in his footsteps.
Seagoing spectacle with strong characters; all concerned show Hollywood in its most professional form, but the film somehow fails to catch the imagination or live in the memory.

w John Lee Mahin, Sy Bartlett *d* Henry Hathaway *ph Joe MacDonald m* Alfred Newman

Lionel Barrymore, Dean Stockwell, Richard Widmark, *Cecil Kellaway*, Gene Lockhart

Downhill Racer*
US 1969 101m Technicolor
Paramount / Wildwood (Richard Gregson)

An ambitious American skier gains a place on the team competing in Europe.
Virtually plotless, casually assembled study of a man and a sport, good to look at, often exciting, but just as frequently irritating in its throwaway style.

w James Salter, *novel* Oakley Hall *d* Michael Ritchie *ph Brian Probyn m* Kenyon Hopkins

Robert Redford, Gene Hackman, Camilla Sparv, Joe Jay Jalbert, Timothy Kirk, Dabney Coleman

Dracula***
US 1930 84m bw
Universal (Carl Laemmle Jnr)

A Transylvanian vampire count gets his come-uppance in Yorkshire.
A film which has much to answer for. It started its star and its studio off on horror careers, and it launched innumerable sequels (see below). In itself, after two eerie reels, it becomes a pedantic and slow transcription of a stage adaptation, and its climax takes place offscreen; but for all kinds of reasons it remains full of interest.

w Garrett Fort, *play* Hamilton Deane, John Balderston, *novel Bram Stoker d Tod Browning ph Karl Freund m* none

Bela Lugosi, Helen Chandler, David Manners, *Dwight Frye, Edward Van Sloan*

'A too literal adaptation of the play (*not* the book) results in a plodding, talkative development, with much of the vital action taking place off-screen.'—*William K. Everson*

'The mistiest parts are the best; when the lights go up the interest goes down.'—*Ivan Butler*

† Sequels include *Dracula's Daughter* (qv), *Son of Dracula* (qv); the later Hammer sequence consists of *Dracula* (see below), *Brides of Dracula* (qv), *Dracula Prince of Darkness* (qv), *Dracula Has Risen From the Grave* (qv), *Taste the Blood of Dracula* (qv), *Scars of Dracula* (qv), *Dracula AD 1972* (qv), *The Satanic Rites of Dracula* (qv). Other associated films in which the Count or a disciple appears include (all qv) *Return of the Vampire* (1944), *House of Frankenstein* (1945), *House of Dracula* (1945), *Abbott and Costello Meet Frankenstein* (1948), *The Return of Dracula* (1958), *Kiss of the Vampire* (1963), *The Fearless Vampire Killers* (1967), *Count Yorga Vampire* (1969), *Countess Dracula* (1970), *Vampire Circus* (1970), *The House of Dark Shadows* (1970), *Vampire Lovers* (1971), *Blacula* (1972). Minor potboilers are legion.

Dracula***
GB 1958 82m Technicolor
Hammer (Anthony Hinds)
US title: *Horror of Dracula*

A remake of the 1930 film.
Commendably brief in comparison with the later Hammer films, this was perhaps the best horror piece they turned out as well as the most faithful to its original. Decor and colour were well used, and the leading performances are striking.

w Jimmy Sangster d Terence Fisher ph Jack Asher m James Bernard ad Bernard Robinson

Peter Cushing (as Van Helsing), *Christopher Lee* (as Dracula), Melissa Stribling, Carol Marsh, Michael Gough, John Van Eyssen, Valerie Gaunt, Miles Malleson

Dracula AD 1972
GB 1972 95m Eastmancolor
Warner / Hammer (Josephine Douglas)

Dracula reappears among Chelsea teenagers practising black magic.
Depressed attempt to update a myth; the link with modern sin makes it seem not only tarnished but tasteless, and the film itself is lamentably short on excitement.

w Don Houghton *d* Alan Gibson *ph* Richard Bush *m* Michael Vickers

Peter Cushing, Christopher Lee, Stephanie Beacham, Michael Coles, Christopher Neame, William Ellis

Dracula Has Risen from the Grave
GB 1968 92m Technicolor
Hammer (Aida Young)

Dracula again terrorizes the village in the shadow of his castle, and is routed by a bishop.
Tedious, confined and repetitive shocker with little conventional action and an unusual emphasis on sex.

w John Elder (Anthony Hinds) *d* Freddie Francis *ph* Arthur Grant *m* James Bernard

Christopher Lee, Rupert Davies, Veronica Carlson, Barbara Ewing, Barry Andrews, Ewan Hooper

'A bloody bore.'—*Judith Crist*

Dracula Prince of Darkness
GB 1965 90m Techniscope
Warner / Hammer (Anthony Nelson Keys)

Stranded travellers are made welcome at the late count's castle by his sinister butler, who proceeds to use the blood of one of them to revivify his master.
Ingenious rehash of incidents from the original story, largely dissipated by poor colour and unsuitable wide screen.

w John Sansom *d* Terence Fisher *ph* Michael Reed *m* James Bernard

Christopher Lee, *Philip Latham*, Barbara Shelley, Thorley Walters, Andrew Keir, Francis Matthews, Suzan Farmer, Charles Tingwell

'Run-of-the-coffin stuff... only for ardent fang-and-cross fans.'—*Judith Crist*

Dracula's Daughter**
US 1936 70m bw
Universal

The daughter of the old count follows his remains to London.
Lively sequel which develops in the manner of a Sherlock Holmes story.

w Garrett Fort *d Lambert Hillyer* *ph* George Robinson

Otto Kruger, Marguerite Churchill, Edward Van Sloan, Gloria Holden, Irving Pichel, Nan Grey, Hedda Hopper, Gilbert Emery, Claud Allister, E. E. Clive, Halliwell Hobbes, Billy Bevan

Dragnet*
US 1954 93m Warnercolor
Mark VII (Jack Webb)

Sgt Joe Friday solves the murder of an ex-convict.
Moderately interesting but overlong attempt to transfer television techniques to the big screen; laconic dialogue, question and answer, cheap sets, close-ups and convenient Los Angeles locations.

w Richard Breen *d Jack Webb* *ph* Edward Colman

Jack Webb, Ben Alexander, Richard Boone, Stacy Harris, Ann Robinson, Virginia Gregg

Dragnet*
US 1969 97m Technicolor TVM
Universal / Jack Webb
GB title: *The Big Dragnet*

Sgt Joe Friday investigates the murder of several models.
Enjoyable rehash of the old *Dragnet* formula.

w Richard L. Breen *d* Jack Webb

Jack Webb, Harry Morgan, Vic Perrin, Virginia Gregg, Gene Evans

Dragon Seed*
US 1944 144m bw
MGM (Pandro S. Berman)

Chinese peasants fight the Japs.
Ill-advised attempt to follow the success of *The Good Earth*; badly cast actors mouth propaganda lines in a mechanical script which provokes more boredom and unintentional laughter than sympathy.

w Marguerite Roberts, Jane Murfin, *novel* Pearl S. Buck *d* Jack Conway, Harold S. Bucquet *ph* Sidney Wagner *m* Herbert Stothart

Katharine Hepburn, Walter Huston, Turhan Bey, Aline MacMahon, Akim Tamiroff, Hurd Hatfield, Frances Rafferty, Agnes Moorehead, Henry Travers, J. Carrol Naish

Dragonwyck*
US 1946 103m bw
TCF (Darryl F. Zanuck)

In the 1840s a farmer's daughter marries her rich cousin, not knowing that he has poisoned his first wife.
Good-looking but rather tedious romance of the Jane Eyre/Rebecca school: tyrannical recluse, mystery upstairs, spooky house, etc. Heavy going.

w Joseph L. Mankiewicz, *novel* Anya Seton *d* Joseph L. Mankiewicz *ph Arthur Miller* *m* Alfred Newman

Gene Tierney, Vincent Price, Glenn Langan, Walter Huston, Anne Revere, Spring Byington, Henry Morgan, Jessica Tandy

Drake of England
GB 1935 104m bw
Wardour (Walter C. Mycroft)
US title: *Drake the Pirate*

Sir Francis Drake is knighted by Queen Elizabeth for his seafaring exploits, and defeats the Spanish Armada.
Stiffly moving historical pageant; you can smell the mothballs.

w Clifford Grey, Akos Tolney, Marjorie Deans, Norman Watson *d* Arthur Woods

Matheson Lang, Athene Seyler, Jane Baxter, Donald Wolfit, Henry Mollison, George Merritt, Amy Veness, Sam Livesey, Ben Webster

Dramatic School*
US 1938 80m bw
MGM

Young actresses compete for success.
Another, less lively, *Stage Door*; tolerable but not exciting.

w Ernst Vadja, Mary McCall Jnr, *play* School of Drama by Hans Szekely, Zoltan Egyed *d* Robert B. Sinclair Jnr *ph* William Daniels

Luise Rainer, Paulette Goddard, Alan Marshal, Lana Turner, Anthony Allan (later John Hubbard), Henry Stephenson, Genevieve Tobin, Gale Sondergaard, Melville Cooper, Erik Rhodes, Ann Rutherford, Margaret Dumont, Virginia Grey, Hans Conried

Drango
US 1957 92m bw
UA / Hall Bartlett

After the Civil War, a Union Army officer is assigned to bring law and order to a Georgia community.
Eccentric, downbeat semi-western with aspirations to be some kind of *film noir*; does not come off.

wd Hall Bartlett *ph James Wong Howe*
m Elmer Bernstein

Jeff Chandler, Ronald Howard, Joanne Dru, Julie London, Donald Crisp, John Lupton, Morris Ankrum

A Dream for Christmas*
US 1973 100m colour TVM
Lorimar

A black parson moves from the midwest to Los Angeles, and finds a whole new set of problems.
Pleasing family fare.

w John McGreevy *d* Ralph Senensky

Hari Rhodes, Beah Richards, Lynn Hamilton, George Spell

Dream Girl
US 1947 86m bw
Paramount (P. J. Wolfson)

A girl revels in her own romantic dreams, one of which nearly comes true.
Potentially pleasant comedy about a female Walter Mitty does not work because the director has run out of ideas, the star is miscast and Hollywood has insisted on making the girl rich to begin with, which robs the dreams of any point.

w Arthur Sheekman, *play* Elmer Rice *d* Mitchell Leisen *ph* Daniel L. Fapp *m* Victor Young

Betty Hutton, Macdonald Carey, Walter Abel, Patric Knowles, Virginia Field, Peggy Wood, Lowell Gilmore

The Dream Makers*
US 1975 74m colour TVM
MGM (Charles Robert McLain)

A college professor becomes a recording executive.
Unusual contemporary drama, not very exciting but convincingly done.

w Bill Svanoe *d* Boris Sagal

James Franciscus, Diane Baker, John Astin, Kenny Rogers, Mickey Jones

A Dream of Kings
US 1969 110m Technicolor
National General (Jules Schermer)

Episodes in the life of an improvident, lusty, poetical Chicago Greek with a dying son.
The part screamed for Anthony Quinn and got him, with the result that it has all been seen before, too frequently. Well made, with strong appeal to Chicago Greeks.

w Harry Mark Patrakis, Ian Hunter, *novel* Harry Mark Patrakis *d* Daniel Mann *ph* Richard H. Kline *m* Alex North

Anthony Quinn, Irene Papas, Inger Stevens, Sam Levene, Val Avery, Tamara Daykarhanova

Dream Wife
US 1953 99m bw
MGM (Dore Schary)

An executive leaves his ambitious wife for a sheik's daughter schooled in the art of pleasing men, but naturally finds drawbacks.
Very moderate comedy with strained situations and few laughs. The stars work hard.

w Sidney Sheldon, Herbert Baker, Alfred L. Levitt *d* Sidney Sheldon *ph* Milton Krasner *m* Conrad Salinger

Cary Grant, Deborah Kerr, Walter Pidgeon, Betta St John, Eduard Franz, Buddy Baer, Les Temayne

Dreamboat*
US 1952 83m bw
TCF (Sol C. Siegel)

A romantic star of the silent film era is embarrassed when his old movies turn up on television.
Hollywood rather blunderingly makes fun of its arch enemy in this sometimes sprightly but often disappointing comedy which should have been a bulls-eye.

wd Claude Binyon *ph* Milton Krasner *m* Cyril Mockridge

Clifton Webb, Ginger Rogers, Anne Francis, Jeffrey Hunter, Elsa Lanchester, Fred Clark, Ray Collins, Paul Harvey

Dreaming Lips*
GB 1937 94m bw
Trafalgar (Paul Czinner)

The wife of an invalid musician has an affair with another man and commits suicide.
Standard star fare, possibly Miss Bergner's most notable film, also available in a German version.

w Margaret Kennedy, Lady Cynthia Asquith, Carl Mayer, *play* Henry Bernstein *d* Paul Czinner, Lee Garmes *ph* Lee Garmes

Elisabeth Bergner, Romney Brent, Raymond Massey, Joyce Bland, Sydney Fairbrother, Felix Aylmer, Donald Calthrop

Dreyfus*
GB 1931 90m bw
Wardour (F. W. Kraemer)

In 1894 France, a Jewish officer is accused of spying.
Primitive version of a much-filmed story (cf *The Life of Emile Zola, I Accuse*).

w Rehfisch Herzog, Reginald Berkeley, Walter C. Mycroft *d* F. W. Kraemer, Milton Rosmer

Cedric Hardwicke, George Merritt (as Zola), Charles Carson, Sam Livesey, Garry Marsh (as Esterhazy), Randle Ayrton, George Zucco

Drive a Crooked Road
US 1954 82m bw
Columbia (Jonie Taps)

A garage mechanic falls in with bank robbers.
Terse crime melodrama, quite watchable.

w Blake Edwards *d* Richard Quine *ph* Charles Lawton Jnr *m* Ross di Maggio

Mickey Rooney, Kevin McCarthy, Dianne Foster

Drive Hard, Drive Fast
US 1969 95m Technicolor TVM
Universal (Jo Swerling Jnr)

A womanizing racing driver gets involved in a murder plot in Mexico City.
Unconvincing rigmarole padded out with local colour.

w Matthew Howard *d* Douglas Heyes

Brian Kelly, Joan Collins, Henry Silva, Joseph Campanella

Drive He Said
US 1970 90m colour
Columbia / Drive Productions / BBS (Steve Blauner)

An easygoing college basketball star is helped by an eccentric rebel to ensure his own unfitness for military service. Both run into trouble.
Flabby celebration of against-the-government attitudes, expressed partly through sex and bad language. Defiantly hard to like.

w Jeremy Larner, Jack Nicholson *d* Jack Nicholson *ph* Bill Butler *m* David Shire

Michael Margotta, William Tepper, Bruce Dern, Karen Black, Robert Towne, Henry Jaglom

Drop Dead Darling
GB 1966 100m Technicolor Panavision
Seven Arts (Ken Hughes)
US title: *Arriverderci Baby*

A con man who marries and murders rich women meets a con lady with similar intentions.
Loud, restless black comedy which squanders its moments of genuine inventiveness among scenes of shouting, confusion and action for action's sake.

wd Ken Hughes, *story* The Careful Man by Richard Deeming *ph* Denys Coop *m* Dennis Farnon

Tony Curtis, Rosanna Schiaffino, Lionel Jeffries, Zsa Zsa Gabor, Nancy Kwan, Fenella Fielding, Anna Quayle, Warren Mitchell, Mischa Auer

The Drowning Pool
US 1975 108m Technicolor Panavision
Warner / Coleytown (Lawrence Turman, David Foster)

Private eye Lew Harper goes to New Orleans to investigate an anonymous letter which ends in murder.
Dreary sequel to *Harper* (qv), full of boring characters uninventively deployed.

w Tracy Keenan Wynn, Lorenzo Semple Jnr, Walter Hill, *novel* John Ross MacDonald

d Stuart Rosenberg *ph* Gordon Willis
m Michael Small

Paul Newman, Joanne Woodward, Coral Browne, Tony Franciosa, Murray Hamilton, Gail Strickland, Linda Hayes, Richard Jaeckel

'The impenetrable mystery is not particularly gripping; and the general air of pointlessness is only intensified by the sudden rush of clarifications at the end.'—*Tom Milne*

'It recycles every private eye cliché known to civilized man as it crawls through Louisiana talking all the way.'—*Paul D. Zimmermann*

The Drum*
GB 1938 96m Technicolor
London Films (Alexander Korda)
US title: *Drums*

The British army helps an Indian prince to resist his usurping uncle.
Reasonably entertaining story of the Raj, with adequate excitement after a meandering start.

w Lajos Biro, Arthur Wimperis, Patrick Kirwan, Hugh Gray *d* Zoltan Korda *ph* Georges Périnal *m* John Greenwood, Miklos Rozsa

Sabu, Roger Livesey, Raymond Massey, Valerie Hobson, Desmond Tester, David Tree, Francis L. Sullivan, Roy Emerton, Edward Lexy

Drumbeat
US 1954 111m Warnercolor
Jaguar (no producer credited)

An Indian fighter sets out to make peace with a renegade.
Long, dull western, stolid all round.

wd Delmer Daves *ph* J. Peverell Marley
m Victor Young

Alan Ladd, Audrey Dalton, Marisa Pavan, Robert Keith, Rodolpho Acosta, Charles Bronson, Warner Anderson, Elisha Cook Jnr, Anthony Caruso

Drums along the Mohawk***
US 1939 103m Technicolor
TCF (Raymond Griffith)

Colonists survive Indian attacks in upstate New York during the Revolutionary War.
Patchy, likeable period adventure story with domestic and farming interludes; in its way a key film in the director's canon.

w Lamar Trotti, Sonya Levien, *novel* Walter Edmonds *d John Ford ph Bert Glennon, Ray Rennahan* *m* Alfred Newman

Claudette Colbert, Henry Fonda, *Edna May Oliver*, Eddie Collins, John Carradine, Dorris Bowdon, Jessie Ralph, Arthur Shields, Robert Lowery, Roger Imhof, Ward Bond

Dubarry Was a Lady
US 1943 101m Technicolor
MGM (Arthur Freed)

A New Yorker imagines himself back at the court of Louis XIV.
Dull, stiff adaptation of a Broadway musical comedy, with changed songs.

w Irving Brecher, *book* B. G. De Sylva, Herbert Fields *d* Roy del Ruth *ph* Karl Freund
songs various

Gene Kelly, Lucille Ball, Red Skelton, Virginia O'Brien, Zero Mostel, Rags Ragland, Tommy Dorsey and his Orchestra

The Duchess and the Dirtwater Fox
US 1976 104m De Luxe Panavision
TCF (Melvin Frank)

A Barbary Coast con man and a saloon singer have various hectic adventures.
Wild and woolly spoof western which fires off aimlessly in a variety of styles and becomes merely tiresome despite good scenes.

w Melvin Frank, Barry Sandler *d* Melvin Frank *ph* Joseph Biroc *m* Charles Fox

George Segal, Goldie Hawn, Conrad Janis, Thayer David, Roy Jenson, Bob Hoy, Bennie Dobbins

'The classic western has now been shot to death by Sam Peckinpah, laughed to death by Mel Brooks and pondered to death by Arthur Penn, and Frank is like a scavenger picking up stray relics from its body.'—*Newsweek*

The Duchess of Idaho
US 1950 98m Technicolor
MGM (Joe Pasternak)

Romantic misunderstandings among candidates for Miss Idaho Potato.
Lightweight musical, quite pleasant if routine, with guest spots.

w Dorothy Cooper, Jerry Davis *d* Robert Z. Leonard *ph* Charles Schoenbaum *md* Georgie Stoll

Esther Williams, Van Johnson, John Lund, Paula Raymond, Clinton Sundberg; guests Red Skelton, Eleanor Powell, Lena Horne

Duck Soup****
US 1933 68m bw
Paramount

An incompetent becomes President of Fredonia and wages war on its scheming neighbour.
The satirical aspects of this film are fascinating but appear to have been unintentional. Never mind, it's also the most satisfying and undiluted Marx Brothers romp, albeit the one without

instrumental interludes. It does include the lemonade stall, the mirror sequence, and an endless array of one-liners and comedy choruses.

w Bert Kalmar, Harry Ruby, Arthur Sheekman, Nat Perrin d Leo McCarey ph Henry Sharp *m/ly Bert Kalmar, Harry Ruby ad Hans Dreier, Wiard Ihnen*

The Four Marx Brothers, Margaret Dumont, Louis Calhern, Edgar Kennedy, Raquel Torres

Duel***
US 1971 74 or 90m Technicolor TVM
Universal (George Eckstein)

A car driver on the back roads of California is menaced by a petrol tanker.
Overlong (even longer for theatrical release) but brilliantly made TV movie which started its director off on a successful career. A simple suspenser, it pits one man against a huge anonymous threat as unexplained as the menace in *The Birds*.

w Richard Matheson d Steven Spielberg ph Jack A. Marta m Billy Goldenberg

Dennis Weaver (the others are bit parts)

Duel at Diablo*
US 1965 103m De Luxe
UA / Nelson / Engel / Cherokee / Rainbow / Brien

White and black man fight together as apaches attack.
Well-paced, old-fashioned, shoot-em-up star western.

w Marvin H. Albert, Michel M. Grilikhes *d* Ralph Nelson *ph* Charles F. Wheeler *m* Neal Hefti

Sidney Poitier, James Garner, Bibi Andersson, Bill Travers, William Redfield, John Hoyt, John Hubbard

Duel in the Jungle
GB 1954 101m Technicolor
ABP / Marcel Hellman

An African explorer intends to defraud an insurance company and sets traps for the investigator who pursues him.
Lackadaisical romp in the studio jungle, none of it with much style or film sense.

w Sam Marx, T. J. Morrison *d* George Marshall *ph* Erwin Hillier *m* Mischa Spoliansky

Dana Andrews, Jeanne Crain, David Farrar, Patrick Barr

Duel in the Sun***
US 1946 135 or 138m Technicolor
David O. Selznick

A half-breed girl causes trouble between two brothers.
Massive western, dominated and fragmented by its producer, who bought the best talent and proceeded to interfere with it, so that while individual scenes are marvellous, the narrative has little flow. The final gory shoot-up between two lovers was much discussed at the time.

w David O. Selznick, Oliver H. P. Garrett, *novel* Niven Busch *d King Vidor* (and others) *second unit B. Reeves Eason, Otto Brower ph Lee Garmes, Harold Rosson, Ray Rennahan m Dmitri Tiomkin ad James Basevi pd J. McMillan Johnson*

Jennifer Jones, Joseph Cotten, Gregory Peck, Lionel Barrymore, Lillian Gish, Walter Huston, Herbert Marshall, Charles Bickford, Tilly Losch, Joan Tetzel, Harry Carey, Otto Kruger, Sidney Blackmer

Duffy
GB 1968 101m Technicolor
Columbia / Martin Manulis

Two half-brothers plan to rob their millionaire father.
Would-be with-it caper film, all flashy fragments and pop art, like sitting through a feature-length commercial. Exasperating.

w Donald Cammell, Harry Joe Brown Jnr *d* Robert Parrish *ph* Otto Heller *m* Ernie Freeman

James Coburn, James Mason, James Fox, Susannah York, John Alderton, Guy Deghy, Tutte Lemkow, Carl Duering, Marne Maitland

Duffy's Tavern
US 1945 97m bw
Paramount (Danny Dare)

The owner of a bar is helped by Hollywood stars.
Flat comedy based on a radio show and not helped by dismal guest star appearances.

w Melvin Frank, Norman Panama *d* Hal Walker *ph* Lionel Lindon

Ed Gardner, Victor Moore, Marjorie Reynolds, Barry Sullivan and guests including Bing Crosby, Bob Hope, Betty Hutton, Alan Ladd, Dorothy Lamour, Veronica Lake, William Bendix, Joan Caulfield

The Duke of West Point*
US 1938 112m bw
Edward Small

An extrovert army cadet finds the going tough.
Dated romantic flagwaver which pleased at the time.

w George Bruce *d* Alfred E. Green *ph* Robert Planck

Louis Hayward, Joan Fontaine, Tom Brown, Richard Carlson, Alan Curtis, Donald Barry, Gaylord Pendleton, Jed Prouty, Marjorie Gateson

Dulcima
GB 1971 98m Technicolor
EMI (Basil Rayburn)

A farmer's daughter reluctantly moves in with a persistent, lecherous old miser.
Weird sex melodrama from *Cold Comfort Farm* country, more risible than interesting.

wd Frank Nesbitt, *story* H. E. Bates *ph* Tony Imi *m* Johnny Douglas

John Mills, Carol White, Stuart Wilson, Bernard Lee, Dudley Foster

Dumbo***
US 1941 64m Technicolor
Walt Disney

A baby circus elephant finds that his big ears have a use after all.
Delightful cartoon feature notable for set pieces such as the drunken nightmare and the crows' song.

w various *d* Ben Sharpsteen

Dunkirk**
GB 1958 135m bw
MGM / Ealing (Michael Balcon)

In 1940 on the Normandy beaches, a small group gets detached from the main force.
Sober, small-scale approach to an epic subject; interesting but not inspiring, with performances to match.

w W. P. Lipscomb, David Divine *d* Leslie Norman *ph* Paul Beeson *m* Malcolm Arnold

John Mills, Richard Attenborough, Bernard Lee, Robert Urquhart, Ray Jackson

The Dunwich Horror*
US 1970 90m Movielab
AIP (Roger Corman, Jack Bohrer)

A young warlock plans to use his girl friend in a fertility rite.
Bookish horror story, quite well done against a village background.

w Curtis Lee Hanson, Henry Rosenbaum, Ronald Silkosky, *story* H. P. Lovecraft *d Daniel Haller* *ph* Richard C. Glouner *m* Les Baxter

Dean Stockwell, Sandra Dee, Ed Begley, Sam Jaffe, Lloyd Bochner

Dust Be My Destiny*
US 1939 88m bw
Warner (Lou Edelman)

A young misfit tries to find himself in the country.
Dated but well made social melodrama.

w Robert Rossen, *story* Jerome Odlum *d* Lewis Seiler *ph* James Wong Howe *m* Max Steiner

John Garfield, Priscilla Lane, Alan Hale, Frank McHugh, John Litel, Charles Grapewin, Billy Halop, Bobby Jordan, Stanley Ridges

Dutchman*
GB 1966 56m bw
Gene Persson

On a New York subway train a woman humiliates a black man and finally knifes him.
An allegory for addicts who can ferret out the meaning; on the surface, vaguely Pinterish and mainly boring.

w LeRoi Jones, from his play *d* Anthony Harvey *ph* Gerry Turpin *m* John Barry

Shirley Knight, Al Freeman Jnr

Dying Room Only*
US 1973 73m colour TVM
Lorimar

A woman's husband mysteriously disappears from the washroom of a roadside café.
Adequate suspenser.

w Richard Matheson *d* Philip Leacock

Cloris Leachman, Ross Martin, Ned Beatty, Louise Latham

Dynamite**
US 1929 129m bw
Paramount (Cecil B. de Mille)

In order to gain an inheritance, a socialite marries a man about to be executed . . . but he is reprieved.
Dated but still dynamic social melodrama of the early talkie period.

w Jeanie Macpherson *d* Cecil B. de Mille *ph* Peverell Marley *m* Herbert Stothart

Kay Johnson, Charles Bickford, Conrad Nagel, Julia Faye, Joel McCrea

'Exuberant, wonderfully vigorous, the film skilfully evokes the look and character of the Jazz Age.'—*Charles Higham*

Dynasty*
US 1976 100m colour TVM
David Frost

Problems of an Ohio pioneer family who become

rich between the 1820s and the 1880s.
Satisfying through-the-years family drama with pioneer background: a projected series did not go.

w Sidney Carrol, *novel* James A. Michener
d Lee Phillips
Sarah Miles, Stacy Keach, Harris Yulin, Harrison Ford, Tony Swartz

E

Each Dawn I Die*
US 1939 84m bw
Warner (David Lewis)

A crusading reporter is framed for manslaughter and becomes a hardened prisoner.
Efficient, vigorous yet slightly disappointing star vehicle; the talents are in the right background, but the script is wobbly.

w Norman Reilly Raine, Warren Duff, Charles Perry, *novel* Jerome Odlum *d* William Keighley *ph* Arthur Edeson *m* Max Steiner

James Cagney, George Raft, Jane Bryan, George Bancroft, Maxie Rosenbloom, Stanley Ridges, Alan Baxter, Victor Jory

The Eagle and the Hawk**
US 1933 72m bw
Paramount

In 1918 France, two American army fliers dislike each other but come together before the death of one of them.
Dawn Patrol melodrama, well done with unusually vivid dialogue and acting.

w Bogart Rogers, Seton I. Miller, *story* John Monk Saunders *d* Stuart Walker *ph* Harry Fischbeck

Fredric March, Cary Grant, Carole Lombard, Sir Guy Standing, Jack Oakie, Forrester Harvey

Eagle in a Cage*
GB 1970 103m Eastmancolor
Group W / Ramona (Millard Lampell, Albert Schwarz)

In 1815, a professional soldier becomes governor of St Helena and jailer to Napoleon.
Talkative, anecdotal, heavily serious historical reconstruction with good acting but little control.

w Millard Lampell *d* Fielder Cook *ph* Frano Vodopivec *m* Marc Wilkinson

John Gielgud, Ralph Richardson, Kenneth Haigh, Billie Whitelaw, Moses Gunn, Ferdy Mayne, Lee Montague

Eagle Squadron
US 1942 102m bw
Universal (Walter Wanger)

During World War II, American fliers join the RAF.
Studio-bound air epic, leavened with conventional romance but little humour or sympathy.

w Norman Reilly Raine, *story* C. S. Forester *d* Arthur Lubin *ph* Stanley Cortez *m* Frank Skinner

Robert Stack, Diana Barrymore, John Loder, Eddie Albert, Nigel Bruce, Leif Erickson, Edgar Barrier, Jon Hall, Evelyn Ankers, Isobel Elsom, Alan Hale Jnr, Don Porter, Frederick Worlock, Gladys Cooper

The Earl of Chicago*
US 1940 87m bw
MGM (Victor Saville)

An American gangster accedes to an English earldom but is tried for murder.
Unusual but unsatisfactory comedy-drama which rambles to a dismal conclusion but has entertaining passages.

w Lesser Samuels, *novel* Brock Williams *d* Richard Thorpe *m* Werner Heymann

Robert Montgomery, Edward Arnold, Reginald Owen, Edmund Gwenn

The Early Bird
GB 1965 98m Eastmancolor
Rank / Hugh Stewart

A milkman gets involved in an inter-company war.
Star farcical comedy; not the worst of Wisdom, but overlong and mainly uninventive.

w Jack Davies, Norman Wisdom, Eddie Leslie, Henry Blyth *d* Robert Asher *ph* Jack Asher *m* Ron Goodwin

Norman Wisdom, Edward Chapman, Jerry Desmonde, Paddie O'Neil, Bryan Pringle, Richard Vernon, John Le Mesurier, Peter Jeffrey

Earth II
US 1971 97m Metrocolor TVM
MGM / Wabe (William Reed Woodfield, Allan Balter)

A vast American space station is menaced by a Red Chinese nuclear weapon.

For its length probably the most expensive TV movie ever, scuttled by an entirely dull script and lack of humour.

w William Reed Woodfield, Allan Balter *d* Tom Gries *ph* Michel Hugo *m* Lalo Schifrin

Gary Lockwood, Scott Hylands, Hari Rhodes, Anthony Franciosa, Mariette Hartley, Gary Merrill, Inga Swenson, Lew Ayres

Earthquake*
US 1974 123m Technicolor
Panavision
Universal / Jennings Lang / Mark Robson

Various personal stories intertwine in a Los Angeles earthquake.
Dreary drama with very variable special effects, gimmicked up by Sensurround. A box office bonanza.

w George Fox, Mario Puzo *d* Mark Robson *ph* Philip Lathrop *m* John Williams *pd* Alexander Golitzen *sp* Albert Whitlock

Charlton Heston, Ava Gardner, Lorne Greene, Marjoe Gortner, Barry Sullivan, George Kennedy, Richard Roundtree, Geneviève Bujold, Walter Matthau (under the alias of his real name)

East of Eden**
US 1954 115m Warnercolor
Cinemascope
Warner (Elia Kazan)

In a California farming valley in 1913 a wild adolescent rebels against his stern father and discovers that his mother, believed dead, runs a nearby brothel.
Turgid elaboration of Genesis with strong character but nowhere to go. Heavily over-directed and rousingly acted.

w Paul Osborn, *novel* John Steinbeck *d Elia Kazan* *ph* Ted McCord *m* Leonard Rosenman *ad* James Basevi, Malcolm Bert

Raymond Massey, James Dean (his first star role), Julie Harris, Dick Davalos, *Jo Van Fleet*, Burl Ives, Albert Dekker

'The first distinguished production in Cinemascope.'—*Eugene Archer*

East of Sudan
GB 1964 94m Techniscope
Columbia / Ameran (Charles H. Schneer)

A trooper, a governess and others escape downriver from one of General Gordon's outposts.
Shameless borrowing of plot from *The African Queen* and footage from *The Four Feathers*. The purest hokum.

w Jud Kinberg *d* Nathan Juran *ph* Wilkie Cooper *m* Laurie Johnson

Anthony Quayle, Sylvia Syms, Jenny Agutter.

'Nathan Juran could direct this kind of thing blindfold, and for once would appear to have done so.'—*MFB*

East of Sumatra*
US 1953 82m Technicolor
U-I (Albert J. Cohen)

A mining engineer has trouble with the ruthless chief of a Pacific island.
A good example of routine Hollywood hokum, efficiently staged and acted.

w Frank Gill Jnr *d Budd Boetticher* *ph* Clifford Stine

Jeff Chandler, Anthony Quinn, Marilyn Maxwell, John Sutton

East Side West Side*
US 1949 108m bw
MGM (Voldemar Veltuguin)

A New York businessman is torn between his wife and another woman.
High class soap opera with all the production stops pulled out; generally well acted and reasonably entertaining.

w Isobel Lennart, *novel* Marcia Davenport *d* Mervyn Le Roy *ph* Charles Rosher *m* Miklos Rozsa

James Mason, Barbara Stanwyck, Van Heflin, Ava Gardner, *Gale Sondergaard*, Cyd Charisse, Nancy Davis, William Conrad

'No company is quite so adept as MGM at presenting basically uninteresting material with such style, and such a strong cast, that it cannot fail to entertain.'—*Penelope Houston*

Easter Parade**
US 1948 109m Technicolor
MGM (Arthur Freed)

A song and dance man quarrels with one partner but finds another.
A musical which exists only in its numbers, which are many but variable. All in all, an agreeable lightweight entertainment without the style to put it in the top class.

w Sidney Sheldon, Frances Goodrich, Albert Hackett *d* Charles Walters *ph* Harry Stradling *m/ly Irving Berlin*

Fred Astaire, Judy Garland, Ann Miller, Peter Lawford, Clinton Sundberg, Jules Munshin

Easy Living***
US 1937 91m bw
Paramount (Arthur Hornblow Jnr)

A fur coat is thrown out of a window and lands on a typist . . .
Amusing romantic comedy with farcical trimmings; it now stands among the classic crazy comedies of the thirties.

w Preston Sturges d Mitchell Leisen ph Ted Tetzlaff *m* Boris Morros

Jean Arthur, Ray Milland, *Edward Arnold*, Luis Alberni, Mary Nash, Franklin Pangborn, William Demarest, Andrew Tombes

Easy Living
US 1949 77m bw
RKO (Robert Sparks)

An ageing football star wants to retire but has to satisfy the living standards of his ambitious wife.
Dim drama.

w Charles Schnee, *story* Irwin Shaw *d* Jacques Tourneur *ph* Harry J. Wild *m* Roy Webb

Victor Mature, Lucille Ball, Lizabeth Scott, Sonny Tufts, Lloyd Nolan, Paul Stewart, Jack Paar, Jeff Donnell

Easy Money
GB 1948 93m bw
GFD / Gainsborough (A. Frank Bundy)

Four people win big prizes on the football pools.
Short story compendium; very average.

w Muriel and Sydney Box, *play* Arnold Ridley *d* Bernard Knowles

Edward Rigby, Greta Gynt, Dennis Price, Jack Warner, Mervyn Johns, Petula Clark, Marjorie Fielding, Bill Owen, Raymond Lovell

Easy Rider***
US 1969 94m Technicolor
Columbia / Pando / Raybert (Peter Fonda)

Two drop-outs ride across America on motorcycles.
Happening to please hippies and motor-cycle enthusiasts as well as amateur politicians, this oddball melodrama drew freakishly large audiences throughout the world and was much imitated though never equalled in its casual effectiveness, nor did promising careers ensue for the actors mainly concerned.

w Peter Fonda, Dennis Hopper, Terry Southern *d* Dennis Hopper *ph* Laszlo Kovacs *m* various recordings

Peter Fonda, Dennis Hopper, *Jack Nicholson*

'*Cinéma-vérité* in allegory terms.'—*Peter Fonda*

'Ninety-four minutes of what it is like to swing, to watch, to be fond, to hold opinions and to get killed in America at this moment.'—*Penelope Gilliatt*

Easy to Love
US 1953 96m Technicolor
MGM (Joe Pasternak)

The romances of an aqua-queen in Florida's Cypress Gardens.
Thin, humourless and forgettable musical vehicle sustained by spectacular water ballets.

w Laslo Vadnay, William Roberts *d* Charles Walters *ph* Ray June *m* Lennie Hayton, Georgie Stoll numbers; staged by *Busby Berkeley*

Esther Williams, Tony Martin, Van Johnson

Easy to Wed*
US 1946 110m Technicolor
MGM (Jack Cummings)

A socialite threatens a newspaper editor with libel; he postpones his own wedding and sets a friend to compromise her.
Bright but tasteless remake of *Libelled Lady*, with a second team cast trying hard.

w Dorothy Kingsley, Maurine Watkins, Howard Emmett Rogers, George Oppenheimer *d* Edward Buzzell *ph* Harry Stradling *m* Johnny Green

Van Johnson, Esther Williams, *Lucille Ball*, Keenan Wynn, Cecil Kellaway, Carlos Ramirez, Ben Blue, Ethel Smith

Ebb Tide**
US 1937 92m Technicolor
Paramount (Lucien Hubbard)

Sailors are stranded with a dangerous fanatic on a South Sea island.
Interesting adaptation of Stevenson, notable both for its early colour and its genuinely sour, anti-romantic mood, almost unique for Hollywood in this period.

w Bertram Millhauser, *novel* R. L. Stevenson and Lloyd Osbourne *d* James Hogan *ph* Leo Tover *m* Victor Young

Ray Milland, Frances Farmer, Oscar Homolka, Barry Fitzgerald, Lloyd Nolan

The Eddie Cantor Story
US 1953 116m Technicolor Cinemascope
Warner (Sidney Skolsky)

After a tough childhood on New York's east side, Israel Iskowitz becomes a famous entertainer.
Deliberately patterned after the success of *The Jolson Story*, this is an unhappy example of how close are success and failure; the elements are the

same, but this film suffers from unsure timing, lack of humour, rather apologetic numbers, a really dismal script and a caricature performance in the lead.

w Jerome Weidman, Ted Sherdeman, Sidney Skolsky *d* Alfred E. Green *ph* Edwin DuPar *md* Ray Heindorf *songs* various *ch* Le Roy Prinz

Keefe Brasselle, Marilyn Erskine, Aline MacMahon, Arthur Franz, Alex Gerry, Gerald Mohr, William Forrest (as Ziegfeld), Will Rogers Jnr (as Will Rogers), and Eddie Cantor (who also sings the songs off screen)

The Eddy Duchin Story
US 1955 123m Technicolor Cinemascope
Columbia (Jonie Taps, Jerry Wald)

The success story of a pianist who died of leukemia.
Predictable, glossy, sentimental musical biopic.

w Samuel Taylor *d* George Sidney *ph* Harry Stradling *md* George Duning *piano* Carmen Cavallero

Tyrone Power, Kim Novak, *Victoria Shaw*, James Whitmore, Shepperd Strudwick, Frieda Inescort, Gloria Holden, Larry Keating

Edge of Darkness*
US 1943 124m bw
Warner (Henry Blanke)

Norwegian village patriots resist the Nazis.
High-intentioned, ambitiously cast but ultimately bathetic resistance melodrama, high principled down to its tragic finale but compromised by backlot shooting and the presence of Errol Flynn.

w Robert Rossen *d* Lewis Milestone *ph* Sid Hickox *m* Franz Waxman

Errol Flynn, Ann Sheridan, Walker Huston, Judith Anderson, Ruth Gordon, Nancy Coleman, Helmut Dantine, Morris Carnovsky, Charles Dingle, John Beal, Richard Fraser, Helene Thimig

Edge of Doom
US 1950 97m bw
Samuel Goldwyn
GB title: *Stronger than Fear*

A desperate youth kills a priest and struggles with his conscience.
A sanctimonious weirdie, extremely odd coming from this producer, and unhappily re-edited before release. Someone was interested enough to want to make it, but it seems to have been killed by the cast and the front office.

w Philip Yordan, *novel* Leo Brady *d* Mark Robson *ph* Harry Stradling *m* Hugo Friedhofer

Dana Andrews, Farley Granger, Joan Evans, Robert Keith, Paul Stewart, Mala Powers, Adele Jergens, Harold Vermilyea, Mabel Paige

Edge of Eternity*
US 1959 80m Technicolor Cinemascope
Columbia / Thunderbird (Kendrick Sweet)

A Grand Canyon sheriff traces three murders to an ownership struggle over a disused mine.
Routine but suspenseful thriller with splendid locations.

w Knut Swenson, Richard Collins *d Don Siegel ph Burnett Guffey* *m* Daniele Amfitheatrof

Cornel Wilde, Victoria Shaw, Edgar Barrier, Mickey Shaughnessy, Jack Elam

Edge of the City**
US 1957 85m bw
MGM / Jonathan (David Susskind, Jim di Ganci)
GB title: *A Man is Ten Feet Tall*

Racial tensions lead to tragedy in the railroad yards of New York's waterfront.
Tense, brutal melodrama, which has historical interest as an effective opening-up in cinematic terms of a TV play, in its imitation of *On the Waterfront*, and in its rebel hero and relaxed black friend.

w Robert Alan Arthur, from his play *d Martin Ritt* *ph* Joseph Brun *m* Leonard Rosenman

Sidney Poitier, John Cassavetes, Jack Warden, Kathleen Maguire, Ruby Dee, Robert Simon, Ruth White

Edge of the World**
GB 1937 80m bw
GFD / Rock (Joe Rock)

Life, love and death on Foula, a remote Shetland island.
Rare for its time, a vigorous location drama in the Flaherty tradition; sometimes naïve, usually exhilarating.

wd Michael Powell

Niall MacGinnis, Belle Chrystal, John Laurie, Finlay Currie, Eric Berry

Edison the Man**
US 1940 107m bw
MGM (John W. Considine Jnr)

Edison struggles for years in poverty before becoming famous as the inventor of the electric light bulb.
Standard, well-made biopic following on from

Young Tom Edison; reasonably absorbing, but slightly suspect in its facts.

w Dore Schary, Talbot Jennings, Bradbury Foote, Hugo Butler *d Clarence Brown* *m* Herbert Stothart

Spencer Tracy, Rita Johnson, Lynne Overman, Charles Coburn, Gene Lockhart, Henry Travers, Felix Bressart

Edward My Son
GB 1948 112m bw
MGM (Edwin H. Knopf)

A rich, unscrupulous man remembers the people he has made unhappy, and the son to whom he never behaved as a father should.
Unsatisfactory, rather ugly-looking adaptation of a gripping piece of theatre, with casting and direction remarkably uncertain from such professionals.

w Donald Ogden Stewart, *play* Robert Morley *d* George Cukor

Spencer Tracy, Deborah Kerr, Ian Hunter, James Donald, Leueen McGrath, Mervyn Johns

The Effect of Gamma Rays on Man-in-the-Moon Marigolds
US 1972 101m De Luxe
Newman–Foreman

A slatternly middle-aged woman dreams of better times for herself and her children.
Well-written but essentially banal and pretentious domestic drama, the kind of film that only gets made when powerful stars see in it a juicy role.

w Alvin Sargent, *play* Paul Zendel *d* Paul Newman *ph* Adam Holender *m* Maurice Jarre
Joanne Woodward, Nell Potts, Roberta Wallach, Judith Lowry

The Egg and I*
US 1947 104m bw
U-I (Chester Erskine)

A city couple try to become gentleman farmers.
Mild, pleasant comedy notable chiefly for introducing a hillbilly couple, Ma and Pa Kettle, who went on, in the personae of Main and Kilbride, to make several later features. (See under Kettles.)

w Chester Erskine, Fred Finkelhoffe, *novel* Betty Macdonald *d* Chester Erskine *ph* Milton Krasner *m* Frank Skinner

Claudette Colbert, Fred MacMurray, *Marjorie Main, Percy Kilbride*, Louise Allbritton, Richard Long, Billy House, Ida Moore, Donald MacBride

The Egyptian*
US 1954 140m De Luxe
Cinemascope
TCF (Darryl F. Zanuck)

In ancient Egypt an abandoned baby grows up to be physician to the pharaoh.
More risible than reasonable, sounding more like a parody than the real thing, this pretentious epic from a bestseller flounders helplessly between its highlights but has moments of good humour and makes an excellent example of the pictures they don't make 'em like any more.

w Philip Dunne, Casey Robinson, *novel* Mika Waltari *d* Michael Curtiz *ph* Leon Shamroy *m* Bernard Herrmann, Alfred Newman *ad* Lyle Wheeler, George W. Davis

Edmund Purdom, Victor Mature, *Peter Ustinov*, Bella Darvi, Gene Tierney, Michael Wilding, Jean Simmons, Judith Evelyn, Henry Daniell, John Carradine, Carl Benton Reid

'The novel . . . supplied the reader with enough occurrences and customs of Akhnaton's time . . . to hide some of the more obvious contrivances of the story. The film does not do this.'—*Carolyn Harrow, Films in Review*

The Eiger Sanction*
US 1975 125m Technicolor
Panavision
Universal / Malpaso (Jennings Lang)

An art teacher returns to the CIA as an exterminator, and finds himself in a party climbing the Eiger.
Silly spy melodrama with some breathtaking mountain sequences.

w Warren B. Murphy, Hal Dresner, Rod Whitaker, *novel* Trevanian *d* Clint Eastwood *ph* Frank Stanley, John Cleare, Jeff Schoolfield, Peter Pilafian, Pete White *m* John Williams

Clint Eastwood, George Kennedy, Vonetta McGee, Jack Cassidy, Heidi Bruhl, Thayer David

'All the villains have been constructed from prefabricated Bond models.'—*Richard Combs*

Eight Iron Men
US 1952 80m bw
Columbia / Stanley Kramer

In the ruins of an Italian village, eight American infantrymen wait for relief.
Quickie war film in which everyone talks a lot and they all survive; from the time when Kramer was discovering how fast he could turn 'em out.

w Harry Brown, from his play A Sound of Hunting *d* Edward Dmytryk *ph* Roy Hunt *m* Leith Stevens *pd* Rudolph Sternad

Bonar Colleano, Lee Marvin, Arthur Franz, Richard Kiley, Nick Dennis, James Griffith, Dick Moore, George Cooper

Eighty Thousand Suspects*
GB 1963 113m bw Cinemascope
Rank / Val Guest

A smallpox epidemic terrorizes the city of Bath.
Predictable melodrama which adequately passes the time.

w Val Guest, *novel* Pillars of Midnight by Elleston Trevor *d* Val Guest *ph* Arthur Grant *m* Stanley Black

Claire Bloom, Richard Johnson, Yolande Donlan, Cyril Cusack, Michael Goodliffe, Mervyn Johns, Kay Walsh, Basil Dignam, Ray Barrett

El Cid*
US / Spain 1961 184m Super Technirama
Samuel Bronston

A legendary 11th-century hero drives the Moors from Spain.
Endless glum epic with splendid action sequences as befits the high budget.

w Frederic M. Frank, Philip Yordan *d* Anthony Mann *ph* Robert Krasker *m* Miklos Rozsa

Charlton Heston, Sophia Loren, Raf Vallone, Geraldine Page, John Fraser, Gary Raymond, Herbert Lom, Hurd Hatfield, Massimo Serato, Andrew Cruickshank, Michael Hordern, Douglas Wilmer, Frank Thring

El Dorado*
US 1966 126m Technicolor
Paramount / Laurel (Howard Hawks)

A gunfighter and a drunken sheriff tackle a villainous cattle baron.
Easy-going, semi-somnolent, generally likeable but disappointing western . . . an old man's movie all round.

w Leigh Brackett, *novel* The Stars in their Courses by Harry Joe Brown *d* Howard Hawks *ph* Harold Rosson *m* Nelson Riddle

John Wayne, Robert Mitchum, James Caan, Charlene Holt, Michele Carey, Ed Asner, Arthur Hunnicutt,
R. G. Armstrong, Paul Fix, Christopher George

'A rumbustious lament for the good days of the bad old west.'—*Tom Milne*

'A claustrophobic, careless and cliché-ridden thing, wavering constantly between campy self-deprecation and pretentious pomposity.'—*Richard Schickel*

Eleanor and Franklin**
US 1976 100m x 2 colour TVM
Talent Associates

After Franklin Roosevelt's death his wife looks back on their years together.
Careful saga of a political marriage, well though not excitingly presented.

w James Costigan, *book* Joseph P. Nash
d Daniel Petrie

Edward Herrmann, Jane Alexander, Ed Flanders, Rosemary Murphy

Electra Glide in Blue*
US 1973 113m De Luxe Panavision
UA / James William Guercio / Rupert Hitzig

A small-town motor-cycle cop becomes disillusioned.
Agreeable desert melodrama in the wake of *Easy Rider*, freshly observed with mordant humour, marred by a fashionable downbeat ending.

w Robert Boris d/m James William Guercio *ph Conrad Hall*

Robert Blake, Billy Green Bush, Mitch Ryan, Jeannine Riley, Elisha Cook Jnr, Royal Dana

Elephant Boy**
GB 1937 80m bw
Alexander Korda

In India, a boy elephant keeper helps government conservationists.
Documentary drama which seemed fresh and extraordinary at the time, has dated badly since, but did make an international star of Sabu.

w John Collier, Akos Tolnay, Marcia de Sylva *d Robert Flaherty, Zoltan Korda*

Sabu, Walter Hudd, Allan Jeayes, W. E. Holloway, Wilfrid Hyde White

'This is a fractured film, its skeleton is awry, its bones stick out through the skin.'—*Richard Griffith, 1941*

Elephant Walk*
US 1954 103m Technicolor
Paramount (Irving Asher)

The owner of a Ceylon tea plantation takes back an English wife who finds the atmosphere strange and turns to a friendly overseer for comfort.
Echoes of *Jane Eyre* and *Rebecca*, with stampeding elephants instead of a mad or dead wife. Grade A fiction for ladies.

w John Lee Mahin, *novel* Robert Standish *d* William Dieterle *ph* Loyal Griggs *m* Franz Waxman

Elizabeth Taylor, Peter Finch, Dana Andrews, Abraham Sofaer

'The climactic elephant stampede's a rouser—if you're still awake.'—*Judith Crist*

The Elevator*
US 1974 74m Technicolor TVM
Universal (William Frye)

A variety of people including an escaping thief are trapped in a high rise elevator.
Tolerable panic situation melodrama which does not quite thrill as it should.

w Bruce Shelly, David Ketchum, Rhoda Blecker *d* Jerry Jameson

James Farentino, Myrna Loy, Teresa Wright, Roddy McDowall, Carol Lynley, Don Stroud, Craig Stevens

Eleven Harrowhouse*
GB 1974 108m De Luxe Panavision
TCF / Harrowhouse (Elliott Kastner)

An American diamond merchant is robbed of a valuable jewel, and finds himself in the middle of an ingenious plot.
Amusing caper story marred by sudden changes of mood.

w Jeffrey Bloom, *novel* Gerald A. Browne *d* Aram Avakian *ph* Arthur Ibbetson *m* Michael J. Lewis

Charles Grodin, *James Mason*, Trevor Howard, John Gielgud, Candice Bergen, Peter Vaughan, Helen Cherry, Jack Watson, Jack Watling

Elizabeth of Ladymead
GB 1948 97m Technicolor
BL / Imperadio (Herbert Wilcox)

Four husbands of different generations come home from war (1854, 1903, 1919, 1946) to find their wives altered.
Thin star vehicle turns into an amateur-night compendium with a few funny moments.

w Frank Harvey, from his play *d* Herbert Wilcox

Anna Neagle, Hugh Williams, Bernard Lee, Michael Laurence, Nicholas Phipps, Isobel Jeans, Michael Shepley, Jack Allen

Ellery Queen

The debonair detective created by Manfred B. Lee and Frederic Dannay was seen in several unremarkable second features, usually with his secretary Nikki and his police inspector father. The first two were made for Republic, the rest for Columbia.

1935: THE SPANISH CAPE MYSTERY with Donald Cook
1936: THE MANDARIN MYSTERY (Eddie Quillan)
1940: ELLERY QUEEN MASTER DETECTIVE (Ralph Bellamy)
1941: ELLERY QUEEN'S PENTHOUSE MYSTERY, ELLERY QUEEN AND THE PERFECT CRIME, ELLERY QUEEN AND THE MURDER RING (all Bellamy)
1942: A CLOSE CALL FOR ELLERY QUEEN, A DESPERATE CHANCE FOR ELLERY QUEEN, ENEMY AGENTS MEET ELLERY QUEEN (all William Gargan)
In 1971 Peter Lawford starred in a TV pilot, *Don't Look Behind You*, and in 1975 a one-season series starred Jim Hutton. The books, pseudonymously authored by Ellery Queen, were far more popular than any of the movies.

Ellery Queen: Don't Look behind You
US 1971 95m Technicolor TVM
Universal

Ellery catches a mad strangler known as the Hydra.
Passable, over-padded mystery with nice locations.

w Ted Leighton, *novel* Cat O'Nine Tails by Ellery Queen *d* Barry Shear

Peter Lawford, Stefanie Powers, Harry Morgan, E. G. Marshall, Colleen Gray, Skye Aubrey

Ellery Queen
US 1975 100m Technicolor TVM
Universal
GB title: *The Ellery Queen Whodunit*

Ellery finds the murderer of a fashion designer.
Rather tedious pilot nicely set in the forties: the resultant series lasted one season.

w Richard Levinson, William Link *d* David Greene

Jim Hutton, Ray Milland, David Wayne, Kim Hunter, Monte Markham

Elmer Gantry**
US 1960 146m Eastmancolor
UA / Bernard Smith

The exploits of an American evangelist in the twenties.
Mainly gripping but overlong exposé of commercialized small-town religion

wd Richard Brooks, novel Sinclair Lewis *ph John Alton m* André Previn *ad Edward Carrere*

Burt Lancaster, Jean Simmons, Arthur Kennedy, *Shirley Jones*, Dean Jagger, Edward Andrews, Patti Page, John McIntire

Elopement
US 1952 82m bw
TCF (Fred Kohlmar)
A girl student eloping with her professor is chased by her father.
Unconvincing domestic comedy with some lively chase sequences.
w Bess Taffell *d* Henry Koster *ph* Joseph La Shelle
Clifton Webb, Charles Bickford, Anne Francis, William Lundigan, Margalo Gillmore, Evelyn Varden, Reginald Gardiner

Elstree Calling**
GB 1930 86m bw and colour
BIP / Wardour
A film studio mounts a television show.
Slender excuse for an all-star revue which luckily preserves much light entertainment talent of the time.
w Adrian Brunel, Walter C. Mycroft, Val Valentine *d* Adrian Brunel, Alfred Hitchcock, Jack Hulbert, André Charlot, Paul Murray
Tommy Handley, Jack Hulbert, Cicely Courtneidge, Will Fyffe, Lily Morris, Teddy Brown, Anna May Wong, Gordon Harker, Donald Calthrop, John Longden, Jameson Thomas, Bobbie Comber

The Elusive Pimpernel*
GB 1950 109m Technicolor
BL / London Films (Michael Powell, Emeric Pressburger)
A foppish 18th-century London dandy is actually the hero who rescues French aristocrats from the guillotine.
Expensive remake of *The Scarlet Pimpernel* which fails to please, apparently because the talents were not congenial to the subject. Interesting detail, though.
wd Michael Powell, Emeric Pressburger, *novel* Baroness Orczy *ph* Christopher Challis *m* Brian Easdale *ph* Hein Heckroth
David Niven, Margaret Leighton, Cyril Cusack, Jack Hawkins, David Hutcheson, Robert Coote
'The quality of excitement which should carry the film is quite lost. *The Elusive Pimpernel* is highly—often too highly—coloured, and has an artificiality quite different in character from that of the original.'—*Penelope Houston*

Embassy*
US 1972 90m colour
Hemdale / Triad / Weaver (Mel Ferrer)
At the US Embassy in Beirut, a Soviet official seeking asylum is in danger from a KGB killer.
Goodish suspenser with reasonably literate dialogue and several Hitchcockian sequences.
w William Fairchild d Gordon Hessler
ph Raoul Coutard *m* Jonathan Hodge
Richard Roundtree, Chuck Connors, Max Von Sydow, Broderick Crawford, Ray Milland

Emergency
US 1971 100m Technicolor TVM
Universal / Jack Webb
Adventures of a paramedic unit supervised by the city hospital and fire departments.
Rather dull multi-storied ambulance-chasing action drama which spawned a five-year series.
w Harold Jack Bloom *d* Christian Nyby
Rudolph Mantooth, Robert Fuller, Julie London, Bobby Troup

Emil and the Detectives*
GB 1935 70m bw
Gaumont / Richard Wainwright
A 10-year-old boy and some street urchins track down the thief of a wallet.
Reasonably lively children's film.
w Cyrus Brooks, Margaret Carter, Frank Launder, *novel* Erich Kaestner *d* Milton Rosmer
George Hayes, Mary Glynne, John Williams (as Emil), Clare Greet, George Merritt

Emil and the Detectives*
US 1964 100m Technicolor
Walt Disney (Peter V. Harald)
Modest, likeable remake filmed on location in Germany.
w A. J. Carothers *d* Peter Tewkesbury
ph Gunter Sentleben *m* Heinz Schreiter
Bryan Russell, Walter Slezak, Heinz Schubert, Roger Mobley

Emma*
US 1932 73m bw
MGM
A servant marries into the family.
Predictably cosy family drama tailored for its star.
w Frances Marion, Leonard Praskins, Zelda Sears *d* Clarence Brown *ph* Oliver T. Marsh
Marie Dressler, Richard Cromwell, Jean Hersholt, Myrna Loy, John Miljan, Purnell E. Pratt

Emperor of the North Pole*
US 1973 119m De Luxe
TCF / Inter Hemisphere (Robert Aldrich)
GB title: *Emperor of the North*

In 1933 Oregon, freeloading hobos are brutally attacked by a sadistic train guard.
Unlikely melodrama with vicious but exhilarating high spots separating acres of verbiage.

w Christopher Knopf *d* Robert Aldrich
ph Joseph Biroc *m* Frank de Vol

Lee Marvin, Ernest Borgnine, Keith Carradine, Charles Tyner, Malcolm Atterbury, Elisha Cook Jnr

'It's hard, contrived, pointless in its thesis, repulsive in its people, and it's singularly joyless and contemptible in its glorification of the bum and freeloader.'—*Judith Crist*

The Emperor Waltz
US 1948 106m Technicolor
Paramount (Charles Brackett)

In 1901 Austria, a countess falls for an American phonograph salesman.
Thin to the point of emaciation, this witless comedy with music, dully set-bound, proved its director's strangest and most unsatisfactory choice.

w Charles Brackett, Billy Wilder *d* Billy Wilder
ph George Barnes *m* Victor Young
songs Johnny Burke, James Van Heusen
ad Hans Dreier, Franz Bachelin

Bing Crosby, Joan Fontaine, Roland Culver, Lucile Watson, Richard Haydn, Harold Vermilyea, Sig Rumann, Julie Dean

The Emperor's Candlesticks*
US 1937 89m bw
MGM (John Considine Jnr)

In old Russia, spies on opposite sides fall in love.
Lavish romantic comedy drama, generally well handled; superior Hollywood moonshine.

w Monckton Hoffe, Herman J. Mankiewicz, Harold Goldman, *novel* Baroness Orczy
d George Fitzmaurice *ph* Harold Rosson
m Franz Waxman

William Powell, Luise Rainer, Maureen O'Sullivan, Robert Young, Frank Morgan, Douglass Dumbrille

The Enchanted Cottage*
US 1945 92m bw
RKO

A plain girl and a disfigured man are beautiful to each other.
Wartime updating of a sentimental old play; insufficiently well considered to be more than tolerable.

w De Witt Bodeen, Herman J. Mankiewicz, *play* Sir Arthur Wing Pinero *d* John Cromwell
ph Ted Tetzlaff *m* Roy Webb

Dorothy McGuire, Robert Young, Herbert Marshall, Mildred Natwick

The Enchanted Forest*
US 1945 77m Cinecolor
PRC

Old John the Hermit talks to trees and animals, and rescues a lost child.
Surprising piece of Victorian whimsy, remarkably effective in its unambitious way, especially as a product of this studio. The best known example of Cinecolor.

w Robert Lee Johnson, John Le Bar, Lou Brock
d Lew Landers *ph* Marcel Le Picard *m* Alfred Hay Malotte

Harry Davenport, Edmund Lowe, Brenda Joyce, Billy Severn

Enchanted Island
US 1958 94m Technicolor
Waverly (Benedict Bogeaus)

In the 1840s two sailors jump ship and settle on what they later discover to be a cannibal island.
Tame adaptation of a minor classic, with the actors all at sea.

w James Leicester, Harold Jacob Smith, *novel* Typee by Herman Melville *d* Allan Dwan
ph George Stahl *m* Raul Lavista

Jane Powell (an unconvincing Polynesian), Dana Andrews, Don Dubbins, Arthur Shields, Ted de Corsia, Friedrich Ledebur

Enchantment**
US 1948 101m bw
Samuel Goldwyn

A London house tells the story of three generations.
Yes, a house tells the story, and the leading characters are called Rollo and Lark, but this is a very appealing piece of period romantic nonsense, with the highest possible gloss upon it.

w John Patrick, novel A Fugue in Time by Rumer Godden *d Irving Reis ph Gregg Toland*
m Hugo Friedhofer

David Niven, Teresa Wright, Evelyn Keyes, Farley Granger, Jayne Meadows, Leo G. Carroll

Encore*
GB 1951 88m bw
GFD / Two Cities

Three more Somerset Maugham short stories introduced by the author.
The final follow-up to the success of *Quartet* and *Trio*; television playlets quickly made this kind of short story seem old-fashioned, but the standard here was high.

w T. E. B. Clarke, Arthur Macrae, Eric Ambler, *stories* The Ant and the Grasshopper, Winter Cruise, Gigolo and Gigolette *d* Pat Jackson, Anthony Pelissier, Harold French *ph* Desmond Dickinson *m* Richard Addinsell

Nigel Patrick, Roland Culver, *Kay Walsh*, Noel Purcell, Ronald Squire, John Laurie, Glynis Johns, Terence Morgan, David Hutcheson

The End of the Affair
GB 1954 106m bw
Columbia / Coronado (David Lewis)

In wartime London, a repressed wife has an affair with a writer but develops religious guilt which leads indirectly to her death.
Glum sinning in Greeneland; over-ambitious, miscast, and poor-looking.

w Lenore Coffee, *novel* Graham Greene
d Edward Dmytryk *ph* Wilkie Cooper
w Benjamin Frankel

Deborah Kerr, Van Johnson, Peter Cushing, John Mills, Stephen Murray, Nora Swinburne, Charles Goldner

The End of the River*
GB 1947 83m bw
GFD / The Archers (Michael Powell, Emeric Pressburger)

A South American Indian boy flees to the outside world and finds life in the city as dangerous as in the jungle.
Strange but oddly impressive departure for British film-makers at this time. A commercial and critical disaster.

w Wolfgang Wilhelm *d* Derek Twist
ph Christopher Challis *m* Lambert Williamson

Sabu, Esmond Knight, Bibi Ferreira, Robert Douglas, Antoinette Cellier, Raymond Lovell, Torin Thatcher

The End of the Road*
GB 1954 77m bw
Group Three (Alfred Shaughnessy)

A retired engineer becomes frustrated by idleness, and his family contemplate sending him to an old people's home.
Reasonably absorbing study of old age, suffering from a contrived end.

w James Forsyth, Geoffrey Orme *d* Wolf Rilla
ph Arthur Grant *m* John Addison

Finlay Currie, Duncan Lamont, Naomi Chance, David Hannaford

Endless Night*
GB 1971 99m Eastmancolor
BL / EMI (Leslie Gilliat)

An American girl buys an English stately home and marries a chauffeur, but is later frightened to death.
Bumpy British thriller, structurally weak and peopled by the dullest conceivable characters, but with watchably scary sequences.

wd Sidney Gilliat, *novel* Agatha Christie
ph Harry Waxman *m* Bernard Herrmann

Hayley Mills, Hywel Bennett, George Sanders, Britt Ekland, Per Oscarsson, Lois Maxwell

The Enemy Below*
US 1957 98m Technicolor Cinemascope
TCF (Dick Powell)

During World War II an American destroyer in the South Atlantic is involved in a cat-and-mouse operation with a U-boat.
Well-staged, unsurprising naval thriller with good pace and a pat let's-not-be-nasty-to-each-other ending.

w Wendell Mayes, *novel* Commander D. A. Rayner *d Dick Powell* *ph* Harold Rosson
m Leigh Harline

Robert Mitchum, Curt Jurgens, Theodore Bikel, David Hedison

The Enemy General
US 1960 74m bw
Columbia (Sam Katzman)

An American officer takes revenge on the German general who executed his fiancée.
Routine World War II heroics with a plot deserving a rather better production.

w Dan Pepper, Burt Picard *d* George Sherman
ph Basil Emmott *m* Mischa Bakaleinikoff

Van Johnson, Jean-Pierre Aumont, John Van Dreelen, Dany Carrel, Françoise Prévost

The Enforcer***
US 1950 87m bw
United States Pictures (Milton Sperling)
GB title: *Murder, Inc*

A crusading District Attorney tracks down the leader of a gang which murders for profit.
Extremely suspenseful and well-characterized police yarn based on fact. One of the very best of its kind.

w Martin Rackin *d Bretaigne Windust*
ph Robert Burks *m* David Buttolph

Humphrey Bogart, Everett Sloane, Zero Mostel, Ted de Corsia, Roy Roberts, King Donovan

'A tough, very slickly-made thriller with a host of fine character parts.'—*NFT, 1969*

England Made Me**
GB 1972 100m Eastmancolor
Hemdale / Atlantic (Jack Levin)

In 1935 a sponging Englishman becomes involved through his sister with a German financier.
Somewhat altered from the novel, this unusual film remains a lively, intelligent character melodrama.

w Desmond Cory, Peter Duffell, *novel* Graham Greene *d Peter Duffell ph* Ray Parslow *m* John Scott

Peter Finch, Michael York, Hildegarde Neil, *Michael Hordern*, Joss Ackland

English without Tears*
GB 1944 89m bw
GFD / Two Cities (Anatole de Grunwald, Sydney Box)
US title: *Her Man Gilbey*

World War II: a rich ATS girl falls for her butler who has become a lieutenant.
Wispy satirical comedy with amusing moments, chiefly interesting for the pre-war League of Nations sequences.

w Terence Rattigan, Anatole de Grunwald *d* Harold French

Lilli Palmer, Michael Wilding, *Margaret Rutherford*, Penelope Dudley Ward, Albert Lieven, Roland Culver, Peggy Cummins

Ensign Pulver
US 1964 104m Technicolor Panavision
Warner (Joshua Logan)

Further naval misadventures of the character from *Mr Roberts*.
Threadbare naval comedy with every expected cliché.

w Joshua Logan, Peter S. Feibleman, *play* Joshua Logan, Thomas Heggen *d* Joshua Logan *ph* Charles Lawton *m* George Duning

Robert Walker, Burl Ives, Walter Matthau, Tommy Sands, Millie Perkins, Kay Medford, Larry Hagman, James Farentino, James Coco, Al Freeman Jnr

Enter Laughing*
US 1967 111m Technicolor
Columbia / Acre / Sajo (Carl Reiner, Joseph Stein)

In New York in the thirties, a young man about to train as a pharmacist decides to become an actor instead.
Strident Jewish comedy based on the writer-director's own youthful experiences, which might have been more effectively strained by another hand. The talent is there, though.

w Joseph Stein, Carl Reiner, *play* Carl Reiner *d* Carl Reiner *ph* Joseph Biroc *m* Quincy Jones

Reni Santoni, Jose Ferrer, Shelley Winters, Elaine May, Jack Gilford, Janet Margolin, David Opatoshu, Michael J. Pollard

Enter the Dragon**
US/Hong Kong 1973 99m Technicolor Panavision
Warner / Concord (Fred Weintraub, Paul Heller)

A master of martial arts is enlisted by British intelligence to stop opium smuggling.
The first Hollywood-based Kung Fu actioner; not bad, on the lines of a more violent James Bond.

w Michael Allin *d* Robert Clouse *ph* Gilbert Hubbs *m* Lalo Schifrin

Bruce Lee, John Saxon, Shih Kien, Jim Kelly, Bob Wall

The Entertainer*
GB 1960 96m bw
BL / Bryanston / Woodfall / Holly (John Croydon)

A faded seaside comedian reflects on his failure as an entertainer and as a man.
Even with Olivier repeating his stage triumph, or perhaps because of it, this tragi-comedy remains defiantly theatrical and doesn't take wing on film.

w John Osborne, Nigel Kneale, *play* John Osborne *d* Tony Richardson *ph* Oswald Morris *m* John Addison

Laurence Olivier, Joan Plowright, Brenda de Banzie, *Roger Livesey*, Alan Bates, Shirley Anne Field, Albert Finney, Thora Hird, Daniel Massey

'No amount of deafening sound effects and speciously busy cutting can remove one's feeling that behind this distracting façade of heightened realism lurks a basic lack of confidence.'—*Peter John Dyer*

The Entertainer*
US 1976 100m colour TVM
Robert Stigwood

American TV adaptation of the above: it only springs into life when Ray Bolger's around.

m Marvin Hamlisch

Jack Lemmon, *Ray Bolger*, Sada Thompson

Entertaining Mr Sloane*
GB 1969 94m Technicolor
Pathe / Canterbury (Douglas Kentish)

A lodger attracts the amorous attention of both the middle-aged daughter and older son of the house.
A Gothic *tour de force* of bad taste which worked better on the stage but has its moments.

w Clive Exton, *play* Joe Orton *d* Douglas Hickox *ph* Wolfgang Suschitsky *m* Georgie Fame

Beryl Reid, Harry Andrews, Peter McEnery, Alan Webb

Eric*
US 1975 100m colour TVM
Lorimar

The last year of a young man dying of cancer.
One may suspect the motive and the point, but the thing is nicely done.

novel Doris Lund *d* James Goldstone

John Savage, Patricia Neal, Claude Akins, Sian Barbara Allen, Nehemiah Persoff

The Errand Boy
US 1961 92m bw
Paramount / Jerry Lewis

A dimwit paperhanger causes havoc in a Hollywood studio but is eventually signed up as a comic to rival Jerry Lewis.
Feeble comedy with the star at his self-satisfied worst.

wd Jerry Lewis *ph* W. Wallace Kelley

Jerry Lewis, Brian Donlevy, Sig Rumann, Fritz Feld, Isobel Elsom, Iris Adrian

Escapade
US 1935 87m bw
MGM (Bernard Hyman)

Affairs of a Viennese artist.
Turgid romantic drama copied from the more successful German film *Maskerade*.

w Herman J. Mankiewicz, *original* Walter Reisch *d* Robert Z. Leonard *ph* Ernest Haller *n* Bronislau Kaper, Walter Jurmann

William Powell, Luise Rainer, Virginia Bruce, Mady Christians, Reginald Owen, Frank Morgan, Laura Hope Crews, Henry Travers

Escapade*
GB 1955 87m bw
Pinnacle (Daniel Angel)

Parents row with a headmaster when their three sons steal an aeroplane, but all is well when it turns out that they are on a peace mission.
Whimsical comedy-drama with a rather foolish point; the cast however can hardly fail to provide entertaining moments.

w Gilbert Holland (Donald Ogden Stewart), *play* Roger MacDougall *d* Philip Leacock *ph* Eric Cross *m* Bruce Montgomery

John Mills, Alastair Sim, Yvonne Mitchell, Colin Gordon, Marie Lohr

Escapade in Florence
US 1962 80m Technicolor
Walt Disney (Bill Anderson)

Two American students in Florence uncover art thefts.
Cheerful adventure for children, well enough produced on location, but quite unmemorable.

w Maurice Tombragel *d* Steve Previn *ph* Kurt Grigoleit *m* Buddy Baker

Ivan Desny, Tommy Kirk, Annette Alliotto, Nino Castelnuovo

Escapade in Japan
US 1957 93m Technirama
RKO (Arthur Lubin)

An American boy survives a plane crash in Tokyo and the crisis reunites his parents.
Nicely photographed travelogue with a thread of plot; pleasant but hardly sustaining.

w Winston Miller *d* Arthur Lubin *ph* William Snyder *m* Max Steiner

Cameron Mitchell, Teresa Wright, Jon Prevost, Philip Ober

Escape**
US 1940 104m bw
MGM

An American gets his mother out of a Nazi concentration camp before World War II.
Ingenious but somewhat slow-moving melodrama with an exciting climax and good production values.

w Arch Oboler, Marguerite Roberts, *novel* Ethel Vance *d Mervyn Le Roy* *m* Franz Waxman

Norma Shearer, Robert Taylor, *Conrad Veidt*, *Nazimova*, Felix Bressart, Albert Basserman, Philip Dorn, Bonita Granville

'It takes an hour to get started and makes just another feeble fable from headlines.'—*Otis Ferguson*

Escape
GB 1948 79m bw
TCF (William Perlberg)

A convict escapes from Dartmoor prison and falls in love with a girl who helps him.
Wholly artificial, predictable and uninterestingly made melodrama from a dated play which at least had something to say.

w Philip Dunne, *play* John Galsworthy *d* Joseph L. Mankiewicz *ph* Frederick A. Young *m* William Alwyn

Rex Harrison, Peggy Cummins, William Hartnell, Norman Wooland, Jill Esmond

Escape
US 1971 74m colour TVM
Paramount

An escapologist becomes a spy.
Silly comic strip adventures with entertainingly hare-brained action climaxes.

w Paul Playdon *d* John Llewellyn Moxey

Christopher George, Avery Schreiber, Marlyn Mason, Gloria Grahame, William Windom, John Vernon, William Schallert

Escape from East Berlin
Germany / US 1962 94m bw
MGM / Walter Wood / Hans Albin
aka: *Tunnel 28*

An East German chauffeur is persuaded to help an escape attempt by digging and tunnelling under the Berlin Wall.
Cheerless escape melodrama, thinly based on fact but without much suspense.

w Gabrielle Upton, Peter Berneis, Millard Lampell *d* Robert Siodmak *ph* Georg Krause *m* Hans-Martin Majewski

Don Murray, Christine Kaufmann, Werner Klemperer, Ingrid van Bergen

Escape from Fort Bravo*
US 1953 98m Anscocolor
MGM (Nicholas Nayfack)

A girl helps her Confederate lover to escape from a Yankee fort in Arizona; the commander then tries to save them from Indians.
Grade A western, effectively shot in Death Valley.

w Frank Fenton *d* John Sturges *ph* Robert Surtees *m* Jeff Alexander

William Holden, Eleanor Parker, John Forsythe, William Demarest

Escape from the Dark
GB 1976 104m Technicolor
Walt Disney (Ron Miller)

In 1909 Yorkshire, two boys save pit ponies from the slaughterhouse.
Efficient family fare with plenty of suspense and good character cameos.

w Rosemary Anne Sisson *d* Charles Jarrott *ph* Paul Beeson *m* Ron Goodwin

Alastair Sim, Peter Barkworth, Maurice Colbourne, Susan Tebbs, Geraldine McEwan, Prunella Scales, Leslie Sands, Joe Gladwin

Escape from the Planet of the Apes see Planet of the Apes

Escape from Zahrain
US 1961 93m Technicolor Panavision
Paramount (Ronald Neame)

Prisoners escape across the desert from an oil sheikdom.
Slow, boring adventure film; good to look at, with James Mason unbilled in a tiny part.

w Robin Estridge *d* Ronald Neame *ph* Ellsworth Fredericks *m* Lyn Murray

Yul Brynner, Sal Mineo, Madlyn Rhue, Jack Warden, Jay Novello

Escape in the Desert
US 1945 81m bw
Warner (Alex Gottlieb)

An American flier outwits renegade Nazis.
Oddball remake of *The Petrified Forest*, with Nazis sitting in for gangsters. Of no interest in itself.

w Thomas Job, *play* Robert E. Sherwood *d* Edward A. Blatt *ph* Robert Burks *m* Adolph Deutsch

Philip Dorn, Helmut Dantine, Alan Hale, Jean Sullivan, Irene Manning, Samuel S. Hinds

Escape Me Never*
GB 1935 95m bw
B and D (Herbert Wilcox)

The mother of an illegitimate baby marries a composer who loves someone else.
Archetypal romantic weepie which has probably the star's most memorable and likeable performance.

w Carl Zuckerman, Robert Cullen, *play* Margaret Kennedy *d* Paul Czinner

Elisabeth Bergner, Hugh Sinclair, Griffith Jones, Penelope Dudley Ward, Irene Vanbrugh, Leon Quartermaine, Lyn Harding

Escape Me Never
US 1947 104m bw
Warner (Henry Blanke)

Muddled remake of the above with shifted emphasis. So ill-conceived it's like watching through frosted glass.

w Thomas Williamson, *play* Margaret Kennedy *d* Peter Godfrey *ph* Sol Polito *m* Erich Wolfgang Korngold

Errol Flynn, Ida Lupino, Eleanor Parker, Gig Young, Reginald Denny, Isobel Elsom, Albert Basserman, Ludwig Stossel, Helene Thimig

Escape to Burma
US 1955 88m Technicolor Superscope
Benedict Bogeaus

An adventurer suspected of murder hides out on the tea plantation of an indomitable American woman.
Far Eastern hokum in which the heroine has a way with elephants.

w Talbot Jennings, Herbert Donovan *d* Allan Dwan *ph* John Alton *m* Louis Forbes

Barbara Stanwyck, Robert Ryan, David Farrar, Murvyn Vye, Reginald Denny

Escape to Glory
US 1940 74m bw
Columbia (Sam Bischoff)
aka: *Submarine Zone*

A merchant ship with a variety of passengers is stalked by a Nazi submarine.
Minor *Grand Hotel* afloat: quite brisk and watchable.

w P. J. Wolfson *d* John Brahm *ph* Franz Planer

Pat O'Brien, Constance Bennett, John Halliday, Alan Baxter, Melville Cooper, Edgar Buchanan, Marjorie Gateson

Escape to Mindanao
US 1968 95m Technicolor TVM
Universal (Jack Leewood)

Two Americans escape from a Japanese POW camp.
Routine war action.

w Harold Livingston *d* Don McDougall

George Maharis, Willi Coopman, Nehemiah Persoff, James Shigeta

Escape to Witch Mountain*
US 1974 97m Technicolor
Walt Disney (Jerome Courtland)

Two mysterious orphan children have extraordinary powers, are chased by a scheming millionaire, and prove to come from another planet.
Mildly ingenious story frittered away by poor scripting and special effects. A stimulating change in children's films, however.

w Robert Malcolm Young, *novel* Alexander Key *d* John Hough *ph* Frank Phillips *m* Johnny Mandel *sp* Art Cruickshank, Danny Lee

Ray Milland, Donald Pleasance, Eddie Albert, Kim Richards, Ike Eisenmann, Walter Barnes, Reta Shaw, Denver Pyle

Espionage*
US 1937 67m bw
MGM (Harry Rapf)

Spies and counter spies mingle on the Orient Express.
Lively second feature on familiar lines.

w Manuel Seff, Leonard Lee, Ainsworth Morgan, *play* Walter Hackett *d* Kurt Neumann *ph* Ray June

Edmund Lowe, Madge Evans, Paul Lukas, Ketti Gallian, Skeets Gallagher, Leonid Kinskey, Barnett Parker, Frank Reicher

Espionage Agent
US 1939 83m bw
Warner (Louis F. Edelmann)

An American diplomat falls in love with a spy.
Anti-isolationist, semi-documentary exposé, a rather sketchy cross between *Foreign Correspondent* and *Confessions of a Nazi Spy.*

w Warren Duff, Michael Fessier, Frank Donaghue, Robert Buckner *d* Lloyd Bacon *ph* Charles Rosher

Joel McCrea, Brenda Marshall, Jeffrey Lynn, George Bancroft, Stanley Ridges, James Stephenson, Nana Bryant

Esther and the King
US 1960 109m Technicolor Cinemascope
TCF / Galatea (Raoul Walsh)

A Persian king selects a new bride who helps defend him from his enemies.
Tedious biblical hokum with a muddled script and the usual co-production deficiencies.

w Raoul Walsh, Michael Elkins *d* Raoul Walsh *ph* Mario Bava *m* Francesco Lavagnino

Richard Egan, Joan Collins, Dennis O'Dea, Sergei Fantoni, Rik Battaglia

Esther Waters
GB 1947 108m bw
GFD / Wessex (Ian Dalrymple)

In the 1870s, a maid is seduced by a squire but insists on bringing up her child without help.
Faded costumer with tentative performances and little else to recommend it.

w Michael Gordon, William Rose, Gerard Tyrrell, *novel* George Moore *d* Ian Dalrymple, Peter Proud *ph* C. Pennington-Richards, H. E. Fowle *m* Gordon Jacob

Kathleen Ryan, Dirk Bogarde, Cyril Cusack, Ivor Barnard, Fay Compton, Mary Clare, Morland Graham

The Eternal Sea
US 1955 96m bw
Republic (John H. Auer)

The career of an aircraft carrier captain in World War II and Korea.
Solemn biopic of John Hoskins: competent but quite uninspired.

w Allen Rivkin *d* John H. Auer *ph* John L. Russell Jnr *m* Elmer Bernstein

Sterling Hayden, Alexis Smith, Dean Jagger, Virginia Grey

Eternally Yours*
US 1939 95m bw
Walter Wanger

A magician's wife thinks he is too interested in his tricks.
Slightly scatty romantic comedy, amiable if not quite good enough to stand the test of time, but with a great cast.

w Gene Towne, Graham Baker *d* Tay Garnett *ph* Merritt Gerstad *m* Werner Janssen

Loretta Young, David Niven, Broderick Crawford, Hugh Herbert, Billie Burke, C. Aubrey Smith, Raymond Walburn, Zasu Pitts, Virginia Field, Eve Arden, Herman the Rabbit

Eureka Stockade
GB 1948 103m bw
Ealing (Leslie Norman)

In 1850, Australian gold miners revolt against a harsh governor.
Unconvincingly made historical actioner from Ealing's antipodean period.

w Harry Watt, Walter Greenwood, Ralph Smart *d* Harry Watt

Chips Rafferty, Jane Barrett, Gordon Jackson, Jack Lambert, Peter Illing, Ralph Truman, Peter Finch

The Eve of St Mark
US 1944 95m bw
TCF

A small-town boy goes to war and his sweetheart waits for him.
Poetic propaganda based on a sticky play which however had a tragic ending which the film eschews. Smartly made is all one can say.

w George Seaton, *play* Maxwell Anderson *d* John M. Stahl *ph* Joseph La Shelle *m* Cyril Mockridge

William Eythe, Anne Baxter, Michael O'Shea, Vincent Price, Ruth Nelson, Ray Collins, Stanley Prager, Henry Morgan

Evel Knievel
US 1971 90m Metrocolor
(MGM) Fanfare (George Hamilton)

Episodes from the life of a motor-cycle stuntman.
Mildly entertaining ragbag of action sequences and fragments of philosophy which might have been more tolerable had EK played himself.

w Alan Caillou, John Milius *d* Marvin Chomsky *ph* David Walsh *m* Pat Williams

George Hamilton, Sue Lyon, Bert Freed, Rod Cameron

Evelyn Prentice
US 1934 80m bw
MGM (John W. Considine Jnr)

The wife of a criminal lawyer has an affair with a man who blackmails her.
Moderate domestic-cum-courtroom melodrama, heavily reliant on its popular stars.

w Lenore Coffee, *novel* W. E. Woodward *d* William K. Howard *ph* Charles G. Clarke *m* Oscar Raclin

Myrna Loy, William Powell, Una Merkel, Harvey Stephens, Isabel Jewell, Rosalind Russell, Henry Wadsworth, Edward Brophy

Evensong*
GB 1934 84m bw
Gaumont (Michael Balcon)

At the turn of the century, an Austrian prima donna gives up her career for love.
Well-made romantic drama of its type, notable as the best of its star's few films.

w Edward Knoblock, Dorothy Farnum, *play* Beverly Nichols *d* Victor Saville

Evelyn Laye, Fritz Kortner, Carl Esmond, Alice Delysia, Emlyn Williams, Muriel Aked

Ever Since Eve
US 1937 80m bw
Warner (Earl Baldwin)

A publisher falls for a pretty girl, not realizing that she is his own plain secretary in disguise.
Silly romantic comedy which sadly lacks wit, style and believability.

w Lawrence Riley, Earl Baldwin, Lillie Hayward *d* Lloyd Bacon *ph* George Barnes *m* Leo F. Forbstein

Marion Davies (her last film), Robert Montgomery, Frank McHugh, Patsy Kelly, Louise Fazenda, Barton MacLane, Mary Treen

Evergreen**
GB 1934 90m bw
Gaumont (Michael Balcon)

A star's daughter takes her mother's place, with romantic complications.
Pleasant musical with more wit and style than might be expected.

w Emlyn Williams, Marjorie Gaffney, *play* Benn W. Levy *d Victor Saville*

Jessie Matthews, Sonnie Hale, Betty Balfour, Barry Mackay, Ivor McLaren, Hartley Power

Every Day's a Holiday*
US 1937 79m bw
Paramount (Emmanuel Cohen)

A confidence girl in the old Bowery sells Brooklyn Bridge to suckers.
The most satisfactory example of post-Legion of Decency Mae West, the smut being replaced by a lively cast of comedians.

w Mae West d A. Edward Sutherland *ph* Karl Struss *songs* various

Mae West, Edmund Lowe, Charles Butterworth, Charles Winninger, Walter Catlett, Lloyd Nolan, Herman Bing, Roger Imhof, Chester Conklin

Every Girl Should be Married
US 1948 84m bw
RKO (Don Hartman, Dore Schary)

A determined girl sets her cap at a bachelor pediatrician.
Woefully thin star comedy with few laughs.

w Stephen Morehouse Avery, Don Hartman *d* Don Hartman *ph* George E. Diskant *m* Constantin Bakaleinikoff

Cary Grant, Betsy Drake, Franchot Tone, Diana Lynn, Alan Mowbray, Elizabeth Risdon, Richard Gaines

'In the past, Cary Grant has shown a talent for quietly underplaying comedy. In this picture, he has trouble finding comedy to play.'—*Time*

Every Little Crook and Nanny
US 1972 92m Metrocolor
MGM (Leonard J. Ackerman)

A Mafia chief finds his child's new nanny has a grudge against him.
Sporadically amusing farce.

w Cy Howard, Jonathan Axelrod, Robert Klane *d* Cy Howard *ph* Philip Lathrop *m* Fred Karlin

Victor Mature, Lynn Redgrave, Paul Sand, Maggie Blye, Austin Pendleton, John Astin, Dom De Luise

Every Man Needs One
US 1972 74m colour TVM
Spelling–Goldberg

A swinging bachelor who steers clear of female attachments is forced to hire a woman assistant who takes him over.
Mild contemporary comedy.

w Carl Kleinschmitt *d* Jerry Paris

Ken Berry, Connie Stevens, Henry Gibson, Louise Sorel

Everybody Does It
US 1949 98m bw
TCF (Nunnally Johnson)

A stage-struck wife is chagrined to see her dull husband accidentally become an opera singer.
Very mild remake of *Wife, Husband and Friend*; everyone tries to be zany, but the result is often just silly.

w Nunnally Johnson *d* Edmund Goulding *ph* Joseph La Shelle *m* Alfred Newman

Paul Douglas, Celeste Holm, Linda Darnell, Charles Coburn, Millard Mitchell, Lucile Watson, John Hoyt, George Tobias, Leon Belasco

Everything But the Truth
US 1956 83m Technicolor
U-I (Howard Christie)

A small boy embarrasses his family by telling the truth at all times.
Dum-dum formula comedy made with jaded professionalism.

w Herb Meadow *d* Jerry Hopper *ph* Maury Gertsman *m* Milton Rosen

Maureen O'Hara, John Forsythe, Tim Hovey, Frank Faylen, Barry Atwater

Everything Happens at Night
US 1939 77m bw
TCF (Harry Joe Brown)

Two reporters fall for the daughter of a Nobel Peace Prize winner on the run from the Gestapo.
The star's sixth American film plays down the music and skating in favour of rather jaded spy comedy. Modest entertainment.

w Art Arthur, Robert Harari *d* Irving Cummings *ph* Edward Cronjager *m* various

Sonja Henie, Ray Milland, Robert Cummings, Maurice Moscovitch, Leonid Kinskey, Alan Dinehart, Fritz Feld, Victor Varconi

Everything I Have is Yours
US 1952 92m Technicolor
MGM (George Wells)

A song and dance team is disrupted when the wife decides to become a mother.
Uninventive but lively musical vehicle for the Champions.

w George Wells *d* Robert Z. Leonard *ph* William V. Skall *md* David Rose *ch* Nick Castle, Gower Champion

Marge and Gower Champion, Dennis O'Keefe, Eduard Franz

Everything You Always Wanted to Know About Sex*
US 1972 87m De Luxe
US/Jack Rollins/Charles H. Joffe/Brodsky/Gould

Seven sketches on sexual themes.
Dishevelled revue with a reasonable number of laughs for broadminded audiences.

wd Woody Allen, *book* Dr David Reuben *ph* David M. Walsh *m* Mundell Lowe *pd* Dale Hennesy

Woody Allen, Lynn Redgrave, Anthony Quayle, John Carradine, Lou Jacobi, Louise Lasser, Tony Randall, Burt Reynolds, Gene Wilder

The Evil of Frankenstein
GB 1964 94m Technicolor
U-I / Hammer (Anthony Hinds)

Frankenstein returns to his derelict castle and finds the Monster preserved in a glacier.
For their third Frankenstein film Hammer made a distribution deal with Universal and thus for the first time were able to use fragments of the old plots as well as something approximating to the Karloff make-up. Production and writing, however, are sadly dispirited except when relying on sadism.

w John Elder (Anthony Hinds) *d* Freddie Francis *ph* John Wilcox *m* John Hollingsworth

Peter Cushing, Peter Woodthorpe, Sandor Eles, Kiwi Kingston (as the monster), Duncan Lamont, Katy Wild, David Hutcheson

Evil Roy Slade*
US 1971 100m Technicolor TVM
Universal (Jerry Belson, Gary Marshall)

The west's meanest outlaw reforms when he falls in love.
Overlong spoof, at its best better than *Blazing Saddles*.

w Jerry Belson, Gary Marshall *d* Jerry Paris

John Astin, Mickey Rooney, Pamela Austin, Dick Shawn, Henry Gibson, Dom De Luise, Edie Adams, Milton Berle

The Ex-Mrs Bradford*
US 1936 87m bw
MGM (Edward Kaufman)

A doctor's scatty ex-wife involves him in solving a murder plot.
Amusing crime comedy, just a little way behind *The Thin Man*.

w Anthony Veiller, James Edward Grant *d* Stephen Roberts *ph* J. Roy Hunt *m* Roy Webb

William Powell, Jean Arthur, James Gleason, Eric Blore, Robert Armstrong, Lila Lee, Grant Mitchell, Ralph Morgan

Excuse My Dust*
US 1951 82m Technicolor
MGM (Jack Cummings)

The inventor of a horseless carriage loves the daughter of a livery stable owner.
Innocuous small-town nineties comedy with a race climax. Quite pleasant.

w George Wells *d* Roy Rowland *ph* Alfred Gilks *m* Arthur Schwarz

Red Skelton, Sally Forrest, Macdonald Carey, William Demarest

The Execution of Private Slovik*
US 1973 120m Technicolor TVM
Universal

During World War II an American soldier is executed for desertion.
Factual case history, earnestly but rather drearily retold.

w Richard Levinson, William Link, *book* William Bradford Huie *d* Lamont Johnson

Martin Sheen, Ned Beatty, Gary Busey, Warren Kemmerling, Mariclare Costello

The Executioner*
GB 1970 107m Technicolor Panavision
Columbia / Ameran (Charles H. Schneer)

A British spy suspects a colleague of being a double agent.
Dour espionage thriller with a reasonably holding narrative and predictable performances.

w Jack Pulman *d* Sam Wanamaker *ph* Denys Coop *m* Ron Goodwin

George Peppard, Nigel Patrick, Joan Collins, Judy Geeson, Oscar Homolka, Charles Gray, Keith Michell, George Baker, Alexander Scourby, Peter Bull, Ernest Clark, Peter Dyneley

'Does not escape from the well-worn shallow groove in which the contemporary spy film is in danger of becoming stuck.'—*Russell Campbell*

Executive Action**
US 1973 91m colour
EA Enterprises / Wakefield Orloff (Edward Lewis)

An imaginative version of the facts behind the 1963 assassination of President Kennedy.
Interesting but rather messy mixture of fact and fiction; makes one sit up while it's unreeling.

w Dalton Trumbo, *story* Mark Lane, Donald Freed *d* David Miller *ph* Robert Steadman *m* Randy Edelman

Burt Lancaster, Robert Ryan, Will Geer, Gilbert Green, John Anderson

Executive Suite***
US 1954 104m bw
MGM (John Houseman)

When the president of a big company dies, the boardroom sees a battle for control.
First of the boardroom films of the fifties, a calculatedly commercial mixture of business ethics and domestic asides, with an all-star cast working up effective tensions.

w Ernest Lehman, novel Cameron Hawley *d Robert Wise* *ph* George Folsey

Fredric March, William Holden, June Allyson, *Barbara Stanwyck*, Walter Pidgeon, Shelley Winters, Paul Douglas, *Louis Calhern*, Dean Jagger, *Nina Foch*, Tim Considine
* A TV series followed in 1976.

The Exile*
US 1948 90m bw
U-I (Douglas Fairbanks Jnr)

The man who is to return to the English throne as Charles II hides in Holland, receives his friends and despatches his enemies.
Curious, talkative swashbuckler with only a few moments of action; the available talents are simply not used, though the director imposes a nice pictorial style.

w Douglas Fairbanks Jnr, *novel* His Majesty the King by Cosmo Hamilton *d Max Ophuls* *ph Franz Planer*

Douglas Fairbanks Jnr, Maria Montez, Paula Corday, Henry Daniell, Nigel Bruce, Robert Coote
† Originally released in sepia.

Exodus*
US 1960 220m Technicolor Super Panavision 70
UA / Carlyle / Alpha (Otto Preminger)

The early years of the state of Israel, seen through various eyes.
Heavy-going modern epic, toned down from a passionate novel.

w Dalton Trumbo, *novel* Leon Uris *d* Otto Preminger *ph* Sam Leavitt *m* Ernest Gold

Paul Newman, Eva Marie Saint, Ralph Richardson, Peter Lawford, Lee J. Cobb, Sal Mineo, John Derek, Hugh Griffith, Gregory Ratoff, Felix Aylmer, David Opatoshu, Jill Haworth, Alexandra Stewart, Martin Benson, Martin Miller

'Professionalism is not enough—after three and a half hours the approach seems more exhausting than exhaustive.'—*Penelope Houston*

† Jewish comedian Mort Sahl, invited by the director to a preview, is said to have stood up after three hours and said: 'Otto—let my people go!'

The Exorcist*
US 1973 122m Metrocolor
Warner / Hoya (William Peter Blatty)

A small girl is unaccountably possessed by the devil and turned into a repellent monster who causes several violent deaths before she is cured.
Spectacularly ludicrous mishmash with uncomfortable attention to physical detail and no talent for narrative or verisimilitude. Its sensational aspects, together with a sudden worldwide need for the supernatural, assured its enormous commercial success.

w William Peter Blatty, from his novel *d* William Friedkin *ph* Owen Roizman *m* George Crumb and others *pd* Bill Malloy

Ellen Burstyn, Max Von Sydow, Jason Miller, Linda Blair, Lee J. Cobb, Kitty Winn, Jack McGowran

'No more nor less than a blood and thunder horror movie, foundering heavily on the rocks of pretension.'—*Tom Milne*

'*The Exorcist* makes no sense, [but] if you want to be shaken, it will scare the hell out of you.'—*Stanley Kauffmann*

Experiment in Terror**
US 1962 123m bw
Columbia / Geoffrey-Kate Productions (Blake Edwards)
GB title: *The Grip of Fear*

An asthmatic stranger threatens the life of a bank

teller and her sister if she does not help him commit a robbery.
Detailed, meticulous police thriller with San Francisco locations. Good stuff, a bit long.

w The Gordons, from their novel Operation Terror *d* Blake Edwards *ph* Philip Lathrop *m* Henry Mancini

Glenn Ford, Lee Remick, Ross Martin

Experiment Perilous*
US 1944 91m bw
RKO (Warren Duff)

A woman's wealthy husband is killed in mysterious circumstances, and she is suspected.
Enjoyable mystery melodrama which takes itself with a pinch of salt.

w Warren Duff, *novel* Margaret Carpenter *d Jacques Tourneur* *ph* Tony Gaudio *m* Roy Webb

Hedy Lamarr, Paul Lukas, George Brent, Albert Dekker, Margaret Wycherly

Expresso Bongo*
GB 1959 111m bw Dyaliscope
BL / Britannia / Conquest (Val Guest)

A Soho agent turns a nondescript teenage singer into an international star.
Heavily vulgarized version of a stage skit on the Tommy Steele rock phenomenon, divested of most of its satirical barbs and only intermittently amusing.

w Wolf Mankowitz, from his play *d* Val Guest *ph* John Wilcox *m/ly* various

Laurence Harvey, Sylvia Syms, Yolande Donlan, Cliff Richard, *Meier Tzelniker*, Gilbert Harding, Ambrosine Philpotts, Eric Pohlmann, Wilfrid Lawson, Hermione Baddeley, Reginald Beckwith, Martin Miller

The Extraordinary Seaman
US 1968 80m Metrocolor Panavision
MGM / John Frankenheimer / Edward Lewis (John H. Cushingham, Hal Dresner)

Four stranded sailors come upon the ghostly Royal Navy captain of a ghostly World War II ship.
Curious sixties attempt at forties fantasy; obviously, from its short running time and fragmented style, something went sadly adrift during its making, and the wide screen does not help, but there are scattered funny moments.

w Philip Rock, Hal Dresner *d* John Frankenheimer *ph* Lionel Lindon *m* Maurice Jarre

David Niven, Faye Dunaway, Alan Alda, Mickey Rooney, Jack Carter, Juano Hernandez, Barry Kelley

Eye of the Cat*
US 1969 102m Technicolor
Universal / Joseph M. Schenck (Bernard Schwarz, Philip Hazelton)

A young man who hates cats goes to stay with his crippled aunt who keeps a house full of them.
Odd, *Psycho*-like thriller (from the same screen writer) with plenty of scary sequences but an inadequate resolution.

w Joseph Stefano *d* David Lowell Rich *ph Russell Metty, Ellsworth Fredericks* *m* Lalo Schifrin *cat trainer* Ray Berwick

Eleanor Parker, Michael Sarrazin, Gayle Hunnicutt, Tim Henry, Laurence Naismith
'Not so much a good film as an extravagantly enjoyable one.'—*MFB*

Eye of the Devil*
GB 1967 92m bw
MGM / Filmways (John Calley, Ben Kadish)

A French nobleman is obsessed by a family tradition of pagan self-sacrifice.
Diabolical goings-on in a spooky castle, not really helped by a glittering supporting cast any more than by miscast stars, sluggish direction or a general atmosphere of gloom rather than suspense.

w Robin Estridge, Dennis Murphy, *novel* Day of the Arrow by Philip Loraine *d* J. Lee-Thompson *ph* Erwin Hillier *m* Gary McFarland

David Niven, Deborah Kerr, Emlyn Williams, Flora Robson, Donald Pleasance, Edward Mulhare, David Hemmings, Sharon Tate, John Le Mesurier, Donald Bisset
'It is hard to say why the total effect is so constantly hilarious.'—*MFB*
† The film had a chequered career. The first attempt to make it was abandoned because of Kim Novak's inadequacy; it then went though three titles and a lot of trouble with the censor.

Eyes in the Night*
US 1942 80m bw
MGM (Jack Chertok)

A blind detective sets out to discover whether a mysterious man engaged to an heiress is really a Nazi spy.
Tolerable wartime puzzler.

w Guy Trosper, Howard Emmett Rogers, *novel* Odor of Violets by Bayard Kendrick *d Fred Zinnemann* *ph* Robert Planck, Charles Lawton *m* Lennie Hayton

Edward Arnold, Ann Harding, Donna Reed, Allen Jenkins, John Emery, Stephen McNally, Reginald Denny, Rosemary de Camp, Stanley Ridges
† Edward Arnold appeared once more as Duncan Maclain, in *The Hidden Eye* (1944).

The Eyes of Charles Sand*
US 1972 75m colour TVM
Warner (Hugh Benson)

A young man with second sight solves a bizarre murder mystery.
Old-fashioned horror comic, well camped up.

w Henry Farrell, Stanford Whitmore *d* Reza S. Badiyi

Peter Haskell, Joan Bennett, Barbara Rush, Sharon Farrell, Bradford Dillman, Adam West

Eye Witness
GB 1956 82m bw
Rank / Sydney Box

A maniacal burglar pursues a witness of his crime into the emergency ward of a local hospital.
Naïve but adequate suspenser with too many character cameos getting in the way of the plot.

w Janet Green *d* Muriel Box ph Reg Wyer *m* Bruce Montgomery

Donald Sinden, Muriel Pavlow, Belinda Lee, Michael Craig, Nigel Stock, Susan Beaumont, David Knight, *Ada Reeve*

Eyewitness*
GB 1970 91m Technicolor
ITC / ABP (Paul Maslansky)

A boy is the sole witness to an assassination, but no one believes him except the assassins.
The Window all over again, the standard clichés being tricked out with fancy photography, sub-Hitchcock set-ups and Mediterranean locations, which make it all very tolerable.

w Ronald Harwood, *novel* Mark Hebden *d* John Hough *ph* David Holmes *m* Fairfield Parlour, David Whitaker

Mark Lester, Lionel Jeffries, Susan George, Tony Bonner, Jeremy Kemp, Peter Vaughan, Peter Bowles, Betty Marsden

F

F.P.1*
GB / Germany 1933 93m bw
Gaumont / UFA (Erich Pommer)

Financiers try to destroy the first floating aerodrome.
'Futuristic' melodrama about an aircraft carrier. Very well done, and shot in two languages, but now dated in most respects.

w Curt Siodmak, Walter Reisch, Robert Stevenson, Peter Macfarlane *d* Karl Hartl

Conrad Veidt, Leslie Fenton, Jill Esmond, George Merritt, Donald Calthrop, Nicholas Hannen, Francis L. Sullivan

The Fabulous Dorseys
US 1947 91m bw
UA (Charles R. Rogers)

Two quarrelling bandleader brothers are reunited on the death of their father.
Slight, comedic biopic with the Dorseys playing well and trying hard.

w Richard English, Art Arthur, Curtis Kenyon *d* Alfred E. Green *ph* James Van Trees *m* Louis Forbes

Tommy Dorsey, Jimmy Dorsey (and their bands), Janet Blair, Paul Whiteman, William Lundigan

The Face at the Window*
GB 1939 65m bw
Pennant / Ambassador (George King)

In 1880 Paris, a murderer uses his moronic half-brother to distract his victims but is foiled when a dead man apparently incriminates him.
Roistering melodrama which provided Tod Slaughter with one of his juiciest roles and is here effectively presented, which is more than can be said for the screen treatments of most of his other vehicles.

w A. R. Rawlinson, Randall Faye, *play* F. Brooke Warren *d* George King

Tod Slaughter, Marjorie Taylor, John Warwick, Leonard Henry, Aubrey Mallalieu

'One of the best English pictures I have seen . . . leaves the American horror films far behind.'—*Graham Greene*

The Face behind the Mask*
US 1941 69m bw
Columbia (Wallace MacDonald)

When his face is disfigured in a fire, an immigrant turns to a life of crime.
Effective second feature melodrama with a good star performance.

w Allen Vincent, Paul Jarrico, *play* Thomas O'Connell *d* Robert Florey *ph* Franz Planer *m* Morris Stoloff

Peter Lorre, Evelyn Keyes, *Don Beddoe*, George E. Stone

A Face in the Crowd***
US 1957 126m bw
(Warner) Newton (Elia Kazan)

A small-town hick becomes a megalomaniac when television turns him into a cracker-barrel philosopher.
Brilliantly cinematic melodrama of its time which only flags in the last lap and paints a luridly entertaining picture of modern show business.

w Budd Schulberg, from his story Your Arkansas Traveller *d Elia Kazan* *ph Harry Stradling, Gayne Rescher* *m* Tom Glazer

Andy Griffith, Lee Remick, Walter Matthau, Patricia Neal, Anthony Franciosa, Percy Waram, Marshall Neilan

'Savagery, bitterness, cutting humour.'—*Penelope Houston*

A Face in the Rain*
US 1963 80m bw
Filmways / Calvic (John Calley)

During World War II an American spy in Italy bungles his mission, and hides in the apartment of a professor's wife.
Offbeat, talkative melodrama with a few neat touches.

w Hugo Butler, Jean Rouverol *d Irvin Kershner* *ph Haskell Wexler* *m* Richard Markowitz

Rory Calhoun, Marina Berti, Niall MacGinnis

Face of a Fugitive*
US 1959 81m Eastmancolor
Columbia / Morningside

A man falsely accused of murder makes a new life in a frontier town.
Lively western melodrama with good atmosphere.

w David T. Chantler *d Paul Wendkos*
ph Wilfrid M. Cline *m* Jerry Goldsmith

Fred MacMurray, Lin McCarthy, Alan Baxter, James Coburn

The Face of Fear*
US 1971 72m colour TVM
Quinn Martin

A young woman who has (she believes) a terminal illness arranges for her own murder. And then . . .
An old chestnut adequately warmed over.

w Edward Hume, *novel* Sally E. V. Cunningham
d George McCowan

Elizabeth Ashley, Ricardo Montalban, Jack Warden, Dane Clark

The Face of Fu Manchu**
GB 1965 96m Techniscope
Anglo–EMI / Hallam (Harry Alan Towers)

In the twenties, Nayland Smith of Scotland Yard links an oriental crime wave with evil mastermind Fu Manchu.
A splendidly light touch and attention to detail make this entertaining spoof like a tuppenny blood come to life.

w Peter Welbeck (Harry Alan Towers) *d Don Sharp* *ph* Ernest Steward *m* Chris Whelan
ad Frank White

Nigel Green, Christopher Lee, Tsai Chin, Howard Marion Crawford

Faces*
US 1968 130m bw
Maurice McEndree

A discontented Los Angeles executive tries but fails to go through with a divorce.
A personal, probing study of middle-aged loneliness, made with the director's usual long-winded relentlessness but quite frequently compelling.

wd John Cassavetes *ph* Al Ruban *m* Jack Ackerman

John Marley, Gena Rowlands, Lynn Carlin, Fred Draper

'The cast are all painfully and overpoweringly real.'—*Jan Dawson*

Faces in the Dark*
GB 1960 85m bw
Rank / Welbeck / Penington Eady (Jon Penington)

A blind man survives a plot against his life.
Unlikely but watchable puzzler, betrayed by lifeless handling. Hitchcock could have worked wonders with such a plot.

w Ephraim Kogan, John Tulley, *novel* Pierre Boileau, Thomas Narcejac *d* David Eady
ph Ken Hodges *m* Edwin Astley

John Gregson, Mai Zetterling, Michael Denison, John Ireland, Tony Wright, Nanette Newman

The Facts of Life*
US 1960 103m bw
(UA) HLP (Norman Panama)

Two middle-aged married suburbanites have an abortive affair.
Star comedy with muted slapstick and earnest acting, a good try, but less effective than their normal pratfalls.

w Norman Panama, Melvin Frank *d* Melvin Frank *ph* Charles Lang Jnr *m* Leigh Harline

Bob Hope, Lucille Ball, Ruth Hussey, Don Defore, Louis Nye, Philip Ober

'Random shots of mockery aimed effectively at the American middle-class way of life.'—*Peter John Dyer*

Fahrenheit 451*
GB 1966 112m Technicolor
Rank / Anglo Enterprise / Vineyard (Lewis M. Allen)

In a fascist future state, a fireman's job is to burn books.
1984 stuff, a little lacking in plot and rather tentatively directed, but with charming moments.

w François Truffaut, Jean-Louis Richard, *novel* Ray Bradbury *d* François Truffaut
ph Nicolas Roeg *m* Bernard Herrmann *design consultant* Tony Walton

Oskar Werner, Julie Christie, Cyril Cusack, Anton Diffring, Jeremy Spenser

Fail Safe***
US 1964 111m bw
Columbia / Max E. Youngstein / Sidney Lumet

An American atomic bomber is accidentally set to destroy Moscow, and the president has to destroy New York in retaliation.
Despite a confusing opening, this deadly earnest melodrama gets across the horror of its situation better than the contemporaneous *Dr Strangelove* which treated the same plot as black comedy.

Here the details are both terrifying and convincing.

w Walter Bernstein, *novel* Eugene Burdick, Harvey Wheeler *d Sidney Lumet ph* Gerald Hirschfeld *m* none

Henry Fonda, Walter Matthau, Dan O'Herlihy, Frank Overton, Fritz Weaver, Edward Binns, Larry Hagman, Russell Collins

The Failing of Raymond*
US 1971 73m Technicolor TVM
Universal (George Eckstein)

An embittered student seeks revenge against the middle-aged lady teacher responsible for his not passing an exam.
Fairly good suspenser.

w Adrian Spies *d* George Eckstein

Jane Wyman, Dean Stockwell, Dana Andrews, Murray Hamilton, Paul Henreid, Tim O'Connor

Fair Wind to Java
US 1952 92m Trucolor
Republic (Joseph Kane)

A sailor with a mutinous crew seeks a South Sea treasure.
Routine adventure culminating in a volcanic explosion.

w Richard Tregaskis, *novel* Garland Roark *d* Joseph Kane *ph* Jack Martin *m* Victor Young

Fred MacMurray, Vera Hruba Ralston, Robert Douglas, Victor McLaglen

Faithless
US 1932 76m bw
MGM

A spoiled rich girl and her beau both descend to working-class level and almost further.
Would-be sensational drama ruined by censorship and miscasting.

w Carey Wilson, *novel* Tinfoil by Mildred Cram *d* Harry Beaumont *ph* Oliver T. Marsh

Tallulah Bankhead, Robert Montgomery, Hugh Herbert, Maurice Murphy, Louise Closser Hale, Lawrence Grant, Henry Kolker

The Falcon

A debonair solver of crime puzzles allegedly created by Michael Arlen but owing much to The Saint and resulting from a need by RKO for more of the same. Helped by a tough/comic manservant, he flourished during the forties in sixteen second features (the last three for Film Classics). After three episodes George Sanders tired of the role and was written out by being 'shot' and having his real-life brother Tom Conway take over as his fictional one. The performances of these two actors are pleasant, though the films are now fairly unwatchable, but John Calvert who took over for the last three was not a success.

1941: THE GAY FALCON, A DATE WITH THE FALCON
1942: THE FALCON TAKES OVER (the plot was borrowed from Raymond Chandler's FAREWELL MY LOVELY), THE FALCON'S BROTHER
1943: THE FALCON STRIKES BACK, THE FALCON AND THE CO-EDS, THE FALCON IN DANGER
1944: THE FALCON IN HOLLYWOOD, THE FALCON IN MEXICO, THE FALCON OUT WEST
1945: THE FALCON IN SAN FRANCISCO
1946: THE FALCON'S ALIBI, THE FALCON'S ADVENTURE
1948: THE DEVIL'S CARGO, APPOINTMENT WITH MURDER, SEARCH FOR DANGER

The Fall of the Roman Empire**
US / Spain 1964 187m Technicolor Ultra Panavision 70
Samuel Bronston

After poisoning the Emperor Marcus Aurelius his mad son Commodus succumbs to dissipation and allows Rome to be ravaged by pestilence and the Barbarians.
Would-be distinguished epic with an intellectual first hour; unfortunately the hero is a priggish bore, the villain a crashing bore, the heroine a saintly bore, and the only interesting character is killed off early. A chariot race, a javelin duel, some military clashes and a mass burning at the stake keep one watching, and the production values are high indeed.

w Ben Barzman, Philip Yordan *d Anthony Mann ph* Robert Krasker, John Moore *m* Dmitri Tiomkin *pd* Venerio Colasanti

Alec Guinness, Christopher Plummer, Stephen Boyd, James Mason, Sophia Loren, John Ireland, Eric Porter, Anthony Quayle, Mel Ferrer, Omar Sharif

'The film works from a restricted palette, and the result is weirdly restraining and severe, a dignified curb on absurdities.'—*John Coleman*

Fallen Angel*
US 1945 97m bw
TCF (Otto Preminger)

A man plans to get rid of his wife and marry another woman, but it is the latter who is murdered.
Oddly sleazy melodrama, not more successful then because it was unexpected than now

because it is miscast. Some good sequences, though.

w Harry Kleiner, *novel* Marty Holland *d Otto Preminger ph Joseph La Shelle m* Emil Newman

Dana Andrews, Alice Faye, Linda Darnell, Charles Bickford, Anne Revere, Bruce Cabot, John Carradine, Percy Kilbride

'It holds you by its undertones of small-town life and frustration.'—*Richard Winnington*

The Fallen Idol***
GB 1948 94m bw
British Lion / London Films

An ambassador's small son nearly incriminates his friend the butler in the accidental death of his shrewish wife.
A near-perfect piece of small-scale cinema, built up from clever nuances of acting and cinematic technique.

w Graham Greene, from his story The Basement Room *d Carol Reed ph Georges Périnal m* William Alwyn

Ralph Richardson, Michèle Morgan, *Bobby Henrey*, Sonia Dresdel, Jack Hawkins

'A short story has become a film which is compact without loss of variety in pace and shape.'—*Dilys Powell*

The Fallen Sparrow*
US 1943 93m bw
RKO (Robert Fellows)

An American veteran of the Spanish Civil War finds himself hounded in New York by Nazis seeking the Spanish flag of freedom.
Obscure melodrama, very good to look at but hardly worth unravelling; a precursor of Hollywood's post-war *films noirs.*

w Warren Duff, *novel* Dorothy B. Hughes *d* Richard Wallace *ph Nicholas Musuraca m* Roy Webb

John Garfield, Maureen O'Hara, Walter Slezak, Martha O'Driscoll, Patricia Morison, Bruce Edwards, John Banner, John Miljan

Fame is the Name of the Game*
US 1966 100m Technicolor TVM
Universal

A magazine reporter on assignment discovers a girl's body and traps her murderer.
Ho-hum glossy melodrama which sparked off a three-season series of telefeatures about the magazine, *The Name of the Game* (qv).

w Ranald MacDougall *d* Stuart Rosenberg

Anthony Franciosa, Jill St John, Jack Klugman, George Macready, Lee Bowman, Nanette Fabray, Jay C. Flippen, Jack Warden

Fame Is the Spur*
US 1947 116m bw
GFD / Two Cities / Charter Films (John Boulting)

The rise to political eminence of a working-class socialist.
Disappointingly flat historical drama from a novel allegedly based on the career of Ramsay MacDonald. Interesting moments.

w Nigel Balchin, *novel* Howard Spring *d* Roy Boulting

Michael Redgrave, Rosamund John, Bernard Miles, Carla Lehmann, Hugh Burden, Marjorie Fielding, Seymour Hicks

A Family Affair*
US 1937 69m bw
MGM (Lucien Hubbard)

A small-town judge faces a few family problems.
The second feature that started the highly successful Hardy family series (qv under *Hardy*). In this case the judge and his wife were played by actors who did not persevere into the series, but the stage was otherwise set for a long run, and the town of Carvel came to mean home to many Americans abroad.

w Kay Van Riper, *play* Skidding by Aurania Rouverol *d* George B. Seitz

Lionel Barrymore, Spring Byington, *Mickey Rooney*, Eric Linden, Cecilia Parker, Sara Haden, Charles Grapewin, Julie Haydon

Family Flight*
US 1972 73m Technicolor TVM
Universal (Harve Bennett)

A light plane crashes in the desert and the family involved needs all its ingenuity to survive.
Taut, efficient action suspenser apparently inspired by *The Flight of the Phoenix.*

w Guerdon Trueblood *d* Marvin Chomsky

Rod Taylor, Dina Merrill, Kristoffer Tabori, Janet Margolin, Gene Nelson

Family Honeymoon
US 1948 90m bw
U-I (John Beck, Z. Wayne Griffin)

A college professor marries a widow whose three children join them on their Grand Canyon honeymoon.
Very ordinary and predictable star comedy.

w Dane Lussier, Homer Croy *d* Claude Binyon *ph* William Daniels *m* Milton Schwarzwald

Claudette Colbert, Fred MacMurray, Rita Johnson, Gigi Perreau, Peter Miles, Jimmy Hunt, Hattie McDaniel, Chill Wills

The Family Jewels
US 1965 100m Technicolor
Paramount / York / Jerry Lewis

A child heiress chooses a new father from among her five uncles.
Unfunny star farce with multiple impersonations.

w Jerry Lewis, Bill Richmond *d* Jerry Lewis *ph* W. Wallace Kelley *m* Pete King

Jerry Lewis, Donna Butterworth, Sebastian Cabot, Robert Strauss

The Family Kovack
US 1974 74m colour TVM
Warner / Playboy

A Chicago family bands together when the son is accused of bribing a city official.
Forgettable family drama distinguished by excellent location atmosphere, which was not enough to turn it into a series.

w Adrian Spies *d* Ralph Senensky

James Sloyan, Sarah Cunningham, Andy Robinson, Richard Gilliland

Family Life**
GB 1971 108m Technicolor
EMI / Kestrel (Tony Garnett)

A 19-year-old girl is driven into a mental collapse by emotional and family problems.
A slice of suburban life and an indictment of it, put together with unknown actors and probing TV techniques. Somewhat too harrowing for fiction, but extraordinarily vivid.

w David Mercer, from his play In Two Minds *d Ken Loach* *ph* Charles Stewart *m* Marc Wilkinson

Sandy Ratcliff, Bill Dean, Grace Cave

The Family Nobody Wanted
US 1975 74m Technicolor TVM
Universal (David Victor)

A minister and his wife adopt a very miscellaneous family of twelve, but find they are resented in a new parish.
Old-fashioned sentimentality, laid on with a trowel.

w Suzanne Clauser, *book* Helen Doss *d* Ralph Senensky

Shirley Jones, James Olson, Woodrow Parfrey, Ann Doran

Family Plot**
US 1976 126m Technicolor
Universal (Alfred Hitchcock)

A fake medium tries for easy money by producing a lost heir.
Talkative, complex, patchy, low-key but always interesting Hitchcock suspenser in an unusually friendly vein.

w Ernest Lehman, *novel* The Rainbird Pattern by Victor Canning *d* Alfred Hitchcock *ph* Leonard J. South *m* John Williams *pd* Henry Bumstead

Karen Black, Bruce Dern, Barbara Harris, William Devane, Ed Lauter, Cathleen Nesbitt

The Family Rico
US 1972 73m colour TVM
CBS / George LeMaire

A crime syndicate leader is in trouble when his younger brother defects.
Shades of *On the Waterfront* and *The Brotherhood*, but actually from a Simenon novel previously filmed as *The Brothers Rico*. Enough is enough.

w David Karp *d* Paul Wendkos

Ben Gazzara, James Farentino, Sal Mineo, Jo Van Fleet, Dane Clark, Jack Carter, Leif Erickson, John Marley

The Family Way*
GB 1966 115m Eastmancolor
BL / Jambox (John Boulting)

There is consternation in a Lancashire family when the son cannot consummate his marriage.
Overstretched domestic farce-drama. Good scenes and performances, but it was all much sharper as a one-hour TV play.

w Bill Naughton, from his play Honeymoon Deferred *d* Roy Boulting *ph* Harry Waxman *m* Paul McCartney

John Mills, *Marjorie Rhodes*, Hywel Bennett, Hayley Mills, *Avril Angers*, Murray Head, Wilfred Pickles, Barry Foster, Liz Fraser

The Fan*
US 1949 79m bw
TCF (Otto Preminger)
GB title: *Lady Windermere's Fan*

Scandal almost results when Lady Windermere loses her fan.
Reasonably polished, rather dull version of an old play, not really helped by modern bookends.

w Walter Reisch, Dorothy Parker, Ross Evans, *play* Lady Windermere's Fan by Oscar Wilde *d* Otto Preminger *ph* Joseph La Shelle *m* Daniele Amfitheatrof

George Sanders, Madeleine Carroll, Jeanne Crain, Richard Greene, Martita Hunt, John Sutton, Hugh Dempster, Richard Ney

Fanatic*
GB 1965 96m Technicolor
Hammer / Seven Arts (Anthony Hinds)
US title: *Die! Die! My Darling*

An American girl in England visits the mother of her dead fiancé and finds herself the prisoner of a religious maniac.
Boringly overlong Grand Guignol which even defeats its gallantly unmade-up and deathly-looking star; mildly notable however as a record of one of her last performances.

w Richard Matheson, *novel* Nightmare by Anne Blaisdell *d* Silvio Narizzano *ph* Arthur Ibbetson *m* Wilfrid Josephs *pd* Peter Proud

Tallulah Bankhead, Stefanie Powers, Peter Vaughan, Yootha Joyce, Donald Sutherland

Fancy Pants**
US 1950 92m Technicolor
Paramount (Robert Welch)

A British actor stranded in the far west poses as a butler.
Lively western comedy remake of *Ruggles of Red Gap* (qv), one of the star's better vehicles.

w Edmund Hartman, Robert O'Brien *d George Marshall ph* Charles Lang Jnr *m* Van Cleave

Bob Hope, Lucille Ball, Bruce Cabot, Jack Kirkwood, Lea Penman, Eric Blore, John Alexander, Norma Varden

Fanny*
US 1960 133m Technicolor
Warner / Mansfield (Joshua Logan)

Life on the Marseilles waterfront, and in particular the story of two old men and two lovers.
Lumbering adaptation of three Pagnol films of the thirties (*Marius, Fanny, César*) previously seen as a 1938 Hollywood film (*Port of Seven Seas*) and later as a Broadway musical. This is the dullest version despite fine photography and a couple of good performances.

w Julius J. Epstein, *play* S. N. Behrman, Joshua Logan, *films* Marcel Pagnol *d* Joshua Logan *ph Jack Cardiff m* Harold Rome

Charles Boyer, Maurice Chevalier, Leslie Caron, Horst Buchholz, Georgette Anys, Salvatore Baccaloni, Lionel Jeffries, Raymond Bussières, Victor Francen

Fanny by Gaslight**
GB 1944 108m bw
GFD / Gainsborough (Edward Black)
US title: *Man of Evil*

The illegitimate daughter of a cabinet minister is saved from a lustful Lord.
Highly-coloured Victorian romantic melodrama, enjoyably put over with no holds barred and a pretty high budget for the time.

w Doreen Montgomery, Aimée Stuart, *novel* Michael Sadleir *d Anthony Asquith*

James Mason, Phyllis Calvert, Stewart Granger, Wilfrid Lawson, John Laurie, Margaretta Scott, Stuart Lindsell, Jean Kent

'Seldom have I seen a film more agreeable to watch, from start to finish.'—*William Whitebait*
† One of several costume melodramas patterned after the success of *The Man in Grey* (qv).

Fantasia****
US 1940 135m Technicolor
Walt Disney

A concert of classical music is given cartoon interpretations. The pieces are:
Bach: Toccata and Fugue in D Minor
Tchaikovsky: The Nutcracker Suite
Dukas: The Sorcerer's Apprentice
Stravinsky: The Rite of Spring
Beethoven: The Pastoral Symphony
Ponchielli: Dance of the Hours
Moussorgsky: Night on a Bare Mountain
Schubert: Ave Maria
Brilliantly inventive for the most part, the cartoons having become classics in themselves. The least part (the Pastoral Symphony) can be forgiven.

Supervisor Ben Sharpsteen *md* Edward H. Plumb

Leopold Stokowski, the Philadelphia Orchestra, Deems Taylor

'Dull as it is towards the end, ridiculous as it is in the bend of the knee before Art, it is one of the strange and beautiful things that have happened in the world.'—*Otis Ferguson*
† Multiplane cameras, showing degrees of depth in animation, were used for the first time.

Fantastic Voyage*
US 1966 100m De Luxe Cinemascope
TCF (Saul David)

When a top scientist is shot and suffers brain damage, a team of doctors and a boat are miniaturized and injected into his blood stream . . . but one is a traitor.
Engagingly absurd science fiction which keeps

its momentum but is somewhat let down by its decor.

w Harry Kleiner *d Richard Fleischer ph* Ernest Laszlo *m* Leonard Rosenman *ad* Dale Hennesy, Jack Martin Smith *sp* L. B. Abbott, Art Cruickshank, Emil Kosa Jnr

Stephen Boyd, Raquel Welch, Edmond O'Brien, Donald Pleasance, Arthur Kennedy, Arthur O'Connell, William Redfield

'The process shots are so clumsily matted . . . that the actors look as if a child has cut them out with blunt scissors.'—*Pauline Kael*

The Far Country*
US 1955 97m Technicolor
U-I (Aaron Rosenberg)

Two cowboys on their way to the Alaska goldfields are beset by swindlers.
Sturdy star western with good production values.

w Borden Chase *d* Anthony Mann *ph* William Daniels *m* Joseph Gershenson

James Stewart, Walter Brennan, Ruth Roman, Corinne Calvet, John McIntire

Far from the Madding Crowd*
GB 1967 175m Technicolor
Panavision 70
EMI / Vic / Appia (Joseph Janni)

In Victorian Wessex a headstrong girl causes unhappiness and tragedy.
Good-looking but slackly handled version of a melodramatic and depressing novel.

w Frederic Raphael, *novel* Thomas Hardy *d* John Schlesinger *ph Nicolas Roeg m* Richard Rodney Bennett *pd* Richard Macdonald

Julie Christie, Peter Finch, Alan Bates, Terence Stamp, Prunella Ransome

'In this rather plodding film the insufficiency of the foreground is partly offset by the winsomeness of the backgrounds. The very sheep are so engaging as to entice our gaze into some extremely amiable woolgathering.'—*John Simon*

The Far Horizons
US 1955 108m Technicolor
Vistavision
(Paramount) Pine–Thomas

The story of Lewis and Clark's 1803 expedition west through the Louisiana Purchase territory.
Flabbily-handled historical hokum; potential interest quickly dissipated.

w Winston Miller, Edmund H. North *d* Rudolph Maté *ph* Daniel L. Fapp *m* Hans Salter

Fred MacMurray, Charlton Heston, Donna Reed, Barbara Hale, William Demarest

Faraday and Company see Mystery Movie

Farewell Again**
GB 1937 85m bw
Pendennis / London Films (Erich Pommer)
US title: *Troopship*

Soldiers returning from India have six hours' shore leave to sort out their problems.
Dated but sharply made compendium drama, a solid success of its time.

w Clemence Dane, Patrick Kirwan *d Tim Whelan*

Flora Robson, Leslie Banks, Robert Newton, René Ray, Patricia Hilliard, Sebastian Shaw, Leonora Corbett, Anthony Bushell, Edward Lexy, Wally Patch, Edmund Willard, Martita Hunt, John Laurie

Farewell My Lovely***
US 1944 95m bw
RKO (Adrian Scott)
aka: *Murder My Sweet*

A private eye searches for an ex-convict's missing girl friend.
A revolutionary crime film in that it was the first to depict the genuinely seedy milieu suggested by its author. One of the first *films noirs* of the mid-forties, a minor masterpiece of expressionist film making, and a total change of direction for a crooner who suddenly became a tough guy.

w John Paxton, novel Raymond Chandler d Edward Dmytryk ph Harry J. Wild m Roy Webb

Dick Powell, Claire Trevor, Anne Shirley, *Mike Mazurki, Otto Kruger*, Miles Mander, Douglas Walton, Ralf Harolde, Don Douglas, Esther Howard

'A nasty, draggled bit of dirty work, accurately observed.'—*C. A. Lejeune*

Farewell My Lovely**
US 1975 95m Technicolor
Avco Embassy / Elliott Kastner / ITC (George Pappas, Jerry Bruckheimer)

A pretty sharp remake of the above, with the plot slightly rewritten but tightened, and an excellent performance from a rather over-age star.

w David Zelag Goodman d Dick Richards ph John A. Alonzo *m* David Shire *pd* Dean Tavouraris

Robert Mitchum, Charlotte Rampling, John Ireland, Sylvia Miles, Anthony Zerbe, Jack O'Halloran, Kate Murtagh

'A moody, bluesy, boozy recreation of Marlowe's tacky, neon-flashed Los Angeles of the early forties.'—*Judith Crist*

A Farewell to Arms**
US 1932 78m bw
Paramount

In World War I, a wounded American ambulance driver falls in love with his nurse. Now very dated but important in its time, this romantic drama was one of the more successful Hemingway adaptations to be filmed.

w Benjamin Glazer, Oliver H. P. Garrett; *novel Ernest Hemingway d Frank Borzage ph* Charles Lang

Gary Cooper, *Helen Hayes*, Adolphe Menjou, Mary Philips, Jack La Rue, Blanche Frederici, Henry Armetta

'Too much sentiment and not enough strength.'—*Mordaunt Hall, New York Times*

'Borzage has invested the war scenes with a strange, brooding expressionist quality . . . indeed, the overall visual style is most impressive.'—*NFT, 1974*

† Remade as *Force of Arms* (qv) and see below.

A Farewell to Arms
US 1957 150m De Luxe Cinemascope
TCF / David O. Selznick

Elaborate ill-fated remake which tried to make an adventure epic out of a low-key war drama. Its failure caused David O. Selznick to produce no more films.

w Ben Hecht *d* Charles Vidor *pd* Alfred Junge *ph* Piero Portalupi, Oswald Morris *m* Mario Nascimbene

Rock Hudson, Jennifer Jones, Vittorio De Sica, Alberto Sordi, Kurt Kasznar, Mercedes McCambridge, Oscar Homolka, Elaine Stritch, Victor Francen

The Farmer Takes a Wife*
US 1935 91m bw
TCF (Winfield Sheehan)

By the Erie Canal in the 1820s, a wandering girl finds security with a farmer.
Pleasantly 'different' romantic drama, quite ably executed and introducing Henry Fonda to the screen.

w Edwin Burke, *play* Frank B. Elser and Marc Connelly, *novel* Rome Haul by Walter D. Edmonds *d* Victor Fleming *ph* John Seitz *m* Arthur Lange

Janet Gaynor, Henry Fonda, Charles Bickford, Slim Summerville, Andy Devine, Roger Imhof, Jane Withers, Margaret Hamilton, Sig Rumann, John Qualen

The Farmer Takes a Wife*
US 1953 81m Technicolor
TCF (Frank P. Rosenberg)

Musical remake with an agreeably stylized look, hampered by a slowish script and dull cast.

w Walter Bulloch, Sally Benson, Joseph Fields *d* Henry Levin *ph* Arthur E. Arling *m* Cyril Mockridge *ad Lyle Wheeler, Addison Hehr*

Betty Grable, Dale Robertson, Thelma Ritter, Eddie Foy Jnr, John Carroll

The Farmer's Daughter
US 1940 60m bw
Paramount (William C. Thomas)

A stage struck country girl tries to horn in on a Broadway musical rehearsing nearby.
Feeble comedy for the sticks.

w Lewis R. Foster, Delmer Daves *d* James Hogan *ph* Leo Tover

Martha Raye, Charles Ruggles, Richard Denning, Gertrude Michael, William Frawley, William Demarest, Jack Norton

The Farmer's Daughter**
US 1947 97m bw
David O. Selznick (Dore Schary)

The Swedish maid of a congressman becomes a political force.
Well-made Cinderella story with a touch of asperity and top notch production values and cast.

w Allen Rivkin, Laura Kerr d H. C. Potter ph Milton Krasner m Constantin Bakaleinikoff

Loretta Young, Joseph Cotten, Ethel Barrymore, Charles Bickford, Rose Hobart, Rhys Williams, Harry Davenport, Tom Powers

Fashions of 1934*
US 1934 78m bw
Warner (Henry Blanke)

A confidence trickster conquers the French fashion world.
Slight musical comedy with a couple of splendid Berkeley numbers.

w F. Hugh Herbert, Carl Brickson *d* William Dieterle *ch Busby Berkeley ph* William Rees *m/ly* Sammy Fain, Irving Kahal *ad* Jack Okey

William Powell, Bette Davis, Verree Teasdale, Frank McHugh, Reginald Owen, Hugh Herbert, Henry O'Neill

Fast and Loose
US 1930 70m bw
Paramount

A spoiled rich girl falls in love with a car mechanic.
Tiresome melodrama, dully scripted.

w Doris Anderson, Jack Kirkland, Preston Sturges, *play* The Best People by Avery Hopwood, David Gray *d* Fred Newmeyer *ph* William Steiner

Miriam Hopkins, Carole Lombard, Frank Morgan, Charles Starrett, Henry Wadsworth, David Hutcheson, Ilka Chase

Fast and Loose*
US 1939 80m bw
MGM (Frederick Stephani)

Married detectives and rare book experts solve the mystery of a missing Shakespeare manuscript.
Pleasing comedy mystery in the wake of *The Thin Man.*

w Harry Kurnitz *d* Edwin L. Marin *ph* George Folsey

Robert Montgomery, Rosalind Russell, Ralph Morgan, Reginald Owen, Etienne Girardot, Alan Dinehart, Joan Marsh, Sidney Blackmer

The Fast Lady**
GB 1962 95m Eastmancolor
Rank / Group Films (Teddy Baird)

A bashful suitor buys an old Bentley, becomes a roadhog, passes his test, captures some crooks and gets the girl.
Spirited if aimless farcical comedy which crams in all the jokes about cars anyone can think of.

w Jack Davies, Henry Blyth *d* Ken Annakin *ph* Reg Wyer *m* Norrie Paramor

Stanley Baxter, James Robertson Justice, Leslie Phillips, Julie Christie, Dick Emery

The Fastest Gun Alive*
US 1956 89m bw
MGM (Clarence Greene)

A mild-mannered western storekeeper proves to be the son of a famous gunfighter, and is put to the test.
Flimsily contrived mini-western helped by good performances.

w Frank D. Gilroy, Russel Rouse *d* Russel Rouse *ph* George Folsey *m* André Previn

Glenn Ford, Broderick Crawford, Jeanne Crain, Russ Tamblyn, Allyn Joslyn, Leif Erickson, John Dehner

Fat City*
US 1972 96m Eastmancolor
Columbia / Rastar (Ray Stark)

In a small Californian town, a has-been boxer tries to get back to the top, but loses his self respect and becomes a hobo.
Vivid but over-casual exploration of failure, with more interest in the characters than the sport.

w Leonard Gardner, from his novel *d* John Huston *ph* Conrad Hall *m* Marvin Hamlisch *pd* Richard Sylbert

Stacy Keach, Jeff Bridges, Susan Tyrell

The Fatal Night*
GB 1948 49m bw
(Columbia) Mario Zampi

A joke haunting has unfortunate consequences.
A small, cheaply-made film which really thrilled.

w Gerald Butler, *story* The Gentleman from America by Michael Arlen *d Mario Zampi* *ph* Cedric Williams *m* Stanley Black

Lester Ferguson, Jean Short, Leslie Armstrong, Brenda Hogan, Patrick MacNee

Fate Is the Hunter
US 1964 106m bw Cinemascope
TCF / Arcola (Aaron Rosenberg)

An airline executive investigates the cause of a fatal crash in which his friend the pilot was a victim.
Watchable how-did-it happen melodrama marred by pretentious dialogue.

w Harold Medford, *novel* Ernest K. Gann *d* Ralph Nelson *ph* Milton Krasner *m* Jerry Goldsmith

Glenn Ford, Rod Taylor, Nehemiah Persoff, Nancy Kwan, Suzanne Pleshette, Jane Russell

Father Brown***
GB 1954 91m bw
(Columbia) Facet (Vivian A. Cox)
US title: *The Detective*

A Catholic clergyman retrieves a priceless church cross from master thief Flambeau.
Delightfully eccentric comedy based closely on the famous character, with a sympathetic if rather wandering script, pointed direction and some delicious characterizations. A thoroughly civilized entertainment.

w Thelma Schnee, story The Blue Cross by G. K. Chesterton *d Robert Hamer* *ph* Harry Waxman *m* Georges Auric

Alec Guinness, Joan Greenwood, Peter Finch, Sidney James, *Cecil Parker, Bernard Lee, Ernest Thesiger,* Marne Maitland

Father Came Too*
GB 1963 93m Eastmancolor
Rank / Independent Artists

Honeymooners agree to live with her overbearing actor manager father.
Less funny sequel to *The Fast Lady*, with comic household disasters striking every couple of minutes. Easy-going, and predictably amusing in spots.

w Jack Davies, Henry Blyth *d* Peter Graham Scott *ph* Reg Wyer *m* Norrie Paramor

Stanley Baxter, James Robertson Justice, Sally Smith, Ronnie Barker, Timothy Bateson, Philip Locke

Father Goose*
US 1964 116m Technicolor
U-I / Granox (Robert Arthur)

During World War II a South Seas wanderer is compelled by the Australian navy to act as sky observer on a small island, where he finds himself in charge of six refugee schoolchildren and their schoolmistress.
Eager-to-please but unsatisfactory film which wanders between farce, adventure and sex comedy, taking too long about all of them.

w Peter Stone, Frank Tarloff *d* Ralph Nelson *ph* Charles Lang Jnr *m* Cy Coleman

Cary Grant, Leslie Caron, Trevor Howard

Father of the Bride**
US 1950 93m bw
MGM (Pandro S. Berman)

A dismayed but happy father surveys the cost and chaos of his daughter's marriage.
Fragmentary but mainly delightful suburban comedy which finds Hollywood in its best light vein and benefits from a strong central performance.

w Frances Goodrich, Albert Hackett, novel Edward Streeter d Vincente Minnelli *ph* John Alton *m* Adolph Deutsch

Spencer Tracy, Joan Bennett, Elizabeth Taylor, Don Taylor, Billie Burke, Moroni Olsen, Leo G. Carroll, Taylor Holmes, Melville Cooper

Father Takes a Wife*
US 1941 80m bw
RKO (Lee S. Marcus)

A famous actress marries a shipping magnate and runs into resentment from his children.
Disappointing comedy with a script too flat for the stars to make interesting.

w Dorothy and Herbert Fields *d* Jack Hively *ph* Robert de Grasse *m* Roy Webb

Gloria Swanson, Adolphe Menjou, Desi Arnaz, John Howard, Helen Broderick, Florence Rice, Neil Hamilton

Father's Little Dividend
US 1951 81m bw
MGM (Pandro S. Berman)

Sequel to the above, in which the newlyweds have a baby.
A very flat follow-up, palatable enough at the time but quite unmemorable.

w Frances Goodrich, Albert Hackett *d* Vincente Minnelli *ph* John Alton *m* Georgie Stoll

Spencer Tracy, Joan Bennett, Elizabeth Taylor, Don Taylor, Billie Burke, Moroni Olsen, Frank Faylen, Marietta Candy, Russ Tamblyn

Fathom
GB 1967 99m De Luxe Franscope
TCF (John Kohn)

Adventures of a glamorous sky-diving spy.
Watchable romp with nothing memorable about it.

w Lorenzo Semple Jnr, *novel* Larry Forrester *d* Leslie Martinson *ph* Douglas Slocombe, Ken Vos *m* Johnny Dankworth

Raquel Welch, Tony Franciosa, Clive Revill, Ronald Fraser, Greta Chi, Richard Briers, Tom Adams

'Belongs not in the category of High Camp but in that of Good Wholesome Fun.'—*MFB*

The FBI Story*
US 1959 149m Technicolor
Warner (Mervyn Le Roy)

An FBI agent thinks back on his career with the bureau.
Predictable mix of domestic sentimentality (very trying) and competent crime capsules: mad bomber, Ku Klux Klan, thirties hoodlums, Nazi spy rings and the cold war.

w Richard L. Breen, John Twist *d* Mervyn Le Roy *ph* Joseph Biroc *m* Max Steiner *ad* John Beckman

James Stewart, Vera Miles, Larry Pennell, Nick Adams, Murray Hamilton

'Insufferably cosy.'—*MFB*

The FBI versus Alvin Karpis, Public Enemy Number One
US 1974 100m colour TVM
Warner / Quinn Martin

J. Edgar Hoover personally joins in the chase for a most wanted criminal of the thirties.
Long and flatly told crime busting epic, one of a

short-lived series of telefeatures which followed the one-hour series *The FBI* which ran nine years. See also: *Attack on Terror*.

w Calvin Clements *d* Marvin Chomsky

Robert Foxworth, Eileen Heckart, Kay Lenz, David Wayne, Harris Yulin, Gary Lockwood, Anne Francis

Fear in the Night**
US 1947 72m bw
Maxwell Shane

A man suffering from a strange nightmare discovers he has been hypnotized into committing a murder.
Intriguing small-scale puzzler later remade to less effect as *Nightmare* (qv). Adequate performances and handling, but the plot's the thing.

wd Maxwell Shane ph Jack Grennhalgh

Paul Kelly, De Forrest Kelley, Ann Doran, Kay Scott

Fear in the Night*
GB 1972 85m Technicolor
Hammer (Jimmy Sangster)

A girl recovering from a nervous breakdown is deluded into committing a murder.
Yet another variant on *Les Diaboliques*, ingeniously worked out with good touches of detail to produce an air of general competence.

w Jimmy Sangster, Michael Syson *d* Jimmy Sangster *ph* Arthur Grant *m* John McCabe

Peter Cushing, Judy Geeson, Joan Collins, Ralph Bates

Fear Is the Key*
GB 1972 108m Technicolor Panavision
EMI / KLK (Alan Ladd Jnr, Elliott Kastner)

A man conceives an elaborate plot to track down those responsible for killing his wife and family in a plane crash.
Reasonably absorbing, surprise-plotted thriller.

w Robert Carrington, *novel* Alistair MacLean *d* Michael Tuchner *ph* Alex Thomson *m* Roy Budd

Suzy Kendall, Barry Newman, John Vernon, Dolph Sweet, Ben Kingsley, Ray McAnally

Fear No Evil
US 1969 98m Technicolor TVM
Universal

A scientist dies after buying an antique mirror: a supernatural expert probes its secret.
Overlong scary suspenser which failed to start a series even after a second pilot, *Ritual of Evil* (qv), was tried.

w Richard Alan Simmons *d* Paul Wendkos

Louis Jourdan, Bradford Dillman, Marsha Hunt, Wilfrid Hyde White, Lynda Day, Carroll O'Connor

Fear on Trial**
US 1975 100m colour TVM
Alan Landsburg (Stanley Chase)

The story of John Henry Faulk, a radio commentator who was caught up in fifties blacklisting but finally won his suit alleging wrongful dismissal.
Fascinating re-creation of recent history with a powerhouse performance from Scott as Louis Nizer.

w David Rintels *d* Lamont Johnson

George C. Scott, William Devane, Dorothy Tristan, William Redfield, David Susskind

Fear Strikes Out
US 1957 100m bw Vistavision
Paramount / Alan Pakula

A father wants his son to become a professional baseball player, and the son in consequence suffers a nervous breakdown.
Rather flat biopic of Jim Piersall well-intentioned and careful in its psychological insights, but too often just plain dull.

w Ted Berkman, Raphael Blau *d* Robert Mulligan *ph* Haskell Boggs *m* Elmer Bernstein

Anthony Perkins, Karl Malden, Norma Moore, Perry Wilson

The Fearless Vampire Killers, or Pardon Me, Your Teeth Are in My Neck*
US 1967 124m Metrocolor Panavision
MGM / Cadre Films / Filmways (Gene Gutowski)
aka: *Dance of the Vampires*

A professor and his assistant stake a Transylvanian vampire.
Heavy, slow spoof of *Dracula*, most of which shows that sense of humour is very personal; a few effective moments hardly compensate for the prevailing stodge.

w Gerard Brach, Roman Polanski *d* Roman Polanski *ph Douglas Slocombe m* Krzystof Komeda *pd* Wilfrid Shingleton

Jack McGowran, Roman Polanski, Alfie Bass, Sharon Tate, *Ferdy Mayne*, Iain Quarrier, Terry Downes

'An engaging oddity . . . long stretches might

have been lifted intact from any Hammer horror.'—*Tom Milne*

The Fearmakers
US 1958 85m bw
Pacemaker (Martin H. Lancer)

A brainwashed Korean War veteran returns to Washington and finds that his PR firm has been taken over by communist racketeers.
Unusual but cheaply made anti-Red propaganda, too talkative to be very entertaining.

w Elliot West, Chris Appley, *novel* Darwin Teilhet *d* Jacques Tourneur *ph* Sam Leavitt *m* Irving Gertz

Dana Andrews, Dick Foran, Mel Tormé

Feather and Father
US 1976 74m colour TVM
Columbia (Larry White)

A smart lady lawyer solves cases with the help of her con man father and his underworld friends.
Dismal rehash of forties routines, a long way from Damon Runyon.

w Bill Driskill *d* Buzz Kulik

Stefanie Powers, Harold Gould, John Forsythe, Frank Delfino, Bettye Ackerman, Jim Backus, Severn Darden

A Feather in Her Hat
US 1935 72m bw
Columbia

A London widow with delusions of grandeur tells her son that his real mother was a famous actress.
Outmoded mother-love drama, interestingly cast.

w Lawrence Hazard, *story* I. A. R. Wylie *d* Alfred Santell *ph* Joseph Walker

Pauline Lord, Basil Rathbone, Louis Hayward, Billie Burke, Wendy Barrie, J. M. Kerrigan, Victor Varconi, Nydia Westman, Thurston Hall

Feet First**
US 1930 88m bw
Harold Lloyd

A shoe salesman gets entangled with crooks and has a narrow escape when hanging from the side of a building.
Very funny early talkie comedy, probably the comedian's last wholly satisfactory film.

w Lex Neal, Felix Adler, Paul Gerard Smith *d Clyde Bruckman ph* Walter Ludin, Henry Kohler

Harold Lloyd, Robert McWade, Barbara Kent

The Female Animal
US 1957 82m bw Cinemascope
U-I (Albert Zugsmith)

A beach bum becomes the lover of a film star, then falls in love with her daughter.
Dreary and humourless melodrama notable only for the comeback appearance of one of the screen's legendary glamour queens.

w Robert Hill *d* Harry Keller *ph* Russell Metty *m* Hans Salter

Hedy Lamarr, Jan Sterling, Jane Powell, George Nader, James Gleason

Female Artillery
US 1972 73m Technicolor TVM
Universal (Winston Miller)

A western fugitive is protected from outlaws by a band of women who have been banished from a wagon train.
Failed mix of comedy and action.

w Bud Freeman *d* Marvin Chomsky

Ida Lupino, Dennis Weaver, Sally Ann Howes, Nina Foch, Linda Evans, Lee Harcourt Montgomery, Albert Salmi

The Female on the Beach
US 1955 97m bw
U-I (Albert Zugsmith)

A wealthy widow visits her late husband's beach house and falls for the gigolo next door, who later seems intent on murdering her.
Absurd and jaded melodrama, a rehash of *Love from a Stranger*, enlivened by some hilarious love-hate dialogue.

w Robert Hill, Richard Alan Simmons *d* Joseph Pevney *ph* Charles Lang *m* Joseph Gershenson

Joan Crawford, Jeff Chandler, Jan Sterling, Cecil Kellaway, Natalie Schaefer

The Feminist and the Fuzz*
US 1970 74m colour TVM
Columbia

A cop and a women's-libber end up sharing an apartment.
Brisk romantic comedy with San Francisco backgrounds.

w Jim Henderson *d* Jerry Paris

David Hartman, Barbara Eden, Joanne Worley, Julie Newmar

Fer de Lance*
US 1975 98m colour TVM
Leslie Stevens (Dominic Frontière)
GB theatrical title: *Death Dive*

A submarine full of scientists is stuck on the

ocean bed and terrorized by poisonous snakes.
Smooth but unlikely thriller.

w Leslie Stevens *d* Russ Mayberry

David Janssen, Hope Lange, Ivan Dixon, Jason Evers, Charles Robinson

Ferry to Hong Kong
GB 1958 113m Eastmancolor Cinemascope
Rank (George Maynard)

An Austrian layabout can land at neither of the Hong Kong ferry's ports of call, but shows his true worth when a typhoon strikes.
Silly storyline and rampant bad acting ruin the Rank Organization's first attempt at an international epic.

w Vernon Harris, Lewis Gilbert *d* Lewis Gilbert *ph* Otto Heller *m* Ken Jones

Curt Jurgens, Sylvia Syms, Orson Welles, Jeremy Spenser, Noel Purcell

A Fever in the Blood
US 1960 117m bw
Warner (Roy Huggins)

Candidates for governor sharpen their campaigns on a murder trial.
Interestingly-cast, flabbily-written melodrama.

w Roy Huggins, Harry Kleiner, *novel* William Pearson *d* Vincent Sherman *ph* J. Peverell Marley *m* Ernest Gold

Efrem Zimbalist Jnr, Angie Dickinson, Don Ameche, Herbert Marshall, Jack Kelly, Ray Danton, Jesse White, Rhodes Reason, Robert Colbert

Fiddler on the Roof**
US 1971 180m Technicolor Panavision 70
UA / Mirisch (Norman Jewison)

In a pre-revolutionary Russian village, Tevye the Jewish milkman survives family and political problems and when the pogroms begin cheerfully emigrates to America.
Self-conscious, grittily realistic adaptation of the stage musical, with slow and heavy patches in its grossly overlong celebration of a vanished way of life. The big moments still come off well though the songs tend to be thrown away and the photography is unnecessarily murky.

w Joseph Stein, from his play and Sholom Aleichem's story Tevye and his Daughters *d* Norman Jewison *ph* Oswald Morris *m Jerry Bock* *pd* Robert Boyle *ly* Sheldon Harnick

Topol, Norma Crane, Leonard Frey, Molly Picon

'Jewison hasn't so much directed a film as prepared a product for world consumption.'—*Stanley Kauffmann*

Fiddlers Three*
GB 1944 87m bw
Ealing (Robert Hamer)

Sailors struck by lightning on Salisbury Plain are transported back to ancient Rome.
Sequel to *Sailors Three*; despite a harsh and unattractive look, every conceivable joke about old Romans is deftly mined and the good humour flows free.

w Diana Morgan, Angus Macphail *d* Harry Watt

Tommy Trinder, Sonnie Hale, Frances Day, Francis L. Sullivan, Ernest Milton, Diana Decker, Elizabeth Welch, Mary Clare

The Fiend Who Walked the West
US 1958 101m bw Cinemascope
TCF (Herbert B. Swope Jnr)

A sadistic killer released from prison tracks down the associates of a cellmate and terrorizes the district.
Western remake of *Kiss of Death*, with babyface Robert Evans in the Widmark role. Violent and dull.

w Harry Brown, Philip Yordan *d* Gordon Douglas *ph* Joe MacDonald *m* Leon Klatzkin

Hugh O'Brian, Dolores Michaels, Robert Evans, Linda Cristal, Stephen McNally, Edward Andrews

The Fiend without a Face
GB 1957 75m bw
Producers' Associates (John Croydon)

A scientist working on materialized thought produces monsters from his own id.
Tepid shocker with well-organized mobile brains.

w H. J. Leder *d* Arthur Crabtree *ph* Lionel Banes *m* Buxton Orr *sp* Ruppel and Nordhoff

Kynaston Reeves, Terry Kilburn, Marshall Thompson

The Fiercest Heart
US 1961 90m De Luxe Cinemascope
TCF (George Sherman)

A British army deserter joins a Boer trek into South Africa.
Pioneer 'western', poorly done but with novelty value.

w Edmund H. North, *novel* Stuart Cloete

d George Sherman *ph* Ellis Carter *m* Irving Gertz

Stuart Whitman, Juliet Prowse, Raymond Massey, Ken Scott, Geraldine Fitzgerald, Rafer Johnson

Fifth Avenue Girl*
US 1939 83m bw
RKO (Gregory La Cava)

An unemployed girl is persuaded by a millionaire to pose as a gold digger and annoy his avaricious family.
Brightish comedy of the Cinderella kind.

w Allan Scott *d* Gregory La Cava *ph* Robert de Grasse

Ginger Rogers, Walter Connolly, Verree Teasdale, Tim Holt, James Ellison, Franklin Pangborn, Kathryn Adams, Louis Calhern

55 Days at Peking*
US / Spain 1962 154m Super Technirama 70
Samuel Bronston

In 1900 Peking, Boxer fanatics are encouraged by the Empress to take over the city and besiege the international diplomatic quarter; an American major leads the defence.
Spasmodically lively action spectacular weighed down by romantic stretches.

w Philip Yordan, Bernard Gordon *d* Nicholas Ray, Andrew Marton *ph* Jack Hildyard, Manuel Berenguer *m* Dmitri Tiomkin *ad* Venerio Colasanti, John Moore

Charlton Heston, David Niven, Ava Gardner, Flora Robson, Robert Helpmann, Leo Genn, Paul Lukas, John Ireland, Harry Andrews, Elizabeth Sellars, Massimo Serrato, Jacques Sernas, Geoffrey Bayldon

Fighter Squadron
US 1948 96m Technicolor
Warner (Seton I. Miller)

In World War II, a dedicated flier risks his friends' lives.
Routine aerial actioner.

w Seton I. Miller *d* Raoul Walsh *ph* Sid Hickox, Wilfrid M. Cline *m* Max Steiner

Edmond O'Brien, Robert Stack, John Rodney, Tom D'Andrea, Henry Hull, Walter Reed, Shepperd Strudwick, Rock Hudson

Fighting Father Dunne
US 1948 93m bw
RKO

A clergyman looks after unfortunate boys.
A slum melodrama which all concerned could have made with their eyes closed, and probably did.

w Martin Rackin, Frank Davis *d* Ted Tetzlaff *ph* George E. Diskant *m* Constantin Bakaleinikoff

Pat O'Brien, Darryl Hickman, Charles Kemper, Una O'Connor

The Fighting Kentuckian
US 1949 100m bw
Republic (John Wayne)

In 1810 a farmer combats land-grabbing criminals.
Standard star western for the family.

wd George Waggner *ph* Lee Garmes *m* George Antheil

John Wayne, Vera Ralston, Oliver Hardy, Philip Dorn, Marie Windsor, Mae Marsh

Fighting Mad
US 1976 90m De Luxe
TCF / Santa Fe (Roger Corman)

A rancher and his son are murdered by a local industrialist who wants their land, and the rancher's city-bred son takes revenge.
Another vigilante western in modern dress, very laborious and violent without being very exciting.

wd Jonathan Demme *ph* Bill Birch *m* Bruce Langhorne

Peter Fonda, Lynn Lowry, John Doucette, Philip Carey, Scott Glen

The Fighting O'Flynn
US 1949 94m bw
U-I (Douglas Fairbanks Jnr)

In 18th-century Ireland, a penniless young adventurer aborts Napoleon's plan for invasion.
Lively minor-league adventure.

w Douglas Fairbanks Jnr, Robert Thoeren, *novel* Justin Huntly McCarthy *d* Arthur Pierson *ph* Arthur Edeson *m* Frank Skinner

Douglas Fairbanks Jnr, Helena Carter, Richard Greene, Patricia Medina, Arthur Shields, J. M. Kerrigan

'Fairbanks plays the irrepressible O'Flynn with unflagging energy and tongue in cheek good humour; the rest of the cast stolidly refuses to see the joke.'—*MFB*

The Fighting Prince of Donegal
GB 1966 104m Technicolor
Walt Disney (Bill Anderson)

Adventures of an Irish rebel in the reign of Elizabeth I.
Adequate Boys' Own Paper romp.

w Robert Westerby, *novel* Red Hugh, Prince of Donegal by Robert T. Reilly *d* Michael O'Herlihy *ph* Arthur Ibbetson *m* George Bruns

Peter McEnery, Susan Hampshire, Tom Adams, Gordon Jackson, Andrew Keir, Norman Woolland, Richard Leech

The Fighting Seabees
US 1944 100m bw
Republic (Albert J. Cohen)

During World War II in the Pacific, construction workers attack the Japanese.
Routine, studio-staged war melodrama, heavily fleshed out with love interest.

w Borden Chase, Aeneas Mackenzie *d* Edward Ludwig *ph* William Bradford *m* Walter Scharf

John Wayne, Susan Hayward, Dennis O'Keefe, William Frawley, Duncan Renaldo, Addison Richards, Leonid Kinskey, Paul Fix

The Fighting 69th*
US 1940 89m bw
Warner (Hal B. Wallis)

During World War I in the trenches, a cocky recruit becomes a hero and loses his life in the process.
Recruiting poster stuff, all well enough done but bewildering in its changes of mood.

w Norman Reilly Raine, Fred Niblo Jnr, Dean Franklin *d* William Keighley *ph* Tony Gaudio

James Cagney, Pat O'Brien, George Brent, Jeffrey Lynn, Alan Hale, Frank McHugh, Dennis Morgan, Dick Foran, William Lundigan, Guinn Williams, John Litel, Henry O'Neill

Figures in a Landscape
GB 1970 110m Technicolor
Panavision
Cinecrest (John Kohn)

Two men on the run are pursued by soldiers and helicopters; only one crosses the frontier.
Portentous Pinterish parable, very long-winded and relentlessly boring though good to look at. Everything is symbolic, nothing is specific, not even the country.

w Robert Shaw, *novel* Barry England *d* Joseph Losey *ph* Henri Alekan *m* Richard Rodney Bennett

Robert Shaw, Malcolm McDowell

The File of the Golden Goose
GB 1969 109m De Luxe
UA / Theme / Caralan / Dador (David E. Rose)

An American agent works with Scotland Yard to track down counterfeiters.
Incredibly predictable spy thriller which almost makes an eccentricity out of collecting so many clichés and so many tourist views of London. Like ten TV episodes cut together.

w John C. Higgins, James B. Gordon *d* Sam Wanamaker *ph* Ken Hodges *m* Harry Robinson

Yul Brynner, Edward Woodward, Charles Gray, John Barrie, Bernard Archard, Ivor Dean, Adrienne Corri, Graham Crowden, Karel Stepanek

'The film plods wearily homewards through an exceptionally uninteresting batch of fights, intrigues and sinister encounters.'—*MFB*

The File on Thelma Jordon*
US 1949 100m bw
Paramount (Hal B. Wallis)
aka: *Thelma Jordon*

A district attorney falls for a murder suspect and has her acquitted by losing the case.
Stylishly made, murkily plotted melodrama and a superior star vehicle of its time.

w Ketti Frings *d* Robert Siodmak *ph* George Barnes *m* Victor Young

Barbara Stanwyck, Wendell Corey, Paul Kelly, Joan Tetzel, Stanley Ridges, Richard Rober, Minor Watson, Barry Kelley

The Final Programme
GB 1973 89m Technicolor
Goodtimes / Gladiole (John Goldstone, Sanford Lieberson)

In the future, when the world is torn by famine and war, a scientist awaits a new messiah.
Intellectualized sci-fi, hard to take as entertainment but very glossy.

wd Robert Fuest, *novel* Michael Moorcock *ph* Norman Warwick *m* Paul Beaver, Bernard Krause

Jon Finch, Jenny Runacre, Sterling Hayden, Hugh Griffith

'Clumsy and almost incomprehensible.'—*Sight and Sound*

The Final Test
GB 1953 90m bw
Rank / ACT (R. J. Minney)

A cricketer looks forward to his last game but is out for a duck; he is however cheered by the crowd and comforted by his son.
Flat character study some way below the author's best style, cluttered up with real cricketers and stymied by lack of action.

w Terence Rattigan *d* Anthony Asquith *ph* Bill McLeod *m* Benjamin Franklin

Jack Warner, Robert Morley, George Relph

Finders Keepers
GB 1966 94m Eastmancolor
UA / Interstate (George H. Brown)

The Americans lose an atomic bomb off the Spanish coast, and it's found by a pop group.
Harmless youth musical without much style. Tunes poor, comedy rather too easy-going.

w Michael Pertwee *d* Sidney Hayers *ph* Alan Hume *m* The Shadows, Norrie Paramor

Cliff Richard, The Shadows, Robert Morley, Peggy Mount, Viviane Ventura, Graham Stark, John Le Mesurier, Robert Hutton

A Fine Madness*
US 1966 104m Technicolor
Warner Seven Arts

A frustrated New York poet has outbursts of violence.
Patchy, interesting, with-it comedy which suffers from too many changes of mood.

w Elliot Baker, from his novel *d* Irvin Kershner *ph Ted McCord* *m* John Addison

Sean Connery, Jean Seberg, Joanne Woodward, Patrick O'Neal, Colleen Dewhurst, Clive Revill

'Straddling a no man's land somewhere between the *nouvelle vague* and the crazy comedies of Old Hollywood.'—*Tom Milne*

Finian's Rainbow*
US 1968 140m Technicolor Panavision 70
Warner Seven Arts (Joseph Landon)

A leprechaun tries to retrieve a crock of gold from an old wanderer who has taken it to America.
Musical whimsy-whamsy, rather a long way after a Broadway success; in this overlong and overblown screen version the elements and the style do not jell and there is too much sentimental chat, but moments of magic shine through.

w E. Y. Harburg, Fred Saidy, from their play *d* Francis Ford Coppola *ph* Philip Lathrop *m* Burton Lane *ly* E. Y. Harburg *pd* Hilyard M. Brown *md* Ray Heindorf

Fred Astaire, Petula Clark, Tommy Steele, Don Francks, Keenan Wynn, Barbara Hancock, Al Freeman Jnr

Finishing School
US 1934 73m bw
RKO (Kenneth MacGowan)

A girl at an exclusive school falls for an intern.
Modest pap for the teenage audience.

w Wanda Tuchock, Laird Doyle *d* Wanda Tuchock, George Nicholls Jnr *ph* J. Roy Hunt *m* Max Steiner

Frances Dee, Ginger Rogers, Billie Burke, Bruce Cabot, John Halliday, Beulah Bondi, Sara Haden

Fire Down Below
GB 1957 116m Technicolor Cinemascope
Columbia / Warwick (Irving Allen, Albert Broccoli)

Partners in a Caribbean fishing and smuggling business fall out over a woman.
Overheated melodrama with thin characters, predictable incident and ill-advised casting.

w Irwin Shaw, *novel* Max Catto *d* Robert Parrish *ph* Desmond Dickinson *m* Arthur Benjamin

Rita Hayworth, Robert Mitchum, Jack Lemmon, Herbert Lom, Bonar Colleano, Bernard Lee, Edric Connor, Peter Illing

Fire Over England**
GB 1936 92m bw
Pendennis (Erich Pommer)

Elizabeth I and her navy overcome the Spanish Armada.
Though the film has a faded air and the action climax was always a bath-tub affair, the splendid cast keeps this pageant afloat and interesting.

w Clemence Dane, Sergei Nolbandov, *novel* A. E. W. Mason *d* William K. Howard *ph* James Wong Howe *m* Richard Addinsell

Flora Robson, Laurence Olivier, Leslie Banks, Vivien Leigh, Raymond Massey, Tamara Desni, Morton Selten, Lyn Harding, James Mason

Fireball Forward
US 1972 98m colour TVM
TCF

In World War II France, a general finds a spy in his division.
Adequate actioner with spy trimmings.

w Edmund North *d* Marvin Chomsky

Ben Gazzara, Eddie Albert, Ricardo Montalban, Dana Elcar, Anne Francis, Morgan Paull, L. Q. Jones

The Firechasers*
GB 1970 74m or 101m colour TVM
ITC (Julian Wintle)

An insurance investigator chases an arsonist.
Lumpy, disjointed, watchable adventures.

w Philip Levene *d* Sidney Hayers

Chad Everett, Keith Barron, Anjanette Comer,

Joanne Dainton, Rupert Davies, Robert Flemyng, Roy Kinnear, John Loder, James Hayter

Firecreek
US 1968 104m Technicolor Panavision
Warner Seven Arts (Philip Leacock)

The people of Firecreek protect themselves from wandering gunmen.
Dour, predictable little western which does not show its stars at their best.

w Calvin Clements *d* Vincent McEveety *ph* William Clothier *m* Alfred Newman

James Stewart, Henry Fonda, Gary Lockwood, Dean Jagger, Ed Begley, Jay C. Flippen, Jack Elam, James Best, Barbara Luna

'This cramped and clumsy western grinds to a standstill in its attempts to give Firecreek symbolic status . . . while the gunmen roister like mad and the townsfolk rhubarb glumly in the background.'—*MFB*

The Firefly*
US 1937 131m bw
MGM (Hunt Stromberg)

Adventures of a Spanish lady spy during the Napoleonic war.
Solid production of a romantic operetta; splendid stuff for connoisseurs.

w Frances Goodrich, Albert Hackett, Ogden Nash *d* Robert Z. Leonard *ph* Oliver Marsh *md* Herbert Stothart *original book/ly* Otto Harbach *m* Rudolf Friml

Jeanette MacDonald, *Allan Jones* (who sings the Donkey Serenade), Warren William, Billy Gilbert, Henry Daniell, George Zucco, Douglass Dumbrille

Firehouse
US 1973 74m colour TVM
Metromedia (Dick Berg)

Racist conflicts erupt in a city fire department during an arson outbreak.
Totally unsurprising action yarn which generated a short-lived series.

w Frank Cucci *d* Alex March

Richard Roundtree, Vince Edwards, Andrew Duggan, Richard Jaeckel

Fireman Save My Child
US 1954 80m bw
U-I (Howard Christie)

In 1910 San Francisco, incompetent firemen accidentally catch a gang of crooks.
Slapstick farce intended for Abbott and Costello, taken over by a new team which did not catch on, played like the Keystone Kops. Mildly funny during the chases.

w Lee Loeb, John Grant *d* Leslie Goodwins *ph* Clifford Stine *m* Joseph Gershenson

Buddy Hackett, Spike Jones and the City Slickers, Hugh O'Brian, Adèle Jergens

First Comes Courage
US 1943 88m bw
Columbia (Harry Joe Brown)

During World War II, a Norwegian girl appears to be a Quisling but is really a spy getting information from the Nazis by fraternizing with them.
Doleful war drama with little to commend it except propaganda.

w Lewis Meltzer, Melvin Levy, *novel* The Commandos by Elliott Arnold *d* Dorothy Arzner *ph* Joseph Walker *m* Ernst Toch

Merle Oberon, Brian Aherne, Carl Esmond, Fritz Leiber, Erik Rolf, Reinhold Schunzel, Isobel Elsom

The First Gentleman*
GB 1948 111m bw
Columbia (Joseph Friedman)
US title: *Affairs of a Rogue*

The affairs and foibles of the Prince Regent.
Dullish adaptation of a successful West End play about 18th-century court life; script and performances still entertain.

w Nicholas Phipps, Reginald Long, *play Norman Ginsbury* *d* Cavalcanti

Cecil Parker, Jean-Pierre Aumont, Joan Hopkins, Margaretta Scott, Jack Livesey, Ronald Squire, Athene Seyler, Hugh Griffith

First Lady*
US 1937 82m bw
Warner (Hal B. Wallis)

The President's wife is a power behind the scenes.
Solidly entertaining Washington comedy.

w Rowland Leigh, *play* George S. Kaufman, Katherine Dayton *d* Stanley Logan *ph* Sid Hickox

Kay Francis, Preston Foster, Anita Louise, Walter Connolly, Verree Teasdale, Victor Jory, Marjorie Rambeau, Louise Fazenda

The First Legion*
US 1951 86m bw
Sedif (Douglas Sirk)

Priests are bewildered when one of their number is the centre of an apparent miracle.

Talkative religious drama of a peculiarly American kind which likes to have its cake and eat it; watchable for the performances.

w Emmet Lavery, from his play *d* Douglas Sirk *ph* Robert de Grasse *m* Hans Sommer

Charles Boyer, William Demarest, Lyle Bettger, Barbara Rush, Leo G. Carroll, Walter Hampden, George Zucco, Taylor Holmes

First Man Into Space
GB 1958 78m bw
Producers' Associates (John Croydon)

An astronaut runs into a cloud of meteor dust and returns to earth a vampirish killer.
Quatermass-like shocker with modest budget but firm control.

w John C. Cooper, Lance Z. Hargreaves *d* Robert Day *ph* Geoffrey Faithfull *m* Buxton Orr

Marshall Thompson, Marla Landi, Bill Edwards

First Men in the Moon*
GB 1964 103m Technicolor Panavision
Columbia / Ameran (Charles H. Schneer)

A Victorian eccentric makes a voyage to the moon and is forced to stay there.
Rather slack in plot development, but an enjoyable schoolboy romp with a good eye for detail and tongue firmly in cheek.

w Nigel Kneale, Jan Read, *novel* H. G. Wells *d* Nathan Juran *ph* Wilkie Cooper *m* Laurie Johnson *sp* Ray Harryhausen

Lionel Jeffries, Edward Judd, Martha Hyer
† Uncredited, Peter Finch played the bit part of a process server.

The First of the Few**
GB 1942 117m bw
Melbourne / British Aviation (Leslie Howard, George King, Adrian Brunel, John Stafford)
US title: *Spitfire*

The story of R. J. Mitchell who saw World War II coming and devised the Spitfire.
Low-key but impressive biopic with firm acting and good dialogue scenes. Production values slightly shaky.

w Anatole de Grunwald, Miles Malleson, Henry C. James, Katherine Strueby *d* Leslie Howard

Leslie Howard, David Niven, Rosamund John, Roland Culver, David Horne

The First Texan
US 1956 82m Technicolor Cinemascope
Allied Artists (Walter Mirisch)

The Governor of Tennessee helps Texas win its independence.
Generally well done biopic of Sam Houston, with the usual western excitements.

w Daniel B. Ullman *d* Byron Haskin *ph* Wilfrid Cline *m* Roy Webb

Joel McCrea, Felicia Farr, Jeff Morrow, Wallace Ford, Abraham Sofaer

The First 36 Hours of Dr Durant
US 1975 74m colour TVM
Columbia (James H. Brown)

A young surgeon reports to a city hospital and learns the realities of his career.
Dr Kildare rides again. Adequate for insomniacs.

w Stirling Silliphant *d* Alexander Singer

Scott Hylands, Lawrence Pressman, Katherine Helmond, Karen Carlson

First to Fight
US 1967 97m Technicolor Panavision
Warner (William Conrad)

A World War II hero is taken home and fêted, but on returning to the front he loses his nerve.
War film in the guise of a psychological study; competently done but very American in its sentiments and a bit shaky on period detail.

w Gene L. Coon *d* Christian Nyby *ph* Harold Wellman *m* Fred Steiner

Chad Everett, Gene Hackman, Dean Jagger, Marilyn Devon, Claude Akins

The First Travelling Saleslady
US 1956 92m Technicolor
RKO (Arthur Lubin)

Two women set out to sell barbed wire in the old west.
Strained comedy with very few effective moments.

w Devery Freeman, Stephen Longstreet *d* Arthur Lubin *ph* William Snyder *m* Irving Gertz

Ginger Rogers, Carol Channing, Barry Nelson, James Arness, David Brian, Clint Eastwood

A Fistful of Dollars*
Italy / Ger / Spain 1964 100m Techniscope
UA / Jolly / Constantin / Ocean (Arrigo Colombo, Georgio Papi)

An avenging stranger, violent and mysterious, cleans up a Mexican border town.
A film with much to answer for: it began the craze for 'spaghetti westerns', took its director to

Hollywood, and made a TV cowboy into a world star. In itself it is simple, noisy, brutish and actionful.

w Sergio Leone, Duccio Tessari *d Sergio Leone ph* Massimo Dallamano *m* Ennio Morricone

Clint Eastwood, Gian Maria Volonte, Marianne Koch

† Direct sequels by Leone, apart from numerous imitations, are *For a Few Dollars More* and *The Good, the Bad and the Ugly*.

A Fistful of Dynamite
Italy 1971 150m Techniscope
UA / Rafran / San Marco / Miura (Fulvio Morsella)

In 1913 a Mexican bandit and an ex-IRA explosives expert join forces to rob a bank.
Overblown action spectacular, far too long to be sustained by its flashes of humour and excitement. A good instance of what happens to a small talent when success goes to its head.

wd Sergio Leone ph Giuseppe Ruzzolini *m* Ennio Morricone

Rod Steiger, James Coburn

Fitzwilly*
US 1967 102m De Luxe Panavision
UA / Dramatic Features Inc / Walter Mirisch
GB title: *Fitzwilly Strikes Back*

A New York butler, in order to keep his lady in style, has to organize the staff into a crime syndicate.
Moderately inventive, good-looking comedy with rather too much plot and not enough funny lines.

w Isobel Lennart, *novel* A Garden of Cucumbers by Poyntz Tyler *d* Delbert Mann *ph* Joseph Biroc *m* Johnny Williams

Dick Van Dyke, Edith Evans, Barbara Feldon, John McGiver, Harry Townes, John Fiedler, Norman Fell, Cecil Kellaway, Anne Seymour, Sam Waterston, Billy Halop

Five
US 1951 89m bw
Columbia (Arch Oboler)

There are only five survivors of an atomic holocaust, and their political and racial tensions soon reduce the number to two.
Gutless talkfest which becomes interesting only when the camera moves out of doors; otherwise, too pretentious and dull by half.

wd Arch Oboler *ph* Lou Stoumen, Ed Spiegel, Sid Lubow *m* Henry Russell

William Phipps, Susan Douglas, James Anderson, Charles Lampkin, Earl Lee

'The talk leaves one with a strong impression that in this case the fittest did not survive.'—*Penelope Houston*

Five Against the House
US 1955 84m bw
Columbia (Sterling Silliphant, John Barnwell)

College students try to rob a casino.
Meandering caper melodrama with too much flabby dialogue.

w Sterling Silliphant, John Barnwell, *novel* Jack Finney *d* Phil Karlson *ph* Leslie White *m* George Duning

Guy Madison, Kim Novak, Brian Keith, Kerwin Mathews, William Conrad

Five Branded Women
Italy / US 1960 100m bw
Paramount / Dino de Laurentiis

Five Yugoslav girls have their heads shaved for associating with German soldiers, and after various adventures join the partisans.
Rough, tough war adventure which makes a few boring points about love and war.

w Ivo Perelli, *novel* Ugo Pirro *d* Martin Ritt *ph* Giuseppe Rotunno *m* Francesco Lavagnino

Silvana Mangano, Van Heflin, Vera Miles, Barbara Bel Geddes, Jeanne Moreau, Richard Basehart, Harry Guardino, Steve Forrest, Alex Nicol

'For the most part the film is devoted to unexciting guerrilla action and uninviting partisan life . . . obstinately unreal despite lashings of blood, mutilation, childbirth and death.'—*MFB*

Five Came Back**
US 1939 75m bw
RKO (Robert Sisk)

A passenger plane crashlands in the jungle. It can carry back only five survivors, and headhunters are coming closer . . .
A minor film which gradually achieved cult status and was remade as *Back to Eternity* as well as being the starting point for many variations. Still gripping in its dated way.

w Jerry Cady, Dalton Trumbo, Nathanael West *d John Farrow ph* Nicholas Musuraca *m* Roy Webb

Chester Morris, Lucille Ball, C. Aubrey Smith, Elizabeth Risdon, Wendy Barrie, John Carradine, Joseph Calleia, Allen Jenkins, Kent Taylor, Patric Knowles

Five Card Stud
US 1968 103m Technicolor
Paramount / Hal. B. Wallis

Members of a lynching party are murdered one by one.
Would-be nonchalant murder mystery western: the stars just about hold it together, but it's an uphill fight.

w Marguerite Roberts, *novel* Ray Gaulden *d* Henry Hathaway *ph* Daniel L. Fapp *m* Maurice Jarre

Dean Martin, Robert Mitchum, Inger Stevens, Roddy McDowall, Katherine Justice, John Anderson, Yaphet Kotto

'Marginally watchable . . . but destined to sink without trace minutes after one leaves the cinema.'—*Gavin Millar*

'So mediocre you can't get mad at it.' —*Judith Crist*

Five Desperate Women
US 1971 73m colour TVM
Aaron Spelling

Five women on holiday find that one of two men on an island with them is a murderer.
Fair goosepimpler.

w Marc Norman, Walter Black *d* Ted Post

Anjanette Comer, Joan Hackett, Denise Nichols, Stefanie Powers, Bradford Dillman, Robert Conrad, Julie Sommars

Five Easy Pieces**
US 1970 98m Technicolor
Columbia / Bert Schneider (Bob Rafelson, Richard Wechsler)

A middle-class drifter jilts his pregnant mistress for his brother's fiancée, but finally leaves both and hitches a ride to nowhere in particular.
Echoes of *Easy Rider, The Graduate* and *Charlie Bubbles* abound in this generally likeable but insubstantial modern anti-drama which at least takes place in pleasant surroundings and is firmly directed.

w Adrien Joyce *d* Bob Rafelson *ph* Laszlo Kovacs *m* various

Jack Nicholson, Karen Black, Susan Anspach, Lois Smith, Billy 'Green' Bush, Fannie Flagg

Five Finger Exercise
US 1962 109m bw
Columbia / Sonnis (Frederick Brisson)

A snobbish wife falls in love with a young house guest, with dire effect on her husband and son.
This West End study of a neurotic family is probably not good film material, certainly not adaptable to California, and above all not suitable to this star's whizzbang dramatics. Numbing hysteria arrives early and stays till the end.

w Frances Goodrich, Albert Hackett, *play* Peter Shaffer *d* Daniel Mann *ph* Harry Stradling *m* Jerome Moross

Rosalind Russell, Jack Hawkins, Maximilian Schell, Richard Beymer

Five Fingers***
US 1952 108m bw
TCF (Otto Lang)

The valet of the British ambassador in Ankara sells military secrets to the Germans, who pay him but never use the information.
Absorbing, lightweight film adaptation of a true story of World War II; civilized suspense entertainment with all talents contributing nicely.

w Michael Wilson, book Operation Cicero by L. C. Moyzich *d Joseph L. Mankiewicz* *ph* Norbert Brodine *m* Bernard Herrmann *ad* Lyle Wheeler, George W. Davis

James Mason, Danielle Darrieux, Michael Rennie, Walter Hampden, Oscar Karlweis, Herbert Berghof, John Wengraf, Michael Pate

'One of the highest, fastest and most absorbing spy melodramas since Hitchcock crossed the Atlantic.'—*Arthur Knight*

Five Graves to Cairo***
US 1943 96m bw
Paramount (Charles Brackett)

During the North Africa campaign, British spies try to destroy Rommel's secret supply dumps.
Intriguing spy melodrama set in a desert hotel, a notable example of Hollywood's ability to snatch polished drama from the headlines.

w Charles Brackett, Billy Wilder, play Lajos Biro *d Billy Wilder* *m* Miklos Rozsa

Franchot Tone, Anne Baxter, *Erich Von Stroheim* (as Rommel), Akim Tamiroff, Peter Van Eyck, Miles Mander

The 500 Pound Jerk
US 1972 73m colour TVM
David Wolper (Stan Margulies)
GB title: *The Strong Man*

A hillbilly giant is groomed as an Olympic weightlifter.
Mild satirical comedy.

w James B. Henderson *d* William Cronick

James Franciscus, Alex Karras, Hope Lange, Howard Cosell, Victor Spinetti

Five Miles to Midnight*
France / Italy 1962 110m bw
UA / Filmsonor / Dear Film (Anatole Litvak)

A neurotic believed dead forces his terrified wife to collect his life insurance.
Hysterical melodrama, smoothly made with all the familiar expressionist devices, but far too long for its content.

w Peter Viertel, Hugh Wheeler *d Anatole Litvak ph Henri Alekan m* Mikis Theodorakis

Sophia Loren, Anthony Perkins, Gig Young, Jean-Pierre Aumont, Yolande Turner, Tommy Norden

'From the polished immediacy of the cars, streets, shop windows and café tables to the off-focus vertigo shots of panic, from the overhead view of neighbours on stairs . . . to the close-ups of hands in filing trays touching off the details of fear and guilt, there is a thread of colour to keep you watching.'—*MFB*

'A well-ordered exercise in mechanical suspense.'—*Arthur Schlesinger Jnr*

The Five Pennies*
US 1959 117m Technicolor
Vistavision
Paramount / Dena (Jack Rose)

The rags-to-riches success story of cornet player Red Nichols.
The only touch of originality in this biopic is that the subject is given touches of irascibility. Production values reach a good standard.

w Jack Rose, Melville Shavelson *d* Melville Shavelson *ph* Daniel L. Fapp *m* Leith Stevens *ad* Hal Pereira, Tambi Larsen *songs* Sylvia Fine *trumpet solos* Red Nichols

Danny Kaye, Barbara Bel Geddes, *Louis Armstrong*, Bob Crosby, Harry Guardino, Tuesday Weld, Ray Anthony

Five Star Final***
US 1931 89m bw
Warner

A sensation-seeking newspaper editor causes tragedy.
Dated but still powerful melodrama which set the pattern for all the newspaper films of the thirties.

w Robert Lord, Byron Morgan, play Louis Weitzenkorn *d Mervyn Le Roy ph* Sol Polito *m* Leo Forbstein

Edward G. Robinson, H. B. Warner, Marian Marsh, Anthony Bushell, George E. Stone, Ona Munson, Aline MacMahon, Boris Karloff

'All the elements to make a hit attraction.'—*Variety*

Five Steps to Danger
US 1956 80m bw
UA / HSK

A girl possessing secret information from her dead scientist brother has a mental breakdown, and is pursued by spies.
Lively if cliché-ridden espionage melodrama, like an old-time serial.

wd Henry S. Kesler, *novel* Donald Hamilton *ph* Kenneth Peach *m* Paul Sawtell, Bert Shefter

Sterling Hayden, Ruth Roman, Werner Klemperer, Richard Gaines

The Five Thousand Fingers of Doctor T**
US 1953 88m Technicolor
Columbia / *Stanley Kramer*

A boy who hates piano lessons dreams of his teacher as an evil genius who keeps five hundred boys imprisoned in a castle of musical instruments.
Badly scripted fantasy with gleaming sophisticated dream sequences which deserve a better frame. A real oddity to come from Hollywood at this time, even though Dr Seuss' books were and are bestsellers.

w Dr Seuss (Theodore Geisel), Alan Scott *d* Roy Rowland *ph Franz Planer m* Frederick Hollander *ly* Dr Seuss *pd Rudolph Sternad ch* Eugene Loring

Hans Conried, Tommy Rettig, Peter Lind Hayes, Mary Healy

Five Weeks in a Balloon
US 1962 101m De Luxe
Cinemascope
TCF (Irving Allen)

In 1862 a professor is financed on a balloon trip into central Africa.
Would-be humorous semi-fantasy which strives to equal *Journey to the Center of the Earth* but unfortunately falls flat on its face despite the interesting talent available. Limp comedy situations, poor production values.

w Charles Bennett, Irving Allen, Albert Gail, *novel* Jules Verne *d* Irving Allen *ph* Winton Hoch *m* Paul Sawtell *ad* Jack Martin Smith, Alfred Ybarra

Cedric Hardwicke, Peter Lorre, Red Buttons, Fabian, Richard Haydn, Billy Gilbert, Herbert Marshall, Reginald Owen, Henry Daniell

Fixed Bayonets
US 1951 93m bw
TCF (Jules Buck)

An American division in Korea fights a rearguard action.

Downbeat war melodrama of a familiar kind, with more characterization than action.

wd Samuel Fuller *ph* Lucien Ballard *m* Roy Webb

Richard Basehart, Gene Evans, Michael O'Shea, Richard Hylton, Craig Hill

The Fixer
US 1968 130m Metrocolor
MGM / Edward Lewis, John Frankenheimer

A Jew in Tsarist Russia denies his race but becomes a scapegoat for various crimes and is imprisoned without trial until he becomes a *cause célèbre*.
Worthy but extremely dreary realist melodrama.

w Dalton Trumbo, *novel* Bernard Malamud *d* John Frankenheimer *ph* Marcel Grignon *m* Maurice Jarre

Alan Bates, Dirk Bogarde, Georgia Brown, Jack Gilford, Hugh Griffith, Elizabeth Hartman, Ian Holm, David Warner, Carol White, Murray Melvin, Peter Jeffrey, Michael Goodliffe

'The kind of film in which one has to admire much of the acting simply because it is all there is to admire.'—*David Pirie*

'A totally false film, devoid of a breath of human life or truth.'—*Arthur Schlesinger Jnr*

The Flame and the Arrow*
US 1950 88m Technicolor
(Warner) Harold Hecht, Frank Ross

In medieval Italy, a rebel leader seeks victory over a tyrant.
Good-humoured Robin Hood stuff with the star at his most acrobatic.

w Waldo Salt *d* Jacques Tourneur *ph* Ernest Haller *m* Max Steiner *ad* Edward Carrere

Burt Lancaster, Virginia Mayo, Robert Douglas, Aline MacMahon, Frank Allenby, Nick Cravat

The Flame and the Flesh
US 1954 104m Technicolor
MGM (Joe Pasternak)

An unscrupulous American woman in Naples has a fatal fascination for the local menfolk.
Dreary remake of *Naples au Baiser du Feu* (France 1937), with the dullest possible handling all round.

w Helen Deutsch, *novel* Auguste Bailly *d* Richard Brooks *ph* Christopher Challis *m* Nicholas Brodszky

Lana Turner, Carlos Thompson, Bonar Colleano, Pier Angeli, Charles Goldner, Peter Illing

Flame in the Streets
GB 1961 93m colour Cinemascope
Rank / Somerset (Roy Baker)

A liberal-minded union man erupts when his daughter proposes to marry a black man.
Predictable East End problem picture, unconvincingly set and acted and boring into the bargain.

w Ted Willis, from his TV play Hot Summer Night *d* Roy Baker *ph* Christopher Challis *m* Phil Green

John Mills, Brenda de Banzie, Sylvia Syms, Earl Cameron, Johnny Sekka, Ann Lynn, Wilfred Brambell

'Its methods belong more to the writer's study than to life.'—*John Gillett*

The Flame of New Orleans*
US 1941 79m bw
Universal (Joe Pasternak)

A European adventuress settles in America.
Fluffy comedy romance with the exiled director scarcely in top form.

w Norman Krasna *d* René Clair *ph* Rudolph Maté *m* Frank Skinner

Marlene Dietrich, Roland Young, Bruce Cabot, Mischa Auer, Andy Devine, Frank Jenks, Eddie Quillan, Laura Hope Crews, Franklin Pangborn

Flame of the Barbary Coast
US 1945 91m bw
Republic (Joseph Kane)

A cattleman's romance with a saloon singer comes to a climax in the 1906 earthquake.
Brawling romantic comedy-drama, adequately produced but not memorable.

w Borden Chase *d* Joseph Kane *ph* Robert de Grasse *m* Morton Scott

Ann Dvorak, John Wayne, Joseph Schildkraut, William Frawley, Virginia Grey

Flaming Star*
US 1960 92m De Luxe Cinemascope
TCF (David Weisbart)

A half-breed family is torn between two loyalties.
Solemn, unusual Civil War western with a downbeat ending.

w Clair Huffaker, Nunnally Johnson *d* Don Siegel *ph* Charles G. Clarke *m* Cyril Mockridge

Elvis Presley, Dolores del Rio, Steve Forrest, Barbara Eden, John McIntire, Rodolpho Acosta

'Despite familiar absurdities, it has more than its share of good moments.'—*MFB*

Flamingo Road*
US 1949 94m bw
Warner (Jerry Wald)

A tough carnival dancer is stranded in a small town and soon affects the lives of the local politicians.
Standard melodrama from a bestseller, absurd but well performed.

w Robert Wilder, from his novel *d* Michael Curtiz *ph* Ted McCord *m* Max Steiner

Joan Crawford, David Brian, Sidney Greenstreet, Zachary Scott, Gladys George, Virginia Huston, Fred Clark

Flap
US 1970 106m Technicolor
Panavision
Warner (Jerry Adler)
GB title: *The Last Warrior*

A drunken Indian on a dilapidated modern reservation starts a public relations war and leads a march on the city.
Unendearing comedy with a tragic end tacked on, not very entertaining as whimsy, farce or social conscience.

w Clair Huffaker, from his novel Nobody Loves a Drunken Indian *d* Carol Reed *ph* Fred Koenekamp *m* Marvin Hamlisch

'A corny, ill-made film full of tedious movie brawls.'—*Stanley Kauffmann*

Flare Up
US 1969 98m Metrocolor
MGM / GMF (Leon Fromkes)

A man kills his wife and threatens her friends who he feels are responsible for the break-up of his marriage.
Sensationally violent melodrama with a plot that goes back to *Sudden Fear* and further. Adequately made.

w Mark Rodgers *d* James Neilson *ph* Andrew J. McIntyre *m* Les Baxter

Raquel Welch, James Stacy, Luke Askew, Don Chastain, Ron Rifkin

Flash Gordon
The hero of the 25th century was created in comic strip form by Alex Raymond and his chief claims to film fame are three wild and woolly serials made by Universal: *Flash Gordon* (1936), *Flash Gordon's Trip to Mars* (1938), and *Flash Gordon Conquers the Universe* (1940), all starring Buster Crabbe with Charles Middleton as the wily Emperor Ming. Their cheap and cheerful futuristic sets and their non-stop action have kept them popular with film buffs through the years.
In 1974 a semi-porno spoof, *Flesh Gordon,* appeared.

A Flea in Her Ear*
US/France 1968 94m De Luxe
Panavision
TCF (Fred Kohlmar)

Various suspicious wives and husbands converge on the notorious Hotel Coq d'Or.
Disappointing filming of a Feydeau farce, which needs to be much more cleverly handled to come over with its full theatrical force.

w John Mortimer, *play* La Puce à l'Oreille by Georges Feydeau *d* Jacques Charon
ph Charles Lang *m* Bronislau Kaper
pd Alexander Trauner

Rex Harrison, Rachel Roberts, Rosemary Harris, Louis Jourdan, John Williams, Grégoire Aslan, Edward Hardwicke, Frank Thornton, Victor Sen Yung

The Fleet's In*
US 1942 93m bw
Paramount (Paul Jones)

A sailor on leave in San Francisco takes a bet that he can kiss the glamorous owner of a swank nightclub.
Mindless wartime musical which happened to set the seal of success on a number of young talents.
Previously a Clara Bow vehicle.

w Walter de Leon, Sid Silvers *d* Victor Schertzinger *ph* William Mellor *m/ly* various

Dorothy Lamour, William Holden, *Eddie Bracken, Betty Hutton*, Cass Daley, Gil Lamb, Leif Erickson, Betty Jane Rhodes

Flesh and Blood
GB 1951 102m bw
BL / Harefield (Anatole de Grunwald)

Three generations of a family suffer from the effects of heredity.
Fragmented Scottish period piece which never settles down long enough to make an impact with any group of characters.

w Anatole de Grunwald, *play* A Sleeping Clergyman by James Bridie *d* Anthony Kimmins *ph* Otto Heller *m* Charles Williams

Richard Todd, Glynis Johns, Joan Greenwood, André Morell, Ursula Howells, Freda Jackson, George Cole, James Hayter, Ronald Howard, Muriel Aked

Flesh and Fantasy*
US 1943 94m bw
Universal (Charles Boyer, Julien Duvivier)

A club bore tells three strange stories.

A portmanteau with ingredients of varying interest, attempting to emulate the success of *Tales of Manhattan*. The fourth episode planned was deleted and turned up as *Destiny* (qv). All quite stylish, the best section being *Lord Arthur Savile's Crime*.

w Ernest Pascal, Samuel Hoffenstein, Ellis St Joseph, *stories* Ellis St Joseph, Oscar Wilde, Laslo Vadnay *d Julien Duvivier ph Paul Ivano, Stanley Cortez* *m* Alexandre Tansman

Robert Benchley, *Edward G. Robinson*, Barbara Stanwyck, Charles Boyer, Betty Field, Robert Cummings, *Thomas Mitchell*, C. Aubrey Smith, Dame May Whitty, Edgar Barrier, David Hoffman

The Flesh and the Fiends
GB 1959 97m bw Dyaliscope
Regal / Triad (Robert Baker, Monty Berman)

In 1820 Edinburgh, 'resurrection men' commit murders to keep anatomists supplied.
Dr Robert Knox rides again, in a version more bloody but less entertaining than *The Body Snatcher*.

w John Gilling, Leon Griffiths *d* John Gilling

Peter Cushing, June Laverick, George Rose, Donald Pleasance, Renée Houston, Billie Whitelaw, Dermot Walsh

Flight Command
US 1940 116m bw
MGM (J. Walter Ruben)

A cocky recruit makes good in the naval air arm.
Routine flagwaver.

w Wells Root, Cmdr Harvey Haislip *d* Frank Borzage *ph* Harold Rosson *m* Franz Waxman

Robert Taylor, Ruth Hussey, Walter Pidgeon, Paul Kelly, Nat Pendleton, Red Skelton, Shepperd Strudwick, Dick Purcell

Flight for Freedom
US 1943 101m bw
RKO (David Hempstead)

Biography of an intrepid aviatrix and her husband.
Patchy job based on the life of Amelia Earhart, suggesting that her final disappearance was on a government mission. Dull production.

w Oliver H. P. Garrett, S. K. Lauren *d* Lothar Mendes *m* Roy Webb

Rosalind Russell, Fred MacMurray, Herbert Marshall, Eduardo Ciannelli, Walter Kingsford

Flight from Ashiya*
US/Japan 1963 102m Eastmancolor Panavision
UA / Harold Hecht / Daiei

When a cargo vessel sinks off the coast of Japan during a typhoon, the helicopter rescue service springs into action.
Conventional Grade A action thriller with flashbacks to earlier disasters in the lives of its heroes.

w Elliot Arnold, Waldo Salt *d* Michael Anderson *ph* Joe MacDonald, Burnett Guffey *m* Frank Cordell *pd* Eugène Lourié

Yul Brynner, Richard Widmark, George Chakiris, Shirley Knight, Daniele Gaubert, Suzy Parker

Flight of the Doves*
US 1971 101m colour
Columbia / Rainbow (Ralph Nelson)

Two children run away from their bullying stepfather to join their Irish grandmother, but are chased by a wicked uncle who knows they are heirs to a fortune.
Pantomimish whimsy which works in fits and starts, but has little real humour or charm.

wd Ralph Nelson, *novel* Walter Macken *ph* Harry Waxman *m* Roy Budd

Ron Moody, Dorothy McGuire, Helen Raye, Dana, Jack Wild, Stanley Holloway, William Rushton

The Flight of the Phoenix*
US 1965 149m De Luxe
TCF / Associates and Aldrich

A cargo passenger plane crashes in the desert, and the survivors try to avert disaster.
Achingly slow character adventure; an all-star cast works desperately hard but the final flight of the rebuilt plane seems almost an anti-climax after the surfeit of personal melodramatics.

w Lukas Heller, *novel* Elleston Trevor *d* Robert Aldrich *ph* Joseph Biroc *m* Frank de Vol

James Stewart, Richard Attenborough, Hardy Kruger, Peter Finch, Dan Duryea, Ernest Borgnine, Ian Bannen, Ronald Fraser, Christian Marquand, George Kennedy

The Flight that Disappeared
US 1961 73m bw
UA / Harvard (Robert E. Kent)

Atomic scientists on an airliner find themselves in 'heaven' being tried by people of the future.
Eccentric anti-bomb curiosity, a second feature *Outward Bound*.

w Ralph Hart, Judith Hart, Owen Harris

d Reginald Le Borg *ph* Gilbert Warrenton *m* Richard La Salle

Gregory Morton, Addison Richards, Craig Hill, Paula Raymond, Dayton Lummis

Flight to Tangier
US 1953 90m Technicolor 3-D
Paramount (Nat Holt)

A female FBI agent chases a three million dollar letter of credit.
Forced and boring action romance without much of either element.

wd Charles Marquis Warren *ph* Ray Rennahan *m* Paul Sawtell

Joan Fontaine, Jack Palance, Corinne Calvet, Robert Douglas, Marcel Dalio, Jeff Morrow, Murray Matheson, John Doucette

The Flim Flam Man*
US 1967 104m De Luxe Panavision
TCF / Lawrence Turman
GB title: *One Born Every Minute*

An army deserter joins forces with an elderly con man.
Folksy comedy in a small-town setting; none of it really comes to the boil after a couple of early chase sequences.

w William Rose, *novel* Guy Owen *d* Irvin Kershner, *Yakima Canutt* *ph* Charles Lang *m* Jerry Goldsmith

George C. Scott, Michael Sarrazin, Sue Lyon, Harry Morgan, Jack Albertson, Alice Ghostley, Albert Salmi

Flipper
US 1963 87m Metrocolor
(MGM) Ivan Tors

A fisherman's son on the Florida Keys befriends a dolphin.
Harmless boy-and-animal adventure which spawned two sequels and a TV series.

w Arthur Weiss *d* James B. Clark *ph* Lamar Boren, Joseph Brun *m* Henry Vars

Chuck Connors, Luke Halpin, Kathleen Maguire, Connie Scott

Flirtation Walk*
US 1934 97m bw
Warner (Frank Borzage)

Love affairs of West Point cadets.
Light musical very typical of its period, with a few agreeable numbers.

w Delmer Daves *d* Frank Borzage *ch* Bobby Connelly *ph* Sol Polito, George Barnes *m/ly* Allie Wrubel, Mort Dixon

Dick Powell, Ruby Keeler, Pat O'Brien, Ross Alexander, John Arledge, Henry O'Neill, Guinn Williams

'A rousing recruiting poster . . . and a splendid laboratory specimen of the adolescent cinema.'—*André Sennwald, New York Times*

Floods of Fear*
GB 1958 84m bw
Rank / Sydney Box

Two escaped convicts, a warder, and a pretty girl are trapped by floods in a lonely house.
Adequate melodrama with impressively gloomy production and performances but not many surprises.

wd Charles Crichton, *novel* Joan and Ward Hawkins *ph* Christopher Challis *m* Alan Rawsthorne

Howard Keel, Anne Heywood, Harry H. Corbett, Cyril Cusack

Flower Drum Song*
US 1961 133m Technicolor Panavision
U-I / Rodgers and Hammerstein / Joseph Fields

Romantic problems among the immigrants in San Francisco's Chinatown.
A Broadway musical which on the screen seems old-fashioned, remorselessly cute, and even insulting to the Chinese characters. Within its limits, however, it is well enough staged and performed.

w Joseph Fields *m/ly* Richard Rodgers, Oscar Hammerstein II *ph Russell Metty* *ad* Alexander Golitzen, Joseph Weight *costumes* Irene Sharaff *ch* Hermes Pan

Nancy Kwan, James Shigeta, Juanita Hall, Myoshi Umeki, James Soo, Sen Yung

Fluffy
US 1964 92m Eastmancolor
U-I / Scarus (Gordon Kay)

A biologist manages to tame a lion.
Mindless, cheerful animal comedy.

w Samuel Rocca *d* Earl Bellamy *ph* Clifford Stine *m* Irving Gertz

Tony Randall, Shirley Jones, Edward Andrews, Ernest Truex, Howard Morris, Jim Backus, Frank Faylen

The Fly
US 1958 94m Eastmancolor Cinemascope
TCF (Kurt Neumann)

A scientist invents a method of transmitting and

reassembling atoms. He transmits himself and does not notice a fly in the compartment . . . Unpleasant horror film which becomes ludicrous but not funny.

w James Clavell *d* Kurt Neumann *ph* Karl Struss *m* Paul Sawtell

David Hedison, Patricia Owens, Herbert Marshall, Vincent Price
† Sequels were *Return of the Fly* (1960) and *Curse of the Fly* (1965), neither worth noting in detail.

The Flying Deuces*
US 1939 67m bw
Boris Morros

Laurel and Hardy join the Foreign Legion. Patchy comedy from the end of the comedians' period of glory, and showing signs of decline.

w Ralph Spence, Harry Langdon, Charles Rogers, Alfred Schiller *d* Edward Sutherland *ph* Art Lloyd, Elmer Dyer

Stan Laurel, Oliver Hardy, Jean Parker, James Finlayson, Reginald Gardiner, Charles Middleton

'Mechanical stuff . . . seemed like *Beau Hunks* and *Bonnie Scotland* all over again.'—*William K. Everson*

Flying Down to Rio**
US 1933 89m bw
RKO (Merian C. Cooper, Lou Brock)

A dance band is a big success in Rio de Janeiro. A thin musical electrified by the finale in which girls dance on the wings of moving airplanes, and by the teaming of Astaire and Rogers for the first time. Now an irresistible period piece.

w Cyril Hume, H. W. Hannemann, Erwin Gelsey, *play* Anne Caldwell *d* Thornton Freeland *ph* J. Roy Hunt *m* Vincent Youmans *ly* Edward Eliscu, Gus Kahn *ch Dave Gould*

Dolores del Rio, Gene Raymond, Raul Roulien, *Ginger Rogers, Fred Astaire*, Blanche Frederici, Walter Walker, Franklin Pangborn, Eric Blore

Flying Fortress
GB 1942 104m bw
Warner

A Canadian becomes a hero of bombing missions over Berlin.
Cardboard propaganda with silly love interest and a hilarious climax in which the hero does his stuff on the wing of a flying plane.

w Brock Williams, Gordon Wellesley, Edward Dryhurst *d* Walter Forde *ph* Gus Drisse, Basil Emmott

Richard Greene, Carla Lehmann, Betty Stockfield, Donald Stewart, Charles Heslop, Sidney King, Basil Radford, John Stuart

Flying Leathernecks
US 1951 102m Technicolor
RKO (Edmund Grainger)

Two marine officers fight the Japs and each other on Guadalcanal.
Empty, violent war actioner full of phoney heroics.

w James Edward Grant *d* Nicholas Ray *ph* William E. Snyder *m* Roy Webb

John Wayne, Robert Ryan, Janis Carter, Don Taylor, Jay C. Flippen, William Harrigan, James Bell

'Ray's treatment is depressingly second rate and does nothing to alleviate the unpleasant impression of this disturbingly violent production.'—*Penelope Houston*

Flying Tigers
US 1942 100m bw
Republic (Edmund Grainger)

American airmen fight the Japs over World War II China.
More mock heroics with noisy but unconvincing action sequences.

w Kenneth Garnet, Barry Trivers *d* David Miller *ph* Jack Marta *m* Victor Young

John Wayne, John Carroll, Anna Lee, Paul Kelly, Mae Clarke

Fog over Frisco***
US 1934 68m bw
Warner (Henry Blanke)

A San Francisco heiress gets herself murdered. Silly whodunnit highly notable for its cinematic style, all dissolves, wipes and quick takes. Probably the fastest moving film ever made, and very entertaining despite its plot inadequacy.

w Robert N. Lee, *novel* George Dyer *d William Dieterle ph* Tony Gaudio *m* Leo Forbstein *editor Harold McLernon*

Bette Davis, Donald Woods, Margaret Lindsay, Lyle Talbot, Hugh Herbert, Arthur Byron, Robert Barrat, Douglass Dumbrille, Henry O'Neill, Irving Pichel, Alan Hale

'It reveals those qualities of pace and velocity and sharpness which make the Hollywood product acceptable even when the shallow content of ideas makes you want to scream.'—*Robert Forsythe*

'Its speed is artificially created by pacing, wipes, opticals, overlapping sound, camera movement and placing of characters, and by its

habit of never having time really to begin or end scenes.'—*William K. Everson*
† Remade 1942 as *Spy Ship*, a second feature.

Folies Bergère***
US 1935 84m bw
Twentieth Century (William Goetz, Raymond Griffith)
GB title: *The Man from the Folies Bergère*
A Parisian banker persuades a music hall artist to impersonate him, but the wife and girl friend become involved in the confusion.
Amusing star vehicle with inventive Berkeleyish numbers and some remarkably sexy dialogue.
w Bess Meredyth, Hal Long, *play* The Red Cat by Rudolph Lothar, Hans Adler *d* Roy del Ruth *ph* Barney McGill, Peverell Marley *md* Alfred Newman *ch Dave Gould*
Maurice Chevalier, Merle Oberon, Ann Dvorak, Eric Blore
† Remade as *That Night in Rio*, with Don Ameche, and *On the Riviera*, with Danny Kaye (both qv).

Follow a Star
GB 1959 104m bw
Rank (Hugh Stewart)
A shy amateur singer allows a fading star to mime to his voice.
Star comedy with an antique plot and a superfluity of pathos.
w Jack Davies, Henry Blyth, Norman Wisdom *d* Robert Asher *ph* Jack Asher *m* Philip Green
Norman Wisdom, Jerry Desmonde, June Laverick, Hattie Jacques, Richard Wattis, John Le Mesurier, Fenella Fielding, Ron Moody
'Such comedy as there is is mostly muffed by the lack of any sense of comic timing.'—*MFB*

Follow Me
GB 1971 93m Technicolor Panavision
Universal/Hal B. Wallis (Paul Nathan)
US title: *The Public Eye*
An eccentric private eye is hired to follow an accountant's wife, and she finds him fascinating.
Dullish, whimsical rendering of a dullish, whimsical one-act play; it never springs to life or interest.
w Peter Shaffer, from his play *d* Carol Reed *ph* Christopher Challis *m* John Barry
Topol, Michael Jayston, Mia Farrow

Follow Me Boys
US 1966 132m Technicolor
Walt Disney (Winston Hibler)
The domestic trials and tribulations of a small-town schoolmaster.
Sentimental family saga full of patriotic fervour.
w Louis Pelletier, *novel* God and My Country by Mackinlay Kantor *d* Norman Tolear *ph* Clifford Stine *m* George Bruns
Fred MacMurray, Vera Miles, Lillian Gish, Charlie Ruggles, Elliott Reid, Kurt Russell, Luana Patten, Ken Murray
'Demands an extremely strong stomach.'—*MFB*

Follow That Dream
US 1962 110m De Luxe Panavision
UA / Mirisch (David Weisbart)
A wandering family sets up house on a Florida beach.
Tiresomely cute comedy vehicle for a resistible star.
w Charles Lederer, *novel* Pioneer Go Home by Richard Powell *d* Gordon Douglas *ph* Leo Tover *m* Hans Salter
Elvis Presley, Arthur O'Connell, Joanna Moore, Anne Helm, Jack Kruschen

Follow the Boys*
US 1944 109m bw
Universal (Charles K. Feldman)
A song and dance man organizes entertainment for the US troops during World War II.
Scrappy, unattractive propaganda tribute by the stars to the stars, enlivened only by a few guest spots.
w Lou Breslow, Gertrude Purcell *d* A. Edward Sutherland *ph* David Abel *m* Leigh Harline and others
George Raft, Vera Zorina, Charley Grapewin, Grace MacDonald, Charles Butterworth, George Macready, Elizabeth Patterson; and Orson Welles, Marlene Dietrich, Jeanette MacDonald, Dinah Shore, Donald O'Connor, Peggy Ryan, W. C. Fields, the Andrews Sisters, Artur Rubenstein, Sophie Tucker, Ted Lewis and his band, etc

Follow the Boys
US 1963 95m Metrocolor Panavision
MGM / Franmet (Laurence P. Bachmann)
An American warship is diverted from Cannes to Santa Margarita, and the waiting wives have to follow by road.
Harmless star comedy musical.
w David T. Chantler, David Osborn *d* Richard Thorpe *ph* Ted Scaife
Connie Francis, Paula Prentiss, Dany Robin, Russ Tamblyn, Richard Long

Follow the Fleet**
US 1936 110m bw
RKO (Pandro S. Berman)

Sailors on shore leave romance a couple of girl singers.
Amiable star musical which makes heavy weather of a listless and overlong script, but has good numbers for those who can wait.

w Dwight Taylor, *play* Shore Leave by Hubert Osborne, Allan Scott *d* Mark Sandrich *ph* David Abel *m/ly Irving Berlin*

Fred Astaire, Ginger Rogers, Randolph Scott, Harriet Hilliard, Astrid Allwyn, Harry Beresford, Lucille Ball, Betty Grable, Tony Martin

Follow the Sun
US 1951 93m bw
TCF (Samuel G. Engel)

Ben Hogan, a professional golfer, recovers slowly and painfully from a car crash and for the first time gains the affection of the crowd.
Modest sporting biopic, generally watchable but rising to no great heights.

w Frederick Hazlitt Brennan *d* Sidney Lanfield *ph* Leo Tover *m* Cyril Mockridge

Glenn Ford, Anne Baxter, Dennis O'Keefe, June Havoc, Larry Keating, Nana Bryant, Roland Winters

Folly to be Wise*
GB 1952 91m bw
London Films / Launder and Gilliat

A brains trust at an army unit starts off a battle of the sexes.
Typical James Bridie comedy which starts brightly and whimsically, then peters out and is saved by the acting.

w Frank Launder, John Dighton, *play* It Depends What You Mean by James Bridie *d* Frank Launder *ph* Jack Hildyard *m* Temple Abady

Alastair Sim, Roland Culver, Elizabeth Allen, Martita Hunt, Colin Gordon

The Food of the Gods
US 1976 88m Movielab
AIP (Bert I. Gordon)

A curious substance which oozes out of the ground turns common beasts into monsters.
Rather crude horror movie which has little affinity with its literary original.

wd Bert I. Gordon, *story* H. G. Wells *ph* Reginald Morris *m* Elliot Kaplan

Marjoe Gortner, Pamela Franklin, Ida Lupino, Ralph Meeker, John McLiam

'Not only sick, but sickening.'—*Arthur Knight*

Fools for Scandal*
US 1938 81m bw
Warner (Mervyn Le Roy)

A Hollywood movie star falls in love with a French nobleman.
Disappointingly leaden romantic comedy.

w Herbert and Joseph Fields, *play* Return Engagement by Nancy Hamilton, Rosemary Casey, James Shute *d* Mervyn Le Roy *ph* Ted Tetzlaff *m* Richard Rodgers, Lorenz Hart

Carole Lombard, Fernand Gravet, Ralph Bellamy, Allen Jenkins, Isabel Jeans, Marie Wilson, Ottola Nesmith

Fools Parade**
US 1971 98m Eastmancolor
Columbia / Stanmore / Penbar (Andrew V. McLaglen)
GB title: *Dynamite Man from Glory Jail*

An ex-con has trouble cashing a cheque for his prison savings, especially as outlaws are after it.
Curious admixture of comedy, adventure and violence with a thirties setting, from the author of *Night of the Hunter*; generally gripping entertainment.

w James Lee Barrett, novel Davis Grubb *d* Andrew V. McLaglen *ph* Harry Stradling Jnr *m* Henry Vars

James Stewart, George Kennedy, Strother Martin, Anne Baxter, Kurt Russell, William Windom, Mike Kellin

'A quintessentially American tribute to the quiet heroism of the self-made man.'—*Nigel Andrews*

Footlight Parade***
US 1933 104m bw
Warner (Robert Lord)

A determined producer of cine-variety numbers gets the show going despite great difficulty.
Classic putting-on-a-show musical distinguished by rapid-fire dialogue, New York setting, star performances and some of the best Busby Berkeley numbers.

w Manuel Seff, James Seymour *d Lloyd Bacon ch Busby Berkeley* *ph* George Barnes *ad Anton Grot, Jack Okey* *m/ly* Harry Warren, Al Dubin, Sammy Fain, Irving Fahal

James Cagney, Joan Blondell, Ruby Keeler, Dick Powell, Frank McHugh, Guy Kibbee, Ruth Donnelly, Hugh Herbert, Claire Dodd, Herman Bing

'Bevies of beauty and mere males disport

themselves in a Honeymoon Hotel, by (and in) a Waterfall, and over several acres of Shanghai.'—*C. A. Lejeune*

Footlight Serenade
US 1942 80m bw
TCF (William LeBaron)

A boxer romances a showgirl.
Indifferent star musical.

w Robert Ellis, Helen Logan, Lynn Starling *d* Gregory Ratoff *ph* Lee Garmes *md* Charles Henderson

Betty Grable, John Payne, Victor Mature, James Gleason, Phil Silvers, Jane Wyman, Cobina Wright Jnr, June Lang, Mantan Moreland

Footsteps
US 1972 74m colour TVM
Metromedia (Dick Berg)

A tough coach is hired to whip a small college football team into shape.
Minor sporting drama.

w Alvin Sargent, Robert, E. Thompson, *novel* Hamilton Maule *d* Paul Wendkos

Richard Crenna, Joanna Pettet, Forrest Tucker, Clu Gulager, Mary Murphy

Footsteps in the Fog*
GB 1955 90m Technicolor
Columbia / Mike Frankovich (Maxwell Setton)

A Victorian murderer plans to eliminate a blackmailing maid.
This variation on *Gaslight* turns into a black comedy without laughs, but it has effective moments and is efficiently if charmlessly made.

w Dorothy Reid, Lenore Coffee, *story* The Interruption by
W. W. Jacobs *d* Arthur Lubin *ph* Christopher Challis *m* Benjamin Frankel *ad* Wilfrid Shingleton

Stewart Granger, Jean Simmons, Bill Travers, Ronald Squire, Finlay Currie, Peter Bull

For the First Time
US 1959 97m Technirama
MGM / Corona / Orion (Alexander Gruter)

A famous tenor slips off incognito to Capri and falls in love with a deaf girl.
Slipshod co-production (with West Germany) with a hoary sentimental plot, a fat star, and some agreeable picture postcard views.

w Andrew Solt *d* Rudolph Maté *ph* Aldo Tonti *md* Georgie Stoll

Mario Lanza, Johanna von Koczian, Kurt Kasznar, Zsa Zsa Gabor, Hans Sohnker

For Heaven's Sake
US 1950 92m bw
TCF (William Perlberg)

Two angels are sent to earth to mend a Broadway producer's marriage.
Silly, flat whimsy of the *Here Comes Mr Jordan* school, and originating from the same author. Stale beer, but historically interesting.

w George Seaton, *play* Harry Segall *d* George Seaton *ph* Lloyd Ahern *m* Alfred Newman

Clifton Webb, Edmund Gwenn, Robert Cummings, Joan Bennett, Joan Blondell, Gigi Perreau, Jack La Rue

For Love of Ivy
US 1968 100m Perfectcolor
Cinerama / Palomar (Edgar J. Scherick, Jay Weston)

An invaluable coloured maid gives notice, and the family blackmails a likeable black ne'er-do-well to make love to her so that she will stay.
Unhappy whimsy with an extremely laboured script and no jokes, notable only as Hollywood's first bow towards a black love affair.

w Robert Alan Aurthur, *story* Sidney Poitier *d* Daniel Mann *ph* Joseph Coffey *m* Quincy Jones

Sidney Poitier, Abby Lincoln, Beau Bridges, Carroll O'Connor, Nan Martin, Lauri Peters

For the Love of Mike*
US 1960 84m De Luxe Cinemascope
TCF / Shergari (George Sherman)
GB title: *None But the Brave*

An Indian boy in New Mexico is helped by a priest to care for sick animals.
Sentimental outdoor film for young people with a pleasantly light touch.

w D. D. Beauchamp *d* George Sherman *ph* Alex Phillips *m* Raul La Vista

Richard Basehart, Stuart Erwin, Arthur Shields, Armando Silvestre

For Love or Money
US 1963 108m Technicolor
U-I (Robert Arthur)

A rich widow hires a lawyer to look after the affairs of her three wayward daughters; he picks the eldest for himself.
Slow, thin, overlong comedy with a surfeit of witless chat.

w Larry Marks, Michael Morris *d* Michael Gordon *ph* Clifford Stine *m* Frank de Vol

Kirk Douglas, Mitzi Gaynor, Thelma Ritter, William Bendix, Gig Young

For Me and My Gal***
US 1942 104m bw
MGM (Arthur Freed)

Just before World War I, a girl vaudevillian chooses between two partners.
A routine musical romance at the time of its production, this film now stands out because of its professional execution, its star value, and the fact that they don't make 'em like that any more.

w Richard Sherman, Sid Silvers, Fred Finkelhoffe *d Busby Berkeley ph William Daniels md* Georgie Stoll

Judy Garland, Gene Kelly, George Murphy, Marta Eggerth, Ben Blue, Richard Quine, Stephen McNally
'A touch of imagination and a deal more than a touch of energy.'—*The Times*

For Pete's Sake*
US 1974 90m Eastmancolor
Columbia / Rastar / Persky–Bright–Barclay (Martin Erlichmann, Stanley Shapiro)

A New York taxi driver's wife borrows money and finds herself heavily committed to work off the debt.
Involved farcical comedy with amusing passages.

w Stanley Shapiro, Martin Richlin *d* Peter Yates *ph* Laszlo Kovacs *m* Artie Butler

Barbra Streisand, Michael Sarrazin, Estelle Parsons, William Redfield, Molly Picon
'Revives memories of how much more inventively they used to do it thirty years ago.'—*Sight and Sound*

For Them That Trespass
GB 1948 93m bw
ABP

A man proves himself innocent of the crime for which he has served fifteen years in prison.
Tedious melodrama which served to introduce Richard Todd to the screen.

w J. Lee-Thompson *d* Alberto Cavalcanti *ph* Derick Williams *m* Philip Green

Richard Todd, Stephen Murray, Joan Dowling, Patricia Plunkett, Michael Laurence, Rosalyn Boulter

For Whom the Bell Tolls**
US 1943 170m Technicolor
Paramount (Sam Wood)

An American joins partisan fighters in the Spanish Civil War and falls in love with a refugee girl before going on a suicide mission.
Portentous, solemn adventure story based on a modern classic but without much cinematic impetus despite careful handling and useful performances. It looks expensive, though.

w Dudley Nichols, *novel* Ernest Hemingway *d* Sam Wood *ph* Ray Rennahan *m* Victor Young *pd* William Cameron Menzies

Gary Cooper, Ingrid Bergman, Akim Tamiroff, Arturo de Cordova, *Katina Paxinou*, Vladimir Sokoloff, Mikhail Rasumny, Victor Varconi, Joseph Calleia, Alexander Granach

Forbidden Cargo
GB 1954 85m bw
Rank / London Independent Productions (Sydney Box)

A customs investigator prevents a large consignment of drugs from reaching its English outlets.
Routine British thick ear.

w Sydney Box *d* Harold French *ph* C. Pennington-Richards *m* Lambert Williamson

Nigel Patrick, Elizabeth Sellars, Terence Morgan, Jack Warner

Forbidden Planet**
US 1956 98m Eastmancolor Cinemascope
MGM (Nicholas Nayfack)

In AD 2200 a space cruiser visits the planet Altair Four to discover the fate of a previous mission.
Intriguing sci-fi with a plot derived from *The Tempest* and a Prospero who unwittingly creates monsters from his own id. High spirits and suspense sequences partially cancelled out by wooden playing from the younger actors and some leaden dialogue.

w Cyril Hume d Fred M. Wilcox ph George Folsey *m* Louis and Bebe Barron *ad* Cedric Gibbons, Arthur Lonergan

Walter Pidgeon, Anne Francis, Leslie Nielsen, Warren Stevens, Jack Kelly, Richard Anderson, Earl Holliman

The Forbin Project**
US 1969 100m Technicolor Panavision
Universal (Stanley Chase)

An enormous computer takes over the defence of the western world; but it goes into collaboration with the Russian one.
Good-looking sci-fi for intellectual addicts.

w James Bridges, *novel* Colossus by D. F. Jones *d* Joseph Sargent *ph* Gene Polito *m* Michel Columbier

Eric Braeden, Gordon Pinsent, Susan Clark, William Schallert

Force Five
US 1975 74m Technicolor TVM
Universal (Michael Gleason, David Levinson)

An undercover police unit is formed to control street crime.
Yet another elite force hopes and fails to make the grade as a series.

w Michael Gleason, David Levinson *d* Walter Grauman

Gerald Gordon, Nick Pryor, William Lucking, James Hampton, Roy Jenson, David Spielberg, Leif Erickson, Bradford Dillman

Force of Arms*
US 1951 100m bw
Warner (Anthony Veiller)

A soldier in the Italian campaign falls in love with his nurse.
Routine variation on *A Farewell to Arms*, adequately but unexcitingly mounted.

w Orin Jannings, *story* Richard Tregaskis *d* Michael Curtiz *ph* Ted McCord *m* Max Steiner

William Holden, Nancy Olson, Frank Lovejoy, Gene Evans, Dick Wesson, Paul Picerni

Force of Evil***
US 1948 78m bw
MGM / Enterprise

A racketeer's lawyer finds that his boss has killed the lawyer's brother.
Involved, atmospheric melodrama about the numbers racket, moodily and brilliantly photographed in New York streets, gloweringly well acted and generally almost as hypnotic as *Citizen Kane*.

w Abraham Polonsky, Ira Wolfert, *novel* Tucker's People by Ira Wolfert *d Abraham Polonsky ph George Barnes m David Raksin*

John Garfield, *Thomas Gomez*, Beatrice Pearson, Marie Windsor

'It credits an audience with intelligence in its ears as well as its eyes.'—*Dilys Powell*

A Foreign Affair**
US 1948 116m bw
Paramount (Charles Brackett)

A deputation of American politicians goes to visit post-war Berlin and a congresswoman finds herself in an emotional triangle with a captain and his German mistress.
Bleakly sophisticated comedy from this team's headline-grabbing period; full of interest and amusement, it never quite sparkles enough to remove the doubtful taste.

w Charles Brackett, Billy Wilder, Richard Breen d Billy Wilder ph Charles Lang Jnr *m* Frederick Hollander

Jean Arthur, Marlene Dietrich, John Lund, Millard Mitchell, Peter Von Zerneck, Stanley Prager

Foreign Correspondent****
US 1940 120m bw
Walter Wanger

An American journalist is sent to Europe in 1938 and becomes involved with spies.
Thoroughly typical and enjoyable Hitchcock adventure with a rambling script which builds up into brilliantly managed suspense sequences: an assassination, a windmill, an attempted murder in Westminster Cathedral, a plane crash at sea. The final speech was an attempt to encourage America into the war.

w Charles Bennett, Joan Harrison, James Hilton, Robert Benchley, from Personal History by Vincent Sheean *d Alfred Hitchcock ph Rudolph Maté m* Alfred Newman *sp* Lee Zavitz *ad* Alexander Golitzen

Joel McCrea, Laraine Day, *Herbert Marshall, Albert Basserman, Edmund Gwenn, George Sanders*, Eduardo Ciannelli, *Robert Benchley, Harry Davenport*, Martin Kosleck

'If you have any interest in the true motion and sweep of pictures, watching that man work is like listening to music . . . If you would like a seminar in how to make a movie travel the lightest and fastest way, in a kind of beauty that is peculiar to movies alone, you can see this once, and then again to see what you missed, and then study it twice.'—*Otis Ferguson*

Foreign Exchange
GB 1969 72m colour TVM
Cohen–Sangster

A private eye is called back into the British Secret Service.
Espionage hokum which with *The Spy Killer* (qv) makes two failed pilots for the same non-series.

w Jimmy Sangster *d* Roy Baker

Robert Horton, Sebastian Cabot, Jill St John, Dudley Foster, Eric Pohlmann

Foreign Intrigue*
US 1956 100m Eastmancolor
UA / Sheldon Reynolds

A press agent investigates the death of a man who had been blackmailing potential traitors.
Location espionage melodrama of the cold war fifties, quite well done in a rather dismal vein, but a long way from *Foreign Correspondent*.

wd Sheldon Reynolds *ph* Bertil Palmgrem *m* Paul Durand

Robert Mitchum, Genevieve Page, Ingrid Thulin, Eugene Deckers

The Foreman Went to France**
GB 1941 87m bw
Ealing (Alberto Cavalcanti)
US title: *Somewhere in France*

Before Dunkirk, a Welsh foreman is sent on a mission to salvage secret French machinery.
Fresh, appealing comedy drama based on a true incident of World War II.

w John Dighton, Angus Macphail, Leslie Arliss, Roger Macdougall, Diana Morgan, *story* J. B. Priestley *d* Charles Frend

Tommy Trinder, Constance Cummings, Clifford Evans, Robert Morley, Gordon Jackson, Ernest Milton

The Forest Rangers*
US 1942 85m Technicolor
Paramount (Robert Sisk)

A socialite marries a district ranger and rescues her disgruntled rival during a forest blaze.
Routine, competent, box office actioner of its time, with popular stars, adequate plot, but precious little inventiveness.

w Harold Shumate *d* George Marshall *ph* Charles Lang

Fred MacMurray, Paulette Goddard, Susan Hayward, Lynne Overman, Albert Dekker, Eugene Pallette, Regis Toomey, Rod Cameron

Forever Amber*
US 1947 137m Technicolor
TCF (William Perlberg)

Adventures of a desirable young lady during the reign of Charles II.
Much-bowdlerized version of a sensational novel of the forties; pretty but rather thin, with a colourless cast, saved by lively action sequences.

w Philip Dunne, Ring Lardner Jnr, *novel* Kathleen Winsor *d* Otto Preminger *ph Leon Shamroy m* Alfred Newman *ad Lyle Wheeler*

Linda Darnell, Cornel Wilde, *George Sanders* (as Charles II), Richard Greene, Glenn Langan, Richard Haydn, Jessica Tandy, Anne Revere, Robert Coote, John Russell, Leo G. Carroll

Forever and a Day**
US 1943 104m bw
RKO (Herbert Wilcox, Victor Saville)

The history of a London house from 1804 to the blitz of World War II.
Made for war charities by a combination of the European talents in Hollywood, this series of sketches was unavoidably patchy but gave good opportunities to several familiar performers and stands as a likeable quick reference to their work at this period.

w Charles Bennett, C. S. Forester, Lawrence Hazard, Michael Hogan, W. P. Lipscomb, Alice Duer Miller, John Van Druten, Alan Campbell, Peter Godfrey, S. M. Herzig, Christopher Isherwood, Gene Lockhart, R. C. Sherriff, Claudine West, Norman Corwin, Jack Hartfield, James Hilton, Emmet Lavery, Frederick Lonsdale, Donald Ogden Stewart, Keith Winter *ph* Robert de Grasse, Lee Garmes, Russell Metty, Nicholas Musuraca *m* Anthony Collins *pd* René Clair, Edmund Goulding, Cedric Hardwicke, Frank Lloyd, Victor Saville, Robert Stevenson, Herbert Wilcox *ad* Albert D'Agostino, Lawrence Williams, Al Herman

Anna Neagle, Ray Milland, *Claude Rains, C. Aubrey Smith*, Dame May Whitty, Gene Lockhart, Ray Bolger, Edmund Gwenn, Charles Coburn, Ian Hunter, *Jessie Matthews, Charles Laughton*, Montagu Love, *Cedric Hardwicke*, Reginald Owen, *Buster Keaton*, Wendy Barrie, Ida Lupino, *Brian Aherne*, Edward Everett Horton, June Duprez, Eric Blore, Merle Oberon, Una O'Connor, Nigel Bruce, *Roland Young, Gladys Cooper*, Robert Cummings, Richard Haydn, Elsa Lanchester, Sara Allgood, Robert Coote, Donald Crisp, Ruth Warrick, Kent Smith, Herbert Marshall, Victor McLaglen, many others in bit parts

'One of the most brilliant casts of modern times has been assembled to bolster up one of the poorest pictures.'—*James Agate*

Forever Darling
US 1956 91m Eastmancolor
MGM / Zanra (Desi Arnaz)

A couple's matrimonial difficulties are solved by her guardian angel.
Cutesy-pie comedy with all concerned embarrassed by their material.

w Helen Deutsch *d* Alexander Hall *ph* Harold Lipstein *m* Bronislau Kaper

Lucille Ball, Desi Arnaz, James Mason (as the angel), John Emery, Louis Calhern, John Hoyt, Natalie Schaefer

Forever Female
US 1953 93m bw
Paramount (Pat Duggan)

A young writer sells his play to a Broadway producer who wants to transform it into a vehicle for his ex-wife; she falls for the writer but eventually discourages him.

Talky romantic comedy without much style or sense of Broadway; a long way from *All About Eve.*

w Julius J. Epstein, Philip G. Epstein, *play* Rosalind by J. M. Barrie *d* Irving Rapper *ph* Harry Stradling *m* Victor Young

Ginger Rogers, William Holden, Paul Douglas, James Gleason, Pat Crowley

The Forgotten Man*
US 1971 73m colour TVM
ABC Circle (Walter Grauman)

Five years after being reported missing, a soldier returns from Vietnam, finds his wife remarried, and becomes desperate.
Well-filmed and rather poignant melodrama.

w Mark Rodgers *d* Walter Grauman

Dennis Weaver, Anne Francis, Lois Nettleton, Andrew Duggan, Percy Rodrigues

Forsaking All Others*
US 1934 84m bw
MGM

A wife nearly breaks up her rather dull marriage, but thinks better of it.
Star power carries this thin comedy drama.

w Joseph L. Mankiewicz, *play* Edward Barry Roberts, Frank Morgan Cavett *d* W. S. Van Dyke *ph* Gregg Toland, George Folsey

Clark Gable, Joan Crawford, Robert Montgomery, *Charles Butterworth*, Billie Burke, Frances Drake, Rosalind Russell, Arthur Treacher

Fort Apache**
US 1948 127m bw
RKO (John Ford, Merian C. Cooper)

In the old west, a military martinet has trouble with his family as well as the Indians.
Rather stiff and unsatisfactory epic western which yet contains sequences in its director's best manner.

w Frank S. Nugent, *story* Massacre by James Warner Bellah *d John Ford* *ph* Archie Stout *m* Richard Hageman

Henry Fonda, John Wayne, Shirley Temple, Pedro Armendariz, Ward Bond, Irene Rich, George O'Brien, John Agar, Victor McLaglen, Anna Lee, Dick Foran, Guy Kibbee

'A visually absorbing celebration of violent deeds.'—*Howard Barnes*

'The whole picture is bathed in a special form of patriotic sentimentality: scenes are held so that we cannot fail to appreciate the beauty of the American past.'—*New Yorker, 1976*

Fort Ti
US 1953 73m Technicolor 3-D
Columbia (Sam Katzman)

In 1759 a platoon of Rogers' Rangers marches north to defend their territory against Indians.
Cheap and feeble western memorable only for the amount of miscellaneous objects thrown at the audience via 3-D photography.

w Robert E. Kent *d* William Castle *ph* Lester E. White, Lathrop B. Worth *m* Ross di Maggio

George Montgomery, Joan Vohs, Irving Bacon, James Seay

'The lack of restraint is remarkable. To the injury of tomahawks, rifle shots, cannon balls, flaming arrows, broken bottles and blazing torches is added the insult of grubby redskins hurled judo style into one's lap.'—*David Robinson*

The Fortune
US 1975 88m Technicolor Panavision
Columbia (Hank Moonjean)

A twenties heiress elopes with her lover and his dim-witted friend but discovers that they mean to murder her for her money.
Bungled black comedy with top talent over-confident of carrying it.

w Adrien Joyce (Carole Eastman) *d* Mike Nichols *ph* John A. Alonzo *m* various songs *pd* Richard Sylbert

Jack Nicholson, Warren Beatty, Stockard Channing, Florence Stanley, Richard B. Shull, John Fiedler

'Like the ill-assorted styles of the film generally, the stars themselves frequently seem to belong in different movies.'—*Richard Combs*

'A silly, shallow, occasionally enjoyable comedy trifle . . . classy 20's production values often merit more attention than the plot.'—*Variety*

Fortune and Men's Eyes
Canada / US 1971 102m Metrocolor
MGM / Cinemex / CFD (Lester Persky, Lewis M. Allen)

Life among homosexuals in a Canadian jail.
A welter of sensational incident outweighs any point the author may have had; this prison seems to be beyond reform.

w John Herbert, from his play *d* Harvey Hart *ph* Georges Dufaux *m* Galt McDermot

Wendell Burton, Michael Greer

The Fortune Cookie*
US 1966 125m bw Panavision
UA / Mirisch / Phalanx / Jalem (Billy Wilder)
GB title: *Meet Whiplash Willie*

A crooked lawyer forces his slightly injured client to sue for a million dollars.
Flat, stretched-out, only occasionally effective comedy which relies too much on mordant attitudes and a single star performance.

w Billy Wilder, I. A. L. Diamond *d* Billy Wilder *ph* Joseph La Shelle *m* André Previn

Walter Matthau, Jack Lemmon, Ron Rich, Cliff Osmond, Lurene Tuttle

Fortune Is a Woman*
GB 1956 95m bw
Columbia / Frank Launder, Sidney Gilliat
US title: *She Played with Fire*

An insurance assessor investigates a fire, finds a murder, marries the victim's widow, and is blackmailed . . .
Slackly-handled mystery thriller, a disappointment from the talents involved.

w Frank Launder, Sidney Gilliat, *novel* Winston Graham *d* Sidney Gilliat *ph* Gerald Gibbs *m* William Alwyn

Jack Hawkins, Arlene Dahl, Dennis Price, Geoffrey Keen, Violet Farebrother, John Robinson, Bernard Miles, Greta Gynt

Forty Carats*
US 1973 109m Metrocolor
Columbia / M. J. Frankovich

A 40-year-old divorcee on holiday in Greece has a brief affair with a 22-year-old man.
Curiously miscast and mishandled comedy for the smart set; scores a laugh or two but never really takes off.

w Leonard Gershe, *play* Pierre Barillet, Jean-Pierre Gredy *d* Milton Katselas *ph* Charles Lang Jnr *m* Michel Legrand

Liv Ullman, Edward Albert, Gene Kelly, Billy 'Green' Bush, Binnie Barnes, Nancy Walker, Deborah Raffin, Don Porter, Natalie Schaefer, Rosemary Murphy

The Forty Eight Hour Mile
US 1970 97m Technicolor TVM
Universal

A private eye pursues a tense triangle situation which leads to murder.
OK who's-following-whom mystery.

d Gene Levitt

Darren McGavin, William Windom, Kathy Brown, Carrie Snodgress

Forty Guns
US 1957 80m bw Cinemascope
TCF / Globe (Samuel Fuller)

A powerful ranchwoman protects her hoodlum brother.
Heavily melodramatic and slow-moving western with a few effective moments.

wd Samuel Fuller *ph* Joseph Biroc *m* Harry Sukman

Barbara Stanwyck, Barry Sullivan, Dean Jagger, Gene Barry, John Ericson

Forty Ninth Parallel***
GB 1941 123m bw
GFD / Ortus (John Sutro, Michael Powell)
US title: *The Invaders*

In Canada, five stranded U-boat men try to escape into the US.
Episodic, effective propaganda piece which develops some nice Hitchcockian touches and allows a range of star actors to make impact.

w Emeric Pressburger, Rodney Ackland d Michael Powell m Ralph Vaughan Williams

Eric Portman, Laurence Olivier, *Anton Walbrook, Leslie Howard, Raymond Massey*, Glynis Johns, Niall MacGinnis, Finlay Currie, Raymond Lovell, John Chandos

Forty Pounds of Trouble*
US 1963 105m Eastmancolor Panavision
U-I / Curtis Enterprises (Stan Margulies)

A casino manager is chased by his ex-wife's detective for alimony payments, and also has to look after an abandoned six-year-old girl.
Standard sentimental comedy with some verve and a lively climactic chase through Disneyland.

w Marion Hargrove *d* Norman Jewison *ph* Joe MacDonald *m* Mort Lindsey

Tony Curtis, Phil Silvers, Suzanne Pleshette, Edward Andrews

Forty-Second Street****
US 1933 89m bw
Warner (Hal B. Wallis)

A Broadway musical producer has troubles during rehearsal but reaches a successful opening night.
Archetypal Hollywood putting-on-a-show musical in which the leading lady is indisposed and a chorus girl is told to get out there and come back a star. The clichés are written and performed with great zest, the atmosphere is convincing, and the numbers when they come are dazzlers.

w James Seymour, Rian James, novel Bradford

Ropes *d Lloyd Bacon ch Busby Berkeley ph Sol Polito m/ly Al Dubin, Harry Warren*

Warner Baxter, Ruby Keeler, Bebe Daniels, George Brent, Una Merkel, Guy Kibbee, Dick Powell, *Ginger Rogers* (as Anytime Annie), *Ned Sparks*, George E. Stone, Allen Jenkins

'The story has been copied a hundred times since, but never has the backstage atmosphere been so honestly and felicitously caught.'—*John Huntley, 1966*

Foster and Laurie*
US 1975 100m colour TVM
Arthur Stolnitz

The true story of two New York cops, shot in the line of duty.
A well-intentioned tribute, but basically the same old mean streets cops and robbers.

w Albert Ruben, *book* Al Silverman *d* John Llewellyn Moxey *m* Lalo Schifrin

Perry King, Dorian Harewood, Talia Shire, Jonelle Allen

The Fountain
US 1934 84m bw
RKO (Pandro S. Berman)

During World War I a British woman is tempted to forsake her mangled German air ace husband for her childhood sweetheart.
A slice of impenetrable gloom from an intractable novel.

w Jane Murfin, Samuel Hoffenstein, *novel* Charles Morgan *d* John Cromwell *ph* Henry W. Gerrard

Ann Harding, Brian Aherne, Paul Lukas, Jean Hersholt, Ralph Forbes, Violet Kemble-Cooper, Sara Haden

'One of the talkiest talkies yet.'—*Variety*

'Long and solemn and wonderfully empty.'—*Otis Ferguson*

The Fountainhead**
US 1949 114m bw
Warner (Henry Blanke)

An idealistic architect clashes with big business.
Overripe adaptation of a rather silly novel, full of Freudian symbols and expressionist techniques with which the star really can't cope; but an enjoyable field day for the director and the rest of the cast.

w Ayn Rand, from her novel *d King Vidor ph Robert Burks m* Max Steiner

Gary Cooper, *Patricia Neal, Raymond Massey*, Kent Smith, Robert Douglas, Henry Hull, Ray Collins, Moroni Olson, Jerome Cowan

Four Daughters***
US 1938 90m bw
Warner (Henry Blanke)

Domestic and romantic adventures of a small-town family.
Standard small-town hearth-fire hokum, impeccably done and really quite irresistible.

w Julius Epstein, Lenore Coffee, *novel* Sister Act by Fannie Hurst *d Michael Curtiz ph* Ernest Haller *m* Max Steiner

Claude Rains, John Garfield (a sensation in his first role), Priscilla Lane, Rosemary Lane, Lola Lane, Gale Page, Jeffrey Lynn, Frank McHugh, *May Robson*, Dick Foran

† An immediate sequel was required, but the Garfield character had been killed off, so to accommodate him a variation was written under the title *Daughters Courageous*; then came two proper sequels without him, *Four Wives* and *Four Mothers*. In 1955 the original was remade as *Young at Heart* (qv).

The Four Feathers**
US 1929 83m bw
Paramount (David O. Selznick)

During the Sudan campaign of the nineties, a stay-at-home receives four white feathers as a symbol of cowardice; but he goes undercover, becomes a hero, and rescues his best friend.
Ambitious early talkie based on a famous adventure novel, partly filmed in Africa; interesting but now very stilted.

w Howard Estabrook, *novel* A. E. W. Mason *d* Lothar Mendes, Merian C. Cooper, Ernest Schoedsack *ph* Robert Kurlle, Merian C. Cooper, Ernest Schoedsack *m* William F. Peters

Richard Arlen, Fay Wray, Clive Brook, William Powell, George Fawcett, Theodore Von Eltz, Noah Beery

The Four Feathers****
GB 1939 130m Technicolor
London (Alexander Korda, Irving Asher)

The standard version of the above, perfectly cast and presented, with battle scenes which have since turned up in a score of other films from *Zarak* to *Master of the World*; also a triumph of early colour.

w R. C. Sheriff, Lajos Biro, Arthur Wimperis *d Zoltan Korda ph* Georges Périnal, Osmond Borradaile, Jack Cardiff *m* Miklos Rozsa

John Clements, Ralph Richardson, C. Aubrey Smith, June Duprez, Allan Jeayes, Jack Allen, Donald Gray, Henry Oscar, John Laurie

'It cannot fail to be one of the best films of the year . . . even the richest of the ham goes

smoothly down, savoured with humour and satire.'—*Graham Greene*
† Remade 1956 as *Storm over the Nile* (qv).

Four for Texas
US 1963 124m Technicolor
Warner / Sam Company (Robert Aldrich)

Two survivors of a stagecoach raid doublecross each other for the loot and become rival saloon owners.
Flabby western comedy, tediously directed and casually performed.

w Teddi Sherman, Robert Aldrich *d* Robert Aldrich *ph* Ernest Laszlo *m* Nelson Riddle

Dean Martin, Frank Sinatra, Anita Ekberg, Ursula Andress, Charles Bronson, Victor Buono, the Three Stooges

'The major laughs come from the Three Stooges doing an ancient routine and an old lady falling out of her wheelchair. Zowie.'—*Judith Crist*

'One suspects that the most amusing antics were those that went on off-screen.'—*Films and Filming*

Four Frightened People*
US 1934 78m bw
Paramount / Cecil B. de Mille

A bubonic plague outbreak on board ship causes four survivors to escape via a lifeboat and trek through dangerous jungle.
Studio-bound but interesting action melodrama, of a type unusual from this director.

w Bartlett Cormack, Lenore Coffee, *novel* E. Arnot Robertson *d Cecil B. de Mille* *ph* Karl Struss *m* Karl Hajos and others

Claudette Colbert, Herbert Marshall, William Gargan, Mary Boland, Leo Carrillo, Nella Walker, Tetsu Komai, Ethel Griffies

Four Girls in Town
US 1956 85m Technicolor
Cinemascope
U-I (Aaron Rosenberg)

Girls from various countries are chosen for Hollywood screen tests.
Formula romantic comedy adequately exposing young talent.

wd Jack Sher *ph* Irving Glassberg *m* Joseph Gershenson

George Nader, Julie Adams, Marianne Cook, Elsa Martinelli, Gia Scala, Sidney Chaplin, Grant Williams, John Gavin

The Four Horsemen of the Apocalypse*
US 1961 153m Metrocolor
Cinemascope
MGM (Julian Blaustein)

The idle grandson of an Argentinian beef tycoon finds his manhood at last as a member of the French resistance during World War II.
Ill-fated modernization of the 1921 Valentino success based on an essentially Victorian-gothic novel complete with visionary skyriding figures of death and pestilence, which simply do not fit in with bombs and concentration camps. Glum acting by a too elderly company, ugly colour and the usual hindrances of Cinemascope.

w Robert Ardrey, John Gay, *novel* Vincente Blasco Ibanez *d* Vincente Minnelli *ph* Milton Krasner *m* André Previn

Glenn Ford, Ingrid Thulin, Charles Boyer, Paul Henreid, Lee J. Cobb, Paul Lukas, Karl Boehm, Yvette Mimieux

'An elephantine helping of hysteria and hokum.'—*Judith Crist, 1973*

Four Hours to Kill**
US 1935 74m bw
Paramount (Arthur Hornblow Jnr)

A psychopathic gangster gets loose during an evening at the theatre.
Tense, well-handled melodrama making full use of its setting.

w Norman Krasna, from his play Small Miracle *d Mitchell Leisen* *ph* Theodor Sparkhul

Richard Barthelmess, Ray Milland, Gertrude Michael, Joe Morrison, Helen Mack, Dorothy Tree, Roscoe Karns, Henry Travers

Four Jills in a Jeep
US 1944 89m bw
TCF (Irving Starr)

Four Hollywood glamour girls entertain the troops.
Condescending, dispirited 'semi-documentary' war musical.

w Robert Ellis, Helen Logan, Snag Werris *d* William A. Seiter *ph* Peverell Marley *md* Emil Newman

Kay Francis, Martha Raye, Carole Landis, Mitzi Mayfair, Jimmy Dorsey and his band, John Harvey, Phil Silvers, Dick Haymes; guest stars Alice Faye, Betty Grable, Carmen Miranda, George Jessel

'It gives the painful impression of having been tossed together in a couple of hours.'—*Bosley Crowther*

The Four Just Men*
GB 1939 85m bw
Ealing–Capad (S. C. Balcon)

To save the Empire, four stalwart Britishers agree to murder a villainous MP.
Bright, unusual but dated thriller from a popular novel.

w Roland Pertwee, Angus Macphail, Sergei Nolbandov, *novel* Edgar Wallace *d* Walter Forde

Hugh Sinclair, Francis L. Sullivan, Frank Lawton, Griffith Jones, Anna Lee, Basil Sidney, Alan Napier, Athole Stewart, Edward Chapman, Garry Marsh, Ellaline Terriss, Lydia Sherwood, George Merritt
† The TV series of the late fifties restrained its heroes from criminal acts; the men were Jack Hawkins, Richard Conte, Dan Dailey, Vittorio De Sica

Four Men and a Prayer**
US 1938 97m bw
TCF (Kenneth MacGowan)

Four young Englishmen set out to clear the name of their dishonoured father.
Pleasantly performed mystery which improves after a slowish start.

w Richard Sherman, Sonya Levien, Walter Ferris, *novel* David Garth *d John Ford*
ph Ernest Palmer *m* Louis Silvers

Loretta Young, Richard Greene, George Sanders, David Niven, William Henry, C. Aubrey Smith, J. Edward Bromberg, John Carradine, Alan Hale, Reginald Denny, Barry Fitzgerald, Berton Churchill, John Sutton

The Four Musketeers (The Revenge of Milady)*
Panama 1974 103m Technicolor
TCF / Film Trust / Este (Alexander Salkind, Michael Salkind)

Athos, Porthos, Aramis and D'Artagnan have a final battle with Rochefort.
Perfunctory sequel to the same team's *The Three Musketeers*; allegedly the two films were intended as one, but if so the first ten reels were by far the best, though this section has its regulation quota of high spirits and lusty action.

w George MacDonald Fraser *d* Richard Lester
ph David Watkin *m* Lalo Schifrin *pd* Brian Eatwell

Michael York, Oliver Reed, Frank Finlay, Richard Chamberlain, Raquel Welch, Faye Dunaway, Charlton Heston, Christopher Lee, Simon Ward, Geraldine Chaplin, Jean-Pierre Cassel, Roy Kinnear
'The whole sleek formula has rolled over to reveal a very soft, very flabby underside.'—*Tony Rayns*

The Four-Poster
US 1952 103m bw
Columbia / Stanley Kramer

The history of a marriage told in a series of bedroom scenes.
Hastily shot and rather tatty looking version of a stage play; unfortunately film can't contrast the comedy of the opening and the tragedy of the close within one small set, and the UPA cartoon bridges, though smart in themselves, are merely an irritation.

w Allan Scott, *play* Jan de Hartog *d* Irving Reis
ph ghal Mohr *m* Dmitri Tiomkin

Rex Harrison, Lilli Palmer

The Four Skulls of Jonathan Drake
US 1959 70m bw
UA / Vogue (Robert E. Kent)

A family is cursed by a head-hunting Equadorian medicine man.
Cheaply made but full-blooded occult horror, rather effectively done by a cast that knows how.

w Orville H. Hampton *d* Edward L. Cahn
ph Maury Gertsman *m* Paul Dunlap

Henry Daniell, Eduard Franz, Valerie French, Grant Richards, Paul Cavanagh
'Amazonian Indians may find the plot a shade far-fetched.'—*MFB*

Four Sons*
US 1940 89m bw
TCF

A Czech family is divided when the Nazis take over.
Predictable po-faced anti-Hitler melodrama released to an indifferent public well before America entered the war. A remake of a silent film set during World War I.

w John Howard Lawson *d* Archie Mayo
ph Leon Shamroy *m* David Buttolph

Don Ameche, Eugenie Leontovich, Mary Beth Hughes, Alan Curtis, George Ernest, Robert Lowery, Sig Rumann, Lionel Royce, Ludwig Stossel

Fourteen Hours***
US 1951 92m bw
TCF (Sol C. Siegel)

A man stands on the ledge of a tall building and threatens to jump.
Well-made documentary drama based on a true occurrence but given a happy ending. First class detail gives an impression of realism.

w John Paxton, article Joel Sayre *d Henry Hathaway ph* Joe MacDonald *m* Alfred Newman

Richard Basehart, Paul Douglas, Barbara Bel Geddes, Debra Paget, Agnes Moorehead, Robert Keith, Howard da Silva, Jeffrey Hunter, Martin Gabel, Jeff Corey

'A model of craftsmanship in all departments.'—*Penelope Houston*

The Fox*
US / Canada 1967 110m De Luxe
Warner / Raymond Stross / Motion Pictures International (Howard Koch)

On an isolated farm, two lesbians are disturbed by the arrival of a wandering seaman.
Rather obvious sexual high jinks full of symbolism and heavy breathing.

w Lewis John Carlino, Howard Koch, *novel* D. H. Lawrence *d* Mark Rydell *ph* Bill Fraker *m* Lalo Schifrin

Anne Heywood, Sandy Dennis, Keir Dullea

Fox Follies of 1929
US 1929 82m bw
Fox
GB title: *Movietone Follies of 1929*

An all-star review.
Every studio had its early talkie musical using up its contract stars; this was perhaps the least interesting.

wd David Butler, William K. Wells *ph* Charles Van Enger

Sue Carol, Lola Lane, Dixie Lee, Sharon Lynn, Stepin Fetchit

The Foxes of Harrow
US 1947 117m bw
TCF (William A. Bacher)

In 1820 New Orleans, a philanderer seeks advancement by breaking up his marriage.
Tolerable but rather flat adaptation of a bestseller, stultified by central miscasting.

w Wanda Tuchock, *novel* Frank Yerby *d* John M. Stahl *ph* Joseph La Shelle *m* Alfred Newman

Rex Harrison, Maureen O'Hara, Richard Haydn, Victor McLaglen, Vanessa Brown, Patricia Medina, Gene Lockhart, Hugo Haas

Foxfire
US 1955 92m Technicolor
U-I (Aaron Rosenberg)

A rich New York girl on holiday in Arizona is attracted to a half-Apache miner.
Romantic melodrama with action asides; watchable for women who like that sort of thing.

w Ketti Frings, *novel* Anya Seton *d* Joseph Pevney *ph* William Daniels *m* Frank Skinner

Jane Russell, Jeff Chandler, Frieda Inescort, Dan Duryea

Foxhole in Cairo
GB 1960 80m bw
Omnia (Steven Pallos, Donald Taylor)

A German agent in Libya is allowed to get back to Rommel with false information.
Interesting true spy story deflated by muddled handling.

w Leonard Mosley, from his book The Cat and the Mice *d* John Moxey *ph* Desmond Dickinson *m* Wolfram Rohrig

James Robertson Justice, Adrian Hoven, Albert Lieven (as Rommel), Niall MacGinnis, Peter Van Eyck, Robert Urquhart, Fenella Fielding

Fra Diavolo**
US 1933 90m bw
MGM / Hal Roach
aka: *The Devil's Brother*

Two incompetent bandits are hired as manservants by a real bandit.
Auber's 1830 operetta becomes a vehicle for Laurel and Hardy, setting a pattern they followed with *Babes in Toyland* and *The Bohemian Girl*. They have excellent sequences, but overall the film lacks pace.

w Jeanie McPherson *d* Hal Roach, Charles Rogers *ph* Art Lloyd, Hap Depew *md* Le Roy Shield

Stan Laurel, Oliver Hardy, Dennis King, *James Finlayson*, Thelma Todd

Fragment of Fear*
GB 1970 95m Technicolor
Columbia (John R. Sloan)

A young writer investigates the murder of his aunt, but finds that he may himself be mad.
What appears to be a whodunnit turns into a flashy, fashionable, sub-Antonioni puzzle with no ending, but despite the considerable irritation this causes, the details and character cameos are excellent.

w Paul Dehn, *novel* John Bingham *d* Richard C. Sarafian *ph* Oswald Morris *m* Johnny Harris

David Hemmings, Gayle Hunnicutt, Roland Culver, Daniel Massey, Flora Robson, Wilfrid Hyde White, Adolfo Celi, Mona Washbourne

The Franchise Affair*
GB 1950 88m bw
ABP (Robert Hall)

A young girl accuses two gentlewomen of kidnapping and ill-treating her.
Unusual and absorbing mystery based on a true 18th-century case; the treatment however is rather too mild.

w Robert Hall, Lawrence Huntington, *novel* Josephine Tey *d* Lawrence Huntington *ph* Gunther Krampf *m* Philip Green

Michael Denison, Dulcie Gray, Anthony Nicholls, Marjorie Fielding, Athene Seyler, Ann Stephens, Hy Hazell, John Bailey, Kenneth More

Francis*
US 1950 90m bw
U-I (Robert Arthur)

An army private makes friends with a talking mule who causes him some embarrassment.
Simple-minded, quite agreeable if rather slow-moving fantasy farce which was popular enough to spawn several sequels and later a TV series called *Mister Ed.*

w David Stern, from his novel *d* Arthur Lubin *ph* Irving Glassberg *m* Frank Skinner

Donald O'Connor, Patricia Medina, Zasu Pitts, Ray Collins, John McIntyre, Eduard Franz, Robert Warwick, and Chill Wills as Francis' voice.

Sequels (the first six with Donald O'Connor):
1951: FRANCIS GOES TO THE RACES
1952: FRANCIS GOES TO WEST POINT
1953: FRANCIS COVERS BIG TOWN
1954: FRANCIS JOINS THE WACS
1955: FRANCIS IN THE NAVY
1956: FRANCIS IN THE HAUNTED HOUSE (with Mickey Rooney)

Francis of Assisi
US 1961 107m De
Luxe Cinemascope
TCF / Perseus (Plato A. Skouras)

The son of a medieval cloth merchant takes a vow of poverty, cares for animals and dies a hermit.
Tedious biopic.

w Eugene Vale, Jack Thomas, James Forsyth *d* Michael Curtiz *ph* Piero Portalupi *m* Mario Nascimbene

Bradford Dillman, Dolores Hart, Stuart Whitman, Eduard Franz, Pedro Armendariz, Cecil Kellaway, Finlay Currie, Mervyn Johns, Athene Seyler

Frankenstein****
US 1931 71m bw
Universal (Carl Laemmle Jnr)

A research scientist creates a living monster from corpses, but it runs amok.
Whole books have been written about this film and its sequels. Apart from being a fascinating if primitive cinematic work in its own right, it set its director and star on interesting paths and established a Hollywood attitude towards horror (mostly borrowed from German silents such as *The Golem*). A seminal film indeed, which at each repeated viewing belies its age.

w Garrett Fort, Francis Edward Faragoh, John L. Balderston, from the play by Peggy Webling and the novel by Mary Wollstonecraft Shelley *d James Whale, ph Arthur Edeson m* none *ad Charles D. Hall*

Boris Karloff, Colin Clive, Mae Clarke, John Boles, *Edward Van Sloan, Frederick Kerr, Dwight Frye*

'Still the most famous of all horror films, and deservedly so.'—*John Baxter, 1968*

† Direct sequels by the same studio (all qv) include *The Bride of Frankenstein, Son of Frankenstein, Ghost of Frankenstein, Frankenstein Meets the Wolf Man, House of Frankenstein, House of Dracula, Abbott and Costello Meet Frankenstein.* The later Hammer series, which told the story all over again in gorier vein, includes *The Curse of Frankenstein* (qv), *The Revenge of Frankenstein, The Evil of Frankenstein, Frankenstein Created Woman, Frankenstein Must be Destroyed, Horror of Frankenstein, Frankenstein and the Monster from Hell.* Other Frankenstein films date from as early as 1908, and scores have been made in various languages. *Young Frankenstein* (qv) is a partly effective spoof on the Hollywood series; *The Munsters* was a sixties comedy series for TV which used the monster as its leading character in a domestic setting.

Frankenstein Meets the Wolf Man**
US 1943 73m bw
Universal

Lawrence Talbot, the wolf man, travels to Vasaria in the hope of a cure, and finds the Frankenstein monster being reactivated.
Once one recovered from the bargain basement combination of two monsters in one picture, this was a horror comic with stylish sequences, weakened by cuts in the script and a miscast Bela Lugosi.

w Curt Siodmak *d Roy William Neill* *ph* George Robinson *m* Hans Salter

Lon Chaney Jnr, Ilona Massey, Bela Lugosi (as the monster), Patric Knowles, *Maria Ouspenskaya*

Frankenstein '70
US 1958 83m bw Cinemascope
Allied Artists (Aubrey Schenck)

Television film-makers descend on Castle Frankenstein; the current Count needs the money to finance some monster making of his own.
Boringly talkative and very silly 'futuristic' blot on an honourable name, apart from a rather frightening pre-credits sequence.

w Richard Landau, G. Worthing Yates *d* Howard W. Koch *ph* Carl Guthrie *m* Paul Dunlap

Boris Karloff, Tom Duggan, Jana Lund

Frankenstein: The True Story
US 1973 200m Technicolor TVM
Universal (Hunt Stromberg Jnr)

It never was a true story anyway, this version doesn't stick to the book any more than the others, and at this length it is just an embarrassment, though good performances flicker through the tedium.

w Christopher Isherwood, Don Bachardy *d* Jack Smight

James Mason, Leonard Whiting, David McCallum, Michael Sarrazin, Jane Seymour, Nicola Pagett, John Gielgud, Margaret Leighton, Ralph Richardson, Michael Wilding, Tom Baker, Agnes Moorehead

Frankie and Johnny*
US 1966 87m Technicolor
UA / F and J (Edward Small)

On a Mississippi riverboat, a gambling singer is the despair of his lady partner.
Mildly amusing pastiche both of the old song and of the various riverboat dramas.

w Alex Gottlieb *d* Frederick de Cordova *ph* John Marquette *m* Fred Karger

Elvis Presley, Donna Douglas, Sue Ane Langdon, Harry Morgan, Nancy Kovack, Audrey Christie, Jerome Cowan

Fraulein
US 1958 100m Eastmancolor Cinemascope
TCF (Walter Reisch)

During World War II an American prisoner of war escapes and is helped by the daughter of a German professor.
Studio-bound war heroics with little conviction achieved or aimed at.

w Lee Townsend, *novel* James McGowan *d* Henry Koster *ph* Leo Tover *m* Daniele Amfitheatrof

Dana Wynter, Mel Ferrer, Margaret Hayes, Dolores Michaels, Theodore Bikel, Helmut Dantine

Freaks**
US 1932 64m bw
MGM (Tod Browning)

A lady trapeze artist marries a midget, then poisons him for his money; his abnormal friends take revenge by turning her into a freak.
Made but disowned by MGM after accusations of tastelessness, this strident and silly melodrama has dated badly but has sequences of great power, especially the final massing of the freaks, slithering to their revenge in a rainstorm. It would have been better as a silent; the dialogue kills it.

w Willis Goldbeck, Leon Gordon, *novel* Spurs by Tod Robbins *d Tod Browning* *ph* Merrit B. Gerstad

Wallace Ford, Olga Baclanova, Leila Hyams, Roscoe Ates

'It is a skilfully presented production but of a character which in consideration of the susceptibilities of mass audiences should be avoided.'—*Martin Quigley*

A Free Soul*
US 1931 91m bw
MGM

An unconventional lawyer regrets allowing his daughter to consort with a gangster.
Heavy melodrama with outdated attitudes, but an impressive example of the studio's style in the early thirties.

w John Meehan, *novel* Adela Rogers St John *d* Clarence Brown *ph* William Daniels

Lionel Barrymore, Norma Shearer, Leslie Howard, Clark Gable, Lucy Beaumont, James Gleason

Freebie and the Bean*
US 1974 113m Technicolor Panavision
Warner (Richard Rush)

Two vaguely incompetent cops try to link a mobster with the numbers racket.
Violent comedy melodrama with a high mortality rate, amoral outlook, and the usual seventies reliance on incoherent plot, bumbled dialogue and excessive background noise. Occasionally funny all the same.

w Richard Kaufman *d* Richard Rush *ph* Laszlo Kovacs *m* Dominic Frontière

Alan Arkin, James Caan, Loretta Swit, Jack Kruschen, Mike Kellin

'It summarizes Hollywood's favourite thematic elements of the early seventies: platonic male love affair, police corruption, comic violence, cynicism in high places, San Francisco, gay villains, the car chase. A return to the Keystone Kops, with character trimmings and lashings of sado-masochistic mayhem.'—*Clyde Jeavons*

'A tasteless film from a spitball script.'—*Variety*

Freedom Radio
GB 1941 95m bw
Columbia / Two Cities (Mario Zampi)
US title: *A Voice in the Night*

In Vienna during World War II, the husband of a Nazi actress runs a secret radio transmitter for Allied propaganda.
Moderate wartime flagwaver.

w Basil Wood, Gordon Wellesley, Louis Golding, Anatole de Grunwald, Jeffrey Dell, Bridget Boland, Roland Pertwee *d* Anthony Asquith

Diana Wynyard, Clive Brook, Raymond Huntley, Joyce Howard, Derek Farr, Howard Marion Crawford, Morland Graham

The French Connection***
US 1971 104m De Luxe
TCF / Philip D'Antoni

New York police track down a consignment of drugs entering the country in a car.
Lively semi-documentary based on the true exploits of a tough cop named Eddie Egan who liked to break a few rules. Most memorable for a car chase scene involving an elevated railway, for showing the seamy side of New York more or less as it is, and for the most mumbled dialogue and the poorest sound track in years.

w Ernest Tidyman, *book* Robin Moore
d William Friedkin *ph* Owen Roizman *m* Don Ellis

Gene Hackman, Roy Scheider, *Fernando Rey*, Tony Lo Bianco

French Connection II
US 1975 119m De Luxe
TCF (Robert L. Rosen)

The New York cop who in *The French Connection* smashed most of a drug ring arrives in Marseilles to track down its elusive leader.
Sleazy, virtually plotless and unattractive sequel which rises to a few good action moments but is bogged down by bad language, unconvincing characterization and an interminable and irrelevant 'cold turkey' sequence.

w Robert Dillon, Laurie Dillon, Alexander Jacobs *d* John Frankenheimer *ph* Claude Renoir *m* Don Ellis

Gene Hackman, Fernando Rey, Bernard Fresson, Jean-Pierre Castaldi

'Visually as well as morally the film makes you uncertain where its feet are.'—*New Yorker*

French Dressing
GB 1963 86m bw
ABP / Kenwood (Kenneth Harper)

A deckchair attendant and a local reporter believe that what Bardot can do for St Tropez they can do for Gormleigh-on-Sea.
Cinema's *enfant terrible* directs this his first theatrical film at breakneck speed with echoes of Tati, Keaton and the Keystone Kops. Alas, lack of star comedians and firm control make its exuberance merely irritating.

w Peter Myers, Ronald Cass, Peter Britt *d Ken Russell* *ph* Ken Higgins *m* Georges Delerue

James Booth, Roy Kinnear, Marisa Mell, Bryan Pringle

The French Line
US 1953 102m Technicolor 3-D
RKO (Edmund Grainger)

A cheery Texas oil heiress finds a husband while travelling to France.
Very thinly plotted but quite attractive light musical with a good-humoured star wearing costumes once thought censorable.

w Mary Loos, Richard Sale *d* Lloyd Bacon *ph* Harry J. Wild *md* Lionel Newman *ch* Jack Cole

Jane Russell, Gilbert Roland, Arthur Hunnicutt, Mary McCarty

'A slouching Amazon, her clothes appear to stay put just as long as she agrees not to burst out of them; essentially a good sort, she has an ever-annihilating sneer for the false, the pretentious and the fresh.'—*MFB*

A French Mistress
GB 1960 98m bw
British Lion / Charter (John Boulting)

An attractive new mistress causes havoc at a boys' school.
Sloppy, predictable comedy with practised performers getting a few easy laughs. The producers tried to excuse its imperfections by promoting it as 'a romp'.

w Roy Boulting, Jeffrey Dell, *play* Robert Monro (Sonnie Hale) *d* Roy Boulting

James Robertson Justice, Cecil Parker, Raymond Huntley, Ian Bannen, Agnes Laurent,

Thorley Walters, Edith Sharpe, Athene Seyler, Kenneth Griffith

French without Tears*
GB 1939 85m bw
Paramount / Two Cities (David E. Rose)

Young Britons at a French crammers fall for the young sister of one of their number.
Pleasant light comedy from a successful West End play.

w Terence Rattigan, Anatole de Grunwald, Ian Dalrymple, *play Terence Rattigan* *d* Anthony Asquith

Ray Milland, Ellen Drew, *Guy Middleton, Ronald Culver*, David Tree, Jim Gerald, Janine Darcy, Kenneth Morgan

Frenchman's Creek**
US 1944 112m Technicolor
Paramount (B. G. De Sylva)

In Restoration England, a lady flees from a lascivious nobleman to her family home in Cornwall, where she falls in love with a French pirate.
Enjoyable Girls' Own Paper romance, dressed to kill and entertaining despite its many palpable absurdities.

w Talbot Jennings, *novel* Daphne du Maurier *d Mitchell Leisen* *ph George Barnes* *m* Victor Young *ad Hans Dreier, Ernest Fegte*

Joan Fontaine, Arturo de Cordova, Basil Rathbone, Nigel Bruce, *Cecil Kellaway*, Ralph Forbes, Moyna McGill

Frenzy*
GB 1972 116m Technicolor
Universal / Alfred Hitchcock

A disillusioned and aggressive ex-RAF officer is suspected through circumstantial evidence of being London's 'necktie murderer'.
Has-been, unconvincing, cliché-ridden thriller, an old man's sex suspenser, which would have been derided if anyone but Hitchcock had made it. As it is, a few comic and suspenseful touches partly atone for the implausibilities and lapses of taste.

w Anthony Shaffer, *novel* Goodbye Piccadilly, Farewell Leicester Square by Arthur La Bern *d* Alfred Hitchcock *ph* Gilbert Taylor *m* Ron Goodwin

Jon Finch, *Alec McCowen, Barry Foster*, Vivien Merchant, Anna Massey

'Hitchcock's most stodgy piece since *Dial M for Murder* and possibly his least interesting film from any period.'—*William S. Pechter*

Freud**
US 1963 140m bw
U-I (Wolfgang Reinhardt)

Vienna 1865; Dr Sigmund Freud, a neurologist, uses hypnotism to treat hysteria, and finds new interest in the case of a boy whose hatred of his father springs from incestuous love of his mother, a failing which Freud finds in himself.
Earnest and competent biopic harking back to Warners' similar films of the thirties, with the addition of franker language. Generally absorbing, but undeniably hard tack.

w Charles Kaufman, Wolfgang Reinhardt *d John Huston* *ph* Douglas Slocombe *m* Jerry Goldsmith

Montgomery Clift, Larry Parks, Susannah York, Eileen Herlie, Susan Kohner, David McCallum

Friday the Thirteenth***
GB 1933 84m bw
Gainsborough (Michael Balcon)

Several people are involved in a bus crash, and we turn back the clock to see how they came to be there.
Highly competent compendium of comedies and dramas looking back to *The Bridge of San Luis Rey* and forward to the innumerable all-star films of the forties.

w G. H. Moresby-White, Sidney Gilliat *d Victor Saville*

Sonnie Hale, Cyril Smith, *Eliot Makeham*, Ursula Jeans, *Emlyn Williams*, Frank Lawton, Belle Chrystal, *Max Miller*, Alfred Drayton, Edmund Gwenn, Mary Jerrold, Gordon Harker, *Robertson Hare*, Martita Hunt, Leonora Corbett, Jessie Matthews, Ralph Richardson

Frieda*
GB 1947 97m bw
Ealing (Michael Relph)

An RAF officer marries and takes home a girl who helped him escape from a POW camp.
Stuffy and dated drama about how one English family learned to love one particular German. Timely when it appeared, however, and well made within its conventions.

w Angus Macphail, Ronald Millar, *play* Ronald Millar *d* Basil Dearden *ph* Gordon Dines

Mai Zetterling, David Farrar, Glynis Johns, Flora Robson, Albert Lieven

Friendly Persuasion**
US 1956 139m De Luxe
AA (William Wyler)

At the outbreak of the Civil War, a family of Quakers has to consider its position.
Sentimental, homespun western fare, well done without being especially engrossing.

w Michael Wilson, *novel* Jessamyn West *d William Wyler ph* Ellsworth Fredericks *m* Dmitri Tiomkin

Gary Cooper, Dorothy McGuire, Anthony Perkins, Marjorie Main, Richard Eyer, Robert Middleton, Walter Catlett

Friendly Persuasion
US 1975 100m colour TVM
International (Herbert B. Leonard)

Modest remake in the hope of a series. The hope was forlorn.

w William P. Woods *d* Joseph Sargent

Richard Kiley, Shirley Knight, Michael O'Keefe, Tracie Savage

Friends
US 1971 102m Technicolor
Paramount (Lewis Gilbert)

Teenage lovers run away to a country cottage and have a child.
Peculiar idyll given corny 'poetic' treatment: a real non-starter.

w Jack Russell, Vernon Harris *d* Lewis Gilbert *ph* Andrew Winding *m* Elton John

Sean Bury, Anicee Alvina, Toby Robbins, Ronald Lewis

The Friends of Eddie Coyle*
US 1973 102m Technicolor Panavision
Paramount (Paul Monash)

An ageing hoodlum agrees to become a police informer and is hunted down by his former associates.
Dour gangster melodrama held together by its central performance.

w Paul Monash, *novel* George V. Higgins *d* Peter Yates *ph* Vernon J. Kemper *m* Dave Grusin

Robert Mitchum, Peter Boyle, Richard Jordan, Steven Keats, Mitch Ryan, Alex Rocco

The Frisco Kid*
US 1935 77m bw
Warner (Samuel Bischoff)

A Shanghaied sailor rises to power among the riff raff of the Barbary Coast in the 1860s.
Fair melodrama with the star in action and (less interestingly) in love.

w Warren Duff, Seton I. Miller *d* Lloyd Bacon *ph* Sol Polito *m* Leo Forbstein

James Cagney, Margaret Lindsay, Ricardo Cortez, Lili Damita, Donald Woods, Barton MacLane, George E. Stone, Addison Richards

Fritz the Cat**
US 1971 78m De Luxe
Fritz Productions / Aurica (Steve Krantz)

An alleycat student in New York seeks new and varied experience.
Cartoon feature which applies the old anthropomorphism to the contemporary scene, and whips up more obscenity and violence than Disney ever dreamed of. A fast-moving orgy of outrage which could never have got by in live form.

wd/animator Ralph Bakshi, comic strip R. H. Crumb

'A bitter and snarling satire that refuses to curl up in anyone's lap.'—*Bruce Williamson*

The Frog*
GB 1937 75m bw
Herbert Wilcox

The mysterious leader of a criminal organization is unmasked.
Lively old-fashioned mystery melodrama.

w Ian Hay, Gerald Elliott, *novel* The Fellowship of the Frog by Edgar Wallace *d* Jack Raymond

Gordon Harker, Carol Goodner, Noah Beery, Jack Hawkins, Richard Ainley, Esmé Percy, Felix Aylmer

† Sequel 1938: *The Return of the Frog.*

The Frogmen
US 1951 96m bw
TCF (Samuel G. Engel)

Underwater demolition experts pave the way for the invasion of a Japanese-held island.
Standard, efficient war fare.

w John Tucker Battle *d* Lloyd Bacon *ph* Norbert Brodine *m* Cyril Mockridge

Richard Widmark, Dana Andrews, Gary Merrill, Jeffrey Hunter, Warren Stevens, Robert Wagner, Harvey Lembeck

'Competent, unpretentious and free from jingoism.'—*MFB*

Frogs*
US 1972 91m Movielab
AIP (George Edwards, Peter Thomas)

A remote, inhabited island in the southern States is overtaken by reptiles.
As Hitchcock might have said, the frogs is coming; instead of monsters, ordinary creepy-

crawlies in their thousands devour most of the cast. Well enough done for those with strong stomachs.

w Robert Hutchison, Robert Blees *d* George McCowan *ph* Mario Tosi *m* Les Baxter

Ray Milland, Joan Van Ark, Sam Elliott, Adam Roarke, Judy Pace

'One of the most remarkable and impressive onslaughts since *King Kong*.'—*David Pirie*

From Beyond the Grave*
GB 1973 98m Technicolor
Warner / Amicus (Milton Subotsky)

The proprietor of an East End antique shop involves his customers in horrific situations.
Reasonably lively portmanteau of tall tales from a familiar stable.

w Robin Clarke, Raymond Christodoulou *d* Kevin Connor *ph* Alan Hume *m* David Gamley *pd* Maurice Carter

David Warner, Donald Pleasance, Ian Bannen, Diana Dors, Margaret Leighton, Ian Carmichael, Nyree Dawn Porter, Ian Ogilvy

From Hell to Texas
US 1958 100m Eastmancolor Cinemascope
TCF (Robert Buckner)
GB title: *Manhunt*

After accidentally killing a man, a cowboy is vengefully pursued by the victim's father.
Competent chase western with a stand against violence.

w Robert Buckner, Wendell Mayes *d* Henry Hathaway *ph* Wilfrid Cline *m* Daniele Amfitheatrof

Don Murray, Diane Varsi, Chill Wills, Dennis Hopper, R. G. Armstrong, Margo, Jay C. Flippen

From Here to Eternity***
US 1953 118m bw
Columbia (Buddy Adler)

Life in a Honolulu barracks at the time of Pearl Harbor.
Cleaned up and streamlined version of a bestseller in which the mainly sexual frustrations of a number of unattractive characters are laid bare. As a production, it is Hollywood in good form, and certainly took the public fancy as well as establishing Sinatra as an acting force.

w Dalton Trumbo, *novel* James Jones *d Fred Zinnemann* *ph* Burnett Guffey *m* George Duning

Burt Lancaster, Deborah Kerr, *Frank Sinatra*, Donna Reed, Ernest Borgnine, Montgomery Clift, Philip Ober, Mickey Shaughnessy

From the Earth to the Moon
US 1958 100m Technicolor
Waverley (Benedict Bogeaus)

In the 1880s an armaments millionaire finances a trip to the moon in a projectile fired by his own invention.
Cardboard science fiction, with an imposing cast at sea in an unspeakable script and an unseaworthy production.

w Robert Blees, James Leicester, *novel* Jules Verne *d* Byron Haskin *ph* Edwin DuPar *m* Louis Forbes *ad* Hal Wilson Cox

Joseph Cotten, George Sanders, Henry Daniell, Carl Esmond, Melville Cooper, Don Dubbins, Debra Paget, Patric Knowles

From Russia with Love***
GB 1963 118m Technicolor
UA / Eon (Harry Saltzman, Albert Broccoli)

A Russian spy joins an international crime organization and develops a plan to kill James Bond and steal a coding machine.
The second Bond adventure and possibly the best, with Istanbul and Venice for backdrops and climaxes involving a speeding train and a helicopter. Arrant nonsense with tongue in cheek, on a big budget.

w Richard Maibaum, Johanna Harwood, novel Ian Fleming *d* Terence Young *ph Ted Moore* *m* John Barry *titles Robert Brownjohn*

Sean Connery, Robert Shaw, Pedro Armendariz, Daniela Bianchi, *Lotte Lenya*, Bernard Lee, Eunice Gayson, Lois Maxwell

From the Terrace
US 1960 144m De Luxe Cinemascope
TCF / Linebrook (Mark Robson)

Life among Pennsylvania's idle rich.
Heavy-going family melodrama from a bestseller peopled with boorish characters.

w Ernest Lehman, *novel* John O'Hara *d* Mark Robson *ph* Leo Tover *m* Elmer Bernstein

Paul Newman, Joanne Woodward, Myrna Loy, Ina Balin, Leon Ames, Felix Aylmer, George Grizzard, Patrick O'Neal, Elizabeth Allen

From This Day Forward***
US 1946 95m bw
RKO (William L. Pereira)

After World War II, a New York couple think back to their early years in the poverty-stricken thirties.

Effective sentimental realism coupled with Hollywood professionalism made this film more memorable than it may sound.

w Hugo Butler, Garson Kanin, *novel* All Brides Are Beautiful by Thomas Bell *d John Berry* *ph George Barnes* *m* Leigh Harline

Joan Fontaine, Mark Stevens, Rosemary de Camp, Henry Morgan, Wally Brown, Arline Judge, Bobby Driscoll, Mary Treen

'Distinguished from the usual film about Young Love and Young Marriage by irony, poetry and realism.'—*Richard Winnington*

The Front Page****

US 1931 101m bw
Howard Hughes

A Chicago reporter wants to retire and marry, but is tricked by his scheming editor into covering one last case.
Brilliant early talkie perfectly transferring into screen terms a stage classic of the twenties. Superficially a shade primitive now, its essential power remains.

w Bartlett Cormack, Charles Lederer, *play Charles MacArthur, Ben Hecht d Lewis Milestone ph* Glen MacWilliams

Adolphe Menjou, Pat O'Brien, Mary Brian, Edward Everett Horton, Walter Catlett, George E. Stone, Mae Clarke, Slim Summerville, Frank McHugh

'The most riproaring movie that ever came out of Hollywood.'—*Pare Lorentz*
† Remade 1940 as *His Girl Friday* (qv).

The Front Page**

US 1974 105m Technicolor Panavision
U-I (Paul Monash)

Disappointing Billy Wilder remake, relying overmuch on bad language and farcical intrusions, while tending to jettison the plot in the latter half. Some laughs nevertheless.

w Billy Wilder, I. A. L. Diamond *d* Billy Wilder *ph* Jordan S. Cronenweth *m* Billy May

Walter Matthau, Jack Lemmon, Susan Sarandon, *David Wayne*, Carol Burnett, Vincent Gardenia, Allen Garfield, Herb Edelmann, Charles Durning, *Austin Pendleton*

'The signs of coarsening in Wilder's comedy technique are unmistakable.'—*MFB*

Front Page Story*

GB 1953 99m bw
British Lion / Jay Lewis

A day in the life of a Fleet Street newspaper, when the editor is torn between several big stories and nearly loses his wife.
Dogged 'slice of life' drama with few excitements but some incidental entertainment and a production of routine competence.

w Jay Lewis, Jack Howells *d* Gordon Parry *ph* Gilbert Taylor *m* Jackie Brown

Jack Hawkins, Elizabeth Allan, Derek Farr, Michael Goodliffe, Martin Miller

Front Page Woman**

US 1935 82m bw
Warner (Samuel Bischoff)

Rival reporters try to outshine each other.
Lively comedy-melodrama very typical of its style and time.

w Laird Doyle, Lillie Hayward, Roy Chanslor *d* Michael Curtiz *ph* Tony Gaudio *m* Leo Forbstein

Bette Davis, George Brent, Roscoe Karns, Wini Shaw,
J. Carrol Naish, Walter Walker

Frontier Gal

US 1945 84m Technicolor
Universal (Michael Fessier, Ernest Pagano)
GB title: *The Bride Wasn't Willing*

An outlaw weds a saloon girl at pistol point; emerging five years later from prison, he finds he has a daughter.
Rambling western with some pretensions to humour and sentiment; not a success, but it established de Carlo as a star.

w Michael Fessier, Ernest Pagano *d* Charles Lamont *ph* George Robinson, Charles Boyle *m* Frank Skinner

Yvonne de Carlo, Rod Cameron, Sheldon Leonard, Andy Devine, Fuzzy Knight, Andrew Tombes, Clara Blandick

The Frozen Limits*

GB 1939 84m bw
Gainsborough (Edward Black)

Six impecunious comedians hear of the Yukon gold rush, and join it . . . forty years too late.
The Crazy Gang not quite at its best, but working hard, with a few hilarious moments and a special assist from Moore Marriott.

w Marriott Edgar, Val Guest, J. O. C. Orton d Marcel Varnel

Flanagan and Allen, Nervo and Knox, Naughton and Gold, *Moore Marriott*, Eileen Bell, Anthony Hulme, Bernard Lee, Eric Clavering

'The funniest English picture yet produced . . . it can bear comparison with *Safety Last* and *The General*.'—*Graham Greene*

Fu Manchu
The Yellow Peril, or evil Oriental master criminal, was created by Sax Rohmer in a 1911 novel, which led to 13 more plus some short stories. A long series of British two-reelers was made in the twenties, and talking films are as follows:

1929: THE MYSTERIOUS DR FU MANCHU, with Warner Oland (Paramount)
1930: THE RETURN OF DR FU MANCHU (ditto)
1931: DAUGHTER OF THE DRAGON (ditto)
1932: THE MASK OF FU MANCHU (qv) with Boris Karloff (MGM)
1939: DRUMS OF FU MANCHU, with Henry Brandon (Republic serial).

The remainder are British productions by Harry Alan Towers, with Christopher Lee:
1965: THE FACE OF FU MANCHU (qv)
1966: BRIDES OF FU MANCHU
1968: THE VENGEANCE OF FU MANCHU
1969: THE BLOOD OF FU MANCHU
1970: THE CASTLE OF FU MANCHU

The Fugitive*
US 1947 104m bw
Argosy (Merian C. Cooper, John Ford)

In an anti-clerical country, a priest is on the run.
Ford's attempt to do a Mexican *Informer* is slow and rather boring, but the pictures are nice to look at even though the original novel has been totally emasculated.

w Dudley Nichols, *novel* The Power and the Glory by Graham Greene *d John Ford ph Gabriel Figueroa m* Richard Hageman

Henry Fonda, Dolores del Rio, Pedro Armendariz, J. Carrol Naish, Leo Carrillo, Ward Bond, Robert Armstrong, John Qualen

'A symphony of light and shade, of deafening din and silence, of sweeping movement and repose.'—*Bosley Crowther*

'The most pretentious travesty of a literary work since *For Whom the Bell Tolls*.'—*Richard Winnington*

The Fugitive Kind
US 1960 121m bw
UA / Martin Jurow / Richard A. Shepherd / Pennebaker

A Mississippi drifter in a small strange town runs into trouble with women.
Doom-laden melodrama, almost a parody of the author's works, full of cancer patients, nympho-dipsos, and cemetery seductions; we are however spared the final castration.

w Tennessee Williams, Meade Roberts, *play* Orpheus Descending by Tennessee Williams *d* Sidney Lumet *ph* Boris Kaufman *m* Kenyon Hopkins *pd* Richard Sylbert

Marlon Brando, Anna Magnani, Joanne Woodward, Victor Jory, Maureen Stapleton, R. G. Armstrong

'A series of mythological engravings, determined by a literary text and a lurid concept of hell on earth.'—*Peter John Dyer*

Full of Life*
US 1956 91m bw
Columbia (Fred Kohlmar)

A poor New York/Italian couple expect a baby.
Domestic comedy drama with good scenes but fatally uncertain mood.

w John Fante, from his novel *d* Richard Quine *ph* Charles Lawton Jnr *m* George Duning

Judy Holliday, Richard Conte, Esther Minciotti, Salvatore Baccaloni

The Full Treatment
GB 1960 109m bw Megascope
Columbia / Hilary / Falcon (Val Guest)
US title: *Stop Me Before I Kill*

A racing driver crashes and subsequently tries to murder his wife; psychiatric help leads to further gruesome goings-on.
Variation on *Les Diaboliques*, with very little mystery and too much talk from boring characters.

w Val Guest, Ronald Scott Thorn, *novel* Ronald Scott Thorn *d* Val Guest *ph* Gilbert Taylor *m* Stanley Black

Ronald Lewis, Diane Cilento, Claude Dauphin, Françoise Rosay, Bernard Braden

The Fuller Brush Girl*
US 1950 85m bw
Columbia (S. Sylvan Simon)

A cosmetics saleslady gets involved in murder.
Fairly amusing slapstick mystery with the star in good form.

w Frank Tashlin d Lloyd Bacon *ph* Charles Lawton *m* Morris Stoloff

Lucille Ball, Eddie Albert, Carl Benton Reid, Gale Robbins, Jeff Connell, John Litel, Jerome Cowan, Lee Patrick

The Fuller Brush Man*
US 1948 93m bw
Columbia (S. Sylvan Simon)
GB title: *That Mad Mr Jones*

A door-to-door salesman gets involved in homicide.
Bright star comedy with slow patches.

w Frank Tashlin, Devery Freeman *d* S. Sylvan Simon *ph* Leslie White *m* Heinz Roemheld

Red Skelton, Janet Blair, Don McGuire, Adele Jergens

Fun and Fancy Free*
US 1947 73m Technicolor
Walt Disney (Ben Sharpsteen)

Cartoon stories told by and to Jiminy Cricket and Edgar Bergen.
Variable Disney ragbag including *Bongo* the Bear, and a lengthy version of *Jack and the Beanstalk*.

w various *d* various

Fun in Acapulco
US 1963 97m Technicolor
Paramount / Hal B. Wallis

A trapeze artist becomes a lifeguard and is pursued by a lady bullfighter.
Dim comedy musical.

w Allan Weiss *d* Richard Thorpe *ph* Daniel Fapp *m* Joseph J. Lilley

Elvis Presley, Ursula Andress, Paul Lukas

Funeral in Berlin*
GB 1967 102m Technicolor
Paramount / Harry Saltzman (Charles Kasher)

Harry Palmer is sent to Berlin to check a story that a Russian colonel wants to defect.
Initially intriguing, finally confusing, always depressing spy yarn in the sixties manner, i.e. with every character devious and no one a hero. Good production.

w Evan Jones, *novel* The Berlin Memorandum by Len Deighton *d* Guy Hamilton *ph* Otto Heller *m* Konrad Elfers *pd* Ken Adam

Michael Caine, *Oscar Homolka*, Eva Renzi, Paul Hubschmid, *Hugh Burden*, Guy Doleman, Rachel Gurney

'So many twists that even Sherlock Holmes might have been baffled . . . before long it becomes difficult to remember who is watching whom and why, or indeed whether anybody *was* watching anybody at any given moment.'—*Tom Milne*

† Second in the Harry Palmer series, of which the first was *The Ipcress File* and the third *Billion Dollar Brain* (both qv).

Funny Face**
US 1956 103m Technicolor
Vistavision
Paramount (Roger Edens)

A fashion editor and photographer choose a shy bookstore attendant as their 'quality woman'.
Stylish, wistful musical with good numbers but drawn-out dialogue; finally a shade too sophisticated and a whole lot too fey.

w Leonard Gershe *d Stanley Donen ph Ray June m/ly George and Ira Gershwin*

Fred Astaire, Audrey Hepburn, Kay Thompson, Michel Auclair, Robert Flemyng

Funny Girl**
US 1968 169m Technicolor
Panavision 70
Columbia / Rastar (Ray Stark)

Fanny Brice, an ugly Jewish girl from New York's east side, becomes a big Broadway star but loses her husband in the process.
Interminable cliché-ridden musical drama relieved by a few good numbers, high production gloss and the unveiling of a new powerhouse star.

w Isobel Lennart, from her play *d* William Wyler *ph* Harry Stradling *m Jule Styne ly* Bob Merrill *pd* Gene Callahan

Barbra Streisand, Omar Sharif, Walter Pidgeon, Kay Medford, Anne Francis, Lee Allen, Gerald Mohr, Frank Faylen

Funny Lady*
US 1975 138m Eastmancolor
Columbia / Rastar / Persky–Bright / Vista (Ray Stark)

Fanny Brice marries Billy Rose.
Unnecessary sequel to the above, entirely predictable and far from the truth, but with the occasional pleasures that a high budget brings.

w Jay Presson Allen, Arnold Schulman *d* Herbert Ross *ph James Wong Howe m/ly* various *pd* George Jenkins

Barbra Streisand, James Caan, *Ben Vereen*, Omar Sharif, Roddy McDowall, Larry Gates

'The plot line is as slackly handled as the milieu.'—*Geoff Brown*

'As Fanny Brice, Streisand is no longer human; she's like a bitchy female impersonator imitating Barbra Streisand.'—*New Yorker*

A Funny Thing Happened on the Way to the Forum**
US 1966 99m De Luxe
UA / Quadrangle (Melvin Frank)

In ancient Rome, a conniving slave schemes to win his freedom.
Bawdy farce from a Broadway musical inspired by Plautus but with a New York Jewish atmosphere. The film pays scant attention to the comic numbers that made the show a hit, but adds some style of its own, including a free-for-all slapstick climax.

w Melvin Frank, Michael Pertwee, *musical*

comedy Burt Shevelove, Larry Gelbart *m/ly Stephen Sondheim d Richard Lester ph Nicolas Roeg pd* Tony Walton *titles* Richard Williams

Zero Mostel, Phil Silvers, Michael Crawford, Jack Gilford, *Michael Hordern*, Buster Keaton, Patricia Jessel, Leon Greene, Beatrix Lehmann

'Actors have to be very fast and very sly to make themselves felt amid the flash and glitter of a characteristic piece of Lester film-mosaic.'—*John Russell Taylor*

'He proceeds by fits and starts and leaves jokes suspended in mid-air . . . like coitus interruptus going on forever.'—*Pauline Kael*

The Furies*
US 1950 109m bw
Paramount / Hal B. Wallis

A cattle baron feuds with his tempestuous daughter.
Interesting but heavy-going western, more solemn than stimulating despite its Freudian excesses.

w Charles Schnee, *novel* Niven Busch *d* Anthony Mann *ph* Victor Milner *m* Franz Waxman

Barbara Stanwyck, *Walter Huston*, Wendell Corey, Judith Anderson, Gilbert Roland, Thomas Gomez, Beulah Bondi, Wallace Ford, Albert Dekker, Blanche Yurka

'An immoral saga, capably mounted, with some pretentious psychological trimmings.'—*MFB*

Fury***
US 1936 94m bw
MGM (Joseph L. Mankiewicz)

A traveller in a small town is mistaken for a murderer and apparently lynched; he escapes in a fire but determines to have his persecutors hanged for his murder.
Powerful drama which becomes artificial in its latter stages but remains its director's best American film.

w Bartlett Cormack, Fritz Lang, *story* Norman Krasna *d Fritz Lang ph Joseph Ruttenberg m* Franz Waxman

Spencer Tracy, Sylvia Sidney, Bruce Cabot, Walter Abel, Edward Ellis, Walter Brennan, Frank Albertson

'The surface of American life has been rubbed away: *Fury* gets down to the bones of the thing and shows them for what they are.'—*C. A. Lejeune*

'Since the screen began to talk, no other serious film except *The Front Page* has so clearly shown that here is a new art and what this new art can do.'—*John Marks*

'Everyday events and people suddenly took on tremendous and horrifying proportion; even the most insignificant details had a pointed meaning.'—*Lewis Jacobs*

Fury at Furnace Creek*
US 1948 88m bw
TCF

A westerner clears the name of his father, a general accused of diverting a wagon train into hostile Indian territory.
Adequate old-fashioned western with a good story line and standard excitements.

w Charles G. Booth *d* H. Bruce Humberstone *ph* Harry Jackson *m* Alfred Newman

Victor Mature, Coleen Gray, Glenn Langan, Reginald Gardiner

Futureworld*
US 1976 107m Metrocolor
AIP (James T. Aubrey Jnr, Paul Lazarus III)

The robot factory seen in *Westworld* (qv) now aims at world domination by duplicating influential figures.
Amusing and fairly suspenseful fantasy with a bigger budget than its predecessor.

w Mayo Simon, George Schenck *d* Richard T. Heffron *ph* Howard Schwarz, Sol Polito *m* Fred Karlin

Peter Fonda, Blythe Danner, Arthur Hill, Yul Brynner, John Ryan, Stuart Margolin, Jim Antonio

Fuzz*
US 1972 93m De Luxe
UA / Filmways / Javelin (Jack Farren)

Detectives of Boston's 87th precinct try to catch a rapist.
A black farce devoted to police incompetence, though taken from a straight 'Ed McBain' story. Brisk and sometimes funny.

w Evan Hunter ('Ed McBain') *d* Richard A. Colla *ph* Jacques Marquette *m* Dave Grusin

Burt Reynolds, Raquel Welch, Jack Weston, Yul Brynner, Tom Skerritt, James McEachin

The Fuzzy Pink Nightgown
US 1957 88m bw
UA / Russ–Field (Robert Waterfield)

A glamorous film star falls in love with her kidnapper.
Unendurable cheap romantic farce.

w Richard Alan Simmons, *novel* Sylvia Tate *d* Norman Taurog *ph* Joseph La Shelle

Jane Russell, Ralph Meeker, Keenan Wynn, Fred Clark

G

GI Blues
US 1960 104m Technicolor
Paramount / Hal B. Wallis (Paul Nathan)

A guitar-playing gunner with the American army in West Germany falls for a cabaret dancer.
Routine star vehicle marking Presley's return from military service.

w Edmund Beloin, Henry Garson *d* Norman Taurog *ph* Loyal Griggs *m* Joseph J. Lilley

Elvis Presley, Juliet Prowse, Robert Ivers, Leticia Roman, Arch Johnson

G Men***
US 1935 85m bw
Warner (Lou Edelman)

A young lawyer becomes a G-man to avenge the murder of his best friend, and finds himself tracking down another old friend who is a gangster.
In the face of mounting criticism of their melodramas making heroes of gangsters, Warners pulled a clever switch by showing the same crimes from a different angle, that of the law enforcer. As an action show it became pretty good after a slow start.

w Seton I. Miller d William Keighley *ph* Sol Polito *m* Leo Forbstein

James Cagney, Ann Dvorak, Margaret Lindsay, Robert Armstrong, Barton MacLane, Lloyd Nolan, William Harrigan

'The gangster is back, racing madly through one of the fastest melodramas ever made.'—*New York Sun*

'The headiest dose of gunplay that Hollywood has unleashed in recent months.'—*André Sennwald, New York Times*

Gabriel over the White House*
US 1933 87m bw
MGM / Walter Wanger

A crook becomes president and mysteriously reforms.
Pleasing, dated New Deal fantasy.

w Carey Wilson, Bertram Bloch, *novel* Rinehard by T. F. Tweed *d* Gregory La Cava *ph* Bert Glennon *m* William Axt

Walter Huston, Karen Morley, Franchot Tone, C. Henry Gordon, Samuel S. Hinds, Jean Parker, Dickie Moore

Gaby
US 1956 97m Eastmancolor
Cinemascope
MGM (Edwin H. Knopf)

Flabby remake of *Waterloo Bridge* (qv); saccharine, fussy and outmoded, despite updated settings and a happy ending.

w Albert Hackett, Frances Goodrich, Charles Lederer *d* Curtis Bernhardt *ph* Robert Planck *m* Conrad Salinger

Leslie Caron, John Kerr, Cedric Hardwicke, Taina Elg, Margalo Gillmore

Gaiety George
GB 1946 98m bw
Embassy (George King)

The career in the London theatre of Irish impresario George Howard in the early part of the century.
Tepid musical biopic.

w Katherine Strueby *d* George King

Richard Greene, Ann Todd, Peter Graves, Hazel Court, Leni Lynn, Ursula Jeans, Morland Graham, Frank Pettingell

Gaily, Gaily**
US 1969 117m De Luxe
UA / Mirisch / Cartier
GB title: *Chicago, Chicago*

The early life on a Chicago newspaper of Ben Hecht.
Busy, farcical, melodramatic, always interesting biopic of the formative years of a celebrated literary figure.

w Abram S. Ginnes, book Ben Hecht d Norman Jewison ph Richard Kline *m* Henry Mancini *pd* Robert Boyle

Beau Bridges, Melina Mercouri, *Brian Keith*, George Kennedy, Hume Cronyn, Margot Kidder, Wilfrid Hyde White, Melodie Johnson, John Randolph

Galileo*
GB 1975 145m Eastmancolor
Ely Landau / Cinevision

In the 17th century, a poor Italian mathematics teacher has trouble establishing his 'heretical' astronomical theories.
Overlong play-on-celluloid for the American Film Theatre: very decently made and acted, it lacks inspiration.

w Barbara Bray, Joseph Losey, *play* Bertolt Brecht *d* Joseph Losey *ph* Michael Reed *m* Hanns Eisler

Topol, Edward Fox, Michel Lonsdale, Richard O'Callaghan, Tom Conti, Judy Parfitt, Patrick Magee, Michael Gough, John Gielgud, Colin Blakely, Margaret Leighton, Clive Revill

The Gallant Hours*
US 1959 115m bw
UA / James Cagney / Robert Montgomery

Episodes in the career of Admiral William F. Halsey.
Adulatory but physically restrained biopic which covers World War II with barely a scene outside control room sets: interesting but finally too talky.

w Beirne Lay Jnr, Frank D. Gilroy *d* Robert Montgomery *ph* Joe MacDonald *m* Roger Wagner

James Cagney, Dennis Weaver, Richard Jaeckel, Ward Costello, Carl Benton Reid

'Imaginatively conceived but erroneously realized.'—*Robert Vas*

Gallant Journey
US 1946 86m bw
Columbia

The life of an early American aviation pioneer.
Curious biopic, very tentatively done, about an inventor so obscure as to be virtually fictitious. Sentimental, artificial, but harmless.

w Byron Morgan, William A. Wellman *d* William A. Wellman *ph* Burnett Guffey *m* Martin Skiles

Glenn Ford, Janet Blair, Charles Ruggles, Henry Travers, Arthur Shields

Gallant Lady
US 1933 84m bw
Darryl F. Zanuck

A woman allows her illegitimate son to be adopted, but years later marries his stepfather.
A tearjerker very typical of its time, moderately well assembled; later remade as *Always Goodbye* (qv).

w Sam Mintz, *story* Gilbert Emery, Doug Doty *d* Gregory La Cava *ph* Peverell Marley

Ann Harding, Clive Brook, Otto Kruger, Tullio Carminati, Dickie Moore, Janet Beecher

The Galloping Major*
GB 1951 82m bw
British Lion / Romulus (Monja Danischewsky)

A group of suburbanites form a syndicate to buy a racehorse.
Rather contrived and imitative sub-Ealing comedy which fails to generate much steam.

w Monja Danischewsky, Henry Cornelius *d* Henry Cornelius *ph* Stan Pavey *m* Georges Auric

Basil Radford, Janette Scott, Hugh Griffith, Jimmy Hanley, René Ray, Joyce Grenfell, Sidney Tafler, Charles Victor, A. E. Matthews

Gambit**
US 1966 109m Techniscope
Universal (Leo L. Fuchs)

A cockney thief conspires with a Eurasian girl to rob a multi-millionaire of a prize statue.
An enjoyably light pattern of cross and double cross is well sustained to the end.

w Jack Davies, Alvin Sargent *d* Ronald Neame *ph* Clifford Stine *m* Maurice Jarre

Michael Caine, Shirley Maclaine, Herbert Lom, John Abbott, Roger C. Carmel, Arnold Moss

The Gambler**
US 1975 111m Eastmancolor
Paramount (Irwin Winkler, Robert Chartoff)

A compulsive gambler has a will to lose.
Flashily made but basically uninteresting sub-Freudian study, vaguely based on Dostoievsky.

w James Tomack *d* Karel Reisz *ph* Victor J. Kemper *m* Mahler *md* Jerry Fielding

James Caan, Paul Sorvino, Lauren Hutton, Morris Carnovsky, Jacqueline Brookes, Burt Young

Gambler from Natchez
US 1954 88m Technicolor
TCF / Panoramic

A professional gambler returns to New Orleans to avenge his father's murder, and disposes of his enemies one by one.
Mildly watchable semi-western with a plot borrowed from *The Count of Monte Cristo*.

w Gerald Drayson Adams, Irving Wallace *d* Henry Levin *ph* Lloyd Ahern *m* Lionel Newman

Dale Robertson, Debra Paget, Thomas Gomez, Kevin McCarthy

Gambling Lady*
US 1934 66m bw
Warner

The daughter of a gambling suicide follows in father's footsteps and becomes involved in murder.
Fast-paced melodrama with a happy ending: smart entertainment of its time.

w Ralph Block, Doris Malloy *d* Archie Mayo *ph* George Barnes

Barbara Stanwyck, Joel McCrea, Pat O'Brien, Claire Dodd, C. Aubrey Smith, Robert Barrat, Philip Reed

A Game of Death
US 1945 72m bw
RKO

Cheap remake of *The Most Dangerous Game* (qv); excitement dissipated by poor handling.

w Norman Houston *d* Robert Wise *ph* J. Roy Hunt *m* Paul Sawtell

John Loder, Audrey Long, Edgar Barrier, Russell Wade, Russell Hicks

Games*
US 1967 100m Techniscope
Universal (George Edwards)

A sophisticated New York couple play complex games, one of which turns out to have a deadly effect.
Tedious variation on *Les Diaboliques*, with interesting moments.

w Gene Kearney *d Curtis Harrington* *ph* William A. Fraker *m* Samuel Matlovsky

Simone Signoret, James Caan, Katharine Ross, Don Stroud, Kent Smith, Estelle Winwood, Marjorie Bennett

The Games*
GB 1970 97m De Luxe Panavision
TCF (Lester Linsk)

Four men in various parts of the world prepare to take part in the marathon at the Rome Olympics.
Tepid multi-drama with good locations and a well-shot and exciting climactic race.

w Erich Segal, *novel* Hugh Atkinson *d* Michael Winner *ph Robert Paynter* *m* Francis Lai

Stanley Baker, Michael Crawford, Ryan O'Neal, Charles Aznavour, Jeremy Kemp, Elaine Taylor, Kent Smith, Mona Washbourne

The Gang That Couldn't Shoot Straight
US 1971 96m Metrocolor
MGM (Robert Chartoff, Irwin Winkler)

Members of the New York Mafia organize a cycle race and start antagonisms that end in mass murder.
Unfunny black comedy with all concerned gesticulating wildly.

w Waldo Salt, *novel* Jimmy Breslin *d* James Goldstone *ph* Owen Roizman *m* Dave Grusin

Jerry Orbach, Leigh Taylor-Young, Jo Van Fleet, Lionel Stander, Robert de Niro, Herve Villechaize, Joe Santos

The Gang's All Here*
GB 1939 77m bw
ABP (Walter C. Mycroft, Jack Buchanan)
US title: *The Amazing Mr Forrest*

An insurance investigator goes undercover among gangsters.
Lively comedy-melodrama.

w Ralph Spence *d* Thornton Freeland

Jack Buchanan, Googie Withers, Edward Everett Horton, Syd Walker, Otto Kruger, Jack La Rue, Walter Rilla

The Gang's All Here**
US 1943 103m Technicolor
TCF (William Le Baron)
GB title: *The Girls He Left Behind*

A serviceman is caught between a fiery entertainer and a Park Avenue socialite.
Frenetic wartime musical with some of Busby Berkeley's most outré choreography (e.g. The Lady in the Tutti Frutti Hat) and gleamingly effective Technicolor.

w Walter Bullock *d/ch Busby Berkeley* *ph Edward Cronjager* *md* Alfred Newman *songs* Leo Robin, Harry Warren

Alice Faye, Carmen Miranda, James Ellison, Phil Baker, Benny Goodman, Charlotte Greenwood, Eugene Pallette, Edward Everett Horton

'Those who consider Berkeley a master consider this film his masterpiece.'—*New Yorker, 1976*

The Garden of Allah**
US 1936 80m Technicolor
David O. Selznick

A disenchanted socialite falls in love with a renegade monk in the Algerian desert.
Arty old-fashioned romantic star vehicle; great to look at, and marking a genuine advance in colour photography, but dramatically a bit of a drag.

w W. P. Lipscomb, Lynn Riggs, *novel* Robert Hichens *d* Richard Boleslawski *ph W. Howard Greene, Harold Rosson m Max Steiner* *ad* Sturges Carne, Lyle Wheeler

Marlene Dietrich, Charles Boyer, Basil Rathbone, Tilly Losch, Edward Boyle

'Hopelessly dated folderol.'—*J. R. Parish*

'The juiciest tale of woe ever, produced in poshly lurid colour, with a Max Steiner score poured on top.'—*Judith Crist*

Garden of Evil*
US 1954 100m Technicolor Cinemascope
TCF (Charles Brackett)

En route to the Californian goldfields an ex-sheriff and a gambler help a woman to rescue her husband from a mine, but are trapped by Indians.
High-flying western melodrama with the principals glowering at each other. Stock situations quite skilfully compiled.

w Frank Fenton *d* Henry Hathaway *ph* Milton Krasner *m Bernard Herrmann*

Susan Hayward, Gary Cooper, Richard Widmark, Hugh Marlowe, Cameron Mitchell

Gargoyles*
US 1972 74m colour TVM
Tomorrow (Roger Gimbel)

An anthropologist and his daughter in Mexico are menaced by ancient legendary creatures.
Foolish but effective horror piece.

w Elinor and Stephen Karpf *d* B. W. L. Norton

Cornel Wilde, Jennifer Salt, Grayson Hall

The Garment Jungle*
US 1957 88m bw
Columbia (Harry Kleiner)

Union and gangster problems abound for a family in the New York clothing business.
Reasonably powerful melodrama fashioned from familiar material in the wake of *On the Waterfront*.

w Harry Kleiner *d* Robert Aldrich, Vincent Sherman *ph* Joseph Biroc *m* Leith Stevens

Lee J. Cobb, Kerwin Mathews, Gia Scala, Richard Boone, Valerie French, Robert Loggia, Joseph Wiseman

Gas! or It Became Necessary to Destroy the World in Order to Save It
US 1970 79m Movielab
AIP / San Jacinto (Roger Corman)

A gas which speeds up the ageing process is accidentally released and kills everyone over twenty-five.
Psychedelic sci-fi for the Easy Rider set. Very mildly diverting.

w Graham Armitage *d* Roger Corman *ph* Ron Dexter *m* Country Joe and the Fish

Robert Corff, Elaine Giftos, Pat Patterson, Graham Armitage, Alex Wilson, Ben Vereen, Bud Cort

Gasbags*
GB 1940 77m bw
Gainsborough (Edward Black)

Airmen stranded in Germany by a barrage balloon return in a captured secret weapon.
Fast-moving knockabout from the Crazy Gang; often inventive despite reach-me-down script and production.

w Val Guest, Marriott Edgar *d* Marcel Varnel

Flanagan and Allen, Nervo and Knox, Naughton and Gold, Moore Marriott, Wally Patch, Peter Gawthorne, Frederick Valk

Gaslight****
GB 1939 88m bw
British National (John Corfield)
US title: *Angel Street*

A Victorian schizophrenic drives his wife insane when she seems likely to stumble on his guilty secret of an old murder and hidden rubies.
Modest but absolutely effective film version of a superb piece of suspense theatre.

w A. R. Rawlinson, Bridget Boland, *play Patrick Hamilton d Thorold Dickinson*

Anton Walbrook, Diana Wynyard, Frank Pettingell, Cathleen Cordell, Robert Newton, Jimmy Hanley

'The electric sense of tension and mid-Victorian atmosphere are entirely cinematic.'—*Sequence, 1950*

Gaslight**
US 1944 114m bw
MGM (Arthur Hornblow Jnr)
GB title: *The Murder in Thornton Square*

Grossly overblown and less effective version of the above, but with moments of power, effective performances and superior production.

w John Van Druten, Walter Reisch, John L. Balderston *d George Cukor ph Joseph Ruttenberg m* Bronislau Kaper *ad Cedric Gibbons*

Charles Boyer, Ingrid Bergman, Joseph Cotten, Dame May Whitty, Barbara Everest, *Angela Lansbury*, Edmund Breon, Halliwell Hobbes

A Gathering of Eagles
US 1962 115m Eastmancolor
U-I (Sy Bartlett)

A colonel becomes unpopular when he strives to improve the efficiency of a Strategic Air Command base.
Tame revamp of *Twelve O'clock High* without the justification of war; all strictly routine and perfectly dull.

w Robert Pirosh *d* Delbert Mann *ph* Russell Harlan *m* Jerry Goldsmith

Rock Hudson, Mary Peach, Rod Taylor, Barry Sullivan, Kevin McCarthy

Gawain and the Green Knight*
GB 1973 93m Technicolor Panavision
UA / Sancrest (Philip Breen)

The medieval legend of a supernatural knight who challenges the king's men to kill him.
Enterprising if unsuccessful low-budget attempt to create a medieval world; too long by half.

w Philip Green, Stephen Weeks *d* Stephen Weeks *ph* Ian Wilson *m* Ron Goodwin
ad Anthony Woollard

Murray Head, Ciaran Madden, Nigel Green, Anthony Sharp, Robert Hardy, Murray Melvin

The Gay Bride
US 1934 80m bw
MGM

A gold-digging chorus girl marries a racketeer but soon becomes a widow.
Misfiring satirical melodrama which quickly becomes tedious.

w Bella and Samuel Spewack, *story* Repeal by Charles Francis Coe *d* Jack Conway *ph* Ray June

Carole Lombard, Chester Morris, Zasu Pitts, Nat Pendleton, Leo Carrillo

The Gay Deception*
US 1935 79m bw
TCF (Jesse L. Lasky)

A Ruritanian prince becomes a doorman at a swank New York hotel, and marries a secretary.
Lightly-handled Cinderella story showing most of its director's accomplishment.

w Stephen Morehouse Avery, Don Hartman
d William Wyler *ph* Joseph Valentine

Francis Lederer, Frances Dee, Benita Hume, Alan Mowbray, Akim Tamiroff, Lennox Pawle, Richard Carle, Lionel Stander

The Gay Desperado**
US 1936 85m bw
Mary Pickford

An heiress is held for ransom by a romantic bandit.
Very light, quite amusing, sometimes irritatingly skittish musical spoof sparked by the director's ideas.

d Rouben Mamoulian *m* Alfred Newman

Ida Lupino, Nino Martini, Leo Carrillo, Harold Huber, Mischa Auer

'One of the best light comedies of the year . . . Mr Mamoulian's camera is very persuasive.'—*Graham Greene*

The Gay Divorcee****
US 1934 107m bw
RKO (Pandro S. Berman)
GB title: *The Gay Divorce*

A would-be divorcee in a Brighton hotel mistakes an author who loves her for a professional co-respondent.
Wildly and hilariously dated comedy musical with splendidly archaic comedy routines supporting Hollywood's great new dance team in their first big success. Not much dancing, but 'The Continental' is a show-stopper.

w George Marion Jnr, Dorothy Yost, Edward Kaufman, *musical comedy* Dwight Taylor
d Mark Sandrich *ph* David Abel *md* Max Steiner *songs* various *sp Vernon Walker*
ad Van Nest Polglase, Carroll Clark

Fred Astaire, Ginger Rogers, Edward Everett Horton, Alice Brady, Erik Rhodes, Eric Blore, Lillian Miles, Betty Grable

Gay Purree*
US 1962 85m Technicolor
UPA

A country cat goes to Paris and is Shanghaied.
Feature cartoon similar to Disney's later *The Aristocats* and about as good, i.e. not quite up to the best standards.

w Dorothy and Chuck Jones *d* Abe Levitow
md Mort Lindsey

voices Judy Garland, Robert Goulet, Hermione Gingold

The Gay Sisters*
US 1942 110m bw
Warner (Henry Blanke)

Three sisters refuse to sell their aristocratic New York mansion to make way for development.
Slowish but quite interesting family drama with Chekhovian touches.

w Lenore Coffee, *novel* Stephen Longstreet
d Irving Rapper *ph* Sol Polito *m* Max Steiner

Barbara Stanwyck, George Brent, Geraldine Fitzgerald, Donald Crisp, *Gig Young* (so named after his part in this film; formerly Byron Barr), Nancy Coleman, Gene Lockhart, Larry Simms, Donald Woods, Grant Mitchell

The Gazebo*
US 1959 102m bw
MGM / Avon (Lawrence Weingarten)

A TV writer kills a blackmailer (he thinks) and hides his body in the garden.
Frenetic black comedy which must have worked better on the stage but produces a few laughs.

w George Wells, *play* Alec Coppel *d* George Marshall *ph* Paul C. Vogel *m* Jeff Alexander

Glenn Ford, Debbie Reynolds, Carl Reiner, John McGiver, Mabel Albertson, Doro Merande, Zasu Pitts, Martin Landau

The Geisha Boy
US 1958 98m Technicolor Vistavision
Paramount (Jerry Lewis)

A third-rate magician joins a USO entertainment tour in Japan.
Disconnected farce which amuses only fitfully, and actively displeases when it becomes sentimental with the star drooling over a baby.

wd Frank Tashlin *ph* Haskell Boggs *m* Walter Scharf

Jerry Lewis, Marie MacDonald, Barton MacLane, Sessue Hayakawa, Suzanne Pleshette

Gemini Man
US 1976 74m Technicolor TVM
Universal

Recasting of the failed *Invisible Man* series; not much better.

w Leslie Stevens *d* Alan Levi

Ben Murphy

The Gene Krupa Story
US 1959 101m bw
Columbia (Philip A. Waxman)
GB title: *Drum Crazy*

A successful jazz drummer is convicted on a drugs charge and falls from grace.
Dreary biopic with the expected music track.

w Orin Jannings *d* Don Weis *ph* Charles Lawton Jnr *m* Leith Stevens

Sal Mineo, Susan Kohner, James Darren, Susan Oliver, Yvonne Craig, Lawrence Dobkin, Celia Lovsky; and Red Nichols, Shelly Manne, Buddy Lester

The General Died at Dawn**
US 1936 93m bw
Paramount

A mercenary in China overcomes an evil warlord and falls in love with a spy.
Heavy-going but very decorative studio-bound intrigue which seems to take place on the old *Shanghai Express* sets with an extra infusion of dry ice. An intellectual's picture of its day.

w Clifford Odets *d Lewis Milestone ph Victor Milner* *m* Werner Janssen, Gerard Carbonara

Gary Cooper, Madeleine Carroll, *Akim Tamiroff, Dudley Digges*, Porter Hall, *William Frawley*

'If it were not for a rather ludicrous ending, this would be one of the best thrillers for some years.'—*Graham Greene*

'In terms of cinematic invention, a fascinating technical exercise.'—*John Baxter, 1968*

'A curious study in exoticism.'—*NFT, 1974*

Genesis II
US 1972 74m colour TVM
Warner (Gene Roddenberry)

A space scientist is buried alive while in a sealed container and awakes in the 21st century, when mankind is formed into two tribes at war with each other.
Boring and unpersuasive sci-fi with one splendid special effect of a shuttle train. Two more pilots were made (*Planet Earth, Strange New World*, qv) but the show never got on the road.

d John Llewellyn Moxey

Alex Cord, Mariette Hartley, Percy Rodrigues, Harvey Jason

Genghis Khan*
US 1964 126m Technicolor Panavision
Columbia / Irving Allen / CCC / Avala

Temujin raises a Mongol army and revenges himself on his old enemy Jamuga.
Meandering epic in which brutality alternates with pantomimish comedy and bouts of sex. Necessarily patchy but reasonably watchable.

w Clarke Reynolds, Beverly Cross *d* Henry Levin *ph* Geoffrey Unsworth *m* Ducan Radic

Omar Sharif, Stephen Boyd, Françoise Dorléac, *James Mason*, Robert Morley, Telly Savalas, Woody Strode, Eli Wallach, Yvonne Mitchell

Genevieve****
GB 1954 86m Technicolor
Rank (Henry Cornelius)

Two friendly rivals engage in a race on the way back from the Brighton veteran car rally.
One of those happy films in which for no very good or expected reason a number of modest elements merge smoothly to create an aura of

high style and memorable moments. A charmingly witty script, carefully pointed direction, attractive actors and locations, an atmosphere of light-hearted British sex and a lively harmonica theme turned it, after a slowish start, into one of Britain's biggest commercial hits and most fondly remembered comedies.

w William Rose d Henry Cornelius ph Christopher Challis *m Larry Adler* (who also played it) *ad* Michael Stringer

Dinah Sheridan, John Gregson, Kay Kendall, Kenneth More, Geoffrey Keen, Joyce Grenfell, Reginald Beckwith, Arthur Wontner

'One of the best things to have happened to British films over the last five years.'—*Gavin Lambert*

The Gentle Sex**
GB 1943 93m bw
Rank / Two Cities / Concanen (Leslie Howard, Derrick de Marney)

Seven girls from different backgrounds are conscripted into the ATS.
Unassuming war propaganda, quite pleasantly done and historically very interesting.

w Moie Charles, Aimée Stuart, Phyllis Rose, Roland Pertwee *d* Leslie Howard, Maurice Elvey

Rosamund John, Joan Greenwood, Joan Gates, Jean Gillie, Lilli Palmer, Joyce Howard, Barbara Waring, John Justin, Frederick Leister, Mary Jerrold, Everley Gregg

A Gentleman after Dark
US 1942 74m bw
Edward Small

A jewel thief comes out of prison to pay back his vindictive wife for shopping him.
Efficient melodrama of a dated kind.

w Patterson McNutt, George Bruce *d* Edwin L. Marin *ph* Milton Krasner *m* Dmitri Tiomkin

Brian Donlevy, Miriam Hopkins, Preston Foster, Harold Huber, Philip Reed, Gloria Holden, Douglass Dumbrille, Ralph Morgan

The Gentle Sergeant
US 1955 85m bw
Columbia (Fred Kohlmar)

A Jap-hating sergeant in Tokyo falls in love with a Japanese girl.
Efficient sentimental drama shot on the spot.

wd Richard Murphy *ph* Burnett Guffey *m* George Duning

Aldo Ray, Phil Carey, Dick York, Chuck Connors, Mitsuko Kimura

Gentleman Jim**
US 1942 104m bw
Warner (Robert Buckner)

The rise to fame of boxer Jim Corbett.
Cheerful biopic of a nineties show-off, mostly played for comedy.

w Vincent Lawrence, Horace McCoy, *book* The Roar of the Crowd by James J. Corbett *d Raoul Walsh ph* Sid Hickox *m* Heinz Roemheld

Errol Flynn, Alan Hale, Alexis Smith, John Loder, Jack Carson, *Ward Bond*, William Frawley, Rhys Williams, Arthur Shields

'Good-natured enough, but it lacks flavour.'—*New Yorker, 1976*

Gentleman's Agreement**
US 1947 118m bw
TCF (Darryl F. Zanuck)

A journalist poses as a Jew in order to write about anti-semitism.
Worthy melodrama which caused a sensation at the time but as a film is alas rather dull and self-satisfied.

w Moss Hart, *novel* Laura Z. Hobson *d* Elia Kazan *ph* Arthur Miller *m* Alfred Newman

Gregory Peck, Dorothy McGuire, *John Garfield*, Celeste Holm, *Anne Revere*, June Havoc, Albert Dekker, Jane Wyatt, Dean Stockwell

Gentlemen Marry Brunettes
US 1955 95m Technicolor Cinemascope
UA / Russ–Field (Richard Sale, Robert Waterfield)

Two American shopgirls seek rich husbands in Paris, and find that their aunts were notorious there.
Jaded sequel to *Gentlemen Prefer Blondes*; it barely raises a smile and the numbers are dismal.

w Mary Loos, Richard Sale *d* Richard Sale *ph* Desmond Dickinson *m* Robert Farnon *ad* Paul Sheriff *ch* Jack Cole

Jane Russell, Jeanne Crain, Alan Young, Scott Brady, Rudy Vallee

Gentlemen Prefer Blondes*
US 1953 91m Technicolor
TCF (Sol. C. Siegel)

A dumb blonde and a showgirl go to Paris in search of rich husbands.
Musicalized and updated version of the twenties satire; no real vigour, but not too bad.

w Charles Lederer, *novel* Anita Loos *d* Howard Hawks *ph* Harry J. Wild *md* Lionel Newman *songs* Jule Styne, Leo Robin *ch* Jack Cole

Jane Russell, Marilyn Monroe, Charles Coburn, Tommy Noonan, Norma Varden, Elliott Reid, George Winslow

Geordie*
GB 1955 99m Technicolor
British Lion / Argonaut (Sidney Gilliat, Frank Launder)

A weakly Scottish boy takes a physical culture course and becomes an Olympic hammer-thrower.
Slight comic fable, good to look at but without the necessary style to follow it through.

w Sidney Gilliat, Frank Launder, *novel* David Walker *d* Frank Launder *ph* Wilkie Cooper *m* William Alwyn

Bill Travers, Alastair Sim

The George Raft Story
US 1961 105m bw
Allied Artists (Ben Schwab)
GB title: *Spin of a Coin*

In twenties New York, a dancer falls in with gangsters, but eludes them when he goes to Hollywood, where his acting career is harmed by temperament.
Tepid, unconvincing biopic, rather shoddily made but with flashes of interest.

w Crane Wilbur *d* Joseph M. Newman *ph* Carl Guthrie *m* Jeff Alexander

Ray Danton, Julie London, Jayne Mansfield, Frank Gorshin, Neville Brand (as Al Capone)

George Washington Slept Here
US 1942 93m bw
Warner (Jerry Wald)

A New York couple move to a dilapidated country house.
Disappointingly stiff and ill-timed version of a play that should have been a natural.

w Everett Freeman, *play* George Kaufman, Moss Hart *d* William Keighley *ph* Ernest Haller *m* Adolph Deutsch

Jack Benny, Ann Sheridan, Percy Kilbride, Charles Coburn, Hattie McDaniel, William Tracy, Lee Patrick, John Emery, Charles Dingle

George White's Scandals*
US 1934 79m bw
Fox (Winfield Sheehan)

Romance blossoms backstage during the production of a big musical.
Revue with minimum plot and some impressive numbers.

w Jack Yellen, from the Broadway show directed by George White *d* Thornton Freeland, Harry Lachman, George White *ph* Lee Garmes, George Schneiderman *songs* various

George White, Rudy Vallee, Alice Faye, Jimmy Durante, Dixie Dunbar, Adrienne Ames, Cliff Edwards, Gertrude Michael, Gregory Ratoff

George White's 1935 Scandals*
US 1935 83m bw
Fox (Winfield Sheehan)

A small-town star is discovered by a Broadway producer.
Again, basic plot serves to introduce some pretty good acts.

w Jack Yellen, Patterson McNutt *d* George White *ph* George Schneiderman *songs* various

George White, Alice Faye, James Dunn, Eleanor Powell, Ned Sparks, Lyda Roberti, Cliff Edwards, Arline Judge

George White's Scandals*
US 1945 95m bw
RKO (Jack J. Gross, Nat Holt, George White)

Ex-Scandals girls get together, and one disappears.
Lively comedy-musical with vaudeville orientations.

w Hugh Wedlock, Parker Levy, Howard Green *d* Felix E. Feist *m* Robert de Grasse *songs* various

Joan Davis, Jack Haley, Philip Terry, Martha Holliday, Ethel Smith, Margaret Hamilton, Glenn Tryon, Jane Greer, Fritz Feld, Rufe Davis

Georgy Girl*
GB 1966 100m bw
Columbia / Everglades (Otto Plaschkes, Robert A. Goldston)

An unattractive girl is fancied by her middle-aged employer but escapes to look after the illegitimate baby of her ungrateful friend.
Frantic black farce which seems determined to shock, but has a few good scenes once you get attuned to the mood. A censorship milestone.

w Margaret Forster, Peter Nichols, *novel* Margaret Forster *d Silvio Narizzano ph* Ken Higgins *m* Alexander Faris

James Mason, Lynn Redgrave, Charlotte Rampling, Alan Bates, Bill Owen, Clare Kelly, Rachel Kempson

'Another swinging London story filled with people running through London late at night, dancing madly in the rain, and visiting deserted children's playgrounds to ride on the roundabouts.'—*MFB*

'So glib, so clever, so determinedly kinky that

everything seems to be devalued.'—*Pauline Kael*

Geronimo*
US 1939 89m bw
Paramount

The seventh cavalry gives the Indians a run for their money.
Muddled western of no discernible merit.

wd Paul H. Sloane *ph* Henry Sharp *m* Gerald Carbonara

Ellen Drew, Preston Foster, Andy Devine, Gene Lockhart, Ralph Morgan

Geronimo
US 1962 101m Technicolor Panavision
UA / Laven–Gardner–Levy

In 1883 Geronimo and his remaining Apaches seek peace but are betrayed.
Moderate western held back by script and performances.

w Pat Fielder *d* Arnold Laven *ph* Alex Phillips *m* Hugo Friedhofer

Chuck Connors, Ross Martin, Kamala Deva

Get Carter*
GB 1971 112m Metrocolor
MGM / Mike Klinger

A racketeer goes to Newcastle to avenge his brother's death at the hands of gangsters. He kills those responsible but is himself shot by a sniper.
Brutal British crime melodrama with faint echoes of Raymond Chandler. Sex and thuggery unlimited, narrative disjointed, rewards few.

wd Mike Hodges, *novel* Jack's Return Home by Ted Lewis *ph* Wolfgang Suschitsky *m* Roy Budd

Michael Caine, John Osborne, Ian Hendry, Britt Ekland

'TV on the big screen—more sex, more violence, but no more attention to motivation or plot logic.'—*Arthur Knight*

Get Christie Love
US 1974 74m colour TVM
David Wolper

Adventures of a black undercover policewoman.
The mixture as before; it led to a one-season series.

w George Kirgo *d* William Graham

Teresa Graves, Harry Guardino, Louise Sorel, Paul Stevens

The Getaway**
US 1972 122m Technicolor Todd-AO 35
Solar / First Artists (David Foster, Mitchell Brower)

A convict leaves jail and promptly joins his wife in a bank robbery.
Violent, amoral, terse and fast-moving action melodrama which generally holds the interest despite its excesses.

w Walter Hill, *novel* Jim Thompson *d Sam Peckinpah* *ph* Lucien Ballard *m* Quincy Jones

Steve McQueen, Faye Dunaway, Ben Johnson, Sally Smithers, Al Lettieri, Slim Pickens

'This pair have no mission or "meaning". As in all romances, *The Getaway* simply extracts one element of reality and dwells on it. Nor is the violence "American". Pictures like this don't fail overseas.'—*Stanley Kauffmann*

Getting Away from It All
US 1971 74m colour TVM
Palomar

Two middle class, middle-aged couples sell up and seek the simple life.
Fairly amusing contemporary comedy.

d Lee Phillips

Barbara Feldon, Jim Backus, Larry Hagman

Getting Straight*
US 1970 125m Eastmancolor
Columbia / The Organization (Richard Rush)

A political activist returns to college in order to teach and discovers the foolishness of most contemporary attitudes.
Modish comedy, too long, far too pleased with itself, and now irrevocably dated.

w Robert Kaufman *novel* Ken Kolb *d* Richard Rush *ph* Laszlo Kovacs *m* Ronald Stein

Elliott Gould, Candice Bergen, Robert F. Lyons, Jeff Corey, Max Julien, Cecil Kellaway

The Ghost and Mr Chicken
US 1965 90m Techniscope
Universal (Edward J. Montagne)

An incompetent small-town reporter finds ghosts in a local murder mansion.
Old-fashioned scare comedy starring a highly resistible comic. A big hit in American small towns.

w James Fritzell, Everett Greenbaum *d* Alan Rafkin *ph* William Margulies *m* Vic Mizzy

Don Knotts, Skip Homeier, Joan Staley, Liam Redmond, Dick Sargent, Reta Shaw

The Ghost and Mrs Muir**
US 1947 104m bw
TCF (Fred Kohlmar)

A widow refuses to be frightened away from her seaside home by the ghost of a sea captain, with whom she falls in love.
Charming sentimental fable in Hollywood's best style.

w Philip Dunne, *novel* R. A. Dick *d* Joseph L. Mankiewicz *ph Charles Lang m Bernard Herrmann ad Richard Day*

Gene Tierney, Rex Harrison, George Sanders, Edna Best, Vanessa Brown, Anna Lee, Robert Coote, Natalie Wood, Isobel Elsom

The Ghost Breakers***
US 1940 85m bw
Paramount (Arthur Hornblow Jnr)

A girl inherits a West Indian castle and finds herself up to her neck in ghosts, zombies and buried treasure.
Archetypal comedy horror, very well done; a follow-up to the success of *The Cat and the Canary*, and just about as entertaining.

w Paul Dickey, Walter de Leon, play Paul Dickey, Charles W. Goddard d George Marshall ph Charles Lang m Ernst Toch ad Hans Dreier

Bob Hope, Paulette Goddard, Paul Lukas, *Willie Best*, Richard Carlson, *Lloyd Corrigan*, Anthony Quinn, Noble Johnson, Pedro de Cordova

The Ghost Goes West***
GB 1936 85m bw
London Films (Alexander Korda)

When a millionaire buys a Scottish castle and transports it stone by stone to America, the castle ghost goes too.
Amusing whimsy which is always pleasant but never quite realizes its full potential; fondly remembered for its star performance.

w Robert E. Sherwood, Geoffrey Kerr, *story* Eric Keown *d René Clair ph* Harold Rosson

Robert Donat, Jean Parker, Eugene Pallette, Elsa Lanchester, Ralph Bunker, Patricia Hilliard, Morton Selten

'Although the film is not cast in the fluid, rapidly paced style of Clair's typical work, it has a sly wit and an adroitness of manner that make it delightful.'—*André Sennwald, New York Times*

The Ghost of St Michael's**
GB 1941 82m bw
Ealing (Basil Dearden)

A school is evacuated to the Isle of Skye, and the local ghost turns out to be an enemy agent.
The star's schoolmaster character is here at its seedy best, and he is well supported in a comedy-thriller plot.

w Angus Macphail, John Dighton d Marcel Varnel

Will Hay, Claude Hulbert, Felix Aylmer, Raymond Huntley, Elliot Mason, Charles Hawtrey, John Laurie, Hay Petrie, Roddy Hughes, Manning Whiley

Ghost Story*
GB 1974 89m Fujicolor
Stephen Weeks

Former college acquaintances spend a weekend at a country house, and one of them is drawn into tragic events of forty years before.
Overlong chiller, ingeniously shot in India but very variably acted; aims for the M. R. James style and sometimes achieves it, but badly needs cutting.

w Rosemary Sutcliff, Stephen Weeks *d* Stephen Weeks *ph* Peter Hurst *m* Ron Geesin

Murray Melvin, Larry Dann, Vivian Mackerall, Marianne Faithfull, Anthony Bate, Leigh Lawson, Barbara Shelley

The Ghost Train***
GB 1931 72m bw
Gainsborough (Michael Balcon)

Passengers stranded at a haunted station in Cornwall include a detective posing as a silly ass in order to trap smugglers.
Excellent early sound version of a comedy-thriller play which has not only been among the most commercially successful ever written but also provided the basic plot for many another comedy: *Oh Mr Porter, The Ghost of St Michael's, Back Room Boy, Hold That Ghost*, etc. Previously filmed as a silent in 1927, with Guy Newall.

w Angus Macphail, Lajos Biro, play Arnold Ridley d Walter Forde

Jack Hulbert, Cicely Courtneidge, Donald Calthrop, Ann Todd, Cyril Raymond, Angela Baddeley, Allan Jeayes

The Ghost Train**
GB 1941 85m bw
Gainsborough (Edward Black)

Adequate remake with the lead split into two characters, which doesn't work quite so well.

w Marriott Edgar, Val Guest, J. O. C. Orton *d* Walter Forde

Arthur Askey, Richard Murdoch, Kathleen

Harrison, Morland Graham, Linden Travers, Peter Murray Hill, *Herbert Lomas*

The Ghosts of Berkeley Square*
GB 1947 89m bw
British National (Louis H. Jackson)

Two 18th-century ghosts are doomed to haunt a London house until royalty visits.
Thin, skittish whimsy with pleasant moments.

w James Seymour, *novel* No Nightingales by S. J. Simon, Caryl Brahms *d* Vernon Sewell

Robert Morley, Claude Hulbert, Felix Aylmer, Yvonne Arnaud, Abraham Sofaer, Ernest Thesiger, Marie Lohr, Martita Hunt, A. E. Matthews, John Longden, Ronald Frankau, Wilfrid Hyde White, Esmé Percy, Mary Jerrold, Wally Patch, Martin Miller

The Ghoul***
GB 1933 79m bw
Gaumont (Michael Balcon)

An Egyptologist returns from the tomb to uncover stolen jewels and a murderer.
Fascinating minor horror piece reminiscent of *The Old Dark House*, with many effective moments and a ripe cast.

w Frank King, Leonard Hines, L. DuGarde Peach, Roland Pertwee, John Hastings Turner, Rupert Downing, *novel* Frank King *d T. Hayes Hunter*

Boris Karloff, Cedric Hardwicke, Ralph Richardson, Kathleen Harrison, Ernest Thesiger, Dorothy Hyson, Anthony Bushell, D. A. Clarke-Smith
† Remade after a fashion as *What A Carve Up* (1962).

The Ghoul*
GB 1975 87m Eastmancolor
Tyburn (Kevin Francis)

In the twenties, a group of stranded travellers is reduced in number when they take shelter in the house of a former clergyman.
Blood-soaked horror without much style, but an interesting mixture of ancient clichés.

w John Elder *d* Freddie Francis *ph* John Wilcox *m* Harry Robinson

Peter Cushing, Alexandra Bastedo, John Hurt, Gwen Watford, Veronica Carlson, Don Henderson

'Peter Cushing brings out his violin for a soothing spot of the classics, the local copper mutters veiled warnings before trundling off on his bike, and thick fog swirls round the exterior sets at the drop of a canister.'—*Geoff Brown*

Giant**
US 1956 197m Warnercolor
Warner (George Stevens, Henry Ginsburg)

The life of a Texas cattle rancher through two generations.
Sprawling, overlong family saga with unconvincing acting but good visual style.

w Fred Guiol, Ivan Moffat, *novel* Edna Ferber *d George Stevens* *ph* William C. Mellor, Edwin DuPar *m Dmitri Tiomkin*

Rock Hudson, Elizabeth Taylor, James Dean, Mercedes McCambridge, Carroll Baker, Chill Wills, Jane Withers, Dennis Hooper, Sal Mineo, Rod Taylor, Judith Evelyn, Earl Holliman, Alexander Scourby, Paul Fix

Gideon's Day*
GB 1958 91m Technicolor
Columbia / John Ford (Michael Killanin)
US title: *Gideon of Scotland Yard*

A Scotland Yard Inspector has an eventful but frustrating day.
Pleasant, ordinary little TV style police yarn showing no evidence of its director's particular talents.

w T. E. B. Clarke, *novel* John Creasey *d* John Ford *ph* Frederick A. Young *m* Douglas Gamley *ad* Ken Adam

Jack Hawkins, Dianne Foster, Anna Lee, Andrew Ray, Anna Massey, Frank Lawton, John Loder, Cyril Cusack

Gidget
US 1959 95m Eastmancolor Cinemascope
Columbia (Lewis J. Rachmil)

A 16-year-old girl falls for a surfer; her parents disapprove until he turns out to be the son of their best friend.
Commercial mixture of domestic comedy and beach athletics, for nice teenagers and their moms and pops.

w Gabrielle Upton, *novel* Frederick Kohner *d* Paul Wendkos *ph* Burnett Guffey *m* Morris Stoloff

Sandra Dee, Cliff Robertson, James Darren, Arthur O'Connell
† Sequels include *Gidget Goes Hawaiian* (1961) with Deborah Walley; *Gidget Goes to Rome* (1962) with Cindy Carol; and two TV movies.

Gidget Gets Married
US 1971 73m colour TVM
Columbia (E. W. Swackhamer)

She was bad enough as a teenager, but the cast helps.

w John McGreevey *d* E. W. Swackhamer

Macdonald Carey, Paul Lynde, Don Ameche, Joan Bennett, Michael Burns, Monie Ellis

Gidget Grows Up
US 1969 74m colour TVM
Columbia (Jerome Courtland)

See above.

w John McGreevey *d* James Sheldon

Karen Valentine, Robert Cummings, Edward Mulhare, Paul Lynde, Nina Foch, Warner Anderson

The Gift Horse*
GB 1952 100m bw
British Lion / Molton (George Pitcher)
US title: *Glory at Sea*

In 1940 an old US destroyer is given to Britain, and an officer reluctantly takes charge of it.
Conventional, popular seafaring war adventure.

w William Fairchild, Hugh Hastings, William Rose *d* Compton Bennett *ph* Harry Waxman *m* Clifton Parker

Trevor Howard, Richard Attenborough, Sonny Tufts, James Donald, Joan Rice, Bernard Lee, Dora Bryan, Hugh Williams, Robin Bailey

The Gift of Love
US 1958 105m Eastmancolor Cinemascope
TCF (Charles Brackett)

A dying wife adopts an orphan girl so that her husband will not be lonely.
Incredibly cloying and miscast remake of *Sentimental Journey* (qv).

w Luther Davis *d* Jean Negulesco *ph* Milton Krasner *m* Cyril Mockridge

Lauren Bacall, Robert Stack, Evelyn Rudie, Lorne Greene

Gigi***
US 1958 119m Metrocolor Cinemascope
MGM (Arthur Freed)

A girl trained as a high society courtesan becomes the mistress of a rich and handsome boulevardier.
Laundered and musicalized version of a favourite French period novel; delightfully set, costumed and performed, but oddly lacking dance numbers.

w/ly Alan Jay Lerner m Frederick Loewe d Vincente Minnelli ph Joseph Ruttenberg md André Previn *pd/cost Cecil Beaton*

Leslie Caron, Louis Jourdan, Maurice Chevalier, Hermione Gingold, Isabel Jeans, Jacques Bergerac, Eva Gabor, John Abbott

'It has the sureness expected when a group of the most sophisticated talents are able to work together on material entirely suited to them.'—*Penelope Houston*

Gigot
US 1962 104m De Luxe
TCF / Seven Arts (Kenneth Hyman)

The mute caretaker of a Montmartre boarding house looks after an ailing prostitute and her child.
From Paris, Hollywood, comes a grotesque piece of self-indulgence, the arch example of the clown who wanted to play Hamlet. Plotless, mawkish and wholly unfunny.

w John Patrick, Jackie Gleason *d* Gene Kelly *ph* Jean Bourgoin *m* Jackie Gleason *ad* Auguste Capelier

Jackie Gleason, Katherine Kath, Gabrielle Dorziat, Jean Lefebvre, Jacques Marin

'Chaplinesque pretensions have proved fatal before to artists who will not accept their own limitations.'—*Gavin Lambert*

Gilda****
US 1946 110m bw
Columbia (Virginia Van Upp)

A gambler in a South American city resumes a love-hate relationship with an old flame . . . but she is now married to his dangerous new boss.
Archetypal Hollywood *film noir*, wholly studio-bound and the better for it, with dialogue that would seem risible if it did not happen to be dealt with in this style and with these actors, who keep the mood balanced between suspense and absurdity.

w Marion Parsonnet, story E. A. Ellington *d Charles Vidor ph Rudolph Maté md* Morris Stoloff, Marvin Skiles

Rita Hayworth, Glenn Ford, George Macready, Steve Geray, Joseph Calleia, Joe Sawyer, Gerald Mohr, Ludwig Donath

'From a quietly promising opening the film settles into an intractable obscurity of narrative through which as in a fog three characters bite off at each other words of hate.'—*Richard Winnington*

The Gilded Lily*
US 1935 80m bw
Paramount (Albert Lewis)

A poor stenographer who meets her reporter boy friend on a park bench is wooed by a British peer.
Good depression era romantic comedy with the heroine inevitably choosing poverty.

w Claude Binyon *d* Wesley Ruggles *ph* Victor Milner

Claudette Colbert, Fred MacMurray, Ray Milland,
C. Aubrey Smith, Luis Alberni, Donald Meek

The Girl Can't Help It*
US 1956 97m Eastmancolor Cinemascope
TCF (Frank Tashlin)

A theatrical agent grooms a gangster's dumb girl friend for stardom.
Scatty, garish pop scene spoof with a plot borrowed from *Born Yesterday* and a lot of jokes about its new star's superstructure. Some scenes are funny, and it puts the first rock and roll stars in pickle for all time.

w Frank Tashlin, Herbert Baker *d Frank Tashlin ph* Leon Shamroy *md* Lionel Newman

Jayne Mansfield, Tom Ewell, Edmond O'Brien, Henry Jones, John Emery; and Julie London, Ray Anthony, Fats Domino, Little Richard, the Platters

Girl Crazy*
US 1943 99m bw
MGM (Arthur Freed)

Romance at a desert college.
Predictable star musical with good tunes.

w Fred F. Finklehoffe, *play* Guy Bolton, Jack McGowan *d* Norman Taurog *ph* William Daniels, Robert Planck *md* Georgie Stoll *songs George and Ira Gershwin*

Judy Garland, Mickey Rooney, Guy Kibbee, Gil Stratton, Robert E. Strickland, Rags Ragland, June Allyson, Nancy Walker, Tommy Dorsey and his band
† Remade 1965 as *When the Girls Meet the Boys*.

The Girl from Manhattan
US 1948 81m bw
UA / Benedict Bogeaus

A model returns home to help her uncle with his mortgaged boarding house.
Mouldy comedy-drama full of kind thoughts, charming failures and worldly priests. Interesting for cast.

w Howard Estabrook *d* Alfred E. Green *ph* Ernest Laszlo *md* David Chudnow

Dorothy Lamour, Charles Laughton, George Montgomery, Ernest Truex, Hugh Herbert, Constance Collier, Sara Allgood, Frank Orth, Howard Freeman, Adeline de Walt Reynolds, George Chandler, Maurice Cass

The Girl from Mexico see Mexican Spitfire

The Girl from Missouri*
US 1934 75m bw
MGM (Bernard H. Hyman)
aka: *100% Pure*

A chorus girl determines to remain virtuous until the right millionaire comes along.
Smart, amusing comedy very typical of its period.

w Anita Loos, John Emerson d Jack Conway *ph* Ray June *m* Dr William Axt

Jean Harlow, Franchot Tone, Lionel Barrymore, Lewis Stone, Patsy Kelly, Alan Mowbray, Clara Blandick, Henry Kolker

'Noisily defiant, rip-roaring and raucous in spots . . . fast and furious adult fare.'—*Photoplay*

The Girl from Tenth Avenue
US 1935 69m bw
Warner (Robert Lord)

A jilted attorney drowns his sorrows and marries on the rebound.
Watchable 'woman's picture'.

w Charles Kenyon, *play* Hubert Henry Davies *d* Alfred E. Green *ph* James Van Trees

Bette Davis, Ian Hunter, Colin Clive, Alison Skipworth, Katherine Alexander, John Eldredge, Philip Reed

Girl Happy
US 1965 96m Metrocolor Panavision
MGM / Euterpe (Joe Pasternak)

A pop singer in Florida is forced to chaperone a group of college girls including a gangster's daughter.
Standard star vehicle, quite professionally made and totally forgettable.

w Harvey Bullock, R. S. Allen *d* Boris Sagal *ph* Philip Lathrop *m* George Stoll

Elvis Presley, Harold J. Stone, Shelley Fabares, Gary Crosby, Nita Talbot

The Girl He Left Behind
US 1956 103m bw
Warner (Frank P. Rosenberg)

The army makes a man of a spoiled youth.
Platitudinous recruiting comedy for dim American teenagers.

w Guy Trosper, *book* Marion Hargrove *d* David Butler *ph* Ted McCord *m* Roy Webb

Tab Hunter, Natalie Wood, Jessie Royce Landis, Jim Backus, Henry Jones, Murray Hamilton, Alan King, James Garner, David Janssen

The Girl Hunters
GB 1963 100m bw Panavision
Present Day (Robert Fellows)

Private eye Mike Hammer solves a few murders plus the disappearance of his own ex-secretary. Comic strip thuggery with the author playing his own slouchy hero; the general incompetence gives this cheap production an air of Kafkaesque menace.

w Mickey Spillane, Roy Rowland, Robert Fellows *d* Roy Rowland *ph* Ken Talbot *m* Phil Green

Mickey Spillane, Shirley Eaton, Lloyd Nolan

A Girl in Every Port
US 1951 87m bw
RKO (Irwin Allen, Irving Cummings Jnr)

Two accident-prone sailors have trouble with a racehorse.
Dismally mechanical farce.

wd Chester Erskine *ph* Nicholas Musuraca *m* Roy Webb

Groucho Marx, William Bendix, Marie Wilson, Don Defore, Gene Lockhart

The Girl in the Headlines*
GB 1963 93m bw
Bryanston / Viewfinder (John Davis)

Scotland Yard investigates the murder of a model.
Standard police mystery, well enough done.

w Vivienne Knight, Patrick Campbell, *novel* The Nose on My Face by Laurence Payne *d* Michael Truman *ph* Stan Pavey *m* John Addison

Ian Hendry, Ronald Fraser, Margaret Johnston, Natasha Parry

The Girl in the News*
GB 1940 78m bw
TCF (Edward Black)

A nurse is framed for the death of her employer.
Easy-going British mystery of the Agatha Christie school.

w Frank Launder, Sidney Gilliat, *novel* Roy Vickers *d* Carol Reed

Margaret Lockwood, Barry K. Barnes, Emlyn Williams, Margaretta Scott, Roger Livesey, Basil Radford, Wyndham Goldie, Irene Handl, Mervyn Johns

The Girl in the Red Velvet Swing*
US 1955 109m De Luxe Cinemascope
TCF (Charles Brackett)

In New York at the turn of the century, a rich unstable man shoots his mistress's former lover.
Plushy but not very interesting recounting of a celebrated murder case in which the victim was a famous architect, Stanford White.

w Walter Reisch, Charles Brackett *d* Richard Fleischer *ph* Milton Krasner *m* Hugo Friedhofer *ad* Lyle R. Wheeler, Maurice Ransford

Ray Milland, Farley Granger, Joan Collins, Glenda Farrell, Luther Adler, Cornelia Otis Skinner, Philip Reed, John Hoyt
'A needlessly long-winded piece of lush sensationalism.'—*Penelope Houston*

The Girl in White*
US 1952 93m bw
MGM (Armand Deutsch)
GB title: *So Bright the Flame*

The story of Dr Emily Dunning, the first woman to become an intern in one of New York's hospitals.
Bland biopic, modestly produced, with predictable plot crises.

w Irmgard Von Cube, Allen Vincent, *book* Bowery to Bellevue by Emily Dunning Barringer *d* John Sturges *ph* Paul C. Vogel *m* David Raksin

June Allyson, Arthur Kennedy, Gary Merrill, Mildred Dunnock, Jesse White, Marilyn Erskine

The Girl Most Likely
US 1956 98m Technicolor RKOscope
RKO (Stanley Rubin)

A girl finds herself engaged to three men at the same time, and envisions marriage with each.
Dully cast, quite brightly handled remake of *Tom, Dick and Harry*, with modest songs and dances.

w Devery Freeman *d* Mitchell Leisen *ph* Robert Planck *m* Nelson Riddle

Jane Powell, Cliff Robertson, Keith Andes, Tommy Noonan, Kaye Ballard, Una Merkel
† For Mitchell Leisen and RKO studios, their last film.

The Girl Most Likely To
US 1973 74m colour TVM
ABC Circle

An ugly college girl tries plastic surgery.
Rather tasteless comedy with obvious situations.

w Joan Rivers, Agnes Gallin, *novel* Joan Rivers *d* Lee Phillips

Stockard Channing, Ed Asner, Warren Berlinger, Jim Backus, Joe Flynn

A Girl Must Live**
GB 1939 92m bw
Gainsborough (Edward Black)

A runaway schoolgirl falls among chorus girls planning to marry into the nobility.
Light, peppery comedy with a strong cast.

w Frank Launder, Austin Melford, *novel* Emery Bonnet *d Carol Reed*

Margaret Lockwood, Renée Houston, Lilli Palmer, George Robey, Hugh Sinclair, Naunton Wayne, Moore Marriott, Mary Clare, David Burns, Kathleen Harrison, Martita Hunt, Helen Haye

A Girl Named Sooner
US 1974 100m colour TVM
TCF

A hillbilly orphan girl inspires the devotion of an unhappy vet.
Slow moving drama.

w Suzanne Clauser from her novel *d* Delbert Mann

Cloris Leachman, Richard Crenna, Lee Remick, Don Murray, Susan Deer, Anne Francis

A Girl Named Tamiko
US 1962 119m Technicolor
Panavision
Paramount / Hal B. Wallis (Paul Nathan)

A Eurasian photographer uses his women in an attempt to get American nationality.
Humdrum romantic melodrama with dim performances.

w Edward Anhalt, *novel* Ronald Kirkbride *d* John Sturges *ph* Charles Lang Jnr *m* Elmer Bernstein

Laurence Harvey, France Nuyen, Martha Hyer, Michael Wilding, Miyoshi Umeki

The Girl Next Door
US 1953 92m Technicolor
TCF (Robert Bassler)

A Broadway musical star falls for her suburban neighbour.
Mild musical linked by UPA cartoon sequences.

w Isobel Lennart *d* Richard Sale *ph* Leon Shamroy *md* Lionel Newman *songs* Josef Myrow, Mack Gordon *ch* Richard Barstow

Dan Dailey, June Haver, Natalie Schaefer, Dennis Day, Cara Williams

The Girl of the Golden West
US 1930 81m bw
Warner (Robert North)

A gun-toting, saloon-owning girl marries an outlaw and saves him from the sheriff.
Straight version of a dusty old Broadway success, later musicalized under the same title (see below).

w Waldemar Young, *play* David Belasco *d* John Francis Dillon *ph* Sol Polito

Ann Harding, James Rennie, Harry Bannister, Ben Hendricks Jnr, J. Farrell MacDonald

The Girl of the Golden West
US 1938 121m bw (sepia release)
MGM (William Anthony McGuire)

In backwoods Canada, a girl loves a bandit who is being chased by the Mounties.
Solemn musical melodrama in which the stars seem miscast and a bit of pep is badly needed. Taken from a hoary David Belasco spectacular, and looks it.

w Isobel Dawn, Boyce DeGaw *d* Robert Z. Leonard *ph* Oliver Marsh *songs* Sigmund Romberg, Gus Kahn

Jeanette MacDonald, Nelson Eddy, Walter Pidgeon, Leo Carrillo, Buddy Ebsen, Olin Howland

The Girl on the Boat
GB 1962 91m bw
UA / Knightsbridge (John Bryan)

On a transatlantic liner in the twenties, two Englishmen fall in love.
Curious attempt to do something different with a star comic, who is clearly outclassed by the lighter talents at hand.

w Reuben Ship, *story* P. G. Wodehouse *d* Henry Kaplan *ph* Denys Coop *m* Kenneth V. Jones

Norman Wisdom, *Richard Briers*, Millicent Martin, Athene Seyler, Sheila Hancock, Philip Locke

The Girl on the Late Late Show
US 1974 74m colour TVM
Columbia

A talk show executive tracks down a mysterious silent film star, and uncovers a guilty secret.
Patchy mystery drama with a muddled plot and too many stops for guest cameos.

w Mark Rodgers *d* Gary Nelson

Don Murray, Laraine Stephens, Gloria Grahame, Walter Pidgeon, Yvonne de Carlo, Van Johnson, Cameron Mitchell, John Ireland

Girl on the Run
US 1958 77m bw TVM
Warner (William T. Orr, Roy Huggins)

A hired killer menaces a beautiful nightclub singer.
Pasted together episodes of *77 Sunset Strip*.

w Marion Hargrove *d* Richard L. Bare

Efrem Zimbalist Jnr, Edd Byrnes, Erin O'Brien, Shepperd Strudwick, Barton MacLane, Vince Barnett

The Girl Rush
US 1955 85m Technicolor Vistavision
Paramount (Frederick Brisson, Robert Alton)

A gambler's daughter inherits a half share in a Las Vegas hotel.
Dull charmless semi-musical vehicle for a star who can't quite carry it.

w Phoebe and Henry Ephron *d* Robert Pirosh *ph* William Daniels *m* Spencer Hagen *ch* Robert Alton

Rosalind Russell, Eddie Albert, Fernando Lamas, James Gleason, Gloria de Haven, *Marion Lorne*

The Girl Who Came Gift-Wrapped
US 1974 74m colour TVM
Spelling–Goldberg

A publisher who has everything is given a beautiful girl for his birthday.
Empty-headed, witless nonsense.

w Susan Silver *d* Bruce Bilson

Richard Long, Karen Valentine, Louise Sorel, Reta Shaw, Dave Madden, Tom Bosley

The Girl Who Had Everything
US 1953 69m bw
MGM (Adolph Deutsch)

The daughter of a wealthy criminal lawyer falls in love with one of her father's crooked clients.
Glossy melodrama of purely superficial interest.

w Art Cohn, *novel* Adela Rogers St John *d* Richard Thorpe *ph* Paul Vogel *m* André Previn

Elizabeth Taylor, William Powell, Fernando Lamas, Gig Young

Girl with Green Eyes**
GB 1963 91m bw
UA / Woodfall (Oscar Lewenstein)

An artless young Dublin girl falls for a middle-aged writer.
Lyrical romance which just about preserves its charm by good location sense.

w Edna O'Brien, from her novel The Lonely Girl *d Desmond Davis ph Manny Wynn m* John Addison

Peter Finch, Rita Tushingham, Lynn Redgrave

Les Girls*
US 1957 114m Metrocolor Cinemascope
MGM (Sol. C. Siegel)

Two members of a girl dancing troupe sue over a memoir written by the third.
Disappointing, talent-laden comedy-musical with a *Rashomon*-like flashback plot and a curious absence of the expected wit and style.

w John Patrick, *novel* Vera Caspary *d* George Cukor *ph* Robert Surtees *m/ly* Cole Porter *ch* Jack Cole

Gene Kelly, *Kay Kendall*, Mitzi Gaynor, Taina Elg, Jacques Bergerac, Leslie Phillips, Henry Daniell, Patrick MacNee

Girls' Dormitory*
US 1936 66m bw
TCF

A college girl falls for her headmaster.
Old-fashioned romance for nice young people, smoothly produced in the Fox mid-thirties manner.

w Gene Markey, *story* Ladislaus Fodor *d* Irving Cummings *m* Arthur Lange

Herbert Marshall, *Simone Simon*, Ruth Chatterton, Constance Collier, J. Edward Bromberg, Dixie Dunbar, Tyrone Power

The Girls of Huntington House*
US 1973 73m colour TVM
Lorimar (Robert L. Jacks)

Problems at a school for unwed mothers.
Well acted soaper.

w Blossom Elfman from her novel *d* Alf Kjellin

Shirley Jones, Mercedes McCambridge, Sissy Spacek, William Windom

Girls, Girls, Girls
US 1962 106m Technicolor
Wallis–Hazen (Hal B. Wallis)

A nightclub singer runs a fishing boat as a hobby.
Empty-headed, lighter than air vehicle for star fans.

w Edward Anhalt, Allan Weiss *d* Norman Taurog *ph* Loyal Griggs *m* Joseph J. Lilley

Elvis Presley, Stella Stevens, Laurel Goodwin, Jeremy Slate

The Girls of Pleasure Island
US 1953 96m Technicolor
Paramount (Paul Jones)

In 1945 the Marines land on a tiny Pacific island, disturbing the life of an English gentleman and his three inexperienced but beautiful daughters.

Tedious and wholly artificial comedy with a leaden touch, devised as a try-out for young talent.

w F. Hugh Herbert *d* F. Hugh Herbert, Alvin Ganzer *ph* Daniel Fapp *m* Lyn Murray

Leo Genn, Gene Barry, Don Taylor, Elsa Lanchester, Dorothy Bromiley, Audrey Dalton, Joan Elan

Give a Girl a Break*
US 1953 84m Technicolor
MGM (Jack Cummings)

A Broadway star walks out on a show and three girls audition as replacements.
Minor musical vehicle for the Champions; an agreeable time-passer.

w Frances Goodrich, Albert Hackett *d* Stanley Donen *ph* William Mellor *md* André Previn *songs* Ira Gershwin, Burton Lane *ch* Stanley Donen, Gower Champion

Marge and Gower Champion, Debbie Reynolds, Bob Fosse, Kurt Kasznar

Give My Regards to Broadway*
US 1948 89m Technicolor
TCF

An old-time vaudevillian yearns to get back into show business.
Pleasantly performed, sentimental family musical with familiar tunes.

w Samuel Hoffenstein, Elizabeth Reinhardt *d* Lloyd Bacon *ph* Harry Jackson

Dan Dailey, *Charles Winninger*, Fay Bainter, Charles Ruggles, Nancy Guild

'Vaudeville is dead. I wish to God someone would bury it.'—*James Agee*

Give Us This Day
GB 1949 120m bw
Plantagenet (Rod E. Geiger, N. A. Bronsten)
US title: *Salt to the Devil*

Depression struggles of an Italian immigrant family in New York.
An unconvincing, self-pitying wallow, a very curious enterprise for a British studio.

w Ben Barzman, *story* Christ in Concrete by Pietro di Donato *d* Edward Dmytryk *ph* C. Pennington Richards *m* Benjamin Frankel

Sam Wanamaker, Lea Padovani, Kathleen Ryan, Charles Goldner, Bonar Colleano, William Sylvester, Karel Stepanek, Sidney James

'Dmytryk insisted on cutting the film himself and he has left in at least three spare reels.'—*Richard Winnington*

Glamorous Night
GB 1937 81m bw
ABP (Walter C. Mycroft)

An opera singer and her gypsy friends save a Ruritanian king from his scheming prime minister.
Modest transcription of a popular stage musical.

w Dudley Leslie, Hugh Brooke, William Freshman, *play* Ivor Novello *m* Ivor Novello

Mary Ellis, Otto Kruger, Victor Jory, Barry Mackay, Trefor Jones

Glamour
US 1934 74m bw
Universal

A day in the life of a Broadway star.
Competent minor entertainment.

w Doris Anderson, *story* Edna Ferber *d* William Wyler *ph* George Robinson

Constance Cummings, Paul Lukas, Philip Reed, Joseph Cawthorne, Doris Lloyd, Olaf Hytten

The Glass Bottom Boat
US 1966 110m Metrocolor
Panavision
MGM / Arwin–Reame (Martin Melcher)

A young widow gets involved with spies.
Frantic spy spoof, pleasantly set on the Californian coast, but overflowing with pratfalls, messy slapstick and pointless guest appearances.

w Everett Freeman *d* Frank Tashlin *ph* Leon Shamroy *m* Frank de Vol

Doris Day, Rod Taylor, Arthur Godfrey, Paul Lynde, John McGiver, Edward Andrews, Eric Fleming, Dom De Luise

The Glass House*
US 1972 73m colour TVM
Tomorrow

Tensions mount between the inmates of a state prison.
Good acting, routine plot.

w Tracy Keenan Wynn, *story* Truman Capote *d* Tom Gries

Alan Alda, Vic Morrow, Clu Gulager, Billy Dee Williams, Dean Jagger, Kristoffer Tabori

The Glass Key**
US 1935 87m bw
Paramount (E. Lloyd Sheldon)

A slightly corrupt but good-natured politician is saved by his henchman from being implicated in a murder.
Lively transcription of a zesty crime novel.

w Kathryn Scola, Kubec Glasmon, Harry

Ruskin, *novel Dashiell Hammett* *d* Frank Tuttle *ph* Henry Sharp

Edward Arnold, George Raft, Claire Dodd, Rosalind Keith, Guinn Williams, Ray Milland

The Glass Key**
US 1942 85m bw
Paramount (Fred Kohlmar)

Nifty remake of the above which finds some limited talents in their best form, helped by a plot which keeps one watching.

w Jonathan Latimer *d Stuart Heisler* *ph Theodor Sparkuhl* *m* Victor Young

Brian Donlevy, Alan Ladd, Veronica Lake, Bonita Granville, *William Bendix*, Richard Denning, Joseph Calleia, Moroni Olsen

The Glass Menagerie**
US 1950 107m bw
Warner (Jerry Wald, Charles K. Feldman)

A shy crippled girl seeks escape from the shabby reality of life in St Louis and from her mother's fantasies.
Pleasantly moody version of one of its author's lighter and more optimistic plays; fluent and good-looking production, memorable performances.

w Tennessee Williams (with Peter Berneis) from his play *d Irving Rapper* *ph Robert Burks* *m* Max Steiner

Gertrude Lawrence, Jane Wyman, Kirk Douglas, Arthur Kennedy

The Glass Menagerie*
US 1973 112m colour TVM
Talent Associates / Norton-Simon

A faded aristocratic lady and her invalid daughter live in hopes of something turning up.
This version lacks the charm of the film, and although Hepburn is always worth watching, she is miscast.

play Tennessee Williams *d* Anthony Harvey

Katharine Hepburn, Sam Waterston, Joanna Miles, Michael Moriarty

The Glass Mountain
GB 1949 98m bw
Victoria (John Sutro, Joseph Janni, Fred Zelnik)

In the Dolomites, a married composer loves an Italian girl who saved his life during the war.
Tedious sudser, ineptly produced; an enormous British box office success because of its theme music.

w Joseph Janni, John Hunter, Emery Bonnet, Henry Cass, John Cousins *d* Henry Cass *m* Nino Rota

Michael Denison, Dulcie Gray, Valentina Cortese, Tito Gobbi, Sebastian Shaw

The Glass Slipper
US 1954 94m Eastmancolor
MGM (Edwin H. Knopf)

The story of Cinderella.
To those used to the pantomime version this is dull, dreary, high-flown stuff: limbo sets, ballets, psychological rationalization and virtually no comedy.

w/ly Helen Deutsch *d* Charles Walters *ph* Arthur E. Arling *m* Bronislau Kaper *ch* Roland Petit

Leslie Caron, Michael Wilding, Elsa Lanchester, Barry Jones, *Estelle Winwood* (as Fairy Godmother)

The Glass Web
US 1954 81m bw 3-D
U-I (A. J. Cohen)

A TV executive kills a blackmailing actress and allows a young scriptwriter to be accused.
Boring thriller set in a TV studio.

w Robert Blees, Leonard Lee *d* Jack Arnold *ph* Maury Gertsman *m* Joseph Gershenson

Edward G. Robinson, John Forsythe, Marcia Henderson, Richard Denning

The Glenn Miller Story**
US 1954 116m Technicolor
U-I (Aaron Rosenberg)

The life of the unassuming trombonist and bandleader whose plane disappeared during World War II.
Competent musical heartwarmer with a well-cast star and successful reproduction of the Miller sound. A big box office hit.

w Valentine Davies, Oscar Brodney *d Anthony Mann* *ph William Daniels* *md* Joseph Gershenson

James Stewart, June Allyson, Harry Morgan, Charles Drake, Frances Langford, Louis Armstrong, Gene Krupa

A Global Affair
US 1963 84m bw
Seven Arts / Hall Bartlett

A United Nations official has to look after an abandoned baby.
Flat sentimental farce which embarrassingly tries to say something about the UN.

w Arthur Marx, Bob Fisher, Charles Lederer

d Jack Arnold *ph* Joseph Ruttenberg *m* Dominic Frontière

Bob Hope, Lilo Pulver, Michèle Mercier, Yvonne de Carlo

'Squaresville incarnate, with a side trip into Leersville.'—*Judith Crist, 1973*

Glorifying the American Girl*
US 1929 87m bw, colour sequence
Paramount (Florenz Ziegfeld)

A chorus girl rejects her boy friend for the sake of stardom.
Archetypal show-must-go-on musical.

w J. P. McEvoy, Millard Webb *d* Millard Webb, John Harkrider *ph* George Folsey *md* Frank Tours

Mary Eaton, Edward Crandall; and as guests Eddie Cantor, Helen Morgan, Rudy Vallee, Florenz Ziegfeld, Adolph Zukor, Otto Kahn, Texas Guinan, Mayor Jimmy Walker, Ring Lardner, Noah Beery, Johnny Weissmuller

Glory
US 1955 100m Technicolor Superscope
RKO (David Butler)

Girl loves horse more than boy.
Conventional young love / Kentucky Derby marshmallow.

w Peter Milne *d* David Butler *ph* Wilfrid Cline *m* Frank Perkins

Margaret O'Brien, Walter Brennan, Charlotte Greenwood, John Lupton

The Glory Brigade
US 1953 82m bw
TCF (William Bloom)

Greek soldiers fight in Korea alongside the Americans.
Modest war adventure with predictable racial tensions.

w Franklin Coen *d* Robert D. Webb *ph* Lucien Andriot *m* Lionel Newman

Victor Mature, Alexander Scourby, Lee Marvin, Richard Egan

The Glory Guys*
US 1965 112m De Luxe Panavision
UA / Levy–Gardner–Laven

Officers of the US cavalry disagree about dealing with the Indians.
Standard big-budget western.

w Sam Peckinpah, *novel* The Dice of God by Hoffman Birney *d* Arnold Laven *ph* James Wong Howe *m* Riz Ortolani

Tom Tryon, Harve Presnell, Senta Berger, Andrew Duggan, James Caan, Slim Pickens, Michael Anderson Jnr

The Gnome-Mobile*
US 1967 90m Technicolor
Walt Disney (James Algar)

A millionaire and his family go for a forest picnic and help a colony of gnomes.
Cheerful adventures for small children, with good trick work.

w Ellis Kadison, *novel* Upton Sinclair *d* Robert Stevenson *ph* Edward Colman *m* Buddy Baker

Walter Brennan, Matthew Garber, Karen Dotrice, Richard Deacon, Sean McClory, Ed Wynn, Jerome Cowan, Charles Lane

Go Ask Alice*
US 1973 74m colour TVM
Metromedia (Gerald I. Isenberg)

The diary of a teenage drug addict from a good family.
If we have to go through all this again, it's well done.

w Ellen Violett, from anonymous book *d* John Korty

William Shatner, Julie Adams, Andy Griffith, Jamie Smith Jackson, Ruth Roman, Wendell Burton

The Go-Between**
GB 1970 116m Technicolor
EMI / World Film Services (John Heyman, Norman Priggen)

Staying at a stately home around the turn of the century, 12-year-old Leo carries love letters from a farmer to his friend's sister.
A rather tiresome plot sustains a rich picture of the Edwardian gentry, a milieu with which however the director is not at home and treats far too slowly and tricksily.

w Harold Pinter, *novel* L. P. Hartley *d* Joseph Losey *ph Geoffrey Fisher* *m* Michel Legrand *ad Carmen Dillon*

Alan Bates, Julie Christie, Michael Redgrave, Dominic Guard, Michael Gough, Margaret Leighton, Edward Fox

The Go-Getter
US 1937 90m bw
Warner (Sam Bischoff)

A one-legged navy veteran is determined that his injury will not prevent him from becoming a success.
Moderate comedy-drama, agreeably played.

w Delmer Daves, Peter B. Kyne *d* Busby

Berkeley *ph* Arthur Edeson *md* Leo F. Forbstein

George Brent, Charles Winninger, Anita Louise, John Eldredge, Henry O'Neill, Willard Robertson, Eddie Acuff

Go for a Take
GB 1972 90m colour
Rank / Century Films (Roy Simpson)

Two waiters in debt to a gangster take refuge in a film studio.
Painful British farce.

w Alan Hackney *d* Harry Booth *ph* Mark McDonald *m* Glen Mason

Reg Varney, Norman Rossington, Sue Lloyd, Dennis Price, Julie Ege, Patrick Newell, David Lodge

Go for Broke
US 1951 93m bw
MGM (Dore Schary)

World War II exploits of Japanese-American soldiers.
Absolutely unsurprising war film with all the anti-Japs converted by the end. Production quite good.

wd Robert Pirosh *ph* Paul C. Vogel *m* Alberto Columbo

Van Johnson, Lane Nakano, George Miki, Akira Fukunaga, Warner Anderson, Don Haggerty

Go into Your Dance**
US 1935 89m bw
Warner (Sam Bischoff)
GB title: *Casino de Paree*

A big-headed star gets his come-uppance and finds happiness.
Moderate backstage musical notable for the only teaming of Jolson and Keeler, who were then married.

w Earl Baldwin *d* Archie Mayo *ph* Tony Gaudio, Sol Polito *songs* Harry Warren, Al Dubin

Al Jolson, Ruby Keeler, Glenda Farrell, Benny Rubin, Phil Regan, Barton MacLane, Sharon Lynne, Akim Tamiroff, Helen Morgan, Patsy Kelly

Go Man Go
US 1954 82m bw
Alfred Palca (Anton M. Leader)

How Abe Saperstein moulded and trained the Harlem Globetrotters basketball team.
Not so much a film as an athletic demonstration with some actors round the edges.

w Arnold Becker *d James Wong Howe* *ph* Bill Steiner *m* Alex North

Dane Clark, Sidney Poitier, Pat Breslin, Edmond Ryan

Go Naked in the World
US 1960 103m Metrocolor Cinemascope
MGM / Arcola (Aaron Rosenberg)

A prostitute causes a rift between son and millionaire father.
Antediluvian melodrama with overblown performances.

wd Ranald MacDougall, *novel* Tom Chanales *ph* Milton Krasner *m* Adolph Deutsch

Gina Lollobrigida, Tony Franciosa, Ernest Borgnine, Luana Patten, Will Kuluva, Philip Ober

'A good example of how the increased liberation of Hollywood can be misused.'—*MFB*

Go to Blazes
GB 1961 84m Technicolor Cinemascope
ABP (Kenneth Harper)

Ex-convicts become firemen, intending to use the engine for smash and grab raids.
Mild comedy ruined by wide screen.

w Patrick Campbell, Vivienne Knight *d* Michael Truman *ph* Erwin Hillier *m* John Addison

Dave King, Daniel Massey, Norman Rossington, Wilfrid Lawson, Maggie Smith, Robert Morley, Coral Browne

Go West**
US 1940 82m bw
MGM (Jack Cummings)

Three zanies tackle a western villain.
Minor Marx comedy with a good start (the ticket office sketch) and a rousing finale as they take a moving train to bits, but some pretty soggy stuff in between.

w Irving Brecher *d* Edward Buzzell *ph* Leonard Smith *m* Georgie Stoll

Groucho, Harpo, Chico, John Carroll, Diana Lewis, Robert Barrat

Go West Young Man
US 1936 80m bw
Paramount (Emmanuel R. Cohen)

A movie star has a car breakdown in Pennsylvania and falls for a local lad.
Cleaned-up Mae West vehicle, all rather boring.

w Mae West, *play* Personal Appearance by Lawrence Riley *d* Henry Hathaway *ph* Karl Struss *m* George Stoll

Mae West, Randolph Scott, Warren William, Lyle Talbot, Alice Brady, Isabel Jewell, Elizabeth Patterson

God Is My Co-Pilot
US 1945 89m bw
Warner (Robert Buckner)

Pacific air adventures during World War II.
Adequate flagwaver.

w Peter Milne, Abem Finkel, *book* Col. Robert Lee Scott Jnr *d* Robert Florey *ph* Sid Hickox *m* Franz Waxman

Dennis Morgan, Dane Clark, Raymond Massey, Alan Hale, Andrea King, John Ridgely, Stanley Ridges, Craig Stevens

The Godchild
US 1974 74m colour TVM
MGM / Mor / Alan Neuman

Three outlaws care for a baby whose mother has died.
Three Godfathers (qv) all over again; enough was enough.

w Ron Bishop *d* John Badham

Jack Palance, Jack Warden, Keith Carradine, Ed Lauter, Jose Perez

The Goddess*
US 1958 105m bw
Columbia (Milton Perlman)

A small-town girl becomes a Hollywood sex symbol and lives to regret it.
Savage attack on the Marilyn Monroe cult, a bit lachrymose and compromised by miscasting, but with interesting detail.

w Paddy Chayevsky d John Cromwell *ph* Arthur J. Ornitz *m* Virgil Thompson

Kim Stanley, Lloyd Bridges, Steven Hill, Betty Lou Holland

The Godfather***
US 1971 175m Technicolor
Paramount / Alfran (Albert S. Ruddy)

When, after ruling for two generations, the Mafia's New York head dies of old age, his son takes over reluctantly but later learns how to kill.
A brilliantly-made film with all the fascination of a snake pit: a warm-hearted family saga except that the members are thieves and murderers. Cutting would help, but the duller conversational sections do heighten the cunningly judged moments of suspense and violence.

w Francis Ford Coppola, Mario Puzo, *novel* Mario Puzo *d Francis Ford Coppola* *ph* Gordon Willis *m* Nino Rota *pd* Dean Tavoularis

Marlon Brando (unintentionally comic in an absurd make-up), *Al Pacino*, Robert Duvall, James Caan, Richard Castellano, Diane Keaton

'The immorality lies in his presentation of murderers as delightful family men—the criminal is the salt of the earth—and to our shame we rub it into the wounds of our Watergate-world morality and even ask for more.'—*Judith Crist, 1974*

'They have put pudding in Brando's cheeks and dirtied his teeth, he speaks hoarsely and moves stiffly, and these combined mechanics are hailed as great acting . . . Like star, like film, the keynote is inflation. *The Godfather* was made from a big bestseller, a lot of money was spent on it, and it runs over three hours. Therefore it's important.'—*Stanley Kauffmann*

The Godfather, Part Two***
US 1974 200m Technicolor
Paramount / the Coppola Company (Francis Ford Coppola

In 1958, Michael Corleone reflects on the problems of himself and his father before him.
Curious rehash of part of the original with new scenes, a shade difficult to follow but full of good scenes and performances.

w Francis Ford Coppola, Mario Puzo *d Francis Ford Coppola* *ph* Gordon Willis *m* Nino Rota *pd* Dean Tavoularis

Al Pacino, *Robert de Niro*, Diane Keaton, Robert Duvall, John Cazale, Lee Strasberg, Michael V. Gazzo

'The complete work is an epic vision of the corruption of America.'—*New Yorker*

God's Country and the Woman
US 1936 80m Technicolor
Warner (Lou Edelman)

The junior partner of a lumber company goes to work undercover in an opponent's camp, causes trouble, and falls in love.
Adequate outdoor melodrama in early colour.

w Norman Reilly Raine, *novel* James Oliver Curwood *d* William Keighley *ph* Tony Gaudio

George Brent, Beverly Roberts, Barton MacLane, Robert Barrat, Alan Hale, Addison Richards, El Brendel, Roscoe Ates, Billy Bevan

God's Little Acre*
US 1958 110m bw
Security (Sidney Harmon)

A poor white farmer in Georgia neglects his land in a fruitless search for gold.
Tobacco Road under another name, and not so lively: bowdlerized and eventually tedious

despite a welter of sensational incident and depraved characters.

w Philip Yordan, *novel* Erskine Caldwell
d Anthony Mann *ph* Ernest Haller *m Elmer Bernstein*

Robert Ryan, Aldo Ray, Tina Louise, Buddy Hackett, Jack Lord, Vic Morrow, Rex Ingram

Godspell*
US 1973 102m TVC color
Columbia / Lansbury / Duncan / Beruh (Edgar Lansbury)

The Gospel according to St Matthew played out musically by hippies in the streets of New York.
Wild and woolly film version of the successful theatrical fantasy, surviving chiefly by virtue of its gleaming photography.

w David Greene, John Michael Tebelak *d David Greene ph Richard G. Heimann m/ly Stephen Schwarz*

Victor Garber, David Haskell, Jerry Sroka, Lynne Thigpen, Robin Lamont

'A patch of terra incognita somewhere between *Sesame Street* and the gospel according to *Laugh-In*.'—*Bruce Williamson*

Gog*
US 1954 85m Color Corporation
Ivan Tors

In an underground laboratory in New Mexico, a giant computer controls two robots, and a spy programmes it to kill.
Brisk, imaginative low-budget sci-fi in gleaming colour, well staged and developed.

w Tom Taggart *d* Herbert B. Strock
ph Lothrop B. Worth *m* Harry Sukman

Richard Egan, Constance Dowling, Herbert Marshall

Going My Way**
US 1944 126m bw
Paramount (Leo McCarey)

A young priest comes to a New York slum parish and after initial friction charms the old pastor he is to succeed.
Sentimental comedy which got away with it wonderfully at the time, largely through careful casting, though it seems thin and obvious now.

w Frank Butler, Frank Cavett, Leo McCarey
d Leo McCarey *ph* Lionel Lindon
songs Johnny Burke, James Van Heusen, J. R. Shannon

Bing Crosby, Barry Fitzgerald, Rise Stevens, Frank McHugh, James Brown, Gene Lockhart, Jean Heather, Porter Hall

† Father O'Malley reappeared in *The Bells of St Mary's* and *Say One for Me* (both qv).

Going to Town*
US 1935 74m bw
Paramount (William Le Baron)

A western oil heiress moves into society.
Reasonably satisfactory Mae West vehicle, the last in fact before the censor killed her style.

w Mae West *d* Alexander Hall *ph* Karl Struss
songs Sammy Fain, Irving Kahal

Mae West, Paul Cavanagh, Ivan Lebedeff, Tito Coral, Marjorie Gateson, Fred Kohler Snr, Monroe Owsley

The Going Up of David Lev
US 1971 74m colour TVM
Hallmark

A boy learns how his father, a Jewish American, died in the Six Day War.
Modest Israeli adventure drama.

w Ernest Kinoy, Ephraim Kishon *d* James F. Collier

Topol, Claire Bloom, Melvyn Douglas, Brandon Cruz

Gold**
GB 1974 124m Technicolor Panavision
Hemdale / Avton (Michael Klinger)

A South African mining engineer falls for the boss's granddaughter and exposes a conspiracy.
Old-fashioned thick ear with spectacular underground sequences and a rousing finale.

w Wilbur Smith, Stanley Price *d Peter Hunt ph Ousama Rawi m* Elmer Bernstein

Roger Moore, Susannah York, Ray Milland, Bradford Dillman, John Gielgud, Tony Beckley

Gold Diggers in Paris*
US 1938 95m bw
Warner (Sam Bischoff)

Three girls chase rich husbands abroad.
A thin end to the series, saved by an agreeable cast.

w Earl Baldwin, Warren Duff *d* Ray Enright
ph Sol Polito, George Barnes *ch Busby Berkeley songs* Harry Warren, Al Dubin, Johnny Mercer

Rudy Vallee, Rosemary Lane, Hugh Herbert, Allen Jenkins, Gloria Dickson, Melville Cooper, Fritz Feld, Ed Brophy, Curt Bois

Gold Diggers of Broadway*
US 1929 98m Technicolor
Warner

Three Broadway chorus girls seek rich husbands. Fascinating primitive musical.

w Robert Lord, *play* The Gold Diggers by Avery Hopwood *d* Roy del Ruth *ph* Barney McGill, Ray Rennahan *songs* Al Dubin, Joe Burke

Nancy Welford, Conway Tearle, Winnie Lightner, Ann Pennington, Lilyan Tashman, William Bakewell, Nick Lucas
† Other versions of the play include *The Gold Diggers* (1923), *Gold Diggers of 1933* (qv), *Painting the Clouds with Sunshine* (qv).

Gold Diggers of 1933***
US 1933 96m bw
Warner (Robert Lord)

Cheerful, competent, well-cast remake of the above; numbers include 'My Forgotten Man', 'We're in the Money' and 'Pettin' in the Park'.

w Erwin Gelsey, James Seymour, David Boehm, Ben Markson *d Mervyn Le Roy ch Busby Berkeley songs Harry Warren, Al Dubin ph Sol Polito*

Warren William, Joan Blondell, *Aline MacMahon*, Ruby Keeler, Dick Powell, Guy Kibbee, Ned Sparks, Ginger Rogers, Clarence Nordstrom

Gold Diggers of 1935**
US 1935 95m bw
Warner (Robert Lord)

A socialite puts on a Broadway show at her country home, and is taken in by a swindler. Heavy-handed but laugh-provoking comedy with familiar faces of the day, climaxed by big numbers including 'Lullaby of Broadway'.

w Manuel Seff, Peter Milne, Robert Lord *d/ch Busby Berkeley ph* George Barnes *songs Al Dubin, Harry Warren*

Dick Powell, Adolphe Menjou, Gloria Stuart, Alice Brady, Hugh Herbert, Glenda Farrell, Frank McHugh, Grant Mitchell, Wini Shaw

'Busby Berkeley, the master of scenic prestidigitation, continues to dazzle the eye and stun the imagination.'—*André Sennwald, New York Times*

'A decidedly heady mixture.'—*Pare Lorentz*

Gold Diggers of 1937*
US 1937 100m bw
Warner (Hal B. Wallis)

A group of insurance salesmen back a show. Mild tailing-off of the Gold Diggers series, though with the accustomed production polish.

w Warren Duff, *play* Richard Maibaum, Michael Wallach, George Haight *d* Lloyd Bacon *ch Busby Berkeley ph* Arthur Edeson *songs* Harry Warren, Al Dubin, E. Y. Harburg, Harold Arlen

Dick Powell, Joan Blondell, Glenda Farrell, Victor Moore, Lee Dixon, Osgood Perkins, Charles D. Brown

Gold Is Where You Find It*
US 1938 90m Technicolor
Warner (Sam Bischoff)

Gold rush miners settle as California farmers. Agreeable western in excellent early colour.

w Warren Duff, Clements Ripley, Robert Buckner *d* Michael Curtiz ph Sol Polito m Max Steiner

George Brent, Olivia de Havilland, Claude Rains, Margaret Lindsay, John Litel, Marcia Ralston, Barton MacLane, Tim Holt, Sidney Toler

Gold of the Seven Saints
US 1961 89m bw Warnerscope
Warner (Leonard Freeman)

Cowboys compete in a search for lost gold. Adequate minor western using TV stars.

w Leigh Brackett, Leonard Freeman *d* Gordon Douglas *ph* Joseph Biroc *m* Howard Jackson

Clint Walker, Roger Moore, Leticia Roman, Robert Middleton, Chill Wills, Gene Evans

The Golden Age of Comedy****
US 1957 78m bw
Robert Youngson Productions

First of the scholarly compilations of silent comedy which saved many negatives from destruction, this is a fast-paced general survey which despite a facetious sound track does provide a laugh a minute. It particularly brought Laurel and Hardy back into public notice, and includes sections from *Two Tars* and *The Battle of the Century.*

wd Robert Youngson narrators Dweight Weist, Ward Wilson *m* George Steiner

Stan Laurel, Oliver Hardy, Harry Langdon, Ben Turpin, Will Rogers, Billy Bevan, Charlie Chase, Andy Clyde

The Golden Blade
US 1953 80m Technicolor
U-I (Richard Wilson)

With the help of a magic sword, Harun saves a princess and captures a rebel.
Standard cut-rate Arabian Nights adventure, very typical of its studio during the fifties.

w John Rich *d* Nathan Juran *ph* Maury Gertsman *m* Joseph Gershenson

Rock Hudson, Piper Laurie, George Macready, Gene Evans, Kathleen Hughes

Golden Boy*
US 1939 101m bw
Columbia (William Perlberg)

A poor boy is torn between two absorbing interests: prizefighting and the violin.
Personalized version of a socially conscious play; moderately effective with smooth production and good cast.

w Lewis Meltzer, Daniel Taradash, Sarah Y. Mason, Victor Heerman, *play* Clifford Odets *d Rouben Mamoulian ph* Nicholas Musuraca, Karl Freund *m* Morris Stoloff

Barbara Stanwyck, *William Holden*, Adolphe Menjou, Joseph Calleia, *Lee J. Cobb*, Sam Levene, Edward Brophy, Don Beddoe

'A slick, swift, exciting but insensitive movie.'—*Gordon Sager*

Golden Earrings*
US 1947 95m bw
Paramount (Harry Tugend)

A British Intelligence officer is helped by a gypsy to sneak a poison gas formula out of Nazi Germany.
One of the silliest stories of all time, despite the presence of Quentin Reynolds asserting that he believed it; also lacking in the humour which might have saved it, but produced with polish and interesting for the two stars at this stage in their careers.

w Abraham Polonsky, Frank Butler, Helen Deutsch, *novel* Yolanda Foldes *d Mitchell Leisen ph* Daniel L. Fapp *m* Victor Young

Ray Milland, Marlene Dietrich, Murvyn Vye, Bruce Lester, Dennis Hoey, Reinhold Schuntzel, Ivan Triesault

'A good deal of torso work goes on which I can't help feeling they're a bit old for.'—*Richard Winnington*

Golden Girl*
US 1951 108m Technicolor
TCF (George Jessel)

The story of Lotta Crabtree, who after the Civil War determined to become a great musical star.
Harmless semi-western biopic with good tunes.

w Walter Bullock, Charles O'Neal, Gladys Lehman *d* Lloyd Bacon *ph* Charles G. Clarke *md* Lionel Newman *ch* Seymour Felix

Mitzi Gaynor, Dale Robertson, Dennis Day, James Barton, Una Merkel, Raymond Walburn, Gene Sheldon

The Golden Head
US / Hungary 1964 115m
Technirama 70
Cinerama / Hungarofilm

Passengers on a Danube pleasure boat become involved in the theft of the golden head of St Laszlo.
Travelogue with a thin plot, somewhat slow moving but suitable for children.

w Stanley Boulder, Ivan Boldizsar *d* Richard Thorpe *ph* Istvan Hildebrand *m* Peter Fenyes

George Sanders, Buddy Hackett, Douglas Wilmer, Jess Conrad, Robert Coote

The Golden Horde
US 1951 76m Technicolor
U-I (Howard Christie)

Crusaders meet Mongols in Samarkand, and Sir Guy wins a princess.
Rather priceless idiocies are perpetrated in this variation on the studio's favourite Arabian Nights theme, but somehow they fail to make one laugh, which should be the only possible response to such a farrago.

w Gerald Drayson Adams *d* George Sherman *ph* Russell Metty *m* Hans Salter

David Farrar, Ann Blyth, George Macready, Henry Brandon, Richard Egan, Marvin Miller

The Golden Mistress*
US 1954 80m Technicolor
UA / RK (Richard Kay, Harry Rybnick)

An American and his girl friend search the sea bed for the forbidden treasure of a Haitian tribe.
Curious independent production, an adventure in the style of silent serials; amateur in many ways, yet with a freshness of photography and location plus some powerful voodoo scenes.

wd Fred Judge *ph William C. Thompson m* Raoul Kraushaar

John Agar, Rosemarie Bowe, Abner Biberman

Golden Needles
US 1974 92m Movielab Panavision
AIP / Sequoia (Fred Weintraub, Paul Heller)

Various factions seek a Hong Kong statue showing seven miraculous acupuncture points.
Youth/sex/Kung Fu/James Bond action amalgam.

w S. Lee Pogostin, Sylvia Schneble *d* Robert Clouse *ph* Gilbert Hubbs *m* Lalo Schifrin

Joe Don Baker, Elizabeth Ashley, Jim Kelly, Burgess Meredith, Ann Sothern

The Golden Voyage of Sinbad*
GB 1973 105m Eastmancolor
Columbia / Morningside (Charles H. Schneer)

Sinbad finds a strange map and crosses swords with a great magician.
Routine, rather uninspired fantasy enlivened by grotesque trick effects.

w Brian Clemens, Ray Harryhausen *d* Gordon Hessler *ph* Ted Moore *m* Miklos Rozsa *sp Ray Harryhausen pd* John Stoll

John Philip Law, Caroline Munro, Tom Baker, Douglas Wilmer, Grégoire Aslan

Goldfinger***
GB 1964 112m Technicolor
UA / Eon (Harry Saltzman, Albert R. Broccoli)

James Bond prevents an international gold smuggler from robbing Fort Knox.
Probably the liveliest and most amusing of the Bond spy spoofs, with a fairly taut plot between the numerous highlights. The big budget is well used.

w Richard Maibaum, Paul Dehn, novel Ian Fleming *d Guy Hamilton ph Ted Moore m John Barry pd Ken Adam titles Robert Brownjohn*

Sean Connery, Honor Blackman, Gert Frobe, Harold Sakata, Shirley Eaton, Bernard Lee, Lois Maxwell, Desmond Llewellyn

'A dazzling object lesson in the principle that nothing succeeds like excess.'—*Penelope Gilliatt*

'A diverting comic strip for grown-ups.'—*Judith Crist*

The Goldwyn Follies**
US 1938 115m Technicolor
Samuel Goldwyn

A Hollywood producer seeks the average girl to test his scripts.
Goldwyn's failure to become Ziegfeld, chiefly due to a lack of humour in the script, still has a soupçon of effective Hollywood satire and some excellent numbers.

w Ben Hecht *d* George Marshall *ph* Gregg Toland *m* various *ch* George Balanchine *ad* Richard Day

Kenny Baker, Vera Zorina, *the Ritz Brothers, Adolphe Menjou*, Edgar Bergen and Charlie McCarthy, Helen Jepson, Phil Baker, Ella Logan, Bobby Clark, Jerome Cowan, Nydia Westman

Gone to Earth
GB 1948 110m Technicolor
London Films / David O. Selznick
US title: *The Wild Heart*

In the 1890s, a wild Shropshire girl is desired by the local squire.
Unintentionally funny film version of an intractable novel.

w/p/d Michael Powell and Emeric Pressburger, *novel* Mary Webb *ph* Christopher Challis *m* Brian Easdale *pd* Hein Heckroth

Jennifer Jones, David Farrar, Cyril Cusack, Esmond Knight, Sybil Thorndike, Edward Chapman, George Cole, Hugh Griffith, Beatrice Varley

Gone with the Wind****
US 1939 220m Technicolor
MGM / *David O. Selznick*

An egotistic Southern girl survives the Civil War but finally loses the only man she cares for.
The only film in history which could be profitably revived for forty years: 'still pure gold', said the *Daily Mirror* in 1975. Whole books have been written about it; its essential appeal is that of a romantic story with strong characters and an impeccable production. The widescreen version produced in the late sixties ruined its composition and colour, but it is to be hoped that the original negative still survives.

w Sidney Howard (and others), *novel Margaret Mitchell d Victor Fleming* (and George Cukor, Sam Wood) *ph Ernest Haller, Ray Rennahan m Max Steiner pd William Cameron Menzies ad Lyle Wheeler*

Clark Gable, Vivien Leigh, Olivia de Havilland, Leslie Howard, Thomas Mitchell, Barbara O'Neil, *Hattie McDaniel, Butterfly McQueen*, Victor Jory, Evelyn Keyes, Ann Rutherford, Laura Hope Crews, Harry Davenport, Jane Darwell, Ona Munson, Ward Bond

'A major event in the history of the industry but only a minor event in motion picture art. There are moments when the two categories meet on good terms, but the long stretches between are filled with mere spectacular efficiency.'—*Franz Hoellering, The Nation*

The Good Companions***
GB 1932 113m bw
Gaumont / Welsh–Pearson (T. A. Welsh, George Pearson)

Three ill-assorted people take to the road and in various capacities join the Dinky Doos pierrot troupe.
Gallant, mini-budgeted version of Priestley's popular picaresque novel. A little faded now, it

retains some of its vigour, and the performances please.

w W. P. Lipscomb, Angus Macphail, Ian Dalrymple, *novel J. B. Priestley* *d* Victor Saville

Edmund Gwenn, Mary Glynne, John Gielgud, *Jessie Matthews*, Percy Parsons, A. W. Baskomb, Dennis Hoey, Richard Dolman, Frank Pettingell, Finlay Currie, *Max Miller*, Jack Hawkins, George Zucco

The Good Companions*
GB 1956 104m Technicolor Cinemascope
ABP (Hamilton Inglis, J. Lee-Thompson)

Faint-hearted remake of the above, unwisely Cinemascoped and leaving no impression.

w T. J. Morrison *d* J. Lee-Thompson *ph* Gilbert Taylor *m* Laurie Johnson

Eric Portman, Celia Johnson, John Fraser, Janette Scott, Hugh Griffith, Bobby Howes, Rachel Roberts, John Salew, Thora Hird

The Good Die Young*
GB 1954 98m bw
Remus (Jack Clayton)

Four crooks, all with private problems, set out to rob a mail van.
Glum all-star melodrama which set a pattern for such things; worth waiting for is the climactic chase through underground stations.

w Vernon Harris, Lewis Gilbert *d* Lewis Gilbert *ph* Jack Asher *m* Georges Auric

Laurence Harvey, Margaret Leighton, Gloria Grahame, Richard Basehart, Joan Collins, John Ireland, René Ray, Stanley Baker, Robert Morley

The Good Earth***
US 1937 138m bw
MGM (*Irving Thalberg*)

A Chinese peasant grows rich but loses his beloved wife.
A massive, well-meaning and fondly remembered production which is nevertheless artificial, unconvincing and pretty undramatic in the second half. The star performances impress to begin with, then wear thin, but the final locust attack is as well done as it originally seemed. Historically valuable as a Hollywood prestige production of the thirties.

w Talbot Jennings, Tess Schlesinger, Claudine West, *play* Owen and Donald Davis, *novel* Pearl S. Buck *d Sidney Franklin* *ph Karl Freund* *m* Herbert Stothart *montage* Slavko Vorkapitch *ad* Cedric Gibbons

Paul Muni, Luise Rainer, Walter Connolly, Tilly Losch, Jessie Ralph, Charley Grapewin, Keye Luke, Harold Huber

'One of the superb visual adventures of the period.'—*John Baxter, 1968*

The Good Fairy**
US 1935 90m bw
Universal (Henry Henigson)

A beautiful but naïve cinema usherette ensnares three rich men.
Delightful romantic comedy using top talent.

w Preston Sturges, play Ferenc Molnar *d William Wyler* *ph* Norbert Brodine

Margaret Sullavan, Herbert Marshall, Frank Morgan, Reginald Owen, Alan Hale, Beulah Bondi, Cesar Romero, Eric Blore, Al Bridge

Good Girls Go To Paris*
US 1939 75m bw
Columbia (William Perlberg)

After several zany adventures, a Greek professor marries a gold digger.
Amusingly crazy comedy, one of the last of its type.

w Gladys Lehman, Ken Englund *d* Alexander Hall *ph* Henry Freulich *md* Morris Stoloff

Melvyn Douglas, Joan Blondell, Walter Connolly, Alan Curtis, Joan Perry, Isabel Jeans, Alexander D'Arcy, Clarence Kolb

The Good Guys and the Bad Guys*
US 1969 90m Technicolor Panavision
Warner (Robert M. Goldstein)

An ageing sheriff and a train robber have one last showdown.
Good-humoured, black-flavoured western set in the early days of automobiles.

w Ronald M. Cohen, Dennis Shyrack *d* Burt Kennedy *ph* Harry Stradling Jnr *m* William Lava

Robert Mitchum, George Kennedy, David Carradine, Tina Louise, Douglas Fowley, Martin Balsam, Lois Nettleton, John Davis Chandler, John Carradine, Marie Windsor

Good Morning Miss Dove
US 1955 107m Eastmancolor Cinemascope
TCF (Samuel G. Engel)

While recovering from an operation, a small-town schoolmistress looks back on her career.
Glutinous old-fashioned drama, no *Mr Chips*.

w Eleanore Griffin, *novel* Frances Gray Patton *d* Henry Koster *ph* Leon Shamroy *m* Leigh Harline

Jennifer Jones, Robert Stack, Robert Douglas, Kipp Hamilton, Peggy Knudsen, Marshall Thompson, Chuck Connors, Mary Wickes

Good Neighbour Sam
US 1964 130m Eastmancolor
Columbia / David Swift

A prissy suburban advertising man becomes innocently involved in a pretence to be the husband of the divorcee next door.
A promising comic idea is here ruined by lengthiness, lack of funny lines, and no apparent idea of how to film a farce. The actors are driven to repeating every trick a dozen times.

w James Fritzell, Everett Greenbaum, David Swift, *novel* Jack Finney *d* David Swift *ph* Burnett Guffey *m* Frank de Vol

Jack Lemmon, Dorothy Provine, Senta Berger, Edward G. Robinson, Mike Connors, Edward Andrews, Louis Nye

Good News*
US 1947 83m Technicolor
MGM (Arthur Freed)

Various college romances hinge on a football game.
Bright, good-humoured minor musical from a venerable stage show.

w Betty Comden, Adolph Green, *musical play* De Sylva, Brown and Henderson *d* Charles Walters *ph* Charles Schoenbaum *ch* Roger Edens

June Allyson, Peter Lawford, Patricia Marshall, *Joan McCracken*, Mel Tormé

Good Sam
US 1948 114m bw
Rainbow (Leo McCarey)

A small-town business man is so charitable that he finds himself bankrupt.
Poor, disjointed, overlong and obvious comedy in the Capra style.

w Ken Englund *d* Leo McCarey *ph* George Barnes *m* Robert Emmett Dolan

Gary Cooper, Ann Sheridan, Ray Collins, Edmund Lowe, Joan Lorring, Ruth Roman

Goodbye Again*
US 1961 120m bw
UA / Mercury / Argus / Anatole Litvak

A woman of forty swaps her rich lover for a young law student.
Melancholy romantic drama, well produced and staged on Paris locations.

w Samuel Taylor, *novel* Aimez-vous Brahms by Françoise Sagan *d* Anatole Litvak *ph Armand Thirard* *m* Georges Auric

Ingrid Bergman, Anthony Perkins, Yves Montand, Jessie Royce Landis, Jackie Lane

'A grey-toned Sagan novella, spread wide and lush over two hours of screen time.'—*MFB*

'The kind of "woman's picture" that gives women a bad name.'—*Judith Crist, 1973*

Goodbye Charlie*
US 1964 116m De Luxe Cinemascope
TCF / Venice (David Weisbart)

A philandering gangster, shot dead by an irate husband, is reincarnated in his friend's house as a dishy blonde.
Overlong but amusing Broadway comedy for wisecrackers, uninventively adapted.

w Harry Kurnitz, *play* George Axelrod *d* Vincente Minnelli *ph* Milton Krasner *m* André Previn

Debbie Reynolds, Pat Boone, Walter Matthau, Tony Curtis

Goodbye Columbus**
US 1969 105m Technicolor
Paramount / Willow Tree (Stanley Jaffe)

A young Jewish librarian has an affair with the wilful daughter of a *nouveau riche* family.
An amusing and well-observed delineation of two kinds of Jewish life in New York; the story, despite its frank talk of penises and diaphragms, leaves much to be desired, and the style is post-*Graduate*.

w Arnold Schulman, *novel* Philip Roth *d Larry Peerce* *ph* Gerald Hirschfeld *m* Charles Fox

Richard Benjamin, Ali MacGraw, Jack Klugman, Nan Martin, Michael Meyers, Lori Shelle

Goodbye Mr Chips***
GB 1939 114m bw
MGM (Victor Saville)

The life of a shy schoolmaster from his first job to his death.
Sentimental romance in MGM's best style, a long-standing favourite for its performances and humour; but the production seems slightly unsatisfactory these days.

w R. C. Sherriff, Claudine West, Eric Maschwitz, *novel* James Hilton *d Sam Wood* *ph* Frederick A. Young *m* Richard Addinsell

Robert Donat, Greer Garson, Paul Henreid, Lyn Harding, Austin Trevor, Terry Kilburn, John Mills, Milton Rosmer, Judith Furse

'The whole picture has an assurance, bears a glow of popularity like the face of a successful candidate on election day. And it is wrong to despise popularity in the cinema.'—*Graham Greene*

Goodbye Mr Chips*
GB 1969 147m Metrocolor
Panavision 70
MGM / APJAC (Arthur P. Jacobs)

Elaborate musical remake of the above. Slow and slushy, with no improvement visible whatever; but a few of the trimmings please.

w Terence Rattigan *d* Herbert Ross *ph* Oswald Morris *m* Leslie Bricusse *pd* Ken Adam

Peter O'Toole, Petula Clark, Michael Bryant, Michael Redgrave, George Baker, Jack Hedley, Sian Phillips, Alison Leggatt

Goodbye My Fancy
US 1951 107m bw
Warner (Henry Blanke)

A congresswoman returns to her old college for an honorary degree, and falls in love.
Tolerable romantic flim-flam.

w Ivan Goff, Ben Roberts, *play* Fay Kanin *d* Vincent Sherman *ph* Ted McCord *m* Ray Heindorf

Joan Crawford, Robert Young, Frank Lovejoy, Eve Arden, Janice Rule

Goodbye My Lady*
US 1956 95m bw
Batjac

A Mississippi swamp boy finds a valuable dog but eventually returns it to its owner.
Reliable, slightly unusual family film.

w Sid Fleischman, *novel* James Street *d* William Wellman *ph* William H. Clothier, Archie Stout *m* Laurindo Almeida, George Field

Brandon de Wilde, Walter Brennan, Phil Harris, Sidney Poitier, William Hopper, Louise Beavers

Goodbye Raggedy Ann*
US 1971 73m colour TVM
Studio Center / Fielder Cook

A Hollywood starlet is driven to the point of suicide.
Well-made but rather obvious and unsympathetic mini-drama.

w Jack Sher *d* Fielder Cook

Mia Farrow, Hal Holbrook, John Colicos, Ed Flanders, Martin Sheen

Goodnight My Love**
US 1972 73m colour TVM
ABC Circle

Two private eyes—one a dwarf—are hired by a beautiful blonde to find her missing boy friend.
Successful spoof of a Chandler forties mystery, with good lines and excellent recreated Los Angeles settings.

wd Peter Hyams

Richard Boone, Michael Dunn, Barbara Bain, Victor Buono, Walter Burke

The Goose Steps Out*
GB 1942 79m bw
Ealing (S. C. Balcon)

To steal a secret weapon, an incompetent teacher is sent into Germany in place of his Nazi double.
Quite amusing star vehicle, not up to his best standards.

w Angus Macphail, John Dighton *d* Will Hay, Basil Dearden

Will Hay, Charles Hawtrey, Frank Pettingell, Julien Mitchell, Peter Croft, Jeremy Hawk, Peter Ustinov, Raymond Lovell, Barry Morse

Gordon's War
US 1973 90m TVC color
Palomar (Robert L. Schaffel)

A black Vietnam veteran returns to Harlem and avenges the death of his wife.
Violent vigilante melodrama with vivid locations.

w Howard Friedlander, Ed Spielman *d* Ossie Davis *ph* Victor J. Kemper *m* Andy Bodale, Al Ellis

Paul Winfield, Carl Lee, David Downing

The Gorgeous Hussy*
US 1936 105m bw
MGM (Joseph L. Mankiewicz)

The love life of Peggy O'Neal, protégée of President Andrew Jackson.
Bowdlerized all-star historical drama; the production values are better than the script.

w Ainsworth Morgan, Stephen Morehouse Avery, *novel* Samuel Hopkins Adams *d Clarence Brown* *ph* George Folsey *m* Herbert Stothart

Joan Crawford, Lionel Barrymore, Franchot Tone, Melvyn Douglas, Robert Taylor, James Stewart, Alison Skipworth, Louis Calhern, Beulah Bondi, Melville Cooper, Sidney Toler, Gene Lockhart

Gorgo
GB 1960 78m Technicolor
King Brothers (Wilfrid Eades)

A prehistoric monster is caught in Irish waters and brought to London, but rescued by its mother.

Amiable monster hokum with a happy ending but not much technical resource.

w John Loring, Daniel Hyatt *d* Eugene Lourié *ph* Frederick A. Young *m* Angelo Lavagnino *sp* Tom Howard

Bill Travers, William Sylvester, Vincent Winter, Christopher Rhodes, Joseph O'Conor, Bruce Seton, Martin Benson

The Gorgon*
GB 1964 83m Technicolor
Hammer (Anthony Nelson Keys)

A castle ruin near a German village is infested by Megaera, the gorgon of ancient myth, whose gaze turns people to stone and who can take over the form of an unknowing villager.
Writhing snakes in the hair-do being too great a challenge to the make-up man, the monster is barely glimpsed and the film becomes a who-is-it, all quite suspenseful despite the central idea being too silly for words.

w John Gilling *d* Terence Fisher *ph* Michael Reed *m* James Bernard

Peter Cushing, Christopher Lee, Barbara Shelley, Richard Pasco, Patrick Troughton

The Gorilla*
US 1939 66m bw
TCF

A murderer blames an escaped gorilla for his crimes.
Spooky house mystery comedy revamped as a Ritz Brothers vehicle; not much suspense, but it all looks good and the cast is highly satisfactory.

w Rian James, Sid Silvers, *play* Ralph Spence *d Allan Dwan ph Edward Cronjager m* David Buttolph

The Ritz Brothers, Bela Lugosi, Lionel Atwill, Patsy Kelly, Joseph Calleia, Anita Louise, Edward Norris, Wally Vernon
† There were two previous versions, in 1927 and 1931.

Gorilla at Large
US 1954 93m Technicolor 3-D
TCF / Panoramic (Robert L. Jacks)

A circus gorilla is used as a cover for murder.
Silly thriller with the gorilla as unconvincing as the story.

w Leonard Praskins, Barney Slater *d* Harmon Jones

Anne Bancroft, Lee J. Cobb, Cameron Mitchell, Lee Marvin, Raymond Burr, Charlotte Austin, Peter Whitney, Warren Stevens

The Gracie Allen Murder Case see Philo Vance

The Graduate***
US 1967 105m Technicolor Panavision
UA / Embassy (Lawrence Turman)

A rich Californian ex-student is led into an affair with the wife of his father's friend, then falls in love with her daughter.
Richly reflecting the anything-goes mood of the late sixties, this lushly-filmed sex comedy opened a few new doors, looked ravishing, was well acted and had a popular music score, so that few people noticed that only the first half was any good.

w Calder Willingham, Buck Henry, *novel Charles Webb d Mike Nichols ph Robert Surtees songs Paul Simon singers Simon and Garfunkel m* Dave Grusin *pd Richard Sylbert*

Dustin Hoffman, Anne Bancroft, Katharine Ross, Murray Hamilton, William Daniels, Elizabeth Wilson

'Seeing *The Graduate* is a bit like having one's most brilliant friend to dinner, watching him become more witty and animated with every moment, and then becoming aware that what one may really be witnessing is the onset of a nervous breakdown.'—*Renata Adler*

'Yes, there are weaknesses . . . But in cinematic skill, in intent, in sheer connection with us, *The Graduate* is a milestone in American film history.'—*Stanley Kauffmann*

Grand Hotel***
US 1932 115m bw
MGM

The lives of various hotel guests become intertwined and reach their climaxes.
It's a little faded now, but much of the magic still works in this first of the portmanteau movies; the production is opulent yet somehow stiff, and the performances have survived with varying success.

w William A. Drake, *novel* Vicki Baum *d Edmund Goulding ph* William Daniels *ad* Cedric Gibbons

Greta Garbo, *John Barrymore*, Lionel Barrymore, Joan Crawford, Wallace Beery, Jean Hersholt, Lewis Stone
† Remade as *Weekend at the Waldorf* (qv).

Grand Prix*
US 1966 179m Metrocolor Super Panavision
MGM (Edward Lewis)

Motor racers converge on Monte Carlo and other European centres.
Seemingly endless montage, mostly in multi-split screens, of motor races, with some very jaded personal footage between. It looks a dream but quickly becomes a bore.

w Robert Alan Aurthur *d John Frankenheimer ph Lionel Lindon m* Maurice Jarre *pd Richard Sylbert*

James Garner, Eva Marie Saint, Brian Bedford, Yves Montand, Toshiro Mifune, Jessica Walter, Françoise Hardy, Adolfo Celi, Claude Dauphin, Genevieve Page

'The same old story with the same types we've seen flying planes and riding horses in dozens of fast, cheap, hour-and-a-quarter movies.'—*Pauline Kael*

'Nothing more nor less than a paean to the racing car . . . off the track, though, the film is firmly stuck in bottom gear.'—*MFB*

The Grapes of Wrath****
US 1940 128m bw
TCF (Nunnally Johnson)

After the dust-bowl disaster of the thirties, Oklahoma farmers trek to California in the hope of a better life.
A superb film which could scarcely be improved upon. Though the ending is softened from the book, there was too much here for filmgoers to chew on. Acting, photography, direction combine to make this an unforgettable experience, a poem of a film.

w Nunnally Johnson, novel John Steinbeck *d John Ford ph Gregg Toland m* Alfred Newman

Henry Fonda, Jane Darwell, John Carradine, Charley Grapewin, Dorris Bowdon, Russell Simpson, Zeffie Tilbury, O. Z. Whitehead, John Qualen, Eddie Quillan, Grant Mitchell

'A genuinely great motion picture which makes one proud to have even a small share in the affairs of the cinema.'—*Howard Barnes*

The Grass Is Greener*
GB 1960 104m Technirama
Grandon (Stanley Donen)

The wife of an English earl falls for an American millionaire tourist.
Heavy-going and unsuitably widescreened version of an agreeable piece of West End fluff. Performances just about save it.

w Hugh and Margaret Williams, from their play *d* Stanley Donen *ph* Christopher Challis *m/ly* Noel Coward *md* Douglas Gamley

Cary Grant, Deborah Kerr, Robert Mitchum, *Jean Simmons, Moray Watson*

'It's too bad Coward couldn't have written the wisecracks too.'—*Philip T. Hartung*

The Grasshopper
US 1969 98m Technicolor
NGP (Jerry Belson, Barry Marshall)

A small-town girl goes from man to man in Los Angeles and Las Vegas, finally becoming a call girl.
The road to ruin in modern dress; nicely made and quite entertaining in its gaudy way.

w Jerry Belson, *novel* The Passing of Evil by Mark MacShane *d* Jerry Paris *ph* Sam Leavitt *m* Billy Goldenberg

Jacqueline Bisset, Jim Brown, Joseph Cotten, Corbett Monica

The Gravy Train
US 1974 96m Eastmancolor
Tomorrow (Jonathan T. Taplin)
aka: *The Dion Brothers*

A canning factory worker throws up his job to hijack a treasury van and open a seafood restaurant.
Old-hat caper story.

w David Whitney, Bill Kirby *d* Jack Starrett *ph* Jerry Hirschfeld *m* Fred Karlin

Stacy Keach, Frederic Forrest, Margot Kidder, Barry Primus

The Great American Beauty Contest
US 1972 73m colour TVM
Spelling–Goldberg (Everett Chambers)

A beauty contest is threatened by scandal.
Acceptable comedy drama.

w Stanford Whitmore *d* Robert Day

Eleanor Parker, Bob Cummings, Louis Jourdan, Barbi Benson, Farrah Fawcett, Tracy Reed

The Great American Broadcast*
US 1941 90m bw
TCF (Kenneth MacGowan)

A romantic triangle set against the burgeoning years of the radio industry.
Pleasant musical, amusing if historically inaccurate.

w Don Ettlinger, Edwin Blum, Robert Ellis, Helen Logan *d* Archie Mayo *ph* Leon Shamroy, Peverell Marley *songs* Mack Gordon, Harry Warren

Alice Faye, John Payne, Jack Oakie, Cesar Romero, The Ink Spots, The Nicholas Brothers, The Wiere Brothers

The Great American Pastime
US 1956 89m bw
MGM (Henry Berman)

A mild lawyer takes over a junior baseball team but incurs parental jealousy.
Thin lower-bracket comedy.

w Nathaniel Benchley *d* Herman Hoffman *ph* Arthur E. Arling *m* Jeff Alexander

Tom Ewell, Anne Francis, Ann Miller, Dean Jones, Raymond Bailey

A Great American Tragedy*
US 1972 74m colour TVM
Metromedia (Gerald I. Isenberg)
GB title: *Man at the Crossroads*

A middle-aged executive loses his job and finds it hard to get another.
Convincing sketch of a familiar situation.

w Caryl Ledner *d* J. Lee-Thompson

George Kennedy, Vera Miles, William Windom, Kevin McCarthy, Natalie Trundy

The Great Bank Robbery*
US 1969 98m colour Panavision
Warner (Malcolm Stuart)

Would-be bank robbers turn up in a western town disguised as priests.
Western spoof without the courage of its convictions, but easy enough to watch.

w William Peter Blatty, novel Frank O'Rourke *d* Hy Averback *ph* Fred J. Koenekamp *m* Nelson Riddle

Kim Novak, Zero Mostel, Clint Walker, Claude Akins, Akim Tamiroff, Larry Storch, John Anderson, Sam Jaffe, Ruth Warrick, Elisha Cook Jnr

The Great Caruso**
US 1950 109m Technicolor
MGM (Joe Pasternak)

Semi-fictional biography of the Italian tenor.
Dramatically flat but opulently staged biopic, turned into a star vehicle and a huge commercial success.

w Sonya Levien, William Ludwig *d* Richard Thorpe *ph* Joseph Ruttenberg *md* Johnny Green

Mario Lanza, Ann Blyth, Dorothy Kirsten, Jarmila Novotna, Carl Benton Reid, Eduard Franz, Richard Hageman, Ludwig Donath, Alan Napier

Great Catherine
GB 1968 98m Technicolor
Warner / Keep Films (Jules Buck)

An English captain visits the court of Catherine the Great.
Chaos results from the attempt to inflate an ill-considered Shavian whimsy into a feature film: the material is simply insufficient and the performances flounder in irrelevant production values.

w Hugh Leonard, *play* Bernard Shaw *d* Gordon Flemyng *ph* Oswald Morris *m* Dmitri Tiomkin *pd* John Bryan

Jeanne Moreau, Peter O'Toole, Zero Mostel, Jack Hawkins, Marie Lohr, Akim Tamiroff, Marie Kean, Kenneth Griffith

Great Day in the Morning
US 1955 92m Technicolor Superscope
RKO (Edmund Grainger)

At the outbreak of the Civil War, Denver has divided loyalties.
Solemn semi-western without much excitement.

w Lesser Samuels, *novel* Robert Hardy Andrews *d* Jacques Tourneur *ph* William Snyder *m* Leith Stevens

Robert Stack, Virginia Mayo, Ruth Roman, Alex Nicol, Raymond Burr, Regis Toomey

The Great Dictator**
US 1940 129m bw
Charles Chaplin

A Jewish barber is mistaken for dictator Adenoid Hynkel.
Chaplin's satire on Hitler has a few funny moments, but the rest is heavy going, the production is cheeseparing, and the final speech to the world is a grave mistake.

wd Charles Chaplin *ph* Karl Struss, Rollie Totheroh *md* Meredith Willson *ad* J. Russell Spencer

Charles Chaplin, Paulette Goddard, *Jack Oakie* (as Napaloni), Reginald Gardiner, Henry Daniell, Billy Gilbert, Maurice Moscovitch

'For this film he takes on more than a mimed representation of common humanity; he states, and accepts, the responsibility of being one of humanity's best and most widely-known representatives.'—*Basil Wright*

The Great Escape**
US 1963 173m De Luxe Panavision
UA / Mirisch / Alpha (John Sturges)

Allied prisoners plan to escape from a German prison camp.
Pretty good but overlong POW adventure with a tragic ending.

w James Clavell, W. R. Burnett, *book* Paul

Brickhill *d* John Sturges *ph Daniel Fapp* *m* Elmer Bernstein

James Garner, *Steve McQueen*, Richard Attenborough, James Donald, Charles Bronson, Donald Pleasance, James Coburn, David McCallum, Gordon Jackson, John Leyton, Nigel Stock

Great Expectations****
GB 1946 118m bw
Rank / Cineguild (Anthony Havelock-Allan)

A boy meets an escaped convict on the Romney Marshes, with strange consequences for both of them.
Despite the inevitable simplifications, this is a superbly pictorial rendering of a much-loved novel, with all the famous characters in safe hands and masterly judgement in every department.

w Ronald Neame, David Lean, Kay Walsh, Cecil McGivern, Anthony Havelock-Allan, *novel Charles Dickens d David Lean ph Ronald Neame ad John Bryan*

John Mills, Bernard Miles, *Finlay Currie, Martita Hunt*, Valerie Hobson, *Jean Simmons*, Alec Guinness, Francis L. Sullivan, Anthony Wager, Ivor Barnard, Freda Jackson, Hay Petrie, O. B. Clarence, George Hayes, Torin Thatcher, Eileen Erskine

'The first big British film to have been made, a film that sweeps our cloistered virtues out into the open.'—*Richard Winnington*

'The best Dickens adaptation, and arguably David Lean's finest film.'—*NFT, 1969*

Great Expectations*
GB 1975 116m colour TVM
ITC (Robert Fryer)

So-so version planned as a musical but with the music removed.

w Sherman Yellen *d* Joseph Hardy *ph* Freddie Young

Michael York, Sarah Miles, James Mason, Margaret Leighton, Robert Morley, Anthony Quayle, Rachel Roberts, Joss Ackland, Andrew Ray, Heather Sears

The Great Garrick**
US 1937 91m bw
Warner (Mervyn Le Roy)

When Garrick goes to act in Paris, members of the Comédie Française take over a wayside inn and try to teach him a lesson, but the plan goes awry.
A pleasant unhistorical conceit makes a rather literary film to have come from Hollywood, but it is all very winning and cast and director keep the fun simmering happily.

w Ernest Vajda d James Whale ph Ernest Haller *m* Adolph Deutsch

Brian Aherne, Edward Everett Horton, Olivia de Havilland, Lionel Atwill, *Melville Cooper, Luis Alberni, Étienne Girardot*, Marie Wilson, Lana Turner, Albert Dekker, Fritz Leiber, Dorothy Tree, Chester Clute

'As elegantly witty as anything Whale ever did.'—*Tom Milne*

'A jestful and romantic piece.'—*Frank S. Nugent, New York Times*

The Great Gatsby*
US 1949 90m bw
Paramount

Events leading to the death of a retired gangster and mysterious Long Island plutocrat.
Rather bland and uninteresting attempt to accommodate a unique author to a formula star.

w Richard Maibaum, *novel* F. Scott Fitzgerald *d* Elliott Nugent *m* Robert Emmett Dolan

Alan Ladd, Macdonald Carey, Betty Field, Barry Sullivan, Howard da Silva

The Great Gatsby**
US 1974 146m Eastmancolor
Paramount / Newdon (David Merrick)

Plush version with lavish production values and pleasing period sense but not much grip on the story or characters. Overlong footage is not made to seem shorter by snail's pace and dull performances.

w Francis Ford Coppola *d* Jack Clayton *ph Douglas Slocombe m* Nelson Riddle *pd* John Box

Robert Redford, Mia Farrow, Karen Black, Scott Wilson, *Sam Waterston*, Lois Chiles

'Pays its creator the regrettable tribute of erecting a mausoleum over his work.'—*Richard Combs*

'Leaves us more involved with $6,500,000's worth of trappings than with human tragedy.'—*Judith Crist*

'A total failure of every requisite sensibility.'—*Stanley Kauffmann*

Great Guns*
US 1941 74m bw
TCF (Sol M. Wurtzel)

A young millionaire's retainers join the army with him.
Disappointing Laurel and Hardy comedy, their first for Fox and the beginning of their decline. A

few good jokes, but no overall control or inventiveness.

w Lou Breslow *d* Monty Banks *ph* Glen MacWilliams

Stan Laurel, Oliver Hardy, Sheila Ryan, Dick Nelson, Edmund Macdonald, Charles Trowbridge, Ludwig Stossel, Mae Marsh

Great Guy*
US 1936 73m bw
Grand National (Douglas Maclean)
GB title: *Pluck of the Irish*

An ex-prizefighter joins the bureau of weights and measures and fights corruption.
Rather tame racket film, Cagney's first independent venture away from Warners. He atones for rather thin production values.

w Henry McCarthy, Henry Johnson, James Edward Grant, Harry Ruskin *d* John G. Blystone *ph* Jack McKenzie *m* Merlin Skiles

James Cagney, Mae Clarke, James Burke, Edward Brophy, Henry Kolker

'It's all typical Cagney stuff, and that's the trouble with it.'—*Variety*

The Great Ice Rip-Off*
US 1974 74m colour TVM
ABC Circle / Dan Curtis

Four jewel thieves get away on an interstate bus.
Lively comedy-thriller.

w Andrew Peter Marin *d* Dan Curtis

Lee J. Cobb, Gig Young, Grayson Hall, Robert Walden

The Great Impersonation*
US 1935 81m bw
Universal (Edmund Grainger)

During World War I, a German murders an English nobleman and, being his double, takes over.
Reliable espionage melodrama with atmospheric country house asides, from a sturdily compelling novel, previously filmed in 1921.

w Frank Wead, Eve Greene, *novel* E. Phillips Oppenheim *d* Alan Crosland *ph* Milton Krasner *m* Franz Waxman

Edmund Lowe, Valerie Hobson, Vera Engels, Henry Mollison, Lumsden Hare, Spring Byington, Charles Waldron, Dwight Frye

The Great Impersonation*
US 1942 71m bw
Universal (Paul Malvern)

Okay quickie updating of the above, serviceable rather than inventive.

w W. Scott Darling *d* John Rawlins *ph* George Robinson *m* Hans Salter

Ralph Bellamy, Evelyn Ankers, Aubrey Mather, Edward Norris, Karen Verne, Henry Daniell, Ludwig Stossel

The Great Imposter*
US 1961 112m bw
U-I (Robert Arthur)

The career of Ferdinand Waldo Demara, a marine and Trappist monk who also impersonated a Harvard research fellow, a prison warden, a naval doctor and a schoolteacher.
Uncertain mood hampers this biopic of a likeable fantasist.

w Liam O'Brien, *book* Robert Crichton *d* Robert Mulligan *ph* Robert Burks *m* Henry Mancini

Tony Curtis, Raymond Massey, Karl Malden, Edmond O'Brien, Arthur O'Connell, Gary Merrill, Frank Gorshin, Joan Blackman, Robert Middleton

The Great John L.
US 1945 96m bw
UA (Frank Mastroly, James Edward Grant)
GB title: *A Man Called Sullivan*

Women in the life of prizefighter John L. Sullivan.
Very mild period biopic without the zest of *Gentleman Jim.*

w James Edward Grant *d* Frank Tuttle *ph* James Van Trees *m* Victor Young

Greg McClure, Linda Darnell, Barbara Britton, Lee Sullivan, Otto Kruger, Wallace Ford, Robert Barrat

The Great Lie***
US 1941 107m bw
Warner (Hal B. Wallis, Henry Blanke)

A determined girl loses the man she loves, believes him dead in a plane crash, and takes over the baby which his selfish wife does not want.
Absurd melodrama becomes top-flight entertainment with all concerned in cracking form and special attention on the two bitchy female leads, splendidly played. Classical music trimmings, too.

w Lenore Coffee, novel Polan Banks *d Edmund Goulding ph Tony Gaudio m Max Steiner*

Bette Davis, Mary Astor, George Brent, Lucile Watson, Hattie McDaniel, Grant Mitchell, Jerome Cowan

The Great Locomotive Chase*
US 1956 76m Technicolor Cinemascope
Walt Disney (Lawrence Edward Watkin)

During the Civil War, Union spies steal a train and destroy track and bridges behind them.
A serious version of Buster Keaton's *The General*, based on a true incident; good sequences but no overall pace.

w Lawrence Edward Watkin *d* Francis D. Lyon *ph* Charles Boyle *m* Paul Smith

Fess Parker, Jeffrey Hunter, Jeff York, John Lupton, Kenneth Tobey

The Great Lover*
US 1949 80m bw
(Paramount) Hope Enterprises (Edmund Beloin)

On a transatlantic liner, a timid scoutmaster catches a strangler.
Amusing suspense comedy, a good star vehicle.

w Edmund Beloin, Melville Shavelson, Jack Rose *d* Alexander Hall *ph* Charles Lang *m* Joseph J. Lilley

Bob Hope, Rhonda Fleming, *Roland Young*, Jim Backus, Roland Culver, George Reeves

The Great Man**
US 1956 92m bw
U-I (Aaron Rosenberg)

A memorial programme to a much-loved TV personality turns into an exposé.
Patchy melodrama with a *Citizen Kane* framework; the best bits are very effective.

w Jose Ferrer, Al Morgan, novel Al Morgan *d* Jose Ferrer *ph* Harold Lipstein *m* Herman Stein

Jose Ferrer, Dean Jagger, Keenan Wynn, *Julie London*, Joanne Gilbert, *Ed Wynn*, Jim Backus

'Its distinction is in its unwavering tone—one of blunt and frequently savage irony and cynicism.'—*MFB*

'The movie is almost over before one realizes what a slick, fast sell it is (resembling nothing so much as what it is attacking).'—*Pauline Kael, 1968*

The Great Man Votes*
US 1939 72m bw
RKO

A drunken professor turns out to have the casting vote in a local election.
Slow-starting but progressively funny political comedy with some favourite talents in good form.

w John Twist, *story* Gordon Malherbe Hillman *d Garson Kanin ph* Russell Metty *m* Roy Webb

John Barrymore, Virginia Weidler, Peter Holden, *William Demarest, Donald MacBride*

The Great Man's Lady*
US 1942 90m bw
Paramount (William A. Wellman)

A western pioneer is inspired and encouraged by his wife.
Adequate but unsurprising flashback family drama starting with its star as a lady of 109.

w W. L. Rivers, *story* Vina Delmar *d* William L. Wellman *ph* William C. Mellor *m* Victor Young

Barbara Stanwyck, Joel McCrea, Brian Donlevy, Katharine Stevens, Thurston Hall, Lloyd Corrigan

The Great Man's Whiskers
US 1971 96m Technicolor TVM
Universal (Adrian Scott)

President-elect Abraham Lincoln agrees with a little girl's suggestion that he should grow a beard.
Whimsy based on fact, far too long for its substance.

w John Paxton, *play* Adrian Scott *d* Philip Leacock

Dennis Weaver, Dean Jones, Ann Sothern, John McGiver

The Great McGinty**
US 1940 83m bw
Paramount

A hobo and a crook have a hectic political career.
Lively comedy-drama which signalled the arrival as director of a new and stimulating Hollywood talent.

wd Preston Sturges m Frederick Hollander

Brian Donlevy, Akim Tamiroff, Muriel Angelus, Louis Jean Heydt, Arthur Hoyt

'This is his first directing job and where has he been all our lives? He has that sense of the incongruous which makes some of the best gaiety.'—*Otis Ferguson*

'The tough dialogue is matched by short, snappy scenes; the picture seems to have wasted no time, no money.'—*Gilbert Seldes*

'A director as adroit and inventive as any in the business . . . it starts like a five-alarm fire and never slackens pace for one moment until its unexpected conclusion.'—*Pare Lorentz*

The Great Mr Handel*
GB 1942 103m Technicolor
Rank / GHW (James B. Sloan)

How the 18th-century composer came to write the Messiah.
Earnest, unlikely biopic, naïve but rather commendable.

w Gerald Elliott, Victor MacClure, *play* L. DuGarde Peach *d* Norman Walker

Wilfrid Lawson, Elizabeth Allan, Malcolm Keen, Michael Shepley, Hay Petrie, A. E. Matthews

The Great Moment**
US 1944 83m bw
Paramount

How anaesthetics may have been invented.
Curious biopic of Dr W. T. G. Morgan, poised somewhere between utter seriousness and pratfall farce. The beginning of its director's decline, but always interesting in itself.

wd Preston Sturges, book Triumph over Pain by René Fulop-Miller *ph* Victor Milner *m* Victor Young

Joel McCrea, Betty Field, William Demarest, Harry Carey, Franklin Pangborn, Grady Sutton, Jimmy Conlin

The Great Niagara*
US 1974 74m colour TVM
Playboy

During the Depression, a river family helps guide those who challenge Niagara Falls.
Unusual, watchable open-air drama.

w Robert E. Thompson *d* William Hale

Richard Boone, Randy Quaid, Jennifer Salt, Michael Sacks, Burt Young

The Great Northfield Minnesota Raid*
US 1971 91m Technicolor
Universal / Robertson and Associates / Jennings Lang

In 1876 a gang of bandits, technically pardoned, plan a bank robbery.
'Realistic' western in which the settings and photography have an impressively rough look but the script leaves much to be desired.

wd Philip Kaufman *ph Bruce Surtees m* Dave Grusin

Cliff Robertson, Robert Duvall, Luke Askew, Elisha Cook Jnr

The Great Profile*
US 1940 82m bw
TCF (Raymond Griffith)

A dissipated actor disgraces his family and becomes an acrobat.
Shapeless farce in which a great talent on his last legs parodies himself.

w Milton Sperling, Hilary Lynn *d* Walter Lang *ph* Ernest Palmer *m* Cyril Mockridge

John Barrymore, Mary Beth Hughes, Gregory Ratoff, Anne Baxter, John Payne, Lionel Atwill, Edward Brophy, Willie Fung

The Great Race***
US 1965 163m Technicolor Super Panavison
Warner / Patricia / Jalem / Reynard (Martin Jurow)

In 1908, the Great Leslie and Professor Fate are leading contenders in the first New York to Paris car race.
Elaborate comedy spectacular with many good moments, notably the early disasters, a western saloon brawl, and a custard pie fight. Elsewhere, there is more evidence of an oversize budget than of wit or finesse, and the entire Prisoner of Zenda spoof could have been omitted. Excellent production detail and general good humour.

w Arthur Ross *d* Blake Edwards *ph Russell Harlan m Henry Mancini pd Fernando Carrere*

Jack Lemmon, Tony Curtis, Peter Falk, Natalie Wood, George Macready, Ross Martin, Vivian Vance, Dorothy Provine

The Great Scout and Cathouse Thursday
US 1976 102m Technicolor
AIP (Jules Buck and David Korda)

While trying to revenge himself on an absconding partner, an old cowboy falls for a young prostitute.
Downright peculiar comedy western which never seems to make up its mind what it's trying to be, and too often is merely embarrassing.

w Richard Shapiro *d* Don Taylor *ph* Alex Phillips Jnr *m* John Cameron *pd* Jack Martin Smith

Lee Marvin, Oliver Reed, Kay Lenz, Robert Culp, Elizabeth Ashley, Strother Martin, Sylvia Miles

The Great Sinner*
US 1949 110m bw
MGM (Gottfried Reinhardt)

A serious young writer becomes a compulsive gambler.
Rather pointless and heavy-handed but extremely good-looking and splendidly cast period drama vaguely based on Dostoievsky.

w Ladislas Fodor, Christopher Isherwood *d* Robert Siodmak *ph George Folsey* *m* Bronislau Kaper *ad Cedric Gibbons, Hans Peck*

Gregory Peck, *Walter Huston*, Ava Gardner, Agnes Moorehead, Ethel Barrymore, Melvyn Douglas, Frank Morgan

The Great Sioux Massacre
US 1965 93m Eastmancolor Cinemascope
Columbia / FF (Leon Fromkess)

Two officers are court-martialled after Custer's last stand.
Fragmentary flashback western let down by production and performances.

w Fred C. Dobbs *d* Sidney Salkow *ph* Irving Lippman *m* Emil Newman, Edward B. Powell

Joseph Cotten, Darren McGavin, Phil Carey, Nancy Kovack, Julie Sommars, Michael Pate

The Great Sioux Uprising
US 1953 80m Technicolor
U-I (Albert J. Cohen)

Indians rebel when their horses are stolen for sale to the commander of Fort Laramie.
Moderate western programmer.

w Richard Breen, Gladys Atwater *d* Lloyd Bacon *ph* Maury Gertsman *m* Joseph Gershenson

Jeff Chandler, Faith Domergue, Lyle Bettger

The Great Victor Herbert*
US 1939 91m bw
Paramount (Andrew L. Stone)

At the turn of the century a famous composer plays cupid to two young singers.
Pleasant minor musical with excellent songs and an infectious cheerfulness.

w Russel Crouse, Robert Lively *d Andrew L. Stone* *ph* Victor Milner

Walter Connolly, Allan Jones, Mary Martin, Susanna Foster, Lee Bowman

The Great Waldo Pepper**
US 1975 108m Technicolor Todd-AO 35
Universal (George Roy Hill)

In the twenties, a World War I flier becomes an aerial stuntman.
Whimsical spectacular which concentrates less on the mystique of flying than on a series of splendid stunts.

w William Goldman *d George Roy Hill* *ph Robert Surtees* *m* Henry Mancini

Robert Redford, Bo Svenson, Bo Brundin, Susan Sarandon, Geoffrey Lewis

'Charged with enthralling balletic precision.'—*Tom Milne*

'One hundred per cent pure plastic adolescent male fantasy.'—*New Yorker*

The Great Waltz***
US 1938 103m bw
MGM (Bernard Hyman)

Young Johann Strauss becomes Vienna's waltz king.
Exhilarating old-fashioned studio-set musical located in Hollywood's endearing vision of Old Vienna, assisted by streamlined production and excellent cast. Musical schmaltz.

w Walter Reisch, Samuel Hoffenstein, *story* Gottfried Reinhardt *d Julien Duvivier*

Fernand Gravet, Luise Rainer, Miliza Korjus, Lionel Atwill, Hugh Herbert, Herman Bing, Curt Bois

The Great Waltz*
US 1972 134m Metrocolor Panavision 70
MGM (Andrew L. Stone)

Heavy-going remake set on real locations and hampered by them, styled in the manner of the same director's *Song of Norway*, i.e. with no real style at all. The music survives.

wd Andrew L. Stone *ph* David Boulton *ad* William Albert Havenmeyer *ch* Onna White

Horst Buchholz, Nigel Patrick, Mary Costa, Rossano Brazzi, Yvonne Mitchell

The Great White Hope**
US 1970 103m De Luxe Panavision
TCF (Lawrence Turman)

In 1910, a black boxer becomes world heavyweight champ but has trouble through his affair with a white girl.
Vivid, slightly whitewashed biopic of Jack Johnson (called Jefferson). Dramatic deficiencies outweighed by excellent period detail and a spellbinding central performance.

w Howard Sackler, from his play *d Martin Ritt* *ph Burnett Guffey* *m* negro traditionals *pd John de Cuir*

James Earl Jones, Jane Alexander, Lou Gilbert, Joel Fluellen, Chester Morris, Robert Webber, Hal Holbrook

The Great Ziegfeld**
US 1936 179m bw
MGM (Hunt Stromberg)

The growth and Broadway fame of impresario Florenz Ziegfeld.
Mammoth biopic which despite a few show-stopping numbers never takes off dramatically and becomes something of an endurance test; interesting, however, as a spectacular of its time.

w William Anthony McGuire *d* Robert Z. Leonard *ph* Oliver T. Marsh, Ray June, George Folsey *md* Arthur Lange *ad* Cedric Gibbons

William Powell, Luise Rainer (as Anna Held), Myrna Loy (as Billie Burke), Frank Morgan, Reginald Owen, Nat Pendleton, Virginia Bruce, *Ray Bolger*, Harriett Hoctor, Ernest Cossart, *Fannie Brice*, Robert Greig, Gilda Gray, Leon Errol, Stanley Morner (Dennis Morgan)

'This huge inflated gas-blown object bobs into the critical view as irrelevantly as an airship advertising somebody's toothpaste at a south coast resort. It lasts three hours. That is its only claim to special attention.'—*Graham Greene*

The Greatest Gift
US 1974 100m Technicolor TVM
Universal

The life of a preacher in the midwest early in the century.
Slow, earnest, rather empty pilot for an unsuccessful series (*Holvak*).

w Abby Mann *d* Boris Sagal

Glenn Ford, Julie Harris, Lance Kerwin

The Greatest Show on Earth*
US 1952 153m Technicolor
Paramount / Cecil B. de Mille (Henry Wilcoxon)

Various dramas come to a head under the big top.
Moribund circus drama with bad acting, stilted production, an irrelevant train crash climax and a few genuinely spectacular and enjoyable moments.

w Fredric M. Frank, Theodore St John, Frank Cavett, Barre Lyndon *d* Cecil B. de Mille *ph* George Barnes, Peverell Marley, Wallace Kelley *m Victor Young* *ad* Hal Pereira, Walter Tyler

Betty Hutton, Cornel Wilde, James Stewart, Charlton Heston, Dorothy Lamour, Gloria Grahame, Lyle Bettger, Henry Wilcoxon, Emmett Kelly, Lawrence Tierney, John Kellogg, John Ringling North

The Greatest Story Ever Told**
US 1965 225m Technicolor Ultra Panavision 70
UA / George Stevens

Solemn spectacular with an elephantine pace, shot in Utah because allegedly it looked more like Palestine than Palestine did. All frightfully elegant and reverent, but totally unmoving, partly because of the fatal casting of stars in bit parts. (John Wayne looks in merely to say 'Truly this man was the son of God.')

w James Lee Barrett, George Stevens, from various sources *d* George Stevens *ph William C. Mellor, Loyal Griggs* *m* Alfred Newman *ad Richard Day, William Creber*

Max Von Sydow, Dorothy McGuire, Claude Rains, Jose Ferrer, David McCallum, Charlton Heston, Sidney Poitier, Donald Pleasance, Roddy McDowall, Gary Raymond, Carroll Baker, Pat Boone, Van Heflin, Sal Mineo, Shelley Winters, Ed Wynn, John Wayne, Telly Savalas, Angela Lansbury, Joseph Schildkraut, Victor Buono, Nehemiah Persoff

'George Stevens was once described as a water buffalo of film art. What this film more precisely suggests is a dinosaur.'—*MFB*

'God is unlucky in *The Greatest Story Ever Told*. His only begotten son turns out to be a bore . . . the photography is inspired mainly by Hallmark Cards . . . as the Hallelujah Chorus explodes around us stereophonically and stereotypically it becomes clear that Lazarus was not so much raised from the tomb as blasted out of it. As for pacing, the picture does not let you forget a single second of its four hours.'—*John Simon*

'No more than three minutes have elapsed before we suspect that Stevens' name and fame have been purchased by the Hallmark Greeting Card Company, and that what we are looking at is really a lengthy catalogue of greeting cards for 1965—for Those Who Care Enough to Send the Very Best.'—*Stanley Kauffmann*

The Greeks Had a Word for Them*
US 1932 77m bw
UA

Adventures of three New York gold diggers.
Smart early talkie which helped launch the *Gold Diggers* series and TCF's parallel *Three Little Mice / Moon over Miami / How to Marry a Millionaire* series.

w Sidney Howard, *play* Zoe Akins *d* Lowell Sherman *ph* George Barnes

Joan Blondell, Madge Evans, Ina Claire, David Manners, Lowell Sherman, Phillips Smalley, Betty Grable

The Green Berets
US 1968 141m Technicolor Panavision
Warner / Batjac (Michael Wayne)

After extensive training, two tough army detachments see service in Vietnam.
Overlong actioner criticized for unquestioningly accepting the Vietnam cause; in itself, violent, exhausting and dull.

w James Lee Barrett, *novel* Robin Moore *d* John Wayne, Ray Kellogg *ph* Winton C. Hoch *m* Miklos Rozsa

John Wayne, David Janssen, Jim Hutton, Aldo Ray, Raymond St Jacques, Jack Soo, Bruce Cabot, Patrick Wayne, Irene Tsu, Jason Evers, Luke Askew

'Propaganda as crude as this can only do damage to its cause.'—*David Wilson*

'A film best handled from a distance and with a pair of tongs.'—*Penelope Gilliatt*

Green Dolphin Street
US 1947 141m bw
MGM

A Channel Islander emigrates to New Zealand and sends home for the wrong bride.
Silly 19th-century romance climaxed by rather a good earthquake. Expensively but falsely produced.

w Samson Raphaelson, *novel* Elizabeth Goudge *d* Victor Saville *ph* George Folsey

Lana Turner, Richard Hart, Edmund Gwenn, Van Heflin, Donna Reed

Green Fire
US 1954 100m Eastmancolor Cinemascope
MGM

Two engineers disagree over their mining of Columbia diamonds.
Routine adventure story with good action highlights including landslide, flood and storm, all deadened by dull dialogue and romantic complications.

w Ivan Goff, Ben Roberts *d* Andrew Marton *ph* Paul Vogel *m* Miklos Rozsa

Stewart Granger, Paul Douglas, Grace Kelly

Green for Danger****
GB 1946 93m bw
Rank / Individual (Frank Launder, Sidney Gilliat)

A mysterious murderer strikes on the operating table at a wartime emergency hospital.
Classic comedy-thriller, with serious detection balanced by excellent jokes and performances, also by moments of fright.

w Sidney Gilliat, Claude Guerney, novel Christianna Brand *d Sidney Gilliat ph Wilkie Cooper*

Alastair Sim, Sally Gray, Rosamund John, Trevor Howard, Leo Genn, Megs Jenkins, Judy Campbell, Ronald Ward, Moore Marriott

The Green Goddess*
US 1930 74m bw
Warner

An Indian potentate holds Britishers prisoner.
Early talkie star vehicle which was also successful on the stage and as a silent but has little appeal now.

w Julian Josephson, *play* William Archer *d* Alfred E. Green *ph* James Van Trees

George Arliss, Alice Joyce, H. B. Warner, Ralph Forbes, David Tearle

Green Hell*
US 1940 87m bw
Universal (Harry Edgington)

Explorers seek Inca treasure in the South American Jungle.
Studio-bound potboiler unworthy of its director but mainly enjoyable as a romp.

w Frances Marion *d* James Whale *ph* Karl Freund

Douglas Fairbanks Jnr, Joan Bennett, George Sanders, Vincent Price, Alan Hale, Gene Garrick, George Bancroft, John Howard
† The temple set was re-used the same year in *The Mummy's Hand.*

The Green Light*
US 1937 85m bw
Warner (Henry Blanke)

A dedicated doctor gives up his practice when a patient dies.
Adequate star melodrama.

w Milton Krims, *novel* Lloyd C. Douglas *d* Frank Borzage *ph* Byron Haskin *m* Max Steiner

Errol Flynn, Anita Louise, Margaret Lindsay, Cedric Hardwicke, Henry O'Neill, Spring Byington

The Green Man*
GB 1956 80m bw
BL / Grenadier (Frank Launder, Sidney Gilliat)

A professional assassin stalks a pompous politician.
Cheerful but not very subtle black comedy,

suffering from the attempt to make a star part out of a very minor character.

w Sidney Gilliat, Frank Launder, from their play Meet a Body *d* Robert Day *ph* Gerald Gibbs *m* Cedric Thorpe Davie

Alastair Sim, George Cole, Jill Adams, Terry-Thomas, Avril Angers, John Chandos, Dora Bryan, Colin Gordon, Raymond Huntley

Green Mansions
US 1959 104m Metrocolor Cinemascope
MGM / Avon (Edmund Grainger)

In a remote Amazon forest an adventurer encounters Rima, a child of nature who takes him on a quest for truth.
Absurd studio-bound Shangri-La story based on an Edwardian fantasy that may well have suited the printed page, but not the wide screen. Dismally photographed in shades of green, with all concerned looking acutely uncomfortable.

w Dorothy Kingsley, *novel* W. H. Hudson *d* Mel Ferrer *ph* Joseph Ruttenberg *m* Bronislau Kaper, Hector Villa-Lobos

Anthony Perkins, Audrey Hepburn, Lee J. Cobb, Henry Silva

The Green Pastures****
US 1936 93m bw
Warner (Henry Blanke)

Old Testament stories as seen through simple-minded negro eyes.
Though recently attacked as setting back the cause of black emancipation, this is a brilliantly sympathetic and humorous film, very cunningly adapted for the screen in a series of dramatic scenes which make the material work even better than it did on the stage.

w Marc Connelly, from his play and stories by Roark Bradford *d William Keighley, Marc Connelly ph Hal Mohr m Erich Wolfgang Korngold*

Rex Ingram, Oscar Polk, Eddie Anderson, Frank Wilson, George Reed

'I imagine God has a sense of humour, and I imagine that He is delighted with *The Green Pastures*.'—*Don Herold*

'That disturbance around the Music Hall yesterday was the noise of shuffling queues in Sixth Avenue and the sound of motion picture critics dancing in the street.'—*Bosley Crowther, New York Times*

The Green Scarf
GB 1954 96m bw
B and A (Bertram Ostrer, Albert Fennell)

An elderly French lawyer takes on the defence of a blind, deaf and dumb murder suspect.
Plodding courtroom drama with familiar faces in unconvincing French guise.

w Gordon Wellesley, *novel* The Brute by Guy des Cars *d* George More O'Ferrall *ph* Jack Hildyard *m* Brian Easdale

Michael Redgrave, Ann Todd, Leo Genn, Kieron Moore

The Green Years*
US 1946 127m bw
MGM (Leon Gordon)

A young boy brought up strictly in Ireland makes friends with his mischievous grandfather.
Period family film in familiar style, sparked only by its scene-stealing star performance.

w Robert Ardrey, Sonya Levien, *novel* A. J. Cronin *d* Victor Saville *ph* George Folsey *m* Herbert Stothart *ad* Cedric Gibbons, Hans Peters

Charles Coburn, Dean Stockwell, Tom Drake, Beverly Tyler, Hume Cronyn, Gladys Cooper, Selena Royle, Jessica Tandy, Richard Haydn, Andy Clyde

'It has been described in the ads as "wonderful" by everyone within Louis B. Mayer's purchasing power except his horses, so I hesitate to ask you to take my word for it: the picture is awful.'—*James Agee*

The Greengage Summer*
GB 1961 99m Technicolor
Columbia / PKL (Victor Saville, Edward Small)
US title: *Loss of Innocence*

A young girl staying at a hotel falls in love with a jewel thief but is accidentally responsible for his capture.
Old-fashioned and not very interesting story with an appeal, one supposes, to well-brought-up young women. Decently made.

w Howard Koch, *novel* Rumer Godden *d* Lewis Gilbert *ph* Frederick A. Young *m* Richard Addinsell

Kenneth More, Danielle Darrieux, Susannah York, Claude Nollier, Jane Asher, Elizabeth Dear, Maurice Denham

Greenwich Village*
US 1944 82m Technicolor
TCF (William Le Baron)

In the twenties, a hick composer in New York allows his concerto to be used in a jazz musical.
Lightweight musical romp.

w Michael Fessier, Ernest Pagano *d* Walter

Lang *ph* Leon Shamroy, Harry Jackson *songs* Leo Robin, Nacio Herb Brown

Carmen Miranda, Don Ameche, William Bendix, Vivian Blaine, Felix Bressart, Tony and Sally De Marco, Adolph Green, Betty Comden, Alvin Hammer, Judy Holliday

Greyfriars Bobby*
GB 1960 91m Technicolor
Walt Disney (Hugh Attwooll)

A Skye terrier keeps persistent vigil over his master's grave and is made a freeman of the city of Edinburgh.
Adequately produced film of a charming old Victorian story.

w Robert Westerby *d* Don Chaffey *ph* Paul Beeson *m* Francis Chagrin

Donald Crisp, Laurence Naismith, Alexander Mackenzie, Kay Walsh, Andrew Cruickshank, Vincent Winter, Moultrie Kelsall, Duncan Macrae

'The better Disney qualities of exact period detail and childlike directness are apparent.'—*MFB*

Griff*
US 1974 102m Technicolor TVM
Universal (David Victor)
aka: *Man on the Outside*

When his private eye son is murdered, an ex-cop takes over the business and hunts down the murderer.
Smooth pilot for an unsuccessful series, which appeared at the same time as the similar and more popular *Barnaby Jones*.

w Larry Cohen *d* Boris Sagal

Lorne Greene, James Olson, Lorraine Gary, Lee H. Montgomery

Grip of the Strangler*
GB 1958 78m bw
Producers' Associates (John Croydon)

A novelist investigating an old murder case finds that he was himself the murderer.
Moderate thriller with a predictable but efficient plot.

w Jan Read *d* Robert Day *ph* Lionel Banes *m* Buxton Orr

Boris Karloff, Elizabeth Allan, Jean Kent, Vera Day, Anthony Dawson

The Grissom Gang
US 1971 128m Metrocolor
Associates and Aldrich / ABC

In 1931, a New York heiress is kidnapped by gangsters and comes to like it.
Unpleasant remake of *No Orchids for Miss Blandish* (previously filmed under that title, incredibly badly, in GB in 1948), with too much footage of lush blonde being slobbered over by psychotic thug, and an inevitable emphasis on violence.

w Leon Griffiths, *novel* James Hadley Chase *d* Robert Aldrich *ph* Joseph Biroc *m* Gerald Fried *ad* James Dowell Vance

Scott Wilson, Kim Darby, Tony Musante, Robert Lansing, Irene Dailey, Connie Stevens, Wesley Addy

'Offensive, immoral and perhaps even lascivious.'—*Vincent Canby*

The Groundstar Conspiracy*
US 1972 96m Technicolor Panavision
Universal / Hal Roach International (Trevor Wallace)

An explosion rips apart a top secret space project, and the surviving scientist loses his memory.
Gimmicky but generally compulsive sci-fi mystery yarn, with an effective though predictable climax.

w Matthew Howard, *novel* The Alien by L. P. Davies *d* Lamont Johnson *ph* Michael Reed *m* Paul Hoffert

George Peppard, Michael Sarrazin, James Olson, Christine Belford, Tim O'Connor, James McEachin

The Group***
US 1966 152m De Luxe
UA / Famous Artists (Sidney Buchman)

The subsequent love lives of a group of girls who graduate from Vassar in 1933.
Patchy but generally fascinating series of interwoven sketches and character studies, with mainly tragic overtones; good attention to period detail, and dazzling array of new talent.

w Sidney Buchman, novel Mary McCarthy d Sidney Lumet ph Boris Kaufman m Charles Gross *pd Gene Callahan*

Joanna Pettet, Candice Bergen, *Jessica Walter, Joan Hackett*, Elizabeth Hartman, Mary Robin-Redd, *Kathleen Widdoes*, Shirley Knight, Larry Hagman, *Hal Holbrook, Robert Emhardt*, Robert Mulligan, James Congdon, James Broderick

'A strange, all-inclusive, no-holds-barred movie.'—*Philip T. Hartung*

Guadalcanal Diary*
US 1943 93m bw
TCF (Byron Foy)

Marines fight for a vital Pacific base.
Standard war propaganda, with good action scenes.

w Lamar Trotti, *book* Richard Tregaskis *d* Lewis Seiler *ph* Charles G. Clarke *m* David Buttolph

Preston Foster, Lloyd Nolan, William Bendix, Richard Conte, Anthony Quinn, Richard Jaeckel, Roy Roberts, Minor Watson, Ralph Byrd, Lionel Stander, Miles Mander, Reed Hadley

The Guardsman*
US 1931 83m bw
MGM

A jealous actor tests his wife's fidelity.
Theatrically effective comedy filmed for the sake of its stars; later remade as a musical, *The Chocolate Soldier* (qv).

w Ernest Vajda, Claudine West, *play* Ferenc Molnar *d* Sidney Franklin *ph* Norbert Brodine

Alfred Lunt, Lynn Fontanne, Roland Young, Zasu Pitts, Maude Eburne, Herman Bing, Ann Dvorak

Guess Who's Coming to Dinner**
US 1967 112m Technicolor
Columbia / Stanley Kramer

A well-to-do San Francisco girl announces that she is going to marry a black man, and her parents find they are less broad-minded than they thought.
The problem picture that isn't really, since everyone is so nice and the prospective bridegroom is so eligible. It looks like a photographed play, but isn't based on one; the set is unconvincing; but the acting is a dream.

w William Rose *d* Stanley Kramer *ph* Sam Leavitt *m* Frank de Vol *pd* Robert Clatworthy

Spencer Tracy, Katharine Hepburn, Katharine Houghton (Hepburn's niece), *Sidney Poitier*, Cecil Kellaway, Roy E. Glenn Snr, Beah Richards, Isabell Sanford, Virginia Christine

'Suddenly everybody's caught up in a kind of integrated drawing-room comedy, and unable to decide whether there's anything funny in it or not.'—*Ann Birstein, Vogue*

Guess Who's Sleeping in My Bed?
US 1973 74m colour TVM
ABC Circle / Mark Carliner

A man and his overwhelming family, including a large dog, turn up to stay with his ex-wife.
Thin, fairly likeable comedy.

w Pamela Herbert Chais *d* Theodore Flicker

Dean Jones, Barbara Eden, Kenneth Mars, Reta Shaw, Suzanne Benton

Guest in the House*
US 1944 121m bw
Hunt Stromberg

A seemingly pleasant young woman is invited to stay with a family and brings tragedy and hatred to them.
Theatrical and rather unconvincing melodrama.

w Ketti Frings, *play* Dear Evelyn by Dale Eunson, Hagar Wilde *d* John Brahm *ph* Lee Garmes *m* Werner Janssen *pd* Nicolai Remisoff

Anne Baxter, Ralph Bellamy, Aline MacMahon, Ruth Warrick, Scott McKay, Jerome Cowan, Marie McDonald, Percy Kilbride, Margaret Hamilton

A Guide for the Married Man**
US 1967 91m De Luxe Panavision
TCF (Frank McCarthy)

A practised wolf explains to a perfect husband how to be unfaithful.
Generally funny revue with as many hilarious moments as flat spots.

w Frank Tarloff *d* Gene Kelly *ph* Joe Macdonald *m* Johnny Williams

Walter Matthau, Inger Stevens, *Robert Morse*, Sue Anne Langdon, Lucille Ball, Art Carney, Jack Benny, Polly Bergen, Joey Bishop, Sid Caesar, Wally Cox, Jayne Mansfield, Carl Reiner, Phil Silvers, Jeffrey Hunter, Terry-Thomas, Ben Blue

The Guilt of Janet Ames
US 1948 83m bw
Columbia

A paralysed war widow seeks to discover whether her husband's sacrifice was worthwhile.
Embarrassing attempt by a comedienne to play Hamlet.

w Louella Macfarlane, Allen Rivkin, Devery Freeman, *story* Lenore Coffee *d* Henry Levin *ph* Joseph Walker *m* Morris Stoloff

Rosalind Russell, Melvyn Douglas, Sid Caesar, Betsy Blair, Nina Foch, Harry Von Zell, Arthur Space

Guilty or Innocent: The Sam Sheppard Murder Case*
US 1975 156m Technicolor TVM
Universal (Harve Bennett)

In 1954, a Cleveland doctor is convicted, then acquitted, of murdering his wife: he later gives up his practice and becomes a professional wrestler.
Pretty absorbing true-life stuff, but this is too

long a time to spend on a tale with no end: the doctor died without revealing the truth.

w Harold Gast *d* Robert Michael Lewis

George Peppard, William Windom, Nina Van Pallandt, Walter McGinn, Barnard Hughes

The Guinea Pig**
GB 1949 97m bw
Pilgrim (The Boultings)
US title: *The Outsider*

The first poor boy to win a scholarship to a famous public school has a hard time.
Enjoyable though unrealistic school drama with chief interest centring on the staff. A rude word ('kick up the arse') ensured its popularity.

w Bernard Miles, Warren Chetham Strode, from the latter's play *d* Roy Boulting *ph* Gilbert Taylor *m* John Wooldridge

Richard Attenborough, *Robert Flemyng, Cecil Trouncer*, Sheila Sim, Bernard Miles, Joan Hickson

The Gumball Rally
US 1976 93m Technicolor
Warner / First Artists (Chuck Bail)

A variety of vehicles take part in a crazy race from New York to Long Beach.
The stuntmen are the real stars of this good-looking but dramatically deficient chase and destruction extravaganza.

w Leon Capetanos *d* Chuck Bail *ph Richard Glouner m* Dominic Frontière *stunt co-ordinator* Eddie Donno

Michael Sarrazin, Normann Burton, Gary Busey, John Durren, Susan Flannery

Gumshoe**
GB 1972 85m Eastmancolor
Columbia / Memorial (David Barber)

A Liverpool bingo caller dreams of becoming a Bogart-like private eye and finds himself in the middle of a murder case.
A likeable spoof which is never quite as funny as it means to be. Billy Liar did it better, but there is plenty of amusing detail.

w Neville Smith *d* Stephen Frears *ph* Chris Menges *m* Andrew Lloyd Webber

Albert Finney, Billie Whitelaw, Fulton Mackay, Frank Finlay, Janice Rule

The Gun
US 1974 74m Technicolor TVM
Universal (Richard Levinson, William Link)

A gun passes from hand to hand.
Shades of *Tales of Manhattan* ... but the mini-stories here are not very interesting.

w Richard Levinson, William Link *d* John Badham

Steven Elliott, Pepe Serna, Edith Diaz, Mariclare Costello, Jean Le Bouvier

The Gun and the Pulpit
US 1974 74m colour TVM
Danny Thomas

A gunslinger on the run masquerades as a preacher.
Hesitant variation on *The Left Hand of God.*

w William Bowers *d* Daniel Petrie

Marjoe Gortner, Estelle Parsons, David Huddleston, Slim Pickens

Gun Crazy*
US 1950 87m bw
King Brothers

A boy and girl set off on a trail of armed robbery and murder.
Modernized Bonnie and Clyde story which has become a minor cult film.

w Mackinlay Kantor, Millard Kaufman *d Joseph H. Lewis ph* Russell Harlan *m* Stuart Fryt

John Dall, Peggy Cummins, Morris Carnovsky, Barry Kroger, Annabel Shaw, Harry Lewis

Gun Fury
US 1953 80m Technicolor 3-D
Columbia (Lewis J. Rachmil)

Outlaws rob a stagecoach and abduct a girl; her fiancé follows and takes revenge.
Adequate western programmer.

w Irving Wallace, Roy Huggins *d* Raoul Walsh *ph* Lester H. White *m* Mischa Bakaleinikoff

Rock Hudson, Donna Reed, Phil Carey, Lee Marvin, Neville Brand

Gun Glory
US 1957 89m Metrocolor
Cinemascope
MGM (Nicholas Nayfack)

A gunfighter returns home to settle down, but finds his wife dead and his son resentful.
Dull, unexciting star western.

w William Ludwig, *novel* Man of the West by Philip Yordan *d* Roy Rowland *ph* Harold J. Marzorati *m* Jeff Alexander

Stewart Granger, Rhonda Fleming, Chill Wills, Steve Rowland, James Gregory

The Gun of Zangara*
US 1961 97m bw TVM
Desilu / Quinn Martin

An assassin's bullet marked for the President hits the Mayor of Chicago.
Solidly entertaining *Untouchables* feature.

w William Spier

Robert Stack, Bruce Gordon, Joe Mantell, Anthony George, Claude Akins

The Gun Runners*
US 1958 82m bw
UA / Seven Arts (Clarence Greene)

The owner of a Florida motor cruiser innocently rents it to a gun merchant.
Modestly effective action melodrama, the third version of *To Have and Have Not* (qv).

w Daniel Mainwaring, Paul Monash *d Don Siegel ph Hal Mohr m* Leith Stevens

Audie Murphy, Eddie Albert, Patricia Owens, Everett Sloane

A Gunfight*
US 1970 94m Technicolor
Harvest / Thoroughbred / Bryna (Ronnie Lubin, Harold Jack Bloom)

Two famous gunfighters on their uppers stage a duel for money.
Austere and anti-climactic western supposedly against popular blood lust.

w Harold Jack Bloom *d* Lamont Johnson *ph* David M. Walsh *m* Laurence Rosenthal

Kirk Douglas, Johnny Cash, Karen Black, Raf Vallone

Gunfight at Dodge City
US 1958 81m De Luxe Cinemascope
UA / Mirisch

After various problems, Bat Masterson is elected sheriff of Dodge City.
Fair standard western with emphasis on plot and character.

w Daniel B. Ullman, Martin M. Goldsmith *d* Joseph M. Newman *ph* Carl Guthrie *m* Hans Salter

Joel McCrea, Julie Adams, John McIntire, Richard Anderson, Nancy Gates

Gunfight at the OK Corral**
US 1957 122m Technicolor Vistavision
Paramount / Hal Wallis

Wyatt Earp and Doc Holliday defeat the Clanton Gang.
Watchable, ambitious, but vaguely disappointing super-western.

w Leon Uris *d* John Sturges *ph* Charles B. Lang *m* Dmitri Tiomkin

Burt Lancaster, Kirk Douglas, Jo Van Fleet, Rhonda Fleming, John Ireland, Frank Faylen, Kenneth Tobey, Earl Holliman

'Carefully and lavishly mounted, but overlong and overwrought.'—*John Cutts*

The Gunfighter**
US 1950 84m bw
TCF (Nunnally Johnson)

A gunfighter fails to shake off his past.
Downbeat, small-scale but very careful adult western set in a believable community.

w William Bowers, William Sellers *d Henry King ph Arthur Miller m* Alfred Newman

Gregory Peck, Helen Westcott, Millard Mitchell, Jean Parker, Karl Malden, Skip Homeier, Mae Marsh

'Preserves throughout a respectable level of intelligence and invention.'—*Lindsay Anderson*

Gunga Din***
US 1939 117m bw
RKO (George Stevens)

Three cheerful army veterans meet adventure on the North-West Frontier.
Rousing period actioner with comedy asides, one of the most entertaining of its kind ever made.

w Joel Sayre, Fred Guiol, Ben Hecht, Charles MacArthur, *poem* Rudyard Kipling *d George Stevens ph Joseph H. August m* Alfred Newman *ad* Van Nest Polglase

Cary Grant, Victor McLaglen, Douglas Fairbanks Jnr, Sam Jaffe, Eduardo Ciannelli, Joan Fontaine, Montagu Love, Robert Coote, Cecil Kellaway, Abner Biberman, Lumsden Hare

'One of the most enjoyable nonsense-adventure movies of all time.'—*Pauline Kael, 1968*

'Bravura is the exact word for the performances, and Stevens' composition and cutting of the fight sequences is particularly stunning.'—*NFT, 1973*

Gunman's Walk*
US 1958 97m Technicolor Cinemascope
Columbia (Fred Kohlmar)

A tough westerner has two sons, one of whom follows too literally in his footsteps.
Competent action melodrama with good characterization.

w Frank Nugent *d* Phil Karlson *ph* Charles Lawton *m* George Duning

Van Heflin, Tab Hunter, James Darren, Kathryn Grant

Gunn*
US 1967 95m Technicolor
Paramount / Geoffrey (Owen Crump)

A private eye is hired to find a gangster's killer.
Tongue-in-cheek violence from the television series, with Craig Stevens doing a Cary Grant imitation.

w Blake Edwards, William Peter Blatty *d* Blake Edwards *ph* Philip Lathrop *m* Henry Mancini

Craig Stevens, Laura Devon, Ed Asner, Sherry Jackson, Helen Traubel, J. Pat O'Malley, Regis Toomey

'Falters between parody and straight action.'—*MFB*

Guns at Batasi*
GB 1964 103m bw Cinemascope
TCF / George H. Brown

The headquarters of an Anglo-African regiment is threatened by rebels.
Basically the old chestnut about a group of disparate types trapped in a dangerous situation, this is given shape and stature by the star's lively performance as the martinet of an RSM.

w Robert Hollis, from his novel The Siege of Battersea *d* John Guillermin *ph* Douglas Slocombe *m* John Addison

Richard Attenborough, Flora Robson, Mia Farrow, Jack Hawkins, Cecil Parker, Percy Herbert, Errol John, John Leyton, Earl Cameron

Guns for San Sebastian
France / Mexico / Italy 1967 111m
Eastmancolor Franscope
MGM / Cipra / Filmes / Ernesto Enriques (Jacques Bar)

In Mexico in 1746, a rebel on the run stays to defend a besieged village.
Multi-national actioner, violent but quite undistinguished.

w Serge Ganz, Miguel Morayta, Ennio de Concini *d* Henri Verneuil *ph* Armand Thirard *m* Ennio Morricone

Anthony Quinn, Charles Bronson, Sam Jaffe, Anjanette Comer, Silvia Pinal

Guns of Darkness
GB 1962 102m bw
ABP / Cavalcade (Thomas Clyde)

A British plantation boss in Latin America escapes with his wife when rebels strike.
Chase/escape film with a few tiny comments about violence.

w John Mortimer, *novel* Act of Mercy by Francis Clifford *d* Anthony Asquith *ph* Robert Krasker *m* Benjamin Frankel

David Niven, Leslie Caron, James Robertson Justice, David Opatoshu

The Guns of Fort Petticoat
US 1957 79m Technicolor
Columbia / Brown-Murphy (Harry Joe Brown)

During the Civil War, a wandering Texan trains townswomen into a fighting force.
Unlikely western which passes the time.

w Walter Doniger *d* George Marshall *ph* Ray Rennahan *m* Mischa Bakaleinikoff

Audie Murphy, Kathryn Grant, Hope Emerson, Jeff Donnell, Isobel Elsom

The Guns of Navarone**
GB 1961 157m Technicolor
Cinemascope
Columbia / Carl Foreman (Cecil F. Ford)

In 1943 a sabotage team is sent to destroy two giant guns on a Turkish Island.
Ambitiously produced Boy's Own Paper heroics, with lots of noise and self-sacrifice; intermittently exciting but bogged down by philosophical chat.

w Carl Foreman, *novel* Alistair Maclean *d* J. Lee-Thompson *ph* Oswald Morris *m* Dmitri Tiomkin *ad* Geoffrey Drake

Gregory Peck, David Niven, Stanley Baker, Anthony Quinn, Anthony Quayle, James Darren, Gia Scala, James Robertson Justice, Richard Harris, Irene Papas, Bryan Forbes

'A desperate imbalance: the moral arguments cut into the action without extending it.'—*Penelope Houston*

Guns of the Timberland
US 1960 91m Technicolor
Jaguar (Aaron Spelling)
GB title: *Stampeded*

Loggers are opposed by cattle interests.
Routine star western with tolerable production values.

w Joseph Petracca, Aaron Spelling *d* Robert D. Webb *ph* John Seitz *m* David Buttolph

Alan Ladd, Jeanne Crain, Gilbert Roland, Frankie Avalon, Lyle Bettger, Noah Beery Jnr

The Guru
US / India 1969 112m De Luxe
TCF / Arcadia (Ismail Merchant)

In India, an English pop singer succumbs to the local atmosphere.

Pleasant, affectionate but forgettable anecdote of modern India.

w Ruth Prawer Jhabvala, James Ivory *d* James Ivory *ph* Subrata Mitra *m* Ustad Vilayat Khan

Michael York, Rita Tushingham, Utpal Dutt, Aparna Sen, Barry Foster

Gus
US 1976 96m Technicolor
Walt Disney (Ron Miller)

A football team co-opts a mule which can kick a hundred yard ball.
Predictable Disney fantasy comedy with a direct line back to *The Absent Minded Professor*.

w Arthur Alsberg, Don Nelson *d* Vincent McEveety *ph* Frank Phillips *m* Robert F. Brunner

Ed Asner, Don Knotts, Gary Grimes, Tim Conway, Liberty Williams, Bob Crane, Harold Gould, Tom Bosley, Dick Van Patten

The Guvnor
GB 1935 88m bw
Gaumont (Michael Balcon)
US title: *Mr Hobo*

By chance a tramp becomes a bank director.
Predictable star vehicle with Arliss a most unlikely tramp.

w Maude Howell, Guy Bolton *d* Milton Rosmer

George Arliss, Gene Gerrard, Viola Keats, Patric Knowles, Frank Cellier, Mary Clare, George Hayes

'His admirers need not fear that he has lost any of his usual refinement or sentiment, his cultured English accent, his Universal certificate.'—*Graham Greene*

A Guy Named Joe
US 1944 120m bw
MGM (Everett Riskin)

A flier is killed but comes back as a ghost to supervise his ex-girl's new romance.
Icky romantic comedy-drama with strong propaganda intent; the stars make it tolerable.

w Dalton Trumbo *d* Victor Fleming *ph* George Folsey, Karl Freund *m* Herbert Stothart

Spencer Tracy, Irene Dunne, Ward Bond, Van Johnson, James Gleason, Lionel Barrymore, Barry Nelson, Don Defore, Henry O'Neill

Guys and Dolls*
US 1955 149m Eastmancolor Cinemascope
Samuel Goldwyn

A New York gangster takes a bet that he can romance a Salvation Army lady.
The artifices of Runyonland are made more so by a defiantly studio-bound production and thoroughly flat handling; but the songs and sometimes the performances survive.

wd Joseph L. Mankiewicz, *musical* Jo Swerling and Abe Burrows, *songs Frank Loesser* *ph* Harry Stradling *ch* Michael Kidd *ad* Joseph Wright *pd* Oliver Smith

Frank Sinatra, Marlon Brando, Jean Simmons, *Vivian Blaine, Stubby Kaye*, B. S. Pully, Robert Keith, Sheldon Leonard, George E. Stone

'Quantity has been achieved only at the cost of quality.'—*Penelope Houston*

Gypsy*
US 1962 149m Technirama
Warner (Mervyn Le Roy)

The early days of stripteaser Gypsy Rose Lee, and the exploits of her ambitious mother.
A vaudeville musical that is nowhere near raucous enough, or brisk enough, for its subject, and is miscast into the bargain. The songs are great, but not here: Miss Russell is as boring as an electric drill in a role that should have been reserved for Ethel Merman.

w Leonard Spiegelgass, *book* Arthur Laurents *d* Mervyn Le Roy *m Jule Styne* *ly Stephen Sondheim* *ph* Harry Stradling *ad* John Beckman

Rosalind Russell, Natalie Wood, *Karl Malden*, James Milhollin

The Gypsy and the Gentleman
GB 1957 107m Eastmancolor
Rank (Maurice Cowan)

A penniless Regency rake marries a tempestuous gypsy, with melodramatic and tragic results.
Expensive and typically mistimed Rank attempt to re-do *The Man in Grey*; a barnstormer notable only for waste of talent.

w Janet Greene, *novel* Darkness I Leave You by Nina Warner Hooke *d* Joseph Losey *ph* Jack Hildyard *m* Hans May *ad* Ralph Brinton

Melina Mercouri, Keith Michell, Patrick McGoohan, June Laverick, Flora Robson, Helen Haye

The Gypsy Moths*
US 1969 110m Metrocolor
MGM (Hal Landers, Bobby Roberts)

Sky-diving stuntmen find love and death on a small-town tour.
Brilliantly breathtaking actioner which too frequently gets grounded, and does not find a reason for being so glum.

w William Hanley, *novel* James Drought *d* John

Frankenheimer *ph* Philip Lathrop *aerial ph Carl Boenisch* *m* Elmer Bernstein

Burt Lancaster, Deborah Kerr, Gene Hackman, Scott Wilson, William Windom, Bonnie Bedelia, Sheree North

Gypsy Wildcat
US 1944 77m Technicolor
Universal (George Waggner)

A Transylvanian gypsy girl is really a long lost countess.

Universal's Frankenstein sets are put to lighter use in a quite incredible piece of downright hokum.

w James Hogan, Gene Lewis, James M. Cain *d* Roy William Neill *ph* George Robinson, W. Howard Greene *m* Edward Ward

Maria Montez, Jon Hall, Leo Carrillo, Gale Sondergaard, Douglass Dumbrille, Nigel Bruce, Peter Coe, Curt Bois

'The picture's so bad, it's bound to make money.'—*Cue*

Hail the Conquering Hero***
US 1944 101m bw
Paramount (Preston Sturges)

An army reject is accidentally thought a hero when he returns to his small-town home.
Skilfully orchestrated Preston Sturges romp, slightly marred by an overdose of sentiment but featuring his repertory of comic actors at full pitch.

wd Preston Sturges *ph* John Seitz *m* Werner Heymann

Eddie Bracken, William Demarest, Ella Raines, *Franklin Pangborn,* Elizabeth Patterson, *Raymond Walburn, Alan Bridge,* Georgia Caine, Freddie Steele, Jimmy Conlin, Torben Meyer

'Mob scenes, rough-houses and sharply serious passages are played for all the pantomime they are worth . . . one of the happiest, heartiest comedies in a twelvemonth.'—*Otis L. Guernsey Jnr*

The Hairy Ape
US 1944 91m bw
Jules Levy

A ship's stoker aims to kill a socialite who has insulted him.
Patchy treatment of an intractable and dated play.

w Jules Levy, *play* Eugene O'Neill *d* Alfred Santell *ph* Lucien Andriot *m* Michel Michelet

William Bendix, Susan Hayward, John Loder, Dorothy Comingore, Roman Bohnen, Alan Napier

Half a Sixpence*
GB 1968 148m Technicolor Panavision
Paramount / Ameran (Charles H. Schneer, George Sidney)

A draper's assistant inherits a fortune and moves into society.
Mildly likeable but limp and overlong musical which would have benefited from more intimate, sharper treatment than the wide screen can give. The period decor and lively numbers seem insufficient compensation for the longueurs.

w Beverly Cross, from his play based on Kipps by H. G. Wells *d* George Sidney *ph* Geoffrey Unsworth *m/ly* David Heneker *pd* Ted Haworth *ch Gillian Lynne*

Tommy Steele, Julia Foster, Cyril Ritchard, Penelope Horner, Elaine Taylor, Hilton Edwards, Pamela Brown, James Villiers

The Halfway House*
GB 1944 99m bw
Ealing (Cavalcanti)

Overnight guests at an inn find it was bombed a year before and they have all been given a supernatural chance to reconsider their lives.
Interesting pattern play which would have benefited from lighter handling.

w Angus Macphail, Diana Morgan, *play* Denis Ogden *d* Basil Dearden

Françoise Rosay, Tom Walls, Alfred Drayton, Sally Ann Howes, Mervyn Johns, Glynis Johns, Esmond Knight, Richard Bird, Guy Middleton

Hallelujah!**
US 1929 106m bw
MGM (King Vidor)

A black cotton worker accidentally kills a man and decides to become a preacher.
Hollywood's unique black melodrama now seems stilted because of its early talkie technique, but at the time its picture of negro life had a freshness and truth which was not reached again for thirty years.

w Wand Tuchock, King Vidor *d King Vidor* *ph* Gordon Avil *md Eva Jessye*

Daniel Haynes, Nina Mae McKinney, William Fountaine, Fannie Belle De Knight, Harry Gray

Hallelujah, I'm a Bum**
US 1933 80m bw
Lewis Milestone
GB titles: *Hallelujah I'm a Tramp; Lazy Bones*

The leader of a group of Central Park tramps smartens himself up for love of a lady who lost her memory. When she recovers it, he becomes a tramp again.
Curious whimsy expressed mainly in recitative, with embarrassing stretches relieved by moments

of visual and verbal inspiration. Very typical of the Depression, with the tramps knowing best how life should be lived.

w S. N. Behrman, Ben Hecht d Lewis Milestone ph Lucien Andriot ad Richard Day *rhymes/m/ly Richard Rodgers, Lorenz Hart*

Al Jolson, Harry Langdon, Madge Evans, Frank Morgan, Chester Conklin

The Hallelujah Trail
US 1965 167m Technicolor Ultra Panavision 70
UA / Mirisch / Kappa (John Sturges)

In 1867 a wagonload of whisky bound for Denver is waylaid by Indians, temperance crusaders and the civilian militia.
Absurdly inflated, prolonged, uninventive comedy western with poor narrative grip; all dressed up and nowhere to go.

w John Gay, *novel* Bill Gulick *d* John Sturges *ph Robert Surtees m* Elmer Bernstein

Burt Lancaster, Lee Remick, Brian Keith, Jim Hutton, Donald Pleasance, Martin Landau

The Halliday Brand*
US 1956 78m bw
UA / Collier Young

A tough farmer/sheriff conflicts with his son over his attitude to Indians.
Dour, reliable western melodrama with a good cast.

w George W. George, George S. Slavin *d* Joseph H. Lewis *ph* Ray Rennahan *m* Stanley Wilson

Joseph Cotten, Viveca Lindfors, Ward Bond, Betsy Blair, Bill Williams, Jay C. Flippen

Halls of Anger
US 1969 99m De Luxe
UA / Mirisch (Herbert Hirschman)

A black basketball star goes to teach in his home town and faces segregation problems.
Schematic melodrama, as well meaning as it is boring.

w John Shaner, Al Ramrus *d* Paul Bogart *ph* Burnett Guffey *m* Dave Grusin

Calvin Lockhart, Janet McLachlan, Jeff Bridges

Halls of Montezuma*
US 1950 113m Technicolor
TCF (Robert Bassler)

Marines fight World War II in the Pacific.
Well-mounted, simple-minded actioner.

w Michael Blankfort *d* Lewis Milestone *ph* Winton C. Hoch, Harry Jackson *m* Lionel Newman

Richard Widmark, Jack Palance, Reginald Gardiner, Robert Wagner, Karl Malden, Richard Hylton, Richard Boone, Skip Homeier, Jack Webb, Bert Freed, Neville Brand, Don Hicks, Martin Milner

Hamlet**
GB 1948 142m bw
Rank / Two Cities (Laurence Olivier)

Prince Hamlet takes too long making up his mind to revenge his father's death.
The play is sharply cut, then time is wasted having the camera prowl pointlessly along gloomy corridors . . . but much of the acting is fine, some scenes compel, and the production has a splendid brooding power.

w William Shakespeare *d* Laurence Olivier *ph Desmond Dickinson pd Roger Furse m* William Walton *ad Carmen Dillon*

Laurence Olivier, Eileen Herlie, Basil Sydney, Jean Simmons, Felix Aylmer, Norman Wooland, Terence Morgan, *Stanley Holloway*, Peter Cushing, Esmond Knight, Anthony Quayle, Harcourt Williams, John Laurie, Niall MacGinnis, Patrick Troughton

Hammerhead
GB 1968 99m Technicolor
Columbia / Irving Allen

An American secret agent captures a master criminal.
Jaded James Bond imitation, full of would-be fashionable detail.

w William Bast, Herbert Baker, *novel* James Mayo *d* David Miller *ph* Kenneth Talbot, Wilkie Cooper *m* David Whitaker

Vince Edwards, Peter Vaughan, Judy Geeson, Diana Dors, Michael Bates, Beverly Adams, Patrick Cargill, Patrick Holt

Hammersmith Is Out*
US 1972 114m Du Art Color
Cinerama / J. Cornelius Cream (Alex Lucas)

With the help of a male nurse, a homicidal mental inmate escapes and becomes the most influential man in the country.
Pretentious updating of Faust into a kind of black farce that seldom amuses but is interesting in fits and starts.

w Stanford Whitmore *d* Peter Ustinov *ph* Richard Kline *m* Dominic Frontière

Richard Burton, Elizabeth Taylor, Peter Ustinov, Beau Bridges, Leon Ames, John Schuck, George Raft

The Hancocks
US 1976 96m colour TVM
Warner (Jerry Thorpe, Philip Mandelker)

Problems of a well-to-do family, especially a young wife who feels she must leave her husband and children for a while.
High-class soap, slow moving and pretentious; the technical sheen and the good life depicted make it look like a feature-length commercial.

w Barbara Turner *d* Jerry Thorpe

Joanna Pettet, Kim Hunter, Anne Archer, John Anderson, Lawrence Casey, Claudette Nevins, Robert Sampson, James Houghton

Hand in Hand*
GB 1960 80m bw
ABP / Helen Winston

The friendship of two 7-year-olds is affected by racial prejudice because one is Catholic and the other Jewish; but after misunderstandings their friendship is confirmed by priest and rabbi.
Pleasant, well-meaning drama apparently intended for older children.

w Diana Morgan *d* Philip Leacock
ph Frederick A. Young *m* Stanley Black

Lorette Parry, Phillip Needs, Sybil Thorndike, John Gregson, Finlay Currie

Handle with Care*
US 1958 82m bw
MGM (Morton Fine)

Small-town college students stage a mock trial and come up with some embarrassing answers.
Interesting melodrama with a disappointing ending; a well done second feature.

w Morton Fine, David Friedkin d David Friedkin ph Harold J. Marzorati *m* Alexander Courage

Dean Jones, Joan O'Brien, Thomas Mitchell, Walter Abel, John Smith

The Hands of Cormac Joyce
Australia 1972 74m colour TVM
Fielder Cook

A killer storm threatens a fishing community off the Irish coast.
Slow, folksy outdoor drama.

w Thomas Rickman, *novel* Leonard Wibberly
d Fielder Cook

Stephen Boyd, Cyril Cusack, Colleen Dewhurst, Dominic Guard

The Hands of Orlac
GB / France 1960 105m colour
Riviera / Pendennis (Steven Pallos. Don Taylor)

A concert pianist's hands are crushed in an accident, and a mad surgeon grafts on those of an executed murderer.
Flatulent remake of the 1926 German silent and the 1935 American *Mad Love*. Stilted, hammy, threadbare and overlong.

w John Baines, Edmond T. Gréville, *novel* Maurice Renard *d* Edmond T. Gréville
ph Desmond Dickinson *m* Claude Bolling

Mel Ferrer, Donald Wolfit, Christopher Lee

Hands across the Table**
US 1935 81m bw
Paramount (E. Lloyd Sheldon)

A manicurist determines to marry a rich man.
Lively romantic comedy, smoothly made and typical of its time.

w Norman Krasna, Vincent Lawrence, Herb Fields *d Mitchell Leisen ph* Ted Tetzlaff
m Sam Coslow, Frederick Hollander

Carole Lombard, Fred MacMurray, Ralph Bellamy, Astrid Allwyn, Ruth Donnelly, Marie Prévost, William Demarest, Ed Gargan

Hands of the Ripper
GB 1971 85m Technicolor
Hammer (Aida Young)

Jack the Ripper stabs his wife to death in view of his small daughter, who grows up a sexually repressed murderess.
Gory Hammer horror with well done scenes.

w L. W. Davidson *d* Peter Sasdy *ph* Kenneth Talbot *m* Christopher Gunning *ad Roy Stannard*

Angharad Rees, Eric Porter, Dora Bryan, Jane Merrow, Derek Godfrey

Handy Andy
US 1934 82m bw
Fox

A midwestern druggist is married to a snob.
Competent star vehicle overflowing with crackerbarrel philosophy.

w William Counselman, Henry Johnson, *play* Merry Andrew by Lewis Beach *d* David Butler
ph Arthur Miller

Will Rogers, Peggy Wood, Conchita Montenegro, Mary Carlisle, Roger Imhof, Robert Taylor (his first film), Paul Harvey

Hang 'em High
US 1967 114m De Luxe
UA / Malpaso / Leonard Freeman

A cowboy is rescued from lynching and takes revenge on his persecutors.
Hollywood's first attempt to imitate the gore and

brutality of spaghetti westerns and to take back its own errant star. Emetic and interminable.

w Leonard Freeman, Mel Goldberg *d* Ted Post *ph* Leonard South, Richard Kline *m* Dominic Frontière

Clint Eastwood, Inger Stevens, Ed Begley, Pat Hingle, James MacArthur, Arlene Golonka, Charles McGraw, Ben Johnson, L. Q. Jones

The Hanged Man
US 1965 87m Technicolor TVM
Universal (Ray Wagner)

A crook fakes his own death and goes undercover.
Complicated thieves-fall-out mystery set against a New Orleans mardi gras festival; a remake of *Ride the Pink Horse* (qv).

w Jack Laird, Stanford Whitmore *d* Don Siegel

Edmund O'Brien, Vera Miles, Gene Raymond, Robert Culp, J. Carrol Naish, Norman Fell, Archie Moore

The Hanged Man
US 1974 74m colour TVM
Bing Crosby Productions

A gunslinger is unjustly hanged, but recovers and becomes a mysterious avenger.
Doom-laden western comic strip which failed to take off as a series.

w Ken Trevey *d* Michael Coffey

Steve Forrest, Cameron Mitchell, Sharon Acker, Dean Jagger, Will Geer

The Hanging Tree*
US 1958 106m Technicolor
Warner / Baroda (Martin Jurow, Richard Shepherd)

Life is tough in a Montana gold-mining camp, especially for a doctor who has killed his unfaithful wife.
Lowering western with a feeling for place and period, plus a welter of melodramatic incident.

w Wendell Mayes, Halstead Welles, *novel* Dorothy M. Johnson *d* Delmer Daves *ph* Ted McCord *m* Max Steiner

Gary Cooper, Maria Schell, Karl Malden, Ben Piazza, George C. Scott

The Hangman
US 1959 86m bw
Paramount (Frank Freeman Jnr)

A marshal with a reputation for getting his man deliberately allows one to escape.
Dour, low-key western, competent but rather flat and uninteresting.

w Dudley Nichols *d* Michael Curtiz *ph* Loyal Griggs *m* Harry Sukman

Robert Taylor, Jack Lord, Fess Parker, Tina Louise, Mickey Shaughnessy

Hangmen Also Die*
US 1943 131m bw
Fritz Lang (T. W. Baumfield)

The Nazis take revenge for the killing of Heydrich.
Disappointingly heavy-handed, though deeply felt war propaganda set in Hollywood's idea of Czechoslovakia. Only moments of interest remain.

w John Wexley, *story* Fritz Lang, Bertolt Brecht *d Fritz Lang* *ph* James Wong Howe *m* Hanns Eisler

Brian Donlevy, Anna Lee, Walter Brennan, Gene Lockhart, Dennis O'Keefe, Alexander Granach, Margaret Wycherly, Nana Bryant, Hans von Twardowski (as Heydrich), Jonathan Hale, Lionel Stander

'Lang, working with American actors on an American theme, has produced *Fury*. Lang trying to recreate his own Central Europe on a Hollywood set is completely at sea.'—*Paul Rotha, 1949*

'Directed with a skill which excites and delights . . . brilliant use of the tiny, shocking detail.'—*Dilys Powell*

Hangover Square*
US 1944 77m bw
TCF (Robert Bassler)

In 1903 London, a psychopathic composer murders pretty women.
This rather empty melodrama has almost nothing to do with the book from which it is allegedly taken, but the Hollywoodian evocation of gaslit London is richly entertaining and good to look at.

w Barre Lyndon, *novel* Patrick Hamilton *d John Brahm ph Joseph La Shelle m Bernard Herrmann ad Lyle Wheeler, Maurice Ransford*

Laird Cregar, Linda Darnell, George Sanders, Glenn Langan, Faye Marlowe, Alan Napier, Frederick Worlock

'Cregar lumbers around with a Karloffian glare in the spacious mists which happily blur the architectural decor.'—*Richard Winnington*

'Distinguished photography gets the last glint of fancy fright out of the pomps and vanities of the turn of the century.'—*Time*

† Tragically, Laird Cregar died after slimming for this role, to which he was in any case unsuited.

Hannibal Brooks
GB 1968 102m De Luxe
UA / Scimitar (Michael Winner)

A British POW in Germany escapes over the Alps with an elephant.
Curious action adventure which seems undecided whether to take itself seriously. Some passable sequences.

w Dick Clement, Ian La Frenais *d* Michael Winner *ph* Robert Paynter *m* Francis Lai

Oliver Reed, Michael J. Pollard, Wolfgang Preiss, Karen Baal

Hannie Caulder
GB 1971 85m colour Panavision
Tigon / Curtwel (Tony Tenser)

Raped by three outlaws who murdered her husband, a western woman takes revenge.
Unintentionally comical action melodrama with the star defeating all comers.

w Z. X. Jones (Burt Kennedy, David Haft) *d* Burt Kennedy *ph* Ted Scaife *m* Ken Thorne

Raquel Welch, Robert Culp, Ernest Borgnine, Strother Martin, Jack Elam, Christopher Lee, Diana Dors

Hans Christian Andersen*
US 1952 112m Technicolor
Samuel Goldwyn

A storytelling cobbler leaves his village to make shoes for the prima ballerina in Copenhagen.
Artificial, sugary confection with little humour and far too little magic of any kind; the star carries it nicely, but he is on his own apart from the songs.

w Moss Hart *songs Frank Loesser d* Charles Vidor *ph* Harry Stradling *md* Walter Scharf *ad Richard Day ch* Roland Petit

Danny Kaye, Jeanmaire, Farley Granger, John Qualen, Joey Walsh

The Happening
US 1967 101m Technicolor
Columbia / Horizon / Dover (Jud Kinberg)

Four young hippies kidnap a wealthy businessman and don't know what to do with him; he turns the tables.
Freewheeling irresponsible comedy which even at the time of swinging cities seemed very irritating.

w Frank R. Pierson, James D. Buchanan, Ronald Austin *d* Eliot Silverstein *ph* Philip Lathrop *m* Frank de Vol *pd* Richard Day

Anthony Quinn, George Maharis, Michael Parks, Faye Dunaway, Robert Walker, Oscar Homolka, Martha Hyer, Milton Berle, Jack Kruschen

'A wacky comedy à la mode, oddly mixed and only spasmodically effective.'—*Variety*

The Happiest Days of Your Life***
GB 1950 81m bw
British Lion / Individual (Frank Launder)

A ministry mistake billets a girls' school on a boys' school.
Briskly handled version of a semi-classic post-war farce, with many familiar talents in excellent form.

w Frank Launder, John Dighton, *play John Dighton d Frank Launder ph* Stan Pavey *m* Mischa Spoliansky

Alastair Sim, Margaret Rutherford, Joyce Grenfell, Richard Wattis, Edward Rigby, Guy Middleton, Muriel Aked, John Bentley, Bernadette O'Farrell

The Happiest Millionaire
US 1967 159m Technicolor
Walt Disney (Bill Anderson)

In 1916, a sporting millionaire has several surprising interests but finds time to sort out family problems.
Drearily inept family entertainment with a couple of good songs and an amusing alligator sequence but acres of yawning boredom in between.

w A. J. Carothers, *play* Kyle Crichton, *book* My Philadelphia Father by Cornelia Drexel Biddle *d* Norman Tokar *ph* Edward Colman *m/ly* Richard M. and Robert B. Sherman

Fred MacMurray, *Tommy Steele*, Greer Garson, John Davidson, Gladys Cooper, Lesley Anne Warren, Geraldine Page, Hermione Baddeley

Happy Anniversary
US 1959 83m bw
UA / Ralph Fields

A television set causes family trouble.
Marital farce designed to take a few sideswipes at TV.

w Joseph Fields, Jerome Chodorov, from their play Anniversary Waltz *d* David Miller *ph* Lee Garmes *m* Sol Kaplan, Robert Allan

David Niven, Mitzi Gaynor, Carl Reiner, Loring Smith, Patty Duke, Phyllis Povah

Happy Birthday Wanda June*
US 1971 105m Technicolor
Columbia

An adventurer believed dead returns just as his wife is about to choose one of two suitors.

A farcical situation becomes in this writer's hands an investigation of the hero cult, with many zany jokes, episodes in heaven, and bad language. Interesting in spots, but it would have worked better with a more fluent cinematic technique.

w Kurt Vonnegut Jnr, from his play *d* Mark Robson

Rod Steiger, Susannah York, George Grizzard, Don Murray

'We can only assume that Mr Robson deserted the filmic instincts that brought him commercial success because here he was, finally, in the presence of Art.'—*Hollis Alpert*

'Nothing more than a miscast film record of the dialogue and plot outline of the stage work.'—*Judith Crist*

The Happy Ending*

US 1969 112m Technicolor Panavision

UA / Pax Films (Richard Brooks)

A middle-aged woman reflects over sixteen years of unhappy marriage.

Sometimes glib, sometimes trenchant sophisticated drama with enough interesting scenes to make it more than merely a 'woman's picture'.

wd Richard Brooks ph Conrad Hall *m* Michel Legrand

Jean Simmons, John Forsythe, Shirley Jones, Lloyd Bridges, Teresa Wright, Dick Shawn, Nanette Fabray, Bobby Darin, Tina Louise

'Packed with punchy little epigrams floating in a vacuum of glossy superficiality.'—*David Wilson*

Happy Ever After*

GB 1954 87m Technicolor

ABP / Mario Zampi

US title: *O'Leary Night*

Irish villagers draw lots for the privilege of murdering their rascally squire.

Fairly hilarious black comedy with a good cast entering into the spirit of the thing.

David Niven, Yvonne de Carlo, A. E. Matthews, Michael Shepley, George Cole, Barry Fitzgerald

Happy Go Lovely

GB 1950 97m Technicolor

ABP (Marcel Hellman)

A chorus girl meets a millionaire during the Edinburgh Festival.

For a semi-official contribution to the Festival of Britain this is a lamentably unspontaneous musical with no use of cinema techniques or natural locales. Even allowing for the flat handling, it is tedious.

w Val Guest *d* Bruce Humberstone *ph* Erwin Hillier *m* Mischa Spoliansky

David Niven, Vera-Ellen, Cesar Romero, Bobby Howes, Diane Hart, Gordon Jackson, Barbara Couper, Gladys Henson, Joyce Carey

Happy Go Lucky

US 1943 81m Technicolor

Paramount (Harold Wilson)

A cigarette girl chases a millionaire to a Caribbean island.

Flimsy musical for those who like the stars.

w Walter de Leon, Melvin Frank, Norman Panama *d* Curtis Bernhardt *ph* Karl Struss, Wilfrid Cline *songs* Frank Loesser, Jimmy McHugh

Mary Martin, Dick Powell, Betty Hutton (singing 'Murder He Says'), Rudy Vallee, Eddie Bracken, Mabel Paige, Eric Blore, Clem Bevans

The Happy Hooker

US 1975 98m Movielab

Double H / Cannon-Happy (Fred Caruso)

A Dutch girl in New York starts a career as a prostitute and finds she enjoys it.

Glum sex comedy based on the supposed exploits of a real madam; crude and not very funny. If this is emancipation, Shirley Temple seems more attractive by the minute.

w William Richert, *book* Xaviera Hollander *d* Nicholas Sgarro *ph* Dick Kratina *m* Don Elliott

Lynn Redgrave (hilariously miscast), Jean-Pierre Aumont, Lovelady Powell, Nicholas Pryor, Elizabeth Wilson, Tom Poston, Conrad Janis, Richard Lynch

Happy Is the Bride*

GB 1957 84m bw

British Lion / Paul Soskin

A couple planning a quiet summer wedding reckon without the intervention of her parents.

Tame remake of *Quiet Wedding*; the right spirit but not much sparkle.

w Jeffrey Dell, Roy Boulting, *play* Dodie Smith *d* Roy Boulting *ph* Ted Scaife *m* Benjamin Frankel

Ian Carmichael, Janette Scott, Cecil Parker, Joyce Grenfell, Terry-Thomas, John Le Mesurier, Eric Barker, Edith Sharpe, Athene Seyler

Happy Land*
US 1943 75m bw
TCF

Grandfather's ghost comes back to comfort a family which has lost its son at war.
Sentimental flagwaver very typical of its time; well made, it ensured not a dry eye in the house.

w Mackinlay Kantor *d* Irving Pichel *ph* Joseph La Shelle

Don Ameche, Frances Dee, Harry Carey, Ann Rutherford, Cara Williams, Henry Morgan, Richard Crane, Dickie Moore

Happy Landing*
US 1938 102m bw
TCF (David Hempstead)

A Norwegian girl falls for an American flier who crashes near her home.
Lightweight skating musical, well put together.

w Milton Sperling, Boris Ingster *d* Roy del Ruth *ph* John Mescall *md* Louis Silvers

Sonja Henie, Don Ameche, Cesar Romero, Ethel Merman, Jean Hersholt, Billy Gilbert, Wally Vernon, El Brendel

The Happy Road*
US / France 1956 100m bw
MGM / Thor (Gene Kelly)

Two children run away from a Swiss school and are pursued by the American father of one of them.
Whimsical peripatetic comedy which fails to come off despite charming passages.

w Arthur Julian, Joseph Morhain, Harry Kurnitz *d* Gene Kelly *ph* Robert Juillard *m* Georges Van Parys

Gene Kelly, Barbara Laage, Michael Redgrave, Bobby Clark, Brigitte Fossey

The Happy Thieves
US 1962 88m bw
UA / Hillworth (James Hill, Rita Hayworth)

A gentleman thief and his accomplice become unwittingly involved in murder.
Dreary comedy which turns into equally dreary drama and makes its European backgrounds look ugly.

w John Gay, *novel* The Oldest Confession by Richard Condon *d* George Marshall *ph* Paul Beeson *m* Mario Nascimbene

Rex Harrison, Rita Hayworth, Grégoire Aslan, Joseph Wiseman, Alida Valli

The Happy Time***
US 1952 94m bw
Columbia / Stanley Kramer (Earl Felton)

Domestic misadventures of a family of French Canadians during the twenties.
Basically concerned with adolescent sexual stirrings, this very agreeable film has a light touch and is most deftly directed and acted.

w Earl Felton, play Samuel A. Taylor *d Richard Fleischer ph Charles Lawton Jnr m* Dmitri Tiomkin *pd Rudolph Sternad*

Charles Boyer, Louis Jourdan, Bobby Driscoll, Marsha Hunt, Marcel Dalio, Kurt Kasznar, Linda Christian, Jeanette Nolan, Jack Raine, Richard Erdman

Hard Contract
US 1969 106m De Luxe Panavision
TCF (Marvin Schwarz)

A professional killer has sexual hang-ups.
Heavy-going modern thriller with lively scenes separated by too much self-analytical chat, not to mention a tour of Europe.

wd S. Lee Pogostin *ph* Jack Hildyard *m* Alex North

James Coburn, Lilli Palmer, Lee Remick, Burgess Meredith, Patrick Magee, Sterling Hayden, Helen Cherry, Karen Black, Claude Dauphin

'Behind it one glimpses a much better film than its surface suggests.'—*MFB*

'Like a flat-footed James Bond story that soaked its feet in a hot bath of existentialism.'—*John Simon*

A Hard Day's Night****
GB 1964 85m bw
UA / Proscenium (Walter Shenson)

Harassed by their manager and Paul's grandpa, the Beatles embark from Liverpool by train for a London TV show.
Comic fantasia with music; an enormous commercial success with the director trying every cinematic gag in the book, it led directly to all the kaleidoscopic swinging London spy thrillers and comedies of the later sixties, and so has a lot to answer for; but at the time it was a sweet breath of fresh air, and the Beatles even seemed willing and likeable.

w Alun Owen d Richard Lester ph Gilbert Taylor songs The Beatles md George Martin

The Beatles, Wilfrid Brambell, Norman Rossington, *Victor Spinetti*

'A fine conglomeration of madcap clowning . . . with such a dazzling use of camera that it tickles the intellect and electrifies the nerves.'—*Bosley Crowther*

Hard, Fast and Beautiful
US 1951 76m bw
RKO / The Filmmakers (Collier Young)

A girl tennis player is influenced by her ambitious mother.
Unusual but not very effective melodrama.

w Martha Wilkerson, *novel* John R. Tunis *d* Ida Lupino *ph* Archie Stout *m* Roy Webb

Claire Trevor, Sally Forrest, Carleton Young, Robert Clarke, Kenneth Patterson, Joseph Kearns.

Hard Times*
US 1975 93m Metrocolor Panavision
Columbia (Lawrence Gordon)
GB title: *The Streetfighter*

In New Orleans in the Depression-hit thirties, a prizefighter and a promoter help each other.
Interesting, atmospheric melodrama on the lone stranger theme.

w Walter Hill, Bryan Gindorff, Bruce Henstell *d* Walter Hill *ph* Philip Lathrop *m* Barry DeVorzon

Charles Bronson, James Coburn, Jill Ireland, Strother Martin, Maggie Blye

Hard to Handle**
US 1933 75m bw
Warner (Robert Lord)

The success story of a cheerful public relations man.
Punchy star comedy with interesting sidelights on the social fads of the early thirties including marathon dancing, get-rich-quick schemes and grapefruit diets.

w Wilson Mizner, Robert Lord *d* Mervyn Le Roy *ph* Barney McGill

James Cagney, Ruth Donnelly, Mary Brian, Allen Jenkins, Claire Dodd

'A violent, slangy, down-to-the-pavement affair which has many a mirthful moment.'—*Mordaunt Hall*

The Hard Way*
US 1942 109m bw
Warner (Jerry Wald)

A strong-willed girl pushes her reluctant sister to the heights of show business.
Unconvincing but well-mounted drama.

w Daniel Fuchs, Peter Viertel *d* Vincent Sherman *ph* James Wong Howe *m* Leo F. Forbstein

Ida Lupino, Joan Leslie, Dennis Morgan, Jack Carson, Gladys George, Faye Emerson, Paul Cavanagh, Roman,Bohnen

Hardcase
US 1971 73m colour TVM
Matt Rapf

A western adventurer returns home to find his ranch sold and his wife run away with a Mexican.
Tolerable quest western.

w Harold Jack Bloom, Sam Rolfe *d* John Llewellyn Moxey

Clint Walker, Stefanie Powers, Alex Karras, Pedro Armendariz Jnr

The Harder They Fall*
US 1956 109m bw
Columbia (Philip Yordan)

A press agent exposes the crooked fight game.
Wearily efficient sporting melodrama.

w Philip Yordan, *novel* Budd Schulberg *d* Mark Robson *ph* Burnett Guffey *m* Hugo Friedhofer
Humphrey Bogart (his last performance), Rod Steiger, Jan Sterling, Mike Lane, Max Baer, Edward Andrews, Harold J. Stone

The Hardy Family
America's favourite fictional characters just before and during World War II were the family of a small-town judge, who seemed to personify all that everyone was fighting for, especially as the young son was always getting into amusing scrapes. Designed by a delighted MGM as low-budgeters, they paid for many an expensive failure, and introduced, as young Andy's girl friends, a series of starlets who went on to much bigger things. The basic family was Lewis Stone, Fay Holden, Mickey Rooney, Cecilia Parker and Sara Haden (as the spinster aunt); but in the very first episode Lionel Barrymore and Spring Byington played the judge and his wife.

A FAMILY AFFAIR (1936); 69m; *d* George B. Seitz; *w* Kay Van Riper, *play* Aurania Rouverol
YOU'RE ONLY YOUNG ONCE (1938); 78m; *d* George B. Seitz; *w* Kay Van Riper; introducing Ann Rutherford (who became a regular)
JUDGE HARDY'S CHILDREN (1938); 78m; *d* George B. Seitz; *w* Kay Van Riper; *with* Ruth Hussey
LOVE FINDS ANDY HARDY (1938); 90m; *d* George B. Seitz; *w* William Ludwig; *with* Judy Garland, Lana Turner
OUT WEST WITH THE HARDYS (1938); 90m; *d* George B. Seitz; *w* Kay Van Riper, Agnes Christine Johnson, William Ludwig
THE HARDYS RIDE HIGH (1939); 81m; *d* George B. Seitz; *w* as above
ANDY HARDY GETS SPRING FEVER (1939); 85m; *d* W. S. Van Dyke II; *w* Kay Van Riper

JUDGE HARDY AND SON (1939); 90m; *d* George B. Seitz; *w* Carey Wilson; *with* June Preisser, Maria Ouspenskaya
ANDY HARDY MEETS A DEBUTANTE (1940); 89m; *d* George B. Seitz; *w* Annalee Whitmore, Thomas Seller; *with* Judy Garland
ANDY HARDY'S PRIVATE SECRETARY (1941); 101m; *d* George B. Seitz; *w* Jane Murfin, Harry Ruskin; *with* Kathryn Grayson, Ian Hunter
LIFE BEGINS FOR ANDY HARDY (1941); 100m; *d* George B. Seitz; *w* Agnes Christine Johnson; *with* Judy Garland
THE COURTSHIP OF ANDY HARDY (1942); 93m; *d* George B. Seitz; *w* Agnes Christine Johnson; *with* Donna Reed
ANDY HARDY'S DOUBLE LIFE (1942); 92m; *d* George B. Seitz; *w* Agnes Christine Johnson; *with* Esther Williams, Susan Peters
ANDY HARDY'S BLONDE TROUBLE (1944); 107m; *d* George B. Seitz; *w* Harry Ruskin, William Ludwig, Agnes Christine Johnson; *with* Bonita Granville, Jean Porter, Herbert Marshall, the Wilde twins
LOVE LAUGHS AT ANDY HARDY (1946); 94m; *d* Willis Goldbeck; *w* Harry Ruskin, William Ludwig; *with* Bonita Granville
ANDY HARDY COMES HOME (1958); 80m; *d* Howard Koch; *w* Edward Everett Hutshing, Robert Morris Donley; *without* Lewis Stone

Harlow
US 1965 125m Technicolor Panavision
Paramount / Embassy / Prometheus (Joseph E. Levine)

In 1929, starlet Jean Harlow is shot to fame by her agent Arthur Landau.
Absurdly whitewashed and excruciatingly boring rags-to-riches yarn with most of the characters fictitious and little to do with the real Jean Harlow. Only the studio scenes are mildly interesting.

w John Michael Hayes *d* Gordon Douglas *ph* Joseph Ruttenberg *m* Neal Hefti *ad* Hal Pereira, Roland Anderson *costumes Edith Head*

Carroll Baker, Peter Lawford, Mike Connors, Red Buttons, Raf Vallone, Angela Lansbury, *Martin Balsam*

'Hollywood once again succeeds in reducing one of its few fascinating realities to the sleazy turgid level of its more sordid fictions.'—*Judith Crist*

† A rather better television tape drama of the same title, starring Carol Lynley and Ginger Rogers, was made almost simultaneously. It was converted to film ('Electronovision') but had few bookings.

The Harness*
US 1971 97m Technicolor TVM
Universal (William Sackheim)

A California farmer finds his toughness gone when his wife becomes ill.
Adequate character drama which outstays its welcome.

w Leon Tokatyan, Edward Hume, *story* John Steinbeck *d* Boris Sagal

Lorne Greene, Louise Latham, Julie Sommars, Murray Hamilton, Lee H. Montgomery

Harold and Maude**
US 1971 92m Technicolor
Paramount / Mildred Lewis / Colin Higgins

A repressed young man, fixated on death and funerals, has an affair with an 80-year-old woman.
Often hilarious black comedy for those who can stand it: the epitome of bad taste, splashed around with wit and vigour, it became a minor cult.

w Colin Higgins d Hal Ashby ph John A. Alonzo *m* Cat Stevens

Bud Cort, Ruth Gordon, Vivian Pickles, Cyril Cusack

Harold Lloyd's Funny Side of Life***
US 1963 99m bw
Harold Lloyd (Duncan Mansfield)

Excerpts from twenties comedies plus a shortened version of *The Freshman* (1925).
Excellent compilation, though the mini-feature makes it a little unbalanced.

w Arthur Ross *m* Walter Scharf

Harold Lloyd

Harold Lloyd's World of Comedy****
US 1962 97m bw
Harold Lloyd

Splendidly hilarious compilation of the best short Harold Lloyd sequences, guaranteed to leave any audience rolling in the aisles.
Films excerpted include *Safety Last, Why Worry, Feet First, Girl Shy, Professor Beware.*

m Walter Scharf

Harper*
US 1966 121m Technicolor Panavision
Warner / Gershwin–Kastner
GB title: *The Moving Target*

A Los Angeles private eye is hired by a rich woman to find her missing husband.
Formula Californian detection distinguished by

its cast rather than by any special talent in the writing or presentation. It seemed likely to produce a new Chandleresque school, but imitations proved very sporadic; the star repeated the role less successfully in *The Drowning Pool* (qv).

w William Goldman, *novel* The Moving Target by John Ross Macdonald *d* Jack Smight *ph* Conrad Hall *m* Johnny Mandel

Paul Newman, Lauren Bacall, Shelley Winters, Arthur Hill, Julie Harris, Janet Leigh, Pamela Tiffin, Robert Wagner, Robert Webber, Strother Martin

'It isn't a bad try, but it never really slips into overdrive.'—*Penelope Houston*

'Nothing needs justification less than entertainment; but when something planned only to entertain fails, it has no justification. A private-eye movie without sophistication and style is ignominious.'—*Pauline Kael, 1968*

Harpy
US 1970 100m colour TVM
Cinema Center

A woman tries to break up her ex-husband's impending re-marriage.
Amusing but overlong romantic comedy.

w William Wood *d* Jerrold Freedman

Elizabeth Ashley, Hugh O'Brian, Tom Nardini, Marlyn Mason, Mark Miller

The Harrad Experiment
US 1973 97m Eastmancolor
Cinerama / Cinema Arts (Dennis F. Stevens)

A college professor conducts a series of tests on sexual relationships.
Low-keyed Kinsey Report for the seventies, pleasantly made but not very stimulating.

w Michael Werner, Ted Cassidy, *novel* Robert H. Rimmer *d* Ted Post *ph* Richard Kline *m* Artie Butler

James Whitmore, Tippi Hedren, Don Johnson, Laurie Walters, Robert Middleton

'Ludicrously sober-sided amalgam of nude yoga and extra-curricular groping, which should set sex educational theory back ten years.'—*Sight and Sound*

Harriet Craig
US 1950 94m bw
Columbia (William Dozier)

A wife's only real love is her meticulously kept and richly appointed house.
Ho-hum remake of a sturdy thirties film *Craig's Wife* (qv).

w Anne Froelick, James Gunn, *play* Craig's Wife by George Kelly *d* Vincent Sherman *ph* Joseph Walker *m* Morris Stoloff

Joan Crawford, Wendell Corey, Allyn Joslyn, Lucile Watson, William Bishop, K. T. Stevens, Raymond Greenleaf

Harry and Tonto*
US 1974 115m De Luxe
TCF (Paul Mazursky)

An elderly New York widower and his cat are evicted and trek to Chicago.
Amiable character study, very watchable but rather pointless.

w Paul Mazursky, Josh Greenfield *d* Paul Mazursky *ph* Michael Butler *m* Bill Conti

Art Carney, Ellen Burstyn, Chief Dan George, Geraldine Fitzgerald, Larry Hagman, Arthur Hunnicutt, Herbert Berghof

'A vivacious and affectionate folk tale.'—*New Yorker*

Harry and Walter go to New York
US 1976 120m Metrocolor
Panavision
Columbia (Don Devlin, Harry Gittes)

In oldtime New York, two carnival entertainers get involved with suffragettes and a safecracker.
Extended period romp in which the high humour soon palls and a general lack of talent makes itself felt.

w John Byrum, Robert Kaufman *d* Mark Rydell *ph* Laszlo Kovacs *m* David Shire
pd Harry Horner

James Caan, Elliott Gould, Michael Caine, Diane Keaton, Charles Durning, Lesley Ann Warren, Jack Gilford

Harry Black and the Tiger
GB 1958 117m Technicolor
Cinemascope
TCF (John Brabourne)

A famous tiger hunter allows his best friend to prove himself a hero, and falls in love with the friend's wife.
Lethargic melodrama with good Indian backgrounds.

w Sydney Boehm, *novel* David Walker *d* Hugo Fregonese *ph* John Wilcox *m* Clifton Parker

Stewart Granger, Anthony Steel, Barbara Rush, *I. S. Johar*

Harry in Your Pocket
US 1973 103m De Luxe Panavision
UA / Cinema Video (Bruce Geller)

Adventures of a young, a middle-aged and an old pickpocket.

Partly pleasant but rather aimless comedy drama, agreeably set in Seattle and Salt Lake City.

w Ron Austin, James Buchanan *d* Bruce Geller *ph* Fred Koenekamp *m* Lalo Schifrin

James Coburn, *Walter Pidgeon*, Michael Sarrazin, Trish Van Devere

Harry O
US 1973 75m colour TVM
Warner

An ex-cop private eye with a bullet in his back lives in a beach shack and takes on occasional cases.
Glum *policier* which took off as a series after the second pilot. *Smile Jenny You're Dead* (qv).

w Howard Rodman *d* Jerry Thorpe

David Janssen, Martin Sheen, Margot Kidder, Sal Mineo, Will Geer

Harvey***
US 1950 104m bw
U-I (John Beck)

A middle-aged drunk has an imaginary white rabbit as his friend, and his sister tries to have him certified.
An amiably batty play with splendid lines is here transferred virtually intact to the screen and survives superbly thanks to understanding by all concerned, though the star is as yet too young for a role which he later made his own.

w Mary Chase (with Oscar Brodney) from her play *d Henry Koster ph* William Daniels

James Stewart, Josephine Hull, Victoria Horne, Peggy Dow, *Cecil Kellaway*, Charles Drake, *Jesse White*, Nana Bryant, Wallace Ford

The Harvey Girls**
US 1946 101m Technicolor
MGM (Arthur Freed)

A chain of 19th-century restaurants hires young ladies to go out west as waitresses.
Sprightly if overlong musical based on fact; a good example of an MGM middle-budget extravaganza.

w Edmund Beloin, Nathaniel Curtis *d* George Sidney *ph* George Folsey *md* Lennie Hayton *songs* Johnny Mercer, Harry Warren

Judy Garland, Ray Bolger, John Hodiak, Preston Foster, Virginia O'Brien, Angela Lansbury, Marjorie Main, Chill Wills, Kenny Baker, Selena Royle

'Anybody who did anything at all in America up to 1900 is liable to be made into a film by MGM.'—*Richard Winnington*

Harvey Middleman Fireman*
US 1965 76m Eastmancolor
Columbia (Robert L. Lawrence)

A frustrated middle-aged fireman begins an affair; the resulting guilt complex drives him to a psychiatrist.
Grotesque satirical comedy from one of the sixties' most fashionable cartoonists. Mild, quite pleasing, occasionally crude.

wd/m Ernest Pintoff ph Karl Malkames

Gene Troobnick, Hermione Gingold, Pat Harty

Has Anybody Seen My Gal?**
US 1952 89m Technicolor
U-I (Ted Richmond)

A multi-millionaire pretends to be poor and moves in with distant relatives to test their worthiness.
Very agreeable comedy set in the twenties and centring on a satisfying star performance.

w Joseph Hoffman *d Douglas Sirk ph* Clifford Stine *m* Joseph Gershenson *ad Bernard Herzbrun, Hilyard Brown*

Charles Coburn, Piper Laurie, Rock Hudson, Gigi Perreau, Lynn Bari, Larry Gates, William Reynolds, Skip Homeier, James Dean

The Hasty Heart*
GB 1949 104m bw
ABP (Vincent Sherman)

At an army hospital in Burma, attitudes to an arrogant young Scot change when it is learned that he has only a few weeks to live.
Flat, adequate filming of a successful sentimental stage play.

w Ranald MacDougall, *play* John Patrick *d* Vincent Sherman *ph* Wilkie Cooper *m* Jack Beaver

Richard Todd, Patricia Neal, Ronald Reagan, Orlando Martins, Howard Marion-Crawford

Hatari!*
US 1962 158m Technicolor
Paramount / Malabar (Howard Hawks)

International hunters in Tanganyika catch game to send to zoos.
Plotless adventure film with good animal sequences but no shape or suspense; a typical folly of its director, whose chief interest is seeing smart men and women in tough action. The elephants steal this overlong show.

w Leigh Brackett *d* Howard Hawks *ph Russell Harlan m Henry Mancini*

John Wayne, Elsa Martinelli, Red Buttons, Hardy Kruger

The Hatchet Man
US 1932 74m bw
Warner
GB title: *The Honourable Mr Wong*

The executioner of a San Francisco tong dutifully kills his best friend but promises to care for his daughter.
Unconvincing Chinese-American melodrama.

w J. Grubb Alexander, *play* Achmed Abdullah, David Belasco *d* William A. Wellman *ph* Sid Hickox

Edward G. Robinson, Loretta Young, Dudley Digges, Leslie Fenton, Edmund Breese, Tully Marshall, J. Carrol Naish, Noel Madison, Blanche Frederici

The Hatfields and the McCoys
US 1975 74m colour TVM
Charles Fries

The story of the hillbilly feud which exploded because two young people wanted to marry.
Surprisingly botched retelling of a story which has so often been told before.

wd Clyde Ware

Jack Palance, Steve Forrest, Richard Hatch, Karen Lamm

A Hatful of Rain*
US 1957 108m bw Cinemascope
TCF / (Buddy Adler)

A war veteran becomes a drug addict and upsets his wife and family.
One of the first drug dramas: straightforward, well acted, and quite powerful.

w Michael V. Gazzo (with Alfred Hayes), from his play *d Fred Zinnemann ph* Joe Macdonald *m* Bernard Herrmann

Eva Marie Saint, Don Murray, Anthony Franciosa, Lloyd Nolan, Howard da Silva

Hatter's Castle**
GB 1941 102m bw
Paramount British (Isadore Goldsmith)

In the nineties, a megalomaniac Scottish hatter ruins the lives of his wife and daughter.
Enjoyable period melodrama with a rampant star performance and pretty good detail.

w Rodney Ackland, *novel* A. J. Cronin *d* Lance Comfort *ph* Max Greene *m* Horace Shepherd

Robert Newton, Deborah Kerr, James Mason, Beatrice Varley, Emlyn Williams, Henry Oscar, Enid Stamp-Taylor, Brefni O'Rourke

The Haunted Palace
US 1963 85m Pathecolor Panavision
AIP / Alta Vista (Roger Corman)

In 1875 a New Englander claims an old mansion as his inheritance and is haunted by his vicious ancestor.
Plodding horror comic, too slow to give opportunities to its stalwart cast.

w Charles Beaumont, from material by H. P. Lovecraft and Edgar Allan Poe *d* Roger Corman *ph* Floyd Crosby *m* Ronald Stein

Vincent Price, Lon Chaney Jnr, Debra Paget, Frank Maxwell, Leo Gordon, Elisha Cook Jnr, John Dierkes

'For those of ghoulish bent, or lovers of the perfectly awful.'—*Judith Crist*

The Haunting*
GB 1963 112m bw Panavision
MGM / Argyle (Robert Wise)

An anthropologist, a sceptic and two mediums spend the weekend in a haunted Boston mansion.
Quite frightening but exhausting and humourless melodrama with a lot of suspense, no visible spooks, and not enough plot for its length. The wide screen is a disadvantage.

w Nelson Gidding, *novel* The Haunting of Hill House by Shirley Jackson *d* Robert Wise *ph David Boulton m* Humphrey Searle *pd* Elliot Scott

Richard Johnson, Claire Bloom, Russ Tamblyn, Julie Harris, Lois Maxwell, Valentine Dyall

Haunts of the Very Rich***
US 1972 73m colour TVM
Lillian Gallo

Holidaymakers at a lush tropical resort find that they may be dead and this may be hell.
Smooth, palatable, exciting updating of *Outward Bound*, only marred by an unnecessarily tricksy and confusing finish.

w William Wood *d Paul Wendkos*

Lloyd Bridges, Cloris Leachman, *Moses Gunn*, Anne Francis, Ed Asner, Tony Bill, Robert Reed, Donna Mills

Hauser's Memory*
US 1970 96m Technicolor TVM
Universal (Jack Laird)

A scientist receives another man's memory by chemical transfer.
Variation on *Donovan's Brain*, quite pacy and likeable.

w Adrian Spies, *novel* Curt Siodmak *d* Boris Sagal

David McCallum, Lilli Palmer, Susan Strasberg, Robert Webber, Leslie Nielsen, Helmut Kautner

Having Wonderful Time
US 1938 70m bw
RKO (Pandro S. Berman)

A New York girl falls in love at a summer camp.
Mild comedy which, robbed of its original Jewish milieu, falls resoundingly flat.

w Arthur Kober, from his play *d* Alfred Santell *ph* Robert de Grasse *m* Roy Webb

Ginger Rogers, Douglas Fairbanks Jnr, Peggy Conklin, Lucille Ball, Lee Bowman, Eve Arden, Red Skelton, Donald Meek, Jack Carson

Hawaii*
US 1966 186m De Luxe Panavision
UA / Mirisch (Lewis J. Rachmil)

In 1820 a pious Yale divinity student becomes a missionary to the Hawaiian islands.
Ambitious attempt to contrast naïve dogma with native innocence, ruined by badly handled sub-plots, storms, a childbirth sequence and other distractions, all fragments of an immense novel. Heavy going.

w Daniel Taradash, Dalton Trumbo, *novel* James A. Michener *d* George Roy Hill *ph* Russell Harlan *m* Elmer Bernstein *2nd unit Richard Talmadge pd* Cary Odell

Max Von Sydow, Julie Andrews, Richard Harris, *Jocelyn la Garde*, Carroll O'Connor, Torin Thatcher, Gene Hackman

'Consistently intelligent humanism gives it a certain stature among the wide screen spectacles.'—*Brenda Davies*

Hawaii Five-O**
US 1968 73m colour TVM
Leonard Freeman

Adventures of a special investigation unit of the Hawaii state government.
Pilot for an immensely successful series.

d Leonard Freeman

Jack Lord, Nancy Kwan, Leslie Nielsen, Andrew Duggan, Lew Ayres, James Gregory

The Hawaiians
US 1970 132m De Luxe Panavision
UA / Mirisch (Walter Mirisch)
GB title: *Master of the Islands*

A young scion of a shipping business leaves after an argument and strikes oil in terrain supposedly barren.
More fragments from Michener, covering 1870 to 1900 and comprising an absolutely uninteresting family chronicle with moments of spectacle.

w James R. Webb *d* Tom Gries *ph* Philip Lathrop *m* Henry Mancini *pd* Cary Odell

Charlton Heston, Tina Chen, Geraldine Chaplin, John Philip Law, Alec McCowen, Mako, Ann Knight, Lyle Bettger, Keye Luke

'A quickfire succession of corruption, revolution, plague, fire and questions of moral responsibility.'—*MFB*

'Total relaxation—preferably of the brain—is recommended.'—*Judith Crist*

Hawkins on Murder*
US 1973 74m colour TVM
MGM (Norman Felton)
aka: *Death and the Maiden*

A famous homespun lawyer defends an heiress of a triple killing.
Careful, unexciting star pilot which ran to a short series of 74m follow-ups under the titles shown below.

w David Karp *d* Jud Taylor

James Stewart, Bonnie Bedelia, Strother Martin, Kate Reid, Robert Webber
Sequels:
DIE, DARLING DIE (*d* Paul Wendkos)
MURDER IN MOVIELAND (*d* Jud Taylor)
A LIFE FOR A LIFE (*d* Jud Taylor)
BLOOD FEUD (*d* Paul Wendkos)
MURDER IN THE SLAVE TRADE (*d* Paul Wendkos)
MURDER ON THE 13TH FLOOR (*d* Jud Taylor)

Hazard
US 1948 95m bw
Paramount (Mel Epstein)

A compulsive lady gambler agrees to marry the winner of a dice game, but runs away and is chased by a private detective.
Silly, unamusing romantic comedy-drama.

w Arthur Sheekman, Roy Chanslor *d* George Marshall *ph* Daniel L. Fapp *m* Frank Skinner

Paulette Goddard, Macdonald Carey, Fred Clark, Stanley Clemens, Maxie Rosenbloom, Charles McGraw

'A good bit this side of inspired.'—*New York Times*

He Laughed Last*
US 1956 77m Technicolor
Columbia (Jonie Taps)

In the twenties, New York gangsters battle for control of a night club.

Small-scale gangster burlesque which comes off rather better than its credits suggest.

wd Blake Edwards *ph* Henry Freulich *m* Arthur Morton

Frankie Laine, Lucy Marlow, Anthony Dexter, *Jesse White*

He Ran All the Way*
US 1951 78m bw
UA / Bob Roberts

A hoodlum on the run from the police virtually picks up a girl and hides in her family's apartment.
Uninteresting situation melodrama helped by intelligent acting and handling.

w Guy Endore, Hugo Butler, *novel* Sam Ross *d John Berry ph James Wong Howe m* Franz Waxman

John Garfield, Shelley Winters, Wallace Ford, Selena Royle, Gladys George, Norman Lloyd, Bobby Hyatt

He Stayed for Breakfast
US 1940 89m bw
Columbia (B. P. Schulberg)

A Parisian communist waiter hides out in the apartment of American capitalists, and learns from them.
Post-*Ninotchka* comedy, not bad but somehow rather uninteresting and mechanical.

w P. J. Wolfson, Michael Fessier, Ernest Vajda, *play* Liberté Provisoire by Michel Duran *d* Alexander Hall *ph* Joseph Walker

Melvyn Douglas, Loretta Young, Alan Marshal, Eugene Pallette, Una O'Connor, Curt Bois, Leonid Kinskey

He Walked by Night*
US 1948 80m bw
Eagle–Lion / Bryan Foy

A burglar becomes a cop-killer and is hunted down by the police.
Interesting if rather flatly handled documentary melodrama in clear imitation of *Naked City*.

w John C. Higgins, Crane Wilbur *d* Alfred Werker *ph John Alton m* Leonid Raab

Richard Basehart, Scott Brady, Roy Roberts, White Bissell

He Who Rides a Tiger
GB 1965 103m bw
British Lion / David Newman

A feckless burglar comes out of prison and returns to the old life.
Cliché crime yarn which tries rather desperately after fresh detail but bogs down in romantic asides.

w Trevor Peacock *d* Charles Crichton *ph* John Von Kotze *m* Alexander Faris

Tom Bell, Judi Dench, Paul Rogers, Kay Walsh, Ray McAnally, Jeremy Spenser

The Healers
US 1974 100m colour TVM
Warner

Life in a medical research hospital.
Boring, rather pretentious pap.

w John Furia Jnr, Howard Dimsdale *d* Tom Gries

John Forsythe, Pat Harrington, John McIntire, Beverly Garland, Anthony Zerbe

The Heart is a Lonely Hunter*
US 1968 123m Technicolor
Warner Seven Arts (Joel Freeman)

Incidents in the life of a gentle deaf mute in a small southern town.
Wispy film of a wistful novel; quite well done but overlong and hard to cheer at.

w Thomas C. Ryan, *novel* Carson McCullers *d* Robert Ellis Miller *ph James Wong Howe m* Dave Grusin

Alan Arkin, Sondra Locke, Stacy Keach, Laurinda Barrett, Chuck McCann, Biff McGuire, Percy Rodriguez, Cicely Tyson

The Heart of the Matter*
GB 1953 105m bw
British Lion / London Films (Ian Dalrymple)

In 1942 in an African colony a police officer has an affair while his wife is away, is blackmailed, and plans suicide despite his staunch Catholic belief.
Rather stodgy attempt to film Graham Greene; perhaps everyone tries a little too hard, and in any case the ending is compromised.

w Ian Dalrymple, Lesley Storm, *novel* Graham Greene *d* George More O'Ferrall *ph* Jack Hildyard *m* African themes

Trevor Howard, Maria Schell, Elizabeth Allan, Denholm Elliott, Peter Finch, Gérard Oury, George Coulouris, Earl Cameron, Michael Hordern, Colin Gordon, Cyril Raymond, Orlando Martins

'A curious choice for commercial filming.'—*Lindsay Anderson*

Heartbeat
US 1946 102m
RKO / Robert and Raymond Hakim

A French gamin released from reform school becomes a professional pickpocket.
Unamusing remake of *Battement de Coeur*, with script and most performances very strained.

w Hans Wilhelm, Max Kolpe, Michel Druan, Morrie Ryskind *d* Sam Wood *ph* Joe Valentine *m* Paul Misraki

Ginger Rogers, Jean-Pierre Aumont, Adolphe Menjou, *Basil Rathbone*, Mikhail Rasumny, Melville Cooper, Mona Maris, Henry Stephenson

'The heartbeat is irregular and sadly ailing.'—*Photoplay*

The Heartbreak Kid*
US 1972 106m De Luxe
(TCF) Palomar (Edgar J. Scherick)

Disappointed with his honeymoon, a sporting goods salesman promptly sets his cap at a richer, prettier prospective spouse.
Heartless modern comedy reminiscent of *The Graduate*; quite well done but unsympathetic and somehow too American to export satisfactorily.

w Neil Simon, *story* A Change of Plan by Bruce Jay Friedman *d* Elaine May *ph* Owen Roizman *m* Garry Sherman

Charles Grodin, Cybill Shepherd, Jeannie Berlin, Eddie Albert, Audra Lindley, William Prince, Art Metrano

'The latest in a relatively new kind of American film—glittery trash.'—*Stanley Kauffmann*

Hearts of the West*
US 1975 103m Metrocolor
MGM / Bill–Zieff (Tony Bill)
GB title: *Hollywood Cowboy*

In the early thirties a naïve mid-westerner almost accidentally becomes a Hollywood star.
Overstretched comedy poking gentle fun at old Hollywood: likeable but finally disappointing, as it obviously needed a Buster Keaton.

w Rob Thompson *d* Howard Zieff *ph* Mario Tosi *m* Ken Lauber

Jeff Bridges, Alan Arkin, Andy Griffith, Blythe Danner, Donald Pleasance, Richard B. Shull, Herb Edelman

Heat of Anger*
US 1971 74m colour TVM
Metromedia (Dick Berg)
aka: *Fitzgerald and Pride*

A lady attorney and her young assistant defend a murderer.
Competent courtroom pilot which did not make it.

w Fay Kanin *d* Don Taylor

Susan Hayward, James Stacy, Lee J. Cobb, Fritz Weaver, Bettye Ackerman

The Heat's On
US 1943 79m bw
Columbia (Milton Carter)
GB title: *Tropicana*

A star seeks financial backing from an elderly angel whose sister runs the Legion of Purity.
Dim musical vehicle for a fading star; her last film for twenty-seven years.

w Fitzroy Davis, George S. George, Fred Schiller *d* Gregory Ratoff *ph* Franz Planer *md* Yasha Bunchuk

Mae West, Victor Moore, William Gaxton, Almira Sessions, Lester Allan, Mary Roche, Hazel Scott, Alan Dinehart, Lloyd Bridges, Xavier Cugat and his Orchestra

Heatwave**
US 1974 74m Technicolor TVM
Universal (Harve Bennett)

An energy crisis topped by a heat wave incapacitates the city and sends people scurrying for the mountains.
Uncomfortably convincing and well-observed social melodrama.

w Peter Allan Fields, Mark Weingart *d* Jerry Jamison

Bonnie Bedelia, Ben Murphy, Lew Ayres, Lionel Johnston, Naomi Stevens, David Huddleston

Heaven Can Wait***
US 1943 112m Technicolor
TCF (Ernst Lubitsch)

On arrival in Hades, an elderly playboy reports his peccadilloes to Satan, who sends him Upstairs.
Charming period piece with fantasy bookends; the essence of the piece is its evocation of American society in the nineties, and in its director's waspish way with a funny scene.

w Samson Raphaelson, play Birthday by Lazlo Bus-Fekete *d Ernst Lubitsch ph Edward Cronjager m* Alfred Newman *ad James Basevi, Leland Fuller*

Don Ameche, Gene Tierney, *Laird Cregar, Charles Coburn, Marjorie Main*, Eugene Pallette, *Allyn Joslyn*, Spring Byington, Signe Hasso, Louis Calhern

'It was so good I half believed Lubitsch could still do as well as he ever did, given half a chance.'—*James Agee*

Heaven Knows Mr Allison*
US 1957 105m Technicolor Cinemascope
TCF (Buddy Adler, Eugene Franks)

Marooned on a small Pacific island during World War II, a marine and a nun, antagonistic to each other, combine to outwit the Japs.
Silly adventure story with predictably well-handled action sequences separated by even more predictable dialogue, lots of it.

w John Lee Mahin, John Huston, *novel* Charles Shaw *d* John Huston *ph* Oswald Morris *m* Georges Auric

Robert Mitchum, Deborah Kerr

Heaven Only Knows
US 1947 98m bw
(UA)

An angel is sent to the old west to reform a bad man.
Whimsical comedy-drama which does not work at all, even as a distant cousin of *Here Comes Mr Jordan*.

w Art Arthur, Rowland Leigh *d* Albert S. Rogell *ph* Karl Struss *m* Heinz Roemheld

Robert Cummings, Brian Donlevy, Marjorie Reynolds, Bill Goodwin, John Litel, Stuart Erwin

The Heavenly Body
US 1943 93m bw
MGM (Arthur Hornblow Jnr)

An astronomer is too busy to notice his wife, so she takes up astrology and meets a dark handsome stranger as predicted.
Thin romantic comedy which despite crazy touches never actually makes one laugh.

w Michael Arlen, Walter Reisch *d* Alexander Hall *ph* Robert Planck *m* Bronislau Kaper

William Powell, Hedy Lamarr, James Craig, Fay Bainter, Henry O'Neill, Spring Byington, Morris Ankrum, Connie Gilchrist

Heavens Above*
GB 1963 118m bw
British Lion / Charter (Roy Boulting)

A northern parson with proletarian sympathies is accidentally appointed to a snobby village where he converts the dowager aristocrat to works of absurd charity. Eventually he has the whole country in an uproar and takes the place of an astronaut.
Patchy satirical comedy which takes unsteady aim at too many targets but scores some predictable laughs.

w Frank Harvey, John Boulting *d* John Boulting *ph* Max Greene *m* Richard Rodney Bennett

Peter Sellers, Isabel Jeans, Cecil Parker, Brock Peters, Ian Carmichael, Irene Handl, Eric Sykes, Bernard Miles

Heidi*
US 1937 88m bw
TCF (Raymond Griffith)

An orphan is sent to stay with her crusty grandfather in a mountain village.
Star-tailored version of a favourite children's story: just what the box office ordered at the time.

w Walter Ferris, Julian Josephson, *novel* Johanna Spyri *d* Allan Dwan *ph* Arthur Miller *md* Louis Silvers

Shirley Temple, Jean Hersholt, Arthur Treacher, Helen Westley, Pauline Moore, Mary Nash, Thomas Beck, Sidney Blackmer, Mady Christians, Sig Rumann, Marcia Mae Jones, Christian Rub

The Heiress**
US 1949 115m bw
Paramount (William Wyler)

A plain but rich young woman takes revenge on her fortune-seeking lover.
Richly-decorated and generally pleasing version of a stage success based on a Henry James story set in the nineties.

w Ruth and Augustus Goetz, from their play and Henry James's Washington Square *d William Wyler* *ph* Leo Tover *m* Aaron Copland *ad John Meehan*

Olivia de Havilland, Ralph Richardson, Montgomery Clift, Miriam Hopkins, Vanessa Brown, Mona Freeman, Ray Collins

The Heist*
US 1973 73m colour TVM
Paramount (Edward J. Milkis)
GB title: *Suspected Person*
aka: *The Caper*

An armoured car guard is framed for the robbery of his vehicle.
Competent routine crime melodrama.

w Lionel E. Siegel *d* Don McDougall

Christopher George, Elizabeth Ashley, Howard Duff, Norman Fell, Cliff Osmond

The Helen Morgan Story
US 1957 118m bw Cinemascope
Warner (Martin Rackin)
GB title: *Both Ends of the Candle*

A young singer rises from vaudeville to

Broadway but becomes an alcoholic.
Moderately truthful biopic with effective twenties trimmings.

w Oscar Saul, Dean Riesner, Stephen Longstreet, Nelson Gidding *d* Michael Curtiz *ph* Ted McCord *m* various *ad* John Beckman

Ann Blyth, Paul Newman, Richard Carlson, Gene Evans, Alan King, Cara Williams, Walter Woolf King (as Ziegfeld)

Helen of Troy
US / Italy 1955 118m Warnercolor Cinemascope
Warner (Robert Wise)

Helen is kidnapped by Paris and regained by use of the Trojan Horse.
Dingy historical spectacular, stultifyingly boring until the final spectacle, with the actors obviously wishing themselves doing anything but mouthing the doggerel dialogue.

w John Twist, Hugh Gray *d* Robert Wise *ph* Harry Stradling *m* Max Steiner

Rosanna Podesta, Jacques Sernas, Cedric Hardwicke, Niall MacGinnis, Stanley Baker, Nora Swinburne, Robert Douglas, Torin Thatcher, Harry Andrews, Janette Scott, Ronald Lewis, Brigitte Bardot

Hell and High Water
US 1954 103m Technicolor Cinemascope
TCF (Raymond A. Klune)

A privately-financed anti-Red scientific expedition sets off for Alaska to prevent a Chinese anti-American plot.
Early scoper which mixes deviously plotted schoolboy fiction with submarine spectacle and cold war heroics.

wd Samuel Fuller *ph* Joe MacDonald *m* Alfred Newman

Richard Widmark, Bella Darvi, Victor Francen, David Wayne, Cameron Mitchell, Gene Evans

Hell Below
US 1933 105m bw
MGM

Tensions mount at a Mediterranean submarine base during World War I.
Adequate war actioner with appropriate trimmings of heroism, tragedy, comedy and romance.

w John Lee Mahin, John Meehan, Laird Doyle, Raymond Schrock, *novel* Pigboats by Commander Edward Ellsberg *d* Jack Conway *ph* Harold Rosson

Robert Montgomery, Walter Huston, Madge Evans, Jimmy Durante, Eugene Pallette, Robert Young, Edwin Styles, John Lee Mahin, Sterling Holloway

Hell below Zero
GB 1954 91m Technicolor
Columbia / Warwick (Irving Allen, Albert Broccoli)

An American adventurer accompanies the daughter of a whaling captain to the Antarctic to discover who killed her father.
Adequate outdoor thick ear with an unusual setting and lively cast.

w Alec Coppel, Max Trell, *novel* The White South by Hammond Innes *d* Mark Robson *ph* John Wilcox *m* Clifton Parker

Alan Ladd, Joan Tetzel, Basil Sydney, Stanley Baker, Jill Bennett, Niall MacGinnis

Hell Divers*
US 1931 113m bw
MGM

Friendly rivalry exists between two officers in the Naval Air Force.
Routine romantic melodrama with action highlights; a crowdpuller of its day.

w Harvey Gates, Malcolm Stuart Boylan, *story* Spig Wead *d* George Hill *ph* Harold Wenstrom

Wallace Beery, Clark Gable, Conrad Nagel, Dorothy Jordan, Marjorie Rambeau, Marie Prévost, Cliff Edwards

'It's a matter of squadron after squadron of planes, the mechanics attached thereto, the cutting in and around newsreel material, which Metro does so well, and Beery's excellent personal performance.'—*Hollywood Reporter*

Hell Drivers*
GB 1957 108m bw Vistavision
Rank / Aqua (Ben Fisz)

Fast driving on death-trap roads is required of rival lorry drivers for a cheapjack haulage firm.
Absurd, violent, hilarious and constantly surprising melodrama with the silliest of premises backed by a good cast and well handled thrill sequences.

w John Kruse, C. Raker Endfield *d* C. Raker Endfield *ph Geoffrey Unsworth* *m* Hubert Clifford

Stanley Baker, Patrick McGoohan, Herbert Lom, Peggy Cummins, William Hartnell, Wilfrid Lawson, Sidney James, Jill Ireland, Alfie Bass, Gordon Jackson

'This extraordinary film may interest future historians for its description of road haulage and masculine social behaviour in the mid-20th century . . . though produced with efficiency and assurance it is disagreeable and occasionally vicious.'—*MFB*

Hell in the Pacific*
US 1969 104m Technicolor Panavision
Cinerama / Selmur (Reuben Bercovitch)

During World War II, an American pilot and a Japanese naval officer who are stranded on the same tiny Pacific island almost become friends.
Highly artificial and pretentious allegorical two-parter which is occasionally well acted and good to look at.

w Alexander Jacobs, Eric Bercovici *d* John Boorman *ph Conrad Hall* *m* Lalo Schifrin

Lee Marvin, Toshiro Mifune

'No real reverberation and no real excitement, intellectual or physical.'—*Tom Milne*

Hell Is a City*
GB 1959 93m bw Hammerscope
ABP / Hammer (Michael Carreras)

A jewel thief breaks jail and is hunted by the Manchester police.
Lively semi-documentary, cameo-filled cop thriller filmed on location.

wd Val Guest, novel Maurice Proctor *ph Arthur Grant* *m* Stanley Black

Stanley Baker, John Crawford, Donald Pleasance, Maxine Audley, Billie Whitelaw, Joseph Tomelty, George A. Cooper, Vanda Godsell

'A hectic pace, with frequent scene changes, mobility of camera and performers, and much rapid, loud, intense dialogue.'—*MFB*

Hell Is for Heroes*
US 1962 90m bw
Paramount (Henry Blanke)

In 1944, embittered GIs fight and die while taking a German pillbox near the Siegfried line.
Fairly routine anti-war film with a strong cast and effectively-directed moments battling a generally artificial look.

w Robert Pirosh, Richard Carr *d* Don Siegel *ph* Harold Lipstein *m* Leonard Rosenman

Steve McQueen, Bobby Darin, Fess Parker, James Coburn, Bob Newhart, Harry Guardino

Hell on Frisco Bay
US 1955 98m Warnercolor Cinemascope
Jaguar (George Berthelon)

An ex-cop sets out to find the man who framed him for manslaughter.
Tedious actioner enlivened by the character parts and a violent climax.

w Sidney Boehm, Martin Rackin, *novel* William P. McGivern *d* Frank Tuttle *ph* John Seitz *m* Max Steiner

Alan Ladd, Edward G. Robinson, Joanne Dru, *Paul Stewart*, William Demarest, Fay Wray

Hell to Eternity
US 1960 132m bw
Allied Artists / Atlantic (Irving H. Levin)

Marine Guy Gabaldon, brought up by Japanese foster parents, has divided loyalties after Pearl Harbor.
Battle-strewn biopic which after two hours seems to lose its point, if it ever had one, but is efficiently made.

w Ted Sherdeman, Walter Roeber Schmidt *d* Phil Karlson *ph* Burnett Guffey *m* Leith Stevens

Jeffrey Hunter, David Janssen, Vic Damone, Patricia Owens, Richard Eyer, Sessue Hayakawa

The Hell with Heroes
US 1968 102m Techniscope
Universal (Stanley Chase)

Air cargo experts find themselves unwittingly smuggling cigarettes into France, and American counter-intelligence steps in.
Unremarkable, totally predictable action melodrama.

w Halsted Welles, Harold Livingston *d* Joseph Sargent *ph* Bud Thackery *m* Quincy Jones

Rod Taylor, Claudia Cardinale, Harry Guardino, Kevin McCarthy, Pete Deuel, William Marshall

Heller in Pink Tights*
US 1960 100m Technicolor Vistavision
Paramount / Ponti–Girosi

Adventures of a dramatic company touring the west in the 1880s.
Genteel spoof western which does not quite come off.

w Dudley Nichols, Walter Bernstein, *novel* Louis L'Amour *d* George Cukor *ph* Harold Lipstein *m* Daniele Amfitheatrof *ad* Hal Pereira, Eugene Allen

Sophia Loren, Anthony Quinn, Steve Forrest, Eileen Heckart, Edmund Lowe, Margaret O'Brien, Ramon Novarro

'It has a welcome individuality which is never quite smothered by its lapses into convention.'—*Penelope Houston*

Hellfighters
US 1969 120m Technicolor Panavision
Universal (Robert Arthur)

Oil well fire-fighting specialists have problems among themselves and with their womenfolk.
Ham-fisted story line and performances are slightly, but only slightly, compensated by excellent special effects.

w Clair Huffaker *d* Andrew V. McLaglen *ph* William H. Clothier *m* Leonard Rosenman

John Wayne, Jim Hutton, Katharine Ross, Vera Miles, Jay C. Flippen, Bruce Cabot, Barbara Stuart

'The overall effect is unpardonably tedious.'—*MFB*

The Hellfire Club*
GB 1960 93m Eastmancolor Dyaliscope
Regal / New World (Robert S. Baker, Monty Berman)

In the 18th century, a nobleman's child escapes from his degenerate father, joins a travelling circus, and later returns to claim his inheritance.
Sprightly historical romantic melodrama lightly based on the nefarious activities of the real Hellfire Club; energetic and entertaining if slightly too jokey.

w Leon Griffiths, Jimmy Sangster *d/ph* Robert S. Baker, Monty Berman *m* Clifton Parker

Keith Michell, Peter Arne, Adrienne Corri, Kai Fischer, Bill Owen, Peter Cushing, David Lodge, Francis Matthews

Hello Dolly**
US 1969 129m De Luxe Todd-AO
TCF / Chenault (Ernest Lehman)

In 1890 New York, a widowed matchmaker has designs on a wealthy grain merchant.
Generally agreeable but overblown musical based on a slight but much worked-over farce, fatally compromised by the miscasting of a too-young star. Some exhilarating moments.

w Ernest Lehman, *musical Jerry Herman (m/ly)* and Michael Stewart (*book*), from *Thornton Wilder's* play The Matchmaker *d Gene Kelly ph Harry Stradling pd John de Cuir ch Michael Kidd*

Barbra Streisand, Walter Matthau, *Michael Crawford, Marianne McAndrew*, E. J. Peaker, Tommy Tune, David Hurst

'The film leaves an oddly negative impression; a good deal of synthetic effervescence . . . but very little real vitality.'—*David Wilson*

Hello Frisco Hello*
US 1943 98m Technicolor
TCF (Milton Sperling)

On the Barbary Coast, a girl singer becomes a star.
Moderately pleasing period musical with plenty going on but nothing very striking.

w Robert Ellis, Helen Logan, Richard Macauley *d* Bruce Humberstone *ph* Charles Clarke, Allen Davey *songs* various *ad James Basevi, Boris Leven*

Alice Faye, John Payne, Jack Oakie, Lynn Bari, Laird Cregar, June Havoc, Ward Bond, Aubrey Mather, George Barbier, Frank Orth

Hello Goodbye
US 1970 101m De Luxe
TCF (André Hakim)

A cheerful young Englishman falls for a mysterious Frenchwoman who turns out to be the wife of a Baron.
Modest, aimless, forgettable romantic comedy, full of old-fashioned clichés imperfectly remembered.

w Roger Marshall *d* Jean Negulesco *ph Henri Decaë* *m* Francis Lai *pd* John Howell *ad* Auguste Capelier

Michael Crawford, Geneviève Gilles, Curt Jurgens, Ira Furstenberg

Hello Sister*
US 1933 62m bw
Fox (Winfield Sheehan)
aka: *Walking down Broadway*

Boy meets girl in New York.
A mild little romance, only notable because it was edited down from an original by Erich Von Stroheim, and touches of his work remain.

w Erich Von Stroheim, Leonard Spiegelgass, *novel* Dawn Powell *d* Erich Von Stroheim, Alfred Werker *ph* James Wong Howe

James Dunn, Boots Mallory, Zasu Pitts, Minna Gombell

Hell's Angels****
US 1930 135m bw (some scenes in colour)
Howard Hughes

Two Americans become fliers in World War I.
Celebrated early talkie spectacular, with zeppelin and flying sequences that still thrill. The dialogue is another matter, but all told this expensive production, first planned as a silent, is a milestone of cinema history.

w Howard Estabrook, Harry Behn *d Howard*

Hughes ph Tony Gaudio, Harry Perry, E. Burton Steene

Ben Lyon, James Hall, Jean Harlow, John Darrow, Lucien Prival

'It is not great, but it is as lavish as an eight-ring circus, and when you leave the theatre you will know you have seen a movie and not a tinny reproduction of a stage show.'—*Pare Lorentz*

Hell's Heroes
US 1930 65m bw
Universal

Three cowboys find an abandoned baby.
Yet another version of *Three Godfathers*; maybe not the best but the shortest.

w Tom Reed, *novel* Peter Kyne *d* William Wyler *ph* George Robinson

Charles Bickford, Raymond Hatton, Fred Kohler, Fritzi Ridgeway

Hell's Island*
US 1955 84m Technicolor Vistavision
Paramount / Pine–Thomas

Crooks congregate on a Caribbean island in search of a famous ruby.
Cheeky rehash of *The Maltese Falcon*, not bad in its own routine way.

w Maxwell Shane *d* Phil Karlson *ph* Lionel Lindon *m* Irvin Talbot

John Payne, Mary Murphy, *Francis L. Sullivan*, Arnold Moss

Hellzapoppin***
US 1942 84m bw
Universal / Mayfair (Glenn Tryon, Alex Gottlieb)

Two incompetent comics make a picture.
Zany modification of a smash burlesque revue; the crazy jokes are toned down and a romantic interest is added (and tentatively sent up). The result is patchy but often hilarious, and the whole is a handy consensus of forties humour and pop music.

w Nat Perrin, Warren Wilson *d H. C. Potter ph* Woody Bredell *md* Charles Previn

Ole Olsen, Chic Johnson, Hugh Herbert, Martha Raye, Mischa Auer, Robert Paige, Jane Frazee, Shemp Howard, Elisha Cook Jnr, Richard Lane

Help!*
GB 1965 92m Eastmancolor
UA / Walter Shenson / Suba Films

An oriental high priest chases the Beatles around the world because one of them has a sacred ring.
Exhausting attempt to outdo *A Hard Day's Night* in lunatic frenzy, which goes to prove that some talents work better on low budgets. The humour is a frantic cross between *Hellzapoppin*, the Goons, Bugs Bunny and the shade of Monty Python to come. It looks good but becomes too tiresome to entertain.

w Charles Wood, Marc Behm *d* Dick Lester *ph David Watkin m The Beatles ad Ray Simm*

The Beatles, Leo McKern, Eleanor Bron, Victor Spinetti

Helter Skelter*
US 1976 100m x 2 colour TVM
Lorimar (Tom Gries)

A fictionalized account of the Manson Murders.
Extremely powerful, *In Cold Blood* type treatment of a case which is certainly not entertaining and should probably have been left in the newspaper files.

w J. P. Miller *d* Tom Gries

Hemingway's Adventures of a Young Man*
US 1962 145m De Luxe Cinemascope
TCF (Jerry Wald)

The son of a weak doctor and a religious mother breaks away from his family circle on a voyage of discovery.
Curious mélange of ill-assimilated Hemingway stories based on his Nick Adams character. The film has good intentions but no shape or style, and the guest stars don't help.

w A. E. Hotchner, *stories* Ernest Hemingway *d* Martin Ritt *ph* Lee Garmes *m* Franz Waxman

Richard Beymer, Diane Baker, Corinne Calvet, Fred Clark, Dan Dailey, James Dunn, Juano Hernandez, Arthur Kennedy, Ricardo Montalban, Susan Strasberg, Paul Newman, Jessica Tandy, Eli Wallach

Hennessy
GB 1975 104m colour
AIP / Marseilles (Peter Snell)

Angered at the death of his family in the Belfast troubles, an Irish revolutionary hurries to London to blow up the Houses of Parliament.
Unattractive, uninventive thriller with a silly script and not an ounce of real suspense.

w John Gay, *story* Richard Johnson *d* Don Sharp *ph* Ernest Steward *m* John Scott *pd* Ray Simm

Rod Steiger, Richard Johnson, Lee Remick, Trevor Howard, Eric Porter, Peter Egan, David Collings

Henry Aldrich
Henry was originally a radio character created by Ezra Stone, an awkward small-town youth who like Andy Hardy was always getting into scrapes. Clifford Goldsmith wrote the original play which hit Broadway as well as the radio waves before starting a Hollywood series of amiable Paramount second features, most of them starring Jimmy Lydon with Charles Smith as his friend Dizzy.

1939: WHAT A LIFE (with Jackie Cooper)
1941: LIFE WITH HENRY (with Jackie Cooper). HENRY ALDRICH FOR PRESIDENT
1942: HENRY AND DIZZY, HENRY ALDRICH EDITOR
1943: HENRY ALDRICH GETS GLAMOUR, HENRY ALDRICH SWINGS IT, HENRY ALDRICH HAUNTS A HOUSE
1944: HENRY ALDRICH BOY SCOUT, HENRY ALDRICH PLAYS CUPID, HENRY ALDRICH'S LITTLE SECRET

Henry V****
GB 1944 137m Technicolor
Rank / Two Cities (Laurence Olivier)

Shakespeare's historical play is seen in performance at the Globe Theatre in 1603; as it develops, the scenery becomes more realistic.
Immensely stirring, experimental and almost wholly successful production of Shakespeare on film, sturdy both in its stylization and its command of more conventional cinematic resources for the battle.

w Laurence Olivier, Alan Dent, *play* William Shakespeare *d Laurence Olivier ph Robert Krasker m William Walton ad Paul Sheriff*

Laurence Olivier, *Robert Newton, Leslie Banks, Esmond Knight*, Renée Asherson, George Robey, *Leo Genn*, Ernest Thesiger, Ivy St Helier, Ralph Truman, Harcourt Williams, Max Adrian, Valentine Dyall, Felix Aylmer, John Laurie, Roy Emerton

Henry VIII and His Six Wives*
GB 1972 125m Technicolor
EMI (Roy Baird)

Dullish historical account of the king's reign, staged as recollections from his deathbed but lacking any of the sparkle of *The Private Life of Henry VIII* made forty years previously.
Accurate sets and costumes fail to compensate for lack of film flair.

w Ian Thorne *d* Waris Hussein *ph* Peter Suschitsky *m* David Munro

Keith Michell, Frances Cuka (Aragon), Charlotte Rampling (Boleyn), Jane Asher (Seymour), Jenny Bos (Cleves), Lynne Frederick (Howard), Barbara Leigh-Hunt (Parr), Donald Pleasance (Thomas Cromwell)
† The production was stimulated by a highly successful BBC TV series of the same name

Her Cardboard Lover*
US 1942 93m bw
MGM (J. Walter Ruben)

A flirtatious lady hires a lover to make her fiancé jealous.
Paper-thin comedy previously filmed in silent days as *The Passionate Plumber* (with Buster Keaton). It did nobody any good, but preserves some style despite a witless script.

w Jacques Deval, John Collier, Anthony Veiller, William H. Wright, *play* Jacques Deval
d George Cukor *ph* Harry Stradling, Robert Planck

Norma Shearer, Robert Taylor, George Sanders, Frank McHugh, Elizabeth Patterson, Chill Wills

Her Highness and the Bellboy
US 1945 112m bw
MGM (Joe Pasternak)

A hotel bellboy forsakes his crippled sweetheart to woo a visiting princess.
Glutinous sentimental mishmash; one waits for musical numbers which never happen.

w Richard Connell, Gladys Lehmann *d* Richard Thorpe *ph* Harry Stradling *m* Georgie Stoll

Hedy Lamarr, Robert Walker, June Allyson, Rags Ragland, Agnes Moorehead, Carl Esmond, Warner Anderson, Ludwig Stossel

Her Husband's Affairs*
US 1947 83m bw
Columbia (Raphael Hakim)

A husband and wife team of advertising agents promote a depilatory which turns out to grow hair instead.
Mildly amiable crazy comedy.

w Ben Hecht *d* S. Sylvan Simon *ph* Charles Lawton Jnr

Lucille Ball, Franchot Tone, Edward Everett Horton, Mikhail Rasumny, Gene Lockhart, Nana Bryant, Jonathan Hale, Mabel Paige

Her Jungle Love*
US 1938 81m Technicolor
Paramount (George M. Arthur)

An aviator crashlands in the jungle, where he is comforted by a lovely lady, a chimp and a lion but distressed by an earthquake, a volcano and assorted villains.
Second of Dorothy Lamour's jungle hokum

shows, and the first in colour; despite its fair technical proficiency, the fact that it once packed 'em in is tribute to the changing tastes of mankind.

w Joseph M. March, Lillie Hayward, Eddie Welch *d* George Archainbaud *ph* Ray Rennahan *m* Gregory Stone

Dorothy Lamour, Ray Milland, Lynne Overman, J. Carrol Naish, Dorothy Howe

Her Twelve Men
US 1954 91m Anscocolor
MGM (John Houseman)

A woman teacher in a boys' school reforms a difficult class.
Predictable, sugary and artificial school story with the star exuding sweetness and light.

w William Roberts, Laura Z. Hobson *d* Robert Z. Leonard *ph* Joseph Ruttenberg *m* Bronislau Kaper

Greer Garson, Robert Ryan, Richard Haydn, Barry Sullivan

Here Come the Girls*
US 1953 78m Technicolor
Paramount (Paul Jones)

In the nineties an ageing chorus boy traps a mysterious murderer.
Spotty, ineptly titled star comedy with music; in fact among the last of his passable vehicles, with excellent production backing.

w Edmund Hartmann, Hal Kanter *d* Claude Binyon *ph* Lionel Lindon *md* Lyn Murray *ad Hal Pereira, Roland Anderson*

Bob Hope, Rosemary Clooney, Tony Martin, Arlene Dahl, Millard Mitchell, Fred Clark, William Demarest, Robert Strauss

Here Come the Huggetts*
GB 1948 93m bw
Rank / Gainsborough (Betty Box)

A suburban family has its ups and downs.
Cosy domestic comedy drama, a presage of TV soap operas to come, or Britain's answer to the Hardys, depending how you look at it. Tolerable at the time.

w Mabel and Denis Constanduros, Muriel and Sydney Box, Peter Rogers *d* Ken Annakin

Jack Warner, Kathleen Harrison, Jane Hylton, Susan Shaw, Petula Clark, Jimmy Hanley, David Tomlinson, Diana Dors, Peter Hammond, John Blythe
† The Huggetts had actually originated in *Holiday Camp* the previous year, and appeared again in *Vote for Huggett* and *The Huggetts Abroad*; Warner and Harrison became an inseparable duo for many years.

Here Come the Waves
US 1944 98m bw
Paramount (Mark Sandrich)

A sailor falls in love with identical twin Waves.
Empty-headed, professionally executed musical recruiting poster.

w Allen Scott, Ken Englund, Zion Myers *d* Mark Sandrich *ph* Charles Lang *md* Robert Emmett Dolan *songs* Harold Arlen, Johnny Mercer

Bing Crosby, Betty Hutton, Sonny Tufts, Ann Doran, Gwen Crawford

Here Comes Mr Jordan***
US 1941 93m bw
Columbia (Everett Riskin)

A prizefighter who is also an amateur saxophonist crashes in his private plane and goes to heaven by mistake: he was supposed to survive and live another forty years.
Unfortunately when he goes back for his body it has been cremated, so he has to find another one, recently deceased . . .
Weird heavenly fantasy which succeeded because of its novelty and because heaven in wartime was a comforting vision. As a movie taken on its own merits, it suffers from illogicalities, a miscast star and a wandering plot, but scene for scene there is enough firmness and control to make it memorable. It certainly had many imitations, including *Angel on My Shoulder, Down to Earth, A Guy Named Joe, Heaven Only Knows, The Horn Blows at Midnight* and *That's the Spirit.*

w Seton I. Miller, Sidney Buchman, play Halfway to Heaven by Harry Segall *d Alexander Hall* *ph* Joseph Walker *m* Morris Stoloff

Robert Montgomery, Evelyn Keyes, Rita Johnson, *Claude Rains, James Gleason, Edward Everett Horton*, John Emery, *Donald MacBride*, Halliwell Hobbes, Don Costello

Here Comes the Groom*
US 1951 114m bw
Paramount (Frank Capra)

A journalist adopts war orphans and reforms his selfish fiancée.
Tired attempt by Capra to recapture his pre-war mood; despite intermittent pleasures it has neither the right style nor the topical substance.

w Virginia Van Upp, Myles Connelly, Liam O'Brien, *story* Robert Riskin *d Frank Capra ph* George Barnes *md* Joseph Lilley *songs* Jay Livingston, Ray Evans

Bing Crosby, Jane Wyman, Franchot Tone, Alexis Smith, James Barton, Connie Gilchrist, Robert Keith, Anna Maria Alberghetti

'The general impression is of a loud, strident, rather vulgar comedy in which technique is used to disappointingly mechanical ends, and which a few bright lines of dialogue cannot rescue from tedium.'—*Penelope Houston*

Here Comes the Navy*
US 1934 86m bw
Warner

An aggressive young naval rating fights with his former friend, now Petty Officer.
Breezy comedy melodrama teaming Cagney and O'Brien for the first time and offering star heroics as a sop to the Legion of Decency.

w Ben Markson, Earl Baldwin *d* Lloyd Bacon *ph* Arthur Edeson *m* Leo F. Forbstein

James Cagney, Pat O'Brien, Dorothy Tree, Gloria Stuart, Frank McHugh, Robert Barrat

'Rapid and reasonably authentic, a satisfactory addition to a series of cinema cartoons which, because their colour and mood are indigenous and timely, may be more interesting twenty years from now.'—*Time*

Here We Go round the Mulberry Bush*
GB 1967 96m Technicolor
UA / Giant (Larry Kramer, Clive Donner)

A school-leaver is obsessed by sex and determines to lose his virginity.
Repetitive comedy which certainly opened new avenues in British humour and seemed pretty permissive at the time (pre*Graduate*). In itself, however, more modish than sympathetic.

w Hunter Davies (with Larry Kramer), from his novel *d Clive Donner* *ph* Alex Thomson *m* various groups

Barry Evans, Judy Geeson, Angela Scoular, Adrienne Posta, Sheila White, Vanessa Howard, Denholm Elliott, Maxine Audley, Moyra Fraser, Michael Bates

'The only incongruity is that it should have been made by adults, so completely does it enter into the teenager's view of himself.'—*MFB*

The Heroes of Telemark*
GB 1965 131m Technicolor Panavision
Rank / Benton (Ben Fisz)

Norwegian resistance workers in World War II help the Allies to smash a heavy water plant.
Ambling narrative with big action sequences which often seem irrelevant, so that the story as a whole fails to excite.

w Ivan Moffat, Ben Barzman *d* Anthony Mann *ph Robert Krasker* *m* Malcolm Arnold

Kirk Douglas, Richard Harris, Ulla Jacobsson, Roy Dotrice, Anton Diffring

Hero's Island*
US 1962 94m Technicolor Panavision
UA / Daystar / Portland (James Mason, Leslie Stevens)

In 1718 bondslaves settle on a Carolina island, are attacked by fishermen and protected by Blackbeard the Pirate.
An oddly personal, patchy, rather mysterious film with a rhetorical script and rather good action sequences.

wd Leslie Stevens *ph* Ted McCord *m* Dominic Frontière

James Mason, Kate Manx, Neville Brand, Rip Torn

Hers to Hold
US 1943 94m bw
Universal (Felix Jackson)

A girl decides whether or not to marry a serviceman.
Limp star vehicle, a sequel to *Three Smart Girls* (qv).

w Lewis R. Foster *d* Frank Ryan *ph* Elwood Bredell *md* Charles Previn *m* Frank Skinner

Deanna Durbin, Joseph Cotten, Charles Winninger, Nella Walker, Gus Schilling, Ludwig Stossel

Hester Street*
US 1974 89m bw
Midwest Films (Raphael D. Silver)

How Jewish immigrants settled in East Side New York in the nineties.
Modest, humorous, but not always smooth or dramatically emphatic chronicle of a familiar background; the detail however is excellent.

wd Joan Micklin Silver, *story* Yeki by Abraham Cahan *ph* Kenneth Van Sickle *m* William Bolcom

Steven Keats, Carol Kane, Mel Howard, Dorrie Kavanaugh, Doris Roberts

'A small, beautifully detailed, slightly shaggy independent film of charm and substance.'—*Judith Crist*

Hey I'm Alive*
US 1975 74m colour TVM
Charles Fries (Lawrence Schiller)

The true account of two people who survived a light plane crash in the frozen Yukon.
A good start, but it gets a bit gruelling and repetitive.

w Rita Lakin, *book* Helen Klauben *d* Larry Schiller

Ed Asner, Sally Struthers

Hi Diddle Diddle*
US 1943 72m bw
Columbia / Andrew Stone
aka: *Try and Find It*

Young lovers are hampered by con artist parents.
Scatty comedy with amusing patches and some zest in the telling.

w Edmund L. Hartmann *d* Andrew L. Stone *ph* Charles Van Enger *m* Hans J. Salter

Adolphe Menjou, Pola Negri, Dennis O'Keefe, Billie Burke, Martha Scott, June Havoc

Hi Gang
GB 1941 100m bw
Rank / Gainsborough (Edward Black)

American expatriates in London get involved in a case of mistaken identity.
Icky farce based faintly on a wartime radio variety series, notable only for preserving the three stars involved.

w Val Guest, Marriott Edgar, J. O. C. Orton, Howard Irving Young *d* Marcel Varnel

Bebe Daniels, Ben Lyon, Vic Oliver, Graham Moffatt, Moore Marriott, Felix Aylmer, Sam Browne

Hi Nellie*
US 1934 79m bw
Warner (Robert Presnell)

An ex-editor is demoted to advice to the lovelorn and gets involved in city rackets.
Minor, effective star comedy-melodrama.

w Abe Finkel, Sidney Sutherland *d* Mervyn Le Roy *ph* Sol Polito

Paul Muni, Glenda Farrell, Ned Sparks, Robert Barrat, Hobart Cavanaugh, Berton Churchill, Donald Meek, Douglass Dumbrille, Edward Ellis

Hickey and Boggs
US 1972 111m De Luxe
UA / Film Guarantors Ltd (Fouad Said)

Two down and out private eyes, hired to find a girl, keep falling over dead bodies.
Extraordinarily confused thriller with moments of humour and well staged action sequences.

w Walter Hill *d* Robert Culp *ph* Wilmer Butler *m* Ted Ashford

Robert Culp, Bill Cosby, Rosalind Cash

The High and the Mighty*
US 1954 147m Warnercolor Cinemascope
Wayne–Fellows

A big passenger plane is in trouble over the Pacific, and its occupants react in various ways to the prospect of a crash landing.
Compendium fiction with even the pilot having a personal problem which could cloud his judgment. Tolerable, well made hokum.

w Ernest K. Gann, from his novel *d* William Wellman *ph* William Clothier *m* Dmitri Tiomkin

John Wayne, Robert Newton, Robert Stack, Doe Avedon, Claire Trevor, Laraine Day, Jan Sterling, Phil Harris, Sidney Blackmer, John Howard

High Barbaree
US 1947 91m bw
MGM

A pilot crashlands in the Pacific and finds himself drifting towards a Utopian island fancifully described by his favourite uncle.
Thin Hollywood mysticism on Shangri-La lines but without the solid virtues of plot, dialogue and imagination.

w Anne Morrison Chapin, Whitfield Cook, Cyril Hume *d* Jack Conway *ph* Sidney Wagner

Van Johnson, June Allyson, Thomas Mitchell, Marilyn Maxwell

The High Bright Sun
GB 1965 114m Technicolor
Rank (Betty Box)
US title: *McGuire Go Home*

In 1957 Cyprus the British army is beleaguered by partisans, and an officer tries to contact a leading rebel.
Confused and boring attempt to make romantic drama out of an intractably sad situation.

w Ian Stuart Black, from his novel *d* Ralph Thomas *ph* Ernest Steward *m* Angelo Lavagnino

Dirk Bogarde, Susan Strasberg, George Chakiris, Denholm Elliott

The High Command*
GB 1936 88m bw
ABFD / Fanfare / Wellesley (Gordon Wellesley)

The general of a West African garrison has a

guilty secret known to his young medical officer. Dated melodrama, rather interestingly performed and directed.

w Katherine Strueby, *novel* The General Goes Too Far by Lewis Robinson *d Thorold Dickinson ph* Otto Heller *m* Ernest Irving

James Mason, Lionel Atwill, Lucie Mannheim, Steve Geray, Leslie Perrins

The High Cost of Loving*
US 1958 87m bw
MGM (Milo O. Frank Jnr)

A happily married middle class couple have doubts about their future.
Pleasant, mildly satirical romantic comedy which doesn't really get anywhere.

w Rip Van Ronkel *d* Jose Ferrer *ph* George J. Folsey *m* Jeff Alexander

Jose Ferrer, Gena Rowlands, Joanne Gilbert, Jim Backus, Bobby Troup, Philip Ober, Edward Platt, Werner Klemperer

High Flight
GB 1958 102m Technicolor
Columbia / Warwick (Phil C. Samuel)

Cadets train at the Royal Air Force College.
Simple-minded peacetime flagwaver.

w Joseph Landon, Ken Hughes *d* John Gilling *ph* Muir Mathieson *m* Kenneth V. Jones, Douglas Gamley

Ray Milland, Bernard Lee, Kenneth Haigh, Anthony Newley, Kenneth Fortescue, Sean Kelly, Helen Cherry

High Noon****
US 1952 85m bw
Stanley Kramer

A marshal gets no help when he determines to defend his town against revengeful badmen.
A minor western with a soft-pedalled message for the world, this turned out to be a classic simply because it was well done, with every scene and performance clearly worked out. Cinematically it was pared to the bone, and the theme tune helped.

w Carl Foreman d Fred Zinnemann ph Floyd Crosby m Dmitri Tiomkin singer Tex Ritter

Gary Cooper, Grace Kelly, Thomas Mitchell, Lloyd Bridges, Katy Jurado, Otto Kruger, Lon Chaney, Henry Morgan

'Like nearly all the Kramer productions, this is a neat, well-finished and literate piece of work, though its limitations are more conventional than most.'—*Gavin Lambert*

'A western to challenge *Stagecoach* for the all time championship.'—*Bosley Crowther*

'A series of crisp and purposeful scenes that interpret each other like the pins on a strategist's war map.'—*Robert L. Hatch*

High Plains Drifter*
US 1972 105m Technicolor Panavision
Universal / Malpaso (Robert Daley)

A mysterious stranger rides into town and terrifies the inhabitants.
Semi-supernatural, mystical revenge western with an overplus of violence. Very watchable, but irritating.

w Ernest Tidyman *d* Clint Eastwood *ph* Bruce Surtees *m* Dee Barton *ad* Henry Bumstead

Clint Eastwood, Verna Bloom, Marianna Hill, Mitch Ryan, Jack Ging

''Ritualized violence and plodding symbolism make for heavy going.'—*Sight and Sound*

'A nervously humorous, self-conscious near-satire on the prototype Eastwood formula.'—*Variety*

High Risk*
US 1976 74m colour TVM
MGM / Danny Thomas (Robert E. Relyea)

A group of professionals with special skills take on impossible missions at a half million dollars a time.
Polished, predictable, highly derivative entertainment.

w Robert Carrington *d* Sam O'Steen

Victor Buono, Don Stroud, Joe Sirola, Joanna Cameron, Ronne Troup, Wolf Roth

High Sierra*
US 1941 96m bw
Warner (Hal. B. Wallis, Mark Hellinger)

An ex-con gangster plans one last heist in the Californian mountains, but is mortally wounded through his involvement with two women.
Rather dreary action melodrama which gave Bogart his first real star part (after George Raft turned it down). Remade 1955 as *I Died a Thousand Times* (qv); also in 1949 as a western, *Colorado Territory*.

w John Huston, W. R. Burnett, *novel* W. R. Burnett *d Raoul Walsh ph* Tony Gaudio *m* Adolph Deutsch

Humphrey Bogart, Ida Lupino, Joan Leslie, Alan Curtis, Arthur Kennedy, Henry Hull, Henry Travers, Jerome Cowan

'The last swallow, perhaps, of the gangsters' summer.'—*William Whitebait*

High Society
US 1956 107m Technicolor Vistavision
MGM (Sol C. Siegel)

A haughty rich girl chooses between several suitors.
Cold, flat, dull musical reworking of *The Philadelphia Story* (qv), with ill-cast performers and just a few bright moments.

w John Patrick *d* Charles Walters *ph* Paul C. Vogel *m/ly* Cole Porter *ad* Cedric Gibbons, Hans Peters

Bing Crosby, Grace Kelly, Frank Sinatra, Celeste Holm, Louis Armstrong, Sidney Blackmer, Margalo Gillmore, Louis Calhern, Lydia Reed, John Lund

High Tide at Noon
GB 1957 111m bw
Rank (Julian Wintle)

Passions run high among lobster fishermen in Nova Scotia.
Neat, clean romantic melodrama in agreeable surroundings.

w Neil Paterson *d* Philip Leacock *ph* Eric Cross *m* John Veale

Betta St John, Michael Craig, Patrick McGoohan, William Sylvester, Flora Robson, Alexander Knox, Peter Arne, Patrick Allen, Susan Beaumont

High Time
US 1960 103m De Luxe Cinemascope
TCF / Bing Crosby

A middle-aged widower goes back to college.
Flaccid comedy-musical with some undergraduatish jokes.

w Tom and Frank Waldman *d* Blake Edwards *ph* Ellsworth Fredericks *m* Henry Mancini *songs* Sammy Cahn, Jimmy Van Heusen

Bing Crosby, Tuesday Weld, Fabian, Richard Beymer, Nicole Maurey

High Treason*
GB 1951 93m bw
GFD / Conqueror (Paul Soskin)

Saboteurs are routed by the London police.
Unconvincing documentary melodrama which moves fast enough to be entertaining.

w Frank Harvey, Roy Boulting *d* Roy Boulting *ph* Gilbert Taylor *m* John Addison

Liam Redmond, André Morell, Anthony Bushell, Kenneth Griffith, Patric Doonan, Joan Hickson, Anthony Nicholls, Mary Morris, Geoffrey Keen, Dora Bryan

High Wall
US 1948 99m bw
MGM

A war veteran is put in an asylum after confessing to killing his wife, but later events prove that he was drugged into saying so.
Adequately entertaining, supremely unconvincing mystery melodrama.

w Sydney Boehm *d* Curtis Marshall *ph* Paul C. Vogel *m* Bronislau Kaper

Robert Taylor, Herbert Marshall, Audrey Totter, Dorothy Patrick, H. B. Warner, Warner Anderson

High, Wide and Handsome*
US 1937 110m bw
Paramount (Arthur Hornblow Jnr)

Pennsylvania 1859: a travelling showgirl falls in love with a farmer.
Disappointingly stilted period musical with most of the talent ill at ease until the final reel.

w Oscar Hammerstein II *d* Rouben Mamoulian *ph* Victor Milner, Theodore Sparkuhl *ch* LeRoy Prinz *songs* Jerome Kern, Oscar Hammerstein II *md* Boris Morros *ad* Hans Dreier, John Goodman

Irene Dunne, Randolph Scott, Dorothy Lamour, Raymond Walburn, Alan Hale, Elizabeth Patterson, Charles Bickford, William Frawley, Akim Tamiroff, Ben Blue, Irving Pichel, Lucien Littlefield

A High Wind in Jamaica*
GB 1965 104m De Luxe Cinemascope
TCF (John Croydon)

In Victorian days, English children en route home from Jamaica are captured by pirates and influence their lives.
Semi-serious adventure story with a highly unlikely ending in which the chief pirate allows himself to be executed for a murder committed by a child. There are however pleasures along the way.

w Stanley Mann, Ronald Harwood, Denis Cannan, *novel* Richard Hughes *d* Alexander Mackendrick *ph* Douglas Slocombe *m* Larry Adler

Deborah Baxter, Anthony Quinn, James Coburn, Isabel Dean, Nigel Davenport, Gert Frobe, Lila Kedrova

Higher and Higher*
US 1943 90m bw
RKO (Tim Whelan)

Servants have an elaborate plan to restore the family fortune.
Unamusing musical which undernourishes several talents.

w Jay Dratler, Ralph Spence, *play* Gladys Hurlbut, Joshua Logan *d* Tim Whelan *ph* Robert de Grasse *md* Constantin Bakaleinikoff *songs* Jimmy McHugh, Harold Adamson

Michele Morgan, Jack Haley, *Frank Sinatra*, Leon Errol, Marcy McGuire, *Victor Borge*, Mary Wickes, Barbara Hale, Elizabeth Risdon

Hijack
US 1973 74m colour TVM
Spelling–Goldberg

A truck driver with a secret cargo has to frustrate several hijack attempts along his route.
Rather sluggish action melodrama

w James D. Buchanan, Ronald Austin *d* Leonard Horn

David Janssen Lee Purcell, Keenan Wynn, Jeanette Nolan, Tom Tully

Hilda Crane
US 1956 87m Technicolor Cinemascope
TCF (Herbert B. Swope Jnr)

An unhappy woman marries for the third time and convinces herself it won't work.
Emotional melodrama of the old school: very moderate in all departments.

wd Philip Dunne, *play* Samson Raphaelson *ph* Joe MacDonald *m* David Raksin

Jean Simmons, Guy Madison, Jean-Pierre Aumont, *Evelyn Varden*, Judith Evelyn, Peggy Knudsen

The Hill**
GB 1965 122m bw
MGM / Seven Arts (Kenneth Hyman)

Prisoners rebel against the harsh discipline of a British military detention centre in North Africa during World War II.
Lurid melodrama which descends fairly quickly into black farce with a number of sweaty actors outshouting each other. Enjoyable on this level when you can hear the dialogue through the poor sound recording.

w Ray Rigby, from his TV play *d* Sidney Lumet *ph* Oswald Morris *m* none

Sean Connery, Harry Andrews, Michael Redgrave, Ian Bannen, Alfred Lynch, *Ossie Davis*, Roy Kinnear, Jack Watson, Ian Hendry

A Hill in Korea
GB 1956 81m bw
British Lion / Wessex (Anthony Squire)

During the Korean war, a small patrol guards a hill.
Minor war talk-piece, shot in Surrey and looking it.

w Ian Dalrymple, Anthony Squire, Ronald Spencer, *novel* Max Catto *d* Julian Amyes *ph* Freddie Francis *m* Malcolm Arnold

George Baker, Harry Andrews, Stanley Baker, Michael Medwin, Ronald Lewis, Stephen Boyd, Victor Maddern, Harry Landis

'Character is adequately sketched into a suitably laconic script.'—*MFB*

The Hindenberg*
US 1975 125m Technicolor Panavision
Universal / Filmmakers (Robert Wise)

In 1937, sabotage causes the airship Hindenberg to crash on arrival at New York.
An extremely uninteresting guess at the cause of this famous disaster. The plot and dialogue are leaden, and such actors as have more than a couple of lines look extremely glum. The special effects, however, are fine despite curious blue-rinse photographic processing.

w Nelson Gidding, *novel* Michael M. Mooney *d* Robert Wise *ph* Robert Surtees *pd* Edward Carfagno *sp Albert Whitlock* *m* David Shire

George C. Scott, Anne Bancroft, Burgess Meredith, William Atherton, Roy Thinnes, Gig Young, Charles Durning, Robert Clary, René Auberjonois

'The tackiest disaster movie yet—a cheap and chaotic collage of painted drops, wooden actors and not-so-special effects that manages to make one of this century's most sensational real-life catastrophes seem roughly as terrifying as a badly stubbed toe.'—*Frank Rich*

The Hired Hand
US 1971 93m Technicolor
Universal / Pando (William Hayward)

Two western drifters avenge the killing of their friend and settle down to work on a farm; but violence follows them.
A potentially enjoyable small-scale western is spoiled by pretentious direction and effects which bore the spectator to death.

w Alan Sharp *d* Peter Fonda *ph* Vilmos Zsigmond *m* Bruce Langhorne

Peter Fonda, Warren Oates, Verna Bloom, Severn Darden

'The first slow-motion western, with endless artsy photography not quite succeeding in obscuring the rambling plot.'—*Judith Crist, 1973*

The Hireling*
GB 1973 108m colour
Columbia / World Film Services (Ben Arbeid)

In the twenties, a lady's chauffeur falls in love with her.
Talkative drama, elegant but not much fun.

w Wolf Mankowitz, *novel* L. P. Hartley *d Alan Bridges ph* Michael Reed *m* Marc Wilkinson *pd Natasha Kroll*

Sarah Miles, Robert Shaw, Peter Egan, Elizabeth Sellars, Caroline Mortimer

His Brother's Wife
US 1936 91m bw
MGM (Lawrence Weingarten)

A young scientist is helped out of trouble by his brother, on condition he disappears; the brother then weds the scientist's girl friend.
Heavy romantic melodrama containing everything including jungle fever, flung together to take advantage of the stars' real-life romance.

w Leon Gordon, John Meehan, *story* George Auerbach *d* W. S. Van Dyke II *ph* Oliver T. Marsh *m* Franz Waxman

Robert Taylor, Barbara Stanwyck, Joseph Calleia, John Eldredge, Jean Hersholt, Samuel S. Hinds, Leonard Mudie, Jed Prouty

His Butler's Sister*
US 1943 94m bw
Universal (Felix Jackson)

A temporary maid falls for her sophisticated boss.
Pleasant comedy musical: no great shakes, but the principals give the air of enjoying themselves.

w Samuel Hoffenstein, Betty Reinhardt *d* Frank Borzage *ph* Elwood Bredell *m* Hans Salter

Deanna Durbin, Franchot Tone, Pat O'Brien, Evelyn Ankers, Walter Catlett, Alan Mowbray, Akim Tamiroff, Else Janssen, Iris Adrian

His Girl Friday****
US 1940 92m bw
Columbia (Howard Hawks)

A remake of *The Front Page* (qv), with Hildy Johnson turned into a woman.
Frantic, hilarious black farce with all participants at their best; possibly the fastest comedy ever filmed, and one of the funniest.

w Charles Lederer, play The Front Page by Ben Hecht, Charles MacArthur *d Howard Hawks ph* Joseph Walker *m* Morris Stoloff

Rosalind Russell, Cary Grant, Ralph Bellamy, Gene Lockhart, Porter Hall, *Ernest Truex,* Cliff Edwards, *Clarence Kolb, Roscoe Karns, Frank Jenks,* Abner Biberman, Frank Orth, John Qualen, Helen Mack, *Billy Gilbert,* Alma Kruger

'The kind of terrific verbal slam-bang that has vanished from current film-making.'—*New Yorker, 1975*

'One of the fastest of all movies, from line to line and from gag to gag.'—*Manny Farber, 1971*

'Overlapping dialogue carries the movie along at breakneck speed; word gags take the place of the sight gags of silent comedy, as this vanished race of brittle, cynical, childish people rush around on corrupt errands.'—*Pauline Kael, 1968*

His Kind of Woman*
US 1951 120m bw
RKO (Howard Hughes, Robert Sparks)

At a remote Mexican ranch resort, a gangster on the run holds up residents including a fortune-hunting girl and a fading matinee idol.
Agreeable tongue-in-cheek melodrama which slightly outstays its welcome but is generally good fun.

w Frank Fenton, *d* John Farrow *ph* Harry J. Wild *m* Constantin Bakaleinikoff

Robert Mitchum, Jane Russell, *Vincent Price,* Raymond Burr, Tim Holt, Charles McGraw, Marjorie Reynolds, Jim Backus

His Majesty O'Keefe
GB 1954 90m Technicolor
Warner / Harold Hecht

Native islanders are taught by an easygoing mariner how to exploit their natural resources and defend themselves against pirates.
Thin adventure romance with too little for its star to do.

w Borden Chase, James Hill *d* Byron Haskin *ph* Otto Heller *m* Robert Farnon

Burt Lancaster, Joan Rice, André Morell, Abraham Sofaer, Benson Fong, Archie Savage

History Is Made at Night*
US 1937 97m bw
Walter Wanger

A divorcee and her new love have trouble from her ex-husband.
Atmospheric, artificial, generally entertaining romantic comedy-drama of a kind which went out of fashion long ago.

w Gene Towne, Graham Baker *d* Frank Borzage *ph* Gregg Toland *m* Alfred Newman

Charles Boyer, Jean Arthur, *Leo Carrillo,* Colin Clive

The History of Mr Polly*
GB 1949 94m bw
GFD / Two Cities (John Mills)

A draper's assistant buys a small shop but tires of his nagging wife and decides the time has come for a change.
Patchy but generally amusing version of a popular comic novel, very English and rather appealingly done.

w Anthony Pelissier, *novel* H. G. Wells
d Anthony Pelissier ph Desmond Dickinson
m William Alwyn

John Mills, Sally Ann Howes, Megs Jenkins, Finlay Currie, Betty Ann Davies, Edward Chapman

Hit!
US 1973 134m Technicolor
Panavision
Paramount (Harry Korshak)

A federal agent takes personal action against a drug ring which caused his daughter's death.
Black vigilante melodrama, very violent and interminably padded out with irrelevancies.

w Alan Trustman, David M. Wolf *d* Sidney J. Furie *ph* John A. Alonzo *m* Lalo Schifrin

Billy Dee Williams, Richard Pryor, Paul Hampton, Gwen Welles

'No more under-the-armpit shots, but obscurity is still the keynote of this Sidney Furie effort in the urban vigilante genre.'—*Sight and Sound*

Hit Lady*
US 1974 74m colour TVM
Spelling–Goldberg

A glamorous lady artist is really a professional killer.
Ludicrously unlikely murder melodrama with predictable twists and glossy presentation.

w Yvette Mimieux *d* Tracy Keenan Wynn

Yvette Mimieux, Dack Rambo, Joseph Campanella, Clu Gulager, Keenan Wynn

Hit the Deck
US 1954 112m Eastmancolor
Cinemascope
MGM (Joe Pasternak)

Romantic adventures of three sailors on shore leave in San Francisco.
Boring situations and performances reduce the temperature of this youth musical which is not another *On the Town*.

w Sonya Levien, William Ludwig, *musical play* Herbert Fields, *novel* Shore Leave by Hubert Osborn *ph* George Folsey *m* Vincent Youmans *ly* Leo Robin *ch* Hermes Pan

Tony Martin, Jane Powell, Ann Miller, Debbie Reynolds, Walter Pidgeon, Vic Damone, Gene Raymond

Hitch-Hike*
US 1974 74m Technicolor TVM
Universal (Jay Benson)

A lady driver unwittingly picks up a murderer.
Simple, predictable, well made study in suspense.

w Yale M. Udoff, Jay Benson, M. K. Landstein
d Gordon Hessler

Cloris Leachman, Michael Brandon, Henry Darrow, Cameron Mitchell

Hitched*
US 1971 73m Technicolor TVM
Universal (Richard Alan Simmons)
GB title: *Westward the Wagon*

Newly weds in the old west face various dangers en route to their new home.
Comedy adventure with some pert moments, but generally not quite hilarious enough.

w Richard Alan Simmons *d* Boris Sagal

Sally Field, Tim Matheson, Don Knight, Neville Brand, Kathleen Freeman, Slim Pickens, John Fiedler

Hitler
US 1961 107m bw
Three Crown / E. Charles Straus

A sex-oriented, semi-fictional biopic of the German dictator, from the murder of his niece to his final madness and suicide.
Enterprising sensationalism which deserves a nod for sheer audacity.

w Sam Neuman *d* Stuart Heisler *ph* Joseph Biroc *m* Hans Salter

Richard Basehart, Maria Emo, Martin Kosleck, John Banner

The Hitler Gang**
US 1944 101m bw
Paramount (B. G. De Sylva)

The rise to power of Hitler and his henchmen.
Though at the time it seemed rather like a serious cabaret turn, this fictionalization of historical fact has some good impersonations and dramatically effective scenes.

w Frances Goodrich, Albert Hackett *d John Farrow ph* Ernest Laszlo *m* David Buttolph

Robert Watson, Martin Kosleck (Goebbels), Victor Varconi (Hess), Luis Van Rooten (Himmler), Alexander Pope (Goering), Roman

Bohnen, Ivan Triesault, Helene Thimig, Reinhold Schunzel, Sig Rumann, Alexander Granach

Hitler—The Last Ten Days
GB / Italy 1973 104m Technicolor
MGM / Wolfgang Reinhardt / Westfilm

With Adolf and Eva in the bunker.
Claustrophobic historical reconstruction with an uncomfortable star.

w Ennio de Concini, Maria Pia Fusco, Wolfgang Reinhardt, Ivan Moffat *d* Ennio de Concini *ph* Ennio Guarnieri *m* Mischa Spoliansky

Alec Guinness, Simon Ward, Doris Kunstmann, Adolfo Celi, Diane Cilento, Eric Porter, Joss Ackland

Hitler's Children*
US 1943 83m bw
RKO (Edward A. Golden)

A family reacts to Hitler and the Hitler Youth.
Artificial melodrama set in an unlikely Germany but successful at the time because of its topicality and its refusal to play the Nazis as idiots, which was the usual Hollywood line.

w Emmet Lavery, *book* Education for Death by Gregor Ziemer *d* Edward Dmytryk *m* Roy Webb

Tim Holt, Bonita Granville, Otto Kruger, Kent Smith, H. B. Warner, Lloyd Corrigan, Erford Gage, Gavin Muir, Hans Conried

HM Pulham Esquire**
US 1940 120m bw
MGM (King Vidor)

A moderately successful Bostonian businessman looks back over his rather stuffy life and has a fling.
Solidly upholstered drama which does not quite do justice to the book on which it is based.

w King Vidor, Elizabeth Hill, *novel* John P. Marquand *d* King Vidor

Robert Young, Ruth Hussey, Hedy Lamarr, Charles Coburn, Van Heflin, Fay Holden, Bonita Granville

HMS Defiant*
GB 1962 101m Technicolor
Cinemascope
Columbia / GW (John Brabourne)
US title: *Damn the Defiant*

Mutiny erupts on an 18th-century British sailing ship.
Rather unpleasant and unenterprising sea fare reminiscent of the goings-on aboard the *Bounty*.
Well enough staged and acted but not very remarkable or memorable.

w Nigel Kneale, Edmund H. North, *novel* Mutiny by Frank Tilsley *d* Lewis Gilbert *ph* Christopher Challis *m* Clifton Parker

Alec Guinness, Dirk Bogarde, Anthony Quayle, Tom Bell, Nigel Stock, Murray Melvin, Victor Maddern, Maurice Denham, Walter Fitzgerald

'It authentically if superficially recreates the days of press gangs, maggots and the cat.'—*Peter John Dyer*

Hobson's Choice***
GB 1953 107m bw
British Lion / London (Norman Spencer)

In the 1890s a tyrannical Lancashire bootmaker is brought to heel by his plain-speaking daughter and her simple-minded husband.
Brilliantly played version of a famous working-class comedy, memorably set and photographed; one regrets only the slight decline of the predictable third act.

w Norman Spencer, Wynard Browne, *play* Harold Brighouse *d David Lean ph Jack Hildyard m Malcolm Arnold ad Wilfrid Shingleton*

Charles Laughton, Brenda de Banzie, John Mills, Richard Wattis, Helen Haye, Daphne Anderson, Prunella Scales

Hoffman
GB 1970 113m Technicolor
ABP / Longstone (Ben Arbeid)

A middle-aged misfit blackmails a typist into spending a week with him.
Interminable sex comedy padded out from a short TV play: it quickly becomes claustrophobic, tasteless, and boring.

w Ernest Gebler, from his novel and play *d* Alvin Rakoff *ph* Gerry Turpin *m* Ron Grainer

Peter Sellers, Sinead Cusack, Jeremy Bulloch, Ruth Dunning

Hold Back the Dawn*
US 1941 115m bw
Paramount (Arthur Hornblow Jnr)

A would-be immigrant into the US via Mexico marries a schoolteacher he does not love.
Surprisingly effective romantic melodrama with a nice style and some mordant lines in the script.

w Charles Brackett, Billy Wilder d Mitchell Leisen ph Leo Tover m Victor Young

Charles Boyer, Olivia de Havilland, Paulette Goddard, Victor Francen, Walter Abel, Curt

Bois, Rosemary de Camp, Nestor Paiva, Mitchell Leisen

Hold That Blonde
US 1945 75m bw
Paramount (Paul Jones)

A psychiatrist suggests that romance may cure a kleptomaniac, but the patient unfortunately chooses a jewel thief.
Thin comedy which erupts into frantic farce, with some energetic slapstick and a Harold Lloyd style finale.

w Walter de Leon, Earl Baldwin, E. Edwin Moran *d* George Marshall *ph* Daniel L. Fapp *m* Werner Heymann

Eddie Bracken, Veronica Lake, Albert Dekker, Frank Fenton, George Zucco, Donald MacBride, Norma Varden, Willie Best

Hold That Co-Ed*
US 1938 80m bw
TCF (David Hempstead)
GB title: *Hold That Girl*

A girl dressed as a boy wins a university football match and thereby helps a governor get re-elected.
Intriguingly-cast crazy comedy which works up into a fine frenzy.

w Karl Tunberg, Don Ettinger, Jack Yellen *d* George Marshall *ph* Robert Planck *md* Arthur Lange

John Barrymore, Joan Davis, George Murphy, Marjorie Weaver, Jack Haley, George Barbier, Donald Meek, Johnny Downs, Guinn Williams

Hold That Ghost*
US 1941 86m bw
Universal (Burt Kelly, Glenn Tryon)

A group of strangers are stranded in an apparently haunted house.
Long thought of as Abbott and Costello's best comedy, this now seems pretty strained and slow to start, but it has its classic moments.

w Robert Lees, Fred Rinaldo, John Grant *d* Arthur Lubin *ph* Elwood Bredell, Joe Valentine *m* Hans Salter

Bud Abbott, Lou Costello, Joan Davis, the Andrews Sisters, Richard Carlson, *Ted Lewis* and his band, Evelyn Ankers, Marc Lawrence, Mischa Auer

Hold Your Man*
US 1933 89m bw
MGM (Sam Wood)

A hard-boiled young woman falls for a confidence man, has his baby, and waits for him to emerge from prison.
Briskly-fashioned star comedy-drama with entertaining moments.

w Anita Loos, Howard Emmett Rogers *d* Sam Wood *ph* Harold Rosson

Jean Harlow, Clark Gable, Stuart Erwin, Dorothy Burgess, Muriel Kirkland, Paul Hurst

'The sudden transition from wise-cracking romance to sentimental penitence provides a jolt.'—*Frank S. Nugent*

A Hole in the Head*
US 1959 120m De Luxe Cinemascope
Sincap (Frank Capra)

A Miami hotelier is threatened with foreclosure and tries to raise the money from his provident elder brother.
Easy-going comedy without much point, but various amusing facets artfully deployed.

w Arnold Shulman, from his TV and stage play *d* Frank Capra *ph* William H. Daniels *m* Nelson Riddle

Frank Sinatra, Edward G. Robinson, Eleanor Parker, Eddie Hodges, Carolyn Jones, Thelma Ritter, Keenan Wynn, Joi Lansing

The Hole in the Wall
US 1929 73m bw
Paramount

A gangster falls for a phony fortune teller intent on a revenge scheme.
Involved melodrama, a primitive talkie notable chiefly for its stars.

w Pierre Collings, *play* Fred Jackson *d* Robert Florey *ph* George Folsey

Edward G. Robinson, Claudette Colbert, David Newell, Nelly Savage, Donald Meek, Louise Closser Hale

Holiday*
US 1930 99m bw
Pathe (E. B. Derr)

A bright-minded rich girl steals her sister's fiancé, a struggling young lawyer.
Competent early talkie version of a hit play.

w Horace Jackson, *play* Philip Barry *d* Edward H. Griffith *ph* Norbert Brodine *m* Josiah Zuro

Ann Harding, Robert Ames, Mary Astor, Edward Everett Horton, Hedda Hopper, Monroe Owsley, William Holden

Holiday***
US 1938 93m bw
Columbia (Everett Riskin)
GB titles: *Free to Live; Unconventional Linda*

Elegant, highly successful remake of the above; still a stage play on film, but subtly devised to make the very most of the lines and performances.

w Donald Ogden Stewart d George Cukor
ph Franz Planer *m* Sidney Cutner

Katharine Hepburn, Cary Grant, Doris Nolan, *Edward Everett Horton* (same role), *Ruth Donnelly, Lew Ayres*, Henry Kolker, Binnie Barnes

Holiday Affair
US 1949 87m bw
RKO (Don Hartman)

A young widow falls for an easy-going boat builder.
Flimsy star-shaped romantic comedy with nice touches.

w Isobel Lennart *d* Don Hartman *ph* Milton Krasner *m* Roy Webb

Robert Mitchum, Janet Leigh, Wendell Corey, Griff Barnett, Esther Dale, Gordon Gebert, Henry O'Neill, Harry Morgan

Holiday Camp*
GB 1947 97m bw
GFD / Gainsborough (Sydney Box)

At a summer holiday camp, a murderer on the prowl affects people's enjoyment in various ways.
Seminal compendium comedy drama, a bore in itself but establishing several post-war norms of the British cinema, including the Huggetts.

w Muriel and Sydney Box, Ted Willis, Peter Rogers, Mabel and Denis Constanduros *d* Ken Annakin

Jack Warner, Kathleen Harrison, Flora Robson, Dennis Price, Hazel Court, Emrys Jones, Yvonne Owen, Esmond Knight, Jimmy Hanley, Peter Hammond, Esma Cannon, John Blythe, Susan Shaw

Holiday for Lovers
US 1959 103m De Luxe Cinemascope
TCF (David Weisbart)

To distract his teenage daughter from boys, a Boston psychiatrist organizes a family holiday in South America.
Frail old-fashioned family comedy with entirely predictable situations culminating in a drunk scene for stuffy father.

w Luther Davis *d* Henry Levin *ph* Charles G. Clarke *m* Leigh Harline

Clifton Webb, Jane Wyman, Paul Henreid, Carol Lynley, Jill St John, Gary Crosby, José Greco

Holiday Inn**
US 1942 101m bw
Paramount (Mark Sandrich)

The joint proprietors of a roadhouse hotel love the same girl.
Plain, simple-minded musical which provided a peg for pleasant performances and good numbers. It hit the box office spot, especially as it introduced 'White Christmas'.

w Claude Binyon, Elmer Rice *d Mark Sandrich*
ph David Abel *m/ly Irving Berlin*

Bing Crosby, Fred Astaire, Walter Abel, Marjorie Reynolds, Virginia Dale, Louise Beavers, Irving Bacon, James Bell

The Holly and the Ivy*
GB 1952 83m bw
British Lion / London (Anatole de Grunwald)

Christmas brings family revelations in a remote Norfolk rectory.
A badly-filmed stage success which succeeds because of its performances.

w Anatole de Grunwald, *play* Wynard Browne *d* George More O'Ferrall *ph* Ted Scaife *m* Malcolm Arnold

Ralph Richardson, Celia Johnson, Margaret Leighton, Denholm Elliott, John Gregson, Hugh Williams, Margaret Halstan, Maureen Delany, William Hartnell, Robert Flemyng, Roland Culver

'This type of direct translation to the screen, using none of the cinema's resources, can only do harm to the play itself.'—*Penelope Houston*

Hollywood Boulevard*
US 1936 75m bw
Paramount (A. M. Botsford)

A washed-up Hollywood actor writes a sensational memoir for publication, but lives to regret it.
Entertaining melodrama with famous names in bit parts.

w Marguerite Roberts *d* Robert Florey *ph* Karl Struss *m* Gregory Stone

John Halliday, Marsha Hunt, Robert Cummings, C. Henry Gordon, Frieda Inescort, Esther Dale; and Gary Cooper, Francis X. Bushman, Maurice Costello, Mae Marsh, Charles Ray, Jane Novak, Bryant Washburn, Jack Mulhall, Creighton Hale, Bert Roach

Hollywood Canteen*
US 1944 123m bw
Warner (Alex Gottlieb)

The stars give their evenings to entertaining soldiers.

Shoddily made but sociologically fascinating record of Hollywood doing its bit in World War II.

wd Delmer Daves *ph* Bert Glennon *md* Leo F. Forbstein

Joan Leslie, Robert Hutton, Dane Clark, Janis Paige; and The Andrews Sisters, Jack Benny, Joe E. Brown, Eddie Cantor, Joan Crawford, Bette Davis, John Garfield, Sidney Greenstreet, Paul Henreid, Peter Lorre, Ida Lupino, Dennis Morgan, Roy Rogers, S. Z. Sakall, Alexis Smith, Barbara Stanwyck, Jane Wyman, etc etc

'The corporal steps slowly backwards, in his eyes that look of glazed ecstasy which Jennifer Jones wore all through *The Song of Bernadette*. He has just been kissed by Joan Leslie.'—*Richard Winnington*

Hollywood Cavalcade**
US 1939 96m Technicolor
TCF (Harry Joe Brown)

The career of an old-time Hollywood producer.
A lively first half with amusing re-staging of early slapstick comedies gives way depressingly to personal melodrama, but there is enough historical interest to preserve the balance.

w Ernest Pascal *d* Irving Cummings *ph* Allen M. Davey, Ernest Palmer *ad* Richard Day, Wiard B. Ihnen *md* Louis Silvers

Don Ameche, Alice Faye, *J. Edward Bromberg*, Alan Curtis, Stuart Erwin, Jed Prouty, Buster Keaton, Donald Meek, and the original Keystone Kops

Hollywood Hotel
US 1937 109m bw
Warner (Sam Bischoff)

A Hollywood radio show has its problems.
Half-hearted, overlong Warner musical with little of the expected zip.

w Jerry Wald, Maurice Leo, Richard Macauley *d* Busby Berkeley *ph* Charles Rosher, George Barnes *m/ly* Johnny Mercer, Richard Whiting

Dick Powell, Rosemary Lane, Lola Lane, Hugh Herbert, Ted Healy, Glenda Farrell, Louella Parsons, Alan Mowbray, Frances Langford, Allyn Joslyn, Benny Goodman, Edgar Kennedy

Hollywood or Bust
US 1956 95m Technicolor Vistavision
(Paramount) Hal Wallis

Two halfwits win a car and drive across country to Hollywood.
Dopey comedy with more misses than hits; the last film of Martin and Lewis as a team.

w Erna Lazarus *d* Frank Tashlin *ph* Daniel Fapp *m* Walter Scharf

Dean Martin, Jerry Lewis, Pat Crowley, Maxie Rosenbloom, Anita Ekberg

Hollywood Party
US 1934 68m bw (Technicolor sequence)
MGM

A mad Russian throws a party which ends in disaster.
Dismal 'all-star' comedy relieved by guest appearances.

w Howard Dietz, Arthur Kober *d* uncredited *ph* James Wong Howe

Laurel and Hardy, Jimmy Durante, Lupe Velez, Charles Butterworth, Eddie Quillan, Ted Healy and the Stooges, Polly Moran

The Hollywood Revue of 1929**
US 1929 116m part-Technicolor
MGM (Harry Rapf)

A variety show featuring most of MGM's tal in slightly surprising acts, this is something of a bore to sit through but an archival must; and jus occasionally it boasts surprising vitality.

w Al Boasberg, Robert E. Hopkins *d* Charles F Reisner *ph* John Arnold, Irving Ries, Maximillian Fabian *ch* Sammy Lee
m/ly various

Jack Benny, Buster Keaton, Joan Crawford, John Gilbert, Norma Shearer, Laurel and Hardy, Marion Davies, Marie Dressler, William Haines, Lionel Barrymore, Conrad Nagel, Bessie Love, Cliff Edwards, Nils Asther

Hollywood Story*
US 1951 76m bw
U-I (Leonard Goldstein)

A young producer solves a 20-year-old studio murder mystery.
Adequate potboiler with a reasonably absorbing plot and glimpses of silent stars.

w Frederick Kohner, Fred Brady *d* William Castle *ph* Carl Guthrie *m* Joseph Gershenson

Richard Conte, Julia Adams, Richard Egan, Henry Hull, Fred Clark, Jim Backus, Paul Cavanagh; and Francis X. Bushman, William Farnum, Betty Blythe, Helen Gibson, Joel McCrea

Holy Matrimony*
US 1943 87m bw
TCF

A famous painter comes back from exile for a knighthood; but when his valet dies of

pneumonia, has him buried as himself in Westminster Abbey.
Slightly stilted but generally warmly amusing version of a favourite novel, with excellent star performances.

w Nunnally Johnson, *novel* Arnold Bennett *d* John Stahl *ph* Lucien Ballard

Monty Woolley, Gracie Fields, Laird Cregar, Eric Blore, Una O'Connor

'A pleasant hour and a half, very well produced and acted.'—*James Agate*

Hombre**
US 1967 111m De Luxe Panavision
TCF / Hombre Productions (Martin Ritt, Irving Ravetch)

Stagecoach passengers at the mercy of a robber are helped by a despised half-caste.
Slow but suspenseful western melodrama which works up to a couple of good climaxes but falls away in an unnecessary tragic ending.

w Irving Ravetch, Harriet Frank, *novel* Elmore Leonard *d Martin Ritt ph James Wong Howe* *m* David Rose

Paul Newman, *Diane Cilento, Fredric March*, Richard Boone, Martin Balsam, Barbara Rush, Cameron Mitchell

'A fine array of quirkish characters . . . and some unusually literate dialogue.'—*Tom Milne*

Home at Seven
GB 1952 85m bw
British Lion / London (Maurice Cowan)
US title: *Murder on Monday*

A clerk suffers a 24-hour loss of memory and may have been involved in a murder.
Intriguing suburban mystery, well acted but all too flatly transferred from the stage.

w Anatole de Grunwald, *play* R. C. Sherriff *d* Ralph Richardson *ph* Jack Hildyard, Edward Scaife

Ralph Richardson, Margaret Leighton, Jack Hawkins, Campbell Singer, Michael Shepley, Margaret Withers, Meriel Forbes, Frederick Piper

'A film with a notable absence of imagination in conception, direction and acting is not vindicated because it was made very cheaply in fifteen days . . . it seems ominous that the technique closely resembles that of television.'—*MFB*

Home before Dark
US 1958 137m bw
Warner (Mervyn Le Roy)

A college professor brings his wife home after a year in a mental hospital, but trouble starts again as the circumstances are unchanged.
Overlong, heavygoing, well-made soap opera, quite unconvincing despite firm performances and a suitably gloomy *mise-en-scène*.

w Eileen and Robert Bassing *d* Mervyn Le Roy *ph* Joseph Biroc *md* Ray Heindorf

Jean Simmons, Efrem Zimbalist Jnr, Dan O'Herlihy, Rhonda Fleming, Mabel Albertson

Home for the Holidays*
US 1972 74m colour TVM
Spelling–Goldberg (Paul Junger Witt)

Four daughters go home for Christmas and murders ensue.
Surprisingly grisly whodunnit, quite exciting once it gets going.

w Joseph Stefano *d* John Llewellyn Moxey

Walter Brennan, Eleanor Parker, Jessica Walter, Julie Harris, Sally Field, Jill Haworth

Home from the Hill
US 1959 150m Metrocolor Cinemascope
MGM / Sol C. Siegel (Edmund Grainger)

A southern landowner with a voracious sexual appetite has trouble with his two sons, legitimate and illegitimate.
Shades of *Cold Comfort Farm* and *Tobacco Road* . . . and this solemn family saga does go on a bit.

w Irving Ravetch, Harriet Frank, *novel* William Humphrey *d* Vincente Minnelli *ph* Milton Krasner *m* Bronislau Kaper

Robert Mitchum, George Hamilton, George Peppard, Luana Patten, Everett Sloane, Constance Ford, Ray Teal

Home in Indiana
US 1944 103m Technicolor
TCF (André Daven)

Farmers compete in trotting races and their progeny fall in love.
Archetypal homespun Americana, well enough made according to its lights, but now like something from another world . . . an innocent one.

w Winston Miller, *novel* The Phantom Filly by George Agnew Chamberlain *d* Henry Hathaway *ph* Edward Cronjager *md* Emil Newman

Jeanne Crain, June Haver, Lon McCallister, Walter Brennan, Charlotte Greenwood, Ward Bond, Charles Dingle, Willie Best

A Home of Our Own
US 1976 100m colour TVM
Quinn Martin

The true story of Father William Wasson, a Catholic priest who provided homes for Mexican orphans.
Well-meaning, uninteresting do-goodery.

d Robert Day

Jason Miller, Pancho Cordova, Pedro Armendariz Jnr

Home of the Brave*
US 1949 86m bw
Stanley Kramer

During World War II, a black man finds himself the butt of racist behaviour from the rest of his platoon.
One of the first films to touch the subject of anti-black bias, this now seems pretty tame and dated, and in fact never was much more than a filmed play (in which the butt was originally a Jew).

w Carl Foreman, *play* Arthur Laurents *d* Mark Robson *ph* Robert de Grasse *m* Dmitri Tiomkin

Frank Lovejoy, Lloyd Bridges, Douglas Dick, James Edwards, Steve Brodie, Jeff Corey, Cliff Clark

Homecoming
US 1948 113m bw
MGM (Sidney Franklin)

A ruthless society doctor is called up in World War II and has his life changed by a brief affair with a nurse who is killed in action.
Ho-hum romantic melodrama which stumbles most badly when it aims to be serious.

w Paul Osborn *d* Mervyn Le Roy *ph* Harold Rosson *md* Charles Previn

Clark Gable, Lana Turner, Anne Baxter, John Hodiak, Ray Collins, Gladys Cooper, Cameron Mitchell, Marshall Thompson
'Its basic substance, like the base of a perfume, has a terrible smell; but to many moviegoers the end-product will seem quite pleasant.'—*Time*

The Homecoming*
US 1971 100m colour TVM
Lorimar (Robert L. Jacks)

Life for a poor country family in 1933.
Christmas sentimentality, slow-moving but well-detailed, this was the springboard for the highly successful series *The Waltons*, which surfaced the following year with a different cast.

w Earl Hamner Jnr, from his novel *d* Fielder Cook

Patricia Neal, Richard Thomas, Andrew Duggan, William Windom
† The original material had also been used as a film, *Spencer's Mountain* (qv).

The Homecoming*
GB 1973 114m colour
American Express / Ely Landau

Tensions mount and sexual revelations abound in the house of a retired London butcher.
Plain treatment of an anything-but-plain Pinter play. The result is a record of a performance rather than a film.

w Harold Pinter, from his play *d* Peter Hall *ph* David Watkin *m* Thelonious Monk *pd* John Bury

Paul Rogers, Cyril Cusack, Michael Jayston, Ian Holm, Vivien Merchant, Terence Rigby
'Shocking in its own lucidity, and fascinating as an arrangement of mutually reflecting prisms . . . the remarkable control of Pinter's language guarantees that the dramatic situations are revealed to be even *more* abstract and diagrammatic as they steadily accumulate psychological density.'—*Jonathan Rosenbaum*

Homeward Borne
US 1957 82m bw TVM
Columbia / Playhouse 90

A pilot back from the war feels unwanted because his wife has adopted an orphan.
Woman's magazine stuff, capably presented.

novel Ruth Chatterton *d* Arthur Hiller

Linda Darnell, Richard Kiley, Keith Andes, Richard Eyer

Homicidal
US 1961 87m bw
Columbia / William Castle

A murderous blonde and a very strange young man both live in the house of a paralysed old lady.
Transvestite horror comic allegedly based on a true case; made on a low budget and played for cheap shocks.

w Robb White *d* William Castle *ph* Burnett Guffey *m* Hugo Friedhofer

Jean Arless, Glenn Corbett, Patricia Breslin, Eugenie Leontovitch, Alan Bunce, Richard Rust
† The film was played with a 'fright break' during which faint-hearted members of the audience might leave before the final onslaught.

Hondo*
US 1954 93m Warnercolor 3-D
Wayne–Fellows

In 1874 New Mexico a cavalry despatch rider stops to defend a lonely widow and her son against Indians.
Overwritten but pleasant-looking western, clearly patterned after *Shane*.

w James Edward Grant *d* John Farrow *ph* Robert Burks, Archie Stout *m* Emil Newman, Hugo Friedhofer

John Wayne, Geraldine Page, Ward Bond, Michael Pate

The Honey Pot*
US 1966 150m Technicolor
UA / Famous Artists (Charles K. Feldman) (Joseph L. Mankiewicz)

A millionaire pretends to be dying in order to trick three former mistresses; but one of them is murdered.
Uneasy variation, via two other variations, on Ben Jonson's *Volpone*; despite bright moments, the mood is fatally inconsistent, and a cloud of pseudo-sophisticated dialogue hangs over the whole thing like a pall.

wd Joseph L. Mankiewicz, *play* Mr Fox of Venice by Frederick Knott, *novel* The Evil of the Day by Thomas Sterling *ph* Gianni di Venanzo *m* John Addison *pd* John De Cuir

Rex Harrison, Susan Hayward, *Maggie Smith*, Cliff Robertson, Capucine, Edie Adams, Adolfo Celi, Herschel Bernardi

'One of the talkiest pictures ever made.'—*Stephen Farber*

Honeymoon
US 1947 74m bw
RKO (Warren Duff)
GB title: *Two Men and a Girl*

An 18-year-old elopes to Mexico City with an army corporal but meets a sophisticated older man.
Emaciated comedy, one of the reasons for Shirley Temple's early retirement.

w Michael Kanin, *story* Vicki Baum *d* William Keighley *ph* Edward Cronjager *m* Leigh Harline

Shirley Temple, Franchot Tone, Guy Madison, Lina Romay, Gene Lockhart, Grant Mitchell

Honeymoon Hotel
US 1964 98m Metrocolor Cinemascope
MGM / Avon (Lawrence Weingarten)

A jilted swain goes off with a philandering friend on what was to have been his honeymoon trip . . . only to be followed by his repentant fiancée.
Rather unattractive farce with insufficient funny moments.

w R. S. Allen, Harvey Bulloch *d* Henry Levin *ph* Harold Lipstein *m* Walter Scharf

Nancy Kwan, Robert Goulet, Robert Morse, Jill St John, Elsa Lanchester, Keenan Wynn

The Honeymoon Machine
US 1961 91m Metrocolor Cinemascope
MGM / Avon (Lawrence Weingarten)

A naval lieutenant uses the ship's computer to break the bank at the Venice casino.
Stolid, expensive-looking comedy which barely raises a laugh.

w George Wells, *play* The Golden Fleecing by Lorenzo Semple Jnr *d* Richard Thorpe *ph* Joseph La Shelle *m* Leigh Harline

Steve McQueen, Brigid Bazlen, Jim Hutton, Paula Prentiss, Dean Jagger, Jack Weston, Jack Mullaney

Honeymoon with a Stranger*
US 1969 74m colour TVM
TCF (Robert L. Jacks)

Some days after marrying an American woman, a wealthy European vanishes. Then an impostor arrives, claiming his rights. . . .
This well-worn story started as an episode of *The Whistler*, was filmed as *Chase a Crooked Shadow*, became a play *Trap for a Lonely Man* and a TV movie *One of My Wives Is Missing*. It always works.

w David Harmon, Henry Slesar *d* John Peyser

Janet Leigh, Rossano Brazzi, Cesare Danova, Barbara Rush

The Honkers*
US 1971 102m De Luxe
UA / Levy–Gardner–Laven

An ageing rodeo rider has trouble with his wife.
Quiet, carefully accomplished study of a man and his milieu.

w Steve Ihnat, Stephen Lodge *d* Steve Ihnat *ph* John Crabe *m* Jimmie Haskell

James Coburn, Lois Nettleton, Slim Pickens, Richard Anderson

Honky Tonk*
US 1941 104m bw
MGM (Pandro S. Berman)

A western con man meets his match in the daughter of a fake judge.
Generally amusing comedy melodrama that ambles along between two styles but leaves a pleasant after-effect.

w Marguerite Roberts, John Sandford *d* Jack Conway *ph* Harold Rosson *m* Franz Waxman

Clark Gable, Lana Turner, Frank Morgan, Claire Trevor, Marjorie Main, Albert Dekker, Henry O'Neill, Chill Wills, Betty Blythe

'A lively, lusty western that makes you wish you had been there.'—*Variety*

Honky Tonk*
US 1974 74m colour TVM
MGM

A con man meets his match in old Nevada.
Acceptable spin-off from the Clark Gable movie: it didn't make a series though.

d Don Taylor

Richard Crenna, Margot Kidder, Will Geer, Stella Stevens

Honor Thy Father*
US 1972 100m colour TVM
Metromedia (Charles Fries)

The everyday life of a New York Mafia family.
A mini-*Godfather*, watered down from a popular novel.

w Lewis John Carlino, *novel* Gay Falese *d* Paul Wendkos

Raf Vallone, Richard Castellano, Brenda Vaccaro, Joe Bologna

An Honourable Murder*
GB 1959 70m bw
Danziger

Boardroom executives scheme to be rid of their chairman.
Oddball, interesting attempt to play *Julius Caesar* in modern dress. Not entirely successful, but full marks for trying.

w Brian Clemens, Eldon Howard *d* Godfrey Grayson

Norman Wooland, Margaretta Scott, Lisa Daniely, Douglas Wilmer, Philip Saville, John Longden

The Hoodlum Priest*
US 1961 100m bw
UA / Don Murray–Walter Wood

A Jesuit teacher tries to help young criminals, especially a condemned murderer.
Moderately well done, very depressing and downbeat chunk of social conscience based on the life of Charles Dismas Clark.

w Don Mankiewicz, Joseph Landon *d* Irvin Kershner *ph* Haskell Wexler *m* Richard Markowitz

Don Murray, Keir Dullea, Larry Gates, Cindi Wood, Logan Ramsey

The Hoodlum Saint
US 1946 93m bw
MGM (Cliff Reid)

A cynical newspaperman turns to religion and succours thieves.
Hard-boiled sentimentality, a downright peculiar and doleful comedy drama in deflated post-war mood.

w Frank Wead, James Hill *d* Norman Taurog *ph* Ray June *m* Nathaniel Shilkret

William Powell, Esther Williams, Angela Lansbury, James Gleason, Lewis Stone, Rags Ragland, Frank McHugh, Slim Summerville, Roman Bohnen, Louis Jean Heydt, Charles Arnt, Charles Trowbridge, Henry O'Neill

Hoodlum Empire
US 1951 98m bw
Republic (Joseph Kane)

A Congressional committee investigates a racketeer.
Moderate semi-documentary potboiler inspired by the Kefauver investigations.

w Bruce Manning, Bob Considine *d* Joseph Kane *ph* Reggie Lanning *m* Nathan Scott

Brian Donlevy, Forrest Tucker, Claire Trevor, Vera Ralston, Luther Adler, John Russell, Gene Lockhart, Grant Withers, Taylor Holmes

The Hook
US 1962 98m bw Panavision
MGM / Perlberg–Seaton

Three GIs escaping from Korea are ordered to execute a prisoner but cannot bring themselves to do it.
Predictable, claustrophobic drama which becomes a slick exercise in morality.

w Henry Denker, from his novel Vahe Katcha *d* George Seaton *ph* Joe Ruttenberg

Kirk Douglas, Robert Walker, Nick Adams, Nehemiah Persoff

Hopalong Cassidy
Cassidy, a creation of Clarence E. Mulford, was a fictitious gentleman cowboy who oddly enough wore black; 26 books about him were published between 1912 and 1956 when Mulford died. 66 films were made starring William Boyd as Hoppy, with either George Gabby Hayes or Andy Clyde as comic sidekick: Harry Sherman produced them, first for Paramount and then for UA, and they were later edited down for TV, in which medium Boyd became a folk hero and

eventually made a further series. The films were easy-going, slow-moving second features which always pointed an admirable moral for children; their main directors were Howard Bretherton, Nate Watt, Lesley Selander and George Archainbaud.

1935: HOPALONG CASSIDY, THE EAGLE'S BROOD, BAR 20 RIDES AGAIN
1936: CALL OF THE PRAIRIE, THREE ON THE TRAIL, HEART OF THE WEST, HOPALONG CASSIDY RETURNS, TRAIL DUST
1937: BORDERLAND, HILLS OF OLD WYOMING, NORTH OF THE RIO GRANDE, RUSTLERS' VALLEY, HOPALONG RIDES AGAIN, TEXAS TRAIL
1938: HEART OF ARIZONA, BAR 20 JUSTICE, PRIDE OF THE WEST, SUNSET TRAIL, THE FRONTIERSMAN, PARTNERS OF THE PLAINS, CASSIDY OF BAR 20
1939: RANGE WAR, LAW OF THE PAMPAS, SILVER ON THE SAGE, RENEGADE TRAIL
1940: SANTA FE MARSHAL, THE SHOWDOWN, HIDDEN GOLD, STAGECOACH WAR, THREE MEN FROM TEXAS
1941: DOOMED CARAVAN, IN OLD COLORADO, BORDER VIGILANTES, PIRATES ON HORSEBACK, WIDE OPEN TOWN, OUTLAWS OF THE DESERT, RIDERS OF THE TIMBERLINE, SECRETS OF THE WASTELAND, STICK TO YOUR GUNS, TWILIGHT ON THE TRAIL
1942: UNDERCOVER MAN
1943: COLT COMRADES, BAR 20, LOST CANYON, HOPPY SERVES A WRIT, BORDER PATROL, THE LEATHER BURNERS, FALSE COLOURS, RIDERS OF THE DEADLINE
1944: MYSTERY MAN, FORTY THIEVES, TEXAS MASQUERADE, LUMBERJACK
1946: THE DEVIL'S PLAYGROUND
1947: FOOL'S GOLD, HOPPY'S HOLIDAY, MARAUDERS, UNEXPECTED GUEST, DANGEROUS VENTURE
1948: SINISTER JOURNEY, SILENT CONFLICT, STRANGE GAMBLE, BORROWED TROUBLE, THE DEAD DON'T DREAM, FALSE PARADISE

The Horizontal Lieutenant
US 1962 90m Metrocolor Cinemascope
MGM / Euterpe (Joe Pasternak)

World War II Hawaii; an amorous intelligence officer accidentally captures a Japanese guerrilla.
Very moderate army farce of no great skill or memorability.

w George Wells *d* Richard Thorpe *ph* Richard Bronner *m* George Stoll

Jim Hutton, Paula Prentiss, Jim Backus, Miyoshi Umeki, Jack Carter

The Horn Blows at Midnight*
US 1945 80m bw
Warner (Mark Hellinger)

An angel is sent to earth to destroy the planet with Gabriel's horn.
Wacky comedy inspired by *Here Comes Mr Jordan*, but on a broader slapstick level; much better than its star always pretended.

w Sam Hellman, James V. Kern *d* Raoul Walsh *ph* Sid Hickox *m* Franz Waxman

Jack Benny, Alexis Smith, Dolores Moran, Allyn Joslyn, Guy Kibbee, Reginald Gardiner, *Franklin Pangborn*, John Alexander, Margaret Dumont

Hornet's Nest
US 1969 109m De Luxe
UA / Triangle (Stanley S. Kanter)

In World War II Italy, a wounded US army demolitions expert is nursed back to health by child partisans, who help him destroy a German-held dam.
Overlong war exploits with the children used as a tiresome gimmick.

w S. S. Schweitzer *d* Phil Karlson *ph* Gabor Pogani *m* Ennio Morricone
Rock Hudson, Sergio Fantoni, Sylva Koscina, Jacques Sernas

Horror at 37,000 Feet*
US 1972 73m colour TVM
Anthony Wilson

An evil power is set loose in a transatlantic jet from stones of an old English abbey which are being shipped to America.
Enjoyably arrant nonsense.

d David Lowell Rich

Buddy Ebsen, Chuck Connors, Tammy Grimes, France Nuyen, Lynn Loring, William Shatner, Roy Thinnes, Paul Winfield

Horse Feathers****
US 1932 69m bw
Paramount

A college needs to win at football, and its corrupt new president knows just how to do it.
Possibly the Marxes' wildest yet most streamlined kaleidoscope of high jinks and

irreverence, with at least one bright gag or line to the minute and lively musical interludes to boot. A classic of zany comedy.

w Bert Kalmar, Harry Ruby, S. J. Perelman, Will B. Johnstone *d* Norman Z. McLeod *ph* Ray June *m/ly Bert Kalmar, Harry Ruby*

Groucho, Chico, Harpo, Zeppo, *Thelma Todd,* Robert Greig

'The current Marx comedy is the funniest talkie since the last Marx comedy, and the record it establishes is not likely to be disturbed until the next Marx comedy comes along. As for comparisons, I was too busy having a good time to make any.'—*Philip K. Scheuer*

The Horse Soldiers*
US 1959 119m De Luxe
UA / Mirisch (John Lee Mahin, Martin Rackin)

In 1863 a Union cavalry officer is sent three hundred miles into Confederate territory to demolish a railroad junction.
Typically sprawling John Ford cavalry western with not too many high spots and more sombre ingredients than usual.

w John Lee Mahin, Martin Rackin *d* John Ford *ph* William Clothier *m* David Buttolph

John Wayne, William Holden, Constance Towers, Hoot Gibson

The Horse without a Head**
GB 1963 89m Technicolor
Walt Disney (Hugh Attwooll)

Stolen money is hidden in an old toy horse, and crooks trying to get it back clash with police and children.
Excellent children's adventure with scenes on trains and in a toy factory.

w T. E. B. Clarke d Don Chaffey ph Paul Beeson *m* Eric Rogers

Leo McKern, Jean-Pierre Aumont, Herbert Lom, Pamela Franklin, Vincent Winter

The Horsemen
US 1970 109m colour Super Panavision
Columbia / John Frankenheimer–Edward Lewis

An Afghan tribesman is determined to rival his father at horsemanship.
Rather tedious variant on *Taras Bulba*; plenty of action but not much characterization, or taste, or interest.

w Dalton Trumbo, *novel* Joseph Kessel *d* John Frankenheimer *ph* Claude Renoir *m* Georges Delerue

Omar Sharif, Jack Palance, Leigh Taylor-Young, Peter Jeffrey, Eric Pohlmann, Despo, David De Keyser

The Horse's Mouth*
GB 1958 93m Technicolor
UA / Knightsbridge (John Bryan)

An obsessive painter is a liability to his friends.
Thin but fitfully amusing light study of a social outcast, with a background of London river and streets. Too slight for real success.

w Alec Guinness, *novel* Joyce Cary *d* Ronald Neame *ph Arthur Ibbetson m* K. V. Jones from Prokofiev *paintings* John Bratby

Alec Guinness, Kay Walsh, Renée Houston, Robert Coote, Arthur Macrae, Michael Gough, Ernest Thesiger

The Hospital***
US 1971 101m De Luxe Panavision
UA / Simcha (Howard Gottfried)

A city hospital is beset by weird mishaps, and it transpires that a killer is on the loose.
Black comedy with the emphasis on sex and medical ethics; in the same genre as *M*A*S*H*, and very funny if you can take it.

w Paddy Chayevsky d Arthur Hiller *ph* Victor Kemper *m* Morris Surdin

George C. Scott, Diana Rigg, Barnard Hughes, Nancy Marchand, Richard Dysart

Hostages
US 1943 88m bw
Paramount

In occupied Prague, the Nazis seize a variety of hostages and threaten them with death as a reprisal for underground activities.
Modest morale-builder, unfortunately padded out with melodramatics and overacting.

w Lester Cole, Frank Butler, *novel* Stefan Heym *d* Frank Tuttle

Luise Rainer, Paul Lukas, William Bendix, Oscar Homolka, Arturo de Cordova, Katina Paxinou, Roland Varno

Hostile Witness
GB 1968 101m De Luxe
UA / Caralan / Dador (David E. Rose)

A barrister suffers a nervous breakdown after the death of his daughter and finds himself accused of murder.
Complex courtroom thriller, filmed in a flatly boring way with stagey sets and performances. The plot is the only interest.

w Jack Roffey, from his play *d* Ray Milland *ph* Gerry Gibbs

Ray Milland, Sylvia Sims, Felix Aylmer, Raymond Huntley, Geoffrey Lumsden, Norman Barrs, Percy Marmont, Ewan Roberts

Hot Blood
US 1955 85m Technicolor Cinemascope
Columbia (Howard Welsch)

A dying gypsy king wants his young brother to get married and succeed him.
What promises to be a boring musical proves to be a boring melodrama. Artificial Romany hokum.

w Jesse Lasky Jnr *d* Nicholas Ray *ph* Ray June *m* Les Baxter

Cornel Wilde, Jane Russell, Joseph Calleia, Helen Westcott, Mikhail Rasumny

Hot Enough for June
GB 1963 98m Eastmancolor
Rank (Betty E. Box)
US title: *Agent 8¾*

A penniless writer is sent to Czechoslovakia on a goodwill mission and finds himself being used as a spy.
Very moderate spoof, neither very funny nor very thrilling.

w Lukas Heller, *novel* The Night before Wenceslas by Lionel Davidson *d* Ralph Thomas *ph* Ernest Steward *m* Angelo Lavagnino

Dirk Bogarde, Sylva Koscina, Robert Morley, Leo McKern, John Le Mesurier

Hot Millions*
US 1968 106m colour TVM
MGM / Mildred Freed Alberg

A confidence trickster makes a fortune out of fictitious companies.
Elaborate, talky, overlong comedy with irresistible star performances.

w Ira Wallach, Peter Ustinov *d* Eric Till

Peter Ustinov, Maggie Smith, Bob Newhart, Karl Malden, Robert Morley, Cesar Romero

The Hot Rock***
US 1972 105m De Luxe Panavision
TCF (Hal Landers, Bobby Roberts)
GB title: *How to Steal a Diamond in Four Easy Lessons*

Four crooks plan to rob the Brooklyn Museum of a priceless diamond.
Enjoyable variation on the caper theme, with relaxed comic performances and highly skilled technical back-up. It's refreshing to come across a film which hits its targets so precisely.

w William Goldman, novel Donald E. Westlake *d Peter Yates ph* Ed Brown *m* Quincy Jones

Robert Redford, George Segal, Zero Mostel, Paul Sand, Ron Leibman, Moses Gunn, William Redfield

'A funny, fast-paced, inventive and infinitely clever crime comedy, almost as if *The French Connection* had been remade as a piece of urban humour.'—*Michael Korda*

Hot Spell*
US 1958 86m bw Vistavision
Paramount / Hal Wallis

In a small southern town, a husband seeks to leave his wife and family for a 20-year-old girl.
Overwrought domestic drama slipping perilously close to farce at times, but a good theatrical vehicle for its stars.

w James Poe, *play* Next of Kin by Lonnie Coleman *d* Daniel Mann *ph* Loyal Griggs *m* Alex North

Anthony Quinn, Shirley Booth, Shirley Maclaine, Earl Holliman, Eileen Heckart

Hot Summer Night*
US 1957 85m bw
MGM (Morton S. Fine)

A foolhardy reporter determines on an interview with a notorious outlaw, and has to be rescued.
Interesting but disappointing low-budget experiment.

w Morton S. Fine, David Friedkin *d* David Friedkin *ph* Harold S. Marcorati *m* André Previn

Leslie Nielsen, Colleen Miller, Edward Andrews, Jay C. Flippen, James Best, Paul Richards, Robert Wilke, Claude Akins

Hotel*
US 1967 124m Technicolor
Warner (Wendell Mayes)

Guests at a luxurious New Orleans hotel have various problems.
Old-fashioned omnibus drama from a bestseller, quite brightly done.

w Wendell Mayes, *novel* Arthur Hailey *d* Richard Quine *ph* Charles Lang *m* Johnny Keating

Rod Taylor, Catherine Spaak, Karl Malden, Melvyn Douglas, Merle Oberon, Richard Conte, Michael Rennie, Kevin McCarthy, Alfred Ryder

Hotel Berlin*
US 1945 98m bw
Warner (Louis F. Edelman)

Various lives intertwine in a Berlin hotel towards the end of the war.
After five years of total war this view of life on the other side can hardly fail to be unconvincing, but the actors gleefully seize on moments of melodrama.

w Thomas Job, *novel* Vicki Baum *d* Peter Godfrey *ph* Carl Guthrie *m* Franz Waxman

Raymond Massey, Peter Lorre, Faye Emerson, Helmut Dantine, Andrea King, Alan Hale, George Coulouris, Henry Daniell, Helene Thimig, Kurt Kreuger, Steve Geray, Frank Reicher

Hotel for Women
US 1939 83m bw
TCF (Raymond Griffith)

Young city gold diggers are encouraged by a matron.
Slight comedy drama notable for the acting debut of hostess Elsa Maxwell.

w Katherine Scola, Darrell Ware *d* Gregory Ratoff *ph* Peverell Marley

Elsa Maxwell, Linda Darnell, Ann Sothern, James Ellison, John Halliday, Lynn Bari, Alan Dinehart

Hotel Imperial
US 1939 67m bw
Paramount

Balkans, 1916: a Polish dancer suspects a Hungarian officer of being responsible for her sister's death.
Dim romantic melodrama with espionage trimmings.

w Gilbert Gabriel, Robert Thoeren, *play* Lajos Biro *d* Robert Florey *ph* William Mellor

Ray Milland, Isa Miranda, Reginald Owen, Gene Lockhart, J. Carrol Naish, Curt Bois, Henry Victor, Albert Dekker

Hotel Paradiso*
US 1966 99m Metrocolor Panavision
MGM (Peter Glenville)

Various romantic affairs come to a head one evening at a seedy hotel.
A famous boulevard farce seems jellied in aspic in this good-looking but very flatly handled film version, in which famous artists are left to caper about on an unsuitable wide screen with no help from the director.

w Peter Glenville, Jean-Claude Carrière, *play* Georges Feydeau *d* Peter Glenville *ph Henri Decaë* *m* Laurence Rosenthal *pd François de Lamothe*

Alec Guinness, Gina Lollobrigida, Robert Morley, Peggy Mount, Douglas Byng, Akim Tamiroff, Robertson Hare

Hotel Reserve
GB 1944 89m bw
RKO (Victor Hanbury)

An Austrian refugee in the south of France is asked by the police to track down a spy among his fellow hotel guests.
Slow, obvious and poorly made suspenser from a good novel.

w John Davenport, *novel* Epitaph for a Spy by Eric Ambler *d* Victor Hanbury, Lance Comfort, Max Greene *ph* Max Greene

James Mason, Lucie Mannheim, Raymond Lovell, Julien Mitchell, Martin Miller, Herbert Lom, Frederick Valk, Valentine Dyall

Hotel Sahara*
GB 1951 96m bw
GFD / Tower (George H. Brown)

In North Africa during World War II, a small hotel changes its loyalties to suit its occupiers.
Overstretched, studio-bound, fitfully amusing comedy.

w George H. Brown, Patrick Kirwan *d* Ken Annakin *ph* David Harcourt *m* Benjamin Franklin

Peter Ustinov, Yvonne de Carlo, David Tomlinson, Roland Culver, Albert Lieven, Bill Owen, Sidney Tafler, Ferdy Mayne

Houdini*
US 1953 106m Technicolor
Paramount (George Pal)

In the 1890s a fairground magician shows a passionate talent for escapology and finally kills himself by undertaking increasingly impossible tricks.
Superficial biopic with more attention to romance than to interesting detail. Some zest in the playing is killed by claustrophobic studio sets.

w Philip Yordan *d* George Marshall *ph* Ernest Laszlo *m* Roy Webb

Tony Curtis, Janet Leigh, Torin Thatcher, Sig Rumann, Angela Clarke

The Hound Dog Man
US 1959 87m bw
TCF / Company of Artists (Jerry Wald)

An irresponsible country boy gets his come-uppance.
Mild, competent backwoods comedy drama introducing a teenage rave.

w Fred Gipson, Winston Miller *d* Don Siegel *ph* Charles G. Clarke *m* Cyril Mockridge

Fabian, Stuart Whitman, Carol Lynley, Arthur O'Connell, Betty Field, Royal Dano, Jane Darwell, Edgar Buchanan, Claude Akins

The Hound of the Baskervilles**
US 1939 80m bw
(TCF) Gene Markey

Sherlock Holmes solves the mystery of a supernatural hound threatening the life of a Dartmoor baronet.
Basil Rathbone's first appearance as Sherlock Holmes is in a painstaking studio production which achieves good atmosphere and preserves the flavour if not the letter of the book but is let down by a curious lack of pace.

w Ernest Pascal, *novel* Arthur Conan Doyle *d* Sidney Lanfield *ph* Peverell Marley *m* Cyril Mockridge *ad* Thomas Little

Basil Rathbone, Nigel Bruce, Richard Greene, Wendy Barrie, Lionel Atwill, Morton Lowry, John Carradine, Barlowe Borland, Beryl Mercer, Ralph Forbes, E. E. Clive, Eily Malyon, Mary Gordon
† For Rathbone's other appearances as Holmes see under *Sherlock Holmes*.

The Hound of the Baskervilles*
GB 1959 86m Technicolor
UA / Hammer (Anthony Hinds)

Spirited remake let down by dogged Hammer insistence on promises of horror and sex; good atmosphere also let down by poor colour.

w Peter Bryan *d* Terence Fisher *ph* Jack Asher *m* James Bernard

Peter Cushing, André Morell, Christopher Lee, Marla Landi, Ewen Solon, Francis de Wolff

The Hound of the Baskervilles
US 1972 73m Technicolor TVM
Universal (Stanley Kallis)

Risible version with stolid acting and the most inappropriate sets.

w Robert E. Thompson *d* Barry Crane

Stewart Granger, William Shatner, Bernard Fox, John Williams, Anthony Zerbe, Jane Merrow

The Hour before the Dawn
US 1944 75m bw
Paramount (William Dozier)

When a pacifist English nobleman discovers during World War II that he has married a Nazi spy, he strangles her and joins the forces.
Stultifyingly absurd, badly made and acted melodrama which its author clearly wished he had never written, as it was later withdrawn from his canon.

w Michael Hogan, Lester Samuels, *novel* W. Somerset Maugham *d* Frank Tuttle *ph* John F. Seitz *m* Miklos Rozsa

Franchot Tone, Veronica Lake, John Sutton, Binnie Barnes, Henry Stephenson, Philip Merivale, Nils Asther, Edmund Breon

Hour of the Gun**
US 1967 101m De Luxe Panavision
UA / Mirisch / Kappa (John Sturges)

After the gunfight at the OK corral, Wyatt Earp tracks down the rest of the Clanton gang.
Vividly set, slowly developed western which makes an ambiguous but forceful figure of Earp. Generally confident and interesting.

w Edward Anhalt d John Sturges ph Lucien Ballard m Jerry Goldsmith

James Garner, Jason Robards Jnr, Robert Ryan, Steve Ihnat, Michael Tolan, Frank Converse, Sam Melville, Monte Markham, Albert Salmi, Jon Voight, William Windom, Charles Aidman

The Hour of Thirteen
GB 1952 78m bw
MGM (Hayes Goetz)

Edwardian London is shocked when policemen are stabbed one by one.
Jaded Hollywood-English thriller, a remake of *The Mystery of Mr X* (qv).

w Leon Gordon, Howard Emmett Rogers, *novel* X vs Rex by Philip MacDonald *d* Harold French *ph* Guy Green *m* John Addison

Peter Lawford, Dawn Addams, Roland Culver, Derek Bond, Leslie Dwyer, Michael Hordern, Colin Gordon, Heather Thatcher

The House across the Bay
US 1940 88m bw
(UA) Walter Wanger

To protect her racketeer husband from his enemies, his wife has him convicted of income tax evasion.
Unpersuasive melodrama, a star potboiler.

w Kathryn Scola *d* Archie Mayo *ph* Merritt Gerstad *m* Werner Janssen

Joan Bennett, George Raft, Lloyd Nolan, Walter Pidgeon, Gladys George, June Knight

A House Divided*
US 1931 70m bw
Universal (Paul Kohner)

A tough widowed fisherman seeks a new wife, but she falls in love with his son.

Glum variation on *Desire under the Elms*, interesting for early Wyler touches.

w John P. Clymer, Dale Van Every, John Huston, *story* Heart and Hand by Olive Edens *d William Wyler* *ph* Charles Stumar

Walter Huston, Kent Douglass, Helen Chandler, Vivian Oakland, Frank Hagney, Mary Foy

The House in Nightmare Park*
GB 1973 95m Technicolor
EMI / Associated London Films

In 1907, a ham actor is asked to perform at an old dark house in the country where an axe murderer prowls during the night.
Standard creepy house comedy thriller, well enough done though it would have been better with Bob Hope.

w Clive Exton, Terry Nation *d* Peter Sykes *ph* Ian Wilson *m* Harry Robinson

Frankie Howerd, Ray Milland, Hugh Burden, Kenneth Griffith, John Bennett, Rosalie Crutchley, Ruth Dunning

The House in the Square*
GB 1951 91m Technicolor (b/w endpieces)
TCF (Sol C. Siegel)
US title: *I'll Never Forget You*

An American atomic chemist living in London becomes his own ancestor of two hundred years ago, and falls in love.
Slow-starting but thereafter quite acceptable remake of *Berkeley Square* (qv), with some interesting dialogue and a genuinely affecting fade-out.

w Ranald MacDougall, *play* John L. Balderston *d* Roy Baker *ph* Georges Périnal *m* William Alwyn *ad* C. P. Norman

Tyrone Power, Ann Blyth, Michael Rennie, Beatrice Campbell, Dennis Price, Raymond Huntley, Irene Browne, Robert Atkins (as Dr Johnson)

A House Is Not a Home
US 1964 98m bw
(Paramount) Embassy (Clarence Greene)

The life story of New York's most famous madam, Polly Adler.
Dismal, unappealing, laundered biopic, cheaply made in an unconvincing period setting.

w Russel Rouse, Clarence Greene *d* Russel Rouse *ph* Harold Stine *m* Joseph Weiss

Shelley Winters, Robert Taylor, Cesar Romero, Ralph Taeger, Broderick Crawford

House of Bamboo
US 1955 102m De Luxe Cinemascope
TCF (Buddy Adler)

Japanese and American authorities move into undercover action against Tokyo gangsters.
Routine big-budget crime drama with only the location in its favour; a time passer, vaguely adapted from *The Street with No Name* (qv).

w Harry Kleiner *d* Samuel Fuller *ph* Joe MacDonald *m* Leigh Harline

Robert Stack, Robert Ryan, Shirley Yagamuchi, Cameron Mitchell, Sessue Hayakawa

House of Cards
US 1968 100m Techniscope
Universal / Westward (Dick Berg)

An American becomes tutor in the Paris household of a French general's widow, and finds himself a pawn in a high-powered game of international intrigue.
Good-looking location thriller which after an intricate opening settles into a *39 Steps*-style chase, but makes little of it.

w James P. Bonner, *novel* Stanley Ellin *d* John Guillermin *ph* Piero Portalupi *m* Francis Lai

George Peppard, Inger Stevens, Orson Welles, Keith Michell, William Job, Maxine Audley, Peter Bayliss

House of Dracula*
US 1945 67m bw
U–I (Paul Malvern)

As a result of being visited in one evening by Count Dracula, the Wolf Man and the Frankenstein monster, a sympathetic doctor goes on the rampage.
Mind-boggling finale to the first Universal monster cycle, with a happy ending for the Wolf Man. Cheaply made and not really inventive, but has to be seen to be believed.

w Edward T. Lowe *d* Erle C. Kenton *ph* George Robinson *m* Edgar Fairchild

Onslow Stevens, John Carradine, Lon Chaney Jnr, Glenn Strange, Lionel Atwill, Martha O'Driscoll, Jane Adams

House of Frankenstein*
US 1944 71m bw
U–I (Paul Malvern)

A mad doctor thaws out the monster and the Wolf Man (frozen at the end of *Frankenstein Meets the Wolf Man*) but comes to a sticky end.
Originally called *Chamber of Horrors*, this was the studio's first attempt to package its monsters (the first two reels are about Dracula). It could

have been pacier in view of the possibilities, but it has its interest.

w Edward T. Lowe, Curt Siodmak *d* Erle C. Kenton *ph* George Robinson *m* Hans Salter

Boris Karloff, John Carradine, Lon Chaney Jnr, George Zucco, J. Carrol Naish, Anne Gwynne, Elena Verdugo, Lionel Atwill, Sig Rumann, Glenn Strange

House of Numbers
US 1957 92m bw Cinemascope
MGM (Charles Schnee)

A man helps his thuggish twin brother escape from prison.
An original melodramatic idea is frittered away through slow pacing.

w Russel Rouse, Don M. Mankiewicz, *novel* Jack Finney *d* Russel Rouse *ph* George J. Folsey *m* André Previn

Jack Palance, Barbara Lang, Harold J. Stone, Edward Platt

The House of Rothschild*
US 1934 87m bw (Technicolor sequence)
Twentieth Century (Darryl F. Zanuck)

The chronicles of the famous banking family at the time of the Napoleonic Wars.
Lavish historical pageant with interesting scenes and performances.

w Nunnally Johnson, *play* George Hembert Westley *d* Alfred Werker *ph* Peverell Marley *m* Alfred Newman

George Arliss, Loretta Young, Boris Karloff, Robert Young, C. Aubrey Smith, Arthur Byron, Helen Westley, Reginald Owen, Florence Arliss, Alan Mowbray, Holmes Herbert

House of Secrets
GB 1956 97m Technicolor Vistavision
Rank / Julian Wintle (Vivian A. Cox)

A naval officer is asked to impersonate a lookalike counterfeiter and work undercover to expose the gang.
Old-hat Boys' Own Paper adventure story, mindlessly watchable.

w Robert Buckner, Bryan Forbes *d* Guy Green *ph* Harry Waxman *m* Hubert Clifford

Michael Craig, Julia Arnall, Brenda de Banzie, David Kossoff, Barbara Bates, Gerard Oury, Geoffrey Keen, Anton Diffring

The House of Seven Gables
US 1940 89m bw
Universal

In 17th-century New England, a jealous brother sends his sister's fiancé to prison.
Flat adaptation of a grim, brooding novel; it never grips.

w Lester Cole, *novel* Nathaniel Hawthorne *d* Joe May *ph* Milton Krasner

George Sanders, Margaret Lindsay, Vincent Price, Alan Napier, Nan Grey, Cecil Kellaway, Dick Foran, Miles Mander

House of the Damned*
US 1963 63m bw
TCF / Associated Producers (Maury Dexter)

An architect is asked to make a survey of an old empty castle, but he and his wife find that someone or something is in hiding there.
Corny but mildly effective second feature with a few neat touches.

w Harry Spalding *d* *Maury Dexter* *ph* John Nickolaus Jnr *m* Henry Vars

Ronald Foster, Merry Anders

House of the Seven Hawks
GB 1959 92m bw
MGM / David E. Rose

An American adventurer becomes involved in a search by criminals for buried Nazi loot.
Cliché-ridden thick ear, adequately produced but of no interest.

w Jo Eisinger, *novel* The House of Seven Flies by Victor Canning *d* Richard Thorpe *ph* Ted Scaife *m* Clifton Parker

Robert Taylor, Nicole Maurey, Linda Christian, Donald Wolfit, David Kossoff, Eric Pohlmann, Gerard Heinz

House of Strangers**
US 1949 101m bw
TCF (Sol C. Siegel)

An Italian-American banker who rigidly controls his three sons is arrested for illegal practices, and the family ties slacken.
Interesting ethnic melodrama with good script and performances; much remade, e.g. as *Broken Lance*.

w *Philip Yordan*, *novel* Jerome Weidman *d* Joseph L. Mankiewicz *ph* Milton Krasner *m* Daniele Amfitheatrof

Edward G. Robinson, *Richard Conte*, Susan Hayward, *Luther Adler*, Paul Valentine, Efrem Zimbalist Jnr, Debra Paget, Hope Emerson, Esther Minciotti, Diana Douglas

House of Usher*
US 1960 85m Eastmancolor
Cinemascope
AIP / Alta Vista (Roger Corman)
GB title: *The Fall of the House of Usher*

The last of the Usher line, prone to catalepsy, is buried alive by her brother and returns to wreak vengeance.
Stylish but grottily-coloured low-budget horror which started the Poe cycle of the sixties. A bit slow, it would have worked better in the standard screen ratio, but there is a tense and spectacular finale.

w Richard Matheson, *story* Edgar Allan Poe *d* Roger Corman *ph* Floyd Crosby *m* Les Baxter *ad* Daniel Haller

Vincent Price, Myrna Fahey, Mark Damon, Harry Ellerbe

House of Wax**
US 1953 88m Warnercolor 3-D
Warner (Bryan Foy)

Mutilated in a fire at his wax museum, a demented sculptor arranges a supply of dead bodies to be covered in wax for exhibition at his new showplace.
Spirited remake of *The Mystery of the Wax Museum* (qv); as a piece of screen narrative it leaves much to be desired, but the sudden shocks are well managed, perhaps because this is the first Grade-A 3-D film, packed with gimmicks irrelevant to the story and originally shown with stereophonic sound.

w Crane Wilbur *d* André de Toth *ph* Bert Glennon *m* David Buttolph

Vincent Price (whose horror career began here), Carolyn Jones, Paul Picerni, Phyllis Kirk, Frank Lovejoy
†The director could not see the 3-D effect, being blind in one eye.

The House on Greenapple Road*
US 1970 113m colour TVM
Quinn Martin

A suburban wife has apparently been savagely murdered . . . or has she?
Efficient and generally holding but awesomely long murder mystery, a premature pilot for the *Dan August* series which later emerged with a different lead.

w George Eckstein, *novel* Harold R. Daniels *d* Robert Day

Christopher George, Janet Leigh, Julie Harris, Tim O'Connor, Walter Pidgeon, Barry Sullivan

House on Haunted Hill
US 1958 75m bw
Allied Artists / William Castle

An old house which has seen several murders is the setting for a millionaire's party.
Gimmick ghost story with some (unexplained) gruesome moments; the most outlandish of its producer's cheapjack trick films (*Thirteen Ghosts, The Tingler, Macabre,* etc), it was originally billed as being in Emergo, which meant that at an appropriately horrific moment an illuminated skeleton on wires was suddenly trundled over the heads of the audience.

w Robb White *d* William Castle *ph* Carl Guthrie *m* Von Dexter

Vincent Price, Richard Long, Carol Ohmart, Alan Marshal, Elisha Cook Jnr

The House on 92nd Street****
US 1945 88m bw
TCF (*Louis de Rochemont)*

During World War II in New York, the FBI routs Nazi spies after the atomic bomb formula.
Highly influential documentary-style "now it can be told" spy drama, which borrowed the feel of its producer's *March of Time* series and applied them to a fairly true story set on genuine locations though with a modicum of fictional mystery and suspense.
Highly effective in its own right, it looked forward to *The Naked City* three years later; the later film unaccountably got most of the credit for taking Hollywood out into the open air.

w Barre Lyndon, Charles G. Booth, John Monks Jnr *d* Henry Hathaway *ph* Norbert Brodine *m* David Buttolph

William Eythe, Lloyd Nolan, Signe Hasso, *Leo G. Carroll*, Gene Lockhart, Lydia St Clair, Harry Bellaver

The House on Telegraph Hill
US 1951 93m bw
TCF (Robert Bassler)

A woman in a concentration camp assumes her dead friend's identity so that on release she can be sent to America; but murder threatens there.
Modernized amalgam of *Gaslight* and *Suspicion*, not as good as either, but the complexities of the story hold adequate interest.

w Elick Moll, Frank Partos, *novel* Dana Lyon *d* Robert Wise *ph* Lucien Ballard *m* Sol Kaplan

Richard Basehart, Valentina Cortesa, William Lundigan, Fay Baker, Gordon Gebert, Steve Geray

The House that Dripped Blood*
GB 1970 102m Eastmancolor
Amicus (Milton Subotsky)

A Scotland Yard man investigating a disappearance is led to a house with a murderous history.
Quartet of stories in *Dead of Night* style, neatly made and generally pleasing despite a low level of originality in the writing.

w Robert Bloch *d Peter John Duffell ph* Robert Parslow *m* Michael Dress

John Bennett, Christopher Lee, Peter Cushing, Denholm Elliott, Joanna Dunham, Nyree Dawn Porter, Jon Pertwee, Ingrid Pitt

The House that Wouldn't Die*
US 1970 72m colour TVM
Aaron Spelling

The owner of a Georgetown house feels threatened by an evil spirit and tries to exorcise it.
Single-minded and adequately chilling ghost story.

w Henry Farrell *d* John Llewellyn Moxey

Barbara Stanwyck, Richard Egan, Michael Anderson Jnr, Mabel Albertson

Houseboat
US 1958 110m Technicolor Vistavision
Paramount / Scribe (Jack Rose)

A widower with three children engages a maid who is really a socialite, and they all set up house on a boat.
Artificial sentimental comedy with A-1 credits but little style or bite.

w Melville Shavelson, Jack Rose *d* Jack Rose *ph* Ray June *m* George Duning

Cary Grant, Sophia Loren, Martha Hyer, Eduardo Ciannelli, Harry Guardino

The Housekeeper's Daughter*
US 1939 71m bw
Warner

A gangster's moll returns to mama for a visit and falls in love with the stuffy son of the household.
Zany crime farce which too often lets its zip fade, but atones in a crazy firework finale.

w Rian James, Gordon Douglas, *novel* Donald Henderson Clarke *d* Hal Roach *ph* Norbert Brodine *m* Amedeo de Filippi

Joan Bennett, John Hubbard, Adolphe Menjou, William Gargan, George E. Stone, Peggy Wood, Donald Meek, Marc Lawrence, Lilian Bond, Victor Mature, Luis Alberni

Housewife
US 1934 69m bw
Warner

For an advertising copywriter, success almost brings divorce.
Modestly efficient romantic programmer of its day.

w Manuel Seff, Lillie Hayward *d* Alfred E. Green *ph* William Rees *m* Leo F. Forbstein

Bette Davis, George Brent, Ann Dvorak, John Halliday, Ruth Donnelly, Hobart Cavanaugh, Robert Barrat, Phil Regan

'The dramatic punches are not merely telegraphed, but radioed.' —*Frank S. Nugent*

Houston, We've Got a Problem
US 1974 74m Technicolor TVM
Universal (Harve Bennett)

A reconstruction of the Apollo 13 mission of 1970.
A rather unnecessary fictionalization of facts which speak for themselves.

w Richard Nelson *d* Lawrence Doheny

Robert Culp, Clu Gulager, Gary Collins, Sandra Dee, Ed Nelson

How Awful about Allan*
US 1970 72m colour TVM
Aaron Spelling

A blind young man in his elder sister's care is tormented by strange voices . . .
Artful mystery chiller in the vein of the author's sagas about Baby Jane and Sweet Charlotte.

w Henry Farrell *d* Curtis Harrington

Anthony Perkins, Julie Harris, Joan Hackett

How Do I Love Thee
US 1970 109m Metrocolor
ABC (Robert Enders, Everett Freeman)

A philosophy professor recalls the odd career of his atheist father.
Curious comedy about an eccentric and his family relationships, a kind of *Cheaper by the Dozen* with religion added. Not on in 1970

w Everett Freeman, *novel* Let Me Count the Ways by Peter De Vries *d* Michael Gordon *ph* Russell Metty *m* Randy Sparks

James Gleason, Maureen O'Hara, Shelley Winters, Rick Lenz, Rosemary Forsyth

How Green Was My Valley***
US 1941 118m bw
TCF (Darryl F Zanuck)

Memories of childhood in a Welsh mining village.

Prettified and unconvincing but dramatically very effective tearjerker in the style which lasted from Cukor's *David Copperfield* to *The Green Years*. High production values here add a touch of extra class, turning the result into a Hollywood milestone despite its intrinsic inadequacies.

w Philip Dunne, *novel* Richard Llewellyn *d John Ford ph Arthur Miller m* Alfred Newman

Walter Pidgeon, Maureen O'Hara, Roddy McDowall, Donald Crisp, Sara Allgood, Anna Lee,John Loder, Barry Fitzgerald, Patric Knowles, Morton Lowry, Arthur Shields, Frederic Worlock

'Perfection of cinematic narrative . . . pure visual action, pictures powerfully composed, dramatically photographed, smoothly and eloquently put together.'—*James Shelley Hamilton*

How I Spent My Summer Vacation
US 1967 96m Technicolor TVM
Universal (Jack Laird)
GB theatrical title: *Deadly Roulette*

A young man accepts an invitation to a summer cruise aboard a millionaire's yacht, and finds himself among members of a crime syndicate.
Puffed-out and tediously flashy comedy adventure which soon wears out its welcome except as a tour round lush backgrounds.

w Gene Kearney *d* William Hale

Robert Wagner, Peter Lawford, Lola Albright, Walter Pidgeon, Jill St John, Michael Ansara

How I Won the War
GB 1967 110m Eastmancolor
UA / Petersham (Richard Lester)

During World War II an earnest young man becomes an officer and survives many tribulations including the death of his comrades.
Appalling kaleidoscope of black comedy and the director's own brand of uncontrolled cinematic zaniness, with echoes of *Candide* and *Oh What a Lovely War!* Just the way to alienate a paying audience.

w Charles Wood, *novel* Patrick Ryan *d* Richard Lester *ph* David Watkin *m* Ken Thorne

Michael Crawford, John Lennon, Roy Kinnear, Lee Montague, Jack McGowran, Michael Hordern, Jack Hedley, Karl Michael Vogler, Ronald Lacey, James Cossins, Alexander Knox

'Pretentious tomfoolery.'—*John Simon*

'One feels that Lester has bitten off more than he can chew . . . the ideas misfire, lost somewhere between the paper on which they were conceived and the celluloid on which they finally appear.'—*MFB*

How Sweet It Is*
US 1968 98m Technicolor Panavision
Warner / Cherokee / National General (Garry Marshall, Jerry Belson)

Suspicious of their son's intentions towards his girl friend on a European holiday, a middle-aged American couple decide to follow.
Good-looking, rather silly comedy, plain spoken in the modern manner but without much entertainment value except when farce gets the upper hand.

w Garry Marshall, Jerry Belson, *novel* The Girl in the Turquoise Bikini by Muriel Resnik *d* Jerry Paris *ph* Lucien Ballard *m* Pat Williams

James Garner, Debbie Reynolds, Maurice Ronet, Paul Lynde, Marcel Dalio, Terry-Thomas, Donald Losby, Hilarie Thompson

'One of those slender marital farces in which the behaviour of the adults is consistently more juvenile than that of the teenagers.'—*MFB*

How the West Was Won*
US 1962 162m Technicolor Cinerama
MGM / Cinerama (Bernard Smith)

Panoramic western following the daughter of a pioneering family from youth (1830) to old age, with several half-relevant stories along the way.
Muddled spectacular with splendid set-pieces but abysmal dullness in between, especially if not seen in three-strip Cinerama (the Cinemascope prints are muddy and still show the dividing lines). An all-star fairground show of its time.

w James R. Webb *d* Henry Hathaway (first half), John Ford (Civil War), George Marshall (train) *ph* William Daniels, Milton Krasner, Charles Lang Jnr, Joseph La Shelle *m* Alfred Newman *ad* George W. Davis, William Ferrari, Addison Hehr

Debbie Reynolds, Carroll Baker, Lee J. Cobb, Henry Fonda, Carolyn Jones, Karl Malden, Gregory Peck, George Peppard, Robert Preston, James Stewart, Eli Wallach, John Wayne, Richard Widmark, Brigid Bazlen, Walter Brennan, David Brian, Andy Devine, Raymond Massey, Agnes Moorehead, Henry Morgan, Thelma Ritter, Russ Tamblyn, Spencer Tracy (narrator)

How to Be Very Very Popular
US 1955 89m De Luxe Cinemascope
TCF (Nunnally Johnson)

Two belly dancers on the run from gangsters hide out in a co-ed college.
Wacky remake of *She Loves Me Not* (qv); tries hard for a vein of freewheeling lunacy but only occasionally achieves it. A few numbers might have helped.

wd Nunnally Johnson *ph* Milton Krasner *m* Cyril Mockridge

Betty Grable, Sheree North, *Charles Coburn*, Robert Cummings, Orson Bean, Fred Clark, Tommy Noonan

How to Commit Marriage
US 1969 98m Technicolor
Cinerama / Naho (Bill Larence)

A couple decide to divorce, with repercussions on their family and in-laws.
Tiresome generation-gap comedy.

w Ben Starr, Michael Kanin *d* Norman Panama *ph* Charles Lang *m* Joseph J. Lilley

Bob Hope, Jackie Gleason, Jane Wyman, Leslie Nielsen, Maureen Arthur, Paul Stewart, Tina Louise

How to Marry a Millionaire**
US 1953 96m Technicolor
Cinemascope
TCF (Nunnally Johnson)

Three girls rent an expensive New York apartment and set out to trap millionaires.
Cinemascope's first attempt at modern comedy was not quite as disastrous as might have been expected, largely because of the expensiveness of everything and the several stars still brightly twinkling, but the handling of this variation on the old *Golddiggers* theme, while entirely amiable, is dramatically very slack.

w Nunnally Johnson *d* Jean Negulesco *ph* Joe MacDonald *md* Alfred Newman

Lauren Bacall, Marilyn Monroe, Betty Grable, *William Powell*, Cameron Mitchell, David Wayne, Rory Calhoun, Alex D'Arcy, Fred Clark

How to Murder a Rich Uncle
GB 1957 80m bw Cinemascope
Columbia / Warwick (Ronald Kinnoch)

An impoverished nobleman decides to murder his rich old uncle.
Feebly-handled black comedy which does not come off at all despite a highly talented cast.

w John Paxton, *play* Il faut tuer Julie by Dider Daix *d* Nigel Patrick *ph* Ted Moore

Nigel Patrick, Charles Coburn, *Katie Johnson*, Wendy Hiller, Anthony Newley, Athene Seyler, Michael Caine, Noel Hood, Kenneth Fortescue

How to Murder Your Wife*
US 1964 118m Technicolor
UA / Murder Inc (George Axelrod)

A strip cartoonist tests out his violent scenes in real life; when his wife disappears he finds himself accused of murder.
Amusing preliminaries give way to dreary plot complications and an overlong courtroom scene. Leave after the first hour.

w George Axelrod *d* Richard Quine *ph* Harry Stradling *m* Neal Hefti *pd Richard Sylbert*

Jack Lemmon, Virna Lisi, *Terry-Thomas, Eddie Mayehoff*, Sidney Blackmer, Claire Trevor

How to Save a Marriage and Ruin Your Life
US 1968 102m Technicolor
Panavision
Columbia / Nob Hill (Stanley Shapiro)

An attorney takes it upon himself to convince his friend of the infidelity of the friend's mistress . . .
Tedious sex antics without any sex; a few smiles are not enough to endear it.

w Stanley Shapiro, Nate Monaster *d* Fielder Cook *ph* Lee Garmes *m* Michel Legrand

Dean Martin, Eli Wallach, Stella Stevens, Anne Jackson, Betty Field, Jack Albertson, Katharine Bard

'Another variation on Hollywood's patent version of the Restoration comedy, which as usual abandons the lustiness of its 17th-century prototype in favour of guilt-ridden lechery and a fundamental respect for the married state.'—*MFB*

How to Steal a Million*
US 1966 127m De Luxe Panavision
TCF / World Wide (Fred Kohlmar)

The daughter of an art forger mistakenly involves a private detective in a robbery.
High-class but rather boring romantic comedy; the credits promise much but interest wanes quickly owing to uncertain handling.

w Harry Kurnitz *d* William Wyler *ph* Charles Lang *m* Johnny Williams

Audrey Hepburn, Peter O'Toole, Charles Boyer, Hugh Griffith, Eli Wallach, Fernand Gravet, Marcel Dalio

How to Steal an Airplane
US 1970 100m Technicolor TVM
Universal (Roy Huggins)
aka: *Only One Day Left before Tomorrow*

Two adventurers pose as tourists in a Latin American country to repossess a Lear jet stolen by the dictator's irresponsible son.
Modest, unremarkable adventure.

w Robert Foster, Philip de Guere Jnr *d* Leslie H. Martinson

Pete Duel, Clinton Greyn, Claudine Longet, Sal Mineo, Julie Sommars

How to Succeed in Business without Really Trying**
US 1967 121m De Luxe Panavision
UA / Mirisch (David Swift)

A window cleaner cajoles his way to the top of a New York company.
Cinematically uninventive but otherwise brisk and glowing adaptation of a sharp, slick Broadway musical.

w David Swift, *musical book* Abe Burrows, Jack Weinstock, Willie Gilbert, *book* Shepherd Mead *d* David Swift *ph* Burnett Guffey *m/ly Frank Loesser ch* Dale Moreda after Bob Fosse

Robert Morse, Rudy Vallee, Michele Lee, Anthony Teague, Maureen Arthur, Murray Matheson

'Shows how taste and talent can succeed in bringing a stage musical to the screen with its virtues intact.'—*John Cutts*

The Howards of Virginia
US 1940 117m bw
Columbia (Frank Lloyd)
GB title: *The Tree of Liberty*

A Virginian surveyor finds himself involved in the Revolutionary War.
Historical cavalcade in which central miscasting seems to cast a shadow of artifice over the whole. Interesting but seldom stimulating.

w Sidney Buchman, *novel* The Tree of Liberty by Elizabeth Page *d* Frank Lloyd *ph* Bert Glennon *m* Richard Hageman

Cary Grant, Martha Scott, Cedric Hardwicke, Alan Marshal, Richard Carlson, Paul Kelly, Irving Bacon, Elizabeth Risdon

A Howling in the Woods*
US 1971 96m Technicolor TVM
Universal

In a creepy house by Lake Tahoe, a girl is menaced by what appears to be a spectral dog, and a murder secret is unearthed.
Enjoyable spinechiller with not quite enough plot for its length.

w Richard de Roy *d* Daniel Petrie

Larry Hagman, Vera Miles, Barbara Eden, John Rubenstein

Huckleberry Finn
US 1931 71m bw
Paramount

The river adventures of Mark Twain's scapegrace hero.
Adequate early talkie family film.

d Norman Taurog

Jackie Coogan, Junior Durkin, Mitzi Green, Jackie Searl, Eugene Pallette

Huckleberry Finn**
US 1939 90m bw
MGM (Joseph L. Mankiewicz)

Solidly competent remake with excellent production values and several entertaining sequences.

w Hugo Butler *d* Richard Thorpe *ph* John Seitz

Mickey Rooney, Walter Connolly, William Frawley, Rex Ingram

Huckleberry Finn*
US 1960 107m Metrocolor
MGM
aka: *The Adventures of Huckleberry Finn*

Another patchy remake.

w James Lee *d* Michael Curtiz

Eddie Hodges, Tony Randall, Archie Moore, Neville Brand, Judy Canova, Buster Keaton, Andy Devine

Huckleberry Finn
US 1974 118m De Luxe Panavision
UA / Apjac / Readers Digest (Robert Greenhut)

Ambitious but lustreless version of the famous story, with songs.

w/ly/m Richard M. Sherman, Robert B. Sherman *d* J. Lee-Thompson *ph* Laszlo Kovacs *pd* Philip Jeffries

Jeff East, Paul Winfield, David Wayne, Harvey Korman, Arthur O'Connell, Gary Merrill, Natalie Trundy

'It expires in a morass of treacle.'—*Tom Milne*

Huckleberry Finn
US 1974 75m Technicolor TVM
ABC Circle (Steven North)

Rough-edged TV version.

w Jean Holloway *d* Robert Totten

Ronny Howard, Jack Elam, Merle Haggard, Donny Most, Sarah Selby, Jean Howard, Clint Howard, Royal Dano

The Hucksters**
US 1947 115m bw
MGM (Arthur Hornblow Jnr)

Back from the war, an advertising executive finds it difficult to put up with his clients' tantrums.

Good topical entertainment which still entertains and gives a good impression of its period.

w Luther Davis, *novel* Frederic Wakeman *d Jack Conway* *ph* Harold Rosson *m* Lennie Hayton

Clark Gable, Deborah Kerr, Ava Gardner, *Sidney Greenstreet*, Adolphe Menjou, Keenan Wynn, Edward Arnold, Aubrey Mather

'A good picture, quick and to the point.'—*Photoplay*

Hud***
US 1963 112m bw Panavision
Paramount / Salem / Dover (Martin Ritt, Irving Ravetch)

Life is hard on a Texas ranch, and the veteran owner is not helped by his sexually arrogant ne'er-do-well son, who is a bad influence on the household.
Superbly set in an arid landscape, this incisive character drama is extremely well directed and acted but somehow lacks the touch of greatness.

w Irving Ravetch, Harriet Frank, novel Horseman Pass By by Larry McMurty *d Martin Ritt* *ph James Wong Howe* *m* Elmer Bernstein

Paul Newman, Patricia Neal, Melvyn Douglas, Brandon de Wilde

Hudson's Bay**
US 1940 95m bw
TCF (Kenneth MacGowan)

Pierre Radisson, a French Canadian trapper, opens up millions of acres of northern wilderness for England.
Well-made historical saga with good production and performances.

w Lamar Trotti *d Irving Pichel* *ph* Peverell Marley, George Barnes *m* Alfred Newman *ad* Richard Day, Wiard B. Ihnen

Paul Muni, Laird Cregar, Gene Tierney, John Sutton, Virginia Field, Vincent Price (as King Charles II), Nigel Bruce, Morton Lowry, Robert Greig, Frederic Worlock, Montagu Love

Hue and Cry***
GB 1946 82m bw
Ealing

East End boys discover that their favourite boys' paper is being used by crooks to pass information.
The first 'Ealing comedy' uses vivid London locations as background for a sturdy comic plot with a climax in which the criminals are rounded up by thousands of boys swarming over dockland.

w T. E. B. Clarke *d Charles Crichton* *ph* Douglas Slocombe, John Seaholme

Alastair Sim, Jack Warner, Harry Fowler, Valerie White, Frederick Piper

'Refreshing, bloodtingling and disarming.'—*Richard Winnington*

Hugo the Hippo
US 1975 78m colour
Brut (Robert Halmi)

An independently-minded hippo combats a Zanzibar magician.
Uninventive cartoon feature, endearing neither in characterization nor in draughtsmanship.

w Thomas Baum *d* William Feigenbaum *md* Bert Keyes

The Human Comedy*
US 1943 117m bw
MGM (Clarence Brown)

In a small town during the war, a telegram boy brings tragedy to others and is touched by it himself.
Gooey, sentimental morale booster in the best MGM tradition, a variant on the Hardy family series but with all the pretensions of its author.

w Howard Estabrook, *novel* William Saroyan *d Clarence Brown*

Mickey Rooney, Frank Morgan, James Craig, Marsha Hunt, Jackie Jenkins, Fay Bainter, Ray Collins, Van Johnson, Donna Reed

'The dignity and simplicity of the ideas shade off into cheap pretentiousness.'—*Bosley Crowther*

'The best one can say of it . . . is that it tries on the whole to be "faithful" to Saroyan; not invariably a good idea.'—*James Agee*

Human Desire
US 1954 90m bw
Columbia (Lewis J. Rachmil)

A jealous railway official forces his wife to help him murder her suspected lover.
Drab and unattractive remake of *La Bête Humaine*.

w Alfred Hayes *d* Fritz Lang *ph* Burnett Guffey *m* Daniele Amfitheatrof

Gloria Grahame, Glenn Ford, Broderick Crawford, Edgar Buchanan

Humoresque**
US 1947 125m bw
Warner (Jerry Wald)

An ambitious violinist gets emotionally involved with his wealthy patroness.
Lush soaper about suffering in high society,

complete with tragic end and lashings of classical music (Isaac Stern on the sound track).

w Clifford Odets, Zachary Gold, *novel* Fannie Hurst *d Jean Negulesco ph Ernest Haller md* Franz Waxman

Joan Crawford, John Garfield, Oscar Levant, J. Carrol Naish, Joan Chandler, Tom D'Andrea, Craig Stevens, Ruth Nelson

The Hunchback of Notre Dame****
US 1939 117m bw
RKO (Pandro S. Berman)

The deformed Notre Dame bellringer rescues a gypsy girl from the evil attentions of his guardian.
This superb remake of the Lon Chaney classic is one of the best examples of Hollywood expertise at work: art direction, set construction, costumes, camera, lighting and above all direction brilliantly support an irresistible story and bravura acting.

w Sonya Levien, Bruno Frank, novel Victor Hugo *d William Dieterle ph Joseph H. August m Alfred Newman ad Van Nest Polglase*

Charles Laughton, Cedric Hardwicke, Maureen O'Hara, Edmond O'Brien, Thomas Mitchell, Harry Davenport, Walter Hampden, Alan Marshal, George Zucco, Katherine Alexander, Fritz Leiber, Rod la Rocque

'Has seldom been bettered as an evocation of medieval life.'—*John Baxter, 1968*

Hungry Hill
GB 1946 92m bw
GFD / Two Cities (William Sistrom)

An Irish family feud spans three generations.
Rather uninteresting costume melodrama.

w Daphne du Maurier, Terence Young, Francis Crowdy d Brian Desmond Hurst

Margaret Lockwood, Dennis Price, Cecil Parker, Michael Denison, F. J. McCormick, Dermot Walsh, Jean Simmons, Eileen Herlie, Siobhan McKenna, Eileen Crowe, Dan O'Herlihy

Hunted*
GB 1952 84m bw
GFD / Independent Artists (Julian Wintle)
US title: *The Stranger in Between*

A runaway boy joins forces with a runaway murderer, and the latter sacrifices himself for the boy's safety.
Predictable pattern melodrama, nicely made and acted.

w Jack Whittingham *d Charles Crichton ph Eric Cross m* Hubert Clifford

Dirk Bogarde, Jon Whiteley, Kay Walsh, Elizabeth Sellars, Frederick Piper, Geoffrey Keen, Julian Somers

Hunted Men*
US 1938 67m bw
Paramount

A killer on the run moves into a private home and is outwitted by the head of the house.
Competent second feature which sticks in the memory.

w Horace McCoy, William R. Lipman *d* Louis King *ph* Victor Milner

Lloyd Nolan, Lynne Overman, Mary Carlisle, J. Carrol Naish, Anthony Quinn, Dorothy Peterson

Hunter
US 1971 73m colour TVM
Unit Productions

Enemy agents try to brainwash a CIA man after he has been hurt in a racetrack accident.
Spies and counterspies; nothing new.

d Leonard Horn

John Vernon, Steve Ihnat, Fritz Weaver, Edward Binns, Barbara Rhoades

The Hunters
US 1958 108m De Luxe Cinemascope
TCF (Dick Powell)

A fearless American pilot is sent to Korea on a special mission.
Standard war thriller, good to look at when airborne but pretty boring on the ground; propaganda element very strong.

w Wendell Mayes *d* Dick Powell *ph* Charles G. Clarke *m* Paul Sawtell

Robert Mitchum, Robert Wagner, Richard Egan, Mai Britt

Hunters Are for Killing*
US 1970 100m colour TVM
Cinema Center (Hugh Benson)

An ex-con finds himself in danger from his own family and his girl friend's father.
Complex suspenser which passes the time.

d Bernard Kowalski

Burt Reynolds, Melvyn Douglas, Martin Balsam, Suzanne Pleshette, Larry Storch

The Hunting Party
US 1971 108m De Luxe
UA / Brighton / Levy–Gardner–Levy

A sadistic Texas baron sets out to shoot one by one the outlaws who have kidnapped his wife.

Crude, brutish and repellent melodrama: the epitome of permissiveness, replete with gore, rape and sadism.

w William Norton, Gilbert Alexander, Lou Morheim *d* Don Medford *ph* Cecilio Paniagua *m* Riz Ortolani

Gene Hackman, Candice Bergen, Oliver Reed

The Hurricane**
US 1937 110m bw
Samuel Goldwyn (Merritt Hulburd)

The simple life on a South Pacific island is disrupted, not only by a vindictive governor but by a typhoon.
Tolerable island melodrama with a spectacular climax and a generally good cast.

w Dudley Nichols, Oliver H. P. Garrett, *novel* Charles Nordhof, James Norman Hall *d John Ford, Stuart Heisler ph Bert Glennon m* Alfred Newman

Dorothy Lamour, Jon Hall, C. Aubrey Smith, Mary Astor, Raymond Massey, Thomas Mitchell, John Carradine, Jerome Cowan

Hurricane
US 1974 74m colour TVM
Metromedia

Several people are caught up in a Gulf Coast hurricane.
Piffling multi-drama making far too obvious use of news footage at the expense of personal involvement.

w Jack Turley *d* Jerry Jameson

Larry Hagman, Martin Milner, Jessica Walter, Barry Sullivan, Michael Learned, Will Geer

Hurricane Smith
US 1952 90m Technicolor
Paramount / Nat Holt

An adventurer charters a boat to find a South Sea treasure but the boat owner turns the tables on him.
Standard thick ear with plenty of action.

w Frank Gruber *d* Jerry Hopper *ph* Ray Rennahan *m* Paul Sawtell

John Ireland, Yvonne de Carlo, James Craig, Forrest Tucker

Hurry Sundown
US 1967 146m Technicolor
Panavision
Paramount / Sigma (Otto Preminger)

Post-war racial problems in Georgia farmland, with degenerate whites and noble blacks.
Incredibly cliché-ridden epic melodrama with action and sex asides, from a rock bottom bestseller. It long outstays its welcome even for unintentional hilarity.

w Thomas C. Ryan, Horton Foote, *novel* K. B. Gilden *d* Otto Preminger *ph* Loyal Griggs, Milton Krasner *m* Hugo Montenegro

Jane Fonda, Michael Caine, Rex Ingram, Diahann Carroll, Burgess Meredith, John Philip Law, Robert Hooks, Faye Dunaway, Beah Richards, George Kennedy, Madeleine Sherwood

'Critic Wilfrid Sheed wrote recently that no film is ever so bad that you can't find some virtue in it. He must not have seen *Hurry Sundown*.'—*Rex Reed*

'To criticize it would be like tripping a dwarf.'—*Wilfrid Sheed*

'A pantomime version of Greek tragedy.'—*MFB*

Husbands*
US 1970 154m De Luxe
Columbia / Faces Music Inc (Al Ruban)

Three married men, shocked by the death of their friend, impulsively get drunk, fly to London and set out on a weekend of dissipation.
Irritatingly rough hewn and insanely overlong, this half-improvised tragi-comedy forces three good actors to overplay embarrassingly; but its best moments are memorable.

wd John Cassavetes ph Victor Kemper *m* none

Peter Falk, John Cassavetes, Ben Gazzara

Hush Hush Sweet Charlotte**
US 1964 133m bw
TCF / Associates and Aldrich

A southern belle lives thirty-seven years in a lonely mansion tormented by nightmarish memories of her fiancé's murder. Suddenly, after a series of apparent hauntings and other strange events, she finds she didn't do it.
Padded but generally enjoyable replay of elements from *Whatever Happened to Baby Jane*, with a large helping of *Les Diaboliques*. The stars help more than the director.

w Henry Farrell, Lukas Heller *d* Robert Aldrich *ph Joseph Biroc m* Frank de Vol *ad* William Glasgow

Bette Davis, Olivia de Havilland, Joseph Cotten, Cecil Kellaway, Victor Buono, William Marshall, Mary Astor, Agnes Moorehead

'The blood is on the cleaver, the madwoman is on the loose, the headless corpse is on the prowl and the Guignol is about as grand as it can get.'—*Judith Crist*

Hustle
US 1975 118m Eastmancolor
Paramount / RoBurt (Robert Aldrich)

A police lieutenant lives with a call girl and is drawn into her corrupt life.
Doleful crime melodrama with both eyes in the gutter.

w Steve Shagan *d* Robert Aldrich *ph* Joseph Biroc *m* Frank de Vol

Burt Reynolds, Catherine Deneuve, Ben Johnson, Paul Winfield, Eileen Brennan, Eddie Albert, Ernest Borgnine, Catherine Bach, Jack Carter

'A fine companion piece to *Kiss Me Deadly* in its vision of a journey to the end of the night in quest of a myth.'—*Tim Milne*

'Even with such a meandering script as this, one expects more than the paltry fare Aldrich offers.'—*Paul Coleman*

The Hustler**
US 1961 135m bw Cinemascope
TCF / Robert Rossen

A pool room con man comes to grief when he falls in love.
Downbeat melodrama with brilliantly handled and atmospheric pool table scenes; the love interest is redundant.

w Robert Rossen, Sidney Carroll, *novel* Walter Tevis *d Robert Rossen ph Eugen Schufftan* *m* Kenyon Hopkins

Paul Newman, Jackie Gleason, George C. Scott, Piper Laurie, Myron McCormick, Murray Hamilton, Michael Constantine

'There is an overall impression of intense violence, and the air of spiritual decadence has rarely been conveyed so vividly.'—*David Robinson*

Hustling*
US 1975 96m colour TVM
Filmways / Lillian Gallo

A woman reporter tries to write the truth about New York prostitution.
Grainy, gritty, true-life semi-documentary. The fuzzy sound recording makes fiction or fact preferable to this well-meant compromise, but it tries hard.

w Fay Kanin, *book* Gail Sheehy *d* Joseph Sargent

Lee Remick, *Jill Clayburgh*, Monte Markham, Alex Rocco

Hysteria
GB 1964 85m bw
MGM / Hammer (Jimmy Sangster)

An American suffering from amnesia is discharged from a London clinic and walks into a murder plot.
Complicated and rather unsympathetic Hammer twister.

w Jimmy Sangster *d* Freddie Francis *ph* John Wilcox *m* Don Banks

Robert Webber, Lelia Goldoni, Anthony Newlands, Jennifer Jayne, *Maurice Denham*, Peter Woodthorpe

I

I Accuse*
GB 1958 99m bw Cinemascope
MGM (Sam Zimbalist)

In 1894 Paris, Alfred Dreyfus is tried for treason and later defended by Emile Zola.
A well tried historical incident is stolidly retold and unsuitably wide-screened; the star cast tends to flounder for lack of assistance.

w Gore Vidal *d* Jose Ferrer *ph* Frederick A. Young *m* William Alwyn

Jose Ferrer (Dreyfus), *Anton Walbrook* (Esterhazy), Emlyn Williams (Zola), Viveca Lindfors, David Farrar, Leo Genn, Herbert Lom, Harry Andrews, Felix Aylmer, George Coulouris, Donald Wolfit

I Aim at the Stars
US 1960 107m bw
Columbia / Morningside / Fama (Charles H. Schneer)

The story of German rocket expert Wernher Von Braun and his later work on American space vehicles.
Shaky biopic of a controversial scientist who changed sides.

w Jay Dratler *d* J. Lee-Thompson *ph* Wilkie Cooper *m* Laurie Johnson

Curt Jurgens, Herbert Lom, James Daly, Gia Scala, Victoria Shaw, Adrian Hoven, Karel Stepanek

'Mannered panning shots and crafty cutting abound, leading to a stylistic St Vitus' Dance.'— *John Gillett*

I Am a Camera
GB 1955 99m bw
Romulus (Jack Clayton)

A young English writer observes life in Berlin in the early thirties, and has a platonic relationship with an amoral and reckless young English girl.
A rather flat and flabby treatment of the stories by Christopher Isherwood and the play by John Van Druten, all better known these days in the form of *Cabaret*. Disappointingly unstylish.

w John Collier *d* Henry Cornelius *ph* Guy Green *m* Malcolm Arnold

Julie Harris, Laurence Harvey, Shelley Winters, Ron Randell, Anton Diffring

I Am a Fugitive from a Chain Gang****
US 1932 90m bw
Warner (Hal B. Wallis)

An innocent man is convicted and after brutal treatment with the chain gang becomes a vicious criminal on the run.
Horrifying story in the semi-documentary manner; a milestone in Hollywood history and still a fairly compelling piece of shock entertainment.

w Sheridan Gibney, Brown Holmes, Robert E. Burns d Mervyn Le Roy ph Sol Polito

Paul Muni, Glenda Farrell, Helen Vinson, Preston Foster, Allen Jenkins, Edward J. Macnamara, Berton Churchill, Edward Ellis

'To be enthusiastically commended for its courage, artistic sincerity, dramatic vigour, high entertainment concept and social message.'— *Wilton A. Barrett*

I Am the Law*
US 1938 83m bw
Columbia (Everett Riskin)

A law professor is asked by a civic leader to become a special prosecutor cleaning up rackets.
Adequate star potboiler, quite enjoyable.

w Jo Swerling *d* Alexander Hall *ph* Henry Freulich *m* Morris Stoloff

Edward G. Robinson, Otto Kruger, John Beal, Barbara O'Neil, Wendy Barrie, Arthur Loft, Marc Lawrence

I Believe in You*
GB 1952 95m bw
Ealing (Michael Relph)

Interwoven stories of probation officers; watchable and reasonable but not very compelling.

w Michael Relph, Basil Dearden, Jack Whittingham, Nicholas Phipps *d* Basil Dearden

Celia Johnson, Cecil Parker, Godfrey Tearle, Harry Fowler, George Relph, Joan Collins, Laurence Harvey, Ernest Jay, Ursula Howells,

Sidney James, Katie Johnson, Ada Reeve, Brenda de Banzie

I Can Get It for You Wholesale*
US 1951 89m bw
TCF (Sol C. Siegel)
GB title: *This Is My Affair*
American TV title: *Only the Best*

An ambitious young mannequin starts her own dressmaking firm and sets her sights high.
Watchable comedy-drama which quickly sheds the edge of satire which might have made it the dressmaker's *All About Eve*.

w Abraham Polonsky, *novel* Jerome Weidman *d* Michael Gordon *ph* Milton Krasner *m* Lionel Newman

Susan Hayward, Dan Dailey, George Sanders, Sam Jaffe, Randy Stuart, Marvin Kaplan, Harry Von Zell

I Confess**
US 1953 94m bw
Warner / Alfred Hitchcock

A priest hears the confession of a murderer and cannot divulge it to the police even though he is himself suspected.
Hitchcock is always worth watching, and although this old chestnut gives him very restricted scope he imbues the story with a strong feeling for its setting (Quebec) and an overpowering sense of doom.

w George Tabori, William Archibald, *play* Paul Anthelme *d Alfred Hitchcock* *ph* Robert Burks *m* Dmitri Tiomkin

Montgomery Clift, Anne Baxter, Brian Aherne, Karl Malden, Dolly Haas, O. E. Hasse

'Whatever its shortcomings, it has the professional concentration of effect, the narrative control, of a story teller who can still make most of his rivals look like amateurs.'—*MFB*

I Could Go on Singing*
GB 1963 99m Eastmancolor
Panavision
UA / Barbican (Lawrence Turman)

An American singing star in Britain looks up an old lover and tries to take over their illegitimate son, but the call of the footlights proves stronger.
The star enjoys her last specially-tailored role; a banal, old-fashioned agreeable one-woman show.

w Mayo Simon *d* Ronald Neame *ph* Arthur Ibbetson *m* Mort Lindsey

Judy Garland, Dirk Bogarde, Aline MacMahon, Jack Klugman

I Cover the Waterfront*
US 1933 75m bw
(UA)

A reporter uses a girl's friendship to expose her father's smuggling activities.
In its time a tough, even daring melodrama, this plot has now become the stuff of every other TV series episode.

w Wells Root, Jack Jevne, Max Miller *d James Cruze* *ph* Ray June

Claudette Colbert, Ben Lyon, Ernest Torrence, Hobart Cavanaugh

'A bit raw and a bit sentimental and a bit routine, the film does let life in through the cracks.'—*Graham Greene*

I Deal in Danger
US 1966 89m colour TVM
TCF

In World War II, a member of the Nazi High Command is really an American spy.
Tall tale put together from bits of the series *The Blue Light*.

w Larry Cohen *d* Walter Grauman

Robert Goulet, Christine Carere, Donald Harron, Horst Frank, Werner Peters

I Died a Thousand Times
US 1955 109m Warnercolor
Cinemascope
Warner (Willis Goldbeck)

An ex-convict plans a big hotel robbery, but things go wrong within his gang.
Overlong, heavygoing, tedious gangster melodrama with too much talk.

w W. R. Burnett *d* Stuart Heisler *ph* Ted McCord *m* David Buttolph

Jack Palance, Shelley Winters, Lori Nelson, Lon Chaney Jnr, Lee Marvin, Gonzales Gonzales, Earl Holliman, Perry Lopez

'This remake of *High Sierra* is scarcely more inspired than its title.'—*MFB*

The I Don't Care Girl*
US 1953 78m Technicolor
TCF (George Jessel)

The life of musical entertainer Eva Tanguay, at her height during World War I, as told by three men in her life.
Breezy, conventional backstage musical biopic.

w Walter Bullock *d* Lloyd Bacon *ph* Arthur Arling *md* Lionel Newman *ch* Jack Cole, Seymour Felix

Mitzi Gaynor, David Wayne, Oscar Levant, *George Jessel*, Warren Stevens

I Don't Want to be Born
GB 1975 94m Eastmancolor
(Rank) Unicapital (Norma Corney)
US title: *The Devil within Her*

An ex-stripper gives birth to a monstrous baby which goes on a murderous rampage.
Sick horror stuff with a high death rate and no notable credits.

w Stanley Price *d* Peter Sasdy *ph* Ken Talbot *m* Ron Grainer

Joan Collins, Ralph Bates, Donald Pleasance, Eileen Atkins, George Claydon

I Dood It!
US 1943 102m bw
MGM (Jack Cummings)
GB title: *By Hook or by Crook*

A tailor falls for a Hollywood star.
Boring star comedy with interpolated musical numbers.

w Sig Herzig, Fred Saidy *d* Vincente Minnelli *ph* Ray June *md* Georgie Stoll

Red Skelton, Eleanor Powell, John Hodiak, Lena Horne, Jimmy Dorsey and his Orchestra, Hazel Scott, Richard Ainley

I Dream Too Much
US 1935 95m bw
RKO (Pandro S. Berman)

A French girl singer marries an American composer.
Forgettable vehicle for an operatic star.

w Edmund North, James Gow *d* John Cromwell *ph* David Abel *songs* Jerome Kern, Dorothy Fields

Lily Pons, Henry Fonda, Eric Blore, Osgood Perkins, Lucien Littlefield, Lucille Ball, Esther Dale, Mischa Auer, Paul Porcasi

I Escaped from Devil's Island
US 1973 81m De Luxe
UA / Roger Corman, Gene Corman

In 1918, a black convict makes his plans for escape.
Rough, brutish melodrama which plainly aimed to beat *Papillon* to the box office.

w Richard L. Adams *d* William Witney *ph* Rosalio Solano *m* Les Baxter

Jim Brown, Christopher George, Rick Ely, James Luisi, Richard Rust

'Exploitation's own *Papillon*, mercifully free from big brother's pretentiousness.'—*Sight and Sound*

I Heard the Owl Call My Name*
US 1973 74m colour TVM
Tomorrow

A sickly young priest is sent to a remote Canadian Indian village and dies there.
Scenic, moving, slightly pointless personal saga.

w Gerald di Pego, *book* Margaret Craven
d Daryl Duke

Tom Courtenay, Dean Jagger

I Know Where I'm Going**
GB 1945 91m bw
GFD / The Archers (Michael Powell, Emeric Pressburger)

A determined girl travels to the Hebrides to marry a wealthy old man, but is stranded on Mull and marries a young naval officer instead.
A strange assembling of attractive but disparate elements: romance, comedy, bleak scenery, a trained hawk and a dangerous whirlpool. At the time it seemed to represent the Elizabethan age of the British cinema, and remains entertaining for its parts though a bit of a puzzle as a whole.

wd Michael Powell, Emeric Pressburger
ph Erwin Hillier

Wendy Hiller, Roger Livesey, Pamela Brown, Nancy Price, Finlay Currie, John Laurie, George Carney, Walter Hudd

I Live for Love
US 1935 83m bw
Warner (Bryan Foy)

A socialite has show business leanings.
Minor musical.

w Jerry Wald, Julius Epstein, Robert Andrews *d/ch* Busby Berkeley *ph* George Barnes *md* Leo F. Forbstein

Dolores del Rio, Everett Marshall, Allen Jenkins, Eddie Conrad, Guy Kibbee, Berton Churchill

I Live in Grosvenor Square
GB 1945 113m bw
ABP (Herbert Wilcox)
US title: *A Yank in London*

A duke's daughter falls in love with an American air force sergeant.
Sloppily-made topical romance which was hot box office at the time and started the producer's 'London' romances: *Piccadilly Incident, Spring in Park Lane, Maytime in Mayfair*, etc.

w Nicholas Phipps, William D. Bayles, Maurice Cowan *d* Herbert Wilcox *ph* Max Greene

Anna Neagle, *Dean Jagger*, Rex Harrison, Robert Morley, Jane Darwell, Nancy Price, Irene Vanbrugh, Edward Rigby, Walter Hudd

I Live My Life
US 1935 85m bw
MGM (Bernard H. Hyman)

A bored society girl falls for a working class archaeologist.
Standard star romance.

w Joseph L. Mankiewicz, *story* Claustrophobia by A. Carter Goodloe *d* W. S. Van Dyke II *ph* George Folsey

Joan Crawford, Brian Aherne, Frank Morgan, Aline MacMahon, Eric Blore, Jessie Ralph, Arthur Treacher, Hedda Hopper, Etienne Girardot, Ed Brophy

I'll Take Romance
US 1937 85m bw
Columbia (Everett Riskin)

When an opera singer refuses to fulfil a South American contract, her impresario kidnaps her.
Moderate star vehicle.

w George Oppenheimer, Jane Murfin *d* Edward H. Griffith *ph* Lucien Andriot *songs* various

Grace Moore, Melvyn Douglas, Helen Westley, Stuart Erwin, Margaret Hamilton, Walter Kingsford, Esther Muir

I Love a Mystery*
US 1945 68m bw
Columbia

An eastern secret society offers a businessman a large sum for his head when he dies, as he resembles their founder whose embalmed head is deteriorating.
Start of a short series of mysteries from a radio series; the production was never up to the ingenious plots.

w Charles O'Neal *d* Henry Levin *ph* Burnett Guffey

George Macready, Jim Bannon, Nina Foch

I Love a Mystery
US 1967 98m Technicolor TVM
Universal (Frank Price)

Three super-detectives seek a missing billionaire.
Woefully unfunny transfer to film of a spoof radio serial.

w Leslie Stevens, *serial* Carlton E. Morse *d* Leslie Stevens

Ida Lupino, Les Crane, David Hartman, Jack Weston, Don Knotts

I Love a Soldier
US 1944 106m bw
Paramount (Mark Sandrich)

A San Francisco girl thinks hard before embarking on a wartime marriage.
Glossy, insubstantial sudser chiefly memorable for casting its leading lady as a welder.

w Allan Scott *d* Mark Sandrich *ph Charles Lang m* Robert Emmett Dolan

Paulette Goddard, Sonny Tufts, Beulah Bondi, Walter Sande, Mary Treen, Ann Doran, Barry Fitzgerald

I Love Melvin*
US 1953 77m Technicolor
MGM (George Wells)

A photographer's assistant falls for a high-born chorus girl.
Zippy little musical with all concerned working hard with thin material.

w George Wells *d* Don Weis *ph* Harold Rosson *md* George Stoll *ch* Robert Alton

Donald O'Connor, Debbie Reynolds, Una Merkel, Allyn Joslyn

I Love My Wife
US 1970 95m Technicolor
Universal (Robert Kaufman)

The affairs of a successful doctor with a guilt complex about sex.
Frantic, fashionable comedy drama with wildly erratic treatment and performances.

w Robert Kaufman *d* Mel Stuart *ph* Vilis Lapenieks *m* Lalo Schifrin

Elliott Gould, Brenda Vaccaro, Angel Tompkins
'A leer-laden, anti-feminist tract disguised as a comedy.'—*Judith Crist*

I Love You Again*
US 1940 99m bw
MGM (Lawrence Weingarten)

A much married man gets amnesia and turns into a gay Lothario.
Sprightly romantic comedy with all concerned letting rip until the pace slows.

w Charles Lederer, George Oppenheimer, Harry Kurnitz *d* W. S. Van Dyke II *ph* Oliver T. Marsh *m* Franz Waxman

William Powell, Myrna Loy, Frank McHugh, Edmund Lowe, Donald Douglas, Nella Walker, Pierre Watkin

I Love You, Alice B. Toklas*
US 1968 93m Technicolor
Warner Seven Arts / Paul Mazursky, Larry Tucker

An asthmatic Los Angeles lawyer escapes his bullying fiancée by joining the flower people.
Quite amusing satirical farce about the dangers of marijuana, Gertrude Stein and Jewish mothers, thrown together with no great sense of

style but achieving hilarious moments among the longueurs.

w Paul Mazursky, Larry Tucker d Hy Averback *ph* Philip Lathrop *m* Elmer Bernstein *pd* Pato Guzman

Peter Sellers, Jo Van Fleet, Joyce Van Patten, Leigh Taylor-Young, David Arkin, Herb Edelman

I Love You . . . Goodbye
US 1974 74m colour TVM
Tomorrow

A suburban housewife leaves her family in an attempt to fulfil herself.
Mildly interesting character study.

w Diana Gould *d* Sam O'Steen

Hope Lange, Earl Holliman, Michael Murphy, Patricia Smith

I Loved a Woman*
US 1933 90m bw
Warner (Henry Blanke)

The career of a Chicago meat packer is hampered by his social-climbing wife.
Potboiling star melodrama which still holds some interest.

w Charles Kenyon, Sidney Sutherland *d* Alfred E. Green *ph* James Van Trees

Edward G. Robinson, Kay Francis, Genevieve Tobin,
J. Farrell MacDonald, Henry Kolker, Robert Barrat

I Married a Monster from Outer Space*
US 1958 78m bw
Paramount / Gene Fowler Jnr

A young man is taken over by alien invaders but his wife helps to destroy them and bring him back to normal.
Decent, plodding, reasonably effective low-budget science fiction on a well-trampled theme; its minor virtues have been effaced by its silly title.

w Louis Vittes *d* Gene Fowler Jnr *ph* Haskell Boggs *sp* John P. Fulton

Tom Tryon, Gloria Talbott, Robert Ivers

I Married a Witch****
US 1942 82m bw
(UA) Cinema Guild / René Clair

A Salem witch and her sorcerer father come back to haunt the descendant of the Puritan who had them burned.
Delightful romantic comedy fantasy which shows all concerned at the top of their form.
Hollywood moonshine, impeccably distilled.

w Robert Pirosh, Marc Connelly, novel The Passionate Witch by Thorne Smith *d René Clair ph* Ted Tetzlaff *m* Roy Webb

Fredric March, Veronica Lake, Cecil Kellaway, Robert Benchley, Susan Hayward, Elizabeth Patterson, Robert Warwick

I Married an Angel
US 1942 84m bw
MGM (Hunt Stromberg)

An attractive angel lures a playboy from his earthly girl friends.
Silly musical fantasy which spelled the end of a great musical star partnership.

w Anita Loos, *play* Vilismary Janos *d* W. S. Van Dyke *m/ly* Richard Rodgers, Lorenz Hart

Jeanette MacDonald, Nelson Eddy, Edward Everett Horton, Binnie Barnes, Reginald Owen, Douglass Dumbrille

I Married a Woman
US 1956 85m bw RKOscope
RKO

A nervous young advertising executive neglects his wife, who determines to make him jealous.
Simple-minded comedy tailored to unsympathetic stars.

w Goodman Ace *d* Hal Kanter *ph* Lucien Ballard *m* Cyril Mockridge

George Gobel, Diana Dors, Adolphe Menjou, Jessie Royce Landis, Nita Talbot

I Met a Murderer*
GB 1939 78m bw
Grand National / Gamma (Roy Kellino, Pamela Kellino, James Mason)

A murderer on the run meets a girl novelist who is touring in her motor caravan.
Semi-professional location melodrama which won commendation at the time but now seems very faded.

w Pamela Kellino, James Mason *d* Roy Kellino *ph* Roy Kellino *m* Eric Ansell

James Mason, Pamela Kellino, Sylvia Coleridge, William Devlin, Peter Coke

'Graceful, gallant, resourceful . . . better and more enjoyable than most studio pictures.'—*James Agee*

'That it has a number of defects does not mean that it is not worthy of serious consideration.'—*Basil Wright*

I Met Him in Paris*
US 1937 86m bw
Paramount (Wesley Ruggles)

A fashion designer spends five years' savings on

a fling in Paris and finds herself pursued to Switzerland by two philanderers.
Not very witty but likeable romantic comedy with polished performers near their best.

w Claude Binyon *d* Wesley Ruggles *ph* Leo Tover *m* Boris Morros

Claudette Colbert, Melvyn Douglas, Robert Young, Lee Bowman, Mona Barrie

'At least half the footage is a perfect scream, and if you miss it you are an old sobersides, and who cares.'—*Otis Ferguson*

I, Mobster
US 1958 80m bw Cinemascope
Edward L. Alperson

A slum teenager becomes a top gangster.
Routine gangland thriller.

w Steve Fisher, *novel* Joseph Hilton Smith *d* Roger Corman *ph* Floyd Crosby *m* Gerald Fried

Steve Cochran, Lita Milan, Robert Strauss, Celia Lovsky, Grant Withers

I, Monster*
GB 1970 75m Eastmancolor
Amicus (Milton Subotsky)

A straight remake of *Dr Jekyll and Mr Hyde*, holding closely to the original novel but mysteriously using different names.
Interesting minor work.

w Milton Subotsky *d* Stephen Weeks *ph* Moray Grant *m* Carl Davis *ad* Tony Curtis

Christopher Lee, Peter Cushing, Richard Hurndall, George Merritt

I Never Sang for My Father**
US 1969 92m Technicolor
Columbia / Jamel (Gilbert Cates)

When his mother dies, a middle-aged widower is saddled with his cantankerous father, who tries to prevent him from remarrying.
Literal transcription of a Eugene O'Neillish play, a fascinating if depressing character study.

w Robert Anderson, from his play *d Gilbert Cates ph* Morris Hartzband, George Stoetzel *m* Al Gorgoni, Barry Mann

Melvyn Douglas, Gene Hackman, Dorothy Stickney, Estelle Parsons

I Passed for White
US 1960 92m bw
Allied Artists (Fred M. Wilcox)

A light-skinned negress comes to New York but fails to achieve happiness by pretending to be white.
Earnest, rather dreary social drama which doesn't get anywhere.

d Fred M. Wilcox

Sonya Wilde, James Franciscus, Pat Michon, Elizabeth Council

I Remember Mama**
US 1948 134m bw
RKO (George Stevens)

A novelist remembers some of the adventures of growing up with her Swedish–American family.
Overlong, but well-upholstered nostalgia: warm-hearted, sentimental, nicely detailed, richly acted but just a little boring in spots.

w De Witt Bodeen, *play* John Van Druten, *book* Mama's Bank Account by Kathryn Forbes *d George Stevens ph* Nicholas Musuraca *m* Roy Webb

Irene Dunne, Barbara Bel Geddes, Oscar Homolka, Edgar Bergen, Philip Dorn, Ellen Corby, Florence Bates, Cedric Hardwicke, Barbara O'Neil, Rudy Vallee

I Saw What You Did
US 1965 82m bw
Universal / William Castle

A murderer thinks that two playful teenagers have witnessed his deed, and sets out to kill them too.
Predictable and long-winded suspenser, very short of inventive detail.

w William McGivern, *novel* Ursula Curtiss *d* William Castle *ph* Joseph Biroc *m* Joseph Gershenson

John Ireland, Joan Crawford, Leif Erickson

I See a Dark Stranger**
GB 1945 112m bw
GFD / Individual
US title: *The Adventuress*

An Irish colleen who hates the English comes to England to spy for the Germans but falls in love with a young English officer.
Slipshod plotting does not quite destroy the jolly atmosphere of this comedy-thriller which has the cheek to take an IRA member as its heroine. Good fun, very well staged.

w Frank Launder, Sidney Gilliat, Wolfgang Wilhelm d Frank Launder ph Wilkie Cooper

Deborah Kerr, Trevor Howard, Raymond Huntley, Norman Shelley, Michael Howard, Brenda Bruce, Liam Redmond, Brefni O'Rourke

'It is the cinematic equivalent of Irish blarney which inspires most of this picture.'—*MFB*

I Stole a Million
US 1939 89m bw
Universal (Burt Kelly)

A cab driver cheated by a finance company becomes a criminal to support his family.
Ho-hum star melodrama.

w Nathanael West, *story* Lester Cole *d* Frank Tuttle *ph* Milton Krasner

George Raft, Claire Trevor, Dick Foran, Henry Armetta, Victor Jory, Joe Sawyer, Stanley Ridges

I Take This Woman
US 1931 74m bw
Paramount

A reckless society girl falls for a cowhand and agrees to live in his ramshackle house.
Patchy romantic comedy–drama of little remaining interest.

w Vincent Lawrence, *novel* Lost Ecstasy by Mary Roberts Rinehart *d* Marion Gering, Slavko Vorkapitch *ph* Victor Milner

Gary Cooper, Carole Lombard, Helen Ware, Lester Vail, Charles Trowbridge, Clara Blandick

I Take This Woman
US 1939 97m bw
MGM (Louis B. Mayer)

A doctor marries a beautiful European and decides too late that he does not love her.
Thin comedy–drama which Louis B. Mayer unaccountably took it into his head to produce personally. The results had to be re-shot so much and so often that Hollywood dubbed the film *I Re-Take This Woman*. It offers little in the way of entertainment.

w James Kevin McGuinness, *story* Charles MacArthur
d W. S. Van Dyke *m* Bronislau Kaper

Spencer Tracy, Hedy Lamarr, Verree Teasdale, Kent Taylor, Laraine Day, Mona Barrie, Jack Carson, Paul Cavanagh, Marjorie Main

I Thank a Fool
GB 1962 100m Metrocolor
Cinemascope
MGM (Anatole de Grunwald)

A woman found guilty of the murder of her lover is offered a fresh start in the home of the prosecutor's family . . . but another nightmare situation builds up.
Jane Eyre melodrama of the loonier type, with good actors struggling through a wild but unrewarding script.

w Karl Tunberg, *novel* Audrey Erskine Lindop *d* Robert Stevens *ph* Harry Waxman *m* Ron Goodwin

Peter Finch, Susan Hayward, Diane Cilento, Cyril Cusack, Kieron Moore, Athene Seyler

I the Jury
US 1953 87m bw 3-D
Parklane (Victor Saville)

Private eye Mike Hammer avenges the murder of his friend.
Charmless toughie, roughly made and devoid of plot or character interest.

wd Harry Essex *ph* John Alton *m* Franz Waxman

Biff Elliott, Peggie Castle, Preston Foster, Elisha Cook Jnr, John Qualen

I Wake Up Screaming**
US 1941 79m bw
TCF (Milton Sperling)
GB and alternative title: *Hot Spot*

A model is murdered and her sister joins forces with the chief suspect to find the real killer.
Moody thriller with plenty going for it including one memorable performance.

w Dwight Taylor, *novel* Steve Fisher *d H. Bruce Humberstone ph Edward Cronjager m* Cyril Mockridge

Betty Grable, Victor Mature, Carole Landis, *Laird Cregar*, William Gargan, Alan Mowbray, Allyn Joslyn, Elisha Cook Jnr
† Remade as *Vicki* (qv).

I Walk Alone*
US 1948 98m bw
Paramount (Hal B. Wallis)

An ex-smuggler comes out seeking vengeance after fourteen years in prison.
Dreary gangster drama unworthy of its stars.

w Charles Schnee, *play* Beggars Are Coming to Town by Theodore Reeves *d* Byron Haskin *ph* Leo Tover *m* Victor Young

Burt Lancaster, Kirk Douglas, Lizabeth Scott, Wendell Corey, Kristine Miller, George Rigaud, Marc Lawrence, Mike Mazurki

I Walk the Line*
US 1970 97m Eastmancolor
Panavision
Columbia / Frankenheimer / Lewis / Halcyon / Atticus (Harold D. Cohen)

A Tennessee sheriff protects moonshiners for the favours of their daughter; when an investigator arrives, bloodshed results.
Competent but uninteresting hothouse

melodrama in which only the plot twists compel attention.

w Alvin Sargent, *novel* An Exile by Madison Jones *d* John Frankenheimer *ph David M. Walsh md* Robert Johnson

Gregory Peck, Tuesday Weld, Estelle Parsons, Ralph Meeker

I Walked with a Zombie*
US 1943 68m bw
RKO (*Val Lewton*)

A nurse is retained by a Caribbean planter to care for his voodoo-sick wife.
Mild horror from the famous Lewton package; some style, but generally thin stuff, the plot having been mirthfully borrowed from *Jane Eyre.*

w Curt Siodmak, Ardel Wray *d Jacques Tourneur ph* J. Roy Hunt *m* Roy Webb

Frances Dee, James Ellison, Tom Conway, Christine Gordon, Edith Barrett, James Bell, Sir Lancelot

I Want a Divorce
US 1940 74m bw
Paramount

A young law student marries rashly, but is prevented from doing anything about it by examples of the unhappiness brought by divorce.
Peculiar comedy-drama which never seems to make up its mind to any particular course.

w Frank Butler, *story* Adela Rogers St John *d* Ralph Murphy

Dick Powell, Joan Blondell, Frank Fay, Gloria Dickson, Jessie Ralph, Conrad Nagel, Harry Davenport, Sidney Blackmer, Louise Beavers

I Want to Live*
US 1958 120m bw
(UA) Walter Wanger

A vagrant prostitute is executed in the gas chamber despite growing doubt as to her guilt.
Sober, harrowing treatment of the Barbara Graham case, uneasily adapted to provide a star role amid the tirade against capital punishment.

w Nelson Gidding, Don Mankiewicz *d* Robert Wise *ph* Lionel Lindon *m* John Mandel

Susan Hayward, Simon Oakland, Virginia Vincent, Theodore Bikel, Wesley Lau, Philip Coolidge

'An inconclusive amalgam of variously unexplored themes.'—*Peter John Dyer*

I Want What I Want
GB 1971 105m Eastmancolor
Marayan (Raymond Stross)

Roy has a sex change operation and becomes Wendy.
Although based on an actual trans-sexual experience, this film confuses more than it informs, and provokes unintentional mirth when its glamorous star is playing a boy.

w Gillian Freeman, *novel* Geoff Brown *d* John Dexter *ph* Gerry Turpin *m* Johnny Harris

Anne Heywood, Paul Rogers, Harry Andrews, Jill Bennett

I Want You
US 1951 101m bw
Samuel Goldwyn

A family reacts to the Korean war.
Glossy small-town flagwaver; no *Best Years of Our Lives.*

w Irwin Shaw *d* Mark Robson *ph* Harry Stradling *m* Leigh Harline *ad Richard Day*

Dorothy McGuire, Dana Andrews, Farley Granger, Peggy Dow, Robert Keith, Ray Collins, Mildred Dunnock, Martin Milner, Jim Backus

'A recruiting picture which seems to accept a third world war almost as a present reality.'—*Penelope Houston*

I Wanted Wings*
US 1941 131m bw
Paramount (Arthur Hornblow Jnr)

The fortunes of three recruits to the American Air Force.
Cheerful, overlong recruiting poster with concessions to melodrama.

w Richard Maibaum, Beirne Lay Jnr, Sig Herzig *d* Mitchell Leisen *ph* Leo Tover, Elmer Dyer *m* Victor Young

Ray Milland, William Holden, Brian Donlevy, Wayne Morris, Veronica Lake, Constance Moore, Harry Davenport, Phil Brown

I Was a Communist for the FBI
US 1951 83m bw
Warner (Bryan Foy)

Matt Cvetic, a Pittsburgh steel worker, is actually an FBI agent working undercover to trap communists.
Crude and shoddy Red-baiting melodrama, a kind of updating of *Confessions of a Nazi Spy* but using a sadly deteriorated technique.

w Crane Wilbur, Matt Cvetic *d* Gordon Douglas *ph* Edwin DuPar

Frank Lovejoy, Dorothy Hart, Phil Carey, James Millican, Richard Webb, Paul Picerni, Konstantin Shayne

'It seems that this is a subject which

Hollywood is incapable of tackling even at its customary level of journalistic efficiency.'—*Penelope Houston*

I Was Happy Here*
GB 1965 91m bw
Partisan (Roy Millichip)
US title: *Time Lost and Time Remembered*

A girl leaves her husband in London and returns to the little Irish port of her childhood.
Nicely made, over-mannered study in nostalgia and lost illusions.

w Edna O'Brien, Desmond Davis *d Desmond Davis ph Manny Wynn m* John Addison

Sarah Miles, Cyril Cusack, Julian Glover, Sean Caffrey, Marie Kean

I Was a Male War Bride**
US 1949 105m bw
TCF (Sol C. Siegel)
GB title: *You Can't Sleep Here*

A WAC in Europe marries a French officer and can't get him home.
High-spirited farce against realistic backgrounds of war-torn Europe, which scarcely accord with Cary Grant's pretending to be a Frenchman (and later a Frenchwoman). Funny, though.

w Charles Lederer, Hagar Wilde, Leonard Spiegelgass *d Howard Hawks ph* Norbert Brodine, Osmond Borradaile *m* Lionel Newman

Cary Grant, *Ann Sheridan*, Marion Marshall, Randy Stuart

I Was Monty's Double**
GB 1958 100m bw
ABP / Maxwell Setton
US title: *Hell, Heaven and Hoboken*

To distract the Nazis in Africa, an actor is hired to pose as General Montgomery.
An amusing and intriguing first hour gives way to spy chases, but the overall provides solid entertainment.

w Bryan Forbes, book M. E. Clifton-James *d John Guillermin ph* Basil Emmott *m* John Addison

John Mills, Cecil Parker, M. E. Clifton-James, Patrick Allen, Leslie Phillips, Michael Hordern, Marius Goring

I Was a Spy**
GB 1933 89m bw
Gaumont (Michael Balcon)

In Belgium 1914, a nurse is trained as a spy.
Good standard war espionage melodrama.

w W. P. Lipscomb, Ian Hay, *book* Marthe McKenna *d* Victor Saville

Madeleine Carroll, Conrad Veidt, Herbert Marshall, Gerald du Maurier, Edmund Gwenn, Donald Calthrop, Nigel Bruce, Anthony Bushell, Martita Hunt

I Was a Teenage Werewolf
US 1957 76m bw
AIP / Sunset (Herman Cohen)

A scientist experiments on an aggressive student and turns him into a werewolf.
Hilarious farrago with a title which achieved a splendour of its own.

w Ralph Thornton *d* Gene Fowler Jnr *ph* Joseph La Shelle *m* Paul Dunlap

Michael Landon, Whit Bissell, Yvonne Leslie

I Will Fight No More Forever*
US 1975 101m colour TVM
Stan Margulies

The story of Indian chief Joseph who in 1877 led his people on a 1600 mile trek rather than live on a reservation.
Earnest historical account, a shade thin for its length.

w Jeb Rosebrook, Theodore Strauss *d* Richard Heffron

James Whitmore, Ned Romero, Sam Elliott

I Wonder Who's Kissing Her Now*
US 1947 104m Technicolor
TCF (George Jessel)

The career of nineties songwriter Joseph E. Howard.
Routine biopic, quite pleasantly handled.

w Lewis R. Foster *d* Lloyd Bacon *ph* Ernest Palmer *md* Alfred Newman *ad* Richard Day, Boris Leven *ch* Hermes Pan

Mark Stevens, June Haver, Martha Stewart, Reginald Gardiner, Lenore Aubert, William Frawley, Gene Nelson

Ice Cold in Alex**
GB 1958 132m bw
APB (W. A. Whittaker)

In 1942 Libya, the commander of a motor ambulance gets his vehicle and passengers to safety despite the hazards of minefields and a German spy.
Engrossing desert adventure with plenty of suspense sequences borrowed from *The Wages of Fear*; long, but very well presented.

w T. J. Morrison, Christopher Landon *d J. Lee-Thompson ph Gilbert Taylor m* Leighton Lucas

John Mills, Sylvia Sims, Anthony Quayle, Harry Andrews

Ice Follies of 1939
US 1939 82m bw (Technicolor sequence)
MGM (Harry Rapf)

A Hollywood star goes east to help her old ice-skating friends put on a show.
The downright peculiar sight of these particular stars on ice is backed by good turns and practically no story.

w Florence Ryerson, Edgar Allan Woolf *d* Reinhold Schunzel *ph* Joseph Ruttenberg, Oliver T. Marsh *m* Roger Edens

Joan Crawford, James Stewart, Lew Ayres, Lewis Stone, Lionel Stander, Bess Ehrhardt, Charles D. Brown, the International Ice Follies

Ice Palace
US 1960 143m Warnercolor Cinemascope
Warner (Henry Blanke)

After World War I, two men set up a fishery business in Alaska, and their subsequent lives are tied up with the political development of the state.
Tedious saga from a bestseller, with entertaining incidents but no real grip.

w Harry Kleiner, *novel* Edna Ferber *d* Vincent Sherman *ph* Joseph Biroc *m* Max Steiner *ad* Malcolm Bert

Richard Burton, Robert Ryan, Martha Hyer, Carolyn Jones, Jim Backus, Ray Danton, Diane McBain, Karl Swenson

Ice Station Zebra
US 1968 148m Metrocolor Super Panavision
MGM / Filmways (James C. Pratt)

Russian and American agents speed towards the North Pole to recover a lost capsule containing vital military information.
Talky and unconvincingly staged spy adventure with a disappointing lack of action and a great many cold war platitudes.

w Douglas Heyes, Harry Julian Fink, *novel* Alistair MacLean *d* John Sturges *ph* Daniel L. Fapp *m* Michel Legrand

Rock Hudson, Patrick McGoohan, Ernest Borgnine, Jim Brown, Tony Bill, Lloyd Nolan, Gerald S. O'Loughlin, Alf Kjellin

'It's terrible in such a familiar way that at some level it's pleasant. We learn to settle for so little, we moviegoers.'—*Pauline Kael*

Ichabod and Mr Toad**
US 1950 68m Technicolor
Walt Disney

Cartoon versions of stories by Washington Irving and Kenneth Grahame.
An uncomfortable double bill; the story of Ichabod, though well narrated by Basil Rathbone, is macabre without being very interesting; *The Wind in the Willows*, however, is charmingly pictured, and Mr Toad is splendidly voiced by Eric Blore.

d Jack Kinney, Clyde Geronimi, James Algar *supervisor* Ben Sharpsteen

I'd Climb the Highest Mountain*
US 1951 88m Technicolor
TCF (Lamar Trotti)

A Methodist preacher and his wife face the problems of life in a remote part of North Georgia.
Pleasant, rambling, adequately serious and old-fashioned family entertainment, well presented in Hollywood's medium style.

w Lamar Trotti, *novel* Corra Harris *d Henry King* *ph* Edward Cronjager *m* Lionel Newman

Susan Hayward, William Lundigan, Rory Calhoun, Barbara Bates, Gene Lockhart, Lynn Bari, Ruth Donnelly, Alexander Knox

I'd Rather Be Rich*
US 1964 96m Eastmancolor
U–I / Ross Hunter

To comfort her dying grandfather, an heiress introduces an eligible stranger as her fiancé . . . but the old man recovers and begins matchmaking.
Reasonably zesty remake of *It Started with Eve*, kept afloat by Chevalier's performance.

w Oscar Brodney, Leo Townsend, Norman Krasna *d* Jack Smight *ph* Russell Metty *m* Percy Faith

Maurice Chevalier, Sandra Dee, Robert Goulet, Andy Williams, Gene Raymond, Hermione Gingold, Charles Ruggles

An Ideal Husband*
GB 1947 96m Technicolor
British Lion / London Films (Alexander Korda)

In the nineties, the career of a London diplomat is threatened by the reappearance of an old flame.
A slight, stiff play is swamped by the cast, the decor, and very garish colour, but there are moments of enjoyment along the way.

w Lajos Biro, *play* Oscar Wilde *d* Alexander Korda *ph* Georges Périnal *m* Arthur Benjamin *ad Vincent Korda* *cost Cecil Beaton*

Paulette Goddard, Hugh Williams, Michael Wilding, Diana Wynyard, *C. Aubrey Smith, Constance Collier*, Glynis Johns, Christine Norden

'The composing and cutting of this fine raw material is seldom above medium grade.'—*James Agee*

Idiot's Delight*
US 1939 105m bw
MGM (Hunt Stromberg)

At the outbreak of World War II, in a hotel on the Swiss border, a hoofer with an all-girl troupe meets an old flame masquerading as a Russian countess.
Interesting but quite unsuccessful film version of a highly artificial play which had been carried off superbly by the Lunts but was now somewhat less well cast, though it did represent an early Hollywood challenge to Hitler. The flagwaving in fact made it more than a little boring.

w Robert E. Sherwood, from his play *d* Clarence Brown *ph* William Daniels

Clark Gable, Norma Shearer, Edward Arnold, Charles Coburn, Burgess Meredith, Joseph Schildkraut, Laura Hope Crews, Skeets Gallagher, Pat Patterson, Fritz Feld

'The fun and excitement are still there, however filtered it may be.'—*Film Daily*

The Idol
GB 1966 111m bw
Embassy (Leonard Lightstone)

A divorced woman falls in love with her son's friend.
Stupefyingly boring generation-gap sex drama.

w Millard Lampell *d* Daniel Petrie *ph* Ken Higgins *m* Johnny Dankworth

Jennifer Jones, Michael Parks, John Leyton, Jennifer Hilary, Guy Doleman, Natasha Pyne

. . . If***
GB 1968 111m Eastmancolor
Paramount / Memorial (Lindsay Anderson, Michael Medwin)

Discontent at a boys' public school breaks out into rebellion.
Allegorical treatment of school life with much fashionable emphasis on obscure narrative, clever cutting, variety of pace, even an unaccountable changing from colour to monochrome and vice versa. Intelligence is clearly at work, but it seems to have suffered from undigested gobs of Pinter, and the film as a whole makes no discernible point.

w David Sherwin d Lindsay Anderson
ph Miroslav Ondricek *m* Marc Wilkinson
pd Jocelyn Herbert

Malcolm McDowell, David Wood, Richard Warwick, Robert Swann, Christine Noonan, Peter Jeffrey, Arthur Lowe, Anthony Nicholls

'The school . . . is the perfect metaphor for the established system all but a few of us continue to accept.'—*David Wilson*

'It's something like the Writing on the Wall.'—*Lindsay Anderson*

'Combines a cold and queasy view of youth with a romantic view of violence.'—*New Yorker*

If I Had a Million**
US 1932 88m bw
Paramount

Various people each receive a million dollars from an eccentric who wants to test their reactions.
Interesting, dated multi-part comedy drama remembered chiefly for the brief sequence in which Laughton blows a raspberry to his boss and Fields chases road hogs. As an entertainment it's patchy, lacking an overall style.

w Claude Binyon, Whitney Bolton, Malcolm Stuart Boylan, John Bright, Sidney Buchman, Lester Cole, Isabel Dawn, Boyce De Gaw, Walter de Leon, Oliver H. P. Garrett, Harvey Gates, Grover Jones, Ernst Lubitsch, Lawton Mackaill, Joseph L. Mankiewicz, William Slavens McNutt, Seton I. Miller, Tiffany Thayer, *story* Robert D. Andrews *d* Ernst Lubitsch, Norman Taurog, Stephen Roberts, Norman Z. McLeod, James Cruze, William A. Seiter, H. Bruce Humberstone

W. C. Fields, *Charles Laughton, May Robson*, Richard Bennett, Alison Skipworth, Gary Cooper, Wynne Gibson, George Raft, Jack Oakie, Frances Dee, Charles Ruggles, Mary Boland, Roscoe Karns, Gene Raymond, Lucien Littlefield

If I Were King*
US 1938 101m bw
Paramount

The 14th-century poet and rascal François Villon matches wits with Louis XI and leads an uprising of the people.
A story which we have grown used to seeing with music as *The Vagabond King* is here well presented but somehow rings hollow, with insufficient derring-do; it is the wrong kind of swashbuckling for its star, who is for once outacted by Rathbone in an unusual wily characterization.

w Preston Sturges *d* Frank Lloyd *m* Richard Hageman

Ronald Colman, *Basil Rathbone*, Frances Dee,

Ellen Drew, C. V. France, Heather Thatcher, Henry Wilcoxon, Sidney Toler

If It's Tuesday, This Must Be Belgium**
US 1969 98m De Luxe
UA / Wolper (Stan Margulies)

A group of American tourists have various adventures during a lightning tour of Europe.
Amusing comedy which does pretty well by a good idea.

w David Shaw *d* Mel Stuart *ph* Vilis Lapenieks *m* Walter Scharf

Suzanne Pleshette, Ian McShane, Mildred Natwick, Murray Hamilton, Michael Constantine, Sandy Baron, Norman Fell, Peggy Cass, Marty Ingels, Pamela Britton, Luke Halpin, Aubrey Morris

If Tomorrow Comes
US 1971 74m colour TVM
Aaron Spelling (Richard Newton)

Before Pearl Harbor, an American girl marries a Japanese . . .
Predictable tearjerker.

w Lew Hunter *d* George McCowan

Patty Duke, Frank Liu, James Whitmore, Anne Baxter, Pat Hingle

If Winter Comes
US 1948 97m bw
MGM (Victor Saville)

A sentimental idealist, unhappily married, finds himself at the mercy of village gossip when he takes in a pregnant girl.
Artificial romantic nonsense, unconvincingly staged and modernized from a very dated bestseller.

w Marguerite Roberts, Arthur Wimperis, *novel* A. S. M. Hutchinson *d* Victor Saville *ph* George Folsey *m* Herbert Stothart

Walter Pidgeon, Deborah Kerr, Janet Leigh, Angela Lansbury, Binnie Barnes, Dame May Whitty, Reginald Owen

If You Knew Susie*
US 1948 90m bw
RKO

A vaudeville couple retire to his ancestral home in New England.
Mild family comedy capitalizing on the team established in *Show Business.*

w Warren Wilson, Oscar Brodney *d* Gordon Douglas *ph* Frank Redman

Eddie Cantor, Joan Davis, Allyn Joslyn, Bobby Driscoll, Charles Dingle

I'll Be Seeing You**
US 1944 85m bw
David O. Selznick (Dore Schary)

A lady convict at home on parole for Christmas meets and falls for a shell-shocked soldier.
Schmaltzy, middle-American romantic drama with some nicely handled moments and plenty of talent on hand. In the Hollywood mainstream.

w Marion Parsonnet, *novel* Charles Martin *d William Dieterle ph Tony Gaudio m* Daniele Amfitheatrof

Ginger Rogers, Joseph Cotten, Shirley Temple, Spring Byington, Tom Tully, Chill Wills

I'll Cry Tomorrow*
US 1955 119m bw
MGM (Lawrence Weingarten)

Lillian Roth, a Broadway/Hollywood star of the early thirties, becomes an alcoholic.
Fictionalized biopic, pretty well done of the True Confessions kind.

w Helen Deutsch, Jay Richard Kennedy, *book* Lillian Roth, Gerold Frank *d* Daniel Mann *d* Arthur E. Arling *m* Alex North

Susan Hayward, Richard Conte, Eddie Albert, Jo Van Fleet, Don Taylor, Ray Danton, Margo

I'll Never Forget Whatshisname*
GB 1967 96m Technicolor
Universal / Scimitar (Michael Winner)

An advertising executive gives up power and money for integrity on a small literary magazine, but is won back by a mogul.
Vivid yet muddled tragi-comedy of the sixties, with splashes of sex and violence in trendy settings, a hero one really doesn't believe in, and a title which seems to have no meaning whatsoever.

w Peter Draper *d Michael Winner ph* Otto Heller *m* Francis Lai

Oliver Reed, Orson Welles, Carol White, Harry Andrews, Michael Hordern, Wendy Craig, Marianne Faithfull

I'll See You in My Dreams*
US 1952 112m bw
Warner (Louis F. Edelman)

The domestic and professional life of songwriter Gus Kahn.
Quiet-toned, well made, quite forgettable musical.

w Melville Shavelson, Jack Rose *d* Michael Curtiz *ph* Ted McCord *md* Ray Heindorf *ch* Le Roy Prinz

Doris Day, Danny Thomas, Frank Lovejoy, Patrice Wymore, James Gleason

I'll Take Sweden
US 1965 96m Technicolor
UA / Edward Small

A widowed oil company executive accepts a Stockholm posting to remove his teenage daughter from an unsuitable attachment.
Feeble comedy which unwisely attempts to be with it, but is bogged down by amateurish handling and wit-wise is sadly without it.

w Nat Perrin, Bob Fisher, Arthur Marx *d* Frederick de Cordova *ph* Daniel L. Fapp *m* Jimmy Haskell

Bob Hope, Tuesday Weld, Frankie Avalon, Dina Merrill, Jeremy Slate, John Qualen, Walter Sande

Illegal*
US 1955 88m bw
Warner (Frank P. Rosenberg)

A disillusioned District Attorney becomes a racketeer's lawyer but finally denounces him at the cost of his own life.
Competent remake of *The Mouthpiece* (qv), a good star melodrama.

w W. R. Burnett, James R. Webb, *story* Frank J. Collins *d* Lewis Allen *ph* Peverell Marley *m* Max Steiner

Edward G. Robinson, Nina Foch, Albert Dekker, Hugh Marlowe, Jayne Mansfield, Howard St John, Ellen Corby

'Hard-hitting stuff in the old gangster tradition.'—*MFB*

Ill Met by Moonlight
GB 1956 104m bw Vistavision
Rank / Vega (Michael Powell, Emeric Pressburger)
US title: *Night Ambush*

In Crete during the German occupation, British agents work with partisans to capture a German general.
Disappointingly dreary war adventure with too many night locations, too little suspense and characterization, and photography which seems to be deliberately unattractive.

wd Michael Powell, Emeric Pressburger, *book* W. Stanley Moss *ph* Christopher Challis *m* Mikis Theodorakis

Dirk Bogarde, Marius Goring, David Oxley, Cyril Cusack, John Cairney, Laurence Payne, Wolfe Morris, Michael Gough

The Illustrated Man*
US 1969 103m Technicolor Panavision
Warner / SKM (Howard B. Kreitsek, Ted Mann)

A strange wanderer tells weird stories based on the tattooed pictures which cover him from tip to toe.
Oddball compendium based rather insecurely on Ray Bradbury stories; in this form they don't amount to much but the presentation is assured.

w Howard B. Kreitsek *d* Jack Smight *ph* Philip Lathrop *m* Jerry Goldsmith *ad* Joel Schiller

Rod Steiger, Claire Bloom, Robert Drivas, Don Dubbins, Jason Evers

'A curiously passionless affair – efficient enough, meaty enough, but without poetry, without charm, without beauty.'—*Philip Strick*

'A pretentious comic strip of maudlin and muddled fantasies.'—*Judith Crist*

I'm All Right Jack***
GB 1960 104m bw
British Lion / Charter (Roy Boulting)

A world-innocent graduate takes a job in industry; by starting at the bottom he provokes a national strike.
Satirical farce which manages to hit most of its widespread targets and finds corruption in high, low and middle places. A not inaccurate picture of aspects of British life in the fifties, and a presage of the satire boom to come with *Beyond the Fringe* and *That Was the Week That Was.*

w Frank Harvey, John Boulting, novel Private Life by *Alan Hackney* *d* John Boulting *ph* Max Greene *m* Ken Hare

Ian Carmichael, Peter Sellers, Irene Handl, Richard Attenborough, *Terry-Thomas*, Dennis Price, Margaret Rutherford, Liz Fraser, *John Le Mesurier*, Sam Kydd

I'm No Angel***
US 1933 88m bw
Paramount (William Le Baron)

A carnival dancer gets off a murder charge, moves into society and sues a man for breach of promise.
The star's most successful vehicle, credited with saving the fortunes of Paramount, remains a highly diverting side show with almost a laugh a minute. Released before the Legion of Decency was formed, it also contains some of Mae's fruitiest lines.

w Mae West *d* Wesley Ruggles *ph* Leo Tover

Mae West, Edward Arnold, Cary Grant,

Gregory Ratoff, Ralf Harolde, Kent Taylor, Gertrude Michael

'The most freewheeling of all Mae's screen vehicles, and the most satisfying of the lot.'—*James Robert Parish*

Images
Eire 1972 101m Technicolor Panavision
Lions Gate / Hemdale (Tommy Thompson)

A semi-hysterical woman is confronted by the images of her former lovers.
Pretentious psycho-drama which might have made a good half-hour.

wd Robert Altman *ph* Vilmos Zsigismond *m* John Williams

Susannah York, René Auberjonois, Marcel Bozzuffi

Imitation General
US 1958 88m bw
MGM (William Hawks)

France 1944: when a general is killed, a sergeant takes his place to preserve morale.
Odd, rather unpalatable war comedy-drama.

w William Bowers *d* George Marshall *ph* George Folsey

Glenn Ford, Red Buttons, Taina Elg, Dean Jones, Kent Smith

Imitation of Life**
US 1934 109m bw
Universal

A woman becomes rich through the pancake recipe of her black servant, but the latter has a tragic life because her daughter passes for white.
Monumentally efficient tearjerker, generally well done.

w William Hurlbut, *novel* Fannie Hurst *d John Stahl* *ph* Merritt Gerstad *m* Heinz Roemheld

Claudette Colbert, Warren William, *Louise Beavers*, Ned Sparks, Rochelle Hudson, Fredi Washington, Alan Hale, Henry Armetta

Imitation of Life*
US 1959 124m Eastmancolor
U-I (Ross Hunter)

Glossy remake of the above with its heroine now an actress; stunningly produced but dully acted, making its racially sensitive plot seem insincere.

w Eleanore Griffin, Allan Scott *d Douglas Sirk* *ph* Russell Metty *m* Frank Skinner

Lana Turner, Juanita Moore, John Gavin, Susan Kohner, Dan O'Herlihy, Sandra Dee, Robert Alda

The Immortal*
US 1969 74m colour TVM
Paramount (Lou Morheim)

Our hero has a rare blood type which gives immunity not only to disease but to ageing . . . Superman rides again. Some fun, but the subsequent series was shortlived.

w Robert Specht *d* Joseph Sargent

Chris George, Barry Sullivan, Jessica Walter, Ralph Bellamy, Carol Lynley

The Immortal Sergeant*
US 1943 90m bw
TCF (Lamar Trotti)

In the North African campaign, a battle-toughened sergeant is killed after inspiring the raw recruits under his command.
'Inspirational' war adventure, quite neatly done but a shade embarrassed by its own poetic leanings.

w Lamar Trotti, *novel* John Brophy *d* John Stahl *ph* Arthur Miller *m* David Buttolph

Henry Fonda, Thomas Mitchell, Maureen O'Hara, Allyn Joslyn, Reginald Gardiner, Melville Cooper, Branwell Fletcher, Morton Lowry

The Impatient Heart
US 1971 95m colour TVM
Universal (William Sackheim)

A lady social worker tries to turn every relationship into a case.
Romantic comedy-drama: strictly for ladies.

w Alvin Sargent *d* John Badham

Carrie Snodgress, Michael Brandon, Michael Constantine, Marian Hailey

The Impatient Years
US 1944 91m bw
Columbia

A soldier finds difficulty in adjusting to his civilian matrimonial state.
Thin star comedy.

w Virginia Van Upp *d* Irving Cummings *ph* Joseph Walker *m* Marlin Skiles

Jean Arthur, Lee Bowman, Charles Coburn, Edgar Buchanan, Harry Davenport, Grant Mitchell, Jane Darwell

The Imperfect Lady
US 1947 97m bw
Paramount (Karl Tunberg)
GB title: *Mrs Loring's Secret*

In nineties London, an MP marries a lady with a past.

Dusty melodrama, adequately produced.

w Karl Tunberg, *story* Ladislas Fodor *d* Lewis Allen *ph* John F. Seitz *m* Victor Young

Ray Milland, Teresa Wright, Cedric Hardwicke, Virginia Field, Anthony Quinn, Reginald Owen, Melville Cooper, George Zucco, Rhys Williams, Charles Coleman, Miles Mander, Edmund Breon, Frederick Worlock

The Impersonator*
GB 1961 64m bw
Bryanston / Herald (Anthony Perry)

Americans at a British air base are suspected when a murderous prowler strikes.
Well made second-feature thriller with effective locations, suspense sequences and village atmosphere.

wd Alfred Shaughnessy ph John Coquillon *m* de Wolfe

John Crawford, Jane Griffith, Patricia Burke, John Salew

The Importance of Being Earnest**
GB 1952 95m Technicolor
Rank / Javelin / Two Cities (Teddy Baird)

Two wealthy and eligible bachelors of the nineties have problems with their marriage prospects.
Disappointingly stagey rendering (when compared, say, with *Occupe-toi d'Amélie*) of Britain's most wondrously witty lighter-than-air comedy of manners. As a record of a theatrical performance, however, it is valuable.

w Anthony Asquith, *play* Oscar Wilde *d* Anthony Asquith *ph* Desmond Dickinson *m* Benjamin Frankel *ad Carmen Dillon*

Michael Redgrave, Michael Denison, Edith Evans, Margaret Rutherford, Joan Greenwood, Miles Malleson, Dorothy Tutin, Walter Hudd

'A more positive decision on style should have been taken. A film of this kind must be either an adaptation or a piece of filmed theatre. This one, being partially both, is not wholly either.'—*Gavin Lambert*

The Impossible Years
US 1968 98m Metrocolor Panavision
MGM / Marten (Lawrence Weingarten)

A university psychiatrist has trouble controlling his nubile 17-year-old daughter.
Wacky farce which veers between the tasteless and the ludicrous, and is never more than momentarily entertaining.

w George Wells, *play* Bob Fisher, Arthur Marx *d* Michael Gordon *ph* William H. Daniels *m* Don Costa

David Niven, Lola Albright, Chad Everett, Ozzie Nelson, Cristina Ferrare, Don Beddoe

The Imposter
US 1974 75m colour TVM
Warner

An actor hires himself out to the security force as an impersonator of famous people.
Tiresome idea, tiresome pilot; no series ensued.

w John Sevorg, Ken August *d* Edward Abrams

Paul Hecht, Nancy Kelly, Ed Asner, Meredith Baxter, John Vernon

In a Lonely Place*
US 1950 93m bw
Columbia / Santana (Robert Lord)

An embittered Hollywood scriptwriter escapes a murder charge but loses his girl friend through his violent temperament.
Curious character melodrama which intrigues without satisfying.

w Andrew Solt, *novel* Dorothy B. Hughes *d* Nicholas Ray *ph* Burnett Guffey *m* George Antheil

Humphrey Bogart, Gloria Grahame, Frank Lovejoy, Carl Benton Reid, Art Smith, Jeff Donnell

'It remains better than average, but lacks the penetration which would make it really interesting.'—*Gavin Lambert*

In Broad Daylight**
US 1971 73m colour TVM
Aaron Spelling (Robert Mirisch)

A blind actor plans to kill his unfaithful wife.
Satisfyingly twisty suspenser.

w Larry Cohen *d* Robert Day

Richard Boone, Suzanne Pleshette, Stella Stevens, John Marley

In Celebration
GB 1974 131m Eastmancolor
Ely Landau / Cinevision

Three sons travel north for their miner father's fortieth wedding anniversary.
Sharply observant but fairly predictable dramatics, plainly filmed.

w David Storey, from his play *d* Lindsay Anderson *ph* Dick Bush *m* Christopher Gunning

Alan Bates, James Bolam, Brian Cox, Constance Chapman, Bill Owen

In Cold Blood*
US 1967 134m bw Panavision
Columbia / Richard Brooks

An account of a real life crime in which an entire family was brutally murdered by wandering gunmen.
Unnecessarily complicated as narrative, and uncompromisingly brutal in treatment, this well-meaning film is hard to take in many ways.

wd Richard Brooks, *book* Truman Capote *ph* Conrad Hall *m* Quincy Jones

Robert Blake, Scott Wilson, John Forsythe, Paul Stewart, Gerald S. O'Loughlin, Jeff Corey

'It marks a slight step up for its director, best remembered for reducing *Lord Jim* to pablum and *The Brothers Karamazov* to pulp.'—*John Simon*

In Enemy Country
US 1968 107m Techniscope
Universal (Harry Keller)

In 1939 Paris, the French secret service evolves an elaborate four-year undercover plan.
Standard, overlong espionage melodrama with no surprises.

w Edward Anhalt, *story* Sy Bartlett *d* Harry Keller *ph* Loyal Griggs *m* William Lava

Tony Franciosa, Anjanette Comer, Guy Stockwell, Paul Hubschmid, Tom Bell, Harry Townes, Michael Constantine, John Marley

In Harm's Way*
US 1965 167m bw Panavision
Paramount / Sigma (Otto Preminger)

The American navy retaliates after Pearl Harbor.
Odd mix of all-star action, spectacle (mostly models) and personal romances, with a few interesting scenes; shorn of colour it seems rather half-hearted.

w Wendell Mayes, *novel* James Bassett *d* Otto Preminger *ph* Loyal Griggs *m* Jerry Goldsmith *titles* Saul Bass

John Wayne, Kirk Douglas, Patricia Neal, Tom Tryon, Paula Prentiss, Brandon de Wilde, Stanley Holloway, Burgess Meredith, Henry Fonda, Dana Andrews, Franchot Tone, Jill Haworth, George Kennedy, Hugh O'Brian, Carroll O'Connor, Patrick O'Neal, Slim Pickens, Bruce Cabot, Larry Hagman, James Mitchum

'Lacks even a touch of the touch.'—*Stanley Kauffmann*

In Like Flint
US 1967 107m De Luxe Cinemascope
TCF (Saul David)

Top agent Derek Flint unmasks a subversive female spy ring which has kidnapped the President.
This sequel to *Our Man Flint* (qv) is silly rather than funny, a spy spoof which becomes irritatingly hard to take.

w Hal Fimberg *d* Gordon Douglas *ph* William Daniels *m* Jerry Goldsmith

James Coburn, Lee J. Cobb, Jean Hall, Andrew Duggan, Anna Lee

'It gently founders in yards of flat dialogue, lavishly uninteresting sets, fuzzy colour processing, and a supporting cast in which all the girls look alarmingly mass produced.'—*MFB*

In Love and War
US 1958 111m Eastmancolor Cinemascope
TCF (Jerry Wald)

Three men from different backgrounds join the US Marines and see service in the Pacific.
Self-conscious propaganda concoction of bare routine interest.

w Edward Anhalt, *novel* Anton Myrer *d* Philip Dunne *ph* Leo Tover *m* Hugo Friedhofer

Jeffrey Hunter, Robert Wagner, Bradford Dillman, Dana Wynter, Hope Lange, Sheree North, France Nuyen

In Name Only*
US 1939 94m bw
RKO (Pandro S. Berman)

A rich man falls in love but his wife refuses a divorce.The stars seem unhappy in this sombre matrimonial drama, but of its kind it's surprisingly well made.

w Richard Sherman, *novel* Memory of Love by Bessie Brewer *d John Cromwell* *ph* J. Roy Hunt *m* Roy Webb

Cary Grant, Carole Lombard, Kay Francis, Charles Coburn, Helen Vinson

'Shot with a refined taste for interior decoration . . . it is oversweetened with the material for tears.'—*Graham Greene*

In Name Only
US 1969 75m colour TVM
Columbia (E. W. Swackhamer)

Marriage brokers discover that ceremonies they performed in the past were not legal, and set out to make them so.
A well-worn theme, lamely tackled.

w Bernard Slade *d* E. W. Swackhamer

Michael Callan, Ann Prentiss, Paul Ford, Eve Arden, Elsa Lanchester, Ruth Buzzi, Chris Connelly

In Old Arizona**
US 1929 95m bw
Fox

Adventures of the Cisco Kid.
Primitive sound western, a sensation in its day but now of purely historical interest.

w Tom Batty, *stories* O. Henry *d* Raoul Walsh, Irving Cummings *ph* Arthur Edeson

Warner Baxter, Edmund Lowe, Dorothy Burgess, J. Farrell MacDonald
†See also *The Cisco Kid.*

In Old Chicago***
US 1938 115m bw
TCF (Kenneth MacGowan)

Events leading up to the great Chicago fire include a torrid romance between a gambler and a café singer.
Spectacular melodrama which with its two-million-dollar budget was a deliberate attempt to outdo *San Francisco*, and only failed because the cast was less interesting. A splendid studio super-production.

w Lamar Trotti, Sonya Levien, *novel* We the O'Learys by Niven Busch *d Henry King, ph Peverell Marley m* Louis Silvers *sp H. Bruce Humberstone, Daniel B. Clark, Fred Sersen, Louis J. Witte ad William Darling*

Tyrone Power, Alice Faye, Don Ameche, *Alice Brady,* Andy Devine, Brian Donlevy, Phyllis Brooks, Tom Brown, Sidney Blackmer, Berton Churchill, Paul Hurst, Rondo Hatton, Eddie Collins

In Our Time*
US 1944 110m bw
Warner (Jerry Wald)

Lovers try to save Poland from the Nazis.
Ambitious, would-be meaningful melodrama that doesn't quite come off.

w Ellis St Joseph, Howard Koch *d* Vincent Sherman *ph* Carl Guthrie *m* Franz Waxman

Ida Lupino, Paul Henreid, Nancy Coleman, *Nazimova*, Mary Boland, Victor Francen, Michael Chekhov

In Person
US 1935 85m bw
RKO (Pandro S. Berman)

A glamorous but exhausted film star tries to escape her public by fleeing incognito to the country.
Mild star comedy.

w Allan Scott, *novel* Samuel Hopkins Adams *d* William A. Seiter *ph* Edward Cronjager

Ginger Rogers, George Brent, Alan Mowbray, Grant Mitchell, Samuel S. Hinds, Spencer Charters

In Search of America*
US 1970 72m colour TVM
Four Star

A family sets out to see the country by van, and to make its own mind up on contemporary values.
Naïve, patchy, sometimes agreeable semi-documentary.

d Paul Bogart

Carl Betz, Vera Miles, Jeff Bridges, Ruth McDevitt, Howard Duff, Kim Hunter, Sal Mineo

In Search of Gregory
GB 1969 90m Technicolor
Universal / Vic Films / Vera Films (Joe Janni, Daniele Senatore)

A girl attends her father's wedding to meet a mysterious guest named Gregory, whom she never quite contacts.
Irritatingly pretentious Pinterish puzzle-drama with apparently no hidden depths except the urge to be clever.

w Tonino Guerra, Lucile Laks *d* Peter Wood *ph* Otto Heller, Giorgio Tonti *m* Ron Grainer

Julie Christie, Michael Sarrazin, John Hurt, Adolfo Celi, Roland Culver, Tony Selby
'Moments in a vacuum: however lively the surface, the centre remains depressingly inert.'—*MFB*

In Search of the Castaways***
GB 1961 100m Technicolor
Walt Disney (Hugh Attwooll)

With the aid of an eccentric professor, three children seek their lost explorer father in some geographically fantastic regions of South America.
Engaging Victorian fantasy which starts realistically but builds up to sequences in the manner of *The Wizard of Oz* and concludes in *Treasure Island* vein. Jaunty juvenile fare.

w Lowell S. Hawley, *novel* Captain Grant's Children by Jules Verne *d* Robert Stevenson *ph* Paul Beeson *m* William Alwyn *ad* Michael Stringer

Maurice Chevalier, Hayley Mills, George Sanders, Wilfrid Hyde White, *Wilfrid Brambell*

In Society*
US 1944 74m bw
U-I

Two incompetent plumbers ruin a mansion.
One of the better A & C romps, with little padding between the comedy highlights, though the trimmings are fearsomely dated.

w John Grant, Hal Finberg, Edmund L. Hartmann *d* Jean Yarbrough *ph* Jerome Ash *m* Edgar Fairchild

Bud Abbott, Lou Costello, Kirby Grant, Ann Gillis, Arthur Treacher, Steve Geray, George Dolenz, Marion Hutton

In Tandem**
US 1974 74m colour TVM
Metromedia / D'Antoni-Weiss
aka: *Movin' On*

A pair of truckers help an orange farmer save his land.
Tense, well-characterized pilot with reminiscences of *Thieves' Highway* and *The Wages of Fear*; the resultant series ran two seasons, under the title *Movin' On.*

w Bob Collins, Herb Meadow *d* Bernard Kowalski

Claude Akins, Frank Converse, Richard Angarola, Ann Coleman

In the Cool of the Day
US 1962 91m Metrocolor Panavision
MGM (John Houseman)

The frail wife of a New York publisher dies in Greece after an affair with his colleague.
Travelogue with romantic asides; a pretty glum business.

w Meade Roberts, *novel* Susan Ertz *d* Robert Stevens *ph* Peter Newbrook *m* Francis Chagrin *ad* Ken Adam

Jane Fonda, Peter Finch, Arthur Hill, Angela Lansbury, Constance Cummings

In the French Style*
US / France 1962 105m bw
Columbia / Casanna / Orsay (Robert Parrish, Irwin Shaw)

An American girl in Paris has affairs with a young boy and with a divorced newspaperman.
Smooth, episodic, romantic character study, well made but with no perceptible dramatic point.

w Irwin Shaw *d* Robert Parrish *ph Michel Kelber* *m* Josef Kosma

Jean Seberg, Stanley Baker, Philippe Fouquet

In the Good Old Summertime*
US 1949 102m Technicolor
MGM (Joe Pasternak)

In a Chicago music store in 1906, a salesgirl corresponds through a dating service with a man who turns out to be the manager she detests.
Cheerful remake of *The Shop around the Corner* (qv), with agreeable music, garish colour and not much style.

w Albert Hackett, Frances Goodrich, Ivan Tors, *play* Miklos Laszlo *d* Robert Z. Leonard *ph* Harry Stradling *md* George Stoll *ad* Randell Duell *ch* Robert Alton

Judy Garland, Van Johnson, S. Z. Sakall, Spring Byington, Clinton Sundberg, Buster Keaton, Lilian Bronson

In the Heat of the Night**
US 1969 109m De Luxe
UA / Mirisch (Walter Mirisch)

In a small southern town, the bigoted and bombastic sheriff on a murder hunt grudgingly accepts the help of a black detective.
Overrated policier in which the personality clash is amusing (and was timely) but the murder puzzle is a complete throwaway.

w Sterling Silliphant *d Norman Jewison* *ph Haskell Wexler* *m* Quincy Jones

Sidney Poitier, Rod Steiger, Warren Oates, Quentin Dean, William Schallert

† Poitier subsequently starred in a couple of very inferior sequels, *They Call Me Mister Tibbs* and *The Organization* (both qv).

In This House of Brede*
GB 1975 105m colour TVM
Tomorrow

A widowed businesswoman becomes a nun.
Sincere, simplified Nun's Story: Good watching.

w James Costigan, *novel* Rumer Godden *d* George Schaefer

Diana Rigg, Judi Bowker, Pamela Brown, Gwen Watford

In This Our Life**
US 1942 101m bw
Warner (David Lewis)

A neurotic girl steals her sister's husband, leaves him in the lurch, dominates her hapless family and is killed while on the run from the police.
Splendid star melodrama with good supporting acting and background detail.

w Howard Koch, novel Ellen Glasgow *d John Huston* *ph* Ernest Haller *m* Max Steiner

Bette Davis, Charles Coburn, Olivia de Havilland, Frank Craven, George Brent, Dennis

Morgan, Billie Burke, Hattie McDaniel, Lee Patrick, Walter Huston (uncredited)

In Which We Serve****
GB 1942 114m bw
Rank / Two Cities (Noel Coward)

Survivors from a torpedoed destroyer recall their life at sea and on leave.
Dated but splendid flagwaver; an archetypal British war film of almost limitless propaganda value.

w Noel Coward d Noel Coward, David Lean
m Noel Coward

Noel Coward, Bernard Miles, *John Mills*, Richard Attenborough, *Celia Johnson*, Kay Walsh, Joyce Carey, Michael Wilding, Penelope Dudley Ward, Kathleen Harrison, Philip Friend, George Carney, Geoffrey Hibbert, James Donald

'One of the screen's proudest achievements at any time and in any country.'—*Newsweek*

Inadmissible Evidence**
GB 1968 96m bw
Paramount / Woodfall (Ronald Kinnoch)

A frustrated 40-year-old solicitor is on the verge of a nervous breakdown.
Interesting and surprisingly successful transcription of a difficult play which was virtually an anti-humanity soliloquy.

w John Osborne, from his play *d Anthony Page*
ph Kenneth Hodges *m* Dudley Moore
ad Seamus Flannery

Nicol Williamson, Eleanor Fazan, Jill Bennett, Peter Sallis, Eileen Atkins, Isobel Dean

'A play that was conceived as an increasingly bad dream has been made into a grittily detailed, naturalistic film.'—*Stanley Kauffmann*

Incendiary Blonde*
US 1945 112m Technicolor
Paramount (Joseph Sistrom)

The life of twenties nightclub queen Texas Guinan.
Laundered biopic with guns, girls and gangsters as well as songs.

w Claude Binyon, Frank Butler *d* George Marshall *ph Ray Rennahan m* Robert Emmett Dolan

Betty Hutton, Arturo de Cordova, Charles Ruggles, Albert Dekker, Barry Fitzgerald, Mary Phillips, Bill Goodwin, Eduardo Ciannelli, Maurice Rocco

Incident in San Francisco
US 1970 98m colour TVM
Quinn Martin

A man tries to help in a street brawl and finds himself accused of murder: he is saved by a crusading journalist.
Efficient but rather tedious melodrama.

w Robert Dozier, *novel* Incident at 125th Street by J. E. Brown *d* Don Medford

Richard Kiley, Chris Connelly, Dean Jagger, Leslie Nielsen, Phyllis Thaxter, Ruth Roman, John Marley

Incident on a Dark Street
US 1972 98m colour TVM
TCF

The US attorney's office makes a stab at organized crime.
Routine crime-fighting melodrama.

w David Gerber *d* Buzz Kulik

James Olson, Richard Castellano, William Shatner, David Canary, Gilbert Roland

The Incredible Journey**
US 1963 80m Technicolor
Walt Disney (James Algar)

Two dogs and a cat, separated from their owners, escape and travel 250 miles home.
A novelty attraction which keeps going purely on its animal interest, which is considerable.

w James Algar, *book* Sheila Burnford *d* Fletcher Markle *ph* Kenneth Peach, Jack Couffer, Lloyd Beebe *m* Oliver Wallace

The Incredible Mr Limpet
US 1964 102m Technicolor
Warner (John C. Rose)

A meek but patriotic clerk is turned down by the navy and turns into a fish. In this form he becomes a radar assistant to a warship.
Sentimental sub-Disney Goo, part animated.

w Jameson Bewer, John C. Rose, *novel* Theodore Pratt *d* Arthur Lubin *ph* Harold Stine *m* Frank Perkins

Don Knotts, Andrw Duggan, Larry Keating, Jack Weston

The Incredible Sarah*
GB 1976 105m Technicolor
Readers Digest (Helen M. Strauss)

The career of French actress Sarah Bernhardt up to the age of thirty-five.
Mildly pleasing old-fashioned biopic with remarkably unreliable detail and a regrettably bland approach to its fascinating subject.

w Ruth Wolff d Richard Fleischer
ph Christopher Challis *m* Elmer Bernstein
pd Elliot Scott

Glenda Jackson, Daniel Massey, Yvonne Mitchell, Douglas Wilmer, David Langton, Simon Williams, John Castle, Edward Judd, Peter Sallis

The Incredible Shrinking Man**
US 1957 81m bw
U-I (Albert Zugsmith)

After being caught in a radioactive mist, a man shrinks inexorably to micro-size.
Horrifyingly inevitable sci-fi with imaginative touches gracing a cheap production.

w Richard Matheson d Jack Arnold *ph* Ellis W. Carter *m* Joseph Gershenson *sp Clifford Stine, Roswell A. Hoffman, Everett H. Bronssard*

Grant Williams, Randy Stuart, April Kent, Paul Langton

'It opens up new vistas of cosmic terror.'—*Peter John Dyer*

The Indian Fighter
US 1955 88m Technicolor Cinemascope
UA / Bryna (William Schorr)

An Indian fighter protects a wagon train from the Sioux.
Simple-minded western with touches of philosophy and not much drive.

w Frank Davis, Ben Hecht *d* André de Toth
ph Wilfrid M. Cline *m* Franz Waxman

Kirk Douglas, Elsa Martinelli, Walter Abel, Walter Matthau, Diana Douglas, Eduard Franz, Lon Chaney Jnr, Alan Hale Jnr, Elisha Cook Jnr

Indict and Convict*
US 1974 100m Technicolor TVM
Universal (David Victor)

The attorney-general's office investigates a murder which may have been committed by a public official.
Reasonably absorbing courtroom drama with attention to detail.

w Winston Miller *d* Boris Sagal

George Grizzard, Reni Santoni, William Shatner, Susan Howard, Eli Wallach, Myrna Loy, Harry Guardino

Indiscreet**
GB 1958 100m Technicolor
Grandon (Stanley Donen)

An American diplomat in London falls in love with an actress but protects himself by saying he is married.
Affairs among the ultra rich, amusing when played by these stars but with imperfect production values which the alarmingly thin plot allows one too much time to consider.

w Norman Krasna, from his play Kind Sir
d Stanley Donen *ph* Frederick A. Young
m Richard Bennett, Ken Jones

Cary Grant, Ingrid Bergman, Phyllis Calvert, Cecil Parker, David Kossoff, Megs Jenkins

'One is often on the point of being bored, but one never is, quite.'—*Richard Roud*

Indiscretion of an American Wife*
Italy / US 1954 75m bw
David O. Selznick (Vittorio De Sica)
Alternative titles: *Terminus Station, Indiscretion*

An American woman and an Italian professor say goodbye in Rome's terminal station.
Strained attempt to re-do *Brief Encounter* against the busy background of a great railway station; moments of interest, but artificiality prevails, and the plot never gets up enough steam.

w Cesare Zavattini, Truman Capote, etc
d Vittorio De Sica *ph* G. R. Aldo *m* Aldo Cicognini

Jennifer Jones, Montgomery Clift, Gino Cervi, Richard Beymer

Inferno**
US 1953 83m Technicolor 3-D
TCF (William Bloom)

When a millionaire breaks his leg in the desert, his wife and her lover leave him to die; but he contrives to catch up with them.
An outdoor melodrama which made better use of 3-D than any other film, suggesting the lone handicapped figure in the vast spaces; but the lovers are dull and the fire climax perfunctory.

w Francis Cockrell *d* Roy Baker *ph Lucien Andriot m* Paul Sawtell

Robert Ryan, William Lundigan, Rhonda Fleming

The Informer****
US 1935 91m bw
RKO (Cliff Reid)

An IRA leader is betrayed by a simple-minded hanger-on who wants money to emigrate; he is hounded by fellow rebels and his own conscience.
A tedious plot is turned into brilliant cinema by full-blooded acting and a highly stylized yet brilliantly effective *mise en scène* which never attempts reality.

w Dudley Nichols, *novel* Liam O'Flaherty

d John Ford ph Joseph H. August m Max Steiner ad Van Nest Polglase

Victor McLaglen, Heather Angel, Margot Grahame, Una O'Connor, Wallace Ford, Preston Foster, J. M. Kerrigan, Joe Sawyer, Donald Meek

'As impressive as *Scarface*, or anything in the whole powerful literature redolent of fog and grime and dreariness which the Germans gave to the Americans.'—*Bardèche and Brasillach*

The Informers
GB 1963 104m bw
Rank (William MacQuitty)
US title: *Underworld Informers*

A police informer is murdered and his brother takes revenge.
Basic police melodrama, with clumsy script and jaded direction.

w Alun Falconer, *novel* Death of a Snout by Douglas Warner *d* Ken Annakin *ph* Reg Wyer *m* Clifton Parker

Nigel Patrick, Colin Blakely, Derren Nesbitt

Inherit the Wind***
US 1960 127m bw
UA / Lomitas (Stanley Kramer)

A fictionalized account of the 1925 Scopes 'monkey trial', when a schoolmaster was accused of teaching the theory of evolution.
Splendid theatrics with fine performances, marred by boring subplots but enhanced by a realistic portrait of a sweltering southern town.

w Nathan E. Douglas, Harold Jacob Smith, *play* Jerome Lawrence, Robert E. Lee *d Stanley Kramer ph Ernest Laszlo m* Ernest Gold

Spencer Tracy, Fredric March, Florence Eldridge, Gene Kelly, Dick York, Donna Anderson, Harry Morgan, Elliott Reid, Claude Akins

The Inn of the Sixth Happiness**
GB 1958 158m De Luxe Cinemascope
TCF (Mark Robson)

An English servant girl becomes a missionary and spends many arduous years in China.
Romanticized biopic of Gladys Aylward, with lots of children, a happy ending, and everyone sensationally miscast. Somehow it all works, even North Wales standing in for China.

w Isobel Lennart, *book* The Small Woman by Alan Burgess *d* Mark Robson *ph* Frederick A. Young *m* Malcolm Arnold

Ingrid Bergman, Curt Jurgens, Robert Donat, Athene Seyler, Ronald Squire, Richard Wattis, Moultrie Kelsall

Inner Sanctum

The title was taken from a radio show featuring mystery stories with a last minute twist. The films were introduced rather oddly by a misshapen head in a crystal ball on the empty table of a boardroom. The head belonged to David Hoffman, and he introduced each film: 'This . . . is the inner sanctum . . .' (The original reference was presumably to the innermost working of the human mind.) The films, made for Universal, all starred Lon Chaney Jnr (who alternated as hero and villain); they were among the most boring and badly made second feature thrillers of the forties.
1943: CALLING DR DEATH
1944: WEIRD WOMAN, DEAD MAN'S EYES
1945: STRANGE CONFESSION (remake of THE MAN WHO RECLAIMED HIS HEAD), THE FROZEN GHOST
1946: PILLOW OF DEATH

Innocent Bystanders*
GB 1972 110m Eastmancolor
Sagittarius (George H. Brown)

The British secret service sends three agents to trace a Russian traitor.
Confused and violent espionage thriller; rather a waste of good production.

w James Mitchell *d* Peter Collinson *ph* Brian Probyn *m* John Keating

Stanley Baker, Geraldine Chaplin, Dana Andrews, Donald Pleasance

Innocent Sinners**
GB 1957 95m bw
Rank (Hugh Stewart)

A 13-year-old London girl builds a garden in the rubble of a bombed church, and gets into trouble with the police.
Likeable, slightly unfinished, mildly astringent little human drama full of well-observed character sketches.

w Neil Paterson, novel An Episode of Sparrows by Rumer Godden *d Philip Leacock ph* Harry Waxman *m* Philip Green

Flora Robson, Catherine Lacey, David Kossoff, Barbara Mullen, June Archer

The Innocents**
GB 1961 99m bw Cinemascope
TCF / Achilles (Jack Clayton)

In Victorian times, a spinster governess in a

lonely house finds her young charges possessed by evil demons of servants now dead.
Elaborate revamping of Henry James' *The Turn of the Screw*, the ghosts being now (possibly) the figments of a frustrated woman's imagination. The frissons would have worked better on a normal-shaped screen, but the decor, lighting and general handling are exceptional.

w William Archibald, Truman Capote *d Jack Clayton ph Freddie Francis ad Wilfrid Shingleton*

Deborah Kerr, Megs Jenkins, Pamela Franklin, Martin Stephens, Michael Redgrave, Peter Wyngarde

Innocents in Paris
GB 1953 102m bw
Romulus (Anatole de Grunwald)

British tourists spend a weekend in the gay city.
Strained compendium of anecdotes which misses an easy target.

w Anatole de Grunwald *d* Gordon Parry *ph* Gordon Lang *m* Josef Kosma

Alastair Sim, Margaret Rutherford, Jimmy Edwards, Claire Bloom, Laurence Harvey, Ronald Shiner

Innocents of Paris
US 1929 69m bw
Paramount

A Parisian junk dealer saves a boy's life and falls for his aunt.
Heavygoing and dated musical comedy which introduced Chevalier to world audiences.

w Ethel Doherty, Ernest Vajda *d* Richard Wallace *ph* Charles Lang *songs* Leo Robin, Richard A. Whiting

Maurice Chevalier, Sylvia Beecher, Russell Simpson, George Fawcett

Inserts*
GB 1975 117m De Luxe
UA / Film and General (Davina Belling, Clive Parsons)

In 1930 Hollywood, a fading silent queen and a has-been director take to drugs.
Curious, interesting semi-porno melodrama with Pinterish asides and an inaccurate but stimulating feel of the film city at its height.

wd John Byrum ph Denys Coop *md* Jessica Harper

Richard Dreyfuss, Jessica Harper, Veronica Cartwright, Bob Hoskins, Stephen Davies

Inside Daisy Clover*
US 1965 128m Technicolor Panavision
Warner / Pakula–Mulligan (Alan J. Pakula)

Tribulations of an adolescent movie star in thirties Hollywood.
Amusing, rather hysterical variant on *A Star Is Born*; agreeably wacky in spots, glum in others. Would have benefited from the greater permissiveness possible a few years later.

w Gavin Lambert, from his novel *d* Robert Mulligan *ph* Charles Lang Jnr *m* André Previn *ch* Herbert Ross *ad* Robert Clatworthy

Natalie Wood, Robert Redford, Ruth Gordon, Christopher Plummer, Roddy MacDowall

'The movie is short on characters, detail, activity, dialogue, even music; it's as if it's so determined to be stylish and sophisticated that rather than risk vulgarity or banality, it eliminates almost everything.'—*Pauline Kael, 1968*

Inside Out*
GB / West Germany 1975 97m Technicolor
Warner / Kettledrum (Judd Bernard)

A German ex-commandant of a POW camp enlists the aid of Americans in a daring plan to kidnap a Nazi war criminal from East Germany and find buried Nazi loot.
Entertaining but very silly actioner with too many changes of mood, though some sequences please.

w Judd Bernard, Stephen Schneck *d* Peter Duffell *ph* John Coquillon *m* Konrad Elfers

Telly Savalas, James Mason, Robert Culp, Aldo Ray, Gunter Meisner, Adrian Hoven, Charles Korvin, Richard Warner

The Inspector*
GB 1961 111m De Luxe Cinemascope
TCF (Mark Robson)
US title: *Lisa*

In 1946 a Dutch policeman rescues a Jewish girl from an ex-Nazi and helps smuggle her to Palestine.
Peripatetic melodrama with surface suspense and subdued thoughts of ideology and race. Moments of interest, but generally dully developed and acted.

w Nelson Gidding, *novel* Jan de Hartog *d* Philip Dunne *ph* Arthur Ibbetson *m* Malcolm Arnold

Stephen Boyd, Dolores Hart, Leo McKern, *Hugh Griffith*, Donald Pleasance, Harry Andrews, Robert Stephens, Marius Goring

'A sluggish mélange of melodrama, romance, mystery and what the inactive might call action.'—*Judith Crist*

An Inspector Calls**
GB 1954 79m bw
British Lion / Watergate

In 1912 a prosperous Yorkshire family is visited by a mysterious inspector who proves that each of them was partly responsible for the death of a young girl.
Tactful, enjoyable record of a celebrated play in its author's most typical manner.

w Desmond Davis, *play J. B. Priestley d Guy Hamilton ph Ted Scaife m* Francis Chagrin *ad* Joseph Bato

Alastair Sim, Jane Wenham, Arthur Young, Olga Lindo, Brian Worth, Eileen Moore, Bryan Forbes

Inspector Clouseau
GB 1968 105m Eastmancolor Panavision
UA / Mirisch (Lewis J. Rachmil)

An incompetent French policeman is brought to London to investigate the aftermath of the Great Train Robbery.
Tiresome charade with all the jokes well telegraphed, and a background of swinging London.

w Tom and Frank Waldman *d* Bud Yorkin *ph* Arthur Ibbetson *m* Ken Thorne

Alan Arkin, Delia Boccardo, Frank Finlay, Patrick Cargill, Beryl Reid, Barry Foster

The Inspector General**
US 1949 101m Technicolor
Warner (Jerry Wald)
aka: *Happy Times*

An assistant elixir salesman with a travelling fair is mistaken by villagers for the dreaded inspector general.
Well wrought but basically boring version of a basically boring classic farce full of rhubarbing Old Russians. Nice production and hilarious moments do not quite atone for the dull stretches.

w Philip Rapp, Harry Kurnitz, *play* Nikolai Gogol *d* Henry Koster *ph* Elwood Bredell *m/ly* Sylvia Fine *ad* Robert Haas

Danny Kaye, Walter Slezak, Barbara Bates, Elsa Lanchester, Gene Lockhart, Alan Hale, Benny Baker, Walter Catlett

Inspector Hornleigh*
GB 1939 87m bw
TCF (Robert T. Kane)

A Scotland Yard man and his lugubrious sergeant discover who stole the Chancellor of the Exchequer's bag.
Lively low-budgeter based on a radio series; the stars also made two sequels, *Inspector Hornleigh on Holiday* and *Inspector Hornleigh Goes to It.*

w Bryan Wallace, Gerald Elliott, Richard Llewellyn, character created by Hans Prewin *d* Eugene Forde

Gordon Harker, Alastair Sim, Hugh Williams, Steve Geray, Wally Patch, Edward Underdown, Ronald Adam, Gibb McLaughlin

Inspiration*
US 1931 74m bw
MGM

A Parisienne demi-mondaine walks out on her true love rather than spoil his life.
Smooth star vehicle, a woman's picture par excellence.

w Gene Markey *d* Clarence Brown *ph* William Daniels

Greta Garbo, Robert Montgomery, Lewis Stone, Marjorie Rambeau, Beryl Mercer, John Miljan, Edwin Maxwell

'Camille without the cough.'—*Motion Picture*

The Intelligence Men
GB 1965 104m Eastmancolor
Rank / Hugh Stewart
US title: *Spylarks*

Two incompetent spies blunder through a series of adventures.
Inept and rather embarrassing big-screen debut for two excellent television comedians.

w S. C. Green, R. M. Hills *d* Robert Asher *ph* Jack Asher *m* Phillip Green

Eric Morecambe, Ernie Wise, William Franklyn, April Olrich, Richard Vernon, David Lodge, Warren Mitchell, Francis Matthews

Intent to Kill*
GB 1958 89m bw Cinemascope
TCF / Zonic (Adrian Worker)

In a Montreal hospital, attempts are made on the life of a South American dictator recovering from a brain operation.
Solidly entertaining suspenser.

w Jimmy Sangster *d* Jack Cardiff *ph* Desmond Dickinson *m* Kenneth V. Jones

Richard Todd, Betsy Drake, Herbert Lom, Warren Stevens, Alexander Knox

Interlude
US 1958 89m Technicolor
Cinemascope
U-I (Ross Hunter)

An American girl in Munich falls in love with an orchestral conductor but leaves him because of his insane wife.
Dull remake of *When Tomorrow Comes* (qv), with poor script and performances.

w Daniel Fuchs, Franklin Coen *d* Douglas Sirk *ph* R. F. Schoengarth *m* Frank Skinner

Rossano Brazzi, June Allyson, Françoise Rosay, Marianne Cook, Keith Andes, Jane Wyatt
'Contains every cliché known to romantic fiction.'—*MFB*

Interlude*
GB 1968 113m Technicolor
Columbia / Domino (David Deutsch, Jack Hanbury)

A girl reporter falls for a celebrated orchestral conductor; they have an affair but he finally goes back to his wife.
Intermezzo remade for the swinging London set, quite agreeable in parts because of the acting but generally rather soggy.

w Lee Langley, Hugh Leonard *d* Kevin Billington *ph Gerry Fisher m* Georges Delerue *pd* Tony Woolard

Oskar Werner, Barbara Ferris, *Virginia Maskell, John Cleese,* Donald Sutherland, Nora Swinburne, Alan Webb
'If you laughed at *Brief Encounter* you will roar over this one.'—*Wilfrid Sheed*
'It's got all the schmaltz and none of the style of the tearjerkers of yesteryear.'—*Judith Crist, 1973*

Intermezzo***
US 1939 69m bw
David O. Selznick
GB title: *Escape to Happiness*

A renowned, married violinist has an affair with his musical protégée.
Archetypal cinema love story, Hollywoodized from a Swedish original but quite perfect in its brief, sentimental way.

w George O'Neil, *original scenario* Gosta Stevens, Gustav Molander *d Gregory Ratoff ph* Gregg Toland *m Robert Henning, Heinz Provost*

Leslie Howard, Ingrid Bergman, John Halliday, Edna Best, Cecil Kellaway

International House*
US 1932 73m bw
Paramount

A weird variety of travellers are quarantined in a Shanghai hotel where a local doctor has perfected television.
Madcap farce which succeeds in hits and misses.

w Francis Martin, Walter de Leon, Lou Heifetz, Neil Brant *d* Edward Sutherland *ph* Ernest Haller

W. C. Fields, George Burns, Gracie Allen, Peggy Hopkins Joyce, Stuart Erwin, Sari Matitza, Bela Lugosi, Edmund Breese, Lumsden Hare, Rose Marie, Rudy Vallee, Sterling Holloway, Cab Calloway and his band, Colonel Stoopnagle and Budd
'Constructed along the lines of a mammoth vaudeville show, the motivating story often is sidetracked entirely to permit a lot of unrelated hokum comedy.'—*Motion Picture Herald*

International Lady*
US 1941 102m bw
Edward Small

An FBI man falls for the lady Axis agent he is chasing.
Cliché-ridden melodrama partially saved by light comedy touches.

w Howard Estabrook *d* Tim Whelan *ph* Hal Mohr *m* Lucien Moraweck

George Brent, Basil Rathbone, Ilona Massey, Gene Lockhart, George Zucco, Francis Pierlot, Martin Kosleck, Marjorie Gateson

International Squadron*
US 1941 87m bw
Warner (Edmund Grainger)

A playboy becomes a fighting air ace.
Standard war story, quite well done; remake of *Ceiling Zero* (qv).

w Barry Trivers, *story* Frank Wead *d* Lothar Mendes *ph* Arthur Edeson

Ronald Reagan, James Stephenson, Julie Bishop, Cliff Edwards, Reginald Denny, Olympe Bradna, William Lundigan, John Ridgely

The Internecine Project*
GB 1974 89m Eastmancolor
Maclean and Co / Lion International / Hemisphere (Barry Levinson, Andrew Donally)

A Harvard professor arranges the mutual extermination of four people who could spoil a politician's presidential chances.
Coldly murderous romp with plenty of style.

w Barry Levinson, Jonathan Lynn, *novel* Mort W. Elkind *d Ken Hughes ph* Geoffrey Unsworth *m* Roy Budd

James Coburn, Lee Grant, Harry Andrews, Ian Hendry, Michael Jayston, Keenan Wynn

Internes Can't Make Money*
US 1937 75m bw
Paramount (Benjamin Glazer)
GB title: *You Can't Take Money*

A hospital doctor persuades a gangster friend to help a woman find her missing child.
Quite interesting minor melodrama, first of the Dr Kildare series which was subsequently recast and restyled by MGM.

w Rian James, Theodore Reed, *story* Max Brand *d Alfred Santell ph* Theodor Sparkuhl *m* Gregory Stone

Joel McCrea, Barbara Stanwyck, Lloyd Nolan, Stanley Ridges, Lee Bowman, Irving Bacon

The Interns*
US 1962 130m bw
Columbia / Interns Co. / Robert Cohn

In an American hospital, newly qualified doctors have personal and career problems.
Birth, abortion, sudden death, drugs and women's lib all figure in this melodramatic compendium which succeeds well enough on its own level and spawned a sequel (*The New Interns*) and an unsuccessful TV series.

w Walter Newman, David Swift, *novel* Richard Frede *d* David Swift *ph* Russell Metty *m* Leith Stevens

Cliff Robertson, Michael Callan, James MacArthur, Nick Adams, Suzy Parker, Buddy Ebsen, Telly Savalas

Interpol
GB 1957 92m bw Cinemascope
Columbia / Warwick (Irving Allen, Albert R. Broccoli)
US title: *Pickup Alley*

The US Anti-Narcotics Squad trails across Europe the insane and ruthless leader of a drug ring.
Drearily routine thick ear electrified by one performance but not helped by wide screen.

w John Paxton *d* John Gilling *ph* Ted Moore *m* Richard Bennett

Victor Mature, Anita Ekberg, *Trevor Howard,* Bonar Colleano, Marne Maitland, Eric Pohlmann, Alec Mango, Peter Illing, Sidney Tafler

The Interrupted Journey*
US 1975 100m Technicolor TVM
Universal
aka: *The UFO Incident*

A black man and his wife claim to have seen a flying saucer and to have been invited aboard.
Overlong fictionalization of an incident reported in a book by John G. Fuller: quite amusing.

d Richard A. Colla

James Earl Jones, Estelle Parsons

Interrupted Melody
US 1955 106m Eastmancolor Cinemascope
MGM (Jack Cummings)

The story of Marjorie Lawrence, an Australian opera singer who fell victim to polio.
Standard biopic which jells less well than some.

w William Ludwig, Sonya Levien *d* Curtis Bernhardt *ph* Joe Ruttenberg, Paul Vogel *music supervisor* Saul Chaplin

Eleanor Parker, Glenn Ford, Roger Moore, Cecil Kellaway, Stephen Bekassy

Intimacy*
US 1965 87m bw
Goldstone (David Heilwell)

A businessman in need of a government contract tries to compromise the official concerned.
Unusual minor melodrama, interesting but not quite successful.

w Eva Wolas *d* Victor Stoloff *ph* Ted Saizis *m* Geordie Hormel

Barry Sullivan, Nancy Malone, Jack Ging, Joan Blackman, Jackie Shannon

The Intimate Stranger*
GB 1956 95m bw
Anglo–Guild (Alec Snowden)

An American film producer in England is plagued by a strange girl who claims to have been his mistress.
Acceptable mystery thriller which holds the interest and has good detail.

w Peter Howard *d* Joseph Walton (Joseph Losey) *m* Trevor Duncan *ph* Gerald Gibbs

Richard Basehart, Mary Murphy, Mervyn Johns, Constance Cummings, Roger Livesey, Faith Brook

The Intruder*
GB 1953 84m bw
British Lion / Ivan Foxwell

An ex-army officer surprises a burglar and

recognizes his old commander who has been ill-served by society.
Watchable but rather mechanical compendium drama in which a series of cameos supposedly sum up the problems of life in post-war Britain.

w Robin Maugham, John Hunter, *novel* Line on Ginger by Robin Maugham *d* Guy Hamilton *ph* Ted Scaife *m* Francis Chagrin

Jack Hawkins, Michael Medwin, Hugh Williams, George Cole, Dennis Price, Dora Bryan

The Intruder*
US 1961 84m bw
Filmgroup (Roger Corman)
GB title: *The Stranger*

A mild-mannered stranger arrives in a southern town and stirs up racist trouble.
Cheaply-made social melodrama with many effective moments.

w Charles Beaumont, from his novel *d Roger Corman* *ph* Taylor Byars, *m* Herman Stein

William Shatner, Frank Maxwell, Beverly Lunsford, Robert Emhardt, Jeanne Cooper, Leo Gordon, Charles Beaumont

Intruder in the Dust***
US 1951 87m bw
MGM (Clarence Brown)

In a southern town, a boy and an old lady solve a mystery and prevent a black man from being lynched.
Excellent character drama which also offers vivid local colour, a murder puzzle and social comment. A semi-classic.

w Ben Maddow, novel William Faulkner *d Clarence Brown* *ph Robert Surtees* *m* Adolph Deutsch

Juano Hernandez, Elizabeth Patterson, David Brian, Claude Jarman Jnr, *Porter Hall*, Will Geer

'It is surely the years of range and experience which have given him a control of the medium so calm, sure and—apparently—easy that he can make a complex story seem simple and straightforward.'—*Pauline Kael*

'A really good movie that is also and incidentally the first honestly worked out "racial" film I have seen.'—*Richard Winnington*

The Intruders
US 1967 95m Technicolor TVM
Universal (Bert Granet)

Western townsfolk look to their reluctant marshal for defence against approaching gunmen.
High Noon style minor western: nothing surprising.

w Dean Riesner *d* William Graham

Edmond O'Brien, Don Murray, John Saxon, Anne Francis

Invaders from Mars
US 1953 82m Cinecolor
Edward L. Alperson

Martian invaders use hypnotized humans as saboteurs.
Poverty Row sci-fi partly redeemed by its erratic but talented designer who provides flashes of visual imagination.

w Richard Blake *d/pd William Cameron Menzies* *ph* John Seitz *m* Raoul Kraushaar

Helena Carter, Arthur Franz, Leif Erickson, Hillary Brooke

Invasion**
GB 1966 82m bw
AA / Merton Park (Jack Greenwood)

An English village is beset one night by invaders from outer space.
Understated, effective little suspenser, well done in all departments.

w Roger Marshall *d Alan Bridges* *ph* James Wilson *m* Bernard Ebbinghouse

Edward Judd, Valerie Gearon, Lyndon Brook, Yoko Tani, Tsai Chin, Barrie Ingham, Arthur Sharp

The Invasion of Johnson County
US 1976 98m Technicolor TVM
Universal (Roy Huggins)
aka: *Brahmin*

A Bostonian con man in Wyoming prevents a private army from routing small-time ranchers.
What begins like a promising reprise of *Maverick* turns into a very limp outdoor drama, protracted way beyond its dramatic possibilities.

w Nicholas E. Baehr *d* Jerry Jameson

Bill Bixby, Bo Hopkins, John Hillerman, Billy Green Bush, Alan Fudge

Invasion of the Body Snatchers****
US 1956 80m bw Superscope
Allied Artists / Walter Wanger

A small American town is imperceptibly taken over by an alien force.
Persuasive, thoroughly satisfying, low-budget science fiction, put across with subtlety and intelligence in every department.

w Daniel Mainwaring, *novel Jack Finney* *d Don*

Siegel ph Ellsworth Fredericks *m* Carmen Dragon

Kevin McCarthy, Dana Wynter, Larry Gates, *King Donovan,* Carolyn Jones, Virginia Christine, Sam Peckinpah

Invasion USA
US 1952 70m bw
Columbia (Albert Zugsmith)

A hypnotist in a New York bar gives a group of people a foretaste of what might happen to them under atomic attack.
Ludicrous, dangerous, hilarious low-budget exploitationer composed mainly of rubber rocks and old newsreels.

w Robert Smith *d* Alfred E. Green *ph* John L. Russell *m* Albert Glasser

Dan O'Herlihy, Gerald Mohr, Peggie Castle

Invisible Boy
US 1957 89m bw
MGM / Pan (Nicholas Nayfack)

A scientist allows his 10-year-old son to repair a robot, which comes under the control of an alien force.
Minor sci-fi utilizing the robot from *Forbidden Planet.*

w Cyril Hume *d* Herman Hoffman *ph* Harold Wellman *m* Les Baxter

Richard Eyer, Philip Abbott, Harold J. Stone, Diane Brewster

The Invisible Man****
US 1933 71m bw
Universal (Carl Laemmle Jnr)

A scientist discovers a means of making himself invisible, but in the process becomes a megalomaniac.
Superb blend of eccentric character comedy, melodrama and trick photography in a Hollywood English setting; remarkably faithful to the spirit of the book. It made a star of Claude Rains in his first film, even though he is seen for only a couple of seconds.

w R. C. Sheriff, Philip Wylie, novel H. G. Wells d James Whale ph Arthur Edeson sp John P. Fulton

Claude Rains, Gloria Stuart, William Harrigan, Henry Travers, *E. E. Clive, Una O'Connor,* Forrester Harvey, Dudley Digges, Holmes Herbert

'Taken either as a technical exercise or as a sometimes profoundly moving retelling of the Frankenstein fable, it is one of the most rewarding of recent films.'—*William Troy*
† Sequels, successively less interesting, were *The Invisible Man Returns* (1939), *Invisible Woman* (qv) (1940), *Invisible Agent* (1942), *The Invisible Man's Revenge* (1944) and *Abbott and Costello Meet the Invisible Man* (qv) (1951). A short-lived TV series followed in 1975: it was restructured as *Gemini Man* in 1976.

The Invisible Man*
US 1975 74m Technicolor TVM
Universal (Harve Bennett, Steven Boshco)

Quite a good updating of the theme; just occasionally it even catches the flavour of the original novel. The tricks are good, but the resultant series didn't work; the following year a variation, *Gemini Man,* was tried.

w Steven Boshco *d* Robert Michael Lewis

David McCallum, Jackie Cooper, Henry Darrow, Melinda Fee

The Invisible Ray*
US 1936 79m bw
Universal

A scientist discovers a superpowerful element which makes him homicidal.
Slow-moving science fiction with a touch of horror, and the pattern for its star's many later roles as a sympathetic man who turns into a monster. Interesting rather than stimulating.

w John Colton, *story* Howard Higgin, Douglas Hodges *d* Lambert Hillyer *ph* George Robinson *m* Franz Waxman *sp John P. Fulton*

Boris Karloff, Bela Lugosi, Frances Drake, Frank Lawton, Walter Kingsford, Beulah Bondi, Violet Kemble Cooper, Nydia Westman

The Invisible Woman*
US 1941 72m bw
Universal (Burt Kelly)

A mad scientist turns a model invisible.
Screwball comedy with a deteriorating star at his hammiest: generally very laboured, but with some funny moments.

w Robert Lees, Fred Rinaldo, Gertrude Purcell *d* A. Edward Sutherland *ph* Elwood Bredell

John Barrymore, Charles Ruggles, Virginia Bruce, John Howard, Oscar Homolka, Donald MacBride, Edward Brophy, Shemp Howard, Margaret Hamilton, Maria Montez

Invitation
US 1952 81m bw
MGM (Lawrence Weingarten)

When a millionaire's daughter believes she is dying, revelations ensue about her beloved husband's original intentions.
Competently idiotic weepie with a happy ending.

w Paul Osborn, *story* Jerome Weidman *d* Gottfried Reinhardt *ph* Ray June *m* Bronislau Kaper

Dorothy McGuire, Van Johnson, Ruth Roman, Louis Calhern, Ray Collins, Michael Chekhov

'The dialogue is stagey and the treatment indeterminate, with overmuch reliance on the dubious emotional reinforcement of loud background music.'—*Penelope Houston*

Invitation to a Gunfighter*
US 1964 92m De Luxe
UA / Stanley Kramer (Richard Wilson)

A small-town tyrant hires a smooth gunfighter to keep down the farmers he has cheated.
Predictable, rather self-satisfied little western with a studio look. Smart script and performances.

w Elizabeth and Richard Wilson *d* Richard Wilson *ph* Joseph MacDonald *m* David Raksin

Yul Brynner, George Segal, Janice Rule, Pat Hingle

Invitation to Happiness
US 1939 95m bw
Paramount (Wesley Ruggles)

A society girl marries a prizefighter.
Routine star romantic drama.

w Claude Binyon *d* Wesley Ruggles *ph* Leo Tover *m* Frederick Hollander

Irene Dunne, Fred MacMurray, Charles Ruggles, Billy Cook, William Collier Snr, Marion Martin

Invitation to the Dance**
GB 1954 92m Technicolor
MGM (Arthur Freed)

Three stories in dance and mime.
Unsuccessful ballet film which closed its star's great period and virtually ended the heyday of the Hollywood musical. The simple fact emerged that European ballet styles were not Kelly's forte; yet there was much to enjoy in *Circus*, *Ring around the Rosy* and *The Magic Lamp*.

w/ch/d Gene Kelly ph Frederick A. Young *m* Jacques Ibert, André Previn, Rimsky-Korsakov *ad* Alfred Junge

Gene Kelly, Igor Youskevitch, Tommy Rall, Belita, Tamara Toumanova

The Ipcress File**
GB 1965 109m Techniscope
Rank / Steven / Lowndes (Harry Saltzman)

An intelligence man traces a missing scientist and finds that one of his own superiors is a spy.
The attempt to present a low-key James Bond (glasses, good at cookery, supermarket shopper) is frustrated by flashy direction and a confused plot. It did herald a new genre though the whole ambiance is now sadly dated, like an old copy of *The Sunday Times* Colour Supplement.

w Bill Canaway, James Doran, *novel* Len Deighton *d* Sidney J. Furie *ph* Otto Heller *m* John Barry *ad* Ken Adam

Michael Caine, Nigel Green, Guy Doleman, Sue Lloyd, Gordon Jackson

† Two sequels appeared starring 'Harry Palmer' (never named in the books): *Funeral in Berlin* and *Billion Dollar Brain* (both qv).

Irene
US 1940 101m bw (colour sequence)
RKO / Imperator (Herbert Wilcox)

A New York Irish shopgirl moves into society.
Fairly dim picturization of the old musical: the cast does its best.

w Alice Duer Miller, *play* James H. Montgomery *d* Herbert Wilcox *ph* Russell Metty *md* Anthony Collins *songs* Harry Tierney, Joseph McCarthy

Anna Neagle, Ray Milland, Roland Young, Alan Marshal, May Robson, Billie Burke, Arthur Treacher, Marsha Hunt, Isabel Jewell, Ethel Griffies

'This pre-camp version tries to be innocuously charming, and the effort is all too evident.'—*New Yorker, 1976*

Irish Eyes Are Smiling**
US 1944 90m Technicolor
TCF (Damon Runyon)

The life and times of a nineties songwriter, Ernest R. Ball.
Standard musical biopic, handsomely mounted.

w Earl Baldwin, John Tucker Battle *d* Gregory Ratoff *ph* Harry Jackson *md* Alfred Newman, Charles Henderson

Dick Haymes, June Haver, Monty Woolley, Anthony Quinn, Beverly Whitney, Maxie Rosenbloom, Veda Ann Borg, Clarence Kolb

The Irish in Us
US 1935 84m bw
Warner (Samuel Bischoff)

Adventures of three New York brothers.
Routine, good-natured star action frolic.

w Earl Baldwin *d* Lloyd Bacon *ph* George Barnes *m* Leo F. Forbstein

James Cagney, Pat O'Brien, Olivia de Havilland, Mary Gordon, Frank McHugh, Allen Jenkins, J. Farrell MacDonald, Thomas Jackson

Irma La Douce*
US 1963 146m Technicolor Panavision
UA / Phalanx / Mirisch / Edward L. Alperson (Billy Wilder)

A Paris policeman falls for a prostitute and becomes her pimp.
A saucy yarn originally presented inventively as a small-scale stage musical becomes a tasteless yawn on the big screen, especially when presented at such length and without the songs. Minor compensations abound but are insufficient.

w Billy Wilder, I. A. L. Diamond *d* Billy Wilder *ph* Joseph La Shelle *md* André Previn *musical themes* Marguerite Monnot *ad* Alexander Trauner

Shirley Maclaine, Jack Lemmon, Lou Jacobi, Herschel Bernardi, Joan Shawlee, Bruce Yarnell

The Iron Curtain
US 1948 87m bw
TCF (Sol C. Siegel)

A Russian official in Ottawa becomes disillusioned and reveals to the US authorities details of a spy ring.
Cold war biopic of Igor Gouzenko; not badly done in the semi-documentary mould.

w Milton Krims *d* William Wellman *ph* Charles G. Clarke *md* Alfred Newman, using Russian themes

Dana Andrews, Gene Tierney, Berry Kroeger, Edna Best

The Iron Duke*
GB 1934 88m bw
Gaumont (Michael Balcon)

After Waterloo, the Duke of Wellington defeats a French scheme to discredit him.
A popular historical star vehicle of its time and a good example of British pre-war production in the Korda mould.

w Bess Meredith, play H. M. Harwood *d* Victor Saville

George Arliss, Gladys Cooper, Emlyn Williams, Ellaline Terriss, A. E. Matthews, Edmund Willard, Felix Aylmer

The Iron Maiden
GB 1962 98m Eastmancolor
AA / GHW (Peter Rogers)

An aircraft designer gets into trouble because of his affection for traction engines.
Feeble attempt to duplicate the success of *Genevieve*, this time starring a steamroller. Very English.

w Vivian Cox, Leslie Bricusse *d* Gerald Thomas *ph* Alan Hume *m* Eric Rogers

Michael Craig, Alan Hale Jnr, Jeff Donnell, Cecil Parker, Noel Purcell, Roland Culver, the Duke of Bedford, Anne Helm

The Iron Man
US 1931 73m bw
Universal (Carl Laemmle Jnr)

A prizefighter is spurred on by his money-hungry wife.
Competent, routine, ringside melodrama.

w Francis Edward Faragoh, *novel* W. R. Burnett *d* Tod Browning *ph* Percy Hilburn

Lew Ayres, Jean Harlow, Robert Armstrong, John Miljan, Eddie Dillon, Ned Sparks

The Iron Mistress
US 1952 107m Technicolor
Warner (Henry Blanke)

The life of westerner Jim Bowie and his famous knife.
Stolid actioner with uninspired script and performances.

w James R. Webb, *novel* Paul I. Wellman *d* Gordon Douglas *ph* John Seitz *m* Max Steiner

Alan Ladd, Virginia Mayo, Joseph Calleia, Phyllis Kirk, Alf Kjellin, Douglas Dick, Tony Caruso, George Voskovec

The Iron Petticoat
GB 1956 96m Technicolor Vistavision
Remus / Harry Saltzman (Betty E. Box)

An American air force officer persuades a Russian lady flier of the advantages of the western way of life.
Feeble imitation of *Ninotchka* with a saucy star team which simply doesn't jell.

w Ben Hecht *d* Ralph Thomas *ph* Ernest Steward

Bob Hope, Katharine Hepburn, James Robertson Justice, Robert Helpmann, David Kossoff, Alan Gifford, Paul Carpenter, Noelle Middleton

Ironside*
US 1967 97m Technicolor TVM
Universal (Collier Young)
GB title: *A Man Called Ironside*

San Francisco's chief of detectives is crippled for life after a shooting, but traps his attacker.
Fair pilot for a series that ran eight years and was usually watchable though seldom stimulating.

w Don M. Mankiewicz, Collier Young *d* James Goldstone

Raymond Burr, Don Galloway, Barbara Anderson, Donald Mitchell, Geraldine Brooks, Wally Cox, Kim Darby

Is Paris Burning?
France / US 1965 165m Panavision bw
Paramount / Transcontinental / Marianne (Paul Graetz)

A multi-storied account of the 1944 liberation of Paris.
Muddled, scribbled, tedious and confusing attempt at a thinking man's all-star war epic.

w Francis Ford Coppola, Gore Vidal *d* René Clément *ph* Marcel Grignon *m* Maurice Jarre

Leslie Caron, Gert Frobe, Charles Boyer, Yves Montand, Orson Welles, Alain Delon, Jean-Pierre Cassel, Jean-Paul Belmondo, Kirk Douglas, Glenn Ford, Claude Dauphin, Daniel Gélin, Anthony Perkins, Simone Signoret, Robert Stack, George Chakiris

Is There Anybody There?
Australia 1976 74m colour TVM
Paramount / Gemini (David Hannay)

Two women are locked in a penthouse for the weekend with a murderer.
Mildly watchable, uninspired psycho-thriller.

w Bruce A. Wishart *d* Peter Maxwell *ph* Russell Boyd

George Lazenby, Wendy Hughes, Tina Grenville, Charles Tingwell

Isadora*
GB 1968 138m Eastmancolor Panavision
Universal (Robert and Raymond Hakim)

Eccentric character dancer Isadora Duncan reflects on her crowded and unconventional life.
Ambitious and expensive but finally unsatisfactory biopic of a controversial figure of the twenties.

w Melvyn Bragg, Clive Exton *d Karel Reisz* *ph* Larry Pizer *m* Maurice Jarre *pd* Jocelyn Herbert *ad* Michael Seymour, Ralph Brinton

Vanessa Redgrave, Jason Robards Jnr, James Fox, Ivan Tchenko, John Fraser, Bessie Love
'A brave attempt at a daunting task.'—*Tom Milne*

The Island at the Top of the World**
US 1974 93m Technicolor
Walt Disney (Winston Hibler)

In 1907, a rich Englishman commissions an airship to take him to a mythical arctic Shangri-La in search of his lost son.
Generally brisk and effective adventure fantasy whose trick effects are sufficiently splendid to redeem a sag in the middle and an overplus of Viking chatter which has to be laboriously translated.

w John Whedon, *novel* The Lost Ones by Ian Cameron *d* Robert Stevenson *ph* Frank Phillips *m* Maurice Jarre *pd Peter Ellenshaw* *sp Art Cruickshank, Danny Lee*

Donald Sinden, David Hartman, Jacques Marin, Mako

Island in the Sky*
US 1953 109m bw
Wayne–Fellows (Robert Fellows)

A transport plane makes a forced landing north of Greenland, and the crew must survive till help comes.
Well made outdoor suspenser shot in the California Sierras.

w Ernest K. Gann, from his novel *d* William Wellman *ph* Archie Stout *m* Emil Newman *ad* James Basevi

John Wayne, Lloyd Nolan, Walter Abel, Allyn Joslyn, Andy Devine, James Arness

Island in the Sun*
GB 1957 119m Technicolor Cinemascope
TCF (Darryl F. Zanuck)

Sexual and racial problems erupt on a West Indian island.
Portmanteau romantic melodrama which generally misfires, especially in an attempt to parallel *Crime and Punishment*; but the cast is interesting.

w Alfred Hayes, *novel* Alec Waugh *d* Robert Rossen *ph* Frederick A. Young *m* Malcolm Arnold

James Mason, Joan Fontaine, Harry Belafonte, John Williams, Dorothy Dandridge, Joan Collins, Michael Rennie, Patricia Owens, Stephen Boyd, Basil Sydney, Diana Wynyard, Ronald Squire, John Justin

Island of Lost Souls*
US 1932 74m bw
Paramount

On a remote South Sea island, mad Dr Moreau transforms animals into humans by vivisection.
Unchilling but interesting thriller with a rolling-eyed star performance.

w Waldemar Young, Philip Wylie, *story* The Island of Dr Moreau by H. G. Wells *d* Erle C. Kenton *ph* Karl Struss

Charles Laughton, Bela Lugosi, Richard Arlen, Kathleen Burke, Leila Hyams

Island of the Blue Dolphins
US 1964 93m Eastmancolor
U-I / Robert B. Radnitz

Two orphaned children grow up alone on a Californian island, protected by wild dogs.
Pleasant if unconvincing family film based on a true story.

w Ted Sherdeman, Jane Klove, *novel* Scott O'Dell *d* James B. Clark *ph* Leo Tover *m* Paul Sawtell

Celia Kaye, Larry Dornasin, George Kennedy

Island of Love
US 1963 101m Technicolor
Panavision
Warner / Belgrave (Morton da Costa)

A gangster finances a film providing his girl friend stars, but when it flops he chases the producers to a Greek island.
Dismally unfunny comedy wasting a talented cast.

w David R. Schwarz *d* Morton da Costa *ph* Harry Stradling *m* George Duning

Robert Preston, Tony Randall, Walter Matthau, Giorgia Moll

Island of Terror
GB 1966 89m Eastmancolor
Planet (Tom Blakeley)

On an Irish island, a scientist makes monsters who thrive on bone.
Horror hokum, moderately done.

w Edward Andrew Mann, Alan Ramsen *d* Terence Fisher *ph* Reg Wyer *m* Malcolm Lockyer *sp* John St John Earl

Peter Cushing, Edward Judd, Carole Gray, Eddie Byrne, Sam Kydd, Niall MacGinnis

Isle of the Dead**
US 1945 72m bw
RKO (*Val Lewton*)

On a Balkan island in 1912 a group of people shelter from the plague and fear that one of their number is a vampire.
Glum, ghoulish melodrama with some neatly handled shocks; quite different from any other horror film.

w Ardel Wray, Josef Mischel *d Mark Robson ph Jack Mackenzie m* Leigh Harline

Boris Karloff, Ellen Drew, Helene Thimig, Marc Cramer, Katherine Emery, Alan Napier, Jason Robards

Isn't It Romantic?*
US 1948 87m bw
Paramount (Daniel Dare)

Romance hits the household of an ex-Civil War colonel in Indiana.
Pleasant but forgettable period semi-musical.

w Theodore Strauss, Josef Mischel, Richard Breen *d* Norman Z. McLeod *ph* Lionel Lindon *m* Joseph J. Lilley

Veronica Lake, Mona Freeman, Mary Hatcher, Roland Culver, Billy de Wolfe, Patric Knowles, Richard Webb, Kathryn Givney, Pearl Bailey

Isn't It Shocking?*
US 1973 73m colour TVM
ABC Circle

In a sleepy New England town, someone is killing off the senior citizens.
Unusual black comedy. It doesn't quite work, but at least it's different.

w Lane Slate, Ron Bernstein, Howard Roseman *d* John Badham

Alan Alda, Ruth Gordon, Louise Lasser, Edmond O'Brien, Lloyd Nolan, Will Geer

Isn't Life Wonderful?*
GB 1952 83m Technicolor
ABP (Warwick Ward)

In 1902, drunken Uncle Willie runs a bicycle shop and manages to reconcile a lovers' quarrel.
Engaging, well cast family comedy.

w Brock Williams *d* Harold French *ph* Erwin Hillier *m* Philip Green *ad* Terence Verity

Donald Wolfit, Eileen Herlie, Cecil Parker, Eleanor Summerfield, Robert Urquhart, Cecil Trouncer

Istanbul
US 1956 84m Technicolor
Cinemascope
U-I (Albert J. Cohen)

Various adventurers and an amnesiac girl seek stolen diamonds in Istanbul.
Dim remake of a flat-footed piece of thick ear called *Singapore*.

w Seton I. Miller, Barbara Gray, Richard Alan Simmons *d* Joseph Pevney *ph* William Daniels *m* Joseph Gershenson

Errol Flynn, Cornell Borchers, John Bentley, Torin Thatcher, Leif Erickson, Martin Benson, Vladimir Sokoloff, Werner Klemperer, Nat King Cole, Peggy Knudsen

Istanbul Express
US 1968 94m Technicolor TVM
Universal (Richard Irving)

Secret information is due to be exchanged on the train from Paris to Istanbul.
Underdeveloped and rather tedious spy caper.

w Richard Levinson, William Link *d* Richard Irving

Gene Barry, John Saxon, Mary Ann Mobley, Jack Kruschen, John Marley, Moustache, Senta Berger

It All Came True*
US 1940 97m bw
Warner (Mark Hellinger)

A gangster hides out in a boarding house and puts it back on its feet.
Competent New York fairy story full of sweetness and light.

w Michael Fessier, Lawrence Kimble, *story* Better Than Life by Louis Bromfield *d* Lewis Seiler *ph* Ernest Haller *m* Heinz Roemheld

Humphrey Bogart, Ann Sheridan, Jeffrey Lynn, Zasu Pitts, Una O'Connor, Jessie Busley, John Litel, Grant Mitchell, Felix Bressart

It Always Rains on Sunday***
GB 1947 92m bw
Ealing

An escaped convict takes refuge in his married mistress's house in East London.
Influential slumland melodrama, now dated—the stuff of every other television play—but at the time electrifyingly vivid and very well done.

w Angus Macphail, Robert Hamer, Henry Cornelius, novel Arthur La Bern d Robert Hamer ph Douglas Slocombe m Georges Auric

Googie Withers, John McCallum, Jack Warner, Edward Chapman, Susan Shaw, Sidney Tafler

It Came from beneath the Sea
US 1955 80m bw
Columbia / Sam Katzman (Charles Schneer)

A giant octopus half destroys San Francisco.
Tepid monster movie; special effects only fair.

w George Worthing Yates, Hal Smith *d* Robert Gordon *ph* Henry Freulich *m* Mischa Bakaleinikoff

Kenneth Tobey, Faith Domergue, Donald Curtis, Ian Keith

It Came from Outer Space**
US 1953 80m bw 3-D
U-I (William Alland)

A young astronomer sees a space ship land in the Arizona desert and tracks down the occupants who can adopt human appearance at will.
Quite bright science fiction, the first to use this theme of borrowing bodies and the first to utilize the western desert locations. 3-D adds a shock moment or two.

w Harry Essex, story Ray Bradbury *d Jack Arnold ph* Clifford Stine *m* Joseph Gershenson

Richard Carlson, Barbara Rush, Charles Drake, Kathleen Hughes

It Couldn't Happen to a Nicer Guy
US 1974 74m colour TVM
Josak (Arne Sultan)

A real estate agent is raped at gunpoint by a mysterious woman.
And it doesn't get any better after that. Silly, tasteless comedy.

w Arne Sultan, Earl Barrett *d* Cy Howard

Paul Sorvino, Michael Learned, Adam Arkin, Ed Barth

It Grows on Trees
US 1952 84m bw
U-I (Leonard Goldstein)

A housewife finds a money tree in her backyard.
Protracted fantasy comedy.

w Leonard Praskins, Barney Slater *d* Arthur Lubin *ph* Maury Gertsman *m* Frank Skinner

Irene Dunne (her last film), Dean Jagger, Joan Evans, Richard Crenna, Edith Meiser, Dee Pollock

It Had To Be You
US 1947 98m bw
Columbia / Don Hartman

A dizzy dame runs out on three prospective husbands and is pursued by an Indian.
Weak sex farce without the courage of its lack of convictions.

w Norman Panama, Melvin Frank *d* Don Hartman, Rudolph Maté *ph* Rudolph Maté *m* Morris Stoloff

Ginger Rogers, Cornel Wilde, Percy Waram, Spring Byington, Thurston Hall, Ron Randell

It Happened at the World's Fair
US 1962 104m Metrocolor Panavision
MGM / Ted Richmond

At the Seattle World's Fair, two crop-dusting pilots have romantic intrigues.
Routine star vehicles.

w Si Rose, Seaman Jacobs *d* Norman Taurog *ph* Joseph Ruttenberg *m* Leith Stevens

Elvis Presley, Gary Lockwood, Joan O'Brien, Yvonne Craig, Ginny Tiu

It Happened Here**
GB 1963 99m bw
UA / Kevin Brownlow, Andrew Mollo

What might have happened if the Germans had invaded England in 1940.
A remarkable semi-professional reconstruction which took seven years to film and is totally convincing in detail, but unfortunately rather confused and padded as drama.

wd Kevin Brownlow, Andrew Mollo ph Peter Suschitsky *m* Jack Beaver

Sebastian Shaw, Pauline Murray, Fiona Lekland, Honor Fehrson

It Happened in Athens
US 1961 100m De Luxe
TCF (James S. Elliott)

At the first revival of the Olympic Games in 1896 a publicity-seeking actress announces that she will marry whoever wins the Marathon.
Witless extravagant romp, well mounted but adding up to zero.

w Laszlo Vadnay *d* Andrew Marton *ph* Curt Courant

Jayne Mansfield, Trax Colton, Bob Mathias

It Happened in Brooklyn*
US 1947 103m bw
MGM

Young New Yorkers with musical talents find their way to fame.
Well-handled routine musical of its time.

w Isobel Lennart *d* Richard Whorf *ph* Robert Planck

Frank Sinatra, Jimmy Durante, Kathryn Grayson, Peter Lawford, Gloria Grahame

It Happened on Fifth Avenue*
US 1947 115m bw
AA

A child of divorce finds amiable squatters in her millionaire father's house.
Curious, overlong, cheerful Capraesque comedy with the mildest of social pretensions.

w Everett Freeman *d* Roy del Ruth *ph* Henry Sharp

Gale Storm, Ann Harding, Victor Moore, Charles Ruggles, Don Defore

It Happened One Night****
US 1934 105m bw
Columbia (Frank Capra)

A runaway heiress falls in love with the reporter who is chasing her across America.
Highly successful and influential romantic comedy, the first to use buses and motels as background and still come up sparkling; it remains superlative in patches, but overall has a faded, dated air.

w Robert Riskin, story Night Bus by Samuel Hopkins Adams *d Frank Capra ph* Joseph Walker *md* Louis Silvers

Clark Gable, Claudette Colbert, Walter Connolly, Roscoe Karns, Alan Hale, Ward Bond, Jameson Thomas, Arthur Hoyt

'It will be a long day before we see so little made into so much.'—*Otis Ferguson*

'Something to revive your faith in a medium which could belong among the great arts.'—*Robert Forsythe*

† Remade 1956 (badly) as *You Can't Run away From It.*

It Happened to Jane
US 1959 98m Technicolor
Cinemascope
Columbia / Arwin (Richard Quine)

A lady lobster dealer becomes involved in a battle with the railroad whose inefficiency affects her business.
Witless, wholesome farce which promises more than it delivers.

w Norman Karkov *d* Richard Quine
ph Charles Lawton Jnr *m* George Duning

Doris Day, Jack Lemmon, *Ernie Kovacs*, Steve Forrest

It Happened Tomorrow***
US 1944 84m bw
(UA) Arnold Pressburger

A reporter meets an old man with the power to show him tomorrow's newspaper headlines, so that he always gets scoops—including his own death . . .
Engaging fantasy, flawlessly made and quietly very entertaining.

w Dudley Nichols, René Clair d René Clair ph Archie Stout m Robert Stolz

Dick Powell, Linda Darnell, Jack Oakie, *John Philliber*, Edgar Kennedy, Ed Brophy, George Cleveland, Sig Rumann

It Happens Every Spring
US 1949 80m bw
TCF (William Perlberg)

A chemistry teacher discovers a formula that makes baseballs repellent to wood.

Smartly produced but rather desperate fantasy comedy.

w Valentine Davies *d* Lloyd Bacon *ph* Joe MacDonald *m* Leigh Harline

Ray Milland, Jean Peters, Paul Douglas, Ed Begley, Ted de Corsia, Ray Collins, Jessie Royce Landis, Alan Hale Jnr

It Happens Every Thursday*

US 1953 80m bw

U-I (Anton Leader)

The new owner of a small-town newspaper becomes unpopular through his attempts to boost the circulation.
Pleasant comedy with amusing scenes.

w Dane Lussier *d* Joseph Pevney *ph* Russell Metty *m* Joseph Gershenson

Loretta Young, John Forsythe, Jimmy Conlin, Frank McHugh, Edgar Buchanan, Jane Darwell

It Should Happen to You**

US 1954 87m bw

Columbia (Fred Kohlmar)

A slightly daffy New York model with an urge to be famous rents a huge billboard and puts her name on it.
Likeable comedy which starts brightly and slowly falls apart, disappointing considering the credentials of the talents involved and the satiric possibilities of the plot.

w Ruth Gordon, Garson Kanin d George Cukor *ph* Charles Lang *m* Frederick Hollander

Judy Holliday, Jack Lemmon, Peter Lawford, Michael O'Shea

It Shouldn't Happen to a Vet

GB 1976 93m Technicolor

EMI / Talent Associates / Readers Digest

Adventures of a Yorkshire vet just before World War II.
Competent sequel to *All Creatures Great and Small* (qv).

w Alan Plater, *books* James Herriot *d* Eric Till *ph* Arthur Ibbetson *m* Laurie Johnson

John Alderton, Colin Blakely, Lisa Harrow, Bill Maynard, Richard Pearson, Raymond Francis, John Barrett, Paul Shelley

It Started in Naples*

US 1960 100m Technicolor Vistavision

Paramount / Capri (Jack Rose)

A Philadelphia lawyer goes to Naples to settle his dead brother's affairs, and falls for his nephew's aunt.
Nicely made, formula romantic comedy which started life as a vehicle for Gracie Fields.

w Melville Shavelson, Jack Rose, Susi Cecchi d'Amico *d* Melville Shavelson *ph* Robert Surtees *m* Alessandro Cicognini

Clark Gable, Sophia Loren, Vittorio De Sica, Marietto, Paulo Carlini

It Started in Paradise

GB 1952 94m Technicolor

GFD / British Film Makers (Leslie Parkyn, Sergei Nolbandov)

The career of an ambitious dress designer.
Stilted and garishly coloured but often amusing backstage melodrama of the fashion world: a Hollywood-style star vehicle which seems faintly surprising as a British product.

w Marghanita Laski *d* Compton Bennett *ph* Jack Cardiff *m* Malcolm Arnold *ad* Edward Carrick

Jane Hylton, Ian Hunter, Terence Morgan, Muriel Pavlow, Brian Worth, *Martita Hunt, Ronald Squire, Harold Lang*, Joyce Barbour, Kay Kendall

It Started with a Kiss

US 1959 104m Metrocolor Cinemascope

MGM / Arcola (Aaron Rosenberg)

An army sergeant posted to Spain is embarrassed when his wife follows him.
Flabby comedy with the emphasis on sex and pratfalls.

w Charles Lederer *d* George Marshall *ph* Robert Bronner *m* Jeff Alexander

Glenn Ford, Debbie Reynolds, Fred Clark, Edgar Buchanan, Eva Gabor

It Started with Eve**

US 1941 93m bw

Universal (Joe Pasternak)

A dying millionaire wants to see his grandson engaged, so a waitress obliges for an hour . . . but the old man recovers.
Charming comedy which was probably the star's best film; remade as *I'd Rather be Rich* (qv).

w Norman Krasna, Leo Townsend *d* Henry Koster *m* Hans J. Salter

Deanna Durbin, Charles Laughton, Robert Cummings, Margaret Tallichet, Guy Kibbee, Walter Catlett, Catherine Doucet

The Italian Job**

GB 1969 100m Eastmancolor Panavision

Paramount / Oakhurst (Michael Deeley)

Crooks stage a traffic jam in Turin in order to pull off a bullion robbery.
Lively caper comedy which provides a good measure of entertainment.

w Troy Kennedy Martin *d* Peter Collinson *ph* Douglas Slocombe, Norman Warwick *m* Quincy Jones

Michael Caine, Noel Coward, Benny Hill, Raf Vallone, Tony Beckley, Rossano Brazzi, Maggie Blye, Irene Handl, John Le Mesurier, Fred Emney

It's a Big Country
US 1952 88m bw
MGM (Robert Sisk)

Seven stories show the diversity of the US and the glory of being one of its citizens.
Stultifying flagwaver memorable chiefly as a waste of good actors.

w William Ludwig, Helen Deutsch, George Wells, Allen Rivkin, Dorothy Kingsley, Isobel Lennart *d* Richard Thorpe, Don Weis, John Sturges, Don Hartman, William Wellman, Charles Vidor *ph* John Alton, Ray June, William Mellor, Joseph Ruttenberg *m* Bronislau Kaper, Rudolph G. Kopp, David Raksin, David Rose

Ethel Barrymore, Keefe Brasselle, Nancy Davis, Van Johnson, Gene Kelly, Janet Leigh, Marjorie Main, Fredric March, George Murphy, William Powell, S. Z. Sakall, Lewis Stone, James Whitmore

It's a Gift**
US 1934 73m bw
Paramount (William Le Baron)

A general store proprietor buys an orange ranch by mail and transports his family to California.
Roughly assembled comedy of disasters which happens to show the star more or less at his best, though the expected climax is lacking.

w Jack Cunningham, *story* W. C. Fields, J. P. McEvoy *d* Norman Z. McLeod *ph* Henry Sharp

W. C. Fields, Kathleen Howard, Jean Rouverol, Julian Madison, Tommy Bupp, Baby LeRoy

It's a Great Feeling*
US 1949 85m Technicolor
Warner (Alex Gottlieb)

No one will direct a Jack Carson movie, so he has to do it himself.
Amiable studio farce with plenty of guest appearances.

w Jack Rose, Mel Shavelson *d* David Butler *ph* Wilfrid M. Cline *m/ly* Jule Styne, Sammy Cahn

Jack Carson, Doris Day, Dennis Morgan, Bill Goodwin, Gary Cooper, Joan Crawford, Errol Flynn, Sidney Greenstreet, Danny Kaye, Patricia Neal, Edward G. Robinson, Jane Wyman, Eleanor Parker, Ronald Reagan

It's a Mad Mad Mad Mad World**
US 1963 192m Technicolor Ultra Panavision 70
UA / Stanley Kramer

An assortment of people including a frustrated cop are overcome by greed when they hear of buried loot.
Three hours of frantic chasing and violent slapstick is too much even when done on this scale and with this cast, but one must observe that scene for scene it is extremely well done and most of the players are in unusually good form though they all outstay their welcome and are upstaged by the stunt men.

w William and Tania Rose *d Stanley Kramer ph Ernest Laszlo m Ernest Gold stunts Carey Loftin titles Saul Bass*

Spencer Tracy, Jimmy Durante, *Milton Berle*, Sid Caesar, Ethel Merman, Buddy Hackett, Mickey Rooney, Dick Shawn, *Phil Silvers, Terry-Thomas*, Jonathan Winters, Edie Adams, Dorothy Provine, Eddie Anderson, Jim Backus, William Demarest, Peter Falk, Paul Ford, Leo Gorcey, Ben Blue, Edward Everett Horton, Buster Keaton, Joe E. Brown, Carl Reiner, the Three Stooges, Zasu Pitts, Sterling Holloway, Jack Benny, Jerry Lewis

'To watch on a Cinerama screen in full colour a small army of actors inflict mayhem on each other with cars, planes, explosives and other devices for more than three hours with stereophonic sound effects is simply too much for the human eye and ear to respond to, let alone the funny bone.'—*Dwight MacDonald*

It's a 2'6" above the Ground World
GB 1972 96m Eastmancolor
British Lion / Welbeck / Betty E. Box–Ralph Thomas
Also known as: *The Love Ban*

A Roman Catholic couple go on the pill.
Smutty, not very funny sex comedy.

w Kevin Laffan, from his play *d* Ralph Thomas *ph* Tony Imi *m* Stanley Myers

Nanette Newman, Hywel Bennett, Russell Lewis, Simon Henderson, Milo O'Shea

It's a Wonderful Life****
US 1946 129m bw
RKO / Liberty Films (Frank Capra)

A man is prevented from committing suicide by an elderly angel, who takes him back through his life to show him what good he has done.
Superbly assembled small-town comedy drama in a fantasy framework; arguably Capra's best and most typical work.

w Frances Goodrich, Albert Hackett, Frank Capra d Frank Capra ph Joseph Walker, Joseph Biroc m Dmitri Tiomkin

James Stewart, Henry Travers, Donna Reed, Lionel Barrymore, Thomas Mitchell, Beulah Bondi, Frank Faylen, Ward Bond, Gloria Grahame, H. B. Warner, Frank Albertson, Samuel S. Hinds, Mary Treen

'One of the most efficient sentimental pieces since *A Christmas Carol.*'—*James Agee*

'The most brilliantly made motion picture of the 1940s, so assured, so dazzling in its use of screen narrative.'—*Charles Higham*

It's a Wonderful World**
US 1939 86m bw
MGM (Frank Davis)

Kidnapped by a suspected murderer, a girl helps him track down the real criminal.
Madcap comedy mystery which now seems much fresher and funnier than it did at the time. A highlight of the crazy comedy cycle.

w Ben Hecht, Herman J. Mankiewicz *d* W. S. Van Dyke II *ph* Oliver Marsh

Claudette Colbert, James Stewart, Guy Kibbee, Nat Pendleton, Frances Drake, Edgar Kennedy, Ernest Truex, Richard Carle, Sidney Blackmer, Andy Clyde, Cliff Clark, Hans Conried

It's Alive
US 1974 91m Technicolor
Warner / Larco (Larry Cohen)

A new-born baby turns out to be a vicious monster.
Exploitation horror flick in the worst of taste, with a good central performance.

wd Larry Cohen *ph* Fenton Hamilton *m* Bernard Herrmann

John Ryan, Sharon Farrell, Andrew Duggan, Guy Stockwell, James Dixon, Michael Ansara

It's Always Fair Weather**
US 1955 101m Eastmancolor Cinemascope
MGM (Arthur Freed)

In 1945 three army veterans vow to meet ten years on, but they find each other dull failures until they go on a wild spree.
Rather dejected New Yorkish comedy with musical sequences; some of it works very well, but the colour is crude and the wide screen doesn't help.

w/ly/m Betty Comden, Adolph Green *d* Gene Kelly, Stanley Donen *ph* Robert Bronner *md* André Previn

Gene Kelly, Dan Dailey, Michael Kidd, Dolores Gray, Cyd Charisse

It's Good to be Alive*
US 1974 100m colour TVM
Metromedia

The story of baseball player Roy Campanella, paralysed after an auto accident.
Another 'inspiring' real life case of the miseries; sympathetically done, but not exactly riveting.

w Steven Gethers *d* Michael Landon

Paul Winfield, Ruby Dee, Lou Gossett, Julian Burton

It's in the Air*
GB 1938 86m bw
ABFD

Adventures of an accident-prone RAF recruit.
Amiable star comedy with good situations and songs.

wd Anthony Kimmins

George Formby, Garry Marsh, Polly Ward, Julien Mitchell, Jack Hobbs, Hal Gordon

It's in the Bag**
US 1945 87m bw
(UA) Manhattan Productions
GB title: *The Fifth Chair*

The owner of a flea circus seeks a legacy hidden in one of five chairs which have been sold to a variety of people.
Patchily amusing, star-studded comedy which was also filmed as *Keep Your Seats Please* and *The Twelve Chairs*. Full enjoyment requires some knowledge of American radio characters.

w Jay Dratler, Alma Reville *d* Richard Wallace *ph* Russell Metty *m* Werner Heymann

Fred Allen, Binnie Barnes, *Jack Benny*, Robert Benchley, Don Ameche, Victor Moore, Rudy Vallee, William Bendix, Jerry Colonna

It's Love I'm After*
US 1937 90m bw
Warner

A beloved stage star couple fight like cat and dog behind the scenes.

Amusing romantic farce which has worn rather less well than might have been expected but does present two stars at their peak.

w Casey Robinson *d* Archie Mayo *ph* James Van Trees *m* Heinz Roemheld

Bette Davis, Leslie Howard, Olivia de Havilland, Patric Knowles, Eric Blore, George Barbier, Spring Byington, Bonita Granville, E. E. Clive

'One of the most delightful and diverting comedies the madcap cinema has yet turned out.'—*New York World Telegram*

'Proceeds like a somewhat deranged *Taming of the Shrew*... [BD and LH] are surrounded by that set of millionaires, valets and heiresses that were at one time as much of a convention in American comedy as the fops of Restoration theatre.'—*American Film institute*

It's Only Money
US 1962 84m bw
Paramount / York / Jerry Lewis Productions (Paul Jones)

A TV repair mechanic hampers his detective friend in a search for a missing heir, which turns out to be himself.
Patchy mystery spoof with the star in rather better form than usual, and a memorable scene in which he is chased by an army of lawnmowers.

w John Fenton Murray *d* Frank Tashlin *ph* W. Wallace Kelley *m* Walter Scharf

Jerry Lewis, Zachary Scott, Joan O'Brien, Jesse White, Jack Weston

It's That Man Again**
GB 1942 84m bw
GFD / Gainsborough (Edward Black)

The Mayor of Foaming-at-the-Mouth puts on a show to save a bombed theatre.
Smart, fast-moving comedy which no longer seems particularly funny in itself but is an invaluable record of the characters and wisecracks of a radio show which proved a prime morale booster during World War II.

w Howard Irving Young, *Ted Kavanagh* *d Walter Forde*

Tommy Handley, Jack Train, Greta Gynt, Dino Galvani, Dorothy Summers, Horace Percival, Sidney Keith, Clarence Wright

Ivanhoe*
GB 1953 106m Technicolor
MGM (Pandro S. Berman)

Derring-do among the knights of medieval England.
Tolerable, big-budget spectacular based on Sir Walter Scott's novel.

w Noel Langley, Aeneas Mackenzie *d* Richard Thorpe
ph F. A. Young *m* Miklos Rozsa

Robert Taylor, Joan Fontaine, Elizabeth Taylor, Emlyn Williams, George Sanders, Robert Douglas, Finlay Currie, Felix Aylmer, Francis de Wolff, Guy Rolfe, Norman Wooland, Basil Sydney

I've Lived Before
US 1956 82m bw
U–I (Howard Christie)

After a plane crash, the pilot recovers but believes himself to be another airman who died in 1918.
Dullish, talky drama which wastes its interesting reincarnation theme.

w Norman Jolley, William Talman *d* Richard Bartlett *ph* Maury Gertsman *m* Herman Stein

Jock Mahoney, Leigh Snowden, Ann Harding, John McIntire, Raymond Bailey, Jerry Paris

Ivy*
US 1947 99m bw
Universal (William Cameron Menzies)

In Edwardian society England, a lady poisoner gets her come-uppance.
Curiously ineffective period thriller in which the star is the elegant but artificial production design: the script is deadly dull.

w Charles Bennett, *novel* Mrs Belloc Lowndes *d Sam Wood ph Russell Metty m* Daniele Amfitheatrof *pd William Cameron Menzies*

Joan Fontaine, Herbert Marshall, Patric Knowles, Richard Ney, Cedric Hardwicke, Lucile Watson, Sara Allgood, Henry Stephenson, Rosalind Ivan, Lilian Fontaine, Una O'Connor, Isobel Elsom. Alan Napier, Paul Cavanagh, Gavin Muir, Norma Varden

J

J. W. Coop*
US 1971 112m Eastmancolor
Columbia / Robertson and Associates (Cliff Robertson)

After ten years in prison, a rodeo rider returns to his home town.
Well-made but rather inconsequential drama with attractive locations.

w Cliff Robertson, Gary Cartwright, Bud Shrake *d* Cliff Robertson *ph* Frank Stanley *m* Don Randi, Louise Shelton

Cliff Robertson, Cristina Ferrare, Geraldine Page, R. G. Armstrong

Jack the Giant Killer**
US 1961 94m Technicolor
Zenith / Edward Small (Robert E. Kent)

Demon Pendragon kidnaps the princess of Cornwall but she is rescued by a farmer's son.
Very creditable fairy tale, with the right style and atmosphere assisted by vigorous acting, good pace and excellent trick effects. Unfortunately it turned out rather scary for a child audience and so fell between two stools.

w Orville Hampton, Nathan Juran d Nathan Juran ph David S. Horsley m Paul Sawtell *sp Howard Anderson ad Fernando Carere, Frank McCoy*

Kerwin Mathews, Judi Meredith, *Torin Thatcher, Don Beddoe*, Walter Burke, Barry Kelley

Jack the Ripper
GB 1958 84m bw
Mid Century (Baker and Berman)

In Victorian London the Ripper murders are finally attributed to a demented surgeon.
Flat and rather flabby treatment of a *cause célèbre,* saved by a reasonably convincing period look.

w Jimmy Sangster *d/ph* Robert S. Baker, Monty Berman *m* Stanley Black

Ewen Solon, Lee Patterson, Eddie Byrne, Betty McDowell, John Le Mesurier

Jack's the Boy*
GB 1932 91m bw
Gainsborough (Michael Balcon)

The police commissioner's son proves his worth in rounding up a smash-and-grab gang.
Dated but lively farce which established its star as a British box office attraction of the thirties.

w W. P. Lipscomb *d* Walter Forde

Jack Hulbert, Cicely Courtneidge, Francis Lister, Winifred Shotter, Peter Gawthorne, Ben Field

The Jackpot**
US 1950 85m bw
TCF (Samuel G. Engel)

A suburban husband finds that life becomes complicated when winning the jackpot on a radio quiz makes him a celebrity.
Modest, skilful comedy in Hollywood's best manner.

w Phoebe and Henry Ephron d Walter Lang ph Joseph La Shelle *m* Lionel Newman

James Stewart, Barbara Hale, James Gleason, Fred Clark, Alan Mowbray, Patricia Medina, Natalie Wood, Tommy Rettig, Robert Gist, Lyle Talbot

Jacqueline*
GB 1957 93m bw
Rank (George H. Brown)

A Belfast shipyard worker cannot stand heights, takes to drink, and is helped by his small daughter.
Convincing, well-made, realistically set domestic comedy-drama.

w Patric Kirwan, Liam O'Flaherty *d* Roy Baker *ph Geoffrey Unsworth m* Cedric Thorpe Davie

John Gregson, Kathleen Ryan, Jacqueline Ryan, Noel Purcell, Cyril Cusack, Marie Kean, Liam Redmond, Maureen Delany

Jailhouse Rock*
US 1957 96m bw Cinemascope
MGM (Pandro S. Berman)

An ex-convict becomes a pop star.

Reasonably competent star vehicle, sourer in tone than most.

w Guy Trosper *d* Richard Thorpe *ph* Robert Bronner *md* Jeff Alexander

Elvis Presley, Judy Tyler, Mickey Shaughnessy, Vaughn Taylor, Dean Jones

Jamaica Inn*
GB 1939 107m bw
Mayflower (Erich Pommer)

In old Cornwall, an orphan girl becomes involved with smugglers.
Stagey, stilted adventure story which never loses its studio feel or takes fire as a Hitchcock picture. The cast keeps it interesting.

w Sidney Gilliat, Joan Harrison, J. B. Priestley *d Alfred Hitchcock* *ph* Harry Stradling, Bernard Knowles *m* Eric Fenby

Charles Laughton, Maureen O'Hara, Leslie Banks, Robert Newton, Emlyn Williams, Wylie Watson, Marie Ney, Morland Graham

'I was irresistibly reminded of an all-star charity matinee.'—*Graham Greene*

Jamaica Run
US 1953 92m Technicolor
Paramount Pine–Thomas

A search for documents, which may apportion a great house to another branch of the family, leads to murder.
Plot-bound romantic mystery in period, with elements of a Caribbean *Rebecca*. Watchable medium-budget hokum.

wd Lewis R. Foster, *novel* Max Murray *ph* Lionel Lindon *m* Lucien Cailliet

Ray Milland, Arlene Dahl, Wendell Corey, Patric Knowles

Jane Eyre***
US 1944 96m bw
TCF (William Goetz)

In Victorian times, a harshly treated orphan girl becomes governess in a mysterious Yorkshire mansion with a brooding master.
Sharply paced, reasonably faithful and superbly staged Hollywood version of Charlotte Bronte's archetypal romantic novel which stimulated so many imitations, including *Rebecca*.

w Aldous Huxley, Robert Stevenson, John Houseman d Robert Stevenson ph George Barnes m Bernard Herrmann sp Fred Sersen ad Wiard B. Ihnen, James Basevi

Joan Fontaine, Orson Welles, Margaret O'Brien, *Henry Daniell,* John Sutton, Agnes Moorehead, Elizabeth Taylor, Peggy Ann Garner, Sara Allgood, Aubrey Mather, Hillary Brooke, Edith Barrett, Ethel Griffies, Barbara Everest, *John Abbott*

'A careful and tame production, a sadly vanilla-flavoured Joan Fontaine, and Orson Welles treating himself to road operatic sculpturings of body, cloak and diction, his eyes glinting in the Rembrandt gloom, at every chance, like side orders of jelly.'—*James Agee*

Jane Eyre*
GB 1971 108m colour TVM
Omnibus (Frederick H. Brogger)

Over-bright teleplay with a strong Rochester and not much else.

w Jack Pulman *d* Delbert Mann *ph* Paul Beeson *m* John Williams *ad* Alex Vetchinsky

George C. Scott, Susannah York, Jack Hawkins, Nyree Dawn Porter, Ian Bannen, Kenneth Griffith, Peter Copley, Rachel Kempson, Jean Marsh, Constance Cummings.

Janie*
US 1944 104m bw
Warner (Alex Gottlieb)

A small-town 16-year-old miss becomes popular with the army and holds a wild party in her parents' home.
Sociologically instructive wartime domestic comedy from a popular play. Well enough made and well cast.

w Agnes Christine Johnston, Charles Hoffman, *play* Josephine Bentham, Herschel Williams *d* Michael Curtiz *ph* Carl Guthrie *m* Heinz Roemheld

Joyce Reynolds, Robert Hutton, Edward Arnold, Ann Harding, Robert Benchley, Alan Hale, Hattie McDaniel, Richard Erdman, Jackie Moran, Ann Gillis
† *Janie Gets Married* followed in 1945.

Japanese War Bride*
US 1952 94m bw
TCF / Bernhard (Joseph Bernhard)

An officer wounded in Korea marries his Japanese nurse and takes her home to California.
Predictable domestic drama very similar to the British *Frieda*, marginally interesting for sociological reasons.

w Catherine Turney *d* King Vidor *ph* Lionel Lindon *m* Emil Newman

Shirley Yamaguchi, Don Taylor, Cameron Mitchell, Marie Windsor, James Bell, Louise Lorimer

Jarrett
US 1973 74m colour TVM
Columbia (David Gerber)

An adventurer combats a wily villain for the possession of rare scrolls.
Foolish comic strip capers with a star far too old for this kind of thing.

w Richard Maibaum *d* Barry Shear

Glenn Ford, Anthony Quayle, Forrest Tucker, Laraine Stephens, Richard Anderson

Jason and the Argonauts***
GB 1963 104m Technicolor
Columbia / Charles H. Schneer

With help and hindrance from the gods, Jason voyages in search of the Golden Fleece and meets all kinds of monsters.
Rambling semi-classic mythological fantasy which keeps its tongue firmly in its cheek and provides a framework for some splendid stop-frame animation.

w Jan Read, Beverly Cross *d Don Chaffey* *ph* Wilkie Cooper *m Bernard Herrmann* *sp Ray Harryhausen*

Todd Armstrong, Honor Blackman, Niall MacGinnis, Andrew Faulds, Nancy Kovack

Jassy
GB 1947 102m Technicolor
GFD / Gainsborough (Sydney Box)

A gypsy servant girl falls in love with her master but is accused of murder.
Period romantic melodrama of the *Man in Grey* school; poor of its kind despite high production values.

w Dorothy and Campbell Christie, Geoffrey Kerr, *novel* Norah Lofts *d* Bernard Knowles *ph* Geoffrey Unsworth

Margaret Lockwood, Patricia Roc, Dennis Price, Basil Sydney, Dermot Walsh, Nora Swinburne, Linden Travers, Ernest Thesiger, Cathleen Nesbitt, John Laurie, Jean Cadell, Clive Morton

Jaws**
US 1975 125m Technicolor Panavision
Universal / Zanuck–Brown (William S. Gilmore Jnr)

A man-eating shark causes havoc off the Long Island coast.
In the exploitation-hungry seventies this film took more money than any other. In itself, despite genuinely suspenseful and frightening sequences, it is a slackly narrated and sometimes flatly handled thriller with an over-abundance of dialogue and, when it finally appears, a pretty unconvincing monster.

w Peter Benchley, Carl Gottlieb, *novel* Peter Benchley *d Steven Spielberg* *ph* Bill Butler *m* John Williams

Robert Shaw, Roy Scheider, *Richard Dreyfuss*, Lorraine Gary, Murray Hamilton, Carl Gottlieb

'A mind-numbing repast for sense-sated gluttons. Shark stew for the stupified.'—*William S. Pechter*

The Jayhawkers
US 1959 110m Technicolor Vistavision
Paramount / Panama and Frank

Before the Civil War, a farmer defeats a militant posse of private raiders.
Unconvincing but rather unusual western, flat patches alternating with striking ones.

w Melvin Frank, Joseph Petracca, Frank Fenton,
A. I. Bezzerides *d* Melvin Frank *ph* Loyal Griggs *m* Jerome Moross

Fess Parker, Jeff Chandler, Nicole Maurey, Henry Silva, Herbert Rudley

The Jazz Singer****
US 1927 89m bw
Warner

A cantor's son makes it big in show business.
Archetypal Jewish weepie which became of absorbing interest as the first talkie film (songs and a few fragments of speech) and in its way, surprisingly, is not half bad.

w Alfred A. Cohn, *play* Samson Raphaelson *d Alan Crosland* *ph* Hal Mohr

Al Jolson, May McAvoy, Warner Oland, Eugenie Besserer, Otto Lederer

'A beautiful period piece, extravagantly sentimental . . . yet entirely compelling in its own conviction.'—*NFT, 1969*

The Jazz Singer
US 1953 107m Technicolor
Warner (Louis F. Edelman)

Ill-considered, schmaltzy remake of the above.

w Frank Davis, Leonard Stern, Lewis Meltzer *d* Michael Curtiz *ph* Carl Guthrie *md* Ray Heindorf

Danny Thomas, Peggy Lee, Mildred Dunnock, Eduard Franz

Jeanne Eagels*
US 1957 114m bw
Columbia (George Sidney)

A sideshow dancer becomes a Broadway star of the twenties but dies of drugs.
Well-upholstered but basically too conventional showbiz biopic.

w Daniel Fuchs, Sonya Levien, John Fante *d George Sidney* *ph Robert Planck* *m* George Duning

Kim Novak, Jeff Chandler, Agnes Moorehead, Charles Drake, Larry Gates, *Virginia Grey*

Jeannie*
GB 1941 101m bw
GFD / Tansa (Marcel Hellman)
US title: *Girl in Distress*

A Scots girl comes into money and takes a European holiday.
Mildly astringent, generally amusing comedy which overcomes shaky production. Remade as *Let's Be Happy* in 1952.

w Anatole de Grunwald, Roland Pertwee, *play* Aimée Stuart *d* Harold French

Barbara Mullen, Michael Redgrave, *Albert Lieven*, Wilfrid Lawson, Kay Hammond, Edward Chapman, Googie Withers, Gus MacNaughton

Jennie Gerhardt
US 1933 85m bw
Paramount (B. P. Schulberg)

An unmarried mother is hard done by but gets the man she loves in the end.
Archetypal weepie, adequately put across.

w Josephine Lovett, Joseph M. March, S. K. Lauren, Frank Portos *d* Marion Gering *ph* Leon Shamroy

Sylvia Sidney, Donald Cook, Mary Astor, Edward Arnold, H. B. Warner, Theodor Von Eltz

Jennifer
US 1953 73m bw
AA (Berman Swarttz)

The lady housekeeper of a California mansion broods on the mysterious disappearance of her predecessor.
Slight, quietly effective suspenser with a let-down ending.

w Virginia Myers *d* Joel Newton *ph James Wong Howe* *m* Ernest Gold

Ida Lupino, Howard Duff, Robert Nicholas, Mary Shipp

Jeopardy
US 1952 69m bw
MGM (Sol Baer Fielding)

A man on a camping holiday falls off a jetty and gets stuck in the timbers while the water rises; his wife frantically seeks help from an escaped convict.
Panic melodrama enjoyable for its clichés.

w Mel Dinelli *d* John Sturges *ph* Victor Milner *m* Dmitri Tiomkin

Barbara Stanwyck, Barry Sullivan, Ralph Meeker

Jeremiah Johnson**
US 1972 107m Technicolor Panavision
Warner (Joe Wizan)

In the 1850s an ex-soldier becomes a mountain trapper.
Splendidly made if rather desultorily plotted adventure story with the feel of raw reality.

w John Milius *d Sydney Pollack* *ph* Andrew Callaghan *m* John Rubinstein, Edward Anhalt

Robert Redford, Will Geer, Allyn McLerie

Jeremy
US 1973 90m De Luxe
UA / Kenasset

A music student falls in love with a ballet dancer.
Sentimental love story with nothing positive to commend it, chiefly interesting because for commercial release it was blown up from 16mm.

wd Arthur Barron *ph* Paul Goldsmith *m* Lee Holdridge

Robby Benson, Glynnis O'Connor, Len Bari, Leonardo Cimino

The Jerusalem File
US / Israel 1971 96m Metrocolor
MGM / Sparta (Ram Ben Efraim)

American archaeologists in Jerusalem become involved in Arab/Israeli espionage.
Muddled mixture of action and politics.

w Troy Kennedy Martin *d* John Stoll *ph* Raoul Coutard *m* John Scott

Bruce Davison, Nicol Williamson, Donald Pleasance, Ian Hendry

Jesse James**
US 1939 106m Technicolor
TCF (Nunnally Johnson)

After the Civil War, two brothers take to train robbing when railroad employees harass their family.
The life of an outlaw turns into family entertainment when Hollywood bathes it in sentiment, soft colour, family background and

warm humour. It works dangerously well, and the action sequences are splendid.

w Nunnally Johnson d Henry King ph George Barnes m Louis Silvers *ad William Darling, George Dudley*

Tyrone Power, Henry Fonda, Nancy Kelly, Jane Darwell, Randolph Scott, Henry Hull, Slim Summerville, Brian Donlevy, J. Edward Bromberg, John Carradine, Donald Meek

† Sequel 1940: *The Return of Frank James.* Remake 1957: *The True Story of Jesse James.*

Jessica

France / Italy / US 1962 105m Technicolor Panavision

UA / Ariane / Dear Film (Jean Negulesco)

The attractive midwife in a Sicilian village causes the women to go on a sex strike.

Synthetic rustic naughtiness showing several influences imperfectly assimilated.

w Edith Sommer, *novel* The Midwife of Pont Clery by Flora Sundstrom *d* Jean Negulesco *ph* Piero Portalupi *m* Mario Nascimbene

Angie Dickinson, Maurice Chevalier, Noel Noel, Gabriele Ferzetti, Sylva Koscina, Agnes Moorehead, Marcel Dalio

Jesus Christ Superstar*

US 1973 107m Technicolor Todd-AO 35

Universal (Norman Jewison, Robert Stigwood)

Young tourists in Israel re-enact episodes of the life of Christ.

Location-set fantasia based on the phenomenally successful rock opera; some of it works, but the original concept was a theatrical one.

w Melvyn Bragg, Norman Jewison, *book* Tim Rice *d* Norman Jewison *m Andrew Lloyd Webber ph Douglas Slocombe md* André Previn

Ted Neeley, Carl Anderson, Yvonne Elliman, Barry Dennen

'One of the true fiascos of modern cinema.'—*Paul D. Zimmerman*

Jet over the Atlantic

US 1958 95m bw

Warner / Inter Continental (Benedict Bogeaus)

A noble British passenger on a plane from Madrid to New York has planted a gas bomb in the luggage compartment.

Mechanical airborne suspenser with the usual assortment of unconvincing types making unconvincing gestures.

w Irving H. Cooper *d* Byron Haskin *ph* George Stahl *m* Lou Forbes

Guy Madison, Virginia Mayo, George Raft, George Macready, Ilona Massey, Anna Lee, Margaret Lindsay, Venetia Stevenson, Mary Anderson, Brett Halsey, Frederic Worlock

Jet Pilot

US 1950–57 112m Technicolor

Howard Hughes (Jules Furthman)

A Russian lady spy falls for an American pilot.

Lamentably dull and stupid romantic actioner of which all concerned should be thoroughly ashamed, especially as it took seven years to complete and is not even technically competent.

w Jules Furthman *d* Josef Von Sternberg (and others) *ph* Winton C. Hoch *m* Bronislau Kaper

John Wayne, Janet Leigh, Jay C. Flippen, Paul Fix, Richard Rober, Roland Winters, Ivan Triesault, Hans Conried

'One of the most childish, tedious and futile cold war spy dramas yet concocted by a Hollywood screenwriter.'—*John Gillett*

Jet Storm*

GB 1959 99m bw

British Lion / Britannia / Pendennis (Steven Pallos)

An airliner in flight from London to New York is discovered to have a bomb on board.

All-star slice-of-life suspenser with competently handled dialogue and situations.

w Cy Endfield, Sigmund Miller *d* Cy Endfield *ph* Jack Hildyard *m* Thomas Rajna

Richard Attenborough, George Rose, Hermione Baddeley, Mai Zetterling, Diane Cilento, Stanley Baker, Harry Secombe, Virginia Maskell, Elizabeth Sellars, Sybil Thorndike, Bernard Braden, Cec Linder, David Kossoff

Jew Suss**

GB 1934 109m bw

Gaumont (Michael Balcon)

US title: *Power*

In 18th-century Wurttemberg a Jew attains power in order to help his race, then finds he cannot use it.

Strongly made, unusual historical melodrama twisted to give an anti-Aryan slant. (Hitler later twisted his version the other way.) A little hard to take, but worthy and powerful.

w Dorothy Farnum, A. R. Rawlinson, *novel* Leon Feuchtwangler *d* Lothar Mendes

Conrad Veidt, Benita Hume, Frank Vosper,

Cedric Hardwicke, Gerald du Maurier, Pamela Ostrer, Joan Maude, Paul Graetz, Mary Clare

Jewel Robbery*
US 1932 68m bw
Warner

A jewel thief and a millionaire's wife fall in love in Vienna.
Good sparkling fun in the shadow of *Trouble in Paradise* (qv).

w Erwin Gelsey, *play* Ladislaus Fodor
d William Dieterle *ph* Robert Kurrle

William Powell, Kay Francis, Hardie Albright, André Luguet, Henry Kolker, Spencer Charters, Alan Mowbray, Helen Vinson, Lawrence Grant

Jezebel***
US 1938 104m bw
Warner (Henry Blanke)

Before the Civil War, a southern belle stirs up trouble among the menfolk by her wilfulness and spite, but atones when a plague strikes.
Superb star melodrama, tossed to her in compensation for losing *Gone with the Wind*, and dealt with in high style by all concerned.

w Clements Ripley, Abem Finkel, John Huston, *play* Owen Davis Snr *d William Wyler* *ph Ernest Haller* *m Max Steiner*

Bette Davis, Henry Fonda, George Brent, Margaret Lindsay, Fay Bainter, Richard Cromwell, Donald Crisp, Henry O'Neill, John Litel, Spring Byington, Eddie Anderson, Gordon Oliver, Irving Pichel

'Its excellences come from many sources—good plotting and writing, a director and photographer who know how to make the thing flow along with dramatic pictorial effect, and a cast that makes its story a record of living people.'—*James Shelley Hamilton*

'Without the zing Davis gave it, it would have looked very mossy indeed.'—*Pauline Kael, 1968*

Jigsaw
US 1949 72m bw
(UA) Tower (The Danzigers)

An assistant District Attorney uncovers a mob stirring up racial hatred.
Undistinguished piece of do-goodery, curiously decorated by guest stars doing bit parts as a gesture of goodwill.

w Fletcher Markle, Vincent McConnor
d Fletcher Markle *ph* Don Malkames *m* Robert Stringer

Franchot Tone, Jean Wallace, Myron McCormick, Marc Lawrence, Marlene Dietrich, Henry Fonda, John Garfield, Marsha Hunt, Leonard Lyons, Burgess Meredith

Jigsaw**
GB 1962 107m bw Cinemascope
British Lion / Britannia / Figaro (Val Guest)

Brighton policemen track down the murderer of a woman found in a lonely house on the beach.
Absorbing and entertaining little murder mystery which sustains its considerable length with interesting detail and plays as fair as can be with the audience. Excellent unassuming entertainment.

wd Val Guest, *play* Sleep Long My Love by Hilary Waugh *ph* Arthur Grant *m* none

Jack Warner, Ronald Lewis, *Michael Goodliffe*, Yolande Donlan, John Barron

Jigsaw*
US 1972 98m Technicolor TVM
Universal (Stanley Kallis)

A disgraced policeman seeks the missing witness who can save him from a murder charge.
Sufficiently engrossing plot and some fine desert chases keep the pot boiling.

w Robert E. Thompson *d* William Graham

James Wainwright, Vera Miles, Andrew Duggan, Edmond O'Brien, Marsha Hunt, Irene Dailey, Richard Kiley

Jim Thorpe, All-American
US 1951 105m bw
Warner (Everett Freeman)
GB title: *Man of Bronze*

A Red Indian becomes a star footballer, but later succumbs to drink.
Adequate sporting biopic.

w Douglas Morrow, Everett Freeman *d* Michael Curtiz *ph* Ernest Haller *m* Max Steiner

Burt Lancaster, Charles Bickford, Steve Cochran, Phyllis Thaxter, Dick Wesson

Jimmy the Gent*
US 1934 67m bw
Warner (Robert Lord)

A racketeer supplies heirs for unclaimed estates.
Adequate star crime comedy.

w Bertram Millhauser *d* Michael Curtiz *ph* Ira Morgan *md* Leo F. Forbstein

Jimmy Cagney, Bette Davis, Alice White, Allen Jenkins, Arthur Hohl, Mayo Methot, Alan Dinehart, Hobart Cavanaugh, Ralf Harolde, Philip Reed, Joe Sawyer

'Fast and flip, rough and rowdy.'—*New York American*

Jitterbugs*
US 1943 75m bw
TCF (Sol M. Wurtzel)

Laurel and Hardy help a nightclub singer to fight off gangsters.
The last Laurel and Hardy film to contain any good scenes, and almost the only one of their TCF films that did.

w Scott Darling *d* Mal St Clair *ph* Lucien Andriot

Stan Laurel, Oliver Hardy, Vivian Blaine, Bob Bailey, Douglas Fowley, Noel Madison, Lee Patrick

Jivaro!
US 1953 91m Technicolor 3-D
(Paramount) Pine–Thomas
GB title: *Lost Treasure of the Amazon*

The owner of a rubber plantation in the Amazon delta sets off into headhunter country in search of a lost treasure, and is followed by friends and enemies.
Secondary thick ear hokum; studio bound, but watchable.

w Winston Miller *d* Edward Ludwig *ph* Lionel Lindon *m* Gregory Stone

Brian Keith, Fernando Lamas, Rhonda Fleming, Lon Chaney Jnr, Richard Denning

Joan of Arc
US 1948 145m Technicolor
Walter Wanger

The last campaign of the Maid of Orleans.
Strictly from Dullsville; one studio-set piece follows another, and a group of talented people clearly thought that prestige would sell itself without the hard work that goes into more commercial productions.

w Maxwell Anderson, Andrew Solt, *play* Joan of Lorraine by Maxwell Anderson *d* Victor Fleming *ph* Joe Valentine *m* Emil Newman *ad* Richard Day

Ingrid Bergman, Jose Ferrer, George Coulouris, Francis L. Sullivan, Gene Lockhart, Ward Bond, John Ireland, Hurd Hatfield, Cecil Kellaway, George Zucco, J. Carrol Naish

'A bad film with one or two good things. It is childishly oversimplified, its battles *papier maché,* its heroine far too worldly, its spiritual content that of a chromo art calendar.'—*Herman G. Weinberg*

Joanna
GB 1968 122m De Luxe Panavision
TCF / Laughlin (Michael S. Laughlin)

A girl art student comes to London and quickly finds the road to ruin.
Antediluvian rubbish tarted up with swinging London settings.

wd Michael Sarne *ph* Walter Lassally *m* Rod McKuen

Genevieve Waite, Christian Doermer, Calvin Lockhart, Donald Sutherland

'An unnecessarily protracted punishing of a very dead quadruped.'—*MFB*

Joe*
US 1970 107m De Luxe
Cannon (David Gil)

A construction worker in a bar meets a businessman who has just killed his daughter's drug addicted lover; they become buddies in their hatred of hippies.
Highly successful in America as a backlash against permissiveness, this rough-hewn opportunistic melodrama is vivid enough but moves in fits and starts.

w Norman Wexler *d/ph* John G. Avildsen *m* Bobby Scott

Peter Boyle, Dennis Patrick, Audrey Caire, Susan Sarandon

'A bad film disfigured by brute strokes of tendentiousness.'—*Penelope Gilliatt*

Joe Butterfly
US 1957 90m Technicolor Cinemascope
U-I (Aaron Rosenberg)

Shortly after World War II, American occupying troops are conned by a Japanese interpreter.
Dull comedy intent on healing old wounds.

w Sy Gomberg, Jack Sher, Marion Hargrove *d* Jesse Hibbs *ph* Irving Glassberg *m* Joseph Gershenson

Burgess Meredith, Audie Murphy, George Nader, Keenan Wynn, Fred Clark, John Agar, Charles McGraw

Joe Kidd
US 1972 87m Technicolor Panavision
Universal / Malpaso (Sidney Beckerman)

A disreputable bounty hunter tracks down the leader of a tribe of Mexican bandits.
Rough and tumble star western with untenable moral attitudes.

w Elmore Leonard *d* John Sturges *ph* Bruce Surtees *m* Lalo Schifrin

Clint Eastwood, Robert Duvall, John Saxon, Don Stroud, James Wainwright

Joe Macbeth
GB 1955 90m bw
Columbia / Frankovich (George Maynard)

A gangster is urged by his wife to rub out his boss.
Almost too bad to be funny, this effort to update Shakespeare has actors behaving as though they were stuck in treacle, and its gimmick quality is quickly dissipated by an indifferent production.

w Philip Yordan *d* Ken Hughes *ph* Basil Emmott *m* Trevor Duncan

Paul Duncan, Ruth Roman, Grégoire Aslan, Bonar Colleano, Sidney James

Joe Smith American*
US 1942 63m bw
MGM (Jack Chertok)
GB title: *Highway to Freedom*

An aircraft factory worker with special knowledge is kidnapped by Nazis but leads the FBI to his captors.
Watchable propaganda thriller credited with easing Americans into a war mood.

w Allen Rivkin, *story* Paul Gallico *d* Richard Thorpe *ph* Charles Lawton Jnr

Robert Young, Marsha Hunt, Darryl Hickman, Harvey Stephens, Jonathan Hale, Noel Madison, Joseph Anthony

'Not a high-powered movie, it is a first rate die for the new propaganda models which Hollywood is readying for mass production.'—*Time*

Joey Boy
GB 1965 91m bw
British Lion / Launder–Gilliat

In 1941, a group of petty crooks join the army.
Abysmal service comedy, incredibly cheap and tatty and the nadir of several of the talents involved.

wd Frank Launder *ph* Arthur Lavis *m* Philip Green

Harry H. Corbett, Stanley Baxter, Bill Fraser, Reg Varney, Percy Herbert, Lance Percival

'As visually shoddy as it is unfunny . . . the final shot (Corbett pulling a lavatory chain) is all too crudely apt.'—*MFB*

John and Julie
GB 1955 82m Eastmancolor
Group Three (Herbert Mason)

Two children run away to see the coronation.
Genial little family comedy full of stock comic characters.

wd William Fairchild *ph* Arthur Grant *m* Philip Green

Colin Gibson, Leslie Dudley, Peter Sellers, Moira Lister, Wilfrid Hyde White, Sidney James, Andrew Cruickshank

John and Mary*
US 1969 92m De Luxe Panavision
TCF / Debrod (Ben Kadish)

Two New Yorkers have a one-night affair and cannot decide whether to continue.
Slight, disappointing sex comedy vehicle for two stars who were very hot at the time.

w John Mortimer, *novel* Mervyn Jones *d* Peter Yates *ph* Gayne Rescher *m* Quincy Jones *pd* John Robert Lloyd

Dustin Hoffman, Mia Farrow, Michael Tolan, Sunny Griffin, Tyne Daly

'The emphasis is not on action but on acting, which although skilful and subtly nuanced does not in this case amount to the same thing as character.'—*Jan Dawson*

'Despite all the "now" sets and surfaces, it's like an old comedy of the thirties—minus the comedy.'—*Judith Crist*

John Goldfarb Please Come Home
US 1965 96m De Luxe Cinemascope
TCF / Steve Palmer / J. Lee-Thompson

An American spy pilot crashlands near the palace of a Middle Eastern potentate at the same time as a girl reporter arrives for an interview.
Would-be satire on the cold war, anti-feminism, American football, American/Arab relations, etc. None of it works for a minute, and the actors' desperation can be plainly seen.

w William Peter Blatty *d* J. Lee-Thompson *ph* Leon Shamroy *m* Johnny Williams

Shirley Maclaine, Richard Crenna, Peter Ustinov, Fred Clark, Wilfrid Hyde White, Jim Backus

John Paul Jones
US 1959 126m Technirama
Warner / Samuel Bronston

At the time of the American revolution a young Scotsman rises to great heights in the American navy.
Fragmented biopic with a succession of guest stars which turn it into a charade almost as silly as *The Story of Mankind*. On that level it is not unentertaining.

wd John Farrow *ph* Michel Kelber *m* Max Steiner

Robert Stack, Charles Coburn (as Benjamin Franklin), Bette Davis (as Catherine the Great), Marisa Pavan, Jean-Pierre Aumont, Peter Cushing, Bruce Cabot, Macdonald Carey

Johnny Allegro*
US 1949 81m bw
Columbia (Irving Starr)
GB title: *Hounded*

A private eye eliminates a counterfeiter and marries his wife.
Cheeky variation on the plot of *Gilda*, with Macready repeating his role; later stages borrow from *The Most Dangerous Game*. All mildly diverting.

w Karen de Wolf, Guy Endore, James Edward Grant *d* Ted Tetzlaff *ph* Joseph Biroc *m* George Duning

George Raft, George Macready, Nina Foch, Will Geer, Ivan Triesault

Johnny Apollo
US 1940 93m bw
TCF (Harry Joe Brown)

A well-heeled young man turns crook.
Moderate crime melo, impeccably turned out.

w Philip Dunne, Rowland Brown *d* Henry Hathaway *ph* Arthur Miller *m* Alfred Newman

Tyrone Power, Dorothy Lamour, Edward Arnold, Lloyd Nolan, Charles Grapewin, Lionel Atwill, Marc Lawrence, Jonathan Hale

Johnny Belinda**
US 1948 103m bw
Warner (Jerry Wald)

In a remote fishing community, a deaf mute girl is raped and the sympathetic local doctor is suspected of being the father of her baby.
Melodrama of the old school which in 1948 seemed oddly to mark a new permissiveness and made a big star of Jane Wyman; the production and locations were also persuasive.

w Irmgard Von Cube, Allen Vincent, *play* Elmer Harris *d Jean Negulesco ph Ted McCord* *md* Leo F. Forbstein

Jane Wyman, Lew Ayres, Charles Bickford, Agnes Moorehead, Stephen McNally, Jan Sterling, Rosalind Ivan, Mabel Paige

Johnny Come Lately*
US 1943 97m bw
William Cagney
GB title: *Johnny Vagabond*

A travelling newspaperman is jailed for vagrancy in a small town and stays to expose corrupt politicians.
A turn-of-the-century folksy drama seemed an odd choice for a Cagney independent production, and it was not very persuasively made, but the star produced moments of his old charisma.

w John Van Druten, *novel* McLeod's Folly by Louis Bromfield *d* William K. Howard *ph* Theodor Sparkuhl *m* Leigh Harline

James Cagney, *Grace George*, Marjorie Main, Marjorie Lord, Hattie McDaniel, Edward McNamara, Bill Henry, Robert Barrat, George Cleveland, Margaret Hamilton, Lucien Littlefield, Irving Bacon

'The kind of business that might result if Jimmy Cagney, the immortal Hollywood movie star, had returned to play the lead in the annual production of his old high school's Masque and Film Club.'—*John T. McManus*

Johnny Concho
US 1956 84m bw
UA / Kent (Frank Sinatra)

A coward runs Cripple Creek because he has a gunfighter brother, but when the latter is shot another gunman takes over.
Unexpected small-scale western, pleasantly made but no *High Noon*.

w David P. Harmon, Don McGuire *d* Don McGuire *ph* William Mellor *m* Nelson Riddle

Frank Sinatra, *William Conrad*, Phyllis Kirk, Wallace Ford, John Qualen

Johnny Cool*
US 1963 101m bw
UA / Chrislaw (William Asher)

A Sicilian bandit is sent to the US on a mission of vengeance.
Chilling gangster thriller, the callousness of which is apparently meant to be counterpointed by the humorous cameo appearances of several well-known faces. This does not work.

w John McPartland, *novel* Joseph Landon *d* William Asher *ph* Sam Leavitt *m* Billy May

Henry Silva, Elizabeth Montgomery, Jim Backus, Marc Lawrence, John McGiver, Sammy Davis Jnr, Mort Sahl, Telly Savalas, Joseph Calleia, Robert Armstrong, Douglass Dumbrille, Elisha Cook Jnr

Johnny Dark
US 1954 85m Technicolor
U-I (William Alland)

A motor company produces a new sports car designed by an employee, who drives it in a race.
Competent, unremarkable action melodrama tailor-made for its star.

w Franklin Coen *d* George Sherman *ph* Carl Guthrie *m* Joseph Gershenson

Tony Curtis, Piper Laurie, Don Taylor, Paul Kelly, Ilka Chase, Sidney Blackmer

Johnny Eager*
US 1941 107m bw
MGM (John W. Considine)

A gangster makes a play for a society girl.
Well-made, rather unattractive gangster melodrama.

w John Lee Mahin, James Edward Grant
d Mervyn Le Roy *ph* Harold Rosson

Robert Taylor, *Van Heflin*, Lana Turner, Edward Arnold, Robert Sterling, Patricia Dane, Glenda Farrell, Henry O'Neill

Johnny Frenchman
GB 1945 111m bw
Ealing (S. C. Balcon)

Rivalry between the fishermen of Cornwall and Brittany prevents the course of true love from running smooth.
Rhubarbing extras and studio sets make this an unreal and disappointing Ealing melodrama, and all the actors look helpless.

w T. E. B. Clarke *d* Charles Frend *ph* Roy Kellino

Françoise Rosay, Tom Walls, Patricia Roc, Paul Dupuis, Ralph Michael, Frederick Piper, Arthur Hambling

Johnny Got His Gun
US 1971 111m colour
World Entertainments Ltd (Bruce Campbell)

In 1918 a soldier is so badly wounded as to lose arms, legs, eyes, ears, mouth and nose, and begs his doctors to kill him.
A horrifying and fascinating premise turns out to have nowhere to go, at least not in this talky treatment which the author has nurtured too long.

wd Dalton Trumbo *ph* Jules Brenner *m* Jerry Fielding

Timothy Bottoms, Jason Robards Jnr, Marsha Hunt, Donald Sutherland, Kathy Fields, Diane Varsi

Johnny Guitar*
US 1953 110m Trucolor
Republic (Nicholas Ray)

In old Arizona, the proprietress of a gambling saloon stakes a claim to valuable land and incurs the enmity of a lady banker.
Weird Freudian western notable for a running catfight between its lady protagonists; the title character is decidedly secondary. Not exactly a good movie, but memorable because it's almost always over the top.

w Philip Yordan, *novel* Roy Chanslor
d Nicholas Ray *ph* Harry Stradling *m* Victor Young

Joan Crawford, Mercedes McCambridge, Sterling Hayden, Ernest Borgnine, Ward Bond, John Carradine, Scott Brady

'A very rum western, with cockeyed feminist attitudes.'—*New Yorker, 1975*

Johnny Tremain
US 1957 81m Technicolor
Walt Disney

In 1773 Boston an apprentice silversmith joins the Sons of Liberty and helps start the War of Independence.
Schoolbook history with little vitality.

w Tom Blackburn, *novel* Esther Forbes
d Robert Stevenson *ph* Charles B. Boyle
m George Bruns

Hal Stalmaster, Luana Patten, Jeff York, Sebastian Cabot, Richard Beymer, Walter Sande

Johnny Trouble
US 1956 88m bw
Clarion (John H. Auer)

An elderly widow becomes involved with a boys' college and thinks she has found her lost grandson.
Sentimental, whimsical star vehicle.

w Charles O'Neal, David Lord *d* John H. Auer
ph Peverell Marley *m* Frank de Vol

Ethel Barrymore, Stuart Whitman, Cecil Kellaway, Carolyn Jones, Jesse White

The Joker Is Wild*
US 1957 126m bw Vistavision
Paramount / Charles Vidor

Joe E. Lewis, a twenties nightclub singer, loses his voice after an attack by gangsters, and becomes a comedian.
Reasonably lively showbiz biopic in jaundiced vein; good atmosphere but far too long.

w Oscar Saul, *book* Art Cohn *d* Charles Vidor
ph Daniel L. Fapp *m* Walter Scharf

Frank Sinatra, Mitzi Gaynor, Eddie Albert, Jeanne Crain, Beverly Garland, Jackie Coogan, Ted de Corsia

The Jokers**
GB 1967 126m Technicolor
Universal / Adastra / Gildor / Scimitar (Maurice Foster Ben Arbeid)

Two young brothers in London society plan to create a sensation by borrowing (and replacing) the crown jewels.
Bright suspense comedy which sums up the

swinging London era pretty well and is generally amusing though it finally lacks aplomb.

w Dick Clement, Ian La Frenais d Michael Winner ph Ken Hodges *m* Johnny Pearson

Michael Crawford, Oliver Reed, Harry Andrews, *James Donald*, Daniel Massey, Michael Hordern, Gabriella Licudi, Frank Finlay, Warren Mitchell, Rachel Kempson, Peter Graves

A Jolly Bad Fellow*
GB 1964 95m bw
British Lion / Pax / Tower / Michael Balcon (Donald Taylor)
US title: *They All Died Laughing*

A brash chemistry don tries a new poison on his enemies.
Interesting but finally irritating comedy of murders with a punnish rather than a donnish script and only moments of genuine sub-Ealing hilarity.

w Robert Hamer, Donald Taylor, *novel* Don Among the Dead Men by C. E. Vulliamy *d* Robert Hamer *ph* Gerald Gibbs *m* John Barry

Leo McKern, Janet Munro, Maxine Audley, Duncan Macrae, Dennis Price, Miles Malleson, Leonard Rossiter

Jolson Sings Again**
US 1949 96m Technicolor
Columbia (Sidney Buchman)

Al Jolson's later career and second marriage to a nurse he met while entertaining troops in World War II.
Breezy, routine, rather empty sequel to the following.

w Sidney Buchman *d* Henry Levin *ph* William Snyder *md* Morris Stoloff

Larry Parks, Barbara Hale, William Demarest, Ludwig Donath, Bill Goodwin, Tamara Shayne, Myron McCormick

The Jolson Story****
US 1946 129m Technicolor
Columbia (Sidney Skolsky)

Asa Yoelson, son of a cantor, becomes Al Jolson, the great entertainer of the twenties; but showbiz success brings marital difficulties.
Whitewashed biopic in impeccable Hollywood style, with everything working shamelessly right, a new star in the leading role, perfect if unambitious production values, and a deluge of the best songs ever written.

w Stephen Longstreet d Alfred E. Green, Joseph H. Lewis ph Joseph Walker *md* Morris Stoloff

Larry Parks (using Jolson's own voice), *William Demarest, Evelyn Keyes, Ludwig Donath, Tamara Shayne*, Bill Goodwin, *Scotty Beckett*, John Alexander

Jonathan Livingston Seagull*
US 1973 114m De Luxe Panavision
Paramount / JLS Partnership / Hall Bartlett

The life of a seagull who aims to fly faster than any of his peers and eventually arrives in a perfect world.
Weird 'family' fantasy based on a phenomenally successful book which clearly could not translate easily to the screen. The bird photography is much more successful than the mysticism.

w Richard Bach, from his book *d* Hall Bartlett *ph Jack Couffer m* Neil Diamond, Lee Holdridge *ph* Boris Leven

'A parable couched in the form of a nature film of overpowering beauty and strength in which, perhaps to our horror, we are forced to recognize ourselves in a seagull obsessed with the heights.'—*Michael Korda*

The Jones Family
Less human, more farcical than the Hardy films (qv), this series was TCF's second feature answer to MGM's money-makers, and pleased a lot of people at the time. Pop was Jed Prouty, Mom was Spring Byington, Grandma was Florence Roberts, and the youngsters included Kenneth Lake, George Ernest, Billy Mahan, June Carlson and June Lang. The first script was from a play by Katharine Cavanaugh, and the principal director was Frank Strayer.

1936: EVERY SATURDAY NIGHT, EDUCATING FATHER, BACK TO NATURE
1937: OFF TO THE RACES, BORROWING TROUBLE, HOT WATER
1938: LOVE ON A BUDGET, TRIP TO PARIS, SAFETY IN NUMBERS, DOWN ON THE FARM
1939: EVERYBODY'S BABY, QUICK MILLIONS, THE JONES FAMILY IN HOLLYWOOD, TOO BUSY TO WORK
1940: ON THEIR OWN

† An earlier series with different actors was abandoned after two episodes: *Young as You Feel* (1931), *Business and Pleasure* (1932).

Josephine and Men
GB 1955 98m Eastmancolor
Charter (John and Roy Boulting)

The three romances of a determined young woman.
Alarmingly thin, old-fashioned romantic comedy

with all resolved in a country cottage. Nothing quite works, especially the colour.

w Nigel Balchin, Roy Boulting, Frank Harvey *d* Roy Boulting *ph* Gilbert Taylor *m* John Addison

Glynis Johns, *Jack Buchanan*, Donald Sinden, Peter Finch, Heather Thatcher, Ronald Squire

The Journey
US 1959 125m Technicolor
MGM / Alby (Anatole Litvak)

During the 1956 Hungarian uprising, a busload of international passengers is detained overnight by a Russian major.
Pretentious, predictable and dull multi-melodrama peopled by uninteresting characters; different handling might have made a *Casablanca* of it.

w George Tabori *d* Anatole Litvak *ph* Jack Hildyard *m* Georges Auric

Yul Brynner, Deborah Kerr, Jason Robards Jnr, Anouk Aimée, Robert Morley, E. G. Marshall, Anne Jackson, David Kossoff, Kurt Kasznar, Gerard Oury

'Ten minutes of this and we know where we are: we are back in the 1930s with Alfred Hitchcock and that glamorous band of international characters trapped in Mitteleuropa.'—*Steven Marcus*

Journey for Margaret*
US 1942 81m bw
MGM (B. P. Fineman)

An American correspondent brings home an orphan from the London blitz.
Efficient tearful propaganda which coincidentally made a star of little Margaret O'Brien.

w David Hertz, William Ludwig, *book* William L. White *d* W. S. Van Dyke *ph* Ray June *m* Franz Waxman

Robert Young, Laraine Day, *Margaret O'Brien*, Billy Severn, Fay Bainter, Signe Hasso, Nigel Bruce, Halliwell Hobbes

Journey from Darkness
US 1975 74m colour TVM
Columbia / Bob Banner

A blind student fights to enter medical school.
Another true weepie, more moving than dramatic.

w Peggy Chantler Dick *d* James Goldstone

Mark Singer, Kay Lenz, Wendell Burton, William Windom, Joseph Campanella, Jack Warden

Journey into Fear***
US 1942 71m bw
RKO (Orson Welles)

A munitions expert finds himself in danger from assassins in Istanbul, and has to be smuggled home.
Highly enjoyable impressionist melodrama supervised by Orson Welles and full of his touches and excesses.

w Joseph Cotten, Orson Welles, novel Eric Ambler d Norman Foster (and *Orson Welles*) *ph Karl Struss m* Constantin Bakaleinikoff

Joseph Cotten, Dolores del Rio, Jack Moss, Orson Welles, Ruth Warrick, Agnes Moorehead

'Brilliant atmosphere, the nightmare of pursuit, eccentric encounters on the way, and when the shock comes it leaps at eye and ear.'—*William Whitebait*

Journey to the Center of the Earth***
US 1959 132m De Luxe Cinemascope
TCF (Charles Brackett)

An Edinburgh professor and assorted colleagues follow an explorer's trail down an extinct Icelandic volcano to the earth's centre.
Enjoyable hokum which gets more and more fantastic but only occasionally misses its footing; it ends splendidly with the team being catapulted out of Stromboli on a tide of lava.

w Walter Reisch, Charles Brackett, novel Jules Verne *d Henry Levin ph* Leo Tover *m Bernard Herrmann ad* Lyle R. Wheeler, Franz Bachelin, Herman A. Blumenthal

James Mason, Arlene Dahl, Pat Boone, Peter Ronson, Diane Baker, Thayer David

'The attraction of a Jules Verne fantasy . . . is in the endearing contrast between the wildest adventures and the staidest Victorian propriety on the part of those undergoing them . . . There is about the whole film a good-natured enjoyment of its own excesses.'—*Penelope Houston*

Journey to the Far Side of the Sun*
GB 1969 99m De Luxe Cinemascope
Universal / Century 21 Productions (Gerry Anderson)
Alternative title: *Doppelganger*

An astronaut on a mission to a hitherto undetected planet discovers it to be an exact duplicate of Earth, and his own double returns in his place.
Intriguing, impeccably produced, but rather dull science fiction.

w Gerry and Sylvia Anderson, Donald James *d* Robert Parrish *ph* John Read *m* Barry Gray *sp* Harry Oakes *models* Derek Meddings

Ian Hendry, Roy Thinnes, Patrick Wymark, Lynn Loring, Herbert Lom, George Sewell, Ed Bishop

Journey Together*
GB 1944 95m bw
RAF Film Unit

Trainee pilots receive instruction in England and America before going on their first bombing mission.
Modest wartime semi-documentary, pleasingly done.

w Terence Rattigan *d* John Boulting *ph* Harry Waxman *m* Gordon Jacob *pd* John Howell

Richard Attenborough, Jack Watling, David Tomlinson, Edward G. Robinson, Hugh Wakefield, Sebastian Shaw, Ronald Adam, Bessie Love

Journey's End*
GB 1930 120m bw
Gainsborough–Welsh–Pearson–Tiffany (George Pearson)

France 1917: personal tensions mount as men die in the trenches.
Primitive early sound version (made in Hollywood because of better equipment) of a justly celebrated play first performed a year earlier. Cinematically uninteresting, with acting generally over the top, but it kept Whale and Clive in Hollywood where they shortly collaborated on *Frankenstein*.

w Joseph Moncure March, Gareth Gundrey, *play R. C. Sheriff* *d* James Whale *ph* Benjamin Kline

Colin Clive, Ian MacLaren, David Manners, Billy Bevan, Anthony Bushell, Robert Adair

'It has been transferred to the screen with the greatest possible tact and discretion.'—*James Agate*

Joy in the Morning
US 1965 103m Metrocolor
MGM (Henry T. Weinstein)

Early episodes in the marriage of a poor teenage student.
Glutinous romantic drama, quite well made.

w Sally Benson, Alfred Hayes, Norman Lessing, *novel* Betty Smith *d* Alex Segal *ph* Ellsworth Fredericks *m* Bernard Herrmann

Richard Chamberlain, Yvette Mimieux, Arthur Kennedy, Oscar Homolka, Joan Tetzel, Sidney Blackmer

Joy of Living*
US 1938 90m bw
RKO (Felix Young)

A practical-minded Broadway songstress succumbs to the charms of an aristocratic freewheeler.
Zany romantic comedy, not quite zippy enough to make one forget its irritating archness, but socio-historically very interesting, in the mould of *You Can't Take It with You.*

w Gene Towne, Allan Scott, Graham Baker *d* Tay Garnett *ph* Joseph Walker *md* Frank Tours

Irene Dunne, Douglas Fairbanks Jnr, Alice Brady, Guy Kibbee, Lucille Ball, Eric Blore, Jean Dixon, Warren Hymer, Billy Gilbert

Juarez**
US 1939 132m bw
Warner (Hal. B. Wallis, Henry Blanke)

A revolutionary leader causes the downfall of Emperor Maximilian of Mexico.
Spectacular historical drama with many fine moments which do not quite coalesce into a dramatic whole, chiefly owing to the lack of a single viewpoint.

w John Huston, Wolfgang Reinhardt, Aeneas Mackenzie *d William Dieterle ph Tony Gaudio m Erich Wolfgang Korngold*

Brian Aherne, Bette Davis, Paul Muni, Claude Rains, John Garfield, Donald Crisp, Gale Sondergaard, Joseph Calleia, Gilbert Roland, Henry O'Neill, Pedro de Cordoba, Montagu Love, Harry Davenport

'A million dollars' worth of ballroom sets, regimentals, gauze shots and whiskers.'—*Otis Ferguson*

'Dramatically by far the most effective of Warners' biographical films of the thirties.'—*Graham Greene*

Jubal
US 1955 101m Technicolor Cinemascope
Columbia (William Fadiman)

A rancher's wife causes trouble when she falls in love with a wandering cowhand.
Solid sex western, moderately interestingly done.

w Russell S. Hughes, Delmer Daves, *novel* Jubal Troop by Paul Wellman *d* Delmer Daves *ph* Charles Lawton *m* David Raksin

Glenn Ford, Ernest Borgnine, Felicia Farr, Rod Steiger, Valerie French, Charles Bronson, Noah Beery Jnr

Jubilee Trail*
US 1954 103m Trucolor
Republic (Joseph Kane)

Jealousy and murder by covered wagon en route from New Orleans to the California gold fields.
Bumpy adventure melodrama, generally quite entertaining.

w Bruce Manning, *novel* Gwen Bristow
d Joseph Kane *ph* Jack Marta *m* Victor Young

Vera Hruba Ralston, Forrest Tucker, Joan Leslie, Pat O'Brien, John Russell, Ray Middleton

The Judge and Jake Wyler
US 1972 100m Technicolor TVM
Universal (Richard Levinson, William Link)

An eccentric lady judge, retired for health reasons, employs an ex-con as her 'legs' to solve murder cases.
Another comical pair of investigators, and this time their heart plainly is not in it: they must have seen the script.

w David Shaw, Richard Levinson, William Link
d Gil Melle

Bette Davis, Doug McClure, Eric Braeden

The Judge Steps Out*
US 1947 91m bw
RKO
GB title: *Indian Summer*

A middle-aged judge leaves his wife and sets off on an aimless journey in the course of which he falls in love with a café proprietress.
A pleasing human story, simply told in a manner which at the time seemed more French than American.

w Boris Ingster, Alexander Knox *d* Boris Ingster

Alexander Knox, Ann Sothern, George Tobias, Sharyn Moffett

Judgment at Nuremberg**
US 1961 190m bw
UA / Roxlom (Stanley Kramer)

A fictionalized version of the 1948 trial of the Nazi leaders for crimes against humanity.
Interminable, heavy-going dramatic documentary expanded from a succinct TV play into a courtroom marathon with philosophical asides. All good stuff, but too much of it.

w Abby Mann, from his play *d* Stanley Kramer
ph Ernest Laszlo *m* Ernest Gold *pd* Rudolph Sternad

Spencer Tracy, Marlene Dietrich, Burt Lancaster, Richard Widmark, *Maximilian Schell*, Judy Garland, Montgomery Clift, William Shatner, Edward Binns, Werner Klemperer, Torben Meyer, Alan Baxter, Ray Teal

'Some believe that by tackling such themes Kramer earns at least partial remission from criticism. How much? 20 per cent off for effort?'—*Stanley Kauffmann*

Judith
US 1965 109m Technicolor Panavision
Paramount / Cumulus / Command

In 1947 Israel, loyalists rescue the wife of an escaped war criminal and ask her to identify him, but she takes her own revenge.
Glowering kibbutz adventures, well enough made but adding up to neither one thing nor the other, and rather confusing to non-Jews.

w Jon Michael Hayes, *story* Lawrence Durrell
d Daniel Mann *ph* John Wilcox *m* Sol Kaplan
pd Wilfrid Shingleton

Sophia Loren, Peter Finch, Jack Hawkins, Hans Verner, André Morell

Juggernaut
GB 1936 64m bw
Ambassador

A scientist lacking funds for his experiments agrees to commit murder.
Tedious melodrama which wastes Karloff's time.

w Cyril Campion, H. Fowler Mear, H. Fraenkel
d Henry Edwards *ph* Sidney Blythe

Boris Karloff, Mona Goya, Joan Wyndham, Arthur Margetson, Anthony Ireland, Morton Selten

Juggernaut**
US 1974 110m De Luxe Panavision
UA / Richard Alan Simmons

A transatlantic liner is threatened by a mad bomber.
Elaborate suspense spectacular, most of which works pretty well.

w Richard Alan Simmons *d* Richard Lester
ph Gerry Fisher *m* Ken Thorne *pd* Terence Marsh

Richard Harris, David Hemmings, Omar Sharif, Anthony Hopkins, Ian Holm, Shirley Knight, Roy Kinnear, Cyril Cusack, Freddie Jones

'However unoriginal its basic ingredients, it hardly ever slackens its pace or diverts attention from its central premise.'—*Jonathan Rosenbaum*

'Jaunty, cynical slapstick.'—*New Yorker*

The Juggler
US 1953 88m bw
Columbia / Stanley Kramer

A Jewish refugee in Palestine has a horror of being imprisoned, and runs away from a transit camp with a small wandering boy.
Well-meaning cheapie, a curiously aimless topical drama which fails to make any of its several points.

w Michael Blankfort, from his novel *d* Edward Dmytryk *ph* Roy Hunt *m* Georges Antheil

Kirk Douglas, Milly Vitale, Paul Stewart, Joey Walsh

Juke Girl
US 1942 90m bw
Warner (Jack Saper, Jerry Wald)

Fruit workers in Florida get involved in murder.
Hokum melodrama with all concerned treading water.

w A. I. Bezzerides, *novel* Theodore Pratt *d* Curtis Bernhardt *ph* Bert Glennon *m* Adolph Deutsch

Ann Sheridan, Ronald Reagan, Richard Whorf, Gene Lockhart, Faye Emerson, George Tobias, Alan Hale, Howard da Silva, Donald McBride, Fuzzy Knight, Willie Best

Julia Misbehaves
US 1948 99m bw
MGM (Everett Riskin)

An actress returns to her stuffy husband when her daughter is about to marry.
Desperate attempt to find a vehicle for a fading star team.

w William Ludwig, Arthur Wimperis, Harry Ruskin, *novel* The Nutmeg Tree by Margery Sharp *d* Jack Conway *ph* Joseph Ruttenberg *m* Adolph Deutsch

Greer Garson, Walter Pidgeon, Elizabeth Taylor, Peter Lawford, Cesar Romero, Lucile Watson, Nigel Bruce, Mary Boland, Reginald Owen, Ian Wolfe, Edmund Breon, Fritz Feld, Aubrey Mather, Henry Stephenson

Julie*
US 1956 97m bw
MGM / Arwin (Marty Melcher)

A concert pianist plans to murder his wife.
Wildly improbable but entertaining suspenser in which the lady finally has to assume control of an airplane.

wd Andrew Stone *ph* Fred Jackman Jnr *m* Leith Stevens

Doris Day, Louis Jourdan, Barry Sullivan, Frank Lovejoy, John Gallaudet

'Some of the dialogue reaches a fine pitch of banality.'—*MFB*

Julius Caesar**
US 1953 121m bw
MGM (John Houseman)

Cassius and Brutus lead the conspirators who murder Caesar, but are themselves routed by Mark Antony.
Straightforward, rather leaden presentation of Shakespeare's play, lit by effective moments in the acting, but the sudden change from talk to battle is not smoothed over.

wd Joseph L. Mankiewicz *ph* Joseph Ruttenberg *m* Miklos Rozsa *ad* Cedric Gibbons, Edward Carfagno

John Gielgud, James Mason, Marlon Brando, Greer Garson, Deborah Kerr, Louis Calhern, Edmond O'Brien, George Macready, Michael Pate, John Hoyt, Alan Napier

Julius Caesar
GB 1969 116m Technicolor Panavision
Commonwealth United (Peter Snell)

Elementary production with a surprising number of faults and very few merits.

w Robert Furnival *d* Stuart Burge *ph* Ken Higgins *m* Michael Lewis *pd* Julia Trevelyan Oman

Richard Johnson, Jason Robards Jnr, *John Gielgud*, Charlton Heston, Robert Vaughn, Richard Chamberlain, Diana Rigg, Jill Bennett, Christopher Lee, Alan Browning, Andrew Crawford

Jumbo*
US 1962 124m Metrocolor Panavision
MGM (Joe Pasternak, Martin Melcher)
Alternative title: *Billy Rose's Jumbo*

In 1910, the daughter of the owner of a shaky circus prevents a take-over bid.
Hoary circus story with music. General effect disappointing: the elephant steals the show.

w Sidney Sheldon, *play* Ben Hecht, Charles MacArthur *d* Charles Walters *ph* William H. Daniels *m/ly* Richard Rodgers, Lorenz Hart *ch Busby Berkeley*

Doris Day, Jimmy Durante, Stephen Boyd, Martha Raye, Dean Jagger

Jump for Glory
GB 1937 89m bw
Criterion (Douglas Fairbanks Jnr, Marcel Hellman)
US title: *When Thief Meets Thief*

Adventures of a cat burglar who accidentally kills his ex-partner.
Curious star comedy drama with pleasing scenes.

w John Meehan Jnr, Harold French, *novel* Gordon MacDonnell *d* Raoul Walsh

Douglas Fairbanks Jnr, Valerie Hobson, Alan Hale, Edward Rigby, Barbara Everest, Jack Melford, Anthony Ireland

Jump into Hell
US 1955 93m bw
Warner (David Weisbart)

Paratroops relieve a fort in Indo-China.
Mediocre semi-documentary war heroics.

w Irving Wallace *d* David Butler *ph* Peverell Marley *m* David Buttolph

Jacques Sernas, Kurt Kasnar, Arnold Moss, Peter Van Eyck, Pat Blake

Jumping Jacks*
US 1952 96m bw
Paramount / Hal B. Wallis

Two cabaret comedians join the paratroops.
Standard star farce, one of Martin and Lewis' best.

w Robert Lees, Fred Rinaldo, Herbert Baker *d* Norman Taurog *ph* Daniel L. Fapp *m* Joseph J. Lilley

Dean Martin, *Jerry Lewis*, Mona Freeman, Robert Strauss, Don Defore

June Bride
US 1948 97m bw
Warner (Henry Blanke)

Two bickering reporters are sent to cover a small-town wedding.
Sloppily structured romantic farce in which nothing ever comes together.

w Ranald MacDougall, *play* Feature for June by Eileen Tighe, Graeme Lorimer *d* Bretaigne Windust *ph* Ted McCord *m* David Buttolph

Bette Davis, Robert Montgomery, Fay Bainter, Tom Tully, Betty Lynn, Barbara Bates, Jerome Cowan, Mary Wickes, Debbie Reynolds

The Jungle Book*
US 1942 109m Technicolor
Alexander Korda (W. Howard Greene)
aka: *Rudyard Kipling's Jungle Book*

Growing up with animals in an Indian forest, a boy forestalls the getaway of three thieves.
High-budgeted but rather boring live action version with stiff-jointed model animals.

w Laurence Stallings, *stories* Rudyard Kipling *d* Zoltan Korda, André de Toth *ph* Lee Garmes

Sabu, Joseph Calleia, John Qualen, Frank Puglia, Rosemary de Camp

Jungle Book*
US 1967 78m Technicolor
Walt Disney

Cartoon version relying less on action than on songs and voices; patchily successful but no classic.

d Wolfgang Reitherman *m/ly* Richard and Robert Sherman, Terry Gilkyson *voices* George Sanders, Phil Harris, Louis Prima, Sabation Cabot, Sterling Holloway

Jungle Jim

When Johnny Weissmuller began to show his middle-age spread, Columbia put him in a jacket and more or less redid his Tarzan thing in a series of second features which appeared to be shot in producer Sam Katzman's back garden and gradually indulged in wilder and wilder plots. None of them has more than curiosity value. Main scriptwriters were Carroll Young, Dwight Babcock, Sam Newman; main directors William Berke, Lee Sholem, Spencer G. Bennet.

1948: JUNGLE JIM
1949: THE LOST TRIBE
1950: CAPTIVE GIRL, MARK OF THE GORILLA, PYGMY ISLAND
1951: FURY OF THE CONGO, JUNGLE MANHUNT
1952: JUNGLE JIM IN THE FORBIDDEN LAND, VOODOO TIGER
1953: SAVAGE MUTINY, VALLEY OF THE HEADHUNTERS, KILLER APE
1954: JUNGLE MANEATERS, CANNIBAL ATTACK
1955: JUNGLE MOON MEN, DEVIL GODDESS

The Jungle Princess*
US 1936 84m bw
Paramount (E. Lloyd Sheldon)

A British hunter is injured on a tropical island and rescued by a native girl and her animal retinue.
Dorothy Lamour's first film role cast her as the female Tarzan she was to play (in a sarong, of course) a dozen times again. This is strictly a programmer, but after its success it was all done again, rather better, as *Her Jungle Love*.

w Cyril Hume, Gerald Geraghty, Gouverneur Morris *d* William Thiele *ph* Harry Fischbeck *md* Morris Stoloff

Dorothy Lamour, Ray Milland, Akim Tamiroff, Lynne Overman, Molly Lamont, Hugh Buckler

'Poor Mr Lynne Overman is expected to lend humorous relief to a film already richly comic.'—*Graham Greene*

Junior Bonner*
US 1972 105m Movielab Todd-AO 35
Joe Wizan / Booth–Gardner / Solar / ABC

An ageing rodeo star returns to his home town and finds his family in trouble.
Well-made, rather downcast and not very interesting drama, remarkably gentle from this director.

w Jeb Rosebrook *d* Sam Peckinpah *ph* Lucien Ballard *m* Jerry Fielding

Steve McQueen, Ida Lupino, Robert Preston, Joe Don Baker, Ben Johnson

Juno and the Paycock*
GB 1930 85m bw
British International (John Maxwell)

During the Irish troubles of the early twenties, tragedy comes to a poor Dublin family.
A plainly done film version of a modern classic whose changes of mood would not in any case have worked well on the screen.

w Alfred Hitchcock, Alma Reville, *play* Sean O'Casey *d* Alfred Hitchcock *ph* Jack Cox

Sara Allgood, Edward Chapman, Maire O'Neill, Sidney Morgan, John Laurie

'A film which completely justifies the talkies.'—*James Agate*

Jupiter's Darling*
US 1954 96m Eastmancolor Cinemascope
MGM (George Wells)

Advancing on Rome, Hannibal falls in love with the dictator's fiancée.
A splendid example of the higher lunacy, with coloured elephants decorating an MGM musical about the fall of the Roman Empire. Small elements can be salvaged, and the gall is enough to be divided into three parts.

w Dorothy Kingsley, *play* The Road to Rome by Robert E. Sherwood *d* George Sidney *ph* Paul C. Vogel, Charles Rosher *m* Burton Lane *ly* Harold Adamson *ch* Hermes Pan *ad* Cedric Gibbons, Uric McCleary

Esther Williams, Howard Keel, George Sanders, Marge and Gower Champion, Richard Haydn, William Demarest

Just for You
US 1952 104m Technicolor
Paramount (Paul Duggan)

A successful songwriter finds that his troublesome teenage son is in love with his own fiancée.
Tiresomely scripted, pleasantly played romantic comedy with music.

w Robert Carson, *novel* Famous by Stephen Vincent Benet *d* Elliott Nugent *ph* George Barnes *md* Emil Newman *songs* Harry Warren, Leo Robin

Bing Crosby, Jane Wyman, Bob Arthur, Ethel Barrymore, Natalie Wood, Cora Witherspoon, Regis Toomey

Just My Luck
US 1957 86m bw
Rank (Hugh Stewart)

A jeweller's assistant becomes involved in horse racing.
Flat star vehicle.

w Alfred Shaughnessy *d* John Paddy Carstairs *ph* Jack Cox *m* Philip Green

Norman Wisdom, Leslie Phillips, Margaret Rutherford, Delphi Lawrence

Justine
US 1969 116m De Luxe Panavision
TCF / Pandro S. Berman

In Alexandria in the thirties, the beautiful wife of a wealthy banker influences the lives of all who meet her.
Disastrous condensed version of a very unusual set of novels whose atmosphere has not translated at all well. The result is like a bad rehearsal for a film, which is not surprising in view of the number of producers variously involved. The author feared 'a sort of *Peyton Place* with camels', and got it.

w Lawrence B. Marcus, *novels* The Alexandria Quartet by Lawrence Durrell *d* George Cukor *ph* Leon Shamroy *m* Jerry Goldsmith

Anouk Aimée, Michael York, Dirk Bogarde, Anna Karina, John Vernon, George Baker, Philippe Noiret, Robert Forster, Jack Albertson, Michael Dunn, Barry Morse, Cliff Gorman, Severn Darden

'Could well stand as a model of what can happen when Hollywood gets to grips with a celebrated literary property.'—*David Wilson*

'Despite leaden forays into homosexuality, transvestitism, incest, and child prostitution, it remains as naively old-fashioned in its emotional and intellectual vocabulary as in its actual verbiage and cinematic technique.'—*John Simon*

K

Kaleidoscope*
GB 1966 103m Technicolor
Warner / Winkast (Elliott Kastner)
Reissue title: *The Bank Breaker*

An American playboy breaks into a playing card factory and marks the designs so that he can win in every European casino.
Would-be swinging comedy-thriller which in fact is entertaining only when it stops trying to dazzle.

w Robert and Jane Howard-Carrington *d* Jack Smight *ph Christopher Challis* *m* Stanley Myers *ad* Maurice Carter

Warren Beatty, Susannah York, Clive Revill, Eric Porter, Murray Melvin

'A "groovie movie" it certainly is, with a battery of fashionable camera tricks, kaleidoscopic dissolves, and virtually every scene introduced from behind an irrelevant piece of furniture.'—*David Wilson*

Kangaroo
US 1952 84m Technicolor
TCF (Robert Bassler)

In old Australia, a con man pretends to be a rancher's long lost heir, then complicates things by falling in love with the rancher's daughter.
Standard romantic action hokum.

w Harry Kleiner *d* Lewis Milestone *ph* Charles G. Clarke *m* Sol Kaplan

Maureen O'Hara, Peter Lawford, Finlay Currie, Richard Boone, Chips Rafferty, Charles Tingwell

Kansas City Bomber
US 1972 99m Metrocolor
MGM / Levy–Gardner–Laven / Raquel Welch (Marty Elfand)

A roller skating star finds time between affairs to beat her rival in a big match.
Vulgar melodrama with good action scenes.

w Thomas Rickman, Calvin Clements *d* Jerrold Freedman *ph* Fred Koenekamp *m* Don Ellis

Raquel Welch, Kevin McCarthy, Norman Alden, Jeanne Cooper

Kansas City Massacre*
US 1975 100m colour TVM
Dan Curtis

Melvin Purvis, the midwestern G-man who captured Dillinger, is ambushed when he transports a prisoner by train.
Pretty good gangster thriller, violent by TV standards.

wd Dan Curtis

Dale Robertson, Bo Hopkins

Kate MacShane
US 1975 100m colour TVM
Paramount (E. Jack Neuman)

A lady lawyer with an Irish family defends a socialite on a murder charge.
Tiresomely talkative and restless courtroom pilot with a highly unconvincing dénouement.

w E. Jack Neuman *d* Marvin Chomsky

Anne Meara, Sean McClory, Christine Belford, Charles Cioffi, Larry Gates

Katherine
US 1975 100m colour TVM
Josak

A young heiress despises her heritage and joins a party of semi-revolutionaries.
Or, Tanya Where Art Thou? One most people could do without.

d Jeremy Kagan

Art Carney, Sissy Spacek, Henry Winkler, Jane Wyatt

Kathleen
US 1941 88m bw
MGM (George Haight)

A neglected daughter finds a new wife for her widowed father.
One of the reasons for Shirley Temple's early retirement.

w Mary McCall Jnr, *story* Kay Van Riper
d Harold S. Bucquet *ph* Sidney Wagner
m Franz Waxman

Shirley Temple, Herbert Marshall, Laraine Day, Gail Patrick, Felix Bressart, Nella Walker, Lloyd Corrigan

Kathy O
US 1958 99m Eastmancolor
Cinemascope
U-I (Sy Gomberg)

A temperamental child star befriends a lonely columnist.
Overlong Hollywood comedy drama with amusing moments.

w Jack Sher, Sy Gomberg *d* Jack Sher *ph* Arthur E. Arling *m* Charles Tobias, Ray Joseph

Matty McCormack, Dan Duryea, Jan Sterling, Sam Levene

The Keegans
US 1975 74m Technicolor TVM
Universal (George Eckstein)

Problems of an Irish family living near Boston.
Predictable to the last drop of blarney, this cosy family drama suddenly turns into a murder plot.

w Dean Riesner *d* John Badham

Adam Roarke, Judd Hirsch, Joan Leslie, Spencer Milligan, Paul Shenar

Keep 'Em Flying
US 1941 86m bw
Universal (Glenn Tryon)

Two incompetents in the Army Air Corps get mixed up with identical twin girls.
A big moneymaker of its day, this comedy now seems especially resistible.

w True Boardman, Nat Perrin, John Grant *d* Arthur Lubin *ph* Joseph Valentine

Bud Abbott, Lou Costello, Martha Raye, Carol Bruce, William Gargan, Dick Foran, Charles Lang

Keep Your Powder Dry
US 1945 93m bw
MGM (George Haight)

Three girls from different backgrounds join the WACS.
Totally uninteresting and unconvincing female flagwaver.

w Mary C. McCall Jnr, George Bruce *d* Edward Buzzell *ph* Ray June *m* David Snell

Lana Turner, Laraine Day, Susan Peters, Agnes Moorehead, Bill Johnson, Natalie Schaefer, June Lockhart, Lee Patrick

Keep Your Seats Please*
GB 1936 82m bw
ATP (Basil Dean)

A prospective heir seeks a fortune hidden in one of six chairs.
Good star comedy on a theme later reworked in *It's in the Bag* (qv) and *The Twelve Chairs* (qv).

w Tom Geraghty, Ian Hay, Anthony Kimmins, *play* Twelve Chairs by Elie Ilf, Eugene Petrov *d* Monty Banks

George Formby, Florence Desmond, Alastair Sim, Gus McNaughton, Harry Tate

Keeper of the Flame*
US 1942 100m bw
MGM (Victor Saville)

A reporter befriends the widow of a politician and forces her to disclose her husband's guilty secret.
Well-acted but over-solemn melodrama which badly needs a sting in the tail.

w Donald Ogden Stewart, *novel* I. A. R. Wylie *d* George Cukor *ph* William Daniels *m* Bronislau Kaper

Spencer Tracy, Katharine Hepburn, Richard Whorf, Margaret Wycherly, Donald Meek, Stephen McNally, Audrey Christie, Frank Craven

Kelly and Me
US 1956 86m Technicolor
Cinemascope
U-I (Robert Arthur)

The ups and downs of a song and dance man and the dog who shares his act.
Mild vaudeville saga with totally predictable twists.

w Everett Freeman *d* Robert Z. Leonard *ph* Maury Gertsman *m* Joseph Gershenson

Van Johnson, Piper Laurie, Martha Hyer, Onslow Stevens

Kelly's Heroes
US / Yugoslavia 1970 143m Metrocolor
Panavision
MGM / The Warriors / Avala (Irving Leonard)

During World War II, an American platoon abducts a German general and accidentally discovers the whereabouts of a fortune in gold.
Crude slam-bang actioner for the obvious market.

w Troy Kennedy Martin *d* Brian G. Hutton *ph* Gabriel Figueroa *m* Lalo Schifrin *2nd unit* Andrew Marton

Clint Eastwood, Telly Savalas, Don Rickles, Donald Sutherland, Carroll O'Connor, Stuart Margolin, Dick Davalos

'Over two hours of consistently devastating explosions, pyrotechnics and demolition.'—*MFB*

'Made for no possible reason other than a

chance to use the Yugoslav army at cut rates.'—*Judith Crist, 1973*

The Kennel Murder Case*
US 1933 73m bw
Warner
Philo Vance proves that an apparent suicide is really murder.
Complex murder mystery, very smartly handled and often cited as a classic of the genre.
w Robert N. Lee, Peter Milner, *novel* S. S. Van Dine *d Michael Curtiz* *ph* William Reese
William Powell, Mary Astor, Eugene Pallette, Ralph Morgan, Helen Vinson, Jack La Rue, Paul Cavanagh, Robert Barrat
† See also *Philo Vance*.

The Kentuckian
US 1955 104m Technicolor Cinemascope
UA / Hecht–Lancaster
A Kentucky backwoodsman takes his small son to settle in Texas.
Ambling mid-western with moments of interest.
w A. B. Guthrie Jnr, *novel* The Gabriel Horn by Felix Holt *d* Burt Lancaster *ph* Ernest Laszlo *m* Roy Webb
Burt Lancaster, Dianne Foster, Diana Lynn, *Walter Matthau*, John McIntire, Una Merkel, John Carradine

Kentucky*
US 1938 95m Technicolor
TCF (Gene Markey)
Horse-breeding rivalry prevents the smooth running of true love.
Harmless family entertainment, more professionally handled than its innumerable later imitations. Remade as *April Love*.
w Lamar Trotti, *novel* The Look of Eagles by John Taintor Foote *d* David Butler *ph* Ernest Palmer *m* Louis Silvers
Loretta Young, Richard Greene, Walter Brennan, Douglass Dumbrille, Karen Morley, Moroni Olsen, Russell Hicks

Kes*
GB 1969 109m Technicolor
UA / Woodfall (Tony Garnett)
In a northern industrial town, a boy learns about life from the fate of his pet bird.
'Realistic' family drama, full of the kind of merit that does not equate with entertainment: hard to take and harder to hear.
w Barry Hines, Ken Loach, Tony Garnet, *novel* A Kestrel for a Knave by Barry Hines *d Ken Loach* *ph* Chris Menges *m* John Cameron
David Bradley, Lynne Perrie, Colin Welland, Freddie Fletcher, Brian Glover
'There emerges a most discouraging picture of life in the industrial north . . . infinitely sad in its total implications, it is also immensely funny in much of its detail.'—*Brenda Davies*

The Kettles
The rustic couple evolved from characters in *The Egg and I* (qv); Marjorie Main and Percy Kilbride went on to play them in a cheap but very popular series for Universal, variously scripted and directed.
1949: MA AND PA KETTLE
1950: MA AND PA KETTLE GO TO TOWN
1951: MA AND PA KETTLE BACK ON THE FARM
1952: MA AND PA KETTLE AT THE FAIR
1953: MA AND PA KETTLE ON VACATION
1954: MA AND PA KETTLE AT HOME
1955: MA AND PA KETTLE AT WAIKIKI
1956: THE KETTLES IN THE OZARKS (Arthur Hunnicutt instead of Kilbride)
1957: THE KETTLES ON OLD MACDONALD'S FARM (Parker Fennelly instead of Kilbride)

The Key*
GB 1958 134m bw Cinemascope
Columbia / Open Road (Carl Foreman)
World War II tugboat skippers, about to embark on dangerous missions, pass on the key to an apartment and a girl to go with it.
Rather foolish symbolic melodrama which never makes its purpose clear but along the way provides fragments of love story, chunks of the supernatural and dollops of war action, rather languidly assembled with great technical competence but little real feeling. The talent occasionally shows through.
w Carl Foreman, *novel* Stella by Jan de Hartog *d* Carol Reed *ph* Oswald Morris *m* Malcolm Arnold
William Holden, Sophia Loren, *Trevor Howard*, Oscar Homolka, Kieron Moore

Key Largo***
US 1948 101m bw
Warner (Jerry Wald)
A returning war veteran fights gangsters on the Florida keys.
Moody melodrama on similar lines to *To Have and Have Not*: it sums up the post-war mood of despair, allows several good acting

performances, and builds up to a pretty good action climax.

w Richard Brooks, John Huston, play Maxwell Anderson *d John Huston ph Karl Freund* *m* Max Steiner

Humphrey Bogart, Lauren Bacall, *Claire Trevor, Edward G. Robinson, Lionel Barrymore*, Thomas Gomez, Marc Lawrence

Key to the City
US 1950 101m bw
MGM (Z. Wayne Griffin)

At a San Francisco convention, two mayors get involved in several escapades and fall in love. Routine romantic comedy.

w Robert Riley Crutcher *d* George Sidney *ph* Harold Rosson *m* Bronislau Kaper

Clark Gable, Loretta Young, Frank Morgan, James Gleason, Marilyn Maxwell, Raymond Burr, Lewis Stone, Raymond Walburn, Pamela Britton

'A comedy made to measure . . . the script concerns itself with wringing every possible laugh from a number of stock situations.'—*Variety*

Key West
US 1972 91m colour TVM
Warner (Anthony S. Martin)

Documents incriminating a US senator are sought by crooks and agents on the Florida keys. Ho-hum hokum.

w Anthony S. Martin *d* Philip Leacock

Stephen Boyd, Woody Strode, Sheree North, Earl Hindman, Tiffany Bolling, William Prince

The Keys of the Kingdom*
US 1944 137m bw
TCF (Joseph L. Mankiewicz)

The life of a 19th-century Scottish priest in China.
Studio-made missionary melodrama, a big hit for its new star but otherwise an undistinguished piece of work with a shuffling pace and not much by way of climax.

w Joseph L. Mankiewicz, Nunnally Johnson, *novel* A. J. Cronin *d* John M. Stahl *ph* Arthur Miller *m* Alfred Newman *ad* James Basevi, William Darling

Gregory Peck, Thomas Mitchell, Vincent Price, Rose Stradner, Roddy McDowall, Edmund Gwenn, Cedric Hardwicke, Peggy Ann Garner, James Gleason, Anne Revere

Khartoum*
GB 1966 134m Technicolor Ultra Panavision
UA / Julian Blaustein

The last years of General Gordon.
Dullish history book stuff which fails to explain Gordon the man but occasionally erupts into glowing action.

w Robert Ardrey *d* Basil Dearden *ph Edward Scaife, Harry Waxman m* Frank Cordell

Charlton Heston, Laurence Olivier, Ralph Richardson, Richard Johnson, Hugh Williams, Alexander Knox, Johnny Sekka, Nigel Green, Michael Hordern

'Academic accuracy and spectacular battles are unhappy partners.'—*MFB*

Kid Blue
US 1973 100m De Luxe Panavision
TCF / Marvin Schwarz Productions

In 1902 Texas a young outlaw tries to go straight.
Deliberately myth-deflating western with agreeably rich detail.

w Edwin Shrake *d* Dennis Hopper *ph* Billy Williams *m* Tim McIntyre, John Rubenstein *pd* Joel Schiller

Dennis Hopper, Warren Oates, Peter Boyle, Ben Johnson, Lee Purcell, Janice Rule, Clifton James

A Kid for Two Farthings*
GB 1955 96m Eastmancolor
London Films (Carol Reed)

Among the colourful characters of London's Petticoat Lane market moves a boy whose pet goat seems to have the magical power of a unicorn.
Whimsical character comedy-drama made with some style but too insubstantial and unconvincing to be affectionately remembered.

w Wolf Mankowitz *d* Carol Reed *ph* Ted Scaife *m* Benjamin Frankel

Celia Johnson, Diana Dors, David Kossoff, Brenda de Banzie, Sidney Tafler, Primo Carnera, Joe Robinson

The Kid from Brooklyn
US 1946 114m Technicolor
Samuel Goldwyn

A timid milkman becomes a prizefighter.
Yawn-provoking comedy, a remake of Harold Lloyd's *The Milky Way*; the first indication that Danny Kaye could be a bore.

w Grover Jones, Frank Butler, Richard Connell *d* Norman Z. McLeod *ph* Gregg Toland *md* Carmen Dragon

Danny Kaye, Virginia Mayo, Vera-Ellen, Steve Cochran, Eve Arden, Walter Abel, Lionel Stander, Fay Bainter, Clarence Kolb

The Kid from Spain**
US 1932 90m bw
Samuel Goldwyn

A simpleton is mistaken for a celebrated bullfighter.
Charmingly dated star musical which, though primitive in some respects, is a splendid reminder of its period.

w William Anthony McGuire, Bert Kalmar, Harry Ruby *d* Leo McCarey *ph* Gregg Toland *ch Busby Berkeley*

Eddie Cantor, Lyda Roberti, Robert Young, Ruth Hall, John Miljan, Noah Beery, J. Carrol Naish, Stanley Fields, Betty Grable, Paulette Goddard

Kid Galahad*
US 1937 101m bw
Warner (Samuel Bischoff)

A bellhop is groomed as a prizefighter.
Good standard prizefight melodrama, remade as *The Wagons Roll at Night* and later as *Kid Galahad* with Elvis Presley (see below).

w Seton I. Miller, *novel* Francis Wallace *d* Michael Curtiz *ph* Tony Gaudio *m* Heinz Roemheld, Max Steiner

Edward G. Robinson, Bette Davis, Wayne Morris, Jane Bryan, Humphrey Bogart, Harry Carey

Kid Galahad
US 1962 96m De Luxe
UA / Mirisch (David Weisbart)

Tolerable light-hearted musical remake of the above.

w William Fay *d* Phil Karlson *ph* Burnett Guffey *m* Jeff Alexander

Elvis Presley, Lola Albright, Gig Young, Joan Blackman, Charles Bronson, Ned Glass, David Lewis, Robert Emhardt

Kid Millions
US 1935 90m bw (Technicolor sequence)
Samuel Goldwyn

An East Side kid inherits a fortune and has the time of his life.
Dated star musical with moments which still please.

w George Oppenheimer, William Anthony McGuire *d* Roy del Ruth *ph* Gregg Toland *m/ly* Bert Kalmar, Harry Ruby *ad* Richard Day

Eddie Cantor, Ethel Merman, Ann Sothern, George Murphy, Warren Hymer

Kidnapped*
US 1938 90m bw
TCF

During the Jacobite rebellion a young boy is sold by his wicked uncle as a slave, and is helped by an outlaw.
Much altered version of a classic adventure story, exciting enough in its own right, and well made in the thirties tradition.

w Sonya Levien, Richard Sherman, Walter Ferris, *novel* Robert Louis Stevenson *d* Alfred L. Werker *m* Arthur Lange

Warner Baxter, Freddie Bartholemew, Arleen Whelan, John Carradine, C. Aubrey Smith, Nigel Bruce, Reginald Owen

Kidnapped*
GB 1971 107m Movielab Panavision
Omnibus (Frederick H. Brogger)

Remake incorporating sections of *Catriona*. Not particularly exciting, but the acting helps.

w Jack Pulman *d* Delbert Mann *ph* Paul Beeson *m* Roy Budd

Michael Caine, Lawrence Douglas, Trevor Howard, Jack Hawkins, Donald Pleasance, Gordon Jackson, Freddie Jones, Jack Watson

The Kidnappers*
GB 1953 95m bw
Rank / Nolbandov–Parkyn
US title: *The Little Kidnappers*

In a Nova Scotian village at the turn of the century a stern old man denies his young grandchildren a pet, so they borrow a baby and hide it in the woods.
Fairly pleasing and popular whimsy for family audiences.

w Neil Paterson *d* Philip Leacock *ph* Eric Cross *m* Bruce Montgomery

Duncan Macrae, Vincent Winter, Jon Whiteley, Theodore Bikel, Jean Anderson

Kiki
US 1931 96m bw
UA / Mary Pickford (Joseph M. Schenck)

Long unseen star musical.

w Sam Taylor, *play* David Belasco *d* Sam Taylor *ph* Karl Struss

Mary Pickford, Reginald Denny, Joseph Cawthorne, Margaret Livingston

Killdozer
US 1974 74m Technicolor TVM
Universal (Herbert F. Solow)

A bulldozer affected by a strange meteorite murderously attacks a construction crew on a remote site.
And they can't run fast enough to get out of its way. Silly nonsense.

w Theodore Sturgeon, Ed MacKillop *d* Jerry London

Clint Walker, James Wainwright, Carl Betz, Neville Brand

The Killer Bees*
US 1974 74m colour TVM
RSO

The elderly matriarch of a strange family is obsessed by bees and can use them to kill.
Flabby, over-talkative suspenser with a couple of good sequences; mainly notable for the reappearance of its star.

w Joyce and John William Corrington *d* Curtis Harrington

Gloria Swanson, Edward Albert, Kate Jackson, Roger Davis, Craig Stevens

Killer by Night*
US 1971 100m colour TVM
Cinema Center 100

A doctor seeks a diphtheria carrier, a cop seeks a killer . . . and they're both looking for the same man.
Didn't this use to be *Panic in the Streets*? Well enough done again, anyway.

d Bernard McEveety

Robert Wagner, Diane Baker, Greg Morris, Theodore Bikel, Robert Lansing, Mercedes McCambridge, Pedro Armendariz Jnr

The Killer Elite
US 1975 120m De Luxe Panavision
UA / Exeter–Persky Bright (Martin Baum, Arthur Lewis)

A private crime fighting organization handles cases which the CIA prefers not to.
Smooth, fashionable violence which seems to proclaim the end of a cycle.

w Marc Norman, Stirling Silliphant, *novel* Monkey in the Middle by Robert Rostand *d* Sam Peckinpah *ph* Philip Lathrop *m* Jerry Fielding

James Caan, Robert Duvall, Arthur Hill, Gig Young, Mako, Bo Hopkins, Burt Young, Tom Clancy

'Merely a commercial chore.'—*Tom Milne*

The Killer That Stalked New York
US 1950 75m bw
Columbia (Robert Cohn)
GB title: *Frightened City*

New York is on the alert for a girl smallpox carrier.
Absurdly-titled minor thriller, quite competent but wholly unsurprising.

w Harry Essex *d* Earl McEvoy *ph* Joseph Biroc *m* Hans Salter

Charles Korvin, Evelyn Keyes, William Bishop, Dorothy Malone, Lola Albright, Barry Kelley, Carl Benton Reid, Ludwig Donath

The Killer Who Wouldn't Die
US 1976 96m colour TVM
Paramount (Ivan Goff, Ben Roberts)
aka: *Ohanian*

An ex-detective takes to his boat when his wife is killed in mistake for himself, but finds himself harbouring a hired killer and avenging the death of a friend.
Lame crime pilot with the star using his own name and his own boat; it's all a mite too relaxed to make suspenseful melodrama.

w Cliff Gould *d* William Hale *m* George Garvarentz

Mike Connors, Samantha Eggar, Patrick O'Neal, Clu Gulager, Grégoire Aslan, Robert Hooks, Robert Colbert, James Shigeta, Mariette Hartley

The Killers***
US 1946 105m bw
U-I (Mark Hellinger)
TV title: *A Man Alone*

In a small sleazy town a gangster waits for two assassins to kill him, and we later find out why.
Elaborate tale of cross and double-cross, stunningly executed.

w Anthony Veiller, story Ernest Hemingway *d Robert Siodmak ph Elwood Bredell m* Miklos Rozsa

Burt Lancaster, Edmond O'Brien, Ava Gardner, Albert Dekker, Sam Levene, John Miljan, Virginia Christine, Vince Barnett, Charles D. Brown, Donald MacBride, Phil Brown, Charles McGraw, William Conrad

'About one tenth is Hemingway's, the rest is Universal-International's.'—*Richard Winnington*

'Seldom does a melodrama maintain the high tension that distinguishes this one.'—*Variety*

The Killers*
US 1964 95m Pathecolor TVM
U-I (Don Siegel)

Zesty, brutal remake intended for TV, but released theatrically because of its violence.

w Gene L. Coon *d* Don Siegel *ph* Richard L. Rawlings *m* Johnny Williams

John Cassavetes, Lee Marvin, Clu Gulager, Angie Dickinson, Ronald Reagan, Claude Akins

Killer's Kiss
US 1955 64m bw
UA / Stanley Kubrick

A prizefighter rescues a girl from her gangster lover, and is marked for death.
Tedious low-budget indie which first brought its director into notice.

w/d/ph Stanley Kubrick *m* Gerald Fried

Frank Silvera, Irene Kane, Jamie Smith

The Killers of Kilimanjaro
GB 1959 91m Technicolor Cinemascope
Columbia / Warwick
US title: *Adamson of Africa*

A railroad engineer helps a girl find her lost father and fiancé.
Old-fashioned safari adventure full of action and animals.

w Richard Maibaum, Cyril Hume *d* Richard Thorpe *ph* Ted Moore *m* William Alwyn

Robert Taylor, Anne Aubrey, Grégoire Aslan, Anthony Newley

The Killing**
US 1956 83m bw
UA / Harris–Kubrick (J. B. Harris)

An ex-convict recruits helpers to steal two million dollars from a racetrack.
Incisive, entertaining, downbeat caper movie clearly influenced by *The Asphalt Jungle* and *Rififi*.

wd Stanley Kubrick, novel Clean Break by Lionel White *ph* Lucien Ballard *m* Gerald Fried

Sterling Hayden, Marie Windsor, Jay C. Flippen, Elisha Cook Jnr, Coleen Gray, Vince Edwards, Ted de Corsia, Joe Sawyer, Tim Carey

'The visual authority constantly dominates a flawed script.'—*Arlene Croce*

'The camera watches the whole shoddy show with the keen eye of a terrier stalking a pack of rats.'—*Time*

The Killing of Sister George*
US 1969 138m Metrocolor
Associates and Aldrich / Palomar

An ageing lesbian actress is fired from a TV serial and her life collapses around her.
Heavily handled film version of an amusing and moving play; everything is clumsily spelt out, including the love scenes, and the actresses are forced to repeat themselves.

w Lukas Heller, *play Frank Marcus* *d* Robert Aldrich *ph* Joseph Biroc *m* Gerald Fried

Beryl Reid, Susannah York, *Coral Browne*, Roland Fraser, Patricia Medina, Hugh Paddick, Cyril Delevanti

'The play was second-rate, but with its nice blend of the homely and the chilling, the absurdist and the perverse, it had the quality of a Kraft-Ebbing comic book. Aldrich and Heller have turned this material into a crawling tear-jerker, the lines spoken at a speed adjusted to non-English or non-language-speaking audiences.'—*John Simon*

Kim*
US 1951 112m Technicolor
MGM (Leon Gordon)

The orphaned son of a British soldier in India has adventures with his horseman friend who belongs to the British secret service.
Colourful Boys' Own Paper high jinks, quite lively but never convincing.

w Leon Gordon, Helen Deutsch, Richard Schayer, *novel* Rudyard Kipling *d* Victor Saville *ph* William Skall *m* André Previn

Errol Flynn, Dean Stockwell, Paul Lukas, Robert Douglas, Thomas Gomez, Cecil Kellaway, Arnold Moss, Reginald Owen

'Ornate, lavish, but curiously lacking in genuine atmosphere, vitality or period sense.'—*Penelope Houston*

Kind Hearts and Coronets***
GB 1949 106m bw
Ealing

An impecunious heir eliminates eight D'Ascoynes who stand between him and the family fortune.
Witty, genteel black comedy well set in the stately Edwardian era and quite deserving of its reputation for wit and style; yet the effect is curiously muffled and several opportunities missed.

w Robert Hamer, John Dighton d Robert Hamer ph Douglas Slocombe

Dennis Price, Alec Guinness (in eight roles), Valerie Hobson, Joan Greenwood, Miles Malleson, Arthur Lowe

'A brilliant misfire for the reason that its plentiful wit is literary and practically never pictorial.'—*Richard Winnington*

'Enlivened with cynicism, loaded with dramatic irony and shot through with a suspicion of social satire.'—*Daily Telegraph*

Kind Lady*
US 1935 76m bw
MGM / Lucien Hubbard
aka: *House of Menace*

A confidence trickster insinuates himself and his criminal friends into the house of an invalid lady.
Unusual but unconvincing melodrama with overwrought leading performances.

w Bernard Schubert, *play* Edward Chodorov, *story* Hugh Walpole *d* George B. Seitz *ph* George Folsey *m* Edward Ward

Basil Rathbone, Aline MacMahon, Mary Carlisle, Frank Albertson, Dudley Digges, Doris Lloyd

Kind Lady*
US 1951 78m bw
MGM (Armand Deutsch)

Edwardian-set remake of the above, rather more subtly acted but failing to extract all possible frissons.

w Jerry Davis, Edward Chodorov, Charles Bennett *d* John Sturges *ph* Joseph Ruttenberg *m* David Raksin

Maurice Evans, Ethel Barrymore, Angela Lansbury, Keenan Wynn, Betsy Blair, John Williams

'A curiously tame melodrama whose shocks, when they do come, are muffled and ineffectual.'—*Penelope Houston*

A Kind of Loving***
GB 1962 112m bw
Anglo-Amalgamated / Vic Films / Waterhall

A young north country draughtsman is forced into marriage, has to live with his dragon-like mother in law, and finally sorts out a relationship with his unhappy wife.
Blunt melodrama with strong kinship to *Saturday Night and Sunday Morning*, strikingly directed and photographed amid urban grime and suburban conformity.

w Keith Waterhouse, Willis Hall, novel Stan Barstow d John Schlesinger ph Denys Coop m Ron Grainer

Alan Bates, June Ritchie, Thora Hird, Bert Palmer, Gwen Nelson

King and Country*
GB 1964 86m bw
BHE (Norman Priggen, Joseph Losey)

In the trenches during World War I, a private is courtmartialled and shot for desertion.
Neat cinematic treatment of a very downbeat play.

w Evan Jones, *play* Hamp by John Wilson *d* Joseph Losey *ph Denys Coop m* Larry Adler *pd* Richard Macdonald

Tom Courtenay, *Dirk Bogarde*, Leo McKern, Barry Foster, James Villiers, Peter Copley

The King and Four Queens
US 1956 86m De Luxe Cinemascope
UA / Russ / Field / Gabco (David Hempstead)

A cowboy braves the wrath of a lady sharpshooter to gain gold and the hand of one of her four daughters.
Tawdry sex western sporadically enlivened by good-humoured playing.

w Margaret Fitts, Richard Alan Simmons *d* Raoul Walsh *ph* Lucien Ballard *m* Alex North

Clark Gable, Eleanor Parker, Jo Van Fleet, Jean Willes, Barbara Nichols, Sara Shane, Roy Roberts

'A superficially cynical exercise in the rival attractions of sex and money.'—*MFB*

The King and I**
US 1956 133m Eastmancolor Cinemascope 55
TCF (Charles Brackett)

Musical remake of *Anna and the King of Siam* (qv), from the highly successful stage production.
The film is opulent in lush detail but quite lacking in style.

w Ernest Lehman *d* Walter Lang *ph* Leon Shamroy *m Richard Rodgers book/ly Oscar Hammerstein II ad* Lyle Wheeler, John de Cuir

Deborah Kerr, Yul Brynner, Rita Moreno, Martin Benson, Alan Mowbray, Geoffrey Toone, Terry Saunders

'Gaiety has something of a struggle to survive.'—*Penelope Houston*

King Creole
US 1958 116m bw Vistavision
Paramount (Hal B. Wallis)

A failed graduate becomes a singer in a New Orleans night club, and gets involved with gangsters.
Disagreeable crook melodrama turned into a musical star vehicle.

w Herbert Baker, Michael V. Gazzo, *novel* A

Stone for Danny Fisher by Harold Robbins
d Michael Curtiz

Elvis Presley, Carolyn Jones, Dean Jagger, Walter Matthau, Dolores Hart, Paul Stewart

A King in New York*
GB 1957 109m bw
Attica (Charles Chaplin)

A penniless European king finds himself at odds with the American way of life.
Feeble Chaplin comedy from his anti-American period; tedious dialogue and poor physical production allow only momentary flashes of the satire intended.

wd/m Charles Chaplin *ph* Georges Périnal

Charles Chaplin, Michael Chaplin, *Oliver Johnson*, Dawn Addams, Jerry Desmonde, Harry Green, Maxine Audley, Sid James

'Unhappily he is a sadder and an older man; the real punch is gone. His dethroned king is an ironically apt image.'—*Marvin Felheim*

King Kong****
US 1933 100m bw
RKO (Merian C. Cooper)

A film producer on safari brings back a giant ape which terrorizes New York.
The greatest monster movie of all, a miracle of trick work and suspense, with some of the most memorable moments in film history.

w James Creelman, Ruth Rose, *story* Edgar Wallace *d Merian C. Cooper, Ernest Schoedsack ph* Edward Linden, Verne Walker, J. O. Taylor *sound effects* Murray Spivak *chief technician Willis J. O'Brien m Max Steiner*

Robert Armstrong, Fay Wray, Bruce Cabot, Frank Reicher

King Lear*
GB / Denmark 1970 137m bw
Columbia / Filmways–Laterna (Michael Birkett)

Tragedy ensues when an old king prematurely divides his kingdom between his daughters.
Miserably photographed in freezing Jutland, this is a deliberately downbeat version which despite its varied points of interest is extremely hard to sit through.

w William Shakespeare (a cut text) *d* Peter Brook *ph* Henning Kristiansen *m* none *pd* Georges Wakhevitch

Paul Scofield, Irene Worth, Alan Webb, Tom Fleming, Susan Engel, Cyril Cusack, Patrick Magee, Jack MacGowran

King of Alcatraz*
US 1938 56m bw
Paramount (William C. Thomas)

Convicts escape on a freighter, but one needs surgery.
Pacy programmer with a stalwart cast.

w Irving Reis *d* Robert Florey *ph* Harry Fischbeck *m* Boris Morros

Gail Patrick, J. Carrol Naish, Lloyd Nolan, Harry Carey, Robert Preston, Anthony Quinn, Dennis Morgan, Porter Hall

King of Burlesque*
US 1936 88m bw
TCF (Kenneth MacGowan)

A vaudeville impresario overcomes his troubles.
Well-written musical with plenty of variety talent.

w James Seymour, Gene Markey, Harry Tugend *d* Sidney Lanfield *ph* Peverell Marley *songs* various

Warner Baxter, Alice Faye, Jack Oakie, Mona Barrie, Arline Judge, Dixie Dunbar, Gregory Ratoff, Herbert Mundin, *Fats Waller*, Kenny Baker

King of Gamblers
US 1937 79m bw
Paramount
aka: *Czar of the Slot Machines*

A ruthless gangster loves a singer who loves a reporter who is out to expose him.
A muddled script mars this pacy lower-berth item.

w Doris Anderson *d* Robert Florey *ph* Harry Fischbeck *m* Boris Morros

Akim Tamiroff, Claire Trevor, Lloyd Nolan, Buster Crabbe, Porter Hall

King of Jazz***
US 1930 101m Technicolor
Universal (Carl Laemmle Jnr)

Musical revue.
Stylish, spectacular, revelatory early musical: a treasure trove.

devised/d John Murray Anderson w Harry Ruskin, Charles MacArthur *pd* Hal Mohr, Ray Rennahan, Jerome Ash *ad Herman Rose*

Paul Whiteman and his orchestra, John Boles, Bing Crosby (with the Rhythm Boys), Laura la Plante, Glenn Tryon, Slim Summerville, Walter Brennan

King of Kings*
US 1961 161m Super Technirama
MGM / Samuel Bronston

The life of Jesus Christ.
Known in the trade as *I Was a Teenage Jesus*, this good-looking but rather tedious film is neither vulgar nor very interesting: a solemn, decent, bible-in-pictures pageant.

w Philip Yordan *d* Nicholas Ray *ph* Franz Planer, Manuel Berenger *m* Miklos Rozsa *ad* Georges Wakhevitch

Jeffrey Hunter, Robert Ryan, Siobhan McKenna, Frank Thring, Hurd Hatfield, Rip Torn, Harry Guardino, Viveca Lindfors, Rita Gam

The King of Marvin Gardens*
US 1972 104m Eastmancolor
Columbia / BBS (Bob Rafaelson)

The host of a late night radio talk show gets embroiled in his brother's schemes.
Thoughtful tragi-comedy overweighted by talk, but with good performances.

w Jacob Brackman *d* Bob Rafaelson *ph* Laszlo Kovacs

Jack Nicholson, Bruce Dern, Ellen Burstyn, Julia Anne Robinson

'Indecipherable dark nonsense about brothers and goals and the American dream. An unqualified disaster.'—*New Yorker*

'Glum news from the people who made *Five Easy Pieces*, which had a lot of good work in it along with some pretentious flab. In their new picture the flab has taken over.'—*Stanley Kauffmann*

King of the Khyber Rifles
US 1954 100m Technicolor Cinemascope
TCF (Frank Rosenberg)

In 1857 a British garrison in India is threatened by the forces of Kuuram Khan but saved by a half-caste officer.
Standard North-West Frontier adventure, old-fashioned and rather dull.

w Ivan Goff, Ben Roberts *d* Henry King *ph* Leon Shamroy *m* Bernard Herrmann

Tyrone Power, Terry Moore, Michael Rennie, Guy Rolfe, John Justin

King of the Roaring Twenties
US 1961 106m bw
Warner / AA / Bischoff–Diamond
GB title: *The Big Bankroll*

A gambler, Arnold Rothstein, becomes powerful among twenties gangsters.
Routine crime drama, shoddily made.

w Jo Swerling *d* Joseph M. Newman *ph* Carl Guthrie *m* Franz Waxman

David Janssen, Dianne Foster, Mickey Rooney, Mickey Shaughnessy, Diana Dors, Dan O'Herlihy, Jack Carson, Keenan Wynn, William Demarest, Joseph Schildkraut, Regis Toomey, Murvyn Vye

'Superficial, shopworn biography of an infamous bookie.'—*MFB*

King, Queen, Knave*
US / West Germany 1972 92m Eastmancolor
Wolper / Maran (Lutz Hengst)

The wife of a Munich bookseller falls for his adolescent nephew.
Amusing, capriciously directed sex comedy.

w David Shaw, David Seltzer, *novel* Vladimir Nabokov *d* Jerzy Skolomowski *ph* Charly Steinberger *m* Stanley Myers

Gina Lollobrigida, David Niven, John Moulder-Brown, Mario Adorf, Carl Fox-Duering

King Rat**
US 1965 134m bw
Columbia / Coleytown (James Woolf)

In Singapore's Changi Gaol during World War II an American corporal lives more comfortably than the other prisoners by shabby dealings with the camp guards.
Overlong but generally gripping character melodrama—'not a story of escape but a story of survival'.

wd Bryan Forbes, novel James Clavell *ph* Burnett Guffey *m* John Barry

George Segal, Tom Courtenay, John Mills, James Fox, Denholm Elliott, Todd Armstrong, Patrick O'Neal, James Donald, Alan Webb, Leonard Rossiter, Geoffrey Bayldon

King Richard and the Crusaders
US 1954 113m Warnercolor Cinemascope
Warner (Henry Blanke)

During the Crusades, the dreaded Saladin arrives in England in disguise and falls in love with Lady Edith . . .
Crudely confected comic strip version of Sir Walter Scott's *The Talisman*, ineptly written and cast, with poor production values.

w John Twist *d* David Butler *ph* Peverell Marley *m* Max Steiner

Rex Harrison (as Saladin), Virginia Mayo, George Sanders, Laurence Harvey, Robert Douglas

'Do not adjust your set—the sound you hear is Sir Walter Scott turning in his grave.'—*Sunday Express*

King Solomon's Mines**
GB 1938 80m bw
Gainsborough (Geoffrey Barkas)

Explorers in Africa persuade an exiled chief to help them find a diamond mine.
Lively, well-cast version of a favourite adventure novel.

w Michael Hogan, A. R. Rawlinson, Roland Pertwee, Ralph Spence, Charles Bennett, *novel* H. Rider Haggard *d Robert Stevenson*

Cedric Hardwicke, *Paul Robeson*, Roland Young, John Loder, Anna Lee, Sydney Fairbrother, Robert Adams

King Solomon's Mines**
US 1950 102m Technicolor
MGM (Sam Zimbalist)

A remake which is largely travelogue with the merest trimmings of story.

w Helen Deutsch *d* Compton Bennett *ph* Robert Surtees

Stewart Granger, Deborah Kerr, Richard Carlson, Hugo Haas, Lowell Gilmore

Kings Go Forth
US 1958 109m bw
UA / Ross–Eton (Frank Ross)

August 1944: two American soldiers fall out over a black French woman who is torn between them.
Heavy-going war melodrama, well enough done for those who can take it.

w Merle Miller, *novel* Joe David Brown *d* Delmer Daves *ph* Daniel Fapp *m* Elmer Bernstein

Frank Sinatra, Tony Curtis, Natalie Wood, Leora Dana, Karl Swenson

Kings of the Sun
US 1963 108m De Luxe Panavision
UA / Mirisch (Lewis J. Rachmil)

A Mayan tribe emigrates from Mexico to Texas and makes peace with the local Indian chief.
Ponderous dark age epic replete with human sacrifice, high-mindedness and solemn pauses. The actors and sets carry it as far as it will go.

w Elliot Arnold, James R. Webb *d* J. Lee-Thompson *ph* Joe MacDonald *m* Elmer Bernstein *ad* Alfred Ybarra

Yul Brynner, George Chakiris, Shirley Anne Field, Richard Basehart, Brad Dexter, Barry Morse

King's Rhapsody
GB 1955 93m Eastmancolor Cinemascope
Everest (Herbert Wilcox)

An exiled Ruritanian king leaves his mistress to return home to a political marriage.
Love versus duty in a ludicrously inept film of Ivor Novello's highly theatrical musical drama, cheaply made and killed stone dead by casting and wide screen.

w Pamela Bower, Christopher Hassall, A. P. Herbert *d* Herbert Wilcox *ph* Max Greene

Errol Flynn, Anna Neagle, Patrice Wymore, Martita Hunt, Finlay Currie

King's Row****
US 1941 127m bw
Warner (David Lewis)

In a small American town during the early years of the century, three children grow up into a world of cruelty and madness.
Superb Hollywood melodrama, a Peyton Place with style and an absorbing if incredible plot and characters.

w Casey Robinson, novel Henry Bellamann *d Sam Wood ph James Wong Howe m Erich Wolfgang Korngold pd William Cameron Menzies*

Ann Sheridan, Robert Cummings, Ronald Reagan, *Claude Rains*, Betty Field, Charles Coburn, Nancy Coleman, *Maria Ouspenskaya*, Harry Davenport, Judith Anderson, Karen Verne

The King's Thief
US 1955 79m Eastmancolor Cinemascope
MGM (Edwin H. Knopf)

The Duke of Brampton plots treason against Charles II but a highwayman robs him of an incriminating notebook.
Dismal swashbuckler with neither zest nor style, just a cast of unhappy-looking actors.

w Charles Knopf *d* Robert Z. Leonard *ph* Robert Planck

David Niven, Edmund Purdom, Ann Blyth, George Sanders, Roger Moore

Kipps***
GB 1941 112m bw
TCF (Edward Black)
US title: *The Remarkable Mr Kipps*

In 1906, a draper's assistant comes into money and tries to crash society.
Charming, unassuming film of a well-loved novel, later musicalized as *Half a Sixpence*.

w Frank Launder, Sidney Gilliat, novel H. G. Wells *d Carol Reed*

Michael Redgrave, Phyllis Calvert, Diana Wynyard, *Arthur Riscoe*, Max Adrian, Helen Haye, Michael Wilding, Lloyd Pearson, Edward Rigby

Kismet
US 1930 90m bw
Warner

An Oriental magician overcomes a wicked vizier.
Rather tame filming of a spectacular which belongs on the stage.

w Howard Estabrook, *play* Edward Knoblock *d* John Francis Dillon *ph* John Seitz

Otis Skinner, Loretta Young, David Manners, Mary Duncan, Sidney Blackmer, Fred Sterling, Edmund Breese, Montagu Love

Kismet*
US 1944 100m Technicolor
MGM (Everett Riskin)

In Old Baghdad, a magician outwits the Grand Vizier.
Hollow and humourless but striking-looking film of an antique Arabian Nights stage success.

w John Meehan, *play* Edward Knoblock *d William Dieterle ph Charles Rosher* *m* Herbert Stothart *ad* Cedric Gibbons, Daniel B. Cathcart

Ronald Colman, Marlene Dietrich, James Craig, Edward Arnold, Hugh Herbert, Joy Ann Page, Florence Bates, Harry Davenport, Hobart Cavanaugh, Robert Warwick

Kismet
US 1955 113m Eastmancolor Cinemascope
MGM (Arthur Freed)

Unlucky musical remake from the stage show with Borodin music.

w Charles Lederer, Luther Davis, from their musical play *d* Vincente Minnelli *ph* Joseph Ruttenberg *ch* Jack Cole *ad* Cedric Gibbons, Preston Ames

Howard Keel, Ann Blyth, Dolores Gray, Vic Damone, Monty Woolley, Sebastian Cabot, Jay C. Flippen, Mike Mazurki, Jack Elam

Kiss and Make Up
US 1934 80m bw
Paramount (B. P. Schulberg)

A Parisian beauty specialist forsakes a rich client for his loyal secretary.
Forgettable romantic comedy.

w Harlan Thompson, George Marion Jnr, *play* Stephen Bekeffi *d* Harlan Thompson *ph* Leon Shamroy

Cary Grant, Genevieve Tobin, Helen Mack, Edward Everett Horton, Lucien Littlefield, Mona Maris

Kiss and Tell*
US 1945 92m bw
Columbia (Sol C. Siegel)

To protect another girl, an irrepressible teenager pretends to be pregnant.
Good-humoured farcical comedy which at the time was thought pretty shocking, especially with the infant darling of the thirties in the lead.

w F. Hugh Herbert, from his play *d* Richard Wallace *ph* Charles Lawton *m* Werner Heymann

Shirley Temple, Robert Benchley, Walter Abel, Jerome Courtland, Katherine Alexander, Porter Hall, Tom Tully

'All brilliantly characteristic of the worst anyone could think of American life.'—*James Agee*

A Kiss before Dying*
US 1956 94m De Luxe Cinemascope
UA / Crown (Robert Jacks)

A college boy kills women who get in his way.
Reasonably absorbing exercise in psychopathology which would have been more effective on a smaller screen.

w Lawrence Roman, *novel* Ira Levin *d* Gerd Oswald *ph* Lucien Ballard *m* Lionel Newman

Jeffrey Hunter, Joanne Woodward, Robert Wagner, Virginia Leith, *Mary Astor*, George Macready

A Kiss for Corliss
US 1949 88m bw
UA / James Nasser
aka: *Almost a Bride*

A teenager develops a crush on a middle-aged *roué*.
Dismal sequel to *Kiss and Tell* in the shadow of *The Bachelor and the Bobby Soxer*.

w Howard Dimsdale *d* Richard Wallace *ph* Robert de Grasse *m* Werner Heymann

David Niven, Shirley Temple, Tom Tully, Darryl Hickman, Virginia Welles

A Kiss in the Dark
US 1949 87m bw
Warner (Harry Kurnitz)

A concert pianist finds romance in a boarding house peopled with zany characters.
Paper-thin romantic comedy.

w Harry Kurnitz *d* Delmer Daves *ph* Robert Burks *m* Max Steiner

David Niven, Jane Wyman, Broderick Crawford, Maria Ouspenskaya, Victor Moore, Wayne Morris, Joseph Buloff, Curt Bois

Kiss Me Deadly
US 1955 105m bw
UA / Parklane (Robert Aldrich)

By helping a girl who is nevertheless murdered, Mike Hammer prevents crooks from stealing a case of radio-active material.
Curiously arty and excruciatingly boring private eye thriller, a ripe piece of cinematic cheese full of tilt shots and symbols: even the titles read from down to up.

w A. I. Bezzerides *d* Robert Aldrich *ph* Ernest Laszlo *m* Frank de Vol

Ralph Meeker, Albert Dekker, Cloris Leachman, Paul Stewart, Juano Hernandez, Wesley Addy, Maxene Cooper

Kiss Me Kate**
US 1953 111m Anscocolor 3-D
MGM (Jack Cummings)

The married leading players of a musical version of *The Taming of the Shrew* lead an equally tempestuous life backstage.
Brisk, bright screen version of the Broadway musical hit.

w Dorothy Kingsley, *play* Samuel and Bella Spewack *d George Sidney ph* Charles Rosher *m/ly Cole Porter ch Hermes Pan*

Howard Keel, Kathryn Grayson, Ann Miller, Keenan Wynn, Bobby Van, Tommy Rall, James Whitmore, Bob Fosse, Kurt Kasznar

Kiss Me Stupid*
US 1964 124m bw Panavision
UA / Mirisch / Phalanx / (Billy Wilder)

A womanizing pop singer stops overnight in a small California desert town and shows interest in an unsuccessful songwriter in order to get at his wife.
Draggy, tasteless, surprisingly unamusing smoking room story, with the actors behaving as though driven against their will (apart from Dean Martin, ideally cast as the idol who gets a headache if he doesn't have sex every night). Some good wisecracks, but it should have been much faster and funnier.

w Billy Wilder, I. A. L. Diamond, *play* L'oro della fantasia by Anna Bonacci *d* Billy Wilder *ph* Joseph La Shelle *m* André Previn *pd* Alexander Trauner *songs* George and Ira Gershwin

Dean Martin, Kim Novak, Ray Walston, Cliff Osmond

'A work of ferocious tastelessness . . . Swiftian in its relentless disgust.' *Peter Barnes*

Kiss of Death**
US 1947 98m bw
TCF

A captured thief informs on his own gang, and a psychopathic killer is sent to extract vengeance.
Gloomy, well-made semi-location thriller which descends into heavy melodrama. Remade as *The Fiend Who Walked the West*.

w Ben Hecht, Charles Lederer *d* Henry Hathaway *ph* Norbert Brodine *m* David Buttolph

Victor Mature, Richard Widmark, Brian Donlevy, Coleen Gray, Karl Malden, Taylor Holmes

Kiss of the Vampire*
GB 1962 88m Eastmancolor
U-I / Hammer (Anthony Hinds)
US title: *Kiss of Evil*

In 1910 a Bavarian disciple of Dracula lures a British honeymoon couple.
This unsubtle variation on *Dracula* is handled in lively fashion, with a splendid climax in which assorted white-robed vampires are destroyed by bats.

w John Elder *d Don Sharp ph* Alan Hume *m* James Bernard

Noel Willman, Clifford Evans, Edward De Souza, Jennifer Daniel, Isobel Black

Kiss the Blood Off My Hands
US 1948 80m bw
Universal (Harold Hecht)
GB title: *Blood on My Hands*

A nurse helps a seaman on the run for murder.
Risible romantic melodrama in never-was London docks setting, with Newton large as life and twice as villainous.

w Leonardo Bercovici, *novel* Gerald Butler *d* Norman Foster *ph* Russell Metty *m* Miklos Rozsa

Joan Fontaine, Burt Lancaster, Robert Newton, Lewis Russell, Aminta Dyne

Kiss the Boys Goodbye*
US 1941 85m bw
Paramount

A Broadway producer falls for one of his chorines.
Moderately smart musical entertainment of its time.

w Harry Tugend, Dwight Taylor, *play* Clare Boothe *d* Victor Shertzinger *m/ly* Victor Shertzinger, Frank Loesser

Don Ameche, Mary Martin, Oscar Levant, Rochester, Raymond Walburn, Connie Boswell, Virginia Dale, Barbara Jo Allen, Elizabeth Patterson

Kiss Them for Me

US 1957 105m Eastmancolor Cinemascope
TCF (Jerry Wald)

Three navy pilots spend a weekend's unofficial leave in San Francisco, and get into various kinds of trouble.
Based on a novel which also served as source for the musical *Hit the Deck*, this very heavy-footed comedy with serious asides is most unsuitably cast and generally ill-timed and unattractive.

w Julius Epstein, *novel* Shore Leave by Frederick Wakeman *d* Stanley Donen *ph* Milton Krasner *m* Lionel Newman

Cary Grant, Jayne Mansfield, Suzy Parker, Ray Walston, Larry Blyden, Leif Erickson, Werner Klemperer

Kiss Tomorrow Goodbye

US 1950 102m bw
United States Pictures (William Cagney)

A violent criminal breaks jail and plans several daring robberies.
Surprisingly brutal star melodrama which failed to repeat the success of *White Heat*.

w Harry Brown, *novel* Horace McCoy *d* Gordon Douglas *ph* Peverell Marley *m* Carmen Dragon

James Cagney, Barbara Payton, Ward Bond, Luther Adler, Helena Carter, Steve Brodie, Rhys Williams, Barton MacLane, Frank Reicher, John Litel

'The mixture as before without an ingredient changed.'—*Otis Guernsey Jnr*

Kisses for My President

US 1964 113m bw
Warner / Pearlayne (Curtis Bernhardt)

America's first woman president causes problems for her husband.
Solidly-carpentered comedy with too few ideas for its length.

w Claude Binyon, Robert G. Kane *d* Curtis Bernhardt *ph* Robert Surtees *m* Bronislau Kaper

Polly Bergen, Fred MacMurray, Arlene Dahl, Eli Wallach, Edward Andrews

Kissin' Cousins

US 1963 96m Metrocolor Panavision
MGM / Four Leaf (Sam Katzman)

The USAF wants to build a missile base on Smokey Mountain, and their PR man discovers that one of the hillbillies is his double.
A feeble production in every sense, even below its star's usual standard.

w Gerald Drayson Adams, Gene Nelson *d* Gene Nelson *ph* Ellis W. Carter *md* Fred Karger

Elvis Presley, Arthur O'Connell, Glenda Farrell, Jack Albertson

The Kissing Bandit

US 1948 102m Technicolor
MGM (Joe Pasternak)

In old California, a young businessman finds he is expected to keep up his bandit father's criminal and romantic reputation.
Silly, witless musical which never settles into gear; mocked by its star as Benny mocked *The Horn Blows at Midnight*.

w Isabel Lennart, John Briard Harding *d* Laslo Benedek *ph* Robert Surtees *m* Georgie Stoll

Frank Sinatra, Kathryn Grayson, J. Carrol Naish, Mildred Natwick, Mikhail Rasumny, Billy Gilbert, Clinton Sundberg

Kitty***

US 1945 103m bw
Paramount (Karl Tunberg)

In 18th-century London, an aristocrat makes a duchess of a guttersnipe.
Well-detailed period *Pygmalion* which works much better than one would expect.

w Darrell Ware, Karl Tunberg, *novel* Rosamund Marshall *d Mitchell Leisen ph Daniel L. Fapp m* Victor Young

Paulette Goddard, Ray Milland, Cecil Kellaway, Constance Collier, Reginald Owen, Patric Knowles, Dennis Hoey, Sara Allgood, Eric Blore, Gordon Richards, Michael Dyne

Kitty Foyle**

US 1940 108m bw
RKO (Harry E. Edgington, David Hempstead)

A white-collar girl has a troubled love life.
Solid entertainment of its time, especially aimed at ambitious young ladies.

w Dalton Trumbo, Donald Ogden Stewart, *novel* Christopher Morley *d* Sam Wood *ph* Robert de Grasse *m* Roy Webb

Ginger Rogers, Dennis Morgan, James Craig, *Eduardo Ciannelli*, Ernest Cossart, Gladys Cooper, Mary Treen

The Klansman
US 1974 112m Technicolor
Paramount / Atlanta (William Alexander)

An Alabama sheriff confronts the Ku Klux Klan.
Violent melodrama, all noise, brutality and bad acting.

w Millard Kaufman, Samuel Fuller, *novel* William Bradford Huie *d* Terence Young *ph* Lloyd Ahern, Aldo Tonti *m* Stax Organisation

Lee Marvin, Richard Burton, Cameron Mitchell, O. J. Simpson, Lola Falana, David Huddleston, Luciana Paluzzi, Linda Evans

'There's not a shred of quality, dignity, relevance or impact in this yahoo-oriented bunk.'—*Variety*

Klondike Annie
US 1936 83m bw
Paramount (William Le Baron)

A torch singer on the run disguises herself as a missionary and revivifies a Klondike mission.
Laundered Mae West vehicle, from her fading period but not too bad.

w Mae West, Marion Morgan, George B. Dowell *d* Raoul Walsh *ph* George Clemer

Mae West, Victor McLaglen, Philip Reed, Helen Jerome Eddy, Harry Beresford, Harold Huber, Esther Howard

Klute***
US 1971 114m Technicolor Panavision
Warner (Alan J. Pakula)

A policeman leaves the force to investigate the disappearance of a research scientist, and takes up with a call girl who is involved.
Excellent adult thriller with attention to detail and emphasis on character.

w Andy K. Lewis, Dave Lewis d Alan J. Pakula ph Gordon Lewis *m* Michael Small

Jane Fonda, Donald Sutherland, Charles Cioffi, Roy Scheider, Rita Gam

The Knack***
GB 1965 84m bw
UA / Woodfall (Oscar Lewenstein)

A sex-starved young teacher lets one room of his house to a successful womanizer, another to an innocent girl from the north.
An excuse for an anarchic series of visual gags, a kaleidoscope of swinging London in which anything goes. Brilliantly done in the style of *A Hard Day's Night.*

w Charles Wood, *play* Ann Jellicoe *d Richard Lester ph David Watkin m* John Barry

Michael Crawford, Ray Brooks, Rita Tushingham, Donal Donnelly

Knave of Hearts*
GB 1954 103m bw
Transcontinental (Paul Graetz)
aka: *Monsieur Ripois et son nemesis*

A born philanderer confesses all his affairs to his wife.
Well-observed though strangely flat and disappointing sex comedy, something of a pioneer in its time and therefore perhaps too diffident in its approach.

w René Clément, Hugh Mills *d* René Clément *ph* Oswald Morris *m* Roman Vlad

Gérard Philipe, Margaret Johnston, Joan Greenwood, Natasha Parry, Valerie Hobson

Knickerbocker Holiday
US 1944 84m bw
UA / Harry Joe Brown / PCA

In old New Amsterdam, a one-legged tyrant finally sees the light.
Artificial musical from a famous stage original, with engaging moments including Charles Coburn singing 'September Song'.

w Thomas Lennon, *stage musical* by *Maxwell Anderson, Kurt Weill ph* Phil Tammura *m* Werner Heymann

Charles Coburn, Nelson Eddy, Constance Dowling, Ernest Cossart, Shelley Winters, Otto Kruger

Knight without Armour**
GB 1937 107m bw
London Films (Alexander Korda)

During the Russian Revolution of 1917, a widowed countess is helped to safety by a British translator.
Underrated romantic adventure with big production values and some splendid moments.

w Lajos Biro, Arthur Wimperis, Frances Marion, *novel* James Hilton *ph Harry Stradling d Jacques Feyder m* Miklos Rozsa

Robert Donat, Marlene Dietrich, Irene Vanbrugh, Herbert Lomas, Austin Trevor, Basil Gill, David Tree, John Clements, Lawrence Hanray

'A first class thriller, beautifully directed, with spare and convincing dialogue and a nearly watertight scenario.'—*Graham Greene*

Knights of the Round Table*
GB 1953 115m Eastmancolor Cinemascope
MGM (Pandro S. Berman)

Lancelot, banished from King Arthur's court for loving Guinevere, returns to defeat the evil Modred.
Disappointingly flat, pageant-like adaptation of the legends, with a few lively strands insufficiently firmly drawn together.

w Talbot Jennings, Jan Lustig, Noel Langley *d* Richard Thorpe *ph* Frederick A. Young, Stephen Dade *m* Miklos Rozsa *ad* Alfred Junge, Hans Peters

Robert Taylor, Mel Ferrer, Ava Gardner, Anne Crawford, Stanley Baker, Felix Aylmer, Robert Urquhart, Niall MacGinnis

Knock on Any Door*
US 1949 100m bw
Columbia (Nicholas Ray)

A defence lawyer pleads with the jury for the life of a slum boy on a murder charge.
Smartly-made but empty melodrama making facile social points.

w Daniel Taradash, John Monks Jnr, *novel* Willard Motley *d* Nicholas Ray *ph* Burnett Guffey *m* George Antheil

Humphrey Bogart, John Derek, George Macready, Allene Roberts

Knock on Wood**
US 1954 103m Technicolor
Paramount (Norman Panama, Melvin Frank)

Stolen plans are hidden inside the dummy of an unsuspecting ventriloquist.
Excellent star comedy with good script and production (but some strange ideas of London's geography).

wd Norman Panama, Melvin Frank *ph* Daniel Fapp *m/ly* Sylvia Fine *ch* Michael Kidd

Danny Kaye, Mai Zetterling, David Burns, Torin Thatcher, Leon Askin, Abner Biberman, Steve Geray

Kona Coast
US 1968 93m colour TVM
Warner / Richard Boone

The South Seas skipper of a fishing boat avenges his daughter's death from drugs.
Listless thick-ear which never made a series.

w Gil Ralston, *novel* John D. MacDonald *d* Lamont Johnson

Richard Boone, Vera Miles, Joan Blondell, Kent Smith

Kongo
US 1932 86m bw
MGM

An embittered African recluse takes revenge on the daughter of his former enemy.
No-holds-barred melodrama which never really exerts the right grip; a remake of the Lon Chaney silent *West of Zanzibar*.

w Leon Gordon, *play* Chester de Vonde, Kilbourn Gordon *d* William Cowen *ph* Harold Rosson

Walter Huston, Lupe Velez, Virginia Bruce, Conrad Nagel, C. Henry Gordon

Kotch**
US 1971 114m Metrocolor
ABC / Kotch Company (Richard Carter)

An eccentric 72-year-old widower is at odds with his family and helps a pregnant babysitter.
Variously amusing, moving and sentimental, this generally likeable film about a crotchety grandpa is sustained by its star performance.

w John Paxton, *novel* Katherine Topkins *d* Jack Lemmon *ph* Richard H. Kline *m* Marvin Hamlisch

Walter Matthau, Deborah Watts, Felicia Farr, Charles Aidman

Krakatoa, East of Java
US 1968 136m Technicolor Cinerama
ABC / Cinerama (Lester A. Sansom)

In 1883 the SS *Batavia Queen* leaves Singapore and is engulfed by the Krakatoa eruption.
Mindless spectacular, technically quite impressive but with no dramatic interest whatsoever.

w Clifford Newton Gould, Bernard Gordon *d* Bernard Kowalski *ph* Manuel Berenguer *m* Frank de Vol *pd/sp Eugene Lourié*

Maximilian Schell, Diane Baker, Brian Keith, Rossano Brazzi, Barbara Werle, John Leyton, Sal Mineo,
J. D. Cannon, Marc Lawrence

'Apparently designed to disprove the old adage, "they don't make them like that any more". At a conservative count it includes such sure-fire cinematic ingredients as hidden treasure, deep-sea divers with shattered lungs and claustrophobia, mutiny *and* fire on board ship, nuns, convicts, a lost orphan boy, girl divers and even a little striptease, climaxing in the biggest explosion and the greatest tidal wave known to history.'—*MFB*

The Kremlin Letter
US 1970 122m De Luxe Panavision
TCF (Carter de Haven, Sam Wiesenthal)

An American intelligence team is sent

undercover to Moscow to retrieve an arms treaty mistakenly signed.
Tediously violent cold war mystifier: a few good performances do not make it worth unravelling.

w John Huston, Gladys Hill, *novel* Noel Behn *d* John Huston *ph* Ted Scaife *m* Robert Drasnin *pd* Ted Haworth

Richard Boone, Orson Welles, Bibi Andersson, Max Von Sydow, Patrick O'Neal, Ronald Radd, George Sanders, Dean Jagger, Nigel Green, Barbara Parkins, Lila Kedrova, Michael MacLiammoir, Sandor Eles, Niall MacGinnis, John Huston

'One of those all-star international spy sagas that trick out an indecipherably tortuous plot with a series of vignettes in which the pleasures of star-spotting are expected to compensate for any narrative longueurs.'—*Nigel Andrews*

Kung Fu***
US 1971 75m colour TVM
Warner (Jerry Thorpe)

In the 1870s a half-American buddhist monk flees to America with a price on his head.
Curious, likeable mixture of Oriental wisdom, western action and martial arts, impeccably photographed and fascinating to watch. The style however wore rather thin over the three years the series ran.

w Ed Spielman, Howard Friedlander *d* Jerry Thorpe

David Carradine, Barry Sullivan, Keye Luke, Albert Salmi, Wayne Maunder

L

The L-Shaped Room*
GB 1962 142m bw
British Lion / Romulus (James Woolf, Richard Attenborough)

A girl intending to have an abortion takes a room in a London suburban house which is none too clean but full of characters.
Watchable, mildly sensational low-life-melodrama of the pre-swinging London era when well-to-dos thought it amusing to live in garrets. Hellishly overlong but enjoyable in patches because of the professionalism with which it is made.

w Bryan Forbes, *novel* Lynne Reid Banks
d Bryan Forbes *ph* Douglas Slocombe
m Brahms, John Barry

Leslie Caron, Tom Bell, *Brock Peters, Cicely Courtneidge*, Bernard Lee, *Avis Bunnage, Patricia Phoenix, Emlyn Williams*

'It would be hard to imagine a more unlikely, or commercially more sure-fire group of lodgers living under a single roof than this pregnant French girl, maladjusted negro, lesbian actress, couple of prostitutes, and unpublished writer who finally commits it all to paper—shades of *I Am a Camera* as well as *A Taste of Honey*.'—*MFB*

Laburnum Grove**
GB 1936 73m bw
ATP (Basil Dean)

A suburban father reveals he is a forger.
Agreeable worm-turns comedy melodrama, much copied since.

w Gordon Wellesley, Anthony Kimmins, *play J. B. Priestley* *d Carol Reed*

Cedric Hardwicke, Edmund Gwenn, Victoria Hopper, Ethel Coleridge, Katie Johnson, Francis James

'Here at last is an English film one can unreservedly praise.'—*Graham Greene*

Ladies Courageous
US 1944 88m bw
Universal (Walter Wanger)

Girls ferry war planes from base to base for the USAF.
Absolutely predictable propaganda potboiler.

w Norman Reilly Raine, Doris Gilbert *d* John Rawlins *ph* Hal Mohr

Loretta Young, Geraldine Fitzgerald, Diana Barrymore, Evelyn Ankers, Anne Gwynne, Philip Terry, David Bruce, Lois Collier, Samuel S. Hinds

Ladies in Love*
US 1936 97m bw
TCF (B. G. De Sylva)

Man-hunting girls in Budapest form a joint plan.
Amusing romantic nonsense.

w Melville Baker, *play* Ladislaus Bus-Fekete
d Edward H. Griffith *ph* Hal Mohr *m* Louis Silvers

Janet Gaynor, Loretta Young, Constance Bennett, Simone Simon, Don Ameche, Paul Lukas, Tyrone Power, Alan Mowbray, Wilfred Lawson, J. Edward Bromberg, Virginia Field

Ladies in Retirement***
US 1941 92m bw
Columbia

A housekeeper murders her employer for the sake of her two mentally disturbed sisters.
Splendidly effective Grand Guignol, from a well-written play but filmically quite interesting.
Remade with lots of gore as *The Mad Room* (qv).

w Reginald Denham, Edward Percy, Garrett Fort, *play* Reginald Denham, Edward Percy
d Charles Vidor *ph* George Barnes *m* Ernst Toch

Ida Lupino, Louis Hayward, Isobel Elsom, Edith Barrett, Elsa Lanchester, Emma Dunn

Ladies Love Brutes
US 1930 83m bw
Paramount

A gangster tries to improve himself to marry a socialite.
Uneasy comedy-drama with good moments.

w Waldemar Young, Herman J. Mankiewicz, *play* Pardon My Glove by Zoe Akins
d Rowland V. Lee *ph* Harry Fischbeck

George Bancroft, Mary Astor, Fredric March, Margaret Quimby, Stanley Fields

Ladies' Man*
US 1931 70m bw
Paramount

A man of the world preys successfully on rich women until one grows jealous when her daughter falls for him.
Vivid, hard melodrama showing the blacker side of early thirties high society living.

w Herman J. Mankiewicz d Lothar Mendes *ph* Victor Milner

William Powell, Kay Francis, Carole Lombard, Gilbert Emery, Olive Tell

Ladies' Man
US 1961 106m Technicolor
Paramount / York (Jerry Lewis)

The adventures of an accident-prone houseboy at a Hollywood hotel for aspiring actresses.
Hit-or-miss collection of comic scraps which might have benefited from being put together on a less grandiose scale.

w Jerry Lewis, Bill Richmond *d* Jerry Lewis *m* Walter Scharf

Jerry Lewis, Helen Traubel, Jack Kruschen, Doodles Weaver, Gloria Jean

'Regression into infantilism cannot be carried much further than this.'—*MFB*

Ladies of the Big House
US 1931 77m bw
Paramount

A married couple are framed on a murder charge and sent to prison.
Melodramatic nonsense in the wake of *The Big House.*

w Louis Weitzenkorn *d* Marion Gering *ph* David Abel

Sylvia Sidney, Gene Raymond, Wynne Gibson, Rockcliffe Fellows, Earle Foxe

Ladies Should Listen
US 1934 63m bw
Paramount (Douglas MacLean)

A knowledgeable switchboard operator helps a financier with his problems.
Moderately beguiling, instantly forgettable romantic frou-frou.

w Claude Binyon, Frank Butler, Guy Bolton *d* Frank Tuttle *ph* Harry Sharp

Cary Grant, Frances Drake, Edward Everett Horton, Rosita Morena, George Barbier, Nydia Westman, Charles Ray

Ladies They Talk About*
US 1933 69m bw
Warner

Trouble in a women's prison.
Entertaining comedy-melodrama which had some brushes with the Hays Office because of its frankly man-hungry characters.

w Sidney Sutherland, Brown Holmes, *play* Women in Prison by Dorothy Mackaye, Carlton Miles *d* Howard Bretherton, William Keighley *ph* John Seitz

Barbara Stanwyck, Lyle Talbot, Preston Foster, Dorothy Burgess, Lillian Roth, Maude Eburne, Ruth Donnelly, Harold Huber

Ladies Who Do
GB 1963 85m bw
British Lion / Bryanston / Fanfare (George H. Brown)

Charladies form a successful company from tips they salvage from wastepaper baskets.
Mild farce sustained by familiar actors.

w Michael Pertwee *d* C. M. Pennington-Richards *ph* Geoffrey Faithfull *m* Ron Goodwin

Peggy Mount, Miriam Karlin, Robert Morley, Harry H. Corbett, Dandy Nichols

The Lady and the Mob
US 1939 65m bw
Columbia (Fred Kohlmar)

A lady bank owner menaced by gangsters forms her own mob.
Weak comedy.

w Richard Maibaum, Gertrude Purcell *d* Ben Stoloff *ph* John Stumar

Fay Bainter, Ida Lupino, Lee Bowman, Henry Armetta, Warren Hymer, Harold Huber

The Lady and the Monster
US 1944 86m bw
Republic (George Sherman)
aka: *Tiger Man*
GB title: *The Lady and the Doctor*

A scientist keeps alive the brain of a mortally injured financier, and it comes to dominate him.
Fair, over-padded version of a much filmed thriller (see also *Donovan's Brain, Vengeance*).

w Dane Lussier, Frederick Kohner, *novel* Donovan's Brain by Curt Siodmak *d* George Sherman *ph* John Alton *m* Walter Scharf

Erich Von Stroheim, Richard Arlen, Vera Hruba Ralston, Mary Nash, Sidney Blackmer, Helen Vinson

Lady and the Tramp**
US 1955 76m Technicolor
Cinemascope
Walt Disney (Erdmann Penner)

A pedigree spaniel falls foul of two stray cats and has a romantic adventure with a mongrel who helps her.
Pleasant cartoon feature in Disney's cutest and most anthropomorphic vein.

d Hamilton Luske, Clyde Geronomi, Wilfred Jackson *m* Oliver Wallace

Lady Be Good*
US 1941 111m bw
MGM (Arthur Freed)

Married songwriters produce a musical.
Thin musical with good talent and tunes; very little connection with the 1924 musical show.

w Jack McGowan, Kay Van Riper, John McClain *d* Norman Z. McLeod *ph* George J. Folsey, Oliver T. Marsh *songs* various

Eleanor Powell, Robert Young, Ann Sothern, Red Skelton, Dan Dailey, Virginia O'Brien, Reginald Owen, John Carroll, Lionel Barrymore, Jimmy Dorsey and his Orchestra

Lady By Choice*
US 1934 78m bw
Columbia

A publicity-mad dancer adopts an old rummy as a Mother's Day stunt.
Amusing sentimental comedy in the wake of *Lady for A Day*.

w Jo Swerling, Dwight Taylor *d* David Burton *ph* Ted Tetzlaff

Carole Lombard, May Robson, Walter Connolly, Roger Pryor, Arthur Hohl, Raymond Walburn, James Burke, Henry Kolker

Lady Caroline Lamb*
GB 1972 123m Eastmancolor
Panavision
EMI / GEC / Pulsar / Video Cinematographica
(Fernando Ghia)

In 1805, impulsive Lady Caroline Ponsonby marries William Lamb, later Lord Melbourne, and then disgraces him by her wildness.
Pale, disappointing historical fiction with good spots but no reverence for fact; slackly written and handled, and not helped by the wide screen.

wd Robert Bolt *ph* Oswald Morris *m* Richard Rodney Bennett *ad* Carmen Dillon

Sarah Miles, Jon Finch, Richard Chamberlain (as Byron), Margaret Leighton, John Mills (as Cobbett), *Ralph Richardson* (as George III), *Laurence Olivier* (as Wellington)

The Lady Eve***
US 1941 97m bw
Paramount (Paul Jones)

A lady cardsharper and her father are outsmarted on a transatlantic liner by a millionaire simpleton; she plans an elaborate revenge.
Hectic romantic farce, the first to show its director's penchant for mixing up sexual innuendo, funny men and pratfalls. There are moments when the pace drops, but in general it's scintillating entertainment, especially after viewing its weak remake *The Birds and the Bees* (qv).

wd Preston Sturges, play Monckton Hoffe *ph* Victor Milner *m* Leo Shuken

Barbara Stanwyck, Henry Fonda, Charles Coburn, Eugène Pallette, William Demarest, Eric Blore, Melville Cooper, Martha O'Driscoll, Janet Beecher, Robert Greig, Luis Alberni, Jimmy Conlin

'The whole theme, with all its variations of keys, is played to one end, to get laughs, and at several different levels it gets them.'—*National Board of Review*

'Preston Sturges, they tell me, is known in Hollywood as "the streamlined Lubitsch". This needn't put you off, because if he goes on producing films as lively as this one he will one day come to be known as Preston Sturges.'—*William Whitebait*

Lady for a Day***
US 1933 95m bw
Columbia

Gangsters help an old apple seller to pose as a rich woman when her daughter visits.
Splendid sentimental comedy full of cinematic resource; the best translation of Runyon to the screen.

w Robert Riskin, story Madame La Gimp by Damon Runyon *d Frank Capra ph* Joseph Walker

May Robson, Warren William, Guy Kibbee, Glenda Farrell, Ned Sparks, Jean Parker, Walter Connolly, Nat Pendleton

Lady for a Night
US 1941 87m bw
Republic (Albert J. Cohen)

The lady owner of a gambling boat determines to break into society.
Moderate period comedy with a belated murder plot.

w Isabel Dawn, Boyce DeGaw *d* Leigh Jason *ph* Norbert Brodine *m* David Buttolph

Joan Blondell, John Wayne, Ray Middleton,

Philip Merivale, Blanche Yurka, Edith Barrett, Leonid Kinskey, Montagu Love

The Lady from Cheyenne
US 1949 87m bw
Universal (Frank Lloyd)

In 1860 Wyoming, a schoolmistress fights for women's rights.
Mild western star romance.

w Kathryn Scola, Warren Duff *d* Frank Lloyd *ph* Milton Krasner *m* Charles Previn

Loretta Young, Robert Preston, Gladys George, Edward Arnold, Frank Craven, Jessie Ralph, Spencer Charters, Alan Bridge

Lady from Louisiana
US 1941 84m bw
Republic (Bernard Vorhaus)

In old Mississippi, a lottery-owner's daughter falls in love with a lawyer employed to make her father's business illegal.
Curious pot-boiler containing everything but the kitchen stove, including murder and a raging storm.

w Vera Caspary, Guy Endore, Michael Hogan *d* Bernard Vorhaus *ph* Jack Marta *m* Cy Feuer

John Wayne, Ona Munson, Ray Middleton, Henry Stephenson, Helen Westley, Dorothy Dandridge, Jack Pennick

The Lady from Shanghai**
US 1948 87m bw
Columbia (Richard Wilson, William Castle)

A seaman becomes involved in the maritime wanderings of a crippled lawyer and his homicidal frustrated wife.
Absurd, unintelligible, plainly much cut and rearranged, this thriller was obviously left too much in Welles' hands and then just as unfairly taken out of them; but whole sequences of sheer brilliance remain, notably the final shoot-out in the hall of mirrors.

wd Orson Welles, novel If I Die Before I Wake by Sherwood King *ph Charles Lawton Jnr* *m* Heinz Roemheld

Orson Welles, Rita Hayworth, *Everett Sloane, Glenn Anders*, Ted de Corsia, Erskine Sanford, Gus Schilling

'The slurred social conscience of the hero leads him to some murky philosophizing, all of which with many individualities of diction clog the issue and the sound track. Sub-titles, I fear, would have helped.'—*Richard Winnington*

The Lady Gambles
US 1949 99m bw
U-I (Michael Kraike)

A happy woman destroys her marriage when she becomes addicted to gambling.
Boring, overwrought, underplotted fiction for women.

w Lewis Meltzer, Oscar Saul *d* Michael Gordon *ph* Russell Metty *m* Frank Skinner

Barbara Stanwyck, Robert Preston, Stephen McNally, Edith Barrett, John Hoyt

'A kind of *Lost Weekend* of the gaming tables.'—*Ella Smith*

Lady Godiva
US 1955 89m Technicolor
U-I (Robert Arthur)

Lord Leofric tames a Saxon shrew but she suspects his motives and rides naked through the streets of Coventry to prove the loyalty of the Saxons.
Comic strip historical legend, reliably turned out for midwestern family audiences.

w Oscar Brodney, Harry Ruskin *d* Arthur Lubin *m* Joseph Gershenson

George Nader, Maureen O'Hara, Vic Morrow, Eduard Franz, Torin Thatcher

Lady Godiva Rides Again
GB 1951 90m bw
British Lion / London Films / Sidney Gilliat, Frank Launder

A waitress wins a local beauty contest and becomes a charm school starlet and later a stripteaser.
Disappointing satirical comedy with good credentials.

w Frank Launder, Val Valentine *d* Frank Launder *ph* Wilkie Cooper *m* William Alwyn

Pauline Stroud, Stanley Holloway, Diana Dors, Alastair Sim, George Cole, Dennis Price, John McCallum, Bernadette O'Farrell, Kay Kendall, Dora Bryan

Lady Hamilton: see That Hamilton Woman

The Lady Has Plans
US 1942 77m bw
Paramount (Fred Kohlmar)

A lady reporter in Lisbon is mistaken for a Nazi spy.
Competent fluff which veers between comedy and melodrama.

w Harry Tugend *d* Sidney Lanfield *ph* Charles Lang

Paulette Goddard, Ray Milland, Albert Dekker,

Roland Young, Margaret Hayes, Cecil Kellaway, Addison Richards, Edward Norris

Lady Ice
US 1973 92m Technicolor Panavision
Tomorrow Entertainment (Harrison Starr)

An insurance investigator steals a diamond and goes into partnership with a gangster's daughter.
Unamusing Miami-based thriller.

w Alan Trustman, Harold Clemins *d* Tom Gries *ph* Lucien Ballard *m* Perry Botkin Jnr

Donald Sutherland, Jennifer O'Neil, Robert Duvall, Patrick Magee

Lady in a Cage
US 1964 97m bw
American Entertainments Corp. (Luther Davis)

A rich widow is trapped by roving marauders in her private elevator.
Unpleasant and boring suspenser with nasty details.

w Luther Davis *d* Walter Grauman *ph* Lee Garmes *m* Paul Glass *pd* Rudolf Sternad

Olivia de Havilland, James Caan, Ann Sothern, Jeff Corey

'The film parades its pretensions on a note of high-pitched hysteria.'—*MFB*

Lady in Cement
US 1968 93m De Luxe Panavision
TCF / Arcola / Millfield (Aaron Rosenberg)

A Florida private eye on his morning swim finds a dead blonde.
Routine private eye stuff with fashionable sex and violence added.

w Marvin H. Albert, Jack Guss *d* Gordon Douglas *ph* Joseph Biroc *m* Hugo Montenegro

Frank Sinatra, Raquel Welch, Richard Conte, Martin Gabel, Lainie Kazan, Pat Henry, Steve Peck

'While *Tony Rome* seemed to herald a return to the forties thriller, *Lady in Cement* marks nothing more exciting than a return to *Tony Rome.*'—*MFB*

The Lady in Question*
US 1940 81m bw
Columbia

A Parisian shopkeeper on a jury is responsible for getting a girl acquitted of a murder charge, but begins to worry when his son falls in love with her.
Stagey but quite satisfying Hollywood remake of the French drama *Gribouille*.

w Lewis Meltzer, *story* Marcel Achard *d* Charles Vidor *ph* Lucien Andriot *m* Morris Stoloff

Brian Aherne, Rita Hayworth, Glenn Ford, Irene Rich, George Coulouris, Lloyd Corrigan, Evelyn Keyes, Edward Norris, Curt Bois, Frank Reicher

The Lady in the Car with Glasses and a Gun
France / US 1969 105m Eastmancolor Panavision
Lira Film / Columbia (Anatole Litvak)

An English secretary in Paris decides to drive to the coast but has various adventures which make her believe she is either mad or amnesiac.
Muddled, tedious suspenser with a totally implausible 'explanation'.

w Richard Harris, Eleanor Perry *d* Anatole Litvak *ph* Claude Renoir *m* Michel Legrand

Samantha Eggar, Oliver Reed, John McEnery, Stéphane Audran

Lady in the Dark**
US 1944 100m Technicolor
Paramount (Richard Blumenthal)

The editress of a fashion magazine is torn between three men, has worrying dreams, and takes herself to a psychoanalyst.
Lush, stylish and frequently amusing version of a Broadway musical, lacking most of the songs; despite its faults, an excellent example of studio spectacle and a very typical forties romantic comedy.

w Frances Goodrich, Albert Hackett, *play* Moss Hart *d Mitchell Leisen ph Ray Rennahan m Kurt Weill ly* Ira Gershwin *sp* Gordon Jennings *ad Hans Dreier*

Ginger Rogers, Warner Baxter, Ray Milland, Jon Hall, *Mischa Auer,* Mary Phillips, Barry Sullivan

Lady in the Lake*
US 1947 103m bw
MGM (George Haight)

A private eye is assigned to find a missing wife . . .
Complex private eye yarn which makes the original Chandler dialogue sound childish by over-reliance on the subjective camera method: we see the hero's face only when he looks in a mirror. An experiment that failed because it was not really understood.

w Steve Fisher, *novel* Raymond Chandler *d* Robert Montgomery *ph* Paul C. Vogel *m* David Snell

Robert Montgomery, Audrey Totter, Lloyd Nolan, Tom Tully, Leon Ames

Lady in the Morgue*
US 1938 70m bw
Universal (Irving Starr)
GB title: *The Case of the Missing Blonde*

A private eye investigates a suicide and finds three murders.
Bright second feature thriller produced under the Crime Club banner.

w Eric Taylor, Robertson White, *novel* Jonathan Latimer *d Otis Garrett ph* Stanley Cortez *m* Charles Previn

Preston Foster, Frank Jenks, Patricia Ellis, Barbara Pepper, Thomas Jackson, Gordon Elliott

The Lady Is a Square
GB 1958 99m bw
ABP / Wilcox–Neagle

An impoverished socialite widow tries to keep her husband's symphony orchestra going and is helped by a pop singer.
Strained attempt to carry on the *Spring in Park Lane* tradition, with a few inspirations from Joe Pasternak and *One Hundred Men and a Girl.* Earnest performances, obvious jokes.

w Harold Purcell, Pamela Bower, Nicholas Phipps *d* Herbert Wilcox *ph* Gordon Dines *md* Wally Stott

Anna Neagle, Frankie Vaughan, Anthony Newley, Janette Scott, Wilfrid Hyde White

The Lady Is Willing
US 1942 91m bw
Columbia (Mitchell Leisen)

A musical comedy star adopts a baby and falls in love with its pediatrician.
Dull mixture of light drama and heavy comedy, with all concerned ill at ease.

w James Edward Grant, Albert McCleery *d* Mitchell Leisen *ph* Ted Tetzlaff *m* W. Frank Harling

Marlene Dietrich, Fred MacMurray, Aline MacMahon, Stanley Ridges, Arline Judge, Marietta Canty

Lady Killer***
US 1933 76m bw
Warner (Henry Blanke)

A cinema usher turns to crime, flees to Hollywood, and becomes a movie star.
Hectic slam-bang action comedy with melodramatic moments. Great fun.

w Ben Markson, *novel* The Finger Man by Rosalind Keating Shaffer *d Roy del Ruth ph* Tony Gaudio *m* Leo F. Forbstein

James Cagney, Mae Clarke, Leslie Fenton, Margaret Lindsay, Henry O'Neill, Willard Robertson, Raymond Hatton, Russell Hopton

'A kind of résumé of everything he has done to date in the movies.'—*New York Evening Post*

Lady L
France / Italy / US 1965 124m
Eastmancolor Panavision
Concordia / Champion / MGM (Carlo Ponti)

An 80-year-old lady recalls her romantic life from her youth as a Paris laundress.
Unhappy, lumbering, styleless attempt to recapture several old forms, indifferently though expensively made and acted.

wd Peter Ustinov, *novel* Romain Gary *ph* Henri Alekan *m* Jean Françaix *ad* Jean D'Eaubonne, Auguste Capelier

Sophia Loren, David Niven, Paul Newman, Peter Ustinov, Claude Dauphin, Philippe Noiret, Michel Piccoli, Marcel Dalio, Cecil Parker, Eugène Deckers

Lady Luck
US 1946 97m bw
RKO (Warren Duff)

The daughter of a long line of ill-fated gamblers marries one and tries to reform him, but the reverse happens.
Tedious comedy drama.

w Lynn Root, Frank Fenton *d* Edwin L. Marin *ph* Lucien Andriot *m* Leigh Harline

Robert Young, Barbara Hale, Frank Morgan, James Gleason, Don Rice, Harry Davenport, Lloyd Corrigan

Lady of Burlesque*
US 1943 91m bw
Hunt Stromberg
GB title: *Striptease Lady*

A burlesque dancer solves a number of backstage murders.
Agreeable murder mystery with strong injections of comedy.

w James Gunn, *novel* The G-String Murders by Gypsy Rose Lee *d* William A. Wellman *ph* Robert de Grasse *m* Arthur Lange

Barbara Stanwyck, Michael O'Shea, J. Edward Bromberg, Iris Adrian, Gloria Dickson, Charles Dingle

Lady of the Tropics
US 1939 92m bw
MGM (Sam Zimbalist)

An American playboy in Saigon marries a half-caste girl but her former admirer prevents her from getting a passport.
Interminable romantic melodrama with stars apparently straight from the taxidermist.

w Ben Hecht *d* Jack Conway *ph* George Folsey *m* Franz Waxman

Robert Taylor, Hedy Lamarr, Joseph Schildkraut, Gloria Franklin, Ernest Cossart

Lady on a Train*
US 1945 84m bw
Universal (Felix Jackson)

A girl arriving in New York by train sees a murder committed and can't make anyone believe her.
Cheerful mystery which starts in the right spirit but does not progress too satisfactorily.

w Edmund Beloin, Robert O'Brien, *novel* Leslie Charteris *d* Charles David *m* Miklos Rozsa

Deanna Durbin, Ralph Bellamy, David Bruce, Edward Everett Horton, George Coulouris, Allen Jenkins, Dan Duryea, Patricia Morison

Lady Possessed
US 1952 86m bw
Republic / Portland (James Mason)

An unbalanced woman imagines she is destined to take the place of a pianist's dead wife.
Weary melodramatic nonsense dating from Hollywood's first obsession with psychiatry.

w Pamela Kellino, James Mason, *novel* Del Palma by Pamela Kellino *d* William Spier, Roy Kellino *ph* Karl Struss *m* Nathan Scott

James Mason, June Havoc, Stephen Dunne, Fay Compton, Pamela Kellino, Steven Geray

Lady Scarface
US 1941 69m bw
RKO (Cliff Reid)

A police lieutenant captures a dangerous female gangster.
Weird gangster second feature with too many domestic comedy asides; notable only for the appearance in it of its dignified lead, fresh from *Rebecca*.

w Armand D'Usseau, Richard Collins *d* Frank Woodruff *ph* Nicholas Musuraca

Judith Anderson, Dennis O'Keefe, Frances Neal, Mildred Coles, Eric Blore, Marc Lawrence

Lady Sings the Blues**
US 1972 144m Eastmancolor Panavision
Paramount / Motown / Weston / Furie (Jay Weston, James S. White)

The disastrous private life of blues singer Billie Holliday.
Old-fashioned showbiz biopic with new-fashioned drugs, sex and squalor.

w Terence McCloy, Chris Clark, Suzanne de Passe *d* Sidney J. Furie *ph* John Alonzo *m* Michel Legrand

Diana Ross, Billy Dee Williams, Richard Pryor, James Callahan, Sid Melton

A Lady Takes a Chance
US 1943 86m bw
RKO (Frank Ross)
aka: *The Cowboy and the Girl*

A New York office girl on holiday in Oregon falls for a rodeo rider.
Slender star action romance.

w Robert Ardrey *d* William A. Seiter *ph* Frank Redman *m* Roy Webb

Jean Arthur, John Wayne, Charles Winninger, Phil Silvers, Mary Field, Don Costello, John Philliber, Grady Sutton, Hans Conried

The Lady Vanishes****
GB 1938 97m bw
Gaumont-British (Edward Black)

En route back to England by train from Switzerland, an old lady disappears and two young people investigate.
The disappearing lady trick brilliantly refurbished by Hitchcock and his screenwriters, who even get away with a horrid model shot at the beginning. Superb, suspenseful, brilliantly funny, meticulously detailed entertainment.

w Sidney Gilliat, Frank Launder, novel The Wheel Spins by Ethel Lina White *d Alfred Hitchcock ph* Jack Cox *m* Louis Levy

Margaret Lockwood, Michael Redgrave, Dame May Whitty, Paul Lukas, Basil Radford, Naunton Wayne, Catherine Lacey, Cecil Parker, Linden Travers, Googie Withers, *Mary Clare*, Philip Leaver

'If it were not so brilliant a melodrama, we should class it as a brilliant comedy.'—*Frank S. Nugent*

'No one can study the deceptive effortlessness with which one thing leads to another without learning where the true beauty of this medium is to be mined.'—*Otis Ferguson*

The Lady with a Lamp*
GB 1951 110m bw
British Lion / Imperadio (Herbert Wilcox)
The life of Florence Nightingale and her work in reforming the nursing service in 19th-century England.
Solid biopic, not quite in accord with history.
w Warren Chetham Strode, *play* Reginald Berkeley *d* Herbert Wilcox *ph* Max Greene *m* Anthony Collins *ad* William C. Andrews
Anna Neagle, Michael Wilding, Gladys Young, Felix Aylmer, Julian D'Albie, Arthur Young, Edwin Styles, Barbara Couper, Cecil Trouncer, Rosalie Crutchley
'A slow, sedate, refined chronicle . . . Herbert Wilcox is a good deal more at ease with the balls and dinners, than with anything that happens later.'—*Penelope Houston*

Lady with Red Hair*
US 1940 78m bw
Warner (Edmund Grainger)
The life of actress Mrs Leslie Carter and her association with impresario David Belasco.
Mildly interesting but unsatisfying biopic of a lady scarcely remembered.
w Charles Kenyon, Milton Krims, N. Brewster Morse, Norbert Faulkner *d* Curtis Bernhardt *ph* Arthur Edeson *m* Heinz Roemheld
Miriam Hopkins, Claude Rains, Richard Ainley, John Litel, Laura Hope Crews, Helen Wesley, Mona Barrie, Victor Jory, Cecil Kellaway, Fritz Leiber, Halliwell Hobbes

A Lady without Passport*
US 1950 84m bw
MGM (Samuel Marx)
A secret service undercover man tracks down aliens being smuggled into the US, and falls in love with one of them.
Routine material, very well handled.
w Howard Dimsdale *d Joseph H. Lewis* *ph* Paul C. Vogel *m* David Raksin
Hedy Lamarr, John Hodiak, James Craig, George Macready, Steve Geray

The Ladykillers*
GB 1955 97m Technicolor
Ealing (Seth Holt)
An old lady takes in a sinister lodger, who with his four friends commits a robbery. When she finds out, they plot to kill her, but are hoist with their own petards.
Overrated comedy in poor colour; those who made it quite clearly think it funnier than it is.
w William Rose *d* Alexander Mackendrick *ph* Otto Heller *m* Tristam Cary
Alec Guinness, *Katie Johnson*, Peter Sellers, Cecil Parker, Herbert Lom, Danny Green, Jack Warner, Frankie Howerd, Kenneth Connor

Lafayette Escadrille
US 1957 93m bw
Warner (William Wellman)
GB title: *Hell Bent for Glory*
Early in World War I, a young American joins the French air force.
The director's valedictory film, on a subject close to his heart, is a curiously disappointing, flat and disjointed affair, partly salvaged by a good period feel.
w A. S. Fleischmann *d* William A. Wellman *ph William Clothier* *m* Leonard Rosenman
Tab Hunter, David Janssen, Clint Eastwood, Will Hutchins, Paul Fix

The Lamp Still Burns
GB 1943 90m bw
GFD / Two Cities (Leslie Howard)
Adventures of wartime probationary nurses.
Understated wartime morale-builder, no longer very interesting.
w Elizabeth Baron, Roland Pertwee, *novel* One Pair of Feet by Monica Dickens *d* Maurice Elvey
Rosamund John, Stewart Granger, Godfrey Tearle, Sophie Stewart, John Laurie, Margaret Vyner, Cathleen Nesbitt, Joyce Grenfell

Lancelot and Guinevere*
GB 1962 117m Eastmancolor Panavision
Emblem (Cornel Wilde)
US title: *Sword of Lancelot*
Sir Lancelot covets the wife of his beloved King Arthur, but after Arthur's death she takes the veil.
Decently made, rather tame transcription of the legends, with all concerned doing quite creditably but not brilliantly.
w Richard Schayer, Jefferson Pascal *d* Cornel Wilde *ph* Harry Waxman *m* Ron Goodwin
Cornel Wilde, Jean Wallace, Brian Aherne, George Baker, John Barrie

Lancer Spy*
US 1937 80m bw
TCF
A German spy is captured and his English double is sent back to replace him.
World War I yarn on the lines of *The Great*

Impersonation (qv). Excellent production and a good beginning and end, but a slow middle.

w Philip Dunne, *novel* Marthe McKenna *d* Gregory Ratoff *ph* Barney McGill *m* Arthur Lange

George Sanders, Dolores del Rio, Peter Lorre, Joseph Schildkraut, Virginia Field, Sig Rumann, Fritz Feld

Land of the Pharaohs*
US 1955 105m Warnercolor Cinemascope
Warner / Continental (Howard Hawks)

Pharaoh is obsessed with life after death and builds a great pyramid for himself and his treasures . . . but his wife is ambitious . . .
Unexpected, interesting excursion into Ancient Egypt, distended by Cinemascope; basically a macabre melodrama with a final spectacular twist. The engineering details would make a fascinating documentary.

w William Faulkner, Harry Kurnitz, H. Jack Bloom *d* Howard Hawks *ph Lee Garmes, Russell Harlan m Dmitri Tiomkin ad Alexander Trauner*

Jack Hawkins, Joan Collins, Alexis Minotis, James Robertson Justice, Sidney Chaplin

The Land That Time Forgot*
GB 1974 91m Technicolor
Amicus (John Dark)

In 1916, survivors from a torpedoed supply ship find themselves on a legendary island full of prehistoric monsters.
Lively old-fashioned adventure fantasy with good technical credits.

w James Cawthorne, Michael Moorcock, *novel* Edgar Rice Burroughs *d* Kevin Connor *ph* Alan Hume *m* Douglas Gamley *pd Maurice Carter sp* Derek Meddings, Roger Dicken

Doug McClure, John McEnery, Susan Penhaligon, Keith Barron, Anthony Ainley

The Land Unknown*
US 1957 78m bw Cinemascope
U-I (William Alland)

A plane is forced down into a strange Antarctic valley where dinosaurs still roam.
Efficient adventure fantasy on *King Kong* lines but without any of that film's panache.

w Laslo Gorog *d* Virgil Vogel *ph* Ellis Carter *m* Joseph Gershenson *sp* Roswell Hoffman, Fred Knoth, Orien Ernest, Jack Kevan

Jock Mahoney, Shawn Smith, William Reynolds, Henry Brandon

The Landlord*
US 1970 110m De Luxe
UA / Mirisch / Carter

A tycoon's son buys a tenement in Brooklyn's black ghetto, and conscience diverts him into improving the lot of his tenants.
Overlong satirical comedy, good on detail but short on structure.

w Bill Gunn, *novel* Kristin Hunter *d Hal Ashby ph* Gordon Willis *m* Al Kooper *pd* Robert Boyle

Beau Bridges, Lee Grant, Pearl Bailey, Diana Sands

'Bad taste from start to finish . . . not an avenue of offensiveness to any race is left unexplored.'—*Judith Crist*

Lanigan's Rabbi
US 1976 98m Technicolor TVM
Universal / Heyday (Leonard B. Stern)

A rabbi with a penchant for detection helps the local police chief solve a murder.
Initially pleasant but overlong and finally undistinguished pilot for a *Mystery Movie* segment.

w Don M. Mankiewicz, Gordon Cotler, *novel* Friday the Rabbi Slept Late by Harry Kemelman *d* Lou Antonio *ph* Andrew Jackson *m* Leonard Rosenman

Stuart Margolin, Art Carney, Janet Margolin, Janis Paige

Larceny
US 1948 89m bw
Universal (Aaron Rosenberg)

A con man fleeces a war widow into paying for a memorial to her husband, but falls in love with her.
Drearily predictable melodrama.

w Herbert F. Margolis, Louis Markein, William Bowers *novel* The Velvet Fleece by Lois Ely, John Fleming *d* George Sherman *ph* Irving Glassberg *m* Leith Stevens

Joan Caulfield, John Payne, Dan Duryea, Shelley Winters, Dorothy Hart, Richard Rober, Dan O'Herlihy

Larceny Inc.
US 1942 95m bw
Warner (Jack Saper, Jerry Wald)

An ex-convict tries to rob a bank but finds that honesty pays best.
Tepid comedy-drama from the period when Warners were taming their gangster image.

w Everett Freeman, Edwin Gilbert, *play* The

Night before Christmas by Laura and S. J. Perelman *d* Lloyd Bacon *ph* Tony Gaudio

Edward G. Robinson, Jane Wyman, Broderick Crawford, Anthony Quinn, Jack Carson, Edward Brophy, Harry Davenport, John Qualen, Barbara Jo Allen, Jackie Gleason, Grant Mitchell, Andrew Tombes

Larry
US 1974 74m colour TVM
Tomorrow

A normally intelligent man of 26 has been considered mentally retarded and hospitalized since infancy.
Interesting case history based on fact.

w David Seltzer *d* William A. Graham

Frederic Forrest, Tyne Daly, Michael McGuire, Robert Walden

The Las Vegas Story
US 1952 88m bw
RKO (Robert Sparks)

When an investment broker and his new wife stop at Las Vegas, her shady past begins to emerge.
So-so programmer with some eccentric talents in average form, capped by a desert helicopter chase.

w Earl Felton, Harry Essex *d* Robert Stevenson *ph* Harry J. Wild *m* Constantin Bakeleinikoff

Jane Russell, Victor Mature, Vincent Price, Hoagy Carmichael, Colleen Miller, Brad Dexter, Jay C. Flippen

Lassie
The official Lassie series, made by MGM, was as follows:

1943: LASSIE COME HOME (qv)
1945: SON OF LASSIE (*d* S. Sylvan Simon *with* Peter Lawford, Donald Crisp, Nigel Bruce)
1946: COURAGE OF LASSIE (*d* Fred M. Wilcox *with* Elizabeth Taylor, Frank Morgan, Tom Drake)
1948: THE HILLS OF HOME[1] (*d* Fred M. Wilcox *with* Edmund Gwenn, Donald Crisp, Tom Drake)
1949: THE SUN COMES UP (*d* Richard Thorpe *with* Jeanette MacDonald, Lloyd Nolan)
1949: CHALLENGE TO LASSIE (*d* Richard Thorpe *with* Edmund Gwenn, Donald Crisp)
1951: THE PAINTED HILLS (*d* Harold F. Kress *with* Paul Kelly, Bruce Cowling)

† Later 'Lassie' features were taken from episodes of the long-running TV series.

[1] (GB title: *Master of Lassie*)

Lassie Come Home*
US 1943 88m Technicolor
MGM (Samuel Marx)

A poor family is forced to sell its beloved dog, but she makes a remarkable journey to return to them.
First of the Lassie films and certainly the best: an old-fashioned heartwarmer.

w Hugo Butler, *novel* Eric Knight *d* Fred M. Wilcox *ph* Leonard Smith *m* Daniele Amfitheatrof

Roddy McDowall, Elizabeth Taylor, Donald Crisp, Edmund Gwenn, Dame May Whitty, Nigel Bruce, Elsa Lanchester, J. Pat O'Malley

'The late Eric Knight wrote this immortal essay in Doggery-Woggery. MGM finished it off.'—*Richard Winnington*

The Last American Hero*
US 1973 95m De Luxe Panavision
TCF / Wizan / Rojo (John Cutts, William Roberts)

The adventures of an illicit whisky distiller with a passion for fast cars.
Observant, amusing hillbilly comedy drama based on the early life of racing driver Elroy Jackson.

w William Roberts *d Lamont Johnson* *ph* George Silano *m* Charles Fox

Jeff Bridges, Valerie Perrine, Geraldine Fitzgerald, Ned Beatty, Art Lund, Gary Busey

The Last Angry Man*
US 1959 100m bw
Columbia (Fred Kohlmar)

An old doctor in a Brooklyn slum is made the subject of a TV documentary.
Self-confidently sentimental wallow which just about works.

w Gerald Green *d* Daniel Mann *ph* James Wong Howe *m* George Duning

Paul Muni, David Wayne, Betsy Palmer, Luther Adler, Dan Tobin, Robert F. Simon

The Last Angry Man
US 1974 74m colour TVM
Columbia

Unnecessary TV remake of the above. Quite flat.

w Gerald Green *d* Jerrold Freedman

Pat Hingle, Lynn Carlin, Tracy Bogart, Michael Margotta, Andrew Duggan, Sorrell Booke

The Last Blitzkrieg
US 1959 84m bw
Columbia / Sam Katzman

During the Battle of the Bulge a German leads a squad of American saboteurs.
Weakly pacifist, technically incompetent war adventure.

w Lou Morheim *d* Arthur Dreifuss *ph* Ted Scaife *m* Hugo de Groot

Van Johnson, Kerwin Mathews, Dick York, Larry Storch

The Last Child*
US 1971 73m colour TVM
Aaron Spelling (William Allyn)

A future government denies married couples the right to more than one child; one family tries to escape.
Orwellian fantasy, rather better than *Zero Population Growth* which it resembles.

w Peter S. Fischer *d* John Llewellyn Moxey

Michael Cole, Janet Margolin, Van Heflin, Harry Guardino, Ed Asner

The Last Command*
US 1955 110m Trucolor
Republic (Frank Lloyd)

Jim Bowie returns to Texas in the 1830s and dies at the Alamo alongside other famous men.
Reasonably interesting western on a subject which has often figured but seldom worked.

w Warren Duff *d* Frank Lloyd *ph* Jack Marta *m* Max Steiner

Ernest Borgnine, Sterling Hayden, Anna Maria Alberghetti, Arthur Hunnicutt, Richard Carlson, J. Carrol Naish

The Last Day*
US 1975 100m colour TVM
Paramount / A. C. Lyles

A retired gunman brings out his weapons to defend his town against the Dalton gang.
Trickily made western which would have played better straight but has some nice conceits and performances.

w Jim Byrnes, Steve Fisher *d* Vincent McEveety

Richard Widmark, Robert Conrad, Barbara Rush, Loretta Swit, Tim Matheson, Christopher Connelly, Richard Jaeckel

The Last Days of Dolwyn*
GB 1949 95m bw
London / BLPA (Anatole de Grunwald)
US title: *Woman of Dolwyn*

A Welsh valley is flooded to make a reservoir and a village has to be evacuated.
Interesting but rather stagey drama based on an actual 19th-century event, with personal melodrama added.

wd Emlyn Williams *ph* Otto Heller *m* John Greenwood

Edith Evans, Emlyn Williams, Richard Burton, Hugh Griffith, Barbara Couper, Allan Aynesworth

'The conventionally picturesque Welsh flavour and mounting probabilities apart, the treatment is stiff and episodic.'—*MFB*

The Last Days of Pompeii**
US 1935 96m bw
RKO (Merian C. Cooper)

In ancient Pompeii, various personal dramas are submerged in the eruption of Vesuvius.
Starchy melodrama capped by a reel of spectacular disaster.

w Ruth Rose, Boris Ingster, *novel* Lord Lytton
d Merian C. Cooper, Ernest Schoedsack
ph Eddie Linden Jnr, Ray June *m* Roy Webb
sp Vernon Walker, Harry Redmond

Preston Foster, Basil Rathbone, Alan Hale, Dorothy Cooper

The Last Detail**
US 1973 104m Metrocolor
Columbia / Acrobat / Persky–Bright (Gerald Ayres)

Two hardened naval petty officers escort a young recruit, sentenced for thieving, from Virginia to a New Hampshire jail, and give him a wild last night.
Foul-mouthed weekend odyssey, with a few well-observed moments for non-prudes. Technically the epitome of Hollywood's most irritating seventies fashion, with fuzzy sound recording, dim against-the-light photography, and a general determination to show up the ugliness of everything around us.

w Robert Towne, *novel* Darryl Ponicsan *d* Hal Ashby *ph* Michael Chapman *m* Johnny Mandel

Jack Nicholson, Otis Young, Randy Quaid, Clifton James, Carol Kane

'Visually it is relentlessly lower-depths gloomy, and the material, though often very funny, is programmed to wrench your heart.'—*New Yorker*

The Last Flight****
US 1931 80m bw
Warner

In 1919, four veteran American fliers stay on in

Paris in the hope of calming their shattered physical and emotional states.
Fascinatingly offhand study on post-war cynicism and the faint hope of a better world, beautifully written and directed in a manner more effective than *The Sun Also Rises*.

w John Monk Saunders, from his novel Single Lady *d William Dieterle* *ph* Sid Hickox

Richard Barthelmess, Helen Chandler, David Manners, John Mack Brown, *Elliott Nugent*, Walter Byron

'A narrative as tight and spare as a Racine tragedy . . . unique in Hollywood of that time in its persistent, calculated understatement.'—*Tom Milne, 1975*

The Last Gangster*
US 1937 81m bw
MGM

A gangster is released from Alcatraz and plans vengeance on his wife for deserting him.
Clean-cut star melodrama which suddenly turns sentimental.

w John Lee Mahin *d* Edward Ludwig *ph* William Daniels *montage Slavko Vorkapitch*

Edward G. Robinson, Rose Stradner, James Stewart, Lionel Stander, Douglas Scott, John Carradine, Sidney Blackmer, Edward Brophy

'A lot of water has flowed under the bridge since *Little Caesar*, but Mr Robinson has breasted the tides to make his impersonation of a 1937 thug as persuasive as was his portrait of a killer in that earlier classic of rats and rackets.'—*Frank Nugent*

The Last Grenade
GB 1969 93m Eastmancolor Panavision
Cinerama / Dimitri de Grunwald / Josef Shaftel

An army mercenary is betrayed by an ex-friend in the Congo and pursues him to Hong Kong.
Violent action melodrama with few redeeming qualities.

w Kenneth Ware, *novel* The Ordeal of Major Grigsby by John Sherlock *d* Gordon Flemyng *ph* Alan Hume *m* Johnny Dankworth

Stanley Baker, Alex Cord, Honor Blackman, Richard Attenborough, Rafer Johnson, Andrew Keir, Ray Brooks, Julian Glover, John Thaw

The Last Hard Men
US 1976 97m De Luxe Panavision
TCF / Belasco–Seltzer–Thatcher

A train robber breaks jail and sets out to revenge himself on the now-retired lawman who committed him.
Tough action adventure without much sense except to paint the end of the golden days of the west.

w Guerdon Trueblood, *novel* Gun Down by Brian Garfield *d* Andrew V. McLaglen *ph* Duke Callaghan *m* Jerry Goldsmith

Charlton Heston, James Coburn, Barbara Hershey, Christopher Mitchum, Michael Parks, Jorge Rivero, Thalmus Rasulala

Last Holiday*
GB 1950 88m bw
ABPC / Watergate (Stephen Mitchell, A. D. Peters, J. B. Priestley)

A man with a short time to live has a thoroughly enjoyable and useful final fling.
Slight, amusing and moving comedy drama spoiled by an unnecessary double twist.

w J. B. Priestley *d* Henry Cass *ph* Ray Elton *m* Francis Chagrin

Alec Guinness, Kay Walsh, Beatrice Campbell, Grégoire Aslan, Bernard Lee, Wilfrid Hyde White, Helen Cherry, Sidney James, Muriel George

Last Hours before Morning*
US 1975 74m colour TVM
MGM / Charles Fries

A hotel house detective is involved in a murder.
Chandleresque murder mystery, quite effectively done; it did not go as a series.

w Robert Garland, George Yanok *d* Joseph Hardy

Ed Lauter, Rhonda Fleming, Robert Alda, Kaz Garas, Peter Donat, Don Porter

The Last Hunt*
US 1955 103m Eastmancolor Cinemascope
MGM (Dore Schary)

Buffalo hunters fall out with each other.
Terse, brutish outdoor western with something to say about old western myths and a famous ending in which the bad guy freezes to death while waiting to gun down the hero.

wd Richard Brooks *ph* Russell Harlan *m* Daniele Amfitheatrof

Stewart Granger, Robert Taylor, Debra Paget, Lloyd Nolan, Russ Tamblyn, Constance Ford

The Last Hurrah***
US 1958 125m bw
Columbia (John Ford)

The political boss of a New England town fights his last campaign.
Enjoyable if disjointed melodrama, an old man's film crammed with cameo performances from familiar faces: important as one of Hollywood's great sentimental reunions.

w Frank Nugent, novel Edwin O'Connor *d John Ford ph* Charles Lawton Jnr

Spencer Tracy, Jeffrey Hunter, Dianne Foster, *Pat O'Brien, Basil Rathbone, Edward Brophy, Donald Crisp, James Gleason, John Carradine, Ricardo Cortez, Wallace Ford, Frank McHugh,* Frank Albertson, Anna Lee, Jane Darwell, Willis Bouchey, Basil Ruysdael

The Last Mile*
US 1932 84m bw
World Wide (E. W. Hammons)

Tensions mount in jail as the execution of Killer Mears approaches.
Strident melodrama which works up quite a head of hysteria.

w Seton I. Miller, *play* John Wexley *d* Sam Bischoff *ph* Arthur Edeson

Preston Foster, Howard Phillips, George E. Stone, Noel Madison

The Last Mile
US 1959 81m bw
UA / Vanguard (Milton Subotsky)

Even more hysterical remake, retaining the original period. A cheerless, though literally electrifying, entertainment.

w Milton Subotsky, Seton I. Miller *d* Howard W. Koch *ph* Joseph Brun *m* Van Alexander

Mickey Rooney, Clifford David, Frank Conroy, Frank Overton, Leon Janney

The Last of Mrs Cheyney
US 1929 94m bw
MGM

A confidence woman in British high society falls in love.
Old theatrical warhorse, much filmed but never very satisfactorily. (See below.)

w Hans Kraly, Claudine West, *play* Frederick Lonsdale *d* Sidney Franklin *ph* William Daniels

Norma Shearer, Basil Rathbone, George Barraud, Hedda Hopper, Maude Turner Gordon, Herbert Bunston

The Last of Mrs Cheyney
US 1937 98m bw
MGM (Lawrence Weingarten)

Adequate, unexciting remake.

w Leon Gordon, Samson Raphaelson, Monckton Hoffe *d* Richard Boleslawski *ph* George Folsey *m* William Axt

Joan Crawford, Robert Montgomery, William Powell, Frank Morgan, Jessie Ralph, Nigel Bruce, Benita Hume, Melville Cooper, Sara Haden

† A further remake was *The Law and the Lady* (qv).

The Last of Sheila*
US 1973 123m Technicolor
Warner (Herbert Ross)

A Hollywood star is killed by a hit-and-run driver; a year later her husband invites six friends to his yacht, and murders begin.
Confused, in-jokey showbiz whodunnit with flashes of interest.

w Stephen Sondheim, Anthony Perkins *d* Herbert Ross *ph* Gerry Turpin *m* Billy Goldenberg *ad* Ken Adam

Richard Benjamin, Dyan Cannon, James Coburn, James Mason, Joan Hackett, Ian MacShane, Raquel Welch

'The most teasing riddles for an audience are likely to be the real identities of the personalities being satirized.'—*MFB*

The Last of the Belles*
US 1974 98m colour TVM
Robert Buzz Burger

How F. Scott Fitzgerald met his wife Zelda.
Odd, underplayed romantic piece, quite out of the normal run.

d George Schaefer

Richard Chamberlain, Blythe Danner, Susan Sarandon

The Last of the Comanches*
US 1953 85m Technicolor
Columbia (Buddy Adler)
GB title: *The Sabre and the Arrow*

Survivors of an Indian raid take refuge in an abandoned mission until help arrives.
Competent western remake of *Sahara* (which was a remake of *The Lost Patrol*).

w Kenneth Gamet *d* André de Toth *ph* Charles Lawton Jnr *m* George Duning

Broderick Crawford, Barbara Hale, Lloyd Bridges, Martin Milner

The Last of the Mohicans
US 1936 91m bw
Edward Small

Incidents during colonial America's French–Indian war.

Vigorous if rough-and-ready western, later remade (poorly) as *Last of the Redmen* and as a Canadian TV series.

w Philip Dunne, John Balderston, Paul Perez, Daniel Moore, *novel* James Fenimore Cooper *d* George B. Seitz *ph* Robert Planck *m* Nathaniel Shilkret

Randolph Scott, Binnie Barnes, Bruce Cabot, Henry Wilcoxon, Heather Angel, Hugh Buckler

The Last of the Powerseekers*
US 1969 101m Technicolor TVM
Universal

Complications and sudden deaths ensue when a banker accuses his son-in-law of embezzlement.
Ingenious stretch-out of several episodes from the unsuccessful Harold Robbins series *The Survivors*; most of the glamorous sequences are included, and the new plot hangs together remarkably well.

wd Walter Doniger, Joseph Leytes, Paul Henreid

Lana Turner, George Hamilton, Ralph Bellamy, Kevin McCarthy, Louis Hayward, Diana Muldaur, Jan-Michael Vincent

Last of the Red Hot Lovers*
US 1972 98m Technicolor
Paramount (Howard W. Koch)

A middle-aged fish restaurateur feels the need for an extra-marital spree.
Modest, plainly-filmed sex comedy from a reliable stable.

w Neil Simon, from his play *d* Gene Saks *ph* Victor J. Kemper *m* Neal Hefti

Alan Arkin, Paula Prentiss, Sally Kellerman, Renée Taylor

The Last Outpost*
US 1935 75m bw
Paramount (E. Lloyd Sheldon)

A British officer is captured by the Kurds and freed by an adventurer whose wife he covets.
Patchy, unusual adventure story with good moments.

w Philip MacDonald, *story* F. Britten Austin *d* Charles Barton, Louis Gasnier *ph* Theodor Sparkuhl

Cary Grant, Claude Rains, Gertrude Michael, Kathleen Burke, Colin Tapley, Akim Tamiroff, Billy Bevan, Jameson Thomas

The Last Picture Show***
US 1971 118m bw
Columbia / LPS / BDS (Stephen J. Friedman)

Teenage affairs in a small Texas town in 1951, ending with the hero's embarkation for Korea and the closing of the tatty cinema.
Penetrating nostalgia with over-emphasis on sex; the detail is the attraction.

w Larry McMurty, Peter Bogdanovich *d Peter Bogdanovich ph Robert Surtees m* original recordings *pd Polly Platt*

Timothy Bottoms, Jeff Bridges, Cybill Shepherd, Ben Johnson, Cloris Leachman, Ellen Burstyn

'The most important work by a young American director since *Citizen Kane*.'—*Paul D. Zimmerman*

'So many things in it are so good that I wish I liked it more.'—*Stanley Kauffmann*

The Last Run*
US 1971 92m Metrocolor Panavision
MGM (Carter de Haven)

An ex-Chicago gangster retired to a Portuguese fishing village undertakes one last fatal job.
Well-made, rather uninteresting downbeat melodrama.

w Alan Sharp *d* Richard Fleischer *ph* Sven Nykvist *m* Jerry Goldsmith

George C. Scott, Tony Musante, Trish Van Devere

The Last Safari
GB 1967 110m Technicolor
Paramount (Henry Hathaway)

A disillusioned white hunter takes on one last safari.
Dullsville adventure story with good animal photography redeeming some of the clichés.

w John Gay, *novel* Gilligan's Last Elephant by Gerald Hanley *d* Henry Hathaway *ph* Ted Moore *m* Johnny Dankworth

Stewart Granger, Kaz Garas, Gabriella Licudi, Johnny Sekka, Liam Redmond, Eugene Deckers

Last Summer*
US 1969 97m Eastmancolor
Alsid / Francis (Alfred Crown, Sidney Beckerman)

Well-to-do teenagers have sexual adventures on a summer seaside holiday.
Striking off-beat melodrama with vividly sketched characters.

w Eleanor Perry, novel Evan Hunter *d Frank Perry ph* Gerald Hirschfeld *m* John Simon

Barbara Hershey, Richard Thomas, Bruce Davison, Cathy Burns, Ernesto Gonzales, Ralph Waite

The Last Sunset
US 1961 112m Eastmancolor
U-I (Brynaprod)

A killer and his hunter learn a lot about each other before the final showdown.
Slow psycho-western with pretensions to tragedy.

w Dalton Trumbo, *novel* Showdown at Crazy Horse by Howard Grigsby *d* Robert Aldrich *ph* Ernest Laszlo *m* Ernest Gold

Rock Hudson, Kirk Douglas, Dorothy Malone, Carol Lynley, Joseph Cotten, Regis Toomey, Neville Brand

The Last Survivors
US 1975 74m colour TVM
Columbia / Bob Banner

After a sea disaster, an officer must decide which passengers shall remain in an overcrowded lifeboat.
Bathtub remake of *Seven Waves Away* (qv). Not as good (or even worse).

w Douglas Day Stewart *d* Lee H. Katzin

Martin Sheen, Diane Baker, Tom Bosley, Christopher George, Bruce Davison, Anne Francis, Percy Rodrigues, Anne Seymour, Bethel Leslie

Last Tango in Paris*
France / Italy / US 1972 129m Technicolor
Les Artistes Associés / PEA / UA (Alberto Grimaldi)

A middle-aged man and a young French girl have a doomed love affair.
Pretentious sex melodrama mainly notable for being banned.

w Bernardo Bertolucci, Franco Arcalli *d* Bernardo Bertolucci *ph* Vittorio Storaro *m* Gato Barbieri

Marlon Brando, Maria Schneider, Jean-Pierre Léaud

The Last Time I Saw Archie
US 1961 98m bw
UA / Mark VII / Manzanita / Talbot (Jack Webb)

Adventures of a con man amid overage civilian pilots at an army/air force base.
Patchy service comedy.

w William Bowers *d* Jack Webb *ph* Joe MacDonald *m* Frank Comstock

Jack Webb, Robert Mitchum, Martha Hyer, France Nuyen, Louis Nye, Jimmy Lydon, Richard Arlen, Don Knotts, Robert Strauss, Joe Flynn

The Last Time I Saw Paris
US 1954 116m Technicolor
MGM

A writer recalls his romance with a wealthy American girl in Paris.
Dull romantic drama which very deadeningly and predictably updates F. Scott Fitzgerald's *Babylon Revisited*.

w Julius J. and Philip G. Epstein, Richard Brooks *d* Richard Brooks *ph* Joseph Ruttenberg *m* Conrad Salinger

Elizabeth Taylor, Van Johnson, Walter Pidgeon, Donna Reed, Eva Gabor

Last Train from Gun Hill*
US 1959 98m Technicolor Vistavision
(Paramount) Hal B. Wallis / Bryna

A marshal tracks down the man who raped and murdered his wife; it turns out to be the son of an old friend.
Good suspense and action western culminating in a *High Noon* situation.

w James Poe *d John Sturges* *ph* Charles Lang Jnr *m* Dmitri Tiomkin

Kirk Douglas, Anthony Quinn, Earl Holliman, Carolyn Jones, Brian Hutton

The Last Train from Madrid
US 1937 85m bw
Paramount (George M. Arthur)

A variety of people escape the fighting in the Spanish Civil War.
Tawdry topical melodrama with cliché characters and situations.

w Louis Stevens, Robert Wyler *d* James Hogan *ph* Harry Fischbeck *md* Boris Morros

Dorothy Lamour, Lew Ayres, Gilbert Roland, Karen Morley, Lionel Atwill, Helen Mack, Robert Cummings, Olympe Bradna, Anthony Quinn, Lee Bowman, George Lloyd

'It is probably the worst film of the decade and should have been the funniest.'—*Graham Greene*

'Simply a topical and different background for a glib little fiction.'—*Frank S. Nugent*

The Last Valley
GB 1970 128m Eastmancolor Todd-AO
ABC / Season / Seamaster (James Clavell)

In 1641 during the Thirty Years War a scholar tries to defend a remote and prosperous Swiss valley against a horde of mercenaries.
Big-scale historical action picture crammed with pillage, torture, rape, death at the stake, throat

cutting and general carnage; reasonably literate for all that, and convincingly set.

wd James Clavell, *novel* J. B. Pick *ph* Norman Warwick *m* John Barry *ad* Peter Mullins

Michael Caine, Omar Sharif, Florinda Bolkan, Nigel Davenport, Per Oscarsson, Arthur O'Connell, Brian Blessed

The Last Voyage*

US 1960 91m Metrocolor

MGM / Andrew and Virginia Stone

A boiler room explosion causes an old passenger liner to sink.

Spectacular if dramatically deficient actioner for which a genuine liner (awaiting scrapping) was sunk.

wd Andrew L. Stone ph Hal Mohr *m* Rudy Schrager

Robert Stack, Dorothy Malone, Edmond O'Brien, George Sanders, Woody Strode, Jack Kruschen

'A prolonged nerve stretcher.'—*MFB*

The Last Wagon

US 1960 99m Eastmancolor Cinemascope

TCF (William B. Hawks)

A half breed wanted for murder joins an 1875 wagon train.

Heavy-going big-scale western.

w James Edward Grant, Delmer Daves, Gwen Bagni *d* Delmer Daves *ph* Wilfrid Cline *m* Lionel Newman

Richard Widmark, Felicia Farr, Tommy Rettig, Susan Kohner, Ray Stricklyn, Nick Adams, Carl Benton Reid

The Late Edwina Black*

GB 1951 78m bw

IFD / Elvey–Gartside

US title: *Obsessed*

When a schoolteacher's wife is found dead, the police have three suspects.

Adequately suspenseful Victorian thriller from a successful play.

w Charles Frank, David Evans, *play* William Dinner, William Morum *d* Maurice Elvey *ph* Stephen Dade *m* Allan Gray

Geraldine Fitzgerald, David Farrar, *Roland Culver*, Jean Cadell, Mary Merrall, Harcourt Williams, Charles Heslop, Ronald Adam

The Late George Apley*

US 1946 96m bw

TCF (Joseph L. Mankiewicz)

The uneventful family life of a Boston blueblood.

Pleasant but tame family comedy-drama, solidly carpentered.

w Philip Dunne, *novel* John P. Marquand *d* Joseph L. Mankiewicz *ph* Joseph La Shelle *m* Cyril Mockridge

Ronald Colman, Edna Best, Vanessa Brown, Richard Haydn, Peggy Cummins, Charles Russell

Latin Lovers

US 1953 104m Technicolor

MGM (Joe Pasternak)

An heiress on holiday in Brazil looks for a man who will love her for herself alone.

Barren romantic drama, flatfooted and drawn out.

w Isobel Lennart *d* Mervyn Le Roy *ph* Joseph Ruttenberg *m* George Stoll

Lana Turner, Ricardo Montalban, John Lund, Louis Calhern, Jean Hagen

Latin Quarter*

GB 1945 80m bw

British National

US title: *Frenzy*

In nineties Paris a mad sculptor murders his fiancée and hides her inside his latest exhibit.

Artificial-looking but melodramatically effective thriller with a chilling climax and a detailed Dégas-period background.

wd Vernon Sewell ph Gunther Krampf, *play* l'Angoisse by Pierre Mills, Charles Vylars

Derrick de Marney, Joan Greenwood, Beresford Egan, Frederick Valk, Lily Kann, Martin Miller

Laughing Anne

GB 1953 90m Technicolor

Republic / Wilcox–Neagle

French Anne and her boxing lover are characters of the Javanese waterfront; he kills her after she has fallen for a sea captain.

Cheap and turgid adaptation of a Joseph Conrad story; the author would not recognize it. Studio settings put the lid on hilariously bad work all round.

w Pamela Bower *d* Herbert Wilcox *ph* Max Greene *m* Anthony Collins

Margaret Lockwood, Forrest Tucker, Ronald Shiner, Wendell Corey, Robert Harris

The Laughing Policeman*

US 1973 112m De Luxe

TCF (Stuart Rosenberg)

GB title: *An Investigation of Murder*

A mad machine-gunner eludes the San Francisco police.

Downbeat, semi-documentary police thriller with pretensions. Too complex by half, with an overplus of characterization, but the location work is excellent.

w Thomas Rickman, *novel* Maj Sjowall, Per Wahloo *d* Stuart Rosenberg *ph* David Walsh *m* Charles Fox

Walter Matthau, Bruce Dern, Lou Gossett, Albert Paulsen, Anthony Zerbe

Laughter**
US 1930 99m bw
Paramount

An ex-Follies girl marries a millionaire but later goes on a spree with the composer she once loved.
Sharply observed, before its time romantic comedy reminiscent now of the later *Philadelphia Story* in its attitudes to wealth and love. A precursor of the smart crazy comedies of the mid-thirties.

w Donald Ogden Stewart d Harry d'Abbabie d'Arrast ph George Folsey

Fredric March, Nancy Carroll, Frank Morgan, Glen Anders, Diane Ellis

'One of the best talking pictures I have ever seen.'—*James Agate*

'A talkie with so fast a pace that it crowds the comprehension of half the customers . . . marked at intervals by superb dialogue and the quick hand of a smart director.'—*Pare Lorentz*

Laughter in Paradise*
GB 1951 93m bw
ABPC (*Mario Zampi*)

An eccentric leaves in his will a fortune for each of his relations providing they will perform certain embarrassing or criminal acts.
A funny idea gets half-hearted treatment, but the good bits are hilarious.

w Michael Pertwee, Jack Davies *d* Mario Zampi *ph* William McLeod *m* Stanley Black

Alastair Sim, Joyce Grenfell, Hugh Griffith, Fay Compton, John Laurie, George Cole, Guy Middleton, Ronald Adam, Leslie Dwyer, A. E. Matthews, Beatrice Campbell

† Remade 1972 as *Some Will, Some Won't.*

Laughter in the Dark*
GB / France 1969 104m De Luxe
UA / Woodfall / Winkast / Marceau (Neil Hartley)

A wealthy art dealer is taken in by an ambitious usherette and her lover, and after being blinded in a car accident tries to kill them.
Unsatisfactory adaptation of a novel with a very specialized appeal: conventional swinging London and Riviera settings only confuse the spectator. Moments do work, though.

w Edward Bond, *novel* Vladimir Nabokov *d* Tony Richardson *ph* Dick Bush *m* Raymond Leppard *ad* Julia Trevelyan Oman

Nicol Williamson, Anna Karina, Jean-Claude Drouot, Peter Bowles, Sian Phillips

'It fails to create the slightest interest in its trio of repulsive characters.'—*Philip Strick*

Laura****
US 1944 85m bw
TCF (Otto Preminger)

A beautiful girl is murdered . . . or is she? A cynical detective investigates.
A quiet, streamlined little murder mystery that brought a new adult approach to the genre and heralded the mature *film noir* of the later forties. A small cast responds perfectly to a classically spare script, and in Clifton Webb a new star is born.

w Jay Dratler, Samuel Hoffenstein, Betty Reinhardt, novel Vera Caspary *d Otto Preminger ph Joseph La Shelle m David Raksin*

Dana Andrews, Clifton Webb, Gene Tierney, Judith Anderson, *Vincent Price*, Dorothy Adams, James Flavin

The Lavender Hill Mob****
GB 1951 78m bw
Ealing (Michael Truman)

A timid bank clerk conceives and executes a bullion robbery.
Superbly characterized and inventively detailed comedy, one of the best ever made at Ealing or in Britain.

w T. E. B. Clarke d Charles Crichton ph Douglas Slocombe m Georges Auric

Alec Guinness, Stanley Holloway, Sidney James, Alfie Bass, Marjorie Fielding, Edie Martin, John Gregson, Gibb McLaughlin

'Amusing situations and dialogue are well paced and sustained throughout: the climax is delightful.'—*MFB*

The Law**
US 1974 120m Technicolor TVM
Universal

The work of a public defender in a murder trial.
Harsh, sometimes quite brilliant drama documentary which goes on too long.

w Joel Oliansky *d* John Badham

Judd Hirsch, John Beck, Bonnie Franklin, Sam Wanamaker

Law and Disorder*
GB 1958 76m bw
British Lion / Hotspur (Paul Soskin)

Crooks rally round a confederate about to be arrested, to prevent his son from learning of his father's real career.
Amusing, well-pointed caper on sub-Ealing lines.

w T. E. B. Clarke, *novel* Smuggler's Circuit by Denys Roberts *d* Charles Crichton *ph* Ted Scaife *m* Humphrey Searle

Michael Redgrave, Robert Morley, Joan Hickson, Lionel Jeffries, Ronald Squire, Elizabeth Sellars

Law and Disorder*
US 1975 102m Technicolor Panavision
Memorial / Leroy Street / Ugo Fadsin (William Richert)

New York suburbanites aghast at escalating violence form themselves into a vigilante patrol.
Bewilderingly uneven comedy drama which starts as satirical comedy and ends with one of the heroes dead and the other moralizing. Sporadically interesting, and certainly topical.

w Ivan Passer, William Richert, Kenneth Harris Fishman *d* Ivan Passer *ph* Arthur J. Ornitz *m* Andy Badale

Ernest Borgnine, Carroll O'Connor, Karen Black, Ann Wedgeworth, Leslie Ackerman, David Spielberg

The Law and Jake Wade*
US 1958 86m Metrocolor Cinemascope
MGM (William Hawks)

A marshal helps an old outlaw friend to escape from jail, and lives to regret it.
Good standard western, enjoyable throughout but with no outstanding merits.

w William Bowers *d* John Sturges *ph* Robert Surtees

Robert Taylor, Richard Widmark, Patricia Owens, Robert Middleton, Henry Silva

Law and Order*
US 1976 144m approx colour TVM
Paramount / PA (E. Jack Neuman)

An Irish Catholic New York cop has troubles stemming from the past as well as the present.
Heavy going if well-detailed crime chronicle with a confusing technique which means that the star always seems either too old or too young.

w E. Jack Neuman, *novel* Dorothy Uhnak *d* Marvin Chomsky *ph* Jack Marquette

Darren McGavin, Suzanne Pleshette, Will Geer, Art Hindle, Keir Dullea, Robert Reed, James Olson, Teri Garr, Biff McGuire, Jeanette Nolan

The Law and the Lady
US 1951 104m bw
MGM (Edwin H. Knopf)

A couple of confidence tricksters inveigle themselves into the house of a vulgar millionairess, but one of them has an attack of conscience.
Dreary remake of *The Last of Mrs Cheyney* (qv) with the locale altered, the plot simplified, and the level of wit diluted.

w Leonard Spiegelgass, Karl Tunberg *d* Edwin H. Knopf *ph* George Folsey *m* Carmen Dragon

Greer Garson, Michael Wilding, Fernando Lamas, Marjorie Main, Hayden Rorke, Margalo Gillmore, Ralph Dumke

Law of the Lawless
US 1963 87m Techniscope
Paramount / A. C. Lyles

A judge arrives in a small western town to conduct the murder trial of a former friend.
Jaded western of interest only for the producer's custom of packing the bit roles with former stars.

w Steve Fisher *d* William F. Claxton *ph* Lester Shorr

Dale Robertson, Yvonne de Carlo, William Bendix, Bruce Cabot, Barton MacLane, John Agar, Richard Arlen, Kent Taylor, Lon Chaney Jnr

The Lawless
US 1949 83m bw
Paramount / Pine–Thomas
GB title: *The Dividing Line*

The editor of a California small-town newspaper defends a Spanish boy who is being victimized by the racist element.
Well-meaning 'realistic' melodrama, unfortunately among the dullest of the socially conscious movies of this period.

w Geoffrey Homes *d* Joseph Losey *ph* Roy Hunt *m* David Chudnow

Macdonald Carey, Gail Russell, John Sands, John Hoyt, Lee Patrick, Lalo Rios

The Lawless Breed
US 1952 83m Technicolor
U-I (William Alland)

The adventures and repentance of badman John Wesley Hardin.
Standard western programmer with the star in an unlikely role.

w Bernard Gordon *d* Raoul Walsh *ph* Irving Glassberg *m* Joseph Gershenson

Rock Hudson, Julie Adams, John McIntire, Dennis Weaver, Hugh O'Brian

Lawman*
US 1970 99m Technicolor
UA / Scimitar (Michael Winner)

When a marshal tracks down drunken cowboys who have killed an old man, the townsfolk's resistance leads to a bloodbath.
Terse, violent western with a good cast.

w Gerald Wilson *d* Michael Winner *ph* Bob Paynter *m* Jerry Fielding

Burt Lancaster, Robert Ryan, Lee J. Cobb, Sheree North, Robert Duvall, Joseph Wiseman, John McGiver, Albert Salmi, J. D. Cannon

Lawrence of Arabia***
GB 1962 221m Technicolor Super Panavision 70
Columbia / Horizon (Sam Spiegel)

An adventurer's life with the Arabs, told in flashbacks after his accidental death in the thirties.
Sprawling epic which manages after four hours to give no insight whatever into the complexities of character of this mysterious historic figure, but is often spectacularly beautiful and exciting along the way.

w Robert Bolt *d David Lean ph Frederick A. Young m Maurice Jarre pd John Box ad John Stoll*

Peter O'Toole, Omar Sharif, Arthur Kennedy, Jack Hawkins, Donald Wolfit, Claude Rains, Anthony Quayle, *Alec Guinness*, Anthony Quinn, Jose Ferrer, Michel Ray, Zia Mohyeddin

'Grandeur of conception is not up to grandeur of setting.'—*Penelope Houston*

The Lawyer*
US 1970 120m Technicolor
Paramount (Brad Dexter)

An ambitious young Italian-American defence lawyer takes on a murder case.
Smartly-scripted, perfectly ordinary courtroom drama in a well-detailed western setting. The star subsequently played the same character in a TV series, *Petrocelli*.

w Sidney J. Furie, Harold Buchman *d Sidney J. Furie ph* Ralph Woolsey *m* Malcolm Dodds

Barry Newman, Harold Gould, Diana Muldaur, Robert Colbert, Kathleen Crowley, Booth Colman

Laxdale Hall
GB 1952 77m bw
Group Three (Alfred Shaughnessy)

MPs are sent to investigate a tiny Hebridean island which refuses to pay road tax.
Thin rehash of *Whisky Galore* put together without the Ealing style. Minor compensations can be found.

w John Eldridge, Alfred Shaughnessy *d* John Eldridge *ph* Arthur Grant *m* Frank Spencer

Raymond Huntley, Ronald Squire, Sebastian Shaw, Fulton Mackay, Kathleen Ryan, Kynaston Reeves

Le Mans*
US 1971 108m De Luxe Panavision
Solar / Cinema Center (Jack N. Reddish)

A sullen American enters for the 24-hour race.
Almost no plot and little documentary examination; what's left is a multitude of racing shots with Steve McQueen at the wheel. For some this may be enough.

w Harry Kleiner *d* Lee H. Katzin *ph* Robert B. Hauser, René Gruissart Jnr *m* Michel Legrand

Steve McQueen, Siegfried Rauch, Elga Andersen, Ronald Leigh-Hunt

The League of Gentlemen***
GB 1960 112m bw
Rank / Allied Film Makers (Michael Relph)

An ex-army officer recruits high-class misfits with guilty secrets to help him in a bank robbery.
Delightfully handled comedy adventure, from the days (alas) when crime did not pay; a lighter ending would have made it a classic.

w Bryan Forbes, novel John Boland *d Basil Dearden ph* Arthur Ibbetson *m* Philip Green

Jack Hawkins, Richard Attenborough, *Roger Livesey, Nigel Patrick*, Bryan Forbes, Kieron Moore, Terence Alexander, *Norman Bird*, Robert Coote, Melissa Stribling, Nanette Newman, Gerald Harper, Patrick Wymark, David Lodge, Doris Hare, Lydia Sherwood

Lease of Life*
GB 1954 94m Eastmancolor
Ealing (Jack Rix)

A poor clergyman is given a year to live, and puts it to good use.
Somewhat depressing but well-acted drama with excellent village atmosphere.

w Eric Ambler *d* Charles Frend *ph* Douglas Slocombe *m* Alan Rawsthorne

Robert Donat, Kay Walsh, Adrienne Corri, Denholm Elliott

The Leather Boys*
GB 1963 108m bw Cinemascope
British Lion / Garrick (Raymond Stross)

Two working-class teenagers marry for sex; she becomes a drudge and he develops a relationship with a homosexual motorcyclist.
Sharply-observed slice of low life which now seems quite dated, the central figures no longer being of the 'heroic' interest given them at the time. Technically the film is tediously and fashionably flashy.

w Gillian Freeman, *novel* Elliot George *d* Sidney J. Furie *ph* Gerald Gibbs *m* Bill McGuffie

Rita Tushingham, Dudley Sutton, Colin Campbell, Gladys Henson

The Leather Saint
US 1955 86m bw Vistavision
Paramount (Norman Retchin)

To provide his parish hospital with medical equipment, a Catholic priest becomes a commercial prizefighter.
Unlikely piece of religiosity, not too badly done.

w Norman Retchin, Alvin Ganzer *d* Alvin Ganzer *ph* Haskell Boggs *m* Irvin Talbot

Paul Douglas, John Derek, Cesar Romero, *Ernest Truex*, Jody Lawrance

Leave Her to Heaven
US 1945 111m Technicolor
TCF (William A. Bacher)

A selfish, jealous woman causes unhappiness for those around her, even in her suicide.
No-holds-barred melodrama of the old school; what seemed lush production at the time now looks tatty.

w Jo Swerling, *novel* Ben Ames Williams *d* John M. Stahl *ph* Leon Shamroy *m* Alfred Newman

Gene Tierney, Cornel Wilde, Jeanne Crain, Vincent Price, Mary Phillips, Ray Collins, Gene Lockhart, Reed Hadley, Chill Wills

The Left Hand of God
US 1955 87m De Luxe Cinemascope
TCF (Buddy Adler)

China, 1947: a Catholic priest newly arrived in a small village proves to be an American flier on the run from a warlord; but he contrives to work a small 'miracle'.
Hollywood religiosity at its most contrived, put together without distinction; the players have a wary look.

w Alfred Hayes, *novel* William E. Barrett *d* Edward Dmytryk *ph* Franz Planer *m* Victor Young

Humphrey Bogart, Gene Tierney, Lee J. Cobb, E. G. Marshall, Agnes Moorehead

The Left Handed Gun*
US 1958 102m bw
Warner / Haroll (Fred Coe)

Billy the Kid sets out to shoot four men who have killed his friend.
'Method'-oriented western, efficiently made but somewhat downcast.

w Leslie Stevens, *TV play* Gore Vidal *d* Arthur Penn *ph* Peverell Marley *m* Alexander Courage

Paul Newman, John Dehner, Lita Milan, Hurd Hatfield

Left Right and Centre*
GB 1959 95m bw
British Lion / Launder and Gilliat

A TV personality becomes Tory candidate at a by-election.
Scrappy political comedy with the saving grace of a large number of comic talents.

w Sidney Gilliat, Val Valentine *d* Sidney Gilliat *ph* Gerald Gibbs *m* Humphrey Searle

Ian Carmichael, Alastair Sim, Patricia Bredin, Richard Wattis, Eric Barker, Gordon Harker, George Benson, Frederick Leister

The Legend of Hell House*
GB 1973 94m De Luxe
TCF / Academy (James H. Nicholson)

Four people arrive at a haunted house in which several psychic investigators have been killed.
Harrowing thriller, a less solemn but more frightening version of *The Haunting*.

w Richard Matheson, from his novel *d John Hough* *ph* Alan Hume *m* Brian Hodgson, Delia Derbyshire

Pamela Franklin, Roddy McDowall, Clive Revill, Gayle Hunnicutt, Roland Culver, Peter Bowles, Michael Gough

The Legend of Lizzie Borden*
US 1975 100m colour TVM
Paramount (George LeMaire)

An account of the Fall River murders of 1892, when the daughter of the house was suspected of having forty whacks at each of her parents . . .
A decently made film which takes a long time to produce no fresh evidence, and goes a bit overboard on the axe murders.

w William Bast *d* Paul Wendkos

Elizabeth Montgomery, Fritz Weaver, Katherine Helmond, Ed Flanders, Don Porter, Fionnuala Flanagan, John Beal

The Legend of Lobo*
US 1962 67m Technicolor
Walt Disney (James Algar)

The life of a forest wolf.
Least attractive of the three True Life Fantasies (the others being *Perri* and *Nikki*). Some nice things in it, though.

w Dwight Hauser, James Algar, *story* Ernest Thompson Seton *d* Jack Couffer

The Legend of Lylah Clare*
US 1968 130m Metrocolor Panavision
MGM / Robert Aldrich

A mad director brings an unknown actress to Hollywood because of her resemblance to a former star, his creation, who had died mysteriously.
Unintentionally risible melodrama with echoes of *Svengali* and *Sunset Boulevard*; not to the public's taste, or anyone else's, in the late sixties.

w Hugo Butler, Jean Rouverol, *TV play* Robert Thom, Edward de Blasio *d* Robert Aldrich *ph* Joseph Biroc *m* Frank de Vol

Peter Finch, Kim Novak, Ernest Borgnine, Coral Browne, Milton Seltzer, Rossella Falk, Gabriele Tinti, Valentina Cortesa, George Kennedy

Legend of the Lost
US 1957 107m Technirama
UA / Batjac / Robert Haggiag / Dear (Henry Hathaway)

Two adventurers and a slave girl seek a lost city in the Sahara.
Tediously vague and underplotted desert adventure with a few attractive moments.

w Robert Presnell Jnr, Ben Hecht *d* Henry Hathaway *ph* Jack Cardiff *m* A. F. Lavagnino

John Wayne, Sophia Loren, Rossano Brazzi

The Legend of the Seven Golden Vampires
GB / Hong Kong 1974 89m Eastmancolor Panavision
Hammer–Shaw (Don Houghton, Vee King Shaw)

In 1904 Chungking, Professor Van Helsing finds his old enemy Dracula behind a Chinese vampire cult.
Hectic, outlandish mix of Hammer horror and Kung Fu; plenty of gusto but not much sense.

w Don Houghton *d* Roy Ward Baker *ph* John Wilcox, Roy Ford *m* James Bernard

Peter Cushing, David Chiang, Julie Ege, Robin Stewart, John Forbes Robertson

The Legend of Tom Dooley
US 1959 77m bw
Columbia / Shpetner

At the end of the Civil War, Confederate youths take the law into their own hands and attack Unionists.
Youthful rebellion in historical mould, decently but rather dully delivered, based on a folk ballad.

w Stan Shpetner *d* Ted Post *ph* Gilbert Warrenton *m* Ronald Stein

Michael Landon, Richard Rust, Jo Morrow

The Legend of Valentino
US 1975 100m colour TVM
Spelling-Goldberg

The alleged life and loves of the silent screen's sex idol.
A foolish fantasy which scarcely touches truth at all.

wd Melville Shavelson *ph* Arch Dalzell

Franco Nero, Suzanne Pleshette, Yvette Mimieux, Judd Hirsch, Lesley Warren, Milton Berle, Harold J. Stone

The Lemon Drop Kid*
US 1951 91m bw
Paramount (Robert A. Welch)

A gangster forces a bookie to find the money which he has lost on a horse through the bookie's incompetence.
Amusing Bob Hope/Runyon vehicle despite heavy sentiment about an old folks' home. The Santa Claus sequences are memorable.

w Edmund Hartman, Frank Tashlin, Robert O'Brien, *story* Damon Runyon *d* Sidney Lanfield *ph* Daniel L. Fapp

Bob Hope, Marilyn Maxwell, Lloyd Nolan, Jane Darwell, Andrea King, Fred Clark, Jay C. Flippen, William Frawley, Harry Bellaver

Lenny**
US 1974 111m bw
UA (Marvin Worth)

The career of obscene comedian Lenny Bruce and his struggles with the law.
Old-fashioned rags-to-riches-to-rags story, rampant with the new permissiveness. Filmically extremely clever, emotionally hollow.

w Julian Barry, from his play *d Bob Fosse* *ph* Bruce Surtees *md* Ralph Burns *pd* Joel Schiller

Dustin Hoffman, Valerie Perrine, Jan Miner, Stanley Beck, Gary Morton

'For audiences who want to believe that Lenny Bruce was a saintly gadfly who was martyred for having lived before his time.'—*New Yorker*

Leo the Last
GB 1969 104m De Luxe
UA / Char / Wink / Boor (Irwin Winkler, Robert Chartoff)

An alienated aristocrat brings his retinue to a London slum and has an effect on most of the inhabitants.
Infuriating symbolic fantasy; only the writer-director (presumably) has any idea what it is about.

w William Stair, John Boorman *d* John Boorman *ph* Peter Suschitsky *m* Dred Myrow *pd* Tony Woollard

Marcello Mastroianni, Billie Whitelaw, Calvin Lockhart, Glenna Forster Jones, Graham Crowden, Gwen Ffrangcon Davies, David de Keyser, Vladek Sheybal, Kenneth J. Warren

The Leopard***
US / Italy 1963 205m Technirama
Fox / Titanus / SNPC / GPC (Goffredo Lombardo)

The family life of an Italian nobleman at the time of Garibaldi.
Elaborate, complex family saga, painted like an old master with great care and attention to detail, but with not much chance outside Italy of delivering its original dramatic force. Visconti had asked for Lancaster, so TCF picked up the international release but could not make head or tail of it commercially; they even ruined its high quality by releasing a dubbed, shortened version in Cinemascope and De Luxe colour of poor standard.

wd Luchino Visconti, novel Giuseppe de Lampedusa *ph Giuseppe Rotunno m* Nino Rota *ad Mario Garbuglia*

Burt Lancaster, Claudia Cardinale, Alain Delon, Paolo Stoppa, Serge Reggiani, Leslie French

The Leopard Man**
US 1943 59m bw
RKO (*Val Lewton*)

Murders in a Mexican border town are attributed to an escaped leopard.
Effective minor piece in the Lewton horror gallery; poor plot countered by highly effective suspense sequences.

w Ardel Wray, Edward Dein, *novel* Black Alibi by Cornell Woolrich *d Jacques Tourneur ph* Robert de Grasse

Dennis O'Keefe, Jean Brooks, Margo, James Bell, Isabel Jewell

Lepke
US 1974 110m De Luxe Panavision
Warner / AmeriEuro Pictures (Menahem Golan)

After World War I a small-time crook becomes head of Murder Incorporated.
Violent but totally uninteresting gangster melodrama; fidelity to fact is not enough.

w Wesley Hau, Tamor Hoffs *d* Menahem Golan *ph* Andrew Davis *m* Ken Wannberg *pd* Jack Degovia

Tony Curtis, Anjanette Comer, Michael Callan, Warren Berlinger, Milton Berle, Gianni Russo
'A kosher version of *The Godfather*.'—*Verina Glaessner*

Les Misérables see under Misérables

Let 'Em Have It*
US 1935 90m bw
Edward Small
GB title: *False Faces*

The FBI go after criminals on a terror spree.
Lively cops and robbers with some starkly effective moments.

w Joseph Moncure March, Elmer Harris *d* Sam Wood
ph J. Peverell Marley, Robert Planck

Richard Arlen, Virginia Bruce, Alice Brady, Bruce Cabot, Harvey Stephens, Eric Linden, Joyce Compton, J. Farrell MacDonald

Let George Do It**
GB 1940 82m bw
Ealing (Basil Dearden)

A ukelele player accidentally goes to Bergen instead of Blackpool and is mistaken for a spy.
Generally thought to be the best George Formby vehicle, with plenty of pace, good situations and catchy tunes.

w John Dighton, Austin Melford, Angus MacPhail, Basil Dearden *d* Marcel Varnel

George Formby, Phyllis Calvert, Garry Marsh, Romney Brent, Bernard Lee, Coral Browne, Torin Thatcher, Hal Gordon

Let No Man Write My Epitaph
US 1960 106m bw
Columbia / Boris D. Kaplan

A slum boy wants to become a concert pianist but falls in with gangsters.
Squalid, predictable melodrama without many redeeming features.

w Robert Presnell Jnr, *novel* Willard Motley *d* Philip Leacock *ph* Burnett Guffey *m* George Duning

James Darren, Shelley Winters, Burl Ives, Sal Mineo, Jean Seberg, Jeanne Cooper, Ricardo Montalban, Ella Fitzgerald

Let the People Sing*
GB 1942 105m bw
British National (John Baxter)

An out-of-work comedian persuades a drunken nobleman to join a protest against the closing of a village hall.
A development of *The Good Companions* which compares quite nicely with the Capra films from across the water: naïve but entertaining, with good star performances.

w John Baxter, Barbara K. Emery, Geoffrey Orme. *novel J. B. Priestley d John Baxter*

Alastair Sim, Fred Emney, Edward Rigby, Patricia Roc, Oliver Wakefield, Marian Spencer, Olive Sloane, Gus McNaughton, Charles Hawtrey

Let's Be Happy
GB 1957 107m Technicolor
ABP / Marcel Hellman

Footling musical remake of *Jeannie* (qv).

w Diana Morgan *d* Henry Levin

Vera-Ellen, Tony Martin, Robert Flemyng, Zena Marshall, Guy Middleton, Katherine Kath, Jean Cadell, Gordon Jackson

'Success still eludes the Anglo-American musical.'—*MFB*

Let's Dance
US 1950 112m Technicolor
Paramount (Robert Fellows)

Show business partners reunite after five years of private life.
Tediously plotted musical with a couple of good numbers.

w Allan Scott, *story* Maurice Zolotow *d* Norman Z. McLeod *ph* George Barnes *songs* Frank Loesser

Fred Astaire, Betty Hutton, Roland Young, Ruth Warrick, Lucile Watson, Barton MacLane, Shepperd Strudwick, Melville Cooper, Harold Huber, George Zucco

Let's Do It Again
US 1953 95m Technicolor
Columbia (Oscar Saul)

A songwriter and his wife plan a divorce but call it off in the nick of time.
Tame musical remake of *The Awful Truth (qv)*, pleasant enough but lacking style and punch.

w Mary Loos, Richard Sale *d* Alexander Hall *ph* Charles Lawton Jnr *md* Morris Stoloff *songs* Lester Lee, Ned Washington

Jane Wyman, Ray Milland, Aldo Ray, Leon Ames

Let's Do It Again
US 1975 113m Technicolor
Warner / First Artists / Verdon (Melville Tucker, Pembroke J. Herring)

Three Atlanta workers conceive a zany plan to raise money for their church by hypnotizing a boxer into winning a big fight.
Lively but overlong farce reassembling the black talents of *Uptown Saturday Night.*

w Richard Wesley *d* Sidney Poitier *ph* Donald M. Morgan *m* Curtis Mayfield

Sidney Poitier, Bill Cosby, Calvin Lockhart, John Amos, Denise Nicholas, Ossie Davis, Jimmy Walker

Let's Face It
US 1943 76m bw
Paramount (Fred Kohlmar)

A smart-alec soldier has a plot involving a ladies' health camp, but finds himself up to his neck in spies.
Tepid star comedy which unaccountably ditches almost all the numbers from the musical on which it was based.

w (uncredited) from the musical play by Dorothy and Herbert Fields and Cole Porter, based on the play Cradle Snatchers by Norma Mitchell and Russell Medcraft *d* Sidney Lanfield *ph* Lionel Lindon *songs* Cole Porter

Bob Hope, Betty Hutton, Eve Arden, Phyllis Povah, Dona Drake, Zasu Pitts, Marjorie Weaver, Raymond Walburn, Joe Sawyer

Let's Kill Uncle
US 1966 92m bw
Universal / William Castle

A boy is threatened by his wicked uncle, and retaliates.
Mildly intriguing black comedy, leadenly handled.

w Mark Rodger, *novel* Rohan O'Grady *d* William Castle *ph* Harold Lipstein *m* Herman Stein

Nigel Green, Mary Badham, Pat Cardi, Robert Pickering

Let's Make Love*
US 1960 118m De Luxe Cinemascope
TCF

A multi-millionaire, learning that he is to be

burlesqued in a Broadway show, joins the cast as an actor.
Complex, moderately sophisticated, occasionally funny musical inspired by *On the Avenue* (qv); lively characterizations but poor numbers.

w Norman Krasna *d* George Cukor *ph* Daniel L. Fapp *ch* Jack Cole *songs* Sammy Cahn, Jimmy Van Heusen

Yves Montand, Marilyn Monroe, Tony Randall, Wilfrid Hyde White, Frankie Vaughan, David Burns, and guests Bing Crosby, Gene Kelly, Milton Berle

Let's Scare Jessica to Death
US 1971 89m colour
Paramount / Jessica Co

Back home after a nervous breakdown, our heroine is troubled by voices and visions, not to mention an ambulant corpse and a vampire or two.
Competent screamie.

w Norman Jonas, Ralph Rose *d* John Hancock *ph* Bob Baldwin *m* Orville Stoeber

Zohra Lampert, Barton Heyman

Let's Switch
US 1975 74m Technicolor TVM
Universal (Bruce Johnson)

A housewife changes roles with her career woman friend.
Overstretched comedy which makes little of its situation.

w Peter Lefcourt, Chubby Williams, Sid Arthur, Ruth Brooks Flippen *d* Alan Rafkin

Barbara Eden, Barbara Feldon, Stuart Margolin, Pat Harrington

The Letter*
US 1929 61m bw
Paramount

Early talkie version of a solid piece of theatre.

story and play W. Somerset Maugham *d* Jean de Limur

Jeanne Eagels, O. P. Heggie, Reginald Owen, Herbert Marshall, Irene Browne

The Letter****
US 1940 95m bw
Warner (Robert Lord)

A rubber plantation owner's wife kills a man in what seems to have been self-defence; but a letter from her proves it to have been a crime of passion, and becomes an instrument of blackmail.
Excellent performances and presentation make this the closest approximation on film to reading a Maugham story of the Far East, though censorship forced the addition of an infuriating moral ending.

w Howard Koch, story W. Somerset Maugham d William Wyler ph Tony Gaudio m Max Steiner

Bette Davis, Herbert Marshall, James Stephenson, Sen Yung, Frieda Inescort, Gale Sondergaard, Bruce Lester, Tetsu Komai

Letter from an Unknown Woman****
US 1948 89m bw
Universal (John Houseman)

A woman wastes her life in unrequited love for a rakish pianist.
Superior 'woman's picture' which gave its director his best chance in America to recreate his beloved Vienna of long ago. Hollywood production magic at its best.

w Howard Koch, novel Stefan Zweig *d Max Ophuls ph Franz Planer m* Daniele Amfitheatrof *ad Alexander Golitzen*

Joan Fontaine, Louis Jourdan, Mady Christians, Art Smith, Marcel Journet

'A film full of snow, sleigh bells, lights gleaming in ornamental gardens and trysts at night.'—*Charles Higham, 1972*

'It is fascinating to watch the sure deft means by which Ophuls sidetracks seemingly inevitable clichés and holds on to a shadowy, tender mood, half buried in the past. Here is a fragile filmic charm that is not often or easily accomplished.'—*Richard Winnington*

Letter of Introduction*
US 1938 100m bw
Universal (John M. Stahl)

A young actress is encouraged by an ageing star whom she does not know is her father.
Commercial melodrama with luxury trimmings, all very neatly packaged.

w Sheridan Gibney, Leonard Spiegelgass *d* John M. Stahl *ph* Karl Freund

Adolphe Menjou, Andrea Leeds, Edgar Bergen (and Charlie McCarthy), George Murphy, Eve Arden, Rita Johnson, Ernest Cossart, Ann Sheridan

A Letter to Three Wives**
US 1949 102m bw
TCF (Sol C. Siegel)

Three wives on a picnic receive word from a friend that she has run off with one of their husbands.

Amusing short-story compendium which seemed more revelatory at the time than it does now, and paved the way for its writer-director's heyday.

wd Joseph L. Mankiewicz, novel John Klempner *ph* Arthur Miller *m* Alfred Newman

Jeanne Crain, Ann Sothern, Linda Darnell, Jeffrey Lynn, Kirk Douglas, *Paul Douglas*, Barbara Lawrence, Connie Gilchrist, Florence Bates, Hobart Cavanaugh, and the voice of Celeste Holm

'A mere shadow of those acid Hollywood comedies of the thirties . . . over-written and under-directed . . . but it has a supply of ironies and makes a certain alkaline comment on present-day American customs and manners.'—*Richard Winnington*

The Letters*
US 1972 73m colour TVM
Spelling–Goldberg

Three important letters are delayed a year in delivery.
Multi-mini-drama, all quite watchable in its predictable way.

w Ellis Marcus, Hal Sitowitz, James G. Hirsch *d* Gene Nelson, Paul Krasny

Barbara Stanwyck, John Forsythe, Dina Merrill, Ida Lupino, Leslie Nielsen, Ben Murphy, Jane Powell

Letters from Three Lovers
US 1973 74m colour TVM
Spelling–Goldberg

More delayed letters have dramatic consequences.
Success means a reprise.

w Ann Marcus, Jerome Kass *d* John Erman

Barry Sullivan, June Allyson, Ken Berry, Juliet Mills, Martin Sheen, Belinda Montgomery, Robert Sterling

Libel*
GB 1959 100m bw
MGM / Comet (Anatole de Grunwald)

An ex-POW baronet is accused of being an impostor.
Old-fashioned courtroom spellbinder, quite adequately done though occasionally creaky.

w Anatole de Grunwald, Karl Tunberg, *play* Edward Wooll *d* Anthony Asquith *ph* Robert Krasker *m* Benjamin Frankel

Dirk Bogarde, Olivia de Havilland, Paul Massie, Wilfrid Hyde White, Robert Morley, Anthony Dawson, Richard Wattis, Martin Miller, Millicent Martin

Libeled Lady**
US 1936 98m bw
MGM (Lawrence Weingarten)

An heiress sues a newspaper, and the editor hires a friend to compromise her.
Lively four-star romantic comedy which sums up its era as well as any.

w Maurine Watkins, Howard Emmett Rogers, George Oppenheimer d Jack Conway ph Norbert Brodine

Jean Harlow, Myrna Loy, Spencer Tracy, William Powell, Walter Connolly, Charley Grapewin, Cora Witherspoon, E. E. Clive, Charles Trowbridge
† Remade as *Easy to Wed* (qv); central situation borrowed for *Man's Favorite Sport* (qv).

The Liberation of L. B. Jones*
US 1970 102m Technicolor
Columbia / Liberation Co (Ronald Lubin)

Racial murder is the result when a black undertaker wants a divorce in a small Tennessee town.
Violent, pointless but well-made melodrama which really does not take matters much further than *Intruder in the Dust*.

w Stirling Silliphant, Jesse Hill Ford, from Ford's novel *d William Wyler ph* Robert Surtees *m* Elmer Bernstein

Lee J. Cobb, Anthony Zerbe, Roscoe Lee Browne, Lola Falana, Lee Majors, Barbara Hershey, Yaphet Kotto, Arch Johnson, Chill Wills

'With its genuinely ferocious climax it adds up to probably the most powerful, if not the most sophisticated, race-war film the commercial studios have yet produced.'—*Nigel Andrews*

Licensed to Kill
GB 1965 97m Eastmancolor
Alistair Films (Estelle E. Richmond)
US title: *The Second Best Secret Agent in the Whole Wide World*

The Foreign Office calls in agent Charles Vine to protect a top international scientist.
Cheap copy of James Bond which wins no laurels but produces a few efficient routine thrills.

w Howard Griffiths, Lindsay Shonteff *d* Lindsay Shonteff *ph* Terry Maher *m* Bertram Chappell

Tom Adams, Veronica Hurst, Karel Stepanek, Felix Felton, Peter Bull

Lies My Father Told Me
Canada 1975 102m colour
Columbia / Pentimento / Pentacle (Anthony Bedrich, Harry Gulkin)

Adventures of a poor Jewish boy and his grandfather in Montreal in the twenties.
Effectively if rather dishonestly sentimental, this is the kind of family picture for which critics are always clamouring but which few people in the seventies will pay to see.

w Ted Allan, from his book *d* Jan Kadar *ph* Paul Van der Linden *m* Sol Kaplan

Yossi Yadin, Len Birman, Marilyn Lightstone, Jeffrey Lynas
† A British low-budgeter was made from the same story in 1940, changing the venue to Ireland and the race to Irish.

Lt Robin Crusoe USN
US 1966 114m Technicolor
Walt Disney (Bill Walsh, Ron Miller)

A navy pilot parachutes on to a Pacific island and gets involved in the local women's lib movement.
Slow-paced family comedy with very few laughs.

w Bill Walsh, Don da Gradi *d* Byron Paul *ph* William Snyder *m* Bob Brunner

Dick Van Dyke, Nancy Kwan, Akim Tamiroff

Lt Schuster's Wife*
US 1972 73m Technicolor TVM
Universal (Steven Bochco)

When a policeman is killed and slandered, his widow goes into action.
Adequate, well-paced pilot which didn't get anywhere.

w Bernie Kukoff, Steven Bochco *d* David Lowell Rich

Lee Grant, Jack Warden, Don Galloway, Paul Burke, Eartha Kitt, Nehemiah Persoff, Murray Matheson

The Life and Death of Colonel Blimp***
GB 1943 163m Technicolor
GFD / Archers (Michael Powell, Emeric Pressburger)
US title: *Colonel Blimp*

A British soldier survives three wars and falls in love with three women.
Not the Blimp of the cartoon strip, but a sympathetic figure in a warm, consistently interesting if idiosyncratic love story against a background of war. The Archers as usual provide a sympathetic German lead (friend of the hero); quite a coup in wartime.

wd Michael Powell, Emeric Pressburger
ph Jack Cardiff *m* Allan Gray *ad* Alfred Junge

Roger Livesey, Anton Walbrook, Deborah Kerr, Roland Culver, James McKechnie, Albert Lieven, Arthur Wontner, A. E. Matthews, David Hutcheson, Ursula Jeans, John Laurie, Harry Welchman

The Life and Times of Judge Roy Bean*
US 1972 124m Technicolor Panavision
National General / Famous Artists (John Foreman)

A fantasia on the famous outlaw judge of the old west.
Sporadically entertaining but schematically messy mixture of burlesqued folklore and violent action, not in the same league as *Butch Cassidy*.

w John Milius *d* John Huston *ph* Richard Moore *m* Maurice Jarre

Paul Newman, Ava Gardner, Jacqueline Bisset, Tab Hunter, Stacy Keach, Roddy McDowall, Anthony Perkins, John Huston

Life at the Top*
GB 1965 117m bw
Columbia / Romulus (James Woolf)

Ten years after marrying into money, Joe Lampton is dissatisfied, and he and his wife both have affairs.
Rough-talking but basically predictable and old-fashioned sequel to *Room at the Top*, a bit compromised by having to reflect the sixties London scene; the early Yorkshire sequences are the best.

w Mordecai Richler *d* Ted Kotcheff *ph* Oswald Morris *m* Richard Addinsell

Laurence Harvey, Jean Simmons, Honor Blackman, Michael Craig, Donald Wolfit, *Margaret Johnston*, Allan Cuthbertson, Ambrosine Philpotts, Robert Morley, Nigel Davenport, George A. Cooper
'Another thoroughly mean-spirited film of a kind which has been taking root in the British cinema.'—*Tom Milne*
†The character of Joe Lampton was later used in a long running TV series called *Man at the Top*, which sprouted a film of its own under that title.

Life Begins
US 1932 72m bw
Warner (Ray Griffith)

A night in a maternity hospital.
Multi-melodrama later remade as *A Child Is Born*. Passable.

w Earl Baldwin, *play* Mary McDougal Axelson *d* James Flood *ph* James Van Trees

Loretta Young, Eric Linden, Aline MacMahon, Preston Foster, Glenda Farrell, Frank McHugh, Clara Blandick, Elizabeth Patterson, Gilbert Roland

Life Begins at Eight Thirty*
US 1942 85m bw
TCF (Nunnally Johnson)
GB title: *The Light of Heart*

A distinguished actor is reduced through drink to being a street corner Santa Claus.
Diluted and sentimentalized version of an agreeable play.

w Nunnally Johnson, *play* Emlyn Williams *d* Irving Pichel *ph* Edward Cronjager *m* Alfred Newman

Monty Woolley, Ida Lupino, Cornel Wilde, Sara Allgood, Melville Cooper, J. Edward Bromberg

Life for Ruth*
GB 1962 91m bw
Rank / Allied Film Makers (Michael Relph, Basil Dearden)

A little girl dies because her parents' religion forbids blood transfusions.
Dramatized from the headlines, this little case history is small beer as film-making, and not exactly entertainment, but absorbing as a comment on human behaviour.

w Janet Green, John McCormick *d* Basil Dearden *ph* Otto Heller *m* Muir Matheson

Michael Craig, Patrick McGoohan, Janet Munro

A Life in the Balance*
US 1954 75m bw
TCF / Panoramic (Leonard Goldstein)

A Mexican widower springs into action when his young son is kidnapped by a murderer.
Taut little melodrama taking place during one night in Mexico City; made with vigour on a low budget.

w Robert Presnell Jnr, Leo Townsend *d Harry Horner ph* J. Gomez Urquiza *m* Raul Lavista

Ricardo Montalban, Anne Bancroft, Lee Marvin

The Life of Emile Zola***
US 1937 116m bw
Warner (Henry Blanke)

The French writer intervenes in the case of Alfred Dreyfus, condemned unjustly to Devil's Island.
The box office success of this solidly-carpentered piece of Hollywood history was compounded in equal parts of star power and the sheer novelty of having such a thing turn up at the local Odeon.

w Heinz Herald, Geza Herczeg, Norman Reilly Raine *d William Dieterle ph Tony Gaudio m* Max Steiner *ad Anton Grot*

Paul Muni, Joseph Schildkraut, Gale Sondergaard, Gloria Holden, Donald Crisp, Erin O'Brien Moore, John Litel, Henry O'Neill, Morris Carnovsky, Ralph Morgan, Louis Calhern, Robert Barrat, Vladimir Sokoloff, Harry Davenport, Robert Warwick, Walter Kingsford

'Along with *Louis Pasteur*, it ought to start a new category—the Warner crusading films, costume division.'—*Otis Ferguson.*

'A grave story told with great dignity and superbly played and produced.'—*Pare Lorentz*

'One of the fine ones which begin as a film and end as an experience.'—*John Grierson*

A Life of Her Own
US 1950 108m bw
MGM (Voldemar Vetluguin)

An innocent girl from Kansas becomes one of New York's top models.
Road to ruin, American style, from the pages of a women's magazine.

w Isabel Lennart *d* George Cukor *ph* George Folsey *m* Bronislau Kaper

Lana Turner, Ray Milland, Tom Ewell, Louis Calhern, Ann Dvorak, Barry Sullivan, Jean Hagen

'This story belongs to the realms of soap opera—extremely artificial, highly moral in tone, and deliberately concocted to combine luxurious settings with an elementary assault on the audience's emotions.'—*MFB*

The Life of Jimmy Dolan
US 1933 85m bw
Warner (Hal B. Wallis)
GB title: *The Kid's Last Fight*

An amiable wanderer is mistaken for a prize-fighter wanted for murder.
Modest character romance, later remade as *They Made Me a Criminal.*

w David Boehm, Erwin Gelsey, *play* Bertram Millhauser, Beulah Marie Dix *d* Archie Mayo *ph* Arthur Edeson

Douglas Fairbanks Jnr, Loretta Young, Aline MacMahon, Guy Kibbee, Lyle Talbot, Fifi D'Orsay, Harold Huber, George Meeker

The Life of Vergie Winters
US 1934 82m bw
RKO (Pandro S. Berman)

A rising politician marries for position but keeps watch over his mistress and their child.
Archetypal soap opera, a cross between *Stella Dallas* and *Back Street.*

w Jane Murfin, *novel* Louis Bromfield *d* Alfred Santell *ph* Lucien Andriot

Ann Harding, John Boles, Helen Vinson, Frank Albertson, Lon Chaney Jnr, Sara Haden, Ben Alexander, Donald Crisp

Life with Father*
US 1947 118m Technicolor
Warner (Robert Buckner)

Turn-of-the-century anecdotes of an irascible well-to-do paterfamilias who won't be baptized.
Well-upholstered screen version of a long running play; oddly tedious considering the talent involved.

w Donald Ogden Stewart, *play* Howard Lindsay, Russel Crouse *d* Michael Curtiz *ph* Peverell Marley, William V. Skall *m* Max Steiner *ad* Robert Hass

William Powell, Irene Dunne, Edmund Gwenn, Zasu Pitts, Elizabeth Taylor, Martin Milner, Jimmy Lydon, Emma Dunn, Moroni Olsen, Elizabeth Risdon
† Censorship of the day absurdly clipped Father's famous last line: 'I'm going to be baptized, damn it!'

Lifeboat**
US 1944 96m bw
TCF (Kenneth MacGowan)

Survivors from a torpedoed passenger ship include the U-Boat commander responsible.
Propaganda gimmick melodrama interesting for the casting and for Hitchcock's response to the challenge of filming in one cramped set.

w Jo Swerling, *story* John Steinbeck *d Alfred Hitchcock* *ph* Glen MacWilliams *m* Hugo Friedhofer

Tallulah Bankhead, Walter Slezak, Henry Hull, John Hodiak, Canada Lee, William Bendix, Mary Anderson, Heather Angel, Hume Cronyn

The Light at the Edge of the World
US / Spain / Lichtenstein 1971 120m Eastmancolor Panavision
Bryna / Jet / Triumfilm (Kirk Douglas, Ilya Salkind)

A lighthouse keeper near Cape Horn resists a band of wreckers.
Pretentious, disaster-prone version of a simple adventure story; one wonders not so much what went wrong as whether anything went right in this international venture.

w Tom Rowe, *novel* Jules Verne *d* Kevin Billington *ph* Henri Decaë *m* Piero Piccioni

Kirk Douglas, Yul Brynner, Samantha Eggar, Jean-Claude Drouot, Fernando Rey, Renato Salvatori

The Light in the Forest
US 1958 92m Technicolor
Walt Disney

Kidnapped by Indians as an infant, a teenager is returned to his parents but finds the white man's ways disturbing.
Modest frontier drama with a moral.

w Lawrence Edward Watkin, *novel* Conrad Richter *d* Herschel Daugherty *ph* Ellsworth Fredericks *m* Paul Smith

James MacArthur, Carol Lynley, Jessica Tandy, Wendell Corey, Fess Parker, Joanne Dru, Joseph Calleia

The Light in the Piazza
GB 1962 101m Metrocolor Cinemascope
MGM (Arthur Freed)

An American matron in Florence tries to marry off her mentally retarded daughter to a wealthy Italian.
Puzzling romantic drama in which one is never quite sure why the characters behave as they do; in the end all one appreciates is the tour of northern Italy.

w Julius J. Epstein, *novel* Dorothy Spencer *d* Guy Green *ph* Otto Heller *m* Mario Nascimbene

Olivia de Havilland, Yvette Mimieux, George Hamilton, Rossano Brazzi, Barry Sullivan

The Light that Failed*
US 1939 97m bw
Paramount

A London artist is going blind as the result of a war wound, and must finish the portrait of the little cockney whom he loves.
Nicely-made but rather boring star romance; no surprises in plot or performance.

w Robert Carson, *story* Rudyard Kipling *d* William Wellman *ph* Theodor Sparkuhl *m* Victor Young

Ronald Colman, Walter Huston, Ida Lupino, Dudley Digges, Muriel Angelus, Fay Helm

Lightning Strikes Twice
US 1951 91m bw
Warner (Henry Blanke)

A woman decides to clear her lover of suspicion of murder, but later has her own doubts.

Silly melodrama with no credibility, little suspense, and too much talk.

w Lenore Coffee, *novel* Margaret Echard *d* King Vidor *ph* Sid Hickox *m* Max Steiner

Richard Todd, Ruth Roman, Mercedes McCambridge, Zachary Scott, Darryl Hickman, Frank Conroy, Kathryn Givney

Lights of New York***
US 1928 57m bw
MGM

A chorus girl becomes involved with gangsters.
The first '100 per cent all-talking' film, dramatically primitive but historically important.

w F. Hugh Herbert, Murray Roth *d* Bryan Foy *ph* E. B. DuPar

Helene Costello, Cullen Landis, Wheeler Oakman, Eugene Pallette, Tom Dugan, Gladys Brockwell, Mary Carr

'100 per cent crude.'—*Variety*

The Likely Lads*
GB 1976 90m bw
EMI (Aida Young)

Two Geordie friends, with wife and mistress, go on a touring holiday.
Valuable as a record of an excellent and long-running TV series, this big screen version finds most of the humour regrettably broadened.

w Dick Clement, Ian La Frenais *d* Michael Tuchner *ph* Tony Imi *m* Mike Hugg

Rodney Bewes, James Bolam, Brigit Forsyth, Mary Tamm, Sheila Fern, Zena Walker

A Likely Story
US 1947 88m bw
RKO (Richard H. Berger)

A man thinks he has only a short time to live, and in trying to do his best for a girl friend gets mixed up with gangsters.
Even a star cast could not have made much of this zany comedy script.

w Bess Taffel *d* H. C. Potter *ph* Roy Hunt *m* Constantin Bakaleinikoff

Barbara Hale, Bill Williams, Lanny Rees, Sam Levene, Dan Tobin, Nestor Paiva

Lil Abner*
US 1959 113m Technicolor Vistavision
Paramount / Panama–Frank (Norman Panama)

The hillbilly town of Dogpatch, tagged the most useless community in America, fights being used as a test site for A-bombs.
Set-bound, intrinsically American, but bright and cheerful film of a stage show about Al Capp's famous comic strip characters.

wd Norman Panama, Melvin Frank from the musical show (*ly Johnny Mercer, words* Gene de Paul) *ph* Daniel L. Fapp *ch Dee Dee Wood, Michael Kidd*

Peter Parrish, Billie Hayes, Howard St John, Stubby Kaye, Stella Stevens, Julie Newmar, Robert Strauss

Lilacs in the Spring
GB 1954 94m Trucolor
Republic / Everest (Herbert Wilcox)
US title: *Let's Make Up*

During the London blitz a young actress is knocked unconscious and dreams of herself as Nell Gwyn, Queen Victoria and her own mother before waking up to deal with her personal problems.
Good-humoured theatrical charade deadened by poorish production and colour, strengthened by the star's game run-through of her staple characters. How Mr Flynn came to be involved is anybody's guess.

w Harold Purcell, from his play The Glorious Days *d* Herbert Wilcox *ph* Max Greene *m* Robert Farnon

Anna Neagle, Errol Flynn, Peter Graves, David Farrar, Kathleen Harrison

Lili*
US 1952 81m Technicolor
MGM (Edwin H. Knopf)

A 16-year-old orphan girl joins a carnival and falls in love with the magician.
Romantic whimsy dependent entirely on treatment, which is sometimes heavy-handed. Charm, ballet and puppets are provided, but a little cheerful song and dance would not have been amiss.

w Helen Deutsch, *novel* Paul Gallico *d/ch* Charles Walters *ph* Robert Planck *m* Bronislau Kaper *ad* Cedric Gibbons, Paul Stroesse

Leslie Caron, Jean-Pierre Aumont, Mel Ferrer, Kurt Kasznar

Lilies of the Field*
US 1963 94m bw
UA / Rainbow / Ralph Nelson

An itinerant black workman in New Mexico helps a group of German nuns to build a chapel.
Liberal, sentimental, under-dramatized little comedy with everyone coming to understand

each other's point of view, so that the audience feels improved if not especially entertained.

w James Poe, *novel* William E. Barrett *d* Ralph Nelson *ph* Ernest Haller *m* Jerry Goldsmith

Sidney Poitier, Lilia Skala

Liliom*
US 1930 94m bw
Fox

A Budapest carnival man is killed in a fight but later comes back from heaven to see how his family is doing.
Ingeniously-staged fantasy, very dated but a lot more interesting than its musical remake *Carousel* (qv).

w S. N. Behrman, *play* Ferenc Molnar *d* Frank Borzage *ph* Chester Lyons *m* Richard Fall

Charles Farrell, Rose Hobart, Estelle Taylor, Lee Tracy, Walter Abel, Guinn Williams, H. B. Warner, Dawn O'Day (Anne Shirley)

Lilith*
US 1964 126m bw
Columbia / Centaur (Robert Rossen)

A trainee therapist at an asylum falls in love with a patient.
Strange, wistful, poetic and rather soporific character melodrama.

wd Robert Rossen, *novel* J. R. Salamanca *ph* Eugen Schufftan *m* Kenyon Hopkins *pd* Richard Sylbert

Warren Beatty, Jean Seberg, Peter Fonda, Kim Hunter, Anne Meacham, James Patterson, Jessica Walter, Gene Hackman

'A remarkable attempt to dig a little deeper in an almost untilled field, and to throw some light on the relationship between madness and the creative imagination.'—*Tom Milne*

Lillian Russell**
US 1940 130m bw
TCF (Gene Markey)

The life and loves of the famous nineties entertainer.
Whitewashed biopic, extremely well made of its kind, and very typical.

w William Anthony McGuire *d* Irving Cummings *ph* Leon Shamroy *md* Alfred Newman

Alice Faye, Don Ameche, Edward Arnold, Warren William, Henry Fonda, Leo Carrillo, Helen Westley, Dorothy Peterson, Ernest Truex, Nigel Bruce, Claud Allister, Lynn Bari, Weber and Fields, Eddie Foy Jnr, Una O'Connor

Limbo*
US 1972 111m Technicolor
Universal (Linda Gottlieb)
aka: *Chained to Yesterday*

Women wait for their husbands to return from Vietnam.
Worthy but dramatically uninteresting multi-storied semi-propaganda piece with an untried cast.

w Joan Silver, James Bridges *d* Mark Robson *ph* Charles Wheeler *m* Anita Kerr

Kate Jackson, Katherine Justice, Stuart Margolin, Hazel Medina, Kathleen Nolan

Limehouse Blues*
US 1935 65m bw
Paramount
aka: *East End Chant*

In London's shady quarter, an oriental roustabout tries to leave his jealous mistress for a girl with a shady past.
Artificial, atmospheric melodrama set in a never-never Limehouse redolent of *Broken Blossoms*. Interesting for its very excesses.

w Arthur Phillips, Cyril Hume, Grover Jones *d* Alexander Hall *ph* Harry Fischbeck

George Raft, Anna May Wong, Jean Parker, Kent Taylor, Billy Bevan

Limelight
GB 1935 80m bw
GFD / Herbert Wilcox

A chorus girl helps a street singer to become a star.
Highly predictable backstage musical drama which made a nine days wonder of 'The Street Singer'.

w Laura Whettier *d* Herbert Wilcox

Anna Neagle, *Arthur Tracy*, Jane Winton, Ellis Jeffreys, Muriel George

Limelight***
US 1952 144m bw
Charles Chaplin

A broken-down music hall comedian is stimulated by a young ballerina to a final hour of triumph.
Sentimental drama in a highly theatrical London East End setting. In other hands it would be very hokey, but Chaplin's best qualities, as well as his worst, are in evidence, and in a way the film sums up his own career.

wd/m Charles Chaplin ph Karl Struss ad Eugene Lourié photographic consultant Rollie Totheroh

Charles Chaplin, Claire Bloom, Buster Keaton, Sydney Chaplin, Nigel Bruce, Norman Lloyd

'From the first reel it is clear that he now wants to talk, that he *loves* to talk . . . where a development in the story line might easily be conveyed by a small visual effect, he prefers to make a speech about it . . . it is a disturbing rejection of the nature of the medium itself.'—*Walter Kerr*

Linda*
US 1973 74m Technicolor TVM
Universal (William Frye)

A woman murders her lover's wife and plots to frame her own husband.
Well-constructed murder drama, a shade padded in the later stages.

w Merwin Gerard *d* Jack Smight

Stella Stevens, Ed Nelson, John McIntire, Jess Walton, John Saxon

The Lindbergh Kidnapping Case*
US 1976 156m colour TVM
Columbia

The 1934 trial of Bruno Hauptmann for the kidnapping and murder of the Lindbergh baby.
Lethargic semi-documentary of a famous trial. The film however has nothing new to say, and expounds the facts without flair.

w J. P. Miller *d* Leonard Horn

Anthony Hopkins, Cliff de Young, Sian Barbara Allen, Walter Pidgeon, Joseph Cotten, Martin Balsam, Keenan Wynn, Laurence Luckinbill

The Lineup*
US 1958 86m bw
Columbia (Frank Cooper)

San Francisco police trap a gunman who is also a drug contact.
Energetic, polished movie version of a popular TV series, *San Francisco Beat*.

w Stirling Silliphant *d Don Siegel* *ph* Hal Mohr *m* Mischa Bakaleinikoff

Warren Anderson, Robert Keith, Eli Wallach

The Lion
GB 1962 96m De Luxe Cinemascope
TCF (Samuel G. Engel)

An American lawyer goes to Africa to visit his ex-wife and their child.
Unabsorbing marital drama with child and animal interest.

w Irene and Louis Kamp, *novel* Joseph Kessel *d* Jack Cardiff *ph* Ted Scaife *m* Malcolm Arnold

William Holden, Trevor Howard, Capucine, Pamela Franklin

'The main fault must be attributed to the spiritless direction of Jack Cardiff, whose recent change of métier has resulted in the industry losing a great lighting cameraman.'—*John Gillett*

The Lion Has Wings*
GB 1939 76m bw
Alexander Korda

A documentary drama tracing the steps leading up to the outbreak of war.
Once-inspiring propaganda piece, now regrettably hilarious. Valuable social history, though.

w Adrian Brunel, E. V. H. Emmett *d* Michael Powell, Brian Desmond Hurst, Adrian Brunel

Merle Oberon, Ralph Richardson, June Duprez, Robert Douglas, Anthony Bushell, Derrick de Marney, Brian Worth, Austin Trevor

The Lion in Winter**
GB 1968 134m Eastmancolor Panavision
Avco Embassy / Haworth (Martin Poll)

Henry II and Eleanor of Aquitaine celebrate Christmas together and have a family row.
An acting feast for two principals and assorted supports, a talking marathon in which not all the talk is good, a smart comedy with sudden lapses into melodrama; stimulating in parts but all rather tiresome by the end, especially as there is not much medieval splendour.

w James Goldman, from his play *d* Anthony Harvey *ph* Douglas Slocombe *m* John Barry

Katharine Hepburn, Peter O'Toole, Jane Merrow, John Castle, Anthony Hopkins, Nigel Terry, Timothy Dalton

'He is not writing a factual movie about the Plantagenets but an interpretation in which he combines their language and ours.'—*Philip T. Hartung*

A Lion Is in the Streets*
US 1953 88m Technicolor
Warner / William Cagney

An itinerant confidence trickster becomes a defender of the people, is nominated for governor, and becomes corrupt.
Busy melodrama which came a bit soon after *All the King's Men* but now seems at least its equal.

w Luther Davis, *novel* Adria Locke Langley *d* Raoul Walsh *ph* Harry Stradling *m* Franz Waxman *pd* Wiard Ihnen

James Cagney, Barbara Hale, Anne Francis,

Warner Anderson, John McIntire, Jeanne Cagney, Lon Chaney Jnr, Frank McHugh, Larry Keating, Onslow Stevens, James Millican, Sara Haden

'A headlong and dynamic drama which offers Mr Cagney one of his most colourful and meaningful roles.'—*Bosley Crowther*

Lipstick
US 1976 90m Technicolor
Paramount / Dino de Laurentiis

A girl is raped but gets nowhere in court until her sister lures the man to rape her too.
Franker but not very interesting extension of a fifties co-feature, with all the developments well telegraphed.

w David Rayfiel *d* Lamont Johnson *ph* Bill Butler *m* Michel Polnareff

Margaux Hemingway, Perry King, Anne Bancroft, Chris Sarandon, Mariel Hemingway, Robin Gammell

The Liquidator*
GB 1965 104m Metrocolor Panavision
MGM / Leslie Elliott (Jon Pennington)

An ex-war hero is recruited by the secret service as an eliminator of security risks.
Fairly lively James Bond spoof which is never quite as funny as it imagines.

w Peter Yeldham, *novel* John Gardner *d* Jack Cardiff *ph* Ted Scaife *m* Lalo Schifrin

Rod Taylor, Trevor Howard, *David Tomlinson*, Jill St John, Wilfrid Hyde White, Derek Nimmo, Eric Sykes, Akim Tamiroff

Lisa Bright and Dark
US 1972 74m colour TVM
Hallmark

A mentally disturbed teenage girl has days when she becomes dangerous.
Cheerless case history, rather well acted.

w John Neufeld, from his novel *d* Jeannot Szwarc *m* Rod McKuen

Kay Lenz, Anne Baxter, John Forsythe, Debralee Scott

Lisbon
US 1956 90m Trucolor Naturama
Republic (Ray Milland)

An international crook negotiates an Iron Curtain prisoner's release, but the man's wife has other ideas.
Glossy international intriguer with smart performances.

w John Tucker Battle *d* Ray Milland *ph* Jack Marta *m* Nelson Riddle

Ray Milland, *Claude Rains*, Maureen O'Hara, Yvonne Furneaux, Francis Lederer, Percy Marmont, Edward Chapman

The List of Adrian Messenger**
US 1963 98m bw
U-I / Joel (Edward Lewis)

An intelligence officer traps a mass murderer with a penchant for disguise.
Old-fashioned mystery thriller, as though Holmes and Watson were combatting a modern Moriarty (and a rough-hewn production). The whole thing is camped up like an end-of-term treat, and as a further gimmick four guest stars allegedly appear under heavy disguise in cameo parts.

w Anthony Veiller, *novel* Philip MacDonald *d* John Huston *ph* Joe MacDonald *m* Jerry Goldsmith

George C. Scott, Kirk Douglas, Clive Brook, Dana Wynter, Jacques Roux, Walter Tony Huston, Herbert Marshall, Bernard Archard, Gladys Cooper; and Robert Mitchum, Frank Sinatra, Burt Lancaster, Tony Curtis

Listen Darling*
US 1938 70m bw
MGM (Jack Cummings)

Children try to find their widowed mother a new husband.
Minor musical full of the studio's upcoming talent.

w Elaine Ryan, Anne Morrison Chapin *d* Edwin L. Marin *ph* Charles Lawton Jnr *m* William Axt, George Stoll

Mary Astor, Judy Garland, Freddie Bartholemew, Walter Pidgeon, Alan Hale, Scotty Beckett

Lisztomania
GB 1975 104m colour Panavision
Warner / VPS / Goodtimes (Roy Baird, David Puttnam)

The life of Liszt seen in terms of a modern pop performer.
The most excessive and obscene of all this director's controversial works, incapable of criticism on normal terms except that it seems unusually poor in production values.

wd Ken Russell *ph* Peter Suschitsky *md* John Forsyth

Roger Daltrey, Sara Kestelman, Paul Nicholas, Fiona Lewis, John Justin, Ringo Starr

'Ken Russell's first completely unmitigated

catastrophe in several years . . . a welter of arbitrary gags, manic self-references and frantic exploitation-movie clichés.'—*Tony Rayns*

'Oscar Wilde once said "Each man kills the thing he loves", and the remark perfectly suits Ken Russell's film treatments of classical composers . . . he has bludgeoned into pulp some of the finest music civilization has produced.'—*Patrick Snyder*

The Little Ark
US 1971 86m De Luxe Panavision
Cinema Center / Robert B. Radnitz

Two war orphans and their pets, trapped in a flood, sail to safety in a houseboat.
Well-meaning, somewhat allegorical family film, too desultory to maintain interest and rather too frightening for children.

w Joanna Crawford, *novel* Jan de Hartog
d James B. Clark *ph* Austin Dempster, Denys Coop *m* Fred Karlin

Theodore Bikel, Philip Frame, Genevieve Ambas

Little Big Horn*
US 1951 86m bw
Lippert (Carl K. Hittleman)
GB title: *The Fighting Seventh*

A cavalry squad sets out to warn Custer about Little Big Horn, but all the men are massacred before Custer arrives.
Dour, impressive low-budget western.

wd Charles Marquis Warren ph Ernest Miller
m Paul Dunlap

Lloyd Bridges, John Ireland, Marie Windsor, Reed Hadley, Hugh O'Brian, Wally Cassell, King Donovan

Little Big Man*
US 1970 147m Technicolor Panavision
Stockbridge / Hiller / Cinema Center (Stuart Millar)

An aged veteran of the old west recounts his life story—with elaborations.
A number of episodes varying from stark tragedy to satirical farce are framed for no good reason by the star in heavy disguise; the intention is hard to guess but there are goodies along the way.

w Calder Willingham, *novel* Thomas Berger
d Arthur Penn *ph Harry Stradling m* John Hammond *pd* Dean Tavoularis

Dustin Hoffman, Martin Balsam, Faye Dunaway, *Chief Dan George*, Richard Mulligan, Jeff Corey

'A hip epic, with an amiable first hour. Then the massacres and messages take over.'—*New Yorker, 1976*

'A tangy and, I think, unique film with American verve, about some of the things American verve has done.'—*Stanley Kauffmann*

Little Boy Lost
US 1953 95m bw
Paramount (William Perlberg)

An American returns to Paris after the war to find his wife dead and his small son missing.
Rather dull tearjerker.

wd George Seaton, *novel* Marghanita Laski
ph George Barnes *m* Victor Young

Bing Crosby, Claude Dauphin, Christian Fourcade, Gabrielle Dorziat, Nicole Maurey

Little Caesar****
US 1930 77m bw
Warner

The rise and fall of a vicious gangster.
Its central character clearly modelled on Al Capone, this also has historical interest as vanguard of a spate of noisy gangster films. The star was forever identified with his role, and the film, though technically dated, moves fast enough to maintain interest nearly fifty years later.

w Francis Faragoh, *novel* W. R. Burnett
d Mervyn Le Roy ph Tony Gaudio

Edward G. Robinson, Douglas Fairbanks Jnr, Glenda Farrell, William Collier Jnr, Ralph Ince, George E. Stone, Thomas Jackson, Stanley Fields, Sidney Blackmer

'It has irony and grim humour and a real sense of excitement and its significance does not get in the way of the melodrama.'—*Richard Dana Skinner*

The Little Colonel**
US 1935 80m bw (colour sequence)
TCF (B. G. De Sylva)

In a southern household after the Civil War, a little girl ends a family feud, plays Cupid to her sister, routs a few villains and mollifies her cantakerous grandfather.
First-class Temple vehicle, the first to boast an expensive production.

w William Conselman, *novel* Annie Fellows Johnson *d* David Butler *ph* Arthur Miller
md Arthur Lange

Shirley Temple, Lionel Barrymore, Evelyn Venable, John Lodge, Bill Robinson, Hattie McDaniel, Sidney Blackmer

Little Fauss and Big Halsy
US 1970 99m Movielab Panavision
Paramount / Alfran / Furie (Albert S. Ruddy)

Two motor cycle track racers team up and have violent adventures round the country.
Rather pointless capers in the wake of *Easy Rider*, neither interesting nor well done.

w Charles Eastman *d* Sidney J. Furie *ph* Ralph Woolsey

Robert Redford, Michael J. Pollard, *Noah Beery Jnr*, Lauren Hutton
'A sort of *Batman and Robin* on wheels.'—*Rex Reed*

The Little Foxes***
US 1941 116m bw
Samuel Goldwyn

A family of schemers in post-Civil War days will stop at nothing to outwit each other.
Superb film of a brilliant play; excellent to look at and listen to, with a compelling narrative line and memorable characters.

w Lillian Hellman, from her play *d William Wyler ph Gregg Toland m* Meredith Willson

Bette Davis, Herbert Marshall, Teresa Wright, Richard Carlson, *Charles Dingle, Dan Duryea, Carl Benton Reid, Patricia Collinge*, Jessica Grayson, Russell Hicks

A Little Game*
US 1971 73m Technicolor TVM
Universal (George Eckstein)

A man suspects that his 11-year-old stepson may be homicidal.
Quite a chilling little melodrama.

w Carol Sobieski, *novel* Fielden Farrington *d* Paul Wendkos

Ed Nelson, Diane Baker, Katy Jurado, Howard Duff

The Little Giant
US 1933 74m bw
Warner

At the end of Prohibition, a beer baron moves to California and tries to break into society.
Disappointingly unfunny gangster comedy which never really gets going.

w Robert Lord, Wilson Mizner *d* Roy del Ruth *ph* Sid Hickox *m* Leo F. Forbstein

Edward G. Robinson, Mary Astor, Helen Vinson, Kenneth Thompson, Russell Hopton, Donald Dillaway

Little Giant
US 1946 91m bw
Universal (Joseph Gershenson)
GB title: *On the Carpet*

Misadventures of a vacuum cleaner salesman.
Curious, unsatisfactory Abbott and Costello comedy in which the boys play separate characters instead of working as a team. They should have waited for a better script before experimenting.

w Paul Jarrico, Richard Collins, Walter de Leon *d* William A. Seiter *ph* Charles van Enger *m* Edgar Fairchild

Bud Abbott, Lou Costello, Brenda Joyce, George Cleveland, Elena Verdugo

The Little House on the Prairie
US 1974 100m colour TVM
Ed Friendly

The struggles of an American pioneer family to tame the wilderness.
Totally predictable family fare with the emphasis on the kids; nicely photographed, but the hardship is not too evident.

w Blanche Hanalis, *book* Laura Ingalls Wilder *d* Michael Landon

Michael Landon, Melissa Gilbert, Melissa Sue Anderson, Vic Mohica
† A long-running series followed.

The Little Hut
US 1957 90m Eastmancolor
MGM / Herbson S A

A man, his wife and her lover are shipwrecked on a desert island.
Sophisticated French farce which falls resoundingly flat in this bowdlerized Hollywood version in bilious colour, fatally compromising itself at the beginning with a 'realistic' London prologue.

w F. Hugh Herbert, *play* André Roussin and Nancy Mitford *d* Mark Robson *ph* Frederick A. Young *m* Robert Farnon *ad* Elliot Scott

Stewart Granger, David Niven, Ava Gardner, Walter Chiari, Finlay Currie, Jean Cadell

The Little Minister
US 1934 110m bw
RKO (Pandro S. Berman)

In 1840 Scotland, the gypsy girl with whom the new pastor falls unsuitably in love is really the local earl's wayward daughter.
Tedious film version of a cloyingly whimsical play.

w Jane Murfin, Sarah Y. Mason, Victor

Heerman, *play* J. M. Barrie *d* Richard Wallace *ph* Henry Gerrard *m* Max Steiner

Katharine Hepburn, John Beal, Alan Hale, Donald Crisp, Lumsden Hare, Andy Clyde, Beryl Mercer, Dorothy Stickney, Frank Conroy, Reginald Denny

Little Miss Broadway
US 1938 70m bw
TCF (David Hempstead)

A small girl is adopted by the owner of a hotel for vaudeville artistes.
One of the child star's more casual vehicles, but quite pleasing.

w Harry Tugend, Jack Yellen *d* Irving Cummings *ph* Arthur Miller *m* Louis Silvers

Shirley Temple, George Murphy, Jimmy Durante, Edna May Oliver, Phyllis Brooks, George Barbier, Edward Ellis, Jane Darwell, El Brendel, Donald Meek, Claude Gillingwater, Russell Hicks

'It can't be old age, but it does look like weariness.'—*New York Times*

Little Miss Marker**
US 1934 80m bw
Paramount (B. P. Schulberg)
GB title: *The Girl in Pawn*

A cynical racetrack gambler is forced to adopt a little girl, who not only softens him but saves him from his enemies.
The twin appeals of Temple (a new hot property) and Runyon made this a big hit of its time.

w William R. Lipman, Sam Hellman, Gladys Lehman, *story* Damon Runyon *d* Alexander Hall *ph* Alfred Gilks

Shirley Temple, Adolphe Menjou, Dorothy Dell, Charles Bickford, Lynne Overman, Frank McGlynn Snr, Willie Best
† Remade as *Sorrowful Jones* (qv).

Little Murders
US 1971 108m De Luxe
TCF / Brodsky–Gould (Jack Brodsky)

A young photographer rises above all the urban horror of New York life, but when his wife is killed by a sniper he takes to violence.
This adaptation of an ultrablack comedy would have worked better as a comic strip, for its characters are satirical puppets, and when played by human beings the whole thing seems violently silly.

w Jules Feiffer, from his play *d* Alan Arkin *ph* Gordon Willis *m* Fred Kaz

Elliot Gould, Marcia Rodd, Elizabeth Wilson, Vincent Gardenia, Alan Arkin

Little Old New York
US 1940 100m bw
TCF (Raymond Griffith)

The story of Robert Fulton and his invention of the steamboat.
Romantic hokum with a veneer of fact; good production.

w Harry Tugend, *play* Rida Johnson Young *d* Henry King *ph* Leon Shamroy *m* Alfred Newman

Alice Faye, Richard Greene, Fred MacMurray, Henry Stephenson, Brenda Joyce, Andy Devine, Fritz Feld, Ward Bond

The Little Prince
US 1974 89m Technicolor
Paramount / Stanley Donen

A small boy leaves the asteroid he rules to learn of life on earth.
A whimsical bestseller turns into an arch musical which falls over itself early on and never recovers; in any case it fatally lacks the common touch, though it has pleasing moments.

w Alan Jay Lerner, *novel* Antoine de St-Exupery *d* Stanley Donen *ph Christopher Challis m/ly* Frederick Loewe, Alan Jay Lerner *pd* John Barry

Richard Kiley, Steven Warner, *Bob Fosse*, Gene Wilder, Joss Ackland, Clive Revill, Victor Spinetti, Graham Crowden

'Handsome production cannot obscure limited artistic achievement.'—*Variety*

The Little Princess**
US 1939 93m Technicolor
TCF (Gene Markey)

In Victorian London a little girl is left at a harsh school when her father goes abroad.
One of the child star's plushest vehicles, a charming early colour film complete with dream sequence and happy ending.

w Ethel Hill, Walter Ferris, *novel* Frances Hodgson Burnett *d* Walter Lang *ph Arthur Miller, William Skall md* Louis Silvers

Shirley Temple, Richard Greene, Anita Louise, Ian Hunter, Cesar Romero, Arthur Treacher, Mary Nash, Sybil Jason, Miles Mander, Marcia Mae Jones, Beryl Mercer, E. E. Clive

Little Women***
US 1933 115m bw
RKO / David O. Selznick (Kenneth MacGowan)

The growing up of four sisters in pre-Civil War America.

Charming 'big picture' of its day, with excellent production and performances.

w Sarah Y. Mason, Victor Heerman, *novel* Louisa May Alcott *d George Cukor ph* Henry Gerrard *m* Max Steiner

Katharine Hepburn, Paul Lukas, Joan Bennett, Frances Dee, Jean Parker, *Spring Byington*, Edna May Oliver, Douglass Montgomery, Henry Stephenson, Samuel S. Hinds, John Lodge, Nydia Westman

'If to put a book on the screen with all the effectiveness that sympathy and good taste and careful artifice can devise is to make a fine motion picture, then *Little Women* is a fine picture.'—*James Shelley Hamilton*

Little Women*
US 1949 122m Technicolor
MGM

Syrupy Christmas-card remake, notably lacking the light touch.

w Andrew Solt, Sarah Y. Mason, Victor Heerman *d* Mervyn Le Roy *ph* Franz Planer *m* Daniele Amfitheatrof

June Allyson, Elizabeth Taylor, Peter Lawford, Margaret O'Brien, Janet Leigh, Mary Astor

'It will raise a smile and draw a tear from the sentimental.'—*MFB*

The Littlest Rebel*
US 1935 70m bw
TCF (B. G. De Sylva)

A small southern girl persuades President Lincoln to release her father.
Charming, archetypal early Temple vehicle, very well produced.

w Edwin Burke, *play* Edward Peple *d* David Butler *ph* John Seitz *m* Cyril Mockridge

Shirley Temple, John Boles, Jack Holt, Karen Morley, *Bill Robinson*, Guinn Williams, Willie Best, Frank McGlynn Snr

Live Again, Die Again*
US 1974 74m colour TVM
Universal (David Victor)

A woman kept frozen for forty years is revived and cured; returning home, she finds that someone is trying to kill her.
Nuthouse melodrama which early abandons its crionics theme and subjects the audience to every trick in the book: colour filters, distorted sound, surrealist montages, the lot. Unfortunately the plot is not sound enough to stand up to it.

w Joseph Stefano *d* Richard A. Colla

Donna Mills, Walter Pidgeon, Vera Miles, Geraldine Page, Cliff Potts, Mike Farrell

Live and Let Die*
GB 1973 121m Eastmancolor
UA / Eon (Harry Saltzman)

James Bond chases a black master criminal and becomes involved in West Indian Voodoo.
Standard tongue-in-cheek spy adventure with a new lightweight star and an air of *déjà vu*. Professional standards high.

w Tom Mankiewicz, *novel* Ian Fleming *d* Guy Hamilton *ph* Ted Moore *m* George Martin *titles* Maurice Binder

Roger Moore, Yaphet Kotto, Jane Seymour, Clifton James, David Hedison, Bernard Lee, Lois Maxwell

'Plot lines have descended further to the level of the old Saturday afternoon serial, and the treatment is more than ever like a cartoon.'—*Variety*

'A Bond movie is not made. It is packaged. Like an Almond Joy. So much coconut to this much chocolate and a dash of raisins.'—*Joseph Gelmis*

Live, Love and Learn
US 1937 78m bw
MGM (Harry Rapf)

A bohemian painter is tamed by marriage.
Tiresome romantic trifle.

w Charles Brackett, Cyril Hume, Richard Maibaum *d* George Fitzmaurice *ph* Ray June

Robert Montgomery, Rosalind Russell, Robert Benchley, Helen Vinson, Mickey Rooney, Monty Woolley, E. E. Clive, Maude Eburne

Live Now, Pay Later
GB 1962 104m bw
(Regal) Woodlands / Jay Lewis (Jack Hanbury)

A credit store salesman is himself heavily in debt, and his private life is in ruins; but even after a chapter of unexpected and tragic events he remains irrepressibly optimistic.
A satirical farce melodrama which lets fly in too many directions at once and has a cumulatively cheerless effect despite funny moments.

w Jack Trevor Story, *novel* All on the Never Never by Jack Lindsay *d* Jay Lewis *ph* Jack Hildyard *m* Ron Grainer

Ian Hendry, John Gregson, June Ritchie, Geoffrey Keen, Liz Fraser

Lives of a Bengal Lancer**
US 1935 1i9m bw
Paramount (Louis D. Lighton)

Adventures on the North-West Frontier.
British army heroics are here taken rather solemnly, but the film is efficient and fondly remembered.

w Waldemar Young, John F. Balderston, Achmed Abdullah, Grover Jones, William Slavens McNut, *book* Francis Yeats-Brown *d* Henry Hathaway *ph* Charles Lang

Gary Cooper, *Franchot Tone, Richard Barthelmess, Sir Guy Standing*, C. Aubrey Smith, Monte Blue, Kathleen Burke, Colin Tapley, *Douglass Dumbrille*, Akim Tamiroff, Noble Johnson

The Lives of Jenny Dolan*
US 1975 100m colour TVM
Paramount / Ross Hunter

A lady journalist investigates four puzzling deaths which prove to be connected.
Sleek, ambitious soaper which doesn't really work.

w Richard Alan Simmons, James Lee *d* Jerry Jameson

Shirley Jones, Stephen Boyd, John Gavin, Dana Wynter, Stephen McNally, James Darren, David Hedison, Farley Granger, Lynn Carlin, George Grizzard, Ian MacShane, Pernell Roberts, Percy Rodrigues

Living Free
GB 1972 92m colour
Columbia / Open Road / High Road

On the death of Elsa the lioness, George and Joy Adamson capture her three cubs and transfer them for their own safety to Serengeti.
Sloppy sequel to *Born Free*, depending very heavily on the appeal of the cubs.

w Maurice Kaufman *d* Jack Couffer *ph* Wolfgang Suschitzky *m* Sol Kaplan

Susan Hampshire, Nigel Davenport, Geoffrey Keen

The Living Idol
Mexico / US 1956 100m Eastmancolor Cinemascope
MGM (Albert Lewin)

A Mexican girl becomes possessed by the spirit of the jaguar to whom local maidens were once sacrificed.
Pretentious but rather enjoyable highbrow hokum of the heady kind expected from this producer.

wd Albert Lewin ph Jack Hildyard *m* Manuel Esperon

James Robertson Justice, Steve Forrest, Liliane Montevecchi

Living in a Big Way
US 1947 103m bw
MGM

A demobbed GI finds he can't get on with his rich selfish wife and opens up a charity home for the families of war casualties.
Odd mixture of comedy, drama and a few songs and dances, not forgetting a message or two. It mostly falls flat on its face.

w Gregory La Cava, Irving Ravetch *d* Gregory La Cava *ph* Harold Rosson *m* Lennie Hayton

Gene Kelly, Marie McDonald, Charles Winninger, Phyllis Thaxter, Spring Byington, Clinton Sundberg

Living It Up*
US 1954 95m Technicolor
Paramount / Hal B. Wallis (Paul Jones)

A suspected victim of radium poisoning is played up by the press into a national hero.
Remake of *Nothing Sacred* with Lewis as Carole Lombard; deserves a mark for cheek.

w Jack Rose, Mel Shavelson *d* Norman Taurog *ph* Daniel Fapp

Dean Martin, Jerry Lewis, Janet Leigh, Edward Arnold, Fred Clark, Sheree North, Sig Rumann

Living on Velvet*
US 1935 77m bw
Warner (Edward Chodorov)

A happy-go-lucky aviator changes his life style when he narrowly escapes death in a crash.
Reasonably interesting 'serious' drama of its period.

w Jerry Wald, Julius Epstein *d* Frank Borzage *ph* Sid Hickox *m* Leo F. Forbstein

George Brent, Kay Francis, Warren William, Helen Lowell, Henry O'Neill, Samuel S. Hinds, Russell Hicks, Edgar Kennedy

Lizzie
US 1957 81m bw
MGM / Bryna (Jerry Bresler)

Murder and rape turn a girl into a triple personality.
Preposterous cash-in on *The Three Faces of Eve*, too silly to be even funny.

w Mel Dinelli, *novel* The Bird's Nest by Shirley Jackson *d* Hugo Haas *ph* Paul Ivano *m* Leslie Stevens

Eleanor Parker, Richard Boone, Joan Blondell, Hugo Haas

'Ruddy peculiar.'—*MFB*

Lloyd's of London**

US 1936 115m bw
TCF (Kenneth MacGowan)

A young messenger boy in the 18th century grows up to found a great insurance company.
Thoroughly well mounted, if unconvincing and slightly boring, historical charade in which the Prince of Wales, Lord Nelson, Dr Johnson and other personages make guest appearances. An archetypal prestige film of its time which also turned out to be box office.

w Ernest Pascal, Walter Ferris, *book* Curtis Kenyon *d Henry King ph Bert Glennon* *m* Louis Silvers

Tyrone Power, Madeleine Carroll, George Sanders, Freddie Bartholemew, C. Aubrey Smith, Guy Standing, Virginia Field, Montagu Love, Gavin Muir, Miles Mander, Una O'Connor, E. E. Clive

'The name of England is so freely on the characters' lips that we recognize at once an American picture. These people live, make love, bear children all from the most patriotic motives, and it's all rather like London in coronation week.'—*Graham Greene*

Lock, Stock and Barrel

US 1970 96m Technicolor TVM
Universal

A runaway couple encounter savage animals, vengeful parents, and natural hazards.
Slow starting adventure comedy featuring the couple later seen married in *Hitched* (qv).

w Richard Alan Simmons *d* Jerry Thorpe

Belinda Montgomery, Tim Matheson, Jack Albertson, Neville Brand, Burgess Meredith, Felicia Farr, John Beck, Robert Emhardt

Lock Up Your Daughters

GB 1969 103m Technicolor
Columbia / Domino (David Deutsch)

In 18th-century London an aristocratic rake and various lower orders are all in search of female companionship and get their wires crossed.
Noisy, vulgar, ill-acted version (without music) of a successful musical based on two old theatrical warhorses.

w Keith Waterhouse, Willis Hall, *play* Bernard Miles based on Rape upon Rape by Henry Fielding and The Relapse by John Vanbrugh *d* Peter Coe *ph* Peter Suschitsky *m* Ron Grainer *pd* Tony Woollard

Christopher Plummer, Roy Kinnear, Georgia Brown, Susannah York, Glynis Johns, Ian Bannen, Tom Bell, Elaine Taylor, Jim Dale, Kathleen Harrison, Roy Dotrice, Vanessa Howard, Fenella Fielding, Peter Bayliss, *Richard Wordsworth,* Peter Bull, Fred Emney

'Subtlety is neither required nor displayed.'—*Jack Ibberson*

The Locket

US 1946 85m bw
RKO

A *femme fatale* is bent on destroying men, and eventually we discover why.
Dark, confusing melodrama very typical of the immediate post-war years; it has little to say but says it dourly, even achieving flashbacks within flashbacks within flashbacks.

w Sheridan Gibney *d* John Brahm *ph* Nicholas Musuraca *m* Roy Webb

Laraine Day, Robert Mitchum, Brian Aherne, Gene Raymond, Ricardo Cortez

Locusts*

US 1974 74m colour TVM
Paramount

A discharged World War II pilot comes home in dejection but finds himself fighting a locust plague.
Very moderate personal drama gives way to very moderate special effects.

w Robert Malcolm Young *d* Richard T. Heffron

Ben Johnson, Ron Howard, Lisa Gerritsen, Katherine Helmond

The Lodger*

GB 1932 85m bw
Twickenham (Julius Hagen)
US title: *The Phantom Fiend*

The upstairs lodger is suspected of being Jack the Ripper . . .
Modernized version of a story already tackled by Hitchcock as a silent and to be done again in costume in 1944. Not bad, for a minor British film of the time.

w Ivor Novello, Miles Mander, Paul Rotha, H. Fowler Mear, *novel* Mrs Belloc Lowndes *d* Maurice Elvey

Ivor Novello, Elizabeth Allan, A. W. Baskomb, Jack Hawkins, Barbara Everest, Peter Gawthorne, Kynaston Reeves

The Lodger*

US 1944 84m bw
TCF (Robert Bassler)

1880s version of the above in which the lodger *is* Jack the Ripper.
Nicely mounted apart from some anachronisms, but a little dull.

w Barre Lyndon *d John Brahm ph Lucien Ballard m* Hugo Friedhofer

Laird Cregar, Merle Oberon, George Sanders, Cedric Hardwicke, Sara Allgood, Aubrey Mather, Queenie Leonard, Helena Pickard, Lumsden Hare, Frederick Worlock

The Log of the Black Pearl
US 1975 100m Technicolor TVM
Universal / Jack Webb

A stockbroker inherits a ship and a clue to sunken treasure.
Rather like a modernized Treasure Island, but not as good.

w Harold Jack Bloom *d* Andrew McLaglen

Jack Kruschen, Glenn Corbett, Ralph Bellamy, John Alderson, Anne Archer, Kiel Martin

Logan's Run*
US 1976 118m Metrocolor Todd-AO
MGM (Saul David)

In the future, people try to escape from a society which dooms everyone to death at thirty.
Interesting and quite exciting fantasy melodrama which mercifully moves instead of preaching.

w David Zelag Goodman, novel William F. Nolan *d* Michael Anderson *ph* Ernest Laszlo *m* Jerry Goldsmith *pd* Dale Hennesy

Michael York, Richard Jordan, Jenny Agutter, Roscoe Lee Browne, Farrah Fawcett-Majors, Peter Ustinov, Michael Anderson Jnr

Lolita**
GB 1962 152m bw
MGM / Seven Arts / AA / Anya / Transworld (James B. Harris)

A middle-aged lecturer falls for a 14-year-old girl and marries her mother to be near her.
Fitfully amusing but slightly plotted and very lengthy screen version of a sensational novel in which the heroine is only twelve, which makes a difference. The flashback introduction and various comic asides are pretentious and alienating.

w Vladimir Nabokov, from his novel *d* Stanley Kubrick *ph* Oswald Morris *m* Nelson Riddle

James Mason, Shelley Winters, Sue Lyon, Peter Sellers

'The director's heart is apparently elsewhere. Consequently, we face the problem without the passion, the badness without the beauty, the agony without the ecstasy.'—*Andrew Sarris*

'A diluted *Blue Angel* with a teenage temptress instead of a tart.'—*Stanley Kauffmann*

Lolly Madonna XXX
US 1973 105m Metrocolor
MGM (Rodney Carr-Smith)
GB title: *The Lolly Madonna War*

Tennessee hillbilly farmers fight over a meadow.
Violent feudin' melodrama, technically accomplished but of limited interest to non-hillbillies.

w Rodney Carr-Smith, Sue Grafton, from her novel *d* Richard C. Sarafian *ph* Philip Lathrop *m* Fred Myrow

Rod Steiger, Robert Ryan, Scott Wilson, Jeff Bridges, Season Hubley

London Belongs to Me**
GB 1948 112m bw
GFD / Individual (Frank Launder, Sidney Gilliat)
US title: *Dulcimer Street*

A young boy is arrested on a murder charge and his boarding-house friends rally to his defence.
Unconvincing but highly entertaining sub-Dickensian comedy-drama with a rousing finish and an abundance of character roles.

w Sidney Gilliat, J. B. Williams, *novel* Norman Collins *d Sidney Gilliat ph* Wilkie Cooper *m* Benjamin Frankel

Alastair Sim, Stephen Murray, Richard Attenborough, Fay Compton, Wylie Watson, Susan Shaw, Ivy St Helier, Joyce Carey, Andrew Crawford, Eleanor Summerfield, Hugh Griffith, Gladys Henson

London Town*
GB 1947 126m Technicolor
GFD / Wesley Ruggles
US title: *My Heart Goes Crazy*

An understudy finally achieves stardom thanks to his daughter's schemes.
Disastrous and expensive attempt to make a major British musical without a single new idea. Tasteless, tawdry and sluggish, but it does record for posterity four of the star's sketches.

w Elliot Paul, Siegfried Herzig, Val Guest *d* Wesley Ruggles

Sid Field, Greta Gynt, Kay Kendall, Tessie O'Shea, Claude Hulbert, Sonnie Hale, Mary Clare, Petula Clark, Jerry Desmonde

'I can't see the point of importing an American director and giving him all the time and money in the world to play with when we can make bad musicals on our own, and quicker.'—*Richard Winnington*

Lone Star
US 1952 90m bw
MGM (Z. Wayne Griffin)

Andrew Jackson enlists the aid of a Texas adventurer to persuade Sam Houston to change his mind about an agreement with Mexico.
Slow-moving semi-western, hard to follow for non-Americans. Production values quite high.

w Borden Chase, Howard Estabrook *d* Vincent Sherman *ph* Harold Rosson *m* David Buttolph

Clark Gable, Ava Gardner, Lionel Barrymore, Broderick Crawford, Ed Begley, Beulah Bondi, James Burke, William Farnum, Lowell Gilmore, Moroni Olsen, Russell Simpson, William Conrad

The Lone Wolf
The jewel thief turned sleuth was created by Louis Joseph Vance and turned up in several silent films. During the talkie period several actors played Michael Lanyard; the role of his valet passed from Raymond Walburn to Eric Blore to Alan Mowbray. All the films were made for Columbia, but only the first was anything like a main feature.

1935: THE LONE WOLF RETURNS (*d* Roy William Neill with Melvyn Douglas)
1938: THE LONE WOLF IN PARIS (*d* Albert S. Rogell with Francis Lederer)
1939: THE LONE WOLF SPY HUNT (*d* Peter Godfrey with Warren William)
1940: THE LONE WOLF STRIKES (*d* Sidney Salkow with Warren William)
1941: THE LONE WOLF MEETS A LADY, THE LONE WOLF TAKES A CHANCE, THE LONE WOLF KEEPS A DATE (all as above), SECRETS OF THE LONE WOLF (*d* Edward Dmytryk; WW)
1943: ONE DANGEROUS NIGHT (*d* Michael Gordon: WW), PASSPORT TO SUEZ (*d* André de Toth: WW)
1946: THE NOTORIOUS LONE WOLF (*d* D. Ross Lederman; with Gerald Mohr)
1947: THE LONE WOLF IN LONDON (*d* Leslie Goodwins: GM), THE LONE WOLF IN MEXICO (*d* D. Ross Lederman: GM)
1949: THE LONE WOLF AND HIS LADY (*d* John Hoffman: GM)

The Loneliness of the Long Distance Runner*
GB 1962 104m bw
British Lion / Bryanston / Woodfall (Tony Richardson)

The only thing a Borstal boy does well is run, and as he trains he thinks back to his depressing life.
Rather pale study of a social outcast; interesting scenes do not quite form a compelling whole.

w Alan Sillitoe, from his short story *d* Tony Richardson *ph* Walter Lassally *m* John Addison

Tom Courtenay, Michael Redgrave, James Bolam, Avis Bunnage, Alec McCowen, Joe Robinson, Julia Foster

Lonely Are the Brave*
US 1962 107m bw Panavision
U-I / Joel (Edward Lewis)

The last of the cowboy rebels is no match for pursuit by jeep and helicopter.
A strange, sad, rather moving fable, with very good performances and action scenes, but a shade too unrelenting in its downbeat tone to become a popular classic.

w Dalton Trumbo, *novel* Brave Cowboy by Edward Abbey *d* David Miller *ph* Philip Lathrop *m* Jerry Goldsmith

Kirk Douglas, Walter Matthau, Gena Rowlands, Michael Kane, Carroll O'Connor, Karl Swenson, George Kennedy, Bill Raisch

The Lonely Man
US 1957 87m bw Vistavision
Paramount (Pat Duggan)

An outlaw hopes to regain social recognition and contacts the son who abhors him.
Dullish psycho western.

w Harry Essex, Robert Smith *d* Henry Levin *ph* Lionel Lindon *m* Van Cleave

Jack Palance, Anthony Perkins, Elaine Aiken, Neville Brand, Lee Van Cleef, Elisha Cook Jnr, Robert Middleton

The Lonely Profession*
US 1969 96m Technicolor TVM
Universal (Jo Swerling Jnr)

A private eye's client is murdered.
Acceptable sub-Chandler goings on.

wd Douglas Heyes

Harry Guardino, Dean Jagger, Troy Donahue, Joseph Cotten, Fernando Lamas, Dina Merrill

Lonelyhearts*
US 1958 103m bw
UA / Dore Schary

A young journalist finds himself engrossed, appalled and sickened by his work on the agony column.
Episodic, occasionally interesting but generally too vaguely liberal; an intellectual reshaping of a despairing novel. The producer as usual is well meaning but doesn't quite make it.

w Dore Schary, *novel* Nathanael West

d Vincent J. Donehue *ph* John Alton *m* Conrad Salinger

Montgomery Clift, Robert Ryan, Myrna Loy, Dolores Hart, Maureen Stapleton

The Long and the Short and the Tall*
GB 1960 105m bw
ABP / Michael Balcon
US title: *Jungle Fighters*

In Malaya during World War II a Japanese scout is captured by a British patrol.
Stark war melodrama with the emphasis on character. Vivid at the time, it now seems very routine.

w Wolf Mankowitz, *play* Willis Hall *d* Leslie Norman
ph Erwin Hillier *m* Stanley Black

Laurence Harvey, Richard Todd, David McCallum, Richard Harris, Ronald Fraser, John Meillon, John Rees, Kenji Takaki

The Long Arm**
GB 1956 96m bw
Ealing (Tom Morahan)
US title: *The Third Key*

A Scotland Yard superintendent solves a series of robberies.
Good straightforward police thriller with careful detail.

w Janet Green, Robert Barr d Charles Frend ph Gordon Dines *m* Gerbrand Schurmann

Jack Hawkins, Dorothy Alison, John Stratton, Michael Brooke, Geoffrey Keen, Sidney Tafler, Meredith Edwards, Ralph Truman, Ursula Howells

'A generally efficient example of popular British film-making.'—*MFB*

The Long Dark Hall
GB 1951 86m bw
British Lion / Five Oceans (Anthony Bushell)

A chorus girl is murdered and her married lover is accused.
Miserable mystery with a trick ending, most inappropriately cast.

w Nunnally Johnson, W. E. C. Fairchild *d* Anthony Bushell, Reginald Beck *ph* Wilkie Cooper *m* Benjamin Frankel

Rex Harrison, Lilli Palmer, Raymond Huntley, Denis O'Dea, Anthony Bushell, Henry Longhurst, Patricia Wayne, Meriel Forbes, Brenda de Banzie, Anthony Dawson

The Long Day's Dying
GB 1968 95m Techniscope
Paramount / Junction Films

Three British paratroopers in Europe are cut off from their unit and die pointlessly.
Violent, irritating anti-war film which resurrects all the clichés and makes itself unpleasant into the bargain.

w Charles Wood, *novel* Alan White *d* Peter Collinson *ph* Brian Probyn *m* none *pd* Disley Jones

David Hemmings, Tom Bell, Tony Beckley, Alan Dobie

'It is typical of all that is wrong with the film that it should end on a frozen frame of a soldier in the act of dying while heavily ironic patriotic music swells on the sound track.'—*David Wilson*

Long Day's Journey into Night**
US 1961 174m bw
Ely Landau

Connecticut 1912: days in the life of an ageing actor, his drug addicted wife and their sons, one of whom is an alcoholic and the other Eugene O'Neill.
Heavy going, nicely handled, superbly acted version of a play which can be a player's triumph and certainly is here; but it still has more effect in the theatre.

w Eugene O'Neill *d Sidney Lumet ph Boris Kaufman m* André Previn *pd Richard Sylbert*

Ralph Richardson, Katharine Hepburn, Jason Robards Jnr, *Dean Stockwell*

'Letting his players have their head, lighted miraculously so that every flicker of emotion is preserved, and pursuing them with Kaufman's unobtrusive camera, Lumet illuminates the play, line by line, and gives it all the impact of a live performance.'—*Brenda Davies*

'A very great play has been not translated to the screen but reverently put behind glass.'—*John Simon*

The Long Duel
GB 1967 115m Technicolor Panavision
Rank (Ken Annakin)

On the North-West Frontier in the twenties, British officers disagree about handling the natives, and one of them forms a strong regard for the native leader.
Unconvincing cut-price Indian adventure with little cohesion and less entertainment value.

w Peter Yeldham *d* Ken Annakin *ph* Jack Hildyard *m* Patrick John Scott

Trevor Howard, Yul Brynner, Harry Andrews, Charlotte Rampling, Virginia North, Andrew Keir, Laurence Naismith, Maurice Denham

'The dialogue seems to have been written by a

computer fed a programme of execrable films on the same theme.'—*MFB*

The Long Goodbye
US 1973 111m Technicolor Panavision
UA / Lions Gate (Jerry Bick)

Philip Marlowe helps an eccentric friend who is suspected of murdering his wife.
Ugly, boring travesty of a well-respected detective novel, the apparent intention being to reverse the author's attitudes completely and to substitute dullness and incomprehensibility.

w Leigh Brackett, *novel* Raymond Chandler *d* Robert Altman *ph* Vilmos Zsigismond *m* John T. Williams

Elliott Gould, Nina Van Pallandt, Sterling Hayden, Mark Rydell, Henry Gibson

'Altman's fragmentation bomb blows up itself rather than the myths he has said he wants to lay to rest.'—*Sight and Sound*

'The trouble is that this Marlowe is an untidy, unshaven, semi-literate dimwit slob who could not locate a missing skyscraper and who would be refused service at a hot dog stand.'—*Charles Champlin*

The Long Gray Line*
US 1955 138m Technicolor Cinemascope
Columbia (Robert Arthur)

The career of an athletics trainer at West Point.
Dim biopic, the kind of true life yarn that Americans like, produced in the cheerful, sentimental, sparring way that John Ford likes.

w Edward Hope, *book* Bring Up the Brass by Merty Maher *d* John Ford *ph* Charles Lawton Jnr *m* Morris Stoloff

Tyrone Power, Maureen O'Hara, Donald Crisp, Ward Bond, Robert Francis, Betsy Palmer, Phil Carey, Harry Carey Jnr, Patrick Wayne, Sean McClory

'Its celebration of the codes and ideals of West Point vexatiously combines sentimental cosiness and a kind of religious awe.'—*Gavin Lambert*

The Long Hot Summer*
US 1958 118m Eastmancolor Cinemascope
TCF (Jerry Wald)

Conflict arises between a Mississippi town boss and a tenant farmer.
Busy Peyton Place-style family brawling saga with sex on the side, flabby as narrative but compulsive as character study.

w Irving Ravetch, Harriet Frank, *stories* William Faulkner *d* Martin Ritt *ph* Joseph La Shelle *m* Alex North

Orson Welles, Paul Newman, Joanne Woodward, Tony Franciosa, Lee Remick, Angela Lansbury

Long John Silver
Australia 1953 106m Eastmancolor Cinemascope
TI Pictures (Joseph Kaufman)

Back from Treasure Island, Silver and Hawkins plan a return visit with fresh clues to the treasure.
Cheaply produced, bitsy-piecy adventure fragments with no one to restrain the star from eye-rolling.

w Martin Rackin *d* Byron Haskin *ph* Carl Guthrie *m* David Buttolph

Robert Newton, Connie Gilchrist, Kit Taylor, Rod Taylor

The Long Long Trailer*
US 1954 96m Anscocolor
MGM (Pandro S. Berman)

A construction engineer and his bride buy a trailer for their honeymoon, and wish they hadn't.
Disaster comedy with long bright periods and the inevitable saggy bits.

w Frances Goodrich, Albert Hackett, *novel* Clinton Twiss *d* Vincente Minnelli *ph* Robert Surtees *m* André Deutsch

Lucille Ball, Desi Arnaz, Marjorie Main, Keenan Wynn, Moroni Olsen

Long Lost Father
US 1934 63m bw
RKO

A restaurant owner saves his daughter from a theft charge.
Competent minor star drama.

w Dwight Taylor, *novel* G. B. Stern *d* Ernest B. Schoedsack

John Barrymore, Helen Chandler, Donald Cook, Alan Mowbray, Claude King

The Long Memory
GB 1952 96m bw
Rank (Hugh Stewart)

An ex-con, framed for a murder he did not commit, plots revenge but instead uncovers a fresh crime.
Slow and dreary melodrama set largely on a barge, never rising to anything like excitement.

w Robert Hamer, Frank Harvey, *novel* Winston Clewes *d* Robert Hamer *ph* Harry Waxman *m* William Alwyn

John Mills, John McCallum, Elizabeth Sellars, Geoffrey Keen

The Long Night*
US 1947 97m bw
(RKO) Anatole Litvak

A young man shoots the seducer of his sweetheart and barricades himself in a room against the police.
Good-looking but empty remake of *Le Jour se Lève*.

w John Wexley, *story* Jacques Viot *d* Anatole Litvak *ph* Sol Polito *m* Dmitri Tiomkin

Henry Fonda, Barbara Bel Geddes, Vincent Price, Ann Dvorak, Queenie Smith
'This film faithfully reproduces the letter while altering the spirit of the original almost beyond recognition.'—*MFB*

The Long Ships
GB / Yugoslavia 1963 126m Technirama
Columbia / Warwick / Avila (Irving Allen)

A Viking adventurer and a Moorish prince fall out over a golden bell.
Stilted medieval epic with some visual compensations but more chat than action.

w Berkely Mather, Beverly Cross, *novel* Frank G. Bengtsson *d* Jack Cardiff *ph* Christopher Challis *m* Dusan Radic

Richard Widmark, Sidney Poitier, Russ Tamblyn, Rosanna Schiaffino, Oscar Homolka, Colin Blakely

The Long Voyage Home**
US 1940 104m bw
Walter Wanger

Merchant seamen on shore leave get drunk, philosophize and have adventures.
Stagey-looking but dramatically interesting amalgam of four one-act plays by Eugene O'Neill, with talent abounding.

w Dudley Nichols *d John Ford* *ph* Gregg Toland *m* Richard Hageman

John Wayne, Thomas Mitchell, Ian Hunter, Ward Bond, Barry Fitzgerald, Wilfrid Lawson, Mildred Natwick, John Qualen, Arthur Shields, Joe Sawyer

The Long Wait
US 1954 93m bw
UA / Parklane (Lesser Samuels)

An amnesia victim returns home to solve a murder in which he was involved.
Flatulent version of a Mickey Spillane novel, over-plotted and inadequately motivated.

w Alan Green, Lesser Samuels *d* Victor Saville *ph* Franz Planer *m* Mario Castelnuovo Tedesco

Anthony Quinn, Charles Coburn, Gene Evans, Peggie Castle, Dolores Donlan

The Longest Day**
US 1972 169m bw Cinemascope
TCF (*Darryl F. Zanuck, Elmo Williams*)

A multi-faceted account of the landings in Normandy in June 1944.
Extraordinarily noisy war spectacular, enjoyable as a violent entertainment once one has caught all the threads, but emotionally unaffecting because every part is played by a star.

w Cornelius Ryan, Romain Gary, James Jones, David Pursall, Jack Seddon, *book* Cornelius Ryan *d* Andrew Marton, Ken Annakin, Bernhard Wicki *ph* Henri Persin, Walter Wottitz, Pierre Levent, Jean Bourgoin *m* Maurice Jarre, Paul Anka

John Wayne, Robert Mitchum, Henry Fonda, Robert Ryan, Rod Steiger, Robert Wagner, Paul Anka, Fabian, Tommy Sands, Richard Beymer, Mel Ferrer, Jeffrey Hunter, Sal Mineo, Roddy McDowall, Stuart Whitman, Steve Forrest, Eddie Albert, Edmond O'Brien, Red Buttons, Tom Tryon, Alexander Knox, Ray Danton, Ron Randell, Richard Burton, Donald Houston, Kenneth More, Peter Lawford, Richard Todd, Leo Genn, John Gregson, Sean Connery, Michael Medwin, Leslie Phillips, Irina Demich, Bourvil, Jean-Louis Barrault, Christian Marquand, Arletty, Curt Jurgens, Paul Hartmann, Gert Frobe, Wolfgang Preiss, Peter Van Eyck, Christopher Lee, Eugene Deckers, Richard Wattis

The Longest Hundred Miles
US 1967 93m Technicolor TVM
Universal

An American soldier in the Philippines leads a civilian flight away from the Japanese invasion.
Routine war adventure.

w Winston Miller *d* Don Weis

Doug McClure, Katharine Ross, Ricardo Montalban

The Longest Night*
US 1972 74m Technicolor TVM
Universal (William Frye)

A girl is kidnapped and buried alive in a coffin with a limited life support system.
Suspenseful crime melodrama based on an actual case.

w Merwin Gerard *d* Jack Smight

David Janssen, James Farentino, Phyllis

Thaxter, Skye Aubrey, Charles McGraw, John Kerr

The Longest Yard
US 1974 122m Technicolor
Paramount / Long Road (Albert S. Ruddy)
GB title: *The Mean Machine*

Imprisoned for drunkenness and car theft, a football star is blackmailed into training a prison football team of hulking misfits.
Violent, meandering comedy-drama with murderous jokes but no narrative grip.

w Tracy Keenan Wynn *d* Robert Aldrich
ph Joseph Biroc *m* Frank de Vol

Burt Reynolds, Eddie Albert, Ed Lauter, Michael Conrad, Jim Hampton

Longstreet
US 1970 74m colour TVM
Paramount (Joseph Sargent)

A New Orleans criminal insurance investigator is blinded in a chase but carries on.
Shades of Edward Arnold in *Eyes in the Night*. This very moderate mystery led to a one-season series.

w Stirling Silliphant *d* Joseph Sargent

James Franciscus, Bradford Dillman, John McIntire, Jeanette Nolan

Look Back in Anger*
GB 1959 99m bw
ABP / Woodfall (Gordon L. T. Scott)

A bad-tempered young man with a grudge against life and the government runs a market stall, lives in a squalid flat, and has an affair with his wife's best friend.
Well-made version of a play whose sheer dreariness was theatrically stimulating but in terms of film realism becomes only depressing and stupid despite competence all round. It also set shoddy standards for its many less proficient imitators.

w Nigel Kneale, *play John Osborne* *d* Tony Richardson *ph Oswald Morris* *m* Chris Barber

Richard Burton, Mary Ure, Claire Bloom, Edith Evans, Gary Raymond, Glen Byam Shaw, Phyllis Neilson-Terry, Donald Pleasance, George Devine

Look for the Silver Lining*
US 1949 106m Technicolor
Warner (William Jacobs)

The life story of twenties stage star Marilyn Miller.
Harmless musical biopic with a sense of humour.

w Phoebe and Henry Ephron, Marian Spitzer, Bert Kalmar, Harry Ruby *d* David Butler
ph Peverell Marley *md* David Buttolph

June Haver, *Ray Bolger, Charles Ruggles*, Gordon Macrae, Rosemary de Camp, S. Z. Sakall, Walter Catlett

The Looking Glass War
GB 1969 107m Technicolor Panavision
Columbia / M. J. Frankovich

The British secret service sends a young Pole into East Germany to find a top secret film.
Jaundiced spy story which aims for irony and tragedy but becomes merely verbose and irritating.

wd Frank R. Pierson, *novel* John Le Carré
ph Austin Dempster *m* Wally Scott

Christopher Jones, Pia Degermark, Ralph Richardson, Anthony Hopkins, Paul Rogers, Susan George, Ray McAnally, Robert Urquhart, Maxine Audley, Anna Massey

'There are a lot of incidental pleasures, but in the final analysis they only add up to half a film.'—*Nigel Andrews*

Loot*
GB 1970 101m Eastmancolor
Performing Arts Ltd (Arthur Lewis)

A crook hides his mother's body and uses the coffin to carry the proceeds of a robbery.
Breakneck black farce which still can't move quite fast enough to cover up its bad taste, though well done by all concerned.

w Ray Galton, Alan Simpson, *play* Joe Orton
d Silvio Narizzano *ph* Austin Dempster
m Keith Mansfield, Richard Willing-Denton
ad Anthony Pratt

Richard Attenborough, Lee Remick, Hywel Bennett, Milo O'Shea, Dick Emery

Lord Jeff
US 1938 78m bw
MGM (Frank Davis)
GB title: *The Boy from Barnardo's*

A well-brought-up boy gets into trouble and is sent under supervision to a naval school.
Adequate family film with absolutely no surprises.

w Bradford Roper, Val Burton, André Boehm
d Sam Wood *ph* John Seitz *m* Edward Ward

Freddie Bartholemew, Mickey Rooney, Charles Coburn, Herbert Mundin, Terry Kilburn, Gale Sondergaard, Peter Lawford

Lord Jim*
GB 1964 154m Technicolor Super Panavision
Columbia / Keep (René Dupont)

Adventures of a sailor who prowls the Far East looking for truth; he helps enslaved natives, is raped by a tribal chief, and finally sacrifices his life.
Lush and very boring farrago of miscellaneous incident, with a central character about whose fate no one can care. However, an expensive production must have its points of interest, and the belated introduction of a gentleman villain gives a little edge.

wd Richard Brooks, *novel* Joseph Conrad *ph Frederick A. Young* *m* Bronislau Kaper *pd* Geoffrey Drake

Peter O'Toole, *James Mason*, Eli Wallach, Paul Lukas, Jack Hawkins, Daliah Lavi, Curt Jurgens, Akim Tamiroff

Lord Love a Duck*
US 1966 105m bw
UA / Charleston (George Axelrod)

A senior Los Angeles student practises hypnotism on his girl friend.
Rather sloppy satire on American culture and fancies, dressed up as crazy comedy; occasional laughs.

w Larry H. Johnson, George Axelrod, *novel* Al Hine *d* George Axelrod *ph* Daniel Fapp *m* Neal Hefti

Roddy McDowall, Tuesday Weld, Lola Albright, Ruth Gordon, Harvey Korman, Max Showalter

Lord of the Flies
GB 1963 91m bw
Allen–Hogdon Productions / Two Arts (Lewis M. Allen)

After a plane crash, a party of English schoolboys are stranded on an uncharted tropical island and gradually turn savage.
Semi-professional production of a semi-poetic novel which worked well on the printed page but on screen seems crude and unconvincing.

wd Peter Brook, *novel* William Golding *ph* Tom Hollyman, Gerald Feil *m* Raymond Leppard

James Aubrey, Tom Chapin, Hugh Edwards, Roger Elwin, Tom Gaman

Lorna Doone**
GB 1934 90m bw
ATP (Basil Dean)

In 1625 on Exmoor, a farmer comes to love an outlaw's daughter who proves to be in reality a kidnapped heiress.
Simple, straightforward, effective version of the famous romance, with refreshing use of exteriors.

w Dorothy Farnum, Miles Malleson, Gordon Wellesley, *novel* R. D. Blackmore *d Basil Dean*

Victoria Hopper, John Loder, Margaret Lockwood, *Roy Emerton*, Edward Rigby, Mary Clare, Roger Livesey, George Curzon, D. A. Clarke-Smith, Lawrence Hanray, Amy Veness, Eliot Makeham

Lorna Doone
US 1951 89m Technicolor
Columbia (Edward Small)

Grotesque remake which treats the story like a cheap western.

w Jesse L. Lasky Jnr, Richard Schayer *d* Phil Karlson *ph* Charles Van Enger *m* George Duning

Barbara Hale, Richard Greene, Anne Howard, William Bishop, Carl Benton Reid, Ron Randell, Sean McClory, Onslow Stevens, Lester Matthews, John Dehner

Lost*
GB 1955 89m Technicolor
Rank (Vivian A. Cox)

The police go on the trail of a stolen child.
Mildly effective semi-documentary police story, with good use of locations.

w Janet Green *d* Guy Green *ph* Harry Waxman *m* Benjamin Frankel

David Farrar, David Knight, Julia Arnall, Anthony Oliver, Thora Hird, Eleanor Summerfield, Marjorie Rhodes, Joan Sims

Lost Angel*
US 1946 91m bw
MGM (Robert Sisk)

A lost little girl is adopted by a reporter.
Good star vehicle for the sentimentally-inclined, with solid production and casting back-up.

w Isabel Lennart *d* Roy Rowland *ph* Robert Surtees *m* Daniele Amfitheatrof

Margaret O'Brien, James Craig, Marsha Hunt, Philip Merivale, Henry O'Neill, Donald Meek, Keenan Wynn

'A beautiful opportunity for true satire is offered and, I regret to say, thrown away. For our little Gulliver is rapidly decivilized by all the familiar bromidic palliatives: love, crooning, fairies and night clubs.'—*Richard Winnington*

Lost Boundaries*
US 1949 105m bw
Film Classics (Louis de Rochemont)

In a New Hampshire town in the forties, a beloved doctor and his wife are found to have negro blood.
Well-meaning but dramatically ineffective racial drama which meanders along allowing an occasional burst of genuine feeling to come through.

w Virginia Shaler, Eugene Ling *d* Alfred Werker *ph* William J. Miller *m* Louis Applebaum

Mel Ferrer, Beatrice Pearson, Richard Hylton, Susan Douglas, Canada Lee, Grace Coppin

'It cannot be said to betray its subject, but is, rather, unequal to it.'—*Gavin Lambert*

Lost Command
US 1966 128m Technicolor Panavision
Columbia / Red Lion (Mark Robson)

Adventures of a French paratroop regiment in Indo-China and Algeria.
Anti-war war adventure; noisy but scarcely inspired.

w Nelson Gidding, *novel* The Centurions by Jean Larteguy *d* Mark Robson *ph* Robert Surtees *m* Franz Waxman

Anthony Quinn, Alain Delon, George Segal, Michèle Morgan, Maurice Ronet, Claudia Cardinale, Grégoire Aslan, Jean Servais

The Lost Continent*
GB 1968 98m Technicolor
Hammer (Michael Carreras)

The captain of a tramp steamer illegally carries dynamite, and he and his passengers are stranded in a weird Sargasso Sea colony run by the Spanish Inquisition.
Hilariously imaginative hokum with splendid art direction and some of the grottiest monsters on film; but memorable moments do not quite add up to a classic of the genre.

w Michael Nash, *novel* Uncharted Seas by Dennis Wheatley *d* Michael Carreras *ph* Paul Beeson *m* Gerard Schurmann *sp* Robert A. Mattey, Cliff Richardson *ad Arthur Lawson*

Eric Porter, Hildegarde Neff, Suzanna Leigh, Tony Beckley, Nigel Stock, Neil McCallum, Jimmy Hanley, James Cossins, Victor Maddern

'One of the most ludicrously enjoyable bad films since *Salome Where She Danced.*'—*MFB*

Lost Flight
US 1969 105m Technicolor TVM
Universal

After a plane crash in an island jungle, the passengers learn to survive.
Memories of *Five Came Back*, and of another ill-fated series called *The New People*. This one did not take—it was not very good—but 1976 brought yet another pilot on the theme.

w Dean Riesner *d* Leonard Horn

Lloyd Bridges, Anne Francis, Bobby Van, Ralph Meeker, Andrew Prine, Linden Chiles

Lost Horizon****
US 1937 130m (released at 118m) bw
Columbia (Frank Capra)

Escaping from an Indian revolution, four people are kidnapped by plane and taken to an idyllic civilization in a Tibetan valley, where the weather is always kind and men are not only gentle to each other but live to a very advanced age.
Much re-cut romantic adventure which leaves out some of the emphasis of a favourite Utopian novel but stands up pretty well on its own, at least as a supreme example of Hollywood moonshine, with perfect casting, direction and music. If the design has a touch of Ziegfeld, that's Hollywood.

w Robert Riskin, novel James Hilton d Frank Capra ph Joseph Walker *m Dmitri Tiomkin ad* Stephen Goosson

Ronald Colman, H. B. Warner, Thomas Mitchell, Edward Everett Horton, Sam Jaffe, Isabel Jewell, Jane Wyatt, Margo, John Howard

'One of the most impressive of all thirties films, a splendid fantasy which, physically and emotionally, lets out all the stops.'—*John Baxter, 1968*

'One is reminded of a British critic's comment on *Mary of Scotland*, "the inaccuracies must have involved tremendous research".'—*Robert Stebbins*

Lost Horizon*
US 1972 143m Panavision Technicolor
Columbia / Ross Hunter

Torpid remake with a good opening followed by slabs of philosophizing dialogue and an unbroken series of tedious songs.

w Larry Kramer *d* Charles Jarrott *ph Robert Surtees m* Burt Bacharach *ad* Preston Ames

Peter Finch, Liv Ullman, Sally Kellerman, *Bobby Van*, George Kennedy, Michael York, Olivia Hussey, James Shigeta, John Gielgud, Charles Boyer

Lost in a Harem**
US 1944 89m bw
MGM

Two travelling entertainers in the Middle East get mixed up with a conniving sultan, who hypnotizes them.
Lively, well-staged romp which shows the comedians at their best and uses astute borrowings from burlesque, pantomime, and Hollywood traditions of fantasy and running jokes.

w Harry Ruskin, John Grant, Harry Crane d Charles Reisner ph Lester White *m* David Snell

Bud Abbott, Lou Costello, Douglass Dumbrille, Marilyn Maxwell, John Conte, Jimmy Dorsey and his Orchestra

The Lost Man
US 1969 113m Technicolor Panavision
Universal (Ernest B. Wehmeyer)

After a robbery, a crook is pursued by the police and goes into hiding.
Odd Man Out made over as a vehicle for polemics about civil rights for blacks: too shiny, too long, too talky to have any grip.

w Robert Alan Aurthur *ph* Jerry Finnerman *m* Quincy Jones

Sidney Poitier, Joanna Shimkus, Al Freeman Jnr, Michael Tolan, Leon Bibb, Richard Dysart, David Steinberg, Paul Winfield

The Lost Moment*
US 1947 89m bw
U-I (Martin Gabel)

An American publisher goes to Venice to recover love letters written by a famous poet to a lady now aged 105.
Slightly absurd but memorable period drama with a guilty secret eventually coming to light, all put across with apparently deliberate artificiality.

w Leonardo Bercovici, *novel* The Aspern Papers by Henry James *d* Martin Gabel *ph Hal Mohr m* Daniele Amfitheatrof

Robert Cummings, Susan Hayward, *Agnes Moorehead*, Joan Lorring, Eduardo Ciannelli

'A compelling piece, highly stylized and very personal, with a beautifully photographed studio recreation of Venice.'—*NFT, 1973*

The Lost Patrol***
US 1934 74m bw
RKO (Cliff Reid)

A small British army group is lost in the Mesopotamian desert under Arab attack.
Much-copied adventure story of a small patrol under attack (compare *Sahara, Bataan* and *The Last of the Comanches* for a start). The original now seems pretty starchy but retains moments of power.

w Dudley Nichols, story Patrol by Philip MacDonald *d John Ford ph Harold Wenstrom m* Max Steiner

Victor McLaglen, Boris Karloff, Wallace Ford, Reginald Denny, J. M. Kerrigan, Billy Bevan, Alan Hale

The Lost People
GB 1949 89m bw
GFD / Gainsborough (Gordon Wellesley)

Displaced persons gather for comfort in a disused German theatre.
Once again a very flat film has been unsuitably made from an effective piece of theatre, with all possible types present and all views represented. Not on.

w Bridget Boland, from her play Cockpit *d* Bernard Knowles *ph* Jack Asher *m* John Greenwood

Richard Attenborough, Mai Zetterling, Siobhan McKenna, Dennis Price, Maxwell Reed, William Hartnell, Gerard Heinz, Harcourt Williams, Marcel Poncin

The Lost Squadron*
US 1932 72m bw
RKO

World War I pilots find work stunting for a movie studio.
Unusual comedy-drama with several points of interest.

w Herman J. Mankiewicz, Wallace Smith *d* George Archainbaud *ph* Leo Tover, Edward Cronjager

Richard Dix, Mary Astor, Erich Von Stroheim, Joel McCrea, Dorothy Jordan, Hugh Herbert, Robert Armstrong

The Lost Weekend****
US 1945 101m bw
Paramount *(Charles Brackett)*

Two days in the life of a young dipsomaniac writer.
Startlingly original on its release, this stark little drama keeps its power, especially in the scenes on New York streets and in a dipso ward. It could scarcely have been more effectively filmed.

w Charles Brackett, Billy Wilder, novel Charles Jackson *d Billy Wilder ph John F. Seitz m* Miklos Rozsa

Ray Milland, Jane Wyman, Philip Terry, *Howard da Silva, Frank Faylen*

The Lost World
US 1960 98m De Luxe Cinemascope
TCF / Saratoga (Irwin Allen)

Professor Challenger is financed by a newspaper to confirm the report of prehistoric life on a South African plateau.
Pitiful attempt to continue the success of *Journey to the Center of the Earth*, with the story idiotically modernized, unconvincing monsters, a script which inserts conventional romance and villainy, and fatal miscasting of the central part.

w Irwin Allen, Charles Bennett, *novel* Sir Arthur Conan Doyle *d* Irwin Allen *ph* Winton C. Hoch *m* Bert Shefter, Paul Sawtell

Claude Rains, *Michael Rennie*, David Hedison, *Richard Haydn*, Fernando Lamas, Jill St John, Ray Stricklyn

'Resembles nothing so much as a ride on a rundown fairground Ghost Train.'—*MFB*

Louis Armstrong, Chicago Style*
US 1975 74m colour TVM
Charles Fries / Dick Berg

The famous musician struggles for his fame and fights the mob.
Presumably true anecdotes, quite well made and entertaining.

w James Lee *d* Lee Phillips

Ben Vereen, Red Buttons, Janet McLachlan, Margaret Avery

Louisiana Purchase*
US 1941 98m Technicolor
Paramount (Harold Wilson)

Efforts are made to compromise a politician.
Quite lively transcription of a Broadway musical success with elements of political satire including a climactic filibuster scene.

w Jerome Chodorov, Joseph Fields, *play* Morrie Ryskind *songs* Irving Berlin *d* Irving Cummings *ph* Harry Hallenberger

Bob Hope, Vera Zorina, *Victor Moore*, Irene Bordoni, Dona Drake, Raymond Walburn, Maxie Rosenbloom, Frank Albertson, Donald MacBride, Andrew Tombes

Love Affair
US 1932 68m bw
Columbia

An heiress falls for a flying instructor.
Mild romantic comedy drama.

w Jo Swerling, *story* Ursula Parrott *d* Thornton Freeland *ph* Ted Tetzlaff

Dorothy Mackaill, Humphrey Bogart, Jack Kennedy, Astrid Allwyn, Halliwell Hobbes, Barbara Leonard

Love Affair***
US 1939 89m bw
Paramount (Leo McCarey)

On a transatlantic crossing, a European man of the world meets a New York girl, but their romance is flawed by misunderstanding and physical accident.
The essence of Hollywood romance, and one of the most fondly remembered films of the thirties, perhaps because of the easy comedy sense of the first half.

w Delmer Daves, Donald Ogden Stewart, story Mildred Cram, Leo McCarey *d Leo McCarey ph* Rudolph Maté

Charles Boyer, Irene Dunne, Maria Ouspenskaya, Lee Bowman, Astrid Allwyn, Maurice Moscovitch

'Those excited over the mastery of form already achieved in pictures, will like to follow this demonstration of the qualities of technique and imagination the films must always have and keep on recruiting to their service.'—*Otis Ferguson*

'Clichés of situation and attitude are lifted almost beyond recognition by a morning freshness of eye for each small thing around.'—*Otis Ferguson*

'McCarey brought off one of the most difficult things you can attempt with film. He created a mood, rather than a story; he kept it alive by expert interpolations; he provided comedy when he needed comedy and poignancy when he needed substance; and he did it with the minimum of effort.'—*Pare Lorentz*

† Remade as *An Affair to Remember (qv).*

Love American Style*
US 1969 74m colour TVM
Paramount

Four comedy sketches on the theme of love: a successful series resulted.

w various *d* Charles Rondeau, Marc Daniels, Gary Marshall, Hy Averback

Don Porter, Marjorie Lord, Michael Callan, Penny Fuller, Greg Morris, Darryl Hickman, Robert Reed, Jeannine Riley

Love among the Ruins**
US 1974 100m colour TVM
ABC Circle

An elderly actress turns to a former love for legal counsel in a breach of promise case.
Splendid people are forced to overact because

this high class taradiddle goes on too long and makes their characters unconvincing. Still, it's a delight to have something so civilized.

w James Costigan, *novel* Angela Thirkell *d* George Cukor

Katharine Hepburn, Laurence Olivier, Richard Pearson, Colin Blakely, Joan Sims, Leigh Lawson, Gwen Nelson, Robert Harris

Love and Death*
US 1975 85m De Luxe
UA / Jack Rollins, Charles H. Joffe

In 1812 Russia, a man condemned reviews the follies of his life.
Personalized comedy fantasia inspired by *War and Peace*, Ingmar Bergman and S. J. Perelman. Basically only for star fans.

wd Woody Allen *ph* Ghislain Cloquet *m* Prokofiev

Woody Allen, Diane Keaton, Georges Adel, Despo, Frank Adu

Love and Hisses*
US 1937 84m bw
TCF (Kenneth MacGowan)

A gossip columnist and a bandleader continue their feud.
Moderate sequel to *Wake Up and Live* (qv); it got by.

w Art Arthur, Curtis Kenyon *d* Sidney Lanfield *ph* Robert Planck

Walter Winchell, Ben Bernie and his orchestra, Joan Davis, Bert Lahr, Simone Simon, Ruth Terry

Love and Pain and the Whole Damn Thing
US 1972 113m Eastmancolor
Columbia / Gus (Alan J. Pakula)

An asthmatic young American on holiday in Spain has an affair with an older woman suffering from an incurable disease.
Dreary doomed romance studiously treated as tourist comedy.

w Alvin Sargent *d* Alan J. Pakula *ph* Geoffrey Unsworth *m* Michael Small

Maggie Smith, Timothy Bottoms

The Love Bug**
US 1968 107m Technicolor
Walt Disney (Bill Walsh)

An unsuccessful racing driver finds that his small private Volkswagen has a mind of its own.
Amusing, pacy period fantasy in the best Disney style.

w Bill Walsh, Don da Gradi *d Robert Stevenson* *ph* Edward Colman *m* George Bruns *sp Eustace Lycett*

David Tomlinson, Dean Jones, Michele Lee, Buddy Hackett, Joe Flynn, Benson Fong, Joe E. Ross

Love Crazy*
US 1941 100m bw
MGM (Pandro S. Berman)

When his wife threatens to divorce him, a businessman hatches all manner of crazy schemes, including disguising himself as his own sister.
Zany romantic comedy, over-stretched but with a fair share of hilarity.

w William Ludwig, Charles Lederer, David Hertz *d* Jack Cummings *ph* Ray June *m* David Snell

William Powell, Myrna Loy, Gail Patrick, Jack Carson, Florence Bates, Sidney Blackmer, Vladimir Sokoloff, Donald MacBride, Sig Rumann, Sara Haden, Elisha Cook Jnr, Kathleen Lockhart

Love from a Stranger**
GB 1937 90m bw
Trafalgar (Max Schach)

A young woman realizes she may have married a maniac.
Stalwart suspenser from a popular novel and play.

w Frances Marion, *play* Frank Vosper, *story* Philomel Cottage by Agatha Christie *d* Rowland V. Lee *ph* Philip Tannura

Ann Harding, Basil Rathbone, Binnie Hale, Bruce Seton, Jean Cadell, Bryan Powley, Joan Hickson, Donald Calthrop

Love from a Stranger
US 1947 81m bw
Eagle Lion (James J. Geller)
GB title: *A Stranger Walked In*

Stilted period remake.

w Philip MacDonald *d* Richard Whorf *ph* Tony Gaudio *m* Irving Friedman

Sylvia Sidney, John Hodiak, Ann Richards, John Howard, Isobel Elsom, Frederick Worlock

Love Happy*
US 1949 85m bw
Lester Cowan / Mary Pickford

A group of impoverished actors accidentally gets possession of the Romanov diamonds.
The last dismaying Marx Brothers film, with Harpo taking the limelight and Groucho loping

in for a couple of brief, tired appearances. A roof chase works, but Harpo tries too hard for sentiment, and the production looks shoddy.

w Ben Hecht, Frank Tashlin, Mac Benoff *d* David Miller *ph* William Mellor

Groucho, Harpo, Chico, Eric Blore, Ilona Massey, Marilyn Monroe

Love Has Many Faces
US 1964 104m Eastmancolor
Columbia / Jerry Bresler

A rich woman marries a beach boy and has an affair with another, who is murdered.
Hilarious but unentertaining sex melodrama built around an overage star.

w Marguerite Roberts *d* Alexander Singer *ph* Joseph Ruttenberg *m* David Raksin

Lana Turner, Cliff Robertson, Hugh O'Brian, Stefanie Powers, Ruth Roman, Virginia Grey
'For connoisseurs of perfectly awful movies.'—*Judith Crist*

Love, Hate, Love
US 1970 72m colour TVM
Aaron Spelling

Newlyweds are violently harassed by the girl's ex-suitor.
Rather unpleasant melodrama.

d George McCowan

Ryan O'Neal, Lesley Warren, Peter Haskell

Love in the Afternoon
US 1957 126m bw
AA (Billy Wilder)

The daughter of a private detective warns an American philanderer in Paris that an enraged husband is en route to shoot him.
Tired and dreary romantic sex comedy, miscast and far too long. With the talent around, there are of course a few compensations.

w Billy Wilder, I. A. L. Diamond, *novel* Claude Anet *d* Billy Wilder *ph* William Mellor *m* Franz Waxman *ad* Alexander Trauner

Gary Cooper, Audrey Hepburn, Maurice Chevalier, John McGiver

Love Is a Ball
US 1962 112m Technicolor Panavision
UA / Oxford / Gold Medal (Martin H. Poll)
GB title: *All This and Money Too*

A Riviera matchmaker recruits instructors to train his star pupil, but one of them walks away with the lady.
Forgettable comedy in which more effort goes into the glamorous background than the script.

w David Swift, Tom and Frank Waldman, *novel* The Grand Duke and Mr Pimm by Lindsay Hardy *d* David Swift
ph Edmond Séchan *m* Michel Legrand

Glenn Ford, Charles Boyer, Hope Lange, Ricardo Montalban, Telly Savalas, Ruth McDevitt, Ulla Jacobsson

Love Is a Many Splendored Thing*
US 1955 102m De Luxe Cinemascope
TCF (Buddy Adler)

During the Korean War, a Eurasian lady doctor in Hong Kong falls in love with a war correspondent.
Self-admittedly sentimental soaper with a tragic ending; the theme tune kept it popular for years.

w John Patrick, *novel* Han Suyin *d* Henry King *ph* Leon Shamroy *m* Alfred Newman

Jennifer Jones, William Holden, Torin Thatcher, Isobel Elsom, Murray Matheson, Virginia Gregg, Richard Loo

Love Is News*
US 1937 78m bw
TCF (Earl Carroll, Harold Wilson)

An heiress marries a scoop-hunting reporter just to show him how embarrassing publicity can be.
Silly romantic comedy with plenty of laughs.

w Harry Tugend, Jack Yellen *d* Tay Garnett *ph* Ernest Palmer

Tyrone Power, Loretta Young, Don Ameche, Slim Summerville, Dudley Digges, Walter Catlett, Jane Darwell, Stepin Fetchit, George Sanders, Frank Conroy, Elisha Cook Jnr
† Remade as *That Wonderful Urge* (qv).

Love Letters*
US 1945 101m bw
Paramount (Hal B. Wallis)

A girl who has lost her memory through war shock is threatened by more physical danger.
Oddly unexciting romantic melodrama directed and designed in heavy but satisfying style.
Typical post-war depressive fare.

w Ayn Rand, *novel* Pity My Simplicity by Chris Massie *d William Dieterle* *ph* Lee Garmes *m Victor Young*

Jennifer Jones, Joseph Cotten, Ann Richards, Gladys Cooper, Anita Louise, Cecil Kellaway, Byron Barr, Reginald Denny, Lumsden Hare

The Love Lottery
GB 1953 83m Technicolor
Ealing (Monja Danischewsky)

A British film star is persuaded to offer himself as first prize in a lottery.
Satirical farce which doesn't come off, mainly owing to paucity of comedy ideas.

w Harry Kurnitz *d* Charles Crichton *ph* Douglas Slocombe *m* Benjamin Frankel *pd* Tom Morahan

David Niven, Herbert Lom, Peggy Cummins, Anne Vernon, Charles Victor, Gordon Jackson, Felix Aylmer, Hugh McDermott

The Love Machine
US 1971 110m Eastmancolor
Columbia / Mike Frankovich

Megalomaniac TV reporter progresses to network programme controller but is finally undone by his vivid sex life.
Stodgy, silly melodrama from a bestseller whose inspiration was well known in TV circles.

w Samuel Taylor, *novel* Jacqueline Susann *d* Jack Haley Jnr *ph* Charles Lang Jnr *m* Artie Butler

John Philip Law, Dyan Cannon, Robert Ryan, Jackie Cooper, David Hemmings, Shecky Greene

Love Me or Leave Me**
US 1955 122m Eastmancolor Cinemascope
MGM (Joe Pasternak)

Twenties singer Ruth Etting is befriended by a racketeer who pushes her to the top but drives her to drink and despair in the process.
Agreeably bitter showbiz biopic which gives the impression of being not too far from the truth.

w Daniel Fuchs, Isabel Lennart *d Charles Vidor* *ph* Arthur E. Arling *md* George Stoll *ad* Cedric Gibbons, Urie McCleary

Doris Day, James Cagney, Cameron Mitchell, Robert Keith, Tom Tully, Harry Bellaver, Richard Gaines

Love Me Tender
US 1959 95m bw Cinemascope
TCF (David Weisbart)

Three brothers fall out over loot they have brought home from the Civil War.
Odd western designed (perhaps after shooting began) as Presley's introductory vehicle; he sings four songs before getting shot, and reappears in ghostly form at the end.

w Robert Buckner *d* Robert D. Webb *ph* Leo Tover *m* Lionel Newman

Richard Egan, Debra Paget, Elvis Presley, Robert Middleton, William Campbell, Neville Brand, Mildred Dunnock, Bruce Bennett, James Drury, Ken Clark, Barry Coe

Love Me Tonight****
US 1932 104m bw
Paramount (Rouben Mamoulian)

A Parisian tailor accidentally moves into the aristocracy.
The most fluently cinematic comedy musical ever made, with sounds and words, lyrics and music, deftly blended into a compulsively and consistently laughable mosaic of sophisticated nonsense; one better than the best of Lubitsch and Clair.

w Samuel Hoffenstein, Waldemar Young, George Marion Jnr d Rouben Mamoulian ph Victor Milner songs Rodgers and Hart

Maurice Chevalier, Jeanette MacDonald, Charles Butterworth, Charles Ruggles, Myrna Loy, C. Aubrey Smith, Elizabeth Patterson, Ethel Griffies, Blanche Frederici, Robert Greig

'Gay, charming, witty, it is everything that the Lubitsch musicals should have been but never were.'—*John Baxter, 1968*

'With the aid of a pleasant story, a good musician, a talented cast and about a million dollars, he has done what someone in Hollywood should have done long ago—he has illustrated a musical score.'—*Pare Lorentz*

'It has that infectious spontaneity which distinguishes the American musical at its best.'—*Peter Cowie, 1970*

'A rich amalgam of filmic invention, witty decoration and wonderful songs.'—*NFT, 1974*

Love on the Dole***
GB 1941 100m bw
British National (John Baxter)

Life among unemployed cotton workers in industrial Lancashire between the wars.
Vividly characterized, old-fashioned social melodrama, well made on a low budget; a rare problem picture for Britain at this time.

w Walter Greenwood, Barbara K. Emery, Rollo Gamble, *novel Walter Greenwood d John Baxter*

Deborah Kerr, Clifford Evans, *George Carney*, Joyce Howard, Frank Cellier, Geoffrey Hibbert, *Mary Merrall*, Maire O'Neill, *Marjorie Rhodes*, A. Bromley Davenport, Marie Ault, Iris Vandeleur, Kenneth Griffith

Love on the Run*
US 1936 81m bw
MGM (Joseph L. Mankiewicz)

Rival newspapermen help an heiress to escape an

unwanted wedding and in the process uncover a ring of spies.
Harebrained star farce, smoothly assembled and still fairly funny.

w John Lee Mahin, Manuel Seff, Gladys Hurlbut *d* W. S. Van Dyke *ph* Oliver T. Marsh

Clark Gable, Joan Crawford, Franchot Tone, Reginald Owen, Mona Barrie, Ivan Lebedeff, William Demarest

'A slightly daffy cinematic item of absolutely no importance.'—*New York Times*

The Love Parade**
US 1929 112m bw
Paramount (Ernst Lubitsch)

The prince of Sylvania marries.
Primitive sound operetta set among the idle European rich, with clear but faded instances of the Lubitsch touch.

w Ernest Vajda, Guy Bolton, *play* The Prince Consort by Leon Xanrof and Jules Chancel *d Ernst Lubitsch ph* Victor Milner *songs* Victor Schertzinger, Clifford Grey

Maurice Chevalier, Jeanette MacDonald, Lupino Lane, Lillian Roth, Edgar Norton, Lionel Belmore, Eugene Pallette

'The first truly cinematic screen musical in America.'—*Theodore Huff*

Love Story
GB 1944 112m bw
GFD / Gainsborough (Harold Huth)
US title: *A Lady Surrenders*

In Cornwall during World War II, a half-blind airman falls for a pianist with a weak heart.
Novelettish love story which became popular because of its Cornish Rhapsody.

w Leslie Arliss, Doreen Montgomery, Rodney Ackland, *novel* J. W. Drawbell *d* Leslie Arliss *m Hubert Bath*

Margaret Lockwood, Stewart Granger, Patricia Roc, Tom Walls, Reginald Purdell, Moira Lister

'A splendid, noble and fatuous piece.'—*C. A. Lejeune*

'In psychology and dialogue this is straight out of *Mabel's Weekly*.'—*Richard Winnington*

Love Story*
US 1970 100m Movielab
Paramount (David Golden)

Two students marry; she dies.
A barrage of ripe old Hollywood clichés spiced with new-fangled bad language. In the circumstances, well enough made, and certainly astonishingly popular.

w Erich Segal, from his novelette *d* Arthur Hiller *ph* Dick Kratina *m* Bach, Mozart, Handel

Ali MacGraw, Ryan O'Neal, Ray Milland, John Marley

Love That Brute
US 1950 85m bw
TCF (Fred Kohlmar)

A ruthless Chicago gangleader is actually a softy, leaving his supposedly rubbed-out enemies in a comfortable cellar; a young governess persuades him to reform.
Rickety, dully-scripted gangster farce.

w Darrell Ware, John Lee Mahin, Karl Tunberg *d* Alexander Hall *ph* Lloyd Ahern *m* Cyril Mockridge

Paul Douglas, Jean Peters, Cesar Romero, Joan Davis, Arthur Treacher

Love under Fire
US 1937 75m bw
TCF (Nunnally Johnson)

A detective catches up with a lady jewel thief in Madrid during the Spanish Civil War.
Adequately entertaining but rather tasteless adventure comedy.

w Gene Fowler, Allen Rivkin, Ernest Pascal, *play* Walter Hackett *d* George Marshall *ph* Ernest Palmer *m* Arthur Lange

Loretta Young, Don Ameche, Frances Drake, Walter Catlett, John Carradine, Borrah Minevitch and his Rascals, Sig Rumann, Harold Huber, E. E. Clive, Katherine de Mille

The Love War**
US 1969 74m colour TVM
Spelling–Thomas
aka: *The Sixth Column*

Killers attacking each other in a small California town are actually aliens from another planet fighting for control of Earth.
Smooth, inventive, good-looking science fiction with plenty of suspense.

w David Kidd, Guerdon Trueblood *d George McCowan*

Lloyd Bridges, Angie Dickinson, Harry Basch, Byron Foulger

Love with the Proper Stranger**
US 1964 100m bw
Paramount / Boardwalk (Alan J. Pakula)

A musician tries to help his pregnant shopgirl friend get an abortion, but they decide to get married instead.
Oddly likeable comedy drama set on New

York's Italian East Side, with an excellent location sense.

w Arnold Schulman *d Robert Mulligan* *ph* Milton Krasner *m* Elmer Bernstein

Steve McQueen, Natalie Wood, Tom Bosley, Edie Adams, Herschel Bernardi

The Loved One*
US 1965 118m bw
MGM / Filmways (Neil Hartley)

A young English poet in California gets a job at a very select burial ground.
A pointed satire on the American way of death has been allowed to get out of hand, with writer and actors alike laying it on too thick; but there are pleasantly waspish moments in a movie advertised as 'the film with something to offend everybody'.

w Terry Southern, Christopher Isherwood, *novel* Evelyn Waugh *d* Tony Richardson *ph Haskell Wexler* *m* John Addison *pd* Rouben Ter-Arutunian

Robert Morse, John Gielgud, Rod Steiger, *Liberace,* Anjanette Comer, Jonathan Winters, Dana Andrews, Milton Berle, James Coburn, Tab Hunter, Margaret Leighton, Roddy McDowall, Robert Morley, Lionel Stander

'Even a chaotic satire like this is cleansing, and it's embarrassing to pan even a bad movie that comes out against God, mother and country.'—*Pauline Kael, 1968*

'A spineless farrago of collegiate gags.'—*Stanley Kauffmann*

Lovely to Look At*
US 1952 102m Technicolor
MGM (Jack Cummings)

Three Broadway producers inherit a Paris fashion house.
Lavish but dullish remake of *Roberta* (qv), in itself no great shakes as a storyline; again the fashions and the numbers are the thing.

w George Wells, Harry Ruby *d* Mervyn Le Roy *ph* George J. Folsey *m* Jerome Kern *ad* Cedric Gibbons, Gabriel Scognamillo

Howard Keel, Kathryn Grayson, Ann Miller, Red Skelton

A Lovely Way to Die
US 1968 98m Techniscope
Universal (Richard Lewis)
GB title: *A Lovely Way to Go*

An ex-cop becomes bodyguard to a suspected murderess, but proves her innocent.
Offbeat mélange of caper comedy, black farce, private eye detection, courtroom drama, spectacular action and routine thick ear. Doesn't work.

w A. J. Russell *d* David Lowell Rich *ph* Morris Hartzband *m* Kenyon Hopkins

Kirk Douglas, Sylva Koscina, Eli Wallach, *Martyn Green,* Kenneth Haigh, Sharon Farrell

'The net result is rather as though Philip Marlowe had met Doris Day on his not very inspiring way to the forum.'—*MFB*

Lover Come Back**
US 1961 107m Eastmancolor
U-I / Seven Pictures / Nob Hill / Arwin

Rival executives find themselves advertising a non-existent product.
Fairly sharp advertising satire disguised as a romantic comedy; the most entertaining of the Day-Hudson charmers.

w Stanley Shapiro, Paul Henning *d* Delbert Mann *ph* Arthur E. Arling *m* Frank de Vol

Doris Day, Rock Hudson, *Tony Randall,* Jack Oakie, Edie Adams

Lovers and Other Strangers***
US 1969 104m Metrocolor
ABC / David Susskind

After living together for eighteen months, Susan and Mike decide to get married, and find their parents have sex problems of their own.
Wise, witty and well acted sex farce, with many actors making the most of ample chances under firm directoral control.

w Renée Taylor, Joseph Bologna, David Zelag Goodman *d Cy Howard* *ph Andrew Laszlo* *m* Fred Karlin

Gig Young, Anne Jackson, Richard Castellano, Bonnie Bedelia, Michael Brandon, *Beatrice Arthur,* Robert Dishy, Harry Guardino, Diane Keaton, Cloris Leachman, Anne Meara, *Marian Hailey*

'An extremely engaging comedy.'—*Gillian Hartnoll*

The Loves of Carmen
US 1948 99m Technicolor
Columbia (Charles Vidor)

In 1820s Seville, a dragoon corporal is enslaved by a gypsy, kills her husband and becomes an outlaw.
Unrewarding version of the original much-filmed story, with both stars plainly wishing they were elsewhere.

w Helen Deutsch, *novel* Prosper Mérimée *d* Charles Vidor *ph* William Snyder *m* Mario Castelnuovo-Tedesco

Rita Hayworth, Glenn Ford, Victor Jory, Ron

Randell, Luther Adler, Arnold Moss, Margaret Wycherly, Bernard Nedell

The Loves of Joanna Godden
GB 1947 89m bw
Ealing (Sidney Cole)

On Romney Marsh at the turn of the century, a woman farmer has three suitors.
Dullish 'woman's picture'.

w H. E. Bates, Angus Macphail, *novel* Sheila Kaye-Smith *d* Charles Frend

Googie Withers, John McCallum, Jean Kent, Derek Bond, Chips Rafferty, Henry Mollison, Sonia Holm, Edward Rigby, Josephine Stuart

Lovin' Molly*
US 1973 98m Movielab
Stephen Friedman (David Golden)

In Texas between 1925 and 1945, two men friends and an accommodating lady have a shifting relationship.
Odd little drama compendium, with fragments told by each in turn; too slight in structure and substance for complete success, but interesting most of the way.

w Stephen Friedman, *novel* Leaving Cheyenne by Larry McMurtry *d Sidney Lumet*
ph Edward Brown *m* Fred Hellerman

Blythe Danner, Anthony Perkins, Beau Bridges, Edward Binns, Susan Sarandon

Loving**
US 1970 90m Eastmancolor
Columbia / Brooks Ltd (Don Devlin)

A commercial artist reaches crisis point with both his wife and his mistress.
Smart New Yorkish sex comedy, typical of many but better than most.

w Don Devlin, novel Brooks Wilson Ltd by J. M. Ryan *d Irvin Kershner ph* Gordon Willis
m Bernardo Segall *pd* Walter Scott Herndon

George Segal, Eva Marie Saint, Sterling Hayden, Keenan Wynn, Nancie Phillips, Janis Young, David Doyle

Loving You
US 1957 101m Technicolor Vistavision
Paramount / Hal B. Wallis

A press agent signs a young hillbilly singer to give zest to her husband's band.
Empty-headed, glossy star vehicle.

w Herbert Baker, Hal Kanter *d* Hal Kanter
ph Charles Lang Jnr

Elvis Presley, Lizabeth Scott, Wendell Corey, Dolores Hart, James Gleason

Lucas Tanner
US 1974 74m Technicolor TVM
Universal (David Victor)

A baseball coach becomes an English teacher.
Dull pilot which became a dull series.

w Jerry McNeely *d* Richard Donner

David Hartman, Joe Garagiola, Kathleen Quinlan, Rosemary Murphy

The Luck of Ginger Coffey*
Canada / US 1964 100m bw
Crawley / Roth–Kershner (Leon Roth)

An Irish layabout in Canada finds it difficult to keep a job or protect his family.
Mildly interesting character study with good background detail of Montreal.

w Brian Moore, from his novel *d* Irvin Kershner
ph Manny Wynn *m* Bernardo Segall

Robert Shaw, Mary Ure, Liam Redmond

The Luck of the Irish*
US 1947 99m bw
TCF (Fred Kohlmar)

A New York newsman's love life is complicated by a helpful leprechaun he meets in Ireland.
Hollywood moonshine, second class: the will and the players are there, but the script is not funny enough.

w Philip Dunne, *novel* There Was a Little Man by Constance and Guy Jones *d* Henry Koster
ph Joseph La Shelle *m* Cyril Mockridge

Tyrone Power, *Cecil Kellaway*, Anne Baxter, Lee J. Cobb, James Todd, Jayne Meadows, J. M. Kerrigan, Phil Brown

Lucky Jim**
GB 1958 95m bw
British Lion / Charter (Roy Boulting)

At a provincial university, an accident-prone junior lecturer has a disastrous weekend with his girl friend and his professor.
Quite funny in its own right, this is a vulgarization of a famous comic novel which got its effects more subtly, with more sense of place, time and character.

w Jeffrey Dell, Patrick Campbell, *novel* Kingsley Amis *d* John Boulting *ph* Max Greene

Ian Carmichael, Hugh Griffith, Terry-Thomas, Sharon Acker, Jean Anderson, Maureen Connell, Clive Morton, John Welsh, Reginald Beckwith, Kenneth Griffith

Lucky Jordan
US 1942 83m bw
Paramount (Fred Kohlmar)

A con man is drafted and overcomes Nazi agents.
Forgettable star cheapie.

w Darrell Ware, Karl Tunberg *d* Frank Tuttle *ph* John F. Seitz

Alan Ladd, Helen Walker, Sheldon Leonard, Marie McDonald, Mabel Paige, Lloyd Corrigan, Dave Willock, Miles Mander

Lucky Lady
US 1975 118m De Luxe
TCF / Gruskoff / Venture (Michael Gruskoff)

A cabaret girl in 1930 Tijuana joins two adventurers in smuggling liquor into the US by boat.
Whatever can be done wrong with such a story has been done, including irritatingly washed out photography, kinky sex, and sudden switches from farce to gore. None of it holds the interest for a single moment.

w Willard Huyck, Gloria Katz *d* Stanley Donen *ph* Geoffrey Unsworth *m* Ralph Burns *pd* John Barry

Liza Minnelli, Gene Hackman, Burt Reynolds, Michael Hordern, Geoffrey Lewis, Robby Benson

'A manic mess that tries to be all things to all people and ends up offering nothing to anyone.'—*Frank Rich*

Lucky Me*
US 1954 100m Warnercolor Cinemascope
Warner (Henry Blanke)

Theatrical entertainers stranded in Florida get a lucky break.
Watchable, forgettable musical.

w James O'Hanlon, Robert O'Brien, Irving Elinson *d* Jack Donohue *ph* Wilfrid M. Cline *md* Ray Heindorf

Doris Day, Robert Cummings, Phil Silvers, Eddie Foy Jnr, Nancy Walker, Martha Hyer, Bill Goodwin, Marcel Dalio

'The first Cinemascope musical . . . pleasant, light-hearted, frothy entertainment.'—*MFB*

Lucky Night
US 1939 90m bw
MGM (Louis D. Lighton)

An heiress goes out into the world to make a life for herself, and falls for a man she finds on a park bench.
Tedious pattern romance which did neither of its stars any good.

w Vincent Laurence, Grover Jones *d* Norman Taurog *ph* Ray June

Myrna Loy, Robert Taylor, Joseph Allen, Henry O'Neill, Douglas Fowley, Marjorie Main, Charles Lane, Bernard Nedell

Lucky Partners*
US 1940 101m bw

Two strangers share a sweepstake ticket and fall in love.
A very thin comedy kept afloat by its stars.

w Allan Scott, John Van Druten, *story* Bonne Chance by Sacha Guitry *d* Lewis Milestone *ph* Robert de Grasse *m* Dmitri Tiomkin

Ronald Colman, Ginger Rogers, Jack Carson, Spring Byington, Cecilia Loftus, Harry Davenport

Lucy Gallant*
US 1955 104m Technicolor Vistavision
Paramount / Pine–Thomas

The success story of a dressmaker who comes to run a group of fashion shops but neglects her love life.
Efficient, smartly-handled woman's picture.

w John Lee Mahin, Winston Miller, *novel* The Life of Lucy Gallant by Margaret Cousins *d* Robert Parrish *ph* Lionel Lindon *m* Van Cleave

Jane Wyman, Charlton Heston, Claire Trevor, Thelma Ritter, William Demarest, Wallace Ford, Tom Helmore, Mary Field

Lullaby of Broadway*
US 1951 92m Technicolor
Warner (William Jacobs)

The daughter of a faded Broadway star becomes the new toast of the town.
Reasonably lively musical with solid production values but little style or wit.

w Earl Baldwin *d* David Butler *ph* Wilfrid Cline *md* Ray Heindorf

Doris Day, Billy de Wolfe, Gene Nelson, Gladys George, Florence Bates, S. Z. Sakall

Lure of the Wilderness
US 1952 92m Technicolor
TCF (Robert L. Jacks)

A man falsely accused of murder hides for eight years in Georgia's Okefenokee swamp.
Remake of *Swamp Water*, with Walter Brennan playing the same part. The plot works fairly well still, but colour doesn't suit the scenery.

w Louis Lantz, *story* Vereen Bell *d* Jean Negulesco *ph* Edward Cronjager *m* Franz Waxman

Jeffrey Hunter, Jean Peters, Walter Brennan, Constance Smith, Jack Elam

Lured*
US 1947 102m bw
(UA) James Nasser
GB title: *Personal Column*

An American dancer stranded in London helps Scotland Yard catch a killer.
Minor murder mystery with a pleasing cast.

w Leo Rosten, from the French film *Pièges* *d* Douglas Sirk *ph* William Daniels *m* Michel Michelet *pd* Nicolai Remisoff

Lucille Ball, George Sanders, Charles Coburn, Boris Karloff, Cedric Hardwicke, Alan Mowbray, George Zucco, Joseph Calleia, Robert Coote, Alan Napier

Lust for a Vampire
GB 1970 95m Technicolor
Hammer (Harry Fine, Michael Style)

In 1830 an English writer discerns that a pupil in an exclusive mid-European girls' school is a reincarnated vampire.
Moderate Hammer horror.

w Tudor Gates, based on J. Sheridan Le Fanu's Carmilla *d* Jimmy Sangster *ph* David Muir *m* Harry Robinson

Ralph Bates, Michael Johnson, Barbara Jefford, Suzanna Leigh, Yutte Stensgaard, Mike Raven, Helen Christie

Lust for Gold
US 1949 90m bw
Columbia (S. Sylvan Simon)

A young man goes to Arizona to search for a lost gold mine discovered by his grandfather.
Moderate western drama consisting largely of flashback.

w Ted Sherdeman, Richard English, *novel* Thunder God's Gold by Barry Storm *d* S. Sylvan Simon *ph* Archie Stout *m* George Duning

Ida Lupino, Glenn Ford, Gig Young, William Prince, Edgar Buchanan, Will Geer, Paul Ford

Lust for Life**
US 1956 122m Metrocolor Cinemascope
MGM (John Houseman)

The life of Vincent Van Gogh.
Fairly absorbing, not inaccurate, but somehow uninspiring biopic, probably marred by poor colour and wide screen; despite good work all round, it simply doesn't fall into a classic category.

w Norman Corwin, *book* Irving Stone *d* Vincente Minnelli *ph* F. A. Young, Russell Harlan *m* Miklos Rozsa *ad* Cedric Gibbons, Hans Peters, Preston Ames

Kirk Douglas, Anthony Quinn (as Gauguin), James Donald, Pamela Brown, Everett Sloane, Niall MacGinnis, Noel Purcell, Henry Daniell, Lionel Jeffries, Madge Kennedy, Jill Bennett, Laurence Naismith

The Lusty Men*
US 1952 113m bw
RKO / Wald–Krasna (Jerry Wald)

Tensions lead to the death of one of a pair of rider friends on a rodeo tour.
Standard melodrama with semi-documentary detail and star performances.

w Horace McCoy, David Dortort *d* Nicholas Ray *ph Lee Garmes* *m* Roy Webb

Robert Mitchum, Arthur Kennedy, Susan Hayward, Arthur Hunnicutt

Luther*
US 1973 112m Eastmancolor
American Express / Ely Landau / Cinevision

In 1525, the teachings of Luther culminate in the Peasants' Revolt.
Hard-to-watch filming by the American Film Theatre of a singularly theatrical play, and not a very good one at that. Some good acting.

w Edward Anhalt, *play* John Osborne *d* Guy Green *ph* Freddie Young *m* John Addison *pd* Peter Mullins

Stacy Keach, Patrick Magee, Hugh Griffith, Robert Stephens, Alan Badel, Julian Glover, Judi Dench, Leonard Rossiter, Maurice Denham

Luv
US 1967 95m Technicolor Panavision
Columbia / Jalem (Martin Manulis)

When a man prevents an old friend from jumping off the Brooklyn Bridge and brings him home, a sexual square dance develops.
A modern comedy that should have stayed in the theatre.

w Elliott Baker, *play* Murray Shisgal *d* Clive Donner *ph* Ernest Laszlo *m* Gerry Mulligan

Jack Lemmon, Peter Falk, Elaine May, Nina Wayne, Eddie Mayehoff, Paul Hartman, Severn Darden

'A light but incisive comedy about the patterns and language of love in a Freud-ridden society has become an inept and lethally unamusing film farce.'—*MFB*

Luxury Liner
US 1933 72m bw
Paramount

Stories of various passengers on a liner bound from New York to Bremerhaven.
Interesting minor multi-drama, like a rough sketch for *Ship of Fools* (qv).

w Gene Markey, Kathryn Scola, *novel* Gina Kaus *d* Lothar Mendes *ph* Victor Milner

George Brent, Zita Johann, Vivienne Osborne, Alice White, Verree Teasdale, C. Aubrey Smith, Frank Morgan, Henry Wadsworth, Billy Bevan

Luxury Liner
US 1948 98m Technicolor
MGM (Joe Pasternak)

The captain of a liner has trouble with his teenage daughter.
Minor shipboard musical with pleasing talents applied.

w Gladys Lehmann, Richard Connell *d* Richard Whorf *ph* Ernest Laszlo *md* George Stoll

George Brent, Jane Powell, Lauritz Melchior, Frances Gifford, Marina Koshetz, Xavier Cugat, Richard Derr, Connie Gilchrist

Lydia*
US 1941 104m bw
Alexander Korda (Lee Garmes)

An ageing lady recalls her former beaux.
Pleasing remake of *Carnet du Bal*, with excellent production values.

w Ben Hecht, Samuel Hoffenstein, *story* Julien Duvivier, Laszlo Bus-Fekete *d Julien Duvivier ph Lee Garmes m* Miklos Rozsa *pd Vincent Korda*

Merle Oberon, Joseph Cotten, Alan Marshal, Edna May Oliver, Hans Yaray, George Reeves, John Halliday, Sara Allgood

Lydia Bailey
US 1952 89m Technicolor
TCF (Jules Schermer)

In 1802 a Boston lawyer visits Haiti to obtain the signature of a wayward heiress, and becomes involved in the negro fight against the French.
Standard adventure romance with plenty of excitements.

w Michael Blankfort, Philip Dunne, *novel* Kenneth Roberts *d* Jean Negulesco *ph* Harry Jackson *m* Hugo Friedhofer

Dale Robertson, Anne Francis, Charles Korvin, William Marshall, Adeline de Walt Reynolds

M

M*
US 1951 82m bw
Columbia (Seymour Nebenzal)

The criminals of a city combine to track down a child murderer.
Faithful but fated remake of the German classic of 1930; without the heavy expressionist techniques, the story seems merely silly and the atmosphere is all wrong.

w Norman Reilly Raine, Leo Katcher *d* Joseph Losey *ph* Ernest Laszlo *m* Michel Michelet

David Wayne, Howard da Silva, Luther Adler, Martin Gabel, Glenn Anders, Karen Morley, Norman Lloyd, Walter Burke

Ma and Pa Kettle*
US 1949 75m bw
U-I (Leonard Goldstein)

Pa Kettle wins a house in a contest and is accused of cheating.
First of a series of low-budget comedies which, based on characters from *The Egg and I* (qv), had astonishing commercial success in America. The standard varied from adequate to painful.

w Herbert Margolis, Louis Morheim, Al Lewis *d* Charles Lamont *ph* Maury Gertsman *m* Milton Schwarzwald

Marjorie Main, Percy Kilbride, Richard Long, Meg Randall

'Not exactly Noel Coward.'—*Leonard Maltin*

† For others in the series, see under *The Kettles*.

Macabre
US 1958 73m bw
AA (William Castle)

When a small-town doctor's daughter is kidnapped, he fears she may have been buried alive in the cemetery.
Genuine but unsuccessful attempt to film a horror comic; incredibly stodgy writing, acting and direction put the lid on it.

w Robb White *d* William Castle *ph* Carl Guthrie *m* Les Baxter

William Prince, Jim Backus, Jacqueline Scott, Philip Tonge, Ellen Corby

'A ghoulish but totally ineffective horror piece, set mainly in undertakers' offices and an atmosphere of graveyards and swirling fog.'—*MFB*

† When first released, admission carried insurance against death by fright. Some said it should have been death by boredom.

Macao
US 1952 81m bw
RKO (Alex Gottlieb)

A wandering American in the Far East helps a detective catch a gangster.
A few flashy decorative touches show the director's hand, otherwise this is routine, murky thick ear.

w Bernard C. Schoenfeld, Stanley Rubin *d* Josef Von Sternberg (and Nicholas Ray) *ph* Harry J. Wild *m* Anthony Collins

Robert Mitchum, Jane Russell, William Bendix, Gloria Grahame, Thomas Gomez

Macbeth*
US 1948 89m bw
Republic (Orson Welles)

A famous—or infamous attempt to film Shakespeare in twenty-one days in papier maché settings running with damp: further hampered by the use of a form of unintelligible bastard Scots. A few striking moments at the beginning remain: the rest should be silence.

d Orson Welles *ph John L. Russell* *m* Jacques Ibert *ad* Fred Ritter

Orson Welles, Jeanette Nolan, Dan O'Herlihy, Roddy McDowall, Edgar Barrier, Robert Coote

Macbeth*
GB 1971 140m Technicolor
Todd-AO 35
Playboy / Caliban (Andrew Braunsberg)

A sharpened and brutalized version; the blood swamps most of the cleverness and most of the poetry.

d Roman Polanski *ph Gilbert Taylor* *m* the Third Ear Band *pd Wilfrid Shingleton*

Jon Finch, Francesca Annis, Martin Shaw, Nicholas Selby, John Stride

McCabe and Mrs Miller
US 1971 120m Technicolor Panavision
Warner (David Foster, Mitchell Brower)

At the turn of the century a gambling gunfighter comes to a northwest mining town and uses his money to set up lavish brothels.
Obscurely scripted, muddy-coloured and harshly recorded western melodrama whose squalid 'realism' comes as close to fantasy as does *The Wizard of Oz*.

w Robert Altman, Brian Mackay, *novel* McCabe by Edmund Naughton *d* Robert Altman *ph* Vilmos Zsigmond *pd* Leon Ericksen

Warren Beatty, Julie Christie, René Auberjonois, Shelley Duvall, John Schuck

'A fleeting, diaphanous vision of what frontier life might have been.'—*Pauline Kael*

'Altman directed *M*A*S*H*, which wandered and was often funny; then *Brewster McCloud*, which wandered and was not funny; now this, which wanders and is repulsive. The thesis seems to be that if you take a corny story, fuzz up the exposition, vitiate the action, use a childishly ironic ending, and put in lots of profanity and nudity, you have Marched On with Time.'—*Stanley Kauffmann*

McCloud see Mystery Movie

The McConnell Story
US 1955 107m Warnercolor Cinemascope
Warner (Henry Blanke)
GB title: *Tiger in the Sky*

The career and accidental death of a jet ace of the Korean war.
Crude, obvious and saccharine biopic.

w Ted Sherdeman, Sam Rolfe *d* Gordon Douglas *ph* John Seitz, Ted McCord *m* Max Steiner

Alan Ladd, June Allyson, James Whitmore, Frank Faylen, Willis Bouchey

McCoy see Mystery Movie

Macho Callahan
US 1970 100m Movielab Panavision
Avco / Felicidad (Bernard Kowalski, Martin C. Schute)

A vengeful cowboy annihilates all who stand in his way.
Squalid Mexican-made western with unremitting emphasis on violence.

w Clifford Newton Gould *d* Bernard Kowalski *ph* Gerry Fisher *m* Pat Williams

David Janssen, Lee J. Cobb, David Carradine, James Booth

MacKenna's Gold*
US 1969 136m Technicolor Super Panavision
Columbia / Highroad (Carl Foreman, Dmitri Tiomkin)

A dying Indian entrusts a sheriff with a map of the legendary Valley of Gold, and when the news breaks the map is in demand.
Curious serial-like western melodrama packed with stars and pretensions above its station. On a lower level, it is quite enjoyable.

w Carl Foreman, *novel* Will Henry *d* J. Lee-Thompson *ph* Joseph MacDonald, Harold Wellman *m* Quincy Jones *pd* Geoffrey Drake

Gregory Peck, Omar Sharif, Telly Savalas, Camilla Sparv, Keenan Wynn, Julie Newmar, Ted Cassidy, Eduardo Ciannelli, Eli Wallach, Edward G. Robinson, Raymond Massey, Burgess Meredith, Anthony Quayle, Lee J. Cobb

'Preposterous hotch-potch of every cliché known to the gold lust book.'—*MFB*

'Twelve-year-olds of all ages might tolerate it.'—*Judith Crist*

'A western of truly stunning absurdity, a thriving example of the old Hollywood maxim about how to succeed by failing big.'—*Vincent Canby*

The McKenzie Break*
GB 1970 106m De Luxe
UA / Levy–Gardner–Laven

During World War II, German prisoners at a Scottish camp stage an escape.
Effective little action suspenser.

w William Norton *d* Lamont Johnson *ph* Michael Reed *m* Riz Ortolani

Brian Keith, Helmut Griem, Ian Hendry, Jack Watson, Patrick O'Connell, Horst Janson

The Mackintosh Man*
GB 1973 99m Technicolor
Warner / Newman–Foreman / John Huston

A government agent is sent to prison to contact a criminal gang.
Convoluted but entertaining spy thriller with good performances and action sequences.

w Walter Hill, *novel* The Freedom Trap by Desmond Bagley *d* John Huston *ph* Oswald Morris *m* Maurice Jarre

Paul Newman, James Mason, Dominique Sanda, Nigel Patrick, Harry Andrews, Michael Hordern, Ian Bannen, Peter Vaughan, Roland Culver, Percy Herbert, Robert Lang, Leo Genn

McLintock*
US 1963 127m Technicolor Panavision
UA / Batjac (Michael Wayne)

A cattle baron can control a whole town but not his termagant wife.
Sub-Ford western farce borrowed from *The Taming of the Shrew*, with much fist-fighting and mud-splattering, and rather too much chat in between.

w James Edward Grant *d* Andrew V. McLaglen *ph* William H. Clothier *m* Frank de Vol

John Wayne, Maureen O'Hara, Yvonne de Carlo, Patrick Wayne, Stefanie Powers, Chill Wills, Bruce Cabot, Jack Kruschen

The McMasters
US 1969 90m Technicolor
JayJen (Dimitri de Grunwald)

A black man returning home from the Civil War gets unexpected help from a tough landowner.
Racial western with black, white and red points of view, all very violently expressed.

w Harold Jacob Smith *d* Alf Kjellin *ph* Lester Shorr *m* Coleridge-Taylor Parkinson

Brock Peters, Burl Ives, David Carradine, Nancy Kwan, Jack Palance, Dane Clark, John Carradine, I.Q. Jones, R. G. Armstrong

McMillan and Wife see Mystery Movie

The Macomber Affair*
US 1947 89m bw
(UA) Benedict Bogeaus (Casey Robinson)

The wife of a bullying big game hunter falls for their guide.
Safari melodrama with a plot which has become a cliché but seemed fresh enough at the time. Goodish writing and acting.

w Casey Robinson, *story* The Short Happy Life of Francis Macomber by Ernest Hemingway *d* Zoltan Korda *ph* Karl Struss *m* Miklos Rozsa

Gregory Peck, Joan Bennett, Robert Preston, Reginald Denny, Carl Harbord, Jean Gillie

Macon County Line
US 1973 89m Eastmancolor
Sam Arkoff / Max Baer

In mid-fifties Louisiana, a couple of hell-raisers are harassed by a local sheriff, and much bloodshed results.
Shapeless melodrama more or less in the wake of *Easy Rider*; an unattractive film which unaccountably had great box-office success.

w Max Baer, Richard Compton *d* Richard Compton *ph* Daniel Lacambre *m* Stu Phillips

Alan Vint, Cheryl Waters, Geoffrey Lewis, Joan Blackman, Jesse Vint, Max Baer

McQ
US 1974 111m Technicolor Panavision
Warner / Batjac / Levy–Gardner

A Seattle police detective goes after the gangster who killed his friend.
Rambling, violent thriller with good sequences but no cohesion.

w Lawrence Roman *d* John Sturges *ph* Harry Stradling Jnr *m* Elmer Bernstein

John Wayne, Eddie Albert, Diana Muldaur, Colleen Dewhurst, Clu Gulager, David Huddleston, Julie Adams

Mad about Music*
US 1938 98m bw
Universal (Joe Pasternak)

A girl at a Swiss school adopts a personable visitor as her father.
Pleasing star vehicle with charm and humour; badly remade as *Toy Tiger* (qv).

w Bruce Manning, Felix Jackson *d* Norman Taurog *ph* Joseph Valentine *m/ly* Harold Adamson, Jimmie McHugh

Deanna Durbin, Herbert Marshall, Gail Patrick, Arthur Treacher, Helen Parrish, Marcia Mae Jones, William Frawley

The Mad Doctor
US 1941 90m bw
Paramount (George Arthur)

A doctor marries wealthy women and then murders them.
Naïve melodrama of little interest except as a vehicle for its star.

w Howard J. Green *d* Tim Whelan *ph* Ted Tetzlaff

Basil Rathbone, Ellen Drew, John Howard, Barbara Allen, Ralph Morgan, Martin Kosleck

The Mad Genius
US 1931 81m bw
Warner

A crippled puppeteer adopts a boy and makes him into a great dancer.
Curious variation on *Trilby*, filmed as *Svengali* the previous year with much the same cast. Not a great success: the script is dreadful.

w J. Grubb Alexander, Harvey Thew, *play* The Idol by Martin Brown *d* Michael Curtiz *ph* Barney McGill *ad Anton Grot*

John Barrymore, Marian Marsh, Donald Cook, Luis Alberni, Carmel Myers, Charles Butterworth, Boris Karloff, Frankie Darro

Mad Love**

US 1935 83m bw
MGM (John Considine Jnr)
GB title: *The Hands of Orlac*

A pianist loses his hands in an accident; a mad surgeon, in love with the pianist's wife, grafts on the hands of a murderer.
Absurd Grand Guignol done with great style which somehow does not communicate itself in viewer interest, only in cold admiration.

w Guy Endore, P. J. Wolfson, John Balderston, *novel* The Hands of Orlac by Maurice Renard *d Karl Freund ph* Chester Lyons, Gregg Toland *m* Oscar Radin

Colin Clive, Peter Lorre, Frances Drake, Ted Healy, Edward Brophy, Isabel Jewell, Sara Haden

The Mad Miss Manton*

US 1938 80m bw
RKO (Pandro S. Berman)

A zany socialite involves her friends in a murder mystery.
Mildly funny comedy-thriller without too much of either, but a good example of the style of thirties craziness at its zenith.

w Philip G. Epstein *d* Leigh Jason *ph* Nicholas Musuraca *m* Roy Webb

Barbara Stanwyck, Henry Fonda, Sam Levene, Frances Mercer, Stanley Ridges, Whitney Bourne, Hattie McDaniel, Miles Mander

The Mad Room

US 1969 92m Berkey Pathecolor
Columbia / Norman Mauer

A companion kills her wealthy employer so that her mentally retarded brother and sister will have a home.
Tasteless remake of *Ladies in Retirement*, in the brutalized vein which audiences are supposed by producers to want. In modern dress and sharp locations, it succeeds only in being nauseating.

w Bernard Girard, A. Z. Martin *d* Bernard Girard *ph* Harry Stradling Jnr *m* Dave Grusin

Stella Stevens, Shelley Winters, Skip Ward, Carol Cole, Severn Darden

Mad Wednesday*

US 1947 77m bw
Howard Hughes

A middle-aged book-keeper is sacked and goes on the town.
Woolly and unattractive farce which proved something of a disaster for all the talents concerned but historically is of considerable interest. It begins with an excerpt from *The Freshman* and continues to comic adventures with a lion.

wd/pd Preston Sturges (re-edited by others) *ph* Robert Pittack *m* Werner Richard Heymann

Harold Lloyd, Jimmy Conlin, Raymond Walburn, Franklin Pangborn, Al Bridge, Margaret Hamilton, Edgar Kennedy

Madame Bovary

US 1949 114m bw
MGM (Pandro S. Berman)

A passionate girl marries a dull husband, takes a lover, and commits suicide.
Dull, emasculated version of a classic.

w Robert Ardrey, *novel* Gustave Flaubert *d* Vincente Minnelli *m* Miklos Rozsa

Jennifer Jones, Van Heflin, James Mason, Louis Jourdan, Christopher Kent, Gene Lockhart, Gladys Cooper, John Abbott, George Zucco

Madame Butterfly

US 1932 88m bw
Paramount

A Japanese geisha commits hara kiri when an American lieutenant passes her up for a western girl.
Drearily modernized version of the opera without its music; an odd idea to say the least.

w Josephine Lovett, Joseph M. March, *play* David Belasco, John Luther Long *d* Marion Gering *m* David Abel

Sylvia Sidney, Cary Grant, Charlie Ruggles, Sandor Kallay, Irving Pichel, Helen Jerome Eddy

Madame Curie*

US 1944 124m bw
MGM (Sidney Franklin)

The life and marriage of the woman who discovered radium.
Dignified and rather dull biopic which well exemplifies MGM's best production style of the forties.

w Paul Osborn, Paul H. Rameau, *book* Eve Curie *d* Mervyn Le Roy *ph* Joseph Ruttenberg *m* Herbert Stothart *ad* Cedric Gibbons, Paul Groesse

Greer Garson, Walter Pidgeon, Henry Travers, Albert Basserman, Robert Walker, C. Aubrey Smith, Dame May Whitty, Victor Francen, Elsa Basserman, Reginald Owen, Van Johnson

'It achieves a notable triumph in making the discovery of a new element seem almost as glamorous as an encounter with Hedy Lamarr.'—*C. A. Lejeune*

Madame Satan*
US 1930 105m bw
MGM (C. B. de Mille)

When her husband strays, a socialite disguises herself as a mysterious *femme fatale* and wins him back.
Abysmal comedy in which both director and principals appear frozen until the closing reels present a crazy, spectacular party on a dirigible which crashes but allows a happy ending.

w Jeanie Macpherson *d* C. B. de Mille
ph Harold Rosson

Kay Johnson, Reginald Denny, Lillian Roth, Roland Young

Madame Sin*
GB 1971 73m colour TVM
ITC (Lou Morheim)

A former CIA agent is brainwashed by a ray gun and forced to work for a female mastermind operating out of a Scottish castle.
High camp for star fans: not much fun for anyone else.

w Barry Oringer, David Greene *d* David Greene *ph* Tony Richmond *m* Michael Gibbs

Bette Davis, Robert Wagner, Denholm Elliott, Gordon Jackson, Dudley Sutton, Catherine Schell

Madame X*
US 1929 95m bw
MGM

After an accidental death, a wealthy woman disappears and goes down in the world; at a subsequent murder trial she is defended by her unrecognizing son.
Two silent versions (with Dorothy Donnelly and Pauline Frederick) had been made of this old theatrical warhorse; two sound versions followed this one. The thing defies criticism.

w Willard Mack, *play* Alexandre Bisson
d Lionel Barrymore

Ruth Chatterton, Raymond Hackett, Mitchell Lewis, Sidney Toler, Carroll Nye, Lewis Stone, Richard Carle

Madame X*
US 1937 72m bw
MGM (James K. McGuinness)

Competent remake with an excellent cast.

w John Meehan *d* Sam Wood *m* David Snell

Gladys George, John Beal, Warren William, Reginald Owen, Lynne Carver, Henry Daniell, Emma Dunn, Ruth Hussey, George Zucco

Madame X
US 1965 100m Technicolor
Universal / Ross Hunter / Eltee

An elaborately dressed remake which suffered from a wooden lead; the more expensive the production, the more obvious the holes in the plot and the psychology.

w Jean Holloway *d* David Lowell Rich
ph Russell Metty *m* Frank Skinner

Lana Turner, John Forsythe, Ricardo Montalban, *Constance Bennett*, Burgess Meredith, Keir Dullea, Virginia Grey, Warren Stevens

'One is free to enjoy a luxurious wallow in emotions that are all the more enjoyable for having no connection whatever with reality.'—*Brenda Davies*

Made for Each Other*
US 1938 90m bw
David O. Selznick

Problems of a lawyer and his new wife culminate in the near-death of their infant son.
Smooth star tearjerker.

w Jo Swerling *d* John Cromwell *ph* Leon Shamroy *m* Lou Forbes *pd* William Cameron Menzies

Carole Lombard, James Stewart, Charles Coburn, Lucile Watson, Harry Davenport, Eddie Quillan, Esther Dale, Louise Beavers

Made for Each Other*
US 1971 107m De Luxe
TCF / Roy Townshend

Romance between two New Yorkers with inferiority complexes.
Elongated cabaret sketch, a Brooklynesque comedy of flashy brilliance but limited general interest.

w Renée Taylor, Joe Bologna *d* Robert B. Bean
ph William Storz

Renée Taylor, Joe Bologna

Madeleine*
GB 1949 114m bw
GFD / David Lean / Cineguild (Stanley Haynes)

In Victorian Glasgow a well-to-do young woman is accused of murdering her lover, but the verdict is 'not proven'.
Dramatically dead because of its ambiguous ending, this lavish and good-looking treatment of a *cause célèbre* was a mistake for all concerned, but its incidental pleasures are considerable.

w Nicholas Phipps, Stanley Haynes *d David Lean ph Guy Green w* William Alwyn *pd John Bryan costumes* Margaret Furse

Ann Todd, Leslie Banks, Elizabeth Sellars, Ivor Barnard, Ivan Desny, Norman Wooland, Edward Chapman, Barbara Everest, André Morell, Barry Jones, Jean Cadell, John Laurie, Eugene Deckers

Madhouse*
GB 1974 92m Eastmancolor
AIP / Amicus (Milton Subotsky)

A reluctant horror actor makes a comeback and finds himself involved in a series of grisly murders.
In-jokey horror piece with clips from old AIP chillers; quite likeable.

w Greg Morrison, *novel* Devilday by Angus Hall *d Jim Clark ph* Ray Parslow *m* Douglas Gamley

Vincent Price, Peter Cushing, Robert Quarry, Adrienne Corri, Natasha Pyne, Linda Hayden, Barry Dennen

Madigan*
US 1968 100m Techniscope
Universal (Frank P. Rosenberg)

A Brooklyn police detective brings in a dangerous escaped criminal at the cost of his own life.
Lively, well-characterized police thriller with excellent locations.

w Henri Simoun, Abraham Polonsky, *novel* The Commissioner by Richard Dougherty *d Don Siegel ph* Russell Metty *m* Don Costa

Richard Widmark, Henry Fonda, Michael Dunn, Inger Stevens, Harry Guardino, James Whitmore, Susan Clark, Steve Ihnat, Don Stroud, Sheree North, Warren Stevens, Raymond St Jacques
† The character was later resurrected for a TV series also starring Richard Widmark: see Mystery Movie.

Madison Avenue
US 1961 94m bw Cinemascope
TCF (Bruce Humberstone)

An advertising executive plans to revenge himself on his treacherous boss.
Predictable melodrama with an adequate plot but dismal acting and presentation.

w Norman Corwin, *novel* The Build-Up Boys by Jeremy Kirk *d* Bruce Humberstone *ph* Charles G. Clarke *m* Harry Sukman

Dana Andrews, Jeanne Crain, Eleanor Parker, Eddie Albert, Howard St John, Henry Daniell, Kathleen Freeman

'Simply nowhere near grand enough.'—*MFB*

Madonna of the Seven Moons
GB 1944 110m bw
GFD / Gainsborough (R. J. Minney)

Affected by childhood rape, a demure lady has a second life as a daring gypsy.
Novelettish balderdash killed stone dead by stilted presentation; but highly successful in its day.

w Roland Pertwee, Brock Williams, *novel* Margery Lawrence *d* Arthur Crabtree

Phyllis Calvert, Stewart Granger, Patricia Roc, Peter Glenville, John Stuart, Jean Kent, Nancy Price, Peter Murray Hill, Reginald Tate

The Madwoman of Chaillot*
GB 1969 142m Technicolor Panavision
Warner / Commonwealth United (Ely Landau)

An eccentric Parisian lady has equally eccentric friends, but her real life is in the past.
A highly theatrical whimsy which somewhat lacks humour, this should never have been considered as a film, certainly not as an all-star extravaganza; but it was, and it falls flat on its face in the first reel of tedious conversation.

w Edward Anhalt, *play* Jean Giraudoux *d* Bryan Forbes *ph* Claude Renoir, Burnett Guffey *m* Michael J. Lewis *pd* Ray Simm

Katharine Hepburn, Yul Brynner, Danny Kaye, Edith Evans, Charles Boyer, Claude Dauphin, John Gavin, Paul Henreid, Nanette Newman, Oscar Homolka, Margaret Leighton, Giulietta Masina, Richard Chamberlain, Donald Pleasance, Fernand Gravet

'One finds oneself too often longing for the drop of the curtain.'—*Brenda Davies*

'The intentions are honourable—defeat is inevitable.'—*Rex Reed*

'One of Giraudoux's less good and most fragile plays has been rewritten, bloated with inept contemporary references, drawn out to gigantic proportions of humourless vacuity, and peopled with a barrelful of nonacting stars.'—*John Simon*

The Maggie**
GB 1953 93m bw
Ealing (Michael Truman)
US title: *High and Dry*

An American businessman is tricked into sending his private cargo to a Scottish island on an old puffer in need of repair.
Mildly amusing comedy about the wily Scots; not the studio at its best, but pretty fair.

w William Rose d Alexander Mackendrick ph Gordon Dines *m* John Addison

Paul Douglas, *Alex Mackenzie*, James Copeland, Abe Barker, Dorothy Alison, Hubert Gregg, Geoffrey Keen, Andrew Keir, Tommy Kearins

The Magic Bow
GB 1946 106m bw
GFD / Gainsborough

Episodes in the life of the violin virtuoso Paganini.
Poor costumer, dramatically and historically unpersuasive.

w Norman Ginsbury, Roland Pertwee *d* Bernard Knowles *ph* Jack Cox *violin solos Yehudi Menuhin*

Stewart Granger, Jean Kent, Phyllis Calvert, Dennis Price, Cecil Parker, Felix Aylmer, Frank Cellier, Marie Lohr, Henry Edwards

The Magic Box*
GB 1951 118m Technicolor
Festival Films (Ronald Neame)

The life of William Friese-Greene, a British cinema pioneer who died in poverty.
A joint British film industry venture to celebrate the Festival of Britain, this rather downbeat and uneventful story takes on the nature of a pageant or a series of charades, with well-known people appearing to no good purpose. But it means well.

w Eric Ambler *d* John Boulting *ph Jack Cardiff m* William Alwyn *pd* John Bryan

Robert Donat, Margaret Johnson, Maria Schell, John Howard Davies, Renée Asherson, Richard Attenborough, Robert Beatty, Michael Denison, Leo Genn, Marius Goring, Joyce Grenfell, Robertson Hare, Kathleen Harrison, Jack Hulbert, Stanley Holloway, Glynis Johns, Mervyn Johns, Barry Jones, Miles Malleson, Muir Mathieson, A. E. Matthews, John McCallum, Bernard Miles, Laurence Olivier, Cecil Parker, Eric Portman, Dennis Price, Michael Redgrave, Margaret Rutherford, Ronald Shiner, Sybil Thorndike, David Tomlinson, Cecil Trouncer, Peter Ustinov, Kay Walsh, Emlyn Williams, Harcourt Williams, Googie Withers

The Magic Carpet*
US 1971 97m Technicolor TVM
Universal (Ranald MacDougall)

A pretty American student in Rome becomes a tourist guide.
A pleasant tour of Italy, with some nonsense going on in the foreground.

w Ranald MacDougall *d* William A. Graham

Susan St James, Robert Pratt, Nanette Fabray, Jim Backus, Wally Cox

The Magic Christian
GB 1970 95m Technicolor
Commonwealth United / Grand Films (Dennis O'Dell)

An eccentric millionaire spends his wealth deflating those who pursue money or power.
A series of variably funny but always unpleasant sketches, climaxing with citizens delving for spoils in a vat of blood and manure. In its aim to be satirical, very typical of its time.

w Terry Southern, Joseph McGrath, Peter Sellers, *novel* Terry Southern *d* Joseph McGrath *ph* Geoffrey Unsworth *m* Ken Thorne *pd* Assheton Gorton

Peter Sellers, Ringo Starr, Richard Attenborough, Laurence Harvey, Christopher Lee, Spike Milligan, Yul Brynner, Roman Polanski, Raquel Welch, Wilfrid Hyde White, Fred Emney, John Le Mesurier, Dennis Price, Patrick Cargill, John Cleese, Graham Chapman

The Magic Face
US 1951 90m bw
Columbia (Mort Briskin, Robert Smith)

A brilliant German impersonator kills Hitler, takes his place, and leads Germany deliberately into defeat.
Hilariously unlikely anecdote 'as told to William Shirer', performed with vigour but handicapped by a shoddy production.

w Mort Briskin, Robert Smith *d* Frank Tuttle *ph* Tony Braun *m* Herschel Burke Gilbert

Luther Adler, Patricia Knight, Ilka Windish, William L. Shirer

'If Shirer believed this story, then he must be the only person in the world to do so.'—*Gavin Lambert*

Magic Fire
US 1954 94m Trucolor
Republic (William Dieterle)

The life and loves of Richard Wagner.
Remarkably boring biopic with much music but little story or characterization. Ugly colour minimizes German locations.

w Bertita Harding, E. A. Dupont, David Chantler *d* William Dieterle *ph* Ernest Haller *md* Erich Wolfgang Korngold

Alan Badel, Yvonne de Carlo, Peter Cushing, Frederick Valk, Carlos Thompson, Valentina Cortesa

The Magic Sword
US 1962 80m Eastmancolor
UA / Bert I. Gordon

The son of a well-meaning witch rescues a princess from the clutches of an evil sorcerer.
Shaky medieval fantasy on too low a budget.

w Bernard Schoenfeld *d* Bert I. Gordon *ph* Paul Vogel *m* Richard Markowitz *sp* Milt Rice

Basil Rathbone, Estelle Winwood, Gary Lockwood, Anne Helm

Magic Town
US 1947 103m bw
William A. Wellman

An opinion pollster discovers a small town which exactly mirrors the views of the USA at large.
A bright Capraesque idea is extraordinarily dully scripted, the production looks dim, and all concerned are operating one degree under.

w Robert Riskin *d* William A. Wellman *ph* Joseph Biroc *m* Roy Webb

James Stewart, Jane Wyman, Kent Smith, Regis Toomey, Donald Meek

The Magician*
US 1973 73m colour TVM
Paramount

A professional magician uses his trickery to outsmart kidnappers.
Polished nonsense which led to a one-season series of the same ilk.

w Laurence Heath *d* Marvin Chomsky

Bill Bixby, Kim Hunter, Barry Sullivan, Elizabeth Ashley, Signe Hasso, Joan Caulfield, Keene Curtis

The Magnet
GB 1950 79m bw
Ealing (Sidney Cole)

A small boy steals a magnet and accidentally becomes a hero.
Very mild Ealing comedy, not really up to snuff.

w T. E. B. Clarke *d* Charles Frend *ph* Lionel Banes *m* William Alwyn

Stephen Murray, Kay Walsh, William Fox, Meredith Edwards, Gladys Henson, Thora Hird, Wylie Watson

The Magnetic Monster*
US 1953 75m bw
UA / Ivan Tors

A new radio-active element causes 'implosions' of increasing size by drawing energy from the area around it.
Well-told low-budget sci-fi with the audience kept abreast of all developments; the undersea lab scenes are borrowed from an old German film, *Gold*.

w Curt Siodmak, Ivan Tors d Curt Siodmak pd George Van Marter

Richard Carlson, King Donovan, Jean Byron, Byron Foulger

The Magnificent Ambersons****
US 1942 88m bw
RKO (Orson Welles)

A proud family loses its wealth and its control of the neighbourhood, and its youngest male member gets his come-uppance.
Fascinating period drama told in brilliant cinematic snippets; owing to studio interference the last reels are weak, but the whole is a treat for connoisseurs, and a delight in its fast-moving control of cinematic narrative.

wd Orson Welles, novel Booth Tarkington *ph Stanley Cortez m Bernard Herrmann ad Mark-Lee Kirr*

Joseph Cotten, Dolores Costello, Agnes Moorehead, Tim Holt, Anne Baxter, Ray Collins, Richard Bennett, Erskine Sanford, Donald Dillaway

'Rich in ideas that many will want to copy, combined in the service of a story that few will care to imitate.'—*C. A. Lejeune*

Magnificent Doll
US 1946 95m bw
Universal (Jack H. Skirball, Bruce Manning)

Dolly Madison, wife of the President, finds that traitor Aaron Burr is a memory from her own past.
Uneasy historical semi-fiction, badly cast and rather boring, yet with some sense of period style.

w Irving Stone *d* Frank Borzage *ph* Joseph Valentine *m* Harry J. Salter

Ginger Rogers, David Niven, Burgess Meredith, Stephen McNally, Peggy Wood, Robert Barrat

The Magnificent Dope
US 1942 83m bw
TCF (William Perlberg)

As a publicity stunt a success school brings the

nation's most complete failure to New York, and he outsmarts them all.
Dim sub-Capra comedy.

w George Seaton *d* Walter Lang *ph* Peverell Marley *m* Emil Newman

Henry Fonda, Lynn Bari, Don Ameche, Edward Everett Horton, George Barbier, Frank Orth, Hobart Cavanaugh

The Magnificent Matador
US 1955 94m Eastmancolor Cinemascope
Edward L. Alperson
GB title: *The Brave and the Beautiful*

A matador trains his illegitimate son to follow in his footsteps but has a premonition of his death in the ring.
Dreary bullfighting drama with romantic interludes.

w Charles Lang *d* Budd Boetticher *ph* Lucien Ballard *m* Raoul Kraushaar

Anthony Quinn, Maureen O'Hara, Manuel Rojas, Richard Denning, Thomas Gomez, Lola Albright

Magnificent Obsession**
US 1935 112m bw
Universal (John M. Stahl)

The playboy who is half-responsible for the death of a woman's husband and for her own blindness becomes a surgeon and cures her.
Absurd soaper which was phenomenally popular and is certainly well done.

w George O'Neil, Sarah Y. Mason, Victor Heerman, *novel Lloyd C. Douglas d John M. Stahl ph* John Mescall

Irene Dunne, Robert Taylor, Ralph Morgan, Sara Haden, Charles Butterworth, Betty Furness, Arthur Hoyt, Gilbert Emery, Arthur Treacher

Magnificent Obsession**
US 1954 108m Technicolor
Universal (*Ross Hunter*)

Glossy remake which sent Ross Hunter to the commercial heights as a remaker of thirties weepies. This one worked best.

w Robert Blees *d Douglas Sirk ph* Russell Metty *m* Frank Skinner

Jane Wyman, Rock Hudson, Agnes Moorehead, Barbara Rush, Otto Kruger, Gregg Palmer, Paul Cavanagh, Sara Shane

The Magnificent Rebel
US 1960 94m Technicolor
Walt Disney (Peter V. Herald)

Episodes in the life of the young Beethoven.
Solid Disney biopic, shot in Vienna with good period detail.

w Joanne Court *d* Georg Tressler *ph* Goran Strindberg *md* Frederick Stark

Karl Boehm, Ernst Nadhering, Ivan Desny, Gabriele Porks

The Magnificent Seven**
US 1960 138m De Luxe Panavision
UA / Mirisch–Alpha (John Sturges)

A Mexican village hires seven American gunmen for protection against bandits.
Popular western based on the Japanese *Seven Samurai*; good action scenes, but the rest is verbose and often pretentious.

w William Roberts *d* John Sturges *ph* Charles Lang Jnr *m Elmer Bernstein*

Yul Brynner, Steve McQueen, Robert Vaughn, *James Coburn, Charles Bronson*, Horst Buchholz, Eli Wallach, Brad Dexter, Vladimir Sokoloff

The Magnificent Seven Deadly Sins
GB 1971 107m colour
Tigon (Graham Stark)

Compendium of comedy sketches, a very variable ragbag of old jokes.

w Bob Larbey, John Esmonde, Dave Freeman, Barry Cryer, Graham Chapman, Graham Stark, Marty Feldman, Alan Simpson, Ray Galton, Spike Milligan *d* Graham Stark *ph* Harvey Harrison Jnr *m* Roy Budd

Bruce Forsyth, Joan Sims, Roy Hudd, Harry Secombe, Leslie Phillips, Julie Ege, Harry H. Corbett, Ian Carmichael, Alfie Bass, Spike Milligan, Ronald Fraser

The Magnificent Seven Ride
US 1972 100m De Luxe
UA / Mirisch (William A. Calihan)

Tired finale to a patchy series (*Return of the Seven, Guns of the Magnificent Seven*) in which the original leader returns to save a Mexican village once again from bandits. Very modest.

w Arthur Rowe *d* George McCowan *ph* Fred Koenekamp *m* Elmer Bernstein

Lee Van Cleef, Stefanie Powers, Mariette Hartley, Pedro Armendariz Jnr, Luke Askew

The Magnificent Thief*
US 1967 100m Technicolor TVM
Universal (Frank Price)
aka: *A Thief Is a Thief Is a Thief*; *It Takes a Thief*

A master thief is promised parole if he becomes a US agent.
Smooth, silly pilot for a long-running series (*It Takes a Thief*).

w Roland Kibbee, Leslie Stevens *d* Leslie Stevens

Robert Wagner, Senta Berger, John Saxon, Susan St James, Malachi Throne

The Magnificent Yankee*
US 1951 88m bw
MGM (Armand Deutsch)
GB title: *The Man with Thirty Sons*

Episodes in the later life of Judge Oliver Wendell Holmes.
Vaguely well-meaning biopic without much dramatic sense.

w Emmet Lavery, from his play *d* John Sturges *ph* Joseph Ruttenberg *m* David Raksin

Louis Calhern, Ann Harding, Eduard Franz, Philip Ober, Richard Anderson, Edith Evanson

Magnum Force*
US 1973 124m Technicolor Panavision
Warner / Malpaso (Robert Daley)

Inspector Harry Callahan has to track down his partner who is slaughtering gangsters in cold blood.
Toned-down sequel to *Dirty Harry*; the violence is still there but the hero no longer commits it. Proficient, exciting and immoral.

w John Milius *d* Ted Post *ph* Frank Stanley *m* Lalo Schifrin

Clint Eastwood, Hal Holbrook, Mitch Ryan, Felton Perry, David Soul

'A ragbag of western mythology and head-on thuggery.'—*Sight and Sound*

The Magus
GB 1968 116m De Luxe Panavision
TCF / Blazer (John Kohn, Jud Kinberg)

An English schoolmaster on a Greek island is influenced by the local magician.
Fashionable philosophical nonsense, an elaborate mystery with no solution; the kind of film that all concerned begin to wish they had never thought of, especially as the presentation has nothing like the panache required, so that not even the critics liked it.

w John Fowles, from his novel *d* Guy Green *ph* Billy Williams *m* John Dankworth *pd* Don Ashton

Michael Caine, Anthony Quinn, Candice Bergen, Anna Karina, Paul Stassino, Julian Glover, George Pastell

'Faintly ludicrous some of the time and painfully unexciting all of the time.'—*MFB*

'This may not be the most misguided movie ever made, but it's in there pitching.'—*Rex Reed*

'There's enough incoherence pretending to be enigma, sex play and chat about existentialism and self-discovery to make teenagers think they're having an experience; for grown-ups it's an ordeal.'—*Judith Crist*

Mahler*
GB 1974 115m Technicolor
Goodtimes Enterprises (Roy Baird)

Fantasia on the life and times of the Jewish composer.
Fairly successful Ken Russell musical biopic on the lines of his early BBC specials.

wd Ken Russell ph Dick Bush

Robert Powell, Georgiana Hale, Richard Morant, Lee Montague, Rosalie Crutchley, Benny Lee, David Collings

Mahogany
US 1975 109m colour Panavision
Paramount / Nikor (Rob Cohen, Jack Ballard)

The love life of a model and fashion designer.
Virtually a Joan Crawford vehicle redesigned for a black heroine who creates her own clothes. Fairly hilarious.

w John Byrum *d* Berry Gordy *ph* David Watkin *m* Michael Masser

Diana Ross, Billy Dee Williams, Anthony Perkins, Jean-Pierre Aumont, Nina Foch, Beah Richards, Marisa Mell

'The level of silliness rises steadily.'—*Geoff Brown*

'Movies as frantically bad as *Mahogany* can be enjoyed on at least one level; the spectacle of a lot of people making fools of themselves.'—*Time*

'What *Mahogany* does so fascinatingly and sometimes hilariously is to pilfer certain stock clichés of 50's Hollywood and adapt them to a black milieu.'—*Molly Haskell*

Maid of Salem*
US 1937 86m bw
Paramount (Frank Lloyd)

In 1692 Salem, a young girl is accused of witchcraft but saved by her lover.
Remarkably solemn period melodrama, unfortunately betrayed by amiable but miscast leads.

w Bradley King, Walter Ferris, Durward Grinstead *d* Frank Lloyd *ph* Leo Tover *m* Victor Young

Claudette Colbert, Fred MacMurray, Harvey

Stephens, Gale Sondergaard, Louise Dresser, Edward Ellis, Beulah Bondi, Bonita Granville

The Maids
GB 1974 95m Technicolor
Ely Landau / Cinevision

Two Paris maids evolve a sado-masochistic ritual involving the death of their employer, but never go through with it.
Unbalanced and dreary film version of an essentially theatrical play.

w Robert Enders, Christopher Miles, *play* Jean Genet *d* Christopher Miles *ph* Douglas Slocombe *m* Laurie Johnson

Glenda Jackson, Susannah York, Vivien Merchant, Mark Burns

Mail Order Bride
US 1963 83m Metrocolor Panavision
MGM (Richard E. Lyons)
GB title: *West of Montana*

An old westerner tries to find a bride for a wild young man in his charge.
Mild western comedy drama; quite tolerable.

wd Burt Kennedy *ph* Paul C. Vogel *m* George Bassman

Buddy Ebsen, Lois Nettleton, Keir Dullea, Warren Oates, Marie Windsor

The Main Attraction
US 1962 90m Metrocolor
Seven Arts (John Patrick)

A wandering singer causes emotional problems backstage at a circus.
Limp melodrama with the star miscast as a fatal charmer.

w John Patrick *d* Daniel Petrie *ph* Geoffrey Unsworth *m* Andrew Adorian

Pat Boone, Mai Zetterling, Nancy Kwan, Yvonne Mitchell, John Le Mesurier

Main Street to Broadway*
US 1953 102m bw
Lester Cowan Productions

After several reverses a young playwright sees his work through to a Broadway opening night; it fails, but he has learned several lessons.
Curious, flat attempt to show the public how Broadway works, with big stars playing themselves in cameo roles.

w Samson Raphaelson *d* Tay Garnett
ph James Wong Howe

Tom Morton, Mary Murphy, Ethel Barrymore, Lionel Barrymore, Shirley Booth, Rex Harrison, Lilli Palmer, Helen Hayes, Henry Fonda, Tallulah Bankhead, Mary Martin, Louis Calhern, John Van Druten, Cornel Wilde, Joshua Logan, Agnes Moorehead, Gertrude Berg

Maisie
US 1939 74m bw
MGM (J. Walter Ruben)

Adventures of a Brooklyn showgirl.
Acceptable programmer which led to a series, all quite watchable and absolutely forgettable.

w Mary McCall Jnr, *novel* Dark Dame by Wilson Collinson *d* Edwin L. Marin
ph Leonard Smith

Ann Sothern, Robert Young, Ian Hunter, Ruth Hussey, Anthony Allan (John Hubbard), Cliff Edwards

The succeeding titles, mostly written by Mary McCall and directed by Marin or Harry Beaumont or Roy del Ruth, were:

1940: CONGO MAISIE (with John Carroll; a remake of RED DUST), GOLD RUSH MAISIE (with Lee Bowman), MAISIE WAS A LADY (with Lew Ayres, Maureen O'Sullivan)
1941: RINGSIDE MAISIE (with George Murphy; GB title CASH AND CARRY)
1942: MAISIE GETS HER MAN (with Red Skelton; GB title SHE GOT HER MAN)
1943: SWING SHIFT MAISIE (with James Craig; GB title THE GIRL IN OVERALLS)
1944: MAISIE GOES TO RENO (with John Hodiak; GB title YOU CAN'T DO THAT TO ME)
1946: UP GOES MAISIE (with George Murphy; GB title UP SHE GOES)

The Major and the Minor**
US 1942 100m bw
Paramount (Arthur Hornblow Jnr)

A girl poses as a child in order to travel half fare on a train, and is helped by an officer who falls for her.
Moderately smart comedy showing the writer director's emergent style. Remade as *You're Never Too Young* (qv).

w Charles Brackett, Billy Wilder *d Billy Wilder*
ph Leo Tover *m* Robert Emmett Dolan

Ginger Rogers, Ray Milland, Rita Johnson, Robert Benchley, Diana Lynn, Edward Fielding, Frankie Thomas, Charles Smith

Major Barbara***
GB 1941 121m bw
Gabriel Pascal

The daughter of an armaments millionaire joins

the Salvation Army but resigns when it accepts her father's donation.
Stagey but compulsive version of a play in which the author takes typical side swipes at anything and everything within reach, allowing for some gorgeous acting (and overacting) by an impeccable cast.
w Anatole de Grunwald, Gabriel Pascal, *play Bernard Shaw* *d* Gabriel Pascal, Harold French, David Lean
Wendy Hiller, Rex Harrison, Robert Morley, Robert Newton, Marie Lohr, Emlyn Williams, Sybil Thorndike, Deborah Kerr, David Tree, Felix Aylmer, Penelope Dudley Ward, Walter Hudd, Marie Ault, Donald Calthrop

'Shaw's ebullience provides an unslackening fount of energy . . . his all-star cast of characters are outspoken as no one else is in films except the Marx Brothers.'—*William Whitebait*

Major Dundee*
US 1965 134m Eastmancolor Panavision
Columbia (Jerry Bresler)

A small group of men from a US cavalry post sets out to annihilate marauding Indians.
Large-scale, rough and ready western which rambles along in humourless vein but rises to some spectacularly bloodthirsty climaxes.
w Harry Julian Fink, Oscar Saul, Sam Peckinpah *d* Sam Peckinpah *ph* Sam Leavitt *m* Daniele Amfitheatrof
Charlton Heston, Richard Harris, Jim Hutton, James Coburn, Michael Anderson Jnr, Warren Oates, Senta Berger, Slim Pickens

A Majority of One
US 1961 156m Technicolor
Warner (Mervyn Le Roy)

A Jewish widow has a shipboard romance with a Japanese businessman.
Interminable stage-bound comedy-drama, boringly assembled and fatally compromised by the casting of stars who are neither Jewish nor Japanese.
w Leonard Spiegelgass, from his play *d* Mervyn Le Roy *ph* Harry Stradling *m* Max Steiner
Rosalind Russell, Alec Guinness, Ray Danton, Madlyn Rhue

Make a Wish
US 1937 75m bw
(RKO) Sol Lesser

A composer discovers a boy singer at a summer camp.
Acceptable family entertainment.
w Gertrude Berg, Bernard Schubert, Earle Snell *d* Kurt Neumann *ph* John Mescall *m* Oscar Straus
Basil Rathbone, Bobby Breen, Marion Claire, Leon Errol, Henry Armetta, Ralph Forbes, Donald Meek

Make Me a Star
US 1932 80m bw
Paramount

A grocery clerk goes to Hollywood and becomes a film star.
Modest remake of a silent success; see also *Merton of the Movies.*
w Sam Wintz, Walter de Leon, Arthur Kober, *novel* Merton of the Movies by Harry Leon Wilson *d* William Beaudine *ph* Allen Siegler
Stuart Erwin, Joan Blondell, Zasu Pitts, Ben Turpin, Florence Roberts; and Tallulah Bankhead, Clive Brook, Garry Cooper, Maurice Chevalier, Claudette Colbert, Fredric March, Jack Oakie, Charlie Ruggles, Sylvia Sidney

Make Me an Offer*
GB 1954 88m Eastmancolor
Group Three (W. P. Lipscomb)

An antique dealer has an ambition to own a famous vase.
Mildly pleasant Jewish comedy with interesting sidelights on the antique business.
w W. P. Lipscomb, *novel* Wolf Mankowitz *d* Cyril Frankel *ph* Denny Densham *m* John Addison
Peter Finch, Adrienne Corri, *Meier Tzelniker*, Rosalie Crutchley, Finlay Currie, *Ernest Thesiger*, Wilfrid Lawson, Alfie Bass

Make Mine Music**
US 1946 74m Technicolor
Walt Disney (Joe Grant)

A programme of cartoon shorts: JOHNNY FEDORA, ALL THE CATS JOIN IN, WITHOUT YOU, TWO SILHOUETTES, CASEY AT THE BAT, THE MARTINS AND THE COYS, BLUE BAYOU, AFTER YOU'VE GONE, WILLIE THE SINGING WHALE.
An insubstantial banquet, sometimes arty and sometimes chocolate boxy, which occasionally rises to the expected heights.
w various *d* various

Make Way for Tomorrow**
US 1937 94m bw
Paramount (Leo McCarey)

An elderly couple are in financial difficulty and

have to be parted because their children will not help.
Sentimental drama which had a devastating effect at the time but now seems oversimplified and exaggerated.

w Vina Delmar, *novel* The Years Are So Long by Josephine Lawrence *d Leo McCarey m* George Antheil

Victor Moore, Beulah Bondi, Thomas Mitchell, Fay Bainter, Porter Hall, Barbara Read, Maurice Moscovitch, Elizabeth Risdon, Gene Lockhart

'The most brilliantly directed and acted film of the year.'—*John Grierson*

Malaya*
US 1949 95m bw
MGM (Pandro S. Berman)
GB title: *East of the Rising Sun*

An adventurer attempts to smuggle rubber out of Japanese-occupied Malaya.
Dour action melodrama, unworthy of its considerable cast but watchable.

w Frank Fenton *d* Richard Thorpe *ph* George Folsey *m* Bronislau Kaper

Spencer Tracy, James Stewart, Sidney Greenstreet, John Hodiak, Valentina Cortesa, Lionel Barrymore, Gilbert Roland

The Male Animal*
US 1942 101m bw
Warner (Wolfgang Reinhardt)

A dry college professor emancipates himself when his wife becomes attracted to a football star.
Stagebound but amusing college comedy with pleasant humour and good performances. Remade as *She's Working Her Way through College* (qv).

w Julius J. and Philip G. Epstein, Stephen Morehouse Avery, *play* James Thurber and Elliot Nugent *d* Elliott Nugent *ph* Arthur Edeson *m* Heinz Roemheld

Henry Fonda, Olivia de Havilland, Jack Carson, Joan Leslie, Eugene Pallette, Don Defore, Herbert Anderson, Hattie McDaniel

Mallory
US 1975 74m Technicolor TVM
Universal
aka: *Circumstantial Evidence*

A lawyer is accused of condoning perjury.
Muddled pilot for a series that did not go, with the star in a fright wig.

w Joel Oliansky *d* Boris Sagal

Raymond Burr, Robert Loggia, Mark Hamill

The Malta Story
GB 1953 103m bw
GFD / British Film Makers (Peter de Sarigny)

An English flier is involved in the defence of Malta during World War II.
Glib propaganda piece which is not very excitingly written or characterized, and fails to convince on any but the most elementary level.

w William Fairchild, Nigel Balchin *d* Brian Desmond Hurst *ph* Robert Krasker *m* William Alwyn

Alec Guinness, Anthony Steel, Muriel Pavlow, Jack Hawkins, Flora Robson, Renée Asherson, Ralph Truman, Reginald Tate, Hugh Burden

The Maltese Falcon**
US 1931 80m bw
Warner

After the death of his partner, private eye Sam Spade is dragged into a quest for a priceless statuette.
Excellent crime melodrama with smart pace and performances. Remade as *Satan Met a Lady* (1936); and see below.

w Maude Fulton, Lucien Hubbard, Brown Holmes, *novel Dashiell Hammett d Roy del Ruth ph* William Rees

Ricardo Cortez, Bebe Daniels, *Dudley Digges,* Dwight Frye, Robert Elliott, Thelma Todd, Oscar Apfel

The Maltese Falcon****
US 1941 101m bw
Warner (Henry Blanke)

A remake which shows the difference between excellence and brilliance; here every nuance is subtly stressed, and the cast is perfection.

wd John Huston ph Arthur Edeson m Adolph Deutsch

Humphrey Bogart, Mary Astor, Sidney Greenstreet, Elisha Cook Jnr, Barton MacLane, Lee Patrick, Peter Lorre, Gladys George, *Ward Bond, Jerome Cowan*

'The first crime melodrama with finish, speed and bang to come along in what seems like ages.'—*Otis Ferguson*

'A work of entertainment that is yet so skilfully constructed that after many years and many viewings, it has the same brittle explosiveness—and some of the same surprise—that it had in 1941.'—*Pauline Kael, 1968*

'The trick which Mr Huston has pulled is a combination of American ruggedness with the suavity of the English crime school—a blend of mind and muscle—plus a slight touch of pathos.'—*Bosley Crowther, New York Times*

Mame*
US 1974 131m Technicolor
Panavision
Warner / ABC (Robert Fryer, James Cresson)

In 1928, a 10-year-old boy goes to live with his eccentric, sophisticated aunt.
Old-fashioned and rather bad film of a much overrated Broadway musical, inept in most departments but with occasional show-stopping moments.

w Paul Zandel, *play* Jerome Lawrence, Robert E. Lee, *book* Patrick Dennis *d* Gene Saks *ph* Philip Lathrop *m/ly* Jerry Herman *pd* Robert F. Boyle

Lucille Ball, Beatrice Arthur, Robert Preston, Bruce Davison, Jane Connell, Joyce Van Patten, John McGiver

'It makes one realize afresh the parlous state of the Hollywood musical, fighting to survive against misplaced superstars and elephantine budgets matched with miniscule imagination.'—*Geoff Brown*

'The cast seem to have been handpicked for their tone-deafness, and Lucille Ball's close-ups are shot blatantly out of focus.'—*Sight and Sound*

Mammy*
US 1930 84m bw
Warner

Murder backstage at a minstrel show.
One of the star's better musicals.

w L. G. Rigby, Joseph Jackson *d* Michael Curtiz *ph* Barney McGill *m* Irving Berlin

Al Jolson, Lowell Sherman, rhobart Bosworth, Louise Dresser, Lee Moran

The Man*
US 1971 100m colour TVM
Lorimar / ABC Circle

The US gets its first black president.
Solid mini-screen adaptation of a successful novel.

w Rod Serling, *novel* Irving Wallace *d* Joseph Sargent

James Earl Jones, Martin Balsam, Burgess Meredith, William Windom, Barbara Rush, Lew Ayres, Anne Seymour

Man about Town*
US 1939 85m bw
Paramount (Arthur Hornblow Jnr)

A Broadway producer in London makes his girlfriend jealous.
Fairly amusing comedy-musical programmer.

w Morrie Ryskind *d* Mark Sandrich *ph* Ted Tetzlaff *md* Victor Young

Jack Benny, Dorothy Lamour, Edward Arnold, Binnie Barnes, Phil Harris, Eddie Anderson, Monty Woolley, Isabel Jeans, Betty Grable, E. E. Clive.

A Man Alone*
US 1955 96m Trucolor
Republic

A wandering gunman is framed by other badmen.
Solemn, slow-moving but generally interesting western, the star's first attempt at direction.

w John Tucker Battle *d Ray Milland ph* Lionel Lindon *m* Victor Young

Ray Milland, Mary Murphy, Ward Bond, Raymond Burr, Arthur Space, Lee Van Cleef, Alan Hale Jnr

Man at the Top*
GB 1973 87m Technicolor
Hammer / Dufton (Peter Charlesworth)

A pharmaceutical executive finds that his firm is marketing an unsafe drug.
Further adventures of the belligerent hero of *Room at the Top* (qv), this time following a popular television series. All very fashionable and predictable.

w Hugh Whitemore *d* Mike Vardy *ph* Bryan Probyn *m* Roy Budd

Kenneth Haigh, Nanette Newman, Harry Andrews, John Quentin, Charlie Williams

The Man Between*
GB 1953 101m bw
British Lion / London Films (Carol Reed)

Ivo Kern operates successfully as a West Berlin racketeer; love causes a softening of his attitudes and leads to his death.
Imitation *Third Man* with an uninteresting mystery and a solemn ending. Good acting and production can't save it.

w Harry Kurnitz *d Carol Reed ph Desmond Dickinson m* John Addison *ad* André Andreiev

James Mason, Hildegarde Neff, Claire Bloom, Geoffrey Toone, Ernst Schroeder

'A cold-hearted film about people with cold feet.'—*Daily Express*

A Man Called Horse*
US 1970 114m Technicolor
Panavision
Cinema Center / Sanford Howard

In 1825 an English aristocrat is captured by

Indians, lives with them and eventually becomes their leader.
Harrowing account of tribal life and customs, with much bloodshed and torture and most of the dialogue in Indian. Occasionally impressive but not exactly entertaining.

w Jack di Witt, *story* Dorothy M. Johnson *d* Elliot Silverstein *ph* Robert Hauser *m* Leonard Rosenman

Richard Harris, Judith Anderson, Jean Gascon, Manu Tupou
† Sequel 1976: *The Return of a Man Called Horse.*

The Man Called Noon
GB / Spain / Italy 1973 95m Technicolor
Frontier / Montana / Finarco (Euan Lloyd)

A western gunslinger loses his memory.
Childish western melodrama in the violent manner.

w Scot Finch, *novel* Louis L'Amour *d* Peter Collinson *ph* John Cabrera *m* Luis Bacalov

Richard Crenna, Stephen Boyd, Rosanna Schiaffino, Farley Granger

A Man Called Peter*
US 1955 119m De Luxe
Cinemascope
TCF (Samuel G. Engel)

The life of Peter Marshall, a Scottish clergyman who became chaplain to the US Senate.
Careful but rather dreary biopic.

w Eleanore Griffin, *book* Catherine Marshall *d* Henry Koster *ph* Harold Lipstein *md* Alfred Newman

Richard Todd, Jean Peters, Marjorie Rambeau, Jill Esmond, Les Tremayne, Robert Burton

A Man Could Get Killed*
US 1966 98m Technicolor Panavision
Universal / Cherokee (Ernest Wehmeyer)

An American businessman in Lisbon is mistaken for a secret agent.
Minor thrill comedy with a confused plot and a willing cast.

w T. E. B. Clarke, Richard Breen, *novel* Diamonds Are Danger by David Walker *d* Ronald Neame, Cliff Owen *ph* Gabor Pogany *m* Bert Kaemfert

James Garner, Melina Mercouri, Sandra Dee, Tony Franciosa, Robert Coote, Roland Culver, Cecil Parker, Grégoire Aslan, Dulcie Gray, Martin Benson, Niall MacGinnis

A Man for All Seasons****
GB 1966 120m Technicolor
Columbia / Highland (Fred Zinnemann)

Sir Thomas More opposes Henry VIII's divorce, and events lead inexorably to his execution.
Irreproachable film version of a play which has had its narrative tricks removed but stands up remarkably well. Acting, direction, sets, locations and costumes all have precisely the right touch.

w Robert Bolt, from his play *d Fred Zinnemann ph Ted Moore m Georges Delerue pd John Box*

Paul Scofield, Wendy Hiller, Susannah York, *Robert Shaw*, Orson Welles, Leo McKern, Nigel Davenport, John Hurt, Corin Redgrave, Cyril Luckham, Jack Gwyllim

Man Friday
GB 1975 115m Eastmancolor
Panavision
Avco-Embassy / ITC / ABC / Keep Films (Jules Buck)

The story of Robinson Crusoe told so that Friday appears the more intelligent.
A pointless and not very entertaining exercise which wears out its welcome very early.

w Adrian Mitchell *d* Jack Gold *ph* Alex Phillips *m* Carl Davis

Peter O'Toole, Richard Roundtree

'Liberal intentions trail sadly through every sequence and cause absurd fluctuations of tone, since no one seems to have decided whether laborious slapstick, heavy portentousness or method acting is the best vehicle for the message.'—*Jill Forbes*

The Man from the Alamo*
US 1953 79m Technicolor
U-I (Aaron Rosenberg)

A survivor of the Alamo is thought to be a deserter but proves his story and exposes a villain.
Satisfying western programmer.

w Steve Fisher, D. D. Beauchamp *d* Budd Boetticher *ph* Russell Metty *m* Frank Skinner

Glenn Ford, Victor Jory, Julia Adams, Hugh O'Brian

The Man from Blankley's
US 1930 67m bw
Warner

A drunken aristocrat goes to the wrong party and teaches those present, and himself, a thing or two.
Amusing star trifle, previously filmed as a silent.

w Harvey Thew, Joseph Jackson, *story* F. Anstey *d* Alfred E. Green *ph* James Van Trees

John Barrymore, Loretta Young, William Austin, Albert Gran, Emily Fitzroy

The Man from Colorado
US 1949 99m Technicolor
Columbia (Jules Schermer)

A maladjusted Civil War veteran becomes a western judge and rules by the gun.
Slightly unusual, watchable star western.

w Robert D. Andrews, Ben Maddow, Borden Chase *d* Henry Levin *ph* William Snyder *m* George Duning

Glenn Ford, William Holden, Ellen Drew, Ray Collins, Edgar Buchanan, Jerome Courtland, James Millican, Jim Bannon

Man from Del Rio
US 1956 82m bw
UA / Robert L. Jacks

A Mexican hobo becomes sheriff and forces the local badman to leave town.
Modest, efficient, rather brutal little western.

w Richard Carr *d* Harry Horner *ph* Stanley Cortez *m* Fred Steiner

Anthony Quinn, Katy Jurado, Peter Whitney, Douglas Fowley

The Man from Laramie**
US 1955 104m Technicolor Cinemascope
Columbia (William Goetz)

A wandering cowman seeks revenge on those who killed his brother.
Grade A western with new-fangled touches of brutality touching off the wide screen spectacle.

w Philip Yordan, Frank Burt *d Anthony Mann* *ph* Charles Lang Jnr *m* Morris Stoloff

James Stewart, Arthur Kennedy, Donald Crisp, Cathy O'Donnell, Alex Nicol, Aline MacMahon, Wallace Ford, Jack Elam

The Man from the Diners' Club*
US 1963 96m bw
Columbia / Dena / Ampersand

A clerk accidentally lets a credit card go to a notorious gangster, and makes desperate efforts to retrieve it.
Minor star comedy with funny moments surviving a slapdash script.

w Bill Blatty *d* Frank Tashlin *ph* Hal Mohr *m* Stu Philips

Danny Kaye, Telly Savalas, Martha Hyer, Cara Williams, Everett Sloane, George Kennedy

The Man from Uncle
This long-running one-hour TV series (1964–8) began as a spoof of James Bond, which was itself a spoof. Not much more serious or convincing than *Batman*, they caused a lot of people to suspend their disbelief. Robert Vaughn played Napoleon Solo, David McCallum Ilya Kuryakin, and Leo G. Carroll Mr Waverly. Several feature films were made up from various episodes, and did well in cinemas in some countries. They were: TO TRAP A SPY, THE SPY WITH MY FACE, THE KARATE KILLERS, THE SPY IN THE GREEN HAT, ONE OF OUR SPIES IS MISSING, THE HELICOPTER SPIES, and HOW TO STEAL THE WORLD

The Man from Yesterday
US 1932 71m bw
Paramount

A man is reported missing in World War I, but years later his wife and her new fiancé find him in Switzerland, dying of gas poisoning.
Enoch Arden rides again, and very boringly.

w Oliver H. P. Garrett *d* Berthold Viertel *ph* Karl Struss

Claudette Colbert, Clive Brook, Charles Boyer, Andy Devine, Alan Mowbray, Christian Rub

Man Hunt**
US 1941 98m bw
TCF (Kenneth MacGowan)

A big game hunter misses a shot at Hitler and is chased back to England by the Gestapo.
Despite hilariously inaccurate English backgrounds, this is perhaps its director's most vivid Hollywood thriller, though watered down in tone from the original novel.

w Dudley Nichols, *novel* Rogue Male by Geoffrey Household *d Fritz Lang* *ph* Arthur Miller *m* Alfred Newman

Walter Pidgeon, Joan Bennett, *George Sanders*, John Carradine, Roddy McDowall, Ludwig Stossel, Heather Thatcher, Frederick Worlock

'A tense and intriguing thriller that is both propaganda and exciting entertainment.'—*Paul M. Jensen, 1969*

† Remade for TV in 1976 as *Rogue Male*.

The Man Hunter
US 1969 98m Technicolor TVM
Universal (Don Roth)

A banker hires an African white hunter to track down and kill the murderer of his son.
Watchable action/chase nonsense.

w Meyer Dolinsky, *novel* Wade Miller *d* Don Taylor

Roy Thinnes, Sandra Dee, Albert Salmi, Sorrell Booke, David Brian

The Man I Love
US 1946 76m bw
Warner (Arnold Albert)

A nightclub singer is involved with a mobster.
Dreary little melodrama which never really gets going.

w Catherine Turney *d* Raoul Walsh *ph* Sid Hickox *m* Max Steiner

Ida Lupino, Robert Alda, Andrea King, Martha Vickers, Bruce Bennett, Alan Hale, Dolores Moran, John Ridgely

The Man I Married*
US 1940 79m bw
TCF (Raymond Griffith)
aka: *I Married a Nazi*

When an American couple take a European vacation, the wife is horrified to find her husband, who is of German parentage, agreeing with the Nazis.
Naïve but striking melodrama exploring attitudes of its time.

w Oliver H. P. Garrett, *novel* Swastika by Oscar Shisgall *d* Irving Pichel *ph* Peverell Marley *m* David Buttolph

Joan Bennett, Francis Lederer, Lloyd Nolan, Anna Sten, Otto Kruger, Maria Ouspenskaya, Ludwig Stossel, Johnny Russell

The Man in Grey**
GB 1943 116m bw
GFD / Gainsborough (Edward Black)

In Regency times, an aristocratic girl's love for her less fortunate friend is repaid by jealousy, treachery and murder.
Rather dully performed flashback costume melodrama which caught the public imagination in the middle of a dreary world war, especially as its evil leading characters were played by stars who rapidly went right to the top. The several imitations which followed, including *The Wicked Lady*, *Jassy* and *Hungry Hill*, became known as the Gainsborough school.

w Margaret Kennedy, Leslie Arliss, Doreen Montgomery, *novel* Lady Eleanor Smith *d* Leslie Arliss *ph* Arthur Crabtree *m* Cedric Mallabey *ad* Walter Murton

James Mason, Margaret Lockwood, Phyllis Calvert, Stewart Granger, Helen Haye, Nora Swinburne, Raymond Lovell, Martita Hunt

'There was not a moment when I would not gladly have dived for my hat.'—*James Agate*

'All the time-tested materials: gypsy fortune-teller; scowling, black-browed villain; gushy diary kept by a doe-eyed girl who munches candied violets; fire-breathing adventuress who dotes on discord and low-cut gowns . . .'—*Time*

The Man in Half Moon Street
US 1944 91m bw
Paramount

A mysteriously handsome young scientist is actually a 90-year-old who has discovered a surgical method of preserving youth.
Boring screen version of a play which was conceived in an almost romantic vein; Hollywood has taken it too literally.

w Charles Kenyon, *play* Barre Lyndon *d* Ralph Murphy *ph* Henry Sharp *m* Miklos Rozsa

Nils Asther, Helen Walker, Brandon Hurst, *Reinhold Schunzel*

† Remade in straight horror vein as *The Man Who Could Cheat Death (qv)*.

Man in the Dark*
US 1953 70m bw 3-D
Columbia (Wallace Macdonald)

A convict submits to a brain operation which will remove his criminal tendencies. Unfortunately it also removes his memory, and on his release he is bewildered when gangsters expect him to know where the loot is hidden.
Silly low-budgeter which is only notable as the 3-D film which most exploited the short-lived medium. Apart from a roller coaster ride, objects hurled at the audience include scissors, spiders, knives, forceps, fists and falling bodies.

w George Bricker, Jack Leonard *d* Lew Landers *ph* Floyd Crosby *m* Ross de Maggio

Edmond O'Brien, Audrey Totter, Ted de Corsia, Horace MacMahon

The Man in the Gray Flannel Suit*
US 1956 152m Eastmancolor Cinemascope
TCF (Darryl F. Zanuck)

A young New York executive is offered a demanding job but decides that his first loyalty is to his wife and children.
An amusingly accurate novel of Madison Avenue mores becomes a marathon emotional melodrama in which the mordant bits quickly give way to domestic problems and a guilt complex about a wartime affair, shown in lengthy flashback. It's all too much.

w Nunnally Johnson, *novel* Sloan Wilson *d* Nunnally Johnson *ph* Charles G. Clarke *m* Bernard Herrmann

Gregory Peck, Fredric March, Jennifer Jones,

Ann Harding, *Arthur O'Connell, Henry Daniell,* Marisa Pavan, Lee J. Cobb, Keenan Wynn, Gene Lockhart, Gigi Perreau, Connie Gilchrist, Joseph Sweeney

The Man in the Iron Mask***
US 1939 119m bw
Edward Small

King Louis XIV keeps his twin brother prisoner.
Exhilarating swashbuckler based on a classic novel, with a complex plot, good acting and the three musketeers in full cry.

w George Bruce, novel Alexandre Dumas *d James Whale ph* Robert Planck *m* Lucien Moraweck

Louis Hayward, Warren William (as D'Artagnan), Alan Hale, Bert Roach, Miles Mander, Joan Bennett, *Joseph Schildkraut,* Walter Kingsford, Marion Martin, Montagu Love, Albert Dekker

† Remade 1976 as a TV movie.

The Man in the Middle*
GB 1964 94m bw Cinemascope
TCF / Pennebaker / Belmont (Walter Seltzer)

In India during World War II, an American lieutenant is indicted for murder and the defence counsel is instructed to lose the case.
Courtroom melodrama with unusual angles; quite intriguing, though the wide screen doesn't help.

w Keith Waterhouse, Willis Hall, *novel* The Winston Affair by Howard Fast *d* Guy Hamilton *ph* Wilkie Cooper *m* John Barry

Robert Mitchum, Trevor Howard, Keenan Wynn, Barry Sullivan, France Nuyen, Alexander Knox

'For once Mitchum seems to have an excuse for keeping his eyes at half mast.'—*Judith Crist*

Man in the Shadow*
US 1957 80m bw Cinemascope
U-I (Albert Zugsmith)
GB title: *Pay the Devil*

The sheriff of a small western town investigates a murder against the wishes of a powerful local rancher.
Mini-social drama in which the honest man wins out at last . . . and who would expect anything different. A brooding melodrama which delivers less than it promises.

w Gene L. Coon *d* Jack Arnold *ph* Arthur E. Arling *m* Joseph Gershenson

Jeff Chandler, Orson Welles, Colleen Miller, John Larch, Joe Schneider, Leo Gordon

The Man in the Sky*
GB 1956 87m bw
Ealing (Seth Holt)
US title: *Decision against Time*

A test pilot refuses to bale out when an engine catches fire; his plight is interwoven with scenes of his family, friends and associates.
Thin suspense drama with some effective moments but too many irrelevant asides.

w William Rose, John Eldridge *d* Charles Crichton *ph* Douglas Slocombe *m* Gerbrand Schurmann

Jack Hawkins, Elizabeth Sellars, Walter Fitzgerald, Eddie Byrne, John Stratton, Victor Maddern, Lionel Jeffries, Donald Pleasance

The Man in the White Suit****
GB 1951 81m bw
Ealing (Sidney Cole)

A scientist produces a fabric that never gets dirty and never wears out. Unions and management are equally aghast.
Brilliant satirical comedy played as farce and put together with meticulous cinematic counterpoint, so that every moment counts and all concerned give of their very best.

w Roger Macdougall, John Dighton, Alexander Mackendrick d Alexander Mackendrick ph Douglas Slocombe m Benjamin Frankel

Alec Guinness, Joan Greenwood, Cecil Parker, Vida Hope, *Ernest Thesiger,* Michael Gough, Howard Marion Crawford, Miles Malleson, *George Benson, Edie Martin*

Man in the Wilderness*
US 1971 105m Technicolor Panavision
Warner / Wilderness (Sanford Howard)

In 1820 in the Canadian northwest, a fur trapper is mauled by a grizzly and left for dead, but he learns to survive and sets out for revenge.
Endurance melodrama modelled after *A Man Called Horse*; a bit stretched and only for the hardened, but taking an agreeably unromantic view of nature.

w Jack di Witt *d* Richard Sarafian *ph* Gerry Fisher *m* Johnny Harris

Richard Harris, John Huston, John Bindon, Prunella Ransome, Henry Wilcoxon, Ben Carruthers

Man Made Monster*
US 1940 57m bw
Universal
GB title: *The Electric Man*

A scientist experiments with a man who is

impervious to electric shock, and turns him into a walking robot.
A smart little semi-horror originally planned for Karloff and Lugosi.

w Joseph West *d* George Waggner *ph* Elwood Bredell *m* Charles Previn

Lon Chaney Jnr, Lionel Atwill, Anne Gwynne, Frank Albertson, Samuel S. Hinds

Man of a Thousand Faces**
US 1957 122m bw Cinemascope
U-I (Robert Arthur)

The rise to fame of silent screen character actor Lon Chaney.
Moderately commendable biopic with a strong sense of period Hollywood, an excellent star performance, but too much sudsy emoting about deaf mute parents and an ungrateful wife.

w R. Wright Campbell, Ivan Goff, Ben Roberts *d* Joseph Pevney *ph* Russell Metty *m* Frank Skinner *ad Alexander Golitzen*

James Cagney, Dorothy Malone, Robert Evans (as Irving Thalberg), Roger Smith, *Marjorie Rambeau*, Jane Greer, Jim Backus

Man of Conquest
US 1939 99m bw
Republic (Sol C. Siegel)

The life of western hero Sam Houston, who became president of Texas.
Competent action/domestic biopic.

w Wells Root, E. E. Paramore Jnr *d* George Nicholls Jnr *ph* Joseph H. August *m* Victor Young

Richard Dix, Joan Fontaine, Gail Patrick, Edward Ellis, Victor Jory, Robert Barrat, George Hayes, Ralph Morgan, Robert Armstrong, C. Henry Gordon, Janet Beecher

Man of La Mancha*
US 1972 132m De Luxe
UA / PEA (Arthur Hiller)

Arrested by the Inquisition and thrown into prison, Miguel de Cervantes relates the story of Don Quixote.
Unimaginative but generally good-looking attempt to recreate on the screen an essentially theatrical experience.

w Dale Wasserman, from his play *d* Arthur Hiller *ph Goffredo Rotunno m Mitch Leigh* *ly* Joe Darion *ad* Luciano Damiani

Peter O'Toole, Sophia Loren, James Coco, Harry Andrews, John Castle, Brian Blessed
'Needful of all the imagination the spectator can muster.'—*Variety*

Man of the West
US 1958 100m De Luxe Cinemascope
UA / Ashton (Walter M. Mirisch)

In 1874 Arizona, a reformed gunman is cajoled by his old buddies to help them rob a bank.
Talkative, set-bound, cliché-ridden star western with minor compensations.

w Reginald Rose, *novel* Will C. Brown *d* Anthony Mann *ph* Ernest Haller *m* Leigh Harline

Gary Cooper, Lee J. Cobb, Julie London, Arthur O'Connell, Jack Lord, John Dehner, Royal Dano, Robert Wilke

Man on a String
US 1960 92m bw
Columbia / Louis de Rochemont
GB title: *Confessions of a Counterspy*

A Russian-born Hollywood producer is asked by the Russians to work as a spy but becomes a double agent.
Slightly unbelievable biopic about Boris Morros, rather childlike in its simplicity and not too entertaining either.

w John Kafka, Virginia Shaler, *book* Ten Years a Counterspy by Boris Morros *d* André de Toth *ph* Charles Lawton Jnr and others *m* George Duning

Ernest Borgnine, Kerwin Mathews, Colleen Dewhurst, Alexander Scourby, Glenn Corbett, Vladimir Sokoloff

Man on a String
US 1971 73m colour TVM
Columbia

An ex-policeman goes undercover with the mob.
So routine you don't even need to watch it.

w Ben Maddow *d* Joseph Sargent

Christopher George, Joel Grey, William Schallert, Jack Warden

Man on a Swing
US 1975 108m Technicolor
Paramount (Howard B. Jaffe)

Investigations into a murder are helped by a would-be medium.
Overlong and confused psycho-mystery with one stand-out performance.

w David Zelag Goodman *d* Frank Perry *ph* Adam Holender *m* Lalo Schifrin

Cliff Robertson, *Joel Grey*, Dorothy Tristan, Peter Masterson
'Runs out of interest long before it runs out of film.'—*Variety*

Man on a Tightrope*
US 1953 105m bw
TCF (Robert L. Jacks)

A Czech circus owner has trouble with the communist authorities and tries to escape.
Adventure story with cold war pretensions which virtually kill it.

w Robert Sherwood *d* Elia Kazan *ph* Georg Krause *m* Franz Waxman

Fredric March, Cameron Mitchell, Adolphe Menjou, Richard Boone, John Dehner, Dorothea Wieck

Man on Fire
US 1957 95m bw
MGM (Sol C. Siegel)

When his wife divorces him, a middle-aged man refuses to hand over their son.
Low-key personal drama of very moderate interest and modest budget.

wd Ranald MacDougall *ph* Joseph Ruttenberg *m* David Raksin

Bing Crosby, Inger Stevens, Mary Fickett, E. G. Marshall

The Man on the Eiffel Tower*
US 1948 82m Anscocolor
A & T (Irving Allen)

A crazy killer defies Inspector Maigret to discover his identity.
Early independent production, an unsatisfactory crime melodrama with international talent and Paris locations. Some quirky acting carries it through.

w Harry Brown, *novel* A Battle of Nerves by Simenon *d* Burgess Meredith *ph* Stanley Cortez

Charles Laughton, Burgess Meredith, Franchot Tone, Robert Hutton, Jean Wallace, Patricia Roc, Wilfrid Hyde White, Belita

The Man on the Flying Trapeze*
US 1935 65m bw
Paramount (William Le Baron)
GB title: *The Memory Expert*

Adventures of an oppressed family man who is useful to his boss because of his prodigious memory.
Plotless rigmarole of shapeless comedy sketches, for star fans.

w Ray Harris, Sam Hardy, Jack Cunningham, Bobby Vernon, *story* Charles Bogle (W. C. Fields) *d* Clyde Bruckman *ph* Al Gilks

W. C. Fields, Kathleen Howard, Mary Brian, Grady Sutton, Vera Lewis, Lucien Littlefield, Oscar Apfel

Man Proof
US 1938 74m bw
MGM (Louis D. Lighton)

In trying to win back her man a woman discovers she really loves someone else.
Modest romantic comedy which leaves its stars at sea.

w Vincent Lawrence, Waldemar Young, George Oppenheimer, *novel* The Four Marys by Fanny Heaslip Lea *d* Richard Thorpe *ph* Karl Freund *m* Franz Waxman

Myrna Loy, Franchot Tone, Walter Pidgeon, Rosalind Russell, Nana Bryant, Ruth Hussey

The Man They Could Not Hang
US 1939 65m bw
Columbia

A scientist working on a mechanical heart causes the death of a volunteer student. He is executed, but his assistant restores him to life and he determines to murder those who convicted him.
Predictable horror hokum which set Karloff on his mad doctor cycle.

w Karl Brown *d* Nick Grinde *ph* Benjamin Kline

Boris Karloff, Lorna Gray, Robert Wilcox, Roger Pryor, Don Beddoe, Byron Foulger

A Man to Remember*
US 1938 80m bw
RKO (Robert Sisk)

At a small-town doctor's funeral, his life is remembered by mourners.
Modestly effective family film.

w Dalton Trumbo, *novel* Failure by Katharine Haviland-Taylor *d* *Garson Kanin* *ph* J. Roy Hunt *m* Roy Webb

Edward Ellis, Anne Shirley, Lee Bowman, William Henry, Granville Bates

The Man Upstairs*
GB 1959 88m bw
British Lion / ACT (Robert Dunbar)

A mild-mannered lodger becomes violent, injures a policeman, and barricades himself in his room.
Character melodrama reminiscent of both *Fourteen Hours* and *Le Jour se Lève*, but not so interesting as either.

w Alun Falconer *d* Don Chaffey *ph* Gerald Gibbs

Richard Attenborough, Bernard Lee, Donald Houston, Dorothy Alison, Maureen Connell, Kenneth Griffith, Virginia Maskell, Patricia Jessel

The Man Who Broke the Bank at Monte Carlo*
US 1935 67m bw
TCF (Nunnally Johnson)

A Russian émigré becomes a taxi driver, wins a fortune at roulette, loses it all again, and returns happily to his cab.
Very mild, unconvincing and not very entertaining malarkey which rested squarely on its star, who carried it with aplomb.

w Nunnally Johnson *d* Stephen Roberts *ph* Ernest Palmer

Ronald Colman, Joan Bennett, Colin Clive, Nigel Bruce, Montagu Love, Frank Reicher, Ferdinand Gottschalk

The Man Who Came to Dinner***
US 1941 112m bw
Warner (Jack Saper, Jerry Wald)

An acid-tongued radio celebrity breaks his hip while on a lecture tour, and terrorizes the inhabitants of the suburban home where he must stay for several weeks.
Delightfully malicious caricature of Alexander Woolcott which, though virtually confined to one set, moves so fast that one barely notices the lack of cinematic variety, and certainly provides more than a laugh a minute, especially for those old enough to understand all the references.

w Julius J. and Philip G. Epstein, *play George S. Kaufman, Moss Hart* *d* William Keighley *ph* Tony Gaudio *m* Frederick Hollander

Monty Woolley, Bette Davis, Ann Sheridan, *Jimmy Durante* (spoofing Harpo Marx), *Reginald Gardiner* (spoofing Noel Coward), Richard Travis, *Billie Burke, Grant Mitchell, Ruth Vivian, Mary Wickes*, George Barbier, Elisabeth Fraser

The Man Who Cheated Himself
US 1950 81m bw
TCF (Jack M. Warner)

A woman shoots her husband and her homicide detective lover covers up for her.
Efficient crime melodrama.

w Seton I. Miller, Philip MacDonald *d* Felix Feist *ph* Russell Harlan *m* Louis Forbes

Lee J. Cobb, Jane Wyatt, John Dall, Terry Frost

The Man Who Could Cheat Death
GB 1959 83m Technicolor
Paramount / Hammer (Anthony Nelson-Keys)

A surgeon looks 35 but is really 104, having had a series of gland operations performed on himself.
Vulgar, gory, gruesomely coloured Hammer version of a rather attractive play, previously filmed under its original title *The Man in Half Moon Street* (qv). The shocks are routine, and entertainment value is minimal.

w Jimmy Sangster, *play* Barre Lyndon *d* Terence Fisher *ph* Jack Asher *m* John Hollingsworth

Anton Diffring, Hazel Court, Christopher Lee, Arnold Marle, Delphi Lawrence, Francis de Wolff

The Man Who Could Talk to Kids
US 1973 73m colour TVM
Tomorrow

A frustrated child finds one adult with whom he can express himself.
Tedious taradiddle, well-meaning but dull.

w Douglas Day Stewart *d* Donald Wrye

Peter Boyle, Robert Reed, Scott Jacoby, Collin Wilcox-Horne

The Man Who Could Work Miracles***
GB 1936 82m bw
London (Alexander Korda)

A city clerk discovers he has the power to work miracles (given him by sportive gods) and nearly causes the end of the earth.
Slow-moving but rather pleasing variation on a simple theme.

w Lajos Biro, *story* H. G. Wells *d* Lothar Mendes *ph* Harold Rosson

Roland Young, Ralph Richardson, Ernest Thesiger, Edward Chapman, Joan Gardner, Sophie Stewart, Robert Cochrane, George Zucco, Lawrence Hanray, George Sanders

The Man Who Cried Wolf
US 1937 66m bw
Universal (E. M. Asher)

A distinguished actor confesses to several murders he did not do so that he will be ignored when he does commit the one he intends.
Ingenious but dated crime suspenser.

w Charles Grayson, Sy Bartlett, *story* Too Clever to Live by Arthur Rothsfel *d* Lewis R. Foster *ph* George Robinson

Lewis Stone, Tom Brown, Barbara Read, Marjorie Main, Jameson Thomas

The Man Who Died Twice*
US 1970 100m colour TVM
Cinema Center

An American artist in Spain finds it convenient to sham dead, which leads to complications.

Slightly unusual, location-shot drama which keeps the interest.

d Joseph Sargent

Stuart Whitman, Brigitte Fossey, Jeremy Slate, Bernard Lee, Severn Darden

The Man Who Fell to Earth*

GB 1976 138m colour Panavision

British Lion (Michael Deeley, Barry Spikings)

A visitor from another planet tries to colonize Earth, but his powers are destroyed and he ends an alcoholic cripple.

A weird piece of intellectual science fiction made weirder by longueurs of all varieties: obscure narrative, voyeuristic sex, pop music and metaphysics. Not an easy film or a likeable one, despite its great technical skill.

w Paul Mayersburg, *novel* Walter Tevis *d* Nicolas Roeg *ph* Anthony Richmond *md* John Phillips

David Bowie, Rip Torn, Candy Clark, Buck Henry

The Man Who Finally Died

GB 1962 100m bw Cinemascope

British Lion / Magna / White Cross (Norman Williams)

A German-born Englishman returns to Bavaria for news of his father, and becomes involved in a spy plot.

Busy adaptation of a TV serial with a convoluted plot which might have been more pacily developed and better explained.

w Lewis Greifer, Louis Marks *d* Quentin Lawrence *ph* Stephen Dade *m* Philip Green

Stanley Baker, Peter Cushing, Mai Zetterling, Eric Portman, Niall MacGinnis, Nigel Green, Barbara Everest, Harold Scott

The Man Who Found Himself

US 1937 67m bw

RKO (Cliff Reid)

A nurse helps a downcast doctor face his problems and renew his enthusiasm for life.

Simple-minded programmer.

w J. Robert Bren, Edmund Hartman, G. V. Atwater *d* Lew Landers *ph* Roy Hunt

John Beal, Joan Fontaine, Philip Huston, Jane Walsh, George Irving

The Man Who Had Power over Women

US 1959 105m Eastmancolor Cinemascope

TCF (Nunnally Johnson)

An arrogant, exhibitionist film producer finally alienates his long-suffering wife.

Something of an aberration, with good scenes submerged in an unholy mixture of sharp comedy and sentimental melodrama.

wd Nunnally Johnson, *novel* Colours of the Day by Romain Gary *ph* Milton Krasner *m* Robert Emmett Dolan

Henry Fonda, Leslie Caron, Myron McCormick, Cesare Danova, Marcel Dalio, Conrad Nagel, Harry Ellerbe

'A pretentious extravaganza on a romantic theme.'—*MFB*

The Man Who Haunted Himself

GB 1970 94m Technicolor

ABP / Excalibur (Michael Relph)

After recovering from a road accident, a staid businessman finds that he has an evil doppelganger who steals his wife and his job.

Mildly effective if inexplicable story idea which served more suitably as a Hitchcock TV half hour and here, despite adequate production, outstays its welcome.

w Basil Dearden, Michael Relph, *story* The Case of Mr Pelham by Anthony Armstrong *d* Basil Dearden *ph* Tony Spratling *m* Michael Lewis

Roger Moore, Hildegarde Neil, Olga-Georges Picot, Anton Rodgers, Freddie Jones, Thorley Walters, John Carson, John Welsh

The Man Who Knew Too Much***

GB 1934 84m bw

GFD / Gaumont British (Ivor Montagu)

A child is kidnapped by spies to ensure her father's silence, but he springs into action.

Splendid early Hitchcock which after a faded start moves into memorable sequences involving a dentist, an East End mission and the Albert Hall. All very stagey by today's standards, but much more fun than the expensive remake.

w A. R. Rawlinson, Charles Bennett, D. B. Wyndham Lewis, Edwin Greenwood, Emlyn Williams *d Alfred Hitchcock* *ph* Curt Courant *m* Arthur Benjamin

Leslie Banks, Edna Best, *Peter Lorre*, Nova Pilbeam, Frank Vosper, Hugh Wakefield, Pierre Fresnay

'The film's mainstay is its refined sense of the incongruous.'—*Peter John Dyer, 1964*

The Man Who Knew Too Much*

US 1956 120m Technicolor Vistavision

(Paramount) Alfred Hitchcock

Flaccid remake of the above, twice as long and half as entertaining, though it does improve after a very slow start.

w John Michael Hayes, Angus MacPhail *d* Alfred Hitchcock *ph* Robert Burks *m* Bernard Herrmann

James Stewart, Doris Day, Bernard Miles, Brenda de Banzie, Daniel Gelin, Ralph Truman, Mogens Wieth, Alan Mowbray, Hillary Brooke

The Man Who Loved Cat Dancing
US 1973 114m Metrocolor Panavision
MGM (Martin Poll, Eleanor Perry)

A runaway wife is kidnapped by train thieves and comes to love one of them.
Outdoor variation on *No Orchids for Miss Blandish*, remarkably lacking in any kind of entertainment value.

w Eleanor Perry, *novel* Marilyn Dunham *d* Richard Sarafian *ph* Harry Stradling Jnr *m* John Williams

Sarah Miles, Burt Reynolds, Lee J. Cobb, Jack Warden, George Hamilton, Bo Hopkins, Robert Donner, Jay Silverheels

'Any number of things have gone wrong with this peculiarly dreary western.'—*Tom Milne*

'Sarah Miles undergoes more perils than Pauline.'—*Variety*

The Man Who Loved Redheads
GB 1954 90m Eastmancolor
British Lion / London Films (Josef Somlo)

Throughout his career, a diplomat seeks women who resemble the redhead with whom in youth he had had an idyllic affair.
West End theatrical moonshine, poorly filmed in ugly colour but saved by the cast.

w Terence Rattigan, from his play Who Is Sylvia? *d* Harold French *ph* Georges Périnal *m* Benjamin Frankel

John Justin, Moira Shearer, *Roland Culver*, Gladys Cooper, Denholm Elliott, Harry Andrews, Patricia Cutts, Moira Fraser, *Joan Benham*, Jeremy Spenser

The Man Who Never Was**
GB 1955 102m De Luxe Cinemascope
TCF / André Hakim

In 1943, the British secret service confuses the Germans by dropping a dead man into the sea with false documents.
Mainly enjoyable true life war story marred by an emotional romantic sub-plot with a double twist but helped by an equally fictitious spy hunt which cheers up the last half hour.

w Nigel Balchin, *book* Ewen Montagu *d* Ronald Neame *ph* Oswald Morris *m* Alan Rawsthorne

Clifton Webb, *Robert Flemyng*, Gloria Grahame, *Stephen Boyd*, Laurence Naismith, Josephine Griffin

The Man Who Played God*
US 1932 81m bw
Warner
GB title: *The Silent Voice*

A musician goes deaf but finds satisfaction in helping a young student.
Stagey but effective star vehicle which Arliss also played as a silent film. Remade as *Sincerely Yours* (qv).

w Julian Josephson, Maude Howell, *play* The Silent Voice by Jules Eckert Goodman *d* John G. Adolfi *ph* James Van Trees

George Arliss, Violet Heming, Ivan Simpson, *Bette Davis*, Louise Closser Hale, Donald Cook, Ray Milland

The Man Who Reclaimed His Head*
US 1934 81m bw
Universal (Henry Henigson)

A writer who feels he has been betrayed and his brain sapped by his publisher takes a gruesome revenge.
Oddball period melodrama tailored rather unsuccessfully for a new star. Remade as *Strange Confession* (see *Inner Sanctum*).

w Jean Bart, Samuel Ornitz, *play* Jean Bart *d* Edward Ludwig

Claude Rains, Joan Bennett, Lionel Atwill, Juanita Quigley, Henry O'Neill, Lawrence Grant

The Man Who Shot Liberty Valance*
US 1962 122m bw
Paramount / John Ford (Willis Goldbeck)

A tenderfoot becomes a hero for shooting a bad man, but the shot was really fired by his friend and protector.
Clumsy, obvious western with the director over-indulging himself but providing some good scenes in comedy vein.

w James Warner Bellah, Willis Goldbeck *d* John Ford *ph* William H. Clothier *m* Cyril Mockridge

James Stewart, John Wayne, Vera Miles, Lee Marvin, Edmond O'Brien, Andy Devine, Jeanette Nolan, John Qualen, Ken Murray, Woody Strode, Lee Van Cleef, Strother Martin, John Carradine

'Like Queen Victoria, John Wayne has become lovable because he stayed in the saddle into a new era.'—*Pauline Kael*

'A heavy-spirited piece of nostalgia.'—*Judith Crist, 1975*

The Man Who Talked Too Much
US 1940 75m bw
Warner (Edmund Grainger)

A smart defence attorney gets the goods on a gangster and decides to turn him in.
Below-par remake of *The Mouthpiece* (qv), later filmed again as *Illegal* (qv).

w Walter de Leon, Tom Reed, *play* The Mouthpiece by Frank J. Collins *d* Vincent Sherman *ph* Sid Hickox

George Brent, Brenda Marshall, Richard Barthelmess, Virginia Bruce, William Lundigan, John Litel, George Tobias, Henry Armetta, Alan Baxter

The Man Who Watched Trains Go By
GB 1952 80m Technicolor
Raymond Stross
aka: *Paris Express*

A clerk steals money in order to fulfil his wish of world travel, and this leads to murder.
Miscast minor Simenon, not exactly badly made but with no spark of excitement or suspense.

wd Harold French, *novel* Georges Simenon *ph* Otto Heller *m* Benjamin Frankel

Claude Rains, Marius Goring, Marta Toren, Anouk Aimée, Herbert Lom, Ferdy Mayne

The Man Who Would Be King*
US 1975 129m colour Panavision
Columbia / Allied Artists / Persky-Bright / Devon (John Foreman)

In India in the 1880s, two adventurers find themselves accepted as kings by a remote tribe, but greed betrays them.
After an ingratiating start this ambitious fable becomes more predictable, and comedy gives way to unpleasantness. Despite its sporadic high quality, one does not remember it with enthusiasm.

w John Huston, Gladys Hill, *story* Rudyard Kipling *d* John Huston *ph* Oswald Morris *m* Maurice Jarre *pd* Alexander Trauner

Sean Connery, Michael Caine, Christopher Plummer (as Kipling), Saeed Jaffrey, Jack May, Shakira Caine

The Man with a Cloak*
US 1951 81m bw
MGM (Stephen Ames)

In 1848 New York, a mysterious stranger (who turns out to be Edgar Allan Poe) helps a young French girl to keep her inheritance.
Curious domestic melodrama set on MGM's choicest sets; its playful literary allusion causes it to fall between suspense thriller and character drama, but the acting keeps one watching.

w Frank Fenton, *story* John Dickson Carr *d Fletcher Markle ph George Folsey m* David Raksin

Joseph Cotten, Barbara Stanwyck, Leslie Caron, Louis Calhern, Joe de Santis, Jim Backus, Margaret Wycherly

The Man with Nine Lives
US 1940 73m bw
Columbia
GB title: *Behind the Door*

Trying to cure cancer by freezing, Dr Kravaal is locked in his own secret ice chamber. But ten years later he is revived, proving his theory.
Less a horror comic than a prophetic piece of science fiction, rather tamely told.

w Karl Brown *d* Nick Grinde *ph* Benjamin Kline

Boris Karloff, Roger Pryor, Jo Ann Sayers, Stanley Brown, Byron Foulger

The Man with the Golden Arm*
US 1956 119m bw
Otto Preminger

A Chicago poker dealer finally kicks the drug habit.
Sensational on its first release, with its cold turkey scenes, this now seems a muddled impressionist melodrama with echoes of the silent German cinema and much over-acting and miscasting all round. But Sinatra is good; and it *is* different . . .

w Walter Newman, Lewis Meltzer, *novel* Nelson Algren *d* Otto Preminger *ph Sam Leavitt m Elmer Bernstein pd* Joe Wright *titles Saul Bass*

Frank Sinatra, Kim Novak, Eleanor Parker, Darren McGavin, Arnold Stang, Robert Strauss, John Conte, Doro Merande, George E. Stone

'Nothing very surprising or exciting . . . a pretty plain and unimaginative look-see at a lower depths character.'—*Bosley Crowther*

'A very inferior film . . . the script is inexcusably clumsy, the sets are unbelievable and the casting is ridiculous.'—*Diana Willing, Films in Review*

'It has the same running time as *Citizen Kane* but it seems a whole lot longer.'—*Robert James*

The Man with the Golden Gun*
GB 1974 125m Eastmancolor
UA / Eon (Harry Saltzman, Albert R. Broccoli)

James Bond goes to the Far East to liquidate a professional assassin named Scaramanga.
Thin and obvious Bond extravaganza with conventional expensive excitements.

w Richard Maibaum, Tom Mankiewicz, *novel* Ian Fleming *d* Guy Hamilton *ph* Ted Moore, Oswald Morris *m* John Barry *pd* Peter Murton

Roger Moore, Christopher Lee, Britt Ekland, Maude Adams, Hervé Villechaize, Clifton James, Richard Loo, Marc Lawrence

'The script lacks satiric insolence and the picture grinds on humourlessly.'—*New Yorker*

The Man With The Gun*
US 1955 84m bw
UA / Formosa (Sam Goldwyn Jnr)
GB title: *The Trouble Shooter*

A gunfighter in search of his estranged wife becomes lawman of a lawless town.
Modest, watchable western.

w N. B. Stone Jnr, Richard Wilson *d* Richard Wilson *ph* Lee Garmes *m* Alex North

Robert Mitchum, Jan Sterling, Karen Sharpe, Henry Hull, Emile Meyer, John Lupton

The Man with Two Faces*
US 1934 72m bw
Warner

An actor takes revenge on a scoundrel who had preyed on his sister.
Pleasing melodrama hinging on disguise; the Hays Office surprisingly allowed the hero to get away with it.

w Tom Reed, Niven Busch, *play* The Dark Tower by George S. Kaufman, Alexander Woolcott *d* Archie Mayo *ph* Tony Gaudio

Edward G. Robinson, Mary Astor, Ricardo Cortez, Louis Calhern, Mae Clarke, John Eldredge

The Man Within*
GB 1947 88m Technicolor
GFD / Production Film Service
US title: *The Smugglers*

An orphan boy discovers that his mysterious new guardian is a smuggler.
Unconvincing period yarn which has managed to drain every vestige of subtlety from the novel, but at least looks good.

w Muriel and Sydney Box, *novel* Graham Greene *d* Bernard Knowles *ph* Geoffrey Unsworth *m* Clifton Parker

Michael Redgrave, Richard Attenborough, Jean Kent, Joan Greenwood

The Man without a Country*
US 1973 73m colour TVM
Norman Rosemont

In the 18th century a young man damns his country and is sentenced never to set foot on it again.
Well-acted presentation of an American fable which in the end seems rather foolish.

w Sidney Carroll, *story* Edward Everett Hale *d* Delbert Mann

Cliff Robertson, Beau Bridges, Peter Strauss, Robert Ryan, Patricia Elliott, Walter Abel

The Man without a Star*
US 1955 89m Technicolor
U-I (Aaron Rosenberg)

A wandering cowboy helps settlers to put up barbed wire against an owner of vast cattle herds.
Conventional but entertaining star western.

w Borden Chase, D. D. Beauchamp, *novel* Dee Linford *d* King Vidor *ph* Russell Metty *m* Joseph Gershenson

Kirk Douglas, Jeanne Crain, Claire Trevor, William Campbell, Jay C. Flippen, Mara Corday, Richard Boone

The Manchurian Candidate***
US 1962 126m bw
UA / MC (Howard W. Koch)

A Korean war 'hero' comes back a brainwashed zombie triggered to kill a liberal politician, his control being his own monstrously ambitious mother.
Insanely plotted but brilliantly handled spy thriller, a mixture of Hitchcock, Welles and *All the King's Men*.

w George Axelrod, *novel* Richard Condon *d John Frankenheimer ph Lionel Lindon* *m* David Amram *pd Richard Sylbert*

Frank Sinatra, Laurence Harvey, Janet Leigh, James Gregory, Angela Lansbury, Henry Silva, John McGiver

'The unAmerican film of the year.'—*Penelope Houston*

'An intelligent, funny, superbly written, beautifully played, and brilliantly directed study of the all-embracing fantasy in everyday social, emotional and political existence.'—*Philip Strick, 1973*

Mandingo
US 1975 126m Technicolor
Dino de Laurentiis (Peter Herald)

On a slave breeding plantation in 1840 Louisiana, passions ride high.
Like *Gone with the Wind* with all the characters on heat, this exuberant and unpleasant melodrama goes several points over the top from start to finish but proved to have wide appeal for the groundlings, in the *Tobacco Road* tradition of a wallow in other people's depravities.

w Norman Wexler, *play* Jack Kirkland, *novel* Kyle Onstott *d* Richard Fleischer *ph* Richard H. Kline *m* Maurice Jarre *pd* Boris Leven

James Mason, Susan George, Perry King, Richard Ward, Brenda Sykes, Ken Norton

Mandy***
GB 1952 93m bw
Ealing (Leslie Norman)
US title: *The Crash of Silence*

A little girl, born deaf, is sent to a special school.
Carefully wrought and very sympathetic little semi-documentary film in which all the adults underplay in concession to a new child star who alas did not last long at the top.

w Nigel Balchin, Jack Whittingham, *novel* This Day Is Ours by Hilda Lewis *d Alexander Mackendrick ph* Douglas Slocombe *m* William Alwyn

Jack Hawkins, Terence Morgan, Phyllis Calvert, *Mandy Miller*, Godfrey Tearle, Dorothy Alison

Maneater
US 1973 74m Technicolor TVM
Universal (Robert F. O'Neil)

Holidaymakers are trapped in a wild animal quarry whose mad owner releases tigers to stalk and kill them.
The Hounds of Zaroff ride again, but not very excitingly.

w Vince Edwards, Marcus Demian, Jimmy Sangster *d* Vince Edwards

Richard Basehart, Ben Gazzara, Sheree North, Kip Niven

Manhandled
US 1949 97m bw
Paramount / Pine–Thomas

The secretary of a bogus psychiatrist becomes involved in a murder and finds herself in danger from all comers.
Modest, overlong suspenser with adequate production values.

w Lewis R. Foster, Whitman Chambers, *novel* The Man Who Stole a Dream by L. S. Goldsmith *d* Lewis R. Foster *ph* Ernest Laszlo *m* David Chudnow

Dorothy Lamour, Dan Duryea, Sterling Hayden, Irene Hervey, Harold Vermilyea, Philip Reed, Alan Napier, Art Smith, Irving Bacon

Manhattan Melodrama**
US 1934 93m bw
MGM (David O. Selznick)

Two slum boys grow up friends, one as district attorney and the other as a gangster.
Archetypal American situation drama (cf *Angels with Dirty Faces, Cry of the City*, etc), with the bad guy inevitably indulging in self-sacrifice at the end. An all-star cast makes it palatable in this case, though the film is inevitably dated.

w Oliver H. P. Garrett, Joseph L. Mankiewicz, *story* Arthur Caesar *d* W. S. Van Dyke *ph* James Wong Howe

William Powell, Clark Gable, Myrna Loy, Leo Carrillo, Nat Pendleton, George Sidney, Isabel Jewell, Thomas E. Jackson
† *Manhattan Melodrama* gained some irrelevant fame as the movie John Dillinger was watching when he was cornered and shot.

Manhunter*
US 1974 74m colour TVM
Quinn Martin

In 1933, when his fiancée is killed by public enemies, an ex-marine becomes a travelling G-man dedicated to their capture.
Dour pilot with a good period feel and a hulking Superman hero; the one-season series which followed was surprisingly dull.

w Sam Rolfe *d* Walter Grauman

Ken Howard, Gary Lockwood, Tim O'Connor, James Olson, Stefanie Powers

Maniac
GB 1963 86m bw Hammerscope
Columbia / Hammer (Jimmy Sangster)

Murders by oxyacetelyne torch in the Camargue, with the wrong lunatic going to the asylum.
Hammer's mark two plot, the shuddery murder mystery in which someone is not quite what he seems; feebly done in this case, with a fatally slow start.

w Jimmy Sangster *d* Michael Carreras *ph* Wilkie Cooper

Kerwin Mathews, Donald Houston, Nadia Gray, Justine Lord

Mannequin
US 1937 95m bw
MGM (Joseph L. Mankiewicz)

The wife of a small-time crook gets a modelling job and falls for a shipping magnate.
Competent star melodrama about a working girl's harassments.

w Lawrence Hazard *d* Frank Borzage
ph George Folsey *m* Edward Ward

Joan Crawford, Spencer Tracy, Alan Curtis, Ralph Morgan, Mary Philips, Elizabeth Risdon, Leo Gorcey

Manpower*
US 1941 103m bw
Warner (Mark Hellinger)

Power linesmen fall out over a nightclub hostess.
Yet another variation on *Tiger Shark*, with vivid fisticuff and storm sequences supporting the star performers.

w Richard Macaulay, Jerry Wald *d* Raoul Walsh *ph* Ernest Haller *m* Adolph Deutsch

Edward G. Robinson, George Raft, Marlene Dietrich, Alan Hale, Frank McHugh, Eve Arden, Barton MacLane, Walter Catlett, Joyce Compton, Ward Bond

'The pace and cutting are those of the best gangster films . . . the climax outdoes anything the Lyceum may have known.'—*William Whitebait*

Man's Castle*
US 1933 75m bw
Columbia

Romance blooms among the unemployed who live in a shanty town on the banks of the East River.
Depression moonshine which at the time was taken for realism; sociologically very interesting but very faded as entertainment.

w Jo Swerling, *play* Lawrence Hazard *d* Frank Borzage *ph* Joseph August

Spencer Tracy, Loretta Young, Glenda Farrell, Walter Connolly, Arthur Hohl, Marjorie Rambeau, Dickie Moore

Man's Favourite Sport?*
US 1963 120m Technicolor
Universal / Gibraltar / Laurel (Howard Hawks)

A star salesman of fishing tackle finds his bluff called when he has to enter a fishing competition.
Over-extended romantic farce drawn by the director from memories of older and better films, such as *Libeled Lady* and his own *Bringing Up Baby*.

w John Fenton Murray *d* Howard Hawks
ph Russell Harlan *m* Henry Mancini

Rock Hudson, Paula Prentiss, Maria Perschy, Charlene Holt, John McGiver, Roscoe Karns

'Hawks' deadpan documentation of a physical gag is as effective as ever, but the overall pace of his direction is curiously contemplative, as though he were savoring all his past jokes for the last time.'—*Andrew Sarris*

Mantrap
US 1961 93m bw Panavision
Paramount / Tiger (Edmond O'Brien, Stanley Frazen)

An honest man is lured by an old Marine friend into a hi-jack attempt which leads to the death of his wife.
Rather uninteresting melodrama, played and directed for more than it's worth.

w Ed Waters, *novel* Taint of the Tiger by John D. Macdonald *d* Edmond O'Brien *ph* Loyal Griggs *m* Leith Stevens

Jeffrey Hunter, David Janssen, Stella Stevens, Hugh Sanders

Manuela*
GB 1957 95m bw
British Lion / Ivan Foxwell

In a South American port, the engineer of a tramp steamer smuggles aboard a half caste girl, but it is the disillusioned captain who falls in love with her.
Downbeat seafaring melodrama, fine for those seeking a mood piece.

w William Woods, from his novel *d* Guy Hamilton *ph* Otto Heller *m* William Alwyn

Trevor Howard, Elsa Martinelli, Pedro Armedariz, Donald Pleasance

Many Rivers to Cross*
US 1955 94m Eastmancolor Cinemascope
MGM (Jack Cummings)

A trapper bound for Canada is helped by a sharp-shooting girl, and in return he saves her from marauding Indians.
Simple-minded, cheerful, quite refreshing western compounded of equal parts comedy and action.

w Harry Brown, Guy Trosper *d* Roy Rowland
ph John Seitz *m* Cyril Mockridge

Robert Taylor, Eleanor Parker, Victor McLaglen, Josephine Hutchinson, Jeff Richards, Russ Tamblyn, James Arness, Alan Hale Jnr

Mara Maru
US 1952 98m bw
Warner (David Weisbart)

A Manila salvage expert locates a sunken treasure and defeats crooks who are also in pursuit of it.
Lethargic but pleasant-looking star vehicle with a plot borrowed from *The Maltese Falcon*.

w N. Richard Nash, Philip Yordan, Sidney Harmon, Hollister Noble *d* Gordon Douglas *ph Robert Burks* *m* Max Steiner

Errol Flynn, Ruth Roman, Raymond Burr, Paul Picerni, Richard Webb

The Marat/Sade*
GB 1966 116m De Luxe
UA / Marat Sade (Michael Birkett)
aka: *The Persecution and Assassination of Jean-Paul Marat as performed by the inmates of the Asylum of Charenton under the direction of the Marquis de Sade*

The title tells all, except that at the end the inmates go berserk.
Fairly plain filming of an Old Vic *succès d'estime* which it became fashionable to announce that one had seen and understood. The film makes no effort to attract the unbeliever.

w Adrian Mitchell, *play* Peter Weiss *d* Peter Brook *ph* David Watkin *m* Richard Peaslee

Glenda Jackson, Patrick Magee, Ian Richardson, Michael Williams, Robert Lloyd, Clifford Rose, Freddie Jones

The Marcus Nelson Murders**
US 1973 148m Technicolor TVM
Universal (Abby Mann)

A New York detective tries to help a black youth wrongly arrested for the murder of two women.
Dour, unrecognizable pilot for *Kojak*: the series was much more escapist in tone than this grimly accurate exploration of New York ghettos.

w Abby Mann, from files on record *d* Joseph Sargent

Telly Savalas, Marjoe Gortner, Gene Woodbury, Jose Ferrer, Ned Beatty

Marcus Welby MD
US 1968 98m Technicolor TVM
Universal (David Victor)
aka: *A Matter of Humanities*

An elderly small-town doctor with heart trouble takes on a young assistant and together they help a small boy who cannot speak or write.
Dullish pilot for long-running series. The star subsequently got a better haircut.

w Don M. Mankiewicz *d* David Lowell Rich

Robert Young, James Brolin, Anne Baxter, Pete Duel, Susan Strasberg, Lew Ayres

Mardi Gras
US 1958 107m De Luxe Cinemascope
TCF (Jerry Wald)

In New Orleans at holiday time, a film star falls for a cadet.
Mindless musical using up available talent.

w Winston Miller, Hal Kanter *d* Edmund Goulding *ph* Wilfrid M. Cline *md* Lionel Newman

Pat Boone, Christine Carere, Sheree North, Tommy Sands, Gary Crosby, Fred Clark, Richard Sargent, Barrie Chase

Margie***
US 1946 94m Technicolor
TCF (Walter Morosco)

A married woman reminisces about her college days, when she married the French teacher despite her tendency to lose her bloomers at the most embarrassing moments.
Wholly pleasing nostalgia, very smartly and brightly handled.

w F. Hugh Herbert, *stories* Ruth McKinney, Richard Bransten *d Henry King* *ph* Charles Clarke *md* Alfred Newman

Jeanne Crain, Glenn Langan, *Alan Young*, Lynn Bari, Barbara Lawrence, Conrad Janis, Esther Dale

Margin for Error*
US 1943 74m bw
TCF (Ralph Dietrich)

Just before World War II, the Nazi consul in New York is murdered in his own office.
Mildly intriguing whodunnit with the case solved by a Jewish cop.

w Lillie Hayward, *play* Clare Boothe Luce *d* Otto Preminger *ph* Edward Cronjager *m* Leigh Harline

Milton Berle, Joan Bennett, Otto Preminger, Carl Esmond, Howard Freeman, Poldy Dur, Hans Von Twardowski

Marie Antoinette*
US 1938 149m bw
MGM (Hunt Stromberg)

The last days of the French court before the revolution.
Too slow by half, and so glamorized and fictionalized as to lack all interest, this long delayed production stands only as an example of MGM's expensive prestige movies of the thirties.

w Claudine West, Donald Ogden Stewart, Ernest Vajda
d W. S. Van Dyke *ph* William Daniels *montage* Slavko Vorkapitch *m* Herbert Stothart *ad* Cedric Gibbons

Norma Shearer, Tyrone Power, John Barrymore, Robert Morley, Gladys George, Anita Louise, Joseph Schildkraut, Henry Stephenson, Reginald Gardiner, Peter Bull, Albert Dekker, Cora Witherspoon, Barnett Parker, Joseph Calleia, Henry Kolker, George Zucco, Henry Daniell, Harry Davenport, Barry Fitzgerald, Mae Busch, Robert Barrat

Marines Let's Go
US 1961 103m De Luxe
Cinemascope
TCF (Raoul Walsh)

Marines fighting in Korea are granted leave in Japan.
Brawling tragi-farce with predictable characters, a long way after *What Price Glory*.

w John Twist, *story* Raoul Walsh *d* Raoul Walsh *ph* Lucien Ballard *m* Irving Gertz

Tom Tryon, David Hedison, Tom Reese, Linda Hutchins, William Tyler

'A typically noisy, insensitive and maudlin tribute to the American Marines.'—*MFB*

Marjorie Morningstar
US 1958 123m Warnercolor
(Warner) United States Pictures (Milton Sperling)

A New York Jewish girl has great ambitions for herself but ends up a suburban housewife.
Stodgy 'woman's picture' with all talents somewhat uneasy in their assignments, mainly because the Jewish quality is imperfectly conveyed.

w Everett Freeman, *novel* Herman Wouk
d Irving Rapper *ph* Harry Stradling *m* Max Steiner

Natalie Wood, Gene Kelly, Claire Trevor, Everett Sloane, Ed Wynn, Martin Milner, Carolyn Jones, George Tobias, Jesse White, Martin Balsam

The Mark*
GB 1961 127m bw Cinemascope
TCF / Raymond Stross / Sidney Buchman

A sexual psychopath finds on emerging from prison that his past still haunts him despite the help of his psychiatrist.
Worthy but evasive social drama which outstays its welcome but provides good performances.

w Sidney Buchman, Stanley Mann *d* Guy Green *ph* Douglas Slocombe *m* Richard Rodney Bennett

Stuart Whitman, Maria Schell, *Rod Steiger*, Brenda de Banzie, Maurice Denham, Donald Wolfit, Paul Rogers, Donald Houston

'There is seriousness and care, but neither boldness nor passion . . . no hint of the truly sordid is allowed to seep through.'—*MFB*

Mark of the Vampire*
US 1935 61m bw
MGM (E. J. Mannix)

A policeman tries to solve an old murder in an eerie house by hiring vaudeville performers to pose as vampires.
Semi-spoof horror which is flawed by lack of pace and a patchy script, but contains splendid visual moments. A remake of the Lon Chaney silent, *London After Midnight*.

w Guy Endore, Bernard Schubert *d Tod Browning ph James Wong Howe*

Lionel Barrymore, Jean Hersholt, Elizabeth Allan, Bela Lugosi, Carol Borland, Lionel Atwill, Henry Wadsworth, Donald Meek, Jessie Ralph, Ivan Simpson, Holmes Herbert

The Mark of Zorro***
US 1940 94m bw
TCF (Raymond Griffith)

After being educated in Spain, Diego de Vega returns to California and finds the country enslaved and his father half-corrupted by tyrants. Disguising himself as a masked bandit, he leads the country to expel the usurpers.
Splendid adventure stuff for boys of all ages, an amalgam of *The Scarlet Pimpernel* and *Robin Hood* to which in this version the director adds an overwhelming pictorial sense which makes it stand out as the finest of all.

w John Tainton Foote, Garrett Fort, Bess Meredyth, *novel* The Curse of Capistrano by Johnston McCulley *d Rouben Mamoulian ph Arthur Miller m Alfred Newman*
ad Richard Day, Joseph C. Wright

Tyrone Power, Basil Rathbone, J. Edward Bromberg, Linda Darnell, Eugene Pallette, Montagu Love, Janet Beecher, Robert Lowery

The Mark of Zorro
US 1974 74m colour TVM
TCF

Modestly competent TV version.

w Brian Taggert *d* Don McDougall

Frank Langella, Ricardo Montalban, Gilbert Roland, Louise Sorel, Yvonne de Carlo, Robert Middleton

Marked Woman*
US 1937 96m bw
Warner (Lou Edelman)

A nightclub girl is persuaded to testify against an underworld boss.
A twist on the usual run of gangster melodramas, performed with the star's accustomed intensity and presented with the studio's usual panache.

w Robert Rossen, Abem Finkel *d* Lloyd Bacon *ph* George Barnes *md* Leo F. Forbstein

Bette Davis, Humphrey Bogart, Jane Bryan, Eduardo Ciannelli, Isabel Jewell, Allen Jenkins, Mayo Methot, Lola Lane, Henry O'Neill

Marlowe*
US 1969 95m Metrocolor
MGM / Katzka–Berne–Cherokee / Beckerman (Sergei Petchnikoff)

Private eye Philip Marlowe is hired by a nervous girl to find her missing brother.
The authentic Chandler atmosphere is caught by this busy thriller, but there seems to be a deliberate attempt to make a confusing plot even more obscure, so that the end result is more tiresome than amusing.

w Stirling Silliphant, *novel* The Little Sister by Raymond Chandler *d* Paul Bogart *ph* William H. Daniels *m* Peter Matz

James Garner, Rita Moreno, Sharon Farrell, Bruce Lee, Gayle Hunnicutt, Carroll O'Connor, William Daniels, Jackie Coogan

'One does wonder whether the simple human squalor of the Bogart–Chandler era can ever be recaptured by an increasingly meretricious Hollywood.'—*MFB*

Marnie*
US 1964 130m Technicolor
Universal / Geoffrey Stanley Inc (Alfred Hitchcock)

A rich man marries a kleptomaniac and cures her, but a nightmare in her past makes her still sexually frigid.
Psychodrama with background crime and suspense, lethargically handled by the old master, who alone knows what he saw in it in the first place, as this heroine does not even have fire under her ice. The production is curiously artificial in many ways, from dummy horses to backcloths to back projection.

w Jay Presson Allen, *novel* Winston Graham *d* Alfred Hitchcock *ph* Robert Burks *m* Bernard Herrmann *pd* Robert Boyle

Tippi Hedren, Sean Connery, Martin Gabel, Diane Baker, Louise Latham

Marooned*
US 1969 134m Technicolor Panavision 70
Columbia / Frankovich–Sturges (Frank Capra Jnr)

Three astronauts are stranded in space, and a rescue mission gets under way.
Very heavy-going space suspenser with all possible technical accomplishment but little life of its own.

w Mayo Simon, *novel* Martin Caidin *d* John Sturges *ph* Daniel Fapp *pd* Lyle R. Wheeler

Gregory Peck, Richard Crenna, David Janssen, James Franciscus, Gene Hackman, Lee Grant, Nancy Kovack, Mariette Hartley, Scott Brady

'In something like the plight of Ironman One, Sturges' work seems on the point of slowing to a standstill as it drifts further into projects of ever-increasing, self-effacing size and anonymous technical dexterity.'—*Richard Combs*

'It has all the zip, zest and zing of a moon walk, and I suspect a computer fed a dictionary could come up with better dialogue.'—*Judith Crist, 1973*

The Marriage Go Round
US 1961 98m De Luxe Cinemascope
TCF (Leslie Stevens)

A Swedish girl suggests to a married American professor that she borrow his body for mating purposes, believing they would produce the perfect child.
Silly, unfunny sex comedy.

w Leslie Stevens *d* Walter Lang *ph* Leo Tover *m* Dominic Frontière

James Mason, Susan Hayward, Julie Newmar, Robert Paige, June Clayworth

'As tedious as it is tasteless.'—*Evening Standard*

Marriage Is a Private Affair
US 1943 116m bw
MGM (Pandro S. Berman)

A spoilt rich girl becomes a petulant wife.
Abysmally slow, uninvolving and poorly acted star fodder.

w David Hertz, Lenore Coffee, *novel* Judith Kelly *d* Robert Z. Leonard *ph* Ray June *m* Bronislau Kaper

Lana Turner, James Craig, John Hodiak, Frances Gifford, Keenan Wynn, Natalie Schaefer, Hugh Marlowe, Paul Cavanagh

The Marriage of a Young Stockbroker**
US 1971 95m De Luxe
TCF / Laurence Turman

A stockbroker who finds his life and his marriage dull tries voyeurism and extra-marital sex.
Sardonic adult comedy of the battle between the sexes, pretty lively from start to finish.

w Lorenzo Semple Jnr, novel Charles Webb *d* Laurence Turman *ph* Laszlo Kovacs *m* Fred Karlin

Richard Benjamin, Joanna Shimkus, Elizabeth Ashley, Adam West, Patricia Barry

Marriage on the Rocks
US 1965 109m Technicolor Panavision
Warner / A-C / Sinatra (William H. Daniels)

An ad man and his wife decide to go to Mexico for a divorce but once there change their minds; she ends up accidentally married to his best friend.
All this talent retreats fearfully from a witless, tasteless script and slow handling. A dismal comedy.

w Cy Howard *d* Jack Donohue *ph* William H. Daniels *m* Nelson Riddle

Frank Sinatra, Dean Martin, Deborah Kerr, Cesar Romero, Hermione Baddeley, Tony Bill, Nancy Sinatra, John McGiver

'A long, coarse, and nearly always unfunny comedy, hammered together for no apparent reason except to make money.'—*New Yorker*

The Marriage Playground
US 1929 70m bw
Paramount

Children of divorced rich parents wander round Europe in a group.
Slightly unusual drama of its day; sound technique very thin.

w J. Walter Rubin, Doris Anderson, *novel* The Children by Edith Wharton *d* Lothar Mendes *ph* Victor Milner

Fredric March, Kay Francis, Mary Brian, Lilyan Tashman, Huntley Gordon, Anita Louise

Marriage: Year One
US 1970 100m Technicolor TVM
Universal / Norman Felton (Stephen Karpf)

Problems of lovers who marry while still at college.
The kind of problems most adult viewers at least can do without.

w Stephen and Elinor Karpf *d* William Graham

Sally Field, Robert Pratt, William Windom, Agnes Moorehead, Neville Brand

The Marrying Kind**
US 1952 93m bw
Columbia (Bert Granet)

A couple seeking divorce tell their troubles to a judge, and change their minds.
Smart, New Yorkish, tragi-comic star vehicle which works pretty well.

w Ruth Gordon, Garson Kanin *d* George Cukor *ph* Joseph Walker *m* Hugo Friedhofer

Judy Holliday, Aldo Ray, Madge Kennedy, Mickey Shaughnessy

The Marseilles Contract
GB / France 1974 89m Eastmancolor
Warner / AIP / Kettledrum / PECF (Judd Bernard)
US title: *The Destructors*

An American narcotics agent in Paris hires an assassin to dispose of a drug smuggler.
Routine action melodrama with a jokey atmosphere not sustained by a downbeat script.

w Judd Bernard *d* Robert Parrish *ph* Douglas Slocombe *m* Roy Budd.

Michael Caine, Anthony Quinn, James Mason, Alexandra Stewart, Marcel Bozzufi, Maurice Ronet

Marty****
US 1955 91m bw
UA / Hecht–Hill–Lancaster (Harold Hecht)

A 34-year-old Brooklyn butcher fears he will never get a girl because he is unattractive, but at a Saturday night dance he meets a girl with similar fears. Unfortunately she is not Italian . . .
The first of the filmed teleplays which in the mid-fifties seemed like a breath of spring to Hollywood (they were cheap) and also brought in a new wave of talent. This is one of the best, its new naturalistic dialogue falling happily on the ear; but it has been so frequently imitated since that its revolutionary appearance is hard to imagine.

w Paddy Chayevsky, from his play *d Delbert Mann ph Joseph La Shelle m* Roy Webb

Ernest Borgnine, Betsy Blair, Esther Minciotti, Joe Mantell, Karen Steele, Jerry Paris

'Something rare in the American cinema today: a subtle, ironic and compassionate study of ordinary human relationships.'—*Gavin Lambert*

Mary Burns Fugitive*
US 1935 84m bw
Paramount (Walter Wanger)

The innocent girl friend of a gangster is

convicted through circumstantial evidence, escapes from prison and finds true love. Competent meshing of well-tried thirties elements, a good typical wish-fulfilment melodrama of its time.

w Gene Towne, Graham Baker, Louis Stevens *d* William K. Howard *ph* Leon Shamroy

Sylvia Sidney, Melvyn Douglas, Alan Baxter, Pert Kelton, Wallace Ford, Brian Donlevy, Esther Dale

Mary Mary
US 1963 126m Technicolor
Warner (Mervyn Le Roy)

A publisher falls in love again with his ex-wife but finds she is being pursued by a film star. Feeble film version of a lighter-than-air Broadway success, with the actors paralysed behind the footlights and the camera asleep in the stalls.

w Richard L. Breen, *play* Jean Kerr *d* Mervyn Le Roy *ph* Harry Stradling *m* Frank Perkins

Debbie Reynolds, Barry Nelson, Michael Rennie, Diane McBain

Mary of Scotland*
US 1936 123m bw
RKO (Pandro S. Berman)

Mary Stuart refuses to give up her claim to the English throne, and is eventually executed. Sombre historical charade with splendid sets and atmosphere but suffering from script and performances that don't quite make it despite effort all round.

w Dudley Nichols, *play* Maxwell Anderson *d* John Ford *ph Joseph H. August m* Nathaniel Shilkret *ad Van Nest Polglase, Carroll Clark*

Katharine Hepburn, Fredric March, Donald Crisp, Florence Eldridge, Douglas Walton, John Carradine, Robert Barrat, Monte Blue, Moroni Olsen, Frieda Inescort, Alan Mowbray

'An unpromising and stagey play is fleshed out into a rich and confident exercise in filmcraft.'—*John Baxter, 1968*

Mary Poppins***
US 1964 139m Technicolor
Walt Disney (Bill Walsh)

In Edwardian London a magical nanny teaches two slightly naughty children to make life enjoyable for themselves and others. Sporadically a very pleasant and effective entertainment for children of all ages, with plenty of brightness and charm including magic tricks, the mixing of live with cartoon adventures, and just plain fun. It suffers, however, from a wandering narrative in the second half (when Miss Poppins scarcely appears) and from Mr Van Dyke's really lamentable attempt at Cockney.

w Bill Walsh, Don da Gradi, *novel* P. L. Travers *d* Robert Stevenson *ph* Edward Colman *m/ly Richard M. and Robert B. Sherman pd* Tony Walton *sp Eustace Lycett, Peter Ellenshaw, Robert A. Mattey*

Julie Andrews, David Tomlinson, Glynis Johns, Dick Van Dyke, Reginald Owen, Ed Wynn, Matthew Garber, Karen Dotrice, Hermione Baddeley, Elsa Lanchester, Arthur Treacher, Jane Darwell

Mary Queen of Scots
GB 1971 128m Technicolor
Panavision
Universal / Hal B. Wallis

The story of Mary Stuart's opposition to Elizabeth I, her imprisonment and execution. Schoolbook history in which none of the characters comes to life; dramatic movement is almost entirely lacking despite the liberties taken with fact.

w John Hale *ph* Christopher Challis *d* Charles Jarrott *m* John Barry

Vanessa Redgrave, Glenda Jackson, Trevor Howard, Patrick McGoohan

M*A*S*H***
US 1970 116m De Luxe Panavision
TCF / Aspen (Ingo Preminger, Leon Ericksen)

Surgeons at a mobile hospital in Korea spend what spare time they have chasing women and bucking authority.
Savage comedy of man's rebellion in the face of death, alternating sex farce with gory operation scenes; hailed as the great anti-everything film, and certainly very funny for those who can take it. It led to a television series which for once did not disgrace its original.

w Ring Lardner Jnr, novel Richard Hooker *d Robert Altman ph* Harold E. Stine *m* Johnny Mandel

Donald Sutherland, Elliott Gould, Tom Skerritt, Sally Kellerman, Robert Duvall, Jo Ann Pflug, René Auberjonois, Gary Burghof

'Bloody funny. A hyper-acute wiretap on mankind's death wish.'—*Joseph Morgenstern*

'The laughter is blood-soaked and the comedy cloaks a bitter and terrible truth.'—*Judith Crist*

The Mask of Dimitrios***
US 1944 99m bw
Warner (Henry Blanke)

A timid Dutch novelist is drawn into a Middle-Eastern intrigue with money at the centre of it. Generally successful international intriguer, moodily shot in evocative sets, and remarkable for its time in that the story is not distorted to fit romantic stars: character actors bear the entire burden.

w Frank Gruber, novel Eric Ambler *d Jean Negulesco ph Arthur Edeson m* Adolph Deutsch

Peter Lorre, Sidney Greenstreet, Zachary Scott, Faye Emerson, *Victor Francen, Steven Geray, Florence Bates, Eduardo Ciannelli, Kurt Katch,* John Abbott, Monte Blue

The Mask of Fu Manchu**

US 1932 70m bw
MGM

Nayland Smith and his party are caught and threatened with torture by the yellow terror.
Highly satisfactory episode in the nefarious adventures of the master criminal, fast moving, humorous and very good to look at.

w John Willard, Edgar Woolf, Irene Kuhn, *stories* Sax Rohmer *d Charles Brabin, Charles Vidor ph Tony Gaudio*

Boris Karloff, Myrna Loy, Lewis Stone, Karen Morley, Charles Starrett, Jean Hersholt, Lawrence Grant

The Mask of Sheba

US 1970 100m colour TVM
MGM

Experts from the Foundation of Man fly to Ethiopia to seek a previous expedition and a priceless heirloom.
Inept adventure hokum which never seems to get going.

w Sam Rolfe *d* David Lowell Rich

Eric Braeden, Stephen Young, Inger Stevens, Joseph Wiseman, Walter Pidgeon, William Marshall

The Masque of the Red Death**

GB 1964 89m Pathecolor
AIP / Alta Vista (George Willoughby)

A medieval Italian prince practises devil worship while the plague rages outside, but when he holds a ball, death is an uninvited guest.
Langorous, overstretched, often visually striking horror piece with some extremely effective touches among its longueurs.

w Charles Beaumont, R. Wright Campbell, *story* Edgar Allan Poe *d Roger Corman ph Nicolas Roeg m* David Lee *ad Robert Jones costumes Laura Nightingale*

Vincent Price, Hazel Court, Jane Asher, Patrick Magee, *John Westbrook*

Masquerade*

GB 1965 101m Eastmancolor
UA / Novus (Michael Relph)

To avert friction between Arab states the young heir to one of them is abducted by a British secret service agent; but one of the plotters has other fish to fry.
Quite a lively spy romp with a spectacular action climax, but the plot is simply too complicated.

w Michael Relph, William Goldman, *novel* Castle Minerva by Victor Canning *d* Basil Dearden *ph* Otto Heller *m* Philip Green *pd* Don Ashton

Cliff Robertson, Jack Hawkins, Charles Gray, Bill Fraser, Marisa Mell, Michel Piccoli, John Le Mesurier

Masquerade in Mexico

US 1945 96m bw
Paramount (Karl Tunberg)

A stranded showgirl is hired by a Mexican banker to entice a gigolo away from his wife.
Talent-starved remake of *Midnight* (qv), which seems second-hand even if you don't know why.

w Karl Tunberg *d* Mitchell Leisen *ph* Lionel Lindon *m* Victor Young

Dorothy Lamour, Arturo de Cordova, Patric Knowles, Ann Dvorak, George Rigaud, Natalie Schaefer, Mikhail Rasumny, Billy Daniels

Massacre at Sand Creek

US 1956 74m bw TVM
Columbia / Playhouse 90

An Indian-hating colonel leads his troops unnecessarily into battle.
Adequate mini-western.

d Arthur Hiller

Everett Sloane, John Derek, Gene Evans, H. M. Wynant

The Master of Ballantrae

GB 1953 89m Technicolor
Warner

Two brothers toss to decide which shall join Bonnie Prince Charlie's 1745 rebellion.
Half-hearted version of a classic adventure novel.

w Herb Meadow, *novel* R. L. Stevenson *d* William Keighley *ph* Jack Cardiff *m* William Alwyn

Errol Flynn, Anthony Steel, Roger Livesey, Beatrice Campbell, Felix Aylmer, Mervyn

Johns, Jacques Berthier, Yvonne Furneaux, Ralph Truman

'All that can be salvaged from this rather unforgivable Anglo-American junket are some pleasant exteriors.'—*Gavin Lambert*

Master of Bankdam*

GB 1947 105m bw

GFD / Holbein (Nat Bronsten, Walter Forde, Edward Dryhurst)

19th-century chronicles of a mill-owning Yorkshire family.

Archetypal 'trouble at t'mill' saga with moderate production, good acting and undeniably compulsive story.

w Edward Dryhurst, Moie Charles, *novel* Thomas Armstrong *d* Walter Forde

Tom Walls, Anne Crawford, Dennis Price, Stephen Murray, Linden Travers, Jimmy Hanley, Nancy Price, David Tomlinson, Herbert Lomas

Master of the World

US 1961 104m Magnacolor

AIP / Alta Vista (James H. Nicholson, Anthony Carras)

In 1848 a mad inventor takes to the air in his magnificent flying machine in the hope of persuading men to stop war.

Aerial version of *Twenty Thousand Leagues under the Sea*, with cheap sets and much use of stock footage; some scenes however have a certain vigour.

w Richard Matheson, *novels* Jules Verne *d* William Witney *ph* Gil Warrenton *m* Les Baxter

Vincent Price, Charles Bronson, Henry Hull, Mary Webster, David Frankham

Mata Hari**

US 1932 92m bw

MGM

The career of the famous lady spy of World War I.

Elaborate melodrama, pictorially satisfying and generally more entertaining than might be supposed, with both star and supporting cast in rich thespian form.

w Benjamin Glazer, Leo Birinski, Doris Anderson, Gilbert Emery *d George Fitzmaurice ph* William Daniels

Greta Garbo, Ramon Novarro, Lionel Barrymore, Lewis Stone, C. Henry Gordon, Karen Morley, Blanche Frederici

The Matchmaker*

US 1958 101m bw Vistavision

Paramount (Don Hartman)

In New York at the turn of the century, a rich merchant decides to marry again but the matchmaker he consults has her own eye on him.

Cold and lifeless version of an amusing play which also served as the basis for the musical *Hello Dolly* (qv).

w John Michael Hayes, *play* Thornton Wilder *d* Joseph Anthony *ph* Charles Lang *m* Adolph Deutsch

Shirley Booth, Paul Ford, Anthony Perkins, Shirley Maclaine, Wallace Ford, Robert Morse, Perry Wilson

'Long static dialogue exchanges are further extended by frequent confidences expressed directly to the audience . . . but in spite of the general lack of pace, lightness and dimension there is still a great deal to enjoy.'—*Peter John Dyer*

The Mating Game

US 1959 96m Metrocolor Cinemascope

MGM (Philip Barry Jnr)

An income-tax inspector becomes involved in the affairs of an unorthodox farming family.

Dismally unfunny adaptation for Americans of a very English novel; everyone works hard to no avail.

w William Roberts, *novel* The Darling Buds of May by H. E. Bates *d* George Marshall *ph* Robert Bronner *m* Jeff Alexander

Debbie Reynolds, Tony Randall, Paul Douglas, Fred Clark, Una Merkel, Philip Ober, Charles Lane, Philip Coolidge

'Every joke is driven past the point of exhaustion.'—*MFB*

The Mating Season

US 1950 101m bw

Paramount (Charles Brackett)

A factory draughtsman marries an ambassador's daughter; his mother loses her job and comes incognito to work for them as a cook.

Uninteresting mechanical domestic comedy in which the young folk are dull and the older ones overplay.

w Walter Reisch, Charles Brackett, Richard Breen *d* Mitchell Leisen *ph* Charles Lang

Gene Tierney, John Lund, Miriam Hopkins, Thelma Ritter, Jan Sterling

Matt Helm
US 1975 74m colour TVM
Columbia

An ex-CIA agent becomes a Los Angeles private eye.
Unrecognizable from the movie series and as routine as can be.

w Sam Rolfe *d* Buzz Kulik

Tony Franciosa, James Shigeta, Patrick MacNee, Laraine Stephens

A Matter of Life and Death****
GB 1946 104m Technicolor
GFD / Archers (Michael Powell, Emeric Pressburger)
US title: *Stairway to Heaven*

A pilot with brain damage after bailing out is torn between this world and the next, but an operation puts things to rights.
Outrageous fantasy which seemed more in keeping after the huge death toll of a world war, and in any case learned the Hollywood lesson of eating its cake and still having it, the supernatural elements being capable of explanation. A mammoth technical job in the heavenly sequences, it deserves full marks for its sheer arrogance, wit, style and film flair.

wd Michael Powell, Emeric Pressburger ph Jack Cardiff m Allan Gray pd Hein Heckroth

David Niven, Roger Livesey, Kim Hunter, Marius Goring, Raymond Massey, Abraham Sofaer

'Powell and Pressburger seem to have reached their heaven at last . . . an illimitable Wembley stadium, surrounded by tinkly music and mists, from which all men of insight, if they were ever careless enough to get there, would quickly blaspheme their way out.'—*Richard Winnington*

A Matter of Who
GB 1961 92m bw
MGM / Foray (Walter Shenson, Milton Holmes)

The World Health Organization tracks down a smallpox outbreak.
Curious blend of semi-documentary with suspense and comedy; not really a starter.

w Milton Holmes *d* Don Chaffey *ph* Erwin Hillier *m* Edwin Astley

Terry-Thomas, Sonja Ziemann, Alex Nicol, Guy Deghy, Richard Briers, Clive Morton, Geoffrey Keen, Martin Benson, Honor Blackman, Carol White

A Matter of Wife and Death
US 1975 74m colour TVM
Columbia
aka: *Shamus*

Adventures of another tough private eye. Boring.

w Don Ingalls *d* Marvin Chomsky

Rod Taylor, Tom Drake, Anita Gillette, Joe Santos

Maya
US 1966 91m Technicolor Panavision
MGM / King Brothers (Mary P. Murray, Herman King)

A teenage American boy arrives in India to visit his disillusioned father, who finally comes to understand him only after he has run away.
Good-looking but otherwise uninteresting animal drama which served as the pilot for a TV series.

w John Fante *d* John Berry *ph* Gunter Senftleben *m* Riz Ortolani

Clint Walker, Jay North, I. S. Johar, Sajid Kanh

Maybe I'll Come Home in the Spring
US 1970 74m colour TVM
Metromedia (Charles Fries)

A teenage runaway comes back home and tries to see her parents' point of view.
Well detailed domestic drama, just a wee bit over earnest.

w Bruce Feldman *d* Russ Metty

Eleanor Parker, Jackie Cooper, Lane Bradbury, Sally Field, David Carradine

Mayerling
France / GB 1968 141m Eastmancolor Panavision
Corona / Winchester (Robert Dorfmann)

In 1888 the heir to the Habsburg Empire is forced into a suicide pact with his mistress.
Tedious dramatization of historical events which in 1936 had made a delicate French film but in these hands seems an endless and boring manipulation of doubtful events into turgid romance.

wd Terence Young, *novel* Claude Anet *ph* Henri Alekan *m* Francis Lai *pd* Georges Wakhevitch

Omar Sharif, Catherine Deneuve, James Mason, Ava Gardner, James Robertson Justice, Genevieve Page, Ivan Desny, Maurice Teynac

The Mayor of Hell*
US 1933 90m bw
Warner

A racketeer becomes superintendent of a reform school, and it changes his life.

Moderate star vehicle with a plot that did yeoman service thereafter in Dead End Kids films.

w Edward Chodorov *d* Archie Mayo
ph Barney McGill *m* Leo F. Forbstein

James Cagney, Madge Evans, Allen Jenkins, Dudley Digges, Frankie Darro

'Propaganda for nothing: like most of what comes out of Hollywood, it is entertaining trash.'—*Time*

Maytime**
US 1937 132m bw (colour sequence) (originally shown in sepia)
MGM (Hunt Stromberg)

An opera star falls in love with a penniless singer but her jealous impresario shoots him.
Lush romantic musical which turns gradually into melodrama and ends in a ghostly reunion for the lovers. If that's what you like, it could scarcely be better done.

w Noel Langley, *operetta* Rida Johnson Young
d Robert Z. Leonard ph Oliver T. Marsh
m Sigmund Romberg md Herbert Sothart

Jeanette MacDonald, Nelson Eddy, John Barrymore, Herman Bing, Lynne Carver, Rafaela Ottiano, Paul Porcasi, Sig Rumann

Me and My Gal*
US 1932 79m bw
Fox
GB title: *Pier 13*

A cop on the beat romances a hashslinger and catches a crook.
Pleasant little programmer, very evocative of its period.

w Arthur Kober *d Raoul Walsh ph* Arthur Miller

Spencer Tracy, Joan Bennett, George Walsh, Marion Burns, J. Farrell MacDonald, Noel Madison, Henry B. Walthall

Me and the Colonel
US 1958 110m bw
Columbia / Court–Goetz (William Goetz)

In 1940 an anti-semitic Polish colonel is obliged to flee from France in the company of a Jewish refugee.
Rather obvious war comedy with predictable but not very entertaining situations, sentiment, action and pathos. The stars cope well enough but the picture never picks up steam.

w S. N. Behrman, George Froeschel, *play* Franz Werfel *d* Peter Glenville *ph* Burnett Guffey
m George Duning

Danny Kaye, Curt Jurgens, Nicole Maurey, Françoise Rosay, Akim Tamiroff, Martita Hunt, Alexander Scourby, Liliane Montevecchi, Ludwig Stossel

Me, Natalie*
US 1969 111m De Luxe
Cinema Center (Stanley Shapiro)

An unattractive 18-year-old girl moves into Greenwich Village and learns to accept herself as she is.
Basically very predictable but rather well done character study with excellent detail.

w A. Martin Zweiback *d Fred Coe ph* Arthur J. Ornitz *m* Henry Mancini

Patty Duke, James Farentino, Martin Balsam, Elsa Lanchester, Salome Jens, Nancy Marchand, Al Pacino

Mean Streets**
US 1973 110m Technicolor
Taplin–Perry–Scorsese (Jonathan T. Taplin)

Four young Italian-Americans use Tony's Bar as a base for drinking, brawling and hustling.
Relentlessly sordid melodrama with a good eye for realistic detail.

w Martin Scorsese, Mardik Martin *d* Martin Scorsese *ph* Norman Gerard

Harvey Keitel, Robert de Niro, David Proval, Amy Robinson, Richard Romanus

'A thicker-textured rot than we have ever had in an American movie, and a deeper sense of evil.'—*New Yorker*

'Lacks a sense of story and structure . . . unless a film-maker respects the needs of his audience, he can't complain if that audience fails to show up.'—*Variety*

'Extraordinarily rich and distinguished on many levels.'—*Joseph Gelmis*

The Mechanic
US 1972 100m Technicolor
UA / Chartoff / Winkler / Carlino

A professional assassin under contract to the Mafia makes his missions look like accidents.
Violent thriller with a few pretensions, but too flashily made to be taken seriously.

w Lewis John Carlino *d* Michael Winner
ph Richard Kline, Robert Paynter *m* Jerry Fielding

Charles Bronson, Jan-Michael Vincent, Keenan Wynn, Jill Ireland

A Medal for Benny*
US 1945 77m bw
Paramount (Paul Jones)

An old rustic is the centre of small town

celebrations in honour of his dead war hero son.
Satirical-sentimental location drama, effective but not memorable.

w Frank Butler, *story* John Steinbeck *d* Irving Pichel *ph* Lionel Lindon *m* Victor Young

Dorothy Lamour, Arturo de Cordova, *J. Carrol Naish*, Mikhail Rasumny, Charles Dingle, Frank McHugh, Grant Mitchell

Medical Story**
US 1975 100m colour TVM
Columbia (David Gerber)

An idealistic intern has some successes but loses his most valued patient.
Sharply made, hard-hitting and realistic hospital drama, pilot for a short-lived series.

w Abby Mann, Gary Nelson

Beau Bridges, Jose Ferrer, Harriet Karr, Shirley Knight, Carl Reiner, Claude Akins

Medium Cool**
US 1969 111m Technicolor
Paramount / H & J Pictures (Tully Friedman)

A TV news cameraman is made apathetic by the events around him.
Stimulating if overlong comment on the quality of life in the sixties, immaculately made and with a rather effective though obvious twist ending.

w/ d/ ph Haskell Wexler *m* Mike Bloomfield *ad* Leon Ericksen

Robert Forster, Verna Bloom, Peter Bonerz, Marianna Hill, Sid McCoy

'A deeply moving questioning of America's violence and voyeurism.'—*Jan Dawson*

Meet Danny Wilson
US 1952 83m bw
U-I (Leonard Goldstein)

An overbearing crooner gets to the top with the help of gangsters.
Fairly abrasive star vehicle, almost amounting to self-parody.

w Don McGuire *d* Joseph Pevney *ph* Maury Gertsman *md* Joseph Gershenson

Frank Sinatra, Shelley Winters, Alex Nicol, Raymond Burr

Meet John Doe***
US 1941 123m bw
Liberty Films (Frank Capra)

A tramp is hired to embody the common man in a phony political drive, and almost commits suicide.
Vividly staged but over-sentimental Capra extravaganza with high spots outnumbering low.

w Robert Riskin d Frank Capra ph George Barnes *m* Dmitri Tiomkin

Gary Cooper, *Barbara Stanwyck*, Edward Arnold, Walter Brennan, James Gleason, Spring Byington, Gene Lockhart, Rod la Rocque, Irving Bacon, Regis Toomey, Ann Doran, Warren Hymer, Andrew Tombes

Meet Me after the Show*
US 1951 88m Technicolor
TCF (George Jessel)

A musical star thinks she has discovered an affair between her husband and his glamorous backer.
Surprisingly bright routine musical.

w Mary Loos, Richard Sale *d Richard Sale ph Arthur E. Arling md* Lionel Newman *songs* Jule Styne, Leo Robin

Betty Grable, Macdonald Carey, Rory Calhoun, Eddie Albert, Irene Ryan

Meet Me at the Fair
US 1952 87m Technicolor
U-I (Albert J. Cohen)

In 1900, an orphan joins a travelling medicine show.
Mildly pleasing open-air comedy drama.

w Irving Wallace, *novel* The Great Companions by Gene Markey *d* Douglas Sirk *ph* Maury Gertsman *md* Joseph Gershenson

Diana Lynn, Dan Dailey, Hugh O'Brian, Chet Allen, Rhys Williams

Meet Me in Las Vegas
US 1956 112m Eastmancolor Cinemascope
MGM (Joe Pasternak)
GB title: *Viva Las Vegas!*

A gambler's luck changes when he grabs the hand of a passing ballerina.
Listless song-and dance extravaganza which wastes a great deal of talent.

w Isabel Lennart *d* Roy Rowland *ph* Robert Bronner *m* Nicholas Brodsky *ly* Sammy Cahn *ch* Eugène Loring, Hermes Pan

Dan Dailey, Cyd Charisse, Agnes Moorehead, Lili Darvas, Paul Henreid, Oscar Karlweis, Lena Horne, Jerry Colonna, Frankie Laine

'A large-scale musical of almost stupefying banality.'—*MFB*

Meet Me in St Louis***
US 1944 113m Technicolor
MGM (Arthur Freed)

Scenes in the life of an affectionate family at the turn of the century.

Patchy but generally highly agreeable musical nostalgia with an effective sense of the passing years and seasons.

w Irving Brecher, Fred F. Finklehoffe, *novel* Sally Benson *d Vincente Minnelli ph* George Folsey *md* Georgie Stoll

Judy Garland, Margaret O'Brien, Tom Drake, Leon Ames, Mary Astor, Lucille Bremer, June Lockhart, *Harry Davenport*, Marjorie Main, Joan Carroll, Hugh Marlowe, Robert Sully, Chill Wills

'A family group framed in velvet and tinsel . . . it has everything a romantic musical should have.'—*Dilys Powell, 1955*

Meet Me Tonight
GB 1952 85m Technicolor
Rank / Anthony Havelock Allan

Three short Noel Coward plays: *Red Peppers, Fumed Oak, Ways and Means.*
Regrettably bald treatment of three playlets which have not lasted well. A thoroughly artificial evening.

w/m Noel Coward *d* Anthony Pelissier *ph* Desmond Dickinson

Ted Ray, Kay Walsh, Stanley Holloway, Betty Ann Davies, Nigel Patrick, Valerie Hobson

Meet Mr Lucifer*
GB 1953 81m bw
Ealing (Monja Danischewsky)

The Demon King in a tatty provincial pantomime dreams he is the devil preventing people from wasting time watching television.
Clean and occasionally amusing piece of topical satire on tellymania; but the prologue is funnier than the sketches.

w Monja Danischewsky, *play* Beggar My Neighbour by Arnold Ridley *d* Anthony Pelissier *ph* Desmond Dickinson *m* Eric Rogers

Stanley Holloway, Peggy Cummins, Jack Watling, Barbara Murray, Joseph Tomelty, Gordon Jackson, Jean Cadell, Kay Kendall, Ian Carmichael, Gilbert Harding, Charles Victor, Humphrey Lestocq

Meet Nero Wolfe*
US 1936 73m bw
Columbia

A corpulent stay-at-home sleuth solves a disappearance and a murder.
The film debut of an engaging crime character, who oddly never made it to a series.

w Howard J. Green, Bruce Manning, Joseph Anthony, *novel* Fer de Lance by Rex Stout *d* Herbert Biberman *ph* Henry Freulich

Edward Arnold, Lionel Stander, Joan Perry, Rita Hayworth, Victor Jory, Nana Bryant, Walter Kingsford, John Qualen

Meet the People
US 1944 100m bw
MGM (E. Y. Harburg)

A Broadway musical star proves she isn't snooty by taking a job in a shipyard.
Thin propaganda musical which wastes a fair amount of talent.

w S. M. Herzig, Fred Saidy, *play* Louis Lantz, Sol and Ben Barzman *d* Charles Reisner *ph* Robert Surtees *songs* various

Lucille Ball, Dick Powell, Virginia O'Brien, Bert Lahr, Rags Ragland, June Allyson, Steve Geray, Phil Regan, Spike Jones and his City Slickers, Vaughn Monroe and his Orchestra

Melba
GB 1953 113m Technicolor
Horizon (Sam Spiegel)

The life of the internationally famous Australian opera singer of Victorian days.
Moderately interesting recreation of a woman and an era, though dramatically rather stodgy.

w Harry Kurnitz *d* Lewis Milestone *ad* André Andreiev *md* Muir Mathieson

Patrice Munsel, Robert Morley, Alec Clunes, Martita Hunt, Sybil Thorndike, John McCallum

Melody
GB 1971 106m Eastmancolor
Hemdale / Sagittarius / Goodtimes
aka: *S.W.A.L.K.*

Calf love at school causes jealousy between two boys.
Tough-sentimental teenage comedy-drama of little interest to adults.

w Alan Parker *d* Waris Hussein *ph* Peter Suschitsky *m* Richard Hewson

Jack Wild, Mark Lester, Tracy Hyde

Melody Time*
US 1948 75m Technicolor
Walt Disney (Ben Sharpsteen)

An unlinked variety show of cartoon segments.
A mainly mediocre selection with the usual moments of high style: *Once upon a Wintertime, Bumble Boogie, Johnny Appleseed, Little Toot, Trees, Blame it on the Samba, Pecos Bill.*

w various *d* various

Melvin Purvis G-Man*
US 1974 74m colour TVM
AIP / Dan Curtis
GB theatrical title: *The Legend of Machine Gun Kelly*

In 1933, a midwestern G-man captures Machine Gun Kelly.
Adequate gangster thriller which did not make a series. See also: *Kansas City Massacre*.

w John Milius, William F. Nolan *d* Dan Curtis *ph* Jacques Marquette *m* Richard Cobert

Dale Robertson, Margaret Blye, Harris Yulin, Dick Sargent, David Canary

The Member of the Wedding*
US 1953 91m bw
Columbia / Stanley Kramer

A 12-year-old girl learns something about life when her sister gets married and a young boy dies.
Boringly contained in a kitchen set, this filmed play has interesting characters but is really not good enough for the talent involved.

w Edna and Edward Anhalt, *play* and *novel* Carson McCullers *d* Fred Zinnemann *ph* Hal Mohr *m* Alex North

Julie Harris, *Ethel Waters*, Brandon de Wilde, Arthur Franz, Nancy Gates, James Edwards

The Men***
US 1950 85m bw
Stanley Kramer

Paraplegic war veterans are prepared for civilian life; the fiancée of one of them helps overcome his problems.
Vivid semi-documentary melodrama, at the time rather shocking in its no-holds-barred treatment of sexual problems.

w Carl Foreman d Fred Zinnemann ph Robert de Grasse *m* Dmitri Tiomkin

Marlon Brando, Teresa Wright, Everett Sloane, Jack Webb, Howard St John
† Later reissued as *Battle Stripe*.

Men Are Not Gods
GB 1937 92m bw
London (Alexander Korda)

An actor playing Othello nearly strangles his wife.
Tepid melodramatic attempt at a theme later used in
A Double Life.

w G. B. Stern, Iris Wright *d* Walter Reisch

Miriam Hopkins, Sebastian Shaw, Rex Harrison, Gertrude Lawrence, A. E. Matthews, Val Gielgud, Laura Smithson

The Men in Her Life
US 1941 90m bw
Columbia (Gregory Ratoff)

A former circus rider becomes a ballerina.
Well-worn rags-to-riches romance of little interest.

w Frederick Kohner, Michael Wilson, Paul Trivers, *novel* Ballerina by Lady Eleanor Smith *d* Gregory Ratoff *ph* Harry Stradling, Arthur Miller *md* David Raksin

Loretta Young, Conrad Veidt, Dean Jagger, Eugenie Leontovich, Shepperd Strudwick, Otto Kruger, Paul Baratoff

Men in War
US 1957 104m bw
Security (Sidney Harmon)

Korea 1950: an infantry platoon is cut off from HQ and tries to take an enemy-occupied hill.
Stereotyped small-scale war heroics; the film makes its points but fails to entertain.

w Philip Yordan *d* Anthony Mann *ph* Ernest Haller *m* Elmer Bernstein

Robert Ryan, Robert Keith, Aldo Ray, Vic Morrow, James Edwardes, Sen Yung

Men in White
US 1934 80m bw
MGM

An ambitious intern is in love with an attractive socialite who resents his devotion to duty.
Popular but obvious star drama.

w Waldemar Young, *play* Sidney Kingsley *d* Richard Boleslawski *ph* George Folsey

Clark Gable, Myrna Loy, Jean Hersholt, Elizabeth Allan, Otto Kruger, C. Henry Gordon, Wallace Ford

Men of Boys' Town
US 1941 106m bw
MGM (John W. Considine Jnr)

Further adventures of Father Flanagan.
Mushy sequel to *Boys' Town* (qv).

w James Kevin McGuinness *d* Norman Taurog *ph* Harold Rosson

Spencer Tracy, Mickey Rooney, Bobs Watson, Larry Nunn, Lee J. Cobb, Mary Nash, Henry O'Neill, Darryl Hickman, Anne Revere

Men of the Dragon**
US 1974 74m colour TVM
David Wolper (Stan Margulies)

A young American in Hong Kong combats a sinister organization to get back his kidnapped sister.

It's well-staged action all the way in this Kung Fu penny dreadful. Great fun.

w Denne Bart Petitclerc *d* Harry Falk *m* Elmer Bernstein

Jared Martin, Joseph Wiseman, Katie Saylor, Robert Ito

Men of the Fighting Lady
US 1954 80m Anscocolor
MGM (Henry Berman)

Adventures of an aircraft carrier during the Korean War.
Tepid war actioner with a few effective semi-documentary sequences of naval tactics.

w Art Cohn *d* Andrew Marton *ph* George Folsey *m* Miklos Rozsa

Van Johnson, Walter Pidgeon, Louis Calhern, Dewey Martin, Keenan Wynn, Frank Lovejoy, Robert Horton

Men of Tomorrow
GB 1932 88m bw
Paramount (Alexander Korda)

Oxford students have more than academic work on their minds.
Dim comedy-drama with an interesting cast.

w Arthur Wimperis, Anthony Gibbs, *play* Young Apollo by Anthony Gibbs *d* Leontine Sagan

Maurice Braddell, Joan Gardner, Emlyn Williams, Merle Oberon, Robert Donat

Men of Two Worlds
GB 1946 109m Technicolor
GFD / Two Cities (John Sutro)
US title: *Witch Doctor*

In Tanganyika, an educated native helps white men to counter the force of witch doctors and persuade tribes to leave an infected area.
Earnest but totally unpersuasive semi-documentary shot in unconvincing sets and garish colour.

w Thorold Dickinson, Joyce Cary, E. Arnot Robertson, Herbert Victor *d* Thorold Dickinson

Eric Portman, Phyllis Calvert, Robert Adams, Orlando Martins, Arnold Marle, Cathleen Nesbitt, David Horne, Cyril Raymond

Men with Wings
US 1938 106m Technicolor
Paramount (William Wellman)

Boyhood friends become civil aviation pioneers but fall out over a girl.
Disappointing epic from the maker of *Wings*, with highly predictable story line, modest acting and ho-hum spectacle.

w Robert Carson *d* William Wellman *ph* W. Howard Greene *m* W. Franke Harling, Gerald Carbonara

Fred MacMurray, Ray Milland, Louise Campbell, Andy Devine, Walter Abel, Virginia Weidler, Donald O'Connor

Men without Women
US 1932 77m bw
Fox

Men in a submarine are trapped on the ocean bed.
Early talkie action drama noted more for its credits than its accomplishment.

w Dudley Nichols *d* John Ford *ph* Joseph H. August

Kenneth MacKenna, Frank Albertson, Paul Page, Pat Somerset, Stuart Erwin, Warren Hymer, John Wayne

The Mephisto Waltz*
US 1971 109m De Luxe
TCF / QM Productions

A satanic concert pianist on the point of death wills his soul into the body of a journalist.
Complex diabolical mumbo-jumbo with plenty of style.

w Ben Maddow, *novel* Fred Mustard Stewart *d Paul Wendkos ph* William W. Spencer *m* Jerry Goldsmith

Alan Alda, Jacqueline Bisset, Curt Jurgens, Barbara Parkins

The Mercenaries
GB 1968 100m Metrocolor
Panavision
MGM / George Englund
US title: *Dark of the Sun*

In the Belgian Congo in 1960 a mercenary officer is ordered to bring back a fortune in diamonds by armoured train.
Basically an old-fashioned thriller about the hazards of a journey beset by brutish villains and damsels in distress, this unpleasant film is notable for the amount of sadistic action it crams into its running time.

w Quentin Werty, Adrian Spies, *novel* Dark of the Sun by Wilbur Smith *d* Jack Cardiff *ph* Edward Scaife *m* Jacques Loussier

Rod Taylor, Yvette Mimieux, Kenneth More, Jim Brown, Peter Carsten, André Morell, Guy Deghy, Calvin Lockhart, Alan Gifford

'The violence done to the human body is matched by violence done to the intelligence by a stock adventure story given a gloss of topicality and social insult.'—*Judith Crist*

Merrill's Marauders
US 1962 98m Technicolor
Cinemascope
Warner / US Pictures (Milton Sperling)

Adventures of a crack US army unit in 1942 Burma.
Physically exhausting war adventure with emphasis on hand-to-hand fighting and much bloodshed.

w Samuel Fuller, Milton Sperling *d* Samuel Fuller *ph* William Clothier *m* Howard Jackson

Jeff Chandler, Ty Hardin, Andrew Duggan, Peter Brown, Will Hutchins

Merrily We Go to Hell
US 1932 78m bw
Paramount

A socialite marries a dipsomaniac journalist.
Glum problem drama.

w Edwin Justin Mayer, *novel* I Jerry Take Thee Joan by Cleo Lucas *d* Dorothy Arzner *ph* David Abel

Sylvia Sidney, Fredric March, Adrienne Allen, Richard Gallagher, Florence Burton, Esther Howard, Kent Taylor

Merrily We Live*
US 1938 90m bw
Hal Roach

A zany family hires a chauffeur who is actually a famous writer posing as a tramp.
Quite likeable compound of *My Man Godfrey* and *You Can't Take It with You*.

w Eddie Moran, Jack Jevne *d* Norman Z. McLeod *ph* Norbert Brodine *md* Marvin Hatley

Constance Bennett, Brian Aherne, Billie Burke, Alan Mowbray, Patsy Kelly, Ann Dvorak, Tom Brown, Bonita Granville, Marjorie Rambeau, Clarence Kolb

Merry Andrew
US 1958 103m Metrocolor
Cinemascope
MGM / Sol C. Siegel

A stuffy teacher in search of an ancient statue joins a travelling circus.
Deliberately charming star comedy which plumps too firmly for whimsy and, despite its professionalism, provokes barely a smile, let alone a laugh.

w Isabel Lennart, I. A. L. Diamond, *story* Paul Gallico *d/ch* Michael Kidd *ph* Robert Surtees *m* Saul Chaplin *ly* Johnny Mercer

Danny Kaye, Pier Angeli, Baccaloni, Noel Purcell, Robert Coote, Patricia Cutts, Rex Evans, Walter Kingsford, Tommy Rall, Rhys Williams

The Merry Monahans
US 1944 90m bw
Universal (Michael Fessier, Ernest Pagano)

Adventures of a family of vaudeville performers.
Acceptable backstage comedy drama with good atmosphere.

w Michael Fessier, Ernest Pagano *d* Charles Lamont *ph* Charles Van Enger *m* Hans Salter

Donald O'Connor, Jack Oakie, Rosemary de Camp, Peggy Ryan, Ann Blyth, Isabel Jewell, John Miljan

The Merry Widow**
US 1934 99m bw
MGM

A bankrupt king orders a nobleman to woo a wealthy American widow.
Patchy, but sometimes sparkling.

w Samson Raphaelson, Ernest Vajda, *libretto* Victor Leon, Leo Stein *d Ernst Lubitsch* *ph* Oliver T. Marsh *m Franz Lehar*

Maurice Chevalier, Jeanette MacDonald, Edward Everett Horton, Una Merkel, George Barbier, Donald Meek, Sterling Holloway, Shirley Ross

The Merry Widow
US 1952 105m Technicolor
MGM (Joe Pasternak)

Chill, empty remake.

w Sonya Levien, William Ludwig *d* Curtis Bernhardt *ph* Robert Surtees

Fernando Lamas, Lana Turner, Richard Haydn, Una Merkel, Thomas Gomez, John Abbott
'Nothing has been omitted (except the spirit of the original).'—*MFB*

Merton of the Movies*
US 1947 82m bw
MGM

An innocent young man in Hollywood becomes a star.
The plot and characterizations of this old chestnut are resistible, but the Hollywood background is well managed and convincing.

w George Wells, Lou Breslow, *novel* Henry Leon Wilson *d* Robert Alton *m* David Snell

Red Skelton, Virginia O'Brien, Alan Mowbray

A Message to Garcia*
US 1936 86m bw
TCF (Raymond Griffith)

During the Spanish–American war a Cuban girl helps an American agent get through to the rebel leader with a diplomatic message.
Agreeable embroidery of a historical incident: good production values and entertaining star performances.

w W. P. Lipscomb, Gene Fowler, *book* Andrew S. Rohan *d* George Marshall *ph* Rudolph Maté *m* Louis Silvers

Wallace Beery, Barbara Stanwyck, John Boles, Alan Hale, Herbert Mundin, Mona Barrie

Message to My Daughter
US 1973 74m colour TVM
Metromedia / Gerald Isenberg

A girl learns much about herself and her stepfather while listening to tapes recorded by her mother, now dead.
Icky and unconvincing weepie.

w Rita Lakin *d* Robert Michael Lewis

Bonnie Bedelia, Martin Sheen, Kitty Wynn, Neva Patterson

Mexican Spitfire
A series of second feature comedies nominally about a young businessman and his temperamental Mexican wife (Donald Woods and Lupe Velez), whose interest shifted firmly to the young man's accident-prone uncle Matt and his aristocratic boss Lord Epping, both of whom were played by the rubber-legged Ziegfeld comic Leon Errol at something near the top of his form. The plots made little sense, but the hectic situations provoked hearty roars of laughter. The films were all made by RKO, and all directed by Leslie Goodwins.

1939: THE GIRL FROM MEXICO, MEXICAN SPITFIRE
1940: MEXICAN SPITFIRE OUT WEST
1941: MEXICAN SPITFIRE'S BABY, MEXICAN SPITFIRE AT SEA
1942: MEXICAN SPITFIRE SEES A GHOST, MEXICAN SPITFIRE'S ELEPHANT
1943: MEXICAN SPITFIRE'S BLESSED EVENT

Michael Shayne
The private eye created by Brett Halliday was featured in several second features starring Lloyd Nolan, mostly directed by Eugene Forde for Fox. They were adequate time-passers without too much sparkle.

1940: MICHAEL SHAYNE PRIVATE DETECTIVE
1941: DRESSED TO KILL, JUST OFF BROADWAY, THE MAN WHO WOULDN'T DIE
1942: TIME TO KILL (a version of Chandler's FAREWELL MY LOVELY), BLUE WHITE AND PERFECT

Mickey One*
US 1965 93m bw
Columbia / Florin / Tatira (Arthur Penn, Harrison Starr)

A nightclub entertainer runs away after an orgy to find some meaning in his life.
Obscure symbolic melodrama whose flashes of talent and interest needed firmer control.

w Alan Surgal *d* Arthur Penn *ph* Ghislain Cloquet *m* Eddie Sauter *pd* George Jenkins

Warren Beatty, Hurd Hatfield, Alexandra Stewart, Franchot Tone, Teddy Hart, Jeff Corey

'Arresting at first, it becomes more and more bogged down by its own pretensions, until one's main interest is simply in seeing it through.'—*MFB*

Midas Run
US 1969 104m Technicolor
Raymond Stross / MPI (Leon Chooluck)
GB title: *A Run on Gold*

An ageing secret service chief plans to hi-jack a bullion shipment.
Incompetently handled caper story with interest unwisely shifted for romantic purposes to the plotter's recruits.

w James D. Buchanan, Ronald Austin, Berne Giler *d* Alf Kjellin *ph* Ken Higgins *m* Elmer Bernstein

Fred Astaire, Richard Crenna, Anne Heywood, Ralph Richardson, Roddy McDowall, Adolfo Celi, Maurice Denham, Cesar Romero

Middle of the Night**
US 1959 118m bw
Columbia (George Justin)

An elderly garment manufacturer falls in love with a young girl.
Serious and moving examination of a human predicament, shot against beautifully observed New York backgrounds.

w Paddy Chayevsky, from his TV play *d* Delbert Mann *ph Joseph Brun m* George Bassman

Fredric March, Kim Novak, Glenda Farrell, Jan Norris, Lee Grant

'A work of greater cogency than his New York play script and of deeper maturity than his *Marty*.'—*Time*

'The best of the TV transformations into film.'—*Stanley Kauffmann*

Midnight
US 1934 80m bw
Universal / All Star (Chester Erskine)
aka: *Call It Murder*

A District Attorney finds his own daughter on the wrong side of the law.
Tepid family melodrama.

wd Chester Erskine, *play* Paul and Claire Sifton

Sidney Fox, O. P. Heggie, Henry Hull, Humphrey Bogart, Margaret Wycherly, Lynne Overman, Richard Whorf, Cora Witherspoon

Midnight***
US 1939 95m bw
Paramount (Arthur Hornblow Jnr)

A girl stranded in Paris is hired by an aristocrat to seduce the gigolo paying unwelcome attention to his wife.
Sparkling sophisticated comedy which barely flags until a slightly disappointing ending; all the talents involved are in excellent form.

w Billy Wilder, Charles Brackett, story Edwin Justus Mayer, Franz Schultz *d Mitchell Leisen ph* Charles Lang *m* Frederick Hollander

Claudette Colbert, Don Ameche, *John Barrymore*, Francis Lederer, Mary Astor, Elaine Barrie, Hedda Hopper, Rex O'Malley

'Leisen's masterpiece, one of the best comedies of the thirties.'—*John Baxter, 1968*

'One of the authentic delights of the thirties.'—*New Yorker 1976*

Midnight Cowboy***
US 1969 113m De Luxe
UA / Jerome Hellman

A slightly dim-witted Texan comes to New York to offer his services as a stud for rich ladies, but spends a hard winter helping a tubercular con man.
Life in the New York gutter, brilliantly if not too accurately observed by a master showman with no heart.

w Waldo Salt, *novel* James Leo Herlihy *d John Schlesinger ph Adam Holender md* John Barry *pd* John Robert Lloyd

Jon Voight, Dustin Hoffman, Brenda Vaccaro, Sylvia Miles, John McGiver

'If only Schlesinger's directorial self-discipline had matched his luminous sense of scene and his extraordinary skill in handling actors, this would have been a far more considerable film.'—*Arthur Schlesinger Jnr (no relation)*

'A great deal besides cleverness, a great deal of good feeling and perception and purposeful dexterity.'—*Stanley Kauffmann*

Midnight Episode
GB 1950 78m bw
Columbia / Triangle (Thomas Lageard)

An old busker stumbles over a dead body and a lot of money.
Tame British version of Raimu's French success *Monsieur La Souris*, saved only by its star performance.

w Rita Barisse, Reeve Taylor, Paul Vincent Carroll, David Evans, William Templeton *d* Gordon Parry *ph* Hone Glendining

Stanley Holloway, Natasha Parry, Leslie Dwyer, Reginald Tate, Meredith Edwards, Wilfrid Hyde White, Joy Shelton

Midnight Lace*
US 1960 108m Eastmancolor
Universal (Ross Hunter, Martin Melcher)

The wife of a rich Londoner is terrorized by threatening phone calls and voices in the fog.
Thoroughly silly rehash of *Gaslight* and *The Boy Who Cried Wolf*; its glamorous accoutrements can't fight a lack of humour or predictable plot development.

w Ivan Goff, Ben Roberts, *play* Matilda Shouted Fire by Janet Green *d* David Miller *ph* Russell Metty *m* Frank Skinner

Doris Day, Rex Harrison, John Gavin, Myrna Loy, Roddy McDowall, Herbert Marshall, Natasha Parry, John Williams, Anthony Dawson, Hermione Baddeley, Richard Ney, Rhys Williams, Doris Lloyd

The Midnight Man
US 1974 117m Technicolor
Universal / Norlan (Roland Kibbee, Burt Lancaster)

An ex-cop, paroled after killing his wife's lover, takes a job as security guard and runs into a murder case.
Muddled mystery with pretentious characterization and bouts of violence.

wd Roland Kibbee, Burt Lancaster, *novel* The Midnight Lady and the Mourning Man by David Anthony *ph* Jack Priestley *m* Dave Grusin

Burt Lancaster, Susan Clark, Cameron Mitchell, Morgan Woodward, Harris Yulin, Robert Quarry, Joan Lorring, Lawrence Dobin, Ed Lauter

'A thriller that has the impenetrability of Chandler but none of the flavour.'—*Tom Milne*

'Efficient enough but lifeless, and burdened with portentous sentiments about solitude, violence and the nature of the beast.'—*Sight and Sound*

A Midsummer Night's Dream***
US 1935 117m bw
Warner (Max Reinhardt)

Two pairs of lovers sort out their problems with fairy help at midnight in the woods of Athens.
Shakespeare's play is treated with remarkable respect in this super-glamorous Hollywood adaptation based on the Broadway production by Max Reinhardt. Much of it comes off, and visually it's a treat.

w Charles Kenyon, Mary McCall Jnr, *play* William Shakespeare *d Max Reinhardt, William Dieterle ph Hal Mohr, Fred Jackman, Byron Haskin, H. F. Koenekamp*
m Mendelssohn *md Erich Wolfgang Korngold ch Bronislawa Nijinska ad Anton Grot*

James Cagney, Dick Powell, Jean Muir, Ross Alexander, Olivia de Havilland, Joe E. Brown, Hugh Herbert, Arthur Treacher, Frank McHugh, Otis Harlan, Dewey Robinson, *Victor Jory*, Verree Teasdale, *Mickey Rooney*, Anita Louise, Grant Mitchell, Ian Hunter, Hobart Cavanaugh

'The publicity push behind the film is tremendous—it is going to be a success or everyone at Warner Brothers is going to get fired.'—*Robert Forsythe*

'Its assurance as a work of film technique is undoubted.'—*John Baxter, 1968*

Midway*
US 1976 132m Technicolor
Panavision Sensurround
Universal (Walter Mirisch)

A reconstruction of the Pacific sea-air battle in June 1942.
Efficient, unsurprising blockbuster.

w Donald S. Sanford *d* Jack Smight *ph* Harry Stradling Jnr *m* John Williams *ad* Walter Tyler

Charlton Heston, Henry Fonda, Glenn Ford, James Coburn, Hal Holbrook, Toshiro Mifune, Robert Mitchum, Cliff Robertson, Robert Wagner, Robert Webber, Ed Nelson, James Shigeta, Monte Markham, Biff McGuire, Chris George, Glenn Corbett, Edward Albert

'It emerges more as a passingly exciting theme park extravaganza than as a quality motion picture action-adventure story.'—*Variety*

Mighty Joe Young*
US 1949 94m bw
RKO (Merian C. Cooper)

A little girl brings back from Africa a pet gorilla which grows to enormous size and causes a city to panic.
Rather tired comic-sentimental follow-up to *King Kong*, with a tedious plot and variable animation but a few endearing highlights.

w Ruth Rose *d* Ernest Schoedsack *ph* J. Roy Hunt *m* Roy Webb *sp* Willis O'Brien, Ray Harryhausen

Terry Moore, Ben Johnson, Robert Armstrong, Frank McHugh, Douglas Fowley

Mildred Pierce**
US 1945 113m bw
Warner (Jerry Wald)

A dowdy housewife leaves her husband, becomes the owner (through hard work) of a restaurant chain, and survives a murder case before true love comes her way.
A woman's picture par excellence, glossily and moodily photographed, with a star suffering in luxury on behalf of the most ungrateful daughter of all time.

w Ranald MacDougall, Catherine Turney, *novel* James M. Cain *d Michael Curtiz ph Ernest Haller m Max Steiner ad Anton Grot*

Joan Crawford, Jack Carson, Zachary Scott, *Eve Arden, Ann Blyth,* Bruce Bennett, George Tobias, Lee Patrick, Moroni Olsen

Miles to Go before I Sleep*
US 1974 75m colour TVM
Tomorrow

A lonely elderly man fulfils himself by helping teenage delinquents.
Yes, very worthy, and well acted, but not exactly compelling.

w Judith Parker, Bill Svanoe *d* Fielder Cook

Martin Balsam, Mackenzie Philips, Kitty Wynn, Elizabeth Wilson

The Milky Way*
US 1936 88m bw
Paramount / Harold Lloyd (Edward Sheldon)

A milkman becomes a prizefighter and overcomes a gang of crooks.
Modest Harold Lloyd comedy towards the end of his career; remade as *The Kid from Brooklyn* (qv).

w Grover Jones, Frank Butler, Richard Connell, *play* Lynn Root, Harry Clark *ph* Alfred Gilks *d* Leo McCarey

Harold Lloyd, Adolphe Menjou, Verree Teasdale, Helen Mack, William Gargan, George Barbier, Lionel Stander

Million Dollar Duck
US 1971 92m Technicolor
Walt Disney (Bill Anderson)

A duck lays eggs with solid gold yolks, which provoke interest from gangsters as well as the government.
Minor Disney fantasy borrowed without permission from *Mr Drake's Duck* (qv).

w Roswell Rogers *d* Vincent McEveety *ph* William Snyder *m* Buddy Baker

Dean Jones, Sandy Dennis, Joe Flynn

Million Dollar Legs*
US 1932 64m bw
Paramount

A mythical sport-ridden country decides to enter the Olympic Games.
The good gags in this film are weighted down by plodding treatment, and the general effect is more doleful than funny.

w Harry Myers, Nick Barrows, Joseph L. Mankiewicz *d* Edward Cline *ph* Arthur Todd

W. C. Fields, Jack Oakie, Andy Clyde, Lyda Roberti, Ben Turpin, Hugh Herbert, Billy Gilbert, George Barbier, Susan Fleming

Million Dollar Legs
US 1939 59m bw
TCF

College students back a favourite horse.
Very modest collegiate comedy.

w Lewis Foster, Richard English *d* Nick Grinde *ph* Harry Fischbeck

Betty Grable, John Hartley, Donald O'Connor, Jackie Coogan, Buster Crabbe, Thurston Hall

Million Dollar Mermaid*
US 1952 115m Technicolor
MGM (Arthur Hornblow Jnr)
GB title: *The One Piece Bathing Suit*

The story of Australian swimmer Annette Kellerman.
Inaccurate biopic with a *raison d'être* in its spectacular aquashow scenes, but nothing at all new in its script.

w Everett Freeman *d* Mervyn Le Roy *ph* George J. Folsey *md* Adolph Deutsch *ch Busby Berkeley*

Esther Williams, Victor Mature, Walter Pidgeon, David Brian, Jesse White, Maria Tallchief, Howard Freeman

The Million Pound Note*
GB 1954 91m Technicolor
GFD / Group Films (John Bryan)
US title: *Man with a Million*

A man inherits a million dollars in the form of a single banknote and finds it difficult to spend.
Fairly pleasing period comedy which wears its one joke pretty thin but is nicely decorated and acted.

w Jill Craigie, *story* Mark Twain *d* Ronald Neame *ph* Geoffrey Unsworth *m* William Alwyn

Gregory Peck, Jane Griffiths, Ronald Squire, Joyce Grenfell, A. E. Matthews, Reginald Beckwith, Hartley Power, Wilfrid Hyde White

A Millionaire for Christy
US 1951 91m bw
TCF (Bert Friedlob)

A lawyer's secretary is sent to Los Angeles to inform an heir of his good fortune, and decides to marry him.
Modest romantic comedy with plenty to be modest about.

w Ken Englund *d* George Marshall *ph* Harry Stradling *m* Victor Young

Eleanor Parker, Fred MacMurray, Richard Carlson, Douglass Dumbrille

The Millionairess*
GB 1960 90m De Luxe Cinemascope
TCF / Dimitri de Grunwald (Pierre Rouve)

The richest woman in the world falls for a poor Indian doctor.
Messy travesty of a Shavian comedy that was never more than a star vehicle to begin with. Hardly any of it works despite the star cast, who are mostly miscast.

w Wolf Mankowitz, *play* Bernard Shaw *d* Anthony Asquith *ph* Jack Hildyard *m* Georges Van Parys

Sophia Loren, Peter Sellers, Alastair Sim, Vittorio De Sica, Dennis Price, Gary Raymond, Alfie Bass, Miriam Karlin, Noel Purcell

'The result, lacking any sort of dramatic cohesion or continuity and seemingly planned less as a film than as a series of haphazard effects, is merely tiring.'—*Peter John Dyer*

Millions like Us**
GB 1943 103m bw
GFD / Gainsborough (Edward Black)

The tribulations of a family in wartime, especially of the meek daughter who goes into war work and marries an airman, who is killed.
Fragmentary but reasonably accurate picture of the Home Front during World War II; a little more humour would not have been out of place, but as propaganda it proved an effective weapon.

wd Frank Launder, Sidney Gilliat

Patricia Roc, Gordon Jackson, Moore Marriott,

Eric Portman, Anne Crawford, Basil Radford, Naunton Wayne, Joy Shelton, Megs Jenkins

'There is an unsentimental warmheartedness which I hope we shall cling to and extend in filmed representations of the British scene.'—*Richard Winnington*

Min and Bill**

US 1930 69m bw
MGM

A boozy old waterfront character and his wife try to keep her daughter from being placed in care.
Well-remembered and much-loved character comedy which led to the even more successful *Tugboat Annie* with the same team.

w Frances Marion, Marion Jackson, *play* Dark Star by Lorna Moon *d* George ghill *ph* Harold Wenstrom

Marie Dressler, Wallace Beery, Dorothy Jordan, Marjorie Rambeau, Donald Dillaway, Russell Hopton

The Mind Benders*

GB 1963 113m bw
Anglo–Amalgamated / Novus (Michael Relph)

A scientist undergoes an experiment aimed at depriving him of all sensation. It works too well; he becomes a sadist; and his colleagues can't reverse the process.
Matter-of-factly played hocus-pocus with spy asides; quite gripping while it's on, but in no way memorable.

w James Kennaway *d* Basil Dearden *ph* Denys Coop *m* Georges Auric

Dirk Bogarde, John Clements, Mary Ure, Michael Bryant

The Mind of Mr Soames

GB 1970 98m Technicolor
Columbia / Amicus (Teresa Bolland)

A man who has lived in a coma for thirty years is cured but faces the world as a new-born infant.
Ill-advised attempt at science fiction with meaning; its earnestness becomes a bore.

w John Hale, Edward Simpson, *novel* Charles Eric Maine *d* Alan Cooke *ph* Billy Williams *m* Michael Dress

Terence Stamp, Robert Vaughn, Nigel Davenport, Donal Donnelly, Christian Roberts, Vickery Turner, Scott Forbes

Mine Own Executioner***

GB 1947 108m bw
London Films

A lay psychiatrist undertakes the care of a mentally disturbed war veteran, but fails to prevent him from murdering his wife.
When this film first appeared it seemed like the first adult drama featuring sophisticated people to emerge from a British studio. Time and television have blunted its impact, but it remains a well told suspense melodrama with memorable characters.

w Nigel Balchin, from his novel *d Anthony Kimmins ph* Wilkie Cooper *m* Benjamin Frankel

Burgess Meredith, Kieron Moore, Dulcie Gray, Barbara White, Christine Norden

'The first psychoanalytical film that a grown-up can sit through without squirming.'—*Richard Winnington*

Ministry of Fear***

US 1944 85m bw
Paramount (Seton I. Miller)

During World War II in England, a man just out of a mental hospital wins a cake at a village fair and finds himself caught up in bewildering intrigues.
Little to do with the novel, but a watchable, well-detailed little thriller on Hitchcock lines, once you forgive the usual phoney Hollywood England.

w Seton I. Miller, *novel* Graham Greene *d Fritz Lang ph Henry Sharp m* Victor Young

Ray Milland, Marjorie Reynolds, Carl Esmond, Hillary Brooke, Dan Duryea, Percy Waram, Alan Napier, Erskine Sanford

'A crisp and efficiently made thriller with no pretension to intellectual content.'—*Paul Jensen*

The Miniver Story

GB 1950 104m bw
MGM (Sidney Franklin)

Mrs Miniver faces the tribulations of post-war Britain.
Glum sequel to *Mrs Miniver*, with the dauntless heroine finally succumbing to a glossy but fatal disease. Well enough made, but very hard to take.

w Ronald Millar, George Froeschel *d* H. C. Potter *ph* Joseph Ruttenberg *m* Herbert Stothart

Greer Garson, Walter Pidgeon, Cathy O'Donnell, John Hodiak, Leo Genn, Reginald Owen, Henry Wilcoxon, William Fox, Anthony Bushell

Minnie and Moskowitz*

US 1971 115m Technicolor
Universal (Al Rubin)

Two lonely Los Angeles misfits have a bumpy courtship.
Enjoyably aimless character comedy.

wd John Cassavetes *ph* Arthur J. Ornitz *m* Bob Harwood

Gena Rowlands, Seymour Cassel

Minstrel Man*
US 1976 98m colour TVM
Tomorrow / First Artists (Mitchell Brower, Bob Lovenheim)

A dramatized account of the 19th-century minstrel shows.
Unusual, well-produced musical period piece.

w Richard and Esther Shapiro *d* William A. Graham

Glynn Turman, Ted Ross, Stanley Clay, Saundra Sharp

The Miracle
US 1959 121m Technirama
Warner (Henry Blanke)

In Spain during the Peninsular War, a nun breaks her vows in order to follow a British soldier, and a statue of the Virgin Mary steps down to take her place.
And that's only the beginning in this very tall tale, full of heavy breathing, violent action and religiosity, from the old Max Reinhardt pageant. Quite incredible, and sloppily done.

w Frank Butler, *play* Karl Vollmoeller *d* Irving Rapper *ph* Ernest Haller *m* Elmer Bernstein

Carroll Baker, Roger Moore, Walter Slezak, Vittorio Gassman, Katina Paxinou, Dennis King, Isobel Elsom, Torin Thatcher

Miracle in Soho
GB 1957 93m Eastmancolor
Rank (Emeric Pressburger)

A Soho roadworker falls for a barmaid.
Rudimentary romantic whimsy in an unconvincing street set, with characters either too voluble or just plain dull.

w Emeric Pressburger *d* Julian Amyes *ph* Christopher Challis *m* Brian Easdale

John Gregson, Belinda Lee, Cyril Cusack

Miracle in the Rain**
US 1954 107m bw
Warner (Frank P. Rosenberg)

A plain New York girl falls for a soldier; when he is killed in action, he keeps their appointment on the church steps as a ghost.
Archetypal Hollywood schmaltz, half acute observation of amusing types, half sentimental whimsy, with a final supernatural touch of eating your cake and having it.

w Ben Hecht d Rudolph Maté ph Russell Metty m Franz Waxman

Janey Wyman, Van Johnson, Fred Clark, Eileen Heckart, William Gargan

The Miracle Man
US 1932 85m bw
Paramount

A gang of crooks is reformed by a faith healer they have exploited.
Adequate remake of the silent Lon Chaney vehicle; no sparks this time.

w Waldemar Young, Samuel Hoffenstein, *play* Frank L. Packard, George M. Cohan *d* Norman Z. McLeod *ph* David Abel

Sylvia Sidney, Chester Morris, Irving Pichel, John Wray, Robert Coogan, Hobart Bosworth, Boris Karloff, Ned Sparks, Virginia Bruce

The Miracle of Morgan's Creek****
US 1944 99m bw
Paramount (Preston Sturges)

Chaos results when a stuttering hayseed tries to help a girl accidentally pregnant by a soldier she met hazily at a dance.
Weird and wonderful one-man assault on the Hays Office and sundry other American institutions such as motherhood and politics; an indescribable, tasteless, roaringly funny mêlée, as unexpected at the time as it was effective, like a kick in the pants to all other film comedies.

wd Preston Sturges ph John Seitz *m* Leo Shuken, Charles Bradshaw

Betty Hutton, Eddie Bracken, William Demarest, Diana Lynn, Porter Hall, Akim Tamiroff, Brian Donlevy, Alan Bridge

'Like taking a nun on a roller coaster.'—*James Agee*

'This film moves in a fantastic and irreverent whirl of slapstick, nonsense, farce, sentiment, satire, romance, melodrama—is there any ingredient of dramatic entertainment except maybe tragedy and grand opera that hasn't been tossed into it?'—*National Board of Review*

The Miracle of Our Lady of Fatima
US 1952 102m Warnercolor
Warner (Bryan Foy)

An account of the 1917 appearance of the Virgin Mary to three Portuguese peasant children.
Poorly staged religious film which manages to be less pro-Catholic than anti-communist, and was clearly seen by Jack L. Warner as a means of atoning for *Mission to Moscow*. A real cold war piece.

w Crane Wilbur, James O'Hanlon *d* John Brahm *ph* Edwin DuPar *m* Max Steiner *ad* Edward Carrere

Gilbert Roland, Frank Silvera, Angela Clarke, Jay Novello

The Miracle of the Bells
US 1948 120m bw
Jesse L. Lasky

The death of a glamorous film star causes a small-town miracle and a nationwide publicity stunt..
One hopes that this oddity was intended as a satire; as a straight entertainment it's more than a little icky, and good production values scarcely help.

w Ben Hecht, *novel* Russell Janney *d* Irving Rapper *ph* Robert de Grasse *m* Leigh Harline

Fred MacMurray, Alida Valli, Frank Sinatra, Lee J. Cobb

'An offensive exhibition of vulgar insensitivity.'—*MFB*

'I hereby declare myself the founding father of the Society for the Prevention of Cruelty to God.'—*James Agee*

The Miracle of the White Stallions*
US 1962 118m Technicolor
Walt Disney (Peter V. Herald)
GB title: *The Flight of the White Stallions*

During World War II the Nazis occupy Vienna and the owner of the Spanish Riding School guides his stallions to safety.
Adequate family adventure fare with a dull hero but interesting backgrounds.

w A. J. Carothers *d* Arthur Hiller *ph* Gunther Anders *m* Paul Smith

Robert Taylor, Lilli Palmer, Eddie Albert, Curt Jurgens

Miracle on Main Street*
US 1936 76m bw
RKO / Jack Skirball

A cabaret dancer finds an abandoned baby but her plans are thwarted by the return of her husband.
Odd, interesting but flatly handled melodrama.

w Sam Ornitz, Boris Ingster, *story* Felix Jackson *d* Steve Sekely *ph* Charles Van Enger

Walter Abel, Margo, William Collier, Jane Darwell, Lyle Talbot, Wynne Gibson

Miracle on 34th Street***
US 1947 94m bw
TCF (William Perlberg)

A department store Santa Claus claims to be the real thing.
Mainly charming comedy fantasy which quickly became an American classic but does suffer from a few dull romantic stretches.

wd George Seaton, story Valentine Davies *ph* Charles Clarke, Lloyd Ahern *m* Cyril Mockridge

Edmund Gwenn, Maureen O'Hara, John Payne, Natalie Wood, Gene Lockhart, Porter Hall, William Frawley, Jerome Cowan, Thelma Ritter

Miracle on 34th Street
US 1973 100m colour TVM
TCF

Dull TV remake with too much footage and inadequate talent.

w Jeb Rosebrook *d* Fielder Cook

Sebastian Cabot, Roddy McDowall, Jane Alexander, David Hartman, Jim Backus, Suzanne Davidson

The Miracle Woman*
US 1932 90m bw
Columbia (Harry Cohn)

A lady evangelist turns confidence trickster.
Mild satirical drama inspired by the career of Aimée Semple Macpherson.

w Jo Swerling, *play* Bless You Sister by Robert Riskin, John Meehan *d Frank Capra m* Joseph Walker

Barbara Stanwyck, Sam Hardy, David Manners, Beryl Mercer, Russell Hopton

The Miracle Worker*
US 1962 106m bw
UA / Playfilms (Fred Coe)

The childhood of Helen Keller, taught by Annie Sullivan after being left blind, deaf and dumb in an illness.
A moving real-life story is given hysterical treatment and the good scenes have a hard task winning through; in any case a documentary might have been more persuasive.

w William Gibson, from his play *d* Arthur Penn *ph* Ernest Caparros *m* Laurence Rosenthal *ad* George Jenkins

Anne Bancroft, Patty Duke, Victor Jory, Inga Swenson, Andrew Prine, Beah Richards

Mirage***
US 1965 109m bw
U-I (Harry Keller)

During a New York power blackout, an executive falls to his death from a skyscraper and a cost accountant loses his memory.

Striking puzzler, rather slowly developed but generally effective and with a strong sense of place and timing.

w Peter Stone, novel Howard Fast *d Edward Dmytryk ph* Joe MacDonald *m* Quincy Jones

Gregory Peck, Diane Baker, Walter Abel, *Walter Matthau*, Leif Erickson, Kevin McCarthy

Miranda*
GB 1947 80m bw
GFD / Gainsborough

A doctor on holiday in Cornwall catches a mermaid and takes her to London disguised as an invalid.
Simple-minded comedy which scores a few easy laughs on obvious targets.

w Peter Blackmore, from his play *d* Ken Annakin *ph* Ray Elton *m* Temple Abady

Glynis Johns, Griffith Jones, Googie Withers, *Margaret Rutherford*, David Tomlinson, Sonia Holm, John McCallum
† Sequel 1949, *Mad about Men.*

Les Misérables****
US 1935 109m bw
Twentieth Century (Darryl F. Zanuck)

Unjustly convicted and sentenced to years in the galleys, Jean Valjean emerges to build up his life again but is hounded by a cruel and relentless police officer.
Solid, telling, intelligent version of a much-filmed classic novel; in adaptation and performance it is hard to see how this film could be bettered.

w W. P. Lipscomb, novel Victor Hugo *d Richard Boleslawski ph Gregg Toland m* Alfred Newman

Fredric March, Charles Laughton, Cedric Hardwicke, Rochelle Hudson, Frances Drake, John Beal, Jessie Ralph, Florence Eldridge

'A superlative effort, a thrilling, powerful, poignant picture.'—*New York Evening Post*

'Deserving of rank among the cinema's finest achievements.'—*New York World Telegram*

Les Misérables**
US 1952 106m bw
TCF (Fred Kohlmar)

Solemn remake, well done but lacking the spark of inspiration.

w Richard Murphy *d* Lewis Milestone *ph* Joseph La Shelle *m* Alex North

Michael Rennie, Robert Newton, Edmund Gwenn, Debra Paget, Cameron Mitchell, Sylvia Sidney, Elsa Lanchester, James Robertson Justice, Joseph Wiseman, Rhys Williams

The Misfits*
US 1961 124m bw
UA / Frank E. Taylor

Cowboys gather in the Nevada desert to rope wild mustangs, and a divorcee becomes involved with one of them.
Ill-fated melodrama whose stars both died shortly afterwards; a solemn, unattractive, pretentious film which seldom stops wallowing in self-pity.

w Arthur Miller *d* John Huston *ph* Russell Metty *m* Alex North

Clark Gable, Marilyn Monroe, Montgomery Clift, Eli Wallach, Thelma Ritter, James Barton, Estelle Winwood, Kevin McCarthy

Miss Annie Rooney
US 1942 86m bw
Edward Small

Poor Irish girl loves rich boy.
A totally routine offering for a teenage star; no wonder she didn't make it.

w George Bruce *d* Edwin L. Marin *ph* Lester White *m* Edward Paul

Shirley Temple, William Gargan, Guy Kibbee, Dickie Moore, Peggy Ryan, Gloria Holden, Jonathan Hale, Mary Field

Miss Grant Takes Richmond*
US 1949 87m bw
Columbia (S. Sylvan Simon)
GB title: *Innocence Is Bliss*

A dumb secretary helps defeat crooks and improve the local housing situation.
Mildly amusing star comedy.

w Nat Perrin, Devery Freeman, FrankTashlin *d* Lloyd Bacon *ph* Charles Lawton Jnr *m* Morris Stoloff

Lucille Ball, William Holden, Janis Carter, James Gleason, Gloria Henry, Frank McHugh, George Cleveland

Miss Marple
Agatha Christie's inquisitive spinster detective was brought to the screen by director George Pollock and star Margaret Rutherford in four increasingly disappointing films for MGM.

1962: MURDER SHE SAID (qv)
1963: MURDER AT THE GALLOP
1964: MURDER MOST FOUL, MURDER AHOY

Miss Pinkerton*
US 1932 66m bw
Warner

A private nurse helps a police detective to solve a murder case.
Pleasing little mystery comedy.

w Lilyan Hayward, Niven Busch, *story* Mary Roberts Rinehart *d* Lloyd Bacon *ph* Barney McGill

Joan Blondell, George Brent, Mae Madison, John Wray, Ruth Hall, C. Henry Gordon, Elizabeth Patterson

Miss Sadie Thompson*
US 1953 91m Technicolor
Columbia (Lewis J. Rachmil)

Vigorous semi-musical remake of *Rain* (qv); a good star vehicle, but not otherwise notable.

w Harry Kleiner *d* Curtis Bernhardt *ph* Charles Lawton *md* George Duning

Rita Hayworth, Jose Ferrer, Aldo Ray, Russell Collins, Harry Bellaver

Miss Susie Slagle's
US 1946 88m bw
Paramount (John Houseman)

Romances of nursing students in 1910 Baltimore.
Modest melodramatic potboiler.

w Anne Froelich, Hugo Butler, *novel* Augusta Tucker *d* John Berry *ph* Charles Lang Jnr *m* Daniele Amfitheatrof

Veronica Lake, Joan Caulfield, Sonny Tufts, Lillian Gish, Ray Collins, Billy de Wolfe, Bill Edwards, Roman Bohnen, Morris Carnovsky, Lloyd Bridges

Miss Tatlock's Millions*
US 1948 101m bw
Paramount (Charles Brackett)

A stunt man impersonates the idiot heir to a fortune.
Tasteless but quite funny comedy with a cast of eccentrics indulging in enjoyable fooling.

w Charles Brackett, Richard L. Breen *d* Richard Haydn *ph* Charles Lang Jnr *m* Victor Young

John Lund, Wanda Hendrix, Monty Woolley, Barry Fitzgerald, Robert Stack, Ilka Chase, Dorothy Stickney

The Missiles of October***
US 1974 125m colour TVM (videotape)
Viacom / ABC

President Kennedy deals with the 1962 Cuban missile crisis.
Absorbing documentary drama which led from *Pueblo* to *Collision Course.*

w Stanley Greenberg *d* Anthony Page

William Devane, Martin Sheen, Howard da Silva

The Missing Are Deadly
US 1974 74m colour TVM
Allen Epstein

A mischievous youth steals a rat from a laboratory and nearly starts a plague.
Obvious, uninteresting suspenser.

w Kathryn and Michael Michaelian *d* Don MacDougall

Ed Nelson, Leonard Nimoy, Jose Ferrer, Marjorie Lord

Mission to Moscow**
US 1943 112m bw
Warner (Robert Buckner)

The Russian career of US Ambassador Joseph E. Davies.
Stodgy but fascinating wartime propaganda piece viewing the Russians as warm-hearted allies; in the later days of the McCarthy witch hunt, Jack L. Warner regretted he had ever allowed it to be made.

w Howard Koch, *book* Joseph E. Davies *d* Michael Curtiz *ph* Bert Glennon *m* Max Steiner

Walter Huston, Ann Harding, Oscar Homolka, George Tobias, Gene Lockhart, Eleanor Parker, Richard Travis, Helmut Dantine, Victor Francen, Henry Daniell, Barbara Everest, Dudley Field Malone, Roman Bohnen, Maria Palmer, Moroni Olsen, Minor Watson

Mississippi*
US 1935 80m bw
Paramount (Arthur Hornblow Jnr)

A showboat singer has a cloud on his reputation.
Mild period musical with occasional stops for comedy.

w Herbert Fields, Claude Binyon, *story* Booth Tarkington *d* Edward A. Sutherland *ph* Charles Lang *m/ly* Rodgers and Hart

Bing Crosby, W. C. Fields, Joan Bennett, Gail Patrick, Claude Gillingwater, John Miljan, Queenie Smith

Mississippi Gambler
US 1953 98m Technicolor
U-I (Ted Richmond)

A showboat gambler has trouble with a bad loser, but finally marries his sister.
Picturesque star melodrama with period settings and not much meat in the story.

w Seton I. Miller *d* Rudolph Maté *ph* Irving Glassberg *m* Frank Skinner

Tyrone Power, Piper Laurie, John McIntyre, Julia Adams, Dennis Weaver

The Missouri Breaks
US 1976 126m De Luxe
UA / Elliott Kastner / Robert B. Sherman

Montana ranchers and rustlers fight over land and livestock, and a hired killer shoots it out with a horse thief.
Savage, dislikeable western with both stars over the top.

w Thomas McGuane *d* Arthur Penn
ph Michael Butler *m* John Williams

Marlon Brando, Jack Nicholson, Randy Quaid, Kathleen Lloyd, Frederic Forrest, Harry Dean Stanton

Mr Ace
US 1946 84m bw
Benedict Bogeaus

A rich, spoiled congresswoman is backed by a gangster but gets religion.
Odd star drama, perfunctorily made.

w Fred Finklehoffe *d* Edwin L. Marin *ph* Karl Struss *m* Heinz Roemheld

Sylvia Sidney, George Raft, Stanley Ridges, Sara Haden, Jerome Cowan

Mr and Mrs Bo Jo Jones*
US 1971 74m colour TVM
TCF (Lester Linsk)

A young couple have to get married, and do well despite parental interference.
Convincing, well-scripted domestic drama.

w William Wood, *novel* Ann Head *d* Robert Day

Desi Arnaz Jnr, Chris Norris, Susan Strasberg, Dan Dailey, Tom Bosley, Dina Merrill, Lynn Carlin

Mr and Mrs Smith*
US 1941 95m bw
RKO (Harry E. Edington)

A much-married couple discover that their marriage wasn't legal.
Smartish matrimonial comedy, surprisingly but not obviously directed by the master of suspense.

w Norman Krasna *d* Alfred Hitchcock
ph Harry Stradling *m* Roy Webb

Carole Lombard, Robert Montgomery, Gene Raymond, Jack Carson, Philip Merivale, Lucile Watson, William Tracy

Mr Belvedere Goes to College*
US 1949 88m bw
TCF (Samuel G. Engel)

A self-styled genius goes back to school and helps a college widow.
Flat follow up to *Sitting Pretty* (qv), with only a few laughs.

w Richard Sale, Mary Loos, Mary McCall Jnr *d* Elliott Nugent *ph* Lloyd Ahern *m* Alfred Newman

Clifton Webb, Shirley Temple, Alan Young, Tom Drake, Jessie Royce Landis, Kathleen Hughes, Taylor Holmes

Mr Belvedere Rings the Bell*
US 1951 87m bw
TCF (André Hakim)

Imperturbable Mr Belvedere enters an old folks' home under false pretences to test his theories of ageing.
A not unagreeable star vehicle for those who can stand the sentiment.

w Ranald MacDougall, *play* The Silver Whistle by Robert E. McEnroe *d* Henry Koster
ph Joseph La Shelle *m* Cyril Mockridge

Clifton Webb, Joanne Dru, Hugh Marlowe, Zero Mostel, Doro Merande

Mr Blandings Builds His Dream House***
US 1948 84m bw
RKO (Norman Panama, Melvin Frank)

A New York advertising man longs to live in the Connecticut countryside, but finds the way to rural satisfaction is hard.
It hasn't the lightness and brightness of the book, but this is a fun film for the middle-aged who like to watch three agreeable stars doing their thing.

w Norman Panama, Melvin Frank, novel Eric Hodgkin d H. C. Potter ph James Wong Howe *m* Constantin Bakaleinikoff

Cary Grant, Myrna Loy, Melvyn Douglas, Reginald Denny, Louise Beavers, Ian Wolfe, Harry Shannon, Nestor Paiva, Jason Robards

'A bulls-eye for middle-class middlebrows.'—*James Agee*

Mister Buddwing
US 1966 99m bw
MGM / DDD / Cherokee (Douglas Laurence, Delbert Mann)
GB title: *Woman without a Face*

An amnesiac wakes up in Central Park and goes in search of his identity.
Rather muddled melodrama in which the characters are so dull that by the time the flashbacks fall into place we scarcely care.

w Dale Wassermann, *novel* Buddwing by Evan Hunter *d* Delbert Mann *ph* Ellsworth Fredericks *m* Kenyon Hopkins

James Garner, Jean Simmons, Angela Lansbury, Suzanne Pleshette, Katharine Ross, George Voskovec, Jack Gilford, Joe Mantell, Raymond St Jacques

Mister Cory
US 1957 92m Eastmancolor Cinemascope
U-I (Robert Arthur)

A small-time gangster leaves the Chicago slums to seek fame and fortune among the country-club set.
Modest star comedy drama.

wd Blake Edwards *ph* Russell Metty *m* Joseph Gershenson

Tony Curtis, Martha Hyer, Charles Bickford, Kathryn Grant

Mr Deeds Goes to Town***
US 1936 118m bw
Columbia (Frank Capra)

A small-town poet inherits a vast fortune and sets New York on its heels by his honesty.
What once was fresh and charming now seems rather laboured in spots, and the production is parsimonious indeed, but the courtroom scene still works, and the good intentions conquer all.

w Robert Riskin, story Opera Hat by Clarence Budington Kelland *d Frank Capra* *ph* Joseph Walker *md* Howard Jackson

Gary Cooper, Jean Arthur, Raymond Walburn, Lionel Stander, Walter Catlett, George Bancroft, Douglass Dumbrille, H. B. Warner, Ruth Donnelly, *Margaret Seddon, Margaret McWade*

'I have an uneasy feeling he's on his way out. He's started to make pictures about themes instead of people.'—*Alistair Cooke*

Mr Denning Drives North
GB 1951 93m bw
London Films (Anthony Kimmins, Stephen Mitchell)

A wealthy man accidentally kills a criminal in love with his daughter; he hides the body, which then disappears.
Initially suspenseful but finally disappointing melodrama which seems to lack a twist or two.

w Alec Coppel *d* Anthony Kimmins *ph* John Wilcox *m* Benjamin Frankel

John Mills, Phyllis Calvert, Sam Wanamaker, Freda Jackson

Mr Drake's Duck**
GB 1950 85m bw
Daniel M. Angel / Douglas Fairbanks

A duck lays a uranium egg, and a gentleman farmer finds himself at the centre of international military disagreement.
Brisk and amusing minor comedy deploying British comic types to good purpose.

wd Val Guest, radio play Ian Messiter *ph* Jack Cox

Douglas Fairbanks Jnr, Yolande Donlan, Wilfrid Hyde White, A. E. Matthews, Jon Pertwee, Reginald Beckwith, Howard Marion-Crawford, Peter Butterworth, Tom Gill

Mister 880**
US 1950 90m bw
TCF (Julian Blaustein)

An elderly counterfeiter perplexes the US Secret Service.
Whimsical star comedy which moves along cheerfully enough to be a good example of the Hollywood programmer at its prime.

w Robert Riskin *d* Edmund Goulding *ph* Joseph La Shelle *m* Sol Kaplan

Edmund Gwenn, Burt Lancaster, Dorothy McGuire, Millard Mitchell

Mr Emmanuel*
GB 1944 97m bw
Two Cities (William Sistrom)

In 1936 an elderly Jew visits Germany in search of the mother of an orphan boy.
Simply made but quite effective and unusual story giving Aylmer his only star part.

w Gordon Wellesley, Norman Ginsburg, *novel* Louis Golding *d* Harold French

Felix Aylmer, Greta Gynt, Walter Rilla, Peter Mullins, Ursula Jeans, Elspeth March, Meier Tzelniker

Mr Forbush and the Penguins*
GB 1971 101m Technicolor
EMI / PGI / Henry Trettin

A biologist is sent to the Antarctic to study penguins, and gets a new understanding of life.
Rather broken-backed animal film with a moral; pleasant enough, its two halves don't fit together.

w Anthony Shaffer, *novel* Graham Billey *d* Roy Boulting, *Arne Sucksdorff* *ph* Harry Waxman, Ted Scaife *m* John Addison

John Hurt, Hayley Mills, Tony Britton

Mr Hobbs Takes a Vacation*
US 1962 116m De Luxe
Cinemascope
TCF (Jerry Wald)

A city dweller takes a seaside house for a family holiday, but it turns out to be a crumbling ruin.
Overlong, sloppy comedy which devotes too much time to teenage romance but manages occasional smiles.

w Nunnally Johnson, *novel* Edward Streeter *d* Henry Koster *ph* W. C. Mellor *m* Henry Mancini

James Stewart, Maureen O'Hara, Fabian, John Saxon, Marie Wilson, Reginald Gardiner, *John McGiver*

Mr Imperium
US 1951 87m Technicolor
MGM (Edwin H. Knopf)
GB title: *You Belong to My Heart*

An exiled king in Hollywood meets a famous film star with whom he once had a romance.
Minor romantic drama with songs.

w Edwin Knopf, Don Hartman *d* Don Hartman *ph* George J. Folsey *m* Harold Arlen

Lana Turner, Ezio Pinza, Marjorie Main, Barry Sullivan, Cedric Hardwicke, Debbie Reynolds

Mr Inside, Mr Outside*
US 1973 74m colour TVM
Metromedia / Phil D'Antoni

One of a pair of cops goes undercover to trap diamond smugglers.
Adequate location *policier*.

w Jerry Coppersmith *d* Alex March

Hal Linden, Tony Lo Bianco, Phil Bruns, Paul Benjamin

Mr Jerico*
GB 1969 85m colour TVM
ITC (Julian Wintle)

Adventures of a con man.
Pleasant chase-and-caper yarn.

w Philip Levene *d* Sidney Hayers

Patrick MacNee, Connie Stevens, Herbert Lom, Marty Allen

Mr Lucky*
US 1943 98m bw
RKO (David Hempstead)

During World War II a gambling ship owner goes straight and instigates Bundles for Britain.
Unconvincing mixture of comedy and drama with the actors looking somewhat bewildered.

w Milton Holmes, Adrian Scott *d* H. C. Potter *ph* George Barnes *m* Roy Webb

Cary Grant, Laraine Day, Charles Bickford, Gladys Cooper, Alan Carney, Henry Stephenson, Paul Stewart, Walter Kingsford
† Remade 1950 as *Gambling House.*

Mr Majestyk*
US 1974 103m De Luxe
UA / Mirisch (Walter Mirisch)

A Colorado melon grower crosses swords with the local Mafia.
Violent but unexpectedly enjoyable action melodrama.

w Elmore Leonard *d* Richard Fleischer *ph* Richard Kline *m* Charles Bernstein

Charles Bronson, Al Lettieri, Linda Cristal, Lee Purcell, Paul Keslo

Mister Moses*
GB 1965 103m Technicolor
Panavision
UA / Frank Ross / Talbot

A quack doctor is the only person who can persuade an African tribe to move before their land is flooded, and he leads them to their promised land.
Adventure spectacle with naïve biblical parallels; quite agreeable.

w Charles Beaumont, Monja Danischewsky, *novel* Max Catto *d* Ronald Neame *ph* Oswald Morris *m* John Barry

Robert Mitchum, Carroll Baker, Ian Bannen, Alexander Knox, Reginald Beckwith, Raymond St Jacques

Mr Moto
The Japanese detective created by John P. Marquand figured in several above-average second features of the late thirties, but the outbreak of war caused him to vanish. The casts were interesting, the TCF production excellent, and the director usually Norman Foster. The 1965 attempt to revive the character with Henry Silva was painfully boring.

1937: THINK FAST MR MOTO (with Virginia Field, Sig Rumann), THANK YOU MR MOTO (with Pauline Frederick, Sidney Blackmer)
1938: MR MOTO'S GAMBLE (with Keye Luke, Lynn Bari), MR MOTO TAKES A CHANCE (with Rochelle Hudson, J. Edward Bromberg), MYSTERIOUS MR MOTO (with Henry Wilcoxon, Erik Rhodes)
1939: MR MOTO'S LAST WARNING (with Ricardo Cortez, George Sanders, Robert Coote, John Carradine), MR MOTO IN DANGER ISLAND (with Jean Hersholt, Warren Hymer),

MR MOTO TAKES A VACATION (with Joseph Schildkraut, Lionel Atwill)
1965: THE RETURN OF MR MOTO

Mr Music*
US 1950 113m bw
Paramount (Robert L. Welch)

A college girl is employed to keep an idle middle-aged songwriter's nose to the grindstone.
Bland musical remake of *Accent on Youth* (qv); pleasant performances, moments of comedy, guest stars.

w Arthur Sheekman *d* Richard Haydn *ph* George Barnes *songs* Johnny Burke, James Van Heusen *ad* Hans Dreier, Earl Hedrick

Bing Crosby, Nancy Olson, Charles Coburn, Ruth Hussey, Marge and Gower Champion, Peggy Lee, Groucho Marx

Mr Peabody and the Mermaid
US 1948 89m bw
U-I (Nunnally Johnson)

A middle-aged husband imagines an affair with a mermaid.
Bone-headed quick-cash-in on *Miranda* (qv); it never begins to work.

w Nunnally Johnson, *novel* Guy and Constance Jones *d* Irving Pichel *ph* Russell Metty *m* Robert Emmett Dolan

William Powell, Ann Blyth, Irene Hervey, Andrea King, Clinton Sundberg

Mr Perrin and Mr Traill*
GB 1948 92m bw
GFD / Two Cities

A handsome young master at a boys' school incurs the jealousy of an embittered colleague.
Flat, over-acted but mildly watchable picturization of a well-known story.

w L. A. G. Strong, *novel* Hugh Walpole *d* Lawrence Huntington *ph* Erwin Hillier *m* Alan Gray

Marius Goring, David Farrar, Greta Gynt, Edward Chapman, Raymond Huntley, Mary Jerrold, Finlay Currie, Ralph Truman

Mister Quilp
GB 1975 119m Technicolor Panavision
Reader's Digest (Helen M. Straus)
aka: The Old Curiosity Shop

In 1840 London, an antique-shop owner is in debt to a hunchback moneylender who has designs on his business.
The novel, with its villainous lead, is a curious choice for musicalizing, and in this treatment falls desperately flat, with no sparkle of imagination visible anywhere.

w Louis Kamp, Irene Kamp, *novel* The Old Curiosity Shop by Charles Dickens *d* Michael Tuchner *ph* Christopher Challis *m* Anthony Newley *pd* Elliot Scott *md* Elmer Bernstein *ch* Gillian Lynne

Anthony Newley, Michael Hordern, David Hemmings, Sarah-Jane Varley, David Warner, Paul Rogers, Jill Bennett

'Another soggy piece of family entertainment from Reader's Digest, who produced the toothless screen musicals of *Tom Sawyer* and *Huckleberry Finn*.'—*Philip French*

Mr Ricco
US 1975 98m Panavision
MGM (Douglas Netter)

A defence counsel risks his life to prove his black client innocent.
Complex urban action thriller with a tired, ageing hero and impenetrable plot.

w Robert Hoban *d* Paul Bogart *ph* Frank Stanley *m* Chico Hamilton

Dean Martin, Eugene Roche, Thalmus Rasulala, Denise Nicholas, Cindy Williams, *Geraldine Brooks*, Frank Puglia

Mister Roberts**
US 1955 123m Warnercolor Cinemascope
Warner / Leland Hayward

Life aboard a World War II cargo ship yearning for action.
A mixture of comedy and sentimentality which has become an American minor classic as a play; this film version is a shambling affair but gets most of the effects over.

w Frank Nugent, Joshua Logan, *play* Thomas Heggen and Joshua Logan, *novel Thomas Heggen* *d* John Ford, Mervyn Le Roy *ph* Winton Hoch *m* Franz Waxman

Henry Fonda, James Cagney, William Powell, Jack Lemmon, Betsy Palmer, Ward Bond, Phil Carey, Ken Curtis, Harry Carey Jnr

Mr Sardonicus
US 1961 90m bw
Columbia / William Castle

A surgeon is lured to an ex-girl friend's remote home to cure her sadistic husband's crippled face.
Flatly handled, boring semi-horror.

w Robb White *d* William Castle

Ronald Lewis, Guy Rolfe, Audrey Dalton, Oscar Homolka

Mr Scoutmaster
US 1953 87m bw
TCF

A TV personality wants to understand children and is persuaded to take over a scout troop.
A star vehicle which starts promisingly enough in the *Sitting Pretty* vein but quickly falls headlong into an abyss of sentimentality.

w Leonard Praskins, Barney Slater *d* Henry Levin *ph* Joseph La Shelle *m* Lionel Newman

Clifton Webb, Edmund Gwenn, George Winslow, Frances Dee, Veda Ann Borg

Mr Skeffington***
US 1944 127m bw
Warner (Julius J. and Philip G. Epstein)

A selfish beauty finally turns to her discarded dull husband; when he is blind, he doesn't mind her faded looks.
Long, patchily made, but thoroughly enjoyable star melodrama.

w Julius J. and Philip G. Epstein, *novel* 'Elizabeth' *d* Vincent Sherman *ph* Ernest Haller *m* Franz Waxman

Bette Davis, Claude Rains, Walter Abel, Richard Waring, George Coulouris, John Alexander, Jerome Cowan

'An endless woman's page dissertation on What To Do When Beauty Fades.'—*James Agee*

Mr Smith Goes to Washington****
US 1939 130m bw
Columbia (Frank Capra)

Washington's youngest senator exposes corruption in high places, almost at the cost of his own career.
Archetypal high-flying Capra vehicle, with the little man coming out top as he seldom does in life. Supreme gloss hides the corn, helter-skelter direction keeps one watching, and all concerned give memorable performances. A cinema classic.

w Sidney Buchman, story Lewis R. Foster *d Frank Capra ph Joseph Walker m Dmitri Tiomkin montage Slavko Vorkapich*

James Stewart, Claude Rains, Jean Arthur, Thomas Mitchell, Edward Arnold, Guy Kibbee, Eugene Pallette, Beulah Bondi, *Harry Carey,* H. B. Warner, Astrid Allwyn, Ruth Donnelly, Charles Lane, Porter Hall

'More fun, even, than the Senate itself . . . not merely a brilliant jest, but a stirring and even inspiring testament to liberty and freedom.'—*Frank S. Nugent, New York Times*

'A totally compelling piece of movie-making, upholding the virtues of traditional American ideals.'—*NFT, 1973*

Mr Winkle Goes to War
US 1944 80m bw
Columbia (Jack Moss)
GB title: *Arms and the Woman*

A middle-aged bank clerk joins the army and becomes a hero.
Agreeable, forgettable propaganda comedy-drama.

w Waldo Salt, George Corey, Louis Solomon, *novel* Theodore Pratt *d* Alfred E. Green *ph* Joseph Walker *m* Carmen Dragon, Paul Sawtell

Edward G. Robinson, Ruth Warrick, Ted Donaldson, Bob Haymes, Richard Lane, Robert Armstrong, Walter Baldwin

Mr Wong
A cheeseparing set of second features from Monogram, based on stories by Hugh Wiley. Boris Karloff was unsuitably cast as a Chinese detective, and in the last film he was replaced by Keye Luke. The films were directed by William Nigh.

1938: MR WONG DETECTIVE
1939: THE MYSTERY OF MR WONG, MR WONG IN CHINATOWN
1940: THE FATAL HOUR, DOOMED TO DIE (GB title: THE MYSTERY OF THE WENTWORTH CASTLE)
1941: PHANTOM OF CHINATOWN

Mrs Mike
US 1949 99m bw
Nassour / Huntingdon Hartford (Edward Gross)

A Mountie takes his new wife to live in the frozen northwest.
Predictable sentimental drama, well enough done to keep interest, but only just.

w Lewis Levitt, De Witt Bodeen *d* Louis King *ph* Joseph Biroc *m* Max Steiner

Dick Powell, Evelyn Keyes, J. M. Kerrigan, Angela Clarke

Mrs Miniver**
US 1942 134m bw
MGM (Sidney Franklin)

An English housewife survives World War II.
This is the rose-strewn English village, Hollywood variety, but when released it proved a beacon of morale despite its false sentiment, absurd rural types and melodramatic situations. It is therefore beyond criticism, except that some of the people involved should have known better.

w Arthur Wimperis, George Froeschel, James Hilton, Claudine West *d* William Wyler *ph* Joseph Ruttenberg *m* Herbert Stothart

Greer Garson, Walter Pidgeon, Teresa Wright, Richard Ney, Dame May Whitty, Henry Travers, Reginald Owen, Henry Wilcoxon, Helmut Dantine, Rhys Williams, Aubrey Mather

Mrs O'Malley and Mr Malone*
US 1950 69m bw
MGM (William H. Wright)

On a train to New York, a radio contest winner and a lawyer help solve a murder.
Lively second feature farce.

w William Powers *d* Norman Taurog *ph* Ray June

Marjorie Main, James Whitmore, Ann Dvorak, Fred Clark, Dorothy Malone, Phyllis Kirk

Mrs Parkington
US 1944 124m bw
MGM (Leon Gordon)

A lady's maid marries a miner who becomes wealthy, and pushes her way into society.
Thoroughly unconvincing three-generation drama, with a bewigged and powdered star giving the boot to her conniving relations. It has production values and nothing else.

w Robert Thoeren, Polly James, *novel* Louis Bromfield *d* Tay Garnett *ph* Joseph Ruttenberg *m* Bronislau Kaper

Greer Garson, Walter Pidgeon, Edward Arnold, Agnes Moorehead, Cecil Kellaway, Gladys Cooper, Frances Rafferty, Tom Drake, Peter Lawford, Dan Duryea, Hugh Marlowe, Selena Royle
† The heroine is shown having a romance with Edward VII when Prince of Wales; special scenes were shot for the European version substituting Cecil Kellaway, who played Edward, by Hugo Haas who played a European king of indeterminate origin.

Mrs Pollifax—Spy
US 1970 110m De Luxe
UA / Mellor (Frederick Brisson)

A respectable American matron offers her services to the CIA and sees active service in Albania.
Incredible comedy-dramatic vehicle for a star who won't give up. An obvious failure from the word go.

w C. A. McKnight, *novel* Dorothy Gilman *d* Leslie Martinson *ph* Joseph Biroc *m* Lalo Schifrin

Rosalind Russell, Darren McGavin

Mrs Sundance
US 1973 74m colour TVM
TCF

The widow of an outlaw tries to go straight and becomes a schoolmistress, then finds she isn't a widow at all.
Disappointing western considering the possibilities: it takes too long to get going.

w Christopher Knopf *d* Marvin Chomsky

Elizabeth Montgomery, Robert Foxworth, L. Q. Jones, Lurene Tuttle, Dean Smith, Arthur Hunnicutt

Mrs Wiggs of the Cabbage Patch*
US 1934 80m bw
Paramount (Douglas MacLean)

Adventures of a poor family who live on the wrong side of the tracks in a broken down old shack.
A Depression fantasy of respectability and optimism, almost incredible to see now, although it plumbed the same never-never milieu as did Chaplin. Moments of comedy still please, but one does long for Mr Fields' delayed entry.

w William Slavens McNutt, Jane Storm, *novel* Alice Hegan Rice *d* Norman Taurog *ph* Charles Lang

Pauline Lord, *Zasu Pitts, W. C. Fields*, Evelyn Venable, Kent Taylor, Charles Middleton, Donald Meek, Edith Fellows, Virginia Weidler, George Breakston
'A nasty all's-right-with-the-world burlesque of poverty, with emotions to tug at such heartstrings as are worn dangling from the mouth.'—*Otis Ferguson*

Mrs Wiggs of the Cabbage Patch
US 1942 80m bw
Paramount

Curiously quick remake, almost word for word, but without the moments of inspiration.

w Doris Anderson, Jane Storm, William Slavens McNutt *d* Ralph Murphy

Fay Bainter, Hugh Herbert, Vera Vague, Barbara Britton, Carl Switzer, Moroni Olsen, Billy Lee

Mix Me a Person
GB 1961 116m bw
Wessex (Sergei Nolbandov)

A barrister's psychiatrist wife takes on one of his failures, a client condemned to death for murder.

Once it gets started, a routine suspense thriller with the wrong man convicted and an espresso bar background. Not a very good one, though.

w Ian Dalrymple, *novel* Jack Trevor Story *d* Leslie Norman *ph* Ted Moore *m* Johnny Worth

Anne Baxter, Donald Sinden, Adam Faith, Walter Brown, Glyn Houston

Mixed Company
US 1974 109m De Luxe
UA / Cornell (Melville Shavelson)

A basketball coach and his wife adopt several children of different races.
Room for One More and then some, but not very interesting.

w Melville Shavelson, Mort Lachman *d* Melville Shavelson *ph* Stan Lazan *m* Fred Karlin *pd* Stan Jolley

Barbara Harris, Joseph Bologna, Lisa Gerritson, Arianne Heller

The Mob*
US 1951 87m bw
Columbia (Jerry Bresler)
GB title: *Remember That Face*

A policeman works undercover to catch a dockside racketeer.
Tough, lively thriller with effectively sustained mystery and a serial-like finale.

w William Bowers d Robert Parrish ph Joseph Walker *m* George Duning

Broderick Crawford, Richard Kiley, Ernest Borgnine, Neville Brand, Charles Bronson

Mobile Two
US 1975 74m Technicolor TVM
Universal / Jack Webb

Adventures of a television news gatherer.
Routine, unexciting competence in the producer's accustomed manner: the resulting series was short-lived.

w David Moessinger, James M. Miller *d* David Moessinger

Jackie Cooper, Julie Gregg, Edd Byrnes, Jack Hogan, Mark Wheeler

Moby Dick*
US 1930 75m bw
Warner

Captain Ahab returns minus a leg from fighting the white whale, and finds that his fiancée is too shocked to love him.
Mangled remake of a fine novel filmed in silent form as *The Sea Beast*.

w J. Grubb Alexander, *novel* Herman Melville *d* Lloyd Bacon *ph* Robert Kurrie

John Barrymore, Joan Bennett, Lloyd Hughes, May Boley, Walter Long

Moby Dick**
GB 1956 116m Technicolor
John Huston

A whaling skipper is determined to harpoon the white whale which robbed him of a leg.
Pretentious period adventure, rather too obsessed with symbolism and certainly too slowly developed, but full of interesting detail which almost outweighs the central miscasting.

w Ray Bradbury, John Huston, *novel* Herman Melville *d* John Huston *ph Oswald Morris* *m* Philip Stainton

Gregory Peck, Richard Basehart, Friedrich Ledebur, Leo Genn, Orson Welles, James Robertson Justice, Harry Andrews, Bernard Miles, Noel Purcell, Edric Connor, Joseph Tomelty, Mervyn Johns

The Model and the Marriage Broker
US 1952 103m bw
TCF (Charles Brackett)

A broker conceals her profession from a friend but gets the friend fixed up.
Moderate, unsurprising comedy somewhat overweighted by talent which can't express itself.

w Charles Brackett, Walter Reisch, Richard Breen *d* George Cukor *ph* Milton Krasner *m* Cyril Mockridge

Thelma Ritter, Jeanne Crain, Scott Brady, Zero Mostel, Michael O'Shea, Nancy Kulp

Modern Times***
US 1936 87m bw
Charles Chaplin

An assembly-line worker goes berserk but can't get another job.
Silent star comedy produced in the middle of the sound period; flashes of genius alternate with sentimental sequences and jokes without punch.

wd/m Charles Chaplin ph Rollie Totheroh, Ira Morgan

Charles Chaplin, Paulette Goddard, Henry Bergman, Chester Conklin, Tiny Sandford

'A feature picture made out of several one- and two-reel shorts, proposed titles being *The Shop, The Jailbird, The Singing Waiter.'—Otis Ferguson*

Modesty Blaise
GB 1966 119m Technicolor
TCF / Modesty Blaise Ltd (Joseph Janni)

Female arch-agent Modesty Blaise defends a shipload of diamonds against a sadistic master criminal.
Comic-strip adventures made by people with no sense of humour; Fu Manchu was much more fun.

w Evan Jones, *comic strip* Peter O'Donnell, Jim Holdaway *d* Joseph Losey *ph* Jack Hildyard *m* Johnny Dankworth

Monica Vitti, Dirk Bogarde, Terence Stamp, Harry Andrews, Michael Craig, Scilla Gabel, Clive Revill, Rossella Falk, Joe Melia

Mogambo*
GB 1954 116m Technicolor
MGM (Sam Zimbalist)

The headquarters of a Kenyan white hunter is invaded by an American showgirl and a British archaeologist and his wife, and they all go off on a gorilla hunt.
Amiable, flabby remake of *Red Dust*, with direction scarcely in evidence and the gorillas out-acting a genial cast.

w John Lee Mahin *d* John Ford *ph* Robert Surtees, F. A. Young

Clark Gable, Ava Gardner, Grace Kelly, Donald Sinden, Laurence Naismith, Philip Stainton
† The story was also made as *Congo Maisie* in 1940.

The Molly Maguires
US 1970 123m Technicolor Panavision
Paramount / Tamm (Martin Ritt, Walter Bernstein)

In the Pennsylvania coalmining district in the 1870s, an undercover detective exposes the leaders of a secret society.
Sober-sided and slow-moving account of actual events which also formed the basis for Conan Doyle's rather more entertaining *The Valley of Fear*. Expensive, nicely photographed, but unpersuasive and empty.

w Walter Bernstein *d* Martin Ritt *ph James Wong Howe m* Henry Mancini

Richard Harris, Sean Connery, Samantha Eggar, Frank Finlay, Anthony Zerbe, Bethel Leslie, Art Lund

'The film's vague sense of grievance and harrowing circumstances hangs in the air like the smoky pall cast up by the anthracite workings.'—*Richard Combs*

'A cold, dry and rather perfunctory film.'—*Arthur Schlesinger Jnr*

Moment to Moment
US 1966 108m Technicolor
Universal (Mervyn Le Roy)

A housewife finds herself with a body on her hands.
Incredibly old-fashioned romantic/melodramatic malarkey set on the French Riviera but scarcely moving a step out of Hollywood. Lush settings made it marketable to women.

w John Lee Mahin, Alec Coppel *d* Mervyn Le Roy *ph* Harry Stradling *m* Henry Mancini

Jean Seberg, *Honor Blackman*, Sean Garrison, Arthur Hill, Grégoire Aslan

Money to Burn
US 1973 74m Technicolor TVM
Universal (Harve Bennett)

A crooked couple work out a counterfeiting caper even though the husband is in prison.
Initially ingenious crime comedy which suddenly peters out.

w Gerald di Pego *d* Robert Michael Lewis

E. G. Marshall, Mildred Natwick, Cleavon Little, Alejandro Rey, David Doyle, Charles McGraw

The Money Trap
US 1966 92m bw Panavision
MGM (Max E. Youngstein, David Karr)

A hard-up policeman turns to crime.
A cheap thriller decorated with waning stars, competent at the lowest level.

w Walter Bernstein, *novel* Lionel White *d* Burt Kennedy *ph* Paul C. Vogel *m* Hal Schaefer

Glenn Ford, Rita Hayworth, Elke Sommer, Ricardo Montalban, Joseph Cotten, Tom Reese, James Mitchum

Mongo's Back in Town*
US 1971 73m colour TVM
Bob Banner

A professional killer is hired by his brother to kill a rival.
Tough, competent gangster thriller.

w Herman Miller, *novel* E. Richard Johnson *d* Marvin Chomsky

Telly Savalas, Sally Field, Anne Francis, Martin Sheen, Joe Don Baker, Charles Cioffi, Ned Glass

The Monk
US 1969 74m colour TVM
Spelling–Thomas

A private eye guards an envelope, but it is stolen and his client killed.

Adequate mystery with San Francisco backgrounds.

w Tony Barrett *d* George McCowan

George Maharis, Janet Leigh, Jack Soo, Raymond St Jacques, Jack Albertson, Carl Betz, Rick Jason

Monkey Business***
US 1931 81m bw
Paramount

Four ship's stowaways crash a society party and catch a few crooks.
The shipboard part of this extravaganza is one of the best stretches of Marxian lunacy, but after the Chevalier impersonations it runs out of steam. Who's grumbling?

w S. J. Perelman, Will B. Johnstone, Arthur Sheekman d Norman Z. McLeod *ph* Arthur L. Todd

Groucho, Chico, Harpo, Zeppo, Thelma Todd, Rockcliffe Fellowes, Ruth Hall, Harry Woods

Monkey Business*
US 1952 97m bw
TCF (Sol C. Siegel)

A chimpanzee in a research lab accidentally concocts an elixir of youth.
Remarkably laboured comedy by and with top people; it can't fail to have funny moments, but they are few and far between.

w Ben Hecht, Charles Lederer, I. A. L. Diamond *d* Howard Hawks *ph* Milton Krasner *m* Leigh Harline

Cary Grant, Ginger Rogers, *Charles Coburn, Marilyn Monroe*, Hugh Marlowe

Monkey on My Back
US 1957 93m bw
UA / Imperial / Edward Small

A Guadalcanal hero is given morphine to relieve malaria and becomes addicted.
Dreary case history sold as exploitation.

w Crane Wilbur, Anthony Veiller, Peter Dudley, from the experiences of Barney Ross *d* André de Toth *ph* Maury Gertsman

Cameron Mitchell, Dianne Foster, Jack Albertson, Paul Richards

Monsieur Beaucaire*
US 1946 93m bw
Paramount (Paul Jones)

King Louis XV's bumbling barber impersonates a court dandy.
What seemed a lively period burlesque has faded somewhat with age, but it still has its moments. Any relation between this and the silent Valentino film is quite accidental.

w Melvin Frank, Norman Panama *d* George Marshall *ph* Lionel Lindon *md* Robert Emmett Dolan

Bob Hope, Joan Caulfield, Patric Knowles, Marjorie Reynolds, Cecil Kellaway, Joseph Schildkraut, Reginald Owen, Constance Collier, Hillary Brooke, Douglass Dumbrille, Mary Nash

'Whether you yawn or rather wearily laugh depends chiefly on your chance state of mind.'—*James Agee*

Monsieur Verdoux**
US 1947 125m bw
Charles Chaplin

A bank cashier marries and murders rich women to support his real wife.
Interesting but unsatisfactory redrafting of the Landru case; the star is more dapper than funny, the moral is unconvincing, and the slapstick sequences too often raise yawns.

wd/m Charles Chaplin *ph* Rollie Totheroh

Charles Chaplin, Martha Raye, Isobel Elsom

The Monster and the Girl
US 1940 64m bw
Paramount

A man is wrongfully executed and his brain is implanted in a gorilla, which goes on the rampage.
Curiously ineffectual considering its plot and cast, this little horror thriller seems to have been the first to use this particular situation, which became very well worn later.

w Stuart Anthony *d* Stuart Heisler *ph* Victor Milner

Paul Lukas, Ellen Drew, Joseph Calleia, George Zucco, Robert Paige, Rod Cameron, Philip Terry, Onslow Stevens, Gerald Mohr

Monte Carlo*
US 1930 94m bw
Paramount

A count passes himself off as a hairdresser to win a gambling lady.
Faded but charming romantic comedy with music, the first to show its director's sound style in full throttle, notably in the final 'Beyond the Blue Horizon' sequence.

w Ernest Vajda, *play* The Blue Coast by Hans Muller, *novel* Monsieur Beaucaire by Booth Tarkington *d Ernst Lubitsch ph* Victor Milner *ad* Hans Dreier

Jack Buchanan, Jeanette MacDonald, Zasu

Pitts, Tyler Brooke, Claud Allister, Lionel Belmore

Monte Walsh*
US 1970 108m Technicolor
Cinema Center (Hal Landis, Bobby Roberts)

Two ageing cowboys find life increasingly hard and hopeless; an old acquaintance kills one and is shot by the other.
'Realistic' western developed in leisurely style with the emphasis on character and on the real drudgery of frontier life.

w David Z. Goodman, Lukas Heller, *novel* Jack Schaefer *d* William A. Fraker *ph* David M. Walsh *m* John Barry

Lee Marvin, Jack Palance, Jeanne Moreau, Mitch Ryan, Jim Davis

Monty Python and the Holy Grail**
GB 1975 90m Technicolor
EMI / Python (Monty) Pictures / Michael White (Mark Forstater)

King Arthur and his knights seek the Holy Grail.
Hellzapoppin-like series of linked sketches on a medieval theme; some slow bits, but often uproariously funny and with a remarkable visual sense of the middle ages.

w Graham Chapman, John Cleese, Terry Gilliam, Eric Idle, Michael Palin *d* Terry Gilliam, Terry Jones *ph* Terry Bedford *animation* Terry Gilliam *m* Neil Innes *pd Roy Smith*

Graham Chapman, John Cleese, Terry Gilliam, Eric Idle, Michael Palin

'The team's visual buffooneries and verbal rigmaroles are piled on top of each other with no attention to judicious timing or structure, and a form which began as a jaunty assault on the well-made revue sketch and an ingenious misuse of television's fragmented style of presentation, threatens to become as unyielding and unfruitful as the conventions it originally attacked.'—*Geoff Brown*

The Moon and Sixpence***
US 1943 85m bw (colour sequence)
Stanley Kramer

A stockbroker leaves his wife and family, spends some selfish years painting in Paris and finally dies of leprosy on a South Sea island.
Pleasantly literary adaptation of an elegant novel based on the life of Gauguin; a little stodgy in presentation now, but much of it still pleases.

w Albert Lewin, *novel* W. Somerset Maugham *d* Albert Lewin *ph* John Seitz *m* Dmitri Tiomkin

George Sanders, Herbert Marshall (as Maugham), *Steve Geray*, Doris Dudley, Elena Verdugo, Florence Bates, Heather Thatcher, Eric Blore, Albert Basserman

'An admirable film until the end, when it lapses into Technicolor and techni-pathos.'—*James Agate*

The Moon Is Blue*
US 1953 99m bw
Otto Preminger

A spry young girl balances the attractions of a middle-aged lover against her young one.
Paper-thin comedy partly set on top of the Empire State Building (and thereafter in a dowdy set); mildly amusing in spots, it gained notoriety, and a Production Code ban, by its use of such naughty words as 'virgin' and 'mistress'.

w F. Hugh Herbert, from his play *d* Otto Preminger *ph* Ernest Laszlo

Maggie McNamara, David Niven, William Holden, Tom Tully, Dawn Addams

'It adds nothing to the art of cinema and certainly does not deserve the attention it will get for flouting the Production Code.'—*Philip T. Hartung*

The Moon Is Down**
US 1943 90m bw

A Norwegian village resists the Nazis.
Sombre, talkative, intelligent little drama, the best of the resistance films, shot on the set of *How Green Was My Valley* (with snow covering).

w Nunnally Johnson, *novel* John Steinbeck *d Irving Pichel* *ph* Arthur Miller *m* Alfred Newman

Henry Travers, Cedric Hardwicke, Lee J. Cobb, Dorris Bowden, Margaret Wycherly, Peter Van Eyck, John Banner

Moon of the Wolf*
US 1972 74m colour TVM
Filmways (Everett Chambers)

A southern town is terrorized by a werewolf.
Horror hokum which looks pretty silly in modern dress, but packs a scare or two.

w Alvin Sapinsley *d* Daniel Petrie

David Janssen, Barbara Rush, Bradford Dillman, John Beradino

Moon over Burma
US 1940 76m bw
Paramount

Jungle lumbermen fight over a standard American entertainer.

Routine adventure romance climaxing in a forest fire.

w Frank Wead, W. P. Lipscomb, Harry Clark *d* Louis King *ph* William Mellor

Dorothy Lamour, Robert Preston, Preston Foster, Doris Nolan, Albert Basserman, Frederick Worlock, Addison Richards

Moon over Miami*
US 1941 92m Technicolor
TCF (Harry Joe Brown)

Two sisters seek rich husbands in Florida.
Musical remake of *Three Blind Mice*, which was suspiciously similar to *Golddiggers of Broadway, The Greeks Had a Word for Them*, etc., and the later *How to Marry a Millionaire* and *Three Little Girls in Blue*. In short, a Hollywood standard, not too badly done.

w Vincent Lawrence, Brown Holmes *d* Walter Lang *ph* Peverell Marley, Leon Shamroy *md* Alfred Newman

Don Ameche, Betty Grable, Carole Landis, Charlotte Greenwood, Jack Haley, Cobina Wright Jnr, Robert Greig

Moon Pilot**
US 1961 98m Technicolor
Walt Disney (Ron Miller)

A reluctant astronaut falls in love with a girl from outer space, who finally accompanies him on his mission.
Engaging science-fiction spoof with good performances.

w Maurice Tombragel, *serial* Robert Buckner *d* James Neilson *ph* William Snyder *m* Peter Smith *sp* Eustace Lycett

Edmond O'Brien, Tom Tryon, Brian Keith

The Moon Spinners*
GB 1964 119m Technicolor
Walt Disney (Bill Anderson)

A young girl holidaying in Crete becomes involved with jewel robbers.
Teenage adventure against attractive locations; quite agreeable but overlong.

w Michael Dyne, *novel* Mary Stewart *d* James Neilson *ph* Paul Beeson *m* Ron Grainer

Hayley Mills, Peter McEnery, Eli Wallach, Joan Greenwood, John Le Mesurier, *Pola Negri*

Moon Zero Two
GB 1969 100m Technicolor
Hammer (Michael Carreras)

In 2021, the moon is being colonized and crooks are trying to get control of an asteroid.
A self-acknowledged 'space western' which has a few bright ideas but suffers from a childish script.

w Michael Carreras, *story* Gavin Lyall, Frank Hardman, Martin Davidson *d* Roy Ward Baker *ph* Paul Beeson *m* Don Ellis

James Olson, Catherina Von Schell, Warren Mitchell, Ori Levy, Adrienne Corri, Dudley Foster, Bernard Bresslaw, Neil McCallum

'It's all just about bad enough to fill older audiences with nostalgia for the inspired innocence of Flash Gordon, or even the good old days of Abbott and Costello in outer space.'—*MFB*

Moonfleet*
US 1955 87m Eastmancolor Cinemascope
MGM (John Houseman)

In Devonshire in 1770 an orphan boy finds that his elegant guardian leads a gang of smugglers.
Period gothic melodrama which nearly, but not quite, comes off; the script simply doesn't build to the right climax, and too many characters come to nothing. But there are splendid moments.

w Margaret Fitts, Jan Lustig, *novel* J. Meade Faulkner *d* Fritz Lang *ph* Robert Planck *m* Miklos Rozsa

Stewart Granger, Jon Whiteley, George Sanders, Joan Greenwood, Viveca Lindfors, Liliane Montevecchi, Melville Cooper, Sean McClory, John Hoyt, Alan Napier

Moonlight Sonata*
GB 1937 90m bw
Pall Mall (Lothar Mendes)

Stranded victims of a plane crash are affected by the art of a famous pianist.
Curious, slight, unexpected play-on-film designed to showcase the talent of Paderewski.

w Edward Knoblock, E. M. Delafield *d* Lothar Mendes

Ignace Paderewski, Eric Portman, *Marie Tempest*, Charles Farrell, Barbara Greene, Binkie Stuart

The Moonlighter
US 1953 77m bw 3-D
Warner (Joseph Bernhard)

A cattle rustler moves towards reforming.
Ho-hum western which offers its stars little to work with and was not even very exciting in 3-D.

w Niven Busch *d* Roy Rowland *ph* Bert Glennon *m* Heinz Roemheld

Fred MacMurray, Barbara Stanwyck, Ward Bond, William Ching, John Dierkes, Morris Ankrum

The Moonraker*
GB 1958 82m Technicolor
ABPC (Hamilton Inglis)

During the English Civil War, a noble highwayman smuggles the king's son into France.
Likeable swashbuckler which confines its second half to suspense at an inn, a who-is-it rather than a whodunnit. Good fun.

w Robert Hall, Wilfred Eades, Alistair Bell, *play* Arthur Watkyn *d* David MacDonald

George Baker, Sylvia Syms, Marius Goring, Peter Arne, Richard Leech, Clive Morton, Paul Whitsun-Jones, Gary Raymond, John Le Mesurier (as Cromwell), Patrick Troughton, Michael Anderson Jnr

Moonrise*
US 1948 90m bw
Republic

A murderer's son is driven into violence by memories and fears of his childhood.
Broody melodrama set against a remote village and swamp background; not a very interesting story, but memorable detail.

w Charles Haas *d Frank Borzage ph* John L. Russell *m* William Lava

Gail Russell, Dane Clark, Ethel Barrymore, Allyn Joslyn, Rex Ingram

The Moon's Our Home*
US 1936 80m bw
Paramount (Walter Wanger)

A headstrong actress marries an adventurer on impulse, and they both try to work it out.
Light, bright romantic comedy with the zany tinge then in fashion.

w Isabel Dawn, Boyce DeGaw, *novel* Faith Baldwin *d* William A. Seiter *ph* Joseph Valentine

Margaret Sullavan, Henry Fonda, Beulah Bondi, Charles Butterworth, Margaret Hamilton, Dorothy Stickney, Lucien Littlefield

The Moonshine War
US 1970 100m Metrocolor Panavision
MGM / Filmways (James C. Pratt, Leonard Blair)

In Kentucky just before the repeal of prohibition, a corruptible revenue agent regrets bringing in a sadistic crook to help confiscate illegal whisky.
Downright peculiar hillbilly melodrama, neither straight nor satirical; interesting only in fits and starts.

w Elmore Leonard, from his novel *d* Richard Quine *ph* Richard H. Kline *m* Fred Karger

Patrick McGoohan, Richard Widmark, Alan Alda, Melodie Johnson, Will Geer

Moontide*
US 1942 94m bw
TCF (Mark Hellinger)

A seaman cares for an unhappy waif.
A Hollywood attempt at romantic melodrama in the French manner. It looks good, and the cast is fine, but everything is just a bit too glum.

w John O'Hara, *novel* Willard Robertson *d* Archie Mayo *ph* Charles G. Clarke *m* Cyril Mockridge, David Buttolph

Jean Gabin, Ida Lupino, Claude Rains, Thomas Mitchell, Jerome Cowan, Sen Yung, Tully Marshall, Helen Reynolds

The Morals of Marcus
GB 1936 75m bw
Gaumont British (W. J. Locke)

A girl escapes from a Middle Eastern harem by stowing away with a British aristocrat.
Feeble 'naughty' comedy, killed by lack of wit and pace.

w Guy Bolton, Miles Mander, *play* W. J. Locke *d* Miles Mander

Lupe Velez, Ian Hunter, Adrienne Allen, Noel Madison,
J. H. Roberts, H. F. Maltby

The More the Merrier***
US 1943 104m bw
Columbia (George Stevens)

In crowded Washington during World War II, a girl allows two men to share her apartment and falls in love with the younger one.
Thoroughly amusing romantic comedy with bright lines and situations; remade less effectively as *Walk Don't Run* (qv).

w Robert Russell, Frank Ross, Richard Flournoy, Lewis R. Foster *d George Stevens* *ph* Ted Tetzlaff *md* Morris Stoloff

Jean Arthur, Joel McCrea, Charles Coburn, Richard Gaines, Bruce Bennett

'The gayest comedy that has come from Hollywood in a long time. It has no more substance than a watermelon, but is equally delectable.'—*Howard Barnes*

Morgan—A Suitable Case for Treatment**
GB 1966 97m bw
British Lion / Quintra (Leon Clore)

A young woman determines to leave her talented

but half-mad artist husband, who has a fixation on gorillas and behaves in a generally uncivilized manner.
Archetypal sixties marital fantasy, an extension of *Look Back in Anger* in the mood of swinging London. As tiresome as it is funny—but it *is* funny.

w David Mercer, from his play *d Karel Reisz ph Larry Pizer, Gerry Turpin m* Johnny Dankworth

Vanessa Redgrave, *David Warner*, Robert Stephens, Irene Handl, Newton Blick, Nan Munro

'Poor Morgan: victim of a satire that doesn't bite, lost in a technical confusion of means and ends, and emerging like an identikit photograph, all bits and pieces and no recognizable face.'—*Penelope Houston*

'The first underground movie made above ground.'—*John Simon*

'I think *Morgan* is so appealing to college students because it shares their self-view: they accept this mess of cute infantilism and obsessions and aberrations without expecting the writer and director to resolve it and without themselves feeling a necessity to sort it out.'—*Pauline Kael*

The Morning After*
US 1974 74m colour TVM
David Wolper (Lawrence Turman, Stan Margulies)

A businessman becomes an alcoholic.
An actor's piece which doesn't really convince.

w Richard Matheson *d* Richard Heffron *m* Pete Carpenter, John Lennon

Dick Van Dyke, Lynn Carlin, Don Porter, Jewel Blanch

Morning Departure*
GB 1950 102m bw
Rank / Jay Lewis (Leslie Parkyn)
US title: *Operation Disaster*

Twelve men are caught in a trapped submarine, and only eight can escape.
Archetypal stiff-upper-lip service tragedy, which moves from briskness to a slow funereal ending.

w William Fairchild, *play* Kenneth Woolard *d* Roy Baker *ph* Desmond Dickinson

John Mills, Richard Attenborough, Nigel Patrick, Lana Morris, Peter Hammond, Helen Cherry, James Hayter, Andrew Crawford, George Cole, Michael Brennan, Wylie Watson, Bernard Lee, Kenneth More

Morning Glory***
US 1933 74m bw
RKO (Pandro S. Berman)

A young actress comes to New York determined to succeed.
Marvellously evocative theatrical drama which provided a strong star part for a fresh young actress and surrounded her with accomplished thespians. Remade to much less effect as *Stage Struck* (qv).

w Howard J. Green, *play* Zoe Akins *d* Lowell Sherman *ph* Bert Glennon

Katharine Hepburn, Douglas Fairbanks Jnr, Adolphe Menjou, Mary Duncan, C. Aubrey Smith, Don Alvarado

Morocco***
US 1930 97m bw
Paramount

A cabaret singer arrives in Morocco and continues her wicked career by enslaving all the men in sight; but true love reaches her at last.
The star's first American film reveals her quintessence, and although wildly dated in subject matter remains a perversely enjoyable entertainment.

w Jules Furthman, *novel* Amy Jolly by Benno Vigny *d Josef Von Sternberg ph* Lee Garmes

Marlene Dietrich, Gary Cooper, Adolphe Menjou, Ullrich Haupt, Juliette Compton, Francis McDonald

'A cinematic pattern brilliant, profuse, subtle, and at almost every turn inventive.'—*Wilton A. Barrett*

The Mortal Storm**
US 1940 100m bw
MGM

A German family in the thirties is split by Nazism.
Solid anti-Nazi melodrama typical of the period before America entered the war; good performances outweigh unconvincing studio sets.

w Claudine West, George Froeschel, Andersen Ellis, *novel* Phyllis Bottome *d Frank Borzage ph* William Daniels *m* Edward Kane

Margaret Sullavan, Robert Young, James Stewart, Frank Morgan, Robert Stack, Bonita Granville, Irene Rich, Maria Ouspenskaya

Moss Rose
US 1947 82m bw
TCF

A Victorian chorus girl suspects her aristocratic admirer of being a murderer.

Absurd, stilted mystery melodrama with a better-looking production than it deserves.

w Jules Furthman, Tom Reed, *d* Gregory Ratoff *ph* Joe MacDonald *m* David Buttolph

Peggy Cummins, Victor Mature, Ethel Barrymore, Vincent Price

The Most Dangerous Game***
US 1932 63m bw
(RKO) Merian C. Cooper
GB title: *The Hounds of Zaroff*

A mad hunter lures guests on to his island so that he can hunt them down like animals.
Dated but splendidly shivery melodrama with moments of horror and mystery and a splendidly photographed chase sequence. Much imitated in curious ways, and not only by direct remakes such as *A Game of Death* and *Run for the Sun* (qv).

w James Creelman, story Richard Connell d Ernest B. Schoedsack, Irving Pichel ph Henry Gerrard m Max Steiner

Leslie Banks, Joel McCrea, Fay Wray, Robert Armstrong, Noble Johnson

The Most Dangerous Man in the World
GB 1969 99m De Luxe Panavision
TCF / APJAC (Mort Abrahams)
US title: *The Chairman*

A top scientist is sent by western intelligence on a mission into Red China, with a transmitter and a detonator implanted in his skull.
Wild Boys' Own Paper adventure which regrettably slows down in the middle for political philosophizing.

w Ben Maddow, *novel* The Chairman by Jay Richard Kennedy *d* J. Lee-Thompson *ph* Ted Moore *m* Jerry Goldsmith

Gregory Peck, Anne Heywood, Arthur Hill, Conrad Yama, Francisca Tu, Keye Luke, Alan Dobie, Ori Levy

Most Wanted*
US 1976 74m colour TVM
Quinn Martin

An elite force is formed and tackles the capture of a maniac who rapes and murders nuns.
What starts as a serious police drama becomes totally conventional and eventually hilariously inept.

w Larry Heath *d* Walter Grauman

Robert Stack, Sheree North

Mother Carey's Chickens
US 1938 82m bw
RKO (Pandro S. Berman)

The tribulations of a small-town family in the nineties.
Modest domestic drama, not totally unpleasing.

w S. K. Lauren, Gertrude Purcell, *novel* Kate Douglas Wiggin *d* Rowland V. Lee *ph* Roy Hunt

Anne Shirley, Ruby Keeler, Fay Bainter, James Ellison, Walter Brennan, Donnie Dunagan, Frank Albertson, Alma Kruger, Jackie Moran, Virginia Weidler, Margaret Hamilton

Mother Didn't Tell Me
US 1950 88m bw
TCF (Fred Kohlmar)

A working girl marries a doctor and their off duty hours don't coincide.
Thin comedy.

wd Claude Binyon, *novel* The Doctor Wears Three Faces by Mary Baird *ph* Joseph La Shelle

Dorothy McGuire, William Lundigan, June Havoc, Gary Merrill, Jessie Royce Landis

Mother, Jugs and Speed
US 1976 98m De Luxe Panavision
TCF (Joseph R. Barbera)

Comic and tragic events in the lives of Los Angeles drivers of private commercial ambulances.
Black comedy of incidents ranging from farcical to sentimental, sometimes funny but basically unacceptable in either vein.

w Tom Mankiewicz *d* Peter Yates *ph* Ralph Woolsey *m* Joel Sill

Bill Cosby, Raquel Welch, Harvey Keitel, *Allen Garfield*, Bruce Davison, Larry Hagman

Mother Riley Meets the Vampire
GB 1952 74m bw
Renown (John Gilling)

An old washerwoman accidentally catches a robot-wielding crook called The Vampire.
Childish farce notable for Lucan's last appearance in his dame role, and Lugosi's last substantial appearance of any kind—two pros at the end of their tether.

w Val Valentine *d* John Gilling *ph* Stan Pavey

Arthur Lucan, Bela Lugosi, Dora Bryan, Richard Wattis

'Stupid, humourless and repulsive.'—*MFB*

Mother Wore Tights*
US 1947 109m Technicolor
TCF (Lamar Trotti)

Recollections of a vaudeville team and their growing family.

Well-mounted, reasonably charming family musical, one of the best of the many TCF examples of this genre.

w Lamar Trotti, *book* Miriam Young *d* Walter Lang *ph* Harry Jackson *md* Alfred Newman, Charles Henderson

Betty Grable, Dan Dailey, Mona Freeman, Connie Marshall, Vanessa Brown, Robert Arthur, Sara Allgood, William Frawley, Ruth Nelson

Moulin Rouge
US 1934 69m bw
RKO (Darryl F. Zanuck)

The wife of a songwriter impersonates her own sister in order to revitalize her marriage and her stage career.
Predictable minor star vehicle, quite competently done.

w Nunnally Johnson, Henry Lehrman, *play* Lyon de Bri *d* Sidney Lanfield *ph* Charles Rosher *md* Alfred Newman

Constance Bennett, Franchot Tone, Tullio Carminati, Helen Westley, Andrew Tombes, Hobart Cavanaugh

Moulin Rouge**
GB 1952 119m Technicolor
Romulus (Jack Clayton)

Fictional biopic of Toulouse Lautrec.
The dramatic emphasis is on the love affairs of the dwarfish artist, but the film's real interest is in its evocation of 19th-century Montmartre, and especially in the first twenty-minute can can sequence. Nothing later can stand up to the exhilaration of this, and the film slowly slides into boredom.

w John Huston, Anthony Veiller, *novel* Pierre La Mure *d* John Huston *ph Oswald Morris* *m* Georges Auric *ad Paul Sheriff*

Jose Ferrer, Zsa Zsa Gabor, Katherine Kath, Colette Marchand

The Mountain*
US 1956 105m Technicolor Vistavision
Paramount (Edward Dmytryk)

After an airplane crash the wreck is difficult to reach. A young man sets off alone to loot it, and his elder brother follows to stop him.
An indeterminate production in which one believes neither the setting, the plot nor the characters, especially not with Vistavision making everything sharply unreal and the brothers seeming two generations apart.

w Ranald MacDougall, *novel* Henri Troyat *d* Edward Dmytryk *ph* Franz Planer *m* Daniele Amfitheatrof

Spencer Tracy, Robert Wagner, Claire Trevor, William Demarest, E. G. Marshall

The Mountain Road
US 1960 102m bw
Columbia / William Goetz

In 1944 China, an American officer helps peasants against the Japanese.
Confused and rather dreary war adventure with pretensions.

w Alfred Hayes, *novel* Theodore White *d* Delbert Mann *ph* Burnett Guffey *md* Morris Stoloff

James Stewart, Lisa Lu, Glenn Corbett, Henry Morgan, Frank Silvera, James Best, Mike Kellin, Frank Maxwell, Alan Baxter

Mourning Becomes Electra*
US 1947 170m bw
RKO / Theatre Guild (Dudley Nichols)

Murder, doom and guilt affect a New England family at the end of the Civil War.
A mark for trying is all. This is a clearly fated attempt to film the unfilmable, a long and lugubrious updating of Sophocles with more than its share of risible moments.

wd Dudley Nichols, *play* Eugene O'Neill *m* Richard Hagemann *ph George Barnes* *ad* Albert D'Agostino

Michael Redgrave, Rosalind Russell, Katina Paxinou, Kirk Douglas, Raymond Massey, Nancy Coleman, Leo Genn

'A star cast fumbles with helpless and sometimes touching ineptitude.'—*Gavin Lambert*

The Mouse on the Moon
GB 1963 85m Eastmancolor
UA / Walter Shenson

The tiny duchy of Grand Fenwick discovers that its home-made wine makes excellent rocket fuel.
Piddling sequel to *The Mouse that Roared*, suffering from a hesitant script, too few jokes, and overacting.

w Michael Pertwee *d* Richard Lester *ph* Wilkie Cooper *m* Ron Grainer

Margaret Rutherford, Ron Moody, Bernard Cribbins, David Kossoff, Terry-Thomas, Michael Crawford

The Mouse that Roared**
GB 1959 85m Technicolor
Columbia / Open Road (Carl Foreman)

The tiny duchy of Grand Fenwick is bankrupt,

and its minister decides to declare war on the United States, be defeated, and receive Marshall Aid.
Lively comedy which sounds rather better than it plays, but has bright moments.

w Roger Macdougall, Stanley Mann, *novel* Leonard Wibberley *d* Jack Arnold *ph* John Wilcox *m* Edwin Astley

Peter Sellers (playing three parts), Jean Seberg, David Kossoff, William Hartnell, Leo McKern, Macdonald Parke, Harold Kasket
'The kind of irrepressible topical satire whose artistic flaws become increasingly apparent but whose merits outlast them.'—*Peter John Dyer*

Mousey*
GB 1973 74m colour TVM
RSO (Beryl Vertue, Aida Young)
GB theatrical title: *Cat and Mouse*

An unhinged schoolteacher taunts his ex-wife with murder threats.
Unusual psychological thriller.

w John Peacock *d* Daniel Petrie *ph* Jack Hildyard *m* Ron Grainer

Kirk Douglas, Jean Seberg, John Vernon, Sam Wanamaker, James Bradford, Bessie Love

The Mouthpiece**
US 1932 90m bw
Warner (Lucien Hubbard)

A prosecuting counsel successfully turns to defence but becomes corrupt.
A hard-hitting and entertaining melodrama allegedly based on the career of William Fallon, a New York lawyer.

w Joseph Jackson, Earl Baldwin *d* James Flood, Elliott Nugent *ph* Barney McGill

Warren William, Sidney Fox, Aline MacMahon, John Wray, Ralph Ince, Guy Kibbee

Move Over Darling**
US 1963 103m De Luxe Cinemascope
TCF / Arcola / Arwin (Aaron Rosenberg, Marty Melcher)

A wife who has spent five years shipwrecked on a desert island returns to find that her husband has just remarried.
Thin but fitfully amusing remake of *My Favorite Wife*; sheer professionalism gets it by.

w Hal Kanter, Jack Sher *d* Michael Gordon *ph* Daniel L. Fapp *m* Lionel Newman

Doris Day, James Garner, Polly Bergen, Thelma Ritter, Chuck Connors, Fred Clark

Movie Crazy***
US 1932 82m bw
Harold Lloyd

A filmstruck young man is mistakenly invited to Hollywood for a film test.
The silent comedian is not quite at his best in this early sound comedy, but it contains his last really superb sequences and its picture of Hollywood is both amusing and nostalgic.

w Harold Lloyd and others *d* Clyde Bruckman *ph* Walter Lundin

Harold Lloyd, Constance Cummings

The Movie Maker**
US 1967 91m Technicolor TVM
Universal (Harry Tatelman)

The last of the old-time movie tycoons finds his life and his career falling apart.
Sympathetic portrait of a Louis B. Mayer or Darryl Zanuck type.

w Rod Serling, Steven Bochco *d* Josef Leytes

Rod Steiger, Robert Culp, James Dunn, Sally Kellerman, Anna Lee

The Movie Murderer*
US 1970 99m Technicolor TVM
Universal (Jack Laird)

An insurance investigator traps an arsonist who tries to destroy the negative of a movie in which he was filmed.
Lively suspense thriller with good performances.

w Stanford Whitmore *d* Boris Sagal

Arthur Kennedy, Tom Selleck, Warren Oates, Jeff Corey, Nita Talbot, Robert Webber, Severn Darden

Moving Violation*
US 1976 91m De Luxe
TCF / Roger Corman

Small-town teenagers are pursued by the sheriff because they saw him commit a murder.
Old hat suspenser with a smart new line in thrills.

w David R. Osterhout, William Norton d Charles S. Dubin ph Charles Correll *m* Don Leake

Stephen McHattie, Kay Lenz, Eddie Albert, Lonnie Chapman, Will Geer
'Probably the most hair-raising pursuit sequences in the history of film.'—*Cleveland Amory*

The Mudlark**
GB 1951 98m bw
TCF (Nunnally Johnson)

A scruffy boy from the docks breaks into

Windsor Castle to see Queen Victoria and ends her fifteen years of seclusion.
A pleasant whimsical legend which could have done without the romantic interest, but which despite an air of unreality provides warm-hearted, well upholstered entertainment for family audiences.

w Nunnally Johnson, novel Theodore Bonnet *d Jean Negulesco ph Georges Périnal* *m* William Alwyn *ad* C. P. Norman

Alec Guinness, Irene Dunne, *Andrew Ray*, Anthony Steel, Constance Smith, *Finlay Currie, Edward Rigby*

The Mummy**
US 1932 72m bw
Universal

An Egyptian mummy comes back to life and covets a young girl.
Strange dreamlike horror film with only fleeting frissons but plenty of narrative interest despite the silliest of stories and some fairly stilted acting.

w John L. Balderston d Karl Freund ph Charles Stumar

Boris Karloff, Zita Johann, David Manners, Arthur Byron, Edward Van Sloan

'It beggars description . . . one of the most unusual talkies ever produced.'—*New York Times*

'Editing very much in the Germanic style, magnificent lighting and a superb performance from Karloff make this a fantasy almost without equal.'—*John Baxter, 1968*

The Mummy*
GB 1959 88m Technicolor
Hammer

A mummy brought back to England by archaeologists wakes up and goes on the rampage.
Typical Hammer vulgarization of a Hollywood legend; starts slowly and unpleasantly, but picks up speed and resource in the last half hour.

w Jimmy Sangster *d* Terence Fisher *ph* Jack Asher *m* Frank Reizenstein

Peter Cushing, Christopher Lee, Yvonne Furneaux, Eddie Byrne, Felix Aylmer, Raymond Huntley, John Stuart
† Hammer sequels, of little interest, were *Curse of the Mummy's Tomb* (1964), *The Mummy's Shroud* (1967) and *Blood from the Mummy's Tomb* (1971).

The Mummy's Hand**
US 1940 67m bw
Universal

The high priest of an evil sect revivifies an Egyptian mummy and uses it to kill off members of an archaeological expedition.
Semi-sequel to 1932's *The Mummy*, economically using the same flashback. It starts off in comedy vein, but the last half hour is among the most scary in horror film history.

w Griffin Jay, Maxwell Shane *d Christy Cabanne ph* Elwood Bredell

Dick Foran, Wallace Ford, *George Zucco*, Cecil Kellaway, Peggy Moran, *Tom Tyler, Eduardo Ciannelli*
† Sequels, of decreasing merit, were *The Mummy's Tomb* (1942) (in which the heroes of *The Mummy's Hand* are killed off), *The Mummy's Ghost* (1944) and *The Mummy's Curse* (1944). See also *Abbott and Costello Meet the Mummy*.

Munster Go Home*
US 1966 96m Technicolor TVM
Universal (Joe Connelly, Bob Mosher)

The family of monsters who want to be just the same as anyone else inherit a British manor house.
Not a pilot, as it came *after* the popular comedy show: the funny folk are a little less amusing in colour.

w George Tibbles, Joe Connelly, Bob Masher *d* Earl Bellamy

Fred Gwynne, Yvonne de Carlo, Al Lewis, Butch Patrick, Debbie Watson, Hermione Gingold, Terry-Thomas

Murder**
GB 1930 92m bw
British International (John Maxwell)

A girl is convicted of murder, but one of the jurors sets out to prove her innocent.
Interesting early Hitchcock, a rare whodunnit for him.

w Alma Reville, *novel* Enter Sir John by Clemence Dane and Helen Simpson *d Alfred Hitchcock ph* Jack Cox

Herbert Marshall, Nora Baring, Phyllis Konstam, Edward Chapman, Miles Mander, Esmé Percy, Donald Calthrop

Murder at the Vanities*
US 1934 89m bw
Paramount (E. Lloyd Sheldon)

Murder backstage at the first night of Earl Carroll's Vanities.
Curious, stylish mixture of musical numbers, broad comedy and mystery. Dated, but fun.

w Carey Wilson, Joseph Gollomb, Sam Hellman *d Mitchell Leisen ph* Leo Tover

Jack Oakie, Victor McLaglen, Carl Brisson, Kitty Carlisle, Dorothy Stickney, Gertrude Michael, Jessie Ralph, Gail Patrick

Murder by Contract*

US 1958 81m bw
Columbia / Orbin (Leon Chooluck)

A professional killer makes a fatal mistake and is shot down by police.
Low-budgeter which seemed stark and original at the time, but television has familiarized its contents. Moody, contrasty photography and restrained style give it a minor distinction.

w Ben Simcoe *d Irving Lerner ph Lucien Ballard m* Perry Borkin

Vince Edwards, Philip Pine, Herschel Bernardi, Caprice Toriel

'Ice cold and completely unsentimental.'—*John Gillett*

Murder by Death*

US 1976 94m Metrocolor
Columbia / Ray Stark

Several (fictional) detectives are invited to stay at the home of a wealthy recluse, and mystery and murder follow.
Sometimes thin but generally likeable spoof of a longstanding genre; the stars seize their opportunities avidly, and the film does not outstay its welcome

w Neil Simon d Robert Moore *ph* David M. Walsh *m* Dave Grusin *pd* Stephen Grimes

Peter Falk, Alec Guinness, Peter Sellers, Truman Capote, Estelle Winwood, Elsa Lanchester, Eileen Brennan, James Coco, David Niven, Maggie Smith, Nancy Walker

Murder by the Clock

US 1931 76m bw
Paramount

Creepy goings on in an old house after the death of a dowager who has built herself a tomb from which she can escape if buried alive.
Tasteless chiller which had the distinction of being withdrawn from British circulation after public protests.

w Henry Myers, Rufus King, Charles Beahan, *play* Charles Beahan, *novel* Rufus King *d* Edward Sloman

Lilyan Tashman, William 'Stage' Boyd, Regis Toomey, Irving Pichel, Blanche Frederici, Walter McGrail

Murder He Says**

US 1945 91m bw
Paramount (E. D. Leshin)

An insurance salesman stays with a homicidal family of hillbillies.
A curious black farce which seems to be compounded of *Cold Comfort Farm* and *The Red Inn.* Very funny, and ahead of its time.

w Lou Breslow *d* George Marshall *ph* Theodor Sparkuhl

Fred MacMurray, Marjorie Main, Helen Walker, Peter Whitney, Jean Heather, Porter Hall, Mabel Paige

Murder in the Cathedral

GB 1951 136m bw
George Hoellering

The 12th-century struggle between Henry II and his archbishop culminates in the assassination of Becket in Canterbury Cathedral.
Plainly filmed, slightly amateur version of the celebrated verse play; scarcely a rewarding cinematic experience.

wd George Hoellering, *play* T. S. Eliot *ph* David Kosky *m* Laszlo Lajtha *ad* Peter Pendrey

Father John Grosner, Alexander Gauge, David Ward, George Woodbridge, Basil Burton, Paul Rogers, Niall MacGinnis, Mark Dignam, Leo McKern

'A curious ordeal for the audience . . . a no-man's-land between cinema and drama has been discovered, rather than any extension of either.'—*Gavin Lambert*

Murder, Incorporated

US 1960 103m bw Cinemascope
TCF (Burt Balaban)

In the thirties, Anastasia and Lepke build up their crime syndicate which spreads terror through New York.
Tedious and poorly made gangster thriller, unforgivable faults considering the many admirable models it has to follow.

w Irve Tunick, Mel Barr *d* Burt Balaban, Stuart Rosenberg *ph* Gayne Rescher *m* Frank de Vol

Stuart Whitman, Mai Britt, Henry Morgan, Peter Falk, David J. Stewart, Simon Oakland, Morey Amsterdam

The Murder Man*

US 1935 84m bw
MGM (Harry Rapf)

A reporter commits murder and frames someone else.
Good low-key melodrama with an interesting cast.

w Tim Whelan, John C. Higgins *d* Tim Whelan

Spencer Tracy, Virginia Bruce, Lionel Atwill, James Stewart, Harvey Stephens, William Collier Snr

Murder My Sweet***
US 1944 95m bw
RKO (Adrian Scott)
GB title: *Farewell My Lovely*

Philip Marlowe investigates a disappearance and almost ends up a murder victim.
Complex thriller which seemed at the time to demonstrate all manner of strikingly new techniques in a *film noir* mood, and certainly marked an astonishing transformation in its star. Thirty years later, the second half has a jaded look.

w John Paxton, novel Raymond Chandler d Edward Dmytryk ph Harry J. Wild m Roy Webb

Dick Powell, Claire Trevor, Anne Shirley, Miles Mander, Otto Kruger, Douglas Walton, Ralf Harolde, *Mike Mazurki*, Don Douglas

Murder on Flight 502*
US 1975 100m colour TVM
Spelling–Goldberg (David Chasman)

Murder on a transatlantic jet: will the killer strike again?
Watchable old-fashioned suspenser.

w David P. Harmon *d* George McCowan

Ralph Bellamy, Polly Bergen, Theodore Bikel, Sonny Bono, Dane Clark, Laraine Day, Fernando Lamas, George Maharis, Hugh O'Brian, Molly Picon, Walter Pidgeon, Robert Stack

Murder on the Orient Express**
GB 1974 131m Technicolor
EMI / GW Films (John Brabourne, Richard Goodwin)

In the early thirties, Hercule Poirot solves a murder on a snowbound train.
Reasonably elegant but disappointingly slackly-handled version of a classic mystery novel. Finney overacts and his all-star support is distracting, while as soon as the train chugs into its snowdrift the film stops moving too, without even a dramatic 'curtain'.

w Paul Dehn, *novel* Agatha Christie *d* Sidney Lumet *ph* Geoffrey Unsworth *m* Richard Rodney Bennett *pd* Tony Walton

Albert Finney, *Ingrid Bergman*, Lauren Bacall, Wendy Hiller, Sean Connery, Vanessa Redgrave, Michael York, Martin Balsam, Richard Widmark, Jacqueline Bisset, Jean-Pierre Cassel, Rachel Roberts, George Coulouris, *John Gielgud*, Anthony Perkins, Colin Blakely, Jeremy Lloyd, Denis Quilley

'Audiences appear to be so hungry for this type of entertainment that maybe it hardly matters that it isn't very good.'—*Judith Crist*

Murder Once Removed*
US 1971 74m colour TVM
Metromedia (Bob Markell)

A doctor finds his wife is unfaithful and plans the 'perfect' murder.
Carefully plotted, very watchable will-he-get-away-with-it suspenser.

w Irving Gaynor Neiman *d* Charles Dulsin

John Forsythe, Richard Kiley, Barbara Bain, Joseph Campanella, Wendell Corey

Murder One
US 1969 97m Technicolor TVM
Universal (Harold Jack Bloom)
aka: *The DA: Murder One*

The District Attorney traps a homicidal nurse.
One of two competent pilots (see *Conspiracy to Kill*) made for a series that didn't go.

w Harold Jack Bloom *d* Boris Sagal

Robert Conrad, Howard Duff, Diane Baker, J. D. Cannon, David Opatoshu

Murder or Mercy?*
US 1974 74m colour TVM
Quinn Martin

An attorney emerges from retirement to defend a man who killed his terminally ill wife.
Good acting in a human drama which isn't especially dramatic.

w Douglas Day Stewart *d* Harvey Hart

Melvyn Douglas, Bradford Dillman, Denver Pyle, Mildred Dunnock, David Birney, Don Porter, Robert Webber, Kent Smith

Murder She Said*
GB 1962 87m bw
MGM (George H. Brown)

An elderly spinster investigates after seeing a woman strangled in a passing train.
Frightfully British and disappointingly tame adaptation of an Agatha Christie character, with only the star (who is somewhat miscast) holding one's attention.

w David Pursall, Jack Seddon, *novel* 4.50 from Paddington by Agatha Christie *d* George Pollock *ph* Geoffrey Faithfull *m* Ron Goodwin

Margaret Rutherford, Charles Tingwell, Muriel Pavlow, Arthur Kennedy, James Robertson

Justice, Thorley Walters, Gerald Cross, Conrad Phillips

† Thanks to Miss Rutherford's popularity, three increasingly poor sequels were made: *Murder at the Gallop* (1963), *Murder Most Foul* (1964), *Murder Ahoy* (1964).

Murderer's Row
US 1966 108m Technicolor
Columbia / Meadway–Claude / Euan Lloyd

Matt Helm tracks down an international villain who has kidnapped an inventor.
Witless and uninventive spy spoof which drags itself wearily along but never attempts an explanation of its own title.

w Herbert Baker, *novel* Donald Hamilton *d* Henry Levin *ph* Sam Leavitt *m* Lalo Schifrin

Dean Martin, Ann-Margret, Karl Malden, Camilla Sparv, James Gregory, Beverly Adams, Tom Reese

Murders in the Rue Morgue*
US 1932 62m bw
Universal

A series of grisly murders prove to be the work of a trained ape.
A distant relation of the original story, mildly interesting for its obvious Caligari influences, but not very good in any way.

w Tom Reed, Dale Van Avery, John Huston, *story* Edgar Allan Poe *d Robert Florey* *ph* Karl Freund

Bela Lugosi, Sidney Fox, Leon Ames, Bert Roach, Brandon Hurst

Murders in the Rue Morgue*
US 1971 86m Foto Film Color
AIP

Poe's story is being presented at a Grand Guignol theatre in Paris, and when murders happen within the company Inspector Vidocq comes to investigate.
Playfully plotted chiller which has more to do with *The Phantom of the Opera* than with Poe. A good time waster for addicts.

w Charles Wicking, Henry Slesar *d Gordon Hessler* *ph* Manuel Berengier *m* Waldo de Los Rios

Jason Robards Jnr, Herbert Lom, Lilli Palmer, Adolfo Celi, Michael Dunn

Murdock's Gang
US 1973 84m colour TVM
Don Fedderson

After serving a prison term, a flamboyant attorney becomes a private eye with a staff of ex-cons.
Unpersuasive time-passer.

w Edmund H. North *d* Charles Dubin

Alex Dreier, Janet Leigh, Murray Hamilton, William Daniels, Harold Gould, Don Knight

Murphy's War*
GB 1971 108m Eastmancolor Panavision
Hemdale / Yates–Deeley (Michael Deeley)

A torpedoed British merchantman in Venezuela devotes himself to bombing a U-boat from a home-made plane.
Modest adventure story with the star in better form than the script.

w Stirling Silliphant, *novel* Max Catto *d* Peter Yates *ph* Douglas Slocombe *m* John Barry

Peter O'Toole, Sian Phillips, Philippe Noiret, Horst Janson

Music for Millions*
US 1944 117m bw
MGM

A small girl helps her pregnant sister who is a member of Jose Iturbi's orchestra.
Dewy-eyed wartime musical, full of popular classics, sentimentality and child interest, all smoothly packaged. As an example of what the public wanted in 1944, quite an eye-opener.

w Myles Connelly *d* Henry Koster *ph* Robert Surtees

Margaret O'Brien, June Allyson, Jose Iturbi, Jimmy Durante, Marsha Hunt, Hugh Herbert, Henry Davenport, Connie Gilchrist

Music in the Air
US 1934 85m bw
Fox

An opera singer is torn between two men.
Heavy-going light entertainment.

w Howard Young, Billy Wilder, *play* Oscar Hammerstein II, Jerome Kern *ph* Ernest Palmer *d* Joe May

Gloria Swanson, John Boles, Douglass Montgomery, June Lang, Al Shean, Reginald Owen, Joseph Cawthorn, Hobart Bosworth

The Music Lovers*
GB 1970 123m Eastmancolor Panavision
UA / Rossfilms (Roy Baird)

Homosexual composer Tchaikovsky is impelled to marry, loses his sponsor, drives his wife into an asylum and dies of cholera.

Absurd fantasia on the life of a great composer, produced in a manner reminiscent of MGM's sillier musicals; up to a point hysterically (and unintentionally) funny, then rather sickening.

w Melvyn Bragg, *book* Beloved Friend by C. D. Bowen, Barbara Van Meck *d Ken Russell* *ph* Douglas Slocombe *md* André Previn

Richard Chamberlain, *Glenda Jackson, Christopher Gable*, Max Adrian, Isabella Telezynska, Maureen Pryor, Andrew Faulds

'Tchaikovsky has been made the excuse for a crude melodrama about sex.'—*Konstantin Bazarov*

The Music Man***
US 1962 151m Technirama
Warner (Morton da Costa)

A confidence trickster persuades a small-town council to start a boys' band, with himself as the agent for all the expenses.
Reasonably cinematic, thoroughly invigorating transference to the screen of a hit Broadway musical. Splendid period 'feel', standout performances, slight sag in second half.

w Marion Hargrove, *book* Meredith Willson *d Morton da Costa* *ph* Robert Burks *md* Ray Heindorf *ch* Onna White *songs Meredith Willson*

Robert Preston, Shirley Jones, Buddy Hackett, *Hermione Gingold*, Pert Kelton, Paul Ford

The Mutations
GB 1974 92m Eastmancolor
Columbia / Getty (Robert D. Weinbach)

A bio-chemist uses circus freaks in his experiments to find the perfect synthesis of plant and animal.
Tasteless horror film with little style of any kind.

w Robert D. Weinbach, Edward Mann *d* Jack Cardiff *ph* Paul Beeson *m* Basil Kirchin

Donald Pleasance, Tom Baker, Brad Harris, Julie Ege, Michael Dunn, Scott Antony, Jill Haworth, Lisa Collings

Mutiny on the Bounty***
US 1935 135m bw
MGM (Irving Thalberg, Albert Lewin)

An 18th-century British naval vessel sets off for South America but during a mutiny the captain is cast adrift and the mutineers settle in the Pitcairn Islands.
A still-entertaining adventure film which seemed at the time like the pinnacle of Hollywood's achievement but can now be seen to be slackly told, with wholesale pre-release editing very evident. Individual scenes and performances are however refreshingly well-handled.

w Talbot Jennings, Jules Furthman, Carey Wilson, *book* Charles Nordhoff, James Hall *d Frank Lloyd* *ph* Arthur Edeson *m* Herbert Stothart

Charles Laughton, Clark Gable, Franchot Tone, Movita, Dudley Digges, Henry Stephenson, Donald Crisp, Eddie Quillan, Francis Lister, Spring Byington, Ian Wolfe

Mutiny on the Bounty
US 1962 185m Technicolor Ultra Panavision 70
MGM / Arcola (Aaron Rosenberg)

Overlong and unattractive remake marred principally by Brando's English accent and various production follies, not to mention his overlong and bloody death scene. The shipboard sadism still works pretty well, but after the landing in Tahiti boredom takes over.

w Charles Lederer *d* Lewis Milestone *ph* Robert Surtees *m* Bronislau Kaper

Trevor Howard, Marlon Brando, Richard Harris, Hugh Griffith, Tarita, Richard Haydn, Percy Herbert, Duncan Lamont, Gordon Jackson, Chips Rafferty, Noel Purcell

My Blood Runs Cold
US 1965 108m bw Panavision
Warner (William Conrad)

A spoilt heiress meets a strange young man who claims she is the reincarnation of a long dead charmer; he turns out to be a madman who has come across an old diary.
Initially intriguing but eventually exhausting melodrama with a weak solution.

w John Mantley *d* William Conrad *ph* Sam Leavitt *m* George Duning

Troy Donahue, Joey Heatherton, Barry Sullivan, Jeanette Nolan

'Not all that bad, but not worth missing *I Love Lucy* for either.'—*Leonard Maltin*

My Blue Heaven
US 1950 96m Technicolor
TCF (Sol C. Siegel)

A pair of troupers want a family, by adoption if not otherwise.
Routine musical drenched in sentimentality.

w Lamar Trotti, Claude Binyon *d* Henry Koster *ph* Alfred E. Arling *songs* Harold Arlen

Betty Grable, Dan Dailey, Mitzi Gaynor, David Wayne, Jane Wyatt, Una Merkel

My Cousin Rachel*
US 1953 98m bw
TCF (Nunnally Johnson)

A Cornish gentleman dies in Italy after marrying a mysterious lady; when she comes to England she arouses the hostility, and love, of her husband's foster son.
Well-wrought but dramatically unsatisfactory Victorian melodrama from a bestseller; plenty of suspicion but no solution makes Rachel a dull girl.

w Nunnally Johnson, *novel* Daphne du Maurier *d* Henry Koster *ph* Joseph La Shelle *m* Franz Waxman

Olivia de Havilland, Richard Burton, John Sutton, Audrey Dalton, Ronald Squire

My Daughter Joy
GB 1950 81m bw
Columbia / Gregory Ratoff
US title: *Operation X*

In order to cement a new trade pact, an international financier plans to marry his daughter to the son of an African sultan.
Turgid melodrama swamping some good actors.

w Robert Thoeren, William Rose, *novel* David Golder by Irene Neirowsky *d* Gregory Ratoff *ph* Georges Périnal

Edward G. Robinson, Peggy Cummins, Nora Swinburne, Richard Greene, Finlay Currie, Gregory Ratoff, Ronald Adam, Walter Rilla, James Robertson Justice, David Hutcheson

My Darling Clementine***
US 1946 98m bw
TCF (Samuel G. Engel)

Wyatt Earp cleans up Tombstone and wipes out the Clanton gang at the OK corral.
Archetypal western mood piece, full of nostalgia for times gone by and crackling with memorable scenes and characterizations.

w Samuel G. Engel, Winston Miller, *book* Wyatt Earp, Frontier Marshal by Stuart N. Lake *d John Ford ph Joe MacDonald m Cyril Mockridge*

Henry Fonda, Victor Mature, Walter Brennan, Linda Darnell, Cathy Downs, Tim Holt, Ward Bond, *Alan Mowbray*, John Ireland, Jane Darwell

'Every scene, every shot is the product of a keen and sensitive eye.'—*Bosley Crowther*

'Considerable care has gone to its period reconstruction, but the view is a poetic one.'—*Lindsay Anderson*

My Dream Is Yours
US 1949 101m Technicolor
Warner

A Hollywood talent scout discovers a new singer.
Competent, forgettable musical.

w Harry Kurnitz, Dane Lussier *d* Michael Curtiz *ph* Ernest Haller *m* Harry Warren *ly* Ralph Blane *ch* Le Roy Prinz.

Doris Day, Jack Carson, Lee Bowman, Adolphe Menjou, Eve Arden, S. Z. Sakall

My Fair Lady***
US 1964 175m Technicolor Super Panavision 70
CBS / Warner (Jack L. Warner)

Musical version of *Pygmalion*, about a flower girl trained by an arrogant elocutionist to pass as a lady.
Careful, cold transcription of a stage success; cinematically quite uninventive when compared with *Pygmalion* itself, but a pretty good entertainment.

w Alan Jay Lerner, *play* Pygmalion by Bernard Shaw *d* George Cukor *ph Harry Stradling m* Frederick Loewe *ch* Hermes Pan *ad* Gene Allen *costumes Cecil Beaton*

Rex Harrison, Audrey Hepburn, *Stanley Holloway*, Wilfrid Hyde White, Gladys Cooper, Jeremy Brett, Theodore Bikel, Isobel Elsom, Mona Washbourne, Walter Burke

'The property has been not so much adapted as elegantly embalmed.'—*Andrew Sarris*

My Father's House*
US 1975 96m colour TVM
Filmways

A high pressure executive has a heart attack and recalls family life with his father who suffered a similar fate.
Watchable but somewhat padded and elementary personal drama.

w David Sontag, David Seltzer, *novel* Philip Kunhardt Jnr *d* Alex Segal

Robert Preston, Cliff Robertson, Rosemary Forsyth, Eileen Brennan

My Favorite Blonde***
US 1942 78m bw
Paramount (Paul Jones)

A burlesque comic travelling by train helps a lady in distress and lives to regret it.
Smartly paced spy comedy thriller, one of its star's best vehicles.

w Don Hartman, Frank Butler, Melvin Frank,

Norman Panama d Sidney Lanfield ph William Mellor *m* David Buttolph

Bob Hope, Madeleine Carroll, Gale Sondergaard, George Zucco, Lionel Royce, Walter Kingsford, Victor Varconi

My Favorite Brunette*
US 1947 87m bw
Paramount (Daniel Dare)

A photographer gets mixed up with mobsters. Pretty fair star vehicle which half-heartedly spoofs *Farewell My Lovely.*

w Edmund Beloin, Jack Rose *d* Elliott Nugent *ph* Lionel Lindon *m* Robert Emmett Dolan

Bob Hope, Dorothy Lamour, Peter Lorre, Lon Chaney Jnr, John Hoyt, Charles Dingle, Reginald Denny

My Favorite Spy*
US 1951 93m bw
Paramount (Paul Jones)

A burlesque comic is asked by the US government to pose as an international spy who happens to be his double.
Moderately funny star vehicle with more willing hands than good ideas. The chase finale however is worth waiting for.

w Edmund Hartmann, Jack Sher *d* Norman Z. McLeod *ph* Victor Milner *m* Victor Young

Bob Hope, Hedy Lamarr, Francis L. Sullivan, Arnold Moss, Mike Mazurki, Luis Van Rooten

My Favorite Wife***
US 1940 88m bw
RKO (Leo McCarey)

A lady explorer returns after several shipwrecked years to find that her husband has married again.
A well-worn situation gets its brightest treatment in this light star vehicle.

w Sam and Bella Spewack, Leo McCarey d Garson Kanin ph Rudolph Maté *m* Roy Webb

Cary Grant, Irene Dunne, Randolph Scott, Gail Patrick, Ann Shoemaker, Donald MacBride

'One of those comedies with a glow on it.'—*Otis Ferguson*

† Other variations (qv): *Too Many Husbands, Our Wife, Three for the Show, Move Over Darling.*

My Foolish Heart*
US 1949 98m bw
Samuel Goldwyn

A woman deceives her husband into thinking her forthcoming child is his.
A 'woman's picture' par excellence, and among the first to benefit from commercial plugging of a schmaltzy theme tune.

w Julius J. and Philip G. Epstein, *story* J. D. Salinger *d* Mark Robson *ph* Lee Garmes *m Victor Young*

Susan Hayward, Dana Andrews, Kent Smith, Robert Keith, Gigi Perreau, Lois Wheeler, Jessie Royce Landis

My Forbidden Past
US 1951 81m bw
RKO (Polan Banks)

A New Orleans beauty seeks vengeance when her cousin prevents her marriage.
Stuffy period melodrama with vigorous performances.

w Marion Parsonnet, *novel* Polan Banks *d* Robert Stevenson *ph* Harry J. Wild *m* Frederick Hollander *ad* Albert S. D'Agostino

Ava Gardner, Melvyn Douglas, Robert Mitchum, Janis Carter, Lucile Watson

My Friend Flicka*
US 1943 89m Technicolor
TCF

Adventures of a young boy and his pet colt.
Winsome boy-and-horse story, one of the most popular family films of the forties. Sequel 1945 with virtually the same cast: *Green Grass of Wyoming.*

w novel Mary O'Hara, from her novel *d* Harold Schuster *m* Alfred Newman

Roddy McDowall, Preston Foster, Rita Johnson, James Bell, Jeff Corey

My Friend Irma*
US 1949 103m bw
Paramount / Hal B. Wallis

Dumb blonde Irma deserts her crooked boy friend and marries a singing soda jerk.
Comic strip humour responsible for the screen debut of Martin and Lewis. Sequel 1950: *My Friend Irma Goes West.*

w Cy Howard, Parke Levy, *radio show* Cy Howard *d* George Marshall *ph* Leo Tover *m* Roy Webb

Marie Wilson, John Lund, Diana Lynn, *Dean Martin, Jerry Lewis,* Don Defore, Hans Conried, Kathryn Givney

My Gal Sal*
US 1942 103m Technicolor
TCF (Robert Bassler)

The career and romances of songwriter Paul Dreiser.

Conventional nineties musical biopic, more vigorous and likeable than most.

w Seton I. Miller, Darrell Ware, Karl Tunberg, *book* My Brother Paul by Theodore Dreiser *d* Irving Cummings *ph* Ernest Palmer *md* Alfred Newman

Rita Hayworth, Victor Mature, John Sutton, Carole Landis, James Gleason, Phil Silvers, Walter Catlett, Mona Maris, Frank Orth

My Geisha
US 1962 120m Technirama
Paramount / Steve Parker

A director makes a film in Japan; his wife disguises herself as a geisha and gets the leading role.
Silly, overstretched comedy with pretty locations.

w Norman Krasna *d* Jack Cardiff *ph* Shunichuro Nakao *m* Franz Waxman

Shirley Maclaine, Yves Montand, Robert Cummings, Edward G. Robinson, Yoko Tani

My Girl Tisa***
US 1948 95m bw
United States Pictures (Milton Sperling)

An immigrant girl in New York in the nineties falls for an aspiring politician, is threatened with deportation but saved by the intervention of Theodore Roosevelt.
Charming period fairy tale with excellent background detail and attractive performances.

w Allen Boretz, *play* Lucille S. Prumbs, Sara B. Smith *d Elliott Nugent* *ph* Ernest Haller *m* Max Steiner

Lilli Palmer, Sam Wanamaker, Alan Hale, Stella Adler, Akim Tamiroff

My Learned Friend***
GB 1943 76m bw
Ealing (Robert Hamer)

A shady lawyer is last on a mad ex-convict's murder list of those who helped get him convicted.
Madcap black farce, plot-packed and generally hilarious; the star's last vehicle, but one of his best, with superbly timed sequences during a pantomime and on the face of Big Ben.

w John Dighton, Angus Macphail d Basil Dearden, Will Hay

Will Hay, Claude Hulbert, Mervyn Johns, Ernest Thesiger, Charles Victor, Lloyd Pearson, Maudie Edwards, G. H. Mulcaster, Gibb McLaughlin

My Life with Caroline*
US 1941 81m bw
RKO (Lewis Milestone)

An understanding husband thinks his high-spirited wife may be having an affair.
Very minor romantic comedy with an agreeable air but no substance whatever.

w John Van Druten, Arnold Belgard *d* Lewis Milestone *ph* Victor Milner *m* Werner Heymann

Ronald Colman, Anna Lee, Reginald Gardiner, Charles Winninger, Gilbert Roland

My Little Chickadee*
US 1939 83m bw
Universal (Lester Cowan)

A shady lady and an incompetent cardsharp unmask a villain in the old west.
A clash of comedy personalities which is affectionately remembered but in truth does not play very well apart from the odd line.

w Mae West, W. C. Fields *d* Edward Cline *ph* Joseph Valentine *md* Charles Previn

Mae West, W. C. Fields, Joseph Calleia, Dick Foran, Margaret Hamilton

'It obstinately refuses to gather momentum.'—*The Times*

'A classic among bad movies . . . the satire never really gets off the ground. But the ground is such an honest mixture of dirt, manure and corn that at times it is fairly aromatic.'—*Pauline Kael, 1968*

My Lucky Star*
US 1938 84m bw
TCF (Harry Joe Brown)

A shopgirl is innocently caught in a compromising situation with the owner's son.
Fluffy comedy, acceptable as a background for skating sequences.

w Harry Tugend, Jack Yellen *d* Roy del Ruth *ph* John Mescall *songs* Mack Gordon, Harry Revel

Sonja Henie, Richard Greene, Joan Davis, Buddy Ebsen, Cesar Romero, Arthur Treacher, George Barbier, Louise Hovick, Billy Gilbert

My Man and I
US 1952 99m bw
MGM (Stephen Ames)

A Mexican farm labourer, proud of his American citizenship, is drawn into trouble.
Eccentric melodrama in which all the native Americans are whores, cheats or murderers; well enough made but not very interesting.

w John Fante, Jack Leonard *d* William Wellman *ph* William Mellor *m* David Buttolph

Ricardo Montalban, Shelley Winters, Claire Trevor, Wendell Corey

My Man Godfrey***

US 1936 90m bw

Universal (Gregory La Cava)

A zany millionaire family invite a tramp to be their butler and find he is richer than they are. Archetypal Depression concept which is also one of the best of the thirties crazy sophisticated comedies, though its pacing today seems somewhat unsure.

w Morrie Ryskind, Eric Hatch, Gregory La Cava d Gregory La Cava ph Ted Tetzlaff

Carole Lombard, William Powell, Alice Brady, Mischa Auer, Eugene Pallette, Gail Patrick, Alan Mowbray, Jean Dixon

My Man Godfrey

US 1957 92m Technicolor Cinemascope

U-I (Ross Hunter)

Tepid remake which without the period background, and in unsuitable wide screen, raises very few laughs.

w Everett Freeman, Peter Berneis, William Bowers *d* Henry Koster *ph* William Daniels *m* Frank Skinner

June Allyson, David Niven, Jessie Royce Landis, Jay Robinson, Robert Keith, Martha Hyer, Eva Gabor

My Name Is Julia Ross**

US 1945 65m bw

Columbia

A girl is kidnapped and forced to impersonate an heiress.

A very good second feature which has been culted into a reputation beyond its worth, though it is undeniably slick and entertaining.

w Muriel Roy Bolton, *novel* The Woman in Red by Anthony Gilbert *d Joseph H. Lewis ph* Burnett Guffey *m* Mischa Bakaleinikoff

Nina Foch, Dame May Whitty, George Macready, Roland Varno, Doris Lloyd

'A superior, well-knit thriller.'—*Don Miller*

My Own True Love

US 1948 84m bw

Paramount

A lonely man home from the war quarrels with his son over a girl twenty years younger than himself.

Minor romantic drama, competently but coldly presented.

w Arthur Kober, *novel* Yolanda Foldes *d* Compton Bennett *ph* Charles Lang *m* Robert Emmett Dolan

Phyllis Calvert, Melvyn Douglas, Philip Friend, Wanda Hendrix, Binnie Barnes

My Reputation

US 1946 96m bw

Warner (Henry Blanke)

A widow is talked about for dispensing too soon with her weeds.

Dim drama, hastily shot on familiar sets with a reach-me-down script.

w Catherine Turney, *novel* Instruct My Sorrows by Clare Jaynes *d* Curtis Bernhardt *ph* James Wong Howe *m* Max Steiner

Barbara Stanwyck, George Brent, Warner Anderson, Lucile Watson, John Ridgely, Eve Arden, Jerome Cowan, Esther Dale, Scotty Beckett

My Sister Eileen*

US 1942 96m bw

Columbia (Max Gordon)

Two Ohio girls come to New York and live with some zany friends in a Greenwich Village basement apartment.

Rather strained high jinks which were, not surprisingly, later musicalized.

w Ruth McKinney, Joseph Fields, Jerome Chodorov, *book* Ruth McKinney *d* Alexander Hall *ph* Joseph Walker *m* Morris Stoloff

Rosalind Russell, Janet Blair, Brian Aherne, Allyn Joslyn, George Tobias, Elizabeth Patterson, June Havoc

My Sister Eileen*

US 1955 108m Technicolor Cinemascope

Columbia (Fred Kohlmar)

Musical version of the above, via a Broadway show. Watchable but hardly stimulating.

w Blake Edwards, Richard Quine, *play* Joseph Fields, Jerome Chodorov *d* Richard Quine *ph* Charles Lawton Jnr *md* Morris Stoloff *songs* Jule Styne, Leo Robin *ch Bob Fosse*

Betty Garrett, Janet Leigh, Jack Lemmon, Bob Fosse, Kurt Kasznar, Horace MacMahon, Dick York

My Six Convicts*

US 1952 104m bw

Columbia / Stanley Kramer

A psychologist joins the staff of an American

prison and gains the trust of six inmates.
Moderately interesting semi-documentary melodrama marred by a conventional prison break climax.

w Michael Blankfort, *book* Donald Powell Wilson *d* Hugo Fregonese *ph* Guy Roe *m* Dmitri Tiomkin

John Beal, *Millard Mitchell, Gilbert Roland*, Marshall Thompson, Regis Toomey

My Six Loves
US 1965 101m Technicolor Vistavision
Paramount / Gant Gaither

A musical comedy star goes to the country for a rest and with the help of the local minister adopts six scruffy children.
Icky sentimental comedy for the easily pleased.

w John Fante, Joseph Calvelli, William Wood *d* Gower Champion *ph* Arthur E. Arling *m* Walter Scharf

Debbie Reynolds, David Janssen, Cliff Robertson, Eileen Heckart

'Enough to make you settle for cyclamates—or cyanide.'—*Judith Crist, 1973*

My Son John
US 1952 122m bw
Paramount (Leo McCarey)

An American Catholic family is horrified when its eldest son is revealed as a communist.
The lower depths of Hollywood's witch hunt cycle are marked by this Goldwynesque family saga, all sweetness and light, in which the commie son is treated as though he had rabies. Purely as entertainment the plot is pretty choppy and defeats all attempts at acting.

w Myles Connelly, Leo McCarey *d* Leo McCarey *ph* Harry Stradling *m* Robert Emmett Dolan

Helen Hayes, Robert Walker, Dean Jagger, Van Heflin, Minor Watson, Frank McHugh, Richard Jaeckel

My Son My Son*
US 1940 117m bw
Edward Small

A man who becomes rich spoils his son and lives to regret it.
Solid narrative from a bestseller.

w Lenore Coffee, *novel* Howard Spring *d* Charles Vidor

Brian Aherne, Madeleine Carroll, Louis Hayward, Laraine Day, Henry Hull

My Sweet Charlie*
US 1970 96m Technicolor TVM
Universal (Bob Banner)

In a deserted beach house a young girl and a black man hide out from society for different reasons.
Well made but slow and pretentious character drama.

w Richard Levinson, William Link, *novel* David Westheimer *d* Lamont Johnson

Patty Duke, Al Freeman Jnr, Ford Rainey

My Teenage Daughter
GB 1956 100m bw
British Lion / Everest (Herbert Wilcox)
US title: *Teenage Bad Girl*

A widow's seventeen-year-old daughter meets an aggressive young man and ends up in court.
Predictable domestic drama, a tame British version of *Rebel without a Cause*.

w Felicity Douglas *d* Herbert Wilcox *ph* Max Greene

Anna Neagle, Sylvia Syms, Kenneth Haigh, Norman Wooland, Wilfrid Hyde White, Julia Lockwood, Helen Haye

My Wife's Best Friend
US 1952 87m bw
TCF (Robert Bassler)

A wife assumes different personalities in an effort to keep her wayward husband.
Moderately lively comedy.

w Isabel Lennart *d* Richard Sale *ph* Leo Tover *m* Leigh Harline

Anne Baxter, Macdonald Carey, Cecil Kellaway, Leif Erickson

My Wild Irish Rose
US 1947 101m Technicolor
Warner

The ups and downs of Irish tenor Chauncey Olcott and his encounters with Lillian Russell.
Inoffensive but not very exciting period musical, rather lacking in humour.

w Peter Milne, *book* Rita Ilcott *d* David Butler *ph* Arthur Edeson *m* Le Roy Prinz

Dennis Morgan, Arlene Dahl, Andrea King, Alan Hale, George Tobias

Myra Breckinridge
US 1970 94m De Luxe Panavision
TCF (Robert Fryer)

After a sex change operation a film critic goes to Hollywood to accomplish the deflation of the American male.

A sharply satirical novel has been turned into a sleazy and aimless picture which became a watershed of permissiveness; after international outcry it was shunned even by its own studio. A few good laughs do emerge from the morass, but even the old clips are misused.

w Mike Sarne, David Giler, *novel* Gore Vidal *d* Mike Sarne *ph* Richard Moore *m* Lionel Newman

Mae West, Raquel Welch, John Huston, Rex Reed, Jim Backus, John Carradine, Andy Devine

Mysterious Island*

GB 1961 101m Technicolor
Columbia / Ameran (Charles Schneer)

Confederate officers escape by balloon and join shipwrecked English ladies on a strange island where they are menaced by prehistoric monsters and helped by Captain Nemo.
Rambling, lively juvenile adventure with good moments and excellent monsters.

w John Prebble, Dan Ullman, Crane Wilbur, *novel* Jules Verne *d* Cy Endfield *ph* Wilkie Cooper *m* Bernard Herrmann *sp* Ray Harryhausen

Joan Greenwood, Michael Craig, Herbert Lom, Michael Callan, Gary Merrill

Mystery Movie

In 1971 Universal began making films for this NBC slot which required either 74 or 97 minutes. Most of the films were too long at either length for their plots, and few were genuine mysteries, but some of the detective characters became household words. They included the shabby police detective COLUMBO, who usually got his man by annoying him; McCLOUD, a policeman who treated New York City like the open west where he came from; McMILLAN AND WIFE, a Thin Man-like pair who banteringly saved San Francisco from violent crime. These heroes were played respectively by Peter Falk, Dennis Weaver, Rock Hudson and Susan St James. Less successful, and shorter-lived, were the New York cop MADIGAN (Richard Widmark); the private eyes FARADAY AND COMPANY (Dan Dailey, James Naughton); the elderly thriller writers THE SNOOP SISTERS (Helen Hayes, Mildred Natwick); the western detective HEC RAMSAY (Richard Boone); the black detective TENAFLY (James McEachin); the con man McCOY (Tony Curtis); the man-for-millionaire-hire in COOL MILLION (James Farentino). A moderate success was the expensive loot finder BANACEK (George Peppard).

The films in the first five seasons were as follows (74m unless otherwise stated):

Columbo (see Prescription Murder)

RANSOM FOR A DEAD MAN (qv)
MURDER BY THE BOOK
DEAD WEIGHT
SHORT FUSE
BLUEPRINT FOR MURDER
SUITABLE FOR FRAMING
LADY IN WAITING
DEATH LENDS A HAND
DAGGER OF THE MIND (96m)
DOUBLE SHOCK
ETUDE IN BLACK (97m)
THE GREENHOUSE JUNGLE
THE MOST CRUCIAL GAME
THE MOST DANGEROUS MATCH
REQUIEM FOR A FALLING STAR
A STITCH IN CRIME
ANY OLD PORT IN A STORM (96m)
CANDIDATE FOR CRIME (96m)
DOUBLE EXPOSURE
LOVELY BUT LETHAL
MIND OVER MAYHEM
PUBLISH OR PERISH
SWAN SONG (97m)
A FRIEND IN NEED (97m)
AN EXERCISE IN FATALITY (97m)
NEGATIVE REACTION (96m)
BY DAWN'S EARLY LIGHT (96m)
PLAYBACK
A DEADLY STATE OF MIND
TROUBLED WATERS (97m)
FORGOTTEN LADY (97m)
A MATTER OF HONOUR
A CASE OF IMMUNITY
IDENTITY CRISIS (98m)
LAST SALUTE TO THE COMMODORE
NOW YOU SEE HIM (89m)

McMillan and Wife (see also Once Upon a Dead Man)

EASY SUNDAY MURDER CASE
MURDER BY THE BARREL
HUSBANDS, WIVES AND KILLERS
THE FACE OF MURDER
DEATH IS A SEVEN-POINT FAVOURITE
TILL DEATH US DO PART
AN ELEMENTARY CASE OF MURDER
BLUES FOR SALLY M
COP OF THE YEAR
THE FINE ART OF STAYING ALIVE
NIGHT OF THE WIZARD
NO HEARTS, NO FLOWERS
TERROR TIMES TWO
TWO DOLLARS ON TROUBLE TO WIN
CROSS AND DOUBLE CROSS (96m)
DEATH OF A MONSTER, BIRTH OF A LEGEND

THE DEVIL YOU SAY
FREE FALL TO TERROR
THE MAN WITHOUT A FACE (96m)
REUNION IN TERROR
DOWNSHIFT TO DANGER (97m)
GAME OF SURVIVAL (97m)
BURIED ALIVE (97m)
GUILT BY ASSOCIATION (98m)
NIGHT TRAIN TO L.A. (97m)
LOVE, HONOUR AND SWINDLE (96m)
DEADLY INHERITANCE (97m)
REQUIEM FOR A BRIDE (97m)
AFTERSHOCK (97m)
SECRETS FOR SALE (97m)
GREED (97m)
POINT OF LAW (97m)
THE DEADLY CURE (98m)

McCloud (see Who Killed Miss U.S.A.?)

ENCOUNTER WITH ARIES
FIFTH MAN IN A STRING QUARTET
SOMEBODY'S OUT TO GET JENNIE
TOP OF THE WORLD, MA
DISPOSAL MAN
A LITTLE PLOT AT TRANQUIL VALLEY
THE BAREFOOT STEWARDESS CAPER (96m)
THE MILLION DOLLAR ROUND-UP (96m)
THE NEW MEXICAN CONNECTION
THE PARK AVENUE RUSTLERS
SHOWDOWN AT THE END OF THE WORLD
BUTCH CASSIDY RIDES AGAIN (96m)
THE COLORADO CATTLE CAPER
THE SOLID GOLD SWINGERS (98m)
COWBOY IN PARADISE (97m)
THIS MUST BE THE ALAMO (96m)
THE 42nd STREET CAVALRY (96m)
THE GANG THAT STOLE MANHATTAN (96m)
THE CONCRETE JUNGLE CAPER (96m)
THE BAREFOOT GIRLS OF BLEECKER STREET (99m)
SHIVAREE ON DELANCY STREET (98m)
THE LADY ON THE RUN (97m)
RETURN TO THE ALAMO
SHARKS (98m)
PARK AVENUE PIRATES (97m)
THREE GUNS FOR NEW YORK (98m)
SHOWDOWN AT TIMES SQUARE (97m)
FIRE! (99m)
OUR MAN IN THE HAREM (98m)
THE DAY NEW YORK TURNED BLUE (98m)
NIGHT OF THE SHARK (98m)

Madigan (see Brock's Last Case)

THE MANHATTAN BEAT
THE MIDTOWN BEAT
THE LISBON BEAT
THE LONDON BEAT
THE NAPLES BEAT
THE PARK AVENUE BEAT

Banacek (see Detour to Nowhere)

THE GREATEST COLLECTION OF THEM ALL
LET'S HEAR IT FOR A LIVING LEGEND
A MILLION THE HARD WAY
NO SIGN OF THE CROSS
PROJECT PHOENIX
TO STEAL A KING
THE TWO MILLION CLAMS OF CAP'N JACK
TEN THOUSAND DOLLARS A PAGE
A HORSE OF A SLIGHTLY DIFFERENT COLOR
IF MAX IS SO SMART, WHY DOESN'T HE TELL US WHERE HE IS?
ROCKET TO OBLIVION
FLY ME—IF YOU CAN FIND ME
NO STONE UNTURNED
NOW YOU SEE IT, NOW YOU DON'T
THE THREE MILLION DOLLAR PIRACY
THE VANISHING CHALICE

Hec Ramsey (see The Century Turns)

THE MYSTERY OF CHALK HILL (96m)
THE MYSTERY OF THE YELLOW ROSE (96m)
THE GREEN FEATHER MYSTERY
HANGMAN'S WAGES
DEAD HEAT (95m)
THE DETROIT CONNECTION
A HARD ROAD TO VENGEANCE (98m)
SCAR TISSUE (97m)
ONLY BIRDS AND FOOLS (96m)

Cool Million (see Cool Million)

THE ABDUCTION OF BAYARD BARNES
ASSAULT ON GAVALONI
HUNT FOR A LONELY GIRL
MILLION DOLLAR MISUNDERSTANDING

Faraday and Company (see Say Hello to a Dead Man)

FIRE AND ICE
A MATTER OF MAGIC
A WHEELBARROW FULL OF TROUBLE

The Snoop Sisters (see The Snoop Sisters/The Female Instinct)

CORPSE AND ROBBERS
A BLACK DAY FOR BLUEBEARD
FEAR IS A FREE THROW
THE DEVIL MADE ME DO IT

McCoy (see The Big Rip-Off)

BLESS THE BIG FISH
DOUBLE TAKE (96m)
IN AGAIN OUT AGAIN (98m)

NEW DOLLAR DAY

Amy Prentiss (see Amy Prentiss aka The Chief)

THE DESPERATE WORLD OF JANE DOE (96m)
PROFILE IN EVIL
BAPTISM OF FIRE (99m)

Tenafly (see Tenafly)

THE CASH AND CARRY CAPER
JOYRIDE TO NOWHERE
MAN RUNNING
THE WINDOW THAT WASN'T

Quincy (see A Star Is Dead)

began 1976

The Mystery of Edwin Drood*
US 1935 85m bw
Universal

In a cathedral town, a drug-addicted choirmaster is his nephew's rival for the hand of Rosa Bud.
Fairly creditable attempt to deal with a famous unfinished novel. Slightly stilted, but good visuals and performances.

w John L. Balderston, Gladys Unger, Bradley King, Leopold Atlas, *novel* Charles Dickens *d Stuart Walker*

Claude Rains, Douglass Montgomery, Heather Angel, David Manners, E. E. Clive, Valerie Hobson

The Mystery of Marie Roget
US 1942 61m bw
Universal (Paul Malvern)

A Parisian music hall star plots to kill her sister but herself disappears.
Ham-fisted, stilted mystery drama relying hardly at all on its original.

w Michael Jacoby, *story* Edgar Allan Poe *d* Phil Rosen *ph* Elwood Bredell

Maria Montez, Patric Knowles, *Maria Ouspenskaya*, Lloyd Corrigan, John Litel, Edward Norris, Frank Reicher

The Mystery of Mr X
US 1934 84m bw
MGM

In foggy London, a jewel thief protects himself by finding the murderer of several policemen.
Passable mystery, later remade as *The Hour of Thirteen.*

w Howard Emmett Rogers, Philip MacDonald, Monckton Hoffe, *novel* X vs Rex by Philip MacDonald *d* Edgar Selwyn *ph* Oliver T. Marsh

Robert Montgomery, Elizabeth Allan, Lewis Stone, Ralph Forbes, Henry Stephenson, Forrester Harvey

The Mystery of the Wax Museum****
US 1933 77m Technicolor
Warner (Henry Blanke)

A sculptor disfigured in a fire builds a wax museum by covering live victims in wax.
Archetypal horror material is augmented by a sub-plot about drug-running and an authoritative example of the wisecracking reporter school of the early thirties. The film is also notable for its highly satisfactory use of two-colour Technicolor and for its splendid art direction. Remade 1953 as *House of Wax* (qv).

w Don Mullally, Carl Erickson, play Charles S. Belden *d* Michael Curtiz *ph Ray Rennahan ad Anton Grot*

Lionel Atwill, Fay Wray, *Glenda Farrell, Frank McHugh*, Gavin Gordon, Allen Vincent, Edwin Maxwell

Mystery Street*
US 1950 93m bw
MGM (Frank E. Taylor)

Harvard medical scientists help solve a murder by examining the victim's bones.
Standard semi-documentary police thriller; well paced and quite entertaining.

w Sidney Boehm, Richard Brooks d John Sturges *ph* John Alton *m* Rudolph Kopp

Ricardo Montalban, Sally Forrest, Elsa Lanchester, Bruce Bennett, Marshall Thompson, Jan Sterling

Mystery Submarine
GB 1962 92m bw
British Lion / Britannia / Bertram Ostrer

A Nazi submarine is captured and sent out again with a British crew.
Routine war adventure.

w Hugh Woodhouse, Bertram Ostrer, Jon Manchip White *d* C. M. Pennington-Richards *ph* Stan Pavey *m* Clifton Parker

Edward Judd, James Robertson Justice, Laurence Payne, Albert Lieven

N

Naked Alibi
US 1954 85m bw
U-I (Ross Hunter)

The police track a homicidal baker to a Mexican border town.
Modest police thriller which sags after it crosses the border.

w Lawrence Roman *d* Jerry Hopper *ph* Russell Metty *m* Joseph Gershenson

Sterling Hayden, Gene Barry, Gloria Grahame, Marcia Henderson, Casey Adams, Chuck Connors

The Naked and the Dead
US 1958 131m Technicolor RKOscope
RKO Teleradio / Gregjac (Paul Gregory)

Adventures of an army platoon in the Pacific war.
Shorn of the four letter words which made the novel notorious, this is a routine war film, neither very good nor very bad.

w Denis and Terry Sanders, *novel* Norman Mailer *d* Raoul Walsh *ph* Joseph La Shelle *m* Bernard Herrmann

Aldo Ray, Cliff Robertson, Raymond Massey, William Campbell, Richard Jaeckel, James Best, Joey Bishop, Robert Gist, Jerry Paris, L. Q. Jones

The Naked City****
US 1948 96m bw
Universal (Mark Hellinger)

New York police track down a killer.
Highly influential documentary thriller which, shot on location in New York's teeming streets, claimed to be giving an impression of city life; actually its real mission was to tell an ordinary murder tale with an impressive accumulation of detail and humour. The narrator's last words became a cliché: 'There are eight million stories in the naked city. This has been one of them.'

w Malvin Wald, Albert Maltz d Jules Dassin ph William Daniels md Milton Schwarzwald

Barry Fitzgerald, Don Taylor, Howard Duff, Dorothy Hart, Ted de Corsia, Adelaide Klein

Naked Earth
GB 1958 96m bw Cinemascope
TCF / Foray Films (Adrian Worker)

In 1895 a young Irish farmer goes to Africa to grow tobacco, but moves on to crocodile hunting.
Predictable and uninteresting epic of endurance; not very convincing either.

w Milton Holmes *d* Vincent Sherman *ph* Erwin Hillier

Richard Todd, Juliette Greco, John Kitzmiller, Finlay Currie, Laurence Naismith, Christopher Rhodes, Orlando Martins

The Naked Edge
GB 1961 100m bw
US / Pennebaker / Baroda (Walter Seltzer, George Glass)

A successful executive is suspected by his wife of an old murder in which he testified against the man who was convicted.
Dreary thriller which piles up red herrings in shoals, then abandons them all for a razor-and-bathroom finale.

w Joseph Stefano, *novel* First Train to Babylon by Max Ehrlich *d* Michael Anderson *ph* Erwin Hillier *m* William Alwyn

Gary Cooper, Deborah Kerr, Peter Cushing, Eric Portman, Diane Cilento, Hermione Gingold, Michael Wilding, Ronald Howard

The Naked Jungle*
US 1954 95m Technicolor
Paramount (Frank Freeman Jnr)

In 1901 a young woman is married by proxy to a South American cocoa planter, and when she arrives at his jungle home she has to conquer not only him but an army of soldier ants.
Mixture of *Rebecca* elements with a more unusual kind of thrill; all quite watchable, and the ant scenes very effective.

w Philip Yordan, Ranald MacDougall, *story* Leiningen Versus the Ants by Carl Stephenson *d* George Pal *ph* Ernest Laszlo *m* Daniele Amfitheatrof

Charlton Heston, Eleanor Parker, William

Conrad, Abraham Sofaer, John Dierkes, Douglas Fowley

The Naked Maja
Italy / US 1959 112m Technirama
MGM / Titanus (Goffredo Lombardo)

Peasant Francisco Goya becomes a famous painter through the influence of the Duchess of Alba.
Boring and unconvincing biopic.

w Giorgio Prosperi, Norman Corwin, Albert Lewin, Oscar Saul *d* Henry Koster
ph Giuseppe Rotunno *m* Francesco Lavagnino

Anthony Franciosa, Ava Gardner, Amedeo Nazzari, Gino Cervi, Lea Padovani, Massimo Serrato

'This travesty of Goya's life, country and period adds up to nothing more entertaining than a perfunctory, heavy-handed pageant.'—*MFB*

The Naked Prey*
US 1964 94m Technicolor Panavision
Paramount / Theodora / Sven Persson (Cornel Wilde)

In 1840, a white hunter becomes brutalized when a tribe hunts him down as though he were a lion.
Savage adventure story with bloodthirsty detail; unusual and certainly effective.

w Clint Johnston, Don Peters *d Cornel Wilde*
ph I. A. R. Thompson *m* Andrew Tracy

Cornel Wilde, Gert Van Den Berg, Ken Gampu

The Naked Runner
GB 1967 104m Techniscope
Warner / Artanis (Brad Dexter)

British intelligence conceive a plan to turn an innocent businessman into a spy killer.
Silly espionage thriller further marred by its director's penchant for making a zany composition of every frame.

w Stanley Mann, *novel* Francis Clifford
d Sidney J. Furie *ph* Otto Heller *m* Harry Sukman

Frank Sinatra, Peter Vaughan, Derren Nesbitt, Nadia Gray, Toby Robins, Cyril Luckham, Edward Fox, Inger Stratton

'It might be a good movie to read by if there were light in the theatre.'—*Pauline Kael*

The Naked Spur*
US 1952 91m Technicolor
MGM (William H. Wright)

A bounty hunter has trouble getting his quarry back to base.
Standard big studio western shot in Colorado, with all characters motivated by greed.

w Sam Rolfe, Harold Jack Bloom *d* Anthony Mann *ph* William Mellor *m* Bronislau Kaper

James Stewart, Robert Ryan, Janet Leigh, Millard Mitchell

The Naked Truth*
GB 1957 92m bw
Rank / Mario Zampi
US title: *Your Past is Showing*

Celebrities band together to kill a blackmailer who threatens to expose unsavoury aspects of their lives.
Frenzied black farce, quite a lot of which comes off.

w Michael Pertwee *d* Mario Zampi *ph* Stan Pavey *m* Stanley Black

Peter Sellers, Terry-Thomas, Peggy Mount, Dennis Price, Shirley Eaton, Georgina Cookson

The Name of the Game
This series of 74-minute movies which sprang from *Fame Is the Name of the Game* (qv) ran three seasons (1968–1970). The films were watchable but almost always over-padded, better on the crime themes than the social concern. Gene Barry played the managing editor, with Robert Stack looking after crime and Tony Franciosa current affairs; they usually appeared on a rotating basis. Susan St James was Barry's secretary.

The titles were as follows:

ORDEAL (RS, Farley Granger, Martha Hyer, Jessica Walter)
WITNESS (GB, RS, Victor Jory, Joan Hackett)
THE BOBBY CURRIER STORY (RS, Brandon de Wilde, Julie Harris)
THE FEAR OF HIGH PLACES (GB, TF, Zsa Zsa Gabor, Jeanne Crain, John Payne)
THE TAKER (GB, TF, Bradford Dillman, Laraine Day, Estelle Winwood)
THE INQUIRY (RS, Barry Sullivan, Jack Kelly, Gia Scala)
SHINE ON, SHINE ON, JESSE GIL (TF, Darren McGavin, Juliet Prowse)
NIGHTMARE (RS, Martin Balsam, Troy Donahue)
THE WHITE BIRCH (GB, Boris Karloff, Lilia Skala, Roddy McDowall)
AN AGENT FOR THE PLAINTIFF (GB, Honor Blackman, Maurice Evans)
THE PROTECTOR (GB, Robert Young, Anne Baxter, Ralph Meeker)
HIGH ON A RAINBOW (RS, June Allyson, Broderick Crawford, Van Johnson)
LOLA IN LIPSTICK (GB, Ed Begley, Dana Wynter, William Windom)
INCIDENT IN BERLIN (GB, Kevin

McCarthy, Dane Clark, Geraldine Brooks)
THE SUNTAN MOB (RS, Suzanne Pleshette, Wilfrid Hyde White)
COLLECTORS' EDITION (TF, John Saxon, Senta Berger, Nina Foch, Paul Lukas)
THE REVOLUTIONARY (GB, Harry Guardino, Simon Oakland)
THE THIRD CHOICE (GB, Shirley Jones, Ossie Davis)
SWINGERS ONLY (RS, Robert Lansing, Ann Blyth, Jack Klugman)
LOVE-IN AT GROUND ZERO (GB, Keenan Wynn, Tisha Sterling)
PINEAPPLE ROSE (GB, Mel Torme, Susan Strasberg)
THE BLACK ANSWER (TF, Abby Lincoln, Ivan Dixon)
THE INCOMPARABLE CONNIE WALKER (TF, GB, Ivan Dixon, Dina Merrill)
A WRATH OF ANGELS (RS, Ricardo Montalban, Edward Andrews)
KEEP THE DOCTOR AWAY (TF, Robert Goulet, Vera Miles)
BREAKOUT TO A FAST BUCK (RS, Barry Nelson, Arthur O'Connell)
GIVE TILL IT HURTS (RS, Diane Baker, Dennis Weaver)
THE GARDEN (RS, Richard Kiley, Anne Francis, Brenda Scott)
CHAINS OF COMMAND (RS, Sidney Blackmer, Dorothy Lamour, Pernell Roberts)
THE CIVILIZED MEN (RS, Jack Kelly, Rod Cameron, Jill St John)
THE EMISSARY (GB, Craig Stevens, Charles Boyer)
THE TAKEOVER (GB, Anne Baxter, David Sheiner, Michael Ansara)
BRASS RING (RS, Celeste Holm, Van Johnson)
MAN OF THE PEOPLE (GB, Fernando Lamas, Vera Miles, Robert Alda)
A HARD CASE OF THE BLUES (RS, Keenan Wynn, Sal Mineo, Russ Tamblyn)
THE POWER (RS, William Conrad, Broderick Crawford, Gene Raymond)
THE SKIN GAME (RS, Rossano Brazzi, Suzanne Pleshette)
GOODBYE HARRY (GB, Darren McGavin, Dane Clark)
LADY ON THE ROCKS (GB, Janice Rule, Nigel Davenport, James R. Justice)
THE TRADITION (GB, Ina Balin, Nico Minardos)
THE PRISONER WITHIN (TF, Steve Forrest, Ron Hayes)
HIGH CARD (GB, Jon Colicos, Gene Raymond, Barry Sullivan)
THE PERFECT IMAGE (GB, Ida Lupino, Hal Holbrook, Clu Gulager)
BLIND MAN'S BLUFF (TF, Broderick Crawford, Jack Klugman)
ISLAND OF GOLD AND PRECIOUS STONES (TF, Lee Meriwether, Henry Jones)
LAURIE MARIE (TF, Mark Richman, Antoinette Bower)
THE OTHER KIND OF A SPY (TF, Ed Begley, Leslie Nielsen, Joseph Campanella)
THE KING OF DENMARK (TF, Joseph Cotten, Margaret Leighton, Noel Harrison)
ECHO OF A NIGHTMARE (RS, Ricardo Montalban, Arthur Hill)
ONE OF THE GIRLS IN RESEARCH (GB, Brenda Vaccaro, Will Geer)
TAROT (GB, William Shatner, Luther Adler, Jose Ferrer)
JENNY WILDE IS DROWNING (TF, Pamela Franklin, Frank Gorshin)
AQUARIUS DESCENDING (GB, William Smithers, Arthur Hill, Hermione Gingold)
THE TIME IS NOW (GB, Jack Klugman, Yaphet Kotto, Roscoe Lee Browne)
A LOVE TO REMEMBER (GB, Lee Grant, Ray Milland, J. D. Cannon)
THE WAR MERCHANTS (RS, Robert Wagner, Scott Brady)
THE BROKEN PUZZLE (GB, Chuck Connors, Pat Crowley, Alex Dreier)
BATTLE AT GANNON'S BRIDGE (RS, Darren McGavin, Jan Murray, Joan Blondell)
WHY I BLEW UP DAKOTA (RS, Jose Ferrer, Carolyn Jones, Clu Gulager)
THE GLORY SHOUTER (RS, William Shatner, Dina Merrill, Howard Duff)
SO LONG, BABY, AND AMEN (RS, Julie Harris, James Gregory)
ALL THE OLD FAMILIAR FACES (GB, Burgess Meredith, Michael Constantine)
THE SAVAGE EYE (RS, Pete Duel, Jim Hutton, Marianne Hill)
CYNTHIA IS ALIVE AND LIVING IN AVALON (GB, Robert Culp, Mickey Rooney, Barbara Feldon)
LITTLE BEAR DIED RUNNING (Robert Culp, Steve Forrest)
THE ENEMY BEFORE US (TF, Orson Welles, Martin Balsam, Katina Paxinou)
A SISTER FROM NAPOLI (Peter Falk, Geraldine Page, Tom Ewell, Kurt Kasznar)
BEWARE OF THE WATCHDOG (RS, Richard Kiley, Pernell Roberts, Diana Muldaur)
LA 2017 (GB, Barry Sullivan, Edmond O'Brien, Paul Stewart)
THE MAN WHO KILLED A GHOST (Robert Wagner, Janet Leigh, David Hartman)
APPOINTMENT IN PALERMO (GB, Brenda Vaccaro, Harry Guardino)
A CAPITOL AFFAIR (GB, Suzanne Pleshette, Larry Hagman, Mercedes McCambridge)

THE SHOWDOWN (GB, Warren Oates, Albert Salmi, Jack Albertson)
SEEK AND DESTROY (RS, Leif Erickson, John Vernon, John McGiver)
I LOVE YOU, BILLY BAKER (two parts) (TF, Sammy Davis Jnr, Joey Bishop)

Nana*
US 1934 89m bw
Samuel Goldwyn

The high life and subsequent degradation of a Parisian demi-mondaine in the nineties.
Stylish yet stolid slice of *le beau monde*, intended to create a new star.

w Willard Mack, Harry Wagstaff Gribble, *novel* Emile Zola *d Dorothy Arzner ph Gregg Toland*

Anna Sten, Lionel Atwill, Phillips Holmes, Richard Bennett, Mae Clarke, Muriel Kirkland, Reginald Owen, Jessie Ralph

Nancy Drew
This series of second features starring Bonita Granville as a teenage small-town detective was moderately well received but quickly forgotten. The character was created in novels by Edward Stratemeyer and his daughter Harriet Evans; the films were all directed by William Clemens for Warners.

1938: NANCY DREW, DETECTIVE
1939: NANCY DREW, REPORTER; NANCY DREW, TROUBLE SHOOTER; NANCY DREW AND THE HIDDEN STAIRCASE

Nancy Goes to Rio
US 1950 99m Technicolor
MGM (Joe Pasternak)

Two actresses, mother and daughter, are both after the same part.
Mild shipboard musical.

w Sidney Sheldon *d* Robert Z. Leonard *ph* Ray June

Jane Powell, Ann Sothern, Carmen Miranda, Barry Sullivan, Louis Calhern, Fortunio Bonanova, Hans Conried

Nancy Steele Is Missing*
US 1938 85m bw
TCF (Nunnally Johnson)

Crooks try to pass off a girl as the long lost heir to a fortune.
Slightly unusual, well cast melodrama.

w Charles Francis Coe *d* George Marshall

Victor McLaglen, Peter Lorre, June Lang, Jane Darwell, John Carradine

The Nanny*
GB 1965 93m bw
ABP / Hammer (Jimmy Sangster)

A ten-year-old boy hates his nanny, and with good reason, for she is a neurotic murderess.
Muted Hammer experiment in psychopathology, with too much equivocation before the dénouement; the star's role allows few fireworks, and the plot is rather unpleasant.

w Jimmy Sangster, *novel* Evelyn Piper *d Seth Holt ph* Harry Waxman *m* Richard Rodney Bennett

Bette Davis, Jill Bennett, William Dix, James Villiers, Wendy Craig, Pamela Franklin, Maurice Denham

Napoleon and Samantha
US 1972 91m Technicolor
Walt Disney (Winston Hibler)

When his old guardian dies, a small boy and his girl friend run away with their pet lion.
Patchy, episodic action drama for older children, with a very sleepy lion.

w Stewart Raffil *d* Bernard McEveety *ph* Monroe Askins

Michael Douglas, Will Geer

The Narrow Margin***
US 1950 70m bw
RKO (Stanley Rubin)

Police try to guard a prosecution witness on a train from Chicago to Los Angeles.
Tight little thriller which takes every advantage of its train setting. What the trade used to call a sleeper, it gave more satisfaction than many a top feature

w Earl Felton *d Richard Fleischer ph George E. Diskant*

Charles McGraw, Marie Windsor, Jacqueline White, Queenie Leonard

Nashville**
US 1975 161m Metrocolor Panavision
Paramount / ABC (Robert Altman)

A political campaign in Nashville organizes a mammoth pop concert to gain support.
Kaleidoscopic, fragmented, multi-storied musical melodrama, a mammoth movie which can be a bore or an inspiration according to taste. Certainly many exciting moments pass by, but the length is self-defeating.

w Joan Tewkesbury *d* Robert Altman *ph* Paul Lohmann *md* Richard Baskin

Geraldine Chaplin, David Arkin, Barbara

Baxley, Ned Beatty, Karen Black, Keith Carradine, Henry Gibson, Keenan Wynn

'A gigantic parody . . . crammed with samples taken from every level of Nashville society, revealed in affectionate detail bordering on caricature in a manner that would surely delight Norman Rockwell.'—*Philip Strick*

The National Health*
GB 1973 97m Eastmancolor
Columbia (Ned Sherrin, Terry Glinwood)

Life in the general men's ward of a large antiquated hospital.
Acerbic comedy from a National Theatre play which mixes tragedy and farce into a kind of *Carry on Dying*.

w Peter Nichols, from his play *d Jack Gold* *ph* John Coquillon *m* Carl David *pd* Ray Simm

Jim Dale, Lynn Redgrave, Eleanor Bron, Sheila Scott-Wilkinson, Donald Sinden, Colin Blakely, Clive Swift

National Velvet*
US 1944 125m Technicolor
MGM (Pandro S. Berman)

Children train a horse to win the Grand National.
A big bestseller from another era; its flaws of conception and production quickly became evident.

w Theodore Reeves, Helen Deutsch, *novel* Enid Bagnold *d* Clarence Brown *ph* Leonard Smith *m* Herbert Stothart

Mickey Rooney, Elizabeth Taylor, *Anne Revere*, Donald Crisp, Angela Lansbury, Jackie Jenkins, Reginald Owen, Terry Kilburn, Norma Varden, Alec Craig, Arthur Shields, Dennis Hoey

Naughty But Nice
US 1939 90m bw
Warner (Sam Bischoff)

A professor of classical music accidentally writes a popular song.
Mildly amusing comedy musical with all the tunes adapted from the classics (cf *That Night with You*).

w Jerry Wald, Richard Macaulay *d* Ray Enright *ph* Arthur L. Todd *songs* Harry Warren, Johnny Mercer

Dick Powell, Ann Sheridan, Ronald Reagan, Gale Page, Zasu Pitts, Jerry Colonna

Naughty Marietta**
US 1935 106m bw
MGM (Hunt Stromberg)

A French princess goes to America and falls in love with an Indian scout.
Period operetta which set the seal of success on the MacDonald-Eddy team. In itself, dated but quite pleasing for those who like the genre.

w John Lee Mahin, Frances Goodrich, Albert Hackett, *operetta* Rida Johnson Young *d* W. S. Van Dyke *ph* William Daniels *m* Victor Herbert *ad* Cedric Gibbons

Jeanette MacDonald, Nelson Eddy, Frank Morgan, Elsa Lanchester, Douglass Dumbrille, Joseph Cawthorn, Cecelia Parker, Walter Kingsford

The Naughty Nineties
US 1945 72m bw
Universal (Edward L. Hartmann, John Grant)

Two incompetents help an old showboat owner.
Dim star comedy apart from the team's rendition of their most famous routine, 'Who's On First'.

w Edmund L. Hartmann, John Grant, Edmund Joseph, Hal Fimburg *d* Jean Yarborough *ph* George Robinson

Bud Abbott, Lou Costello, Henry Travers, Alan Curtis, Rita Johnson, Joe Sawyer

Navy Blues
US 1941 109m bw
Warner (Jerry Wald)

Naval ratings get into trouble in Honolulu.
Undernourished musical comedy with not too much of either commodity.

w Jerry Wald, Richard Macauley, Arthur T. Horman *d* Lloyd Bacon *ph* Tony Gaudio *ch* Seymour Felix *songs* Arthur Scwarz, Johnny Mercer

Ann Sheridan, Jack Oakie, Martha Raye, Jack Haley, Herbert Anderson, Jack Carson, Richard Lane, Jackie Gleason, Howard da Silva

Nazi Agent*
US 1942 84m bw
MGM (Irving Asher)

A German-American is forced by his Nazi twin to help a group of German spies.
Modest suspenser with a plot twist similar to *The Great Impersonation* and *Dead Ringer*.

w Paul Gangelin, John Meehan Jnr *d Jules Dassin*

Conrad Veidt, Ann Ayars, Frank Reicher, Dorothy Tree, Martin Kosleck

Necromancy
US 1973 83m colour
Cinerama (Bert I. Gordon)

Two young people become involved in small-town witchcraft.
Low-key, low-talent thriller overbalanced by its star.

wd Bert I. Gordon *m* Fred Karger

Orson Welles, Pamela Franklin, Michael Onthean, Lee Purcell

Ned Kelly
GB 1970 103m Technicolor
UA / Woodfall (Neil Hartley)

The career of a 19th-century Australian outlaw.
Obstinately unlikeable action picture with some kind of message which never becomes clear amid all the cleverness.

w Tony Richardson, Ian Jones *d* Tony Richardson *ph* Gerry Fisher *m* Shel Silverstein *pd* Jocelyn Herbert

Mick Jagger, Allen Bickford, Geoff Gilmour, Mark McManus

Negatives*
GB 1968 98m Eastmancolor
Crispin / Kettledrum (Judd Bernard)

Three people indulge in sexual fantasies involving Dr Crippen and Baron Von Richthofen.
Smoothly done but impenetrable psychological poppycock: what is fact and what is fancy, only the author knows.

w Peter Everett, Roger Lowry, *novel* Peter Everett *d* Peter Medak *ph* Ken Hodges *m* Basil Kirchin

Glenda Jackson, Peter McEnery, Diane Cilento, Maurice Denham, Steven Lewis, Norman Rossington

Nell Gwyn**
GB 1934 85m bw
B and D (Herbert Wilcox)

The affair of Charles II and an orange seller.
Naïve, vivid account of a famous couple; physically cheap and rather faded, but the best film on the subject and one of the best covering this period.

w Miles Malleson d Herbert Wilcox

Anna Neagle, Cedric Hardwicke, Jeanne de Casalis, Muriel George, Miles Malleson, Esmé Percy, Moore Marriott

The Neon Ceiling*
US 1971 97m Technicolor TVM
Universal (William Sackheim)

A runaway wife and her daughter take temporary refuge in a desert shack with a colourful dropout.
Talkative but ingratiating and very well acted three character drama.

w Carol Sobieski, Henri Simoun *d* Frank Pierson

Gig Young, Lee Grant, Denise Nickerson

The Neptune Factor
Canada 1972 98m De Luxe Panavision
TCF / Quadrant / Bellevue–Pathe (Sanford Howard)
Later retitled: *The Neptune Disaster*

American oceanologists conduct an experiment in underwater living.
Wet 'actioner' in which very little happens except a few porthole views of magnified fish.

w Jack de Witt *d* Daniel Petrie *ph* Harry Makin *m* Lalo Schifrin

Ben Gazzara, Walter Pidgeon, Yvette Mimieux, Ernest Borgnine, Chris Wiggins

Neptune's Daughter*
US 1949 93m Technicolor
MGM (Jack Cummings)

A lady bathing suit designer has a South American romance.
Generally thought one of the better aquatic musicals, and certainly very typical of them and its studio at this time.

w Dorothy Kingsley *d* Edward Buzzell *ph* Charles Rosher *m* George Stoll

Esther Williams, Red Skelton, Ricardo Montalban, Betty Garrett, Keenan Wynn, Xavier Cugat and his Orchestra, Mike Mazurki, Ted de Corsia, Mel Blanc

The Net
GB 1953 86m bw
Rank / Two Cities (Anthony Darnborough)
US title: *Project M7*

Tension among boffins in an aviation research station leads to murder and the discovery of a spy.
Low-key suspenser, quite adequately presented.

w William Fairchild, *novel* John Pudney *d* Anthony Asquith *ph* Desmond Dickinson *m* Benjamin Frankel

Phyllis Calvert, Noel Willman, Herbert Lom, James Donald, Robert Beatty, Muriel Pavlow, Walter Fitzgerald, Maurice Denham

Nevada Smith*
US 1966 131m Eastmancolor Panavision
Avco / Solar (Joe Levine, Henry Hathaway)

A cowboy takes a long revenge on the outlaws who murdered his parents.
Violent, sour, occasionally lively but frequently boring western melodrama on a well worn theme.

w John Michael Hayes, from the 'early life' of a character in The Carpetbaggers by Harold Robbins *d* Henry Hathaway *ph* Lucien Ballard *m* Alfred Newman

Steve McQueen, Karl Malden, Brian Keith, Suzanne Pleshette, Arthur Kennedy, Janet Margolin, Howard da Silva, Raf Vallone, Pat Hingle

Nevada Smith
US 1975 74m colour TVM
MGM / Martin Rackin

Thin pilot with the hero a wandering, sometimes revengeful, do-gooder.

w John Michael Hayes, Martin Rackin *d* Gordon Douglas

Cliff Potts, Lorne Greene

Never a Dull Moment
US 1950 89m bw
RKO (Harriet Parsons)

A lady music critic marries a rodeo cowboy and finds life hard down on the ranch.
Very mild star programmer.

w Lou Breslow, Doris Anderson, *novel* Who Could Ask for Anything More? by Kay Swift *d* George Marshall *ph* Joseph Walker *m* Constantin Bakaleinikoff

Irene Dunne, Fred MacMurray, William Demarest, Andy Devine, Gigi Perreau, Natalie Wood, Philip Ober, Jack Kirkwood

Never a Dull Moment
US 1967 100m Technicolor
Walt Disney (Ron Miller)

An unsuccessful actor is mistaken for a notorious gangster.
Slapstick romp with vigour but not much flair.

w A. J. Carothers, *novel* John Godey *d* Jerry Paris *ph* William Snyder *m* Robert F. Brunner

Dick Van Dyke, Edward G. Robinson, Dorothy Provine, Henry Silva, Joanna Moore, Tony Bill, Slim Pickens, Jack Elam

Never Give a Sucker an Even Break*
US 1941 70m bw
Universal
GB title: *What a Man*

W. C. Fields dives off an aeroplane into the lap of a young woman who has never seen a man; she falls in love with him.
Stupefyingly inept in its scripting and pacing, this comedy is often irresistibly funny because of the anti-everything personality of its writer-star. No one else could have got away with it, or would have been likely to try.

w John T. Neville, Precott Chaplin, *story* Otis Criblecoblis (W. C. Fields) *d* Edward Cline *ph* Charles Van Enger *m* Frank Skinner

W. C. Fields, Gloria Jean, Leon Errol, Butch and Buddy, Franklin Pangborn, Anne Nagel, Mona Barrie, Ann Miller, Margaret Dumont

Never Let Go
GB 1960 91m bw
Rank / Julian Wintle–Leslie Parkin (Peter de Sarigny)

A travelling salesman has his car stolen and stands up to the sadistic gang boss responsible.
Brutishly unattractive thriller, apparently designed for the sole purpose of giving Peter Sellers a villainous part.

w Alun Falconer *d* John Guillermin *ph* Christopher Challis *m* John Barry

Richard Todd, Peter Sellers, Elizabeth Sellars, Adam Faith, Carol White, Mervyn Johns, Noel Willman

Never Let Me Go
GB 1953 94m bw
MGM (Clarence Brown)

After World War II an American correspondent marries a Russian ballerina but is later deported by the authorities.
Ho-hum romantic melodrama, quite interestingly cast.

w Roland Millar, George Froeschel, *novel* Came the Dawn by Roger Bax *d* Delmer Daves *ph* Robert Krasker *m* Hans May

Clark Gable, Gene Tierney, Richard Haydn, Belita, Bernard Miles, Kenneth More, Karel Stepanek, Theodore Bikel, Frederick Valk

Never Love a Stranger
US 1958 93m bw
Harold Robbins / Allied Artists (Peter Gettlinger)

A Catholic boy who has become a gangster helps his Jewish friend who has become assistant district attorney to trap a vicious hoodlum.
The old *Manhattan Melodrama* theme is dusted off once again, this time to very little effect.

w Harold Robbins, Richard Day, *novel* Harold

Robbins *d* Robert Stevens *ph* Lee Garmes *m* Raymond Scott

John Drew Barrymore, Steve McQueen, Robert Bray, Lita Milan, R. G. Armstrong, Salem Ludwig

Never Put it in Writing*
GB 1963 93m bw
MGM / Andrew Stone

A young executive tries to recover from the mails an indiscreet letter he has written to his boss.
Frantic hit-or-miss farcical comedy distinguished by Dublin locations and cast.

wd Andrew Stone *ph* Martin Curtis *m* Frank Cordell

Pat Boone, Fidelma Murphy, Reginald Beckwith, John Le Mesurier, Colin Blakely

Never Say Die*
US 1939 80m bw
Paramount (Paul Jones)

A millionaire hypochondriac is convinced he is dying.
Thin farce with Hope on the very brink of stardom; some bright moments.

w Don Hartman, Frank Butler, Preston Sturges *d* Elliott Nugent *ph* Leo Tover *md* Boris Morros

Martha Raye, Bob Hope, Andy Devine, Alan Mowbray, Gale Sondergaard, Sig Rumann, Ernest Cossart, Monty Woolley, Christian Rub

Never Say Goodbye
US 1956 96m Technicolor
U-I (Albert J. Cohen)

In 1945 Berlin an American army doctor marries a pianist who is later trapped in the Russian zone; they meet years later in America.
Romantic drama aimed at a female audience, remade from *This Love of Ours* (qv).

w Charles Hoffman *d* Jerry Hopper *ph* Maury Gertsman

Rock Hudson, George Sanders, Cornell Borchers, Ray Collins, David Janssen

Never So Few
US 1959 124m Metrocolor
Cinemascope
MGM / Canterbury (Edmund Grainger)

Adventures of World War II Americans commanding Burmese guerrillas.
Jungle actioner with pauses for philosophizing; well enough made but not very interesting.

w Millard Kaufman, *novel* Tom Chamales *d* John Sturges *ph* William H. Daniels *m* Hugo Friedhofer

Frank Sinatra, Gina Lollobrigida, Peter Lawford, Steve McQueen, Paul Henreid, Richard Johnson, Brian Donlevy, Charles Bronson, Dean Jones

Never Steal Anything Small
US 1958 94m Eastmancolor
Cinemascope
U-I (Aaron Rosenberg)

The reformation of a corrupt but sympathetic dockers' union boss.
Curious semi-musical which doesn't come off at all despite excellent credentials.

wd Charles Lederer, *play* The Devil's Hornpipe by Rouben Mamoulian, Maxwell Anderson *ph* Harold Lipstein *m* Allie Wrubel *ly* Maxwell Anderson *ch* Hermes Pan

James Cagney, Shirley Jones, Roger Smith, Cara Williams, Nehemiah Persoff, Royal Dano, Anthony Caruso

Never Take No for an Answer*
GB 1951 82m bw
Anthony Havelock-Allan

A small boy goes to Rome to get permission from the Pope to take his sick donkey to be blessed in the church.
Slight, easy-going whimsy with attractive sunlit locations.

w Paul and Pauline Gallico, *novel* The Small Miracle by Paul Gallico *d* Maurice Cloche, Ralph Smart *ph* Otto Heller *m* Nino Rota

Vittorio Manunta, Denis O'Dea, Guido Cellano, Nerio Bernardi

'The main pleasures of this slender film are visual ones.'—*MFB*

† Remade as a TV movie *Small Miracle.*

Never Too Late
US 1965 104m Technicolor
Panavision
Warner / Lear–Yorkin (Norman Lear)

A well-to-do middle-aged housewife discovers she is pregnant.
Predictable, rather hysterical domestic comedy, flatly developed from a successful play which offered two star parts for old stagers.

w Sumner Arthur Long, from his play *d* Bud Yorkin *ph* Philip Lathrop *m* David Rose

Paul Ford, Maureen O'Sullivan, Connie Stevens, Jim Hutton, Lloyd Nolan, Henry Jones, Jane Wyatt

Never Wave at a WAC
US 1952 87m bw
Independent Artists (Frederick Brisson)
GB title: *The Private Wore Skirts*

A Washington hostess joins the WACs and finds she can't get beyond the rank of private.
Pattern comedy, unconvincing in all respects but with a smattering of funny moments. Flagwaving takes over towards the end.

w Ken Englund *d* Norman Z. McLeod
ph William Daniels *m* Elmer Bernstein

Rosalind Russell, Paul Douglas, Marie Wilson, William Ching, Leif Erickson, Arleen Whelan, Charles Dingle

The New Centurions*
US 1972 103m Eastmancolor Panavision
Columbia / Chartoff–Winkler
GB title: *Los Angeles Precinct 45*

An old cop teaches a new one.
'Realistic' crime prevention saga which spawned the TV series *Police Story* and *Police Woman*. Well done within its limits.

w Stirling Silliphant, *novel* Joseph Wambaugh
d Richard Fleischer *ph* Ralph Woolsey
m Quincy Jones

George C. Scott, Stacy Keach, Jane Alexander, Rosalind Cash, Scott Wilson

The New Daughters of Joshua Cabe
US 1976 74m colour TVM
Spelling–Goldberg

Josh is unjustly imprisoned on a murder charge and his three 'daughters' evolve an escape plan.
Tired time-filler.

w Paul Savage *d* Bruce Bilson

John McIntire, Jeanette Nolan, Jack Elam, Liberty Williams, Renne Jarrett, Lezlie Dalton
† See also *The Daughters of Joshua Cabe.*

New Faces*
US 1954 99m Eastmancolor Cinemascope
Edward L. Alperson (Leonard Sillman)

A revue goes on despite money problems.
Five minutes of plot, ninety-five minutes of revue from the Broadway stage; mostly quite amusing, and chiefly notable for introducing Eartha Kitt with all her standards.

w various *d* Harry Horner *ph* Lucien Ballard
revue deviser John Murray Anderson

Eartha Kitt, Ronny Graham, Alice Ghostley, Robert Clary, Paul Lynde

The New Healers
US 1972 74m colour TVM
Paramount
aka: *The Paramedics, The Storm*

Three ex-armed-forces medical students help the doctor of a rural area and are accepted after a flood.
Predictable, watchable medico-action drama which didn't make a series.

w Stirling Silliphant *d* Bernard L. Kowalski

Leif Erickson, Kate Johnson, Robert Foxworth, Jonathan Lippe, Burgess Meredith, William Windom

The New Interns
US 1964 123m bw
Columbia (Robert Cohn)

Young doctors at a city hospital have trouble saving a rapist and his victim.
Unnecessary sequel to *The Interns*, its 'realism' requiring large pinches of salt.

w Wilton Schiller *d* John Rich *ph* Lucien Ballard *m* Earle Hagen

George Segal, Telly Savalas, Michael Callan, Dean Jones, Inger Stevens, Stefanie Powers, Lee Patrick

A New Kind of Love
US 1963 110m Technicolor
Paramount / Llenroc (Melville Shavelson)

An American dress designer in Paris is softened by a boorish newspaper columnist.
Very thin sex comedy, dressed to kill but with nowhere to go.

wd Melville Shavelson *ph* Daniel Fapp *m* Leith Stevens

Paul Newman, Joanne Woodward, Maurice Chevalier, Thelma Ritter, George Tobias

A New Leaf*
US 1970 102m Movielab
Paramount / Aries / Elkins (Joe Manduke)

A middle-aged playboy, close to bankruptcy, thinks of acquiring a wealthy wife.
Agreeably mordant comedy which sparkles in patches rather than as a whole.

wd Elaine May, story The Green Heart by Jack Ritchie *ph* Gayne Rescher *m* none
pd Richard Fried

Walter Matthau, Elaine May, Jack Weston, George Rose, William Redfield, James Coco

'Unashamedly a thirties fairly tale in modern, but not fashionable, dress.'—*Jan Dawson*

New Moon*
US 1940 105m bw
MGM (Robert Z. Leonard)

Romance in old French Louisiana.
Stalwart adaptation of an operetta previously filmed in 1931 with Lawrence Tibbett and Grace Moore.

w Jacques Deval, Robert Arthur *d* Robert Z. Leonard *ph* William Daniels *m/ly* Sigmund Romberg, Oscar Hammerstein

Jeanette MacDonald, Nelson Eddy, Mary Boland, George Zucco, H. B. Warner, Stanley Ridges, Grant Mitchell

The New Original Wonder Woman
US 1975 74m colour TVM
Warner / Douglas S. Cramer

See *Wonder Woman*. More nonsense adventures, slightly more firmly strung together with a World War II backdrop.

w Stanley Ralph Ross *d* Leonard Horn

Lynda Carter, Cloris Leachman, Lyle Waggoner, Red Buttons, Stella Stevens, Kenneth Mars, John Randolph

New Orleans*
US 1947 89m bw
Jules Levey

How jazz was born, according to the movies.
Routine low-budgeter enlivened by a splendid array of guest musicians.

w Elliot Paul, Dick Irving Hyland *d* Arthur Lubin *ph* Lucien Andriot *md* Nathaniel Finston

Louis Armstrong and his All Stars, Arturo de Cordova, Dorothy Patrick, *Billie Holiday, Meade Lux Lewis, Woody Herman* and his Orchestra

New York Confidential
US 1955 87m bw
Warner / Russel Rouse, Clarence Greene

The head of a crime syndicate is assassinated by his own hired killer.
Unexciting 'realistic' thriller with the gangsters presented as family and businessmen; seventeen years later *The Godfather* did it rather better.

w Clarence Greene, Russel Rouse *d* Russel Rouse *ph* Edward Fitzgerald *m* Joseph Mullendore *pd* Fernando Carrere

Broderick Crawford, Richard Conte, Anne Bancroft, Marilyn Maxwell, Onslow Stevens, J. Carrol Naish, Barry Kelley, Mike Mazurki, Celia Lovsky

Newman's Law
US 1974 99m Technicolor
Universal (Richard Irving)

A cop uses unconventional methods to trap drug smugglers.
Very routine police actioner, just above TV movie level.

w Anthony Wilson *d* Richard Heffron *ph* Vilis Lapenieks *m* Robert Prince

George Peppard, Roger Robinson, Eugene Roche, Gordon Pinsent, Abe Vegoda

The Next of Kin***
GB 1942 102m bw
Ealing (S. C. Balcon)

Careless talk causes loss of life in a commando raid.
A propaganda instructional film which was made so entertainingly that it achieved commercial success and remains an excellent example of how to make a bitter pill palatable.

w Thorold Dickinson, Basil Bartlett, Angus Macphail, John Dighton *d* Thorold Dickinson

Mervyn Johns, Nova Pilbeam, Stephen Murray, Reginald Tate, Basil Radford, Naunton Wayne, Geoffrey Hibbert, Philip Friend, Mary Clare, Basil Sydney

'The detail everywhere is curious and surprising, with something of the fascination of a Simenon crime being unravelled.'—*William Whitebait*

Next Time We Love
US 1936 87m bw
Universal (Paul Kohner)
GB title: *Next Time We Live*

The wife of a war-correspondent has plenty of time for romance.
Romantic drama which badly needs an injection of comedy.

w Melville Baker, *stories* Ursula Parrott *d* Edward H. Griffith *ph* Joseph Valentine

Margaret Sullavan, Ray Milland, James Stewart, Grant Mitchell, Robert McWade

The Next Voice You Hear*
US 1950 83m bw
MGM (Dore Schary)

God speaks to mankind on the radio, and the life of Joe Smith American is changed.
Soppy parable, the archetypal instance of Schary's reign of do-goodery at MGM. (He wrote a book about it, *Case History of a Movie*.) The idea is handled with deadly reverence, and falls quite flat, while the depiction of the inhabitants of American suburbia is depressing.

w Charles Schnee *d* William Wellman *ph* William Mellor *m* David Raksin

James Whitmore, Nancy Davis, Lillian Bronson, Jeff Corey

'The sins of the American working man are singularly uninteresting and their obliteration seems scarcely to require the very voice of God.'—*Henry Hart*

Niagara***
US 1952 89m Technicolor
TCF (Charles Brackett)

While visiting Niagara Falls, a faithless wife is plotting to murder her husband, but he turns the tables.
Excellent suspenser with breathtaking locations; in the best Hitchcock class though slightly marred by the emphasis on Monroe's wiggly walk (it was her first big part).

w Charles Brackett, Walter Reisch, Richard Breen *d Henry Hathaway ph Joe MacDonald m* Sol Kaplan

Joseph Cotten, Jean Peters, *Marilyn Monroe*, Don Wilson, Casey Adams

'A masterly example of fluid screen narrative.'—*Charles Higham*

Nice Girl?*
US 1941 95m bw
Universal

A teenager finds herself in demand by two older men.
Amusing romantic trifle supposed to mark the growing up of Universal's great teenage star.

w Richard Connell, Gladys Lehman *d* William A. Seiter *ph* Joseph Valentine *m* Charles Girl

Deanna Durbin, Franchot Tone, Robert Stack, Walter Brennan, Robert Benchley, Helen Broderick, Ann Gillis

A Nice Girl Like Me
GB 1969 91m Eastmancolor
Anglo Embassy / Partisan (Roy Millichip)

A sheltered young lady sets out to see life but keeps getting pregnant.
Insufferable romantic whimsy, made to look like a marathon TV commercial but never so interesting.

w Anne Piper, Desmond Davis *d* Desmond Davis *ph* Gil Taylor, Manny Wynn *m* Pat Williams

Barbara Ferris, Harry Andrews, Gladys Cooper, Joyce Carey, Bill Hinnant, James Villiers, Christopher Guinee, Fabia Drake

'High-toned woman's magazine nostalgia.'—*MFB*

A Nice Little Bank that should be Robbed
US 1958 87m bw Cinemascope
TCF (Anthony Muto)
GB title: *How to Rob a Bank*

Two incompetent crooks rob a bank and buy a racehorse.
Feeble comedy, a sad waste of its stars.

w Sidney Boehm *d* Henry Levin *ph* Leo Tover

Mickey Rooney, Tom Ewell, Mickey Shaughnessy, Dina Merrill

Nicholas and Alexandra*
US 1971 189m Eastmancolor Panavision
Columbia / Horizon (Sam Spiegel)

The life of Tsar Nicholas II from 1904 to the execution of the family in 1918.
Inflated epic of occasional interest, mainly for its sets; generally heavy going.

w James Goldman, *book* Robert K. Massie *d* Franklin Schaffner *ph Frederick A. Young m* Richard Rodney Bennett *pd John Box*

Michael Jayston, Janet Suzman, Laurence Olivier, Jack Hawkins, Tom Baker, Harry Andrews, Michael Redgrave, Alexander Knox

Nicholas Nickleby**
GB 1947 108m bw
Ealing

The adventures of a Victorian schoolmaster, deprived of his rightful fortune, who joins a band of travelling entertainers.
Quite tasteful and expert but too light-handed potted version of Dickens, which suffered by comparison with the David Lean versions.

w John Dighton, *novel* Charles Dickens *d* Alberto Cavalcanti *ph* Gordon Dines

Derek Bond, *Cedric Hardwicke, Alfred Drayton, Sybil Thorndike*, Stanley Holloway, James Hayter, Sally Ann Howes, Jill Balcon, Cyril Fletcher, Fay Compton

Nicky's World
US 1974 100m colour TVM
Tomorrow

Problems facing a Greek family in America.
Ethnic drama: absorbing for Greeks.

w Edward Adler, Bill Katz *d* Paul Stanley

Charles Cioffi, George Voskovec, Olympia Dukakis, Despo

Night after Night*
US 1932 70m bw
Paramount

An ex-boxer seeking refinement buys a night club and falls for a socialite.
Dim little drama which is remembered for introducing Mae West to the screen with her famous line, 'Goodness had nothing to do with it'.

w Vincent Laurence, *novel* Single Night by Louis Bromfield *d* Archie Mayo *ph* Ernest Haller

George Raft, Constance Cummings, Wynne Gibson, *Mae West*, Alison Skipworth, Roscoe Karns, Louis Calhern

Night and Day*
US 1946 132m Technicolor
Warner (Arthur Schwarz)

The life of Cole Porter.
Or rather, a fictitious story about a composer who happens to be called Cole Porter. A careful but undistinguished musical with pleasant moments.

w Charles Hoffman, Leo Townsend, William Bowers *d* Michael Curtiz *ph* Peverell Marley, William V. Skall *m/ly Cole Porter* *md* Leo Forbstein, Ray Heindorf *ch* Le Roy Prinz

Cary Grant, Alexis Smith, Monty Woolley, Mary Martin, Ginny Simms, Jane Wyman, Eve Arden, Victor Francen, Alan Hale, Dorothy Malone

Night and the City
GB 1950 101m bw
TCF (Samuel G. Engel)

A crooked wrestling promoter is tracked down by an underworld gang.
A fated attempt to extend the success of *Naked City* in a London setting; the surface is accomplished enough, but the plot and characters are just plain dull, especially as little is seen of the police.

w Jo Eisinger, *novel* Gerald Kersh *d* Jules Dassin *ph Max Greene* *m* Benjamin Frankel

Richard Widmark, Gene Tierney, Googie Withers, Hugh Marlowe, Herbert Lom

'Brilliantly photographed, it is an example of neo-expressionist techniques at their most potent.'—*Richard Roud, 1964*

A Night at the Opera****
US 1935 96m bw
MGM (Irving Thalberg)

Three zanies first wreck, then help an opera company.
Certainly among the best of the Marxian extravaganzas, and the first to give them a big production to play with as well as musical interludes by other than themselves for a change of pace. The mix plays beautifully.

w George S. Kaufman, Morrie Ryskind *d Sam Wood* *ph* Merritt Gerstad *md* Herbert Stothart

Groucho, Chico, Harpo (Zeppo absented himself from here on), *Margaret Dumont*, Kitty Carlisle, Allan Jones, Walter Woolf King, *Sig Rumann*

Night Chase
US 1970 100m colour TVM
Cinema Center

A wealthy businessman on the run from police is nearly trapped in Los Angeles.
Overlong chase melodrama with attractive locations.

d Jack Starret

David Janssen, Yaphet Kotto, Victoria Vetri, Elisha Cook Jnr, Joe de Santis

Night Club Scandal
US 1937 74m bw
Paramount

A society doctor murders his wife and incriminates her lover.
Smooth second feature remake of *Guilty as Hell*, chiefly notable for its star's last controlled performance.

w Lillie Hayward, *play* Riddle Me This by Daniel Rubin *d* Ralph Murphy

John Barrymore, Lynne Overman, Charles Bickford, Elizabeth Patterson, Evelyn Brent, Louise Campbell,
J. Carrol Naish

Night Creatures: see Captain Clegg

Night Flight*
US 1933 84m bw
MGM

The president of a civil airline insists that dangerous night flights must continue as a mark of progress.
Spurious, unsatisfactory, multi-star air melodrama lacking both narrative flow and the common touch.

w Oliver H. P. Garrett, *stories* Antoine de St Exupéry *d* Clarence Brown *ph* Oliver T. Marsh, Elmer Dyer, Charles Marshall

John Barrymore, Helen Hayes, Lionel Barrymore, Clark Gable, Robert Montgomery, Myrna Loy, William Gargan, C. Henry Gordon

'It is in the sense it conveys of human beings caught in the swift machinery of modern living that *Night Flight* soars above other pictures of its kind.'—*James Shelley Hamilton*

Night Gallery*
US 1969 98m Technicolor TVM
Universal (William Sackheim)

Three short stories of the supernatural, introduced by Rod Serling through paintings.
Not a bad package: the first is the best. The series ran for two years and repeated most of the plots from *Twilight Zone*.

w Rod Serling *d* Boris Sagal, Steven Spielberg, Barry Shear

Ossie Davis, George Macready, Roddy McDowall, Joan Crawford, Barry Sullivan, Richard Kiley, Sam Jaffe

Night Games
US 1974 74m colour TVM
Paramount (Thomas L. Miller, Edward K. Milkis)

A small-town lawyer defends a socialite on a murder charge.
The pilot for the series *Petrocelli*; routine competence in all departments.

w E. Jack Neuman *d* Don Taylor

Barry Newman, Susan Howard, Albert Salmi, Stefanie Powers, Anjanette Comer, Ralph Meeker, Henry Darrow

Night Hair Child
GB 1971 89m Movielab
Leander / Harry Alan Towers (Graham Harris)

A 12-year-old boy makes sexual advances to his stepmother.
Corrupt voyeuristic weirdie which has to be seen to be believed.

w Trevor Preston *d* James Killy *ph* Harry Waxman *m* Stelvio Cipriani

Mark Lester, Britt Ekland, Hardy Kruger, Harry Andrews, Lilli Palmer

Night Has a Thousand Eyes
US 1948 80m bw
Paramount (André Boehm)

A vaudeville mentalist finds that he really does have the power to predict the future.
Predictable supernatural melodrama closely modelled on *The Clairvoyant* (qv); quite nicely made but simply not exciting.

w Barre Lyndon, Jonathan Latimer, *novel* Cornell Woolrich *d* John Farrow *ph* John F. Seitz *m* Victor Young

Edward G. Robinson, Gail Russell, John Lund, Virginia Bruce, William Demarest, Richard Webb, Jerome Cowan

The Night Has Eyes*
GB 1942 79m bw
ABP (John Argyle)

A young teacher disappears on the Yorkshire moors; her friend goes in search, and comes under the influence of a strange young man and his sinister housekeeper.
Stagey but effective little thriller, with oodles of fog and bog to help the suspense.

w Alan Kennington *d* Leslie Arliss *ph* Gunther Krampf

James Mason, Joyce Howard, *Wilfrid Lawson, Mary Clare,* Tucker McGuire, John Fernald
'Some ingenuity and not a little style.'—*The Times*

The Night Holds Terror*
US 1955 86m bw
Columbia (Andrew Stone)

Three gunmen on the run kidnap a factory worker and hold him to ransom.
Effective, detailed, low-budget police melodrama; its plot may be over familiar now, but at the time it was refreshing and the whole film an intelligent exercise in suspense.

wd Andrew Stone ph Fred Jackman Jnr *m* Lucien Calliet

Jack Kelly, Hildy Parks, John Cassavetes, David Cross, Edward Marr, Jack Kruschen

A Night in Casablanca**
US 1946 85m bw
David L. Loew

Three zanies rout Nazi refugees in a North African hotel.
The last authentic Marxian extravaganza; it starts uncertainly, builds to a fine sustained frenzy, then peters out in some overstretched airplane acrobatics.

w Joseph Fields, Roland Kibbee, Frank Tashlin *d* Archie Mayo *ph* James Van Trees *m* Werner Janssen *pd* Duncan Cramer

Groucho, Chico, Harpo, Sig Rumann, Lisette Verea, Charles Drake, Lois Collier, Dan Seymour

A Night in Paradise
US 1946 84m Technicolor
(Universal) Walter Wanger

Aesop falls in love at the court of King Croesus.
Deadly boring, unintentionally funny Arabian Nights farrago without the saving grace of action.

w Ernest Pascal, Emmet Lavery, *novel* Peacock's Feather by George S. Hellman *d* Arthur Lubin *ph* Hal Mohr *m* Frank Skinner

Merle Oberon, Turhan Bey, Thomas Gomez, Gale Sondergaard, Ray Collins, George Dolenz, John Litel, Ernest Truex, Jerome Cowan, Douglass Dumbrille

Night into Morning
US 1951 86m bw
MGM (Edwin H. Knopf)

A college professor loses his wife and son in an accident; despair drives him to drink and attempted suicide.
Well-made and well meaning melodrama whose virtual absence of plot makes it seem by the end merely maudlin.

w Karl Tunberg, Leonard Spiegelgass *d* Fletcher Markle *ph* George Folsey *m* Carmen Dragon

Ray Milland, Nancy Davis, John Hodiak, Lewis Stone, Jean Hagen, Rosemary de Camp

Night Key
US 1937 67m bw
Universal

An inventor's idea is stolen by his former partner, and he takes an appropriate revenge.
Low-key star melodrama: competent, but no great shakes.

w Tristam Tupper, John C. Moffit *d* Lloyd Corrigan *ph* George Robinson *make up* Jack Pierce

Boris Karloff, Jean Rogers, Warren Hull, Samuel S. Hinds, Alan Baxter, Ward Bond, Edwin Maxwell

Night Monster
US 1942 73m bw
Universal
GB title: *House of Mystery*

Murders are committed in a spooky house by a cripple who produces synthetic legs by self-hypnotism.
Stilted, creaky would-be thriller with a good cast and an impertinent plot.

w Charles Upson Young *d* Ford Beebe *ph* Charles Van Enger

Ralph Morgan, Don Porter, Irene Hervey, Bela Lugosi, Lionel Atwill, Nils Asther, Leif Erickson, Frank Reicher

Night Moves*
US 1975 99m Technicolor
Warner / Hillier / Layton (Robert M. Sherman)

A private eye is engaged to find a runaway teenager.
Apparently a Chandlerish mystery, this is really a Pinterish audience-teaser with obsessions about communication and the meaning of life. A smart-ass entertainment for eager trendies.

w Alan Sharp *d* Arthur Penn *ph* Bruce Surtees *m* Michael Small *pd* George Jenkins

Gene Hackman, Jennifer Warren, Edward Binns, Harris Yulin, Kenneth Mars

'Beneath the complicated unravelling of a mystery, an anti-mystery, with the hero's detection registering as an evasion of his own problems; beneath a densely charted intrigue of betrayals and cross purposes, a cryptic void . . .'—*Jonathan Rosenbaum*

'A suspenseless suspenser . . . there's very little rhyme or reason for the plot's progression.'—*Variety*

Night Must Fall**
US 1937 117m bw
MGM (Hunt Stromberg)

A bland young bellboy who is really a psychopathic murderer attaches himself to the household of a rich old lady.
Unconvincing but memorable Hollywood expansion of an effective British chiller.

w John Van Druten, *play* Emlyn Williams *d* Richard Thorpe *ph* Ray June *m* Edward Ward

Robert Montgomery, Rosalind Russell, *May Whitty*, Alan Marshal, Merle Tottenham, Kathleen Harrison, Matthew Boulton, E. E. Clive

'A pretty little murder play has made a long dim film.'—*Graham Greene*

Night Must Fall
GB 1964 105m bw
MGM (Albert Finney, Karel Reisz)

Dreary remake with a mannered star performance and the emphasis on axe murders.
A mistake from beginning to end.

w Clive Exton *d* Karel Reisz *ph* Freddie Francis *m* Ron Grainer

Albert Finney, Susan Hampshire, Mona Washbourne, Sheila Hancock, Michael Medwin, Joe Gladwin, Martin Wyldeck

'Not so much a thriller as a typically humourless example of that overworked genre known as psychological drama . . . (Finney) constantly recalls a ventriloquist's dummy.'—*MFB*

The Night My Number Came Up*
GB 1954 94m bw
Ealing (Tom Morahan)

A man dreams that his plane will crash, and the dream begins to come true.

Intriguing little melodrama which badly lacks a twist ending and foxes itself by a flashback construction which leaves very little open to doubt. Production generally good.

w R. C. Sheriff *d* Leslie Norman *ph* Lionel Banes *m* Malcolm Arnold

Michael Redgrave, Alexander Knox, Sheila Sim, Denholm Elliott, Ursula Jeans, George Rose, Nigel Stock, Michael Hordern, Ralph Truman, Victor Maddern, Bill Kerr, Alfie Bass

Night Nurse*

US 1931 72m bw
Warner

A nurse uncovers a plot by other members of the household against her patient's children.
Fast-moving melodrama with solid star performances; just what the public wanted in 1931.

w Oliver H. P. Garrett, *novel* Dora Macy *d* William Wellman *ph* Chick McGill

Barbara Stanwyck, Ben Lyon, Joan Blondell, Clark Gable, Charles Winninger, Vera Lewis, Blanche Frederici, Charlotte Merriam

'A conglomeration of exaggerations, often bordering on serial dramatics.'—*Hollywood Reporter*

Night of Terror*

US 1972 73m colour TVM
Paramount (Edward J. Mikis)

A young woman is terrorized by an unknown assailant.
Nothing new, but plenty of suspense and inventive use of locations.

d Jeannot Szwarc

Donna Mills, Eddie Egan, Martin Balsam, Chuck Connors, Agnes Moorehead

Night of the Demon***

GB 1957 82m bw
Columbia / Sabre (Frank Bevis)
US title: *Curse of the Demon*

An occultist despatches his enemies by raising a giant medieval devil.
Despite dim work from the leads, this supernatural thriller is intelligently scripted and achieves several frightening and memorable sequences in the best Hitchcock manner.

w Charles Bennett, Hal E. Chester, story Casting the Runes by *M. R. James d Jacques Tourneur ph* Ted Scaife *m* Clifton Parker *ad* Ken Adam

Dana Andrews, Peggy Cummins, *Niall MacGinnis, Athene Seyler*, Brian Wilde, Maurice Denham, Ewan Roberts, Liam Redmond, Reginald Beckwith

Night of the Eagle**

GB 1961 87m bw
Independent Artists (Albert Fennell)

At a medical school, a jealous witch sets an evil force on her rival.
Pretty good supernatural thriller, let down by leading performances and sustained by character roles and solid production values in creepy sequences.

w Charles Beaumont, Richard Matheson, George Baxt, *novel* Burn Witch Burn by Fritz Leiber *d Sidney Hayers ph* Reg Wyer *m* William Alwyn

Margaret Johnston, Janet Blair, Peter Wyngarde, Anthony Nicholls, Reginald Beckwith, Kathleen Byron

The Night of the Following Day*

US 1969 100m Technicolor
Universal / Gina (Hubert Cornfield)

A young girl arriving in Paris to stay with her father is kidnapped and held to ransom by an eccentric gang.
Straightforward suspense thriller with delusions of grandeur; the second half bogs down in pretentious talk and the end suggests that the whole thing was a dream.

w Hubert Cornfield, Robert Phippeny, *novel* The Snatchers by Lionel White *d Hubert Cornfield ph* Willy Kurant *m* Stanley Myers

Marlon Brando, Richard Boone, Rita Moreno, Pamela Franklin, Jess Hahn

The Night of the Generals**

GB 1967 148m Technicolor Panavision
Columbia / Horizon / Filmsonor (Sam Spiegel)

A German intelligence agent tracks down a psychopathic Nazi general who started killing prostitutes in Warsaw during World War I.
A curiously bumpy narrative which is neither mystery nor character study but does provide a few effective sequences and impressive performances. The big budget seems well spent.

w Joseph Kessel, Paul Dehn, *novel* Hans Helmut Hirst *d* Anatole Litvak *ph* Henri Decaë *m* Maurice Jarre *pd* Alexander Trauner

Peter O'Toole, *Omar Sharif, Tom Courtenay,* Donald Pleasance, Joanna Pettet, *Philippe Noiret*, Charles Gray, Coral Brown, John Gregson, Harry Andrews, Nigel Stock, Christopher Plummer, Juliette Greco

'The "who" is obvious from the first and the "dunit" interminable.'—*Judith Crist, 1973*

The Night of the Grizzly
US 1966 102m Techniscope
Paramount (Burt Dunne)

A Wyoming ex-sheriff kills a marauding bear and earns the respect of his son.
Stout-hearted family film, rather sluggishly made.

w Warren Douglas *d* Joseph Pevney *ph* Harold Lipstein, Loyal Griggs *m* Leith Stevens

Clint Walker, Martha Hyer, Keenan Wynn, Leo Gordon, Kevin Brodie, Nancy Kulp, Ellen Corby, Jack Elam, Ron Ely

The Night of the Hunter***
US 1955 93m bw
UA / Paul Gregory

A psychopathic preacher goes on the trail of hidden money, the secret of which is held by two children.
Weird, manic fantasy in which evil finally comes to grief against the forces of sweetness and light (the children, an old lady, water, animals). Although the narrative does not flow smoothly there are splendidly imaginative moments, and no other film has ever quite achieved its texture.

w James Agee, novel Davis Grubb *d Charles Laughton ph Stanley Cortez m* Walter Schumann

Robert Mitchum, Shelley Winters, Lillian Gish, Don Beddoe, Evelyn Varden, Peter Graves, James Gleason

'One of the most frightening movies ever made.'—*Pauline Kael, 1968*

'A genuinely sinister work, full of shocks and over-emphatic sound effects, camera angles and shadowy lighting.'—*NFT, 1973*

'One of the most daring, eloquent and personal films to have come from America in a long time.'—*Derek Prouse*

The Night of the Iguana***
US 1964 125m bw
MGM / Seven Arts (Ray Stark)

A disbarred clergyman becomes a travel courier in Mexico and is sexually desired by a teenage nymphomaniac, a middle-aged hotel owner and a frustrated itinerant artist.
The author is most tolerable when poking fun at his own types, and this is a sharp, funny picture with a touch of poetry.

w Anthony Veiller, *play Tennessee Williams d John Huston ph Gabriel Figueroa m* Benjamin Frankel *ad* Stephen Grimes

Richard Burton, Deborah Kerr, Ava Gardner, Sue Lyon, *Grayson Hall, Cyril Delevanti*

Night of the Lepus
US 1972 88m Metrocolor
MGM (A. C. Lyles)

A serum meant to control a surplus of rabbits instead produces monster varieties four feet tall.
Tolerable sci-fi tailored to a very tired formula.

w Don Holiday, Gene R. Kearney *d* William F. Claxton *ph* Ted Voigtlander *m* Jimmie Haskell

Stuart Whitman, Rory Calhoun, Janet Leigh, Paul Fix, De Forrest Kelley

'For insomniacs with lax standards.'—*Judith Crist*

Night Passage*
US 1957 90m Technirama
U-I (Aaron Rosenberg)

A railroad worker entrusted with a payroll finds that the bandits trying to rob it are led by his own brother.
Obscurely titled and rather empty western providing standard excitements.

w Borden Chase *d* James Neilson *ph* William Daniels *m* Dmitri Tiomkin

James Stewart, Audie Murphy, Dan Duryea, Brandon de Wilde, Dianne Foster

Night People*
US 1954 93m Technicolor
Cinemascope
TCF (Nunnally Johnson)

When a US corporal stationed in Berlin is kidnapped by the Russians, his influential father flies into action.
Curiously titled cold war suspenser which would have been more memorable if not in Cinemascope; the pace and talent are visible, but the wide screen and poor colour dissipate them.

wd Nunnally Johnson ph Charles G. Clarke *m* Cyril Mockridge

Gregory Peck, Broderick Crawford, Anita Bjork, Walter Abel, Rita Gam, Buddy Ebsen, Jill Esmond, Peter Van Eyck

Night Slaves*
US 1970 74m colour TVM
Bing Crosby Productions (Everett Chambers)

In a small peaceful hotel, a man wakes up to find that his wife has been abducted by alien forces which have taken over the town.
Unexpected, intriguing sci-fi.

w Everett Chambers, Robert Specht *d* Ted Post

James Franciscus, Lee Grant, Leslie Nielsen, Tisha Sterling, Andrew Prine

Night Song
US 1947 101m bw
RKO (Harriet Parsons)

A wealthy socialite falls for a blind pianist and pretends to be blind also, and poor to boot.
Silly, pretentious soaper, moodily photographed.

w Frank Fenton, Irving Hyland, De Witt Bodeen *d* John Cromwell *ph Lucien Ballard* *m* Leith Stevens

Dana Andrews, Merle Oberon, Hoagy Carmichael, Ethel Barrymore, Artur Rubenstein, Eugene Ormandy

The Night Stalker*
US 1971 73m colour TVM
Aaron Spelling

A vampire stalks Las Vegas.
Horror comic with a sense of humour.

w Richard Matheson *d* John Llewellyn Moxey

Darren McGavin, Carol Lynley, Simon Oakland, Claude Akins, Charles McGraw, Barry Atwater, Elisha Cook Jnr, Kent Smith

The Night Strangler*
US 1972 74m colour TVM
Aaron Spelling / Dan Curtis

The reporter who tracked down the night stalker turns his attention to Seattle and a multi-murderer 120 years old.
More horror nonsense, rather less effective than before, but highly watchable. The two films led to a monster series called *Kolchak: The Night Stalker* (which made no sense); a more stylish pilot had been tried in *The Norliss Tapes* (qv).

w Richard Matheson *d* Dan Curtis

Darren McGavin, Jo Ann Pflug, Simon Oakland, Scott Brady, Margaret Hamilton, Wally Cox, John Carradine

The Night that Panicked America**
US 1975 100m colour TVM
Paramount (Anthony Wilson, Joseph Sargent)

An account of Orson Welles' 1938 broadcast of *The War of the Worlds* and the effect it had on the nation.
The studio recreation is excellent, but the film bogs down when it deals with the domestic dramas, which are totally predictable.

w Nicholas Meyer, Anthony Wilson *d* Joseph Sargent

Vic Morrow, Cliff de Young, Michael Constantine, Paul Shenar, Walter McGinn, Meredith Baxter, Tom Bosley, Will Geer

The Night They Raided Minsky's**
US 1968 99m De Luxe
UA / Tandem (Norman Lear)
GB title: *The Night They Invented Striptease*

Various human problems are posed and solved during a night at a burlesque theatre.
Marvellous kaleidoscopic ragbag of brilliant fragments which unfortunately don't cohere in the mind into a really memorable film, though it gives detailed pleasure on every viewing.

w Arnold Schulman, Sidney Michaels, Norman Lear, *book* Rowland Barber *d William Friedkin* *ph Andrew Laszlo* *m Charles Strouse* *pd William Eckar, Jean Eckar* *ch* Danny Daniels *narrator* Rudy Vallee

Jason Robards, Britt Ekland, *Norman Wisdom*, Forrest Tucker, Joseph Wiseman, Bert Lahr, Harry Andrews, Denholm Elliott, Elliot Gould, Jack Burns

A Night to Remember*
US 1941 91m bw
Columbia (Samuel Bischoff)

A Greenwich Village mystery-writing couple try to solve a murder.
Reasonably sparkling comedy whodunnit with a zany tinge.

w Richard Flournoy, Jack Henley *d* Richard Wallace *ph* Joseph Walker *m* Morris Stoloff

Loretta Young, Brian Aherne, Jeff Donnell, William Wright, Sidney Toler, Gale Sondergaard, Donald MacBride, Lee Patrick, Blanche Yurka

A Night to Remember***
GB 1958 123m bw
Rank (William Macquitty)

The story of the 1912 sea disaster when the *Titanic* struck an iceberg.
A major film enterprise featuring hundreds of cameos, none discernibly more important than the other. On this account the film seems alternately stiff and flabby as narrative, but there is much to enjoy and admire along the way, though the sense of awe is dissipated by the final model shots.

w Eric Ambler, book Walter Lord *d Roy Baker* *ph Geoffrey Unsworth* *m* William Alwyn

Kenneth More, Honor Blackman, Michael Goodliffe, David McCallum, George Rose, Anthony Bushell, Ralph Michael, John Cairney, Kenneth Griffith, Frank Lawton, Michael Bryant

'A worthy, long-drawn-out documentary, with noticeably more honesty about human nature than most films, but little shape or style.'—*Kenneth Cavender*

Night Train to Munich***
GB 1940 93m bw
TCF (Edward Black)
aka: *Gestapo; Night Train*

A British agent poses as a Nazi in order to rescue a Czech inventor.
First-rate comedy suspenser obviously inspired by the success of *The Lady Vanishes* and providing much the same measure of thrills and laughs.

w Frank Launder, Sidney Gilliat, novel Gordon Wellesley *d Carol Reed ph* Otto Kanturek *m* Louis Levy

Margaret Lockwood, *Rex Harrison, Basil Radford, Naunton Wayne,* Paul Henreid, Keneth Kent, Felix Aylmer, Roland Culver, *Eliot Makeham, Raymond Huntley*, Wyndham Goldie

'A very nice triumph of skill and maturity in films, and thus a pleasure to have.'—*Otis Ferguson*

Night unto Night*
US 1949 85m bw
Warner (Owen Crump)

An epileptic scientist falls for a girl hallucinated by the ghost of her dead husband.
Cheerless nuthouse melodrama, one of the well-meant aberrations which Hollywood studios used to produce as a sop to conscience.

w Kathryn Scola, *novel* Philip Wylie *d Don Siegel ph* Peverell Marley *m* Franz Waxman

Ronald Reagan, Viveca Lindfors, Rosemary de Camp, Broderick Crawford, Osa Massen, Craig Stevens, Erskine Sanford

The Night Walker*
US 1964 86m bw
U-I / William Castle

The widow of a tough executive, killed and disfigured in an explosion, is haunted in her dreams not only by him but by a mysterious lover who turns up in reality.
Stiff and unconvincing but still fairly frightening low-budget shocker with a plot twist or two.

w Robert Bloch d William Castle *ph* Harold Stine *m* Vic Mizzy

Robert Taylor, *Barbara Stanwyck*, Lloyd Bochner, Rochelle Hudson, Judi Meredith, Hayden Rorke

Night Watch
GB 1973 98m Technicolor
Avco / Brut (David White)

A widow recovering from a nervous breakdown keeps seeing bodies in the night. Her friends try to help, but things are not quite what they seem.
Predictable coiled-spring shocker which goes curiously flat despite a star cast and lashings of blood. Perhaps we have all been here once too often.

w Tony Williamson, *play* Lucille Fletcher *d* Brian G. Hutton *ph* Billie Williams *m* John Cameron

Elizabeth Taylor, Laurence Harvey, Billie Whitelaw, Robert Lang, Tony Britton, Bill Dean

'It has all the trappings of a Joan Crawford vehicle of the forties, with numerous elegant dresses for Miss Taylor, an appropriately unbecoming wardrobe for Miss Whitelaw, and a set which is an art director's dream.'—*Brenda Davies*

Night without Sleep
US 1952 77m bw
TCF (Robert Bassler)

A man reconstructs his drunken actions the night before, and fears he has committed a murder.
Dreary melodrama, all frayed tempers drunkenness and cigarette smoke.

w Frank Partos, Elick Moll *d* Roy Baker *ph* Lucien Ballard

Gary Merrill, Linda Darnell, Hildegarde Neff, Hugh Beaumont, Mae Marsh

The Nightcomers*
GB 1971 96m Technicolor
Scimitar / Kastner–Kanter–Ladd (Michael Winner)

How the ghost-ridden children in *The Turn of the Screw* became evil; they became involved in aberrant sexual activities between the gardener and the housekeeper, and finally murdered the former.
Despite its unexpected literariness this is unpleasant and unconvincing nonsense with a boring script punctuated by shock cuts and very little period feel.

w Michael Hastings *d* Michael Winner *ph* Robert Paynter *m* Jerry Fielding

Stephanie Beacham, Marlon Brando, Thora Hird, Harry Andrews, Verna Harvey, Christopher Ellis

Nightfall*
US 1957 78m bw
Columbia (Ted Richmond)

The police and two bank robbers chase an innocent artist who happens to know that the loot is hidden in a Wisconsin snowdrift.
Occasionally stylish but obscurely narrated suspenser.

w Stirling Silliphant, *novel* David Goodis

d Jacques Tourneur *ph* Burnett Guffey
m George Duning

Anne Bancroft, Aldo Ray, Brian Keith, James Gregory, Jocelyn Brando, Frank Albertson

Nightmare*
US 1956 89m bw
UA / Pine–Thomas / Shane (Maxwell Shane)

A young musician is hypnotized into committing a murder, and reconstructs his actions with the help of his policeman brother-in-law.
Lethargic remake of the ingenious *Fear in the Night* (qv). Watchable.

wd Maxwell Shane, *novel* Cornell Woolrich
ph Joseph Biroc *m* Herschel Burke Gilbert

Edward G. Robinson, Kevin McCarthy, Virginia Christine, Connie Russell

Nightmare*
GB 1964 82m bw Hammerscope
U-I / Hammer (Jimmy Sangster)

18-year-old Janet still has nightmares after seeing her mad mother kill her father six years ago; brought home, even more frightening visions afflict her.
Genuinely scary *Diabolique*-type mystery with the usual Hammer borrowings put to good use.

w Jimmy Sangster *d* Freddie Francis *ph* John Wilcox *m* Don Banks

Moira Redmond, David Knight, Brenda Bruce, John Welsh, *Jennie Linden*

Nightmare*
US 1973 75m colour TVM
Mark Carliner

A man in a Manhattan apartment witnesses a murder and becomes the quarry of the killers.
The old old story, excitingly filmed but foolish in detail.

w David Wiltse *d* William Hale

Richard Crenna, Patty Duke, Vic Morrow

Nightmare Alley**
US 1947 112m bw
TCF

A fairground barker becomes a successful confidence trickster dealing with the supernatural, but finally sinks to the depths.
Unusual road to ruin melodrama, a striking oddity from Hollywood at the time, and still quite interesting and well done.

w Jules Furthman, novel William Lindsay Gresham *d Edmund Goulding* *ph Lee Garmes*
m Cyril Mockridge

Tyrone Power, Coleen Gray, Joan Blondell, *Taylor Holmes*, Helen Walker, Mike Mazurki, Ian Keith

Nightmare in Chicago
US 1964 80m colour TVM
Universal

A hunted killer finds himself trapped by police road blocks and commits more violence in an attempt to escape from the city.
Rough, occasionally vivid police story which eventually becomes tiresome to watch.

w David Moessinger *d* Robert Altman

Robert Ridgeley, Charles McGraw, Philip Abbott

Nightmare in the Sun*
US 1963 81m De Luxe
Afilmco (Marc Lawrence, John Derek)

A rich man kills his wife and blames a hitch-hiker who has had a brief affair with her.
Modest independent melodrama, quite interestingly made though not entirely effective.

w Ted Thomas *d* Marc Lawrence *ph* Stanley Cortez *m* Paul Glass

John Derek, Ursula Andress, Arthur O'Connell, Aldo Ray

Nikki, Wild Dog of the North*
US 1961 74m Technicolor
Walt Disney (Winston Hibler)

The life of a Canadian trapper's wolf dog.
Pleasing 'true life fiction' which didn't quite reach top feature status.

w Ralph Wright, Winston Hibler, *novel* James Oliver Curwood *d* Jack Couffer *m* Oliver Wallace

Emile Genest, Jean Coutu

Nine Girls
US 1944 78m bw
Columbia (Burt Kelly)

College girls are murdered in a sorority house.
Cheapjack whodunnit with a cardboard look and feel.

w Karen de Wolff, Connie Lee, *play* Wilfred H. Pettit *d* Leigh Jason *ph* James Van Trees
m John Leopold

Ann Harding, Evelyn Keyes, Jinx Falkenberg, Anita Louise, Leslie Brooks, Lynn Merrick, Jeff Donnell, Nina Foch, Marcia Mae Jones, William Demarest

Nine Hours to Rama
GB 1962 125m De Luxe Cinemascope
TCF / Red Lion (Mark Robson)

Events leading to the assassination of Mahatma Gandhi.
Fictionalized, sensationalized and very dull, this multi-character drama holds interest only for snatches of acting and location backgrounds.

w Nelson Gidding, *novel* Stanley Wolpert *d* Mark Robson *ph* Arthur Ibbetson *m* Malcolm Arnold

Jose Ferrer, Diane Baker, Robert Morley, J. S. Casshyap, Horst Buchholz, Harry Andrews

'The only interesting line in the movie is the thick brown one visible on the inside of every white collar.'—*John Simon*

1984*
GB 1955 91m bw
Holiday (N. Peter Rathvon)

Europe has become the fascist state of Oceania, ruled by Big Brother; Winston Smith yearns for the old days, and is brainwashed.
The famous prophecy of a dehumanized future is followed with reasonable fidelity apart from the defiant ending, but the novel is too literary for cinematic success and the result is too often both downbeat and boring.

w William P. Templeton, Ralph Bettinson, *novel George Orwell d Michael Anderson ph* C. Pennington Richards *m* Malcolm Arnold

Michael Redgrave, Edmond O'Brien, Jan Sterling, David Kossoff, Mervyn Johns, Donald Pleasance

1900**
US / Italy 1976 320m Technicolor
Paramount–UA–TCF / PEA (Alberto Grimaldi)

Events affecting a modern Italian family as fascism takes hold.
Immensely long domestic epic with brilliant strokes lost in the great voids of time when little seems to happen.

wd Bernardo Bertolucci ph Vittorio Storaro *m* Ennio Morricone

Burt Lancaster, Robert de Niro, Sterling Hayden, Dominique Sanda, Donald Sutherland, Alida Valli

99 and 44/100 Per Cent Dead
US 1974 98m De Luxe Panavision
Joe Wizan / Vashon
aka: *Call Harry Crown*

A losing gang boss hires a trouble shooter.
Violent gangster melodrama apparently intended as a black comedy; if so, as clumsy as its title.

w Robert Dillon *d* John Frankenheimer *ph* Ralph Woolsey *m* Henry Mancini

Richard Harris, Edmond O'Brien, Bradford Dillman, Ann Turkel, Chuck Connors, Constance Ford

'Esthetically, commercially and morally, a quintessential fiasco.'—*Variety*

99 River Street*
US 1953 83m bw
UA / Edward Small

A taxi driver becomes involved in a diamond robbery.
Adequate thick ear with quite good detection and action sequences.

w Robert Smith *d Phil Karlson ph* Franz Planer

John Payne, Evelyn Keyes, Frank Faylen, Brad Dexter, Peggie Castle

Ninotchka***
US 1939 110m bw
MGM (Ernst Lubitsch)

A Paris playboy falls for a communist emissary sent to sell some crown jewels.
Sparkling comedy on a theme which has been frequently explored; delicate pointing and hilarious character comedy sustain this version perfectly until the last half hour, when it certainly sags; but it remains a favourite Hollywood example of this genre.

w Charles Brackett, Billy Wilder, Walter Reisch, story Melchior Lengyel *d Ernst Lubitsch ph William Daniels m* Werner Heymann

Greta Garbo, Melvyn Douglas, Sig Rumann, Alexander Granach, Felix Bressart, Ina Claire, Bela Lugosi

'The Lubitsch style, in which much was made of subtleties—glances, finger movements, raised eyebrows—has disappeared. Instead we have a hard, brightly lit, cynical comedy with the wisecrack completely in control.'—*John Baxter, 1968*

No Blade of Grass
GB 1970 97m Metrocolor Panavision
MGM (Cornel Wilde)

Industrial pollution sets a destructive virus ruining the crops of the world: anarchy spreads through Britain and one family takes refuge in the Lake District.
Apocalyptic sci-fi, moderately well done though so humourless as to be almost funny.

w Sean Forestal, Jefferson Pascal, *novel* John Christopher *d* Cornel Wilde *ph* H. A. R. Thompson *m* Burnell Whibley

Nigel Davenport, Jean Wallace, Patrick Holt, John Hamill

No Deposit, No Return
US 1976 112m Technicolor
Walt Disney (Ron Miller)

Airport confusion causes crooks to abduct (unwittingly) a millionaire's grandchildren; the millionaire gives chase.
Overlong and tedious action comedy which makes little sense.

w Arthur Alsberg, Don Nelson *d* Norman Tokar *ph* Frank Phillips *m* Buddy Baker

David Niven, Darren McGavin, Don Knotts, Herschel Bernardi, Barbara Feldon, John Williams, Vic Tayback, Kim Richards

No Down Payment**
US 1957 105m bw Cinemascope
TCF (Jerry Wald)

Tension among smart suburban couples in a Los Angeles housing development.
Lively domestic melodrama, very useful to sociologists as a mirror of its times.

w Philip Yordan, novel John McPartland *d Martin Ritt ph* Joseph La Shelle *m* Leigh Harline

Joanne Woodward, Tony Randall, Sheree North, Jeffrey Hunter, Cameron Mitchell, Patricia Owens, Barbara Rush, Pat Hingle

No Funny Business
GB 1933 75m bw
John Stafford

Two professional co-respondents are sent to the Riviera; each mistakes the other as his client.
Stagey farce, notable for its unlikely star teaming and its hilariously dated style.

w Victor Hanbury, Frank Vosper, Dorothy Hope *d* John Stafford, Victor Hanbury

Gertrude Lawrence, Laurence Olivier, Jill Esmond, Edmund Breon, Gibb McLaughlin, Muriel Aked

No Highway**
GB 1951 98m bw
TCF (Louis D. Lighton)
US title: *No Highway in the Sky*

During a transatlantic flight, a boffin works out that the plane's tail is about to fall off from metal fatigue.
The central premise of this adaptation from a popular novel is fascinating, but the romantic asides are a distraction and the characters cardboard; the film still entertains through sheer professionalism.

w R. C. Sheriff, Oscar Millard, Alec Coppel, *novel* Nevil Shute *d* Henry Koster *ph* Georges Périnal

James Stewart, Marlene Dietrich, Glynis Johns, Jack Hawkins, Janette Scott, Elizabeth Allan, Kenneth More, Niall MacGinnis, Ronald Squire

No Leave, No Love
US 1946 118m bw
MGM (Joe Pasternak)

Sailors on leave meet an English girl.
Witless, overlong musical extravaganza.

w Charles Martin, Leslie Karkos *d* Charles Martin *ph* Harold Rosson, Robert Surtees *md* Georgie Stoll

Van Johnson, Pat Kirkwood, Keenan Wynn, Guy Lombardo and his Orchestra, Edward Arnold, Marie Wilson, Leon Ames

No Love for Johnnie*
GB 1960 111m bw Cinemascope
Rank / Five Star (Betty E. Box)

The personal and political problems of a Labour MP.
Predictable but quite lively study of ambition and frustration, with good cameos; Cinemascope all but ruins its impact.

w Nicholas Phipps, Mordecai Richler, *novel* Wilfred Fienburgh *d* Ralph Thomas *ph* Ernest Steward *m* Malcolm Arnold

Peter Finch, Mary Peach, *Stanley Holloway*, Donald Pleasance, Billie Whitelaw, Hugh Burden, Rosalie Crutchley, Michael Goodliffe, Mervyn Johns, Geoffrey Keen, Paul Rogers, Dennis Price, Peter Barkworth, Fenella Fielding, Gladys Henson

No Man Is an Island
US 1962 114m Eastmancolor
U-I / Gold Coast (John Monks Jnr, Richard Goldstone)
GB title: *Island Escape*

After the Japanese attack on Guam, a radioman finds refuge in a leper colony and sets up his own resistance unit.
Unexceptionable war adventure in the jungle.

wd John Monks Jnr, Richard Goldstone *ph* Carl Kayser *m* Restie Umali

Jeffrey Hunter, Marshall Thompson, Barbara Perez, Ronald Remy
'Good clean fun for right-minded teenagers.'—*MFB*

No Man of Her Own*
US 1932 98m bw
Paramount

A big-time gambler marries a local girl on a bet and tries to keep her innocent of his activities.

Star romantic comedy drama, quite professionally assembled and played.

w Maurine Watkins, Milton H. Gropper *d* Wesley Ruggles *ph* Leo Tover

Clark Gable, Carole Lombard, Dorothy Mackail, Grant Mitchell, George Barbier, Elizabeth Patterson, J. Farrell MacDonald

'Just about everything that the ordinary picture fan looks for: drama, romance, comedy, strong build-ups, exciting climaxes, a fine line of human interest.'—*Film Daily*

No Man of Her Own*
US 1949 98m bw
Paramount (Richard Maibaum)

A pregnant wanderer is involved in a train crash and assumes the identity of the wife of a dead passenger.
Glossy star melodrama, very watchable.

w Catherine Turney, Sally Benson, Mitchell Leisen *d Mitchell Leisen* *ph* Daniel L. Fapp *m* Hugo Friedhofer

Barbara Stanwyck, John Lund, Lyle Bettger, *Jane Cowl*, Phyllis Thaxter, Henry O'Neill, Richard Denning

No Minor Vices
US 1948 96m bw
(MGM) Enterprise

A doctor brings home an artist friend who proceeds to wreck his household.
Interminable thin comedy which gives no clue as to what the talent involved thought it was doing.

w Arnold Manoff *d* Lewis Milestone *ph* George Barnes *m* Franz Waxman

Dana Andrews, Lilli Palmer, Louis Jourdan, Jane Wyatt, Norman Lloyd

No More Ladies
US 1935 79m bw
MGM

A society girl thinks that by marrying a rake she can reform him.
Breezy sophisticated comedy which doesn't quite maintain its impetus.

w Donald Ogden Stewart, Horace Jackson, *play* A. E. Thomas *d* Edward H. Griffith, George Cukor *ph* Oliver T. Marsh

Joan Crawford, Robert Montgomery, Franchot Tone, Charles Ruggles, Edna May Oliver, Gail Patrick, Reginald Denny, Arthur Treacher

No Orchids for Miss Blandish
GB 1948 102m bw
Renown (A. R. Shipman, Oswald Mitchell)

An heiress is kidnapped by gangsters and falls for their psychopathic leader.
Hilariously awful gangster movie from a bestselling shocker.
Everyone concerned is all at sea, and the result is one of the worst films ever made.

wd St John L. Clowes, *novel* James Hadley Chase *ph* Gerald Gibbs

Jack La Rue, Linden Travers, Hugh McDermott, Walter Crisham, Lily Molnar, Zoe Gail

'This must be the most sickening exhibition of brutality, perversion, sex and sadism ever to be shown on a cinema screen . . . with pseudo-American accents the actors literally battle their way through a script laden with suggestive dialogue.'—*MFB*

† Remade as *The Grissom Gang* (qv).

No Place to Run
US 1972 73m colour TVM
Spelling–Goldberg

An old man flees to Canada with his orphan grandson of whom he can't get legal custody.
Patchy action drama with weepy interludes.

w James G. Hirsch *d* Delbert Mann

Herschel Bernardi, Larry Hagman, Stefanie Powers, Neville Brand, Scott Jacoby

No Questions Asked
US 1951 80m bw
MGM (Nicholas Nayfack)

A young lawyer undertakes shady business and finds himself framed for murder.
Well made second feature on conventional lines.

w Sidney Sheldon *d* Harold Kress *ph* Harold Lipstein *m* Leith Stevens

Barry Sullivan, George Murphy, Arlene Dahl, Jean Hagen, William Reynolds, Mari Blanchard

No Resting Place
GB 1951 77m bw
Colin Lesslie

A wandering Irish tinker accidentally kills a man and is hounded by a Civil Guard.
Interesting attempt at realistic location drama, suffering from a dejected plot and unsympathetic characters.

w Paul Rotha, Colin Lesslie, Michael Orrom, *novel* Ian Niall *ph* Wolfgang Suschitsky *m* William Alwyn

Michael Gough, Noel Purcell, Jack McGowran

No Room at the Inn
GB 1948 82m bw
British National (Ivan Foxwell)

A monstrous woman half-starves evacuees and turns her house into a brothel.
Absurd melodrama from a play which was popular because it offered a full-blooded star performance. The film is less convincing but works pretty well on its level.

w Ivan Foxwell, Dylan Thomas, *play* Joan Temple *d* Dan Birt

Freda Jackson, Joy Shelton, Hermione Baddeley, Joan Dowling, Harcourt Williams, Sydney Tafler, Frank Pettingell, Niall MacGinnis

No Sad Songs for Me
US 1950 89m bw
Columbia (Buddy Adler)

A young wife discovers she has only eight months to live, and spends it planning her husband's future.
Well-meant but rather icky melodrama featuring one of those beautiful illnesses that appear to have no physical effect.

w Howard Koch, *novel* Ruth Southard *d* Rudolph Maté *ph* Joseph Walker *m* George Duning

Margaret Sullavan, Wendell Corey, Viveca Lindfors, Natalie Wood, John McIntire

No Sex Please, We're British*
GB 1973 91m Technicolor
Columbia / BHP (John R. Sloan)

A wrongly addressed parcel of dirty postcards causes chaos when it arrives at a bank.
Archetypal British farce with less plot than one might expect, but quite brightly performed.

w Anthony Marriott, Johnnie Mortimer, Brian Cooke, *play* Anthony Marriott, Alistair Foot *d* Cliff Owen *ph* Ken Hodges *m* Eric Rogers

Ronnie Corbett, Beryl Reid, *Arthur Lowe*, Ian Ogilvy, Susan Penhaligon, David Swift, Michael Bates, Gerald Sim

No Time for Comedy*
US 1940 93m bw
Warner (Robert Lord)

A playwright is depressed by the times and has lost the knack of making people laugh.
Smooth film version of a thoughtful romantic comedy play.

w Julius J. and Philip G. Epstein, *play S. N. Behrman* *d* William Keighley *ph* Ernest Haller *m* Heinz Roemheld

James Stewart, Rosalind Russell, Charles Ruggles, Genevieve Tobin, Allyn Joslyn, Clarence Kolb, Louise Beavers

No Time for Love*
US 1943 83m bw
Paramount (Mitchell Leisen)

A lady photographer falls for the foreman of a crew digging a tunnel under the Hudson.
Agreeable romantic slapstick farce.

w Claude Binyon *d* Mitchell Leisen *ph* Charles Lang Jnr *m* Victor Young

Claudette Colbert, Fred MacMurray, Ilka Chase, Richard Haydn, June Havoc, Marjorie Gateson, Bill Goodwin

No Time for Sergeants
US 1958 111m bw
Warner (Mervyn Le Roy)

Adventures of a hillbilly army conscript.
Heavy-handed adaptation of the stage success, a real piece of filmed theatre with not much sparkle to it.

w John Lee Mahin, *play* Ira Levin, *novel* Mac Hyman *d* Mervyn Le Roy *ph* Harold Rosson *m* Ray Heindorf

Andy Griffith, William Fawcett, Murray Hamilton, Nick Adams, Myron McCormick, Bartlett Robinson

No Trees in the Street
GB 1958 96m bw
ABP / Allegro (Frank Godwin)

Problems of a London slum family in the thirties.
Artificial and unconvincing attempt at a London *Love on the Dole*, dragged up and redigested in a later era when 'realism' was thought to be fashionable.

w Ted Willis, from his play *d* J. Lee-Thompson *ph* Gilbert Taylor *m* Laurie Johnson

Sylvia Syms, Herbert Lom, Joan Miller, Melvyn Hayes, Stanley Holloway, Liam Redmond, Ronald Howard, Carole Lesley, Lana Morris, Lily Kann

'Nothing remains but crude sensationalism and several moments of unconscious humour.'—*MFB*

No Way Out*
US 1950 106m bw
TCF (Darryl F. Zanuck)

A crook stirs up racial feeling against a black doctor in whose hands his brother has died.
Vivid, hard-hitting melodrama with a hospital background and a strong sociological flavour.

w Joseph L. Mankiewicz, Lesser Samuels *d* Joseph L. Mankiewicz *ph Milton Krasner* *m* Alfred Newman

Richard Widmark, Sidney Poitier, Linda

Darnell, Stephen McNally, Harry Bellaver, Stanley Ridges, Ossie Davis, Ruby Dee

No Way to Treat a Lady*
US 1968 108m Technicolor
Paramount / Sol C. Siegel

A mass murderer of women who is also a master of disguise has a running battle with a police detective.
Curious mixture of star show-off piece, murder mystery, black farce, suspense melodrama and Jewish comedy. Bits of it come off very well, but it's a bumpy ride.

w John Gay, *novel* William Goldman *d* Jack Smight *ph* Jack Priestley *m* Stanley Myers

Rod Steiger, George Segal, Lee Remick, Eileen Heckart, Murray Hamilton, Michael Dunn

Nob Hill*
US 1945 95m Technicolor
TCF (André Daven)

In the gay nineties, a San Francisco saloon owner tries to step into society and win one of its most eligible young ladies.
Engaging period musical drama with all talents working well.

w Wanda Tuchock, Norman Reilly Raine *d* Henry Hathaway *ph* Edward Cronjager *md* Emil Newman, Charles Henderson

George Raft, Joan Bennett, Peggy Ann Garner, Vivian Blaine, Alan Reed, B. S. Pully, Edgar Barrier

Nobody Lives Forever
US 1946 100m bw
Warner (Robert Buckner)

A con man fleeces a rich widow, then falls in love with her.
Forgettable romantic melodrama.

w W. R. Burnett *d* Jean Negulesco *ph* Arthur Edeson *m* Adolph Deutsch

John Garfield, Geraldine Fitzgerald, Walter Brennan, Faye Emerson, George Coulouris, George Tobias

Nobody Runs Forever*
GB 1968 101m Eastmancolor
Rank / Selmur (Betty E. Box)
US title: *The High Commissioner*

An Australian detective is sent to arrest the high commissioner in London on a charge of murdering his first wife.
Sub-Hitchcock thriller which comes to life in patches but has a plot and dialogue which obviously embarrass the actors.

w Wilfred Greatorex, *novel* The High Commissioner by Jon Cleary *ph* Ernest Steward *m* Georges Delerue

Rod Taylor, Christopher Plummer, Lilli Palmer, Camilla Sparv, Daliah Lavi, Clive Revill, Lee Montague, Calvin Lockhart, Derren Nesbitt, Leo McKern, Franchot Tone

Nobody's Perfect
US 1968 103m Techniscope
Universal (Howard Christie)

An ex-naval officer returns to Japan to make amends for stealing a buddha.
Flatfooted comedy adventure.

w John D. F. Black, *novel* The Crows of Edwina Hill by Allan R. Bosworth *d* Alan Rafkin *ph* Robert H. Wyckoff *m* Irving Gertz

Doug McClure, Nancy Kwan, Steve Carlson, James Whitmore, David Hartman, Gary Vinson, James Shigeta

Nocturne*
US 1946 87m bw
RKO (Joan Harrison)

A police detective investigates the death of a composer.
Amusingly self-mocking crime thriller, quite smoothly done in all departments.

w Jonathan Latimer d Edwin L. Marin *ph* Harry J. Wild *m* Leigh Harline

George Raft, Lynn Bari, Virginia Huston, Joseph Pevney, Myrna Dell, Edward Ashley, Walter Sande, Mabel Paige

Non Stop New York
GB 1937 71m bw
Gaumont

Gangsters chase a chorus girl witness who stows away on a transatlantic airliner.
Naïve thriller which has some interest for its cast and for preserving an impression of air travel in the thirties.

w Curt Siodmak, Roland Pertwee, J. O. C. Orton, Derek Twist *d* Robert Stevenson

John Loder, Anna Lee, Francis L. Sullivan, Frank Cellier, Desmond Tester, Athene Seyler, Jerry Verno

None But the Brave
US 1965 105m Technicolor Panavision
Warner / Eiga / Toho / Artanis (Frank Sinatra)

During World War II a plane carrying US Marines to the Pacific front crashlands on an island held by Japanese.
Anti-war melodrama in which the action scenes

are more memorable than the admirable sentiments.

w John Twist, Katsuya Susaki *d* Frank Sinatra *ph* Harold Lipstein *m* Johnny Williams

Frank Sinatra, Clint Walker, Tommy Sands, Tony Bill, Brad Dexter

None But the Lonely Heart*

US 1944 113m bw
RKO (David Hempstead)

In the thirties, a cockney drifter finds himself when he learns that his mother is dying.
Wildly astonishing moodpiece to come from Hollywood during World War II; its picture of East End low life is as rocky as its star performance, but it started Miss Barrymore on the west coast career which sustained her old age.

wd Clifford Odets, *novel* Richard Llewellyn *ph* George Barnes *m* Constantin Bakaleinikoff

Cary Grant, *Ethel Barrymore*, June Duprez, Barry Fitzgerald, Jane Wyatt, George Coulouris, Dan Duryea, Konstantin Shayne, Morton Lowry, Helene Thimig

None Shall Escape*

US 1945 85m bw
Columbia (Sam Bischoff)

The career of a Nazi officer shown as flashbacks from his trial as a war criminal.
Taut topical melodrama reflecting the mood of the time.

w Lester Cole *d* André de Toth *ph* Lee Garmes *m* Ernst Toch

Alexander Knox, Marsha Hunt, Henry Travers, Dorothy Morris, Richard Crane

Nora Prentiss*

US 1946 117m bw
Warner (William Jacobs)

A doctor falls for a café singer who ruins his life.
Standard star melodrama aimed at women, and appreciated by them.

w N. Richard Nash, *story* Paul Webster, Jack Sobell *d* Vincent Sherman *ph* James Wong Howe *m* Franz Waxman

Ann Sheridan, Kent Smith, Bruce Bennett, Robert Alda, Rosemary de Camp, John Ridgely, Wanda Hendrix

The Norliss Tapes***

US 1973 74m colour TVM
Metromedia / Dan Curtis

A supernatural investigator looks into the case of a woman whose diabolist husband has risen from the dead a ravening monster.
Smoothly made, fast-paced and genuinely frightening horror movie, an example of what can be done on a low budget.

w William F. Nolan *d Dan Curtis*

Roy Thinnes, Angie Dickinson, Claude Akins, Hurd Hatfield

North by Northwest****

US 1959 136m Technicolor Vistavision
MGM (Alfred Hitchcock)

A businessman is mistaken for a spy, and enemy agents then try to kill him because he knows too much.
Delightful chase comedy-thriller with a touch of sex, a kind of compendium of its director's best work, with memories of *The 39 Steps, Saboteur* and *Foreign Correspondent* among others.

w Ernest Lehman d Alfred Hitchcock ph Robert Burks m Bernard Herrmann

Cary Grant, Eva Marie Saint, James Mason, Leo G. Carroll, Martin Landau, Jessie Royce Landis, Adam Williams

North Star*

US 1943 105m bw
Samuel Goldwyn (William Cameron Menzies)
aka: *Armored Attack*

A Russian village defends itself against the Nazi onslaught.
Highly artificial propaganda piece later disowned by its makers and retitled. Good acting can't make its mark when the Russian steppes become a never-never land.

w Lillian Hellman *d* Lewis Milestone *ph* James Wong Howe *m* Aaron Copland

Anne Baxter, Farley Granger, Jane Withers, Dana Andrews, Walter Brennan, Erich Von Stroheim, Dean Jagger, Ann Harding, Carl Benton Reid, Walter Huston

'Putting American villagers into Russian costumes and calling them by Russian names is never going to deceive this old bird.'—*James Agate*

'Its failure is the case history of every Hollywood film that steps out of its scope.'—*Richard Winnington*

North to Alaska*

US 1960 122m De Luxe Cinemascope
TCF (Henry Hathaway)

In 1900, two successful gold prospectors have woman trouble.
Good-natured brawling adventure story which could do with cutting but is certainly the type of action movie they don't make 'em like any more.

w John Lee Mahin, Martin Rackin, Claude Binyon, *play* Birthday Gift by Ladislas Fodor *d* Henry Hathaway *ph* Leon Shamroy *m* Lionel Newman

John Wayne, Stewart Granger, Fabian, Capucine, Ernie Kovacs, Mickey Shaughnessy, Karl Swenson, Joe Sawyer, John Qualen

Northern Pursuit*

US 1943 94m bw
Warner (Jack Chertok)

A Mountie tracks a stranded Nazi pilot through the Canadian wastes.
Rather unusual star actioner, not badly done.

w Frank Gruber, Alvah Bessie *d* Raoul Walsh *ph* Sid Hickox *m* Adolph Deutsch

Errol Flynn, Helmut Dantine, Julie Bishop, John Ridgely, Gene Lockhart, Tom Tully, Bernard Nedell

Northwest Frontier***

GB 1959 129m Eastmancolor Cinemascope
Rank / Marcel Hellman
US title: *Flame Over India*

In 1905 an English officer during a rebellion escorts a young Hindu prince on a dangerous train journey.
Thoroughly enjoyable Boys' Own Paper adventure story with excellent set pieces and a spot-the-villain mystery.

w Robin Estridge d J. Lee-Thompson ph Geoffrey Unsworth *m* Mischa Spoliansky

Kenneth More, Lauren Bacall, Herbert Lom, Ursula Jeans, Wilfrid Hyde White, I. S. Johar, Eugene Deckers, Ian Hunter

'*Northwest Frontier* seems to have borrowed its eccentric engine from *The General*, its hazardous expedition from *Stagecoach* and its background of tribal violence from *The Drum*.'—*Penelope Houston*

Northwest Mounted Police*

US 1940 125m Technicolor
Paramount (Cecil B. de Mille)

A Texas Ranger seeks a fugitive in Canada.
Typical big-scale action concoction by de Mille, but in this case none of it's very memorable and the detail is poor.

w Alan Le May, Jesse Lasky Jnr, C. Gardner Sullivan *d* Cecil B. de Mille *ph* Victor Milner, Duke Green *m* Victor Young

Gary Cooper, Paulette Goddard, Madeleine Carroll, Preston Foster, Robert Preston, George Bancroft, Lynne Overman, Akim Tamiroff, Walter Hampden, Lon Chaney Jnr, Montagu Love, George E. Stone

Northwest Outpost

US 1940 91m bw
Republic (Allan Dwan)
GB title: *End of the Rainbow*

Adventures of California cavalrymen.
Milk-and-water adventures in a forgettable operetta.

w Elizabeth Meehan, Richard Sale *d* Allan Dwan *ph* Reggie Lanning *m* Rudolf Friml

Nelson Eddy, Ilona Massey, Hugo Haas, Elsa Lanchester

Northwest Passage***
(Part One, Rogers' Rangers)

US 1940 126m Technicolor
MGM (Hunt Stromberg)

Colonial rangers fight it out with hostile Indians.
Part Two was never made, but no one seemed to mind that the characters in Part One never got round to seeking the titular sea route. The adventures depicted had the feel of historical actuality, and the star was well cast.

w Lawrence Stallings, Talbot Jennings, *novel* Kenneth Roberts *d King Vidor* *ph* Sidney Wagner, William V. Skall *m* Herbert Stothart

Spencer Tracy, Robert Young, Ruth Hussey, Walter Brennan, Nat Pendleton, Robert Barrat, Lumsden Hare, Donald MacBride

Norwood

US 1969 95m Technicolor
Paramount / Hal B. Wallis

A Vietnam veteran returns to his Texas home but feels restless and decides to become a radio singer.
A rather ordinary film about an innocent abroad, neither very funny nor very moving.

w Marguerite Roberts *d* Jack Haley Jnr *ph* Robert B. Hauser *m* Al de Lory

Glen Campbell, Kim Darby, Joe Namath, Carol Lynley, Pat Hingle, Tisha Sterling, Dom De Luise, Jack Haley, Cass Daley, Gil Lamb

Not as a Stranger**

US 1955 135m bw
UA / Stanley Kramer

A medical student has professional and personal struggles.
Earnest filming of a bestseller, with all the actors too old for their parts.

w Edna and Edward Anhalt, *novel* Morton Thompson *d* Stanley Kramer *ph* Franz Planer *m* George Antheil *pd* Rudolph Sternad

Robert Mitchum, Olivia de Havilland, Broderick Crawford, Frank Sinatra, Gloria Grahame, Charles Bickford, Myron McCormick, Lon Chaney Jnr, Jesse White, Henry Morgan, Lee Marvin, Virginia Christine

Not of This Earth**
US 1957 72m bw
AA (Roger Corman)

An alien comes to earth in human form in search of blood which may save his planet.
Modestly budgeted minor sci-fi; ruthless, original and competent.

w Charles Griffith, Mark Hanna d Roger Corman ph John Mescall *m* Ronald Stein

Paul Birch, Beverly Garland, Morgan Jones

Not with My Wife You Don't
US 1966 119m Technicolor
Warner / Fernwood / Reynard (Norman Panama, Joel Freeman)

A Korean war veteran is furious when an old rival turns up in London and again makes eyes at his wife.
Extraordinarily flat star comedy of cross and double cross among friends.

w Norman Panama, Larry Gelbart, Peter Barnes *d* Norman Panama *ph* Charles Lang, Paul Beeson *m* Johnny Williams

Tony Curtis, George C. Scott, Virna Lisi, Carroll O'Connor, Richard Eastham

'About as frothy as a tin of dehydrated milk.'—*MFB*

'It has all the verve, subtlety and sophistication of its title.'—*Judith Crist*

Nothing But the Best**
GB 1964 99m Eastmancolor
Anglo Amalgamated / Domino (David Deutsch)

An ambitious clerk learns to fight his way to the top by cheek and one-upmanship.
Hard, skilful, rather unattractive comedy with interesting social comments on its time.

w Frederic Raphael d Clive Donner ph Nicolas Roeg *m* Ron Grainer *ad* Reece Pemberton

Alan Bates, Denholm Elliott, Harry Andrews, Millicent Martin, Pauline Delany

Nothing But the Night*
GB 1972 90m Eastmancolor
Rank / Charlemagne (Anthony Nelson Keys)

The trustees of an orphanage die off mysteriously, and it seems that the orphans themselves are responsible.
Convoluted murder mystery with horror elements and a twist hardly worth waiting for; earnest performances help.

w Brian Hayles, *novel* John Blackburn *d* Peter Sasdy *ph* Ken Talbot *m* Malcolm Williamson

Christopher Lee, Peter Cushing, Diana Dors, Georgia Brown, Keith Barron, John Robinson

Nothing But Trouble
US 1945 70m bw
MGM (B. F. Ziedman)

A chef and butler accidentally prevent a poison plot against a young king.
Feebly-devised star comedy, their last for a big studio.

w Russel Rouse, Ray Golden *d* Sam Taylor *ph* Charles Salerno Jnr *m* Nathaniel Shilkret

Stan Laurel, Oliver Hardy, Mary Boland, Henry O'Neill, David Leland

Nothing Sacred****
US 1937 77m Technicolor
David O. Selznick

A girl thought to be dying of a rare disease is built up by the press into a national heroine; but the diagnosis was wrong.
Hollywood's most bitter and hilarious satire, with crazy comedy elements and superb wisecracks; a joy.

w Ben Hecht d William Wellman ph W. Howard Greene *m* Oscar Levant

Carole Lombard, Fredric March, Walter Connolly, Charles Winninger, Sig Rumann, Frank Fay, Maxie Rosenbloom, Margaret Hamilton, Hedda Hopper, Monty Woolley, Hattie McDaniel, Olin Howland, John Qualen

Notorious***
US 1946 101m bw
David O. Selznick (Barbara Keon)

In Rio, a notorious lady marries a Nazi renegade to help the US government but finds herself falling in love with her contact.
Superb romantic suspenser containing some of Hitchcock's best work.

w Ben Hecht d Alfred Hitchcock ph Ted Tetzlaff *m* Roy Webb

Cary Grant, Ingrid Bergman, Claude Rains, Louis Calhern, Leopoldine Konstantin, Reinhold Schunzel

'Velvet smooth in dramatic action, sharp and sure in its characters, and heavily charged with the intensity of warm emotional appeal.'—*Bosley Crowther*

'The suspense is terrific.'—*New Yorker, 1976*

The Notorious Landlady
GB 1962 127m bw
Columbia / Kohlmar / Quine (Fred Kohlmar)

An American diplomat in London takes rooms with a murder suspect; after many mysterious happenings he helps to clear her.
Flatly whimsical goings on in comical old London, complete with fog and eccentrics. The actors all try hard but are deflated by the script.

w Larry Gelbart, Richard Quine *d* Richard Quine *ph* Arthur E. Arling *m* George Duning

Kim Novak, Jack Lemmon, Fred Astaire, Lionel Jeffries, Estelle Winwood, Maxwell Reed

Now and Forever*
US 1934 82m bw
Paramount (Louis D. Lighton)

A jewel thief and his mistress are taught a thing or two by his small daughter.
Odd mixture of comedy and drama which was box office at the time but seems pretty dated after forty years, though technically very smooth.

w Vincent Lawrence, Sylvia Thalberg *d* Henry Hathaway *ph* Harry Fischbeck

Gary Cooper, Carole Lombard, Shirley Temple, Guy Standing, Charlotte Granville, Gilbert Emery, Henry Kolker

Now I'll Tell
US 1934 72m bw
Fox (Winfield Sheehan)
GB title: *When New York Sleeps*

The story of Arnold Rothstein, gambler-racketeer of the twenties, as told by his widow.
Competent crime/domestic programmer.

wd Edwin Burke *ph* Ernest Palmer *m* Hugo Friedhofer

Spencer Tracy, Helen Twelvetrees, Hobart Cavanaugh, Alice Faye, G. P. Huntley Jnr, Shirley Temple, Leon Ames

'In spite of the breezy sequences with which it starts, it quickly gets improbable and goes from bad to maudlin.'—*Otis Ferguson*

Now Voyager***
US 1942 117m bw
Warner (Hal B. Wallis)

A dowdy frustrated spinster takes the psychiatric cure and embarks on a doomed love affair.
A basically soggy script still gets by, and how, through the romantic magic of its stars, who were all at their best; and suffering in mink went over very big in wartime.

w Casey Robinson, *novel* Olive Higgins Prouty *d Irving Rapper* *ph* Sol Polito *m* Max Steiner

Bette Davis, Claude Rains, Paul Henreid, Gladys Cooper, John Loder, Bonita Granville, Ilka Chase, Lee Patrick, Charles Drake, Franklin Pangborn

'If it were better it might not work at all . . . this way it's a vulgar classic.'—*New Yorker, 1976*

Now You See Him Now You Don't
US 1972 88m Technicolor
Walt Disney

Two students discover an elixir of invisibility and help prevent a gangster from taking over the college.
Flat Disney frolic with fair trick effects.

w Joseph L. McEveety *d* Robert Butler *ph* Frank Phillips *m* Robert F. Brunner *sp* Eustace Lycett, Danny Lee

Kurt Russell, Cesar Romero, Joe Flynn, Jim Backus, William Windom, Edward Andrews, Richard Bakalyan

Now You See It, Now You Don't
US 1967 96m Technicolor TVM
Universal (Roland Kibbee)
aka: *Midnight Oil*

An art appraiser plans to sell a fake Rembrandt to a Middle Eastern prince.
Woebegone, overlong comedy with much mugging from the star.

w Roland Kibbee *d* Don Weis

Jonathan Winters, Luciana Paluzzi, Steve Allen, Jayne Meadows, Jack Weston

The Nun and the Sergeant
US 1962 74m bw
UA / Springfield

In Korea, a tough sergeant commanding a 'dirty dozen' mission is joined by a schoolgirl and a nun.
Minor war adventure, moderately well done but highly unconvincing.

w Don Cerveris *d* Franklin Adreon *ph* Paul Ivano *m* Jerry Fielding

Anna Sten, Robert Webber, Leo Gordon, Hari Rhodes

The Nun's Story***
US 1959 151m Technicolor
Warner (Henry Blanke)

A Belgian girl joins a strict order, endures hardship in the Congo, and finally returns to ordinary life.
The fascinating early sequences of convent routine are more interesting than the African adventures, but this is a careful, composed and

impressive film with little Hollywood exaggeration.

w Robert Anderson, book Kathryn C. Hulme d Fred Zinnemann ph Franz Planer m Franz Waxman

Audrey Hepburn, Peter Finch, Edith Evans, Peggy Ashcroft, Dean Jagger, Mildred Dunnock, Patricia Collinge, Beatrice Straight

Nurse on Wheels
GB 1963 86m bw
Anglo Amalgamated / GHW (Peter Rogers)

Adventures of a young District Nurse.
Part sentimental, part Carry On; watchable of its curious kind.

w Norman Hudis, *novel* Nurse Is a Neighbour by Joanna Jones *d* Gerald Thomas *ph* Alan Hume *m* Eric Rogers

Juliet Mills, Ronald Lewis, Joan Sims, Raymond Huntley, Athene Seyler

The Nutty Professor
US 1963 107m Technicolor
Paramount / Jerry Lewis (Ernest D. Glucksman)

An eccentric chemistry professor discovers an elixir which turns him into a pop idol.
Long dreary comedy which contains patches of its star at somewhere near his best; but even *Dr Jekyll and Mr Hyde* is funnier.

w Jerry Lewis, Bill Richmond *d* Jerry Lewis *ph* W. Wallace Kelley *m* Walter Scharf

Jerry Lewis, Stella Stevens, Howard Morris, Kathleen Freeman

O

O. Henry's Full House**
US 1952 117m bw
TCF (André Hakim)
GB title: *Full House*

John Steinbeck introduces five stories by O. Henry.
Modelled on the success of *Quartet* (qv), this compendium was less successful because these turn-of-the century tales of New York depend less on character than on the sting in the tail; but the cast and production were lavish.

m Alfred Newman

THE COP AND THE ANTHEM *w* Lamar Trotti *d* Henry Koster *ph* Lloyd Ahern
Charles Laughton, David Wayne, Marilyn Monroe
THE CLARION CALL *w* Richard Breen *d* Henry Hathaway *ph* Lucien Ballard
Dale Robertson, Richard Widmark
THE LAST LEAF *w* Ivan Goff, Ben Roberts *d* Jean Negulesco *ph* Joe MacDonald
Anne Baxter, Jean Peters, Gregory Ratoff
THE RANSOM OF RED CHIEF *w* uncredited *d* Howard Hawks *ph* Milton Krasner
Fred Allen, Oscar Levant
THE GIFT OF THE MAGI *w* Walter Bullock *d* Henry King *ph* Joe MacDonald
Jeanne Crain, Farley Granger

O Lucky Man**
GB 1973 174m Eastmancolor
Warner / Memorial / Sam

The odyssey of a trainee salesman who after a while as an international financier settles down to be a do-gooder.
Modern revue-style version of *Candide/ Decline and Fall*; very hit or miss in style and effect, and hellishly overlong, but with good things along the way.

w David Sherwin *d* Lindsay Anderson *ph* Miroslav Ondricek *m Alan Price* *pd* Jocelyn Herbert

Malcolm McDowell, Arthur Lowe, Ralph Richardson, Rachel Roberts, Helen Mirren, Mona Washbourne, Dandy Nichols

'A sort of mod *Pilgrim's Progress*.'—*New Yorker*

OSS*
US 1946 107m bw
Paramount

American spies are parachuted into France in 1943.
Espionage heroics with an unhappy ending and a slight documentary flavour. Not bad of its kind.

w Richard Maibaum *d Irving Pichel* *ph* Lionel Lindon

Alan Ladd, Geraldine Fitzgerald, Patric Knowles, John Hoyt, Don Beddoe

Objective Burma*
US 1944 142m bw
Warner (Jerry Wald)

Exploits of an American platoon in the Burma campaign.
Overlong but vivid war actioner which caused a diplomatic incident by failing to mention the British contribution.

w Ranald MacDougall, Lester Cole, Alvah Bessie *d Raoul Walsh* *ph* James Wong Howe *m* Franz Waxman

Errol Flynn, James Brown, William Prince, George Tobias, Henry Hull, Warner Anderson, John Alwin

The Oblong Box
GB 1969 95m Eastmancolor
AIP (Gordon Hessler)

One of two 19th-century brothers is mysteriously disfigured and buried alive; he recovers and runs amok.
Nastily effective horror film with a frail story but good background detail.

w Lawrence Huntington *d Gordon Hessler* *ph* John Coquillon *m* Harry Robinson

Vincent Price, Christopher Lee, Alastair Williamson, Hilary Dwyer, Peter Arne, Maxwell Shaw, Rupert Davies

'A pervasive aura of evil.'—*MFB*

Obsession**
US 1976 98m Technicolor Panavision
Columbia (Robert S. Bremson)

A widower with guilt feelings meets the double of

his dead wife and is drawn into a strange plot. Hitchcockian adventure with a few unwise attempts at seriousness, à la *Don't Look Now*. Generally entertaining, skilled and quite rewarding.

w Paul Schrader d Brian de Palma ph Vilmos Zsigmond m Bernard Herrmann

Cliff Robertson, Geneviève Bujold, John Lithgow, Sylvia Williams, Wanda Blackman, Patrick McNamara

Ocean's Eleven*
US 1960 128m Technicolor Panavision
Warner (Lewis Milestone)

A gang of friends plan to rob a Las Vegas casino. Self-indulgent and overlong caper comedy which marked Hollywood's entry into a subsequently much overworked field. In this case the plot stops all too frequently for guest spots and in-jokes.

w Harry Brown, Charles Lederer *d* Lewis Milestone *ph* William H. Daniels *m* Nelson Riddle

Frank Sinatra, Peter Lawford, Sammy Davis Jnr, Richard Conte, Dean Martin, Angie Dickinson, Cesar Romero, Joey Bishop, Patrice Wymore, Akim Tamiroff, Henry Silva, Ilka Chase

The October Man**
GB 1947 98m bw
GFD / Two Cities (Eric Ambler)

After an accident which causes a head injury and subsequent depression, a lonely man staying at a small hotel is suspected of a local murder.
Nice blend of character study, mystery and suspense, with excellent attention to suburban detail.

w Eric Ambler d Roy Baker ph Erwin Hillier

John Mills, Joan Greenwood, Edward Chapman, Kay Walsh, Catherine Lacey, Joyce Carey, Adrianne Allen, Felix Aylmer

The Odd Couple**
US 1968 105m Technicolor Panavision
Paramount (Howard W. Koch)

A fussy divorce-shocked newswriter moves in with his sloppy sportscaster friend, and they get on each other's nerves.
Straight filming of a funny play which sometimes seems lost on the wide screen, but the performances are fine.

w Neil Simon, from his play *d* Gene Saks *ph* Robert B. Hauser *m* Neal Hefti

Jack Lemmon, Walter Matthau, John Fiedler, Herb Edelman, David Sheiner, Larry Haines, Monica Evans, Carole Sheely, Iris Adrian

Odd Man Out***
GB 1946 115m bw
GFD / Two Cities (Carol Reed)
US title: *Gang War*

An IRA gunman, wounded and on the run in Belfast, is helped and hindered by a variety of people.
Superbly crafted but rather empty dramatic charade, visually and emotionally memorable but with nothing whatever to say.

w F. L. Green, R. C. Sheriff, *novel* F. L. Green *d Carol Reed ph Robert Krasker m* William Alwyn

James Mason, Robert Newton, Kathleen Ryan, F. J. McCormick, Cyril Cusack, Robert Beatty, Fay Compton, Dan O'Herlihy, Denis O'Dea, Maureen Delany, Joseph Tomelty, William Hartnell

'The story seems to ramify too much, to go on too long, and at its unluckiest to go arty. Yet detail by detail *Odd Man Out* is made with great skill and imaginativeness and with a depth of ardour that is very rare.'—*James Agee*

Odds against Tomorrow*
US 1959 96m bw
UA / Harbel (Robert Wise)

Three crooks plan to rob a bank, but two of them cause the enterprise to fail because of their own racist hatreds.
Sour, glossy crime thriller with elementary social significance.

w John O. Killens, Nelson Gidding, *novel* John P. McGivern *d Robert Wise ph Joseph Brun m* John Lewis

Robert Ryan, Harry Belafonte, *Ed Begley,* Shelley Winters, Gloria Grahame, Will Kuluva, Kim Hamilton

'An efficient but unnecessarily portentous thriller.'—*Penelope Houston*

The Odessa File**
GB 1974 129m Eastmancolor Panavision
Columbia / Domino / Oceanic (John Woolf)

In 1963, a young German reporter tracks down a gang of neo-Nazis.
Elaborate but uninvolving suspenser with several excellent cliffhanging sequences and a let-down climax.

w Kenneth Ross, George Markstein, *novel* Frederick Forsyth *d* Ronald Neame *ph* Oswald Morris *m* Andrew Lloyd Webber *pd* Rolf Zeherbauer

Jon Voight, Maria Schell, Maximilian Schell, Mary Tamm, Derek Jacobi, Peter Jeffrey, *Noel Willman*

Odette*
GB 1950 123m bw
Herbert Wilcox

A Frenchwoman with an English husband spies for the French resistance, is caught and tortured. Deglamorized true life spy story with emotional moments let down by generally uninspired handling, also by the too well-known image of its star, who however gives a remarkable performance.

w Warren Chetham Strode, *book* Jerrard Tickell *d* Herbert Wilcox *ph* Max Greene

Anna Neagle, Trevor Howard, Peter Ustinov, Marius Goring

Of Human Bondage**
US 1934 83m bw
(RKO)

A well-to-do Englishman is brought down by his infatuation with a sluttish waitress.
This version of the famous novel brought Bette Davis to prominence but is not otherwise any better than the others.

w Lester Cohen, *novel* W. Somerset Maugham *d* John Cromwell *ph* Henry W. Gerrard

Leslie Howard, Bette Davis, Frances Dee, Reginald Owen, Reginald Denny, Kay Johnson, Alan Hale

Of Human Bondage*
US 1946 105m bw
Warner (Henry Blanke)

Good-looking but thoroughly dull remake.

w Catherine Turney *d* Edmund Goulding *ph* Peverell Marley *m* Erich Wolfgang Korngold

Paul Henreid, Eleanor Parker, Alexis Smith, Edmund Gwenn, Patric Knowles, Janis Paige, Henry Stephenson

Of Human Bondage
GB 1964 99m bw
Seven Arts / MGM (James Woolf)

Disastrous remake with both star roles miscast.

w Bryan Forbes *d* Henry Hathaway, Ken Hughes *ph* Oswald Morris *m* Ron Goodwin *pd* John Box

Laurence Harvey, Kim Novak, Nanette Newman, Roger Livesey, Jack Hedley, Robert Morley, Siobhan McKenna, Ronald Lacey

Of Human Hearts*
US 1938 100m bw
MGM (John Considine Jnr)

A 19th-century idyll of middle America and especially of a preacher and his wayward son.
Curious all-American moral fable, splendidly made and acted.

w Bradbury Foote, *novel* Benefits Forgot by Honoré Morrow *d* Clarence Brown *ph* Clyde de Vinna *m* Herbert Stothart

Walter Huston, James Stewart, Beulah Bondi, Gene Reynolds, Charles Coburn, Guy Kibbee, John Carradine, Gene Lockhart, Ann Rutherford

Of Love and Desire
US 1963 97m De Luxe
New World (Victor Stoloff)

An engineer in Mexico takes up with the boss's nymphomaniac sister.
Unwise sensationalist vehicle for an ageing leading lady who is past such carryings on.

w Laslo Gorag, Richard Rush *d* Richard Rush *ph* Alex Phillips *m* Ronald Stein

Merle Oberon, Steve Cochran, John Agar, Curt Jurgens

Of Mice and Men***
US 1939 107m bw
Hal Roach (Lewis Milestone)

An itinerant worker looks after his mentally retarded brother, a giant who doesn't know his own strength.
A strange and unexpected tragedy which has strength and is very persuasively made but seems somehow unnecessary.

w Eugene Solow, *novel* John Steinbeck *d Lewis Milestone ph Norbert Brodine m* Aaron Copland

Burgess Meredith, Lon Chaney Jnr, Betty Field, Charles Bickford, Roman Bohnen, Bob Steele, Noah Beery Jnr

The Offence*
GB 1972 113m De Luxe
UA / Tantallon

A tough police inspector bullies a suspected child molester.
Tortuous psychological study on the fringe of hysteria; good performances.

w John Hopkins, from his play This Story of Yours *d* Sidney Lumet *ph* Gerry Fisher *m* Harrison Birtwhistle

Sean Connery, Trevor Howard, Ian Bannen, Vivien Merchant

Off Limits
US 1953 89m bw
Paramount
GB title: *Military Policemen*

A boxing manager trains a young fighter in the military police.
Flat star comedy.

w Hal Kanter, Jack Sher *d* George Marshall
ph Peverell Marley *m* Van Cleave

Bob Hope, Mickey Rooney, Marilyn Maxwell, Marvin Miller

Oh Dad, Poor Dad, Mamma's Hung You in the Closet and I'm Feelin' So Sad
US 1966 86m Technicolor
Paramount / Seven Arts (Ray Stark, Stanley Rubin)

A dead father helps his son to get married despite his mother's influence to the contrary.
Zany black comedy which never really worked on the stage, let alone the screen.

w Ian Bernard, *play* Arthur Kopit *d* Richard Quine *ph* Geoffrey Unsworth *m* Neal Hefti

Rosalind Russell, Jonathan Winters, Robert Morse, Hugh Griffith, Barbara Harris, Lionel Jeffries, Cyril Delevanti, Hiram Sherman

Oh Men! Oh Women!
US 1957 90m Eastmancolor
Cinemascope
TCF (Nunnally Johnson)

A psychoanalyst discovers that his wife is involved with two of his patients.
Scatty Broadway comedy which strains the patience.

wd Nunnally Johnson, *play* Edward Chodorov
ph Charles G. Clarke *m* Cyril Mockridge

David Niven, Ginger Rogers, Dan Dailey, Barbara Rush, Tony Randall

Oh Mr Porter****
GB 1937 84m bw
GFD / Gainsborough (Edward Black)

The stationmaster of an Irish halt catches gun-runners posing as ghosts.
Marvellous star comedy showing this trio of comedians at their best, and especially Hay as the seedy incompetent. The plot is borrowed from *The Ghost Train*, but each line and gag brings its own inventiveness. A delight of character comedy and cinematic narrative.

w Marriott Edgar, Val Guest, J. O. C. Orton d Marcel Varnel

Will Hay, Moore Marriott, Graham Moffat, Dave O'Toole, Dennis Wyndham

'That rare phenomenon: a film comedy without a dud scene.'—*Peter Barnes, 1964*

Oh Rosalinda!
GB 1955 105m Technicolor
Cinemascope
ABP / Powell and Pressburger

A playboy in four-power Vienna plays a practical joke on four officers and the flirtatious wife of one of them.
Lumbering attempt to modernize *Die Fledermaus*, unsuitably wide-screened and totally lacking the desired Lubitsch touch. A monumental step in the decline of these producers, and a sad stranding of a brilliant cast.

wd Michael Powell, Emeric Pressburger
ph Christopher Challis *m* Johann Strauss
ad Hein Heckroth

Anton Walbrook, Michael Redgrave, Anthony Quayle, Mel Ferrer, Dennis Price, Ludmilla Tcherina

Oh What a Lovely War**
GB 1969 144m Technicolor
Panavision
Paramount / Accord (Brian Duffy, Richard Attenborough)

A fantasia with music on World War I.
A brave all-star attempt which comes off only in patches; the pier apparatus from the stage show really doesn't translate, the piece only works well when it becomes cinematic, as in the recruiting song and the final track-back from the graves. But there are many pleasures, as well as yawns, along the way.

w Len Deighton, *stage show* Joan Littlewood, Charles Chilton *d* Richard Attenborough
ph Gerry Turpin *m* various *md* Alfred Ralston
pd Don Ashton

Ralph Richardson, Meriel Forbes, John Gielgud, Kenneth More, John Clements, Paul Daneman, Joe Melia, Jack Hawkins, John Mills, Maggie Smith, Michael Redgrave, Laurence Olivier, Susannah York, Dirk Bogarde, Phyllis Calvert, Vanessa Redgrave

Oh You Beautiful Doll*
US 1949 93m Technicolor
TCF (George Jessel)

Fred Fisher wants to write opera but is more successful with pop songs.
Standard turn of the century biopic, very pleasantly handled and performed.

w Albert and George Lewis *d* John M. Stahl
ph Harry Jackson *md* Alfred Newman

S. Z. Sakall, Mark Stevens, June Haver,

Charlotte Greenwood, Jay C. Flippen, Gale Robbins

O'Hara US Treasury
US 1971 98m Technicolor TVM
Universal / Jack Webb
aka: *Operation Cobra*

Suddenly widowed by an accident, a deputy sheriff from the midwest becomes a customs agent and cracks a narcotics ring.
Semi-documentary thick ear which led to a moderately successful series.

w James E. Moser *d* Jack Webb

David Janssen, Lana Wood, Jerome Thor, Gary Crosby, William Conrad

Oil for the Lamps of China*
US 1935 98m bw
Warner (Robert Lord)

The career in China of an American oil company representative.
Adequate general audience picture from a bestseller.

w Laird Doyle, *novel* Alice Tisdale Hobart *d* Mervyn Le Roy *ph* Tony Gaudio *m* Leo F. Forbstein

Pat O'Brien, Josephine Hutchinson, Jean Muir, Lyle Talbot, Arthur Byron, John Eldredge, Henry O'Neill, Donald Crisp

'Far above average in performance, direction and content.'—*John Baxter, 1968*

Oklahoma!**
US 1955 143m Technicolor Todd-AO
Rodgers and Hammerstein (Arthur Hornblow Jnr)

A cowboy wins his girl despite the intervention of a sinister hired hand.
Much of the appeal of the musical was in its simple timeworn story and stylized sets; the film makes the first merely boring and the latter are replaced by standard scenery, not even of Oklahoma. The result is efficient rather than startling or memorable.

w Sonya Levien, William Ludwig, *'book'* Oscar Hammerstein, *play* Green Grow the Rushes by Lynn Riggs *d* Fred Zinnemann *ph* Robert Surtees *m Richard Rodgers ly* Oscar Hammerstein *pd* Oliver Smith

Gordon Macrae, Shirley Jones, Rod Steiger, Gloria Grahame, Charlotte Greenwood, Gene Nelson, Eddie Albert

Oklahoma Crude*
US 1973 111m Technicolor
Columbia / Stanley Kramer

In 1913, a drifting oil man stops to help a girl develop her rig.
Dour, downbeat melodrama with restricted action and much bad language; within its lights quite entertaining, but odd.

w Marc Norman *d* Stanley Kramer *ph* Robert Surtees *m* Henry Mancini *pd* Alfred Sweeney

Faye Dunaway, George C. Scott, John Mills, Jack Palance, Woodrow Parfrey

The Oklahoma Kid**
US 1939 80m bw
Warner (Samuel Bischoff)

During the settlement of the Cherokee Strip a cowboy avenges the unjust lynching of his father.
Competent but slightly disappointing star western memorable for the clash in this guise of its protagonists, more usually seen as gangsters.

w Warren Duff, Robert Buckner, Edward E. Paramore *d* Lloyd Bacon *ph* James Wong Howe *m* Max Steiner

James Cagney, Humphrey Bogart, Rosemary Lane, Donald Crisp, Harvey Stephens, Charles Middleton, Edward Pawley, Ward Bond

'There's something entirely disarming about the way he has tackled horse opera, not pretending for a minute to be anything but New York's Jimmy Cagney all dressed up as a Robin Hood of the old west.'—*Frank Nugent*

Old Acquaintance**
US 1943 110m bw
Warner (Henry Blanke)

Two jealous lady novelists interfere in each other's love lives.
A dated but rather splendid battle of the wild cats, with two stars fighting their way through a plush production and a rather overlong script.

w John Van Druten, Lenore Coffee, *play* John Van Druten *d* Vincent Sherman *ph* Sol Polito *m* Franz Waxman

Bette Davis, Miriam Hopkins, Gig Young, John Loder, Dolores Moran, Philip Reed, Roscoe Karns, Anne Revere

'The odd thing is that on the screen such trash can seem mature and even adventurous.'—*James Agee*

Old Bones of the River*
GB 1938 90m bw
GFD / Gainsborough (Edward Black)

A teacher in Africa accidentally quells a native rising.
Tediously funny star comedy; enough said.

w Marriott Edgar, Val Guest, J. O. C. Orton *character* Edgar Wallace *d* Marcel Varnel *ph* Arthur Crabtree *m* Louis Levy *ad Vetchinsky*

Will Hay, Moore Marriott, Graham Moffat, Robert Adams, Jack Livesey

The Old Curiosity Shop*
GB 1934 95m bw
BIP / Wardour

The lives of a gambler and his granddaughter are affected by a miserly dwarf.
Heavy-going Dickens novel given reasonably rich production and well enough acted; sentimentality prevented a remake until the unsuccessful *Mister Quilp* (qv) in 1975.

w Margaret Kennedy, Ralph Neale, *novel* Charles Dickens *d* Thomas Bentley

Hay Petrie, Ben Webster, Elaine Benson, Beatrice Thompson, Gibb McLaughlin, Reginald Purdell, Polly Ward

The Old Dark House ****
US 1932 71m bw
Universal

Stranded travellers take refuge in the house of a family of eccentrics.
Marvellous horror comedy filled with superb grotesques and memorable lines, closely based on a Priestley novel but omitting the more thoughtful moments. A stylist's and connoisseur's treat.

w Benn W. Levy, R. C. Sherriff, novel Benighted *by J. B. Priestley d James Whale ph Arthur Edeson*

Melvyn Douglas, Charles Laughton, Raymond Massey, Boris Karloff, Ernest Thesiger, Eva Moore, Gloria Stuart, Lilian Bond, Brember Wills, John Dudgeon (Elspeth Dudgeon)

'An unbridled camp fantasy directed with great wit.'—*Charles Higham*

'Each threat as it appears is revealed to be burlap and poster paint . . . despite storm, attempted rape and a remarkable final chase, the film is basically a confidence trick worked with cynical humour by a brilliant technician.'—*John Baxter, 1968*

†The 1963 Hammer 'remake' is best forgotten.

The Old Fashioned Way*
US 1934 74m bw
Paramount / (William Le Baron)

Adventures of The Great McGonigle and his troupe of travelling players.
Period comedy tailored for its star and incorporating fragments of *The Drunkard.* Not so funny as it might be, but essential for students.

w Garnett Weston, Jack Cunningham, Charles Bogle (W. C. Fields) *d* William Beaudine *ph* Benjamin Reynolds *m* Harry Revel

W. C. Fields, Joe Morrison, Judith Allen, Jan Duggan, Jack Mulhall, Baby Leroy

The Old Maid**
US, 1939 95m bw
Warner (Henry Blanke)

When her suitor is killed in the Civil War, an unmarried mother lets her childless cousin bring up her daughter as her own.
A 'woman's picture' par excellence, given no-holds-barred treatment by all concerned but a little lacking in surprise.

w Casey Robinson, *play* Zoe Akins, *novel* Edith Wharton *d Edmund Goulding ph Tony Gaudio m* Leo F. Forbstein

Bette Davis, Miriam Hopkins, George Brent, Jane Bryan, Donald Crisp, Louise Fazenda, Henry Stephenson, Jerome Cowan, William Lundigan, Rand Brooks

'It is better than average and sticks heroically to its problem, forsaking all delights and filling a whole laundry bag with wet and twisted handkerchiefs.'—*Otis Ferguson*

The Old Man and the Sea*
US 1958 89m Technicolor
Warner / Leland Hayward

An old fisherman dreams of hooking a great fish.
Expensive but poor-looking and stultifyingly dull one-character drama with variable production effects, a low key *Moby Dick.* Interesting but not effective.

w Ernest Hemingway, from his novel *d* John Sturges *ph* James Wong Howe, Floyd Crosby, Tom Tutweiler, Lamar Boren *m* Dmitri Tiomkin

Spencer Tracy, Felipe Pazos, Harry Bellaver

'A literary property about as suited for the movie medium as *The Love Song of J. Alfred Prufrock.*'—*Time*

The Old Man Who Cried Wolf*
US 1970 74m colour TVM
Aaron Spelling

An old man sees his friend beaten to death but the police do not believe him: only the killer does.
Modestly effective, predictable suspenser.

w Luther Davis *d* Walter Grauman

Edward G. Robinson, Martin Balsam, Diane Baker, Ruth Roman, Percy Rodrigues

Old Mother Riley

This Irish washerwoman with flailing arms and a nice line in invective was a music hall creation of Arthur Lucan, a variation of a pantomime dame. His wife Kitty Macshane played Mother Riley's daughter, and despite personal difficulties they were top of the bill for nearly 30 years. The films were very cheaply made and the padding is difficult to sit through, but Lucan at his best is a superb comedian: they were made for small independent companies such as Butler's and usually directed by Maclean Rogers.

1937: OLD MOTHER RILEY
1938: OLD MOTHER RILEY IN PARIS
1939: OLD MOTHER RILEY MP, OLD MOTHER RILEY JOINS UP
1940: OLD MOTHER RILEY IN BUSINESS, OLD MOTHER RILEY'S GHOSTS
1941: OLD MOTHER RILEY'S CIRCUS
1942: OLD MOTHER RILEY IN SOCIETY
1943: OLD MOTHER RILEY DETECTIVE
1944: OLD MOTHER RILEY AT HOME
1945: OLD MOTHER RILEY HEADMISTRESS
1947: OLD MOTHER RILEY'S NEW VENTURE
1949: OLD MOTHER RILEY'S JUNGLE TREASURE
1952: MOTHER RILEY MEETS THE VAMPIRE

Old Yeller*

US 1957 83m Technicolor
Walt Disney

The love of a boy for his dog.
Archetypal family movie set in a remote rural area.

w Fred Gipson, William Tubberg, *novel* Fred Gipson *d* Robert Stevenson *ph* Charles P. Boyle *m* Oliver Wallace

Dorothy McGuire, Fess Parker, Tommy Kirk, Kevin Corcoran, Jeff York, Chuck Connors

Oliver!***

GB 1968 146m Technicolor
Panavision 70
Columbia / Warwick / Romulus (John Woolf)

A musical version of *Oliver Twist*.
The last, perhaps, of the splendid film musicals which have priced themselves out of existence; it drags a little in spots but on the whole it does credit both to the show and the original novel, though eclipsed in style by David Lean's straight version.

w Vernon Harris, *play* Lionel Bart, *novel Charles Dickens d Carol Reed ph Oswald Morris m* Lionel Bart *md* John Green *pd John Box ch Onna White*

Ron Moody, Oliver Reed, Harry Secombe, *Mark Lester*, Shani Wallis, *Jack Wild*, Hugh Griffith, Joseph O'Conor, Leonard Rossiter, Hylda Baker, Peggy Mount, Megs Jenkins

'Only time will tell if it is a great film but it is certainly a great experience.'—*Joseph Morgenstern*

'There is a heightened discrepancy between the romping jollity with which everyone goes about his business and the actual business being gone about . . . such narrative elements as the exploitation of child labour, pimping, abduction, prostitution and murder combine to make *Oliver!* the most non-U subject ever to receive a U certificate.'—*Jan Dawson*

Oliver Twist****

GB 1948 116m bw
GFD / Cineguild

A foundling falls among thieves but is rescued by a benevolent old gentleman.
Simplified, brilliantly cinematic version of a voluminous Victorian novel, beautiful to look at and memorably played, with every scene achieving the perfect maximum impact.

w David Lean, Stanley Haynes, novel Charles Dickens d David Lean ph Guy Green m Arnold Bax pd John Bryan

Alec Guinness, Robert Newton, Francis L. Sullivan, John Howard Davies, Kay Walsh, Anthony Newley, Henry Stephenson, Mary Clare, Gibb McLaughlin, Diana Dors

'A thoroughly expert piece of movie entertainment.'—*Richard Winnington*

Omar Khayyam

US 1956 101m Technicolor
Vistavision
Paramount (Frank Freeman Jnr)

The Persian poet and philosopher defends his Shah against the Assassins.
Clean but dull Arabian Nights fantasy with pantomime sets and no humour.

w Barre Lyndon *d* William Dieterle *ph* Ernest Laszlo *m* Victor Young

Cornel Wilde, Michael Rennie, Raymond Massey, John Derek, Yma Sumac, Sebastian Cabot, Debra Paget

The Omega Man*

US 1971 98m Technicolor Panavision
Warner / Walter Seltzer

In 1977 a plague resulting from germ warfare has decimated the world's population; in Los

Angeles, one man wages war against loathsome carriers of the disease.
'Realistic' version of a novel which was about vampires taking over, and was previously filmed unsatisfactorily as *The Last Man on Earth*. This nasty version rises to a few good action sequences but is bogged down by talk in between.

w John William Corrington and Joyce M. Corrington, *novel* I Am Legend by Richard Matheson *d* Boris Sagal *ph* Russell Metty *m* Ron Grainer

Charlton Heston, Rosalind Cash, Anthony Zerbe

The Omen**
US 1976 111m De Luxe Panavision
TCF (Harvey Bernhard)

The adopted child of an ambassador to Great Britain shows unnerving signs of being diabolically inspired.
Commercially successful variation on *The Exorcist*, quite professionally assembled and more enjoyable as entertainment than its predecessor.

w David Seltzer *d Richard Donner ph* Gil Taylor *m* Jerry Goldsmith

Gregory Peck, Lee Remick, David Warner, Billie Whitelaw, Leo McKern, Harvey Stevens, Patrick Troughton, Anthony Nicholls, Martin Benson

On a Clear Day You Can See For Ever*
US 1970 129m Technicolor Panavision
Paramount (Howard Koch)

A psychiatric hypnotist helps a girl to stop smoking, and finds that in trances she remembers previous incarnations.
Romantic musical which tries, and fails, to substitute wispy charm for its original Broadway vitality. There are compensations.

w Alan Jay Lerner, from his play *d* Vincente Minnelli *ph* Harry Stradling *m* Burton Lane

Barbra Streisand, Yves Montand, Bob Newhart, Larry Blyden, Jack Nicholson, Simon Oakland

On an Island with You
US 1948 104m Technicolor
MGM

A film actress on location in the South Seas is chased by a naval officer.
Below par musical which far outstays its welcome.

w Dorothy Kingsley, Dorothy Cooper, Charles Martin, Hans Wilhelm *d* Richard Thorpe *ph* Charles Rosher

Esther Williams, Peter Lawford, Jimmy Durante, Ricardo Montalban, Cyd Charisse, Xavier Cugat and his Orchestra

On Approval***
GB 1943 80m bw
(GFD) Clive Brook

An Edwardian duke and an American heiress plan a chaperoned trial marriage in a remote Scottish castle.
Sparkling comedy of manners made even more piquant by careful casting and mounting; a minor delight.

w Clive Brook, Terence Young, play Frederick Lonsdale d Clive Brook

Clive Brook, Beatrice Lillie, Googie Withers, Roland Culver, O. B. Clarence, Lawrence Hanray, Hay Petrie

'Totally diverting, highly cinematic.'—*NFT, 1974*

'There has probably never been a richer, funnier anthology of late-Victorian mannerisms.'—*Time*

On Borrowed Time*
US 1939 98m bw
MGM (Sidney Franklin)

An old man refuses to die and chases Death up the apple tree.
Amiable, very American fantasy with much sentiment and several effective moments.

w Alice Duer Miller, Frank O'Neill, Claudine West, *novel* Lawrence Edward Watkin *d* Harold S. Bucquet *m* Franz Waxman

Lionel Barrymore, Bobs Watson, Beulah Bondi, *Cedric Hardwicke* (as Mr Brink), Una Merkel, Ian Wolfe, Philip Terry, Eily Malyon

'A weird, wild, totally unpredictable fantasy with dream sequences more like Bunuel than anything in the cinema.'—*John Russell Taylor, 1965*

On Dangerous Ground
US 1951 82m bw
RKO (John Houseman)

A tough cop falls in love with the blind sister of a mentally defective murderer.
Pretentious Hollywood *film noir* in the Gabin manner, partly redeemed by its glossy surface.

w A. I. Bezzerides, *novel* George Butler *d* Nicholas Ray *ph George E. Diskant m* Bernard Herrmann

Robert Ryan, Ida Lupino, Ward Bond, Ed Begley, Cleo Moore, Charles Kemper

On Her Majesty's Secret Service**
GB 1969 140m Technicolor
Panavision
UA / Eon / Danilaq (Harry Saltzman, Albert R. Broccoli)

James Bond tracks down master criminal Blofeld in Switzerland.
Perhaps to compensate for no Sean Connery and a tragic ending, the producers of this sixth Bond opus shower largesse upon us in the shape of no fewer than four protracted and spectacular climaxes. Splendid stuff, but too much of it, and the lack of a happy centre does show.

w Richard Maibaum, *novel* Ian Fleming *d* Peter Hunt *ph* Michael Reed, Egil Woxholt, Roy Ford, John Jordan *m* John Barry *pd* Syd Cain

George Lazenby, Diana Rigg, Telly Savalas, Ilse Steppat, Gabriele Ferzetti, Yuri Borienko, Bernard Lee, Lois Maxwell

On Moonlight Bay**
US 1951 95m Technicolor
Warner (William Jacobs)

Family crises, to do with growing up and young love, in a 1917 Indiana town.
Pleasant musical, competently made, from the Penrod stories, with the emphasis switched to big sister.

w Melville Shavelson, Jack Rose, *stories* Booth Tarkington *d* Roy del Ruth *ph* Ernest Haller *md* Ray Heindorf

Doris Day, Gordon Macrae, Leon Ames, Rosemary de Camp, Billy Gray
† See also *By the Light of the Silvery Moon*, a companion piece.

On Our Merry Way*
US 1948 107m bw
Benedict Bogeaus, Burgess Meredith

A reporter is urged by his wife to dig up some human interest stories.
Frail compendium of anecdotes which barely work.

w Laurence Stallings, *story* Arch Oboler *d* King Vidor, Leslie Fenton *ph* Joseph August, Gordon Avil, John Seitz, Edward Cronjager *md* David Chudnow, Skitch Henderson

Burgess Meredith, Paulette Goddard, Fred MacMurray, Hugh Herbert, James Stewart, Dorothy Lamour, Victor Moore, Henry Fonda, William Demarest

On the Avenue**
US 1937 89m bw
TCF (Gene Markey)

An heiress rages because she is being satirized in a revue, but later falls in love with the star.
Bright musical which keeps moving and uses its talents wisely.

w Gene Markey, William Conselman d Roy del Ruth ph Lucien Andriot *m/ly Irving Berlin* *ch* Seymour Felix

Dick Powell, Madeleine Carroll, The Ritz Brothers, George Barbier, Alice Faye, Walter Catlett, Joan Davis, E. E. Clive
† Revamped as *Let's Make Love* (qv).

On the Beach**
US 1959 134m bw
US / Stanley Kramer

When most of the world has been devastated by atomic waste, an American atomic submarine sets out to investigate.
Gloomy prophecy which works well in spasms but is generally too content to chat rather than imagine. A solid prestige job nevertheless.

w John Paxton, James Lee Barrett, *novel* Nevil Shute *d Stanley Kramer ph Giuseppe Rotunno, Daniel Fapp* *m* Ernest Gold *pd Rudolph Sternad*

Gregory Peck, Ava Gardner, *Fred Astaire*, Anthony Perkins, Donna Anderson, John Tate, Lola Brooks

'Its humanism is clearly of the order that seeks the support of a clamorous music score. The characters remain little more than spokesmen for timid ideas and Salvation Army slogans, their emotions hired from a Hollywood prop room; which is all pretty disturbing in a film about nothing less than the end of the world.'—*Robert Vas*

On the Beat
GB 1962 105m bw
Rank (Hugh Stewart)

A Scotland Yard car park attendant manages to capture some crooks and become a policeman.
Busy but flat comedy vehicle, never very likeable.

w Jack Davies *d* Robert Asher *ph* Geoffrey Faithfull *m* Philip Green

Norman Wisdom, Jennifer Jayne, Raymond Huntley, David Lodge

On the Buses
GB 1971 88m Technicolor
EMI / Hammer (Ronald Woolfe, Ronald Chesney)

Women drivers cause trouble at a bus depot.
Grotesque, ham-handed farce from a TV series which was sometimes funny; this is merely vulgar.

w Ronald Woolfe, Ronald Chesney *d* Harry Booth *ph* Mark MacDonald *m* Max Harris

Reg Varney, Doris Hare, Anna Karen, Michael Robbins, Stephen Lewis

On the Double*

US 1961 92m Technicolor Panavision
Paramount / Dena–Capri (Jack Rose)

During World War II, an American private is asked to impersonate a British intelligence officer.
From the plot and the talents it seems one might start laughing at this while still in the queue, but in fact most of it goes sadly awry and it never quite comes to the boil.

w Jack Rose, Melville Shavelson *d* Melville Shavelson *ph* Harry Stradling, Geoffrey Unsworth *m* Leith Stevens

Danny Kaye, Dana Wynter, Wilfrid Hyde White, Diana Dors, Margaret Rutherford, Allan Cuthbertson, Jesse White

On the Fiddle*

GB 1961 97m bw
Anglo-Amalgamated / S. Benjamin Fisz
US title: *Operation Snafu*

A wide boy and a slow-witted gypsy have comic and other adventures in the RAF.
Curious mixture of farce and action, more on American lines than British, but quite entertainingly presented.

w Harold Buchman, *novel* Stop at a Winner by R. F. Delderfield *d* Cyril Frankel *ph* Ted Scaife *m* Malcolm Arnold

Alfred Lynch, Sean Connery, Cecil Parker, Wilfrid Hyde White, Kathleen Harrison, Alan King, Eleanor Summerfield, Eric Barker, Terence Longdon, John Le Mesurier, Harry Locke

On the Night of the Fire*

GB 1939 94m bw
GFD / G & S (Josef Somlo)
US title: *The Fugitive*

A barber kills the blackmailer of his wife.
Dour little drama, rather unusual for pre-war British studios.

w Brian Desmond Hurst, Terence Young, *novel* F. L. Green *d* Brian Desmond Hurst

Ralph Richardson, Diana Wynyard, Romney Brent, Mary Clare, Henry Oscar, Frederick Leister

On the Riviera**

US 1951 90m Technicolor
TCF (Sol C. Siegel)

A cabaret artist is persuaded to pose as a philandering businessman.
Remake of *Folies Bergère* and *That Night in Rio* (see also *On the Double*); disliked at the time and accused of tastelessness, it now seems smarter and funnier than comparable films of its era.

w Valentine Davies, Phoebe and Henry Ephron *d Walter Lang ph* Leon Shamroy

Danny Kaye, Corinne Calvet, Gene Tierney, Marcel Dalio, Jean Murat

On the Threshold of Space

US 1956 96m Eastmancolor Cinemascope
TCF (William Bloom)

The USAF medical corps explores human reactions at high altitudes.
Semi-documentary flagwaver with dreary domestic asides; very dated now, and of no particular nostalgic interest.

w Simon Wincelberg, Francis Cockrill *d* Robert D. Webb *ph* Joe MacDonald

Guy Madison, Virginia Leith, John Hodiak, Dean Jagger, Warren Stevens

On the Town****

US 1949 98m Technicolor
MGM (*Arthur Freed*)

Three sailors enjoy twenty-four hours' leave in New York.
Most of this brash location musical counts as among the best things ever to come out of Hollywood; the serious ballet towards the end tends to kill it, but it contains much to be grateful for.

w Betty Comden, Adolph Green, ballet Fancy Free by Leonard Bernstein *d/ch Gene Kelly, Stanley Donen ph Harold Rosson m* Lennie Hayton *songs* various

Gene Kelly, Frank Sinatra, Jules Munshin, Vera-Ellen, Betty Garrett, Ann Miller, Tom Dugan, Florence Bates, Alice Pearce

'A film that will be enjoyed more than twice.' *Lindsay Anderson*

'So exuberant that it threatens at moments to bounce right off the screen.'—*Time*

On the Waterfront***

US 1954 108m bw
Columbia / Sam Spiegel

After the death of his brother, a young stevedore breaks the hold of a waterfront gang boss.
Intense, broody dockside thriller with 'method' performances; very powerful of its kind, and much imitated.

w Budd Schulberg, from his novel *d Elia Kazan ph Boris Kaufman m* Leonard Bernstein

Marlon Brando, Eva Marie Saint, *Lee J. Cobb*, Rod Steiger, Karl Malden, Pat Henning, Leif Erickson, James Westerfield, John Hamilton

'An uncommonly powerful, exciting and imaginative use of the screeen by gifted professionals.'—*New York Times (AW)*

On with the Show
US 1929 98m Technicolor (two-colour)
Warner

Crude early talkie musical revue with historical interest.

w Robert Lord, *play* Shoestring by Humphrey Pearson *d* Alan Crosland *ph* Tony Gaudio *songs* Grant Clarke, Harry Akst

Betty Compson, Louise Fazenda, Sally O'Neil, Joe E. Brown, Ethel Waters, Arthur Lake

On Your Toes*
US 1939 94m bw
Warner (Robert Lord)

Backstage jealousies at the ballet.
Smooth film version of a top Broadway show of its time.

w Jerry Wald, Richard Macaulay, *play* George Abbott *d* Ray Enright *ph* James Wong Howe, Sol Polito *m/ly Richard Rodgers, Lorenz Hart*

Vera Zorina, Eddie Albert, Alan Hale, Frank McHugh, James Gleason, Donald O'Connor, Gloria Dickson

Once a Jolly Swagman*
GB 1948 100m bw
GFD / Wessex (Ian Dalrymple)
US title: *Maniacs on Wheels*

A factory worker becomes a speedway rider.
Competent sporting drama of no particular interest.

w William Rose, Jack Lee *d* Jack Lee *ph* H. E. Fowle *m* Bernard Stevens

Dirk Bogarde, Renée Asherson, Bonar Colleano, Bill Owen

Once a Thief
US 1965 107m bw Panavision
MGM / Cipra / RN / Fred Engel (Jacques Bar)

An ex-convict is hounded by a vengeful cop.
Glum crime melodrama gleamingly photographed but otherwise quite routine.

w Zekial Marko *d* Ralph Nelson *ph Robert Burks m* Lalo Schifrin

Alain Delon, Ann-Margret, Van Heflin, Jack Palance, John David Chandler

Once in a Lifetime**
US 1933 80m approx bw
Universal

How a script was sold in old-time Hollywood.
Half good-humoured, half-scathing satire on Hollywood; technique dated, content still amusing.

w Seton I. Miller, *play* Moss Hart, George S. Kaufman *d* Russell Mack *ph* George Robinson

Jack Oakie, Sidney Fox, Aline MacMahon, Russell Hopton, Zasu Pitts, Louise Fazenda, Gregory Ratoff, Onslow Stevens

Once Is Not Enough
US 1975 122m Movielab Panavision
Paramount / Sujac / Aries (Howard W. Koch)
aka: *Jacqueline Susann's Once Is Not Enough*

The daughter of a movie producer is corrupted by his circle.
Old-fashioned jet-set melodrama with new-fashioned sexual novelties.

w Julius J. Epstein, *novel* Jacqueline Susann *d* Guy Green *ph* John A. Alonzo *m* Henry Mancini *pd* John de Cuir

Kirk Douglas, Alexis Smith, David Janssen, George Hamilton, Melina Mercouri, Gary Conway, Brenda Vaccaro, Deborah Raffin

Once More My Darling
US 1949 92m bw
Universal (Joan Harrison)

A young girl is romantically pursued by an older man.
Tame comedy.

w Robert Carson *d* Robert Montgomery *ph* Franz Planer *m* Elizabeth Firestone

Robert Montgomery, Ann Blyth, Jane Cowl, Taylor Holmes, Charles McGraw

Once More with Feeling
GB 1960 92m Technicolor
Columbia / Stanley Donen

The volatile private life of an orchestral conductor.
Thin comedy from a West End play, something between a shouting match and a fashion show.

w Harry Kurnitz, from his play *d* Stanley Donen *ph* Georges Périnal *md* Muir Mathieson *pd* Alexander Trauner

Yul Brynner, Kay Kendall, Geoffrey Toone, Maxwell Shaw, Mervyn Johns, Martin Benson, Gregory Ratoff

Once Upon a Dead Man**
US 1971 100m Technicolor TVM
Universal (Leonard B. Stern)

San Francisco's police chief and his zany wife uncover an art racket.
Easily digestible, hard-to-follow mystery climaxing in a cycle chase. Pilot for the *McMillan and Wife* series.

w Leonard B. Stern, Chester Krumholtz *d* Leonard B. Stern

Rock Hudson, Susan St James, Jack Albertson, René Auberjonois, Kurt Kazsnar, Jonathan Harris, Herb Edelman, John Schuck, James Wainwright

Once Upon a Honeymoon*
US 1942 116m bw
RKO (Leo McCarey)

An American radio correspondent and an ex-burlesque queen cheat the Nazis—and her husband—in Europe during World War II.
Smooth but curious mixture of comedy and drama, a satisfactory but unmemorable star vehicle.

w Sheridan Gibney, Leo McCarey *d* Leo McCarey *ph* George Barnes *m* Robert Emmett Dolan

Cary Grant, Ginger Rogers, Walter Slezak, Albert Dekker, Albert Bassermann, Ferike Boros, Harry Shannon
'The attempt to play for both laughs and significance against a terrifying background of Nazi aggression is on the whole a little disappointing.'—*Newsweek*

Once Upon a Time*
US 1944 89m bw
Columbia (Louis Edelman)

A luckless producer makes a sensation out of a boy and his dancing caterpillar.
Thin whimsical comedy, too slight to come off given such standard treatment, but with nice touches along the way.

w Lewis Meltzer, Oscar Saul, *radio play* My Client Curley by Norman Corwin, Lucille F. Herrmann *d* Alexander Hall *ph* Franz Planer *m* Frederick Hollander

Cary Grant, Janet Blair, James Gleason, Ted Donaldson, Howard Freeman, William Demarest, Art Baker, John Abbott
'There just isn't enough material here for a full-length feature.'—*Philip T. Hartung*

Once Upon a Time in the West*
Italy / US 1969 165m Techniscope
Paramount / Rafran / San Marco (Fulvio Morsella)

A lonely woman in the old west is in danger from a band of gunmen.
Immensely long and convoluted epic western marking its director's collaboration with an American studio and his desire to make serious statements about something or other. Beautifully made, empty, and very violent.

w Sergio Leone, Sergio Donati *d* Sergio Leone *ph* Tonino Delli Colli *m* Ennio Morricone

Henry Fonda, Claudia Cardinale, Jason Robards, Charles Bronson, Gabriele Ferzetti, Keenan Wynn, Paolo Stoppa, Lionel Stander, Jack Elam, Woody Strode

One Day in the Life of Ivan Denisovich*
GB 1971 105m Eastmancolor
Group W (Caspar Wrede)

Life in a Siberian labour camp in 1950.
A fairly successful book adaptation, as far as mere pictures can cope with the harrowing detail.

w Ronald Harwood, *novel* Alexander Solzhenitsyn *d* Caspar Wrede *ph Sven Nykvist* *m* Arne Nordheim

Tom Courtenay, Espen Skjonberg, James Maxwell, Alfred Burke, Eric Thompson, Matthew Guinness
'The film's general air of earnestness deflects rather than stimulates involvement.'—*David Wilson*

One Desire
US 1955 94m Technicolor
U-I (Ross Hunter)

The romantic career of the lady owner of a gambling saloon.
Tawdry nineties drama which never really gets going.

w Lawrence Roman, Robert Blees, *novel* Tacey Cromwell by Conrad Richter *d* Jerry Hopper *ph* Maury Gertsman *m* Joseph Gershenson

Anne Baxter, Rock Hudson, Julia Adams, Natalie Wood, Barry Curtis, William Hopper, Carl Benton Reid
'The standards of writing and characterization belong to a Victorian servant girl's paper-covered romance.'—*MFB*

One Eyed Jacks
US 1961 141m Technicolor Vistavision
Paramount (Frank P. Rosenberg)

An outlaw has a running battle with an old friend.
Grossly self-indulgent western controlled (unwisely) by its star, full of solemn pauses and bouts of violence.

w Guy Trosper, Calder Willingham, *novel* The Authentic Death of Hendry Jones by Charles

Neider *d* Marlon Brando *ph* Charles Lang Jnr *m* Hugo Friedhofer

Marlon Brando, Karl Malden, Pina Pellicier, Katy Jurado, Slim Pickens, Ben Johnson, Timothy Carey, Elisha Cook Jnr

One Flew over the Cuckoo's Nest***
US 1975 134m De Luxe
UA / Fantasy Films (Paul Zaentz, Michael Douglas)

A cheerful immoralist imprisoned for rape is transferred for observation to a state mental hospital.
Wildly and unexpectedly commercial film of a project which had lain dormant for fourteen years, this amusing and horrifying film conveniently sums up anti-government attitudes as well as make love not war and all that. It's certainly impossible to ignore.

w Laurence Hauben, Bo Goldman, *novel Ken Kesey d Milos Forman ph* Haskell Wexler *m* Jack Nitzche *pd* Paul Sylbert

Jack Nicholson, Louise Fletcher, William Redfield, Will Sampson, Brad Dourif, Christopher Lloyd

'Lacks the excitement of movie art, but the story and the acting make the film emotionally powerful.'—*New Yorker*

One Foot in Heaven*
US 1941 108m bw
Warner (Robert Lord, Irving Rapper)

The small-town doings of a methodist minister.
Slow but pleasing chronicle, nicely assembled.

w Casey Robinson, *biography* (of his father) Hartzell Spence *d* Irving Rapper *ph* Charles Rosher *m* Max Steiner

Fredric March, Martha Scott, Beulah Bondi, Gene Lockhart, Elizabeth Fraser, Harry Davenport, Laura Hope Crews, Grant Mitchell, Moroni Olsen, Ernest Cossart, Jerome Cowan

'A clean, sweet, decent picture.'—*Cecilia Ager*

One Hour with You***
US 1932 84m bw
Paramount (*Ernst Lubitsch*)

The affairs of a philandering Parisian doctor.
Superbly handled comedy of manners in Lubitsch's most inventive form, handled by a most capable cast. Unique entertainment of a kind which is, alas, no more.

w Samson Raphaelson, play Only a Dream by Lothar Schmidt *d George Cukor, Ernst Lubitsch ph* Victor Milner *m Oscar Straus, Richard Whiting ly Leo Robin ad Hans Dreier*

Maurice Chevalier, Jeanette MacDonald, Genevieve Tobin, Roland Young, Charles Ruggles, George Barbier

'A brand new form of musical entertainment . . . he has mixed verse, spoken and sung, a smart and satiric musical background, asides to the audience, and sophisticated dialogue, as well as lilting and delightful songs . . . The result is something so delightful that it places the circle of golden leaves jauntily upon the knowing head of Hollywood's most original director.'—• *Philadelphia Inquirer*

† A remake of Lubitsch's silent success *The Marriage Circle.*

One Hundred and One Dalmatians***
US 1960 79m Technicolor
Walt Disney

The dogs of London help save puppies which are being stolen for their skins by a cruel villainess.
Disney's last really splendid feature cartoon, with the old flexible style cleverly modernized and plenty of invention and detail in the story line. The London backgrounds are especially nicely judged.

w Bill Peet, *novel* Dodie Smith *d* Wolfgang Reitherman, Hamilton S. Luske, Clyde Geronimi

One Hundred Men and a Girl***
US 1937 84m bw
Universal (*Joe Pasternak*)

A young girl persuades a great conductor to form an orchestra of unemployed musicians.
Delightful and funny musical fable, an instance of the Pasternak formula of sweetness and light at its richest and best.

w Bruce Manning, Charles Kenyon, Hans Kraly d Henry Koster ph Joseph Valentine *songs* various

Deanna Durbin, Adolphe Menjou, Leopold Stokowski, Alice Brady, Mischa Auer, Eugene Pallette, Billy Gilbert, Alma Kruger, Jed Prouty, Frank Jenks, Christian Rub

100 Rifles*
US 1969 109m De Luxe
TCF / Marvin Schwartz

In war-torn Mexico, a black American sheriff and his prisoner become involved in a girl's fight for vengeance after her father's death.
Blood-soaked adventure with plenty of tough action and tight pace. A little too purposeful in its unpleasantness to be very entertaining.

w Clair Huffaker, Tom Gries, *novel* Robert MacLeod *d Tom Gries ph* Cecilio Paniagua *m* Jerry Goldsmith

Jim Brown, Raquel Welch, Burt Reynolds, Fernando Lamas, Dan O'Herlihy, Hans Gudegast

One in a Million**

US 1937 94m bw
TCF (Raymond Griffith)

The daughter of a Swiss innkeeper becomes an Olympic ice-skating champion.
Sonja Henie's film debut shows Hollywood at its most professional, making entertainment out of the purest moonshine with considerable injections of novelty talent.

w Lenore Praskins, Mark Kelly *d* Sidney Lanfield *ph* Edward Cronjager *md* Louis Silvers

Sonja Henie, Don Ameche, *The Ritz Brothers*, Jean Hersholt, Ned Sparks, Arline Judge, Dixie Dunbar, Borrah Minnevitch and his Rascals, Montagu Love

One Is a Lonely Number*

US 1972 97m Metrocolor
MGM (Stan Margulies)

When her husband leaves her, a woman tries to develop new interests.
Satirical sentimental view of American divorce, with interesting moments.

w David Seltzer, *novel* Rebecca Morris *d* Mel Stuart *ph* Michel Hugo *m* Michel Legrand

Trish Van Devere, Monte Markham, Michael Douglas, Janet Leigh

One Little Indian

US 1973 91m Technicolor
Walt Disney (Winston Hibler)

A cavalry corporal escapes from jail and falls in with a ten-year-old Indian.
Sentimental semi-western, a bit dull for Disney apart from a camel.

w Harry Spalding *d* Bernard McEveety *ph* Charles F. Wheeler *m* Jerry Goldsmith

James Garner, Vera Miles, Pat Hingle, Morgan Woodward, John Doucette

One Million BC*

US 1939 80m bw
Hal Roach
GB title: *Man and His Mate*
aka: *The Cave Dwellers*

Life between warring tribes of primitive man in the stone age.
Impressive-looking but slow-moving grunt-and-groan epic originally based on D. W. Griffith's *Man's Genesis* and on which Griffith did some work. The totally unhistoric dinosaurs (which had disappeared long before man arrived) are impressively concocted by magnifying lizards.

w Mickell Novak, George Baker, Joseph Frickert *d* Hal Roach, Hal Roach Jnr, D. W. Griffith *ph Norbert Brodine* *m* Werner R. Heymann

Victor Mature, Carole Landis, Lon Chaney Jnr, John Hubbard, Nigel de Brulier, Conrad Nagel

One Million Years BC*

GB 1966 100m Technicolor
Hammer (Michael Carreras)

A vague remake of the above, with animated monsters. Not badly done, with some lively action.

w Michael Carreras *d* Don Chaffey *ph* Wilkie Cooper *m* Mario Nascimbene

John Crawford, Raquel Welch, Robert Brown, Percy Herbert, Martine Beswick

'Very easy to dismiss the film as a silly spectacle; but Hammer production finesse is much in evidence and Don Chaffey has done a competent job of direction. And it is all hugely enjoyable.'—*David Wilson*

One Minute to Zero

US 1952 105m bw
RKO (Edmund Grainger)

In Korea a US colonel is evacuating American civilians but is forced to bomb refugees.
Flat war film with Something To Say and the star at his most humourless.

w Milton Krims, William Haines *d* Tay Garnett *ph* William E. Snyder *m* Constantin Bakaleinikoff

Robert Mitchum, Ann Blyth, William Talman, Charles McGraw, Richard Egan

One More River*

US 1934 88m bw
Universal (James Whale)
GB title: *Over the River*

A wife runs away from her husband, and he sets detectives on her and her lover.
Old-fashioned, well made picturization of a novel.

w R. C. Sheriff, *novel* John Galsworthy *d* James Whale *ph* John Mescall *m* W. Franke Harling

Colin Clive, Diana Wynyard, C. Aubrey Smith, Jane Wyatt, Lionel Atwill, Mrs Patrick Campbell, Frank Lawton, Reginald Denny, C. Aubrey Smith, Henry Stephenson, Alan Mowbray, E. E. Clive

'Taste, elegance, narrative drive and a deliberate nostalgia for the Galsworthy period.'—*Peter John Dyer, 1966*

One More Spring*
US 1935 87m bw
Fox (Winfield Sheehan)

Three strangers, in reduced circumstances due to the Depression, meet in Central Park and pool their resources.
Topical serio-comedy which looks pretty dated but still serves as a summation of American mid-thirties attitudes.

w Edwin Burke, novel Robert Nathan *d* Henry King *ph* John Seitz *md* Arthur Lange

Janet Gaynor, Warner Baxter, Walter Woolf King, Grant Mitchell, Jane Darwell, Roger Imhof, John Qualen, Dick Foran, Stepin Fetchit

One More Time
GB 1969 93m De Luxe
UA / Chrislaw–Tracemark (Milton Ebbins)

More crime-solving adventures of Salt and Pepper.
Even less funny than before; see *Salt and Pepper*.

w Michael Pertwee *d* Jerry Lewis *ph* Ernest Steward *m* Les Reed

Peter Lawford, Sammy Davis Jnr, Esther Anderson, Maggie Wright

One More Tomorrow*
US 1946 89m bw
Warner (Henry Blanke)

A wealthy playboy marries a left-wing photographer and buys up her magazine.
An interesting but dated play fails to come to life because neither cast nor director seem to understand what it's about.

w Charles Hoffman, Catherine Turney, Julius J. and Philip G. Epstein, *play* The Animal Kingdom by Philip Barry *d* Peter Godfrey *ph* Bert Glennon *d* Max Steiner

Ann Sheridan, Dennis Morgan, Jack Carson, Alexis Smith, Jane Wyman, Reginald Gardiner, John Loder, Marjorie Gateson

One More Train to Rob
US 1971 108m Technicolor
Universal (Robert Arthur)

A train robber comes out of prison and warily takes up with his old partners.
Undistinguished western which tries to be funny and serious at the same time.

w Don Tait, Dick Nelson *d* Andrew V. McLaglen *ph* Alric Edens *m* David Shire

George Peppard, Diana Muldaur, John Vernon, France Nuyen, Steve Sandor

One Night in Lisbon
US 1941 97m bw
Paramount (Edward H. Griffith)

During World War II an American flier falls for a British socialite who is being used by the government as a decoy for spies.
Flabby romantic comedy-drama which mostly wastes a good cast.

w Virginia Van Upp *d* Edward H. Griffith

Madeleine Carroll, Fred MacMurray, Edmund Gwenn, Patricia Morison, Billie Burke, John Loder, Dame May Whitty, Reginald Denny, Billy Gilbert

One Night in the Tropics
US 1940 69m bw
Universal (Leonard Spiegelgass)

Holidays on a Caribbean island lead to a double wedding.
Very lightweight comedy-musical notable only for introducing Abbott and Costello.

w Gertrude Purcell, Charles Grayson, *play* Love Insurance by Earl Derr Biggers *d* A. Edward Sutherland *ph* Joseph Valentine *md* Charles Previn *songs* Oscar Hammerstein II, Jerome Kern, Otto Harbach, Dorothy Fields

Allan Jones, Nancy Kelly, Bud Abbott, Lou Costello, Robert Cummings, Leo Carillo, Peggy Moran, Mary Boland

One Night of Love**
US 1934 95m bw
Columbia (Harry Cohn)

An opera star rebels against her demanding teacher.
Light classical musical which was a surprising box office success and brought Hollywood careers for Lily Pons, Gladys Swarthout, Miliza Korjus, etc.

w Dorothy Speare, Charles Beahan, S. K. Lauren, James Gow, Edmund North *d Victor Schertzinger* *ph* Joseph Walker *md* Pietro Cimini

Grace Moore, Tullio Carminati, Lyle Talbot, Mona Barrie, Nydia Westman, Jessie Ralph, Luis Alberni, Jane Darwell

One of My Wives Is Missing**
US 1975 97m colour TVM
Spelling–Goldberg (Barney Rosenzweig)

A man arrives at a holiday resort and reports to the police that his wife has vanished. A woman he has never seen before then turns up claiming to be his wife. . . .
Satisfying what's-it-all-abouter which plays pretty fair and deals suspicion like a pack of

cards. The plot is borrowed from *Chase a Crooked Shadow* and other sources.

w Peter Stone, *play* Trap for a Lonely Man by Robert Thomas *d* Glen Jordan

James Franciscus, Jack Klugman, Elizabeth Ashley, Joel Fabiani

One of Our Aircraft Is Missing*
GB 1941 102m bw
British National (Michael Powell, Emeric Pressburger)

A bomber is grounded after a raid and its crew is helped by the Dutch resistance.
Efficient propaganda piece which starts vigorously but gets bogged down in talk.

wd Michael Powell, Emeric Pressburger

Godfrey Tearle, Eric Portman, Hugh Williams, Bernard Miles, Hugh Burden, Emrys Jones, Googie Withers, Pamela Brown, Peter Ustinov, Joyce Redman, Hay Petrie, Robert Helpmann, Alec Clunes

One of Our Dinosaurs Is Missing*
US 1975 94m Technicolor
Walt Disney (Bill Walsh)

In the 1920s a strip of secret microfilm is smuggled out of China and hidden in a dinosaur's skeleton in the Natural History Museum.
Unexceptionable family comedy with everyone trying hard; somehow it just misses, perhaps because it is told through talk rather than cinematic narrative.

w Bill Walsh, *novel* The Great Dinosaur Robbery by David Forrest *d* Robert Stevenson *ph* Paul Beeson *m* Ron Goodwin

Helen Hayes, Peter Ustinov, Derek Nimmo, Clive Revill, Joan Sims, Bernard Bresslaw, Roy Kinnear, Deryck Guyler, Richard Pearson

One of Our Own
US 1975 98m Technicolor TVM
Universal (Matthew Rapf, Jack Laird)

The chief of a large hospital faces numerous crises.
Predictable pilot for the unsuccessful series *Doctors' Hospital.*

w Jack Laird *d* Richard Sarafian

George Peppard, Oscar Homolka, William Daniels, Louise Sorel, Stother Martin, Zohra Lampert, Albert Paulsen

One Sunday Afternoon**
US 1933 93m bw
Paramount (Louis D. Lighton)

In 1910, a Brooklyn dentist feels he has married the wrong girl, but discovers that his choice was the right one.
Pleasant period comedy drama which was twice remade; as *The Strawberry Blonde* (qv) and see below.

w William Slavens McNutt, Grover Jones, *play* James Hagan *d* Stephen Roberts *ph* Victor Milner

Gary Cooper, Frances Fuller, Fay Wray, Neil Hamilton, Roscoe Karns

One Sunday Afternoon
US 1948 90m Technicolor
Warner (Jerry Wald)

Pleasant but undistinguished musical remake of the above.

w Robert L. Richards *d* Raoul Walsh *ph* Sid Hickox, Wilfrid M. Cline *m* Ralph Blane *ad* Anton Grot

Dennis Morgan, Dorothy Malone, Janis Paige, Don Defore, Ben Blue

The One That Got Away**
GB 1957 111m bw
Rank (Julian Wintle)

A German flier, Franz Von Werra, is captured and sent to various British prisoner-of-war camps, from all of which he escapes.
True-life biopic, developed in a number of suspense and action sequences, all very well done.

w Howard Clewes, book Kendal Burt, James Leasor *d Roy Baker ph* Eric Cross *m* Hubert Clifford

Hardy Kruger, Michael Goodliffe, Colin Gordon, *Alec McCowen*

One Third of a Nation*
US 1939 79m bw
Federal Theatre (Dudley Murphy)

A shopgirl persuades a landlord to tear down his dangerous slums and put up good buildings.
Naïve do-goodery, not too persuasively managed.

w Dudley Murphy, Oliver H. P. Garrett, *play* Arthur Arent *d* Dudley Murphy *ph* William Miller

Sylvia Sidney, Leif Erickson, Myron McCormick, Hiram Sherman, Sidney Lumet, Percy Waram

One Touch of Venus*
US 1948 82m bw
Universal / Lester Cowan

In a fashionable department store, a statue of

Venus comes to life and falls for a window dresser.
Pleasant satirical comedy, watered down from the Broadway original.

w Harry Kurnitz, Frank Tashlin, *play* S. J. Perelman, Ogden Nash *d* William A. Seiter *ph* Franz Planer *songs* Kurt Weill *ad* Bernard Herzbrun, Emrich Nicholson

Ava Gardner, Robert Walker, Eve Arden, Dick Haymes, Olga San Juan, Tom Conway

One, Two, Three***
US 1961 115m bw Panavision
UA / Mirisch / Pyramid

An executive in West Berlin is trying to sell Coca Cola to the Russians while preventing his boss's daughter from marrying a communist.
Back to *Ninotchka* territory, but this time the tone is that of a wild farce which achieves fine momentum in stretches but also flags a lot in between, teetering the while on the edge of taste.

w Billy Wilder, I. A. L. Diamond, *play* Ferenc Molnar *d Billy Wilder ph* Daniel Fapp *m* André Previn

James Cagney, Horst Buchholz, Arlene Francis, Pamela Tiffin, Lilo Pulver, Howard St John, Leon Askin

'A sometimes bewildered, often wonderfully funny exercise in nonstop nuttiness.'—*Time*

'This first-class featherweight farce is a serious achievement.'—*Stanley Kauffmann*

One Way Passage*
US 1932 69m bw
Warner (Robert Lord)

On an ocean voyage, a dying girl falls in love with a crook going home to face a life sentence.
Pattern melodrama which stood Hollywood in good stead.

w Wilson Mizner, Joseph Jackson, Robert Lord *d* Tay Garnett *ph* Robert Kurrie

William Powell, Kay Francis, Frank McHugh, Aline MacMahon, Warren Hymer, Herbert Mundin, Roscoe Karns, Stanley Fields
† Remade as *'Til We Meet Again* (qv).

One Way Pendulum
GB 1964 85m bw
UA / Woodfall (Michael Deeley)

A suburban clerk leads a dream existence; his son teaches speak-your-weight machines to sing, while he sets an imaginary murder trial in motion.
A nonsense play (which has many adherents) resists the literalness of the camera eye.

w N. F. Simpson, from his play *d* Peter Yates *ph* Denys Coop *m* Richard Rodney Bennett

Eric Sykes, George Cole, Peggy Mount, Alison Leggatt, Mona Washbourne

One Way Street
US 1950 79m bw
U-I / Leonard Goldstein (Sam Goldwyn Jnr)

A disillusioned doctor steals a fortune and hides out in a Mexican village, where he regains his self-respect.
Thin and pointless melodrama.

w Lawrence Kimble *d* Hugo Fregonese *ph* Maury Gertsman *m* Frank Skinner

James Mason, Marta Toren, Dan Duryea, William Conrad, King Donovan, Jack Elam

'It is reported that James Mason chooses his own parts, and if this is true I have to report that he is a glutton for punishment.'—*Daily Herald*

'One of the dullest, most stupid films of the year.'—*Sunday Pictorial*

Onionhead
US 1958 110m bw
Warner (Jules Schermer)

Adventures of a ship's cook in the US Coastguard.
Service comedy that must have seemed funnier in the US than in Britain.

w Nelson Gidding, *novel* Weldon Hill *d* Norman Taurog *ph* Harold Rosson *md* Ray Heindorf

Andy Griffith, Felicia Farr, Walter Matthau, Erin O'Brien, Joe Mantell, Ray Danton, Roscoe Karns, James Gregory, Tige Andrews
† An attempt to cash in on the success of *No Time for Sergeants*.

Only Angels Have Wings**
US 1939 121m bw
Columbia (Howard Hawks)

Tension creeps into the relationships of the men who fly cargo planes over the Andes when a stranded showgirl sets her cap at the boss.
For an action film this is really too restricted by talk and cramped studio sets, and its theme was more entertainingly explored in *Red Dust*. Still, it couldn't be more typical of the Howard Hawks film world, where men are men and women have to be as tough as they are.

wd Howard Hawks ph Joseph Walker, Elmer Dyer *md* Morris Stoloff

Cary Grant, Jean Arthur, Rita Hayworth, Richard Barthelmess, Thomas Mitchell, Sig Rumann, Victor Kilian, John Carroll, Allyn Joslyn

'All these people did the best they could with what they were given—but look at it.'—*Otis Ferguson*

The Only Game in Town
US 1969 113m De Luxe
TCF (Fred Kohlmar)

A Las Vegas chorus girl and a piano player have an unhappy life because of his gambling fever. Uninteresting two-header from a play that didn't make it; no light relief, no action, and not even very good acting.

w Frank D. Gilroy, from his play *d* George Stevens *ph* Henri Decäe *m* Maurice Jarre

Elizabeth Taylor, Warren Beatty, Charles Braswell, Hank Henry

'It epitomises the disaster the studio and star systems foist on films . . . the only two-character tale around to cost $11 million.'—*Judith Crist*

Only the Valiant
US 1950 105m bw
William Cagney

A tough cavalry officer in a lonely fort wins a battle against Indians.
Standard top-of-the-bill western; competent but not very gripping.

w Edmund H. North, Harry Brown *d* Gordon Douglas *ph* Lionel Lindon *m* Franz Waxman

Gregory Peck, Ward Bond, Gig Young, Lon Chaney Jnr, Barbara Payton, Neville Brand

Only Two Can Play***
GB 1962 106m bw
British Lion / Vale (Launder and Gilliat)

A much married assistant librarian in a Welsh town has an abortive affair with a councillor's wife.
Well characterized and generally diverting 'realistic' comedy which slows up a bit towards the end but contains many memorable sequences and provides its star's last good character performance.

w Bryan Forbes, novel That Uncertain Feeling by *Kingsley Amis d Sidney Gilliat ph* John Wilcox *m* Richard Rodney Bennett *ad* Albert Witherick

Peter Sellers, Mai Zetterling, Virginia Maskell, Richard Attenborough, Raymond Huntley, John Le Mesurier, *Kenneth Griffith*

The Only Way Out Is Dead
Canada 1970 100m colour TVM
Palomer
aka: *The Man Who Wanted to Live Forever*

A man determined to live forever selects other people's organs for his future use.
A talky rather than gruesome, but still rather tasteless suspenser.

w Henry Denker *d* John Trent

Burl Ives, Sandy Dennis, Stuart Whitman, Ron Hartman, Robert Goodier

Only When I Larf*
GB 1968 103m Eastmancolor
Paramount / Beecord (Len Deighton, Brian Duffy, Hugh Attwooll)

The adventures of three confidence tricksters. Quite likeable but unmemorable 'with it' comedy of the sixties; the tricks are more amusing than the characterization.

w John Salmon, *novel* Len Deighton *d* Basil Dearden *ph* Anthony Richmond *m* Ron Grainer

Richard Attenborough, David Hemmings, Alexandra Stewart, Nicholas Pennell, Melissa Stribling, Terence Alexander, Edric Connor, Calvin Lockhart, Clifton Jones

Only with Married Men*
US 1974 74m colour TVM
Spelling–Goldberg

A sexy girl who only wants to date married men meets a sly bachelor who pretends to be married so as not to get involved.
Brash, bright sex comedy which sustains well for most of its length.

w Jerry Davis *d* Jerry Paris

David Birney, Michele Lee, John Astin, Judy Carne, Dom De Luise

Ooh, You Are Awful*
GB 1972 97m Eastmancolor
British Lion / Quintain (E. M. Smedley Aston)

A London con man seeks a fortune, the clue to which is tattooed on the behind of one of several girls.
Amusing star vehicle with plenty of room for impersonations and outrageous jokes.

w John Warren, John Singer *d Cliff Owen* *ph* Ernest Stewart *m* Christopher Gunning

Dick Emery, Derren Nesbitt, Ronald Fraser, Pat Coombs, William Franklyn, Brian Oulton, Norman Bird

Open Season
US / Spain / Switzerland 1974 104m Eastmancolor Panavision
Impala / Arpa (George H. Brown, Jose S. Vicuna)

Three young criminals hunt human prey, but one of their victims takes his own revenge.
Rough, flashy, violent melodrama which pretends to have something to say but in fact is merely sensationalist.

w David Osborn, Liz Charles Williams *d* Peter Collinson *ph* Fernando Arribas *m* Ruggero Cini

Peter Fonda, Cornelia Sharp, John Phillip Law, Richard Lynch, Albert Mendoza, William Holden

'Both patience and the plot line are severely strained by the artiness Collinson frequently indulges, with frozen shots to mark the moments of truth and a meaningless punctuation throughout of long shots, angles and flashes.'—*Tom Milne*

'An offensive, gamy potboiler.'—*Variety*

Operation Amsterdam*
GB 1958 104m bw
Rank / Maurice Cowan

In 1940 spies are sent into Holland to prevent the invading Germans from finding Amsterdam's stock of industrial diamonds.
Semi-documentary war adventure, well mounted and played.

w Michael McCarthy, John Eldridge, *book* Adventure in Diamonds by David Walker *d Michael McCarthy ph* Reg Wyer, *m* Philip Green

Peter Finch, Tony Britton, Eva Bartok, Alexander Knox, Malcolm Keen, Tim Turner, John Horsley, Melvyn Hayes, Christopher Rhodes

Operation Crossbow*
GB 1965 116m Metrocolor Panavision
MGM / Carlo Ponti
aka: *The Great Spy Mission*

In World War II, trained scientists are parachuted into Europe to destroy the Nazi rocket-making plant at Peenemunde.
Unlikely, star-packed war yarn with more passing tragedy than most, all obliterated by a shoot-em-up James Bond finale.

w Robert Imrie (Emeric Pressburger), Derry Quinn, Ray Rigby *d* Michael Anderson *ph* Erwin Hillier *m* Ron Goodwin

George Peppard, Tom Courtenay, John Mills, Sophia Loren, Lilli Palmer, Anthony Quayle, Patrick Wymark, Jeremy Kemp, Paul Henreid, Trevor Howard, Sylvia Sims, Richard Todd

Operation Daybreak
US 1975 119m Technicolor
Warner / Howard R. Schuster / American Allied (Carter de Haven)

In 1941, Czech patriots kill the hated Nazi Heydrich and are hunted down.
Curiously-timed evocation of wartime resistance adventures, too realistic for the squeamish and certainly not very entertaining despite a fair level of professionalism.

w Ronald Harwood, *novel* Seven Men at Daybreak by Alan Burgess *d* Lewis Gilbert *ph* Henri Decaë *m* David Hentschel

Timothy Bottoms, Martin Shaw, Joss Ackland, Nicola Pagett, Anthony Andrews, Anton Diffring, Carl Duering, Diana Coupland

Operation Heartbeat*
US 1969 100m colour TVM
MGM (A. C. Ward)
aka: *U.M.C.*

Life at a university medical center.
Competent pilot for the long-running series *Medical Centre.*

w A. C. Ward *d* Boris Sagal

Richard Bradford, James Daly, Edward G. Robinson, Maurice Evans, Kevin McCarthy, William Windom, Kim Stanley, J. D. Cannon

Operation Mad Ball*
US 1957 105m bw
Columbia (Jed Harris)

American troops in Normandy are forbidden to fraternize with nurses, but a clandestine dance is arranged.
Madcap army farce which keeps promising to be funnier than it is.

w Arthur Carter, Jed Harris, Blake Edwards, *play* Arthur Carter *d Richard Quine ph* Charles Lawton Jnr *m* George Duning

Jack Lemmon, Ernie Kovacs, Kathryn Grant, Mickey Rooney, James Darren, Arthur O'Connell

Operation Pacific
US 1950 109m bw
Warner (Louis F. Edelmann)

Adventures of a submarine commander in the Pacific war.
Routine war heroics, tolerably done but overstretched.

wd George Waggner *ph* Bert Glennon *m* Max Steiner

John Wayne, Patricia Neal, Ward Bond, Scott Forbes, Phil Carey, Paul Picerni, William Campbell, Martin Milner

Operation Petticoat*
US 1959 124m Eastmancolor
Universal / Granart (Robert Arthur)

During World War II, a crippled submarine is refloated by fair means and foul, and a party of nurses is taken aboard.

Flabby comedy with good moments, but not many.

w Stanley Shapiro, Maurice Richlin *d* Blake Edwards *ph* Russell Harlan *m* David Rose

Cary Grant, Tony Curtis, Joan O'Brien, Dina Merrill, Gene Evans, Arthur O'Connell, Richard Sargent

'Grant is a living lesson in getting laughs without lines.'—*Variety*

Operation Secret
US 1952 108m bw
Warner (Henry Blanke)

A traitor in the French resistance movement shoots a colleague, and the wrong man is accused.
Belated World War II adventure which gives the impression of having been discarded by Errol Flynn.

w James R. Webb, Harold Medford *d* Lewis Seiler *ph* Ted McCord m Roy Webb

Cornel Wilde, Steve Cochran, Paul Picerni, Karl Malden

Operator 13
US 1933 86m bw
MGM / Cosmopolitan (Lucien Hubbard)
GB title: *Spy 13*

During the Civil War an actress becomes a Union spy.
Elaborate period romance with action highlights.

w Harry Thew, Zelda Sears, Eve Greene *d* Richard Boleslawski *ph George Folsey* *m* William Axt

Marion Davies, Gary Cooper, Jean Parker, Katherine Alexander, Ted Healy, Russell Hardie, Henry Wadsworth, Douglass Dumbrille

The Opposite Sex
US 1956 116m Metrocolor Cinemascope
MGM (Joe Pasternak)

A New York socialite divorces her unfaithful husband but finally takes him back.
Softened, musicalized version of *The Women* (qv); very patchy, shapeless, and not nearly sharp enough.

w Fay and Michael Kanin, *play* Clare Boothe *d* David Miller *m* George Stoll *songs* Nicholas Brodsky, Sammy Cahn

June Allyson, Dolores Gray, Joan Collins, Ann Sheridan, Agnes Moorehead, Joan Blondell, Barbara Jo Allen, Charlotte Greenwood

The Optimists of Nine Elms*
GB 1973 110m Eastmancolor
Chettah / Sagittarius (Adrian Gaye, Victor Lyndon)

Children of a London slum make friends with an old busker.
Gentle, sentimental, quite well-observed piece of wistful melancholia, falsified by its star performance.

wd Anthony Simmons, from his novel *co-w* Tudor Gates *ph* Larry Pizer *m* George Martin

Peter Sellers, Donna Mullane, John Chaffey, David Daker, Marjorie Yates

The Oracle
GB 1952 83m bw
Group Three (Colin Lesslie)

A reporter discovers that a village well in Ireland contains an oracle which can predict the future.
Weak sub-Ealing comedy which aims to please and gets a few laughs. All very British.

w Patrick Campbell *d* C. M. Pennington-Richards *ph* Wolfgang Suschitsky *m* Temple Abady

Robert Beatty, Virginia McKenna, Mervyn Johns, Gilbert Harding

Orchestra Wives**
US 1942 97m bw
TCF (William Le Baron)

A small-town girl marries the singer of a travelling swing band.
Fresh and lively musical of its period, full of first-class music and amusing backstage backbiting.

w Karl Tunberg, Darrell Ware *d* Archie Mayo *ph* Lucien Ballard *md* Alfred Newman

Ann Rutherford, George Montgomery, Lynn Bari, *Glenn Miller and his Orchestra*, Carole Landis, Jackie Gleason

Ordeal*
US 1973 74m colour TVM
TCF

An injured businessman is left for dead in the desert by his wife and her lover.
Remake of *Inferno*, considerably less effective.

w Francis Cockrell, Leon Tokatyan *d* Lee H. Katzin

Arthur Hill, Diana Muldaur, James Stacy, Michael Ansara, Macdonald Carey

Orders to Kill*
GB 1958 111m bw
British Lion / Lynx (Anthony Asquith, Anthony Havelock-Allan)

During World War II a bomber pilot undertakes a mission to parachute into occupied France and kill a double agent, who turns out afterwards to have been innocent.
Strong, hard-to-take but well made war story about the effect of war on conscience.

w Paul Dehn d Anthony Asquith ph Desmond Dickinson *m* Benjamin Frankel

Paul Massie, Irene Worth, James Robertson Justice, *Leslie French*, Eddie Albert, Lillian Gish, John Crawford, Jacques Brunius, Lionel Jeffries

The Oregon Trail
US 1975 100m Technicolor TVM
Universal

A pioneeer family heads west.
Talky mini-western, pilot for a series that never was, making lavish use of clips from older and better movies.

w Michael Gleason *d* Boris Sagal

Rod Taylor, Blair Brown, Douglas Fowley, Andrew Stevens

The Organization
US 1971 108m De Luxe
UA / Mirisch (Walter Mirisch)

San Francisco policemen combat an international drug smuggling organization.
The third and weakest adventure of Virgil Tibbs, black policeman of *In the Heat of the Night*. Absolutely routine.

w James R. Webb *d* Don Medford *ph* Joseph Biroc *m* Gile Melle

Sidney Poitier, Barbara McNair, Sheree North, Gerald S. O'Loughlin

The Oscar*
US 1966 118m Pathecolor
Paramount / Greene–Rouse

On the night of the Academy Awards his friend recalls a heel's rise to stardom.
Squalid, sensationalist account of Hollywood mores; one hopes it isn't quite true.

w Harlan Ellison, Russel Rouse, Clarence Greene, *novel* Richard Sale *d* Russel Rouse *ph* Joseph Ruttenberg *m* Percy Faith

Stephen Boyd, Elke Sommer, Tony Bennett, Eleanor Parker, Milton Berle, Joseph Cotten, Jill St John, Edie Adams, Ernest Borgnine, Ed Begley, Walter Brennan, Broderick Crawford, James Dunn, Peter Lawford, Edith Head, Hedda Hopper, Merle Oberon, Bob Hope, Frank Sinatra

'This is the sort of film that only Hollywood could make, and on that level it is preposterously enjoyable.'—*David Wilson*

'That true movie rarity—a picture that attains a perfection of ineptitude quite beyond the power of words to describe.'—*Richard Shickel*

Oscar Wilde**
GB 1959 96m bw
Vantage (William Kirby)

Scandal strikes Oscar Wilde through his involvement with Lord Alfred Douglas.
Competent, well acted version of well-known events of the nineties, with Morley in his original stage role; generally more satisfactory than *The Trials of Oscar Wilde* which was shot simultaneously.

w Jo Eisinger *d* Gregory Ratoff *ph* Georges Périnal *m* Kenneth V. Jones

Robert Morley, John Neville, Phyllis Calvert, *Ralph Richardson*, Dennis Price, Alexander Knox, Edward Chapman, Martin Benson, Robert Harris, Henry Oscar, William Devlin

Othello*
US / France 1951 91m bw
Mercury / Films Marceau

Shakespeare's play as rearranged by Orson Welles at the start of his European wanderings; modest budget, flashes of brilliance, poor technical quality, variable acting. Not really the best way to film Shakespeare.

w Orson Welles, *play* William Shakespeare *d* Orson Welles *ad* Alexander Trauner

Orson Welles, Micheal MacLiammoir, Fay Compton, Robert Cook, Suzanne Cloutier, Michael Laurence, Hilton Edwards, Doris Dowling

Othello*
GB 1965 166m Technicolor Panavision
BHE (Richard Godwin)

A record of the National Theatre production, disappointing in terms of cinema but a valuable record of a famous performance.

d Stuart Burge *ph* Geoffrey Unsworth *md* Richard Hampton

Laurence Olivier, Frank Finlay, Joyce Redman, Maggie Smith, Derek Jacobi, Robert Lang, Anthony Nicholls

The Other*
US 1972 100m De Luxe
TCF / Rex-Benchmark (Tom Tryon)

A boy insists that his dead twin is responsible several unexplained deaths.

Subtle family ghost story for intellectuals; a bit pretentious and restrained for popular success.

w Tom Tryon, from his novel *d* Robert Mulligan *ph* Robert Surtees *m* Jerry Goldsmith *pd* Albert Brenner

Uta Hagen, Diana Muldaur, Chris Connelly, Victor French

The Other Love
US 1947 96m bw
Enterprise (David Lewis)

At a Swiss sanatorium, a lady concert pianist who is dying falls in love with her doctor. Fairly icky 'woman's picture' with uncomfortable performances.

w Ladislas Fodor, Harry Brown, *story* Erich Maria Remarque *d* André de Toth *ph* Victor Milner *m* Miklos Rozsa

Barbara Stanwyck, David Niven, Richard Conte, Gilbert Roland, Joan Lorring, Lenore Aubert

The Other Man*
US 1970 99m Technicolor TVM
Universal (William Frye)

An ex-convict hatches a complex revenge plot on the attorney responsible for his conviction.
Cold, complex suspenser which slightly overreaches itself.

w Michael Blankfort, Eric Bercovici *d* Richard A. Colla

Roy Thinnes, Arthur Hill, Joan Hackett, Tammy Grimes

The Other Side of the Mountain
US 1975 102m Technicolor
Universal / Filmways / Larry Peerce (Edward S. Feldman)
GB title: *A Window to the Sky*

A girl skiing champion is paralysed by polio.
Maudlin tearjerker based on a real case; altogether too much of a good thing.

w David Seltzer, *book* A Long Way Up by E. G. Valens *d* Larry Peerce *ph* David M. Walsh *m* Charles Fox

Marilyn Hassett, Beau Bridges, Belinda Montgomery, Nan Martin, William Bryant, Dabney Coleman

Otley**
GB 1968 91m Technicolor
Columbia / Open Road (Bruce Cohn Curtis)

An inoffensive Londoner falls in with spies and murderers.
Semi-spoof comedy thriller taking in James Bondery and the swinging London set. Generally pretty funny, but not entirely certain of its own motives.

w Ian La Frenais, Dick Clement, *novel* Martin Waddell *d* Dick Clement *ph* Austin Dempster *md* Stanley Myers

Tom Courtenay, Romy Schneider, Alan Badel, James Villiers, Leonard Rossiter, Freddie Jones, James Bolam, Fiona Lewis

Our Betters*
US 1933 82m bw
RKO (David O. Selznick)

An American woman in London finds her titled husband is unfaithful and sets about causing society scandals.
Dimly adapted West End success makes an interesting but unamusing film.

w Jane Murfin, Harry Wagstaff Gribble, *play* W. Somerset Maugham *d* George Cukor *ph* Charles Rosher *md* Max Steiner

Constance Bennett, Violet Kemble Cooper, Alan Mowbray, Gilbert Roland, Phoebe Foster, Charles Starrett, Grant Mitchell, Anita Louise, Minor Watson, Hugh Sinclair

'One of those familiar dreams of high life in which we are asked to admire even while we condemn the superb immorality of our almost godlike betters.'—*The Times*

Our Blushing Brides
US 1930 74m bw
MGM

Department store shopgirls and mannequins share an apartment.
Would-be shocking exposé of the love life of young people in 1930, following on the star's silent successes *Our Dancing Daughters* and *Our Modern Maidens*.

w Bess Meredyth, John Howard Lawson *d* Harry Beaumont *ph* Merritt B. Gerstad

Joan Crawford, Robert Montgomery, Anita Page, Dorothy Sebastian, Raymond Hackett, John Miljan, Edward Brophy

Our Hearts Were Young and Gay*
US 1944 81m bw
Paramount (Sheridan Gibney)

Two well-to-do flappers of the twenties find fun and romance in Paris.
A pleasant, undemanding piece of nostalgia based on a popular biography; in 1946 a less successful sequel, *Our Hearts Were Growing Up*, involved the young ladies with bootleggers at Princeton.

w Sheridan Gibney, *book* Cornelia Otis Skinner,

Emily Kimbrough *d* Lewis Allen *ph* Theodor Sparkuhl *m* Werner Heymann

Gail Russell, Diana Lynn, Charles Ruggles, Dorothy Gish, Beulah Bondi, James Brown, Bill Edwards, Jean Heather

Our Little Girl
US 1935 63m bw
TCF (Edward Butcher)

A doctor's daughter brings her parents together.
One of the child star's thinner and more sentimental vehicles.

w Stephen Morehouse Avery, Allen Rivkin, Jack Yellen, *story* Heaven's Gate by Florence Leighton Pfalzgraf *d* John Robertson *ph* John Seitz *md* Oscar Bradley

Shirley Temple, Joel McCrea, Rosemary Ames, Lyle Talbot, Erin O'Brien-Moore

Our Man Flint*
US 1965 108m De Luxe Cinemascope
TCF (Saul David)

An American secret agent and super stud fights an organization bent on controlling the world through its weather.
Comic strip imitation of James Bond; in its wild way the first instalment scored a good many laughs, but the sequel, *In Like Flint* (qv), quickly ended the series.

w Hal Fimberg, Ben Starr *d* Daniel Mann *ph* Daniel L. Fapp *m* Jerry Goldsmith

James Coburn, Lee J. Cobb, Gila Golan, Edward Mulhare, Benson Fong, Sigrid Valdis

'Despite the fact that everyone from designers to actors seems to be having a ball, the film somehow goes over the edge of parody—ultimately it looks suspiciously like a case of wish-fulfilment.'—*John Gillett*

Our Man in Havana*
GB 1959 112m bw Cinemascope
Columbia / Kingsmead (Carol Reed)

A British vacuum cleaner salesman in Havana allows himself to be recruited as a spy, and wishes he hadn't.
The wry flavour of the novel does not really translate to the screen, and especially not to the wide screen, but a few lines and characters offer compensation.

w Graham Greene, from his novel *d* Carol Reed *ph* Oswald Morris *m* Hermanos Deniz Cuban Rhythm Band

Alec Guinness, *Noel Coward*, Burl Ives, Maureen O'Hara, Ernie Kovacs, *Ralph Richardson*, Jo Morrow, Paul Rogers, Grégoire Aslan, Duncan Macrae

'The main weakness is the absence of economic, expressive cutting and visual flow. As a result . . . stretches of dialogue become tedious to watch; and the essential awareness of the writer's shifting tensions yields disappointingly to the easier mannerisms of any conventional comedy-thriller.'—*Peter John Dyer*

Our Miss Fred*
GB 1972 96m Technicolor
EMI / Willis World Wide (Josephine Douglas)

In World War II France, an actor escapes in women's clothes when his troupe is captured by the Nazis.
A carefully nurtured vehicle for Britain's top female impersonator somehow doesn't come off; celluloid both constrains his range and reveals his inadequacies.

w Hugh Leonard *d* Bob Kellett *ph* Dick Bush *m* Peter Greenwell

Danny La Rue, Alfred Marks, Lance Percival, Lally Bowers, Frances de la Tour, Walter Gotell

Our Mother's House*
GB 1967 105m Metrocolor
MGM / Filmways (Jack Clayton)

When mother dies, seven children, who don't want to go to an orphanage, bury her in the garden. Then their ne'er-do-well father turns up.
Unpleasant and rather boring melodrama, too silly to have much dramatic impact.

w Jeremy Brooks, Haya Harareet, *novel* Julian Gloag *d* Jack Clayton *ph* Larry Pizer *m* Georges Delerue

Dirk Bogarde, Margaret Brooks, Pamela Franklin, Mark Lester, Yootha Joyce, Anthony Nicholls

'The children begin to display an alarming variety of accents . . . and when Dirk Bogarde enters, doing a rich Bill Sykes act as the long lost wicked father to a predominantly genteel family, the whole structure collapses.'—*Tom Milne*

Our Relations***
US 1936 65m bw
Hal Roach / Stan Laurel Productions

Two sailors entrusted with a diamond ring get mixed up with their long lost and happily married twin brothers.
A fast-moving comedy which contains some of Laurel and Hardy's most polished work as well as being their most satisfying production.

w Richard Connell, Felix Adler, Charles Roger,

Jack Jevne, *story* The Money Box by W. W. Jacobs *d Harry Lachman ph Rudolph Maté*

Stan Laurel, Oliver Hardy, James Finlayson, Alan Hale, Sidney Toler, Daphne Pollard, Iris Adrian, Noel Madison, Ralf Harolde, *Arthur Housman*

Our Town**
US 1940 90m bw
Principal Artists / Sol Lesser

Birth, life and death in a small New Hampshire community.
One of the main points of the play, the absence of scenery, is abandoned in this screen version, and the graveyard scene has to be presented as a dream, but the film retains the narrator and manages to make points of its own while absorbing the endearing qualities which made the play a classic.

w Thornton Wilder, Frank Craven, Harry Chantlee, *play* Thornton Wilder *d Sam Wood ph* Bert Glennon *m* Aaron Copland *pd William Cameron Menzies*

Frank Craven, William Holden, *Martha Scott, Thomas Mitchell, Fay Bainter, Guy Kibbee, Beulah Bondi*, Stuart Erwin

Our Very Own
US 1950 93m bw
Samuel Goldwyn

A girl is shocked to discover that she is adopted.
Another Goldwyn foray into chintzy, middle-class, small-town America, but not a winning example.

w F. Hugh Herbert *d* David Miller *ph* Lee Garmes *m* Victor Young *ad* Richard Day

Ann Blyth, Farley Granger, Joan Evans, Jane Wyatt, Ann Dvorak, Donald Cook, Natalie Wood, Gus Schilling, Phyllis Kirk

Our Vines Have Tender Grapes*
US 1945 105m bw
MGM (Robert Sisk)

Life in a Norwegian farm community in southern Wisconsin.
Unexceptionable family picture produced in MGM's best manner.

w Dalton Trumbo, *novel* George Victor Martin *d* Roy Rowland *ph* Robert Surtees *m* Bronislau Kaper

Edward G. Robinson, Margaret O'Brien, James Craig, Agnes Moorehead, Jackie 'Butch' Jenkins, Morris Carnovsky, Frances Gifford, Sara Haden

Our Wife
US 1941 95m bw
Columbia (John M. Stahl)

A composer is romantically torn between a lady scientist and his own ex-wife.
Middling romantic comedy of a kind very familiar at the time.

w P. J. Wolfson, *play* Lillian Day by Lyon Mearson *d* John M. Stahl *ph* Franz Planer *m* Leo Shuken

Melvyn Douglas, Ruth Hussey, Ellen Drew, Charles Coburn, John Hubbard, Harvey Stephens

Out of Season*
GB 1975 90m Technicolor
EMI / Lorimar

One winter in an English seaside resort, an old love is rekindled.
Restrained sexual fireworks in the old French manner, well enough done with excellent atmosphere but a shade overlong and marred by the need to indulge in modern tricks such as a deliberately ambiguous ending.

w Reuben Bercovitch, Eric Bercovici *d Alan Bridges ph* Arthur Ibbetson *m* John Cameron

Cliff Robertson, Vanessa Redgrave, Susan George, Edward Evans

Out of the Clouds*
GB 1954 88m Eastmancolor
Ealing (Michael Relph, Basil Dearden)

Several personal stories mesh against a background of London airport during a fog.
A dull compendium of stories with a background of documentary detail which is now fascinating because it's so dated.

w John Eldridge, Michael Relph *d* Michael Relph, Basil Dearden *ph* Paul Beeson *m* Richard Addinsell

Anthony Steel, Robert Beatty, David Knight, Margo Lorenz, James Robertson Justice, Eunice Gayson, Isabel Dean, Gordon Harker, Bernard Lee, Michael Howard, Marie Lohr, Esme Cannon, Abraham Sofaer

'The film relies considerably on small-time players and marginal incidents; the detail, however, never looks like adding up to a satisfactory whole.'—*Penelope Houston*

Out of the Fog*
US 1941 86m bw
Warner (Henry Blanke)

Gangsters move in to terrorize an innocent Brooklyn family.

Standard exploration of a situation which became routine.

w Robert Rossen, Jerry Wald, Richard Macaulay, *play* The Gentle People by Irwin Shaw *d* Anatole Litvak *ph* James Wong Howe

Ida Lupino, John Garfield, Thomas Mitchell, Eddie Albert, George Tobias, Aline MacMahon. Jerome Cowan, John Qualen, Leo Gorcey

Out of the Past**
US 1947 97m bw
RKO (Warren Duff)
GB title: *Build My Gallows High*

A private detective is hired by a hoodlum to find his homicidal girl friend; he does, and falls in love with her.
Moody *film noir* with Hollywood imitating French models; plenty of snarling and a death-strewn climax.

w Geoffrey Homes, from his novel Build My Gallows High *d Jacques Tourneur* *ph* Nicholas Musuraca *m* Roy Webb

Robert Mitchum, Jane Greer, Kirk Douglas, Rhonda Fleming, Richard Webb, Steve Brodie, Virginia Huston, Dickie Moore

'Is this not an outcrop of the national masochism induced by a quite aimless, newly industrialized society proceeding rapidly on its way to nowhere?'—*Richard Winnington*

Out of this World
US 1945 96m bw
Paramount (Sam Coslow)

A Western Union messenger becomes a hit crooner and a national phenomenon.
Very mild comedy with the gimmick that Bing Crosby dubbed the singing.

w Walter de Leon, Arthur Phillips *d* Hal Walker *ph* Stuart Thompson *m* Victor Young

Eddie Bracken, Veronica Lake, Diana Lynn, Cass Daley, Parkyakarkus, Donald MacBride, Florence Bates, Carmen Cavallero

The Out of Towners*
US 1970 98m Movielab
Paramount / Jalem (Paul Nathan)

An executive and his wife fly into New York for an interview, but their encounter with the city is a mounting series of traumatic disasters.
A love-hate relationship with a city demonstrated by a resident is something of an in-joke and becomes increasingly hysterical and unsympathetic, but there are bright moments in this company.

w Neil Simon *d* Arthur Hiller *ph* Andrew Laszlo *m* Quincy Jones

Jack Lemmon, Sandy Dennis

Outback*
Australia 1970 109m Technicolor
NIT / Group W (George Willoughby)

A young teacher becomes involved in the rougher side of life in a remote Australian village.
A convincingly brutal picture of a community whose interests range from homosexuality to a bloody kangaroo hunt.

w Evan Jones, *novel* Wake in Fright by Kenneth Cook *d Ted Kotcheff* *ph* Brian West *m* John Scott

Gary Bond, Donald Pleasance, Chips Rafferty

An Outcast of the Islands**
GB 1951 102m bw
London Films (Carol Reed)

A shiftless trader finds a secret Far Eastern trading post where he can be happy – but even here he becomes an outcast.
An interesting but not wholly successful attempt to dramatize a complex character study. It looks great and is well acted.

w William Fairchild, *novel* Joseph Conrad *d* Carol Reed *ph John Wilcox* *m* Brian Easdale

Trevor Howard, Ralph Richardson, Kerima, Robert Morley, Wendy Hiller, George Coulouris, Frederick Valk, Wilfrid Hyde White, Betty Ann Davies

'The script is so overwhelmed by the narrative itself that the characters and relationships fail to crystallize . . . while the handling is often intelligent, ingenious, and has its effective moments, no real conception emerges.'—*Gavin Lambert*

The Outcasts of Poker Flat
US 1937 68m bw
RKO (Robert Sisk)

Four undesirables are run out of town and stuck in a mountain cabin during a snowstorm.
Overstretched anecdote with a predictably downbeat finale and not much action.

w John Twist, Harry Segall, *story* Bret Harte *d* Christy Cabanne *ph* Rudolph Maté

Preston Foster, Jean Muir, Van Heflin

The Outcasts of Poker Flat
US 1952 80m bw
TCF (Julian Blaustein)

Good-looking but equally undramatic remake of the above.

w Edmund H. North *d* Joseph M. Newman *ph* Joseph La Shelle *m* Hugo Friedhofer

Dale Robertson, Anne Baxter, Cameron Mitchell, Miriam Hopkins

The Outfit
US 1973 103m Metrocolor
MGM (Carter de Haven)

A criminal just out of prison finds himself in danger from the Syndicate.
Unattractive rehash of *Point Blank* with much gratuitous violence.

wd John Flynn, *novel* Richard Stark *ph* Bruce Surtees *m* Jerry Fielding

Robert Duvall, Karen Black, Robert Ryan, Joe Don Baker, Timothy Carey, Richard Jaeckel, Sheree North, Marie Windsor, Jane Greer, Elisha Cook Jnr

'A nice profusion of Hollywood character actors makes up for the overall lack of drive.'—*Sight and Sound*

The Outlaw*
US 1943 126m bw
Howard Hughes

Billy the Kid, Doc Holliday and Pat Garrett meet up at a way station and quarrel over a half-breed girl.
Half-baked western with much pretentious chat and the main interest squarely focused on the bosom of the producer's new discovery. This aspect kept censorship ballyhoo going for six years before the film was finally released in truncated form, and audiences found it not worth the wait, though it does look good.

w Jules Furthman *d* Howard Hughes *ph Gregg Toland md* Victor Young

Jack Beutel, Jane Russell, Thomas Mitchell, Walter Huston

The Outlaw Josey Wales*
US 1976 135m De Luxe Panavision
Warner (Robert Daley)

A westerner gradually avenges the death of his wife at the hands of bandits.
Bloodthirsty actioner in the star's usual mould; likely to prove unintentionally funny for hardened addicts.

w Phil Kaufman, Sonia Chernus, *novel* Gone to Texas by Forrest Carter *d* Clint Eastwood *ph* Bruce Surtees *m* Jerry Fielding

Clint Eastwood, Chief Dan George, Sandra Locke, John Vernon, Bill McKinney

Outpost in Morocco
US 1949 92m bw
Joseph N. Ermolieff

A romantic Foreign Legion officer falls for the daughter of an enemy Arab.
Despite authentic locations and the co-operation of the Legion this is a stolid piece of work, too dull even for children's matinees.

w Charles Grayson, Paul de St Columbe *d* Robert Florey *ph* Lucien Andriot

George Raft, Akim Tamiroff, Marie Windsor, John Litel, Eduard Franz

Outrage
US 1950 75m bw
Filmmakers (Collier Young)

A girl who has been raped is almost unhinged by the experience.
Well-meaning low-budgeter, thin in entertainment value.

w Ida Lupino, Collier Young, Marvin Wald *d* Ida Lupino *ph* Archie Stout *m* Constantin Bakaleinikoff *pd* Harry Horner

Mala Powers, Tod Andrews, Robert Clarke, Raymond Bond, Lilian Hamilton

'An unconvincing mixture of sensationalism, sentiment and half-baked sociology.'—*MFB*

The Outrage*
US 1964 97m bw Panavision
MGM / Harvest / February / Ritt / Kayos (A. Ronald Lubin)

Conflicting views of a western murder.
Wildly ineffective remake of *Rashomon,* with everyone strangely overacting and little sense of the west as it is normally depicted.

w Michael Kanin *d* Martin Ritt *ph* James Wong Howe *m* Alex North

Paul Newman, Edward G. Robinson, Laurence Harvey, Claire Bloom, William Shatner, Albert Salmi

Outrage**
US 1973 74m colour TVM
ABC Circle / Michael Green

A well-to-do businessman is harassed at home by marauding teenagers and finds himself powerless to do anything about it.
Based on a true case of a man who finally took the law into his own hands, this is a chilling and well-observed piece of unpleasantness.

w William Wood *d* Richard Heffron

Robert Culp, Marlyn Mason, Beah Richards, Thomas Leopold

The Outriders
US 1950 93m Technicolor
MGM (Richard Goldstone)

Three Confederate soldiers escape from a yankee prison camp.
Competent star western with solid production values.

w Irving Ravetch *d* Roy Rowland *ph* Charles Schoenbaum *m* André Previn

Joel McCrea, Arlene Dahl, Barry Sullivan, Claude Jarman Jnr, Ramon Novarro

The Outsider
US 1961 108m bw
U-I (Sy Bartlett)

Ira Hayes, a simple Red Indian, becomes a war hero but cannot reconcile himself to living in a white society.
Prolonged biopic which proves a shade too much for an eager star; it's all earnest and mildly interesting but not cinematically compulsive.

w Stewart Stern *d* Delbert Mann *ph* Joseph La Shelle *m* Leonard Rosenman

Tony Curtis, James Franciscus, Bruce Bennett, Gregory Walcott, Vivian Nathan, Edmund Hashim, Stanley Adams

The Outsider*
US 1967 98m Technicolor TVM
Universal (Roy Huggins)

A Los Angeles private eye takes on a surveillance job, is promptly mugged in Chinatown, and finds his suspect dead.
Adequate copy of many obvious models from Marlowe to Harper.

w Roy Huggins *d* Michael Ritchie

Darren McGavin, Sean Garrison, Shirley Knight, Edmond O'Brien, Ann Sothern, Ossie Davis

Outward Bound*
US 1930 82m bw
Warner

Passengers on a strange liner discover that they are all dead and heading for purgatory.
Early sound version of a popular twenties play which does not translate too well to cinematic forms and now seems very dated apart from a couple of performances; remade as *Between Two Worlds* (qv).

w J. Grubb Alexander, *play* Sutton Vane
d Robert Milton *ph* Hal Mohr

Leslie Howard, Douglas Fairbanks Jnr, Alec B. Francis, Helen Chandler, Beryl Mercer, Alison Skipworth, Montagu Love, Dudley Digges

The Over the Hill Gang*
US 1969 74m colour TVM
Spelling–Thomas

Retired – really retired – Texas Rangers bring law and order to a corrupt town.
Mildly amusing comedy western full of old faces.

w Jameson Brewer *d* Jean Yarborough

Pat O'Brien, Walter Brennan, Chill Wills, Edgar Buchanan, Jack Elam, Andy Devine, Gypsy Rose Lee, Rick Nelson, Edward Andrews

The Over the Hill Gang Rides Again
US 1970 74m colour TVM
Spelling–Thomas

Three retired Texas Rangers rescue a drunken friend and make him a marshal.
More of the above, not exactly inspired.

w Richard Carr *d* George McCowan

Walter Brennan, Fred Astaire, Edgar Buchanan, Chill Wills, Andy Devine

Over the Moon
GB 1937 78m Technicolor
London Films (Alexander Korda)

A poor girl comes into a fortune but this does not help her romance with a proud young doctor.
Insubstantial comedy which turns itself into a European travelogue before petering out.

w Anthony Pelissier, Arthur Wimperis, Alec Coppel *d* Thornton Freeland *ph* Harry Stradling *m* Mischa Spoliansky

Merle Oberon, Rex Harrison, Ursula Jeans, Robert Douglas, Louis Borell, Zena Dare, Peter Haddon, David Tree

Over Twenty-One
US 1945 102m bw
Columbia (Sidney Buchman)

A famous lady screenwriter copes with wartime domestic problems while her husband is off at the war.
Thin star comedy based on Ruth Gordon's play about her own predicament; not for the wider audience, and not very good anyway.

w Sidney Buchman, *play* Ruth Gordon
d Alexander Hall *ph* Rudolph Maté *m* Marlin Skiles

Irene Dunne, Alexander Knox, Charles Coburn, Jeff Donnell, Lee Patrick, Phil Brown, Cora Witherspoon

The Overlanders**
Australia 1946 91m bw
Ealing

In 1943 a drover saves a thousand head of cattle

from the Japanese by taking them two thousand miles across country.
Attractive, easy-going semi-western, the first and best of several films made by Ealing Studios in Australia.

wd Harry Watt ph Osmond Borradaile

Chips Rafferty, John Heyward, Daphne Campbell

Overlord*
GB 1975 83m bw
EMI / Jowsend (James Quinn)

An eighteen-year-old is called up in early 1944 and killed in the D-Day landings.
Semi-documentary recreating a time in history (with much aid from newsreels) but making no discernible point. Interesting, though.

w Stuart Cooper, Christopher Hudson *d* Stuart Cooper *ph* John Alcott *m* Paul Glass

Brian Stirner, Davyd Harries, Nicholas Ball, Julie Neesam

Owd Bob*
GB 1938 78m bw
GFD / Gainsborough (Edward Black)
US title: *To the Victor*

A Cumberland farmer's faithful dog is accused of killing sheep.
Sentimental yarn with good location backgrounds; the plot was later reused as a Lassie vehicle.

w Michael Hogan, J. B. Williams, *novel* Alfred Olivant *d* Robert Stevenson

Will Fyffe, John Loder, Margaret Lockwood, Moore Marriott, Graham Moffatt, Wilfred Walter, Elliot Mason

Owen Marshall: Counselor at Law
US 1971 100m Technicolor TVM
Universal (Douglas Benton)

A California lawyer defends a young man accused of rape and murder.
Comfortable, over-prolonged courtroom stuff which turned into a one-year series.

w Jerry McNeely *d* Buzz Kulik

Arthur Hill, Vera Miles, Joseph Campanella, William Shatner, Bruce Davison

The Owl and the Pussycat*
US 1970 96m Eastmancolor Panavision
Columbia / Rastar (Ray Stark)

A bookstore assistant reports a fellow tenant for prostitution, and when she is evicted she moves in with him.
Wacky, bawdy double act which starts promisingly but outstays its welcome. A solid step forward in permissiveness, with kinky behaviour as well as four-letter words.

w Buck Henry, *play* Bill Manhoff *d* Herbert Ross *ph* Harry Stradling, Andrew Laszlo *m* Richard Halligan

Barbra Streisand, George Segal, Robert Klein, Allen Garfield

The Ox-Bow Incident**
US 1942 75m bw
TCF (Lamar Trotti)
GB title: *Strange Incident*

A cowboy is unable to prevent three wandering travellers being unjustly lynched for murder.
Stark lynch law parable, beautifully made but very depressing.

w Lamar Trotti, *novel* Walter Van Tilburg Clark *d William Wellman ph Arthur Miller* *m* Cyril Mockridge

Henry Fonda, Henry Morgan, Jane Darwell, Anthony Quinn, Dana Andrews, Mary Beth Hughes, William Eythe, Harry Davenport, *Frank Conroy*

'Realism that is as sharp and cold as a knife.'—*Frank S. Nugent, New York Times*

P

P.J.
US 1967 109m Techniscope
Universal (Edward J. Montagne)
GB title: *New Face in Hell*

A down-at-heel private eye takes a job as bodyguard to a boorish businessman.
Routine thick-ear with a predictable turnabout plot.

w Philip Reisman Jnr *d* John Guillermin *ph* Loyal Griggs *m* Neal Hefti

George Peppard, Gayle Hunnicutt, Raymond Burr, Susan St James, Coleen Gray, Jason Evers, Wilfrid Hyde White, Severn Darden

'Enough action to keep you from noticing that the plot doesn't make any sense.'—*Judith Crist*

Pacific Blackout
US 1942 76m bw
Paramount (Sol C. Siegel)

An inventor escapes from jail and proves his innocence during a practice air raid blackout.
Minor melo which proved profitably topical, being released shortly after the Japanese attack on Pearl Harbor.

w Lester Cole, W. P. Lipscomb *d* Ralph Murphy *ph* Theodor Sparkuhl

Robert Preston, Martha O'Driscoll, Philip Merivale, Eva Gabor, Louis Jean Heydt, Thurston Hall

Pacific Destiny
GB 1956 97m Eastmancolor Cinemascope
James Lawrie

Experiences of a British colonial servant in the South Seas.
Pleasant episodic drama which needed a firmer hand all round.

w Richard Mason, *autobiography* A Pattern of Islands by Sir Arthur Grimble *d* Wolf Rilla *ph* Martin Curtis *m* James Bernard

Denholm Elliott, Susan Stephen, Michael Hordern

Pack Up Your Troubles*
US 1931 68m bw
Hal Roach

Two World War I veterans try to look after their late pal's orphan daughter.
Patchy comedy vehicle in which too many gags are not fully thought out or timed.

w H. M. Walker *d* George Marshall, Ray McCarey *ph* Art Lloyd

Stan Laurel, Oliver Hardy, Donald Dillaway, Mary Carr, Charles Middleton, Dick Cramer, James Finlayson, Tom Kennedy, Billy Gilbert

The Pad, and How to Use It*
US 1966 86m Technicolor
Universal (Ross Hunter)

A shy young man has his first date.
Pleasant, odd little comedy apparently made in emulation of *The Knack*.

w Thomas C. Ryan, Benn Starr, *play* The Private Ear by Peter Shaffer *d* Brian C. Hutton *ph* Ellsworth Fredericks *m* Russ Garcia

Brian Bedford, James Farentino, Julie Sommars, Edy Williams, Nick Navarro

Paddy the Next Best Thing
US 1933 75m bw
Fox

Adventures of an Irish tomboy in New York.
Modest star comedy from a popular play.

w Edwin Burke, *play* Gertrude Page *d* Harry Lachman *ph* John Seitz

Janet Gaynor, Warner Baxter, Walter Connolly, Harvey Stephens, Margaret Lindsay

Pagan Love Song
US 1950 76m Technicolor
MGM (Arthur Freed)

An American schoolteacher marries a Tahitian girl.
Very mild musical potboiler using familiar talents.

w Robert Nathan, Jerry Davis *d* Robert Alton *ph* Charles Rosher *m* Harry Warren *ly* Arthur Freed

Esther Williams, Howard Keel, Rita Moreno, Minna Gombell

Page Miss Glory*
US 1935 90m bw
Warner / Cosmopolitan

A con man wins a beauty contest with a composite photograph of a non-existent girl.
Amusing comedy-musical, unjustly forgotten.

w Delmer Daves, Robert Lord, *play* Joseph Schrank, Philip Dunning *d* Mervyn Le Roy *ph* George Folsey *m/ly* Harry Warren, Al Dubin

Dick Powell, Marion Davies, Frank McHugh, Pat O'Brien, Mary Astor, Lyle Talbot, Patsy Kelly, Allen Jenkins, Barton MacLane

Paid*
US 1930 80m bw
MGM

A woman sent to prison unjustly plots revenge on those responsible.
Reliable melodrama with the heroine eventually forgiving and forgetting.

w Charles MacArthur, Lucien Hubbard, *play* Within the Law by Bayard Veiller *d* Sam Wood *ph* Charles Rosher

Joan Crawford, Douglass Montgomery, Robert Armstrong, Marie Prévost, John Miljan, Polly Moran

Paid in Full
US 1950 105m bw
Paramount / Hal B. Wallis

A woman is responsible for the death of her sister's child, and becomes pregnant herself in the knowledge that giving birth will be fatal to her.
Stolid, contrived tearjerker.

w Robert Blees, Charles Schnee *d* William Dieterle *ph* Leo Tover *m* Walter Lang, Victor Young

Lizabeth Scott, Diana Lynn, Robert Cummings, Eve Arden, Ray Collins, Frank McHugh, Stanley Ridges, Louis Jean Heydt

Paint Your Wagon*
US 1969 164m Technicolor
Panavision 70
Paramount / Alan Jay Lerner (Tom Shaw)

During the California Gold Rush, two prospectors set up a Mormon menage with the same wife.
Good-looking but uncinematic and monumentally long version of an old musical with a new plot and not much dancing. There are minor pleasures, but it really shouldn't have been allowed.

w Paddy Chayevsky, *musical play* Alan Jay Lerner, Frederick Loewe *d* Joshua Logan *ph* William A. Fraker *pd* John Truscott

Lee Marvin, Clint Eastwood, Jean Seberg, Harve Presnell, Ray Walston

'One of those big movies in which the themes are undersized and the elements are juggled around until nothing fits together right and even the good bits of the original show you started with are shot to hell.'—*Pauline Kael*

The Painted Veil*
US 1934 84m bw
MGM

In China, a doctor's wife gives up her lover to join her husband fighting an epidemic.
Soulful melodrama which seemed much more acceptable in this version than in the summer stock style remake *The Seventh Sin*.

w John Meehan, Salka Viertel, Edith Fitzgerald, *novel* W. Somerset Maugham *d* Richard Boleslawski *ph* William Daniels

Greta Garbo, George Brent, Herbert Marshall, Warner Oland, Jean Hersholt

Painting the Clouds with Sunshine
US 1951 86m Technicolor
Warner (William Jacobs)

Three singing sisters go to Las Vegas in search of rich husbands.
Yet another revamp of the original *Gold Diggers* (qv), and not a very lively one.

w Henry Clark, Roland Kibbee, Peter Milne *d* David Butler *ph* Wilfred Cline

Virginia Mayo, Gene Nelson, Dennis Morgan, S. Z. Sakall, Lucille Norman, Tom Conway

The Pajama Game***
US 1957 101m Warnercolor
Warner / George Abbott

Workers in a pajama factory demand a pay rise, but their lady negotiator falls for the new boss.
Brilliantly conceived musical on an unlikely subject, effectively concealing its Broadway origins and becoming an expert, fast-moving, hard-hitting piece of modern musical cinema.

w George Abbott, Richard Bissell, book Seven and a Half Cents by Richard Bissell *d Stanley Donen ph* Harry Stradling, *songs Richard Adler, Jerry Ross ch Bob Fosse*

Doris Day, John Raitt, *Eddie Foy Jnr,* Reta Shaw, Carol Haney

Pal Joey**
US 1957 109m Technicolor
Columbia / Essex–Sidney (Fred Kohlmar)

The rise of a nightclub entertainer who is also a heel.
Smart musical which begins very brightly indeed but slides off alarmingly into conventional sentiment.

w Dorothy Kingsley, *play* John O'Hara, *stories* John O'Hara *d* George Sidney *ph* Harold Lipstein *songs Richard Rodgers, Lorenz Hart*

Frank Sinatra, Rita Hayworth, Kim Novak, Bobby Sherwood, Hank Henry, Elizabeth Patterson, Barbara Nichols

The Paleface***
US 1948 91m Technicolor
Paramount (Robert L. Welch)

Calamity Jane undertakes an undercover mission against desperadoes, and marries a timid dentist as a cover.
Splendid wagon train comedy western with the stars in excellent form. Sequel, *Son of Paleface* (qv); remake, *The Shakiest Gun in the West* (1968).

w Edmund Hartman, Frank Tashlin d Norman Z. McLeod *ph* Ray Rennahan *m* Victor Young

Bob Hope, Jane Russell, Robert Armstrong, Iris Adrian, Robert Watson, Jack Searle, Joe Vitale, Clem Bevans, Charles Trowbridge

The Palm Beach Story***
US 1942 88m bw
Paramount (Paul Jones)

The wife of a penurious engineer takes off for Florida to set her sights on a millionaire.
Flighty comedy, inconsequential in itself, but decorated with scenes, characters and zany touches typical of its creator, here at his most brilliant if uncontrolled.

wd Preston Sturges ph Victor Milner

Claudette Colbert, Joel McCrea, Rudy Vallee, Mary Astor, Sig Arno, Robert Warwick, Torben Meyer, Jimmy Conlin, William Demarest, Jack Norton, Robert Greig, Roscoe Ates, Chester Conklin, Franklin Pangborn, Alan Bridge, *Robert Dudley*

'Surprises and delights as though nothing of the kind had been known before . . . farce and tenderness are combined without a fault.'—*William Whitebait*

Palm Springs Weekend
US 1963 100m Technicolor
Warner (Michael Hoey)

Various holidaymakers at Palm Springs get romantically involved.
Youth-oriented farce, better produced than most but basically a depressing experience.

w Earl Hanmer Jnr *d* Norman Taurog *ph* Harold Lipstein *m* Frank Perkins

Troy Donahue, Ty Hardin, Connie Stevens, Stefanie Powers, Robert Conrad, Jack Weston, Andrew Duggan

Palmy Days
US 1932 77m bw
Samuel Goldwyn

Shady fortune tellers find a willing stooge.
Dated star comedy.

w Eddie Cantor, Mornie Ryskind, David Greenman *d* A. Edward Sutherland *ph* Gregg Toland *ch* Busby Berkeley

Eddie Cantor, Charlotte Greenwood, Charles Middleton, George Raft, Walter Catlett

Pan-Americana*
US 1945 85m bw
RKO (Sid Rogell)

A New York magazine sends editors around South America to choose the prettiest girl of each nation.
Slick, mindless musical with good numbers.

w Laurence Kimble *d* John H. Auer *ph* Frank Redman *md* Constantin Bakaleinikoff *ch* Charles O'Curran

Audrey Long, Philip Terry, Robert Benchley, Eve Arden, Ernest Truex, Marc Cramer

Panache*
US 1976 76m colour TVM
Warner

Adventures of a 'second team' of the king's musketeers in 17th-century France.
A mark for trying, but both acting and production are very laboured.

w Duke Vincent *d* Gary Nelson

René Auberjonois, David Healy, Charles Seibert

Panama Hattie
US 1942 79m bw
MGM (Arthur Freed)

A showgirl in Panama helps to capture Nazis.
Dim film version of a Broadway musical, stripped of most of its music and more like a *Maisie* comedy.

w Jack McGowan, Wilkie Mahoney, *musical play* Herbert Fields, B. G. De Sylva, Cole Porter *d* Norman Z. McLeod *ph* George Folsey *md* George Stoll

Ann Sothern, Dan Dailey, Red Skelton, Marsha Hunt, Rags Ragland, Virginia O'Brien, Alan Mowbray, Ben Blue, Carl Esmond

Pancho Villa
Spain 1972 93m Technicolor
Granada Films (Bernard Gordon)

In 1916 Villa is rescued from execution and starts a reign of terror.
Mexican banditry played half for laughs and half for real; not a successful compromise.

w Julian Halevy *d* Eugenio Martin *ph* Allejandro Ulloa *m* Anton Garcia-Abril

Telly Savalas, Clint Walker, Chuck Connors

Pandora and the Flying Dutchman*
GB 1950 122m Technicolor
Romulus (Albert Lewin)

A cold but beautiful American woman in Spain falls for a mystery man who turns out to be a ghostly sea captain; she dies so as to be with him.
Pretentious, humourless, totally unpersuasive fantasy of the kind much better done in *Portrait of Jennie*. The writer-director wears Omar Khayyam's moving finger to the bone, and the actors look thoroughly unhappy; even the colour is a bit thick.

wd Albert Lewin ph Jack Cardiff *m* Alan Rawsthorne *ad* John Bryan

James Mason, Ava Gardner, Harold Warrender, Nigel Patrick, Sheila Sim, Mario Cabre, John Laurie, Pamela Kellino, Marius Goring

'Conspicuous in its confident assumption of scholarship and its utter poverty of imagination and taste.'—*C. A. Lejeune*

'It might have been enjoyably silly but for Lewin's striving to be classy and an air of third-rate decadence that hangs about it. This is an Anglo-American co-production and one of the occasions, I think, when we might be generous and let Hollywood have all the credit.'—*Richard Winnington*

The Panic in Needle Park
US 1971 110m De Luxe
Gadd Productions (Dominick Dunne)

Drug addiction problems in a New York ghetto.
Vivid, intimate but overlong and unsympathetic account of a junkie and his mistress.

w Joan Didion, John Gregory Dunne, *novel* James Mills *d* Jerry Schatzberg *ph* Adam Holender *m* none

Al Pacino, Kitty Winn, Adam Vint, Richard Bright, Kiel Martin

Panic in the Streets***
US 1950 96m bw
TCF (Sol C. Siegel)

On the New Orleans waterfront, public health officials seek a carrier of bubonic plague.
Semi-documentary suspenser in the *Naked City* manner; location Hollywood at its best.

w Richard Murphy, Edward and Edna Anhalt *d Elia Kazan ph Joe MacDonald m* Alfred Newman

Richard Widmark, Jack Palance, Paul Douglas, Barbara Bel Geddes, Zero Mostel

Panic in Year Zero*
US 1962 93m bw Cinemascope
AIP (Lou Rusoff, Arnold Houghland)

Adventures of a family on a fishing trip in the mountains when Los Angeles is blasted by a nuclear attack.
Mildly interesting catalogue of predictable events—thugs, looting, fear of fall-out—in a simple-minded script finishing with a hopeful meeting of the UN.

w Jay Simms, John Morton *d* Ray Milland *ph* Gil Warrenton *m* Les Baxter

Ray Milland, Jean Hagen, Frankie Avalon, Joan Freeman

Panic on the 5.22*
US 1974 74m colour TVM
Quinn Martin

Wealthy train passengers are terrorized by three incompetent hoodlums who are exasperated at finding credit cards instead of money.
Smooth, odd little suspenser which goes on too long and submerges in cliché philosophy. Some smart moments, though.

w Eugene Price *d* Harvey Hart

Lynda Day George, Laurence Luckinbill, Ina Balin, Andrew Duggan, Bernie Casey, Linden Chiles, Dana Elcar, Eduard Franz, Reni Santoni

Papa's Delicate Condition
US 1963 98m Technicolor
Paramount / Amro (Jack Rose)

At the turn of the century in a small Texas town an amiable family man gets into scrapes when he drinks too much.
Basically pleasing period comedy which suffers from slow, stiff treatment.

w Jack Rose, *book* Corinne Griffith *d* George Marshall *ph* Loyal Griggs *m* Joseph J. Lilley

Jackie Gleason, Glynis Johns, Charles Ruggles, Charles Lane, Laurel Goodwin, Juanita Moore, Elisha Cook Jnr, Murray Hamilton

The Paper Chase*
US 1973 111m De Luxe Panavision
TCF (Robert C. Thompson, Rodrick Paul)

A Harvard law graduate falls in love with the divorced daughter of his tetchiest professor.

A thoughtful analysis of attitudes to learning turns into just another youth movie.

wd James Bridges, *novel* John Jay Osborn Jnr *ph* Gordon Willis *m* John Williams

Timothy Bottoms, Lindsay Wagner, *John Houseman*, Graham Bickel

'A slightly unfocused account of conformism and milk-mild rebellion on the campus.'—*Sight and Sound*

Paper Man*
US 1971 74m colour TVM
TCF (Tony Wilson)

A computer accidentally issues a bogus credit card and three students create an identity to fit it. Complicated melodrama which finally loses the interest after a very smart beginning.

w James D. Buchanan, Ronald Austin *d* Walter Grauman

Dean Stockwell, Stefanie Powers, James Stacy, James Olson, Elliott Street

Paper Moon**
US 1973 103m bw
Paramount / Saticoy (Peter Bogdanovich)

In the American midwest in the thirties, a bible salesman and a plain little girl make a great con team.
Unusual but overrated comedy, imperfectly adapted from a very funny book, with careful but disappointing period sense and photography. A lot more style and gloss was required.

w Alvin Sargent, *novel* Addie Pray by *Joe David Brown* *d* Peter Bogdanovich *ph* Laszlo Kovacs *m* popular songs and recordings

Ryan O'Neal, Tatum O'Neal, Madeleine Kahn, John Hillerman

'I've rarely seen a film that looked so unlike what it was about.'—*Stanley Kauffmann*

'At its best the film is only mildly amusing, and I'm not sure I could recall a few undeniable highlights if pressed on the point.'—*Gary Arnold*

Paper Tiger
GB 1975 99m Technicolor
Maclean and Co (Euan Lloyd)

An ageing Englishman becomes tutor to the son of the Japanese ambassador in a Pacific state, and finds he has to live his heroic fantasies in reality.
Uneasy adventure comedy drama which might, given more skilled handling, have been much better than it is.

w Jack Davies *d* Ken Annakin *ph* John Cabrera *m* Roy Budd

David Niven, Toshiro Mifune, Hardy Kruger, Ando, Ivan Desny, Irene Tsu, Miiko Taka, Ronald Fraser, Jeff Corey

Papillon*
US 1973 150m Technicolor Panavision
Papillon Partnership / Corona / General Production Co (Robert Dorfmann)

Filmed autobiography of life on Devil's Island. Overlong and rather dreary film of a bestseller; it determinedly rubs the audience's nose in ordure from the start, and the final successful escape is one try too many.

w Dalton Trumbo, Lorenzo Semple Jnr, *book* Henri Charrière *d* Franklin Schaffner *ph* Fred Koenekamp *m* Jerry Goldsmith

Steve McQueen, Dustin Hoffman, Don Gordon, Anthony Zerbe, George Coulouris, Woodrow Parfrey

'A 2½-hour epic trampling the corn growing round the theme of man's inhumanity to man.'—*Sight and Sound*

'Papillon offers torture as entertainment but winds up making entertainment a form of torture . . . a tournament of brutality unrelieved by imagination.'—*Paul D. Zimmermann*

The Paradine Case**
US 1947 115m bw
Selznick

A barrister falls in love with his client, a murder suspect who, it turns out, is actually guilty.
A stodgy and old-fashioned script is given gleaming treatment; this and the acting make it seem better thirty years later than it did on release.

w David O. Selznick, *novel* Robert Hichens *d Alfred Hitchcock ph Lee Garmes m* Franz Waxman

Gregory Peck, *Alida Valli*, Ann Todd, Louis Jourdan, *Charles Laughton*, Charles Coburn, Ethel Barrymore, Leo G. Carroll

'This is the wordiest script since the death of Edmund Burke.'—*James Agee*

'The characters and their problems don't make much imprint on a viewer; if you can't remember whether you've seen the picture or not, chances are you did and forgot it.'—*New Yorker, 1976*

The Parallax View*
US 1974 102m Technicolor Panavision
Paramount / Gus / Harbour / Doubleday

Witnesses to a political assassination are

systematically killed, despite the efforts of a crusading journalist.
Stylish, persuasive political thriller with a downbeat ending; the villains win.

w David Giler, Lorenzo Semple Jnr, *novel* Loren Singer *d* Alan J. Pakula *ph* Gordon Willis *m* Michael Small

Warren Beatty, Paula Prentiss, William Daniels, Hume Cronyn, Walter McGinn

Paramount on Parade*
US 1930 102m bw (Technicolor sequence)
Paramount (Elsie Janis)

A revue featuring Paramount contract stars.
A ragged affair by any standard, but worth a look for a couple of Chevalier's numbers.

w various *d* Dorothy Arzner, Otto Brower, Edmund Goulding, Victor Heerman, Edwin H. Knopf, Rowland V. Lee, Ernst Lubitsch, Lothar Mendes, Victor Schertzinger, Edward Sutherland, Frank Tuttle *ph* Harry Fischbeck, Victor Milner *m* various

Richard Arlen, Jean Arthur, George Bancroft, Clara Bow, Nancy Carroll, Ruth Chatterton, Maurice Chevalier, Gary Cooper, Leon Errol, Kay Francis, Harry Green, Mitzi Green, Dennis King, Fredric March, Nino Martini, Jack Oakie, Charles 'Buddy' Rogers, Lillian Roth, Fay Wray, Clive Brook, Warner Oland, Eugene Pallette, William Powell

Paranoiac*
GB 1963 80m bw Cinemascope
U-I / Hammer (Anthony Hinds)

An heiress is saved from a suicide attempt by a young man claiming to be her dead brother.
A complex maze of disguise, mistaken identity, family curses and revelations of something nasty in the woodshed, out of *Psycho* by *Taste of Fear*. Not very good in itself, but interesting in its borrowings.

w Jimmy Sangster *d* Freddie Francis *ph* Arthur Grant *m* Elisabeth Lutyens

Oliver Reed, Janette Scott, Alexander Davion, Sheila Burrell, Liliane Brousse, Maurice Denham, John Bonney

Pardners
US 1956 88m Technicolor Vistavision
Paramount (Paul Jones)

An incompetent idiot goes west and accidentally cleans up the town.
Stiff western star burlesque, a remake of *Rhythm on the Range*.

w Sidney Sheldon *d* Norman Taurog *ph* Daniel Fapp *songs* Sammy Cahn, Jimmy Van Heusen

Dean Martin, Jerry Lewis, Agnes Moorehead, Lori Nelson, John Baragrey, Jeff Morrow, Lon Chaney Jnr

Pardon My Past*
US 1945 88m bw
Columbia

A man unwittingly takes on the problems of his double, a shady playboy.
Amusing mistaken identity comedy.

w Earl Felton, Karl Kamb *d* Leslie Fenton *ph* Russell Metty

Fred MacMurray, Marguerite Chapman, Akim Tamiroff, Rita Johnson, William Demarest, Harry Davenport

Pardon Us*
US 1931 55m bw
Hal Roach
aka: *Jailbirds*

Two zany bootleggers find themselves in and out of prison.
Patchy star comedy which finds the boys on the whole not in quite their best form.

w H. M. Walker *d* James Parrott *ph* Jack Stevens

Stan Laurel, Oliver Hardy, Wilfred Lucas, Walter Long, James Finlayson

The Parent Trap*
US 1961 129m Technicolor
Walt Disney (George Golitzen)

Twin daughters of separated parents determine to bring the family together again.
Quite bright but awesomely extended juvenile romp.

wd David Swift, *novel* Das Doppelte Lottchen by Erich Kastner *ph* Lucien Ballard *m* Paul Smith

Hayley Mills, Maureen O'Hara, Brian Keith, Charles Ruggles, Leo G. Carroll, Una Merkel, Joanna Barnes, Cathleen Nesbitt, Ruth McDevitt, Nancy Kulp

Paris Blues*
US 1961 98m Technicolor
UA / Pennebaker / Diane / Jason / Monica / Monmouth (Sam Shaw)

Two jazz musicians have romantic problems in Paris.
Semi-serious mini-drama with emphasis on the music; one is not quite sure what the actors thought they were up to.

w Jack Sher, Irene Kamp, Walter Bernstein, *novel* Harold Flender *d* Martin Ritt *ph* Christian Matras *m* Duke Ellington

Paul Newman, Joanne Woodward, Sidney Poitier, Louis Armstrong, Diahann Carroll, Serge Reggiani, Barbara Laage

Paris Calling
US 1941 95m bw
Universal / Charles K. Feldman

When the Nazis invade Paris, a woman discovers that her husband is a traitor.
Totally predictable flagwaver.

w Benjamin Glazer, Charles Kaufmann *d* Edwin L. Marin *ph* Milton Krasner *m* Richard Hageman

Elizabeth Bergner, Basil Rathbone, Randolph Scott, Gale Sondergaard, Lee J. Cobb, Eduardo Ciannelli, Charles Arnt

Paris Holiday*
US 1957 101m Technirama
UA / Tolda (Bob Hope)

An American comedian meets a French one in Paris, and both have narrow escapes because their script contains the clue to a gang of counterfeiters.
Amiable location romp with the stars in pretty good form.

w Edmund Beloin, Dean Riesner *d* Gerd Oswald *ph* Roger Hubert *m* Joseph J. Lilley

Bob Hope, Fernandel, Anita Ekberg, Martha Hyer, André Morell, Maurice Teynac, Jean Murat, Preston Sturges

Paris Underground
US 1945 97m bw
(UA) Constance Bennett
GB title: *Madame Pimpernel*

Two women caught in Paris when the Nazis invade continue their resistance activities.
Artificial and not very exciting flagwaver.

w Boris Ingster, Gertrude Purcell, *novel* Etta Shiber *d* Gregory Ratoff *ph* Lee Garmes *m* Alexander Tansman

Constance Bennett, Gracie Fields, George Rigaud, Kurt Kreuger, Leslie Vincent

Paris When It Sizzles
US 1963 110m Technicolor
Paramount (Richard Quine, George Axelrod)

A film writer tries out several script ideas with his secretary as heroine and himself as hero or villain.
As a French film called *La Fête à Henriette* this was a charming whimsy, but Hollywood made it heavy-handed and boring, especially as no one in it seems to be having much fun.

w George Axelrod, *screenplay* Julien Duviver, Henri Jeanson *d* Richard Quine *ph* Charles Lang Jnr *m* Nelson Riddle

William Holden, Audrey Hepburn, Grégoire Aslan, Noel Coward, Raymond Bussières

Park Row
US 1952 83m bw
UA / Samuel Fuller

Conflict breaks out between two newspapers in 1886 New York.
Earnest but flat low-budgeter of a rather unusual kind.

wd Samuel Fuller *ph* Jack Russell *ad* Ray Robinson

Gene Evans, Mary Welch, Herbert Hayes, Forrest Taylor

Parnell*
US 1937 96m bw
MGM

A 19th-century Irish politician comes to grief through his love for a married woman.
Well made but miscast biopic, a resounding thud at the box office.

w John Van Druten, S. N. Behrman, *play* Elsie T. Schauffler *d* John M. Stahl *ph* Karl Freund *m* William Axt

Clark Gable, Myrna Loy, Edmund Gwenn, Edna May Oliver, Alan Marshal, Donald Crisp, Billie Burke, Berton Churchill, Donald Meek, Montagu Love, George Zucco

'A singularly pallid, tedious and unconvincing drama.'—*Frank Nugent*

Parrish
US 1961 137m Technicolor
Warner (Delmer Daves)

A young tobacco plantation worker has an ample sex life and the luck to become boss.
Predictable trudge through scenes from a bestselling novel, less offensive than most such adaptations.

wd Delmer Daves, *novel* Mildred Savage *ph* Harry Stradling *m* Max Steiner

Troy Donahue, Claudette Colbert, Karl Malden, Dean Jagger, Connie Stevens, Diane McBaine, Sharon Hugueny

The Parson of Panamint
US 1941 84m bw
Paramount (Harry Sherman)

A gold rush mountain town is corrupted by

success until a two-fisted parson puts things right.
Middling western morality play.

w Harold Shumate, Adrian Scott, *novel* Peter B. Kyne *d* William McGann

Charles Ruggles, Ellen Drew, Philip Terry, Joseph Schildkraut, Henry Kolker, Janet Beecher, Paul Hurst

Partners in Crime
US 1973 74m Technicolor TVM
Universal (Jon Epstein)

A retired lady judge and a reformed crook set up a detective agency.
A recast version of *The Judge and Jake Wyler* (qv) with a plot about an amnesiac robber who can't find his own loot. Still no takers.

w David Shaw *d* Jack Smight, Jon Epstein

Lee Grant, Lou Antonio, Harry Guardino, Richard Jaeckel, Bob Cummings, Lorraine Gary, Charles Drake

The Party*
US 1968 98m De Luxe Panavision
UA / Mirisch / Geoffrey (Blake Edwards)

An accident-prone Indian actor is accidentally invited to a swank Hollywood party and wrecks it.
Would-be Tatiesque comedy of disaster, occasionally well-timed but far too long for all its gloss.

w Blake Edwards, Tom and Frank Waldman *d* Blake Edwards *ph* Lucien Ballard *m* Henry Mancini *pd* Fernando Carrere

Peter Sellers, Claudine Longet, Marge Champion, Fay McKenzie, Steve Franken, Buddy Lester

'One thing the old movie makers did know is that two reels is more than enough of this stuff.'—*Wilfred Sheed*

'It is only rarely that one laughs or even smiles; mostly one just chalks up another point for ingenuity.'—*Tom Milne*

Party Girl
US 1958 98m Metrocolor
Cinemascope
MGM / Euterpe (Joe Pasternak)

In twenties Chicago, a lawyer wins a girl from a gangster.
Heavy-handed Scarface-style saga which at one time won a curious reputation for being a satire.

w George Wells *d* Nicholas Ray *ph* Robert Bronner *m* Jeff Alexander

Robert Taylor, Cyd Charisse, Lee J. Cobb, John Ireland, Kent Smith, Claire Kelly, Corey Allen

The Party's Over
GB 1963 94m bw
Tricastle (Anthony Perry)

An American girl joins a group of Chelsea beatniks and dies in a fall from a balcony; her father investigates.
Tasteless and boring swinging London trash which became notorious when its producers (Rank) disowned it because it features a party at which a man makes love to a dead girl. An unattractive display of moral squalor.

w Marc Behm *d* Guy Hamilton *ph* Larry Pizer *m* John Barry

Oliver Reed, Eddie Albert, Ann Lynn, Louise Sorel

Passage Home
GB 1955 102m bw
GFD / Group Films (Julian Wintle)

In 1931, tensions run high on a merchant ship when the captain accepts an attractive girl as passenger from South America.
Obvious melodrama complete with drunken captain and storm at sea; not badly done if it must be done at all.

w William Fairchild, *novel* Richard Armstrong *d* Roy Baker *ph* Geoffrey Unsworth *m* Clifton Parker

Peter Finch, Anthony Steel, Diane Cilento, Cyril Cusack, Geoffrey Keen, Hugh Griffith, Duncan Lamont, Bryan Forbes, Gordon Jackson, Michael Craig

Passage to Marseilles*
US 1944 110m bw
Warner (Hal B. Wallis)

Convicts escape from Devil's Island and join the Free French.
The only known film to have flashbacks within flashbacks within flashbacks, this confusing if sometimes entertaining all-star saga is done to death by its unconvincing flagwaving endpapers which prevent it from being at all comparable with *Casablanca*, as was clearly intended.

w Casey Robinson, Jack Moffitt, *story* Charles Nordhoff, James Hall *ph* James Wong Howe *d* Michael Curtiz *m* Max Steiner

Humphrey Bogart, Michèle Morgan, Claude Rains, Philip Dorn, Sidney Greenstreet, Peter Lorre, Helmut Dantine, George Tobias, John Loder, Victor Francen, Eduardo Ciannelli

The Passing of the Third Floor Back*
GB 1935 90m bw
Gaumont (Ivor Montagu)

A Christ-like visitor stays at a London boarding house and changes the lives of the inmates.
Competent film version of a famous, sentimental, dated play.

w Michael Hogan, Alma Reville, *play* Jerome K. Jerome *d* Berthold Viertel

Conrad Veidt, René Ray, Anna Lee, Frank Cellier, Mary Clare, Beatrix Lehmann, Cathleen Nesbitt, Sara Allgood

The Passionate Friends**
GB 1948 91m bw
GFD / Cineguild (Eric Ambler)
US title: *One Woman's Story*

A woman marries an older man, then meets again her young lover.
A simple and obvious dramatic situation is tricked out with flashbacks and the inimitable high style of its director to make a satisfying entertainment.

w Eric Ambler, *novel* H. G. Wells *d* David Lean *ph Guy Green* *m* Richard Addinsell

Ann Todd, Trevor Howard, Claude Rains, Betty Ann Davies, Isabel Dean, Arthur Howard, Wilfrid Hyde White

The Passionate Stranger
GB 1956 97m
part bw, part Eastmancolor
British Lion / Beaconsfield
(Peter Rogers, Gerald Thomas)
US title: *A Novel Affair*

A lady novelist bases a character on her virile chauffeur; he reads the book and thinks she fancies him.
Feeble comedy, half of it consisting of a dramatization of the heroine's very dull novel.

w Muriel and Sydney Box *d* Muriel Box *ph* Otto Heller *m* Humphrey Searle

Ralph Richardson, Margaret Leighton, Carlo Justini, Patricia Dainton, Marjorie Rhodes, Thorley Walters, Frederick Piper

Passionate Summer
GB 1958 104m Eastmancolor
Rank / Kenneth Harper

A divorced headmaster at a Jamaican school is loved by three women.
Silly melodrama with splendid backgrounds ruined by poor colour.

w Joan Henry, *novel* The Shadow and the Peak by Richard Mason *d* Rudolph Cartier *ph* Ernest Steward *m* Angelo Lavagnino

Virginia McKenna, Bill Travers, Yvonne Mitchell, Alexander Knox, Ellen Barrie, Carl Mohner.

'The climactic hurricane does little to dispel the overall feeling of emotional suffocation.'—*MFB*

Passport to Pimlico****
GB 1949 84m bw
Ealing (E. V. H. Emmett)

Part of a London district is discovered to belong to Burgundy, and the inhabitants find themselves free of rationing restrictions.
A cleverly detailed little comedy which inaugurated the best period of Ealing, its preoccupation with suburban man and his foibles. Not exactly satire, but great fun, and kindly with it.

w T. E. B. Clarke *d Henry Cornelius* *ph* Lionel Banes *m Georges Auric*

Stanley Holloway, *Margaret Rutherford*, Basil Radford, Naunton Wayne, Hermione Baddeley, John Slater, Paul Dupuis, Jane Hylton, Raymond Huntley, Betty Warren, Barbara Murray, Sidney Tafler

The Password Is Courage*
GB 1962 116m bw
MGM / Andrew and Virginia Stone

In Europe during World War II, Sgt-Major Charles Coward has a career of escapes and audacious anti-Nazi exploits.
Lively, slightly over-humorous account of one man's war, well mounted and shot entirely on location.

wd Andrew L. Stone, *biography* John Castle *ph* David Boulton

Dirk Bogarde, Maria Perschy, Alfred Lynch, Nigel Stock, Reginald Beckwith

'The experiences are, it seems, mainly true but they do not seem so.'—*Guardian*

Pastor Hall*
GB 1940 97m bw
Charter (John Boulting)

The story of German village pastor Niemoller, who in 1934 was shot for denouncing the Nazis.
A courageous film of its time, not very interesting dramatically or cinematically.

w Leslie Arliss, Haworth Bromley, Anna Reiner, *play* Ernst Toller *d* Roy Boulting

Wilfrid Lawson, Nova Pilbeam, Seymour Hicks, Marius Goring, Percy Walsh, Brian Worth, Peter Cotes, Hay Petrie

Pat and Mike**
US 1952 95m bw
MGM (Lawrence Weingarten)

A small-time sports promoter takes on a female intellectual multi-champion.
A comedy which amuses because of its star playing, but doesn't really develop. All very easy going, with guest appearances from sporting personalities.

w Ruth Gordon, Garson Kanin *d* George Cukor *ph* William Daniels *m* David Raksin

Spencer Tracy, Katharine Hepburn, Aldo Ray, William Ching, Sammy White, Jim Backus, Phyllis Povah

A Patch of Blue*
US 1966 105m bw Panavision
MGM / Pandro S. Berman

A blind girl who lives in a slum is helped by a negro with whom she falls in love without realizing his colour.
Polished tearjerker with racial overtones; nicely done for those who can take it.

wd Guy Green, *novel* Be Ready with Bells and Drums by Elizabeth Kata *ph* Robert Burks *d* Jerry Goldsmith

Sidney Poitier, Elizabeth Hartman, Shelley Winters, Wallace Ford, Ivan Dixon, Elizabeth Fraser, John Qualen

Pat Garrett and Billy the Kid
US 1973 106m Metrocolor Panavision
MGM (Gordon Carroll)

Blood-spattered version of a western legend, with violence always to the fore, accentuated by the impossibility of listening to the dialogue because of poor direction and recording.

w Rudolph Wurlitzer *d* Sam Peckinpah *ph* John Coquillon *m* Bob Dylan

James Coburn, Kris Kristofferson, Bob Dylan, Richard Jaeckel, Katy Jurado, Slim Pickens, Chill Wills, Jason Robards Jnr

'A sombre, intense, downbeat essay on the truth behind the legend and the legend behind the the truth.'—*Sight and Sound*

'Shows what Peckinpah can do when he doesn't put his mind to it.'—*Stanley Kauffmann*

'A rash adventure in inadvertent self-parody.'—*William S. Pechter*

Paths of Glory****
US 1957 86m bw
UA / Bryna (James B. Harris)

In 1916 in the French trenches, three soldiers are courtmartialled for cowardice.
Incisive melodrama chiefly depicting the corruption and incompetence of the high command; the plight of the soldiers is less interesting. The trench scenes are the most vivid ever made, and the rest is shot in genuine castles, with resultant difficulties of lighting and recording; the overall result is an overpowering piece of cinema.

w Stanley Kubrick, Calder Willingham, Jim Thompson, *novel* Humphrey Cobb *d Stanley Kubrick ph George Krause m* Gerald Fried

Kirk Douglas, Adolphe Menjou, George Macready, Wayne Morris, Richard Anderson, Ralph Meeker, Timothy Carey

'A bitter and biting tale, told with stunning point and nerve-racking intensity.'—*Judith Crist*

'Beautifully performed, staged, photographed, cut and scored.'—*Colin Young*

Patrick the Great*
US 1945 88m bw
Universal (Howard Benedict)

An actor whose career is waning is jealous of his young son.
Slick teenage family comedy, virtually a one-man show for O'Connor.

w Jane Hall, Bertram Millhauser, Dorothy Bennett, Frederick and Ralph Block *d* Frank Ryan *ph* Frank Redman *m* Hans Salter

Donald O'Connor, Donald Cook, Peggy Ryan, Frances Dee, Eve Arden, Thomas Gomez, Gavin Muir, Andrew Tombes

The Patsy
US 1964 101m Technicolor
Paramount

Hollywood executives try to mould a bellboy to replace a deceased comedian.
A few mildly funny scenes scarcely atone for a long raucous comedy in which the star upstages his betters.

wd Jerry Lewis *ph* Wallace Kelley *m* David Raksin

Jerry Lewis, Everett Sloane, Peter Lorre, John Carradine, Phil Harris, Hans Conried

Patterns***
US 1956 88m bw
UA / Jed Harris, Michael Myerberg
GB title: *Patterns of Power*

The tough boss of a New York corporation forces a showdown between a young executive and the older ineffectual man who he hopes will resign.
Tense little boardroom melodrama with domestic asides, one of the best of the filmed TV plays of the mid-fifties.

w Rod Serling, from his play *d Fielder Cook ph* Boris Kaufman

Van Heflin, Everett Sloane, Ed Begley, Beatrice Straight, Elizabeth Wilson

Patton***
US 1969 171m De Luxe Dimension 150
TCF (Frank McCarthy)
GB title: *Patton—Lust for Glory*

World War II adventures of an aggressive American general.
Brilliantly handled wartime character study which is also a spectacle and tries too hard to have it both ways, but as a piece of film-making is hard to beat.

w Francis Ford Coppola, Edmund H. North *d Franklin Schaffner ph Fred Koenekamp m Jerry Goldsmith*

George C. Scott, Karl Malden, Michael Bates, Stephen Young, Michael Strong, Frank Latimore

'Here is an actor so totally immersed in his part that he almost makes you believe he is the man himself.'—*John Gillett*

Paula
US 1952 80m bw
Columbia (Buddy Adler)
GB title: *The Silent Voice*

A barren wife causes a boy's deafness in an accident; she cures and adopts him.
Adequate woman's picture, a vehicle for a star and a luxuriant wardrobe.

w James Poe, William Sackheim *d* Rudolph Maté *ph* Charles Lawton Jnr *m* George Duning

Loretta Young, Kent Smith, Alexander Knox, Tommy Rettig

The Pawnbroker**
US 1965 114m bw
Landau–Unger (Worthington Miner)

A Jew in slummy New York is haunted by his experiences in Nazi prison camps.
Engrossing, somewhat over-melodramatic character study, generally well done.

w David Friedkin, Morton Fine, *novel* Edward Lewis Wallant *d* Sidney Lumet *ph* Boris Kaufman *m* Quincy Jones

Rod Steiger, Brock Peters, Geraldine Fitzgerald, Jaime Sanchez, Thelma Oliver, Juano Hernandez

Pay or Die!*
US 1960 109m bw
Allied Artists (Richard Wilson)

In 1906, a New York Italian police detective forms a special squad to combat the Black Hand.
Tough, convincing period melodrama.

w Richard Wilson, Bertram Millhauser *d Richard Wilson ph* Lucien Ballard *m* David Raksin *ad* Fernando Carrere

Ernest Borgnine, Alan Austin, Zohra Lampert, Robert F. Simon, Renata Vanni

Payday
US 1972 103m colour
Cinerama / Pumice / Fantasy (Ralph J. Gleason)

An over-age pop singer has personal problems which erupt into violence.
Well made, dislikeable melodrama.

w Don Carpenter *d* Daryl Duke *ph* Richard C. Glouner *md* Ed Bogas

Rip Torn, Ahna Capri, Elayne Heilveil, Michael C. Gwynn

Payment Deferred*
US 1932 75m bw
MGM

A man desperate for money poisons his wealthy nephew.
Watchable photographed play.

w Ernest Vajda, Claudine West, *play* Jeffrey Dell *d* Lothar Mendes *ph* Merritt Gerstad

Charles Laughton, Maureen O'Sullivan, Ray Milland, Dorothy Peterson, Veree Teasdale, Billy Bevan, Halliwell Hobbes

Payment on Demand*
US 1951 90m bw
RKO / Jack H. Skirball

A happy wife and mother is appalled when her husband asks for a divorce.
A star suffers her way through luxury to a happy ending; good enough stuff for its intended audience.

w Bruce Manning, Curtis Bernhardt *d* Curtis Bernhardt *ph* Leo Tover *m* Victor Young

Bette Davis, Barry Sullivan, Jane Cowl, Kent Taylor, Betty Lynn, John Sutton, Frances Dee, Otto Kruger

Payroll*
GB 1961 105m bw
Anglo Amalgamated / Lynx (Norman Priggen)

Small-time crooks snatch £100,000, but after the getaway things begin to go wrong.
Tense, vivid, thoroughly predictable *Rififi*-style thriller, handled with solid professionalism.

w George Baxt, *novel* Derek Bickerton *d Sidney Hayers ph Ernest Steward m* Reg Owen

Michael Craig, Billie Whitelaw, Françoise Prévost, Kenneth Williams, William Lucas, Tom Bell, Barry Keegan, Joan Rice, Glyn Houston

Peeper
US 1975 87m De Luxe Panavision
TCF / Chartoff–Winkler (Ron Buck)

In 1947 Los Angeles, a poor British private eye gets into trouble when he seeks a man's lost daughter.
Semi-spoofing Chandleresque caper which is never quite funny or quite thrilling enough.

w W. D. Richter, *novel* Deadfall by Keith Laumer *d* Peter Hyams *ph* Earl Rath *m* Richard Clements

Michael Caine, Natalie Wood, Kitty Winn, Thayer David, Liam Dunn
'Flimsy whimsy.'—*Variety*

Peeping Tom
GB 1959 109m Eastmancolor
Anglo Amalgamated / Michael Powell

A film studio focus puller is obsessed by the lust to murder beautiful women and photograph the fear on their faces.
Thoroughly disagreeable suspenser, a kind of compendium of the bad taste the director showed in flashes during his career.

w Leo Marks *d* Michael Powell *ph* Otto Heller *m* Brian Easdale

Carl Boehm, Moira Shearer, Anna Massey, Maxine Audley, Esmond Knight, Michael Goodliffe, Shirley Ann Field, Jack Watson

Peking Express
US 1951 90m bw
Paramount / Hal B. Wallis

In communist China, an assortment of people are aboard a train which is diverted by outlaws.
Pot-boiling remake of *Shanghai Express* (qv); an adequate time-passer.

w John Meredyth Lucas *d* William Dieterle *ph* Charles Lang *m* Dmitri Tiomkin

Joseph Cotten, Corinne Calvet, Edmund Gwenn, Marvin Miller
'Lacks flavour or distinction.'—*Leonard Maltin*

The Penalty
US 1941 81m bw
MGM (Jack Chertok)

The son of a gangster is regenerated by farm life and turns against his father.
Antediluvian sweetness and light which wastes a good cast.

w Harry Ruskin, John C. Higgins *d* Harold S. Bucquet

Edward Arnold, Lionel Barrymore, Marsha Hunt, Robert Sterling, Gene Reynolds

Pendulum*
US 1969 102m Technicolor
Columbia / Pendulum (Stanley Niss)

A convicted murderer and rapist is freed on appeal and kills the wife of the detective who arrested him.
Heavy-going police melodrama, efficient but not very interesting.

w Stanley Niss *d* George Schaefer *ph* Lionel Lindon *m* Walter Scharf

George Peppard, Jean Seberg, Richard Kiley, Charles McGraw, Robert F. Lyons, Madeleine Sherwood

Penelope
US 1966 98m Metrocolor Panavision
MGM / Euterpe (Joe Pasternak, Arthur Loew Jnr)

The wife of a bank vice-president is a bank robber and kleptomaniac.
Would be cute comedy which only sickens one for wasting its talent.

w George Wells, *novel* E. V. Cunningham *d* Arthur Hiller *ph* Harry Stradling *m* Johnny Williams

Natalie Wood, Ian Bannen, Dick Shawn, Peter Falk, Jonathan Winters, Lila Kedrova, Lou Jacobi, Norma Crane, Arthur Malet, Jerome Cowan

Penny Princess
GB 1952 94m Technicolor
Rank / Conquest (Frank Godwin)

A New York shopgirl inherits a tiny European state and boosts its economy by marketing a mixture of cheese and schnapps.
Thin, spoofy comedy with mild moments of fun.

wd Val Guest *ph* Geoffrey Unsworth *m* Philip Martell

Dirk Bogarde, Yolande Donlan, A. E. Matthews, Anthony Oliver, Edwin Styles, Reginald Beckwith, Kynaston Reeves, Peter Butterworth, Laurence Naismith, Mary Clare, Desmond Walter-Ellis

Penny Serenade*
US 1941 120m bw
Columbia (Fred Guiol)

Courtship, marriage and the death of two children are recollected by a woman contemplating divorce.

Well-played but uneasy film which veers suddenly and disconcertingly from light comedy into tragedy.

w Morrie Ryskind *d* George Stevens *ph* Joseph Walker *m* Morris Stoloff

Cary Grant, Irene Dunne, Beulah Bondi, Edgar Buchanan, Ann Doran

'To make something out of very little, and that so near at hand, is one of the tests of artistry.'—*Otis Ferguson*

The Penthouse
GB 1967 96m Eastmancolor
Paramount / Tahiti (Harry Fine)

Illicit lovers in an unfinished block of flats are terrorized by intruders.
Thoroughly objectionable and unpleasant melodrama with no attractive characters and no attempt to explain itself.

wd Peter Collinson, *play* The Meter Man by J. Scott Forbes *ph* Arthur Lavis *m* John Hawkesworth

Suzy Kendall, Terence Morgan, Tony Beckley, Norman Rodway, Martine Beswick

'Pornography in Pinter's clothing.'—*MFB*

The People*
US 1971 74m colour TVM
Metromedia

A young teacher takes a job in a remote town and finds that her employers and pupils are aliens from another planet.
Quiet, understated science fiction with plenty of charm but not enough get up and go.

w James M. Miller *d* John Korty

Kim Darby, Dan O'Herlihy, William Shatner, Diane Varsi

The People against O'Hara*
US 1952 102m bw
MGM (William H. Wright)

An ex-alcoholic defence lawyer sacrifices himself to prove his client's innocence.
Formula drama, well made and entertainingly performed, with snatches of bright dialogue.

w John Monks Jnr, *novel* Eleanor Lipsky *d* John Sturges *ph* John Alton *m* Carmen Dragon

Spencer Tracy, Diana Lynn, Pat O'Brien, John Hodiak, James Arness, Arthur Shields, Eduardo Ciannelli, Louise Lorimer

The People Next Door
US 1970 93m De Luxe
Avco Embassy (Herb Brodkin)

Suburban parents have trouble with their drug-addicted teenage daughter.
Hysterical melodrama with good credentials.

w J. P. Miller, from his TV play *d* David Greene *ph* Gordon Willis *m* Don Sebesky

Eli Wallach, Julie Harris, Hal Holbrook, Cloris Leachman, Stephen McHattie, Nehemiah Persoff

'As unlovely a picture of suburban living as one is likely to see.'—*Judith Crist*

People Will Talk**
US 1951 110m bw
TCF (Darryl F. Zanuck)

A surgeon's unorthodox psychological methods cause jealousy among his colleagues, especially when he falls in love with a pregnant patient.
Oddly entertaining jumble of melodrama, comedy, romance, speeches and a little mystery, all quite typical of its director.

wd Joseph L. Mankiewicz, play Dr Praetorius by Curt Goetz *ph* Milton Krasner *md* Alfred Newman

Cary Grant, Jeanne Crain, Finlay Currie, Hume Cronyn, Walter Slezak, Sidney Blackmer, Basil Ruysdael

'A picture so mature and refreshingly frank as to hold that an erring young woman might be rewarded with a wise and loving mate is most certainly a significant milestone in the moral emancipation of American films.'—*New York Times*

Pepe
US 1960 195m Eastmancolor
Cinemascope
Columbia / George Sidney (Jacques Gelman)

A Mexican peasant in Hollywood gets help from the stars.
Feeble and seemingly endless extravaganza in which the boring stretches far outnumber the rest, and few of the guests have anything worthwhile to do.

w Dorothy Kingsley, Claude Binyon *d* George Sidney *ph* Joe MacDonald *md* Johnny Green

Cantinflas, Dan Dailey, Shirley Jones, Ernie Kovacs, Jay North, William Demarest, Michael Callan, Maurice Chevalier, Bing Crosby, Richard Conte, Bobby Darin, Sammy Davis Jnr, Jimmy Durante, Zsa Zsa Gabor, Hedda Hopper, Joey Bishop, Peter Lawford, Janet Leigh, Jack Lemmon, Kim Novak, André Previn, Donna Reed, Debbie Reynolds, Greer Garson, Edward G. Robinson, Cesar Romero, Frank Sinatra, Billie Burke, Tony Curtis, Dean Martin, Charles Coburn

Percy
GB 1971 103m Eastmancolor
Anglo EMI / Welbeck (Betty E. Box)

After an unfortunate accident, a young man undergoes a successful penis transplant, and sets out to discover who the donor was.
Barrage of phallic jokes, some quite funny, but mostly as witless as the whole idea.

w Hugh Leonard, *novel* Raymond Hitchcock *d* Ralph Thomas *ph* Ernest Steward *m* Ray Davies

Hywel Bennett, Elke Sommer, *Denholm Elliott*, Britt Ekland, Cyd Hayman

Percy's Progress
GB 1974 101m Eastmancolor
EMI (Betty E. Box)

A chemical causes impotence in all males except the owner of the first transplanted penis.
Percy dug deep, but this is really the bottom of the barrel.

w Sid Colin *d* Ralph Thomas *ph* Tony Imi *m* Tony Macauley

Leigh Lawson, Elke Sommer, Denholm Elliott, Judy Geeson, Harry H. Corbett, Vincent Price, Adrienne Posta, Julie Ege, James Booth

Perfect Friday*
GB 1970 95m Eastmancolor
London Screenplays / Sunnymede (Dimitri de Grunwald)

A bank manager engages aristocratic help to rob his own bank.
Middling comedy caper.

w Anthony Greville-Bell, J. Scott Forbes *d* Peter Hall *ph* Alan Hume *m* Johnny Dankworth *pd* Terence Marsh

Stanley Baker, Ursula Andress, David Warner, Patience Collier, T. P. McKenna, David Waller, Joan Benham, Julian Orchard

The Perfect Furlough
US 1958 93m Eastmancolor Cinemascope
U-I (Robert Arthur)
GB title: *Strictly for Pleasure*

To help morale at a remote Arctic army unit, one of the men is selected to enjoy the perfect leave in Paris on behalf of the others.
Amiable farce which entertains while it's on but is quickly forgotten.

w Stanley Shapiro *d* Blake Edwards *ph* Philip Lathrop *m* Frank Skinner

Tony Curtis, Janet Leigh, Elaine Stritch, Keenan Wynn, Troy Donahue, King Donovan, Linda Cristal

The Perfect Marriage
US 1946 88m bw
Paramount / Hal B. Wallis

On their tenth wedding anniversary, a happy couple have a row and start divorce proceedings.
Wispy comedy, unmemorable and rather tiresome.

w Leonard Spiegelgass, *play* Samson Raphaelson *d* Lewis Allen *ph* Russell Metty *m* Frederick Hollander

David Niven, Loretta Young, Eddie Albert, Nona Griffith, Virginia Field, Jerome Cowan, Rita Johnson, Charles Ruggles, Nana Bryant, Zasu Pitts

'Another film about disillusionment and reconciliation in a mansion with constant evening dress.'—*Sunday Times*

The Perfect Specimen
US 1937 98m bw
Warner (Harry Joe Brown)

The grandmother of a rich young man brings him up uncontaminated by the world, but when a girl crashes her car into his fence he proves fitted to deal with the situation.
Fantasticated comedy a long way after *Mr Deeds* and too slow by half.

w Norman Reilly Raine, Lawrence Riley, Brewster Morse, Fritz Falkenstein, Samuel Hopkins Adams *d* Michael Curtiz *ph* Charles Rosher

Errol Flynn, Joan Blondell, Hugh Herbert, Edward Everett Horton, May Robson, Dick Foran, Beverly Roberts, Allen Jenkins

Perfect Strangers**
GB 1947 102m bw
MGM / London Films (Alexander Korda)
US title: *Vacation from Marriage*

A downtrodden clerk and his dowdy wife go to war, and come back unrecognizably improved.
Pleasant comedy with good actors; but the turnabout of two such caricatures really strains credibility.

w Clemence Dane, Anthony Pelissier *d* Alexander Korda

Robert Donat, Deborah Kerr, Glynis Johns, Ann Todd, Roland Culver, Elliot Mason, Eliot Makeham, Brefni O'Rourke, Edward Rigby

Perfect Strangers
US 1950 87m bw
Warner (Jerry Wald)
GB title: *Too Dangerous to Love*

Two jurors on a murder case fall in love.
Talkative, unlikely, and rather boring potboiler.

w Edith Sommer, *play* Ladies and Gentlemen by Charles MacArthur, Ben Hecht *d* Bretaigne Windust *ph* Peverell Marley *m* Leigh Harline

Ginger Rogers, Dennis Morgan, Thelma Ritter, Margalo Gillmore, Howard Freeman, Alan Reed, Paul Ford, George Chandler

Perfect Understanding*
GB 1933 80m bw
Gloria Swanson British Pictures Ltd

A couple agree to marry on condition that they will never disagree with each other.
Silly comedy with a unique star combination looking acutely uncomfortable.

w Miles Malleson, Michael Powell *d* Cyril Gardner *ph* Curt Courant

Gloria Swanson, Laurence Olivier, John Halliday, Nigel Playfair, Michael Farmer, Genevieve Tobin, Nora Swinburne

Performance*
GB 1970 105m Technicolor
Warner / Goodtimes (Donald Cammell)

A vicious gangster moves in with an ex-pop star.
Dense, Pinterish melodrama about alter egos; not really worth the trouble it takes, but superficially very flashily done.

w Donald Cammell *d Nicolas Roeg, Donald Cammell ph Nicolas Roeg md* Randy Newman

James Fox, Mick Jagger, Anita Pallenberg, Michèle Breton, Stanley Meadows, Allan Cuthbertson

A Perilous Journey
US 1953 87m bw
Republic (W. J. O'Sullivan)

A party of women sail to the California goldfields to sell themselves into marriage.
Reasonably lively action drama.

w Richard Wormser, *novel* The Golden Tide by Virgie Roe *d* R. G. Springsteen *ph* Jack Marta *m* Victor Young

Vera Ralston, David Brian, Charles Winninger, Scott Brady, Virginia Grey, Ben Cooper

Perilous Voyage
US 1969 97m Technicolor TVM
Universal (Jack Laird)

A revolutionary hijacks a ship and its cargo of machine guns.
Highly-coloured adventure story with plenty of action but not much sense.

w Oscar Millard, Sid Stebel, Robert Weverka *d* William Graham

William Shatner, Lee Grant, Michal Parks, Michael Tolan, Frank Silvera, Louise Sorel

The Perils of Pauline*
US 1947 96m Technicolor
Paramount (Sol C. Siegel)

The career of silent serial queen Pearl White.
An agreeable recreation of old time Hollywood, with plenty of slapstick chases but a shade too much sentiment also.

w P. J. Wolfson *d* George Marshall *ph* Ray Rennahan *md* Robert Emmett Dolan

Betty Hutton, John Lund, Billy de Wolfe, William Demarest, Constance Collier, Frank Faylen, William Farnum, Paul Panzer, Snub Pollard, Creighton Hale, Chester Conklin, James Finlayson, Hank Mann, Bert Roach, Francis McDonald, Chester Clute

The Perils of Pauline*
US 1967 98m Technicolor TVM
Universal (Herbert B. Leonard)

An orphan girl has international adventures but finally marries the richest man in the world.
Sometimes engaging burlesque of the silent serial, afflicted by an attack of the cutesy-poos.

w Albert Beich *d* Herbert B. Leonard, Joseph Shelley *ph* Jack Marta *m* Vic Mizzy

Pat Boone, Pamela Austin, Terry-Thomas, Edward Everett Horton, Kurt Kasznar, Leon Askin

Period of Adjustment
US 1962 122m bw Panavision
MGM / Marton (Lawrence Weingarten)

A Korean War veteran has the shakes and his sexual adequacy is affected, as his wife furiously discovers.
Comedy of maladjustment, tolerably witty but unsuitably widescreened.

w Isabel Lennart, *play* Tennessee Williams *d* George Roy Hill *ph* Paul C. Vogel *m* Lyn Murray

Tony Franciosa, Jane Fonda, Jim Hutton, Lois Nettleton

Permission to Kill
US / Austria 1975 97m Technicolor Panavision
Warner / Sascha (Paul Mills)

British agents try to stop a communist returning home from the west.
Prolonged, confusing and boring spy melodrama in which everyone looks understandably glum.

w Robin Estridge, from his novel *d* Cyril

Frankel *ph* Freddie Young *m* Richard Rodney Bennett

Bekim Fehmiu, Dirk Bogarde, Ava Gardner, Timothy Dalton, Frederic Forrest

'Pretentious political mishmash.'—*MFB*

Perri**
US 1957 75m Technicolor
Walt Disney (Winston Hibler)

The life of a squirrel.
Disney's first True Life Fantasy, in which live footage of animals is manipulated against artificial backgrounds to produce an effect as charming and unreal as a cartoon.

w Ralph Wright, Winston Hibler, *novel* Felix Salten *d* Ralph Wright *ph* various *m* Paul Smith

Persecution
GB 1974 96m Eastmancolor
Fanfare / Tyburn (Kevin Francis)

A rich American woman in England is hated by her son and fearful that her murky past will be revealed.
Rich but not engrossing nonsense, somewhat à la *Baby Jane*, with hazy script and stolid production.

w Robert B. Hutton, Rosemary Wootten *d* Don Chaffey *ph* Ken Talbot *m* Paul Ferris

Lana Turner, Ralph Bates, Olga Georges-Picot, Trevor Howard, Suzan Farmer, Ronald Howard, Patrick Allen

Personal Affair
GB 1953 83m bw
Rank / Two Cities (Anthony Darnborough)

A schoolmaster and his neurotic wife run into trouble when a girl pupil develops a crush on him.
Preposterous domestic drama making much ado about nothing.

w Lesley Storm, from her play *d* Anthony Pelissier *ph* Reg Wyer *m* William Alwyn

Leo Genn, Gene Tierney, Glynis Johns, Pamela Brown

Personal Property*
US 1937 84m bw
MGM (John W. Considine Jnr)
GB title: *The Man in Possession*

An American widow in England, in financial straits, falls for the bailiff sent to keep an eye on her.
Moderate star comedy which still amuses.

w Hugh Mills, Ernest Vajda, *play* The Man in Possession by H. M. Harwood *d* W. S. Van Dyke II *ph* William Daniels *m* Franz Waxman

Jean Harlow, Robert Taylor, Reginald Owen, Una O'Connor, Henrietta Crosman, E. E. Clive, Cora Witherspoon, Barnett Parker

Persons in Hiding*
US 1939 71m bw
Paramount

A bored girl absconds with gangsters and becomes a public enemy.
Interesting programmer which led to several sequels using the same book as source; this one was vaguely inspired by the story of Bonnie and Clyde.

w William R. Lipman, Horace McCoy, *book* J. Edgar Hoover *d* Louis King *ph* Harry Fischbeck *m* Boris Morros

Patricia Morison, J. Carrol Naish, Lynne Overman, William Henry, Helen Twelvetrees, William Frawley

Pete 'n Tillie*
US 1972 100m Technicolor
Panavision
Universal (Julius J. Epstein)

The tragi-comic marriage of two eccentrics.
Curious: plain drama treated as comedy, with surprisingly satisfactory results, but not an example to be followed.

w Julius J. Epstein, *novel* Witch's Milk by Peter de Vries *d* Martin Ritt *ph* John Alonzo *m* John T. Williams

Walter Matthau, Carol Burnett, Geraldine Page, René Auberjonois, Barry Nelson, Henry Jones

'For the most part an amusing, moving, sentimental comedy. The wisecracks stay on this side of human possibility – that is, we don't feel, as we do so often with Neil Simon, that the characters have private gag writers in their homes.'—*Stanley Kauffmann*

Pete Kelly's Blues*
US 1955 95m Warnercolor
Cinemascope
Warner (Jack Webb)

Jazz musicians in the twenties get involved with gangsters.
Minor cult film, mainly for the score; dramatically it is not exactly compelling.

w Richard L. Breen *d* Jack Webb *ph* Hal Rosson *ph* Harper Goff *m* Sammy Cahn, Ray Heindorf, Arthur Hamilton, Matty Matlock

Jack Webb, Edmond O'Brien, Janet Leigh, Peggy Lee, Andy Devine, *Ella Fitzgerald,* Lee Marvin, Martin Milner

'Concerned with striking attitudes and establishing an atmosphere rather than developing anything very coherent in the way of narrative . . . one remains aware of an over-deliberate straining after effect.'—*Penelope Houston*

Peter Ibbetson*
US 1935 85m bw
Paramount (Louis D. Lighton)

Childhood sweethearts meet again as adults, are separated when he is imprisoned for her husband's murder, but are reunited in heaven.
Downright peculiar romantic fantasy, even more oddly cast, but extremely well produced.

w Vincent Lawrence, Waldemar Young, Constance Collier, *novel* George du Maurier *d* Henry Hathaway *ph* Charles Lang *m* Ernst Toch

Gary Cooper, Ann Harding, Ida Lupino, John Halliday, Douglass Dumbrille, Virginia Weidler, Dickie Moore, Doris Lloyd

Peter Pan***
US 1952 76m Technicolor
Walt Disney

Three London children are taken into fairyland by a magic flying boy who cannot grow up.
Solidly crafted cartoon version of a famous children's play; not Disney's best work, but still miles ahead of the competition.

supervisor Ben Sharpsteen *d* Wilfred Jackson, Clyde Geronomi, Hamilton Luske

The Petrified Forest**
US 1936 83m bw
Warner (Henry Blanke)

Travellers at a way station in the Arizona desert are held up by gangsters.
Rather faded melodrama (it always was), which is important to Hollywood for introducing such well used figures as the poet idealist hero and the gangster anti-hero, and for giving Bogart his first meaty role. Otherwise, the settings are artificial, the acting theatrical, the development predictable and the dialogue pretentious.

w Charles Kenyon, Delmer Daves, *play* Robert E. Sherwood *d* Archie Mayo *ph* Sol Polito *md* Leo F. Forbstein

Leslie Howard, Bette Davis, *Humphrey Bogart,* Genevieve Tobin, Dick Foran, Joe Sawyer, Porter Hall, Charley Grapewin

'Drama slackens under the weight of Mr Sherwood's rather half-baked philosophy.'—*Alistair Cooke*

†Remade as *Escape in the Desert* (qv).

Petticoat Fever
US 1936 80m bw
MGM (Frank Davis)

A girl and her stuffy fiancé crash land their plane in sub-Arctic Labrador and are helped by a wireless operator who has not seen a woman for two years.
Pert, slightly unusual comedy which comes off pretty well.

w Harold Goldman, *play* Mark Reed *d* George Fitzmaurice *ph* Ernest Haller

Robert Montgomery, Myrna Loy, Reginald Owen, Winifred Shotter

Petulia*
US 1968 105m Technicolor
Warner / Petersham (Raymond Wagner)

A doctor's life is disrupted by his meeting and loving a kooky girl who has family problems.
Swinging London melodrama which happens to be set in San Francisco. All very flashy, and occasionally arresting or well acted, but adding up to nothing.

w Lawrence B. Marcus, *novel* Me and the Arch Kook Petulia by John Haase *d* Richard Lester *ph* Nicolas Roeg *m* John Barry

George C. Scott, Julie Christie, Richard Chamberlain, Joseph Cotten, Arthur Hill, Shirley Knight, Kathleen Widdoes, Pippa Scott

'A sad and savage comment on the ways we waste our time and ourselves in upper-middle-class America.'—*Richard Schickel*

'A soulless, arbitrary, attitudinizing piece of claptrap.'—*John Simon*

Peyton Place**
US 1957 157m De Luxe Cinemascope
TCF (Jerry Wald)

Sex, frustration and violence ferment under the placid surface of a small New England town.
Well-made film of what was at the time a scandalous bestseller, one of the first to reveal those nasty secrets of 'ordinary people'.

w John Michael Hayes, *novel* Grace Metalious *d* Mark Robson *ph* William Mellor *m* Franz Waxman

Lana Turner, Arthur Kennedy, Hope Lange, Lee Philips, Lloyd Nolan, Diane Varsi, RussTamblyn, Terry Moore, Barry Coe, David Nelson, Betty Field, Mildred Dunnock, Leon Ames, Lorne Greene

Phaedra*
US / Greece 1961 116m bw
UA Melinafilm (Jules Dassin)

A tycoon's wife falls in love with her stepson.

Ludicrous, awesomely folly-filled attempt to modernize and sex up Greek tragedy.

wd Jules Dassin *ph* Jacques Natteau *m* Mikis Theodorakis

Melina Mercouri, Anthony Perkins, Raf Vallone, Elizabeth Ercy

'Unfortunately unforgettable.'—*John Simon*

Phantom Lady**
US 1944 87m bw
Universal

A man is accused of murder and his only alibi is a mysterious lady he met in a bar.
Odd little thriller which doesn't really hold together but is made for the most part with great style.

w Bernard C. Schoenfeld, *novel* William Irish *d* Robert Siodmak

Franchot Tone, Alan Baxter, Ella Raines, Elisha Cook Jnr, Fay Helm, Andrew Tombes

Phantom of Crestwood*
US 1932 77m bw
RKO (David O. Selznick)

Murder strikes when a blackmailer assembles her victims.
Lively mystery with spoof elements.

w Bartlett Cormack, J. Walter Ruben *d* J. Walter Ruben

Ricardo Cortez, H. B. Warner, Anita Louise, Karen Morley, Pauline Frederick, Robert McWade, Skeets Gallagher

The Phantom of Hollywood*
US 1974 74m colour TVM
MGM

When a film studio's back lot is bulldozed, mysterious deaths are caused by a masked figure.
Cheeky transplanting of *The Phantom of the Opera;* unfortunately the script isn't quite up to it.

w George Schenck *d* Gene Levitt

Jack Cassidy, Peter Lawford, Skye Aubrey, Jackie Coogan, Broderick Crawford, Peter Haskell, John Ireland

The Phantom of the Opera**
US 1943 92m Technicolor
Universal (George Waggner)

A composer haunts the sewers under the Paris Opera House after his face has been scarred by acid.
This long-accepted but nonsensical story was a famous vehicle for Lon Chaney in 1925. This version is more decorous and gentlemanly, with much attention paid to the music, but it certainly has its moments.

w Erich Taylor, Samuel Hoffenstein, *novel* Gaston Leroux *d* Arthur Lubin *ph Hal Mohr, W. Howard Greene* *m* Edmund Ward *ad John B. Goodman, Alexander Golitzen*

Claude Rains, Nelson Eddy, Susanna Foster, Edgar Barrier, Leo Carrillo, J. Edward Bromberg, Jane Farrar, Hume Cronyn

Phantom of the Opera
GB 1962 90m Technicolor
U-I / Hammer (Anthony Hinds)

Stodgy remake with the accent on shock.

w John Elder *d* Terence Fisher *ph* Arthur Grant *m* Edwin Astley

Herbert Lom, Edward de Souza, Heather Sears, Thorley Walters, Michael Gough, Ian Wilson, Martin Miller, John Harvey, Miriam Karlin

Phantom of the Paradise*
US 1974 91m Movielab
TCF / Pressman Williams (Edward R. Pressman)

A modern satirical remake of *Phantom of the Opera* in rock opera terms, set in a pop music palace. Not bad in spots, but it doesn't really know where it's going.

wd Brian de Palma *ph* Larry Pizer *m* Paul Williams *pd* Jack Fisk

Paul Williams, William Finley, Jessica Harper, George Memmoli, Gerrit Graham

'Too broad in its effects and too bloated in style to cut very deeply as a parody ... closer to the anything goes mode of a *Mad* magazine lampoon.'—*Richard Combs*

Phantom of the Rue Morgue
US 1954 84m Warnercolor 3-D
Warner (Henry Blanke)

In old Paris, a killer of pretty girls turns out to be an ape.
Dull revamping of a rather dull story, with boring characters and little horror.

w Harold Medford, James R. Webb, *story* Murders in the Rue Morgue by Edgar Allan Poe *d* Roy del Ruth *ph* Peverell Marley *m* David Buttolph

Karl Malden, Claude Dauphin, Steve Forrest, Patricia Medina, Allyn McLerie, Dolores Dorn

The Phantom President*
US 1932 78m bw
Paramount

A fast-talking quack doubles for a lacklustre presidential candidate.

A likely but in fact unsuccessful film debut for a famous Broadway star: many points of interest.

w Walter de Leon, Harlan Thompson
d Norman Taurog *ph* David Abel
songs Richard Rodgers, Lorenz Hart

George M. Cohan, Claudette Colbert, Jimmy Durante, George Barbier, Sidney Toler, Jameson Thomas, Paul Hurst, Alan Mowbray

The Phantom Tollbooth**
US 1969 90m Metrocolor
MGM / Animation Visual Arts

A bored boy goes through a magic tollbooth to land beyond his wildest imagination, rescues Rhyme and Reason, and defeats the Demons of Ignorance.
Ambitious and well-devised, though rather slow-starting, cartoon feature which falls in style somewhere between *Alice in Wonderland* and *The Wizard of Oz* but is more intellectual than either and would be beyond the reach of most children. Discerning adults may have a ball.

w Chuck Jones, Sam Rosen, *novel* Norton Juster *d* Chuck Jones, Abe Levitow *ph* Maurice Noble

Butch Patrick

Phase IV
GB 1973 84m Technicolor
Paramount / Alced (Paul B. Radin)

In the Arizona desert, ants attack a scientific installation.
Oddly effective if repulsive science fiction; the ants are all the more unpleasant because they stay the normal size.

w Mayo Simon *d Saul Bass* *ph* Dick Bush
m Brian Gascoyne

Nigel Davenport, Lynne Frederick, Michael Murphy, Alan Gifford

The Phenix City Story*
US 1955 100m bw
Allied Artists (Sam Bischoff, David Diamond)

A young lawyer fights the racketeers who control his town.
Goodish example of the semi-documentary melodramas of small-town corruption which swarmed out of Hollywood following the Kefauver investigations.

w Crane Wilbur, Dan Mainwaring *d Phil Karlson* *ph* Harry Neumann *m* Harry Sukman

Richard Kiley, *Edward Andrews,* John McIntire, Kathryn Grant

Phffft
US 1954 91m bw
Columbia (Fred Kohlmar)

The title refers to the sound of an expiring match; the story tells of a couple who get divorced and try to find out what they have been missing.
Champagne comedy with no bubbles.

w George Axelrod *d* Mark Robson *ph* Charles Lang *m* Frederick Hollander

Jack Lemmon, Judy Holliday, Kim Novak, Jack Carson, Luella Gear, Donald Randolph, Donald Curtis, Merry Anders

The Philadelphia Story****
US 1940 112m bw
MGM (Joseph L. Mankiewicz)

A stuffy heiress, about to be married for the second time, turns human and returns gratefully to number one.
Hollywood's most wise and sparkling comedy, with a script which is even an improvement on the original play. Cukor's direction is so discreet you can hardly sense it, and all the performances are just perfect.

w Donald Ogden Stewart, play Philip Barry
d George Cukor *ph* Joseph Ruttenberg
m Franz Waxman *ad* Cedric Gibbons

Katharine Hepburn, Cary Grant, James Stewart, Ruth Hussey, Roland Young, John Halliday, Mary Nash, Virginia Weidler, John Howard, Henry Daniell

Philo Vance

The smooth sleuth created by S. S. Van Dine was a popular film hero of the thirties, for several different companies and with several different actors. As a series it was very variable indeed.

1929: THE CANARY MURDER CASE (Paramount: William Powell); THE GREENE MURDER CASE (Paramount: William Powell)
1930: THE BISHOP MURDER CASE (MGM: Basil Rathbone); THE BENSON MURDER CASE (Paramount: William Powell)
1933: THE KENNEL MURDER CASE (qv) (Warner: William Powell)
1934: THE DRAGON MURDER CASE (Warner: Warren William)
1935: THE CASINO MURDER CASE (MGM: Paul Lukas)
1936: THE GARDEN MURDER CASE (MGM: Edmund Lowe)
1937: NIGHT OF MYSTERY (Paramount: Grant Richards)
1939: THE GRACIE ALLEN MURDER CASE (Paramount: Warren William);

CALLING PHILO VANCE (Warner: James Stephenson)
1947: PHILO VANCE RETURNS (PRC: William Wright); PHILO VANCE'S GAMBLE (PRC: Alan Curtis); PHILO VANCE'S SECRET MISSION (PRC: Alan Curtis)

Phone Call from a Stranger
US 1952 96m bw
TCF (Nunnally Johnson)

Of four airplane acquaintances, only one survives a crash; he visits the families of the others.
Four stories with an unlikely link. (The compendium craze, which had started in 1948 with *Quartet,* was now straining itself.) Nothing to remember except Miss Davis.

w Nunnally Johnson *d* Jean Negulesco *ph* Milton Krasner *m* Franz Waxman

Bette Davis, Gary Merrill, Michael Rennie, Shelley Winters, Keenan Wynn, Evelyn Varden, Warren Stevens, Craig Stevens
'A cinematic party line on which several conversations are going at once, none of them coming across very distinctly.'—*Time*

Piccadilly Incident*
GB 1946 102m bw
ABP (Herbert Wilcox)

During World War II, a girl believed drowned returns from the front to find her husband remarried.
The Enoch Arden theme again, and the first of the Wilcox-Neagle 'London' films, though untypically a melodrama with a sad ending. Efficient enough for its chosen audience.

w Nicholas Phipps *d* Herbert Wilcox *ph* Max Greene

Anna Neagle, Michael Wilding, Michael Laurence, Frances Mercer, Coral Browne, A. E. Matthews, Edward Rigby, Brenda Bruce

Piccadilly Jim*
US 1936 100m bw
MGM (Harry Rapf)

A cartoonist helps his father to marry by making the bride's stuffy family objects of ridicule.
Amiable comedy with a diverting London setting.

w Charles Brackett, Edwin Knopf, *novel* P. G. Wodehouse *d* Robert Z. Leonard *ph* Joseph Ruttenberg *m* William Axt

Robert Montgomery, Madge Evans, Frank Morgan, Billie Burke, Eric Blore, Robert Benchley, Ralph Forbes, Cora Witherspoon, E. E. Clive

Pick a Star
US 1937 67m bw
Hal Roach / MGM

An innocent girl in Hollywood achieves stardom with the help of a publicity man.
Perfectly awful Cinderella story with interesting glimpses behind the studio scenes and (if you can wait that long) a couple of good Laurel and Hardy sequences.

w Richard Flournoy, Arthur Vernon Jones, Thomas J. Dugan *d* Edward Sedgwick *ph* Norbert Brodine

Rosina Lawrence, Jack Haley, Patsy Kelly, Mischa Auer, *Stan Laurel, Oliver Hardy,* Charles Halton, Lyda Roberti

Pick Up
US 1951 78m bw
Columbia (Hugo Haas)

A lonely middle-aged man falls for a tart who is interested only in his money.
Modest variation on *The Blue Angel*, the first of several second features made by Haas to feature himself as a second Emil Jannings. They got progressively more maudlin.

wd Hugo Haas ph Paul Ivano

Hugo Haas, Beverly Michaels, Allan Nixon, Howard Chamberlin

Pickup on South Street*
US 1953 80m bw
TCF (Jules Schermer)

A pickpocket steals a girl's wallet and finds himself up to his neck in espionage.
Over-rich mixture of crime, violence and anti-communism, smartly made without being very interesting.

wd Samuel Fuller *ph* Joe MacDonald *m* Leigh Harline

Richard Widmark, Jean Peters, *Thelma Ritter,* Richard Kiley
† Remade 1968 as *Capetown Affair.*

The Pickwick Papers*
GB 1952 115m bw
George Minter (Bob McNaught)

Various adventures of the Pickwick Club culminate in Mrs Bardell's suit for breach of promise.
Flatly conceived and loosely constructed Dickensian comedy; good humour and lots of well-known faces do not entirely atone for lack of artifice.

wd Noel Langley *ph* Wilkie Cooper *m* Anthony Hopkins *ad* Fred Pusey

James Hayter, James Donald, Donald Wolfit,

Hermione Baddeley, Hermione Gingold, Kathleen Harrison, *Nigel Patrick*, Alexander Gauge, Lionel Murton

Picnic***
US 1956 113m Technicolor
Cinemascope
Columbia (Fred Kohlmar)

A brawny wanderer causes sexual havoc one summer in a small American town.
Seminal melodrama setting new directions for Hollywood and illustrating the side of life the Hardy family never showed. Generally quite compulsive despite some overacting.

w Daniel Taradash, *play William Inge* *d* Joshua Logan *ph James Wong Howe* *pd* Jo Mielziner *ad* William Flannery *m* George Duning

William Holden, Kim Novak, Rosalind Russell, *Susan Strasberg*, Arthur O'Connell, Cliff Robertson, Betty Field, Verna Felton, Reta Shaw

Picnic at Hanging Rock*
Australia 1975 115m Eastmancolor
Picnic Productions / Australia Film Corporation (Hal and Jim McElroy)

In 1900, schoolgirls set out for a picnic; some disappear and are never found.
An intriguing but finally irritating puzzle with no answer; the atmosphere is nicely calculated, but as in *L'Avventura* the whole thing outstays its welcome.

w Cliff Green, *novel* Joan Lindsay *d* Peter Weir *ph* Russell Boyd *m* Bruce Smeaton

Rachel Roberts, Dominic Guard, Helen Morse, Jacki Weaver, Vivean Gray, Kirsty Child

The Picture of Dorian Gray***
US 1945 110m bw
MGM

A Victorian gentleman keeps in the attic a picture of himself, which shows his age and depravity while he stays eternally young.
Elegant variation on *Dr Jekyll and Mr Hyde*, presented in portentous style which suits the subject admirably.

wd Albert Lewin, novel Oscar Wilde *m* Herbert Stothart

George Sanders, Hurd Hatfield, Donna Reed, Angela Lansbury, Peter Lawford

'Respectful, earnest, and, I'm afraid, dead.'—*James Agee*

'Loving and practised hands have really improved Wilde's original, cutting down the epigrammatic flow . . . and rooting out all the preciousness which gets in the way of the melodrama.'—*Richard Winnington*

The Picture Snatcher**
US 1933 77m bw
Warner

An ex-racketeer just out of prison becomes a scandal photographer.
Lively star vehicle, interesting for period detail.

w Allen Rivkin, P. J. Wolfson *d* Lloyd Bacon *ph* Sol Polito *md* Leo F. Forbstein

James Cagney, Ralph Bellamy, Patricia Ellis, Alice White, Ralf Harolde, Robert Emmett O'Connor, Robert Barrat

'A vulgar but generally funny collection of blackouts.'—*Time*

'Fast, snappy, tough and packed with action.'—*New York Herald Tribune*

The Pied Piper**
US 1942 86m bw
TCF (Nunnally Johnson)

An elderly man who hates children finds himself smuggling several of them out of occupied France.
Smart, sentimental, occasionally funny war adventure.

w Nunnally Johnson, *novel* Nevil Shute *d* Irving Pichel *ph* Edward Cronjager *m* Alfred Newman

Monty Woolley, Anne Baxter, Roddy McDowall, Otto Preminger, J. Carrol Naish, Lester Matthews, Jill Esmond, Peggy Ann Garner

The Pied Piper
GB 1971 90m Eastmancolor
Panavision
Sagittarius / Goodtimes (David Puttnam, Sanford Lieberson)

In 1349 a strolling minstrel rids Hamelin of a plague of rats.
Paceless, slightly too horrific, and generally disappointing fantasy, especially from this director; poor sets and restricted action.

w Jacques Demy, Mark Peploe, Andrew Birkin *d* Jacques Demy *ph* Peter Suschitsky *m* Donovan *pd* Assheton Gorton

Donovan, Donald Pleasance, Michael Hordern, Jack Wild, Diana Dors, John Hurt

The Pigeon
US 1969 70m colour TVM
Spelling–Thomas

A black private eye tries to protect a family from the Mafia.
Unoriginal detection caper.

w Edward Lask *d* Earl Bellamy

Sammy Davis Jnr, Dorothy Malone, Ricardo

Montalban, Pat Boone, Roy Glenn Snr, Victoria Vetri

The Pigeon That Took Rome
US 1962 101m bw Panavision
Paramount / Llenroc (Melville Shavelson)

American undercover agents are smuggled into Rome during the German occupation.
Heavy-going war comedy-drama with bright sequences countered by too little wit and too many voluble Italians.

wd Melville Shavelson, *novel* The Easter Dinner by Donald Downes *ph* Daniel Fapp *m* Alessandro Cicognini

Charlton Heston, Elsa Martinelli, Brian Donlevy, Harry Guardino, Baccaloni

Pigskin Parade
US 1936 93m bw
TCF (Bogart Rogers)

A country farmer becomes a college football hero.
Livelier-than-average college comedy.

w Harry Tugend, Jack Yellen, William Conselman *d* David Butler *ph* Arthur Miller *md* David Buttolph

Stuart Erwin, Patsy Kelly, Jack Haley, Johnny Downs, Betty Grable, Arline Judge, Dixie Dunbar, Judy Garland, Tony Martin, Elisha Cook Jnr

Pillars of the Sky
US 1956 95m Technicolor Cinemascope
U-I (Robert Arthur)
GB title: *The Tomahawk and the Cross*

An indian scout and a missionary help bring peace between cavalry and indians.
Modest western, adequately done.

w Sam Rolfe *d* George Marshall *ph* Harold Lipstein *m* Joseph Gershenson

Jeff Chandler, Dorothy Malone, Ward Bond, Keith Andes, Lee Marvin, Sydney Chaplin, Michael Ansara, Willis Bouchey

Pillow Talk**
US 1959 110m Eastmancolor Cinemascope
U-I (Ross Hunter, Martin Melcher)

Two people who can't stand each other fall in love via a party line.
Slightly elephantine romantic comedy which nevertheless contains a number of funny scenes and was notable for starting off the Hudson-Day partnership and a run of similar comedies which survived the sixties.

w Stanley Shapiro, Maurice Richlin *d* Michael Gordon *ph* Arthur E. Arling *m* Frank de Vol

Doris Day, Rock Hudson, Tony Randall, Thelma Ritter, Nick Adams, Julia Meade, Allen Jenkins, Marcel Dalio, Lee Patrick

Pillow to Post
US 1945 96m bw
Warner (Alex Gottlieb)

A girl poses as a soldier's wife to get a hotel room.
World War II comedy on a familiar theme (*The More the Merrier, Standing Room Only, The Doughgirls,* etc). Uninspired.

w Charles Hoffman, *play* Pillar to Post by Rose Simon Kohn *d* Vincent Sherman *ph* Wesley Anderson *m* Frederick Hollander

Ida Lupino, Sidney Greenstreet, William Prince, Stuart Erwin, Ruth Donnelly, Barbara Brown, Frank Orth

Pilot Number Five
US 1943 71m bw
MGM (B. P. Fineman)

A pilot in the South Pacific volunteers for a desperate mission because—we learn in flashback—he hates fascists.
Rather unpalatable propaganda encased in dim drama.

w David Hertz *d* George Sidney

Franchot Tone, Gene Kelly, Marsha Hunt, Van Johnson, Alan Baxter, Dick Simmons, Steve Geray

Pimpernel Smith**
GB 1941 121m bw
British National (Leslie Howard)
US title: *Mister V*

A professor of archaeology goes into war-torn Europe to rescue refugees.
The Scarlet Pimpernel unassumingly and quite effectively brought up to date, with memorable scenes after a slow start.

w Anatole de Grunwald, Roland Pertwee, Ian Dalrymple *d* Leslie Howard

Leslie Howard, Mary Morris, Francis L. Sullivan, Hugh McDermott, Raymond Huntley, Manning Whiley, Peter Gawthorne, David Tomlinson

Pin Up Girl
US 1944 83m Technicolor
TCF (William Le Baron)

A Washington secretary becomes a national celebrity when she meets a navy hero.

Adequate star flagwaver, mildly interesting for its new streamlined set designs.

w Robert Ells, Helen Logan, Earl Baldwin *d* Bruce Humberstone *ph* Ernest Palmer *md* Emil Newman, Charles Henderson *ch Hermes Pan ad James Basevi, Joseph C. Wright*

Betty Grable, John Harvey, Martha Raye, Joe E. Brown, Eugene Pallette, Dave Willcock, Charles Spivak and his Orchestra

'A spiritless blob of a musical, and a desecration of a most inviting theme.'—*Bosley Crowther*

The Pink Jungle
US 1968 104m Techniscope
Universal / Cherokee (Stan Margulies)

A photographer and his model are stranded in a South American village and become involved in a diamond hunt.
Curious mixture of adventure and light comedy that works only in patches.

w Charles Williams, *novel* Snake Water by Alan Williams *d* Delbert Mann *ph* Russell Metty *m* Ernie Freeman

James Garner, Eva Renzi, George Kennedy, Nigel Green, Michael Ansara, George Rose

The Pink Panther**
US 1963 113m Technirama
UA / Mirisch (Martin Jurow)

An incompetent *sureté* inspector is in Switzerland on the trail of a jewel thief called The Phantom.
Sporadically engaging mixture of pratfalls, Raffles, and Monsieur Hulot, all dressed to kill and quite palatable for the uncritical. Inspector Clouseau later became a cartoon character and also provoked three sequels, *Inspector Clouseau, The Return of the Pink Panther* and *The Pink Panther Strikes Again.*

w Maurice Richlin, Blake Edwards *d* Blake Edwards· *ph* Philip Lathrop *m* Henry Mancini *ad* Fernando Carrere *animation* De Patie-Freleng

David Niven, Peter Sellers, Capucine, Claudia Cardinale, Robert Wagner, Brenda de Banzie, Colin Gordon

Pink String and Sealing Wax*
GB 1945 89m bw
Ealing (S. C. Balcon)

In 1880 Brighton, a publican's wife plans to have her husband poisoned.
Unusual, carefully handled period crime melodrama which needed a slightly firmer grip.

w Diana Morgan, Robert Hamer, *play* Roland Pertwee *d* Robert Hamer

Googie Withers, Mervyn Johns, Gordon Jackson, Sally Ann Howes, Mary Merrall, John Carol, Catherine Lacey, Gary Marsh

Pinky**
US 1949 102m bw
TCF (Darryl F. Zanuck)

In the American south, a negro girl who passes for white has romantic problems.
Rather blah problem picture which seemed brave at the time; a highly professional piece of work nevertheless.

w Philip Dunne, Dudley Nichols, *novel* Quality by Cid Ricketts Summer *d Elia Kazan ph Joe MacDonald m* Alfred Newman

Jeanne Crain, Ethel Barrymore, Ethel Waters, William Lundigan, Basil Ruysdael, Nina Mae McKinney, Frederick O'Neal, Evelyn Varden

Pinocchio****
US 1940 77m Technicolor
Walt Disney

The blue fairy breathes life into a puppet, which has to prove itself before it can turn into a real boy.
Charming, fascinating, superbly organized and streamlined cartoon feature without a single second of boredom.

supervisors Ben Sharpsteen, Hamilton Luske *m/ly Leigh Harline, New Washington, Paul J. Smith*

'There isn't a snail or puppy dog's tail that a Disney animator couldn't give character and expression to.'—*Otis Ferguson*

'A film of amazing detail and brilliant conception.'—*Leonard Maltin*

Pioneer Woman*
US 1973 74m colour TVM
Filmways

Even after her husband is killed, a western-bound woman sets up house with her family.
Earnest sodbusting epic which unfortunately never made a series: it's convincingly done.

w Suzanne Clouser *d* Buzz Kulik

Joanna Pettet, David Janssen, William Shatner, Lance Le Gault

The Pirate**
US 1948 102m Technicolor
MGM (Arthur Freed)

In a West Indian port, a girl imagines that a wandering player is a famous pirate, who in fact is her despised and elderly suitor.

Minor MGM musical with vivid moments and some intimation of the greatness shortly to come; all very set-bound, but the star quality is infectious.

w Albert Hackett, Frances Goodrich, *play* S. N. Behrman *d* Vincente Minnelli *ph* Harry Stradling *m/ ly* Cole Porter

Gene Kelly, Judy Garland, Walter Slezak, Gladys Cooper, Reginald Owen, George Zucco, *the Nicholas Brothers*

Pirates of Blood River*
GB 1961 84m Technicolor Hammerscope
Hammer (Anthony Nelson Keys)

Pirates in search of gold terrorize a Huguenot settlement.
Land-locked blood and thunder for tough schoolboys.

w John Hunter, John Gilling *d* John Gilling *ph* Arthur Grant

Christopher Lee, Andrew Keir, Kerwin Mathews, Glenn Corbett, Peter Arne, Oliver Reed, Marla Landi, Michael Ripper

The Pit and the Pendulum*
US 1961 85m Pathecolor Panavision
AIP / Alta Vista (Roger Corman)

Lovers plan to drive her brother mad; he responds by locking them in his torture chamber.
The centrepiece only is borrowed from Poe; the rest is lurid but mostly ineffective. Still, its commercial success started the Poe cycle of the sixties.

w Richard Matheson *d* Roger Corman *ph* Floyd Crosby *m* Les Baxter

Vincent Price, Barbara Steele, John Kerr

'As in *House of Usher*, the quality of the film is its full-blooded feeling for Gothic horror—storms and lightning, mouldering castles and cobwebbed torture chambers, bleeding brides trying to tear the lids from their untimely tombs.'—*David Robinson*

Pitfall
US 1948 85m bw
Samuel Bischoff

An insurance investigator proves easy prey for a grasping woman.
Modest suspenser, quite efficiently made.

w Jay Dratler, from his novel *d* André de Toth *ph* Harry Wild *md* Louis Forbes

Dick Powell, Lizabeth Scott, Jane Wyatt, Raymond Burr, John Litel, Byron Barr, Ann Doran

Pittsburgh
US 1942 91m bw
Universal (Charles K. Feldman)

A coal miner's daughter has two loves, all of them trying to improve their social status as Pittsburgh becomes a world centre of steel production.
Routine melodrama ending as a flagwaver, and allowing none of its stars any opportunity.

w Kenneth Gamet, Tom Reed *d* Lewis Seiler *ph* Robert de Grasse *m* Hans Salter

Marlene Dietrich, Randolph Scott, John Wayne, Frank Craven, Louise Allbritton, Shemp Howard, Ludwig Stossel, Thomas Gomez

A Place in the Sun**
US 1951 122m bw
Paramount / George Stevens

A poor young man, offered the chance of a rich wife, allows himself to be convicted and executed for the accidental death of his former fiancée.
Overblown, overlong and over-praised melodrama from a monumental novel of social guilt; sometimes visually striking, this version alters the stresses of the plot and leaves no time for sociological detail. A film so clearly intended as a masterpiece could hardly fail to be boring.

w Maurice Wilson, Harry Brown, *novel* An American Tragedy by Theodore Dreiser *d George Stevens ph William C. Mellor* *m* Franz Waxman *ad* Hans Dreier, Walter Tyler

Montgomery Clift, Elizabeth Taylor, Shelley Winters, Anne Revere, Keefe Brasselle, Fred Clark, Raymond Burr, Frieda Inescort, Shepperd Strudwick, Kathryn Givney, Walter Sande

'An almost incredibly painstaking work . . . mannered enough for a very fancy Gothic murder mystery. This version gives the story a modern setting, but the town is an arrangement of symbols of wealth, glamour and power versus symbols of poor, drab helplessness—an arrangement far more suitable to the thirties than to the fifties.'—*Pauline Kael*

A Place of One's Own**
GB 1944 92m bw
GFD / Gainsborough (R. J. Minney)

In Edwardian times, an old house is taken over by an elderly couple, and their young companion is possessed by the spirit of a murdered girl.
Charming little ghost story, not quite detailed enough to be totally effective.

w Brock Williams, *novel* Osbert Sitwell *d* Bernard Knowles *ph Stephen Dade* *m* Louis Levy

James Mason, Barbara Mullen, Margaret Lockwood, Dennis Price, Helen Haye, Michael Shepley, Dulcie Gray, Moore Marriott

'A fine piece of work . . . gripping, marvellous, outstanding, eerie, perky, beautiful, lovely and different.'—*C. A. Lejeune*

'One comes away with an impression of elegance which has not so far been frequent in the British cinema.'—*Dilys Powell*

A Place to Go
GB 1963 86m bw
British Lion / Excalibur (Michael Relph, Basil Dearden)

A young man depressed by his urban environment turns to crime.
Panorama of London low life, efficiently varied and well made but not in any way memorable. *It Always Rains on Sunday,* fifteen years earlier, wears better.

w Michael Relph, Clive Exton, *novel* Bethnal Green by Michael Fisher *d* Basil Dearden *ph* Reg Wyer *m* Charles Blackwell

Rita Tushingham, Mike Sarne, Doris Hare, John Slater, Bernard Lee, Barbara Ferris, Roy Kinnear

The Plague of the Zombies*
GB 1965 91m Technicolor
Hammer (Anthony Nelson Keys)

A voodoo-practising Cornish squire raises zombies from the dead and uses them to work his tin mine.
They don't explain why he didn't simply hire the living; apart from that this is Hammer on its better side, with a charming elderly hero and good suspense sequences.

w Peter Bryan *d* John Gilling *ph* Arthur Grant *m* James Bernard

André Morell, John Carson, Diane Clare, Brook Williams, Jacqueline Pearce, Alex Davion, Michael Ripper

'Visually the film is splendid . . . the script manages several offbeat strokes.'—*MFB*

The Plainsman**
US 1936 113m bw
Paramount / Cecil B. de Mille

The life of Wild Bill Hickok and his friends Buffalo Bill and Calamity Jane.
Standard big-scale thirties western; narrative lumpy, characters idealized, spectacle impressive, technical credits high.

w Waldemar Young, Lynn Riggs, Harold Lamb *d Cecil B. de Mille* *ph* Victor Milner, George Robinson *md* Boris Morros

Gary Cooper, James Ellison, Jean Arthur, Charles Bickford, Helen Burgess, Porter Hall, Paul Harvey, Victor Varconi

The Plainsman
US 1966 92m Technicolor TVM
Universal

Tame remake of the above, with a happy ending.

w Michael Blankfort *d* David Lowell Rich *ph* Bud Thackery

Guy Stockwell, Don Murray, Abby Dalton, Bradford Dillman, Henry Silva, Leslie Nielsen

Planet Earth
US 1974 75m colour TVM
Warner

A modern man in the 22nd century finds that women rule.
Boring sci-fi. See *Genesis II.*

w Gene Roddenberry *d* Marc Daniels

John Saxon, Diana Muldaur, Janet Margolin, Chris Cary, Ted Cassidy

Planet of the Apes***
US 1968 119m De Luxe Panavision
TCF / Apjac (Mort Abrahams)

Astronauts caught in a time warp land on a planet which turns out to be Earth in the distant future, when men have become beasts and the apes have taken over.
Stylish, thoughtful science fiction which starts and finishes splendidly but suffers from a sag in the middle. The ape make-up is great.

w Michael Wilson, Rod Serling, novel Monkey Planet by Pierre Boulle *d Franklin Schaffner* *ph Leon Shamroy* *m* Jerry Goldsmith

Charlton Heston, Roddy McDowall, *Kim Hunter,* Maurice Evans, James Whitmore, James Daly, Linda Harrison

'One of the most telling science fiction films to date.'—*Tom Milne*

†Sequels, in roughly descending order of interest, were BENEATH THE PLANET OF THE APES (1969), ESCAPE FROM THE PLANET OF THE APES (1970), CONQUEST OF THE PLANET OF THE APES (1972) and BATTLE FOR THE PLANET OF THE APES (1973). A TV series followed in 1974, and a cartoon series in 1975.

The Planter's Wife
GB 1952 91m bw
Rank / Pinnacle (John Stafford)
US title: *Outpost in Malaya*

Malaya under the terrorists. A wife is planning to

leave but changes her mind after she and her husband defend their home in a siege.
Superficial studio-bound melodrama unworthy of its subject but a good star vehicle.

w Peter Proud, Guy Elmes *d* Ken Annakin *ph* Geoffrey Unsworth *m* Allan Gray

Claudette Colbert, Jack Hawkins, Ram Gopal, Jeremy Spenser, Tom Macauley, Helen Goss

Play Dirty*
GB 1969 118m Technicolor Panavision
UA / Lowndes (Harry Saltzman)

During World War II, a squad of ex-criminals is given the job of destroying an enemy oil depot in North Africa.
Small-scale dirty dozen with would-be ironic twists; well made entertainment for the stout-hearted.

w Lotte Colin, Melvyn Bragg *d* André de Toth *ph* Edward Scaife *m* Michel Legrand

Michael Caine, Nigel Davenport, Nigel Green, Harry Andrews, Bernard Archard, Daniel Pilon

Play It Again Sam*
US 1972 86m Technicolor Panavision
Paramount / Apjac

A neurotic film critic is abandoned by his wife and seeks fresh companionship, with help from the shade of Humphrey Bogart.
Random comedy for star fans, mainly quite lively and painless.

w Woody Allen, from his play *d* Herbert Ross *ph* Owen Roizman *m* Billy Goldenberg

Woody Allen, Diane Keaton, Jerry Lacy, Susan Anspach

Play Misty for Me*
US 1971 102m Technicolor
Universal / Malpaso (Robert Daley)

A radio disc jockey is pestered by a girl who turns out to be homicidally jealous.
Smartly made if over-extended psycho melodrama with good suspense sequences and a fair quota of shocks.

w Jo Heims, Dean Reisner *d* Clint Eastwood *ph* Bruce Surtees *m* Dee Barton

Clint Eastwood, Jessica Walter, Donna Mills, John Larch

Playmates*
US 1941 96m bw
RKO (Cliff Reid)

For the sake of a lucrative radio contract, John Barrymore agrees to turn bandleader Kay Kyser into a Shakespearian actor.
Barrymore's last film is a weird comedy concoction, awesome in its waste of his talents but fairly funny in a high school kind of way.

w James V. Kern *d* David Butler *ph* Frank Redman *songs* James Van Heusen, Johnny Burke

Kay Kyser and his Band, *John Barrymore*, Ginny Simms, Lupe Velez, May Robson, Patsy Kelly, Peter Lind Hayes, George Cleveland

Playmates**
US 1972 74m colour TVM
Lillian Gallo

Two divorced men from different backgrounds become friends when taking their kids to the park. Later each begins to date the other's ex-wife.
Amusing modern comedy, smartly scripted and edited.

w Richard Baer *d* Theodore J. Flicker

Alan Alda, Doug McClure, Connie Stevens, Barbara Feldon

Plaza Suite*
US 1971 114m Technicolor
Paramount (Howard B. Koch)

Three sketches set in the same suite at New York's Plaza Hotel, with Walter Matthau appearing in all three but in different character.
A highly theatrical entertainment which was bound to seem flattened on the screen, but emerges with at least some of its laughs intact.

w Neil Simon, from his play *d* Arthur Hiller *ph* Jack Marta *m* Maurice Jarre

Walter Matthau, Maureen Stapleton, Barbara Harris, Lee Grant, Louise Sorel

Please Believe Me
US 1947 87m bw
MGM (Val Lewton)

An English girl inherits an American ranch and is chased by a millionaire, a con man and a lawyer.
Dullsville comedy which failed to establish its star in America.

w Nathaniel Curtis *d* Norman Taurog *ph* Robert Planck

Deborah Kerr, Robert Walker, Mark Stevens, Peter Lawford, James Whitmore, Spring Byington

Please Don't Eat the Daisies
US 1960 111m Metrocolor Panavision
MGM (Joe Pasternak)

The family of a drama critic move to the country.

Thin, obvious comedy, all dressed up but with nowhere to go.

w Isobel Lennart, *book* Jean Kerr *d* Charles Walters *ph* Robert Bronner *m* David Rose

Doris Day, David Niven, Janis Paige, Spring Byington, Patsy Kelly, Richard Haydn, Jack Weston, John Harding, Margaret Lindsay

Please Murder Me
US 1956 78m bw
DCA (Donald Hyde)

An attorney defends an accused murderess, at great cost to himself.
Adequate Poverty Row suspenser with a foreseeable trick ending.

w Al C. Ward, Donald Hyde *d* Peter Godfrey *ph* Allen Stensvold

Angela Lansbury, Raymond Burr, Dick Foran, John Dehner, Lamont Johnson, Denver Pyle

Please Sir
GB 1971 101m Eastmancolor
Rank / LWL / Leslie Grade (Andrew Mitchell)

The masters and pupils of Fenn Street school go on an annual camp.
Grossly inflated, occasionally funny big-screen version of the TV series.

w John Esmonde, Bob Larbey *d* Mark Stuart *ph* Wilkie Cooper *m* Mike Vickers

John Alderton, Deryck Guyler, Joan Sanderson, Noel Howlett, Eric Chitty, Richard Davies

The Pleasure Girls
GB 1965 88m bw
Compton Tekli

Girl flatmates in London have trouble with their boy friends.
The road to ruin sixties style, hackneyed but quite well observed.

wd Gerry O'Hara ph Michael Reed *m* Malcolm Lockyer

Ian McShane, Francesca Annis, Tony Tanner, Klaus Kinski, Mark Eden, Suzanna Leigh

The Pleasure of His Company
US 1961 114m Technicolor
Paramount / Perlberg–Seaton

An ageing playboy arrives unexpectedly in San Francisco for his daughter's wedding.
Tame family comedy, very flatly adapted from the stage; dressed to kill, but with no narrative or cinematic drive.

w Samuel Taylor, *play* Samuel Taylor, Cornelia Otis Skinner *d* George Seaton *ph* Robert Burks *m* Alfred Newman

Fred Astaire, Lilli Palmer, Debbie Reynolds, Charles Ruggles, Tab Hunter, Gary Merrill, Harold Fong

'Smart comedy in its most diluted form.'—*MFB*

The Pleasure Seekers
US 1964 107m De Luxe Cinemascope
TCF (David Weisbart)

Three girls in Madrid find boy friends.
Dim remake of *Three Coins in the Fountain,* adequate but unstimulating on all levels.

w Edith Sommer *d* Jean Negulesco *ph* Daniel L. Fapp *m* Lionel Newman

Ann-Margret, Tony Franciosa, Carol Lynley, Gene Tierney, Brian Keith, Gardner McKay, Isobel Elsom

The Plough and the Stars*
US 1936 72m bw
RKO (Cliff Reid, Robert Sisk)

In 1916, a Dublin marriage is threatened by the husband's appointment as commander of the citizen army.
Rather elementary film version of the play about the Troubles; interesting for effort rather than performance, and for the talent involved.

w Dudley Nichols, *play* Sean O'Casey *d* John Ford *ph* Joseph August *m* Roy Webb

Barbara Stanwyck, Preston Foster, Barry Fitzgerald, Denis O'Dea, Eileen Crowe, F. J. McCormick, Arthur Shields, Una O'Connor, Moroni Olsen, J. M. Kerrigan, Bonita Granville

Plunder of the Sun*
US 1953 81m bw
Warner (Robert Fellows)

Various criminal elements seek buried treasure among the Mexican Aztec ruins.
Interestingly located, well made, unconvincingly scripted melodrama, yet another borrowing from *The Maltese Falcon.*

w Jonathan Latimer, *novel* David Dodge *d* John Farrow *ph* Jack Draper *m* Antonio D. Conde

Glenn Ford, Diana Lynn, Francis L. Sullivan, Patricia Medina, Sean McClory, Douglass Dumbrille, Eduardo Noriega

The Plunderers
US 1960 94m bw
Allied Artists / August (Joseph Pevney)

In the old west, four juvenile delinquents take over a town.
The Wild One in period dress. Nothing in particular.

w Bob Barbash *d* Joseph Pevney *ph* Eugene Polito *m* Leonard Rosenman

Jeff Chandler, John Saxon, Ray Sticklyn, Roger Torrey, Dee Pollock, Marsha Hunt, Dolores Hart, Jay C. Flippen, James Westerfield

Plymouth Adventure*
US 1952 105m Technicolor
MGM (Dore Schary)

The Pilgrim Fathers sail from Plymouth on the Mayflower and spend their first months ashore on the coast of America.
Well-meaning schoolbook history, totally unconvincing and very dull despite obvious effort all round. One or two of the actors have their moments.

w Helen Deutsch, *novel* Ernest Gebler
d Clarence Brown *ph* William Daniels
m Miklos Rozsa

Spencer Tracy, Gene Tierney, Van Johnson, Leo Genn, Dawn Addams

'It demonstrates how Hollywood can dull down as well as jazz up history.'—*Judith Crist, 1973*

Pocket Money
US 1972 100m Technicolor
First Artists / Coleytown

Two slow-thinking Arizona cowboys try to make money herding cattle.
Peculiar modern western comedy drama which doesn't work.

w Terry Malick, *novel* Jim Kane by J. K. S. Brown *d* Stuart Rosenberg *ph* Laszlo Kovacs *m* Alex North

Paul Newman, Lee Marvin, Strother Martin, Kelly Jean Peters, Wayne Rogers

Pocketful of Miracles
US 1961 136m Technicolor Panavision
UA / Franton (Frank Capra)

Kindly gangsters help an old apple seller to persuade her long lost daughter that she is a lady of means.
Boring, overlong remake of *Lady for a Day*, showing that Capra's touch simply doesn't work on the wide screen, that his themes are dated anyway, and that all the fine character actors in Hollywood are a liability unless you find them something to do.

w Hal Kanter, Harry Tugend, *scenario* Robert Riskin, *story* Damon Runyon *d* Frank Capra *ph* Robert Bronner *m* Walter Scharf

Bette Davis, Glenn Ford, Hope Lange, Arthur O'Connell, Peter Falk, Thomas Mitchell, Edward Everett Horton, Sheldon Leonard, Barton MacLane, Jerome Cowan, Fritz Feld, Snub Pollard, David Brian, Ann-Margret, John Litel, Jay Novello, Willis Bouchey, George E. Stone, Mike Mazurki, Jack Elam, Mickey Shaughnessy, Peter Mann, Frank Ferguson

'The effect is less one of whimsy than of being bludgeoned to death with a toffee apple.'—*Peter John Dyer*

'The story has enough cracks in it for the syrup to leak through.'—*Playboy*

Point Blank*
US 1967 92m Metrocolor Panavision
MGM / Judd Bernard, Irwin Winkler

A gangster takes an elaborate revenge on his cheating partner.
Extremely violent gangster thriller, well shot on location and something of a cult, but with irritating pretentiousness and obscure plot points.

w Alexander Jacobs, David Newhouse, Rafe Newhouse, *novel* The Hunter by Richard Stark *d* John Boorman *ph Philip Lathrop* *m* Johnny Mandel

Lee Marvin, Angie Dickinson, Keenan Wynn, Carroll O'Connor, Lloyd Bochner, Michael Strong, John Vernon, Sharon Acker

†*The Outfit* (qv) is a kind of sequel / reprise.

Poison Pen*
GB 1939 79m bw
ABP (Walter C. Mycroft)

A village community is set at odds by a writer of vindictive anonymous letters.
Effective minor drama, with good location atmosphere.

w Doreen Montgomery, William Freshman, N. C. Hunter, Esther McCracken, *play* Richard Llewellyn *d* Paul Stein

Flora Robson, Reginald Tate, Robert Newton, Ann Todd, Geoffrey Toone, Belle Chrystal, Edward Chapman, Edward Rigby

Police Story*
US 1972 74m colour TVM
Columbia / David Gerber

A policeman outsmarts a cocky criminal.
Routine big city cop stuff which led to an anthology series 'created' by Joseph Wambaugh, author of *The New Centurions*.

w E. Jack Neuman *d* William Graham
ph Robert Morrison *m* Jerry Goldsmith

Vic Morrow, Ed Asner, Chuck Connors, Diane Baker, Harry Guardino

Polly of the Circus
US 1932 72m bw
MGM

A trapeze artiste falls for the local minister, but incurs disapproval from his bishop.
Elementary romance reminiscent of silent drama.

w Carey Wilson, *play* Margaret Mayo *d* Alfred Santell *ph* George Barnes

Marion Davies, Clark Gable, C. Aubrey Smith, Raymond Hatton, David Landau, Maude Eburne, Guinn Williams, Ray Milland

Pollyanna*
US 1960 134m Technicolor
Walt Disney (George Golitzen)

A 12-year-old orphan girl cheers up the grumps of the small town where she comes to live.
Well cast but overlong and rather humourless remake of a children's classic from an earlier age.

wd David Swift, *novel* Eleanor Porter *ph* Russell Harlan *m* Paul Smith *ad* Carroll Clark, Robert Clatworthy

Hayley Mills, Jane Wyman, Karl Malden, Nancy Olson, Adolphe Menjou, Donald Crisp, Agnes Moorehead, Richard Egan, Kevin Corcoran, James Drury, Reta Shaw, Leora Dana

'Even Hayley Mills can neither prevent one from sympathizing with the crusty aunts, hermits, vicars and hypochondriacs who get so forcibly cheered up, nor from feverishly speculating whether films like this don't run the risk of inciting normally kind and gentle people into certain excesses of violent crime – child murder, for instance.'—*MFB*

Pony Express*
US 1953 101m Technicolor
Paramount (Nat Holt)

In 1860 Buffalo Bill Cody and Wild Bill Hickok are sent to establish pony express stations across California.
Standard western which tells a factual tale adequately if rather slowly.

w Charles Marquis Warren *d* Jerry Hopper *ph* Ray Rennahan *m* Paul Sawtell

Charlton Heston, Forrest Tucker, Rhonda Fleming, Jan Sterling

Pony Soldier
US 1952 82m Technicolor
TCF (Samuel G. Engel)
GB title: *MacDonald of the Canadian Mounties*

The mounties settle the hash of Canadian Indian renegades who have been causing trouble on the American border.
Mediocre outdoor adventure.

w John C. Higgins *d* Joseph M. Newman *ph* Harry Jackson *m* Alex North

Tyrone Power, Cameron Mitchell, Robert Horton, Thomas Gomez, Penny Edwards, *Adeline de Walt Reynolds*

Pool of London
GB 1950 85m bw
Ealing (Michael Relph)

A smuggling sailor gets involved in murder.
Routine semi-documentary police thriller with locations in London docks decorating a standard piece of thick ear.

w Jack Whittingham, John Eldridge *d* Basil Dearden *ph* Gordon Dines

Bonar Colleano, Susan Shaw, Earl Cameron, Renée Asherson, Moira Lister, Max Adrian, James Robertson Justice, Joan Dowling

Poor Cow*
GB 1967 101m Eastmancolor
Anglo Amalgamated / Vic / Fenchurch (Joe Janni)

The dismal life of a young London mother who lives in squalor with her criminal husband.
Television-style fictional documentary determined to rub one's nose in the mire.
Innovative and occasionally striking but not very likeable.

w Nell Dunn, Ken Loach, *novel* Nell Dunn *d Ken Loach* *ph* Brian Probyn *m* Donovan

Carol White, Terence Stamp, John Bindon, Kate Williams, Queenie Watts

'A superficial, slightly patronizing excursion into the nether realms of social realism.'—*Jan Dawson*

Poor Devil
US 1972 73m colour TVM
Paramount

An aide of Satan fails to persuade a book-keeper to sign one of his contracts.
Grimly unfunny heavenly pantomime with all concerned ill at ease.

w Arne Sultan, Earl Barrett, Richard Baer *d* Robert Scheerer

Sammy Davis Jnr, Christopher Lee, Jack Klugman

Poor Little Rich Girl*
US 1936 79m bw
TCF (Darryl F. Zanuck)

A child is separated from her father and joins a radio singing act.
Pleasing star vehicle with all the expected elements, adapted from a Mary Pickford vehicle of 1917.

w Sam Hellman, Gladys Lehman, Harry Tugend *d* Irving Cummings *ph* John Seitz *songs* Mack Gordon, Harry Revel

Shirley Temple, Jack Haley, Alice Faye, Gloria Stuart, Michael Whalen, Sara Haden, Jane Darwell, Claude Gillingwater, Henry Armetta

Pope Joan
GB 1972 132m Eastmancolor Panavision
Big City Productions / Kurt Unger
aka: *The Devil's Imposter*

The legend of a 9th-century German semi-prostitute who discovered a vocation to preach and was made Pope.
Uninspiring pageant, brutish and rather silly, full of would-be medieval sensationalism.

w John Briley *d* Michael Anderson *ph* Billy Williams *m* Maurice Jarre *pd* Elliott Scott

Liv Ullman, Trevor Howard, Olivia de Havilland, Maximilian Schell, Keir Dullea, Robert Beatty, Franco Nero, Patrick Magee

Popi*
US 1969 113m De Luxe
UA / Leonard Films (Herbert B. Leonard)

Adventures of a cheerful inhabitant of New York's Puerto Rican ghetto.
Ethnic comedy-drama of the kind that has since found its way in abundance into American TV series. Very competently done for those who like it, e.g. Puerto Ricans.

w Tina and Lester Pine *d* Arthur Hiller *ph* Ross Lowell *m* Dominic Frontière

Alan Arkin, Rita Moreno, Miguel Alejandro, Ruben Figuero

'An appropriately disenchanted view of an immigrant's struggling ambitions in the Promised Land.'—*Richard Combs*

Poppy*
US 1936 74m bw
Paramount (Paul Jones)

An itinerant medicine-seller sets up his stall in a small town where his daughter falls in love with the mayor's son.
Clumsily but heavily plotted vehicle for W. C. Fields, who as usual has great moments but seems to rob the show of its proper pace.

w Waldemar Young, Virginia Van Upp, *play* Dorothy Donnelly *d* A. Edward Sutherland *ph* William Mellor

W. C. Fields, Rochelle Hudson, Richard Cromwell, Granville Bates, Catherine Doucet, Lynne Overman, Maude Eburne

'Antique hokum trussed up for a Fields vehicle.'—*Literary Digest*

The Poppy Is Also a Flower
US 1966 105m colour TVM
Comet / Euan Lloyd / TelsUN
GB title: *Danger Grows Wild*

United Nations agents destroy a narcotics ring.
All-star do-goodery sponsored by the United Nations; not much of a film.

w Jo Eisinger, *theme* Ian Fleming *d* Terence Young

Yul Brynner, Omar Sharif, Trevor Howard, Angie Dickinson, Rita Hayworth, E. G. Marshall, Gilbert Roland, Anthony Quayle, Eli Wallach, Stephen Boyd, Jack Hawkins, Marcello Mastroianni

Porgy and Bess*
US 1959 138m Technicolor Todd-AO
Samuel Goldwyn

A slum girl falls in love with a crippled beggar.
Negro opera about the inhabitants of Catfish Row; full of interest for music lovers, but not lending itself very readily to screen treatment.

w N. Richard Nash, *libretto* Du Bose Heyward, *play* Porgy by Du Bose and Dorothy Heyward *d* Otto Preminger *ph* Leon Shamroy *m George Gershwin* *ch* Hermes Pan

Sidney Poitier, Dorothy Dandridge, Sammy Davis Jnr, Pearl Bailey, Brock Peters, Diahann Carroll, Clarence Muse

Pork Chop Hill*
US 1959 97m bw

The Americans in Korea take a vital hill but the colonel in command finds it difficult to hold.
Ironic war film with vivid spectacle separated by much talk.

w James R. Webb *d Lewis Milestone* *ph Sam Leavitt* *m* Leonard Rosenman *pd* Nicolai Remisoff

Gregory Peck, Harry Guardino, George Shibata, Woody Strode, James Edwards, Rip Torn, George Peppard, Barry Atwater, Robert Blake

Port of New York*
US 1949 82m bw
Eagle Lion (Aubrey Schenck)

A woman narcotics smuggler determines to betray her colleagues to the authorities.
Good routine semi-documentary thick ear, notable for an early appearance by Yul Brynner as villain-in-chief.

w Eugene Ling *d* Laslo Benedek *ph* George E. Diskant

Scott Brady, Richard Rober, K. T. Stevens, Yul Brynner

Port of Seven Seas*
US 1938 81m bw
MGM (Henry Henigson)

Love on the Marseilles waterfront.
Stagey Hollywoodization of Pagnol's *Marius* trilogy: some vigour shows through.

w Preston Sturges *d* James Whale *ph* Karl Freund

Wallace Beery, Frank Morgan, Maureen O'Sullivan, John Beal, Jessie Ralph, Cora Witherspoon

Portnoy's Complaint
US 1972 101m Technicolor Panavision
Warner / Chehnault (Ernest Lehman)

A young New York Jewish boy has mother and masturbation problems.
Foolhardy attempt to film a fashionably sensational literary exercise; one of Hollywood's last attempts – thank goodness – to be 'with it'.

wd Ernest Lehman, *novel* Philip Roth *ph* Philip Lathrop *m* Michel Legrand

Richard Benjamin, Karen Black, Lee Black, Jack Somack, Jill Clayburgh, Jeannie Berlin

'The spectator is forced into the doubly uncomfortable position of a voyeur who can't actually see anything.'—*Jan Dawson*

Portrait in Black*
US 1960 113m Eastmancolor
U-I / Ross Hunter

An elderly shipping tycoon is murdered by his wife and doctor, but they are blackmailed.
Absurd old-fashioned melodrama of dark doings among the idle rich. Quite entertaining for addicts.

w Ivan Goff, Ben Roberts *d* Michael Gordon *ph* Russell Metty *m* Frank Skinner

Lana Turner, Anthony Quinn, Richard Basehart, Anna May Wong, Lloyd Nolan, Sandra Dee, John Saxon, Ray Walston, Virginia Grey

'Connoisseurs of the higher tosh should find it irresistible.'—*Penelope Houston*

Portrait of a Mobster
US 1961 108m bw
Warner

The career of twenties gangster Dutch Schultz.
Over-familiar, warmed over racketeering stuff with no particular edge or style.

w Howard Browne *d* Joseph Pevney *ph* Eugene Polito *m* Max Steiner

Vic Morrow, Leslie Parrish, Peter Breck, Ray Danton (repeating as Legs Diamond), Norman Alden, Ken Lynch

Portrait of Clare
GB 1950 98m bw
ABPC (Leslie Landau)

In 1900, a woman looks back on her three marriages.
High school novelette for easily pleased female audiences.

w Leslie Landau, Adrian Arlington, *novel* Francis Brett Young *d* Lance Comfort *ph* Gunther Krampf *ad* Don Ashton

Margaret Johnston, Richard Todd, Robin Bailey, Ronald Howard, Mary Clare, Marjorie Fielding, Anthony Nicholls, Lloyd Pearson

Portrait of Jennie***
US 1948 86m bw
David O. Selznick
GB title: *Jennie*

A penniless artist meets a strange girl who seems to age each time he sees her; they fall in love and he discovers that she has long been dead, though she finally comes to life once more during a sea storm like the one in which she perished.
A splendid example of the higher Hollywood lunacy: a silly story with pretensions about life and death and time and art, presented with superb persuasiveness by a first-class team of actors and technicians.

w Peter Berneis, Paul Osborn, Leonard Bernovici, *novel* Robert Nathan *d William Dieterle ph Joseph August m Dmitri Tiomkin*

Jennifer Jones, Joseph Cotten, Ethel Barrymore, David Wayne, Lillian Gish, Henry Hull, Florence Bates

'Though the story may not make sense, the pyrotechnics, joined to the dumbfounded silliness, keeps one watching.'—*New Yorker 1976*

The Poseidon Adventure**
US 1972 117m De Luxe Panavision
TCF / Kent (Irwin Allen)

A luxury liner is capsized, and trapped

passengers have to find their way to freedom via an upside down world.
Tedious disaster movie which caught the public fancy and started a cycle. Spectacular moments, cardboard characters, flashes of imagination.

w Stirling Silliphant, Wendell Mayes, *novel* Paul Gallico *ph* Harold Stine *d* Ronald Neame *m* John Williams *pd* William Creber

Gene Hackman, Ernest Borgnine, Shelley Winters, Red Buttons, Carol Lynley, Leslie Nielson, Arthur O'Connell

'The script is the only cataclysm in this waterlogged *Grand Hotel*.'—*New Yorker*

Posse**
US 1975 93m Technicolor Panavision
Paramount / Bryna (Kirk Douglas)

A US marshal seeking higher office vows to capture a railroad bandit, but the tables are smartly turned.
Unusual minor western, quite pleasing in all departments and neither mindless nor violent.

w William Roberts, Christopher Knopf d Kirk Douglas ph Fred Koenekamp *m* Maurice Jarre

Kirk Douglas, Bruce Dern, Bo Hopkins, James Stacy, Luke Askey, David Canary

Possessed*
US 1931 76m bw
MGM

A factory girl goes to New York in search of riches.
Reasonably gutsy Depression melodrama which moves at a fair pace.

w Lenore Coffee, *play* The Mirage by Edgar Selwyn *d* Clarence Brown *ph* Oliver T. Marsh

Joan Crawford, Clark Gable, Wallace Ford, Skeets Gallagher, Frank Conroy, Marjorie White, John Miljan

'Lots of luxury; lots of charm; lots of smooth talk about courage and marriage and what women want.'—*James R. Quirk*

Possessed*
US 1947 108m bw
Warner (Jerry Wald)

An emotionally unstable nurse marries her employer but retains a passionate love for an engineer whom she kills when he does not respond.
Extremely heavy, almost Germanic, flashback melodrama with everyone tearing hammer and tongs at the rather ailing script. Fun if you're in that mood, and an interesting example of the American *film noir* of the forties.

w Silvia Richards, Ranald MacDougall, *novel* One Man's Secret by Rita Weiman *d Curtis Bernhardt ph Joseph Valentine m* Franz Waxman

Joan Crawford, Raymond Massey, Van Heflin, Geraldine Brooks, Stanley Ridges, John Ridgely, Moroni Olsen

'Acting with bells on.'—*Richard Winnington*

'Miss Crawford performs with the passion and intelligence of an actress who is not content with just one Oscar.'—*James Agee*

The Possession of Joel Delaney*
US 1971 108m Eastmancolor
ITC / Haworth (George Justin)

A wealthy New York divorcee tries to save her brother from death at the hands of a Puerto Rican occult group who believe in ritual murder and demonic possession.
Unpleasant, frightening and overlong horror film with some kind of message struggling to get out but precious little entertainment value.

w Matt Robinson, Grimes Grice, *novel* Ramona Stewart *d* Waris Hussein *ph* Arthur J. Ornitz *m* Joe Ragoso

Shirley Maclaine, Perry King, Lisa Kohane, David Ellacott

The Postman Always Rings Twice*
US 1946 113m bw
MGM (Carey Wilson)

A guilty couple murder her husband but get their come-uppance.
Pale shadow of *Double Indemnity,* efficient but not interesting or very suspenseful.

w Harry Ruskin, Niven Busch, *novel* James M. Cain *d* Tay Garnett *ph Sidney Wagner m* George Basserman

Lana Turner, John Garfield, Cecil Kellaway, Hume Cronyn, Leon Ames, Audrey Totter, Alan Reed

Postman's Knock*
GB 1961 88m bw
MGM (Ronald Kinnoch)

A village postman is transferred to London, finds life and work bewildering, but captures some crooks and ends up a hero.
Mildly amusing star vehicle rising to good comic climaxes.

w John Briley, Jack Trevor Story *d* Robert Lynn *ph* Gerald Moss *m* Ron Goodwin

Spike Milligan, Barbara Shelley, Wilfrid Lawson

Pot O'Gold
US 1941 87m bw
(UA) James Roosevelt
GB title: *The Golden Hour*

A radio giveaway show finds work for idle musicians.
Thin Capraesque comedy which needed more determined handling.

w Walter de Leon *d* George Marshall *ph* Hal Mohr *md* Lou Forbes

James Stewart, Paulette Goddard, Horace Heidt, Charles Winninger, Mary Gordon, Frank Melton, Jed Prouty

Powder Keg*
US 1970 93m colour TVM
Filmways

In the 1914 southwest, two car-driving troubleshooters agree to get back from Mexico a hijacked train.
Ambitious pilot which flags between the action highlights. The resulting series, *Bearcats,* was shortlived.

wd Douglas Heyes

Rod Taylor, Dennis Cole, Michael Ansara, Fernando Lamas, Tisha Sterling, John McIntire, Luciana Paluzzi, Reni Santoni

The Power*
US 1967 109m Metrocolor Cinemascope
MGM / George Pal

Scientists researching into human endurance are menaced by one of their number who has developed the ability to kill by will power.
Interesting but finally unexciting and exasperating science fiction which badly lacks a gimmick one can actually see.

w John Gay, *novel* Frank M. Robinson *d* Byron Haskin *ph* Ellsworth Fredericks *m* Miklos Rozsa

Michael Rennie, George Hamilton, Suzanne Pleshette, Nehemiah Persoff, Earl Holliman, Arthur O'Connell, Aldo Ray, Barbara Nichols, Yvonne de Carlo, Richard Carlson, Gary Merrill, Ken Murray, Miiko Taka, Celia Lovsky

The Power and the Glory*
US 1933 76m bw
Fox (Jesse L. Lasky)

The flashback story of a tycoon who rose from nothing and was corrupted by power.
Often noted as a forerunner of *Citizen Kane,* this is in fact a disappointing film with a very thin script and a general sense of aimlessness. 'Presented in narratage' meant that the characters voice their unspoken thoughts. Most interesting for its credits.

w Preston Sturges *d* William K. Howard

Spencer Tracy, Colleen Moore, Ralph Morgan, Helen Vinson

The Power and the Prize*
US 1956 98m bw Cinemascope
MGM (Nicholas Nayfack)

An ambitious company executive is criticized by his president for wanting to marry a European refugee, but the other executives support him.
Unconvincing big business fairy tale which passes the time competently enough, though Taylor is a humourless hero.

w Robert Ardrey, *novel* Howard Swiggett *d* Henry Koster *ph* George Folsey *m* Bronislau Kaper

Robert Taylor, Elizabeth Mueller, Mary Astor, Burl Ives, Charles Coburn, Cedric Hardwicke

The Powers Girl
US 1942 92m bw
UA / Charles R. Rogers
GB title: *Hello Beautiful*

Girls come to New York to become models for John Robert Powers.
Extremely thin and forgettable musical.

w Edwin Moran, Harry Segall, *book* John Robert Powers *d* Norman Z. McLeod *ph* Stanley Cortez *md* Louis Silvers

George Murphy, Anne Shirley, Carole Landis, Alan Mowbray (as Powers), Dennis Day, Benny Goodman and his Orchestra, Mary Treen

Practically Yours
US 1944 89m bw
Paramount (Mitchell Leisen)

A war hero comes back after being supposed dead, and finds himself with a fiancée he never met.
Silly romantic comedy which never gets going.

w Norman Krasna *d* Mitchell Leisen *ph* Charles Lang Jnr *m* Victor Young

Claudette Colbert, Fred MacMurray, Gil Lamb, Cecil Kellaway, Robert Benchley, Rosemary de Camp, Tom Powers, Jane Frazee

Pray for the Wildcats*
US 1974 100m colour TVM
ABC / Tony Wilson

Four business associates take a motor cycle trip into a remote region, but they end up fighting natural obstacles and each other.

A timid version of *Deliverance:* not bad on its level.

w Jack Turley *d* Robert Michael Lewis

Andy Griffith, Marjoe Gortner, Robert Reed, William Shatner, Angie Dickinson, Janet Margolin, Lorraine Gary

Prelude to Fame
GB 1950 88m bw
Rank / Two Cities (Donald B. Wilson)

The health of a child musical prodigy is endangered by an ambitious woman who pushes him to the top.
Banal drama with classical music, generally overacted by the adults.

w Robert Westerby, *story* Young Archimedes by Aldous Huxley *d* Fergus McDonell *ph* George Stretton

Jeremy Spenser, Guy Rolfe, Kathleen Ryan, Kathleen Byron, James Robertson Justice, Henry Oscar, Rosalie Crutchley

The Premature Burial
US 1961 81m Eastmancolor Panavision
AIP (Roger Corman)

A man afraid of being buried alive suffers just that fate, but later comes to and wreaks revenge on his tormentors.
Gloomy Gothic horror based vaguely on Edgar Allan Poe: the ultimate in graveyard ghoulishness.

w Charles Beaumont, Ray Russell *d* Roger Corman *ph* Floyd Crosby *m* Ronald Stein *ad* Daniel Haller

Ray Milland, Heather Angel, Hazel Court, Richard Ney, Alan Napier, John Dierkes

Prescription Murder**
US 1967 99m Technicolor TVM
Universal (Richard Irving)

A smoothie doctor murders his wife, but a dim-looking police lieutenant is on his trail.
Actually the first *Columbo* (see *Mystery Movie)* made four years before the series proper began. One of the best, with the formula intact.

w Richard Levinson, William Link, from their play *d* Richard Irving

Peter Falk, Gene Barry, Katharine Justice, Nina Foch, William Windom

Presenting Lily Mars*
US 1943 104m bw
MGM (Joe Pasternak)

A girl from the sticks hits it big on Broadway.
No, the plot wasn't new, but some of the numbers were nice.

w Richard Connell, Gladys Lehman, *novel* Booth Tarkington *d* Norman Taurog *ph* Joseph Ruttenberg *md* George Stoll

Judy Garland, Van Heflin, Fay Bainter, Richard Carlson, Martha Eggerth, Spring Byington, Bob Crosby and his band, Tommy Dorsey and his band

The President's Analyst*
US 1967 104m Technicolor Panavision
Paramount / Panpiper (Stanley Rubin)

A psychiatrist who has been asked to treat the President is pursued by spies of every nationality.
Wild political satirical farce which finally unmasks as its chief villain the telephone company. Laughs along the way, but it's all rather too much.

wd Theodore J. Flicker *ph* William A. Fraker *m* Lalo Schifrin *ph* Pato Guzman

James Coburn, Godfrey Cambridge, Severn Darden, Joan Delaney, Pat Harrington, Eduard Franz, Will Geer

The President's Lady*
US 1953 96m bw
TCF (Sol C. Siegel)

An account of the early career of Andrew Jackson, a lawyer whose frail wife died shortly after he became president.
Well-produced political historical romance.

w John Patrick, *novel* Irving Stone *d* Henry Levin *ph Leo Tover* *m Alfred Newman*

Charlton Heston, Susan Hayward, John McIntire, Fay Bainter, Carl Betz

The President's Plane Is Missing*
US 1971 94m colour TVM
ABC Circle

Air Force One disappears with the President aboard . . .
Rather mild political suspenser which disappoints.

w Mark Carliner, Ernest Kinoy *d* Daryl Duke

Buddy Ebsen, Peter Graves, Arthur Kennedy, Rip Torn, Raymond Massey, Tod Andrews, Mercedes McCambridge, Joseph Campanella

Pressure Point*
US 1962 89m bw
UA / Larcas / Stanley Kramer

A black prison psychiatrist has longstanding trouble with a violent racist inmate.

Curious, quite compelling case history, told in pointless and confusing flashback; sharply made and photographed, melodramatically acted.

w Hubert Cornfield, S. Lee Pogositin *d Hubert Cornfield ph Ernest Haller m* Ernest Gold

Sidney Poitier, Bobby Darin, Peter Falk, Carl Benton Reid

Pretty Baby*
US 1950 92m bw
Warner (Harry Kurnitz)

A girl finds it easier to get a seat on the subway if she is carrying a (dummy) baby, but gets into complications when she meets a baby food king.
Silly but quite pleasant comedy variation on *Bachelor Mother*.

w Everett Freeman, Harry Kurnitz *d* Bretaigne Windust *ph* Peverell Marley *m* David Buttolph

Betsy Drake, Edmund Gwenn, Dennis Morgan, Zachary Scott, William Frawley

Pretty Boy Floyd
US 1974 74m Technicolor TVM
Universal (Jo Swerling Jnr)

The hunt for a 1930s public enemy.
Routine law-and-gangster stuff.

wd Clyde Ware

Martin Sheen, Michael Parks, Kim Darby, Ellen Corby

Pretty Maids All in a Row*
US 1971 95m Metrocolor
MGM (Gene Roddenbury)

High school girl students are being murdered by their guidance counsellor.
Uneasy murder comedy with few laughs, casting its star as a most unlikely villain. An interesting if unsuccessful attempt to be different.

w Gene Roddenberry, *novel* Francis Pollini *d* Roger Vadim *ph* Charles Rosher *m* Lalo Schifrin

Rock Hudson, Angie Dickinson, Telly Savalas, Roddy McDowall, Keenan Wynn

Pretty Poison**
US 1968 89m De Luxe
TCF / Lawrence Turman / Mollino (Marshal Backlar, Noel Black)

A psychotic arsonist enlists the aid of a teenager but soon discovers she is kinkier than he and has murder in mind.
Bizarre black comedy-melodrama, quite successfully mixed and served.

w Lorenzo Semple Jnr, *novel* She Let Him Continue by Stephen Geller *d Noel Black ph* David Quaid *m* Johnny Mandel

Anthony Perkins, Tuesday Weld, Beverly Garland, John Randolph, Dick O'Neill, Clarice Blackburn

Pretty Polly
GB 1967 102m Techniscope
Universal / George W. George, Frank Granat
US title: *A Matter of Innocence*

On a world tour with her vulgar aunt, a timid maiden finds romance in Singapore.
Slight romantic fable decked out with travel guide backgrounds and at odds with the cynicism of the short story from which it originates.

w Keith Waterhouse, Willis Hall, *story* Noel Coward *d* Guy Green *ph* Arthur Ibbetson *m* Michel Legrand

Hayley Mills, Trevor Howard, Shashi Kapoor, Brenda de Banzie, Dick Patterson, Peter Bayliss, Patricia Routledge, Dorothy Alison

'It came and went this winter, leaving a slight trace of camphor and old knitting needles.'—*Wilfrid Sheed*

Pride and Prejudice***
US 1940 116m bw
MGM (Hunt Stromberg)

An opinionated young lady of the early 19th-century wins herself a rich husband she had at first despised for his pride.
A pretty respectable version of Jane Austen's splendid romantic comedy, with a generally excellent cast; full of pleasurable moments.

w Aldous Huxley, Jane Murfin, *play* Helen Jerome, *novel Jane Austen d Robert Z. Leonard*

Laurence Olivier, Greer Garson, Edmund Gwenn, Mary Boland, Melville Cooper, Edna May Oliver, Karen Morley, Frieda Inescort, Bruce Lester, Edward Ashley, Ann Rutherford, Maureen O'Sullivan, E. E. Clive, Heather Angel, Marsha Hunt

'The most deliciously pert comedy of old manners, the most crisp and crackling satire in costume that we in this corner can remember ever having seen on the screen.'—*Frank S. Nugent, New York Times*

The Pride and the Passion*
US 1957 131m Technicolor Vistavision
UA / Stanley Kramer

In 1810 Spain a British naval officer helps Spanish guerrillas, by reactivating an old cannon, to win their fight against Napoleon.
Stolid, miscast adventure spectacle, its main

interest being the deployment of the gun across country by surging throngs of peasants.

w Edna and Edward Anhalt, *novel* The Gun by C. S. Forester *d* Stanley Kramer *ph Franz Planer* *m* Georges Antheil

Cary Grant, Sophia Loren, Frank Sinatra, Theodore Bikel, John Wengraf, Jay Novello, Philip Van Zandt

'The whirr of the cameras often seems as loud as the thunderous cannonades. It evidently takes more than dedication, co-operative multitudes and four million dollars to shoot history in the face.'—*Time*

The Pride of St Louis
US 1952 93m bw
TCF (Jules Schermer)

The life of baseball star Dizzy Dean, who injured himself and became a commentator.
Sporting biopic of clearly restricted interest; modestly well done.

w Herman J. Mankiewicz *d* Harmon Jones *ph* Leo Tover *m* Arthur Lange

Dan Dailey, Joanne Dru, Richard Haydn, Richard Crenna, Hugh Sanders

Pride of the Marines*
US 1945 120m bw
Warner (Jerry Wald)
GB title: *Forever in Love*

The story of Marine Al Schmid, blinded while fighting the Japanese.
Over-dramatic, sudsy biopic which is well enough mounted to carry quite an impact in the flagwaving Hollywood style.

w Albert Maltz *d* Delmer Daves *ph* Peverell Marley *m* Franz Waxman

John Garfield, Eleanor Parker, Dane Clark, John Ridgely, Rosemary de Camp, Ann Doran, Warren Douglas, Tom D'Andrea

The Pride of the Yankees*
US 1942 128m bw
Samuel Goldwyn

The story of baseball star Lou Gehrig, who died of leukemia at the height of his powers.
Standard sporting biopic ending on Gehrig's famous speech to the crowd; emotion covers the film's other deficiencies.

w Jo Swerling, Herman J. Mankiewicz, *story* Paul Gallico *d* Sam Wood *ph* Rudolph Maté *m* Leigh Harline *pd* William Cameron Menzies

Gary Cooper, Teresa Wright, Babe Ruth, Walter Brennan, Dan Duryea, Elsa Janssen, Ludwig Stossel, Virginia Gilmore

The Priest Killer*
US 1971 100m Technicolor TVM
Universal

San Francisco's law forces combine to catch a madman who murders Catholic priests.
Oddball cop show in which Ironside meets Sarge, and between them they get their man. Originally intended as two episodes of *Ironside*.

w Robert Van Scoyk, Joel Oliansky *d* Richard A. Colla

Raymond Burr, George Kennedy, Don Galloway, Louise Jeffries, Don Mitchell, Anthony Zerbe

Prime Cut
US 1972 91m Technicolor Panavision
Cinema Center (Joe Wizan)

A Kansas gangster incurs the wrath of his Chicago bosses, and a hired killer is sent to eliminate him.
Gory cat-and-mouse chase melodrama with no interest save its excesses.

w Robert Dillon *d* Michael Ritchie *ph* Gene Polito *m* Lalo Schifrin

Gene Hackman, Lee Marvin, Angel Tompkins, Sissy Spacek

The Prime Minister*
GB 1940 109m bw
Warner (Max Milder)

Episodes in the life of Disraeli.
Modestly budgeted historical pageant notable only for performances.

w Brock Williams, Michael Hogan *d* Thorold Dickinson

John Gielgud, Diana Wynyard, Will Fyffe, Stephen Murray, Owen Nares, Fay Compton (as Queen Victoria), Lyn Harding, Leslie Perrins

The Prime of Miss Jean Brodie*
GB 1969 116m De Luxe
TCF (Robert Fryer)

A sharp-minded Edinburgh schoolmistress of the thirties is a bad influence on her more easily-swayed pupils.
Interesting but slackly handled and maddeningly played character drama.

w Jay Presson Allen, *novel* Muriel Spark *d* Ronald Neame *ph* Ted Moore *m* Rod McKuen *pd* John Howell

Maggie Smith, Robert Stephens, Pamela Franklin, Celia Johnson, Gordon Jackson, Jane Carr

'The novel lost a good deal in its stage simplification, and loses still more in its movie reduction of that stage version.'—*John Simon*

The Primrose Path
US 1940 92m bw
RKO (Gregory La Cava)

The youngest of a family of shanty-town prostitutes falls in love with an honest hamburger stand proprietor.
Downright peculiar melodrama for its day and age, and not very entertaining either, spending most of its time being evasive.

w Allan Scott, Gregory La Cava, *play* Robert Buckner, Walter Hart, *novel* February Hill by Victoria Lincoln *d* Gregory La Cava *ph* Joseph H. August *m* Werner Heymann

Ginger Rogers, Joel McCrea, Marjorie Rambeau, Henry Travers, Miles Mander, Queenie Vassar, Joan Carroll

The Prince and the Pauper*
US 1937 118m bw
Warner (Robert Lord)

In Tudor London, young Edward VI changes places with a street urchin who happens to be his double.
Well-produced version of a famous story; it never quite seems to hit the right style or pace, but is satisfying in patches.

w Laird Doyle, *novel* Mark Twain *d* William Keighley *ph* Sol Polito *m Erich Wolfgang Korngold*

Errol Flynn, Claude Rains, Billy and Bobby Mauch, Henry Stephenson, Barton MacLane, Alan Hale, Eric Portman, Montagu Love (as Henry VIII), Lionel Pape, Halliwell Hobbes, Fritz Leiber

The Prince and the Showgirl*
GB 1957 117m Technicolor
Warner / Marilyn Monroe Productions (Laurence Olivier)

In London for the 1911 coronation, a Ruritanian prince picks up a chorus girl and they come to understand and respect each other.
Heavy-going comedy, rich in production values but weak in dramatic style and impact.

w Terence Rattigan, from his play The Sleeping Prince *d* Laurence Olivier *ph* Jack Cardiff *m* Richard Addinsell *pd* Roger Furse *ad* Carmen Dillon

Laurence Olivier, Marilyn Monroe, Sybil Thorndike, Richard Wattis, Jeremy Spenser, Esmond Knight, Rosamund Greenwood, Maxine Audley

The Prince of Central Park*
US 1975 74m colour TVM
Lorimar

Two children run away from home and decide to live in the city park.
Pleasing modern fable which New Yorkers will take with a very large pinch of salt.

novel Evan H. Rhodes *d* Harvey Hart

T. J. Hargrave, Lisa Richard, Ruth Gordon

Prince of Foxes*
US 1949 107m bw
TCF (Sol. C. Siegel)

A wandering adventurer in medieval Italy gets mixed up with the Borgias.
Good-looking historical fiction with a slight edge to it.

w Milton Krims, *novel* Samuel Shellabarger *d* Henry King *ph* Leon Shamroy *m* Alfred Newman

Tyrone Power, Orson Welles, Wanda Hendrix, Felix Aylmer, Everett Sloane, Katina Paxinou, Marina Berti

'Plot, counterplot, action and vengeance.'—*MFB*

Prince of Players*
US 1955 102m De Luxe Cinemascope
TCF (Philip Dunne)

Episodes in the life of actor Edwin Booth, brother of the man who killed Abraham Lincoln.
Earnest but ham-fisted biopic more notable, as a Hollywood entertainment, for its dollops of straight Shakespeare than for any dramatic interest.

w Moss Hart, *book* Eleanor Ruggles *d* Philip Dunne *ph* Charles G. Clarke *m* Bernard Herrmann

Richard Burton, Eva Le Gallienne, Maggie McNamara, John Derek, Raymond Massey, Charles Bickford, Elizabeth Sellars, Ian Keith

Prince Valiant*
US 1954 100m Technicolor Cinemascope
TCF (Robert L. Jacks)

The son of the exiled king of Scandia seeks King Arthur's help against the usurper, and becomes involved in a court plot.
Agreeable historical nonsense for teenagers, admittedly and sometimes hilariously from a comic strip.

w Dudley Nichols, *comic strip* Harold Foster *d* Henry Hathaway *ph* Lucien Ballard *m* Franz Waxman

Robert Wagner, James Mason, Debra Paget, Sterling Hayden, Victor McLaglen, Donald

Crisp, Brian Aherne, Barry Jones, Primo Carnera

The Prince Who Was a Thief
US 1951 88m Technicolor
U-I (Leonard Goldstein)

An Arabian Nights prince is lost as a baby and brought up by thieves, but finally fights back to his rightful throne.
Given the synopsis, any viewer can write the script himself. Standard eastern western romp.

w Gerald Drayson Adams, Aeneas Mackenzie, *story* Theodore Dreiser *d* Rudolph Maté *ph* Irving Glassberg *m* Hans Salter

Tony Curtis, Piper Laurie, Everett Sloane, Jeff Corey

The Princess and the Pirate*
US 1944 94m Technicolor
Samuel Goldwyn (Don Hartman)

An impostor is on the run from a vicious pirate.
Typical star costume extravaganza with fewer laughs than you'd expect.

w Don Hartman, Melville Shavelson, Everett Freeman *d* David Butler *ph* William Snyder, Victor Milner *m* David Rose

Bob Hope, Virginia Mayo, Victor McLaglen, Walter Slezak, Walter Brennan, Marc Lawrence, Hugo Haas, Maude Eburne

The Princess Comes Across*
US 1936 76m bw
Paramount (Arthur Hornblow Jnr)

A starstruck Brooklyn girl makes a transatlantic liner voyage disguised as a princess, and finds herself involved in a murder mystery.
Zany comedy thriller with plenty of jokes.

w Walter de Leon, Frances Martin, Frank Butler, Don Hartman, Philip MacDonald, *novel* Louis Lucien Rogger *d* William K. Howard *ph* Ted Tetzlaff

Carole Lombard, Fred MacMurray, Alison Skipworth, Douglass Dumbrille, William Frawley, Porter Hall, George Barbier, Lumsden Hare, Sig Rumann, Mischa Auer, Tetsu Komai

Princess O'Rourke
US 1943 94m bw
Warner (Hal B. Wallis)

An ace pilot falls for a princess and causes diplomatic complications.
Very thin wartime comedy with a propaganda ending involving Franklin Roosevelt.

wd Norman Krasna *ph* Ernest Haller *m* Frederick Hollander

Olivia de Havilland, Robert Cummings, Charles Coburn, Jack Carson, Jane Wyman, Harry Davenport, Gladys Cooper, Minor Watson, Curt Bois

The Prisoner*
GB 1955 91m bw
(Columbia) Facet / London Independent Producers (Vivian A. Cox)

In a European totalitarian state, a Cardinal is tortured and brainwashed.
Virtually a two-character talkpiece from an offbeat play which should have stayed in the theatre.

w Bridget Boland, from her play *d* Peter Glenville *ph* Reg Wyer *m* Benjamin Frankel

Alec Guinness, Jack Hawkins, Wilfrid Lawson, Kenneth Griffith, Ronald Lewis, Raymond Huntley

The Prisoner of Second Avenue*
US 1975 98m Technicolor Panavision
Warner (Melvin Frank)

A New York clerk and his wife are driven to distraction by the problems of urban living.
Gloomier-than-usual (from this author) collection of one-liners which almost turns into a psychopathic melodrama and causes its amiable leading players to overact horrendously.

w Neil Simon, from his play *d* Melvin Frank *ph* Philip Lathrop *m* Marvin Hamlisch

Jack Lemmon, Anne Bancroft, Gene Saks, Elizabeth Wilson

The Prisoner of Shark Island**
US 1936 95m bw
TCF (Darryl F. Zanuck)

The story of the doctor who treated the assassin of President Lincoln.
Well-mounted historical semi-fiction with excellent detail.

w Nunnally Johnson d John Ford ph Bert Glennon md Louis Silvers

Warner Baxter, Gloria Stuart, Joyce Kay, Claude Gillingwater, Douglas Wood, Harry Carey, Paul Fix, John Carradine

Prisoner of War
US 1954 81m bw
MGM (Henry Berman)

Life in a communist prison camp in Korea.
Sensational propaganda, reduced to comic strip level.

w Allen Rivkin *d* Andrew Marton *ph* Robert Planck *m* Jeff Alexander

Ronald Reagan, Steve Forrest, Dewey Martin, Oscar Homolka, Robert Horton, Paul Stewart, Henry Morgan, Stephen Bekassy

'It presents its catalogue of horrors in a manner unworthy of the cause it attempts to uphold.'—*John Gillett*

The Prisoner of Zenda****
US 1937 101m bw
David O. Selznick

An Englishman on holiday in Ruritania finds himself helping to defeat a rebel plot by impersonating the kidnapped king at his coronation.
A splendid schoolboy adventure story is perfectly transferred to the screen in this exhilarating swashbuckler, one of the most entertaining films to come out of Hollywood.

w John Balderston, Wills Root, Donald Ogden Stewart, novel Anthony Hope d John Cromwell ph James Wong Howe m Alfred Newman

Ronald Colman, Douglas Fairbanks Jnr, Madeleine Carroll, David Niven, Raymond Massey, Mary Astor, *C. Aubrey Smith*, Byron Foulger, Montagu Love
† Previously filmed in 1913 and 1922.

The Prisoner of Zenda*
US 1952 100m Technicolor
MGM (Pandro S. Berman)

A costly scene-for-scene remake which only goes to show that care and discretion are no match for the happy inspiration of the original.

w John Balderston, Noel Langley *d* Richard Thorpe *ph* Joseph Ruttenberg *m Alfred Newman*

Stewart Granger, James Mason, Deborah Kerr, Robert Coote, Robert Douglas, Jane Greer, Louis Calhern, Francis Pierlot, Lewis Stone

The Private Affairs of Bel Ami*
US 1947 119m bw
UA / David L. Loew (Ray Heinz)

In nineties Paris, a career journalist climbs to fame over the ruined lives of his friends.
Tame and stuffy adaptation of an incisive novel, rather poorly produced.

wd Albert Lewin, *novel* Guy de Maupassant *ph* Russell Metty *m* Darius Milhaud

George Sanders, Angela Lansbury, Ann Dvorak, Frances Dee, John Carradine, Hugo Haas, Marie Wilson, Albert Basserman, Warren William

Private Angelo
GB 1949 106m bw
Pilgrim (Peter Ustinov)

An Italian soldier hates war and spends World War II on the run from both sides.
Listless satirical comedy that just isn't funny enough.

w Peter Ustinov, Michael Anderson, *novel* Eric Linklater *d* Peter Ustinov *ph* Erwin Hillier

Peter Ustinov, Godfrey Tearle, Robin Bailey, Maria Denis, Marjorie Rhodes, James Robertson Justice, Moyna McGill

The Private Life of Don Juan
GB 1934 90m bw
London Films (Alexander Korda)

In 17th-century Spain, the famous lover fakes death and makes a comeback in disguise.
Lacklustre frolic by an overage star through dismal sets. The production was meant to extend the success of *The Private Life of Henry VIII*, but totally failed to do so.

w Lajos Biro, Frederick Lonsdale, *play* Henri Bataille *d* Alexander Korda *ph* Georges Périnal *m* Mischa Spoliansky

Douglas Fairbanks, Merle Oberon, Binnie Barnes, Benita Hume, Joan Gardner, Melville Cooper, Athene Seyler, Owen Nares

The Private Life of Henry VIII***
GB 1933 97m bw
London Films (*Alexander Korda*)

How Henry beheaded his second wife and acquired four more.
This never was a perfect film, but certain scenes are very funny and its sheer sauciness established the possibility of British films making money abroad, as well as starting several star careers. It now looks very dated and even amateurish in parts.

w Lajos Biro, Arthur Wimperis d Alexander Korda *ph* Georges Périnal *m* Kurt Schroeder

Charles Laughton, Elsa Lanchester, Robert Donat, Merle Oberon, Binnie Barnes, Franklin Dyall, Miles Mander, Wendy Barrie, Claud Allister, Everly Gregg

The Private Life of Sherlock Holmes***
GB 1970 125m De Luxe Panavision
UA / Phalanx / Mirisch / Sir Nigel (Billy Wilder)

A secret Watson manuscript reveals cases in which Sherlock Holmes became involved with women.
What started as four stories is reduced to two, one brightly satirical and the other no more than

a careful and discreet recreation, with the occasional jocular aside, of the flavour of the stories themselves. A very civilized and pleasing entertainment except for the hurried rounding-off which is a let-down.

w Billy Wilder, I. A. L. Diamond d Billy Wilder *ph* Christopher Challis *m* Miklos Rozsa *ad Alexander Trauner*

Robert Stephens, Colin Blakely, Genevieve Page, Clive Revill, Christopher Lee, Catherine Lacey, Stanley Holloway

'Affectionately conceived and flawlessly executed.'—*NFT, 1974*

Private Lives*
US 1931 92m bw
MGM

Ex-marrieds desert their intended new spouses to try each other again.
An essentially theatrical comedy, and a great one, seems somewhat slow-witted on film.

w Hans Kraly, Richard Schayer, *play* Noel Coward *d* Sidney Franklin *ph* Ray Binger

Norma Shearer, Robert Montgomery, Reginald Denny, Una Merkel, Jean Hersholt

The Private Lives of Elizabeth and Essex**
US 1939 106m Technicolor
Warner (Robert Lord)

Elizabeth I falls in love with the Earl of Essex, but events turn him into a rebel and she has to order his execution.
Unhistorical history given the grand treatment; a Hollywood picture book, not quite satisfying dramatically despite all the effort.

w Norman Reilly Raine, Aeneas Mackenzie, *play* Elizabeth the Queen by Maxwell Anderson *d* Michael Curtiz *ph* Sol Polito *m* Erich Wolfgang Korngold

Bette Davis, Errol Flynn, Olivia de Havilland, Donald Crisp, Vincent Price, Alan Hale, Henry Stephenson, Henry Daniell, Leo G. Carroll, Nanette Fabray, Robert Warwick, John Sutton

'A rather stately, rigorously posed and artistically technicolored production.'—*Frank S. Nugent*

Private Number
US 1936 80m bw
TCF (Raymond Griffith)

A wealthy young man keeps a secret of his marriage to a housemaid.
Warmed-over class melodrama previously filmed in 1930 as *Common Clay*. Adequate within its lights.

w Gene Markey, William Conselman, *play* Common Clay by Cleves Kinkead *d* Roy del Ruth *ph* Peverell Marley

Loretta Young, Robert Taylor, Basil Rathbone, Patsy Kelly, Marjorie Gateson, Paul Harvey, Monroe Owsley, John Miljan

Private Potter
GB 1962 89m bw
MGM / Ben Arbeid

A young soldier is court-martialled for cowardice but claims he had a vision of god.
Stilted morality play, unpersuasively made and acted.

w Ronald Harwood, from his TV play *d* Caspar Wrede *ph* Arthur Lavis *m* George Hall

Tom Courtenay, Mogens Wieth, Ronald Fraser, James Maxwell, Ralph Michael, Brewster Mason

The Private War of Major Benson
US 1955 105m Technicolor
Cinemascope
U-I (Howard Pine)

A soldier with outspoken views is sent to cool off as commander of a military academy run by an order of nuns.
Cute and sentimental nonsense with unlikely situations, with a martinet becoming soft-centred and a happy-ever-after finale.

w William Roberts, Richard Alan Simmons *d* Jerry Hopper *ph* Harold Lipstein *m* Joseph Gershenson

Charlton Heston, Julie Adams, Tim Hovey, William Demarest, Tim Considine, Sal Mineo, Nana Bryant, Milburn Stone, Mary Field

Private Worlds*
US 1935 84m bw
Paramount (Walter Wanger)

Romance among the doctors at a mental hospital.
Melodrama treated with what was at the time unexpected seriousness.

w Lynn Starling, *novel* Phyllis Bottome *d* Gregory La Cava *ph* Leon Shamroy

Claudette Colbert, Charles Boyer, Joel McCrea, Joan Bennett, Helen Vinson, Esther Dale, Samuel S. Hinds

A Private's Affair
US 1959 92m De Luxe Cinemascope
TCF (David Weisbart)

Three army recruits form a close harmony trio and get into various scrapes.
Thin service comedy for the 'new' youth audience.

w Winston Miller *d* Raoul Walsh *ph* Charles G. Clarke *m* Cyril Mockridge

Sal Mineo, Christine Carere, Barry Coe, Barbara Eden, Gary Crosby, Terry Moore, Jim Backus, Jessie Royce Landis

Private's Progress***
GB 1956 97m bw
British Lion / Charter (Roy Boulting)

An extremely innocent young national serviceman is taught a few army dodges and becomes a dupe for jewel thieves.
Celebrated army farce with satirical pretensions; when released it had something to make everyone in Britain laugh.

w Frank Harvey, John Boulting, novel Alan Hackney *d John Boulting ph* Eric Cross *m* John Addison

Ian Carmichael, Terry-Thomas, Richard Attenborough, *Dennis Price,* Peter Jones, William Hartnell, Thorley Walters, Ian Bannen, Jill Adams, Victor Maddern, Kenneth Griffith, Miles Malleson, *John Le Mesurier*

Privilege*
GB 1967 103m Technicolor
Universal / Worldfilm / Memorial (John Heyman)

The publicity campaign for a pop star turns him into a religious messiah.
Rather hysterical fable for our time, undeniably forceful in spots and yawnful in others.

w Norman Bogner, *story* Johnny Speight *d Peter Watkins ph* Peter Suschitsky *m* Mike Leander

Paul Jones, Jean Shrimpton, Mark London, Max Bacon, Jeremy Child, James Cossins, Victor Henry

'Everything in it goes wrong, and one can do little but catalogue the failures.'—*MFB*

The Prize***
US 1963 135m Metrocolor Panavision
MGM / Roxbury (Pandro S. Bergman)

In Stockholm during the Nobel Prize awards, a drunken American author stumbles on a spy plot.
Whatever the original novel is like, the film is a Hitchcock pastiche which works better than most Hitchcocks: suspenseful, well characterized, fast moving and funny from beginning to end.

w Ernest Lehman, novel Irving Wallace *d Mark Robson ph* William Daniels *m* Jerry Goldsmith

Paul Newman, Elke Sommer, *Edward G. Robinson,* Diane Baker, Kevin McCarthy, *Leo G. Carroll,* Micheline Presle

A Prize of Arms
GB 1961 105m bw
British Lion / Interstate (George Maynard)

An ex-army officer and an explosives expert plan to steal an army payroll.
Standard, pacy caper melodrama offering nothing at all new.

w Paul Ryder *d* Cliff Owen *ph* Gilbert Taylor *m* Robert Sharples

Stanley Baker, Tom Bell, Helmut Schmid, John Phillips

A Prize of Gold
GB 1955 100m Technicolor
Columbia / Warwick (Phil C. Samuel)

An American army sergeant in Berlin decides to steal a cargo of Nazi loot.
Routine caper thriller with sentimental leanings.

w Robert Buckner, John Paxton, *novel* Max Catto *d* Mark Robson *ph* Ted Moore *m* Malcolm Arnold

Richard Widmark, Mai Zetterling, Nigel Patrick, George Cole, Donald Wolfit, Andrew Ray, Joseph Tomelty, Karel Stepanek

The Prizefighter and the Lady
US 1933 102m bw
MGM (Hunt Stromberg)
GB title: *Every Woman's Man*

A boxer falls for a high class gangster's girl.
Plodding romantic melodrama, popular because it starred a real boxer.

w John Meehan, John Lee Mahin *d* W. S. Van Dyke

Myrna Loy, Max Baer, Otto Kruger, Walter Huston, Jack Dempsey, Primo Carnera

Probe**
US 1972 97m colour TVM
Warner (Leslie Stevens)
aka: *Search*

CIA agents are monitored by implanted radio devices.
Childlike James Bond stuff which works very well because it has a sense of humour and the bigger than usual budget is well spent. The resultant series, however, fell apart because of rotating leads.

wd Russell Mayberry

Hugh O'Brian, John Gielgud, Angel Tompkins, Elke Sommer, Burgess Meredith, Lilia Skala, Kent Smith

The Prodigal
US 1955 115m Eastmancolor
Cinemascope
MGM (Charles Schnee)

The sons of a Hebrew farmer falls for the high priestess of a pagan cult.
Wildly apochryphal 'biblical' story of obvious expensiveness but no merit.

w Maurice Zimm *d* Richard Thorpe *ph* Joseph Ruttenberg *m* Bronislau Kaper

Lana Turner, Edmund Purdom, Louis Calhern, James Mitchell, Walter Hampden, Francis L. Sullivan, Joseph Wiseman, Audrey Dalton, Taina Elg, Neville Brand, Cecil Kellaway

'A few lines of dialogue derive from the Bible; the rest is pure Hollywood, but Hollywood in its mood of sham solemnity when even the unintentional jokes are not funny.'—*MFB*

The Producers*
US 1967 88m Pathecolor
Avco / Springtime / MGM / Crossbow (Sidney Glazier)

A Broadway producer seduces elderly widows to obtain finance for his new play, sells 25000 per cent in the expectation that it will flop, and is horrified when it succeeds.
Dismally unfunny satire except for the play itself, *Springtime for Hitler,* which is neatly put down. This has, however, become a cult film, so that criticism is pointless.

wd Mel Brooks *ph* Joseph Coffey *m* John Morris

Zero Mostel, Gene Wilder, Kenneth Mars, Estelle Winwood, Renee Taylor, Dick Shawn

'Over and over again promising ideas are killed off, either by over-exposure or bad timing.'—*Tom Milne*

'An almost flawless triumph of bad taste, unredeemed by wit or style.'—*Arthur Schlesinger Jnr*

The Profane Comedy
US 1969 96m Technicolor TVM
Universal (Roy Huggins)
aka: *Set This Town on Fire*

A convict is pardoned and announces that he will run for Lieutenant Governor.
Hard-to-like, awkwardly paced and obscurely narrated melodrama.

w John Thomas James *d* David Lowell Rich

Chuck Connors, Carl Betz, Lynda Day George, John Anderson, Jeff Corey

Professional Soldier
US 1936 75m bw
TCF (Darryl F. Zanuck)

A kidnapper befriends the young prince who is his victim.
Predictable, polished family film.

w Gene Fowler, Howard Willis Smith, *story* Damon Runyon *d* Tay Garnett *ph* Rudolph Maté *m* Louis Silvers

Victor McLaglen, Freddie Bartholemew, Constance Collier, Gloria Stuart, Michael Whalen

Professional Sweetheart
US 1933 70m bw
RKO (Merian C. Cooper)
GB title: *Imaginary Sweetheart*

A radio 'purity girl' seeks some real life romance.
Modestly smart comedy of no lasting merit.

w Maurine Watkins *d* William Seiter *ph* Edward Cronjager

Ginger Rogers, Betty Furness, Gregory Ratoff, Sterling Holloway, Frank McHugh, Zasu Pitts, Allen Jenkins, Norman Foster, Edgar Kennedy, Franklin Pangborn

The Professionals**
US 1966 123m Technicolor
Panavision
Columbia / Pax (Richard Brooks)

Skilled soldiers of fortune are hired by a millionaire rancher to get back his kidnapped wife.
Strong-flavoured star western with good suspense sequences.

wd Richard Brooks, novel A Mule for the Marquesa by Frank O'Rourke *ph* Conrad Hall *m* Maurice Jarre

Burt Lancaster, Lee Marvin, Robert Ryan, Jack Palance, Ralph Bellamy, Claudia Cardinale, Woody Strode

'After the *Lord Jim* excursion, it is good to see Brooks back on his own professional form, filming the tight, laconic sort of adventure which usually seems to bring out the best in Hollywood veterans.'—*Penelope Houston*

'It has the expertise of a cold old whore with practised hands and no thoughts of love.'—*Pauline Kael, 1968*

Project X*
US 1968 97m Technicolor
Paramount / William Castle

In the year 2118, a man is scientifically induced to think he lives in the 1960s so that he can recover a lost secret.

Fearsomely complex science fiction, cheaply made but on the whole intriguingly imagined.

w Edmund Morris, *novels* Leslie P. Davies *d* William Castle *ph* Harold Stine *m* Van Cleave

Christopher George, Greta Baldwin, Henry Jones, Monte Markham, Harold Gould

Promise at Dawn
US / France 1970 102m De Luxe
Avco / Nathalie (Jules Dassin)

The boyhood of novelist Romain Gary and the last years of his fearsome Russian Jewish actress mother with whom he traipses around Europe.
Scrappy star vehicle and unnecessary biopic in a variety of indulgent styles.

w Jules Dassin, *play* First Love by Samuel Taylor *d* Jules Dassin *ph* Jean Badal *m* Georges Delerue

Melina Mercouri, Assef Dayan

Promise Her Anything
GB 1966 97m Technicolor
Seven Arts (Stanley Rubin)

A mail order movie maker falls for a young French widow in the next flat.
Scatty comedy set in Greenwich Village and aiming in vain for a kind of frantic bohemian charm, with a baby as deus ex machina.

w William Peter Blatty *d* Arthur Hiller *ph* Douglas Slocombe *m* Lynn Murray

Warren Beatty, Leslie Caron, Hermione Gingold, Lionel Stander, Robert Cummings, Keenan Wynn, Cathleen Nesbitt

Promise Him Anything
US 1975 74m colour TVM
Seven Arts (Stanley Rubin)

Having suggested on her computer dating card that 'anything goes', a girl is taken to court when she doesn't produce.
The comedy doesn't produce either.

w David Freeman *d* Edward Parone

Eddie Albert, Meg Foster, Frederic Forrest, William Schallert, Tom Ewell

The Proud and Profane
US 1956 112m bw Vistavision
Paramount (William Perlberg)

In the Pacific War a Roman Catholic widow falls for a tough Lieutenant Colonel. ('My pleasure is physical; my men call me The Beast.')
Unlikely romantic melodrama with a certain amount of plain speaking, otherwise routine.

wd George Seaton, *novel* The Magnificent Bastards by Lucy Herndon Crockett *ph* John F. Warren *m* Victor Young

William Holden, Deborah Kerr, Thelma Ritter, Dewey Martin, William Redfield

The Proud Ones
US 1956 94m Eastmancolor Cinemascope
TCF (Robert L. Jacks)

A marshal cleans up a crooked town despite the hazards of his own physical disability and a deputy who hates him.
Entertaining though rather foolishly scripted western.

w Edmund North, Joseph Patracca *d* Robert L. Webb *ph* Lucien Ballard *m* Lionel Newman

Robert Ryan, Jeffrey Hunter, Vera Miles, Robert Middleton

The Proud Rebel
US 1958 103m Technicolor
MGM / Sam Goldwyn Jnr

After the Civil War, a southerner wanders the Yankee states in search of a doctor to cure his mute son; he falls for a lady farmer and his son finds his voice at a crucial moment.
Pretty dim family western for pretty dim families; everything happens precisely according to plan.

w Joseph Patracca, Lillie Hayward *d* Michael Curtiz *ph* Ted McCord *m* Jerome Moross

Alan Ladd, Olivia de Havilland, David Ladd, Dean Jagger, Cecil Kellaway, Dean Stanton, Henry Hull, John Carradine, James Westerfield

The Proud Valley*
GB 1939 76m bw
Ealing (Sergei Nolbandov)

A black stoker helps unemployed Welsh miners reopen their pits.
Neat little propaganda drama.

w Roland Pertwee, Louis Golding, Jack Jones *d Pen Tennyson*

Paul Robeson, Edward Chapman, Edward Rigby, *Rachel Thomas*, Simon Lack, Clifford Evans, Allan Jeayes

The Prowler*
US 1951 92m bw
Horizon (Sam Spiegel)

A discontented wife thinks she sees a prowler and calls a cop; they have an affair and murder her husband.
Another variant on *Double Indemnity* and *The Postman Always Rings Twice*; the script is terse and the actors well-handled.

w Hugo Butler *d Joseph Losey ph* Arthur Miller
Van Heflin, Evelyn Keyes, John Maxwell, Katharine Warren
'A rivetingly cool, clean thriller.'—*NFT, 1973*

Prudence and the Pill*
GB 1968 92m De Luxe
TCF / Kenneth Harper, Ronald Kahn
A girl borrows her mother's contraceptive pills and replaces them with aspirin, causing no end of complications.
Self-consciously naughty sex comedy with a long dénouement and some stiff patches to affect one's enjoyment of the brighter moments.
w Hugh Mills, from his play *d* Fielder Cook *ph* Ted Moore *m* Bernard Ebbinghouse
David Niven, Deborah Kerr, Edith Evans, Keith Michell, Robert Coote, Irina Demick, Joyce Redman, Judy Geeson
'Everybody winds up pregnant to clutter the earth, apparently, with people as obnoxious as their progenitors.'—*Judith Crist*

Psyche 59
GB 1964 94m bw
Columbia / Troy / Schenck (Philip Hazelton)
A wife recovering from blindness realizes that her husband is in love with her sister.
Pretentious melodrama with stuffy dialogue, pompous direction and irritating characters.
w Julian Halevy, *novel* Françoise de Ligneris *d* Alexander Singer *ph* Walter Lassally *m* Kenneth V. Jones
Patricia Neal, Curt Jurgens, Samantha Eggar, Ian Bannen, Beatrix Lehmann

The Psychiatrist: God Bless the Children
US 1970 97m Technicolor TVM
Universal (Edgar Small, Norman Felton)
A psychoanalyst helps a small town fight a school drug epidemic.
Ho-hum social conscience stuff.
w Jerrold Freedman *d* Daryl Duke
Roy Thinnes, Pete Duel, Luther Adler, Katherine Justice

Psycho***
US 1960 109m bw
Shamley / Alfred Hitchcock
At a lonely motel vicious murders take place and are attributed to the manic mother of the young owner.
Curious shocker devised by Hitchcock as a tease and received by most critics as an unpleasant horror piece in which the main scene, the shower stabbing, was allegedly directed not by Hitchcock but by Saul Bass. After enormous commercial success it achieved classic status over the years; despite effective moments of fright, it has a childish plot and script, and its interest is that of a tremendously successful confidence trick, made for very little money by a TV crew.
w Joseph Stefano, *novel* Robert Bloch *d Alfred Hitchcock* (and *Saul Bass) ph* John L. Russell *m Bernard Herrmann*
Anthony Perkins, Vera Miles, John Gavin, Janet Leigh, John McIntire, Martin Balsam, Simon Oakland
'Probably the most visual, most cinematic picture he has ever made.'—*Peter Bogdanovich*
†When asked by the press what he used for the blood in the bath, Mr Hitchcock said: 'Chocolate sauce'.

Psychomania
GB 1972 91m Technicolor
Benmar (Andrew Donally)
A Hells Angels motor cyclist commits suicide and returns from the dead an invulnerable monster.
Arrant nonsense of the macabre sort, sometimes irresistibly amusing.
w Armand d'Usseau *d* Don Sharp *ph* Ted Moore *m* David Whitaker
George Sanders, Nicky Henson, Beryl Reid, Robert Hardy

The Psychopath
GB 1966 83m Techniscope
Paramount / Amicus (Milton Subotsky)
Men are found dead in London, each with a doll beside him.
Complicated horror thriller in which the actors go further over the top the more the plot winds down.
w Robert Bloch *d* Freddie Francis *ph* John Wilcox *m* Philip Martell
Patrick Wymark, Margaret Johnston, John Standing, Alexander Knox, Judy Huxtable, Don Borisenko, Thorley Walters, Colin Gordon

PT 109
US 1963 140m Technicolor Panavision
Warner (Brian Foy)
Adventures of president-to-be John F. Kennedy when he was a naval lieutenant in the Pacific during World War II.
Extraordinarily protracted and very dull action story which seems to have been overawed by its subject.

w Richard L. Breen *d* Leslie H. Martinson *ph* Robert Surtees *m* William Lava, David Buttolph

Cliff Robertson, Ty Hardin, James Gregory, Robert Blake

The Public Enemy***
US 1931 84m bw
Warner
GB title: *Enemies of the Public*

Two slum boys begin as bootleggers, get too big for their boots, and wind up dead.
Although it doesn't flow as a narrative, this early gangster film still has vivid and startling scenes and was most influential in the development of the urban American crime film.

w Kubec Glasmon, John Bright *d William Wellman ph Dev Jennings*

James Cagney, Edward Woods, Jean Harlow, Joan Blondell, Beryl Mercer, Donald Cook, Mae Clarke, Leslie Fenton

'The real power of *The Public Enemy* lies in its vigorous and brutal assault on the nerves and in the stunning acting of James Cagney.'—*James Shelley Hamilton*

Public Enemy's Wife
US 1935 78m bw
Warner (Sam Bischoff)
GB title: *G-Man's Wife*

Lower-berth gangster thrills culminating in a chase climax; neatly enough done.

w Abem Finkel, Harold Buckley, *story* David O. Selznick,
P. J. Wolfson *ph* Ernest Haller *d* Nick Grinde

Pat O'Brien, Margaret Lindsay, Robert Armstrong, Cesar Romero, Dick Foran, Dick Purcell

Public Hero Number One
US 1935 89m bw
MGM (Lucien Hubbard)

A G-man goes undercover to track down the Purple Gang.
Moderate thick ear dating from the time when studios tried to smother public outcry against gangster films by presenting the cop as the hero.

w Wells Root *d* J. Walter Ruben *ph* Gregg Toland

Chester Morris, Jean Arthur, Joseph Calleia, Lionel Barrymore, Paul Kelly, Lewis Stone, Paul Hurst

Pueblo**
US 1973 100m colour
TVM (videotape)
Titus

An American ship is seized by the North Koreans.
Dramatic documentary, very powerfully made.

Hal Holbrook, Andrew Duggan, Richard Mulligan, George Grizzard, Gary Merrill, Mary Fickett

Pufnstuf
US 1970 98m Technicolor
Universal / Krofft Enterprises

A dejected boy is led by his talking flute on a talking boat to Living Island, full of strange but friendly animals in fear of an incompetent witch.
Amalgam of a TV series using life-size puppets to project a mildly pleasing variation on *The Wizard of Oz*, without quite achieving the right blend of wit and charm.

w John Fenton Murray, Si Rose
d Hollingsworth Morse *ph* Kenneth Peach
m Charles Fox *ad Alexander Golitzen*

Jack Wild, Billie Hayes, Martha Raye, Mama Cass

Pulp*
GB 1972 95m colour
UA / Klinger–Caine–Hodges (Michael Klinger)

An ex-funeral director now living in the Mediterranean as a successful pulp fiction writer gets involved with gangsters and weirdos.
Occasionally funny pastiche which sorely lacks shape and is sustained by guest appearances and zany ideas.

wd Mike Hodges ph Ousama Rawi *m* George Martin

Michael Caine, *Mickey Rooney*, Lizabeth Scott, Lionel Stander, Nadia Cassini, Al Lettieri, Dennis Price

'Various eccentrics act out their "turns", but never quite lift a light comedy-thriller through the more playful and productive inversions of parody.'—*Richard Combs*

The Pumpkin Eater***
GB 1964 118m bw
Columbia / Romulus (James Woolf)

A compulsive mother (of eight children) finds her third marriage rocking when she gets evidence of her husband's affairs.
Brilliantly made if basically rather irritating kaleidoscope of vivid scenes about silly people,

all quite recognizable as sixties Londoners; very well acted.

w Harold Pinter, *novel* Penelope Mortimer *d Jack Clayton ph Oswald Morris m* Georges Delerue

Anne Bancroft, Peter Finch, James Mason, Maggie Smith, Cedric Hardwicke, Richard Johnson, Eric Porter

'There never was a film so rawly memorable.'—*Evening Standard*

'It is solid, serious, intelligent, stylish. It is also, for the most part, quite dead.'—*The Times*

Punch and Jody
US 1974 74m colour TVM
Metromedia

An executive leaves his wife and joins the circus as a clown. Fifteen years later his daughter comes looking for him.
Drippy drama, awash in sentimentality and self-pity.

w John McGreevey *d* Barry Shear

Glenn Ford, Pam Griffin, Ruth Roman, Kathleen Widdoes.

The Punch and Judy Man*
GB 1962 96m bw
(ABP) Macconkey (Gordon L. T. Scott)

A seashore children's entertainer tries and fails to establish himself as an important citizen.
Melancholy comedy of failure which did not please its star's adherents and indeed just missed the style it was seeking.

w Philip Oakes, Tony Hancock *d* Jeremy Summers *ph* Gilbert Taylor *m* Derek Scott, Don Banks

Tony Hancock, Sylvia Syms, Ronald Fraser, Barbara Murray, John Le Mesurier, Hugh Lloyd

Puppet on a Chain*
GB 1970 98m Technicolor
Big City (Kurt Unger)

An American Interpol agent hunts down drug smugglers in Amsterdam.
Sadistic adventure thriller, a toughened version of James Bond, climaxing in a splendid boat chase through Amsterdam.

w Alistair MacLean, Don Sharp, Paul Wheeler, *novel* Alistair MacLean *d* Geoffrey Reeve, *Don Sharp ph* Jack Hildyard, Skeets Kelly *m* Piero Piccioni

Sven Bertil Taube, Barbara Parkins, Patrick Allen, Alexander Knox, Vladek Sheybal

'One suspects that a marionette also sat in for Alistair MacLean.'—*Judith Crist*

The Purple Heart*
US 1944 99m bw
TCF (Darryl F. Zanuck)

American prisoners of war in Japan are tried and executed.
Relentlessly sombre flagwaver, extremely persuasively presented.

w Jerome Cady, Darryl F. Zanuck *d Lewis Milestone ph* Arthur Miller *m* Alfred Newman

Dana Andrews, Richard Conte, Farley Granger, Kevin O'Shea, Sam Levene, Don Barry, Richard Loo

The Purple Mask
US 1955 82m Technicolor Cinemascope
U-I (Howard Christie)

In 1802 Paris the Royalist resistance to Napoleon is led by the mysterious Purple Mask, who also disguises himself as a foppish dandy.
Cheeky rewrite of *The Scarlet Pimpernel*, with plenty of gusto but not much style.

w Oscar Brodney *d* Bruce Humberstone *ph* Irving Glassberg *m* Joseph Gershenson

Tony Curtis, Dan O'Herlihy, Colleen Miller, Gene Barry, Angela Lansbury, George Dolenz, John Hoyt

'Sir Percy, one feels, would have personally conducted this lot to the guillotine.'—*MFB*

The Purple Plain*
GB 1954 100m Technicolor
GFD / Two Cities (John Bryan)

During the Burma campaign, a Canadian squadronleader regains his shattered nerves during an arduous trek across country.
Psychological study and eastern adventure combined; not the best of either, but a potent crowd-puller.

w Eric Ambler, *novel* H. E. Bates *d* Robert Parrish *ph* Geoffrey Unsworth *m* John Veale

Gregory Peck, Maurice Denham, Win Min Than, Lyndon Brook, Brenda de Banzie, Bernard Lee, Anthony Bushell, Ram Gopal

Pursued*
US 1947 101m bw
(Warner) United States (Milton Sperling)

A revenge-seeking cowboy accidentally causes a tragedy in his adopted family.
Glum, good-looking revenge western.

w Niven Busch *d* Raoul Walsh *ph James Wong Howe m* Max Steiner

Robert Mitchum, Teresa Wright, Judith Anderson, Dean Jagger, Alan Hale, Harry Carey Jnr

Pursuit**
US 1972 73m colour TVM
Lee Rich (Robert L. Jacks)

A political madman steals a deadly nerve gas and plans to destroy San Diego in the middle of a convention.
Well-devised, smartly-detailed nailbiter with a tense climax.

w Robert Dozier, *novel* Michael Crichton
d Michael Crichton

Ben Gazzara, E. G. Marshall, William Windom, Joseph Wiseman, Martin Sheen

The Pursuit of Happiness
US 1934 75m bw
Paramount (Arthur Hornblow Jnr)

In 1776 Connecticut a Puritan maid falls for a Hessian soldier.
Mildly pleasing romantic comedy centring on the ancient practice of 'bundling' in which betrothed couples might sleep together fully clothed.

w Stephen Morehouse Avery, Jack Cunningham, J. P. McEvoy, Virginia Van Upp, *play* Lawrence Langner, Armina Marshall
d Alexander Hall *ph* Karl Struss

Francis Lederer, Joan Bennett, Charles Ruggles, Mary Boland, Walter Kingsford, Minor Watson

The Pursuit of Happiness*
US 1970 98m Eastmancolor
Columbia / TA Films / Norton–Simon (David Susskind)

A New York college dropout is sent to prison after a hit and run accident.
Smooth, watchable but empty youth movie.

w Sidney Carroll, George L. Sherman *d* Robert Mulligan *ph* Dick Kratina *m* Dave Grusin

Michael Sarrazin, Barbara Hershey, Robert Klein, Ruth White, E. G. Marshall, Arthur Hill

Pushover*
US 1954 91m bw
Columbia (Jules Schermer)

An honest policeman involves himself in murder for loot.
Another variation on *Double Indemnity*, smoothly carpentered as the first appearance of newly-groomed star Kim Novak. The events of a night were familiar and watchable.

w Roy Huggins, *novels* The Night Watch by Thomas Walsh, Rafferty by William S. Ballinger
d Richard Quine *ph* Lester B. White *m* Arthur Morton

Fred MacMurray, Kim Novak, Phil Carey, Dorothy Malone, E. G. Marshall

Puzzle of a Downfall Child
US 1970 104m Technicolor
Universal / Newman–Foreman

Fantasy reminiscences of a top fashion model.
Pretentious, fashionable, seemingly interminable collage of sex and high living.

w Adrian Joyce *d Jerry Schatzberg* *ph* Adam Holender *m* Michael Small

Faye Dunaway, Barry Primus, Viveca Lindfors, Barry Morse, Roy Scheider

Pygmalion****
GB 1938 96m bw
Gabriel Pascal

A professor of phonetics takes a bet that he can turn a cockney flower seller in six months into a lady who can pass as a duchess.
Perfectly splendid Shavian comedy of bad manners, extremely well filmed and containing memorable lines and performances; subsequently turned into the musical *My Fair Lady* (qv). One of the most heartening and adult British films of the thirties.

w Anatole de Grunwald, W. P. Lipscomb, Cecil Lewis, Ian Dalrymple, *play Bernard Shaw*
d Anthony Asquith, Leslie Howard *m Arthur Honegger*

Leslie Howard, Wendy Hiller, Wilfrid Lawson, Scott Sunderland, Marie Lohr, David Tree, Esmé Percy, Everley Gregg, Jean Cadell

'An exhibition of real movie-making – of a sound score woven in and out of tense scenes, creating mood and tempo and characterization.'—*Pare Lorentz*

Q

QB VII**
US 1974 312m colour TVM
Columbia / Douglas S. Cramer

A Jewish novelist accuses a Polish doctor of crimes against humanity while he was working in a Nazi concentration camp. The doctor sues.
Insanely long tele-epic intended to be screened in two parts. There are several good things in it, but half the time would have done, especially as it comes to no clear conclusion and an excellent documentary on the true facts lasted an hour.

w Edward Anhalt, novel Leon Uris *d* Tom Gries

Anthony Hopkins, Ben Gazzara, Leslie Caron, Edith Evans, Jack Hawkins, John Gielgud, Dan O'Herlihy, Juliet Mills, Lee Remick, Signe Hasso, Sam Jaffe, Milo O'Shea

Q Planes**
GB 1939 82m bw
Harefield / London Films (Irving Asher, Alexander Korda)
US title: *Clouds over Europe*

A secret ray helps spies to steal test aircraft during proving flights.
Lively comedy thriller distinguished by a droll leading performance.

w Brock Williams, Jack Whittingham, Arthur Wimperis *d Tim Whelan*

Ralph Richardson, Laurence Olivier, Valerie Hobson, George Merritt, George Curzon, Gus McNaughton, David Tree

Quackser Fortune Has a Cousin in the Bronx*
US 1970 90m Eastmancolor
UMC (John H. Cushingham)

An Irish layabout strikes up an acquaintance with an American student.
Likeable if plotless Dublin comedy, pleasantly photographed.

w Gabriel Walsh *d* Waris Hussein *ph* Gil Taylor *m* Michael Dress

Gene Wilder, Margot Kidder, Eileen Colgen, Seamus Ford

Quality Street*
US 1937 84m bw
RKO (Pandro S. Berman)

When an officer returns from the Napoleonic wars, he does not recognize his sweetheart, whose beauty has faded, so she masquerades as her own capricious niece.
Fairly successful attempt to capture on screen the essence of Barrie whimsy; everyone tries hard, anyway.

w Mortimer Offner, Allan Scott, *play* J. M. Barrie *d* George Stevens *ph* Robert de Grasse *m* Roy Webb

Katharine Hepburn, Franchot Tone, Fay Bainter, Eric Blore, Cora Witherspoon, Estelle Winwood, Florence Lake, Joan Fontaine

Quarantined
US 1970 74m colour TVM
Paramount

A case of cholera hits a hospital just as a kidney donor is needed.
Medical suspenser, not very interesting.

w Norman Katkov *d* Leo Penn

John Dehner, Gary Collins, Sharon Farrell, Wally Cox, Sam Jaffe

The Quare Fellow
GB 1962 90m bw
Anthony Havelock-Allan

Life in a Dublin prison when two men are to be hanged, as experienced by a new young warder.
Watered-down version of a rumbustious stage tragi-comedy, with not much but the gloom left.

wd Arthur Dreifuss, *play* Brendan Behan *ph* Peter Hennessey *m* Alexander Faris

Patrick McGoohan, Sylvia Syms, Walter Macken, Dermot Kelly, Hilton Edwards

Quartet***
GB 1948 120m bw
GFD / Gainsborough (Anthony Darnborough)

Four stories introduced by the author.
This entertaining production began the compendium fashion (*Full House, Phone Call from a Stranger,* etc) and is fondly remembered,

though all the stories had softened endings and the middle two did not work very well as drama. Subsequent Maugham compilations were *Trio* and *Encore* (both qv).

w R. C. Sherriff, stories W. Somerset Maugham m John Greenwood

THE FACTS OF LIFE *d* Ralph Smart *ph* Ray Elton

Basil Radford, Naunton Wayne, Mai Zetterling, Jack Watling, James Robertson Justice

THE ALIEN CORN *d* Harold French *ph* Ray Elton

Dirk Bogarde, Françoise Rosay, Raymond Lovell, Honor Blackman, Irene Browne

THE KITE *d* Arthur Crabtree *ph* Ray Elton

George Cole, Hermione Baddeley, Susan Shaw, Mervyn Johns, Bernard Lee

THE COLONEL'S LADY *d* Ken Annakin *ph* Reg Wyer

Cecil Parker, Linden Travers, Nora Swinburne, Ernest Thesiger, Felix Aylmer, Henry Edwards, Wilfrid Hyde White

Quatermass and the Pit**

GB 1967 97m Technicolor
Hammer / Anthony Nelson Keys
US title: *Five Million Years to Earth*

Prehistoric skulls are unearthed during London Underground excavations, and a weird and deadly force makes itself felt.
The third film of a Quatermass serial is the most ambitious, and in many ways inventive and enjoyable, yet spoiled by the very fertility of the author's imagination: the concepts are simply too intellectual to be easily followed in what should be a visual thriller. The climax, in which the devil rears over London and is 'earthed', is satisfactorily harrowing.

w Nigel Kneale, from his TV serial *d Roy Ward Baker ph* Arthur Grant *m* Tristam Cary

Andrew Keir, James Donald, Barbara Shelley, Julian Glover, Duncan Lamont, Edwin Richfield, Peter Copley

The Quatermass Experiment**

GB 1955 82m bw
Exclusive / Hammer (Anthony Hinds)
US title: *The Creeping Unknown*

When a rocketship returns from space, two of its three crew members have disappeared and the third is slowly taken over by a fungus which thrives on blood.
Intelligent science fiction based on a highly successful BBC TV serial; the film version is generally workmanlike despite its obvious low budget.

w Richard Landau, Val Guest, *serial Nigel Kneale d* Val Guest *ph* Jimmy Harvey

Brian Donlevy, Jack Warner, Margia Dean, *Richard Wordsworth,* David King Wood, Thora Hird, Gordon Jackson

Quatermass II**

GB 1957 85m bw
Hammer (Anthony Hinds)
US title: *Enemy from Space*

A research station operating under military secrecy is supposed to be making synthetic foods, but is in fact an acclimatization centre for invaders from outer space.
Simplified version of a TV serial, a bit stodgy in the talk scenes, but building into sequences of genuine alarm and based on an idea of lingering persuasiveness.

w Nigel Kneale, Val Guest, *serial Nigel Kneale d Val Guest ph* Gerald Gibbs *m* James Bernard

Brian Donlevy, John Longden, Sidney James, Bryan Forbes, William Franklyn, Charles Lloyd Pack, Percy Herbert, Tom Chatto

Queen Bee*

US 1955 95m bw
Columbia (Jerry Wald)

A wealthy woman has a compulsion to dominate everyone around her.
Claustrophobic southern-set melodrama obviously created for its star.

wd Ranald MacDougall, *novel* Edna Lee *ph* Charles Lang *m* Morris Stoloff

Joan Crawford, Barry Sullivan, Betsy Palmer, John Ireland, Lucy Marlow, William Leslie, Fay Wray

Queen Christina****

US 1933 101m bw
MGM (Walter Wanger)

The queen of 17th-century Sweden, distressed at the thought of a political marriage, goes wandering through her country in men's clothes and falls in love with the new Spanish ambassador.
The star vehicle par excellence, superb to look at and one of its star's most fondly remembered films. Historically it's nonsense, but put across with great style.

w Salka Viertel, H. M. Harwood, S. N. Behrman d Rouben Mamoulian ph William Daniels m Herbert Stothart

Greta Garbo, John Gilbert, Ian Keith, Lewis Stone,
C. Aubrey Smith, Reginald Owen, Elizabeth Young

'Garbo, as enchanting as ever, is still enveloped by her unfathomable mystery.'—*Photoplay*

Queen of Hearts*
GB 1936 80m bw
ATP (Basil Dean)

A working girl poses as a socialite and wins a matinee idol.
Stalwart romantic comedy with its star slightly more glamorized than usual.

w Clifford Grey, H. F. Maltby, Douglas Furber, Anthony Kimmins, Gordon Wellesley *d* Monty Banks

Gracie Fields, John Loder, Enid Stamp Taylor, Fred Duprez, Edward Rigby, Hal Gordon

The Queen of Spades***
GB 1948 96m bw
ABP / World Screen Plays

A Russian officer tries to wrest from an ancient countess the secret of winning at cards, in return for which he has sold her soul to the devil; but she dies of fright and haunts him.
Disappointingly slow-moving but splendidly atmospheric recreation of an old Russian story with all the decorative stops out; the chills when they come are quite frightening, the style is impressionist and the acting suitably extravagant.

w Rodney Ackland, Arthur Boys, *novel* Alexander Pushkin *d Thorold Dickinson ph Otto Heller m Georges Auric ad Oliver Messel*

Anton Walbrook, Edith Evans, Ronald Howard, Yvonne Mitchell, Mary Jerrold

Queen of the Mob*
US 1940 61m bw
Paramount

A murderess and her three sons are captured by the FBI.
Pacy crime melodrama from the *Persons in Hiding* series, based on the exploits of Ma Barker.

w Horace McCoy, William R. Lippmann *d* James Hogan *ph* Theodor Sparkuhl

Blanche Yurka, Ralph Bellamy, Jack Carson, Richard Denning, Paul Kelly, J. Carrol Naish, Jeanne Cagney, William Henry, James Seay, Hedda Hopper

Queen of the Stardust Ballroom**
US 1975 109m colour TVM
Robert Christianson, Rick Rosenberg

A middle-aged Bronx widow finds a new interest in life – the local dance hall.
Charming, well-written, homely drama reminiscent of *Marty*.

w Jerome Cass *d* Sam O'Steen

Maureen Stapleton, Charles Durning, Michael Brandon, Michael Strong

The Queen's Guards
GB 1960 112m Technicolor Cinemascope
TCF / Imperial (Michael Powell)

Reminiscences during trooping the colour of father and son guardsmen.
Incredibly old-fashioned family melodrama complete with skeleton in family closet; despite its date it has a decidedly pre-war air, except that it might have been more smartly done then.

w Roger Milner *d* Michael Powell *ph* Gerald Turpin *m* Brian Easdale

Raymond Massey, Daniel Massey, Robert Stephens, Ursula Jeans, Judith Stott, Elizabeth Shepherd, Duncan Lamont, Ian Hunter, Jack Watling

'This flagwaving museum piece would be distressing if it weren't so inept . . . [the actors] battle manfully with dialogue and characters as dated as a Crimean cavalry charge. The film could scarcely be taken as a tribute to the Guards except, just possibly, by elderly aunts in Cheltenham.'—*MFB*

Queimada!
France / Italy 1968 132m De Luxe
PEA / PPA (Alberto Grimaldi)
aka: *Burn!*

A diplomat is sent to a Caribbean island to break the Portuguese sugar monopoly and becomes involved with revolutionaries.
An indigestible attempt to combine adventure with the film of ideas; very tedious.

w Franco Solinas, Giorgio Arlorio *d* Gillo Pontecorvo *ph* Marcello Gatti *m* Ennio Morricone

Marlon Brando, Renato Salvatori, Norman Hill, Evaristo Marquez

Quentin Durward*
GB 1955 101m Eastmancolor Cinemascope
MGM (Pandro S. Berman)
aka: *The Adventures of Quentin Durward*

An elderly English lord sends his nephew to woo a French lady on his behalf; but the boy falls in love with her himself.
Haphazardly constructed and produced, but

quite enjoyable, period romp, with a bold black villain and several rousing set pieces including a final set-to on bell ropes.

w Robert Ardrey, *novel* Sir Walter Scott *d* Richard Thorpe *ph* Christopher Challis *m* Bronislau Kaper

Robert Taylor, Kay Kendall, Robert Morley, Alec Clunes, Marius Goring, Wilfrid Hyde White, Ernest Thesiger, Duncan Lamont, Harcourt Williams, Laya Raki, George Cole

The Quest*
US 1976 100m colour TVM
Columbia / David Gerber (Christopher Morgan)

Two brothers seek their sister who years ago was abducted by Indians.
Expensive pilot for a series which could go in any direction: the opener is simply glum.

w Tracy Keenan Wynn *d* Lee H. Katzin

Kurt Russell, Tim Matheson, Brian Keith, Neville Brand, Cameron Mitchell, Keenan Wynn, Will Hutchins

Quest for Love*
GB 1971 90m Eastmancolor
Rank / Peter Rogers Productions (Peter Eton)

After an explosion during an experiment, a young physicist finds himself living a different life, in love with a dying girl; returning to normal, he finds the girl and saves her.
Pleasing variation on *Berkeley Square*, quite well staged and played.

w Terence Feely, *story* Random Quest by John Wyndham Ralph Thomas *ph* Ernest Steward *m* Eric Rogers

Tom Bell, Joan Collins, Denholm Elliott, Laurence Naismith, Lyn Ashley

The Questor Tapes
US 1973 100m Technicolor TVM
Universal

A superstrong robot is partly human but has no emotions.
A rather boring bit of science fiction which was elbowed out of the series stakes by *Six Million Dollar Man*.

w Gene Roddenberry, Gene L. Coon *d* Richard A. Colla

Robert Foxworth, Mike Farrell, John Vernon, Lew Ayres, Dana Wynter, James Shigeta

Quick before It Melts
US 1964 97m Metrocolor Panavision
MGM / Biography (Douglas Lawrence, Delbert Mann)

A journalist is sent to cover a naval enterprise in the Antarctic, and gets a scoop despite his shyness.
Noisy service comedy with precious little plot.

w Dale Wasserman, *novel* Philip Benjamin *d* Delbert Mann *ph* Russell Harlan *m* David Rose

George Maharis, Robert Morse, Anjanette Comer, James Gregory, Howard St John, Janine Gray, Michael Constantine

'The combination of romantic dalliance, service high jinks and hectic journalism remains uniformly flat all through.'—*MFB*

Quick Let's Get Married
US 1965 100m colour
Golden Eagle (William Marshall)
aka: *The Confession, Seven Different Ways*

The voice of a sneak thief in a ruined church is taken by an unwed mother as a miracle.
Downright peculiar mishmash wasting interesting stars; an independent production by Rogers and husband in Jamaica.

w Allen Scott *d* William Dieterle *ph* Robert Bronner *m* Michael Colicchio

Ginger Rogers, Ray Milland, Barbara Eden, Walter Abel, Cecil Kellaway, Elliott Gould, Michael Ansara, David Hurst

Quick Millions**
US 1931 69m bw
Fox

An ambitious truck driver becomes a ruthless racketeer.
Fast-moving, otherwise naïve early gangster melodrama notable for Tracy's first star performance.

w Courtney Terrett, Rowland Brown, John Wray *d Rowland Brown* *ph* Joseph August

Spencer Tracy, Marguerite Churchill, Sally Eilers, Robert Burns, John Wray, George Raft

The Quiet American**
US 1957 122m bw
UA / Figaro (Joseph L. Mankiewicz)

An American in Saigon has naïve ideas for ending the war; he saves the life of a journalist who for various reasons becomes jealous and is duped into betraying the American to the communists.
Semi-successful excursion into the territory of Graham Greene, who as in *Brighton Rock* has allowed his ironic ending to be totally re-emphasized, here making the film anti-communist instead of anti-American.

wd Joseph L. Mankiewicz, novel Graham

Greene *ph* Robert Krasker *m* Mario Nascimbene

Michael Redgrave, Audie Murphy, Claude Dauphin, Giorgia Moll, Bruce Cabot, Fred Sadoff, Richard Loo

The Quiet Man***
US 1952 129m Technicolor
Republic / Argosy (John Ford, Merian C. Cooper)

An Irish village version of *The Taming of the Shrew*, the tamer being an ex-boxer retired to the land of his fathers and in need of a wife.
Archetypal John Ford comedy, as Irish as can be, with everything but leprechauns and the Blarney Stone on hand. Despite some poor sets the film has a gay swing to it, much brawling vigour and broad comedy, while the actors all give their roistering best.

w Frank Nugent, story Maurice Walsh *d John Ford ph Winton C. Hoch, Archie Stout m Victor Young*

John Wayne, Maureen O'Hara, Barry Fitzgerald, Victor McLaglen, Ward Bond, Mildred Natwick, Francis Ford, Arthur Shields, Eileen Crowe, Sean McClory, Jack McGowran

Quiet Please, Murder*
US 1943 70m bw
TCF (Ralph Dietrich)

Nazis and art thieves cause a high death rate in a public library.
Unusual, stylish second feature.

wd John Larkin ph Joe MacDonald

George Sanders, Kurt Katch, Gail Patrick, Richard Denning, Lynne Roberts, Sidney Blackmer, Byron Foulger

Quiet Wedding***
GB 1940 80m bw
Paramount / Conqueror (Paul Soskin)

Middle-class wedding preparations are complicated by family guests.
A semi-classic British stage comedy is admirably filmed with a splendid cast.

w Terence Rattigan, Anatole de Grunwald, play Esther McCracken d Anthony Asquith

Margaret Lockwood, Derek Farr, *A. E. Matthews, Marjorie Fielding, Athene Seyler, Peggy Ashcroft,* Margaretta Scott, Frank Cellier, Roland Culver, Jean Cadell, David Tomlinson, Bernard Miles
†Remade as *Happy is The Bride* (qv).

The Quiller Memorandum*
GB 1966 105m Eastmancolor Panavision
Rank / Ivan Foxwell / Carthay

A British secret service man is sent to Berlin to combat a neo-Nazi organization.
Disappointingly thin but smooth and watchable spy story.

w Harold Pinter, *novel* The Berlin Memorandum by Adam Hall (Elleston Trevor) *d* Michael Anderson *ph Erwin Hillier m* John Barry

George Segal, Max Von Sydow, Alec Guinness, Senta Berger, George Sanders, Robert Helpmann, Robert Flemyng

'In disposing of most of the storyline Pinter has virtually thrown out the baby with the bathwater; all that remains is a skeleton plot which barely makes sense and is totally lacking in excitement.'—*Brenda Davies*

Quo Vadis**
US 1951 171m Technicolor
MGM (Sam Zimbalist)

A Roman commander under Nero falls in love with a Christian girl and jealous Poppea has them both thrown to the lions.
Spectacular but stagey and heavy-handed Hollywood version of a much-filmed colossus which shares much of its plot line with *The Sign of the Cross.* Three hours of solemn tedium with flashes of vigorous acting and a few set pieces to take the eye; but the sermonizing does not take away the bad taste of the emphasis on physical brutality.

w John Lee Mahin, S. N. Behrman, Sonya Levien *d* Mervyn Le Roy *ph* Robert Surtees, William V. Skall *m* Miklos Rozsa *ad* Cedric Gibbons, Edward Carfagno, William Horning

Robert Taylor, Deborah Kerr, *Peter Ustinov, Leo Genn, Patricia Laffan,* Finlay Currie, Abraham Sofaer, Marina Berti, Buddy Baer, Felix Aylmer, Nora Swinburne, Ralph Truman, Norman Wooland

R

RPM (Revolutions Per Minute)
US 1970 97m colour
Columbia / Stanley Kramer

At an American college, a middle-aged professor teaches liberal ideas.
Dim, thankfully forgotten addition to the *Strawberry Statement* cycle.

w Erich Segal *d* Stanley Kramer *ph* Michel Hugo, Perry Botkin Jnr *m* Barry de Vorzon

Anthony Quinn, Ann-Margret, Gary Lockwood, Paul Winfield, Alan Hewitt

Rabbit, Run
US 1970 94m Technicolor Panavision
Warner

A man leaves his pregnant wife for a prostitute.
Uninteresting sex melodrama without any of the wit which distinguishes the book; hard to sit through.

w Howard B. Kreitsek, *novel* John Updike *d* Jack Smight *ph* Philip Lathrop *m* Ray Burton, Brian King

James Caan, Anjanette Comer, Arthur Hill, Jack Albertson, Carrie Snodgress

The Rabbit Trap*
US 1959 76m bw
UA / Canon (Harry Kleiner)

A hardworking draughtsman finally defies his boss and completes his holiday with his family.
Watchable minor drama just about marking the end of Hollywood's infatuation with TV plays which had begun with *Marty*; the moral and family problems of ordinary people were beginning to prove a shade lacking in excitement.

w J. P. Miller, from his TV play *d Philip Leacock ph* Irving Glassberg *m* Jack Marshall

Ernest Borgnine, Bethel Leslie, David Brian, Kevin Corcoran

Race with the Devil
US 1975 88m De Luxe
TCF / Saber / Maslansky (Wes Bishop)

Holidaymakers witness a black mass and are pursued by the diabolists.
Silly melodrama which resolves into a wild car chase and much violence.

w Lee Frost, Wes Bishop *d* Jack Starrett *ph* Robert Jessup *m* Leonard Rosenman

Peter Fonda, Warren Oates, Loretta Swit, Lara Parker, R. G. Armstrong

The Racers
US 1955 112m De Luxe Cinemascope
TCF (Julian Blaustein)
GB title: *Such Men Are Dangerous*

A Monte Carlo Rally contestant is financed by an attractive lady gambler.
Routine racing car melodrama, totally unmemorable but impersonally efficient.

w Charles Kaufman, *novel* Hans Ruesch *d* Henry Hathaway *ph* Joe MacDonald *m* Alex North

Kirk Douglas, Bella Darvi, Gilbert Roland, Cesar Romero, Lee J. Cobb, Katy Jurado, Charles Goldner, George Dolenz

Rachel and the Stranger*
US 1948 92m bw
RKO (Richard H. Berger)

A western farmer feels real love for his wife for the first time when an attractive stranger seems likely to take her away from him.
Modestly appealing romantic drama in a western setting.

w Martin Rackin, *novel* Howard Fast *d* Norman Foster *ph* Maury Gertsman *m* Constantin Bakaleinikoff

Loretta Young, Robert Mitchum, William Holden, Gary Gray, Tom Tully, Sara Haden, Frank Ferguson

Rachel, Rachel**
US 1968 101m Eastmancolor
Warner / Kayos (Paul Newman)

Events in the life of a middle-aged schoolmistress in a small New England town.
Appealing and freshly observed study of a limited personality in a small community.

w Stewart Stern, novel A Jest of God by

Margaret Laurence *d Paul Newman ph Gayne Rescher m* Jerome Moross

Joanne Woodward, Estelle Parsons, James Olson, Kate Harrington, Donald Moffat, Geraldine Fitzgerald, Bernard Barrow

'It could all very easily degenerate into a woman's weepy; and the fact that it doesn't is due largely to Newman's refusal to treat Manawaka as another Peyton Place.'—*Jan Dawson*

The Rack
US 1956 100m bw
MGM (Arthur M. Loew Jnr)

A veteran of the Korean War is courtmartialled for collaborating with the enemy under torture.
Dullish courtroom melodrama overstretched from a TV play.

w Stewart Stern, from his TV play *d* Arnold Laven *ph* Paul Vogel *m* Adolph Deutsch

Paul Newman, Walter Pidgeon, Edmond O'Brien, Lee Marvin, Cloris Leachman, Wendell Corey

The Racket*
US 1951 88m bw
RKO / Edmund Grainger

Police break up the empire of a powerful gangster.
Oddly timed and rather weak remake of the 1928 film; glossy but very old-fashioned in treatment.

w William Wister Haines, *play* Bartlett Cormack *d* John Cromwell *ph* George E. Diskant *m* Constantin Bakaleinikoff

Robert Ryan, Robert Mitchum, Ray Collins, Lizabeth Scott, William Talman

Raffles*
US 1940 72m bw
Samuel Goldwyn

Raffles the famous cricketer is also a compulsive and daring amateur thief.
Slight, modernized version of the turn-of-the century stories; very palatable, but it could have been better.

w John Van Druten, Sydney Howard, *novel* Raffles the Amateur Cracksman by E. W. Hornung *d* Sam Wood *ph* Gregg Toland *m* Victor Young

David Niven, Olivia de Havilland, *Dudley Digges*, May Whitty, Douglas Walton, Lionel Pape, E. E. Clive, Peter Godfrey

Rage
US 1966 103m Technicolor
Columbia / Joseph M. Schenck / Cinematografico Jalisco (Gilberto Gazcon)

A drunken doctor finds a new will to live during a difficult journey to avert a rabies epidemic.
Pattern melodrama with no surprises, but gripping most of the way.

w Teddi Sherman, Gilberto Gazcon, Fernando Mendez *d* Gilberto Gazcon *ph* Rosalio Solano *m* Gustavo Cesar Carreon

Glenn Ford, Stella Stevens, David Reynoso, Armando Silvestre

Rage
US 1972 99m De Luxe Panavision
Warner (Fred Weintraub)

A father takes revenge when his son dies after a chemical warfare accident.
Well-meaning but turgid and boring melodrama.

w Philip Friedman, Dan Kleinman *d* George C. Scott *ph* Fred Koenekamp *m* Lalo Schrifrin

George C. Scott, Richard Basehart, Martin Sheen, Barnard Hughes, Stephen Young

'Sluggish, tired and tiring.'—*Variety*

Rage in Heaven
US 1941 82m bw
MGM (Gottfried Reinhardt)

An unstable millionaire becomes jealous of his wife and arranges his own death so that her supposed lover will be suspected.
Stilted melodrama with the stars more or less at sea.

w Christopher Isherwood, Robert Thoeren, *novel* James Hilton *d* W. S. Van Dyke II *ph* Oliver T. Marsh *m* Bronislau Kaper

Robert Montgomery, Ingrid Bergman, George Sanders, Lucile Watson, Oscar Homolka, Philip Merivale, Matthew Boulton, Aubrey Mather

A Rage to Live
US 1965 101m bw Panavision
UA / Mirisch (Lewis J. Rachmil)

The unhappy college and married life of a nymphomaniac.
Well made but deliberately 'daring' case history which becomes too obvious and silly.

w John T. Kelley, *novel* John O'Hara *d* Walter Grauman *ph* Charles Lawton *m* Nelson Riddle

Suzanne Pleshette, Bradford Dillman, Ben Gazzara, Peter Graves, Bethel Leslie, James Gregory, Ruth White

'Stuff like this needs the exuberance of grand

opera; sadly, all it gets here is a blue note.'— *MFB*

The Raging Moon*
GB 1970 111m Technicolor
EMI (Bruce Cohn Curtis)
aka: *Long Ago Tomorrow*

A love affair develops between two inmates of a home for the physically handicapped.
Appealing romantic drama which nearly became a big commercial success.

wd Bryan Forbes, novel Bruce Marshall *ph* Tony Imi *m* Stanley Myers

Malcolm McDowell, Nanette Newman, Georgia Brown, Bernard Lee, Gerald Sim, Michael Flanders

The Raging Tide
US 1951 93m bw
U-I (Aaron Rosenberg)

A San Francisco gangster stows away on a fishing trawler and redeems himself when he perishes saving the life of a fisherman.
Fearfully old-fashioned seafaring melodrama, rather well made.

w Ernest K. Gann, from his novel Fiddler's Green *d* George Sherman *ph Russell Metty* *m* Frank Skinner

Richard Conte, Charles Bickford, Shelley Winters, Stephen McNally, Alex Nicol, Jesse White, John McIntire

The Ragman's Daughter
GB 1972 94m Technicolor
TCF / Penelope (Harold Becker)

A Nottingham layabout falls in love with an exciting middle-class girl; they fail to overcome parental opposition and she is killed in a road accident.
Wispy drama framed in pointless flashbacks; done on the cheap, it never seems to get anywhere and even fails to use its locations to advantage.

w Alan Sillitoe, from his short story *d* Harold Becker *ph* Michael Seresin *m* Kenny Clayton

Simon Rouse, Victoria Tennant, Patrick O'Connell, Leslie Sands

The Raid*
US 1954 83m Technicolor
TCF (Robert L. Jacks)

In 1864 six confederate soldiers escape from a union prison, and from a Canadian refuge carry out a revenge raid on a small Vermont town.
Interesting little action drama, crisply characterized and plotted, and based on a historical incident.

w Sidney Boehm, story Affair at St Albans by Herbert Ravenal Sass *d Hugo Fregonese* *ph Lucien Ballard* *m* Roy Webb

Van Heflin, Anne Bancroft, Richard Boone, Lee Marvin, Tommy Rettig, Peter Graves, Douglas Spencer, Will Wright, John Dierkes

Raid on Rommel
US 1971 99m Technicolor
Universal (Harry Tatelman)

In North Africa during World War II, a British officer releases prisoners of war and leads them in an assault on Tobruk.
Dispirited low-budget actioner apparently first intended for television.

w Richard Bluel *d* Henry Hathaway *ph* Earl Rath *m* Hal Mooney

Richard Burton, John Colicos, Clinton Greyn, Wolfgang Preiss

The Raiders
US 1964 75m Technicolor TVM
Universal

Bushwhacked cattle drivers get some famous westerners to help them.
Mildly fanciful western.

w Gene L. Coon *d* Herschel Daugherty

Robert Culp, Brian Keith, Judi Meredith, Alfred Ryder, Simon Oakland

The Railway Children***
GB 1971 108m Technicolor
EMI (Robert Lynn)

Three Edwardian children and their mother move into Yorkshire when their father is imprisoned as a spy, and have adventures on the railway line while helping to prove his innocence.
Fresh and agreeable family film with many pleasing touches to compensate for its meandering plot.

wd Lionel Jeffries, novel E. Nesbit *ph Arthur Ibbetson* *m* Johnny Douglas

Dinah Sheridan, William Mervyn, Jenny Agutter, Bernard Cribbins, Iain Cuthbertson, Gary Warren

Rain*
US 1932 92m bw
(UA)

Stranded passengers in Pago Pago during an epidemic include a prostitute and a missionary who lusts after her.
Early talkie version of a much filmed story;

interesting but not very entertaining now that the sensational aspects have worn off.

w Maxwell Anderson, *play* John Colton, Clemence Randolph, *story* W. Somerset Maugham *d* Lewis Milestone *ph* Oliver T. Marsh

Joan Crawford, Walter Huston, William Gargan, Beulah Bondi, Matt Moore, Guy Kibbee, Walter Catlett

† Other versions: *Sadie Thompson* (1928) with Gloria Swanson; *Miss Sadie Thompson* (1953) (qv).

Rainbow Island
US 1944 95m Technicolor
Paramount (I. D. Leshin)

A white girl brought up by her doctor father on a Pacific island is pursued by three sailors escaping from the Japanese.
Cheerful spoof of the sarong cycle with the star seeing the joke; otherwise a silly service farce with South Sea trimmings.

w Walter de Leon, Seena Owen, Arthur Phillips *d* Ralph Murphy *ph* Karl Struss *m* Roy Webb

Dorothy Lamour, Eddie Bracken, Gil Lamb, Barry Sullivan, Forrest Orr, Anne Revere, Reed Hadley, Marc Lawrence

The Rainbow Jacket
GB 1954 99m Technicolor
Ealing (Michael Relph)

A boy jockey is blackmailed into losing a big race.
Disappointing racecourse drama which packs in all the expected ingredients.

w T. E. B. Clarke *d* Basil Dearden

Kay Walsh, Bill Owen, Edward Underdown, Robert Morley, Wilfrid Hyde White, Charles Victor, Honor Blackman, Sidney James

The Rainmaker
US 1956 121m Technicolor
Vistavision
Paramount / Hal B. Wallis (Paul Nathan)

In 1913 Kansas, a fake rainmaker has more success melting the heart of a confirmed spinster.
Such a whimsical play is too talky to make a good movie, especially as the actors are over-age, their performances are mannered, the dialogue seems interminable and the production is too stagey.

w N. Richard Nash, from his play *d* Joseph Anthony *ph* Charles Lang Jnr *m* Alex North

Katharine Hepburn, Burt Lancaster, Wendell Corey, Lloyd Bridges, Earl Holliman, Cameron Prud'homme, Wallace Ford

The Rains Came***
US 1939 103m bw
TCF

High-class parasites in India during the Raj redeem themselves when a flood disaster strikes.
Wholly absorbing disaster spectacular in which the characterization and personal plot development are at least as interesting as the spectacle, and all are encased in a glowingly professional production.

w Philip Dunne, Julien Josephson, novel Louis Bromfield *d Clarence Brown ph Arthur Miller m Alfred Newman sp Fred Sersen*

Myrna Loy, *George Brent*, Tyrone Power, Brenda Joyce, *Maria Ouspenskaya, Joseph Schildkraut*, H. B. Warner, Nigel Bruce, Mary Nash, Jane Darwell, Marjorie Rambeau, Henry Travers

'It would be difficult to improve on the direction, the outbreak of the monsoon, a certain billowing in the breeze, a lamp casting the shadow of latticework against white silk, servants scattering for cover . . .'—*Charles Higham, 1972*

The Rains of Ranchipur
US 1955 104m Eastmancolor
Cinemascope
TCF (Frank Ross)

Dismal remake of *The Rains Came*, with bored actors and inferior production, all the character of the original being wiped out by badly processed wide-screen spectacle.

w Merle Miller *d* Jean Negulesco *ph* Milton Krasner *m* Hugo Friedhofer

Lana Turner, Fred MacMurray, Richard Burton, Joan Caulfield, Eugenie Leontovich, Michael Rennie

Raintree County
US 1958 166m Technicolor
Panavision (Camera 65)
MGM (David Lewis)

During the Civil War a southern belle gets the man she thinks she wants, but subsequently finds life as a schoolmaster's wife boring.
Dreary attempt by MGM to out-do *Gone with the Wind*, with neither characters nor plot one third as interesting and the production values merely expensive.

w Millard Kaufman, *novel* Ross Lockridge *d* Edward Dmytryk *ph* Robert Surtees *m* Johnny Green

Montgomery Clift, Elizabeth Taylor, Eva Marie Saint, Nigel Patrick, Lee Marvin, Rod Taylor,

Agnes Moorehead, Walter Abel, Jarma Lewis, Tom Drake, Gardner McKay, Rhys Williams

A Raisin in the Sun*
US 1961 128m bw
Columbia / Paman–Doris (David Susskind, Philip Rose)

The life of a struggling black family in a cramped Chicago flat.
Earnest but claustrophobic play-on-film which long outstays its welcome but contains good performances.

w Lorraine Hansberry, from her play *d* Daniel Petrie *ph* Charles Lawton Jnr *m* Laurence Rosenthal

Sidney Poitier, Ruby Dee, Claudia McNeil, Diana Sands, Ivan Dixon, John Fielder, Lou Gossett

The Rake's Progress**
GB 1945 123m bw
GFD / Individual (Frank Launder, Sidney Gilliat)
US title: *Notorious Gentleman*

The career of a cheerful ne'er-do-well playboy of the thirties.
The road to ruin played for light comedy, with silly endpapers in which, quite out of character, the rake becomes a war hero. Generally good production, witty script.

w Frank Launder, Sidney Gilliat d Sidney Gilliat

Rex Harrison, Lilli Palmer, Margaret Johnston, Godfrey Tearle, Griffith Jones, Guy Middleton, Jean Kent, Marie Lohr, Garry Marsh, David Horne, Alan Wheatley

Rally Round the Flag Boys
US 1958 106m De Luxe Cinemascope
TCF (Leo McCarey)

A small community protests at the siting nearby of a missile base.
Raucous service and sex comedy which becomes frenetic without ever being very funny.

w Claude Binyon, Leo McCarey, *novel* Max Shulman *d* Leo McCarey *ph* Leon Shamroy *m* Cyril Mockridge

Paul Newman, Joanne Woodward, Joan Collins, Jack Carson, Dwayne Hickman, Tuesday Weld, Gale Gordon, Murvyn Vye

Ramona
US 1936 90m Technicolor
TCF (Sol M. Wurtzel)

A half-breed girl and an Indian chief's son combat the greed of white pioneers.
Old-fashioned, stuffy adventure romance, much filmed in silent days.

w Lamar Trotti, *novel* Helen Hunt Jackson *d* Henry King *ph* William Skall, Chester Lyons *m* Alfred Newman

Loretta Young, Don Ameche, Kent Taylor, Pauline Frederick, Jane Darwell, Katherine de Mille, Victor Kilian, John Carradine

Rampage
US 1963 98m Technicolor
Warner Seven Arts / Talbot (William Fadiman)

Two white hunters love the same girl; one releases a tiger to harm the other, but it escapes.
Silly, unconvincing, old-style melodrama in which even the animals seem to overact.

w Robert Holt, Marguerite Roberts, *novel* Alan Caillou *d* Phil Karlson *ph* Harold Lipstein *m* Elmer Bernstein

Robert Mitchum, Jack Hawkins, Elsa Martinelli, Sabu, Emile Genest

Ramrod
US 1947 94m bw
UA (Harry Sherman)

A predatory lady ranch owner hires a tough foreman and her ruthlessness causes several deaths and a stampede.
Ho-hum minor western with fading stars.

w Jack Moffit, Graham Baker, Cecile Kramer, *story* Luke Short *d* André de Toth *ph* Russell Harlan *m* Adolph Deutsch

Veronica Lake, Joel McCrea, Preston Foster, Charles Ruggles, Donald Crisp, Arleen Whelan, Lloyd Bridges

Rancho De Luxe
US 1974 95m De Luxe
UA / EK (Anthony Ray)

Cheerful cattle rustlers go on a binge and end up in prison.
Modern anti-everything western; it's anti-entertainment as well.

w Thomas McGuane *d* Frank Perry *ph* William A. Fraker *m* Jimmy Buffett

Sam Waterston, Jeff Bridges, Elizabeth Ashley, Charlene Dallas, Clifton James, Slim Pickens

Rancho Notorious
US 1952 89m Technicolor
RKO / Fidelity (Howard Welsch)

A cowboy seeking revenge for his girl friend's murder follows a clue to a lonely ranch run by a saloon singer.

Curious western which seems to have been intended as another *Destry Rides Again* but is made in a hard inflexible style which prevents it from appealing.

w Daniel Taradash *d* Fritz Lang *ph* Hal Mohr *m* Emil Newman

Marlene Dietrich, Arthur Kennedy, Mel Ferrer, Gloria Henry, William Frawley, Jack Elam

Random Harvest***
US 1942 126m bw
MGM (Sidney Franklin)

A shell-shocked officer in the 1914–18 war escapes from an asylum, marries a music hall singer and is idyllically happy until a shock makes him remember that he is the head of a noble family. His wife, whom he does not now remember, dutifully becomes his secretary and years later another shock brings memory and happiness back.
A silly enough story works remarkably well in this rather splendid, no holds barred, roses round the door romance in Hollywood's best style with incomparable stars. A triumph of the Peg's Paper syndrome, and hugely enjoyable because it is done so enthusiastically.

w Claudine West, George Froeschel, Arthur Wimperis, *novel* James Hilton *d Mervyn Le Roy ph* Joseph Ruttenberg *m* Herbert Stothart

Ronald Colman, Greer Garson, Susan Peters, Philip Dorn, Reginald Owen, Edmund Gwenn, Henry Travers, Margaret Wycherly, Bramwell Fletcher, Arthur Margetson

'I would like to recommend this film to those who can stay interested in Ronald Colman's amnesia for two hours and who could with pleasure eat a bowl of Yardley's shaving soap for breakfast.'—*James Agee*

The Rangers
US 1974 74m Technicolor TVM
Universal / Jack Webb (Edwin Self)
aka: *Sierra*

Problems of rangers in Yosemite National Park.
Typical Webb multi-drama in which the more exciting rescue bits look fake. The resulting series, *Sierra*, was a dead loss.

w Robert A. Cinader, Michael Donovan, Preston Wood *d* Chris Nyby Jnr

James G. Richardson, Colby Chester, Jim B. Smith, Laurence Delaney

Ransom*
US 1955 104m bw
MGM (Nicholas Nayfack)

A rich man takes desperate measures to rescue his son from a kidnapper.
Solid but overlong suspenser, virtually a vehicle for a star at his twitchiest and most dogged.

w Cyril Hume, Richard Maibaum *d* Alex Segal *ph* Arthur E. Arling *m* Jeff Alexander

Glenn Ford, Donna Reed, Leslie Nielsen, Juano Hernandez, Robert Keith

Ransom*
GB 1975 98m Eastmancolor
Lion International (Peter Rawley)

A British ambassador to Scandinavia is kidnapped by terrorists and a Norwegian security chief gives chase.
Topical but unconvincing action thriller with unfamiliar detail; builds up to exciting sequences but is quickly forgotten.

w Paul Wheeler *d* Caspar Wrede *ph Sven Nykvist m* Jerry Goldsmith

Sean Connery, Ian McShane, Norman Bristow, John Cording, Isabel Dean, William Fox, Robert Harris

Ransom for a Dead Man**
US 1970 100m Technicolor TVM
Universal (Dean Hargrove)

A shabby police lieutenant outwits a murderous lady lawyer.
Second pilot for Columbo, and a good one. See *Prescription Murder*.

w Dean Hargrove *d* Richard Irving

Peter Falk, Lee Grant, John Fink, Harold Gould, Patricia Mattick

Rapture
US / France 1965 104m bw
International Classics / TCF (Christian Ferry)

A mentally unstable girl has a tragic romance with a fugitive murderer.
Gloomy all the way, and if it's art it needs explaining.

w Stanley Mann, *novel* Rapture in My Rags by Phyllis Hastings *d* John Guillermin *ph* Marcel Grignon

Patricia Gozzi, Dean Stockwell, Melvyn Douglas, Gunnel Lindblom

The Rare Breed
US 1966 97m Technicolor Panavision
Universal (William Alland)

An English bull is taken by its woman owner to St Louis to breed with American longhorns, and various frictions are caused among the ranchers.
Amusing western idea which misses fire by not coming down firmly as either drama or comedy; it does however pass the time amiably enough.

w Ric Hardman *d* Andrew V. McLaglen *ph* William H. Clothier *m* Johnny Williams

James Stewart, Maureen O'Hara, Brian Keith, Juliet Mills, Don Galloway, David Brian, Jack Elam, Ben Johnson

Rasputin and the Empress*
US 1932 133m bw
MGM (Irving Thalberg)

The story of the last years of the Russian court, when a sinister monk gained influence over the empress.
An unhappy film which was besieged by lawsuits and never generated much drama of its own despite starring the three Barrymores, who all seemed to be acting in separate rooms.
Production values are the most impressive thing about it.

w Charles MacArthur *d* Richard Boleslawski *ph* William Daniels *m* Herbert Stothart

John Barrymore, Ethel Barrymore, Lionel Barrymore, Diana Wynyard, Ralph Morgan, C. Henry Gordon, Edward Arnold, Jean Parker, Gustav Von Seyffertitz, Anne Shirley (Dawn O'Day)

The Rat Race*
US 1960 105m Technicolor
Paramount / Perlberg–Seaton

A young jazz musician and a dance hall hostess share a flat and face the adversities of New York.
A kind of sour fairy tale of the big city which has neither enough jokes nor enough incident but purveys the kind of charm that grows on one despite oneself.

w Garson Kanin, from his play *d* Robert Mulligan *ph* Robert Burks *m* Elmer Bernstein

Tony Curtis, Debbie Reynolds, Jack Oakie, Kay Medford, Don Rickles

'The New Yorkers of *The Rat Race* – noisy soft-hearted landlady, philosophical bartender, backchatting taxi driver – are as familiar as the settings of shabby apartment house and quiet little bar across the street. Film makers no longer need to invent here – they simply move in for a few weeks.'—*Penelope Houston*

Rattle of a Simple Man
GB 1964 95m bw
Sydney Box (William Gell)

A shy football supporter in London spends the night with a tart for a bet.
Archetypal farcical situation with sentiment added to string it out to twice its proper length.
Production values modest but adequate.

w Charles Dyer, from his play *d* Muriel Box *ph* Reg Wyer *m* Stanley Black

Harry H. Corbett, *Diane Cilento*, Thora Hird, Charles Dyer

The Raven*
US 1935 61m bw
Universal

A doctor obsessed by Poe-inspired torture devices transforms a gangster on the run into a hideous mutant.
Silly but quite effective horror film with memorable sequences.

w David Boehm *d* Lew Landers *ph* Charles Stumar

Bela Lugosi, Boris Karloff, Samuel S. Hinds, Irene Ware, Lester Matthews

The Raven*
US 1963 86m Pathecolor Panavision
AIP / Alta Vista (Roger Corman)

Two 15th-century conjurors fight a deadly duel of magic.
The rather splendid duel is a long time coming; the preliminaries are largely confined to chat in a single set, and the random jokes do not quite atone for the boredom.

w Richard Matheson *d* Roger Corman *ph Floyd Crosby* *m* Les Baxter

Vincent Price, Peter Lorre, Boris Karloff, Hazel Court, Jack Nicholson

Raw Wind in Eden
US 1958 93m Eastmancolor Cinemascope
U-I (William Alland)

A model is stranded on a Sardinian island, and falls in love with a mysterious American who turns out to be a disillusioned millionaire.
Wish-fulfilment woman's picture with the occasional relief of a smart line.

w Elizabeth and Richard Wilson *d* Richard Wilson *ph* Enzo Serafin *m* Hans Salter

Esther Williams, Jeff Chandler, Carlos Thompson, Rossana Podesta, Eduardo de Filippo, Rik Battaglia

Rawhide**
US 1950 86m bw
TCF (Samuel G. Engel)

Four escaped convicts terrorize a stagecoach stop.
Good suspense western with excellent technical credits.

w Dudley Nichols d Henry Hathaway ph Milton Krasner m Sol Kaplan

Tyrone Power, Susan Hayward, Hugh Marlowe, Jack Elam, Dean Jagger, George Tobias, Edgar Buchanan, Jeff Corey

The Razor's Edge*
US 1947 146m bw
TCF (Darryl F. Zanuck)

A well-to-do young man spends the years between the wars first idling, then looking for essential truth.
The novel was an empty parable with amusing trimmings. In the film the trimmings seem less amusing, but the presentation is glossy.

w Lamar Trotti, *novel* W. Somerset Maugham *d* Edmund Goulding *ph* Arthur Miller *m* Alfred Newman *ad* Richard Day, Nathan Juran

Tyrone Power, Gene Tierney, *Clifton Webb, Herbert Marshall,* John Payne, Anne Baxter, Lucile Watson, Frank Latimore, Elsa Lanchester, Fritz Kortner

'I like Somerset Maugham when he's looking through keyholes or down cracks, not at vistas.'—*Richard Winnington*

Reach for Glory*
GB 1962 86m bw
Columbia / Blazer (John Kohn, Jud Kinberg)

During World War II, evacuee boys play war games and a German refugee is accidentally killed.
Grim and unpalatable parable, competently rather than excitingly made.

w John Rae, from his novel The Custard Boys *d* Philip Leacock *ph* Bob Huke *m* Bob Russell

Kay Walsh, Harry Andrews, Michael Anderson Jnr, Oliver Grimm, Alexis Kanner, Martin Stephenson, Richard Vernon

Reach for the Sky*
GB 1956 135m bw
Rank / Pinnacle (Daniel M. Angel)

Douglas Bader loses both legs in a 1931 air crash, learns to walk on artificial limbs and flies again in World War II.
Box office exploitation of one man's personal heroism, adequately but not inspiringly put together with many stiff upper lips and much jocular humour.

wd Lewis Gilbert, *book* Paul Brickhill *ph* Jack Asher *m* John Addison

Kenneth More, Muriel Pavlow, Lyndon Brook, Lee Patterson, Alexander Knox, Dorothy Alison, Sydney Tafler, Howard Marion Crawford

Ready Willing and Able
US 1937 93m bw
Warner (Samuel Bischoff)

Two songwriters import an English leading lady for their new show.
Lightweight star musical with no outstanding qualities.

w Sig Herzig, Jerry Wald, Warren Duff *d* Ray Enright *ph* Sol Polito *ch* Bobby Connelly *songs* Johnny Mercer, Richard Whiting

Ruby Keeler, Ross Alexander, Lee Dixon, Wini Shaw, Jane Wyman, Allen Jenkins

The Real Glory*
US 1939 96m bw
Samuel Goldwyn

Soldiers of fortune help the American Army to quell a terrorist uprising in the Philippines just after the Spanish-American War.
Well made Gunga Dinnery.

w Jo Swerling, Robert R. Presnell *d* Henry Hathaway *ph* Rudolph Maté *m* Alfred Newman *ad* James Basevi

Gary Cooper, David Niven, Broderick Crawford, Andrea Leeds, Reginald Owen, Kay Johnson, Russell Hicks, Vladimir Sokoloff

Reap the Wild Wind**
US 1942 124m Technicolor
Paramount / Cecil B. de Mille

Seafaring salvage engineers fight over a southern belle.
Georgia-set period adventure; intended as another *Gone with the Wind,* it simply doesn't have the necessary, but on its level it entertains solidly, climaxing with the famous giant squid fight.

w Alan le May, Jesse Lasky Jnr *d Cecil B. de Mille ph* Victor Milner, Dewey Wrigley, William V. Skall *m* Victor Young *ad* Hans Dreier, Roland Anderson

Ray Milland, John Wayne, *Paulette Goddard,* Raymond Massey, Robert Preston, Lynne Overman, Susan Hayward, Charles Bickford, Walter Hampden, Louise Beavers, Martha O'Driscoll, Hedda Hopper

Rear Window***
US 1954 112m Technicolor
Alfred Hitchcock

A news photographer, confined to his room by a broken leg, sees a murder committed in a room on the other side of the court.
Artificial but fairly gripping suspenser of an unusual kind; with such restricted settings, all

depends on the script and the acting, and they generally come up trumps.

w John Michael Hayes, novel Cornell Woolrich *d Alfred Hitchcock ph* Robert Burks *m* Franz Waxman

James Stewart, Grace Kelly, Raymond Burr, Judith Evelyn, Wendell Corey, Thelma Ritter

Rebecca****
US 1940 130m bw
David O. Selznick

The naïve young second wife of a Cornish landowner is haunted by the image of his glamorous first wife Rebecca.
The supreme Hollywood entertainment package, set in Monte Carlo and Cornwall, with generous helpings of romance, comedy, suspense, melodrama and mystery, all indulged in by strongly-drawn characters, and directed by the new English wizard for the glossiest producer in town, from a novel which sold millions of copies. It really couldn't miss, and it didn't.

w Robert E. Sherwood, Joan Harrison, novel Daphne du Maurier d Alfred Hitchcock ph George Barnes m Franz Waxman

Laurence Olivier, Joan Fontaine, George Sanders, Judith Anderson, Nigel Bruce, Gladys Cooper, Florence Bates, Reginald Denny, C. Aubrey Smith, Melville Cooper, Leo G. Carroll, Leonard Carey

Rebecca of Sunnybrook Farm
US 1938 80m bw
TCF (Raymond Griffith)

A child performer becomes a pawn in the fight to exploit her talents on radio.
Unrecognizable revamping of a famous story makes a very thin star vehicle.

w Karl Tunberg, Don Ettlinger, *novel* Kate Douglas Wiggin *d* Allan Dwan *ph* Arthur Miller *songs* various

Shirley Temple, Randolph Scott, Jack Haley, Gloria Stuart, Phyllis Brooks, Helen Westley, Slim Summerville, Bill Robinson

The Rebel*
GB 1960 105m Technicolor
Associated British (W. A. Whitaker)
US title: *Call Me Genius*

A suburban businessman goes to Paris to become an artist.
A kind of farcical *The Moon and Sixpence,* insufficiently well tailored to the requirements of a very specialized comic, but occasionally diverting none the less.

w Alan Simpson, Ray Galton *d* Robert Day *ph* Gilbert Taylor *m* Frank Cordell

Tony Hancock, George Sanders, Paul Massie, Margit Saad, Grégoire Aslan, Dennis Price, Irene Handl, Mervyn Johns, Peter Bull, John Le Mesurier, Nanette Newman, Oliver Reed, John Wood

'The more prosaic the setting, the funnier Hancock seems; transplanted into a conventionally silly screen art world, he is submerged among the other grotesques.'—*Penelope Houston*

Rebel without a Cause**
US 1955 111m Warnercolor Cinemascope
Warner (David Weisbart)

The adolescent son of a well-to-do family gets into trouble with other kids and the police.
The first film to suggest that juvenile violence is not necessarily bred in the slums, this somewhat dreary melodrama also catapulted James Dean to stardom as the prototype fifties rebel.

w Stewart Stern d Nicholas Ray *ph* Ernest Haller *m* Leonard Rosenman

James Dean, Natalie Wood, Jim Backus, Sal Mineo, Ann Doran, Dennis Hopper, Nick Adams

Reckless
US 1935 96m bw
MGM (David O. Selznick)

A theatrical agent loves the glamorous star he represents, but she marries a drunken millionaire.
Remarkably flat backstage melodrama with music, based on the life of Libby Holman.

w P. J. Wolfson *d* Victor Fleming *ph* George Folsey *songs* various

Jean Harlow, William Powell, Franchot Tone, May Robson, Ted Healy, Nat Pendleton, Rosalind Russell, Henry Stephenson

The Reckless Moment*
US 1949 82m bw
Columbia (Walter Wanger)

A woman accidentally kills her daughter's would-be seducer, and is then trailed by a blackmailer.
Uninteresting melodrama electrified by Ophuls' direction, which might have been applied to something more worthwhile.

w Henry Garson, R. W. Soderborg, *novel* The Blank Wall by Elizabeth Sanxay Holding *d Max Ophuls ph* Burnett Guffey *m* Morris Stoloff

Joan Bennett, James Mason, Geraldine Brooks, Henry O'Neill, Shepperd Strudwick

'Swift, sure narrative and solidly pleasurable detail.'—*Richard Winnington*

The Reckoning**

GB 1969 108m Technicolor
Columbia / Ronald Shedlo (Hugh Perceval)

A tough London executive with a Liverpool-Irish background has a brutal streak and a self-destructive urge, but goes on narrowly averting misfortune.
Interesting melodrama of a man disgusted with both bourgeois and working-class values; slickly made and fast-moving.

w John McGrath, novel The Harp That Once by Patrick Hall *d Jack Gold ph Geoffrey Unsworth m* Malcolm Arnold

Nicol Williamson, Rachel Roberts, Paul Rogers, Zena Walker, Ann Bell, Gwen Nelson, J. G. Devlin

The Red Badge of Courage**

US 1951 69m bw
MGM (Gottfried Reinhardt)

A youth called up during the Civil War gets his first taste of battle.
Fresh, poetic, but dramatically unsatisfactory filming of a classic American novel. The story of its production is fascinatingly told in *Picture,* a book by Lillian Ross.

wd John Huston, novel Stephen Crane *ph Harold Rosson m Bronislau Kaper*

Audie Murphy, Bill Mauldin, Douglas Dick, Royal Dano, John Dierkes, Andy Devine, Arthur Hunnicutt

The Red Badge of Courage*

US 1974 74m colour TVM
TCF / Norman Rosemont

During the American Civil War, a shy youth gets his first taste of battle.
Adequate, uninspired TV remake.

w John Gay *d* Charles B. Fitzsimons

Richard Thomas, Michael Brandon, Wendell Burton, Warren Berlinger, Charles Aidman

Red Ball Express

US 1952 83 bw
U-I (Aaron Rosenberg)

A supply column runs from the Normandy beachhead to Patton's army on the outskirts of Paris.
Standard war adventure, not too convincingly mounted but providing the usual excitements.

w John Michael Hayes *d* Budd Boetticher *ph* Maury Gertsman

Jeff Chandler, Sidney Poitier, Alex Nicol, Judith Braun, Hugh O'Brian, Jack Kelly, Jack Warden

The Red Beret

GB 1953 88m Technicolor
Warwick (Irving Allen, Albert R. Broccoli)
US title: *Paratrooper*

In 1940, an American with a guilt complex joins the British paratroopers.
Routine war action flagwaver; good battle scenes, rubbish in between.

w Richard Maibaum, Frank Nugent, *book* Hilary St George Saunders *d* Terence Young *ph* John Wilcox *m* John Addison

Alan Ladd, Susan Stephen, Leo Genn, Harry Andrews, Donald Houston, Anthony Bushell, Patric Doonan, Stanley Baker, Lana Morris

The Red Danube

US 1950 119m bw
MGM (Carey Wilson)

In occupied Vienna, citizens are being returned to Russia against their will.
Tedious and silly Red-baiting cold war charade.

w Gina Kaus, Arthur Wimperis, *novel* Vespers in Vienna by Bryan Marshall *d* George Sidney *ph* Charles Rosher m Miklos Rozsa

Ethel Barrymore, Walter Pidgeon, Janet Leigh, Peter Lawford, Francis L. Sullivan, Angela Lansbury, Louis Calhern, Melville Cooper

Red Dust***

US 1932 86m bw
MGM

On a rubber plantation in Indo-China, the overseer is pursued by his engineer's bride but himself falls for a stranded prostitute.
Vigorous romantic melodrama with echoes of *Rain;* remade as *Congo Maisie* and *Mogambo.*

w John Lee Mahin, *play* Wilson Collison *d Victor Fleming ph* Harold Rosson

Clark Gable, Jean Harlow, Mary Astor, Gene Raymond, Donald Crisp, Tully Marshall, Forrester Harvey

'Gable and Harlow have full play for their curiously similar sort of good-natured toughness.'—*Time*

Red Garters**

US 1954 91m Technicolor
Paramount (Pat Duggan)

Various familiar types congregate in the western town of Paradise Lost, and settle matters by the Code of the West.
Amusing western musical spoof slightly deadened by its pretty but finally boring

theatrically stylized scenery. Songs are catchy, performances good natured.

w Michael Fessier d George Marshall *ph Arthur E. Arling* *m* Joseph J. Lilley *songs Jay Livingston, Ray Evans*

Rosemary Clooney, Guy Mitchell, Gene Barry, Jack Carson, Pat Crowley, Cass Daley, Frank Faylen, Reginald Owen

'A musical of considerable freshness and gaiety.'—*MFB*

Red Headed Woman*
US 1932 74m bw
MGM

A shopgirl marries the boss but is rejected in his social circles.
Unconvincing but occasionally entertaining melodrama.

w Anita Loos, *novel* Katharine Brush *d* Jack Conway *ph* Harold Rosson

Jean Harlow, Chester Morris, Lewis Stone, Leila Hyams, Una Merkel, Henry Stephenson, Charles Boyer, May Robson

The Red House*
US 1947 100m bw
Sol Lesser

A moody farmer's guilty obsession with an old house in the woods is that he murdered his parents in it.
Psycho-like suspense melodrama, too extended for comfort and too restricting for the actors, but effective in spurts.

wd Delmer Daves, *novel* George Agnew Chamberlain *ph* Bert Glennon *m* Miklos Rozsa

Edward G. Robinson, Judith Anderson, Lon McCallister, Allene Roberts, Rory Calhoun, Julie London, Ona Munson

Red Line 7000
US 1965 110m Technicolor
Paramount / Laurel (Howard Hawks)

The career and loves of a stock car racer.
Very routine romantic actioner full of the director's favourite situations but failing to find any fresh slant.

w George Kirgo *d* Howard Hawks *ph* Milton Krasner *m* Nelson Riddle

James Caan, Laura Devon, Gail Hire, Charlene Holt, John Robert Crawford

Red Mountain
US 1951 84m Technicolor
Paramount / Hal B. Wallis

A Confederate captain joins Quantrell's Raiders but is horrified by their brutality.
Fast-moving action western.

w John Meredyth Lucas, George W. George, George F. Slavin *d* William Dieterle *ph* Charles Lang Jnr *m* Franz Waxman

Alan Ladd, Lizabeth Scott, Arthur Kennedy, John Ireland, Jeff Corey, James Bell

Red Planet Mars
US 1952 87m bw
UA / Donald Hyde, Anthony Veiller

Americans and Russians both tune in to Mars and learn that it is a powerful Christian planet; the news causes first panic, then a religious revival and a determination to live more harmoniously on earth.
Lunatic farrago that has to be seen to be believed.

w Anthony Veiller, John L. Balderston *d* Harry Horner *ph* Joseph Biroc *m* David Chudnow *ad* Charles D. Hall

Herbert Berghof, Peter Graves, Andrea King, Marvin Miller

The Red Pony
US 1949 88m Technicolor
Republic (Lewis Milestone)

When his pet pony dies after an illness, a farmer's son loses faith in his father.
Sincere but rather obvious little fable which although capably made does not make inspiring film drama.

w John Steinbeck *d* Lewis Milestone *ph* Tony Gaudio *m* Aaron Copland pd Nicolai Remisoff

Myrna Loy, Robert Mitchum, Peter Miles, Louis Calhern, Shepperd Strudwick, Margaret Hamilton

The Red Pony*
US 1973 100m colour TVM
Universal / Omnibus (Frederick Brogger)

Well-meaning, overlong and dullish TV remake.

w Robert Totten, Ron Bishop *d* Robert Totten

Henry Fonda, Maureen O'Hara, Ben Johnson, Clint Howard

Red River**
US 1948 133m bw
UA / Monterey (Howard Hawks)

How the Chisholm Trail was developed as a cattle drive.
Brawling western, a bit serious and long drawn out but with splendid action sequences.

w Borden Chase, Charles Schnee *d Howard Hawks ph Russell Harlan m Dmitri Tiomkin*

John Wayne, Montgomery Clift, Joanne Dru,

Walter Brennan, Colleen Gray, John Ireland, Noah Beery Jnr, Harry Carey Jnr

Red Salute*
US 1935 78m bw
Edward Small
aka: *Runaway Daughter*; GB title: *Arms and the Girl*

A college girl with communist leanings takes a cross country trip with an American soldier.
Odd little romantic comedy modelled on *It Happened One Night*; it was picketed for its inconsequential attitude to politics.

w Humphrey Pearson, Manuel Seff *d* Sidney Lanfield *ph* Robert Planck

Barbara Stanwyck, Robert Young, Hardie Albright, Cliff Edwards, Ruth Donnelly, Gordon Jones, Henry Kolker

The Red Shoes****
GB 1948 136m Technicolor
GFD / The Archers *(Michael Powell, Emeric Pressburger)*

A girl student becomes a great ballet star but commits suicide when torn between love and her career.
Never was a better film made from such a penny plain story so unpersuasively written and performed; the splendour of the production is in the intimate view it gives of life backstage in the ballet world with its larger-than-life characters. The ballet excerpts are very fine, and the colour discreet; the whole film is charged with excitement.

wd Michael Powell, Emeric Pressburger ph Jack Cardiff m Brian Easdale pd Hein Heckroth

Anton Walbrook, Moira Shearer, Marius Goring, Robert Helpmann, Albert Basserman, Frederick Ashton, Leonide Massine, Ludmilla Tcherina, Edmond Knight

Red Skies of Montana
US 1952 99m Technicolor
TCF (Samuel G. Engel)

Tension among firefighting crews in the mountains of Montana.
Adequate, routine action melodrama with semi-documentary touches.

w Harry Kleiner *d* Joseph M. Newman *ph* Charles G. Clarke *m* Sol Kaplan

Richard Widmark, Jeffrey Hunter, Constance Smith, Richard Boone, Richard Crenna

Red Sky at Morning
US 1970 113m Technicolor
Universal / Hal Wallis

During World War II the family of an officer on active service find life in New Mexico not what they've been used to.
Peyton Place by any other name, well produced but of little real interest.

w Marguerite Roberts, *novel* Richard Bradford *d* James Goldstone *ph* Vilmos Zsigismond *m* Billy Goldenberg

Claire Bloom, Richard Thomas, Richard Crenna, Catherine Burns, Desi Arnaz Jnr, John Colicos, Harry Guardino

The Red Tent*
Italy / USSR 1970 121m Technicolor
Paramount / Vides / Mosfilm (Franco Cristaldi)

The story of General Nobile's ill-fated 1928 expedition by dirigible to the Arctic.
Stiffly-conceived international spectacular with one striking sequence but not much good cheer.

w Ennio de Concini, Richard Adams *d* Mikhail Kalatozov *ph Leonid Kalashnikov m* Ennio Morricone

Peter Finch, Sean Connery, Hardy Kruger, Claudia Cardinale, Mario Adorf, Massimo Girotti

Reflection of Fear
US 1971 90m Eastmancolor
Columbia (Howard B. Jaffe)

A retarded teenage girl kills her mother and her grandmother.
Psycho thriller of little interest or suspense.

w Edward Hume, Lewis John Carlino, *novel* Go to Thy Deathbed by Stanton Forbes *d* William A. Fraker *ph* Laszlo Kovacs *m* Fred Myrow

Robert Shaw, Mary Ure, Signe Hasso, Sondra Locke, Mitch Ryan

Reflections in a Golden Eye*
US 1967 108m Technicolor
Warner / Seven Arts (Ray Stark)

Repressions at a peacetime army camp in Georgia. A private soldier rides nude on horseback, a major has the hots for him, the major's wife has an affair with their neighbour, whose wife has cut off her nipples with garden shears.
A film as idiotic as its story line, but smoothly marshalled so that at least it's more amusing than boring.

w Chapman Mortimer, Gladys Hill, *novel* Carson McCullers *d John Huston ph Aldo Tonti* *pd* Stephen Grimes *m* Toshiro Mayuzumi

Marlon Brando, Elizabeth Taylor, Brian Keith, Julie Harris, Robert Forster, Zorro David

'One feels trapped in a huge overheated hothouse containing nothing but common snapdragons.'—*John Simon*

'Nothing more than nutty people and pseudo porn.'—*Judith Crist*

'Pedestrian, crass, and uninvolving to the point of repellence.'—*John Simon*

'Too much expressionistic foliage on the screen and too much declamatory thunder on the sound track.'—*Pauline Kael*

Reflections of Murder
US 1974 96m colour TVM
ABC Circle (Aaron Rosenberg)

At a remote boys' school, the headmaster's wife and mistress plot to murder him.
Dismal remake of *Les Diaboliques*, totally without pace or atmosphere.

w Carol Sobieski *d* John Badham

Sam Waterston, Joan Hackett, Tuesday Weld, Lucille Benson

The Reformer and the Redhead*
US 1950 90m bw
MGM (Norman Panama, Melvin Frank)

A small-town reform candidate abandons his crooked protector and wins under his own steam, helped by the daughter of the zoo superintendent.
Scatty sub-Capra comedy with a lightweight script but good production and playing.

wd Norman Panama, Melvin Frank *ph* Ray June *m* David Raksin

Dick Powell, June Allyson, Cecil Kellaway, David Wayne, Ray Collins, Robert Keith, Marvin Kaplan

Reign of Terror*
US 1949 88m bw
U-I
aka: *The Black Book*

During the French Revolution, a secret organization strives to overthrow Robespierre.
Unhistorical but quite stylish melodrama with an unusual cast and flavour.

w Philip Yordan, Aeneas Mackenzie *d Anthony Mann* *ph* John Alton *m* Sol Kaplan

Robert Cummings, Arlene Dahl, Richard Basehart, Richard Hart, Arnold Moss, Beulah Bondi

The Reincarnation of Peter Proud
US 1974 104m Technicolor
Avco Embassy / Bing Crosby (Frank P. Rosenberg)

A history professor is troubled by recurring dreams of his former existence.
Hysterical psychic melodrama which pretty well ruins its own chances by failing to explain its plot.

w Max Ehrlich, from his novel *d* J. Lee-Thompson *ph* Victor J. Kemper *m* Jerry Goldsmith

Michael Sarrazin, Jennifer O'Neill, Margot Kidder, Cornelia Sharpe, Paul Hecht

'It may well be the silliest approach to the subject in any medium ... all flashbacks trampling the action with the finesse of a rogue elephant.'—*Tom Milne*

The Reivers*
US 1970 111m Technicolor Panavision
Cinema Center / Duo / Solar (Irving Ravetch)

In Mississippi at the turn of the century a hired hand borrows the new family auto for a trip into Memphis with the grandson of the family and a black stablehand.
Pleasant but insubstantial yarn of more gracious days; most attractive to look at, it entertains gently without ever reaching a point.

w Irving Ravetch, Harriet Frank Jnr, *novel* William Faulkner *d* Mark Rydell *ph Richard Moore* *m* John Williams

Steve McQueen, Sharon Farrell, Will Geer, Rupert Crosse, Mitch Vogel, Michael Constantine, Juano Hernandez, Clifton James

The Reluctant Debutante*
US 1958 96m Metrocolor Cinemascope
MGM / Avon (Pandro S. Berman)

A noble couple have difficulty in steering their American-educated daughter through the intricacies of the London season.
A slight but pleasing British comedy has become a rather strident example of lease-lend, but still affords minor pleasures.

w William Douglas Home, from his play *d* Vincente Minnelli *ph* Joseph Ruttenberg *md* Eddie Warner *ad* Jean d'Aubonne

Rex Harrison, Kay Kendall, Sandra Dee, Peter Myers, Angela Lansbury, John Saxon, Diane Clare

The Reluctant Dragon**
US 1941 72m Technicolor
Walt Disney

A tour of the Disney Studios affords some glimpses of how cartoons are made.
Amiable pot-pourri of cartoon shorts *(Baby Weems, How to Ride a Horse* and the title story) linked by a studio tour of absorbing interest.

w various *d* Alfred Werker (live action), various

Robert Benchley, Frances Gifford, Nana Bryant

Reluctant Heroes*
GB 1951 80m bw
Byron (Henry Halstead)

Comedy of national servicemen and their misdemeanors.
Simple-minded army farce which was popular for years as play and film.

w Colin Morris, from his play *d* Jack Raymond

Brian Rix, Ronald Shiner, Derek Farr, Christine Norden, Larry Noble

The Reluctant Heroes
US 1971 73m colour TVM
Aaron Spelling
aka: *The Egghead on Hill 656*

A knowledge of history helps a lieutenant on foot patrol during the Korean War.
Thin war comedy, a long way before *M*A*S*H.*

w Herman Hoffman, Ernie Frankel *d* Robert Day

Ken Berry, Cameron Mitchell, Warren Oates, Jim Hutton, Ralph Meeker

The Reluctant Widow
GB 1950 91m bw
Rank / Two Cities (Gordon Wellesley)

During the Napoleonic wars a governess is co-opted as a spy.
Thin romantic drama which despite nice art direction never really sparks into life.

w Gordon Wellesley, J. B. Boothroyd, *novel* Georgette Heyer *d* Bernard Knowles *ph* Jack Hildyard *ad Carmen Dillon*

Jean Kent, Guy Rolfe, Kathleen Byron, Paul Dupuis, Lana Morris, Julian Dallas, Peter Hammond, Andrew Cruickshank

Remains to be Seen
US 1953 88m bw
MGM (Arthur Hornblow Jnr)

The manager of an apartment house finds a dead body, and before the police arrive someone sticks a knife into it.
Flabby comedy-thriller giving the cast little to work on.

w Sidney Sheldon, *play* Howard Lindsay, Russel Crouse *d* Don Weis *ph* Robert Planck *md* Jeff Alexander

June Allyson, Van Johnson, Angela Lansbury, Louis Calhern, John Beal, Dorothy Dandridge

The Remarkable Andrew*
US 1942 80m bw
Paramount (Richard Blumenthal)

A young municipal bookkeeper is framed by local politicians but helped by the ghost of Andrew Jackson and friends.
Pleasant, rather faded, whimsical comedy which also managed to be propaganda for the war effort.

w Dalton Trumbo *d* Stuart Heisler *ph* Theodor Sparkuhl

William Holden, Ellen Drew, Brian Donlevy, Rod Cameron, Richard Webb, Porter Hall, Frances Gifford, Nydia Westman, Montagu Love

The Remarkable Mr Pennypacker
US 1959 87m Technicolor Cinemascope
TCF

A Pennsylvania businessman leads two lives with two separate families.
Feeble and obvious period comedy of bigamy; very few laughs.

w Walter Reisch, *play* Liam O'Brien *d* Henry Levin *ph* Milton Krasner *m* Leigh Harline

Clifton Webb, Dorothy McGuire, Charles Coburn, Ray Stricklyn, Jill St John, Ron Ely, David Nelson

Rembrandt****
GB 1937 85m bw
London Films (Alexander Korda)

Episodes in the life of the 17th-century painter.
Austerely comic, gently tragic character piece, superbly staged and photographed, with a great performance at its centre.

w Lajos Biro, June Head, Carl Zuckmayer d Alexander Korda

Charles Laughton, Elsa Lanchester, Gertrude Lawrence, Edward Chapman, Walter Hudd, Roger Livesey, Herbert Lomas, Allan Jeayes, Sam Livesey, Raymond Huntley, John Clements

'Amazingly full of that light which the great master of painting subdued to his supreme purpose.'—*James Agate*

Remember?
US 1939 83m bw
MGM (Milton Bren)

A newly married couple do not get on, so a friend gives them a potion which makes them lose their

memories and fall in love all over again.
Silly, witless comedy which did no good for anyone concerned.

w Corey Ford, Norman Z. McLeod *d* Norman Z. McLeod *ph* George Folsey

Robert Taylor, Greer Garson, Lew Ayres, Billie Burke, Reginald Owen, George Barbier, Henry Travers, Richard Carle, Laura Hope Crews, Halliwell Hobbes, Sig Rumann

Remember Last Night?**
US 1936 80m bw
Universal

Socialites with hangovers find that murder was committed during their party.
Ingenious but overlong mixture of styles: farce, *Thin Man* comedy, murder mystery, satire, fantasy. Very well worth looking at.

w Harry Clark, Dan Totheroh, Doris Malloy, *novel* The Hangover Murders by Adam Hobhouse *d* James Whale *ph* Joseph Valentine

Robert Young, Edward Arnold, Arthur Treacher, Constance Cummings, Robert Armstrong, Sally Eilers, Reginald Denny, Ed Brophy, Jack La Rue, Gustav Von Seyffertitz, Gregory Ratoff

Remember the Day*
US 1941 86m bw
TCF (William Perlberg)

An elderly schoolteacher recollects her past life.
Pleasant sentimental drama, very well mounted.

w Tess Schlesinger, Frank Davis, Allan Scott, *play* Philo Higley *d* Henry King *ph* George Barnes

Claudette Colbert, John Payne, Shepperd Strudwick, Jane Seymour, Anne Revere, Frieda Inescort

Remember the Night*
US 1940 94m bw
Paramount (Mitchell Leisen)

An assistant district attorney takes a lady shoplifter home with him for Christmas.
Eccentric but winning blend of comedy, romance and drama, deftly mixed by master chefs.

w Preston Sturges d Mitchell Leisen ph Ted Tetzlaff *m* Frederick Hollander

Barbara Stanwyck, Fred MacMurray, Beulah Bondi, Elizabeth Patterson, Sterling Holloway, Paul Guilfoyle, Willard Robertson

Remember When*
US 1973 96m colour TVM
Danny Thomas

Problems of a Connecticut family in wartime.
Rather untidily assembled nostalgia with a warmly sentimental core.

w Herman Raucher *d* Buzz Kulik

Jack Warden, Nan Martin, William Schallert

Rendezvous
US 1935 106m bw
MGM (Lawrence Weingarten)

A decoding expert breaks an enemy spy ring.
Agreeable light romantic comedy drama with an espionage plot.

w Bella and Samuel Spewack, *novel* Black Chamber by Herbert Yardley *d* William K. Howard *ph* William Daniels *m* William Axt

William Powell, Rosalind Russell, Binnie Barnes, Lionel Atwill, Cesar Romero, Samuel S. Hinds, Henry Stephenson, Frank Reicher

Rentadick
GB 1972 94m Eastmancolor
Rank / Paradise / Virgin (Ned Sherrin)

Incompetent private eyes become involved in the battle for a deadly nerve gas.
Ineffective crazy comedy which never takes shape, preferring to aim barbs of satire in all directions.

w John Cleese, Graham Chapman *d* Jim Clark *ph* John Coquillon *m* Carl Davis

James Booth, Richard Briers, Julie Ege, Donald Sinden, Roy Kinnear

Repeat Performance*
US 1947 93m bw
Eagle / Lion

People in trouble find they can repeat the previous year.
Adequate flashback fantasy, very dated now.

w Walter Bullock *d* Alfred L. Werker *ph* Lew O'Connell

Louis Hayward, Joan Leslie, Tom Conway, Richard Basehart, Virginia Field

Report to the Commissioner
US 1974 112m Metrocolor
UA / M. J. Frankovich
GB title: *Operation Undercover*

A policeman's son follows in father's footsteps but finds life around Times Square dismaying.
Realistic, concerned crime melodrama with nothing very new to say.

w Abby Mann, Ernest Tidyman, *novel* James Mills *d* Milton Katselas *ph* Mario Tosi *m* Elmer Bernstein

Michael Moriarty, Yaphet Kotto, Susan Blakely, Hector Elizondo, Tony King, Michael McGuire

'A clear also-ran in the police thriller stakes.' —*Verina Glaessner*

The Reptile*
GB 1966 90m Technicolor
Hammer (Anthony Nelson Keys)

A Cornish village is terrified by several mysterious and unpleasant deaths; it turns out that the daughter of the local doctor, victim of a Malayan sect, periodically turns into a deadly snake.
Silly horror story most effectively filmed as a mixture of chills, detection and good characterization.

w John Elder d John Gilling ph Arthur Grant *m* Don Banks

Noel Willman, Jennifer Daniel, Ray Barrett, Jacqueline Pearce, Michael Ripper, John Laurie, Marne Maitland

Repulsion**
GB 1965 105m bw
Compton / Tekli (Gene Gutowski)

A Belgian manicurist in London is driven by pressures into neurotic withdrawal; terrified above all by sex, she locks herself up in her gloomy flat and murders her boy friend and landlord when they try to approach her.
Weird, unmotivated but undeniably effective Grand Guignol in the form of a case history; little dialogue, which is just as well as the director at that time clearly had no ear for the language.

w Roman Polanski, Gerard Brach *d Roman Polanski ph Gilbert Taylor m* Chico Hamilton

Catherine Deneuve, Ian Hendry, John Fraser, Patrick Wymark, Yvonne Furneaux

Requiem for a Heavyweight*
US 1962 87m bw
Columbia (David Susskind)
GB title: *Blood Money*

The last bouts of a prizefighter who will not realize his career is over.
Tough, effective melodrama, extremely well acted.

w Rod Serling, from his TV play *d Ralph Nelson ph Arthur J. Ornitz m* Laurence Rosenthal

Anthony Quinn, *Jackie Gleason, Mickey Rooney,* Julie Harris, Stan Adams, Madame Spivy, Jack Dempsey, Cassius Clay

Resurrection
US1931 81m bw
Universal

In 1870s Russia, a peasant girl is seduced by a prince and bears his child.
Unremarkable version of a much-filmed melodrama.

w Finis Fox, *novel* Leo Tolstoy *d* Edwin Carewe *ph* Robert B. Kurrie, Al Green *m* Dmitri Tiomkin

Lupe Velez, John Boles, Nance O'Neil, William Keighley, Rose Tapley
† See also: *We Live Again.*

Retreat, Hell!
US 1952 95m bw
(Warner) United States (Milton Sperling)

Adventures of a Marine unit in the Korean War.
Standard war film.

w Milton Sperling, Ted Sherdeman *d* Joseph H. Lewis *ph* Warren Lynch *m* William Lava

Frank Lovejoy, Richard Carlson, Anita Louise, Russ Tamblyn

Return from the Ashes*
GB 1965 104m bw Panavision
UA / Mirisch (J. Lee-Thompson)

A woman returns from Dachau to find that her husband is living with her step-daughter and that they plan to murder her.
Broken-backed thriller melodrama, the first half of which is quite irrelevant to the second. The whole is modestly inventive for those who don't mind a mixture of *Enoch Arden, Psycho* and *Dial M for Murder* with a touch of the concentration camps and a background of post-war misery.

w Julius J. Epstein, *novel* Hubert Monteilhet *d* J. Lee-Thompson *ph Christopher Challis* *m* Johnny Dankworth

Ingrid Thulin, Maximilian Schell, Samantha Eggar, Herbert Lom

The Return of a Man Called Horse*
US 1976 125m De Luxe Panavision
UA / Sandy Howard / Richard Harris

The English nobleman of *A Man Called Horse* goes back to the west to save his adopted Indian tribe from extinction.
Another 'realistic' action adventure with torture highlights; nicely made, but not for the squeamish.

w Jack de Witt *d* Irvin Kershner *ph Owen Roizman m Laurence Rosenthal*

Richard Harris, Gale Sondergaard, Geoffrey Lewis, Bill Lucking, Jorge Luke
†At 17 minutes, this pre-title sequence must be the longest so far.

The Return of Dr X*
US 1939 62 bw
Warner (Bryan Foy)

A modern vampire terrorizes the city.
Minor thriller which doesn't get going till the last reel; only notable for Bogart's appearance as the monster. Nothing to do with *Dr X*.

w Lee Katz, *novel* The Doctor's Secret by William J. Makin *d* Vincent Sherman *ph* Sid Hickox

Dennis Morgan, Rosemary Lane, Wayne Morris, Humphrey Bogart, Olin Howland, John Litel

The Return of Dracula*
US 1958 77m bw
UA / Gramercy (Jules V. Levy, Arthur Gardner)
GB title: *The Fantastic Disappearing Man*

A European vampire makes his way to an American small town in the guise of a refugee Iron Curtain painter.
Quite nicely made low-budget horror film with a good balance of the supernatural and the ordinary.

w Pat Fielder *d Paul Landres ph* Jack McKenzie *m* Gerald Fried

Francis Lederer, Norma Eberhardt, Ray Stricklyn, Jimmie Baird, John Wengraf

The Return of Frank James*
US 1940 92m Technicolor
TCF (Darryl F. Zanuck)

A sequel to *Jesse James (*qv).
Moody, nicely photographed western in which Jesse's brother avenges his murder.

w Sam Hellman *d Fritz Lang ph* George Barnes, William V. Skall *m* David Buttolph

Henry Fonda, Gene Tierney, Jackie Cooper, Henry Hull, John Carradine, J. Edward Bromberg, Donald Meek, Eddie Collins, George Barbier

The Return of Joe Forrester*
US 1975 74m colour TVM
Columbia

Problems of a cop on the beat.
Adequate pilot for an adequate series, relying heavily on its star.

w Mark Rodgers *d* Virgil W. Vogel

Lloyd Bridges, Pat Crowley, Jim Backus, Dane Clark, Charles Drake, Dean Stockwell, Della Reese, Janis Paige, Edie Adams, Tom Drake, Eddie Egan, Hari Rhodes

The Return of the Bad Men
US 1948 90m bw
RKO (Nat Holt)

A farmer tries to reform the female leader of a terrorist outlaw gang, but she is killed in a bank raid.
Standard, well shot western which contrives to introduce a number of well-known historical bandits.

w Charles O'Neal, Jack Netteford, Luci Ward *d* Ray Enright *ph* J. Roy Hunt *m* Constantin Bakaleinikoff

Randolph Scott, Robert Ryan, Anne Jeffreys, Jacqueline White, Steve Brodie

The Return of the Gunfighter
US 1967 98m colour TVM
MGM
aka: *As I Rode Down from Laredo*

An ex-gunslinger avenges the death of a Mexican girl's parents.
Sluggish low-budget western.

w Robert Buckner *d* James Neilson

Robert Taylor, Chad Everett, Ana Martin, Lyle Bettger, Michael Pate

The Return of the Pink Panther*
GB 1974 113m De Luxe Panavision
UA / Jewel / Pimlico / Mirisch / Geoffrey (Blake Edwards)

When the Pink Panther diamond – national treasure of the Eastern state of Lugash – is once again stolen, bungling Inspector Clouseau is called in.
Rehash of jokes from *The Pink Panther* (qv), not bad in parts but a rather tedious whole.

w Frank Waldman, Blake Edwards *d* Blake Edwards *ph* Geoffrey Unsworth *m Henry Mancini*

Peter Sellers, Christopher Plummer, Herbert Lom, Catherine Schell, Peter Arne, Peter Jeffrey, Grégoire Aslan, David Lodge, Graham Stark

'The film never comes fully to the boil, but simmers in a series of self-contained, self-destructing little set pieces.'—*Richard Combs*

The Return of the Scarlet Pimpernel*
GB 1937 94m bw
London Films (Alexander Korda, Arnold Pressburger)

Sir Percy Blakeney saves his wife and other French aristos from the guillotine.
Predictable, stylish revolutionary romance, much thinner in plot and performance than its predecessor.

w Lajos Biro, Arthur Wimperis, Adrian Brunel *d* Hans Schwarz

Barry K. Barnes, Sophie Stewart, Margaretta Scott, James Mason, *Henry Oscar,* Francis Lister, Anthony Bushell

The Return of the Seven
US 1966 95m Technicolor Panavision
UA / Mirisch / CB (Ted Richmond)

The seven gunmen, slightly reconstituted, fight again to rescue some kidnapped farmers.
The mixture as before (see *The Magnificent Seven*); adequate but scarcely inspired.

w Larry Cohen *d* Burt Kennedy *ph* Paul Vogel *m* Elmer Bernstein

Yul Brynner, Robert Fuller, Julian Mateos, Warren Oates, Claude Akins, Virgilio Texeira, Emilio Fernandez, Jordan Christopher

The Return of the Vampire*
US 1943 69m bw
Columbia

Dracula reappears amid the London blitz.
Surprisingly well made and complexly plotted horror film; it looks good and only lacks humour. The wolf man, however, is a regrettable intrusion.

w Griffin Jay *d Lew Landers ph John Stumar, L. J. O'Connell m* Morris Stoloff

Bela Lugosi, Nina Foch, Frieda Inescort, Miles Mander, Matt Willis, Roland Varno, Ottola Nesmith

The Return of the World's Greatest Detective
US 1976 74m Technicolor TVM
Universal (Roland Kibbee, Dean Hargrove)
aka: *Alias Sherlock Holmes*

A motor cycle cop has an accident and recovers believing himself to be Sherlock Holmes.
Inept spoof apparently inspired by *They Might Be Giants* (qv), and originally intended to become a series within *Mystery Movie.* No way.

w Roland Kibbee, Dean Hargrove *d* Dean Hargrove *ph* William Mendenhall *m* Dick de Benedictus

Larry Hagman, Jenny O'Hara, Nicholas Colasanto, Woodrow Parfrey, Ivor Francis

Return to Macon County
US 1975 89m Movielab
AIP / Macon Service Company (Eliot Schick)

In the fifties, two wandering youths pick up a waitress and have serious trouble with a manic policeman in America's unfriendliest area.
Slam-bang sequel to *Macon County Line,* rather unintentionally comic.

wd Richard Compton *ph* Jacques Marquette *m* Robert O. Ragland

Nick Nolte, Don Johnson, Robin Mattson, Robert Viharo

Return to Paradise*
US 1953 109m Technicolor
UA / Aspen (Theron Warth)

A peace seeker settles on a tiny South Sea island and leaves when his wife dies; he returns after World War II with his daughter.
Curious idyll, slow but not displeasing.

w Charles Kaufman, *novel* James Michener *d* Mark Robson *ph* Winton Hoch *m* Dmitri Tiomkin

Gary Cooper, Barry Jones, Roberta Haynes, Moira MacDonald

Return to Peyton Place*
US 1961 122m De Luxe Cinemascope
TCF / API (Jerry Wald)

Constance Mackenzie's daughter writes a novel about Peyton Place and falls in love with the publisher.
More closets are unlocked, more skeletons fall out; for addicts, the sequel does not disappoint, and it's all very glossy.

w Ronald Alexander *d* Jose Ferrer *ph* Charles G. Clarke *m* Franz Waxman

Jeff Chandler, Carol Lynley, Eleanor Parker, *Mary Astor,* Robert Sterling, Luciana Paluzzi, Brett Halsey, Tuesday Weld

'Enough soap suds to pollute the Mississippi along with the mind.'—*Judith Crist, 1973*

Returning Home
US 1976 75m colour TVM
Lorimar

After World War II, three veterans pick up their lives in a small midwestern town.
Pointless potted version of *The Best Years of Our Lives* (qv); it did not make a series.

w John McGreevey, Bill Svanoe *d* Daniel Petrie

Dabney Coleman, Tom Selleck, Joan Goodfellow, Whitney Blake, James Miller

Reunion in France
US 1943 104m bw
MGM (Joseph L. Mankiewicz)
GB title: *Mademoiselle France*

A selfish Parisian dress designer gradually realizes that her world has changed when the Nazis invade and she is asked to help an American flier.

Action flagwaver which tries also to be a woman's picture and goes pretty soppily about it.

w Jan Lustig, Marvin Borowsky, Marc Connelly, *story* Ladislas Bus-Fekete *d* Jules Dassin *ph* Robert Planck *m* Franz Waxman

Joan Crawford, John Wayne, Philip Dorn, Reginald Owen, Albert Basserman, John Carradine, Ann Ayars, J. Edward Bromberg, Henry Daniell, Moroni Olsen, Howard da Silva

'Miss Crawford isn't making all the sacrifices implied in the script... Dressing like a refugee is certainly not in her contract.'—*New York Herald Tribune*

Reunion in Vienna*

US 1933 100m bw
MGM

A long-exiled nobleman tries to take up an old romance even though the lady is married.
Lacklustre adaptation of a play which must have style; the performances remain interesting.

w Ernest Vajda, Claudine West, *play* Robert E. Sherwood *d* Sidney Franklin *ph* George Folsey

John Barrymore, Diana Wynyard, Frank Morgan, May Robson, Eduardo Ciannelli, Una Merkel, Henry Travers

Revenge

GB 1971 89m Eastmancolor
Rank / Peter Rogers Productions (George H. Brown)

When children are raped and murdered in a north country town, two men take the law into their own hands.
Crude melodrama set in Cold Comfort Farm country; efficient but unrewarding.

w John Kruse *d* Sidney Hayers *ph* Ken Hodges *m* Eric Rodgers

Joan Collins, Sinead Cusack, James Booth, Ray Barrett, Kenneth Griffith

Revenge!

US 1971 73m colour TVM
Aaron Spelling (Mark Carliner)

A man is lured and locked up in a cellar by a crazy woman who thinks he has wronged her.
Heavy-going melodrama with the star well over the top.

w Joseph Stefano, *novel* Elizabeth Davis *d* Jud Taylor

Shelley Winters, Bradford Dillman, Carol Rossen, Stuart Whitman

The Revenge of Frankenstein

GB 1958 89m Technicolor
Columbia / Hammer (Anthony Hinds)

Baron Frankenstein evades the guillotine and makes a new creature with the brain of a homicidal dwarf.
Dullish horror farrago with a few indications of quirkish humour.

w Jimmy Sangster, Hurford Janes *d* Terence Fisher *ph* Jack Asher *m* Leonard Salzedo

Peter Cushing, Michael Gwynn, Oscar Quitak, Francis Matthews, Eunice Gayson, John Welsh, Lionel Jeffries, Richard Wordsworth, Charles Lloyd Pack, John Stuart, Arnold Diamond

† This second Hammer Frankenstein set the tone for the rest; see *The Curse of Frankenstein.*

The Revengers

US 1972 108m De Luxe Panavision
Cinema Center / Martin Rackin

A rancher gathers a posse to hunt down the Indians who have allegedly murdered his wife and family.
Standard major western with a dismal script which echoes *The Dirty Dozen* and *The Wild Bunch*: sometimes repulsive, seldom exciting.

w Wendell Mayes *d* Daniel Mann *ph* Gabriel Torres *m* Pino Calvi

William Holden, Ernest Borgnine, Susan Hayward, Woody Strode, Roger Hanin

The Revolt of Mamie Stover

US 1956 93m Eastmancolor Cinemascope
TCF (Buddy Adler)

A dance hall girl leaves San Francisco for Honolulu, makes money there but reforms for love of a rich novelist.
Absurdly bowdlerized and boring film version of a novel about a sleazy prostitute; hardly worth making at all in this form, especially as the cast seems well capable of a raunchier version.

w Sidney Boehm, *novel* William Bradford Huie *d* Raoul Walsh *ph* Leo Tover *m* Hugo Friedhofer

Jane Russell, Agnes Moorehead, Richard Egan, Joan Leslie

The Revolutionary

US 1970 101m Technicolor
(UA) Pressman–Williams (Edward R. Pressman)

Episodes in the life of a revolutionary, from distributing leaflets to attempted assassination.
A rather casual study of one man's radicalism, in no particular time or place; no doubt of great interest to other revolutionaries.

w Hans Konigsberger *d* Paul Williams *ph* Brian Probyn *m* Michael Small

Jon Voight, Jennifer Salt, Robert Duvall

The Reward
US 1965 92m De Luxe Cinemascope
TCF / Aaron Rosenberg

A mixed group of adventurers set out across the desert to capture a murderer; but thieves fall out. Pretentious and talky melodrama which quickly scuttled its director's chances in Hollywood. Little action, obvious outcome, attractive Death Valley locations.

w Serge Bourgignon, Oscar Mullard, *novel* Michael Barrett *d* Serge Bourgignon *ph Joe MacDonald* *m* Elmer Bernstein

Max Von Sydow, Efrem Zimbalist Jnr, Yvette Mimieux, Gilbert Roland, Emilio Fernandez, Henry Silva

Rex Harrison Presents Three Stories of Love
US 1974 100m Technicolor TVM
Universal
aka: *Three Faces of Love*

Three stories ranging from uninteresting to inept. *Epicac* by Kurt Vonnegut, *Kiss Me Again Stranger* by Daphne du Maurier, *The Fortunate Painter* by Somerset Maugham. Harrison doesn't help.

w Liam O'Brien, Arthur Dales, John T. Kelley *d* John Badham, Arnold Laven, Jeannot Szwarc

Julie Sommars, Bill Bixby, Roscoe Lee Browne, Lorne Greene, Leonard Nimoy, Juliet Mills, Agnes Moorehead

Rhapsody
US 1954 116m Technicolor
MGM (Lawrence Weingarten)

A wealthy woman affects the lives of two quite different musicians, each of whom has his weakness.
Tedious romantic drama which vainly attempted a smart veneer but boasted a splendid musical sound track.

w Fay and Michael Kanin, *novel* Maurice Guest by Henry Handel Richardson *d* Charles Vidor *ph* Robert Planck *md* Johnny Green, Bronislau Kaper *pianist* Claudio Arrau *violinist* Michael Rabin

Elizabeth Taylor, Vittorio Gassman, John Ericson, Louis Calhern, Michael Chekhov, Barbara Bates, Celia Lovsky, Richard Hageman

Rhapsody in Blue**
US 1945 139m bw
Warner (Jesse L. Lasky)

The life story of composer George Gershwin. No more trustworthy on factual matters than other Hollywood biopics of its era, this rather glum saga at least presented the music and the performers to excellent advantage.

w Howard Koch, Elliot Paul *d Irving Rapper* *ph Sol Polito* *md* Leo F. Forbstein *ch* Le Roy Prinz *ad* Anton Grot, John Hughes

Robert Alda, Joan Leslie, Alexis Smith, Charles Coburn, Julie Bishop, *Albert Basserman, Oscar Levant, Herbert Rudley*, Rosemary de Camp, Morris Carnovsky, *Al Jolson, Paul Whiteman*, George White, Hazel Scott

Rhino
US 1964 91m Metrocolor
MGM / Ivan Tors (Ben Chapman)

A scientist working with white rhinos is joined by an unscrupulous big game hunter.
Inoffensive African adventure.

w Art Arthur, Arthur Weiss *d* Ivan Tors *ph* Sven Persson, Lamar Boren *m* Lalo Schifrin

Harry Guardino, Robert Culp, Shirley Eaton

Rhodes of Africa*
GB 1936 91m bw
Gaumont (Geoffrey Barkas)
US title: *Rhodes*

A rough-hewn diamond miner becomes Prime Minister of Cape Colony.
Heavy-going but generally interesting historical drama shot on location.

w Michael Barringer, Leslie Arliss, Miles Malleson, *book* Sarah Millin *d* Berthold Viertel

Walter Huston, Oscar Homolka, Basil Sydney, Peggy Ashcroft, Frank Cellier, Bernard Lee, Lewis Casson

Rhubarb
US 1951 94m bw
Paramount (Perlberg–Seaton)

A millionaire leaves his fortune, including a baseball team, to a wild ginger cat, which means problems for his publicity agent.
Typical scatty farce of the early fifties, held together by the splendid performance of the disdainful feline in the title role rather than by any special merit in the handling.

w Dorothy Reid, Francis Cockrill, *novel* H. Allen Smith *d* Arthur Lubin *ph* Lionel Lindon *m* Van Cleave

Ray Milland, Jan Sterling, Gene Lockhart, William Frawley

Rhythm on the Range*
US 1936 87m bw
Paramount (Benjamin Glazer)

A hired hand saves the boss's daughter when she is kidnapped by local badmen.
Easy-going musical comedy with a western background, later remade as *Pardners* (qv).

w John C. Moffett, Sidney Salkow, Walter de Leon, Francis Martin *d* Norman Taurog *ph* Karl Struss *songs* various

Bing Crosby, Martha Raye, Frances Farmer, Bob Burns, Lucile Watson, Samuel S. Hinds, George E. Stone, Warren Hymer

Rhythm on the River*
US 1940 92m bw
Paramount (William Le Baron)

A song writer employs 'ghosts' to produce his music and lyrics; they discover this fact and go into business for themselves.
Cheerful musical with strong billing.

w Dwight Taylor, Billy Wilder, Jacques Théry *d* Victor Schertzinger *ph* Ted Tetzlaff *m* Johnny Burke, James V. Monaco

Bing Crosby, Mary Martin, Basil Rathbone, Oscar Levant, Oscar Shaw, Charley Grapewin, William Frawley

Rich and Strange*
GB 1932 83m bw
BIP (John Maxwell)

A young couple come into money and take a trip around the world.
Slight, agreeable early talkie with a few Hitchcock touches.

w Alma Reville, Val Valentine, Alfred Hitchcock *d Alfred Hitchcock* *ph* Jack Cox, Charles Martin *m* Hal Dolphe

Henry Kendall, Joan Barry, Percy Marmont, Betty Amann, Elsie Randolph

The Rich Are Always with Us
US 1932 73m bw
Warner (Sam Bischoff)

A socialite determines on a divorce but her new love is annoyed by her concern for her ex-husband.
Cocktail drama of a kind which totally disappeared from the screen.

w Austin Parker, *novel* E. Pettit *d* Alfred E. Green *ph* Ernest Haller *m* W. Franke Harling

Ruth Chatterton, George Brent, John Miljan, Bette Davis, Adrienne Dore, Mae Madison, Robert Warwick

Rich Man, Poor Man**
US 1976 550m approx Technicolor TVM
Universal (Harve Bennett)

The contrasting lives of two sons of a baker after World War II.
Designed to be shown as a serial in hour or two-hour parts, this mammoth enterprise has its importance as the first attempt by American commercial television to serialize a novel (which Britain had been doing for years). As a production it is average: the narrative, especially the sexier parts of it, is what keeps one watching.

w Dean Riesner, *novel* Irwin Shaw *d* David Greene

Nick Nolte, Peter Strauss, Susan Blakely, Dorothy McGuire, *Ed Asner*, Ray Milland, Gloria Grahame, Bill Bixby, Van Johnson, Dorothy Malone, Robert Reed, Lynda Day George, George Maharis, Kim Darby, Kay Lenz, Murray Hamilton, Craig Stevens

Rich Man's Folly
US 1931 80m bw
Paramount

A rich man has no time for his children.
Curious updating of Dickens' *Dombey and Son*; not really a success.

w Grover Jones, Edward Paramore Jnr *d* John Cromwell *ph* David Abel

George Bancroft, Frances Dee, Robert Ames, Juliette Compton, Dorothy Peterson

Rich, Young and Pretty
US 1951 95m Technicolor
MGM (Joe Pasternak)

A Texas rancher takes his young daughter to Paris, where she meets her real mother.
Moderate musical.

w Dorothy Cooper, Sidney Sheldon *d* Norman Taurog *ph* Robert Planck *m* Nicholas Brodsky *ly* Sammy Cahn *ch* Nick Castle

Danielle Darrieux, Wendell Corey, Jane Powell, Fernando Lamas, Vic Damone

Richard III***
GB 1956 161m Technicolor Vistavision
London Films (Laurence Olivier)

Shakespeare's play about Richard Crookback, his seizure of the throne and his defeat at Bosworth.
Theatrical but highly satisfying filming of a splendidly melodramatic view of history. Interesting but not fussy camera movement,

delightful sets (followed by a disappointingly 'realistic' battle) and superb performances.

w William Shakespeare (adapted by Laurence Olivier, Alan Dent, with additions) *d Laurence Olivier ph Otto Heller ph Roger Furse m William Walton ad Carmen Dillon*

Laurence Olivier, Claire Bloom, *Ralph Richardson, Cedric Hardwicke*, Stanley Baker, Alec Clunes, John Gielgud, Mary Kerridge, Pamela Brown, Michael Gough, Norman Wooland, Helen Haye, Patrick Troughton, Clive Morton, Andrew Cruickshank

The Ride Back*

US 1957 79m bw
UA / Associates and Aldrich (William Conrad)

A lawman arrests an outlaw wanted for murder, but has the problem of getting him back to base. Slightly offbeat low-budget western, well enough done if it had to be done at all.

w Anthony Ellis *d* Allen H. Miner *ph* Joseph Biroc *m* Frank de Vol

Anthony Quinn, William Conrad, George Trevino, Lita Milan

Ride beyond Vengeance

US 1966 100m Technicolor
Columbia / Tiger / Goodson / Todman / Sentinel / Fenady

A young westerner, accused of cattle rustling and branded, vows revenge.
Dourly brutal but studio-bound and very padded western; if there is any entertainment value it doesn't emerge for more than a few moments.

w Andrew J. Fenady, *novel* The Night of the Tiger by Al Dewlen *d* Bernard McEveety *ph* Lester Shorr *m* Richard Markowitz

Chuck Connors, Michael Rennie, Kathryn Hays, Claude Akins, Bill Bixby, Paul Fix, Gary Merrill, Joan Blondell, Gloria Grahame, Ruth Warrick, Arthur O'Connell, Frank Gorshin, James MacArthur
† Probably intended as a TV movie and found too violent.

Ride the High Country**

US 1962 94m Metrocolor Cinemascope
MGM (Richard E. Lyons)
GB title: *Guns in the Afternoon*

Two retired lawmen help transport gold from a mining camp to the bank, but one has ideas of his own.
Thoughtful western graced by ageing star presences; generally well done.

w N. B. Stone Jnr *d Sam Peckinpah ph* Lucien Ballard *m* George Bassman

Joel McCrea, Randolph Scott, Edgar Buchanan, Mariette Hartley, James Drury

'A nice little conventional unconventional western.'—*Stanley Kauffmann*

Ride the Pink Horse*

US 1947 101m bw
U-I

An ex-serviceman visits a New Mexican town in search of the gangster who killed his buddy. Dour, complex melodrama with a certain amount of style but not enough substance.

w Charles Lederer, *novel* Dorothy B. Hughes *d* Robert Montgomery *ph* Russell Metty *m* Frank Skinner

Robert Montgomery, Wanda Hendrix, Andrea King, Thomas Gomez, Fred Clark, Art Smith

Ride the Wild Surf

US 1964 101m Eastmancolor
Columbia / Jana (Jo and Art Napoleon)

Surf riders go to Hawaii and find romance. Pleasant, overlong, open air fun and games.

w Jo and Art Napoleon *d* Don Taylor *ph* Joseph Biroc *m* Stu Phillips

Fabian, Shelley Fabares, Tab Hunter, Barbara Eden

Ride the Wind

US 1965 95m colour TVM
NTA / NBC

The Cartwright family gets involved with the expansion of the Pony Express.
Bonanza material telescoped into a feature.

w Paul Schneider *d* William Witney

Lorne Greene, Dan Blocker, Michael Landon, Victor Jory, Rod Cameron

Ride, Vaquero

US 1953 90m Anscocolor
MGM (Stephen Ames)

Ranchers settling in New Mexico after the Civil War cause some natives to turn bandit; one of them has a mysterious American associate called Rio.
Very mildly interesting western with the stars rather swamping a humourless script.

w Frank Fenton *d* John Farrow *ph* Robert Surtees *m* Bronislau Kaper

Robert Taylor, Ava Gardner, Howard Keel, Anthony Quinn, Charlita

Riders to the Stars*

US 1954 81m Color Corporation
UA / Ivan Tors

Rocket scientists investigate the problems of cosmic bombardment.
Enjoyably straightforward science fiction with no monsters or political problems; it has decided historic interest as a record of what scientists in 1954 thought rocket travel would be like.

w Curt Siodmak *d* Richard Carlson *ph* Stanley Cortez *m* Harry Sukman

Richard Carlson, Herbert Marshall, William Lundigan, Dawn Addams, Martha Hyer, Robert Karnes, Lawrence Dobkin

Riding High
US 1943 88m Technicolor
Paramount (Fred Kohlmar)

A burlesque queen goes home to Arizona and helps ranchers by performing at a dude ranch.
Dim formula musical with exuberance but neither wit nor style.

w Walter de Leon, Arthur Phillips, Art Arthur, *play* Ready Money by James Montgomery *d* George Marshall *ph* Karl Struss, Harry Hallenberger *md* Victor Young

Dorothy Lamour, Dick Powell, Victor Moore, Gil Lamb, Cass Daley, Bill Goodwin, Rod Cameron, Glenn Langan, Andrew Tombes, Tim Ryan, Douglas Fowley, Milt Britton and his Band

Riding High*
US 1950 112m bw
Paramount (Frank Capra)

An easygoing racing man forsakes the chance of wealth to train his beloved horse for the Imperial Derby.
The director's familiar ingredients—farce, sentimentality, fast cutting, nice people and a lot of noise—seem a shade too tried and tested in this remake of his 1934 success *Broadway Bill*. Despite the cast, the result is only moderately entertaining.

w Robert Riskin *d* Frank Capra *ph* George Barnes, Ernest Laszlo *m* James Van Heusen *ly* Johnny Burke

Bing Crosby, Coleen Gray, Charles Bickford, Raymond Walburn, James Gleason, Oliver Hardy, Frances Gifford, William Demarest, Ward Bond, Clarence Muse, Percy Kilbride, Harry Davenport, Margaret Hamilton, Douglass Dumbrille, Gene Lockhart

Riff Raff
US 1935 90m bw
MGM (Irving Thalberg)

A con man and his wife end up on the wrong side of the law.
Modest comedy drama that never quite sparks.

w Frances Marion, H. W. Haneman, Anita Loos *d* Robert Z. Leonard

Jean Harlow, Spencer Tracy, Joseph Calleia, Una Merkel, Mickey Rooney, Victor Kilian, J. Farrell MacDonald

Riff Raff*
US 1947 80m bw
RKO

A dying man hands a Panama City con man a map to valuable oil deposits, and various shady people are after it.
Rather heavy but well made comedy-drama with some striking scenes.

w Martin Rackin *d* Ted Tetzlaff *ph* George E. Diskant *m* Roy Webb

Pat O'Brien, Walter Slezak, Anne Jeffreys, Percy Kilbride, Jerome Cowan

The Right Approach
US 1961 92m bw Cinemascope
TCF (Oscar Brodney)

A Hollywood opportunist tries to make it as a star.
A potentially witty Hollywood story is sabotaged by a style which is as naïve as it is dismal; and Mr Vaughan's hopes of stardom unfairly ended right here.

w Fay and Michael Kanin, *play* Garson Kanin *d* David Butler *ph* Sam Leavitt *m* Dominic Frontière

Frankie Vaughan, Martha Hyer, Juliet Prowse, Gary Crosby, David MacLean, Jesse White, Jane Withers

Right Cross
US 1950 90m bw
MGM (Armand Deutsch)

A boxing champion injures his hand and has to abandon his career.
Rather dull sporting melodrama with a Mexican background, saved by good production values.

w Charles Schnee *d* John Sturges *ph* Norbert Brodine *m* David Raksin

Dick Powell, June Allyson, Lionel Barrymore, Ricardo Montalban

The Ring
US 1952 79m bw
King Brothers

A young Mexican becomes a prizefighter in the hope of winning greater respect for Mexican-Americans.
Well-meant low-budget programmer.

w Irving Shulman *d* Kurt Neumann *ph* Russell Harlan *m* Herschel Burke Gilbert

Gerald Mohr, Lalo Rios, Rita Moreno, Robert Arthur

Ring of Bright Water*
GB 1969 107m Technicolor
Palomar / Brightwater (Joseph Strick)

A civil servant buys a pet otter and moves to a remote cottage in the western Highlands.
Disneyesque fable for animal lovers, from a bestselling book.

w Jack Couffer, Bill Travers, *book* Gavin Maxwell *d* Jack Couffer *ph* Wolfgang Suschitsky *m* Frank Cordell

Bill Travers, Virginia McKenna, Peter Jeffrey, Roddy McMillan, Jameson Clark

Ring of Fear
US 1954 88m Warnercolor Cinemascope
Warner / Wayne–Fellows (Robert M. Fellowes)

A homicidal maniac returns to the circus where he used to work and causes various 'accidents'.
Tediously predictable circus melodrama with a curious but not very likeable cast.

w Paul Fix, Philip MacDonald, James Edward Grant *d* James Edward Grant *ph* Edwin DuPar *m* Emil Newman, Arthur Lange

Clyde Beatty, Pat O'Brien, Mickey Spillane, Sean McClory, Marion Carr, John Bromfield, Pedro Gonzalez Gonzalez, Emett Lynn

Ring of Fire
US 1961 90m Metrocolor
MGM / Andrew and Virginia Stone

An Oregon sheriff is kidnapped by teenage delinquents but manages to lead them into both a police trap and a forest fire.
Outdoor action thriller with a plot which is ludicrously unconvincing in detail, though the fire scenes impress.

wd Andrew L. Stone *ph* William H. Clothier *m* Duane Eddy

David Janssen, Joyce Taylor, Frank Gorshin, Joel Marston

Ring of Spies*
GB 1963 90m bw
British Lion (Leslie Gilliatt)
US title: *Ring of Treason*

How the Portland spy ring was tracked down.
Documentary drama, rather less intriguing, somehow, than the actual facts; but the sheer thought of spies in the suburbs keeps interest going.

w Frank Launder, Peter Barnes *d* Robert Tronson *ph* Arthur Lavis

Bernard Lee, Margaret Tyzack, David Kossoff, Nancy Nevinson, William Sylvester

The Ringer*
GB 1952 78m bw
BL / London (Hugh Perceval)

A dangerous criminal known only as The Ringer threatens to kill the crooked lawyer responsible for his sister's death.
Artful old-fashioned mystery, quite well restaged, and in fact the best extant example of filmed Wallace.

w Val Valentine, *novel* and *play* Edgar Wallace *d* Guy Hamilton *ph* Ted Scaife *m* Malcolm Arnold

Donald Wolfit, Mai Zetterling, Herbert Lom, Greta Gynt, William Hartnell, Norman Wooland

Rings on Her Fingers*
US 1942 85m bw
TCF (Milton Sperling)

The front girl for a couple of confidence tricksters falls in love with their first victim.
Lively comedy which drags into drama in its second half.

w Ken Englund *d* Rouben Mamoulian *ph* George Barnes *m* Cyril Mockridge

Gene Tierney, Henry Fonda, Laird Cregar, Spring Byington, Shepperd Strudwick, Frank Orth, Henry Stephenson, Marjorie Gateson

Rio
US 1939 78m bw
Universal

A crooked financier escapes from Devil's Island to join his wife in Rio, only to find she has been unfaithful.
Modest but well made melodrama.

w Stephen Morehouse Avery, Frank Partos, Edwin Justus Mayer, Abem Kandel, Jean Negulesco *d John Brahm* *ph* Hal Mohr *m* Charles Previn

Basil Rathbone, Victor McLaglen, Sigrid Gurie, Robert Cummings, Leo Carrillo, Billy Gilbert, Irving Bacon, Irving Pichel

Rio Bravo**
US 1959 141m Technicolor
Warner (Howard Hawks)

A wandering cowboy and a drunken sheriff hold a town against outlaws.

Cheerfully overlong and slow-moving western in which everybody, including the director, does his thing. All very watchable for those with time to spare, but more a series of revue sketches than an epic.

w Jules Furthman, Leigh Brackett *d Howard Hawks* *ph* Russell Harlan *m* Dmitri Tiomkin

John Wayne, Dean Martin, Ricky Nelson, Angie Dickinson, Walter Brennan, Ward Bond, John Russell, Pedro Gonzalez Gonzalez, Claude Akins, Harry Carey Jnr, Bob Steele

Rio Conchos*
US 1964 107m De Luxe Cinemascope
TCF (David Weisbart)

Two thousand rifles are stolen from an army command port and traced to the hide-out of a former Confederate colonel who wants to continue the Civil War.
Good standard western which shares much of its story line with *The Comancheros.*

w Clair Huffaker, Joseph Landon *d* Gordon Douglas *ph* Joe MacDonald *m* Jerry Goldsmith

Richard Boone, Edmond O'Brien, Stuart Whitman, Tony Franciosa

Rio Grande*
US 1950 105m bw
Republic (John Ford, Merian C. Cooper)

A Cavalry unit on the Mexican border in the 1880s conducts a vain campaign against marauding Indians.
Thin Ford western on his favourite theme, with too many pauses for song, too many studio sets, and too little plot. *Aficianodos*, however, will find much to admire.

w James Kevin McGuinness, *story* James Warner Bellah *d* John Ford *ph* Bert Glennon, Archie Stout *m* Victor Young

John Wayne, Maureen O'Hara, Ben Johnson, Claude Jarman Jnr, Harry Carey Jnr, Chill Wills, J. Carrol Naish, Victor McLaglen

Rio Lobo*
US 1970 114m Technicolor
Cinema Center (Howard Hawks)

A union colonel near the end of the Civil War recovers a gold shipment and exposes a traitor.
Rambling western with traces of former glory, enjoyable at least for its sense of humour.

w Leigh Brackett, Burton Wohl *d* Howard Hawks *ph* William Clothier *m* Jerry Goldsmith

John Wayne, Jorge Rivero, Jennifer O'Neill, *Jack Elam,* Victor French, Chris Mitchum, Mike Henry

Rio Rita
US 1929 135m bw and Technicolor
RKO (William Le Baron)

Romance on a ranch near the Mexican border.
Very early talkie version of a popular Broadway operetta of the twenties; historical interest only.

w Luther Reed, Russell Mack, *book* Guy Bolton, Fred Thomson, as produced by Florenz Ziegfeld *d* Luther Reed *ph* Robert Kurle, Lloyd Knetchel *md* Victor Baravalle *songs* Harry Tierney, Joe McCarthy

Bebe Daniels, John Boles, Bert Wheeler, Robert Woolsey, Dorothy Lee, Don Alvarado, George Renavent

Rio Rita
US 1942 91m bw
MGM (Pandro S. Berman)

Flat-footed remake bringing in Nazi spies; poor comedy even by Abbott and Costello standards.

w Richard Connell, Gladys Lehman *d* S. Sylvan Simon *ph* George J. Folsey

Bud Abbott, Lou Costello, John Carroll, Kathryn Grayson, Tom Conway, Barry Nelson

Riot
US 1968 98m Technicolor
Paramount / William Castle

While the warden is away, thirty-five convicts take over a state penitentiary and are violently subdued.
Strikingly bloody melodrama set in an actual prison in Arizona; well made, but less entertaining than Cagney and Raft used to be.

w James Poe, *novel* Frank Elli *d* Buzz Kulik *ph* Robert B. Hauser *m* Christopher Komeda

Gene Hackman, Jim Brown, Ben Carruthers, Mike Kellin, Gerald O'Loughlin, Clifford David

Riot in Cell Block Eleven*
US 1954 80m bw
Allied Artists / Walter Wanger

In a big American prison three convicts seize their guards, free the other prisoners and barricade themselves in their block.
Socially concerned low-budgeter, quite nicely made and persuasive of the need for prison reform.

w Richard Collins d Don Siegel ph Russell Harlan *m* Herschel Burke Gilbert

Neville Brand, *Emile Meyer,* Frank Faylen, Leo Gordon, Robert Osterloh, Paul Frees, Don Keefer

'As a compassionate, angry, unsensational account of an episode of violence it makes

considerably more impact than many of the overblown melodramas currently in fashion.'
—*Penelope Houston*

Riptide*
US 1934 90m bw
MGM (Irving Thalberg)

A British diplomat weds a Manhattan chorus girl, but she later falls for an old flame.
Elegantly set, star-packed drawing-room drama which somehow didn't click.

wd Edmund Goulding *ph* Ray June *m* Herbert Stothart

Norma Shearer, Robert Montgomery, Herbert Marshall, Mrs Patrick Campbell, Skeets Gallagher, Ralph Forbes, Lilyan Tashman, Helen Jerome Eddy, George K. Arthur, Halliwell Hobbes

The Rise and Fall of Legs Diamond
US 1960 101m bw
Warner / United States (Milton Sperling)

The career of a New York hoodlum of the twenties.
Inspired, like *King of the Roaring Twenties*, by the TV success of *The Untouchables*, this was part of a brief attempt by Warners to recapture its pre-war gangster image. Alas, stars and style were equally lacking.

w Joseph Landon *d* Budd Boetticher *ph* Lucien Ballard *m* Leonard Rosenman

Ray Danton, Karen Steele, Elaine Stewart, Jesse White, Simon Oakland, Robert Lowery, Warren Oates, Judson Pratt

The Rise and Rise of Michael Rimmer
GB 1970 101m Technicolor
Warner / David Frost (Harry Fine)

An efficiency expert takes over an advertising agency and is soon an MP, a cabinet minister, and PM.
Satirical comedy which quickly goes overboard and is only occasionally funny; it does, however, mark the final death throes of the swinging sixties, and the changeover to *Monty Python*.

w Peter Cook, John Cleese, Kevin Billington, Graham Chapman *d* Kevin Billington *ph* Alex Thompson *m* John Cameron

Peter Cook, John Cleese, Arthur Lowe, Denholm Elliott, Ronald Fraser, Vanessa Howard, George A. Cooper, Harold Pinter, James Cossins, Roland Culver, Dudley Foster, Julian Glover, Dennis Price, Ronnie Corbett

Rise and Shine
US 1941 93m bw
TCF (Mark Hellinger)

A dumb but brilliant football player is kidnapped by the other side.
Drab collegiate comedy, disappointing considering the credits.

w Herman J. Mankiewicz, *novel* My Life and Hard Times by James Thurber *d* Allan Dwan *ph* Edward Cronjager *m* Emil Newman

Linda Darnell, Jack Oakie, George Murphy, Walter Brennan, Milton Berle, Sheldon Leonard, Donald Meek, Ruth Donnelly, Donald MacBride, Raymond Walburn, Emma Dunn

The Rising of the Moon
Eire 1957 81m bw
Warner / Four Provinces (Lord Killanin)

Three Irish short stories.
Curiously dull John Ford portmanteau with the Abbey players.

w Frank Nugent, *stories* Frank O'Connor, Malcolm J. McHugh, Lady Gregory *d* John Ford *ph* Robert Krasker *m* Eamonn O'Gallagher *narrator* Tyrone Power

Maureen Connell, Eileen Crowe, Cyril Cusack, Maureen Delany, Donal Donelly, Frank Lawton, Edward Lexy, Jack MacGowran, Denis O'Dea, Jimmy O'Dea, Noel Purcell

Ritual of Evil
US 1969 98m Technicolor TVM
Universal (David Levinson)

A psychiatrist who is also a supernatural investigator loses one of his patients to a witchcraft ritual.
An interesting theme is spun out too long and becomes nonsense.

w Robert Presnell Jnr *d* Robert Day

Louis Jourdan, Anne Baxter, Diana Hyland, John McMartin, Belinda Montgomery

The Ritz*
US 1976 90m Technicolor
Warner (Denis O'Dell)

A comedy of mistaken identities in a gay New York turkish bath.
An adaptation of a stage success which doesn't seem nearly as funny as it thinks it is; but some of it does work.

w Terrance McNally, from his play *d* Richard Lester *ph* Paul Wilson *m* Ken Thorne *pd* Phillip Harrison

Jack Weston, Rita Moreno, Jerry Stiller, Kaye Ballard, Bessie Love, George Couloris, F. Murray Abrahams, Treat Williams

The River*
India 1951 87m Technicolor
Oriental / International / Theatre Guild (Kenneth McEldowney)

Episodes in the life of a small English community living on the banks of the Ganges.
A slight and surprising work from this director, superbly observed and a pleasure to watch but dramatically very thin.

w Rumer Godden, Jean Renoir, *novel* Rumer Godden *d Jean Renoir ph Claude Renoir m* M. A. Partha Sarathy *ph Eugene Lourié*

Nora Swinburne, Esmond Knight, Arthur Shields, Adrienne Corri

River of Gold
US 1970 74m colour TVM
Aaron Spelling

Two American divers in Mexico become involved in the undersea search for a relic.
Below average adventure hokum.

w Salvatore C. Puedes *d* David Friedkin

Dack Rambo, Roger Davis, Ray Milland, Suzanne Pleshette, Melissa Newman

River of Mystery
US 1969 96m Technicolor TVM
Universal (Steve Shagan)

Two oil wildcatters in Brazil are lured into helping rebels.
Jungle thick ear: quite unremarkable.

w Albert Ruben *d* Paul Stanley

Vic Morrow, Claude Akins, Niall MacGinnis, Edmond O'Brien, Nico Minardos, Louise Sorel

River of No Return*
US 1954 91m Technicolor Cinemascope
TCF (Stanley Rubin)

During the California gold rush a widower and his 10-year-old son encounter a saloon singer with a gold claim.
Cheerful, clichéd star western designed to exploit the splendours of early Cinemascope, and very adequate for this purpose.

w Frank Fenton *d* Otto Preminger *ph* Joseph La Shelle *m* Lionel Newman

Robert Mitchum, Marilyn Monroe, Tommy Rettig, Rory Calhoun, Murvyn Vye

The River's Edge
US 1956 87m Eastmancolor
Cinemascope
TCF (Benedict Bogeaus)

A fugitive bank robber forces a farmer to guide him over the mountains into Mexico.
Sluggish open-air character melodrama.

w Harold J. Smith *d* Allan Dwan *ph* Harold Lipstein *m* Lou Forbes

Ray Milland, Anthony Quinn, Debra Paget, Byron Foulger

The Road Back**
US 1937 97m bw
Universal (James Whale)

After World War I, German soldiers go home to problems and disillusion.
A major work, intended as a sequel to *All Quiet on the Western Front*. Despite impressive sequences, it doesn't quite reach inspiring heights.

w R. C. Sherriff, Charles Kenyon, *novel* Erich Maria Remarque *d James Whale ph John Mescall, George Robinson m* Dmitri Tiomkin *ad* Charles D. Hall

Richard Cromwell, John King, Slim Summerville, Andy Devine, Barbara Read, Louise Fazenda, Noah Beery Jnr, Lionel Atwill, John Emery, Etienne Girardot, Spring Byington, Laura Hope Crews
† The film is said to have been extensively reshot after protests from the German consul in Los Angeles. No 35mm negative now exists, as it reverted to Remarque and was lost.

Road House*
US 1948 95m bw
TCF

A road house owner is jealous of his manager and frames him for murder.
Dated but watchable *film noir* of its era, with all characters cynical or homicidal.

w Edward Chodorov *d* Jean Negulesco *ph* Joseph La Shelle *m* Cyril Mockridge

Richard Widmark, Ida Lupino, Cornel Wilde, Celeste Holm

Road Show*
US 1941 86m bw
Hal Roach

A young man wrongly committed to an insane asylum escapes with other inmates and joins a travelling circus.
Engaging scatty comedy on familiar Roach lines which suffers from lame pacing but manages some likeable moments.

w Arnold Beldard, Harry Langdon, Mickell Novak, *novel* Eric Hatch *d* Gordon Douglas

John Hubbard, Adolphe Menjou, Carole Landis, Patsy Kelly, George E. Stone

The Road to Glory*
US 1936 103m bw
TCF (Darryl F. Zanuck)

Adventures of a French regiment in World War I.
Meticulously produced war movie which bears comparison with *All Quiet on the Western Front*.

w Joel Sayre, William Faulkner *d Howard Hawks* *ph Gregg Toland* *m* Louis Silvers

Fredric March, Warner Baxter, Lionel Barrymore, June Lang, Gregory Ratoff, Victor Kilian, John Qualen, Julius Tannen, Leonid Kinskey

Road to Singapore*
US 1940 84m bw
Paramount (Harlan Thompson)

Two rich playboys swear off women until they quarrel over a Singapore maiden.
The first Hope–Crosby–Lamour 'road' picture is basically a light romantic comedy and quite forgettable; the series got zanier as it progressed.

w Don Hartman, Frank Butler, *story* Harry Hervey *d* Victor Schertzinger *ph* William C. Mellor *m* Victor Young

Bing Crosby, Bob Hope, Dorothy Lamour, Charles Coburn, Judith Barrett, Anthony Quinn, Jerry Colonna

The others:

Road to Zanzibar**
US 1941 92m bw
Paramount (Paul Jones)

The trio on safari in Africa, with *Hellzapoppin* gags breaking in and an anything-goes atmosphere.

w Frank Butler, Sy Bartlett *d* Victor Schertzinger *ph* Ted Tetzlaff *songs* Johnny Burke, Jimmy Van Heusen

Hope, Crosby, Lamour, Una Merkel, Eric Blore, Luis Alberni, Douglass Dumbrille

Road to Morocco**
US 1942 83m bw
Paramount (Paul Jones)

Hollywood Arab palaces, a captive princess, topical gags and talking camels.

w Frank Butler, Don Hartman *d* David Butler *ph* William C. Mellor *md* Victor Young *songs* Johnny Burke, Jimmy Van Heusen

Hope, Crosby, Lamour, Anthony Quinn, Dona Drake

Road to Utopia**
US 1945 89m bw
Paramount (Paul Jones)

The California gold rush, with all the previous gag styles in good order, capped by a cheeky epilogue and constant explanatory narration by Robert Benchley.

w Norman Panama, Melvin Frank *d* Hal Walker *ph* Lionel Lindon *m* Leigh Harline *songs* Johnny Burke, Jimmy Van Heusen

Hope, Crosby, Lamour, Douglass Dumbrille, Hillary Brooke, Jack La Rue

Road to Rio**
US 1947 100m bw
Paramount (Daniel Dare)

Guest stars are given their head, plot intrudes again in the shape of a hypnotized heiress, and the style is more constrained (but still funny).

w Edmund Beloin, Jack Rose *d* Norman Z. McLeod *ph* Ernest Laszlo *md* Robert Emmett Dolan *songs* Johnny Burke, Jimmy Van Heusen

Hope, Crosby, Lamour, Gale Sondergaard, Frank Faylen, the Wiere Brothers, the Andrews Sisters

Road to Bali*
US 1952 91m Technicolor
Paramount (Harry Tugend)

In and around the South Seas, with colour making the sets obvious and the gags only tediously funny. The team's zest was also flagging.

w Frank Butler, Hal Kanter, William Morrow *d* Hal Walker *ph* George Barnes *md* Joseph J. Lilley *songs* Johnny Burke, Jimmy Van Heusen

Hope, Crosby, Lamour, Murvyn Vye, Peter Coe

Road to Hong Kong
GB 1962 91m bw
UA / Melnor (Norman Panama)

Curious, slightly dismal-looking attempt to continue the series in a British studio and on a low budget. A few good gags, but it's all very tired by now, and the space fiction plot makes it seem more so.

w Norman Panama, Melvin Frank *d* Melvin Frank *ph* Jack Hildyard *m* Robert Farnon *pd* Roger Furse

Hope, Crosby, Lamour, Joan Collins, Robert Morley, Walter Gotell, Felix Aylmer and guests Peter Sellers, David Niven, Frank Sinatra, Dean Martin, Jerry Colonna

Roadhouse Nights*
US 1930 71m bw
Paramount

A reporter exposes a gangster operating from a country nightclub.
Experimental mingling of elements which later become very familiar.

w Garrett Fort, *story* Ben Hecht *d* Hobart Henley *ph* William Steiner

Helen Morgan, Charles Ruggles, Fred Kohler, Jimmy Durante, Fuller Mellish Jnr

The Roaring Twenties***
US 1939 106m bw
Warner (Hal B. Wallis)

A World War I veteran returns to New York, innocently becomes involved in bootlegging, builds up an empire and dies in a gang war.
Among the last of the Warner gangster cycle, this was perhaps the best production of them all, despite the familiar plot line: stars and studio were in cracking form.

w Jerry Wald, Richard Macaulay, Robert Rossen, *story* Mark Hellinger *d Raoul Walsh, Anatole Litvak ph Ernest Haller*

James Cagney, Humphrey Bogart, Priscilla Lane, Jeffrey Lynn, Gladys George, Frank McHugh, Paul Kelly, Elizabeth Risdon

Rob Roy the Highland Rogue
GB 1953 81m Technicolor
Walt Disney (Perce Pearce)

After the defeat of the clans in the 1715 rebellion, their leader escapes and after several adventures is granted a royal pardon.
A kind of Scottish Robin Hood, so stiffly acted and made that it might as well—or better—be a cartoon.

w Lawrence E. Watkin *d* Harold French *ph* Guy Green *m* Cedric Thorpe Davie

Richard Todd, Glynis Johns, James Robertson Justice, Michael Gough, Finlay Currie, Geoffrey Keen, Archie Duncan

Robbery*
GB 1967 113m Eastmancolor
Joseph E. Levine / Oakhurst (Michael Deeley, Stanley Baker)

Criminals conspire to rob the night mail train from Glasgow.
Heavy-going fictionalized account of the famous train robbery of 1963; best seen as standard cops and robbers, with some good chase sequences.

w Edward Boyd, Peter Yates, George Markstein *d Peter Yates ph* Douglas Slocombe *m* Johnny Keating

Stanley Baker, James Booth, Frank Finlay, Joanna Pettet, Barry Foster, William Marlowe, Clinton Greyn, George Sewell

Robbery under Arms
GB 1957 99m Eastmancolor
Rank (Joe Janni)

In 19th-century Australia, two farming brothers join the notorious outlaw Captain Starlight.
Howlingly dull film version of a semi-classic adventure novel; a rambling story with no unity of viewpoint is saved only by excellent photography.

w Alexander Baron, W. P. Lipscomb, *novel* Rolf Boldrewood *d* Jack Lee *ph Harry Waxman m* Matyas Seiber

Peter Finch, David McCallum, Ronald Lewis, Maureen Swanson, Jill Ireland, Laurence Naismith, Jean Anderson

The Robe**
US 1953 135m Technicolor Cinemascope
TCF (Frank Ross)

Followers and opponents of Jesus are affected by the robe handed down by him at his crucifixion.
The first film in Cinemascope was, surprisingly, a biblical bestseller, but the crowded Roman sets hid most of the flaws in the process. The film itself was competent and unsurprising in the well-tried *Sign of the Cross* manner.

w Philip Dunne, *novel* Lloyd C. Douglas *d* Henry Koster *ph Leon Shamroy m* Alfred Newman

Richard Burton, Jean Simmons, Michael Rennie, *Victor Mature*, Jay Robinson, Torin Thatcher, Dean Jagger, Richard Boone, Betta St John, Jeff Morrow, Ernest Thesiger, Dawn Addams

Roberta*
US 1935 105m bw
RKO (Pandro S. Berman)

An American inherits a Parisian fashion house.
Thin and remarkably flatly-handled musical romance of the old school, charged only by the occasional appearances in supporting roles of Astaire and Rogers, then on the brink of stardom.

w Jane Murfin, Sam Mintz, Allan Scott, *play* Otto Harbach, *book* Gowns by Roberta by Alice Duer Miller *d* William A. Seiter *ph* Edward Cronjager *m Jerome Kern md* Max Steiner *ch* Fred Astaire *ad* Van Nest Polglase

Irene Dunne, *Fred Astaire, Ginger Rogers*, Randolph Scott, Helen Westley, Claire Dodd, Victor Varconi, Torben Meyer
† Remade as *Lovely to Look At* (qv).

Robin and Marian*
US 1976 107m Technicolor
Columbia / Rastar (Dennis O'Dell)

Robin Hood returns from the Crusades and finds conditions in Britain depressing; he finally conquers the evil Sheriff but dies in the attempt.
A kind of serious parody of medieval life, after the fashion of *The Lion in Winter* but much glummer; in fact, nothing to laugh at at all.

w James Goldman *d* Richard Lester *ph* David Watkin *m* John Barry *pd* Michael Stringer

Sean Connery, Audrey Hepburn, Robert Shaw, Ronnie Barker, Nicol Williamson, Richard Harris, Denholm Elliott, Kenneth Haigh, Ian Holm, Bill Maynard, Esmond Knight, Peter Butterworth

'Surface realism only hides a core of mush, suddenly revealed when the hero and heroine settle down for love-making in a field of corn.' —*Geoff Brown*

Robin and the Seven Hoods*
US 1964 123m Technicolor Panavision
Warner / PC (Howard W. Koch, William H. Daniels)

A spoof of the Robin Hood legend set in gangland Chicago of the twenties.
Too flabby by far to be as funny as it thinks it is, this farrago of cheerful jokes has effective moments and lively routines, but most of them are nearly swamped by flat treatment and the wide screen.

w David Schwartz *d* Gordon Douglas *ph* William H. Daniels *m* Nelson Riddle *songs* Sammy Cahn, James Van Heusen

Frank Sinatra, Dean Martin, Bing Crosby, Sammy Davis Jnr, Peter Falk, Barbara Rush, Edward G. Robinson, Victor Buono, Barry Kelley, Jack La Rue, Allen Jenkins, Sig Rumann, Hans Conried

Robin Hood see The Adventures of Robin Hood, The Story of Robin Hood

Robin Hood
US 1973 83m Technicolor
Walt Disney (Wolfgang Reitherman)

Alarmingly poor cartoon feature with all the characters 'played' by animals; songs especially dim and treatment quite lifeless.

w Larry Clemmons, Ken Anderson, others *d* Wolfgang Reitherman *voices* Brian Bedford, Peter Ustinov, Terry-Thomas, Phil Harris, Andy Devine, Pat Buttram

Robinson Crusoe on Mars**
US 1964 110m Techniscope
Paramount / Devonshire (Aubrey Schenck)

An astronaut lands on Mars and learns to survive until rescue comes.
Remarkably close to Defoe (Man Friday being a refugee in an interplanetary war) this is an absorbing, entertaining and well-staged piece of science fiction, strikingly shot in Death Valley.

w Ib Melchior, John C. Higgins *d Byron Haskin ph Winton C. Hoch m* Van Cleave *sp Lawrence Butler ad* Hal Pereira, Arthur Lonergan

Paul Mantee, Adam West, Vic Lundin

Rock a Bye Baby
US 1958 107m Technicolor Vistavision
Paramount (Jerry Lewis)

A film star asks her devoted schoolday admirer to look after her triplets by a secret marriage.
Tasteless jazzing-up of *The Miracle of Morgan's Creek* by talents distinctly unsympathetic.

wd Frank Tashlin *ph* Haskell Boggs *m* Walter Scharf

Jerry Lewis, Marilyn Maxwell, Reginald Gardiner, Salvatore Baccaloni, Hans Conried, Isobel Elsom, James Gleason, Isa Moore, Connie Stevens

Rock around the Clock*
US 1956 74m bw
Columbia (Sam Katzman)

A band playing a new form of jive—rock 'n roll—becomes a nationwide sensation.
A cheap second feature with guest artists, this cheerful little movie deserved at least a footnote in the histories because it spotlights the origins and the leading purveyors of rock 'n roll. It also caused serious riots in several countries. A sequel in 1957, *Don't Knock the Rock*, was merely cheap.

w Robert E. Kent, James B. Gordon *d* Fred F. Sears *ph* Benjamin H. Kline

Bill Haley and the Comets, the Platters, Little Richard, Tony Martinez and his Band, Freddie Bell and the Bellboys, Johnny Johnson, Alan Freed, Lisa Gaye, Alix Talton

Rockets Galore
GB 1958 94m Technicolor
Rank / Relph and Dearden

The Scottish island of Todday resists the installation of a rocket-launching site.
Amiable but disappointingly listless sequel to *Whisky Galore*.

w Monja Danischewsky *d* Michael Relph *ph* Reg Wyer *m* Cedric Thorpe Davie

Jeannie Carson, Donald Sinden, Roland Culver, Noel Purcell, Ian Hunter, Duncan Macrae, Jean Cadell, Carl Jaffe, Gordon Jackson, Catherine Lacey

Rocketship XM*
US 1950 79m bw
Lippert (Kurt Neumann)

An expedition to the moon lands by accident on Mars.
The first post-war space adventure is sheer hokum, quite likeable for its cheek though not for its cheap sets.

wd Kurt Neumann *ph* Karl Struss *m* Ferde Grofe

Lloyd Bridges, Osa Massen, John Emery, Hugh O'Brian

The Rockford Files*
US 1974 74m Technicolor TVM
Universal (Meta Rosenberg)

An ex-con private eye investigates 'closed' cases and helps a young woman to find out whether her father was murdered.
Lively pilot for a moderately successful series, shot in Los Angeles and the desert and maintaining a nice sense of humour.

w Stepehn J. Cannell *d* Richard Heffron

James Garner, Lindsay Wagner, Noah Beery Jnr, William Smith

The Rocking Horse Winner*
GB 1949 90m bw
Rank / Two Cities (John Mills)

A boy discovers he can predict winners while riding an old rocking horse; his mother's greed has fatal results.
A very short story is fatally over-extended and becomes bathetic; but the production is solid and the film deserves a mark for trying.

wd Anthony Pelissier, *story* D. H. Lawrence *ph* Desmond Dickinson *m* William Alwyn *ad* Carmen Dillon

John Mills, Valerie Hobson, John Howard Davies, Ronald Squire, Hugh Sinclair, Cyril Smith

Rocky Mountain
US 1950 83m bw
Warner (William Jacobs)

A Confederate horseman gets involved in an Indian war.
Routine star western with unusual tragic ending.

w Winston Miller, Alan le May *d* William Keighley *ph* Ted McCord *m* Max Steiner

Errol Flynn, Patrice Wymore, Scott Forbes, Guinn Williams, Slim Pickens

Rogue Cop
US 1954 92m bw
MGM (Nicholas Nayfack)

A police detective is on the payroll of a crime syndicate.
Uncompelling star melodrama.

w Sidney Boehm, *novel* William P. McGivern *d* Roy Rowland *ph* John Seitz *m* Jeff Alexander

Robert Taylor, George Raft, Janet Leigh, Steve Forrest, Anne Francis

'Another of the sour, disillusioned crime stories which have recently been coming into fashion.' —*Penelope Houston*

Rogue's March
US 1953 84m bw
MGM (Leon Gordon)

A British army officer is unjustly accused of espionage but becomes a hero in India.
Victorian comedy adventure set on a never-never frontier. Not much.

w Leon Gordon *d* Allan Davis *ph* Paul C. Vogel *m* Alberto Columbo

Peter Lawford, Richard Greene, Janice Rule, Leo G. Carroll, John Abbott, Patrick Aherne

Rogues of Sherwood Forest*
US 1950 80m Technicolor
Columbia (Fred M. Packard)

Robin Hood's son helps the barons to force the signing of Magna Carta.
Satisfactory action adventure.

w George Bruce *d* Gordon Douglas *ph* Charles Lawton Jnr *m* Heinz Roemheld, Harold MacArthur

John Derek, Diana Lynn, George Macready, Alan Hale, Paul Cavanagh, Lowell Gilmore, Billy House

Rogues' Regiment
US 1948 86m bw
U-I

An intelligence man joins the French Foreign Legion in Saigon to track down an ex-Nazi.
Keen but rather muddled actioner.

w Robert Buckner *d* Robert Florey *ph* Maury Gertsman *m* Daniele Amfitheatrof

Dick Powell, Marta Toren, Vincent Price, Stephen McNally

Roll, Freddy, Roll
US 1975 74m colour TVM
Persky–Denoff

In order to win a place in the Guinness Book of Records, a mild-mannered computer programmer lives for seven days on roller skates. Slow-starting but finally quite hilarious comedy.

w Bill Persky, Sam Denoff *d* Bill Persky

Tim Conway, Jan Murray, Henry Jones, Scott Brady, Ruta Lee

Rollerball*
US 1975 129m Technicolor Scope
UA / Norman Jewison

In the 21st century an ultra-violent game is used to release the anti-social feelings of the masses. A one-point parable, and an obvious point at that, is stretched out over more than two hours of violence in which the rules of the game are not even explained. A distinctly unlikeable film.

w William Harrison *d* Norman Jewison *ph* Douglas Slocombe *md* André Previn *pd* John Box

James Caan, John Houseman, Ralph Richardson, Maud Adams, John Beck, Moses Gunn

'A classic demonstration of how several millions of dollars can be unenjoyably wasted.' —*Jonathan Rosenbaum*

Rolling Man*
US 1972 73m colour TVM
Aaron Spelling

An ex-con tries to find his sons who have been farmed out to foster homes.
Efficient, slightly unusual melodrama.

w Steve and Elinor Karpf *d* Peter Hyams

Dennis Weaver, Don Stroud, Agnes Moorehead, Donna Mills, Jimmy Dean, Sheree North

Roman Grey
US 1975 74m Technicolor TVM
Universal (Richard Irving)
aka: *The Art of Crime*

A New York gypsy antique dealer tries to save a friend on a murder charge.
Uninspired and rather desperate pilot which didn't go.

w Martin Smith, Bill Davidson *d* Richard Irving

Ron Liebman, Jose Ferrer, David Hedison, Jill Clayburgh, Eugene Roche

Roman Holiday**
US 1953 118m bw
Paramount (William Wyler)

A princess on an official visit to Rome slips away incognito and falls in love with a newspaperman. Wispy, charming, old-fashioned romantic comedy shot in Rome and a little obsessed by the locations; one feels that a studio base would have resulted in firmer control of the elements. The stars, however, made it memorable.

w Ian McLellan Hunter, John Dighton *d William Wyler* *ph* Franz Planer, Henri Alekan *m* Georges Auric

Gregory Peck, Audrey Hepburn, Eddie Albert, Hartley Power, Harcourt Williams

Roman Scandals**
US 1933 93m bw
Samuel Goldwyn

A troubled young man dreams himself back in ancient Rome.
Musical farce which is not only pretty entertaining on its own account but remains interesting for a number of reasons; as its star's best vehicle, for its Depression bookends, as a spoof on *The Sign of the Cross* and the inspiration of scores of other comedies in which the heroes dreamed themselves back into other times. Note also the musical numbers, the chariot race finale, and the rare appearance of Ruth Etting.

w William Anthony McGuire, George Oppenheimer, Arthur Sheekman, Nat Perrin, *story* George S. Kaufman, Robert E. Sherwood *d* Frank Tuttle *chariot sequence Ralph Cedar* *ph Gregg Toland* *ch Busby Berkeley* *songs* various

Eddie Cantor, Gloria Stuart, Ruth Etting, Edward Arnold, Alan Mowbray, Verree Teasdale

The Roman Spring of Mrs Stone*
GB 1961 104m Technicolor
Warner Seven Arts / AA (Louis de Rochemont)

A widowed American actress in Rome begins to drift into lassitude and moral decline.
Vivien Leigh gets degraded again in this rambling novella complete with mysterious dark stranger waiting at the end. Nice to look at, and occasionally compelling, but unsuccessful as a whole.

w Gavin Lambert, *novel* Tennessee Williams *d* José Quintero *ph* Harry Waxman *m* Richard Addinsell *pd* Roger Furse *ad* Herbert Smith

Vivien Leigh, Warren Beatty, Lotte Lenya, Jeremy Spenser, Coral Browne, Ernest Thesiger

The Romance of Rosy Ridge
US 1947 103m bw
MGM (Jack Cummings)

After the Civil War, farmers make their own peace.
Mild period romance with everything settled by a betrothal.

w Lester Cole, *novel* Mackinlay Kantor *d* Roy Rowland

Van Johnson, Thomas Mitchell, Janet Leigh, Selena Royle, Marshall Thompson, Dean Stockwell
'Rustic charm spread through it like molasses.'—*Douglas Eames*

Romance on the High Seas*
US 1948 99m Technicolor
Warner (Alex Gottleib, George Amy)
GB title: *It's Magic*

Various romances mesh on an ocean voyage.
Lightweight musical which introduces Doris Day and generally manages to keep afloat.

w Julius J. and Philip G. Epstein, I. A. L. Diamond *d* Michael Curtiz *ph* Elwood Bredell *songs* Jule Styne, Sammy Cahn

Jack Carson, Janis Paige, Don Defore, Doris Day, Oscar Levant, S. Z. Sakall, Eric Blore, Franklin Pangborn, Fortunio Bonanova

Romanoff and Juliet*
US 1961 103m Technicolor
U-I / Pavla (Peter Ustinov)

Both Americans and Russians woo the tiny country of Concordia, and war threatens while the ambassadors' children fall in love.
Despite the author's wit this pattern comedy became something of a bore as a stylized stage piece, and the film is not smartly enough handled to be anything but a yawn; the humour never becomes cinematic.

wd Peter Ustinov, from his play *ph* Robert Krasker *m* Mario Nascimbene *ad* Alexander Trauner

Peter Ustinov, Sandra Dee, John Gavin, Akim Tamiroff, Tamara Shayne, John Phillips, Alix Talton, Peter Jones

The Romantic Englishwoman*
GB 1975 116m Eastmancolor
Dial / Meric–Matalon (Daniel M. Angel)

A discontented woman, holidaying at Baden Baden, falls in love with a stranger while her husband completes a novel on the same theme.
Almost as ambiguous as *Last Year in Marienbad*, this annoying film wastes good actors in a script which hovers uncertainly between fantasy, melodrama and reality, intending one supposes to make humourless and obvious comparisons between romance and life.

w Tom Stoppard, Thomas Wiseman, *novel* Thomas Wiseman *d* Joseph Losey *ph* Gerry Fisher *m* Richard Hartley

Glenda Jackson, Michael Caine, Helmut Berger, Marcus Richardson, Kate Nelligan, René Kolldehoff, Michael Lonsdale
'The central trio bite off their lines, play deviously with hypocrisies and humiliations, and seem slightly aware that they're creations by artifice out of artificiality.'—*Penelope Houston*

Rome Express***
GB 1932 94m bw
Gaumont (Michael Balcon)

Thieves and blackmail victims are among the passengers on an express train.
Just a little faded now as sheer entertainment, this remains the prototype train thriller from which *The Lady Vanishes, Murder on the Orient Express* and a hundred others are all borrowed; it also spawned a myriad movies in which strangers are thrown together in dangerous situations. Technically it still works very well, though the script needs modernizing.

w Clifford Grey, Sidney Gilliat, Frank Vosper, Ralph Stock *d* Walter Forde

Conrad Veidt, Gordon Harker, Esther Ralston, Joan Barry, Harold Huth, Cedric Hardwicke, Donald Calthrop, Hugh Williams, Finlay Currie, Frank Vosper, Muriel Aked, Eliot Makeham
†Remade 1948 as *Sleeping Car to Trieste* (qv).

Romeo and Juliet*
US 1936 127m bw
MGM (Irving Thalberg)

Hollywood Shakespeare with a super production and a rather elderly cast. Not entertaining in the strict sense, but full of interest.

w Talbot Jennings *d* George Cukor *ph* William Daniels *m* Herbert Stothart *ad* Cedric Gibbons

Leslie Howard, Norma Shearer, John Barrymore, Basil Rathbone, Edna May Oliver, Henry Kolker, C. Aubrey Smith, Violet Kemble-Cooper, Robert Warwick, Virginia Hammond, Reginald Denny, Ralph Forbes, Andy Devine, Conway Tearle

Romeo and Juliet
GB 1954 138m Technicolor
Rank / Verona (Joe Janni, Sandro Ghenzi)

Good-looking but extremely boring version shot on Italian locations with quite unacceptable leads.

wd Renato Castellani *ph* Robert Krasker *m* Roman Vlad

Laurence Harvey, Susan Shentall, Aldo Zollo, Enzo Fiermonte, Flora Robson, Mervyn Johns, Sebastian Cabot, Lydia Sherwood, Giulio Garbinetti, Nietta Zocchi, Bill Travers, Norman Wooland, John Gielgud as prologue speaker

Romeo and Juliet*
GB 1968 152m Technicolor
Paramount / BHE / Verona / Dino de Laurentiis (Anthony Havelock-Allan, John Brabourne, Richard Goodwin)

The with-it version for modern youngsters; unfortunately the admirably rapid style does not suit the verse, and long before the much-deferred end the thing becomes just as tiresome as the other versions.

w Franco Brusati, Masolino D'Amico *d* Franco Zeffirelli *ph* Pasquale de Santis *m* Nino Rota

Leonard Whiting, Olivia Hussey, John McEnery, Michael York, Pat Heywood, Milo O'Shea, Paul Hardwick, Natasha Parry, Antonio Pierfederici, Esmeralda Ruspoli, Bruce Robinson, Roberto Bisacco, Laurence Olivier as prologue speaker

Rookery Nook**
GB 1930 76m bw
British and Dominions (Herbert Wilcox)

A nervous husband on holiday tries to hide a runaway girl who has asked for protection against her stepfather.
Primitive talkie technique cannot entirely conceal the brilliance of the original Aldwych farce team in their most enduring vehicle.

w Ben Travers, from his play *d* Tom Walls

Ralph Lynn, Tom Walls, Robertson Hare, Winifred Shotter, Mary Brough, Ethel Coleridge, Griffith Humphreys, Margot Grahame

The Rookies*
US 1971 73m colour TVM
Aaron Spelling

Recruits adjust to police life in a big city.
Semi-documentary cop show, tersely narrated. It led to a four-year series.

w William Blinn *d* Jud Taylor

Darren McGavin, Cameron Mitchell, Paul Burke

Room at the Top***
GB 1958 117m bw
Remus (John and James Woolf)

An ambitious young clerk causes the death of his real love but manages to marry into a rich family.
Claimed as the first British film to take sex seriously, and the first to show the industrial north as it really was, this melodrama actually cheats on both counts but scene for scene is vivid and entertaining despite a weak central performance.

w Neil Paterson, novel John Braine *d Jack Clayton ph Freddie Francis m* Mario Nascimbene

Laurence Harvey, *Simone Signoret,* Heather Sears, Donald Wolfit, Ambrosine Philpotts, Donald Houston, Raymond Huntley, John Westbrook, Allan Cuthbertson, Hermione Baddeley, Mary Peach

'A drama of human drives and torments told with maturity and precision.'—*Stanley Kauffmann*

Room for One More
US 1952 95m bw
Warner (Henry Blanke)

A married couple adopt several underprivileged children.
Slightly mawkish family movie redeemed by star performances.

w Jack Rose, Melville Shavelson *d* Norman Taurog *ph* Robert Burks *m* Max Steiner

Cary Grant, Betsy Drake, Lurene Tuttle, Randy Stuart, George Winslow

Room Service*
US 1938 78m bw
RKO (Pandro S. Berman)

Penniless theatricals find ways of staying in a hotel until they can find a backer.
Claustrophobic Broadway farce unsuitably adapted for the Marx Brothers, who are constrained by having to play characters with a passing resemblance to human beings.

w Morrie Ryskind, *play* John Murray, Allen Boretz *d* William A. Seiter *ph* Russell Metty *m* Roy Webb

Groucho, Chico, Harpo, Lucille Ball, *Donald MacBride, Frank Albertson, Ann Miller, Philip Loeb*

'It should also be noted . . . that there is a scene in which a turkey is chased around a room. Not everybody will care for this.'—*MFB*

† Remade as *Step Lively* (qv).

Rooney*
GB 1958 88m bw
Rank (George H. Brown)

Adventures of a bachelor Irish dustman.
Moderately charming, though unconvincing, Dublin comedy.

w Patrick Kirwan, *novel* Catherine Cookson *d* George Pollock *ph* Christopher Challis *m* Philip Green

John Gregson, Barry Fitzgerald, Muriel Pavlow, June Thorburn, Noel Purcell, Marie Kean, Liam Redmond, Jack MacGowan, Eddie Byrne

Rooster Cogburn*
US 1975 108m Technicolor Panavision
Universal (Paul Nathan)

An elderly marshal after a gang of outlaws is helped by the Bible-thumping daughter of a priest.
Disappointing western too obviously patterned after *True Grit* and *The African Queen*. Having had the idea for outrageous star casting, the producers obviously decided erroneously that the film would make itself.

w Martin Julien *d* Stuart Millar *ph* Harry Stradling Jnr *m* Laurence Rosenthal

John Wayne, Katharine Hepburn, Anthony Zerbe, Richard Jordan, John McIntyre, Strother Martin

The Roots of Heaven*
US 1958 125m Eastmancolor Cinemascope
TCF / Darryl F. Zanuck

A white man in central Africa dedicates himself to prevent the slaughtering of elephants.
Curiously patchy version of a novel which was a strange choice for filming; so many side issues are introduced that at times it takes on the look of another jolly safari adventure.

w Romain Gary, Patrick Leigh-Fermor, *novel* Romain Gary *d* John Huston *ph* Oswald Morris *m* Malcolm Arnold

Trevor Howard, Juliette Greco, Errol Flynn, Eddie Albert, Orson Welles, Paul Lukas, Herbert Lom, Grégoire Aslan, Friedrich Ledebur, Edric Connor

'The Huston who did *Sierra Madre* would have lighted his cigar with this script.'—*Stanley Kauffmann*

Rope**
US 1948 80m Technicolor
Transatlantic (Sidney Bernstein, Alfred Hitchcock)

Two homosexuals murder a friend for the thrill of it and conceal his body in a trunk from which they serve cocktails to a party including his father and girl friend.
An effective piece of Grand Guignol on the stage, this seemed rather tasteless when set in a New York skyscraper, especially when the leading role of the investigator was miscast and Hitch had saddled himself with the ten-minute take, a short-lived technique which made the entire action (set in one room) cinematically continuous (and dizzy-making). Of considerable historic interest, nevertheless.

w Arthur Laurents, *play* Patrick Hamilton *d Alfred Hitchcock* *ph* Joseph Valentine, William V. Skall *m* Leo F. Forbstein

James Stewart, John Dall, Farley Granger, Joan Chandler, Cedric Hardwicke, Constance Collier, Edith Evanson, Douglas Dick

Rope of Sand*
US 1949 105m bw
Paramount (Hal B. Wallis)

Various factions seek hidden diamonds in a prohibited South African area.
Ham-fisted adventure story which suggests at times that a violent parody of *Casablanca* was intended. The stars carry it through.

w Walter Doniger *d* William Dieterle *ph* Charles Lang *m* Franz Waxman

Burt Lancaster, Paul Heinreid, Claude Rains, Peter Lorre, Corinne Calvet, Sam Jaffe

Rosalie*
US 1938 118m bw
MGM (William Anthony McGuire)

A college football hero falls for an incognito Balkan princess.
Ambitious light musical with a wispy plot but satisfying numbers.

w William Anthony McGuire, *play* William Anthony McGuire, Guy Bolton *d* W. S. Van Dyke *ph* Oliver T. Marsh *songs* Cole Porter

Nelson Eddy, Eleanor Powell, Frank Morgan, Ray Bolger, Ilona Massey, Reginald Owen, Edna May Oliver, Jerry Colonna

Rose Marie*
US 1936 113m bw
MGM (Hunt Stromberg)

A Canadian Mountie gets his man— and a lady.
Backwoods romance from a stage success, filmed mostly on location and quite successfully.

w Frances Goodrich, Albert Hackett, Alice Duer Miller, *play* Otto Harbach, Oscar Hammerstein II *d* W. S. Van Dyke *ph* William Daniels *md* Herbert Stothart *songs* various

Nelson Eddy, Jeanette MacDonald, James Stewart, Reginald Owen, Allan Jones, Gilda Gray, George Regas, Alan Mowbray, Robert

Greig, Una O'Connor, Alan Mowbray, David Niven, Herman Bing
† Previously filmed in 1928—and see below.

Rose Marie
US 1954 115m Technicolor Cinemascope
MGM (Mervyn Le Roy)

Dull remake with stodgy handling and poor sets.

w Ronald Millar *d* Mervyn Le Roy *ph* Paul C. Vogel *md* George Stoll *ch* Busby Berkeley

Howard Keel, Ann Blyth, Fernando Lamas, Bert Lahr, Marjorie Main, Ray Collins

Rose of Washington Square**
US 1939 86m bw
TCF (Nunnally Johnson)

Tribulations of a Broadway singer in love with a worthless husband.
Revamping of the Fanny Brice story; smartly done, but the material interpolated for Jolson is what makes the film notable.

w Nunnally Johnson *d* Gregory Ratoff *ph* Karl Freund *m* Louis Silvers *songs* various

Alice Faye, Tyrone Power, *Al Jolson, Hobart Cavanaugh,* William Frawley, Joyce Compton, Louis Prima and his band

The Rose Tattoo
US 1955 117m bw Vistavision
Paramount / Hal B. Wallis

A Sicilian woman on the gulf coast is tormented by the infidelity of her dead husband, but a brawny truckdriver makes her forget him.
Heavily theatrical material, unsuited to the big screen for all the powerful acting (or perhaps because of it).

w Tennessee Williams, from his play *d* Daniel Mann *ph* James Wong Howe *m* Alex North

Anna Magnani, Burt Lancaster, Marisa Pavan, Ben Cooper, Virginia Grey, Jo Van Fleet

Roseanna McCoy
US 1949 89m bw
Samuel Goldwyn

In old Virginia the Hatfields and the McCoys continue their feud with tragic results.
Hillbilly Romeo and Juliet saga, a shade too cornfed despite the credits.

w John Collier *d* Irving Reis *ph* Lee Garmes *m* David Buttolph

Joan Evans, Farley Granger, Charles Bickford, Raymond Massey, Richard Basehart, Aline MacMahon

Rosebud
US 1975 126m Eastmancolor Panavision
UA / Otto Preminger

Five girls of wealthy families are kidnapped by the Palestine Liberation Army.
Overlong topical suspenser which goes awry by not being very suspenseful, and by packing in too many irrelevant satirical jibes.

w Erik Lee Preminger, *novel* Joan Hemingway, Paul Bonnecarrere *d* Otto Preminger *ph* Denys Coop *m* Terry Sharratt *titles* Saul Bass

Peter O'Toole, Richard Attenborough, Cliff Gorman, Claude Dauphin, John V. Lindsay, Peter Lawford, Raf Vallone, Adrienne Corri

Rosemary's Baby**
US 1968 137m Technicolor
Paramount / William Castle

After unwittingly becoming friendly with diabolists, an actor's wife is impregnated by the Devil.
Seminal gothic melodrama which led in due course to the excesses of *The Exorcist*; in itself well done in a heavy-handed way, the book being much more subtle.

wd Roman Polanski, *novel Ira Levin* *ph* William Fraker *m* Krzysztof Komeda *pd* Richard Sylbert

Mia Farrow, John Cassavetes, Ruth Gordon, Sidney Blackmer, Patsy Kelly, Ralph Bellamy, Maurice Evans, Angela Dorian, Elisha Cook, Charles Grodin

Rosie
US 1967 98m Techniscope
Universal / Ross Hunter (Jacque Mapes)

A rich woman spends wildly and her daughters try to have her committed to safeguard their inheritance.
Hopelessly muddled comedy drama which flits from one mood to the other without making a success of either.

w Samuel Taylor, *play* Ruth Gordon, *French original* Les Joies de la Famille by Philippe Heriat *d* David Lowell Rich *ph* Clifford Stine *m* Lyn Murray

Rosalind Russell, Brian Aherne, Sandra Dee, Vanessa Brown, Audrey Meadows, James Farentino, Leslie Nielsen, Margaret Hamilton, Reginald Owen, Juanita Moore, Virginia Grey
'A mawkish mixture of *Auntie Mame* and *King Lear.*'—*MFB*

Rotten to the Core
GB 1965 88m bw Panavision
BL / Tudor (The Boulting Brothers)

Ex-convicts plan an army payroll robbery.
Routine caper comedy, unsuitably widescreened, with a few good jokes along the way.

w Jeffrey Dell, Roy Boulting, John Warren, Len Heath *d* John Boulting *ph* Freddie Young *m* Michael Dress

Anton Rodgers, *Thorley Walters*, Eric Sykes, Kenneth Griffith, Charlotte Rampling, Ian Bannen, Avis Bunnage, Raymond Huntley
†The original title, *Rotten to the Corps*, was more apt but plainly seemed too subtle.

The Rough and the Smooth
GB 1959 99m bw
Renown (George Minter)

An archaeologist about to marry the niece of a press lord falls for a mysterious nymphomaniac.
Preposterous melodrama about unreal people; its very excesses become enjoyable for those who can stay the course.

w Audrey Erskine-Lindop, Dudley Leslie, *novel* Robin Maugham *d* Robert Siodmak *ph* Otto Heller *md* Muir Mathieson

Tony Britton, Najda Tiller, William Bendix, Natasha Parry, Norman Wooland, Donald Wolfit, Tony Wright, Adrienne Corri, Joyce Carey

'The script is never even on nodding terms with life, and tries to make up for this deficiency by a candidly explosive vocabulary which gives the production a weirdly old-fashioned air.'—*MFB*

Rough Night in Jericho
US 1967 97m Techniscope
Universal (Martin Rackin)

A stagecoach man rids a cattle town of a villain.
Totally uninteresting star western with glum performances.

w Sidney Boehm, Marvin H. Albert, *novel* The Man in Black by Marvin H. Albert *d* Arnold Laven *ph* Russell Metty *m* Don Costa

George Peppard, Dean Martin, Jean Simmons, John McIntire, Slim Pickens, Don Galloway, Brad Weston

Rough Shoot*
GB 1952 86m bw
Raymond Stross
US title: *Shoot First*

A retired US officer in Dorset thinks he has shot a poacher—but the dead man is a spy, and someone else shot him.
Minor Hitchcock-style thriller with a climax in Madame Tussaud's. Generally efficient and entertaining.

w Eric Ambler, novel Geoffrey Household *d Robert Parrish ph* Stan Pavey *m* Hans May

Joel McCrea, Evelyn Keyes, Marius Goring, Roland Culver, Frank Lawton, Herbert Lom

Roughly Speaking*
US 1945 117m bw
Warner (Henry Blanke)

Oddball, overlong domestic comedy drama about father's wild and impractical schemes.

w Louise Randall Pierson, from her book *d* Michael Curtiz *ph* Joseph Walker *m* Max Steiner

Rosalind Russell, Jack Carson, Robert Hutton, Jean Sullivan, Alan Hale, Donald Woods, Andrea King, Ray Collins, Kathleen Lockhart

The Rounders
US 1965 85m Metrocolor Panavision
MGM (Richard E. Lyons)

Two modern cowboys mean to settle down but never get around to it.
Pale comedy western which never gets going.

wd Burt Kennedy, *novel* Max Evans *ph* Paul C. Vogel *m* Jeff Alexander

Henry Fonda, Glenn Ford, Chill Wills, Sue Anne Langdon, Edgar Buchanan

Roustabout
US 1964 101m Techniscope
Hal B. Wallis

A wandering tough guy joins a travelling carnival.
Dreary star vehicle momentarily salvaged by its co-star.

w Allan Weiss, Anthony Lawrence *d* John Rich *ph* Lucien Ballard *m* Joseph L. Lilley

Elvis Presley, Barbara Stanwyck, Sue Ann Langdon, Joan Freeman, Leif Erickson

Roxie Hart**
US 1942 72m bw
TCF (Nunnally Johnson)

A twenties showgirl confesses for the sake of publicity to a murder of which she is innocent.
Crowded Chicago burlesque which now seems less funny than it did but is full of smart moments.

w Nunnally Johnson, play Chicago by Maurine Watkins *d William Wellman ph Leon Shamroy*

Ginger Rogers, George Montgomery, *Adolphe Menjou*, Lynne Overman, Nigel Bruce, Spring Byington, Sara Allgood, William Frawley

'A masterpiece of form, of ensemble acting, of powerhouse comedy and scripting.'—*NFT, 1974*

The Royal Family of Broadway*
US 1930 82m bw
Paramount
GB title: *Theatre Royal*

The off-stage escapades of a famous family of actors.
Fairly funny lampoon of the Barrymores, primitively staged and very talky but still entertaining for those in the joke.

w Herman J. Mankiewicz, Gertrude Purcell, *play* George S. Kaufman, Edna Ferber *d* George Cukor, Cyril Gardner *ph* George Folsey

Fredric March, Henrietta Crosman, Ina Claire, Mary Brian, Charles Starrett, Frank Conroy

'Lionel does not come into the burlesque at all, and I can quite believe that he is the most damaged of the entire family.'—*James Agate*

Royal Flash
GB 1975 118m Technicolor
TCF / Two Roads (David V. Picker, Denis O'Dell)

A Victorian bully and braggart has various adventures in Europe and Ruritania.
A rather unsatisfactory romp which takes pot shots at every 19th-century person and object in the encyclopaedia, but is never as funny as it intends to be.

w George Macdonald Fraser, from his novel *d* Richard Lester *ph* Geoffrey Unsworth *m* Ken Thorpe *ph* Terence Marsh

Malcolm McDowall, Oliver Reed, Alan Bates, Florinda Bolkan, Britt Ekland, Lionel Jeffries, Tom Bell, Joss Ackland, Leon Greene, Richard Hurndall, Alastair Sim, Michael Hordern

A Royal Scandal
US 1945 94m bw
TCF (Ernst Lubitsch)
GB title: *Czarina*

The illicit loves of Catherine the Great.
Censored romps around some chilly court sets; very few moments of interest, and none of the style of the silent version *Forbidden Paradise*.

w Edwin Justus Mayer, *play* Lajos Biro, Melchior Lengyel *d* Otto Preminger *ph* Arthur Miller *m* Alfred Newman

Tallulah Bankhead, Charles Coburn, Anne Baxter, William Eythe, Vincent Price, Mischa Auer, Sig Rumann, Vladimir Sokoloff

Royal Wedding
US 1951 93m Technicolor
MGM (Arthur Freed)
GB title: *Wedding Bells*

Journalists congregate in London for the royal wedding.
Thin musical with acceptable numbers.

w Alan Jay Lerner *d* Stanley Donen *ph* Robert Planck *md* Johnny Green *songs* Alan Jay Lerner, Burton Lane

Fred Astaire, Jane Powell, Sarah Churchill, Peter Lawford, Keenan Wynn

Ruby Gentry
US 1952 82m bw
David O. Selznick (Joseph Bernhard, King Vidor)

A tempestuous girl, brought up as a boy in the Carolina swamps, has a love-hate relationship with a local aristocrat, revenges herself on the people who scorn her, loses her lover in a swamp shooting, and becomes a sea captain.
Richly absurd sex melodrama typical of its director and star yet not very entertaining.

w Sylvia Richards *d* King Vidor *ph* Russell Harlan *m* Heinz Roemheld *ad* Dan Hall

Jennifer Jones, Charlton Heston, Karl Malden, Josephine Hutchinson

Ruggles of Red Gap**
US 1935 90m bw
Paramount (Arthur Hornblow Jnr)

A British butler has a startling effect on the family of an American rancher who takes him out west.
A famous comedy which seemed hilarious at the time but can now be seen as mostly composed of flat spots; the performances however are worth remembering.

w Walter de Leon, Harlan Thompson, Humphrey Pearson, *novel* Harry Leon Wilson *d* Leo McCarey *ph* Alfred Gilks

Charles Laughton, Mary Boland, Charles Ruggles, Zasu Pitts, Roland Young, Leila Hyams, James Burke, Maude Eburne, Lucien Littlefield

'A sane, witty, moving and quite unusual picture of Anglo-American relations.' —*C. A. Lejeune*

† Remade as *Fancy Pants* (qv).

Rulers of the Sea*
US 1939 96m bw
Paramount (Frank Lloyd)

Problems surround the first steamship voyage across the Atlantic.

Well-made period action drama.

w Talbot Jennings, Frank Cavett, Richard Collins *d* Frank Lloyd

Douglas Fairbanks Jnr, Margaret Lockwood, Will Fyffe, Montagu Love, George Bancroft, Mary Gordon, Alan Ladd

The Ruling Class*
GB 1971 155m De Luxe
Keep Films (Jules Buck, Jack Hawkins)

The fetishistic Earl of Gurney is succeeded by his mad son Jack who believes he is God.
An overlong satirical play with brilliant patches is hamfistedly filmed but boasts some bright performances. The hits are as random as the misses, however.

w Peter Barnes, from his play *d* Peter Medak *ph* Ken Hodges *m* John Cameron

Peter O'Toole, Harry Andrews, *Arthur Lowe, Alastair Sim,* Coral Browne, Michael Bryant
'This irritating and unsatisfying film is worth being irritated and unsatisfied by.'—*Stanley Kauffmann*

Rumba*
US 1935 71m bw
Paramount (William Le Baron)

A society girl has a yen for a Broadway hoofer.
Streamlined star vehicle which attempts to recapture the success of *Bolero* (qv).

w Howard J. Green *d* Marion Gering *ph* Ted Tetzlaff

Carole Lombard, George Raft, Margo, Lynne Overman, Monroe Owsley, Iris Adrian, Gail Patrick, Samuel S. Hinds, Jameson Thomas

Run a Crooked Mile
GB 1969 100m Technicolor TVM
Universal (Ian Lewis)

An amnesiac is manipulated by a mysterious group of businessmen on whose secret he has accidentally stumbled.
Absurd sub-Hitchcock hokum with the hero disbelieved by everybody until . . .

w Trevor Wallace *d* Gene Levitt

Louis Jourdan, Mary Tyler Moore, Wilfrid Hyde White, Stanley Holloway, Alexander Knox, Laurence Naismith

Run for Cover*
US 1955 92m Technicolor Vistavison
Paramount (William H. Pine)

An ex-convict becomes innocently involved in a train robbery.
Adequate star western.

w William C. Thomas, *story* Harriet Frank Jnr, Irving Ravetch *d* Nicholas Ray *ph* Daniel Fapp *md* Howard Jackson

James Cagney, Viveca Lindfors, John Derek, Jean Hersholt, Grant Withers, Ernest Borgnine, Jack Lambert

Run for the Sun
US 1956 99m Technicolor Superscope
UA / Russ–Field (Harry Tatelman)

Crashlanding in the Mexican jungle, a disillusioned author and a lady journalist find themselves at the mercy of renegade Nazis.
Tame remake of *The Most Dangerous Game* with Count Zaroff replaced by Lord Haw-Haw. Sluggish plot development mars the action.

w Dudley Nichols, Roy Boulting *d* Roy Boulting *ph* Joseph La Shelle *m* Fred Steiner

Richard Widmark, Jane Greer, Trevor Howard, Peter Van Eyck

A Run for Your Money*
GB 1949 83m bw
Ealing (Leslie Norman)

Welsh Rugby supporters have various adventures on their one day in London.
Slight, bright, British chase comedy with characterizations as excellent as they are expected.

w Richard Hughes, Charles Frend, Leslie Norman *d* Charles Frend *ph* Douglas Slocombe *m* Ernest Irving

Alec Guinness, Meredith Edwards, Moira Lister, Donald Houston, Hugh Griffith, Clive Morton, Joyce Grenfell

Run of the Arrow
US 1956 85m Technicolor RKOscope
Global (Samuel Fuller)

An ex-Civil War soldier is captured by Indians and accepted by them, but sickened by their violence.
Bloody little western in the accustomed Fuller vein of unpleasantness.

wd Samuel Fuller *ph* Joseph Biroc *m* Victor Young

Rod Steiger, Sarita Montiel, Charles Bronson, Tim McCoy, Ralph Meeker

Run Silent Run Deep*
US 1958 93m bw
UA / Hecht- Hill–Lancaster (William Schorr)

Antagonisms flare up between the officers of a US submarine in Tokyo Bay during World War II.

Competent, unsurprising war actioner trading on its stars.

w John Gay *d* Robert Wise *ph* Russell Harlan *m* Franz Waxman

Clark Gable, Burt Lancaster, Jack Warden, Brad Dexter, Nick Cravat, Joe Maross, H. M. Wynant

'Mostly good sea fights. Otherwise it's damn the torpedoes, half speed ahead.'—*Time*

Run Simon Run
US 1970 74m colour TVM
Universal

An ex-con Indian seeks revenge against the real murderer of his mother.
Tedious but good-looking open-air melodrama which shifts from suspense to racial discussions.

w Lionel E. Siegel *d* George McGowan

Burt Reynolds, Inger Stevens, James Best, Royal Dano

Run Wild, Run Free*
GB 1969 98m Technicolor
Columbia / Irving Allen (John Danischewsky)

A mute boy living on Dartmoor gains self-confidence through the love of animals.
Rather vaguely developed family film with agreeable sequences.

w David Rook, from his novel The White Colt *d* Richard C. Sarafian *ph* Wilkie Cooper *m* David Whitaker

John Mills, Sylvia Syms, Mark Lester, Bernard Miles, Gordon Jackson, Fiona Fullerton

Runaway*
US 1973 74m Technicolor TVM
Universal (Harve Bennett)

A ski train carrying holidaymakers down a mountain has no brakes.
Modestly effective mini-disaster movie, quite watchable.

w Gerald di Pego *d* David Lowell Rich

Ben Murphy, Ben Johnson, Vera Miles, Martin Milner, Ed Nelson, Darleen Carr, Lee Harcourt Montgomery

The Runaway Barge
US 1975 75m colour TVM
Lorimar
aka: *The Rivermen*

Three men earning a living on a Mississippi boat become involved in a kidnapping.
Slow starting, heavily accented adventure which didn't make a series.

w Sanford Whitmore *m* Nelson Riddle *d* Boris Sagal

Bo Hopkins, Tim Matheson, Jim Davis, Nick Nolte, James Best, Clifton James

The Runaway Bus*
GB 1954 78m bw
Eros / Conquest–Guest (Val Guest)

Passengers at London Airport are fogbound, and a relief bus driver takes some of them to Blackbushe. Incognito among them are robbers and detectives . . .
Vaguely plotted variation on *The Ghost Train*, with fair production, a good smattering of jokes, and a hilarious view of a great airport in its earlier days.

wd Val Guest *ph* Stan Pabey *m* Ronald Binge

Frankie Howerd, Margaret Rutherford, George Coulouris, Petula Clark, Terence Alexander, Toke Townley, Belinda Lee

The Runaways
US 1975 74m colour TVM
Lorimar

A teenage boy and a leopard meet in the wilderness: both have run away from insoluble problems . . .
Silly-serious extravaganza which looks good but dramatically makes little impact.

novel Victor Canning *d* Harry Harris

Dorothy McGuire, Van Williams, John Randolph, Neva Patterson, Josh Albee

The Running Man*
GB 1963 103m Technicolor Panavision
Columbia / Peet (Carol Reed, John R. Sloan)

A private airline pilot fakes an accident and disappears, leaving his wife to collect the insurance and meet him in Spain.
Flabby, expensive suspenser; both plot and character take a back seat to scenic views.

w John Mortimer, *novel* The Ballad of the Running Man by Shelley Smith *d* Carol Reed *ph* Robert Krasker *m* William Alwyn

Laurence Harvey, Alan Bates, Lee Remick, Felix Aylmer, Eleanor Summerfield, Allan Cuthbertson

'There seems to be something about the panoramic screen that seduces film-makers into filling it with irrelevant local colour and drawing the whole proceedings out to a length that matches its width.'—*Brenda Davies*

Running Scared
GB 1972 98m Technicolor Panavision
Paramount / Wigan / Hemmings / O'Toole (Gareth Wigan)

A university student is generally condemned for allowing his friend to commit suicide; eventually he takes his own life.
Depressing and rather pointless exercise in death wish complicated by a doomed love affair.

w Clive Exton, David Hemmings, *novel* Gregory MacDonald *d* David Hemmings *ph* Ernest Day *m* Michael J. Lewis

Robert Powell, Gayle Hunnicutt, Barry Morse, Stephanie Bidmead, Edward Underdown, Maxine Audley, Georgia Brown

Russian Roulette
US 1975 90m Eastmancolor
ITC / Elliott Kastner / Bulldog

Real and fake secret agents shoot it out when the Russian premier is about to visit Vancouver.
Fast-moving but impossible to follow location thriller which resolves itself into a series of chases.

w Tom Ardies, Stanley Mann, Arnold Margolin, *novel* Kosygin is Coming by Tom Ardies *d* Lou Lombardo *ph* Brian West *m* Michael J. Lewis

George Segal, Gordon Jackson, Denholm Elliott, Cristina Raines, Richard Romanus, Louise Fletcher, Nigel Stock

'A stale, mechanical espionage caper that wastes its star.'—*Kevin Thomas*

The Russians Are Coming, The Russians Are Coming*
US 1966 126m De Luxe Panavision
UA / Mirisch (Norman Jewison)

Russian submariners make a forced landing on a Connecticut holiday island and cause panic.
'Daring' cold war comedy which turns out to be of the most elementary and protracted nature, saved from boredom only by a few cameos.

w William Rose, *novel* The Off-Islanders by Nathaniel Benchley *d* Norman Jewison *ph* Joseph Biroc *m* Johnny Mandel

Carl Reiner, Eva Marie Saint, Alan Arkin, John Philip Law, Paul Ford, Tessie O'Shea, Brian Keith, Jonathan Winters, Theodore Bikel, Ben Blue

Ruthless*
US 1948 104m bw
Eagle Lion / Arthur S. Lyons

A conniver breaks several lives on his way to the top.
Rich melodrama with some entertaining moments.

w S. K. Lauren, Gordon Kahn, *novel* Prelude to Night by Dayton Stoddert *d* Edgar G. Ulmer *ph* Bert Glennon *m* Werner Janssen

Zachary Scott, Sidney Greenstreet, Diana Lynn, Louis Hayward, Martha Vickers, Lucille Bremer, Edith Barrett, Raymond Burr, Dennis Hoey

Ryan's Daughter**
GB 1971 206m Metrocolor Panavision 70
MGM / Faraway (Anthony Havelock-Allan)

1916 Ireland: a village schoolmaster's wife falls for a British officer.
A modestly effective pastoral romantic melodrama, stretched on the rack of its director's meticulous film-making technique and unnecessarily big budget. A beautiful, impressive, well-staged and well-acted film, but not really four hours' worth of drama.

w Robert Bolt *d David Lean ph Frederick A. Young m* Maurice Jarre *pd* Stephen Grimes (who created an entire village)

Sarah Miles, Robert Mitchum, Chris Jones, John Mills, Trevor Howard, Leo McKern

S

SOS Pacific*
GB 1959 91m bw
Rank / Sydney Box (John Nasht, Patrick Filmer-Sankey)

Survivors of a Pacific plane crash await rescue on a small island which is the site of an imminent H-bomb test.
Satisfactory open-air thick ear with strongly deployed types and a suspense climax.

w Robert Westerby *d* Guy Green *ph* Wilkie Cooper

Eddie Constantine, Pier Angeli, John Gregson, Richard Attenborough, Eva Bartok, Clifford Evans, Jean Anderson, Cec Linder

Saadia
US 1953 87m Technicolor
MGM (Albert Lewin)

A young French doctor in the Sahara has trouble with the local witch doctor.
Pretentious and ill-considered multi-national romance from the champion of Omar's Rubaiyat.

wd Albert Lewin, *novel* Echec au Destin by Francis D'Autheville *ph* Christopher Challis *m* Bronislau Kaper

Cornel Wilde, Mel Ferrer, Rita Gam, Michel Simon, Wanda Rotha, Cyril Cusack, Marcel Poncin, Peter Bull

Sabotage***
GB 1936 76m bw
Gaumont British (Michael Balcon, Ivor Montagu)
US title: *A Woman Alone*

The proprietor of a small London cinema is a dangerous foreign agent.
Unattractively plotted but fascinatingly detailed Hitchcock suspenser with famous sequences and a splendidly brooding melodramatic atmosphere.

w Charles Bennett, Ian Hay, Helen Simpson, E. V. H. Emmett, *novel* The Secret Agent by Joseph Conrad *d Alfred Hitchcock ph* Bernard Knowles *m* Louis Levy

Oscar Homolka, Sylvia Sidney, John Loder, Desmond Tester, Joyce Barbour, Matthew Boulton

'Tightly packed, economical, full of invention and detail.'—*NFT, 1961*

Saboteur***
US 1942 108m bw
Universal (Frank Lloyd, Jack H. Skirball)

A war worker unjustly suspected of sabotage flees across the country and unmasks a spy ring.
Flawed Hitchcock action thriller, generally unsatisfactory in plot and pace but with splendid sequences at a ball, in Radio City Music Hall, and atop the Statue of Liberty.

w Peter Viertel, Joan Harrison, Dorothy Parker, *story* Alfred Hitchcock *d Alfred Hitchcock ph* Joseph Valentine *m* Charles Previn, Frank Skinner

Robert Cummings, Patricia Lane, Otto Kruger, Alan Baxter, Alma Kruger, *Norman Lloyd*

The Saboteur, Code Name Morituri*
US 1965 122m bw
TCF / Arcola / Colony (Aaron Rosenberg)

In 1942 a German pacifist working for the allies is actually a German spy.
Dreary as a whole, suspenseful in snatches, this shipboard melodrama is full of irrelevancies and is in any case played much more seriously than the matter demands.

w Daniel Taradash, *novel* Werner Jeorg Kosa *d* Bernhard Wicki *ph* Conrad Hall *m* Jerry Goldsmith

Yul Brynner, Marlon Brando, Trevor Howard, Janet Margolin

Sabrina*
US 1954 113m bw
Paramount (Billy Wilder)
GB title: *Sabrina Fair*

The chauffeur's daughter is wooed by both her brother employers.
Superior comedy, rather uneasily cast.

w Billy Wilder, *play* Samuel Taylor *d* Billy Wilder *ph* Charles Lang Jnr *m* Frederick Hollander

Humphrey Bogart, William Holden, Audrey Hepburn, Walter Hampden, John Williams, Martha Hyer, Joan Vohs, Marcel Dalio

The Sad Sack
US 1957 98m bw Vistavision
Paramount (Paul Nathan)

Adventures of an army misfit.
Resistible star comedy.

w Edmund Beloin, Nate Monaster, *cartoon* George Baker *d* George Marshall *ph* Loyal Griggs *m* Walter Scharf

Jerry Lewis, David Wayne, Phyllis Kirk, Peter Lorre, Joe Mantell, Gene Evans, George Dolenz, Liliane Montvecchi, Shepperd Strudwick

Saddle the Wind*
US 1958 84m Metrocolor
Cinemascope
MGM (Armand Deutsch)

A reformed gunman's young brother gets into bad company.
Modestly effective, humourless western drama.

w Rod Serling *d* Robert Parrish *ph* George J. Folsey *m* Elmer Bernstein

Robert Taylor, John Cassavetes, Julie London, Donald Crisp, Charles McGraw, Royal Dano, Richard Erdman

Sadie McKee*
US 1934 88m bw
MGM (Lawrence Weingarten)

A maid at various times loves her master, a young ne'er-do-well, and a middle-aged millionaire.
Solidly carpentered millgirl's romance of the period.

w John Meehan, *story* Vina Delmar *d* Clarence Brown *ph* Oliver T. Marsh

Joan Crawford, Franchot Tone, Gene Raymond, Edward Arnold, Esther Ralston, Jean Dixon, Leo Carrillo, Akim Tamiroff

'The stuff the fans cry for.'—*Hollywood Reporter*

Safari
GB 1956 91m Technicolor
Cinemascope
Warwick (Adrian Worker)

A white hunter falls in love with the wife of his employer and luckily the latter is killed by the Mau Mau.
Feeble adventure story exploiting political tensions.

w Anthony Veiller *d* Terence Young *ph* John Wilcox, Fred Ford, Ted Moore *m* William Alwyn

Victor Mature, Janet Leigh, Roland Culver, John Justin, Earl Cameron, Liam Redmond, Orlando Martins

The Safecracker
GB 1958 96m bw
MGM / Coronado (David E. Rose)

A safecracker is released to help in a commando raid during World War II.
One-twelfth of a dirty dozen, with a long indecisive lead-up and not much pull as drama or comedy.

w Paul Monash, *story* Rhys Davies *d* Ray Milland *ph* Gerald Gibbs *m* Richard Rodney Bennett

Ray Milland, Barry Jones, Jeanette Sterke, Victor Maddern, Ernest Clark, Cyril Raymond, Melissa Stribling

Sahara**
US 1943 97m bw
Columbia

During the retreat from Tobruk a group of men of mixed nationality find water for themselves and harass the Nazis.
Good, simple war actioner with a realistic feel and strong characters deployed in melodramatic situations.

w John Howard Lawson, Zoltan Korda *d Zoltan Korda* *ph* Rudolph Maté *m* Miklos Rozsa

Humphrey Bogart, Bruce Bennett, Lloyd Bridges, Rex Ingram, J. Carrol Naish, Dan Duryea, Kurt Kreuger

Saigon
US 1948 93m bw
Paramount (P. J. Wolfson)

Veteran airmen in Saigon are offered half a million to help in a robbery.
Tired studio-set star actioner.

w P. J. Wolfson, Arthur Sheekman *d* Leslie Fenton *ph* John Seitz *m* Robert Emmett Dolan

Alan Ladd, Veronica Lake, Douglas Dick, Wally Cassell, Luther Adler, Morris Carnovsky, Mikhail Rasumny

Sail a Crooked Ship
US 1961 88m bw
Columbia / Philip Barry Jnr

A shipowner unwittingly takes on a crew of crooks intending to use the boat as a getaway after a bank robbery.
Flimsy comedy sustained by a star comedian.

w Ruth Brooks Flippen, Bruce Geller, *novel* Nathaniel Benchley *d* Irving Brecher *ph* Joseph Biroc *m* George Duning

Robert Wagner, *Ernie Kovacs*, Dorothy Hart, Carolyn Jones, Frank Gorshin

Sailor Beware
US 1952 103m bw
Paramount / Hal B. Wallis

Martin and Lewis in the navy.
Unlovable star antics.

w James Allardice, Martin Rackin, *play* Kenyon Nicholson, Charles Robinson *d* Hal Walker *ph* Daniel L. Fapp *m* Joseph J. Lilley

Dean Martin, Jerry Lewis, Corinne Calvet, Marion Marshall, Robert Strauss, Leif Erickson

Sailor Beware*
GB 1956 80m bw
Romulus (Jack Clayton)

A young sailor has trouble with his mother-in-law-to-be.
Plain but adequate film version of a successful lowbrow stage farce about an archetypal female dragon.

w Philip King and Falkland L. Cary, from their play *d* Gordon Parry *ph* Douglas Slocombe *m* Peter Akister

Peggy Mount, Esma Cannon, Cyril Smith, Shirley Eaton, Ronald Lewis

The Sailor Who Fell from Grace with the Sea
GB 1976 105m Technicolor
AVCO / Sailor Company (Martin Poll)

A precocious boy interferes with his widowed mother's affair with a sailor by castrating the latter.
Weird and unattractive sex fantasy set in Dartmouth of all places and not helped by tiresome sex scenes.

wd Lewis John Carlino, *novel* Gogo No Eiko by Mishima Yukio *ph* Douglas Slocombe *m* John Mandel

Sarah Miles, Kris Kristofferson, Jonathan Kahn, Margo Cunningham, Earl Rhodes

Sailors Three**
GB 1940 86m bw
Ealing (Culley Forde)
US title: *Three Cockeyed Sailors*

Drunken sailors capture a German battleship by mistake.
Low service comedy which keeps moving, is brightly played and reaches a good standard.
Sequel: *Fiddlers Three* (qv).

w Angus Macphail, John Dighton, Austin Melford *d* Walter Forde

Tommy Trinder, Claude Hulbert, Michael Wilding, Carla Lehmann, Jeanne de Casalis, James Hayter, John Laurie

The Saint
Leslie Charteris' famous character, the reformed British gentleman crook who becomes a Robin Hood of crime, has been most popular in the long-running sixties TV series starring Roger Moore. The films which featured him never seemed to hit quite the right note, and now seem slow. All but one were made for RKO, who later switched allegiance to THE FALCON (qv).

1938: THE SAINT IN NEW YORK
1939: THE SAINT STRIKES BACK, THE SAINT IN LONDON
1940: THE SAINT'S DOUBLE TROUBLE, THE SAINT TAKES OVER
1941: THE SAINT IN PALM SPRINGS, THE SAINT'S VACATION
1943 (Republic): THE SAINT MEETS THE TIGER
1954: THE SAINT'S GIRL FRIDAY

Louis Hayward played the role in the first and last; Hugh Sinclair in VACATION and TIGER; George Sanders in the rest.

St Benny the Dip
US 1951 79m bw
Danzigers

Gamblers learn to escape the law by dressing as priests, but circumstance converts them to good works.
Unfunny comedy notable only for its cast.

w John Roeburt *d* Edgar G. Ulmer *ph* Don Malkames *m* Robert Stringer

Freddie Bartholemew, Roland Young, Dick Haymes, Lionel Stander, Nina Foch

St Ives
US 1973 93m Technicolor
Warner (Pancho Kohner, Stanley Kanter)

An ex-police reporter gets involved in a complex murder puzzle.
Soporific suspenser with every tired situation in the book.

w Barry Beckerman, *novel* The Procane Chronicle by Oliver Bleeck *d* J. Lee-Thompson *ph* Lucien Ballard *m* Lalo Schifrin

Charles Bronson, Harry Guardino, John Houseman, Jacqueline Bisset, Maximilian

Schell, Harris Yulin, Dana Elcar, Elisha Cook Jnr

Saint Joan
GB 1957 110m bw
Otto Preminger
Glumly assembled screen version of the brilliantly argumentative play about the Maid of Orleans. Plenty of talent, but neither wit nor style.
w Graham Greene, *play* Bernard Shaw *d* Otto Preminger *ph* Georges Périnal *m* Mischa Spoliansky *pd* Roger Furse
Jean Seberg, Anton Walbrook, Richard Widmark, John Gielgud, Felix Aylmer, Harry Andrews, Richard Todd

St Louis Blues*
US 1939 92m bw
Paramount (Jeff Lazarus)
A Broadway musical star finds new fame down south.
Moderate star entertainment with good guest artists.
w John C. Moffitt, Malcolm Stuart Boylan, Frederick Hazlitt Brennan *d* Raoul Walsh *ph* Theodor Sparkuhl *songs* Frank Loesser, Burton Lane
Dorothy Lamour, Lloyd Nolan, Tito Guizar, Jerome Cowan, Jessie Ralph, William Frawley, the King's Men, Matty Melneck and his Orchestra

St Martin's Lane**
GB 1938 85m bw
Mayflower (Erich Pommer)
US title: *Sidewalks of London*
A middle-aged busker falls in love with a brilliant girl dancer who becomes a star.
Well-made romantic drama with star performances and interesting theatrical background.
w Clemence Dane *d* Tim Whelan
Charles Laughton, Vivien Leigh, Rex Harrison, Tyrone Guthrie, Larry Adler, Gus MacNaughton

The St Valentine's Day Massacre
US 1967 99m De Luxe Panavision
TCF / Los Altos (Roger Corman)
The twenties gang war between Al Capone and Bugs Moran.
The director's first big studio film is disappointing; stagey, poorly developed, unconvincing-looking and overacted.
w Howard Browne *d* Roger Corman *ph* Milton Krasner *m* Lionel Newman, Fred Steiner
Jason Robards Jnr, George Segal, Ralph Meeker, Jean Hale, Clint Ritchie, Joseph Campanella, Richard Bakalyan, David Canary, Bruce Dern, Harold J. Stone, Kurt Kreuger, John Agar, Alex D'Arcy

The Sainted Sisters
US 1948 89m bw
Paramount (Richard Maibaum)
Two New York con girls find themselves taken in by the inhabitants of the small town in which they are hiding out.
Unfunny period comedy which misses on all cylinders.
w Harry Clark *d* William D. Russell *ph* Lionel Lindon *m* Van Cleave
Veronica Lake, Joan Caulfield, Barry Fitzgerald, William Demarest, George Reeves, Beulah Bondi, Chill Wills, Darryl Hickman

Sally and St Anne
US 1952 90m bw
U-I (Leonard Goldstein)
When an Irish-American family is threatened with eviction, the daughter appeals to St Anne for help.
Whimsical comedy, quite nimbly performed.
w James O'Hanlon, Herb Meadow *d* Rudolph Maté *ph* Irving Glassberg *m* Frank Skinner
Ann Blyth, Edmund Gwenn, Hugh O'Brian, John McIntire, Jack Kelly

Sally in Our Alley*
GB 1931 77m bw
Basil Dean
Poor girl loves wounded soldier.
Early talkie drama with music which made Gracie Fields a star and gave her a theme song.
w Miles Malleson, Archie Pitt, Alma Reville, *play* The Likes of 'Er by Charles McEvoy *d* Maurice Elvey
Gracie Fields, Ian Hunter, Florence Desmond, Ivor Barnard

Sally, Irene and Mary
US 1938 72m bw
TCF (Gene Markey)
Three girls try to break into show business.
Simple-minded romantic comedy-musical, well enough done.
w Harry Tugend, Jack Yellen *d* William A. Seiter *ph* Peverell Marley *md* Arthur Lange
Alice Faye, Tony Martin, Fred Allen, Jimmy

Durante, Gregory Ratoff, Joan Davis, Marjorie Weaver, Gypsy Rose Lee

Salome
US 1953 103m Technicolor
Columbia (Buddy Adler)

Princess Salome of Galilee eludes her licentious stepfather, falls in love with a secret Christian, and leaves home when her dancing fails to save the life of John the Baptist.
Distorted biblical hokum with an interesting cast frozen into unconvincing attitudes.

w Harry Kleiner, Jesse Lasky Jnr *d* William Dieterle *ph* Charles Lang *m* Daniele Amfitheatrof *ad* John Meehan

Rita Hayworth, Charles Laughton, Stewart Granger, Judith Anderson, Cedric Hardwicke, Alan Badel, Basil Sydney, Maurice Schwartz, Rex Reason, Arnold Moss

Salome Where She Danced*
US 1945 90m Technicolor
Universal (Walter Wanger, Alexander Golitzen)

During the Austro-Prussian war a dancer is suspected of being a spy and flees to Arizona, where she affects the lives of the citizenry.
Absurdly plotted and stiffly played romantic actioner whose sheer creakiness made it a minor cult film.

w Laurence Stallings, *story* Michael J. Phillips *d* Charles Lamont· *ph* Hal Mohr, W. Howard Green *m* Edward Ward

Yvonne de Carlo, Rod Cameron, Albert Dekker, David Bruce, Walter Slezak, Marjorie Rambeau, J. Edward Bromberg, Abner Biberman, John Litel, Kurt Katch

Salt and Pepper
GB 1968 101m De Luxe
UA / Chrislaw / Tracemark (Milton Ebbins)

Soho nightclub proprietors solve a murder.
Infuriating throwaway star vehicle set in the dregs of swinging London. The sequel, *One More Time* (1970), was quite unnecessary.

w Michael Pertwee *d* Richard Donner *ph* Ken Higgins *m* Johnny Dankworth

Sammy Davis Jnr, Peter Lawford, Michael Bates, Ilona Rodgers, John Le Mesurier, Graham Stark, Ernest Clark

The Salzburg Connection
US 1972 93m De Luxe Panavision
TCF (Ingo Preminger)

An American lawyer on holiday in Salzburg finds himself suspected by spies of both sides.
Turgid, routine action thriller with attractive locations.

w Oscar Millard, *novel* Helen MacInnes *d* Lee H. Katzin *ph* Wolfgang Treu *md* Lionel Newman

Barry Newman, Anna Karina, Maria Brandauer, Karen Jensen, Wolfgang Preiss
'So dull you can't tell the CIA agents from the neo-Nazis or double agents—or the inept actors from the blocks and stones in the handsome Austrian locales.'—*Judith Crist*

Sam Whiskey
US 1969 96m De Luxe
UA / Brighton (Jules Levy, Arthur Gardner Arnold Laven)

An itinerant gambler is paid to recover a fortune in gold bars from the bottom of a Colorado river.
Easy-going but rather slackly-handled western.

w William W. Norton *d* Arnold Laven *ph* Robert Moreno *m* Herschel Burke Gilbert

Burt Reynolds, Clint Walker, Ossie Davis, Angie Dickinson, Rick Davis, William Schallert

Sammy Going South*
GB 1963 128m Eastmancolor Cinemascope
Bryanston (Hal Mason)
US title: *A Boy Ten Feet Tall*

A 10-year-old boy is orphaned in Port Said and hitch-hikes to his aunt in Durban.
Disappointing family-fodder epic in which the mini-adventures follow each other too predictably.

w Denis Cannan, *novel* W. H. Canaway *d* Alexander Mackendrick *ph* Erwin Hillier *m* Tristam Cary

Fergus McClelland, Edward G. Robinson, Constance Cummings, Harry H. Corbett

Samson and Delilah
US 1949 128m Technicolor
Paramount / Cecil B. de Mille

Delilah, rejected by religious strong man Samson, cuts his hair and delivers him to his enemies.
Absurd biblical hokum, stodgily narrated and directed, monotonously photographed and edited, and notable only for the 30-second destruction of the temple at the end.

w Jesse L. Lasky Jnr, Fredric M. Frank *d* Cecil B. de Mille *ph* George Barnes *m* Victor Young *ad* Hans Dreier, Walter Tyler

Hedy Lamarr, Victor Mature, Angela Lansbury.

George Sanders, Henry Wilcoxon, Olive Deering, Fay Holden, Russ Tamblyn

San Antonio*
US 1945 109m Technicolor
Warner (Robert Buckner)

A cowboy incurs the jealousy of a saloon owner.
Typically thinly-plotted Warner star western which works well enough sequence by sequence, climaxing with a fight in the deserted Alamo.

w Alan le May, W. R. Burnett *d* David Butler *ph* Bert Glennon *m* Max Steiner

Errol Flynn, Alexis Smith, Paul Kelly, Victor Francen, S. Z. Sakall, John Litel, Florence Bates, Robert Shayne, Monte Blue, Robert Barrat

San Diego I Love You*
US 1944 83m bw
Universal (Michael Fessier, Ernest Pagano)

A family travels to San Diego to promote father's inventions.
Pleasing, easy-come-easy-go comedy full of memorable incident and characterization.

w Michael Fessier, Ernest Pagano *d* Reginald Le Borg

Louise Allbritton, Edward Everett Horton, Jon Hall, Eric Blore, *Buster Keaton*, Irene Ryan

San Francisco****
US 1936 117m bw
MGM (John Emerson, Bernard Hyman)

The loves and career problems of a Barbary Coast saloon proprietor climax in the 1906 earthquake.
Incisive, star-packed, superbly-handled melodrama which weaves in every kind of appeal and for a finale has some of the best special effects ever conceived.

w Anita Loos, story Robert Hopkins *d W. S. Van Dyke ph Oliver T. Marsh md Herbert Stothart montage John Hoffman*

Clark Gable, Spencer Tracy, Jeanette MacDonald, Jack Holt, Jessie Ralph, Ted Healy, Shirley Ross, Al Shean, Harold Huber

'Prodigally generous and completely satisfying.'—*Frank S. Nugent*

San Francisco International Airport**
US 1970 96m Technicolor TVM
Universal (Frank Price)

A day's problems for the manager of a big airport.
No mad bomber, otherwise a mini-*Airport* and quite slick and entertaining.

w William Read Woodfield, Allan Balter *d* John Llewellyn Moxey

Pernell Roberts, Clu Gulager, Beth Brickell, Van Johnson, Nancy Malone, David Hartman, Cliff Potts, Tab Hunter

The San Francisco Story*
US 1952 90m bw
Warner / Fidelity–Vogue (Howard Welsch)

In 1856, a wanderer bound for China stops in San Francisco to get involved in politics.
Lively melodrama with good period feel.

w D. D. Beauchamp, *novel* Richard Summers *d* Robert Parrish *ph* John Seitz *m* Emil Newman

Joel McCrea, Yvonne de Carlo, Sidney Blackmer, Florence Bates

San Quentin*
US 1937 70m bw
Warner (Sam Bischoff)

A convict's sister loves the warden.
Standard tough prison melodrama, competently done.

w Peter Milne, Humphrey Cobb *d* Lloyd Bacon *ph* Sid Hickox

Pat O'Brien, Ann Sheridan, Humphrey Bogart, Barton MacLane, Joseph Sawyer, Veda Ann Borg

Sanctuary
US 1960 90m bw Cinemascope
TCF (Richard D. Zanuck)

The governor's daughter is seduced by a bootlegger, and her life goes from one tragedy to another.
Confused adaptation of unadaptable material, full of pussyfoot daring but little sense.

w James Poe, *novel* William Faulkner *d* Tony Richardson *ph* Ellsworth Fredericks *m* Alex North

Lee Remick, Bradford Dillman, Yves Montand, Odetta, Harry Townes, Howard St John, Reta Shaw, Strother Martin

The Sand Pebbles*
US 1966 193m De Luxe Panavision
TCF / Argyle / Solar (Robert Wise)

In 1926 an American gunboat patrolling the Yangtze river gets involved with Chinese warlords.
Confused action blockbuster with Vietnam parallels for those who care to pick them up; pretty thinly stretched entertainment despite the tons of explosive.

w Robert Anderson, *novel* Richard McKenna

d Robert Wise *ph* Joseph MacDonald *m* Jerry Goldsmith

Steve McQueen, Candice Bergen, Richard Attenborough, Richard Crenna, Marayat Andriane, Mako, Larry Gates, Simon Oakland

'If it had been done twenty years ago, it would have been fast and unpretentious, with some ingeniously faked background shots . . . and we would never have asked for larger historical meanings.'—*Pauline Kael*

Sanders of the River*
GB 1935 98m bw
London (Alexander Korda)

Problems of a British colonial servant in keeping peace among the tribes.
Much-caricatured African adventure of the very old school, helped by Robeson's personality.

w Lajos Biro, Jeffrey Dell, Arthur Wimperis *d* Zoltan Korda

Leslie Banks, Paul Robeson, Nina Mae McKinney, Robert Cochran

The Sandpiper
US 1965 116m Metrocolor Panavision
MGM / Filmways (John Calley)

An artist lives with her illegitimate son in a Monterey beach shack; when she is forced to send the boy to school he attracts the attention of the minister in charge.
Absurd novelettish love story basically copied from *The Garden of Allah;* pretty seascapes are the most rewarding aspect.

w Dalton Trumbo, Michael Wilson *d* Vincente Minnelli *ph* Milton Krasner *m* Johnny Mandel

Elizabeth Taylor, Richard Burton, Eva Marie Saint, Charles Bronson, Robert Webber

'Straight Louisa May Alcott interlarded with discreet pornographic allusions.'—*John Simon*

Sands of Iwo Jima*
US 1949 109m bw
Republic (Edmund Grainger)

During World War II in the Pacific, a tough sergeant of marines moulds raw recruits into fighting men but is himself shot by a sniper.
Celebrated star war comic, still quite hypnotic in its flagwaving way.

w Harry Brown, James Edward Grant *d* Allan Dwan *ph* Reggie Lanning *m* Victor Young

John Wayne, John Agar, Adele Mara, Forrest Tucker, Arthur Franz, Julie Bishop, Richard Jaeckel

'The battle sequences are terrifyingly real . . . but the personal dramatics make up a compendium of war-picture clichés.'—*Variety*

Sands of the Kalahari
GB 1965 119m Technicolor Panavision
Pendennis (Cy Endfield, Stanley Baker)

Survivors of a plane crash trek across the desert and are menaced by baboons and each other.
Hysterical melodrama with predictable heebie-jeebies by all concerned and the baddie finally left to the mercy of the monkeys. For hardened sensationalists.

wd Cy Endfield, *novel* William Mulvihill *ph* Erwin Hillier *m* Johnny Dankworth

Stanley Baker, Stuart Whitman, Harry Andrews, Susannah York, Theodore Bikel, Nigel Davenport, Barry Lowe

Sangaree
US 1953 95m Technicolor 3-D
Paramount / Pine-Thomas

Trouble ensues when a plantation owner wills his wealth to the son of a slave.
Period skullduggery rather hammily presented.

w David Duncan, *novel* Frank G. Slaughter *d* Edward Ludwig *ph* Lionel Lindon, W. Wallace Kelley *m* Lucien Caillet

Fernando Lamas, Arlene Dahl, Patricia Medina, Francis L. Sullivan, Charles Korvin, Tom Drake, John Sutton, Willard Parker, Lester Matthews

Santa Fe Trail**
US 1940 110m bw
Warner (Robert Fellows)

A cavalry officer is responsible for the final capture of John Brown.
The most solemn western from star or studio has impressive patches amid routine excitements.

w Robert Buckner *d Michael Curtiz ph* Sol Polito *m* Max Steiner

Errol Flynn, Olivia de Havilland, Raymond Massey, Ronald Reagan, Alan Hale, Van Heflin, Gene Reynolds, Henry O'Neill

Santee
US 1972 93m colour
Vagabond (Deno Paoli Edward Platt)

A boy goes west to find his father and befriends the bounty hunter who has killed him.
Personable, violent western with adequate style and performances.

w Brand Bell *d* Gene Nelson *ph* Donald Morgan *m* Don Randi

Glenn Ford, Michael Burns, Dana Wynter, Jay Silverheels, Harry Townes, John Larch

Santiago
US 1956 92m Warnercolor Cinemascope
Warner (Martin Rackin)
GB title: *The Gun Runner*

A Mississippi paddle-boat sets out for Cuba with a consignment of guns for the rebels.
Stiff period actioner of no particular merit.

w Martin Rackin, John Twist *d* Gordon Douglas *ph* John Seitz *m* David Buttolph

Alan Ladd, Rossana Podesta, Lloyd Nolan, Chill Wills, Paul Fix, L. Q. Jones, Frank de Kova

Sapphire**
GB 1959 92m Eastmancolor
Rank / Artna (Michael Relph)

Scotland Yard solves the murder of a coloured music student.
Efficient police thriller with a strong race angle.

w Janet Green *d* Basil Dearden *ph* Harry Waxman *m* Philip Green

Nigel Patrick, Michael Craig, Yvonne Mitchell, Paul Massie, Bernard Miles, Olga Lindo, Earl Cameron, Gordon Heath, Robert Adams

Saps at Sea
US 1940 60m bw
Hal Roach

Olly needs a rest after working in a horn factory, so he and Stan take a boating holiday but are kidnapped by a gangster.
Disappointing star comedy with gags too few and too long drawn out.

w Charles Rogers, Harry Langdon, Gil Pratt, Felix Adler *d* Gordon Douglas *ph* Art Lloyd

Stan Laurel, Oliver Hardy, James Finlayson, Dick Cramer, Ben Turpin

Sara T.: Portrait of a Teenage Alcoholic*
US 1975 100m Technicolor TVM
Universal (David Levinson)

A case history of a schoolgirl alcoholic.
Sensationalized documentary drama, the most popular TV movie of its year in America.

w Richard and Esther Shapiro *d* Richard Donner

Linda Blair, Verna Bloom, William Daniels, Larry Hagman

Saraband for Dead Lovers*
GB 1948 96m Technicolor
Ealing (Michael Relph)

The tragic love affair of Konigsmark and Sophie Dorothea, wife of the Elector of Hanover who later became George I of England.
Gloomy but superb-looking historical love story: it just misses being a memorable film.

w John Dighton, Alexander Mackendrick, *novel* Helen Simpson *d* Basil Dearden, Michael Relph *ph Douglas Slocombe* *m* Alan Rawsthorne

Stewart Granger, Joan Greenwood, Françoise Rosay, Flora Robson, Peter Bull

'Suspense, romance, interest and excitement in full measure.'—*MFB*

Sarah and Son
US 1930 85m bw
Paramount

A widow seeks the baby her husband took away from her.
Mother love saga: soppy but with good credits.

w Zoe Akins, *novel* Timothy Shea *d* Dorothy Arzner *ph* Charles Lang

Ruth Chatterton, Fredric March, Fuller MmMellish Jnr, Gilbert Emery, Doris Lloyd

Saratoga*
US 1937 102m bw
MGM (Bernard H Hyman)

A bookmaker helps the daughter of a horse breeder.
Forgettable racetrack drama notable chiefly as the last film of Jean Harlow who died before it was completed.

w Anita Loos, Robert Hopkins *d* Jack Conway *ph* Ray June *m* Edward Ward

Clark Gable, Jean Harlow, Lionel Barrymore, Frank Morgan, Walter Pidgeon, Una Merkel, Cliff Edwards, George Zucco, Jonathan Hale

'Glib, forthright, knowing and adroit.'—*Time*

Saratoga Trunk*
US 1943 135m bw
Warner (Hal B Wallis)

A notorious woman comes back to New Orleans and falls for a cowboy helping a railroad combine against their rivals.
Curious, unsatisfactory, miscast and overlong film version of a bestseller: there are enjoyable sequences, but it simply fails to come alive.

w Casey Robinson, *novel* Edna Ferber *d* Sam Wood *ph Ernest Haller* *m* Max Steiner
ph Joseph St Amaad

Ingrid Bergman, Gary Cooper, Flora Robson, Jerry Austin, Florence Bates, John Warburton, John Abbott, Curt Bois, Ethel Griffies

'It lacks a logical pattern of drama and

character . . . a piece of baggage labelled solely for the stars.'—*Bosley Crowther*

Saskatchewan
US 1954 87m Technicolor
U-I (Aaron Rosenberg)
GB title: *O'Rourke of the Royal Mounted*

A mountie helps the lady survivor of an Indian attack.
Standard star actioner.

w Gil Doud *d* Raoul Walsh *ph* John Seitz *m* Joseph Gershenson

Alan Ladd, Shelley Winters, J. Carrol Naish, Hugh O'Brian, Robert Douglas, Richard Long, Jay Silverheels

The Satan Bug*
US 1965 114m De Luxe Panavision
UA / Mirisch / Kappa (John Sturges)

At a top-secret desert research station, one scientist is a traitor, and a deadly virus has been stolen for use by a mad millionaire.
Slow-moving, portentous, gadget-filled actioner which looks good but seldom stimulates.

w James Clavell, Edward Anhalt, *novel* Alistair MacLean *d* John Sturges *ph Robert Surtees* *m* Jerry Goldsmith

George Maharis, Richard Basehart, Anne Francis, Dana Andrews, Ed Asner

Satan Met a Lady*
US 1936 74m bw
Warner (Henry Blanke)

Various crooks and a private detective pursue a rare artifact.
Perversely rewritten version of *The Maltese Falcon* (qv). Fascinating but not really successful.

w Brown Holmes *w* William Dieterle *ph* Arthur Edeson *m* Leo F. Forbstein

Bette Davis, Warren William, Alison Skipworth, Arthur Treacher, Wini Shaw, Marie Wilson, Porter Hall

'One lives through it in constant expectation of seeing a group of uniformed individuals appear suddenly from behind the furniture and take the entire cast into protective custody.'—*Bosley Crowther*

Satan Never Sleeps
US / GB 1962 126m De Luxe Cinemascope
TCF / Leo McCarey
GB title: *The Devil Never Sleeps*

In the late forties in China, Catholic missionaries defy the communists.
Failed anti-Red imitation of *Inn of the Sixth Happiness* with the priests from *Going My Way*. Has to be seen to be believed.

w Claude Binyon, Leo McCarey *d* Leo McCarey *ph* Oswald Morris *m* Richard Rodney Bennett

Clifton Webb, William Holden, France Nuyen, Weaver Lee, Athene Seyler, Martin Benson

The Satanic Rites of Dracula
GB 1973 88m Technicolor
Hammer (Roy Skeggs)

When vampires infest London, a property speculator proves to be Dracula himself.
Intriguingly plotted screamer with more mystery than horror.

w Don Houghton *d* Alan Gibson *ph* Brian Probyn *m* John Cacavas

Peter Cushing, Christopher Lee, Michael Coles, William Franklyn, Freddie Jones, Richard Vernon, Patrick Barr

Satan's School for Girls
US 1973 74m colour TVM
Spelling–Goldberg

A schoolmistress fights the devil for control of a girl's school.
Lunatic farrago which might have been more suspensefully narrated and produced.

w Arthur A. Ross *d* David Lowell Rich

Roy Thinnes, Kate Jackson, Pamela Franklin, Jo Van Fleet, Lloyd Bochner

Satan's Skin
GB 1970 93m Eastmancolor
Tigon / Chilton (Tony Tenser)
aka: *Blood on Satan's Claw*

In 1670 a farmer unearths a skull with one eye intact, and a devil creature subsequently terrifies the village.
Implausible, unpleasant but occasionally rather stylish horror picture.

w Robert Wynne-Simmons *d* Piers Haggard *ph* Dick Bush *m* Marc Wilkinson

Patrick Wymark, Linda Hayden, Barry Andrews, Avice Landon, Tamara Ustinov

Satan's Triangle*
US 1975 74m colour TVM
James Rokos–Danny Thomas

Dead bodies are found in a drifting boat in the Bermuda mystery area.
Good-looking hocus pocus which doesn't make much dramatic sense.

w William Read Woodfield *d* Sutton Roley

Kim Novak, Doug McClure, Alejandro Rey, Jim Davis, Ed Louter

Satellite in the Sky
GB 1956 85m Warnercolor Cinemascope
Warner / Tridelta / Danziger

A rocketship is ordered to lose a tritonium bomb in space, but the device attaches itself to the side of the ship.
Boringly talkative low-budget science fiction with ideas beyond its station but not enough talent to put them over.

w John Mather, J. T. McIntosh, Edith Dell *d* Paul Dickson *ph* Georges Périnal *m* Albert Elms

Kieron Moore, Lois Maxwell, Donald Wolfit, Bryan Forbes, Jimmy Hanley, Alan Gifford

Saturday Island
GB 1951 102m Technicolor
Coronado (David E. Rose)
US title: *Island of Desire*

In 1943 a supply boat is torpedoed and a Canadian nurse finds romance on a desert island with a US marine and a one-armed RAF pilot.
Unlikely, conversational, old-fashioned love story.

wd Stuart Heisler, *novel* Hugh Brooke *ph* Oswald Morris *m* William Alwyn

Linda Darnell, Tab Hunter, Donald Gray

Saturday Night and Sunday Morning****
GB 1960 89m bw
Bryanston / Woodfall (Harry Salzman, Tony Richardson)

A Nottingham factory worker is dissatisfied with his lot, gets into trouble through an affair with a married woman, but finally settles for convention.
Startling when it emerged, this raw working-class melodrama, with its sharp detail and strong comedy asides, delighted the mass audience chiefly because of its strong central character thumbing his nose at authority. Matching the mood of the times, and displaying a new attitude to sex, it transformed British cinema and was much imitated.

w Alan Sillitoe, from his novel *d Karel Reisz ph Freddie Francis m* Johnny Dankworth

Albert Finney, Shirley Anne Field, *Rachel Roberts,* Bryan Pringle, Norman Rossington, Hylda Baker

Saturday's Children
US 1940 101m bw
Warner (Henry Blanke)

An impractical young inventor marries an ambitious young woman, but depressed finances lead to discord.
Glum, dated rehash of a 1929 silent; watchable but not compelling.

w Julius J. and Philip G. Epstein, *play* Maxwell Anderson *d* Vincent Sherman *ph* James Wong Howe

John Garfield, Claude Rains, Anne Shirley, Lee Patrick, George Tobias, Roscoe Karns, Elizabeth Risdon, Berton Churchill

Savage*
US 1972 74m Technicolor TVM
Universal (Paul Mason)

Adventures of the hard-hitting front man of a news commentary team.
Smooth topical melodrama which didn't run to a series.

w Mark Rodgers, William Link, Richard Levinson
d Steven Spielberg

Martin Landau, Barbara Bain, Will Geer, Barry Sullivan, Louise Latham, Pat Hingle, Susan Howard

The Savage
US 1952 95m Technicolor
Paramount (Mel Epstein)

A white boy grows up with Indians and later suffers from divided loyalties.
Solemn, rather tedious but well produced western.

w Sidney Boehm, *novel* L. L. Foreman *d* George Marshall *ph* John F. Seitz *m* Paul Sawtell

Charlton Heston, Susan Morrow, Peter Hanson, Joan Taylor, Richard Rober, Don Porter

The Savage Innocents
GB / France / Italy 1960 107m Super Technirama 70
Joseph Janni / Magic Film / Playart / Gray Films (Maleno Malenotti)

Trials of an Eskimo and his wife in Canada's frozen north.
Conscientious, determined and very boring account of Eskimo life played by actors talking pidgin English. Not a success despite the magnificent photography.

w Nicholas Ray, *novel* Top of the World by Hans Ruesch *d* Nicholas Ray, Baccio Bandini *ph Aldo Tonti, Peter Hennessy m* Angelo Lavagnino

Anthony Quinn, Yoko Tani, Marie Yang, Peter

O'Toole, Carlo Justini, Anna May Wong, Lee Montague, Ed Devereaux

Savage Messiah*
GB 1972 103m Metrocolor
MGM / Russ-Arts (Ken Russell)

The life together (1910–14) of the 18-year-old painter Gaudier and 38-year-old Sophie Brzeska.
Intense, fragmentary art film about two eccentrics; would have better suited TV.

w Christopher Logue, *book* H. S. Ede *d* Ken Russell *ph* Dick Bush *m* Michael Garrett *pd* Derek Jarman

Dorothy Tutin, Scott Anthony, Helen Mirren, Lindsay Kemp, Michael Gough, John Justin

Savage Pampas
Spain / Argentina / US 1967 108m
Eastmancolor Superpanorama
Jaime Prados–Dasa–Sam Bronston

In 19th-century Argentina the commander of an isolated fort finds that a bandit is bribing his men to desert.
Densely plotted semi-western, sometimes good to look at but slow and lugubrious.

w Hugo Fregonese, John Melson *d* Hugo Fregonese *ph* Marcel Berenguer *m* Waldo de los Rios

Robert Taylor, Ron Randell, Ty Hardin, Rosenda Monteros, Marc Lawrence

Savage Sam*
US 1962 104m Technicolor
Walt Disney (Bill Anderson)

The youngest son of a homesteading family has a troublesome dog which redeems itself by tracking down Apaches.
Folksy boy-and-dog western, good of its kind, with adequate suspense and scenery.

w Fred Gipson, William Tunberg *d* Norman Tokar *ph* Edward Colman *m* Oliver Wallace

Brian Keith, Tommy Kirk, Kevin Corcoran, Dewey Martin, Jeff York

'A cadet edition of the best of Ford.'—*MFB*

Savages
US 1972 106m colour
Angelika / Merchant–Ivory (Joseph Saleh)

Forest wanderers take over a deserted mansion and begin to feel its civilizing influence.
Mild fable which needed a Bunuel to do it justice; a few lively moments.

w George Swift Trow, Michael O'Donoghue *d* James Ivory *ph* Walter Lassally *m* Joe Raposo

Louis Stadlen, Anne Francine, Thayer David, Salome Jens, Neil Fitzgerald

Savages*
US 1974 74m colour TVM
Spelling–Goldberg

An unarmed youth in the desert flees from a deranged hunter.
Adventure suspense, not badly done.

w William Wood, *novel* Death Watch by Robb White *d* Lee H. Katzin

Andy Griffith, Sam Bottoms, Noah Beery Jnr, James Best, Randy Boone

Save the Tiger*
US 1972 100m Movielab
Paramount / Jalem / Filmways / Cirandinha (Steve Shagan)

A middle-aged businessman regrets the slack morality of modern America.
Self-adulatory drama which really has little point but gets a few marks for meaning well and for vivid scenes.

w Steve Shagan *d* John G. Avildsen *ph* Jim Crabe *m* Marvin Hamlisch

Jack Lemmon, Jack Gilford, Laurie Heineman, Norman Burton, Thayer David

'A scathing indictment of the US, of materialism, war, marriage—the works. Wordy, literate and deeply felt.'—*NFT, 1974*

The Saxon Charm
US 1948 88m bw
Universal (Joseph Sistrom)

A Broadway impresario dominates the lives of those around him.
Rather heavy-going comedy drama which could have done with more malicious wit; allegedly based on Jed Harris.

wd Claude Binyon, *novel* Frederick Wakeman *ph* Milton Krasner *m* Walter Scharf

Robert Montgomery, Susan Hayward, John Payne, Audrey Totter, Henry Morgan, Harry Von Zell, Cara Williams, Chill Wills, Heather Angel

Say Goodbye, Maggie Cole*
US 1972 73m colour TVM
Spelling–Goldberg

A widow returns to medical practice in a tough slum area.
Efficient woman's tearjerker.

w Sandor Stern *d* Jud Taylor

Susan Hayward, Darren McGavin, Michael Constantine, Dane Clark, Beverly Garland

Say Hello to a Dead Man*
US 1972 73m Technicolor TVM
Universal

Escaping from twenty-five years in a South American jungle prison, a private eye returns to his old practice (which is being run by his son) and finds it difficult to adjust.
A silly premise at least provides some good jokes and chases. Pilot for *Faraday and Company* (see *Mystery Movie*).

d Gary Nelson

Dan Dailey, James Naughton, Sharon Glass, Craig Stevens, Geraldine Brooks, David Wayne, Howard Duff

Say Hello to Yesterday
GB 1970 92m Eastmancolor
Josef Shaftel (William Hill)

A middle-aged married woman goes to London for shopping and is pursued by a strange young man whom she allows to seduce her.
Unattractive 'with it' romantic drama with a swinging London setting, a long way after *Brief Encounter*.

w Alvin Rakoff, Peter King *d* Alvin Rakoff *ph* Geoffrey Unsworth *m* Riz Ortolani

Jean Simmons, Leonard Whiting, *Evelyn Laye*, John Lee, Jack Woolgar

Say One for Me
US 1959 117m De Luxe Cinemascope
TCF / Bing Crosby (Frank Tashlin)

Adventures of a parish priest in New York's theatrical quarter.
Unconvincing, unattractive imitation of *Going My Way* which counters bad taste with religiosity.

w Robert O'Brien *d* Frank Tashlin *ph* Leo Tover *songs* Sammy Cahn, James Van Heusen

Bing Crosby, Robert Wagner, Debbie Reynolds, Ray Walston, Les Tremayne, Connie Gilchrist, Frank McHugh, Joe Besser, Sebastian Cabot

Sayonara**
US 1957 147m Technirama
Goetz Pictures–Pennebaker (William Goetz)

An American air force major in Tokyo after the war falls in love with a Japanese actress.
A lush travelogue interrupted by two romances, one tragic and one happy. A great success at the time, though mainly of interest to Americans; now vaguely dated.

w Paul Osborn, *novel* James A. Michener *d* Joshua Logan *ph Ellsworth Fredericks* *m* Franz Waxman *ad* Ted Haworth

Marlon Brando, Miyoshi Umeki, Miiko Taka, Red Buttons, Ricardo Montalban, Patricia Owens, Kent Smith, Martha Scott, James Garner

Scalawag
US / Italy 1973 93m Technicolor
Bryna / Inex–Oceania (Anne Douglas)

Mexico 1840: a one-legged pirate and a boy try to trace a hidden treasure.
Flagrant reworking of *Treasure Island*, heavily overdone by stars and rhubarbing extras alike.

w Albert Maltz, Sid Fleischman *d* Kirk Douglas *ph* Jack Cardiff *m* John Cameron

Kirk Douglas, Mark Lester, Neville Brand, David Stroud, Lesley-Anne Down, Phil Brown

The Scalphunters*
US 1968 102m De Luxe Panavision
UA / Bristol / Norlan (Levy–Gardner–Laven)

An old cowboy and a black ex-slave track down a gang who kill Indians for their scalps.
Vigorous, aimless, likeable comedy western with the emphasis on brawling.

w William Norton *d* Sidney Pollack *ph* Duke Callaghan, Richard Moore *m* Elmer Bernstein

Burt Lancaster, Ossie Davis, Telly Savalas, Shelley Winters, Nick Cravat, Paul Picerni

'It is the sort of frolic where bodies litter the ground, but you know they'll get up and draw their pay. And where even a villain can crack a joke without losing face.'—*Robert Ottaway*

Scalplock
US 1967 100m colour TVM
Columbia

A gambler wins a railroad.
Western pilot for *The Iron Horse* series.
Prolonged but watchable.

w Stephen Kandel *d* James Goldstone

Dale Robertson, Robert Random, Diana Hyland

Scandal at Scourie
US 1953 90m Technicolor
MGM (Edwin H. Knopf)

The wife of the Protestant reeve of a Scottish-Canadian protestant community adopts a Catholic child.
Sentimental whimsy with no holds barred, but with rather jaded acting and production.

w Norman Corwin, Leonard Spiegelgass, Karl Tunberg *d* Jean Negulesco *ph* Robert Planck *m* Daniele Amfitheatrof

Greer Garson, Walter Pidgeon, Agnes Moorehead, Arthur Shields, Philip Ober

A Scandal in Paris *
US 1946 100m bw
UA / Arnold Pressburger
aka: *Thieves' Holiday*

Adventures of Vidocq, a 19th-century rogue who became Paris chief of police.
The actors look uneasy in their costumes, and the sets are cardboard, but there is fun to be had from this light comedy-drama.

w Ellis St Joseph *d* Douglas Sirk *ph* Guy Roe

George Sanders, Signe Hasso, Carole Landis, Akim Tamiroff, Gene Lockhart

Scandal Sheet
US 1952 81m bw
Columbia (Edward Small)
GB title: *The Dark Page*

An editor has to allow his star reporter to expose a murderer—himself.
Obvious, reasonably holding melodrama with familiar characters.

w Ted Sherdeman, Eugene Ling, James Poe, *novel* Samuel Fuller *d* Phil Karlson *ph* Burnett Guffey *m* George Duning

Broderick Crawford, John Derek, Donna Reed, Rosemary de Camp, Henry O'Neill, Henry Morgan

Scandalous John
US 1971 117m Technicolor
Walt Disney (Bill Walsh)

The elderly owner of a derelict ranch resists all efforts to close him up.
Unsatisfactory Disney attempt to capture a more adult audience than usual; overlong, repetitious and dreary.

w Bill Walsh, Don da Gradi, *novel* Richard Gardner *d* Robert Butler *ph* Frank Phillips *m* Rod McKuen

Brian Keith, Alfonso Arau, Michele Carey, Rick Lenz, Henry Morgan, Simon Oakland

The Scapegoat *
GB 1959 92m bw
MGM / Du Maurier-Guinness (Dennis Van Thal)

A quiet bachelor on a French holiday is tricked into assuming the identity of a lookalike aristocrat who wants to commit a murder.
Disappointing adaptation of a good story, with much evidence of re-cutting and an especially slack middle section.

w Gore Vidal, Robert Hamer, *novel* Daphne du Maurier *d* Robert Hamer *ph* Paul Beeson *m* Bronislau Kaper

Alec Guinness, Bette Davis, Irene Worth, Nicole Maurey, Pamela Brown, Geoffrey Keen

The Scar
US 1948 83m bw
Eagle Lion (Bryan Foy, Paul Henreid)
aka: *Hollow Triumph*

A fugitive kills his psychoanalyst double and takes his place, but is caught for the double's crimes.
Cheap suspense thriller with no suspense and no surprises.

w Daniel Fuchs, *novel* Murray Forbes *d* Steve Sekely *ph* John Alton *m* Sol Kaplan

Joan Bennett, Paul Henreid, Eduard Franz, Leslie Brooks, John Qualen, Mabel Paige, Herbert Rudley

Scaramouche **
US 1952 115m Technicolor
MGM (Carey Wilson)

A young man disguises himself as an actor to avenge the death of his friend at the hands of a wicked marquis.
Cheerful swashbuckler set in French revolutionary times, first filmed in the twenties with Ramon Novarro. MGM costume production at somewhere near its best.

w Ronald Millar, George Froeschel, *novel* Rafael Sabatini *d* George Sidney *ph* Charles Rosher *m* Victor Young *ad Cedric Gibbons, Hans Peters*

Stewart Granger, Mel Ferrer, Eleanor Parker, Janet Leigh, Henry Wilcoxon, Nina Foch, Lewis Stone, Robert Coote, Richard Anderson

Scarecrow *
US 1973 112m Technicolor Panavision
Warner (Robert M. Sherman)

Two of the world's losers hitch-hike across America.
Well-shot but eventually dreary parable of friendship, a pedestrian *Easy Rider*.

w Garry Michael White *d* Jerry Schatzberg *ph* Vilmos Zsigmond *m* Fred Myrow

Gene Hackman, Al Pacino

'Here's a picture that manages to abuse two American myths at once—the Road and the Male Pair.'—*Stanley Kaufmann*

Scared Stiff
US 1953 108m bw
Paramount (Hal B. Wallis)

Nightclub entertainers get involved with a girl who has inherited a spooky castle off the Cuban coast.

Stretched-out remake of *The Ghost Breakers*; the last half hour, being closest to the original, is the most nearly funny.

w Herbert Baker, Walter de Leon *d* George Marshall, Ed Simmons, Norman Lear *ph* Ernest Laszlo *md* Joseph J. Lilley

Dean Martin, Jerry Lewis, Lizabeth Scott, Carmen Miranda, George Dolenz, Dorothy Malone, William Ching, Jack Lambert

The Scarf
US 1951 86m bw
UA / Gloria (I. G. Goldsmith)

A man escapes from a lunatic asylum and proves himself innocent of the crime for which he was committed.
Glum and pretentious murder mystery with a pictorial style to match its flowery dialogue.

wd E. A. Dupont *ph* Franz Planer *m* Herschel Burke Gilbert

John Ireland, Mercedes McCambridge, Emlyn Williams, James Barton, Lloyd Gough, Basil Ruysdael

Scarface****
US 1932 99m bw
Howard Hughes
aka: *The Shame of a Nation*

The life and death of a Chicago gangster of the twenties.
Obviously modelled on Al Capone, with an incestuous sister thrown in, this was perhaps the most vivid film of the gangster cycle, and its revelling in its own sins was not obscured by the subtitle, *The Shame of a Nation*.

w Ben Hecht, Seton I. Miller, John Lee Mahin, W. R. Burnett, Fred Pasley, *novel* Armitage Traill *d Howard Hawks ph Lee Garmes, L. W. O'Connell*

Paul Muni, Ann Dvorak, George Raft, Boris Karloff, Osgood Perkins, Karen Morley, C. Henry Gordon, Vince Barnett, Henry Armetta, Edwin Maxwell

'More brutal, more cruel, more wholesale than any of its predecessors.'—*James Shelley Hamilton*

The Scarface Mob*
US 1958 96m bw
Desilu (Quinn Martin)

Al Capone's empire thrives while he is in Alcatraz, and prohibition agent Eliot Ness recruits a tough squad to fight the gangsters.
Though released theatrically, this was in effect a pilot film for the successful TV series *The Untouchables*, well enough done within its limits.

w Paul Monash, *novel* The Untouchables by Eliot Ness *d* Phil Karlson *ph* Charles Straumer *m* Wilbur Hatch

Robert Stack, Neville Brand, Keenan Wynn, Barbara Nichols, Joe Mantell, Pat Crowley, Bruce Gordon, Paul Picerni, Abel Fernandez

Scarlet Angel
US 1952 81m Technicolor
U-I (Leonard Goldstein)

A saloon hostess presents herself to a wealthy family as their dead son's wife.
Modest, satisfactorily plotted woman's picture with action interludes.

w Oscar Brodney *d* Sidney Salkow *ph* Russell Metty *m* Joseph Gershenson

Yvonne de Carlo, Rock Hudson, Richard Denning, Henry O'Neill, Amanda Blake

The Scarlet Blade*
GB 1963 82m Technicolor
Hammerscope
Hammer (Anthony Nelson Keys)
US title: *The Crimson Blade*

In 1648, a Cromwellian colonel plans to hang every royalist rebel.
Adequate swashbuckler.

wd John Gilling ph Jack Asher *m* Gary Hughes

Lionel Jeffries, Oliver Reed, Jack Hedley, June Thorburn, Duncan Lamont

The Scarlet Coat
US 1955 99m Eastmancolor
Cinemascope
MGM (Nicholas Nayfack)

During the American War of Independence, an American officer deserts to the British in order to unmask a traitor.
Rather talky historical actioner with too much time spent on friendship and romance.

w Karl Tunberg *d* John Sturges *ph* Paul C. Vogel *m* Conrad Salinger

Cornel Wilde, Michael Wilding, George Sanders, Anne Francis, Robert Douglas, Bobby Driscoll, John McIntire

The Scarlet Empress***
US 1934 109m bw
Paramount

A fantasia on the love life of Catherine the Great.
A marvellous, overwhelming, dramatically insubstantial but pictorially brilliant homage to a star; not to everyone's taste, but a film to remember.

w Manuel Komroff *d Josef Von Sternberg ph Bert Glennon md* W. Franke Harling, John

M. Leipold, Milan Roder *ad Hans Dreier, Peter Ballbusch, Richard Kollorsz*

Marlene Dietrich, John Lodge, Sam Jaffe, Louise Dresser, C. Aubrey Smith, Gavin Gordon, Jameson Thomas

'She's photographed behind veils and fishnets, while dwarfs slither about and bells ring and everybody tries to look degenerate.'—*New Yorker, 1975*

'A ponderous, strangely beautiful, lengthy and frequently wearying production.'—*Mordaunt Hall, New York Times*

The Scarlet Hour
US 1955 93m bw Vistavision
Paramount (Michael Curtiz)

A bored wife persuades her lover to turn thief; her husband misconstrues the situation and is accidentally killed.
Complex suspenser designed to introduce new talent; rather too smooth, and pretty boring.

w Rip van Ronkel, Frank Tashlin, Meredyth Lucas *d* Michael Curtiz *ph* Lionel Lindon *m* Leith Stevens

Carol Ohmart, Tom Tryon, James Gregory, Jody Lawrance, E. G. Marshall, *Elaine Stritch*

The Scarlet Pimpernel***
GB 1934 98m bw
London Films (Alexander Korda)

In the early days of the French revolution, an apparently foppish Englishman leads a daring band in rescuing aristocrats from the guillotine.
First-class period adventure with a splendid and much imitated plot, strong characters, humour and a richly detailed historical background.

w Robert E. Sherwood, Sam Berman, Arthur Wimperis, Lajos Biro, *novel* Baroness Orczy *d Harold Young*

Leslie Howard, Merle Oberon, Raymond Massey, Nigel Bruce, Bramwell Fletcher, Anthony Bushell, Joan Gardner, Walter Rilla

'One of the most romantic and durable of all swashbucklers.'—*New Yorker, 1976*

'A triumph for the British film world.'—*Sunday Times*

Scarlet Street**
US 1946 103m bw
Universal / Diana (Walter Wanger)

A prostitute is murdered by her client and her pimp is executed for the crime.
Daring but rather gloomy Hollywood melodrama, the first in which a crime went unpunished (though the culprit was shown suffering remorse). Interesting and heavily Teutonic, but as entertainment not a patch on the similar but lighter *The Woman in the Window*, which the same team had made a year previously.

w Dudley Nichols, *play* La Chienne by George de la Fouchardière (filmed by Jean Renoir in 1932) *d Fritz Lang ph* Milton Krasner *m* Hans Salter *ad* Alexander Golitzen

Edward G. Robinson, Joan Bennett, Dan Duryea, Jess Barker, Margaret Lindsay, Rosalind Ivan, Samuel S. Hinds, Arthur Loft

'The director unerringly chooses the right sound and image to assault the spectator's sensibilities.'—*C. A. Lejeune*

Scars of Dracula
GB 1970 96m Technicolor
Hammer / EMI (Aida Young)

A young man on the run finds himself an unwitting guest of Count Dracula.
Overpadded vampire saga, its few effective moments stemming directly from the original novel.

w John Elder *d* Roy Ward Baker *ph* Moray Grant *m* James Bernard

Christopher Lee, Dennis Waterman, Christopher Matthews, Jenny Hanley, Patrick Troughton, Michael Gwynn, Bob Todd

School for Husbands
GB 1937 71m bw
Wainwright (Richard Wainwright)

A romantic novelist annoys the husbands of his adoring fans.
Would-be champagne comedy which bubbles pretty well for most of its length.

w Frederick Jackson, Gordon Aherry, Austin Melford, *play* Frederick Jackson *d* Andrew Marton *ph* Phil Tannura

Rex Harrison, Henry Kendall, Romney Brent, Diana Churchill, June Clyde

School for Scoundrels*
GB 1960 94m bw
ABP / Guardsman (Hal E. Chester)

A failure reports to the College of One-Upmanship and his life is transformed.
Amusing trifle, basically a series of sketches by familiar comic actors.

w Patricia Mayes, Hal E. Chester, *books* Stephen Potter *d* Robert Hamer *ph* Erwin Hillier *m* John Addison

Ian Carmichael, Alastair Sim, Terry-Thomas, Janette Scott, Dennis Price, Peter Jones, Edward Chapman, John Le Mesurier

School for Secrets
GB 1946 108m bw
Rank / Two Cities (George H. Brown, Peter Ustinov)
US title: *Secret Flight*

The boffins who invented radar find themselves in a little war action of their own.
An unsatisfactory entertainment which, with the best intentions, shuffles between arch comedy, character drama, war action and documentary, doing less than justice to any of these aspects.

wd Peter Ustinov

Ralph Richardson, Raymond Huntley, Richard Attenborough, Marjorie Rhodes, John Laurie, Ernest Jay, David Tomlinson, Finlay Currie

Scorpio
US 1972 114m Technicolor
UA / Scimitar (Walter Mirisch)

CIA agents doublecross each other.
Incredibly complex spy thriller in which it's difficult to know, or care, who's following whom. The brutalities, however, are capably staged.

w David W. Rintels, Gerald Wilson *d* Michael Winner *ph* Robert Paynter *m* Jerry Fielding

Burt Lancaster, Alain Delon, Paul Scofield, John Colicos, Gayle Hunnicutt, J. D. Cannon
'Strictly zoom and thump.'—*Sight and Sound*

The Scorpio Letters
US 1967 98m colour TVM
MGM

British government agencies compete to smash a blackmailing ring.
Ho-hum spy hokum.

w Adrian Spies, Jo Eisinger *d* Richard Thorpe

Alex Cord, Shirley Eaton, Laurence Naismith

Scotland Yard
US 1941 68m bw
TCF (Sol M. Wurtzel)

The Nazis capture a London banker and use his double to turn funds over to them.
Outlandish spy melodrama which certainly keeps the interest.

w Samuel G. Engel, John Balderston, *play* Deniston Clift *d* Norman Foster *ph* Virgil Miller

Nancy Kelly, Edmund Gwenn, Henry Wilcoxon, John Loder, Melville Cooper, Gilbert Emery, Norma Varden

Scott of the Antarctic**
GB 1948 111m Technicolor
Ealing (Sidney Cole)

After long preparation, Captain Scott sets off on his ill-fated 1912 expedition to the South Pole.
The stiff-upper-lip saga par excellence; inevitable knowledge of the end makes it pretty downbeat, and the actors can only be sincere; but the snowscapes, most of them artificial, are fine.

w Ivor Montagu, Walter Meade, Mary Hayley Bell *d* Charles Frend

John Mills, James Robertson Justice, Derek Bond, Harold Warrender, Reginald Beckwith, Kenneth More, James McKechnie, John Gregson

The Scoundrel**
US 1935 74m bw
Paramount (Ben Hecht, Charles MacArthur)

A famous writer dies; his ghost comes back to find the meaning of love.
Unique thirties supernatural melodrama with barbs of dated wit despatched by a splendid cast. Nonsense, but great nonsense.

wd Ben Hecht, Charles MacArthur

Noel Coward, Alexander Woolcott, Julie Haydon, Stanley Ridges, Eduardo Ciannelli
'An unmistakeable whiff from a gossip column world which tries hard to split the difference between an epigram and a wisecrack.'—*William Whitebait*

Scream and Scream Again*
GB 1969 94m Eastmancolor
AIP / Amicus (Milton Subotsky)

Murders are traced to superhuman composite beings created by a mad scientist.
Energetic and well-staged though rather humourless shocker.

w Christopher Wicking, *novel* The Disorientated Man by Peter Saxon *d* Gordon Hessler *ph* John Coquillon *m* David Whittaker *ad* Don Mingaye

Vincent Price, Christopher Lee, Peter Cushing, Alfred Marks, Anthony Newlands, David Lodge

Scream of the Wolf*
US 1974 74m colour TVM
Metromedia–Dan Curtis
aka: *The Hunter*

What appears to be a mad killer animal is actually a werewolf.
Adequately scary piece with not much sense in its script.

w Richard Matheson *d* Dan Curtis

Clint Walker, Peter Graves, Jo Ann Pflug, Phil Carey

Scream, Pretty Peggy*
US 1973 74m Technicolor TVM
Universal (Lou Morheim)

A girl student takes a summer job in a sinister house, and chooses the wrong allies.
Fairly obvious but well presented Grand Guignol.

w Jimmy Sangster, Arthur Hoffe *d* Gordon Hessler

Bette Davis, Ted Bessell, Sian Barbara Allen, Charles Drake

The Screaming Woman*
US 1971 73m Technicolor TVM
Universal (William Frye)

A woman recently ill thinks there is a woman buried somewhere in the grounds of her house. And there is.
Predictable suspenser with a nice cast.

w Merwin Gerard, *story* Roy Bradbury *d* Jack Smight

Olivia de Havilland, Joseph Cotten, Walter Pidgeon, Ed Nelson, Laraine Stephens

Scrooge***
GB 1951 86m bw
Renown (Brian Desmond Hurst)

A Victorian miser is reformed by ghostly visitations on Christmas Eve.
By far the best available version of the classic parable; casting, art direction, pace and general handling are as good as can be.

w Noel Langley, *novel* Charles Dickens *d Brian Desmond Hurst ph C. Pennington-Richards*
m Richard Addinsell

Alastair Sim, Mervyn Johns, Kathleen Harrison, Jack Warner, Michael Hordern, Hermione Baddeley, George Cole, Miles Malleson

Scrooge*
GB 1970 113m Technicolor Panavision
Cinema Center / Waterbury

Dim musical version, darkly coloured and quite lost on the wide screen; but it has its macabre moments of trick photography.

w/m/ly Leslie Bricusse *d* Ronald Neame
ph Oswald Morris *pd* Terry Marsh

Albert Finney, Michael Medwin, Alec Guinness, Edith Evans, Kenneth More, David Collings, Laurence Naismith, Kay Walsh

Scudda Hoo, Scudda Hay
US 1948 98m Technicolor
TCF (Walter Morosco)
GB title: *Summer Lightning*

A farmer's son is less interested in girls than in the welfare of his two mules.
Antediluvian rural romance for the simple-minded.

wd F. Hugh Herbert, *novel* George Agnew Chamberlain *ph* Ernest Palmer *m* Cyril Mockridge

June Haver, Lon McCallister, Walter Brennan, Anne Revere, Natalie Wood, Robert Karnes, Henry Hull, Tom Tully, Marilyn Monroe

The Sea Chase*
US 1955 117m Warnercolor
Cinemascope
Warner (John Farrow)

In 1939 a German freighter tries to make it from Sydney harbour back to Germany.
Unusual but not very compelling naval melodrama, chiefly because the leads are miscast.

w James Warner Bellah, John Twist, *novel* Andrew Geer *d* John Farrow *ph* William Clothier *m* Roy Webb

John Wayne, Lana Turner, David Farrar, Lyle Bettger, Tab Hunter, James Arness, Dick Davalos, John Qualen

'A film compounded of monotonously familiar ingredients.'—*Penelope Houston*

Sea Devils
GB 1953 90m Technicolor
Coronado (David E. Rose)

Spies prevent Napoleon's invasion of England.
Cheerful, forgettable swashbuckler.

w Borden Chase *d* Raoul Walsh *ph* Wilkie Cooper *m* Richard Addinsell

Yvonne de Carlo, Rock Hudson, Maxwell Reed, Denis O'Dea, Michael Goodliffe, Bryan Forbes, Ivor Barnard, Arthur Wontner

Sea Fury
GB 1958 97m bw
Rank (Benjamin Fisz)

Rivalry strikes up between an old and a young sailor on tugboats plying between Spain and England.
Shapeless, leery melodrama with strong performances and an exciting storm-at-sea climax.

w John Kruse, Cy Endfield *d* Cy Endfield
ph Reg Wyer *m* Philip Green

Stanley Baker, Victor McLaglen, Luciana Paluzzi, Grégoire Aslan, Francis de Wolff, David Oxley, Rupert Davies, Robert Shaw

The Sea Gull*
GB 1968 141m Technicolor
Warner / Sidney Lumet
Loves and hates on a 19th-century Russian estate.
Rather heavily star-studded, but certainly proficient film version of a Chekhov favourite.
w Moura Budberg, *play* Anton Chekhov *d* Sidney Lumet *ph* Gerry Fisher *m* none *pd* Tony Walton
James Mason, Simone Signoret, Vanessa Redgrave, David Warner, Harry Andrews, Ronald Radd, Eileen Herlie, Kathleen Widdoes, Denholm Elliott, Alfred Lynch

The Sea Hawk***
US 1940 122m bw
Warner (Hal B. Wallis, Henry Blanke)
Elizabeth I encourages one of her most able captains to acts of piracy against the Spanish.
Wobbly-plotted but stirring and exciting seafaring actioner, with splendid battle and duel scenes.
w Seton I. Miller, Howard Koch *d Michael Curtiz ph Sol Polito m Erich Wolfgang Korngold ad Anton Grot*
Errol Flynn, Flora Robson, Brenda Marshall, *Henry Daniell,* Claude Rains, Donald Crisp, Alan Hale, Una O'Connor, James Stephenson, Gilbert Roland, William Lundigan

The Sea of Grass
US 1947 131m bw
MGM (Pandro S. Berman)
A cattle tycoon is so obsessed by his work that he alienates his family.
Brooding, overlong semi-western with an unexpected cast.
w Marguerite Roberts, Vincent Lawrence, *novel* Conrad Richter *d* Elia Kazan *ph Harry Stradling m* Herbert Stothart
Spencer Tracy, Katharine Hepburn, Melvyn Douglas, Phyllis Thaxter, Robert Walker, Edgar Buchanan, Harry Carey, Ruth Nelson, James Bell
'An epically dreary film.'—*Time*

Sea of Sand*
GB 1958 98m bw
Rank / Tempean (Robert Baker, Monty Berman)
Just before Alamein an Eighth Army desert group plans to destroy one of Rommel's last petrol dumps.
Good standard war suspenser.
w Robert Westerby *d* Guy Green *ph* Wilkie Cooper *m* Clifton Parker
Richard Attenborough, John Gregson, Vincent Ball, Percy Herbert, Michael Craig, Barry Foster, Andrew Faulds, Dermot Walsh

The Sea Shall Not Have Them
GB 1954 93m bw
Eros / Daniel M. Angel
Survivors of a seaplane crash await rescue in a dinghy.
Rather dim computerized compendium of flashback mini-dramas.
w Lewis Gilbert, Vernon Harris *d* Lewis Gilbert *ph* Stephen Dade *m* Malcolm Arnold
Dirk Bogarde, Michael Redgrave, Bonar Colleano, Jack Watling, Anthony Steel, Nigel Patrick, James Kenney, Sidney Tafler, George Rose

Sea Wife
GB 1957 82m De Luxe Cinemascope
TCF / Sumar (André Hakim)
Survivors of a shipwreck near Singapore in 1942 are rescued, not before the bosun has fallen in love with the only lady, not knowing she is a nun.
Flashbacked, uncertain, intermittently effective film of a popular minor novel.
w George K. Burke, *novel* Sea Wyf and Biscuit by J. M. Scott *d* Bob McNaught *ph* Ted Scaife *m* Kenneth V. Jones, Leonard Salzedo
Richard Burton, Joan Collins, Basil Sydney, Cy Grant

The Sea Wolf**
US 1941 90m bw
Warner (Henry Blanke)
Survivors of a ferry crash in San Francisco Bay are picked up by a psychopathic freighter captain who keeps them captive.
Much filmed action suspenser which in this version looks great but overdoes the talk. See also *Barricade,* a disguised western version.
w Robert Rossen, *novel* Jack London *d Michael Curtiz ph Sol Polito m Erich Wolfgang Korngold*
Edward G. Robinson, Alexander Knox, Ida Lupino, John Garfield, Gene Lockhart, Barry Fitzgerald, Stanley Ridges, David Bruce, Howard da Silva
'A Germanic, powerful work almost devoid of compromise.'—*Charles Higham, 1972*

Seagulls over Sorrento
GB 1954 92m bw
MGM (John and Roy Boulting)
US title: *Crest of the Wave*

Life on a naval research station on a small Scottish island.
A long-running British service comedy has been Americanized to little effect, but it remains just about watchable.

w Frank Harvey, Roy Boulting, *play* Hugh Hastings *d* John and Roy Boulting *ph* Gilbert Taylor *m* Miklos Rozsa

Gene Kelly, John Justin, Bernard Lee, Sidney James, Jeff Richards, Patric Doonan, Patrick Barr

Sealed Verdict
US 1948 83m bw
Paramount (Robert Fellows)

An American officer in Germany falls in love with the ex-girl friend of a Nazi war criminal.
Routine melodrama, as boring as it sounds.

w Jonathan Latimer, *novel* Lionel Shapiro *d* Lewis Allen *ph* Leo Tover *m* Hugo Friedhofer

Ray Milland, Florence Marly, Broderick Crawford, John Hoyt, John Ridgely, Ludwig Donath

Seance on a Wet Afternoon*
GB 1964 121m bw
Rank / Allied Film Makers (Richard Attenborough, Bryan Forbes, Jack Rix)

A fake medium persuades her husband to kidnap a child so that she can become famous by revealing its whereabouts in a trance.
Overlong character melodrama in which the suspense is better than the psychopathology. A mannered performance from the lady, a false nose from the gentleman, and a general air of gloom.

wd Bryan Forbes ph Gerry Turpin *m* John Barry

Kim Stanley, Richard Attenborough, Nanette Newman, Patrick Magee

The Search*
US / Switzerland 1948 105m bw
MGM / Praesens Film (Lazar Wechsler)

An American soldier in Germany cares for a war orphan.
Vivid semi-documentary post-war drama which falls down in its elementary dramatics but sent audiences home wiping away tears.

w Richard Schweizer, David Wechsler, Paul Jarrico *d Fred Zinnemann pd Emil Berna ph* Robert Blum

Montgomery Clift, Aline MacMahon, Ivan Jandl, Wendell Corey

The Search for Bridey Murphy*
US 1956 84m bw Vistavision
Paramount (Pat Duggan)

A Colorado businessman and amateur hypnotist finds a lady neighbour so good a subject that he is able to delve into her previous incarnation as a long-dead Irish peasant.
Adequately presented with alienation effects, but mainly consisting of two-shots and fuzzy flashbacks, this treatment of an actual case (subsequently discredited) works up to a fine pitch of frenzy when the subject seems unable to come back from her previous life.

wd Noel Langley, book Morey Bernstein *ph* John F. Warren *m* Irving Talbot

Teresa Wright, Louis Hayward, Kenneth Tobey, Nancy Gates, Richard Anderson

The Search for Green Eyes
US 1976 100m colour TVM
Lorimar

A black soldier goes back to Vietnam to seek his native wife and child.
Documentary style tearjerker with lots to say about the tragedy of war.

d John Erman

Paul Winfield, Rita Tushingham

Search for the Gods*
US 1975 100m colour TVM
Warner / Douglas S. Cramer

A rare medallion sends three adventurers seeking evidence of ancient visitors to earth.
Overstretched action hokum with pleasing moments.

w Herman Miller, Ken Pettus *d* Jud Taylor

Kurt Russell, Stephen McHattie, Ralph Bellamy, Victoria Racimo, Raymond St Jacques

The Searchers**
US 1956 119m Technicolor Vistavision
Warner / C. V. Whitney (Merian C. Cooper)

A Confederate war veteran tracks down the Indians who have slaughtered his brother and sister-in-law and carried off their daughter.
Desultory, easy-going, good-looking western in typical Ford style: a bit more solemn than usual.

w Frank S. Nugent, *novel* Alan le May *d John Ford ph Winton C. Hoch m* Max Steiner

John Wayne, Jeffrey Hunter, Natalie Wood, Vera Miles, Ward Bond, John Qualen, Henry Brandon, Antonio Moreno

The Searching Wind*
US 1946 107m bw
Paramount (Hal B. Wallis)

Affairs of an American diplomat in Europe during the thirties.
Earnest melodrama which would have been better timed six years earlier. Excellent production, though.

w Lillian Hellman, from her play *d* William Dieterle *ph* Lee Garmes *m* Victor Young *ad* Hans Dreier, Franz Bachelin

Robert Young, Sylvia Sidney, Ann Richards, Douglas Dick, Dudley Digges, Albert Basserman, Dan Seymour

Sebastian
GB 1968 100m Eastmancolor
Paramount/Maccius (Herb Brodkin, Michael Powell)

An Oxford professor and code expert is appointed to the secret service.
Mildly spoofy spy yarn: style but not much substance.

w Gerald Vaughan-Hughes *d David Greene* *ph* Gerry Fisher *m* Jerry Goldsmith *pd* Wilfred Shingleton

Dirk Bogarde, *John Gielgud,* Lilli Palmer, Susannah York, Janet Munro, Margaret Johnston, Nigel Davenport, Ronald Fraser

'One of the problems with this kind of movie is the enormous pressure put on the audience to have a good time over practically nothing.'—*Renata Adler*

Second Chance
US 1953 82m Technicolor 3-D
RKO (Edmund Grainger)

In South America, a professional killer stalks a gangster's moll.
Comic strip antics with a climax on a stalled cable car.

w Oscar Millard, Sidney Boehm, *story* D. M. Marshman Jnr *d* Rudolph Maté *ph* William Snyder *m* Roy Webb

Robert Mitchum, Linda Darnell, Jack Palance, Reginald Sheffield, Roy Roberts

Second Chance
US 1971 74m colour TVM
Metromedia

A stockbroker buys a Nevada ghost town and decks it out as a new community for people like himself.
Sluggish comedy drama.

w Michael Morris *d* Peter Tewkesbury

Brian Keith, Elizabeth Ashley, Juliet Prowse, Rosie Greer, Pat Carroll, William Windom

Second Chorus
US 1941 84m bw
Paramount (Boris Morros)

Two trumpeters and their lady manager hit Broadway.
Mild musical.

w Elaine Ryan, Ian McClellan Hunter, Frank Cavett *d* H. C. Potter *ph* Theodor Sparkuhl *songs* various

Fred Astaire, Burgess Meredith, Paulette Goddard, Charles Butterworth, Artie Shaw and his Band, Frank Melton, Jimmy Conlon

Second Fiddle
US 1939 86m bw
TCF (Gene Markey)

A Minnesota skating schoolteacher goes to Hollywood and becomes a star.
Routine star vehicle.

w Harry Tugend *d* Sidney Lanfield *ph* Leon Shamroy *md* Louis Silvers

Sonja Henie, Tyrone Power, Edna May Oliver, Rudy Vallee, Mary Healy, Lyle Talbot, Alan Dinehart

The Second Greatest Sex
US 1955 87m Technicolor Cinemascope
U-I (Albert J. Cohen)

Western women emulate Lysistrata to stop their men from feuding.
Flat attempt to cash in on *Seven Brides for Seven Brothers*; some good acrobatic dancing but no style.

w Charles Hoffman *d* George Marshall *ph* Wilfrid M. Cline *md* Joseph Gershenson *ch* Lee Scott

Jeanne Crain, George Nader, Bert Lahr, Kitty Kallen, Paul Gilbert, Keith Andes, Mamie Van Doren, Tommy Rall

Second Honeymoon
US 1937 79m bw
TCF (Raymond Griffith)

A man tries to win back his ex-wife.
Moderate star romantic comedy.

w Kathryn Scola, Darrell Ware, *story* Philip Wylie *d* Walter Lang *ph* Ernest Palmer

Tyrone Power, Loretta Young, Stuart Erwin, Claire Trevor, Marjorie Weaver, Lyle Talbot, J. Edward Bromberg

The Second Mrs Tanqueray
GB 1952 75m bw
Vandyke (Roger Proudlock)

A Victorian society widower marries a notorious lady.
Stiff-backed penny-pinching version of an interestingly antiquated play.

play Arthur Wing Pinero *d* Dallas Bower

Pamela Brown, Hugh Sinclair, Ronald Ward, Virginia McKenna, Andrew Osborn

The Second Time Around
US 1961 99m De Luxe Cinemascope
TCF / Cummings / Harman (Jack Cummings)

In 1912 Arizona, a widow stands for sheriff and has plenty of choice for a husband.
Light-hearted western fun mixed with family sentimentality.

w Oscar Saul, Cecil Van Heusen, *novel* Richard Emery Roberts *d* Vincent Sherman *ph* Ellis W. Carter *m* Gerald Fried

Debbie Reynolds, Steve Forrest, Andy Griffith, Juliet Prowse, Thelma Ritter, Ken Scott, Isobel Elsom

'Keep a lemon handy for sucking to ward off an attack of the terminal cutesies.'—*Judith Crist, 1973*

Seconds**
US 1966 106m bw
Paramount / Joel / Gibraltar (Edward Lewis)

A secret organization sells a special service to the jaded rich; apparent death followed by physical rejuvenation.
An intriguing half-hour is followed by a glum new life for our hero, capped by a horrifying finale in which, dissatisfied, he learns he is to become one of the corpses necessary to the organization's continuance.

w Lewis John Carlino, *novel* David Ely *d John Frankenheimer ph James Wong Howe m* Jerry Goldsmith *titles* Saul Bass

Rock Hudson, *John Randolph, Will Geer*, Salome Jens, Jeff Corey, Richard Anderson, Murray Hamilton, Wesley Addy

The Secret Agent**
GB 1936 83m bw
Gaumont British (Michael Balcon, Ivor Montagu)

A reluctantly recruited spy is ordered to kill a man.
Unsatisfactory in casting and writing, this Hitchcock suspenser nevertheless has many typically amusing moments.

w Charles Bennett, *play* Campbell Dixon, *story* Ashenden by Somerset Maugham *d Alfred Hitchcock ph* Bernard Knowles *m* Louis Levy

John Gielgud, Robert Young, *Peter Lorre*, Madeleine Carroll, Percy Marmont, Lilli Palmer, Michael Redgrave, Florence Kahn

'As uncommon as it is unsentimentally cruel.'—*Peter John Dyer, 1964*

'Many sequences which show Hitchcock at his very best: the fake funeral, the murder on the mountainside, the riverside café, and the climax in a chocolate factory.'—*NFT, 1961*

The Secret beyond the Door
US 1948 98m bw
Universal / Walter Wanger (Fritz Lang)

An heiress marries a moody millionaire with a death fixation, and comes to think of herself as his next potential victim.
Silly melodrama with much chat and little suspense.

w Sylvia Richards, *story* Rufus King *d* Fritz Lang *ph* Stanley Cortez *m* Miklos Rozsa

Joan Bennett, Michael Redgrave, Anne Revere, Barbara O'Neil, Natalie Schaefer, Paul Cavanagh

'A dog-wagon *Rebecca* with a seasoning of psychiatrics.'—*Otis L. Guernsey Jnr*

The Secret Bride
US 1935 63m bw
Warner

A District Attorney is secretly married to the daughter of the politician he is trying to convict.
Dismal melodrama, tritely scripted.

w Tom Buckingham, F. Hugh Herbert, Mary McCall Jnr, *play* Concealment by Leonard Ide *d* William Dieterle *ph* Ernest Haller

Barbara Stanwyck, Warren William, Glenda Farrell, Grant Mitchell, Arthur Byron, Henry O'Neill, Douglass Dumbrille

Secret Ceremony
GB 1969 109m Eastmancolor
Universal / World Films / Paul M. Heller (John Heyman, Norman Priggen)

A prostitute mothers a young girl with a strange past.
Nuthouse melodrama for devotees of the director.

w George Tabori, *short story* Marco Denevi *d* Joseph Losey *ph* Gerry Fisher *m* Richard Rodney Bennett

Elizabeth Taylor, Robert Mitchum, Mia Farrow, Pamela Brown, Peggy Ashcroft

'This piece of garbage is so totally ridiculous that I can't imagine why anyone would want to be in it, let alone see it.'—*Rex Reed*

Secret Command
US 1944 92m bw
Columbia (Phil L. Ryan)

An ex-foreign correspondent goes undercover at a shipyard to track down saboteurs.
Routine wartime thick ear.

w Roy Chanslor, *story* The Saboteurs by John and Ward Hawkins *d* Eddie Sutherland *ph* Franz Planer *m* Paul Sawtell

Pat O'Brien, Carole Landis, Chester Morris, Ruth Warrick, Barton MacLane, Tom Tully, Wallace Ford, Howard Freeman

The Secret Fury
US 1950 86m bw
RKO (Jack H. Skirball, Bruce Manning)

A successful pianist is deliberately driven insane by her fiancé.
Derivative melodrama of no great interest.

w Lionel House *d* Mel Ferrer *ph* Leo Tover *m* Constantin Bakaleinikoff

Claudette Colbert, Robert Ryan, Jane Cowl, Paul Kelly, Philip Ober, Elizabeth Risdon, Doris Dudley

The Secret Garden*
US 1949 92m bw (Technicolor sequence)
MGM

An orphan girl goes to stay with her moody uncle and brightens up the lives of those around her.
Subdued, richly produced, rather likeable Victorian fable with the same moral as *The Bluebird* and *The Wizard of Oz*: happiness is in your own back yard.

w Robert Ardrey, *novel* Frances Hodgson Burnett *d* Fred M. Wilcox *ph* Ray June *m* Bronislau Kaper

Margaret O'Brien, Herbert Marshall, Gladys Cooper, Elsa Lanchester, Dean Stockwell, Brian Roper

The Secret Heart
US 1946 97m bw
MGM (Edwin H. Knopf)

A widow has problems with her emotionally disturbed daughter.
Old-fashioned woman's picture.

w Rose Franken, William Brown Meloney *d* Robert Z. Leonard *ph* George Folsey *m* Bronislau Kaper

Claudette Colbert, Walter Pidgeon, June Allyson, Robert Sterling, Marshall Thompson, Elizabeth Patterson, Richard Derr, Patricia Medina

' "There are three things you can't hide," says Walter Pidgeon in one of his bantering moments; "love, smoke, and a man riding a camel." I would add a fourth—that old MGM touch.'—*Richard Winnington*

The Secret Invasion
US 1964 98m De Luxe Panavision
UA / San Carlos (Gene Corman)

During World War II five convicted criminals become commandos.
Cut price *Dirty Dozen*, quite well made and exciting.

w R. Wright Campbell *d* Roger Corman *ph* Arthur E. Arling *m* Hugo Friedhofer

Stewart Granger, Raf Vallone, Henry Silva, Mickey Rooney, Edd Byrnes, William Campbell, Peter Coe

The Secret Life of an American Wife**
US 1968 92m De Luxe
TCF / Charlton (George Axelrod)

A bored suburban housewife sets out to seduce a movie star.
Sympathetic comedy of sixties suburban manners.

wd George Axelrod *ph* Leon Shamroy *m* Billy May

Walter Matthau, Anne Jackson, Patrick O'Neal, Edy Williams

'Both a first-class satire on American mores and a compassionate study of wish-fulfilment.' —*NFT, 1970*

The Secret Life of Walter Mitty**
US 1947 110m Technicolor
Samuel Goldwyn

A mother's boy dreams of derring-do, and eventually life catches up with fiction.
This pleasantly remembered star comedy, though it never had much to do with Thurber, can now be seen to have missed most of its opportunities, though the nice moments do tend to compensate.

w Ken Englund, Everett Freeman, *story* James Thurber *d* Norman Z. McLeod *ph* Lee Garmes *m* David Raksin

Danny Kaye, Virginia Mayo, Boris Karloff, Florence Bates, Fay Bainter, *Thurston Hall*, Ann Rutherford, Gordon Jones, Reginald Denny

Secret Mission
GB 1942 94m bw
GFD / Marcel Hellman / Excelsior

During World War II four British Intelligence officers are landed in occupied France to discover the truth about German defences.
Stilted war suspenser.

w Anatole de Grunwald, Basil Bartlett, Terence Young *d* Harold French *ph* Bernard Knowles *m* Mischa Spoliansky

Hugh Williams, Carla Lehmann, James Mason, Roland Culver, Nancy Price, Michael Wilding, Percy Walsh

The Secret Night Caller*
US 1975 74m colour TVM
Charles Fries / Penthouse

An otherwise respectable man has a compulsion to make obscene phone calls . . .
Fairly interesting psycho-drama.

w Robert Presnell Jnr *d* Jerry Jameson

Robert Reed, Hope Lange, Michael Constantine, Sylvia Sidney, Elaine Giftos

The Secret of Blood Island
GB 1964 84m Technicolor
U-I / Hammer

A girl parachutist secret agent is smuggled into a Japanese POW camp and out again.
Absurd blood and thunder, almost perversely enjoyable—but not quite.

w John Gilling *d* Quentin Lawrence *ph* Jack Asher *m* James Bernard

Barbara Shelley, Jack Hedley, Charles Tingwell, Bill Owen, Lee Montague

The Secret of Convict Lake*
US 1951 83m bw
TCF (Frank P. Rosenberg)

In the 1870s, escaped convicts take over a California town.
Brooding, snowy, set-bound western melodrama; predictable but watchable.

w Oscar Saul *d* Michael Gordon *ph* Leo Tover *m* Lionel Newman

Glenn Ford, Gene Tierney, Ann Dvorak, Ethel Barrymore, Zachary Scott, Barbara Bates, Cyril Cusack, Jeanette Nolan, Ruth Donnelly

The Secret of My Success
GB 1965 105m Metrocolor Panavision
MGM / Andrew and Virginia Stone

A village policeman follows his mother's dictum that he should not think ill of others, and accidentally goes from success to success.
Flabby portmanteau comedy full of in-jokes and flat-footed farce; satire is not evident.

wd Andrew L. Stone *ph* David Boulton *m* Roland Shaw, Lucien Caillet

James Booth, Lionel Jeffries, *Amy Dalby*, Stella Stevens, Honor Blackman, Shirley Jones, Joan Hickson

The Secret of Santa Vittoria*
US 1969 140m Technicolor Panavision
UA / Stanley Kramer

In 1945 an Italian village hides its wine from the occupying Germans.
Expected, exhausting epic comedy with everyone talking at once.

w William Rose, Ben Maddow, *novel* Robert Crichton *d* Stanley Kramer *ph* Giuseppe Rotunno *m* Ernest Gold

Anthony Quinn, Anna Magnani, Virna Lisi, Hardy Kruger, Sergio Franchi, Renato Rascel

'A brainless farrago of flying rolling pins and rotten vegetables, filled with the kind of screaming, belching, eye-rolling fictional Italians only Stanley Kramer could invent.'—*Rex Reed*

The Secret of the Incas
US 1954 101m Technicolor
Paramount (Mel Epstein)

Various adventurers seek a priceless Inca jewel.
Boys' Own Paper yarn which sounds a good deal more exciting than it is: too much talk and a few choice studio backcloths drop the tension alarmingly, and the script lacks humour and conciseness.

w Ranald MacDougall, Sidney Boehm *d* Jerry Hopper *ph* Lionel Lindon *m* David Buttolph

Charlton Heston, Robert Young, Thomas Mitchell, Nicole Maurey, Yma Sumac, Glenda Farrell, Michael Pate

The Secret Partner*
GB 1961 91m bw
MGM (Michael Relph)

A blackmailing dentist is visited by a mysterious hooded stranger who forces him to rob one of his businessman victims.
Complex puzzle thriller, neatly made in sub-Hitchcock style.

w David Pursall, Jack Seddon *d* Basil Dearden *ph* Harry Waxman *m* Philip Green

Stewart Granger, Haya Harareet, Bernard Lee, Hugh Burden, Melissa Stribling, Norman Bird, Conrad Philips

The Secret People*
GB 1951 96m bw
Ealing (Sidney Cole)

European refugees in London during the thirties become members of a ring of anarchists.
Downbeat political melodrama which pleased neither the masses nor the highbrows, despite plaudits for sensitive direction and performances.

w Thorold Dickinson, Wolfgang Wilhelm
d Thorold Dickinson *ph* Gordon Dines
m Roberto Gerhard

Valentina Cortese, Serge Reggiani, Audrey Hepburn, Charles Goldner, Megs Jenkins, Irene Worth, Athene Seyler, Reginald Tate

'The tension and power of the film make it one of the most remarkable British productions for some time.'—*Penelope Houston*

'That *Secret People*, despite the creative agonies recorded by Mr Lindsay Anderson [in a book on the making of the film] should turn out to be a confused, unco-ordinated spy thriller concealing a tentative message deep down below some strained effects of style is another tragedy of British film hopes.'—*Richard Winnington*

The Secret Six*
US 1931 83m bw
MGM

A syndicate of businessmen finance two reporters to get evidence against a gang of bootleggers.
Solidly carpentered gangster thriller.

w Frances Marion *d* George Hill *ph* Harold Wenstrom

Wallace Beery, Lewis Stone, Clark Gable, John Mack Brown, Jean Harlow, Marjorie Rambeau, Paul Hurst, Ralph Bellamy, John Miljan

The Secret War of Harry Frigg
US 1967 109m Techniscope
Universal / Albion (Hal E. Chester)

In 1943 a private engineers the escape of five captured generals.
Unattractive war comedy; slow, uninventive and overlong.

w Peter Stone, Frank Tarloff *d* Jack Smight
ph Russell Metty *m* Carlo Rustichelli

Paul Newman, *John Williams*, Sylva Koscina, Andrew Duggan, Tom Bosley, Charles D. Gray, Vito Scotti, James Gregory

The Secret Ways*
US 1961 112m bw
U-I / Heath (Richard Widmark)

An American reporter is recruited to rescue a scholar from communist Hungary.
Pretentious Iron Curtain melodrama, quite good to look at but overlong and no *Third Man*.

w Jean Hazelwood, *novel* Alistair MacLean
d Phil Karlson *ph* Max Greene *m* Johnny Williams

Richard Widmark, Sonja Ziemann, Charles Regnier, Walter Rilla, Howard Vernon, Senta Berger

See Here Private Hargrove*
US 1944 102m bw
MGM (George Haight)

Adventures of a raw recruit in the US army.
Standard transcription of a humorous bestseller which did its best to make the war painless for Americans.

w Harry Kurnitz, *book* Marion Hargrove
d Wesley Ruggles *ph* Charles Lawton *m* David Snell

Robert Walker, Donna Reed, Robert Benchley, Keenan Wynn, Bob Crosby, Ray Collins, Chill Wills, Grant Mitchell
† Sequel 1945: *What Next, Corporal Hargrove?*

See How They Run*
US 1965 100m Technicolor TVM
Universal (Jack Laird)

The children of a spy are menaced by neo-Nazis and helped by a G-man.
Lively chase adventure with good use of New York locations.

w Michael Blankfort *d* David Lowell Rich

John Forsythe, Senta Berger, Franchot Tone, Jane Wyatt, Leslie Nielsen

See the Man Run**
US 1971 73m Technicolor TVM
Universal (Stan Shpetner)

An actor devises a means of easy money but finds himself in the middle of a kidnap plot.
Ingenious suspenser which starts well and keeps its end up.

w Mann Rubin *d Corey Allen*

Robert Culp, Angie Dickinson, June Allyson, Eddie Albert, Charles Cioffi

The Seekers
GB 1954 90m Eastmancolor
GFD / Fanfare (George H. Brown)
US title: *Land of Fury*

In 1820 a British sailor and his family emigrate to New Zealand.

Stilted epic which never gains the viewer's sympathy or interest.

w William Fairchild *d* Ken Annakin *ph* Geoffrey Unsworth *m* William Alwyn

Jack Hawkins, Glynis Johns, Inia Te Wiata, Noel Purcell, Kenneth Williams, Laya Raki

The Sellout
US 1951 82m bw
MGM (Nicholas Nayfack)

A newspaper editor exposes a corrupt administration.
Competent melodrama with no surprises.

w Charles Palmer *d* Gerald Mayer *ph* Paul Vogel *m* David Buttolph

Walter Pidgeon, John Hodiak, Audrey Totter, Thomas Gomez, Everett Sloane, Cameron Mitchell, Karl Malden, Paula Raymond

The Senator Was Indiscreet*
US 1947 95m bw
U-I (Nunnally Johnson)
GB title: *Mr Ashton Was Indiscreet*

A foolish politician determines to become president and hires a press agent.
Satirical political farce which hurls its shafts wide and doesn't seem to mind how few of them hit.

w Charles MacArthur, *story* Edwin Lanham *d* George S. Kaufman *ph* William Mellor *m* Daniele Amfitheatrof

William Powell, Ella Raines, Peter Lind Hayes, Ray Collins, Arleen Whelan, Allen Jenkins, Hans Conried, Charles D. Brown

Send Me No Flowers*
US 1964 100m Technicolor
U-I / Martin Melcher (Harry Keller)

A hypochondriac mistakenly thinks he is dying and tries to provide another spouse for his wife.
A timeworn farcical situation is handled in the glossy Doris Day manner; it all starts quite brightly but gradually fizzles out.

w Julius Epstein, *play* Norman Barrasch, Carroll Moore *d* Norman Jewison *ph* Daniel Fapp *m* Frank de Vol *ad* Alexander Golitzen, Robert Clatworthy

Doris Day, Rock Hudson, Tony Randall, Paul Lynde, Clint Walker, Hal March, Edward Andrews

Senior Year
US 1974 74m Technicolor TVM
Universal

Family and college problems in 1955

Inspired by *American Graffiti*, this became a tedious but brief series called *Sons and Daughters*.

w M. Charles Cohen *d* Richard Donner

Gary Frank, Glynnis O'Connor, Scott Columby, Barry Livingston

Sensations of 1945
US 1944 87m bw
Andrew L. Stone

Father and son disagree over the handling of their publicity agency.
Slim plot holds together a ragbag of variety acts, some quite choice.

w Dorothy Bennett *d* Andrew L. Stone *ph* Peverell Marley, John Mescall *md* Mahlon Merrick

Eleanor Powell, W. C. Fields, Sophie Tucker, Dennis O'Keefe, Eugene Pallette, C. Aubrey Smith, Lyle Talbot, Dorothy Donegan, Cab Calloway and his band, Woody Herman and his band

Sentimental Journey
US 1946 94m bw
TCF (Walter Morosco)

An actress who knows she is dying arranges for a little orphan girl to take her place in her husband's affections.
Hollywood's most incredible three-handkerchief picture; nicely made, but who dared to write it?

w Samuel Hoffenstein, Elizabeth Reinhardt, *story* Nelia Gardner White *d* Walter Lang *ph* Norbert Brodine *m* Cyril Mockridge

Maureen O'Hara, John Payne, William Bendix, Cedric Hardwicke, Glenn Langan, Mischa Auer, Connie Marshall, Kurt Kreuger

'In twenty years of filmgoing I can't remember being so slobbered at: the apotheosis of the weepie.'—*Richard Winnington*

† Remade as *The Gift of Love* (qv).

Separate Tables**
US 1958 98m bw
UA / Hecht–Hill–Lancaster (Harold Hecht)

Emotional tensions among the boarders at a British seaside guest house.
The genteel melodramas seem less convincing on the Hollywood screen than they did on the London stage, but the handling is thoroughly professional.

w Terence Rattigan, John Gay, *play* Terence Rattigan *d* Delbert Mann *m* David Raksin

Burt Lancaster, Rita Hayworth, *David Niven*, Deborah Kerr, *Wendy Hiller*, *Gladys Cooper*,

Cathleen Nesbitt, Felix Aylmer, Rod Taylor, Audrey Dalton, *May Hallatt*

September Affair
US 1950 104m bw
Paramount (Hal B. Wallis)

Two married people fall in love and a plane crash in which they are reported dead gives them their chance.
Turgid romantic melodrama, not very well made despite the background tour of Capri; what made it a hit was the playing of the old Walter Huston record of the title song.

w Robert Thoeren *d* William Dieterle *ph* Charles B. Lang *m* Victor Young

Joseph Cotten, Joan Fontaine, Françoise Rosay, Jessica Tandy, Robert Arthur, Jimmy Lydon
'A smooth surface mirrors the film's essential superficiality.'—*Penelope Houston*

September Storm
US 1960 110m De Luxe Cinemascope 3-D
TCF / Alco (Edward L. Alperson)

A New York model and two adventurers search for sunken treasure off an uncharted Mediterranean island.
Thin actioner originally intended to marry 3-D and Cinemascope, but failed to do so.

w W. R. Burnett, *novel* The Girl in the Red Bikini by Steve Fisher *d* Byron Haskin *ph* Jorge Stahl Jnr, Lamar Boren *m* Edward L. Alperson Jnr

Joanne Dru, Mark Stevens, Robert Strauss

Serenade
US 1956 121m Warnercolor
Warner (Henry Blanke)

A vineyard worker becomes a successful opera singer and is desired by two women.
Cliché success story with plot taking second place to singing.

w Ivan Goff, Ben Roberts, John Twist, *novel* James M. Cain *d* Anthony Mann *ph* Peverell Marley *md* Nicholas Brodsky

Mario Lanza, Joan Fontaine, Sarita Montiel, Vincent Price, Joseph Calleia, Harry Bellaver, Vince Edwards, Silvio Minciotti

The Sergeant
US 1968 108m Technicolor
Warner / Robert Wise (Richard Goldstone)

France, 1952. In a dreary army camp, a tough army sergeant with a guilt complex is brought face to face with his own homosexuality.
Well-made but very ponderous and limited melodrama which could have been told in half the time.

w Dennis Murphy, from his novel *d* John Flynn *ph* Henri Persin *m* Michel Mayne

Rod Steiger, John Philip Law, Frank Latimore, Ludmila Mikael

Sergeant Madden
US 1939 90m bw
MGM (J. Walter Ruben)

A policeman's son becomes a gangster.
Routine crime melodrama with sentimental trimmings, quite untypical of its director.

w Wells Root, *story* A Gun in His Hand by William A. Ulman *d* Josef Von Sternberg *ph* John Seitz *m* William Axt

Wallace Beery, Tom Brown, Alan Curtis, Laraine Day, Fay Holden, Marc Lawrence, Marion Martin

Sergeant Rutledge*
US 1960 111m Technicolor
Warner / John Ford (Willis Goldbeck, Patrick Ford)

In 1881 a black army sergeant is on trial for rape and murder, but his defence counsel reveals the real culprit.
Flashback western; not the director's best, but generally of some interest.

w James Warner Bellah, Willis Goldbeck *d* John Ford *ph* Bert Glennon *m* Howard Jackson

Woody Strode, Jeffrey Hunter, Constance Towers, Willis Bouchey, Billie Burke, Carleton Young, Juano Hernandez, Mae Marsh

Sergeant Ryker
US 1963 85m Pathecolor TVM
Universal (Frank Telford)

In Korea, army lawyers prepare the trial of a sergeant accused of being a traitor.
Muddled courtroom drama which began life as two episodes of the anthology series *Crisis* and also served as pilot for a one-hour series *Counsellors at War*, also known as *Court Martial*.

w Seeleg Lester, William D. Gordon *d* Buzz Kulik

Lee Marvin, Bradford Dillman, Peter Graves, Vera Miles, Lloyd Nolan, Murray Hamilton, Norman Fell

Sergeant York**
US 1941 134m bw
Warner (Jesse L. Lasky)

The story of a gentle hillbilly farmer who became a hero of World War I.

Standard real-life fiction given the big treatment; a key Hollywood film of its time in several ways.

w Abem Finkel, Harry Chandler, Howard Koch, John Huston *d Howard Hawks ph Sol Polito m Max Steiner*

Gary Cooper, Joan Leslie, Walter Brennan, George Tobias, David Bruce, Stanley Ridges, Margaret Wycherly, Dickie Moore, Ward Bond

Sergeants Three
US 1961 112m Technicolor Panavision
(UA) Essex–Claude (Frank Sinatra)

Just after the Civil War three cavalry sergeants, with the help of an ex-slave bugler, dispose of some hostile Indians.
High-spirited but exhausting parody of *Gunga Din*, with bouts of unfunny bloodthirstiness separated by tedious slabs of dialogue.

w W. R. Burnett *d* John Sturges *ph* Winton Hock, Carl Guthrie *m* Billy May

Frank Sinatra, Dean Martin, Peter Lawford, Sammy Davis Jnr, Joey Bishop, Henry Silva, Ruta Lee

'The participants have a better time than the onlookers.'—*Judith Crist, 1973*

Serious Charge
GB 1959 99m bw
Alva (Mickey Delamar)

A small-town troublemaker, accused by his priest of being responsible for the death of a young girl, amuses himself by accusing the priest of making homosexual advances.
A sensational play of its time makes a dull film despite earnest performances.

w Guy Elmes, Mickey Delamar, *play* Philip King *d* Terence Young *ph* Georges Périnal *m* Leighton Lucas

Anthony Quayle, Andrew Ray, Sarah Churchill, Irene Browne, Percy Herbert, Cliff Richard

The Serpent
France / Italy / Germany 1974 124m colour
Films La Boetie (Henri Verneuil)

A top KGB official defects to the west.
Complicated, humourless, multi-lingual spy capers.

w Henri Verneuil, Gilles Perrault, *novel* Pierre Nord *d* Henri Verneuil *ph* Claude Renoir *m* Ennio Morricone

Yul Brynner, Henry Fonda, Dirk Bogarde, Philippe Noiret, Farley Granger, Virna Lisi

Serpico*
US 1973 130m Technicolor
Paramount / Artists Entertainment Complex / Dino de Laurentiis (Martin Bregman)

A New York cop reveals police corruption and is eventually forced to leave the country.
A harrowing true story played with authentic gloom and violence.

w Waldo Salt, Norman Wexler, *book* Peter Maas *d Sidney Lumet ph* Arthur J. Ornitz *m* Mikis Theodorakis

Al Pacino, John Randolph, Jack Kehoe, Biff McGuire

'There's nothing seriously wrong with *Serpico* except that it's unmemorable, and not even terribly interesting while it's going on.'—*Stanley Kauffmann*

Serpico
US 1976 98m colour TVM
Paramount / Emmet Lavery
aka: *The Deadly Game*

TV remake/pilot, dour in mood and hard to follow: for New Yorkers who enjoy having their noses rubbed in the dirt.

w Robert Collins, David Birney, Tom Atkins

The Servant**
GB 1963 116m bw
Elstree / Springbok (Joseph Losey, Norman Priggen)

A rich, ineffectual young man is gradually debased and overruled by his sinister manservant and his sexy 'sister'.
Acclaimed in many quarters on its first release, this downbeat melodrama now seems rather naïve and long drawn out; its surface gloss is undeniable, but the final orgy is more risible than satanic.

w Harold Pinter, *novel* Robin Maugham *d* Joseph Losey *ph Douglas Slocombe* *m* Johnny Dankworth

Dirk Bogarde, James Fox, Sarah Miles, Wendy Craig, Catherine Lacey, Richard Vernon

'Moodily suggestive, well acted, but petering out into a trickle of repetitious unmeaningful nastiness.'—*John Simon*

Servants' Entrance
US 1934 88m bw
Fox

A maid falls in love with a chauffeur.
Upstairs downstairs style comedy drama; passable.

w Samson Raphaelson, *novel* Sigrid Boo
d Frank Lloyd *ph* Hal Mohr

Janet Gaynor, Lew Ayres, Walter Connolly, G. P. Huntley Jnr, Sig Rumann, Louise Dresser, Astrid Allwyn, Ned Sparks

Service for Ladies
GB 1932 93m bw
Paramount (Alexander Korda)
US title: *Reserved for Ladies*

A waiter has a way with his rich lady clients.
Tenuous satirical comedy, a variation on the American silent *The Grand Duchess and the Waiter*.

w Eliot Crawshay-Williams, Lajos Biro, *novel* The Head Waiter by Ernst Vajda *d* Alexander Korda

Leslie Howard, George Grossmith, Benita Hume, Elizabeth Allan, Morton Selten, Cyril Ritchard, Martita Hunt, Merle Oberon

The Set Up***
US 1949 72m bw
RKO (Richard Goldstone)

An ageing boxer refuses to pull his last fight, and is beaten up by gangsters.
One of the most brilliant little *films noirs* of the late forties; thoroughly studio-bound, yet evoking a brilliant feeling for time and place. Photography, direction, editing, acting are all of a piece.

w Art Cohn, *poem* Joseph Moncure March
d Robert Wise ph Milton Krasner
m Constantin Bakaleinikoff

Robert Ryan, Audrey Totter, George Tobias, Alan Baxter, Wallace Ford

Seven Brides for Seven Brothers**
US 1954 104m Anscocolor Cinemascope
MGM (Jack Cummings)

In the old west, seven hard-working brothers decide they need wives, and carry off young women from the villages around.
Disappointingly studio-bound western musical, distinguished by an excellent score and some brilliant dancing, notably the barn-raising sequence.

w Frances Goodrich, Albert Hackett, *story* Sobbin' Women by Stephen Vincent Benet
d Stanley Donen ph George Folsey *ch Michael Kidd songs Johnny Mercer, Gene de Paul*

Howard Keel, Jane Powell, Jeff Richards, Russ Tamblyn, Tommy Rall, Howard Petrie, Marc Platt, Jacques d'Amboise, Matt Mattox

Seven Cities of Gold*
US 1955 103m De Luxe Cinemascope
TCF (Robert D. Webb, Barbara McLean)

In 1796, a Spanish expedition sets out from Mexico to annex California, but with it goes Father Junipero Serra . . .
A semi-historical, semi-religious western which ends up not being much of anything but has interesting sequences.

w Richard L. Breen, John C. Higgins, *novel* Isabelle Gibson Ziegler *d* Robert D. Webb
ph Lucien Andriot *m* Hugo Friedhofer

Michael Rennie, Richard Egan, Anthony Quinn, Rita Moreno, Jeffrey Hunter, Eduardo Noriega, John Doucette

Seven Days in May***
US 1964 120m bw
Seven Arts / Joel / John Frankenheimer (Edward Lewis)

An American general's aide discovers that his boss intends a military takeover because he considers the President's pacifism traitorous.
Absorbing political mystery drama marred only by the unnecessary introduction of a female character. Stimulating entertainment.

w Rod Serling, novel Fletcher Knebel, Charles W. Bailey II *d John Frankenheimer*
ph Ellsworth Fredericks m Jerry Goldsmith

Kirk Douglas, Burt Lancaster, *Fredric March*, Ava Gardner, Martin Balsam, *Edmond O'Brien*, George Macready, John Houseman

'A political thriller which grips from start to finish.'—*Penelope Houston*

'It is to be enjoyed without feelings of guilt, there should be more movies like it, and there is nothing first class about it.'—*John Simon*

Seven Days Leave
US 1929 83m bw
Paramount (Louis D. Lighton)
GB title: *Medals*

A London charlady 'adopts' a soldier, and both their lives are changed.
Sentimental melodrama which suited the times and confirmed Cooper's stardom.

w John Farrow, Dan Totheroh, *play* The Old Lady Shows Her Medals by J. M. Barrie
d Richard Wallace *ph* Charles Lang

Gary Cooper, Beryl Mercer, Daisy Belmore, Nora Cecil, Tempe Piggott, Arthur Hoyt, Basil Radford

Seven Days Leave
US 1942 87m bw
RKO (Tim Whelan)

In order to inherit a hundred thousand dollars, a soldier must marry within a week.
Cheerful frivolity featuring radio stars of the time.

w William Bowers, Ralph Spence, Curtis Kenyon, Kenneth Earl *d* Tim Whelan *ph* Robert de Grasse *md* Constantin Bakaleinikoff

Lucille Ball, Victor Mature, Harold Peary, Mary Cortes, Ginny Simms, Ralph Edwards, Peter Lind Hayes, Marcy McGuire, Wallace Ford

Seven Days to Noon**
GB 1950 94m bw
London Films (The Boulting Brothers)

A professor engaged on atomic research threatens to blow up London unless his work is brought to an end.
Persuasively understated suspense piece which was subsequently much copied, so that it now seems rather obvious.

w Frank Harvey, Roy Boulting, Paul Dehn, James Bernard d John Boulting ph Gilbert Taylor *m* John Addison

Barry Jones, Olive Sloane, André Morell, Joan Hickson, Sheila Manahan, Hugh Cross, Ronald Adam, Marie Ney

'A first rate thriller that does not pretend to a serious message, but yet will leave a query in the mind.'—*Richard Winnington*

711 Ocean Drive*
US 1950 102m bw
Columbia (Frank N. Seltzer)

A wireless expert is drawn into the bookie racket.
Overlong but vigorous crime exposé melodrama with excellent location sequences, notably a climax on Hoover Dam.

w Richard English, Francis Swann *d Joseph H. Newman ph* Franz Planer *m* Sol Kaplan

Edmond O'Brien, Joanne Dru, Otto Kruger, Don Porter, Sammy White, Dorothy Patrick, Barry Kelley, Howard St John

Seven Faces of Dr Lao*
US 1964 100m Metrocolor
MGM / George Pal

An elderly Chinaman with a penchant for spectacular disguise solves the problems of a western desert town.
A pleasant idea and excellent production are submerged in a sloppily sentimental and verbose script.

w Charles G. Finney, from his novel *d* George Pal *ph* Robert Bronner *m* Leigh Harline *make up* William Tuttle

Tony Randall, Arthur O'Connell, John Ericson, Barbara Eden, Noah Beery Jnr, Lee Patrick, Minerva Urecal, John Qualen

Seven Hills of Rome
US / Italy 1957 104m Technirama
MGM / Titanus (Lester Welch)

An American singer in Italy is pursued by the fiancée with whom he has quarrelled.
Thin travelogue with several halts for the star to sing; production very patchy.

w Art Cohn, Giorgio Prosperi *d* Roy Rowland *ph* Tonino Delli Colli *md* George Stoll

Mario Lanza, Renato Rascel, Marisa Allasio, Peggie Castle

Seven in Darkness
US 1969 74m colour TVM
Paramount

A chartered plane crashes in a mountainous region, and all the survivors are blind.
For connoisseurs of unlikely situations.

w John W. Bloch, *novel* Against Heaven's Hand by Leonard Bishop *d* Michael Caffey

Milton Berle, Dina Merrill, Sean Garrison, Arthur O'Connell, Alejandro Rey, Lesley Ann Warren

Seven Keys to Baldpate*
US 1935 69m bw
RKO

An old theatrical warhorse also filmed in 1926 and 1947. None is as amusing as a good stage production.

play George M. Cohan, *story* Earl Derr Biggers *d* William Hamilton, Edward Killy *ph* Robert de Grasse

Gene Raymond, Margaret Callahan, Eric Blore, Grant Mitchell, Moroni Olsen, Henry Travers

The Seven Little Foys*
US 1955 95m Technicolor Vistavision
Paramount (Jack Rose)

The story of a family vaudeville act.
Routine showbiz biopic, a little heavy on the syrup.

w Melville Shavelson, Jack Rose *d* Melville Shavelson *ph* John F. Warren *md* Joseph J. Lilley

Bob Hope, Milly Vitale, George Tobias, Angela Clarke, Herbert Heyes, *James Cagney* as George M. Cohan

Seven Men from Now
US 1956 78m Warnercolor
Batjac (Andrew V. McLaglen, Robert E. Morrison)

A sheriff seeks revenge when his wife is killed by bandits.
Good western programmer.

w Burt Kennedy *d* Budd Boetticher *ph* William H. Clothier *m* Henry Vars

Randolph Scott, Gail Russell, Lee Marvin, Walter Reed, Don Barry, John Larch

The Seven Minutes
US 1971 102m De Luxe
TCF (Russ Meyer)

A bookseller is arrested for distributing an obscene novel, and many people are unexpectedly involved in the court case.
A fascinating piece of old-fashioned hokum, full of 'daring' words and cameo performances.

w Richard Warren Lewis, *novel* Irving Wallace *d* Russ Meyer *ph* Fred Mandl *m* Stu Philips

Wayne Maunder, Marianne MacAndrew, Yvonne de Carlo, Phil Carey, Jay C. Flippen, Edy Williams, Lyle Bettger, Ron Randell, David Brian, Charles Drake, John Carradine, Harold J. Stone

Seven Nights in Japan
GB / France 1976 104m Eastmancolor
EMI–Marianne (Lewis Gilbert)

The heir to the British throne has shore leave in Tokyo and falls in love with a geisha.
Tediously daring romance with a banal script which seems over impressed by its own barely-existent controversial qualities.

w Christopher Wood *d* Lewis Gilbert *ph Henri Decaë* *m* David Hentschel

Michael York, Hidemi Aoki, James Villiers, Peter Jones, Charles Gray

Seven Seas to Calais
US / Italy 1962 103m Eastmancolor Cinemascope
MGM / Adelphia

In 1577, Sir Francis Drake follows the Spanish treasure route.
Ho-hum swashbuckler with a background of schoolboy history.

w Filippo Sanjust *d* Rudolph Maté *ph* Giulio Gianini *m* Franco Mannino

Rod Taylor, Keith Michell, Irene Worth, Anthony Dawson, Basil Dignam

Seven Sinners*
GB 1936 70m bw
Gaumont (Michael Balcon)
US title: *Doomed Cargo*

Gunrunners wreck trains to cover traces of murder.
Fascinatingly dated comedy suspenser with excellent sub-Hitchcock sequences, the whole thing having a strong flavour of *The 39 Steps*.

w Frank Launder, Sidney Gilliat, L. DuGarde Peach, Austin Melford, *play* The Wrecker by Arnold Ridley, Bernard Merivale *d Albert de Courville*

Edmund Lowe, Constance Cummings, Thomy Bourdelle, Henry Oscar, Felix Aylmer, Allan Jeayes, O. B. Clarence

Seven Sinners*
US 1940 86m bw
Universal (Joe Pasternak)
GB title: *Café of Seven Sinners*

A cabaret singer is deported from several South Sea islands for causing too many fights among the naval officers.
Ho-hum hokum with an amiable cast and a good-natured final free-for-all.

w John Meehan, Harry Tugend *d* Tay Garnett *ph* Rudolph Maté *m* Frank Skinner

Marlene Dietrich, John Wayne, Albert Dekker, Broderick Crawford, Mischa Auer, Billy Gilbert, Oscar Homolka, Anne Lee, Samuel S. Hinds

Seven Sweethearts
US 1942 98m bw
MGM (Joe Pasternak)

Seven daughters must marry in sequence, eldest first.
Period musical frou-frou inspired by *Pride and Prejudice*. So light it almost floats.

w Walter Reisch, Leo Townsend *d* Frank Borzage *ph* George Folsey *m* Franz Waxman

Kathryn Grayson, Marsha Hunt, Van Heflin, Cecelia Parker, S. Z. Sakall, Peggy Moran, Isobel Elsom, Diana Lewis, Donald Meek, Louise Beavers

Seven Thieves*
US 1960 102m bw Cinemascope
TCF (Sidney Boehm)

An elderly crook conceives a last plan to rob the Monte Carlo casino.
Routine caper story, efficiently presented with some humour.

w Sidney Boehm, *novel* Lions at the Kill by Max Catto *d* Henry Hathaway *ph* Sam Leavitt *m* Dominic Frontière

Edward G. Robinson, Rod Steiger, Joan Collins, Eli Wallach, Michael Dante, Alexander Scourby, Berry Kroeger, Sebastian Cabot

The Seven-Ups
US 1973 103m TVC De Luxe
TCF / Philip D'Antoni

Gangsters are hunted down by a secret force of the New York police.
Formulary realistic rough stuff in the wake of *The French Connection.*

w Albert Ruben, Alexander Jacobs *d* Philip D'Antoni *ph* Urs Furrer *m Don Ellis*

Roy Scheider, Victor Arnold, Jerry Leon, Tony Lo Bianco, *Richard Lynch*

Seven Waves Away
GB 1956 95m bw
Columbia / Copa (John R. Sloan)
US title: *Abandon Ship*

After the sinking of a luxury liner, the officer in charge of a lifeboat has to make life or death decisions.
Initially gripping but finally depressing open sea melodrama derived from *Souls at Sea* and later remade for TV as *The Last Survivors.*

wd Richard Sale *ph* Wilkie Cooper *m* Arthur Bliss

Tyrone Power, Mai Zetterling, Lloyd Nolan, Stephen Boyd, Moira Lister, James Hayter, Marie Lohr, Moultrie Kelsall, Noel Willman, Gordon Jackson, Clive Morton, John Stratton

'Eventually one is bludgeoned into a grudging admiration for the film's staying power.'—*Peter John Dyer*

Seven Women*
US 1966 100m Metrocolor Panavision
MGM / John Ford / Bernard Smith

In 1935, an isolated Chinese mission staffed by American women is overrun by bandits.
Dusty melodrama which might have appealed in the thirties but was quite out of tune with the sixties. Well enough made and acted, but a strange choice for Ford's last film.

w Janet Green, John McCormick, *story* Chinese Finale by Norah Lofts *d John Ford ph* Joseph La Shelle *m* Elmer Bernstein

Anne Bancroft, Flora Robson, Margaret Leighton, Sue Lyon, Mildred Dunnock, Betty Field, Anna Lee, Eddie Albert, Mike Mazurki, Woody Strode, Irene Tsu

The Seven Year Itch*
US 1955 105m De Luxe Cinemascope
TCF (Charles K. Feldman, Billy Wilder)

A married man has a fling with the girl upstairs.
An amusing theatrical joke, with dream sequences like revue sketches, is really all at sea on the big screen, especially as the affair remains unconsummated, but direction and performances keep the party going more or less.

w Billy Wilder, George Axelrod, *play* George Axelrod *d Billy Wilder ph* Milton Krasner *m* Alfred Newman

Tom Ewell, Marilyn Monroe, Sonny Tufts, Evelyn Keyes, Robert Strauss, Oscar Homolka, Marguerite Chapman, Victor Moore

1776*
US 1972 141m Eastmancolor Panavision
Columbia / Jack L. Warner

The thirteen American colonies prepare to declare their independence of Great Britain.
Plain, low-key filming of the successful Broadway musical showing the domestic lives of the historical figures concerned. Splendid moments alternate with stretches of tedium.

w Peter Stone, from his play *d* Peter Hunt *ph* Harry Stradling Jnr *m/ly* Sherman Edwards *ad* George Jenkins

William Daniels, Howard da Silva, Ken Howard, Donald Madden, Blythe Danner

Seventh Cavalry
US 1956 75m Technicolor
Columbia / Scott–Brown

An officer accused of cowardice volunteers to bring back General Custer's body after Little Big Horn.
Lively co-feature with a good traditional action climax.

w Peter Packer *d* Joseph H. Lewis *ph* Ray Rennahan *m* Mischa Bakaleinikoff

Randolph Scott, Barbara Hale, Jay C. Flippen, Jeanette Nolan, Frank Faylen

The Seventh Cross**
US 1944 112m bw
MGM (Pandro S. Berman)

Seven Germans escape from a concentration camp, and the Nazis threaten to execute them all. Just one escapes.
Impressive melodrama, brilliantly limiting its escape/suspense story to studio sets. Old-style Hollywood production at its best; but a rather obviously contrived story.

w Helen Deutsch, *novel* Anna Seghers *d Fred Zinnemann ph Karl Freund m* Roy Webb *ad Cedric Gibbons, Leonid Vasian*

Spencer Tracy, Signe Hasso, Hume Cronyn,

Jessica Tandy, Agnes Moorehead, Felix Bressart, George Macready, George Zucco

The Seventh Dawn
GB 1964 123m Technicolor
UA / Holden / Charles K. Feldman (Karl Tunberg)

In the early fifties a Malayan rubber planter finds that his best friend is a leading terrorist.
Doom-laden romantic adventure drama with a lot of suffering and too little entertainment value.

w Karl Tunberg, *novel* The Durian Tree by Michael Keon *d* Lewis Gilbert *ph* Freddie Young *m* Riz Ortolani

William Holden, Tetsuro Tamba, Capucine, Susannah York, Michael Goodliffe, Allan Cuthbertson, Maurice Denham

'Echoes of *The Ugly American, Love Is a Many-Splendored Thing*, and many another adventure East of Sumatra, with every character running absolutely true to form.'—*MFB*

'An interminable melange of political, racial and romantic clichés, with performances and dialogue as overripe as the jungle setting.' —*Judith Crist, 1973*

Seventh Heaven*
US 1937 102m bw
TCF (Raymond Griffith)

A Parisian waif loves a street-cleaner, but he goes off to war.
Dewy-eyed remake of famous silent romance; the mood is antediluvian but the production impresses.

w Melville Baker, *play* Austin Strong *d Henry King ph Merritt Gerstad m* Louis Silvers *ad William Darling*

James Stewart, Simone Simon, Jean Hersholt, Gale Sondergaard, J. Edward Bromberg, Gregory Ratoff, John Qualen, Victor Kilian, Sig Rumann, Mady Christians

The Seventh Sin
US 1957 94m bw Cinemascope
MGM (David Lewis)

A faithless wife accompanies her bacteriologist husband to fight a Chinese cholera epidemic, and regains her self-respect.
Tatty remake of a Garbo vehicle which was dated even in 1934. (See *The Painted Veil.)*

w Karl Tunberg, *novel* The Painted Veil by Somerset Maugham *d* Ronald Neame *ph* Ray June *m* Miklos Rozsa

Eleanor Parker, Bill Travers, George Sanders, Jean-Pierre Aumont, Françoise Rosay

The Seventh Veil***
GB 1945 94m bw
Theatrecraft / Sydney Box / Ortus

A concert pianist is romantically torn between her psychiatrist, her guardian, and two other fellows.
A splendid modern melodrama in the tradition of *Jane Eyre* and *Rebecca*; it set the seal of moviegoing approval on psychiatry, classical music, and James Mason, and it is the most utter tosh.

w Muriel and Sydney Box d Compton Bennett ph Reg Wyer *m Benjamin Frankel*

James Mason, Ann Todd, Herbert Lom, Albert Lieven, Hugh McDermott, Yvonne Owen, David Horne, Manning Whiley

'An example of the intelligent, medium-priced picture made with great technical polish which has represented for Hollywood the middle path between the vulgar and the highbrow.' —*Spectator*

'A popular film that does not discard taste and atmosphere.'—*Daily Mail*

'A rich, portentous mixture of Beethoven, Chopin, Kitsch and Freud.'—*Pauline Kael, 1968*

The Seventh Victim*
US 1943 71m bw
RKO (*Val Lewton*)

A girl goes to New York in search of her sister, who is under the influence of Satanists.
Much praised but in effect rather boring little thriller, with rather stately acting and ponderous direction and dialogue. Censorship made the plot so obscure that it's difficult to follow.

w Charles O'Neal, De Witt Bodeen *d* Mark Robson *ph* Nicholas Musuraca *m* Constantin Bakaleinikoff

Kim Hunter, Tom Conway, Jean Brooks, Hugh Beaumont, Erford Gage, Isabel Jewell, Evelyn Brent

'It is the almost oppressive mood, the romantic obsession with death-in-life, which dominates the film.'—*NFT, 1973*

† Note the use in the first scene of the staircase from *The Magnificent Ambersons*.

The Seventh Voyage of Sinbad*
US 1958 89m Technicolor
Columbia / Morningside (Charles Schneer)

Sinbad seeks a roc's egg which will restore his fiancée from the midget size to which an evil magician has reduced her.
Lively fantasy with narrative drive and excellent effects.

w Kenneth Kolb *d* Nathan Juran *ph* Wilkie

Cooper *m* Bernard Herrmann *sp Ray Harryhausen*

Kerwin Mathews, Kathryn Grant, Torin Thatcher, Richard Eyer, Alec Mango

A Severed Head*
GB 1970 98m Technicolor
Columbia / Winkast (Alan Ladd Jnr)

A wine merchant has a long-standing affair which he thinks is secret, but is annoyed when his wife tries the same game.
Unwisely boisterous screen version of a slyly academic novel; tolerably sophisticated for those who don't know the original.

w Frederic Raphael, *novel* Iris Murdoch *d* Dick Clement *ph* Austin Dempster *m* Stanley Myers *pd* Richard Macdonald

Lee Remick, Richard Attenborough, Ian Holm, Claire Bloom, Jennie Linden, Clive Revill

Sex and the Single Girl
US 1964 114m Technicolor
Warner / Richard Quine / Reynard (William T. Orr)

A journalist worms his way into the life of a lady sexologist in order to unmask her—but guess what.
Coy sex comedy with noise substituting for wit and style, all pretence being abandoned in a wild chase climax.

w Joseph Heller, David R. Schwarz, *book* Helen Gurley Brown *d* Richard Quine *ph* Charles Lang Jnr *m* Neal Hefti

Natalie Wood, Tony Curtis, Henry Fonda, Lauren Bacall, Mel Ferrer, Fran Jeffries, Edward Everett Horton, Otto Kruger

'For those willing to devote two hours of their lives to a consideration of Natalie Wood's virginity.'—*Judith Crist, 1973*

The Sex Symbol
US 1974 98m or 110m colour TVM
Columbia / Douglas S. Cramer

The private life of a Hollywood glamour queen.
Obsessively silly exposé obviously patterned after Marilyn Monroe.

w Alvah Bessie, from his novel The Symbol *d* David Lowell Rich *ph* J. J. Jones *m* Jeff Alexander

Connie Stevens, Shelley Winters, Don Murray, William Smith, James Olson, Nehemiah Persoff, Jack Carter

Shack Out on 101*
US 1955 80m bw
AA / William F. Broidy

A waitress at a café near a research establishment unmasks two spies.
Modest suspenser which seemed at the time to have some fresh and realistic attitudes.

w Ed and Mildred Dein *d Ed Dein ph Floyd Crosby m* Paul Dunlap

Frank Lovejoy, Lee Marvin, Keenan Wynn, Terry Moore, Whit Bissell

Shadow in the Sky
US 1951 78m bw
MGM (William H. Wright)

A shell-shocked marine moves from a psychiatric hospital to live with his sister.
Low-key drama, plainly but quite well done, though of little continuing interest.

w Ben Maddow *d* Fred M. Wilcox *ph* George Folsey *m* Bronislau Kaper

Ralph Meeker, Nancy Davis, James Whitmore, Jean Hagen

Shadow in the Streets*
US 1975 74m colour TVM
Playboy

A tough ex-convict becomes a parole agent.
Routine socially conscious melodrama, well put together.

w John D. F. Black *d* Richard Donner

Tony Lo Bianco, Sheree North, Dana Andrews, Ed Lauter, Jesse Welles

Shadow of a Doubt***
US 1943 108m bw
Universal (Jack H. Skirball)

A favourite uncle comes to visit his family in a small Californian town. He is actually on the run from police, who know him as the Merry Widow murderer.
Hitchcock's quietest film is memorable chiefly for its depiction of small-town life; but the script is well written and keeps the suspense moving slowly but surely.

w Thornton Wilder, Sally Benson, Alma Reville, story Gordon McDonell *d Alfred Hitchcock ph* Joe Valentine *m* Dmitri Tiomkin

Joseph Cotten, Teresa Wright, Hume Cronyn, Macdonald Carey, Patricia Collinge, Henry Travers, Wallace Ford

Shadow of the Cat
GB 1961 79m bw
U-I / BHP

A cat appears to wreak vengeance on those who murdered its mistress.
Tolerable old dark house shocker with an amusing theme not too well sustained.

w George Baxt *d* John Gilling *ph* Alec Grant *m* Mikis Theodorakis

André Morell, William Lucas, Barbara Shelley, Conrad Phillips, Alan Wheatley, Vanda Godsell, Richard Warner, Freda Jackson

Shadow on the Land*
US 1968 97m colour TVM
Columbia (Matthew Rapf)

America is taken over by a totalitarian government, and rebels strike.
An Awful Warning of the hysterical kind makes fair action melodrama.

w Ned Young *d* Richard Sarafian

Jackie Cooper, John Forsythe, Carol Lynley, Gene Hackman, Janice Rule

Shadow on the Wall
US 1949 84m bw
MGM (Robert Sisk)

A child is traumatized by the accidental witnessing of the murder of her unpleasant stepmother.
Forgettable melodramatic suspenser.

w William Ludwig *d* Pat Jackson *ph* Ray June *m* André Previn

Ann Sothern, Zachary Scott, Gigi Perreau, Nancy Davis, Kristine Miller, John McIntire

The Shadow on the Window
US 1957 73m bw
Columbia (Jonie Taps)

Three teenage thugs break into a lonely house, murder its owner and hold a girl hostage.
Routine crime programmer, rather boringly unravelled.

w Leo Townsend, David Harmon *d* William Asher *ph* Kit Carson *m* George Duning

Betty Garrett, Phil Carey, John Barrymore Jnr, Corey Allen, Gerald Saracini

Shadow over Elveron*
US 1968 100m Technicolor TVM
Universal (Jack Laird)

An evil local midwestern sheriff commits murder and is unmasked by the new young doctor.
Heavy melodrama on familiar lines, with *Hot Spot* and *The Tattered Dress* for models.

w Chester Krumholz, *novel* Michael Kingsley *d* James Goldstone

Leslie Nielsen, James Franciscus, Shirley Knight, Franchot Tone, James Dunn, Don Ameche

Shadows*
US 1959 81m bw
Cassavetes / Cassel / Maurice McEndree

Two blacks and their sister find their identities in Manhattan.
16mm realistic drama which began a new and essentially dreary trend of grainily true-life pictures with improvised dialogue and little dramatic compression.

w the cast *d* John Cassavetes *ph* Erich Kollmar *m* Charles Mingus

Ben Carruthers, Leila Goldoni, Hugh Hurd, Rupert Crosse, Anthony Ray

Shaft*
US 1971 100m Metrocolor
MGM / Shaft Productions (Joel Freeman)

A black private eye finds himself at odds with a powerful racketeer.
Violent, commercial action thriller which spawned two sequels and a tele-series as well as stimulating innumerable even more violent imitations.

w Ernest Tidyman, John D. F. Black *d* Gordon Parks *ph* Urs Furrer *m* Isaac Hayes

Richard Roundtree, Moses Gunn, Charles Cioffi, Christopher St John

'Relentlessly supercool dialogue, all throwaway colloquialisms and tough Chandlerian wisecracks.'—*MFB*

Shaft in Africa
US 1973 112m Metrocolor Panavision
(MGM) Shaft Productions (Roger Lewis)

Shaft is kidnapped by an Ethiopian emir who wants him to track down a gang of slavers.
More miscellaneous violence, rather shoddily assembled, with a few good jokes.

w Stirling Silliphant *d* John Guillermin *ph* Marcel Grignon *m* Johnny Pate

Richard Roundtree, Frank Finlay, Vonetta McGee

Shaft's Big Score
US 1972 105m Metrocolor Panavision
MGM / Shaft Productions (Richard Lewis, Ernest Tidyman)

Shaft avenges the death of a friend and comes up against the numbers racket.
Violent footage and an incomprehensible plot.

w Ernest Tidyman *d* Gordon Parks *ph* Urs Furrer *m* Gordon Parks

Richard Roundtree, Moses Gunn, Drew Bundini Brown, Joseph Mascolo

The Shaggy Dog*
US 1959 101m bw
Walt Disney (Bill Walsh)

A small boy turns into a big shaggy dog and catches some crooks.
Simple-minded, overlong Disney comedy for kids and their indulgent parents; good laughs in the chase scenes.

w Bill Walsh, Lillie Hayward, *novel* The Hound of Florence by Felix Salten *d* Charles Barton *ph* Edward Colman *m* Paul Smith

Fred MacMurray, Jean Hagen, Tommy Kirk, Cecil Kellaway, Annette Funicello, Tim Considine, Kevin Corcoran, Alexander Scourby

Shake Hands with the Devil*
Eire 1959 110m bw
UA / Troy / Pennebaker (Michael Anderson)

In 1921 Dublin a surgeon is the secret leader of the IRA, and comes to cherish violence as an end rather than a means.
Downbeat action melodrama, politically very questionable but well made.

w Ivan Goff, Ben Roberts, *novel* Rearden Connor *d* Michael Anderson *ph* Erwin Hillier *m* William Alwyn
James Cagney, Glynis Johns, Don Murray, Dana Wynter, Michael Redgrave, Sybil Thorndike, Cyril Cusack, Niall MacGinnis, Richard Harris, Ray McAnally, Noel Purcell

Shakedown
US 1950 80m bw
U-I (Ted Richmond)

A ruthless press photographer becomes a blackmailer.
Routine crime melodrama, adequately done.

w Alfred Lewis, Martin Goldsmith *d* Joseph Pevney *ph* Irving Glassberg *m* Joseph Gershenson

Howard Duff, Brian Donlevy, Anne Vernon, Peggy Dow, Lawrence Tierney, Bruce Bennett

The Shakedown
GB 1959 92m bw
Rank / Alliance / Ethiro (Norman Williams)

A Soho vice boss photographs prominent people in compromising situations and blackmails them.
A semi-remake set in the squalid London so beloved of film makers at the time, before it became 'swinging'. Of no interest or entertainment value.

w Leigh Vance *d* John Lemont *ph* Brendan J. Stafford *m* Philip Green

Terence Morgan, Hazel Court, Donald Pleasance, Bill Owen, Robert Beatty, Harry H. Corbett, Gene Anderson, Eddie Byrne

The Shakiest Gun in the West
US 1967 101m Techniscope
Universal (Edward J. Montagne)

A cowardly dentist becomes a western hero.
Dreary farce, an unsubtle remake of *The Paleface*.

w Jim Fritzell, Everett Greenbaum *d* Alan Rafkin *ph* Andrew Jackson *m* Vic Mizzy

Don Knotts, Barbara Rhoades, Jackie Coogan, Don Barry

Shalako
GB 1968 118m Technicolor Franscope
Kingston / Dimitri de Grunwald (Euan Lloyd)

New Mexico, 1880: a cowboy acts as guide to European aristocratic big game hunters, but the Indians become annoyed and attack.
A cute idea is given routine treatment; though packed with stars, the action never becomes very exciting despite incidental brutalities.

w J. J. Griffith, Hal Hopper, Scot Finch, *novel* Louis L'Amour *d* Edward Dmytryk *ph* Ted Moore *m* Robert Farnon

Sean Connery, Brigitte Bardot, Jack Hawkins, Stephen Boyd, Peter Van Eyck, Honor Blackman, Eric Sykes, Alexander Knox, Woody Strode, Victor French

Shall We Dance?**
US 1937 116m bw
RKO (Pandro S. Berman)

Dancing partners pretend to be married but are not; until they both get the same idea.
A light musical which was full of good things but nevertheless began the decline of Astaire-Rogers films; repetition was obvious, as was ostentation for its own sake, and the audience was expecting too much.

w Allan Scott, Ernest Pagano *d* Mark Sandrich *ph* David Abel *m/ly George and Ira Gershwin* *md* Nathaniel Shilkret *ad* Van Nest Polglase

Fred Astaire, Ginger Rogers, Edward Everett Horton, Eric Blore, Harriet Hoctor, Jerome Cowan, Ketti Gallian, Ann Shoemaker

Shampoo*
US 1975 110m Technicolor
Columbia / Persky–Bright / Vista (Warren Beatty)

A Beverly Hills hairdresser seduces his most glamorous clients.
Ugly little sex farce with few laughs but much dashing about and bad language. Its setting on

election eve 1968 has made some people think it a political satire.

w Robert Towne, Warren Beatty *d* Hal Ashby *ph* Laszlo Kovacs *m* Paul Simon

Warren Beatty, Julie Christie, Lee Grant, Goldie Hawn, Jack Warden, Tony Bill, Jay Robinson

'It has the bursting-with-talent but fuzziness-of-effect aspect of a movie made by a group of friends for their own amusement.'—*Richard Combs*

Shamus
US 1972 98m Eastmancolor
Columbia / Robert M. Weitman

A private eye is hired by a wealthy man to recover stolen jewels and find a murderer.
A forties retread with seventies violence; junky stuff, with a few laughs for buffs who can spot the in-jokes.

w Barry Beckerman *d* Buzz Kulik *ph* Victor J. Kemper *m* Jerry Goldsmith

Burt Reynolds, Dyan Cannon, John Ryan, Joe Santos, Giorgio Tozzi, Ron Weyland

'Very hectic, very vividly New York and as idiotic as Reynolds' physical resiliency.'—*Judith Crist*

Shane***
US 1953 118m Technicolor
Paramount (George Stevens, Ivan Moffat)

A mysterious stranger helps a family of homesteaders.
Archetypal family western, but much slower and statelier than most, as though to emphasize its own quality, which is evident anyway.

w A. B. Guthrie Jnr, *novel* Jack Schaefer *d George Stevens* *ph* Loyal Griggs *m* Victor Young

Alan Ladd, Jean Arthur, Van Heflin, *Jack Palance*, Brandon de Wilde, Ben Johnson, Edgar Buchanan, Emile Meyer, Elisha Cook Jnr, John Dierkes

'A kind of dramatic documentary of the pioneer days of the west.'—*MFB*

'Westerns are better when they're not too self-importantly self-conscious.'—*New Yorker, 1975*

Shanghai
US 1935 77m bw
Paramount (Walter Wanger)

A visiting American lady falls in love with a half caste.
Romantic drama programmer.

w Gene Towne, Graham Baker, Lynn Starling *d* James Flood *ph* James Van Trees

Loretta Young, Charles Boyer, Warner Oland, Alison Skipworth, Fred Keating, Charles Grapewin, Walter Kingsford

Shanghai Express***
US 1932 84m bw
Paramount

A British officer and his old flame meet on a train which is waylaid by Chinese bandits.
Superbly pictorial melodrama which set the pattern for innumerable train movies to come, though none matched its deft visual quality and few sketched in their characters so neatly. Plot and dialogue are silent style, but refreshingly so.

w Jules Furthman d Josef Von Sternberg ph Lee Garmes ad Hans Dreier

Marlene Dietrich, Clive Brook, Warner Oland, Anna May Wong, Eugene Pallette, Lawrence Grant, Louise Closser Hale, Gustav Von Seyffertitz

'A limited number of characters, all meticulously etched, highly atmospheric sets and innumerable striking photographic compositions.'—*Curtis Harrington, 1964*

The Shanghai Gesture*
US 1941 90m bw
Arnold Pressburger (Albert de Courville)

The proprietress of a Shanghai gambling casino taunts her ex-husband by showing him his daughter in a state of degradation; but he proves that the girl is her daughter also.
An ancient theatrical shocker was completely bowdlerized and chopped into nonsense for the screen; but the director's hand showed in the handling of the vast casino set.

w Josef Von Sternberg, Geza Herczeg, Karl Vollmoeller, Jules Furthman, *play* John Colton *d Josef Von Sternberg* *ph* Paul Ivano *m* Richard Hageman *ad Boris Leven*

Ona Munson, Victor Mature, Walter Huston, Gene Tierney, Albert Basserman, Phyllis Brooks, Maria Ouspenskaya, Eric Blore, Ivan Lebedeff, Mike Mazurki

'The effect of a descent into a maelstrom of iniquity.'—*Curtis Harrington, 1962*

'In spite of all the changes necessitated by the Hays Office, seldom have decadence and sexual depravity been better suggested on the screen.' —*Richard Roud, 1966*

The Sharkfighters
US 1956 72m Technicolor Cinemascope
(UA) Formosa (Samuel Goldwyn Jnr)

To save the lives of fliers forced down into the sea, navy scientists experiment with a shark repellent.

Straightforward semi-documentary with suspenseful action sequences.

w Lawrence Roman, John Robinson *d* Jerry Hopper *ph* Lee Garmes *m* Jerome Moross

Victor Mature, Karen Steele, James Olson, Claude Akins

Shark's Treasure*
US 1974 95m De Luxe
UA / Symbol (Cornel Wilde)

Treasure hunters seek buried gold in the Caribbean where sharks abound.
Fairly thrilling action hokum.

wd Cornel Wilde *ph* Jack Atcheler, Al Giddings *m* Robert O. Ragland

Cornel Wilde, Yaphet Kotto, John Neilson, David Canary, Cliff Osmond

'Wilde maintains his reputation for making the most likeable bad movies around.'—*Tom Milne*

She*
US 1935 89m bw
RKO (Merian C. Cooper)

Ancient papers lead a Cambridge professor and his friends to the lost city where dwells a queen who cannot die—until she falls in love.
The producers have the right spirit for this Victorian fantasy, but tried too hard to emulate the mood of their own *King Kong*, and it was a mistake to transfer the setting from Africa to the Arctic. One for connoisseurs, though.

novel H. Rider Haggard *d* Ernest Schoedsack

Randolph Scott, Nigel Bruce, Helen Gahagan

'To an unrepentant Haggard fan it does sometimes seem to catch the thrill as well as the childishness of his invention.'—*Graham Greene*

She
GB 1965 105m Technicolor Hammerscope
ABP / Hammer (Aida Young)

Flat, uninventive and tedious remake which reverts to Africa but does nothing else right; it ignores the essential Cambridge prologue and ignores all suggestions of fantasy.

w David T. Chantler *d* Robert Day *ph* Harry Waxman *m* James Bernard

Peter Cushing, Ursula Andress, Christopher Lee, John Richardson, Bernard Cribbins, André Morell, Rosenda Monteros

'The stagey decor of Kor is in the art deco style of Radio City Music Hall, and you keep expecting the Rockettes to turn up . . . the picture is deadly slow, and the lovebirds could try anyone's patience, but camp like this is a rarity.'—*New Yorker, 1976*

She Cried Murder*
US 1973 74m Technicolor TVM
Universal (William Frye)

A model witnesses a murder, and the policeman who comes to investigate is the murderer.
A ripe chestnut, nicely shot on New York locations.

w Merwin Gerard *d* Herschel Daugherty

Telly Savalas, Lynda Day George, Mike Farrell

She Didn't Say No!
GB 1958 97m Technicolor
ABP (Sergei Nolbandov)

A young Irish widow has five illegitimate children, each by a different father.
Coyly daring comedy full of stage Oirishisms and obvious jokes, a few of which work.

w T. J. Morison, Una Troy, from her novel We Are Seven *d* Cyril Frankel *ph* Gilbert Taylor *m* Tristam Cary

Eileen Herlie, Jack MacGowran, Perlita Neilson, Niall MacGinnis, Ian Bannen

She Done Him Wrong***
US 1933 68m bw
Paramount (William Le Baron)

A lady saloon keeper of the Gay Nineties falls for the undercover cop who is after her.
As near undiluted Mae West as Hollywood ever came: fast, funny, melodramatic and pretty sexy; also a very atmospheric and well-made movie.

w Mae West, from her play Diamond Lil (with help on the scenario from Harry Thew, John Bright) *d Lowell Sherman ph* Charles Lang *songs* Ralph Rainger

Mae West, Cary Grant, Owen Moore, Gilbert Roland, Noah Beery, David Landau, Rafaela Ottiano, Rochelle Hudson, Dewey Robinson

She Gets Her Man*
US 1945 73m bw
Universal (Warren Wilson)

A country girl in New York tracks down a blowgun murderer.
Disarming mystery farce which tries every slapstick situation known to gag writers, and gets away with it.

w Warren Wilson, Clyde Bruckman *d* Erle C. Kenton *ph* Jerry Ash

Joan Davis, William Gargan, Leon Errol, Milburn Stone, Russell Hicks

She Had to Say Yes
US 1952 89m bw
RKO (Robert Sparks)
GB title: *Beautiful But Dangerous*

An heiress returns to the town of her childhood to distribute anonymous gifts to those who had helped her.
Moderate Capraesque comedy which doesn't quite come off.

w D. D. Beauchamp, William Bowers, Richard Flournoy *d* Lloyd Bacon *ph* Harold J. Wild *m* Roy Webb

Jean Simmons, Robert Mitchum, Arthur Hunnicutt, Edgar Buchanan, Wallace Ford, Raymond Walburn

She Lives
US 1973 74m colour TVM
ABC Circle

College newlyweds find that the wife is dying of a rare disease.
Dreary copy of *Love Story*.

w Paul Neimark *d* Stuart Hagmann

Season Hubley, Desi Arnaz Jnr

She Loves Me Not*
US 1934 85m bw
Paramount (Benjamin Glazer)

A showgirl murder witness takes refuge in a men's college.
Larky musical farce later remade as *True to the Army* and *How to be Very Very Popular*; this first version is perhaps the most nearly amusing.

w Ben Glazer, *novel* Edward Hope, *play* Howard Lindsay *d* Elliott Nugent *ph* Charles Lang *songs* various

Bing Crosby, Miriam Hopkins, Kitty Carlisle, Edward Nugent, Lynne Overman, Henry Stephenson, Warren Hymer, George Barbier

She Waits*
US 1971 74m colour TVM
Metromedia

A bride is possessed by the evil spirit of her husband's first wife.
Obvious ghost story with a few frissons and a good cast.

w Arthur Wallace *d* Delbert Mann

Dorothy McGuire, Patty Duke, David McCallum, Lew Ayres, Beulah Bondi

She Wore a Yellow Ribbon**
US 1949 103m Technicolor
RKO

Problems of a cavalry officer about to retire.
Fragmentary but very enjoyable western with all Ford ingredients served piping hot.

w Frank Nugent, Laurence Stallings, *story* James Warner Bellah *d John Ford ph Winton C. Hoch m* Richard Hageman

John Wayne, Joanne Dru, John Agar, Ben Johnson, Harry Carey Jnr, Victor McLaglen, Mildred Natwick, George O'Brien, Arthur Shields

The Sheepman*
US 1958 91m Metrocolor
Cinemascope
MGM (Edmund Grainger)

A tough sheep farmer determines to settle in a cattle town.
Easy-going western with humorous moments.

w William Bowers, James Edward Grant *d* George Marshall *ph* Robert Bronner *m* Jeff Alexander

Glenn Ford, Shirley Maclaine, Leslie Nielsen, Mickey Shaughnessy, Edgar Buchanan

The Sheik Steps Out
US 1937 68m bw
Republic (Herman Schlom)

A modern sheik has a riotous time in the big city.
Uninventive spoof of the Valentino myth.

w Adele Buffington, Gordon Kahn *d* Irving Pichel *ph* Jack Marta *md* Alberto Columbo

Ramon Novarro, Lola Lane, Gene Lockhart, Kathleen Burke, Stanley Fields

Shell Game*
US 1975 74m colour TVM
TCF

A con man fleeces the crooked head of a charity fund.
Pleasant comedy suspenser on the lines of *It Takes a Thief*.

w Harold Jack Bloom *d* Glenn Jordan

John Davidson, Tommy Atkins, Marie O'Brien, Jack Kehoe, Joan Van Ark

Shenandoah**
US 1965 105m Technicolor
Universal (Robert Arthur)

How the American Civil War affected the lives of a Virginia family.
Surprisingly hard-centred and moving semi-western for the family; excellent performances and well-controlled mood.

w James Lee Barrett d Andrew V. McLaglen ph William Clothier *m* Joseph Gershenson

James Stewart, Rosemary Forsyth, Doug

McClure, Glenn Corbett, Katharine Ross, Philip Alford

The Sheriff*
US 1970 74m colour TVM
Columbia (Jon Epstein)

A black sheriff gets into race trouble on a rape case.
Routine adequately-made melodrama.

w Arnold Perl *d* David Lowell Rich

Ossie Davis, Ruby Dee

The Sheriff of Fractured Jaw
GB 1959 103m Eastmancolor Cinemascope
TCF / Daniel M. Angel

A London gunsmith in the old west accidentally becomes a hero.
Tame, predictable comedy with a clear lack of invention.

w Arthur Dales *d* Raoul Walsh *ph* Otto Heller *m* Robert Farnon

Kenneth More, Jayne Mansfield, Robert Morley, Ronald Squire, David Horne, Henry Hull, Eynon Evans, Bruce Cabot, William Campbell

Sherlock Holmes
The innumerable Sherlock Holmes films are noted in *Filmgoer's Companion*, and in this volume the appropriate films are listed under their own titles with the exception of the modernized dozen made in the forties by Universal, starring Basil Rathbone as Holmes and Nigel Bruce as Watson. These followed on from Fox's two period pieces, THE HOUND OF THE BASKERVILLES and THE ADVENTURES OF SHERLOCK HOLMES (qv). The series started and ended somewhat lamely but several of the episodes remain highly enjoyable, for performances and dialogue rather than plot or pacing. All but the first were directed by Roy William Neill.

1942: SHERLOCK HOLMES AND THE VOICE OF TERROR (*d* John Rawlins *with* Reginald Denny, Thomas Gomez); SHERLOCK HOLMES AND THE SECRET WEAPON* (with Lionel Atwill as Moriarty)
1943: SHERLOCK HOLMES IN WASHINGTON* (*with* Henry Daniell, George Zucco); SHERLOCK HOLMES FACES DEATH** (*with* Halliwell Hobbes, Dennis Hoey)
1944: SHERLOCK HOLMES AND THE SPIDER WOMAN** (*with* Gale Sondergaard, Dennis Hoey); THE SCARLET CLAW** *(with* Gerald Hamer); THE PEARL OF DEATH** (*with* Miles Mander, Dennis Hoey, Rondo Hatton)
1945: THE HOUSE OF FEAR* (*with* Aubrey Mather, Dennis Hoey); THE WOMAN IN GREEN* (*with* Henry Daniell as Moriarty); PURSUIT TO ALGIERS (*with* Martin Kosleck)
1946: TERROR BY NIGHT* (*with* Alan Mowbray), DRESSED TO KILL (GB title: SHERLOCK HOLMES AND THE SECRET CODE; *with* Patricia Morison)

Sherlock Holmes*
US 1932 68m bw
Fox

Moriarty brings Chicago gangsters into London.
Interesting but rather unsatisfactory Holmes adventure.

w Bertram Milhauser *d* William K. Howard *ph* George Barnes

Clive Brook, Reginald Owen, Ernest Torrence, Miriam Jordan, Alan Mowbray, Herbert Mundin

She's Working Her Way through College
US 1952 101m Technicolor
Warner (William Jacobs)

A burlesque queen goes to college and brings out the beast in an English professor.
Limp and vulgar musical remake of a well-liked play and film; just about gets by as a lowbrow timekiller.

w Peter Milne, *play* The Male Animal by James Thurber, Elliott Nugent *d* Bruce Humberstone *ph* Wilfrid Cline *md* Ray Heindorf *ch* Le Roy Prinz *songs* Sammy Cahn, Vernon Duke

Virginia Mayo, Ronald Reagan, Don Defore, Gene Nelson, Phyllis Thaxter, Patrice Wymore
† Sequel 1953: *She's Back on Broadway.*

Shine on Harvest Moon*
US 1944 112m bw (Technicolor sequence)
Warner (William Jacobs)

The life and times of vaudeville singer Nora Bayes.
Standard ragtime biopic, very adequately made.

w Sam Hellman, Richard Weil, Francis Swan, James Kern *d* David Butler *ph* Arthur Edeson *md* Heinz Roemheld

Ann Sheridan, Dennis Morgan, Jack Carson, Irene Manning, S. Z. Sakall, Marie Wilson, Robert Shayne

Shining Victory
US 1941 80m bw
Warner (Robert Lord)

A psychiatrist is torn between love and duty.
Adequate romantic programmer.

w Howard Koch, Ann Froelick, *play* Jupiter Laughs by A. J. Cronin *d* Irving Rapper *ph* James Wong Howe

James Stephenson, Geraldine Fitzgerald, Donald Crisp, Barbara O'Neil, Montagu Love, Sig Rumann

Ship Ahoy
US 1942 95m bw
MGM (Jack Cummings)

On a trip to Puerto Rico, a tap dancer is enlisted as a spy.
Tepid musi-comedy.

w Harry Clark *d* Eddie Buzzell *ph* Leonard Smith *md* Merrill Pye

Eleanor Powell, Red Skelton, Bert Lahr, Virginia O'Brien, William Post Jnr, James Cross

Ship of Fools***
US 1965 150m bw
Columbia / Stanley Kramer

In 1933 a German liner leaves Vera Cruz for Bremerhaven with a mixed bag of passengers.
Ambitious, serious, quite fascinating slice-of-life shipboard multi-melodrama. Capable mounting, memorable performances and a bravura finale erase memories of padding and symbolic pretensions.

w Abby Mann, novel Katherine Anne Porter *d Stanley Kramer ph Ernest Laszlo m Ernest Gold*

Vivien Leigh, Simone Signoret, Oskar Werner, Heinz Ruhmann, Jose Ferrer, Lee Marvin, Elizabeth Ashley, *Michael Dunn*, George Segal, Jose Greco, Charles Korvin, Alf Kjellin, Werner Klemperer, John Wengraf, Lilia Skala, Karen Verne

The Ship That Died of Shame
GB 1955 91m bw
Ealing (Michael Relph, Basil Dearden)

The wartime crew of a motor gunboat buy the vessel and go into postwar business as smugglers.
Thin and rather obvious melodramatic fable.

w John Whiting, Michael Relph, Basil Dearden, *novel* Nicholas Monsarrat *d* Michael Relph, Basil Dearden *ph* Gordon Dines *m* William Alwyn

Richard Attenborough, George Baker, Bill Owen, Virginia McKenna, Roland Culver, Bernard Lee, Ralph Truman, John Chandos

'A sentimental fantasy tacked on to a basically conventional thriller.'—*Penelope Houston*

Ships with Wings*
GB 1941 103m bw
Ealing (S. C. Balcon)

Aircraft carriers prepare for World War II.
Historically interesting, dramatically insubstantial flagwaver.

w Sergei Nolbandov, Patrick Kirwan, Austin Melford, Diana Morgan *d* Sergei Nolbandov

John Clements, Leslie Banks, Jane Baxter, Ann Todd, Basil Sydney, Edward Chapman, Hugh Williams, Frank Pettingell, Michael Wilding

The Shiralee*
GB 1957 99m bw
Ealing (Jack Rix)

An Australian swagman leaves his wife and takes to the road with his small daughter.
Episodic character comedy-drama throwing a fairly sharp light on the Australian scene.

w Neil Paterson, Leslie Norman, *novel* D'Arcy Niland *d Leslie Norman ph* Paul Beeson *m* John Addison

Peter Finch, Dana Wilson, Elizabeth Sellars, George Rose, Russell Napier, Nial MacGinnis, Tessie O'Shea

Shirts/Skins*
US 1973 74m colour TVM
MGM

Six young businessmen turn themselves into competing teams on a crazy bet.
Spasmodically funny, erratically scripted comedy.

d William Graham

René Auberjonois, Bill Bixby, Leonard Frey, Doug McClure, McLean Stevenson, Robert Walden, Loretta Swit

Shock
US 1946 70m bw
TCF

A girl in a hotel sees a murder committed, and an elaborate plan is concocted to silence her.
Flat treatment ruins a good suspense situation.

w Eugene Ling *d* Alfred Werker *ph* Glen MacWilliams, Joe MacDonald

Vincent Price, Lynn Bari, Frank Latimore, Annabel Shaw

'Extreme improbabilities and a general lack of finish.'—*MFB*

Shock Corridor
US 1963 101m Technicolor
Leon Fromkess / Sam Firks (Samuel Fuller)

A journalist gets himself admitted to a mental asylum to solve the murder of an inmate.
Sensational melodrama, a cinematic equivalent of the yellow press, and on that level quite lively.

wd Samuel Fuller

Peter Breck, Constance Towers, Gene Evans, James Best, Hari Rhodes, Philip Ahn

Shock Treatment
US 1964 94m bw
Warner (Aaron Rosenberg)

Murders are committed in a mental institution.
Tasteless thriller, not even very arresting as a yarn.

w Sidney Boehm *d* Denis Sanders *ph* Sam Leavitt *m* Jerry Goldsmith

Lauren Bacall, Roddy MacDowall, Carol Lynley, Ossie Davis, Stuart Whitman, Douglass Dumbrille

The Shocking Miss Pilgrim
US 1946 85m Technicolor
TCF (William Perlberg)

In 1894 Boston, a lady typist (stenographer) fights for women's rights.
Period comedy with music; not nearly as sharp as it thinks it is.

wd George Seaton *ph* Leon Shamroy *ad* James Basevi, Boris Leven *songs* George and Ira Gershwin

Betty Grable, Dick Haymes, Anne Revere, Allyn Joslyn, Gene Lockhart, Elizabeth Patterson, Arthur Shields, Elizabeth Risdon

The Shoes of the Fisherman**
US 1968 157m Metrocolor Panavision
MGM (George Englund)

After twenty years as a political prisoner, a Russian bishop becomes Pope.
Predigested but heavy-going picturization of a bestseller; big budget, big stars, big hopes. In fact a commercial dud, with plenty of superficial interest but more dramatic contrivance than religious feeling.

w John Patrick, James Kennaway, *novel* Morris West *d Michael Anderson ph Erwin Hiller m* Alex North *ad Edward Carfagno, George W. Davis*

Anthony Quinn, David Janssen, Laurence Olivier, Oskar Werner, John Gielgud, Barbara Jefford, Leo McKern, Vittorio de Sica, Clive Revill, Paul Rogers

'A splendidly decorated curate's egg.'—*MFB*

The Shooting
US 1966 82m De Luxe
Santa Clara (Jack Nicholson, Monte Hellman)

An ex-bounty hunter is trailed by a hired killer.
Simplistic semi-professional western which achieves some power despite poor technical quality and a deliberately obscure ending.

w Adrien Joyce *d* Monte Hellman *ph* Gregory Sandor *m* Richard Markowitz

Warren Oates, Will Hutchins, Jack Nicholson, Millie Perkins

The Shootist**
US 1976 100m Technicolor Panavision
Paramount / Frankovich-Self

In 1901, a dying ex-gunfighter arrives in a small town to set his affairs in order.
Impressive semi-western melodrama, very well written and acted all round; the kind of solidly entertaining and thoughtful movie one imagined they didn't make any more.

w Miles Hood Swarthout, Scott Hale, novel Glendon Swarthout *d Don Siegel ph* Bruce Surtees *m* Elmer Bernstein

John Wayne, Lauren Bacall, James Stewart, Ron Howard, Bill McKinney, Richard Boone, John Carradine, Scatman Crothers, Harry Morgan, Hugh O'Brian, Sheree North

'Just when it seemed that the western was an endangered species, due for extinction because it had repeated itself too many times, Wayne and Siegel have managed to validate it once more.' —*Arthur Knight*

Shootout
US 1971 94m Technicolor
Universal (Hal B. Wallis)

After seven years in prison, a bank robber seeks out his betrayer.
Routine, flatly-handled revenge western.

w Marguerite Roberts, *novel* The Lone Cowboy by Will James *d* Henry Hathaway *ph* Earl Rath *m* Dave Grusin

Gregory Peck, Pat Quinn, Robert F. Lyons, Susan Tyrell, Jeff Corey, James Gregory, Rita Gam

Shootout in a One Dog Town*
US 1973 74m colour TVM
Hanna–Barbera

A banker prepares a dangerous scheme to protect his money from outlaws.
Offbeat, entertaining western.

wd Burt Kennedy

Richard Crenna, Jack Elam, Richard Egan, Dub

Taylor, Gene Evans, Stefanie Powers, Michael Ansara

The Shop around the Corner**
US 1940 97m bw
MGM (Ernst Lubitsch)

In a Budapest shop, the new floorwalker and a girl who dislikes him find they are pen pals.
Pleasant period romantic comedy which holds no surprises but is presented with great style.

w Samson Raphaelson, play Nikolaus Laszlo *d Ernst Lubitsch ph* William Daniels *m* Werner Heymann

James Stewart, Margaret Sullavan, *Frank Morgan*, Joseph Schildkraut, Sara Haden, *Felix Bressart*, William Tracy

'It's not pretentious but it's a beautiful job of picture-making, and the people who did it seem to have enjoyed doing it just as much as their audiences will enjoy seeing it.'—*James Shelley Hamilton*

'An agreeably bittersweet example of light entertainment.'—*Charles Higham, 1972*

† Remade as *In The Good Old Summertime* (qv).

Shopworn Angel*
US 1928 90m approx bw part-talkie
Paramount (Louis D. Lighton)

A showgirl meets a naïve young soldier off to war and forsakes her man about town.
Hard-boiled, soft-centred romantic drama remade as below and later as *That Kind of Woman* (qv).

w Howard Estabrook, Albert Shelby Le Vino, *play* Private Pettigrew's Girl by Dana Burnet *d* Richard Wallace *ph* Charles Lang

Nancy Carroll, Gary Cooper, Paul Lukas, Emmett King

Shopworn Angel*
US 1938 85m bw
MGM (Joseph L. Mankiewicz)

Smooth, close remake of the above.

w Waldo Salt *d* H. C. Potter *ph* Joseph Ruttenberg *montage* Slavko Vorkapitch

Margaret Sullavan, James Stewart, Walter Pidgeon, Hattie McDaniel, Sam Levene

Short Cut to Hell
US 1957 89m bw Vistavision
Paramount (A. C. Lyles)

A racketeer hires a gunman to commit a double murder, then doublecrosses him.
Rough and ready remake of *This Gun for Hire* (qv), less arresting than the original.

w Ted Berkeman, Raphael Blau, W. R. Burnett, *novel* A Gun for Sale by Graham Greene *d James Cagney ph* Haskell Boggs *m* Irvin Colbert

Robert Ivers, Georgeann Johnson, William Bishop, Murvyn Vye

Short Walk to Daylight*
US 1972 73m Technicolor TVM
Universal (Edward J. Montagne)

Eight people are trapped in the New York subway by an earthquake.
Unfortunately most of the excitement is at the beginning, but at least it's a good idea.

w Philip H. Reisman Jnr, Steven Bochco, Gerald di Pego *d* Barry Shear

James Brolin, Don Mitchell, James McEachin, Abby Lincoln, Brooke Bundy

A Shot in the Dark*
US 1964 101m De Luxe Panavision
UA / Mirisch / Geoffrey (Blake Edwards)

A woman is accused of shooting her lover; accident-prone Inspector Clouseau investigates.
Further adventures of the oafish, Tatiesque clodhopper from *The Pink Panther*; mildly funny for those in the mood for pratfalls.

w Blake Edwards, William Peter Blatty *d* Blake Edwards *ph* Christopher Challis *m* Henry Mancini *pd* Michael Stringer

Peter Sellers, Elke Sommer, George Sanders, Herbert Lom, Tracy Reed, Graham Stark

Shout at the Devil*
GB 1976 147m Technicolor Panavision
Tonav (Michael Klinger)

In 1913 Zanzibar, a hard-drinking American and an old Etonian Englishman join forces to rout a brutal German commissioner who resents their poaching ivory in his territory.
The main characters are respectively repellent, effete, and just plain nasty, but the action scenes are vivid and the production is mainly notable as an expensive old-fashioned British film made at a time when there were few British films of any kind.

w Wilbur Smith, Stanley Price, Alastair Reid, *novel* Wilbur Smith *d* Peter Hunt *ph* Mike Reed *m* Maurice Jarre

Lee Marvin, Roger Moore, Barbara Parkins, René Kolldehoff, Ian Holm, Karl Michael Vogler, Maurice Denham, Jean Kent, Robert Lang, Murray Melvin, George Coulouris

Show Business***
US 1944 92m bw
RKO (Eddie Cantor)

The careers of four friends in vaudeville.
Lively low-budget period musical which probably presents the best picture of what old-time vaudeville was really like; a lot of fun when the plot doesn't get in the way.

w Joseph Quillan, Dorothy Bennett *d Edwin L. Marin* *ph* Robert de Grasse, Vernon L. Walker *md* Constantin Bakaleinikoff *ch Nick Castle*

Eddie Cantor, Joan Davis, George Murphy, Constance Moore, Don Douglas, Nancy Kelly
'Bits of archaic vaudeville which give off a moderately pleasant smell of peanuts and cigar smoke.'—*James Agee*

Show of Shows**
US 1929 128m Technicolor
Warner (Darryl F. Zanuck)

A big musical show put on by Warner contract artists.
Primitive early talkie, of vital historical interest but mostly photographed from a seat in the stalls.

w/m various *d* John G. Adolfi *ph* Barney McGill

Frank Fay, H. B. Warner, Monte Blue, Lupino Lane, Ben Turpin, Chester Morris, Ted Lewis and his band, Georges Carpentier, Patsy Ruth Miller, Beatrice Lillie, Winnie Lightner, Irene Bordoni, Myrna Loy, Douglas Fairbanks Jnr, John Barrymore, Betty Compson
'Colour photography of the crudest, most garish kind, the resulting impression being that a child of seven has been let loose with a shilling box of paints.'—*James Agate*

Show Them No Mercy*
US 1935 76m bw
TCF (Raymond Griffith)

Kidnappers are rounded up by G-men.
Lively crime thriller typical of its time.

w Kubec Glasmon, Henry Lehrman *d* George Marshall *ph* Bert Glennon

Rochelle Hudson, Cesar Romero, Bruce Cabot, Edward Norris, Edward Brophy, Warren Hymer

Showboat***
US 1936 110m bw
Universal (Carl Laemmle Jnr)

Lives and loves of the personnel on an old-time Mississippi showboat.
Great style and excellent performances mark this version, which still suffers from longueurs in the middle followed by the rapid passage of many years to provide a happy ending.

w Oscar Hammerstein II, from his book for the Broadway musical from Edna Ferber's novel *d James Whale* *ph John Mescall* *m Jerome Kern* *ly Oscar Hammerstein II*

Irene Dunne, Allan Jones, Helen Morgan, Paul Robeson, Charles Winninger, Hattie McDaniel, Donald Cook, Sammy White
† A primitive talkie version of *Showboat*, now lost, was made in 1929.

Showboat**
US 1951 108m Technicolor
MGM (Arthur Freed)

Vigorous remake with good ensemble dancing; otherwise inferior to the 1936 version.

w John Lee Mahin *d* George Sidney *ph* Charles Rosher *ch Robert Alton*

Kathryn Grayson, *Howard Keel*, Ava Gardner, William Warfield, *Joe E. Brown*, Robert Sterling, Marge and Gower Champion, Agnes Moorehead

Showdown
US 1972 99m Technicolor Todd-AO 35
Universal (George Seaton)

A sheriff finds that his old friend is leader of an outlaw gang.
Routine star western adequately done.

w Theodore Taylor *d* George Seaton *ph* Ernest Laszlo *m* David Shire

Rock Hudson, Dean Martin, Susan Clark, Donald Moffat, Don McLiam

The Shrike
US 1955 88m bw
U-I (Aaron Rosenberg)

A brilliant theatre man has a nervous breakdown because his wife is a vindictive harpy.
Theatrical two-hander, aridly filmed, of little interest except to show that both stars are capable of sustained emotional acting.

w Ketti Frings, *play* Joseph Kramm *d* Jose Ferrer *ph* William Daniels *m* Frank Skinner *titles Saul Bass*

Jose Ferrer, June Allyson, Joy Page, Jacqueline de Wit, Kendall Clark
'The film is unvaryingly paced, the result, one feels, of a respectable but far from invigorating honesty of purpose.'—*MFB*

The Shuttered Room
GB 1967 110m Technicolor
Warner / Troy–Schenck (Philip Hazelton)

Returning to her childhood home on an island off the New England coast, a girl and her husband are subjected to terror and violence.
Stretched out suspenser which looks good and is carefully made but fails in its effort to combine the menace of teenage yobboes with that of the monster lurking upstairs.

w D. B. Ledrov, Nathaniel Tanchuck, *story* H. P. Lovecraft, August Derleth *d David Greene ph Ken Hodges m* Basil Kirchin

Gig Young, Carol Lynley, Flora Robson, Oliver Reed, William Devlin

Side Street
US 1950 83m bw
MGM (Sam Zimbalist)

A petty thief finds himself involved with big-time crooks.
Well-made but rather boring crime melodrama with an excellent car chase finale.

w Sidney Boehm *d* Anthony Mann *ph* Joseph Ruttenberg *m* Lennie Hopkins

Farley Granger, Cathy O'Donnell, James Craig, Paul Kelly, Jean Hagen, Edmon Ryan, Paul Harvey

Sidekicks
US 1974 75m colour TVM

A black and a white con man get in and out of scrapes in the old west.
Rather dreary action comedy based on *The Skin Game* (qv). No go as a series.

w William Bowers *d* Burt Kennedy

Lou Gossett, Larry Hagman, Blythe Danner, Jack Elam

Sidewalks of New York*
US 1931 73m bw
MGM (Lawrence Weingarten)

The playboy owner of some tenement apartments falls in love with the daughter of one of the tenants.
Interesting rather than wholly successful early sound comedy which marked the beginning of Keaton's decline; he was not allowed full control and the comedy scenes are thinly spaced.

w George Landy, Paul Gerard Smith, Eric Hatch, Robert E. Hopkins *d* Jules White, Zion Myers *ph* Leonard Smith

Buster Keaton, Anita Page, Cliff Edwards, Frank Rowan

The Siege of Pinchgut
GB 1959 104m bw
Ealing (Eric Williams)

Escaped convicts take over a small island in Sydney harbour.
Disappointingly obvious location melodrama with routine excitements.

w Harry Watt, Jon Cleary *d* Harry Watt *ph* Gordon Dines *m* Kenneth V. Jones

Aldo Ray, Heather Sears, Neil McCallum, Victor Maddern, Carlo Justini

The Siege at Red River
US 1954 86m Technicolor
TCF / Panoramic (Leonard Goldstein)

During the American Civil War a Confederate agent behind northern lines defeats a treacherous helper and escapes to the south.
Modest, generally watchable, and quite forgettable western.

w Sidney Boehm *d* Rudolph Maté *ph* Edward Cronjager *m* Lionel Newman

Van Johnson, Joanne Dru, Richard Boone, Milburn Stone, Jeff Morrow, Craig Hill

The Siege of Sidney Street*
GB 1960 92m bw Dyaliscope
Midcentury (Robert S. Baker, Monty Berman)

An account of the anarchists who infiltrated London in 1912.
Detailed but not dramatically absorbing historical reconstruction with unsatisfactory fictional trimmings.

w Jimmy Sangster, Alexander Baron *d/ph* Robert S. Baker, Monty Berman *m* Stanley Black

Peter Wyngarde, Donald Sinden, Nicole Berger, Kieron Moore, Leonard Sachs, Tutte Lemkow

The Siege of the Saxons
GB 1963 85m Technicolor
Columbia / Ameran (Jud Kinberg)

When King Arthur is ill, the Saxons plot his overthrow but are foiled by a handsome outlaw.
Comic strip adventure with action highlights borrowed from older and better films.

w John Kohn, Jud Kinberg *d* Nathan Juran *ph* Wilkie Cooper, Jack Willis

Ronald Lewis, Janette Scott, Ronald Howard, Mark Dignam, John Laurie, Richard Clarke, Jerome Willis

The Sign of the Cross***
US 1932 123m bw
Paramount (Cecil B. de Mille)

In the days of Nero, a Roman officer is converted to Christianity.
A heavily theatrical play becomes one of de Mille's most impressive films, the genuine horror

of the arena mingling with the debauched humour of the court. A wartime prologue added in 1943 prolongs the film without improving it.

w Waldemar Young, Sidney Buchman, *play* Wilson Barrett *d Cecil B. de Mille ph Karl Struss*

Fredric March, Elissa Landi, *Charles Laughton, Claudette Colbert*, Ian Keith, Harry Beresford, Arthur Hohl, Nat Pendleton

'A beautiful film to watch ... a triumph of popular art.'—*Charles Higham, 1972*

'However contemptible one may find de Mille's moralizing, it is impossible not to be impressed by *The Sign of the Cross*.'—*John Baxter, 1968*

'De Mille's bang-them-on-the-head-with-wild-orgies-and-imperilled-virginity style is at its ripest.'—*New Yorker, 1976*

'Preposterous, but the laughter dies on the lips.'—*NFT, 1974*

The Sign of the Pagan
US 1954 92m Technicolor Cinemascope
U-I (Albert J. Cohen)

Attila the Hun is defeated by the Romans.
Historic horse opera, rather cheaply done.

w Oscar Brodney, Barre Lyndon *d* Douglas Sirk *ph* Russell Metty *m* Frank Skinner

Jeff Chandler, Jack Palance, Rita Gam, Ludmilla Tcherina, Jeff Morrow, George Dolenz, Eduard Franz, Alexander Scourby

Signpost to Murder
US 1967 74m bw Panavision
MGM / Martin (Lawrence Weingarten)

A convicted murderer escapes after ten years and a lonely wife promises to help him.
Tricksy mystery set in a never-never English village.

w Sally Benson, *play* Monte Doyle *d* George Englund *ph* Paul C. Vogel *m* Lyn Murray

Joanne Woodward, Stuart Whitman, Edward Mulhare, Alan Napier, Murray Matheson

The Silence*
US 1975 74m colour TVM
Palomar

For violating West Point's honour code, a cadet is shunned by his associates.
Mildly interesting story based on fact.

d Joseph Hardy

Richard Thomas, Gunnel Lindblom, Jorgen Lindstrom

The Silencers*
US 1966 103m Technicolor
Columbia / Irving Allen (Jim Schmerer)

Adventures of a sexy secret agent.
Or, James Bond sent up rotten. Plenty of fun along the way, with in-jokes and characters like Lovey Kravezit, but the plot could have done with more attention, and the sequels (*Murderers Row, The Ambushers, Wrecking Crew*) were uncontrolled disaster areas.

w Oscar Saul, *novel* Donald Hamilton *d* Phil Karlson *ph* Burnett Guffey *m* Elmer Bernstein

Dean Martin, Stella Stevens, Victor Buono, Daliah Lavi, Cyd Charisse, Robert Webber, James Gregory, Nancy Kovack

The Silent Enemy
GB 1958 112m bw
Romulus (Bertram Ostrer)

The World War II exploits of a naval frogman in the Mediterranean.
Stereotyped naval underwater adventures, adequately presented.

wd William Fairchild *ph* Egil Woxholt, Otto Heller *m* William Alwyn

Laurence Harvey, John Clements, Michael Craig, Dawn Addams, Sidney James, Alec McCowen, Nigel Stock

The Silent Gun*
US 1969 74m colour TVM
Paramount (Bruce Lansbury)

A former gunfighter who has shunned weapons is appointed sheriff of his home town.
Adequate minor western.

w Clyde Ware *d* Michael Caffey

Lloyd Bridges, John Beck, Ed Begley, Edd Byrnes, Pernell Roberts, Susan Howard

Silent Movie*
US 1976 87m De Luxe
TCF (Michael Hertzberg)

An alcoholic producer gets the idea that a silent movie would be a great novelty, and tries to get stars to take part.
Fairly lively spoof with the talents concerned in variable form. The shortage of laughter made it a hit in the seventies, but at no time does it approach the Keaton or Laurel and Hardy level.

w Mel Brooks, Ron Clark, Rudy de Luca, Barry Levinson *d* Mel Brooks *ph* Paul Lohmann *m* John Morris

Mel Brooks, Marty Feldman, Dom De Luise, Bernardette Peters, Sid Caesar, Harold Gould, Fritz Feld, Harry Ritz, Henny Youngman *guest stars* Anne Bancroft, Paul Newman, Burt

Reynolds, James Caan, Liza Minnelli, Marcel Marceau

Silent Night, Lonely Night*
US 1969 98m Technicolor TVM
Universal (Jack Farren)

Two lonely people with problems fall in love at Christmas in a small New England inn.
Acceptable rueful love story.

w John Vlahos, *play* Robert Anderson *d* Daniel Petrie

Lloyd Bridges, Shirley Jones, Carrie Snodgress, Lynn Carlin

Silent Running*
US 1971 90m Technicolor
Universal / Michel Gruskoff / Douglas Trumbull

Members of a space station crew in 2001 are space gardening to replenish nuclear-devasted earth.
Sombre futuristic fantasy, well made but slow and muddled in development.

w Deric Washburn, Mike Cimino, Steve Bocho *d* Douglas Trumbull *ph* Charles F. Wheeler *m* Peter Schickele

Bruce Dern, Cliff Potts, Ron Rifkin, Jesse Vint

Silk Stockings*
US 1957 116m Metrocolor Cinemascope
MGM (Arthur Freed)

A Russian composer in Paris agrees to write music for a Hollywood film; a lady commissar is sent to get him back.
Musical rewrite of *Ninotchka* via a Broadway show; good moments but generally very stretched.

w Leonard Gershe, Leonard Spiegelgass, *play* George S. Kaufman, Leueen McGrath, Abe Burrows, *original play* Melchior Lengyel *d* Rouben Mamoulian *ph* Robert Bronner *m/ly* Cole Porter *md* André Previn

Fred Astaire, Cyd Charisse, Peter Lorre, Janis Paige, George Tobias, Jules Munshin, Joseph Buloff

The Silken Affair
GB 1956 96m bw
Dragon (Fred Feldkamp)

An accountant decides to live it up, and finds himself on trial for manipulating the firm's books.
Unsatisfactory mix of comedy and fantasy, with a dim plot and virtually no comic ideas.

w Robert Lewis Taylor *d* Roy Kellino *ph* Gilbert Taylor *m* Peggy Stuart

David Niven, Genevieve Page, Wilfrid Hyde White, Ronald Squire, Beatrice Straight, Howard Marion Crawford, Dorothy Alison

The Silver Chalice
US 1955 142m Warnercolor Cinemascope
Warner (Victor Saville)

Adventures of a slave freed by Luke the apostle to fashion a chalice to hold the cup used at the Last Supper.
Po-faced biblical hokum, slower and deadlier than most, with howlingly bad casting and direction. On reflection, interesting things are being attempted with limbo set design, but in this sea of boredom the attempt only raises an eyebrow.

w Lesser Samuels, *novel* Thomas B. Costain *d* Victor Saville *ph* William V. Skall *m* Franz Waxman *pd Rolf Gerard*

Paul Newman, Pier Angeli, Jack Palance, Virginia Mayo, Walter Hampden, Joseph Wiseman, Alexander Scourby, Lorne Greene, Michael Pate, E. G. Marshall

The Silver Fleet*
GB 1943 87m bw
GFD / Archers (Michael Powell, Emeric Pressburger, Ralph Richardson)

In occupied Holland, a shipping magnate destroys his new U-boat and himself and his Nazi mentors with it.
Slow-starting, rather stilted melodrama which when it gets into its stride provides good acting and gripping propaganda.

wd Vernon Sewell, Gordon Wellesley

Ralph Richardson, Esmond Knight, Googie Withers, Beresford Egan, Frederick Burtwell, Kathleen Byron

Silver Queen
US 1942 80m bw
UA / Harry Sherman

A chivalrous western gambler rescues a girl from the wiles of a villain.
Standard romantic melodrama mainly set in saloons.

w Bernard Schubert, Cecile Kramer *d* Lloyd Bacon *ph* Russell Harlan

George Brent, Priscilla Lane, Bruce Cabot, Lynne Overman, Eugene Pallette, Janet Beecher, Guinn Williams, Roy Barcroft

Simba
GB 1955 99m Eastmancolor
GFD / Group Film (Peter de Sarigny)

An English farmer in Kenya fights the Mau Mau. Savagely topical melodrama which tends to cheapen a tragic situation.

w John Baines *d* Brian Desmond Hurst *ph* Geoffrey Unsworth *m* Francis Chagrin

Dirk Bogarde, Donald Sinden, Virginia McKenna, Basil Sydney, Marie Ney, Joseph Tomelty, Earl Cameron, Orlando Martins

Simon and Laura*
GB 1955 91m Technicolor Vistavision
GFD / Group Films (Teddy Baird)

The actors who play husband and wife in a TV series are married in reality and hate each other, a fact that shows in the live Christmas episode. Adequate film of a reasonably sophisticated West End comedy; good lines and performances.

w Peter Blackmore, *play* Alan Melville *d* Muriel Box *ph* Ernest Steward *m* Benjamin Frankel

Peter Finch, Kay Kendall, Ian Carmichael, Alan Wheatley, Richard Wattis, Muriel Pavlow, Maurice Denham, Hubert Gregg

Sinbad the Sailor
US 1947 117m Technicolor
RKO (Stephen Ames)

Sinbad sets off on his eighth voyage to find the lost treasure of Alexander.
Well-staged but humourless Arabian Nights swashbuckler.

w John Twist *d* Richard Wallace *ph* George Barnes *m* Roy Webb

Douglas Fairbanks Jnr, Walter Slezak, Maureen O'Hara, Anthony Quinn, George Tobias, Jane Greer, Mike Mazurki, Sheldon Leonard

Since You Went Away***
US 1944 172m bw
David O. Selznick

When hubby is away at the war, his wife and family adopt stiff upper lips.
Elaborate flagwaving investigation of the well-heeled American home front in World War II, with everyone brimming with goodwill and not a dry eye in the place. Absolutely superbly done, if it must be done at all, and a symposium of Hollywood values and techniques of the time.

w David O. Selznick, *book* Margaret Buell Wilder *d John Cromwell ph Stanley Cortez, Lee Garmes m* Max Steiner *pd William L. Pereira*

Claudette Colbert, Joseph Cotten, Jennifer Jones, Shirley Temple, Agnes Moorehead, Monty Woolley, Lionel Barrymore, Guy Madison, Robert Walker, Hattie McDaniel, Craig Stevens, Keenan Wynn, Albert Basserman, Nazimova, Lloyd Corrigan

'A deft, valid blend of showmanship, humour, and yard-wide Americanism.'—*James Agee*

'The whole litany of that middle-class synthetic emotionalism, meticulously annotated over a decade by tough and sentimental experts, has been procured for us.'—*Richard Winnington*

'A rather large dose of choking sentiment.' —*Bosley Crowther*

'It is not an average US reality. It is an average US dream.'—*Time*

Sincerely Yours
US 1955 115m Warnercolor Cinemascope
Warner (Henry Blanke)

A concert pianist goes deaf and retires to his penthouse, but with the help of binoculars lipreads the humble folk below. Helping them anonymously gives him courage to have an operation.
Absurd updating for a modern non-star of a creaky old George Arliss vehicle *The Man Who Played God.*

w Irving Wallace *d* Gordon Douglas *ph* William H. Clothier *m adviser* George Liberace

Liberace, Joanne Dru, Dorothy Malone, Alex Nicol, William Demarest

Sinful Davey
GB 1968 95m Eastmancolor Panavision
UA / Mirisch / Webb (William N. Graf)

In 1821 a young Scotsman determines to become a criminal like his father, but falls in love. Thin imitation of *Tom Jones*, highly implausible but played with some zest.

w James R. Webb, based on the autobiography of David Haggart *d* John Huston *ph* Ted Scaife, Freddie Young *m* Ken Thorne *pd* Stephen Grimes

John Hurt, Pamela Franklin, Nigel Davenport, Ronald Fraser, Robert Morley, Maxine Audley, Noel Purcell

Sing As We Go***
GB 1934 80m bw
ATP (Basil Dean)

An unemployed millgirl gets various holiday jobs in Blackpool.
A splendid, pawky star vehicle which is also the

best picture we have of industrial Lancashire in the thirties. Great fun.

w J. B. Priestley, Gordon Wellesley d Basil Dean

Gracie Fields, John Loder, *Frank Pettingell*, Dorothy Hyson, Stanley Holloway

'We have an industrial north that is bigger than Gracie Fields running around a Blackpool fun fair.'—*C. A. Lejeune*

Sing You Sinners**
US 1938 88m bw
Paramount (Wesley Ruggles)

The adventures of a happy-go-lucky family and their racehorse.
Cheerful family musical with amiable cast and good tunes.

w Claude Binyon *d* Wesley Ruggles *ph* Karl Struss *md* Boris Morros

Bing Crosby, Donald O'Connor, Fred MacMurray, Elizabeth Patterson, Ellen Drew, John Gallaudet

The Singer Not the Song
GB 1960 132m colour Cinemascope
Rank (Roy Baker)

In an isolated Mexican town a priest defies an outlaw who oddly respects him.
Lengthy character drama with little action or humour but a great deal of moody introspection and a suggestion of homosexuality.

w Nigel Balchin, *novel* Audrey Erskine Lindop *d* Roy Baker *ph* Otto Heller *m* Philip Green

John Mills, Dirk Bogarde, Mylene Demongeot, John Bentley, Laurence Naismith, Eric Pohlmann

'A rewarding film, as startling as a muffled scream from the subconscious.'—*Peter John Dyer*

The Singing Fool**
US 1928 110m bw
Warner

A successful singer goes on the skids when his small son dies.
Early talkie musical, a sensation because of its star's personality, but a pretty maudlin piece of drama.

w C. Graham Baker, *play* Leslie S. Barrows *d* Lloyd Bacon *ph* Byron Haskin *songs* Lew Brown, Ray Henderson, B. G. De Sylva

Al Jolson, Davey Lee, Betty Bronson, Josephine Dunn, Arthur Housman

'Obvious and tedious as the climax is, when the black-faced comedian stands before the camera and sings "Sonny Boy" you know the man is greater, somehow, than the situation, the story or the movie.'—*Pare Lorentz*

Singin' in the Rain****
US 1952 102m Technicolor
MGM (Arthur Freed)

When talkies are invented, the reputation of one female star shrivels while another grows.
Brilliant comic musical, the best picture by far of Hollywood in transition, with the catchiest tunes, the liveliest choreography, the most engaging performances and the most hilarious jokes of any musical.

w Adolph Green, Betty Comden d/ch Gene Kelly, Stanley Donen ph Harold Rosson m Nacio Herb Brown md Lennie Hayton ly Arthur Freed

Gene Kelly, Donald O'Connor, Debbie Reynolds, Millard Mitchell, Jean Hagen, Rita Moreno, Cyd Charisse, *Douglas Fowley*

'Perhaps the most enjoyable of all movie musicals.'—*New Yorker, 1975*

The Singing Nun
US 1966 98m Metrocolor Panavision
MGM (Jon Beck)

Adventures of a nun who takes her music to the outside world.
Icky musical drama based on a true character.

w Sally Benson, John Furia *d* Henry Koster *ph* Milton Krasner *md* Harry Sukman *songs* Soeur Sourire

Debbie Reynolds, Greer Garson, Ricardo Montalban, Agnes Moorehead, Chad Everett, Katharine Ross, Ed Sullivan, Juanita Moore

Sink the Bismarck**
GB 1960 97m bw Cinemascope
TCF / John Brabourne

In 1941, Britain's director of naval operations arranges the trapping and sinking of Germany's greatest battleship.
Tight little personal drama which would have been better on a standard screen, as its ships are plainly models and much of the footage stretched-out newsreel. Nevertheless, a good example of the stiff-upper-lip school.

w Edmund H. North *d* Lewis Gilbert *ph* Christopher Challis *m* Muir Mathieson

Kenneth More, Dana Wynter, Karel Stepanek, Carl Mohner, Laurence Naismith, Geoffrey Keen, Michael Hordern, Maurice Denham, Esmond Knight

The Sins of Rachel Cade
US 1960 123m Technicolor
Warner (Henry Blanke)

An American missionary nurse in the Belgian Congo falls in love with a crashed flier and has a baby.
Romantic melodrama which starts like *The Nun's Story* and ends like Peg's Paper; competent on its level.

w Edward Anhalt, *novel* Charles Mercer *d* Gordon Douglas *ph* Peverell Marley *m* Max Steiner

Angie Dickinson, Roger Moore, Peter Finch, Errol John, Woody Strode, Juano Hernandez, Frederick O'Neal, Mary Wickes

Sirocco
US 1951 98m bw
Columbia / Santana (Robert Lord)

In 1925 Damascus, an American runs guns for the rebels.
Tedious romantic drama in the *Casablanca* vein but with none of the magic.

w A. I. Bezzerides, Hans Jacoby, *novel* Coup de Grâce by Joseph Kessel *d* Curtis Bernhardt *ph* Burnett Guffey *m* George Antheil

Humphrey Bogart, Marta Toren, Lee J. Cobb, Everett Sloane, Gerald Mohr, Zero Mostel, Onslow Stevens

Sister Kenny*
US 1946 116m bw
RKO

The career of a nurse who instigated treatment for polio.
Standard, well-done biopic.

w Dudley Nichols, Alexander Knox, Mary McCarthy *d* Dudley Nichols *ph* George Barnes

Rosalind Russell, Alexander Knox, Dean Jagger, Philip Merivale, Beulah Bondi, Dorothy Peterson

The Sisters*
US 1938 98m bw
Warner (Hal B. Wallis)

The marriages of three sisters from a small Montana town.
Well-made potboiler for women; it even brings in the San Francisco earthquake, and the star teaming is piquant to say the least.

w Milton Krims, *novel* Myron Brinig *d* Anatole Litvak *ph* Tony Gaudio *m* Max Steiner

Bette Davis, Errol Flynn, Anita Louise, Ian Hunter, Donald Crisp, Beulah Bondi, Jane Bryan, Alan Hale, Dick Foran, Henry Travers, Patric Knowles, Lee Patrick, Harry Davenport

Sitting Pretty*
US 1933 85m bw
Paramount (Charles R. Rogers)

Two songwriters strike it rich in Hollywood.
Cheerful comedy musical, interesting for its backgrounds.

w Jack McGowan, S. J. Perelman, Lou Breslow *d* Harry Joe Brown *ph* Milton Krasner *songs* Mack Gordon, Harry Revel

Jack Oakie, Jack Haley, Ginger Rogers, Thelma Todd, Gregory Ratoff, Lew Cody, Harry Revel, Mack Gordon

Sitting Pretty***
US 1948 84m bw
TCF (Samuel G. Engel)

A young couple acquire a most unusual male baby sitter, a self-styled genius who sets the neighbourhood on its ears by writting a novel about it.
Out of the blue, a very funny comedy which entrenched Clifton Webb as one of Hollywood's great characters and led to two sequels, *Mr Belvedere Goes to College* and *Mr Belvedere Rings the Bell* (qv).

w F. Hugh Herbert, novel Belvedere by Gwen Davenport *d* Walter Lang *ph* Norbert Brodine *m* Alfred Newman

Clifton Webb, Robert Young, Maureen O'Hara, *Richard Haydn*, Louise Allbritton, Ed Begley, Randy Stuart, Larry Olsen

Sitting Target
GB 1972 92m Metrocolor
MGM (Barry Kulick)

A violent criminal breaks out of jail to kill his faithless wife.
Rough, tough action thriller; passes the time for hardened addicts.

w Alexander Jacobs, *novel* Lawrence Henderson *d* Douglas Hickox *ph* Ted Scaife *m* Stanley Myers *pd* Jonathan Barry

Oliver Reed, Jill St John, Edward Woodward, Frank Finlay, Ian McShane, Freddie Jones, Robert Beatty

Situation Hopeless But Not Serious
US 1965 97m bw
Paramount / Castle (Gottfried Reinhardt)

In 1944, two American fliers are captured by a friendly, lonely mild-mannered German, who keeps them in his cellar and hasn't the heart to tell them when the war is over . . .
Flat little comedy which leaves a talented cast no room for manoeuvre.

w Silvia Reinhardt, *novel* The Hiding Place by

Robert Shaw *d* Gottfried Reinhardt *ph* Kurt Hasse *m* Harold Byrne

Alec Guinness, Robert Redford, Mike Connors, Anita Hoefer

Six Bridges to Cross
US 1955 96m bw
U-I (Aaron Rosenberg)

The criminal career of a young hoodlum in Boston in the thirties.
Public Enemy reprise with a sentimental veneer, smooth but uninteresting.

w Sidney Boehm, *novel* They Stole Two and a Half Million Dollars and Got Away with It by Joseph F. Dineen *d* Joseph Pevney *ph* William Daniels *m* Joseph Gershenson

Tony Curtis, George Nader, Julie Adams, Jay C. Flippen, Sal Mineo, Jan Merlin

Six Day Bike Rider
US 1934 69m bw
Warner (Sam Bischoff)

One of life's failures impresses his girl by entering a cycling contest.
One of the star's stronger comedy vehicles.

w Earl Baldwin *d* Lloyd Bacon *ph* Warren Lynch

Joe E. Brown, Maxine Doyle, Frank McHugh, Gordon Westcott

The Six Million Dollar Man*
US 1972 74m Technicolor TVM
Universal (Richard Irving)

An astronaut injured in a crash is remade with powerful artificial limbs and becomes a superhuman, bionic spy.
A slow starter for an immensely popular science fiction series which injected love interest by later spinning off *The Bionic Woman*. Two other 74-minute starters were made before the show settled down into a one-hour slot; *Wine, Women and War* and *The Solid Gold Kidnapping*.

w Henri Simoun, *novel* Cyborg by Martin Caiden *d* Richard Irving

Lee Majors, Darren McGavin, Martin Balsam, Barbara Anderson

Six of a Kind*
US 1934 69m bw
Paramount

Comic adventures of six people driving across America.
Minor comedy which doesn't come off as a whole but adequately displays the talents of its stars.

w Walter de Leon, Harry Ruskin *d* Leo McCarey *ph* Henry Sharp *m* Ralph Rainger

Charles Ruggles, Mary Boland, W. C. Fields, Alison Skipworth, George Burns, Gracie Allen

633 Squadron*
GB 1964 94m Technicolor Panavision
UA / Mirisch (Cecil F. Ford)

In 1944 Mosquito aircraft try to collapse a cliff overhanging a munitions factory in a Norwegian fjord.
Standard war heroics with enough noise and disorder to keep most audiences hypnotized.

w James Clavell, Howard Koch, *novel* Frederick E. Smith *d* Walter Grauman *ph* Ted Scaife, John Wilcox *m Ron Goodwin*

Cliff Robertson, George Chakiris, Maria Perschy, Harry Andrews, Donald Houston, Michael Goodliffe

Sixty Glorious Years**
GB 1938 95m Technicolor
Imperator (Herbert Wilcox)
US title: *Queen of Destiny*

Scenes from the life of Queen Victoria.
A stately pageant apparently composed of material which couldn't be fitted into the previous year's black-and-white success *Victoria the Great*. Fascinating, though the camerawork is not very nimble.

w Robert Vansittart, Miles Malleson, Charles de Grandcourt *d* Herbert Wilcox *ph* Frederick A. Young

Anna Neagle, Anton Walbrook, C. Aubrey Smith, Walter Rilla, Charles Carson, Felix Aylmer, Lewis Casson
† The two films were edited together in 1943 to make a new selection called *Queen Victoria*, and in the process the original negatives were accidentally destroyed, so that both films now have to be printed from unattractive dupes.

The Ski Raiders
US 1972 90m Technicolor Panavision
Warner (Edward L. Rissien)
aka: *Snow Job*

An alpine ski instructor devises a scheme to rob a bank.
Very medium caper thriller with a breathtaking opening sequence.

w Ken Kolb, Jeffrey Bloom *d* George Englund *ph* Gabor Pogany, Willy Bogner *m* Jacques Loussier

Jean Claude Killy, Cliff Potts, Vittorio De Sica, Daniele Gaubert

Skidoo
US 1968 98m Technicolor Panavision
Paramount / Sigma (Otto Preminger)

Active and reformed gangsters get involved with hippies and preach universal love.
Abysmal mishmash with top talent abused; clearly intended as satirical farce, but in fact one of the most woebegone movies ever made.

w Doran William Cannon *d* Otto Preminger *ph* Leon Shamroy *m* George Tipton

Jackie Gleason, Carol Channing, Groucho Marx, Frankie Avalon, Fred Clark, Michael Constantine, Frank Gorshin, John Philip Law, Peter Lawford, Burgess Meredith, George Raft, Cesar Romero, Mickey Rooney

The Skin Game*
US 1971 102m Technicolor Panavision
Warner / Cherokee (Harry Keller)

A white and a black con man have near escapes in many a western town.
Amusing comedy western with good pace and a few shafts of wit.

w Peter Stone, Richard Alan Simmons *d* Paul Bogart *ph* Fred Koenekamp *m* David Shire

James Garner, Lou Gossett, Susan Clark, Brenda Sykes, Ed Asner, Andrew Duggan, Henry Jones, Neva Patterson

Skippy*
US 1931 88m bw
Paramount

The young son of a local health inspector makes friends in the slums.
Standard, blameless family entertainment.

w Joseph L. Mankiewicz, Norman McLeod, *comic strip* Percy Crosby *d* Norman Taurog *ph* Karl Struss

Jackie Cooper, Robert Coogan, Mitzi Green, Jackie Searl, Willard Robertson

Skirts Ahoy
US 1952 105m Technicolor
MGM (Joe Pasternak)

Three girls join the navy and get their men.
Musical recruiting poster, quite devoid of interest.

w Isobel Lennart *d* Sidney Lanfield *ph* William Mellor *m* Harry Warren *ly* Ralph Blane *ch* Nick Castle

Esther Williams, Vivian Blaine, Joan Evans, Barry Sullivan, Keefe Brasselle, Dean Miller, Debbie Reynolds, Bobby Van, Billy Eckstine

The Skull
GB 1965 83m Techniscope
Paramount / Amicus (Milton Subotsky)

The skull of the Marquis de Sade haunts two antiquarians.
Clodhopping horror with very visible wires.

w Milton Subotsky, *story* Robert Bloch *d* Freddie Francis *ph* John Wilcox *m* Elisabeth Lutyens

Peter Cushing, Christopher Lee, Patrick Wymark, Jill Bennett, Nigel Green, Michael Gough, George Coulouris

Skullduggery
US 1969 105m Technicolor Panavision
Universal (Saul David)

Archaeologists and adventurers clash on a trek in New Guinea.
Fashionable oddball adventure about the discovery of an unspoiled primitive tribe; the elements don't jell.

w Nelson Gidding *d* Gordon Douglas *ph* Robert Moreno *m* Oliver Nelson

Burt Reynolds, Susan Clark, Roger C. Carmel, Paul Hubschmid, Chips Rafferty, Alexander Knox, Edward Fox, Wilfrid Hyde White, Rhys Williams

Sky Full of Moon
US 1952 73m bw
MGM (Sidney Franklin Jnr)

A rodeo cowboy wins money and a showgirl in Las Vegas.
Ambling comedy with an agreeable air of innocence.

wd Norman Foster *ph* Ray June *m* Paul Sawtell

Carleton Carpenter, Jan Sterling, Keenan Wynn

Sky Heist*
US 1975 100m colour TVM
Warner / Jack Webb

Holidaymakers rescued by the Aero Bureau of the Los Angeles County Sheriff's office turn out to be criminals with a major robbery in hand.
Exciting but overlong caper yarn intended as a pilot for a helicopter series.

w William F. Nolan, Rick Rosner *d* Lee H. Katzin

Don Meredith, Joseph Campanella, Larry Wilcox, Ken Swofford, Stefanie Powers, Frank Gorshin, Shelley Fabares

Sky Riders*
US 1976 91m De Luxe Todd-AO 35
TCF (Terry Morse Jnr)

In Athens, the family of an American businessman is kidnapped by terrorists and rescued by hang gliders led by a soldier of fortune.
Old-fashioned actioner with new-fashioned political concern.

w Jack de Witt, Stanley Mann, Gary Michael White, Hall T. Sprague, Bill McGaw *d* Douglas Hickox *ph* Ousama Rawi *m* Lalo Schifrin

James Coburn, Susannah York, Robert Culp, Charles Aznavour, Werner Pochath, Kenneth Griffith, Harry Andrews

Sky West and Crooked
GB 1965 102m Eastmancolor
Rank / John Mills
US title: *Gypsy Girl*

A mentally retarded girl falls in love with a gypsy.
Eccentric rural melodrama with echoes of *Cold Comfort Farm* and *Les Jeux Interdits*. Interesting, but scarcely a runaway success.

w Mary Hayley Bell, John Prebble *d* John Mills *ph* Arthur Ibbetson *m* Malcolm Arnold

Hayley Mills, Ian McShane, Laurence Naismith, *Geoffrey Bayldon*, Annette Crosbie, Norman Bird

'Behind the overwhelming feyness of it all lurk assumptions which in cold blood look almost sinister.'—*MFB*

Skyjacked*
US 1972 101m Metrocolor Panavision
MGM / Walter Seltzer

A Boeing 707 on a flight from Los Angeles to Minneapolis is forced by a mad bomber to fly to Moscow.
Shamelessly hackneyed aeroplane adventure with quite enjoyable elements.

w Stanley R. Greenberg, *novel* Hijacked by David Harper *d* John Guillermin *ph* Harry Stradling Jnr *m* Perry Botkin Jnr

Charlton Heston, Yvette Mimieux, James Brolin, Claude Akins, Jeanne Crain, Rosey Grier, Walter Pidgeon, Leslie Uggams

Skylark
US 1941 94m bw
Paramount (Mark Sandrich)

A wife decides on her fifth anniversary that she is tired of being secondary to her husband's career, and needs a fling.
Formula matrimonial comedy; plenty of talent but no sparkle.

w Z. Myers, *play* Samson Raphaelson *d* Mark Sandrich *ph* Charles Lang

Claudette Colbert, Ray Milland, Brian Aherne, Binnie Barnes, Walter Abel, Grant Mitchell, Mona Barrie, Ernest Cossart

The Sky's the Limit*
US 1943 89m bw
RKO (David Hempstead)

A flier on leave meets and falls for a news photographer.
Thin musical with incidental compensations.

w Frank Fenton, Lynn Root *d* Edward H. Griffith *ph* Russell Metty *m* Leo Forbstein *songs* Harry Warren, Al Dubin

Fred Astaire, Joan Leslie, *Robert Benchley*, Robert Ryan, Elizabeth Patterson

Skyway to Death*
US 1974 74m Technicolor TVM
Universal (Lou Morheim)

A mountain cable car gets stuck with passengers aboard.
Routine disaster/suspense adventure, dullish when everyone talks, okay when the action begins.

w David Spector *d* Gordon Hessler

Bobby Sherman, Stefanie Powers, John Astin, Joseph Campanella, Ross Martin

Slander
US 1956 81m bw
MGM (Armand Deutsch)

Revelations about a film star in a scandal magazine lead to blackmail and murder.
Unlikely melodrama, routinely assembled, based on the Confidential Magazine lawsuits.

w Jerome Weidman *d* Roy Rowland *ph* Harold J. Marzerati *m* Jeff Alexander

Van Johnson, Ann Blyth, Steve Cochran, *Marjorie Rambeau*, Harold J. Stone

Slattery's Hurricane
US 1949 87m bw
TCF (William Perlberg)

Loves of a storm-spotting pilot with the US Weather Bureau in Florida.
Forgettable programmer with good storm sequences.

w Herman Wouk, Richard Murphy, *novel* Herman Wouk *d* André de Toth *ph* Charles G. Clarke *m* Lionel Newman

Richard Widmark, Linda Darnell, Veronica

Lake, John Russell, Gary Merrill, Walter Kingsford

Slaughter
US 1972 90m De Luxe Todd-AO 35
AIP / Slaughter United (Monroe Sachson)

A black Vietnam veteran hunts down the underworld syndicate which killed his mother and father.
Hectic crime yarn with a pitilessly violent hero and not enough style to relieve the unappetizing monotony.

w Mark Hanna, Don Williams *d* Jack Starrett *ph* Rosanio Solano *m* Luchi de Jesus

Jim Brown, Rip Torn, Don Gordon, Cameron Mitchell
'The cast perform their trigger-happy tasks with all the passionate conviction of a team of well-oiled robots.'—*Jan Dawson*

Slaughter on Tenth Avenue
US 1957 103m bw
U-I (Albert Zugsmith)

The New York DA's office investigates union murders on the docks.
Uninteresting imitation of *On the Waterfront.*

w Lawrence Roman, *novel* The Man Who Rocked the Boat by William J. Keating, Richard Carter *d* Arnold Laven *ph* Fred Jackman *m* Richard Rodgers

Richard Egan, Jan Sterling, Dan Duryea, Julie Adams, Walter Matthau, Charles McGraw, Sam Levene, Mickey Shaughnessy, Harry Bellaver

Slaughter's Big Rip-Off
US 1973 93m Movielab Todd-AO 35
AIP (Monroe Sachson)

Still on the run from gangsters who have killed his best friend, Slaughter violently disposes of a number of adversaries.
More routine black violence, a rampage of senseless brutality against sunny Los Angeles backgrounds.

w Charles Johnson *d* Gordon Douglas *ph* Charles Wheeler *m* Jim Brown, Fred Wesley

Jim Brown, Ed MacMahon, Brock Peters, Don Stroud

Slaughterhouse Five*
US 1972 104m Technicolor
Universal / Vanadas (Paul Monash)

A suburban optometrist has nightmare space/time fantasies involving Nazi POW camps and a strange futuristic planet.
Interesting but infuriating anti-war fantasy for intellectuals.

w Stephen Geller, *novel* Kurt Vonnegut Jnr *d* George Roy Hill *ph* Miroslav Ondricek *m* Glen Gould *pd Henry Bumstead*

Michael Sacks, Ron Leibman, Eugène Roche, Sharon Gans, Valerie Perrine, Sorrell Booke, John Dehner
'A lot of good makings in this picture; but very little is made.'—*Stanley Kauffmann*

Slave Girl
US 1947 79m Technicolor
U-I (Michael Fessier, Ernest Pagano)

In the early 1800s, a diplomat is sent to Tripoli to ransom sailors held by the power-mad potentate.
Criticism would be superfluous: when the film was finished it was obviously so bad that executives ordered the addition of a talking camel and other *Hellzapoppin*-type jokes in order to turn it into a comedy.

w Michael Fessier, Ernest Pagano *d* Charles Lamont *ph* George Robinson, W. Howard Greene *m* Milton Rosen

George Brent, Yvonne de Carlo, Albert Dekker, Broderick Crawford, Lois Collier, Andy Devine, Carl Esmond, Arthur Treacher

Slave Girls
GB 1966 95m Technicolor Cinemascope

A hunter seeking white rhinoceros finds himself in a lost valley ruled by a tribe of women.
Feebly preposterous comic strip farrago without the saving grace of humour.

wd Michael Carreras *ph* Michael Reed *m* Carlo Mantelli

Michael Latimer, Martine Beswick, Edina Ronay

Slaves
US 1969 110m Eastmancolor
Slaves Company / Theatre Guild / Walter Reade (Philip Langner)

In 1850 Kentucky a slave stands up for his rights and plans escape.
Well-meaning but muddled and old-fashioned melodrama, hardly well enough done to raise comparison with *Gone with the Wind.*

wd Herbert J. Biberman *ph* Joseph Brun *m* Bobby Scott

Stephen Boyd, Ossie Davis, Dionne Warwick, Shepperd Strudwick, Nancy Coleman, David Huddleston, Gale Sondergaard

Slay Ride*
US 1972 97m colour TVM
TCF

A New Mexico sheriff clears an Indian of a murder charge.
Competent outdoor murder mystery originally shown as two episodes of *Cade's County*.

w Anthony Silson, Rick Husky *d* Marvin Chomsky

Glenn Ford, Edgar Buchanan, Victor Campos, Peter Ford, Tony Bill

Sleep My Love*
US 1948 96m bw
(UA) Mary Pickford (Charles 'Buddy' Rogers)

A man plots to murder his wife, but is foiled.
Thin suspenser, rather splendidly photographed in the expressionist manner.

w St Clair McKelway, *novel* Leo Rosten *d Douglas Sirk ph Joseph Valentine m* Rudy Schrager

Claudette Colbert, Don Ameche, Robert Cummings, Rita Johnson, George Coulouris, Hazel Brooks, Keye Luke

Sleeper*
US 1973 88m De Luxe
UA / Charles Rollins, Charles Joffe (Jack Greenberg)

A health food store owner is deep frozen after an operation and wakes two hundred years in the future.
Predictable star vehicle with an agreeable string of bright gags.

w Woody Allen, Marshall Brickman d Woody Allen *ph* David M. Walsh *m* Woody Allen *pd* Dale Hennesy

Woody Allen, Diane Keaton, John Beck, Mary Gregory

The Sleeping Beauty*
US 1958 75m Technirama 70
Walt Disney (Ken Peterson)

Rather stodgy, unwisely Cinemascoped feature cartoon of the old legend; very fashionable and detailed, but somehow lifeless.

d Clyde Geronomi *md* George Bruns *pd* Don da Gradi, Ken Anderson

Sleeping Car to Trieste*
GB 1948 95m bw
GFD / Two Cities

Spy melodrama, a slow-starting but generally entertaining remake of *Rome Express* (qv).

w Allan Mackinnon *d* John Paddy Carstairs *ph* Jack Hildyard *m* Benjamin Frankel

Albert Lieven, Jean Kent, David Tomlinson, David Hutcheson, Rona Anderson, Paul Dupuis, Finlay Currie, *Alan Wheatley*, Derrick de Marney, Grégoire Aslan, Hugh Burden

The Sleeping City**
US 1950 85m bw
U-I (Leonard Goldstein)

A policeman disguises himself as a medical student to learn more about a murder in a general hospital.
A location melodrama of modest excellence.

w Jo Eisinger d George Sherman ph William Miller m Frank Skinner

Richard Conte, Richard Taber, Coleen Gray, John Alexander, Peggy Dow, Alex Nicol

The Sleeping Tiger
GB 1954 89m bw
Anglo-Amalgamated / Insignia (Victor Hanbury)

A psychiatrist overpowers a criminal and takes him home as a guinea pig; the criminal then falls in love with the psychiatrist's wife.
Turgid and unconvincing melodrama, a thoroughgoing bore.

w Harold Buchman, Carl Foreman, *novel* Maurice Moiseiwitch *d* Joseph Losey *ph* Harry Waxman *m* Malcolm Arnold

Dirk Bogarde, Alexander Knox, Alexis Smith, Hugh Griffith, Maxine Audley, Glyn Houston, Billie Whitelaw

The Slender Thread*
US 1966 98m bw
Paramount / Athene (Stephen Alexander)

A volunteer social worker tries to prevent a woman from committing suicide while police track her down from their phone conversations.
Acceptable star melodrama, curiously artificially styled.

w Stirling Silliphant *d Sydney Pollack ph* Loyal Griggs *m* Quincy Jones

Anne Bancroft, Sidney Poitier, Steven Hill, Telly Savalas

Sleuth**
GB 1972 139m colour
Palomar (Morton Gottlieb)

A successful thriller writer invents a murder plot which rebounds on himself.
Well-acted version of a highly successful piece of stage trickery; despite hard work all round it seems much less clever and arresting on the screen, and the tricks do show.

w Anthony Shaffer, from his play *d* Joseph L.

Mankiewicz *ph* Oswald Morris *m* John Addison

Laurence Olivier, Michael Caine

A Slight Case of Murder***
US 1938 85m bw
Warner (Sam Bischoff)

When a beer baron tries to go legitimate his colleagues attempt to kill him, but end up shooting each other.
Amusing black farce, remade to less effect as *Stop, You're Killing Me* (qv).

w Earl Baldwin, Joseph Schrank, *play* Damon Runyon, Howard Lindsay *d Lloyd Bacon* *ph* Sid Hickox *m* M. K. Jerome, Jack Scholl

Edward G. Robinson, Jane Bryan, Willard Parker, *Ruth Donnelly,* Allen Jenkins, John Litel, Harold Huber, Edward Brophy, Bobby Jordan

'The complications crazily mount, sentiment never raises its ugly head, a long nose is made at violence and death.'—*Graham Greene*

Slightly Honorable
US 1940 85m bw
UA (Tay Garnett)

Lawyer partners set out to break a crime syndicate.
Fair crime thriller which can't decide whether it's comedy or drama.

w John Hunter Lay, Robert Tallman, Ken Englund, *novel* Send Another Coffin by F. G. Presnell *d* Tay Garnett *ph* Merritt Gerstad *m* Werner Janssen

Pat O'Brien, Broderick Crawford, Edward Arnold, Eve Arden, Claire Dodd, Ruth Terry, Bernard Nedell, Alan Dinehart, Douglass Dumbrille, Ernest Truex

Slightly Scarlet
US 1956 92m Technicolor Superscope
(RKO) Benedict Bogeaus

The mayor's secretary loves the leader of a criminal gang.
Competent but uninteresting crime romance.

w Robert Blees, *novel* James A. Cain *d* Allan Dwan *ph* John Alton *m* Louis Forbes

Arlene Dahl, John Payne, Rhonda Fleming, Kent Taylor, Ted de Corsia

'So complicated that it is difficult to sort out which characters are supposed to be sympathetic.'—*MFB*

The Slipper and the Rose*
GB 1976 146m Technicolor Panavision
Paradine Co-Productions (David Frost, Stuart Lyons)

The story of Cinderella.
The elements are charming, but the treatment is fussy yet uninventive and the film is immensely overlong and lacking in magic and wit. Alas, not the renaissance of the family film that was hoped for.

w Bryan Forbes, Robert and Richard Sherman *d* Bryan Forbes *ph* Tony Imi *songs* Robert and Richard Sherman *pd Ray Simm*

Richard Chamberlain, Gemma Craven, Kenneth More, Michael Hordern, Edith Evans, Annette Crosbie, Margaret Lockwood, *Christopher Gable*, Julian Orchard, Lally Bowers, John Turner

Slither*
US 1972 96m Metrocolor
MGM / Talent Associates / Jack Sher

An ex-con, some gangsters, and a few mobile homes are involved in a chase across California for some hidden loot.
Wackily with-it comedy-thriller ranging from violence to slapstick, the former always undercut into the latter. Pretty funny, once you get the idea.

w W. D. Richter *d* Howard Zieff *ph* Laszlo Kovacs *m* Tom McIntosh

James Caan, Peter Boyle, Sally Kellerman, Louise Lasser

The Small Back Room**
GB 1949 106m bw
London Films / The Archers

A bomb expert with a lame foot and a drink problem risks his life dismantling a booby bomb and returns to his long-suffering girl friend.
Rather gloomy suspense thriller with ineffective personal aspects but well-made location sequences and a fascinating background of boffins at work in post-war London.

wd Michael Powell, Emeric Pressburger *ph Christopher Challis* *m* Brian Easdale

David Farrar, Kathleen Byron, Jack Hawkins, Leslie Banks, Robert Morley, Cyril Cusack

Small Miracle*
US 1973 74m colour TVM
Hallmark

Remake of *Never Take No for an Answer* (qv), about a small boy who takes his sick donkey to the Pope.

w John Patrick, Arthur Dales, *novel* Paul Gallico *d* Jeannot Szwarc *m* Ernest Gold

Marco della Cava, Vittorio De Sica, Raf Vallone

Small Town Girl*
US 1936 90m bw
MGM (Hunt Stromberg)

A girl traps a handsome stranger into offering marriage when he's drunk, then sets out to win him when he's sober.
Thin but adequate romantic comedy, a good example of MGM's production line of the mid-thirties, with established star and character players helping upcoming talents.

w John Lee Mahin, Edith Fitzgerald, *novel* Ben Ames Williams *d* William A. Wellman *ph* Charles Rosher

Janet Gaynor, Robert Taylor, James Stewart, Binnie Barnes, Frank Craven, Elizabeth Patterson, Lewis Stone, Andy Devine, Isabel Jewell, Charley Grapewin, Robert Greig, Agnes Ayres

Small Town Girl*
US 1953 93m Technicolor
MGM (Joe Pasternak)

Musical remake of the above.
Willing hands make the most of it, but the songs are not the best.

w Dorothy Cooper, Dorothy Kingsley *d* Leslie Kardos *ph* Joseph Ruttenberg *m* Leo Robin, Nicholas Brodsky

Jane Powell, Farley Granger, *Bobby Van,* Ann Miller, Robert Keith, Billie Burke, S. Z. Sakall, Fay Wray, Nat King Cole

The Small Voice*
GB 1948 83m bw
British Lion / Constellation (Anthony Havelock-Allan)
US title: *Hideout*

Escaped convicts hold up a playwright and his wife in their country cottage.
Gripping, well-characterized version of a very well worn plot.

w Derek Neame, Julian Orde, *novel* Robert Westerby *d* Fergus McDonell

James Donald, Valerie Hobson, Howard Keel, David Greene, Michael Balfour, Joan Young

The Small World of Sammy Lee
GB 1962 107m bw
Bryanston / Seven Arts / Ken Hughes (Frank Godwin)

A small-time Soho crook tries desperately to raise money to pay off threatening bookies.
Overlong 'realist' comedy-melodrama based on a TV play and filled with low-life 'characters'; vivid but cursed with a tedious hero.

wd Ken Hughes, from his TV play *ph* Wolfgang Suschitsky *m* Kenny Graham *ad* Seamus Flannery

Anthony Newley, Julia Foster, Robert Stephens, Wilfrid Brambell, Warren Mitchell, Miriam Karlin, Kenneth J. Warren

The Smallest Show on Earth*
GB 1957 81m bw
British Lion / Launder and Gilliat (Michael Relph)
US title: *Big Time Operators*

Two young marrieds inherit a decayed cinema and make it pay.
Amiable caricature comedy with plenty of obvious jokes and a sentimental attachment to old cinemas but absolutely no conviction, little plot, and a very muddled sense of the line between farce and reality.

w William Rose, John Eldridge *d* Basil Dearden *ph* Douglas Slocombe *m* William Alwyn

Bill Travers, Virginia McKenna, Margaret Rutherford, Bernard Miles, Peter Sellers, Leslie Phillips, Francis de Wolff

Smart Money
US 1931 90m bw
Warner

A gambler hits the big time but finally goes to jail.
Rather ordinary crime drama, a distinct letdown for its star after *Little Caesar*.

w Kubec Glasmon, John Bright, Lucien Hubbard, Joseph Jackson *d* Alfred E. Green *ph* Robert Kurrie

Edward G. Robinson, James Cagney, Evalyn Knapp, Ralf Harolde, Noel Francis, Margaret Livingstone, Boris Karloff, Billy House
† This film marks the only teaming of Robinson and Cagney.

Smart Woman
US 1948 93m bw
Monogram (Hal E. Chester)

A crafty lady lawyer becomes romantically involved with a crusading district attorney.
What to Monogram was a high-class production would have been a very routine programmer from anyone else.

w Alvah Bessie, Louise Morheim, Herbert Margolis *d* Edward A. Blatt *ph* Stanley Cortez *m* Constantin Bakaleinikoff

Constance Bennett, Brian Aherne, Barry

Sullivan, Michael O'Shea, James Gleason, Otto Kruger, Isobel Elsom, Taylor Holmes, John Litel

Smash-up
US 1947 113m bw
U-I
GB title: *A Woman Destroyed*

The story of a lady alcoholic.
Tedious distaff side of *The Lost Weekend*.

w John Howard Lawson *d* Stuart Heisler *ph* Stanley Cortez

Susan Hayward, Lee Bowman, Eddie Albert, Marsha Hunt, Carl Esmond, Carleton Young, Charles D. Brown

Smashing Time
GB 1967 96m Eastmancolor
Paramount / Partisan / Carlo Ponti (Ray Millichip)

Two north country girls have farcical adventures in swinging London, including paint squirting and pie throwing.
Horrendous attempt to turn two unsuitable actresses into a female Laurel and Hardy; plenty of coarse vigour but no style or sympathy.

w George Melly *d* Desmond Davis *ph Manny Wynn* *m* John Addison

Rita Tushingham, Lynn Redgrave, Ian Carmichael, Anna Quayle, Michael York, Irene Handl, Jeremy Lloyd

Smile*
US 1975 113m De Luxe
UA (Michael Ritchie)

A bird's eye view of the Young Miss America pageant in a small California town.
A witty series of sketches in the form of a drama-documentary or satirical mosaic.
Highly polished fun for those who can stay the course.

w Jerry Belson d Michael Ritchie ph Conrad Hall *m* various

Bruce Dern, Barbara Feldon, Michael Kidd, Geoffrey Lewis, Nicholas Pryor

Smile Jenny, You're Dead*
US 1974 90m colour TVM
Warner

A private eye protects a cover girl from murder.
Second pilot for *Harry O* (qv); smoothly made.

w Howard Rodman *d* Jerry Thorpe

David Janssen, Andrea Marcovicci, Jodie Foster, Zalman King, Clu Gulager

Smiley*
GB 1957 97m Technicolor Cinemascope
TCF / London Films (Anthony Kimmins)

An adventurous Australian boy has various adventures and finally gets the bicycle he wants.
An open-air 'William'-type story for children, quite nicely made and generally refreshing.
Smiley Gets a Gun was a less effective sequel.

w Moore Raymond, Anthony Kimmins *d* Anthony Kimmins *ph* Ted Scaife, Russ Wood *m* William Alwyn

Colin Petersen, Ralph Richardson, Chips Rafferty, John McCallum

Smilin' Through**
US 1932 97m bw
MGM (Irving Thalberg)

Three generations of complications follow when a Victorian lady is accidentally killed by a jealous lover on her wedding day.
Archetypal sentimental romantic drama, wholly absorbing to the mass audience and extremely well done; originally a 1922 Norma Talmadge vehicle.

w Ernest Vajda, Claudine West, Donald Ogden Stewart, J. B. Fagan, *play* Jane Cowl, Jane Murfin *d* Sidney Franklin *ph Lee Garmes*

Norma Shearer, Leslie Howard, Fredric March, O. P. Heggie, Ralph Forbes, Beryl Mercer

'A sensitive and beautiful production distinguished by excellent settings and rich photography.'—*New York Mirror*

Smilin' Through*
US 1941 100m bw
MGM (Victor Saville)

Flat but adequate remake of the above.

w Donald Ogden Stewart, John Balderston *d* Frank Borzage

Jeanette MacDonald, Gene Raymond, Brian Aherne, Ian Hunter, Frances Robinson, Patrick O'Moore

The Smiling Lieutenant***
US 1931 88m bw
Paramount (Ernst Lubitsch)

A Viennese guards officer leaves his mistress to become consort to a visiting princess.
A sophisticated soufflé in Lubitsch's best style, naughty but quite nice, with visual effects largely replacing dialogue.

w Ernest Vajda, Samson Raphaelson, *operetta* A Waltz Dream *d Ernst Lubitsch ph* George Folsey *m* Oscar Straus *md* Adolph Deutsch

Maurice Chevalier, Miriam Hopkins, Claudette

Colbert, Charles Ruggles, George Barbier, Elizabeth Patterson

'All the shrewd delights that were promised in *The Love Parade* all realized with an economy and sureness that give it a luster which no other American-made comedy satire has achieved. One must look to *Le Million* to find its peer.' —*Richard Watts, New York Post*

The Smugglers
US 1968 100m Technicolor TVM
Universal (Norman Lloyd)

American ladies on holiday in Europe are pawns for an international smuggling ring.
Lively adventure comedy.

w Alfred Hayes, *novel* Elizabeth Hely *d* Norman Lloyd

Shirley Booth, Gayle Hunnicutt, Michael J. Pollard, Kurt Kasznar, Carol Lynley, David Opatoshu

The Snake Pit**
US 1948 108m bw
TCF (Anatole Litvak, Robert Bassler)

A girl becomes mentally deranged and has horrifying experiences in an institution.
A headline-hitting film which made a stirring plea for more sympathetic treatment of mental illness. Very well made, and arrestingly acted, but somehow nobody's favourite movie.

w Frank Partos, Millen Brand, *novel* Mary Jane Ward *d Anatole Litvak* *ph* Leo Tover *m* Alfred Newman

Olivia de Havilland, Leo Genn, Mark Stevens, Celeste Holm, Glenn Langan, Leif Erickson, Beulah Bondi, Lee Patrick, Natalie Schaefer

Snatched*
US 1972 73m colour TVM
Spelling–Goldberg

The wives of three wealthy businessmen are kidnapped for ransom.
Slick, tough action melodrama.

d Sutton Roley

Howard Duff, Leslie Nielsen, Sheree North, Barbara Parkins, Robert Reed, John Saxon

The Sniper**
US 1952 87m bw
Columbia / Stanley Kramer (Edna and Edward Anhalt)

A psychopath kills a succession of blondes with a high-powered rifle.
Semi-documentary police drama which was quite startling and influential when released but seems quite routine now.

w Harry Brown *d Edward Dmytryk* *ph* Burnett Guffey *m* George Antheil

Adolphe Menjou, Arthur Franz, Gerald Mohr, Richard Kiley, Frank Faylen, Marie Windsor

The Snoop Sisters
US 1972 96m Technicolor TVM
Universal (Douglas Benton)
aka: *The Female Instinct*

Two elderly lady mystery writers annoy their policeman nephew by investigating the death of a film star.
A promising format didn't really work despite the talent applied. See *Mystery Movie* for subsequent episodes.

w Leonard B. Stern, Hugh Wheeler *d* Leonard B. Stern

Helen Hayes, Mildred Natwick, Art Carney, Paulette Goddard (in a minuscule role), Craig Stevens, Bill Dana

The Snorkel
GB 1958 80m bw
Columbia / Hammer (Michael Carreras)

A man murders his wife and is given away by his observant young stepdaughter.
Tenuous suspenser which outstays its welcome.

w Peter Myers, Jimmy Sangster, Anthony Dawson *d* Guy Green *ph* Jack Asher

Peter Van Eyck, Mandy Miller, William Franklyn, Grégoire Aslan

Snow Treasure
US 1968 95m Eastmancolor
Sagittarius (Irving Jacoby)

In Nazi-occupied Norway a teenage boy finds gold hidden in the snow; an underground agent helps him get it to safety.
Curiously undernourished but attractively made adventure film.

w Irving Jacoby, Peter Hansen, *novel* Marie McSwigan *d* Irving Jacoby *ph Sverre Bergli* *m* Egil Monn-Iversen

James Franciscus, Paul Anstad, Paoul Oyen, Randi Borch

Snow White and the Seven Dwarfs****
US 1937 82m Technicolor
Walt Disney

In Disney's first feature cartoon, a mammoth enterprise which no one in the business thought would work. The romantic leads were wishy-washy but the splendid songs and the marvellous comic and villainous characters turned the film into a world-wide box office bombshell which is almost as fresh today as when it was made.

w Ted Sears, Otto Englander, Earl Hurd, Dorothy Ann Blank, Richard Creedon, Dick Richard, Merrill de Maris, Webb Smith, from the fairy tale by the brothers Grimm *supervising director David Hand* *m* Frank Churchill, Leigh Harline, Paul Smith *songs Larry Morey, Frank Churchill*

'The first full-length animated feature, the turning point in Disney's career, a milestone in film history, and a great film.'—*Leonard Maltin*

Snow White and the Three Stooges*
US 1961 107m De Luxe Cinemascope
(TCF) Chanford (Charles Wick)
GB title: *Snow White and the Three Clowns*

The old story retold as a vehicle for a champion skater and three veteran clowns. Surprisingly tolerable as a holiday attraction, once you get over the shock.

w Noel Langley, Elwood Ullman *d* Walter Lang *ph* Leon Shamroy *m* Lyn Murray *ad* Jack Martin Smith, Maurice Ransford

Carol Heiss, Moe Howard, Larry Fine, Joe de Rita, Edson Stroll, Patricia Medina, Guy Rolfe, Buddy Baer, Edgar Barrier

Snowball Express
US 1972 99m Technicolor
Walt Disney (Ron Miller)

An insurance accountant inherits a dilapidated skiing hotel in the Colorado Rockies.
Uninspired family comedy with slapstick on the snow slopes.

w Don Tait, Jim Parker, Arnold Margolin, *novel* Château Bon Vivant by Frankie and John O'Rear *d* Norman Tokar *ph* Frank Phillips *m* Robert F. Brunner

Dean Jones, Nancy Olson, Henry Morgan, Keenan Wynn, Mary Wickes, Johnny Whittaker

'As wholesome and bland as that old American favourite the peanut butter and jelly sandwich.' —*MFB*

The Snows of Kilimanjaro**
US 1952 117m Technicolor
TCF (Darryl F. Zanuck)

A hunter lies wounded in Africa and while waiting for help looks back over his life and loves.
Hollywood version of a portable Hemingway, with reminiscences of several novels stirred into a lush and sprawling mix of action and romance, open spaces and smart salons. A big popular star film of its time, despite constricted and unconvincing characters.

w Casey Robinson, *story* Ernest Hemingway *d Henry King* *ph* Leon Shamroy *m* Bernard Herrmann

Gregory Peck, Susan Hayward, Ava Gardner, Hildegard Neff, Leo G. Carroll, Torin Thatcher, Marcel Dalio

'A naïve kind of success story with a conventional boy-meets-lots-of-girls plot.' —*Karel Reisz*

So Big*
US 1932 80m bw
Warner (Lucien Hubbard)

A schoolteacher marries a farmer, has trouble with her son, falls in love with a sculptor.
Watchable, superficial, top-talented adaptation of a best-seller, first filmed in 1925 with Colleen Moore.

w J. Grubb Alexander, Robert Lord, *novel* Edna Ferber *d* William Wellman *ph* Sid Hickox

Barbara Stanwyck, George Brent, Dickie Moore, Guy Kibbee, Bette Davis, Hardie Albright

So Big
US 1953 101m bw
Warner (Henry Blanke)

By the time this inflated remake came along, the story was just too corny despite careful production.

w John Twist *d* Robert Wise *ph* Ellsworth Fredericks *m* Max Steiner

Jane Wyman, Sterling Hayden, Richard Beymer, Nancy Olson, Steve Forrest, Elizabeth Fraser, Martha Hyer

So Dear to My Heart*
US 1948 84m Technicolor
Walt Disney

Life on a country farm in 1903.
Live action nostalgia with a few cartoon segments; well enough done, but mainly appealing to well brought up children.

w John Tucker Battle, *novel* Midnight and Jeremiah by Sterling North *d* Harold Schuster *ph* Winton C. Hoch *m* Paul Smith

Burl Ives, Beulah Bondi, Harry Carey, Luana Patten, Bobby Driscoll

So Ends Our Night*
US 1941 120m bw
(UA) David L. Loew, Albert Lewin

Refugees from Nazi Germany are driven from country to country and meet persecution everywhere.
Worthy but rather drab and unfocused melodrama from the headlines.

w Talbot Jennings, *novel* Flotsam by Erich Maria Remarque *d* John Cromwell *ph* William Daniels *m* Louis Gruenberg

Fredric March, Margaret Sullavan, Glenn Ford, Frances Dee, Anna Sten, Erich Von Stroheim, Joseph Cawthorn, Leonid Kinskey, Alexander Granach, Sig Rumann

'It ought to be a great picture but it isn't.' *—Archer Winsten, New York Post*

So Evil My Love*
US 1948 100m bw
Paramount (Hal B. Wallis)

A missionary's widow is enticed into a life of crime and immorality by a scoundrelly artist.
Curious Victorian melodrama with a Wildean flavour; doesn't quite come off.

w Leonard Spiegelgass, Ronald Miller, *novel* Joseph Shearing *d* Lewis Allen *ph* Max Greene *m* Victor Young, William Alwyn

Ray Milland, Ann Todd, Geraldine Fitzgerald, Leo G. Carroll, Raymond Huntley, Martita Hunt, Moira Lister, Raymond Lovell, Muriel Aked, Finlay Currie, Hugh Griffith

So Goes My Love
US 1946 88m bw
(U-I) Jack H. Skirball / Bruce Manning
GB title: *A Genius in the Family*

The domestic life of inventor Hiram Maxim.
Formula period family film with pleasant moments.

w Bruce Manning, James Clifden *d* Frank Ryan *ph* Joseph Valentine

Myrna Loy, Don Ameche, Rhys Williams, Bobby Driscoll, Richard Gaines

So Little Time
GB 1952 88m bw
ABP / Mayflower (Aubrey Baring, Maxwell Setton)

In occupied Belgium an aristocratic lady falls in love with a Nazi colonel.
Doomed love story with musical accompaniment; tolerable but slow.

w John Cresswell *d* Compton Bennett *ph* Oswald Morris *m* Robert Gill

Marius Goring, Maria Schell, Gabrielle Dorziat, Barbara Mullen

So Long at the Fair*
GB 1950 86m bw
Rank / Gainsborough / Sydney Box (Betty E. Box)

During the 1889 Paris Exposition a girl books into a hotel with her brother, and next day finds that he has totally disappeared and his existence is denied by all concerned.
Straightforward version of an old yarn which has turned up in such varied forms as *The Lady Vanishes* and *Bunny Lake is Missing*. This modest production is pleasant enough but badly lacks drive.

w Hugh Mills, Anthony Thorne *d* Terence Fisher, Anthony Darnborough *ph* Reginald Wyer *m* Benjamin Frankel *ad* Cedric Dawe

Jean Simmons, Dirk Bogarde, David Tomlinson, Marcel Poncin, Cathleen Nesbitt, Honor Blackman, Betty Warren, Felix Aylmer, André Morell

So Proudly We Hail*
US 1943 125m bw
Paramount (Mark Sandrich)

The self-sacrifice of war nurses in the Pacific.
Fairly harrowing and well-meant but studio-bound and unconvincing flagwaver.

w Allan Scott *d* Mark Sandrich *ph* Charles Lang *m* Miklos Rozsa

Claudette Colbert, Paulette Goddard, Veronica Lake, George Reeves, Barbara Britton, Walter Abel, Sonny Tufts, John Litel

'Probably the most deadly accurate picture ever made of what war looks like through the lenses of a housewives' magazine romance.' *—James Agee*

'The stars are devotedly, almost gallantly, deglamorized and dishevelled but they cannot escape the smell of studio varnish.'*—Richard Winnington*

So Red the Rose*
US 1935 82m bw
Paramount (Douglas MacLean)

The life of a southern family during the Civil War.
Quiet, pleasing historical romance.

w Laurence Stallings, Maxwell Anderson, Edwin Justus Mayer, *novel* Stark Young *d* King Vidor *ph* Victor Milner *m* W. Franke Harling

Margaret Sullavan, Randolph Scott, Walter Connolly, Elizabeth Patterson, Janet Beecher, Robert Cummings

So Soon to Die
US 1957 74m bw TVM
Columbia / Playhouse 90

An unemployed actor is employed to kill a girl, but falls for his prey.
Obvious, old-hat melodrama.

d John Brahm

Richard Basehart, Anne Bancroft, Sebastian Cabot, Torin Thatcher

So This Is Love
US 1953 101m Technicolor
Warner (Henry Blanke)
GB title: *The Grace Moore Story*

Events leading up to Grace Moore's debut at the Metropolitan Opera in 1928.
Acceptable musical biopic full of the usual Hollywood contrivances.

w John Monks Jnr, from Grace Moore's autobiography *d* Gordon Douglas *ph* Robert Burks *md* Ray Heindorf, Max Steiner *ch* Le Roy Prinz *ad* Edward Carrere

Kathryn Grayson, Merv Griffin, Joan Weldon, Walter Abel, Rosemary de Camp, Jeff Donnell, Douglas Dick, Mabel Albertson, Fortunio Bonanova

So This Is New York*
US 1948 78m bw
Stanley Kramer / Enterprise

In 1919 some country cousins who have come into money have a big time in the gay city.
Curious, sporadically effective, silent-style comedy which doesn't quite come off.

w Carl Foreman, Herbert Baker, *novel* The Big Town by Ring Lardner *d* Richard Fleischer *ph* Jack Russell

Henry Morgan, Rudy Vallee, Hugh Herbert, Bill Goodwin, Virginia Grey, Dona Drake, Leo Gorcey

So This Is Paris
US 1955 96m Technicolor
U-I (Albert J. Cohen)

Three American sailors on leave in Paris meet girls and help war orphans.
Very thin imitation of *On the Town*, bogged down by sentimentality and lack of sparkle. The musical numbers, however, are not bad.

w Charles Hoffman *d* Richard Quine *ph* Maury Gertsman *md* Joseph Gershenson *ch* Gene Nelson, Lee Scott

Tony Curtis, Gloria de Haven, Gene Nelson, *Corinne Calvet*, Paul Gilbert, Mara Corday, Allison Hayes

So Well Remembered*
GB 1947 114m bw
(RKO) Alliance (Adrian Scott)

The ambitious daughter of a mill-owner marries a rising politician but almost ruins his life.
Rather routine treatment of a three-decker north country novel; humdrum incident and unsympathetic characters, but full of minor British virtues.

w John Paxton, *novel* James Hilton *d* Edward Dmytryk *ph* Frederick A. Young

John Mills, Martha Scott, Trevor Howard, Patricia Roc, Richard Carlson

Soak the Rich*
US 1935 74m bw
Paramount (Ben Hecht, Charles MacArthur)

A rebellious rich girl is cured when she is rescued from kidnapping.
Smartly written social comedy-melodrama.

wd Ben Hecht, Charles MacArthur *ph* Leon Shamroy

Walter Connolly, John Howard, Mary Taylor, Lionel Stander, Ilka Chase

Sodom and Gomorrah
Italy / France 1962 154m colour
Titanus / S. N. Pathe (Gottfredo Lombardo)

Lot and the Hebrews become involved in a Helamite plan to take over the rich sinful cities of Sodom and Gomorrah.
Dreary biblical blood-and-thunder; an international muddle, tedious in the extreme outside a few hilariously misjudged moments.

w Hugo Butler, Giorgio Prosperi *d* Robert Aldrich *ph* Silvano Ippoliti, Cyril Knowles *m* Miklos Rozsa *ad* Ken Adam

Stewart Granger, Stanley Baker, Pier Angeli, Anouk Aimée, Rossana Podesta

Soft Beds, Hard Battles
GB 1973 107m colour
Rank / Charter (John Boulting)

Inhabitants of a Paris brothel help to win World War II.
Ragbag of poor sketches and dirty jokes, with the star in several ineffective roles including Hitler.

w Leo Marks, Roy Boulting *d* Roy Boulting *ph* Gil Taylor *m* Neil Rhoden

Peter Sellers, Lila Kedrova, Curt Jurgens, Gabriella Licudi, Jenny Hanley

Sol Madrid
US 1968 90m Metrocolor Panavision
MGM / Gershwin–Kastner (Hall Bartlett)
GB title: *The Heroin Gang*

An undercover narcotics agent is assigned to track down an elusive Mafia executive.
Humdrum, predictable, brutishly violent international crime caper.

w David Karp, *novel* Fruit of the Poppy by

Robert Wilder *d* Brian G. Hutton *ph* Fred Koenekamp *m* Lalo Schifrin

David McCallum, Telly Savalas, Stella Stevens, Ricardo Montalban, Rip Torn, Pat Hingle, Paul Lukas, Perry Lopez, Michael Ansara.

Soldier Blue*
US 1970 114m Technicolor Panavision
Avco (Gabriel Katzka, Harold Loeb)

A paymaster's detachment of the US cavalry is attacked by Indians seeking gold, and two white survivors trek through the desert.
Extremely violent 'anti-violence' western with a particularly nauseating climax following clichés all the way. From a director with pretensions.

w John Gay, *novel* Arrow in the Sun by Theodore V. Olsen *d* Ralph Nelson *ph* Robert Hauser *m* Roy Budd

Candice Bergen, Peter Strauss, Donald Pleasence

'One is more likely to be sickened by the film itself than by the wrongs it tries to right.'—*Tom Milne*

Soldier in the Rain
US 1963 87m bw
AA / Cedar / Solar (Martin Jurow)

Two army sergeants have wild plans for their demob, but one dies.
Curious sentimental tragi-comedy which misfires on all cylinders.

w Blake Edwards, Martin Richlin, *novel* William Goldman *d* Ralph Nelson *ph* Philip Lathrop *m* Henry Mancini

Steve McQueen, Jackie Gleason, Tuesday Weld, Tony Bill, Tom Poston, Ed Nelson, John Hubbard

Soldier of Fortune*
US 1955 96m De Luxe Cinemascope
TCF (Buddy Adler)

When a photographer disappears in Red China, his wife comes to Hong Kong to institute a search, enlists the aid of an amiable smuggler.
Cheerful Boys' Own Paper adventure romance with attractive locations and some silly anti-Red dialogue.

w Ernest K. Gann, from his novel *d* Edward Dmytryk *ph* Leo Tover *m* Hugo Friedhofer

Clark Gable, Susan Hayward, Gene Barry, Alex D'Arcy, Michael Rennie, Tom Tully, Anna Sten, Russell Collins, Leo Gordon

'A very good adventure film but not one of the Gable smashes.'—*Hollywood Reporter*

Soldiers Three
US 1951 87m bw
MGM (Pandro S. Berman)

Adventures of three roistering British officers on the North-West Frontier.
A kind of unofficial remake of *Gunga Din* without the title character; one suspects it was meant seriously and found to be so bad that the only way out was strenuously to play it for laughs.

w Marguerite Roberts, Tom Reed, Malcolm Stuart Boylan *d* Tay Garnett *ph* William Mellor *m* Adolph Deutsch

Stewart Granger, David Niven, Robert Newton, Walter Pidgeon, Cyril Cusack, Greta Gynt, Frank Allenby, Robert Coote, Dan O'Herlihy

The Sole Survivor*
US 1969 100m colour TVM
Cinema Center

A brigadier general helps to investigate the crash seventeen years earlier of a plane which he navigated.
Interesting mystery drama.

w Guerdon Trueblood *d* Paul Stanley

Vince Edwards, William Shatner, Richard Basehart

The Solid Gold Cadillac**
US 1956 99m bw
Columbia (Fred Kohlmar)

A very minor stockholder upsets the crooked board of a large corporation.
Vaguely Capraesque comedy which begins brightly but peters out; performances sustain passing interest.

w Abe Burrows, *play* George S. Kaufman, Howard Teichmann *d* Richard Quine *ph* Charles Lang *m* Cyril Mockridge

Judy Holliday, Paul Douglas, *John Williams*, *Fred Clark*, Hiram Sherman, Neva Patterson, Ralph Dumke, Ray Collins, Arthur O'Connell

Solomon and Sheba*
US 1959 142m Super Technirama 70
UA / Edward Small (Ted Richmond)

When David names his younger son as heir, his older son plots revenge.
Dullish biblical spectacle, alternating between pretentiousness and cowboys and Indians.

w Anthony Veiller, Paul Dudley, George Bruce *d* King Vidor *ph* Frederick A. Young *m* Mario Nascimbene *ad* Richard Day, Alfred Sweeney

Yul Brynner, Gina Lollobrigida, George Sanders, Marisa Pavan, David Farrar, John

Crawford, Laurence Naismith, Alejandro Rey, Harry Andrews

Sombrero
US 1953 103m Technicolor
MGM (Jack Cummings)

Two Mexican villages feud over the burial place of a famous poet.
Rather self-consciously unusual musical which never catches fire but certainly keeps one watching its incredible mixture of music and melodrama.

w Norman Foster, Josefina Niggli, from her novel A Mexican Village *d* Norman Foster *ph* Ray June *m* Leo Arnaud

Ricardo Montalban, Pier Angeli, Yvonne de Carlo, Nina Foch, Cyd Charisse, Rick Jason, Jose Greco, Thomas Gomez, Kurt Kasznar, Walter Hampden, John Abbott

'Staggering is the only word for the hokum of this extraordinary film.'—*Gavin Lambert*

Some Call It Loving
US 1973 103m Technicolor
Pleasant Pastures / James B. Harris

A young man buys a 'sleeping beauty' at a fair but is sorry when he wakes her up.
Fashionable fantasy, amplified from a slender, winning short story.

wd James B. Harris, *story* Sleeping Beauty by John Collier *ph* Mario Tosi *m* Richard Hazard

Zalman King, Carol White, Tisa Farrow, Richard Pryor, Veronica Anderson

Some Came Running
US 1959 136m Metrocolor
Cinemascope
MGM / Sol C. Siegel

A disillusioned writer returns after service to his home town and takes up with a gambler and a prostitute.
Strident and rather pointless melodrama with solid acting and production values.

w John Patrick, Arthur Sheekman, *novel* James Jones *d* Vincente Minnelli *ph* William H. Daniels *m* Elmer Bernstein

Frank Sinatra, Dean Martin, Shirley Maclaine, Martha Hyer, Arthur Kennedy, Nancy Gates, Leora Dana

Some Girls Do
GB 1969 93m Eastmancolor
Rank / Ashdown (Betty E. Box)

Bulldog Drummond traces the sabotage of a supersonic airliner to a gang of murderous women.
Abysmal spoof melodrama in the swinging sixties mould; a travesty of a famous character.

w David Osborn, Liz Charles-Williams *d* Ralph Thomas *ph* Ernest Steward *m* Charles Blackwell

Richard Johnson, Daliah Lavi, Bebi Loncar, James Villiers, Sydne Rome, Robert Morley, Maurice Denham, Florence Desmond, Ronnie Stevens

Some Kind of a Nut
US 1969 89m De Luxe
UA / Mirisch / TFT / DFI (Walter Mirisch)

When a bank teller grows a beard because of an unsightly bee sting, he is thought to be flouting authority and his whole life changes.
Laboured, cliché-ridden anti-establishment comedy, a waste of the talent involved.

wd Garson Kanin *ph* Burnett Guffey, Gerald Hirschfeld *m* Johnny Mandel

Dick Van Dyke, Angie Dickinson, Rosemary Forsyth, Zohra Lampert, Elliot Reid, Dennis King

Some Like It Hot
US 1939 65m bw
Paramount

A sideshow owner runs out of money.
Very mild comedy, one of several which helped to establish Hope's star potential.

w Lewis R. Foster, *play* Wilkie C. Mahoney, Ben Hecht, Gene Fowler *d* George Archainbaud *ph* Karl Struss

Bob Hope, Shirley Ross, Una Merkel, Gene Krupa, Richard Denning

Some Like It Hot***
US 1959 122m bw
UA / Mirisch (Billy Wilder)

Two unemployed musicians accidentally witness the St Valentine's Day Massacre and flee to Miami disguised as girl musicians.
Overstretched but sporadically very funny comedy which constantly flogs its central idea to death and then recovers with a smart line or situation. It has in any case become a milestone of film comedy.

w Billy Wilder, I. A. L. Diamond d Billy Wilder ph Charles Lang Jnr *m* Adolph Deutsch

Jack Lemmon, Tony Curtis, Marilyn Monroe, Joe E. Brown, George Raft, Pat O'Brien, Nehemiah Persoff, George E. Stone, Joan Shawlee

Some May Live
GB / US 1966 100m colour TVM
(RKO) Foundation Pictures (Philip N. Krasne)

A woman army intelligence agent in Saigon passes classified information to her husband, a communist.
Boring political espionage adventure.

w David T. Chantler *d* Vernon Sewell *ph* Ray Parslow *m* Cyril Ornadel

Joseph Cotten, Martha Hyer, Peter Cushing, John Ronane

Some People
GB 1962 93m Eastmancolor
Vic Films (James Archibald)

Troublesome teenage factory workers are helped by a church organist and become model citizens.
Bland propaganda for the Duke of Edinburgh's Award scheme for young people, quite acceptably presented, with pop music ad lib.

w John Eldridge *d* Clive Donner *ph* John Wilcox *m* Ron Grainer

Kenneth More, Ray Brooks, Annika Wells, David Andrews, Angela Douglas, David Hemmings, Harry H. Corbett

Some Will, Some Won't
GB 1969 90m Technicolor
ABP / Transocean (Giulio Zampi)

In order to inherit under an eccentric will, four people have to perform tasks out of character.
Thin remake of *Laughter in Paradise* (qv); funny moments extremely few.

w Lew Schwarz *d* Duncan Wood *ph* Harry Waxman *m* Howard Blake

Ronnie Corbett, Thora Hird, Michael Hordern, Leslie Phillips, Barbara Murray, James Robertson Justice, Dennis Price, Wilfrid Brambell, Eleanor Summerfield, Arthur Lowe

Somebody Loves Me
US 1952 97m Technicolor
Paramount / Perlberg–Seaton

First successful in San Francisco at earthquake time, Blossom Seeley climbs to Broadway success with her partner Benny Fields, then retires to become his wife.
Adequate, unsurprising star musical of the second or third rank.

wd Irving Brecher *ph* George Barnes *songs* Jay Livingston, Ray Evans

Betty Hutton, Ralph Meeker, Robert Keith, Adele Jergens, Billie Bird, Sid Tomack, Ludwig Stossel

Somebody Up There Likes Me*
US 1956 112m bw
MGM (Charles Schnee)

An East Side kid with reform school experience becomes middleweight boxing champion of the world.
A sentimental fantasia on the life of Rocky Graziano, expertly blending violence, depression, prizefight sequences and fake uplift.

w Ernest Lehman *d* Robert Wise *ph* Joseph Ruttenberg *m* Bronislau Kaper

Paul Newman, Pier Angeli, Everett Sloane, Eileen Heckart, Sal Mineo, Joseph Buloff, Harold J. Stone, Robert Loggia

Someone I Touched*
US 1975 74m colour TVM
Charles Fries

A woman and her husband come to terms with each other when they find they have venereal disease.
Adequate 'outspoken' social melodrama.

w James Henderson *d* Lou Antonio

Cloris Leachman, James Olson, Glynnis O'Connor, Andy Robinson, Allyn Ann McLerie, Kenneth Mars

Something Big
US 1971 108m Technicolor
Cinema Center / Stanmore and Penbar (Andrew V. McLaglen)

A retiring cavalry colonel has a last battle with his old enemy.
Wry serio-comic western in the Ford tradition.

w James Lee Barrett *d* Andrew V. McLaglen *ph* Harry Stradling Jnr *m* Marvin Hamlisch

Dean Martin, Brian Keith, Honor Blackman, Carol White, Ben Johnson, Albert Salmi, Denver Pyle

Something Evil*
US 1971 73m colour TVM
Bedford Productions

A young couple and family move into a haunted farmhouse.
Flashy supernatural thriller with not enough plot.

w Robert Clouse *d* Steven Spielberg

Sandy Dennis, Darren McGavin, Ralph Bellamy

Something for a Lonely Man
US 1968 98m Technicolor TVM
Universal (Richard E. Lyons)

An old steam-engine brings prosperity to a western town.

Mildly enjoyable family western.

w John Fante, Frank Fenton *d* Don Taylor

Dan Blocker, Susan Clark, John Dehner, Warren Oates, Don Stroud

Something for Everyone*
US 1970 110m colour
National General (John Flaxman)
GB title: *Black Flowers for the Bride*

A young con man insinuates himself into the household of a widowed Austrian countess.
Unusual black comedy which doesn't quite come off.

w Hugh Wheeler, *novel* The Cook by Harry Kressing *d* Harold Prince *ph* Walter Lassally *m* John Kander

Angela Lansbury, Michael York, Anthony Corlan, Heidelinde Weis

'Nothing much for anyone, actually.'—*New Yorker*

Something for the Birds
US 1952 81m bw
TCF (Samuel G. Engel)

An elderly fraud is of help to a Washington girl trying to save a bird sanctuary.
Derivative, competent but slightly boring political whimsy on Capra lines.

w I. A. L. Diamond, Boris Ingster *d* Robert Wise *ph* Joseph La Shelle *m* Sol Kaplan

Edmund Gwenn, Victor Mature, Patricia Neal, Larry Keating, Christian Rub

Something for the Boys
US 1944 87m Technicolor
TCF (Irving Starr)

A southern plantation is turned into a retreat for army wives.
Modest musical, vaguely based on a Broadway success.

w Robert Ellis, Helen Logan, Frank Gabrielson, *musical comedy* Cole Porter, Herbert and Dorothy Fields *d* Lewis Seiler *ph* Ernest Palmer *songs* Cole Porter

Carmen Miranda, Michael O'Shea, Vivian Blaine, Phil Silvers, Sheila Ryan, Perry Como, Glenn Langan, Cara Williams

Something in the Wind
US 1946 89m bw
U-I (Joseph Sistrom)

A lady disc jockey is mistaken for her aunt, who has been seeing too much for the heirs' liking of a wealthy old man.
Poorish star musical comedy

w Harry Kurnitz, William Bowers *d* Irving Pichel

Deanna Durbin, Donald O'Connor, John Dall, Charles Winninger, Helena Carter

Something Money Can't Buy
GB 1952 82m bw
Rank / Vic (Joe Janni)

After World War II a young couple find civilian life difficult and dreary, but finally start a catering and secretarial business.
Weakly contrived comedy which makes nothing of its possibilities and is limply handled all round.

w Pat Jackson, James Lansdale Hodson *d* Pat Jackson *ph* C. Pennington-Richards *m* Nino Rota

Patricia Roc, Anthony Steel, A. E. Matthews, Moira Lister, David Hutcheson, Michael Trubshawe, Diane Hart, Charles Victor, Henry Edwards

Something of Value
US 1957 113m bw
MGM (Pandro S. Berman)

A young African with many English friends is initiated into the Kikuyu.
An attempt to see all sides in the case of the African ritual murders of the fifties; bloodthirsty and unconvincing as well as dull.

wd Richard Brooks, *novel* Robert Ruark *ph* Russell Harlan *m* Miklos Rozsa

Rock Hudson, Sidney Poitier, Dana Wynter, Wendy Hiller, Robert Beatty, Juano Hernandez, William Marshall, Walter Fitzgerald, Michael Pate

Something to Live For
US 1952 89m bw
Paramount (George Stevens)

A commercial artist member of Alcoholics Anonymous falls for a dipsomaniac actress but refuses to break up his marriage.
Glossy romantic melodrama with some style but no depth; the casting makes it seem like a sequel to *The Lost Weekend*.

w Dwight Taylor *d* George Stevens *ph* George Barnes *m* Victor Young

Ray Milland, Joan Fontaine, Teresa Wright, Richard Derr, Douglas Dick

'The victory over alcohol becomes a somewhat woebegone business.'—*Penelope Houston*

Something Wild
US 1961 112m bw
(UA) Prometheus (George Justin)

A girl's life and attitudes change after she is

raped, and she moves in with a garage mechanic. A bit of a wallow, with much method acting but no clear analysis of the central relationship.

w Jack Garfein, Alex Karmel, *novel* Mary Ann by Alex Karmel *d* Jack Garfein *ph* Eugene Schufftan *m* Aaron Copland *ad* Richard Day

Carroll Baker, Ralph Meeker, Mildred Dunnock, Charles Watts, Martin Kosleck, Jean Stapleton

Sometimes a Great Notion*
US 1971 114m Technicolor Panavision
Universal / Newman–Foreman
GB title: *Never Give an Inch*

In a small Oregon township, trouble is caused by an independent family of lumberjacks.
Freewheeling but unsatisfactorily eccentric comedy-melodrama which never quite jells but has flashes of individuality.

w John Gay, *novel* Ken Kesey *d Paul Newman ph* Richard Moore *m* Henry Mancini

Paul Newman, Henry Fonda, Lee Remick, Michael Sarrazin, Richard Jaeckel, Linda Lawson, Cliff Potts

Somewhere I'll Find You*
US 1942 108m bw
MGM (Pandro S. Berman)

Brother war correspondents quarrel over a girl and later find her in Indo-China smuggling Chinese babies to safety.
Absurd but satisfactory star vehicle of the second rank, with the theme designed to prepare America for war.

w Marguerite Roberts, *story* Charles Hoffman *d* Wesley Ruggles *ph* Harold Rosson *m* Bronislau Kaper

Clark Gable, Lana Turner, Robert Sterling, Patricia Dane, Reginald Owen, Lee Patrick, Charles Dingle, Rags Ragland, William Henry

Somewhere in England
GB 1940 79m bw
Mancunian (John E. Blakeley)

High jinks among army recruits staging a show.
One of a series of misshapen and badly made regional comedies which afflicted British cinemas in the forties and should be mentioned for their immense popularity, their new-style vulgarity (later to be refined by the Carry On series) and their highly popular stars.

w Arthur Mertz, Rodney Parsons *d* John E. Blakeley

Frank Randle, Harry Korris, Robbie Vincent, Winki Turner, Dan Young

† Subsequently released, or allowed to escape, between 1941 and 1949 were *Somewhere in Camp, Somewhere on Leave, Somewhere in Civvies* and *Somewhere in Politics.*

Somewhere in the Night*
US 1946 111m bw
TCF

An amnesiac war veteran tries to discover his true identity and discovers he is a crook with much-wanted information.
Overlong suspenser with a tentative *film noir* atmosphere. A few nice touches partly atone for a tediously conversational plot.

w Howard Dimsdale, Joseph L. Mankiewicz *d* Joseph L. Mankiewicz *ph* Norbert Brodine *m* David Buttolph

John Hodiak, Nancy Guild, Lloyd Nolan, Richard Conte, Josephine Hutchinson, *Fritz Kortner*

Son of Ali Baba
US 1952 75m Technicolor
U-I (Leonard Goldstein)

A cadet of the military academy outwits a wicked caliph.
Routine Arabian Nights hokum.

w Gerald Drayson Adams *d* Kurt Neumann *ph* Maury Gertsman *m* Joseph Gershenson

Tony Curtis, Piper Laurie, Sebastian Cabot, Victor Jory

Son of Dracula*
US 1943 80m bw
Universal

A mysterious stranger named Alucard, with a penchant for disappearing in puffs of smoke, turns up on a southern plantation.
Stolid series entry with a miscast lead; nicely handled moments.

w Eric Taylor *d Robert Siodmak ph George Robinson m* Hans Salter

Lon Chaney Jnr, Louise Allbritton, Robert Paige, Samuel S. Hinds, Evelyn Ankers, Frank Craven, J. Edward Bromberg
† The title cheats: he isn't the son of, but the old man himself . . .

Son of Frankenstein***
US 1939 99m bw
Universal (Rowland V. Lee)

The old baron's son comes home and starts to dabble, with the help of a broken-necked and vindictive shepherd.
Handsomely mounted sequel to *Bride of Frankenstein* and the last of the classic trio. The

monster is less interesting, but there are plenty of other diversions, including the splendid if impractical sets.

w Willis Cooper d Rowland V. Lee ph George Robinson m Frank Skinner ad Jack Otterson

Basil Rathbone, Boris Karloff, Bela Lugosi, Lionel Atwill, Josephine Hutchinson, Donnie Dunagan, Emma Dunn, *Edgar Norton,* Lawrence Grant

Son of Fury*
US 1942 102m bw
TCF (William Perlberg)

An 18th-century Englishman is deprived of his inheritance, flees to a South Sea island but comes back seeking restitution.
Elaborate costumer which suffers from loss of suspense during the central idyll. Much to enjoy along the way.

w Philip Dunne, *novel* Benjamin Blake by Edison Marshall *d John Cromwell ph* Arthur Miller *m* Alfred Newman

Tyrone Power, Gene Tierney, George Sanders, Frances Farmer, Roddy McDowall, John Carradine, Elsa Lanchester, *Dudley Digges,* Harry Davenport, Halliwell Hobbes
† Remade as *Treasure of the Golden Condor* (qv).

Son of Kong*
US 1933 69m bw
RKO (Merian C. Cooper)

After Kong has wrecked New York, producer Carl Denham flees from his creditors and finds more monsters on the old island.
Hasty sequel to the splendid *King Kong*; the results were so tame and unconvincing that the film was sold as a comedy, but it does have a few lively moments after four reels of padding.

w Ruth Rose *d* Ernest B. Schoedsack *ph* Eddie Linden, Vernon Walker, J. O. Taylor *m* Max Steiner *sp Willis O'Brien*

Robert Armstrong, Helen Mack, Frank Reicher, John Marston, Victor Wong

Son of Monte Cristo*
US 1940 102m bw
(UA) Edward Small

The masked avenger who quashes a dictatorship in 1865 Lichtenstein is none other than the son of Edmond Dantes.
Cheerful swashbuckler of the second class.

w George Bruce *d* Rowland V. Lee *ph* George Robinson *m* Edward Ward

Louis Hayward, Joan Bennett, George Sanders, Florence Bates, Lionel Royce, Montagu Love, Clayton Moore, Ralph Byrd

Son of Paleface*
US 1952 95m Technicolor
(Paramount) Bob Hope (Robert L. Welch)

A tenderfoot and a government agent compete for the attentions of a lady bandit.
Gagged-up sequel to *The Paleface*; much of the humour now seems self-conscious and dated in the *Road* tradition which it apes, but there are still moments of delight.

w Frank Tashlin, Joseph Quillan, Robert L. Welch *d* Frank Tashlin *ph* Harry J. Wild *m* Lyn Murray

Bob Hope, Roy Rogers, Jane Russell, Trigger, Douglass Dumbrille, Harry Von Zell, Bill Williams, Lloyd Corrigan

Son of Robin Hood
GB 1958 77m Eastmancolor Cinemascope
TCF / Argo (George Sherman)

Robin's daughter joins with the Regent's brother to overthrow the Black Duke.
Empty-headed romp, more or less in the accepted tradition.

w George George, George Slavin *d* George Sherman *ph* Arthur Grant *m* Leighton Lucas

David Hedison, June Laverick, David Farrar, Marius Goring, Philip Friend, Delphi Lawrence, George Coulouris, George Woodbridge

Son of Sinbad*
US 1955 88m Technicolor Superscope
RKO (Robert Sparks)

Sinbad and Omar Khayyam are imprisoned by the Caliph but escape with the secret of green fire.
Arabian Nights burlesque, mainly quite bright, with the forty thieves played by harem girls.

w Aubrey Wisberg, Jack Pollexfen *d* Ted Tetzlaff *ph* William Snyder *m* Victor Young

Dale Robertson, Vincent Price, Sally Forrest, Lili St Cyr, Mari Blanchard, Leon Askin, Jay Novello

A Song Is Born*
US 1948 113m Technicolor
Samuel Goldwyn

Flat remake of *Ball of Fire* (qv), graced by an array of top-flight musical talent.

w Harry Tugend *d* Howard Hawks *ph* Gregg Toland *md* Emil Newman

Danny Kaye, Virginia Mayo, Hugh Herbert,

Steve Cochran, Felix Bressart, J. Edward Bromberg, Mary Field, Ludwig Stossel, Louis Armstrong, Charlie Barnet, Benny Goodman, Lionel Hampton, Tommy Dorsey, Mel Powell

The Song of Bernadette**
US 1943 156m bw
TCF (William Perlberg)

A peasant girl has a vision of the Virgin Mary at what becomes the shrine of Lourdes.
Hollywood religiosity at its most commercial; but behind the lapses of taste and truth is an excellent production which was phenomenally popular and created a new star.

w George Seaton, *novel* Franz Werfel *d Henry King ph Arthur Miller m* Alfred Newman *ad James Basevi, William Darling*

Jennifer Jones, William Eythe, Charles Bickford, Vincent Price, Lee J. Cobb, Gladys Cooper, Anne Revere, Roman Bohnen, Patricia Morison, Aubrey Mather, Charles Dingle, Mary Anderson, Edith Barrett, Sig Rumann

'A tamed and pretty image, highly varnished, sensitively lighted, and exhibited behind immaculate glass, the window at once of a shrine and of a box office.' *James Agee*

Song of Freedom*
GB 1936 80m bw
Hammer (J. Fraser Passmore)

A black London docker becomes an opera singer, then goes to Africa to free the tribe of which he has discovered himself to be the head.
A weird fable but a good star vehicle and a surprisingly smart production for the time.

w Fenn Sherie, Ingram d'Abbes, Michael Barringer, Philip Lindsay *d* J. Elder Wills

Paul Robeson, Elizabeth Welch, George Mosart, Esmé Percy

Song of Love*
US 1947 118m bw
MGM (Clarence Brown)

The story of Clara and Robert Schumann and their friend Johannes Brahms.
Dignified musical biopic which unfortunately falls into most of the pitfall clichés of the genre. Dull it may be, but it looks good and the music is fine.

w Ivan Tors, Irmgard Von Cube, Allen Vincent, Robert Ardrey *d* Clarence Brown *ph* Harry Stradling *md* Bronislau Kaper *ad* Cedric Gibbons *piano* Artur Rubenstein

Katharine Hepburn, Paul Henreid, Robert Walker, Henry Daniell, Leo G. Carroll, Else Janssen, Gigi Perreau

'This is how Brahms and the Schumanns might very possibly have acted if they had realized that later on they would break into the movies.' *Time*

Song of Norway*
US 1970 141m De Luxe Super Panavision 70
ABC / Andrew and Virginia Stone

A fantasia on the life of Grieg.
Multinational hodgepodge, mostly in the *Sound of Music* style but with everything from cartoons to Christmas cracker backgrounds. Quite watchable, and the landscapes are certainly splendid.

wd Andrew Stone *ph* Davis Boulton *stage musical* Milton Lazarus *(book)* Robert Wright, George Forrest *(m/ly)*

Toralv Maurstad, Florence Henderson, Christina Schollin, Frank Poretta, Harry Secombe, Edward G. Robinson, Robert Morley, Elizabeth Larner, Bernard Archard, Oscar Homolka, Richard Wordsworth

Song of Russia
US 1944 107m bw
MGM (Joe Pasternak)

An American symphony conductor is in Russia when hostilities begin, and watches the citizens' war effort with admiration.
A terrible big-budget film which followed the wartime propaganda line but five years later was heavily criticized by the Unamerican Activities Committee (for the wrong reasons).

w Paul Jarrico, Richard Collins *d* Gregory Ratoff *m* Herbert Stothart

Robert Taylor, Susan Peters, John Hodiak, Robert Benchley, Felix Bressart, Michael Chekhov, Darryl Hickman

'Film makers have evolved a new tongue the broken accent deriving from no known language to be used by foreigners on all occasions.' *Richard Winnington*

Song of Scheherezade
US 1947 107m Technicolor
Universal (Edward Kaufman)

In 1865 naval cadet Rimsky-Korsakov falls in love with a dancer.
Yet another composer takes a drubbing in this dull and unconvincing hodgepodge.

wd Walter Reisch *ph* Hal Mohr, William V. Skall *md* Miklos Rozsa *ch* Tilly Losch *ad* Jack Otterson

Yvonne de Carlo, Jean-Pierre Aumont, Brian

Donlevy, Eve Arden, Charles Kullman, John Qualen, Richard Lane, Terry Kilburn

Song of Songs*
US 1933 89m bw
Paramount (Rouben Mamoulian)

A German peasant girl falls for a sculptor but marries a lecherous baron.
Pretentious romantic nonsense, made fairly palatable by the director's steady hand.

wd Rouben Mamoulian, *play* Edward Sheldon, *novel* Das hohe Lied by Hermann Sudermann *ph* Victor Milner *m* Karl Hajos, Milien Rodern *ad* Hans Dreier

Marlene Dietrich, Brian Aherne, Lionel Atwill, Alison Skipworth, Hardie Albright
'An ornate and irresistible slice of outright hokum.'—*Peter John Dyer, 1966*

Song of Surrender
US 1949 93m bw
Paramount (Richard Maibaum)

In turn-of-the-century New England, a sophisticated visitor from New York falls for the wife of the museum curator.
Ho-hum romantic drama, well enough presented.

w Richard Maibaum *d* Mitchell Leisen *ph* Daniel L. Fapp *m* Victor Young

Wanda Hendrix, Claude Rains, Macdonald Carey, Andrea King, Henry Hull, Elizabeth Patterson, Art Smith

Song of the Islands*
US 1942 75m Technicolor
TCF (William Le Baron)

On a South Sea island, the daughter of an Irish beachcomber falls for the son of an American cattle king.
Wispy musical with agreeable settings and lively songs.

w Joseph Schrank, Robert Pirosh, Robert Ellis, Helen Logan *d* Walter Lang *ph* Ernest Palmer *md* Alfred Newman *songs* various

Betty Grable, Victor Mature, Jack Oakie, Thomas Mitchell, *Hilo Hattie*, Billy Gilbert, George Barbier

Song of the South*
US 1947 94m Technicolor
Walt Disney (Perce Pearce)

On a long-ago southern plantation, small boys listen to the Brer Rabbit stories from an elderly black servant.
Too much Uncle Remus and not enough Brer Rabbit, we fear, but children liked it. The cartoons were actually very good.

w Dalton Raymond *d* Harve Foster *ph* Gregg Toland *cartoon credits* various

Ruth Warrick, Bobby Driscoll, James Baskett, Luana Patten, Lucile Watson, Hattie McDaniel
'The ratio of live to cartoon action is approximately two to one, and that is the ratio of the film's mediocrity to its charm.'—*Bosley Crowther*

A Song to Remember**
US 1945 113m Technicolor
Columbia (Louis F. Edelman)

The life and death of Chopin and his liaison with Georges Sand.
Hilarious classical musical biopic which was unexpectedly popular and provoked a flood of similar pieces. As a production, not at all bad, but the script . . .

w Sidney Buchman *d* Charles Vidor *ph* Tony Gaudio *md* Morris Stoloff *piano José Iturbi* *ad* Lionel Banks, Van Nest Polglase

Cornel Wilde, Merle Oberon, Paul Muni, Stephen Bekassy, Nina Foch, George Coulouris, Sig Arno, Howard Freeman, George Macready
'It is the business of Hollywood to shape the truth into box-office contours.'—*Richard Winnington*

Song without End
US 1960 142m Eastmancolor
Cinemascope
Columbia (William Goetz)

The life and loves of Franz Liszt.
What worked at the box office for Chopin failed disastrously for Liszt; famous people are turned into papier maché dullards. Again, the production is elegance itself.

w Oscar Millard *d* Charles Vidor, George Cukor *ph* James Wong Howe *md* Morris Stoloff *piano* Jorge Bolet *ad Walter Holscher*

Dirk Bogarde, Capucine, Genevieve Page, Patricia Morison, Ivan Desny, Martita Hunt, Lyndon Brook, Alex Davion (as Chopin)

Sons and Lovers***
GB 1960 103m bw Cinemascope
TCF / Company of Artists / Jerry Wald

A Nottingham miner's son learns about life and love.
Well-produced and generally absorbing, if unsurprising, treatment of a famous novel.

w Gavin Lambert, T. E. B. Clarke, novel D. H. Lawrence *d Jack Cardiff ph Freddie Francis* *m* Lambert Williamson

Dean Stockwell, Trevor Howard, Wendy Hiller, Mary Ure, Heather Sears, William Lucas, Donald Pleasence, Ernest Thesiger

'An album of decent Edwardian snapshots.' —*Peter John Dyer*

The Sons of Katie Elder*
US 1965 122m Technicolor Panavision
Paramount / Hal B. Wallis (Paul Nathan)

At Katie Elder's funeral, her four troublesome wandering sons find themselves on the verge of further trouble.
Sluggish all-star western with predictable highlights.

w Allan Weiss, William H. Wright, Harry Essex *d* Henry Hathaway *ph* Lucien Ballard *m* Elmer Bernstein

John Wayne, Dean Martin, Michael Anderson Jnr, Earl Holliman, Martha Hyer, Jeremy Slate, James Gregory, George Kennedy, Paul Fix

Sons of the Desert****
US 1934 68m bw
Hal Roach
GB title: *Fraternally Yours*

Stan and Ollie want to go to a Chicago convention, but kid their wives that they are going on a cruise for health reasons.
Archetypal Laurel and Hardy comedy, unsurpassed for gags, pacing and sympathetic characterization.

w Frank Craven, Byron Morgan d William A. Seiter ph Kenneth Peach

Stan Laurel, Oliver Hardy, Charlie Chase, Mae Busch, Dorothy Christie

Sorrowful Jones
US 1949 88m bw
Paramount (Robert L. Welch)

A racetrack tout unofficially adopts an orphan girl.
Heavy-going sentimental comedy peopled by comic gangsters, a remake of *Little Miss Marker* with the emphasis changed.

w Melville Shavelson, Edmund Hartmann, Jack Rose, *story* Damon Runyon *d* Sidney Lanfield *ph* Daniel L. Fapp *m* Robert Emmett Dolan

Bob Hope, Lucille Ball, William Demarest, Bruce Cabot, Thomas Gomez, Tom Pedi, Houseley Stevenson, Mary Jane Saunders

Sorry Wrong Number**
US 1948 89m bw
Paramount (Hal B. Wallis, Anatole Litvak)

A bedridden neurotic woman discovers she is marked for murder and tries to summon help.
Artificial but effective suspenser, extended from a radio play.

w Lucille Fletcher, from her play *d* Anatole Litvak *ph* Sol Polito *m* Franz Waxman

Barbara Stanwyck, Burt Lancaster, Ann Richards, Wendell Corey, Ed Begley, Harold Vermilyea, Leif Erickson, William Conrad

Souls at Sea*
US 1937 93m bw
Paramount

In a 19th-century shipwreck an intelligence officer must save himself, and his mission, at the cost of other lives, and is courtmartialled.
A lively seafaring melodrama produced on a fairly impressive scale.

w Grover Jones, Dale Van Every *d* Henry Hathaway *ph* Charles Lang Jnr *md* Boris Morros

Gary Cooper, George Raft, Frances Dee, Henry Wilcoxon, Harry Carey, Olympe Bradna, Robert Cummings, Porter Hall, George Zucco, Virginia Weidler, Joseph Schildkraut, Gilbert Emery

The Sound and the Fury
US 1959 117m Eastmancolor Cinemascope
TCF / Jerry Wald

A once proud southern family has sunk low in finance and moral stature, and a stern elder son tries to do something about it.
Heavy melodrama with performances to match.

w Irving Ravetch, Harriet Frank Jnr, *novel* William Faulkner *d* Martin Ritt *ph* Charles G. Clarke *m* Alex North

Yul Brynner, Joanne Woodward, Margaret Leighton, Stuart Whitman, Ethel Waters, Jack Warden, Françoise Rosay, John Beal, Albert Dekker

'A fourth carbon copy of Chekhov in Dixie.' —*Stanley Kauffmann*

The Sound Barrier**
GB 1952 118m bw
London Films (David Lean)
US title: *Breaking the Sound Barrier*

An aircraft manufacturer takes risks with the lives of his family and friends to prove that the sound barrier can be broken.
Riveting, then topical, melodrama with splendid air sequences; a bit upper crust, but with well-drawn characters.

w Terence Rattigan d David Lean ph Jack Hildyard m Malcolm Arnold

Ralph Richardson, Nigel Patrick, Ann Todd,

John Justin, Dinah Sheridan, Joseph Tomelty, Denholm Elliott

The Sound of Anger
US 1968 100m Technicolor TVM
Universal (Roy Huggins)

A team of lawyers defend teenage lovers accused of murdering the girl's father.
Moderate pilot for the series *The Bold Ones*. It achieves its purpose.

w Dick Nelson *d* Michael Ritchie

Burl Ives, James Farentino, Dorothy Provine

The Sound of Fury**
US 1951 92m bw
(UA) Robert Stillman

Two men are arrested for kidnapping and murder, and a journalist stirs the small town to lynch fury.
Harrowing, relentless melodrama, possibly the best on this subject.

w Jo Pagano, from his novel The Condemned *d Cyril Endfield ph* Guy Roe *m* Hugo Friedhofer

Frank Lovejoy, Lloyd Bridges, Kathleen Ryan, Richard Carlson, Katherine Locke, Adele Jergens, Art Smith

'The characterization and the handling of the drama are remarkable, at times reaching a complexity rare in films of this type.'—*Gavin Lambert*

The Sound of Music***
US 1965 172m De Luxe Todd-AO
TCF / Argyle (Robert Wise)

In 1938 Austria, a trainee nun becomes governess to the Trapp family, falls in love with the widower father, and helps them all escape from the Nazis.
Slightly muted, very handsome version of an enjoyably old-fashioned stage musical with splendid tunes.

w Ernest Lehman, *book* Howard Lindsay, Russel Crouse *d Robert Wise ph Ted McCord m/ly Richard Rodgers, Oscar Hammerstein II pd Boris Leven*

Julie Andrews, Christopher Plummer, Richard Haydn, Eleanor Parker, *Peggy Wood*, Anna Lee, Marni Nixon

'. . . sufficient warning to those allergic to singing nuns and sweetly innocent children.' —*John Gillett*

Sound Off
US 1952 83m Supercinecolor
Columbia (Jonie Taps)

An entertainer is recruited into the army and has predictable difficulties.
Dishevelled service farce with funny moments.

w Blake Edwards, Richard Quine *d* Richard Quine *ph* Ellis Carter *m* Morris Stoloff

Mickey Rooney, Anne James, Sammy White, John Asher, Gordon Jones

Sounder*
US 1972 105m De Luxe Panavision
TCF / Radnitz–Mattel (Robert B. Radnitz)

During the thirties Depression, black sharecroppers in the deep south endure various tribulations.
Well made liberated family movie . . . but not very exciting.

w Lonnie Elder III, *novel* William H. Armstrong *d* Martin Ritt *ph* John Alonzo *m* Taj Mahal

Paul Winfield, Cicely Tyson, Kevin Hooks, Carmen Mathews, James Best, Taj Mahal

Sounder
US 1976 74m colour TVM
ABC Circle

More adventures of the *Sounder* family: a TV pilot that didn't take.

d William Graham

Ebony Wright, Harold Sylvester, Daryl Young

South of Algiers
GB 1952 95m Technicolor
ABP / Mayflower (Aubrey Baring, Maxwell Setton)
US title: *The Golden Mask*

Archaeologists and thieves search the Sahara for a priceless mask.
Schoolboy adventure story with a straightforward plot and plenty of local colour.

w Robert Westerby *d* Jack Lee *ph* Oswald Morris *m* Robert Gill

Van Heflin, Wanda Hendrix, Eric Portman, Charles Goldner, Jacques François, Jacques Brunius, Alec Mango, Marne Maitland

South Pacific**
US 1958 170m Technicolor Todd-AO
Magna / S. P. Enterprises (Buddy Adler)

In 1943 an American navy nurse on a South Pacific island falls in love with a middle-aged French planter who becomes a war hero.
Overlong, solidly produced film of the musical stage hit, with great locations, action climaxes and lush photography (also a regrettable tendency to use alarming colour filters for dramatic emphasis).

w Paul Osborn, Richard Rodgers, Oscar Hammerstein II, Joshua Logan, *stories* Tales of the South Pacific by James A. Michener *d* Joshua Logan *ph Leon Shamroy* *m/ly Richard Rodgers, Oscar Hammerstein II* *ch* Le Roy Prinz

Mitzi Gaynor, Rossano Brazzi, Ray Walston, John Kerr, France Nuyen, Juanita Hall

South Riding**
GB 1937 91m bw
London Films (Alexander Korda, Victor Saville)

A schoolmistress in a quiet Yorkshire dale exposes crooked councillors and falls for the depressed local squire.
Dated but engrossing multi-drama from a famous novel; a good compact piece of film-making.

w Ian Dalrymple, Donald Bull, novel Winifred Holtby d Victor Saville

Ralph Richardson, Edna Best, Edmund Gwenn, Ann Todd, Glynis Johns, John Clements, Marie Lohr, Milton Rosmer, Edward Lexy

South Sea Woman
US 1953 89m bw
Warner (Sam Bischoff)

Adventures of a fight-loving marine in the Pacific war.
Unlovable mixture of brawling, romancing and war-winning.

w Edwin Blum, *play* William M. Rankin *d* Arthur Lubin *ph* Ted McCord *m* David Buttolph

Burt Lancaster, Virginia Mayo, Chuck Connors, Arthur Shields, Barry Kelley, Leon Askin

The Southern Star*
GB / France 1968 105m Techniscope
Columbia / Eurofrance / Capitole

In French West Africa in 1912, a penniless American finds a huge diamond which several crooks are after.
Quite a likeable adventure romp, with good suspense sequences and convincing jungle settings.

w David Pursall, Jack Seddon, *novel* Jules Verne *d* Sidney Hayers *ph* Raoul Coutard *m* Georges Garvarentz

George Segal, Ursula Andress, Orson Welles, Ian Hendry, Michael Constantine, Johnny Sekka, Harry Andrews

A Southern Yankee*
US 1948 90m bw
MGM (Paul Jones)
GB title: *My Hero*

During the Civil War a southern bellboy masquerades as a spy and finds himself behind enemy lines.
A rather feeble reworking of Buster Keaton's *The General*, with some excellent gags supervised by the master himself.

w Harry Tugend *d* Edward Sedgwick *ph* Ray June *m* David Snell

Red Skelton, Brian Donlevy, Arlene Dahl, George Coulouris, Lloyd Gough, John Ireland, Minor Watson, Charles Dingle

The Southerner***
US 1945 91m bw
(UA) David Loew, Robert Hakim

Problems of penniless farmers in the deep south.
Impressive, highly pictorial outdoor drama, more poetic than *The Grapes of Wrath* and lacking the acting strength.

wd Jean Renoir, novel Hold Autumn in Your Hand by George Sessions Perry *ph Lucien Andriot* *m* Werner Janssen

Zachary Scott, Betty Field, *Beulah Bondi*, J. Carrol Naish, Percy Kilbride, Blanche Yurka, Norman Lloyd

'I cannot imagine anybody failing to be spellbound by this first successful essay in Franco-American screen collaboration.'
—*Richard Winnington*

Soylent Green*
US 1973 97m Metrocolor Panavision
MGM (Walter Seltzer, Russell Thatcher)

In 2022, the population of New York exists in perpetual heat on synthetic foods; a policeman hears from his elderly friend about an earlier time when things were better.
Lively futuristic yarn with a splendid climax revealing the nature of the artificial food; marred by narrative incoherence and by direction which fails to put plot points clearly across.

w Stanley R. Greenberg, *novel* Make Room, Make Room by Harry Harrison *d* Richard Fleischer *ph* Richard H. Kline *m* Fred Myrow

Charlton Heston, *Edward G. Robinson*, Leigh Taylor-Young, Chuck Connors, Brock Peters, Joseph Cotten

Spanish Affair
US 1958 92m Technicolor Vistavision
Paramount / Nomad (Bruce Odlum)

An American architect in Madrid falls in love

with his interpreter and is pursued by her lover. Curiously plotless excuse for a travelogue, lushly photographed but not exactly gripping.

w Richard Collins *d* Don Siegel *ph* Sam Leavitt *m* Daniele Amfitheatrof

Richard Kiley, Carmen Sevilla, Jose Guardiola

The Spanish Gardener
GB 1956 97m Technicolor Vistavision
Rank (John Bryan)

The British consul in Spain is annoyed when his young son develops a strong friendship with the gardener.
Slow, understated study in human relationships which doesn't come off; any sexual relevance is well concealed.

w Lesley Storm, John Bryan, *novel* A. J. Cronin *d* Philip Leacock *ph* Christopher Challis *m* John Veale

Dirk Bogarde, Michael Hordern, Jon Whiteley, Cyril Cusack, Geoffrey Keen, Maureen Swanson, Lyndon Brook, Josephine Griffin, Bernard Lee, Rosalie Crutchley

The Spanish Main*
US 1945 101m Technicolor
RKO (Robert Fellows)

In the Caribbean, the fiancée of the Spanish viceroy is kidnapped by a pirate who determines to tame her before marrying her.
Slightly tongue-in-cheek pirate hokum; generally good value for the easily amused.

w George Worthing Yates, Herman J. Mankiewicz *d* Frank Borzage *ph* George Barnes *m* Constantin Bakaleinikoff

Paul Henreid, Maureen O'Hara, Binnie Barnes, Walter Slezak, John Emery, Barton MacLane, J. M. Kerrigan, Nancy Gates, Fritz Leiber, Jack La Rue, Mike Mazurki, Victor Kilian

Spare the Rod
GB 1961 93m bw
British Lion / Bryanston / Weyland (Victor Lyndon)

At an East End school, a novice master wins the confidence of tough pupils.
A British *Blackboard Jungle*, paving the way for *To Sir with Love*; not exciting on its own account.

w John Cresswell, *novel* Michael Croft *d* Leslie Norman *ph* Paul Beeson *m* Laurie Johnson

Max Bygraves, Geoffrey Keen, Donald Pleasance, Richard O'Sullivan, Betty McDowall, Eleanor Summerfield, Mary Merrall

Sparrows Can't Sing
GB 1962 94m bw
Elstree / Carthage

Returning after two years at sea, a sailor searches for his wife and threatens vengeance on her lover.
Relentlessly caricatured cockney comedy melodrama, too self-conscious to be effective, and not at all likeable anyway.

w Stephen Lewis, Joan Littlewood *d* Joan Littlewood *ph* Mac Greene *m* James Stevens

James Booth, Barbara Windsor, Roy Kinnear, Avis Bunnage, George Sewell, Barbara Ferris, Murray Melvin, Arthur Mullard

Spartacus**
US 1960 196m Super Technirama 70
U-I / Bryna (Edward Lewis)

The slaves of ancient Rome revolt and are quashed.
Long, well-made, downbeat epic with deeper than usual characterization and several bravura sequences.

w Dalton Trumbo, *novel* Howard Fast *d Stanley Kubrick ph Russell Metty m* Alex North *pd* Alexander Golitzen

Kirk Douglas, Laurence Olivier, Charles Laughton, Tony Curtis, Jean Simmons, Peter Ustinov, John Gavin, Nina Foch, Herbert Lom, John Ireland, John Dall, Charles McGraw, Woody Strode

'Everything is depicted with a lack of imagination that is truly Marxian.'—*Anne Grayson*

'A lot of first-rate professionals have pooled their abilities to make a first-rate circus.'—*Stanley Kauffmann*

Spawn of the North**
US 1938 110m bw
Paramount (Albert Lewin)

In 1890s Alaska, American fishermen combat Russian poachers. Solidly carpentered all-star action melodrama, a sizzler of its day. Remade 1953 as *Alaska Seas.*

w Talbot Jennings, Jules Furthman *d Henry Hathaway ph Charles Lang m* Dmitri Tiomkin

George Raft, Henry Fonda, Dorothy Lamour, *John Barrymore*, Akim Tamiroff, Louise Platt, Lynne Overman, Fuzzy Knight, Vladimir Sokoloff, Duncan Renaldo, John Wray

Speak Easily*
US 1932 83m bw
MGM

A professor inherits a Broadway musical and falls for the lure of the bright lights.
Interesting Keaton talkie at the point of his decline.

w Ralph Spence, Lawrence E. Johnson, *novel* Footlights by Clarence Budington Kellad *d* Edward Sedgwick *ph* Harold Wentstrom

Buster Keaton, Jimmy Durante, Hedda Hopper

Special Delivery
US 1976 99m De Luxe
TCF / Bing Crosby Productions (Richard Berg)

Three disabled Vietnam veterans rob a bank, and the consequences are complicated.
Unremarkable suspenser which takes itself too seriously.

w Don Gazzaniga *d* Paul Wendkos *ph* Harry Stradling Jnr *m* Lalo Schifrin

Bo Svenson, Cybill Shepherd, Michael C. Gwynne, Vic Tayback, Sorrell Booke

The Specialists
US 1974 74m Technicolor TVM
Universal (Robert A. Cinader)

US public health experts trace an epidemic.
Lacklustre pilot.

w Preston Wood, R. A. Cinader *d* Richard Quine

Robert York, Jack Hogan, Maureen Reagan, Kyle Anderson, Tom Scott

The Specter of the Rose*
US 1946 90m bw
Republic

A schizophrenic ballet dancer lives his role and nearly murders his wife.
A rather hilarious bid for culture: hard to sit through without laughing, but unique.

wd Ben Hecht *ph* Lee Garmes *m* Georges Antheil

Viola Essen, Ivan Kirov, Michael Chekhov

Spellbound
GB 1940 82m bw
Pyramid Amalgamated (R. Murray Leslie)
aka: *Passing Clouds*; US title: *The Spell of Amy Nugent*

A young man is in despair when his fiancée dies, and nearly goes mad when a medium materializes her from the dead.
Very odd, very naïve, but somehow rather winning.

w Miles Malleson, *novel* The Necromancers by Robert Benson *d* John Harlow

Derek Farr, Vera Lindsay, Frederick Leister, Hay Petrie, Diana King, Felix Aylmer

Spellbound***
US 1945 111m bw
David O. Selznick

The new head of a mental institution is an impostor and an amnesiac; a staff member falls in love with him and helps him recall the fate of the real Dr Edwardes.
Enthralling and rather infuriating psychological mystery; the Hitchcock touches are splendid, and the stars shine magically, but the plot could have stood a little more attention.

w Ben Hecht, Angus MacPhail, *novel* The House of Dr Edwardes by Francis Beeding *d Alfred Hitchcock ph George Barnes dream sequence Salvador Dali* *m* Miklos Rozsa *ad* James Basevi

Ingrid Bergman, Gregory Peck, Leo G. Carroll. Michael Chekhov, Rhonda Fleming, John Emery, Norman Lloyd, Steve Geray

'Just about as much of the id as could be safely displayed in a Bergdorf Goodman window.'—*James Agee*

'Bergman's apple-cheeked sincerity has rarely been so out of place as in this confection whipped up by jaded chefs.'—*New Yorker, 1976*

Spencer's Mountain*
US 1963 121m Technicolor Panavision
Warner (Delmer Daves)

Life in rural America in the thirties with a poor quarry worker and his family of nine.
Sentimental rose-tinted hokum which later became TV's *The Waltons*. Expertly concocted, Hollywood style.

wd Delmer Daves, *novel* Earl Hanmer Jnr *ph* Charles Lawton, H. F. Koenekamp *m* Max Steiner

Henry Fonda, Maureen O'Hara, James MacArthur, Donald Crisp, Wally Cox, Mimsy Farmer, Lilian Bronson

The Spikes Gang
US 1974 96m De Luxe
UA / Mirisch / Duo / Sanford

Three boys shelter a bank robber and join his gang.
Doom-laden, violent western with a few comic lines.

w Irving Ravetch, Harriet Frank Jnr, *novel* The Bank Robber by Giles Tippette *d* Richard Fleischer *ph* Brian West *m* Fred Karlin

Lee Marvin, Gary Grimes, Ron Howard,

Charles Martin Smith, Arthur Hunnicutt, Noah Beery Jnr

Spinout
US 1966 93m Metrocolor Panavision
MGM / Euterpe (Joe Pasternak)
GB title: *California Holiday*

A carefree touring singer agrees to drive an experimental car in a road race.
Mild star musical which at least stays in the open air.

w Theodore J. Flicker, George Kirgo *d* Norman Taurog *ph* Daniel L. Fapp *md* Georgie Stoll

Elvis Presley, Shelley Fabares, Carl Betz, Cecil Kellaway, Diane McBain, Deborah Walley, Jack Mullaney, Will Hutchins, Una Merkel

The Spiral Road
US 1962 145m Eastmancolor
U-I (Robert Arthur)

In 1936 Java, an atheist medical man fights a leprosy epidemic and eventually becomes a missionary.
A long slog through jungle/religious clichés, with a hilariously miscast star and an almost Victorian script.

w John Lee Mahin, Neil Paterson, *novel* Jan de Hartog *d* Robert Mulligan *ph* Russell Harlan *m* Jerry Goldsmith

Rock Hudson, Burl Ives, Geoffrey Keen, Gena Rowlands, Will Kuluva, Neva Patterson, Philip Abbott

The Spiral Staircase***
US 1946 83m bw
David O. Selznick

A small town in 1906 New England is terrorized by a psychopathic killer of deformed girls.
Archetypal old dark house thriller, superbly detailed and set during a most convincing thunderstorm. Even though the identity of the villain is pretty obvious, this is a superior Hollywood product.

w Mel Dinelli, novel Some Must Watch by Ethel Lina White *d Robert Siodmak ph Nicholas Musuraca m Roy Webb ad Albert S. D'Agostino, Jack Okey*

Dorothy McGuire, George Brent, Kent Smith, Ethel Barrymore, Rhys Williams, Rhonda Fleming, Gordon Oliver, Sara Allgood, James Bell

'A nice, cosy and well-sustained atmosphere of horror.'—*C. A. Lejeune*

The Spiral Staircase
GB 1975 89m Technicolor
Warner / Raven (Peter Shaw)

Modernized remake of the above using virtually the same script, and apparently determined to prove how badly it can be presented.

w Allan Scott, Chris Bryant *d* Peter Collinson *ph* Ken Hodges *m* David Lindup

Jacqueline Bisset, Christopher Plummer, Sam Wanamaker, Mildred Dunnock, Gayle Hunnicutt, Sheila Brennan, Elaine Stritch, John Ronane, Ronald Radd

The Spirit Is Willing
US 1966 100m Technicolor
Paramount / William Castle

A family finds that its holiday home is haunted by the ghosts of a *crime passionel.*
Overlong, overlayed and witless farce with virtually no opportunity well taken.

w Ben Starr, *novel* The Visitors by Nathaniel Benchley *d* William Castle *ph* Hal Stine *m* Vic Mizzy

Sid Caesar, Vera Miles, John McGiver, Cass Daley, John Astin, Mary Wickes, Jesse White

The Spirit of St Louis*
US 1957 135m Warnercolor Cinemascope
Warner (Leyland Hayward)

In 1927 Charles Lindbergh flies a specially constructed plane 3,600 miles nonstop New York to Paris in $33\frac{1}{2}$ hours.
Impeccably in its period, this needlessly Cinemascoped reconstruction can scarcely avoid dull patches since for long stretches its hero is on screen solo apart from a fly, and his monologues become soporific.

w Billy Wilder, Wendell Mayes, *book* Charles Lindbergh *d* Billy Wilder *ph* Robert Burks, Peverell Marley *m* Franz Waxman

James Stewart, Murray Hamilton, Marc Connelly

Spitfire*
US 1934 88m bw
RKO (Pandro S. Berman)

An Ozark mountain girl believes herself to be a faith healer and is driven from the community.
Curious star melodrama with effective moments.

w Jane Murfin, *play* Trigger by Lula Vollmer *d* John Cromwell *ph* Edward Cronjager *m* Max Steiner

Katharine Hepburn, Robert Young, Ralph Bellamy, Martha Sleeper, Louis Mason

Splendor
US 1935 77m bw
Samuel Goldwyn

The son of a once-wealthy Park Avenue family marries a poor girl.
Dated romantic drama.

w Rachel Crothers, from her play *d* Elliott Nugent *ph* Gregg Toland *md* Alfred Newman

Joel McCrea, Miriam Hopkins, Helen Westley, Katherine Alexander, David Niven, Paul Cavanagh, Billie Burke, Arthur Treacher

Splendor in the Grass*
US 1961 124m Technicolor
Warner / NBI (Elia Kazan)

Adolescent love in a small Kansas town in the twenties.
Impressive though curiously unmemorable addition to a nostalgic young sex cycle which was already played out; production and performances well up to scratch.

w Wiliam Inge *d Elia Kazan* *ph* Boris Kaufman *m* David Amram

Natalie Wood, Warren Beatty, Pat Hingle, Audrey Christie, Barbara Loden, Zohra Lampert, Sandy Dennis

'Less like a high-school version of *Summer and Smoke* than [like] an Andy Hardy story with glands.'—*Stanley Kauffmann*

The Split
US 1968 90m Metrocolor Panavision
MGM / Spectrum (Robert Chartoff, Irwin Winkler)

A black criminal plans to rob the Los Angeles Coliseum during a football match.
Busy, brutal crime thriller, well enough done but totally unsympathetic.

w Robert Sabarpff, *novel* The Seventh by Richard Stark *d* Gordon Flemyng *ph* Burnett Guffey *m* Quincy Jones

Jim Brown, Diahann Carroll, Ernest Borgnine, Julie Harris, Gene Hackman, Jack Klugman, Warren Oates, James Whitmore, Donald Sutherland

Split Second
US 1953 85m bw
RKO (Edmund Grainger)

An escaped convict hides out with four hostages in an Arizona ghost town which has been cleared in preparation for an atom bomb test.
Routine suspenser.

w William Bowers, Irving Wallace *d* Dick Powell *ph* Nicholas Musuraca *m* Roy Webb

Stephen McNally, Alexis Smith, Jan Sterling, Keith Andes, Arthur Hunnicutt, Paul Kelly, Richard Egan, Robert Paige

The Spoilers*
US 1930 86m bw
Paramount

In Alaska during the gold rush, crooked government officials begin despoiling the richest claims.
Early talkie version of a famous brawling saga.

w Bartlett Cormack, Agnes Brand Leahy, *novel* Rex Beach *d* Edward Carewe *ph* Harry Fischbeck

Gary Cooper, William 'Stage' Boyd, Betty Compson, Kay Johnson, Harry Green, Slim Summerville

The Spoilers**
US 1942 87m bw
Universal (Frank Lloyd)

Two adventurers in the Yukon quarrel over land rights and a saloon entertainer.
Well-packaged mixture of saloon brawls, romance and adventure, much filmed as a silent.

w Lawrence Hazard, Tom Reed *d* Ray Enright *ph* Milton Krasner *m* Hans Salter *ad* Jack Otterson

Marlene Dietrich, Randolph Scott, John Wayne, Margaret Lindsay, Harry Carey, Richard Barthelmess, George Cleveland, Samuel S. Hinds

The Spoilers*
US 1955 82m Technicolor
U-I (Ross Hunter)

Adequate, unmemorable remake of the above.

w Oscar Brodney, Charles Hoffman *d* Jesse Hibbs *ph* Maury Gertsman *m* Joseph Gershenson

Anne Baxter, Jeff Chandler, Rory Calhoun, Barbara Britton, Carl Benton Reid, Ray Danton, John McIntire, Raymond Walburn, Wallace Ford

Spring and Port Wine
GB 1970 101m Technicolor
EMI / Memorial (Michael Medwin)

A Lancashire family runs into trouble when stern father insists that teenage daughter should eat a meal she refuses.
A popular old-fashioned stage comedy which simply doesn't work on film, partly from being set in a too-real town (Bolton) and partly because of a miscast lead.

w Bill Naughton, from his play *d* Peter

Hammond *ph* Norman Warwick *m* Douglas Gamley *pd* Reece Pemberton

James Mason, Diana Coupland, Susan George, Rodney Bewes, Hannah Gordon, Adrienne Posta, Arthur Lowe

Spring in Park Lane**
GB 1948 92m bw
British Lion / Herbert Wilcox

A diamond merchant's niece falls for a footman who just happens to be an impoverished lord in disguise.
Flimsy but highly successful romantic comedy which managed to get its balance right and is still pretty entertaining, much more so than its sequel *Maytime in Mayfair*.

w Nicholas Phipps, play Come Out of the Kitchen by Alice Duer Miller *d Herbert Wilcox ph* Max Greene

Anna Neagle, Michael Wilding, Tom Walls, Nicholas Phipps, Peter Graves, Marjorie Fielding, *Nigel Patrick*, Lana Morris

'A never-failing dream of Olde Mayfaire and its eternally funny butlers and maids, its disguised lords and ladies.'—*Richard Winnington*

Spring Parade*
US 1940 89m bw
Universal (Joe Pasternak)

A single baker's assistant falls for a prince.
Pleasing, artificial Austrian frou-frou with star and support in good escapist form.

w Bruce Manning, Felix Jackson, *story* Ernst Marischka *d* Henry Koster *ph* Joseph Valentine *m* Robert Stolz

Deanna Durbin, Robert Cummings, S. Z. Sakall, Mischa Auer, Henry Stephenson, Anne Gwynne, Butch and Buddy

Spring Reunion
US 1957 79m bw
UA / Bryna (Jerry Bresler)

College classmates fall in love all over again at a reunion fifteen years later.
Romantic fiction for the middle-aged, performed with bare competence.

wd Robert Pirosh *ph* Harold Lipstein *m* Herbert Spencer, Earle Hagen

Betty Hutton, Dana Andrews, Jean Hagen, Robert Simon, James Gleason, Laura La Plante, Irene Ryan

Springfield Rifle
US 1952 93m Warnercolor
Warner (Louis E. Edelman)

A Union officer gets himself cashiered, joins the Confederates as a spy, and unmasks a traitor.
Stolid Civil War western with Grade A production but not much individuality.

w Charles Marquis Warren, Frank Davis *d* André de Toth *ph* Edwin DuPar *m* Max Steiner

Gary Cooper, Phyllis Thaxter, David Brian, Lon Chaney Jnr, Paul Kelly, Phil Carey, James Millican, Guinn Williams

Springtime in the Rockies
US 1942 91m Technicolor
TCF (Darryl F. Zanuck)

Romances blossom on a mountain holiday.
Flimsily-plotted, studio-bound, absolutely routine musical.

w Walter Bullock, Ken Englund *d* Irving Cummings *ph* Ernest Palmer *songs* Mack Gordon, Harry Warren

Betty Grable, John Payne, Carmen Miranda, Edward Everett Horton, Cesar Romero, Charlotte Greenwood, Frank Orth, Harry James and his Music Makers

Spy Hunt*
US 1950 74m bw
Universal (Ralph Dietrich)
GB title: *Panther's Moon*

Secret microfilm is stowed in the collar of one of two panthers being transported out of Europe by train for circus use.
Slick minor espionage thriller.

w George Zuckerman, Leonard Lee, *novel* Panther's Moon by Victor Canning *d* George Sherman, *ph* Irving Glassberg *m* Joseph Gershenson

Howard Duff, Marta Toren, Philip Friend, Robert Douglas, Philip Dorn, Walter Slezak, Kurt Kreuger

The Spy in Black**
GB 1939 82 bw
Harefield / Alexander Korda (Irving Asher)
US title: *U-Boat 29*

In the Orkneys in 1917, German spies don't trust each other.
Unusual romantic melodrama which provided an unexpectedly interesting romantic team.

w Emeric Pressburger, Roland Pertwee, novel J. Storer Clouston *d Michael Powell*

Conrad Veidt, Valerie Hobson, Hay Petrie, Helen Haye, Sebastian Shaw, Marius Goring, June Duprez, Athole Stewart, Cyril Raymond

The Spy Killer
GB 1969 74m colour TVM
Cohen–Sangster

An ex-secret agent is blackmailed into looking for a mysterious notebook.
Companion piece to *Foreign Exchange* (qv); no better.

w Jimmy Sangster *d* Roy Baker

Robert Horton, Sebastain Cabot, Jill St John, Eleanor Summerfield, Barbara Shelley

The Spy Who Came in from the Cold**
GB 1966 112m bw
Paramount / Salem (Martin Ritt)

A British master spy is offered a chance to get even with his East German opponent by being apparently sacked, disillusioned, and open for recruitment.
The old undercover yarn with trimmings of such sixties malaises as death wish, anti-establishmentism and racial problems. As a yarn, quite gripping till it gets too downbeat, but very harshly photographed.

w Paul Dehn, Guy Trosper, *novel* John Le Carré *d* Martin Ritt *ph* Oswald Morris *m* Sol Kaplan *pd* Tambi Larsen

Richard Burton, Claire Bloom, *Oskar Werner*, Peter Van Eyck, Sam Wanamaker, Rupert Davies, George Voskovec, Cyril Cusack, Michael Hordern, Robert Hardy, Bernard Lee, Beatrix Lehmann

The Spy with a Cold Nose
GB 1966 93m Eastmancolor
Paramount / Associated London / Embassy (Robert Porter)

A fashionable vet is blackmailed by MI5 into inserting a radio transmitter into a bulldog.
Rather painful, overacted and overwritten farce full of obvious jokes masquerading as satire.

w Ray Galton, Alan Simpson *d* Daniel Petrie *ph* Kenneth Higgins *m* Riz Ortolani

Lionel Jeffries, Laurence Harvey, Daliah Lavi, Eric Sykes, Eric Portman, Colin Blakely, Denholm Elliott, Robert Flemyng, Paul Ford, Bernard Lee, June Whitfield, Bernard Archard

S*P*Y*S
GB 1974 100m Technicolor
Dymphana / C-W / American Film Properties (Irwin Winkler, Robert Chartoff)

Clumsy CIA agents in Paris come across a list of KGB agents in China.
Surprisingly dull and unfashionable parade of comic spy clichés; the talents involved obviously intended something closer to M*A*S*H.

w Malcolm Marmorstein, Lawrence J. Cohen, Fred Freeman *d* Irwin Kershner *ph* Gerry Fisher *m* John Scott

Elliott Gould, Donald Sutherland, Zouzou, Joss Ackland, Kenneth Griffith, Vladek Sheybal

'Seems to have arrived several years too late to find its true niche.'—*Sight and Sound*

Squadron Leader X
GB 1942 100m bw
RKO (Victor Hanbury)

A Nazi hero poses as a British pilot but has difficulty getting back home.
Tall war story with dreary romantic trimmings.

w Wolfgang Wilhelm, Miles Malleson *d* Lance Comfort

Eric Portman, Ann Dvorak, Walter Fitzgerald, Barry Jones, Henry Oscar, Beatrice Varley

The Square Jungle
US 1955 85m bw
U-I (Albert Zugsmith)

A conceited boxer gets his come-uppance.
Tailor-made studio co-feature.

w George Zuckerman *d* Jerry Hopper *ph* George Robinson *m* Heinz Roemheld

Tony Curtis, Ernest Borgnine, Pat Crowley, Jim Backus, Paul Kelly

The Square Peg*
GB 1958 89m bw
Rank (Hugh Stewart)

An army recruit finds he is the double of a German general.
Slam-bang star slapstick, shorter than usual and with a few jokes that can't fail.

w Jack Davies *d* John Paddy Carstairs *ph* Jack Cox *m* Philip Green

Norman Wisdom, Edward Chapman, Campbell Singer, Hattie Jacques, Brian Worth, Terence Alexander

The Squaw Man
US 1931 106m bw
MGM (Cecil B. de Mille)
GB title: *The White Man*

An Indian maiden saves the life of a British aristocrat, bears his child and commits suicide.
Third outing for a hoary miscegenation drama filmed in 1914 with Dustin Farnum and Red Wing, and in 1918 with Elliott Dexter and Ann Little. This talkie version sank without trace.

w Lucien Hubbard, Lenore Coffee, *play* Edwin Milton Royle *d* Cecil B. de Mille *ph* Harold Rosson

Warner Baxter, Lupe Velez, Charles Bickford, Eleanor Boardman, Roland Young, Paul Cavanagh, Raymond Hatton

The Squeaker*
GB 1937 77m bw
London Films (Alexander Korda)
US title: *Murder on Diamond Row*

A dangerous diamond fence is unmasked by a discredited policeman.
Typical Edgar Wallace who-is-it, performed with old-fashioned bravura.

w Edward O. Berkman, Bryan Wallace, *novel* Edgar Wallace *d* William K. Howard

Edmund Lowe, Sebastian Shaw, Ann Todd, Tamara Desni, Alastair Sim, Robert Newton, Allan Jeayes, Stewart Rome

Squirm
US 1976 92m Movielab
AIP / The Squirm Company (Edgar Lansbury, Joseph Beruh)

A power cable cut in a storm turns worms into maneaters.
Revolting shocker with a few funny moments for those who can take it.

wd Jeff Lieberman *ph* Joseph Mangine *m* Robert Prince

John Scardino, Patricia Pearcy, R. A. Dow, Jean Sullivan

Stage Door***
US 1937 93m bw
RKO (Pandro S. Berman)

Life in a New York theatrical boarding house for girls.
Melodramatic, sharply comedic, always fascinating slice of stagey life from a Broadway hit; the performances alone make it worth preserving.

w Morrie Ryskind, Anthony Veiller, play Edna Ferber, George S. Kaufman d Gregory La Cava ph Robert de Grasse *m* Roy Webb *ad* Van Nest Polglase

Katharine Hepburn, Ginger Rogers, Adolphe Menjou, Gail Patrick, Constance Collier, Andrea Leeds, Lucille Ball, Samuel S. Hinds, Jack Carson, Franklin Pangborn, Eve Arden

'It is a long time since we have seen so much feminine talent so deftly handled.'—*Otis Ferguson*

'Zest and pace and photographic eloquence.' —*Frank S. Nugent, New York Times*

'A rare example of a film substantially improving on a stage original and a remarkably satisfying film on all levels.'—*NFT, 1973*

Stage Door Canteen*
US 1963 132m bw
Sol Lesser (Barnett Briskin)

How the stars in New York entertained the armed forces during World War II.
Nothing as a film, mildly interesting as sociology and for some rarish appearances.

w Delmer Daves *d* Frank Borzage *ph* Harry Wild *m* Freddie Rich *pd* Harry Horner

Cheryl Walker, Lon McCallister, Judith Anderson, Tallulah Bankhead, Ray Bolger, Katherine Cornell, Helen Hayes, George Jessel, Alfred Lunt, Harpo Marx, Yehudi Menuhin, Elliott Nugent, Cornelia Otis Skinner, Ethel Waters, May Whitty, William Demarest, Gracie Fields, Katharine Hepburn, Gertrude Lawrence, Ethel Merman, Merle Oberon, Johnny Weissmuller, Edgar Bergen, Jane Cowl, Lynn Fontanne, Paul Muni, Gypsy Rose Lee, George Raft, etc; Count Basie, Benny Goodman, Xavier Cugat, Guy Lombardo, Kay Kyser and their bands

Stage Fright*
GB 1950 110m bw
Warner (Alfred Hitchcock)

A man is on the run for a backstage murder, and his girl friend takes a job as maid to the great star he says is responsible.
Creaky Hitchcock thriller in which you can see all the joins and the stars seem stuck in treacle; but a few of the set pieces work well enough.

w Whitfield Cook, *novel* Man Running by Selwyn Jepson *d* Alfred Hitchcock *ph* Wilkie Cooper *m* Leighton Lucas

Marlene Dietrich, Jane Wyman, Richard Todd, Alastair Sim, Michael Wilding, Sybil Thorndike, Kay Walsh, Miles Malleson

Stage Struck
US 1936 95m bw
Warner (Robert Lord)

Young people put on a show and become instant hits.
Dim musical oddly shorn of production numbers.

w Tom Buckinham, Pat C. Flick, Robert Lord *d/ch* Busby Berkeley *ph* Byron Haskin *m* Leo F. Forbstein *songs* Harold Arlen, E. Y. Harburg

Dick Powell, Joan Blondell, Jeanne Madden, the Yacht Club Boys, Warren William, Frank McHugh

Stage Struck**
US 1957 95m Technicolor
RKO (Stuart Millar)

A young actress comes to New York intent on stardom . . .
Careful, slightly arid remake of *Morning Glory* marred by a tiresome central performance; good theatrical detail.

w Ruth and Augustus Goetz, *play* Zoe Akins *d Sidney Lumet ph Franz Planer m* Alex North *ad* Kim Edgar Swados

Susan Strasberg, Henry Fonda, Herbert Marshall, *Joan Greenwood*, Christopher Plummer

Stage to Thunder Rock
US 1964 89m Techniscope
Paramount / A. C. Lyles

An ageing sheriff takes a bank robber back to jail by stagecoach.
Acceptable lower-berth western with the producer's usual roster of half-forgotten character actors.

w Charles Wallace *d* William F. Claxton *ph* W. Wallace Kelley *m* Paul Dunlap

Barry Sullivan, Marilyn Maxwell, Scott Brady, Keenan Wynn, Allan Jones, Lon Chaney Jnr, John Agar, Wanda Hendrix, Anne Seymour, Robert Lowery

Stagecoach****
US 1939 99m bw
(UA) Walter Wanger

Various western characters board a stagecoach in danger from an Indian war party.
What looked like a minor western, with a plot borrowed from Maupassant's *Boule de suif*, became a classic by virtue of the firm characterization, restrained writing, exciting climax and the scenery of Monument Valley. Whatever the reasons, it damn well works.

w Dudley Nichols, story Stage to Lordsburg by Ernest Haycox *d John Ford ph* Bert Glennon, Ray Binger *m Boris Morros*

Claire Trevor, John Wayne, Thomas Mitchell, George Bancroft, Andy Devine, *Berton Churchill*, Louise Platt, *John Carradine, Donald Meek*, Tim Holt, Chris-Pin Martin

'Grand Hotel on wheels.'—*New Yorker, 1975*

'The basic western, a template for everything that followed.'—*John Baxter, 1968*

'A motion picture that sings a song of camera.'—*Frank S. Nugent, New York Times*

Stagecoach
US 1966 114m De Luxe Cinemascope
TCF / Martin Rackin

Absolutely awful remake of the above; costly but totally spiritless, miscast and uninteresting.

w Joseph Landon *d* Gordon Douglas
ph William H. Clothier *m* Jerry Goldsmith

Ann-Margret, Alex Cord, Bing Crosby, Van Heflin, Slim Pickens, Robert Cummings, Stefanie Powers, Michael Connors, Red Buttons, Keenan Wynn

Staircase*
US /France 1969 101m De Luxe Panavision
TCF / Stanley Donen

The problems of two ageing homosexual hairdressers.
Unsatisfactorily opened-out and over-acted version of an effective two-hander play. Oddly made in France, so that the London detail seems all wrong.

w Charles Dyer, from his play *d* Stanley Donen *ph* Christopher Challis *m* Dudley Moore

Richard Burton, Rex Harrison, Cathleen Nesbitt, Beatrix Lehmann

'The shape is smashed . . . no longer a graceful duet, it becomes a waddling tale, spattered with ugliness, that falls into the biggest sentimental trap for homosexual material: it pleads for pity.'—*Stanley Kauffmann*

Stakeout on Dope Street*
US 1958 83m bw
Warner (Andrew J. Fenady)

Three young men find a briefcase containing heroin and are attacked by the gangsters who lost it.
Lively little crime morality, uneven but worth a look.

w Irwin Schwartz, Irvin Kershner, Andrew J. Fenady *d Irvin Kershner ph Mark Jeffrey* *m* Richard Markowitz

Yale Wexler, Jonathon Haze, Morris Miller, Abby Dalton

Stalag 17**
US 1953 120m bw
Paramount (Billy Wilder)

Comedy and tragedy for American servicemen in a Nazi prisoner-of-war camp.
High jinks, violence and mystery in a sharply calculated mixture; an atmosphere quite different from the understated British films on the subject.

w Billy Wilder, Edwin Blum, play Donald Bevan, Edmund Trzinski *d* Billy Wilder *ph* Ernest Laszlo *m* Franz Waxman

William Holden, Don Taylor, Otto Preminger, *Robert Strauss*, Harvey Lembeck, Richard

Erdman, Peter Graves, Neville Brand, Sig Rumann

'A facility for continuous rapid-fire action which alternately brings forth the laughs and tingles the spine.'—*Otis L. Guernsey Jnr*

The Stalking Moon*
US 1968 109m Technicolor Panavision
National General / Stalking Moon Company (Alan J. Pakula)

An ageing scout escorts home a white woman who has escaped from the Indians, and kills a murderous Apache.
Slow, thoughtful western with effective moments.

w Alvin Sargent, *novel* Theodore V. Olsen *d* Robert Mulligan *ph* Charles Lang *m* Fred Karlin

Gregory Peck, Eva Marie Saint, Robert Forster, Frank Silvera

Stallion Road
US 1947 97m bw
Warner (Alex Gottlieb)

An outbreak of anthrax threatens a racing stable.
Routine romantic drama with sporting background.

w Stephen Longstreet *d* James V. Kern *ph* Arthur Edeson *m* Frederick Hollander

Ronald Reagan, Alexis Smith, Zachary Scott, Peggy Knudsen, Patti Brady, Harry Davenport, Frank Puglia

Stamboul Quest
US 1934 88m bw
Warner

During World War I, Germany's most notorious lady spy falls for an American medical student.
Modest variation on the true story twice filmed as *Fräulein Doktor*; standard Hollywood values.

w Herman J. Mankiewicz *d* Sam Wood *ph* James Wong Howe

Myrna Loy, George Brent, Lionel Atwill, C. Henry Gordon, Douglass Dumbrille, Mischa Auer

Stand by for Action
US 1943 109m bw
MGM (Robert Z. Leonard, Orville O. Dull)
GB title: *Cargo of Innocents*

A Harvard graduate learns the realities of war on an old destroyer.
Studio-bound war heroics slurping into sentiment.

w George Bruce, Herman J. Mankiewicz, John L. Balderston *d* Robert Z. Leonard *ph* Charles Rosher

Robert Taylor, Charles Laughton, Brian Donlevy, Walter Brennan, Marilyn Maxwell, Henry O'Neill

Stand In*
US 1937 90m bw
Walter Wanger

An efficiency expert is sent to save a Hollywood studio from bankruptcy.
Amusing satire which could have done with sharper scripting and firmer control but is pleasantly remembered.

w Gene Towne, Graham Baker, *serial* Clarence Budington Kelland *d* Tay Garnett *ph* Charles G. Clarke *m* Heinz Roemheld

Leslie Howard, Joan Blondell, Humphrey Bogart, Alan Mowbray, Marla Shelton, C. Henry Gordon, Jack Carson, Tully Marshall

Stand Up and Be Counted*
US 1971 99m Eastmancolor
Columbia / Mike Frankovich

An international woman journalist returns to Denver and becomes involved in women's lib.
A glamoured-up flirtation with a fashionable theme, quite nicely done but instantly dated—and sociologically interesting.

w Bernard Slade *d* Jackie Cooper *ph* Fred Koenekamp *m* Ernie Wilkins

Jacqueline Bisset, Stella Stevens, Steve Lawrence, Gary Lockwood, *Loretta Swit*, Lee Purcell, Madlyn Rhue

Stand Up and Cheer*
US 1934 80m bw
Fox (Winfield Sheehan)

The new US Secretary of Amusement attempts to shake the country's Depression blues by staging a mammoth revue.
Naïve propaganda, but the whole world was swept away to cloud nine—by Shirley Temple.

w Will Rogers, Philip Klein *d* Hamilton McFadden *ph* Ernest Palmer *md* Arthur Lange

Warner Baxter, Madge Evans, Nigel Bruce, Stepin Fetchit, Frank Melton, Lila Lee, Ralph Morgan, James Dunn, *Shirley Temple*, John Boles, George K. Arthur

Stand Up and Fight*
US 1939 99m bw
MGM (Mervyn Le Roy)

A southern aristocrat comes into conflict with a

stagecoach operator used as transportation for stolen slaves.
Superior star action piece with plenty of vigorous brawls.

w James M. Cain, Jane Murfin, Harvey Ferguson *d W. S. Van Dyke II ph* Leonard Smith *m* William Axt

Wallace Beery, Robert Taylor, Florence Rice, Helen Broderick, Charles Bickford, Barton MacLane, Charley Grapewin, John Qualen

Standing Room Only*
US 1944 83m bw
Paramount (Paul Jones)

Hotel rooms being hard to find in wartime Washington, a resourceful secretary hires out herself and her boss as a servant couple.
Moderate romantic farce with a few good laughs.

w Darrell Ware, Karl Tunberg *d* Sidney Lanfield *ph* Charles Lang *m* Robert Emmett Dolan

Paulette Goddard, Fred MacMurray, Edward Arnold, Roland Young, Hillary Brooke, Porter Hall, Clarence Kolb, Anne Revere

Stanley and Livingstone***
US 1939 101m bw
TCF (Kenneth MacGowan)

An American journalist goes to Africa to find a lost Victorian explorer.
A prestige picture which played reasonably fair with history and still managed to please the masses.

w Philip Dunne, Julien Josephson *d Henry King ph George Barnes m* Alfred Newman *ad* Thomas Little

Spencer Tracy, Cedric Hardwicke, Richard Greene, Nancy Kelly, Walter Brennan, Charles Coburn, Henry Hull, Henry Travers, Miles Mander, Holmes Herbert

Star!**
US 1968 194m De Luxe Todd-AO
TCF / Robert Wise (Saul Chaplin)

Revue artist Gertrude Lawrence rises from poverty to international stardom and a measure of happiness.
Elephantiasis finally ruins this patient, detached, generally likeable recreation of a past theatrical era. In the old Hollywood style, it would probably have been even better on a smaller budget; but alas the star would still have been ill at ease with the drunken termagant scenes.

w William Fairchild *d Robert Wise ph* Ernest Laszlo *md* Lennie Hayton *ch* Michael Kidd *pd* Boris Leven

Julie Andrews, Richard Crenna, Michael Craig, *Daniel Massey* (as Noel Coward), John Collin, Robert Reed, Bruce Forsyth, Beryl Reid, Jenny Agutter

The Star*
US 1952 91m bw
TCF / Bert E. Friedlob

A once famous Hollywood star is financially and psychologically on her uppers.
A movie apparently tailor-made for its star turns out to be a disappointingly plotless wallow.

w Katherine Albert, Dale Eunson *d* Stuart Heisler *ph* Ernest Laszlo *m* Victor Young

Bette Davis, Sterling Hayden, Natalie Wood, Warner Anderson, Minor Watson

Star Dust*
US 1940 85m bw
TCF (Kenneth MacGowan)

A talent scout discovers a new Hollywood star.
Light, amusing studio comedy, a pleasing addition to Hollywood mythology.

w Robert Ellis, Helen Logan *d* Walter Lang *ph* Peverell Marley *m* David Buttolph

Linda Darnell, John Payne, Roland Young, Charlotte Greenwood, William Gargan, Mary Beth Hughes, Donald Meek, Jessie Ralph

A Star Is Born***
US 1937 111m Technicolor
David O. Selznick

A young actress meets Hollywood success and marries a famous leading man, whose star wanes as hers shines brighter.
Abrasive romantic melodrama which is also the most accurate study of Hollywood ever put on film.

w Dorothy Parker, Alan Campbell, Robert Carson, story William A. Wellman, based partly on *What Price Hollywood* (1932) (qv)
d William A. Wellman ph W. Howard Greene m Max Steiner

Janet Gaynor, Fredric March, Adolphe Menjou, Lionel Stander, Andy Devine, May Robson, Owen Moore, Franklin Pangborn

'Good entertainment by any standards.'—*Frank S. Nugent, New York Times*

'A peculiar sort of masochistic self-congratulatory Hollywood orgy.'—*New Yorker, 1975*

A Star Is Born**
US 1954 181m Technicolor Cinemascope
Warner (Sidney Luft)

Musical version of the above which begins very strongly and has two splendid performances, but suffers in the second half from a lack of writing strength and heavy post-production cutting. The numbers add very little except length.

w Moss Hart *d George Cukor* *ph* Sam Leavitt *md Ray Heindorf*

Judy Garland, James Mason, Charles Bickford, Jack Carson, Tommy Noonan, Amanda Blake, Lucy Marlow

'Maintains a skilful balance between the musical and the tear jerker.'—*Penelope Houston*

A Star Is Dead
US 1976 74m Technicolor TVM
Universal (Lou Shaw)
aka: *Quincy*

A pathologist investigates the death of a young actress.
Pilot for a new Mystery Movie character: brisk, amusing and efficient but not exciting.

w Lou Shaw, Michael Kozoll *d* Noel Black

Jack Klugman, Donna Mills, Robert Foxworth, June Lockhart, William Daniels

The Star Maker*
US 1939 94m bw
Paramount (Charles R. Rodgers)

A songwriter makes the big time by organizing kid acts.
Pleasant minor musical based on the career of Gus Edwards.

w Frank Butler, Don Hartman, Arthur Caesar *d* Roy del Ruth

Bing Crosby, Louise Campbell, Linda Ware, Ned Sparks, Laura Hope Crews, Janet Waldo, Walter Damrosch

Star of Midnight**
US 1935 90m bw
RKO (Pandro S. Berman)

A New York attorney solves the disappearance of a leading lady.
Wisecracking, debonair murder mystery modelled on *The Thin Man.*

w Howard J. Green, Anthony Veiller, Edward Kaufman *d* Stephen Roberts *ph* J. Roy Hunt *m* Max Steiner

William Powell, Ginger Rogers, Paul Kelly, Gene Lockhart, Ralph Morgan, Leslie Fenton, J. Farrell MacDonald

'It is all suavity and amusement, pistol shots and cocktails.'—*Graham Greene*

'One of the best sophisticated comedy-mysteries in a period full of such films.'—*NFT, 1973*

The Star Spangled Girl
US 1971 92m colour
Paramount (Howard W. Koch)

A sweet old-fashioned girl is fought for by two young radicals.
Unamusingly 'with it' comedy from an unsuccessful play.

w Arnold Margolin, Jim Parker, *play* Neil Simon *d* Jerry Paris *ph* Sam Leavitt *m* Charles Fox

Sandy Duncan, Tony Roberts, Todd Susman, Elizabeth Allen

Star Spangled Rhythm***
US 1942 99m bw
Paramount (Joseph Sistrom)

The doorman of Paramount Studios pretends to his sailor son that he is a big producer.
Frenetic farce involving most of the talent on Paramount's payroll and culminating in an 'impromptu' show staged for the navy. A good lighthearted glimpse of wartime Hollywood.

w Harry Tugend *d* George Marshall *ph* Leo Tover, Theodor Sparkuhl *md* Robert Emmett Dolan *songs* Johnny Mercer, Harold Arlen

Betty Hutton, Eddie Bracken, *Victor Moore, Walter Abel,* Anne Revere, Cass Daley, Gil Lamb, Macdonald Carey, Bob Hope, Bing Crosby, Paulette Goddard, Veronica Lake, Dorothy Lamour, Vera Zorina, Fred MacMurray, Ray Milland, Lynne Overman, Franchot Tone, Dick Powell, *Walter Dare Wahl and Co, Cecil B. de Mille, Preston Sturges,* Alan Ladd, Rochester, Katherine Dunham, Susan Hayward

The Star Witness*
US 1931 68m bw
Warner

An old man witnesses a crime and is threatened by gangsters.
Pacy melodrama with good performances.

w Lucien Hubbard *d* William Wellman *ph* James Van Trees

Walter Huston, Chic Sale, Grant Mitchell, Frances Starr, Sally Blane

Stars and Stripes Forever*
US 1952 89m Technicolor
TCF (Lamar Trotti)
GB title: *Marching Along*

In the 1890s John Philip Sousa, a bandmaster who wants to write ballads, finds success as a writer of marches.
Low-key musical biopic with predictably noisy numbers.

w Lamar Trotti, from Sousa's autobiography
d Henry Koster *ph* Charles G. Clarke
md Alfred Newman

Clifton Webb, Debra Paget, Robert Wagner, Ruth Hussey, Finlay Currie, Roy Roberts, Lester Matthews

The Stars Are Singing
US 1952 99m Technicolor
Paramount (Irving Asher)

A Polish refugee girl illegally enters the US and becomes an opera star.
Painless Cinderella fantasy in which everybody sings.

w Liam O'Brien *d* Norman Taurog *ph* Lionel Lindon *md* Victor Young

Anna Maria Alberghetti, Lauritz Melchior, Rosemary Clooney, Fred Clark, Mikhail Rasumny

Stars in My Crown*
US 1950 89m bw
MGM (William H. Wright)

A two-gun parson brings peace to a Tennessee town after the Civil War.
Sentimental family western, quite pleasantly made and performed.

w Margaret Pitts, *novel* Joe David Brown
d Jacques Tourneur *ph* Charles Schoenbaum
m Adolph Deutsch

Joel McCrea, Ellen Drew, Dean Stockwell, Juano Hernandez, James Mitchell, Lewis Stone, Alan Hale, Amanda Blake

The Stars Look Down**
GB 1939 110m bw
Grafton (Isadore Goldschmidt)

The son of a coal miner struggles to become an MP.
Economically but well made social drama from a popular novel, with good pace and backgrounds.

w J. B. Williams, A. J. Cronin, novel A. J. Cronin
d Carol Reed

Michael Redgrave, Margaret Lockwood, Edward Rigby, Emlyn Williams, Nancy Price, Allan Jeayes, Cecil Parker, Linden Travers

Stars over Broadway
US 1935 89m bw
Warner (Sam Bischoff)

Unremarkable musical, with unusual talent.

w Jerry Wald, Julius J. Epstein, Pat C. Flick
d William Keighley *ph* George Barnes
md Leo F. Forbstein *ch* Busby Berkeley, Bobby Connolly *songs* Harry Warren, Al Dubin

James Melton, Jane Froman, Pat O'Brien, Jean Muir, Frank McHugh, Marie Wilson, Frank Fay

Starsky and Hutch*
US 1975 75m colour TVM
Spelling–Goldberg

Two undercover cops are subject to murder attempts, and want to find out why.
Rough-and-tumble cop show with lots of car chases; it led to a successful series.

w William Blinn *d* Barry Lear

David Soul, Paul Michael Glaser, Buddy Lester, Richard Lynch

Start the Revolution without Me*
US 1969 90m Technicolor
Warner / Norbud

Two sets of twins get mixed up at the court of Louis XVI.
Historical spoof of the kind subsequently made familiar by Mel Brooks; the script might have suited Abbott and Costello better than these two actors.

w Fred Freeman, Lawrence J. Cohen *d* Bud Yorkin *ph* Jean Tournier *m* John Addison

Donald Sutherland, Gene Wilder, Hugh Griffith, Jack McGowran, Billie Whitelaw, Victor Spinetti, Ewa Aulin

State Fair**
US 1933 80m bw
Fox (Winfield Sheehan)

Dad wants his prize pig to win at the fair, but the younger members of his family have romance in mind.
Archetypal family film, much remade but never quite so pleasantly performed.

w Paul Green, Sonya Levien, *novel* Phil Stong
d Henry King *ph* Hal Mohr *md* Louis de Francesco

Will Rogers, Janet Gaynor, Lew Ayres, Sally Eilers, Norman Foster, Louise Dresser, Frank Craven, Victor Jory, Hobart Cavanaugh

'A pungent, good-humoured motion picture.' *Pare Lorentz*

'Vigour, freshness and sympathy abound in its admittedly idealized fantasy treatment of small-town life.' *Charles Higham, 1972*

State Fair**
US 1945 100m Technicolor
TCF (William Perlberg)

Musical remake with an amiable cast and a rousing score.

w/ly Oscar Hammerstein II *d* Walter Lang

ph Leon Shamroy *m Richard Rodgers*
md Alfred Newman

Charles Winninger, Jeanne Crain, Dana Andrews, Vivian Blaine, Dick Haymes, Fay Bainter, Frank McHugh, Percy Kilbride, Donald Meek

'Surely the sort of theme that clamours for movie treatment. But no, say Twentieth Century Fox: let's make the fair look like a night club. Let's look around for stars of pristine nonentity. Let's screw the camera down to the studio floor. The result, "an epic that sings to the skies . . . with glorious, glamorous new songs".'—*Richard Winnington*

State Fair
US 1962 118m De Luxe Cinemascope
TCF (Charles Brackett)

Dullsville modernized version, condescending towards the rurals and peopled by unattractive youngsters.

w Richard Breen *d* Jose Ferrer *ph* William C. Mellor *md* Alfred Newman

Pat Boone, Alice Faye, Tom Ewell, Pamela Tiffin, Ann-Margret, Bobby Darin, Wally Cox

State of the Union***
US 1948 110m bw
(MGM) Liberty Films (Frank Capra)

An estranged wife rejoins her husband when he is running for president.
Brilliantly scripted political comedy which unfortunately goes soft at the end but offers stimulating entertainment most of the way.

w Anthony Veiller, Myles Connelly, *play Howard Lindsay, Russel Crouse d Frank Capra ph* George J. Folsey *m* Victor Young

Spencer Tracy, Katharine Hepburn, Adolphe Menjou, Van Johnson, Angela Lansbury, Lewis Stone, Howard Smith, Raymond Walburn, Charles Dingle

'A triumphant film, marked all over by Frank Capra's artistry.'—*Howard Barnes*

State Secret**
GB 1950 104m bw
British Lion / London (Frank Launder, Sidney Gilliat)
US title: *The Great Manhunt*

In a Ruritanian country, spies pursue a surgeon, the only man who knows that the dictator is dead.
Hitchcockian chase comedy-thriller which is well detailed and rises to the heights on occasion.

wd Sidney Gilliat *ph* Robert Krasker
m William Alwyn

Douglas Fairbanks Jnr, Glynis Johns, Herbert Lom, Jack Hawkins, Walter Rilla, Karel Stepanek, Carl Jaffe

Station Six Sahara
GB 1962 101m bw
British Lion / CCC / Artur Brauner (Victor Lyndon)

Five men working on a remote Saharan pipeline quarrel over the favours of an American girl whose car crashes nearby.
Raging old-fashioned melodrama with the courage of its lack of convictions.

w Bryan Forbes, Brian Clemens *d* Seth Holt
ph Gerald Gibbs *m* Ron Grainer

Carroll Baker, Ian Bannen, Peter Van Eyck, Denholm Elliott, Mario Adorf, Jorg Felmy, Biff McGuire

Station West
US 1948 91m bw
RKO (Robert Sparks)

A saloon queen is the secret head of a gang of gold robbers.
Predictable but well made western patterned after *Destry Rides Again.*

w Frank Fenton, Winston Miller, *novel* Luke Short *d* Sidney Lanfield *ph* Harry J. Wild
m Heinz Roemheld

Dick Powell, Jane Greer, Agnes Moorehead, Burl Ives, Tom Powers, Gordon Oliver, Steve Brodie, Guinn Williams, Raymond Burr, Regis Toomey

The Statue
US 1970 89m Eastmancolor
Cinerama / Josef Shaftel (Anis Nohra)

A languages professor is embarrassed when his sculptress wife makes an immense nude statue of him—with someone else's private parts.
Strained phallic comedy which doesn't even make the most of its one joke.

w Alec Coppel, Denis Norden *d* Rod Amateau
ph Piero Portalupi *m* Riz Ortolani

David Niven, Virna Lisi, Robert Vaughn, Ann Bell, John Cleese, Hugh Burden

Stay Away Joe
US 1968 102m Metrocolor Panavision
MGM (Douglas Lawrence)

An Indian rodeo rider returns to his reservation, makes several romantic conquests, and helps a government rehabilitation scheme.
Thin if surprising vehicle for a singing star; all rather tedious.

w Michael A. Hoey, *novel* Dan Cushman

d Peter Tewkesbury *ph* Fred Koenekamp *m* Jack Marshall

Elvis Presley, Burgess Meredith, Joan Blondell, Katy Jurado, Thomas Gomez, Henry Jones, L. Q. Jones

Stay Hungry
US 1976 102m De Luxe
UA / Outov (Harold Schneider, Bob Rafaelson)

The heir to an Alabama estate annoys the locality by assembling a curious bunch of friends and making unexpected use of his money.
Rather obvious and pointless fable; well made but not very stimulating.

w Charles Gaines, Bob Rafaelson, *novel* Charles Gaines *d* Bob Rafaelson *ph* Victor Kemper *m* Bruce Langhorne, Byron Berline

Jeff Bridges, Sally Field, Arnold Schwarzenegger, R. G. Armstrong, Robert Englund, Roger E. Mosley

Steamboat Round the Bend*
US 1935 80m bw
TCF (Sol M. Wurtzel)

A Mississippi steamboat captain defeats his rival and finds evidence to clear his nephew of a murder charge.
Rather heavily-scripted star vehicle which sacrifices fun for atmosphere but is often good to look at.

w Dudley Nichols, Lamar Trotti, *novel* Ben Lucien Berman *d John Ford* *ph* George Schneiderman *m* Samuel Kaylin

Will Rogers, Anne Shirley, Eugene Pallette, John McGuire, Irvin S. Cobb, Berton Churchill, Stepin Fetchit, Roger Imhof, Raymond Hatton

The Steel Bayonet
GB 1957 85m bw Hammerscope
(UA) Hammer (Michael Carreras)

During the assault on Tunis a battle-weary platoon holds a farm against enemy attack.
Dreary cliché-ridden war melodrama peopled by all the usual types.

w Howard Clewes *d* Michael Carreras *ph* Jack Asher *m* Leonard Salzedo

Leo Genn, Kieron Moore, Michael Medwin, Robert Brown, Michael Ripper, John Paul, Bernard Horsfall

Steel Town
US 1952 84m Technicolor
U-I (Leonard Goldstein)

A steel president's nephew joins the company as a furnace hand.
Routine drama with an unusual background.

w Gerald Drayson Adams, Lou Breslow *d* George Sherman *ph* Charles P. Boyle *m* Joseph Gershenson

Ann Sheridan, John Lund, Howard Duff, James Best, Nancy Kulp

The Steel Trap*
US 1952 85m bw
TCF / Thor (Bert E. Friedlob)

An assistant bank manager steals half a million dollars from the vault but is troubled by conscience and manages to put it back before the loss is discovered.
Solidly competent little suspenser with plenty of movement.

wd Andrew Stone *ph* Ernest Laszlo *m* Dmitri Tiomkin

Joseph Cotten, Teresa Wright, Jonathan Hale, Walter Sande

Steelyard Blues
US 1972 92m Technicolor
Warner / S. B. Productions (Tony Bill, Michael and Julia Phillips)

An ex-con and his call-girl friend are an embarrassment to his DA brother.
Bits and pieces of anti-establishment comedy are tacked on to a thin plot; a few of them work.

w David S. Ward *d* Alan Myerson *ph* Laszlo Kovacs, Steven Larner *m* Nick Gravenites

Donald Sutherland, Jane Fonda, Peter Boyle, Howard Hesseman

Stella Dallas*
US 1937 106m bw
Samuel Goldwyn

A crude, common woman embarrasses her blueblood husband and smothers her daughter with mother-love.
Antediluvian silent weepie quite fashionably remade with excellent talent; 1937 audiences came to sneer and stayed to weep.

w Victor Heerman, Sara Y. Mason *d King Vidor* *ph* Rudolph Maté *m* Alfred Newman

Barbara Stanwyck, John Boles, Anne Shirley, Barbara O'Neil, Alan Hale, Marjorie Main, Tim Holt

Step Down to Terror
US 1959 76m bw
U-I (Joseph Gershenson)
GB title: *The Silent Stranger*

A man returns to his home town and is discovered to be a psychopathic killer on the run.

Dismal reworking of *Shadow of a Doubt*; strictly second feature stuff.

w Mel Dinelli, Czenzi Ormonde, Chris Cooper *d* Harry Keller *ph* Russell Metty *m* Joseph Gershenson

Charles Drake, Coleen Miller, Rod Taylor, Josephine Hutchinson, Jocelyn Brando

Step Lively*
US 1944 88m bw
RKO (Robert Fellows)

Gleaming musical remake of *Room Service* (qv); all very efficient if witless.

w Warren Duff, Peter Milne *d* Tim Whelan *ph* Robert de Grasse *md* Constantin Bakaleinikoff *songs* Jule Styne, Sammy Cahn

Frank Sinatra, George Murphy, Adolphe Menjou, Gloria de Haven, Anne Jeffreys, Walter Slezak, Eugene Pallette

A Step Out of Line*
US 1970 100m colour TVM
Cinema Center

Korean War buddies use their skills in a daring civilian robbery.
Okay crime comedy.

d Bernard McEveety

Vic Morrow, Peter Falk, Peter Lawford, Jo Ann Pflug

The Stepford Wives*
US 1974 110m colour
Palomar (Edgar J. Scherick)

In a small Connecticut community, the bored wives are all taken over by an alien force.
Drawn out suspenser with a rather silly explanation.

w William Goldman, *novel* Ira Levin *d* Bryan Forbes *ph* Owen Roizman *m* Michael Small

Katharine Ross, Nanette Newman, Paula Prentiss, Peter Masterson

Steptoe and Son
GB 1972 98m Technicolor
EMI / Associated London Films (Aida Young)

Harold gets married, mislays his wife but thinks he is a father.
Strained attempt to transfer the TV rag-and-bone comedy (which in the US became *Sanford and Son*) to the big screen. Not the same thing at all.

w Ray Galton, Alan Simpson *d* Cliff Owen *ph* John Wilcox *m* Roy Budd, Jack Fishman

Wilfrid Brambell, Harry H. Corbett, Carolyn Seymour, Arthur Howard, Victor Maddern

† *Steptoe and Son Ride Again*, which followed in 1973, was even more crude and out of character.

The Sterile Cuckoo
US 1969 107m Technicolor
Paramount / Boardwalk (Alan J. Pakula)
GB title: *Pookie*

A talkative but insecure college girl has her first sexual adventures.
Rather tiresome comedy drama with good scenes; general handling far too restrained.

w Alvin Sargent, *novel* John Nicholson *d* Alan J. Pakula *ph* Milton Krasner *m* Fred Karlin

Liza Minnelli, Tim McIntire, Wendell Burton, Austin Green, Sandra Faison

Stiletto
US 1969 99m Berkey–Pathe
Avco / Harold Robbins

A wealthy playboy racing driver is in fact a Mafia executioner.
Dreary, violent, fashionable Mafioso melodrama with international jet set trimmings.

w A. J. Russsell, *novel* Harold Robbins *d* Bernard Kowalski *ph* Jack Priestly *m* Sid Ramin

Alex Cord, Britt Ekland, Barbara McNair, Patrick O'Neal, Joseph Wiseman, John Dehner, Eduardo Ciannelli, Roy Scheider

The Sting**
US 1973 129m Technicolor
Universal / Richard Zanuck, David Brown (Tony Bill, Michael S. Phillips)

In twenties Chicago, two con men stage an elaborate revenge on a big time gangster who caused the death of a friend.
Bright, likeable, but overlong, unconvincingly studio-set and casually developed comedy suspenser cashing in on star charisma but riding to enormous success chiefly on its tinkly music and the general lack of simple entertainment.

w David S. Ward *d George Roy Hill* *ph* Robert Surtees *m Scott Joplin* (arranged by Marvin Hamlisch) *ad* Henry Bumstead

Paul Newman, *Robert Redford*, Robert Shaw, Charles Durning, Ray Walston, Eileen Brennan

'A visually claustrophobic, mechanically plotted movie that's meant to be a roguishly charming entertainment.'—*New Yorker*

'It demonstrates what can happen when a gifted young screenwriter has the good fortune to fall among professionals his second time out.'—*Judith Crist*

A Stitch in Time
GB 1963 94m bw
Rank (Hugh Stewart)

A butcher's boy goes into hospital and falls for a nurse.
Thin star slapstick; all one can say is that it's marginally preferable to Jerry Lewis.

w Jack Davies *d* Robert Asher *ph* Jack Asher *m* Philip Green

Norman Wisdom, Edward Chapman, Jerry Desmonde, Jeanette Sterke, Jill Melford

Stolen Hours
GB 1963 97m De Luxe
UA / Mirisch / Barbican (Denis Holt)

An American divorcee with only a year to live falls in love with her surgeon.
Tired remake of *Dark Victory*; pleasant Cornish backgrounds.

w Jessamyn West *d* Daniel Petrie *ph* Harry Waxman *m* Mort Lindsey

Susan Hayward, Michael Craig, Diane Baker, Edward Judd, Paul Rogers

A Stolen Life*
GB 1938 91m bw
(Paramount) Orion (Anthony Havelock-Allan)

In Brittany, a woman deceives her husband by exchanging identities with her dead twin.
An actress's showcase, quite satisfactorily mounted.

w Margaret Kennedy, George Barraud, *novel* Karel J. Benes *d* Paul Czinner

Elisabeth Bergner, Michael Redgrave, Wilfrid Lawson, Richard Ainley, Mabel Terry-Lewis, Clement McCallin

A Stolen Life*
US 1946 107m bw
Warner (Bette Davis)

Enjoyable if slightly disappointing remake with New England backgrounds.

w Catherine Turney *d* Curtis Bernhardt *ph* Sol Polito, Ernest Haycox *m* Max Steiner

Bette Davis, Glenn Ford, Dane Clark, Walter Brennan, Charles Ruggles, Bruce Bennett, Peggy Knudsen, Esther Dale

'A distressingly empty piece of show-off.'—*Bosley Crowther*

'What I'm waiting for is a film about beautiful identical quintuplets who all love the same man.'—*Richard Winnington*

The Stone Killer*
US 1973 96m Technicolor
Columbia / Dino de Laurentiis (Michael Winner)

A brutal Los Angeles police detective takes on the Mafia.
Fast-moving amalgam of chases and violence with a downbeat hero.

w Gerald Wilson, *novel* A Complete State of Death by John Gardner *d* Michael Winner *ph* Richard Moore *m* Roy Budd

Charles Bronson, Martin Balsam, Ralph Waite, David Sheiner, Norman Fell

'Film-making as painting by numbers.'—*Sight and Sound*

The Stooge
US 1951 100m bw
Paramount / Hal B. Wallis

In 1930 a conceited song and dance man fails to realize that his moronic stooge is the act's real attraction.
Typical, and particularly resistible, Martin and Lewis concoction: whenever one thinks of laughing, a dollop of sentimentality comes along and promptly quashes the idea.

w Fred Finkelhoffe, Martin Rackin *d* Norman Taurog *ph* Daniel L. Fapp *m* Joseph J. Lilley

Dean Martin, Jerry Lewis, Polly Bergen, Marie McDonald, Eddie Mayehoff, Marion Marshall, Richard Erdman

Stop You're Killing Me
US 1953 86m Warnercolor
Warner (Louis F. Edelman)

At the end of prohibition a beer baron decides to go straight, but finds his house filled with the corpses of rival gangsters.
Frantic remake of *A Slight Case of Murder* with a few musical numbers added; all rather messy.

w James O'Hanlon *d* Roy del Ruth *ph* Ted McCord *md* Ray Heindorf

Broderick Crawford, Claire Trevor, Virginia Gibson, Bill Hayes, Sheldon Leonard, Joe Vitale, Howard St John, Henry Morgan, Margaret Dumont

Stopover Tokyo
US 1957 100m Eastmancolor Cinemascope
TCF (Walter Reisch)

An American spy in Tokyo seeks to capture a communist undercover man.
Sprawling espionage stuff with frequent halts for scenic tours.

· Richard L. Breen, Walter Reisch, *novel* John

P. Marquand *d* Richard L. Breen *ph* Charles G. Clarke *m* Paul Sawtell

Robert Wagner, Joan Collins, Edmond O'Brien, Ken Scott, Larry Keating

The Stork Club
US 1945 98m bw
Paramount (B. G. De Sylva)

A nightclub hat-check girl saves an elderly millionaire from drowning.
Very light comedy with music, a great ad for a once famous night haunt.

w B. G. De Sylva, John McGowan *d* Hal Walker *ph* Charles Lang Jnr *md* Robert Emmett Dolan

Betty Hutton, Barry Fitzgerald, Don Defore, Robert Benchley, Bill Goodwin, Iris Adrian, Mary Young, Mikhail Rasumny

Storm Center
US 1956 87m bw
Columbia / Phoenix (Julian Blaustein)

A small-town librarian is dismissed when she refuses to remove a communist book from the shelves.
Formula anti-McCarthy melodrama originally designed for Mary Pickford's comeback; not very absorbing and rather dingily produced.

w Daniel Taradash, Elick Moll *d* Daniel Taradash *ph* Burnett Guffey *m* George Duning

Bette Davis, Brian Keith, Kim Hunter, Paul Kelly, Joe Mantell

Storm Fear
US 1955 88m bw
(UA) Theodora (Cornel Wilde)

Three fugitives from justice hide in a mountain cabin, but all meet violent deaths.
Gloomy, strenuous melodrama, partly shot outdoors.

w Horton Foote, *novel* Clinton Seeley *d* Cornel Wilde *ph* Joseph La Shelle *m* Elmer Bernstein

Cornel Wilde, Jean Wallace, Dan Duryea, Lee Grant, Steven Hill, Dennis Weaver

Storm in a Teacup*
GB 1936 87m bw
Alexander Korda / Victor Saville

A national sensation ensues when a Scottish provost fines an old lady for not licensing her dog, and she refuses to pay.
Early Ealing-type comedy, a bit emaciated by later standards.

w Ian Dalrymple, Donald Bull, *play* Sturm in Wasserglass by Bruno Frank *d* Ian Dalrymple, Victor Saville *ph* Max Greene

Vivien Leigh, Rex Harrison, Cecil Parker, Sara Allgood, Ursula Jeans, Gus McNaughton, Arthur Wontner

Storm over Lisbon
US 1944 86m bw
Republic (George Sherman)

An international spy mastermind runs a Lisbon night club and sells documents to the highest bidder.
Feeble copy of *Casablanca*.

w Doris Gilbert, Dane Lussier *d* George Sherman *ph* John Alton *m* Walter Scharf

Vera Hruba Ralston, Erich Von Stroheim, Richard Arlen, Mary Nash, Sidney Blackmer, Helen Vinson, Bill Henry

Storm over the Nile
GB 1955 107m Technicolor Cinemascope
Independent / London (Zoltan Korda)

Feeble remake of *The Four Feathers* (qv), using most of that film's action highlights stretched out to fit the wide screen.

w R. C. Sheriff *d* Zoltan Korda *ph* Ted Scaife, Osmond Borradaile *m* Benjamin Frankel

Anthony Steel, Laurence Harvey, Ronald Lewis, Ian Carmichael, James Robertson Justice, Mary Ure, Geoffrey Keen, Jack Lambert, Ferdy Mayne, Michael Hordern

'The material appears not so much dated as fossilized within its period.'—*Penelope Houston*

Storm over Tibet
US 1951 87m bw
Columbia / Summit (Ivan Tors, Laslo Benedek)

An explorer steals a holy mask which brings bad luck.
Slight adventure yarn ingeniously built around an old German documentary.

w Ivan Tors, Sam Mayer *d* Andrew Marton *ph* George E. Diskant, Richard Angst *m* Arthur Honegger

Rex Reason, Diana Douglas, Myron Healey

Storm Warning*
US 1950 93m bw
Warner (Jerry Wald)

A New York model goes south to visit her sister, and finds that her brother-in-law is an oversexed brute and a Ku Klux Klan killer.
Heavy melodrama disguised as a social document; sufficiently arresting for its purposes.

w Daniel Fuchs, Richard Brooks *d* Stuart

Heisler *ph* Carl Guthrie *m* Daniele Amfitheatrof

Ginger Rogers, Doris Day, *Steve Cochran*, Ronald Reagan, Hugh Sanders, Raymond Greenleaf, Ned Glass

Stormy Weather***
US 1943 77m bw
TCF (Irving Mills)

A backstage success story lightly based on the career of Bill Robinson.
Virtually a high-speed revue with all-black talent, and what talent! The production is pretty slick too.

w Frederick Jackson, Ted Koehler *d Andrew Stone ph Leon Shamroy, Fred Sersen md Benny Carter ch* Clarence Robinson

Bill Robinson, Lena Horne, Fats Waller, Ada Brown, Cab Calloway, Katherine Dunham and her Dancers, Eddie Anderson, Flournoy Miller, *The Nicholas Brothers*, Dooley Wilson

The Story of a Woman
US / Italy 1969 101m Technicolor
Universal / Westward (Leonardo Bercovici)

A Swedish girl pianist in Rome falls in love with a fashionable doctor, then back in Sweden meets an American diplomat.
Intermezzo-type romantic drama with colour supplement trappings. Tolerable of its kind.

wd Leonardo Bercovici *ph* Piero Portalupi *m* John Williams

Robert Stack, Bibi Andersson, James Farentino, Annie Girardot, Frank Sundstrom

The Story of Alexander Graham Bell**
US 1939 97m bw
TCF (Kenneth MacGowan)
GB title: *The Modern Miracle*

The inventor of the telephone marries a deaf girl.
Acceptable history lesson with dullish principals but excellent production.

w Lamar Trotti *d* Irving Cummings *ph* Leon Shamroy

Don Ameche, Henry Fonda, Loretta Young, Charles Coburn, Gene Lockhart, Spring Byington, Bobs Watson

A Story of David
GB 1960 99m Eastmancolor TVM
William Goetz / Scoton / Mardeb (George Pitcher)

David's trouble with King Saul.
Competent biblical mini-epic.

w Gerry Day, Terence Maple d Bob McNaught *ph* Arthur Ibbetson *m* Kenneth V. Jones

Jeff Chandler, Basil Sydney, David Knight, Barbara Shelley, Richard O'Sullivan, Donald Pleasence

The Story of David
US 1976 200m colour TVM
Columbia / Milburg Theatrical (Mildred Freed Alburg)

David's life from his battle with Goliath to the end of his reign.
Ho-hum religious biopic, overlong and sententious.

w Ernest Kinoy *d* Alex Segal, David Lowell Rich *m* Laurence Rosenthal

Timothy Bottoms, Keith Michell, Anthony Quayle, Jane Seymour, Susan Hampshire, Norman Rodway, Brian Blessed, Barry Morse

The Story of Dr Wassell*
US 1944 140m Technicolor
Paramount / Cecil B. de Mille

The adventures of a naval doctor who heroically saved men during the Pacific war.
Long, slogging, glamorized account of real events which is typical de Mille and very unconvincing physically, but keeps one watching simply as a story.

w Alan le May, Charles Bennett, *book* James Hilton *d* Cecil B. de Mille *ph* Victor Milner, William Snyder *m* Victor Young

Gary Cooper, Laraine Day, Signe Hasso, Dennis O'Keefe, Carol Thurston, Carl Esmond, Paul Kelly, Stanley Ridges

'The director has taken a true story of heroism . . . and jangled it into a cacophony of dancing girls, phoney self-sacrifice and melodramatic romance.'—*Howard Barnes*

The Story of Esther Costello*
GB 1957 103m bw
Columbia / Romulus (James Woolf)
US title: *The Golden Virgin*

A blind Irish deaf mute girl is adopted by an American socialite and her plight becomes an international cause.
Rich melodrama develops from this unlikely premise and the star enjoys it hugely.

w Charles Kaufman, *novel* Nicholas Monsarrat *d* David Miller *ph* Raoul Kraushaar *m* Georges Auric

Joan Crawford, Heather Sears, Rossano Brazzi, Ron Randell, Lee Patrick, Fay Compton, John Loder, Dennis O'Dea, Sidney James, Maureen Delany

The Story of GI Joe**
US 1945 108m bw
(UA) Lester Cowan (David Hall)
aka: *War Correspondent*

Journalist Ernie Pyle follows fighting men into the Italian campaign.
Slow, convincing, sympathetic war film with good script and performances; not by any means the usual action saga.

w Leopold Atlas, Guy Endore, Philip Stevenson, *book Ernie Pyle* *d William A. Wellman* *ph Russell Metty* *m* Ann Ronell, Louise Applebaum

Burgess Meredith, Robert Mitchum, Freddie Steele, Wally Cassell, Jimmy Lloyd, Jack Reilly

'It is humorous, poignant and tragic, an earnestly human reflection of a stern life and the dignity of man.'—*Thomas M. Pryor*

'A tragic and eternal work of art.'—*James Agee*

The Story of Gilbert and Sullivan*
GB 1953 109m Technicolor
British Lion / London Films (Frank Launder, Sidney Gilliat)

In 1875 a young composer named Arthur Sullivan and a librettist named William Gilbert come together under the auspices of Rupert D'Oyly Carte and write the Savoy Operas.
Light, accurate, well-cast and well-produced Victorian musical which somehow fails to ignite despite the immense talent at hand.

w Sidney Gilliat, Leslie Baily *d* Sidney Gilliat *ph* Christopher Challis *md* Sir Malcolm Sargent *pd* Hein Heckroth

Robert Morley, Maurice Evans, Peter Finch, Eileen Herlie, Dinah Sheridan, Isabel Dean, Wilfrid Hyde White, Muriel Aked

The Story of Jacob and Joseph
US 1974 100m colour TVM
Columbia / Milburg Theatrical (Mildred Freed Alburg)

Another biblical biopic, rather patchy and obliquely narrated.

w Ernest Kinoy *d* Michael Cacoyannis *m* Mikis Theodorakis

Keith Michell, Tony Lo Bianco, Colleen Dewhurst, Herschel Bernardi, Harry Andrews, Alan Bates (narrator)

The Story of Louis Pasteur***
US 1935 85m bw
Warner (Henry Blanke)

How the eminent 19th-century French scientist overcomes obstacles in finding cures for various diseases.
Adequate biopic which caused a sensation and started a trend; some of the others were better but this was the first example of Hollywood bringing schoolbook history to box office life.

w Sheridan Gibney, Pierre Collins *d William Dieterle* *ph* Tony Gaudio *m Erich Wolfgang Korngold*

Paul Muni, Josephine Hutchinson, Anita Louise, Donald Woods, Fritz Leiber, Henry O'Neill, Porter Hall, Akim Tamiroff, Walter Kingsford

'What should be vital and arresting has been made hollow and dull . . . we are tendered something that is bright and stagey for something out of life.'—*Otis Ferguson*

'More exciting than any gangster melodrama.' —*C. A. Lejeune*

The Story of Mankind
US 1957 100m Technicolor
Warner / Cambridge (Irwin Allen)

A heavenly tribunal debates whether to allow man to destroy himself, and both the Devil and the Spirit of Man cite instances from history.
Hilarious charade, one of the worst films ever made, but full of surprises, bad performances, and a wide range of stock shots.

w Irwin Allen, Charles Bennett, *book* Henrik Van Loon *d* Irwin Allen *ph* Nicholas Musuraca *m* Paul Sawtell

Ronald Colman, Vincent Price, Cedric Hardwicke, the Marx Brothers, Hedy Lamarr, Agnes Moorehead, Reginald Gardiner, Peter Lorre, Virginia Mayo, Charles Coburn, Francis X. Bushman

The Story of Robin Hood and his Merrie Men
GB 1952 84m Technicolor
Walt Disney (Perce Pearce)

When Prince John starts a ruthless taxation campaign, Robert Fitzooth turns outlaw.
Fairly competent but quite forgettable version of the legend, softened for children.

w Laurence E. Watkin *d* Ken Annakin *ph* Guy Green *m* Clifton Parker

Richard Todd, Joan Rice, James Hayter, Hubert Gregg, James Robertson Justice, Martita Hunt, Peter Finch

The Story of Ruth
US 1960 132m De Luxe Cinemascope
TCF (Samuel G. Engel)

Ruth becomes the favourite of a pagan king but eventually flees to Israel.
Tedious, portentous bible-in-pictures, of virtually no interest or entertainment value.

w Norman Corwin *d* Henry Koster *ph* Arthur E. Arling *m* Franz Waxman

Elana Eden, Peggy Wood, Viveca Lindfors, Stuart Whitman, Tom Tryon, Jeff Morrow, Thayer David, Eduard Franz

The Story of Seabiscuit
US 1949 98m Technicolor
Warner (William Jacobs)
GB title: *Pride of Kentucky*

The success story of a racehorse.
Blue grass vapidities, the kind of family entertainment that drove the families away.

w John Taintor Foote *d* David Butler *ph* Wilfrid Cline *md* David Buttolph

Shirley Temple, Barry Fitzgerald, Lon McCallister, Rosemary de Camp, Donald McBride, Pierre Watkin

The Story of Temple Drake*
US 1933 71m bw
Paramount

A neurotic southern flapper is abducted by gangsters, and likes it.
Deliberately shocking melodrama of its time, restructured from a notorious book later filmed under its own title. Very dated, but interesting.

w Oliver H. P. Garrett, *novel* Sanctuary by William Faulkner *d* Stephen Roberts *ph* Karl Struss

Miriam Hopkins, Jack La Rue, William Gargan, William Collier Jnr, Irving Pichel, Guy Standing, Elizabeth Patterson, Florence Eldridge

The Story of Three Loves
US 1953 122m Technicolor
MGM (Sidney Franklin)

Three love stories concerning the passengers on a transatlantic liner.
Three bits of old-fashioned kitsch, one tragic, one whimsical, one melodramatic, all rather slow and dull though well produced.

w John Collier, Jan Lustig, George Froeschel *d* Gottfried Reinhardt, Vincente Minnelli *ph* Charles Rosher, Harold Rosson *m* Miklos Rozsa

Ethel Barrymore, James Mason, Moira Shearer, Pier Angeli, Leslie Caron, Kirk Douglas, Farley Granger, Agnes Moorehead, Zsa Zsa Gabor

The Story of Vernon and Irene Castle**
US 1939 93m bw
RKO (George Haight, Pandro S. Berman)

The story of a husband and wife dance team who had their first success in Paris and became influential international celebrities before he was killed as a flier in World War I.
Pleasant understated musical with very agreeable dance sequences and a firm overall style. The last of the main stream of Astaire-Rogers musicals.

w Richard Sherman, Oscar Hammerstein II, Dorothy Yost, *books* Irene Castle *d H. C. Potter ph Robert de Grasse md* Victor Baravalle *ch Hermes Pan ad Van Nest Polglase*

Fred Astaire, Ginger Rogers, Edna May Oliver, Walter Brennan, Lew Fields, Etienne Girardot, Donald MacBride

The Story of Will Rogers
US 1950 109m Technicolor
Warner (Robert Arthur)

A wild west performer becomes a Ziegfeld star and pop philosopher.
Bland, unshaped biopic of one of American show business's best loved figures, who died in an air crash in 1935.

w Frank Davis, Stanley Roberts *d* Michael Curtiz *ph* Wilfrid M. Cline *md* Victor Young

Will Rogers Jnr, Jane Wyman, James Gleason, Eddie Cantor (as himself), Carl Benton Reid

The Story on Page One
US 1960 123m bw Cinemascope
TCF / Company of Artists

A lawyer undertakes the defence of a woman who with her lover is charged with the murder of her husband.
Long drawn out and not very interesting courtroom drama, performed and presented with some style.

wd Clifford Odets *ph* James Wong Howe *m* Elmer Bernstein

Rita Hayworth, Tony Franciosa, Gig Young, Mildred Dunnock, Hugh Griffith, Sanford Meisner, Alfred Ryder

Stowaway*
US 1936 86m bw
TCF (Earl Carroll, Harold Wilson)

The orphan daughter of a Shanghai missionary stows away on an American pleasure ship.
Very good star vehicle in which Shirley performs some of her best musical numbers.

w William Conselman, Arthur Sheekman, Nat

Perrin *d* William A. Seiter *ph* Arthur Miller *md* Louis Silvers

Shirley Temple, Robert Young, Alice Faye, Eugene Pallette, Helen Westley, Arthur Treacher, J. Edward Bromberg, Astrid Allwyn

Stowaway to the Moon
US 1974 100m colour TVM
TCF (John Cutts)

An 11-year-old boy stows away on a space flight.
Prolonged juvenile adventure.

w William R. Shelton, Jon Boothe *d* Andrew V. McLaglen

Lloyd Bridges, Michael Link, John Carradine, Pete Conrad, Jeremy Slate

Straight on Till Morning
GB 1972 96m Technicolor
EMI / Hammer (Roy Skeggs)

A Liverpool girl in London meets a dangerous psychotic.
Unattractive suspenser, wildly directed.

w Michael Peacock *d* Peter Collinson *ph* Brian Probyn *m* Roland Shaw

Rita Tushingham, Shane Briant, Tom Bell, Annie Ross, James Bolam

Strait Jacket
US 1963 92m bw
Columbia / William Castle

A woman who murdered her faithless husband with an axe is released twenty years later, and more axe murders occur.
Dull and unattractive shocker in which all concerned lean over backwards to conceal the trick ending.

w Robert Bloch *d* William Castle *ph* Arthur E. Arling *m* Van Alexander

Joan Crawford, Diane Baker, Leif Erickson, Howard St John, Rochelle Hudson, George Kennedy

The Strange Affair
GB 1968 106m Techniscope
Paramount (Howard Harrison, Stanley Mann)

A young London policeman finds that his superiors are almost as corrupt as the villains.
Stylishly made melodrama of despair, with a sexy nymphet heroine straight from swinging London. It all leaves a sour taste in the mouth.

w Stanley Mann, *novel* Bernard Toms *d David Greene* *ph* Max Thompson *m* Basil Kirchin

Michael York, Jeremy Kemp, Susan George, Jack Watson, George A. Cooper

The Strange and Deadly Occurrence*
US 1975 74m colour TVM
Alpine / Charles Fries

A couple feel that their brand new house is haunted.
Stylish but rather strained suspenser with a lame ending.

w Sandor Stern *d* John Llewellyn Moxey

Robert Stack, Vera Miles, L. Q. Jones, Herb Edelman, Margaret Willock

Strange Bedfellows
US 1965 99m Technicolor
U-I / Panama–Frank (Melvin Frank)

An American executive in London nearly divorces his fiery Italian wife.
Frantic sex comedy with picture postcard background; fatiguing rather than funny, but with minor compensations.

w Melvin Frank, Michael Pertwee *d* Melvin Frank *ph* Leo Tover

Rock Hudson, Gina Lollobrigida, Gig Young, Edward Judd, Howard St John, Arthur Haynes, Dave King, Terry-Thomas

'The grind of predictable situations is further afflicted by considerable lapses in taste.'—*MFB*

Strange Cargo*
US 1940 105m bw
MGM (Joseph L. Mankiewicz)

Eight convicts escape from Devil's Island and are influenced by a Christ-like fugitive.
One of Hollywood's occasional lunacies; one doubts whether even the author knew the point of this cockamamy parable, but it was well produced and acted.

w Lawrence Hazard, *novel* Not Too Narrow, Not Too Deep by Richard Sale *d* Frank Borzage *ph* Robert Planck *m* Franz Waxman

Clark Gable, Joan Crawford, Ian Hunter, Peter Lorre, Paul Lukas, Albert Dekker, J. Edward Bromberg, Eduardo Ciannelli, Frederick Worlock

The Strange Door*
US 1951 81m bw
U-I (Ted Richmond)

A young nobleman, passing through the one-way door of a castle, finds himself the prisoner of a madman.
Torture-chamber suspenser, adequately if rather tediously developed, with most of its interest reposing in the cast.

w Jerry Sackheim, *story* The Sire de Maletroit's Door by Robert Louis Stevenson *d* Joseph

Pevney *ph* Irving Glassberg *m* Joseph Gershenson

Charles Laughton, Boris Karloff, Michael Pate, Sally Forrest, Richard Stapley, Alan Napier

Strange Homecoming
US 1974 74m colour TVM
Alpine / Charles Fries

A burglar and murderer goes home for the first time in years and his family think him charming.
Anyone seen *Shadow of a Doubt* lately? It was better.

w Eric Bercovici *d* Lee H. Katzin

Robert Culp, Glen Campbell, Barbara Anderson, Whitney Blake

Strange Interlude**
US 1932 110m bw
MGM (Irving Thalberg)

Problems of an unfulfilled wife and her lover.
Surprising film version of a very heavy modern classic, complete with asides to the audience; very dated now, but a small milestone in Hollywood's development.

w Bess Meredyth, C. Gardner Sullivan, *play* Eugene O'Neill *d* Robert Z. Leonard *ph* Lee Garmes

Norma Shearer, Clark Gable, May Robson, Alexander Kirkland, Ralph Morgan, Robert Young, Maureen O'Sullivan, Henry B. Walthall

'A cinematic novelty to be seen by discerning audiences.'—*Film Weekly*

'More exciting than a thousand "action" movies.'—*Pare Lorentz*

Strange Intruder
US 1957 78m bw
AA (Lindsley Parsons)

A psychopathic ex-POW menaces the children of his dead friend's wife.
Gloomy second feature melodrama, rather well presented.

w David Evans, Warren Douglas, *novel* Helen Fowler *d* Irving Rapper *ph* Ernest Haller *m* Paul Dunlap

Edmund Purdom, Ida Lupino, Ann Harding, Jacques Bergerac, Carl Benton Reid

Strange Lady in Town
US 1955 118m Warnercolor Cinemascope
Warner (Mervyn Le Roy)

Adventures of a woman doctor in 1880 Santa Fe.
Quaint western drama which is never any more convincing than its star.

w Frank Butler *d* Mervyn Le Roy *ph* Harold Rosson *m* Dmitri Tiomkin

Greer Garson, Dana Andrews, Cameron Mitchell, Lois Smith, Walter Hampden

The Strange Love of Martha Ivers**
US 1946 116m bw
Paramount / Hal B. Wallis

A murderous child becomes a wealthy woman with a spineless lawyer husband; the melodrama starts when an ex-boy friend returns to town.
Irresistible star melodrama which leaves no stone unturned; compulsive entertainment of the old school.

w Robert Rossen *d* Lewis Milestone *ph* Victor Milner *m* Miklos Rozsa

Barbara Stanwyck, Van Heflin, Kirk Douglas, Lizabeth Scott, Judith Anderson, Roman Bohnen

Strange New World
US 1975 100m colour TVM
Warner

Three scientists return to earth after 200 years in a time capsule and find things very changed: women rule.
Third attempt at a new space fiction format. The other pilots were *Genesis II* and *Planet Earth*, and after this one they gave up.

w Al Ramrus, Ronald F. Graham, Walon Green *d* Robert Butler

John Saxon, Kathleen Miller, Keene Curtis, James Olson, Martine Beswick

The Strange One*
US 1957 99m bw
Columbia / Sam Spiegel
GB title: *End as a Man*

A sadistic cadet causes trouble at a southern military college.
A weird and unsavoury but rather compelling melodrama which unreels like a senior version of *Tom Brown's Schooldays*.

w Calder Willingham, from his novel End as a Man *d* Jack Garfein *ph* Burnett Guffey *m* Kenyon Hopkins

Ben Gazzara, George Peppard, Mark Richman, Pat Hingle, Arthur Storch, Paul Richards, Geoffrey Horne, James Olson

'The film's brilliance is in its persuasive depiction of a highly controversial, artificially organized world; its failure is to make any dramatic statement about it.'—*MFB*

The Strange Woman
US 1946 100m bw
(UA) Hunt Stromberg (Jack Chertok)

A scheming woman plays with the lives of three men.
Star wish-fulfilment; otherwise a hammy costume piece.

w Herb Meadows, *novel* Ben Ames Williams *d* Edgar G. Ulmer *ph* Lucien Andriot *m* Carmen Dragon

Hedy Lamarr, George Sanders, Louis Hayward, Gene Lockhart, Hillary Brooke

The Stranger*
US 1946 95m bw
(RKO) Sam Spiegel

An escaped Nazi criminal marries an American woman and settles in a Connecticut village.
Highly unconvincing and artificial melodrama enhanced by directorial touches, splendid photography and no-holds-barred climax involving a church clock.

w Anthony Veiller, *story* Victor Trivas, Decia Dunning *d Orson Welles ph Russell Metty* *m* Bronislau Kaper

Edward G. Robinson, Orson Welles, Loretta Young, Philip Merivale, Richard Long, Konstatin Shayne

'Some striking effects, with lighting and interesting angles much relied on.'—*Bosley Crowther*

The Stranger*
US 1972 98m colour TVM
Bing Crosby Productions (Alan A. Armer)

An astronaut crashes on another planet and becomes a fugitive from the authorities.
Lively chase pilot which just didn't catch on.

w Gerald Sanford *d* Lee H. Katzin

Glenn Corbett, Cameron Mitchell, Lew Ayres, Sharon Acker, Dean Jagger, Tim O'Connor, George Coulouris

Stranger at My Door
US 1956 85m bw
Republic (Sidney Picker)

A gunman takes refuge in the house of a preacher who tries to convert him.
Odd, sentimental little western morality play, not badly presented.

w Barry Shipman *d* William Witney *ph* Bud Thackery *m* Dale Butts

Macdonald Carey, Skip Homeier, Patricia Medina, Louis Jean Heydt

A Stranger in My Arms
US 1958 88m bw Cinemascope
U-I (Ross Hunter)

A test pilot falls in love with his dead friend's widow and helps her face up to her in-laws.
Dreary romantic drama.

w Peter Berneis, *novel* And Ride a Tiger by Robert Wilder *d* Helmut Kautner *ph* William Daniels *m* Joseph Gershenson

June Allyson, Jeff Chandler, *Mary Astor*, Sandra Dee, Charles Coburn, Conrad Nagel, Peter Graves

Stranger on the Run*
US 1967 97m Technicolor TVM
Universal (Richard E. Lyons)

A tramp arrives in a western town and becomes a murder suspect.
Routine western with the usual messages about goodwill towards men.

w Dean Riesner, *story* Reginald Rose *d* Don Siegel

Henry Fonda, Michael Parks, Anne Baxter, Dan Duryea, Sal Mineo

The Stranger Who Looks Like Me
US 1974 74m colour TVM
Filmways

An adopted girl searches for her real mother.
Efficient tearjerker.

w Gerald di Pego *d* Larry Peerce

Meredith Baxter, Beau Bridges, Whitney Blake, Walter Brooke, Neva Patterson

The Stranger Within*
US 1974 74m colour TVM
Lorimar

A pregnant mother is bizarrely controlled by her own unborn child.
The start of the monstrous baby cycle (*The Devil within Her, It's Alive, I Don't Want to Be Born*, etc). More subtle than most.

w Richard Matheson *d* Lee Philips

Barbara Eden, George Grizzard, Joyce Van Patten, David Doyle, Nehemiah Persoff

The Strangers in 7A*
US 1972 75m colour TVM
Palomar / Mark Carliner

The superintendent of an apartment building becomes a hostage in a robbery plot.
Adequate suspenser.

w Eric Roth, *novel* Fielden Farrington *d* Paul Wendkos

Andy Griffith, Ida Lupino, Michael Brandon, Suzanne Hildur

Strangers on a Train***
US 1951 101m bw
Warner (Alfred Hitchcock)

A tennis star is pestered on a train by a psychotic who wants to swap murders, and proceeds to carry out his part of the bargain.
This quirky melodrama has the director at his best, sequence by sequence, but the story is basically unsatisfactory. It makes superior suspense entertainment, however.

w Raymond Chandler, Czenzi Ormonde, *novel* Patricia Highsmith *d Alfred Hitchcock ph Robert Burks m Ray Heindorf*

Farley Granger, *Robert Walker*, Ruth Roman, Leo G. Carroll, Patricia Hitchcock, *Marion Lorne*, Howard St John, Jonathan Hale, Laura Elliott

Stranger on the Third Floor*
US 1940 64m bw
RKO

A reporter finds that he was wrong in the well-intentioned testimony which helps convict an innocent man for murder.
Stylish B feature with a striking dream scene and a curious fleeting performance by Lorre as the real murderer.

w Frank Partos *d* Boris Ingster *ph* Nicholas Musuraca *m* Roy Webb

Margaret Tallichet, Peter Lorre, John McGuire, Charles Waldron, Elisha Cook Jnr, Charles Halton, Ethel Griffies

Strangers May Kiss
US 1931 82m bw
MGM

A sophisticated wife takes love and fidelity lightly.
Dated romantic drama.

w John Meehan, *novel* Ursula Parrott *d* George Fitzmaurice *ph* William Daniels

Norma Shearer, Robert Montgomery, Neil Hamilton, Marjorie Rambeau, Irene Rich

Strangers When We Meet*
US 1960 117m Technicolor Cinemascope
Columbia / Bryna (Richard Quine)

A successful architect starts an affair with a beautiful married neighbour.
Beverly Hills soap opera with lots of romantic suffering in luxury. Lumpy but generally palatable.

w Evan Hunter, from his novel *d* Richard Quine *ph* Charles Lang Jnr *m* George Duning

Kirk Douglas, Kim Novak, *Ernie Kovacs, Walter Matthau,* Barbara Rush, Virginia Bruce, Helen Gallagher, Kent Smith

The Strangler
US 1963 80m bw
AA

An obese lab technician murders nurses who help his hated mother.
Modest, lively shocker.

w Bill S. Ballinger *d* Burt Topper *ph* Jacques Marquette *m* Martin Skiles

Victor Buono, David McLean, Ellen Corby, Diane Sayer

The Stranglers of Bombay
GB 1959 81m bw Megascope
Columbia / Hammer (Anthony Hinds)

In 1826 travellers are waylaid and sacrificially killed by a cult of stranglers.
Semi-historical parade of atrocities, repellent but scarcely exciting.

w David Z. Goodman *d* Terence Fisher *ph* Arthur Grant *m* James Bernard

Guy Rolfe, Allan Cuthbertson, Andrew Cruickshank, Marne Maitland, Jan Holden, George Pastell, Paul Stassino

Strategic Air Command
US 1955 114m Technicolor Vistavision
Paramount (Samuel J. Briskin)

A baseball player is recalled to air force duty.
Sentimental flagwaver featuring the newest jets of the fifties.

w Valentine Davies, Beirne Lay Jnr *d* Anthony Mann *ph* William Daniels *m* Victor Young

James Stewart, June Allyson, Frank Lovejoy, Barry Sullivan, Alex Nicol, Bruce Bennett, Jay C. Flippen, James Millican, James Bell

Strategy of Terror
US 1967 90m Technicolor TVM
Universal

A New York police officer thwarts a plot to murder a UN leader.
Adequate chase thriller, originally a two-parter in the *Crisis* anthology.

w Robert L. Joseph *d* Jack Smight

Hugh O'Brian, Barbara Rush, Neil Hamilton, Harry Townes

The Stratton Story
US 1949 106m bw
MGM (Sam Wood)

An amateur baseball enthusiast becomes a famous professional, but suffers an accident which involves the amputation of a leg.
Mild sentimental biopic, well made but not very interesting.

w Douglas Morrow, Guy Trosper *d* Sam Wood *ph* Harold Rosson *m* Adolph Deutsch

James Stewart, June Allyson, Frank Morgan, Agnes Moorehead, Bill Williams

Straw Dogs
GB 1971 118m Eastmancolor
Talent Associates / Amerbroco (Daniel Melnick)

In a Cornish village, a mild American university researcher erupts into violence when taunted by drunken villagers who commit sustained assaults on himself and his wife.
Totally absurd, poorly contrived, hilariously overwritten Cold Comfort Farm melodrama with farcical violence.

w David Zelag Goodman, Sam Peckinpah *novel* The Siege of Trencher's Farm by Gordon M. Williams *d* Sam Peckinpah *ph* John Coquillon, *m* Jerry Fielding

Dustin Hoffman, Susan George, Peter Vaughan, David Warner, T. P. McKenna, Colin Welland

The Strawberry Blonde**
US 1941 97m bw
Warner (William Cagney)

A dentist in turn-of-the-century Brooklyn wonders whether he married the right woman.
Pleasant period comedy drama, a remake of *One Sunday Afternoon* (qv).

w Julius J. and Philip G. Epstein *d* Raoul Walsh *ph James Wong Howe* *m* Heinz Roemheld

James Cagney, Olivia de Havilland, *Rita Hayworth, Alan Hale,* George Tobias, Jack Carson, Una O'Connor, George Reeves

'It not only tells a very human story, it also creates an atmosphere, recreates a period.'—*New York Sun*

The Strawberry Statement
US 1970 109m Metrocolor
MGM / Robert Chartoff, Irwin Winkler

Student rebels occupy a university administration building.
One of a short-lived group of student anti-discipline films of the early seventies, and about the most boring.

w Israel Horowitz, *novel* James Simon Kunen *d* Stuart Hagmann *ph* Ralph Woolsey *m* Ian Freebairn Smith

Bruce Davison, Kim Darby, Bud Cort, Murray MacLeod

Street Corner
GB 1953 94m bw
Rank / LIP / Sydney Box
US title: *Both Sides of the Law*

Days in the lives of the women police of Chelsea.
Patter-plotted female *Blue Lamp*; just about watchable.

w Muriel and Sydney Box *d* Muriel Box *ph* Reg Wyer *m* Temple Abady

Rosamund John, Anne Crawford, Peggy Cummins, Terence Morgan, Barbara Murray, Sarah Lawson, Ronald Howard, Eleanor Summerfield, Michael Medwin

Street of Chance
US 1930 78m bw
Paramount

A New York gambler gets his come-uppance.
Dullish family melodrama with gangsters as *dei ex machina.*

w Lenore Coffee *d* John Cromwell *ph* Charles Lang

William Powell, Kay Francis, Regis Toomey, Jean Arthur

Street Scene*
US 1931 80m bw
Samuel Goldwyn

In a New York slum street on a hot summer night, an adulterous woman is shot by her husband.
Slice-of-life drama from an influential play; never much of a film, and very dated.

w Elmer Rice, from his play *d* King Vidor *ph* George Barnes

Sylvia Sidney, William Collier Jnr, Max Mantor, David Landau, Estelle Taylor, Russell Hopton

The Street with No Name*
US 1948 93m bw
TCF

An FBI man goes undercover to unmask a criminal gang.
The oldest crime plot in the world, applied with vigour to the documentary realism of *The House on 92nd Street* and built around the *Kiss of Death* psychopathic character created by Richard Widmark.

w Harry Kleiner *d* William Keighley *ph Joe MacDonald* *m* Lionel Newman

Richard Widmark, Mark Stevens, Lloyd Nolan, Barbara Lawrence, Ed Begley

A Streetcar Named Desire**
US 1951 122m bw
Charles K. Feldman / Elia Kazan

A repressed southern widow is raped and driven mad by her brutal brother-in-law.
Reasonably successful, decorative picture from a highly theatrical but influential play; unreal sets and atmospheric photography vaguely Sternbergian.

w Tennessee Williams, from his play *d Elia Kazan ph Harry Stradling m* Alex North *ad* Richard Day

Vivien Leigh, Marlon Brando, Kim Hunter, Karl Malden

Streets of Laredo
US 1949 92m Technicolor
Paramount

Two of three bandit friends become Texas Rangers.
Adequate star western, a remake of *The Texas Rangers*.

w Charles Marquis Warren *d* Leslie Fenton *ph* Ray Rennahan *m* Victor Young

William Holden, William Bendix, Macdonald Carey, Mona Freeman

The Streets of San Francisco**
US 1972 98m colour TVM
Warner / Quinn Martin

An old and a young police detective discover who murdered a young girl.
Highly efficient pilot for long-running location series.

w Edward Hume, *novel* Poor Poor Ophelia by Carolyn Weston *d* Walter Grauman

Karl Malden, Michael Douglas, Robert Wagner, Kim Darby

Strictly Dishonourable
US 1951 94m bw
MGM (Melvin Frank, Norman Panama)

A young girl falls in love with a rakish Italian opera star; he is such a sentimentalist that he marries her.
Emasculated sentimental version of the sharp Preston Sturges comedy.

wd Norman Panama, Melvin Frank *ph* Ray June

Ezio Pinza, Janet Leigh, Millard Mitchell, Maria Palmer

Strike Force*
US 1975 75m colour TVM
D'Antoni–Weitz

An elite police force is set up to counter organized crime.
Rough, tough, realistic cop show which didn't take.

w Roger Hirson *d* Barry Shear

Cliff Gorman, Donald Blakely, Richard Gere, Edward Grover

Strike Me Pink*
US 1936 104m bw
Samuel Goldwyn

A timid amusement park owner is threatened by crooks.
Acceptable star comedy with music.

w Frank Butler, Walter de Leon, Francis Martin *d* Norman Taurog *ph* Gregg Toland, Merritt Gerstad

Eddie Cantor, Sally Eilers, Ethel Merman, William Frawley, Parkyakarkus

Strike Up the Band*
US 1940 120m bw
MGM (Arthur Freed)

A high-school band takes part in a nationwide radio contest.
Rather tiresomely high-spirited musical with the stars at the top of their young form.

w Fred Finklehoffe, John Monks Jnr *d/ch* Busby Berkeley *ph* Ray June *md* Georgie Stoll, Roger Edens

Judy Garland, Mickey Rooney, Paul Whiteman and his Orchestra, June Preisser, William Tracy, Larry Nunn

The Strip*
US 1951 85m bw
MGM (Joe Pasternak)

A band drummer is accused of the murder of a racketeer.
Minor mystery melodrama intriguingly set on Sunset Strip, with jazz accompaniment.

w Allen Rivkin *d* Leslie Kardos *ph* Robert Surtees *m* George Stoll

Mickey Rooney, Sally Forrest, William Demarest, James Craig, Kay Brown; and Louis Armstrong, Earl Hines, Jack Teagarden

The Stripper*
US 1963 95m bw Cinemascope
TCF (Jerry Wald)
GB title: *Woman of Summer*

An ageing beauty queen returns to her Kansas

hometown and has an affair with a 19-year-old garage hand.
Downbeat character melodrama typical of its time and its author; competent but sterile and rather tedious.

w Meade Roberts, *play* A Loss of Roses by William Inge *d Franklin Schaffner* *ph* Ellsworth Fredericks *m* Jerry Goldsmith

Joanne Woodward, Richard Beymer, *Claire Trevor*, Carol Lynley, Robert Webber, Louis Nye, Gypsy Rose Lee, Michael J. Pollard

The Strongest Man in the World
US 1976 92m Technicolor
Walt Disney (Bill Anderson)

An accident in a science lab gives a student superhuman strength.
Formula comedy for older children.

w Joseph L. McEveety, Herman Groves *d* Vincent McEveety *ph* Andrew Jackson *m* Robert F. Brunner

Kurt Russell, Joe Flynn, Eve Arden, Cesar Romero, Phil Silvers, Dick Van Patten, Harold Gould, William Schallert, James Gregory, Roy Roberts, Fritz Feld, Raymond Bailey, Eddie Quillan, Burt Mustin

Strongroom*
GB 1961 80m bw
Bryanston / Theatrecraft (Guido Coen)

Two car breakers plan a once-for-all bank robbery but get involved with potential murder when their hostages get locked in.
Suspenseful second feature with gloss and pace.

w Max Marquis, René Harris *d Vernon Sewell* *ph* Basil Emmott *m* Johnny Gregory

Colin Gordon, Ann Lynn, Derren Nesbitt, Keith Faulkner

The Student Prince
US 1954 107m Anscocolor Cinemascope
MGM (Joe Pasternak)

A prince studies in Heidelberg and falls for a barmaid.
Ruritanian operetta, lumpishly filmed, with Mario Lanza providing only the voice of the hero as he got too fat to play the part.

w William Ludwig, Sonya Levien, *play* Old Heidelberg by Wilhelm Meyer-Foerster *operetta* Dorothy Donnelly *d* Richard Thorpe *ph* Paul C. Vogel *m Sigmund Romberg* *md* George Stoll

Edmund Purdom, Ann Blyth, John Williams, Edmund Gwenn, S. Z. Sakall, John Ericson, Louis Calhern, Betta St John, Evelyn Varden

A Study in Terror*
GB 1965 95m Eastmancolor
Compton–Tekli / Sir Nigel (Henry E. Lester)

Sherlock Holmes discovers the identity of Jack the Ripper.
A reasonably good Holmes pastiche marred by a surfeit of horror and over-riotous local colour; quite literate, but schizophrenic.

w Donald and Derek Ford, *novel* Ellery Queen *d* James Hill *ph* Desmond Dickinson *m* John Scott *ad* Alex Vetchinsky

John Neville, Donald Houston, John Fraser, Robert Morley, Cecil Parker, Anthony Quayle, Barbara Windsor, Adrienne Corri, Judi Dench, Frank Finlay, Barry Jones, Kay Walsh, Georgia Brown

The Subject Was Roses*
US 1968 107m Metrocolor
MGM (Edgar Lansbury)

A young war veteran finds he can't communicate with his parents, and vice versa.
Photographed play notable for its performances.

w Frank D. Gilroy, from his play *d* Ulu Grosbard

Patricia Neal, Jack Albertson, Martin Sheen, Don Saxon, Elaine Williams

Submarine Command
US 1951 87m bw
Paramount (John Farrow, Joseph Sistrom)

A submarine officer who considers himself a coward becomes a hero in Korea.
Very routine soul-searching actioner.

w Jonathan Latimer *d* John Farrow *ph* Lionel Lindon *m* David Buttolph

William Holden, Don Taylor, Nancy Olsen, William Bendix, Moroni Olsen, Peggy Webber

Submarine X-I
GB 1967 90m Eastmancolor
UA / Mirisch (John C. Champion)

A submarine commander in World War II trains men to attack the *Lindendorf* in midget submarines.
Belated quota quickie, routine in every department.

w Donald S. Sanford, Guy Elmes *d* William Graham *ph* Paul Beeson

James Caan, Norman Bowler, David Sumner

Subterfuge
GB 1968 92m colour TVM
Intertel / Commonwealth United

An American agent runs into trouble in London.
Second-rate espionage thick ear.

d Peter Graham Scott

Gene Barry, Joan Collins, Michael Rennie, Suzanna Leigh, Richard Todd

The Subterraneans
US 1960 89m Metrocolor Cinemascope
MGM (Arthur Freed)

The love affairs of San Francisco bohemians.
A boring oddity with lashings of eccentric behaviour and sexual hang-ups; MGM venturing very timidly outside its field.

w Robert Thom, *novel* Jack Kerouac *d* Ranald MacDougall *ph* Joseph Ruttenberg *m* André Previn

George Peppard, Leslie Caron, Janice Rule, Roddy McDowall, Anne Seymour, Jim Hutton

Subway in the Sky
GB 1958 87m bw
Sydney Box (John Temple-Smith, Patrick Filmer-Sankey)

A Berlin cabaret star finds her landlady's ex-husband, a deserter, hiding in her apartment and sets out to prove his innocence of drug smuggling.
Tedious photographed play with precious few points of dramatic interest.

w Jack Andrews, *play* Ian Main *d* Muriel Box *ph* Wilkie Cooper *m* Mario Nascimbene

Hildegarde Neff, Van Johnson, Katherine Kath, Cec Linder, Albert Lieven, Edward Judd

Such Good Friends*
US 1971 102m Movielab
Paramount / Sigma (Otto Preminger)

A successful man has a mysterious illness and his wife enlists help from his friends.
Satirical parable which alternates between sex comedy and medical exposé; generally heavy-going but with good moments.

w Elaine May, *novel* Louis Gould *d* Otto Preminger *ph* Gayne Rescher *m* Thomas Z. Shepherd

Dyan Cannon, James Coco, Jennifer O'Neil, Nina Foch, Laurence Luckinbill, Ken Howard, Burgess Meredith, Louise Lasser, Sam Levene, Rita Gam, Nancy Guild

Sudden Fear**
US 1952 111m bw
RKO / Joseph Kaufman

A playwright heiress finds that her husband is plotting to kill her.
Archetypal star suspenser, glossy and effectively climaxed.

w Lenore Coffee, Robert Smith *d David Miller* *ph Charles Lang Jnr* *m* Elmer Bernstein

Joan Crawford, Jack Palance, Gloria Grahame, Bruce Bennett, Chuck Connors

Suddenly*
US 1954 75m bw
UA / Robert Bassler

Gunmen take over a suburban house and plan to assassinate the President who is due to pass by.
Moderately effective minor suspenser with rather too much psychological chat.

w Richard Sale *d* Lewis Allen *ph* Charles G. Clarke *m* David Raksin

Frank Sinatra, Sterling Hayden, James Gleason, Nancy Gates, Kim Charney

Suddenly It's Spring
US 1947 87m bw
Paramount (Claude Binyon)

A WAC captain comes home to find that her husband wants a divorce.
Tired romantic comedy with no fizz at all.

w Claude Binyon *d* Mitchell Leisen *ph* Daniel L. Fapp *m* Victor Young

Paulette Goddard, Macdonald Carey, Fred MacMurray, Arleen Whelan, Lillian Fontaine, Frank Faylen, Victoria Horne

Suddenly Last Summer*
GB 1959 114m bw
Columbia / Horizon (Sam Spiegel)

A homosexual poet's young cousin goes mad when she sees him raped and murdered by beach boys.
Arty flashback talk-piece from a one-act play, padded out with much sub-poetic mumbo jumbo; it takes too long to get to the revelation, which is ambiguously presented anyway.

w Gore Vidal, *play* Tennessee Williams *d* Joseph L. Mankiewicz *ph Jack Hildyard* *m* Buxton Orr, Malcolm Arnold *pd Oliver Messel*

Katharine Hepburn, Elizabeth Taylor, Montgomery Clift, Albert Dekker, Mercedes McCambridge, Gary Raymond

Suddenly Single*
US 1971 73m colour TVM
Chris–Rose

A newly divorced man joins a California singles community.

Reasonably amusing contemporary comedy.

w Elinor and Stephen Karpf *d* Jud Taylor

Hal Holbrook, Agnes Moorehead, Barbara Rush, Harvey Korman, Margot Kidder, Michael Constantine

Suez*
US 1938 104m bw
TCF (Darryl F. Zanuck)

The career of French engineer Ferdinand de Lesseps, who built the Suez Canal.
Superbly mounted but rather undramatic fictionalized biopic.

w Philip Dunne, Julien Josephson *d* Allan Dwan *ph* Peverell Marley *m* Louis Silvers

Tyrone Power, Annabella, Loretta Young, J. Edward Bromberg, Joseph Schildkraut, Henry Stephenson, Sidney Blackmer, Maurice Moscovitch, Sig Rumann, Nigel Bruce, Miles Mander, George Zucco, Leon Ames, Rafaela Ottiano

Sugarland Express**
US 1974 110m Technicolor Panavision
Universal (Richard Zanuck, David Brown)

A convict's wife persuades him to escape because their baby is being adopted, and they inadvertently leave behind them a trail of destruction, ending in tragedy.
Mainly comic adventures with a bitter aftertaste, very stylishly handled.

w Hal Barwood, Matthew Robbins *d Steven Spielberg ph* Vilmos Zsigmond *m* John Williams

Goldie Hawn, Ben Johnson, Michael Sacks, William Atherton

'*Ace in the Hole* meets *Vanishing Point.'—Sight and Sound*

The Sullivans*
US 1944 111m bw
TCF (Sam Jaffe)

Five sons of the same family are killed in World War II.
Inspirational true story which had a wide appeal.

w Mary C. McCall Jnr *d* Lloyd Bacon *ph* Lucien Andriot *m* Alfred Newman

Anne Baxter, Thomas Mitchell, Selena Royle, Edward Ryan, Trudy Marshall, John Campbell, James Cardwell, John Alvin, George Offerman Jnr, Roy Roberts

Sullivan's Empire
US 1967 90m Technicolor TVM
Universal

Three sons seek their missing father in the South American jungle.
Watchable adventure hokum.

w Frank Chase *d* Harvey Hart, Thomas Carr

Martin Milner, Linden Chiles, Don Quine, Clu Gulager, Karen Jensen

Sullivan's Travels****
US 1941 90m bw
Paramount (Paul Jones)

A Hollywood director tires of comedy and goes out to find real life.
Marvellously sustained tragi-comedy which ranges from pratfalls to the chain gang and never loses its grip or balance.

wd Preston Sturges ph John Seitz m Leo Shuken

Joel McCrea, Veronica Lake, Robert Warwick, William Demarest, Franklin Pangborn, Porter Hall, Byron Foulger, Eric Blore, Robert Greig, Torben Meyer, *Jimmy Conlin*, Margaret Hayes

'A brilliant fantasy in two keys—slapstick farce and the tragedy of human misery.'—*James Agee*

Summer and Smoke
US 1961 118m Technicolor Vistavision
Paramount / Hal B. Wallis

In a small Mississippi town in 1916, the minister's spinster daughter nurses an unrequited love for the local rebel.
Wearisome screen version, in hothouse settings, of a pattern play about earthly and spiritual love.

w James Poe, Meade Roberts, *play* Tennessee Williams *d* Peter Glenville *ph* Charles Lang Jnr *m* Elmer Bernstein *ad* Walter Tyler

Geraldine Page, Laurence Harvey, Una Merkel, John McIntire, Pamela Tiffin, Rita Moreno, Thomas Gomez, Casey Adams, Earl Holliman, Lee Patrick, Malcolm Atterbury

Summer Holiday**
US 1948 92m Technicolor
MGM (Arthur Freed)

Life for a small-town family at the turn of the century.
Musical version of a famous play: excellent individual numbers, warm playing and sympathetic scenes, but a surprising lack of overall style.

w Frances Goodrich, Albert Hackett, Ralph Blane, *play* Ah Wilderness by Eugene O'Neill *d Rouben Mamoulian ph Charles Schoenbaum md* Lennie Hayton *ch Charles Walters*

Walter Huston, Mickey Rooney, Frank Morgan, Agnes Moorehead, Butch Jenkins,

Selena Royle, Marilyn Maxwell, Gloria de Haven, Anne Francis

Summer Holiday*
GB 1962 109m Technicolor Cinemascope
ABP / Ivy (Kenneth Harper)

Four young London Transport mechanics borrow a double decker bus for a continental holiday.
Pacy, location-filmed youth musical with plenty of general appeal.

w Peter Myers, Ronnie Cass *d Peter Yates* *ph* John Wilcox *md* Stanley Black

Cliff Richard, Lauri Peters, Melvyn Hayes, Una Stubbs, Teddy Green, Ron Moody, Lionel Murton, David Kossoff

Summer Magic*
US 1962 104m Technicolor
Walt Disney (Ron Miller)

Children help their widowed mother in 1912 Boston.
Amiable remake of *Mother Carey's Chickens*, irreproachably presented.

w Sally Benson *d* James Neilson *ph* William Snyder *m* Buddy Baker *songs* the Sherman Brothers

Hayley Mills, Burl Ives, Darren McGavin, Deborah Walley, Una Merkel, Eddie Hodges, Michael J. Pollard

Summer of '42*
US 1971 103m Technicolor
Warner (Richard Alan Roth)

Adolescents make sexual explorations on a New England island in 1942.
Well-observed indulgence in the new permissiveness.

w Herman Raucher *d* Robert Mulligan *ph* Robert Surtees *m* Michel Legrand

Jennifer O'Neill, Gary Grimes, Jerry Houser, Oliver Conant, Lou Frizell

Summer of the Seventeenth Doll
US / Australia 1959 94m bw
UA / Hecht–Hill–Lancaster (Leslie Norman)
US title: *Season of Passion*

Two cane-cutters on their annual city lay-off have woman trouble.
Miscast and unsatisfactory rendering of a good play; the humour has evaporated.

w John Dighton, *play* Ray Lawler *d* Leslie Norman *ph* Paul Beeson *m* Benjamin Frankel

Ernest Borgnine, John Mills, Angela Lansbury, Anne Baxter, Vincent Ball

A Summer Place
US 1959 130m Technicolor
Warner (Delmer Daves)

Romantic summer adventures of teenagers and their elders on an island off the coast of Maine.
Sex among the idle rich: a routine piece of Hollywood gloss, bowdlerized from a bestseller.

wd Delmer Daves, *novel* Sloan Wilson *ph* Harry Stradling *m* Max Steiner

Richard Egan, Dorothy McGuire, Sandra Dee, Arthur Kennedy, Troy Donahue, Constance Ford, Beulah Bondi

Summer Stock*
US 1950 109m Technicolor
MGM (Joe Pasternak)
GB title: *If You Feel Like Singing*

A theatre troupe takes over a farm for rehearsals, and the lady owner gets the bug.
Likeable but halting musical with the star's weight problems very obvious.

w George Wells, Sy Gomberg *d* Charles Walters *ph* Robert Planck *md* Johnny Green *ch* Nick Castle

Judy Garland, Gene Kelly, Gloria de Haven, Carleton Carpenter, Eddie Bracken, Phil Silvers, Hans Conried

Summer Storm*
US 1944 106m bw
UA (Seymour Nebenzal)

In 1912 Russia, a provincial judge falls for a local mancatcher.
One of Hollywood's occasional aberrations, an attempt to do something very European in typical west coast style. An interesting failure.

w Rowland Lee, *story* The Shooting Party by Anton Chekhov *d* Douglas Sirk *ph* Archie Stout *md* Karl Majos

George Sanders, Linda Darnell, *Edward Everett Horton*, Anna Lee, Hugo Haas, John Philiber, Sig Rumann, André Charlot

Summer Wishes, Winter Dreams*
US 1973 88m Technicolor
Columbia / Rastar (Jack Brodsky)

A neurotic New York housewife goes to pieces when her mother dies but finds a new understanding of her husband when she accompanies him on a trip to the World War II battlefields.
Menopausal melodrama, well observed but disappointingly wispy and underdeveloped.

w Stewart Stern *d* Gilbert Cates *ph* Gerald Hirschfeld *m* Johnny Mandel

Joanne Woodward, Martin Balsam, Sylvia Sidney, Dori Brenner, Win Forman

A Summer Without Boys*
US 1973 74m colour TVM
Playboy

At a holiday resort during World War II, a woman becomes involved with a younger man and her daughter resents it.
Adequate woman's picture.

w Rita Lakin *d* Jeannot Szwarc

Barbara Bain, Michael Moriarty, Kay Lenz, Mildred Dunnock

Summertime***
US 1955 99m Eastmancolor
Ilya Lopert / Alexander Korda
GB title: *Summer Madness*

An American spinster has a holiday in Venice and becomes romantically involved.
Delightful, sympathetic travelogue with dramatic asides, great to look at and hinging on a single superb performance.

w David Lean, H. E. Bates, *play* The Time of the Cuckoo by Arthur Laurents *d David Lean* *ph Jack Hildyard* *m* Sandro Cicogini

Katharine Hepburn, Rossano Brazzi, Isa Miranda, Darren McGavin, Mari Aldon, André Morell

'The eye is endlessly ravished.'—*Dilys Powell*

Summertree
US 1971 88m Eastmancolor
Warner / Bryna (Kirk Douglas)

A bored student learns about life and becomes a Vietnam casualty.
Well-made, rather tedious character study; good social observation.

w Edward Hume, Stephen Yafa, *play* Ron Cowen *d* Anthony Newley *ph* Richard C. Glouner *m* David Shire

Michael Douglas, Brenda Vaccaro, Jack Warden, Barbara Bel Geddes

The Sun Also Rises**
US 1957 129m Eastmancolor Cinemascope
TCF (Darryl F. Zanuck)

In Paris after World War I an impotent journalist meets a nymphomaniac lady of title, and they and their odd group of friends have various saddening adventures around Europe.
Not a bad attempt to film a difficult novel, though Cinemascope doesn't help and the last half hour becomes turgid. *The Last Flight* (qv) conveyed the same atmosphere rather more sharply.

w Peter Viertel, *novel* Ernest Hemingway *d Henry King* *ph* Leo Tover *m* Hugo Friedhofer

Tyrone Power, Ava Gardner, *Errol Flynn*, Eddie Albert, Mel Ferrer, Robert Evans, Juliette Greco, Gregory Ratoff, Marcel Dalio, Henry Daniell

The Sun Never Sets
US 1939 98m bw
Universal (Rowland V. Lee)

Two brothers in the African colonial service prevent a munitions baron from plunging the world into war.
Stiff upper lip melodrama, very dated.

w W. P. Lipscomb *d* Rowland V. Lee *ph* George Robinson *m* Charles Previn

Basil Rathbone, Douglas Fairbanks Jnr, Virginia Field, Lionel Atwill, Barbara O'Neil, C. Aubrey Smith, Melville Cooper

The Sun Shines Bright**
US 1953 92m bw
Republic / Argosy (John Ford, Merian C. Cooper)

Forty years after the Civil War, the judge of a Kentucky town still has trouble quelling the Confederate spirit.
Mellow anecdotes of time gone by, scrappily linked but lovingly polished; a remake of a Will Rogers vehicle *Judge Priest*.

w Lawrence Stallings, *stories* Irwin S. Cobb *d John Ford* *ph Archie Stout* *m Victor Young*

Charles Winninger, Arleen Whelan, John Russell, Stepin Fetchit, Milburn Stone, Grant Withers, Russell Simpson

'Passages of quite remarkable poetic feeling ... alive with affection and truthful observation.'—*Lindsay Anderson*

Sun Valley Serenade*
US 1941 86m bw
TCF (Milton Sperling)

The band manager at an Idaho ice resort takes care of a Norwegian refugee.
Simple-minded musical which still pleases because of the talent involved.

w Robert Ellis, Helen Logan *d* H. Bruce Humberstone *ph* Edward Cronjager *songs* Mack Gordon, Harry Revel

Sonja Henie, *Glenn Miller and his Orchestra*, John Payne, *Milton Berle*, Lynn Bari, Joan

Davis, *The Nicholas Brothers*, Dorothy Dandridge

Sunday, Bloody Sunday***
GB 1971 110m De Luxe
UA / Vectia (Joseph Janni)

A young designer shares his sexual favours equally between two loves of different sexes, a Jewish doctor and a lady executive.
Stylishly made character study with melodramatic leanings, rather self-conscious about its risky subject but, scene by scene, both adult and absorbing, with an overpowering mass of sociological detail about the way we live.

w Penelope Gilliatt d John Schlesinger ph Billy Williams m Ron Geesin *pd* Luciana Arrighi

Glenda Jackson, Peter Finch, Murray Head, Peggy Ashcroft, Maurice Denham, Vivian Pickles, Frank Windsor, Tony Britton, Harold Goldblatt

Sunday Dinner for a Soldier*
US 1944 86m bw
TCF (Walter Morosco)

A poor family living on a derelict Florida houseboat scrape together enough money to invite a soldier for a meal.
Sentimental little flagwaving romance, quite sympathetically presented and agreeably underacted.

w Wanda Tuchock, Melvin Levy *d* Lloyd Bacon *ph* Joe MacDonald *m* Alfred Newman

Anne Baxter, John Hodiak, Charles Winninger, Anne Revere, Connie Marshall, Chill Wills, Bobby Driscoll, Jane Darwell

'Simple, true and tender, the best propaganda America has put out in the current year.'—*Richard Winnington*

Sunday in New York*
US 1963 105m Metrocolor
MGM / Seven Arts (Everett Freeman)

Complications in the love life of a brother and sister, each of whom thinks the other is very moral.
Fresh, fairly adult sex comedy with New York backgrounds.

w Norman Krasna, from his play *d* Peter Tewkesbury *ph* Leo Tover *m* Peter Nero

Cliff Robertson, Rod Taylor, Jane Fonda, Robert Culp, Jo Morrow, Jim Backus

Sundown
US 1941 91m bw
Walter Wanger

The adopted daughter of an Arab trader assists British troops in Africa during World War II.
Artificial-looking romantic actioner with good cast.

w Barre Lyndon *d* Henry Hathaway *ph* Charles Lang *m* Miklos Rozsa

Gene Tierney, Bruce Cabot, George Sanders, Harry Carey, Joseph Calleia, Cedric Hardwicke, Carl Esmond, Reginald Gardiner

The Sundowners**
GB / Australia 1960 133m Technicolor
Warner (Gerry Blatner)

In the twenties an Irish sheepdrover and his family travel from job to job in the Australian bush.
Easygoing, often amusing but lethargically developed family film with major stars somewhat ill at ease. Memorable sequences.

w Isabel Lennart, *novel* Jon Cleary *d Fred Zinnemann ph* Jack Hildyard *m* Dmitri Tiomkin

Robert Mitchum, Deborah Kerr, *Glynis Johns, Peter Ustinov*, Michael Anderson Jnr, Dina Merrill, *Wylie Watson*, Chips Rafferty

'For all Zinnemann's generous attention to character, the hints of longing, despair and indomitable spirit, the overall impression remains one of sheer length and repetition and synthetic naturalism.'—*Richard Winnington*

Sunny*
US 1930 81m bw
Warner

A showgirl falls for a rich young man.
Tinny early musical notable for its star.

w Humphrey Pearson, Henry McCarthy, *musical play* Otto Harbach, Oscar Hammerstein II, Jerome Kern *ph* Ernest Haller *d* William A. Seiter

Marilyn Miller, Lawrence Grey, Jack Donahue, Mackenzie Ward, O. P. Heggie

Sunny*
US 1941 97m bw
RKO / Imperator (Herbert Wilcox)

Adequate remake of the above.

w Sig Herzig *d* Herbert Wilcox *ph* Russell Metty *m* Anthony Collins

Anna Neagle, Ray Bolger, John Carroll, Edward Everett Horton, Frieda Inescort, Grace and Paul Hartman

Sunny Side Up*
US 1929 80m bw
Fox

A slum girl falls for the son of a rich Southampton family.
Typical early musical of the softer kind; rewarding for those who can project themselves back.

w/m/ly B. G. De Sylva, Lew Brown, Ray Henderson *d* David Butler *ph* Ernest Palmer

Janet Gaynor, Charles Farrell, El Brendel, Marjorie White, Sharon Lynn

Sunrise at Campobello*
US 1960 143m Technicolor
Warner / Dore Schary

The early life of Franklin Roosevelt, including his battle against polio and return to politics.
Static filming of a rather interesting Broadway success and of a memorable performance.

w Dore Schary, from his play *d* Vincent J. Donehue *ph* Russell Harlan *m* Franz Waxman

Ralph Bellamy, Greer Garson, Ann Shoemaker, Hume Cronyn, Jean Hagen

Sunset Boulevard***
US 1950 110m bw
Paramount (Charles Brackett)

A luckless Hollywood scriptwriter goes to live with a wealthy older woman, a slightly dotty and extremely possessive relic of the silent screen.
Incisive melodrama with marvellous moments but a tendency to overstay its welcome; the first reels are certainly the best, though the last scene is worth waiting for and the malicious observation throughout is a treat.

w Charles Brackett, Billy Wilder, D. M. Marshman Jnr d Billy Wilder ph John F. Seitz m Franz Waxman

Gloria Swanson, William Holden, Erich Von Stroheim, Fred Clark, Nancy Olson, Jack Webb, Lloyd Gough, *Cecil B. de Mille*, H. B. Warner, Anna Q. Nilsson, Buster Keaton, Hedda Hopper

'That rare blend of pungent writing, expert acting, masterly direction and unobtrusively artistic photography which quickly casts a spell over an audience and holds it enthralled to a shattering climax.'—*New York Times (T.M.P.)*

Sunshine*
US 1973 121m Technicolor TVM
Universal

A young wife finds she is dying of cancer.
Unbearably icky sudser which was popular among teenagers and sparked a shortlived series.

w Carol Sobieski *d* Joseph Sargent *ph* Bill Butler *m* John Denver

Cliff de Young, Brenda Vaccaro, Christina Raines

† A sequel, *My Sweet Lady*, released in 1976, was made up from segments of a TV series which had briefly surfaced meanwhile.

The Sunshine Boys*
US 1975 111m Metrocolor
MGM / Rastar (Ray Stark)

Two feuding old vaudeville comedians come together for a television spot, and ruin it.
Over-extended sketch in which one main role is beautifully underplayed, the other hammed up, and the production lacks any kind of style. The one-liners are good, though.

w Neil Simon, from his play *d* Herbert Ross *ph* David M. Walsh *md* Harry V. Lojewski

Walter Matthau, *George Burns*, Richard Benjamin, Carol Arthur

The Sunshine Patriot*
US 1968 98m Technicolor TVM
Universal (Joel Rogosin)

A Russian secret agent takes the place of his double, an American businessman.
Adequate espionage suspenser.

w Gustave Field, Joel Rogosin, John Kneubuhl *d* Joseph Sargent

Cliff Robertson, Dina Merrill, Wilfrid Hyde White, Lilia Skala, Antoinette Bower, Donald Sutherland, Luther Adler

Sunstruck
Australia 1972 92m Eastmancolor
Immigrant (Jack Neary, James Grafton)

A shy Welsh schoolmaster emigrates to the Australian outback.
Simple-minded, uninspired, predictable family comedy for star fans.

w Stan Mars *d* James Gilbert *ph* Brian West *m* Peter Knight

Harry Secombe, Maggie Fitzgibbon, John Meillon, Dawn Lake

Superfly
US 1972 98m Technicolor
Warner (Sig Shore)

The New York adventures of black cocaine peddlers.
'Sensational' comedy with violence in which the pushers exit laughing. Tedious and deplorable.

w Philip Fenty *d* Gordon Parks *ph* James Signorelli *m* Jeff Alexander

Ron O'Neal, Carl Lee, Sheila Frazier

'It suggests that New York is now nothing more than a concrete junkieyard.'—*Philip Strick*

Supernatural*
US 1933 67m bw
Paramount

A girl is possessed by the soul of a dead murderess.
Mad doctor nonsense, interestingly but not very successfully styled.

w Harvey Thew, Brian Marlow *d Victor Halperin ph* Arthur Martinelli

Carole Lombard, H. B. Warner, Randolph Scott, Vivienne Osborne, Alan Dinehart

Support Your Local Gunfighter
US 1971 92m De Luxe
UA / Cherokee / Brigade (Burt Kennedy)

A con man jumps a train at a small mining town and is mistaken for a dreaded gunfighter.
Disappointing sequel to the following; just a couple of good jokes.

w James Edward Grant *d* Burt Kennedy *ph* Harry Stradling Jnr *m* Jack Elliott, Allyn Ferguson

James Garner, Suzanne Pleshette, Joan Blondell, Jack Elam, Chuck Connors, Harry Morgan, Marie Windsor, Henry Jones, John Dehner

Support Your Local Sheriff**
US 1968 92m Technicolor
UA / Cherokee (William Bowers)

Gold is found near a western village, and the resulting influx of desperate characters causes problems for the sheriff.
Amusing comedy, drawing on many western clichés.

w William Bowers d Burt Kennedy ph Harry Stradling Jnr *m* Jeff Alexander

James Garner, Joan Hackett, Walter Brennan, Jack Elam, Henry Morgan, Bruce Dern, Henry Jones

'It rejuvenates a stagnating genre by combining just the right doses of parody and affectionate nostalgia.'—*Jan Dawson*

Suppose They Gave a War and Nobody Came
US 1969 114m De Luxe
Engel–Auerbach / ABC (Fred Engel)

Three accident-prone PROs try to give the army a good name in a town which wishes it would go away; they eventually cause panic by arriving at a dance in a tank.
Muddled farce which may have hoped to be satire.

w Don McGuire, Hal Captain *d* Hy Averback *ph* Burnett Guffey *m* Jerry Fielding

Tony Curtis, Brian Keith, Ernest Borgnine, Ivan Dixon, Suzanne Pleshette, *Tom Ewell*, Bradford Dillman, Arthur O'Connell, Robert Emhardt, John Fiedler, Don Ameche

Surprise Package
GB 1960 100m bw
Columbia / Stanley Donen

An American gangster is deported to the same Mediterranean island as an exiled European king, whose crown gets stolen.
Flat and feeble comedy which defeats its stars.

w Harry Kurnitz, *novel* Art Buchwald *d* Stanley Donen *ph* Christopher Challis *m* Benjamin Frankel

Yul Brynner, Noel Coward, Mitzi Gaynor, Bill Nagy, Eric Pohlmann, George Coulouris, Warren Mitchell

Susan and God*
US 1940 117m bw
MGM (Hunt Stromberg)
GB title: *The Gay Mrs Trexel*

A flighty society woman gets religion but fails to practise what she preaches.
Unusual comedy-drama for MGM to tackle, but a fairly successful one for high class audiences.

w Anita Loos, play Rachel Crothers *d George Cukor ph* Robert Planck *m* Herbert Stothart

Joan Crawford, Fredric March, Ruth Hussey, John Carroll, Rita Hayworth, Nigel Bruce, Bruce Cabot, Rita Quigley, Rose Hobart, Constance Collier, Gloria de Haven, Marjorie Main

Susan Lenox, Her Fall and Rise*
US 1931 76m bw
MGM
GB title: *The Rise of Helga*

A farm girl flees to the city when her father tries to marry her off to a brute.
Moderate star melodrama with the star somewhat miscast.

w Wanda Tuchock, novel David Graham Phillips *d* Robert Z. Leonard *ph* William Daniels

Greta Garbo, Clark Gable, Jean Hersholt, John Miljan, Alan Hale

Susan Slade
US 1961 116m Technicolor
Warner (Delmer Daves)

An engineer brings his family back to San

Francisco from Chile, and his teenage daughter runs into problems of the heart.
Stilted, busy sudser.

w Delmer Daves, *novel* Doris Hume *d* Delmer Daves *ph* Lucien Ballard *m* Max Steiner

Connie Stevens, Troy Donahue, Dorothy McGuire, Lloyd Nolan, Brian Aherne, Natalie Schaefer, Grant Williams, Bert Convy, Kent Smith

Susan Slept Here
US 1954 98m Technicolor
RKO (Harriet Parsons)

The Hollywood scriptwriter of a film about youth problems agrees to look after a delinquent teenage girl.
Skittish, would-be piquant comedy; quite unattractive.

w Alex Gottlieb *d* Frank Tashlin *ph* Nicholas Musuraca *md* Leigh Harline

Dick Powell, Debbie Reynolds, Anne Francis, Glenda Farrell, Alvy Moore, Horace MacMahon

Susannah of the Mounties*
US 1939 78m bw
TCF (Kenneth MacGowan)

A little girl who is the only survivor of a wagon train massacre is looked after by the Canadian Mounties.
Adequate star action romance, Shirley's last real success.

w John Taintor Foote, Philip Dunne *d* Sidney Lanfield *ph* Bert Glennon *m* Louis Silvers

Shirley Temple, Randolph Scott, Margaret Lockwood, J. Farrell MacDonald, Maurice Moscovitch, Moroni Olsen, Victor Jory

The Suspect*
US 1944 84m bw
Universal

A henpecked husband kills his wife and is blackmailed.
Efficient studio-bound suspenser with theatrically effective acting.

w Bertram Millhauser, *novel* James Ronald *d* Robert Siodmak *ph* Paul Ivano

Charles Laughton, Henry Daniell, Rosalind Ivan, Ella Raines, Molly Lamont, Dean Harens

'High marks for tension, local colour, story.' —*William Whitebait*

Suspect*
GB 1960 81m bw
The Boulting Brothers / British Lion

Government research chemists find a traitor in their midst.
Entertaining but fairly routine spy melodrama, shot on an experimental low budget but confined to lower berth bookings.

w Nigel Balchin, from his novel Sort of Traitors *d* Roy and John Boulting *ph* Max Greene *m* John Wilkes

Tony Britton, Virginia Maskell, Peter Cushing, Ian Bannen, Raymond Huntley, Donald Pleasance, Thorley Walters, Spike Milligan, Kenneth Griffith

'A better standard of second feature film is badly needed, but the way to do it is not by making pictures which look as though they have strayed from TV.'—*Penelope Houston*

Suspicion**
US 1941 99m bw
RKO

A sedate young girl marries a playboy, and comes to suspect that he is trying to murder her.
Rather artificial and stiff Hitchcock suspenser, further marred by an ending suddenly switched to please the front office. Full of the interesting touches one would expect.

w Samson Raphaelson, Alma Reville, Joan Harrison, *novel* Before the Fact by Francis Iles *d Alfred Hitchcock* *ph* Harry Stradling *m* Franz Waxman

Joan Fontaine, Cary Grant, Nigel Bruce, Cedric Hardwicke, May Whitty, Isabel Jeans, Heather Angel, Leo G. Carroll

Suzy*
US 1936 95m bw
MGM (Maurice Revnes)

A French air ace of World War I marries an American showgirl; they then find that her former husband, thought dead, is still alive.
Proficient star comedy-drama with romance, action, comedy and a complex plot. A showcase for its stars.

w Dorothy Parker, Alan Campbell, Horace Jackson, Lenore Coffee, *novel* Herbert Gorman *d* George Fitzmaurice *ph* Ray June *m* William Axt

Jean Harlow, Cary Grant, Franchot Tone, Benita Hume, Lewis Stone

Svengali**
US 1931 81m bw
Warner

In nineties Paris, a hypnotist turns a girl into a great opera singer but she does not reciprocate his love.

Victorian fantasy melodrama with a great grotesque part for the star and interesting artwork.

w J. Grubb Alexander, *novel* Trilby by George du Maurier *d Archie Mayo* *ph* Barney McGill

John Barrymore, Marian Marsh, Luis Alberni, Lumsden Hare, Donald Crisp, Paul Porcasi

Svengali
GB 1954 82m Eastmancolor
Renown / Alderdale (Douglas Pierce)

Flatulent remake which does have the virtue of following the original book illustrations but is otherwise unpersuasive.

wd Noel Langley *ph* Wilkie Cooper *m* William Alwyn *ad Fred Pusey*

Donald Wolfit, Hildegarde Neff, Terence Morgan, Derek Bond, Paul Rogers, David Kossoff, Hubert Gregg, Noel Purcell, Alfie Bass, Harry Secombe

Swallows and Amazons
GB 1974 92m Eastmancolor
EMI / Theatre Projects

In the twenties four children have adventures in the Lake District.
Mild family film, great to look at but lacking in real excitement or style.

w David Wood, *novel* Arthur Ransome *d* Claude Whatham *ph* Denis Lewiston *m* Wilfred Josephs

Virginia McKenna, Ronald Fraser, Simon West, Sophie Neville, Zanna Hamilton, Stephen Grenville

Swamp Water**
US 1941 90m bw
TCF (Irving Pichel)
GB title: *The Man Who Came Back*

A fugitive holds out for years in the Okenfenokee swamp, and affects the lives of the local township.
A strange little story, not very compelling as drama but with striking photography and atmosphere. Remade more straightforwardly as *Lure of the Wilderness* (qv).

w Dudley Nicholas, *story* Vereen Bell *d Jean Renoir* *ph Peverell Marley* *m* David Buttolph

Walter Huston, Walter Brennan, Anne Baxter, Dana Andrews, Virginia Gilmore, John Carradine, Eugene Pallette, Ward Bond, Guinn Williams

The Swan*
US 1956 108m Eastmancolor Cinemascope
MGM (Dore Schary)

In 1910 Hungary, a girl of noble stock is groomed to marry the crown prince.
Interesting chiefly for a typical Hollywood reaction to a news event; about to lose their top star to a real life prince, MGM dusted off this old and creaky property for her last film. The star cast can't make much of it and the treatment is very heavy.

w John Dighton, *play* Ferenc Molnar *d* Charles Vidor *ph* Robert Surtees *m* Bronislau Kaper *ad* Cedric Gibbons, Randall Duell

Grace Kelly, Alec Guinness, Louis Jourdan, Agnes Moorehead, Jessie Royce Landis, Brian Aherne, Leo G. Carroll, *Estelle Winwood*, Robert Coote

'Balancing between artificial comedy and a no less artificial romantic theme, the film ultimately requires considerably greater finesse and subtlety in the handling.'—*Penelope Houston*

Swanee River**
US 1939 84m Technicolor
TCF (Darryl F. Zanuck)

The life and loves of Stephen Foster.
Attractive, unsurprising family film in rich early colour, sparked by Jolson as E. P. Christy.

w John Taintor Foote, Philip Dunne *d* Sidney Lanfield

Don Ameche, *Al Jolson*, Andrea Leeds, Felix Bressart, Russell Hicks

Swashbuckler*
US 1976 101m Technicolor
Universal / Elliott Kastner (Jennings Lang)
GB title: *The Scarlet Buccaneer*

Rival pirates help a wronged lady.
Uninspired reworking of some old Errol Flynn ideas; the idea was pleasant, but the old style is sadly lacking.

w Jeffrey Bloom *d* James Goldstone *ph* Philip Lathrop *m* John Addison *pd* John Lloyd

Robert Shaw, James Earl Jones, Peter Boyle, Geneviève Bujold, Beau Bridges, Geoffrey Holder

'This tacky pastepot job can't make up its mind whether it's serious, tongue-in-cheek, satirical, slapstick, burlesque, parody or travesty; but be assured it is all of the above.'—*Variety*

SWAT*
US 1973 97m colour TVM
Spelling–Goldberg
aka: *SWAT Squad*

Rookie cops are temporarily assigned to a unit skilled in the use of special weapons and tactics, and prevent the robbery of a condominium.
A pilot for the successful series which was rebuked for showing police violence, this originally played as a double episode of *The Rookies*. As entertainment, it's fast and suspenseful.

w Robert Hamner *d* E. W. Swackhamer

Steve Forrest, George Stanford Brown, Sam Melville, Gerald S. O'Loughlin, Leslie Nielsen, Barbara Rush, Donna Mills, Lloyd Bochner, Arte Johnson

Sweeney!*
GB 1976 89m Technicolor
EMI / Euston (Tom Childs)

Scotland Yard's Flying Squad investigates a suicide and uncovers an elaborate political blackmail scheme.
Enjoyable big screen version of a pacy, violent TV cop show.

w Ranald Graham *d* David Wickes *ph* Dusty Miller *m* Denis King

John Thaw, Denis Waterman, Barry Foster, Ian Bannen, Colin Welland, Michael Coles, Joe Melia

Sweeney Todd, the Demon Barber of Fleet Street*
GB 1936 68m bw
George King

A barber kills his customers and makes them into 'mutton pies' for sale at the shop next door.
Decent version of a famous old melodrama; stilted as film-making, but preserving a swaggering star performance.

w Frederick Hayward, H. F. Maltby, *play* George Dibdin-Pitt *d* George King

Tod Slaughter, Bruce Seton, Eve Lister, Stella Rho, Ben Soutten

Sweet Adeline
US 1935 85m bw
Warner (Edward Chodorov)

In the nineties, the daughter of a beer garden owner attracts the attention of a composer and becomes a Broadway star.
Unexceptionable, and quite forgotten, adaptation of a pleasant, old-fashioned Broadway musical.

w Erwin S. Gelsey, *play* Jerome Kern, Oscar Hammerstein II, Harry Armstrong, Dick Gerard *d* Mervyn Le Roy *m/ly* Jerome Kern, Oscar Hammerstein II *ph* Sol Polito *ch* Bobby Connolly *ad* Robert Haas

Irene Dunne, Donald Woods, Ned Sparks, Hugh Herbert, Wini Shaw, Louis Calhern, Nydia Westman, Joseph Cawthorn

Sweet Bird of Youth*
US 1961 120m Metrocolor Cinemascope
MGM / Roxbury (Pandro S. Berman)

A Hollywood drifter brings an ageing glamour star back to his home town, but runs into revenge from the father of a girl he had seduced.
Emasculated version of an overwrought play with the author's usual poetic squalor; comatose patches alternate with flashes of good acting and diverting dialogue, but the wide screen and heavy colour don't direct the attention.

wd Richard Brooks, *play* Tennessee Williams *ph* Milton Krasner *md* Robert Armbruster

Paul Newman, Geraldine Page, *Ed Begley*, Mildred Dunnock, Rip Torn, Shirley Knight, Madeleine Sherwood

Sweet Charity*
US 1969 149m Technicolor Panavision 70
Universal (Robert Arthur)

A New York taxi dancer dreams of love.
A revue-type musical bowdlerized from Fellini's *Le notti di Cabiria* accords ill with real New York locations, especially as its threads of plot come to nothing; but behind the camera are sufficient stylists to ensure striking success with individual numbers.

w Peter Stone, *play* Neil Simon *d Robert Fosse ph Robert Surtees m Cy Coleman ly David Fields*

Shirley Maclaine, Ricardo Montalban, John McMartin, *Chita Rivera*, Paula Kelly, Stubby Kaye, Sammy Davis Jnr

'The kind of platinum clinker designed to send audiences flying towards the safety of their television sets.'—*Rex Reed*

Sweet November
US 1968 113m Technicolor
Warner Seven Arts / Jerry Gershwin, Elliott Kastner

An English tycoon in New York meets a girl who takes a new lover every month because she hasn't long to live.
Irritating exercise in eccentric sentimentality, not helped by twitchy stars.

w Herman Raucher *d* Robert Ellis Miller *ph* Daniel L. Fapp *m* Michel Legrand

Anthony Newley, Sandy Dennis, Theodore Bikel, Burr de Benning

The Sweet Ride
US 1967 110m De Luxe Panavision
TCF (Joe Pasternak)

Surfers and drop-outs on a California beach have woman trouble.
Teenage melodrama, well produced but abysmal of content.

w Tom Mankiewicz, *novel* William Murray *d* Harvey Hart *ph* Robert B. Hauser *m* Pete Rugolo

Jacqueline Bisset, Tony Franciosa, Michael Sarrazin, Bob Denver, Michael Wilding

Sweet Rosie O'Grady*
US 1943 79m Technicolor
TCF (William Perlberg)

A Police Gazette reporter tries to uncover the past of a musical comedy star.
Pleasant nineties musical with plenty of zest but a lack of good numbers. A typical success of the war years.

w Ken Englund *d* Irving Cummings *ph Ernest Palmer* *ch* Hermes Pan *songs* Mack Gordon, Harry Warren *ad James Basevi, Joseph C. Wright*

Betty Grable, Robert Young, Adolphe Menjou, Reginald Gardiner, Virginia Grey, Phil Regan, Sig Rumann, Hobart Cavanaugh, Alan Dinehart

Sweet Smell of Success***
US 1957 96m bw
UA / Norma / Curtleigh (James Hill)

A crooked press agent helps a megalomaniac New York columnist break up his sister's marriage.
Moody, brilliant, Wellesian melodrama put together with great artificial style; the plot matters less than the photographic detail and the skilful manipulation of decadent characters, bigger than life-size.

w Clifford Odets, Ernest Lehman *d Alexander Mackendrick* *ph James Wong Howe* *m Elmer Bernstein* *ad* Edward Carrere

Burt Lancaster, *Tony Curtis*, Martin Milner, Sam Levene, Susan Harrison, Barbara Nichols, *Emile Meyer*

Sweet Sweet Rachel*
US 1971 73m colour TVM
Stan Shpetner

An ESP expert tries to find out how a beautiful woman is being driven mad.
Reasonably chilling semi-supernatural thriller.

w Anthony Lawrence *d* Sutton Roley

Alex Dreier, Stefanie Powers, Pat Hingle, Louise Latham, Brenda Scott

Sweethearts**
US 1938 120m Technicolor
MGM (Hunt Stromberg)

Two stars of the musical stage never stop fighting each other.
The lightest and most successful of the MacDonald/Eddy musicals, with an excellent script, production and cast.

w Dorothy Parker, Alan Campbell *d W. S. Van Dyke* *ph* Oliver Marsh *m* Victor Herbert

Jeanette MacDonald, Nelson Eddy, Frank Morgan, Ray Bolger, Florence Rice, Mischa Auer, Fay Holden, Reginald Gardiner, Herman Bing, Allyn Joslyn, Raymond Walburn, Lucile Watson, Gene Lockhart

The Swimmer**
US 1968 94m Technicolor
Columbia / Horizon / Dover (Frank Perry, Roger Lewis)

A man clad only in trunks swims his way home via the pools of his rich friends, and arrives home to find that his success is a fantasy.
Strange but compelling fable, too mystifying for popular success, about the failure of the American dream. Annoyingly inexplicit, but well made and sumptuously photographed in a variety of Connecticut estates.

w Eleanor Perry, short story John Cheever *d* Frank Perry, Sydney Pollack *ph David L. Quaid* *m* Marvin Hamlisch

Burt Lancaster, Janice Rule, Kim Hunter, Diana Muldaur, Cornelia Otis Skinner, Marge Champion

Swing High Swing Low**
US 1937 97m bw
Paramount (Arthur Hornblow Jnr)

A talented trumpeter goes on a bender but is rescued by his wife.
Backstage comedy-drama, a beautifully cinematic version of a very tedious story also filmed as *Dance of Life* (1929) and *When My Baby Smiles at Me* (1948).

w Virginia Van Upp, Oscar Hammerstein II, *play* Burlesque by George Manker Walters, Arthur Hopkins *d Mitchell Leisen* *ph* Ted Tetzlaff *m* Boris Morros

Carole Lombard, Fred MacMurray, Charles

Butterworth, Jean Dixon, Dorothy Lamour, Harvey Stephens, Franklin Pangborn, Anthony Quinn

'Enough concentrated filmcraft to fit out half a dozen of those gentlemen who are always dashing around in an independent capacity making just the greatest piece of cinema ever.' —*Otis Ferguson*

Swing Time**
US 1936 103m bw
RKO (Pandro S. Berman)

A dance team can't get together romantically because he has a commitment to a girl back home.
Satisfactory but unexciting musical vehicle for two stars at the top of their professional and box-office form.

w Howard Lindsay, Allan Scott *d* George Stevens *ph* David Abel *md* Nathaniel Shilkret *songs* Jerome Kern, Dorothy Fields

Fred Astaire, Ginger Rogers, Victor Moore, Helen Broderick, Eric Blore, Betty Furness, Georges Metaxa

Swing Your Lady*
US 1937 77m bw
Warner (Sam Bischoff)

A promoter gets involved in the problems of a hillbilly wrestler.
Minor comedy with some laughs.

w Joseph Scrank, Maurice Leo, *story* Toehold on Artemus by H. R. Marsh *d* Ray Enright *ph* Arthur Edeson *m* Adolph Deutsch

Humphrey Bogart, Louise Fazenda, Nat Pendleton, Frank McHugh, Penny Singleton, Allen Jenkins, Ronald Reagan, The Weaver Brothers and Elviry

The Swinger
US 1966 81m Technicolor
Paramount / George Sidney

When a girl writer's wholesome stories are rejected, she pretends to have a naughty past.
With-it comedy which audiences preferred to be without.

w Lawrence Roman *d* George Sidney *ph* Joseph Biroc *m* Marty Paich

Ann-Margret, Tony Franciosa, Robert Coote, Yvonne Romain, Horace MacMahon, Nydia Westman

'A hectically saucy mixture of lechery, depravity, perversion, voyeurism and girlie magazines . . . a heavy, witless pudding.'—*MFB*

The Swiss Family Robinson
US 1940 93m bw
(RKO) Gene Towne, Graham Baker

A shipwrecked family builds a new home on a desert island.
Pleasing low-budgeter.

w Gene Towne, Graham Baker, Walter Ferris, *novel* Johann Wyss *d* Edward Ludwig *ph* Nicholas Musuraca

Thomas Mitchell, Edna Best, Freddie Bartholemew, Tim Holt, Terry Kilburn

'In outlook, dialogue and manner it is frankly old-fashioned.'—*MFB*

The Swiss Family Robinson*
GB 1960 126m Technicolor Panavision
Walt Disney (Bill Anderson, Basil Keys)

A family of emigrants are shipwrecked after a skirmish with pirates, and learn to live on a desert island.
Quite pleasing comedy adventure from the children's classic.

w Lowell S. Hawley, *novel* Johann Wyss *d* Ken Annakin *ph* Harry Waxman *m* William Alwyn

John Mills, Dorothy McGuire, James MacArthur, Tommy Kirk, Kevin Corcoran, Janet Munro, Sessue Hayakawa, Cecil Parker

The Swiss Family Robinson
US 1975 74m colour TVM
TCF / Irwin Allen
GB title: *Island of Adventure*

Abysmal remake heralding a likewise series.

w Ken Trevey *d* Harry Harris

Martin Milner, Cameron Mitchell, Pat Delaney, Michael Wixted, John Vernon

Swiss Miss*
US 1938 73m bw
(MGM) Hal Roach

Two mousetrap salesmen in Switzerland run into trouble with a cook, a gorilla and two opera singers.
Operetta style vehicle which constrains its stars, since their material is somewhat below vintage anyway. Not painful to watch, but disappointing.

w James Parrott, Felix Adler, Charles Nelson *d* John G. Blystone *ph* Norbert Brodine

Stan Laurel, Oliver Hardy, Walter Woolf King, Della Lind, Eric Blore

Switch**
US 1975 74m Technicolor TVM
Universal (Glen A. Larson)

A con man and an ex-cop are partners in an investigation agency and pull the wool over the eyes of a conniving police officer.
Fast moving, funny, not very comprehensible pilot based on the appeal of *The Sting*. Unfortunately the resultant series disappointed.

w Glen A. Larson *d* Robert Day

Robert Wagner, Eddie Albert, Charles Durning, Sharon Glass

The Sword and the Rose
GB 1952 91m Technicolor
Walt Disney (Perce Pearce)

The romantic problems of young Mary Tudor.
Unhistorical charade not quite in the usual Disney vein, and not very good.

w Laurence E. Watkin, *novel* When Knighthood Was in Flower by Charles Major *d* Ken Annakin *ph* Geoffrey Unsworth *m* Clifton Parker

Richard Todd, Glynis Johns, James Robertson Justice, Michael Gough, Jane Barrett, Peter Copley, Rosalie Crutchley, Jean Mercure, D. A. Clarke-Smith

The Sword in the Stone**
US 1963 80m Technicolor
Walt Disney (Ken Peterson)

In the Dark Ages, a young forest boy named Wart becomes King Arthur.
Feature cartoon with goodish sequences but disappointingly showing a flatness and economy of draughtsmanship.

w Bill Peet, *novel* The Once and Future King by T. H. White *d* Wolfgang Reitherman *m* George Bruns *songs* The Sherman Brothers

Sword of Sherwood Forest
GB 1960 80m Technicolor Megascope
Columbia / Hammer / Yeoman (Richard Greene, Sidney Cole)

Robin Hood reveals the villainy of the Sheriff of Nottingham and the Earl of Newark.
This big-screen version of a popular TV series makes a rather feeble addition to the legend, but the actors try hard.

w Alan Hackney *d* Terence Fisher *ph* Ken Hodges *m* Alan Hoddinott

Richard Greene, Peter Cushing, Richard Pasco, Niall MacGinnis, Jack Gwyllim, Sarah Branch, Nigel Green

Sylvia
US 1964 115m bw
Paramount / Joseph E. Levine

A millionaire with a mysterious fiancée hires a detective to discover the truth about her past.
Improbable story of a high-minded prostitute, sluggishly narrated and variably acted.

w Sidney Boehm, *novel* E. V. Cunningham *d* Gordon Douglas *ph* Joseph Ruttenberg *m* Walter Scharf

Carroll Baker, George Maharis, Peter Lawford, Joanne Dru, Ann Sothern, Viveca Lindfors, Edmond O'Brien, Aldo Ray

Sylvia Scarlett*
US 1935 94m bw
RKO (Pandro S. Berman)

A girl masquerades as a boy in order to escape to France with her crooked father.
Strange, peripatetic English comedy-adventure which failed to ring any bells but preserves aspects of interest.

w Gladys Unger, John Collier, Mortimer Offner, *novel* Compton Mackenzie *d* George Cukor *ph* Joseph August *m* Roy Webb

Katharine Hepburn, Cary Grant, Edmund Gwenn, Brian Aherne, Lennox Pawle

Symphony of Six Million
US 1932 94m bw
RKO (Pandro S. Berman)
GB title: *Melody of Life*

A doctor drags himself from New York's slums to Park Avenue, but feels guilty and demoralized when he can't save the life of his own father.
Monumental tearjerker, not badly done.

w Bernard Schubert, J. Walter Ruben, *novel* Fannie Hurst *d* Gregory La Cava *ph* Leo Tover *m* Max Steiner

Irene Dunne, Ricardo Cortez, Gregory Ratoff, Anna Appel, Noel Madison, Julie Haydon

The System
US 1953 90m bw
Warner (Sam Bischoff)

A crime leader is softened by love, and allows himself to be convicted.
Strange nonsense inspired by the Kefauver investigations into American society; neither edifying nor entertaining.

w Jo Eisinger *d* Lewis Seiler *ph* Edwin DuPar *m* David Buttolph

Frank Lovejoy, Joan Weddon, Bob Arthur, Paul Picerni, Don Beddoe

The System

GB 1964 90m bw

British Lion / Bryanston / Kenneth Shipman

US title: *The Girl-Getters*

Seaside layabouts have a system for collecting and sharing rich girl visitors, but one of the latter traps the leader at his own game.
Adequate sexy showcase for some looming talents; all very unattractive, but smoothly directed in a number of imitated styles.

w Peter Draper *d Michael Winner ph Nicolas Roeg m* Stanley Black

Oliver Reed, Jane Merrow, Barbara Ferris, Julia Foster, Ann Lynn, Guy Doleman, Andrew Ray, David Hemmings, John Alderton, Derek Nimmo, Harry Andrews

T

Tail Spin
US 1938 83m bw
TCF (Harry Joe Brown)

The interwoven private lives of lady civilian air pilots.
Predictable romantic goings on; a tear, a smile, a song, etc.

w Frank Wead *d* Roy del Ruth *ph* Karl Freund *m* Louis Silvers

Alice Faye, Constance Bennett, Joan Davis, Nancy Kelly, Charles Farrell, Jane Wyman, Kane Richmond, Wally Vernon, Harry Davenport

Take a Giant Step
US 1958 100m bw
UA / Sheila / Hecht–Hill–Lancaster (Julius J. Epstein)

A young black person brought up in a white town feels ill at ease and runs into adolescent troubles.
Well-meaning racial drama with good detail but no real feeling.

w Louis S. Peterson, Julius J. Epstein *d* Philip Leacock *ph* Arthur Arling *m* Jack Marshall

Johnny Nash, Estelle Hemsley, Ruby Dee, Frederick O'Neal

Take a Girl Like You
GB 1970 101m Eastmancolor
Columbia / Albion (Hal E. Chester)

A north country girl comes to teach in London and has man trouble.
Old-fashioned novelette with sex trimmings and neither zest nor humour.

w George Melly, *novel* Kingsley Amis *d* Jonathan Miller *ph* Dick Bush *m* Stanley Myers

Hayley Mills, Oliver Reed, Noel Harrison, Sheila Hancock, John Bird, Aimi MacDonald

Take a Letter, Darling**
US 1942 94m bw
Paramount (Fred Kohlmar)
GB title: *Green-Eyed Woman*

A woman executive hires a male secretary.
Smartish romantic comedy.

w Claude Binyon d Mitchell Leisen ph John Mescall *m* Victor Young

Rosalind Russell, Fred MacMurray, Macdonald Carey, Constance Moore, Cecil Kellaway, Charles Arnt, Kathleen Howard, Dooley Wilson

Take Care of My Little Girl
US 1951 93m Technicolor
TCF (Julian Blaustein)

A university freshwoman gets into trouble with her sorority.
Ho-hum exposé of college conventions, of routine interest at best.

w Julius J. and Philip G. Epstein, *novel* Peggy Goodwin *d* Jean Negulesco *ph* Harry Jackson *m* Alfred Newman

Jeanne Crain, Mitzi Gaynor, Dale Robertson, Jean Peters, Jeffrey Hunter

'As is customary in college pictures, it appears that Tri U recruits most of its strength from the chorus.'—*Penelope Houston*

Take Her, She's Mine*
US 1963 98m De Luxe Cinemascope
TCF (Henry Koster)

A lawyer protects his teenage daughter from boys and causes.
Routine Hollywood family comedy with some laughs and an agreeable cast.

w Nunnally Johnson, *play* Phoebe and Henry Ephron *d* Henry Koster *ph* Lucien Ballard *m* Jerry Goldsmith

James Stewart, Sandra Dee, Robert Morley, Audrey Meadows, Philippe Forquet, John McGiver

Take Me High
GB 1973 90m Technicolor
EMI (Kenneth Harper)

A bank manager helps an unsuccessful restaurant to launch a new hamburger.
Jaded youth musical with no dancing but some zip and bounce to commend it to mums and dads if not to its intended young audience.

w Christopher Penfold *d* David Askey *ph* Norman Warwick *m/songs* Terry Cole

Cliff Richard, Debbie Watling, Hugh Griffith, George Cole, Anthony Andrews, Richard Wattis

Take Me Out to the Ball Game***
US 1949 93m Technicolor
MGM (Arthur Freed)

A woman takes over a baseball team and the players are antagonistic.
Lively, likeable nineties comedy musical which served as a trial run for *On the Town* and in its own right is a fast-moving, funny, tuneful delight with no pretensions.

w Harry Tugend, George Wells d Gene Kelly, Stanley Donen ph George Folsey *md* Adolph Deutsch *songs Betty Comden, Adolph Green, Roger Edens*

Gene Kelly, Frank Sinatra, Esther Williams, *Betty Garrett*, Jules Munshin, Edward Arnold, Richard Lane, Tom Dugan

Take Me to Town
US 1953 81m Technicolor
U-I (Ross Hunter)

The three sons of a backwoods widower import a vaudeville artiste as their new mother.
Old-fashioned family schmaltz containing every known cliché professionally stitched into the plot.

w Richard Morris *d* Douglas Sirk *ph* Russell Metty *m* Joseph Gershenson

Ann Sheridan, Sterling Hayden, Philip Reed, Lee Patrick, Lee Aaker, Harvey Grant, Dusty Henley

Take My Life**
GB 1947 79m bw
GFD / Cineguild (Anthony Havelock-Allan)

A man is suspected of murdering an ex-girl friend, and his wife journeys to Scotland to prove him innocent.
Hitchcock-style thriller with excellent detail and performances.

w Winston Graham, Valerie Taylor *d Ronald Neame ph Guy Green m* William Alwyn

Hugh Williams, Greta Gynt, Marius Goring, Francis L. Sullivan, Rosalie Crutchley, Henry Edwards, Ronald Adam

Take One False Step*
US 1949 94m bw
U-I (Chester Erskine)

An innocent middle-aged man who has befriended a girl is hunted by the police when she is murdered.
Fairly absorbing and well-cast chase thriller in a minor key.

w Irwin Shaw, Chester Erskine, *story* Night Call *by* Irwin and David Shaw *d* Chester Erskine *ph* Franz Planer *m* Walter Scharf

William Powell, Shelley Winters, Marsha Hunt, Dorothy Hart, James Gleason, Felix Bressart, Art Baker, Sheldon Leonard

Take the High Ground
US 1953 101m Anscocolor
MGM (Dore Schary)

A tough sergeant trains army conscripts for action in Korea.
Very routine flagwaver.

w Millard Kaufman *d* Richard Brooks *ph* John Alton *m* Dmitri Tiomkin

Richard Widmark, Karl Malden, Carleton Carpenter, Elaine Stewart, Russ Tamblyn, Jerome Courtland, Steve Forrest, Robert Arthur

Take the Money and Run
US 1968 85m Technicolor
Palomar (Charles H. Joffe)

A social misfit becomes a bungling crook.
A torrent of middling visual gags, not the star's best vehicle.

wd Woody Allen *ph* Lester Shorr *m* Marvin Hamlisch

Woody Allen, Janet Margolin, Marcel Hillaire

The Taking of Pelham 123*
US 1974 104m Technicolor Panavision
UA / Palomar / Palladium (Gabriel Katzka)

Four ruthless gunmen hold a New York subway train to ransom and have an ingenious plan for escape.
Entertaining crime caper made less enjoyable by all the fashionable faults; the script is deliberately hard to follow and full of four letter words, the sound track hard to hear, and the visuals ugly.

w Peter Stone, *novel* John Godey *d* Joseph Sargent *ph* Owen Roizman *m* David Shire

Walter Matthau, Robert Shaw, Martin Balsam, Hector Elizondo, Earl Hindman, James Broderick

'Full of noise and squalling and dirty words used for giggly shock effects.'—*New Yorker*

Taking Off**
US 1971 92m Movielab
Universal (Alfred W. Crown, Michael Hausman)

Suburban parents seek their errant daughter among the hippies, and gradually lose their own inhibitions.
Slight, formless, but amusing revue-style comment by a Czech director on the American scene.

w Milos Forman, John Guare, Jean-Claude Carrière, John Klein *d Milos Forman*
ph Miroslav Ondricek

Lynn Carlin, Buck Henry, Linnea Heacock

A Tale of Five Cities
GB 1951 99m bw
Grand National (Alexander Paal)
US title: *A Tale of Five Women*

An amnesiac American seeks clues to his past in Rome, Vienna, Paris, Berlin and London.
Tedious pattern drama remarkable only for its then untried cast.

w Patrick Kirwan, Maurice J. Wilson
d Montgomery Tully *ph* Gordon Lang *m* Hans May

Bonar Colleano, Gina Lollobrigida, Barbara Kelly, Lana Morris, Anne Vernon, Eva Bartok

A Tale of Two Cities**
US 1935 121m bw
MGM (David O. Selznick)

A British lawyer sacrifices himself to save another man from the guillotine.
Richly detailed version of the classic melodrama, with production values counting more than the acting.

w W. P. Lipscomb, S. N. Behrman, *novel* Charles Dickens *d Jack Conway* *ph* Oliver T. Marsh *m* Herbert Stothart

Ronald Colman, Elizabeth Allan, Basil Rathbone, Edna May Oliver, Blanche Yurka, Reginald Owen, Henry B. Walthall, Donald Woods, Walter Catlett, H. B. Warner, Claude Gillingwater, Fritz Leiber

A Tale of Two Cities*
GB 1958 117m bw
Rank (Betty E. Box)

Modest but still costly remake with good moments but a rather slow pace.

w T. E. B. Clarke *d* Ralph Thomas *ph* Ernest Steward *m* Richard Addinsell

Dirk Bogarde, Dorothy Tutin, Christopher Lee, Athene Seyler, Rosalie Crutchley, Ernest Clark, Stephen Murray, Paul Guers, Donald Pleasance, Ian Bannen, Cecil Parker, Alfie Bass
'Serviceable rather than imaginative.'—*MFB*

Tales from the Crypt*
GB 1972 92m Eastmancolor
Metromedia / Amicus (Milton Subotsky)

Five people get lost in catacombs and are shown the future by a sinister monk who turns out to be Satan.
Fair ghoulish fun; a quintet of stories with a recognizable Amicus link.

w Milton Subotsky, from comic strips by William Gaines *d* Freddie Francis *ph* Norman Warwick *m* Douglas Gamley

Ralph Richardson, Geoffrey Bayldon, Peter Cushing, Joan Collins, Ian Hendry, Robin Phillips, Richard Greene, Barbara Murray, Roy Dotrice, Nigel Patrick, Patrick Magee

Tales of Beatrix Potter**
GB 1971 90m Technicolor
EMI (Richard Goodwin)
US title: *Peter Rabbit and the Tales of Beatrix Potter*

Children's stories danced by the Royal Ballet in animal masks.
A charming entertainment for those who can appreciate it, though hardly the most direct way to tell these stories.

w Richard Goodwin, Christine Edward
d Reginald Mills *ph* Austin Dempster *m* John Lanchbery *ch Frederick Ashton masks Rotislav Doboujinsky* *pd* Christine Edward

The Tales of Hoffman**
GB 1953 127m Technicolor
British Lion / London / Michael Powell, Emeric Pressburger

The poet Hoffman, in three adventures, seeks the eternal woman and is beset by eternal evil.
Overwhelming combination of opera, ballet, and rich production design, an indigestible hodgepodge with flashes of superior talent.

wd Michael Powell, Emeric Pressburger
ph Christopher Challis *m Jacques Offenbach*
pd Hein Heckroth

Robert Rounseville, Robert Helpmann, Pamela Brown, Moira Shearer, Frederick Ashton, Leonide Massine, Ludmilla Tcherina, Ann Ayars, Mogens Wieth; music conducted by Sir Thomas Beecham with the Royal Philharmonic Orchestra
'The most spectacular failure yet achieved by Powell and Pressburger, who seem increasingly to dissipate their gifts in a welter of aimless ingenuity.'—*Gavin Lambert*

Tales of Manhattan**
US 1942 118m bw
TCF (Boris Morros, Sam Spiegel)

Separate stories of a tail coat, which passes from owner to owner.
The stories are all rather disappointing in their different veins, but production standards are high and a few of the stars shine. A sequence starring W. C. Fields was deleted before release.

w Ben Hecht, Ferenc Molnar, Donald Ogden Stewart, Samuel Hoffenstein, Alan Campbell, Ladislas Fodor, Laslo Vadnay, Laszlo Gorog, Lamar Trotti, Henry Blankfort *d Julien Duvivier ph* Joseph Walker *m* Sol Kaplan

Charles Boyer, Rita Hayworth, Thomas Mitchell, Eugene Pallette; Ginger Rogers, Henry Fonda, Cesar Romero, Gail Patrick, Roland Young; *Charles Laughton*, Elsa Lanchester, Victor Francen, Christian Rub; *Edward G. Robinson*, George Sanders, James Gleason, Harry Davenport; Paul Robeson, Ethel Waters, Eddie Anderson

† Duvivier was clearly chosen to make this film because of his success with the similar *Carnet de Bal*; he and Boyer went on to make the less successful *Flesh and Fantasy* on similar lines.

Tales of Terror*
US 1962 90m Pathecolor Panavision
AIP (Roger Corman)

'Morella': a dying girl discovers the mummified body of her mother. 'The Black Cat': a henpecked husband kills his wife and walls up the body. 'The Facts in the Case of M Valdemar': an old man is hypnotized at the moment of death.
Tolerable short story compendium, rather short on subtlety and style.

w Richard Matheson, *stories* Edgar Allan Poe *d* Roger Corman *ph* Floyd Crosby *m* Les Baxter

Vincent Price, *Peter Lorre*, Basil Rathbone, Debra Paget

Tales That Witness Madness
GB 1973 90m colour
Paramount / Amicus (Milton Subotsky, Norman Priggen)

Five ghostly tales linked by an old bookshop.
Average example of the Amicus compendiums.

w Jay Fairbank *d* Freddie Francis *ph* Norman Warwick *m* Bernard Ebbinghouse

Jack Hawkins, Donald Pleasance, Georgia Brown, Donald Houston, Suzy Kendall, Peter McEnery, Joan Collins, Michael Jayston, Kim Novak, Michael Petrovitch, Mary Tamm

Talk About a Stranger*
US 1952 65m bw
MGM (Richard Goldstone)

In a small town, gossip is unjustly aroused over a mysterious stranger who is suspected of various crimes.
Unusual though rather naïve second feature, directed for more than its worth.

w Margaret Fitts, *novel* Charlotte Armstrong *d* David Bradley *ph* John Alton *m* David Buttolph

George Murphy, Nancy Davis, Lewis Stone, Billy Gray, Kurt Kasznar

The Talk of the Town***
US 1942 118m bw
Columbia (George Stevens, Fred Guiol)

A girl loves both a suspected murderer and the lawyer who defends him.
Unusual mixture of comedy and drama, delightfully handled by three sympathetic stars.

w Irwin Shaw, Sidney Buchman d George Stevens ph Ted Tetzlaff *m* Frederick Hollander

Roland Colman, Cary Grant, Jean Arthur, Edgar Buchanan, Glenda Farrell, Charles Dingle, Emma Dunn, Rex Ingram

'A rip-roaring, knock-down-and-drag-out comedy about civil liberties.'—*John T. McManus*

The Tall Headlines
GB 1952 100m bw
Grand National / Raymond Stross
aka: *The Frightened Bride*

A family is affected when the eldest son is executed for murder.
Glum, boring, badly cast, badly written and generally inept melodrama.

w Audrey Erskine Lindop (from her novel), Dudley Leslie *d* Terence Young *ph* C. M. Pennington-Richards *m* Hans May

Flora Robson, Michael Denison, Mai Zetterling, Jane Hylton, André Morell, Dennis Price, Mervyn Johns, Naunton Wayne

'A falsity which will surely surprise even those familiar with the conventions of British middle-class cinema.'—*Lindsay Anderson*

Tall in the Saddle
US 1944 87m bw
RKO (Robert Fellows)

The newly-arrived ranch foreman finds that his boss has been murdered.
Quite a watchable, and forgettable, mystery western.

w Michael Hogan, Paul J. Fix *d* Edwin L.

Marin *ph* Robert de Grasse *m* Constantin Bakaleinikoff

John Wayne, Ella Raines, Ward Bond, George 'Gabby' Hayes, Audrey Long, Elizabeth Risdon, Don Douglas, Paul Fix, Russell Wade

The Tall Men*
US 1955 122m De Luxe Cinemascope
TCF (William A. Bacher, William B. Hawks)

After the Civil War, two Texans head north for the Montana goldfields.
Solid star western.

w Sidney Boehm, Frank Nugent, *novel* Clay Fisher *d* Raoul Walsh *ph* Leo Tover *m* Victor Young

Clark Gable, Jane Russell, Robert Ryan, Cameron Mitchell, Juan Garcia, Harry Shannon, Emile Meyer

'A big action feast and value for anyone's money.'—*Newsweek*

Tall Story
US 1960 91m bw
Warner / Mansfield (Joshua Logan)

A college basketball player faces various kinds of trouble when he marries.
Dislikeable campus comedy with leading players miscast.

w Julius J. Epstein, *novel* The Homecoming Game by Howard Nemoor *d* Joshua Logan *ph* Ellsworth Fredericks *m* Cyril Mockridge

Anthony Perkins, Jane Fonda, Ray Walston, Anne Jackson, Marc Connelly, Murray Hamilton, Elizabeth Patterson

The Tall T*
US 1957 78m Technicolor
Columbia / Scott–Brown (Harry Joe Brown)

Three bandits hold up a stagecoach and take a hostage, but are outwitted by a rancher.
Good small-scale suspense western with plenty of action and a blood-spattered finale.

w Burt Kennedy d Budd Boetticher ph Charles Lawton Jnr

Randolph Scott, Richard Boone, Maureen O'Sullivan, Arthur Hunnicutt, Skip Homeier, John Hubbard, Henry Silva

The Tall Target**
US 1951 78m bw
MGM (Richard Goldstone)

A discredited police officer tries to stop the assassination of Abraham Lincoln on a train to Washington.
Lively period suspenser with excellent attention to detail and much of the attraction of *The Lady Vanishes*. The plot slightly relaxes its hold before the end.

w George Worthing Yates, Art Cohn d Anthony Mann ph Paul C. Vogel ad Cedric Gibbons, Eddie Imazu

Dick Powell, Adolphe Menjou, Paula Raymond, Marshall Thompson, *Ruby Dee*, Richard Rober, Will Geer, Florence Bates

'An intelligent minor picture which makes good use of its material.'—*MFB*

Tamahine
GB 1962 95m Technicolor
Cinemascope
ABP (John Bryan)

The headmaster of a boys' school is visited by his glamorous half-caste Polynesian cousin.
Simple-minded school comedy with predictable situations.

w Denis Cannan, *novel* Thelma Niklaus *d* Philip Leacock *m* Malcolm Arnold

John Fraser, Nancy Kwan, Dennis Price, Derek Nimmo, Justine Lord, James Fox, Coral Browne, Michael Gough, Allan Cuthbertson

The Tamarind Seed*
GB 1974 125m Eastmancolor
Panavision
Jewel / Lorimar / Pimlico (Ken Wales)

While holidaying in Barbados, a British widow falls for a Russian military attaché.
Old-fashioned romance which turns into a mild spy caper. A well-heeled time-passer.

w Blake Edwards, *novel* Evelyn Anthony *d* Blake Edwards *ph* Frederick A. Young *m* John Barry

Julie Andrews, Omar Sharif, Sylvia Syms, Dan O'Herlihy, Anthony Quayle, Oscar Homolka

The Taming of the Shrew*
US 1967 122m Technicolor
Panavision
Columbia / Royal / FAI (Richard McWhorter)

Petruchio violently tames his shrewish wife.
Busy version of one of Shakespeare's more proletarian comedies; the words in this case take second place to violent action and rioting colour.

w Suso Cecchi d'Amico, Paul Dehn, Franco Zeffirelli *d Franco Zeffirelli ph* Oswald Morris, Luciano Trasatti *m* Nino Rota

Richard Burton, Elizabeth Taylor, Michael York, Michael Hordern, Cyril Cusack, Alfred Lynch, Natasha Pyne, Alan Webb, Victor Spinetti

'As entertainment *Kiss Me Kate* is infinitely

better but then Cole Porter was a real artist and Burton is a culture vulture.'—*Wilfrid Sheed*

'The old warhorse of a comedy has been spanked into uproarious life.'—*Hollis Alpert*

Tammy*
US 1957 89m Technicolor
Cinemascope
U-I (Ross Hunter)

A backwoods tomboy falls for a stranded flier. Whimsical romance for middle America, which started Hollywood's last series of proletarian family appeal before the family was entirely forsaken for four letter words.

w Oscar Brodney *d* Joseph Pevney *ph* Arthur E. Arling *m* Joseph Gershenson

Debbie Reynolds, Walter Brennan, Leslie Nielsen, Mala Powers, Fay Wray, Sidney Blackmer, Mildred Natwick

Tammy and the Doctor
US 1963 88m Eastmancolor
U-I / Ross Hunter

Tammy leaves her riverboat to accompany an old lady who needs an operation in the big city. More artless family fodder.

w Oscar Brodney *d* Harry Keller *ph* Russell Metty *m* Frank Skinner

Sandra Dee, Peter Fonda, Macdonald Carey, Beulah Bondi, Margaret Lindsay, Reginald Owen, Adam West

'The aura of simple religion and naïve philosophy remains singularly charmless.'—*MFB*

Tammy Tell Me True
US 1961 97m Eastmancolor
U-I (Ross Hunter)

Tammy gets a college education and charms all comers.
Sugar-coated sequel to the above.

w Oscar Brodney *d* Harry Keller *ph* Clifford Stine *m* Percy Faith

Sandra Dee, John Gavin, Charles Drake, Virginia Grey, *Beulah Bondi*, Julia Meade, Cecil Kellaway, Edgar Buchanan

'The heroine appears to be not so much old-fashioned as positively retarded.'—*MFB*

Tampico
US 1944 75m bw
TCF (Robert Bassler)

A tanker captain picks up survivors from a torpedoed ship and finds himself involved with spies.
Very minor action melodrama, efficiently made.

w Kenneth Gamet, Fred Niblo Jnr, Richard Macaulay *d* Lothar Mendes *ph* Charles G. Clarke

Edward G. Robinson, Lynn Bari, Victor McLaglen, Marc Lawrence, E. J. Ballentine, Mona Maris

Tap Roots
US 1948 109m Technicolor
U-I

A southern family tries to remain neutral in the Civil War.
Minor *Gone with the Wind* saga, quite expensively produced but not very exciting.

w Alan le May, *novel* James Street *d* George Marshall *ph* Winton C. Hoch, Lionel Lindon *m* Frank Skinner

Susan Hayward, Van Heflin, Boris Karloff, Julie London, Whitfield Connor

Tarantula
US 1955 80m bw
U-I (William Alland)

Scientists working on an artificial food become grossly misshapen, and an infected spider escapes and grows to giant size.
Moderate monster hokum with the desert setting which became a cliché; the grotesque faces are more horrific than the spider, which seldom seems to touch the ground.

w Robert M. Fresco, Martin Berkeley *d* Jack Arnold *ph* George Robinson *m* Joseph Gershenson

Leo G. Carroll, John Agar, Mara Corday, Nestor Paiva

Taras Bulba*
US 1962 124m Eastmancolor
Panavision
UA / H-H / Avala (Harold Hecht)

A cossack leader has bitter disagreements with his rebellious son.
Violent action epic based on a well-worn story; plenty of spectacular highlights.

w Waldo Salt, Karl Tunberg, *novel* Nicolai Gogol *d* J. Lee-Thompson *ph* Joe MacDonald *m* Franz Waxman *pd* Edward Carrere

Yul Brynner, Tony Curtis, Christine Kaufmann, Sam Wanamaker, Guy Rolfe, George Macready, Vladimir Sokoloff, Abraham Sofaer

Target Risk
US 1975 74m Technicolor TVM
Universal

Bonded couriers combat thieves and blackmailers.

Abysmal crime pilot marking a desperate shortage of style and ideas.

w Don Carlos Dunaway *d* Robert Scheerer

Bo Svenson, Meredith Baxter, John P. Ryan, Robert Coote, Lee Paul

Target Zero
US 1955 93m bw
Warner (David Weisbart)

An infantry patrol in Korea is cut off behind enemy lines.
Routine battle exploits with a highly unlikely superimposed romance.

w Sam Rolfe *d* Harmon Jones *ph* Edwin DuPar *m* David Buttolph

Richard Conte, Charles Bronson, Richard Stapley, Chuck Connors, L. Q. Jones, Peggie Castle

Targets*
US 1967 90m Pathecolor
(Paramount) Peter Bogdanovich

An elderly horror film star confronts and disarms a mad sniper at a drive-in movie.
Oddball melodrama apparently meant to contrast real and fantasy violence; it doesn't quite work despite effective moments, and the low budget shows.

wd Peter Bogdanovich *ph* Laszlo Kovacs

Boris Karloff, Tim O'Kelly, James Brown, Sandy Baron

The Tarnished Angels
US 1957 91m bw Cinemascope
U-I (Albert Zugsmith)

A reporter falls in with a self-torturing family of circus air aces.
Unsatisfactory attempt to reunite the talents of *Written on the Wind*; a dull story, very boringly presented.

w George Zuckerman, *novel* Pylon by William Faulkner *d* Douglas Sirk *ph* Irving Glassberg *m* Joseph Gershenson

Rock Hudson, Robert Stack, Dorothy Malone, Jack Carson, Robert Middleton

Tarzan
The talkie *Tarzans* began with Johnny Weissmuller and tailed off from there. (See *Filmgoer's Companion* for the silents.) The 1932 version more or less followed the original Edgar Rice Burroughs novel, and all the MGM entries had a special vivid quality about them, but subsequently the productions, usually produced under the aegis of Sol Lesser, tailed off towards the standard of the TV series of the sixties starring Ron Ely.

1932: TARZAN THE APE MAN** (MGM: Weissmuller with Maureen O'Sullivan: *d* W. S. Van Dyke: 99m)
1933: TARZAN THE FEARLESS (Principal: Buster Crabbe: *d* Robert Hill: 73m)
1934: TARZAN AND HIS MATE*** (MGM: Weissmuller with Maureen O'Sullivan: *d* Cedric Gibbons: 105m)
1935: THE NEW ADVENTURES OF TARZAN (Burroughs: Herman Brix: *d* Edward Kull: 75m)
1936: TARZAN ESCAPES** (MGM: Weissmuller with Maureen O'Sullivan: *d* Richard Thorpe: 95m)
1938: TARZAN'S REVENGE (Sol Lesser: Glenn Morris: *d* D. Ross Lederman: 70m); TARZAN AND THE GREEN GODDESS (Principal: Herman Brix: *d* Edward Kull: 72m: largely a re-edit of NEW ADVENTURES)
1939: TARZAN FINDS A SON (MGM: Weissmuller with O'Sullivan: Richard Thorpe: 90m)
1941: TARZAN'S SECRET TREASURE (MGM: Weissmuller with O'Sullivan: *d* Richard Thorpe: 81m)
1942: TARZAN'S NEW YORK ADVENTURE (MGM: Weissmuller with O'Sullivan: *d* Richard Thorpe: 71m)
1943: TARZAN ESCAPES (RKO: Weissmuller: *d* William Thiele: 78m); TARZAN'S DESERT MYSTERY (RKO: Weissmuller: *d* William Thiele: 70m)
1945: TARZAN AND THE AMAZONS (RKO: Weissmuller: *d* Kurt Neumann: 76m)
1946: TARZAN AND THE LEOPARD WOMAN (RKO: Weissmuller: *d* Kurt Neumann: 72m)
1947: TARZAN AND THE HUNTRESS (RKO: Weissmuller: *d* Kurt Neumann: 72m)
1948: TARZAN AND THE MERMAIDS (RKO: *d* Robert Florey: Weissmuller: 68m)
1949: TARZAN'S MAGIC FOUNTAIN (RKO: Lex Barker: *d* Lee Sholem: 73m)
1950: TARZAN AND THE SLAVE GIRL (RKO: Lex Barker: *d* Lee Sholem: 74m)
1951: TARZAN'S PERIL (RKO: Lex Barker: *d* Byron Haskin: 79m)
1952: TARZAN'S SAVAGE FURY (RKO: Lex Barker: *d* Cy Endfield: 80m)
1953: TARZAN AND THE SHE-DEVIL (RKO: Lex Barker: *d* Kurt Neumann: 76m)
1955: TARZAN'S HIDDEN JUNGLE (RKO: Gordon Scott: *d* Harold Schuster: 73m)
1957: TARZAN AND THE LOST SAFARI (colour) (MGM: Gordon Scott: *d* Bruce Humberstone: 84m)
1958: TARZAN'S FIGHT FOR LIFE (colour)

(MGM: Gordon Scott: *d* Bruce Humberstone: 86m)
1959: TARZAN'S GREATEST ADVENTURE (colour) (MGM: Gordon Scott: *d* John Guillermin: 90m)
1959: TARZAN THE APE MAN (colour: remake of the original story) (MGM: Denny Miller: *d* Joseph Newman: 82m)
1960: TARZAN THE MAGNIFICENT (colour) (Paramount: Gordon Scott: *d* Robert Day: 88m)
1962: TARZAN GOES TO INDIA (colour) (MGM: Jock Mahoney: *d* John Guillermin: 86m)
1963: TARZAN'S THREE CHALLENGES (colour) (MGM: Jock Mahoney: *d* Robert Day: 92m)
1966: TARZAN AND THE VALLEY OF GOLD (colour) (NatGen: Mike Henry: Robert Day: 90m)
1967: TARZAN AND THE GREAT RIVER (colour) (Paramount: Mike Henry: *d* Robert Day: 88m)
1968: TARZAN AND THE JUNGLE BOY (colour) (Paramount: Mike Henry: *d* Robert Day: 90m)

The Tartars
Italy 1960 105m Technicolor
Totalscope
Lux (Riccardo Gualino)

Viking settlers on the Russian steppes fight Tartar invaders.
Action-packed comic strip.

d Richard Thorpe *ph* Amerigo Genarelli

Orson Welles, Victor Mature, Folco Lulli, Arnoldo Foa

Task Force
US 1949 116m bw (Technicolor sequences)
Warner (Jerry Wald)

An admiral about to retire recalls his struggle to promote the cause of aircraft carriers.
Stilted and long-drawn-out flagwaver with too much chat and action highlights borrowed from wartime newsreel.

wd Delmer Daves *ph* Robert Burks, Wilfrid M. Cline *m* Franz Waxman

Gary Cooper, Walter Brennan, Jane Wyatt, Wayne Morris, Julie London, Bruce Bennett, Stanley Ridges, Jack Holt

A Taste of Evil**
US 1971 73m colour TVM
Aaron Spelling

After seven years in a mental home, a girl goes home to find she is being driven mad again.
Reworking of the same author's *Taste of Fear*; not bad.

w Jimmy Sangster *d* John Llewellyn Moxey

Barbara Stanwyck, Barbara Parkins, William Windom, Arthur O'Connell, Roddy McDowall

A Taste of Excitement
GB 1968 99m Eastmancolor
Trio Films (George Willoughby)

An English girl holidaying on the Riviera suspects that someone is trying to kill her.
Standard frightened lady/'they won't believe me' mystery with enough twists to satisfy addicts.

w Brian Carton, Don Sharp, *novel* Waiting for a Tiger by Ben Healey *d* Don Sharp *ph* Paul Beeson

Eva Renzi, David Buck, Peter Vaughan, Sophie Hardy, Paul Hubschmid, Kay Walsh

Taste of Fear**
GB 1961 82m bw
Columbia / Hammer (Jimmy Sangster)
US title: *Scream of Fear*

A crippled heiress visits her long-lost father and is haunted by his corpse.
Smartly tricked-out sub-Hitchcock screamer with sudden shocks among the Riviera settings and a plot which Hammer borrowed from *Les Diaboliques* and used again and again.

w Jimmy Sangster d Seth Holt ph Douglas Slocombe m Clifton Parker

Susan Strasberg, Ann Todd, Ronald Lewis, Christopher Lee, Leonard Sachs

'All those creaking shutters, flickering candles, wavering shadows and pianos playing in empty rooms still yield a tiny frisson.'—*Penelope Houston*

A Taste of Honey***
GB 1961 100m bw
British Lion / Bryanston / Woodfall (Tony Richardson)

Adventures of a pregnant Salford teenager, her sluttish mother, black lover and homosexual friend.
Fascinating offbeat comedy drama with memorable characters and sharply etched backgrounds.

w Shelagh Delaney, Tony Richardson, *play* Shelagh Delaney *d Tony Richardson ph Walter Lassally m* John Addison

Rita Tushingham, Dora Bryan, Murray Melvin, Robert Stephens, Paul Danquah

'Tart and lively around the edges and bitter at the core.'—*Peter John Dyer*

Taste the Blood of Dracula
GB 1969 95m Technicolor
Hammer (Aida Young)

A depraved peer involves three Victorian businessmen in the reactivation of Dracula.
Latterday vampire saga, initially lively but mainly dreary.

w John Elder *d* Peter Sasdy *ph* Arthur Grant *m* James Bernard

Christopher Lee, Geoffrey Keen, Gwen Watford, Linda Hayden, Peter Sallis, Anthony Corlan, John Carson, Ralph Bates

The Tattered Dress
US 1957 93m bw Cinemascope
U-I (Albert Zugsmith)

While conducting a murder defence, a criminal lawyer annoys a vindictive small-town sheriff, who plots revenge.
Silly melodrama which rapidly loses interest after a promising start.

w George Zuckerman *d* Jack Arnold *ph* Carl Guthrie *m* Frank Skinner

Jeff Chandler, Jack Carson, Jeanne Crain, Gail Russell, George Tobias, Edward Andrews, Philip Reed

A Tattered Web**
US 1971 74m colour TVM
Metromedia (Bob Markell)

A police detective protects himself by taking the law into his own hands.
Complex, satisfying crime melodrama with a twist or two.

w Art Wallace *d* Paul Wendkos

Lloyd Bridges, Broderick Crawford, Murray Hamilton, Ann Helm

Tawny Pipit*
GB 1944 85m bw
GFD / Two Cities (Bernard Miles)

The life of a village in wartime is disrupted when two rare birds nest in a local meadow.
Pleasant, thin little comedy, a precursor of the Ealing school.

w Bernard Miles *d* Bernard Miles, Charles Saunders

Bernard Miles, Rosamund John, Niall MacGinnis, Jean Gillie, Christopher Steele, Lucie Mannheim, Brefni O'Rourke, Marjorie Rhodes

'Almost unimaginably genteel.'—*James Agee*

'Not quite dry enough for the epicures nor sweet enough for the addicts.'—*C. A. Lejeune*

Taxi
US 1952 77m bw
TCF (Samuel G. Engel)

A taxi driver helps a young mother find her husband, and falls for her himself.
Practised sentimental guff, Hollywoodized from the French film *Sans Laisser d'Adresse*.

w D. M. Marshman Jnr, Daniel Fuchs *d* Gregory Ratoff *ph* Milton Krasner *m* Leigh Harline

Dan Dailey, Constance Smith, Neva Patterson, Blanche Yurka, Walter Woolf King

Taxi Driver***
US 1976 114m Metrocolor
Columbia / Italo–Judeo (Michael and Julia Philips)

A lonely Vietnam veteran becomes a New York taxi driver and allows the violence and squalor around him to explode in his mind.
The epitome of the sordid realism of the seventies, this unlovely but brilliantly made film haunts the mind and paints a most vivid picture of a hell on earth. Unfortunately the plot in the latter stages makes no sense.

w Paul Schraeder d Martin Scorsese ph Michael Chapman m Bernard Herrmann

Robert de Niro, Jodie Foster, Cybill Shepherd, Peter Boyle, Leonard Harris, Harvey Keitel

Tea and Sympathy
US 1956 122m Metrocolor Cinemascope
MGM (Pandro S. Berman)

A sensitive teenage schoolboy is scorned by his tougher classmates, but his housemaster's wife takes him in hand . . .
Overblown and bowdlerized version of a quiet little Broadway play; impeccable production values, but no spark.

w Robert Anderson (and the Hays office), from his play *d* Vincente Minnelli *ph* John Alton *m* Adolph Deutsch

Deborah Kerr, *John Kerr*, Leif Erickson, Edward Andrews, Darryl Hickman

Tea for Two*
US 1950 97m Technicolor
Warner (William Jacobs)

A nearly bankrupt financier promises his niece 25,000 dollars for her new musical show if she can say no to every question for twenty-four hours.
Tinkly, quite amusing light musical which has little to do with *No No Nanette* on which it is allegedly based.

w Henry Clark *d* David Butler *ph* Wilfrid Cline *md* Ray Heindorf

Doris Day, Gordon Macrae, Gene Nelson, Eve Arden, Billy de Wolfe, S. Z. Sakall, Bill Goodwin, Patrice Wymore

Teacher's Pet*
US 1957 120m bw Vistavision
Paramount / Perlberg–Seaton (William Perlberg)

A tough city editor falls for a lady professor of journalism and enrols as a student.
Overlong one-joke comedy which quickly reneges on its early promise; but the principals play up divertingly.

w Fay and Michael Kanin *d* George Seaton *ph* Haskell Boggs *m* Roy Webb

Clark Gable, Doris Day, Gig Young, Mamie Van Doren, Nick Adams

The Teahouse of the August Moon*
US 1956 123m Metrocolor Cinemascope
MGM (Jack Cummings)

Okinawa 1944: a wily interpreter helps American troops succumb to the oriental way of life.
Adequate, well-acted screen version of a Broadway comedy which succeeded largely because of its theatricality. A few good jokes remain.

w John Patrick, from his play *d* Daniel Mann *ph* John Alton *m* Saul Chaplin

Marlon Brando, Glenn Ford, Eddie Albert, *Paul Ford*, Michiko Kyo, Henry Morgan

Teenage Rebel
US 1956 94m bw Cinemascope
TCF (Charles Brackett)

A wealthy California woman is visited by her teenage daughter from a former marriage; the girl proceeds to make difficulties for everyone.
The first film in black-and-white Cinemascope is a tedious drama of unreal people.

w Walter Reisch, Charles Brackett, *play* Edith Sommer *d* Edmund Goulding *ph* Joe MacDonald *m* Leigh Harline

Ginger Rogers, Michael Rennie, Mildred Natwick, Betty Lou Keim, Warren Berlinger, Louise Beavers, Irene Hervey

Tell Me That You Love Me, Junie Moon
US 1969 113m Technicolor
Paramount / Sigma (Otto Preminger)

A disfigured girl, a homosexual paraplegic and an introvert epileptic set up house together.
Absurd tragicomedy which remains disturbingly icky in conception and execution.

w Marjorie Kellogg, from her novel *d* Otto Preminger *ph* Boris Kaufman *m* Philip Springer

Liza Minnelli, Ken Howard, Robert Moore, Kay Thompson, Leonard Frey, James Coco, Fred Williamson

Tell Me Where it Hurts
US 1974 74m colour TVM
Tomorrow

A middle-aged housewife discovers women's lib.
Amusing contemporary comedy which should have been shorter.

w Fay Kanin *d* Paul Bogart

Maureen Stapleton, Paul Sorvino, Ayn Ruyman

Tell No Tales**
US 1938 68m bw
MGM (Edward Chodorov)

A managing editor seeks a big scoop to save his newspaper, and solves a kidnap-murder case.
Intriguingly written and handled second feature, with excellent pace, performance and entertainment value.

w Lionel Houser d Leslie Fenton ph Joseph Ruttenberg *m* William Axt

Melvyn Douglas, Louise Platt, Gene Lockhart, Douglass Dumbrille, Zeffie Tilbury, Halliwell Hobbes

Tell Them Willie Boy is Here*
US 1969 97m Technicolor
Universal (Philip A. Waxman)

In 1909 an Indian turned cowboy comes up against old prejudices and is pursued into the desert after an accidental death.
Boringly predictable story of white man's guilt, very professionally made.

wd Abraham Polonsky, novel Willie Boy by Harry Lawton *ph Conrad Hall m* Dave Grusin

Robert Redford, Robert Blake, Katharine Ross, Susan Clark, Barry Sullivan, Charles McGraw, Charles Aidman, John Vernon

Tempest
Italy / France / Yugoslavia 1958 123m Technirama
(Paramount) Dino de Laurentiis / Gray / S. N Pathe / Bosnia

Adventures of a Russian ensign banished by Catherine the Great.
Expensive but sloppy epic which fails to generate much interest.

w Louis Peterson, Alberto Lattuada, Ivo Perelli, *novel* The Captain's Daughter by Alexander Pushkin *d* Alberto Lattuada *ph Aldo Tonti* *m* Piero Piccioni

Van Heflin, Geoffrey Horne, Silvana Mangano, Oscar Homolka, Viveca Lindfors, Robert Keith, Vittorio Gassman, Finlay Currie, Agnes Moorehead, Helmut Dantine, Laurence Naismith

Temptation
US 1946 92m bw
Universal (Edward Small)

An archaeologist's wife takes to poisoning both her husband and her blackmailing lover.
Hoary Edwardian melodrama, unpersuasively restaged.

w Robert Thoeren, *novel* Bella Donna by Robert Hichens *d* Irving Pichel *ph* Lucien Ballard *m* Daniele Amfitheatrof

Merle Oberon, George Brent, Charles Korvin, Paul Lukas, Lenore Ulric, Arnold Moss, Ludwig Stossel, Gavin Muir, Ilka Gruning, André Charlot

Temptation Harbour
GB 1946 104m bw
ABP (Victor Skutesky)

A railway signalman finds and keeps stolen money.
Well-presented but boringly predictable melodrama with an overwrought leading performance set against yards of studio fog.

w Victor Skutesky, Frederic Gotfurt, Rodney Ackland, *novel* Newhaven–Dieppe by Georges Simenon *d* Lance Comfort

Robert Newton, Simone Simon, William Hartnell, Marcel Dalio, Margaret Barton, Edward Rigby, Joan Hopkins, Charles Victor, Kathleen Harrison

The Ten Commandments*
US 1956 219m Technicolor Vistavision
Paramount / Cecil B. de Mille (Henry Wilcoxon)

The life of Moses and his leading of the Israelites to the Promised Land.
Popular but incredibly stilted and verbose bible-in-pictures spectacle. A very long haul along a monotonous route, with the director at his pedestrian worst.

w Aeneas Mackenzie, Jesse L. Lasky Jnr, Jack Gariss, Frederic M. Frank *d* Cecil B. de Mille *ph* Loyal Griggs *m* Elmer Bernstein

Charlton Heston, Yul Brynner, Edward G. Robinson, Anne Baxter, Nina Foch, Yvonne de Carlo, John Derek, H. B. Warner, Henry Wilcoxon, Judith Anderson, John Carradine, Douglass Dumbrille, Cedric Hardwicke, Martha Scott, Vincent Price

Ten Days in Paris
GB 1939 82m bw
Columbia (Jerome J. Jackson)
US titles: *Missing Ten Days/Spy in the Pantry*

An amnesiac wakes up in Paris and finds he has been involved in espionage activities.
Modest, quite likeable little comedy suspenser.

w John Meehan Jnr, James Curtis, *novel* The Disappearance of Roger Tremayne by Bruce Graeme *d* Tim Whelan *ph* Otto Kanturek

Rex Harrison, Karen Verne, Leo Genn, Joan Marion, Anthony Holles, John Abbott, Hay Petrie

Ten Gentlemen from West Point**
US 1942 104m bw
TCF (William Perlberg)

Adventures in Indian territory, and back at West Point, of the first recruits to that military academy in the early 1800s.
Likeable mixture of comedy and flagwaving adventure, with excellent production values and a dominating performance.

w Richard Maibaum, George Seaton *d* Henry Hathaway *ph* Leon Shamroy *m* Alfred Newman

Laird Cregar, George Montgomery, Maureen O'Hara, John Sutton, Shepperd Strudwick, Victor Francen, Harry Davenport, Ward Bond, Douglass Dumbrille, Ralph Byrd, Louis Jean Heydt

Ten Little Indians*
GB 1966 91m bw
Tenlit (Harry Alan Towers)

Ten people, including two servants invited to a remote house in the Austrian Alps are murdered one by one.
Fair copy of a classic whodunnit.

w Peter Yeldham, Harry Alan Towers, *novel* Agatha Christie *d* George Pollock *ph* Ernest Steward *m* Malcolm Lockyer

Wilfrid Hyde White, Dennis Price, Stanley Holloway, Leo Genn, Shirley Eaton, Hugh O'Brian, Daliah Lavi, Fabian, Mario Adorf, Marianne Hoppe
† Made also in 1945 and 1975, as *And Then There Were None* (qv).

Ten North Frederick*
US 1958 102m bw Cinemascope
TCF (Charles Brackett)

At the funeral of a local politico, his family and friends think back to the events of his life.
Small beer, but a generally adult and entertaining family drama despite a miscast lead.

wd Philip Dunne, novel John O'Hara *ph* Joe MacDonald *m* Leigh Harline

Gary Cooper, Geraldine Fitzgerald, Diane Varsi, Stuart Whitman, Suzy Parker, Tom Tully, Ray Stricklyn, John Emery

Ten Rillington Place*
GB 1970 111m Eastmancolor
Columbia / Filmways (Basil Appleby)

An account of London's sordid Christie murders of the forties.
Agreeably seedy reconstruction of a *cause célèbre*, carefully built around the star part of a murderous aberrant landlord. Too long, however, and finally too lacking in detail.

w Clive Exton, *book* Ludovic Kennedy *d* Richard Fleischer *ph* Denys Coop

Richard Attenborough, *John Hurt*, Judy Geeson, Pat Heywood, Isobel Black, Geoffrey Chater, André Morell, Robert Hardy

Ten Seconds to Hell
US 1959 93m bw
Hammer / Seven Arts (Michael Carreras)

Bomb disposal experts in post-war Berlin quarrel over a girl.
Boring, harsh, hollow melodrama, so artificially constructed that no one can possibly care who gets exploded.

w Robert Aldrich, Teddi Sherman, *novel* The Phoenix by Lawrence Bachmann *d* Robert Aldrich *ph* Ernest Laszlo *m* Kenneth V. Jones

Jack Palance, Jeff Chandler, Martine Carol, Robert Cornthwaite, Dave Willock, Wesley Addy

Ten Tall Men
US 1951 97m Technicolor
Columbia / Norma (Harold Hecht)

A Foreign Legion patrol prevents a Riff attack.
Comic strip adventures, efficiently handled.

w Roland Kibbee, Frank Davis *d* Willis Goldbeck *ph* William Snyder *m* David Buttolph

Burt Lancaster, Gilbert Roland, Kieron Moore, John Dehner, Jody Lawrance, George Tobias, Mike Mazurki

10.30 pm Summer
US / Spain 1966 85m Technicolor
UA / Jorill / Argos (Jules Dassin, Anatole Litvak)

The neurotic Greek wife of an Englishman travelling in Spain becomes obsessed with a murderer on the run.
Preposterously overwrought romantic melodrama.

w Jules Dassin, Marguerite Duras, *novel* Marguerite Duras *d* Jules Dassin *ph* Gabor Pogany *m* Christobel Hallfter

Peter Finch, Melina Mercouri, Romy Schneider, Julian Mateos

Ten Thousand Bedrooms
US 1956 114m Metrocolor Cinemascope
MGM (Joe Pasternak)

An American millionaire finds romance when he buys a Rome hotel.
Old-fashioned, unfunny comedy sadly lacking pace and style.

w Laslo Vadnay, Art Cohn, William Ludwig, Leonard Spiegelgass *d* Richard Thorpe *ph* Robert Bronner *m* George Stoll *songs* Nicholas Brodsky, Sammy Cahn

Dean Martin, Eva Bartok, Anna Maria Alberghetti, Walter Slezak, Paul Henreid, Jules Munchin, Marcel Dalio

Ten Who Dared
US 1960 92m Technicolor
Walt Disney (James Algar)

In 1869 a scientific expedition sets out to chart the Colorado River.
Tedious and unconvincing adventures.

w Lawrence E. Watkin, from the journal of Major John Wesley Powell *d* William Beaudine

Brian Keith, John Beal, James Drury, R. G. Armstrong, Ben Johnson, L. Q. Jones

Tenafly*
US 1972 74m Technicolor TVM
Universal / Levinson–Link (Jon Epstein)
aka: *Everybody's Looking*

A black private eye with domestic problems solves the murder of the wife of a talk show host.
Adequate pilot for what became a one-season addition to *Mystery Movie* (qv).

w Richard Levinson, William Link *d* Richard A. Colla

James McEachin, Mel Ferrer, Ed Nelson, John Ericson

Tender Comrade
US 1943 101m bw
RKO (David Hempstead)

Lady welders whose husbands are fighting men keep their chins up during World War II.
Dim tearjerker.

w Dalton Trumbo *d* Edward Dmytryk
ph Russell Metty *m* Leigh Harline

Ginger Rogers, Robert Ryan, Ruth Hussey, Patricia Collinge, Mady Christians, Kim Hunter, Jane Darwell

Tender Is the Night*
US 1961 146m De Luxe Cinemascope
TCF (Henry T. Weinstein)

Adventures around Europe between the wars of a rich American psychiatrist who has married his patient.
Patchy, fairly literal transcription of a patently unfilmable novel about defiantly unreal people in what would now be the jet set. About half the result is superficially entertaining.

w Ivan Moffat, *novel* F. Scott Fitzgerald
d Henry King *ph* Leon Shamroy *m* Bernard Herrmann

Jennifer Jones, Jason Robards Jnr, *Joan Fontaine, Tom Ewell*, Cesare Danova, Jill St John, Paul Lukas

The Tender Trap*
US 1955 111m Eastmancolor Cinemascope
MGM (Lawrence Weingarten)

A smart New York agent has a way with women which annoys his friend; but Casanova gets his come-uppance when he sets his sights on an apparently naïve young actress.
Thin comedy with agreeable moments, not helped by the wide screen.

w Julius J. Epstein, *play* Max Shulman, Robert Paul Smith *d* Charles Walters *ph* Paul Vogel *m* Jeff Alexander

Frank Sinatra, Debbie Reynolds, David Wayne, Celeste Holm, Lola Albright, Carolyn Jones

Tennessee Johnson*
US 1943 102m bw
MGM (J. Walter Ruben)
GB title: *The Man on America's Conscience*

The rise and the problems of President Andrew Johnson.
Sincere, straightforward, well-produced historical drama which failed to set the Thames —or the Hudson—on fire.

w John Balderston, Wells Root *d* William Dieterle *ph* Harold Rosson *m* Herbert Stothart

Van Heflin, Ruth Hussey, Lionel Barrymore, Marjorie Main, Regis Toomey, Montagu Love, Porter Hall, Charles Dingle, J. Edward Bromberg

'Dieterle's customary high-minded, high-polished mélange of heavy touches and intelligent performances.'—*James Agee*

Tension
US 1950 91m bw
MGM (Robert Sisk)

A chemist plans the perfect murder of his wife's lover, loses his nerve, then finds himself suspected when the man is murdered after all.
Disappointing suspenser which starts well but outstays its welcome.

w Allen Rivkin *d* John Berry *ph* Harry Stradling *m* André Previn

Richard Basehart, Audrey Totter, Barry Sullivan, Cyd Charisse, Lloyd Gough, Tom d'Andrea

Tenth Avenue Angel
US 1948 74m bw
MGM (Ralph Wheelwright)

The little daughter of poor parents loses her faith in life.
Icky sentimental piece for a waning child star.

w Angna Enters, Craig Rice, Harry Ruskin, Eleanore Griffin *d* Roy Rowland *ph* Robert Surtees *m* Rudolph G. Kopp

Margaret O'Brien, Angela Lansbury, George Murphy, Phyllis Thaxter, Rhys Williams, Warner Anderson, Audrey Totter, Connie Gilchrist

Teresa**
US 1951 101m bw
MGM (Arthur M. Loew)

A soldier with mother problems brings home an Italian bride.
Careful, sensitive, intelligent variation on a problem frequently considered by films of this period (*Frieda, Fräulein, Japanese War Bride*).

w Stewart Stern d Fred Zinnemann
ph William J. Miller *m* Louis Applebaum

Pier Angeli, John Ericson, Patricia Collinge, Richard Bishop, Peggy Ann Garner, Ralph Meeker, Bill Mauldin

Term of Trial*
GB 1962 130m bw
Romulus (James Woolf)

An unsuccessful schoolmaster is accused of rape by a nymphomaniac schoolgirl he has scorned.
Rather flabby 'adult' drama, too schematic to be

really interesting despite the best that acting can do.

wd Peter Glenville, *novel* The Burden of Proof by James Barlow *ph* Oswald Morris *m* Jean-Michel Demase *ad* Antony Woolard

Laurence Olivier, Sarah Miles, Simone Signoret, Hugh Griffith, Terence Stamp, Roland Culver, Frank Pettingell, Thora Hird, Dudley Foster, Norman Bird

A Terrible Beauty
GB 1960 90m bw
UA / Raymond Stross
US title: *Night Fighters*

In a north Irish village, the IRA revive their activities on the outbreak of World War II.
Heavily Oirish melodrama with a muddled message.

w Robert Wright Campbell, *novel* Arthur Roth *d* Tay Garnett *ph* Stephen Dade *m* Cedric Thorpe Davie

Robert Mitchum, Anne Heywood, Dan O'Herlihy, Cyril Cusack, Richard Harris, Marianne Benet

The Terror
US 1928 82m approx bw
Warner

A mysterious killer lurks in the cellars of a country house.
Primitive talkie which attempted a few new styles but showed that more were needed, also that some silent actors could not make the transfer.

w Harvey Gates, *novel* and *play* Edgar Wallace *d* Roy del Ruth

May McAvoy, Edward Everett Horton, Louise Fazenda, Alec B. Francis

† Remade 1938 (GB) as *The Gaunt Stranger*. *Return of the Terror* (US 1934) has little to do with it.

The Terror
US 1963 81m Pathecolor
AIP / Filmgroup (Roger Corman, Francis Ford Coppola)

A baron lives for twenty years in a creepy castle, mourning the death of his wife . . .
Shoddy horror improvised over a weekend on the set of *The Raven*. It looks it.

w Leo Gordon, Jack Hill *d* Roger Corman *ph* John Nickolaus *m* Ronald Stein

Boris Karloff, Jack Nicholson, Sandra Knight, Dorothy Neumann

Terror in a Texas Town*
US 1958 81m bw
UA / Frank N. Seltzer

A Swedish seaman arrives in a small western town and avenges the death of his brother.
Stylish second feature western, a genuine sleeper which holds the interest throughout.

w Ben L. Perry *d Joseph H. Lewis ph Ray Rennahan m* Gerald Fried

Sterling Hayden, Sebastian Cabot, Carol Kelly, Eugene Martin, Ned Young

Terror in the Sky*
US 1971 74m colour TVM
Paramount (Matthew Rapf)

All the crew of a jet liner are stricken with food poisoning and the plane has to be brought down by a passenger.
Competent remake of *Zero Hour* (qv).

From the novel Flight to Danger by Arthur Hailey *d* Bernard Kowalski

Leif Erickson, Doug McClure, Roddy McDowall, Keenan Wynn, Lois Nettleton, Kenneth Tobey

Terror in the Wax Museum
US 1973 94m De Luxe
Bing Crosby Productions / Fenady Associates (Andrew J. Fenady)

In Victorian London a waxworks owner is murdered . . .
Cheaply produced murder mystery (even the waxworks can't stand still) with horror asides and a cast of elderly hams.

w Jameson Brewer *d* George Fenady *ph* William Jurgensen *m* George Duning

Ray Milland, Broderick Crawford, Elsa Lanchester, Louis Hayward, John Carradine, Shani Wallis, Maurice Evans, Patric Knowles

The Terror of the Tongs
GB 1960 79m Technicolor
Hammer / Merlin

In 1910 Hong Kong a merchant avenges the death of his daughter at the hands of a villainous secret society.
Gory melodrama with dollops of screams, torture and vaguely orgiastic goings-on.

w Jimmy Sangster *d* Anthony Bushell *ph* Arthur Grant *m* James Bernard

Geoffrey Toone, Christopher Lee, Yvonne Monlaur, Brian Worth, Richard Leech

Terror on the Beach
US 1973 74m colour TVM
TCF
A family outing is ruined by violence from beach bums.
Unsurprising melodrama.
w Bill Svanoe *d* Paul Wendkos
Dennis Weaver, Estelle Parsons, Susan Dey, Kristoffer Tabori, Scott Hylands

Terror on the Fortieth Floor*
US 1974 74m colour TVM
Metromedia / Charles Fries (Ed Montagne)
A skyscraper is engulfed by fire.
The mini-screen's *Towering Inferno*; some say it's better.
w Jack Turley *d* Jerry Jameson
John Forsythe, Anjanette Comer, Joseph Campanella, Don Meredith

Tess of the Storm Country
US 1932 80m bw
Fox
A retired sea captain's daughter loves the lord of the manor.
Antiquated tushery first filmed as a Mary Pickford silent.
w S. N. Behrman, Sonya Levien, Rupert Hughes, *novel* Grace Miller White *d* Alfred Santell *ph* Hal Mohr
Janet Gaynor, Charles Farrell, Dudley Digges, June Clyde, George Meeker

Test Pilot**
US 1938 118m bw
MGM (Louis D. Lighton)
A brilliant but unpredictable test pilot is helped by his wife and his self-sacrificing friend.
A big box-office star vehicle of its time, still interesting as a highly efficient product.
w Waldemar Young, Vincent Lawrence, *story* Frank Wead *d Victor Fleming ph* Ray June *m* Franz Waxman
Clark Gable, Myrna Loy, Spencer Tracy, Lionel Barrymore, Samuel S. Hinds, Marjorie Main, Gloria Holden

'The picture is so noisy with sure-fire elements box office cast, violent excitement, glycerine tears and such—that it may be hard to keep the ear attuned to the quieter, more authentically human things in it.'—*James Shelley Hamilton*

The Texan
US 1930 79m bw
Paramount
The Llano Kid absolves his bandit past.
Early sound western, an interesting curiosity.
w Daniel Nathan Rufin, *story* The Double-Dyed Deceiver by O. Henry *d* John Cromwell *ph* Victor Milner
Gary Cooper, Fay Wray, Emma Dunn, Oscar Apfel

The Texans
US 1938 92m bw
Paramount (Lucien Hubbard)
Problems of the post-Civil War years include new railroads, the Ku Klux Klan, and the new cattle drive routes.
Formula western with fairly well staged excitements backing a routine romantic triangle.
w Bertram Millhauser, Paul Sloane, William Wister Haines *d* James Hogan *ph* Theodor Sparkuhl *m* Gerard Carbonara
Joan Bennett, Randolph Scott, May Robson, Walter Brennan, Robert Cummings, Raymond Halton, Robert Barrat, Francis Ford

Texas
US 1941 94m bw (released in sepia)
Columbia (Sam Bischoff)
Two veteran Civil War southerners head for Texas to set up a cattle business.
Western vehicle for two young stars, now very ordinary-looking.
w Horace McCoy, Lewis Meltzer, Michael Blankfort *d* George Marshall *ph* George Meehan
William Holden, Glenn Ford, Claire Trevor, George Bancroft, Edgar Buchanan, Don Beddoe, Andrew Tombes, Addison Richards

Texas across the River
US 1966 101m Techniscope
Universal (Harry Keller)
A Texan, an Indian and a Spanish nobleman on the run from jealous rivals have various adventures.
Sloppy western which seems to have had jokes added when someone realized it wasn't good enough to be taken seriously.
w Wells Root, Harold Greene, Ben Starr *d* Michael Gordon *ph* Russell Metty *m* Joseph Gershenson
Dean Martin, Alain Delon, Joey Bishop, Rosemary Forsyth, Tina Marquand, Peter Graves, Andrew Prine, Michael Ansara

Texas Carnival
US 1951 77m Technicolor
MGM (Jack Cummins)

A fairground showman is mistaken for a millionaire and runs up debts.
Very thin comedy musical relying entirely on its stars.

w Dorothy Kingsley *d* Charles Walters *ph* Robert Planck *m* Harry Warren *ly* Dorothy Fields *ch* Hermes Pan

Esther Williams, Red Skelton, Howard Keel, Ann Miller, Paula Raymond, Keenan Wynn, Tom Tully

Texas Lady
US 1955 85m Technicolor Superscope
RKO (Nat Holt)

A lady newspaper owner runs an anti-corruption campaign.
Mild family western.

w Horace McCoy *d* Tim Whelan *ph* Ray Rennahan *m* Paul Sawtell

Claudette Colbert, Barry Sullivan, Grey Walcott, James Bell, Horace MacMahon, Ray Collins, Walter Sande, Douglas Fowley

The Texas Rangers*
US 1936 95m bw
Paramount (King Vidor)

Three wandering ne'er-do-wells break up; two join the Texas Rangers and hunt down the third, who is an outlaw.
Pleasantly remembered star western, later remade as *The Streets of Laredo* (qv).

w Louis Stevens *d* King Vidor *ph* Edward Cronjager

Fred MacMurray, Jack Oakie, Lloyd Nolan, Jean Parker, Edward Ellis

Thank You, Jeeves*
US 1936 57m bw
TCF (Sol M. Wurtzel)

A valet helps prevent his master from becoming involved in gun-running.
Competent second feature notable as Niven's first leading role; also one of the very few attempts to film Wodehouse.

w Joseph Hoffman, Stephen Gross, *story* P. G. Wodehouse *d* Arthur Greville Collins *ph* Barney McGill

David Niven, Arthur Treacher, Virginia Field, Lester Matthews, Colin Tapley

Thank Your Lucky Stars***
US 1943 127m bw
Warner (Mark Hellinger)

Eddie Cantor and his double get involved in planning a patriotic show.
All-star wartime musical with some unexpected turns and a generally funny script.

w Norman Panama, Melvin Frank, James V. Kern *d* David Butler *ph Arthur Edeson* *md* Leo F. Forbstein *ch* Le Roy Prinz *songs Frank Loesser, Arthur Schwartz*

Eddie Cantor, Dennis Morgan, Joan Leslie, Edward Everett Horton, S. Z. Sakall, Humphrey Bogart, Jack Carson, *Bette Davis*, Olivia de Havilland, *Errol Flynn*, John Garfield, Alan Hale, Ida Lupino, *Ann Sheridan*, Dinah Shore, George Tobias, Spike Jones and his City Slickers, Willie Best, Hattie McDaniel

Thanks a Million**
US 1935 87m bw
TCF (Darryl F. Zanuck)

A crooner runs for governor.
Smart, amusing political musical.

w Nunnally Johnson d Roy del Ruth *ph* Peverell Marley *songs* Arthur Johnston, Gus Kahn

Dick Powell, Fred Allen, Ann Dvorak, Patsy Kelly, Phil Baker, Paul Whiteman and his band, the Yacht Club Boys, Benny Baker, Raymond Walburn, Alan Dinehart

Thanks for the Memory*
US 1938 75m bw
Paramount

A smart novelist has trouble with his marriage.
Light, agreeable domestic comedy on familiar lines.

w Lynn Starling, *play* Up Pops the Devil by Frances Goodrich, Albert Hackett *d* George Archainbaud

Bob Hope, Shirley Ross

Thark*
GB 1932 79m bw
British and Dominion (Herbert Wilcox)

The heir to an old mansion spends a night in it to prove it is not haunted.
Very funny Aldwych farce, plainly transferred to the screen with the original stage team intact. One's only regret is that it peters out at the end.

w Ben Travers, from his play *d* Herbert Wilcox

Ralph Lynn, Tom Walls, Robertson Hare, Mary Brough, Claude Hulbert, Gordon James

That Certain Age*
US 1938 95m bw
Universal (Joe Pasternak)

A girl gets a crush on an older man.
Pleasant, well-cast star musical for the family.

w Bruce Manning *d* Edward Ludwig *ph* Joseph

Valentine *songs* Jimmy McHugh, Harold Adamson

Deanna Durbin, Melvyn Douglas, Jackie Cooper, Irene Rich, Nancy Carroll, John Halliday, Juanita Quigley, Jackie Searl, Charles Coleman

That Certain Feeling
US 1956 102m Technicolor Vistavision
Paramount (Melvin Frank, Norman Panama)

An arrogant comic strip artist loses his touch and hires a 'ghost'—the ex-husband of his secretary/fiancée.
Arid comedy from a mild Broadway play, totally miscast and lacking any kind of interest.

w Norman Panama, Melvin Frank, I. A. L. Diamond, William Altman, *play* King of Hearts by John Kerr, Eleanor Brooke *d* Norman Panama, Melvin Frank *ph* Loyal Griggs *m* Joseph J. Lilley

Bob Hope, George Sanders, Eva Marie Saint, Pearl Bailey, Al Capp

That Certain Summer**
US 1972 74m Technicolor TVM
Universal (Harve Bennett)

A teenager discovers that his father is a homosexual.
Much acclaimed drama: TV comes of age, etc. Actually it takes a while to get started, but the acting is fine.

w Richard Levinson, William Link *d* Lamont Johnson

Hal Holbrook, Hope Lange, Scott Jacoby, Martin Sheen, Joe Don Baker, Marlyn Mason, James McEachin

That Certain Woman*
US 1937 91m bw
Warner (Hal B. Wallis)

A gangster's widow goes straight but runs into complex marriage trouble.
Self-sacrifice and mother love are rewarded by two convenient deaths and a happy ending in this routine romantic melodrama remade from a silent sucess.

wd Edmund Goulding, from his original screen play The Trespasser *ph* Ernest Haller *m* Max Steiner

Bette Davis, Henry Fonda, Ian Hunter, Anita Louise, Donald Crisp, Katherine Alexander, Mary Philips, Minor Watson

That Cold Day in the Park
Canada 1969 115m Eastmancolor
(Commonwealth United) Donald Factor / Robert Altman / Leon Mirrell

A spinster invites a lonely wandering boy into her home, makes him a prisoner and becomes possessively jealous.
A companion piece to *The Collector*, rather better done for those who like morbid psychology.

w Gillian Freeman, *novel* Richard Miles *d* Robert Altman *ph* Laszlo Kovacs *m* Johnny Mandel

Sandy Dennis, Michael Burns, Suzanne Benton, Luana Anders, John Garfield Jnr

'About as pretentious, loathsome and stupid as a film can get.'—*John Simon*

That Darn Cat!*
US 1965 116m Technicolor
Walt Disney (Bill Walsh, Ron Miller)

A troublesome cat inadvertently helps to trail bank robbers.
Overlong but generally pleasing small-town comedy with well-paced sequences and a fascinating feline hero.

w The Gordons, Bill Walsh, *novel* Undercover Cat by the Gordons *d Robert Stevenson* *ph* Edward Colman *m* Bob Brunner

Hayley Mills, Dean Jones, Dorothy Provine, Roddy McDowall, Neville Brand, Elsa Lanchester, William Demarest, Frank Gorshin, Grayson Hall, Ed Wynn

That Forsyte Woman*
US 1949 114m Technicolor
MGM (Leon Gordon)
GB title: *The Forsyte Saga*

The wife of an Edwardian man of property falls in love with her niece's fiancé.
Moderately successful American attempt to film the first part of a very British novel sequence; so genteel, however, that it becomes dull.

w Jan Lustig, Ivan Tors, James B. Williams, *novel* A Man of Property by John Galsworthy *d* Compton Bennett *ph* Joseph Ruttenberg *m* Bronislau Kaper

Greer Garson, *Errol Flynn*, Robert Young, Janet Leigh, Walter Pidgeon, Harry Davenport, Aubrey Mather

That Funny Feeling
US 1965 92m Technicolor
U-I (Harry Keller)

A maid pretends she lives in her boss's apartment.

Makeshift romantic comedy which barely takes the attention even while it's on.

w David R. Schwarz *d* Richard Thorpe *ph* Clifford Stine *m* Joseph Gershenson

Sandra Dee, Bobby Darin, Donald O'Connor, Nita Talbot, Larry Storch, Leo G. Carroll, James Westerfield

That Girl from Paris
US 1936 105m bw
RKO (Pandro S. Berman)

A Paris opera singer falls for a swing band leader and stows away on a transatlantic liner to be near him.
Comedy-accented musical romance: not bad but not memorable.

w P. J. Wolfson, Dorothy Yost, Jane Murfin *d* Leigh Jason *ph* J. Roy Hunt *md* Nathaniel Shilkret

Lily Pons, Gene Raymond, Jack Oakie, Herman Bing, Lucille Ball, Mischa Auer, Frank Jenks

That Hagen Girl
US 1947 83m bw
Warner (Alex Gottlieb)

A girl is convinced she is the illegitimate daughter of her teacher.
Stale teenage drama with odd anti-establishment overtones.

w Charles Hoffman, *novel* Edith Kneipple Roberts *d* Peter Godfrey *ph* Karl Freund *m* Franz Waxman

Shirley Temple, Ronald Reagan, Rory Calhoun, Lois Maxwell, Dorothy Peterson, Charles Kemper, Conrad Janis, Harry Davenport

That Hamilton Woman**
US 1942 128m bw
London Films (Alexander Korda)
GB title: *Lady Hamilton*

The affair of Lord Nelson and Emma Hamilton.
Bowdlerized version of a famous misalliance; coldly made but quite effective scene by scene, with notable performances.

w Walter Reisch, R. C. Sherriff *d* Alexander Korda *ph* Rudolph Maté *m* Miklos Rozsa

Laurence Olivier, Vivien Leigh, Gladys Cooper, Alan Mowbray, Sara Allgood, Henry Wilcoxon, Halliwell Hobbes

That Kind of Woman
US 1953 92m bw
Paramount / Ponti–Girosi

World War II remake of *Shopworn Angel* (qv); rather well made but basically dated and dull.

w Walter Bernstein *d* Sidney Lumet *ph* Boris Kaufman *m* Daniele Amfitheatrof

Sophia Loren, Tab Hunter, George Sanders, Jack Warden, Barbara Nicholas, Keenan Wynn

'The romantic reunion of Tab Hunter and Sophia Loren resembles nothing so much as a sea scout given a luxury liner for Christmas.' —*Peter John Dyer*

That Lady
GB 1955 100m Eastmancolor Cinemascope
TCF / Atlanta (Sy Bartlett)

A noble widow at the court of Philip II of Spain loves a minister but incurs the king's jealous hatred.
Tepid historical romance which never flows as a film should.

w Anthony Veiller, Sy Bartlett, *novel* Kate O'Brien *d* Terence Young *ph* Robert Krasker *m* John Addison

Olivia de Havilland, Gilbert Roland, *Paul Scofield*, Françoise Rosay, Dennis Price, Anthony Dawson, Robert Harris, Peter Illing, Christopher Lee

'Somehow, somewhere, one feels, something went very wrong.'—*MFB*

That Lady in Ermine
US 1948 89m Technicolor
TCF (Ernst Lubitsch)

Two generations of European noblewomen learn to repel invaders.
Cheerless musical comedy which never gets started, what with the director dying during production and unsuitable stars lost in tinselly sets; the result can have appealed to no one.

w Samson Raphaelson *d* Ernst Lubitsch, Otto Preminger *ph* Leon Shamroy *songs* Leo Robin, Frederick Hollander

Betty Grable, Douglas Fairbanks Jnr, Cesar Romero, Walter Abel, Reginald Gardiner, Harry Davenport

That Lucky Touch
GB 1975 93m Technicolor
Rank / Gloria (Dimitri de Grunwald)

During NATO war games in Brussels, a lady correspondent falls for an arms dealer.
Dim romantic farce which gives the impression of emanating from a dog-eared script written for the kind of stars who no longer shine.

w John Briley, *story* Moss Hart *d* Christopher Miles *ph* Douglas Slocombe *m* John Scott

Roger Moore, Susannah York, Lee J. Cobb,

Shelley Winters, Jean-Pierre Cassel, Raf Vallone, Sydne Rome, Donald Sinden

That Man Bolt
US 1973 103m Technicolor
Universal (Bernard Schwarz)

Adventures of a professional black courier skilled in the martial arts.
Black Kung Fu hokum from a major company; tolerable of its debased kind.

w Quentin Werty, Charles Johnson *d* Henry Levin, David Lowell Rich *ph* Gerald Perry Finnerman *m* Charles Bernstein

Fred Williamson, Bryon Webster, Miko Mayama, Teresa Graves

'Gives every indication of having been devised by a computer fed with a variety of ingredients currently thought to guarantee box office success.'—*John Raisbeck, MFB*

That Midnight Kiss
US 1949 98m Technicolor
MGM (Joe Pasternak)

An unknown becomes a great singing star.
Simple-minded vehicle for the first appearance of Mario Lanza.

w Bruce Manning, Tamara Hovey *d* Norman Taurog *ph* Robert Surtees *m* Bronislau Kaper

Kathryn Grayson, Ethel Barrymore, Jose Iturbi, Mario Lanza, Keenan Wynn, J. Carrol Naish, Jules Munshin, Thomas Gomez, Marjorie Reynolds

That Night*
US 1957 88m bw
Galahad (Himan Brown)

An overwhelmed TV writer has a heart attack, and recovers after a series of medical setbacks.
Impressive minor case history, hardly entertainment but quite arresting.

w Robert Wallace, Burton J. Rowles *d* John Newland *ph* Maurice Hartzband *m* Mario Nascimbene

John Beal, Augusta Dabney, Shepperd Strudwick, Ralph Murphy

That Night in Rio*
US 1941 90m Technicolor
TCF (Fred Kohlmar)

A nightclub entertainer is paid to impersonate a lookalike count, but this causes complications with the countess.
Zippy musical based on a story first used in *Folies Bergère* (qv) and later in *On the Riviera* (qv).

w George Seaton, Bess Meredyth, Hal Long, *play* Rudolph Lothar, Hans Adler *d* Irving Cummings *ph* Leon Shamroy *songs* Mack Gordon, Harry Warren

Don Ameche, Alice Faye, Carmen Miranda, S. Z. Sakall, J. Carrol Naish, Curt Bois, Leonid Kinskey, Maria Montez

That Riviera Touch
GB 1966 98m Eastmancolor
Rank (Hugh Stewart)

Two tourists in the south of France get mixed up with jewel thieves.
Disappointing star comedy ending in a surfboard chase.

w S. C. Green, R. M. Hills, Peter Blackmore *d* Cliff Owen *ph* Otto Heller *m* Ron Goodwin

Eric Morecambe, Ernie Wise, Suzanne Lloyd, Paul Stassino, Armand Mestral

That Touch of Mink**
US 1962 99m Eastmancolor Panavision
U-I / Granley / Arwin / Nob Hill (Stanley Shapiro, Martin Melcher)

Bachelor tycoon pursues virginal secretary.
Jaded sex comedy (or what passed for it in nudge-nudge 1962) enlivened by practised star performances and smart timing.

w Stanley Shapiro, Nate Monaster *d* Delbert Mann *ph* Russell Metty *m* George Duning

Cary Grant, Doris Day, Gig Young, Audrey Meadows, Dick Sargent, *John Astin*

That Uncertain Feeling*
US 1941 84m bw
Ernst Lubitsch

A wife with insomnia and hiccups befriends a wacky concert pianist who proceeds to move into her home.
Although Lubitsch had made this story before, as the silent *Kiss Me Again*, the elements didn't really jell in this version, which seemed silly rather than funny.

w Donald Ogden Stewart, Walter Reisch, *play* Divorçons by Victorien Sardou, Emile de Najac *d Ernst Lubitsch ph* George Barnes *m* Werner Heymann *pd* Alexander Golitzen

Merle Oberon, Melvyn Douglas, Burgess Meredith, Alan Mowbray, Olive Blakeney, Harry Davenport, Eve Arden, Sig Rumann

That Way With Women
US 1947 84m bw
Warner (Charles Hoffman)

A millionaire amuses himself by playing Cupid to a young couple.

Routine remake of *The Millionaire*: just about watchable.

w Leo Townsend *d* Frederick de Cordova *ph* Ted McCord *m* Frederick Hollander

Sidney Greenstreet, Dane Clark, Martha Vickers, Alan Hale, Craig Stevens, Barbara Brown

That Woman Opposite
GB 1957 83m bw
Monarch (William Gell)
US title: *City after Midnight*

In a small French town, a killer returns to silence a witness.
Slow-paced semi-mystery, reasonably well done.

wd Compton Bennett, *story* The Emperor's Snuff Box by John Dickson Carr *ph* Lionel Banes *m* Stanley Black

Phyllis Kirk, Dan O'Herlihy, Wilfrid Hyde White, Petula Clark, Jack Watling, William Franklyn, Margaret Withers

That Wonderful Urge
US 1948 82m bw
TCF (Fred Kohlmar)

A newspaperman is forced into marriage with a publicity-shy heiress.
Tepid romantic comedy, a remake of *Love Is News* (qv).

w Jay Dratler *d* Robert B. Sinclair *ph* Charles Clarke *m* Cyril Mockridge

Gene Tierney, Tyrone Power, Reginald Gardiner, Arleen Whelan, Lucile Watson, Gene Lockhart, Porter Hall, Taylor Holmes

That'll Be the Day*
GB 1973 91m Technicolor
EMI / Goodtimes (David Puttnam, Sanford Lieberson)

In 1958, a young drifter becomes a fairground worker, and eventually walks out on his wife and family to become a pop star.
Spirited return to British realism, with well-sketched cameos, a likeable dour viewpoint, and a cheerful pop music background.

w Ray Connolly *d* Claude Whatham *ph* Peter Suschitsky *md* Neil Aspinall, Keith Moon

David Essex, Ringo Starr, Rosemary Leach, James Booth, Billy Fury, Keith Moon, Rosalind Ayres

'As insubstantial as one of its own attempts at a statement.'—*Tony Rayns*

That's Entertainment**
US 1974 137m Metrocolor
70mm (blown up) / scope
MGM (Daniel Melnick, Jack Haley Jnr)

Fred Astaire, Gene Kelly, Elizabeth Taylor, James Stewart, Bing Crosby, Liza Minnelli, Donald O'Connor, Debbie Reynolds, Mickey Rooney and Frank Sinatra introduce highlights from MGM's musical past.
A slapdash compilation which was generally very big at the box office and obviously has fascinating sequences, though the narration is sloppily sentimental and the later wide-screen sequences let down the rest.

wd Jack Haley Jnr *ph* various *m* various

principal stars as above plus Judy Garland, Esther Williams, Eleanor Powell, Clark Gable, Ray Bolger

'While many ponder the future of MGM, none can deny that it has one hell of a past.'—*Variety*

That's Entertainment Part Two**
US 1976 133m Metrocolor
70mm (blown up) / scope
MGM (Saul Chaplin, Daniel Melnick)

More of the above, introduced by Fred Astaire and Gene Kelly, with comedy and drama sequences as well as musical.

d Gene Kelly *titles Saul Bass* *ph* various

Principal stars as above plus Jeanette MacDonald, Nelson Eddy, the Marx Brothers, Laurel and Hardy, Jack Buchanan, Judy Garland, Ann Miller, Mickey Rooney, Oscar Levant, Louis Armstrong, etc.

That's My Boy
US 1951 98m bw
Paramount / Hal B. Wallis (Cy Howard)

An athletic father tries to press his hypochondriac teenage son into the same mould.
American college comedy of no international interest.

w Cy Howard *d* Hal Walker *ph* Lee Garmes *m* Leigh Harline

Dean Martin, Jerry Lewis, Eddie Mayehoff, Ruth Hussey, Polly Bergen, John McIntire

Theatre of Blood*
GB 1973 102m De Luxe
UA / Cineman (John Kohn, Stanley Mann)

A Shakespearean actor uses appropriate murder methods on the various critics who have ridiculed his performances.
Spoof horror picture which goes too far with some sick visuals; the idea and some of the performances are fine.

w Anthony Greville-Bell *d* Douglas Hickox *ph* Wolfgang Suschitsky *m* Michael J. Lewis *pd* Michael Seymour

Vincent Price, Diana Rigg, Ian Hendry, Harry Andrews, Coral Browne, Robert Coote, Jack Hawkins, Michael Hordern, Arthur Lowe, Robert Morley, Dennis Price, Diana Dors, Joan Hickson, Renée Asherson, Milo O'Shea, Eric Sykes

Thelma Jordon
US 1950 100m bw
Paramount / Hal B. Wallis
aka: *The File on Thelma Jordon*

An assistant DA falls for a woman accused of murder and has her acquitted . . . but she is really guilty.
Adequate star melodrama.

w Ketti Frings *d* Robert Siodmak *ph* George Barnes *m* Victor Young

Barbara Stanwyck, Wendell Corey, Paul Kelly, Joan Tetzel, Stanley Ridges, Richard Rober, Minor Watson

Them!***
US 1954 94m bw
Warner (David Weisbart)

Atomic bomb radiation causes giant ants to breed in the New Mexico desert.
Among the first, and certainly the best, of the post-atomic monster animal cycle, this durable thriller starts with several eerie desert sequences and builds up to a shattering climax in the Los Angeles sewers. A general air of understatement helps a lot.

w Ted Sherdeman, *story* George Worthing Yates *d Gordon Douglas ph Sid Hickox* *m* Bronislau Kaper

Edmund Gwenn, James Whitmore, Joan Weldon, James Arness, Onslow Stevens

Then Came Bronson
US 1968 95m colour TVM
MGM

Adventures of a drop-out who is motorcycling around America.
Slow-moving, amiable pilot for a one-season series.

w Denne Bart Petitclerc *d* William A. Graham

Michael Parks, Bonnie Bedelia, Sheree North, Akim Tamiroff, Gary Merrill

Theodora Goes Wild*
US 1936 94m bw
Columbia (Everett Riskin)

A small-town girl writes a titillating bestseller.
Mildly crazy comedy which helped develop the trend for stars performing undignified antics but today seems rather slow and dated.

w Sidney Buchman, story Mary McCarthy *d* Richard Boleslawski *ph* Joseph Walker *m* Morris Stoloff

Irene Dunne, Melvyn Douglas, Thomas Mitchell, Thurston Hall, Rosalind Keith, Spring Byington, Elizabeth Risdon, Nana Bryant

There Goes My Heart
US 1938 91m bw
Hal Roach

A reporter is assigned to track down a runaway heiress.
Very pale imitation of *It Happened One Night*.

w Jack Jevne, Eddie Moran *d* Norman Z. McLeod *ph* Norbert Brodine *m* Marvin Hatley

Fredric March, Virginia Bruce, Patsy Kelly, Nancy Carroll, Eugene Pallette, Claude Gillingwater, Arthur Lake, Harry Langdon, Etienne Girardot

There Was a Crooked Man*
GB 1960 107m bw
UA / Knightsbridge (John Bryan)

An ex-safecracker outwits the crooked mayor of an industrial town.
Semi-happy attempt to humanize a knockabout clown; good supporting performances and production.

w Reuben Ship *d* Stuart Burge *ph* Arthur Ibbetson *m* Kenneth V. Jones

Norman Wisdom, Andrew Cruickshank, Alfred Marks, Susannah York, Reginald Beckwith

There Was a Crooked Man*
US 1970 126m Technicolor Panavision
Warner Seven Arts (Joseph L. Mankiewicz)

In 1883 Arizona a murderer tries to escape from jail and recover hidden loot but is constantly thwarted by the sheriff who arrested him, now a warden.
Curious black comedy melodrama with lots of talent going nowhere in particular; hard to endure as a whole but with entertaining scenes.

w David Newman, Robert Benton *d* Joseph L. Mankiewicz *ph* Harry Stradling Jnr *m* Charles Strouse *ad* Edward Carrere

Kirk Douglas, Henry Fonda, Hume Cronyn, Warren Oates, Burgess Meredith, John Randolph, Arthur O'Connell, Martin Gabel, Alan Hale

There's a Girl in My Soup*
GB 1970 96m Eastmancolor
Columbia / Ascot (John Boulting)

A randy TV personality finds himself outplotted by a waif he picks up.
Flimsy screen version of a long-running sex comedy; some laughs, but the star is uncomfortably miscast.

w Terence Frisby, from his play *d* Roy Boulting *ph* Harry Waxman *m* Mike D'Abo

Peter Sellers, Goldie Hawn, Tony Britton, Nicky Henson, John Comer, Diana Dors, Judy Campbell

There's Always Tomorrow
US 1956 84m bw
Universal (Ross Hunter)

A married man falls for another woman.
Very flat variation on *Brief Encounter*, with stars going through mechanical paces.

w Bernard Schoenfeld, *story* Ursula Parrott *d* Douglas Sirk *ph* Russell Metty *m* Herman Stein, Heinz Roemheld

Barbara Stanwyck, Fred MacMurray, Joan Bennett, Pat Crowley, William Reynolds, Gigi Perreau, Jane Darwell

There's No Business like Show Business**
US 1954 117m De Luxe Cinemascope
TCF (Sol C. Siegel)

The life and times of a family of vaudevillians.
Mainly entertaining events and marvellous tunes make up this very Cinemascoped musical, in which the screen is usually filled with six people side by side.

w Phoebe and Henry Ephron *d Walter Lang* *ph* Leon Shamroy *m/ly Irving Berlin* *ad* John de Cuir, Lyle Wheeler

Ethel Merman, Dan Dailey, Marilyn Monroe, Donald O'Connor, Johnny Ray, Mitzi Gaynor, Hugh O'Brian, Frank McHugh

These Dangerous Years
GB 1957 92m bw
British Lion / Anna Neagle

A Liverpool teenage gang leader is called up and becomes a better guy.
Dim drama with music marking the debut of a singing star.

w John Trevor Story *d* Herbert Wilcox *ph* Gordon Dines *m* Stanley Black

Frankie Vaughan, George Baker, Carole Lesley, Jackie Lane, Katherine Kath, Eddie Byrne, Kenneth Cope

These Thousand Hills
US 1958 96m Eastmancolor Cinemascope
TCF (David Weisbart)

A successful cattle rancher finds that his best friend is a rustler.
Large-scale but somehow unimpressive western variant on *The Virginian*, cluttered with sub-plots.

w Alfred Hayes, *novel* A. B. Guthrie Jnr *d* Richard Fleischer *ph* Charles G. Clarke *m* Leigh Harline

Richard Egan, Stuart Whitman, Don Murray, Lee Remick, Albert Dekker, Harold J. Stone, Patricia Owens

These Three**
US 1936 93m bw
Samuel Goldwyn

A lying schoolgirl accuses two schoolmistresses of scandalous behaviour.
Bowdlerized version of a famous play (instead of lesbianism we have extra-marital affairs). It worked well enough at the time but now seems dated; oddly enough when the play was filmed full strength in 1962 it didn't work at all.

w Lillian Hellman, from her play *The Children's Hour* *d* William Wyler *ph* Gregg Toland *m* Alfred Newman

Merle Oberon, Miriam Hopkins, Joel McCrea, *Bonita Granville*, Catherine Doucet, Alma Kruger, Marcia Mae Jones, Margaret Hamilton, Walter Brennan

These Wilder Years
US 1956 91m bw
MGM (Jules Schermer)

A wealthy industrialist returns to his home town to trace his illegitimate son.
Modest sentimental drama with practised stars.

w Frank Fenton *d* Roy Rowland *ph* George Folsey *m* Jeff Alexander

James Cagney, Barbara Stanwyck, Walter Pidgeon, Betty Lou Keim, Don Dubbins, Edward Andrews

They All Kissed the Bride
US 1942 86m bw
Columbia (Edward Kaufman)

A woman executive falls in love with the crusading writer who is out to expose working conditions in her company.
No surprises are expected or provided in this very ho-hum romantic comedy.

w P. J. Wolfson *d* Alexander Hall *ph* Joseph Walker *m* Morris Stoloff

Joan Crawford, Melvyn Douglas, Roland Young, Billie Burke, Allen Jenkins, Andrew Tombes, Helen Parrish, Mary Treen

They Call It Murder
US 1971 97m colour TVM
TCF / Parsons (Walter Grauman)

The District Attorney investigates a swimming pool murder.
Smooth pilot which got nowhere, featuring Erle Stanley Gardner's DA character.

w Sam Rolfe *d* Walter Grauman

Jim Hutton, Lloyd Bochner, Jessica Walter, Carmen Matthews, Leslie Nielsen, Nita Talbot, Robert J. Wilke, Ed Asner

They Call Me Mister Tibbs!
US 1970 108m De Luxe
UA / Mirisch (Herbert Hirshman)

A San Francisco police lieutenant suspects a crusading local minister of murder.
Flat, dispirited police melodrama with irrelevant domestic asides, a long way after *In the Heat of the Night* which introduced the main character. (*The Organization* was the third and last in the so-called series.)

w Alan R. Trustman, James R. Webb *d* Gordon Douglas *ph* Gerald Finnerman *m* Quincy Jones

Sidney Poitier, Martin Landau, Barbara McNair, Anthony Zerbe, Jeff Corey, Juano Hernandez, Ed Asner

They Came to a City*
GB 1944 77m bw
Ealing (Sidney Cole)

Assorted people find themselves outside the gates of a mysterious city.
The *Outward Bound* format applied to post-war reconstruction, with characters deciding what kind of a world they want. Good talk and good acting, but not quite cinema.

w Basil Dearden, Sidney Cole, *play J. B. Priestley* *d* Basil Dearden

Googie Withers, John Clements, Raymond Huntley, Renée Gadd, A. E. Matthews, Mabel Terry-Lewis, *Ada Reeve*, Norman Shelley, Frances Rowe

They Came to Cordura*
US 1959 123m Technicolor Cinemascope
Columbia / Goetz–Baroda (William Goetz)

In 1916 Mexico, six American military heroes are recalled to base, but the hardships of the journey reveal their true colours.
Watchable adventure epic, not so arresting as was intended but quite professional.

w Ivan Moffat, Robert Rossen, *novel* Glendon Swarthout *d* Robert Rossen *ph* Burnett Guffey *m* Elie Siegmeister

Gary Cooper, Rita Hayworth, Van Heflin, Richard Conte, Tab Hunter, Michael Callan, Dick York, Robert Keith

They Came to Rob Las Vegas*
Spain / France / Germany / Italy 1969 128m Techniscope
Warner / Isasi / Capitoli / Eichberg / Franca

Criminals ambush a security truck in the Nevada desert.
Long-winded, flashily directed, gleamingly photographed, occasionally lively, frequently violent, finally tedious caper melodrama with a multi-lingual cast.

w Anthony Isasi, Jo Eisinger *d* Anthony Isasi *ph Juan Gelpi* *m* Georges Gavarentz

Jack Palance, Lee J. Cobb, Elke Sommer, Gary Lockwood, Georges Geret, Jean Servais

They Dare Not Love
US 1941 76m bw
Columbia (Sam Bischoff)

An Austrian prince flees the Nazis, but they force him to return and he has to leave his fiancée in America.
Curiously naïve romantic propaganda from this director; not at all memorable.

w Charles Bennett, Ernest Vajda *d* James Whale *ph* Franz Planer *m* Morris Stoloff

George Brent, Martha Scott, Paul Lukas, Egon Brecher, Roman Bohnen, Edgar Barrier, Frank Reicher

They Died with Their Boots On**
US 1941 140m bw
Warner (Robert Fellows)

The life of General Custer and his death at Little Big Horn.
It seems it all happened because of an evil cadet who finished up selling guns to the Indians. Oh, well! The first half is romantic comedy, the second steels itself for the inevitable tragic outcome, but it's all expertly mounted and played in the best old Hollywood style.

w Wally Kline, Aeneas Mackenzie *d Michael Curtiz* *ph Bert Glennon*

Errol Flynn, Olivia de Havilland, Arthur Kennedy, Charles Grapewin, Anthony Quinn, Sidney Greenstreet, Gene Lockhart, Stanley Ridges, John Litel, Walter Hampden, Regis Toomey, Hattie McDaniel

They Drive by Night**
GB 1938 84m bw
Warner (Jerome Jackson)

An ex-convict is helped by lorry drivers to solve the silk stocking murders of which he is suspected.
Excellent, little-seen British suspenser of the Hitchcock school.

w Derek Twist, novel James Curtis *d* Arthur Woods

Emlyn Williams, Ernest Thesiger, Anna Konstam, Allan Jeayes, Antony Holles, Ronald Shiner

'Dialogue, acting and direction put this picture on a level with the French cinema.'—*Graham Greene*

They Drive by Night**
US 1940 97m bw
Warner (Mark Hellinger)
GB title: *The Road to Frisco*

A truck driver loses his brother in an accident, and in an attempt to improve his lot becomes involved with a scheming murderess.
Solid melodramatic entertainment which borrows the second half of its plot from *Bordertown*.

w Jerry Wald, Richard Macaulay, *novel* Long Haul by A. I. Bezzerides *d Raoul Walsh md* Adolph Deutsch

George Raft, Humphrey Bogart, *Ann Sheridan, Ida Lupino*, Gale Page, Alan Hale, Roscoe Karns, John Litel, Henry O'Neill, George Tobias

They Flew Alone*
GB 1941 103m bw
RKO / Imperator (Herbert Wilcox)
US title: *Wings and the Woman*

The story of Amy Johnson and Jim Mollison, married flying pioneers of the thirties.
Adequate fictionalized history with interesting historical detail.

w Miles Malleson *d* Herbert Wilcox

Anna Neagle, Robert Newton, Edward Chapman, Nora Swinburne, Joan Kemp-Welch, Charles Carson, Brefni O'Rourke

They Gave Him a Gun
US 1937 94m bw
MGM (Harry Rapf)

Despite the efforts of his friend, a war-hardened veteran turns to crime and comes to a sticky end.
Dullish moral melodrama with its stars looking as though stuck in glue.

w Cyril Hume, Richard Maibaum, Maurice Rapf, *novel* William Joyce Cowan *d* W. S. Van Dyke II *ph* Harold Rosson

Spencer Tracy, Franchot Tone, Gladys George, Edgar Dearing, Mary Treen, Cliff Edwards

They Got Me Covered**
US 1943 93m bw
Samuel Goldwyn

An incompetent foreign correspondent inadvertently breaks up a spy ring in Washington.
One of Hope's better and most typical comedy-thriller vehicles.

w Harry Kurnitz *d* David Butler *ph* Rudolph Maté *m* Leigh Harline

Bob Hope, Dorothy Lamour, Otto Preminger, Lenore Aubert, Eduardo Ciannelli, Marion Martin, Donald Meek, Donald MacBride, Walter Catlett, John Abbott, Florence Bates, Philip Ahn

They Knew What They Wanted**
US 1940 96m bw
RKO (Erich Pommer)

A waitress agrees by mail to marry a California-Italian vineyard owner, but is aghast when she arrives to discover that he sent his handsome foreman's photograph.
First-rate minor drama, expertly handled by stars and production team alike.

w Robert Ardrey, *play* Sidney Howard *d Garson Kanin ph* Harry Stradling *m* Alfred Newman

Charles Laughton, Carole Lombard, William Gargan, Harry Carey, Frank Fay

They Live by Night*
US 1948 96m bw
RKO

A young man imprisoned for an accidental killing escapes with two hardened criminals and is forced to take part in their crimes.
Well-made if basically uninteresting melodrama with a draggy romantic interest; its 'realistic' yet impressionist style drew attention on its first release, and it was remade in the seventies as *Thieves like Us* (qv).

w Charles Schnee *d Nicholas Ray ph George E. Diskant*

Farley Granger, Cathy O'Donnell, Howard da Silva

They Made Me a Criminal*
US 1939 92m bw
Warner (Benjamin Glazer)

When he thinks he has killed a boxing opponent,

a young man flees to the west and settles on a farm.
Competent remake of *The Life of Jimmy Dolan*, a tribute to the American way.

w Sig Herzig *d* Busby Berkeley *ph* James Wong Howe

John Garfield, Claude Rains, Gloria Dickson, May Robson, Billy Halop, Bobby Jordan, Leo Gorcey, Huntz Hall, Gabriel Dell, Ann Sheridan

They Made Me a Fugitive*
GB 1947 104m bw
Warner / Alliance (Nat Bransten, James Carter)
US title: *I Became a Criminal*

An ex-RAF pilot is drawn into black marketeering. Framed for a killing, he escapes from Dartmoor and takes revenge on the gang leader.
Deliberately squalid thriller which began a fashion for British realism, but now seems only momentarily entertaining.

w Noel Langley, *novel* A Convict Has Escaped by Jackson Budd *d* Alberto Cavalcanti *ph* Otto Heller

Trevor Howard, Sally Gray, *Griffith Jones*, René Ray, Mary Merrall, Vida Hope, Ballard Berkeley, Phyllis Robins

They Met in Bombay*
US 1941 86m bw
MGM (Hunt Stromberg)

Jewel thieves on the run in the East fall in love.
A rather unusual romantic comedy chase which provides pretty satisfactory star entertainment.

w Edwin Justus Mayer, Anita Loos, Leon Gordon *d Clarence Brown* *ph* William Daniels *m* Herbert Stothart

Clark Gable, Rosalind Russell, Peter Lorre, Reginald Owen, Jessie Ralph, Matthew Boulton, Eduardo Ciannelli, Luis Alberni

They Might be Giants*
US 1972 88m Technicolor
Universal / Paul Newman, John Foreman

A lawyer imagines he is Sherlock Holmes, and is taken in hand by Dr Mildred Watson.
Curious fantasy comedy which rather tentatively satirizes modern life and the need to retreat into unreality. Mildly pleasing entertainment for intellectuals.

w James Goldman, from his play *d* Anthony Harvey *ph* Victor Kemper *m* John Barry

George C. Scott, Joanne Woodward, Jack Gilford, Lester Rawlins

They Only Come Out at Night
US 1975 74m colour TVM
TCF (Everett Chambers, Bob Monroe)
aka: *Jigsaw John*

A murder is solved by San Francisco's veteran police officer who has never fired a shot.
Modest cop show leading to a short series, *Jigsaw John.*

w Al Martinez *d* Daryl Duke

Jack Warden, Madeleine Sherwood, Tim O'Connor, Joe Mantell

They Only Kill Their Masters*
US 1972 98m Metrocolor
MGM (William Belasco)

A village police chief doggedly solves a series of murders.
Atmospheric, serio-comic murder mystery with a cast of old hands.

w Lane Slate *d* James Goldstone *ph* Michel Hugo *m* Perry Botkin Jnr

James Garner, Katharine Ross, Hal Holbrook, June Allyson, Harry Guardino, Tom Ewell, Peter Lawford, Ann Rutherford, Chris Connelly, Edmond O'Brien, Art Metrano, Arthur O'Connell

They Shall Have Music
US 1939 105m bw
Samuel Goldwyn
GB title: *Melody of Youth*

Jascha Heifetz conducts a charity concert to help a music school for slum children.
Formula family film given the best possible production.

w John Howard Lawson, Irmgard Von Cube *d* Archie Mayo *ph* Gregg Toland *md* Alfred Newman

Joel McCrea, Jascha Heifetz, Andrea Leeds, Gene Reynolds, Walter Brennan, Porter Hall, Terry Kilburn, Diana Lynn (Dolly Loehr)

They Shoot Horses, Don't They?*
US 1969 129m De Luxe Panavision
Palomar / Chartoff–Winkler–Pollack

Tragedy during a six-day marathon dance contest in the early thirties.
An unrelievedly harrowing melodrama about dreary people, confused by 'flashforwards' but full of skilled technique, entertaining detail, and one brilliant performance.

w James Poe, Robert E. Thompson, *novel* Horace McCoy *d Sydney Pollack* *ph Philip Lathrop* *m* John Green *pd* Harry Horner

Gig Young, Jane Fonda, Susannah York,

Michael Sarrazin, Red Buttons, Bonnie Bedelia, Bruce Dern

They Were Expendable*
US 1945 135m bw
MGM (John Ford, Cliff Reid)

Life in and around motor torpedo boats in the Pacific War.
Long drawn out flagwaver with some nice moments.

w Frank Wead, *book* William L. White *d* John Ford *ph* Joseph H. August *m* Herbert Stothart

John Wayne, Robert Montgomery, Donna Reed, Jack Holt, Ward Bond, Marshall Thompson, Leon Ames, Cameron Mitchell, Jeff York

They Were Not Divided*
GB 1951 102m bw
Rank / Two Cities (Earl St John)

The life of a Guards officer is paralleled with that of his American friend; they both die on a reconnaissance during the advance on Berlin.
Odd mixture of barrack room comedy, semi-documentary action, propaganda and the most appalling sentimentality. No one questioned it at the box office, though.

wd Terence Young *ph* Harry Waxman *m* Lambert Williamson

Edward Underdown, Ralph Clanton, Helen Cherry, Stella Andrews, Michael Brennan, Michael Trubshaw, R.S.M. Brittain

'It is a rather curious experience to see a film made with all the best trappings of realism containing so many of the clichés of the studio.'—*Gavin Lambert*

They Were Sisters
GB 1945 115m bw
GFD / Gainsborough (Harold Huth)

The problems of three married sisters.
Flatly handled multi-melodrama, the chief attraction being 'wicked' James Mason as a sadist.

w Roland Pertwee, *novel* Dorothy Whipple *d* Arthur Crabtree *ph* Jack Cox *m* Louis Levy

James Mason, Phyllis Calvert, Dulcie Gray, Hugh Sinclair, Anne Crawford, Peter Murray Hill, Pamela Kellino

They Who Dare
GB 1953 107m Technicolor
British Lion / Mayflower

During World War II a group of British soldiers are sent on a raiding expedition to Rhodes.
Grimmish war actioner with plenty of noise but not much holding power.

w Robert Westerby *d* Lewis Milestone *ph* Wilkie Cooper *m* Robert Gill

Dirk Bogarde, Denholm Elliott, Akim Tamiroff, Gérard Oury, Eric Pohlmann, Alec Mango

They Won't Believe Me*
US 1947 95m bw
RKO (Joan Harrison)

A playboy finds himself on trial for murder because of his philandering with three women.
Unusual suspenser with Hitchcock touches; quite neatly packaged, complete with twist ending.

w Jonathan Latimer *d* Irving Pichel *ph* Harry J. Wild *m* Roy Webb

Robert Young, Susan Hayward, Rita Johnson, Jane Greer, Tom Powers, Don Beddoe, Frank Ferguson

They Won't Forget***
US 1937 94m bw
Warner (Mervyn Le Roy)

The murder of a girl in a southern town leads to a lynching.
Finely detailed social drama, a classic of American realism; harrowing to watch.

w Robert Rossen, Aben Kandel, novel Death in the Deep South by Ward Greene *d Mervyn Le Roy ph* Arthur Edeson, Warren Lynch *m* Leo F. Forbstein

Claude Rains, Gloria Dickson, Edward Norris, Otto Kruger, Allyn Joslyn, Linda Perry, Elisha Cook Jnr, Lana Turner, Cy Kendall, Elizabeth Risdon

'Not only an honest picture, but an example of real movie-making.'—*Pare Lorenz*

The Thief*
US 1952 86m bw
Harry M. Popkin (Clarence Greene)

A nuclear physicist is on the run from the FBI, who suspect him of being a spy.
Curious attempt to produce a thriller with no dialogue whatever; parts are well done, but the strain eventually shows, as the makers are not quite clever enough to flesh out the trickery with human interest.

w Clarence Greene, Russel Rouse *d* Russel Rouse *ph Sam Leavitt m* Herschel Gilbert

Ray Milland, Martin Gabel, Rita Gam, Harry Bronson, John McKutcheon

Thief*
US 1971 74m colour TCF
Metromedia (Dick Berg)

A smooth jewel thief outsmarts himself.
What seems to start as a light comedy later goes sour; a curious mixture.

w John D. F. Black *d* William Graham

Richard Crenna, Angie Dickinson, Cameron Mitchell

The Thief of Baghdad****
GB 1940 109m Technicolor
London Films (Alexander Korda)

A boy thief helps a deposed king thwart an evil usurper.
Marvellous blend of magic, action and music, the only film to catch on celluloid the overpowering atmosphere of the Arabian Nights.

w Miles Malleson, Lajos Biro d Michael Powell, Ludwig Berger, Tim Whelan ph Georges Périnal, Osmond Borradaile m Miklos Rozsa sp Lawrence Butler

Conrad Veidt, Sabu, John Justin, June Duprez, Morton Selten, Miles Malleson, *Rex Ingram*, Mary Morris

'The true stuff of fairy tale.'—*Basil Wright*

'Both spectacular and highly inventive.'—*NFT, 1969*

Thief of Damascus
US 1952 78m Technicolor
Columbia / Sam Katzman

The wicked ruler of Damascus is deposed by his own general, in league with Sinbad, Aladdin, and Scheherezade.
Mindless bosh, interesting only for its liberal use of scenes from *Joan of Arc*; the mind boggles at the costume compromise.

w Robert E. Kent *d* Will Jason *ph* Ellis W. Carter *m* Mischa Bakaleinikoff

Paul Henreid, Lon Chaney Jnr, Jeff Donnell, John Sutton, Elena Verdugo

The Thief Who Came to Dinner
US 1973 105m De Luxe
Warner / Tandem (Bud Yorkin)

A computer analyst determines to become a jewel thief.
Tedious comedy aping the *Raffles* school but saddled with a complex plot and listless script.

w Walter Hill, *novel* Terence L. Smith *d* Bud Yorkin *ph* Philip Lathrop *m* Henry Mancini

Ryan O'Neal, Jacqueline Bisset, Warren Oates, Jill Clayburgh, Charles Cioffi

Thieves' Highway**
US 1949 94m bw
TCF (Robert Bassler)

A truck driver tracks down the racketeers who cheated and maimed his father.
Glossy, highly professional thick ear shedding a convincing light into one of America's less salubrious corners.

w A. I. Bezzerides, from his novel Thieves' Market *d Jules Dassin ph Norbert Brodine* *m* Alfred Newman

Richard Conte, Valentina Cortesa, Lee J. Cobb, Jack Oakie, Millard Mitchell, Joseph Pevney, Barbara Lawrence, Hope Emerson

Thin Ice*
US 1937 78m bw
TCF (Raymond Griffith)
GB title: *Lovely to Look At*

A skating instructress at an Alpine resort falls in love with a visiting prince.
Light-hearted musical vehicle for Hollywood's newest novelty – a skating star.

w Boris Ingster, Milton Sperling, *novel* Der Komet by Attilla Orbok *d* Sidney Lanfield *ph* Robert Planck, Edward Cronjager *md* Louis Silvers

Sonja Henie, Tyrone Power, Arthur Treacher, Raymond Walburn, Joan Davis, Sig Rumann, Alan Hale, Melville Cooper

The Thin Man****
US 1934 93m bw
MGM (Hunt Stromberg)

In New York over Christmas, a tipsy detective with his wife and dog solves the murder of an eccentric inventor.
Fast-moving, alternately comic and suspenseful mystery drama developed in brief scenes and fast wipes. It set a sparkling comedy career for two stars previously known for heavy drama, it was frequently imitated, and it showed a wisecracking, affectionate married relationship almost for the first time.

w Frances Goodrich, Albert Hackett, novel Dashiell Hammett d W. S. Van Dyke ph James Wong Howe *m* William Axt

William Powell, Myrna Loy, Maureen O'Sullivan, Nat Pendleton, Minna Gombell, Edward Ellis, Porter Hall, Henry Wadsworth, William Henry, Harold Huber, Cesar Romero, Edward Brophy

'A strange mixture of excitement, quips and hard-boiled sentiment . . . full of the special touches that can come from nowhere but the

studio, that really make the feet a movie walks on.'—*Otis Ferguson*
† Sequels, on the whole of descending merit, included the following, all made at MGM with the same star duo: 1936: *After the Thin Man* (110m). 1939: *Another Thin Man* (102m). 1941: *Shadow of the Thin Man* (97m). 1944: *The Thin Man Goes Home* (100m). 1947: *Song of the Thin Man* (86m).

The Thin Red Line
US 1964 99m bw Cinemascope
Security / ACE (Sidney Harmon)

Raw recruits land on Guadalcanal and most of them are killed.
Weary, routine, realistic war drama.

w Bernard Gordon, *novel* James Jones
d Andrew Marton *ph* Manuel Berenguer
m Malcolm Arnold

Keir Dullea, Jack Warden, James Philbrook, Kieron Moore

The Thing from Another World**
US 1951 87m bw
RKO / Winchester (Howard Hawks)

A US scientific expedition in the Arctic is menaced by a ferocious being they inadvertently thaw out from a spaceship.
Curiously drab suspense shocker mainly set in corridors, with insufficient surprises to sustain its length. It does, however, contain the first space monster on film, and is quite nimbly made, though it fails to use the central gimmick from its original story.

w Charles Lederer, *story* Who Goes There by J. W. Campbell Jnr *d* Christian Nyby (with mysterious help, either Hawks or Orson Welles) *ph* Russell Harlan *m* Dmitri Tiomkin

Robert Cornthwaite, Kenneth Tobey, Margaret Sheridan, Bill Self, Dewey Martin, James Arness (as the thing)

'There seems little point in creating a monster of such original characteristics if he is to be allowed only to prowl about the North Pole, waiting to be destroyed by the superior ingenuity of the US Air Force.'—*Penelope Houston*

'A monster movie with pace, humour and a collection of beautifully timed jabs of pure horror.'—*NFT, 1967*

Things in Their Season
US 1974 75m colour TVM
Tomorrow

A Wisconsin farm woman learns that she has leukemia at a time when the family has other problems.
Another undramatic dying fall. *Dark Victory* has a lot to answer for.

w John Gay *d* James Goldstone

Patricia Neal, Ed Flanders, Marc Singer, Meg Foster

Things to Come****
GB 1936 113m bw
London Films (Alexander Korda)

War in 1940 is followed by plague, rebellion, a new glass-based society, and the first rocketship to the moon.
Fascinating, chilling and dynamically well-staged vignettes tracing mankind's future. Bits of the script and acting may be wobbly, but the sets and music are magnificent, the first part of the prophecy chillingly accurate, and the whole mammoth undertaking almost unique in film history.

w H. G. Wells, from his book The Shape of Things to Come *d/pd William Cameron Menzies ph Georges Périnal m Arthur Bliss sp Harry Zech, Ned Mann ad Vincent Korda*

Raymond Massey, Edward Chapman, Ralph Richardson, Margaretta Scott, Cedric Hardwicke, Sophie Stewart, Derrick de Marney, John Clements

'An amazingly ingenious technical accomplishment, even if it does hold out small hope for our race . . . the existence pictured is as joyless as a squeezed grapefruit.'—*Don Herold*

'A leviathan among films . . . a stupendous spectacle, an overwhelming, Dorean, Jules Vernesque, elaborated *Metropolis*, staggering to eye, mind and spirit, the like of which has never been seen and never will be seen again.'—*The Sunday Times*

The Third Day
US 1965 119m Technicolor Panavision
Warner (Jack Smight)

An amnesiac learns that he is a rich unpopular tycoon facing a major crisis.
Glum melodrama which suggests domestic mystery but provides only interminable chat.

w Burton Wohl, Robert Presnell Jnr, *novel* Joseph Hayes *d* Jack Smight *ph* Robert Surtees *m* Percy Faith

George Peppard, Elizabeth Ashley, Roddy McDowall, Herbert Marshall, Mona Washbourne, Robert Webber, Charles Drake, Sally Kellerman, Arte Johnson, Vincent Gardenia

Third Finger Left Hand
US 1940 96m bw
MGM (John W. Considine Jnr)

A lady fashion editor fends off unwanted suitors by saying she is already married, but a commercial artist trumps this card by claiming to be the long lost husband of her invention. Cheerful but overstretched romantic comedy.

w Lionel Houser *d* Robert Z. Leonard
ph George Folsey *m* David Snell

Myrna Loy, Melvyn Douglas, Lee Bowman, Bonita Granville, Raymond Walburn, Felix Bressart, Sidney Blackmer

Third Girl from the Left*
US 1973 73m colour TVM
Playboy

An ageing nightclub chorus girl tries to improve her lot.
Smart but not very interesting comedy drama.

w Dory Previn *d* Peter Medak

Tony Curtis, Kim Novak, Michael Brandon

The Third Man****
GB 1949 100m bw
British Lion / London Films / David O. Selznick / Alexander Korda (Carol Reed)

An unintelligent but tenacious writer of westerns arrives in post-war Vienna to join his old friend Harry Lime, who seems to have met with an accident . . . or has he?
Totally memorable and irresistible romantic thriller. Stylish from the first to the last, with inimitable backgrounds of zither music and war-torn buildings pointing up a then-topical black market story full of cynical characters but not without humour. Hitchcock with feeling, if you like.

w Graham Greene d Carol Reed ph Robert Krasker m Anton Karas

Joseph Cotten, Trevor Howard, Alida Valli, Orson Welles, Bernard Lee, Wilfrid Hyde White, Ernst Deutsch, Siegfried Breuer, Erich Ponto, Paul Hoerbiger

'Sensitive and humane and dedicated, [Reed] would seem to be enclosed from life with no specially strong feelings about the stories that come his way other than that they should be something he can perfect and polish with a craftsman's love.'—*Richard Winnington*

'Crammed with cinematic plums which could do the early Hitchcock proud.'—*Time*

Third Man on the Mountain
GB 1959 103m Technicolor
Walt Disney (Bill Anderson)

In 1865 a Swiss dishwasher dreams of conquering the local mountain, and befriends a distinguished mountaineer.
Handsomely photographed boys' adventure story.

w Eleanore Griffin, *novel* Banner in the Sky by James Ramsay Ullman *d* Ken Annakin
ph Harry Waxman, *George Tairraz* *m* William Alwyn

James MacArthur, Michael Rennie, Janet Munro, James Donald, Herbert Lom, Laurence Naismith, Walter Fitzgerald, Nora Swinburne

The Third Secret
GB 1964 103m bw Cinemascope
TCF / Hubris (Robert L. Joseph)

A psychiatrist apparently commits suicide; a patient who has relied on his strength finds the truth by interviewing other patients.
Pretentious package of short stories, only one of which is relevant to the frame (yet another one featuring Patricia Neal was shot but discarded); full of philosophical conversations on a Thames mudbank and other absurdities, but well enough put together.

w Robert L. Joseph d Charles Crichton
ph Douglas Slocombe *m* Richard Arnell

Stephen Boyd, *Pamela Franklin*, Jack Hawkins, Richard Attenborough, Rachel Kempson, Diane Cilento, Paul Rogers, Freda Jackson

'An unappealing and irritatingly muddled scribble of a film, thoroughly lacking in suspense, veracity and justification.'—*MFB*

The Third Voice**
US 1959 80m bw Cinemascope
TCF (Maury Dexter, Hubert Cornfield)

A woman kills her wealthy lover and an accomplice impersonates him through a series of complex negotiations.
Superstylish minor thriller, with a plot fascinating as it unfolds and a climax which is only a slight letdown.

wd Hubert Cornfield, novel All the Way by Charles Williams *ph* Ernest Haller *m* Johnny Mandel

Edmond O'Brien, Laraine Day, Julie London

Thirteen Ghosts
US 1960 88m Technicolor
Columbia / William Castle

A penniless scholar inherits a haunted house.
Childish thriller for which the audience was issued with a 'ghost viewer' (anaglyph spectacles) so that they could see the 'spirits'. The gimmick was called Illusion-O.

w Robb White *d* William Castle *ph* Joseph Biroc *m* Von Dexter

Charles Herbert, Jo Morrow, Martin Milner,

Rosemary de Camp, Donald Woods, Margaret Hamilton

Thirteen Hours by Air*
US 1936 80m bw
Paramount (E. Lloyd Sheldon)

A transcontinental plane is hijacked by an ex-convict.
Solidly carpentered minor thriller which is also an interesting record of the early days of commercial aviation.

w Bogart Rogers, Kenyon Nicholson *d Mitchell Leisen ph* Theodor Sparkhul

Fred MacMurray, Joan Bennett, Zasu Pitts, Alan Baxter, Fred Keating, Brian Donlevy, John Howard, Ruth Donnelly, Dean Jagger

13 Rue Madeleine*
US 1946 95m bw
TCF (Louis de Rochemont)

Four trained American espionage agents locate a Nazi rocket site in France.
Semi-documentary spy stuff in the tradition of *The House on 92nd Street* but rather less satisfactory despite excellent technique.

w John Monks Jnr, Sy Bartlett *d* Henry Hathaway *ph* Norbert Brodine *m* Alfred Newman

James Cagney, Annabella, Richard Conte, Frank Latimore, Walter Abel, Malville Cooper, Sam Jaffe, Blanche Yurka

'Far and away the roughest, toughest spy chase yet gleaned from the bulging files of the OSS.'—*Time*

13 West Street*
US 1962 80m bw
Columbia / Ladd Enterprises

An engineer is attacked on the street by teenage hoodlums and becomes obsessed by revenge.
Competent, darkly photographed, rather dislikeable little thriller, a kind of trial run for *Death Wish.*

w Bernard Schoenfeld, Robert Presnell Jnr *d* Philip Leacock *ph* Charles Lawton Jnr *m* George Duning

Alan Ladd, Rod Steiger, Dolores Dorn, Michael Callan, Kenneth MacKenna, Margaret Hayes

The Thirteenth Guest*
US 1932 70m bw
Monogram (M. H. Hoffman)

A haunted house, a will at midnight, and a frightened lady.
Archetypal comedy thriller, shot on Poverty Row but still watchable.

w Francis Hyland, Arthur Hoerl, *novel* Armitage Traill *ph* Albert Ray *ph* Harry Neumann, Tom Galligan

Ginger Rogers, Lyle Talbot, J. Farrell MacDonald, James Eagles, Eddie Phillips, Erville Alderson

The Thirteenth Letter*
US 1951 85m bw
TCF (Otto Preminger)

A small French-Canadian town suffers from an outbreak of poison pen letters.
Moderate transcription of a memorable French film, *Le Corbeau*; in this version the events seem all too predictable and the performances dull.

w Howard Koch *d* Otto Preminger *ph* Joseph La Shelle *m* Alex North

Charles Boyer, Linda Darnell, Constance Smith, Michael Rennie, Françoise Rosay, Judith Evelyn

–30–
US 1959 96m bw
Warner / Mark VII (Jack Webb)
GB title: *Deadline Midnight*

A night in the newsroom of a paper preoccupied with scoops.
Not very dramatic, oddly titled and rather pretentious newspaper melodrama confined largely to one set.

w William Bowers *d* Jack Webb *ph* Edward Colman *m* Ray Heindorf

Jack Webb, William Conrad, David Nelson, Whitney Blake, James Bell, Nancy Valentine

Thirty Day Princess*
US 1934 74m bw
Paramount (B. P. Schulberg)

An actress is hired to impersonate a princess who gets mumps while visiting New York in hope of a loan.
Modest comedy which needed a wittier script but is stylishly played.

w Preston Sturges, Frank Partos, *novel* Clarence Budington Kelland *d* Marion Gering *ph* Leon Shamroy

Sylvia Sidney, Cary Grant, Edward Arnold, Henry Stephenson, Vince Barnett, Edgar Norton, Lucien Littlewood

Thirty Is a Dangerous Age, Cynthia
GB 1967 84m Technicolor
Columbia / Walter Shenson

A timid nightclub pianist has trouble with women but sells his first musical.

Mild star vehicle for a very mild star, basically a few thin sketches, frantically overdirected.

w Dudley Moore, Joe McGrath, John Wells *d* Joe McGrath *ph* Billy Williams *m* Dudley Moore *titles* Richard Williams

Dudley Moore, Eddie Foy Jnr, Suzy Kendall, John Bird, Duncan Macrae, Patricia Routledge, John Wells

The Thirty-Nine Steps****
GB 1935 81m bw
Gaumont British (Ivor Montagu)

A spy is murdered; the man who has befriended her is suspected, but eludes the police until a chase across Scotland produces the real villains.
Marvellous comedy thriller with most of the gimmicks found not only in Hitchcock's later work but in anyone else's who has tried the same vein. It has little to do with the original novel, and barely sets foot outside the studio, but it makes every second count, and is unparalleled in its use of timing, atmosphere and comedy relief.

w Charles Bennett, Alma Reville, novel John Buchan *d Alfred Hitchcock ph Bernard Knowles m* Louis Levy

Robert Donat, Madeleine Carroll, Godfrey Tearle, Lucie Mannheim, Peggy Ashcroft, John Laurie, *Wylie Watson, Helen Haye*, Frank Cellier

'A narrative of the unexpected – a humorous, exciting, dramatic, entertaining, pictorial, vivid and novel tale told with a fine sense of character and a keen grasp of the cinematic idea.'
—Sydney W. Carroll

The Thirty-Nine Steps*
GB 1960 93m Eastmancolor
Rank (Betty E. Box)

Just to show that stars and story aren't everything, this scene-for-scene remake muffs every opportunity for suspense or general effectiveness, and is practically a manual on how not to make a thriller.

w Frank Harvey *d* Ralph Thomas *ph* Ernest Steward *m* Clifton Parker

Kenneth More, Taina Elg, Barry Jones, Faith Brook, Brenda de Banzie, Duncan Lamont, James Hayter, Michael Goodliffe, Reginald Beckwith

Thirty Seconds over Tokyo**
US 1944 138m bw
MGM (Sam Zimbalist)

How the first American attack on Japan was planned.
Sturdy World War II action flagwaver, with Tracy guesting as Colonel Dolittle.

w Dalton Trumbo *d* Mervyn Le Roy *m* Herbert Stothart

Spencer Tracy, Van Johnson, Robert Walker, Phyllis Thaxter, Tim Murdock, Don Defore, Robert Mitchum

Thirty-Six Hours*
US 1964 115m bw Panavision
MGM / Perlberg–Seaton / Cherokee (William Perlberg)

In 1944 an American major is kidnapped by the Nazis and after drugging is made to think that the war is over.
Well-detailed spy suspenser.

wd George Seaton, *stories* Roald Dahl, Carl K. Hittleman *ph* Philip Lathrop *m* Dmitri Tiomkin

James Garner, Rod Taylor, Eva Marie Saint, Werner Peters, John Banner

This above All*
US 1942 110m bw
TCF (Darryl F. Zanuck)

A surgeon's daughter on active service during World War II falls in love with a conscientious objector who is also an army deserter: he proves his bravery during an air raid.
Superior studio-set war romance.

w R. C. Sheriff, *novel* Eric Knight *d* Anatole Litvak *ph* Arthur Miller *m* Alfred Newman

Tyrone Power, Joan Fontaine, Thomas Mitchell, Henry Stephenson, Nigel Bruce, Gladys Cooper, Philip Merivale, Alexander Knox, Melville Cooper

This Could Be the Night
US 1957 104m bw Cinemascope
MGM (Joe Pasternak)

A schoolteacher becomes secretary to a gangster in his Broadway night club.
Unlikely romantic melodrama with music, like a more solemn *Guys and Dolls.*

w Isabel Lennart, *story* Cornelia Baird Gross *d* Robert Wise *ph* Russell Harlan *m* George Stoll

Jean Simmons, Paul Douglas, Tony Franciosa, Julie Wilson, Joan Blondell, J. Carrol Naish, Zasu Pitts

This Day and Age*
US 1933 98m bw
Paramount / Cecil B. de Mille

During a youth week, boys put a gangster on trial and by his own methods force him to confess to murder.
A curious aberration for de Mille, this fairly

powerful movie was condemned in some quarters as an incitement to fascism.

w Bartlett Cormack *d* Cecil B. de Mille *ph* Peverell Marley *m* Howard Jackson, L. W. Gilbert, Abel Baer

Charles Bickford, Richard Cromwell, Judith Allen, Harry Green, Ben Alexander

'Loaded with that power which excites emotional hysteria . . . should stimulate audiences to the same pitch of enthusiasm as it did the preview crowd.'—*Motion Picture Herald*

This Earth Is Mine
US 1959 124m Technicolor Cinemascope
U-I / Vintage (Casey Robinson, Claude Heilman)

A French-American vineyard owner in California brings out his granddaughter from England in the hope that she will consolidate his dynasty.
Solidly efficient film of a solidly efficient novel.

w Casey Robinson, *novel* The Cup and the Sword by Alice Tisdale Hobart *d* Henry King *ph* Winton Hoch, Russell Metty *m* Hugo Friedhofer

Jean Simmons, *Claude Rains*, Rock Hudson, Dorothy McGuire, Kent Smith, Anna Lee, Ken Scott

This Gun for Hire***
US 1942 81m bw
Paramount (Richard M. Blumenthal)

A professional killer becomes involved in a fifth columnist plot.
Efficient Americanization of one of its author's more sombre entertainments. The melodrama has an authentic edge and strangeness to it, and it established the star images of both Ladd and Lake, as well as being oddly downbeat for a Hollywood product of this jingoistic time.

w Albert Maltz, W. R. Burnett, novel A Gun for Sale by *Graham Greene d Frank Tuttle ph John Seitz m* David Buttolph

Alan Ladd, Veronica Lake, Robert Preston, *Laird Cregar*, Tully Marshall, Mikhail Rasumny, Marc Lawrence

This Happy Breed**
GB 1944 114m Technicolor
GFD / Two Cities / Cineguild (Noel Coward, Anthony Havelock-Allan)

Life between the wars for a London suburban family.
Coward's domestic epic is unconvincingly written and largely miscast, but sheer professionalism gets it through, and the decor is historically interesting.

w David Lean, Ronald Neame, Anthony Havelock-Allan, *play* Noel Coward *d David Lean*

Robert Newton, Celia Johnson, Stanley Holloway, John Mills, Kay Walsh, Amy Veness, Alison Leggatt

This Happy Feeling
US 1958 92m Eastmancolor Cinemascope
U-I (Ross Hunter)

An ageing actor is invigorated by a mild affair with his secretary.
Flat romantic comedy: the bubbles obstinately refuse to rise.

wd Blake Edwards, *play* For Love or Money by F. Hugh Herbert *ph* Arthur E. Arling *m* Frank Skinner

Curt Jurgens, Debbie Reynolds, John Saxon, Alexis Smith, *Mary Astor, Estelle Winwood*

This Is My Affair**
US 1937 102m bw
TCF (Kenneth MacGowan)
GB title: *His Affair*

When President McKinley is assassinated, one of his top undercover agents is suspected of being a criminal, and threatened with execution.
Jolly good romantic melodrama with excellent period trappings; Hollywood of the thirties at its routine best.

w Allen Rivkin, Lamar Trotti d William A. Seiter ph Robert Planck md Arthur Lange

Robert Taylor, Barbara Stanwyck, Victor McLaglen, Brian Donlevy, Sidney Blackmer, John Carradine, Sig Rumann, Alan Dinehart, Douglas Fowley

'The best American melodrama of the year . . . admirable acting, quick and cunning direction . . . a sense of doom, of almost classic suspense.' —*Graham Greene*

This Is My Street
GB 1963 94m bw
Anglo-Amalgamated / Adder (Jack Hanbury)

A Battersea wife has a fling with her mother's lodger.
Unremarkable low-life drama.

w Bill MacIlwraith, *novel* Nan Maynard *d* Sidney Hayers *ph* Alan Hume *m* Eric Rogers

June Ritchie, Ian Hendry, Avice Landon, Meredith Edwards, Madge Ryan, John Hurt, Mike Pratt, Tom Adams

This Is the Army**
US 1943 121m Technicolor
Warner (Jack L. Warner, Hal B. Wallis)

Army recruits put on a musical revue.
Mammoth musical flagwaver.

w Casey Robinson, Claude Binyon *d* Michael Curtiz *ph* Bert Glennon, Sol Polito *m/ly Irving Berlin*

George Murphy, Joan Leslie, Irving Berlin, George Tobias, Alan Hale, Charles Butterworth, Rosemary de Camp, Dolores Costello, Una Merkel, Stanley Ridges, Ruth Donnelly, Kate Smith, Frances Langford, Gertrude Niesen, Ronald Reagan, Joe Louis

This Is the West That Was
US 1974 74m colour TVM
Universal (Roy Huggins, Jo Swerling Jnr)

Wild Bill Hickok, Calamity Jane and Buffalo Bill fight each other and the baddies.
Lame western spoof.

w Sam H. Rolfe, Jo Swerling Jnr *d* Fielder Cook

Ben Murphy, Kim Darby, Matt Clark, Jane Alexander, Tony Franciosa, Stuart Margolin

This Island Earth**
US 1955 86m Technicolor
U-I (William Alland)

Scientists at a mysterious research station are really visitors from a planet in outer space, to which they kidnap brilliant minds who they hope can help them.
Absorbing science fiction mystery with splendid special effects and only one mutant monster to liven the last reels.

w Franklin Coen, Edward G. O'Callaghan, novel Raymond F. Jones *d Joseph Newman ph/sp Clifford Stine, David S. Horsley m Joseph Gershenson ad Alexander Golitzen, Richard H. Riedel*

Jeff Morrow, Faith Domergue, Rex Reason, Lance Fuller, Russell Johnson, Robert Nicholas, Karl Lindt

This Land Is Mine*
US 1943 103m bw
RKO (Jean Renoir, Dudley Nichols)

A European village fights for freedom under occupying Nazis, and a schoolmaster becomes a hero.
Rather superfluous flagwaver with good performances wasted in a totally predictable and rather uninspiring script which gives the director little scope.

w Dudley Nichols *d* Jean Renoir *ph* Frank Redman *m* Lothar Perl

Charles Laughton, Maureen O'Hara, George Sanders, Walter Slezak, Una O'Connor, Kent Smith, Philip Merivale, Thurston Hall, George Coulouris

'Directed with the same Zolaesque intensity, the same excited obsession with locomotives, the same exquisite pictorial sense, that informed *La Bête humaine.'—Guardian*

This Love of Ours
US 1945 90m bw
U-I (Edward Dodds)

A jealous doctor leaves his wife but years later saves her from an unhappy second marriage.
Stupid romantic melodrama with characters in whose idiotic behaviour one can take no interest.
Remade as *Never Say Goodbye* (qv).

w Bruce Manning, John Klorer, Leonard Lee, *play* Comè Prima Meglio di Prima by Luigi Pirandello *d* William Dieterle *ph* Lucien Ballard *m* Hans Salter

Merle Oberon, Charles Korvin, Claude Rains, Carl Esmond, Jess Barker, Harry Davenport, Ralph Morgan, Fritz Leiber

'About as captivating as a funeral dirge.'—*Thomas M. Pryor, New York Times*

'A juicy example of masochistic team work . . my favourite bad film in two years.'—*Richard Winnington*

This Man Is News**
GB 1938 77m bw
(Paramount) Pinebrook (Anthony Havelock-Allan)

A reporter tracks down jewel thieves.
Thoroughly brisk and lively comedy-thriller on *Thin Man* lines. *This Man in Paris* followed two years later.

w Allan MacKinnon, Roger Macdougall, Basil Dearden d David MacDonald

Barry K. Barnes, Valerie Hobson, Alastair Sim, John Warwick, Garry Marsh

This Modern Age
US 1931 68m bw
MGM

The socialite child of divorced parents goes to Paris to stay with her sophisticated mother.
Mildly daring melodrama typical of its star and year.

w Sylvia Thalberg, Frank Butler, *story* Mildred Cram *d* Nick Grinde *ph* Charles Rosher

Joan Crawford, Pauline Frederick, Monroe Owsley, Neil Hamilton, Hobart Bosworth, Emma Dunn

This Property Is Condemned*
US 1966 110m Technicolor
Paramount / Seven Arts / Ray Stark (John Houseman)

Sexual adventures of a tubercular but beautiful girl in her mother's boarding house in a Mississippi town.
The Tennessee Williams mixture as before, quite well done but almost entirely resistible.

w Francis Ford Coppola, Fred Coe, Edith Sommer, *play* Tennessee Williams *d* Sydney Pollack *ph* James Wong Howe *m* Kenyon Hopkins

Natalie Wood, Robert Redford, Mary Badham, Kate Reid, Charles Bronson, Jon Provost, John Harding, Alan Baxter, Robert Blake

This Sporting Life**
GB 1963 134m bw
Rank / Independent Artists (Karel Reisz)

A tough miner becomes a successful rugby player, but his inner crudeness and violence keep contentment at bay.
Skilful movie-making around an unattractive hero in dismal settings; for all the excellent detail, we do not care sufficiently for the film to become any kind of classic.

w David Storey *d Lindsay Anderson ph Denys Coop m* Roberto Gerhard

Richard Harris, Rachel Roberts, Alan Badel, William Hartnell, Colin Blakely, Vanda Godsell, Arthur Lowe

This Thing Called Love*
US 1941 98m bw
Columbia (William Perlberg)
GB title: *Married But Single*

A lady executive insists on proving that marriage is best if the partners start out just good friends.
Amusing comedy which at the time seemed a little saucy, and got itself banned by the Legion of Decency.

w George Seaton, Ken Englund, P. J. Wolfson *d* Alexander Hall *ph* Joseph Walker *m* Morris Stoloff

Rosalind Russell, Melvyn Douglas, Binnie Barnes, Allyn Joslyn, Gloria Dickson, Lee J. Cobb, Gloria Holden, Don Beddoe

This Time for Keeps
US 1947 105m Technicolor
MGM (Joe Pasternak)

The son of a famous singer falls in love with a swimming star.
Dim star musical with no outstanding sequences.

w Gladys Lehman *d* Richard Thorpe *ph* Karl Freund *songs* various

Esther Williams, Jimmy Durante, Lauritz Melchior, Johnnie Johnston, Xavier Cugat and his Orchestra

This Woman Is Dangerous
US 1952 97m bw
Warner (Robert Sisk)

A woman gangster goes blind and falls in love with her doctor.
Glossy hokum without much dramatic movement; strictly for star fans.

w Geoffrey Homes, George Worthing Yates *d* Felix Feist *ph* Ted McCord *m* David Buttolph

Joan Crawford, David Brian, Dennis Morgan, Mari Aldon, Phil Carey

The Thomas Crown Affair**
US 1968 102m De Luxe Panavision
UA / Mirisch / Simkoe / Solar (Norman Jewison)

A bored property tycoon masterminds a bank robbery and is chased by a glamorous insurance investigator.
Not so much a movie as an animated colour supplement, this glossy entertainment makes style its prime virtue, plays cute tricks with multiple images and has a famous sexy chess game, but is not above being boring for the rest of the way.

w Alan R. Trustman *d Norman Jewison ph Haskell Wexler m* Michel Legrand *ad Robert Boyle*

Steve McQueen, Faye Dunaway, Paul Burke, Jack Weston, Yaphet Kotto

'Jewison and Wexler seem to have gone slightly berserk, piling up tricks and mannerisms until the film itself sinks out of sight, forlorn and forgotten.'—*Tom Milne*

'A glimmering, empty film reminiscent of an *haute couture* model stunning on the surface, concave and undernourished beneath.'—*Stefan Kanter*

Thoroughly Modern Millie*
US 1967 138m Technicolor
Universal (Ross Hunter)

In the twenties, a young girl comes to New York, becomes thoroughly modern, falls for her boss, and has various adventures unmasking a white slave racket centring on a Chinese laundry.
Initially most agreeable but subsequently very patchy spoof of twenties fads and films, including a Harold Lloyd thrill sequence which just doesn't work and a comedy performance from Beatrice

Lillie which does. Tunes and performances are alike variable.

w Richard Morris *d* George Roy Hill
ph Russell Metty ad Alexander Golitzen, George Webb *m* Elmer Bernstein
ch Joe Layton *songs* various

Julie Andrews, Mary Tyler Moore, *John Saxon*, James Fox, Carol Channing, *Beatrice Lillie*, Jack Soo, Pat Morita, Anthony Dexter

'What a nice 65-minute movie is buried therein!'—*Judith Crist*

Those Calloways
US 1964 131m Technicolor
Walt Disney (Winston Hibler)

Adventures of a marsh trapper and his family who live near a Maine village and try to protect wild geese from hunters.
Predictable family saga with pleasant backgrounds.

w Louis Pelletier, *novel* Swift Water by Paul Annixter *d* Norman Tokar *ph* Edward Colman *m* Max Steiner

Brian Keith, Vera Miles, Brandon de Wilde, Walter Brennan, Ed Wynn, Linda Evans, Philip Abbott, John Larkin, John Qualen

Those Daring Young Men in Their Jaunty Jalopies
US / Italy / France 1969 125m Technicolor Panavision
Paramount / Dino de Laurentiis / Marianne (Ken Annakin, Basil Keys)
GB title: *Monte Carlo or Bust*

Accidents befall various competitors in the Monte Carlo Rally.
Rough-edged imitation of *The Great Race* and *Those Magnificent Men in Their Flying Machines*, much feebler than either but with the waste of a big budget well in evidence.

w Jack Davies, Ken Annakin *d* Ken Annakin
ph Gabor Pogany *m* Ron Goodwin

Peter Cook, Dudley Moore, Tony Curtis, Bourvil, Walter Chiari, Terry-Thomas, Gert Frobe, Susan Hampshire, Jack Hawkins, Eric Sykes

Those Magnificent Men in Their Flying Machines, or How I Flew from London to Paris in 25 hours and 11 Minutes**
GB 1965 133m Technicolor Todd-AO
TCF (Stan Marguilies, Jack Davies)

In 1910, a newspaper owner sponsors a London to Paris air race.
Long-winded, generally agreeable knockabout comedy with plenty to look at but far too few jokes to sustain it.

w Jack Davies, Ken Annakin *d Ken Annakin*
ph Christopher Challis m Ron Goodwin
pd Tom Morahan

Sarah Miles, Stuart Whitman, Robert Morley, Eric Sykes, Terry-Thomas, James Fox, Alberto Sordi, Gert Frobe, Jean-Pierre Cassel, Karl Michael Vogler, Irina Demich, Benny Hill, Flora Robson, Sam Wanamaker, Red Skelton, Fred Emney, Cicely Courtneidge, Gordon Jackson, John Le Mesurier, Tony Hancock, William Rushton

'There is many a likely gag, but none that survives the second or third reprise. It could have been a good bit funnier by being shorter: the winning time is 25 hours 11 minutes, and by observing some kind of neo-Aristotelian unity the film seems to last exactly as long.'—*John Simon*

Those Were the Days**
GB 1934 80m bw
BIP (Walter C. Mycroft)

In the nineties, a magistrate seeks out his teenage stepson in a music hall.
Lively comedy which is valuable as giving the screen's best recreation of an old-time music hall.

w Fred Thompson, Frank Miller, Frank Launder, Jack Jordan, *play* The Magistrate by Arthur Wing Pinero *d Thomas Bentley*

Will Hay, John Mills, Iris Hoey, Angela Baddeley, Claud Allister, George Graves, Jane Carr, H. F. Maltby

Those Were the Days
US 1940 74m bw
Paramount (J. Theodore Reed)

During their 40th anniversary celebrations, a married couple look back to their courtship days at college.
Pleasant, light, nostalgic escapades.

w Don Hartman, *stories* George Fitch *d* J. Theodore Reed *ph* Victor Milner

William Holden, Bonita Granville, Ezra Stone, Judith Barrett, Vaughan Glazer, Lucien Littlefield, Richard Denning

A Thousand Clowns*
US 1965 115m bw
UA / Harell (Fred Coe)

A New Yorker who has abdicated from work leads a cheerful, useless life with his young nephew, but the school board have their doubts.
Imitative nonconformist comedy with frequent reminiscences of older, better plays such as *You Can't Take It with You*. Good lines occasionally make themselves felt, but the overall effect is patchy, the lead is miscast, and the location

montages only emphasize the basic one-room set.

w Herb Gardner, from his play *d* Fred Coe *ph* Arthur J. Ornitz *m* Don Walker

Jason Robards, Martin Balsam, Barry Gordon, Barbara Harris, *William Daniels*, Gene Saks

Thousands Cheer*
US 1943 126m Technicolor
MGM (Joe Pasternak)

An army base stages an all-star variety show.
Ho-hum studio extravaganza with some good numbers.

w Paul Jarrico, Richard Collins *d* George Sidney *ph* George Folsey *md* Herbert Stothart *songs* various

Kathryn Grayson, Gene Kelly, John Boles, Mary Astor, Jose Iturbi, Kay Kyser and his Orchestra, Lionel Barrymore, Margaret O'Brien, June Allyson, Mickey Rooney, Judy Garland, Red Skelton, Eleanor Powell, Bob Crosby and his Orchestra, Lena Horne, Frank Morgan

Three Blind Mice*
US 1938 75m bw
TCF (Raymond Griffith)

Three Kansas girls in the big city seek rich husbands.
Mild comedy remade as *Three Little Girls in Blue* and *How to Marry a Millionaire*, and not all that different from any of the *Gold Diggers* comedy musicals.

w Brown Holmes, Lynn Starling *d* William A. Seiter *ph* Ernest Palmer

Loretta Young, Joel McCrea, David Niven, Stuart Erwin, Marjorie Weaver, Pauline Moore, Binnie Barnes, Jane Darwell, Leonid Kinskey

Three Brave Men*
US 1956 88m bw Cinemascope
TCF (Herbert B. Swope Jnr)

A civilian employee in the US Navy is suspended as a security risk and it takes a lawsuit to set things straight.
Semi-factual anti-McCarthy drama proving that America is a great place to live—when you're winning. Good courtroom scenes.

wd Philip Dunne, *articles* Anthony Lewis *ph* Charles G. Clarke *m* Hans Salter

Ray Milland, Ernest Borgnine, Nina Foch, Dean Jagger, Frank Lovejoy, Edward Andrews, Frank Faylen, James Westerfield, Joseph Wiseman

The Three Caballeros***
US 1945 70m Technicolor
Walt Disney (Norman Ferguson)

A programme of shorts about South America, linked by Donald Duck as a tourist.
Rapid-fire mélange of fragments supporting the good neighbour policy, following the shorter *Saludos Amigos* of 1943. The kaleidoscopic sequences and the combination of live action with cartoon remain of absorbing interest.

w various *d* various

† Stories include Pablo the Penguin, Little Gauchito, a Mexican sequence and some adventures with Joe Carioca.

Three Came Home**
US 1950 106m bw
TCF (Nunnally Johnson)

In 1941 writer Agnes Newton Keith tries to escape from Borneo but is interned and ill-used by the Japanese.
Well-made, harrowing war adventure.

w Nunnally Johnson, *book* Agnes Newton Keith *d Jean Negulesco ph Milton Krasner* *m* Lionel Newman

Claudette Colbert, Patric Knowles, Sessue Hayakawa, Florence Desmond, Sylvia Andrew, Phyllis Morris

Three Cases of Murder*
GB 1954 99m bw
British Lion / Wessex / London Films (Ian Dalrymple, Hugh Perceval)

'In the Picture': a painting comes to life. 'You Killed Elizabeth': a man suspects himself of his faithless fiancée's murder. 'Lord Mountdrago': the foreign secretary dreams of killing an MP he hates.
Unlinked compendium, in which the first and third stories are quite interesting and well done, the second very commonplace.

w Donald Wilson, Sidney Caroll, Ian Dalrymple (original stories Roderick Wilkinson, Brett Halliday, W. Somerset Maugham) *d* Wendy Toye, David Eady, George More O'Ferrall *ph* Georges Périnal *m* Doreen Carwithen

Alan Badel, Hugh Pryse, Leueen MacGrath, Elizabeth Sellars, John Gregson, Emrys Jones, Orson Welles, André Morell

Three Cheers for the Irish
US 1940 100m bw
Warner (Sam Bischoff)

An Irishman's daughter causes family trouble when she falls for a Scot.

Pleasant, unpretentious but overlong romantic comedy.

w Richard Macaulay, Jerry Wald *d* Lloyd Bacon *ph* Charles Rosher

Thomas Mitchell, Priscilla Lane, Dennis Morgan, Alan Hale, Virginia Grey, Irene Hervey, William Lundigan

Three Coins in the Fountain**
US 1954 102m De Luxe Cinemascope
TCF (Sol C. Siegel)

Three American girls find romance in Rome. An enormous box office hit, the pattern of which was frequently repeated against various backgrounds; it was actually remade in Madrid as *The Pleasure Seekers*. In itself a thin entertainment, but the title song carried it.

w John Patrick, *novel* John H. Secondari *d* Jean Negulesco *ph Milton Krasner m* Victor Young *song Jule Styne, Sammy Cahn*

Clifton Webb, Dorothy McGuire, Louis Jourdan, Jean Peters, Rossano Brazzi, Maggie McNamara, Howard St John, Kathryn Givney, Cathleen Nesbitt

Three Comrades**
US 1938 98m bw
MGM (Joseph L. Mankiewicz)

In twenties Germany, three friends find life hard but derive some joy from their love for a high-spirited girl who is dying of tuberculosis. Despairing romance becomes a sentimental tearjerker with all the stops out; immaculately produced and very appealing to the masses, but prevented by censorship from being the intended indictment of Nazi Germany. The final scene in which the two surviving comrades are joined in the churchyard by their ghostly friends still packs a wallop.

w F. Scott Fitzgerald, Edward A. Paramore, novel Erich Maria Remarque *d Frank Borzage ph* Joseph Ruttenberg *m* Franx Waxman

Margaret Sullavan, Robert Taylor, Robert Young, Franchot Tone, Guy Kibbee, Lionel Atwill, Henry Hull, Charley Grapewin

Three Cornered Moon*
US 1933 72m bw
Paramount

A newly-poor Depression family has trouble finding work.
Slightly screwball romantic comedy, a predecessor of *You Can't Take It with You*; the humour now seems very faded, but it was a signpost of its day.

w S. K. Lauren, Ray Harris *d* Elliott Nugent *ph* Leon Shamroy

Claudette Colbert, Mary Boland, Richard Arlen, Wallace Ford, Lyda Roberti, Tom Brown, Hardie Albright

Three Daring Daughters
US 1948 115m Technicolor
MGM (Joe Pasternak)
GB title: *The Birds and the Bees*

Three girls are dismayed to hear that their mother is remarrying.
Cheerful comedy with music, but nothing to write home about.

w Albert Mannheimer, Frederick Kohner, Sonya Levien, John Meehan *d* Fred M. Wilcox

Jeanette MacDonald, Jose Iturbi, Jane Powell, Ann Todd, Mary Elinor Donahue, Larry Adler, Edward Arnold, Harry Davenport, Moyna MacGill

Three Days of the Condor**
US 1975 118m Technicolor Panavision
Paramount / Dino de Laurentiis / Wildwood (Stanley Schneider)

An innocent researcher for a branch of the CIA finds himself marked for death by assassins employed by another branch.
Entertaining New York-based thriller which shamelessly follows most of the twists of *The 39 Steps*. It is just possible to follow its complexities, and the dialogue is smart.

w Lorenzo Semple Jnr, David Rayfiel, novel Six Days of the Condor by James Grady *d Sydney Pollack ph* Owen Roizman m Dave Grusin

Robert Redford, Faye Dunaway, Cliff Robertson, Max Von Sydow, John Houseman, Walter McGinn

Three Faces East*
US 1931 71m bw
Warner (Darryl F. Zanuck)

The butler to the British war minister is a German spy, and the German nurse sent to help him is really a British agent . . .
Slow, melodramatic remake of a 1926 silent, later turned into a Karloff vehicle, *British Intelligence* (qv).

w Oliver H. P. Garrett, Arthur Caesar, *play* Anthony Paul Kelly *d* Roy del Ruth *ph* Chick McGill

Constance Bennett, Erich Von Stroheim, Anthony Bushell, William Holden

The Three Faces of Eve**
US 1957 95m bw Cinemascope
TCF (Nunnally Johnson)

A psychiatrist discovers that a famale patient has three distinct personalities: a drab housewife, a good time girl and a mature sophisticated woman.
Alistair Cooke introduces this tall tale as if he believed it; as presented, it is entertaining but not very convincing. Its box office success was sufficient to start a schizophrenia cycle.

w Nunnally Johnson, *book* Corbett H. Thigpen MD, Hervey M. Cleckley MD *d Nunnally Johnson ph Stanley Cortez m* Robert Emmett Dolan

Joanne Woodward, Lee J. Cobb, David Wayne, Nancy Kulp, Edwin Jerome

Three Faces West
US 1940 79m bw
Republic (Sol C. Siegel)

A dust bowl community is helped by an Austrian doctor fleeing from the Nazis, but his daughter is followed by a Nazi suitor.
Unusual modern western, blandly told.

w F. Hugh Herbert, Joseph Moncure March, Samuel Ornitz *d* Bernard Vorhaus *ph* John Alton *m* Victor Young

John Wayne, Charles Coburn, Sigrid Gurie, Roland Varno, Spencer Charters, Sonny Bupp

Three for Bedroom C
US 1952 74m Natural Color
Brenco (Edward L. Alperson Jnr)

Confusion reigns on a train when a film star takes a compartment booked for a Harvard scientist.
Inept farce which never rises above mediocrity and coasts along well below it.

wd Milton H. Bren *ph* Ernest Laszlo *m* Heinz Roemheld

Gloria Swanson, Fred Clark, James Warren, Hans Conried, Steve Brodie, Margaret Dumont

Three for Jamie Dawn
US 1956 81m bw
AA (Hayes Goetz)

A crooked lawyer bribes three members of a murder jury.
Minor courtroom melodrama, limply developed.

w John Klempner *d* Thomas Carr *ph* Duke Green
m Walter Scharf

Laraine Day, Ricardo Montalban, Richard Carlson, June Havoc

Three for the Road
US 1975 74m colour TVM
Mary Tyler Moore

A photographer widower travels across America on jobs, with his two sons in a camper.
Acceptable family fare which led to a short series.

w Jerry McNeely *d* Boris Sagal *m* David Shire

Alex Rocco, Vincent Van Patten, Leif Garrett, Julie Sommars

Three for the Show*
US 1955 93m Technicolor Cinemascope
Columbia (Jonie Taps)

A married Broadway star finds that her first husband is still alive.
Adequate musical remake of *Too Many Husbands* (qv); not bad, not good.

w Edward Hope, Leonard Stern, *play* Too Many Husbands by W. Somerset Maugham *d* H. C. Potter *ph* Arthur E. Arling *ch* Jack Cole *songs* various

Betty Grable, Jack Lemmon, Marge Champion, Gower Champion, Myron McCormick, Paul Harvey

Three Girls about Town*
US 1942 71m bw
Columbia

Three sisters in New York find a corpse in their hotel bedroom.
A funny 'B' picture: fast paced and lively from start to finish.

w Richard Carroll *d* Leigh Jason *ph* Franz Planer

Joan Blondell, Binnie Barnes, Janet Blair, John Howard, Robert Benchley, Eric Blore, Una O'Connor

Three Godfathers*
US 1948 106m Technicolor
MGM / Argosy (John Ford)

Three outlaws escaping across the desert take charge of an orphan baby.
'Orrible sentimental parable partly redeemed by splendid scenery.

w Laurence Stallings, Frank S. Nugent, *story* Frank B. Kyne *d John Ford ph Winton Hoch m* Richard Hageman

John Wayne, Pedro Armendariz, Harry Carey Jnr, Ward Bond
† The story was told in several silent versions and as recently as 1975 in a TV movie *The Godchild* (qv).

Three Guns for Texas
US 1968 99m Technicolor TVM
Universal

Adventures of three Texas Rangers.
Low-grade western fodder spliced together from episodes of *Laredo*.

w John D. F. Black *d* David Lowell Rich

Neville Brand, Peter Brown, Martin Miller, William Smith

The 300 Spartans*
US 1962 114m De Luxe Cinemascope
TCF (Rudolph Maté, George St George)

Sparta leads the ancient Greek states against Persia's attack at Thermopylae.
Quite a lively epic with some dignity.

w George St George *d* Rudolph Maté
ph Geoffrey Unsworth *m* Manos Hadjikakis

Richard Egan, Ralph Richardson, David Farrar, Diane Baker, Barry Coe, Donald Houston, Kieron Moore, John Crawford, Robert Brown

Three Husbands
US 1950 76m bw
UA / Gloria (I. G. Goldsmith)

Three husbands receive letters from a dead friend claiming that he had affairs with each of their wives.
Silly copy of *A Letter to Three Wives*, with neither style nor sophistication.

w Vera Caspary, Edward Eliscu *d* Irving Reis
ph Franz Planer *m* Herschel Burke Gilbert

Emlyn Williams, Eve Arden, Howard da Silva, Ruth Warrick, Shepperd Strudwick, Vanessa Brown, Billie Burke, Jonathan Hale

Three in the Attic
US 1968 90m Pathecolor
AIP / Hermes (Richard Wilson)

A college Casanova is locked in an attic by three girls who seduce him by rota until he cries for mercy.
One of the first outspoken comedies of the sexual revolution, but not a particularly funny one.

w Stephen Yafa, from his novel Paxton Quigley's Had the Course *d* Richard Wilson *ph* J. Burgi Contner *m* Chad Stuart

Chris Jones, Yvette Mimieux, Judy Pace, Maggie Turett, Nan Martin

Three into Two Won't Go*
GB 1969 100m Technicolor
Universal (Julian Blaustein)

An executive has an affair with a girl hitch-hiker who later moves into his house to his wife's astonishment.
Palatable sex drama with good performances, rather flabbily written and directed.

w Edna O'Brien, *novel* Andrea Newman *d* Peter Hall *ph* Walter Lassally *m* Christian Gaubert

Rod Steiger, Claire Bloom, Judy Geeson, Peggy Ashcroft, Paul Rogers

Three Little Girls in Blue
US 1946 90m Technicolor
TCF (Mack Gordon)

Musical remake of *Three Blind Mice* (qv); adequate and quite forgettable.

w Valentine Davies *d* Bruce Humberstone
ph Ernest Palmer *songs* Mack Gordon, Joseph Myrow

June Haver, George Montgomery, Vivian Blaine, Celeste Holm, Vera-Ellen, Frank Latimore, Charles Smith, Charles Halton

Three Little Words*
US 1950 102m Technicolor
MGM (Jack Cummings)

The careers of songwriters Bert Kalmar and Harry Ruby.
Disappointingly ordinary musical in which two witty people are made to seem dull, and the plot allows Fred Astaire only one dance.

w George Wells *d* Richard Thorpe *ph* Harry Jackson *md* André Previn *ch* Hermes Pan *songs Bert Kalmar, Harry Ruby* and various collaborators

Fred Astaire, Red Skelton, Vera-Ellen, Arlene Dahl, Keenan Wynn, Gale Robbins, Gloria de Haven, Phil Regan, *Debbie Reynolds*

The Three Lives of Thomasina
GB 1963 97m Technicolor
Walt Disney

In a Scottish village in 1912, a vet finds that his methods are no match for a local girl who treats animals by giving them love.
Syrupy film for children: the animals are the main interest and one of them narrates . . .

w Robert Westerby, *novel* Thomasina by Paul Gallico *d* Don Chaffey *ph* Paul Beeson *m* Paul Smith

Susan Hampshire, Patrick McGoohan, Karen Dotrice, Vincent Winter, Laurence Naismith, Finlay Currie, Wilfrid Brambell

Three Loves Has Nancy
US 1938 69m bw
MGM (Norman Krasna)

A jilted bride takes her time about her next selection.
Adequate star comedy.

w Bella and Sam Spewack, George Oppenheimer, David Hertz *d* Richard Thorpe *ph* William Daniels

Janet Gaynor, Robert Montgomery, Franchot Tone, Guy Kibbee, Claire Dodd, Reginald Owen, Charley Grapewin, Emma Dunn, Cora Witherspoon

Three Men in a Boat
GB 1956 94m Eastmancolor
Cinemascope
Romulus (Jack Clayton)

In the 1890s, misadventures befall three men holidaying on the Thames.
Flabby burlesque of a celebrated comic novel whose style is never even approached.

w Hubert Gregg, Vernon Harris, *novel* Jerome K. Jerome *d* Ken Annakin *ph* Eric Cross *m* John Addison *ad* John Howell

David Tomlinson, Jimmy Edwards, Laurence Harvey, Shirley Eaton, Robertson Hare, Jill Ireland, Lisa Gastoni, Martita Hunt, A. E. Matthews, Ernest Thesiger, Adrienne Corri

Three Men on a Horse*
US 1936 85m bw
Warner (Sam Bischoff)

A timid Brooklynite finds he can always pick winners, and gangsters get interested.
Smooth New Yorkish comedy which pleased at the time.

w Laird Doyle, *play* John Cecil Holm, George Abbott *d* Mervyn Le Roy *ph* Sol Polito

Frank McHugh, Sam Levene, Joan Blondell, Guy Kibbee, Carol Hughes, Allen Jenkins, Edgar Kennedy, Eddie Anderson, Harry Davenport

The Three Mesquiteers

A three-man cowboy team who operated in popular B features at the Hopalong Cassidy level. The make-up of the team varied: the actors most often found in it were John Wayne, Max Terhune, Bob Livingston, Ray Corrigan, Bob Steele, Rufe Davis, Tom Tyler, Raymond Hatton, Duncan Renaldo and Jimmy Dodd. The first film was made for RKO, all the rest for Republic: most frequent directors were George Sherman, Mack V. Wright, Joseph Kane, John English and Lester Orlebeck.

1935: POWDERSMOKE RANGE, THE THREE MESQUITEERS.
1936: GHOST TOWN, GOLD, ROARIN' LEAD.
1937: RIDERS OF THE WHISTLING SKULL, HIT THE SADDLE, GUNSMOKE RANCH, COME ON COWBOYS, RANGE DEFENDERS, HEART OF THE ROCKIES, THE TRIGGER TRIO, WILD HORSE RODEO
1938: THE PURPLE VIGILANTES, CALL THE MESQUITEERS, CALL OF THE MESQUITEERS, OUTLAWS OF SONORA, RIDERS OF THE BLACK HILLS, HEROES OF THE HILLS, PALS OF THE SADDLE, OVERLAND STAGE RAIDERS, SANTA FE STAMPEDE, RED RIVER RANGE
1939: THE NIGHT RIDERS, THREE TEXAS STEERS, WYOMING OUTLAW, NEW FRONTIER, THE KANSAS TERRORS, COWBOYS FROM TEXAS
1940: HEROES OF THE SADDLE, PIONEERS OF THE WEST, COVERED WAGON DAYS, ROCKY MOUNTAIN RANGERS, OKLAHOMA RENEGADES, UNDER TEXAS SKIES, THE TRAIL BLAZERS, LONE STAR RAIDERS
1941: PRAIRIE PIONEERS, PALS OF THE PECOS, SADDLEMATES, GANGS OF SONORA, OUTLAWS OF THE CHEROKEE TRAIL, GAUCHOS OF EL DORADO, WEST OF CIMARRON
1942: CODE OF THE OUTLAW, RIDERS OF THE RANGE, WESTWARD HO, THE PHANTOM PLAINSMAN, SHADOWS ON THE SAGE, VALLEY OF HUNTED MEN
1943: THUNDERING TRAILS, THE BLOCKED TRAIL, SANTA FE SCOUTS, RIDERS OF THE RIO GRANDE

The Three Musketeers**
US 1939 73m bw
TCF
GB title: *The Singing Musketeer*

A burlesque of the familiar story with pauses for song.
A very satisfactory entertainment with all concerned in top form.

w M. M. Musselman, William A. Drake, Sam Hellman *d Allan Dwan ph* Peverell Marley

Don Ameche, the Ritz Brothers, Binnie Barnes, *Joseph Schildkraut*, Lionel Atwill, Miles Mander, Gloria Stuart, Pauline Moore, John Carradine

The Three Musketeers***
US 1948 125m Technicolor
MGM (Pandro S. Berman)

High-spirited version of the famous story, with duels and fights presented like musical numbers. Its vigour and inventiveness is a pleasure to behold.

w Robert Ardrey *d George Sidney ph Robert Planck m Herbert Stothart*

Gene Kelly, Lana Turner, June Allyson, Frank Morgan, Van Heflin, Angela Lansbury, Vincent Price, Keenan Wynn, John Sutton, Gig Young, Robert Coote, Reginald Owen, Ian Keith, Patricia Medina

The Three Musketeers (The Queen's Diamonds)**
Panama 1973 107m Technicolor
Film Trust (Alex Salkind)

Jokey version with realistic blood; despite very lively highlights it wastes most of its high production cost by not giving its plot a chance; but money was saved by issuing the second half separately as *The Four Musketeers* (*The Revenge of Milady*). The latter section was less attractive.

w George MacDonald Fraser *d Richard Lester ph David Watkin m* Michel Legrand *pd Brian Eatwell*

Michael York, Oliver Reed, Richard Chamberlain, Frank Finlay, Raquel Welch, Geraldine Chaplin, Spike Milligan, Faye Dunaway, Charlton Heston, Christopher Lee, Jean-Pierre Cassel

'It's one dragged-out forced laugh. No sweep, no romance, no convincing chivalric tradition to mock.'—*Stanley Kauffmann*

Three on a Match
US 1932 63m bw
Warner (Sam Bischoff)

Three schoolgirl friends meet again in the big city, after which their paths cross melodramatically.
Predictable, watchable multi-story dramatics with an ironic twist: remade in 1938 as *Broadway Musketeers*.

w Lucien Hubbard *d* Mervyn Le Roy *ph* Sol Polito

Joan Bondell, Bette Davis, Ann Dvorak, Warren William, Grant Mitchell, Lyle Talbot, Humphrey Bogart, Glenda Farrell, Clara Blandick

Three Ring Circus
US 1954 103m Technicolor Vistavision
Paramount / Hal B. Wallis

Ex-army veterans join a circus.
The mixture as before from Martin and Lewis: variety acts interspersed with sentiment and heavy mugging.

w Don McGuire, Joseph Pevney *ph* Loyal Griggs *d* Joseph Pevney *m* Walter Scharf

Dean Martin, Jerry Lewis, Joanne Dru, Zsa Zsa Gabor, Wallace Ford, Sig Rumann, Gene Sheldon, Nick Cravat, Elsa Lanchester

Three Sailors and a Girl
US 1953 95m Technicolor
Warner (Sammy Cahn)

A ship's funds are unofficially invested in a musical show.
Undernourished comedy musical.

w Roland Kibbee, Devery Freeman, *play* The Butter and Egg Man by George S. Kaufman *d* Roy del Ruth *ph* Carl Guthrie *songs* Sammy Fain, Sammy Cahn

Jane Powell, Gordon Macrae, Gene Nelson, Sam Levene, George Givot, Veda Ann Borg

Three Secrets*
US 1949 98m bw
(Warner) US Pictures (Milton Sperling)

Three women wait anxiously to find out whose child survived a plane crash.
Well-made, formula woman's picture.

w Martin Rackin, Gina Kaus *d Robert Wise ph Sid Hickox m* Davis Buttolph

Eleanor Parker, Patricia Neal, Ruth Roman, Frank Lovejoy, Leif Erickson, Ted de Corsia, Edmon Ryan, Larry Keating

The Three Sisters*
GB 1970 165m Eastmancolor
Alan Clore Films

At the turn of the century, three fatherless sisters dream of abandoning Russian provincial life for the big city.
Filmed Chekhov, better than most but still lacking cinematic vigour.

translator Moura Budberg *d* Laurence Olivier *ph* Geoffrey Unsworth *m* William Walton

Laurence Olivier, Joan Plowright, Jeanne Watts, Louise Purnell, Derek Jacobi, Alan Bates, Roland Pickup

Three Smart Girls**
US 1936 86m bw
Universal (Joe Pasternak)

Three sisters bring their parents back together.
Pleasant, efficient family film which made a world star of Deanna Durbin.

w Adele Comandini, Austin Parker *d* Henry Koster *ph* Joseph Valentine *md* Charles Previn

Deanna Durbin, Barbara Read, Nan Grey, Charles Winninger, Binnie Barnes, Ray Milland, Alice Brady, Mischa Auer, Ernest Cossart, Hobart Cavanaugh

'The awkward age has never been so laundered and lavendered and laid away.'—*Graham Greene*

Three Smart Girls Grow Up*
US 1939 87m bw
Universal (Joe Pasternak)

A girl helps her sisters to find beaus.
More of the same, quite palatable but inevitably warmed over.

w Bruce Manning, Felix Jackson *d* Henry Koster *ph* Joe Valentine

Deanna Durbin, Helen Parrish, Nan Grey, Charles Winninger, Robert Cummings, William Lundigan, Ernest Cossart, Nella Walker

Three Strangers*
US 1945 92m bw
Warner (Wolfgang Reinhardt)

A sweepstake ticket brings fortune and tragedy to three ill-assorted people.
Humdrum pattern play: the stars work hard to bring a little magic to it.

w John Huston, Howard Koch *d* Jean Negulesco *ph* Arthur Edeson *m* Adolph Deutsch

Sidney Greenstreet, Peter Lorre, Geraldine Fitzgerald, Joan Lorring, Robert Shayne, Marjorie Riordan, Arthur Shields

Three Stripes in the Sun
US 1955 93m bw
Columbia (Fred Kohlmar)
GB title: *The Gentle Sergeant*

After World War II, a Japanese-hating sergeant in the US occupation forces helps a poverty-stricken orphanage.
Predictable sentimentality based on fact, with good background detail.

wd Richard Murphy, *articles* E. J. Kelly *ph* Burnett Guffey *m* George Duning

Aldo Ray, Phil Carey, Dick York, Chuck Connors, Mitsuko Kimura

3.10 to Yuma**
US 1957 92m bw
Columbia (David Heilwell)

A sheriff has to get his prisoner on to a train despite the threatening presence of the prisoner's outlaw friends.
Tense, well-directed but rather talky low-budget western: excellent performances and atmosphere flesh out an unconvincing physical situation.

w Halsted Welles *d Delmer Daves ph Charles Lawton Jnr* *m* George Duning

Glenn Ford, Van Heflin, Felicia Farr, Leora Dana, Henry Jones, Richard Jaeckel, Robert Emhardt

Three Violent People
US 1956 100m Eastmancolor Vistavision
Paramount (Hugh Brown)

Brother ranchers quarrel over the wife of one of them, an ex-saloon hostess.
Characterless 'character' western, a long way after *Duel in the Sun*.

w James Edward Grant *d* Rudolph Maté *ph Loyal Griggs* *m* Walter Scharf

Charlton Heston, Anne Baxter, *Gilbert Roland*, Tom Tryon, Bruce Bennett, Forrest Tucker, Elaine Stritch, Barton MacLane

Three Wise Fools
US 1946 90m bw
MGM (William Wright)

Three crusty old gents adopt an orphan, who softens them.
Antediluvian whimsy without the expected fun, remade from a silent.

w John McDermott, James O'Hanlon, *play* Austin Strong *d* Edward Buzzell

Margaret O'Brien, Lionel Barrymore, Thomas Mitchell, Edward Arnold, Lewis Stone, Jane Darwell, Harry Davenport, Cyd Charisse

Three Wise Girls
US 1932 80m approx bw
Columbia

Three small-town girls gain wisdom in New York.
Three millgirls' romances for the price of one.
Adequate, predictable romantic fodder of its time.

w Robert Riskin, Agnes C. Johnson *d* William Beaudine *ph* Ted Tetzlaff

Jean Harlow, Mae Clarke, Walter Byron, Marie Prevost, Andy Devine, Natalie Moorhead, Jameson Thomas

The Three Worlds of Gulliver
US / Spain 1959 100m Technicolor
Columbia / Morningside (Charles Schneer)

Gulliver's adventures in Lilliput and Brobdingnag.
Flat treatment of marvellous material, with all the excitement squeezed out of it and not even much pizazz in the trick photography.

w Arthur Ross, Jack Sher *d* Jack Sher *m* Bernard Herrmann *sp* Ray Harryhausen

Kerwin Mathews, Basil Sydney, Mary Ellis, Jo Morrow, June Thorburn, Grégoire Aslan, Charles Lloyd Pack, Martin Benson

Three's a Crowd
US 1969 74m colour TVM
Columbia

Erroneously thinking his first wife dead in a plane crash, a businessman remarries . . .
My Favourite Wife revamped; each time to less effect.

w Buck Henry *d* James Frawley

Larry Hagman, E. J. Peaker, Jessica Walter, Norman Fell, Harvey Korman

Thrill of a Romance
US 1945 105m Technicolor
MGM (Joe Pasternak)

A lady swimmer falls for a returning serviceman.
Empty musical vehicle with nothing memorable about it except the waste of time and money.

w Richard Connell, Gladys Lehmann *d* Richard Thorpe *ph* Harry Stradling *md* George Stoll

Esther Williams, Van Johnson, Lauritz Melchior, Frances Gifford, Henry Travers, Spring Byington, Tommy Dorsey

The Thrill of it All*
US 1963 104m Eastmancolor
U-I / Ross Hunter / Arwin (Ross Hunter, Marty Melcher)

The wife of a gynaecologist becomes an advertising model, and work pressures disrupt her marriage.
Glossy matrimonial farce which starts brightly but eventually flags and becomes exhausting. Its better jokes linger in the memory.

w Carl Reiner *d* Norman Jewison *ph* Russell Metty *m* Frank de Vol

Doris Day, James Garner, Anne Francis, Edward Andrews, Reginald Owen, Zasu Pitts, Elliot Reid

'Pleasantly reminiscent of some of the screwball comedies of the thirties.'—*MFB*

Thumb Tripping*
US 1972 94m De Luxe
Avco (Robert Chartoff, Irwin Winkler)

A boy and a girl hitch-hiker in California have a variety of violent adventures.
Tail end of the *Easy Rider* fashion, with odd moments of interesting detail.

w Don Mitchell, from his novel *d* Quentin Masters *ph* Harry Stradling Jnr *m* Bob Thompson

Michael Burns, Meg Foster, Marianna Hill, Bruce Dern

Thunder Bay*
US 1953 102m Technicolor
U-I (Aaron Rosenberg)

An engineer is convinced that oil can be raised from the Louisiana sea-bed.
Well-produced outdoor actioner.

w Gil Doud, John Michael Hayes *d* Anthony Mann *ph* William Daniels *m* Frank Skinner

James Stewart, Joanne Dru, Dan Duryea, Jay C. Flippen, Anthony Moreno, Gilbert Roland, Marcia Henderson

Thunder in the City
GB 1937 88m bw
Atlantic (Akos Tolnay, Alexander Esway)

An American salesman in London helps a penniless duke promote a non-existent metal.
Mild satire on British and American idiosyncrasies, now very faded.

w Robert Sherwood, Abem Kandel, Akos Tolnay *d* Marion Gering *ph* Al Gilks

Edward G. Robinson, Lulu Deste, Ralph Richardson, Nigel Bruce, Constance Collier, Arthur Wontner

Thunder in the East
US 1951 98m bw
Paramount (Everett Riskin)

When India becomes independent in 1947, an American wanting to sell arms clashes with the peace-loving chief of a principality, but the arms are needed when rebels attack.
Artificial and boring action melodrama with platitudinous conversations.

w Jo Swerling, *novel* Rage of the Vulture by Alan Moorehead *d* Charles Vidor *ph* Lee Garmes

Alan Ladd, Charles Boyer, Deborah Kerr, Corinne Calvet, Cecil Kellaway

Thunder in the Sun
US 1958 81m Technicolor
Seven Arts / Carollton (Clarence Greene)

In 1847 an Indian scout guides a group of Basques to California with their vines.
Overwritten and melodramatic wagon train story.

wd Russel Rouse *ph* Stanley Cortez *m* Cyril Mockridge

Susan Hayward, Jeff Chandler, Jacques Bergerac, Blanche Yurka, Carl Esmond

A Thunder of Drums*
US 1961 97m Metrocolor Cinemascope
MGM (Robert J. Enders)

Trouble with Apaches at a frontier post in 1870.
Solid, unexciting first feature western, some way after Ford.

w James Warner Bellah *d* Joseph Newman *ph* William Spencer *m* Harry Sukman

Richard Boone, George Hamilton, Arthur O'Connell, Luana Patten, Richard Chamberlain, Charles Bronson

Thunder on the Hill
US 1951 84m bw
U-I (Michael Kraike)
GB title: *Bonaventure*

In Norfolk, a nun solves a murder mystery during a flood.
Modest whodunnit with an unusual background but not much suspense.

w Oscar Saul, André Solt, *play* Bonaventure by Charlotte Hastings *d* Douglas Sirk *ph* William Daniels *m* Hans Salter

Claudette Colbert, Ann Blyth, Robert Douglas, Anne Crawford, Philip Friend, Gladys Cooper, John Abbott, Connie Gilchrist, Gavin Muir

Thunder Road*
US 1958 92m bw
UA / DRM

Hillbilly bootleggers defy a Chicago gangster.
Downbeat but actionful crime melodrama with an unusual background and plenty of car chases.

w James Arlee Philips, Walter Wise *d Arthur Ripley* *ph* Alan Stensvold *m* Jack Marshall

Robert Mitchum, Gene Barry, Jacques Aubuchon, Keely Smith

Thunder Rock***
GB 1942 112m bw
Charter Films (John Boulting)

A journalist disgusted with the world of the thirties retires to a lighthouse on Lake Michigan and is haunted by the ghosts of immigrants drowned a century before.
Subtle adaptation of an impressive and topical anti-isolationist play, very well acted and presented.

w Jeffrey Dell, Bernard Miles, *play Robert Ardrey* *d Roy Boulting* *ph* Mutz Greenbaum (Max Greene) *m* Hans May

Michael Redgrave, Lilli Palmer, Barbara Mullen, James Mason, Frederick Valk, Frederick Cooper, Finlay Currie, Sybilla Binder

'Boldly imaginative in theme and treatment.' —*Sunday Express*

'More interesting technically than anything since *Citizen Kane*.'—*Manchester Guardian*

Thunderball**
GB 1965 132m Technicolor Panavision
UA / Eon / Kevin McClory

James Bond goes underwater.
Commercially the most successful Bond, but certainly not the best despite a plethora of action sequences.

w Richard Maibaum, John Hopkins, *novel* Ian Fleming *d* Terence Young *ph Ted Moore* *m* John Barry

Sean Connery, Adolfo Celi, Claudine Auger, Luciana Paluzzi, Rik Van Nutter, Bernard Lee, Lois Maxwell

'The screenplay stands on tiptoe at the outermost edge of the suggestive and gazes yearningly down into the obscene.'—*John Simon*

Thunderbird Six
GB 1968 90m Techniscope
UA / AP / Century 21 (Gerry and Sylvia Anderson)

International Rescue combats the Black Phantom.
Bright, suspenseful puppetoon based on the TV series.

w Gerry and Sylvia Anderson *d* David Lane *ph* Harry Oakes *m* Barry Gray *ad* Bob Bell

'Holds some charm for adults, or at least for those who enjoy playing with miniature trains.' —*MFB*

Thunderbirds
US 1942 79m Technicolor
TCF (Lamar Trotti)

Problems of Arizona flight instructors during World War II.
Very minor flagwaver.

w Lamar Trotti *d* William A. Wellman *ph* Ernest Palmer

Gene Tierney, Preston Foster, John Sutton, Jack Holt, May Whitty, George Barbier, Richard Haydn, Reginald Denny, Ted North

Thunderbirds
US 1952 99m bw
Republic (John H. Auer)

An Oklahoma unit covers itself in glory during World War II.
Scrappy, noisy war actioner with much newsreel footage.

w Mary McCall Jnr *d* John H. Auer *ph* Reggie Lanning *m* Victor Young

John Derek, John Barrymore Jnr, Mona Freeman, Ward Bond, Gene Evans

Thunderbolt**
US 1929 94m bw
Paramount

A gangster is caught, tried, and repents.
Gloomy melodrama with interesting style and credits.

w Jules Furthman, Herman J. Mankiewicz *d Josef Von Sternberg* *ph* Henry Gerrard

George Bancroft, Fay Wray, Richard Arlen, Tully Marshall, Eugénie Besserer

Thunderbolt and Lightfoot*
US 1974 115m De Luxe Panavision
UA / Malpaso (Robert Daley)

A bank robber escapes prison, disguises himself as a preacher, befriends a young drifter, and discovers that a new building stands on the spot where the loot is hidden.
Violent melodrama reworking an ancient comedy situation; well made on its level.

wd Michael Cimino *ph* Frank Stanley *m* Dee Barton

Clint Eastwood, Jeff Bridges, George Kennedy, Geoffrey Lewis, Catherine Bach

Thunderhead, Son of Flicka*
US 1945 78m Technicolor
TCF (Robert Bassler)

More where *My Friend Flicka* came from.
Unexceptionable family film with excellent outdoor photography.

w Dwight Cummins, Dorothy Yost, *novel* Mary O'Hara *d* Louis King *ph Charles Clarke* *m* Cyril Mockridge

Roddy McDowall, Preston Foster, Rita Johnson, James Bell, Carleton Young

Thunderstorm
GB 1955 88m bw
Hemisphere / Binnie Barnes

A Spanish fisherman rescues a mysterious girl from a derelict yacht and falls in love with her although the villagers regard her as a witch.
Heady stuff on a low budget, quite smoothly done for lovers of peasant drama.

w George St George, Geoffrey Holmes *d John Guillermin* *ph* Manuel Berenguer *m* Paul Misraki

Linda Christian, Carlos Thompson, Charles Korvin

Thursday's Game*
US 1974 96m colour TVM
ABC Circle

Two married men get into trouble on their once-a-week night with the boys.
Fairly sparkling domestic comedy.

w James Brooks *d* Robert Moore

Bob Newhart, Gene Wilder, Ellen Burstyn, Cloris Leachman, Nancy Walker, Valerie Harper

THX 1138*
US 1970 95m Technicolor / scope
Warner / American Zoetrope (Francis Ford Coppola, Lawrence Sturhahn)

In a future society, computer programmed and emotionless, an automated human begins to break the rules.
Orwellian science fiction; a thoughtful, rather cold affair which is always good to look at.

w George Lucas, Walter Murch *d George Lucas* *ph* Dave Meyers, Albert Kihn *m* Lalo Schifrin

Robert Duvall, Donald Pleasance, Pedro Colley, Maggie McOmie, Ian Wolfe

Tiara Tahiti*
GB 1962 100m Eastmancolor
Rank / Ivan Foxwell

An up-from-the-ranks colonel and an aristocratic smoothie captain continue their antipathy in peacetime Tahiti, where one is nearly murdered and the other gets his come-uppance.
Uneasy mixture of light comedy and character drama; enjoyable in parts, but flabbily assembled and muddily photographed.

w Geoffrey Cotterell, Ivan Foxwell, *novel* Geoffrey Cotterell *d* William T. Kotcheff *ph* Otto Heller *m* Philip Green

John Mills, James Mason, Herbert Lom, Claude Dauphin, Rosenda Monteros

Tick, Tick, Tick . . .*
US 1969 100m Metrocolor Panavision
MGM / Nelson-Barrett (Ralph Nelson, James Lee Barrett)

The first black sheriff in a southern community has trouble with murder and rape cases.
Socially conscious suspenser, well enough m from predictable elements and leading surprisingly to an upbeat ending.

w James Lee Barrett *d* Ralph Nelson *ph* Loy Griggs *m* Jerry Stynes

Jim Brown, George Kennedy, Fredric Mar , Lynn Carlin, Don Stroud, Clifton James

A Ticket to Tomahawk*
US 1950 90m Technicolor
TCF (Robert Bassler)

A stagecoach line defies the new western railroad.
Would-be satirical western which doesn't quite have the stamina and after some pleasing touches settles for dullness.

w Mary Loos *d* Richard Sale *ph* Harry Jackson *m* Cyril Mockridge

Anne Baxter, Dan Duryea, Rory Calhoun, Walter Brennan, Charles Kemper, Connie Gilchrist, Arthur Hunnicutt, Sen Yung

Tickle Me
US 1965 90m De Luxe Panavision
AA (Ben Schwalb)

An unemployed rodeo star accepts a job at a health ranch and helps a girl escape from villains after hidden treasure.
Wispy star vehicle with an unexpected haunted ghost town climax.

w Elwood Ullman, Edward Bernds *d* Norman Taurog *ph* Loyal Griggs *m* Walter Scharf

Elvis Presley, Julia Adams, Jocelyn Lane, Jack Mullaney, Merry Anders, Connie Gilchrist

A Ticklish Affair
US 1963 95m Metrocolor Panavision
MGM / Euterpe (Joe Pasternak)

A naval commander in San Diego falls for a widow with several children.
Thin romantic comedy with too many juvenile antics.

w Ruth Brooks Flippen *d* George Sidney *ph* Milton Krasner *m* George Stoll, Robert Van Eyps

Shirley Jones, Gig Young, Red Buttons, Carolyn Jones, Edgar Buchanan

Tiger Bay**
GB 1959 105m bw
Rank / Wintle–Parkyn (John Hawkesworth)

A Polish seaman in Cardiff kills his faithless girl friend and kidnaps a child who proves more than a match for him.
Generally very proficient police chase melodrama with strong characterizations: a considerable box office success of its time.

w John Hawkesworth, Shelley Smith *d J. Lee-Thompson ph Eric Cross m* Laurie Johnson

Hayley Mills, John Mills, Horst Buchholz, Megs Jenkins, Anthony Dawson, Yvonne Mitchell

Tiger in the Smoke*
GB 1956 94m bw
Rank (Leslie Parkyn)

Ex-commando criminals comb London for hidden loot and threaten a young girl.
Odd little melodrama with a complex plot and a different, Graham Greene-like atmosphere.

w Anthony Pelissier, *novel* Marjorie Allingham *d* Roy Baker *ph* Geoffrey Unsworth *m* Malcolm Arnold

Tony Wright, Muriel Pavlow, Donald Sinden, Bernard Miles, Alec Clunes, Laurence Naismith, Christopher Rhodes, Kenneth Griffith, Beatrice Varley

The Tiger Makes Out*
US 1967 94m Technicolor
Columbia / Elan (George Justin)

A middle-aged New York postman takes revenge on society by kidnapping a young girl—who rather enjoys the experience.
Semi-surrealist comedy misguidedly extended from a two-character play; frantic pace prevents more than a few effective moments.

w Murray Shisgal, from his play *d* Arthur Hiller *ph* Arthur J. Ornitz *m* Milton Rogers

Eli Wallach, Anne Jackson, Bob Dishy, David Burns, Charles Nelson Reilly

Tiger Shark*
US 1932 80m bw
Warner

A tuna fisherman who has lost a hand to a shark marries the daughter of an old friend, finds she loves someone else, and is conveniently killed by another shark.
Vivid melodrama with a plot partly borrowed from *Moby Dick* and itself partly borrowed by innumerable other Warner films including *Kid Galahad, The Wagons Roll at Night* and *Manpower*.

w Wells Root, *story* Tuna by Houston Branch *d Howard Hawks ph* Tony Gaudio

Edward G. Robinson, J. Carrol Naish, Zita Johann

A Tiger Walks*
US 1963 91m Technicolor
Walt Disney (Ron Miller)

In a small western town, a tiger escapes from the circus.
A splendid animal and a happy ending help to make this a pretty good film for children.

w Lowell S. Hawley, *novel* Ian Niall *d* Norman Tokar *ph* William Snyder *m* Buddy Baker

Sabu, Brian Keith, Vera Miles, Pamela Franklin, Kevin Corcoran, Edward Andrews, Una Merkel, Frank McHugh

'The Disney message runs true to form—grown-ups should practise what they preach and children are right about animals.'—*MFB*

Tight Spot
US 1955 97m bw
Columbia (Lewis J. Rachmil)

A material witness in the trial of a gangster is released from prison in the custody of an attorney.
Fairly routine crime melodrama with unexciting star performances.

w William Bowers, *play* Dead Pigeon by Leonard Kantor *d* Phil Karlson *ph* Burnett Guffey *m* Morris Stoloff

Edward G. Robinson, Ginger Rogers, Brian Keith, Lorne Greene, Lucy Marlow, Katherine Anderson

Till Death Us Do Part*
GB 1969 100m Eastmancolor
British Lion / Associated London Films (Jon Pennington)

From the thirties to the sixties with loud-mouthed, bigoted Londoner Alf Garnett.
Unremarkable and frequently misguided opening-up of a phenomenally successful TV series, adapted for the US as *All in the Family*. The original cast wades cheerfully enough through a bitty script; the sequel, *The Alf Garnett Saga*, defeated them.

w Johnny Speight *d* Norman Cohen *ph* Harry Waxman *m* Wilfrid Burns

Warren Mitchell, Dandy Nichols, Anthony Booth, Una Stubbs, Liam Redmond, Bill Maynard, Sam Kydd, Brian Blessed

Till the Clouds Roll By**
GB 1946 137m Technicolor
MGM (Arthur Freed)

The life and times of composer Jerome Kern.
Better-than-average biopic with better-than-average tunes and stars.

w Myles Connolly, Jean Holloway *d* Richard Whorf *ph* Harry Stradling, George J. Folsey *md* Lennie Hayton

Robert Walker, Judy Garland, Lucille Bremer, Van Heflin, Mary Nash, Dinah Shore, Van Johnson, *June Allyson*, Tony Martin, Kathryn Grayson, *Lena Horne, Frank Sinatra, Virginia O'Brien*

Till the End of Time*
US 1946 105m bw
RKO

Three returning GIs find romance and problems in their small town.
Downbeat variation on *The Best Years of Our Lives* with a theme tune which puts words to a Chopin Polonaise.

w Allen Rivkin *d* Edward Dmytryk *ph* Harry J. Wild *m* Leigh Harline

Dorothy McGuire, Guy Madison, Robert Mitchum

'Til We Meet Again
US 1939 99m bw
Warner (David Lewis)

On a ship bound from Hong Kong to San Francisco, a dying woman falls for a crook about to be executed.
Stolid remake of *One Way Passage* (qv).

w Warren Duff, *story* Robert Lord *d* Edmund Goulding *ph* Tony Gaudio

Merle Oberon, George Brent, Frank McHugh, Pat O'Brien, Geraldine Fitzgerald, Eric Blore, Binnie Barnes, Henry O'Neill, George Reeves

Till We Meet Again
US 1944 88m bw
Paramount (David Lewis)

A French nun helps an American aviator escape from the Nazis.
Very moderate, nicely photographed, romantic war actioner.

w Lenore Coffee, *play* Alfred Maury *d* Frank Borzage *ph Theodor Sparkuhl* *m* David Buttolph

Ray Milland, Barbara Britton, Walter Slezak, Lucile Watson, Konstantin Shayne, Vladimir Sokoloff, Mona Freeman

Tillie and Gus*
US 1933 61m bw
Paramount (Douglas MacLean)

Two middle-aged cardsharps return home, help their niece and nephew win an inheritance, and come first in a paddleboat race.
Jumbled comedy with good moments and a rousing climax.

w Walter de Leon, Francis Martin *d* Francis Martin *ph* Benjamin Reynolds

W. C. Fields, Alison Skipworth, Baby Le Roy, Jacqueline Wells, Clifford Jones, Clarence Wilson, Edgar Kennedy, Barton MacLane

Time Bomb*
GB 1952 72m bw
MGM (Richard Goldstone)
US title: *Terror on a Train*

A saboteur places a bomb on a goods train travelling from the north of England to Portsmouth.
Tolerable suspenser padded out with domestic asides.

w Ken Bennett *d* Ted Tetzlaff *ph* Frederick A. Young *m* John Addison

Glenn Ford, Anne Vernon, Maurice Denham, Harcourt Williams, Harold Warrender, Bill Fraser, John Horsley, Victor Maddern

A Time for Killing
US 1967 83m Pathecolor Panavision
Columbia / Sage Western (Harry Joe Brown)
GB title: *The Long Ride Home*

Confederate prisoners escape from a Union fort and the commander sets off in pursuit.
Fairly savage western with Something to Say about the corruption of war.

w Halsted Welles, *novel* Southern Blade by Nelson and Shirley Wolford *d* Phil Karlson *ph* Kenneth Peach *m* Mundell Lowe

Glenn Ford, George Hamilton, Inger Stevens, Max Baer, Paul Petersen, Timothy Carey, Todd Armstrong

A Time for Love
US 1973 100m colour TVM
Paramount (Stirling Silliphant)

Two love stories of different types.
A format which didn't jell, even after the success of *Love Story*. No takers.

w Stirling Silliphant *d* George Schaefer, Joseph Sargent

Jack Cassidy, Bonnie Bedelia, John Davidson, Lauren Hutton, Christopher Mitchum

A Time for Loving
GB 1971 104m colour
London Screen Plays / Mel Ferrer

Short romantic comedies set at different times in the same Paris flat.
Portmanteau ooh-la-la, quite neat but pitifully undernourished; certainly no *Plaza Suite*.

w Jean Anouilh *d* Christopher Miles *ph* Andreas Winding *m* Michel Legrand *pd* Theo Meurisse

Joanna Shimkus, Mel Ferrer, Britt Ekland, Philippe Noiret, Lila Kedrova, Robert Dhery, Michael Burns

Time Gentlemen Please
GB 1952 83m bw
Group Three (Herbert Mason)

A lazy tramp is the one blot on a prize-winning English village.
Artificial, thinly scripted and overlit sub-Ealing comedy with familiar characters and situations.

w Peter Blackmore, *novel* Nothing to Lose by R. J. Minney *d* Lewis Gilbert *ph* Wilkie Cooper *m* Antony Hopkins

Eddie Byrne, Hermione Baddeley, Jane Barrett, Robert Brown, Raymond Lovell, Marjorie Rhodes, Dora Bryan, Thora Hird, Sidney James, Edie Martin, Ivor Barnard, Sidney Tafler

'Quite a nice little picture.'—*Karel Reisz*

Time Limit*
US 1957 95m bw
UA / Richard Widmark, William Reynolds

During the Korean war an officer is courtmartialled for suspected collaboration.
Suspenseful talk piece from a somewhat intellectualized play.

w Henry Denker, *play* Henry Denker, Ralph Berkey *d* *Karl Malden* *ph* Sam Leavitt *m* Fred Steiner

Richard Widmark, Richard Basehart, Dolores Michaels, June Lockhart, Carl Benton Reid, Martin Balsam, Rip Torn

'The tightly constructed story leads logically and unfalteringly to a tense climax.'—*Lindsay Anderson*

Time Lock*
GB 1957 73m bw
Romulus (Peter Rogers)

A small boy is trapped in a bank vault just as it is being locked for the weekend.
Acceptable expansion of a Canadian TV suspenser.

w Peter Rogers, *play* Arthur Hailey *d* Gerald Thomas *ph* Peter Hennessy *m* Stanley Black

Robert Beatty, Betty McDowall, Vincent Winter, Lee Patterson, Alan Gifford, Robert Ayres

The Time Machine*
US 1960 103m Metrocolor
MGM / Galaxy (George Pal)

A Victorian scientist builds a machine which after some trial and error transports him into the year 802701.
Surprisingly careful recreation of a period, and an undeniably charming machine, go for little when the future, including the villainous Morlocks, is so dull.

w David Duncan, *novel* H. G. Wells *d* George Pal *ph* Paul C. Vogel *m* Russell Garcia *ad George W. Davis, William Ferrari*

Rod Taylor, Yvette Mimieux, Alan Young, Sebastian Cabot, Tom Helmore, Whit Bissell, Doris Lloyd

The Time of Their Lives*
US 1946 82m bw
Universal (Val Burton)

Revolutionary ghosts haunt a country estate.
Unusual, quite effective Abbott and Costello vehicle with the comedians not playing as a team.

w Val Burton, Walter de Leon, Bradford Ropes, John Grant *d* Charles Barton *ph* Charles Van Enger *m* Milton Rosen

Bud Abbott, Lou Costello, Marjorie Reynolds, Binnie Barnes, Gale Sondergaard, John Shelton

The Time of Your Life*
US 1948 109m bw
William Cagney

A group of lovable eccentrics spend much of their time philosophizing in a San Francisco bar.
Not really a film at all, this essence of Saroyan contains much to enjoy or to annoy. The performances are pretty good.

w Nathaniel Curtis, *play William Saroyan* *d* H. C. Potter *ph* James Wong Howe *m* Carmen Dragon

James Cagney, William Bendix, Wayne Morris, Jeanne Cagney, Gale Page, Broderick Crawford, *James Barton*, Ward Bond, Paul Draper, James Lydon, Richard Erdman, Natalie Schaefer

'They have done so handsomely by Saroyan that in the long run everything depends on how much of Saroyan you can take.'—*Time*

Time out of Mind
US 1947 88m bw
U-I

The housekeeper's daughter finances music studies for the master's ungrateful son.
Silly romantic melodrama with few visible compensations.

w Abem Finkel, Arnold Phillips, *novel* Rachel Field *d* Robert Siodmak *ph* Maury Gertsman

Phyllis Calvert, Robert Hutton, Ella Raines, Eddie Albert, Leo G. Carroll

The Time, the Place and the Girl
US 1946 105m Technicolor
Warner (Alex Gottlieb)

Two nightclub owners have problems.
Lightweight musical, indistinguishable from a dozen others.

w Francis Swann, Agnes Christine Johnson, Lynn Starling *d* David Butler *ph* William V. Skall *m* Arthur Schwartz

Dennis Morgan, Jack Carson, Janis Paige, Martha Vickers, S. Z. Sakall, Alan Hale, Donald Woods, Angela Greene, Florence Bates

A Time to Love and a Time to Die*
US 1958 132m Eastmancolor Cinemascope
U-I (Robert Arthur)

During World War II, a German officer on his last leave solves problems at home but is killed on his return to the front.
Interesting but preachy and generally misguided attempt, by the studio which made *All Quiet on the Western Front* and *The Road Back*, to repeat the dose in colour and wide screen.

w Orin Jannings, *novel* Erich Maria Remarque *d* Douglas Sirk *ph* Russell Metty *m* Miklos Rozsa

John Gavin, Lilo Pulver, Keenan Wynn, Jock Mahoney, Thayer David, Agnes Windeck, Erich Maria Remarque

The Time Travelers*
US 1964 84m Pathecolor
AIP / Dobie (William Redlin)

Scientists venture 107 years into the future, and on escaping find themselves in a time trap.
Ingenious and lively low-budget science fiction with a sobering ending.

wd Ib Melchior *ph* William Zsigismond *m* Richard La Salle

Preston Foster, Phil Carey, Merry Anders, John Hoyt, Joan Woodbury

Time without Pity*
GB 1957 88m bw
Harlequin (John Arnold, Anthony Simmons)

An alcoholic arrives in London to seek new evidence which will prevent his son from being executed for murder.
Heavy-going, introspective, hysterical, downbeat melodrama which takes itself with a seriousness which is almost deadly.

w Ben Barzman *play* Someone Waiting by Emlyn Williams *d* Joseph Losey *ph* Freddie Francis *m* Tristam Cary

Michael Redgrave, Alec McCowen, Leo McKern, Renée Houston, Ann Todd, Peter Cushing, Paul Daneman, Lois Maxwell, George Devine, Richard Wordsworth, Joan Plowright

'It hammers home its effects with the concentration of a heavyweight out for the kill.' —*Philip Oakes*

Timetable*
US 1955 79m bw
(UA) Mark Stevens

An insurance investigator is assigned to a train robbery which he actually committed himself.

Concise suspenser with good script and treatment.

w Aben Kandel *d* Mark Stevens *ph* Charles Van Enger

Mark Stevens, Felicia Farr, King Calder, Wesley Addy

Tin Pan Alley***
US 1940 95m bw
TCF (Kenneth MacGowan)

During World War I and after, two dancing girls love the same composer.
Archetypal musical, full of Broadway clichés, razzmatazz and zip. Remade 1950 as *I'll Get By*, not to such peppy effect.

w Robert Ellis, Helen Logan *d Walter Lang ph Leon Shamroy ch* Seymour Felix *songs* Mack Gordon, Harry Revel

Alice Faye, Betty Grable, John Payne, Jack Oakie, Allen Jenkins, Esther Ralston, The Nicholas Brothers, John Loder, Elisha Cook Jnr

The Tin Star*
US 1957 93m bw Vistavision
Paramount / Perlberg–Seaton

An ex-sheriff turned bounty hunter helps a new young sheriff to catch bandits.
Dignified and well-characterized western with customary pleasures.

w Dudley Nichols d Anthony Mann ph Loyal Griggs *m* Elmer Bernstein

Henry Fonda, Anthony Perkins, Betsy Palmer, Michel Ray, Neville Brand, John McIntire

The Tingler
US 1959 82m bw
Columbia / William Castle

Fear (it says here) can create on the spinal column a parasite removable only by screaming. A scientist isolates it and it runs amok in a silent cinema.
Ridiculous shocker with generally dull handling but effective moments.

w Robb White *d* William Castle *ph* Wilfrid Cline *m* Von Dexter

Vincent Price, Judith Evelyn, Darryl Hickman, Patricia Cutts

'The sheer effrontery of this piece of hokum is enjoyable in itself.'—*MFB*

Tip on a Dead Jockey
US 1957 99m bw
MGM (Edwin H. Knopf)
GB title: *Time for Action*

A flier loses his nerve and turns international smuggler, but reforms.
Gloomy, pedestrian star melodrama, dully cast

w Charles Lederer, *novel* Irwin Shaw *d* Richard Thorpe *m* Miklos Rozsa

Robert Taylor, Dorothy Malone, Gia Scala, Martin Gabel, Marcel Dalio, Jack Lord

Titanic*
US 1953 98m bw
TCF (Charles Brackett)

Personal dramas aboard the *Titanic* in 1912 come to a head as the ship hits an iceberg.
An excellent example of studio production is squandered on a dim script which arouses no excitement.

w Charles Brackett, Walter Reisch, Richard Breen *d* Jean Negulesco *ph Joe MacDonald m* Sol Kaplan *ad* Lyle Wheeler, Maurice Ransford

Clifton Webb, Barbara Stanwyck, Robert Wagner, Audrey Dalton, Thelma Ritter, Brian Aherne, Richard Basehart, Allyn Joslyn

The Titfield Thunderbolt***
US 1952 84m Technicolor
Ealing (Michael Balcon)

When a branch railway line is threatened with closure, the villagers take it over as a private concern.
Undervalued on its release in the wake of other Ealing comedies, this now seems among the best of them as well as an immaculate colour production showing the England that is no more; the script has pace, the whole thing is brightly polished and the action works up to a fine climactic frenzy.

w T. E. B. Clarke d Charles Crichton ph Douglas Slocombe m Georges Auric

Stanley Holloway, George Relph, John Gregson, Godfrey Tearle, *Edie Martin*, Naunton Wayne, Gabrielle Brune, Sidney James, Jack McGowran, Ewan Roberts, Reginald Beckwith

To All My Friends on Shore
US 1971 74m colour TVM
Bill Cosby

A black businessman discovers his young son has a fatal illness.
One wonders how dying has suddenly acquired such an appeal. This one is such a star weepie that it's hard to be sympathetic.

w Allan Sloane *d* Gilbert Cater

Bill Cosby, Gloria Foster, Dennis Hines

To Be or Not to Be****
US 1942 99m bw
(Alexander Korda) Ernst Lubitsch

Warsaw actors get involved in an underground plot and an impersonation of invading Nazis, including Hitler.
Marvellous free-wheeling entertainment which starts as drama and descends through romantic comedy and suspense into farce; accused of bad taste at the time, but now seen as an outstanding example of Hollywood moonshine, kept alight through sheer talent and expertise.

w Edwin Justus Mayer, story Ernst Lubitsch, Melchior Lengyel *d Ernst Lubitsch ph Rudolph Maté m Werner Heymann ad Vincent Korda*

Jack Benny, Carole Lombard, Robert Stack, *Stanley Ridges, Felix Bressart, Lionel Atwill, Sig Rumann, Tom Dugan,* Charles Halton

'As effective an example of comic propaganda as *The Great Dictator* and far better directed.' —*Charles Higham, 1972*

'Based on an indiscretion, but undoubtedly a work of art.'—*James Agee*

To Catch a Thief*
US 1955 97m Technicolor Vistavision
Paramount / Alfred Hitchcock

A famous cat burglar who has retired to the Riviera catches a thief who is imitating his old style.
Very slow, floppy and rather boring entertainment enlivened by the scenery and the odd Hitchcock touch.

w John Michael Hayes, *novel* David Dodge *d* Alfred Hitchcock *ph* Robert Burks *m* Lyn Murray

Cary Grant, Grace Kelly, *Jessie Royce Landis, John Williams,* Charles Vanel, Brigitte Auber

To Each His Own**
US 1946 100m bw
Paramount (Charles Brackett)

During World War II, a middle-aged woman in London meets the soldier who is her own illegitimate and long-since-adopted-son.
The woman's picture par excellence, put together with tremendous Hollywood flair and extremely enjoyable to watch.

w Charles Brackett, Jacques Théry d Mitchell Leisen ph Daniel L. Fapp *m Victor Young ad* Hans Dreier, Roland Anderson

Olivia de Havilland, John Lund, Roland Culver, Mary Anderson, Philip Terry, Bill Goodwin, Virginia Welles, Virginia Horne

To Find a Man*
US 1971 93m Eastmancolor
Columbia / Rastar (Irving Pincus)

The spoiled daughter of a rich family becomes pregnant and is helped by a young chemist.
Quiet, well-made minor drama about maturity, with good small-town atmosphere.

w Arnold Schulman, novel S. J. Wilson *d* Buzz Kulik *ph* Andy Laszlo *m* David Shire

Pamela Martin, Darrell O'Connor, *Lloyd Bridges,* Phyllis Newman, Tom Ewell, Tom Bosley

To Have and Have Not**
US 1945 100m bw
Warner (Howard Hawks)

An American charter boat captain in Martinique gets involved with Nazis.
Fairly routinely made studio adventure notable for first pairing of Bogart and Bacall, as an imitation of *Casablanca,* and for its consistent though not outstanding entertainment value.
Remade later as *The Breaking Point* (qv) and *The Gun Runners* (qv), and not dissimilar from *Key Largo* (qv).

w Jules Furthman, William Faulkner, novel Ernest Hemingway *d Howard Hawks ph* Sid Hickox *m* Leo F. Forbstein

Humphrey Bogart, Lauren Bacall, Walter Brennan, Hoagy Carmichael, Dolores Moran, Sheldon Leonard, Dan Seymour, Marcel Dalio

'Remarkable for the ingenuity and industry with which the original story and the individualities of Ernest Hemingway have been rendered down into Hollywood basic.'—*Richard Winnington*

'Sunlight on the lattice, sex in the corridors, a new pianist at the café, pistol shots, the fat sureté man coming round after dark.'—*William Whitebait*

To Hell and Back
US 1955 106m Technicolor Cinemascope
U-I (Aaron Rosenberg)

The war career of America's most decorated infantryman.
Routine war story which happens to be about a fellow who later became a film star.

w Gil Doud, *book* Audie Murphy *d* Jesse Hibbs *ph* Maury Gertsman *m* Joseph Gershenson

Audie Murphy, Marshall Thompson, Charles Drake, Gregg Palmer, Jack Kelly, Paul Picerni, Susan Kohner

'The emotion is congealed and there is no real personal response to the anguish of war.'—*John Gillett*

To Kill a Clown
GB 1971 104m De Luxe
Palomar (Theodore Sills)

A painter and his wife move to a New England isle and are menaced by a crippled Vietnam veteran and his vicious dogs.
Pretentious, politically oriented rehash of *The Most Dangerous Game* (qv), carefully made but too slow for suspense.

w George Bloomfield, I. C. Rapoport, *novel* Master of the Hounds by Algis Budrys *d* George Bloomfield *ph* Walter Lassally *m* Richard Hill, John Hawkins

Alan Alda, Blyth Danner, Heath Lamberts, Eric Clavering

To Kill a Mockingbird**
US 1963 129m bw
U-I (Alan Pakula)

A lawyer in a small southern town defends a black man accused of murder.
Familiar dollops of social conscience, very well presented with a child interest and excellent atmosphere, but a mite overlong.

w Horton Foote, *novel* Harper Lee *d Robert Mulligan* *ph* Russell Harlan *m* Elmer Bernstein

Gregory Peck, Mary Badham, Philip Alford, John Megna, Frank Overton, Rosemary Murphy, Ruth White, Brock Peters

To Paris with Love
GB 1954 78m Technicolor
GFD / Two Cities (Anthony Darnborough)

A middle-aged widower and his son go to Paris on holiday and devise matrimonial plans for each other.
Thin, disappointing taradiddle which is short but seems long.

w Robert Buckner *d* Robert Hamer *ph* Reg Wyer *m* Edwin Astley

Alec Guinness, Vernon Gray, Odile Versois, Jacques François, Elina Labourdette, Austin Trevor

'The general impression is somehow too aimless, too muted.'—*Gavin Lambert*

To Please a Lady*
US 1951 91m bw
MGM (Clarence Brown)

A ruthless midget-car racer falls for the lady journalist who is hounding him.
Good action programmer with no frills.

w Barre Lyndon, Marge Decker *d* Clarence Brown *ph* Harold Rosson *m* Bronislau Kaper

Clark Gable, Barbara Stanwyck, Adolphe Menjou, Will Geer, Roland Winters, Emory Parnell, Frank Jenks

To Sir with Love
GB 1967 105m Technicolor
Columbia (James Clavell)

A West Indian teacher comes to a tough East End school.
Sentimental non-realism patterned after *The Blackboard Jungle* but much softer; its influence led to a TV situation comedy, *Please Sir*.

w James Clavell, *novel* E. R. Braithwaite *d* James Clavell *ph* Paul Beeson *m* Ron Grainer

Sidney Poitier, Christian Roberts, Judy Geeson, Suzy Kendall, Lulu, Faith Brook, Geoffrey Bayldon, Patricia Routledge

'The sententious script sounds as if it has been written by a zealous Sunday school teacher after a particularly exhilarating boycott of South African oranges.'—*MFB*

To the Devil a Daughter
GB / Germany 1975 93m Technicolor
EMI / Hammer–Terra Filmkunst (Roy Skeggs)

An occult novelist is asked to take care of a girl who has been 'promised' to a group of Satanists.
Confusingly told, high camp diabolic thriller.

w Chris Wicking, *novel* Dennis Wheatley *d* Peter Sykes *ph* David Watkin *m* Paul Glass

Richard Widmark, Christopher Lee, Denholm Elliott, Honor Blackman, Michael Goodliffe, Anthony Valentine, Derek Francis, Nastassja Kinski

To the Ends of the Earth**
US 1948 107m bw
Columbia (Sidney Buchman)

A government agent follows a world-wide trail after a narcotics gang.
Thoroughly riveting conventional thriller, nicely made and photographed.

w Jay Richard Kennedy *d Robert Stevenson* *ph Burnett Guffey*

Dick Powell, Signe Hasso, Ludwig Donath, Vladimir Sokoloff, Edgar Barrier

To the Shores of Tripoli
US 1942 82m Technicolor
TCF (Milton Sperling)

A cocky playboy becomes a tough marine.
Despite the title, this modest flagwaver with romantic trimmings never moves out of the San Diego training grounds.

w Lamar Trotti *d* Bruce Humberstone *ph* Edward Cronjager *m* Alfred Newman

Maureen O'Hara, John Payne, Randolph Scott,

Nancy Kelly, William Tracy, Maxie Rosenbloom, Henry Morgan, Russell Hicks, Minor Watson

To the Victor
US 1948 100m bw
Warner (Jerry Wald)

French collaborators stand trial for war crimes. Glum melodrama with inadequate cast.

w Richard Brooks *d* Delmer Daves *ph* Robert Burks *m* David Buttolph

Dennis Morgan, Viveca Lindfors, Bruce Bennett, Victor Francen, Dorothy Malone, Tom d'Andrea, Eduardo Ciannelli, Joseph Buloff, Luis Van Rooten, William Conrad

The Toast of New Orleans
US 1950 97m Technicolor
MGM (Joe Pasternak)

A Bayou villager becomes a star of the New Orleans opera.
Very ordinary setting for a new singing star.

w Sy Gomberg, George Wells *d* Norman Taurog *ph* William Snyder *md* George Stoll *ch* Eugene Loring

Kathryn Grayson, David Niven, Mario Lanza, J. Carrol Naish, James Mitchell, Richard Hageman, Clinton Sundberg, Sig Arno

The Toast of New York**
US 1937 109m bw
RKO (Edward Small)

A 19th-century medicine showman becomes a notorious Wall Street financier.
Smart biopic of Jim Fisk; good entertainment with accomplished production.

w Dudley Nichols, John Twist, Joel Sayre *d* Rowland V. Lee *ph* Peverell Marley *m* Nathaniel Shilkret

Edward Arnold, Cary Grant, Frances Farmer, Jack Oakie, Donald Meek, Clarence Kolb, Thelma Leeds

Tobacco Road***
US 1941 84m bw
TCF (Jack Kirkland, Harry H. Oshrin)

Poor whites in Georgia are turned off their land. This bowdlerized version of a sensational book and play has superbly orchestrated farcical scenes separated by delightfully pictorial quieter moments: it isn't what was intended, but in its own way it's quite marvellous.

w Nunnally Johnson, novel Erskine Caldwell, *play* Jack Kirkland *d John Ford ph Arthur Miller m David Buttolph*

Charley Grapewin, Elizabeth Patterson, Dana Andrews, Gene Tierney, *Marjorie Rambeau*, Ward Bond, William Tracy, Zeffie Tilbury, Slim Summerville, Grant Mitchell, Russell Simpson, Spencer Charters

Tobruk
US 1967 110m Techniscope
Universal / Corman / Gibraltar (Gene Corman)

During the North African war, a British major and some German Jews try to blow up the Nazi fuel bunkers.
Routine war adventure, quite tough and spectacular but undistinguished.

w Leo V. Gordon *d* Arthur Hiller *ph* Russell Harlan *m* Bronislau Kaper

Rock Hudson, George Peppard, Nigel Green, Guy Stockwell, Jack Watson, Liam Redmond, Leo Gordon, Norman Rossington, Percy Herbert

Toby Tyler*
US 1959 96m Technicolor
Walt Disney (Bill Walsh)

In 1910, a young orphan runs away to join a travelling circus in the midwest, and with the help of a chimp becomes a famous star.
Acceptable, predictable family fare.

w Bill Walsh, Lillie Hayward, *novel* James Otis Kaler *d* Charles Barton *ph* William Snyder *m* Buddy Baker

Kevin Corcoran, Henry Calvin, Gene Sheldon, Bob Sweeney, James Drury

Today We Live*
US 1933 113m bw
MGM (Howard Hawks)

During World War I, an aristocratic English girl and her three lovers all find themselves at the front, and two fail to return.
Stilted romantic melodrama with imposing credentials.

w Edith Fitzgerald, Dwight Taylor, William Faulkner, *story* Turnabout by William Faulkner *d* Howard Hawks *ph* Oliver T. Marsh

Joan Crawford, Gary Cooper, Robert Young, Franchot Tone, Roscoe Karns, Louise Closser Hale, Rollo Lloyd

The Todd Killings*
US 1970 93m Technicolor Panavision
National General (Barry Shear)

In a small American town, a 23-year old youth starts out on a rampage of rape and murder.
Violent psychological melodrama, based on fact, with inventive direction.

w Dennis Murphy, Joe L. Oliansky *d Barry*

Shear ph Harold E. Stine *m* Leonard Rosenman

Robert F. Lyons, Richard Thomas, Belinda Montgomery, Barbara Bel Geddes, Gloria Grahame

'The most striking of the many recent film versions of the souring of the American dream.' —*Tony Rayns*

Together Again
US 1944 93m bw
Columbia (Virginia Van Upp)

The widow of a New England mayor commissions a statue in his honour.
The title refers to the reteaming of the stars who were so popular in *Love Affair* and *When Tomorrow Comes*, which is a sign of the lack of invention elsewhere. A comedy without laughs.

w Virgina Van Upp, F. Hugh Herbert *d* Charles Vidor *ph* Joseph Walker *m* Werner Heymann

Charles Boyer, Irene Dunne, Charles Coburn, Mona Freeman, Jerome Courtland, Elizabeth Patterson, Charles Dingle, Walter Baldwin

Tokyo Joe
US 1949 88m bw
Columbia / Santana (Robert Lord)

A former nightclub owner returns to postwar Japan to reclaim his fortune and his ex-wife.
Dispirited star melodrama.

w Cyril Hume, Bertram Millhauser *d* Stuart Heisler *ph* Charles Lawton Jnr *m* George Antheil

Humphrey Bogart, Florence Marly, Alexander Knox, Sessue Hayakawa, Lora Lee Michel, Jerome Courtland

Tom Brown's Schooldays*
US 1940 86m bw
(RKO) The Play's the Thing (Gene Towne, Graham Baker)

Tom Brown finds life at Rugby brutal, but helps to become a civilizing influence.
Pretty lively Hollywood version of a rather unattractive semi-classic.

w Walter Ferris, Frank Cavell, *novel* Thomas Hughes *d* Robert Stevenson *ph* Nicholas Musuraca *m* Anthony Collins

Jimmy Lydon, Cedric Hardwicke, Billy Halop, Freddie Bartholemew, Gale Storm, Josephine Hutchinson

Tom Brown's Schooldays
GB 1951 96m bw
Renown (George Minter)

Unexciting remake featuring one surprisingly strong performance.

w Noel Langley *d* Gordon Parry *ph* C. Pennington-Richards *m* Richard Addinsell

Robert Newton, John Howard Davies, Diana Wynyard, Francis de Wolff, Kathleen Byron, Hermione Baddeley, James Hayter, Rachel Gurney, Amy Veness, Max Bygraves, Michael Hordern, John Charlesworth, John Forrest

Tom, Dick and Harry**
US 1940 86m bw
RKO (Robert Sisk)

A girl daydreams about her three boy friends, but can't make up her mind.
Brightly-handled comedy which became a minor classic but does seem to have faded a little.
Remade as *The Girl Most Likely* (qv).

w Paul Jarrico d Garson Kanin ph Merrit Gerstad *m* Roy Webb

Ginger Rogers, Burgess Meredith, Alan Marshal, George Murphy, *Phil Silvers*, Joe Cunningham, Jane Seymour, Lenore Lonergan

'Foot by foot the best made picture of this year.'—*Otis Ferguson*

Tom Jones***
GB 1963 129m Eastmancolor
UA / Woodfall (Tony Richardson)

In 18th-century England a foundling is brought up by the squire and marries his daughter after many adventures.
Fantasia on Old England, at some distance from the original novel, with the director trying every possible jokey approach against a meticulously realistic physical background. Despite trade fears, the *Hellzapoppin* style made it an astonishing box office success (the sex helped), though it quickly lost its freshness and was much imitated.

w John Osborne, *novel* Henry Fielding *d Tony Richardson ph Walter Lassally, Manny Wynn m John Addison pd Ralph Brinton*

Albert Finney, Susannah York, Hugh Griffith, Edith Evans, Joan Greenwood, Diane Cilento, George Devine, Joyce Redman, David Warner, Wilfrid Lawson, Freda Jackson, Rachel Kempson

'Uncertainty, nervousness, muddled method . . . desperation is writ large over it.'—*Stanley Kauffmann*

'Much of the time it looks like a home movie, made with sporadic talent by a group with more enthusiasm than discipline.'—*Tom Milne*

'It is as though the camera had become a method actor: there are times when you wish you could buy, as on certain juke boxes, five minutes' silence . . . Obviously a film which elicits such lyric ejaculations from the reviewers cannot be all good.'—*John Simon*

Tom Sawyer
US 1973 103m De Luxe Panavision
UA / Readers Digest (Arthur P. Jacobs)

Reverential, rather tediously over-produced version for family audiences of the seventies, with brief songs and real Mississippi locations.

w/m/ly Richard and Robert Sherman *d* Don Taylor *ph* Frank Stanley *pd* Philip Jefferies

Johnnie Whitaker, Celeste Holm, Warren Oates, Jeff East, Jodie Foster

Tom Sawyer
US 1975 74m colour TVM

A plain, even homely, version of the famous tale.

w Jean Holloway *d* James Neilson

Buddy Ebsen, Jane Wyatt, Vic Morrow, John McGiver, Josh Albee, Jeff Tyler

Tom Thumb*
GB 1958 98m Eastmancolor
MGM / Galaxy (George Pal)

A tiny forest boy outwits a couple of thieves.
Slight musicap built round the legend of a two-inch boy; good trickwork and songs make it a delightful film for children.

w Ladislas Fodor *d* George Pal *ph* Georges Périnal *m* Douglas Gamley, Kenneth V. Jones *sp Tom Howard*

Russ Tamblyn, Jessie Matthews, Peter Sellers, Terry-Thomas, Alan Young, June Thorburn, Ian Wallace

Toma*
US 1972 74m Technicolor TVM
Universal (Earl A. Glick, Trevor Wallace)
GB title: *Man of Many Faces*

Adventures of an undercover cop with a penchant for disguise.
A series resulted, but after one season the star bowed out and the whole thing changed into *Baretta.*

w Edward Hume, Gerald di Pego *d* Richard T. Heffron

Tony Musante, Susan Strasberg, Simon Oakland, Nick Colasanto, Abe Vigoda, Dave Toma

The Tomb of Ligeia**
GB 1964 81m Eastmancolor
Cinemascope
American International (Roger Corman)

A brooding Victorian metamorphoses his dead wife into a cat, then into the beautiful Lady Rowena.
Complex but rather fascinating horror suspenser which rejogs familiar elements into something new; the best of the Corman Poes.

w Robert Towne, story Edgar Allan Poe *d Roger Corman ph Arthur Grant m* Kenneth V. Jones

Vincent Price, Elizabeth Shepherd, John Westbrook, Oliver Johnson, Richard Johnson, Derek Francis

Tomorrow at Ten*
GB 1962 80m bw
Mancunian (Tom Blakeley)

A crook kidnaps a small boy and locks him up with a time bomb while he makes his demands in person. When the kidnapper is killed, the police have to hunt against time.
Tense second feature, well acted and efficiently done.

w Peter Millar, James Kelly *d Lance Comfort ph* Basil Emmott *m* Bernie Fenton

Robert Shaw, John Gregson, Alec Clunes, Alan Wheatley, Ernest Clark, Kenneth Cope

Tomorrow Is Forever*
US 1946 105m bw
RKO–International (David Lewis)

A man supposed dead in the war returns with an altered face to find his wife has remarried.
Enoch Arden rides again in a rampant woman's picture which is well enough made to be generally entertaining.

w Lenore Coffee *d* Irving Pichel *ph* Joe Valentine *m* Max Steiner

Orson Welles, Claudette Colbert, George Brent, Lucile Watson, Richard Long, Natalie Wood

Tomorrow the World*
US 1944 86m bw
UA / Lester Cowan

A college professor adopts his orphaned German nephew, who turns out to be an ardent 12-year-old Nazi.
Adequate, predictable screen version of a once-topical play.

w Ring Lardner Jnr, Leopold Atlas, *play* James Gow, Armand D'Usseau *d* Leslie Fenton *m* Louis Applebaum

Fredric March, Betty Field, *Skip Homeier,* Agnes Moorehead, Joan Carroll

Tomorrow We Live
GB 1942 85m bw
British Aviation (George King)
US title: *At Dawn We Die*

French villagers help a spy escape to Britain.
Minor flagwaver marred by cheap sets.

w Anatole de Grunwald, Katherine Strueby *d* George King

John Clements, Greta Gynt, Hugh Sinclair, Judy Kelly, Godfrey Tearle, Yvonne Arnaud, Bransby Williams

Tonight or Never
US 1931 80m bw
Samuel Goldwyn

A prima donna falls for a man she thinks is a Venetian gigolo, but he turns out to be an impresario from New York.
Flimsy comedy which turned out to be its star's last vehicle of any consequence for twenty years.

w Ernest Vajda, *play* Lily Hatvany *d* Mervyn Le Roy *ph* Gregg Toland *md* Alfred Newman

Gloria Swanson, Melvyn Douglas (debut), Ferdinand Gottschalk, Robert Greig, Alison Skipworth, Boris Karloff

Tonight and Every Night
US 1945 92m Technicolor
Columbia (Victor Saville)

The lives and loves of London showgirls during the blitz.
Ludicrous concoction looking nothing like London and certainly nothing like the Windmill, the theatre to which it allegedly pays tribute. There are some tolerable numbers along the way.

w Lesser Samuels, Abem Finkel, *play* Heart of a City by Lesley Storm *d* Victor Saville *ph* Rudolph Maté *md* Morris Stoloff

Rita Hayworth, Lee Bowman, Janet Blair, Marc Platt, Leslie Brooks, Dusty Anderson, Florence Bates, Ernest Cossart

Tonight We Sing*
US 1953 109m Technicolor
TCF (George Jessel)

Sol Hurok stifles his own talent to become a great musical impresario.
Blameless uppercrust biopic, with plenty of well-staged guest talent.

w Harry Kurnitz, George Oppenheimer *d* Mitchell Leisen *ph* Leon Shamroy *md* Alfred Newman *ch* David Lichine

David Wayne, Anne Bancroft, Ezio Pinza (Chaliapin), Roberta Peters, Tamara Toumanova (Pavlova), Isaac Stern (Eugene Ysaye), Jan Peerce

Tonka
US 1958 97m Technicolor
Walt Disney

A Sioux Indian tames a magnificent white horse, and after many adventures is reunited with him at Little Big Horn.
Unremarkable and overlong adventure story.

w Lewis R. Foster, Lillie Hayward, *novel* Comanche by David Appel *d* Lewis R. Foster *ph* Loyal Griggs

Sal Mineo, Phil Carey, Jerome Courtland, Rafael Campos, H. M. Wynant

Tony Rome*
US 1967 111m De Luxe Panavision
TCF / Arcola / Millfield (Aaron Rosenberg)

A seedy Miami private eye runs into murder when he guards a millionaire's daughter.
Complex old-fashioned murder mystery decorated with the new amorality and fashionable violence. Tolerable for its backgrounds and professional expertise. Sequel: *Lady in Cement* (qv).

w Richard L. Breen, *novel* Miami Mayhem by Marvin H. Albert *d* Gordon Douglas *ph* Joe Biroc *m* Billy May

Frank Sinatra, Jill St John, Richard Conte, Gena Rowlands, Simon Oakland, Jeffrey Lynn, Lloyd Bochner, Sue Lyon

Too Hot to Handle*
US 1938 105m bw
MGM (Lawrence Weingarten)

Adventures of a scoop-seeking newsreel cameraman.
Boisterous comedy-melodrama with as many sags as highlights but generally making a cheerful star entertainment.

w Laurence Stallings, John Lee Mahin *d* Jack Conway *ph* Harold Rosson *m* Franz Waxman

Clark Gable, Myrna Loy, Walter Connolly, Walter Pidgeon, Leo Carrillo, Johnny Hines, Virginia Weidler

'It's like an old-fashioned serial . . . no one can call it dull.'—*Howard Barnes*

'Breathlessly paced, witty, and violent, this is one of the more acid comedies to have been produced by the Thirties.'—*John Baxter*

Too Hot to Handle
GB 1960 100m Eastmancolor
ABP / Wigmore (Selim Cattan)

Two Soho strip club owners join forces to hunt down a blackmailer.
Rotten, hilarious British gangster film set in a

totally unreal underworld and very uncomfortably cast.

w Herbert Kretzmer *d* Terence Young *ph* Otto Heller *m* Eric Spear

Leo Genn, Jayne Mansfield, Karl Boehm, Danik Patisson, Christopher Lee, Patrick Holt

Too Late Blues
US 1961 100m bw
Paramount (John Cassavetes)

A jazz musician falls for a neurotic girl and has fears of going commercial.
Uninteresting professional feature from a director whose reputation was made with the amateur *Shadows*.

w John Cassavetes, Richard Carr *d* John Cassavetes *ph* Lionel Lindon *m* David Raksin

John Cassavetes, Stella Stevens, Bobby Darin, Everett Chambers, Nick Dennis, Rupert Crosse, Vince Edwards

Too Late for Tears
US 1949 99m bw
(UA) Hunt Stromberg

A lady bluebeard disposes of both husbands and boyfriends.
Silly melodrama, poorly cast.

w Roy Huggins *d* Byron Haskin *ph* William Mellor *m* Dale Butts

Lizabeth Scott, Don Defore, Arthur Kennedy, Dan Duryea, Kristine Miller, Barry Kelley

Too Late the Hero*
US 1969. 144m Technicolor 70mm
Associates and Aldrich / Palomar

In World War II the Japanese hold one end of a small Pacific island, British and Americans the other.
Semi-cynical, long and bloody war adventure of competence but no great merit.

w Robert Aldrich, Lukas Heller *d* Robert Aldrich *ph* Joseph Biroc *m* Gerald Fried

Michael Caine, Cliff Robertson, Ian Bannen, Henry Fonda, Harry Andrews, Denholm Elliott, Ronald Fraser, Percy Herbert

Too Many Crooks*
GB 1958 87m bw
Rank / Mario Zampi

Incompetent crooks plot a kidnapping.
Agreeable farce with black edges and an excellent chase sequence.

w Michael Pertwee *d* Mario Zampi *ph* Stan Pavey *m* Stanley Black

Terry-Thomas, George Cole, Brenda de Banzie, Bernard Bresslaw, Sidney James, Joe Melia, Vera Day, John Le Mesurier

Too Many Girls
US 1940 85m bw
RKO (Harry Edgington, George Abbott)

The father of a wealthy co-ed hires four football heroes to protect her.
Witless nonsense, flabbily derived from a Broadway show.

w John Twist, *play* George Marion Jnr, Richard Rodgers, Lorenz Hart *d* George Abbott *ph* Frank Redman *songs* Rodgers and Hart

Lucille Ball, Desi Arnaz, Richard Carlson, Ann Miller, Eddie Bracken, Frances Langford, Harry Shannon

† The film on which Ball and Arnaz first met.

Too Many Husbands*
US 1940 84m bw
Columbia (Wesley Ruggles)

Allegedly drowned on a boat cruise, a man turns up again after his wife has remarried.
Modest variation on a familiar theme, professional but unexciting; later remade as *Three for the Show* (qv).

w Claude Binyon, *play* Home and Beauty by W. Somerset Maugham *d* Wesley Ruggles *ph* Joseph Walker

Jean Arthur, Melvyn Douglas, Fred MacMurray, Harry Davenport, Dorothy Peterson, Melville Cooper, Edgar Buchanan

Too Many Thieves
US 1966 95m colour TVM
Filmways / Mayo (Richard Alan Simmons)

A New York attorney helps ransom a priceless Middle Eastern treasure stolen from its shrine.
Would-be-funny rigmarole that outstays its welcome, adapted from episodes of a TV series *The Trials of O'Brien*.

w George Bellak *d* Abner Biberman

Peter Falk, Britt Ekland, Elaine Stritch, David Carradine, Nehemiah Persoff, Joanna Barnes, Pierre Olaf, George Coulouris, Ludwig Donath

Too Much Too Soon*
US 1958 121m bw
Warner (Henry Blanke)

Young actress Diana Barrymore goes to Hollywood to look after her alcoholic father John, but mild success goes to her head and she too turns to drink.
Rather dismal and murkily photographed

account of an absorbing real-life situation; one performance holds the first half together.

wd Art Napoleon, *memoirs* Diana Barrymore *ph* Nicholas Musuraca, Carl Guthrie *m* Ernest Gold *ad* George James Hopkins

Dorothy Malone, *Errol Flynn*, Efrem Zimbalist Jnr, Neva Patterson, Martin Milner, Ray Danton, Murray Hamilton

Too Young to Kiss
US 1951 89m bw
MGM (Sam Zimbalist)

A girl pianist poses as an infant prodigy, and falls for the impresario who wants to adopt her.
Dull conveyor belt comedy.

w Frances Goodrich, Albert Hackett *d* Robert Z. Leonard *ph* Joseph Ruttenberg *m* Johnny Green

June Allyson, Van Johnson, Gig Young, Paula Corday, Larry Keating, Hans Conried

Too Young to Love
GB 1959 89m bw
Rank / Welbeck (Herbert Smith)

A 15-year-old prostitute is brought before a Brooklyn juvenile court.
Tepid filming of a popular exploitation play of the fifties, mysteriously made in England.

w Sydney and Muriel Box, *play* Pick Up Girl by Elsa Shelley *d* Muriel Box *ph* Gerald Gibbs *m* Bruce Montgomery

Thomas Mitchell, Pauline Hahn, Joan Miller, Austin Willis, Jess Conrad, Bessie Love, Alan Gifford

Top Banana*
1953 100m Color Corporation
Roadshow / Harry M. Popkin

A TV comedian invites an attractive salesgirl to join his show.
A wisp of plot is the excuse for a revue, and the interest is in the old-time burlesque acts, some of which survive the generally shoddy treatment.

w Gene Towne *d* Alfred E. Green *ph* William Bradford *m/ly* Johnny Mercer

Phil Silvers, Rose Marie, Danny Scholl, Jack Albertson

Top Hat****
US 1935 100m bw
RKO (Pandro S. Berman)

The path of true love is roughened by mistaken identities.
Marvellous Astaire-Rogers musical, with a more or less realistic London supplanted by a totally artificial Venice, and show stopping numbers in a style which is no more separated by amusing plot complications lightly handled by a team of deft *farceurs.*

w Dwight Taylor, Allan Scott d Mark Sandrich ph David Abel, Vernon Walker m/ly Irving Berlin ch Hermes Pan ad Van Nest Polglase, Carroll Clark

Fred Astaire, Ginger Rogers, Edward Everett Horton, Helen Broderick, Eric Blore, Erik Rhodes

'In 25 years *Top Hat* has lost nothing of its gaiety and charm.'—*Dilys Powell, 1960*

Top o'the Morning
US 1949 100m bw
Paramount (Robert L. Welch)

Investigations follow the theft of the Blarney Stone.
More Irish whimsy from the *Going My Way* stars.

w Edmund Beloin, Richard Breen *d* David Miller *ph* Lionel Lindon *m* James Van Heusen

Bing Crosby, Barry Fitzgerald, Ann Blyth, Hume Cronyn, Eileen Crowe, John McIntire

Top Secret*
GB 1952 94m bw
ABP (Mario Zampi)
US title: *Mr Potts Goes to Moscow*

A sanitary engineer, mistaken for a spy, is kidnapped to Moscow when his blueprints are taken for atomic secrets.
Farcical satire full of chases and lavatory humour; much of it comes off nicely.

w Jack Davies, Michael Pertwee d Mario Zampi ph Stan Pavey *m* Stanley Black

George Cole, Oscar Homolka, Nadia Gray, Frederick Valk, Wilfrid Hyde White, Geoffrey Sumner, Ronald Adam

Top Secret Affair*
US 1956 100m bw
Warner / United States (Martin Rackin)
GB title: *Their Secret Affair*

A female news publisher tries to discredit a military diplomat but falls in love with him.
Curious comedy adaptation of a rather heavy novel, moderately skilled in all departments.

w Roland Kibbee, Allan Scott, *novel* Melville Goodwin USA by John P. Marquand *d* H. C. Potter *ph* Stanley Cortez *m* Roy Webb

Kirk Douglas, Susan Hayward, Jim Backus, Paul Stewart, John Cromwell, Roland Winters

Topaz*
US 1969 124m Technicolor
Universal / Alfred Hitchcock

In 1962 the CIA enlists a French agent to break up a Russian spy ring.
Oddly halting, desultory and unconvincing spy thriller shot mainly in flat TV style, with just a few short sequences in its director's better manner. A measure of its unsatisfactoriness is that three different endings were shot and actually used at various points of release.

w Samuel Taylor, *novel* Leon Uris *d* Alfred Hitchcock *ph* Jack Hildyard *m* Maurice Jarre

Frederick Stafford, John Forsythe, John Vernon, *Roscoe Lee Browne*, Dany Robin, Karin Dor, Michel Piccoli, Philippe Noiret

'A larger, slower, duller version of the spy thrillers he used to make in the thirties.'—*New Yorker, 1975*

Topaze*
US 1933 78m bw
David O. Selznick

A simple schoolmaster allows himself to be exploited.
Interesting little comedy with the star playing against type: remade as *Mr Topaze* (qv).

w Benn W. Levy, *play* Marcel Pagnol *d* Harry d'Abbabie d'Arrast *ph* Lucien Andriot *m* Max Steiner

John Barrymore, Myrna Loy, Jobyna Howland, Jackie Searl

Topkapi*
US 1964 119m Technicolor
UA / Filmways (Jules Dassin)

International thieves try to rob the Istanbul museum.
Light-hearted caper story which gets out of control because of the variety of styles and accents, the director's impression that his wife can do no wrong, and the general slowness and lack of wit; but there are bright moments, colourful backgrounds, and a final suspense sequence in the *Rififi* manner.

w Monja Danischewsky, *novel* The Light of Day by Eric Ambler *d* Jules Dassin *ph Henri Alekan* *m* Manos Hadjidakis

Melina Mercouri, Maximilian Schell, Peter Ustinov, Robert Morley, Akim Tamiroff, Gilles Segal, Jess Hahn

Topper**
US 1937 96m bw
Hal Roach

A stuffy banker is haunted by the ghosts of his sophisticated friends the Kirbys, who are visible only to him.
Influential supernatural farce, still pretty funny and deftly acted though a shade slow to get going.

w Jack Jevne, Eric Hatch, Eddie Moran, *novel* The Jovial Ghosts by Thorne Smith *d* Norman Z. McLeod *ph* Norbert Brodine *md* Arthur Morton

Cary Grant, Constance Bennett, Roland Young, Billie Burke, Alan Mowbray, Eugene Pallette, Arthur Lake, Hedda Hopper

Topper Returns***
US 1941 87m bw
Hal Roach

A girl ghost helps Topper solve her own murder.
Spirited supernatural farce which spoofs murder mysteries, spooky houses, frightened servants, dumb cops, etc, in a pacy, accomplished and generally delightful manner.

w Jonathan Latimer, Gordon Douglas, with additional dialogue by Paul Gerard Smith *d* Roy del Ruth

Roland Young, Joan Blondell, Eddie Anderson, Carole Landis, Dennis O'Keefe, *H. B. Warner,* Billie Burke, *Donald McBride,* Rafaela Ottiano

Topper Takes a Trip*
US 1939 85m bw
Hal Roach

Ghostly Mrs Kirby helps Topper to save his wife from a Riviera philanderer.
Mildly pleasant follow-up, with a dog replacing Cary Grant who had become too expensive.

w Eddie Moran, Jack Jevne, Corey Ford *d* Norman Z. McLeod *ph* Norbert Brodine

Constance Bennett, Roland Young, Billie Burke, Alan Mowbray, Verree Teasdale, Franklin Pangborn, Alexander D'Arcy

Tora! Tora! Tora!*
US 1970 144m De Luxe Panavision
TCF (Elmo Williams)

A reconstruction from both sides of the events leading up to Pearl Harbor.
Immense, largely studio-bound, calcified war spectacle with much fidelity to the record but no villains and no hero, therefore no drama and no suspense.

w Larry Forrester, Hideo Oguni, Ryuzo Kikushima *d* Richard Fleischer, Ray Kellogg, Toshio Masuda, Kinji Fukasaku *ph* Charles F. Wheeler and Japanese crews *sp L. B. Abbott, Art Cruickshank*

Martin Balsam, Joseph Cotten, James

Whitmore, Jason Robards, Edward Andrews, Leon Ames, George Macready, Soh Yamamura, Takahiro Tamura

'One of the least stirring and least photogenic historical epics ever perpetrated on the screen.' —*Gary Arnold*

Torch Singer
US 1933 72m bw
Paramount

An unwed mother supports her child by singing in night clubs.
Banal melodrama.

w Lenore Coffee, Lynn Starling, *play* Mike by Grace Perkins *d* Alexander Hall *ph* Karl Struss

Claudette Colbert, Ricardo Cortez, David Manners, Lyda Roberti, Baby LeRoy, Florence Roberts, Ethel Griffies, Helen Jerome Eddy

Torch Song
US 1953 90m Technicolor
MGM (Henry Berman, Sidney Franklin Jnr)

A temperamental musical comedy star falls for a blind pianist.
Ossified star vehicle which looks great but is too often unintentionally funny.

w John Michael Hayes, Jan Lustig, *story* Why Should I Cry? by I. A. R. Wylie *d* Charles Walters *ph* Robert Planck *m* Adolph Deutsch

Joan Crawford, Michael Wilding, Gig Young, Marjorie Rambeau, Henry Morgan, Dorothy Patrick

'Here is Joan Crawford all over the screen, in command, in love and in color.'—*Otis L. Guernsey Jnr*

Torchy Blane
Glenda Farrell played the hard-boiled girl reporter and Barton MacLane the tough police inspector who puts up with her in seven out of the nine second features made by Warners in the late thirties. The characters were created in short stories by Frederick Nebel, and the films were mostly directed by William Beaudine or Frank McDonald.

1936: SMART BLONDE
1937: FLY AWAY BABY, THE ADVENTUROUS BLONDE
1938: BLONDES AT WORK, TORCHY BLANE IN PANAMA (with Lola Lane, Paul Kelly), TORCHY GETS HER MAN
1939: TORCHY BLANE IN CHINATOWN, TORCHY RUNS FOR MAYOR, TORCHY PLAYS WITH DYNAMITE (with Jane Wyman, Allen Jenkins)

Torn Curtain**
US 1966 119m Technicolor
Universal / Alfred Hitchcock

A defector who is really a double agent is embarrassed when his wife follows him into East Germany.
Patchy Hitchcock with some mechanically effective suspense sequences, a couple of efforts at something new, a few miscalculations, some evidence of carelessness, and a little enjoyable repetition of old situations.

w Brian Moore *d Alfred Hitchcock* *ph* John F. Warren *m* John Addison

Paul Newman, Julie Andrews, *Wolfgang Kieling*, Ludwig Donath, Lila Kedrova, Hans-Joerg Felmy, Tamara Toumanova

Torpedo Run*
US 1958 98m Metrocolor Cinemascope
MGM (Edmund S. Grainger)

A US submarine in World War II destroys a Japanese aircraft carrier in Tokyo Bay.
Well-staged potboiler with excellent action sequences marred slightly by excessive platitudinizing.

w Richard Sale, William Wister Haines *d* Joseph Pevney *ph* George J. Folsey

Glenn Ford, Ernest Borgnine, Diane Brewster, Dean Jones

Torrid Zone**
US 1940 88m bw
Warner (Mark Hellinger)

In Central America, a banana plantation manager is tricked by his boss into staying on, and helps a wandering showgirl as well as foiling bandits.
Enjoyable, fast-paced hokum with a plot borrowed from both *The Front Page* and *Red Dust*.

w Richard Macaulay, Jerry Wald *d* William Keighley *ph* James Wong Howe *m* Adolph Deutsch

James Cagney, Pat O'Brien, Ann Sheridan, Helen Vinson, Andy Devine, Jerome Cowan, George Tobias, George Reeves

Tortilla Flat*
US 1942 106m bw
MGM (Sam Zimbalist)

The problems of poor Mexican half-breeds in California.
Expensive but unappealing variation on *The Grapes of Wrath*, with none of the cast quite

getting under the skin of their parts, and no sense of reality, rather that of a musical without music.

w John Lee Mahin, Benjamin Glazier, *novel* John Steinbeck *d* Victor Fleming *m* Franz Waxman

Spencer Tracy, Hedy Lamarr, John Garfield, Frank Morgan, Akim Tamiroff, Connie Gilchrist, John Qualen, Sheldon Leonard, Donald Meek, Allen Jenkins, Henry O'Neill

Torture Garden*
GB 1967 93m Technicolor
Columbia / Amicus (Milton Subotsky)

Five fairground visitors are told their future by the mysterious Dr Diablo.
Crude but effective horror portmanteau including one story about the resurrection of Edgar Allan Poe.

w Robert Bloch *d* Freddie Francis

Burgess Meredith, Jack Palance, Peter Cushing, Beverly Adams, Michael Bryant, John Standing

The Touch*
Sweden / US 1970 112m Eastmancolor
ABC / Cinematograph AB (Lars-Owe Carlburg)

The wife of a provincial surgeon falls in love with an archaeologist.
Freedom versus security: the Bergman treatment is given to a familiar love story, but the expected finesse is lacking.

wd Ingmar Bergman *ph* Sven Nykvist *m* Jan Johansson

Bibi Andersson, Elliott Gould, Max Von Sydow

Touch and Go
GB 1956 85m Technicolor
Ealing (Seth Holt)

A family has doubts about its decision to emigrate to Australia.
Very mild comedy which fails to engage sympathy because the characters don't seem real.

w William Rose *d* Michael Truman *ph* Douglas Slocombe *m* John Addison

Jack Hawkins, Margaret Johnston, June Thorburn, John Fraser, Roland Culver, Alison Leggatt, James Hayter

A Touch of Class**
GB 1972 106m Technicolor Panavision
Avco / Brut / Gordon Films (Melvin Frank)

A married American businessman in London has a hectic affair with a dress designer.
Amiable and very physical sex farce with hilarious highlights and a few longueurs between: the playing keeps it above water.

w Melvin Frank, Jack Rose *d* Melvin Frank *ph* Austin Dempster *m* John Cameron

Glenda Jackson, George Segal, Paul Sorvino, Hildegarde Neil

'Machine-tooled junk.'—*William S. Pechter*

Touch of Evil**
US 1958 95m or 114m bw Cinemascope
U-I (Albert Zugsmith)

A Mexican narcotics investigator honeymooning in a border town clashes with the local police chief over a murder.
Overpoweringly atmospheric melodrama crammed with Wellesian touches, but very cold and unsympathetic, with rather restrained performances (especially his) and a plot which takes some following. Hardly the most auspicious return to Hollywood for a wanderer, but now becoming a cult classic.

wd Orson Welles, novel Badge of Evil by Whit Masterson *ph Russell Metty* *m* Henry Mancini

Charlton Heston, Orson Welles, Janet Leigh, Marlene Dietrich, Akim Tamiroff, Joseph Calleia, Ray Collins, Dennis Weaver

A Touch of Larceny*
GB 1959 92m bw
Paramount / Ivan Foxwell

A naval commander mysteriously disappears in the hope that he will be branded a traitor and can sue for libel.
Fairly amusing light comedy with lively performances.

w Roger MacDougall, Guy Hamilton, Ivan Foxwell, *novel* The Megstone Plot by Andrew Garve *d* Guy Hamilton *ph* John Wilcox *m* Philip Green

James Mason, Vera Miles, George Sanders, Robert Flemyng, Ernest Clark, Duncan Lamont, Peter Barkworth

'A beguilingly polished comedy, reminiscent in its style, urbanity and sheen of the sort of thing Lubitsch was doing in the 30s.'—*Daily Mail*

A Touch of Love
GB 1969 107m Eastmancolor
Amicus / Palomar (Milton Subotsky)
US title: *Thank You All Very Much*

A pregnant London student tries to get an abortion but later decides against it.
Curious bid for serious drama by horror producers; all very conscientious but rather dreary.

w Margaret Drabble, from her novel The Millstone *d* Waris Hussein *ph* Peter Suschitsky *m* Michael Dress

Sandy Dennis, Ian McKellen, Michael Coles, John Standing, Eleanor Bron

A Touch of the Sun
GB 1956 80m bw
Eros / Raystro (Raymond Stross)

A hall porter is left a fortune but after living it up for a while returns to his old hotel which is on the rocks.
Limp comedy vehicle.

w Alfred Shaughnessy *d* Gordon Parry *ph* Arthur Grant *m* Eric Spear

Frankie Howerd, Ruby Murray, Dorothy Bromiley, Gordon Harker, Reginald Beckwith, Richard Wattis, Dennis Price, Alfie Bass, Willoughby Goddard

Toughest Man in Arizona
US 1952 90m Trucolor
Republic (Sidney Picker)

In 1861 a US marshal falls in love with the wife of an outlaw.
Easy-going, pleasant western aimed at the top half of a double bill.

w John K. Butler *d* R. G. Springsteen *ph* Reggie Lanning *m* Dale Butts

Vaughn Monroe, Joan Leslie, Edgar Buchanan, Victor Jory, Jean Parker, Henry Morgan

Tovarich**
US 1937 98m bw
Warner (Robert Lord)

A royal Russian husband and wife flee the revolution to Paris and take jobs as servants in an eccentric household.
A lively comedy of its time; though many of the jokes now seem obvious, the playing preserves its essential quality.

w Casey Robinson, *play adaptation Robert E. Sherwood, original* Jacques Deval *d* Anatole Litvak *ph* Charles Lang *m* Max Steiner

Claudette Colbert, Charles Boyer, Basil Rathbone, Anita Louise, Melville Cooper, Isabel Jeans, Maurice Murphy, Morris Carnovsky, Gregory Gaye, Montagu Love, Fritz Feld

Toward the Unknown
US 1956 115m Warnercolor Warnerscope
Warner / Toluca (Mervyn Le Roy)
GB title: *Brink of Hell*

An over-age officer takes part in the X2 experiments with rocket-firing aircraft.
Humourless flagwaver, very forgettable.

w Beirne Lay Jnr *d* Mervyn Le Roy *ph* Harold Rosson *m* Paul Baron

William Holden, Lloyd Nolan, Virginia Leith, Charles McGraw, Murray Hamilton, L. Q. Jones, James Garner, Paul Fix, Karen Steele

Tower of London**
US 1939 92m bw
Universal (Rowland V. Lee)

With the help of Mord the executioner, Richard Crookback kills his way to the throne but is destroyed at Bosworth.
The Shakespearean view of history played as a horror comic: despite an overall lack of pace, spirited scenes and good performances win the day.

w Robert N. Lee *d* Rowland V. Lee *ph George Robinson* *m* Charles Previn

Basil Rathbone, Boris Karloff, Barbara O'Neil, Ian Hunter, Vincent Price, Nan Grey, John Sutton, Leo G. Carroll, Miles Mander

Tower of London*
US 1962 79m bw
AIP / Admiral (Gene Corman)

A variation on the same events, with Price graduating from Clarence to Crookback, and the addition of ghostly visions. All very cheap, but occasionally vivid melodrama, despite intrusive American accents.

w Leo V. Gordon, Amos Powell, James B. Gordon *d* Roger Corman *ph* Arch Dalzell *m* Michael Anderson

Vincent Price, Michael Pate, Joan Freeman, Robert Brown, Justice Eatson, Sara Salby, Richard McCauly, Bruce Gordon

The Towering Inferno***
US 1974 165m De Luxe Panavision
TCF / Warner (Irwin Allen)

The world's tallest building is destroyed by fire on the night of its inauguration.
Showmanlike but relentlessly padded disaster spectacular, worth seeing for its cast of stars, its sheer old-fashioned expertise, and its special effects.

w Stirling Silliphant, *novels* The Tower by Richard Martin Stern, The Glass Inferno by Thomas M. Scortia, Frank M. Robinson *d John Guillermin, Irwin Allen* *ph Fred Koenekamp* *sp Bill Abbott* *pd William Creber*

Paul Newman, Steve McQueen, William Holden, Faye Dunaway, Fred Astaire, Susan

Blakely, Richard Chamberlain, Robert Vaughn, Jennifer Jones, O. J. Simpson, Robert Wagner

'Several generations of blue-eyed charmers act their roles as if each were under a separate bell jar.'—*Verina Glaessner*

'Each scene of someone horribly in flames is presented as a feat for the audience's delectation.'—*New Yorker*

A Town Called Bastard
GB 1971 97m Technicolor Franscope
Benmar / Zurbano (Ben Fisz)
aka: *A Town Called Hell*

Mexican revolutionaries massacre a priest and his congregation and take over the town. Ten years later a widow arrives seeking vengeance.
Sadistic western with an opening massacre followed by twenty-two killings (count 'em). Pretty dull otherwise.

w Richard Aubrey *d* Robert Parrish *ph* Manuel Berenguer *m* Waldo de Los Rios

Robert Shaw, Stella Stevens, Telly Savalas, Martin Landau, Michael Craig, Fernando Rey, Dudley Sutton

A Town like Alice**
GB 1956 117m bw
Rank / Vic Films (Joseph Janni)
US title: *The Rape of Malaya*

Life among women prisoners of the Japanese in Malaya, especially one who is finally reunited with her Australian lover.
Genteelly harrowing war film, formlessly adapted from the first part of a popular novel; a big commercial success of its day.

w W. P. Lipscomb, Richard Mason, *novel* Nevil Shute *d* Jack Lee *ph* Geoffrey Unsworth *m* Matyas Seiber

Virginia McKenna, Peter Finch, Takagi, Marie Lohr, Maureen Swanson, Jean Anderson, Renée Houston, Nora Nicholson

Town on Trial*
GB 1956 96m bw
Columbia / Marksman (Maxwell Setton)

A police inspector solves the murder of a girl after a tennis club dance in a British country town.
Straightforward murder mystery shot in Weybridge, with a wide variety of suspects having something to hide; settings and characters are quite realistic and also a little dreary.

w Ken Hughes, Robert Westerby *d John Guillermin ph* Basil Emmott *m* Tristam Cary

John Mills, Charles Coburn, Derek Farr, Barbara Bates, Alec McCowen, Geoffrey Keen, Elizabeth Seal, Margaretta Scott, Fay Compton

Town without Pity*
US / Switzerland / Germany 1961 103m bw
UA / Mirisch / Osweg / Gloria (Gottfried Reinhardt)

A German girl is raped and four American soldiers are accused; the defence counsel's wiles lead to the girl's suicide.
Dour drama with overpowering expressionist technique but not much real sympathy, interest or surprise.

w Silvia Reinhardt, George Hurdalek, *novel* The Verdict by Manfred Gregor *d* Gottfried Reinhardt *ph* Kurt Hasse *m* Dmitri Tiomkin

Kirk Douglas, E. G. Marshall, Christine Kaufmann, Barbara Rutting, Robert Blake, Richard Jaeckel

Toy Tiger
US 1956 88m Technicolor Cinemascope
U-I (Howard Christie)

The imaginative small son of a widow 'adopts' her business friend as his father.
Flat sentimental comedy off the studio's conveyor belt, a remake of *Mad about Music.*

w Ted Sherdeman *d* Jerry Hopper *ph* George Robinson *m* Joseph Gershenson

Jeff Chandler, Laraine Day, Tim Hovey, Cecil Kellaway, Richard Haydn, David Janssen

The Toy Wife*
US 1938 95m bw
MGM (Merian C. Cooper)
GB title: *Frou Frou*

In the early 19th century in Louisiana, a flirtatious girl causes jealousy and tragedy.
Another bid in the *Jezebel/Gone with the Wind* stakes, this handsome production proved a commercial misfire and hastened the end of its star's career.

w Zoe Akins *d* Richard Thorpe *ph* Oliver T. Marsh *m* Edward Ward

Luise Rainer, Melvyn Douglas, Robert Young, Barbara O'Neil, H. B. Warner, Alma Kruger, Walter Kingsford

Toys in the Attic*
US 1963 90m bw Panavision
UA / Claude / Mirisch

In a shabby New Orleans home, two ageing spinsters struggle to look after their ne'er-do-well brother.

Play into film doesn't go in this case, but the script and acting are interesting.

w James Poe, play Lillian Hellman *d* George Roy Hill *ph* Joseph Biroc *m* George Duning *ad* Cary Odell

Geraldine Page, Wendy Hiller, Dean Martin, Yvette Mimieux, Gene Tierney, Larry Gates

Track of the Cat*
US 1954 102m Warnercolor Cinemascope
Warner / Wayne–Fellows / Batjac (Robert Fellows)

In the northern California backwoods one winter in the 1880s a farming family is menaced by a marauding mountain lion.
With the lion a symbol of evil, this is real Cold Comfort Farm country and despite good intentions all round becomes irresistibly funny before the end, largely because everyone moves and speaks so s-l-o-w-l-y. The bleached colour is interesting but would suit only snowy settings.

w A. I. Bezzerides, *novel* Walter Van Tilburg Clark *d William A. Wellman ph William H. Clothier* *m* Roy Webb

Robert Mitchum, Diana Lynn, Beulah Bondi, Teresa Wright, Tab Hunter, Philip Tonge, William Hopper, Carl Switzer

'Cinemascope's first genuine weirdie . . . the script is redolent of Eugene O'Neill, and to its presentation the director brings a touch of Poe . . . Despair hangs in the air like a curse . . . unfortunately ambition overreaches itself, and the film topples over into barnstorming melodrama.'—*MFB*

The Trackers
US 1971 73m colour TVM
Aaron Spelling

A posse depends on a black man to find a murderer.
Unremarkable western.

w Gerald Gaiser *d* Earl Bellamy

Sammy Davis Jnr, Ernest Borgnine, Julie Adams, Jim Davis, Connie Kreski, Arthur Hunnicutt

Trackdown
US 1976 98m De Luxe
UA / Essaness (Bernard Schwarz)

A Montana rancher follows his sister to Los Angeles and avenges her ill-treatment there by gangsters.
Routine action thriller with fashionable realism and violence.

w Paul Edwards *d* Richard T. Heffron *ph* Gene Polito *m* Charles Bernstein

Jim Mitchum, Karen Lamm, Anne Archer, Erik Estrada, Cathy Lee Crosby, Vince Cannon

Trade Winds
US 1939 93m bw
Walter Wanger

A girl who thinks she has committed murder flees to the Far East, and a cynical detective is sent to bring her back. Guess what happens.
Smartly written mixture of comedy, drama, mystery and travelogue which comes off only in spots; it needed a firmer hand.

w Dorothy Parker, Alan Campbell, Frank R. Adams *d* Tay Garnett *ph* Rudolph Maté

Fredric March, Joan Bennett, Ralph Bellamy, Ann Sothern, Sidney Blackmer, Thomas Mitchell, Robert Elliott

Trader Horn*
US 1931 120m bw
MGM

An experienced African trader overcomes tribal hostility.
Primitive talkie for which second units were sent to Africa amid much publicity hoo-ha. After forty-five years, nothing of interest remains to be seen.

w Richard Schayer, Dale Van Every, Thomas Neville, *novel* Alfred Aloysius Horn, Etheldreda Lewis *w* W. S. Van Dyke *ph* Clyde de Vinna

Harry Carey, Edwina Booth, Duncan Renaldo, Mutia Omoolu, C. Aubrey Smith

Trader Horn
US 1973 105m Metrocolor
MGM (Lewis J. Rachmil)

Pitiful remake patched together largely from stock footage.

w William Norton, Edward Harper *d* Reza Badiyi *ph* Ronald W. Browne *m* Shelly Manne

Rod Taylor, Anne Heywood, Jean Sorel

'Laughably inept . . . it cannot face word of mouth for long.'—*Variety*

The Trail of the Lonesome Pine*
US 1936 102m Technicolor
Paramount (Walter Wanger)

A hillbilly girl goes back home when her brother is killed in a family feud.
Antediluvian Ozarkian melodrama, notable as the first outdoor film to be shot in three-colour Technicolor.

w Grover Jones, Horace McCoy, Harvey Thew, *novel* John Fox Jnr *d* Henry Hathaway *ph Howard Green* *m* Hugo Friedhofer, Gerrard Carbonara

Sylvia Sidney, Fred MacMurray, Henry Fonda, Fred Stone, Nigel Bruce, Beulah Bondi, Robert Barrat, Spanky McFarland, Fuzzy Knight

'Unnatural as it is, the colour does no serious damage to the picture. This moldy bit of hokum . . . takes movies back to the days of their childhood.'—*Newsweek*

The Train**
US 1965 140m bw
UA / Ariane / Dear (Jules Bricken)

In 1944, the French resistance tries to prevent the Nazis from taking art treasures back to Germany on a special train.
Proficient but longwinded suspense actioner with spectacular sequences; a safe bet for train enthusiasts.

w Franklin Coen, Frank Davis, Walter Bernstein *d John Frankenheimer* *ph* Jean Tournier, Walter Wottitz *m* Maurice Jarre

Burt Lancaster, *Paul Scofield*, Jeanne Moreau, Michael Simon, Wolfgang Preiss, Suzanne Flon

Train of Events
GB 1949 89m bw
Ealing (Michael Relph)

Portmanteau of stories à la Friday the 13th or Dead of Night, linked by a train disaster.
A rather mechanical entertainment, proficiently made.

w Basil Dearden, T. E. B. Clarke, Ronald Millar, Angus MacPhail *d* Basil Dearden, Charles Crichton, Sidney Cole *ph* Lionel Banes, Gordon Dines *m* Leslie Bridgewater

Valerie Hobson, John Clements, Jack Warner, Gladys Henson, Peter Finch, Irina Baronova, Susan Shaw, Patric Doonan, Joan Dowling, Laurence Payne, Mary Morris

The Train Robbers
US 1973 92m Technicolor Panavision
Warner / Batjac (Michael Wayne)

A widow asks three gunmen to help her clear her husband's name by retrieving gold he had stolen.
Shaggy dog western, sadly lacking in comic situation and detail.

wd Burt Kennedy *ph* William Clothier *m* Dominic Frontière

John Wayne, Ann-Margret, Rod Taylor, Ben Johnson, Bobby Vinton, Christopher George

The Traitor*
GB 1957 88m bw
New Realm (E. J. Fancey)

At the annual reunion of a resistance group, the host announces that one of their number was a traitor.
Heavy-handed theatrical melodrama, helped by a stout plot and some directional flair.

wd Michael McCarthy *ph* Bert Mason *m* Jackie Brown

Donald Wolfit, Robert Bray, Jane Griffiths, Carl Jaffe, Anton Diffring, Oscar Quitak, Rupert Davies, John Van Eyssen

The Traitors*
GB 1962 69m bw
Ello (Jim O'Connelly)

A top scientist is killed and MI5 springs into action.
Commendable second feature with narrative virtues absent in most big films.

w Jim O'Connelly *d Robert Tronson* *ph* Michael Reed *m* Johnny Douglas

Patrick Allen, James Maxwell, Ewan Roberts, Zena Walker

Traitor's Gate
GB 1965 80m bw
Columbia / Summit (Ted Lloyd)

A London businessman organizes a gang to steal the Crown Jewels.
Modest caper melodrama, routine but watchable.

w John Sansom, *novel* Edgar Wallace *d* Freddie Francis *ph* Denys Coop

Albert Lieven, Gary Raymond, Margot Trooger, Klaus Kinski, Catherina Von Schell, Edward Underdown

The Trap*
US 1958 84m Technicolor
Paramount / Parkwood–Heath (Melvin Frank, Norman Panama)
GB title: *The Baited Trap*

A lawyer helps a vicious killer to escape into Mexico, but the plan backfires.
Reasonably tense action thriller with desert backgrounds.

w Richard Alan Simmons, Norman Panama *d* Norman Panama *ph* Daniel L. Fapp *m* Irvin Talbot

Richard Widmark, Lee J. Cobb, Earl Holliman, Tina Louise, Carl Benton Reid, Lorne Green

Trapeze**
US 1956 105m De Luxe Cinemascope
UA / Hecht–Lancaster (James Hill)

A circus partnership almost breaks up when a voluptuous third member is engaged.
Concentrated, intense melodrama filmed almost entirely within a French winter circus and giving a very effective feel, almost a smell, of the life therein. Despite great skill in the making, however, the length is too great for a wisp of plot that goes back to *The Three Maxims* and doubtless beyond.

w James R. Webb *d Carol Reed ph Robert Krasker m* Malcolm Arnold

Burt Lancaster, Tony Curtis, Gina Lollobrigida, Thomas Gomez, Johnny Puleo, Katy Jurado, Sidney James

Trapped**
US 1973 74m Technicolor TVM
Universal (Richard Irving, Gary L. Messenger)
GB theatrical title: *Doberman Patrol*

Department store doors close on a man who has been mugged, and he finds himself at the mercy of vicious guard dogs.
Rather silly but suspenseful melodrama.

wd Frank de Felitta

James Brolin, Susan Clark, Earl Holliman

Trapped beneath the Sea
US 1974 100m colour TVM
ABC Circle

Four men are running out of oxygen at the bottom of the sea in a mini-sub.
Predictable, well-managed suspense.

w Stanford Whitmore *d* William Graham

Lee J. Cobb, Martin Balsam, Joshua Bryant, Paul Michael Glaser

The Travelling Executioner*
US 1970 95m Metrocolor Panavision
MGM (Jack Smight)

In 1918 an ex-carnival showman travels the American south with his portable electric chair and charges a hundred dollars per execution, but falls for one of his proposed victims.
Oddball fable without apparent moral; neither fantastic nor funny enough.

w Garrie Bateson *d* Jack Smight *ph* Philip Lathrop *m* Jerry Goldsmith

Stacy Keach, Mariana Hill, Bud Cort, Graham Jarvis

Travels with My Aunt*
US 1972 109m Metrocolor Panavision
MGM (Robert Fryer, James Cresson)

A staid bank accountant is landed in a series of continental adventures by his eccentric life-loving aunt.
Busy but fairly disastrous adaptation of a delightful novel, ruined by ceaseless chatter, lack of characterization, shapeless incident and an absurdly caricatured central performance.

w Jay Presson Allen, Hugh Wheeler, *novel* Graham Greene *d* George Cukor *ph* Douglas Slocombe *m* Tony Hatch *pd* John Box

Maggie Smith, *Alec McCowen*, Lou Gossett, Robert Stephens, Cindy Williams

Travis Logan DA
US 1970 100m colour TVM
Quinn Martin

A DA upsets a murderer's careful plans.
Adequate courtroom job.

d Paul Wendkos

Vic Morrow, Hal Holbrook, Brenda Vaccaro, George Grizzard

Tread Softly Stranger*
GB 1958 91m bw
Alderdale (George Minter)

In a north country town, two brothers in love with the same girl rob a safe.
Hilarious murky melodrama full of glum faces, with a well-worn trick ending; rather well photographed.

w George Minter, Denis O'Dell, *play* Jack Popplewell *d* Gordon Parry *ph Douglas Slocombe m* Tristam Cary

George Baker, Terence Morgan, Diana Dors, Wilfrid Lawson, Patrick Allen, Jane Griffith, Joseph Tomelty, Norman Macowan

Treasure Hunt
GB 1952 79m bw
Romulus (Anatole de Grunwald)

The eccentric middle-aged members of an Irish family find their father's fortune is missing.
Theatrical comedy with some charm and humour, but very much a photographed play.

w Anatole de Grunwald, *play* M. J. Perry *d* John Paddy Carstairs *ph* C. Pennington-Richards *m* Mischa Spoliansky

Jimmy Edwards, *Martita Hunt, Athene Seyler*, Naunton Wayne, June Clyde, Susan Stephen, Brian Worth

Treasure Island**
US 1934 105m bw
MGM

An old pirate map leads to a long sea voyage, a mutiny, and buried treasure.
Nicely mounted Hollywood version of a classic adventure story, a little slow in development but meticulously produced.

w John Lee Mahin, novel Robert Louis Stevenson *d* Victor Fleming *ph* Ray June, Clyde de Vinna, Harold Rosson *m* Herbert Stothart

Wallace Beery, Jackie Cooper, Lewis Stone, *Lionel Barrymore*, Otto Kruger, Douglass Dumbrille, Nigel Bruce, Chic Sale

Treasure Island*
GB 1950 96m Technicolor
Walt Disney (Perce Pearce)

Cheerful Disney remake, poor on detail but transfixed by a swaggeringly overplayed and unforgettable leading performance.

w Lawrence Edward Watkin *d* Byron Haskin *ph* F. A. Young *m* Clifton Parker *pd* Thomas Morahan

Robert Newton, Bobby Driscoll, Walter Fitzgerald, Basil Sydney, Denis O'Dea, Geoffrey Wilkinson, Ralph Truman

'Serviceable rather than imaginative.'
—*Lindsay Anderson*

Treasure Island
GB / France / Germany / Spain 1971 95m colour
Massfilms / FDL / CCC / Eguiluz (Harry Alan Towers)

Spiritless and characterless international remake with poor acting, production and dubbing.

w Wolf Mankowitz, O. W. Jeeves (Welles) *d* John Hough *ph* Cicilio Paniagua *m* Natal Massara

Orson Welles, Kim Burfield, Lionel Stander, Walter Slezak, Rik Battaglia

The Treasure of Lost Canyon
US 1952 82m Technicolor
U-I (Leonard Goldstein)

A small boy robbed of his inheritance finds it with the help of an old tramp.
Modest juvenile adventure, rather boringly narrated.

w Brainerd Duffield, Emerson Crocker, *story* by Robert Louis Stevenson *d* Ted Tetzlaff *ph* Russell Metty *m* Joseph Gershenson

William Powell, Julia Adams, Charles Drake, Rosemary de Camp, Henry Hull, Tommy Ivo

Treasure of Matecumbe
US 1976 116m Technicolor
Walt Disney (Bill Anderson)

Two boys seek buried gold in the Florida keys.
Cheerful adventure tale with a few nods to *Treasure Island*; all very competent in the Disney fashion.

w Don Tait *d* Vincent McEveety *ph* Frank Phillips *m* Buddy Baker

Robert Foxworth, Joan Hackett, Peter Ustinov, Vic Morrow, Jane Wyatt, Johnny Duran, Billy Attmore

The Treasure of Pancho Villa
US 1955 96m Technicolor Superscope
RKO / Edmund Grainger

Mexico 1915: an American adventurer becomes involved with the revolutionary Pancho Villa; both seek a gold consignment but it is buried in an avalanche.
Modestly well made, routine action drama.

w Niven Busch *d* George Sherman *ph* William Snyder *m* Leith Stevens

Rory Calhoun, Shelley Winters, *Gilbert Roland*, Joseph Calleia

Treasure of San Teresa
GB 1959 81m bw
Orbit (John Nasht, Patrick Filmer-Sankey)

An American secret service agent finds Nazi loot in a Czech convent.
Roughly-made, watchable actioner.

w Jack Andrews, Jeffrey Dell *d* Alvin Rakoff *ph* Wilkie Cooper *m* Philip Martell

Eddie Constantine, Dawn Addams, Marius Goring, Christopher Lee, Walter Gotell

Treasure of the Golden Condor
US 1952 93m Technicolor
TCF

A young Frenchman flees to the South Seas but returns to discredit his wicked uncle.
Ineffectual remake of *Son of Fury* (qv) with Guatemalan backgrounds and no punch at all.

wd Delmer Daves *ph* Edward Cronjager *m* Sol Kaplan

Cornel Wilde, Finlay Currie, Constance Smith, George Macready, Walter Hampden, Anne Bancroft, Fay Wray, Leo G. Carroll

The Treasure of the Sierra Madre**
US 1948 126m bw
Warner (Henry Blanke)

Three gold prospectors come to grief through greed.
Well-acted but partly miscast action fable on the oldest theme in the world; rather tedious and studio-bound for a film with such a high reputation.

wd John Huston, *novel* B. Traven *ph* Ted McCord *m* Leo F. Forbstein

Humphrey Bogart, Walter Huston, Tim Holt, Alfonso Bedoya, John Huston, Bruce Bennett, Barton MacLane

'This bitter fable is told with cinematic integrity and considerable skill.'—*Henry Hart*

'The faces of the men, in close-up or in a group, achieve a kind of formal pattern and always dominate the screen.'—*Peter Ericsson*

A Tree Grows in Brooklyn****
US 1945 128m bw
TCF (Louis D. Lighton)

Life for an Irish family with a drunken father in New York's teeming slums at the turn of the century.
A superbly-detailed studio production of the type they don't make any more: a family drama with interest for everybody.

w Tess Slesinger, Frank Davis, novel Betty Smith d Elia Kazan ph Leon Shamroy m Alfred Newman

Peggy Ann Garner, James Dunn, Dorothy McGuire, Joan Blondell, Lloyd Nolan, Ted Donaldson, James Gleason, Ruth Nelson, John Alexander, Adeline de Walt Reynolds, Charles Halton

'He tells a maximum amount of story with a minimum of film. Little touches of humour and human understanding crop up throughout.' —*Frank Ward, NBR*

A Tree Grows in Brooklyn
US 1974 74m colour TVM
TCF

Unaffecting remake, all too brightly coloured.

w Blanche Hanalis *d* Joseph Hardy

Cliff Robertson, Diane Baker, Nancy Malone, James Olson, Pamela Ferdin, Michael-James Wixted

Trent's Last Case
GB 1952 90m bw
Wilcox–Neagle (Herbert Wilcox)

A journalist suspects that the death of a tycoon was murder.
Desultory version of a famous novel, with none of the original style and a few naïveties of its own.

w Pamela Bower, *novel* E. C. Bentley *d* Herbert Wilcox *ph* Max Greene *m* Anthony Collins

Michael Wilding, Margaret Lockwood, Orson Welles, John McCallum, Miles Malleson

Trial*
US 1955 109m bw
MGM (Charles Schnee)

A young lawyer defends a Mexican boy accused of rape and murder.
Stereotyped but pacy and watchable racial drama with political overtones, Our Hero having to resist bigots, Commies *and* McCarthyites.

w Don M. Mankiewicz, from his novel *d* Mark Robson *ph* Robert Surtees *m* Daniele Amfitheatrof

Glenn Ford, Dorothy McGuire, Arthur Kennedy, John Hodiak, Katy Jurado, Rafael Campos, Juano Hernandez, Robert Middleton, John Hoyt

Trial by Combat
GB 1976 90m Technicolor
Warner / Combat (Fred Weintraub, Paul Heller)
aka: *Choice of Weapons*

An apparently harmless secret society of 'medieval knights' rededicates itself to the ritual execution of criminals who have escaped the law.
A rare specimen of comic macabre apparently inspired by the TV series *The Avengers*. Sadly, not much of it really works.

w Julian Bond, Steven Rossen, Mitchell Smith *d* Kevin Conner *ph* Alan Hume *m* Frank Cordell *pd* Edward Marshall

John Mills, Donald Pleasance, Peter Cushing, Barbara Hershey, David Birney, Margaret Leighton, Brian Glover

The Trial of Chaplain Jensen*
US 1975 74m colour TVM
TCF

A naval chaplain is courtmartialled for adultery.
True-life courtroom drama, discreetly scripted.

w Loring Mandel, *book* Andrew Jensen *d* Robert Day

James Franciscus, Joanna Miles, Charles Durning, Lynda Day George

Trial Run
US 1969 98m Technicolor TVM
Universal (Jack Laird)

An ambitious lawyer overreaches himself.
Overlong courtroom drama.

w Chester Krumholz *d* William Graham

James Franciscus, Leslie Nielsen, Janice Rule, Diane Baker

The Trials of Oscar Wilde**
GB 1960 123m Super Technirama 70
Warwick / Viceroy (Harold Huth)
US title: *The Man with the Green Carnation*

Oscar Wilde fatally sues the Marquis of Queensberry for libel, and loses; he is then prosecuted for sodomy.
Plush account of a fascinating event; narrative drive is unfortunately lacking, but one is left with interesting performances.

wd Ken Hughes ph Ted Moore *m* Ron Goodwin *ad* Ken Adam, Bill Constable

Peter Finch, Yvonne Mitchell, *John Fraser*, Lionel Jeffries, *Nigel Patrick*, James Mason, Emrys Jones, Maxine Audley, Paul Rogers, James Booth

The Tribe
US 1974 Technicolor TVM
Universal (George Eckstein)

Problems of cro-magnon man.
Some Universal executive must have had a brainstorm: the result isn't highbrow, it's paralysingly boring.

w Lane Slate *d* Richard A. Colla

Victor French, Warren Vanders, Henry Wilcoxon, Adriana Shaw

Tribes*
US 1970 74m colour TVM
TCF / Marvin Schwarz
GB theatrical title: *The Soldier Who Declared Peace*

A hippie is called up and has a varying relationship with his drill sergeant.
Mildly amusing contemporary comedy.

w Tracy Keenan Wynn, Marvin Schwarz *d* Joseph Sargent *ph* Russell Metty

Darren McGavin, Jan-Michael Vincent, Earl Holliman

Tribute to a Bad Man
US 1956 95m Eastmancolor Cinemascope
MGM (Sam Zimbalist)

A Wyoming horse breeder is callous in his treatment of rustlers, and wins the woman he wants when he becomes more understanding.
Somewhere behind an unsympathetic story and hesitant development lies a convincing picture of life in the old west.

w Michael Blankfort, *story* Jack Schaefer *d* Robert Wise *ph* Robert Surtees *m* Miklos Rozsa

James Cagney, Irene Papas, Don Dubbins, Stephen McNally, Vic Morrow, Royal Dano, Lee Van Cleef

Trilogy of Terror
US 1975 74m colour TVM
ABC Circle / Dan Curtis

Women have the problems in three strange stories.
Grab-bag of hauntings and neuroses; not exactly compulsive.

w William Nolan, Richard Matheson *d* Dan Curtis

Karen Black (in four roles), Robert Burton, John Karlin, George Gaynes

Trio*
GB 1950 91m bw
Rank / Gainsborough (Antony Darnborough)

Following *Quartet* (qv), three more stories from Somerset Maugham: 'The Verger', 'Mr Knowall', and 'Sanatorium'.
An enjoyable package, unpretentiously handled but with full weight to the content.

w W. Somerset Maugham, R. C. Sherriff, Noel Langley, *stories* W. Somerset Maugham *d* Ken Annakin, Harold French *ph* Reg Wyer, Geoffrey Unsworth *m* John Greenwood *ad* Maurice Carter

James Hayter, Kathleen Harrison, Michael Hordern, Felix Aylmer; *Nigel Patrick*, Anne Crawford, Naunton Wayne, Wilfrid Hyde White; Michael Rennie, Jean Simmons, *John Laurie, Finlay Currie*, Roland Culver, Betty Ann Davies, Raymond Huntley, André Morell

The Trip*
US 1967 85m Pathecolor
AIP (Roger Corman)

A director of TV commercials tries LSD and has hallucinations.
Much-banned plotless wallow, the ultimate opt-out movie; well done for those who can take it.

w Jack Nicholson *d* Roger Corman *ph Arch Dalzell psychedelic effects Peter Gardiner montage Dennis Jakob*

Peter Fonda, Susan Strasberg, Bruce Dern, Salli Sachse, Dennis Hopper

Triple Cross
GB 1967 140m colour
Warner / Fred Feldkamp

A small-time crook imprisoned on Jersey at the

start of World War II offers to spy for the Nazis but reports to the English.
Ho-hum biopic of double agent Eddie Chapman; effective scenes merely interrupt the general incoherence.

w René Hardy, *book* The Eddie Chapman Story by Frank Owen *d* Terence Young *ph* Henri Alekan *m* Georges Garvarentz

Christopher Plummer, Yul Brynner, Trevor Howard, Romy Schneider, Gert Frobe, Claudine Auger

Triple Echo*
GB 1972 94m colour
Hemdale

In 1942, a soldier's wife welcomes another soldier to her farm for tea; he deserts and poses as her sister.
Foolish story which would possibly have worked as a TV play but hardly justifies a film despite the talent on hand.

w Robin Chapman, *novel* H. E. Bates *d* Michael Apted *ph* John Coquillon *m* Marc Wilkinson

Glenda Jackson, Brian Deacon, Oliver Reed

Trog
GB 1970 91m Technicolor
Warner / Herman Cohen

A man-ape is discovered in a pothole and trained by a lady scientist.
Ridiculous semi-horror film which degrades its star.

w Aben Kandel *d* Freddie Francis *ph* Desmond Dickinson *m* John Scott

Joan Crawford, Michael Gough, Bernard Kay, David Griffin

The Trojan Women*
US 1971 111m Eastmancolor
Josef Shaftel (Michael Cacoyannis, Anis Nohra)

Troy has fallen to the Greeks and its women bemoan their fate.
And oh, how they bemoan! Even with this cast, Greek tragedy does not fill the big screen.

w Michael Cacoyannis, *play* Euripides *d* Michael Cacoyannis *ph* Alfio Contini *m* Mikis Theodorakis

Katharine Hepburn, Vanessa Redgrave, Geneviève Bujold, Irene Papas, Patrick Magee, Brian Blessed, Pauline Letts

Trooper Hook
US 1957 92m bw
UA / Sol Baer Fielding

A woman prisoner of the Indians has a half-breed son and becomes an outcast when returned to her people.
Peculiar western with good moments, but generally very slow and downbeat.

w Charles Marquis Warren, David Victor, Herbert Little Jnr, *story* Jack Schaefer *d* Charles Marquis Warren *ph* Ellsworth Fredericks *m* Gerald Fried

Barbara Stanwyck, Joel McCrea, Earl Holliman, Edward Andrews, John Dehner, Susan Kohner, Royal Dano

Trottie True*
GB 1949 98m Technicolor
GFD / Two Cities (Hugh Stewart)
US title: *The Gay Lady*

Adventures of a Gaiety girl who married a lord.
Self-conscious period comedy which could have been highly diverting but manages only to be sporadically charming in a whimsically amateurish way.

w C. Denis Freeman, *novel* Caryl Brahms, S. J. Simon *d* Brian Desmond Hurst *ph* Harry Waxman *m* Benjamin Frankel *ad* Ralph Brinton

Jean Kent, James Donald, Hugh Sinclair, Bill Owen, Andrew Crawford, Lana Morris

Trouble along the Way
US 1953 110m bw
Warner (Melville Shavelson)

A famous football coach is co-opted to help a bankrupt college but some of his methods are not quite above board.
American college comedy with dollops of religiosity—a double threat.

w Melville Shavelson, Jack Rose *d* Michael Curtiz *ph* Archie Stout *m* Max Steiner

John Wayne, Donna Reed, Charles Coburn, Tom Tully, Sherry Jackson, Marie Windsor
'No opportunites for a laugh or a tear are missed by the entire cast.'—*MFB*

Trouble Comes to Town
US 1972 73m colour TVM
ABC Circle (Everett Chambers)

Racial problems erupt in a small southern town.
Obvious social melodrama.

w David Westheimer *d* Daniel Petrie

Lloyd Bridges, Pat Hingle, Hari Rhodes, Janet McLachlan, Sheree North

Trouble for Two*
US 1936 75m bw
MGM
GB title: *The Suicide Club*

A European prince in London for an arranged wedding gets involved with an ingenious organization for murder.
Light-hearted, black-edged Victorian literary spoof which starts nicely but can't quite keep up the pace.

w Manuel Seff, Edward Paramore Jnr, *stories* New Arabian Nights by Robert Louis Stevenson *d* J. Walter Rubin *ph* Charles G. Clarke *m* Franz Waxman

Robert Montgomery, Rosalind Russell, *Reginald Owen*, Frank Morgan, *Louis Hayward*, E. E. Clive, Walter Kingsford

Trouble in Paradise****
US 1932 86m bw
Paramount (Ernst Lubitsch)

Jewel thieves insinuate themselves into the household of a rich Parisienne, and one falls in love with her.
A masterpiece of light comedy, with sparkling dialogue, innuendo, great performances and masterly cinematic narrative. For connoisseurs, it can't be faulted, and is the masterpiece of American sophisticated cinema.

w Samson Raphaelson, Grover Jones, play The Honest Finder by Laszlo Aladar *d Ernst Lubitsch ph* Victor Milner

Herbert Marshall, Miriam Hopkins, Kay Francis, Edward Everett Horton, Charles Ruggles, C. Aubrey Smith, Robert Greig, Leonid Kinskey

'One of the gossamer creations of Lubitsch's narrative art . . . it would be impossible in this brief notice to describe the innumerable touches of wit and of narrative skill with which it is unfolded.'—*Alexander Bakshy*

'A shimmering, engaging piece of work . . . in virtually every scene a lively imagination shines forth.'—*New York Times*

'An almost continuous musical background pointed up and commented on the action. The settings were the last word in modernistic design.'—*Theodor Huff, 1948*

Trouble in Store*
GB 1953 85m bw
GFD / Two Cities (Maurice Cowan)

A stock assistant causes chaos in a department store.
First, simplest and best of the Wisdom farces.

w John Paddy Carstairs, Maurice Cowan, Ted Willis *d* John Paddy Carstairs *ph* Ernest Steward *m* Mischa Spoliansky

Norman Wisdom, Jerry Desmonde, Margaret Rutherford, Moira Lister, Derek Bond, Lana Morris, Megs Jenkins, Joan Sims

Trouble in the Glen
GB 1954 91m Trucolor
Republic / Wilcox–Neagle (Stuart Robertson)

An Argentinian laird in a Scottish glen causes ill-feeling.
Heavy-handed Celtic comedy whose predictability and sentimentality could have been forgiven were it not for the most garish colour ever seen.

w Frank S. Nugent, *novel* Maurice Walsh *d* Herbert Wilcox *ph* Max Greene *m* Victor Young

Margaret Lockwood, Orson Welles, Forrest Tucker, Victor McLaglen, John McCallum, Eddie Byrne, Archie Duncan, Moultrie Kelsall

The Trouble with Angels
US 1966 112m Pathecolor
Columbia / William Frye

Two mischievous new pupils cause trouble at a convent school.
Fun with the nuns, for addicts only.

w Blanche Hanalis, *novel* Life with Mother Superior by Jane Trahey *d* Ida Lupino *ph* Lionel Lindon *m* Jerry Goldsmith

Rosalind Russell, Hayley Mills, June Harding, Marge Redmond, Binnie Barnes, Gypsy Rose Lee, Camilla Sparv, Mary Wickes, Margalo Gillmore

'A relentless series of prankish escapades.' —*MFB*

The Trouble with Girls
US 1969 105m Metrocolor Panavision
MGM (Lester Welch)

In the twenties the manager of a travelling chautauqua (educational medicine show) gets involved in a small-town murder.
Curious vehicle for a very bored singing star, with some interesting background detail.

w Arnold and Lois Peyser, *novel* The Chautauqua by Day Keene, Dwight Babcock *d* Peter Tewksbury *ph* Jacques Marquette *m* Billy Strange

Elvis Presley, Marlyn Mason, Nicole Jaffe, Sheree North, Edward Andrews, John Carradine, Vincent Price, Joyce Van Patten

The Trouble with Harry**
US 1955 99m Technicolor Vistavision
(Paramount) Alfred Hitchcock

In the New England woods, various reasons cause various people to find and bury the same body.
Black comedy which never quite, despite bright

moments, catches the style of the book; however, it is finely performed and the autumnal backgrounds are splendid.

w John Michael Hayes, *novel* Jack Trevor Story *d Alfred Hitchcock ph Robert Burks m* Bernard Herrmann

Edmund Gwenn, Mildred Natwick, John Forsythe, Shirley Maclaine, Mildred Dunnock

True as a Turtle
GB 1956 96m Eastmancolor
Rank (Peter de Sarigny)

Honeymooners join a variety of friends on a yacht crossing the Channel, and get involved in smuggling.
Artless, undemanding comedy for those who like messing about in boats.

w Jack Davies, John Coates, Nicholas Phipps *d* Wendy Toye *ph* Reg Wyer *m* Robert Farnon

John Gregson, June Thorburn, Cecil Parker, *Elvi Hale*, Keith Michell, Avice Landone

True Confession**
US 1937 85m bw
Paramount (Albert Lewin)

A fantasy-prone girl confesses to a murder she didn't commit, and her upright lawyer husband defends her.
Archetypal crazy comedy with fine moments despite longueurs and a lack of cinematic inventiveness. Remade as *Cross My Heart* (qv).

w Claude Binyon, *play* Mon Crime by Louis Verneuil, George Berr *d* Wesley Ruggles *ph* Ted Tetzlaff *m* Frederick Hollander

Carole Lombard, Fred MacMurray, *John Barrymore*, Una Merkel, Porter Hall, Edgar Kennedy, Lynne Overman, Fritz Feld, *Irving Bacon*

'The best comedy of the year.'—*Graham Greene*

True Grit*
US 1969 128m Technicolor
Paramount / Hal B. Wallis (Paul Nathan)

In the old west, a young girl wanting to avenge her murdered father seeks the aid of a hard-drinking old marshal.
Disappointingly slow-moving and uninventive semi-spoof western with a roistering performance from a veteran star, who won a sentimental Oscar for daring to look fat and old.

w Marguerite Roberts, *novel* Charles Portis *d* Henry Hathaway *ph* Lucien Ballard *m* Elmer Bernstein

John Wayne, Kim Darby, Glen Campbell, Dennis Hopper, Jeremy Slate, Robert Duvall, Strother Martin, Jeff Corey

'Readers may remember it as a book about a girl, but it's a film about John Wayne.'—*Stanley Kauffmann*

The True Story of Jesse James
US 1956 92m Eastmancolor Cinemascope
TCF (Herbert Swope Jnr)
GB title: *The James Brothers*

After the Civil War, Jesse and Frank James become outlaws and train robbers.
Fairly slavish remake of *Jesse James*, without the style.

w Walter Newman *d* Nicholas Ray *ph* Joe MacDonald *m* Leigh Harline

Robert Wagner, Jeffrey Hunter, Hope Lange, Agnes Moorehead, John Carradine, Alan Hale Jnr, Alan Baxter

The Truth about Women
GB 1957 107m Eastmancolor
British Lion / Beaconsfield (Sydney Box)

An old roué recounts to his son-in-law his early amorous adventures.
Tedious charade with neither wit nor grace.

w Muriel and Sydney Box *d* Muriel Box *ph* Otto Heller *m* Bruce Montgomery

Laurence Harvey, Julie Harris, Diane Cilento, Mai Zetterling, Eva Gabor, Michael Denison, Derek Farr, Roland Culver, Wilfrid Hyde White, Christopher Lee, Marius Goring, Thorley Walters, Ernest Thesiger, Griffith Jones

The Truth about Spring*
GB 1964 102m Technicolor
U-I / Quota Rentals (Alan Brown)

The bored nephew of a millionaire cruising in the Caribbean jumps at the chance to join friends on a scruffy yacht, but they all get involved with pirates.
Pleasing family film with good scenery and a friendly cast.

w James Lee Barrett, *novel* H. de Vere Stacpoole *d* Richard Thorpe *ph Ted Scaife m* Robert Farnon

Hayley Mills, James MacArthur, David Tomlinson, Lionel Jeffries, John Mills, Harry Andrews, Niall MacGinnis

The Trygon Factor*
GB 1966 88m Technicolor
Rank / Rialto Film / Preben Phillipsen (Ian Warren)

Bogus nuns plan a million pound bank raid.

When you get used to its mixture of styles, this Anglo-German production is pretty good imitation Edgar Wallace, with bags of mystery and melodramatic goings-on involving larger than life characters most of whom come to sticky ends.

w Derry Quinn, Stanley Munro, Kingsley Amis *d* Cyril Frankel *ph* Harry Waxman *m* Peter Thomas

Stewart Granger, Susan Hampshire, Cathleen Nesbitt, Robert Morley, James Culliford, Brigitte Horney, Sophie Hardy, James Robertson Justice

Tugboat Annie••
US 1933 88m bw
MGM

An elderly waterfront lady and her boozy friend smooth out the path of young love.
Hilarious and well-loved comedy vehicle for two great stars of the period.

w Zelda Sears, Eve Greene, *stories* Norman Reilly Raine *d* Mervyn Le Roy *ph* Gregg Toland

Marie Dressler, Wallace Beery, Robert Young, Maureen O'Sullivan, Willard Robertson, Paul Hurst

Tulsa•
US 1949 88m Technicolor
Eagle–Lion (Walter Wanger)

The daughter of a cattle owner builds an oil empire.
Splendid Hollywood hokum of the second grade, very predictable but well-oiled.

w Frank Nugent, Curtis Kenyon *d* Stuart Heisler *ph* Winton Hoch *m* Frank Skinner

Susan Hayward, Robert Preston, Pedro Armendariz, Lloyd Gough, Chill Wills, Ed Begley

Tunes of Glory••
GB 1960 107m Technicolor
UA / Knightsbridge (Albert Fennell)

The new disciplinarian CO of a highland regiment crosses swords with his lax, hard-drinking predecessor.
Wintry barracks melodrama, finely acted and well made with memorable confrontation scenes compensating for a somewhat underdeveloped script.

w James Kennaway, from his novel *d Ronald Neame ph Arthur Ibbetson*

Alec Guinness, John Mills, Susannah York, Dennis Price, Kay Walsh, *Duncan Macrae,* Gordon Jackson, John Fraser, Allan Cuthbertson

The Tunnel•
GB 1935 94m bw
Gaumont (Michael Balcon)
US title: *Transatlantic Tunnel*

Crooked finances mar the completion of an undersea tunnel to America.
A rare example of British science fiction, and sadly the negative seems to be lost along with all known prints.

w Curt Siodmak, L. DuGarde Peach, Clemence Dane, *novel* Bernard Kellerman *d* Maurice Elvey

Richard Dix, Leslie Banks, Madge Evans, Helen Vinson, C. Aubrey Smith, George Arliss, Walter Huston, Basil Sydney, Jimmy Hanley

The Tunnel of Love
US 1958 98m bw Cinemascope
MGM / Joseph Fields

A husband applying to adopt an orphan thinks he may, while drunk, have seduced the glamorous orphan agency official.
Tasteless and not very funny comedy, somewhat miscast.

w Joseph Fields, *play* Joseph Fields, Peter de Vries, *novel* Peter de Vries *d* Gene Kelly *ph* Robert Bronner

Richard Widmark, Doris Day, Gig Young, Gia Scala, Elizabeth Fraser, Elizabeth Wilson

Turn the Key Softly
GB 1953 81m bw
GFD / Chiltern (Maurice Cowan)

The problems of three women released from prison.
Soppy formula multi-drama with contrived and uninteresting plots and characters.

w Jack Lee, Maurice Cowan, *novel* John Brophy *d* Jack Lee *ph* Geoffrey Unsworth *m* Mischa Spoliansky

Yvonne Mitchell, Terence Morgan, Joan Collins, Kathleen Harrison, Thora Hird, Dorothy Alison, Glyn Houston, Geoffrey Keen, Clive Morton

Turnabout•
US 1940 83m bw
Hal Roach

A benevolent god enables a quarrelsome couple to change bodies and see how they like it.
"The man's had a baby instead of the lady", said the ads. Well, not quite, but it did seem pretty

daring at the time, and it still provides a hilarious moment of two.

w Mickell Novak, Berne Giler, Jonn McLain, *novel* Thorne Smith *d* Hal Roach *ph* Norbert Brodine

Adolphe Menjou, John Hubbard, Carole Landis, Mary Astor, Verree Teasdale, Donald Meek, William Gargan, Joyce Compton

The Turning Point
US 1952 85m bw
Paramount (Irving Asher)

A young lawyer is appointed by the state governor to smash a crime syndicate.
Familiar exposé drama of its time, quite crisply done.

w Warren Duff *w* William Dieterle *ph* Lionel Lindon *m* Irving Talbot

William Holden, Alexis Smith, Edmond O'Brien, Tom Tully, Ray Teal

The Turning Point of Jim Malloy***
US 1975 74m colour TVM
Columbia
aka: *Gibbsville*

A troublesome youth settles down as reporter on his hometown paper, in 1940s Pennsylvania.
Thoroughly competent blend of *Peyton Place* and *King's Row*, with fast pace, excellent acting, and most of the old Hollywood skills in evidence. A series resulted in 1976.

wd Frank D. Gilroy, novel John O'Hara

John Savage, Gig Young, Biff McGuire, Kathleen Quinlan, Janis Paige

Twelve Angry Men****
US 1957 95m bw
(UA) Orion–Nova (Henry Fonda, Reginald Rose)

A murder case jury about to vote guilty is convinced otherwise by one doubting member.
Though unconvincing in detail, this is a brilliantly tight character melodrama which is never less than absorbing to experience. Acting and direction are superlatively right, and the film was important in helping to establish television talents in Hollywood.

w Reginald Rose, from his play *d Sidney Lumet ph Boris Kaufman m* Kenyon Hopkins

Henry Fonda, Lee J. Cobb, E. G Marshall, Jack Warden, Ed Begley, Martin Balsam, John Fiedler, Jack Klugman, George Voskovec, Robert Webber, Edward Binns, Joseph Sweeney

The Twelve Chairs
US 1970 93m Movielab
UMC / Crossbow (Michael Hertzberg)

A Russian bureaucrat chases twelve dining chairs, in one of which is hidden the family jewels.
Tedious Mel Brooks romp with not too many laughs, from a yarn better handled in *Keep Your Seats Please* and *It's in the Bag*, from both of which he might have learned something about comedy timing.

w Mel Brooks, *novel* Ilf and Petrov *d* Mel Brooks *ph* Dorde Nikolic *m* John Morris

Ron Moody, Frank Langella, Dom De Luise, Bridget Brice, Diana Coupland, Mel Brooks

Twelve O'Clock High***
US 1949 132m bw
TCF (Darryl F. Zanuck)

During World War II, the commander of a US bomber unit in Britain begins to crack under the strain.
Absorbing character drama, justifiably a big box office success of its day, later revived as a TV series. All production values are excellent.

w Sy Bartlett, Beirne Lay Jnr d Henry King ph Leon Shamroy m Alfred Newman

Gregory Peck, Hugh Marlowe, Gary Merrill, Millard Mitchell, Dean Jagger, Robert Arthur, Paul Stewart, John Kellogg

Twentieth Century***
US 1934 91m bw
Columbia

A temperamental Broadway producer trains an untutored actress, but when a star she proves a match for him.
Though slightly lacking in pace, this is a marvellously sharp and memorable theatrical burlesque, and the second half, set on the train of the title, reaches highly agreeable peaks of insanity.

w Ben Hecht, Charles MacArthur, play Napoleon of Broadway by Charles Bruce Millholland *d Howard Hawks ph* Joseph August

John Barrymore, Carole Lombard, Roscoe Karns, Walter Connolly, Ralph Forbes, *Etienne Girardot,* Charles Lane, Edgar Kennedy

'Notable as the first comedy in which sexually attractive, sophisticated stars indulged in their own slapstick instead of delegating it to their inferiors.'—*Andrew Sarris, 1963*

Twenty-Four Hours of a Woman's Life
GB 1952 90m Technicolor
ABPC (Ivan Foxwell)

A young widow tries to reform an inveterate gambler, but he kills himself.
Stilted, over-literary romantic melodrama with philosophical dialogue, flashback framing and Riviera settings.

w Warren Chetham Strode, *novel* Stefan Zweig *d* Victor Saville *ph* Christopher Challis *m* Robert Gill, Philip Green

Merle Oberon, Leo Genn, Richard Todd, Stephen Murray, Peter Illing, Isabel Dean

Twenty Million Miles to Earth
US 1957 82m bw
Columbia (Charles Schneer)

An American rocket ship returning from Venus breaks open and a scaly monster escapes into the Mediterranean and is cornered in the Roman coliseum.
Cheeseparing monster fiction which doesn't wake up till the last five minutes, and looks pretty silly even then.

w Bob Williams, Chris Knopf *d* Nathan Juran *ph* Irving Lippmann *m* Mischa Bakaleinikoff *sp* Ray Harryhausen

William Hopper, Joan Taylor, Frank Puglia, John Zaremba

Twenty Million Sweethearts
US1934 89m bw
Warner

Singing radio sweethearts are kept apart because of their images.
Thin musical with moderate numbers, remade as *My Dream Is Yours.*

w Warren Duff, Harry Sauber *d* Ray Enright *ph* Sid Hickox *songs* Harry Warren, Al Dubin

Dick Powell, Ginger Rogers, Pat O'Brien, the Mills Brothers, Ted Fio Rito and his band, the Radio Rogues, Allen Jenkins, Grant Mitchell

Twenty-One Days*
GB 1937 75m bw
London Films (Alexander Korda)
aka: *The First and the Last*

A barrister's brother accidentally kills a man and lets an old eccentric take the blame.
Watchable but very stilted melodrama with interesting early performances by Olivier and Leigh and a few good moments.

w Graham Greene, *play* John Galsworthy *d* Basil Dean

Laurence Olivier, Vivien Leigh, Leslie Banks, Hay Petrie, Francis L. Sullivan, Esmé Percy, Robert Newton, Victor Rietti

Twenty Thousand Leagues under the Sea**
US 1954 122m Technicolor Cinemascope
Walt Disney

Victorian scientists at sea are wrecked and captured by the mysterious captain of a futuristic submarine.
Pretty full-blooded adaptation of a famous yarn, with strong performances and convincing art and trick work.

w Earl Felton, *novel Jules Verne d Richard Fleischer ph* Franz Lehy, Ralph Hammeras, Till Gabbani *m* Paul Smith *ad John Meehan*

Kirk Douglas, James Mason, Paul Lukas, Peter Lorre, Robert J. Wilke, Carlton Young, Ted de Corsia

Twenty Thousand Years in Sing Sing**
US 1932 77m bw
Warner (Robert Lord)

A tough criminal escapes from prison but his girl kills a man during the attempt, and he takes the blame.
Dated but fast-moving and still-powerful crime melodrama, remade to less effect as *Castle on the Hudson* (qv).

w Wilson Mizner, Brown Holmes, *book* Lewis E. Lawes *d Michael Curtiz ph* Barney McGill *m* Bernhard Kaun

Spencer Tracy, Bette Davis, Arthur Byron, Lyle Talbot, Louis Calhern, Warren Hymer, Sheila Terry, Edward McNamara

Twenty-Three Paces to Baker Street*
US 1956 103m Eastmancolor Cinemascope
TCF (Henry Ephron)

A blind playwright in a pub overhears a murder plot and follows the trail to the bitter end despite attacks on his life.
Sufficiently engrossing murder mystery with a weird idea of London's geography: the hero's Portman Square apartment has a balcony overlooking the Thames two miles away. Perhaps this is part of the script's light touch.

w Nigel Balchin, *novel* Philip MacDonald *d* Henry Hathaway *ph* Milton Krasner *m* Leigh Harline

Van Johnson, Vera Miles, *Cecil Parker,* Patricia Laffan, Maurice Denham, *Estelle Winwood,* Liam Redmond

Twice in a Lifetime
US 1974 74m colour TVM
Martin Rackin

A retired navy cook in San Pedro operates his own salvage tugboat.
Easy-going family comedy-drama.

w Martin Rackin d Herschel Daugherty

Ernest Borgnine, Della Reese, Arte Johnson, Slim Pickens, Herb Jeffries, Vito Scotti

Twice round the Daffodils
GB 1962 89m bw
Anglo Amalgamated / GHW (Peter Rogers)

Comic and serious episodes in the lives of male patients at a TB sanatorium.
Acceptable broadening, almost in *Carry On* style, of a modestly successful play.

w Norman Hudis, *play* Ring for Catty by Patrick Cargill, Jack Beale *d* Gerald Thomas *ph* Alan Hume *m* Bruce Montgomery

Juliet Mills, Donald Sinden, Donald Houston, Kenneth Williams, Ronald Lewis, Joan Sims, Andrew Ray, Lance Percival, Jill Ireland, Sheila Hancock, Nanette Newman

Twilight for the Gods
US 1958 120m Eastmancolor
U-I (Gordon Kay)

The captain of an old sailing ship takes her for a last voyage from Mexico to Tahiti.
Dull and miscast adventure story lacking the spark of the original novel; watchable only for the travelogue elements.

w Ernest K. Gann, from his novel *d* Joseph Pevney *ph* Irving Glassberg *m* Joseph Gershenson

Rock Hudson, Cyd Charisse, Arthur Kennedy, Leif Erickson, Charles McGraw, Ernest Truex, Richard Haydn, Wallace Ford, Celia Lovsky, Vladimir Sokoloff

'Rock Hudson has difficulty in suggesting a dedicated seaman who has served under sail for thirty years.'—*MFB*

Twilight of Honor
US 1963 115m bw Panavision
MGM / Perlsea
GB title: *The Charge Is Murder*

A young small-town lawyer defends a neurotic no-good on a murder charge.
Modest courtroom melodrama in which the detail is better than the main plot.

w Henry Denker, *novel* Al Dewlen *d* Boris Sagal *ph* Philip Lathrop *m* John Green

Richard Chamberlain, *Claude Rains*, Joey Heatherton, Nick Adams, Joan Blackman, James Gregory, Pat Buttram, Jeanette Nolan

Twin Beds*
US 1942 84m bw
Edward Small

A married couple are embarrassed by the antics of a drunken neighbour.
Slight pretext for a pretty funny old-fashioned farce.

w Curtis Kenyon, Kenneth Earl, E. Edwin Moran, *play* Margaret Mayo, Edward Salisbury Field *d Tim Whelan ph* Hal Mohr *m* Dmitri Tiomkin

George Brent, Joan Bennett, *Mischa Auer*, Una Merkel, Glenda Farrell, Ernest Truex, Margaret Hamilton, Charles Coleman

The Twinkle in God's Eye
US 1955 73m bw
Republic (Mickey Rooney)

A parson rebuilds a church in a western town where his father was killed by Indians.
Amiable if unlikely western drama with the star more convincing than one might expect.

w P. J. Wolfson *d* George Blair *ph* Bud Thackery *m* Van Alexander

Mickey Rooney, Hugh O'Brian, Colleen Gray, Michael Connors, Don Barry

Twinky
GB 1969 98m Technicolor
Rank / World Film Services (Clive Sharp)
US title: *Lola*

A 16-year-old London schoolgirl marries a dissolute 40-year-old American author.
Dreary sex comedy drama, the fag end of London's swinging sixties.

w Norman Thaddeus Vane *d* Richard Donner *ph* Walter Lassally *m* John Scott

Charles Bronson, Susan George, Trevor Howard, Michael Craig, Honor Blackman, Robert Morley, Jack Hawkins

Twins of Evil
GB 1971 87m Eastmancolor
Rank / Hammer (Harry Fine, Michael Style)

Identical Austrian twins become devotees of a vampire cult.
Vampire-chasing Puritans add a little flavour to a routine Hammer horror.

w Tudor Gates *d* John Hough *ph* Dick Bush *m* Harry Robinson

Madeleine and Mary Collinson, Peter Cushing, Kathleen Byron, Dennis Price, Isobel Black

Twist around the Clock
US 1961 83m bw
Columbia / Sam Katzman

An astute manager discovers a small-town dance called the twist and promotes it nationally.
Rock around the Clock revisited, with an even lower budget and fewer shreds of talent.

w James B. Gordon *d* Oscar Rudolph
ph Gordon Avil *md* Fred Karger

Chubby Checker, the Marcels, Dion, John Cronin, Mary Mitchell

A Twist of Sand
GB 1968 91m De Luxe
UA / Christina (Fred Engel)

An ill-matched set of criminals seek hidden diamonds on Africa's skeleton coast.
Pattern melodrama of thieves falling out, quite nicely put together but with performances too high pitched.

m Marvin H. Albert, *novel* Geoffrey Jenkins
d Don Chaffey ph John Wilcox *m* Tristam Cary

Richard Johnson, Honor Blackman, Roy Dotrice, Peter Vaughan, Jeremy Kemp

Twisted Nerve
GB 1968 118m Eastmancolor
British Lion / Charter (John Boulting)

A rich, disturbed young man disguises himself as a retarded teenager in order to kill his hated stepfather.
Absurd, unpleasant, longwinded and naïvely scripted shocker, rightly attacked because it asserted that brothers of mongoloids are apt to become murderers. A long way behind the worst Hitchcock.

w Leo Marks, Roy Boulting *d* Roy Boulting
ph Harry Waxman *m* Bernard Herrmann

Hayley Mills, Hywel Bennett, Phyllis Calvert, Billie Whitelaw, Frank Finlay, *Barry Foster*, Salmaan Peer

Two a Penny
GB 1967 98m Eastmancolor
World Wide (Frank R. Jacobson)

An idle art student becomes involved in the drug racket but finally sees the light.
Naïve religious propaganda sponsored by the Billy Graham movement and featuring the evangelist in a cameo. A curiosity.

w Stella Linden *d* James F. Collier *ph* Michael Reed *m* Mike Leander

Cliff Richard, Dora Bryan, Ann Holloway, Avril Angers, Geoffrey Bayldon, Peter Barkworth

Two against the World
US 1936 64m bw
Warner (Bryan Foy)
GB title: *The Case of Mrs Pembroke*

A gutter newspaper unnecessarily digs up a sordid murder case and causes the suicide of two people involved.
Remake of *Five Star Final* with the interest boringly shifted to the do-gooders who *don't* want to publish the story.

w Michel Jacoby, *play* Louis Weitzenkorn
d William McGann *ph* Sid Hickox *m* Heinz Roemheld

Humphrey Bogart, Beverly Roberts, Helen MacKellar, Henry O'Neill, Linda Perry, Virginia Brissac

Two and Two Make Six
GB 1961 89m bw
Bryanston / Prometheus (Monja Danischewsky)

Two motor cycling couples almost accidentally swap partners.
Reasonably fresh little romantic comedy.

w Monja Danischewsky *d* Freddie Francis
ph Desmond Dickinson, Ronnie Taylor
m Norrie Paramor

George Chakiris, Janette Scott, Alfred Lynch, Jackie Lynch, Malcolm Keen, Ambrosine Philpotts, Bernard Braden

The Two Faces of Dr Jekyll
GB 1960 88m Technicolor Megascope
Hammer (Anthony Nelson-Keys)
US title: *House of Fright*

A variation on the much-filmed story: the schizo's evil half is the more handsome.
Surprisingly flat and tedious remake.

w Wolf Mankowitz, *novel* Robert Louis Stevenson *d* Terence Fisher *m* Jack Asher
m John Hollinsworth

Paul Massie, Dawn Addams, Christopher Lee, David Kossoff, Francis de Wolff

Two-Faced Woman*
US 1941 90m bw
MGM (Gottfried Reinhardt)

A ski instructress who fears she may be losing her publisher husband to another woman poses as her own more vivacious twin sister.
The failure of this scatterbrained comedy is alleged to be the reason for Garbo's premature retirement. Looked at half a century later, it is no great shakes but harmless and eager to please; what sabotages it is a shoddy production and flagging pace.

w S. N. Behrman, Salka Viertel, George Oppenheimer *d* George Cukor *ph* Joseph Ruttenberg *m* Bronislau Kaper

Greta Garbo, Melvyn Douglas, *Constance Bennett*, Roland Young, Robert Sterling, Ruth Gordon, George Cleveland

'It is almost as shocking as seeing your mother drunk.'—*Time*

Two Flags West*
US 1950 92m bw
TCF (Casey Robinson)

Sixty Confederate prisoners of war are granted an amnesty and go west to fight the Indians.
Laboured but good-looking Civil War western.

w Casey Robinson *d Robert Wise ph Leon Shamroy m* Hugo Friedhofer

Joseph Cotten, Jeff Chandler, Linda Darnell, Cornel Wilde, Dale Robertson, Jay C. Flippen, Noah Beery Jnr, Harry Von Zell

'Its period reconstruction is remarkable.'—*Gavin Lambert*

Two for the Money*
US 1971 73m colour TVM
Aaron Spelling

Two policemen become private detectives and hunt down a mass murderer.
Adequate failed pilot.

w Howard Rodman *d* Bernard L. Kowalski

Robert Hooks, Stephen Brooks, Walter Brennan, Neville Brand, Catherine Burns, Mercedes McCambridge

Two for the Road
GB 1967 113m De Luxe Panavision
TCF / Stanley Donen

An architect and his wife motoring through France recall the first twelve years of their relationship.
Fractured, fashionable light romantic comedy dressed up to seem of more significance than the gossamer thing it really is; and some of the gossamer has a Woolworth look.

w Frederic Raphael *d* Stanley Donen *ph Christopher Challis m* Henry Mancini

Albert Finney, Audrey Hepburn, Eleanor Bron, William Daniels, Claude Dauphin

Two for the Seesaw
US 1962 120m bw Panavision
UA / Seesaw / Mirisch / Argyle / Talbot (Robert Wise)

A New York dance instructress has a tempestuous affair with a Wyoming doctor on the verge of divorce.
Serious comedy or light drama, meticulously detailed but immensely long for its content and too revealing of its stage origins.

w Isabel Lennart, *play* William Gibson *d* Robert Wise *ph* Ted McCord *m* André Previn *ad* Boris Leven

Robert Mitchum, Shirley Maclaine

Two Girls and a Sailor**
US 1944 124m bw
MGM (Joe Pasternak)

The title says it all.
Loosely-linked wartime musical jamboree with first-class talent; a lively entertainment of its type.

w Richard Connell, Gladys Lehman *d* Richard Thorpe *ph* Robert Surtees *m* George Stoll *songs* various

June Allyson, Gloria de Haven, Van Johnson, Xavier Cugat and his Orchestra, *Jimmy Durante*, Tom Drake, Lena Horne, Carlos Ramirez, Harry James and his Orchestra, Jose Iturbi, *Gracie Allen*, Virginia O'Brien, Albert Coates

The Two-Headed Spy*
GB 1958 93m bw
Columbia (Hal E. Chester)

A bogus Nazi worms his way into the Gestapo hierarchy.
Adequate, not too exciting biopic of Colonel Alex Schottland; standard production values.

w James O'Donnell *d* André de Toth *ph* Ted Scaife *m* Bernard Schurmann

Jack Hawkins, Gia Scala, Alexander Knox, Erik Schumann, Felix Aylmer, Laurence Naismith, Donald Pleasance, Kenneth Griffith

Two Lane Blacktop
US 1971 103m Technicolor scope
Universal / Michael S. Laughlin

In the American southwest, the aimless owners of two souped-up cars have an interminable race.
Occasionally arresting, generally boring eccentricity by a big studio looking for another *Easy Rider*.

w Rudolph Wurlitzer, Will Corry *d* Monte Hellman *ph* Jack Deerson *m* Billy James

James Taylor, Warren Oates, Laurie Bird, Dennis Wilson

Two Left Feet
GB 1963 93m bw
British Lion / Roy Baker (Leslie Gilliat)

A callow 19-year-old has girl trouble.

Ponderous sex comedy with no apparent purpose but some well observed scenes.

w Roy Baker, John Hopkins, *novel* In My Solitude by David Stuart Leslie *d* Roy Baker *ph* Wilkie Cooper *m* Philip Green

Michael Crawford, Nyree Dawn Porter, Julia Foster, David Hemmings, Dilys Watling, David Lodge, Bernard Lee

Two Loves
US 1961 100m Metrocolor Cinemascope
MGM / Julian Blaustein
GB title: *Spinster*

An American teacher in New Zealand teaches Maoris and whites and falls for two men.
Pretentious romantic drama with unspeakable dialogue and eccentric characters.

w Ben Maddow, *novel* Sylva Ashton Warner *d* Charles Walters *ph* Joseph Ruttenberg *m* Bronislau Kaper

Shirley Maclaine, Jack Hawkins, Laurence Harvey, Nobu McCarthy

The Two Mrs Carrolls
US 1945 (released 1947) 99m bw
Warner (Mark Hellinger)

A psychopathic artist paints his wives as the Angel of Death, then murders them with poisoned milk.
Stilted film of an old warhorse of a play, unhappily cast but working up some last-minute tension.

w Thomas Job, *play* Martin Vale *d* Peter Godfrey *ph* Peverell Marley *m* Franz Waxman

Barbara Stanwyck, Humphrey Bogart, Alexis Smith, Nigel Bruce, Isobel Elsom, Pat O'Moore, Peter Godfrey

Two Mules for Sister Sara
US 1969 116m Technicolor Panavision
Universal / Malpaso (Martin Rackin)

A wandering cowboy kills three men trying to rape a nun, but she is not what she seems.
Vaguely unsatisfactory western with patches of nasty brutality leading to an action-packed climax.

w Albert Maltz, Budd Boetticher *d* Don Siegel *ph* Gabriel Figueroa, Gabriel Torres *m* Ennio Morricone

Clint Eastwood, Shirley Maclaine, Manolo Fabregas, Alberto Morin

Two of a Kind
US 1951 75m bw
Columbia (William Dozier)

A man is picked up by a glamorous girl who involves him in an elaborate scheme to defraud an elderly couple.
Modest suspenser.

w Lawrence Kimble, James Grunn *d* Henry Levin *ph* Burnett Guffey *m* George Duning

Edmond O'Brien, Lizabeth Scott, Terry Moore, Alexander Knox, Griff Barnett, Virginia Brissac

Two on a Bench
US 1971 73m Technicolor TVM
Universal / Link-Levinson

One of two eccentrics is known to be a spy, so the CIA brings them together and watches.
Muddled comedy.

w Richard Levinson, William Link *d* Jerry Paris

Patty Duke, Ted Bessell, Andrew Duggan, John Astin, Alice Ghostley

Two on a Guillotine*
US 1965 107m bw Panavision
Warner (William Conrad)

An illusionist arranges to be chained into his coffin at his funeral but promises to return from the dead.
Longwinded and unconvincing shocker with some effectively scary sequences.

w Henry Slesar, John Kneubuhl *d* William Conrad *ph Sam Leavitt* *m* Max Steiner

Connie Stevens, Dean Jones, Cesar Romero, Parley Baer, Virginia Gregg, Connie Gilchrist, John Hoyt

Two People
US 1973 100m Technicolor
Universal (Robert Wise)

An army deserter returns home and falls for a fashion photographer.
Solemn, inconsequential topical drama which made no impact whatever.

w Richard de Roy *d* Robert Wise *ph* Gerald Hirschfeld *m* David Shire

Peter Fonda, Lindsay Wagner, Estelle Parsons, Alan Fudge

'Sluggish pacing, lifeless looping and terminally ludicrous dialogue eventually turn the film into a travesty of its own form.'—*Variety*

Two Rode Together
US 1961 109m Technicolor
Columbia / John Ford / Shpetner

An army commander and a tough marshal negotiate with Comanches for the return of prisoners.
Substandard Ford, moderately good-looking but uninteresting of plot and dreary of development.

w Frank Nugent, *novel* Will Cook *d* John Ford *ph* Charles Lawton Jnr *m* George Duning

James Stewart, Richard Widmark, Shirley Jones, Linda Cristal, Andy Devine, John McIntire

Two Seconds*
US 1932 68m bw
Warner

In the last two seconds of his life a criminal reviews the events leading up to his execution.
Competent, pacy crime melodrama.

w Harvey Thew, *play* Elliott Lester *d Mervyn Le Roy ph* Sol Polito

Edward G. Robinson, Preston Foster, Vivienne Osborne, J. Carrol Naish, Guy Kibbee, Adrienne Dare

'A film that compels attention.'—*Mordaunt Hall, New York Times*

Two Sisters from Boston*
US 1946 112m bw
MGM (Joe Pasternak)

Two girls visiting New York find work in a Bowery saloon.
Nicely-detailed turn-of-the-century musical with pleasant talent.

w Myles Connolly *d* Henry Koster *ph* Robert Surtees *md* Charles Previn *songs* Sammy Fain, Ralph Freed

June Allyson, Kathryn Grayson, Lauritz Melchior, Jimmy Durante, Peter Lawford, Ben Blue

Two Smart People
US 1946 93m bw
MGM (Ralph Wheelwright)

A con man on parole in New Orleans is chased by a lady crook in search of his hidden loot.
Dog-eared comedy drama.

w Ethel Hill, Leslie Charteris *d* Jules Dassin *ph* Karl Freund *m* George Bassman

Lucille Ball, John Hodiak, Lloyd Nolan, Hugo Haas, Lenore Ulric, Elisha Cook Jnr, Lloyd Corrigan, Vladimir Sokoloff

2001: A Space Odyssey***
GB 1968 141m Metrocolor Panavision
MGM / Stanley Kubrick (Victor Lyndon)

From ape to modern space scientist, mankind has striven to reach the unattainable.
A lengthy montage of brilliant model work and obscure symbolism, this curiosity slowly gathered commercial momentum and came to be cherished by longhairs who used it as a trip without LSD.

w Stanley Kubrick, Arthur C. Clarke, *story* The Sentinel by Arthur C. Clarke *d* Stanley Kubrick *ph Geoffrey Unsworth, John Alcott m* various classics *pd Tony Masters, Harry Lange, Ernie Archer ad* John Hoesli

'Somewhere between hypnotic and immensely boring.'—*Renata Adler*

'Morally pretentious, intellectually obscure and inordinately long . . . intensely exciting visually, with that peculiar artistic power which comes from obsession . . . a film out of control, an infuriating combination of exactitude on small points and incoherence on large ones.'—*Arthur Schlesinger Jnr*

Two Thousand Women
GB 1944 97m bw
GFD / Gainsborough (Edward Black)

Two pilots try to rescue British women from a French concentration camp.
Routine mix of laughter and tears; hardly an outstanding film of its time, but mildly entertaining.

w Frank Launder, Sidney Gilliat *d* Frank Launder

Phyllis Calvert, Flora Robson, Patricia Roc, Renée Houston, Anne Crawford, Jean Kent, James McKechnie, Reginald Purdell, Robert Arden, Thora Hird, Dulcie Gray, Carl Jaffe, Muriel Aked

Two Tickets to Broadway
GB 1951 106m Technicolor
RKO

Small-town college girl finds romance and success in the big city.
Very mild musical with TV studio backdrop.

w Sid Silvers, Hal Kanter *d* James V. Kern *ph* Edward Cronjager, Harry J. Wild *m* Walter Scharf

Janet Leigh, Eddie Bracken, Gloria de Haven, Tony Martin, Barbara Lawrence, *Joe Smith and Charlie Dale*

Two Way Stretch**
GB 1960 87m bw
British Lion / Shepperton (M. Smedley Aston)

Three convicts break jail to rob a maharajah.
Amusing comedy with good performances and situations, unofficially borrowed in part from *Convict 99*.

w John Warren, Len Heath d Robert Day ph Geoffrey Faithfull *m* Ken Jones

Peter Sellers, *Lionel Jeffries*, Wilfrid Hyde White, Bernard Cribbins, David Lodge, Maurice

Denham, Beryl Reid, Liz Fraser, Irene Handl, George Woodbridge

Two Weeks in Another Town*
US 1962 107m Metrocolor Cinemascope
MGM (John Houseman)

An ex-alcoholic film director gets his comeback chance in Rome but is plagued by old memories.
Self-indulgent melodrama with entertaining patches for *cinéastes*, especially those who saw *The Bad and the Beautiful*.

w Charles Schnee, novel Irwin Shaw *d* Vincente Minnelli *ph* Milton Krasner *m* David Raksin

Kirk Douglas, Edward G. Robinson, Cyd Charisse, Daliah Lavi, George Hamilton, Claire Trevor, Rosanna Schiaffino, James Gregory, George Macready

Two Weeks with Love*
US 1950 92m Technicolor
MGM (Jack Cummings)

Adventures on a family summer holiday at the turn of the century.
Pleasant family musical.

w John Larkin, Dorothy Kingsley *d* Roy Rowland *ph* Al Gilks *m* Georgie Stoll

Jane Powell, Ricardo Montalban, Louis Calhern, Ann Harding, Phyllis Kirk, Debbie Reynolds, Carleton Carpenter, Clinton Sundberg

Two Years before the Mast*
US 1946 98m bw
Paramount

In the mid-19th century, a writer becomes a sailor to expose bad conditions.
Well-made but unconvincing-looking picturization of a famous book.

w Seton I. Miller, George Bruce, *book* Richard Henry Dana *d* John Farrow *ph* Ernest Laszlo *m* Victor Young

Alan Ladd, Brian Donlevy, William Bendix, Barry Fitzgerald, Howard da Silva, Albert Dekker, Luis Van Rooten, Darryl Hickman

Tycoon
US 1947 129m Technicolor
RKO

An engineer is hired to drive a tunnel through the Andes, and starts a feud with his boss when he falls in love with his daughter.
Boring, studio-set action saga with too many stops for romance.

w Borden Chase, John Twist *d* Richard Wallace *ph* Harry J. Wild *m* Leigh Harline

John Wayne, Cedric Hardwicke, Laraine Day, James Gleason, Judith Anderson, Anthony Quinn, Grant Withers

Typhoon
US 1940 70m Technicolor
Paramount (Anthony Veiller)

On a Dutch Guianan island, two sailors find a girl who has been a castaway since childhood.
One of Lamour's several sarongers, quite entertaining in its way and commendably brisk.

w Allen Rivkin *d* Louis King *ph* William Mellor *m* Frederick Hollander

Dorothy Lamour, Robert Preston, Lynne Overman, J. Carrol Naish, Frank Reicher

U

The Ugly American
US 1962 120m Eastmancolor
U-I / George Englund

A publisher is made ambassador to a south-east Asian state.
Self-dating anti-communist drama which was muddled and boring when new.

w Stewart Stern, *novel* William J. Lederer, Eugene Burdick *d* George Englund

Marlon Brando, Eiji Okada, Sandra Church, Pat Hingle, Arthur Hill, Jocelyn Brando, *Kukrit Pramoj*

The Ugly Dachshund*
US 1965 93m Technicolor
Walt Disney (Winston Hibler)

A dachshund bitch fosters among its puppies an orphan Great Dane.
Cheerful, fast-moving animal farce.

w Albert Aley, *novel* G. B. Stern *d* Norman Tokar *ph* Edward Colman *m* George Bruns

Dean Jones, Suzanne Pleshette, Charles Ruggles, Kelly Thordsen, Parley Baer, Mako, Charles Lane

The Ultimate Warrior
US 1975 94m Technicolor
Warner (Fred Weintraub, Paul Heller)

In AD 2012 New York is ruled by a gangster, the atmosphere is poisoned, and the only hope is a new community on an island off North Carolina.
Curious pretentious fantasy without the courage of its convictions or much entertainment value.

wd Robert Clouse *ph* Gerald Hirschfeld *m* Gil Melle

Yul Brynner, Max Von Sydow, Joanna Miles, William Smith, Richard Kelton, Stephen McHattie

'Less a prophetic vision than a kind of thick-ear *West Side Story.'—Richard Combs*

Ulysses*
Italy 1954 103m Technicolor
Lux Film / Ponti–de Laurentiis (Fernando Cinquini)

Ulysses and his crew sail under the curse of Cassandra, and encounter Circe, the sirens and the cyclops.
Peripatetic adventure yarn not too far after Homer; narrative style uncertain but highlights good.

w Franco Brusati, Mario Camerini, Ennio de Concini, Hugh Gray, Ben Hecht, Ivo Perelli, Irwin Shaw, *poem* The Odyssey by Homer *d* Mario Camerini *ph Harold Rosson* *m* Alessandro Cicognini

Kirk Douglas, Silvana Mangano, Anthony Quinn, Rosanna Podesta

Ulysses*
GB 1967 132m bw Panavision
Walter Reade (Joseph Strick)

Twenty-four hours in Dublin with a young poet and a Jewish newspaper man.
A pleasant enough literary exercise, a decent précis of an unmanageably prolix classic novel, this specialized offering would have passed unnoticed were it not for its language, which got it banned in many places but now seems mild indeed.

w Joseph Strick, Fred Haines, *novel* James Joyce *d* Joseph Strick *ph Wolfgang Suschitsky* *m* Stanley Myers

Maurice Roeves, Milo O'Shea, Barbara Jefford, T. P. McKenna, Anna Manahan, Maureen Potter

'No amount of pious invoking of Joyce's name can disguise the fact that a cheaply produced film is being sold at exorbitant prices so that someone can make his boodle off "culture".'—*John Simon*

'An act of homage in the form of readings from the book plus illustrated slides.'—*Pauline Kael*

'A facile and ludicrous reduction.'—*Stanley Kauffmann*

Ulzana's Raid
US 1972 103m Technicolor
Universal / Carter de Haven / Robert Aldrich

An ageing Indian fighter and a tenderfoot officer lead a platoon sent out to counter a murderous Apache attack.

Bloodthirsty, reactionary western with unpleasant shock moments.

w Alan Sharp *d* Robert Aldrich *ph* Joseph Biroc *m* Frank de Vol

Burt Lancaster, Bruce Davison, Jorge Luke, Richard Jaeckel, Lloyd Bochner

Uncensored
GB 1942 108m bw
GFD / Gainsborough (Edward Black)

In Brussels during the Nazi occupation, the leader of a toe-the-line paper secretly leads the patriots.
Unconvincing underground melodrama with stilted presentation and performances.

w Wolfgang Wilhelm, Terence Rattigan, Rodney Ackland, *novel* Oscar Millard *d* Anthony Asquith

Eric Portman, Phyllis Calvert, Griffith Jones, Raymond Lovell, Peter Glenville, Irene Handl, Carl Jaffe, Felix Aylmer

Uncertain Glory
US 1944 102m bw
Warner (Robert Buckner)

During World War II, a French playboy sacrifices himself for his country.
Tame star vehicle needing more action and less philosophy.

w Laszlo Vadnay, Max Brand *d* Raoul Walsh *ph* Sid Hickox *m* Adolph Deutsch

Errol Flynn, Paul Lukas, Jean Sullivan, Lucile Watson, Faye Emerson, James Flavin, Douglass Dumbrille, Dennis Hoey

Unchained
US 1955 75m bw
Warner / Hall Bartlett

A new governor experiments with a prison without bars.
Decent documentary drama which reaches no great heights.

wd Hall Bartlett, *book* Prisoners Are People by Kenyon J. Scudder *ph* Virgil Miller *m* Alex North

Chester Morris, Elroy Hirsch, Barbara Hale, Todd Duncan, Johnny Johnston, Peggy Knudsen, Jerry Paris, John Qualen

Uncle Silas*
GB 1947 103m bw
GFD / Two Cities (Josef Somlo, Laurence Irving)
US title: *The Inheritance*

A young Victorian heiress finds herself menaced by her uncle and his housekeeper.
Slow-starting but superbly made period suspenser; unfortunately the characters are all sticks.

w Ben Travers, *novel* Sheridan Le Fanu *d* Charles Frank

Jean Simmons, Derrick de Marney, Katina Paxinou, Derek Bond, Esmond Knight, Sophie Stewart, Manning Whiley, Reginald Tate, Marjorie Rhodes

Unconquered
US 1947 146m Technicolor
Paramount / Cecil B. de Mille

An 18th-century English convict girl is deported to the American colonies and suffers various adventures before marrying a Virginia militiaman.
Cardboard epic, expensive and noisy but totally unpersuasive despite cannon, arrows, fire and dynamite.

w Charles Bennett, Frederic M. Frank, Jesse Lasky Jnr, *novel* Neil H. Swanson *d* Cecil B. de Mille *ph* Ray Rennahan *m* Victor Young

Paulette Goddard, Gary Cooper, Boris Karloff, Howard da Silva, Cecil Kellaway, Ward Bond, Katherine de Mille, Henry Wilcoxon, C. Aubrey Smith, Victor Varconi, Virginia Grey, Porter Hall, Mike Mazurki

'De Mille bangs the drum as loudly as ever but his sideshow has gone cold on us.'—*Richard Winnington*

'A five-million dollar celebration of Gary Cooper's virility, Paulette Goddard's femininity, and the American frontier spirit.'—*Time*

The Undefeated
US 1969 119m De Luxe Panavision
TCF (Robert L. Jacks)

After the Civil War, two colonels from opposite sides meet on the Rio Grande.
Sprawling, lethargic star western with moments of glory.

w James Lee Barrett *d* Andrew V. McLaglen *ph* William H. Clothier *m* Hugo Montenegro

John Wayne, Rock Hudson, Lee Meriwether, Tony Aguilar, Roman Gabriel

Under Capricorn
GB 1949 117m Technicolor
Transatlantic (Sidney Bernstein, Alfred Hitchcock)

In Australia in 1830 an English immigrant stays with his cousin Henrietta, who has become a dipsomanic because of her husband's cruelty.
Cardboard 'woman's picture' with elements of *Rebecca,* shot with vestiges of Hitch's ten-minute take. A pretty fair disaster.

w James Bridie, *novel* Helen Simpson *d* Alfred Hitchcock *ph* Jack Cardiff, Paul Beeson, Ian Craig *m* Richard Addinsell

Ingrid Bergman, Joseph Cotten, Michael Wilding, Margaret Leighton, Jack Watling, Cecil Parker, Denis O'Dea

Under Milk Wood*
GB 1971 88m Technicolor
Timon (Hugo French, Jules Buck)

Life in the Welsh village of Llareggub, as seen by the poet's eye.
Attractive but vaguely unsatisfactory screen rendering of an essentially theatrical event (originally a radio play); everything is much too literal, a real place instead of a fantasy.

wd Andrew Sinclair, *play Dylan Thomas* *ph* Bob Huke *m* Brian Gascoigne

Richard Burton, Elizabeth Taylor, Peter O'Toole, Glynis Johns, Vivien Merchant, Sian Phillips, Victor Spinetti, Rachel Thomas, Angharad Rees, Ann Beach

Under My Skin
US 1949 86m bw
TCF (Casey Robinson)

A crooked jockey is idolized by his son and finally reforms rather than disillusion the boy.
Hokey sentimental melodrama with racetrack backgrounds.

w Casey Robinson, *short story* My Old Man by Ernest Hemingway *d* Jean Negulesco *ph* Joseph La Shelle *m* Daniele Amfitheatrof

John Garfield, Micheline Presle, Luther Adler, Orley Lindgren, Ann Codee

Under Ten Flags
US 1960 92m bw
Paramount / Dino de Laurentiis

In World War II, a German surface raider in disguise menaces British shipping.
Muddled naval epic with too many allegiances.

w Vittorio Petrilli, Duilio Coletti, Ulrich Mohr, William Douglas Home *d* Duilio Coletti, Silvio Narizzano *ph* Aldo Tonti *m* Nino Rota

Van Heflin, Charles Laughton, John Ericson, Mylène Demongeot, Cecil Parker, Folco Lulli, Alex Nicol, Liam Redmond

Under the Red Robe*
GB 1937 82m bw
(TCF) Robert T. Kane

A hell-raising nobleman is persuaded by Cardinal Richelieu to unmask the ringleader of an anti-monarchist conspiracy.
Smart, unusual swashbuckler on the lines of *The Prisoner of Zenda,* modestly but quite effectively made.

w Lajos Biro, Philip Lindsay, J. L. Hodson, *novel* Stanley J. Weyman *d Victor Sjostrom* *ph* Georges Périnal

Conrad Veidt, Raymond Massey, Annabella, Romney Brent, Sophie Stewart, Wyndham Goldie, Lawrence Grant

Under the Yum Yum Tree
US 1963 110m Eastmancolor
Columbia / Sonnis / Swift (Frederick Brisson)

Two college students have a trial marriage in an apartment block with a lecherous landlord.
Coy, non-erotic and extremely tedious comedy which runs out of jokes after reel one.

w Lawrence Roman, David Swift *d* David Swift *ph* Joseph Biroc *m* Frank de Vol

Jack Lemmon, Carol Lynley, Dean Jones, Imogene Coca, Edie Adams, Paul Lynde, Robert Lansing

Under Two Flags*
US 1936 111m bw
TCF (Raymond Griffith)

A dashing French Foreign Legionaire is helped by a café girl.
Despite a highly predictable plot (of *Destry Rides Again)* this was a solidly-produced epic with a nice deployment of star talent.

w W. P. Lipscomb, Walter Ferris, *novel* 'Ouida' *d Frank Lloyd* *ph* Ernest Palmer *m* Louis Silvers

Ronald Colman, Claudette Colbert, Rosalind Russell, Victor McLaglen, J. Edward Bromberg, Nigel Bruce, Herbert Mundin, Gregory Ratoff, C. Henry Gordon, John Carradine, Onslow Stevens

Under Your Hat*
GB 1940 79m bw
Grand National (Jack Hulbert)

Film stars chase spies and recover a stolen carburettor.
Light-hearted adaptation of a stage musical, showing the stars in their best film form.

w Rodney Ackland, Anthony Kimmins, *play* Jack Hulbert, Archie Menzies, Geoffrey Kerr, Arthur Macrae *d* Maurice Elvey

Jack Hulbert, Cicely Courtneidge, Austin Trevor, Leonora Corbett, Cecil Parker, H. F. Maltby, Glynis Johns, Charles Oliver

Undercover Man*
US 1949 89m bw
Columbia (Robert Rossen)

US treasury agents indict a gang leader for tax evasion.
Good semi-documentary crime melodrama based on the Al Capone case.

w Sidney Boehm, Malvin Wald *d Joseph H. Lewis ph* Burnett Guffey *m* George Duning

Glenn Ford, Nina Foch, Barry Kelley, James Whitmore, David Wolf, Esther Minciotti

Undercurrent*
US 1946 116m bw
MGM (Pandro S. Berman)

A professor's daughter marries an industrialist and is frightened and finally endangered by the mystery surrounding his brother.
Overlong suspenser with solid performances and production values; a variation on *Gaslight.*

w Edward Chodorov, *story* Thelma Strabel *d* Vincente Minnelli *ph* Karl Freund *m* Herbert Stothart

Katharine Hepburn, Robert Taylor, Robert Mitchum, Edmund Gwenn, Marjorie Main, Jayne Meadows, Clinton Sundberg, Dan Tobin

Underground
US 1941 95m bw
Warner (William Jacobs)

Underground leaders in Germany during World War II send out radio messages under the noses of the Nazis.
Forgotten actioner, quite solidly made.

w Charles Grayson *d* Vincent Sherman *ph* Sid Hickox *m* Adolph Deutsch

Jeffrey Lynn, Philip Dorn, Karen Verne, Mona Maris, Frank Reicher, Martin Kosleck, Ilka Gruning

Underground
US 1970 100m De Luxe
UA / Levy–Gardner–Laven

An American paratrooper joins a French resistance group to kidnap a Nazi general.
Routine war actioner.

w Ron Bishop, Andy Lewis *d* Arthur H. Nader *ph* Ken Talbot *m* Stanley Myers

Robert Goulet, Danièle Gaubert, Laurence Dobkin, Carl Duering

The Underground Man
US 1974 100m colour TVM
Paramount (Philip L. Parslow)
aka: *Archer*

A private eye seeks a missing husband and father-in-law.
Dull adaptation of a John Ross Macdonald novel. A series, *Archer,* ensued but was quickly scuttled.

w Douglas Heyes *d* Paul Wendkos

Peter Graves, Celeste Holm, Sharon Farrell, Jim Hutton, Jack Klugman, Kay Lenz, Vera Miles, Judith Anderson

Underworld USA*
US 1960 99m bw
Columbia / Globe (Samuel Fuller)

A young gangster takes elaborate revenge for the killing of his father.
Violent syndicate melodrama with a semi-documentary veneer and some brutal scenes. Well done but heavy going.

wd Samuel Fuller ph Hal Mohr m Harry Sukman

Cliff Robertson, Beatrice Kay, Larry Gates, Dolores Dorn, *Robert Emhardt,* Paul Dubov, Richard Rust

The Undying Monster*
US 1943 63m bw
TCF
GB title: *The Hammond Mystery*

A curse hangs over the English ancestral home of the Hammonds.
Silly but well-photographed and directed minor horror on wolf man lines.

w Lillie Hayward, Michel Jacoby, *novel* Jessie D. Kerruish *d John Brahm ph Lucien Ballard m* Emil Newman, David Raksin

James Ellison, John Howard, Heather Angel, Bramwell Fletcher, Heather Thatcher, Eily Malyon, Halliwell Hobbes, Aubrey Mather

Unearthly Stranger*
GB 1963 75m bw
Independent Artists (Julian Wintle, Leslie Parkyn, Albert Fennell)

Scientists working on a time-space formula find that the bride of one of them is an alien in search of their secret.
Surprisingly effective minor science fiction, in some ways all the better for its modest, TV-style production values.

w Rex Carlton d John Krish ph Reg Wyer *m* Edward Williams

John Neville, Gabriella Licudi, Philip Stone, Jean Marsh, Patrick Newell, Warren Mitchell

The Unfaithful*
US 1947 109m bw
Warner (Jerry Wald)

A wife gets involved in a murder while her husband is out of town.

Glossy romantic melodrama, an unofficial remake of *The Letter*.

w David Goodis, James Gunn *d* Vincent Sherman *ph* Ernest Haller *m* Max Steiner

Ann Sheridan, Zachary Scott, Lew Ayres, Eve Arden, Steve Geray, Jerome Cowan, John Hoyt

Unfaithfully Yours**
US 1948 105m bw
TCF (Preston Sturges)

An orchestral conductor believes his wife is unfaithful, and while conducting a concert thinks of three different ways of dealing with the situation.
A not entirely happy mixture of romance, farce, melodrama and wit, but in general a pretty entertaining concoction and the last major film of its talented writer-director.

wd Preston Sturges ph Victor Milner *m* Alfred Newman

Rex Harrison, Linda Darnell, Barbara Lawrence, Rudy Vallee, Kurt Kreuger, Lionel Stander, *Edgar Kennedy, Al Bridge*, Julius Tannen, Torben Meyer, Robert Greig

Unfinished Business
US 1941 95m bw
Universal (Gregory La Cava)

A wife has thoughts that she should have married her husband's brother.
Smooth but disappointing romantic comedy; the detail is good enough, but it sadly lacks drive.

w Eugene Thackery *d* Gregory La Cava *ph* Joseph Valentine *m* Franz Waxman

Irene Dunne, Robert Montgomery, Eugene Pallette, Preston Foster, Walter Catlett, June Clyde, Phyllis Barry, Esther Dale, Samuel S. Hinds

The Unfinished Dance
US 1947 101m Technicolor
MGM

The young star of a ballet school becomes jealous of a talented newcomer, and causes her injury in an accident.
The delicacies of the French original, *La Mort du Cygne*, give way to standard Hollywood hokum and produce an accomplished but totally uninteresting film.

w Myles Connolly, *story* Paul Morand *d* Henry Koster *ph* Robert Surtees *md* Herbert Stothart

Margaret O'Brien, Cyd Charisse, Karin Booth, Danny Thomas, Esther Dale

'The same old story, with pathos, humour and ballet substituted for pathos, humour and chorus girls.'—*MFB*

The Unforgiven*
US 1960 125m Technicolor Panavision
UA / James Productions / Hecht–Hill–Lancaster (James Hill)

A rancher's daughter is suspected of being an Indian orphan, and violence results.
Good-looking, expensive but muddled racist western, hard to enjoy.

w Ben Maddow, *novel* Alan le May *d* John Huston *ph Franz Planer m* Dmitri Tiomkin

Burt Lancaster, Audrey Hepburn, Audie Murphy, Lillian Gish, Charles Bickford, Doug McClure, John Saxon, Joseph Wiseman, Albert Salmi

'How much strain can a director's reputation take? Of late, John Huston seems to have been trying to find out. I think he has carried the experiment too far with *The Unforgiven* . . . a work of profound phoniness, part adult western, part that *Oklahoma!* kind of folksy Americana.'—*Dwight MacDonald*

'Ludicrous . . . a hodgepodge of crudely stitched sententiousness and lame story-conference inspirations.'—*Stanley Kauffmann*

The Unguarded Moment
US 1956 85m Technicolor
U-I (Gordon Kay)

A schoolmistress who receives anonymous love notes from a psychotic pupil is discredited by his even more unbalanced father.
Well-meaning but boring melodrama with the star attractively out of her usual element.

w Herb Meadow, Larry Marcus, *story* Rosalind Russell *d* Harry Keller *ph* William Daniels *m* Herman Stein

Esther Williams, George Nader, John Saxon, *Edward Andrews*, Jack Albertson

Unholy Partners*
US 1941 95m bw
MGM (Samuel Marx)

The editor of a sensational newspaper has to accept finance from a gangster, but friction results when the newspaper exposes some of the gangster's activities.
Agreeable twenties melodrama with two solid stars battling it out.

w Earl Baldwin, Lesser Samuels, Bartlett Cormack *d* Mervyn Le Roy *ph* George Barnes *m* David Snell

Edward G. Robinson, Edward Arnold, Laraine Day, Marsha Hunt, William T. Orr, Don Beddoe, Charles Dingle, Walter Kingsford, Marcel Dalio

The Unholy Three*
US 1930 75m bw
MGM

A ventriloquist, a strong man and a dwarf plot a series of crimes.
Curious early talkie first made in 1925 with the same star, whose last film this is.

w J. C. Nugent, Elliott Nugent, *play* Clarence Aaron Robbins *d* Jack Conway *ph* Percy Hilburn

Lon Chaney, Harry Earles, Lila Lee, Elliott Nugent, John Miljan, Ivan Linow

The Unholy Wife
US 1957 94m Technicolor RKOscope
RKO (John Farrow)

A bored wife shoots a friend in mistake for her husband but is sentenced for the accidental death of her mother-in-law.
Totally uninteresting melodrama in the *Double Indemnity* style, professionally made but turgid.

w Jonathan Latimer *d* John Farrow *ph* Lucien Ballard *m* Daniele Amfitheatrof

Diana Dors, Rod Steiger, Tom Tully, Beulah Bondi, Marie Windsor, Arthur Franz, Luis Van Rooten

The Uninvited**
US 1944 98m bw
Paramount (Charles Brackett)

A girl returns to her family house and is haunted by her mother's spirit, which seems to be evil.
One of the cinema's few genuine ghost stories, and a good one, though encased in a rather stiff production; it works up to a fine pitch of frenzy.

w Dodie Smith, novel Uneasy Freehold by Dorothy Macardle *d Lewis Allen ph* Charles Lang *m* Victor Young

Ray Milland, Ruth Hussey, *Gail Russell*, Donald Crisp, Cornelia Otis Skinner, Dorothy Stickney, Barbara Everest, Alan Napier

'Thirty-five first-class jolts, not to mention a well-calculated texture of minor frissons.' *—James Agee*

'Still manages to ice the blood with its implied horrors . . . you can almost smell the ghostly mimosa.'*—Peter John Dyer, 1966*

Union Pacific**
US 1939 133m bw
Paramount / Cecil B. de Mille

Indians and others cause problems for the railroad builders.
Standard big-scale western climaxing in a spectacular wreck; not exactly exciting, but very watchable.

w Walter de Leon, C. Gardner Sullivan, Jesse Lasky Jnr *d Cecil B. de Mille ph* Victor Milner, Dewey Wrigley *m* George Antheil *ad* Hans Dreier, Roland Anderson

Barbara Stanwyck, Joel McCrea, Akim Tamiroff, Robert Preston, Lynne Overman, Brian Donlevy, Robert Barrat, Anthony Quinn, Stanley Ridges, Henry Kolker, Evelyn Keyes, Regis Toomey

Union Station**
US 1950 80m bw
Paramount (Jules Schermer)

Kidnappers nominate a crowded railroad station as their ransom collection point.
Compelling little thriller modelled after *Naked City*, with real locations and plenty of excitement.

w Sidney Boehm, *novel* Thomas Walsh *d Rudolph Maté ph* Daniel L. Fapp *m* Irvin Talbot

William Holden, *Barry Fitzgerald*, Nancy Olson, *Lyle Bettger*, Jan Sterling, Allene Roberts

Universal Soldier
GB 1971 96m colour
Appaloosa / Ionian (Frank J. Schwarz, Donald L. Factor)

A mercenary returns to London but can't escape his past.
Solemnly meaningful melodrama on a tight budget.

wd Cy Endfield *ph* Tony Imi *m* Philip Goodhand-Tait

George Lazenby, Edward Judd, Benito Carruthers, Germaine Greer, Rudolph Walker

The Unknown Man
US 1951 86m bw
MGM (Robert Thomsen)

A civil court lawyer of high principles successfully undertakes a criminal case, finds his client was really guilty, and sets matters straight.
Contrived but entertaining morality with standard production and performances.

w Ronald Millar, George Froeschel *d* Richard Thorpe *ph* William Mellor *m* Conrad Salinger

Walter Pidgeon, Ann Harding, Lewis Stone, Barry Sullivan, Keefe Brasselle, Eduard Franz, Richard Anderson, Dawn Addams

Unman, Wittering and Zigo
GB 1971 102m colour
Paramount / Mediarts

A nervous schoolmaster discovers that his predecessor was murdered by the boys.

Macabre school story which overreaches itself and peters out.

w Simon Raven, *TV play* Giles Cooper *d* John Mackenzie *ph* Geoffrey Unsworth *m* Michael J. Lewis

David Hemmings, Douglas Wilmer, Hamilton Dyce, Carolyn Seymour

Unpublished Story
GB 1942 91m bw
Columbia / Two Cities (Anthony Havelock-Allan)

A reporter exposes the Nazis behind a pacifist organization.
Ho-hum formula flagwaver with generally stilted production.

w Anatole de Grunwald, Patrick Kirwan *d* Harold French

Valerie Hobson, Richard Greene, Basil Radford, Roland Culver, Brefni O'Rourke, Miles Malleson, George Carney, André Morell

The Unsinkable Molly Brown*
US 1964 128m Metrocolor Panavision
MGM / Marten (Lawrence Weingarten)

Western orphan Molly Brown grows up determined to become a member of Denver society.
Semi-western comedy-musical about a real lady who wound up surviving the *Titanic*. Bouncy and likeable but not at all memorable.

w Helen Deutsch, *musical play* Richard Morris *d* Charles Walters *ph* Daniel L. Fapp *md* Robert Armbuster *ad* George W. Davis, Preston Ames

Debbie Reynolds, Harve Presnell, *Ed Begley*, Jack Krischen, Hermione Baddeley, Martita Hunt

The Unsuspected*
US 1947 103m bw
Warner (Charles Hoffman)

A writer-producer of radio crime shows commits a murder and is forced to follow the clues on air.
Sleek, new look mystery thriller with a disappointing plot which gives its interesting cast little to do, and allows itself to peter out in chases.

w Ranald MacDougall, *novel* Charlotte Armstrong *d Michael Curtiz ph Woody Bredell m* Leo F. Forbstein *ad* Anton Grot

Claude Rains, Joan Caulfield, Audrey Totter, Constance Bennett, Michael North, Hurd Hatfield, Fred Clark

Untamed
US 1955 109m Technicolor Cinemascope
TCF (Bert E. Friedlob, William A. Bacher)

A Dutchman and an Irish girl meet again on a Boer trek to South Africa, and survive Zulu attacks.
A long and involved epic-style plot provides standard excitements and predictable romantic complications.

w Talbot Jennings, Michael Blankfort, Frank Fenton, *novel* Helga Moray *d* Henry King *ph* Leo Tover *m* Franz Waxman

Tyrone Power, Susan Hayward, Richard Egan, John Justin, Agnes Moorehead, Rita Moreno, Hope Emerson, Brad Dexter, Henry O'Neill

'A not unenjoyable essay in hokum.'—*MFB*

Untamed Frontier
US 1952 78m Technicolor
U-I (Leonard Goldstein)

The son of an unpopular Texan landowner commits murder.
Stolid minor western.

w Gerald Drayson Adams, Gwen and John Bagni *d* Hugo Fregonese *ph* Charles P. Boyle *m* Hans Salter

Joseph Cotten, Shelley Winters, Scott Brady, Suzan Ball, Minor Watson

Until They Sail
US 1957 95m bw Cinemascope
MGM (Charles Schnee)

Four New Zealand sisters have wartime romances.
Solid 'woman's picture', well enough presented.

w Robert Anderson, *novel* James A. Michener *d* Robert Wise *ph* Joseph Ruttenberg *m* David Raksin

Jean Simmons, Joan Fontaine, Paul Newman, Piper Laurie, Charles Drake, Wally Cassell, Sandra Dee

Unwed Father
US 1974 74m colour TVM
David Wolper (Lawrence Turman, Stan Margulies)

A teenager wants custody of his illegitimate child.
What will they think of next? Something more entertaining, one hopes.

w W. Hermanos, Carol McKeand *d* Jeremy Kagan

Joe Bottoms, Kay Lenz, Joseph Campanella, Beverly Garland, Kim Hunter

Up from the Beach*
US 1965 98m bw Cinemascope
TCF / Panoramic (Christian Ferry)

Just after D-Day, GIs have trouble in a Normandy village.
A kind of subdued sequel to *The Longest Day*, well made for war action addicts, but barely memorable.

w Stanley Mann, Claude Brule, *novel* Epitaph for an Enemy by George Barr *d Robert Parrish ph Walter Wottitz m* Edgar Cosma

Cliff Robertson, Red Buttons, Françoise Rosay, Marius Goring, Irina Demick, Broderick Crawford, James Robertson Justice, Slim Pickens

Up in Arms**
US 1944 106m Technicolor
Samuel Goldwyn

A hypochondriac joins the army.
Loose, generally pleasant introductory vehicle for Danny Kaye.

w Don Hartman, Robert Pirosh, Allen Boretz *d* Elliott Nugent *ph* Ray Rennahan *md* Ray Heindorf, Louis Forbes

Danny Kaye, Dinah Shore, Constance Dowling, Dana Andrews, Louis Calhern, Lyle Talbot

Up in Central Park
US 1948 88m bw
U-I

In turn-of-the-century New York, an Irish girl becomes involved in a crooked political set up.
Stiff and unyielding star musical.

w Karl Tunberg *d* William A. Seiter *ph* Milton Krasner *songs* Sigmund Romberg

Deanna Durbin, Vincent Price, Dick Haymes, Albert Sharpe, Tom Powers

Up in the Cellar
US 1970 94m Movielab
AIP (William J. Immerman)

A dejected freshman tries various schemes to revenge himself on the college president.
Youth satire aimed at a number of targets which quickly became obsolete; mildly interesting sociologically.

wd Theodore J. Flicker, *novel* The Late Boy Wonder by Angus Hall *ph* Earl Roth *m* Don Randi

Wes Stern, Joan Collins, Larry Hagman, Judy Pace

Up in the World
GB 1956 91m bw
Rank (Hugh Stewart)

A window cleaner becomes friendly with a boy millionaire.
Slow and unattractive comedy star vehicle.

w Jack Davies, Henry Blyth, Peter Blackmore *d* John Paddy Carstairs *ph* Jack Cox *m* Philip Green

Norman Wisdom, Martin Carida, Jerry Desmonde, Maureen Swanson, Ambrosine Philpotts, Colin Gordon

Up Periscope
US 1959 111m bw
Warner / Lakeside (Aubrey Schenck)

During World War II a submarine frogman is landed on a Pacific island to steal a Japanese code book.
Stock adventure story given stock presentation.

w Richard Landau, *novel* Robb White *d* Gordon Douglas *ph* Carl Guthrie *m* Ray Heindorf

James Garner, Edmond O'Brien, Alan Hale Jnr, Carleton Carpenter

Up Pompeii
GB 1971 90m Technicolor

A wily slave outwits Nero and escapes the eruption of Vesuvius.
Yawnmaking spinoff of a lively TV comedy series: the jokes just lie there, and die there.

w Sid Colin *d* Bob Kellett *ph* Ian Wilson *m* Carl Davis

Frankie Howerd, Patrick Cargill, Michael Hordern, Barbara Murray, Lance Percival, Bill Fraser, Adrienne Posta
† Sequels: *Up the Front, Up the Chastity Belt* (qv).

Up the Chastity Belt*
GB 1971 94m Technicolor
EMI / Associated London Films (Ned Sherrin)

Medieval adventures of the serf Lurkalot and his master Sir Coward de Custard.
Patchy pantomime which doesn't always have the courage of its own slapdash vulgarity.

w Sid Colin, Ray Galton, Alan Simpson *d* Bob Kellett *ph* Ian Wilson *m* Carl Davis

Frankie Howerd, Graham Crowden, Bill Fraser, Roy Hudd, Hugh Paddick, Anna Quayle, Eartha Kitt, Dave King, Fred Emney

Up the Creek*
GB 1958 83m bw Hammerscope
Byron (Henry Halsted)

A none-too-bright naval lieutenant is assigned command of a broken-down shore establishment.
Cheeky remake of *Oh Mr Porter*. Jokes fair, atmosphere cheerful and easy-going.

wd Val Guest *ph* Arthur Grant

David Tomlinson, Peter Sellers, Wilfrid Hyde White, Vera Day, Tom Gill, Michael Goodliffe, Reginald Beckwith, Lionel Jeffries
† Sequel: *Further Up the Creek.*

Up the Down Staircase*
US 1967 124m Technicolor
Warner / Pakula–Mulligan

Problems of a schoolteacher in one of New York's tough sections.
Earnest, well-acted, not very likeable melodrama.

w Tad Mosel, *novel* Bel Kaufman *d* Robert Mulligan *ph* Joseph Coffey *m* Fred Karlin

Sandy Dennis, Patrick Bedford, Eileen Heckart, Ruth White, Jean Stapleton, Sorrel Booke, Roy Poole

Up the Front
GB 1972 89m Technicolor
EMI / Associated London Films (Ned Sherrin)

A footman is hypnotized into enlisting in World War I and has an enemy 'plan' tattooed on his buttocks.
Threadbare end-of-the-pier romp.

w Sid Colin, Eddie Braben *d* Bob Kellett *ph* Tony Spratling *m* Patrick Greenwell *ad* Seamus Flannery

Frankie Howerd, Bill Fraser, Zsa Zsa Gabor, Stanley Holloway, Hermione Baddeley, Robert Coote, Lance Percival, Dora Bryan

Up the Junction
GB 1967 119m Techniscope
Paramount / Collinson–Crasto

A well-off girl crosses London's river to live among the workers of Clapham.
Socially obsolete sensationalism based on a television semi-documentary. An irritating heroine moves hygenically among motorbikes, discos and mild orgies.

w Roger Smith, *book* Nell Dunn *d* Peter Collinson *ph* Arthur Lavis *m* Mike Hugg, Manfred Mann

Suzy Kendall, Dennis Waterman, Adrienne Posta, Maureen Lipman, Michael Gothard, Liz Fraser, Hylda Baker, Alfie Bass

Up the River
US 1930 80m bw
Fox

An ex-convict is threatened with exposure, but his two pals escape to help him.
Very minor comedy with interesting credits.

w Maurine Watkins *d* John Ford *ph* Joseph August

Spencer Tracy, Warren Hymer, Claire Luce, Humphrey Bogart, William Collier Snr

Up the Sandbox
US 1972 98m Technicolor
Barwood / First Artists (Robert Chartoff, Irwin Winkler)

A professor's wife finds she is pregnant again and fantasizes about her future life.
Muddled comedy-drama with little point and less entertainment value.

w Paul Zindel, *novel* Anne Richardson Roiphe *d* Irwin Kershner *ph* Gordon Willis, Andy Marton *m* Billy Goldenberg *ad* Harry Horner

Barbra Streisand, David Selby, Ariane Heller, Jane Hoffman

'A magical mystery tour through the picture book mind of one Manhattan housewife.'—*Richard Combs*

Up Tight
US 1968 104m Technicolor
Paramount / Marlukin (Jules Dassin)

A black street cleaner betrays his criminal pals for money and is hunted down by them.
Ponderous black remake of *The Informer*, too schematic to make any dramatic or human impression.

w Jules Dassin, Ruby Dee, Julian Mayfield *d* Jules Dassin *ph Boris Kaufman* *m* Booker T. Jones *pd* Alexander Trauner

Raymond St Jacques, Ruby Dee, Julian Mayfield, Frank Silvera, Roscoe Lee Browne, Juanita Moore

Upstairs and Downstairs
GB 1959 101m Eastmancolor
Rank (Betty E. Box)

Newlyweds have trouble with maids and au pair girls.
Glossy, cheerful, empty-headed domestic comedy.

w Frank Harvey, *novel* Ronald Scott Thorn *d* Ralph Thomas

Michael Craig, Anne Heywood, Mylène Demongeot, James Robertson Justice, Sidney James, Daniel Massey, Claudia Cardinale, Joan Hickson, Joan Sims

Uptown Saturday Night*
US 1974 104m Technicolor
Warner / Verdon / First Artists (Melville Tucker)

Three friends pursue crooks who have inadvertently stolen a winning lottery ticket. Witless but high-spirited star comedy for blacks, with a variety of sordid backgrounds.

w Richard Wesley *d* Sidney Poitier *ph* Fred J. Koenekamp *m* Tom Scott

Sidney Poitier, Bill Cosby, Harry Belafonte, Flip Wilson, Roscoe Lee Browne, Richard Pryor, Rosalind Cash, Paula Kelly

'If it had been filmed with a white cast this collection of atrophied comedy routines would have been indistinguishable from a Monogram farce of the forties.'—*David McGillivray*

The Upturned Glass*
GB 1947 86m bw
GFD / Triton (Sydney Box, James Mason)

A Harley Street surgeon murders the woman responsible for the death of the girl he loved. Rather pointless psychopathology with an ill-explained title; an interesting example of a top star not knowing what's best for him.

w Jon P. Monaghan, Pamela Kellino *d* Lawrence Huntington *ph* Reg Wyer *m* Bernard Stevens

James Mason, Pamela Kellino, Rosamund John, Ann Stephens, Henry Oscar, Morland Graham, Brefni O'Rourke

'The psychology is genuine; so too is the tension; the camera plays some good quiet tricks.'—*William Whitebait*

V

The Vagabond King
US 1956 88m Technicolor Vistavision
Paramount (Pat Duggan)

The life and loves of French medieval poet and rebel François Villon.
Shiny, antiseptic studio-set remake of an old musical warhorse. (The 1930 version is lost; a straight version was made in 1938 as *If I Were King*.)

w Ken Englund, Noel Langley, *operetta* Rudolf Friml *d* Michael Curtiz *ph* Robert Burks *md* Victor Young, *songs* Rudolf Friml

Oreste, Kathryn Grayson, Rita Moreno, *Walter Hampden*, Leslie Nielsen, Cedric Hardwicke, William Prince

The Valachi Papers
France / Italy 1972 127m Technicolor
Euro France / de Laurentiis Intermarco (Dino de Laurentiis)

A convicted gangster talks to an FBI agent about his life in the Mafia.
Rough, violent gangster melodrama, none the better for being based on actual events.

w Stephen Geller, *book* Peter Maas *d* Terence Young *ph* Aldo Tonti *m* Riz Ortolani

Charles Bronson, Fred Valleca, Gerald S. O'Loughlin, Lino Ventura, Walter Chiari, Amedeo Nazzari, Joseph Wiseman

Valdez Is Coming
US 1970 90m De Luxe
UA / Norlan / Ira Steiner

A Mexican confronts a rancher who has double-crossed him.
Simply-conceived western which doesn't quite manage to be the classic intended.

w Roland Kibbee, David Rayfiel *d* Edwin Sherin *ph* Gabor Pogany *m* Charles Gross

Burt Lancaster, Susan Clark, Jon Cypher, Barton Heyman, Frank Silvera

Valentino
US 1951 105m Technicolor
Columbia (Edward Small)

An Italian immigrant to the US becomes a world-famous romantic film star but dies young.
Disastrously flat attempt to recapture the feel of Hollywood in the twenties as a background to a flatulent romance.

w George Bruce *d* Lewis Allen *ph* Harry Stradling *m* Heinz Roemheld

Anthony Dexter, Eleanor Parker, Richard Carlson, Patricia Medina, Joseph Calleia, Dona Drake, Lloyd Gough, Otto Kruger

'One can almost see the decorated border round the words . . . it mixes fact, speculation, needless inaccuracy and bathos.'—*Gavin Lambert*

Valerie
US 1957 80m bw
UA / Hal R. Makelim

A western rancher is accused of wounding his wife and murdering her parents.
Curious little *Rashomon*-like courtroom melodrama, quite well made and acted.

w Leonard Heidemann, Emmett Murphy *d* Gerd Oswald *ph* Ernest Laszlo *m* Albert Glasser

Anita Ekberg, Sterling Hayden, Anthony Steel, John Wengraf

The Valiant
GB/Italy 1961 89m bw
(UA) BHP / Euro International

During World War II, a battleship in Alexandria harbour is mined, and the captain tries desperately to avert disaster.
Ill-made war fodder, of no interest at any level.

w Keith Waterhouse, Willis Hall *d* Roy Baker *ph* Wilkie Cooper, Egil Woxholt *m* Christopher Whelen

John Mills, Ettore Manni, Robert Shaw, Liam Redmond, Ralph Michael, Colin Douglas, Dinsdale Landen

Valiant Is the Word for Carrie
US 1936 110m bw
RKO (Wesley Ruggles)

A childless woman devotes her life to orphan children.
Tedious soap opera.

w Claude Binyon, *novel* Barry Benefield *d* Wesley Ruggles *ph* Leo Tover

Gladys George, John Howard, Dudley Digges, Arline Judge, Harry Carey, Isabel Jewell

The Valley of Decision*
US 1945 119m bw
MGM

In old Pittsburgh, an Irish housemaid marries the master's son.
Trouble at t'mill epic romance, American style; starrily cast but not excitingly made.

w John Meehan, Sonya Levien, *novel* Marcia Davenport *d* Tay Garnett *ph* Joseph Ruttenberg *m* Herbert Stothart

Greer Garson, Gregory Peck, Lionel Barrymore, Donald Crisp, Preston Foster, Gladys Cooper, Marsha Hunt, Reginald Owen, Dan Duryea, Jessica Tandy, Barbara Everest, Marshall Thompson

The Valley of Gwangi
US 1968 95m Technicolor
Warner / Morningside

Cowboys and scientists discover prehistoric monsters in a 'forbidden' Mexican valley.
Tedious adventure yarn enhanced by good special effects.

w William E. Bast *d* James O'Connelly *ph* Erwin Hillier *m* Jerome Moross *sp Ray Harryhausen*

Richard Carlson, Laurence Naismith, James Franciscus, Gila Golan, Freda Jackson

Valley of Mystery
US 1967 90m Technicolor TVM
Universal

Survivors of a plane crash fight for survival in a South American jungle.
Or, *Five Came Back* and back and back and back . . . This version isn't even entertaining.

w Dick Nelson, Lowell Barrington *d* Josef Leytes

Richard Egan, Peter Graves, Joby Baker, Lois Nettleton, Harry Guardino, Julie Adams, Fernando Lamas

Valley of the Dolls*
US 1967 123m De Luxe Panavision
TCF / Red Lion (David Weisbart)

An innocent young actress is corrupted by Broadway and Hollywood, and takes to drugs.
Cliché-ridden but good-looking road-to-ruin melodrama from a bitchy bestseller; production values high, but the whole thing goes over the top at the end.

w Helen Deutsch, Dorothy Kingsley, *novel* Jacqueline Susann *d* Mark Robson *ph William H. Daniels* *m* John Williams *ad* Jack Martin Smith, Richard Day

Barbara Parkins, Patty Duke, Susan Hayward, Paul Burke, Sharon Tate, Martin Milner, Tony Scotti, Charles Drake, Alex Davion, Lee Grant, Robert H. Harris

Valley of the Kings
US 1954 86m Eastmancolor
MGM

Archaeologists fight looters in the tomb of a Pharaoh.
Thin as drama, with little action or suspense and dispirited acting, this hokum piece nevertheless benefits from splendid locations.

w Robert Pirosh, Karl Tunberg *d* Robert Pirosh *ph* Robert Surtees *m* Miklos Rozsa

Robert Taylor, Eleanor Parker, Carlos Thompson, Kurt Kasznar, Victor Jory

Valley of the Sun
US 1942 79m bw
RKO (Graham Baker)

A government spy in old Arizona outwits a crooked Indian agent.
Cheapjack western with nothing to commend it.

w Horace McCoy, *story* Clarence Budington Kelland *d* George Marshall *ph* Harry J. Wild *m* Paul Sawtell

James Craig, Lucille Ball, Dean Jagger, Billy Gilbert, Cedric Hardwicke, Peter Whitney, Tom Tyler, Antonio Moreno, George Cleveland

Value for Money
GB 1955 93m Technicolor Vistavision
Rank / Group Films (Sergei Nolbandov)

A Yorkshire businessman determines to broaden his outlook, and falls in love with a London showgirl.
Highly undistinguished north country romantic farce which wastes a good production and cast.

w R. F. Delderfield, William Fairchild, *novel* Derick Boothroyd *d* Ken Annakin *ph* Geoffrey Unsworth *m* Malcolm Arnold

John Gregson, Diana Dors, Susan Stephen, Derek Farr, Frank Pettingell, Jill Adams, *Ernest Thesiger*, Charles Victor, Joan Hickson

Vampira
GB 1974 88m colour
Columbia / Jack H. Wiener
US title: *Old Dracula*

A vampire count lures beauty-contest winners to

his castle and uses their blood to revive his dead wife.
Would-be spoof which falls flat on its fangs.

w Jeremy Lloyd *d* Clive Donner *ph* Tony Richmond *m* David Whitaker

David Niven, Teresa Graves, Peter Bayliss, Jennie Linden, Linda Hayden, Nicky Henson, Bernard Bresslaw, Veronica Carlson

The Vampire
US 1957 74m bw
UA / Gardner–Levy

A research scientist takes bat essence and becomes a vampire.
Silly attempt to turn a legend into science fiction: more risible than sinister.

w Pat Fielder *d* Paul Landres *ph* Jack Mackenzie *m* Gerald Fried

John Beal, Coleen Gray, Kenneth Tobey, Lydia Reed

The Vampire Bat
US 1933 71m bw
Majestic

A mad doctor kills townsfolk in search of 'blood substitute'.
Primitive but vigorous low budget chiller.

w Edward Lowe *d* Frank Strayer *ph* Ira Morgan

Lionel Atwill, Fay Wray, Melvyn Douglas, Maude Eburne, George E. Stone, Dwight Frye, Lionel Belmore

Vampire Circus
GB 1971 87m colour
Hammer (Wilbur Stark)

In 1825 a plague-ridden village is visited by a circus of animal vampires.
Silly but quite inventive horror thriller.

w Judson Kinberg *d* Robert Young *ph* Moray Grant *m* Philip Martell *ad* Scott MacGregor

Adrienne Corri, Laurence Payne, Thorley Walters, John Moulder Brown, Elizabeth Seal, Lynne Frederick, Robert Tayman, Robin Hunter

The Vampire Lovers
GB 1970 91m Technicolor
Hammer / AIP (Harry Fine, Michael Style)

A lady vampire worms her way into several noble households.
Reasonably close retelling of Sheridan Le Fanu's *Carmilla*, complete with lesbian love scenes.
Adequate production but not much spirit.

w Tudor Gates, Harry Fine, Michael Style, *novel* Carmilla by Sheridan Le Fanu, *d* Roy Ward Baker

Ingrid Pitt, Peter Cushing, Pippa Steele, Madeleine Smith, George Cole, Dawn Addams, Douglas Wilmer, Kate O'Mara

Vanessa, Her Love Story
US 1935 76m bw
MGM (David O. Selznick)

When her husband becomes insane, a Victorian lady falls for a gypsy.
Very dated romance which finished Helen Hayes's star career, for thirty years at least.

w Lenore Coffee, *novel* Hugh Walpole *d* William K. Howard *ph* Ray June

Helen Hayes, Robert Montgomery, May Robson, Otto Kruger, Lewis Stone, Henry Stephenson, Violet Kemble-Cooper, Jessie Ralph

Vanished**
US 1970 98m x 2 Technicolor TVM
Universal

The President's top adviser goes missing and is revealed as a homosexual.
Reasonably absorbing, well acted and sharply written political melodrama on the lines of *Seven Days in May*.

w Dean Riesner, *novel* Fletcher Knebel *d* Buzz Kulik

Richard Widmark, Robert Young, James Farentino, Skye Aubrey, Tom Bosley, Stephen McNally, Sheree North, Larry Hagman, Murray Hamilton, Arthur Hill, Robert Hooks, E. G. Marshall, Eleanor Parker, William Shatner

Vanishing Point*
US 1971 107m De Luxe
TCF / Cupid (Norman Spencer)

An ex-racing driver who delivers cars for a living becomes hepped up on benzedrine and leads police a rare chase through the Nevada desert.
Strange, fashionable action suspenser which is better to look at than to understand.

w Guillermo Cain *d Richard Sarafian ph John A. Alonzo md* Jimmy Brown

Barry Newman, Cleavon Little, Dean Jagger, Victoria Medlin, Paul Koslo, Bob Donner

'Uncomfortably reminiscent of *Easy Rider* as an odyssey through an unknown America in its discovery of strange alliances and unpredictable hostilities.'—*Tom Milne*

The Vanishing Virginian
US 1941 97m bw
MGM

A conservative Virginian finds that he harbours suffragettes in his household.
Life with Father in another setting; rather yawn-provoking.

w Jan Fortune, *novel* Rebecca Yancey Williams *d* Frank Borzage

Frank Morgan, Spring Byington, Kathryn Grayson, Elizabeth Patterson, Louise Beavers

Variety Girl
US 1947 83m bw
Paramount (Daniel Dare)

Of all the young hopefuls arriving in Hollywood, one girl becomes a star.
The slightest of excuses for a tour of the Paramount studios, with all the contract stars doing bits. It doesn't add up to much.

w Edmund Hartmann, Frank Tashlin, Monte Brice, Robert Welch *d* George Marshall *ph* Lionel Lindon, Stuart Thompson *md* Joseph J. Lilley, Troy Saunders

Mary Hatcher, Olga San Juan, De Forrest Kelley, Glenn Tryon; and Bob Hope, Bing Crosby, Gary Cooper, Ray Milland, Alan Ladd, Barbara Stanwyck, Paulette Goddard, Dorothy Lamour, Veronica Lake, Sonny Tufts, Joan Caulfield, William Holden, Lizabeth Scott, Burt Lancaster, Gail Russell, Diana Lynn, Sterling Hayden, Robert Preston, William Bendix, Barry Fitzgerald, Billy de Wolfe, George Pal Puppetoons, Cecil B. de Mille, Mitchell Leisen, George Marshall, Spike Jones and his City Slickers, etc

Varsity Show
US 1937 80m bw
Warner (Louis F. Edelman)

Collegians stage a revue.
Mild musical.

w Warren Duff, Richard Macaulay, Jerry Wald, Sig Herzig *d* William Keighley *ph* Sol Polito, George Barnes *ch* Busby Berkeley *songs* Richard Whiting, Johnny Mercer

Dick Powell, Priscilla Lane, Rosemary Lane, Fred Waring and his Pennsylvanians, Buck and Bubbles, Johnny 'Scat' Davis, Ted Healy

Vault of Horror*
GB 1973 86m Eastmancolor
Metromedia / Amicus (Milton Subotsky)

Five men trapped in the basement of a skyscraper tell of their recurring dreams.
All-star horror omnibus, plainly but well staged.

w Milton Subotsky, *stories* William Gaines *d* Roy Ward Baker *ph* Denys Coop *m* Douglas Gamley

Daniel Massey, Anna Massey, Terry-Thomas, Glynis Johns, Curt Jurgens, Dawn Addams, Michael Craig, Edward Judd, Tom Baker, Denholm Elliott

The Velvet Touch*
US 1948 97m bw
(RKO) Independent Artists

A famous actress murders her producer and is struck by conscience but allows a detective to find his own way to the truth.
Solid murder melodrama with an excellent theatrical atmosphere.

w Leo Rosten *d* John Gage *ph* Joseph Walker *m* Leigh Harline

Rosalind Russell, Leo Genn, Sidney Greenstreet, Claire Trevor, Leon Ames, Frank McHugh

Vendetta
US 1950 84m bw
RKO / Howard Hughes

The daughter of an esteemed Corsican family takes vengeance on her father's enemies.
Outmoded ethnic melodrama with nothing to recommend it.

w W. R. Burnett, *novel* Columba by Prosper Mérimée *d* Mel Ferrer *ph* Franz Planer, Al Gilks *m* Constantin Bakaleinikoff

Faith Domergue, George Dolenz, Donald Buka, Hilary Brooke, Nigel Bruce, Joseph Calleia, Hugo Haas

The Venetian Affair
US 1966 92m Metrocolor Panavision
MGM / Jerry Thorpe

A reporter investigates the death in Venice of an American diplomat.
Uninteresting and complicated spy thriller with pleasant locations.

w E. Jack Neuman, *novel* Helen MacInnes *d* Jerry Thorpe *ph* Milton Krasner, Enzo Serafin *m* Lalo Schifrin

Robert Vaughn, Karl Boehm, Elke Sommer, Ed Asner, Boris Karloff, Felicia Farr, Roger C. Carmel, Luciana Paluzzi, Joe de Santis

Venetian Bird*
GB 1952 95m bw
Rank / British Film Makers (Betty E. Box)
US title: *The Assassin*

A private detective goes to Venice to reward a wartime partisan, who turns out to have become a notorious criminal.
Standard action fare with a nod to *The Third Man* but not much excitement or sense of place.

w Victor Canning, from his novel *d* Ralph Thomas *ph* Ernest Steward *m* Nino Rota

Richard Todd, Eva Bartok, John Gregson, George Coulouris, Margot Grahame, Walter Rilla, Sidney James

Vengeance
GB / Germany 1962 83m bw
CCC / Raymond Stross

After a fatal accident, the brain of a tycoon is kept alive and persuades a doctor to find his murderer.
Twisty remake of *Donovan's Brain* (qv), not too badly done.

w Robert Stewart, Philip Mackie *d* Freddie Francis *ph* Bob Hulke *m* Ken Jones

Anne Heywood, Peter Van Eyck, Cecil Parker, Bernard Lee, Maxine Audley, Jeremy Spenser, Miles Malleson

The Vengeance of Fu Manchu
GB 1967 92m Eastmancolor
Anglo Amalgamated / Harry Alan Towers

The Yellow Peril plans a crime syndicate to counter Interpol, and creates a double for Nayland Smith . . .
Limp addition to a series which started well, but was subsequently robbed of period flavour.

w Harry Alan Towers, *novels* Sax Rohmer *d* Jeremy Summers *ph* John Von Kotze *m* Malcolm Lockyer

Christopher Lee, Douglas Wilmer, Tony Ferrer, Tsai Chin, Howard Marion Crawford, Wolfgang Kieling

The Vengeance of She
GB 1967 101m Technicolor
Hammer (Aida Young)

A girl is possessed by the spirit of long-dead Queen Ayesha.
Grotesquely unpersuasive reincarnation melodrama, a long long way from its inspiration.

w Peter O'Donnell *d* Cliff Owen *ph* Wolfgang Suschitsky *m* Mario Nascimbene

John Richardson, Olinka Berova, Edward Judd, Colin Blakely, Derek Godfrey, Noel Willman, André Morell, Jill Melford

Vengeance Valley
US 1951 82m Technicolor
MGM (Nicholas Nayfack)

A western rancher keeps his foster-brother's misdeeds from their father.
Well-made character western, a little short on action.

w Irving Ravetch, *novel* Luke Short *d* Richard Thorpe *ph* George Folsey *m* Rudolph G. Kopp

Burt Lancaster, Robert Walker, Ray Collins, Joanne Dru, Sally Forrest, John Ireland, Carleton Carpenter, Ted de Corsia

Vera Cruz***
US 1953 94m Technicolor Superscope
UA / Hecht–Hill–Lancaster (James Hill)

Adventurers in 1860 Mexico become involved in a plot against Emperor Maximilian.
Terse, lively western melodrama with unusual locations and comedy and suspense touches. Great outdoor entertainment.

w Roland Kibbee, James R. Webb, Borden Chase d Robert Aldrich ph Ernest Laszlo m Hugo Friedhofer

Gary Cooper, Burt Lancaster, Denise Darcel, Cesar Romero, George Macready, Sarita Montiel, Ernest Borgnine, Morris Ankrum, Charles Bronson

The Verdict*
US 1946 86m bw
Warner (William Jacobs)

A retired Scotland Yard inspector continues to work on a case which vexes him.
Victorian murder mystery with very unconvincing Hollywood sets and curious casting, but rather nicely detailed.

w Peter Milne, *novel* The Big Bow Mystery by Israel Zangwill *d Don Siegel ph* Ernest Haller *m* Frederick Hollander

Sidney Greenstreet, Peter Lorre, Joan Lorring, George Coulouris, Rosalind Ivan, Paul Cavanagh, Arthur Shields

Vertigo**
US 1958 128m Technicolor Vistavision
(Paramount) Alfred Hitchcock

A detective with a fear of heights is drawn into a complex plot in which a girl he loves apparently falls to her death. Then he meets her double . . .
Double identity thriller which doesn't really hang together but has many sequences in Hitchcock's best style despite central miscasting.

w Alec Coppel, Samuel Taylor, *novel* D'entre les Morts by Pierre Boileau, Thomas Narcejac *d Alfred Hitchcock ph Robert Burks m Bernard Herrmann*

James Stewart, Kim Novak, Barbara Bel Geddes, Tom Helmore, Henry Jones

The Very Edge
GB 1962 89m bw Cinevision
British Lion / Garrick / Raymond Stross

An obsessive young man menaces a mother-to-be.
Rather unpleasant suspenser, adequately presented.

w E. J. Howard *d* Cyril Frankel *ph* Bob Huke *m* David Lee

Anne Heywood, Richard Todd, Jack Hedley, Jeremy Brett, Nicole Maurey, Barbara Mullen, Maurice Denham, William Lucas

Very Important Person**
GB 1961 98m bw
Rank / Independent Artists (Julian Wintle, Leslie Parkyn)
US title: *A Coming-Out Party*

A senior British scientist is caught by the Nazis and has to be rescued.
Very satisfactory British comedy with a few suspense scenes; POW fare with a difference.

w Jack Davies *d* Ken Annakin *ph* Ernest Steward *m* Reg Owen

James Robertson Justice, Stanley Baxter, Leslie Phillips, Eric Sykes, Richard Wattis, Colin Gordon

A Very Missing Person
US 1972 73m Technicolor TVM
Universal (Edward J. Montagne)
aka: *Hildegarde Withers*

A lady sleuth and her policeman friend follow the disappearance of a young woman.
A bad stab at recasting the old Hildegarde Withers films.

w Philip Reisman *d* Russell Mayberry

Eve Arden, James Gregory, Julie Newmar, Skye Aubrey

A Very Special Favor*
US 1965 105m Technicolor
Universal / Lankershim (Robert Arthur)

A Frenchman with a spinster daughter asks an American lawyer to 'initiate' her.
Tasteless, smirking comedy with several funny scenes, glossily photographed in the lap of luxury and interesting in its early use of homosexuality as a comedy subject.

w Nate Monaster, Stanley Shapiro *d* Michael Gordon *ph Leo Tover* *m* Vic Mizzy

Rock Hudson, Charles Boyer, Leslie Caron, *Nita Talbot*, Dick Shawn, *Walter Slezak*, Larry Storch

The Very Thought of You
US 1944 99m bw
Warner (Jerry Wald)

Problems of a wartime marriage.
Tepid romantic potboiler.

w Alvah Bessie, Delmer Daves *d* Delmer Daves *ph* Bert Glennon *m* Franz Waxman

Dennis Morgan, Eleanor Parker, Dane Clark, Faye Emerson, Beulah Bondi, Henry Travers, William Prince, Andrea King

Vessel of Wrath***
GB 1938 93m bw
Mayflower (Erich Pommer)
US title: *The Beachcomber*

In the Dutch East Indies, the missionary's spinster sister falls for a drunken beachcomber.
First-rate character comedy, remade as *The Beachcomber* (qv).

w Bartlett Cormack, B. Van Thal, *story W. Somerset Maugham* *d* Erich Pommer

Charles Laughton, Elsa Lanchester, Robert Newton, Tyrone Guthrie, Dolly Mollinger, Eliot Makeham

Vice Squad
US 1953 88m bw
UA / Jules Levy, Arthur Gardner
GB title: *The Girl in Room 17*

A police captain tracks down two bank robbers who have killed a cop.
A day in the life of a police captain, quite watchable but scarcely engrossing.

w Lawrence Roman, *novel* Harness Bull by Leslie T. White *d* Arnold Laven *ph* Joseph C. Biroc *m* Herschel Burke Gilbert

Edward G. Robinson, Paulette Goddard, K. T. Stevens, Porter Hall, Adam Williams, Edward Binns, Lee Van Cleef

Vice Versa*
GB 1947 111m bw
Rank / Two Cities (Peter Ustinov, George H. Brown)

A magic stone enables an unhappy Victorian boy to change places with his pompous father.
Funny moments can't disguise the fact that this overlong comedy is a bit of a fizzle, its talented creator not being a film-maker. A pity, as British films have so rarely entered the realms of fancy.

w Peter Ustinov, *novel* F. Anstey *d* Peter Ustinov

Roger Livesey, Kay Walsh, Anthony Newley, *James Robertson Justice*, David Hutcheson, Petula Clark, Joan Young

The Vicious Circle*
GB 1957 84m bw
Romulus (Peter Rogers)

An actress is found dead in Dr Latimer's flat and the weapon turns up in the boot of his car . . .
Entertaining whodunnit from a TV serial.

w Francis Durbridge, from his serial The Brass Candlestick *d* Gerald Thomas *ph* Otto Heller *m* Stanley Black

John Mills, Derek Farr, Noelle Middleton, Roland Culver, Wilfrid Hyde White, Mervyn Johns, René Ray, Lionel Jeffries, Lisa Daniely

Vicki*
US 1953 85m bw
TCF (Leonard Goldstein)

A girl model is murdered, and her sister proves that her boy friend is innocent, despite the efforts of a brutal detective.
Very competent if uninspired remake of *I Wake Up Screaming* (qv).

w Dwight Taylor *d* Harry Horner *ph* Milton Krasner *m* Leigh Harline

Jeanne Crain, Jean Peters, Richard Boone, Elliott Reid, Casey Adams, Alex D'Arcy, Carl Betz, Aaron Spelling

Victim***
GB 1962 100m bw
Rank / Allied Film Makers / Parkway (Michael Relph)

A barrister with homosexual inclinations tracks down a blackmailer despite the risk to his own reputation.
A plea for a change in the law is very smartly wrapped up as a murder mystery which allows all aspects to be aired, and the London locations are vivid.

w Janet Green, John McCormick d Basil Dearden ph Otto Heller m Philip Green

Dirk Bogarde, Sylvia Syms, John Barrie, Norman Bird, Peter McEnery, Anthony Nicholls, Dennis Price, *Charles Lloyd Pack*, Derren Nesbitt, John Cairney, Hilton Edwards, Peter Copley, Donald Churchill, Nigel Stock

The Victim**
US 1972 73m Technicolor TVM
Universal (William Frye)
aka: *The Storm*

A girl visits her sister during a storm, and finds a dead body and a lurking killer.
A very adequate *Psycho*-ish chiller using all the old tricks.

w Merwin Gerard *d* Herschel Daugherty

Elizabeth Montgomery, George Maharis, Sue Ann Langdon, Eileen Heckart

Victoria the Great***
GB 1937 112m bw
British Lion / Imperator / Herbert Wilcox

Episodes in the life of Queen Victoria.
A decent film with all the British virtues, and a milestone in the cinema of its time. Script and performances are excellent; production sometimes falters a little.

w Robert Vansittart, Miles Malleson, plays Victoria Regina by Laurence Housman *d* Herbert Wilcox

Anna Neagle, Anton Walbrook, H. B. Warner, Walter Rilla, Mary Morris, C. V. France, Charles Carson, Felix Aylmer, Derrick de Marney

The Victors*
GB 1963 175m bw Panavision
Columbia / Open Road (Carl Foreman)

World War II adventures of an American infantry platoon.
Patchy compendium with moral too heavily stressed but plenty of impressive scenes and performances along the way. The mixture of realism and irony, though, doesn't really mix.

w Carl Foreman, *novel* The Human Kind by Alexander Baron *d* Carl Foreman *ph* Christopher Challis *m* Sol Kaplan

George Peppard, George Hamilton, Albert Finney, Melina Mercouri, Eli Wallach, Vince Edwards, Rosanna Schiaffino, James Mitchum, *Jeanne Moreau*, Elke Sommer, Senta Berger, Peter Fonda, Michael Callan

'Doggerel epic.'—*John Coleman*

'War has revealed Mr Foreman as a pompous bore.'—*John Simon*

'Having made a point through an image it continually feels the need to state it all over again by way of dialogue.'—*Penelope Houston*

Victory*
US 1940 77m bw
Paramount (Anthony Veiller)

A Dutch East Indies recluse rescues a girl and is menaced by three villains who think he is wealthy.
Curious, ineffective but occasionally compelling attempt to translate the untranslatable to the screen.

w John L. Balderston, *novel* Joseph Conrad *d* John Cromwell *ph* Leo Tover *m* Frederick Hollander

Fredric March, Betty Field, *Cedric Hardwicke*, Sig Rumann, Margaret Wycherly, Jerome Cowan, Fritz Feld, Rafaela Ottiano

Victory through Air Power***
US 1943 65m Technicolor
Walt Disney
The history of aviation and the theories of Major Alexander de Seversky.
What was thought by many to be propaganda was in fact a demonstration of Disney's own fascination with the theories of a controversial figure. The cartoon segments are put together with the studio's accustomed brilliance.
w various *d* H. C. Potter (live action), various

The View from Pompey's Head*
US 1955 97m Eastmancolor Cinemascope
TCF (Philip Dunne)
GB title: *Secret Interlude*
A New York lawyer returns on a case to the small town of his youth, and falls in love again with his old sweetheart.
Routine Marquand-type novelette, long on atmosphere and short on plot.
wd Philip Dunne, *novel* Hamilton Basso *ph* Joe MacDonald *m* Elmer Bernstein
Richard Egan, Dana Wynter, Cameron Mitchell, *Sidney Blackmer, Marjorie Rambeau*

Vigil in the Night
US 1940 96m bw
RKO (George Stevens)
Two nurses are attracted to the same doctor; one dies during an epidemic.
Dull, downbeat romantic melodrama with a miscast lead.
w Fred Guiol, P. J. Wolfson, Rowland Leigh, *novel* A. J. Cronin *d* George Stevens *ph* Robert de Grasse *m* Alfred Newman
Carole Lombard, Anne Shirley, Brian Aherne, Julien Mitchell, Robert Coote, Peter Cushing, Ethel Griffies

The Viking Queen
GB 1967 91m Technicolor
Warner / Hammer (John Temple-Smith)
During the first century AD, the queen of the Iceni tries to keep peace with the occupying Romans but has trouble with hot-headed Druids.
Stuff and nonsense from the Dark Ages; light should not have been shed upon it.
w Clarke Reynolds *d* Don Chaffey *ph* Stephen Dade *m* Gary Hughes
Don Murray, Carita, Donald Houston, Andrew Keir, Patrick Troughton, Adrienne Corri, Niall MacGinnis, Wilfrid Lawson, Nicola Pagett

The Vikings***
US 1958 116m Technirama
UA / KD Productions (Jerry Bresler)
Two Viking half-brothers quarrel over the throne of Northumbria.
Slightly unpleasant and brutal but extremely well-staged and good-looking epic in which you can almost feel the harsh climate. Fine colour, strong performances, natural settings, vivid action, and all production values as they should be.
w Calder Willingham, *novel* The Viking by Edison Marshall *d Richard Fleischer ph Jack Cardiff m Mario Nascimbene credits titles United Productions of America narrator* Orson Welles
Kirk Douglas, Tony Curtis, Ernest Borgnine, Janet Leigh, Frank Thring, James Donald, Maxine Audley, Eileen Way

Villa Rides!
US 1968 125m Technicolor Panavision
Paramount (Ted Richmond)
1912 Mexico: an American pilot who has been gun-running for the rebels is pressed into more active service.
Bang-bang actioner which pauses too often for reflection and local colour.
w Robert Towne, Sam Peckinpah *d* Buzz Kulik *ph* Jack Hildyard *m* Maurice Jarre *ad* Ted Howarth
Yul Brynner, Robert Mitchum, Charles Bronson, Grazia Bucetta, Herbert Lom, Alexander Knox, Fernando Rey

Village of Daughters
GB 1961 86m bw
MGM (George H. Brown)
An unemployed commercial traveller in an Italian village finds himself choosing a bride for a successful emigré.
Voluble, gesticulating minor comedy.
w David Pursall, Jack Seddon *d* George Pollock *ph* Geoffrey Faithfull *m* Ron Goodwin
Eric Sykes, Warren Mitchell, Scilla Gabel, Carol White, Grégoire Aslan, John Le Mesurier

Village of the Damned**
GB 1960 78m bw
MGM (Ronald Kinnoch)
Children born simultaneously in an English village prove to be super-intelligent and deadly beings from another planet.
Modestly made but absorbing and logical science fiction, cleanly presented.

w Stirling Silliphant, Wolf Rilla, Geoffrey Barclay, novel The Midwich Cuckoos by *John Wyndham d Wolf Rilla ph* Geoffrey Faithfull *m* Ron Goodwin

George Sanders, Barbara Shelley, Michael Gwynn, Martin Stephens, Laurence Naismith
† Sequel: *Children of the Damned* (qv).

Villain
GB 1971 98m Technicolor Panavision
EMI / Kastner / Ladd / Kanter

The come-uppance of a cowardly, sadistic, homosexual East End gang boss with a mother fixation.
Very unpleasant and unentertaining British low life shocker, plainly inspired by *White Heat*.

w Dick Clement, Ian La Frenais, *novel* The Burden of Proof by James Barlow *d* Michael Tuchner *ph* Christopher Challis *m* Jonathan Hodge

Richard Burton, Ian MacShane, Nigel Davenport, Joss Ackland, Cathleen Nesbitt, Donald Sinden, T. P. McKenna, Fiona Lewis

The Villain Still Pursued Her*
US 1940 66m bw
(RKO) Harold B. Franklin

An innocent family suffers at the hands of a villainous landlord.
Clumsy burlesque of old time melodrama, interesting that it was done at all and with this cast.

w Elbert Franklin *d* Edward Cline *ph* Lucien Ballard *m* Frank Tours

Buster Keaton, Alan Mowbray, Anita Louise, Hugh Herbert, Joyce Compton, Margaret Hamilton, Billy Gilbert

The Vintage
US 1957 92m Metrocolor
Cinemascope
MGM (Edwin H. Knopf)

Two fugitives from justice cause trouble when they become grape pickers.
Steamy drama with an unconvincing French setting; a Hollywood aberration.

w Michael Blankfort, *novel* Ursula Keir *d* Jeffrey Hayden *ph* Joseph Ruttenberg *m* David Raksin

Mel Ferrer, John Kerr, Michèle Morgan, Pier Angeli, Theodore Bikel, Leif Erickson

The Violent Enemy
GB 1968 98m Eastmancolor
Trio / Group W. (Wilfrid Eades)

An IRA explosives expert escapes from a British jail but quarrels with his leaders.
Dullish political melodrama needlessly rubbing salt in old wounds.

w Edmund Ward, *novel* A Candle for the Dead by Hugh Marlowe *d* Don Sharp *ph* Alan Hume *m* Martin Skiles

Tom Bell, Ed Begley, Susan Hampshire, Noel Purcell, Michael Standing

The Violent Men*
US 1955 96m Technicolor
Columbia (Lewis J. Rachmil)

A crippled cattle baron drives small landowners from his valley, while his wife has an affair with his younger brother.
So much snarling goes on that this seems like a gangster film in fancy dress, but it does hold the attention.

w Harry Kleiner, *novel* Donald Hamilton *d* Rudolph Maté *ph* Burnett Guffey, W. Howard Greene *m* Max Steiner

Edward G. Robinson, Barbara Stanwyck, Glenn Ford, Brian Keith, Dianne Foster, May Wynn, Warner Anderson, Basil Ruysdael

The Violent Ones*
US 1967 90m Eastmancolor
Madison / Harold Goldman

In a small Mexican town, three American hobos are interrogated after the rape and murder of a local girl.
Rather well shot murder mystery with emphasis on character, leading to a desert chase climax.

w Doug Wilson, Charles Davis *d Fernando Lamas ph Fleet Southcott m* Martin Skiles

Fernando Lamas, Aldo Ray, David Carradine, Tommy Sands

Violent Playground
GB 1958 108m bw
Rank (Michael Relph)

A junior liaison officer in the Liverpool slums falls in love with the sister of a fire-raiser.
'Realistic' melodrama sabotaged by an entirely schematic and predictable plot; enervatingly dull until the siege climax.

w James Kennaway *d* Basil Dearden *ph Reg Wyer m* Philip Green

Stanley Baker, Anne Heywood, David McCallum, Peter Cushing, John Slater, Clifford Evans

Violent Saturday*
US 1955 90m De Luxe Cinemascope
TCF (Buddy Adler)

Crooks move quietly into a small town with the intention of robbing the bank.
Interesting little melodrama which the wide screen robs of its proper tension. Adequate presentation and performance.

w Sidney Boehm *d* Richard Fleischer
ph Charles G. Clarke *m* Hugo Friedhofer

Richard Egan, Victor Mature, Stephen McNally, Sylvia Sidney, Virginia Leith, Tommy Noonan, Lee Marvin, Margaret Hayes, J. Carrol Naish, Ernest Borgnine

The VIPs**
GB 1963 119m Metrocolor
Panavision
MGM (Anatole de Grunwald)

Passengers at London Airport are delayed by fog and spend the night at a hotel.
Multi-story compendium cunningly designed to exploit the real-life Burton–Taylor romance. In itself, competent rather than stimulating.

w Terence Rattigan *d* Anthony Asquith
ph Jack Hildyard *m* Miklos Rozsa

Richard Burton, Elizabeth Taylor, Maggie Smith, Rod Taylor, *Margaret Rutherford*, Louis Jourdan, Elsa Martinelli, Orson Welles, Linda Christian, Dennis Price, Richard Wattis, David Frost, Robert Coote, Joan Benham, Michael Hordern, Lance Percival, Martin Miller

'If Mr Rattigan's Aunt Edna still goes to the pictures she should like his latest offering, especially if she has a good lunch first.'—*Brenda Davies*

The Virgin and the Gypsy*
GB 1970 95m colour
Kenwood / Dimitri de Grunwald (Kenneth Harper)

A Midlands clergyman's daughter falls in love with a gypsy fortune teller.
Slow, sensitive, stylish picturization of a Lawrence novella, with generally good performances.

w Alan Plater, story D. H. Lawrence
d Christopher Miles ph Robert Huke *m* Patrick Gowers *pd* Terence Knight

Joanna Shimkus, Franco Nero, Honor Blackman, Michael Burns, Maurice Denham, Fay Compton, Kay Walsh, Norman Bird

Virgin Island
GB 1958 94m Eastmancolor
British Lion / Countryman (Leon Clore, Graham Tharp)

A young couple set up house on a tiny Caribbean island.
Pleasant comedy slowed down by lack of plot and too much conversation.

w Philip Rush, Pat Jackson, *book* Our Virgin Island by Robb White *d* Pat Jackson
ph Freddie Francis *m* Clifton Parker

Virginia Maskell, John Cassavetes, Sidney Poitier, Isabel Dean, Colin Gordon

The Virgin Queen*
US 1955 92m De Luxe Cinemascope
TCF (Charles Brackett)

The relationship of Queen Elizabeth I and Sir Walter Raleigh.
Unhistorical charade, quite pleasantly made and worth noting for its star performance.

w Harry Brown, Mindret Lord *d* Henry Koster
ph Charles G. Clarke *m* Franz Waxman

Bette Davis, Richard Todd, Joan Collins, Herbert Marshall, Jay Robinson, Dan O'Herlihy, Robert Douglas, Romney Brent

The Virgin Soldiers**
GB 1969 96m Technicolor
Columbia / Carl Foreman (Leslie Gilliat, Ned Sherrin)

Serio-comic adventures of recruits in the British army in 1960 Singapore.
Autobiographical fragments, mostly from below the belt, sharply observed and often very funny.

w John Hopkins, novel Leslie Thomas d John Dexter ph Ken Higgins m Peter Greenwell

Hywel Bennett, Nigel Patrick, *Lynn Redgrave*, Nigel Davenport, *Rachel Kempson*, Michael Gwynn, Tsai Chin

'A kind of monstrous mating of *Private's Progress* and *The Family Way*, with bits of *The Long and the Short and the Tall* thrown in for good measure.'—*David Pirie*

† Sequel 1977: *Stand Up Virgin Soldiers.*

Virginia City*
US 1940 121m bw
Warner (Robert Fellows)

A dance hall girl is really a southern spy helping a rebel colonel to steal a gold shipment from her Yankee boy friend.
Lumpy western in Warner's best budget but worst manner: the stars look unhappy and the plot progresses in fits and starts.

w Robert Buckner *d* Michael Curtiz *ph* Sol Polito *m* Max Steiner

Errol Flynn, Randolph Scott, Miriam Hopkins, Humphrey Bogart, Frank McHugh, Alan Hale, Guinn Williams, John Litel, Moroni Olsen, Russell Hicks, Douglass Dumbrille

The Virginia Hill Story**
US 1974 74m colour TVM
RSO (Aaron Rosenberg)

After the 1947 killing of gangster Bugsy Siegel, his girl friend testifies before the Kefauver commission.
Well-written crime exposé with good performances.

w Joel Schumacher, Juleen Compton *d* Joel Schumacher

Dyan Cannon, Harvey Keitel, Alan Garfield, Robby Benson

The Virginian*
US 1929 95m bw
Paramount

A stalwart ranch foreman has to see his best friend hanged for rustling, and defeats the local bad man.
Standard western with famous clichés, e.g. 'Smile when you say that . . .'

w Edward E. Paramore Jnr, Howard Estabrook, *novel* Owen Wister *d* Victor Fleming *ph* J. Roy Hunt

Gary Cooper, Walter Huston, Richard Arlen, Mary Brian, Chester Conklin, Eugene Pallette

The Virginian
US 1946 90m Technicolor
Paramount

Forgettable remake of the above.

d Stuart Gilmore

Joel McCrea, Brian Donlevy, Sonny Tufts, Barbara Britton, William Frawley, Henry O'Neill, Fay Bainter

The Virginian*

This series of 74-minute TV westerns ran seven seasons, from 1962 to 1969, and though mostly boring it did recruit a large number of interesting guest stars who held the attention, despite leisurely production and strong family ambience. It had little to do with the original story: the Virginian (James Drury) was a slightly mysterious but impeccably natured ranch foreman, Trampas (Doug McClure) was an impulsive pal rather than a villain, and most of the stories centred on the judge, played first by Charles Bickford, then by Lee J. Cobb. Here is a selection of the more interesting episodes and guest stars:

THE BRAZEN BELL: George C. Scott
IMPASSE: Eddie Albert
THE DREAM OF STAVROS KARAS: Michael Constantine
ROAR FROM THE MOUNTAIN: Jack Klugman
THE EXECUTIONERS: Hugh O'Brian
THE SMALL PARADE: David Wayne
THE ACCOMPLICE: Bette Davis
IT TAKES A BIG MAN: Ryan O'Neal
THE EVIL THAT MEN DO: Robert Redford
THE BIG DEAL: Ricardo Montalban
THE NOBILITY OF KINGS: Charles Bronson
MEN WITH GUNS: Telly Savalas
OLD COWBOY: Franchot Tone
THE INVADERS: Ed Begley
A TIME REMEMBERED: Yvonne de Carlo
STRANGERS AT SUNDOWN: Harry Morgan
DUEL AT SHILOH: Brian Keith
IT TOLLS FOR THEE: Lee Marvin
THE FORTUNES OF J. J. JONES: Pat O'Brien

The Virtuous Sin
US 1930 81m bw
Paramount

A girl tries to help her student husband when war takes him away from bacteriology.
Stilted romantic drama.

w Martin Brown, Louise Long, *novel* Lajos Zilahy *d* George Cukor, Louis Gasnier *ph* David Abel

Walter Huston, Kay Francis, Kenneth MacKenna, Paul Cavanagh

Visions*
US 1972 73m colour TVM
Leonard Freeman
aka: *Visions of Death*

A clairvoyant professor has a vision of a building being dynamited, and though the police scoff he is suspected when it comes true.
Adequate, predictable TV suspenser.

w Paul Playdon *d* Lee Katzin

Monte Markham, Barbara Anderson, Telly Savalas, Tim O'Connor

The Visit
US 1964 100m bw Cinemascope
TCF / Deutschefox / Cinecittà / Dear Film / Films du Siècle / PECF (Julien Derode, Anthony Quinn)

A millionairess offers a fortune to her home town, providing someone will kill her ex-lover.
A realistic production ill befits an essentially theatrical play, and all the effort goes for nothing.

w Ben Barzman, *play* Friedrich Durrenmatt
d Bernhard Wicki *ph* Armando Nannuzzi
m Hans-Martin Majewski

Ingrid Bergman, Anthony Quinn, Paolo Stoppa, Hans- Christian Vlech, Valentina Cortesa, Irina Demick, Claude Dauphin, Eduardo Ciannelli

Visit to a Chief's Son
US 1974 92m De Luxe Panavision
UA / Robert Halmi

An American anthropologist and his son hope to film the rituals of an African tribe.
Minor adventure film with a happy resolution, based on a photomontage by the producer, a *Life* photographer.

w Albert Ruben *d Lamont Johnson ph* Ernest Day *m* Francis Lai

Robert Mulligan, Johnny Sekka, John Philip Hodgdon

Visit to a Small Planet
US 1959 101m bw
Paramount / Wallis–Hazen

A young man from outer space takes a look at Earth and falls in love.
A satirical play disastrously adapted for the moronic comedy of an unsuitable star.

w Edmund Beloin, Henry Garson, *play* Gore Vidal *d* Norman Taurog *ph* Loyal Griggs *m* Leigh Harline

Jerry Lewis, Joan Blackman, Earl Holliman, Fred Clark, John Williams, Jerome Cowan, Gavin Gordon, Lee Patrick

Viva Las Vegas
US 1964 85m Metrocolor
MGM (Jack Cummins, George Sidney)

A sports car racer has fun in the gambling city.
Tolerable star musical.

w Sally Benson *d* George Sidney *ph* Joseph Biroc *md* George bstoll

Elvis Presley, Ann-Margret, Cesare Danova, William Demarest, Nicky Blair, Jack Carter

Viva Max
US 1969 93m Eastmancolor
Commonwealth United / Mark Carliner

A Mexican general marches his troops into Texas and seizes the Alamo.
Flat comedy with mildly amusing passages but too much noise, bluster and sentiment.

w Elliott Baker, *novel* James Lehrer *d* Jerry Paris *ph* Jack Richards *m* Hugo Montenegro

Peter Ustinov, *John Astin,* Pamela Tiffin, Jonathan Winters, Keenan Wynn, Henry Morgan, Alice Ghostley

Viva Villa**
US 1934 110m bw
MGM (David O. Selznick)

The career of a Mexican rebel.
Gutsy action drama with some smoothing over of fact in the name of entertainment. A big, highly competent production of its year.

w Ben Hecht d Jack Conway ph James Wong Howe, Charles G. Clarke m Herbert Stothart

Wallace Beery, Fay Wray, Leo Carrillo, Donald Cook, Stuart Erwin, George E. Stone, Joseph Schildkraut, Henry B. Walthall, Katherine de Mille

'A strange poem of violence.'—*John Baxter, 1968*

'A glorified horse opera . . . the spectator's excitement is incited by the purely physical impact of the furious riding and war sequences, by the frequent sadism, and by the lively musical score.'—*Irving Lerner*

Viva Zapata**
US 1952 113m bw
TCF (Darryl F. Zanuck)

A Mexican revolutionary is finally betrayed by a friend.
Moody, good-looking star vehicle taking a romanticized but glum view of history.

w John Steinbeck *d Elia Kazan ph Joe MacDonald m* Alfred Newman

Marlon Brando, Jean Peters, Joseph Wiseman, Anthony Quinn, Arnold Moss, Margo, *Frank Silvera*

Vivacious Lady*
US 1938 90m bw
RKO (George Stevens)

A nightclub singer marries a botany professor and has trouble with his parents.
Pleasant romantic comedy for two popular stars.

w P. J. Wolfson, Ernest Pagano *d* George Stevens *ph* Robert de Grasse *m* Roy Webb

Ginger Rogers, James Stewart, Charles Coburn, Beulah Bondi, James Ellison, Frances Mercer, Franklin Pangborn, Grady Sutton, Jack Carson

Vogues of 1938*
US 1937 108m Technicolor
Walter Wanger

Rival fashion houses compete at the Seven Arts Ball.
A fashion show with threads of plot, interesting for clothes and cast, all working hard.

w Bella and Samuel Spewack *d* Irving Cummings *ph* Ray Rennahan *md* Boris Morros *ch* Seymour Felix

Joan Bennett, Walter Baxter, Helen Vinson, Mischa Auer, Alan Mowbray, Jerome Cowan, Alma Kruger, Marjorie Gateson, Penny Singleton, Hedda Hopper

The Voice of Bugle Ann*
US 1936 70m bw
MGM (John Considine Jnr)

When a dog is killed its embittered owner seeks revenge.
Old-fashioned country tale, rather heavy-going but emotionally strong.

w Harvey Gates, Samuel Hoffenstein, *novel* Mackinlay Kantor *d* Richard Thorpe

Lionel Barrymore, Maureen O'Sullivan, Eric Linden, Dudley Digges, Spring Byington, Charley Grapewin
'A very fine movie indeed.'—*Pare Lorentz*

The Voice of Merrill
GB 1952 84m bw
Tempean (Robert Baker, Monty Berman)
US title: *Murder Will Out*

Three men are suspected of murder but one becomes a potential victim.
Complicated murder thriller which intrigues but hardly satisfies.

wd John Gilling *ph* Monty Berman *m* Frank Cordell

Valerie Hobson, James Robertson Justice, Edward Underdown, Henry Kendall, Garry Marsh, Sam Kydd

The Voice of the Turtle**
US 1948 103m bw
Warner (Charles Hoffman)
aka: *One for the Book*

A girl shares her apartment with a soldier on leave.
A three-character play is smoothly filmed, slightly broadened, and burnished till its pale wit glows nicely.

w John Van Druten, from his play *d Irving Rapper ph* Sol Polito *m* Max Steiner

Eleanor Parker, Ronald Reagan, *Eve Arden,* Wayne Morris, Kent Smith

Voices
GB 1973 91m Technicolor
(Hemdale) Warden (Robert Enders)

A young couple in an old country house are haunted by the voice of their dead son.
Twisty little ghost story which would have been more effective at one third of its length.

w George Kirgo, Robert Enders, *play* Richard Lortz *d* Kevin Billington *ph* Geoffrey Unsworth *m* Richard Rodney Bennett

Gayle Hunnicutt, David Hemmings

Voltaire*
US 1933 72m bw
Warner (Ray Griffith)

The life and times of the 18th-century French wit.
One of the better Arliss charades, because the film is as stagey as his performance.

w Paul Green, Maude T. Howell, *novel* George Gibbs, E. Laurence Dudley *d* John Adolfi *ph* Tony Gaudio

George Arliss, Doris Kenyon, Margaret Lindsay, Reginald Owen, Alan Mowbray, David Torrence, Douglass Dumbrille, Theodore Newton

Von Richthofen and Brown
US 1971 97m De Luxe
UA / Roger Corman (Gene Corman)
GB title: *The Red Baron*

During World War I, a Canadian pilot takes on Germany's air ace.
The airplanes are nice, but the film is grounded by plot and dialogue.

w John and Joyce Corrington *d* Roger Corman *ph* Michael Reed *m* Hugo Friedhofer

John Phillip Law, Don Stroud, Barry Primus, Karen Huston, Corin Redgrave, Hurd Hatfield

Von Ryan's Express**
US 1965 117m De Luxe Cinemascope
TCF (Saul David)

In an Italian POW camp during World War II, an unpopular American captain leads English prisoners in a train escape.
Exhilarating action thriller with slow spots atoned for by nail-biting finale, though the downbeat curtain mars the general effect.

w Wendell Mayes, Joseph Landon, *novel* Davis Westheimer *d Mark Robson ph* William H. Daniels, Harold Lipstein *m* Jerry Goldsmith

Frank Sinatra, Trevor Howard, Sergio Fantoni, Edward Mulhare, Brad Dexter, John Leyton, Wolfgang Preiss, James Brolin, Adolfo Celi

The Voyage of the Yes*
US 1972 73m colour TVM
Fenady–Crosby

Teenagers embark on a dangerous sea journey.
Mildly pleasing adventure with racial overtones.

w William Stratton *d* Lee H. Katzin

Desi Arnaz Jnr, Mike Evans, Beverly Garland, Skip Homeier, Della Reese

Voyage to the Bottom of the Sea*
US 1961 105m De Luxe Cinemascope
TCF / Windsor (Irwin Allen)

USN Admiral Nelson takes scientists in his futuristic atomic submarine to explode a belt of radiation.

Childish but sometimes entertaining science fiction which spawned a long-running TV series.

w Irwin Allen, Charles Bennett *d* Irwin Allen *ph* Winton Hoch, John Lamb *m* Paul Sawtell, Bert Shefter *ad J. M. Smith, Herman A. Blumenthal*

Walter Pidgeon, Robert Sterling, Joan Fontaine, Peter Lorre, Barbara Eden, Michael Ansara, Henry Daniell, Regis Toomey, Frankie Avalon

W
US 1973 95m De Luxe
Bing Crosby Productions (Mel Ferrer)

A young wife is threatened by her psychotic first husband.
Tedious rehash of several frightened lady themes, all rather sick.

w Gerald di Pego, James Kelly *d* Richard Quine *ph* Gerry Hirschfeld *m* Johnny Mandell

Twiggy, Michael Witney, Eugene Roche, Dirk Benedict, John Vernon

The W Plan*
GB 1930 105m bw
BIP / Wardour (Victor Saville)

A British spy helps destroy Germany's secret tunnels.
Slightly fantasticated spy/war action which was a big popular success at the time.

w Victor Saville, Miles Malleson, Frank Launder, *novel* Graham Seton *d* Victor Saville

Brian Aherne, Madeleine Carroll, Gordon Harker, Gibb McLaughlin, George Merritt, Mary Jerrold

'Fast, spectacular action, fine acting and notably realistic war scenes.'—*NFT, 1971*

WW and the Dixie Dancekings
US 1975 94m TVC
TCF (Stanley S. Canter)

In a southern state in the 1950s, a crook uses a travelling band as an alibi and stays to promote them.
Combination of *American Graffiti* and *Easy Rider*, either tiresome or tolerable according to one's mood. Very flashy, anyway.

w Thomas Rickman *d* John G. Avildsen *ph* Jim Crabe *m* Dave Grusin

Burt Reynolds, Art Carney, Conny Van Dyke, Jerry Reed, Ned Beatty

Wabash Avenue*
US 1950 92m Technicolor
TCF (William Perlberg)

During the Chicago World's Fair of 1892, a shimmy dancer is pursued by two men.
Bright rehash of *Coney Island* (qv), with solid tunes and performances.

w Harry Tugend, Charles Lederer *d* Henry Koster *ph* Arthur E. Arling *md* Lionel Newman

Betty Grable, Victor Mature, Phil Harris, Reginald Gardiner, Margaret Hamilton, James Barton, Barry Kelley

The Wackiest Ship in the Army
US 1960 99m Technicolor
Cinemascope
Columbia / Fred Kohlmar

In the South Pacific during World War II a decrepit sailing ship with an inexperienced crew manages to confuse Japanese patrols and land a scout behind enemy lines.
Slapstick war comedy with fragments of action; effect rather muddled.

wd Ralph Murphy, *story* Herbert Carlson *ph* Charles Lawton *m* George Duning

Jack Lemmon, Ricky Nelson, John Lund, Chips Rafferty, Tom Tully, Joby Baker, Warren Berlinger, Richard Anderson

Wagonmaster**
US 1950 86m bw
RKO / Argosy (John Ford, Merian C. Cooper)

Adventures of a Mormon wagon train journeying towards Utah in 1879.
Low-key Ford western, essentially a collection of incidents, fondly and enjoyably presented.

w Frank Nugent, Patrick Ford *d John Ford* *ph* Bert Glennon *m* Richard Hageman

Ben Johnson, Joanne Dru, Harry Carey Jnr, Ward Bond, Charles Kemper, Alan Mowbray, Jane Darwell, Russell Simpson

'The feel of the period, the poetry of space and of endeavour, is splendidly communicated.'—*Lindsay Anderson*

The Wagons Roll at Night
US 1941 83m bw
Warner (Harlan Thompson)

The sweetheart of a circus owner makes a pass at the new young lion-tamer.
Dull remake of *Kid Galahad* (qv), whose plot

was borrowed from *Tiger Shark* (qv). Warners were good at this kind of retreading, but gradually poor quality began to show.

w Fred Niblo Jnr, Barry Trivers *d* Ray Enright *ph* Sid Hickox *m* Heinz Roemheld

Humphrey Bogart, Sylvia Sidney, Eddie Albert, Joan Leslie, Sig Rumann, Cliff Clark, Frank Wilcox

Waikiki Wedding*
US 1937 89m bw
Paramount (Arthur Hornblow Jnr)

A press agent in Hawaii promotes a Pineapple Queen contest.
Light-hearted, empty-headed musical very typical of this studio . . . except that this one is quite good.

w Frank Butler, Walter de Leon, Don Hartman, Francis Martin *d* Frank Tuttle *ph* Karl Struss *md* Boris Morros

Bing Crosby, Shirley Ross, Bob Burns, Martha Raye, George Barbier, Leif Erickson, Grady Sutton, Granville Bates, Anthony Quinn

Wait til the Sun Shines, Nellie*
US 1952 108m Technicolor
TCF (George Jessel)

The life of a small-town barber, from marriage through tragedy to retirement.
Amiable, leisurely family drama with pleasant settings; small beer, but oddly compulsive.

w Allan Scott, *novel* Ferdinand Reyher *d* Henry King *ph* Leon Shamroy *m* Alfred Newman

David Wayne, Jean Peters, Hugh Marlowe, Albert Dekker, Alan Hale Jnr, Helene Stanley

Wait until Dark**
US 1967 108m Technicolor
Warner Seven Arts (Mel Ferrer)

A photographer unwittingly smuggles a drug-filled doll into New York, and his blind wife, alone in their flat, is terrorized by murderous crooks in search of it.
Sharp suspenser with shock moments, from a successful play; in this case the claustrophobic atmosphere helps, though a lack of light relief makes itself felt.

w Robert and Jane Howard-Carrington, *play* Frederick Knott *d* Terence Young *ph* Charles Lang *m* Henry Mancini *ad* George Jenkins

Audrey Hepburn, Alan Arkin, Richard Crenna, Efrem Zimbalist Jnr, Jack Weston

Wake Island*
US 1942 78m bw
Paramount (Joseph Sistrom)

During World War II, marines fight to hold an American base on a small Pacific island.
Terse, violent flagwaver, well done within its limits.

w W. R. Burnett, Frank Butler *d* John Farrow *ph* Theodor Sparkuhl, William C. Mellor *m* David Buttolph

Brian Donlevy, Macdonald Carey, Robert Preston, William Bendix, Albert Dekker, Walter Abel, Mikhail Rasumny, Rod Cameron, Barbara Britton

Wake Me When It's Over
US 1960 126m De Luxe Cinemascope
TCF / Mervyn Le Roy

Soldiers holding a Pacific island build a de luxe hotel from surplus war material.
Aptly-titled army farce on the lines of *The Teahouse of the August Moon* but constructed from inferior material. Yawningly tedious.

w Richard Breen, *novel* Howard Singer *d* Mervyn Le Roy *ph* Leon Shamroy *m* Cyril Mockridge

Ernie Kovacs, Dick Shawn, Jack Warden, Margo Moore, Nobu McCarthy, Don Knotts, Robert Emhardt

Wake Me When the War Is Over
US 1969 74m colour TVM
Spelling–Thomas

In the closing days of World War II an American is captured by a German baroness, who keeps him in luxury long after the war.
Smoking room story, a little funnier than *Situation Hopeless But Not Serious*; though not much.

w Frank Peppiatt, John Aylesworth *d* Gene Nelson

Ken Berry, Eva Gabor, Werner Klemperer, Jim Backus, Hans Conried

Wake of the Red Witch**
US 1948 106m bw
Republic (Edmund Grainger)

The owner and captain of a ship settle their differences to seek treasure on an East Indian island.
Rattling good action yarn told in flashback, with adequate production and performances.

w Harry Brown, Kenneth Gamet, novel Garland Roark *d* Edward Ludwig *ph* Reggie Lanning *m* Nathan Scott

John Wayne, *Luther Adler*, Gail Russell, Gig

Young, Adele Mara, Eduard Franz, Grant Withers, Henry Daniell, Paul Fix, Dennis Hoey

Wake Up and Dream
US 1946 92m Technicolor
TCF (Walter Morosco)

A little girl is determined to find her brother who is missing in action in World War II.
Ambitious but unappealing whimsy which descends into sentimentality; either way it bewildered audiences and critics.

w Elick Moll, *novel* The Enchanted Voyage by Robert Nathan *d* Lloyd Bacon *ph* Harry Jackson *md* Emil Newman

June Haver, John Payne, Connie Marshall, Charlotte Greenwood, John Ireland, Clem Bevans, Lee Patrick

Wake Up and Live*
US 1937 91m bw
TCF (Kenneth MacGowan)

Success and failure in the radio world as a commentator and a bandleader fight a verbal duel in public.
Fast-moving spoof in which something is always happening, and usually something funny.

w Harry Tugend, Jack Yellen, *book* Dorothea Brande *d* Sidney Lanfield *ph* Edward Cronjager *m* Louis Silvers

Walter Winchell, Ben Bernie and his band, Alice Faye, Jack Haley, Patsy Kelly, Ned Sparks, Grace Bradley, Walter Catlett, Joan Davis, Douglas Fowley, Miles Mander, Etienne Girardot

Walk a Crooked Mile
US 1948 91m bw
Columbia (Edward Small)

British and American agents investigate the leakage of atomic secrets.
Moderate semi-documentary spy thriller.

w George Bruce *d* Gordon Douglas *ph* George Robinson *m* Paul Sawtell

Louis Hayward, Dennis O'Keefe, Louise Allbritton, Carl Esmond, Raymond Burr, Onslow Stevens

Walk a Crooked Path
GB 1969 88m Eastmancolor
Hanover (John Brason)

A housemaster at a boys' school is accused of homosexuality.
Po-faced melodrama in a minor key; reasonably effective but not exciting.

w Barry Perowne *d* John Brason *ph* John Taylor *m* Leslie Bridgewater

Tenniel Evans, Faith Brook, Christopher Coll, Patricia Haines, Pat Endersby, Margery Mason, Peter Copley

Walk, Don't Run*
US 1966 114m Technicolor Panavision
Columbia (Sol C. Siegel)

In Tokyo during the Olympics accommodation is hard to find, and two men move in with a girl.
Witless reprise of *The More the Merrier*, notable only for the Tokyo backgrounds and for Cary Grant's farewell appearance.

w Sol Saks *d* Charles Walters *ph* Harry Stradling *m* Quincy Jones

Cary Grant, Samantha Eggar, Jim Hutton, *John Standing*, Miiko Taka

Walk East on Beacon*
US 1952 98m bw
Columbia (Louis de Rochemont)
GB title: *The Crime of the Century*

The FBI exposes communist spies in the US.
Fast-moving semi-documentary spy thriller modelled on the same producer's *The House on 92nd Street.*

w Leo Rosten *d* Alfred Werker *ph* Joseph Brun *m* Jack Shaindlin

George Murphy, Finlay Currie, Virginia Gilmore, Karel Stepanek, Louisa Horton

A Walk in the Spring Rain
US 1969 98m Technicolor Panavision
Columbia / Pingee (Stirling Silliphant)

A college lecturer's wife, on holiday in the mountains, falls in love with a local man.
Romance for the middle-aged, nicely done if lacking in surprise.

w Stirling Silliphant, *novel* Rachel Maddox *d* Guy Green *ph* Charles B. Lang *m* Elmer Bernstein

Ingrid Bergman, Anthony Quinn, Fritz Weaver, Katherine Crawford

'Not one line or scene is believably written or acted and the direction is so lazy it appears to have been mailed in during the postal strike.'
—*Richard Roud*

A Walk in the Sun***
US 1946 117m bw
Lewis Milestone Productions

The exploits of a single army patrol during the Salerno landings of 1943, on one vital morning.
Vivid war film in a minor key, superbly disciplined and keenly acted.

w Robert Rossen, novel Harry Brown *d Lewis*

Milestone ph Russell Harlan m Fredric Efrem Rich

Dana Andrews, Richard Conte, Sterling Holloway, John Ireland, George Tyne, Herbert Rudley, Richard Benedict, Norman Lloyd, Lloyd Bridges, Huntz Hall

'Concerned with the individual rather than the battlefield, the film is finely perceptive, exciting, and very moving.'—*Penelope Houston*

'A swiftly overpowering piece of work.' —*Bosley Crowther*

'A notable war film, if not the most notable war film to come from America.'—*Richard Winnington*

Walk like a Dragon
US 1960 95m bw
Paramount / James Clavell

In 1870 San Francisco, a cowboy sets free a Chinese slave girl but incurs racial intolerance when he takes her home.
Curious 'liberated' western which gets itself in a muddle and doesn't come off at all.

w James Clavell, Dan Mainwaring *d* James Clavell *ph* Loyal Griggs *m* Paul Dunlap

Jack Lord, James Shigeta, Nobu McCarthy, Mel Tormé, Josephine Hutchinson, Rodolfo Acosta

Walk on the Wild Side
US 1962 114m bw
Columbia / Famous Artists (Charles K. Feldman)

In the thirties, a penniless farmer finds the girl he once loved working in a New Orleans brothel.
A brilliant title sequence heralds the dreariest and most verbose of self-conscious melodramas, quite missing the sensational effect promised by the advertising.

w John Fante, Edmund Morris, *novel* Nelson Algren *d* Edward Dmytryk *ph* Joe MacDonald *m* Elmer Bernstein *credits Saul Bass*

Jane Fonda, Capucine, Barbara Stanwyck, Laurence Harvey, Anne Baxter, Richard Rust

'Since the film prides itself in calling a spade a spade, it is surprising to find all concerned reacting to their material as though they were up to their waists in a quagmire.'—*MFB*

Walk Softly Stranger
US 1950 81m bw
RKO (Robert Sparks)

A crook on the run falls for a crippled girl, who promises to wait for him.
Dismal love-conquers-all melodrama.

w Frank Genton *d* Robert Stevenson *ph* Harry J. Wild *m* Frederick Hollander

Alida Valli, Joseph Cotten, Spring Byington, Paul Stewart, Jack Paar, Jeff Donnell, John McIntire

Walk the Proud Land
US 1956 88m Technicolor Cinemascope
U-I (Aaron Rosenberg)

An Indian agent persuades the army to use less violent methods.
Fair standard western with a thoughtful and sympathetic attitude.

w Gil Doud, Jack Sher *d* Jesse Hibbs *ph* Harold Lipstein *m* Joseph Gershenson

Audie Murphy, Anne Bancroft, Pat Crowley, Robert Warwick, Charles Drake, Tommy Rall, Jay Silverheels

Walkabout*
Australia 1970 100m Eastmancolor
Max L. Raab / Si Litvinoff

A man kills himself in the desert and his small children trek among the aborigines to safety.
Eerily effective contrast of city with native life, a director's and photographer's experimental success.

w Edward Bond, *novel* James Vance Marshall *d/ph Nicolas Roeg m* John Barry

Jenny Agutter, Lucien John, David Gimpell

The Walking Dead*
US 1936 66m bw
Warner

A man is revived after electrocution and takes revenge on his enemies.
Dour but well mounted horror thriller in a shadowy style very typical of its director.

w Ewart Adamson, Peter Milne, Robert Adams, Lillie Hayward *d Michael Curtiz ph Hal Mohr*

Boris Karloff, Edmund Gwenn, Marguerite Churchill, Ricardo Cortez, Barton MacLane, Warren Hull, Henry O'Neill

Walking My Baby Back Home*
US 1953 95m Technicolor
U-I (Ted Richmond)

Ex-army musicians hit on a combination of symphonic and dixieland jazz.
The lightest of light musicals, this highly polished offering remains mildly pleasing though thinly written throughout.

w Don McGuire, Oscar Brodney *d* Lloyd Bacon *ph* Irving Glassberg *md* Joseph Gershenson

Donald O'Connor, Janet Leigh, Buddy Hackett,

Lori Nelson, Scat Man Crothers, Kathleen Lockhart, George Cleveland, John Hubbard

The Walking Stick*
GB 1970 101m Metrocolor Panavision
MGM / Winkast (Alan Ladd Jnr)

A repressed girl polio victim falls reluctantly in love with a painter who involves her in his criminal schemes.
Slow moving character romance which has its heart in the right place but too often promises suspense which never comes, and is made in a chintzy cigarette commercial style.

w George Bluestone, *novel* Winston Graham *d* Eric Till *ph* Arthur Ibbetson *m* Stanley Myers

David Hemmings, Samantha Eggar, Phyllis Calvert, Ferdy Mayne, Emlyn Williams, Francesca Annis, Dudley Sutton

Walking Tall*
US 1973 125m De Luxe
Bing Crosby Productions (Mort Briskin)

A Tennessee farmer-sheriff meets violence with violence and becomes a local hero.
True story of an American vigilante, made with modest competence; its great commercial success may have been due to the support of the righteous, or of those who revel in violence.

w Mort Briskin *d* Phil Karlson *ph* Jack Marta *m* Walter Scharf

Joe Don Baker, Elizabeth Hartman, Gene Evans, Noah Beery Jnr

'A terrifying image of Nixon's silent majority at work.'—*Gareth Jones*

'It generates a primitive, atavistic sort of power: it awakens more apprehension and dredges up more complicated and contradictory emotions than one anticipates.'—*Gary Arnold*

† Sequel 1976: *Part Two Walking Tall.* (GB title: *Legend of the Lawman.*)

Wall of Noise
US 1963 112m bw
Warner (Joseph Landon)

A racehorse trainer falls for the boss's wife.
Complex but predictable melodrama of the old school, adequately presented and performed.

w Joseph Landon, *novel* Daniel Michael Stein *d* Richard Wilson *ph* Lucien Ballard *m* William Lava

Suzanne Pleshette, Ty Hardin, Dorothy Provine, Ralph Meeker, Simon Oakland, Murray Matheson, Robert F. Simon

The Walls of Jericho
US 1948 106m bw
TCF (Lamar Trotti)

An influential small-town newspaperman is undermined by his vindictive wife.
Filmed novel of standard competence but minimum interest, ending in a courtroom scene.

w Lamar Trotti, *novel* Paul Wellman *d* John M. Stahl *ph* Arthur Miller *m* Cyril Mockridge

Cornel Wilde, Linda Darnell, Anne Baxter, Kirk Douglas, Ann Dvorak, Marjorie Rambeau, Henry Hull, Colleen Townsend

The Waltons' Crisis
US 1973 100m colour TVM
Lorimar

In the thirties, a mother slowly recovers from polio.
A seasonal special shown in the middle of the series *The Waltons*; very padded out, but showing the virtues and vices of the show.

w John McGreevey

Richard Thomas, Michael Learned, Will Geer, Ellen Corby, Ralph Waite

The Waltz King
US 1963 95m Technicolor
Walt Disney (Peter V. Herald)

The life of young Johann Strauss in 1850s Vienna.
Medium-budget international family musical, tolerably well done.

w Maurice Tombragel *d* Steve Previn *ph* Gunther Anders *md* Helmuth Froschauer

Kerwin Mathews, Brian Aherne, Senta Berger, Peter Kraus, Fritz Eckhardt

The Waltz of the Toreadors*
GB 1962 105m Technicolor
Rank / Wintle–Parkyn (Peter de Sarigny)

A lecherous retired general finds his past creeping up on him and loses his young mistress to his son.
Lukewarm adaptation of a semi-classic comedy, disastrously translated to English settings and characters.

w Wolf Mankowitz, *play* Jean Anouilh *d John Guillermin ph* John Wilcox *m* Richard Addinsell *pd* Wilfrid Shingleton

Peter Sellers, Margaret Leighton, Dany Robin, John Fraser, Cyril Cusack, Prunella Scales

Waltzes from Vienna
GB 1933 80m bw
GFD / Gaumont
US title: *Strauss's Great Waltz*

A romance of the Strausses.
There is very little music and very little Hitchcock in this extremely mild romantic comedy.

w Alma Reville, Guy Bolton, *play* Guy Bolton *d* Alfred Hitchcock

Jessie Matthews, Esmond Knight, Frank Vosper, Fay Compton, Edmund Gwenn, Robert Hale, Hindle Edgar

The Wandering Jew*
GB 1933 111m bw
Gaumont / Twickenham (Julius Hagen)

A Jew is condemned to live forever, but dies in the Spanish Inquisition.
Ambitious fantasy which comes off pretty well for those in the mood, but was a curious choice for a British studio at the time.

w H. Fowler Mear, *play* E. Temple Thurston *d* Maurice Elvey

Conrad Veidt, Marie Ney, Basil Gill, Anne Grey, Dennis Hoey, John Stuart, Peggy Ashcroft, Francis L. Sullivan, Felix Ayler, Abraham Sofaer

Wanted for Murder*
GB 1946 103m bw
Marcel Hellman

A man, obsessed with the fact that his father was the public hangman, becomes a murderer himself.
Curiously stagey melodrama with intermittent use of London backgrounds; an interesting curiosity.

w Emeric Pressburger, Rodney Ackland, Maurice Cowan *d* Lawrence Huntington

Eric Portman, Dulcie Gray, Derek Farr, Roland Culver, Stanley Holloway, Barbara Everest, Bonar Colleano, Kathleen Harrison

The War against Mrs Hadley*
US 1942 86m bw
MGM (Irving Asher)

A Washington matron tries to ignore the war and preserve her social life.
Efficient little propaganda piece with a middle-aged heroine.

w George Oppenheimer *d* Harold S. Bucquet

Fay Bainter, Edward Arnold, Richard Ney, Jean Rogers, Sara Allgood, Spring Byington, Van Johnson, Isobel Elsom, Halliwell Hobbes, Miles Mander, Frances Rafferty, Connie Gilchrist

War and Peace**
US / Italy 1956 208m Technicolor Vistavision
Carlo Ponti / Dino de Laurentiis

A Russian family's adventures at the tim Napoleon's invasion.
Despite miscasting and heavy dubbing, the pictorial parts of this précis of a gargantuan novel are powerful and exciting enough; the human side drags a little.

w Bridget Boland, Robert Westerby, King Vidor, Mario Camerini, Ennio de Concini, Ivo Perelli, *novel* Leo Tolstoy *d King Vidor*, (battle scenes) *Mario Soldati ph Jack Cardiff*, (battle scenes) *Aldo Tonti m* Nino Rota *ad Mario Chiari*

Audrey Hepburn, Henry Fonda, Mel Ferrer, *Herbert Lom*, John Mills, Oscar Homolka, Wilfrid Lawson, Vittorio Gassman, Anita Ekberg, Helmut Dantine, Milly Vitale, Barry Jones

'The film has no more warmth than pictures in an art gallery.'—*Philip T. Hartung*

The War between Men and Women
US 1972 105m Technicolor Panavision
National General / Jalem / Llenroc / 4D (Danny Arnold)

A half-blind cartoonist marries a divorcee and is troubled by her ex-husband.
Semi-serious comedy vaguely based on Thurber, but not so that you'd notice, apart from the blind hero; generally neither funny nor affecting.

w Mel Shavelson, Danny Arnold, based on the writings of James Thurber *d* Melville Shavelson *ph* Charles F. Wheeler *m* Marvin Hamlisch *pd* Stan Jolley

Jack Lemmon, Barbara Harris, Jason Robards Jnr, Herb Edelman, Lisa Gerritsen

War Hunt
US 1961 83m bw
TD Enterprises (Terry Sanders)

Korea 1953: a kill-crazy private is befriended by a war orphan but finally has to be shot.
Vaguely commendable but not very expert indictment of the realities of war.

w Stanford Whitmore *d* Denis Sanders *ph* Ted McCord *m* Bud Shank

John Saxon, Robert Redford, Sidney Pollack, Charles Aidman, Tommy Matsuda

The War Lord**
US 1965 121m Technicolor Panavision
Universal / Court (Walter Seltzer)

An officer of the Duke of Normandy has trouble with Druids and the law of *droit de seigneur*.
Complex medieval melodrama with an air of fantasy about it; generally likeably strange, but the production should have been more stylized and fanciful.

w John Collier, Millard Kaufman, *play* The Lovers by Leslie Stevens *d Franklin Schaffner ph Russell Metty m* Jerome Moross *ad* Alexander Golitzen, Henry Bumstead

Charlton Heston, Richard Boone, Rosemary Forsyth, Maurice Evans, Guy Stockwell, Niall MacGinnis, Henry Wilcoxon, James Farentino

The War Lover
GB 1962 105m bw
Columbia / Arthur Hornblow Jnr

In 1943, a Flying Fortress commander based in East Anglia has the wrong ideas about women and war.
Solemn character drama punctuated by aerial battles.

w Howard Koch, *novel* John Hersey *d* Philip Leacock *ph* Bob Huke *m* Richard Addinsell

Steve McQueen, Shirley Anne Field, Robert Wagner, Gary Cockrell, Michael Crawford

A War of Children*
US 1973 73m colour TVM
Tomorrow (Roger Gimbel)

Problems of an Irish family in the present troubles.
Well-made but astonishingly anti-British lowlife drama.

w James Costigan *d* George Schaefer

Vivien Merchant, Jenny Agutter, John Ronane, Anthony Andrews

The War of the Worlds*
US 1952 85m Technicolor
Paramount / George Pal

Terrifying aliens invade Earth via the American midwest.
Spectacular battle scenes are the mainstay of this violent fantasy, which goes to pieces once the cardboard characters open their mouths.

w Barre Lyndon, *novel* H. G. Wells *d* Byron Haskin *ph* George Barnes *ad* Hal Pereira, Albert Nozaki

Gene Barry, Ann Robinson, Les Tremayne, Bob Cornthwaite, Sandra Giglio

The War Wagon**
US 1967 99m Technicolor Panavision
Universal / Batjac (Marvin Schwartz)

Two cowboys and an Indian plan to ambush the gold wagon of a crooked mining contractor.
Exhilarating but simply-plotted action western with strong comedy elements and a cast of old reliables.

w Clair Huffaker, from his novel Badman *d Burt Kennedy ph* William H. Clothier *m* Dmitri Tiomkin

John Wayne, Kirk Douglas, Howard Keel, Robert Walker, Keenan Wynn, Bruce Cabot, Gene Evans, Bruce Dern

'It all works splendidly.'—*MFB*

The Ware Case*
GB 1938 79m bw
Ealing / Capad (S. C. Balcon)

A nobleman is suspected of murdering his wife's rich brother.
Courtroom melodrama twice filmed as a silent; stagey but reasonably compelling in its way.

w Robert Stevenson, Roland Pertwee, E. V. H. Emmett, *play* G. P. Bancroft *d* Robert Stevenson

Clive Brook, Jane Baxter, Barry K. Barnes, C. V. France, Francis L. Sullivan, Frank Cellier, Edward Rigby, Peter Bull, Athene Seyler, Ernest Thesiger

Warlock*
US 1959 123m De Luxe Cinemascope
TCF (Edward Dmytryk)

The cowardly citizens of a small western town hire a gunman as their unofficial marshal.
Overlong, talkative and somewhat pretentious star western with good sequences.

w Robert Alan Aurthur, *novel* Oakley Hall *d* Edward Dmytryk *ph* Joe MacDonald *m* Leigh Harline

Henry Fonda, Richard Widmark, Anthony Quinn, Dorothy Malone, Dolores Michaels, Wallace Ford, Tom Drake, Richard Arlen, Regis Toomey, Don Beddoe, De Forrest Kelley

A Warm December
GB / US 1972 101m Technicolor
First Artists / Verdon (Melville Tucker)

A widowed American doctor in London falls for a mysterious African girl who turns out to be the dying niece of a diplomat.
Weird mishmash of *Love Story, Brief Encounter* and *Dark Victory*, getting the worst of all worlds.

w Lawrence Roman *d* Sidney Poitier *ph Paul Beeson m* Coleridge-Taylor Parkinson

Sidney Poitier, Esther Anderson, George Baker, Johnny Sekka, Earl Cameron

Warning Shot*
US 1966 100m Technicolor
Paramount / Bob Banner (Buzz Kulik)

While looking for a psychopathic killer, a cop shoots dead a man who draws a gun on him. But the dead man's gun cannot be found, and the officer is suspended . . .
Watchable mystery decked out with guest stars; possibly intended as a TV movie.

w Mann Rubin, *novel* 711 Officer Needs Help by Whit Masterson *d* Buzz Kulik *ph* Joseph Biroc *m* Jerry Goldsmith

David Janssen, Lillian Gish, Ed Begley, Keenan Wynn, Sam Wanamaker, Eleanor Parker, Stefanie Powers, Walter Pidgeon, George Sanders, George Grizzard, Steve Allen, Carroll O'Connor, Joan Collins

Warpath
US 1951 93m Technicolor
Paramount (Nat Holt)

An ex-army captain tracks down the outlaws who murdered his girl.
Goodish standard western.

w Frank Gruber *d* Byron Haskin *ph* Ray Rennahan *m* Paul Sawtell

Edmond O'Brien, Dean Jagger, Forrest Tucker, Harry Carey Jnr, Wallace Ford, Polly Bergen

Washington Story
US 1952 82m bw
MGM (Dore Schary)
GB title: *Target for Scandal*

A lady reporter goes to Washington to expose corruption, but falls for an honest congressman.
Standard flagwaver which takes itself a shade too seriously.

wd Robert Pirosh *ph* John Alton *m* Conrad Salinger

Van Johnson, Patricia Neal, Louis Calhern, Sidney Blackmer, Philip Ober, Patricia Collinge, Elizabeth Patterson, Moroni Olsen

Watch on the Rhine**
US 1943 114m bw
Warner (Hal B. Wallis)

A German refugee and his family are pursued by Nazi agents in Washington.
Talky play doesn't make much of a film, though the talk is good talk and the performances outstanding; but it made a prestige point or two for Hollywood.

w Dashiell Hammett, *play Lillian Hellman* *d* Herman Shumlin *ph* Merritt Gerstad, Hal Mohr *m* Max Steiner

Paul Lukas, Bette Davis, Lucile Watson, *George Coulouris*, Donald Woods, Geraldine Fitzgerald, Beulah Bondi, Henry Daniell

Waterhole Three
US 1967 100m Techniscope
Paramount

Sheriff, crooks and a gambler seek buried loot.
Rather irritatingly immoral western with a hero who defines rape as assault with a friendly weapon; in between it tries hard for the ballad style.

w Joseph Steck, Robert R. Young *d* William Graham *ph* Robert Burks *m* Dave Grusin

James Coburn, Carroll O'Connor, Margaret Blye, Claude Akins, Joan Blondell, Timothy Carey

Waterloo*
Italy / USSR 1970 132m Technicolor Panavision
Columbia / DDL / Mosfilm (Dino de Laurentiis)

Historical events leading up to the 1815 battle.
The battle forms the last hour of this historical charade, and looks both exciting and splendid, though confusion is not avoided. The rest is a mixed blessing.

w H. A. L. Craig, Sergei Bondartchuk *d Sergei Bondartchuk ph Armando Nannuzzi m* Nino Rota *pd* Mario Garbuglia

Rod Steiger, Christopher Plummer, Orson Welles, Jack Hawkins, Virginia McKenna, Dan O'Herlihy, Rupert Davies, Ian Ogilvy, Michael Wilding

Waterloo Bridge*
US 1931 72m bw
Universal (Carl Laemmle Jnr)

An army officer marries a ballerina; when he is reported missing his family ignore her and she sinks into prostitution.
One for the ladies, who lapped it up.

w Tom Reed, Benn W. Levy, *play* Robert E. Sherwood *d* James Whale *ph* Arthur Edeson

Mae Clarke, Kent Douglass, Doris Lloyd, Ethel Griffies, Enid Bennett, Frederick Kerr, Bette Davis

Waterloo Bridge**
US 1940 103m bw
MGM (Sidney Franklin)

Lush, all-stops-out remake of the above; for yet another version see *Gaby*.

w S. N. Behrman, Hans Rameau, George Froeschel *d* Mervyn Le Roy *ph Joseph Ruttenberg m* Herbert Stothart

Vivien Leigh, Robert Taylor, Lucile Watson, Virginia Field, Maria Ouspenskaya, C. Aubrey Smith, Steffi Duna

Waterloo Road
US 1944 76m bw
GFD / Gainsborough (Edward Black)

A soldier whose wife is enamoured of a petty crook absents himself to settle matters.
What at the time seemed cheerful realism now seems chronically forced, but amusing moments can still be found.

w Val Valentine, Sidney Gilliat *d* Sidney Gilliat

John Mills, Stewart Granger, Joy Shelton, Alastair Sim, Beatrice Varley, Alison Leggatt, *Jean Kent*

'The harsh rattle of trains over a viaduct, the clamour of the street market, the wailing of sirens and the crash of bombs are the accompaniment of this wartime love story.'—*Richard Winnington*

Watermelon Man
US 1970 100m Technicolor
Columbia / Johanna

A bigoted insurance salesman wakes up one morning to find he has turned into a black man.
Spasmodically funny racial comedy, compromised by the impossibility of a black man playing white even with heavy make-up.

w Herman Raucher *d* Melvin Van Peebles
ph W. Wallace Kelley *m* Melvin Van Peebles

Godfrey Cambridge, Estelle Parsons, Howard Caine, Mantan Moreland

Watusi
US 1959 85m Technicolor
MGM (Al Zimbalist)

Harry Quartermain retraces his father's footsteps to King Solomon's Mines.
Skilful re-use of *King Solomon's Mines* footage; acceptable Boys' Own Paper stuff.

w James Clavell *d* Kurt Neumann *ph* Harold E. Wellman

George Montgomery, Taina Elg, David Farrar, Rex Ingram, Dan Seymour

The Way Ahead***
GB 1944 115m bw
GFD / Two Cities (John Sutro, Norman Walker)

Adventures of a platoon of raw recruits during World War II.
Memorable semi-documentary originally intended as a training film; the warm humour of the early scenes, however, never leads quite naturally into the final action and tragedy.

w Eric Ambler, Peter Ustinov *d Carol Reed*
ph Guy Green

David Niven, Stanley Holloway, Raymond Huntley, *William Hartnell*, James Donald, John Laurie, Leslie Dwyer, Hugh Burden, Jimmy Hanley, Renée Asherson, Penelope Dudley Ward, Reginald Tate, Leo Genn, Mary Jerrold, Peter Ustinov

Way Down East
US 1935 85m bw
TCF (Winfield Sheehan)

A New England maiden is suspected of immorality.
Tedious and unwise remake of the silent classic, complete with ice floe climax.

w Howard Estabrook, William Hurlbut, *play* Lottie Blair Parker *d* Henry King

Rochelle Hudson, Henry Fonda, Slim Summerville, Edward Trevor, Margaret Hamilton, Andy Devine, Spring Byington, Russell Simpson, Sara Haden

Way for a Sailor
US 1930 83m bw
MGM

Adventures of a tough seafarer and a pet seal.
Thin vehicle for a declining star whose talkie voice was at odds with his image.

w Laurence Stallings, W. L. River, *novel* Albert Richard Wetjen *d* Sam Wood *ph* Percy Hilburn

John Gilbert, Wallace Beery, Leila Hyams, Jim Tully, Polly Moran, Doris Lloyd

Way of a Gaucho
US 1952 91m Technicolor
TCF (Philip Dunne)

An Argentine gaucho joins the militia and fig Indians.
Mildly interesting western-in-disguise.

w Philip Dunne, *novel* Herbert Childs *d* Jacques Tourneur *ph* Harry Jackson *m* Sol Kaplan

Rory Calhoun, Gene Tierney, Richard Boone, Hugh Marlowe, Everett Sloane, Enrique Chaico

Way Out West****
US 1937 66m bw
Hal Roach (Stan Laurel)

Laurel and Hardy come to Brushwood Gulch to deliver the deed to a gold mine.
Seven reels of perfect joy, with the comedians at their very best in brilliantly-timed routines, plus two song numbers as a bonus.

w Jack Jevne, Charles Rogers, James Parrott, Felix Adler d James Horne ph Art Lloyd, Walter Lundin

Stan Laurel, Oliver Hardy, James Finlayson, Sharon Lynne, Rosina Lawrence

'Not only one of their most perfect films, it ranks with the best screen comedy anywhere.' —*David Robinson, 1962*

The Way to Love
US 1933 80m bw
Paramount (Benjamin Glazer)

A would-be Paris tourist guide works as a pavement hawker and helps a showgirl evade her knife-thrower partner.
Thin star vehicle with a few pleasant moments.

w Gene Fowler, Benjamin Glazer *d* Norman Taurog *ph* Charles Lang *m/ly* Ralph Rainger, Leo Robin

Maurice Chevalier, Edward Everett Horton, Ann Dvorak, Arthur Pierson, Minna Gombell, Blanche Frederici, Douglass Dumbrille, John Miljan

The Way to the Gold
US 1957 94m bw Cinemascope
TCF (David Weisbart)

An ex-convict seeks hidden loot but is pursued by competitors.
Gloomy, self-pitying melodrama.

w Wendell Mayes, *novel* Wilber Steele *d* Robert D. Webb *ph* Leo Tover *m* Lionel Newman

Jeffrey Hunter, Sheree North, Barry Sullivan, Walter Brennan, Ruth Donnelly, Neville Brand

The Way to the Stars****
GB 1945 109m bw
Two Cities (Anatole de Grunwald)
US title: *Johnny in the Clouds*

World War II as seen by the guests at a small hotel near an airfield.
Generally delightful comedy drama suffused with tragic atmosphere but with very few flying shots, one of the few films which instantly bring back the atmosphere of the war in Britain for anyone who was involved.

w Terence Rattigan, Anatole de Grunwald poem John Pudney d Anthony Asquith

John Mills, Rosamund John, Michael Redgrave, Douglass Montgomery, Basil Radford, Stanley Holloway, Joyce Carey, Renée Asherson, Felix Aylmer, Bonar Colleano, Trevor Howard, Jean Simmons

Way Way Out
US 1966 105m De Luxe Cinemascope
TCF / Coldwater / Jerry Lewis (Malcolm Stuart)

In 1994 a weather expert on the moon has woman trouble.
Dismal sex farce with an unusual backdrop; painful to sit through.

w William Bowers, Laslo Vadnay *d* Gordon Douglas *ph* William H. Clothier *m* Lalo Schifrin

Jerry Lewis, Connie Stevens, Robert Morley, Dick Shawn, Anita Ekberg, Dennis Weaver, Howard Morris, Brian Keith

The Way We Were**
US 1973 118m Eastmancolor Panavision
Columbia / Rastar (Ray Stark)

The romance and marriage of an upper-crust young novelist and a Jewish bluestocking girl, from college to Hollywood in the thirties, forties and fifties.
Instant nostalgia for Americans, some fun and a lot of boredom for everybody is provided by this very patchy star vehicle which makes a particular mess of the McCarthy witch hunt sequence but has undeniable moments of vitality.

w Arthur Laurents, from his novel *d* Sydney Pollack *ph* Harry Stradling Jnr *m* Marvin Hamlisch

Barbra Streisand, Robert Redford, Patrick O'Neal, Viveca Lindfors, Bradford Dillman, Lois Chiles, Allyn Ann McLerie, Herb Edelman, Murray Hamilton

'Not one moment of the picture is anything but garbage under the gravy of false honesty.'—*Stanley Kauffmann*

The Way West*
US 1967 122m De Luxe Panavision
UA / Harold Hecht

Hazards of a wagon train between Missouri and Oregon in 1843.
Semi-spectacular western which looks good but falls apart dramatically, especially in its insistence on a sub-plot about a most unlikely nymphet.

w Ben Maddow, Mitch Lindemann, *novel* A. B. Guthrie Jnr *d* Andrew V. McLaglen *ph William H. Clothier m* Bronislau Kaper

Kirk Douglas, Robert Mitchum, Richard Widmark, Lola Albright, Michael Witney, Sally Field, Stubby Kaye, Jack Elam

'A jerk's idea of an epic; big stars, big landscapes, bad jokes, folksy-heroic music to

plug up the holes, and messy hang-ups.'
—*Pauline Kael*

The Wayward Bus
US 1957 89m bw Cinemascope
TCF (Charles Brackett)

A landslide strands an assortment of bus passengers in a lonely farmhouse . . .
. . . but not the old dark house, unfortunately: this lot does nothing but talk, and the plot never really forms.

w Ivan Moffat, *novel* John Steinbeck *d* Victor Vicas *ph* Charles G. Clarke *m* Leigh Harline

Dan Dailey, Jayne Mansfield, Joan Collins, Rick Jason, Dolores Michaels, Larry Keating, Betty Lou Keim

We Are Not Alone*
US 1939 112m bw
Warner (Henry Blanke)

A man having an innocent affair is accused of murdering his wife.
Gloomy, well-acted drama with a rather uneasy English setting.

w James Hilton, Milton Krims, *novel* James Hilton *d* Edmund Goulding *ph* Tony Gaudio *m* Max Steiner

Paul Muni, Jane Bryan, Flora Robson, Raymond Severn, Una O'Connor, Henry Daniell, Montagu Love, James Stephenson, Cecil Kellaway

We Dive at Dawn
GB 1943 98m bw
GFD / Gainsborough (Edward Black)

World War II adventures of a British submarine disabled in the Baltic.
Fairly routine war suspenser.

w J. P. Williams, Val Valentine, Frank Launder *d* Anthony Asquith

John Mills, Eric Portman, Reginald Purdell, Niall MacGinnis, Joan Hopkins, Josephine Wilson, Jack Watling

We Joined the Navy
GB 1962 105m Eastmancolor Cinemascope
Dial / Daniel M. Angel

A carefree naval commander and three cadets get involved in the affairs of a small Mediterranean country.
Desperate naval farce which sinks from script malnutrition in reel two.

w Arthur Dales, *novel* John Winton *d* Wendy Toye *ph* Otto Heller *m* Ron Grainer

Kenneth More, Lloyd Nolan, Mischa Auer, Joan O'Brien, Jeremy Lloyd, Dinsdale Landen, Derek Fowlds

We Live Again*
US 1934 85m bw
Samuel Goldwyn

A Russian prince is brought up in the country and falls in love with a servant girl whose life later takes a downward path.
Beautifully made but dramatically uninteresting version of a Russian classic.

w Preston Sturges, Maxwell Anderson, Leonard Praskins, *novel* Resurrection by Leo Tolstoy *d Rouben Mamoulian ph Gregg Toland* *m* Alfred Newman

Fredric March, Anna Sten, Jane Baxter, C. Aubrey Smith, Ethel Griffies, Jessie Ralph, Sam Jaffe

We Were Dancing
US 1942 93m bw
MGM (Robert Z. Leonard, Orville Dull)

A Polish princess elopes from her engagement party with a gigolo.
Leaden romantic comedy produced in high style.

w Claudine West, Hans Rameau, George Froeschel, partly based on the play Tonight at 8.30 by Noel Coward *d* Robert Z. Leonard *ph* Robert Planck *m* Bronislau Kaper

Norma Shearer, Melvyn Douglas, Gail Patrick, Lee Bowman, *Marjorie Main,* Reginald Owen, Alan Mowbray, Florence Bates, Sig Rumann, Dennis Hoey, Heather Thatcher, Connie Gilchrist

We Were Strangers*
US 1949 105m bw
Columbia / Horizon (Sam Spiegel)

Cuban rebels in the thirties plan to assassinate a politician and have to build a tunnel through a cemetery.
Well-made but very downbeat adventure story, too cheerless to be exciting.

w Peter Viertel, John Huston, *novel* Rough Sketch by Robert Sylvester *d John Huston* *ph* Russell Metty *m* Georges Antheil

John Garfield, Jennifer Jones, Pedro Armendariz, Gilbert Roland, Wally Cassell, Ramon Novarro, David Bond, Jose Perez

'There is so much about this film I cannot swallow – the implausibilities of detail, the convention of broken accents, the literary conversaziones, the naïve doctrines of revolution . . . [but] it continues to haunt the mind and has therefore had its say.'—*Richard Winnington*

The Weapon
GB 1956 81m bw Superscope 235
Penclean (Frank Bevis)

A boy finds a loaded revolver on a bomb site and mistakenly thinks he has killed someone with it. Standard suspenser with a cast worthy of something more interesting.

w Fred Freiburger *d* Val Guest *ph* Reg Wyer *m* James Stevens

Lizabeth Scott, Steve Cochran, George Cole, Herbert Marshall, Nicole Maurey, Jon Whiteley, Laurence Naismith

The Web*
US 1947 87m bw
U-I

A financier hires a young lawyer as his bodyguard and lures him into committing murder.
Modestly well staged and glossy thriller.

w William Bowers, Bertram Millhauser *d* Michael Gordon *ph* Irving Glassberg *m* Hans Salter

Edmond O'Brien, Vincent Price, Ella Raines, William Bendix

The Webster Boy
GB 1961 83m bw
Emmet Dalton

A teenager suffers at the hands of a sadistic schoolmaster.
Curious, totally unbelievable melodrama.

w Ted Allen *d* Don Chaffey *ph* Gerald Gibbs *m* Wilfrid Joseph

Richard O'Sullivan, John Cassavetes, David Farrar, Elizabeth Sellars, Niall MacGinnis

The Wedding Night*
US 1935 83m bw
Samuel Goldwyn

A Connecticut author causes tragedy when he takes an interest in the local Polish immigrant farmers and especially in the daughter of one of them.
Interesting and unusual but slightly tediously told drama.

w Edith Fitzgerald *d* King Vidor *ph* Gregg Toland *m* Alfred Newman

Gary Cooper, Anna Sten, Sig Rumann, Helen Vinson, Ralph Bellamy, Esther Dale

Wedding Present*
US 1936 81m bw
Paramount (B. P. Schulberg)

A pair of crack newspaper reporters take their jobs and themselves lightly.
Whimsical star comedy with some funny scenes.

w Joseph Anthony, *story* Paul Gallico *d* Richard Wallace *ph* Leon Shamroy

Cary Grant, Joan Bennett, George Bancroft. Conrad Nagel, Gene Lockhart, William Demarest, Edward Brophy

Wedding Rehearsal
GB 1932 84m bw
Ideal / Alexander Korda

A Guards officer foils his grandmother's plans to get him married by finding suitors for all the young ladies offered.
Frail comedy with unsure technique.

w Lajos Biro, Arthur Wimperis *d* Alexander Korda

Roland Young, George Grossmith, John Loder, Lady Tree, Wendy Barrie, Maurice Evans, Joan Gardner, Merle Oberon, Kate Cutler, Edmund Breon

Wee Willie Winkie**
US 1937 99m bw
TCF (Gene Markey)

A small girl becomes the mascot of a British regiment in India.
Vaguely based on a Kipling tale, this was the most expensive Temple vehicle and a first-rate family action picture with sentimental asides.

w Ernest Pascal, Julien Josephson, *story* Rudyard Kipling *d John Ford ph Arthur Miller*

Shirley Temple, Victor McLaglen, C. Aubrey Smith, June Lang, Michael Whalen, Cesar Romero, Constance Collier, Gavin Muir

Weekend at the Waldorf*
US 1945 130m bw
MGM (Arthur Hornblow Jnr)

Four stories about guests at New York's largest hotel.
Disguised version of *Grand Hotel,* with the same stories twisted; the talent at hand, however, is serviceable rather than inspiring.

w Sam and Bella Spewack *d* Robert Z. Leonard *ph* Robert Planck *md* Johnny Green

Ginger Rogers, Walter Pidgeon, Van Johnson, Lana Turner, Robert Benchley, Edward Arnold, Constance Collier, Leon Ames, Warner Anderson, Phyllis Thaxter, Keenan Wynn, Porter Hall, Samuel S. Hinds, George Zucco, Xavier Cugat

Weekend in Havana
US 1941 80m Technicolor
TCF (William Le Baron)

A shopgirl in Havana falls for a shipping executive.
Routine Fox musical showcasing familiar talents: adequate wartime escapist fare.

w Karl Tunberg, Darrell Ware *d* Walter Lang *ph* Ernest Palmer *md* Alfred Newman

Alice Faye, John Payne, Carmen Miranda, Cesar Romero, Cobina Wright Jnr, George Barbier, Sheldon Leonard, Leonid Kinskey

The Weekend Nun
US 1972 75m colour TVM
Paramount

A young nun is a parole officer during the week.
Beyond comment: some people will like it.

w Ken Trevey *d* Jeannot Szwarc

Joanna Pettet, Vic Morrow, Beverly Garland, Ann Sothern, James Gregory, Barbara Werle, Kay Lenz

Weekend of Terror*
US 1970 74m colour TVM
Paramount

Two young killers accidentally kill a hostage and search for a lookalike to replace her.
Fast-moving suspenser.

w Lionel E. Siegel *d* Jud Taylor

Robert Conrad, Lois Nettleton, Lee Majors, Carol Lynley, Jane Wyatt

Weekend with Father
US 1951 83m bw
U-I (Ted Richmond)

A widow and a widower fall in love when taking their respective children to a summer camp.
Mechanical comedy of upsets and embarrassments.

w Joseph Hoffman *d* Douglas Sirk *ph* Clifford Stine *m* Frank Skinner

Van Heflin, Patricia Neal, Gigi Perreau, Virginia Field, Richard Denning

Welcome Danger*
US 1929 110m bw
Harold Lloyd

The meek son of a police chief gets involved in a tong war.
Moderate early talkie comedy showing the star in some trouble with pace and dialogue.

w Clyde Bruckman, Lex Neal, Felix Adler, Paul Gerard Smith *d* Clyde Bruckman *ph* Walter Lundin, Henry Kohler

Harold Lloyd, Barbara Kent, Noah Young, Charles Middleton

Welcome Home Johnny Bristol**
US 1971 100m colour TVM
Cinema Center

A wounded Vietnam veteran seeks the hometown he dreamed of, but finds only mystery.
A good, gripping puzzler.

d George McCowan

Martin Landau, Jane Alexander, Brock Peters, Forrest Tucker, Martin Sheen, Pat O'Brien, Mona Freeman

Welcome Stranger
US 1947 107m bw
Paramount (Sol C. Siegel)

A genial young doctor fills in for a crusty old one on vacation in a small town.
Formula sentimental comedy, one of several reuniting the stars of *Going My Way.*

w Arthur Sheekman *d* Elliott Nugent *ph* Lionel Lindon *m* Robert Emmett Dolan

Bing Crosby, Barry Fitzgerald, Joan Caulfield, Wanda Hendrix, Frank Faylen, Elizabeth Patterson, Robert Shayne, Percy Kilbride

Welcome to Hard Times*
US 1967 103m Metrocolor
MGM / Max E. Youngstein, David Carr
GB title: *Killer on a Horse*

A small western town arms itself against a mysterious bandit.
Curiously likeable, almost symbolic suspense western which has a good start and middle but not much idea how to end.

wd Burt Kennedy, novel E. L. Doctorow *ph* Harry Stradling Jnr *m* Harry Sukman

Henry Fonda, Janice Rule, Keenan Wynn, Janis Paige, John Anderson, Warren Oates, Fay Spain, Edgar Buchanan, Aldo Ray, Lon Chaney Jnr, Elisha Cook Jnr

Welcome to the Club
GB 1970 · 88m bw
Welcome (Sam Lomberg)

Hiroshima 1945; an American Quaker sergeant upsets military protocol.
Pale satirical comedy shot in Copenhagen.

w Clement Biddle Wood, from his novel *d* Walter Shenson *ph* Mikael Salomon *m* Ken Thomas

Brian Foley, Jack Warden, Lee Meredith, Andy Jarrett

The Well*
US 1951 85m bw
Cardinal / Harry M. Popkin (Clarence Greene, Leo Popkin)

A black child falls down a well, and the town unites to save her.
Forceful high-pitched melodrama, cut to a do-gooder pattern which became very familiar.

w Russel Rouse, Clarence Greene *d* Leo Popkin, Russel Rouse *ph* Ernest Laszlo *m* Dmitri Tiomkin

Richard Rober, Henry Morgan, Barry Kelley, Christine Larson

The Well Groomed Bride*
US 1946 75m bw
Paramount (Fred Kohlmar)

A naval officer searches San Francisco for a magnum of champagne with which to launch a ship.
Thin but cheerful star comedy.

w Claude Binyon, Robert Russell *d* Sidney Lanfield *ph* John F. Seitz *m* Roy Webb

Ray Milland, Olivia de Havilland, Sonny Tufts, James Gleason, Constance Dowling, Percy Kilbride, Jean Heather

Wells Fargo*
US 1937 115m bw
Paramount (Frank Lloyd)

How the express delivery service was built up.
Large-scale, entertaining western with overmuch emphasis on domestic issues.

w Paul Schofield, Gerald Geraghty, John Boland, *story* Stuart N. Lake *d* Frank Lloyd *ph* Theodor Sparkuhl *m* Victor Young

Joel McCrea, Bob Burns, Frances Dee, Lloyd Nolan, Henry O'Neill, Mary Nash, Ralph Morgan, John Mack Brown, Porter Hall, Clarence Kolb

Went the Day Well?*
GB 1942 92m bw
Ealing (S. C. Balcon)
US title: *Forty-eight Hours*

Villagers resist when German paratroopers invade an English village and the squire proves to be a quisling.
Could-it-happen melodrama which made excellent wartime propaganda; generally well staged.

w Angus MacPhail, John Dighton, Diana Morgan, *story* Graham Greene *d* Cavalcanti

Leslie Banks, Elizabeth Allen, Frank Lawton, Basil Sydney, Valerie Taylor, Mervyn Johns, Edward Rigby, Marie Lohr, C. V. France, David Farrar

We're No Angels*
US 1954 106m Technicolor Vistavision
Paramount (Pat Duggan)

Whimsical, overstretched period comedy suffering from miscasting but with some pleasantries along the way.
Three escaped Devil's Island convicts help a downtrodden storekeeper and his family to outwit a scheming relative.

w Ranald MacDougall, *play* La Cuisine des Anges by Albert Husson *d* Michael Curtiz *ph* Loyal Griggs *m* Frederick Hollander

Humphrey Bogart, *Peter Ustinov,* Aldo Ray, Joan Bennett, Basil Rathbone, Leo G. Carroll, John Smith

We're Not Dressing*
US 1934 77m bw
Paramount (Benjamin Glazer)

A spoiled heiress shipwrecked on a Pacific island is tamed by an easy-going sailor.
Pleasant, madly dated, light-hearted variation on a much-filmed play, resolving itself into a series of comic turns.

w Horace Jackson, Francis Martin, George Marion Jnr, *play* The Admirable Crichton by J. M. Barrie *d* Norman Taurog *ph* Charles Lang *songs* Harry Revel, Mack Gordon

Bing Crosby, Carole Lombard, George Burns, Gracie Allen, Leon Errol, Ethel Merman, Jay Henry, Ray Milland

We're Not Married*
US 1952 85m bw
TCF (Nunnally Johnson)

Six couples find that they were never legally married.
Amiable, smartly-played compendium of sketches on a familiar theme.

w Nunnally Johnson *d* Edmund Goulding *ph* Leo Tover *m* Cyril Mockridge

Ginger Rogers, Fred Allen, Victor Moore, Paul Douglas, Eve Arden, Marilyn Monroe, David Wayne, Louis Calhern, Zsa Zsa Gabor, Mitzi Gaynor, Eddie Bracken, James Gleason, Jane Darwell

The Werewolf
US 1956 80m bw
Columbia / Clover (Sam Katzman)

In a small mountain town, a victim of radiation

exposure periodically becomes a werewolf and is hounded down.
Absurd and tedious thriller which wastes an interesting background.

w Robert E. Kent, James B. Gordon *d* Fred F. Sears *ph* Edwin Linden *m* Mischa Bakaleinikoff

Steven Ritch, Don McGowan, Joyce Holden

Werewolf of London*
US 1935 75m bw
Universal

Werewolves fight for a rare Tibetan flower with curative properties.
Patchy horror film which lurches from excellent suspense scenes to tedious chunks of superfluous dialogue. In many ways a milestone in the history of its kind.

w Robert Harris *d Stuart Walker ph Charles Stumar*

Henry Hull, Warner Oland, Valerie Hobson, Spring Byington, Lester Matthews, Zeffie Tilbury, Ethel Griffies

West Eleven
GB 1963 93m bw
(ABP) Daniel M. Angel (Vivian Cox)

A young London drifter is offered £10,000 to commit murder.
Dingy but not very convincing 'realist' melodrama with a jazzy style which induces weariness.

w Keith Waterhouse, Willis Hall, *novel* The Furnished Room by Laura del Rivo *ph* Otto Heller *m* Stanley Black, Acker Bilk

Alfred Lynch, Eric Portman, Kathleen Harrison, Diana Dors, Kathleen Breck, Freda Jackson, Finlay Currie, Harold Lang

West Point of the Air
US 1935 90m bw
MGM (Monta Bell)

The army sergeant father of an air cadet has great hopes for him.
Routine sentimental flagwaver.

w James J. McGuinness, John Monk Saunders, Frank Wead, Arthur J. Beckhard *d* Richard Rosson *ph* Clyde de Vinna, Charles A. Marshall, Elmer Dyer

Wallace Beery, Robert Young, Maureen O'Sullivan, Lewis Stone, James Gleason, Rosalind Russell, Russell Hardie, Henry Wadsworth, Robert Taylor

West Point Story*
US 1950 107m bw
Warner (Louis F. Edelman)
GB title: *Fine and Dandy*

A Broadway producer stages a show at the military academy.
Thin and rather tedious musical saved by its irrepressible star.

w John Monks Jnr, Charles Hoffman, Irving Wallace *d* Roy del Ruth *ph* Sid Hickox *md* Ray Heindorf *songs* Sammy Cahn, Jule Styne

James Cagney, Virginia Mayo, Doris Day, Gordon Macrae, Gene Nelson, Alan Hale Jnr, Roland Winters, Jerome Cowan

West Side Story***
US 1961 155m Technicolor Panavision 70
(UA) Mirisch / Seven Arts (Robert Wise)

The Romeo and Juliet story in a New York dockland setting.
The essentially theatrical conception of this entertainment is nullified by determinedly realistic settings which make much of it seem rather silly, but production values are fine and the song numbers electrifying.

w Ernest Lehman, *play* Arthur Laurents, after Shakespeare *d Robert Wise, Jerome Robbins ph* Daniel L. Fapp *m Leonard Bernstein ly Stephen Sondheim pd* Boris Leven

Natalie Wood (sung by Marni Nixon), Richard Beymer (sung by Jimmy Bryant), Russ Tamblyn, *Rita Moreno*, George Chakiris

Western Union**
US 1941 94m Technicolor
TCF (Harry Joe Brown)

Politicians and crooks hamper the laying of cross country cables.
First rate western with familiar excitements.

w Robert Carson, *novel* Zane Grey *d* Fritz Lang *ph* Edward Cronjager *m* David Buttolph

Randolph Scott, Robert Young, Dean Jagger, Virginia Gilmore, Slim Summerville, John Carradine, Chill Wills, Barton MacLane

The Westerner**
US 1940 99m bw
Samuel Goldwyn

Judge Roy Bean comes to grief through his love for Lily Langtry.
Moody melodramatic western with comedy touches; generally entertaining, the villain more so than the hero.

w Jo Swerling, Niven Busch, *story* Stuart N.

Lake *d William Wyler ph Gregg Toland m* Dmitri Tiomkin

Gary Cooper, *Walter Brennan*, Doris Davenport, Fred Stone, Paul Hurst, Chill Wills, Charles Halton, Forrest Tucker, Dana Andrews, Lilian Bond, Tom Tyler

Westward Ho the Wagons
US 1956 85m Technicolor Cinemascope
Walt Disney (Bill Walsh)

A wagon train defends itself against Indians.
Slow and simple-minded family western.

w Tom Blackburn *d* William Beaudine *ph* Charles Boyle *m* George Bruns

Fess Parker, Kathleen Crowley, Jeff York, David Stollery, Sebastian Cabot, George Reeves

Westward Passage
US 1932 73m bw
RKO (David O. Selznick)

A wealthy girl weds a poor novelist but wants the rich full life for their children.
Dogged romantic drama with only the casting of interest.

w Bradley and Humphrey King, *novel* Margaret Ayer Barnes *d* Robert Milton *ph* Lucien Andriot *m* Max Steiner

Ann Harding, Laurence Olivier, Zasu Pitts, Irving Pichel, Juliette Compton, Florence Roberts

Westward the Women*
US 1951 118m bw
MGM (Dore Schary)

In the 1850s an Indian scout leads 150 Chicago women to meet husbands in California.
Good-looking episodic western, apparently intended mainly to amuse but seldom rising to the occasion.

w Charles Schnee *d* William Wellman *ph William Mellor m* Jeff Alexander

Robert Taylor, Denise Darcel, John McIntire, Marilyn Erskine, Hope Emerson, Lenore Lonergan, Julie Bishop

Westworld**
US 1973 89m Metrocolor Panavision
MGM (Paul N. Lazarus III)

In a millionaire holiday resort which recreates the past, a western badman robot goes berserk and relentlessly attacks two visitors.
Unusual and amusing but under-produced melodrama with slipshod story development and continuity, atoned for by memorable moments and underlying excitement.

wd Michael Crichton ph Gene Polito *m* Fred Karlin *ad* Herman Blumenthal

Yul Brynner, Richard Benjamin, James Brolin, Norman Bartold, Alan Oppenheimer

The Wet Parade*
US 1932 122m bw
MGM (Hunt Stromberg)

A politician points to the corruption caused by prohibition.
Sociologically interesting melodrama.

w John Lee Mahin, *novel* Upton Sinclair *d* Victor Fleming *ph* George Barnes

Walter Huston, Myrna Loy, Neil Hamilton, Lewis Stone, Jimmy Durante, Wallace Ford, Dorothy Jordan, John Miljan, Robert Young

What a Way to Go*
US 1963 111m De Luxe Cinemascope
TCF / APJAC / Orchard (Arthur P. Jacobs)

An immensely rich girl tells her psychiatrist how all her husbands proved not only successful but accident-prone.
Wild, mainly agreeable, star-and-gag-laden black comedy which starts on too high a note and fails to sustain.

w Betty Comden, Adolph Green *d* J. Lee-Thompson *ph* Leon Shamroy *m* Nelson Riddle *ly* Comden and Green *songs* Jule Styne

Shirley Maclaine, Bob Cummings, Dick Van Dyke, Robert Mitchum, Gene Kelly, Dean Martin, Paul Newman, Reginald Gardiner, Margaret Dumont

What Are Best Friends For?
US 1973 74m colour TVM
ABC Circle

A man thrown out by his wife moves in with his best friends.
Underwritten treatment of a pleasant idea.

w Rubin Carson, J. A. Vapors *d* Jay Sandrich

Ted Bessell, Lee Grant, Larry Hagman, Barbara Feldon, Nita Talbot

What Became of Jack and Jill?
GB 1971 90m De Luxe
Palomar / Amicus (Milton Subotsky)

A young man tries to hasten his grandmother's death but she has the last laugh.
Feeble suspenser with a dim ending.

w Roger Marshall, *novel* The Ruthless Ones by Laurence Moody *d* Bill Bain *ph* Gerry Turpin *m* Carl Davis

Vanessa Howard, Paul Nicholas, Mona Washbourne, Peter Copley, Peter Jeffrey

What Changed Charley Farthing
GB 1975 101m Eastmancolor
Patina–Hidalgo (Tristam Cones)

A philandering sailor has adventures in Cuba.
Weirdly ineffective comedy actioner which never gets started and should never have been thought of.

w David Pursall, Jack Seddon, *novel* Mark Hebdon *d* Sidney Hayers *ph* Graham Edgar *m* Angela Arteaga

Doug McClure, Lionel Jeffries, Warren Mitchell, Hayley Mills, Dilys Hamlett, Fernando Sancho

What Did You Do in the War, Daddy?
US 1966 115m De Luxe Panavision
UA / Mirisch / Geoffrey (Owen Crump, Blake Edwards)

In 1943, an Italian town surrenders readily to the Americans providing its wine festival and football match can take place.
Silly war comedy with insufficient jokes for its wearisome length. The performances are bright enough.

w William Peter Blatty *d* Blake Edwards *ph* Philip Lathrop *m* Henry Mancini

James Coburn, Dick Shawn, Sergio Fantoni, Giovanni Ralli, Aldo Ray, Harry Morgan, Carroll O'Connor, Leon Askin

What Price Glory?*
US 1952 111m Technicolor
TCF (Sol. C. Siegel)

In 1917 France Captain Flagg and Sergeant Quirt spar for the same girl.
Stagey remake of the celebrated silent film and play; watchable if not exactly inspired.

w Phoebe and Henry Ephron, *play* Maxwell Anderson, Lawrence Stallings *d* John Ford *m* Alfred Newman

James Cagney, Dan Dailey, Corinne Calvet, William Demarest, Robert Wagner, Marisa Pavan, James Gleason

What Price Hollywood?*
US 1932 87m bw
RKO (Pandro S. Berman)

A waitress becomes a film star with the help of a drunken director who later commits suicide.
Fairly trenchant early study of the mores of the film city, later revamped as *A Star Is Born*.

w Jane Murfin, Ben Markson, Gene Fowler, Rowland Brown, *story* Adela Rogers St John *d George Cukor* *ph* Charles Rosher *m* Max Steiner *montage* Slavko Vorkapitch

Constance Bennett, Lowell Sherman, Neil Hamilton, Gregory Ratoff, Brooks Bendict, Louise Beavers, Eddie Anderson

Whatever Happened to Aunt Alice?*
US 1969 101m Metrocolor
Associates and Aldrich / Palomar

A genteel widow murders her housekeepers for their private incomes.
Ladylike shocker with some black humour and good performances.

w Theodore Apstein, *novel* The Forbidden Garden by Ursula Curtiss *d* Lee H. Katzin *ph* Joseph Biroc *m* Gerald Fried

Geraldine Page, Ruth Gordon, Rosemary Forsyth, Robert Fuller, Mildred Dunnock

Whatever Happened to Baby Jane?*
US 1962 132m bw
Warner Seven Arts / Associates and Aldrich (Robert Aldrich)

In middle age, a demented ex-child star lives in an old Hollywood mansion with her invalid sister, and tension leads to murder.
Famous for marking the first time Hollywood's ageing first ladies stooped to horror, and followed by *Hush Hush Sweet Charlotte* and the other *Whatevers*, this dreary looking melodrama only occasionally grabs the attention and has enough plot for about half its length. The performances, however, are striking.

w Lukas Heller *d* Robert Aldrich *ph* Ernest Haller *m* Frank de Vol

Bette Davis, Joan Crawford, Victor Buono, Anna Lee

'It goes on and on, in a light much dimmer than necessary, and the climax, when it belatedly arrives, is a bungled, languid mingling of pursuers and pursued . . .'—*New Yorker*

What's a Nice Girl Like You . . .?**
US 1971 73m Technicolor TVM
Universal (Norman Lloyd)

A working girl impersonates a socialite and is drawn into an elaborate plot.
Sharply written and acted gangster comedy.

w Howard Fast, novel E. V. Cunningham *d* Jerry Paris

Brenda Vaccaro, Vincent Price, Jack Warden, Roddy McDowall, Edmond O'Brien, Jo Ann Worley

What's Good for the Goose
GB 1969 104m Eastmancolor
Tigon (Tony Tenser, Norman Wisdom)

An assistant bank manager falls for a girl hitch-hiker and tries to recover his youth.

Embarrassing attempt to build a sexy vehicle for a star whose sentimental mugging always appealed mainly to children.

w Norman Wisdom *d* Menahem Golan *ph* William Brayne *m* Reg Tilsley

Norman Wisdom, Sally Geeson, Sally Bazeley, Derek Francis, Terence Alexander

What's New Pussycat?
US / France 1965 108m Technicolor
UA / Famous Artists (Charles K. Feldman)

A fashion editor is distracted by beautiful girls. Zany sex comedy with many more misses than hits, a product of the wildly swinging sixties when it was thought that a big budget and stars making fools of themselves would automatically ensure a success.

w Woody Allen *d* Clive Donner *ph* Jean Badal *m Burt Bacharach*

Peter O'Toole, Peter Sellers, Woody Allen, Ursula Andress, Romy Schneider, Capucine, Paula Prentiss

'Unfortunately for all concerned, to make something enjoyably dirty a lot of taste is required.'—*John Simon*

What's So Bad About Feeling Good?
US 1965 94m Technicolor
Universal (George Seaton)

A 'happy virus' is carried into New York by a toucan, and affects the lives of various people. Flimsy pretext for a comedy, further hampered by a less than sparkling script. The actors have their moments.

w George Seaton, Robert Pirosh *d* George Seaton *ph* Ernesto Caparros *m* Frank de Vol

George Peppard, Mary Tyler Moore, Dom De Luise, John McMartin, Susan St James, Don Stroud, Charles Lane

What's the Matter with Helen?*
US 1971 101m De Luxe
Filmways / Raymax (George Edwards, James C. Pratt)

In 1934 Hollywood, two women run a dancing school for child stars; one of them is a killer. More *Baby Jane* melodramatics, quite lively and with interesting period detail.

w Henry Farrell *d* Curtis Harrington *ph* Lucien Ballard *m* David Raksin *pd Eugene Lourié*

Debbie Reynolds, Shelley Winters, Micheal MacLiammoir, Dennis Weaver, Agnes Moorehead

'A cast of seasoned troupers cannot quite alter the impression that they are all working to revive a stiff.'—*Bruce Williamson*

What's Up, Doc?**
US 1972 94m Technicolor
Warner / Saticoy (Peter Bogdanovich)

In San Francisco, an absent-minded young musicologist is troubled by the attentions of a dotty girl who gets him involved with crooks and a series of accidents.
Madcap comedy, a pastiche of several thirties originals. Spectacular stapstick and willing players are somewhat let down by exhausted patches and a tame final reel.

w Buck Henry, David Newman, Robert Benton *d Peter Bogdanovich* *ph* Laszlo Kovacs *m* Artie Butler *pd* Polly Pratt

Barbra Streisand, Ryan O'Neal, Kenneth Mars, Austin Pendleton, Madeleine Kahn, Mabel Albertson, Sorrell Booke

'A comedy made by a man who has seen a lot of movies, knows all the mechanics, and has absolutely no sense of humour. Seeing it is like shaking hands with a joker holding a joy buzzer: the effect is both presumptuous and unpleasant.'—*Jay Cocks*

'It's all rather like a 19th-century imitation of Elizabethan blank verse drama.'—*Stanley Kauffmann*

Wheeler and Murdoch*
US 1970 70m colour TVM
Paramount

Seattle private eyes take on an assignment to guard money that proves to belong to the Syndicate.
Routine cops and robbers with an agreeably fresh and rainy location and a whiff in the script of *The Maltese Falcon*. It didn't make a series for all that.

w Jerry Ludwig, Eric Bercovici *d* Joseph Sargent

Jack Warden, Christopher Stone, Van Johnson, Charles Cioffi, Jane Powell, Diane Baker

The Wheeler Dealers
US 1963 106m Metrocolor Panavision
MGM / Filmways
GB title: *Separate Beds*

A Texas tycoon with a flair for the stock market sets Wall Street agog by manipulating a mysterious and non-existent new product.
Fun for financiers, but barely worth following for the rest. A slick, loud, hollow show.

w G. J. W. Goodman, Ira Wallach *d* Arthur Hiller *ph* Charles Lang Jnr *m* Frank de Vol

James Garner, Lee Remick, Phil Harris, Chill Wills, Jim Backus, Louis Nye, John Astin

When Dinosaurs Ruled the Earth
GB 1969 100m Technicolor
Hammer (Aida Young)

In prehistoric times, a girl is swept out to sea by a cyclone and adopted by a dinosaur.
Sequel to *One Million Years BC*, all very silly but tolerably well done.

wd Val Guest *ph* Dick Bush *m* Mario Nascimbene *sp* Jim Danforth

Victoria Vetri, Patrick Allen, Robin Hawdon, Patrick Holt, Imogen Hassall

When Eight Bells Toll*
GB 1971 94m Eastmancolor
Panavision
Winkast (Elliott Kastner)

A naval secret service agent investigates the pirating of gold bullion ships off the Scottish coast.
Acceptable kill-happy thriller: humourless James Bondery graced by splendid Scottish landscapes.

w Alistair MacLean, from his novel *d* Etienne Perier *ph* Arthur Ibbetson *m* Wally Stott

Anthony Hopkins, Robert Morley, Corin Redgrave, Jack Hawkins, Ferdy Mayne, Derek Bond, Nathalie Delon

When I Grow Up*
US 1951 90m bw
Horizon (S. P. Eagle)

A boy about to run away changes his mind after reading his grandfather's diaries.
Pleasant, sentimental family film with an unusual approach.

wd Michael Kanin *ph* Ernest Laszlo *m* Jerome Moross

Bobby Driscoll, Robert Preston, Charley Grapewin, Martha Scott, Ralph Dumke

When in Rome
US 1952 78m bw
MGM (Clarence Brown)

A gangster in Rome steals a priest's clothes and is accepted in his place.
Typically American religious comedy, nicely made but straying somewhat over the top when the gangster reforms and becomes a monk.

w Charles Schnee, Dorothy Kingsley, Robert Buckner *d* Clarence Brown *ph* William Daniels *m* Carmen Dragon

Van Johnson, Paul Douglas, Joseph Calleia, Carlo Rizzo, Tudor Owen, Aldo Silvani, Dono Nardi

When Ladies Meet*
US 1933 73m bw
RKO

A successful lady novelist falls in love with her married publisher.
Smartish comedy of manners which still has a sting.

w John Meehan, Leon Gordon, *play* Rachel Crothers *d* Harry Beaumont *ph* Ray June

Ann Harding, Robert Montgomery, *Myrna Loy, Alice Brady*, Frank Morgan, Margaret Burton, Luis Alberni

When Ladies Meet
US 1941 108m bw
MGM (Robert Z. Leonard, Orville O. Dull)

Over-produced and very talkative remake of the above.

w S. K. Lauren, Anita Loos *d* Robert Z. Leonard *ph* Robert Planck *m* Bronislau Kaper

Joan Crawford, Robert Taylor, Greer Garson, Spring Byington, Herbert Marshall, Rafael Strom, Olaf Hytten

When Michael Calls**
US 1971 74m colour TVM
TCF (Gil Shiva)

A woman is terrorized by phone calls which appear to come from a dead child.
Chilling suspenser which plays pretty fair and moves smartly along.

w James Bridges *d* Philip Leacock

Michael Douglas, Ben Gazzara, Elizabeth Ashley, Karen Pearson

When My Baby Smiles at Me
US 1948 98m Technicolor
TCF (George Jessel)

A vaudevillian goes on the skids but is saved by his wife.
Routine musical handling of a dreary drama previously filmed as *Dance of Life* (1929) and *Swing High Swing Low* (qv).

w Lamar Trotti, *play* Burlesque by George Manker Walters, Arthur Hopkins *d* Walter Lang *ph* Harry Jackson *md* Alfred Newman

Betty Grable, Dan Dailey, Jack Oakie, June Havoc, Richard Arlen, James Gleason, Jean Wallace

When Strangers Marry*
US 1944 67m bw
Monogram
aka: *Betrayed*

A young bride in New York discovers that she may have married a murderer.
Much-praised second feature: a bit stodgy now, but still entertaining.

w Philip Yordan, Dennis Cooper *d William Castle* *ph* Ira Morgan *m* Dmitri Tiomkin

Dean Jagger, Kim Hunter, Robert Mitchum, Neil Hamilton, Lou Lubin, Milt Kibbee, Dewey Robinson

'The obviousness of the low budget is completely overcome by the solid craftsmanship of the direction, script, music, editing and performances.'—*Don Miller*

When the Daltons Rode*
US 1940 80m bw
Universal

Adventures of the Dalton Gang.
Good standard western with whitewashed bad men for heroes.

d George Marshall *m* Frank Skinner

Randolph Scott, Kay Francis, Brian Donlevy, Andy Devine, George Bancroft, Stuart Erwin

When the Legends Die*
US 1972 105m De Luxe
Sagoponack (Stuart Millar)

A young Indian boy, frustrated by life on the reservations, is helped by an old rodeo rider who becomes his guardian.
Dour modern western, rather stylishly done and an eloquent plea for freedom, but dramatically uncompelling.

w Robert Dozier, *novel* Hal Borland *d* Stuart Millar *ph* Richard Kline *m* Glenn Paxton

Richard Widmark, Frederic Forrest, Luana Anders, Vito Scotti

When Tomorrow Comes**
US 1939 82m bw
Universal (John M. Stahl)

A waitress falls for a concert pianist with a mad wife.
Fascinating star romantic drama, a successful follow-up to *Love Affair*; full of clichés, but impeccably set and acted. The stuff that Hollywood dreams were made of.

w Dwight Taylor, *story* James M. Cain *d John M. Stahl* *ph* John Mescall

Charles Boyer, Irene Dunne, Barbara O'Neil, Nydia Westman, Onslow Stevens
† The same story was remade twice in 1956, as *Serenade* and *Interlude*, and in 1968 as *Interlude* (all qv).

When We Are Married**
GB 1942 98m bw
British National (John Baxter)

In 1890s Yorkshire, three couples celebrating their silver wedding are told they were never legally married.
A very funny play smartly filmed with a superb cast of character actors.

w Austin Melford, Barbara K. Emery, *play J. B. Priestley* *d* Herbert Mason

Raymond Huntley, Marian Spencer, Lloyd Pearson, Olga Lindo, Ernest Butcher, Ethel Coleridge, Sydney Howard, Barry Morse, Lesley Brook, Marjorie Rhodes, Charles Victor, Cyril Smith, George Carney

When Willie Comes Marching Home*
US 1949 82m bw
TCF (Fred Kohlmar)

During World War II, events suddenly transform a small-town air training instructor into a war hero.
Awkwardly paced comedy which could have been much funnier but does amuse in fits and starts.

w Mary Loos, Richard Sale *d* John Ford *ph* Leo Tover *m* Alfred Newman

Dan Dailey, Colleen Townshend, Corinne Calvet, William Demarest, Evelyn Varden, James Lydon, Mae Marsh, Lloyd Corrigan

When Worlds Collide
US 1951 82m Technicolor
Paramount (George Pal)

Another planet is found to be rushing inevitably towards earth, but before the collision a few people escape in a space ship.
Stolid science fiction with a spectacular but not marvellous climax following seventy minutes of inept talk.

w Sidney Boehm, *novel* Philip Wylie, Edwin Balmer *d* Rudolph Maté *ph* John Seitz, W. Howard Greene *m* Leith Stevens

Richard Derr, Barbara Rush, Larry Keating, Peter Hanson, John Hoyt

When You're in Love*
US 1937 110m bw
Columbia (Everett Riskin)
GB title: *For You Alone*

A European opera singer takes on a husband in order to get into the United States.
Pleasing musical star vehicle with comedy touches.

wd Robert Riskin *ph* Joseph Walker *md* Alfred Newman

Grace Moore, Cary Grant, Aline MacMahon, Henry Stephenson, Thomas Mitchell, Catherine Doucet, Luis Alberni, Emma Dunn

Where Angels Go, Trouble Follows
US 1968 95m Eastmancolor
Columbia / William Frye

Nuns from a convent school take pupils to a California youth rally, and learn a thing or two.
Peripatetic comedy, rather frantically assembled; a sequel to *The Trouble with Angels*.

w Blanche Hanalis *d* James Neilson *ph* Sam Leavitt *m* Lalo Schifrin

Rosalind Russell, Stella Stevens, Binnie Barnes, Mary Wickes, Milton Berle, Arthur Godfrey, Robert Taylor, Van Johnson, Susan St James

Where Danger Lives
US 1950 84m bw
RKO (Irving Cummings Jnr)

A doctor falls in love with a murderous patient and is drawn into her schemes.
Standard *film noir* of its time, competent enough in its depressing way.

w Charles Bennett *d* John Farrow *ph* Nicholas Musuraca *m* Roy Webb

Faith Domergue, Robert Mitchum, Claude Rains, Maureen O'Sullivan, Charles Kemper

Where Do We Go from Here?*
US 1945 77m Technicolor
TCF (William Perlberg)

A writer stumbles on a genie who takes him through periods of American history, including a voyage with Christopher Columbus.
Well-staged and rather funny charade with at least one memorable song.

w Morrie Ryskind *d* Gregory Ratoff *ph* Leon Shamroy *songs* Kurt Weill, Ira Gershwin

Fred MacMurray, June Haver, Joan Leslie, Gene Sheldon, Anthony Quinn, Carlos Ramirez, Fortunio Bonanova, Alan Mowbray, Herman Bing, Otto Preminger

'Nine parts heavy facetiousness to one part very good fun.'—*James Agee*

Where Does it Hurt?
US 1971 88m colour
Josef Shaftel (Rod Amateau, William Schwarz)

Adventures of a profiteering hospital adminstrator.
Dislikeable, plodding smut in the form of black comedy.

wd Rod Amateau, *novel* The Operator by Budd Robinson, Rod Amateau *ph* Brick Marquard *m* Keith Allison

Peter Sellers, Jo Ann Pflug, Rick Lenz, Eve Druce

Where Eagles Dare**
GB 1969 155m Metrocolor Panavision 70
MGM / Winkfast (Elliott Kastner)

During World War II, seven British paratroopers land in the Bavarian Alps to rescue a high-ranking officer from an impregnable castle.
Archetypal schoolboy adventure, rather unattractively photographed but containing a sufficient variety of excitements.

w Alistair MacLean, from his novel *d* Brian G. Hutton *ph* Arthur Ibbetson, H. A. R. Thompson *m* Ron Goodwin

Richard Burton, Clint Eastwood, Mary Ure, Patrick Wymark, Michael Hordern, Donald Houston, Peter Barkworth, Robert Beatty

Where Have All the People Gone?*
US 1974 74m colour TVM
Metromedia / Charles Fries

A solar flare kills off most of the people on earth and the rest have a struggle for survival.
Having read the synopsis, there isn't much need to see the picture, but it's well enough done.

w Lewis John Carlino, Sander Stern *d* John Llewellyn Moxey

Peter Graves, Verna Bloom, George O'Hanlon Jnr, Kathleen Quinlan, Michael-James Wixted

Where It's At
US 1969 106m De Luxe
UA / Frank Ross

The owner of a Las Vegas gambling hotel tries to make his son take an interest in the business.
Flaccid comedy drama which belies its credits.

wd Garson Kanin *ph* Burnett Guffey *m* Benny Olsen

David Janssen, Rosemary Forsyth, Robert Drivas, Brenda Vaccaro

Where Love Has Gone*
US 1964 114m Techniscope
Paramount / Embassy (Joseph E. Levine)

A middle-aged man is appalled to hear that his teenage daughter has killed her mother's lover.
Squalid, glossy pulp fiction lightly based on the Lana Turner case, distinguished only by the game performances of its leading ladies.

w John Michael Hayes, *novel* Harold Robbins

d Edward Dmytryk *ph* Joe MacDonald *m* Walter Scharf

Susan Hayward, Bette Davis, Mike Connors, Joey Heatherton, Jane Greer, George Macready

'A typical Robbins pastiche of newspaper clippings liberally shellacked with sentiment and glued with sex.'—*Newsweek*

Where No Vultures Fly*
GB 1951 107m Technicolor
Ealing (Leslie Norman)
US title: *Ivory Hunter*

Adventures of an East African game warden. Pleasantly improving family film, nicely shot on location; a sequel, *West of Zanzibar*, was less impressive.

w W. P. Lipscomb, Ralph Smart, Leslie Norman *d* Harry Watt *ph* Geoffrey Unsworth *m* Alan Rawsthorne

Anthony Steele, Dinah Sheridan, Harold Warrender, Meredith Edwards

Where the Boys Are
US 1960 99m Metrocolor Cinemascope
MGM / Euterpe (Joe Pasternak)

Four college girls spend the Easter vacation near a Florida military post in search of conquests. Mindless, frothy youth musical, quite smoothly done.

w George Wells, *novel* Glendon Swarthout *d* Henry Levin *ph* Robert Bronner *m* George Stoll

George Hamilton, Dolores Hart, Paula Prentiss, Jim Hutton, Yvette Mimieux, Connie Francis, Frank Gorshin, Chill Wills, Barbara Nichols

Where the Sidewalk Ends
US 1950 95m bw
TCF (Otto Preminger)

A tough policeman accidentally kills a suspect and tries to implicate a gang leader. Gloomy *policier* with curious moral values.

w Rex Connor (Ben Hecht), *novel* William L. Stuart *d* Otto Preminger *ph* Joseph La Shelle *m* Cyril Mockridge

Dana Andrews, Gene Tierney, Gary Merrill, Bert Freed, Tom Tully, Karl Malden, Ruth Donnelly, Craig Stevens, Robert Simon

Where Were You When the Lights Went Out?*
US 1966 94m Metrocolor Panavision
MGM (Everett Freeman, Martin Melcher)

New York's famous electrical blackout in 1965 has its effect on the life of a musical comedy star.
Cheerful sex farce with intriguing beginnings; the later confinement to one set is just a bit harmful.

w Everett Freeman, Karl Tunberg, *play* Claude Magnier *d* Hy Averback *ph* Ellsworth Fredericks *m* Dave Grusin

Doris Day, Terry-Thomas, Patrick O'Neal, Robert Morse, Lola Albright, Jim Backus, Ben Blue

Where's Charley?*
GB 1952 97m Technicolor
Warner

An Oxford undergraduate impersonates the rich aunt of his best friend.
Slow and rather stately musical version of the famous farce *Charley's Aunt*, unsatisfactorily shot on a mixture of poor sets and sunlit Oxford locations; worth cherishing for the ebullient performance of its over-age star.

w John Monks Jnr, *play* Brandon Thomas (via stage musical, *book* George Abbott *m* Frank Loesser) *d* David Butler *ph* Erwin Hillier *ch* Michael Kidd

Ray Bolger, Robert Shackleton, Mary Germaine, Allyn McLerie, Margaretta Scott, Horace Cooper

Where's Jack?*
GB 1968 119m Eastmancolor
Paramount / Oakhurst (Stanley Baker)

In 18th-century London Jack Sheppard becomes a romantic highwayman at the behest of underworld leader Jonathan Wild.
Deliberately unromantic, squalid and 'realistic' period piece which takes no hold on the fancy despite the considerable care which was obviously taken in all departments.

w Rafe and David Newhouse *d* James Clavell *ph John Wilcox* *m* Elmer Bernstein *pd Cedric Dawe*

Tommy Steele, Stanley Baker, Fiona Lewis, Alan Badel, Dudley Foster, Sue Lloyd, Noel Purcell

Where's Poppa?*
US 1970 82m De Luxe
Jerry Tokovsky / Martin Worth

A Jewish lawyer's aged mother constantly harms his love life, and he considers various means of getting rid of her.
Much-censored black comedy which might have been funnier in a complete form. Even so, it has its moments.

w Robert Klane, from his novel *d* Carl Reiner *ph* Jack Priestly *m* Jack Elliott

George Segal, Ruth Gordon, Trish Van Devere, Ron Leibman

Where's That Fire?*
GB 1939 73m bw
TCF (Edward Black)

An incompetent village fire brigade accidentally saves the crown jewels from thieves.
Routine but not despicable star comedy, long thought lost; flat patches are well separated by hilarious sequences.

w Marriott Edgar, Val Guest, J. O. C. Orton *d* Marcel Varnel

Will Hay, Moore Marriott, Graham Moffatt, Peter Gawthorne, Eric Clavering, Charles Hawtrey

While I Live
GB 1947 85m bw
Edward Dryhurst

A Cornishwoman believes an amnesiac girl to be the reincarnation of her dead sister.
Silly melodrama which achieved phenomenal popularity, despite poor production, because of its haunting theme tune *The Dream of Olwen*.

w John Harlow, Doreen Montgomery, *play* This Same Garden by Robert Bell *d* John Harlow

Tom Walls, Sonia Dresdel, Carol Raye, Clifford Evans, Patricia Burke, John Warwick, Edward Lexy

While the City Sleeps
US 1956 100m bw
RKO (Bert Friedlob)

Three chief executives of a newspaper empire are pitted against each other in a search for a murder scoop.
Star-packed but leaden-paced news bureau melodrama; a major disappointment considering the talent.

w Casey Robinson, *novel* The Bloody Spur by Charles Einstein *d* Fritz Lang *ph* Ernest Laszlo *m* Herschel Burke Gilbert

Dana Andrews, George Sanders, Ida Lupino, Sally Forrest, Thomas Mitchell, Rhonda Fleming, Vincent Price, Howard Duff, James Craig, Robert Warwick, John Barrymore Jnr

The Whip Hand
US 1951 82m bw
RKO (Lewis J. Rachmil)

A fisherman finds himself unwelcome in a lonely town run by ex-Nazi, now communist, bacteriologists.
Preposterous, pretentious anti-communist low-budgeter, mildly enjoyable for its sheer gall.

w George Bricker, Frank L. Moss *d/pd* William Cameron Menzies *ph* Nicholas Musuraca *m* Paul Sawtell

Elliott Reid, Carla Balenda, Edgar Barrier, Raymond Burr

Whiplash
US 1948 90m bw
Warner (William Jacobs)

A painter becomes a prizefighter.
Hokey, unpersuasive romantic melodrama.

w Maurice Geraghty, Harriet Frank Jnr *d* Lewis Seiler *ph* Peverell Marley *m* Franz Waxman

Dane Clark, Alexis Smith, Zachary Scott, Eve Arden, Jeffrey Lynn, S. Z. Sakall, Alan Hale, Douglas Kennedy

Whipsaw*
US 1935 88m bw
MGM (Harry Rapf)

A G-man infiltrates a gang by wooing its girl member.
Fairly snappy romantic drama which further established both its stars.

w Howard Emmett Rogers *d* Sam Wood *m* William Axt

Spencer Tracy, Myrna Loy, Harvey Stephens, Clay Clements, William Harrigan

Whirlpool*
US 1950 98m bw
TCF (Otto Preminger)

A girl is accused of a murder committed by her hypnotist, who has willed himself out of a hospital bed.
Silly murder melodrama; glossy production makes it entertaining.

w Lester Barstow, Andrew Solt, *novel* Guy Endore *d* Otto Preminger *ph* Arthur Miller *m* David Raksin

Gene Tierney, *Jose Ferrer,* Richard Conte, Charles Bickford, Barbara O'Neil, Eduard Franz, Fortunio Bonanova

'It is sometimes difficult to discover from Miss Tierney's playing whether she is or is not under hypnosis.'—*MFB*

Whirlpool
GB 1959 95m Eastmancolor
Rank (George Pitcher)

A killer escapes in Cologne; his girl friend separates from him and gets a lift down the Rhine in a barge; the trip reforms her and she betrays her lover.
Modestly attractive travelogue with the burden of a very boring melodrama.

w Lawrence P. Bachmann *d* Lewis Allen *ph* Geoffrey Unsworth *m* Ron Goodwin

Juliette Greco, O. W. Fischer, William Sylvester, Marius Goring, Muriel Pavlow

Whisky Galore****
GB 1948 82m bw
Ealing
US title: *Tight Little Island*

During World War II, a ship full of whisky is wrecked on a small Hebridean island, and the local customs and excise man has his hands full.
Marvellously detailed, fast-moving, well-played and attractively photographed comedy which firmly established the richest Ealing vein.

w Compton Mackenzie, Angus Macphail, novel Compton Mackenzie *d Alexander Mackendrick ph Gerald Gibbs m Ernest Irving*

Basil Radford, Joan Greenwood, Jean Cadell, Gordon Jackson, James Robertson Justice, Wylie Watson, John Gregson, Morland Graham, Duncan Macrae, Catherine Lacey, Bruce Seton, Henry Mollinson, Compton Mackenzie, A. E. Matthews

The Whisperers*
GB 1966 106m bw
UA / Seven Pines (Michael S. Laughlin, Ronald Shedlo)

An old lady hears voices and is put upon by her son, her wandering husband, and various others.
Interesting but cold and finally unsatisfactory character melodrama; even the acting, though in a sense admirable, is too genteel.

w Bryan Forbes, *novel* Robert Nicolson *d* Bryan Forbes *ph* Gerry Turpin *m* John Barry

Edith Evans, Eric Portman, Avis Bunnage, Nanette Newman, Gerald Sim, Ronald Fraser

Whispering Smith*
US 1948 88m Technicolor
Paramount (Mel Epstein)

A government agent investigating robberies finds his friend is implicated.
Fairly entertaining detective western.

w Frank Butler, Karl Lamb, *novel* Frank H. Spearman *d* Leslie Fenton *ph* Ray Rennahan *m* Adolph Deutsch

Alan Ladd, Robert Preston, Brenda Marshall, Donald Crisp, William Demarest, Fay Holden, Murvyn Vye, Frank Faylen

The Whistle at Eaton Falls*
US 1951 96m bw
Columbia (Louis de Rochemont)
GB title: *Richer than the Earth*

The story of a strike at a small-town plastics factory.
Reasonably absorbing semi-documentary with a final 'solution' which rather evades the issues.

w Lemist Esler, Virginia Shaler *d* Robert Siodmak *ph* Joseph Brun *m* Louis Applebaum

Lloyd Bridges, Dorothy Gish, Carleton Carpenter, Murray Hamilton, James Westerfield, Lenore Lonergan

Whistle Down the Wind*
GB 1961 99m bw
Rank / Allied Film Makers / Beaver (Richard Attenborough)

Three north country children think a murderer on the run is Jesus Christ.
Charming allegorical study of childhood innocence, extremely well made, amusing, and avoiding sentimentality.

w Keith Waterhouse, Willis Hall, novel Mary Hayley Bell *d Bryan Forbes ph* Arthur Ibbetson *m* Malcolm Arnold

Hayley Mills, Bernard Lee, Alan Bates, Norman Bird, Elsie Wagstaff, Alan Barnes

The Whistler

Originally a radio series of suspense stories introduced by someone whistling the theme tune, this was turned into a fairly workmanlike series of second features quite unrelated to each other except for the leading actor, Richard Dix, who alternated as hero and villain, and William Castle, who directed or produced most of them.

1944: THE WHISTLER, THE MARK OF THE WHISTLER
1945: THE POWER OF THE WHISTLER
1946: THE VOICE OF THE WHISTLER
1947: MYSTERIOUS INTRUDER, THE SECRET OF THE WHISTLER, THE 12th HOUR
1948: THE RETURN OF THE WHISTLER

The White Angel*
US 1935 91m bw
Warner (Henry Blanke)

The life of Florence Nightingale.
Starchy biopic; the Victorian atmosphere is never quite caught.

w Mordaunt Shairp, Michael Jacoby *d* William Dieterle *ph* Tony Gaudio

Kay Francis, Ian Hunter, Donald Woods, Nigel Bruce, Donald Crisp, Henry O'Neill, Billy Mauch, Halliwell Hobbes

White Banners*
US 1938 88m bw
Warner (Henry Blanke)

A social worker tries to solve the problems of a troubled family.
Moderate middle-class drama.

w Lenore Coffee, Cameron Rogers, Abem Finkel *d* Edmund Goulding *ph* Charles Rosher *m* Max Steiner

Fay Bainter, Claude Rains, Jackie Cooper, Bonita Granville, Henry O'Neill, James Stephenson, Kay Johnson

White Cargo*
US 1942 90m bw
MGM (Victor Saville)

White rubber planters are driven mad with desire for a scheming native girl.
Antediluvian melodrama previously filmed in 1930. Good for laughing at, and the star looked great as Tondelayo.

w Leon Gordon, from his play and *novel* Hell's Playground by Vera Simonton *d* Richard Thorpe *m* Bronislau Kaper

Hedy Lamarr, Walter Pidgeon, Richard Carlson, Frank Morgan, Bramwell Fletcher, Richard Ainley, Reginald Owen

White Christmas*
US 1954 120m Technicolor Vistavision
Paramount (Robert Emmett Dolan)

Two entertainers boost the popularity of a winter resort run by an old army buddy.
Humdrum musical lifted only by its stars; a revamp of *Holiday Inn,* which was much better.

w Norman Krasna, Norman Panama, Melvin Frank *d* Michael Curtiz *ph* Loyal Griggs *songs* Irving Berlin

Bing Crosby, Danny Kaye, Rosemary Clooney, Vera-Ellen, Dean Jagger, Mary Wickes, Sig Rumann, Grady Sutton

The White Cliffs of Dover*
US 1944 126m bw
MGM (Sidney Franklin)

An American girl who marries into the British aristocracy loses a husband in World War I and a son in World War II.
Tearful flagwaver with some entertaining scenes in the first half and the general sense of an all-stops-out production.

w Claudine West, Jan Lustig, George Froeschel, *poem* Alice Duer Miller *d* Clarence Brown *ph* George Folsey *m* Herbert Stothart

Irene Dunne, Alan Marshal, Frank Morgan, May Whitty, Roddy McDowall, C. Aubrey Smith, Gladys Cooper, Peter Lawford, Van Johnson

White Corridors*
GB 1951 102m bw
GFD / Vic (Joseph Janni, John Croydon)

Life in a small Midlands hospital.
Competent multi-drama which found a big audience.

w Jan Read, Pat Jackson, *novel* Yeoman's Hospital by Helen Ashton *d* Pat Jackson *ph* C. Pennington-Richards

James Donald, Googie Withers, Godfrey Tearle, Petula Clark, Jack Watling, Moira Lister, Barry Jones, Megs Jenkins, Basil Radford

'This quality of professionalism is comparatively rare in British films.'—*Gavin Lambert*

White Feather*
US 1955 100m Technicolor Cinemascope
TCF / Panoramic (Robert L. Jacks)

A cavalry colonel tries to hold back gold prospectors until the Cheyenne have moved on to their new reservations.
Old-fashioned cowboys and (sympathetic) Indians, very efficiently done.

w Delmer Daves, Leo Townsend *d* Robert Webb *ph* Lucien Ballard *m* Hugo Friedhofer

Robert Wagner, John Lund, Jeffrey Hunter, Debra Paget, Eduard Franz, Noah Beery Jnr, Hugh O'Brian, Virginia Leith, Emile Meyer

White Heat***
US 1949 114m bw
Warner (Louis F. Edelman)

A violent, mother-fixated gangster gets his come-uppance when a government agent is infiltrated into his gang.
This searing melodrama reintroduced the old Cagney and then some: spellbinding suspense sequences complemented his vivid and hypnotic portrayal.

w Ivan Goff, Ben Roberts, *story* Virginia Kellogg *d Raoul Walsh* *ph* Sid Hickox *m* Max Steiner

James Cagney, Edmond O'Brien, *Margaret Wycherly,* Virginia Mayo, Steve Cochran, John Archer

'The most gruesome aggregation of brutalities ever presented under the guise of entertainment.'—*Cue*

White Savage
US 1943 75m Technicolor
Universal (George Waggner)
GB title: *White Captive*

The queen of beautiful South Sea island has trouble with shark hunters and crooks after her mineral deposits.
Self-admitted hokum strung loosely and colourfully around its star: big box office in the middle of the war.

w Richard Brooks *d* Arthur Lubin *ph* Lester White, William Snyder *m* Frank Skinner

Maria Montez, Jon Hall, Sabu, Thomas Gomez, Sidney Toler, Paul Guilfoyle, Turhan Bey, Don Terry

The White Sister
US 1933 110m bw
MGM

When her lover is reported killed in the war, an Italian noblewoman takes the veil . . . but he comes back.
Tiresome romantic drama from another age, a big prestige production of its time.

w Donald Ogden Stewart, *novel* F. Marion Crawford, Walter Hackett *d* Victor Fleming *ph* William Daniels *m* Herbert Stothart

Helen Hayes, Clark Gable, Lewis Stone, Louise Closser Hale, May Robson, Edward Arnold

The White Tower
US 1950 98m Technicolor
RKO (Sid Rogell)

Various people have personal reasons for climbing an Alpine mountain.
Pretentiously symbolic melodrama with some good action sequences and curiously stilted performances.

w Paul Jarrico, *novel* James Ramsay Ullman *d* Ted Tetzlaff *ph* Ray Rennahan *m* Roy Webb

Glenn Ford, Claude Rains, Alida Valli, Oscar Homolka, Cedric Hardwicke, Lloyd Bridges, June Clayworth

'The main interest is a curiosity as to who will fall over which precipice when.'—*Penelope Houston*

The White Unicorn
GB 1947 97m bw
GFD / John Corfield (Harold Huth)
US title: *Bad Sister*

In a home for delinquent girls, the worst offender exchanges reminiscences with the warden.
Peg's Paper melodrama in complex flashback form.

w Robert Westerby, A. R. Rawlinson, Moie Charles, *novel* Flora Sandstrom *d* Bernard Knowles *ph* Reg Wyer *m* Bretton Byrd

Margaret Lockwood, Joan Greenwood, Ian Hunter, Dennis Price, Guy Middleton, Catherine Lacey, Mabel Constanduros, Paul Dupuis

White Witch Doctor
US 1953 96m Technicolor
TCF (Otto Lang)

A nurse in the Congo converts a gold-seeking adventurer.
Stale hokum in which the animals are the most interesting feature.

w Ivan Goff, Ben Roberts, *novel* Louise A. Stinetorf *d* Henry Hathaway *ph* Leon Shamroy *m* Bernard Herrmann

Susan Hayward, Robert Mitchum, Walter Slezak, Timothy Carey

White Woman
US 1933 68m bw
Paramount

A cockney overseer in the Malaysian jungle takes back a cabaret singer as his bride.
Risible melodrama with an obvious outcome.

w Norman Reilly Raine, Frank Butler *d* Stuart Walker *ph* Harry Fischbeck

Charles Laughton, Carole Lombard, Kent Taylor, Charles Bickford, Percy Kilbride, Charles Middleton, James Bell

White Zombie**
US 1932 74m bw
Halperin

Haitian zombies work a sugar mill for a white schemer.
Genuinely eerie horror film with a slow, stagey, out-of-this world quality coupled with an interesting sense of composition.

w Garnett Weston *d* Victor Halperin *ph* Arthur Martinelli

Bela Lugosi, Madge Bellamy, John Harron, Joseph Cawthorn

'A Gothic fairy tale filled with dreamlike imagery, traditional symbols, echoes of Romanticism, and (probably unintentional) pyschosexual overtones.'—*Carlos Clarens*

Who Done It?
GB 1956 85m bw
Ealing (Michael Relph, Basil Dearden)

An ice-rink sweeper sets up as a private eye and captures a ring of spies.
Lively but disappointing film debut for a star comic whose screen personality proved too bland.

w T. E. B. Clarke *d* Basil Dearden *ph* Otto Heller *m* Philip Green

Benny Hill, Belinda Lee, David Kossoff, Garry Marsh, Ernest Thesiger, Thorley Walters

Who Goes There?
GB 1952 85m bw
British Lion / London Films (Anthony Kimmins)
US title: *The Passionate Sentry*

In a Grace and Favour house near St James' Palace, a guardsman is involved in a trail of romantic intrigue.
Very British romantic farce, dully and quickly filmed from a West End success.

w John Dighton, from his play *d* Anthony Kimmins *ph* John Wilcox, Ted Scaife *m* Muir Mathieson

Peggy Cummins, Valerie Hobson, George Cole, Nigel Patrick, A. E. Matthews, Anthony Bushell

Who Is Harry Kellerman and Why Is He Saying These Terrible Things About Me?
US 1971 108m De Luxe
Cinema Center (Ulu Grosbard, Herb Gardner)

A New York composer is persecuted by a mysterious figure which turns out to be himself.
Wild, shapeless, satirical psycho-comedy-melodrama. Not very good.

w Herb Gardner *d* Ulu Grosbard *ph* Victor Kemper *pd* Harry Horner

Dustin Hoffman, Barbara Harris, Jack Warden, David Burns, Gabriel Dell, Dom De Luise

Who Is the Black Dahlia?*
US 1975 96m colour TVM
Douglas S. Cramer

The unsolved 1947 murder case of a 22-year-old girl found on waste ground.
Interesting and well made, but like all unsolved cases a bit of a let-down.

w Robert W. Lenski *d* Joseph Pevney

Lucie Arnaz, Efrem Zimbalist Jnr, Ronny Cox, Macdonald Carey, Linden Chiles, Mercedes McCambridge, Tom Bosley, Gloria de Haven, John Fiedler, Rick Jason, Henry Jones, June Lockhart, Donna Mills

Who Killed Mary What's Her Name?
US 1971 90m De Luxe
Cannon (George Manasse)

An ex-boxer determines to solve the murder of a prostitute.
Old-fashioned whodunnit with something to say grafted on every five minutes: an unsatisfactory mix.

w John O'Toole *d* Ernest Pintoff *ph* Greg Sandor *m* Gary McFarland

Red Buttons, Alice Playten, Sylvia Miles, Sam Waterston

Who Killed Miss USA?*
US 1971 98m Technicolor TVM
Universal (Leslie Stevens)
aka: *McCloud: Who Killed Miss USA?*
GB title: *Who Killed Merri-Ann?*

A New Mexican marshal loses a murder suspect in New York, but recovers him and stays for further training in metropolitan methods.
Based on *Coogan's Bluff* (qv), this is the pilot for one of *Mystery Movie's* more popular segments; the plot makes no great sense, but technically it is well put together.

w Stanford Whitmore, Richard Levinson, William Link *d* Richard A. Colla

Dennis Weaver, Craig Stevens, Mark Richman, Diana Muldaur, Julie Newmar

Who Killed the Mysterious Mr Foster?
US 1973 98m Technicolor TVM
Universal (Jo Swerling Jnr)
aka: *Sam Hill: Who Killed the Mysterious Mr Foster?*

A western sheriff finds the body of the town's new minister.
Failed comedy western pilot which never really gets going.

w Richard Levinson, William Link *d* Fielder Cook

Ernest Borgnine, Judy Geeson, Will Geer, J. D. Cannon, Bruce Dern, Sam Jaffe, John McGiver, Slim Pickens, Jay C. Flippen

Who Slew Auntie Roo?
GB 1972 91m Movielab
AIP / Hemdale (John Pellatt)

A madwoman menaces two orphan children.
Pointless and slenderly plotted adaptation of *Hansel and Gretel*, crude in all departments.

w Robert Blees, Jimmy Sangster *d* Curtis Harrington *ph* Desmond Dickinson *m* Ken Jones

Shelley Winters, Ralph Richardson, Mark Lester, Lionel Jeffries, Chloe Franks, Hugh Griffith, Rosalie Crutchley, Pat Heywood

'Not content with being a delicate fantasy of childish nightmare, it tries to add a totally inappropriate seasoning of Grand Guignol.' —*Tom Milne*

Who Was That Lady?*
US 1960 115m bw
Columbia / Ansark / George Sidney

A professor seen kissing a student persuades a friend to tell his wife that they are both FBI agents on duty. Foreign spies believe them . . .
Agreeably wacky comedy with a strained and prolonged middle section leading to a totally zany climax.

w Norman Krasna, from his play *d* George Sidney *ph* Harry Stradling *m* André Previn

Tony Curtis, Dean Martin, Janet Leigh, James Whitmore, John McIntire, Barbara Nichols, Larry Keating

The Whole Town's Talking*
US 1935 86m bw
Columbia (Lester Cowan)

A gangster finds it convenient occasionally to pose as his double, a meek little clerk.
Pleasingly neat comedy, well staged and acted.

w Jo Swerling, Robert Riskin, *novel* W. R. Burnett *d* John Ford *ph* Joseph August

Edward G. Robinson, Jean Arthur, Arthur Hohl, Wallace Ford, Arthur Byron, Donald Meek, Edward Brophy, Etienne Girardot

'A lively and satisfactory combination of farce and melodrama.'—*Richard Watts Jnr*

The Whole Truth*
GB 1958 84m bw
Columbia / Romulus (Jack Clayton)

A jealous husband poses as a detective in order to murder his wife and incriminate a film producer.
A filmed play, but quite a solidly carpentered murder thriller with a couple of neat twists.

w Jonathan Latimer, *play* Philip Mackie *d* John Guillermin *ph* Wilkie Cooper *m* Mischa Spoliansky

Stewart Granger, George Sanders, Donna Reed, Gianna Maria Canale

The Whole World Is Watching
US 1969 97m Technicolor TVM
Universal (Jo Swerling Jnr)

During a campus revolt, a policeman is killed.
Another pilot (see *The Sound of Anger*) for the lawyer section of *The Bold Ones*.

w Richard Levinson, William Link *d* Richard A. Colla

Burl Ives, James Farentino, Joseph Campanella, Hal Holbrook, Steve Ihnat, Carrie Snodgress

Whoopee*
US 1930 94m Technicolor
Samuel Goldwyn, Florenz Ziegfeld

A timid young man is catapulted into various adventures.
Early sound musical from a popular Broadway show, later remade as *Up in Arms* (qv).

w William Conselman, *musical play* William Anthony McGuire, *play* The Nervous Wreck by Owen Davis *d* Thornton Freeland *ph* Lee Garmes, Ray Rennahan, Gregg Toland *ch* Busby Berkeley

Eddie Cantor, Eleanor Hunt, Paul Gregory, Jack Rutherford, Ethel Shutta

Who's Afraid of Virginia Woolf?***
US 1966 129m bw
Warner (Ernest Lehman)

A college professor and his wife have an all-night shouting match and embarrass their guests.
As a film of a play, fair to middling; as a milestone in cinematic permissiveness, very important; as an entertainment, sensational for those in the mood.

w Ernest Lehman, *play Edward Albee* *d* Mike Nichols ph Haskell Wexler *m* Alex North

Richard Burton, Elizabeth Taylor, George Segal, Sandy Dennis

'A magnificent triumph of determined audacity.'—*Bosley Crowther*

'One of the most scathingly honest American films ever made.'—*Stanley Kauffmann*

Who's Been Sleeping in My Bed?
US 1963 103m Technicolor Panavision
Paramount / Amro (Jack Rose)

A TV matinee idol finds he is a sex symbol also in his private life.
Coy bedroom farce with no real action but a smattering of jokes.

w Jack Rose *d* Daniel Mann *ph* Joseph Ruttenberg *m* George Duning

Dean Martin, Elizabeth Montgomery, Martin Balsam, Jill St John, Richard Conte, Carol Burnett, Louis Nye, Yoko Tani, Elizabeth Fraser

Who's Got the Action?
US 1962 93m Technicolor Panavision
Paramount / Amro (Jack Rose)

A bored wife and her law partner husband have remarkable success betting on horses.
Badly cast and rather slow comedy with flashes of wit.

w Jack Rose, *novel* Four Horse Players Are Missing by Alexander Rose *d* Daniel Mann *ph* Joseph Ruttenberg *m* George Duning

Dean Martin, Lana Turner, Eddie Albert, Walter Matthau, Nita Talbot, Margo, Paul Ford, John McGiver

Who's Minding the Mint?*
US 1967 97m Technicolor
Columbia / Norman Maurer

An employee of the US mint and his friends find a means of printing bills at night.
Smartly-made action comedy with good performances.

w R. S. Allen, Harvey Bullock *d* Howard Morris *ph* Joseph Biroc *m* Lalo Schifrin

Jim Hutton, Dorothy Provine, Milton Berle, Joey Bishop, Bob Denver, Walter Brennan, Victor Buono, Jack Gilford

Who's Minding the Store?*
US 1963 90m Technicolor
Paramount / York / Jerry Lewis (Paul Jones)

An accident-prone young man gets a job in a department store.
Better-than-average star comedy, slapstick being allowed precedence over sentimentality.

w Frank Tashlin, Harry Tugend *d* Frank Tashlin *ph* W. Wallace Kelley *m* Joseph J. Lilley

Jerry Lewis, Jill St John, Agnes Moorehead, John McGiver, Ray Walston, Nancy Kulp

Wicked as They Come
GB 1957 94m bw
Columbia / Film Locations (Maxwell Setton)
US title: *Portrait in Smoke*

A beauty contest winner from the slums makes money and luxury her goal.
Busy melodrama which interests without edifying.

wd Ken Hughes *co-w* Robert Westerby, Sigmund Miller *ph* Basil Emmott *m* Malcolm Arnold

Arlene Dahl, Herbert Marshall, Phil Carey, Michael Goodliffe, David Kossoff, Sidney James, Ralph Truman, Faith Brook

The Wicked Lady*
GB 1945 104m bw
GFD / Gainsborough (R. J. Minney)

In the days of Charles II, Lady Skelton befriends a highwayman and takes to crime.
The most commercially successful of the Gainsborough costume charades because of its atmosphere of gloomy sin. Dramatically turgid and surprisingly poorly acted and directed, but with good period detail. It had to be reshot for America because of the ladies' décolletage.

wd Leslie Arliss, *novel* The Life and Death of the Wicked Lady Skelton by Magdalen King-Hall *ph* Jack Cox *m* Louis Levy

Margaret Lockwood, James Mason, Griffith Jones, Patricia Roc, Michael Rennie, Enid Stamp-Taylor, Felix Aylmer, Martita Hunt, David Horne

'A mixture of hot passion and cold suet pudding.'—*Manchester Guardian*

A Wicked Woman
US 1934 71m bw
MGM (Harry Rapf)
GB title: *A Woman in Her Thirties*

A woman kills her drunken husband to protect her children, later confesses and is exonerated.
The tail end of the mother love saga, better made than most.

w Florence Ryerson, Zelda Sears, *novel* Anne Austin *d* Charles Brabin *ph* Lester White

Mady Christians, Charles Bickford, Betty Furness, William Henry, Jackie Searle, Robert Taylor, Paul Harvey

The Wicker Man*
GB 1973 86m Eastmancolor
British Lion (Peter Snell)

A policeman flies to a remote Scottish isle to investigate the death of a child, and finds himself in the hands of diabolists.
Old-fashioned but remarkably well made scare story, with effective shock moments.

w Anthony Shaffer d Robin Hardy ph Harry Waxman *m* Paul Giovanni *ad* Seamus Flannery

Edward Woodward, Britt Ekland, Christopher Lee, Ingrid Pitt, Diane Cilento

'An encouraging achievement for those who had begun to despair of the British cinema.' —*David McGillivray*

Widow*
US 1975 96m colour TVM
Lorimar

The first year of widowhood for an attractive woman with a family.
Glossy but moving domestic drama.

w Barbara Turner, *book* Lynn Caine *d* J. Lee-Thompson

Michael Learned, Bradford Dillman, Robert Lansing, Louise Sorel, Farley Granger, Carol Rossen

Wife, Doctor and Nurse*
US 1937 84m bw
TCF (Raymond Griffith)

A romantic triangle as the title suggests.
Agreeable fluff with a mildly surprising end (for 1937) suggesting a *ménage à trois*.

w Kathryn Scola, Darrell Ware, Lamar Trotti *d* Walter Lang *ph* George Cronjager *m* Arthur Lange

Loretta Young, Warner Baxter, Virginia Bruce, Jane Darwell, Sidney Blackmer, Maurice Cass, Minna Gombell, Elisha Cook Jnr, Lon Chaney Jnr

Wife, Husband and Friend*
US 1939 80m bw
TCF (Nunnally Johnson)

A man sabotages his wife's efforts to become a professional singer.
Modestly agreeable romantic comedy later remade as *Everybody Does It* (qv).

w Nunnally Johnson, *story* James M. Cain *d* Gregory Ratoff *ph* Ernest Palmer

Loretta Young, Warner Baxter, Binnie Barnes, Cesar Romero, George Barbier, J. Edward Bromberg, Eugene Pallette, Helen Westley

The Wife Takes a Flyer
US 1942 86m bw
Columbia (B. P. Schulberg)
GB title: *A Yank in Dutch*

A Dutchwoman whose husband is in the asylum takes in a fugitive USAF pilot in his place although a Nazi officer is billeted on the household.
Downright peculiar World War II comedy which at the time seemed the height of bad taste—and no laughs.

w Gina Kaus, Jay Dratler *d* Richard Wallace *ph* Franz Planer

Joan Bennett, Franchot Tone, Allyn Joslyn, Cecil Cunningham, Lloyd Corrigan, Georgia Caine

'Kicks in the pants, belching, and exaggerated face-making are lifted from burlesque to decorate this feeble attempt.'—*New York Post*

Wife versus Secretary*
US 1936 88m bw
MGM (Hunt Stromberg)

A publisher's wife starts to believe rumours about his attention to his secretary.
Practised star comedy drama which provided thoroughly satisfactory entertainment of a kind the cinema seems to have forgotten.

w Norman Krasna, Alice Duer Miller, John Lee Mahin, *novel* Faith Baldwin *d* Clarence Brown *ph* Ray June *m* Herbert Stothart, Edward Ward

Clark Gable, Myrna Loy, Jean Harlow, May Robson, George Barbier, James Stewart, Hobart Cavanaugh

'See this picture if you enjoy the spectacle of three clever stars shining for all they are worth.' —*Film Weekly*

The Wilby Conspiracy*
GB 1975 105m De Luxe
UA / Optimus / Baum–Dantine (Stanley Sopel)

A British mining engineer is persuaded to help a black revolutionary in his flight from Cape Town to Johannesburg.
Reasonably exciting political chase thriller with a sufficiency of twists and action sequences; philosophy is present but secondary.

w Rod Amateau, Harold Nebenzal, *novel* Peter Driscoll *d* Ralph Nelson *ph* John Coquillon *m* Stanley Myers

Sidney Poitier, Michael Caine, Nicol Williamson, Prunella Gee, Saeed Jaffrey, Persis Khambatta

The Wild Affair*
GB 1965 87m bw
Seven Arts (Richard Patterson)

An office Christmas party nearly turns into an orgy.
Curious little comedy drama which plays almost like the Road to Ruin and has an attractive but miscast leading lady. Interesting elements.

wd John Krish, *novel* The Last Hours of Sandra Lee by William Sansom *ph* Arthur Ibbetson *m* Martin Slavin

Nancy Kwan, Terry-Thomas, Jimmy Logan, Bud Flanagan, Betty Marsden, Gladys Morgan, Paul Whitsun-Jones, Donald Churchill, Victor Spinetti

The Wild and the Willing
GB 1962 112m bw
Rank / Box–Thomas (Betty E. Box)

A troublesome student at a provincial university seduces the wife of his professor.
Watchable sex melodrama with an interesting background on which no one seems to have quite enough grip; 'realism' is simply there to be exploited.

w Nicholas Phipps, Mordecai Richler, *play* The Tinker by Laurence Dobie, Robert Sloman *d* Ralph Thomas *ph* Ernest Steward *m* Norrie Paramor

Virginia Maskell, Paul Rogers, Ian McShane, Samantha Eggar, John Hurt, Catherine Woodville, John Standing, Jeremy Brett

Wild and Wonderful
US 1963 88m Eastmancolor
U-I / Harold Hecht

A French film star poodle makes friends with an American gambler.
Amiable zany comedy in a set-bound Gay Paree.

w Larry Markes, Michael Morris, Waldo Salt *d* Michael Anderson *ph* Joseph La Shelle *m* Morton Stevens

Tony Curtis, Christine Kaufmann, Larry Storch, Marty Ingels, Jacques Aubuchon, Jules Munshin

The Wild Angels*
US 1966 85m Pathecolor Panavision
AIP (Roger Corman)

A Californian motorcycle gang is run on semi-religious, ritualistic, Nazi lines.
Much-banned melodrama, cheaply made but vigorously handled and of some interest on social and historical levels.

w Charles B. Griffith *d* Roger Corman *ph* Richard Moore *m* Mike Curb

Peter Fonda, Nancy Sinatra, Bruce Dern, Michael J. Pollard

The Wild Blue Yonder
US 1952 98m bw
Republic (Herbert J. Yates)

Incidents in the lives of bomber pilots in the Pacific during World War II.
Routine action flagwaver.

w Richard Tregaskis *d* Allan Dwan *ph* Reggie Lanning *m* Victor Young

Wendell Corey, Vera Hruba Ralston, Forrest Tucker, Phil Harris, Walter Brennan, Ruth Donnelly

Wild Boys of the Road*
US 1933 88m bw
Warner (Robert Presnell)
GB title: *Dangerous Days*

Boys of poor families take to the road in gangs.
Vivid social melodrama of its day, now rather overstated.

w Earl Baldwin *d* William Wellman *ph* Arthur Todd

Frankie Darro, Rochelle Hudson, Edwin Philips, Arthur Hohl

The Wild Bunch***
US 1969 145m Technicolor Panavision 70
Warner Seven Arts (Phil Feldman)

In 1914, Texas bandits are ambushed by an old enemy and die bloodily in defence of one of their number against a ruthless Mexican revolutionary.
Arguably the director's best film, and one which set a fashion for blood-spurting violence in westerns. Undeniably stylish, thoughtful, and in places very exciting.

w Walon Green, Sam Peckinpah *d Sam Peckinpah ph Lucien Ballard m* Jerry Fielding *ad* Edward Carrere

William Holden, Ernest Borgnine, Robert Ryan, Edmond O'Brien, Warren Oates, Jaime Sanchez, Ben Johnson, Strother Martin, L. Q. Jones, Albert Dekker

'A western that enlarged the form aesthetically, thematically, demonically.' —*Stanley Kauffmann, 1972*

'We watch endless violence to assure us that violence is not good.'—*Judith Crist, 1976*

The Wild Country
US 1970 100m Technicolor
Walt Disney (Ron Miller)

In the late 1880s a farmer buys a dilapidated Wyoming ranch and falls foul of a local rancher who controls the water supply.
Predictable family western in the familiar Disney style.

w Calvin Clements Jnr, Paul Savage, *novel* Little Britches by Ralph Moody *d* Robert Totten *ph* Frank Phillips *m* Robert Bronner

Steve Forrest, Vera Miles, Jack Elam, Ronny Howard, Morgan Woodward

Wild Geese Calling
US 1941 77m bw
TCF (Harry Joe Brown)

A young adventurer in Oregon weds the girl friend of a conniving gambler.
Minor semi-western which never really finds a style.

w Horace McCoy, *novel* Stewart Edward White *d* John Brahm *ph* Lucien Ballard

Joan Bennett, Henry Fonda, Warren William, Ona Munson, Barton MacLane, Russell Simpson, Iris Adrian

Wild Harvest
US 1947 92m bw
Paramount (Robert Fellows)

A romantic triangle develops among wheat harvesters on the western plains.
Standard star hokum.

w John Monks Jnr *d* Tay Garnett *ph* John F. Seitz *m* Hugo Friedhofer

Alan Ladd, Dorothy Lamour, Robert Preston,

Lloyd Nolan, Dick Erdman, Allen Jenkins, Will Wright

Wild in the Country
US 1961 114m De Luxe Cinemascope
TCF / Company of Artists (Jerry Wald)

A rebellious hillbilly is involved with three women.
Weird confection designed to show the star in all his facets.

w Clifford Odets, *novel* The Lost Country by J. R. Salamanca *d* Philip Dunne *ph* William C. Mellor *m* Kenyon Hopkins

Elvis Presley, Hope Lange, Tuesday Weld, Millie Perkins, John Ireland, Gary Lockwood

'One can't help feeling he was better off prior to this misguided bid for class.'—*MFB*

Wild in the Sky
US 1971 83m colour
AIP / Bald Eagle (William T. Naud, Dick Gautier)

Three young offenders skyjack a B52 jet bomber.
Black comedy melodrama, uncontrolled but with some engaging absurdities.

w William T. Naud, Dick Gautier *d* William T. Naud *ph* Thomas E. Spalding *m* Jerry Styner

Brandon de Wilde, Keenan Wynn, Dick Gautier, Tim O'Connor, James Daly, Robert Lansing

Wild in the Streets*
US 1968 97m Perfectcolor
AIP (Jack Cash)

In the imminent future, a pop singer becomes president and launches a campaign for teenage emancipation.
Satirical melodrama with a profusion of wild gags, some of which hit the target.

w Robert Thom *d* Barry Shear *ph* Richard Moore *m* Les Baxter

Shelley Winters, Chris Jones, Diane Varsi, Hal Holbrook, Millie Perkins

Wild Is the Wind
US 1957 114m bw Vistavision
Paramount / Hal B. Wallis

A widowed Italian sheep rancher in Nevada marries his wife's sister from Italy, but she falls for his adopted son.
Intense Cold Comfort Farm melodrama with a strong similarity to *They Knew What They Wanted*; the strain shows, and the performances are tiresomely noisy.

w Arnold Schulman *d* George Cukor *ph* Charles Lang Jnr *m* Dmitri Tiomkin

Anna Magnani, Anthony Quinn, Tony Franciosa, Dolores Hart, Joseph Calleia

The Wild North
US 1951 97m Anscocolor
MGM (Stephen Ames)

Standard adventure story with avalanche and wolf attacks.
A mountie gets his man but needs his help getting back to base.

w Frank Fenton *d* Andrew Marton *ph* Robert Surtees *m* Bronislau Kaper

Stewart Granger, Wendell Corey, Cyd Charisse

The Wild One**
US 1954 79m bw
Columbia / Stanley Kramer

Hoodlum motorcyclists terrorize a small town.
Brooding, compulsive, well-made little melodrama which was much banned because there was no retribution. As a narrative it does somewhat lack dramatic point.

w John Paxton, *story* The Cyclists' Raid by Frank Rooney *d Laslo Benedek ph* Hal Mohr *m* Leith Stevens

Marlon Brando, Lee Marvin, Mary Murphy, Robert Keith, Jay C. Flippen

The Wild Party
US 1956 81m bw
UA / Security (Sidney Harmon)

An ex-football player and some Los Angeles layabouts plot a kidnap.
Unpleasant melodrama laced with sex, violence and loud music.

w John McPartland *d* Harry Horner *ph* Sam Leavitt *m* Buddy Bregman

Anthony Quinn, Carol Ohmart, Jay Robinson, Arthur Franz, Nehemiah Persoff, Kathryn Grant, Paul Stewart

The Wild Party
US 1974 91m Movielab
AIP (Edgar Lansbury, Joseph Beruh)

In 1929, a silent film comedian on the skids throws a party to show his latest movie.
Evocative of its period but virtually confined to a single set which becomes boring, this collection of unlikely events and tedious people has only obvious points to make and its final descent into tragedy is not compelling.

w Walter Marks, *poem* Joseph Moncure March *d* James Ivory *ph* Walter Lassally *m* Larry Rosenthal

James Coco, Raquel Welch, Perry King, Tiffany

Bolling, Royal Dano, David Dukes, Dena Dietrich

'Seems to promise a pointillist precision about its characters and milieu which it never quite delivers.'—*Jonathan Rosenbaum*

Wild River*
US 1960 115m De Luxe Cinemascope
TCF (Elia Kazan)

In 1933 a Tennessee Valley Authority inspector incurs the wrath of a local matriarch who will not leave her valley even though it is to be flooded.
Interesting liberal-minded sociological drama marred by an added love story, as the similar *Last Days of Dolwyn* was marred by melodrama. Well made but somehow unmemorable.

w Paul Osborn, *novels* Borden Deal, William Bradford Huie *d* Elia Kazan *ph* Ellsworth Fredericks *m* Kenyon Hopkins

Montgomery Clift, *Jo Van Fleet*, Lee Remick, Albert Salmi, Jay C. Flippen, James Westerfield, Bruce Dern

Wild Rovers
US 1971 132m Metrocolor
Panavision 70
MGM / Geoffrey (Blake Edwards, Ken Wales)

A middle-aged cowboy, depressed with the state of his life, joins with a younger man to become a bank robber.
Fashionable, derivative, quite unsuccessful western tragi-comedy mixing in shades of every director from Ford to Peckinpah.

wd Blake Edwards *ph* Philip Lathrop *m* Jerry Goldsmith

William Holden, Ryan O'Neal, Karl Malden, Lynn Carlin, Tom Skerritt, Joe Don Baker, Rachel Roberts, Leora Dana, Moses Gunn

Wild Women
US 1970 74m colour TVM
Aaron Spelling

Army engineers on a secret mission disguise themselves as a wagon train and use women borrowed from the local jail.
Oddball comedy western, not really very good.

w Vincent Fotre *d* Don Taylor

Hugh O'Brian, Anne Francis, Marilyn Maxwell, Marie Windsor

Will Penny**
US 1967 109m Technicolor
Paramount / Fred Engel / Walter Seltzer / Tom Gries

A middle-aged cowpuncher falls foul of a family of maniacal cut-throats.
Realistically spare, laconic, uncomforting western with a curiously melodramatic set of villains.

wd Tom Gries *ph* Lucien Ballard *m* David Raksin

Charlton Heston, Joan Hackett, Donald Pleasance, Lee Majors, Bruce Dern, Anthony Zerbe, Clifton James, Ben Johnson

Will Success Spoil Rock Hunter?
US 1957 95m Eastmancolor
Cinemascope
TCF (Frank Tashlin)
GB title: *Oh! For a Man!*

A timid advertising executive is touted for a publicity stunt as the world's greatest lover.
A too-wild satire on TV commercials: less frenzied direction and gag-writing would have prised more humour from the situations.

w Frank Tashlin, *play* George Axelrod *d* Frank Tashlin *ph* Joe MacDonald *m* Cyril Mockridge

Jayne Mansfield, Tony Randall, Betsy Drake, Joan Blondell, John Williams, Henry Jones, Mickey Hargitay

Willard*
US 1971 95m De Luxe
Cinerama / Bing Crosby

A shy, withdrawn young man breeds and trains rats to kill his enemies.
Modest, rather unusual suspenser which builds well after a slow start; only horrifying to people who can't stand rats. A sequel, *Ben* (qv), later appeared.

w Gilbert Ralston, *novel* Ratman's Notebooks by Stephen Gilbert *d* Daniel Mann *ph* Robert B. Hauser *m* Alex North *rat trainer* Moe de Sesso

Bruce Davison, Elsa Lanchester, Ernest Borgnine, Sondra Locke, Michael Dante, J. Pat O'Malley

Willy Wonka and the Chocolate Factory*
US 1971 100m Technicolor
David Wolper

A boy wins a tour of the local chocolate factory and finds himself in the power of a magician.
Semi-satiric Grimms Fairy Tale pastiche which looks good but never seems quite happy with itself.

w Roald Dahl, from his novel *d* Mel Stuart *ph* Arthur Ibbetson *songs* Leslie Bricusse, Anthony Newley *ad Harper Goff*

Gene Wilder, Jack Albertson, Peter Ostrum, Roy Kinnear, Aubrey Woods

Wilson***
US 1944 154m Technicolor
TCF (Darryl F. Zanuck)

The rise and fall of an American president. Admirably careful biopic which raises no particular excitement but entertains and instructs on various levels.

w Lamar Trotti d Henry King ph Leon Shamroy m Alfred Newman ad James Basevi, Wiard Ihnen

Alexander Knox, Charles Coburn, Cedric Hardwicke, Geraldine Fitzgerald, Thomas Mitchell, Ruth Nelson, William Eythe, Vincent Price, Mary Anderson, Ruth Ford, Sidney Blackmer, Stanley Ridges, Eddie Foy Jnr, Charles Halton, Thurston Hall, J. M. Kerrigan, Francis X. Bushman

Winchester 73**
US 1950 92m bw
U-I (Aaron Rosenberg)

Long-time enemies settle an old grudge. Entertaining, popular, hard-riding, hard-shooting western of the old school.

w Robert L. Richards, Borden Chase, *story* Stuart N. Lake *d Anthony Mann ph William Daniels m* Joseph Gershenson

James Stewart, Shelley Winters, Dan Duryea, Stephen McNally, Millard Mitchell, Charles Drake, John McIntire, Will Geer, Jay C. Flippen, Rock Hudson, Tony Curtis, John Alexander, Steve Brodie

Winchester 73
US 1967 97m Technicolor TVM
Universal (Richard E. Lyons)

Flat television remake.

w Stephen Kandell, Richard L. Adams *d* Herschel Daugherty

Tom Tryon, John Saxon, Dan Duryea, John Drew Barrymore, John Dehner, Joan Blondell

Wind across the Everglades
US 1958 93m Technicolor
(Warner) Schulberg Productions (Stuart Schulberg)

Florida 1900: a young schoolteacher tracks down those responsible for hunting rare birds for their feathers, and becomes a game warden. Dull, meandering adventure story with a purpose, relying heavily on violence and eccentric characters.

w Budd Schulberg *d* Nicholas Ray *ph* Joseph Brun

Christopher Plummer, Burl Ives, Gypsy Rose Lee, Emmett Kelly, George Voskovec, Tony Galento, Mackinlay Kantor

The Wind and the Lion
US 1975 119m Metrocolor Panavision
Columbia / MGM (Herb Jaffe, Phil Rawlins)

In 1904 Tangier, an American widow and her children are kidnapped by a Riffian chief, and the eyes of the world are focused on the incident. Basing itself very lightly on an actual event, this adventure story is both confused as a narrative and unexciting as an action piece: the camera stops too often to look at sunsets, the plot stops too often for philosophizing, and there are too many underexplained characters and incidents fitting into the international jigsaw.

wd John Milius *ph* Billy Williams *m* Jerry Goldsmith

Sean Connery, Candice Bergen, Brian Keith, John Huston, Geoffrey Lewis, Steve Kanaly, Vladek Sheybal

The Wind Cannot Read
GB 1958 115m Eastmancolor
Rank (Betty E. Box)

In India and Burma during World War II, a flying officer falls in love with a Japanese language instructor suffering from a brain disease.
Or, love is a many-splendored dark victory. Old-fashioned romance for addicts, well enough produced.

w Richard Mason, from his novel *d* Ralph Thomas *ph* Ernest Steward *m* Angelo Lavagnino

Dirk Bogarde, Yoko Tani, Ronald Lewis, John Fraser, Anthony Bushell, Michael Medwin

Windom's Way*
GB 1957 108m Technicolor
Rank (John Bryan)

A doctor on a Far Eastern island tries to quell a native uprising.
Tolerably well intentioned action melodrama, topical because of Malaya; dramatically rather sober and predictable.

w Jill Craigie, *novel* James Ramsay Ullman *d* Ronald Neame *ph* Christopher Challis *m* James Bernard

Peter Finch, Mary Ure, Natasha Parry, Robert Flemyng, Michael Hordern

The Window***
US 1949 73m bw
RKO

A New York slum boy is always telling tall tales, so no one believes him when he actually witnesses a murder . . . except the murderer.
Classic little second feature, entertaining and suspenseful; unfortunately it had few successful imitators.

w Mel Dinelli d Ted Tetzlaff ph William Steiner *m* Roy Webb

Bobby Driscoll, Barbara Hale, Arthur Kennedy, Paul Stewart, Ruth Roman

'Logical, well-shaped, cohesive, admirably acted, beautifully photographed and cut to a nicety.'—*Richard Winnington*

Wing and a Prayer*
US 1944 97m bw
TCF

Life aboard an aircraft carrier.
Standard action flagwaver.

w Jerome Cady *d* Henry Hathaway *ph* Glen MacWilliams

Don Ameche, Cedric Hardwicke, Dana Andrews, Charles Bickford, Richard Jaeckel, Henry Morgan

Winged Victory**
US 1944 130m bw
TCF (Darryl F. Zanuck)

During World War II, pilots are inducted, trained and sent on dangerous missions.
Solid, competent, best-foot-forward flagwaver of the highest inspirational intention.

w Moss Hart, from his play *d* George Cukor *ph* Glen MacWilliams *m* David Rose

Lon McCallister, Jeanne Crain, Edmond O'Brien, Jane Ball, Mark Daniels, Don Taylor, Lee J. Cobb, Judy Holliday, Peter Lind Hayes, Alan Baxter, Red Buttons, Barry Nelson, Gary Merrill, Karl Malden, Martin Ritt, Jo-Carroll Dennison

Wings for the Eagle
US 1942 85m bw
Warner (Robert Lord)

Aircraft workers do their bit during World War II.
Home Front propaganda, well enough produced.

w Byron Morgan, Harrison Orkow *d* Lloyd Bacon *ph* Tony Gaudio

Ann Sheridan, Dennis Morgan, Jack Carson, George Tobias, Don Defore

Wings in the Dark*
US 1935 75m bw
Paramount (Arthur Hornblow Jnr)

Embittered after being blinded in an accident, a research flier finally leaps into action when his stranded girl friend needs help.
Satisfactory romantic melodrama.

w Jack Kirkland, Frank Partos *d* James Flood *ph* William C. Mellor

Cary Grant, Myrna Loy, Roscoe Karns, Hobart Cavanaugh, Dean Jagger, Bert Hanlon, Samuel S. Hinds

The Wings of Eagles*
US 1957 110m Metrocolor Cinemascope
MGM (Charles Schnee)

A navy flier breaks his neck in an accident and on recovery becomes a Hollywood writer.
Sentimental biopic of Frank 'Spig' Wead, a routine, easy-going assignment for its director (who is caricatured by Ward Bond as John Dodge).

w Frank Fenton, William Wister Haines *d* John Ford *ph* Paul C. Vogel *m* Jeff Alexander

John Wayne, Maureen O'Hara, Ward Bond, Dan Dailey, Ken Curtis, Edmund Lowe, Kenneth Tobey, Sig Rumann, Henry O'Neill

Wings of Fire
US 1967 99m Technicolor TVM
Universal (David Lowell Rich)

The daughter of an air freight service owner enters an air race.
Moderate old-fashioned romantic drama with aerial trimmings; rather a bore.

w Stirling Silliphant *d* David Lowell Rich

Suzanne Pleshette, James Farentino, Lloyd Nolan, Juliet Mills, Jeremy Slate, Ralph Bellamy

Wings of the Hawk
US 1953 81m Technicolor 3-D
U-I (Aaron Rosenberg)

Mexico 1911: a gold miner falls into the hands of revolutionaries.
Routine bang-bang, rather sloppily produced.

w James E. Moser *d* Budd Boetticher *ph* Clifford Stine *m* Frank Skinner

Van Heflin, Julie Adams, George Dolenz, Pedro Gonzales-Gonzales, Rodolfo Acosta, Antonio Moreno, Abbe Lane

Wings of the Morning*
GB 1937 89m Technicolor
TCF (Robert T. Kane)

In 1899, a gypsy princess marries an Irish nobleman; in 1937, romance again blooms between their descendants.
Britain's first Technicolor film was great to look at and quite charming, though slight; its major attractions being horse races, songs from John McCormack, and a heroine dressed for plot purposes as a boy.

w Tom Geraghty, *story* Donn Byrne *d* Harold Schuster

Henry Fonda, *Annabella*, Stewart Rome, John McCormack, Leslie Banks, Irene Vanbrugh, Harry Tate, Edward Underdown, Helen Haye

'A wholesome, refreshing and altogether likeable little romance.'—*Frank S. Nugent*

Wings of the Navy
US 1939 89m bw
Warner (Lou Edelman)

The loves and careers of navy pilots.
Competent animated recruiting poster.

w Michael Fessier *d* Lloyd Bacon *ph* Arthur Edeson, Elmer Dyer

George Brent, Olivia de Havilland, John Payne, Frank McHugh, John Litel, Victor Jory, Henry O'Neill, John Ridgely

Winner Take All
US 1975 100m colour TVM
Jozak

A housewife becomes addicted to gambling.
Domestic drama moving in well-defined grooves.

w Caryl Ledner *d* Paul Bogart

Shirley Jones, Laurence Luckinbill, Sam Groom, Joan Blondell, Joyce Van Patten, Sylvia Sidney

Winning*
US 1969 123m Technicolor Panavision 70
Universal / Newman–Foreman (John Foreman)

A racing driver's professional problems strain his relationship with his wife.
Cliché track melodrama with pretensions, well but needlessly made.

w Howard Rodman *d* James Goldstone *ph Richard Moore* *m* Dave Grusin

Paul Newman, Joanne Woodward, Richard Thomas, Robert Wagner, David Sheiner, Clu Gulager

The Winning Team
US 1952 98m bw
Warner (Bryan Foy)

A telephone linesman becomes a great baseball player despite trouble with his vision after an accident.
Standard biopic of Grover Cleveland Alexander; all very pleasant but no surprises.

w Ted Sherdeman, Seeleg Lester, Merwin Gerard *d* Lewis Seiler *ph* Sid Hickox *m* David Buttolph

Doris Day, Ronald Reagan, Frank Lovejoy, Eve Miller, James Millican, Russ Tamblyn

The Winslow Boy***
GB 1948 117m bw
British Lion / London Films (Anatole de Grunwald)

A naval cadet is expelled for stealing a postal order; his father spends all he had on proving his innocence.
Highly enjoyable middle-class British entertainment based on an actual case; performances and period settings are alike excellent, though the film is a trifle overlong.

w Terence Rattigan, Anatole de Grunwald, play Terence Rattigan *d Anthony Asquith* *ph* Frederick Young *m* William Alwyn

Robert Donat, Cedric Hardwicke, Margaret Leighton, Frank Lawton, Jack Watling, Basil Radford, Kathleen Harrison, Francis L. Sullivan, Marie Lohr, Neil North, Wilfrid Hyde White, Ernest Thesiger

Winter Carnival
US 1939 89m bw
UA

College romances over a holiday weekend.
Nondescript romantic comedy.

d Charles Riesner

Ann Sheridan, Richard Carlson, Helen Parrish, Virginia Gilmore, Robert Walker

Winter Kill**
US 1974 100m colour TVM
MGM

Inexplicable but connected murders strike a mountain resort community.
This fairly gripping, nicely photographed and vividly narrated murder mystery was intended as a pilot for a series which never happened, *Adams of Eagle Lake*. It was inspired by the movie *They Always Kill their Masters* but took its plot without permission from an old Sherlock Holmes movie *The Scarlet Claw*.

w John Michael Hayes *d* Jud Taylor

Andy Griffith, Sheree North, John Larch, John Calvin, Tim O'Connor, Louise Latham. Joyce Van Patten

Winter Meeting
US 1948 104m bw
Warner (Henry Blanke)

A repressed spinster falls for a naval hero intent on becoming a priest.
Dreary talk marathon which did its star's career no good at all.

w Catherine Turney, *novel* Ethel Vance *d* Bretaigne Windust *ph* Ernest Haller *m* Max Steiner

Bette Davis, James Davis, Janis Paige, John Hoyt, Florence Bates, Walter Baldwin

Winterset**
US 1936 78m bw
RKO

On the New York waterfront, a drifter determines to avenge his father's death.
Very dated poetic melodrama, here given a talky, artificial production which at the time impressed many critics but is now fairly difficult to endure.

w Anthony Veiller, *play* Maxwell Anderson *d* Alfred Santell *ph* Peverell Marley *md* Nathaniel Shilkret

Burgess Meredith, Eduardo Ciannelli, Margo, Paul Guilfoyle, John Carradine, Edward Ellis, Stanley Ridges, Maurice Moscovitch, Myron McCormick, Mischa Auer

Wintertime
US 1943 82m bw
TCF (William Le Baron)

A Norwegian skating star comes to Canada where her uncles's winter resort is on its uppers.
The last of the star's Fox musicals is pure routine.

w Edward Moran, Jack Jevne, Lynn Starling *d* John Brahm *ph* Glen MacWilliams *md* Charles Henderson

Sonja Henie, Jack Oakie, Cesar Romero, S. Z. Sakall, Carole Landis, Cornel Wilde, Woody Herman and his Band

The Wistful Widow of Wagon Gap*
US 1947 78m bw
U-I (Robert Arthur)

In old Montana, an accident-prone wayfarer accidentally kills a man and has to look after his family.
Tame and disappointing comedy vehicle.

w D. D. Beauchamp, William Bowers *d* Charles T. Barton, Robert Lees, Frederic I. Rinaldo, John Grant *ph* Charles Van Enger *m* Walter Shumann

Bud Abbott, Lou Costello, Marjorie Main, Audrey Young, George Cleveland

Witchcraft*
GB 1964 79m bw
TCF / Lippert (Robert Lippert, Jack Parsons)

A family of witches take revenge on their longtime enemies.
Spasmodically arresting horror film spoiled by too complex a plot line and some variable acting.

w Harry Spaulding *d Don Sharp ph* Arthur Lavis *m* Carlo Martelli

Jack Hedley, Lon Chaney Jnr, Marie Ney, Jill Dixon, David Weston

'Unpretentious and uncommonly gripping.' —*MFB*

The Witches
GB 1967 90m Technicolor
Hammer (Anthony Nelson Keys)
US title: *The Devil's Own*

A schoolmistress finds witchcraft in an English village.
Chintzy horror with predictable development and risible climax.

w Nigel Kneale, *novel* The Devil's Own by Peter Curtis *d* Cyril Frankel *ph* Arthur Grant *m* Richard Rodney Bennett

Joan Fontaine, Kay Walsh, Alec McCowen, Gwen Ffrangcon Davies, Ingrid Brett, John Collin, Michèle Dotrice, Leonard Rossiter, Martin Stephens, Carmel McSharry

Witchfinder General*
GB 1968 87m Eastmancolor
Tigon (Arnold Miller)
US title: *The Conqueror Worm*

In 1645 a villainous lawyer finds it profitable to travel the country instigating witch hunts.
Savage, stylish minor horror melodrama with a growing reputation as the best work of its young director. Not for the squeamish despite its pleasing countryside photography.

w Michael Reeves, Tom Baker, *novel* Ronald Bassett *d Michael Reeves ph John Coquillon* *m* Paul Ferris, Jim Morahan

Vincent Price, Rupert Davies, Ian Ogilvy, Patrick Wymark, Hilary Dwyer

With a Song in My Heart*
US 1952 117m Technicolor
TCF (Lamar Trotti)

Singer Jane Froman is crippled in a plane crash but finally makes a comeback.
Romanticized showbiz biopic with the singer providing voice only. Adequate production and plenty of familiar tunes made this a successful mass appeal sob story.

w Lamar Trotti *d* Walter Lang *ph* Leon Shamroy *md* Alfred Newman

Susan Hayward, David Wayne, Rory Calhoun, Thelma Ritter, Una Merkel, Robert Wagner, Helen Westcott

With Six You Get Egg Roll
US 1968 99m De Luxe Panavision
Cinema Center / Arwin (Martin Melcher)

A widow with three sons marries a widower with one daughter.
Quite a bright and inventive family comedy.

w Gwen Bagni, Paul Dubov *d* Howard Morris *ph* Ellsworth Fredericks, Harry Stradling Jnr

Doris Day, Brian Keith, Pat Carroll, Barbara Hershey

Without Love*
US 1945 111m bw
MGM (Lawrence Weingarten)

The housing shortage in wartime Washington causes a widow to allow a scientist to move in with her, quite platonically.
Altered version of a popular play; rather long-drawn-out and disappointing considering the talent on hand.

w Donald Ogden Stewart, *play* Philip Barry *d* Harold S. Bucquet *ph* Karl Freund *m* Bronislau Kaper

Spencer Tracy, Katharine Hepburn, Lucille Ball, Keenan Wynn, Carl Esmond, Patricia Morison, Felix Bressart, Gloria Grahame

'One of those glossy conversation pieces that MGM does up so handsomely.'—*Rose Pelswick*

Without Reservations
US 1946 101m bw
RKO / Jesse L. Lasky

A famous woman writer heads for Hollywood by train and meets a marine who seems ideal for her male lead.
Would-be zany romantic comedy à la *It Happened One Night*; doesn't quite come off.

w Andrew Solt *d* Mervyn Le Roy *ph* Milton Krasner *m* Roy Webb

Claudette Colbert, John Wayne, Don Defore, Phil Brown, Frank Puglia

Without Warning
US 1952 70m bw
UA / Allart

A sex maniac murders a succession of blondes.
Semi-documentary, low-budget police thriller with all elements adequate for their purpose.

w Bill Raynor *d* Arnold Laven *ph* Joseph Biroc *m* Herschel Burke Gilbert

Adam Williams, Edward Binns, Meg Randall

Witness for the Prosecution***
US 1957 114m bw
UA / Theme / Edward Small (Arthur Hornblow Jnr)

A convalescent QC takes on a murder defence and finds himself in a web of trickery.
Thoroughly likeable though relentlessly over-expanded movie version of a clever stage thriller. Some miscasting and artificiality is condoned by smart dialogue and handling, one celebrated performance, and a handful of surprises.

w Billy Wilder, Harry Kurnitz, play Agatha Christie d Billy Wilder ph Russell Harlan *m* Matty Melneck

Charles Laughton, Tyrone Power, Marlene Dietrich, John Williams, Henry Daniell, Elsa Lanchester, Norma Varden, Una O'Connor, Ian Wolfe

Witness to Murder*
US 1954 81m bw
UA / Chester Erskine

A lonely woman sees a strangling in the flat across the street; the police don't believe her but the murderer does.
Predictable but quite effective screamer with a nick-of-time dénouement.

w Chester Erskine *d* Roy Rowland *ph* John Alton *m* Herschel Burke Gilbert

Barbara Stanwyck, George Sanders, Gary Merrill, Jesse White, Harry Shannon, Claire Carleton

Wives and Lovers
US 1963 103m bw
(Paramount) Hal B. Wallis

A successful author moves his family into Connecticut, where sex rears its ugly head.
Would-be sophisticated comedy with insufficient bubbles.

w Edward Anhalt, *play* The First Wife by Jay Presson Allen *d* John Rich *ph* Lucien Ballard *m* Lyn Murray

Van Johnson, Janet Leigh, Ray Walston, Shelley Winters, Martha Hyer, Jeremy Slate

The Wizard of Oz***
US 1939 102m Technicolor
MGM (Mervyn Le Roy)

Unhappy Dorothy runs away from home, has adventures in a fantasy land, but finally decides

that happiness was in her own back yard all the time.
Classic fairy tale given vigorous straightforward treatment, made memorable by performances, art direction and hummable tunes.

w Noel Langley, Florence Ryerson, Edgar Allan Wolfe, *book* Frank L. Baum *d Victor Fleming ph* Harold Rosson *songs E. Y. Harburg, Harold Arlen ad Cedric Gibbons, William A. Horning*

Judy Garland, Frank Morgan, Ray Bolger, Jack Haley, Bert Lahr, Margaret Hamilton, Billie Burke, Charley Grapewin, Clara Blandick

Wolf Larsen
US 1958 83m bw
AA (Lindsley Parsons)

Serviceable remake of *The Sea Wolf* (qv) without the Nietzschean overtones.

w Jack de Witt, Turnley Walker *d* Harlan Jones *ph* Floyd Crosby *m* Paul Dunlap

Barry Sullivan, Peter Graves, Thayer David, Gita Hall

The Wolf Man**
US 1940 70m bw
Universal

The son of an English squire comes home, is bitten by a gypsy werewolf, and becomes one himself.
Dazzlingly cast, moderately well staged, but dramatically very disappointing horror piece which established a new Universal monster who later met Frankenstein, Abbott and Costello, and several other eccentrics.

w Curt Siodmak *d* George Waggner *ph Joseph Valentine m* Charles Previn

Lon Chaney Jnr, Claude Rains, Warren William, Ralph Bellamy, Bela Lugosi, *Maria Ouspenskaya*, Patric Knowles, Evelyn Ankers, Fay Helm

Woman Accused*
US 1933 73m bw
Paramount

A woman kills her ex-lover in a struggle and goes on the run.
Intriguing rigmarole written as a magazine serial by ten well-known authors contributing a chapter each. The result confirms the method.

w Bayard Veiller, *serial* Rupert Hughes, Vicki Baum, Zane Grey, Vina Delmar, Irvin S. Cobb, Gertrude Atherton, J. P. McEvoy, Ursula Parrott, Polan Banks, Sophie Kerr *d* Paul Sloane *m* Karl Struss

Nancy Carroll, Cary Grant, John Halliday, Irving Pichel, Louis Calhern, Jack La Rue, John Lodge

Woman Hater
GB 1948 105m bw
GFD / Two Cities

An English nobleman tries to disprove a film star's statement that she hates men and loves solitude.
Incredibly slight material is interminably stretched out, well beyond an excellent cast's ability to help.

w Robert Westerby, Nicholas Phipps *d* Terence Young *ph* André Thomas *m* Lambert Williamson

Stewart Granger, Edwige Feuillère, Ronald Squire, Mary Jerrold, Jeanne de Casalis

The Woman Hunter
US 1972 74m colour TVM
Jerome L. Epstein

An international jewel thief and murderer seems to be on the trail of a wealthy woman.
Crime in the luxury classes, suffering from obscure narration.

w Brian Clemens *d* Bernard L. Kowalski

Barbara Eden, Robert Vaughn, Stuart Whitman, Sydney Chaplin, Larry Storch

The Woman I Love*
US 1937 85m bw
RKO (Albert Lewis)
GB title: *The Woman Between*

In World War I France, a pilot loves his superior officer's wife.
Well-made romantic action melodrama from a well-praised original.

w Mary Borden, French film L'Equipage and novel of same name by Joseph Kessel *d Anatole Litvak ph* Charles Rosher *m* Arthur Honegger, Maurice Thiriet

Paul Muni, Miriam Hopkins, Louis Hayward, Colin Clive, Minor Watson, Elizabeth Risdon, Paul Guilfoyle, Mady Christians

Woman in a Dressing Gown*
GB 1957 94m bw
Godwin / Willis / J. Lee-Thompson

After twenty years of marriage, a wife's slatternly ways alienate her once devoted husband, and he asks for a divorce.
Classic British TV play adequately filmed but now rather dated and irritating.

w Ted Willis, from his play *d* J. Lee-Thompson *ph* Gilbert Taylor *m* Louis Levy

Yvonne Mitchell, Anthony Quayle, Sylvia Syms, Andrew Ray, Carole Lesley

Woman in Hiding
US 1949 92m bw
U-I (Michael Kraike)

After escaping her husband's attempts to murder her, a woman goes into hiding while evidence is being accumulated against her.
Modest suspenser with too many near escapes and not much else.

w Oscar Saul *d* Michael Gordon *ph* William Daniels *m* Frank Skinner

Ida Lupino, Howard Duff, Stephen McNally, John Litel, Taylor Holmes, Irving Bacon, Peggy Dow, Joe Besser, Don Beddoe

The Woman in Question*
GB 1949 88m bw
GFD / Javelin (Teddy Baird)
US title: *Five Angles on Murder*

Police investigating a woman's death build up several different impressions of her.
Multi-flashback melodrama which somehow doesn't quite come off despite effort all round.

w John Cresswell *d* Anthony Asquith *ph* Desmond Dickinson *m* John Wooldridge

Jean Kent, Dirk Bogarde, Susan Shaw, John McCallum, Hermione Baddeley, Charles Victor, Duncan Macrae, Lana Morris, Vida Hope

The Woman in the Window***
US 1944 95m bw
International (Nunnally Johnson)

A grass widow professor befriends a girl who gets him involved with murder.
A refreshingly intelligent little thriller which was criticized at the time for a cop-out ending; this can now be seen as a decorative extra to a story which had already ended satisfactorily. Good middlebrow entertainment.

w Nunnally Johnson, novel Once Off Guard by J. H. Wallis *d Fritz Lang ph Milton Krasner* *m* Arthur Lang

Edward G. Robinson, Joan Bennett, *Raymond Massey, Dan Duryea,* Edmund Breon, Thomas Jackson, Dorothy Peterson, Arthur Loft

'A perfect example of its kind, and a very good kind too.'—*James Shelley Hamilton*

'The accumulation of tiny details enlarged as though under a district attorney's magnifying glass gives reality a fantastic and anguishing appearance.'—*Jacques Bourgeois*

The Woman in White**
US 1948 109m bw
Warner (Henry Blanke)

The new tutor of a strange household finds himself among eccentrics, villains and ill-used ladies.
A Victorian thriller which is long on atmosphere but not so hot on suspense or plot development. The cast helps a lot.

w Stephen Morehouse Avery, *novel* Wilkie Collins *d* Peter Godfrey *ph Carl Guthrie* *m* Max Steiner

Gig Young, Eleanor Parker, *Sidney Greenstreet,* Alexis Smith, Agnes Moorehead, John Emery, *John Abbott,* Curt Bois

'The Wilkie Collins novel is given the studious, stolid treatment ordinarily reserved for the ritual assassination of a great classic. This is not intended as a recommendation.'—*James Agee*

'Greenstreet and others move through the murky passages of the story like visitors in some massive Gothic museum, and they move, on the whole, with stately discretion, and do not scribble on the objects or show anything but the greatest veneration for them.'—*C. A. Lejeune*

Woman Obsessed
US 1959 102m De Luxe Cinemascope
TCF (Sidney Boehm)

In the Canadian Rockies, a pioneer woman's small son does not take to his new stepfather.
Antediluvian pulp fiction with quicksand and a forest fire for highlights. Shades of D. W. Griffith, and badly done into the bargain.

w Sidney Boehm, *novel* John Mantley *d* Henry Hathaway *ph* William C. Mellor *m* Hugo Friedhofer

Susan Hayward, Stephen Boyd, Dennis Holmes, Theodore Bikel, Barbara Nichols, Ken Scott, Arthur Franz

A Woman of Distinction
US 1950 85m bw
Columbia (Buddy Adler)

The lady dean of a New England school falls for a British astronomer.
Pratfall farce for ageing stars. No go.

w Charles Hoffman *d* Edward Buzzell *ph* Joseph Walker *m* Morris Stoloff

Rosalind Russell, Ray Milland, Edmund Gwenn, Janis Carter, Mary Jane Saunders, Francis Lederer, Jerome Courtland

Woman of Straw*
GB 1964 114m Eastmancolor
UA / Novus (Michael Relph)

A rich old man's nurse conspires with his nephew in a murder plot.
Rather half-hearted but good-looking star melodrama which ventures into Hitchcock territory.

w Robert Muller, Stanley Mann, Michael Relph, *novel* Catherine Arley *d* Basil Dearden *ph* Otto Heller *m* Muir Mathieson *pd* Ken Adam

Gina Lollobrigida, Sean Connery, *Ralph Richardson,* Johnny Sekka, Laurence Hardy, Alexander Knox

Woman of the North Country
US 1952 90m Trucolor
Republic (Joseph Kane)

Minnesota 1890: rivalry over an iron ore mine erupts between a young engineer and an ambitious woman.
Standard western.

w Norman Reilly Raine *d* Joseph Kane *ph* Jack Marta *m* R. Dale Butts

Ruth Hussey, Rod Cameron, John Agar, Gale Storm, Jim Davis, J. Carrol Naish

Woman of the Year***
US 1942 114m bw
MGM (Joseph L. Mankiewicz)

A sports columnist marries a lady politician; they have nothing in common but love.
Simple, effective, mildly sophisticated comedy which allows two splendid stars, in harness for the first time, to do their thing to the general benefit.

w Ring Lardner Jnr, Michael Kanin d George Stevens ph Joseph Ruttenberg *m* Franz Waxman

Spencer Tracy, Katharine Hepburn, Fay Bainter, Reginald Owen, William Bendix, Dan Tobin, Minor Watson, Roscoe Karns

'Between them they have enough charm to keep any ball rolling.'—*William Whitebait*

Woman of the Year
US 1975 100m colour TVM
MGM (Hugh Benson)

Disappointing TV remake . . . as what remake wouldn't be?

w Joseph Bologna, Renee Taylor, Bernie Kahn *d* Gene Kelly

Renee Taylor, Joe Bologna, Dick O'Neill, Anthony Holland

The Woman on Pier 13
US 1949 73m bw
RKO (Jack J. Gross)
aka: *I Married a Communist*

A shipping executive is blackmailed by communists, who know of a youthful crime, into helping them spy.
Laboured witch-hunt melodrama.

w Charles Grayson, Robert Hardy Andrews *d* Robert Stevenson *ph* Nicholas Musuraca *m* Leigh Harline

Laraine Day, Robert Ryan, John Agar, Thomas Gomez, Janis Carter, Richard Rober, William Talman

Woman on the Beach
US 1947 71m bw
RKO (Jack J. Gloss)

A mentally ailing coastguard meets a *femme fatale* and comes between her and her sadistic husband.
Nuthouse melodrama which neither convinces nor compels for a moment.

w Frank Davis, Jean Renoir, *novel* None So Blind by Mitchell Wilson *d* Jean Renoir *ph* Leo Tover, Harry Wild *m* Hanns Eisler

Joan Bennett, Robert Ryan, Charles Bickford, Nan Leslie, Walter Sande

A Woman Rebels*
US 1936 88m bw
RKO (Pandro S. Berman)

A Victorian miss fights for women's rights and has an illegitimate baby.
Interesting, half-forgotten star drama.

w Anthony Veiller, Ernest Vajda, *novel* Portrait of a Rebel by Netta Syrett *d* Mark Sandrich *ph* Robert de Grasse *m* Roy Webb *ad* Van Nest Polglase

Katharine Hepburn, Herbert Marshall, Elizabeth Allan, Donald Crisp, Doris Dudley, David Manners, Van Heflin, Lucile Watson, Eily Malyon

Woman Times Seven
US / France 1967 99m De Luxe
TCF / Embassy (Arthur Cohn)

Seven sketches, in each of which a woman behaves typically of her sex.
Humourless after-dinner entertainment.

w Cesare Zavattini *d* Vittorio De Sica *ph* Christian Matras *m* Riz Ortolani

Shirley Maclaine, Peter Sellers, Rossano Brazzi, Vittorio Gassman, Lex Barker, Elsa Martinelli, Robert Morley, Adrienne Corri, Patrick Wymark, Alan Arkin, Michael Caine, Anita Ekberg, Philippe Noiret

A Woman under the Influence*
US 1974 146m colour
Faces International (Sam Shaw)

A white collar worker's marriage goes sour. Insanely long case history in close up, with all parties constantly on the brink of hysteria. Often sharply observed, but hard to sit through.

wd John Cassavetes *ph* Mitch Breit *m* Bo Harwood

Peter Falk, Gena Rowlands

The Woman's Angle
GB 1952 86m bw
ABP / Leslie Arliss / Bow Belles (Walter Mycroft)

In a divorce court three flashbacks tell of the life of a composer.
Damp little formula drama for matinee audiences, refashioned from a successful silent film.

wd Leslie Arliss, *novel* Three Cups of Coffee by Ruth Feiner *ph* Erwin Hillier *m* Robert Gill; the Mansell Concerto by Kenneth Leslie Smith

Edward Underdown, Cathy O'Donnell, Lois Maxwell, Claude Farrell, Peter Reynolds, Marjorie Fielding

A Woman's Face**
US 1941 105m bw
MGM (Victor Saville)

A scarred and embittered woman turns to crime but jibs at murder.
Curious, unexpected but very entertaining melodrama with a courtroom frame, Swedish settings, an excellent cast and some bravura sequences.

w Donald Ogden Stewart, *play* Il Était une Fois by Francis de Croisset *d George Cukor ph Robert Planck m* Bronislau Kaper

Joan Crawford, Melvyn Douglas, *Conrad Veidt,* Osa Massen, Reginald Owen, Albert Basserman, Marjorie Main, Donald Meek, Connie Gilchrist

A Woman's Secret
US 1949 85m bw
RKO (Herman J. Mankiewicz)

An ex-singer grooms a girl as her successor but lives to regret it.
Downright peculiar little *film noir* by the co-author of *Citizen Kane* (though not so that you'd notice).

w Herman J. Mankiewicz, *novel* Mortgage on Life by Vicki Baum *d* Nicholas Ray *ph* George Diskant *m* Constantin Bakaleinikoff

Maureen O'Hara, Gloria Grahame, Melvyn Douglas, Bill Williams, Victor Jory, Mary Phillips

A Woman's Vengeance*
US 1948 96m bw
U-I

A man is convicted for the murder of his invalid wife, actually committed by a jealous woman in love with him but later spurned.
Interesting but very stagey melodrama from one of its author's more commercial ventures.

w Aldous Huxley, from his story and play The Gioconda Smile *d* Zoltan Korda *ph* Russell Metty

Charles Boyer, Jessica Tandy, Ann Blyth, Cedric Hardwicke, Mildred Natwick

Woman's World**
US 1954 94m Technicolor Cinemascope
TCF (Charles Brackett)

Three top salesmen and their wives are summoned to New York by the boss, who seeks to choose a new general manager.
Amusing, superficial pattern comedy-drama for an all-star cast, backed by all-round technical competence.

w Claude Binyon, Mary Loos, Richard Sale *d Jean Negulesco ph* Joe MacDonald *m* Cyril Mockridge

Clifton Webb, Lauren Bacall, Van Heflin, June Allyson, Fred MacMurray, Arlene Dahl, Cornel Wilde, Elliott Reid, Marhalo Gillmore

The Women***
US 1939 132m bw
MGM (Hunt Stromberg)

A New York socialite gets a divorce but later thinks better of it.
Bitchy comedy drama distinguished by an all-girl cast ('135 women with men on their minds'). An over-generous slice of real theatre, skilfully adapted, with rich sets, plenty of laughs, and some memorable scenes between the fighting ladies.

w Anita Loos, Jane Murfin, play Clare Boothe d George Cukor ph Oliver T. Marsh, Joseph Ruttenberg *m* Edward Ward, David Snell

Norma Shearer, Joan Crawford, *Rosalind Russell,* Mary Boland, Paulette Goddard, Joan Fontaine, Lucile Watson, Phyllis Povah, Virginia Weidler, Ruth Hussey, Margaret Dumont, Marjorie Main, Hedda Hopper

'Whether you go or not depends on whether you can stand Miss Shearer with tears flowing steadily in all directions at once, and such an endless damn back fence of cats.' —*Otis Ferguson*

Women in Chains
US 1971 74m colour TVM
Bernard Kowalski (Edward J. Mikis)

A probation officer has herself imprisoned to help research, but her only confidant dies . . .
Not exactly a new plot, but the old melodramatics suffice.

w Rita Lakin *d* Bernard Kowalski

Ida Lupino, Lois Nettleton, Jessica Walter, Belinda Montgomery, John Larch, Penny Fuller

Women in Love***
GB 1969 130m De Luxe
UA / Brandywine (Larry Kramer)

Two girls have their first sexual encounters in the Midlands during the twenties.
Satisfactory rendering of a celebrated novel, with excellent period detail atoning for rather irritating characters. The nude wrestling scene was a famous first.

w Larry Kramer, *novel D. H. Lawrence d Ken Russell ph Billy Williams m* Georges Delerue

Glenda Jackson, Jennie Linden, Alan Bates, Oliver Reed, Michael Gough, Alan Webb
'They should take all the pretentious dialogue off the soundtrack and call it Women in Heat.' —*Rex Reed*

Women of All Nations
US 1931 72m bw
Fox

Flagg and Quirt, back in the Marines, have amorous adventures in Sweden, Nicaragua and Egypt.
Routine fun and games with the heroes of *What Price Glory.*

w Barry Connors *d* Raoul Walsh *ph* Lucien Andriot *m* Reginald H. Bassett

Edmund Lowe, Victor McLaglen, Greta Nissen, El Brendel, Fifi D'Orsay, Bela Lugosi, Humphrey Bogart

Women of Twilight
GB 1952 89m bw
Romulus (Daniel M. Angel)

Unmarried mothers are victimized by a professional baby farmer.
Sordid, claustrophobic and ham-handed version of an exploitation play designed to provide another monstrous part for its star.

w Anatole de Grunwald, *novel* Sylvia Rayman *d* Gordon Parry *ph* Jack Asher *m* Alan Gray

Freda Jackson, René Ray, Lois Maxwell, Joan Dowling, Dora Bryan, Vida Hope, Mary Germaine, Laurence Harvey

Won Ton Ton, the Dog Who Saved Hollywood
US 1976 92m colour
Paramount / David V. Picker, Arnold Schulman, Michael Winner

In twenties Hollywood, a lost Alsatian dog becomes a movie star but later suffers some ups and downs before being reunited with his mistress.
Scatty, unlikeable comedy with too frantic a pace, apparently in desperation at the dearth of funny lines and situations. The sixty 'guest stars' barely get a look in; the director seems to think (erroneously) that their appearance makes some kind of point even though they have nothing to do. Altogether, an embarrassment.

w Arnold Schulman, Cy Howard *d* Michael Winner *ph* Richard H. Kline *m* Neal Hefti

Madeleine Kahn, Art Carney, Bruce Dern, Ron Leibman; and Dennis Morgan, William Demarest, Virginia Mayo, Rory Calhoun, Henry Wilcoxon, Ricardo Montalban, Jackie Coogan, Johnny Weissmuller, Aldo Ray, Ethel Merman, Joan Blondell, Yvonne de Carlo, Andy Devine, Broderick Crawford, Richard Arlen, Jack La Rue, Dorothy Lamour, Phil Silvers, Gloria de Haven, Stepin Fetchit, Rudy Vallee, George Jessel, Ann Miller, Janet Blair, the Ritz Brothers, Victor Mature, Fernando Lamas, Cyd Charisse, Huntz Hall, Edgar Bergen, Peter Lawford, Regis Toomey, Alice Faye, Milton Berle, John Carradine, Walter Pidgeon, etc.

Wonder Bar**
US 1934 84m bw
Warner (Robert Lord)

Love and hate backstage at a Paris night club.
Curious musical drama with an interesting cast and fairly stunning numbers.

w Earl Baldwin, *play* Geza Herczeg, Karl Farkas, Robert Katscher *d* Lloyd Bacon *ch Busby Berkeley songs* Harry Warren, Al Dubin *ad* Jack Okey

Al Jolson, Kay Francis, Dolores del Rio, Ricardo Cortez, Dick Powell, Guy Kibbee, Ruth Donnelly, Hugh Herbert, Louise Fazenda, Fifi D'Orsay

Wonder Man***
US 1945 97m Technicolor
Samuel Goldwyn

A mild-mannered student is persuaded by the ghost of his dead twin to avenge his murder.

Smooth, successful mixture of *Topper*, a nightclub musical, a gangster drama and the star's own brand of fooling; this is possibly his best vehicle.

w Don Hartman, Melville Shavelson, Philip Rapp, story Arthur Sheekman *d Bruce Humberstone ph* Victor Milner, William Snyder *md* Louis Forbes *sp* John Fulton

Danny Kaye, Vera-Ellen, Virginia Mayo, Steve Cochran, S. Z. Sakall, Allen Jenkins, Ed Brophy, Donald Woods, Otto Kruger, Richard Lane, Natalie Schaefer

Wonder Woman
US 1974 75m colour TVM
Warner

Wonder Woman leaves Paradise Island to undertake a special mission for the CIA.
Abysmal comic strip adventures lacking in logic or even action.

w John D. F. Black *d* Vincent McEveety

Cathy Lee Crosby, Ricardo Montalban, Andrew Prine, Kaz Garas

The Wonderful Country
US 1959 96m Technicolor
UA / DRM (Chester Erskine)

A wandering gunman is offered a job by the Texas Rangers.
Complexly plotted western offering a range of familiar exploits.

w Robert Ardrey, *novel* Tom Lea *d* Robert Parrish *ph* Floyd Crosby, Alex Phillips

Robert Mitchum, Julie London, Pedro Armendariz, Gary Merrill, Jack Oakie, Albert Dekker, Charles McGraw, John Banner, Jay Novello

Wonderful Life*
GB 1964 113m Techniscope
EMI / Elstree Distributors / Ivy (Kenneth Harper)

Four entertainers on a luxury liner are hired by a film crew in Africa.
Slight but zestful youth musical with highly illogical detail; the highlight is a ten-minute spoof history of the movies.

w Peter Myers, Ronald Cass *d* Sidney J. Furie *ph* Ken Higgins *pd* Stanley Dorfman

Cliff Richard, Walter Slezak, Susan Hampshire, Melvyn Hayes, Richard O'Sullivan, Una Stubbs, Derek Bond, Gerald Harper, the Shadows

The Wonderful World of the Brothers Grimm*
US 1962 134m Technicolor Cinerama
MGM / Cinerama / George Pal

An account of the lives of the German fairy tale writers is supplemented by three of their stories, *The Dancing Princess, The Cobbler and the Elves* and *The Singing Bone.*
Saccharine, heavy-handed pantomime with insufficient comedy, menace or spectacle.

w David P. Harmon, Charles Beaumont, William Roberts *d* Henry Levin, George Pal *ph* Paul C. Vogel *m* Leigh Harline *ad* George W. Davis, Edward Carfagno

Laurence Harvey, Karl Boehm, Claire Bloom, Barbara Eden, Walter Slezak, Oscar Homolka, *Martita Hunt,* Russ Tamblyn, Yvette Mimieux, *Jim Backus,* Beulah Bondi, Terry-Thomas, Buddy Hackett, Otto Kruger

The Wonders of Aladdin
Italy 1961 92m Technicolor Cinemascope
Embassy / Lux

With the help of a genie, Aladdin defeats a usurper and wins the princess's hand.
Flat and disappointing pantomime with virtually no charm.

w Luther Davis *d* Henry Levin, Mario Bava *ph* Tonino Delli Colli *m* Angelo Lavagnino

Donald O'Connor, Vittorio De Sica, Aldo Fabrizi, Michèle Mercier

The Wooden Horse**
GB 1950 101m bw
British Lion / Wessex / London Films (Ian Dalrymple)

During World War II, British prisoners escape from Stalag Luft III by tunnelling under a vaulting horse.
Standard, solid POW drama with predictable but exciting and occasionally moving developments.

w Eric Williams, from his novel *d* Jack Lee *ph* C. Pennington-Richards *m* Clifton Parker

Leo Genn, David Tomlinson, Anthony Steele, David Greene, Michael Goodliffe, Bryan Forbes, Jacques Brunius

Words and Music**
US 1948 121m Technicolor
MGM *(Arthur Freed)*

The songwriting collaboration of Richard Rodgers and Lorenz Hart.
Musical biopic which packs in a lot of good

numbers and manages a script which is neither too offensive nor too prominent.

w Fred Finklehoffe *d* Norman Taurog *ph* Charles Rosher, Harry Stradling *md* Lennie Hayton *ch* Robert Alton, Gene Kelley

Tom Drake, Mickey Rooney, Perry Como, *Mel Tormé,* Betty Garrett, *June Allyson,* Lena Horne, Ann Sothern, Allyn McLerie, *Gene Kelly,* Vera-Ellen, Cyd Charisse, Janet Leigh, Marshall Thompson

Work Is a Four-Letter Word
GB 1968 93m Technicolor
Universal / Cavalcade (Thomas Clyde)

A power station attendant is interested only in growing mushrooms, which have a chaotic effect on his private life.
Weakly futuristic industrial fantasy which the author would probably claim to be about lack of communication. Bored audiences might have a similar view.

w Jeremy Brooks, *play* Eh? by Henry Livings *d* Peter Hall *ph* Gilbert Taylor *m* Guy Woolfenden

David Warner, Cilla Black, Elizabeth Spriggs, Zia Mohyeddin, Joe Gladwin

The World Changes*
US 1933 91m bw
Warner (Robert Lord)

A simple farmer becomes a powerful executive, and success goes to his head.
Adequate moral drama of its time, well staged and acted.

w Edward Chodorov *d* Mervyn Le Roy *ph* Tony Gaudio

Paul Muni, Aline MacMahon, Mary Astor, Donald Cook, Patricia Ellis, Jean Muir, Margaret Lindsay, Guy Kibbee, Alan Dinehart

The World in His Arms*
US 1952 104m Technicolor
Universal (Aaron Rosenberg)

In old San Francisco, a seal-poaching sea captain meets a Russian countess.
Romantic melodrama with plushy period backgrounds and a fair measure of action, climaxing in a boat race.

w Borden Chase *d* Raoul Walsh *ph* Russell Metty *m* Frank Skinner

Gregory Peck, Ann Blyth, Anthony Quinn, John McIntire, Andrea King, Carl Esmond, Eugenie Leontovitch

World in My Corner*
US 1955 85m bw
U-I (Aaron Rosenberg)

A penniless would-be prizefighter becomes the protégé of a millionaire and wins his daughter but not the crucial fight.
Well-done minor melodrama.

w Jack Sher *d* Jesse Hibbs *ph* Maury Gertsman *m* Joseph Gershenson

Audie Murphy, Barbara Rush, Jeff Morrow, John McIntire, Tommy Rall, Howard St John

The World Moves On*
US 1934 90m bw
Fox (Winfield Sheehan)

The saga of a Louisiana family up to World War I.
Careful, good-looking general entertainment.

w Reginald C. Berkeley *d* John Ford *ph* George Schneiderman *m* Max Steiner

Madeleine Carroll, Franchot Tone, Reginald Denny, Stepin Fetchit, Lumsden Hare, Louise Dresser, Sig Rumann

The World of Henry Orient**
US 1964 106m De Luxe Panavision
UA / Pan Arts (Jerome Hellman)

Two rich 14-year-old New York girls build fantasies around a concert pianist.
Charming, immaculately mounted, refreshingly unusual but overlong comedy.

w Nora and Nunnally Johnson, novel Nora Johnson *d George Roy Hill* *ph* Boris Kaufman, Arthur J. Ornitz *m* Elmer Bernstein *pd James Sullivan*

Tippy Walker, Merri Spaeth, Peter Sellers, Angela Lansbury, Paula Prentiss, Phyllis Thaxter, Tom Bosley, Bibi Osterwald

The World of Suzie Wong
GB 1960 129m Technicolor
Paramount / Ray Stark (Hugh Perceval)

A Hong Kong prostitute falls in love with the artist for whom she poses.
Dull, set-bound romantic melodrama without much gusto.

w John Patrick, *play* Paul Osborn *d* Richard Quine *ph* Geoffrey Unsworth *m* George Duning

William Holden, *Nancy Kwan,* Sylvia Syms, Michael Wilding, Laurence Naismith, Jackie Chan

'Maybe one day it will all make the grade as a musical.'—*MFB*

World Premiere*
US 1940 70m bw
Paramount

A zany film producer thinks up some wild publicity schemes for his new film and accidentally traps some Nazi spies.
Occasionally amusing farce mainly notable for its star.

w Earl Felton *d* Ted Tetzlaff

John Barrymore, Ricardo Cortez, Frances Farmer, Sig Rumann, Fritz Feld, Eugene Pallette, Luis Alberni, Virginia Dale, Don Castle

The World Ten Times Over
GB 1963 93m bw
Cyclops (Michael Luke)

Two semi-prostitutes try to improve their lot.
Dreary, derivative low-life drama with flashy technique.

wd Wolf Rilla *ph* Larry Pizer *m* Edwin Astley

Sylvia Syms, June Ritchie, Edward Judd, William Hartnell, Francis de Wolff

The World, the Flesh and the Devil*
US 1959 95m bw Cinemascope
MGM / Sol C. Siegel / Harbel

Trapped for five days in a mine cave-in, a man struggles to the surface to find a dead world devastated by atomic war; but still alive are the elements of an eternal triangle . . .
Enterprising but rather disappointing fantasy which tends to become merely glum and rather self-consciously carries a panic button message.

wd Ranald MacDougall *ph* Harold J. Marzorati *m* Miklos Rozsa *ad* William A. Horning, Paul Groesse

Harry Belafonte, Inger Stevens, Mel Ferrer

World without End
US 1956 80m Technicolor
Cinemascope
AA (Richard Heermance)

A space ship breaks the time barrier and returns to earth in 2508, to find that intelligent humans have been driven underground by mutants.
Reasonably lively sci-fi with horror elements, and a plot borrowed from H. G. Wells.

wd Edward Bernds *ph* Ellsworth Fredericks *m* Leith Stevens

Hugh Marlowe, Nancy Gates, Rod Taylor

The World's Greatest Athlete
US 1973 92m Technicolor
Walt Disney (Bill Walsh)

An American sports coach on an African holiday finds a young Tarzan with amazing powers.
Simple-minded comedy with lame tomfoolery and trickwork.

w Gerald Gardiner, Dee Caruso *d* Robert Scheerer *ph* Frank Phillips *m* Marvin Hamlisch

Tim Conway, John-Michael Vincent, John Amos, Roscoe Lee Browne

Worm's Eye View
GB 1951 77m bw
ABFD / Byron (Henry Halsted)

Incidents in the lives of a group of RAF billetees.
Plotless comedy from a highly successful stage romp; plainly made and empty-headed but not disagreeable.

w R. F. Delderfield, from his play *d* Jack Raymond *ph* James Wilson *m* Tony Lowry, Tony Fones

Ronald Shiner, Garry Marsh, Diana Dors, Eric Davis, John Blythe

The Wrath of God
US 1972 111m Metrocolor Panavision
MGM / Rainbow / Cineman (William S. Gilmore Jnr)

During a twenties Central American revolution, a bootlegger joins forces with a defrocked priest.
Noisy, violent adventure yarn which works up to a gory climax but does not take itself too seriously.

wd Ralph Nelson, *novel* James Graham *ph* Alex Phillips Jnr *m* Lalo Schifrin

Robert Mitchum, Frank Langella, Rita Hayworth, Victor Buono, John Colicos

The Wreck of the Mary Deare*
US 1959 108m Metrocolor
Cinemascope
MGM / Blaustein–Baroda (David Blaustein)

An insurance fraud comes to light when a salvage boat is rescued from high seas.
Curious, star-studded amalgam of seafaring action and courtroom melodrama, originally intended for Hitchcock.

w Eric Ambler, *novel* Hammond Innes
d Michael Anderson *ph* Joseph Ruttenberg, F. A. Young *m* George Duning

Charlton Heston, Gary Cooper, Michael Redgrave, Emlyn Williams, Cecil Parker, Alexander Knox, Virginia McKenna, Richard Harris

The Wrecking Crew
US 1968 104m Technicolor
Columbia / Meadway / Claude (Irving Allen)

Special agent Matt Helm recovers bullion stolen from a Danish train.
Camped-up spy buffoonery with the usual nubile ladies and a production which seeks to be flashy but succeeds only in being tatty.

w William McGivern, *novel* Donald Hamilton *d* Phil Karlson *ph* Sam Leavitt *m* Hugo Montenegro

Dean Martin, Elke Sommer, Sharon Tate, Nancy Kwan, Nigel Green, Tina Louise

Written on the Wind**
US 1956 99m Technicolor
U-I (Albert Zugsmith)

A secretary marries her oil tycoon boss and finds herself the steadying force in a very rocky family.
The sheerest Hollywood moonshine: high-flying melodramatic hokum which moves fast enough to be very entertaining.

w George Zuckerman, *novel* Robert Wilder *d Douglas Sirk ph Russell Metty m* Frank Skinner

Lauren Bacall, *Robert Stack, Dorothy Malone*, Rock Hudson, Robert Keith, Grant Williams

The Wrong Arm of the Law*
GB 1962 94m bw
Romulus / Robert Verlaise (Aubrey Baring, E. M. Smedley Aston)

London gangsters plan retaliation against Australian interlopers, and offer Scotland Yard a temporary truce.
Forgettable but pretty funny crook comedy in the British vein, with pacy script and excellent comedy timing.

w John Warren, Len Heath *d Cliff Owen ph* Ernest Steward *m* Richard Rodney Bennett

Peter Sellers, Lionel Jeffries, Bernard Cribbins, Davy Kaye, Nanette Newman, Bill Kerr, John Le Mesurier

The Wrong Box*
GB 1966 110m Technicolor
Columbia / Salamander (Bryan Forbes)

Two elderly Victorian brothers are the last survivors of a tontine (an involved form of lottery) and try to murder each other.
Well-intentioned and star-studded black farce in which the excellent period trappings and stray jokes completely overwhelm the plot.

w Larry Gelbart, Burt Shevelove, *novel* Robert Louis Stevenson, Lloyd Osbourne *d* Bryan Forbes *ph Gerry Turpin m* John Barry *ad Ray Simm*

Ralph Richardson, John Mills, Michael Caine, *Wilfrid Lawson*, Nanette Newman, Peter Cook, Dudley Moore, Peter Sellers, Tony Hancock, Thorley Walters, Cicely Courtneidge, Irene Handl, John Le Mesurier, Gerald Sim, Norman Bird, Tutte Lemkow

'A slapdash affair in which anything goes, irrespective of whether or not it fits.'—*Tom Milne*

The Wrong Man*
US 1957 105m bw
Warner (Herbert Coleman)

A New York musician is mistaken by police for an armed bandit, and both witnesses and circumstances prevent the truth from emerging.
True but downbeat story from the headlines, filmed with remarkably little persuasion; not its director's *métier* despite evidence of his usual thoroughness.

w Maxwell Anderson, Angus MacPhail *d* Alfred Hitchcock *ph Robert Burks m* Bernard Herrmann

Henry Fonda, Vera Miles, Anthony Quayle, Harold J. Stone, Esther Minciotti

WUSA*
US 1970 117m Technicolor Panavision
Paramount / Mirror / Coleytown / Stuart Rosenberg (Paul Newman, John Foreman)

A penniless wanderer causes chaos when he becomes the announcer for a right-wing radio station.
A farcical melodrama for the intelligentsia, and for the most part a thoroughgoing bore. The last part offers a compensation or two.

w Robert Stone, from his novel Hall of Mirrors *d* Stuart Rosenberg *ph* Richard Moore *m* Lalo Schifrin

Paul Newman, Joanne Woodward, Laurence Harvey, Anthony Perkins, Pat Hingle, Cloris Leachman, Don Gordon, Robert Quarry, Bruce Cabot, Moses Gunn, Wayne Rogers

Wuthering Heights****
US 1939 104m bw
Samuel Goldwyn

The daughter of an unhappy middle-class Yorkshire family falls passionately in love with a gypsy who has been brought up with her.
Despite American script and settings, this wildly romantic film makes a pretty fair stab at capturing the power of at least the first half of a classic Victorian novel, and in all respects it's superb Hollywood production of its day and a typical one, complete with ghostly finale and a first-rate cast.

w Ben Hecht, Charles MacArthur, novel Emily

Brontë d William Wyler ph Gregg Toland m Alfred Newman

Laurence Olivier, Merle Oberon, David Niven, Hugh Williams, Flora Robson, Geraldine Fitzgerald, Donald Crisp, Leo G. Carroll, Cecil Kellaway, *Miles Mander*

'Unquestionably one of the most distinguished pictures of the year.'—*Frank S. Nugent, New York Times*

'A pattern of constant forward motion, with overtones maintained throughout the rise of interest and suspense.'—*Otis Ferguson*

Wuthering Heights*
GB 1970 105m Movielab
AIP (John Pellatt)

Somewhat rewritten and overkeen to find a 1970 mood and interpretation for what can only be a period piece, this disappointing version marks a Z-film company's first determined effort to enter the big-time.

w Patrick Tilley *d* Robert Fuest *ph John Coquillon m* Michel Legrand

Anna Calder-Marshall, Timothy Dalton, Harry Andrews, Pamela Brown, Judy Cornwell, James Cossins, Rosalie Crutchley, Julian Glover, Hugh Griffith, Ian Ogilvy, Aubrey Woods

X—The Man with X-Ray Eyes
US 1963 80m Pathecolor 'Spectarama'
AIP (Roger Corman)
GB title: *The Man with the X-Ray Eyes*

A scientist gives himself X-ray vision and goes mad.
Interesting but rather unpleasant horror story with moments of cleverness but a general air of disappointment.

w Robert Dillon, Ray Russell *d Roger Corman* *ph* Floyd Crosby *m* Les Baxter

Ray Milland, Diana Van Der Vlis, Harold J. Stone, John Hoyt, Don Rickles, John Dierkes

'When the dialogue suggests that Xavier is being driven insane by strange and satanic visions, what one actually sees is rather a comedown.'—*MFB*

'Concise, confident, and not an ounce overweight.'—*NFT, 1967*

X the Unknown*
GB 1956 81m bw
Hammer (Anthony Hinds)

A mysterious force feeds on radiation from a research station on a Scottish moor, and becomes a seeping mass.
Minor sci-fi horror with a monster like liquid lino, rushed into release to cash in on *The Quatermass Experiment*.

w Jimmy Sangster *d* Leslie Norman *ph* Gerald Gibbs *m* James Bernard

Dean Jagger, Edward Chapman, Leo McKern, William Lucas, John Harvey, Peter Hammond, Michael Ripper, Anthony Newley

Y

Yangtse Incident*
GB 1957 113m bw
British Lion / Wilcox–Neagle (Herbert Wilcox)
US title: *Battle Hell*; aka: *Escape of the Amethyst*

In 1949 a British frigate is shelled and held captive by communist shore batteries in the Yangtse.
Stalwart but not very exciting British war heroics.

w Eric Ambler, *book* Franklin Gollings *d* Michael Anderson *ph* Gordon Dines *m* Leighton Lucas

Richard Todd, William Hartnell, Akim Tamiroff, Donald Houston, Keye Luke, Sophie Stewart, Robert Urquhart, James Kenney, Barry Foster

The Yakuza
US 1975 112m Technicolor Panavision
Warner (Sydney Pollack, Michael Hamilburg)

Japanese gangsters kidnap the daughter of a Los Angeles shipping magnate.
Violent thriller roughly exploiting an ancient Japanese genre.

w Paul Schrader, Robert Towne *d* Sydney Pollack *ph* Okazaki Kozo, Duke Callaghan *m* Dave Grusin

Robert Mitchum, Takakura Ken, Brian Keith, Kishi Keilo, Okada Eiji

'No more than a curious footnote to the western exploitation of oriental action movies.'—*Tony Rayns*

A Yank at Eton
US 1942 88m bw
MGM (John Considine Jnr)

A rich, wild American boy is sent to Eton to cool down.
Tame, tasteless imitation of *A Yank at Oxford* with younger participants.

w George Oppenheimer, Lionel Houser, Thomas Phipps *d* Norman Taurog

Mickey Rooney, Freddie Bartholemew, Ian Hunter, Edmund Gwenn, Alan Mowbray, Tina Thayer, Marta Linden, Alan Napier, Terry Kilburn

A Yank at Oxford**
GB 1938 105m bw
MGM (Michael Balcon)

A cocky young American student comes to Oxford and meets all kinds of trouble.
A huge pre-war success which now seems naïve, this was the first big Anglo-American production from a team which went on to make *The Citadel* and *Goodbye Mr Chips* before war stymied them.

w Malcolm Stuart Boylan, Walter Ferris, George Oppenheimer, Leon Gordon, Roland Pertwee, John Monk Saunders, Sidney Gilliat, Michael Hogan *d* Jack Conway

Robert Taylor, Vivien Leigh, Maureen O'Sullivan, Lionel Barrymore, Robert Coote, Edmund Gwenn, C. V. France, Griffith Jones, Morton Selten

A Yank in the RAF*
US 1941 98m bw
TCF (Lou Edelman)

An American chorine stranded in London falls for the titular gentleman.
Silly but entertaining wartime flagwaver.

w Karl Tunberg, Darrell Ware, *story* Melville Crossman (Zanuck) *d* Henry King *ph* Leon Shamroy *m* Alfred Newman

Tyrone Power, Betty Grable, John Sutton, Reginald Gardiner, Donald Stuart, Morton Lowry, Richard Fraser, Bruce Lester

A Yank on the Burma Road
US 1942 66m bw
MGM (Samuel Marx)

A tough truck driver in the Far East abandons profit for heroism when he hears of Pearl Harbor.
Crass action flagwaver.

w George Kahn, Hugo Butler, David Lang *d* George B. Seitz

Barry Nelson, Laraine Day, Stuart Crawford, Keye Luke, Sen Yung

'Glib humbug, playing tiddleywinks with high stakes.'—*Theodore Strauss*

Yankee Doodle Dandy****
US 1942 126m bw
Warner (Hal B. Wallis, William Cagney)

The life story of dancing vaudevillian George M. Cohan.
Outstanding showbiz biopic, with unassuming but effective production, deft patriotic backdrops and a marvellous, strutting, magnetic star performance.

w Robert Buckner, Edmund Joseph *d Michael Curtiz ph James Wong Howe md* Leo F. Forbstein *songs George M. Cohan*

James Cagney, Joan Leslie, *Walter Huston*, Rosemary de Camp, Richard Whorf, George Tobias, Jeanne Cagney, Irene Manning, S. Z. Sakall, George Barbier, Frances Langford, Walter Catlett, Eddie Foy Jnr

The Yearling**
US 1946 134m Technicolor
MGM (Sidney Franklin)

The son of an old-time country farmer is attached to a stray deer.
Excellent family film for four-handkerchief patrons.

w Paul Osborn, *novel* Marjorie Kinnan Rawlings *d Clarence Brown ph* Charles Rosher, Leonard Smith *m* Herbert Stothart

Gregory Peck, Jane Wyman, Claude Jarman Jnr, Chill Wills, Clem Bevans, Margaret Wycherly, Henry Travers, Forrest Tucker

The Years Between
GB 1946 100m bw
GFD / Sydney Box

An MP returns after being presumed dead in the war and finds his wife has been elected in his place.
Stilted variation on the Enoch Arden theme; plot and performances alike unpersuasive.

w Muriel and Sydney Box, *play* Daphne du Maurier *d* Compton Bennett

Michael Redgrave, Valerie Hobson, Flora Robson, Felix Aylmer, James McKechnie, Dulcie Gray, Edward Rigby

The Yellow Balloon
GB 1952 80m bw
ABP (Victor Skuzetsky)

A small boy who thinks he has killed his friend is terrorized by a murderer.
Tense but not especially rewarding suspenser, clearly borrowed from *The Window*.

w Anne Burnaby, J. Lee-Thompson *d* J. Lee-Thompson *ph* Gilbert Taylor *m* Philip Green

Kenneth More, William Sylvester, Kathleen Ryan, Andrew Ray, Bernard Lee, Veronica Hurst

The Yellow Cab Man
US 1950 84m bw
MGM (Richard Goldstone)

A taxi-driving inventor is pursued by crooks after his secret formula.
Moderate star comedy.

w Devery Freeman, Albert Beich *d* Jack Donohue *ph* Harry Stradling *m* Scott Bradley

Red Skelton, Gloria de Haven, Walter Slezak, Edward Arnold, James Gleason, Paul Harvey, Jay C. Flippen

Yellow Canary*
GB 1943 98m bw
RKO / Imperator (Herbert Wilcox)

A socialite suspected of being a Nazi sympathizer is really a British spy.
Mild wartime melodrama chiefly notable for allotting an apparently unsympathetic part to the beloved Miss Neagle.

w De Witt Bodeen, Miles Malleson, *story* Pamela Bower *d* Herbert Wilcox *ph* Max Greene

Anna Neagle, Richard Greene, Nova Pilbeam, Lucie Mannheim, Cyril Fletcher, Albert Lieven, Margaret Rutherford, Marjorie Fielding

Yellow Canary
US 1963 93m bw Cinemascope
TCF / Cooga Mooga (Maury Dexter)

The baby son of a singing idol is kidnapped.
Rather dreary suspenser with too much dialogue.

w Rod Serling, *novel* Easy Come Easy Go by Whit Masterson *d* Buzz Kulik *ph* Floyd Crosby *m* Kenyon Hopkins

Pat Boone, Barbara Eden, Steve Forrest, Jack Klugman, Jesse White, John Banner, Jeff Corey

Yellow Dog
GB 1973 101m Eastmancolor
Scotia–Barber / Akari (Terence Donovan)

A Japanese agent in London keeps watch on a mysterious scientist.
Incoherent spy thriller with a few hybrid oddities.

w Shinobu Hashimoto *d* Terence Donovan *ph* David Watkin *m* Ron Grainer

Jiro Tamiya, Robert Hardy, Carolyn Seymour, Joseph O'Conor

Yellow Jack*
US 1938 83m bw
MGM (Jack Cummings)

In 1899 Cuba a marine offers himself as a guinea pig to combat yellow fever.
Solid, unsurprising, period medical melodrama with conventional romantic sidelights.

w Edward Chodorov, *play* Sidney Howard, Paul de Kruif *d* George B. Seitz *ph* Lester White *m* William Axt

Robert Montgomery, Virginia Bruce, Lewis Stone, Andy Devine, Henry Hull, Charles Coburn, Buddy Ebsen, Henry O'Neill, Janet Beecher

The Yellow Rolls Royce*
GB 1964 122m Metrocolor Panavision
MGM (Anatole de Grunwald)

Three stories about the owners of an expensive car; an aristocrat, a gangster, and a wandering millionairess.
Lukewarm all-star concoction lacking either good stories or a connecting thread.

w Terence Rattigan *d* Anthony Asquith *ph* Jack Hildyard *m* Riz Ortolani *pd* Vincent Korda

Rex Harrison, Jeanne Moreau, Edmund Purdom, Moira Lister, Roland Culver, Shirley Maclaine, George C. Scott, Alain Delon, Art Carney, Ingrid Bergman, Omar Sharif, Joyce Grenfell

'Tame, bloodless, smothered in elegance and the worst kind of discreetly daring good taste.' —*Peter John Dyer*

Yellow Sky**
US 1948 98m bw
TCF (Lamar Trotti)

Outlaws on the run take over a desert ghost town.
Gleaming, stylish western melodrama which benefits from its unusual and confined setting.

w Lamar Trotti, *story* W. R. Burnett *d William Wellman ph Joe MacDonald m* Alfred Newman

Gregory Peck, Anne Baxter, Richard Widmark, Robert Arthur, John Russell, Henry Morgan, James Barton

Yellow Submarine*
GB 1968 87m De Luxe
King Features / Apple (Al Brodax)

The happy kingdom of Pepperland is attacked by the Blue Meanies.
Way-out cartoon fantasia influenced by Beatlemania and the swinging sixties; hard to watch for non-addicts.

w Lee Minoff, Al Brodax, Jack Mendelsohn, Erich Segal *d* George Duning *m* John Lennon, Paul McCartney

The Yellow Ticket*
US 1931 76m bw
Fox
GB title: *The Yellow Passport*

In Russia during the pogroms, a Jewish girl pretends to be a prostitute in order to get a travel permit to see her dying father.
Curious anti-Russian melodrama deriving its plot from *La Tosca*.

w Jules Furthman, Guy Bolton, play Michael Morton *d* Raoul Walsh *ph* James Wong Howe

Elissa Landi, Laurence Olivier, Lionel Barrymore, Walter Byron, Sarah Padden, Mischa Auer, Boris Karloff

Yellowstone Kelly
US 1959 91m Technicolor
Warner

A fur trapper prevents war between Indians and whites.
Standard western with routine excitements and a cast of TV faces.

w Burt Kennedy *d* Gordon Douglas *ph* Carl Guthrie *m* Howard Jackson

Clint Walker, Edd Byrnes, John Russell, Ray Danton, Claude Akins

Yes My Darling Daughter
US 1939 86m bw
Warner (Ben Glazer)

Lovers elope and are pursued by her family.
Mildly amusing domestic comedy.

w Casey Robinson, *play* Mark Reed *d* William Keighley *ph* Charles Rosher

Priscilla Lane, Jeffrey Lynn, Roland Young, Fay Bainter, May Robson, Genevieve Tobin, Ian Hunter

Yes Sir, That's My Baby
US 1949 82m Technicolor
U-I (Leonard Goldstein)

Ex-service undergraduates and their wives have trouble settling down to studies.
Witless and exhausting college comedy.

w Oscar Brodney *d* George Sherman *ph* Irving Glassberg *m* Walter Scharf

Donald O'Connor, Gloria de Haven, Charles Coburn, Barbara Brown, Joshua Shelley

Yesterday's Enemy
GB 1959 95m bw Megascope
Columbia / Hammer (T. S. Lyndon-Haynes)

In 1942 Burma, a British unit violently takes over a village and finds an unsolved puzzle.
Would-be ironic war suspenser, economically made but quite effective in putting its message across.

w Peter R. Newman, from his TV play *d* Val Guest *ph* Arthur Grant *m* none

Stanley Baker, Guy Rolfe, Leo McKern, Philip Ahn, Gordon Jackson, David Oxley, Richard Pasco, Russell Waters, Bryan Forbes, David Lodge, Percy Herbert

Yield to the Night*
GB 1956 99m bw
ABP (Kenneth Harper)

A condemned murderess relives the events which led to her arrest.
Gloomy prison melodrama vaguely based on the Ruth Ellis case and making an emotional plea against capital punishment.

w John Cresswell, Joan Henry, *novel* Joan Henry *d* J. Lee-Thompson *ph* Gilbert Taylor *m* Ray Martin

Diana Dors, Yvonne Mitchell, Michael Craig, Marie Ney, Athene Seyler, Geoffrey Keen

Yolanda and the Thief*
US 1945 108m Technicolor
MGM (Arthur Freed)

A con man poses as the guardian angel of a naïve heiress.
Laboured musical fantasy with arty Mexican settings; not a success in any way, but with a few effective moments.

w Irving Brecher, *story* Ludwig Bemelmans, Jacques Théry *d* Vincente Minnelli *ph* Charles Rosher *m* Lennie Hayton *songs* Harry Warren, Arthur Freed

Fred Astaire, Lucille Bremer, Frank Morgan, Leon Ames, Mildred Natwick

You and Me
US 1938 90m bw
Paramount (Fritz Lang)

A department store owner employs ex-convicts, one of whom has not quite reformed.
Curious comedy drama which never has a hope of coming off.

w Virginia Van Upp, *story* Norman Krasna *d* Fritz Lang *ph* Charles Lang Jnr

Sylvia Sidney, George Raft, Harry Carey, Barton MacLane, Warren Hymer, Roscoe Karns, George E. Stone, Adrian Morris

You Belong to Me*
US 1941 94m bw
Columbia (Wesley Ruggles)
GB title: *Good Morning, Doctor*

A playboy becomes jealous of the male patients of his doctor wife.
Mild comedy for two stars who are well capable of keeping it afloat.

w Claude Binyon, Dalton Trumbo *d* Wesley Ruggles *ph* Joseph Walker *m* Frederick Hollander

Barbara Stanwyck, Henry Fonda, Edgar Buchanan, Roger Clark, Ruth Donnelly, Melville Cooper, Maude Eburne

You Came Along
US 1945 103m bw
Paramount (Hal B. Wallis)

A girl from the treasury department falls in love with one of three GIs she takes on a war bond tour, but he dies of leukemia.
Weird mishmash of farce and sentimentality; quite watchable in its way, but an odd showcase for a new female star.

w Robert Smith, Ayn Rand *d* John Farrow *ph* Daniel L. Fapp *m* Victor Young

Lizabeth Scott, Robert Cummings, Don Defore, Charles Drake, Julie Bishop, Kim Hunter, Rhys Williams, Franklin Pangborn, Minor Watson

You Can't Cheat an Honest Man*
US 1939 79m bw
Universal (Lester Cowan)

Trials and tribulations of a circus owner.
Flat, desultory and generally disappointing comedy vehicle for an irresistible star combination.

w George Marion Jnr, Richard Mack, Everett Freeman, *story* Charles Bogle (W. C. Fields) *d* George Marshall *ph* Milton Krasner *m* Charles Previn

W. C. Fields, Edgar Bergen (with Charlie McCarthy and Mortimer Snerd), Constance Moore, Mary Forbes, Thurston Hall, Charles Coleman, Edward Brophy

You Can't Get Away with Murder
US 1939 78m bw
Warner (Sam Bischoff)

A juvenile delinquent teams up with a gangster and takes a prison rap for him.
Standard post-Dead End crime melodrama with no surprises.

w Robert Buckner, Don Ryan, Kenneth Gamet, *play* Chalked Out by Lewis Lawes, Jonathan Finn *d* Lewis Seiler *ph* Sol Polito

Humphrey Bogart, Billy Halop, Gale Page, John Litel, Henry Travers, Harvey Stephens, Harold Huber

You Can't Have Everything*
US 1937 99m bw
TCF (Lawrence Schwab)

A failed play is turned into a musical.
Lively backstage comedy with good moments.

w Harry Tugend, Jack Yellen, Karl Tunberg *d* Norman Taurog *ph* Lucien Andriot *md* David Buttolph

Alice Faye, *the Ritz Brothers,* Don Ameche, Charles Winninger, Gypsy Rose Lee, Tony Martin, Arthur Treacher, Louis Prima, Tip Tap and Toe, Wally Vernon

You Can't Have Everything
US 1970 90m Eastmancolor
Koala (Lou Brandt)

An 18-year-old virgin GI is about to leave for Vietnam when he picks up a girl and spends a happy but platonic twenty-four hours.
An agreeably understated little love story for those absorbed by teenage sex problems.

wd Martin Zweibach *ph* David M. Walsh *m* Joe Parnello

Richard Thomas, Mary Layne, Lucille Benson, Oscar Beregi

You Can't Run Away from It
US 1956 96m Technicolor Cinemascope
Columbia (Dick Powell)

An heiress runs away from a marriage arranged by her father, and falls for an amiable reporter.
Flat remake of *It Happened One Night,* with practically no comic sense or talent.

w Claude Binyon, Robert Riskin *d* Dick Powell *ph* Charles Lawton Jnr *m* Morris Stoloff

June Allyson, Jack Lemmon, Charles Bickford, Jim Backus, Stubby Kaye, Paul Gilbert, Allyn Joslyn

You Can't Take It with You**
US 1938 127m bw
Columbia (Frank Capra)

The daughter of a highly eccentric New York family falls for a rich man's son.
A hilarious, warm and witty play is largely changed into a tirade against big business, but the Capra expertise is here in good measure and the stars all pull their weight.

w Robert Riskin, *play* George S. Kaufman, Moss Hart *d Frank Capra* *ph* Joseph Walker *m* Dmitri Tiomkin

Jean Arthur, Lionel Barrymore, James Stewart, Edward Arnold, Spring Byington, Mischa Auer, Ann Miller, Samuel S. Hinds, Donald Meek, H. B. Warner, Halliwell Hobbes, Mary Forbes, Dub Taylor, Lillian Yarbo, Eddie Anderson, *Harry Davenport*

'Shangri-La in a frame house.'—*Otis Ferguson*

You Can't Win 'em All
GB 1970 99m Technicolor Panavision
Columbia / SRO (Gene Corman)

In 1922, two rival American mercenaries have adventures in the Mediterranean.
Hectic, overplotted comedy actioner.

w Leo V. Gordon *d* Peter Collinson *ph* Ken Higgins *m* Bert Kaempfert

Tony Curtis, Charles Bronson, Michèle Mercier, Grégoire Aslan, Patrick Magee

You for Me
US 1952 71m bw
MGM (Henry Berman)

A millionaire patient is courted by a needy hospital and falls for a popular nurse.
Cheerful but thin little programme-filler.

w William Roberts *d* Don Weis *ph* Virgil Vogel *m* Alberto Columbo

Peter Lawford, Jane Greer, Gig Young, Paula Corday, Elaine Stewart

You Gotta Stay Happy
US 1948 100m bw
Universal (Karl Tunberg)

A runaway heiress joins cargo pilots on a transcontinental hop with some very queer passengers.
Ho-hum imitation of a Capra comedy; the effort shows.

w Karl Tunberg, *story* Robert Carson *d* H. C. Potter *ph* Russell Metty *m* Daniele Amfitheatrof

Joan Fontaine, James Stewart, Eddie Albert, Roland Young, Willard Parker, Percy Kilbride, Porter Hall, Paul Cavanagh, Halliwell Hobbes

You Lie So Deep My Love
US 1975 74m Technicolor TVM
Universal (David Lowell Rich)

Murder results when a girl is convinced that her husband is a crook and philanderer.
Muddled and slow-starting suspenser.

w William L. Stuart, Robert Hamner, John Neufeld *d* David Lowell Rich

Barbara Anderson, Don Galloway, Walter Pidgeon, Angel Tompkins

You Must Be Joking*
GB 1965 100m bw
Columbia / Ameran (Charles H. Schneer)

Assorted army personnel vie in an extended initiative test.
Slam-bang location comedy with more hits than misses: cheerful entertainment.

w Alan Hackney *d* Michael Winner *ph* Geoffrey Unsworth *m* Laurie Johnson

Terry-Thomas, Lionel Jeffries, Michael Callan, Gabriella Licudi, *Denholm Elliott*, Lee Montague, Bernard Cribbins, Wilfrid Hyde White, James Robertson Justice, Richard Wattis, James Villiers

You Never Can Tell*
US 1951 78m bw
U-I (Leonard Goldstein)
GB title: *You Never Know*

An Alsatian dog is murdered and is sent back from heaven in the guise of a private detective to expose his killer.
Self-confidently outrageous comedy fantasy in the wake of *Here Comes Mr Jordan;* not badly done if you accept the premise.

w Lou Breslow, David Chandler *d* Lou Breslow *ph* Maury Gertsman *m* Hans Salter

Dick Powell, Peggy Dow, Charles Drake, Joyce Holden, Albert Sharpe, Sara Taft

You Only Live Once**
US 1937 85m bw
Walter Wanger

A petty crook framed for murder breaks out of prison and tries to escape to Canada with his wife.
Gloomy melodrama partly based on Bonnie and Clyde and incorporating a plea for justice; very well made and acted.

w Graham Baker, *story* Gene Towne *d Fritz Lang* *ph* Leon Shamroy *m* Alfred Newman

Sylvia Sidney, Henry Fonda, Barton MacLane, Jean Dixon, William Gargan, Jerome Cowan, Chic Sale, Margaret Hamilton, Warren Hymer

'Again and again in this film we find what can only be described as camera style, the use of the pictorial image to narrate with the maximum of emotional impact.'—*Dilys Powell*

You Only Live Twice**
GB 1967 117m Technicolor
Panavision
UA / Eon (Harry Saltzman, Albert R. Broccoli)

James Bond goes to Japan.
The Bond saga at its most expensive and expansive, full of local colour and in-jokes, with an enormously impressive set for the climactic action.

w Roald Dahl, *novel* Ian Fleming *d* Terence Young *ph* Freddie Young, Bob Huke *m* John Barry *pd Ken Adam*

Sean Connery, Tetsuro Tamba, Akiko Wakabayashi, Mie Hama, Karin Dor, Bernard Lee, Lois Maxwell, Desmond Llewellyn, *Charles Gray, Donald Pleasance*

You Were Meant for Me
US 1948 92m bw
TCF (Fred Kohlmar)

A small-town girl marries a bandleader.
Mildly pleasing, muted, musical romance, with good twenties atmosphere.

w Elick Moll, Valentine Davies *d* Lloyd Bacon *ph* Victor Milner *md* Lionel Newman *songs* various

Jeanne Crain, Dan Dailey, Oscar Levant, Barbara Lawrence, Selena Royle, Percy Kilbride, Herbert Anderson

You Were Never Lovelier*
US 1942 97m bw
Columbia (Louis F. Edelman)

An Argentinian hotel tycoon tries to interest his daughter in marriage by creating a mysterious admirer.
Pleasing musical, a follow up for the stars of *You'll Never Get Rich.*

w Michael Fessier, Ernest Pagano, Delmer Daves *d* William A. Seiter *ph* Ted Tetzlaff *songs* Jerome Kern, Johnny Mercer

Fred Astaire, Rita Hayworth, Adolphe Menjou, Leslie Brooks, Adele Mara, Isobel Elsom, Gus Schilling, Xavier Cugat and his Orchestra, Larry Parks

You'll Find Out*
US 1940 97m bw
RKO

Kay Kyser's band is hired to play for a 21st birthday party at a gloomy mansion; they help save the life of the girl concerned.
Cheerful if slow-starting spooky house send-up with a splendid trio of villains.

w James V. Kern, David Butler *d* David Butler *ph* Frank Redman *songs* James McHugh, Johnny Mercer

Kay Kyser, Boris Karloff, Peter Lorre, Bela Lugosi, Dennis O'Keefe, Ginny Simms, Helen Parrish, Alma Kruger, Ish Kabibble

You'll Like My Mother
US 1972 92m Technicolor
Universal / Bing Crosby Productions (Mort Briskin)

Pregnant widow visits neurotic mother-in-law in a snowbound mansion.
Predictable frightened lady shocker aiming somewhere between *Psycho* and *Fanatic*; of strictly routine interest.

w Jo Heims, *novel* Naomi Hintze *d* Lamont Johnson *ph* Jack Marta *m* Gil Melle

Rosemary Murphy, Patty Duke, Richard Thomas, Sian Barbara Allen

You'll Never Get Rich*
US 1941 88m bw
Columbia (Sam Bischoff)

A Broadway dance director helps his philandering producer by taking a romantically-inclined showgirl off his hands.
Smart comedy-musical which set its female lead as a top star.

w Michael Fessier, Ernest Pagano *d* Sidney Lanfield *ph* Philip Tannura *ch* Robert Alton *songs* Cole Porter

Fred Astaire, Rita Hayworth, Robert Benchley, John Hubbard, Osa Massen, Frieda Inescort, Guinn Williams, Donald MacBride

You'll Never See Me Again
US 1973 74m Technicolor TVM
Universal (Harve Bennett)

A wife disappears after a quarrel and may have been murdered.
Standard suspenser.

w William Wood, Gerald di Pego *d* Jeannot Szwarc

David Hartman, Joseph Campanella, Jane Wyatt, Ralph Meeker, Jess Walton, Bo Swenson

Young America
US 1932 74m bw

Two young boys get into trouble with the law.
Dog-eared domestic flagwaver.

w William Conselman, *play* John Frederick Ballard *d* Frank Borzage *ph* George Schneiderman

Spencer Tracy, Doris Kenyon, Tommy Conlon, Ralph Bellamy, Beryl Mercer, Sarah Padden

Young and Innocent***
GB 1937 80m bw
GFD / Gainsborough (Edward Black)

A girl goes on the run with her boy friend when he is suspected of murder.
Pleasant, unassuming chase melodrama with a rather weak cast but plenty of its director's touches.

w Charles Bennett, Alma Reville, *novel* A Shilling for Candles by Josephine Tey *d Alfred Hitchcock* *ph* Bernard Knowles *m* Louis Levy

Nova Pilbeam, Derrick de Marney, Mary Clare, Edward Rigby, Basil Radford, George Curzon, Percy Marmont, John Longden

Young and Willing
US 1942 83m bw
UA (made by Paramount) (Edward H. Griffith)

Impecunious actors in a New York boarding house hit on a great play.
Very mild, innocuous comedy which passed quickly from the public memory.

w Virginia Van Upp, *play* Francis Swann *d* Edward H. Griffith *ph* Leo Tover

William Holden, Susan Hayward, Eddie Bracken, Robert Benchley, Martha O'Driscoll, Barbara Britton, James Brown,, Mabel Paige

Young at Heart**
US 1954 117m Warnercolor
(Warner) Arwin (Henry Blanke)

The daughters of a small-town music teacher have romantic problems.
Softened, musicalized remake of *Four Daughters* (qv), an old-fashioned treat with roses round the door and a high standard of proficiency in all departments.

w Julius J. Epstein, Lenore Coffee, *novel* Fannie Hurst *d* Gordon Douglas *ph* Ted McCord

Doris Day, Frank Sinatra, Ethel Barrymore, Gig Young, Dorothy Malone, Robert Keith, Elizabeth Fraser, Alan Hale Jnr

Young Bess*
US 1953 112m Technicolor
MGM (Sidney Franklin)

The early years of Elizabeth I and her romance with Tom Seymour.
Historical fiction, wildly unreliable as to fact and dramatically not very rewarding. The character actors have the best of it.

w Arthur Wimperis, Jan Lustig, *novel* Margaret Irwin *d* George Sidney *ph* Charles Rosher *m* Miklos Rozsa

Jean Simmons, Stewart Granger, Charles Laughton (as Henry VIII), Kay Walsh, Deborah Kerr, Guy Rolfe, Kathleen Byron, Cecil Kellaway, Robert Arthur, Leo G. Carroll, Elaine Stewart, Dawn Addams, Rex Thompson

Young Billy Young
US 1969 89m De Luxe
UA / Talbot–Youngstein (Max Youngstein)

A young western gunman is helped out of scrapes by a mysterious stranger bent on revenge.
Good-looking but rather ineffective western which throws away good production values.

wd Burt Kennedy, *novel* Who Rides with Wyatt by Will Henry *ph* Harry Stradling Jnr *m* Shelly Manne

Robert Mitchum, Angie Dickinson, Robert Walker Jnr, David Carradine, John Anderson, Paul Fix

Young Cassidy*
GB 1964 110m Technicolor
MGM / Sextant (Robert D. Graff, Robert Emmett Ginna)

A romantic view of the early Dublin life of writer Sean O'Casey.
Ambling, unconvincing but generally interesting picture of a past time.

w John Whiting, from the writings of Sean O'Casey *d* Jack Cardiff, John Ford *ph* Ted Scaife *m* Sean O'Riada

Rod Taylor, Maggie Smith, Edith Evans, Flora Robson, Michael Redgrave, Julie Christie, Jack MacGowran, Sian Phillips, T. P. McKenna

The Young Country*
US 1970 74m Technicolor TVM
Universal (Roy Huggins)

A young gambler gets worried when he finds a fortune in a saddlebag and no one will acknowledge ownership.
Pleasant light western.

wd Roy Huggins

Roger Davis, Walter Brennan, Joan Hackett, Wally Cox, Pete Duel

Young Dillinger
US 1964 102m bw
Alfred Zimbalist

An embittered young convict becomes Public Enemy Number One.
Fantasized, forgettable biopic with violent moments.

w Arthur Hoerl, Don Zimbalist *d* Terry Morse *ph* Stanley Cortez *m* Shorty Rogers

Nick Adams, John Ashley, Robert Conrad, Mary Ann Mobley, Victor Buono, John Hoyt, Reed Hadley

The Young Doctors*
US 1961 102m bw
UA / Drexel / Stuart Millar / Laurence Turman

Old Dr Pearson resents his modern young assistant and almost causes a tragedy.
Routine medical melo of the Kildare/Gillespie kind, given a Grade A production and cast.

w Joseph Hayes, *novel* The Final Diagnosis by Arthur Hailey *d* Phil Karlson *ph* Arthur J. Ornitz *m* Elmer Bernstein

Fredric March, Ben Gazzara, Dick Clark, Eddie Albert, Ina Balin, Aline MacMahon, Edward Andrews, Arthur Hill, George Segal, Rosemary Murphy

Young Eagles*
US 1930 71m bw
Paramount

The adventures of American aviators in World War I.
Spirited early sound actioner.

w William McNutt, Grover Jones *d* William Wellman *ph* Archie Stout

Charles Rogers, Jean Arthur, Paul Lukas, Stuart Erwin, Virginia Bruce, James Finlayson

Young Frankenstein**
US 1974 108m bw
TCF / Gruskoff / Venture / Jouer / Crossbow (Michael Gruskoff)

Young Frederick Frankenstein, a brain surgeon, goes back to Transylvania and pores over his grandfather's notebooks.
The most successful of Mel Brooks' parodies, Mad Magazine style; the gleamingly reminiscent photography is the best of it, the script being far from consistently funny, but there are splendid moments.

w Gene Wilder, Mel Brooks *d* Mel Brooks *ph Gerald Hirschfeld m* John Morris *ad Dale Hennesy*

Gene Wilder, Marty Feldman, Madeleine Kahn, *Peter Boyle*, Cloris Leachman, Kenneth Mars, Gene Hackman, Richard Haydn

The Young in Heart***
US 1938 91m bw
David O. Selznick

A family of charming confidence tricksters move in on a rich old lady but she brings out the best in them.
Delightful, roguish romantic comedy, perfectly cast and pacily handled.

w Paul Osborn, Charles Bennett, novel The Gay Banditti by I. A. R. Wylie *d Richard Wallace ph* Leon Shamroy *m* Franz Waxman

Douglas Fairbanks Jnr, Janet Gaynor, Roland Young, Billie Burke, Minnie Dupree, Paulette Goddard, Richard Carlson, Henry Stephenson

The Young Land
US 1957 89m Technicolor
(Columbia) C. V. Whitney (Patrick Ford)

A young sheriff arrests a gunman and after the trial has to save him from lynching.
Rather stiff attempt at a youth western.

w Norman Shannon Hall *d* Ted Tetzlaff
ph Winton C. Hoch, Henry Sharp

Dan O'Herlihy, Patrick Wayne, Yvonne Craig, Dennis Hopper

The Young Lawyers
US 1969 74m colour TVM
Paramount

A Boston corporation lawyer takes over a legal aid office run by students.
A very predictable pilot.

wd Harvey Hart

Jason Evers, Louise Lathan, Keenan Wynn, Michael Parks, Anjanette Comer

The Young Lions**
US 1958 167m bw Cinemascope
TCF (Al Lichtman)

World War II adventures of two Americans and a German skiing instructor.
Three strands are loosely interwoven into a would-be modern epic; the result is well mounted and generally absorbing but uneven and decidedly overlong.

w Edward Anhalt, *novel* Irwin Shaw *d* Edward Dmytryk *ph* Joe MacDonald *m* Hugo Friedhofer

Marlon Brando, Montgomery Clift, Dean Martin, Hope Lange, Barbara Rush, May Britt, Maximilian Schell, Lee Van Cleef

The Young Lovers*
GB 1954 96m bw
GFD / Group Films (Anthony Havelock-Allan)
US title: *Chance Meeting*

A US Embassy man in London falls in love with the daughter of an Iron Curtain minister.
Romeo and Juliet, cold war style, quite nicely put together with a thriller climax.

w Robin Estridge, *story* George Tabori
d Anthony Asquith

Odile Versois, David Knight, David Kossoff, Joseph Tomelty, Paul Carpenter, Theodore Bikel, Jill Adams

Young Man with a Horn*
US 1950 112m bw
Warner (Jerry Wald)

The professional and romantic tribulations of a trumpet player.
Overwrought character melodrama based on the life of Bix Beiderbecke; quite absorbing though occasionally risible.

w Carl Foreman, Edmund H. North, *novel* Dorothy Baker *d* Michael Curtiz *ph* Ted McCord *m* Ray Heindorf

Kirk Douglas, Lauren Bacall, Doris Day, Hoagy Carmichael, Juano Hernandez, Jerome Cowan, Mary Beth Hughes, Nestor Paiva

Young Man with Ideas*
US 1952 84m bw
MGM (Gottfried Reinhardt, William H. Wright)

A small-town lawyer tries to better himself in Los Angeles.
Modestly likeable comedy which doesn't add up to much.

w Arthur Sheekman *d* Mitchell Leisen
ph Joseph Ruttenberg *m* David Rose

Glenn Ford, Ruth Roman, Nina Foch, Denise Darcel, Donna Corcoran, Mary Wickes, Sheldon Leonard

Young Mr Lincoln***
US 1939 100m bw
TCF (Kenneth MacGowan)

Abraham Lincoln as a young country lawyer stops a lynching and proves a young man innocent of murder.
Splendid performances and period atmosphere are rather nipped in the bud by second-feature courtroom twists, but this is a marvellous old-fashioned entertainment with its heart in the right place.

w Lamar Trotti *d John Ford ph Bert Glennon*
w Alfred Newman

Henry Fonda, Alice Brady, Marjorie Weaver, Arleen Whelan, Eddie Collins, Richard Cromwell, Donald Meek, Eddie Quillan, Spencer Charters

'Its simple good faith and understanding are an expression of the country's best life that says as much as forty epics.'—*Otis Ferguson*

'Period details are lovingly sketched in - a log splitting contest, a tug of war, a tar barrel rolling match . . .'—*Charles Higham*

'Its source is a womb of popular and national spirit. This could account for its unity, its artistry, its genuine beauty.'—*Sergei Eisenstein*

The Young Mr Pitt*
GB 1942 118m bw
TCF (Edward Black)

Britain's youngest prime minister quells the threat of invasion by Napoleon.
Shapeless and overlong but generally diverting historical pastiche timed as wartime propaganda against Hitler.

w Frank Launder, Sidney Gilliat *d* Carol Reed

Robert Donat, Robert Morley, Phyllis Calvert, John Mills, Raymond Lovell, Max Adrian, Felix Aylmer, Albert Lieven

The Young Ones*
GB 1961 108m Technicolor Cinemascope
ABP (Kenneth Harper)

The son of a tycoon starts a youth club and puts on a musical to raise funds.
A shopworn idea is the springboard for a brave try in a field where Britain was presumed to have failed; despite the enthusiasm with which it was greeted at the time, it has dated badly.

w Peter Myers, Ronald Cass *d* Sidney J. Furie *ph* Douglas Slocombe *m* Stanley Black

Cliff Richard, Robert Morley, Carole Grey, Richard O'Sullivan, Melvyn Hayes, Gerald Harper, Robertson Hare

The Young Philadelphians*
US 1959 136m bw
Warner (producer not credited)
GB title: *The City Jungle*

A forceful young lawyer pushes his way to the top of the snobbish Philadelphia heap despite threats to expose his illegitimacy.
Novel on film, gleamingly done and acted with assurance.

w James Gunn, *novel* The Philadelphian by Richard Powell *d* Vincent Sherman *ph* Harry Stradling *m* Ernest Gold

Paul Newman, Barbara Rush, Alexis Smith, Brian Keith, Billie Burke, John Williams, Otto Kruger, Diane Brewster, Robert Vaughn, Paul Picerni, Robert Douglas

Young Pioneers*
US 1975 100m colour TVM
ABC Circle

In 1873, newlywed teenagers travel west.
Standard pioneering saga, well enough made.

novels Rose Wilder Lane *d* Michael O'Herlihy

Roger Kern, Linda Purl

The Young Savages*
US 1961 103m bw
UA / Contemporary (Pat Duggan)

An assistant DA prosecutes three hoodlums for murder but begins to feel that one is not guilty.
Tough, realistic melodrama of the New York slums, with roughhouse climaxes and a political conscience.

w Edward Anhalt, J. P. Miller, *novel* A Matter of Conviction by Evan Hunter *d John Frankenheimer* *ph* Lionel Lindon *m* David Amram

Burt Lancaster, Shelley Winters, John David Chandler, Dina Merrill, Edward Andrews, Telly Savalas

The Young Stranger*
US 1957 84m bw
RKO (Stuart Millar)

The 16-year-old son of a film executive gets into trouble with the police.
Reasonably stimulating film of a TV play about the kind of causeless rebel who quickly became a cliché.

w Robert Dozier *d* John Frankenheimer *ph* Robert Planck *m* Leonard Rosenman

James MacArthur, Kim Hunter, James Daly, James Gregory, Whit Bissell

Young Tom Edison*
US 1940 82m bw
MGM (John Considine Jnr)

First of a two-parter (see *Edison the Man*) tracing Edison's first experiments.
Reasonably factual and absorbing junior biopic.

w Bradbury Foote, Dore Schary, Hugo Butler *d* Norman Taurog *ph* Sidney Wagner *m* Edward Ward

Mickey Rooney, Eugene Pallette, George Bancroft, Fay Bainter, Virginia Weidler, Victor Kilian, Lloyd Corrigan

The Young Widow
US 1946 100m bw
UA / Hunt Stromberg

The widow of a World War II flier returns to the Virginia farm where they had spent happy hours.
Glum sudser with talent all at sea.

w Richard Macaulay, Margaret Buell Wilder, *novel* Clarissa Fairchild Cushman *d* Edwin L. Marin *ph* Lee Garmes *m* Carmen Dragon *pd* Nicolai Remisoff

Jane Russell, Louis Hayward, Faith Domergue, Marie Wilson, Kent Taylor, Penny Singleton, Connie Gilchrist, Cora Witherspoon

Young Winston**
GB 1972 157m Eastmancolor Panavision
Columbia / Open Road / Hugh French (Carl Foreman)

The adventurous life of Winston Churchill up to his becoming an MP.
Generally engaging if lumpy film which switches too frequently from action to family drama to politics to character study and is not helped by irritating directorial tricks.

w Carl Foreman, *book* My Early Life by Winston Churchill *d* Richard Attenborough *ph* Gerry Turpin *m* Alfred Ralston *pd* Don Ashton, Geoffrey Drake

Simon Ward, Robert Shaw, Anne Bancroft, Jack Hawkins, Ian Holm, *Anthony Hopkins*, John Mills, Patrick Magee, Edward Woodward

Youngblood Hawke
US 1964 137m bw
Warner (Delmer Daves)

A Kentucky truck driver becomes a successful novelist and is spoiled by New York success.
Absurdly archetypal soap opera from a bestseller, spilling over with every imaginable cliché; some of its excesses are glossily entertaining.

w Delmer Daves, *novel* Herman Wouk *d* Delmer Daves *ph* Charles Lawton *m* Max Steiner

James Franciscus, Genevieve Page, Suzanne Pleshette, Eva Gabor, *Mary Astor*, Lee Bowman, Edward Andrews, John Emery, Don Porter

The Youngest Profession
US 1943 82m bw
MGM (B. F. Ziedman)

Teenage autograph hounds cause trouble at the MGM studio.
Innocuous comedy with guest stars.

w George Oppenheimer, Charles Lederer, Leonard Spiegelgass, *book* Lillian Day *d* Edward Buzzell *ph* Charles Lawton *m* David Snell

Virginia Weidlerrr, Jean Porter, Edward Arnold, John Carroll, Agnes Moorehead, Greer Garson, William Powell, Lana Turner, Walter Pidgeon, Robert Taylor

Your Money or Your Wife
US 1972 74m colour TVM
Bentwood

A scriptwriter's plot turns into an almost perfect crime.
Rather talkative comedy suspenser.

w J. P. Miller, *novel* If You Want to See Your Wife Again . . . by John Gay *d* Allen Reisner

Ted Bessell, Elizabeth Ashley, Jack Cassidy, Betsy Von Furstenberg

Your Witness*
GB 1950 100m bw
Warner (David E. Rose, Joan Harrison)
US title: *Eye Witness*

An American lawyer comes to an English village to defend a war buddy on a murder charge.
Interesting but ineffective blend of comedy and courtroom procedure intended to contrast English and American ways.

w Hugo Butler, Ian Hunter, William Douglas Home *d* Robert Montgomery *ph* Gerald Young *m* Malcolm Arnold

Robert Montgomery, Leslie Banks, Patricia Cutts, Felix Aylmer, Andrew Cruickshank, Harcourt Williams, Jenny Laird, Michael Ripper

You're a Big Boy Now*
US 1967 96m Eastmancolor
Warner Seven Arts (William Fadiman)

A young assistant librarian discovers girls.
Freewheeling semi-surrealist comedy with exhilarating moments and the inevitable letdowns associated with this kind of campy high style.

wd Francis Ford Coppola, *novel* David Benedictus *ph Andy Laszlo* *m* Bob Prince

Peter Kastner, Elizabeth Hartman, Geraldine Page, Julie Harris, Rip Torn, Tony Bill, Karen Black, Michael Dunn

You're a Sweetheart
US 1937 96m bw
Universal (B. G. De Sylva)

A Broadway star suffers from her press agent's bright ideas.
Muffed musical with all concerned ill at ease with below par material.

w Monte Brice, Charles Grayson *d* David Butler *ph* George Robinson *md* Charles Previn *songs* various

Alice Faye, George Murphy, Ken Murray, William Gargan, Frances Hunt, Frank Jenks, Andy Devine, Charles Winninger, Donald Meek

You're in the Army Now**
US 1941 79m bw
Warner (Ben Stoloff)

Two incompetent vacuum cleaner salesmen accidentally join the army.
An excellent vehicle for two star comedians who

have often suffered from poor material, with a silent-comedy-style climax involving a house on wheels.

w Paul Gerard Smith, George Beatty *d* Lewis Seiler *ph* James Van Trees

Jimmy Durante, Phil Silvers, Donald MacBride, Jane Wyman, Regis Toomey

You're in the Navy Now*
US 1951 93m bw
TCF (Fred Kohlmar)
aka: *USS Teakettle*

Trouble results when the navy instals steam turbines in an experimental patrol craft.
Amusing service comedy with good script touches and capable performances.

w Richard Murphy *d* Henry Hathaway *ph* Joe MacDonald *m* Cyril Mockridge

Gary Cooper, Millard Mitchell, Jane Greer, Eddie Albert, John McIntire, Ray Collins, Harry Von Zell, Jack Webb, Richard Erdman

You're My Everything*
US 1949 94m Technicolor
TCF (Lamar Trotti)

A Boston socialite marries a hoofer and becomes a movie star.
Pleasant twenties comedy with good period detail and lively performances.

w Lamar Trotti, Will Hays Jnr *d* Walter Lang *ph* Arthur E. Arling *m* Alfred Newman

Anne Baxter, Dan Dailey, Anne Revere, Stanley Ridges, Shari Robinson, Henry O'Neill, Selena Royle, Alan Mowbray, Buster Keaton

You're Never Too Young
US 1955 103m Technicolor Vistavision
Paramount / Hal B. Wallis (Paul Jones)

An apprentice barber on the run from a murderer poses as a 12-year-old child to travel half fare.
Unattractive revamping of *The Major and the Minor* (qv), with the star team trying too obviously to make bricks with inferior straw.

w Sidney Sheldon *d* Norman Taurog *ph* Daniel L. Fapp *m* Arthur Schwarz

Dean Martin, Jerry Lewis, Diana Lynn, Nina Foch, Raymond Burr, Veda Ann Borg

You're Only Young Once see The Hardy Family

You're Only Young Twice
GB 1952 81m bw
Group Three (Terry Bishop)

The puritanical head of a Scottish university is laid low by circumstance and his own folly.
Misfire eccentric comedy which deserves marks for trying but fails to amuse.

w Reginald Beckwith, Lindsay Galloway, Terry Bishop, *play* What Say They by James Bridie *d* Terry Gilbert *ph* Jo Jago

Duncan Macrae, Charles Hawtrey, Joseph Tomelty, Patrick Barr, Diane Hart, Robert Urquhart

You're Telling Me*
US 1934 66m bw
Paramount

A small-town inventor meets a princess and makes the social grade.
Meaninglessly-titled star vehicle which is often defiantly unamusing but does include the famous golf routine.

w Walter de Leon, Paul M. Jones *d* Erle C. Kenton *ph* Alfred Gilks *m* Arthur Johnston

W. C. Fields, Larry 'Buster' Crabbe, Joan Marsh, Adrienne Ames, Louise Carter

Yours Mine and Ours*
US 1968 111m Technicolor
UA / Desilu / Walden (Robert F. Blumofe)

A widower with nine children marries a widow with eight, and they settle in an old San Francisco house.
Generally appealing comedy, based on fact and well suited to its stars.

w Mel Shavelson, Mort Lachman *d* Mel Shavelson *ph* Charles Wheeler *m* Fred Karlin

Lucille Ball, Henry Fonda, Van Johnson

Yuma*
US 1970 70m colour TVM
Aaron Spelling

A tough lawman tackles the wildest town in the old west.
Conventional, enjoyable western.

d Ted Post

Clint Walker, Barry Sullivan, Edgar Buchanan, Kathryn Hays

Z

Zabriskie Point
US 1969 112m Metrocolor
Panavision
MGM / Carlo Ponti

A rebellious Los Angeles student steals a private airplane, meets an aimless girl, and finds a revelation in Death Valley . . .
Highly self-indulgent and unattractive fantasy about escape from the crudities of our over-civilized world. An expensive failure and an awful warning of what happens if you give an arty director carte blanche.

wd Michelangelo Antonioni *ph* Alfio Contini
m pop songs

Mark Frechette, Daria Halprin, Rod Taylor, Paul Fix

'Not even a good tourist's notebook . . . from the choice of Death Valley as a symbol of American civilization to the inclusion of gag signs on bar-room walls to the shots of garish billboards, this film sticks to the surface, stranded.'—*Stanley Kauffman*

Zandy's Bride
US 1974 116m Technicolor
Panavision
Warner (Harry Matofsky)

Life for a frontier family.
Dour semi-western.

w Marc Norman, *novel* The Stranger by Lillian Bos Ross *d* Joan Troell *ph* Jordan Cronenweth
m Fred Karlin

Gene Hackman, Liv Ullmann, Eileen Heckart, Harry Dean Stanton, Joe Santos, Frank Cady

Zarak*
GB 1956 99m Technicolor
Cinemascope
Columbia / Warwick

An Afghan outlaw finally saves a British officer at the cost of his own life.
Box-office actioner, shot in Morocco with a weird cast and the help of old movie clips.

w Richard Maibaum *d* Terence Young *2nd unit* Yakima Canutt *ph* John Wilcox, Ted Moore, Cyril Knowles *ad* John Box

Victor Mature, Michael Wilding, Anita Ekberg, Bonar Colleano, Finlay Currie, Bernard Miles, Eunice Gayson, Peter Illing, Frederick Valk, André Morell

Zardoz
GB 1973 105m De Luxe Panavision
TCF / John Boorman

Life in 2293, when the earth has become wasteland and a mass of Brutals are ruled by a few Exterminators who have both memory and intelligence.
Pompous, boring fantasy for the so-called intelligentsia.

wd John Boorman *ph* Geoffrey Unsworth
m David Munrow *pd* Anthony Pratt

Sean Connery, Charlotte Rampling, John Alderton

Zebra in the Kitchen
US 1965 93m Metrocolor
MGM / Ivan Tors

A young boy tries to improve the lot of zoo animals.
Pleasing family film.

w Art Arthur *d* Ivan Tors

Jay North, Martin Milner, Andy Devine, Joyce Meadows, Jim Davis

Zee and Co.*
GB 1971 109m colour
Columbia / Zee Films (Kastner–Ladd–Kanter)
US title: *X, Y and Zee*

A successful architect battles with his termagant wife and seeks an affair.
Overwritten but entertaining sexual melodrama about an absolute bitch. The flow of bad language was new at the time.

w Edna O'Brien *d* Brian G. Hutton *ph* Billy Williams *m* Stanley Myers *ad* Peter Mullins

Elizabeth Taylor, Michael Caine, Susannah York, Margaret Leighton, John Standing

'Miss Taylor is rapidly turning into a latterday Marie Dressler.'—*Tom Milne*

'A slice-of-jet-set-life nightmare far beyond the dreams of the piggiest male chauvinist . . . the distinction of this film is that its characters are repulsive, its style vulgar, its situations beyond belief and its dialogue moronic.'—*Judith Crist*

Zeppelin*
GB 1971 97m Technicolor Panavision
Warner / Getty and Fromkess (Owen Crump)

In 1915, the British need to steal secrets from the zeppelin works at Friedrichshafen.
Undistinguished but entertaining period actioner with adequate spectacle but wooden performances.

w Arthur Rowe, Donald Churchill *d* Etienne Périer *ph* Alan Hume *m* Roy Budd *sp* Wally Veevers

Michael York, Elke Sommer, Peter Carsten, Marius Goring, Anton Diffring, Andrew Keir, Rupert Davies

Zero Hour!
US 1957 83m bw
(Paramount) Bartlett / Champion (John Champion)

Half the passengers and all the crew of a jet plane are stricken with food poisoning and a shell-shocked ex-fighter pilot has to land the plane.
Adequate air melodrama with a premise which later served for *Terror in the Sky* (TV) and *Airport 75*.

w Arthur Hailey, John Champion, Hall Bartlett, *teleplay* Flight into Danger by Arthur Hailey *d* Hall Bartlett *ph* John F. Warren *m* Ted Baker

Dana Andrews, Linda Darnell, Sterling Hayden, Elroy Hirsch, Jerry Paris

Zero Population Growth
US 1971 96m Eastmancolor
Sagittarius (Thomas F. Madigan)

In the 21st century there is a death penalty for having children, but a young couple defy the authorities.
Good sci-fi quickly develops into sticky sentimentality.

w Max Ehrlich, Frank de Felita *d* Michael Campus *ph* Michael Reed *m* Jonathan Hodge *pd* Tony Masters

Oliver Reed, Geraldine Chaplin, Diane Cilento, Don Gordon, Bill Nagy, Aubrey Woods

Ziegfeld Follies**
US 1944 (released 1946) 110m Technicolor
MGM (Arthur Freed)

In heaven, Florenz Ziegfeld dreams up one last spectacular revue.
A rather airless all-star entertainment in which the comedy suffers from the lack of an audience but some of the production numbers are magnificently stylish.

w various *d Vincente Minnelli ph George Folsey, Charles Rosher m* various *ad* Cedric Gibbons, Merrill Pye, Jack Martin Smith

Fred Astaire, Lucille Ball, Bunin's Puppets, William Powell, Jimmy Durante, Edward Arnold, *Fannie Brice*, Lena Horne, Lucille Bremer, Esther Williams, Judy Garland, *Red Skelton, Gene Kelly*, James Melton, Hume Cronyn, Victor Moore, Marion Bell

'Between opening and closing is packed a prodigious amount of material, some of which is frankly not deserving of the lavish treatment accorded it.'—*Film Daily*

Ziegfeld Girl*
US 1941 131m bw
MGM (Pandro S. Berman)

The professional and romantic problems of Ziegfeld chorus girls.
Adequate big-budget drama with music.

w Marguerite Roberts, Sonya Levien *d* Robert Z. Leonard *ph* Ray June *m* Herbert Stothart *ch* Busby Berkeley *songs* various

James Stewart, Judy Garland, Hedy Lamarr, Lana Turner, Tony Martin, Jackie Cooper, Ian Hunter, *Charles Winninger*, *Al Shean*, Edward Everetttt Horton, Philip Dorn, Paul Kelly, Eve Arden, Dan Dailey, Fay Holden, Felix Bressart

'Heaping portions of show life in the opulent days of Flo Ziegfeld, the man who wanted bigger and better staircases.'—*C. A. Lejeune*

Zigzag*
US 1970 104m Metrocolor Panavision
MGM / Freeman–Enders
GB title: *False Witness*

A dying man frames himself for an unsolved murder so that the reward money, claimed under another name, will go to his wife.
Complex thriller which sustains itself pretty well most of the way, but lacks humour and character.

w John T. Kelley *d* Richard A. Colla *ph* James A. Crabe *m* Oliver Nelson

George Kennedy, Anne Jackson, Eli Wallach, Steve Ihnat, William Marshall, Joe Maross

Zoo in Budapest*
US 1933 83m bw
Fox (Jesse Lasky)

An orphan waif runs away to live with a zookeeper.

Curious little romance remembered for its luminescent photography.

w Dan Totheroh, Louise Long, Rowland V. Lee *d* Rowland V. Lee *ph Lee Garmes*

Loretta Young, Gene Raymond, O. P. Heggie, Wally Albright, Paul Fix

'Richly composed impressionistic images, assisted by highly imaginative use of sound and background music, create a poem that Murnau himself would have envied.'—*NFT, 1971*

Zorba the Greek**

GB 1964 142m bw

TCF / Rockley / Cacoyannis

A young English writer in Crete is befriended by a huge gregarious Greek who comes to dominate his life.

A mainly enjoyable character study of a larger-than-life character, this film made famous by its music does not really hang together dramatically and has several melodramatic excrescences.

wd Michael Cacoyannis, novel Nikos Kazantzakis *ph Walter Lassally m Mikis Theodorakis*

Anthony Quinn, Alan Bates, Lila Kedrova, Irene Papas

'For all its immense length, the film never gets down to a clear statement of its theme, or comes within measuring distance of its vast pretensions.'—*Brenda Davies*

Zotz!

US 1962 87m bw

Columbia / William Castle

A professor finds a rare coin with occult powers. Footling farce patterned after *The Absent-Minded Professor*. Poor, to say the least.

w Ray Russell, *novel* Walter Karig *d* William Castle *ph* Gordon Avil *m* Bernard Green

Tom Poston, Fred Clark, Jim Backus, Cecil Kellaway, Margaret Dumont

Zulu*

GB 1964 135m Technirama

Paramount / Diamond (Stanley Baker, Cyril Endfield)

In 1879 British soldiers stand fast against the Zulus at Rorke's Drift.

Standard period heroics, well presented and acted.

w John Prebble, Cy Endfield *d* Cy Endfield *ph* Stephen Dade *m* John Barry

Stanley Baker, Jack Hawkins, *Michael Caine,* Ulla Jacobsson, James Booth, Nigel Green, Ivor Emmanuel, Paul Daneman

The Decline and Fall of the Movie

It is only fair that the author of a book which categorizes forty-five years of films should give some account of his own prejudices. I have spent more than forty years seeing, talking about and writing about films, so my affection for the medium in its 'golden age' can hardly be doubted. Even then, however, the worthwhile movies were the tip of the iceberg: probably eighty per cent of what was produced was ghastly rubbish, which is why this book deals with eight thousand movies, not all of them good, out of a total output of four times that number. The best kind of film buff loves the movie business for what it can be at its best, not for its journeyman 'B' features, its crackpot experiments, its cheapjack exploitation screamies or those relentlessly boring bottom-of-the-bill fillers.

Jonathan Swift said in 1725: 'I hate and detest that animal called man, although I heartily love John, Peter, Thomas and so forth.' This book encapsulates my Johns, my Peters and my Thomases; this essay complains bitterly that they have lately been so few in number, and attempts, admittedly by some slight use of exaggeration, to throw light on a confused and unhappy segment of cinema history.

When Sam Peckinpah made *Straw Dogs* from a novel called *The Siege of Trencher's Farm* he thought it unnecessary to explain to his audience the significance of his new title which, his publicists informed us on request, was taken from an old Chinese proverb. And when Stanley Kubrick made *A Clockwork Orange* he did not bother to retain the section of the Anthony Burgess novel which explained why it was so called. These almost identical incidents exemplify the kind of arrogance which besets film-makers in the seventies. Steeped in the history of Hollywood's golden age, they have no idea what made it work so well, and as soon as they become successful they begin to despise their audiences and are concerned only to over-spend enourmous budgets while putting across some garbled self-satisfying message which is usually anti-establishment, anti-law-and-order and anti-entertainment.

In this they are assisted by such long-haired publications as *Sight and Sound* and a variety of earnest critics who bend over backwards to see 'significance' where none exists and to ascribe all the film's virtues and faults to the director, or in the current jargon the *auteur*. (Would any theatrical critic dream of judging a play solely on the director's contribution, or a literary critic of reviewing a book solely on the basis of its layout on the printed page?) If cinema, which is the creation of so many people, can be an art at all, it must be a folk art which appeals to innocent and sophisticate alike, and can be easily appreciated by both. This happy state of affairs was reached thirty-five years ago by unpretentious and slick productions of the studio system such as *The Maltese Falcon* and *Stagecoach*, which used every camera trick in the book without blinding the audience to the characters and the plot. Nowadays one has to fight one's way through the thick showy surface in order to get to a story which all too often is not worth following.

One problem is that modern films are largely made by people with no sense of humour, people who do not realize that they must please the mass audience if the industry in which they work is to survive. Oldtime screenwriters such as Ben Hecht, Dudley Nichols and Lamar Trottie would no doubt be viewed by these young men as cynical hacks, but at least they took pains to please their audience with all the expertise at their command, and they still expressed their own views in a vein of sardonic humour which ran through most of the scripts of the thirties and forties and was there to please and satisfy the minority of filmgoers who sought it out.

The absurd pretensions of some modern film-makers certainly cause amusement wherever sensible people congregate, but the advocates of sanity are in no position to have the last word. The present set-up of the film industry encourages wilder and wickeder sensations, from homicidal sharks to diabolical babies, as these are the only subjects which lure large audiences. The successes, however, are all one-offs: no one is much interested in sequels, preferring to wait for horrors of some other variety. The result is that only one film in twenty or thirty makes a profit, but the custodians of the cash have no option but to go on investing in the hope that the occasional fluke will make a fortune, which will then be quickly dissipated by a string of failures. Universal's phenomenally successful *Jaws*, for instance, was immediately followed by such commercial duds as *Gable and Lombard, W. C. Fields and Me, The Great Waldo Pepper* and *The Hindenberg*, and the studio is still looking for another hit. The sad fact is that no policy can be devised because the people in charge of the money have no idea what is likely to appeal, and they are forced to put their faith in reputedly brilliant directors who have no idea either but are quite prepared to spend large sums of other people's money in flying their own flimsy kites. The flimsiness is sometimes astonishing. The director of an abysmal 1976 comedy called *Harry and Walter go to New York* announced to the press, as a selling point, that it was 'Laurel and Hardy with real people'. Had he inquired of his mass audience, he would surely have been told that Stan and Ollie had more reality in their little fingers than was to be found in the entire crew of *Harry and Walter go to New York*, whether before or behind the camera.

One should of course add that many films these days are not supposed to make money. The adage which used to run 'you're only as good as your last picture' has been changed to 'you're only as big as your last budget', and it is no trick to get a big budget when many films are conceived by industrialists as tax losses: all you have to do is get in the news by holding outlandish views or even making pornography, and Hollywood these days opens its doors to you because at least you must have learnt how to point a camera or arrest public attention. The ones to suffer are the audiences, who have foisted upon them material which they have every right to expect to be professional, and which all too often is not, just the result of untalented exhibitionists spending someone else's money in whatever way happens to divert them most. Even if there is a profit, their habit is to take the money and run, not to invest it in better production facilities as used to happen in the good old days.

Work is thus produced for a small group of jet-setters; meanwhile that patient paying audience discovers that not only the films but the standards of physical cinema comfort are far worse than they were thirty years ago; since then the cost of admission has risen at a phenomenal rate, the average cost in Britain now being twenty times more than in 1956. What other commodity has risen in price to this extent? Television is infinitely cheaper and can be viewed in the comfort of one's own home: no wonder so many people prefer it.

So the movie industry hastens on its way to perdition and catastrophe, a fate which surely cannot be delayed more than another few years, and for which simple-minded greed, lack of foresight and a large measure of incompetence are chiefly responsible. Those of us who are old enough and who still care about the movies sigh frequently for the halcyon days when Harry Cohn and Louis B. Mayer sat in their front offices, for their intellectual limitations were far less harmful and sometimes far more stimulating to the medium than the excesses of the present incumbents, who seldom stay long enough to make their presences felt and certainly not long enough for any sense of continuity to develop. There is for instance no continuity of employment, which makes the unions tougher and tougher to deal with in an industry which was always volatile in its labour relations: every film is a fresh project for which cast and crew have to be accumulated, and the way things are there is no bank of trained talent to fall back on. As Billy Wilder said, you spend eighty per cent of your time making deals and twenty per cent making pictures. The old moguls had enough common sense and business acumen to keep the system working so that costs were comparatively low and one could afford the occasional interesting failure to please the intellectuals.

How did the movie world go so wrong? You can trace it to the restlessness after World War II, when the regular audience declined and television was a coming threat and the bosses knew that new trends had to be found but no one knew what they might be a glum and depressed world. When actors began to want a say in production and seemed willing to risk their own money, the bosses were delighted to share the possible losses; instead they found themselves being eased out and their profits halved, their studios no longer vast employment centres with a constant production line but simply enclosed space and facilities which could be rented out to the highest bidder.

The old moguls were getting older and couldn't fight the developing situation, the new young ones were businessmen who often backed the wrong horse because they didn't understand the industry. Meanwhile the old showmen had one last irrelevant fling. If television was the enemy, they reasoned, then give the paying public what television cannot provide. Technology now allowed films to be shot on real locations, which was splendid but had two handicaps. First, the units were away from central control for a long time, and the costs were phenomenal; second, the magic was lost, for the real Paris was by no means so romantic or mysterious as Paramount's backlot which had served as Paris for so many years, nor could the lighting of it be so carefully controlled. The new realistic films were slower, because the travel costs had to be justified and travelogue largely took the place of drama (Did anyone complain about the lack of shots of San Francisco in *The Maltese Falcon*?)

The other way to combat television was to change the shape and effect of the entertainment screen, 3-D was tried, but audiences hated wearing polaroid glasses in order to get a three-dimensional image which producers largely utilized by hurling knives, tennis balls, spiders and even grubby redskins into the audience's lap: this was fairground stuff. Cinemascope was then seized upon by Hollywood; twice as wide as the ordinary image and capable of the most spectacular effects. There is no record that the paying audience ever especially liked Cinemascope, or could even remember whether or not a film was in the process, but once the expensive equipment was installed in theatres there was no turning back. Unfortunately the technique involved a reversion in many cinematic effects to the days of D. W. Griffith. The compression of the wide image on to the film and its subsequent expansion in the projector made the photography grainy, especially in black and white, which was henceforth virtually abandoned. (At about the same time a transference to safety stock lost us the glamorous luminescent 'feel' which had been possible with nitrate and which can still be seen in old prints.) The new shape was impossible to compose for, as Fritz Lang said, it was fine for funerals, but what painter through the ages had ever selected it unless to cut up into a triptych? Editing was cut to a minimum because on an image so large each cut made the audience jump. Instead, and cheaper, the camera stayed still while the cast roved around the empty spaces in front of it, and there was an absurd number of shots in which the leading actors reclined so as better to fit the frame. Close-ups and subtle nuances were forgotten; no longer did the camera direct you to the drama, you had to look around and find it yourself. It is rather astonishing that directors with an eye to their reputations still persist in using the scope format, for after initial release the future of any film these days is on the television, and no scope film, will satisfactorily adapt to the TV screen.

In many cinemas Cinemascope was even a fraud, for it had to be on a screen smaller in area than the old image, which was now being referred to sneeringly as 'postage stamp'. This happened when the old screen had already occupied all the width allowed by the cinema's structure: to get the Cinemascope shape, if you could not go any wider, height had to be sacrificed, and audiences wondered why suddenly they were looking at a ribbon of picture across the middle of the space which the fine old screen had occupied.

Cinemascope was patented by Fox, so the other companies all hastened to produce their own variations: Warnerscope, Metroscope, Techniscope, Superscope, Megascope, Camerascope, Panavision, each with its own cheap colour process. Projectionists all over the world were confused by these new names, and seldom knew whether they were projecting a film as they were supposed to. The results were often truly appalling, with lack of focus, too much brightness and wrong screen masking among the most common faults. Paramount's Vistavision, a non-anamorphic process, used the full frame ratio but was intended for projection at anything between 1·33:1 and 2:1, so that the essential action had to take place in a strip along the centre of the picture; consequently, to see a Vistavision print on a 1·33:1 screen was painful indeed, as all the action seemed to take place in the middle distance with great areas of unused space at the top and bottom of the image, and composition, which any painter knows to be all-important, was no longer possible. By the mid-fities, however, 1·33:1 was no longer generally available, as 'wide screen' had become *de rigueur* even for non-anamorphic films: these cut off the top and bottom of the frame and magnified the rest. This meant that revivals were impossible unless one was prepared to suffer dancers without feet and actors without heads!

The result of all this technical uncertainty was that by the mid-fifties movies were in danger of becoming mere expensive sideshows, uninteresting to anyone of sensitivity. At the same time, an element of sophistication crept away from the popular arts: whereas in the thirties and forties smooth and educated idols had been set up for general approbation, the fifties and sixties showed an alarming tendency not merely to make heroes of 'people like us' but to rub our noses firmly in the gutter by devising stories whose leading characters had few redeeming features. Censorship had been absurdly tight and must obviously relax, but it was unwise and unexpected that the floodgates should open as they did, to admit movies which would previously have been considered anti-social rubbish. It was right, for instance, for Otto Preminger to fight the idiocies of the Production Code with his *The Moon Is Blue* and *The Man with the Golden Arm*, but it was a pity he won his battle with a leaden piece of schoolboy smut and an absurdly melodramatic updating of The Road to Ruin. Such films simply made one yearn to go back to the days of *Trouble in Paradise* and *The Palm Beach Story*, or for the true social concern expressed in the considered, powerful and moving masterpieces of Frank Capra, John Ford, or the early Chaplin.

The talents which had made Hollywood great were certainly nearing retirement by now, but it was perhaps unwise as well as churlish for the new wave to pension them off quite as hurriedly as they did, because there was no comparable talent to take their place. Great art directors like Anton Grot and Hans Dreier, great cameramen like Arthur Miller and James Wong Howe, great directors like Michael Curtiz and William Dieterle were either tossed aside or forced to work on material totally unsuited to their talents and not at all comparable to the films which had made their names. The results were big-budget disasters such as *The Egyptian* and *Omar Khayyam*; meanwhile the young directors were copying low-budget television techniques which for every *Marty* produced a dozen flatly realistic bores.

By the early sixties Hollywood had decided on a new image, but it had lost its old loyalties – the golden age audiences as well as the talents were getting older – and had to appeal deliberately to the 'emancipated' young generation. This meant a virtual abolition of censorship, and from the release of *Who's Afraid of Virginia Woolf?* in 1966 to that of *The Texas Chainsaw Massacre* and *The Devil in Miss Jones* ten years later is but a short step. The film is no longer an art, or even a craft: after a brief 'swinging' period it became an exploitation industry designed to take quick money from suckers, led by maverick Ken Russells rather than conscientious Irving Thalbergs, to plaudits from irresponsible critics whenever some totally untalented new director 'does his thing'. There is no justification except box office for films like *The Exorcist* or *Mandingo*, none except self-indulgence for a $12 million coffee-table film like *Barry Lyndon*, while the popularity even in sophisticated circles of shoddy pornography like *Deep Throat* and *Death Weekend* should stand as an awful warning to the leaders of our society that a vivid young art form has overreached itself and is well and truly on the verge of disaster. It is all very well to say in defence of such films that large numbers of people flock to see them: so they did once bear-baiting and public executions and witch hunts, but the human race long ago prided itself on having passed that stage.

The movies will be lucky if, in their search for sensationalism, they do not check themselves out altogether. Audiences have dwindled rapidly and are still dwindling; so is the number of cinemas. The lush old two-thousand seaters have turned into supermarkets, and instead each city has its ineptly-run boxes of mini-cinemas, the effect of which is rather like sitting in cheaply decorated funeral parlours and paying through the nose for the privilege. The family outing to the cinema is a thing of the past: few families can afford it or can find a suitable film, except once or twice a year when the Disney organization stirs itself; and *their* standards are by no means as high as they were, as a comparison of *Robin Hood* with *Bambi* or *Pinocchio* will immediately show. (The fact that such an uninventive computerized cartoon as *Robin Hood* can do well at the box office is an instance of how starved the public is for the older, gentler forms of entertainment.)

Another problem besetting the cinema in the sixties was its adoption by verbose and pompous critics who were determined to turn it into serious art. True art is the work of one man, or at least his personal vision; each film is the work of several hundred people. Of these, admittedly the director has the most control, but to assign to him the role of *auteur* and to ignore the contribution of producer, writer, photographer, composer and editor is arrant nonsense, except possibly in the cases of such as Hitchcock and Kubrick who do control almost every aspect of their output. The new cinema journalism simply encouraged the worst motives of the new breed of film-maker, who came to know that whatever idiocy he perpetrated would be staunchly defended, researched and psychoanalysed by one of these mercenaries in search of a cause. If a character spat on the pavement this would be taken as his final shedding of his working-class upbringing; if he went to bed with a girl it would symbolize his treachery to his own beliefs and his giving in to the snares of Mammon. Listen to a modern critic in the British Film Institute's *Monthly Film Bulletin*, once a terse and reliable guide to film trends, on *Alice Doesn't Live Here Any More*: 'What Scorsese has done, however, is to rescue an American cliché from the bland, flat but much more portentous naturalism of such as *Harry and Tonto* and restore it to an emotional and intellectual complexity through is particular brand of baroque realism.' Or on Rafelson's *Stay Hungry*: 'What distinguishes him from other film-makers of the "head" generation is both the poetic sureness of his fragmentary, allusive style, and the elliptical observation which prevents his social themes from being spiked too easily on the cultural antitheses of that bygone era.' Spare us.

Some of the elements missing from modern cinema are to be found in television, certainly in the UK with its brilliant documentaries, sharp comedies, serious art programmes and single plays; Americans are less lucky except on their public broadcasting system. But television is a private enjoyment, and one inevitably misses the sense of comradeship, of sharing a pleasure, that the cinema used to fulfil. Who having experienced them can forget the feeling of a full house being pleasurably chilled by *The Cat and the Canary*, or rolling in the aisles at Laurel and Hardy, or hoping against hope that Colman will find his *Lost Horizon*? What modern films can produce the sheer entertainment value and unforgettable, vivid scenes of such as *The Philadelphia Story, Stagecoach, Rebecca, Camille, Casablanca, Citizen Kane, Singin' in the Rain, A Night at the Opera, The Lady Vanishes,* and *The Third Man*? These were all intelligent films, all made for the despised mass audience, and they all made money because they were produced with impeccable professionalism and star talent, and because to these qualities they added heart and good humour. Where is the good humour in *Jaws*? Where is the heart in *The Exorcist*? These are rides on fairground ghost trains: one pays for the thrill, but one comes out more depressed than uplifted.

Of course there are some genuine talents at work in films today. One respects the likes of Jack Nicholson and Ellen Burstyn and Al Pacino and Glenda Jackson, but they are all depressingly committed to their own self-expression and to the depiction of mankind with warts and all, not to pleasing, stimulating or improving the public. They need control; but where are the likes of Lubitsch to control them? Of Sturges? Of Ben Hecht? Of James Whale? Of Donald Ogden Stewart? Of S. J. Perelman? Of Robert Benchley and Dorothy Parker? The films produced by Altman and Scorsese and Ashby are doubtless stimulating in their violent, abrasive way but they are not the whole of life. David Lean and John Schlesinger and Arthur Penn are meticulous craftsmen, but they are driven by commerce into the excesses of *Ryan's Daughter* and *Marathon Man* and *The Missouri Breaks*. In the acting league, where are our up-and-coming replacements for David Niven, Cary Grant, Melvyn Douglas, Katharine Hepburn, Ronald Colman? When again will it be the turn of grace and elegance? When indeed will actors want to work? Steve McQueen, Elizabeth Taylor and their like prefer to demand an impossibly high fee, and if they do not get it to sit comfortably at home on the proceeds of their previous hits.

Hollywood at its best – and for Hollywood also read Ealing and Tobis Klangfilm and Svenske Filmindustri – was the purveyor of an expensive and elegant craft which at times touched art, though seldom throughout a whole film. Reality was seldom sought, but why should it be? Real life is not dramatic anyway: even *Taxi Driver* is a heightening, a selection, an emphasis. So are all the great realist films from *The Battleship Potemkin* to *The Grapes of Wrath*. And so are the great works of Beethoven, of Rembrandt, of Michelangelo. Film stands to life as poetry to prose, and its comments were at their most apt and stylish when movies were confined to the sound stage and the backlot. Freedom from that confinement has not made them any better: it has only made them diffuse and patchy and overlong, and colour has made things worse because it apes reality whereas black and white conjured up its own mood and its own comment. Today's screens are too large for the eye to take in. Sound tracks are so 'realistic' as to be incoherent. Big budgets are wasted on movies which would have been ten times as effective if a little imagination had been used or required. Kaleidoscopic effects dazzle the eye and befuddle the brain; immensely long pre-credits sequences make one think the film is nearly over before it actually starts; characterization flies out the window because sex and violence must be fitted in somehow. Plot doesn't matter: since swinging London was invented every film has become a 'happening': which is another way of saying that anything goes and lack of professionalism cannot be criticized.

All right, this essay is a deliberate hatchet job by a disappointed fan who has turned devil's advocate. Some of the new films clearly have virtues which the old ones didn't possess: one is grateful for *The Graduate* and *Charlie Bubbles* and *Cabaret* and *One Flew over the Cuckoo's Nest*, which for various reasons could never have been made in the old Hollywood. But if my thesis were not largely true, how would one explain the enormous popularity of old movies on television, or the recent deluge of books about them? Why, out of more than sixty films on British television over the Christmas of 1976, were *White Heat* (1948), *A Night at the Opera* (1935) and *Yankee Doodle Dandy* (1942) the most discussed and appreciated? Nostalgia is only a trendy word to describe something which people have at last learned to appreciate because it has been taken away from them. No one in his right mind would be nostalgic for PRC second features or for much of the pure assembly line product which inevitably poured out of the studios when they were working at full pitch. And one must progress. But surely not to the wasteful ineptitude which confront us at the cinema these days. Not to *Lucky Lady, Mother Jugs and Speed, At Long Last Love* or *Harry and Walter go to New York*. Most modern audiences really put up with inane or violent rubbish and appear to enjoy it simply because they are supposed not to know any better? We may not be able to get the golden age back, but we can cry for it. If 'they' fail to respond we can at least appreciate the best of it, and learn from that best. This book, I hope, may help a few people to do that.

Alphabetical Index of Alternative Titles

If the film you seek does not appear in the main section of the book and you suspect it to have more than one title, check it here.

N.B. This constitutes a fairly comprehensive list of title changes and it may be that one or two of the less important films mentioned do not appear in the Guide.

Abandon Ship *see* Seven Waves Away
Abbott and Costello Meet the Ghosts *see* Abbott and Costello Meet Frankenstein
Abdulla's Harem *see* Abdulla the Great
Adamson of Africa *see* The Killers of Kilimanjaro
Adventure for Two *see* The Demi-Paradise
The Adventures of Sadie *see* Our Girl Friday
Adventures of a Young Man *see* Hemingway's Adventures of a Young Man
The Adventuress *see* I See a Dark Stranger
Affairs of a Rogue *see* A Scandal in Paris
African Fury *see* Cry the Beloved Country
After Midnight *see* Captain Carey USA
Agent 8¾ *see* Hot Enough For June
Alias Bulldog Drummond *see* Bulldog Jack
All at Sea *see* Barnacle Bill
All This and Money Too *see* Love is a Ball
The Anatolian Smile *see* America, America
Angel Street *see* Gaslight
Angels and the Pirates *see* Angels in the Outfield
Armored Attack *see* North Star
Arms and the Girl *see* Red Salute
Arms and the Woman *see* Mr Winkle Goes to War
Arouse and Beware *see* The Man from Dakota
Arrivederci Baby *see* Drop Dead Darling
The Assassin *see* Venetian Bird
At Dawn We Die *see* Tomorrow We Live
The Avengers *see* The Day Will Dawn

The Baby Vanishes *see* Broadway Limited
Bachelor Bait *see* Adventure in Baltimore
Bachelor Girl Apartment *see* Any Wednesday
Bachelor Girls *see* The Bachelor's Daughters
Bachelor Knight *see* The Bachelor and the Bobbysoxer
Bad Sister *see* The White Unicorn
The Baited Trap *see* The Trap
The Bank Detective *see* The Bank Dick
Battle Hell *see* Yangtse Incident
The Battle for Anzio *see* Anzio
Battle Stripe *see* The Men
The Beachcomber *see* Vessel of Wrath
The Beasts of Marseilles *see* Seven Thunders
The Beautiful Cheat *see* What a Woman
Bend of the River *see* Where the River Bends
Bengal Rifles *see* Bengal Brigade
Beyond the River *see* The Bottom of the Bottle
The Big Bankroll *see* King of the Roaring Twenties
The Big Carnival *see* Ace in the Hole
Big Deal at Dodge City *see* A Big Hand for the Little Lady
The Big Heart *see* Miracle on 34th Street
Big Time Operators *see* The Smallest Show on Earth
The Black Book *see* Reign of Terror
Black Flowers for the Bride *see* Something for Everyone
The Blonde Reporter *see* Sob Sister
Blonde Sinner *see* Yield to the Night
Blood Money *see* Requiem for a Heavyweight
Blood on My Hands *see* Kiss the Blood Off My Hands
Blood on Satan's Claw *see* Satan's Skin
Blue Jeans *see* Blue Denim
Bombsight Stolen *see* Cottage to Let
Bonaventure *see* Thunder on the Hill

Borderlines *see* The Caretakers
Born for Glory *see* Brown on Resolution
Both Ends of the Candle *see* The Helen Morgan Story
Both Sides of the Law *see* Street Corner
The Boy from Barnardo's *see* Lord Jeff
A Boy is Ten Feet Tall *see* Sammy Going South
The Brave and the Beautiful *see* The Magnificent Matador
Breaking the Sound Barrier *see* The Sound Barrier
Break to Freedom *see* Albert RN
Brink of Hell *see* Toward the Unknown
Broadway Singer *see* Torch Singer
Build My Gallows High *see* Out of the Past
Burn! *see* Queimada!
Burn Witch Burn *see* Night of the Eagle
By Hook or by Crook *see* I Dood It

Café of Seven Sinners *see* Seven Sinners
California Holiday *see* Spinout
Call Me Genius *see* The Rebel
Cargo of Innocents *see* Stand By for Action
Caribbean Gold *see* Caribbean
Carnival of Thieves *see* The Caper of the Golden Bulls
The Case of Mrs Pembroke *see* Two Against the World
Cash and Carry *see* Maisie (Ringside Maisie)
Cash on Delivery *see* To Dorothy a Son
Casino de Paree *see* Go Into Your Dance
The Cave Dwellers *see* One Million BC
The Chairman *see* The Most Dangerous Man in the World
Chance Meeting *see* The Young Lovers
The Charge is Murder *see* Twilight of Honor
Charley's American Aunt *see* Charley's Aunt
Chicago, Chicago *see* Gaily, Gaily
Chicago Masquerade *see* Little Egypt
Choose Your Partners *see* Two Girls on Broadway
City After Midnight *see* That Woman Opposite
The City Jungle *see* The Young Philadelphians
Clouds Over Europe *see* Q Planes
Colonel Blimp *see* The Life and Death of Colonel Blimp
Colt 45 *see* Thundercloud
Company of Cowards *see* Advance to the Rear
The Concrete Jungle *see* The Criminal
Confessions of a Counterspy *see* Man on a String
The Conqueror Worm *see* Witchfinder General
The Contact Man *see* Alias Nick Beal
Contest Girl *see* The Beauty Jungle
Convicts Four *see* Reprieve
Cop Out *see* Stranger in the House
Court Martial *see* Carrington VC
The Courtney Affair *see* The Courtneys of Curzon Street
The Crash of Silence *see* Mandy
The Creeping Unknown *see* The Quatermass Experiment
Crest of the Wave *see* Seagulls over Sorrento
Crime of the Century *see* Walk East on Beacon
Curse of the Demon *see* Night of the Demon
Czarina *see* A Royal Scandal

Damn the Defiant *see* HMS Defiant
Dance of the Vampires *see* The Fearless Vampire Killers
Danger Grows Wild *see* The Poppy is Also a Flower
Dangerous Days *see* Wild Boys of the Road
Daniel and the Devil *see* All That Money Can Buy
Dark of the Sun *see* The Mercenaries
The Dark Rage *see* Scandal Sheet
A Date with Destiny *see* The Mad Doctor
The Day They Gave Babies Away *see* All Mine to Give
Dead Image *see* Dead Ringer
Deadline *see* Deadline USA
Deadline Midnight *see* –30–
Decision Against Time *see* The Man in the Sky
The Detective *see* Father Brown
The Devil's Impostor *see* Pope Joan
The Devil Never Sleeps *see* Satan Never Sleeps
The Devil on Wheels *see* Indianapolis Speedway
The Devil Takes the Count *see* The Devil is a Sissy

The Devil's Brother *see* Fra Diavolo
The Devil's Own *see* The Witches
Die Die My Darling *see* Fanatic
The Dividing Line *see* The Lawless
Doomed Cargo *see* Seven Sinners
Doppelganger *see* Journey to the Far Side of the Sun
Dressed to Kill *see* Sherlock Holmes and the Secret Code
Drum Crazy *see* The Gene Krupa Story
Drums *see* The Drum
Dulcimer Street *see* London Belongs To Me
Dynamite Man from Glory Jail *see* Fools Parade

East of Java *see* South Sea Sinner
East of Shanghai *see* Rich and Strange
East of the Rising Sun *see* Malaya
Edge of Divorce *see* Background
The Electric Man *see* Man Made Monster
Elephants Never Forget *see* Zenobia
Ellen *see* The Second Woman
End as a Man *see* The Strange One
End of the Rainbow *see* Northwest Outpost
Eneimies of the Public *see* The Public Enemy
Enemy from Space *see* Quatermass II
Escape to Happiness *see* Intermezzo
Everybody's Cheering *see* Take Me Out to the Ball Game
Every Minute Counts *see* Count the Hours
Every Other Inch a Lady *see* Dancing Co-Ed
Every Woman's Man *see* The Prizefighter and the Lady
Evils of Chinatown *see* Confessions of an Opium Eater
Experiment in Terror *see* The Grip of Fear
Eye Witness (1950) *see* Your Witness

The Fall of the House of Usher *see* House of Usher
Falstaff *see* Chimes at Midnight
The Fantastic Disappearing Man *see* The Return of Dracula
The Fifth Chair *see* It's in the Bag
The Fighting Seventh *see* Little Big Horn
Fine and Dandy *see* West Point Story
The First Rebel *see* Allegheny Uprising
Fitzwilly Strikes Back *see* Fitzwilly
Five Angles on Murder *see* The Woman in Question
Five Million Years to Earth *see* Quatermass and the Pit
Flame over India *see* Northwest Frontier
The Flight of the White Stallions *see* The Miracle of the White Stallions
For You Alone *see* When You're in Love
Forbidden Alliance *see* The Barretts of Wimpole Street
The Forbidden Street *see* Britannia Mews
Forever in Love *see* Pride of the Marines
The Forsyte Saga *see* That Forsyte Woman
Forty Eight Hours *see* Went the Day Well?
Four Against Fate *see* Derby Day
Fraternally Yours *see* Sons of the Desert
Free to Live *see* Holiday
The Frightened Bride *see* The Tall Headlines
The Frightened City *see* The Killer That Stalked New York
Frou Frou *see* The Toy Wife
The Fugitive (1940) *see* On the Night of the Fire
Full House *see* O. Henry's Full House
Fuss over Feathers *see* Conflict of Wings

G Man's Wife *see* Public Enemy's Wife
Gang War *see* Odd Man out
The Gay Falcon *see* The Falcon Takes Over
The Gay Lady *see* Trottie True
The Gay Mrs Trexel *see* Susan and God
A Genius in the Family *see* So Goes My Love
The Gentle Sergeant *see* Three Stripes in the Sun
Get Off My Back *see* Synanon
Gideon of Scotland Yard *see* Gideon's Day
The Girl Getters *see* The System
Girl in Distress *see* Jeannie
The Girl ih Overalls *see* Maisie (Swing Shift Maisie)
The Girl in Room 17 *see* Vice Squad
The Girl in the Painting *see* Portrait from Life
Girl of the Year *see* The Petty Girl
A Girl Was Young *see* Young and Innocent
The Girls He Left Behind *see* The Gang's All Here
Glory at Sea *see* Gift Horse
The Golden Hour *see* Pot o' Gold
The Golden Virgin *see* The Story of Esther Costello

Good Girl *see* Good Dame
Good Morning Doctor *see* You Belong to Me
The Grace Moore Story *see* So This Is Love
The Great Manhunt (GB) *see* The Doolins of Oklahoma
The Great Manhunt (US) *see* State Secret
Green Eyed Woman *see* Take a Letter Darling
The Guest *see* The Caretaker
The Gun Runner *see* Santiago
Guns in the Afternoon *see* Ride the High Country
Guns of Wyoming *see* Cattle King

Hallelujah I'm a Bum *see* Hallelujah I'm a Tramp
The Hammond Mystery *see* The Undying Monster
The Hands of Orlac (1935) *see* Mad Love
Happy Times *see* The Inspector General
The Haunted and the Hunted *see* Dementia 13
Haunted Honeymoon *see* Busman's Honeymoon
Having a Wild Weekend *see* Catch Us If You Can
The Heist *see* Dollars
Hell Bent for Glory *see* Lafayette Escadrille
Hell, Heaven and Hoboken *see* I Was Monty's Double
Hello Beautiful *see* The Powers Girl
Her Man Gilbey *see* English without Tears
The Heroin Gang *see* Sol Madrid
The Hidden Room *see* Obsession
The Hideout *see* The Small Voice
High and Dry *see* The Maggie
High Fury *see* White Cradle Inn
His Affair *see* This is My Affair
His Other Woman *see* Desk Set
Hold That Girl *see* Hold That Co-Ed
The Honourable Mr Wong *see* The Hatchet Man
Horror Hotel *see* City of the Dead
Horror of Dracula *see* Dracula (1958)
Hot Spot *see* I Wake Up Screaming
Hounded *see* Johnny Allegro
The Hounds of Zaroff *see* The Most Dangerous Game
Hours of Glory *see* The Small Back Room
House of Doom *see* The Black Cat
House of Fright *see* The Two Faces of Dr Jekyll
House of Mystery *see* Night Monster
How to Steal a Diamond *see* The Hot Rock
The Human Monster *see* Dark Eyes of London

I Like Money *see* Mr Topaze
I Shall Return *see* An American Guerrilla in the Philippines
If You Feel Like Singing *see* Summer Stock
I'll Never Forget You *see* The House in the Square
Imaginary Sweetheart *see* Professional Sweetheart
Immortal Battalion *see* The Way Ahead
Indiscretion *see* Christmas in Connecticut
The Inheritance *see* Uncle Silas
Innocence is Bliss *see* Miss Grant Takes Richmond
The Invaders *see* 49th Parallel
An Investigation of Murder *see* The Laughing Policeman
The Iron Road *see* Buckskin Frontier
Island Escape *see* No Man is an Island
Island of Desire *see* Saturday Island
Island Rescue *see* Appointment with Venus
It Started in Tokyo *see* Twenty Plus Two
It's Magic *see* Romance on the High Seas
Ivory Hunter *see* Where No Vultures Fly
Jacqueline Susann's Once is Not Enough *see* Once is not Enough
Jailbirds *see* Pardon Us
The James Brothers *see* The True Story of Jesse James
Jennie *see* Portrait of Jennie
John Doe, Dynamite *see* Meet John Doe
Johnny in the Clouds *see* The Way to the Stars
Johnny Vagabond *see* Johnny Come Lately
Jungle Fighters *see* The Long the Short and the Tall

The Kid's Last Fight *see* The Life of Jimmy Dolan
Killer Dino *see* Dino
Killer on a Horse *see* Welcome to Hard Times
Kiss of Evil *see* Kiss of the Vampire

The Lady from Boston *see* Pardon My French

Lady Hamilton *see* That Hamilton Woman
Lady in Distress *see* A Window in London
Lady of Deceit *see* Born to Kill
Lady of the Boulevards *see* Nana
A Lady Surrenders *see* Love Story (1944)
Lady Windermere's Fan *see* The Fan
Land of Fury *see* The Seekers
Larceny Lane *see* Blonde Crazy
The Last Frontier *see* Savage Wilderness
The Last Warrior *see* Flap
Laurel and Hardy in Toyland *see* Babes in Toyland
Lazybones *see* Hallelujah I'm a Bum
Let's Make Up *see* Lilacs in the Spring
Life After Dark *see* Girls in the Night
Lights Out *see* Bright Victory
Lisa *see* The Inspector
The Little Kidnappers *see* The Kidnappers
The Long Ride Home *see* A Time for Killing
Los Angeles Precinct 45 *see* The New Centurions
Loss of Innocence *see* The Greengage Summer
Lost Treasure of the Amazon *see* Jivaro
The Loudest Whisper *see* The Children's Hour
Love in Las Vegas *see* Viva Las Vegas
Lovely to Look At (1937) *see* Thin Ice
A Lovely Way to Go *see* A Lovely Way to Die
Lucky Nick Cain *see* I'll Get You for This

MacDonald of the Canadian Mounties *see* Pony Soldier
McGuire Go Home *see* The High Bright Sun
Mad Little Island *see* Rockets Galore
Madame Pimpernel *see* Paris Underground
Mademoiselle France *see* Reunion in France
The Magic Bullet *see* The Story of Dr Ehrlich's Magic Bullet
The Magnificent Showman *see* Circus World
Man and His Mate *see* One Million BC
Man at the Crossroads *see* A Great American Tragedy
A Man Called Sullivan *see* The Great John L
The Man from the Folies Bergère *see* Folies Bergère
Man of Bronze *see* Jim Thorpe, All American
Man of Evil *see* Fanny by Gaslight
The Man on America's Conscience *see* Tennessee Johnson
The Man Who Came Back *see* Swamp Water
Man with a Million *see* The Million Pound Note
The Man with Thirty Sons *see* The Magnificent Yankee
The Man with X-Ray Eyes *see* X – The Man with X-Ray Eyes
Maniacs on Wheels *see* Once a Jolly Swagman
Marching Along *see* Stars and Stripes Forever
Marie Walewska *see* Conquest
Married but Single *see* This Thing Called Love
Master of the Islands *see* The Hawaiians
A Matter of Innocence *see* Pretty Polly
The Mean Machine *see* The Longest Yard
Medals *see* Seven Days Leave
Meet Whiplash Willie *see* The Fortune Cookie
Melody of Life *see* Symphony of Six Million
Melody of Youth *see* They Shall Have Music
The Memory Expert *see* Man on the Flying Trapeze
Military Policemen *see* Off Limits
Million Dollar Mermaid *see* The One Piece Bathing Suit
Mr Arkadin *see* Confidential Report
Mr Ashton Was Indiscreet *see* The Senator Was Indiscreet
Mr Griggs Returns *see* The Cockeyed Miracle
Mr Potts Goes to Moscow *see* Top Secret
Mister V *see* Pimpernel Smith
Mrs Loring's Secret *see* The Imperfect Lady
The Modern Miracle *see* The Story of Alexander Graham Bell
Money for Jam *see* It Aint Hay
Monsieur Repois *see* Knave of Hearts
Monster of Terror *see* Die Monster Die
Monte Carlo or Bust *see* Those Daring Young Men in Their Jaunty Jalopies
The Moving Target *see* Harper
Murder Inc *see* The Enforcer

The Murder in Thornton Square *see* Gaslight
Murder My Sweet *see* Farewell My Lovely
Murder on Diamond Row *see* The Squeaker
Murder on Monday *see* Home at Seven
My Heart Goes Crazy *see* London Town
My Son Alone *see* American Empire
My Two Husbands *see* Too Many Husbands

The Navy Steps Out *see* A Girl a Guy and a Gob
The Nelson Affair *see* Bequest to the Nation
The Nelson Touch *see* Corvette K 225
Never Give an Inch *see* Sometimes a Great Notion
The New Adventures of Don Juan *see* The Adventures of Don Juan
New Face in Hell *see* P.J.
Next Time We Live *see* Next Time We Love
Night Ambush *see* Ill Met by Moonlight
Night Creatures *see* Captain Clegg
Night Fighters *see* A Terrible Beauty
The Night is Ending *see* Paris After Dark
The Night They Invented Striptease *see* The Night They Raided Minsky's
Nine Days a Queen *see* Tudor Rose
No Highway in the Sky *see* No Highway
No Sleep Till Dawn *see* Bombers B 52
Notorious Gentlemen *see* The Rake's Progress

Obsessed *see* The Late Edwina Black
Oh for a Man *see* Will Success Spoil Rock Hunter?
On the Carpet *see* Little Giant
One Against Seven *see* Counter Attack
One Born Every Minute *see* The Flim Flam Man
One for the Book *see* The Voice of the Turtle
One Hour till Doomsday *see* City beneath the Sea
One Hundred Per Cent Pure *see* The Girl from Missouri
One Man Mutiny *see* The Court Martial of Billy Mitchell
One Woman's Story *see* The Passionate Friends
Operation Disaster *see* Morning Departure
Operation Snafu *see* On the Fiddle
Operation Undercover *see* Report to the Commissioner
Operation X *see* My Daughter Joy
O'Rourke of the Royal Mounted *see* Saskatchewan
Outpost in Malaya *see* The Planter's Wife
The Outsider (US 1948) *see* The Guinea Pig
Over the River *see* One More River

Panic in the Parlor *see* Sailor Beware
Paradise Lagoon *see* The Admirable Crichton
Paratrooper *see* The Red Beret
Paris Express *see* The Man Who Watched Trains Go By
The Passionate Sentry *see* Who Goes There?
Passport to Fame *see* The Whole Town's Talking
Patterns of Power *see* Patterns
Pay the Devil *see* Man in the Shadow
Personal Column *see* Lured
Pickup Alley *see* Interpol
The playgirl and the War Minister *see* The Amorous Prawn
Pluck of the Irish *see* Great Guy
Polly Fulton *see* BF's Daughter
Pookie *see* The Sterile Cuckoo
The Private Wore Skirts *see* Never Wave at a WAC
Project M 7 *see* The Net
The Promoter *see* The Card
The Public Eye *see* Follow Me
Pursuit of the Graf Spee *see* The Battle of the River Plate
Pussycat Alley *see* The World Ten Times Over

Queen of Destiny *see* Sixty Glorious Years

The Randolph Family *see* Dear Octopus
Remember That Face *see* The Mob
Rendezvous *see* Darling How Could You?
The Rich Full Life *see* Cynthia
Richer than the Earth *see* The Whistle at Eaton Falls
The Rise of Helga *see* Susan Lenox, Her Fall and Rise
Road to Frisco *see* They Drive by Nignt
Rommel Desert Fox *see* The Desert Fox
Rookies *see* Buck Privates

HALLIWELL'S FILMGOER'S BOOK OF QUOTES

Hollywood wisdom in barbs of pure gold – from Abbot & Costello to Darryl Zanuck

Another essential movie-maniac's reference book from Leslie Halliwell

'A must for every fan'
Mark Kahn, Sunday Mirror

'Indispensable'
Films Illustrated

The *Filmgoer's Book of Quotes* is packed with classic remarks spoken by, to and about the stars

'What we want is a story that starts with an earthquake and builds up to a climax'
Sam Goldwyn

'Is that your sword, or are you just pleased to see me?'
Mae West

'You've got the brain of a four-year-old boy, and I bet he was glad to get rid of it'
Groucho Marx

'Bogart's a helluva nice guy until 11.30 p.m. After that he thinks he's Bogart'
Dave Chasen

Halliwell's Filmgoer's Book of Quotes, including Movie Quizzes for addicts

NOSTALGIA ISN'T WHAT IT USED TO BE

Simone Signoret

Her international bestselling autobiography
'A splendid self-portrait – frank, warm, funny and exceedingly interesting'
Publishers Weekly

Simone Signoret, France's most famous actress, is the great beauty with a mind of her own who shook up the sleeping British cinema with her shatteringly sensual performance in *Room at the Top*. This is the story of a glittering career and a fascinating marriage also – to another of the great figures of the cinema, Yves Montand – it is the story of a star, but a star who never lost touch with reality, the story of a life full of glamour, but also a life full of guts.

'Lovers of life, of the theatre, and particularly of the cinema, will positively revel in this autobiography with its wealth of detail, its anecdotes, its warmth, its humour'
Evening News

'No-one is more typically French than Simone Signoret . . . a very liberated attitude towards love affairs . . . intelligent . . . discreet'
Daily Express

'Compulsively readable'
Scotsman

'Very enjoyable'
Daily Telegraph

PANTHER £1.50p

A POSTILLION STRUCK BY LIGHTNING

Dirk Bogarde

'A childhood brilliantly recalled'
Daily Telegraph

This is Dirk Bogarde's story, a delightful encounter with a world-famous actor, in which he affectionately recalls his early life in Sussex, the tough days at a Glasgow technical school, his time at Chelsea Polytechnic, his arrival in Hollywood.

To read this absorbing autobiography is not just to trace the first steps of a talented young actor, it is also to discover a fine and gifted writer. For the childhood scenes Bogarde evokes – of a happy and sufficient country life, of the unspoilt harmony of summer days – are brilliantly caught, spiced with a natural humour. It is these moments above all which make the book so memorable and so appealing.

'What emerges . . . is a whole life. Whole in the sense that the sensitive, shy, brilliant human being called Dirk Bogarde speaks to you as you read'
Dilys Powell, Sunday Times

'A powerful, poignant book'
Cosmopolitan

THE GREAT BRITISH PICTURE SHOW

George Perry

From the 90s to the 70s

The show's been going on now for nearly eighty years. There have been heady days of naïve success and dismal waves of cringingly poor films, and despite its superficial emulation of all things Hollywood, the British cinema has until recently been insular and nationalistic.

The entire ethos of the British cinema – the things which stir us, excite us and make us laugh – is examined in this enormously thorough and affectionate book. George Perry discusses every major British film and the people who made them. He shows how the British cinema has transcended blandness and trivia, parasites and charlatans, continuing crises and slumps to produce a fine tradition of satire and documentary, comedy and drama. He places it in its social and political context, examining particularly the British obsession with class that has so often pervaded the industry.

All the major writers, directors, actors and producers of the British film industry are listed in a comprehensive checklist at the end of the book.

THE LONG VIEW

Basil Wright

An international history of the cinema
Fully revised and updated edition

Cinema has been seen as art, as propaganda, as escapism and as documentary. *The Long View* brilliantly draws together these cross-connecting strands. Recurring obsessions of film-makers – war, erotica, patriotism, horror, realism, fantasy and propaganda – are celebrated, and a cohesive history of world cinema since 1895 emerges.

Basil Wright has worked as a documentary film-maker and lecturer since the 1920s. His view of the cinema is as subjective, unique, witty and vast as his experience.

'There can be few more comprehensive histories of the art of the cinema than Basil Wright's *The Long View*'
Daily Telegraph

'The book has the impact of a life-work . . . Splendid'
Dilys Powell, Sunday Times

'Very difficult to put down'
The Guardian

'The virtue of the book lies in its ability to combine an intelligent approach with a readable and often witty writing style'
Financial Times

NORMA JEAN

Fred Lawrence Guiles

The biography of Marilyn Monroe

Help Help
Help I feel life coming closer
When all I want is to die
Marilyn Monroe

Work on this biography – still recognized as the most complete and thoughtful – was begun in 1962, before Marilyn's death. Much material for it was obtained from her close friend and press agent, from two of her husbands, from four of her most important directors and from others associated with her from her childhood to her death. An accurate portrait is drawn of her childhood – her father and family situation – and of her adulthood – her struggles with husbands, film directors and drugs.

But above all this is the story of the love affair which alienated Marilyn from her three husbands and finally destroyed her. And that affair was not with any other man, but with the film camera.

Illustrated

BOGIE

Joe Hyams

The authorized biography of Humphrey Bogart, introduced by Lauren Bacall

Humphrey Bogart, the man in the trenchcoat and the soft felt hat. Off screen as tough a guy as on, always larger than life, Bogie was Hollywood's sweet-water dose of late-night rum, who at the darkest hour would intoxicate an entire culture and by acting out a generation's dreams earn himself immortality.

He was Sam Spade, Philip Marlow, Duke Mantee, Rick, Captain Queeg.

He married four times, most violently to Mayo Methot, who tried to carve him up with a kitchen-knife; most happily to Lauren Bacall, 25 years his junior. This is his story, the *real* legend of Bogie.

'It is an authorised biography, and surprisingly frank, with a loving introduction'
Daily Mirror

Illustrated

MAYFLOWER £0.75

THE CITIZEN KANE BOOK

Raising Kane: Pauline Kael
The Shooting Script: Herman J Mankiewicz and Orson Welles

'Get hold of this book – it's dynamite'
Ken Russell

This is the true-life history of *Citizen Kane* – the film that was 'designed to astonish' (Kenneth Tynan), perhaps the most controversial and yet best-loved film in the history of Hollywood. An $842,000 bribe and the concentrated wrath of the Hearst newspaper empire combined in an attempt to strangle its distribution; and the authorship of the script is still the subject of conflicting and acrimonious gossip.

Pauline Kael's long essay, *Raising Kane*, dissects a maze of fresh Hollywood lore to re-evaluate these and many other fascinating stories about the making of the film. Her account is followed by the complete shooting script illustrated with 81 frames from the film, and the full, shot-by-shot script of the final film. Together they make a unique book, a chronicle of Hollywood in a period of change and a portrait of one of its most gifted, if wayward, children.

'It has become a commonplace in America to include Miss Kael in the excellent tradition of Ferguson, Tyler and Agee. I would go further than that by saying that she is easily the finest film critic yet to appear, and already belongs among the critical writers whose aesthetic principles – usually implicit – comprise the undeclared philosophical wealth of the last three-quarters of a century'
Clive James, The Listener

'Pauline Kael's introduction . . . is generally one of the finest articles on the cinema I have read in the last couple of years'
Philip French, The Times

'I would urge you to rush out and buy this book'
The Spectator

Illustrated

PALADIN £1.25